# A Step-by-step guide to using your Six County Atlas

**1** To locate any street in your Six County Atlas, first select the specific city, town or township from the alphabetical listing below. At the right of the listing, note the section or sections.

**2** Turn to the end of the color coded section to find the complete street index for that section. Under the specific city, town or township heading, locate the street you wish to find and note both its page numer and grid coordinates.

**3** Turn to the map and locate the alpha coordinate along the top of the page and the numeric coordinate along the side of the page. The street will be located on the map where the coordinated intersect.

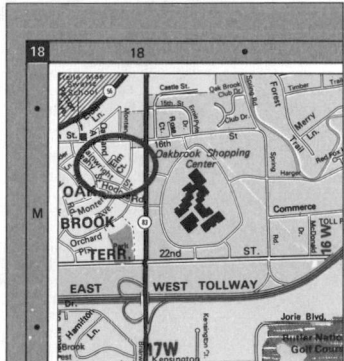

| | |
|---|---|
| Naperville Twp. | Sec. 3 |
| New Lenox | Sec. 8 |
| New Lenox Twp. | Sec. 8 |
| North Aurora | Sec. 4 |
| Oak Brook | Sec. 3 |
| Oakbrook Terrace | Sec. 3 |
| Pingree Grove | Sec. 4 |
| Plainfield | Sec. 8 |
| Plainfield Twp. | Sec. 8 |
| Plato Center | Sec. 4 |
| Plato Twp. | Sec. 4 |
| Richardson | Sec. 4 |
| Ridgewood | Sec. 8 |
| Rockdale | Sec. 8 |
| Romeoville | Sec. 8 |
| Roselle | Sec. 3 |
| Rutland Twp. | Sec. 4 |
| Schaumburg | Sec. 5 |
| Scraper-Moecherville | Sec. 4 |

### OAKBROOK TERRACE
Pages 11,12,17,18
**STREETS**

| Street | Page | Grid |
|---|---|---|
| Buttercup | Pg.17 | M17 |
| Butterfield Rd. | Pg.17 | M16 |
| Cermak Rd. | Pg.17 | M17 |
| Drury Ln. | Pg.12 | L18 |
| Eisenhower Rd. | Pg.17 | M17 |
| Elder Ln. | Pg.17,18 | M18 |
| Elm Ct. | Pg.18 | M18 |
| Elm Pl. | Pg.17 | M17 |
| Halsey Rd. | Pg.17 | M17 |
| Hodges Rd. | Pg.18 | M18 |
| Karban Rd. | Pg.17 | M17 |
| Kolberg Ct. | Pg.12 | L18 |
| Leahy St. | Pg.18 | M18 |
| Lincoln Ave. | Pg.17 | M16 |

## Index to cities, towns and townships
Unincorporated areas indexed under respective townships

| City • Town • Twp | Section |
|---|---|
| Abbott Park | Sec.6 |
| Addison | Sec.3 |
| Addison Township | Sec.3 |
| Alden | Sec.7 |
| Alden Township | Sec.7 |
| Algonquin | Sec.5,7 |
| Algonquin Township | Sec.7 |
| Alsip | Sec.1 |
| Antioch | Sec.6 |
| Antioch Township | Sec.6 |
| Aptakisic | Sec.6 |
| Arbury Hills | Sec.8 |
| Arlington Heights | Sec.2 |
| Aurora | Sec.3,4 |
| Aurora Township | Sec.4 |
| Avon Township | Sec.6 |
| Baldmond | Sec.4 |
| Bannockburn | Sec.6 |
| Barrington | Sec.2,6 |
| Barrington Hills | Sec.2,5, 6,7 |
| Barrington Township | Sec.2,5 |
| Bartlett | Sec.3,5 |
| Batavia | Sec.4 |
| Batavia Township | Sec.4 |
| Beach Park | Sec.6 |
| Bedford Park | Sec.1 |
| Belden | Sec.7 |
| Bellwood | Sec.1 |
| Bensenville | Sec.3 |
| Benton Township | Sec.6 |
| Berkeley | Sec.1 |
| Berwyn | Sec.1 |
| Big Foot | Sec.7 |
| Big Rock | Sec.4 |
| Big Rock Township | Sec.4 |
| Blackberry Township | Sec.4 |
| Bloom Township | Sec.2 |
| Bloomingdale | Sec.3 |
| Bloomingdale Township | Sec.3 |
| Blue Island | Sec.1 |
| Bolingbrook | Sec.3,8 |

| City • Town • Twp | Section |
|---|---|
| Bowes | Sec.4 |
| Bremen Township | Sec.2 |
| Bridgeview | Sec.1 |
| Broadview | Sec.1 |
| Brookfield | Sec.1 |
| Buffalo Grove | Sec.2,6 |
| Bull Valley | Sec.7 |
| Burbank | Sec.1 |
| Burlington | Sec.4 |
| Burlington Township | Sec.4 |
| Burnham | Sec.1 |
| Burr Ridge | Sec.3 |
| Burton Township | Sec.7 |
| Burtons Bridge | Sec.7 |
| Calumet City | Sec.1 |
| Calumet Park | Sec.1 |
| Campton Township | Sec.4 |
| Carney Corners | Sec.6 |
| Carol Stream | Sec.3 |
| Carpentersville | Sec.5 |
| Cary | Sec.7 |
| Cedar Lake | Sec.6 |
| Channel Lake | Sec.6 |
| Chemung | Sec.7 |
| Chemung Township | Sec.7 |
| Chicago | Sec.1 |
| Chicago Heights | Sec.2 |
| Chicago Ridge | Sec.2 |
| Cicero | Sec.1 |
| Clarendon Hills | Sec.3 |
| Coral | Sec.7 |
| Coral Township | Sec.7 |
| Country Club Hills | Sec.2 |
| Countryside | Sec.1 |
| Coynes | Sec.8 |
| Crest Hill | Sec.8 |
| Crestwood | Sec.1 |
| Crystal Lake | Sec.7 |
| Cuba Township | Sec.6 |
| Darien | Sec.3 |
| Deep Lake | Sec.6 |
| Deer Park | Sec.2,6 |

| City • Town • Twp | Section |
|---|---|
| Deerfield | Sec.6 |
| Deerfield Township | Sec.6 |
| Des Plaines | Sec.2 |
| Diamond Lake | Sec.6 |
| Dixmoor | Sec.1 |
| Dolton | Sec.1 |
| Dorr Township | Sec.7 |
| Downers Grove | Sec.3 |
| Downers Grove Township | Sec.3,8 |
| Du Page Township | Sec.3,8 |
| Dundee Township | Sec.4,5 |
| Dunham Township | Sec.7 |
| East Chicago, IN | Sec.1 |
| East Dundee | Sec.5 |
| East Hazelcrest | Sec.2 |
| Eddy | Sec.6 |
| Ela Township | Sec.6 |
| Elburn | Sec.4 |
| Elgin | Sec.5 |
| Elgin Township | Sec.4,5 |
| Elk Grove Township | Sec.2 |
| Elk Grove Village | Sec.2,3 |
| Elmhurst | Sec.3 |
| Elmwood Park | Sec.1 |
| Evanston | Sec.2 |
| Evanston Township | Sec.2 |
| Evergreen Park | Sec.1 |
| Fairfield | Sec.6 |
| Flossmoor | Sec.2 |
| Flowerfield | Sec.3 |
| Ford Heights | Sec.2 |
| Forest Park | Sec.1 |
| Forest View | Sec.1 |
| Fox Lake | Sec.6,7 |
| Fox Lake Hills | Sec.6 |
| Fox River Grove | Sec.7 |
| Fox River Valley Gardens | Sec.7 |
| Frankfort | Sec.8 |
| Frankfort Township | Sec.8 |
| Franklin Park | Sec.1 |
| Franklinville | Sec.7 |
| Fremont Township | Sec.6 |

| City • Town • Twp | Section |
|---|---|
| Gages Lake | Sec.6 |
| Geneva | Sec.4 |
| Geneva Township | Sec.4 |
| Genoa City, WI | Sec.4 |
| Gilberts | Sec.4 |
| Gilmer | Sec.6 |
| Glen Ellyn | Sec.3 |
| Glencoe | Sec.2 |
| Glendale Heights | Sec.3 |
| Glenview | Sec.2 |
| Glenwood | Sec.2 |
| Golf | Sec.2 |
| Grafton Township | Sec.7 |
| Grant Township | Sec.6 |
| Grayslake | Sec.6 |
| Green Oaks | Sec.6 |
| Greenwood | Sec.7 |
| Greenwood Township | Sec.7 |
| Gurnee | Sec.6 |
| Hainesville | Sec.6 |
| Half Day | Sec.6 |
| Hammond, IN | Sec.1 |
| Hampshire | Sec.4 |
| Hampshire Township | Sec.4 |
| Hanover Park | Sec.2,3,5 |
| Hanover Township | Sec.5 |
| Harmony | Sec.7 |
| Hartland | Sec.7 |
| Hartland Township | Sec.7 |
| Harvard | Sec.7 |
| Harvey | Sec.1 |
| Harwood Heights | Sec.1 |
| Hawthorn Woods | Sec.6 |
| Hazel Crest | Sec.2 |
| Hebron | Sec.7 |
| Hebron Township | Sec.7 |
| Hickory Hills | Sec.2 |
| Highland Park | Sec.6 |
| Highwood | Sec.6 |
| Hillside | Sec.1 |
| Hinsdale | Sec.3 |
| Hodgkins | Sec.1 |

**D**

| City • Town • Twp | Section | City • Town • Twp | Section | City • Town • Twp | Section | City • Town • Twp | Section |
|---|---|---|---|---|---|---|---|
| Hoffman Estates | Sec.2,5 | Marengo Township | Sec.7 | Park Ridge | Sec.1,2 | Stickney | Sec.1 |
| Holiday Hills | Sec.7 | Markham | Sec.1 | Phoenix | Sec.1 | Stone Park | Sec.1 |
| Homer Township | Sec.8 | Marywood | Sec.4 | Pingree Grove | Sec.4 | Streamwood | Sec.2,5 |
| Hometown | Sec.1 | Matteson | Sec.2 | Plainfield | Sec.8 | Sugar Grove | Sec.4 |
| Homewood | Sec.2 | Maywood | Sec.1 | Plainfield Township | Sec.8 | Sugar Grove Township | Sec.4 |
| Huntley | Sec.4,7 | McCook | Sec.1 | Plato Center | Sec.4 | Summit | Sec.1 |
| Indian Creek | Sec.6 | McCullom Lake | Sec.7 | Plato Township | Sec.4 | Sylvan Lakes | Sec.6 |
| Indian Head Park | Sec.1 | McHenry | Sec.7 | Posen | Sec.1 | Third Lake | Sec.6 |
| Ingals Park | Sec.8 | McHenry Township | Sec.7 | Prairie Grove | Sec.7 | Thornton | Sec.2 |
| Ingleside | Sec.6 | McQueens | Sec.4 | Prairie View | Sec.6 | Thornton Township | Sec.2 |
| Inverness | Sec.2 | Medinah | Sec.3 | Prospect Heights | Sec.2 | Tinley Park | Sec.2,8 |
| Island Lake | Sec.6,7 | Melrose Park | Sec.1 | Proviso Township | Sec.1 | Tower Lakes | Sec.6 |
| Itasca | Sec.3 | Merrionette Park | Sec.1 | Quentin's Corners | Sec.6 | Troxel | Sec.4 |
| Ivanhoe | Sec.6 | Mettawa | Sec.6 | Rich Township | Sec.2 | Troy Township | Sec.8 |
| Johnsburg | Sec.7 | Midlothian | Sec.1 | Richardson | Sec.4 | Twin Lakes | Sec.7 |
| Joliet | Sec.8 | Millburn | Sec.6 | Richmond | Sec.7 | Udina | Sec.4 |
| Joliet Township | Sec.8 | Milton Township | Sec.3 | Richmond Township | Sec.7 | Union | Sec.7 |
| Justice | Sec.2 | Mokena | Sec.8 | Richton Park | Sec.2 | Valley View | Sec.4 |
| Kaneville | Sec.4 | Monaville | Sec.6 | Ridgefield | Sec.7 | Vernon Hills | Sec.6 |
| Kaneville Township | Sec.4 | Montgomery | Sec.4 | Ridgewood | Sec.8 | Vernon Township | Sec.6 |
| Kenilworth | Sec.2 | Mooseheart | Sec.4 | Riley | Sec.7 | Villa Park | Sec.3 |
| Kildeer | Sec.6 | Morton Grove | Sec.2 | Riley Township | Sec.7 | Virgil | Sec.4 |
| La Fox | Sec.4 | Mount Prospect | Sec.2 | Ringwood | Sec.8 | Virgil Township | Sec.4 |
| LaGrange | Sec.1 | Mundelein | Sec.6 | River Forest | Sec.1 | Volo | Sec.6 |
| LaGrange Park | Sec.1 | Mylith Park | Sec.6 | River Grove | Sec.1 | Wadsworth | Sec.6 |
| Lake Barrington | Sec.6 | Naperville | Sec.3,8 | Riverdale | Sec.1 | Warren Township | Sec.6 |
| Lake Bluff | Sec.6 | Naperville Township | Sec.3 | Riverside | Sec.1 | Warrenville | Sec.3 |
| Lake Forest | Sec.6 | New Lenox | Sec.8 | Riverwoods | Sec.6 | Wasco | Sec.4 |
| Lake Villa | Sec.6 | New Lenox Township | Sec.8 | Robbins | Sec.1 | Wauconda | Sec.6 |
| Lake Villa Township | Sec.6 | New Trier Township | Sec.2 | Rockdale | Sec.8 | Wauconda Township | Sec.6 |
| Lake Zurich | Sec.6 | Newport Township | Sec.6 | Rolling Meadows | Sec.2 | Waukegan | Sec.6 |
| Lake in the Hills | Sec.7 | Niles | Sec.2 | Romeoville | Sec.8 | Waukegan Township | Sec.6 |
| Lakemoor | Sec.6,7 | Niles Township | Sec.2 | Rosecrans | Sec.6 | Wayne | Sec.3,4,5 |
| Lakewood | Sec.7 | Norridge | Sec.1 | Roselle | Sec.2,3 | Wayne Township | Sec.3,5 |
| Lambs Corners | Sec.6 | North Aurora | Sec.4 | Rosemont | Sec.1,2 | West Chicago | Sec.3 |
| Lansing | Sec.2 | North Barrington | Sec.6 | Round Lake | Sec.6 | West Deerfield Township | Sec.6 |
| Lawrence | Sec.7 | North Chicago | Sec.6 | Round Lake Beach | Sec.6 | West Dundee | Sec.5 |
| Lemont | Sec.8 | North Riverside | Sec.1 | Round Lake Heights | Sec.6 | Westchester | Sec.1 |
| Lemont Township | Sec.3,8 | Northbrook | Sec.2 | Round Lake Park | Sec.6 | Western Springs | Sec.1 |
| Leyden Township | Sec.1 | Northfield | Sec.2 | Russell | Sec.6 | Westmont | Sec.3 |
| Libertyville | Sec.6 | Northfield Township | Sec.2 | Rutland Township | Sec.4 | Wheatland Township | Sec.3,8 |
| Libertyville Township | Sec.6 | Northlake | Sec.1 | Sauk Village | Sec.2 | Wheaton | Sec.3 |
| Lily Cache | Sec.8 | Nunda Township | Sec.6 | Schaumburg | Sec.2,5 | Wheeling | Sec.2 |
| Lily Lake | Sec.4 | Oak Brook | Sec.3 | Schaumburg Township | Sec.2 | Wheeling Township | Sec.2 |
| Lilymoor | Sec.7 | Oak Forest | Sec.2 | Schiller Park | Sec.1 | Wildwood | Sec.6 |
| Lincolnshire | Sec.6 | Oak Lawn | Sec.1 | Scraper-Moecherville | Sec.4 | Williams Park | Sec.6 |
| Lincolnwood | Sec.1 | Oak Park | Sec.1 | Seneca Township | Sec.7 | Willow Springs | Sec.1,2 |
| Lincolnwood Hills | Sec.8 | Oakbrook Terrace | Sec.3 | Shields Township | Sec.6 | Willowbrook | Sec.2 |
| Lindenhurst | Sec.6 | Oakwood Hills | Sec.7 | Shorewood | Sec.8 | Wilmette | Sec.2 |
| Lisle | Sec.3 | Old Mill Creek | Sec.6 | Skokie | Sec.2 | Wilson | Sec.6 |
| Lisle Township | Sec.3 | Olympia Fields | Sec.2 | Sleepy Hollow | Sec.5 | Winfield | Sec.3 |
| Lockport | Sec.8 | Orland Hills | Sec.2 | Solon Mills | Sec.7 | Winfield Township | Sec.3 |
| Lockport Township | Sec.8 | Orland Park | Sec.2,8 | South Barrington | Sec.2,5 | Winnetka | Sec.2 |
| Lombard | Sec.3 | Orland Township | Sec.2 | South Chicago Heights | Sec.2 | Winthrop Harbor | Sec.6 |
| Long Grove | Sec.6 | Oswego | Sec.4 | South Elgin | Sec.4,5 | Wonder Lake | Sec.7 |
| Long Lake | Sec.6 | Palatine | Sec.2 | South Holland | Sec.1 | Wood Dale | Sec.3 |
| Loon Lake | Sec.6 | Palatine Township | Sec.2 | South Park | Sec.4 | Woodridge | Sec.3,8 |
| Lynwood | Sec.2 | Palos Heights | Sec.2 | Spaulding Corners | Sec.6 | Woodstock | Sec.7 |
| Lyons | Sec.1 | Palos Hills | Sec.2 | Spring Grove | Sec.7 | Worth | Sec.2 |
| Lyons Township | Sec.1,2 | Palos Park | Sec.2 | St. Charles | Sec.4 | Worth Township | Sec.2 |
| Maine Township | Sec.2 | Palos Township | Sec.2 | St. Charles Township | Sec.4 | York Township | Sec.3 |
| Maple Park | Sec.4 | Park City | Sec.6 | Starks | Sec.4 | Zion | Sec.6 |
| Marengo | Sec.7 | Park Forest | Sec.2 | Steger | Sec.2 | | |

# CITY OF CHICAGO

## SECTION 1

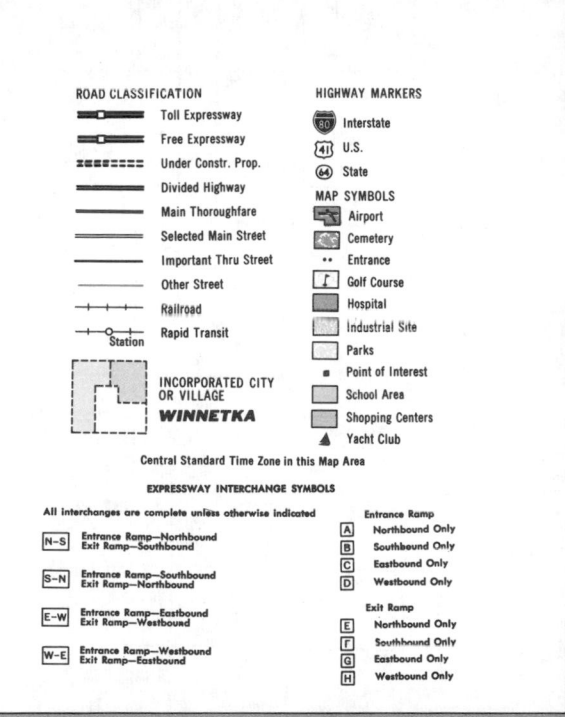

ROAD CLASSIFICATION

Toll Expressway

Free Expressway

Under Constr. Prop.

Divided Highway

Main Thoroughfare

Selected Main Street

Important Thru Street

Other Street

Railroad

Rapid Transit
Station

INCORPORATED CITY OR VILLAGE

**WINNETKA**

HIGHWAY MARKERS

Interstate

U.S.

State

MAP SYMBOLS

Airport

Cemetery

Entrance

Golf Course

Hospital

Industrial Site

Parks

Point of Interest

School Area

Shopping Centers

Yacht Club

Central Standard Time Zone in this Map Area

EXPRESSWAY INTERCHANGE SYMBOLS

All interchanges are complete unless otherwise indicated

N-S Entrance Ramp—Northbound
Exit Ramp—Southbound

S-N Entrance Ramp—Southbound
Exit Ramp—Northbound

E-W Entrance Ramp—Eastbound
Exit Ramp—Westbound

W-E Entrance Ramp—Westbound
Exit Ramp—Eastbound

Entrance Ramp

A Northbound Only

B Southbound Only

C Eastbound Only

D Westbound Only

Exit Ramp

E Northbound Only

F Southbound Only

G Eastbound Only

H Westbound Only

**TURN PAGE FOR ORIENTATION MAP**

# SECTION 1
## ORIENTATION MAP

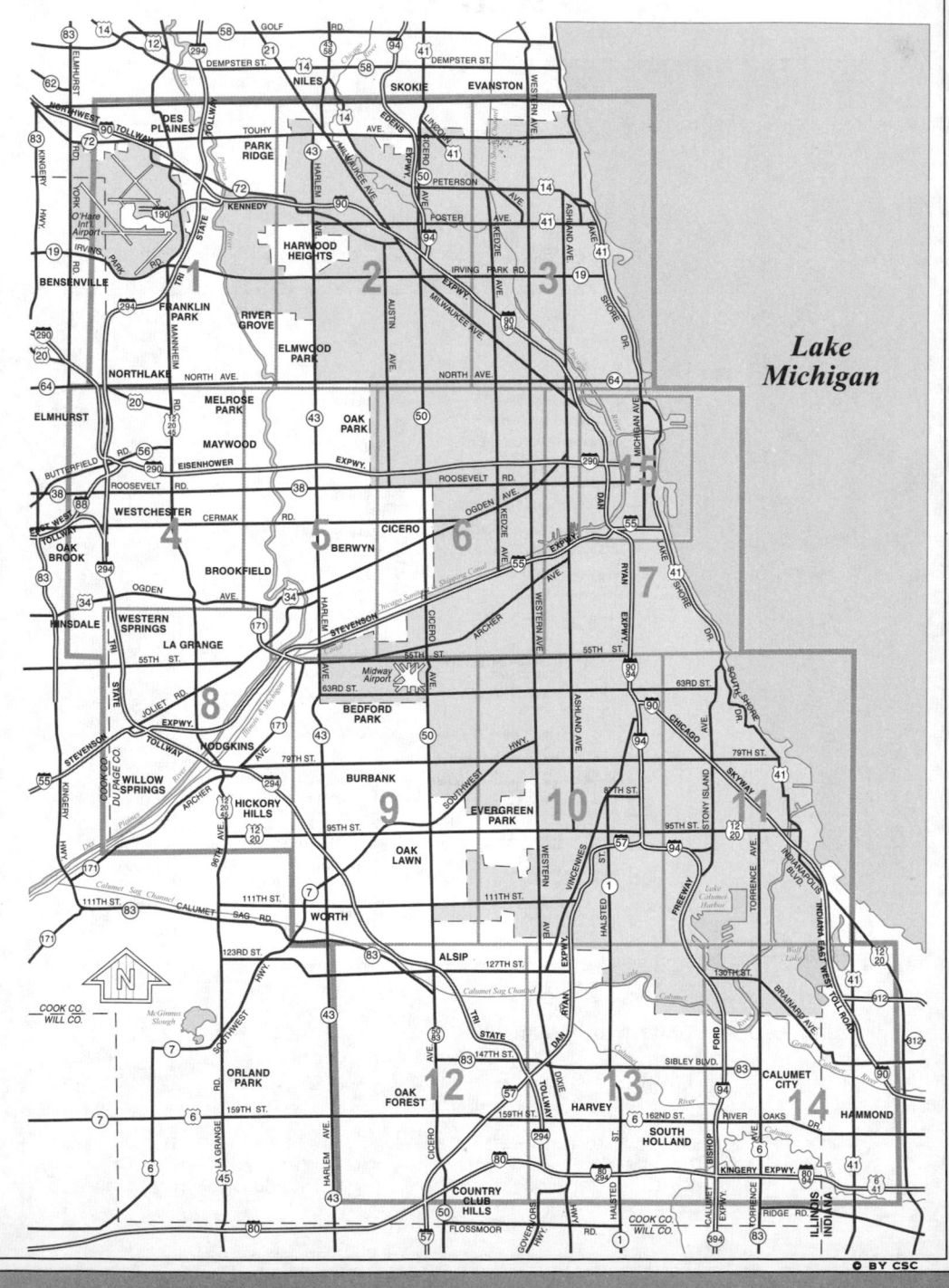

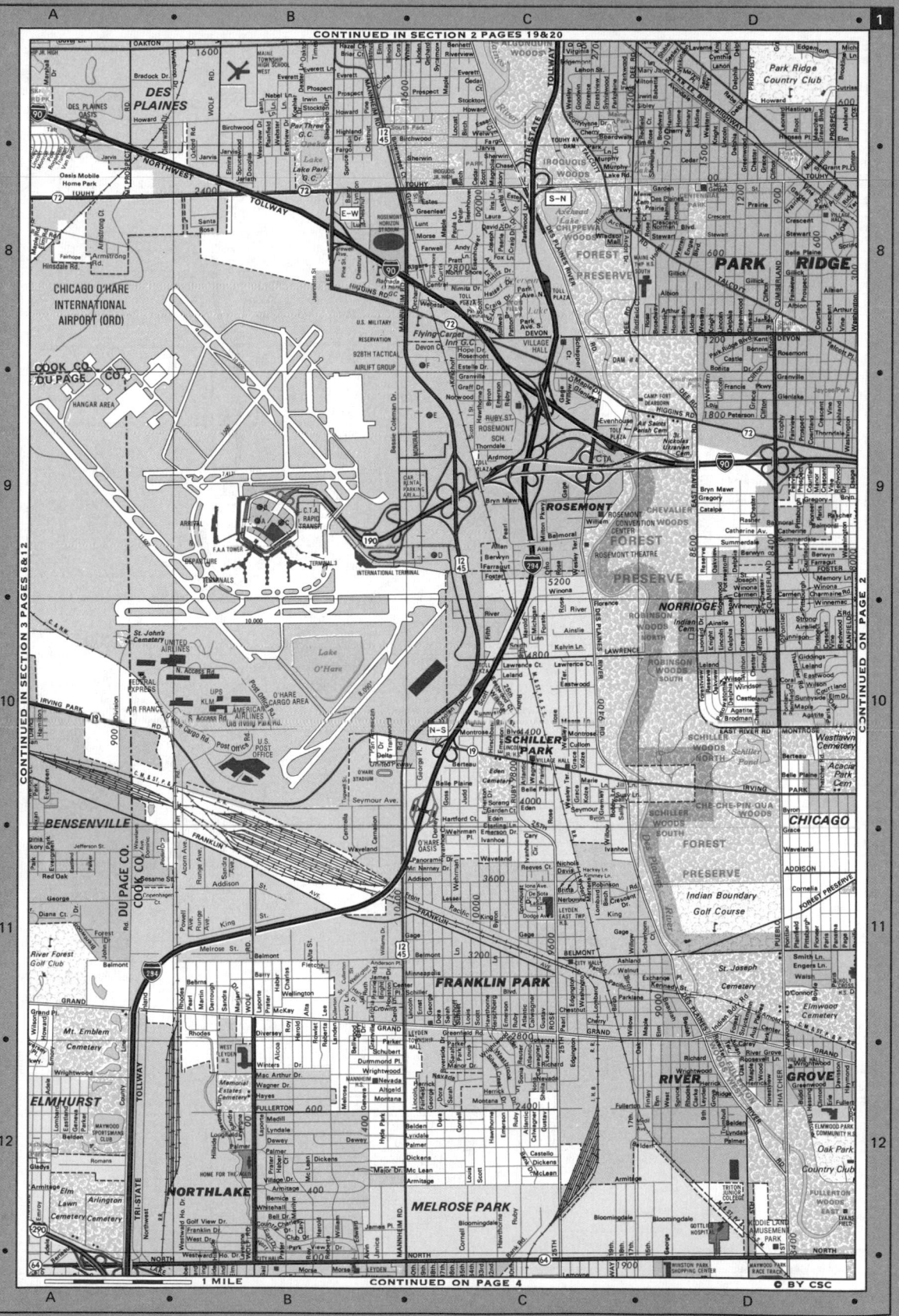

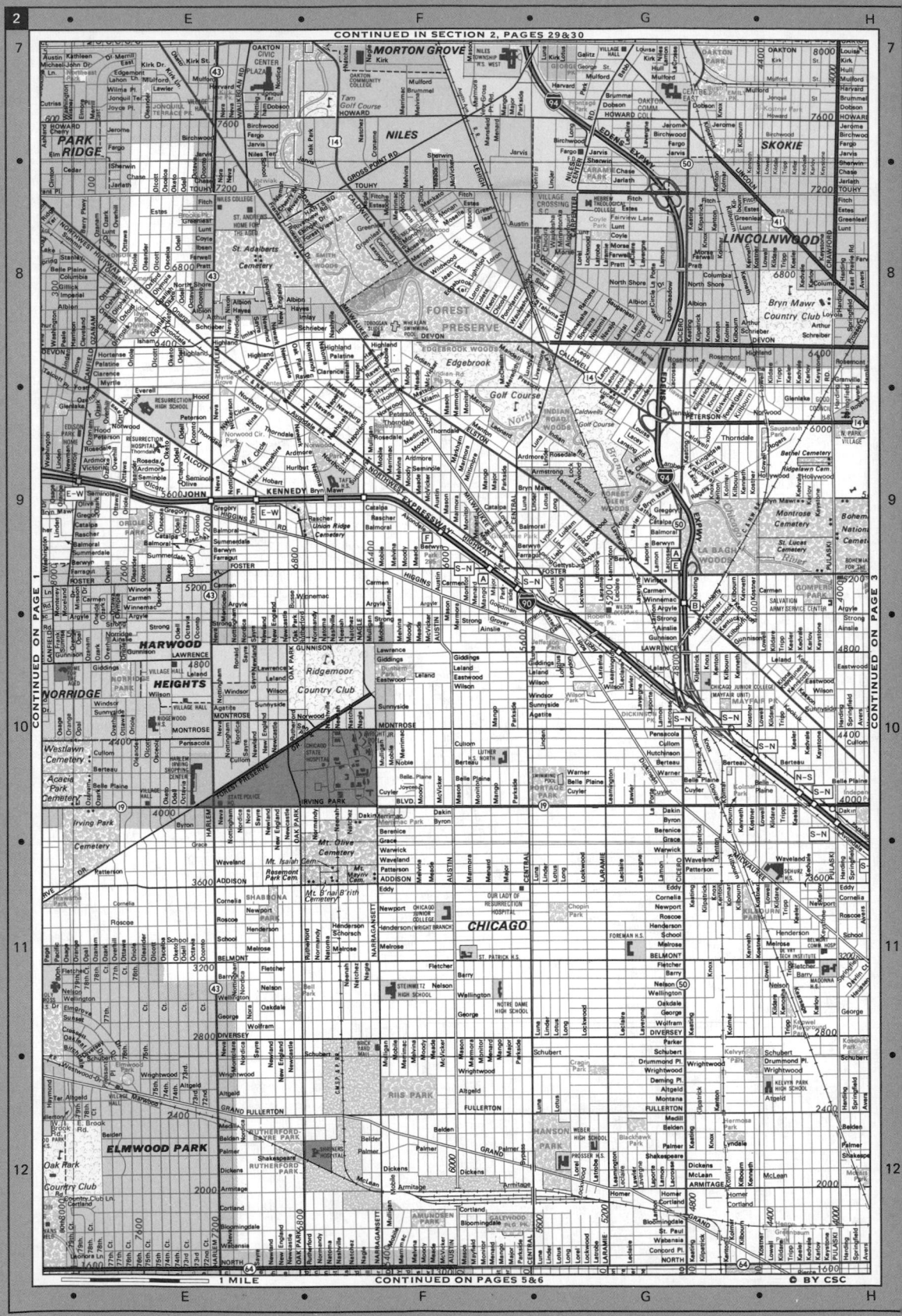

1 MILE

© BY CSC

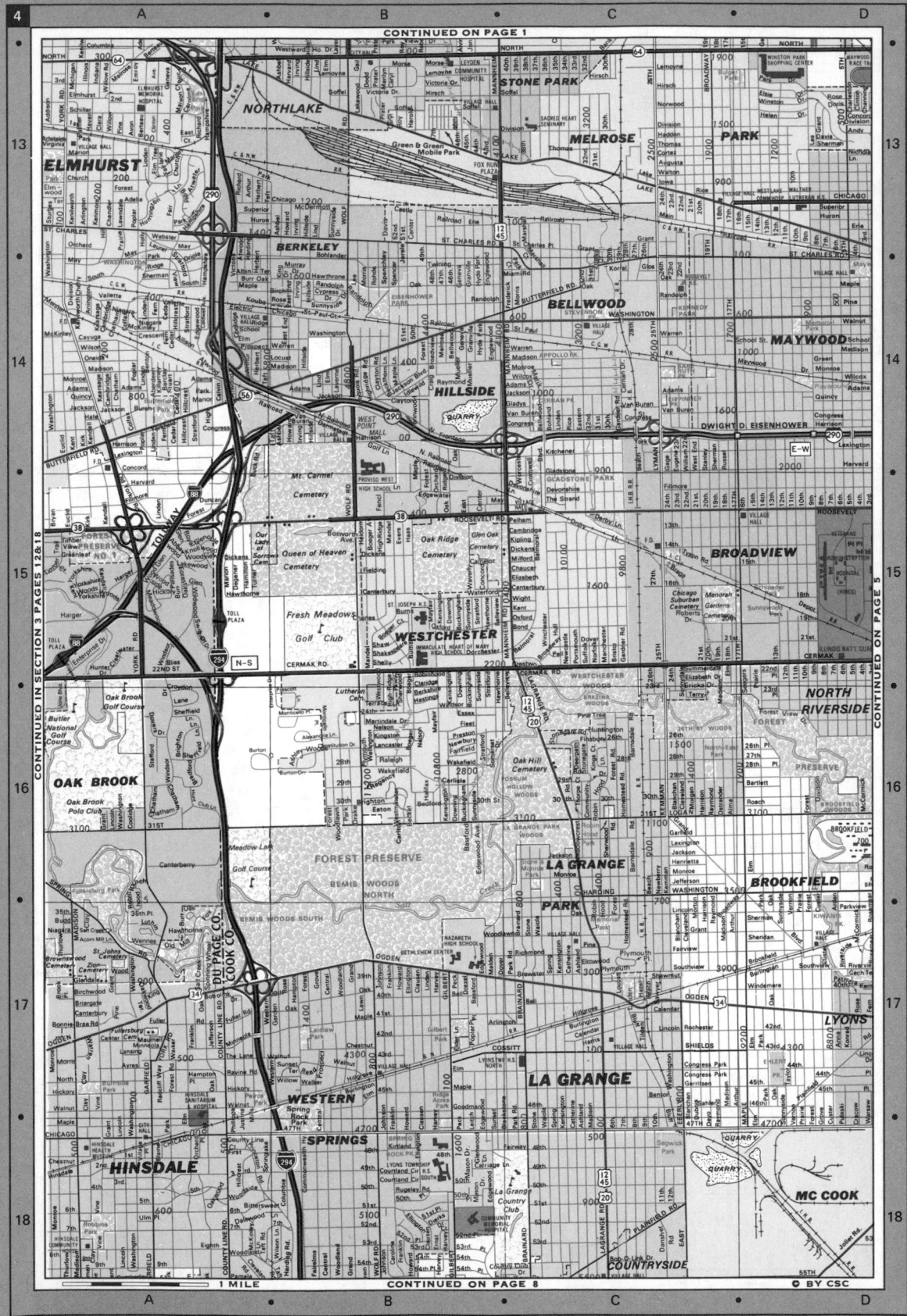

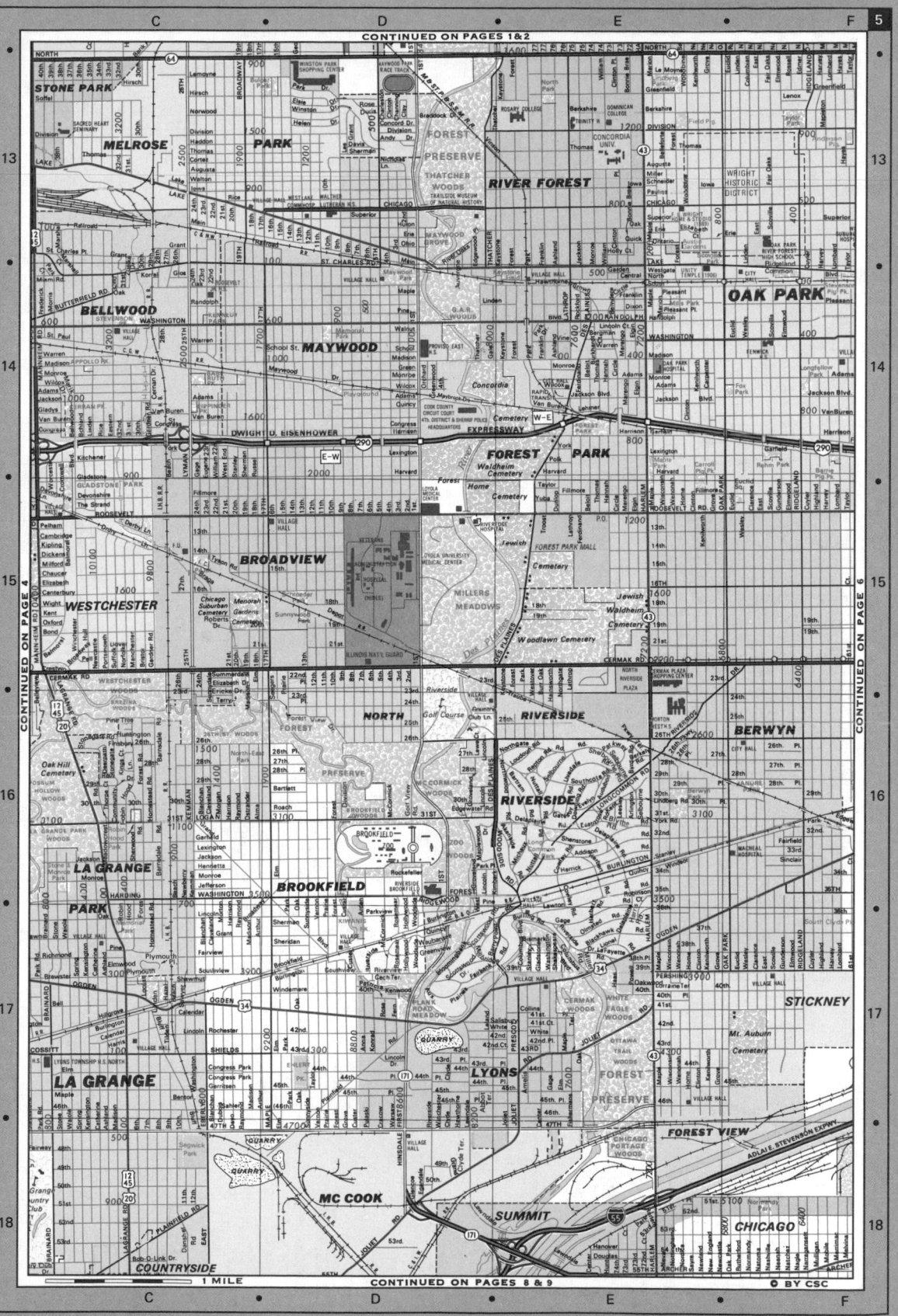

© BY CSC

1 MILE

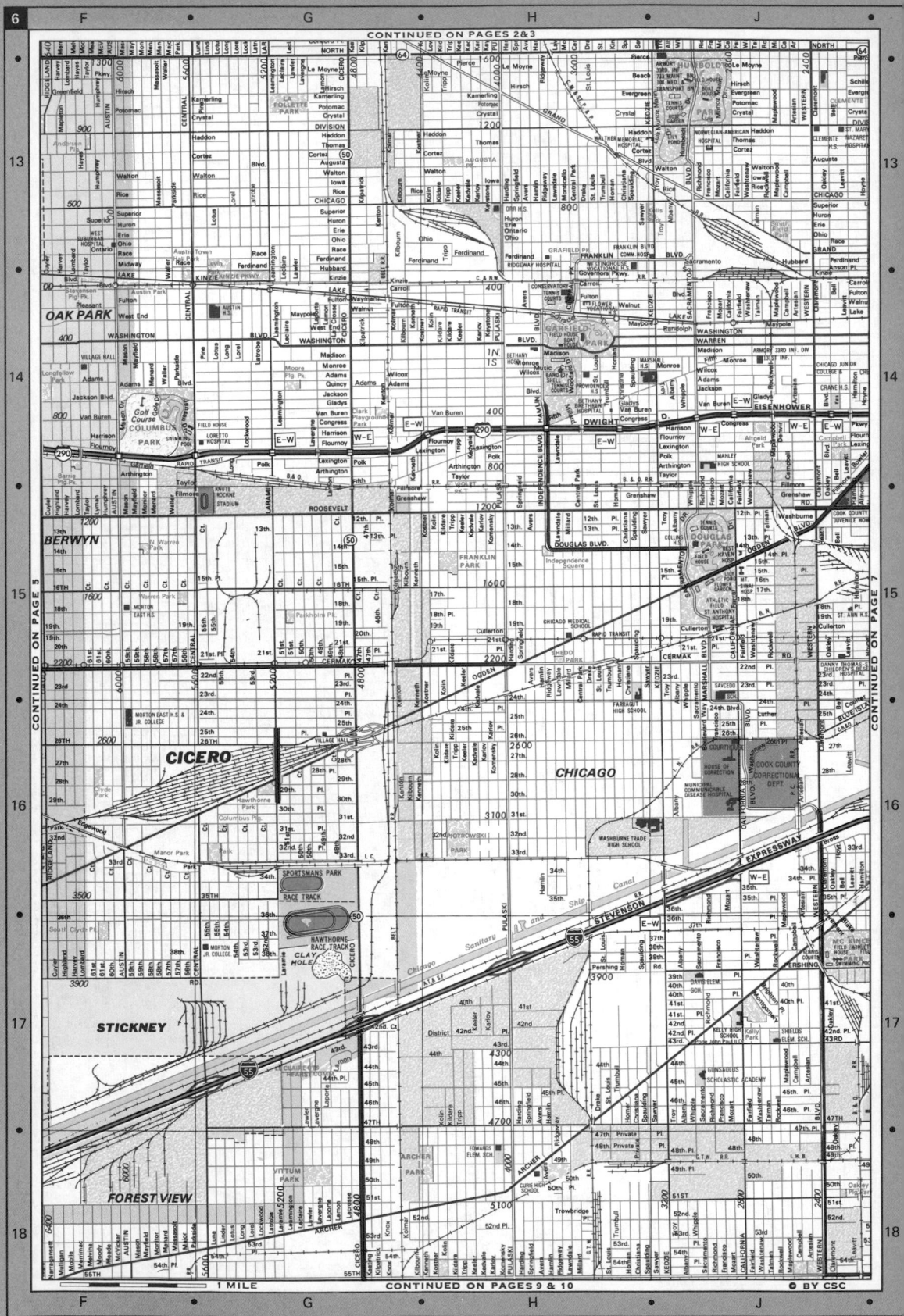

CONTINUED ON PAGE 5
CONTINUED ON PAGE 7

OAK PARK

BERWYN

CICERO

CHICAGO

STICKNEY

FOREST VIEW

1 MILE

© BY CSC

Lake
Michigan

CHICAGO

© BY CSC

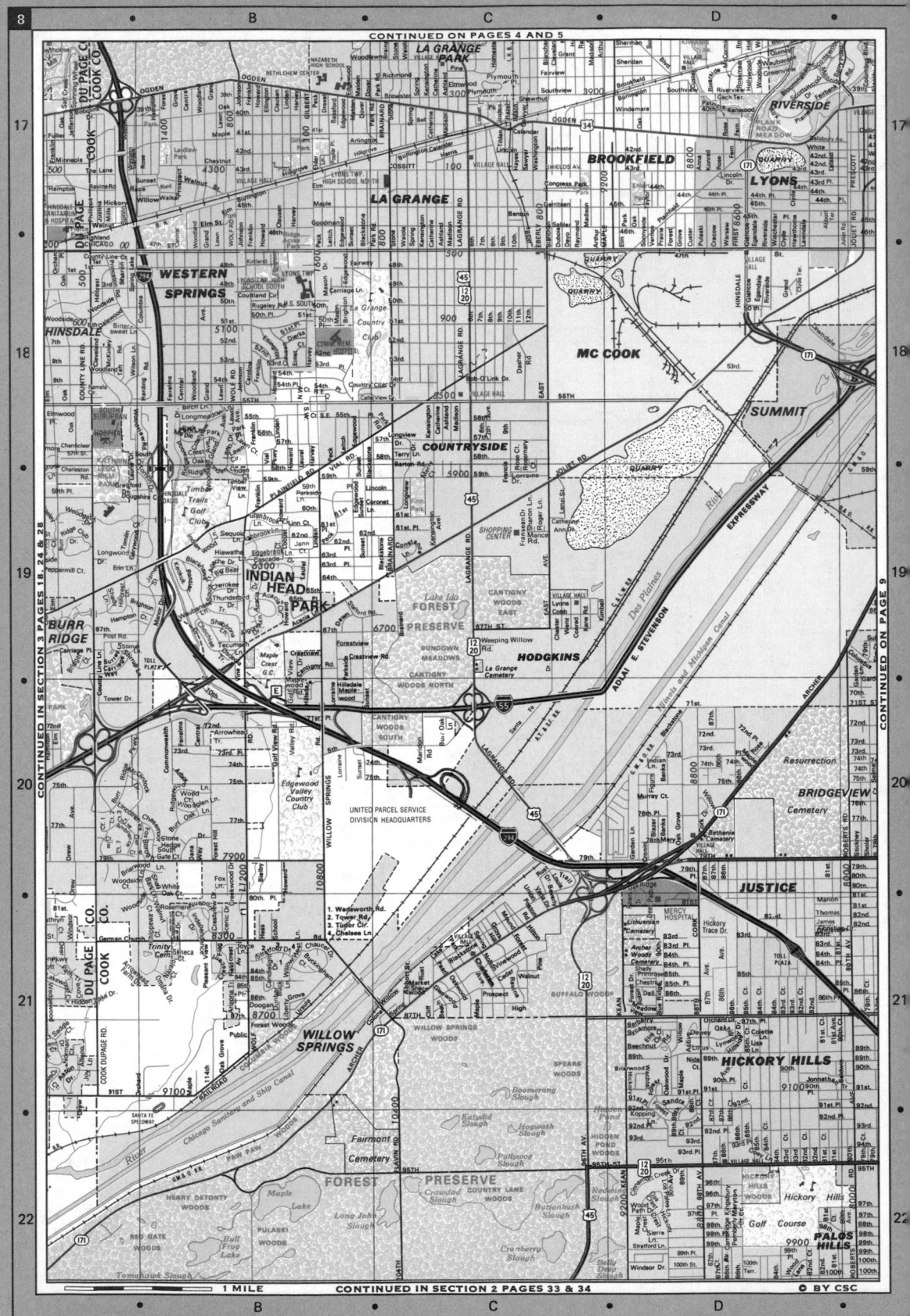

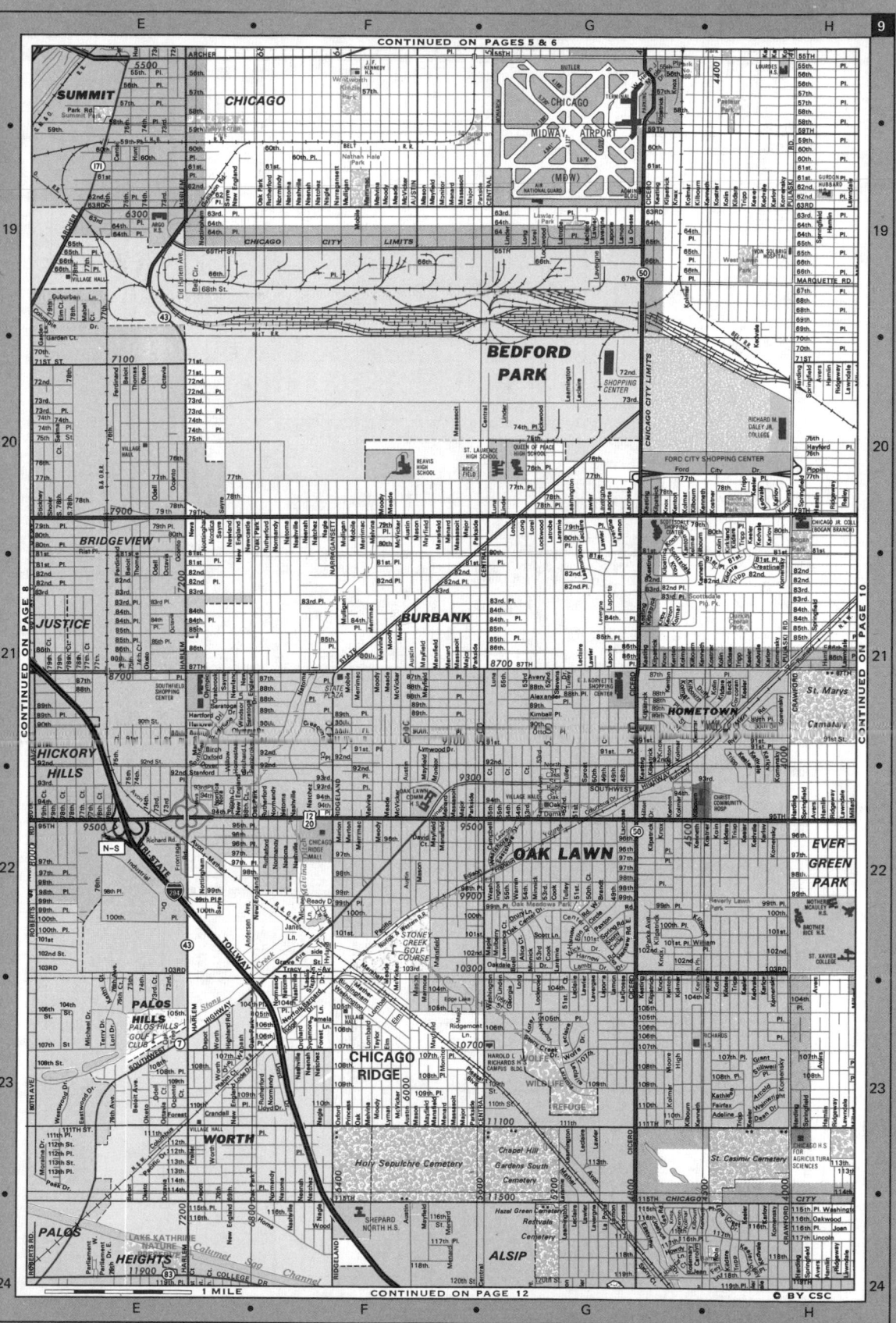

CONTINUED ON PAGE 8
CONTINUED ON PAGE 10

SUMMIT

CHICAGO

CHICAGO MIDWAY AIRPORT (MDW)

CHICAGO CITY LIMITS

BEDFORD PARK

BRIDGEVIEW

JUSTICE

BURBANK

HICKORY HILLS

HOMETOWN

OAK LAWN

EVER GREEN PARK

PALOS HILLS

CHICAGO RIDGE

WORTH

ALSIP

PALOS HEIGHTS

1 MILE

© BY CSC

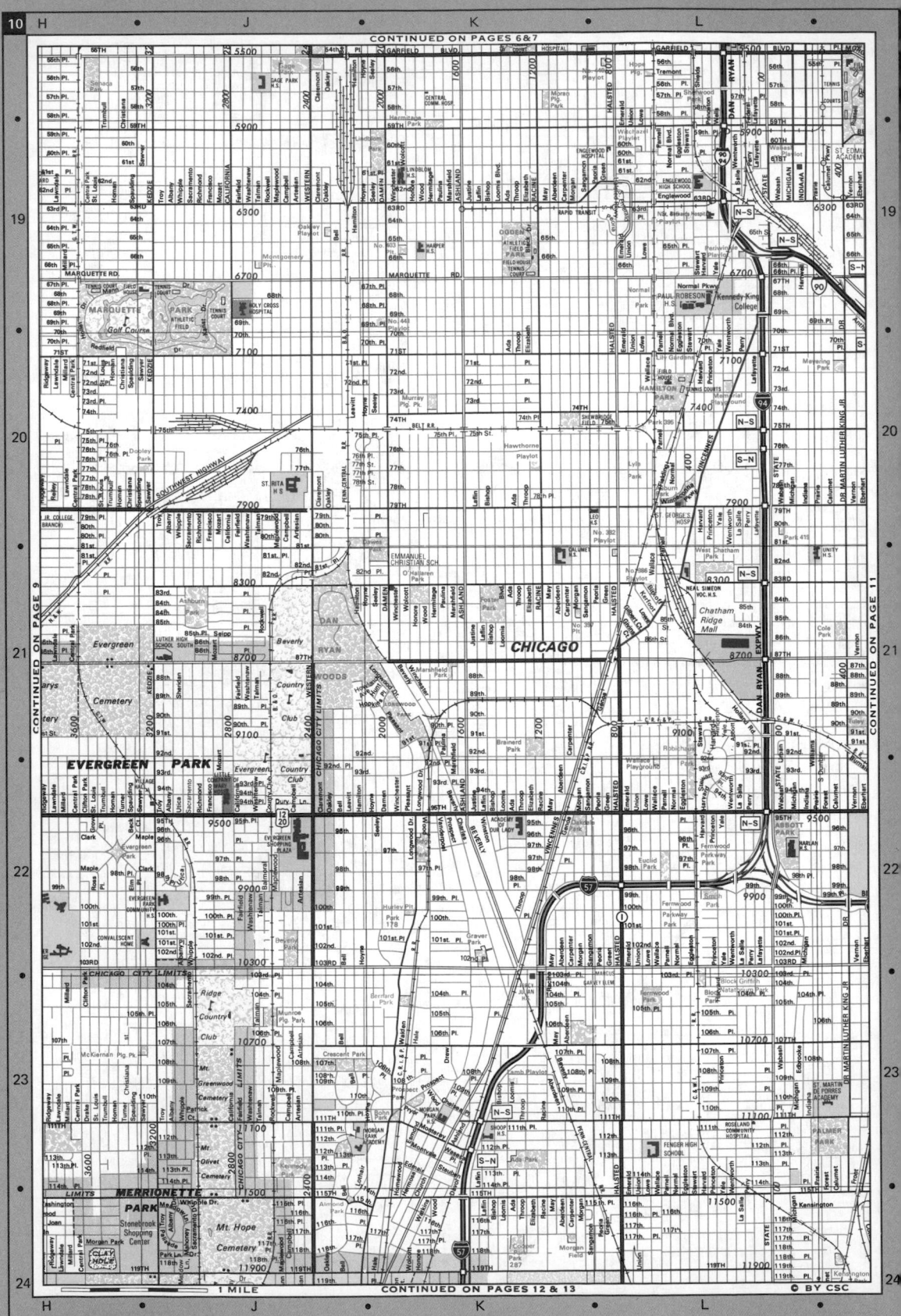

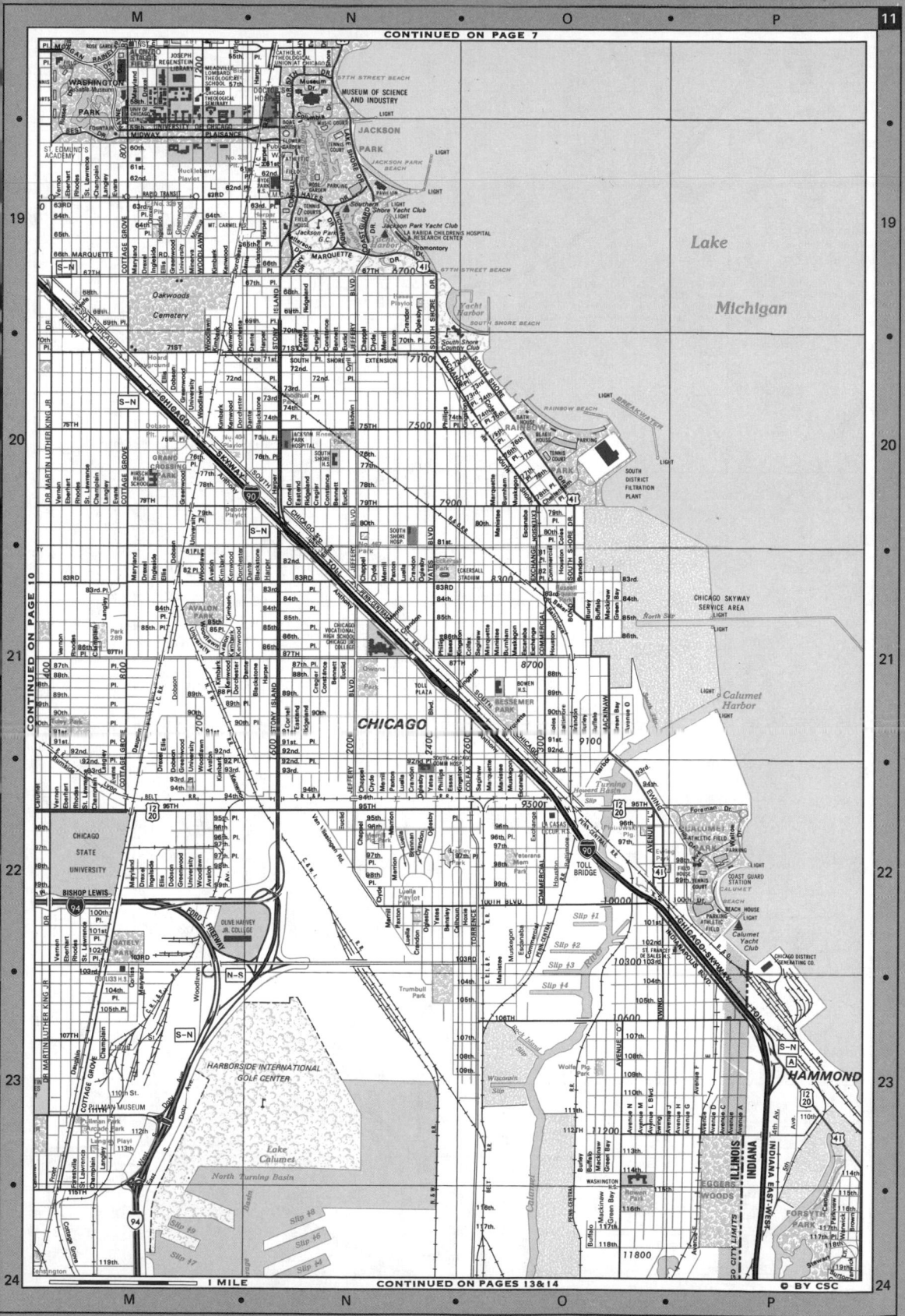

CONTINUED ON PAGE 10

1 MILE

© BY CSC

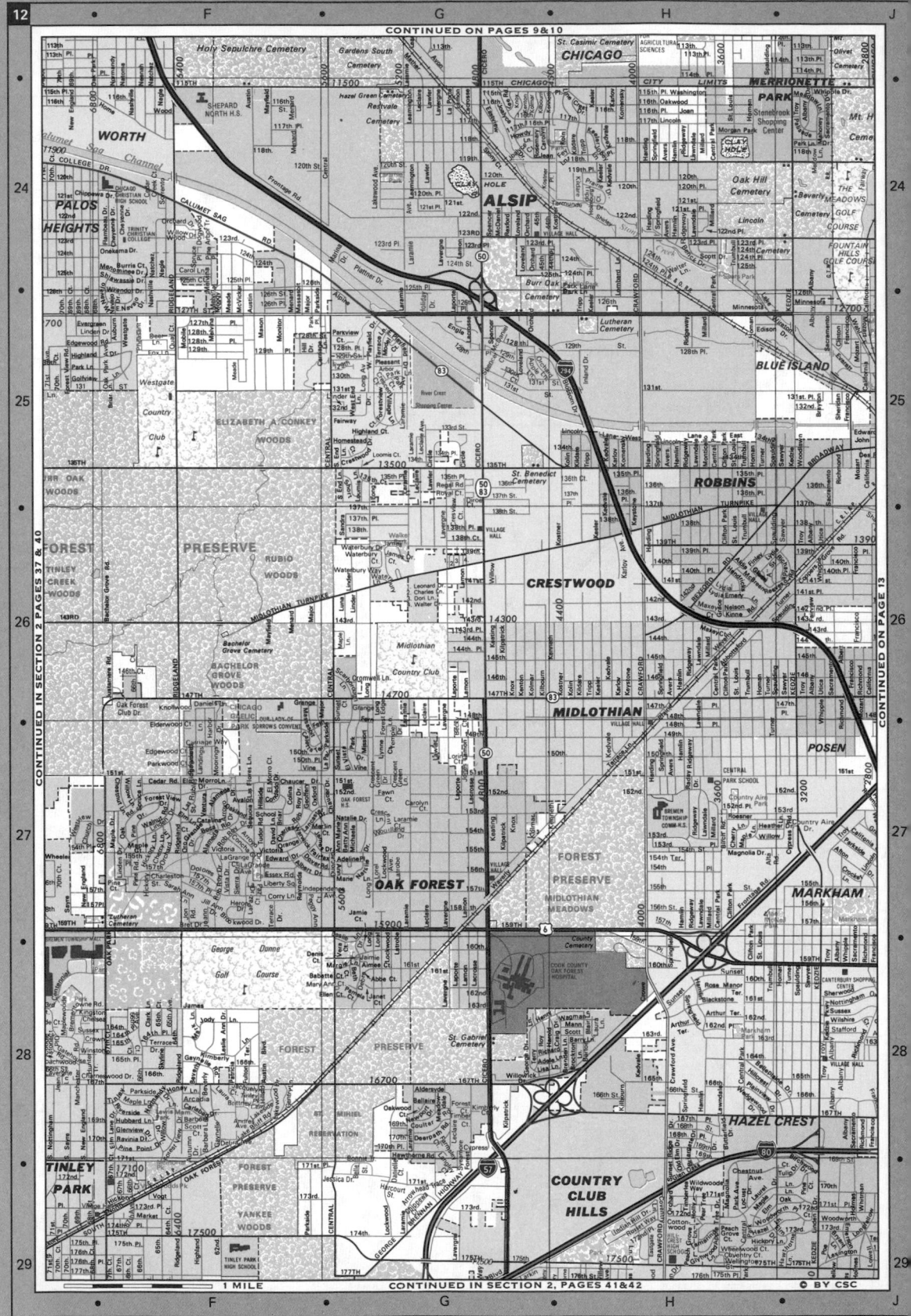

CONTINUED ON PAGE 11

CONTINUED ON PAGE 13

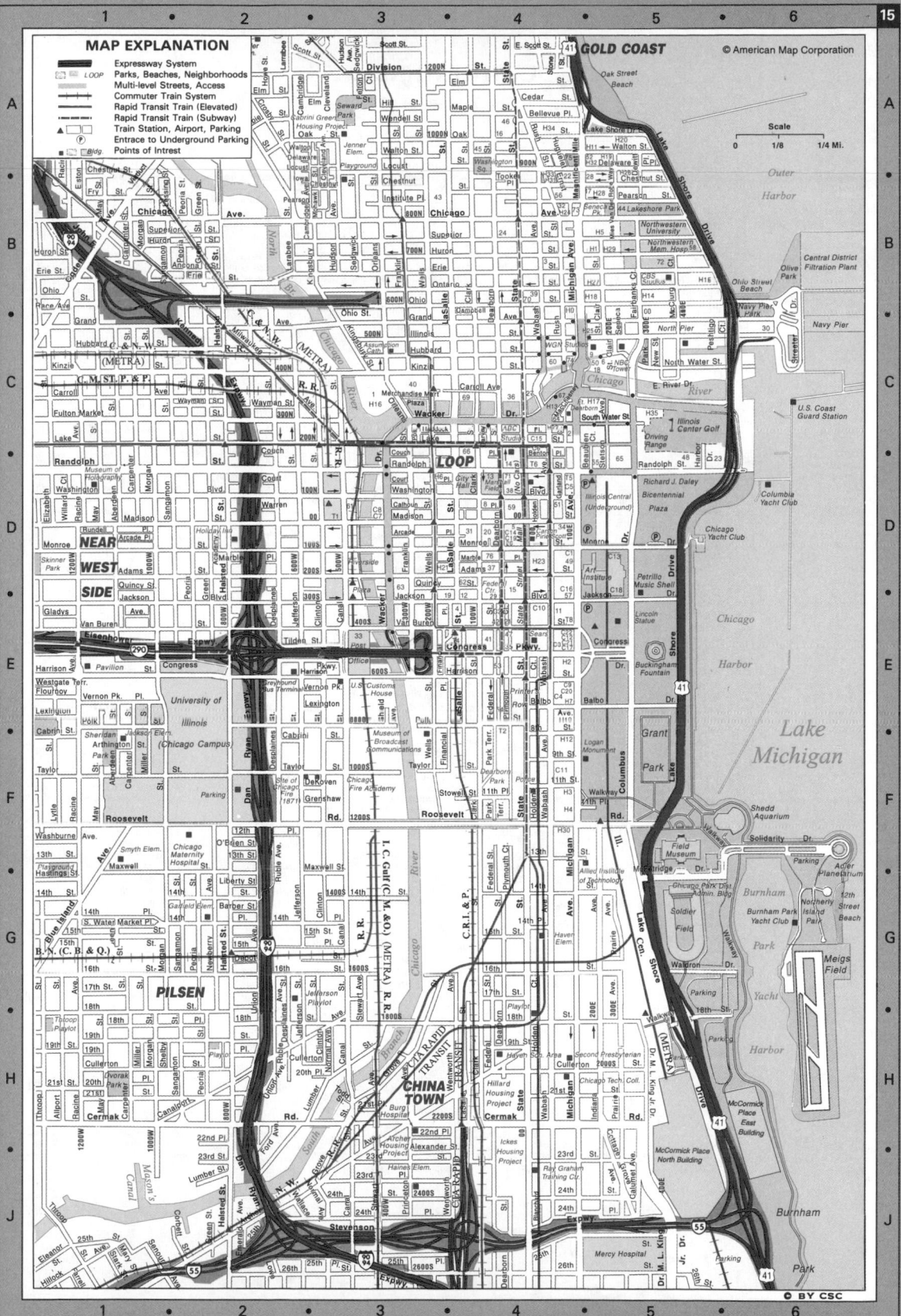

# DOWNTOWN INDEX
## See Map Page 15

**STREETS**

Aberdeen St. . . . . . . . . . D,G1
Academy Pl. . . . . . . . . . . . D2
Adams . . . . . . . . . . . . . . D1,4
Adlai Stevenson Expwy. . . J3,5
Alexander St. . . . . . . . . . . . H3
Allport St. . . . . . . . . . . . . . H1
Ancona St. . . . . . . . . . . . . B2
Arcade Pl. . . . . . . . . . . . . . D1
Archer Ave. . . . . . . . . . . J2,H3
Arthington St. . . . . . . . . . . F1
Astor St. . . . . . . . . . . . . . . A4
Balbo Ave. . . . . . . . . . . . . E4
Balbo Dr. . . . . . . . . . . . . . E5
Barber St. . . . . . . . . . . . . G2
Beaubien Ct. . . . . . . . . . . D4
Bellevue Pl. . . . . . . . . . . . A4
Benton St. . . . . . . . . . . . . C4
Blanchard Ct. . . . . . . . . . . J4
Blue Island Ave. . . . . . . . . G1
Cabrini St. . . . . . . . . . . . F1,2
Calhoun Pl. . . . . . . . . . . . D3
Calumet Ave. . . . . . . . . . . J5
Cambridge Ave. . . . . . . . . B2
Campbell Pl. . . . . . . . . . . . B4
Canal St. . . . . . . . . . . . . E,J3
Canalport Ave. . . . . . . . . H1,3
Carpenter St. . . . . . . . . B,F,H1
Carroll Ave. . . . . . . . . . . C1,4
Cedar St. . . . . . . . . . . . . . A4
Cermak Rd. . . . . . . . . . . H1,4
Chestnut St. . . . . . . . . . B3,5
Chicago Ave. . . . . . . . . . . B1,3
Clark St. . . . . . . . . . . B,D,H4
Cleveland Ave. . . . . . . . . . A3
Clinton St. . . . . . . . . . . . E,H3
Columbus Dr. . . . . . . . . . . F5
Congress Dr. . . . . . . . . . . E5
Congress Pkwy. . . . . . . . . E1,4
Congress Plaza Dr. . . . . . . E5
Corbett St. . . . . . . . . . . . . J2
Cottage Grove Ave. . . . . H,J5
Couch Pl. . . . . . . . . . . . . . C2
Court Pl. . . . . . . . . . . . . . . D2
Cullerton St. . . . . . . . . . . H1,5
Dan Ryan Expwy. . . . . . F,G,H2
DeKoven St. . . . . . . . . . . F2,3
Dearborn St. . . . . . . . . B,E,J4
Delaware Pl. . . . . . . . . . . A2,5
Depot St. . . . . . . . . . . . . . G2,3
Des Plaines St. . . . . . . . . E,H2
Dewitt Pl. . . . . . . . . . . . . . A5
Division St. . . . . . . . . . . . A3,4
Dr. M. L. King Jr. Dr. . . . . H,J5
E. River Dr. . . . . . . . . . . . . C5
Eisenhower Expwy. . . . . . E1,3
Eleanor St. . . . . . . . . . . . . J1
Elizabeth St. . . . . . . . . . . . D1
Elm St. . . . . . . . . . . . . . . A3,4
Emerald Ave. . . . . . . . . . . J2
Erie St. . . . . . . . . . . . . . . B1,3
Ernst Ct. . . . . . . . . . . . . . B4
Fairbanks Ct. . . . . . . . . . . B5
Federal St. . . . . . . . . . . . E,H4
Felton Ct. . . . . . . . . . . . . A3
Field Blvd. . . . . . . . . . . . . C5
Field Plaza Dr. . . . . . . . . . F5
Financial Pl. . . . . . . . . . . E,F3
Flournoy St. . . . . . . . . . . . E1
Ford Ave. . . . . . . . . . . . . . H2
Franklin . . . . . . . . . . . . . B,D3
Fulton Market . . . . . . . . . . C1
Garland Ct. . . . . . . . . . . . D4
Garvey St. . . . . . . . . . . . . C4
Gladys Ave. . . . . . . . . . . . E1
Grand Ave. . . . . . . . . . . . C1,3
Green St. . . . . . . . . . . . B,E,J2
Grenshaw St. . . . . . . . . . . F3
Grove St. . . . . . . . . . . . . H,J3
Haddock Pl. . . . . . . . . . . . C3
Halsted St. . . . . . . . . . C,G,J2
Harbor Dr. . . . . . . . . . . . . C5
Harrison St. . . . . . . . . . . E1,4
Hastings St. . . . . . . . . . . . G1
Hill St. . . . . . . . . . . . . . . . A3
Hillock Ave. . . . . . . . . . . . J1
Holden Ct. . . . . . . . . . . D,F,H4
Hubbard St. . . . . . . . . . . C1,3

Hudson Ave. . . . . . . . . . . A,B3
Huguelet Pl. . . . . . . . . . . . A4
Huron St. . . . . . . . . . . . . B1,3
Illinois St. . . . . . . . . . . . . C3
Indiana Ave. . . . . . . . . . . . H5
Institute Pl. . . . . . . . . . . . B3
Iowa St. . . . . . . . . . . . . . . B2
Jackson Blvd. . . . . . . . . . E1,3
Jackson Dr. . . . . . . . . . . . E5
Jefferson St. . . . . . . . . . . E,H2
John F. Kennedy Expwy. . B1,C2
Kingsbury St. . . . . . . . . . B,C3
Kinzie St. . . . . . . . . . . . . C1,3
LaSalle St. . . . . . . . . B3,E,H4
Lake Park Ave. . . . . . . . . . J5
Lake Shore Drive . . A,E,G5
Lake St. . . . . . . . . . . . . . C1,3
Larabee St. . . . . . . . . . . . B2
Lexington St. . . . . . . . . . E1,3
Liberty St. . . . . . . . . . . . . G2
Locust St. . . . . . . . . . . . . A3
Lowe Ave. . . . . . . . . . . . . J2
Lumber St. . . . . . . . . . . H3,J2
Lytle St. . . . . . . . . . . . . . . F1
MacChesney Ct. . . . . . . . . C4
Madison St. . . . . . . . . . . D1,3
Magnificent Mile . . . . . . . A,B4
Maple St. . . . . . . . . . . . . . A4
Marble Pl. . . . . . . . . . . . . D2
Mary St. . . . . . . . . . . . . . . J1
Maxwell St. . . . . . . . . . . . F1,3
May St. . . . . . . . . . . . . D,F,H1
McClurg Ct. . . . . . . . . . . . B5
McFetridge Dr. . . . . . . . . . G5
Merchandise Mart Plaza . . C3
Michigan Ave. . . . . . . . A,F,H4
Mies Van Der Rohe Way . . B5
Miller St. . . . . . . . . . . . . . F,H1
Milwaukee Ave. . . . . . . . . A3
Mohawk St. . . . . . . . . . . . B3
Monroe Dr. . . . . . . . . . . . . D5
Monroe St. . . . . . . . . . . . D1,4
Morgan St. . . . . . . . . . B,D,H1
New St. . . . . . . . . . . . . . . C5
Newberry Ave. . . . . . . . . . G2
Normal Ave. . . . . . . . . . H,J3
North Water St. . . . . . . . . . C5
O'Brien St. . . . . . . . . . . . . F2
Oak St. . . . . . . . . . . . . . . A2,4
Ogden Ave. . . . . . . . . . . . B1
Ohio St. . . . . . . . . . . . . . B1,3
Ontario St. . . . . . . . . . . . . B3
Orleans St. . . . . . . . . . . . . B3
Park Terr. . . . . . . . . . . . . . F4
Pearson St. . . . . . . . . . . B2,5
Peoria St. . . . . . . . . . . B,D,H2
Peshtigo Ct. . . . . . . . . . . . C5
Plymouth Ct. . . . . . . . . . . E,G4
Polk St. . . . . . . . . . . . . . . E1,3
Post Pl. . . . . . . . . . . . . . . C3
Prairie Ave. . . . . . . . . . . . H5
Princeton Ave. . . . . . . . . . J3
Quincy St. . . . . . . . . . . . D1,3
Race Ave. . . . . . . . . . . . . B1
Racine Ave. . . . . . . . . . D,F,H1
Randolph St. . . . . . . . . . D1,5
Roosevelt Dr. . . . . . . . . . . F5
Roosevelt Rd. . . . . . . . . . F1,3
Ruble Ave. . . . . . . . . . . G,H2
Rundell Pl. . . . . . . . . . . . . D1
Rush St. . . . . . . . . . . . . . A,C4
Sangamon St. . . . . . . B,D1,G2
Scott St. . . . . . . . . . . . . . A2,3
Sedgwick St. . . . . . . . . . . A,B3
Seneca St. . . . . . . . . . . . . C5
Senour Ave. . . . . . . . . . . . J1
Shelby St. . . . . . . . . . . . . H1
Shield Ave. . . . . . . . . . . . E3
Solidarity Dr. . . . . . . . . . . F6
South Water Market Pl. . . . G1
St. Clair St. . . . . . . . . . . B,C5
Stark St. . . . . . . . . . . . . . J1
State St. . . . . . . . . . A,F,H4
Stetson Ave. . . . . . . . . . . C,D5
Stewart Ave. . . . . . . . . G,H,J3
Stone St. . . . . . . . . . . . . . A4
Stowell St. . . . . . . . . . . . . F4
Streeter Dr. . . . . . . . . . . . C6

Superior St. . . . . . . . . . . . B1,3
Taylor St. . . . . . . . . . . . . F1,3
Throop St. . . . . . . . . . . . H,J1
Tilden St. . . . . . . . . . . . . . E2
Todd St. . . . . . . . . . . . . . . H3
Tooker Pl. . . . . . . . . . . . . B4
Union Ave. . . . . . . . . . . . . H2
Van Buren St. . . . . . . . . . E1,3
Vernon Pk. Pl. . . . . . . . . . E1,3
Wabash Ave. . . . . . . . B,E,H4
Wacker Dr. . . . . . . . . . C3,5,E3
Wacker Pl. . . . . . . . . . . . . C5
Waldron Dr. . . . . . . . . . . . G5
Wallace St. . . . . . . . . . . . J2
Walton St. . . . . . . . . . . . A2,5
Warren Ave. . . . . . . . . . . C2
Washburne Ave. . . . . . . . . F1
Washington Blvd. . . . . . . D1,3
Water St. . . . . . . . . . . . . . C5
Wayman St. . . . . . . . . . . . C2
Wells St. . . . . . . . . . . . . B,F3
Wendell St. . . . . . . . . . . . A3
Wentworth Ave. . . . . . . . H,J4
Westgate Terr. . . . . . . . . . E1
Willard Ct. . . . . . . . . . . . . D1
8th St. . . . . . . . . . . . . . . . E4
9th St. . . . . . . . . . . . . . . . F4
11th Pl. . . . . . . . . . . . . . . F4,5
11th St. . . . . . . . . . . . . . . F4
12th Pl. . . . . . . . . . . . . . . F2
13th St. . . . . . . . . . . . . . . F1,4
14th Pl. . . . . . . . . . . . . . . G1,4
14th St. . . . . . . . . . . . . . . G1,4
15th Pl. . . . . . . . . . . . . . . G2,3
15th St. . . . . . . . . . . . . . . G1,4
16th St. . . . . . . . . . . . . . . G1,4
17th St. . . . . . . . . . . . . . . G1,4
18th Pl. . . . . . . . . . . . . . . H1,2
18th St. . . . . . . . . . . . . . G1,H4
19th Pl. . . . . . . . . . . . . . . H1,2
19th St. . . . . . . . . . . . . . . H1,4
20th Pl. . . . . . . . . . . . . . . H1,3
21st Pl. . . . . . . . . . . . . . . H3
21st St. . . . . . . . . . . . . . . H1,4
22nd Pl. . . . . . . . . . . . . . . H2,3
23rd Pl. . . . . . . . . . . . . . . J3
23rd St. . . . . . . . . . . . . H5,6,J2
24th Pl. . . . . . . . . . . . . . . J3,5
24th St. . . . . . . . . . . . . . . J3,4
25th Pl. . . . . . . . . . . . . . . J2,3
25th St. . . . . . . . . . . . . . . J1
26th St. . . . . . . . . . . . . . J2,5

**CULTURAL FACILITIES**

Adler Planetarium & Astronomy
   Museum . . . . . . . . . . . F6
American Conservatory of
   Music,C1 . . . . . . . . . . D4
ArchiCenter,C2 . . . . . . . . . E4
Art Institute . . . . . . . . . . . D5
Auditorium Theatre,C3 . . . . E4
Blackstone Theatre,C4 . . . . E4
Chicago Public Library &
   Cultural Center,C5 . . . . D4
Chicago Theatre,C6 . . . . . . C4
Civic Opera House,C7 . . . . D3
Civic Theatre,C8 . . . . . . . . D3
Drury Lane Theatre at Water
   Tower Place,17 . . . . . . . B5
Eleventh (11th) Street
   Theatre,C11 . . . . . . . . . F4
Field Museum of Natural History
   . . . . . . . . . . . . . . . . . F5
Fine Arts Bldg.,C12 . . . . . . E4
Goodman Theatre,C13 . . . . D5
HOT TIX Booth,C14 . . . . . . D4
Harold Washington Library . E4
Museum of Contemporary
   Art,44 . . . . . . . . . . . . . B5
Newberry Library,45 . . . . . . A4
Orchestra Hall,C16 . . . . . . D4
Petrillo Music Shell . . . . . . D5
Shedd Aquarium . . . . . . . . F6
Shubert Theatre,C19 . . . . . D4
Spertus College & Museum of
   Judaica,C20 . . . . . . . . E4
Studebaker Theatre,C21 . . . E4
World Playhouse,C22 . . . . E4

**DRAINAGE**

Burnham Park Yacht Harbor
   . . . . . . . . . . . . . . . . G,H6
Chicago Harbor . . . . . . . . . E6
Chicago River . . . . . . . . . C3,5
Lake Michigan . . . . . . . . . . F6
Mason's Canal . . . . . . . . . J1
North Branch Chicago
   River . . . . . . . . . . . B2,C3
Ogden Slip . . . . . . . . . . . . C5
Outer Harbor (Lake Michigan)
   . . . . . . . . . . . . . . . A5,6,B6
South Branch Chicago River
   . . . . . . . . . . . . . . D,F3,J1
Turning Basin (Chicago River)
   . . . . . . . . . . . . . . . . . . C3
Turning Basin (Lake Michigan)
   . . . . . . . . . . . . . . . . . . C6

**HOTELS**

Allerton,H1 . . . . . . . . . . . . B5
Americana Congress,H2 . . . E4
Ascot House,H3 . . . . . . . . . F4
Avenue Hotel,H4 . . . . . . . . F4
Barclay Chicago,H5 . . . . . . B5
Bismarck,H6 . . . . . . . . . . . D3
Blackstone,H7 . . . . . . . . . . E4
Chicago Hilton,H10 . . . . . . . E4
Chicago Lakeshore,H8 . . . . B5
Chicago Marriott,H9 . . . . . . B4
Drake,H11 . . . . . . . . . . . . A5
Essex Inn,H12 . . . . . . . . . . F4
Executive House,H13 . . . . . C4
Holiday Inn . . . . . . . . . . . . D2
Holiday Inn Chicago City
   Centre,H14 . . . . . . . . . B5
Holiday Inn Lake Shore
   Drive,H15 . . . . . . . . . . B5
Holiday Inn Mart Plaza,H16  C3
Hyatt Regency Chicago,H17 C5
Inn of Chicago,H18 . . . . . . B5
Knickerbocker Chicago,H19 A5
Mayfair Regent,H20 . . . . . . A5
Midland,H21 . . . . . . . . . . . D3
Oxford House,H22 . . . . . . . C4
Palmer House,H23 . . . . . . . D4
Park Hyatt on Water Tower
   Square,H24 . . . . . . . . . B4
Radisson Chicago,H25 . . . . C5
Raphael,H26 . . . . . . . . . . . B5
Richmont,H27 . . . . . . . . . . B5
Ritz-Carlton,H28 . . . . . . . . B5
Sheraton-Plaza,H29 . . . . . . B5
Travelodge Downtown,H30 . N4
Tremont,H31 . . . . . . . . . . . B4
Westin Chicago,H32 . . . . . . A5
Westin River North Hotel,H34
   . . . . . . . . . . . . . . . . . . C4
Whitehall,H33 . . . . . . . . . . B4

**POINTS OF INTEREST**

ABC Studios . . . . . . . . . . . C4
Apparel Center,1 . . . . . . . . C3
Archer Housing Project . . . . H3
Assumption Roman Catholic
   Church . . . . . . . . . . . . C3
Bloomingdale's,75 . . . . . . . A5
Buckingham Fountain . . . . . E5
Burnham Park Yacht Club . . G6
CBS Studios . . . . . . . . . . . B5
CNA Plaza,11 . . . . . . . . . . E4
Cabrini Green Housing Project
   . . . . . . . . . . . . . . . . . . A3
Carbide & Carbon Bldg.,2 . . C4
Carson Pirie Scott . . . . . . . D4
Cathedral of St. James,3 . . . B4
Central District Filtration Plant
   . . . . . . . . . . . . . . . . . . B6
Chicago Board of Trade,4 . . E4
Chicago Building,5 . . . . . . . D4
Chicago Park District
   Administration Bldg. . . G5,6
Chicago Sun Times Building,7
   . . . . . . . . . . . . . . . . . . C4
Chicago Temple,8 . . . . . . . D4
Chicago Tribune Tower,9 . . . C5
Chicago Yacht Club . . . . . . D5

China Town . . . . . . . . . . . . H3
City Hall/County Bldg.,10 . . . D4
Columbia Yacht Club . . . . . D6
Continental Illinois National
   Bank,12 . . . . . . . . . . . . E4
Daley Center (New Civic
   Center),13 . . . . . . . . . . D4
Daley Plaza . . . . . . . . . . . D5
Delaware Building,14 . . . . . D4
Dirksen Federal Bldg.,15 . . D4
Equitable Building,18 . . . . . C5
Federal Center . . . . . . . . . E4
Federal Reserve Bank,19 . . E3
First National Plaza,20 . . . . D4
Fisher Building,21 . . . . . . . E4
Fourth Presbyterian Church,22
   . . . . . . . . . . . . . . . . . . B4
Gold Coast . . . . . . . . . . . . A5
Harbor Point,23 . . . . . . . . . D5
Hillard Housing Project . . . . H4
Holy Name Cathedral,24 . . . B4
IBM Building,27 . . . . . . . . . C4
Ickes Housing Project . . . H,J4
Inland Steel Bldg.,26 . . . . . D4
John Hancock Center,28 . . . B5
Kluczynski Federal Building,29
   . . . . . . . . . . . . . . . . . . E4
Lake Point Tower,30 . . . . . . C6
Lincoln Statue . . . . . . . . . . E5
Logan Monument . . . . . . . . F5
Loop . . . . . . . . . . . . . . . D3,4
Loop Synagogue,31 . . . . . . D4
Main Post Office,33 . . . . . . E3
Mallers Building,34 . . . . . . D4
Manhattan Bldg.,35 . . . . . . E4
Marina City,36 . . . . . . . . . . C4
Marquette Bldg.,37 . . . . . . . D4
Marshall Field . . . . . . . . . . D4
McCarthy Bldg.,38 . . . . . . . D4
McCormick Place . . . . . . . . H6
Medinah Temple,39 . . . . . . B4
Meigs Field . . . . . . . . . . . . G6
Merchandise Mart,40 . . . . . C3
Mercy Hospital . . . . . . . . . . J5
Metropolitan Correctional
   Center,41 . . . . . . . . . . E4
Monadnock Bldg.,42 . . . . . E4
Moody Bible Institute,43 . . . B3
Museum of Broadcast
   Communications . . . . . . F3
Museum of Holography . . . . D1
NBC Tower . . . . . . . . . . . . C5
Navy Pier . . . . . . . . . . . . . C6
Near West Side . . . . . . . . . D1
Neiman Marcus,76 . . . . . . . B5
Newberry Plaza,44 . . . . . . . A4
North Pier . . . . . . . . . . . . . C5
Northwestern Mem. Hosp. . B5
Old Colony Bldg.,47 . . . . . . E4
Original Site of Fort Dearborn
   . . . . . . . . . . . . . . . . . . C4
Outer Drive East,48 . . . . . . C5
Pavilion . . . . . . . . . . . . . . E1
Peoples Gas Bldg.,49 . . . . . D4
Pilsen . . . . . . . . . . . . . . G1,2
Pioneer Court,50 . . . . . . . . C5
Pittsfield Building,51 . . . . . . D4
Playboy Building,52 . . . . . . A5
Pontiac Building,53 . . . . . . . E4
Printer's Row . . . . . . . . . . . E4
Printer's Row Printing
   Museum,54 . . . . . . . . . E4
Prudential Bldg.,55 . . . . . . . D5
Quigley Seminary North,56 . B4
Railway Exchange Building,57
   . . . . . . . . . . . . . . . . . . E4
Rehabilitation Institute of
   Chicago,58 . . . . . . . . . B5
Reliance Building,59 . . . . . . D4
River Plaza,60 . . . . . . . . . . D4
Riverside Plaza,61 . . . . . . . D3
Rookery,62 . . . . . . . . . . . . E4
Sears . . . . . . . . . . . . . . . . D4
Sears Tower,63 . . . . . . . . . D3
Second Presbyterian . . . . . H4
Seventeenth Church of Christ
   Scientist,64 . . . . . . . . . C4

Site of Chicago Fire in 1871  F2
Soldier Field . . . . . . . . . . . G5
Standard Oil Bldg.,65 . . . . . D5
State of Illinois Bldg.,66 . . . C4
Stone Container Bldg.,67 . . . C4
Time-Life Building,68 . . . . . C5
Traffic Court,69 . . . . . . . . . C4
Tree Studios,70 . . . . . . . . . B4
U.S. Coast Guard Station . . C6
U.S. Custom's House . . . . . E3
Unity Building,71 . . . . . . . . D4
V.A. Lakeside Medical
   Center,72 . . . . . . . . . . B5
WGN Studios . . . . . . . . . . C5
WMAQ Studios . . . . . . . . . C3
Water Tower Visitors
   Center,73 . . . . . . . . . . B4
Wrigley Building,74 . . . . . . . C4
Xerox Centre,75 . . . . . . . . . D4

**PARKS**

Burnham Park . . . . . . . . G,J6
Dvorak Park . . . . . . . . . . . H1
Grant Park . . . . . . . . . . . E,F5
Jane Addams Memorial Park
   . . . . . . . . . . . . . . . . . . B6
Jefferson Playlot . . . . . . . . G3
Lakeshore Park . . . . . . . . . B5
Metro Golf Illinois Center . . C5
Navy Pier Park . . . . . . . . . B6
Northerly Island Park . . . . . G6
Oak Street Beach . . . . . . . A5
Ohio Street Beach . . . . . . . B6
Playground . . . . . . . . . . A3,F1
Playlot . . . . . . . . . . . . . . . H2
Seneca Park . . . . . . . . . . . B5
Seward Park . . . . . . . . . . . A3
Sheridan Park . . . . . . . . . . F1
Skinner Park . . . . . . . . . . . D1
Throop Playlot . . . . . . . . . . H1
Washington Square . . . . . . A4
12th Street Beach . . . . . . . G6

**SCHOOLS**

Allied Institute of Technology
   . . . . . . . . . . . . . . . F4,G5
Chicago Fire Academy . . . . F3
Chicago Technical College
   . . . . . . . . . . . . . . . . H4,5
Columbia College,C9 . . . . . E4
DePaul University (Loop
   Campus),C10 . . . . . . . . E4
Dr. Scholl College of Podiatric
   Medicine,16 . . . . . . . . . A4
Loop College,C15 . . . . . . . C4
Loyola University (Water Twr.
   Campus),32 . . . . . . . . . B4
Moody Bible Institute,43 . . . B3
Northwestern University . . . B5
Dental Sch. . . . . . . . . . . . . B5
J.L. Kellogg Grad Sch. of
   Management . . . . . . . . . B5
Law School . . . . . . . . . . . . B5
Medical Sch. . . . . . . . . . . . B5
Quigley Seminary North,56 . B4
Ray Graham Training Ctr. . . J4
Roosevelt University,C17 . . E4
School of the Art Institute of
   Chicago,C18 . . . . . . . . D5
Spertus College & Museum of
   Judaica,C20 . . . . . . . . E4
University of Illinois (Chicago
   Campus) . . . . . . . . . . . E2

**TRANSPORTATION**

Burnham Parking Area . . G,H5
Chicago & North Western
   Station,T1 . . . . . . . . . . D3
Dearborn Street Station,T2 . E4
Greyhound Terminal . . . . . . D4
Ill. Central Commuter Sta. . D,E
LaSalle Street Station,T4 . . E4
Parking . . . . . . . . . . D4,5,E4
Randolph Street Station,T5 . D4
Union Station,T7 . . . . . . . . D3
Van Buren Street Station,T8 . E4

# INDEX TO CHICAGO AND SURROUNDING CITIES
## See Map Pages 1-14

**ALSIP**
Pages 9,12
STREETS
Alpine . . . . . . . Pg.12 . . . G25
Apple Ln. . . . . Pg.12 . . . G25
Austin . . . . . . Pg.12 . . . F24
Avers . . . . . . Pg.12 . . . H24
Avon . . . . . . . Pg.9 . . . G23
Benck Ct. . . . . Pg.12 . . . H24
Benck Dr. . . . . Pg.12 . . . H24
Blossom Dr. . . . Pg.12 . . . H25
Calumet Sag Rd.
. . . . . . . . . Pg.12 . . . F24
Carolyn . . . . . Pg.12 . . . G24
Central . . . . . Pg.12 . . . G24
Central Park Ave.
. . . . . . . . . Pg.12 . . H24,25
Cicero Ave. . . . Pg.12 . . . G24
Crawford . . . . Pg.12 . . H24,25
Eastview . . . . Pg.12 . . . G24
Engel Rd. . . . . Pg.12 . . . G25
Fey Ln. . . . . . Pg.12 . . . H24
Frontage Rd. . . Pg.12 . . . F24
Hamlin . . . . . . Pg.12 . . . H24
Harding . . . . . Pg.12 . . . H24
Holiday Dr. . . . Pg.12 . . . G25
Holmburg Ct. . . Pg.12 . . . H24
Homan Ave. . . . Pg.12 . . . H25
Howdy Ln. . . . . Pg.12 . . . G24
Inland Dr. . . . . Pg.12 . . . H25
Jean . . . . . . . Pg.12 . . . G24
Joalyce Ct. . . . Pg.12 . . . G24
Joalyce Dr. . . . Pg.12 . . . G24
Jobey Ln. . . . . Pg.12 . . . H24
Karlov . . . . . . Pg.12 . . . H24
Kedvale . . . . . Pg.12 . . . H24
Kedzie . . . . . . Pg.12 . . . J25
Keeler . . . . . . Pg.12 . . H24,25
Kenneth . . . . . Pg.12 . . . G24
Kenton . . . . . . Pg.12 . . . G24
Kilbourne . . . . Pg.12 . . . G24
Kildare . . . . . Pg.12 . . . H24
Knox . . . . . . . Pg.12 . . . G24
Kolmar . . . . . . Pg.12 . . . H24
Komensky . . . . Pg.12 . . . H24
Kostner Ave. . . Pg.12 . . . G24
Kostner Pl. . . . Pg.12 . . . G24
La Porte . . . . . Pg.12 . . . G24
Lacrosse . . . . Pg.12 . . C24,25
Lake Ave. . . . . Pg.12 . . . G24
Lamon . . . . . . Pg.12 . . . G24
Laramie . . . . . Pg.9,12 . . G25
Lavergne . . . . Pg.12 . . . G24
Lawler . . . . . . Pg.9,12 . G23,24
Lawndale . . . . Pg.12 . . . H24
Leamington . . . Pg.9,12 . G23,24
Leclaire . . . . . Pg.9,12 . G23,24
Line Crest Dr. . . Pg.12 . . . H24
Lockwood Ave. . Pg.12 . . . G24
Lombard Ln. . . . Pg.12 . . . H24
Loveland Ave. . . Pg.12 . . . G24
Loveland St. . . . Pg.12 . . . G25
Marina Dr. . . . . Pg.12 . . . G25
Mather . . . . . . Pg.9 . . . G23
Mayfield . . . . . Pg.12 . . . F24
McDaniel Ave. . . Pg.12 . . . G24
McDaniel St. . . . Pg.12 . . . G25
Menard . . . . . . Pg.12 . . . F24
Millard . . . . . . Pg.12 . . H24,25
Orchard Ln. . . . Pg.12 . . . H24
Orchard St. . . . Pg.12 . . . G24
Park Lane Dr. . . Pg.12 . . . H24
Plattner Dr. . . . Pg.12 . . . G24
Prairie Dr. . . . . Pg.12 . . . H24
Rexford . . . . . Pg.12 . . . F24
Ridgeland . . . . Pg.12 . . . F24
Ridgeway . . . . Pg.12 . . H24,25
Rosemary . . . . Pg.12 . . . G24
Scott Dr. . . . . . Pg.12 . . . H24
Shirley Ln. . . . . Pg.12 . . . H24
Spencer Ct. . . . Pg.12 . . . G24
Spencer St. . . . Pg.12 . . . G25
Springfield . . . . Pg.12 . . . H24
Stony Ct. . . . . Pg.12 . . . G24
Termunde Dr. . . Pg.12 . . . H24
Tripp . . . . . . . Pg.12 . . H24,25
Trumbull . . . . . Pg.12 . . . H24
Walter Ln. . . . . Pg.12 . . . H24
44th Pl. . . . . . Pg.12 . . . G24
45th St. . . . . . Pg.12 . . . G24
111th Pl. . . . . Pg.9 . . . G23
113th St. . . . . Pg.12 . . . G23
115th Pl. . . . . Pg.12 . . G,H24
115th St. . . . . Pg.12 . . F,H24
116th Pl. . . . . Pg.12 . . F,H24
116th St. . . . . Pg.12 . . . H24
117th Pl. . . . . Pg.12 . . F,G24
117th St. . . . . Pg.12 . . F,H24
118th St. . . . . Pg.12 . . F,H24
119th Pl. . . . . Pg.12 . . . H24
119th St. . . . . Pg.12 . . . G24
120th Pl. . . . . Pg.12 . . G,H24
120th St. . . . . Pg.12 . . G,H24
121st Pl. . . . . Pg.12 . . G,H24
121st St. . . . . Pg.12 . . G,H24
122nd St. . . . . Pg.12 . . . H24
123rd Pl. . . . . Pg.12 . . G,H24

123rd Pl. . . . . Pg.12 . . . G24
123rd St. . . . . Pg.12 . . . G24
124th Pl. . . . . Pg.12 . . G,H24
124th St. . . . . Pg.12 . . F,H24
125th Pl. . . . . Pg.12 . . . G25
125th St. . . . . Pg.12 . . G,H24
126th Pl. . . . . Pg.12 . . F,H25
126th St. . . . . Pg.12 . . F,H25
127th St. . . . . Pg.12 . . . G25
128th Pl. . . . . Pg.12 . . . H25
128th St. . . . . Pg.12 . . . G25
129th St. . . . . Pg.12 . . G,H25
130th St. . . . . Pg.12 . . . G25
131st St. . . . . Pg.12 . . G,H25
CEMETERIES
Burr Oak Cem. . Pg.12 . . . G24
Chapel Hill Gardens South Cem.
. . . . . . . . . Pg.9 . . . G23
Hazel Green Cem.
. . . . . . . . . Pg.12 . . . G24
Holy Sepulchre Cem.
. . . . . . . . . Pg.9 . . . F23
Lincoln Cem. . . Pg.12 . . . H24
Lutheran Cem. . Pg.12 . . . H25
Oak Hill Cem. . . Pg.12 . . . H24
Restvale Cem. . Pg.12 . . . G24
PARKS
Laramie Pk. . . . Pg.12 . . . G24
SCHOOLS
Moraine Valley Comm. Jr.
College . . . Pg.12 . . . F24
Shephard North H.S. . . . . F24
MISCELLANEOUS
Village Hall . . . . Pg.12 . . . G24

**BEDFORD PARK**
Page 9
STREETS
Archer . . . . . . . . . . . . . E19
Austin . . . . . . . . . . . . . F19
Belt Cir. . . . . . . . . . . . . E19
Central . . . . . . . . . . G19,20
Harlem Ave. . . . . . . . . . E19
Lavergne . . . . . . . . . . . G19
Leamington . . . . . . . . . G20
Leclaire . . . . . . . . . . . . G20
Linder . . . . . . . . . . . . . G20
Lockwood . . . . . . . . . . G20
Major . . . . . . . . . . . . . F19
Massasoit . . . . . . . . . . F20
Melvina . . . . . . . . . . . . F19
Menard . . . . . . . . . . . . F19
Narragansett . . . . . . . . F19
Nashville . . . . . . . . . . . F19
Natchez . . . . . . . . . . . . F19
Oak Park . . . . . . . . . . . F19
Old Harlem Ave. . . . . . . E19
State . . . . . . . . . . . . . G20
64th Pl. . . . . . . . . . . . . E19
64th St. . . . . . . . . . . . . E19
65th St. . . . . . . . . . . . . E19
65th Pl. . . . . . . . . . . E-G19
66th Pl. . . . . . . . . . . E-G19
66th St. . . . . . . . . . . E-G19
67th St. . . . . . . . . . . . G19
68th St. . . . . . . . . . . . . E19
71st St. . . . . . . . . . . . E20
72nd St. . . . . . . . . . . . G20
73rd St. . . . . . . . . . . F,G20
74th Pl. . . . . . . . . . . . G20
75th St. . . . . . . . . . . E,G20
77th Ave. . . . . . . . . . . E19
78th Ave. . . . . . . . . . . E19
SHOPPING CENTERS
Shopping Center . . . . . . . G20
MISCELLANEOUS
Village Hall . . . . . . . . . E19

**BELLWOOD**
Pages 4,5
STREETS
Adams . . . . . . . . . . . . C14
Bellwood . . . . . . . . C13,14
Bohland . . . . . . . . . C13,14
Butterfield Rd. . . . . . . . C14
Castle Dr. . . . . . . . . . . B13
Center Ave. . . . . . . . . . B13
Cernan Dr. . . . . . . . . . C14
Congress . . . . . . . . . . C14
Davis Dr. . . . . . . . . . . B13
Eastern . . . . . . . . . C13,14
Englewood Ave. . . . . B13,14
Erie St. . . . . . . . . . . . B13
Frederick . . . . . . . . . . C14
Gardner Rd. . . . . . . . . C14
Geneva Ave. . . . . . . . . B14
Gladys . . . . . . . . . . . C14
Glos . . . . . . . . . . . . . C14
Grant . . . . . . . . . . . . C13
Granville Ave. . . . . . . . B14
Hyde Park Ave. . . . . . . B14
Jackson . . . . . . . . . . C14
Korrel . . . . . . . . . . . . B14
Linden . . . . . . . . . C13,14

Madison . . . . . . . . . . . C14
Mannheim Rd. . . . . . C13,14
Marik Dr. . . . . . . . . . . . C13
Marshall Ave. . . . . . . . . C13
Marshall Ct. . . . . . . . . . C14
Miami Rd. . . . . . . . . . . C14
Monroe . . . . . . . . . . . . C14
Morris . . . . . . . . . . C13,14
Oak St. . . . . . . . . . . B,C14
Park Ct. . . . . . . . . . . . C14
Railroad Ave. . . . . . . B,C13
Randolph . . . . . . . . . B,C14
Rice . . . . . . . . . . . C13,14
St. Charles Pl. . . . . . . . C13
St. Charles Rd. . . . . . . . C14
St. Paul . . . . . . . . . . . C14
Twining . . . . . . . . . . . B14
Van Buren . . . . . . . . . . C14
Warren . . . . . . . . . . . . C14
Washington Blvd. . . . . . . C14
Wilcox . . . . . . . . . . . . C14
Zuelke Dr. . . . . . . . . . . C14
22nd Ave. . . . . . . . . C13,14
23rd Ave. . . . . . . . . C13,14
24th Ave. . . . . . . . . C13,14
25th St. . . . . . . . . . C13,14
26th Ave. . . . . . . . . . . C13
27th Ave. . . . . . . . . . . C13
28th Ave. . . . . . . . . . . C13
29th Ave. . . . . . . . . . . C13
30th Ave. . . . . . . . . C13,14
31st Ave. . . . . . . . . . . C14
32nd Ave. . . . . . . . . . . C14
46th Ave. . . . . . . . . B13,14
47th Ave. . . . . . . . . . . B14
48th Ave. . . . . . . . . . . B14
49th Ave. . . . . . . . . . . B13
50th Ave. . . . . . . . . . . B13
51st Ave. . . . . . . . . . . B13
52nd Ave. . . . . . . . . . . B13
PARKS
Playground . . . . . . . . . . C14
MISCELLANEOUS
Village Hall . . . . . . . . . C14

**BERKELEY**
Page 4
STREETS
Albin Terr. . . . . . . . . . . A14
Arthur . . . . . . . . . . A13,14
Ashbel . . . . . . . . . . . . B13
Atwood . . . . . . . . . . A13,14
Birch Ct. . . . . . . . . . . . B14
Bohlander . . . . . . . . . . B13
Burr Oak . . . . . . . . . . . A14
Calvin . . . . . . . . . . . . . A14
Chicago . . . . . . . . . . . B13
Coolidge . . . . . . . . . . . A14
Electric . . . . . . . . . . . . A14
Elm . . . . . . . . . . . . . . A14
Harding . . . . . . . . . . . . A14
Hawthorne . . . . . . . . . . A14
Herbert . . . . . . . . . . A13,14
Hillside . . . . . . . . . . . . B13
Howard . . . . . . . . . . . . B13
Huron . . . . . . . . . . . . . A13
Irving . . . . . . . . . . . . . A14
Jerele . . . . . . . . . . . . . B13
King Dr. . . . . . . . . . . . . A14
Kouba . . . . . . . . . . . . . A14
Lee . . . . . . . . . . . . . . D14
Lind . . . . . . . . . . . . . . A14
Maple . . . . . . . . . . . . . A14
McDermott . . . . . . . . . . B13
Morris . . . . . . . . . . . . . A13
Murray Dr. . . . . . . . . . . A14
Park . . . . . . . . . . . . . . A13
Prospect . . . . . . . . . . . A14
Richard . . . . . . . . . . . . A14
Ridge . . . . . . . . . . . . . A14
Rohde . . . . . . . . . . . . . B14
Rose . . . . . . . . . . . . . . A14
School . . . . . . . . . . . . . A14
Spencer . . . . . . . . . . . . B14
Spenchley . . . . . . . . . . A14
St. Charles Rd. . . . . . . . B13
Sunnyside Dr. . . . . . . . . B13
Superior . . . . . . . . . . . A13
Taft . . . . . . . . . . . . A13,14
Victoria . . . . . . . . . . . . A14
Wolf Rd. . . . . . . . . . . . B13
SCHOOLS
MacArthur Senior H.S. . . . A14
Sunnyside Elem. Sch. . . . B13
MISCELLANEOUS
City Hall . . . . . . . . . . . A14

**BERWYN**
Pages 5,6
STREETS
Cermak Rd. . . . . . . . . . E15
Clarence . . . . . . . . . F15-17
Clinton . . . . . . . . . . E15-17
Cuyler . . . . . . . . . . . F15-17

East . . . . . . . . . . . . F15-17
Elmwood . . . . . . . . . F15-17
Euclid . . . . . . . . . . . F15-17
Fairfield . . . . . . . . . . . . F16
Grove . . . . . . . . . . . E15-17
Gunderson . . . . . . . . F15-17
Harvey . . . . . . . . . . . F15-17
Highland . . . . . . . . . . F16-17
Home . . . . . . . . . . . E15-17
Kenilworth . . . . . . . . E15-17
Lombard . . . . . . . . . E15-17
Maple . . . . . . . . . . . E15-17
Oak Park . . . . . . . . . E15-17
Ogden . . . . . . . . . . . . . E17
Park . . . . . . . . . . . . . . F16
Ridgeland . . . . . . . . . F15-17
Riverside Dr. . . . . . . . . . E16
Roosevelt Rd. . . . . . . . . E15
Scoville . . . . . . . . . . F15-17
Sinclair . . . . . . . . . . . . F16
Stanley . . . . . . . . . . . . E16
Wenonah . . . . . . . . . E15-17
Wesley . . . . . . . . . . F15-17
Windsor . . . . . . . . . . . . E16
Wisconsin . . . . . . . . . E15-17
13th St. . . . . . . . . . . . E15
14th St. . . . . . . . . . . . E15
15th St. . . . . . . . . . . . E15
16th St. . . . . . . . . . . . E15
18th St. . . . . . . . . . . . E15
19th St. . . . . . . . . . . . E15
21st St. . . . . . . . . . . . E15
23rd St. . . . . . . . . . . . E15
24th St. . . . . . . . . . . . F16
25th St. . . . . . . . . . . . F16
26th Pkwy. . . . . . . . . . E16
26th Pl. . . . . . . . . . . . E16
26th St. . . . . . . . . . . . E16
27th Pl. . . . . . . . . . . . E16
27th St. . . . . . . . . . . . E16
28th Pl. . . . . . . . . . . . F16
28th St. . . . . . . . . . . . F16
29th Pl. . . . . . . . . . . . E16
29th St. . . . . . . . . . . E,F16
30th Pl. . . . . . . . . . . . E16
30th St. . . . . . . . . . . . E16
31st St. . . . . . . . . . . . E16
32nd St. . . . . . . . . . . E,F16
33rd St. . . . . . . . . . . . F16
34th St. . . . . . . . . . . . E16
35th St. . . . . . . . . . . . E16
36th St. . . . . . . . . . . . E16
37th St. . . . . . . . . . . . E17
38th St. . . . . . . . . . . . E17
39th St. . . . . . . . . . . . E17
PARKS
Berwyn Park . . . . . . . . . E16
SCHOOLS
Morton West H.S. . . . E16
SHOPPING CENTERS
Cermak Plaza . . . . . . . . E15
MISCELLANEOUS
City Hall . . . . . . . . . . . F16
MacNeal Hosp. . . . . . . . F16

**BLUE ISLAND**
Pages 12,13
STREETS
Ann . . . . . . . . . . . . J24,25
Artesian . . . . . . . . . J24,26
Ashland Ave. . . . . . . . . K25
Berrien . . . . . . . . . . . . K25
Birdsall . . . . . . . . . . . . J25
Broadway . . . . . . . . . . J25
Burr Oak . . . . . . . . . . . J25
California . . . . . . . . . J25,26
Calumet . . . . . . . . . . . K25
Canal . . . . . . . . . . . . . J25
Cass . . . . . . . . . . . . . K25
Central Park . . . . . . . . . H25
Chatham . . . . . . . . . J25,26
Chicago . . . . . . . . . . . J25
Clinton . . . . . . . . . . . . J25
Cochran . . . . . . . . . . . J24
Collins . . . . . . . . . . . . J24
Concord . . . . . . . . . . . K25
Coopers Grove Rd. . . . . K25
Des Plaines . . . . . . . J,K25
Division . . . . . . . . . . K24-26
Duane . . . . . . . . . . . . K25
Edison Dr. . . . . . . . . . . H25
Edward . . . . . . . . . . . J25
Elm Dr. . . . . . . . . . . . J24
Elm St. . . . . . . . . . . J24,25
Everett . . . . . . . . . . . . J25
Fairview . . . . . . . . . . . J25
Florence . . . . . . . . . . . J24
Francisco . . . . . . . . . J25,26
Fulton . . . . . . . . . . . . J25
Girard St. . . . . . . . . . . K25
Greenwood . . . . . . . . . J25
Gregory . . . . . . . . . . J24,25
Grove . . . . . . . . . . . . J25
Gruenwald . . . . . . . . . . J24
Hadley . . . . . . . . . . . . K25

High . . . . . . . . . . . . J,K25
Highland . . . . . . . . . . . J25
Homan . . . . . . . . . . . . H25
Honore . . . . . . . . . . . . K25
Hoyne . . . . . . . . . . . . K25
Illinois . . . . . . . . . . . . K25
Irving . . . . . . . . . . . J24,25
Jamco . . . . . . . . . . . . J26
John . . . . . . . . . . . . . J25
Kedzie Ave. . . . . . . . . . J25
Kruger . . . . . . . . . . . . J24
Lewis . . . . . . . . . . . . . J24
Lincoln . . . . . . . . . . . . K25
Longwood Dr. . . . . . . . . J24
Main St. . . . . . . . . . . . K26
Maple . . . . . . . . . . . J24,25
Market . . . . . . . . . . . . K25
Minnesota . . . . . . . . . H,J25
Mozart . . . . . . . . . . . . J25
New . . . . . . . . . . . . . J25
Oak . . . . . . . . . . . . . . J25
Olive . . . . . . . . . . . . . K25
Orange . . . . . . . . . . . . K25
Orchard . . . . . . . . . . . J24
Portland . . . . . . . . . . . J25
Prairie . . . . . . . . . . . . K25
Rexford . . . . . . . . . . . J25
Sacramento . . . . . . . . . J25
Sanders St. . . . . . . . . . J25
Seeley . . . . . . . . . . . . K25
Shamrock Ln. . . . . . . . . J26
Sheridan . . . . . . . . . . . K25
Sycamore . . . . . . . . . . K25
Thornton . . . . . . . . . . . K25
Union . . . . . . . . . . . J,K25
Vermont . . . . . . . . . . . K25
Vernon . . . . . . . . . . . . J25
Vincennes . . . . . . . . . . J25
Vine St. . . . . . . . . . . . K25
Walnut . . . . . . . . . . . J,K25
Western . . . . . . . . . . . K25
Whipple . . . . . . . . . . . J26
Winchester . . . . . . . . . . K25
Wireton . . . . . . . . . . . . J25
Wood . . . . . . . . . . . K24,25
York . . . . . . . . . . . . . . K25
119th St. . . . . . . . . . . J24
120th Pl. . . . . . . . . . . J24
120th St. . . . . . . . . . . J24
121st Pl. . . . . . . . . . . J24
121st St. . . . . . . . . . . J24
122nd Pl. . . . . . . . . . . J24
122nd St. . . . . . . . . . . J24
123rd Pl. . . . . . . . . . . J24
123rd St. . . . . . . . . . . J24
127th St. . . . . . . . . . . J25
131st St. . . . . . . . . . . J25
135th Pl. . . . . . . . . . . J25
135th St. . . . . . . . . . . J25
136th St. . . . . . . . . . . J25
138th St. . . . . . . . . . . J25
139th Pl. . . . . . . . . . . J26
139th St. . . . . . . . . . . J25
140th Pl. . . . . . . . . . . J26
140th St. . . . . . . . . . . J26
141st Pl. . . . . . . . . . . J26
141st St. . . . . . . . . . . J26
142nd Pl. . . . . . . . . . . J26
143rd St. . . . . . . . . . . J26
PARKS
Central Park . . . . . . . . . J25
Memorial Park . . . . . . . . J25
SCHOOLS
Eisenhower H.S. (New) . . J25
Mother of Sorrows H.S. . . J26
MISCELLANEOUS
St. Francis Hosp. . . . . . . J25

**BRIDGEVIEW**
Pages 8,9
STREETS
Beloit . . . . . . . . . . . E20,21
Birch . . . . . . . . . . . . . E21
Cambridge . . . . . . . . . . E21
Columbia Dr. . . . . . . . . . E19
Cranbrook . . . . . . . . . . E21
Dover . . . . . . . . . . . . . E21
Elm Ct. . . . . . . . . . . . . E19
Fairlane . . . . . . . . . . . . E21
Ferdinand . . . . . . . . . E20,21
Frontage Rd. . . . . . . . . . E22
Garden Ct. . . . . . . . . . . E20
Garden Ln. . . . . . . . . . . E21
Hanover . . . . . . . . . . . . E21
Harlem Ave. . . . . . . . . . E21
Hartford . . . . . . . . . . . . E21
Homestead . . . . . . . . . . E21
Industrial Dr. . . . . . . . . . E22
Mabel Ct. . . . . . . . . . . E19
Marin . . . . . . . . . . . . . E21
Oak Park . . . . . . . . . . . E21
Oconto . . . . . . . . . . . E20,21
Octavia Ave. . . . . . . . E20,21
Odell . . . . . . . . . . . . E20,21
Oketo . . . . . . . . . . . E20,21

Olympic Dr. . . . . . . . . . . E21
Orchard Ln. . . . . . . . . . . E21
Oxford . . . . . . . . . . . . . E21
Pembroke Ln. . . . . . . . . E21
Richard Rd. . . . . . . . . . . E22
Roberts Rd. . . . . . . . . . . E20
Saratoga Dr. . . . . . . . . . E21
Sayre . . . . . . . . . . . . . E20
Selma Pl. . . . . . . . . . . . E20
Sholer . . . . . . . . . . . . . E20
Southfield Dr. . . . . . . . . E21
Stanford Dr. . . . . . . . . . E21
Stickney . . . . . . . . . . . E20
Suburban Ln. . . . . . . . . E19
Thomas . . . . . . . . . . E20,21
Willow . . . . . . . . . . . . . E21
Windsor . . . . . . . . . . . . E21
70th St. . . . . . . . . . . . E20
71st St. . . . . . . . . . . . E20
72nd St. . . . . . . . . . . . E20
73rd Ave. . . . . . . . . . E21,22
73rd Ct. . . . . . . . . . . E20-22
73rd Pl. . . . . . . . . . . . E20
73rd St. . . . . . . . . . . . E20
74th Ave. . . . . . . . . . . E22
74th Ct. . . . . . . . . . . E20-22
74th Pl. . . . . . . . . . . . E20
75th Ave. . . . . . . . . . . E22
75th Ct. . . . . . . . . . . . C21
75th St. . . . . . . . . . . . E20
76th Ave. . . . . . . . . . . E20
76th St. . . . . . . . . . . . E20
77th Pl. . . . . . . . . . . . E19
77th Ct. . . . . . . . . . . . E20
77th St. . . . . . . . . . . . E20
78th Ave. . . . . . . . . . E19-21
78th Ct. S . . . . . . . . . . E20
78th St. . . . . . . . . . . . E20
79th Ave . . . . . . . . . . . F19
79th Pl. . . . . . . . . . . . E20
79th St. . . . . . . . . . . . E20
80th Pl. . . . . . . . . . . . E20
80th St. . . . . . . . . . . . E21
81st Pl. . . . . . . . . . . . E21
81st St. . . . . . . . . . . . E21
82nd Pl. . . . . . . . . . . . E21
82nd St. . . . . . . . . . . . E21
83rd Pl. . . . . . . . . . . . E21
83rd St. . . . . . . . . . . . E21
84th Pl. . . . . . . . . . . . E21
84th St. . . . . . . . . . . . E21
85th Pl. . . . . . . . . . . . E21
85th St. . . . . . . . . . . . E21
86th Pl. . . . . . . . . . . . E21
86th St. . . . . . . . . . . . E21
87th Pl. . . . . . . . . . . . E21
87th St. . . . . . . . . . . . E21
88th St. . . . . . . . . . . . E21
89th St. . . . . . . . . . . . E21
90th Pl. . . . . . . . . . . . E21
90th St. . . . . . . . . . . . E21
91st St. . . . . . . . . . . . E21
92nd Pl. . . . . . . . . . . . E22
92nd St. . . . . . . . . . . . E21
93rd St. . . . . . . . . . . . E22
95th St. . . . . . . . . . . . E22
98th Pl. . . . . . . . . . . . E22
100th Pl. . . . . . . . . . . . E22
103rd St. . . . . . . . . . . E22
SHOPPING CENTERS
Southfield Shopping Ctr. . . E21
MISCELLANEOUS
City Hall . . . . . . . . . . . E20

**BROADVIEW**
Pages 4,5
STREETS
Beach . . . . . . . . . . . . . C14
Braga Dr. . . . . . . . . . . . C15
Cermak Rd. . . . . . . . . . C15
Depot . . . . . . . . . . . . . D15
Elizabeth Dr. . . . . . . . . . C15
Ericka Dr. . . . . . . . . . . . C15
Filmore . . . . . . . . . . . . C15
Gardner Rd. . . . . . . . C14,15
Harvard . . . . . . . . . . . . C15
Lexington . . . . . . . . . . . D14
Lyman . . . . . . . . . . . . . C14
Roberts Dr. . . . . . . . . . . C15
Roosevelt Rd. . . . . . . . . C15
Summerdale . . . . . . . . . C15
Sunnydale . . . . . . . . . . C15
Terry . . . . . . . . . . . . . . C16
Tyson Rd. . . . . . . . . . . . C15
York . . . . . . . . . . . . . . C14
9th Ave. . . . . . . . . . . . D15
10th Ave. . . . . . . . . . . . D15
11th Ave. . . . . . . . . . . . D15
12th Ave. . . . . . . . . . . . D15
13th Ave. . . . . . . . . . . . D15
13th St. . . . . . . . . . . C,D15
14th Ave. . . . . . . . . . . . D15
14th St. . . . . . . . . . . . . D15
15th Ave. . . . . . . . . . . . D15
15th St. . . . . . . . . . . . . C15

## BROADVIEW

16th Ave. . . . . . . . . . . . D15
16th Ave. . . . . . . . . . . . C15
17th Ave. . . . . . . . . . . . D15
18th Ave. . . . . . . . . . . . C15
18th St. . . . . . . . . . . . . C15
19th Ave. . . . . . . . . . . . C15
19th St. . . . . . . . . . . . . C15
20th Ave. . . . . . . . . . . . C15
20th St. . . . . . . . . . . . . C15
21st Ave. . . . . . . . . . . . C15
21st St. . . . . . . . . . . . . C15
22nd Ave. . . . . . . . . . . . C15
23rd Ave. . . . . . . . . . . . C15
23rd St. . . . . . . . . . . . . C15
24th Ave. . . . . . . . . . . . C15
25th Ave. . . . . . . . . . . . C15
26th Ave. . . . . . . . . . . . C15
27th Ave. . . . . . . . . . . . C15

**PARKS**
Schroeder Park . . . . . . . . . D15
Sunnywood Park . . . . . . . . D15

**MISCELLANEOUS**
Village Hall . . . . . . . . . . . D15

## BROOKFIELD
Page 5
**STREETS**
Arden . . . . . . . . . . . . . . D17
Arthur . . . . . . . . . . . . . . C17
Bartlett . . . . . . . . . . . . . D16
Blanchan . . . . . . . . . C17,18
Broadway . . . . . . . . . . . . C17
Brookfield . . . . . . . . . . . D17
Burlington . . . . . . . . . . . D17
Cleveland . . . . . . . . . . . . C17
Congress Park . . . . . . . . . C17
Cossit . . . . . . . . . . . . . . C17
Custer . . . . . . . . . . D17,18
Deye . . . . . . . . . . . . . . C18
Division . . . . . . . . . . . . D16
Dubois . . . . . . . . . . C17,18
Elm . . . . . . . . . . . . D16,17
Fairview . . . . . . . . . . . . C17
Forest . . . . . . . . . . . D17,18
Garfield . . . . . . . . . . . . C16
Gerritsen . . . . . . . . . . . . C17
Golf View Rd. . . . . . . . . . D16
Grand Blvd. . . . . . . . . C16,17
Grant . . . . . . . . . . . . . . C17
Grove . . . . . . . . . . . D17,18
Harrison . . . . . . . . . . . . C17
Henrietta . . . . . . . . . . . . C16
Hollywood . . . . . . . . . . . D17
Jackson . . . . . . . . . . . . C16
Jefferson . . . . . . . . . . . . C16
Lexington . . . . . . . . . . . . C16
Lincoln . . . . . . . . . . . . . C17
Madison . . . . . . . . . . . . C17
Maple . . . . . . . . . . . . . D18
McCormick . . . . . . . . C16,17
Monroe . . . . . . . . . . . . . C16
Morton . . . . . . . . . . . . . C17
Oak . . . . . . . . . . . . . . . C18
Ogden Blvd. . . . . . . . . . . C17
Park . . . . . . . . . . . . D16,17
Parkview . . . . . . . . . . . . D17
Plainfield Rd. . . . . . . . . . D17
Prairie . . . . . . . . . . . D17,18
Quincy . . . . . . . . . . . . . C17
Raymond . . . . . . . . . C17,18
Ridgewood . . . . . . . . . . . D16
Riverside . . . . . . . . . . . . D17
Riverview Terr. . . . . . . . . . D17
Roach . . . . . . . . . . . . . D16
Rochester . . . . . . . . . . . C17
Rockefeller . . . . . . . . . . . D16
Rosemear . . . . . . . . . . . D17
Sahler . . . . . . . . . . . . . C17
Sheridan . . . . . . . . . . . . D17
Sherman . . . . . . . . . . . . D17
Southview . . . . . . . . . . C,D17
Sunnyside . . . . . . . . . D17,18
Taylor . . . . . . . . . . . . . D17
Vernon . . . . . . . . . . . D17,18
Washington . . . . . . . . . . . C16
Waubansee . . . . . . . . . . . D17
Windmere . . . . . . . . . . . . D17
Woodside . . . . . . . . . . . . D17
26th Pl. . . . . . . . . . . . . D16
26th St. . . . . . . . . . . . . D16
27th St. . . . . . . . . . . . . D16
28th Pl. . . . . . . . . . . . . D16
31st St. . . . . . . . . . . . . D16
42nd St. . . . . . . . . . . . . D17
43rd St. . . . . . . . . . . . . D17
44th Pl. . . . . . . . . . . . . D17
44th St. . . . . . . . . . . . . D17
45th Pl. . . . . . . . . . . . . D17
45th St. . . . . . . . . . . . . D17
46th St. . . . . . . . . . . . . C17
47th St. . . . . . . . . . . . . C18

**SCHOOLS**
Riverside Brookfield H.S. . . . D16

**MISCELLANEOUS**
Brookfield Woods . . . . . . . . D16
Brookfield Zoo . . . . . . . . . D16
Village Hall . . . . . . . . . . . D17

## BURBANK
Page 9
**STREETS**
Austin . . . . . . . . . . . F20,21
Central . . . . . . . . . . . . . G21
Cicero Ave. . . . . . . . . G20,21
Harlem Ave. . . . . . . . . . . E21
Lacrosse . . . . . . . . . . . . G20
Lamon . . . . . . . . . . . . . G20
Laporte . . . . . . . . . . G20,21
Latrobe . . . . . . . . . . . . . G20
Lavergne . . . . . . . . . . G20,21
Lawler . . . . . . . . . . . G20,21
Leamington . . . . . . . . G20,21
Leclaire . . . . . . . . . . G20,21
Linder . . . . . . . . . . . . . G20
Lockwood . . . . . . . . . . . G20
Long . . . . . . . . . . . . . . G20
Lorel . . . . . . . . . . . . . . G20
Lotus . . . . . . . . . . . . . . G20
Luna . . . . . . . . . . . . . . G20
Major . . . . . . . . . . . F20,21
Mansfield . . . . . . . . . F20,21
Mason . . . . . . . . . . . . . F20
Massasoit . . . . . . . . . F20,21
Mayfield . . . . . . . . . . F20,21
McVicker . . . . . . . . . . . . F20
Meade . . . . . . . . . . . F20,21
Melvina . . . . . . . . . . F20,21
Menard . . . . . . . . . . F20,21
Merrimac . . . . . . . . . F20,21
Mobile . . . . . . . . . . . . . F20
Moody . . . . . . . . . . . F20,21
Mulligan . . . . . . . . . . F20,21
Nagle . . . . . . . . . . . . . . F20
Narragansett . . . . . . . . . . F20
Nashville . . . . . . . . . . . . E20
Natchez . . . . . . . . . . . . . F20
Natoma . . . . . . . . . . . . . F20
Neenah . . . . . . . . . . . . . E20
Neva . . . . . . . . . . . . . . E20
New England . . . . . . . . . . E20
Newcastle . . . . . . . . . . . . E20
Newland . . . . . . . . . . . . E20
Nordica . . . . . . . . . . . . . E20
Normandy . . . . . . . . . . . . E20
Nottingham . . . . . . . . . . . E20
Oak Park . . . . . . . . . . . . F20
Parkside . . . . . . . . . . F20,21
Rutherford . . . . . . . . . . . F20
Sayre . . . . . . . . . . . . . . E20
State . . . . . . . . . . . . . . F21
71st Pl. . . . . . . . . . . . . E20
71st St. . . . . . . . . . . . . E20
72nd Pl. . . . . . . . . . . . . E20
72nd St. . . . . . . . . . . . . E20
73rd Pl. . . . . . . . . . . . . E20
73rd St. . . . . . . . . . . . . E20
74th Pl. . . . . . . . . . . . . E20
74th St. . . . . . . . . . . . . E20
75th St. . . . . . . . . . . . E,G20
76th Pl. . . . . . . . . . . . . G20
76th St. . . . . . . . . . . . . G20
77th Pl. . . . . . . . . . . . . G20
77th St. . . . . . . . . . . . E-G20
78th Pl. . . . . . . . . . . . . G20
78th St. . . . . . . . . . . . E-G20
79th Pl. . . . . . . . . . . . . G20
79th St. . . . . . . . . . . . E-G20
80th Pl. . . . . . . . . . . . . G20
80th St. . . . . . . . . . . . E-G20
81st Pl. . . . . . . . . . . . E-G21
81st St. . . . . . . . . . . . E-G21
82nd Pl. . . . . . . . . . . . E-G21
82nd St. . . . . . . . . . . . F,G21
83rd Pl. . . . . . . . . . . . F,G21
83rd St. . . . . . . . . . . . E-G21
84th Pl. . . . . . . . . . . . E-G21
84th St. . . . . . . . . . . . F,G21
85th Pl. . . . . . . . . . . . F,G21
85th St. . . . . . . . . . . . E-G21
86th Pl. . . . . . . . . . . . F,G21
86th St. . . . . . . . . . . . E-G21
87th St. . . . . . . . . . . . E-G21

**SCHOOLS**
Queen of Peace H.S. . . . . . G20
Reavis H.S. . . . . . . . . . . . F20
St. Laurence H.S. . . . . . . F,G20

## BURNHAM
Page 14
**STREETS**
Bensley Ave. . . . . . . . . . . N26
Brainard Ave. . . . . . . . . . . P26
Burnham Ave. . . . . . . . . . . O26
Calhoun Ave. . . . . . . . . . . N26
Centre . . . . . . . . . . . . . . O26
Chippewa . . . . . . . . . . . . O26
Croissant . . . . . . . . . . . . N26
Exchange Ave. . . . . . . . . . O26
Goodrich Ave. . . . . . . . . . . N26
Greenbay Ave. . . . . . . . . . . O26
Hammond Ave. . . . . . . . . . N26
Hoxie Ave. . . . . . . . . . . . . N26
Kettleson St. . . . . . . . . . . O26
Mackinaw Ave. . . . . . . . . . O26
Manistee Ave. . . . . . . . . . O26
Marquette Ave. . . . . . . . . . O26
Muskegon Ave. . . . . . . . . . O26

## BURR RIDGE
Page 8
(For additional listings,
see Section 3)
**STREETS**
Arrowhead Farm Dr. . . . . . . B21
Bridget St. . . . . . . . . . . . A19
Chippewa Ct. . . . . . . . . . . B21
Commerce St. . . . . . . . . . A20
Fieldstone Dr. . . . . . . . . . A19
High Grove Ct. . . . . . . . . . A20
International St. . . . . . . . . . A19
Mallory Ct. . . . . . . . . . . . A19
Navajo Ct. . . . . . . . . . . . B21
Omaha Dr. . . . . . . . . . . . B21
Seneca Ct. . . . . . . . . . . . B21

**PARKS**
Harvester Park . . . . . . . . . A20
Katherine Legg Mem. Park . . A19

## CALUMET CITY
Page 14
**STREETS**
Allen Ln. . . . . . . . . . . . . N26
Arthur St. . . . . . . . . . . O26-28
Baker St. . . . . . . . . . . . . O27
Balmoral Ave. . . . . . . . . . O28
Bensley Ave. . . . . . . . . . . N27
Buffalo Ave. . . . . . . . . . O27,28
Burnham Ave. . . . . . . . . O26-28
Calhoun Ave. . . . . . . . . . . N27
Calumet Expwy. . . . . . . . . N27
Campbell Ave. . . . . . . . O26,27
Cedar . . . . . . . . . . . . . . O26
Chappel Ave. . . . . . . . . . . N27
Chestnut St. . . . . . . . . . . N28
Cleveland Ave. . . . . . . . . . N26
Clyde Ave. . . . . . . . . . . . N27
Commercial Ave. . . . . . . . . O27
Cornell Ave. . . . . . . . . . . N27
Crandon Ave. . . . . . . . . . . N27
Dawn Ln. . . . . . . . . . . . . O26
Detroit St. . . . . . . . . . . . P28
Dogwood Ct. . . . . . . . . . . N28
Dolton (State St.) . . . . . . . N26
Douglas Ave. . . . . . . . . . . P27
Downs Dr. . . . . . . . . . . . N26
East-West St. . . . . . . . . . N28
Edgewood Dr. . . . . . . . . . O28
Elizabeth St. . . . . . . . . . . P27
Elm Ct. . . . . . . . . . . . . . N28
Escanaba . . . . . . . . . . . . O27
Euclid St. . . . . . . . . . . . . O27
Exchange Ave. . . . . . . . . . O27
Forest Ave. . . . . . . . . . . . P28
Forest Dale Ave. . . . . . . . . P28
Forest Hill . . . . . . . . . . . . O28
Forest Ln. . . . . . . . . . . . . P28
Forest Pl. . . . . . . . . . . . . O28
Forsythe Ave. . . . . . . . . . P27
Freeland Ave. . . . . . . . . O26-28
Garfield Ave. . . . . . . . . . . O27
George, S. . . . . . . . . . . . O26
Golf Ct. . . . . . . . . . . . . . N28
Gordon Ave. . . . . . . . . O27,28
Greenbay Ave. . . . . . . . O27,28
Greenwood Rd. . . . . . . . . . N28
Harbor Ave. . . . . . . . . . . . N26
Harding Ave. . . . . . . . . . . N27
Harmess St. . . . . . . . . . . . O27
Harrison St. . . . . . . . . . . . O27
Henry St. . . . . . . . . . . . . O27
Hickory Ct. . . . . . . . . . . . N28
Highland St. . . . . . . . . . . O27
Hirsch Ave. . . . . . . . . . O27,28
Hirsch Blvd. . . . . . . . . . . . O28
Houston Ave. . . . . . . . . . . N27
Hoxie Ave. . . . . . . . . . . . N27
Imperial Ave. . . . . . . . . . . O28
Ingraham . . . . . . . . . . . . P27
Jeffery Ave. . . . . . . . . . . . N27
Jennifer Ln. . . . . . . . . . . . O26
Kenilworth Dr. . . . . . . . . . P28
Lincoln Ave. . . . . . . . . O28,P27
Lincoln Pl. . . . . . . . . . . . O28
Locust St. . . . . . . . . . . . . N28
Lucas St. . . . . . . . . . . . . O27
Luella . . . . . . . . . . . . N26,27
Mackinaw Ave. . . . . . . . O26-28
Madison Ave. . . . . . . . . . . N27
Manistee . . . . . . . . . . . . O27

## CHICAGO
**STREETS**
Marquette Ave. . . . . . . . . . O27
Mason St. . . . . . . . . . . . . P27
Memorial Dr. . . . . . . . . . . O27
Merrill Ave. . . . . . . . . . . . N27
Michigan City Rd. . . . . . . N-P27
Muskegon . . . . . . . . . . . . O27
Oglesby . . . . . . . . . . . N26,27
Patricia Pl. . . . . . . . . . . . N26
Patton Ln. . . . . . . . . . . . . N26
Paxton . . . . . . . . . . . O26-28
Prairie Ave. . . . . . . . . . . . N26
Price Ave. . . . . . . . . . O27,28
Pulaski Rd. . . . . . . . . . . . N27
Ridgeland Ave. . . . . . . . . . N27
Ring Rd. . . . . . . . . . . . . . N28
River Dr. . . . . . . . . . . . . . O28
River Oaks Dr. . . . . . . . . . O28
Rudolph . . . . . . . . . . . . . O27
Ruth . . . . . . . . . . . . . O,P27
Saginaw Ave. . . . . . . . . . . O27
Schrum . . . . . . . . . . . . . P28
Shirley Dr. . . . . . . . . . . . . P28
Sibley Blvd. . . . . . . . . . . N-P27
Stanley Blvd. . . . . . . . . . . O28
State Line Rd. . . . . . . . . . . P27
State St. . . . . . . . . . . . N-P26
Stewart Ave. . . . . . . . . . . N26
Superior Ave. . . . . . . . . O27,28
Sycamore Ct. . . . . . . . . . . N28
Timothy Ln. . . . . . . . . . . . O27
Torrence . . . . . . . . . . . O26,27
Twilight Ln. . . . . . . . . . . . O26
Virginia St. . . . . . . . . . . . O27
Wabash Ave. . . . . . . . . . . O27
Waltham . . . . . . . . . . . P27,28
Warren . . . . . . . . . . . . . O27
Webb St. . . . . . . . . . . . . O27
Wentworth Ave. . . . . . . . . . P27
West Dr. . . . . . . . . . . . . . O28
William . . . . . . . . . . . . . . O28
Willow Ct. . . . . . . . . . . . . N28
Wilson Ave. . . . . . . . . . O,P27
Woodview . . . . . . . . . . . . O28
Yates Ave. . . . . . . . . . . . N27
142nd St. . . . . . . . . . . . N26
151st St. . . . . . . . . . . . . O27
152nd Pl. . . . . . . . . . . . O27
152nd St. (Memorial Dr.) . . . N27
153rd Pl. . . . . . . . . . . . . O27
153rd St. . . . . . . . . . . . . N27
154th Pl. . . . . . . . . . . . . O27
155th Pl. . . . . . . . . . . . . O27
155th St. . . . . . . . . . . . . O27
156th Pl. . . . . . . . . . . . . O27
156th St. . . . . . . . . . . . . O27
157th Pl. . . . . . . . . . . . . O27
157th St. . . . . . . . . . . . . O27
158th Pl. . . . . . . . . . . . . N28
159th St. . . . . . . . . . . . . O28
160th Pl. . . . . . . . . . . . M29
160th St. . . . . . . . . . . . . O28
161st St. . . . . . . . . . . N18,H18
162nd Pl. . . . . . . . . . . . . P28
162nd St. . . . . . . . . . . O28,E-L9
163rd Pl. . . . . . . . . . . . . O28
163rd St. . . . . . . . . . . O,P28
164th Pl. . . . . . . . . . . . . P28
164th St. . . . . . . . . . . O,P28
165th Pl. . . . . . . . . . . . . P28
165th St. . . . . . . . . . . O,P28
166th Pl. . . . . . . . . . . . . O28
166th St. . . . . . . . . . . O,P28
167th Pl. . . . . . . . . . . . . P28
167th St. . . . . . . . . . . . . P21

**CEMETERIES**
Oakland Cem. . . . . . . . . . N27

**FOREST PRESERVES**
River Oaks G.C. . . . . . . . . N28

**PARKS**
Calumet City Pk. . . . . . . . . P27
Forestdale Pk. . . . . . . . . . P28

**SCHOOLS**
Dirksen Jr. H.S. . . . . . . . . . N27
Schrum Mem. Jr. H.S. . . . . . O28
Sibley Sch. . . . . . . . . . . . N27
Thornton Frac. Twp. H.S. . . . O27
Wentworth Jr. H.S. . . . . . . . O27
Wilson Sch. . . . . . . . . . . . P27

**SHOPPING CENTERS**
River Oaks . . . . . . . . . . . O28

**MISCELLANEOUS**
City Hall . . . . . . . . . . . . . P27

## CALUMET PARK
Page 13
**STREETS**
Aberdeen, S. . . . . . . . K24,25
Ada, S. . . . . . . . . . . . . . K25
Ashland . . . . . . . . . . . . . K25
Bishop, S. . . . . . . . . . . . K25
Burr Oak Ave. . . . . . . K24,25
Carpenter, S. . . . . . . . K24,25
Elizabeth, S. . . . . . . . . . . K25
Green . . . . . . . . . . . . L24,25
Halsted . . . . . . . . . . . . . L24
High . . . . . . . . . . . . . . . K24
Honore . . . . . . . . . . . . . K25

Justine, S. . . . . . . . . . . . K25
Laflin, S. . . . . . . . . . . . . K25
Lincoln . . . . . . . . . . . . . K25
Loomis, S. . . . . . . . . . . . K25
Marshfield . . . . . . . . . . . K25
May, S. . . . . . . . . . . . K24,25
Morgan . . . . . . . . . . . K24,25
Page . . . . . . . . . . . . K24,25
Paulina, S. . . . . . . . . . K24,25
Peoria . . . . . . . . . . . . L24,25
Racine, S. . . . . . . . . . . . K25
Sangamon . . . . . . . . . K24,25
Throop, S. . . . . . . . . . . . K25
Vermont . . . . . . . . . . . . . L24
Winchester . . . . . . . . . . . K25
Wood . . . . . . . . . . . . K24,25
York . . . . . . . . . . . . . . . K24
119th St. . . . . . . . . . . . . K24
120th St., W. . . . . . . . . . . K24
121st St., W. . . . . . . . . . . K24
122nd St., W. . . . . . . . . . . K24
123rd St., W. . . . . . . . . . . K24
124th St., W. . . . . . . . . . . K24
125th St., W. . . . . . . . . . . K24
126th St., W. . . . . . . . . . . K25
127th St. . . . . . . . . . K,L26
128th St., W. . . . . . . . . . . K25

**CEMETERIES**
Cedar Park Cem. . . . . . . . K24

**MISCELLANEOUS**
Raceway Park . . . . . . . . . K25
Village Hall & Fire Dept. . . . . K24

## CHICAGO
**STREETS**
Abbott . . . . . . Pg.10 . . . L21
Aberdeen . . Pg.7,13 . . K13-24
Ada . . . . . . . . Pg.3 . . K12-24
Adams . . . . . . Pg.6 . . . F-L14
Adams Blvd. . . . Pg.6 . . . . F14
Addison . . . . . Pg.1 . . D-L11
Agatite . . . . . . Pg.2 . . . F-L10
Ainslie . . . . . . Pg.2 . . . F-L10
Albany . . . . . . Pg.3 . . . J7-24
Albion . . . . . . Pg.2 . . . E-K8
Aldine . . . . . . Pg.3 . . . K-L11
Alexander . . . . Pg.7 . . . . L15
Algonquin . . . . Pg.2 . . . . . G8
Allen . . . . . . . Pg.3 . . . . H11
Allport . . . . . . Pg.7 . . . . K15
Almond . . . . . . Pg.6 . . . . J14
Alta Vista Ter . . Pg.3 . . K10-11
Altgeld . . . . . . Pg.2 . . E-L12
Anacona . . . . . Pg.7 . . . . K13
Anson Pl. . . . . Pg.6 . . . . J13
Anthony . . . . Pg.11 . M19,O21
Arbour Pl. . . . . Pg.7 . . . . K14
Arcade Pl. . . . . Pg.7 . . . . K14
Arch . . . . . . . Pg.7 . . L15,H18
Archer . . . . . . Pg.7 . . L15,H18
Ardmore . . . . . Pg.2 . . . E-K9
Argyle . . . . . . Pg.1 . . D10,E-L9
Armitage . . . . Pg.2 . . E-K12
Armour . . . . . . Pg.7 . . . . K13
Armstrong . . . . Pg.2 . . . . . G9
Artesian . . . . . Pg.3 . . . J7-24
Arthington . . . . Pg.6 . . . F-L14
Arthur . . . . . . Pg.2 . . . E-K8
Ashland . . . . . Pg.3 . . . K7-22
Astor . . . . . . . Pg.7 . . . . L13
Attrill . . . . . . . Pg.3 . . . . J12
Augusta Blvd. . . Pg.6 . . . C-K13
Austin . . . . . . Pg.2 . . . Pg.9
Avalon . . . . . . Pg.10 . M21-22
Avenue A . . . . Pg.11 . . . P23
Avenue B . . . . Pg.11 . . . P23
Avenue C . . . . Pg.11 . . . P23
Avenue D . . . . Pg.11 . . . P23
Avenue E . . . . Pg.11 . P22-23
Avenue F . . . . Pg.11 . P23-24
Avenue G . . . . Pg.11 . P22-23
Avenue H . . . . Pg.11 . . O25
Avenue J . . . . Pg.11 . . O25
Avenue K . . . . Pg.14 . . O25
Avenue L . . . . Pg.11 . O22-25
Avenue M . . . . Pg.11 . O23-25
Avenue N . . . . Pg.11 . O23-25
Avenue O . . . . Pg.11 . O21-25
Avers . . . . . . Pg.2,3,6,9
. . . . . . . . . . . . . . . . H9-23
Avondale . . . . Pg.2 . E8,J-K12
Baker . . . . . . Pg.11 . . O21
Balbo Dr. . . . . Pg.7 . . M-L14
Baldwin . . . . . Pg.11 . . . N20
Balmoral . . . . Pg.2 . . F-L10
Baltimore . . . . Pg.11 . O21-25
Banks . . . . . . Pg.7 . . . . L13
Barber . . . . . . Pg.7 . . . . K14
Barry . . . . . . Pg.2 . . E-L11
Bauwans . . . . Pg.7 . . . . K13
Beach . . . . . . Pg.6 . H-K13
Beacon . . . . . Pg.3 . . . K10
Beaubien Ct. . . Pg.7 . . . . L14
Belden . . . . . Pg.2 . . E-K12
Bell . . . . . . . Pg.3 . . . J7-24
Belle Plaine . . Pg.1 . . L-D10
Bellevue Pl. . . Pg.7 . . . . L13
Belmont . . . . Pg.2 . . E-L11

Belmont Harbor Dr.
. . . . . . . . . . Pg.3 . . . . L11
Bennett . . . . Pg.11 . . N19-22
Bensley . . . . . Pg.11 . N22-25
Benson . . . . . Pg.7 . . . . K16
Berenice . . . . Pg.2 . . F-K10
Berkeley . . . . Pg.7 . . . . M17
Bernard . . . . . Pg.3 . . H9-12
Berteau . . . . . Pg.1 . . D-K10
Berwyn . . . . . Pg.1 . . . E-K9
Besly Ct. . . . . Pg.3 . . . . K12
Best Dr. . . . . . Pg.11 . . . M19
Beverly . . . . . Pg.10 . K21-23
Bingham . . . . Pg.3 . . . . J12
Birchwood Ave. . Pg.2 . . . E-K7
Birkoff . . . . . . Pg.10 . . . L21
Bishop . . . . . Pg.7 . . K13-24
Bissell . . . . . . Pg.3 . . K-L12
Bittersweet Pl. . Pg.3 . . . . L10
Blackhawk . . . Pg.7 . . K-L13
Blackstone . . . Pg.7 . . N18-22
Blake . . . . . . Pg.6 . . . . J17
Blanchard Ct. . Pg.7 . . . . L16
Bliss . . . . . . . Pg.7 . . . . K13
Bloomingdale . Pg.2 . . E-K12
Blue Island . . . Pg.6 . . J-K15
Bonaparte . . . Pg.7 . . . . K16
Bond . . . . . . Pg.11 . . O21
Bonfield . . . . . Pg.7 . . . . K16
Bosak Ave. . . . Pg.10 . . . J22
Bosworth . . . . Pg.3 . . K7-13
Boulevard Way . Pg.6 . . . . J16
Bowen . . . . . Pg.2 . . . . M17
Bowler . . . . . . Pg.6 . . . . J14
Bowmanville . . Pg.3 . . . . . J9
Bradley Pl. . . . Pg.3 . . J-L11
Brainard . . . . Pg.14 . . O25
Brandon . . . . Pg.11 . O20-25
Brayton . . . . . Pg.13 . . . L24
Brennan . . . . Pg.11 . . N22
Briar Pl. . . . . . Pg.3 . . . . L11
Brighton Pl. . . Pg.6 . . . . J17
Broad . . . . . . Pg.7 . . . . K16
Broadway . . . . Pg.3 . . K9,L11
Brodman . . . . Pg.1 . . . D10
Brompton . . . . Pg.3 . . . . L11
Bross . . . . . . Pg.6 . . . . J16
Browning . . . . Pg.7 . . . . M16
Bryn Mawr . . . Pg.1 . . D-K9
Buckingham Pl. . Pg.3 . . K-L11
Buena . . . . . . Pg.3 . . K-L10
Buffalo . . . . . Pg.11 . O21-25
Burley . . . . . . Pg.11 . O21-25
Burling . . . . . Pg.3 . . L11-12
Burling St. . . . Pg.3 . . . . K13
Burling St. . . . Pg.3 . . . . K13
Burnham . . . . Pg.11 . O20-21
Burnside . . . . Pg.10 . . M21
Burton Pl. . . . . Pg.7 . . . . L13
Busse . . . . . . Pg.2 . . . . . E9
Butler Dr. . . . . Pg.13 . . M-N25
Bypass . . . . . Pg.7 . . . . F12
Byron . . . . . . Pg.1 . . K-D10
Cabrini . . . . . Pg.6 . . K-L14
Caldwell . . . . Pg.2 . . F8,G9
Calhoun . . . . Pg.11 . N22-25
California . . . . Pg.3 . J8-23,L11
Calumet . . . . Pg.11 . M15-25
Cambridge . . . Pg.3 . . L11-13
Campbell . . . . Pg.3 . . J7-24
Canal . . . . . . Pg.7 . . . . K15
Canalport . . . . Pg.7 . . . L-K15
Canfield . . . . . Pg.2 . . . E8-9
Carmen . . . . . Pg.1 . . D-L9
Carondolet . . . Pg.14 . . O25
Carpenter . . . Pg.7 . . K13-24
Carpenter Rd. . Pg.2 . . . . G8
Carroll . . . . . . Pg.6 . . G-L14
Castleisland Ave.
. . . . . . . . . . Pg.1 . . . D10
Castlewood Ter. . Pg.3 . . K-L10
Catalpa . . . . . Pg.1 . . . E-K9
Caton . . . . . . Pg.3 . . . . J12
Cedar . . . . . . Pg.7 . . . . L13
Central . . . . . Pg.2 . . G8-19
Central Park . . Pg.3 . . H8-24
Cermak Rd. . . Pg.6 . . G-M15
Champlain . . . Pg.7 . . M17-23
Chanay . . . . . Pg.3 . . . . J12
Chappel . . . . Pg.11 . N19-25
Charles . . . . . Pg.10 . K22-23
Charleston . . . Pg.3 . . . . J12
Chase Ave. . . . Pg.2 . . . E-K8
Chelsea Pl. . . . Pg.10 . . K23
Cheltenham Pl. . Pg.11 . . O20
Cherry . . . . . Pg.7 . . . . K13
Chester . . . . . Pg.11 . D9-10
Chestnut . . . . Pg.7 . . K-L13
Chicago . . . . Pg.6 . . G-M13
Chicago Beach Dr. (Pvt)
. . . . . . . . . . . . . . . . N18
Chicora . . . . . Pg.2 . . F-G8
Chippewa . . . Pg.14 . . N24
Christiana . . . Pg.3 . . H9-20
Church . . . . . Pg.10 . . K23
Churchill . . . . Pg.3 . . . . J12
Cicero . . . . . Pg.2 . . G8-23
Circle Ave., E. & W.
. . . . . . . . . . Pg.2 . . . . . E9
Cityfront Plaza Dr.
. . . . . . . . . . Pg.7 . . . . L14
Claremont . . . Pg.3 . . J8-23

CHICAGO 19 CHICAGO


Clarence ... Pg.2 ... E-F8
Clarendon ... Pg.3 ... L10
Clark St. ... Pg.3
... K7-11,L11-15
Cleaver ... Pg.7 ... K13
Cleveland ... Pg.7 ... L13
Clifford ... Pg.2 ... G9
Clifton ... Pg.3 ... K10-12
Clifton Park ... Pg.10 ... H23
Clinton ... Pg.7 ... L14-15
Clover ... Pg.2 ... G10
Clybourn ... Pg.3 .. J11-K12
Clyde ... Pg.11 .. N19-25
Coast Guard Dr. Pg.11 ... N19
Coles ... Pg.11 .. O20-21
Colfax ... Pg.11 .. O20-21
Columbia ... Pg.3 ... K8
Columbia Dr. .. Pg.11 ... N18
Columbus Ave. Pg.10 ... J20
Columbus Dr. . Pg.7 ... N18
Commercial ... Pg.11 .. O21-25
Commonwealth Pg.3 ... L11-12
Concord Pl. ... Pg.2,3,7 .. G-L12
Congress Pkwy. Pg.6 ... G-L14
Constance ... Pg.11 ... N19-22
Corbett ... Pg.7 ... K15-16
Corliss ... Pg.11 .. M23-25
Cornelia ... Pg.1 ... D-L11
Cornell ... Pg.7 ... N18-21
Cortez Dr. ... Pg.6 ... G-K13
Cortland ... Pg.2 ... E-K12
Cottage Grove . Pg.7 ... M15-25
Couch Pl. ... Pg.7 ... L14
Court Pl. ... Pg.7 ... L14
Coyle Ave. ... Pg.2 ... E-J8
Crandon ... Pg.11 .. N19-25
Cregier ... Pg.11 .. N19-21
Crestline ... Pg.9 ... H21
Crilly ... Pg.3 ... L12
Crosby ... Pg.7 ... L13
Crowell ... Pg.7 ... K16
Crystal ... Pg.6 ... G-K13
Cullerton ... Pg.6 ... H-L15
Cullom ... Pg.2 ... F-K10
Cumberland ... Pg.1 ... D10
Cuyler ... Pg.2 ... F-L10
Cyril ... Pg.11 ... N20
Dakin ... Pg.2 ... F-L10
Damen ... Pg.3 ... K7-22
Daniel Dr. ... Pg.13 .. L-M25
Dante ... Pg.11 .. N19-21
Dauphin ... Pg.10 .. M21-23
Davlin Ct. ... Pg.3 ... H11
Davol ... Pg.10 ... K23
Dawson ... Pg.3 ... H11
Dayton ... Pg.3 ... K10-12
Dean ... Pg.7 ... K13
Dearborn ... Pg.7 ... L13-18
Dekoven ... Pg.7 ... L14
Delaware Pl. ... Pg.7 ... L13
Delphia Ave. .. Pg.1 ... D10
Deming Pl. ... Pg.2 ... G-L12
Denvir ... Pg.6 ... J14
Depot Pl. ... Pg.7 ... L15
Des Plaines ... Pg.7 ... L13-15
Devon ... Pg.2 ... F-K8
Dewitt Pl. ... Pg.7 ... L13
Dickens ... Pg.2 ... E-L12
Dickinson ... Pg.2 ... G10
District ... Pg.6 ... H17
Diversey ... Pg.2 ... E-L11
Diversey Dr. ... Pg.3 ... L11
Diversey Pkwy. Pg.3 ... K11
Division ... Pg.6 ... F-L13
Dobson ... Pg.11 .. M20-25
Dominick ... Pg.3 ... K12
Dorchester ... Pg.7 ... M17-22
Douglas Blvd. . Pg.6 ... H15
Dover ... Pg.3 ... K10
Dowagiac ... Pg.2 ... G8
Dr. M. L. King Dr.
... Pg.7,10,11,13
... M15-25
Drake ... Pg.3 ... H9-17
Draper ... Pg.3 ... K12
Drew ... Pg.10 ... K23
Drexel ... Pg.7 ... M17-25
Drexel Blvd. ... Pg.7 ... M17
Drexel Sq. Dr. . Pg.7 ... M18
Drummond Pl. . Pg.2 ... G-L12
Dunbar, S. ... Pg.10 .. M21-22
Early ... Pg.3 ... K9
East End ... Pg.11 ... N20
East River Rd. . Pg.1 ... D9-10
Eastlake Terr. .. Pg.3 ... K7
Eastman ... Pg.7 ... K-L13
Eastview Pk. .. Pg.7 ... N18
Eastwood ... Pg.1 ... D-L10
Eberhart ... Pg.7,10,11,13
... M16-25
Edbrooke ... Pg.13 ... L25-27
Eddy ... Pg.2 ... F-K11
Edgebrook Ter. Pg.2 ... F8
Edgewater ... Pg.3 ... K9
Edmaire ... Pg.10 ... K23
Edmund ... Pg.2 ... F-G10
Edward Ct. ... Pg.3 ... L12
Eggleston ... Pg.10 .. L19-25
Elaine Pl. ... Pg.3 ... L11
Elbridge ... Pg.3 ... H11
Eleanor ... Pg.7 ... K16
Elias Ct. ... Pg.7 ... K16
Elizabeth ... Pg.7 ... K13-24
Elk Grove ... Pg.3 ... K12-13
Ellen ... Pg.7 ... K13
Elliot ... Pg.11 ... N20
Ellis ... Pg.7 ... M16-25
Ellsworth Dr. .. Pg.7 ... M18
Elm ... Pg.7 ... L13
Elmdale ... Pg.3 ... K9
Elston ... Pg.2,3,7
... F9,H11,J12,K13
Emerald ... Pg.7 ... L16-25
Emerald S. ... Pg.10 ... L19
Emmett ... Pg.3 ... H11
Englewood ... Pg.10 ... L19
Erie ... Pg.6 ... F-L13
Ernst Ct. ... Pg.7 ... L13
Escanaba ... Pg.11 .. O20-24
Esmond ... Pg.10 ... K23
Essex ... Pg.11 .. N21-22
Estes Ave. ... Pg.2 ... E-K8
Euclid ... Pg.11 .. N19-22
Eugenie ... Pg.3 ... L12
Evans ... Pg.7 ... M17-25
Evans Ct. ... Pg.7 ... L13
Everett ... Pg.7 ... N18
Evergreen ... Pg.2,6,7
... E8,H-L13
Ewing ... Pg.11 .. O22-23
Exchange ... Pg.11 .. O20-25
Fair Pl. ... Pg.7 ... L13
Fairbanks Ct. .. Pg.7 ... L13
Fairfield ... Pg.3 ... J7-24
Fairway Dr. ... Pg.10 ... J24
Fargo Ave. ... Pg.2 ... E-K7
Farragut ... Pg.1 ... E-K9
Farrell ... Pg.7 ... K16
Farwell Ave. ... Pg.2 ... E-K8
Federal ... Pg.7 ... L14-19
Felton Ct. ... Pg.7 ... L13
Ferdinand ... Pg.6 ... G-J13
Fern Ct. ... Pg.3 ... L12
Field Plaza Dr. . Pg.7 ... M15
Fielding ... Pg.10 ... L20
Fifth ... Pg.6 ... G-J14
Fillmore ... Pg.6 ... G-K14
Financial ... Pg.7 ... L14
Fitch Ave. ... Pg.2 ... E-J8
Fletcher ... Pg.1 ... E-L11
Flournoy ... Pg.6 ... G-K14
Ford ... Pg.7 ... L15
Ford City Dr. ... Pg.9 ... G20
Forest ... Pg.10 ... M21-24
Forest Glen ... Pg.2 ... G9
Forest Preserve Pg.1 .. D11,E10
Forrestville ... Pg.7 ... M17-25
Foster ... Pg.2 ... E-L9
Foster Pl. ... Pg.2 ... E9
Francis Pl. ... Pg.3 ... J12
Francisco ... Pg.3,6,10,12,13
... J7-21
Franklin ... Pg.7 ... L14
Franklin Blvd. ... Pg.6 ... J-H13
Fremont ... Pg.3 ... K10-13
Front ... Pg.10,11,13
... M23
Frontier ... Pg.3 ... L10
Fry ... Pg.7 ... K13
Fuller ... Pg.7 ... K16
Fullerton ... Pg.2 ... E-L12
Fulton ... Pg.6 ... E-L14
Fulton Blvd. ... Pg.6 ... H14
Gale ... Pg.2 ... G10
Garfield ... Pg.6 ... F14
Garfield Blvd. ... Pg.6,7,10 K-L18
Garland Ct. ... Pg.7 ... L14
Geneva Ter. ... Pg.3 ... L12
Genoa ... Pg.10 ... L21-22
George ... Pg.2 ... E-L11
Germania Pl. ... Pg.7 ... L13
Gettysburg ... Pg.2 ... G9
Giddings ... Pg.1 ... E-K10
Gilbert Ct. ... Pg.10 ... L21
Giles ... Pg.7 ... M16
Givins Ct. ... Pg.10 ... L21
Gladys ... Pg.6 ... G-L14
Glenlake ... Pg.2 ... E-K9
Glenwood ... Pg.3 ... K8-9
Goethe ... Pg.7 ... L13
Goodman ... Pg.2 ... F9
Gordon Ter. ... Pg.3 ... K-L10
Governor's Pkwy.
... Pg.6 ... H14
Grace ... Pg.1 ... D-L10
Grady Ct. ... Pg.7 ... K16
Grand ... Pg.2,6,7
... E-G12,J-L13
Grant Pl. ... Pg.3 ... L12
Granville ... Pg.2 ... H-K8
Gratten ... Pg.7 ... K16
Green ... Pg.7 ... L14-25
Green Bay ... Pg.11 .. O21-25
Greenleaf ... Pg.2 ... E-K8
Greenview ... Pg.3 ... K7-13
Greenwood ... Pg.7 ... M17-25
Gregory ... Pg.1 ... D-K9
Grenshaw ... Pg.6 ... G-L15
Gresham ... Pg.3 ... H11
Grove ... Pg.7 ... L15
Grover ... Pg.2 ... F10
Gunnison ... Pg.1 ... F-L10
Haddon ... Pg.6 ... G-K13
Haft ... Pg.2 ... F8
Haines ... Pg.7 ... L13
Hale ... Pg.10 .. K23-24
Halsted ... Pg.3 ... L11-25
Halsted Pkwy. ... Pg.10 ... L19
Hamilton ... Pg.3,6,7,10
... J8-22
Hamlin ... Pg.6 ... H8-23
Hamlin Blvd. ... Pg.6 ... H14
Hampden Ct. ... Pg.3 ... L11-12
Harbor ... Pg.11 ... O22
Harbor Dr. ... Pg.7 ... M14
Harding ... Pg.2 ... H8-23
Harlem ... Pg.2 ... E8-19
Harper ... Pg.7 ... N18-20
Harrison ... Pg.6 ... G-L14
Hart ... Pg.2 ... F8
Hartland Ct. ... Pg.7 ... K13
Hartwell ... Pg.10 ... L19
Harvard ... Pg.10 ... L19-25
Haskins ... Pg.3 ... K7
Hastings ... Pg.7 ... J-K15
Hawthorne Pl. .. Pg.3 ... L11
Hayes ... Pg.2 ... E-F8
Hayes Dr. ... Pg.11 ... N19
Hayford Pl. ... Pg.9 ... H20
Haynes Ct. ... Pg.7 ... K16
Hazel ... Pg.3 ... K10
Heath ... Pg.6 ... J15
Helen Mikols Dr. Pg.9 ... G19
Henderson ... Pg.2 ... E-K11
Henry Ct. ... Pg.3 ... J12
Hermione ... Pg.2 ... F8
Hermitage ... Pg.3 ... K8-21
Hermosa ... Pg.10 ... K23
Hiawatha ... Pg.2 ... F8-G9
Hickory ... Pg.7 ... K13
Higgins ... Pg.1 ... B8,F9
Higgins Rd. ... Pg.1 .. B-C8,E9
Highland ... Pg.2 ... E-K8
Hill ... Pg.7 ... L13
Hillock ... Pg.7 ... K16
Hirsch ... Pg.6 ... F-J13
Hobart ... Pg.2 ... E-F9
Hobbie ... Pg.7 ... L13
Hobson ... Pg.3 ... K12
Hoey ... Pg.7 ... K16
Holbrook ... Pg.2 ... F9
Holland Rd. ... Pg.10 ... L21
Hollett Dr. ... Pg.10 .. H19-20
Holly ... Pg.3 ... K12
Hollywood ... Pg.2 ... G-K9
Homan ... Pg.6 ... H13-24
Homer ... Pg.2 ... G-K12
Homewood ... Pg.10 ... K23
Honore ... Pg.3 ... K8-24
Hood ... Pg.2 ... E-K9
Hooker ... Pg.7 ... K13
Hopkins Pl. ... Pg.10 ... K21
Horner ... Pg.3 ... J12
Hortense ... Pg.2 ... E8
Houston ... Pg.11 .. O21-25
Howard St. ... Pg.2 ... E-K7
Howe ... Pg.3 ... L12-13
Howland ... Pg.10 ... K21
Hoxie ... Pg.11 .. O22-25
Hoyne Ave. ... Pg.3,6,7,10
... J8-23
Hoyt ... Pg.6 ... J16
Hubbard ... Pg.6 ... G-L13
Hudson ... Pg.3 ... L11-13
Huguelet Pl. ... Pg.7 ... L13
Humboldt Blvd. Pg.3 ... J12
Humboldt Dr. .. Pg.6 ... J13
Hunt Pl. ... Pg.10 ... K21
Huntington ... Pg.2 ... F8
Hurlbut ... Pg.2 ... E-F9
Huron ... Pg.6 ... F-M13
Hutchinson ... Pg.2 ... F-L10
Hyacinth ... Pg.2 ... F9
Hyde Park Blvd. Pg.7 ... M-N18
Ibsen ... Pg.2 ... E8
Illinois ... Pg.7 ... L13
Imlay ... Pg.2 ... E-F8
Independence Blvd.
... Pg.6 ... H14
Indian Rd. ... Pg.2 ... F8,G9
Indiana ... Pg.7 ... L15-25
Indianapolis ... Pg.11 .. P22-23
Ingleside ... Pg.7 ... M17-25
Institute Pl. ... Pg.7 ... L13
Ionia ... Pg.2 ... G8-9
Iowa ... Pg.6 ... G-K13
Irene ... Pg.3 ... J11
Iron ... Pg.7 ... K16-17
Irving Park Rd. Pg.1 ... D-L10
Isham ... Pg.2 ... E8
Jackson Blvd. ... Pg.6 ... J-L14
Jackson Dr. ... Pg.7 ... L-M14
Jaenssen Blvd. Pg.3 ... K11
James ... Pg.7 ... K18
Jarlath Ave. ... Pg.2 ... E-J8
Jarvis Ave. ... Pg.2 ... E-K7
Jasper Pl. ... Pg.7 ... K16,17
Jean ... Pg.2 ... F8
Jefferson ... Pg.7 ... L14-15
Jeffery ... Pg.14 .. N24-25
Jeffery Blvd. ... Pg.11 .. N19-22
Jerome ... Pg.2 ... E-J7
Jersey ... Pg.3 ... H9
Jessie Ct. ... Pg.6 ... J13-14
Jones ... Pg.3 ... J12
Jonquil Ter. ... Pg.3 ... K7
Jourdan Ct. ... Pg.7 ... L15
Joyce ... Pg.2 ... F10
Julia Ct. ... Pg.3 ... J12
Julian ... Pg.7 ... K13
Juneway Ter. ... Pg.3 ... K7
Junior Ter. ... Pg.3 ... L10
Justine ... Pg.7 ... K14-22
Kamerling ... Pg.6 ... G-H13
Karlov ... Pg.2 ... H8-21
Kasson ... Pg.2 ... H10
Kearsage ... Pg.2 ... H11
Keating ... Pg.2 ... G8-21
Kedvale ... Pg.2 ... H8-21
Kedzie Ave. ... Pg.2,3,6,10
... J7-23
Kedzie Blvd. ... Pg.3 ... J12
Keefe ... Pg.11 ... M19
Keeler ... Pg.2 ... H8-21
Keeley ... Pg.7 ... K16
Keene ... Pg.2 ... G8
Keller Dr. ... Pg.9 ... H8-21
Kemper Pl. ... Pg.3 ... L12
Kenmore ... Pg.3 ... K8-12
Kenneth ... Pg.2 ... G9-21
Kennicott ... Pg.2 ... H10
Kennison ... Pg.2 ... G9-10
Kenosha ... Pg.2 ... H11
Kensington ... Pg.10 ... L-M24
Kenton ... Pg.2 ... G8-21
Kentucky ... Pg.2 ... G10
Kenwood ... Pg.7 ... M17-22
Keokuk ... Pg.3 ... H10
Keota ... Pg.2 ... F8
Kerbs ... Pg.2 ... G9
Kercheval ... Pg.2 ... G9
Kerfoot ... Pg.10 ... L21
Kewanee ... Pg.2 ... H10
Keystone ... Pg.2 ... H8-14
Kilbourn ... Pg.2 ... G9-21
Kildare ... Pg.2 ... H9-21
Kilpatrick ... Pg.2 ... G8-21
Kimball ... Pg.3 ... H8-12
Kimbark ... Pg.7 ... M17-22
Kimberly ... Pg.2 ... G9
Kingsbury ... Pg.3 ... K12-14
Kingsdale ... Pg.2 ... G9
Kingston ... Pg.11 .. O20-22
Kinzie ... Pg.6 ... F-L14
Kinzua ... Pg.2 ... G8
Kiona ... Pg.2 ... H10
Kirby ... Pg.2 ... G9
Kirkland ... Pg.9 ... H20
Kirkwood ... Pg.2 ... G8-9
Knox ... Pg.2 ... G9-21
Kolin ... Pg.6 ... H13-21
Kolmar ... Pg.2 ... G9-21
Komensky ... Pg.6 ... H16-21
Kostner ... Pg.2 ... G9-21
Kruger ... Pg.2 ... G10
LaCrosse ... Pg.2 ... G9-19
LaSalle St. ... Pg.7 ... L18
Lacey ... Pg.2 ... G9
Lafayette ... Pg.7 ... L17-24
Laflin ... Pg.7 ... K14-24
Lake ... Pg.6 ... F-L14
Lake Park ... Pg.7 ... M16-18
Lake Shore Dr. . Pg.3
... K9,L13,M17,N19
Lake Shore Dr. E.
... Pg.3 ... L11
Lake View ... Pg.3 ... L11-12
Lakeside Pl. ... Pg.3 ... K-L10
Lakewood ... Pg.3 ... K8-12
Lambert ... Pg.2 ... G9
Lamed ... Pg.2 ... G9
Lamon ... Pg.2 ... G9-19
Landers ... Pg.2 ... G8-9
Langley ... Pg.7 ... M17
Lansing ... Pg.2 ... G9
Laporte ... Pg.2 ... G9-19
Laramie ... Pg.2 ... G9-18
Larchmont ... Pg.3 ... K10
Larned ... Pg.2 ... G9
Larrabee ... Pg.3 ... L12-13
LasCasas ... Pg.2 ... G9
Latham ... Pg.2 ... G9
Latrobe ... Pg.2 ... G9-19
Lavergne ... Pg.2 ... G9-19
Lawler ... Pg.2 ... G9-19
Lawndale ... Pg.3,6,9,10,12
... H8-23
Lawrence ... Pg.2 ... F-L10
Lawrence Dr. ... Pg.3 ... L10
Le Mai ... Pg.2 ... G8
Le Moyne ... Pg.6 ... F-K13
Leader ... Pg.2 ... G8-9
Leamington ... Pg.2 ... G9-18
Leavenworth ... Pg.2 ... G9
Leavitt ... Pg.3 ... J8-22
Leclaire ... Pg.2 ... G9-19
Lee Pl. ... Pg.7 ... J-K13
Legett ... Pg.2 ... G8-9
Lehigh ... Pg.2 ... G9
Lehmann Ct. ... Pg.3 ... L11
Leland ... Pg.1 ... D-L10
Lemont ... Pg.2 ... G8-9
Lenox ... Pg.2 ... G8-9
Leona ... Pg.2 ... G8
Leonard ... Pg.2 ... F-G9
Leoti ... Pg.2 ... F8,G9
Leroy ... Pg.2 ... G8
Lessing ... Pg.7 ... K13
Lester ... Pg.2 ... G9-10
Levee ... Pg.7 ... K16
Lexington ... Pg.6 ... G-L14
Leyden ... Pg.13 ... M25
Liano ... Pg.2 ... G9
Libbey ... Pg.2 ... G10
Liberty ... Pg.7 ... K-L15
Lieb ... Pg.2 ... G9
Lightfoot ... Pg.2 ... F8
Lill ... Pg.3 ... K12
Lincoln ... Pg.3
... H8,J10,K11,L12
Lincoln Park W. Pg.3 ... L12
Lind ... Pg.2 ... G9
Linden Pl. ... Pg.3 ... D9,J12
Linder ... Pg.2 ... G9-19
Lipps ... Pg.2 ... G10
Lister ... Pg.3 ... K12
Lituanica ... Pg.7 ... K16
Livermore ... Pg.2 ... G8
Lloyd ... Pg.7 ... K16
Lock ... Pg.7 ... K16
Lockwood ... Pg.2 ... G9-19
Locust ... Pg.7 ... L13
Logan Blvd. ... Pg.3 ... J12
Loleta ... Pg.2 ... F8
London ... Pg.2 ... G10
Long ... Pg.2 ... G9-19
Longwood Dr. . Pg.10 .. K21-24
Loomis ... Pg.7 ... K14-24
Loomis Blvd. ... Pg.10 .. K19-22
Loomis Pl. ... Pg.7 ... K16,17
Lorel ... Pg.2 ... G12-19
Loring ... Pg.2 ... G9
Loron ... Pg.2 ... G8
Lothair ... Pg.10 .. J23-24
Lotus ... Pg.2 ... G9-18
Louis Munoz Marin Dr.
... Pg.6 ... J13
Louise ... Pg.2 ... F8,G9
Lovejoy ... Pg.2 ... F9
Lowe ... Pg.7 ... L15-18
Lowell ... Pg.2 ... H8-12
Loyola ... Pg.3 ... K8
Lucerne ... Pg.2 ... G9
Ludlam ... Pg.2 ... G9
Luella ... Pg.11 .. N20-25
Lumber ... Pg.7 ... K-L15
Luna ... Pg.2 ... G9-18
Lundy ... Pg.2 ... F8
Lunt Ave. ... Pg.2 ... E-K8
Luther Pl. ... Pg.6 ... J16
Lyman ... Pg.7 ... K16
Lynch ... Pg.2 ... G9
Lyndale ... Pg.2 ... G-J12
Lyon ... Pg.11 ... M22
Lytle ... Pg.7 ... K14-15
Mackinaw ... Pg.11 .. O21-25
Madison ... Pg.6 ... F-L14
Madison Ave. Pk. E.
... Pg.7 ... M18
Magnet ... Pg.2 ... F9
Magnolia ... Pg.3 ... K8-12
Major ... Pg.2 ... F9-19
Malden ... Pg.3 ... K10
Mandel ... Pg.2 ... F8
Mango ... Pg.2 ... F9-12
Manila ... Pg.2 ... F9
Manistee ... Pg.11 .. O20-25
Mankato ... Pg.2 ... F8
Mann Dr. ... Pg.10 ... H-J19
Manor ... Pg.3 ... D9,J10
Mansfield ... Pg.7 ... K15
Manton ... Pg.2 ... F9
Maple ... Pg.7 ... L13
Maplewood ... Pg.3 ... J7-24
Marcey ... Pg.3 ... K12
Margate Ter. ... Pg.3 ... K-L9
Marine Dr. ... Pg.3 ... L9-10
Marion ... Pg.2 ... F9
Marion Ct. ... Pg.7 ... K13
Market St. ... Pg.13 ... L25
Markham ... Pg.2 ... F9
Marmora ... Pg.2 ... F9-12
Marquette ... Pg.11 .. O20-25
Marquette Dr. . Pg.11 ... N19
Marquette Rd. . Pg.9 ... G-N19
Marshall Blvd. . Pg.6 ... J15
Marshfield ... Pg.3 ... K7-22
Mary ... Pg.7 ... K16
Maryland ... Pg.11 .. M18-23
Mason ... Pg.2 ... F9-19
Massasoit ... Pg.6 ... F13-19
Matson ... Pg.2 ... F9
Maud ... Pg.3 ... K12
Mautene Ct. ... Pg.7 ... K13
Maxwell ... Pg.7 ... K-L15
May ... Pg.7 ... K13-24
Mayfield ... Pg.2 ... F12-19
Maypole ... Pg.6 ... G-K14
McAlpin ... Pg.2 ... F8
McClellan ... Pg.2 ... F8
McClurg Ct. ... Pg.7 ... M13
McCook ... Pg.2 ... F9
McCormick Blvd.
... Pg.3 ... H6-8
McDowell ... Pg.7 ... K17
McFetrige Dr. .. Pg.7 ... M15
McLean ... Pg.2 ... F-K12
McLeod ... Pg.2 ... F9
McVicker ... Pg.2 ... F8-19
Meade ... Pg.2 ... F8-19
Medford ... Pg.2 ... F8
Medill ... Pg.2 ... E-K12
Medina ... Pg.2 ... F9
Meis Van Der Rohe
... Pg.7 ... L13
Melrose ... Pg.2 ... E-L11
Melvina ... Pg.2,5,6,9 F8-12
Menard ... Pg.2 ... F9-19
Mendell ... Pg.2 ... F8,K12
Mendota ... Pg.2 ... F8
Menominee ... Pg.3 ... L12
Meredith ... Pg.2 ... F8
Merrill Ave. ... Pg.11 .. N19-26
Merrimac ... Pg.2,5,6,9 F8-19
Merrion ... Pg.11 ... N22
Meyer ... Pg.3 ... L12
Miami ... Pg.2 ... F9
Michigan ... Pg.7 ... L13-25
Midway ... Pg.6 ... F13
Midway Plaisance
... Pg.11 .. M-N19
Mildred ... Pg.3 ... K11
Millard ... Pg.6,8,10,12
... H14-23
Miller ... Pg.7 ... K14-15
Miltimore ... Pg.2 ... F9
Milwaukee ... Pg.2,3,7
... E7,H11,K13
Minerva ... Pg.11 ... M19
Minnehaha ... Pg.2 ... G8
Minnetonka ... Pg.2 ... F8
Mobile ... Pg.2,5,6,9 F8-19
Moffat ... Pg.3 ... J-K12
Mohawk ... Pg.3 ... L12
Monon Ave. ... Pg.2 ... F8
Monotor ... Pg.2 ... F9-19
Monroe ... Pg.6 ... G-L14
Monroe Dr. ... Pg.7 ... L-M14
Montana ... Pg.2 ... G-K12
Montclare ... Pg.2 .. E9,11-12
Monterrey ... Pg.10 ... K23
Montgomery ... Pg.6 ... J17
Monticello ... Pg.3 ... H8-13
Montrose ... Pg.1 ... D-L10
Montrose Harbor Dr.
... Pg.3 ... L10
Montvale ... Pg.10 ... K23
Moody ... Pg.2 ... F8-19
Moore ... Pg.7 ... L13
Moorman ... Pg.7 ... K13
Morgan ... Pg.7 ... K14-25
Morse Ave. ... Pg.2 ... G-K8
Moselle ... Pg.2 ... F8
Mozart ... Pg.3 ... J8-21
Mulligan ... Pg.2,5,6,9 F9-19
Museum Dr. ... Pg.11 ... N18
Muskegon ... Pg.11 .. O20-25
Myrtle ... Pg.2 ... E8
N. Access Rd. ... B10
Nada ... Pg.7 ... K13
Nagle ... Pg.2 ... F8-19
Naper ... Pg.2 ... F8-9
Naples ... Pg.2 ... F8-9
Napoleon ... Pg.2 ... F9
Narragansett Pg.2,5,6,9
... F10-19
Nashotah ... Pg.2 ... F9
Nashville ... Pg.2 ... F8-19
Nassau ... Pg.2 ... F8-9
Natchez ... Pg.2 ... F9-19
Natoma ... Pg.2 ... F8-19
Navajo ... Pg.2 ... G8
Navarre ... Pg.2 ... E-F9
Neenah ... Pg.2 ... F8-19
Nelson ... Pg.2 ... E-L11
Neola ... Pg.2 ... F8-10
Nettleton ... Pg.2 ... E8-9
Neva ... Pg.2 ... E8-18
New ... Pg.7 ... M13-14
New England ... Pg.2 ... E8-19
New Hampshire Pg.2 ... E9
Newark ... Pg.2 ... E8-9
Newberry ... Pg.7 ... L15
Newburg ... Pg.7 ... L15
Newcastle ... Pg.2 ... E8-19
Newgard ... Pg.3 ... K8
Newland ... Pg.2 ... E8-19
Newport ... Pg.2 ... E-L11
Newton ... Pg.2 ... E9
Niagara ... Pg.2 ... E8-9
Nickerson ... Pg.2 ... E8-9
Nicolet ... Pg.2 ... E9
Nina ... Pg.2 ... E9
Nixon ... Pg.2 ... E8
Nobel ... Pg.2 ... F10
Noble ... Pg.3 ... K12-13
Nokomis ... Pg.2 ... G8
Nora ... Pg.2 ... E10-11
Nordica ... Pg.2 ... E8-18
Normal ... Pg.7 ... L15-24
Normal Blvd. ... Pg.10 ... L19-20
Normal Pkwy. ... Pg.10 ... L19
Normandy ... Pg.2 ... F8-19
North ... Pg.2,3,5,7 E-L12
North Branch .. Pg.7 ... K13
North Park ... Pg.3 ... L12-13

# CHICAGO

Caldwells G.C. . Pg.2 . . . . . . . G9
Columbus Park G.C.
. . . . . . . . Pg.6 . . . . . . . F14
Edgebrook G.C. Pg.2 . . . . F9
Fountain Hills G.C.
. . . . . . . . Pg.13 . . . . . . . J24
Harborside Int'l. Golf Center
. . . . . . . . Pg.11 . . . . . . N23
Indian Boundary G.C.
. . . . . . . . Pg.1 . . . . . . . D11
Jackson Park G.C.
. . . . . . . . Pg.11 . . . . . . N19
Marquette Park G.C.
. . . . . . . . Pg.10 . . . . . . H19
Metro Golf Illinois Center
. . . . . . . . Pg.7 . . . . . . . M14
Ridge C.C. . Pg.10 . . . . J23
South Shore C.C.
. . . . . . . . Pg.11 . . . . . . N20
The Meadows G.C.
. . . . . . . . Pg.13 . . . . . . J24
Waveland G.C. Pg.3 . . . . L10

## HOSPITALS

Alexian Bros. Med. Ctr.
. . . . . . . . Pg.3 . . . . . . . K12
American Hosp. Pg.3 . . . . K10
Augustana Hosp.
. . . . . . . . Pg.3 . . . . . . . L12
Belmont Comm. Hosp.
. . . . . . . . Pg.2 . . . . . . . H11
Bethany Hosp. . Pg.6 . . . . H14
Bethany Meth. Hosp.
. . . . . . . . Pg.3 . . . . . . . K9
Cabrini Hosp. . Pg.7 . . . . K14
Central Comm. Hosp.
. . . . . . . . Pg.10 . . . . . . K18
Chicago Osteopathic Hosp.
. . . . . . . . Pg.7 . . . . . . . M18
Chicago State Hospital
. . . . . . . . Pg.2 . . . . . . . F10
Chicago-Lake Shore Hosp.
. . . . . . . . Pg.3 . . . . . . . L10
Children's Mem. Hosp.
. . . . . . . . Pg.3 . . . . . . . L12
Columbus Hosp.
. . . . . . . . Pg.3 . . . . . . . L12
Cook Co. Hosp. Pg.7 . . . . K14
Cuneo Hosp. . Pg.3 . . . . L10
Doctor's Hosp.
. . . . . . . . Pg.7 . . . . . . . N18
Edgewater Hosp.
. . . . . . . . Pg.3 . . . . . . . K9
Franklin Blvd. Comm. Hosp.
. . . . . . . . Pg.6 . . . . . . . H13
Grant Hospital . Pg.3 . . . . L12
Halco Hospital . Pg.7 . . . . L13
Holy Cross Hospital
. . . . . . . . Pg.10 . . . . . . J19
Ill. Masonic Med. Ctr.
. . . . . . . . Pg.3 . . . . . . . K11
Jackson Park Hosp.
. . . . . . . . Pg.11 . . . . . . N20
LaRabida Children's Hosp. &
Research Ctr. Pg.11 . . . . N19
Loretto Hosp. . Pg.6 . . . . G14
Louis Burg Hosp.
. . . . . . . . Pg.7 . . . . . . . L15
Martha Washington Hosp.
. . . . . . . . Pg.3 . . . . . . . J10
Mary Thompson Hosp.
. . . . . . . . Pg.7 . . . . . . . K14
Mercy Hosp. . Pg.7 . . . . M16
Michael Reese Med. Ctr.
. . . . . . . . Pg.7 . . . . . . . M16
Mt. Sinai Hospital Med. Ctr.
. . . . . . . . Pg.6 . . . . . . . J15
Mun. Communicable Disease
Hosp. . . . . Pg.6 . . . . . J16
Mun. T.B. Sanitarium
. . . . . . . . Pg.3 . . . . . . . H9
Nicholas J. Pritzker Children's
Hosp. . . . . Pg.7 . . . . . M16
Northeast Comm. Hosp.
. . . . . . . . Pg.3 . . . . . . . K8
Northwestern Mem. Hosp.
. . . . . . . . Pg.7 . . . . . . . L13
Norwegian Amer. Hosp.
. . . . . . . . Pg.6 . . . . . . . J13
Our Lady of Ressurection
Hospital . . . Pg.2 . . . . . F11
Pinel Hosp. . Pg.3 . . . . L11
Provident Hosp. Pg.7 . . . . M18
Ravenswood Hosp.
. . . . . . . . Pg.3 . . . . . . . K10
Rest Haven Hosp.
. . . . . . . . Pg.6 . . . . . . . J15
Resurrection Hosp.
. . . . . . . . Pg.2 . . . . . . . E9
Ridgeway Hosp.
. . . . . . . . Pg.6 . . . . . . . H13
Roosevelt Mem. Hosp.
. . . . . . . . Pg.3 . . . . . . . L12
Roseland Comm. Hosp.
. . . . . . . . Pg.10 . . . . . . L23
Rush Presby. St. Luke's
Med. Ctr . . . Pg.7 . . . . . K14
Sheridan Rd. Hosp.
. . . . . . . . Pg.3 . . . . . . . K9
Shriners Hosp. Pg.2 . . . . F12
South Chicago Comm. Hosp.
. . . . . . . . Pg.11 . . . . . . N22

---

South Shore Hosp.
. . . . . . . . Pg.11 . . . . . . N20
St. Anthony's Hosp.
. . . . . . . . Pg.6 . . . . . . . J15
St. Bernard's Hosp.
. . . . . . . . Pg.10 . . . . . . L19
St. Elizabeth's Hosp.
. . . . . . . . Pg.6 . . . . . . . J13
St. Georges Hosp.
. . . . . . . . Pg.10 . . . . . . L20
St. Joseph Hosp.
. . . . . . . . Pg.3 . . . . . . . L11
St. Mary of Nazareth Hosp.
. . . . . . . . Pg.6 . . . . . . . J13
State T.B. Hosp. Pg.7 . . . . K15
Swedish Covenant Hosp.
. . . . . . . . Pg.3 . . . . . . . J9
Thorek Hosp. . Pg.3 . . . . K10
U. of Chicago Clinics
. . . . . . . . Pg.11 . . . . . . M18
U. of IL. Med. Ctr.
. . . . . . . . Pg.7 . . . . . . . K14
Veterans Admin. Hosp.
. . . . . . . . Pg.7 . . . . . . . K14
Veterans Admin. Research
Hosp. . . . . Pg.7 . . . . . M13
Von Solbrig Hosp.
. . . . . . . . Pg.9 . . . . . . . H19
Walther Mem. Hosp.
. . . . . . . . Pg.6 . . . . . . . H13
Weiss Mem. Hosp.
. . . . . . . . Pg.3 . . . . . . . L10

## PARKS

Burnham Park . Pg.7 . . . . M10
Calumet Park . Pg.11 . . . . P22
Columbus Bark Pg.6 . . . . F14
Douglas Park . Pg.6 . . . . J15
Garfield Park . Pg.6 . . . . H14
Grant Park . . Pg.7 . . . . M14
Hamilton Park . Pg.10 . . . . L20
Hanson Park . Pg.2 . . . . G12
Harlod Wahington Park
. . . . . . . . Pg.7 . . . . . . . N18
Horner Park . Pg.3 . . . . J10
Humboldt Park Pg.6 . . . . J13
Jackson Park . Pg.11 . . . . N19
Lincoln Park . Pg.3 . . . . L12
Loyola Park . Pg.3 . . . . K8
Marquette Park Pg.10 . . . . H19
McKinley Park . Pg.6 . . . . J17
Ogden Park . Pg.10 . . . . K19
Oriole Park . Pg.2 . . . . E9
Portage Park . Pg.2 . . . . G10
Rainbow Park . Pg.11 . . . . O20
Riis Park . . . Pg.2 . . . . F12
Rogers Park . Pg.3 . . . . J8
Sherman Park . Pg.10 . . . . K18
Warren Park . Pg.3 . . . . J8
Washington Park
. . . . . . . . Pg.11 . . . . . . M18
Washington Square Park
. . . . . . . . Pg.7 . . . . . . . L13

## SCHOOLS

Academy of Our Lady
. . . . . . . . Pg.10 . . . . . . K22
Amundson H.S. Pg.3 . . . . J9
Austin H.S. . . Pg.6 . . . . G14
Bowen H.S. . Pg.11 . . . . O21
Brother Rice H.S.
. . . . . . . . Pg.9 . . . . . . . H22
Calumet H.S. . Pg.10 . . . . K21
Carver H.S. . Pg.11 . . . . M25
Catholic Theo. Union of
Chicago . . . Pg.11 . . . . N18
Chicago Bible College
. . . . . . . . Pg.3 . . . . . . . K11
Chicago H.S. for Agri. Sci.
. . . . . . . . Pg.9 . . . . . . . H23
Chicago Jr. College (Bogan Branch)
. . . . . . . . Pg.9 . . . . . . . H20
Chicago Jr. College
(Mayfair Unit) Pg.2 . . . . G10
Chicago Jr. College (Wright
Branch) . . . Pg.2 . . . . . F11
Chicago Medical Sch.
. . . . . . . . Pg.6 . . . . . . . H15
Chicago State Univ.
. . . . . . . . Pg.11 . . . . . . M22
Chicago Tech. College
. . . . . . . . Pg.7 . . . . . . . L15
Chicago Theological
Seminary . . Pg.11 . . . . M18
Chicago Voc. H.S.
. . . . . . . . Pg.11 . . . . . . N21
Clemente H.S. Pg.6 . . . . J13
Collins H.S. . Pg.6 . . . . J15
Corliss H.S. . Pg.11 . . . . M22
Crane H.S. . Pg.6 . . . . J14
Cregier Voc. H.S.
. . . . . . . . Pg.7 . . . . . . . K14
Curie H.S. . . Pg.6 . . . . H18
Daley Jr. College
. . . . . . . . Pg.9 . . . . . . . H20
De LaSalle H.S. Pg.7 . . . . L16
DePaul Univ. . Pg.3 . . . . K12
DeVry Inst. of Tech.
. . . . . . . . Pg.2 . . . . . . . H11
Dr. M. L. King Jr. H.S.
. . . . . . . . Pg.7 . . . . . . . M17
Du Sable H.S. Pg.7 . . . . L18

---

Dunbar Voc. H.S.
. . . . . . . . Pg.7 . . . . . . . M16
Englewood H.S. Pg.10 . . . . L19
Farragut H.S. . Pg.6 . . . . H16
Fenger H.S. . Pg.10 . . . . L23
Flower Voc. H.S.
. . . . . . . . Pg.6 . . . . . . . H14
Foreman H.S. . Pg.2 . . . . G11
Good Council H.S.
. . . . . . . . Pg.2 . . . . . . . H9
Gordon Tech. H.S.
. . . . . . . . Pg.3 . . . . . . . J11
Gunsaulus Sch. Acad.
. . . . . . . . Pg.3 . . . . . . . J17
Gurden Hubbard H.S.
. . . . . . . . Pg.9 . . . . . . . H19
Hales Franciscan H.S.
. . . . . . . . Pg.7 . . . . . . . M18
Hanna Saeks H.S.
. . . . . . . . Pg.3 . . . . . . . J8
Harlan H.S. . . Pg.10 . . . . L22
Harold Washington Coll.
. . . . . . . . Pg.7 . . . . . . . L14
Harper H.S. . Pg.10 . . . . K19
Hirsch H.S. . Pg.11 . . . . M20
Holy Trinity H.S. Pg.7 . . . . K13
House of the Good Shepherd
H.S. . . . . . Pg.3 . . . . . K10
Hyde Park H.S. Pg.11 . . . . N19
Ida Crown H.S. Pg.3 . . . . J8
Ill. Coll. of Optometry
. . . . . . . . Pg.7 . . . . . . . L16
Illinois Institute of
Technology . Pg.7 . . . . . L16
Jones Comm. H.S.
. . . . . . . . Pg.7 . . . . . . . L14
Juarez H.S. . Pg.7 . . . . K15
Kelly H.S. . . Pg.6 . . . . J17
Kelvyn Park H.S.
. . . . . . . . Pg.2 . . . . . . . H12
Kennedy H.S. . Pg.9 . . . . F18
Kennedy-King Coll.
. . . . . . . . Pg.10 . . . . . . L19
Kenwood H.S. Pg.7 . . . . N18
King H.S. . . Pg.7 . . . . M17
La Casas Occup. H.S.
. . . . . . . . Pg.11 . . . . . . O22
Lake View H.S. Pg.3 . . . . K10
Lane Tech. H.S. Pg.3 . . . . J11
Leo H.S. . . . Pg.10 . . . . L20
Lindblom H.S. . Pg.10 . . . . K19
Lourdes H.S. . Pg.9 . . . . H18
Loyola Univ. . Pg.3 . . . . K8
Luther H.S. North
. . . . . . . . Pg.2 . . . . . . . F10
Luther H.S. South
. . . . . . . . Pg.10 . . . . . . J21
Madonna H.S. Pg.2 . . . . H11
Malcolm X Coll. Pg.7 . . . . K14
Manley H.S. . Pg.6 . . . . J14
Marshall H.S. . Pg.6 . . . . H14
Mather H.S. . Pg.3 . . . . J9
Meadville Lombard Theo. Sch.
. . . . . . . . Pg.11 . . . . . . M18
Montay College Pg.3 . . . . H8
Moody Bible Inst.
. . . . . . . . Pg.7 . . . . . . . L14
Morgan Park Academy
. . . . . . . . Pg.10 . . . . . . K23
Mother McAuley H.S
. . . . . . . . Pg.9 . . . . . . . H22
Mt. Carmel H.S. Pg.11 . . . . M19
Mundelein Coll. Pg.3 . . . . K8
North Park Coll. & Theo. Sem
. . . . . . . . Pg.3 . . . . . . . H9
Northeastern Ill. Univ.
. . . . . . . . Pg.3 . . . . . . . H9
Northwestern Bus. Coll.
. . . . . . . . Pg.3 . . . . . . . J12
Northwestern Univ. (Chicago
Campus) . . Pg.7 . . . . . M13
Notre Dame H.S.
. . . . . . . . Pg.2 . . . . . . . F11
Olive-Harvey Coll.
. . . . . . . . Pg.11 . . . . . . M22
Orr H.S. . . . Pg.6 . . . . H13
Phillips H.S. . Pg.7 . . . . M17
Prosser H.S. . Pg.2 . . . . G12
Providence H.S. Pg.6 . . . . H14
Quigley Prep. Seminary
. . . . . . . . Pg.7 . . . . . . . L13
Resurrection H.S.
. . . . . . . . Pg.2 . . . . . . . E9
Richards Voc. H.S.
. . . . . . . . Pg.6 . . . . . . . K18
Roosevelt H.S. Pg.3 . . . . H10
Roosevelt Univ. Pg.7 . . . . L14
Savcedo H.S. . Pg.6 . . . . J15
Schurz H.S. . Pg.2 . . . . H11
Senn H.S. . . Pg.3 . . . . K9
Shoop H.S. . Pg.10 . . . . K23
Simeon Voc. H.S.
. . . . . . . . Pg.10 . . . . . . L21
South Shore H.S.
. . . . . . . . Pg.11 . . . . . . N20
Spaulding H.S. Pg.7 . . . . K14
St. Alphonsus Comm. H.S.
. . . . . . . . Pg.3 . . . . . . . K11
St. Ann H.S. . Pg.6 . . . . J15
St. Barbara H.S. Pg.7 . . . . K16

---

St. Benedict H.S.
. . . . . . . . Pg.3 . . . . . . . J10
St. Elizabeth H.S.
. . . . . . . . Pg.7 . . . . . . . L17
St. Francis DeSales H.S.
. . . . . . . . Pg.11 . . . . . . P22
St. Ignatius H.S. Pg.7 . . . . K15
St. Patrick H.S. Pg.3 . . . . F11
St. Rita H.S. . Pg.10 . . . . J20
St. Scholastica H.S.
. . . . . . . . Pg.3 . . . . . . . J7
St. Xavier University
. . . . . . . . Pg.9 . . . . . . . H22
Steinmetz H.S. . Pg.2 . . . . F11
Sullivan H.S. . Pg.3 . . . . K8
Taft H.S. . . Pg.2 . . . . F9
Tilden Tech. H.S.
. . . . . . . . Pg.7 . . . . . . . L17
Unity H.S. . . Pg.10 . . . . M21
Univ. of Chicago
. . . . . . . . Pg.11 . . . . . . M18
Univ. of Ill. (Chicago Campus)
. . . . . . . . Pg.7 . . . . . . . L14
Vandercook College of Music
. . . . . . . . Pg.7 . . . . . . . L16
Von Steuben H.S.
. . . . . . . . Pg.3 . . . . . . . H9
Washburne Trade H.S.
. . . . . . . . Pg.6 . . . . . . . H16
Washington H.S.
. . . . . . . . Pg.11 . . . . . . O23
Wells H.S. . . Pg.6 . . . . K13
Westinghouse Voc. H.S.
. . . . . . . . Pg.6 . . . . . . . H13
Wilson Occup. H.S.
. . . . . . . . Pg.2 . . . . . . . G9
Child Development Inst.
. . . . . . . . Pg.7 . . . . . . . M18
Emmanuel Christian Sch.
. . . . . . . . Pg.10 . . . . . . K21
Paul Robeson H.S.
. . . . . . . . Pg.10 . . . . . . L19
St. Ambrose Sch.
. . . . . . . . Pg.7 . . . . . . . M17
St. Edmonds Academy
. . . . . . . . Pg.11 . . . . . . M19

## SHOPPING CENTERS

Brickyard Mall . Pg.2 . . . . F11
Century Mall . Pg.3 . . . . L11
Ford City . . . Pg.9 . . . . G20
Lake Meadows Pg.7 . . . . M16
Scottsdale S.C. Pg.9 . . . . G20
Chatman Ridge Mall
. . . . . . . . Pg.10 . . . . . . L21

## TRANSPORTATION

Chicago & Northwestern
R.R. Sta. . . Pg.7 . . . . . L14
Chicago Midway Airport
. . . . . . . . Pg.9 . . . . . . . G18,19
Columbia Yacht Club
. . . . . . . . Pg.7 . . . . . . . M14
Dearborn St. R.R. Sta.
. . . . . . . . Pg.7 . . . . . . . L14
I.C. Station . Pg.7 . . . . L14
LaSalle St. R.R. Sta.
. . . . . . . . Pg.7 . . . . . . . L14
Meigs Field . Pg.7 . . . . M15
O'Hare Int'l Airport
. . . . . . . . Pg.1 . . . . . . . B9
Union R.R. Sta. Pg.7 . . . . L14

## MISCELLANEOUS

Adler Planetarium
. . . . . . . . Pg.7 . . . . . . . M15
Aero Space Institute
. . . . . . . . Pg.7 . . . . . . . L13
Air France . . Pg.1 . . . . B10
Alonzo Stagg Field
. . . . . . . . Pg.7 . . . . . . . M18
American Airlines
. . . . . . . . Pg.1 . . . . . . . B10
Art Institute . . Pg.7 . . . . L14
Buckingham Fountain
. . . . . . . . Pg.7 . . . . . . . L14
Burnham Park Yacht Club
. . . . . . . . Pg.7 . . . . . . . M15
Calumet Yacht Club
. . . . . . . . Pg.11 . . . . . . P22
Chicago Acad. of Sciences
. . . . . . . . Pg.3 . . . . . . . L12
Chicago Board of Trade
. . . . . . . . Pg.7 . . . . . . . K17
Chicago Corinthian Yacht Club
. . . . . . . . Pg.3 . . . . . . . L10
Chicago Hist. Society
. . . . . . . . Pg.3 . . . . . . . L12
Chicago Lighthouse for
the Blind . . . Pg.7 . . . . . K15
Chicago Nursery & Orphan Asylum
. . . . . . . . Pg.3 . . . . . . . J9
Chicago Public Library
. . . . . . . . Pg.7 . . . . . . . L14
Chicago Water Reclaimation
Sanitary Dist. Pg.11 . . . . M25
Chicago Yacht Club
. . . . . . . . Pg.7 . . . . . . . M14
Chinatown . . Pg.7 . . . . L15
City Hall . . . Pg.7 . . . . L14
Coast Guard Sta.
. . . . . . . . Pg.7 . . . . . . . M14,P22

---

St. Benedict H.S.
. . . . . . . . Pg.3 . . . . . . . J10
Comiskey Park (White Sox)
. . . . . . . . Pg.7 . . . . . . . L16
Cook Co. Correctional Dept.
. . . . . . . . Pg.6 . . . . . . . J16
Cook Co. Juvenile Home
. . . . . . . . Pg.6 . . . . . . . J15
County Building
. . . . . . . . Pg.7 . . . . . . . L14
Courthouse . . Pg.6 . . . . J16
Daley Center . Pg.7 . . . . L14
Diversey Yacht Club
. . . . . . . . Pg.3 . . . . . . . L12
Douglas Tomb State Mem.
. . . . . . . . Pg.7 . . . . . . . M16
DuSable Museum
. . . . . . . . Pg.11 . . . . . . M18
Eckersall Stadium
. . . . . . . . Pg.11 . . . . . . N21
Federal Bldg. . Pg.7 . . . . L14
Federal Express
. . . . . . . . Pg.1 . . . . . . . B10
Field Museum of Natural History
. . . . . . . . Pg.7 . . . . . . . L15
Filtration Plant . Pg.11 . . . . U20
Ford Motor Company
. . . . . . . . Pg.14 . . . . . . O25
Grant Monument
. . . . . . . . Pg.3 . . . . . . . L12
Home for the Aged
. . . . . . . . Pg.1 . . . . . . . H9
Hull House Museum
. . . . . . . . Pg.7 . . . . . . . L14
Ill. Air Nat'l. Guard
. . . . . . . . Pg.9 . . . . . . . G19
Int'l Amphitheatre
. . . . . . . . Pg.7 . . . . . . . L17
Jackson Park Y.C.
. . . . . . . . Pg.11 . . . . . . N19
KLM . . . . . Pg.1 . . . . B10
Knute Rockne Sta.
. . . . . . . . Pg.6 . . . . . . . G15
Lawrence Hall Youth Service
Center . . . . Pg.3 . . . . . J10
Lincoln Monument Statues
. . . . . . . . Pg.3 . . . . . . . L12
Lincoln Park Archery Club
. . . . . . . . Pg.3 . . . . . . . L12
Lincoln Park Bird Sanctuary
. . . . . . . . Pg.3 . . . . . . . L11
Lincoln Park Conservatory
. . . . . . . . Pg.3 . . . . . . . L12
Lincoln Park Totem Pole
. . . . . . . . Pg.3 . . . . . . . L11
Lincoln Park Zoo
. . . . . . . . Pg.3 . . . . . . . L12
McCormick Place Expo. Center
. . . . . . . . Pg.7 . . . . . . . M15
Merchandise Mart
. . . . . . . . Pg.7 . . . . . . . L14
Museum of Science & Industry
. . . . . . . . Pg.11 . . . . . . N18
Navy Pier . . . Pg.7 . . . . M13
Newberry Library
. . . . . . . . Pg.7 . . . . . . . L13
Opera House . Pg.7 . . . . L14
Port of Chicago Calumet Harbor
. . . . . . . . Pg.14 . . . . . . N25
Post Office-Main
. . . . . . . . Pg.7 . . . . . . . L14
Post Office-O'Hare Airport
. . . . . . . . Pg.1 . . . . . . . B10
Pulman Museum
. . . . . . . . Pg.11 . . . . . . M23
Regenstein Lib. Pg.11 . . . . M18
Rosemont Horizon
. . . . . . . . Pg.1 . . . . . . . B8
Shedd Aquarium
. . . . . . . . Pg.7 . . . . . . . M15
Soldier Field . Pg.7 . . . . M15
South District Filtration Plant
. . . . . . . . Pg.11 . . . . . . O20
Southern Shore Y.C.
. . . . . . . . Pg.7 . . . . . . . N19
Tribune Tower . Pg.7 . . . . L13
U.S. Customs House
. . . . . . . . Pg.7 . . . . . . . L14
U.S. Military Res.
. . . . . . . . Pg.14 . . . . . . P24
UPS . . . . . Pg.1 . . . . B10
United Airlines . Pg.1 . . . . A10
United Center . Pg.7 . . . . K14
Water Tower . Pg.7 . . . . L13
Wrigley Building
. . . . . . . . Pg.7 . . . . . . . L13
Wrigley Field (Cubs)
. . . . . . . . Pg.3 . . . . . . . K11
YMCA . . . . Pg.11 . . . . N19

## CHICAGO RIDGE

Page 9
(For additional listings,
see Section 2)

## STREETS

Andersen Ave. . . . . . . . E22
Austin Ave. . . . . . . . . . F23
Barnard Dr. . . . . . . . . . F23
Birmingham St. . . . . . . F23
Central Ave. . . . . . . . . G23
Fireside Dr. . . . . . . . . . F23
Forest Ln. . . . . . . . . . . F23
Grove St. . . . . . . . . . . F22

---

# CICERO

Hyland Pl. . . . . . . . . . . F22
Janet Ln. . . . . . . . . . . F22
Leslie Ln. . . . . . . . . . . F22
Lombard Ave. . . . . . . . F23
Lyman Ave. . . . . . . . . . F23
Major Ave. . . . . . . . . . F22
Mansfield Ave. . . . . . . F23
Marshall Ave. . . . . . . . F22
Mason Ave. . . . . . . . . . F23
Massasoit Ave. . . . . . . F23
Mather Ave. . . . . . . . . E22,F23
Mayfield Ave. . . . . . . . F22,23
McVicker Ave. . . . . . . . F22,23
Meade Ave. . . . . . . . . . F22
Melvina . . . . . . . . . . . F23
Menard Ave. . . . . . . . . F23
Monitor Ave. . . . . . . . . F23
Moody Ave. . . . . . . . . . F23
Nashville Ave. . . . . . . . F22,23
Natoma Ave. . . . . . . . . F22,23
New England Ave. . . . . E22
Norfolk Av. . . . . . . . . . F22
Normandy Ave. . . . . . . F22,23
Nottingham Ave. . . . . . E22
O'Connell St. . . . . . . . . E22
Oak Ave. . . . . . . . . . . F23
Oak Park Ave. . . . . . . . F22
Orchard Ln. . . . . . . . . . F23
Oxford Ave. . . . . . . . . . F23
Pacific Ave. . . . . . . . . . F22
Pamela Ln. . . . . . . . . . F23
Parkside Ave. . . . . . . . F23
Pleasant Blvd. . . . . . . . F23
Princess Ave. . . . . . . . F23
Ridge Dr. . . . . . . . . . . F23
Ridgeland Ave. . . . . . . F22
Ridgemont Ln. . . . . . . . F23
Sayre . . . . . . . . . . . . E22
Southwest Hwy. . . . . . . E23
Stephen Dr. . . . . . . . . F22
Sycamore . . . . . . . . . . F23
Tracy Ave. . . . . . . . . . F23
Washington St. . . . . . . F23
97th Pl. . . . . . . . . . . . E22
98th St. . . . . . . . . . . . E22
99th Pl. . . . . . . . . . . . E22
99th St. . . . . . . . . . . . E22
100th St. . . . . . . . . . . E22
101st St. . . . . . . . . . . F22
103rd St. . . . . . . . . . . F23
104th Pl. . . . . . . . . . . F23
104th St. . . . . . . . . . . F23
105th St. . . . . . . . . . . F23
106th Pl. . . . . . . . . . . F23
106th St. . . . . . . . . . . F23
107th Pl. . . . . . . . . . . F23
107th St. . . . . . . . . . . F23
108th Pl. . . . . . . . . . . F23
108th St. . . . . . . . . . . F23
109th Pl. . . . . . . . . . . F23
110th Pl. . . . . . . . . . . F23
111th St. . . . . . . . . . . F23

## GOLF COURSES

Stoney Creek G.C. . . . . F22

## PARKS

Memorial Park . . . . . . . F23

# CICERO

Page 6

## STREETS

Austin . . . . . . . . . . . . F15
Central Ave. . . . . . . . . G15-17
Cermak Rd. . . . . . . . . F,G16
Cicero . . . . . . . . . . . . G15-17
Edgewood . . . . . . . . . F16
Laramie . . . . . . . . . . . G15,16
Lombard . . . . . . . . . . F15
Ogden Ave. . . . . . . . . F16
Park . . . . . . . . . . . . . F16
Pershing Rd. . . . . . . . . F17
Roosevelt Rd. . . . . . . . F,G15
12th Pl. . . . . . . . . . . . G15
13th Pl. . . . . . . . . . . . G15
13th St. . . . . . . . . . . . F,G15
14th St. . . . . . . . . . . . F,G15
15th Pl. . . . . . . . . . . . G15
15th St. . . . . . . . . . . . F,G15
16th St. . . . . . . . . . . . F,G15
18th St. . . . . . . . . . . . F17
19th Pl. . . . . . . . . . . . F17
19th St. . . . . . . . . . . . G15
20th St. . . . . . . . . . . . G15
21st Pl. . . . . . . . . . . . G15
21st St. . . . . . . . . . . . G15
22nd Pl. . . . . . . . . . . . F,G15
23rd Pl. . . . . . . . . . . . G15
23rd St. . . . . . . . . . . . G15
24th Pl. . . . . . . . . . . . F,G16
24th St. . . . . . . . . . . . F,G15
25th Pl. . . . . . . . . . . . G16
25th St. . . . . . . . . . . . F,G16
26th St. . . . . . . . . . . . F,G16
27th St. . . . . . . . . . . . F16
28th Pl. . . . . . . . . . . . G16
28th St. . . . . . . . . . . . G16
29th Pl. . . . . . . . . . . . G15
29th St. . . . . . . . . . . . G16
30th Pl. . . . . . . . . . . . G16
30th St. . . . . . . . . . . . G16
31st Pl. . . . . . . . . . . . G16

## CICERO

31st St. F,G16
32nd Pl. G16
32nd St. G16
33rd St. F,G16
34th St. F,G16
35th St. F,G16
36th St. F,G17
37th St. F,G17
38th St. F,G17
46th Ct. G15
46th St. G15
47th Ct. G15
47th St. G15
48th Ct. G15
49th Ct. G15
49th St. G15
50th Ct. G15,16
50th St. G15,16
51st Ct. G15
51st St. G15
52nd St. G15-17
53rd Ct. G17
53rd St. G15-17
54th Ct. G17-17
54th St. G17-17
55th Ct. G15-17
55th St. G15-17
56th Ct. F15-17
56th St. G15
57th Ct. F15-17
57th St. F15-17
58th Ct. F15-17
58th St. F15-17
59th Ct. F15-17
59th St. F15-17
60th Ct. F15-17
61st Ct. F15-17
61st St. F15-17

**PARKS**
Clyde Park F16
Columbus Playground G16
Hawthorne Park G16
Manor Park F16
N. Warren Park F15
Parkholm Park G15
South Clyde Park F17
Warren Park F15

**SCHOOLS**
Morton East H.S. & Jr. Coll. F16

**MISCELLANEOUS**
Hawthorne Race Track G17
Sportsmans Park Race Track G16
Village Hall G16

## COUNTRYSIDE

Page 8

**STREETS**
Ashland C18
Barton Rd. C19
Bob-O-Link Dr. C18
Brainard Ave. C19
Cantigny B19
Catherine C18
Constance Ln. C19
Crestview Rd. B19
Dasher Rd. C18
Dawn B19
East Ave. C18
Edgewood B18
Forestview B19
Francis C19
Golf View Dr. B19
Hillsdale B20
Joliet Rd. C19
Kensington Ave. C18,19
La Grange Rd. C19
Leitch B18
Longview Dr. C18,19
Lorraine Dr. B20,C19
Madison C18
Maplewood Rd. B20
Merry Court C19
Park Rd. C18
Parkside B19
Peck B18
Plainfield Rd. B,C18
Rose Ct. C19
Rosemary Ct. C19
S.E. Ct. B18
Stafford Rd. B19
Sunset B20
Terry Ln. C18
Vail Rd. B,C18
Willow Springs Rd. B19,20
5th St. B20
6th Ave. C18
7th Ave. C18
8th Ave. C18
9th Ave. C18
10th Ave. C18
51st St. C18
53rd St. C18
54th St. C18
55th Pl. B18
55th St. B,C18
56th St. C18
57th St. C18
58th St. C18
59th St. C19
61st Pl. C19
61st St. C19
63rd St. C19
67th St. B19
71st Pl. B20
74th St. C20
75th St. C20

**MISCELLANEOUS**
Village Hall C18

## CRESTWOOD

Page 12

**STREETS**
Arbor Ln. G25
Calumet Sag Rd. G25
Carriage Ln. G25
Central Ave. G25,26
Charles Ln. G26
Cicero Ave. G25
Circle Ave. G25
Circle Ct. G25
Crawford Ave. H26
Crescent Ct. G25
Crestview Ct. G26
Crestwood Ct. G25
Crestwood Dr. G25
Di Roe Ct. G25
Dori Ln. G26
Fairway Dr. G25
Forestview Ct. G25
Forestview Ln. G25
Harding H26
Highland Ct. G25
Hill St. F25
Homestead Dr. G25
James Ct. G26
James Dr. G26
Karlov Ave. H26
Karlov Ave. H26
Keeler H25
Kenton Ave. G25
Kildare Ave. H26
Kilpatrick Ave. G26
Kolmar Ln. H26
Kostner H25
Lamon Ave. G26
Laramie Ave. G25
Lavergne Ave. G26
Lawler Ave. G25
Leclaire Ave. G25
Leonard Dr. G26
Linder St. G25
Long Ave. G25
Loomis Ave. G25
Loomis Ct. G25
Loomis Ln. G25
Midlothian Tpke. H26
Model Ct. G25
Park Ct. G25
Park Ln. G25
Parkview Ct. G25
Playfield Dr., W. G25
Pleasant Ct. G25
Pleasant Ln. G25
Regal Rd. G25
Royal Ct. G25
S. End Ln. G26
Sandra Ln. G26
Short Dr. G25
Springfield Ave. H26
Terrace Ln. G25
Village Ct. G25
Village Ln. G25
Walter Dr. G26
Waterbury Ct. G26
Waterbury Dr. G26
Waterbury Ln. G26
Waterbury Way G26
West End Ln. G25
Willow Ln. G26
127th St. G25
128th Pl. G25
128th St. F25
129th Pl. G25
129th St. G25
130th St. G25
131st St. G25
132nd St. G25
133rd St. G25
134th Pl. G25
135th Ct. G25
135th Pl. G25
135th St. G25
136th Ct. H25
136th St. G25
137th Pl. G,H25
137th St. G25
138th Ct. G26
138th Pl. G26
138th St. G26
139th St. H26
140th Pl. G26
140th St. G,H26
141st St. G,H26
142nd St. G,H26
143rd St. G,H26

**CEMETERIES**
St. Benedict Cem. G25

**PARKS**
Walker Park G26

**SCHOOLS**
Southwest Area Tech Sch. H26

**SHOPPING CENTERS**
Rivercrest S.C. G25

**MISCELLANEOUS**
Village Hall G26

## DES PLAINES

Page 1
(For additional listings, see Section 2)

**STREETS**
Alden Ln. C8
Andy Ct. C8
Andy Ln. C8
Armstrong Ct. A8
Armstrong Rd. A8
Ash B7
Bending Ct. B5
Bennett Pl. C7
Birch St. C7,8
Birchwood Ave. B,C7
Bittersweet Ct. B7
Bradock Dr. A7
Briar Ct. B7
Callen Ln. B5
Carlow Dr. B5
Castlerea Ln. B5
Cedar Ct. C7
Cedar St. C8
Central Ave. C8
Chase Ave. C8
Chestnut St. B7
Circle Dr. C5
Circle St. B7
Clearwater Dr. A7
College Dr. C5
Cora St. B7
Craig Dr. C8
Curtis St. C8
Dale St. C8
David Dr. C8
Des Plaines River Rd. C8
Devon Ave. C8
Dexter Ln. B7
Douglas Ave. B8
Dursey Ln. B5
Eastview Dr. B8
Eisenhower Ct. C8
Eisenhower Dr. C8
Elm St. B7
Elmira Ave. B8
Esser Ct. C7
Estes Ave. C8
Everett Ave. B,C7
Everett Ln. B7
Fargo Ave. B8,C7
Farwell Ave. C8
Fox Ln. C8
Frontage Rd. B8
Greco Ave. C8
Greenleaf C8
Halsey Dr. C8
Hazel Ct. B7
Hickory St. C8
Higgins Rd. A,C8
Highland Dr. B7
Hinsdale Rd. A8
Howard Ave. A,C7
Illinois St. B7
Iris Ln. C8
Irwin Ave. B7
Jariath B8
Jarvis Ave. A-C8
Joseph Ave. C8
Kenmare Ct. B5
Kenmare Dr. B5
Kennicott Ct. C7
Koehler Dr. B7
Kylemore Ct. B5
Kylemore Dr. B5
Laura Ln. C8
Linden St. C7
Locust St. C7
Longford Dr. B5
Lunt Ave. C8
Magnolia St. C8
Mannheim Rd. B7,8
Maple St. C7,8
Marshall Dr. A6,7
Middleton Ct. B5
Middleton Ln. B5
Morse Ave. C8
Mt. Prospect Rd. A8
Nebel Ln. B7
Nimitz Dr. C8
North Shore Ave. C8
Northwest Tollway C8
Oakton Pl. B7
Oakton St. A-C7
Orchard St. C7,8
Oxford Rd. B8
Park Ave. C8
Parkwood Ln. C8
Patton Dr. C8
Paula Ln. C8
Pearle Dr. C8
Peter Rd. C8
Pine St. B7
Plainfield Dr. B7
Pratt Ave. C8
Prospect Ave. B,C7
Prospect Ln. B7
Riverview Ave. C7
Rusty Dr. C8
Santa Rosa Dr. B8
Scott St. C8
Shepard Dr. B7
Sherwin Ave. C8
South Ct. C8
Spruce Ave. B8
Sprucewood Ave. B8
Stillwell Dr. C8
Stockton Ave. B,C7
Sunset Ave. C8
Sycamore St. C7,8
Times Dr. B7
Touhy Ave. A,C8
Tri-State Tollway C8
Tures Ln. B7
Waterford Ct. B5
Webster Ave. C8
Webster Ln. B7
Welwyn Ave. C7
Westview Dr. B8
Wexford Ct. B5
White St. C7
Willie Rd. A7
Winthrop Dr. A7

**PARKS**
Eton Field C8
Majewski Metro Park A7
Seminole Park C8
South Park B7

**SCHOOLS**
Maine Twp. H.S. West B7

**MISCELLANEOUS**
Opeka Lake B7

## DIXMOOR

Page 13

**STREETS**
Ashland K26
Calumet K26
Circle Dr. K26
Cooper K26,27
Davis Ave. J26
Davis Ct. J26
Division St. K26
Dixie Hwy. J26
Elm K26
Honore K26
Hoyne K27
Joliet J27
Leavitt K26
Lincoln K26
Maple K26
Marshfield K26
Norris J,K26
Oak K26
Oakley J26
Page Ave. K26
Paulina Ave. K26
Prairie K26
Robey K27
Seeley K27
Sibley Blvd. K27
Spaulding Ave. K26
Vail K26
Walnut K26
Western J26
Winchester K27
Wood K26
139th St. J,K26
140th St. K26
141st St. K26
142nd St. K26
143rd St. K26
144th St. K26
145th St. J,K26
146th St. K26

**MISCELLANEOUS**
Village Hall K26

## DOLTON

Pages 13,14

**STREETS**
Adams St. M26
Ann St. M26
Arthur Ct. M26
Atlantic Ave. L26
Avalon N26
Beachview M26,27
Blackstone N26,27
Blouin Dr. M27
California M26
Calumet Ave. N26
Calumet Expwy. N26,27
Catalpa Ln. M26
Center Ave. M26
Champlain M26,27
Chicago M26,27
Clark Ave. L27
Clausen Ct. M26
Clyde Ave. N27
Cornell N27
Cottage Grove M26-28
Dante N26,27
Dearborn L27
Diekman Ct. N27
Dilner Pl. M26
Dobson M26,27
Dorchester N26,27
Drexel Ave. M26,27
East End N27
Edbrooke Ave. L27
Ellis M26,27
Empire M26
Engle M26
Evans M26,27
Evers M26,27
Forest M26
Grant St. M26,27
Greenwood Rd. M26,27
Harding M,N27
Harper N26,27
Harvard L26
Hastings Dr. M27
Indiana Ave. M26,27
Ingleside M26,27
Irving M26,27
Jackson Ave. M26
Jefferson St. M26
Kanawha M26
Kasten Dr. N26
Kenwood N26
Kimbark M26,27
La Salle Ave. L26
Lakeside M26
Langley M26,27
Lincoln Hwy. M26
Madison Ave. N27
Main St. L,M26
Manor Ct. M26
Margaret M26
Maryland Ave. M26,27
McArthur Ct. M26
Meadow Ln. M27
Memorial Dr. M26
Michigan Ave. L27
Michigan City Rd. M26
Minerva M26,27
Monroe St. M26
Murray M26
Oak St. M26,27
Ohio M26
Park Ave. M26
Parkside Dr. L26
Pennsylvania N26
Pohlers M26
Princeton Ave. L26
Riverside Dr., N. L26
Sanderson St. M26
Shepard Dr. M26
Sheridan St. M26
Sibley Blvd. L-N27
State St. L27
Stein St. L26
Stewart M,N26
Sunset Dr. N27
University M26,27
Vanburen M26
Wabash Ave. L27
Washington St. M26
Wentworth L26
Woodlawn M26,27
139th Pl. M26
140th Pl. L26
141st Pl. L26
142nd Pl. L26
143rd St. M,N26
144th Pl. M26
144th St. M,N26
145th St. M,N26
146th St. M,N26
147th Pl. M26
147th St. L-N26
148th St. L,M26
149th St. M27
151st St. M,N27
152nd St. M,N27
153rd St. M,N27
154th Pl. N27
154th St. M,N27
155th Pl. N27
155th St. M27
156th St. M27
157th St. M27
158th St. M,N27

**PARKS**
Dolton Park M26

**SCHOOLS**
Thornridge H.S. M27

**MISCELLANEOUS**
City Hall M26

## EAST CHICAGO, IN

Page 14

**STREETS**
Beacon Q26
Columbus Dr. Q26
Exchange Q26
Homer Lee Q27
Kosciusko Q27
Northcote Q26
Reading Q26,27
Ruth Q26,27
Shell Q27
Walsh Q26,27
Wegg Q26,27
142nd Q26
143rd Q26
144th Q26
148th Q26
151st Q27

**SCHOOLS**
Indiana Univ. of East Chicago Q26

## ELMWOOD PARK

Page 2

**STREETS**
Armitage E12
Atgeld E12
Barry St. E11
Belden E12
Belmont Ave. E11
Birchdale E11
Bloomingdale E12
Brook Rd. D12
Cortland E12
Country Club Ln. E12
Cresset E11
Dickens E12
Diversey E11
Elmgrove Dr. E11
Fletcher D11
George St. E11
Grand Ave. E12
Harlem Ave. E12
Marwood E12
Medill E12
Nelson D11
Oakleaf E11
Pacific D11
Palmer E12
Pleasant Pl. E12
Schubert E12
Sunset E11
Thatcher Rd. D12
Wabansia E12
Wellington E11
Westwood Dr. E12
Wrightwood E12
72nd Ct. E12,13
73rd Ave. E12,13
73rd Ct. E12,13
74th Ave. E12,13
74th Ct. E12,13
75th Ave. E12,13
75th Ct. E12,13
76th Ave. E11-13
76th Ct. E11-13
77th Ave. E11-13
77th Ct. E11-13
78th Ave. E11-13
78th Ct. E11-13
79th Ave. E11-13
79th Ct. D11-13
80th Ave. D12

**MISCELLANEOUS**
Village Hall E12

## EVERGREEN PARK

Pages 9,10

**STREETS**
Albany J21,22
Avers H22
Balmoral J22
Beck Ct. H22
California J22
Campbell J22
Central Park H22
Clark H22
Clifton Park H22
Country Club J22
Crawford Ave. H21,22
Elm Pl. H22
Fairfield J21
Francisco J22
Grove Pl. H22
Hamlin H22
Harding H22
Homan H22
Lawndale H22
Maple H22
Maplewood J22
Millard H22
Mozart J22
Richmond J22
Ridgeway H22
Ross Pl. H22
Sacramento J22
Sawyer J22
Sheridan J21
Spaulding H22
Springfield H22
St. Louis H22
Talman J21
Troy J22
Trumbull H22
Turner H22
Utica J22
Washtenaw J21,22

## EVERGREEN PARK

Western Ave. ... J21,22
87th St. ... J21
88th St. ... J21
89th Pl. ... J21
89th St. ... J21
90th Pl. ... J21
90th St. ... J21
91st St. ... J21
92nd St. ... J21
93rd Pl. ... J22
93rd St. ... J22
94th Pl. ... J22
04th St. ... J22
95th Pl. ... J22
95th St. ... J22
96th Pl. ... J22
96th St. ... J22
97th Pl. ... J22
97th St. ... H,J22
98th Pl. ... H,J22
98th St. ... H,J22
99th Pl. ... J22
99th St. ... H,J22
100th Pl. ... J22
100th St. ... H,J22
101st Pl. ... J22
101st St. ... H22
102nd Pl. ... J22
102nd St. ... H,J22

### GOLF COURSES
Beverly C.C. ... J21
Evergreen C.C. ... J22

### PARKS
Evergreen Park ... H22

### SCHOOLS
Brother Rice H.S. ... H22
Evergreen Pk. Comm. H.S. ... J22
Fox College ... J22
Luther H.S. South ... J21
Mother McAuley H.S. ... H22
St. Xavier College ... H22

### SHOPPING CENTERS
Evergreen Shopping Plaza ... J22

### MISCELLANEOUS
Convalescent Home ... H22
Little Company of Mary Hosp. ... J22
Village Hall ... J22

## FOREST PARK
Page 5
### STREETS
Adams ... E14
Beloit ... E14,15
Belvidere ... E14
Bergman ... E14
Brown ... E14
Burkhardt Ct. ... E14
Central ... E14
Cermak Rd. ... E15
Circle ... E14,15
Des Plaines ... E14,15
Dixon ... E14
Dunlop ... E15
Elgin ... E14,15
Ferdinand ... E14,15
Fillmore ... E15
Franklin ... E14
Hannah ... E14,16
Harlem ... E15
Harrison ... E14
Harvard ... E14
Jackson Blvd. ... E14
Lathrop ... E14,15
Lehmer ... E14
Lincoln Ct. ... E14
Madison ... E14
Marengo ... E14,15
Monroe ... E14
Polk ... E14
Randolph ... E14
Rockford ... E15
Roosevelt Rd. ... E15
Taylor ... E14
Thomas ... E14,15
Troost ... E15
Van Buren ... E14
Warren ... E14
Washington ... E14
Wilcox ... E14
York ... E14
Yuba ... E15
13th St. ... E14
14th St. ... E15
15th St. ... E15
16th St. ... E15

### PARKS
Forest Park ... E14

### SHOPPING CENTERS
Forest Park Plaza ... D15
Forest Park Mall ... E15

### MISCELLANEOUS
City Hall ... E14
Post Office ... E15
Riverside Hosp. ... D15

## FOREST VIEW
Pages 5,6
### STREETS
Austin ... F18
Central ... G18
Clinton ... E17
East ... E17
Grove ... E17
Harlem Ave. ... E17
Home ... E17
Kenilworth ... E17
Laramie ... F18
Latrobe ... G18
Lockwood ... G18
Long ... G18
Lorel ... G18
Major ... F18
Maple ... E17
Mason ... F18
Meade ... F18
Menard ... F18
Merrimac ... F18
Monitor ... F18
Oak Park ... E17
Ridgeland ... E17
Wenonah ... E17
Wisconsin ... E17
47th St. ... G17
51st St. ... G18

### MISCELLANEOUS
Village Hall ... E17

## FRANKLIN PARK
Page 1
### STREETS
Acorn Ln. ... B11
Addison Ave., W. ... B,C11
Alta St. ... B11
Anderson Pl. ... B11
Ashland ... C11
Atlantic ... C11,12
Belmont Ave. ... A-C11
Birch ... B11
Bright ... B11
Britta ... C11
Byron ... C11
Calwagner ... C11,12
Carnation ... B11
Carol Ln. ... B11
Center Ave. ... B11
Centralia Blvd. ... B11
Cherry ... C11
Chestnut ... C11
Copenhagen Ct. ... A11
County Line Rd. ... C11
Crescent Dr. ... C11
Crown Rd. ... B11
Cullerton St. ... B11
Davis ... C11
DeSota Ct. ... C11
Dodge Ave. ... C11
Dora ... C11,12
Edgington ... C11,12
Elder Ln. ... C12
Elm ... D11
Emerson ... C11
Ernst ... C11
Exchange Pl. ... D11
Fairfield ... C12
Finley ... C12
Fleetwood Ln. ... B10
Fletcher ... B11
Franklin ... B,C11
Front ... C12
Fullerton ... C12
Gage ... C11
George ... C11,12
Grand ... C11
Greenfield Rd. ... C11
Gustav ... C11
Hackey Ln. ... C11
Hart Dr. ... B11
Hawthorne ... C12
Herrick ... C12
Herschberg ... C11
Houston Dr. ... B11
Iona Ave. ... C11
James ... B11
Jill ... B11
Johanna ... C12
Kimmey Ln. ... C11
King Ave., W. ... B11
Kirschoff ... C12
LaSalle Ct. ... C11
Latoria ... B11
Lee St. ... B10
Leona ... C12
Lesser ... C11
Leyden ... C11
Lincoln ... C11,12
Lombard ... C11
Lonquist Dr. ... C11
Louis ... C11
Lucy Ln. ... B11
Mannheim Rd. ... C12
Maple ... D11
Martens ... C11
McNerney Dr. ... C11
Medill ... D12
Melrose Ave. ... B11
Minneapolis ... C11
Montana ... C12
Nerbonne ... C12
Nevada ... C12
Nichols ... C11
Nona ... C12
Oak ... C12
Pacific ... C,D11
Panoramic Dr. ... C12
Park ... C11
Parker ... C11
Parklane Ave. ... C11
Pearl ... C11
Podlin Dr. ... A11
Powell St. ... B11
Prairie Rd. ... B11
Reeves Ct. ... C11
Reuter ... C12
Richard ... C11
Riverside Dr. ... C12
Robinson Rd. ... C11
Rose ... C11
Ruby ... C11
Runge St. ... B11
Ruth ... B11
Sandra St. ... B11
Sarah ... C11,12
Schierhorn Ct. ... D11
Schiller Blvd. ... C11
Scott ... C11
Seymour ... B10
Sheila ... C12
Silver Creek Dr. ... C12
Surita ... C11
Sunset ... C11
Tugwell St. ... B10
United Pkwy. ... B10
Walnut ... C11
Washington ... C11
Waveland ... C11
Wehrman ... C11
Wellington ... C11
Westbrook ... C12
Williams Dr. ... C11
Willow ... C11
Wolf Rd. ... B11
Wrightwood ... C12
25th Ave. ... C11

### SCHOOLS
Leyden East Twp. H.S. ... C11
Mannheim Sch. ... B11

### MISCELLANEOUS
City Hall ... C11
Leyden Comm. Ext. Care Ctr. ... B11
Leyden Fire Station ... C11
Leyden Twp. Hall ... C11
O'Hare Stadium ... B10

## HAMMOND, IN
Page 14
### STREETS
Alice ... P27
Ames ... P29
Ann ... P27
Ash ... Q26
Atlas ... Q27
Baltimore ... P25,26
Raring ... Q29
Bauer ... P27
Beall ... P27
Becker ... P27
Beech ... Q27,29
Belmont ... Q29
Benjamin ... P24
Bertram ... Q28,29
Birch ... P27-29
Brown ... P24
Brunswick ... P26
Burton Ct. ... P24
Calumet ... P24,26,29
Cameron ... P26
Caroline ... P24
Carroll ... P,Q27
Catalpa ... Q27,29
Cedar ... P26
Cherry ... P28
Chesapeake ... Q28
Chestnut ... Q27,29
Chicago ... P26
Clark ... P26
Claude ... P27
Cleveland ... P,Q28
Clinton ... P27
Columbia ... Q27,29
Columbus Dr. ... P27
Condit ... P27
Conkey ... P28
Coolidge ... P27
Crescent ... P27
Dearborn ... P26
Doty ... P27
Douglas ... P27
Drackert ... P28
Dyer ... P28
Eaton ... Q26
Elm ... Q26
Erie ... P27
Euclid ... P27
Fernwood ... P28
Field ... Q28
Florence ... P28
Forest ... P28
Garfield ... P28
Glendale ... P28
Golf Way ... Q29
Gostlin ... P26
Grover ... P26
Hanover ... P26
Hanson Ct. ... Q28
Harrison ... P28,29
Havana ... P29
Henry ... P25,26
Hickory ... P27
Highland ... P,Q28
Hoffman ... P26
Hohman ... P26,27
Howard ... Q27-29
Hudson ... P26
Huehn ... P26
Hump Rd. ... Q27
Hyslop ... P28
Indiana ... P,Q27
Indiana East-West Toll Road ... P25
Jackson ... P28,29
Jarnecke ... Q29
Jefferson ... P28,29
Jessie ... P27
Johnson ... P25,26
Kane ... P27
Kent ... Q27
Kenwood ... P28
Lawndale ... P28
Lewis ... P28
Linden ... Q27,29
Logan ... P,Q27
Lyman ... P29
Lyons ... P26
Madison ... P27-29
Magnolia ... Q27-29
Malden ... P24
Maplewood ... P29
Marble ... P26
May ... P27
Maywood ... P27
Meadow Ln. ... P28,29
Merrill ... Q28
Michigan ... P27
Molsberger ... Q27
Monroe ... P28,29
Moraine ... P28
Morris ... Q28
Morton Ct. ... P27
Moss ... Q28
Muenich Ct. ... P27
Mulberry ... P28
Murray ... Q27
Nobel ... Q28
Northcote ... Q28
Oak ... Q26
Oakdale ... Q29
Oakley ... P27
Oakwood ... P28
Ogden ... P27
Park ... P29
Park Pl. ... P28
Parkview ... P24
Paxton ... P27
Pine ... P26
Plummer ... P27
Porter Rd. ... Q27
Price ... P27
Ray ... Q28
Rhode ... P28
Ridge ... P28
Ridgeland ... Q28
Rimbach ... P27
Roosevelt ... P24,Q27
Roselawn ... P28
Rosewood ... P28
Russell ... P27
Sheffield ... P25,26
Shell ... Q27
Sherman ... Q27
Sirley ... P27
Sohl ... P27
Southeastern ... Q28
Southmoor ... P29
Spruce ... P28
State ... P27
State Line Rd. ... P28
Stewart ... P24
Summer ... P27
Tapper ... P29,Q28
Tell ... Q27
Thornton ... P27
Tilly Dr. ... Q29
Torrence ... P25,26
Towle ... P26
Truman ... P,Q27
Van Buren ... P28,29
Victoria ... P26
Vine ... P28
Vine Ct. ... P28
Wabash ... P26
Wallace ... Q27
Walnut ... Q27-29
Walter ... P27
Warwick ... P24
Washington ... P28
Webb ... P27
Webster ... P27
White Oak ... Q27,29
White Oak Pl. ... Q29
Wilcox ... P,Q27
Wildwood Rd. ... P28
Willard ... Q28
Williams ... P27
Willis ... Q27
Willow Ct. ... P27
Wood ... P27
Woodlawn ... P29
114th ... P23
115th ... P24
116th ... P24
117th ... P24
117th Pl. ... P24
118th ... P24
119th ... P24
129th ... P25
133rd ... P25
134th ... P25
136th ... P25
137th ... P25
138th ... P26
139th ... P26
140th ... P26
141st ... P26
142nd ... P26
143rd ... P,Q26
145th ... Q26
149th ... P27
150th ... P27
164th Pl. ... Q28
165th ... Q28
16/th ... P,Q28
169th ... P,Q28
169th Pl. ... P28
170th ... P,Q28
170th Pl. ... Q28
171st ... P,Q28,Q29
171st Pl. ... Q29
172nd ... P,Q29
172nd Pl. ... P29
173rd ... P,Q29
173rd Pl. ... P,Q29
174th ... P,Q29
174th Pl. ... P,Q29
175th ... P29
175th Pl. ... P29
176th ... P29
177th ... Q29
177th Pl. ... P29

### CEMETERIES
Concordia Cemetery ... P28
Elmwood Cemetery ... Q28
Oak Hill Cemetery ... P28

### PARKS
Columbia Park ... Q27
Douglas Park ... P26
Edison Park ... P28
Forsyth Park ... P24
Harrison Park ... P27
Maywood Park ... P28
Turner Park ... P27

### SCHOOLS
Don Gavitt H.S. ... Q29
Hammond H.S. ... P27
Technical H.S. ... P27

### MISCELLANEOUS
City Hall ... P27
Columbia Center Housing Project ... Q29
Kennedy Memorial Center ... P27
St. Margaret Hosp. ... P27

## HARVEY
Page 13
### STREETS
Artesian ... J27
Ashland ... K27,28
Belden ... L28
Broadway ... K27
California ... L28
Calumet Blvd. ... K,L26
Campbell ... J27,28
Carol ... L28
Carse ... L28
Center ... K27,28
Clairemont Ave. ... J27
Clairemont Ct. ... J27
Clinton ... L27,28
Commercial ... K27
Cooper ... K27
Des Plaines ... L27
Dixie Hwy. ... J27,K28
Emerald ... L28
Fairfield ... J27
Finch ... L28
Fisk ... K28
Gauger ... K28
Geneva ... L28
Green ... L28
Halsted ... K27
Harvey ... K27
Honore ... K27
Hoyne ... K28
Jefferson ... L27,28
Justine ... K28
Kentucky ... K27
Lathrop ... L28
Leavitt ... K27
Lexington ... K27,28
Lincoln ... K27
Loomis ... K27,28
Lowe ... L28
Madison ... L27
Main ... L27
Maplewood ... J27
Markham Dr. ... L27
Marshfield ... K28
Morgan ... L27
Myrtle ... K28
Oakdale ... L27
Oakley Ave. ... J27
Oakley Ct. ... J27
Page ... K28
Park ... K28
Parkside ... L27
Parnell ... L27
Paulina ... K28
Peoria ... K27
Rockwell ... J27
Sangamon ... K26
Seeley ... K27
Sherman Pl. ... L28
Shore Dr. ... L26
Sibley Blvd. ... J-L27
Streamside Dr. ... L26
Talman ... K27
Thornton Rd. ... K27
Turlington ... K28
Union ... L27
Vail Ave. ... K27
Vincennes ... L27
Vine ... K28
Wallace ... L27,28
Washington ... L27
Washtenaw ... J27
Wells ... K26
West ... K28
Western ... J27
Willard ... L28
Winchester ... K27
Wood ... K27,28
Woodbridge ... L28
144th Ct. ... K26
144th St. ... K26
145th St. ... J-L26
146th St. ... J-L26
147th Pl. ... L27
147th St. ... L27
148th Pl. ... J,L27
148th St. ... J,K27
149th Pl. ... J27
149th St. ... J,K27
150th Pl. ... J27
150th St. ... J,K27
151st Ct. ... J27
151st Pl. ... J27
151st St. ... J27
151st Terr. ... J27
152nd Ct. ... J27
152nd Pl. ... J27
152nd St. ... J-L27
153rd St. ... J,K27
154th Pl. ... J,L27
154th St. ... J,K27
155th Pl. ... K27
155th St. ... K27
156th Pl. ... K27
156th St. ... K27
157th Pl. ... K27
157th St. ... K27
158th Pl. ... K28
158th St. ... K28
159th St. ... K28
160th Pl. ... K28
160th St. ... K,L28
161st St. ... K,L28
162nd St. ... L28
163rd St. ... L28
164th St. ... L28
165th St. ... L28
166th St. ... L28
167th Pl. ... L28
167th St. ... L28
168th Pl. ... L28
168th St. ... L28
171st St. ... K29

### PARKS
Ashland Park ... K27
Holmes Park ... L28
Lexington Park ... K27
Holmes Park ... L28
Honore Park ... K28
Kiwanis Park ... K28
Lincoln Park ... K28
Radio Station Park ... J27
Taft Park ... L28

### SCHOOLS
Thornton Twp. H.S. ... L27
James W. Riley Sch. ... K28
Maya Angelo Sch. ... K28

### SHOPPING CENTERS
Dixie Square Mall ... K27

### MISCELLANEOUS
City Hall ... K27
Ingalls Memorial Hospital ... K27

## HARWOOD HEIGHTS
Page 2
### STREETS
Ainsley E10
Argyle E10
Carmen E10
Foster Pl. E10
Gunnison E,F10
Harlem Ave. E10
Lawrence E10
Leland E10
Montrose F10
Mulligan F10
Nagle F10
Narragansett F10
Nashville F10
Natchez F10
Neenah F10
New England E10
Newcastle E10
Newland E10
Norridge E10
Norwood F10
Oak Park E10
Oconto E10
Octavia E10
Odell E10
Oketo E9
Oriole E10
Ronald E10
Rutherford E10
Sayre E10
Senior Pl. E10
Strong E10
Sunnyside E,F10
Wilson E10
Winnemac E10
Winona E10
### GOLF COURSES
Ridgemoor C.C. F10
### MISCELLANEOUS
Village Hall E10

## HILLSIDE
Page 4
### STREETS
Adams B14
Ashbel B14
Bellwood B14
Berkeley B14
Bosworth Ave. B15
Broadview B14
Buckthorn Rd. B14
Butterfield Rd. C14
Canterbury C15
Center B15
Charles C15
Chicago B14
Clayton Rd. B14
Craig B14
Cypress Ct. B14
Cypress Dr. B14
Darmstadt B14
Dickens B14
Division B15
East B15
East End B14
Edgewater B15
Electric Ave. B14
Elm B14
Englewood B14
Fencl Ln. B15
Fenwood Ln. B14
Fielding B15
Forest B14,15
Frontage Rd. B14
Geneva B14
Golf Ln. B14
Granville Ave. B14
Harrison B14
Hawthorne B14
High Ridge Rd. B14
Hillside B14
Howard B14
Hyde Park B14
Idlewild B14
Iroquois Rd. B14
Irving B14
Jackson Blvd. B14
Laverne B14
Lee B14
Lind B14
Locust B14
Madison B14
Mannheim Rd. C14
Maple Ave. B14
Maple Ln. B14
May B15
Melrose B15
Morris B14
Mueller B14
Oak B14
Oak Ridge B15
Orchard B15
Railroad B,C14
Randolph B14
Raymond B14
Ridge Ave. A14
Rohde B14
Roosevelt Rd. B15
School St. A14
Spenchley B14
St. Paul Ct. B14
Sunnyside Dr. B14
Taft B14
Terrace Ln. B16
Van Buren B14
Vanna Ct. B14
Warren B14
Washington Blvd. C14
Washington St. B14
Westwood B16
Wolf Rd. B15
50th Ave. B15
51st Ave. B14
53rd Ave. B14
### PARKS
Eisenhower Pk. B14
### SCHOOLS
Hillside Sch. B14
Proviso West H.S. B14
### SHOPPING CENTERS
West Point Mall B14
### MISCELLANEOUS
Village Hall B14

## HODGKINS
Page 8
### STREETS
Belfast Ln. C19
Cantigny Rd. C19
Catherine Ann Dr. C19
Chester C19
Cobb C19
Conrad C19
East Ave. C19
Fransean Dr. C19
Kane Rd. C19
Kimball C19
Lagrange Rd. C19,20
Lenzi C19
Lyons C19
Mance Rd. C19
Normandy Ln. C19
Roger Ln. C19
Santa Fe C19,20
Sharon Ln. C19
Stratford Ct. C19
Weeping Willow Rd. C19
Wenz C19
Westgate C19
67th St. C19
### SHOPPING CENTERS
Shopping Center C19
### MISCELLANEOUS
Village Hall C19

## HOMETOWN
Page 9
### STREETS
Beck H21
Corcoran H21
Duffy G21
Keeler H21
Kenton G21
Kilbourn G21
Kildare H21
Kilpatrick G21
Kolin H21
Kolmar G21
Komensky H21
Kostner G21
Main H21
Ryan H21
Southwest Hwy. G,H21
87th Pl. G,H21
87th St. G,H21
88th Pl. G,H21
88th St. G21
89th Pl. G,H21
89th St. G21
90th Pl. G,H21
90th St. H21
91st St. G,H21
### MISCELLANEOUS
Village Hall H21

## INDIAN HEAD PARK
Page 8
### STREETS
Acacia Cir. B19
Acacia Dr. B19
Acacia Ln. B19
Algonquin Dr. B19
Apache Dr. B19
Arrowhead Tr. B20
Ashbrook Ln. B19
Big Bear Ct. B19
Big Bear Dr. B19
Blackhawk Trail B19
Cascade Dr. B19
Cherokee Dr. B19
Cochise Dr. B19
Edgebrook Ct. B19
Edgebrook Ln. B19
Edgewood View Rd. B20
Glenbrook Ct. B19
Glenbrook Ln. B19
Golf View Rd. B20
Hiawatha Ln. B19
Howard Ave. B19
Indian Wood Ln. B19
Joliet Rd. B19
Keokuk B19
Laurel Ave. B19
Mohawk Ct. B19
Osceola Terr. B19
Plainfield Rd. B19
Pontiac Dr. B19
Sequoia Ln. B19
Shabbona Ln. B19
Sioux Tr. B19
Tecumseh Ln. B19
Thunderbird Dr. B19
Vine St. B19
Waubansee Ln. B19
Willow Springs Rd. B19
Wolf Rd. B19
63rd St. B19
65th Pl. B19
65th St. B19
70th Pl. B20
72nd St. B20
Deer Path D21
Hickory Trace Dr. D21
Marion St. D21
Oak Ridge Dr. D21
Pawn Tr. D21
Thomas St. D21
79th Ave. D20
79th Ct. D20
79th Pl. D20
80th Ave. D21
80th St. D20
81st Ave. D21
81st St. D21
82nd Ave. D21
82nd St. D21
83rd Ave. D21
83rd Pl. D21
83rd St. D21
84th Ave. D21
84th Ct. D21
84th Pl. D21
84th St. D21
85th Ave. D21
85th Ct. D21
85th Pl. D21
85th St. D21
86th Ave. D21
86th Ct. D21
86th St. D21
87th Ave. D21
87th St. D21
### MISCELLANEOUS
Mercy Hosp. D21

## LA GRANGE
Page 4
### STREETS
Arlington B17
Ashland C17
Bassford B17
Beach C17
Bell C17
Benton C17
Blacktone B17
Bluff C17
Brainard C17
Brewster C17
Brighton B18
Burlington C17
Calendar C17
Calle View Dr. C18
Carriage Ln. B18
Catherine C17
Cossitt C17
Country Club Dr. C18
Dover B17
Drexel B17
East Ave. C18
Eberly C17
Edgewood B17,18
Elder Ln. B17
Elm B17
Fairway B18
Gilbert B17
Goodman B17
Harris C17
Hayes C17
Hazel C17
Hillgrove Ave. B17
Kensington C17
La Grange Rd. C17,18
Leitch B17
Lincoln C17
Linden C17
Locust C17
Madison C17
Malden B17
Maple C17
Mason Dr. B18
Newberry C17
Ogden Ave. B17
Park Ave. C17
Peck B17
Poplar Pl. B17
Sawyer C17
Shawmut C17
Southview C17
Spring C17
Stone C17
Sunset B17
Tilden C17
Waiola C17
Washington C17
6th Ave. C17,18
7th Ave. C17,18
8th Ave. C17,18
9th Ave. C17,18
10th Ave. C17,18
11th Ave. C18
12th Ave. C18
47th St. B,C18
48th St. C18
49th St. C18
50th Pl. B18
50th St. C18
51st St. C18
52nd Pl. B18
52nd St. C18
53rd Pl. B18
53rd St. C18
54th Pl. B18
54th St. C18
55th St. C18
### GOLF COURSES
La Grange C.C. B,C18
### PARKS
Gilbert Park B17
### SCHOOLS
Lyons Twp. H.S. North C17
### MISCELLANEOUS
Community Mem. Hosp. B18
Village Hall B17

## LA GRANGE PARK
Page 4
### STREETS
Alma C16
Ashland C17
Barnesdale Rd. C16
Beach C16
Blanchan C16
Brainard C17
Brewster C17
Catherine C17
Cleveland C16
Community Dr. C16
Deerpath C16
Dover B17
Edgewood B17
Elmwood C17
Fairview C17
Finsbury Ln. C16
Forest Rd. C16,17
Garfield C16
Grant C17
Harding C16
Harrison C16
Homestead Rd. C16,17
Huntington Ct. C16
Jackson C16
Kemman C16
Kensington C17
Kings Ct. C16
La Grange Rd. C16
Lincoln C17
Logan Blvd. C16
Malden B17
Meadowcrest C16
Monroe C16
Morgan C16
Newberry C16
Oak C17
Ogden Ave. B17
Ostrander C16
Park Rd. C17
Pine C17
Pine Tree C16
Plymouth Pl. C17
Raymond C16
Richmond C17
Robinhood Ln. C16,17
Scotdale C16
Sherwood Rd. C16
Southview C17
Spring C17
Stone C17
Stonegate Rd. C16
Thorpe Ct. C16
Timber Ln. C16
Waiola C17
Woodlawn B17
Woodside Rd. C16
26th St. C16
28th St. C16
29th St. C16
30th St. C16
31st St. (Logan Blvd.) C16
### PARKS
Memorial Park C17
North-East Park C16
Robin Hood Park C16
Stone Monroe Park C16
### SCHOOLS
Nazareth H.S. B17
### MISCELLANEOUS
Village Hall C17

## LEYDEN TOWNSHIP
Page 1
### STREETS
Alcoa B12
Alta B11
Altgeld B12
Armitage C12
Atlantic C12
Balmoral D9
Barry B11
Behrns B11
Belden C12
Belmont B11
Belwood B12
Bryn Mawr D9
Calwagner C12
Catalpa D9
Charles B11
Cornell C12
Courtland D9
Crescent D9
Crown B11
Derrough B11
Dickens C12
Diversey B11
Dora C12
Drummond Pl. B12
Emerson C12
Fairview D9
Fleetwood Ln. B10
Fletcher B11
Franklin B11
Fullerton B12
Gary Dr. B11
Geneva B12
Geneva B12
Grand B11
Granville B11
Gregory D9
Gustav C12
Haber B11
Harold B11
Hawthorne C12
Hyde Park B12
Inland Dr. A11
Landan Dr. B11
Laporte B11
Lee B11
Louis C12
Lyndale C12
Mannheim Rd. B12
Manor D9
Manor Dr. C12
Marian B11
Martin B11
McDonough St. A10
McKay B11
McLean C12
Medill B12
Melrose B12
Montana B12
Nevada B12
Palmer C12
Park C12
Parker B12,12
Pearl B11
Prater B11
Prospect D9
Rascher D9
Redwood D9
Rhodes B11
Roberta Ave. B11
Rowlet B11
Roy B11
Ruby C12
Sandra B11
Sarah C12
Schubert B12
Scott C12
Summerdale D9
Taft Ave. B10
Valor Rd. A10
Vine D9
Washington D9
Wellington B11
Winters Dr. B12
Wolf Rd. B11
Wrightwood B12
### CEMETERIES
All Saints Parish Cem. D9
St. Nickolas Ukranian Cem. D9
### PARKS
West Dale Park B11
### SCHOOLS
Apostle Sch. B11
### MISCELLANEOUS
Camp Fort Dearborn D9
Kiddieland Amusement Park D12

## LINCOLNWOOD
Pages 2,3
### STREETS
Albion G,H8
Arthur G,H8
Avers H8
Carpenter Rd. G8
Central Park H8
Chase Ave. H8
Christiana Ave. H8
Cicero G8
Cicero Ave., N. G8
Columbia G8
Crawford Ave. H8
Devon H8
Drake H8
East Prairie Rd. H8
Estes Ave. H8
Farwell G,H8
Fitch Ave. G,H8
Greenleaf G,H8
Hamlin Ave. H8
Harding H8
Jarlath St. H8
Karlov Ave. H7,8
Keating G8
Keating, N. G8
Kedvale Ave. H7,8
Keeler Ave. H7,8
Kenneth Ave. G8
Kenton Ave. G8
Keystone Ave. H7,8
Kilbourn G8
Kildare H7,8
Kilpatrick G8
Kimball Ave. H8
Knox G8
Kolmar G8
Kostner G8
La Porte G8
Lawndale H8
Lemay G8
Leroy G8
Lincoln St. G7,H8
Longmeadow G8
Lowell H7,8
Loyola H8
Lunt Ave. G,H8
Minehaha G8
Morse Ave. G,H8
Nakomis G8
Navajo G8
North Shore G,H8
Pratt G8
Proesel H8
Ramona G8
Range Terr. H8
Ridgeway H8
Sauganash G8
Schreiber G,H8
Sherwin Ave. H8
Spaulding H8
Spokane G8
Springfield H8
St. Louis H8
Tower Circle Dr. G8
Tower Ct. G8
Tripp Ave. H7,8
Trumbull H8
Wallen H8
### GOLF COURSES
Bryn Mawr C.C. H8
### SCHOOLS
Todd Sch. H8
### MISCELLANEOUS
Police Dept. H8

## LYONS
Page 5
### STREETS
Abbot Terr. D17
Amelia E17
Anna D17
Barrypoint Rd. E17
Center E17
Clyde D17
Collins E17
Cracow D17
Custer D17
Elm E17
Fern D17
First D17
Fishermans Terr. E17
Gage E17
Haas E17
Hawthorne D17
Joliet Ave. E17
Joliet Rd. E17
Kenwood D17
Konrad D17
Lawndale D17
Leland D17
Lincoln Dr. D17
Maple E17
Oak Ave. E17
Ogden Ave. E17
Patricia D17
Plainfield Rd. D17
Powell E17

Prescott E17
Pulaski D17
Riverside D17
Rose D17
Salisbury E17
Warsaw D17
White E17
Winchester D17
38th Pl. E17
39th St. E17
40th St. D,E17
41st Ct. E17
41st Pl. E17
42nd Ct. E17
42nd Pl. E17
42nd St. E17
43rd Pl. D17
43rd St. D17
44th Pl. D17
44th St. D,E17
45th Pl. D,E17
45th St. D,E17
46th St. E17
47th St. D18

**MISCELLANEOUS**

Village Hall E17

## LYONS TOWNSHIP

Page 8
(For additional listings, see Section 2)

**STREETS**

Acacia Ln. B19
Arbor B20
Barton Rd. C18
Bielby Ave. B20
Blackstone C19
Brainard C19
Burr Oak Ln. C20
Central B20
Circle Dr. B20
Commonwealth B20
Coronet Ln. C19
County Line Rd. B20,21
Dana Way B20
Edgewood B19,20
Fairelms B20
Franklin B18,19
German Church B21
Golf View B19
Harvey Ave. B18
Howard B18-20
Jann Ct. B19
Joliet Rd. C19
Laurel B18,19
Lincoln C19
Linden B19
Linn Ct. B19
Locust B19
Lorraine D20
Maple Ave. B21
Marion C20
N.E. Ct. B18
N.W. Ct. B18
Oak Grove B21
Orchard St. B21
Parkside Ln. B19
Peck C19
Plainfield Rd. B19
Pleasant View B21
Public St. B21
Railroad Ave. (91st St.) B21
S.W. Ct. B18
Sunset B18,19
Terry Ln. C18
Timber View Ln. B19
Valley Rd. B20
Vial Pkwy. B18
Vine B19
Willow Springs B20
Wolf Rd. B21
52nd Pl. B18
53rd Pl. B18
54th Pl. B18
54th St. B18
55th Pl. B18
55th St. B18
56th St. B18
57th St. B18
58th Pl. B18
58th St. B19
59th Pl. B19
59th St. B19
60th St. B19
61st Pl. B19
61st St. B19
62nd Pl. B19
62nd St. B19
63rd Pl. B19
63rd St. B19
64th St. B19
70th St. B20
71st Pl. B20
72nd St. B20
73rd Pl. B20
74th St. B20
75th St. B20
77th St. B20
79th St. A20
80th Pl. B21
87th St. B21
114th Ave. B21

**GOLF COURSES**

Edgewood Valley C.C. B20
Maple Crest G.C. B19
Par Three G.C. B19
Timber Trails G.C. B19

**MISCELLANEOUS**

Santa Fe Speedway B22

## MARKHAM

Pages 12,13

**STREETS**

Afton Dr. J27
Albany Ave. J28
Alta Rd. H27
Arthur Terr. H28
Ashland Ave. K28
Belleplaine Dr. H28
Berkshire Dr. J28
Birch Rd. H27
Blackstone Ave. H28
California Ave. J28
Cambridge Dr. J28
Central Park Ave. H27,28
Cherry Ln. H27
Circle Dr. J28
Clifton Park Ave. H27,28
Country Aire Dr. J27
Crawford Ave. H27,28
Crocket Ln. J27
Cypress Rd. J27
Damen Ave. K28
Dixie Hwy. K28
Frontage Rd. H27
Hamlin Ave. H27,28
Heather Dr. H27
Hermitage Ave. K28
Hillcrest Dr. H28
Homan Ave. J27,28
Honore Ave. K28
Hoyne K28
Justine St. K28
Kedzie Ave. J27,28
Laflin St. K28
Lancaster Dr., E. J28
Lathrop Ave. K28
Lawndale Ave. H27,28
Lincoln Dr. J27
Magnolia Dr. H27
Maple Ln. H27
Marshfield Ave. K28
Millard Ave. H27
Mozart St. J28
Nottingham Ave. J28
Oakley J28
Oxford Dr. J28
Parkside Dr. J27
Paulina St. K28
Plainview Dr. H28
Plymouth Dr. J28
Richmond Ave. J28
Ridgeway Ave. H27
Rockwell St. J27
Roesner Dr. H27
Rose Manor Terr. H28
Sacramento Ave. J28
Sawyer Ave. J27,28
Sherwood Ave. J28
Spaulding Ave. J27,28
Springfield Ave. H28
St. Louis Ave. H27,28
Stafford Ave. N21
Sunset Ave. H28
Sussex Ave. J28
Sussex Ct. J28
Troy Ave. J27,28
Trumbull Ave. H27,28
Turner Ave. J27,28
Wedgewood Dr. H28
Western Ave. J28
Whipple St. J28
Willow Ln. H27
Wilshire Ave. J28
Wilshire Ct. J28
Winchester K28
Wolcott Ave. K28
Wood Ave. K28
149th St. H,J27
151st St. H27
152nd St. J27
154th Pl. H27
154th St. H27
155th St. H,J27
156th St. H,J27
157th St. H,J27
158th Pl. J28
158th St. J28
159th Pl. H28
159th St. J28
160th St. H28
161st St. H28
162nd Pl. H28
162nd St. H-K28
163rd Pl. J,K28
163rd St. H-K28
164th St. H-K28
165th St. J28
166th St. H,J28
167th St. H,J28
168th St. H,J28

**PARKS**

Country Aire Park H27
Mae McNeil Park H27
Markham Park H28
Martin Luther King Park K28
Roesner Park J28

**SHOPPING CENTERS**

Canterbury S.C. J28

**MISCELLANEOUS**

City Hall J28

## MAYWOOD

Pages 4,5

**STREETS**

Adams D14
Augusta D13
Chicago D13
Congress D14
Erie D13
Eugene C14
Gage C14
Green D14
Greenwood D14
Harrison D14
Harvard D14
Huron D13
Iowa D13
Lake St. D13
Lexington D14
Madison D14
Main D13
Maple D14
Maywood Dr. D14
Monroe D14
Oak C14
Ohio D13
Orchard D14
Pine D14
Quincy D14
Randolph C14
Russel C14
School St. D14
Sherman C14
Stanley C14
Superior D13
Van Buren C14
Walnut D14
Walton D13
Warren C14
Washington C14
West End C14
Wilcox D14
William C14
1st Ave. D13,14
2nd Ave. D13,14
3rd Ave. D13,14
4th Ave. D13,14
5th Ave. D13,14
6th Ave. D13,14
7th Ave. D13,14
8th Ave. D13,14
9th Ave. D13,14
10th Ave. D13,14
11th Ave. D13,14
12th Ave. D13,14
13th Ave. D13,14
14th Ave. D13
15th Ave. D13
16th Ave. D13
17th Ave. D13
18th Ave. C13
19th Ave. C13
20th Ave. C13
21st Ave. C13
22nd Ave. C14
23rd Ave. C14

**PARKS**

Maywood Grove D13
Maywood Park D14
Memorial Park D14
Playground C,D14

**SCHOOLS**

Proviso East H.S. D14

**MISCELLANEOUS**

Loyola University Medical Ctr. D15
Veterans Administration Hosp. (Hines) D15
Village Hall D14

## MC COOK

Page 8

**STREETS**

Clyde Terr. D18
East Ave. C18
Egandale D18
Glencoe D18
Grand D18
Hinsdale D18
Joliet Rd. C18
Lawndale D18
Plainfield Rd. D18
Riverside D18
47th St. D18
50th D18
53rd D18
55th C18
71st D20

**MISCELLANEOUS**

Village Hall D18

## MELROSE PARK

Pages 1,4,5

**STREETS**

Alvin Pg.1 B12
Andy Dr. Pg.5 D13
Armitage Pg.1 C12
Augusta Pg.4,5 C13
Bank Rd. Pg.4 B13
Belden Pg.1 C,D12
Bloomingdale Pg.1 C,D12
Braddock Dr. Pg.5 D13
Broadway Pg.4 C13
Caryl Pg.4 B13
Channing Ct. Pg.4,5 D13
Charleston Ct. Pg.4,5 D13
Chicago Pg.4,5 D13
Clay Ct. Pg.5 D13
Clinton Ct. Pg.4,5 D13
Concord Dr. Pg.5 D13
Cornell Pg.1 C12
Cortez Pg.4,5 C13
Davis Pg.4,5 D13
Division Pg.4,5 C,D13
Doris Pg.5 D13
Elsie Pg.4,5 D13
Geneva Pg.1 B12
George Pg.1 B12
Grant Pg.4,5 D13
Haddon Pg.4 C13
Harold Pg.4 B13
Hawthorne Pg.1 C12
Helen Dr. Pg.4,5 D13
Hirsch Pg.4 C13
Iowa Pg.4 C13
James Pl. Pg.1 B12
Janice Pg.1 B12
Lake Pg.4 C13
Lee Pg.4,5 D13
Lemoyne Pg.4 C13
Main Pg.4,5 C,D13
Mannheim Pg.1 B12
North Pg.4 B13
Norwood Pg.4 C13
Park Pg.4,5 D13
Rice Pg.4 C13
Roberta Pg.1 B12
Rose Pg.5 D13
Roy Pg.4 B13
Ruby Pg.1 C12
Sherman Pg.4,5 D13
Soffel Pg.4,5 C13
Superior Pg.4,5 D13
Thomas Pg.4 C13
Walton Pg.4 C13
Winston Dr. Pg.4,5 D13
1st Ave. Pg.5 D13
9th Ave. Pg.4,5 D13
10th Ave. Pg.4,5 D13
11th Ave. Pg.4,5 D13
12th Ave. Pg.4,5 D13
13th Ave. Pg.4,5 D13
14th Ave. Pg.4,5 D13
15th Ave. Pg.1,4 D12,13
16th Ave. Pg.4,5 C13
17th Ave. Pg.1,4 C12,13
18th Ave. Pg.1,4 C12,13
19th Ave. Pg.1,4 C12,13
20th Ave. Pg.4,5 C13
21st Ave. Pg.4,5 C13
22nd Ave. Pg.4,5 C13
23rd Ave. Pg.4,5 C13
24th Ave. Pg.4,5 C13
25th Ave. Pg.1 C12
30th Ave. Pg.4,5 C13
31st Ave. Pg.4,5 C13
32nd Ave. Pg.4,5 C13
33rd Ave. Pg.4,5 C13
34th Ave. Pg.4,5 C13
35th Ave. Pg.4,5 C13
36th Ave. Pg.4,5 C13
37th Ave. Pg.4,5 C13
38th Ave. Pg.4,5 C13
43rd Ave. Pg.4 B13
44th Ave. Pg.4 B13
45th Ave. Pg.4 B13
46th Ave. Pg.4 B13
47th Ave. Pg.4 B13

**PARKS**

Bulger Park Pg.4,5 D13

**SHOPPING CENTERS**

Winston Park S.C. Pg.4,5 D13

**MISCELLANEOUS**

Gottlieb Hosp. Pg.1 D12
Maywood Park Racetrack Pg.4,5 D13
Village Hall Pg.4 D13
Walther Lutheran Hosp. Pg.4 D13
Westlake Comm. Hosp. Pg.4 D13

## MERRIONETTE PARK

Page 10

**STREETS**

Albany Dr. J24
Central Park H24
Homan Ave. H24
Kedzie J24
Lincoln H24
Mahoney J24
Meadow J24
Morgan Park H24
Palisade Dr. J24
Park Lane Dr., S. J24
Sacramento Dr. J24
St. Louis H24
Troy J24
Whipple Dr. J24
113th Pl. J23
113th St. J23
114th Pl. J23
114th St. J23
115th St. J24
118th St. J24
119th St. J24

**CEMETERIES**

Beverly Cem. H24
Mt. Hope Cem. J24
Mt. Olivet Cem. J23
Oak Hill Cem. H24

**SHOPPING CENTERS**

Stone Brook Plaza H24

## MIDLOTHIAN

Page 12

**STREETS**

Avers Ave. H26,27
Central Park Ave. H26
Clifton Park Ave. H26
Crawford Ave. H26
Hamlin Ave. H26,27
Harding Ave. H27
Homan Ave. H26
Karlov Ave. H26
Keating Ave. G26
Kedvale Ave. H26,27
Kedzie Ave. J26
Keeler Ave. H26
Kenneth Ave. H26,27
Kenton G26
Keystone Ave. H26
Kilbourn Ave. G26
Kildare Ave. H26
Kilpatrick Ave. G26
Knox Ave. G26
Kolin Ave. H26
Kolmar Ave. G26,27
Kostner H26
LaPorte Ave. G26
Lawndale Ave. H26,27
Maple Ln. G26
Maxey Ct. H26
Millard H26,27
Raday Dr. H27
Ridgeway Ave. H26,27
Sawyer Ave. J26
Spaulding Ave. H26
Springfield Ave. H26
St. Louis Ave. H26
Terrace Ln. H27
Tripp Ave. H26
Trumbull Ave. H26
Turner H26
Waverly H26
143rd Pl. G,H26
143rd St. G,H26
144th Pl. G26
144th St. G,H26
145th St. G,H26
146th St. G,H26
147th Pl. H,J26
147th St. G,H26
148th Pl. H26
148th St. G,H26
149th St. G,H27
150th St. G,H27
151st St. H27
152nd St. H27
153rd Pl. H27
153rd St. H27
154th St. H27

**GOLF COURSES**

Midlothian C.C. G26

**SCHOOLS**

Bremen Twp. Community H.S. H27
Central Park Sch. H27

**MISCELLANEOUS**

Village Hall H27

## NILES

Page 2
(For additional listings, see Section 2)

**STREETS**

Albion E8
Austin Ave. F8
Birchwood Ave. E7
Brummel F7
Caldwell F8
Central Ave. G8
Cherry E8
Concord Ln. F8
Croname Rd. F7
Days Terr. F8
Dobson St. E7
Ebinger Ave. E8
Evergreen E8
Fargo Ave. E7
Forest View Ave. E8
Franks Ave. E8
Greenleaf Ave. F8
Gross Point Rd. F8
Harlem Ave. E7
Harts Rd. F8
Harvard St. E7
Howard St. F7
Jarvis Ave. E7$F7
Jarvis St. E7
Jonquil Terr. E7
Kirk Dr. E7
Kirk Ln. E7
Kirk St. E7
Lawler Ave. E7
Lehigh F8
Lexington Ln. F8
Mason F7
Melvina Ave. F8
Menard Ave. F7
Merrimac Ave. F7
Mulford St. E,F7
Natchez Ave. E7
Neva Ave. E7
Nieman Ave. E8
Niles Ter. E7
Nora Ave. E7
Nordica E7
Nottingham E7
Oak Park Ave. E7
Oakton Ct. E7
Oakton St. E7
Oconto Ave. E7,8
Octavia Ave. E7,8
Odell Ave. E7,8
Oketo Ave. E7,8
Olcott Ave. E7,8
Oleander Ave. E7
Oriole Ave. E7
Osceola Ave. E7,8
Riverside Dr. E8
Riverview Ave. E8
Rosemary Ave. E8
School St. E8
Touhy Ave. F8
Vapor Ln. F7
Waukegan Rd. E7

**CEMETERIES**

St. Adalberts Cem. E8

**GOLF COURSES**

Tam Golf Course F7

**FOREST PRESERVES**

Smith Woods F8

**PARKS**

Jazwiak Park E8
Jonquil Terrace Park E7
Kirk Lane Park E7

**SCHOOLS**

Niles College E8
Niles Twp. H.S. West F7
Oakton Comm. College F7

**SHOPPING CENTERS**

Civic Center Plaza E7

**MISCELLANEOUS**

Village Hall E8

## NORRIDGE

Pages 1,2

**STREETS**

Agatite D,E10
Ainslie D10
Argyle D,E10
Belle Plaine E10
Berteau E10
Canfield D10
Carmen D,E9
Charmaine Rd. D9
Chester D9
Coral Dr. D10
Courtland D10
Crescent D10
Cullom E10
Delphia D10
Denal D10
Eastwood D10
Elm Dr. D10
Forest Preserve Dr. E10
Frank D10
Giddings D,E10
Greenwood D10
Gunnison D,E10
Irving Park F10
Knight D10
Leland D10
Leonard Dr. D10
Lincoln D10
Maple D10

Memory Ln. D9
Mission Dr. E9
Monterey D10
Montrose E10
Moreland D9
Neva E10
Newland E10
Nordica E10
Nottingham E10
Oak D10
Octavia E10
Odell E10
Oketo E10
Olcott E10
Oleander E10
Oneida E10
Opal E10
Orange Dr. E10
Oriole E10
Osage D10
Osceola E10
Ottawa E10
Overhill E10
Ozanam E10
Ozark E10
Paris D10
Pensacola E10
Pittsburgh D10
Plainfield D10
Pontiac D10
Prospect D10
Redwood Dr. D10
Ridgewood D10
Sayre E10
Strong D,E10
Sunnyside D,E10
Sunrise Ln. D10
Thatcher Rd. D10
Vine D10
Wilson D,E10
Windsor E10
Winnemac D10
Winona D9

**CEMETERIES**
Acacia Park Cem. D10
Irving Park Cem. E10
Westlawn Cem. D10

**PARKS**
Norridge Park E10

**SCHOOLS**
Ridgewood H.S. E10

**SHOPPING CENTERS**
Harlem Irving S.C. E10

**MISCELLANEOUS**
Chicago State Hosp. F10
Norridge Home for the Aged D10
State Police Headquarters E10
Village Hall E10

## NORTH RIVERSIDE

Page 5

**STREETS**
Burr Oak E15
Cermak Rd. E15
Country Club Ln. E16
Des Plaines E15,16
Edgewater Rd. D16
Elm D15
Forest E15
Forest View Dr. D16
Groveland D16
Hainsworth E15
Harlem Ave. E15
Keystone E15
Lathrop E15
Lewe Ct. D16
Lincoln D16
Madison D15
Northgate E15
Park E15
Prairie D15
Traube E15
Westover E15
1st Ave. E15
2nd Ave. D15
3rd Ave. D15
4th Ave. D15
5th Ave. D15
6th Ave. D15
7th Ave. D15
8th Ave. D15
9th Ave. D15
10th Ave. D15
11th Ave. D15
12th Ave. D15
13th Ave. D15
17th Ave. D15
22nd Pl. D15
23rd Pl. D16
23rd St. D15
24th St. D16
25th St. D,E16
26th St. D16
27th St. D16
28th St. D16
30th St. D16
31st St. D16

**GOLF COURSES**
Riverside G.C. D16

**SHOPPING CENTERS**
Shopping Center E15

**MISCELLANEOUS**
Village Hall D16

## NORTHLAKE

Pages 1,4

**STREETS**
Alvin Pg.1 B12
Armitage Pg.1 B12
Ashbel Pg.4 B13
Belle Dr. Pg.1 B12
Bernice Pg.1 B12
Caryl Pg.1,4 B12,13
Charles Dr. Pg.1 B12
Country Club Dr. Pg.1 B12
Dewey Pg.1 B12
Dickens Pg.1 B12
Diversey Pg.1 B11
Dodd Pg.4 B13
East Dr. Pg.1 B12
Edward Pg.1 B12
Elm Pg.4 B13
Franklin Dr. Pg.1 B12
Fullerton Pg.1 B12
Gail Pg.4 B13
Geneva Pg.1 B12
Golf View Pg.1 B12
Grand Ave. Pg.1 B11
Haber Ct. Pg.1 B12
Harold Pg.1 B12
Harvard Pg.4 B13
Hayes Pg.1 B12
Hillside Pg.1,4 B12,13
Hirsch Pg.4 B13
Irving Pg.4 B13
Jerome Pg.1 B12
Lake Pg.4 A13
Lakewood Pg.4 B13
Landen Dr. Pg.1 B12
Laporte Pg.1 B12
Lavergne Pg.1 B12
Lemoyne Pg.4 B13
Lind Pg.4 B13
Longfield Pg.1 B12
Lyndale Pg.1 B12
MacArthur Dr. Pg.1 B12
Major Dr. Pg.1 B12
Maplewood Pg.4 B13
Marilyn Pg.1,4 B12,13
McLean Pg.1 B12
Medill Pg.1 B12
Morse Pg.1,4 B13
North Ave. Pg.1,4 B13
Northwest Ave. Pg.1 A12
Palmer Pg.1 B12
Parkview Dr. Pg.1 B12
Prater Pg.1,4 B12,13
Railroad Ave. Pg.1 B12
Rhodes Pg.1 B11
Roberta Pg.1 B12
Roy Pg.1 B12
Sandra Pg.1 B12
Soffel Pg.4 B13
Tri-State Tollway Pg.1 A12
Victoria Dr. Pg.4 B13
Village Dr. Pg.1 B12
Wagner Dr. Pg.1 B12
West Dr. Pg.1 B12
Westward Ho Dr. Pg.1 B12
Whitehall Pg.1 B12
William Pg.1 B12
Winters Dr. Pg.1 B12
Wolf Rd. Pg.1 B12
43rd Ave. Pg.4 B13
44th Ave. Pg.4 B13
45th Ave. Pg.4 B13

**CEMETERIES**
Memorial Estates Cemetery Pg.1 B12

**PARKS**
Grant Park Pg.1 B12
Park Pg.1 B12

**SCHOOLS**
Ben Franklin Sch. Pg.1 B12
Mark Twain Sch. Pg.4 B13
Riley Sch. Pg.4 B13
Roy Sch. Pg.1 B12
St. John Sch. Pg.1 B12
West Leyden H.S. Pg.1 B12
Westdale Sch. Pg.1 B11
Whittier Sch. Pg.1 B12

**MISCELLANEOUS**
City Hall Pg.4 B13
Fire Dept. Pg.1 B12
Home for the Aged Pg.1 B12
Library Pg.4 B13
Northlake Community Hosp. Pg.1 B13
Public Works Pg.4 B13

## OAK LAWN

Page 9
(For additional listings, see Section 2)

**STREETS**
Adeline H23
Alexander G21
Alice Ct. G22
Arnold H23
Austin F22
Avery G21
Brandt G22
Buell G22
Campbell G22
Cass G22
Center Dr. G22
Cicero G21-23
Circle G22
Columbus Dr. G22
Cook G22
Cranbrook E21
Crescent Ct. F21
David Ct. F22
Dean Dr. H23
Drury Ln. G22
Dumke G22
Eastshore Dr. G22
Edgelake F23
Edison F22
Elm G22
Fairfax H23
Franklin G22
Georgia G23
Grant H23
Harlem Ave. E22
Harnew Rd. G22
Hartford E21
High G23
Hilton Dr. G22
James F22
Karlov H21-23
Kathleen H23
Keating G21,23
Kedvale H21-23
Keeler H21-23
Kenneth Ave. G22
Kenneth Pl. G23
Kenton G21-23
Kilbourn G22,23
Kildare H22,23
Kilpatrick G21-23
Kimball Pl. G21
Knox G21-23
Kolin H22,23
Kolmar G21-23
Komensky H21-23
Kostner H22,23
Lacrosse G23
Lamb Dr. G22
Lamon G23
Laporte G23
Laramie G22,23
Lavergne G23
Lawler G23
Lawrence Ct. G22
Lawton G22
Leclaire G23
Linder G22
Lockwood G23
Long G23
Lorel G23
Luna G21
Lynwood Dr. F21
Major F21-23
Mansfield F22
Maple G22
Marion F22
Marmora F23
Mason F22,23
Massasoit F22
Mayfield F21,22
McVicker F21,22
Meade F21,22
Melvina F22
Menard F22
Merrimac F21,22
Merton F22
Minnick G22
Mobile F21
Monitor F22
Moody F21,22
Moore G23
Mulberry G22
Mulligan Dr. F21
Nashville F22
Natchez F22
Natoma F21,22
Neva E22
New England E21,22
Newland E21
Nora E22
Nordica E22
Normandy F22
North St. G21
Oak G22
Oak Center Dr. G22
Oak Park E22
Oakdale Dr. G22
Olympic E21
Otto Pl. G21
Pacific F22
Park G22
Parkside F22
Paxton Rd. G22
Raymond Ave. G22
Ridgeland F22
Ruby G22
Rumsey G22
Rutherford F22
Sayre E21
Scott Ln. G22
Southwest Hwy. G22
Spring Rd. G22
Stevens Dr. G21
Stilwell Pl. H23
Stony Circle G22
Stony Creek Dr. G23
Tripp H21-23
Tulley G21,22
Wainwright H23
Warren G22
Washington G22,23
Westshore Dr. G22
Wick Dr. G22
William Pl. G22
Wolfe Dr. G23
Yourell G22
48th St. G22
49th Ct. G22
49th St. G22
50th Ct. G22
50th St. G22
51st Ct. G23
51st St. G22
52nd St. G22
53rd Ct. G21,22
53rd St. G21,22
54th Ct. G21,22
54th St. G21,22
55th Ct. G21,22
55th St. G21,22
68th Ct. E22
69th Ct. E22
87th Pl. E,F21
87th St. E-G21
88th Pl. E,F21
88th St. E,F21
89th Pl. E,F21
90th Pl. E,F21
90th St. E,F21
91st Pl. E-G21
91st St. E-G21
92nd Pl. E-G22
92nd St. E-G22
93rd Pl. E-G22
93rd St. E-G22
94th Pl. E-G22
94th St. E-G22
95th St. E-G22
96th Pl. E-G22
96th St. E-G22
97th Pl. E-G22
97th St. E-G22
98th Pl. F-H22
98th St. F-H22
99th Pl. F-H22
99th St. F-H22
100th Pl. F-H22
100th St. F-H22
101st Pl. F-H22
101st St. F-H22
102nd Pl. F-H22
102nd St. F-H22
103rd St. F-H22
104th St. F-H23
105th Pl. F-H23
105th St. F-H23
106th Pl. F-H23
106th St. F-H23
107th Pl. G,H23
107th St. G,H23
108th Pl. F,G23
108th St. F,G23
109th St. F,G23
110th Pl. F,G23
110th St. F,G23
111th St. F,G23

**PARKS**
Beverly Lawn Park H22
Oak Meadows Park G22

**SCHOOLS**
Oak Lawn Comm. H.S. F22
Richards H.S. Campus Bldg. F23
Richards H.S. N.E. Bldg. H23

**SHOPPING CENTERS**
Shopping Center G21
State Plaza F21

**MISCELLANEOUS**
Christ Comm. Hosp. H22
Village Hall G22

## OAK PARK

Pages 5,6

**STREETS**
Adams E,F14
Augusta Blvd. E13
Austin Blvd. F13-15
Belleforte E13
Berkshire E13
Carpenter E14
Chicago E13
Clarence E14,15
Clinton E15
Columbian F13
Common F14
Cuyler F13,14
Division E13
East F13-15
Edmer F13
Elizabeth Ct. E13
Elmwood F13-15
Erie E13
Euclid F13-15
Fair Oaks F13
Fillmore E15
Flournoy F14
Forest E13
Garfield E14
Greenfield E,F13
Grove E13,14
Gunderson F15
Harlem E13,14
Harrison F14
Harvard E14
Harvey F13-15
Hayes F13
Highland F15
Home E15
Humphrey F13
Iowa E13
Jackson Blvd. E,F14
Kenilworth E13,14
Lake E13
Le Moyne Pkwy. E,F13
Lenox F13
Lexington E,F14
Linden F13,14
Lombard F13-15
Lyman F15
Madison E,F14
Maple E15
Mapleton F13
Marion E13,14
Miller E13
Monroe E14
North Ave. E13
Oak Park E12-15
Ontario E,F13
Paulina E13
Pleasant E,F14
Pleasant Pl. E14
Randolph E14
Ridgeland F13-15
Roosevelt Rd. E15
Rossell F13
Schneider E13
Scoville F14,15
South Blvd. E14
Superior E,F13
Taylor F13-15
Thomas E13
Van Buren E,F14
Washington Blvd. E14
Wenonah E15
Wesley F14,15
Westgate E14
Wisconsin E15
Woodbine E13

**PARKS**
Anderson Playground F13
Austin Gardens E13
Barrie Plg. Park F14
Carroll Plg. Park E14
Field Park E13
Fox Park F14
Lindberg Park E13
Longfellow Park F14
Maple Park E14
Mills Park E14
Rehm Park F14
Scoville Park E13
Stevenson Plg. Park F14
Taylor Park F13

**SCHOOLS**
Fenwick H.S. F14
Oak Park River Forest H.S. F13

**MISCELLANEOUS**
City Hall F14
Euclid Sq. F15
Frank Lloyd Wright Home E13
Oak Park Hospital E14
Unity Temple E13
West Suburban Hosp. F13
Wright Hist. Dist. F13

## PARK RIDGE

Pages 1,2
(For additional listings, see Section 2)

**STREETS**
Albion D8
Aldine D7,8
Archbury Ln. C8
Arthur D8
Ascot Dr. C8
Ashland D7-9
Austin D7
Avondale D7
Babetta D7
Belle Plaine D8
Berry Pkwy. E8
Bonita Dr. D8
Bonnie D8
Bouterse D7
Broadway D7,8
Brophy D9
Busse Hwy. D7
Canfield Rd. E8
Carolyn D7
Castle Dr. D8
Cedar C,D8
Cherry C,D7
Chester D7,8
Cleveland E8
Clifton D7-9
Clinton D8
Columbia D8
Courtland D8,9
Crescent D8,9
Cumberland D7,8
Curtiss D7
Cynthia D7
Dee Rd. C7,D9
Delphia D7,8
Des Plaines D8
Devon D8
East E7
Edgemont Ln. C-E7
Ellison D7
Elm C,D7
Elmore E7
Engel Blvd. D8
Euclid D8
Fairview D8,9
Florence C7
Forestview C7
Frances Pkwy. D9
Garden D8
Gillick D8
Glenlake D9
Goodwin C7
Grace D7-9
Grand Blvd. D7
Grant Pl. D7
Granville D9
Greenwood D7,8
Grove E8
Hamlin D7,8
Hansen Pl. D7
Harrison E8
Hastings D7
Higgins Rd. D9
Home D7,8
Imperial D8
Irwin D7
James Pl. D8
Jonquil Terr. E7
Joyce Pl. E7
Kathleen E7
Kent D8
Knight D7,8
Lahon C-E7
Lake D8
Laverne D7
Leonard D7
Lincoln D7-9
Linden D8,9
Lois D9
Marvin Pl. D7
Mary Jane D7
Meacham D7
Merrill E7
Michael John Dr. D7
Milton D7
Morris D8
Newton D9
Norman D8
Northwest Hwy. C7,E8
Ozanam E8
Park Pl. D8
Park Ridge Blvd. D8
Parkplaine C7
Parkwood C7
Peale D8
Peterson D9
Prairie D8
Prospect D7-9
Rabe D7
Redfield Ct. D7,8
Ridge Terr. D8
Root D7
Rose Ct. D7,8
Rosemont D8
Rowe D7
Scottylynne Dr. C7
Seeley D7
Seminary D7,8
Sibley D7
Spring D8
Stanley D8
Stewart D8
Summit E8
Sylviawood C7
Talcott Pl. D8
Talcott Rd. C7
Thames Pkwy. C8
Thorndale D9

## PARK RIDGE

Touhy . . . . . . . . . . . . . . . . . . D8
Vine . . . . . . . . . . . . . . . . . . D8,9
Virginia . . . . . . . . . . . . . . . . C7
Warren . . . . . . . . . . . . . . . . . D8
Washington . . . . . . . . . . . . D7-9
Wesley . . . . . . . . . . . . . . . . C7
Western . . . . . . . . . . . . . . . D7-9
Wilkinson Pkwy. . . . . . . . . . . D7
Wilma Pl. . . . . . . . . . . . . . . . E7
Yost . . . . . . . . . . . . . . . . . . E9

### GOLF COURSES
Park Ridge C.C. . . . . . . . . . . . D7

### PARKS
Centennial Park . . . . . . . . . . D8
Hinkley Park . . . . . . . . . . . . . D8
Jaycee Park . . . . . . . . . . . . . D9
Maine Park . . . . . . . . . . . . . . C7
Northeast Park . . . . . . . . . . . E7
South Park . . . . . . . . . . . . . . D8
Southwest Park . . . . . . . . . . D9

### SCHOOLS
Maine Twp. H.S. South . . . . . . D8

### MISCELLANEOUS
Camp Ft. Dearborn . . . . . . . . D9
Lutheran Boys Home . . . . . . . E9
Village Hall . . . . . . . . . . . . . . D8

## PHOENIX
Page 13

### STREETS
Frances St. . . . . . . . . . . . . . . L27
Halsted St. . . . . . . . . . . . . . . L27
Vandrunen Rd. . . . . . . . . . . . L27
Vincennes . . . . . . . . . . . . . . L27
Wallace . . . . . . . . . . . . . . . . L27
Welton . . . . . . . . . . . . . . . . . L27
1st Ave. . . . . . . . . . . . . . . . . L27
2nd Ave. . . . . . . . . . . . . . . . L27
3rd Ave. . . . . . . . . . . . . . . . . L27
4th Ave. . . . . . . . . . . . . . . . . L27
5th Ave. . . . . . . . . . . . . . . . . L27
6th Ave. . . . . . . . . . . . . . . . . L27
7th Ave . . . . . . . . . . . . . . . . L27
8th Ave. . . . . . . . . . . . . . . . . L27
9th Ave. . . . . . . . . . . . . . . . . L27
149th . . . . . . . . . . . . . . . . . . L27
151st Pl. . . . . . . . . . . . . . . . . L27
151st St. . . . . . . . . . . . . . . . L27
153rd St. . . . . . . . . . . . . . . . L27
154th Pl. . . . . . . . . . . . . . . . L27
154th St. . . . . . . . . . . . . . . . L27
155th Pl. . . . . . . . . . . . . . . . L27
155th St. . . . . . . . . . . . . . . . L27
156th St. . . . . . . . . . . . . . . . L27

### MISCELLANEOUS
Village Hall . . . . . . . . . . . . . . L27

## POSEN
Pages 12,13

### STREETS
Albany . . . . . . . . . . . . . . . . . J26
Albert . . . . . . . . . . . . . . . . . . J26
Ash . . . . . . . . . . . . . . . . . . . J26
Blaine . . . . . . . . . . . . . . . . . J26
California . . . . . . . . . . . . . . . J26
Campbell . . . . . . . . . . . . . . . J26
Cleveland . . . . . . . . . . . . . . . J26
Division . . . . . . . . . . . . . . . . J26
Elm . . . . . . . . . . . . . . . . . . . J26
Francisco . . . . . . . . . . . . . . . J26
Grove . . . . . . . . . . . . . . . . . J26
Harrison . . . . . . . . . . . . . . . . J26
Kedzie . . . . . . . . . . . . . . . . . J26
Maple . . . . . . . . . . . . . . . . . J26
McKinley . . . . . . . . . . . . . . . J26
Mozart . . . . . . . . . . . . . . . . . J26
Palmer . . . . . . . . . . . . . . . . J26
Richmond . . . . . . . . . . . . . . J26
Sacramento . . . . . . . . . . . . . J26
Sherman . . . . . . . . . . . . . . . J26
Short . . . . . . . . . . . . . . . . . . J26
Troy . . . . . . . . . . . . . . . . . . J26
Utica . . . . . . . . . . . . . . . . . . J26
Western Ave. . . . . . . . . . . . . J26
Whipple . . . . . . . . . . . . . . . . J26
139th Pl. . . . . . . . . . . . . . . . J26
139th St. . . . . . . . . . . . . . . . J26
140th St. . . . . . . . . . . . . . . . J26
141st St. . . . . . . . . . . . . . . . J26
142nd St. . . . . . . . . . . . . . . . J26
143rd St. . . . . . . . . . . . . . . . J26
144th St. . . . . . . . . . . . . . . . J26
145th St. . . . . . . . . . . . . . . . J26
146th St. . . . . . . . . . . . . . . . J26
148th St. . . . . . . . . . . . . . . . J26
149th St. . . . . . . . . . . . . . . . J26
150th St. . . . . . . . . . . . . . . . J26

### MISCELLANEOUS
Village Hall . . . . . . . . . . . . . . J26

## PROVISO TOWNSHIP
Page 4

### STREETS
Alexandria . . . . . . . . . . . . . . B16
Buck Rd. . . . . . . . . . . . . . . . A14
Burton Ct. . . . . . . . . . . . . . . A16
Concord St. . . . . . . . . . . . . . A15

Degener . . . . . . . . . . . . . . . . A15
Dickens . . . . . . . . . . . . . . . . A15
Duncan St. . . . . . . . . . . . . . . A15
Hamilton . . . . . . . . . . . . . . . A15
Harvard . . . . . . . . . . . . . . . . A15
Hawthorne . . . . . . . . . . . . . . A15
Marion . . . . . . . . . . . . . . . . . A15
Monticello Pl. . . . . . . . . . . . . B16
Turner . . . . . . . . . . . . . . . . . A15

### GOLF COURSES
Fresh Meadow G.C. . . . . . . . . B15
Meadowlark G.C. . . . . . . . . . B16

## RIVER FOREST
Page 5

### STREETS
Ashland . . . . . . . . . . . . . . . . E14
Auvergne Pl. . . . . . . . . . . . . . F13
Berkshire . . . . . . . . . . . . . . . E13
Bonnie Brae . . . . . . . . . . . . . E13
Central . . . . . . . . . . . . . . . . . E14
Chicago . . . . . . . . . . . . . . . . E13
Clinton . . . . . . . . . . . . . . . . . E14
Clinton. Pl. . . . . . . . . . . . . . . E13
Edgewood Pl. . . . . . . . . . . . . F13
Forest . . . . . . . . . . . . . . . E13,14
Franklin . . . . . . . . . . . . . . . . E14
Gale . . . . . . . . . . . . . . . . . . D14
Garden . . . . . . . . . . . . . . . . D14
Harlem Ave. . . . . . . . . . . . . . E13
Hawthorne . . . . . . . . . . . . . . E14
Holly Ct. . . . . . . . . . . . . . . . . E13
Iowa . . . . . . . . . . . . . . . . . . E13
Jackson . . . . . . . . . . . . . . . . C14
Keystone . . . . . . . . . . . . E13,14
Lathrop . . . . . . . . . . . . . . . . E14
Linden . . . . . . . . . . . . . . . . . E14
Monroe . . . . . . . . . . . . . . . . E14
North Ave. . . . . . . . . . . . . . . E13
Oak . . . . . . . . . . . . . . . . . . . E13
Park Ave. . . . . . . . . . . . . . . . E14
Park Dr. . . . . . . . . . . . . . . . . E14
Quick . . . . . . . . . . . . . . . . . . E13
River Oaks . . . . . . . . . . . . . . F13
Thatcher . . . . . . . . . . . . . . . D13
Thomas . . . . . . . . . . . . . . . . E13
Vine . . . . . . . . . . . . . . . . . . . E14
Washington Blvd. . . . . . . . . . E14
William . . . . . . . . . . . . . . E13,14

### PARKS
Keystone Field . . . . . . . . . . . E14
North Park . . . . . . . . . . . . . . E13

### SCHOOLS
Concordia University . . . . . . . E13
Rosary College . . . . . . . . . . . E13
Trinity H.S. . . . . . . . . . . . . . . E13

### MISCELLANEOUS
Village Hall . . . . . . . . . . . . . . E14

## RIVER GROVE
Pages 1,2

### STREETS
Arnold . . . . . . . . . . . . . . . . . D11
Ashland Ave. . . . . . . . . . . . . D11
Aux Plaines . . . . . . . . . . . . . D11
Belden . . . . . . . . . . . . . . . . . D12
Belmont Ave. . . . . . . . . . . . . D11
Beulah . . . . . . . . . . . . . . . . . D11
Boyle . . . . . . . . . . . . . . . . . . D12
Budd . . . . . . . . . . . . . . . . . . D12
Carey . . . . . . . . . . . . . . . . . D12
Center . . . . . . . . . . . . . . . . . D11
Cherry . . . . . . . . . . . . . . . . . D11
Chestnut . . . . . . . . . . . . . . . D11
Clarke . . . . . . . . . . . . . . . . . D12
Clinton . . . . . . . . . . . . . . . . . D12
Davisson . . . . . . . . . . . . . . . D12
Des Plaines River Rd. . . . . . . D12
Elm . . . . . . . . . . . . . . . . . . . D12
Enger . . . . . . . . . . . . . . . . . D11
Erie . . . . . . . . . . . . . . . . . . . D12
Finley . . . . . . . . . . . . . . . . . D12
Forest . . . . . . . . . . . . . . . . . D11
Forestview . . . . . . . . . . . . . . D11
Franklin St. . . . . . . . . . . . . . . D11
Fullerton . . . . . . . . . . . . . . . D12
Grand Ave. . . . . . . . . . . . . . . D12
Greenwood Terr. . . . . . . . . . . D11
Grove . . . . . . . . . . . . . . . . . D12
Haymond . . . . . . . . . . . . . . . D12
Herrick . . . . . . . . . . . . . . . . . D12
Hessing . . . . . . . . . . . . . . . . D12
Indian Bdry. Rd. . . . . . . . . . . D11
Julian Terr. . . . . . . . . . . . . . . D11
Kennedy St . . . . . . . . . . . . . D11
Leyden . . . . . . . . . . . . . . . . D12
Lyndale . . . . . . . . . . . . . . . . D12
Maple . . . . . . . . . . . . . . . . . D11
Marwood . . . . . . . . . . . . . . . D11
O'Connor Dr. . . . . . . . . . . . . D11
Oak . . . . . . . . . . . . . . . . . . . D11
Pacific . . . . . . . . . . . . . . . . . D11
Palmer . . . . . . . . . . . . . . . . D11
Paris . . . . . . . . . . . . . . . . . . D11
Park . . . . . . . . . . . . . . . . . . D11
Rhodes . . . . . . . . . . . . . . . . D12
Richard . . . . . . . . . . . . . . . . D12

Ridge . . . . . . . . . . . . . . . . . D12
River Grove . . . . . . . . . . . . . D12
Roosevelt Ln. . . . . . . . . . . . . D12
Smith Ln. . . . . . . . . . . . . . . . D11
Spruce . . . . . . . . . . . . . . . . D11
Struckmann . . . . . . . . . . . . . D11
Thatcher Ave. . . . . . . . . . . . . D11
Trumbull . . . . . . . . . . . . . . . D12
Walnut . . . . . . . . . . . . . . . . . D11
Walsh . . . . . . . . . . . . . . . . . D11
West . . . . . . . . . . . . . . . . . . D12
Wood . . . . . . . . . . . . . . . . . D12
Wrightwood . . . . . . . . . . . . . D12
5th Ave. . . . . . . . . . . . . . . . . D12

### SCHOOLS
Holy Cross H.S. . . . . . . . . . . . D11
St. Theo Guerin H.S. . . . . . . . D11
Triton Jr. Coll. . . . . . . . . . . . . D12

### MISCELLANEOUS
Village Hall . . . . . . . . . . . . . . D12

## RIVERDALE
Page 13

### STREETS
Acme . . . . . . . . . . . . . . . . . . L25
Ashland . . . . . . . . . . . . . . . . K26
Atlantic St. . . . . . . . . . . . . L25,26
Blue Island-Riverdale Rd. . . . . L25
Clark . . . . . . . . . . . . . . . . . . L26
Dan Ryan Expwy. . . . . . . . . . K25
Dearborn St. . . . . . . . . . . . . . L26
Edbrooke Ave. . . . . . . . . . . . L26
Eggleston . . . . . . . . . . . . . . . L26
Emerald . . . . . . . . . . . . . . . . L26
Forestview . . . . . . . . . . . . . . L26
Halsted St. . . . . . . . . . . . L25,26
Illinois St. . . . . . . . . . . . . . . . L26
Indiana Ave. . . . . . . . . . . L25,26
Jackson . . . . . . . . . . . . . . . . K25
La Salle . . . . . . . . . . . . . . . . L26
Lowe Ave. . . . . . . . . . . . . L25,26
Normal Ave. . . . . . . . . . . . L25,26
Pacesetter Pkwy . . . . . . . K,L26
Parnell Ave. . . . . . . . . . . L25,26
Perry Ave. . . . . . . . . . . . . . . L25
Roll . . . . . . . . . . . . . . . . . . . K25
School . . . . . . . . . . . . . . . L25,26
State St. . . . . . . . . . . . . . . . . L25
Stewart Ave. . . . . . . . . . . . . . L25
Tracy . . . . . . . . . . . . . . . . . . L26
Union . . . . . . . . . . . . . . . . . . L26
Wabash . . . . . . . . . . . . . . . . L25
Wallace Ct. . . . . . . . . . . . L25,26
Wentworth . . . . . . . . . . . . . . L26
135th Pl. . . . . . . . . . . . . . . . L25
136th Pl. . . . . . . . . . . . . . . . L25
136th St. . . . . . . . . . . . . . . . L26
137th Pl. . . . . . . . . . . . . . . . L25
137th St. . . . . . . . . . . . . . . . L25
138th St. . . . . . . . . . . . . . K,L26
139th St. . . . . . . . . . . . . . . . L26
140th Ct. . . . . . . . . . . . . . . . L26
140th St. . . . . . . . . . . . . . . . L26
141st St. . . . . . . . . . . . . . K,L26
142nd St. . . . . . . . . . . . . . . . L26
143rd St. . . . . . . . . . . . . . . . L26
144th St. . . . . . . . . . . . . . . . L26
145th St. . . . . . . . . . . . . . . . L26
146th St. . . . . . . . . . . . . . . . L26

### GOLF COURSES
Pipe O'Peace G.C. . . . . . . . . . K25

### FOREST PRESERVES
Kickapoo Meadows . . . . . . . . K26

### PARKS
Ivanhoe Park . . . . . . . . . . . . L26
Riverdale Park . . . . . . . . . . . . L26

### SCHOOLS
Patton Sch. . . . . . . . . . . . . . . L25

### MISCELLANEOUS
Calumet Boating Ctr. . . . . . . . K25
Kickapoo Boat Launch . . . . . . K26
Village Hall & Fire Dept. . . . . . L26

## RIVERSIDE
Page 5

### STREETS
Addison Rd. . . . . . . . . . . . . . E16
Akenside Rd. . . . . . . . . . . . . E16
Arlington . . . . . . . . . . . . . . . . E16
Audubon Pkwy. . . . . . . . . . . E16
Barrypoint . . . . . . . . . . . . . . D17
Bartram Rd. . . . . . . . . . . . . . E16
Berkley Rd. . . . . . . . . . . . . . . E16
Black Hawk Rd. . . . . . . . . . . . E17
Bloomingbank . . . . . . . . . . . . D17
Blythe Rd. . . . . . . . . . . . . . . . E16
Burling Rd. . . . . . . . . . . . . . . E16
Burlington . . . . . . . . . . . . D17,E16
Byrd Rd. . . . . . . . . . . . . . . . . E16
Columbus Blvd. . . . . . . . . . . . E17
Cowley Rd. . . . . . . . . . . . . . . E16
Delaplaine Rd. . . . . . . . . . E16,17
Des Plaines . . . . . . . . . . . . . D16
Downing Rd. . . . . . . . . . . . . . E16
East Grove Rd. . . . . . . . . . . . E16
Evelyn . . . . . . . . . . . . . . . . . E16
Fairbank Rd. . . . . . . . . . . . . . D17

Forest . . . . . . . . . . . . . . . . . D16
Gage Rd. . . . . . . . . . . . . . . . E17
Gatesby Rd. . . . . . . . . . . . . . E16
Gladstone . . . . . . . . . . . . . . E17
Groveland . . . . . . . . . . . . . . . D16
Haas Ave. . . . . . . . . . . . . . . . E17
Harlem Ave. . . . . . . . . . . . . . E17
Harris Rd. . . . . . . . . . . . . . . . E17
Herbert Rd. . . . . . . . . . . . E16,17
Herrick Rd. . . . . . . . . . . . . . . E16
Kent . . . . . . . . . . . . . . . . . . . E16
Kimbark . . . . . . . . . . . . . . . . E16
La Fayette Rd. . . . . . . . . . . . . E17
Lawton Rd. . . . . . . . . . . . . . . E16
Leesley . . . . . . . . . . . . . . . . E16
Lincoln . . . . . . . . . . . . . . . . . D16
Lindberg Rd. . . . . . . . . . . . . . E16
Lionel Rd. . . . . . . . . . . . . . . . E17
Long Common Rd. . . . . . . . . . E16
Loudoun Rd. . . . . . . . . . . . . . E16
Maplewood Dr. . . . . . . . . . . . D16
Michaux Rd. . . . . . . . . . . . . . E16
Miller Rd. . . . . . . . . . . . . . . . E17
Northgate Rd. . . . . . . . . . . . . E16
Northwood Rd. . . . . . . . . . . . E16
Nuttall Rd. . . . . . . . . . . . . . . E16
Ogden Ave. . . . . . . . . . . . . . . E17
Olmsted Rd. . . . . . . . . . . . . . E16
Park Pl. . . . . . . . . . . . . . . D,E16
Parkway Rd. . . . . . . . . . . . . . E16
Pine . . . . . . . . . . . . . . . . . . . D16
Quincy . . . . . . . . . . . . . D17,E16
Quincy . . . . . . . . . . . . . . . . . E16
Repton Rd. . . . . . . . . . . . . . . E16
Ridgewood . . . . . . . . . . . . . . D16
Riverside Dr. . . . . . . . . . . . . . E17
Robinson Ct. . . . . . . . . . . . . . E17
Scottswood . . . . . . . . . . . . . D17
Selbourne Rd. . . . . . . . . . . . . E16
Shakespeare . . . . . . . . . . . . . E17
Shenstone Rd. . . . . . . . . . . . E16
Southcote Rd. . . . . . . . . . . . . E16
Stanley . . . . . . . . . . . . . . . . E17
Uvedale Rd. . . . . . . . . . . . . . E16
Washington . . . . . . . . . . . . . . E17
Waubansee . . . . . . . . . . . . . D17
West . . . . . . . . . . . . . . . . . . D16
Woodside Rd. . . . . . . . . . . . . E16
York Rd. . . . . . . . . . . . . . . . . E16
39th St. . . . . . . . . . . . . . . . . E17

### PARKS
Long Common Park . . . . . . . . E16

### SHOPPING CENTERS
North Riverside Mall . . . . . . . E16

### MISCELLANEOUS
Village Hall . . . . . . . . . . . . . . E17

## ROBBINS
Page 12

### STREETS
A St. . . . . . . . . . . . . . . . . . . H26
Albany . . . . . . . . . . . . . . . . . J26
Aldia . . . . . . . . . . . . . . . . . . H26
Avers . . . . . . . . . . . . . . . . . . H25
Broadway . . . . . . . . . . . . . . . J25
Central Park . . . . . . . . . . . . . H25
Clifton Park . . . . . . . . . . . H25,26
Emery Ln. . . . . . . . . . . . . . . . H26
Finley . . . . . . . . . . . . . . . . . . H26
Francisco Ave. . . . . . . . . . . . . J25
Glenn . . . . . . . . . . . . . . . . . . H26
Grace . . . . . . . . . . . . . . . . . H26
Hamlin . . . . . . . . . . . . . . . . . H25
Harding . . . . . . . . . . . . . . . . H25
Hendricks . . . . . . . . . . . . . . . H26
Homan . . . . . . . . . . . . . . . . . H25
Karlov . . . . . . . . . . . . . . . . . H25
Kedvale . . . . . . . . . . . . . . . . H25
Kedzie . . . . . . . . . . . . . . . . . J25
Keystone . . . . . . . . . . . . . . . H26
Kildare . . . . . . . . . . . . . . . . . H25
Kinne Rd . . . . . . . . . . . . . . . H26
Kolin . . . . . . . . . . . . . . . . . . H25
Kostner Ave. . . . . . . . . . . . . . H25
Lawndale . . . . . . . . . . . . . . . H25
Lincoln Ln., E. & W. . . . . . . . . H25
Lydia . . . . . . . . . . . . . . . . . . H26
Lydia Ct. . . . . . . . . . . . . . . . . H26
Maxey Ct. . . . . . . . . . . . . . . . H26
McBreen . . . . . . . . . . . . . . . . H25
Midlothian Tpk. . . . . . . . . . H25,26
Monticello . . . . . . . . . . . . . . H25
Nelson Ave. . . . . . . . . . . . . . H26
Reeves Rd. . . . . . . . . . . . . . . H26
Rexford . . . . . . . . . . . . . . . . H26
Richardson . . . . . . . . . . . . . . J26
Richmond . . . . . . . . . . . . . . . J25
Ridgeway . . . . . . . . . . . . . . . H25
Sacramento . . . . . . . . . . . . . J25
Sawyer . . . . . . . . . . . . . . . . J25
Spaulding . . . . . . . . . . H25,H,J26
Springfield . . . . . . . . . . . . . . H25
St. Louis . . . . . . . . . . . . . H25,26
Tripp . . . . . . . . . . . . . . . . . . H25
Troy . . . . . . . . . . . . . . . . . . . J26
Trumbull . . . . . . . . . . . . . H25,26
Turner . . . . . . . . . . . . . . . . . J26
Utica . . . . . . . . . . . . . . . . . . J26
Woodlawn . . . . . . . . . . . . . . . J25

134th Pl. . . . . . . . . . . . . . . . H25
134th St. . . . . . . . . . . . . . . . H25
135th Pl. . . . . . . . . . . . . . . . H25
135th St. . . . . . . . . . . . . . . . H25
136th Pl. . . . . . . . . . . . . . . . H25
136th St. . . . . . . . . . . . . . H,J25
137th St. . . . . . . . . . . . . . H,J25
138th St. . . . . . . . . . . . . . H,J26
139th Pl. . . . . . . . . . . . . . H,J26
139th St. . . . . . . . . . . . . . . . H26
140th St. . . . . . . . . . . . . . . . H26
141st St. . . . . . . . . . . . . . . . H26
143rd St. . . . . . . . . . . . . . . . H26

### MISCELLANEOUS
Village Hall . . . . . . . . . . . . . . H26

## ROSEMONT
Page 1
(For additional listings,
see Section 2)

### STREETS
Allen . . . . . . . . . . . . . . . . . . C9
Ardmore . . . . . . . . . . . . . . . . C9
Barry . . . . . . . . . . . . . . . . . . B8
Berwyn . . . . . . . . . . . . . . . . . C9
Bryn Mawr . . . . . . . . . . . . . . C9
Byron . . . . . . . . . . . . . . . . . . C9
Chestnut . . . . . . . . . . . . . . . B8
Des Plaines River Rd. . . . . . . . C8
Devon . . . . . . . . . . . . . . . . . C8
Devon Ct. . . . . . . . . . . . . . . . C8
Emerson . . . . . . . . . . . . . . . . C9
Estelle Dr. . . . . . . . . . . . . . . C8
Evenhouse . . . . . . . . . . . . . . C9
Farragutt . . . . . . . . . . . . . . . C9
Gage . . . . . . . . . . . . . . . . . . C9
Glenlake . . . . . . . . . . . . . . . . C9
Graff Dr. . . . . . . . . . . . . . . . . C9
Granville . . . . . . . . . . . . . . . . C9
Hawthorne . . . . . . . . . . . . . . C9
Higgins Rd. . . . . . . . . . . . . . . B8
Hope Dr. . . . . . . . . . . . . . . . C8
Kirschoff . . . . . . . . . . . . . . . . C8
Lee St. . . . . . . . . . . . . . . . . . B8
Lunt . . . . . . . . . . . . . . . . . . . B8
Lyndon . . . . . . . . . . . . . . . . . B8
Mannheim Rd. . . . . . . . . . . . B8
Maple Dr. . . . . . . . . . . . . . . . B8
Milton Ct. . . . . . . . . . . . . . . . C9
Milton Pkwy. . . . . . . . . . . . . . C9
Morse . . . . . . . . . . . . . . . . . B8
Norwood . . . . . . . . . . . . . . . C9
Otto . . . . . . . . . . . . . . . . . . . C9
Pearl . . . . . . . . . . . . . . . . . . C9
Rose . . . . . . . . . . . . . . . . . . C9
Rosemont . . . . . . . . . . . . . . C9
Ruby . . . . . . . . . . . . . . . . . . C9
Schaffer Ct . . . . . . . . . . . . . . C9
Scott . . . . . . . . . . . . . . . . . . C8
Thorndale . . . . . . . . . . . . . . . C9
Touhy . . . . . . . . . . . . . . . . . B8
Wesley Ter. . . . . . . . . . . . . . . C9
William . . . . . . . . . . . . . . . . . C9
Willow Creek Dr. . . . . . . . . . . C9

### SCHOOLS
Ruby St. Rosemont Sch. . . . . . C9

### MISCELLANEOUS
Rosemont Theatre . . . . . . . . . C9
Village Hall . . . . . . . . . . . . . . C9

## SCHILLER PARK
Page 1

### STREETS
Agitite Ave. . . . . . . . . . . . . . . C10
Agitite Ct. . . . . . . . . . . . . . . . C10
Ainslie . . . . . . . . . . . . . . . . . C10
Atlantic . . . . . . . . . . . . . . . . C10
Belle Plaine . . . . . . . . . . . . . C10
Berteau . . . . . . . . . . . . . . . . C10
Bobby Ln. . . . . . . . . . . . . . . . C10
Byron St. . . . . . . . . . . . . . . . C10
Cary . . . . . . . . . . . . . . . . . . C11
Cora (Foster) Ave. . . . . . . . . . C10
Cullom . . . . . . . . . . . . . . . . . C10
Delta Pkwy. . . . . . . . . . . . . . B10
Des Plaines River Rd. . . . . . . . C10
Eastwood Ave. . . . . . . . . . . . C10
Eastwood Ct. . . . . . . . . . . . . C10
Eden . . . . . . . . . . . . . . . . . . C10
Emerson Ave. . . . . . . . . . . . . C10
Emerson Dr. . . . . . . . . . . . . . C10
Fifth . . . . . . . . . . . . . . . . . . . C10
Florence . . . . . . . . . . . . . . . . C9
Foster . . . . . . . . . . . . . . . . . C10
Garden Ct. . . . . . . . . . . . . . . C10
Goss . . . . . . . . . . . . . . . . . . C10
Grace . . . . . . . . . . . . . . . . . C10
Gremley . . . . . . . . . . . . . . . . C10
Harold . . . . . . . . . . . . . . . . . C10
Hartford Ct. . . . . . . . . . . . . . . C10
Hirschberg . . . . . . . . . . . . . . C10
Indian Trail . . . . . . . . . . . . . . C10
Irving Park Rd. . . . . . . . . . . . . C10
Ivanhoe Ave. . . . . . . . . . . . . C11
Ivanhoe Cir. . . . . . . . . . . . . . C11
Ivanhoe Ct. . . . . . . . . . . . . . C11
Ivanhoe St. . . . . . . . . . . . . . . C11
Jill Ln. . . . . . . . . . . . . . . . . . C10

## SKOKIE

Judd . . . . . . . . . . . . . . . . . . C10
Kelvin Ln. . . . . . . . . . . . . . . . C10
Kolze . . . . . . . . . . . . . . . . . . C10
Lawrence . . . . . . . . . . . . . . . C10
Lawrence Ct. . . . . . . . . . . . . C10
Leland . . . . . . . . . . . . . . . . . C10
Linn . . . . . . . . . . . . . . . . . . . C10
Marie Ln. . . . . . . . . . . . . . . . C10
Michigan . . . . . . . . . . . . . . . C10
Montrose Blvd. . . . . . . . . . . . C10
Moore Ln. . . . . . . . . . . . . . . . C10
Pan American Dr. . . . . . . . . . B10
Panoramic Dr. . . . . . . . . . . . . C11
Prairie . . . . . . . . . . . . . . . . . C10
River . . . . . . . . . . . . . . . . . . C10
Rose . . . . . . . . . . . . . . . . . . C10
Ruby (9th) . . . . . . . . . . . . . . C10
Sally . . . . . . . . . . . . . . . . . . C10
Scott (5th) Ave. . . . . . . . . . . . C10
Scott St. . . . . . . . . . . . . . . . . C10
Seymour . . . . . . . . . . . . . . . C10
South . . . . . . . . . . . . . . . . . C10
Sterling Ln. . . . . . . . . . . . . . . C10
Sunnyside . . . . . . . . . . . . . . C10
Susy Ln. . . . . . . . . . . . . . . . . C10
Transworld Rd. . . . . . . . . . . . B10
United Pkwy. . . . . . . . . . . . . . B10
Wagner . . . . . . . . . . . . . . . . C10
Waveland Ave. . . . . . . . . . . . C11
Wehrman Pl. . . . . . . . . . . . . . C11
Wesley Terr. . . . . . . . . . . . . . C10
Willow . . . . . . . . . . . . . . . . . C11
Wilson . . . . . . . . . . . . . . . . . C10
Winona . . . . . . . . . . . . . . . . C9
25th Ave. . . . . . . . . . . . . . . . C11

### MISCELLANEOUS
Village Hall . . . . . . . . . . . . . . C10

## SKOKIE
Pages 2,3
(For additional listings,
see Section 2)

### STREETS
Austin Ave. . . . . . . . . . . . . . . F7
Babb Ave. . . . . . . . . . . . . . . G7
Birchwood . . . . . . . . . . . . . G,H7
Birchwood Ave. . . . . . . . . . G,H7
Brummel St. . . . . . . . . . . . . G,H7
Carpenter Rd. . . . . . . . . . . . . G8
Central Ave. . . . . . . . . . . . . . G8
Central Park Ave. . . . . . . . . . . H8
Chase Ave. . . . . . . . . . . . . . . G8
Coyle Ave. . . . . . . . . . . . . . . G8
Crawford Ave. . . . . . . . . . . . . H7
Dobson . . . . . . . . . . . . . . . . G,H7
East Prairie Rd. . . . . . . . . . . . H7
Edens Expwy. . . . . . . . . . . . G7,8
Estes Ave. . . . . . . . . . . . . . . G8
Fairview Ln. . . . . . . . . . . . . . G8
Fargo Ave. . . . . . . . . . . . . . G,H7
Farwell Ave. . . . . . . . . . . . . . G8
Fitch Ave. . . . . . . . . . . . . . . . G8
Galitz Ave. . . . . . . . . . . . . . . G7
George St. . . . . . . . . . . . . . . G7
Harvard St. . . . . . . . . . . . . . G,H7
Howard St. . . . . . . . . . . . . . F-H7
Hull St. . . . . . . . . . . . . . . . . G8
Jarlath Ave. . . . . . . . . . . . . G,H8
Jarvis Ave. . . . . . . . . . . . . . G,H7
Jerome Ave. . . . . . . . . . . . . G,H7
Joneway Terr. . . . . . . . . . . . . G7
Jonquil Terr. . . . . . . . . . . . . . H7
Karlov Ave. . . . . . . . . . . . . . . H7
Kedvale Ave. . . . . . . . . . . . . . H7
Keeler Ave. . . . . . . . . . . . . . . H7
Kenneth Ave. . . . . . . . . . . . . G7
Kenton Ave. . . . . . . . . . . . . . G7
Keystone Ave. . . . . . . . . . . . . H7
Kilbourn Ave. . . . . . . . . . . . . H7
Kildare Ave. . . . . . . . . . . . . . H7
Kilpatrick Ave. . . . . . . . . . . . . H7
Kirk St. . . . . . . . . . . . . . . . . G,H7
Knox Ave. . . . . . . . . . . . . . . . G7
Kolmar Ave. . . . . . . . . . . . . . H7
Kostner Ave. . . . . . . . . . . . . . H7
LaCrosse Ave. . . . . . . . . . . . . G7
Lamon Ave. . . . . . . . . . . . . . G8
Laramie Ave. . . . . . . . . . . . . G8
Latrobe Ave. . . . . . . . . . . . . . G8
Lavergne Ave. . . . . . . . . . . . G7,8
Lawndale Ave. . . . . . . . . . . . H8
LeClaire Ave. . . . . . . . . . . . G7,8
Linder Ave. . . . . . . . . . . . . . . G8
Lockwood Ave. . . . . . . . . . . . G8
Long Ave. . . . . . . . . . . . . . . . G8
Lorel Ave. . . . . . . . . . . . . . . . G8
Louise St. . . . . . . . . . . . . . . G,H7
Lunt Ave. . . . . . . . . . . . . . . . G8
Major Ave. . . . . . . . . . . . . . . F7
Mango Ave. . . . . . . . . . . . . . F7
Marmora Ave. . . . . . . . . . . . . F7
Mason Ave. . . . . . . . . . . . . . F7
McCormick Blvd. . . . . . . . . . . H7
Menard Ave. . . . . . . . . . . . . . F7
Monticello Ave. . . . . . . . . . . . H8
Morse Ave. . . . . . . . . . . . . . . G8
Mulford St. . . . . . . . . . . . . . G,H7
New Gross Point Rd. . . . . . . . F7
Niles Ave. . . . . . . . . . . . . . . . G7
Niles Center Rd. . . . . . . . . . . G8

## SKOKIE

| | |
|---|---|
| Oakton St. | G,H7 |
| Park Ave. | G7 |
| Parkside Ave. | F7 |
| Pratt | G8 |
| Ridgeway Ave. | H8 |
| Sherwin Ave. | G8 |
| Skokie Blvd. | G7 |
| St. Louis Ave. | H8 |
| Touhy Ave. | G8 |

**PARKS**

| | |
|---|---|
| Birch Park | G7 |
| Coyle Park | G8 |
| Emily Park | G7 |
| Frontage Park | G7 |
| George Park | G7 |
| Hamlin Park | H7 |
| Kostner Park | H7 |
| Laramie Park | G8 |
| Little League Park | H7 |
| Oakton Park | G7 |

**SCHOOLS**

| | |
|---|---|
| Hebrew Theological College | G8 |
| Niles Twp. H.S. West | F7 |
| Oakton Comm. College | G7 |

**MISCELLANEOUS**

| | |
|---|---|
| Centre East | G7 |
| Village Hall | G7 |

## SOUTH HOLLAND

Pages 13,14

**STREETS**

| | |
|---|---|
| Avalon Ave. | M27,28 |
| Bennet Ave. | N29 |
| Bernice Rd. | N29 |
| Betty Ln. | M28 |
| Calumet Ave. | L27 |
| Calumet Expwy. | M27,28 |
| Canal St. | L28 |
| Caryn Cir. | M28 |
| Champlain St. | M27 |
| Cherry St. | M27 |
| Church Dr. | M27 |
| Claire Ln. | M28 |
| Clark | L27 |
| Clyde | N28,29 |
| Constance Ave. | N29 |
| Cornell Ave. | N28 |
| Cottage Grove Ave. | M27,28 |
| Cregier Ave. | N29 |
| Dante Dr. | N27 |
| Dearborn | L27 |
| Debbie Ln. | M27,28 |
| Dobson Ave. | M27-29 |
| Dorchester | N27 |
| Drexel Ave. | M27-29 |
| Ellis Ave. | M27,28 |
| Ellis Ct. | M28,29 |
| Elm Ct. | M28 |
| Elm St. | M28 |
| Evans Ave. | M28,29 |
| Evans Ct. | M28 |
| Everett Ave. | N29 |
| Godwens Ln. | M27 |
| Grant St. | M27 |
| Greenwood Ave. | M28,29 |
| Halsted Dr. | L29 |
| Hanley Blvd. | M27 |
| Holland Ave. | M28 |
| Indiana Ave. | L28 |
| Ingleside Ave. | M27,28 |
| Ingleside Ct. | M28 |
| Joyce Cir. | M28 |
| Joyce Ct. | M28 |
| Kenwood Ave. | M27-29 |
| Kenwood Ct. | M28 |
| Kimbark | M27,28 |
| King Ct. | M27 |
| King Dr. | M27 |
| La Salle | L27 |
| Langley Ave. | M28,29 |
| Louis Ave. | M28,29 |
| Louis Ct. | M29 |
| Lowell Ave. | M28 |
| Luella Ave. | N28 |
| Maple Ct. | M28 |
| Maple St. | M27,28 |
| Marian Dr. | M27,28 |
| Maryland Ave. | M28,29 |
| Merrill | N28 |
| Michigan Ave. | M28 |
| Minerva | M28 |
| Mutual Terr. | M27 |
| Naughton Dr. | M27 |
| Orchid Dr. | M27 |
| Park Ln. | M27 |
| Parkside Ave. | M27-29 |
| Parkside Ct. | M28 |
| Paxton Ave. | N28 |
| Perry | L27 |
| Prairie Ave. | L28 |
| Prince Dr. | N27 |
| Riverside Dr. | L,M27 |

| | |
|---|---|
| Riverside Dr., E. & W. | L28 |
| Riverview St. | M27 |
| Robin Ln. | L27 |
| Rose Dr. | M27 |
| School St. | M27-29 |
| Shirley Ct. | M28 |
| Sibley Blvd. | L27 |
| South Park Ave. | M27-29 |
| State St. | L27,28 |
| Suntone Rd. | L27,28 |
| Taft Dr. | L28 |
| Thornton Ave. | L28 |
| Thornton-Blue Island Rd. | L28 |
| Thornwood Dr. | M28,29 |
| Tulip Ct. | M27 |
| Union St. | L29 |
| University Ct. | M28 |
| Vandrunen | L27,28 |
| Vincennes Rd. | L27,28 |
| Volbrecht Dr. | N29 |
| Volbrecht Rd. | N29 |
| Wabash Ave. | L27,28 |
| Wabash Ct. | L27 |
| Wallace Ave. | L28 |
| Waterman Dr. | M27 |
| Wausau Ave. | M28,29 |
| Wausau Ct. | M28 |
| Wentworth Ave. | L27 |
| Westview Ave. | L29 |
| Woodlawn Ave. | M27 |
| Woodlawn Ave., E. | M27 |
| Yates Ave. | N29 |

## STONE PARK

Pages 4,5

**STREETS**

| | |
|---|---|
| Division | C13 |
| Lake | C13 |
| Lemoyne | C13 |
| Mannheim Rd. | B13 |
| North | C13 |
| Soffel | C13 |
| 32nd Ave. | C13 |
| 33rd Ave. | C13 |
| 34th Ave. | C13 |
| 35th Ave. | C13 |
| 36th Ave. | C13 |
| 37th Ave. | C13 |
| 38th Ave. | C13 |
| 39th Ave. | C13 |
| 40th Ave. | C13 |
| 43rd Ave. | B13 |
| 44th Ave. | B13 |
| 45th Ave. | B13 |

**SCHOOLS**

| | |
|---|---|
| Sacred Heart Seminary | C13 |

**MISCELLANEOUS**

| | |
|---|---|
| Village Hall | B13 |

## SUMMIT

Pages 5,8,9

**STREETS**

| | |
|---|---|
| Archer | Pg.5,9 . . E18,19 |
| Center | Pg.5,9 . . E18,19 |
| Douglas | Pg.5 . . E18 |
| Hanover | Pg.5 . . E18 |
| Harlem | Pg.5,9 . . E18,19 |
| Hunt | Pg.9 . . E18,19 |
| Lawndale | Pg.5,8 . . D,E18 |
| Park Ave. | Pg.9 . . E18 |
| 53rd St. | Pg.9 . . E18 |
| 55th St. | Pg.9 . . E18 |
| 56th Pl. | Pg.9 . . E18 |
| 57th Pl. | Pg.9 . . E18 |
| 57th St. | Pg.9 . . E18 |
| 58th Pl. | Pg.9 . . E19 |
| 58th St. | Pg.9 . . E19 |
| 59th Pl. | Pg.9 . . E19 |
| 59th St. | Pg.5,8,9 . . E19 |
| 60th Pl. | Pg.9 . . E19 |
| 60th St. | Pg.9 . . E19 |
| 61st Pl. | Pg.9 . . E19 |
| 61st St. | Pg.9 . . E19 |
| 62nd Pl. | Pg.9 . . E19 |
| 62nd St. | Pg.9 . . E19 |
| 63rd Pl. | Pg.9 . . E19 |
| 63rd St. | Pg.9 . . E19 |
| 64th Pl. | Pg.9 . . E19 |
| 64th St. | Pg.9 . . E19 |
| 72nd Ct. | Pg.5 . . E18 |
| 73rd Ave. | Pg.5,9 . . E18,19 |
| 73rd Ct. | Pg.5 . . E18 |
| 74th Ave. | Pg.5,9 . . E18,19 |
| 75th Ave. | Pg.5,9 . . E18,19 |
| 76th Ave. | Pg.9 . . E19 |

**PARKS**

| | |
|---|---|
| Summit Park | Pg.9 . . E18 |

**SCHOOLS**

| | |
|---|---|
| Argo H.S. | Pg.9 . . E19 |

## STICKNEY

Pages 5,6

**STREETS**

| | |
|---|---|
| Central | G17 |
| Cicero | G17 |
| Clarence | F17 |
| Clinton | E17 |

| | |
|---|---|
| East | F17 |
| Elmwood | F17 |
| Euclid | F17 |
| Grove | E17 |
| Gunderson | E17 |
| Harlem Ave. | E17 |
| Home | E17 |
| Kenilworth | E17 |
| Laramie | G17 |
| Lorraine Terr. | E17 |
| Maple | F17 |
| Oak Park | F17 |
| Pershing Rd. | F17 |
| Ridgeland | F17 |
| Scoville | F17 |
| Wenonah | F17 |
| Westley | F17 |
| Wisconsin | F17 |
| 39th St. | E17 |
| 40th Pl. | E17 |
| 40th St. | E17 |
| 41st St. | E17 |
| 42nd St. | E17 |
| 43rd St. | E17 |
| 44th St. | F17 |
| 45th St. | F17 |

**MISCELLANEOUS**

| | |
|---|---|
| Village Hall | F17 |

## WESTCHESTER

Pages 4,5

**STREETS**

| | |
|---|---|
| Alexandria Ln. | B16 |
| Ashley Woods | B16 |
| Balmoral Blvd. | C15 |
| Bassford | B16 |
| Beckett | B16 |
| Bedford | B16 |
| Belleview | B15 |
| Berkshire | B16 |
| Boeger Ave. | B15,16 |
| Boeger Ct. | B16 |
| Bond | C15 |
| Brighton | B16 |
| Bristol | C15 |
| Broadway | C15 |
| Buckingham | B15,16 |
| Burns | B16 |
| Burton Dr. | B16 |
| Cambridge | C15 |
| Camelot | C15 |
| Canterbury | B,C15 |
| Carlisle | B16 |
| Cermak Rd. | B15 |
| Charles | B15 |
| Chaucer | C15 |
| Claridge | B15 |
| Concord | C15 |
| Constitution Dr. | B16 |
| Crestwood | C15 |
| Cromwell | C15 |
| Denton | B16 |
| Derby Ln. | C15 |
| Devonshire Ln. | C15 |
| Devonshire St. | C15 |
| Dickens | B,C15 |
| Dorchester | B15 |
| Dover | C15 |
| Downing | B15,16 |
| Drake | B16 |
| Drury Ln. | C15 |
| Eaton | B16 |
| Edgewood Ave. | B16 |
| Elizabeth | C15 |
| Enterprise Dr. | B16 |
| Essex | B16 |
| Evers | B15 |
| Fairfield | B16 |
| Fielding | B15 |
| Fleet | B16 |
| Forest | B15 |
| Gardner Rd. | C15 |
| Gladstone | C15 |
| Haas | B15 |
| Halifax | B15 |
| Hastings | B16 |
| Hawthorne | B15 |
| Heidorn | B15 |
| High Ridge Pkwy. | B15,16 |
| Hull | C15 |
| Kensington | B15,16 |
| Kent | B16 |
| Kings | B16 |
| Kingston | C15 |
| Kipling | C15 |
| Kitchener | C15 |
| La Grange Rd. | C16 |
| Lancaster | B16 |
| Manchester | C15 |
| Mandel | B15 |
| Mandel Ct. | B15 |
| Mannheim Rd. | C15 |
| Martindale Dr. | B15 |
| Mayfair | B15,16 |
| Millford | B16 |
| Monticello | B16 |
| Nelson Sq. | C15 |
| Nelson St. | C15 |
| Newbury | B16 |
| Newcastle | C15 |
| Norfolk | B15 |
| Oxford | B,C15 |
| Park | B16 |
| Pelham | C15 |
| Pell | C15 |
| Plymouth | C15 |
| Portsmouth | C15 |
| Prescott | B16 |
| Preston | B16 |
| Princess | B16 |
| Queens | B16 |
| Raleigh | B16 |
| Regency | B16 |
| Robinhood | C15 |
| Roosevelt Rd. | B,C15 |
| Shakespeare | B15 |
| Shaw | B15 |
| Shelly | B15 |
| Sherwood | B16 |
| Somerset Dr. | B16 |
| Stratford | B15,16 |
| Suffolk | C15 |
| Sunnyside | B15,16 |

| | |
|---|---|
| Terrace Ln. | B16 |
| The Strand | C15 |
| Wakefield | B16 |
| Waterford | B15 |
| Waverly | B15 |
| Wellington | B16 |
| Westminster | B16 |
| Westwood | B16 |
| Wight | C15 |
| Winchester | C15 |
| Windsor | B16 |
| Wolf Rd. | B15 |
| Woodlawn | B16 |
| Worcester | C15 |
| 24th St. | B16 |
| 26th St. | B16 |
| 28th St. | B16 |
| 29th St. | B16 |
| 30th St. | B16 |
| 31st St. | B16 |

**CEMETERIES**

| | |
|---|---|
| Glenn Oak Cem. | B15 |
| Oak Ridge Cem. | B15 |

**PARKS**

| | |
|---|---|
| Gladstone Park | C15 |

**SCHOOLS**

| | |
|---|---|
| High Ridge Sch. | B15 |
| Immaculate Heart of Mary H.S. | B15 |
| St. Joseph H.S. | B15 |

**MISCELLANEOUS**

| | |
|---|---|
| Village Hall | C15 |

## WESTERN SPRINGS

Page 8

**STREETS**

| | |
|---|---|
| Birch Ln. | B17,18 |
| Burlington | B17 |
| Caroline | B17 |
| Central | B17,18 |
| Chestnut | B17 |
| Clausen | B17,18 |
| Commonwealth | B18 |
| Courtland Cir. | B18 |
| Crest Ln. | B18 |
| Crestview | B18 |
| Dierks Dr. | B18 |
| Ellington | B17,18 |
| Elm Ave. | B17 |
| Ernst Ct. | B18 |
| Fairelms | B17 |
| Forest | B17 |
| Franklin | B17,18 |
| Garden | B17 |
| Gilbert | B17 |
| Grand | B17,18 |
| Grove | B17 |
| Hampton | B17 |
| Harvey Ave. | B17,18 |
| Hillgrove | B17 |
| Howard | B17,18 |
| Johnson | B17,18 |
| Kirkland Ave. | B18 |
| Lawn Ave. | B17,18 |
| Lawn Cir. | B18 |
| Lawn Ct. | B18 |
| Lawn Dr. | B18 |
| Linden Ave. | B17,18 |
| Linden Cir. | B19 |
| Linden Ct. | B18 |
| Linden Ln. | B19 |
| Longmeadow Ln. | B18 |
| Maple Ln. | B18 |
| Maple St. | B17 |
| Oak Ln. | B19 |
| Oak St. | B17 |
| Ogden | B17 |
| Park Ln. | B18 |
| Park Pl. | B17 |
| Prospect | B17 |
| Race St. | B17 |
| Ridge Ln. | B19 |
| Ridgewood Dr. | B18 |
| Ried St. | B17 |
| Rose | B17 |
| Rugeley Rd. | B18 |
| Sunset Terr. | B17 |
| Walker | B17 |
| Walnut | B18 |
| Western | A17 |
| Willow St. | B17 |
| Wolf Rd. | B17,18 |
| Woodland | B17-19 |
| 39th St. | B17 |
| 40th St. | B17 |
| 41st St. | B17 |
| 42nd St. | B17 |
| 43rd St. | B17 |
| 45th St. | B17 |
| 46th St. | B17 |
| 47th St. | B17 |
| 48th St. | B18 |

| | |
|---|---|
| 49th St. | B18 |
| 50th St. | B18 |
| 50th Pl. | B18 |
| 51st Pl. | B18 |
| 51st St. | B18 |
| 52nd St. | B18 |
| 53rd St. | B18 |
| 54th Pl. | B18 |
| 54th St. | B18 |
| 55th St. | B18 |

**PARKS**

| | |
|---|---|
| Laidlaw Park | B17 |
| Ridge Acres Park | B17 |
| Spring Rock Park | B17 |

**SCHOOLS**

| | |
|---|---|
| Lyons Twp. H.S. South | B18 |

**MISCELLANEOUS**

| | |
|---|---|
| Village Hall | B17 |
| Courtesy Ln. | B3 |
| Plant Rd. | B3 |
| Sumac Ln. | B3 |

## WILLOW SPRINGS

Page 8
(For additional listings, see Section 2)

**STREETS**

| | |
|---|---|
| Abbott St. | C21 |
| Archer Ave. | B21 |
| Arizona Tr. | B21 |
| Beech St. | C21 |
| Beverly Ln. | C21 |
| Blackstone Ave. | C21 |
| Buck Ln. | B21 |
| Buckingham Ct. | B21 |
| Candlelight Dr., E. | B21 |
| Cedar St. | C21 |
| Charlton Ave. | C21 |
| Chaucer Dr. | B21 |
| Chelsea Ln. | C21 |
| Cliff St. | C21 |
| Colonel Ave. | C21 |
| Columbia Woods Dr. | B21 |
| Crescent Ct. | C21 |
| Crestview Dr. | B21 |
| Crown Cir. | B21 |
| Crown St. | B21 |
| Doogan Ave. | B21 |
| Dunbar St. | C21 |
| Elm St. | C21 |
| Fieldcrest Ave. | B21 |
| Flag Ave. | B21 |
| Forest Ave. | C21 |
| German Church Rd. | B21 |
| Glenwood St. | C21 |
| Hess Ave. | B21 |
| High St. | C21 |
| Hill St. | C21 |
| Hilton St. | C21 |
| Independence Dr. | B21 |
| Joyce Ln. | B21 |
| Lake St. | C21 |
| Liberty Grove Dr. | B21 |
| Louis Dr. | C20 |
| Maple Ave. | C21 |
| Market St. | C21 |
| Mound St. | C21 |
| Nolton Ave. | C21 |
| Nueport Ct. | B21 |
| Nueport Dr. | B21 |
| Oakwood Ave. | C21 |
| Park St. | C21 |
| Pearl St. | C21 |
| Pine St. | C21 |
| Pleasantview | C21 |
| Poston Rd. | C21 |
| Prospect Ave. | C21 |
| Ravine Ave. | C21 |
| Regency Ct. | B21 |
| Rosemere Ct. | B21 |
| Rust St. | C21 |
| Rust Trail | C20 |
| Scenic Dr. | B21 |
| School Ave. | B21 |
| Sherwood St. | C21 |
| Spring St. | C21 |
| Stratford Dr. | C21 |
| Tower Rd. | C21 |
| Tudor Cir. | C21 |
| Union St. | C21 |
| Ursala Dr. | B21 |
| Vana Dr. | C21 |
| Vinewood Ave. | B21 |
| Wadsworth Rd. | B21 |
| Walnut St. | C21 |
| Wentworth St. | B21 |
| Willow Springs Rd. | B21 |
| Willow St. | C21 |
| Willow West Dr. | B21 |
| 84th Pl. | B21 |
| 85th St. | B21 |
| 86th St. | B21 |
| 87th St. | B,C21 |

# COOK CO. SUBURBS

## SECTION 2

## LEGEND

| | | | |
|---|---|---|---|
| ▬▬▬ | EXPRESSWAY FREE & TOLL | 🛡 | INTERSTATE |
| ▬▬▬ | MULTI-LANE DIVIDED | 🛡 | U.S. |
| ▬▬▬ | PRIMARY THROUGH ROUTE | ⬤ | STATE |
| ═══ | OTHER THRU ROADS | ▭ | PARK |
| ─── | OTHER STREETS | ▭ | FOREST PRESERVE |
| ┼┼┼┼┼ | RAILROAD | ▬ | GOLF COURSE |
| ～～ | RIVER OR LAKE | ▨ | CEMETERY |
| | | ▬ | AIRPORT |

**TURN PAGE FOR ORIENTATION MAP**

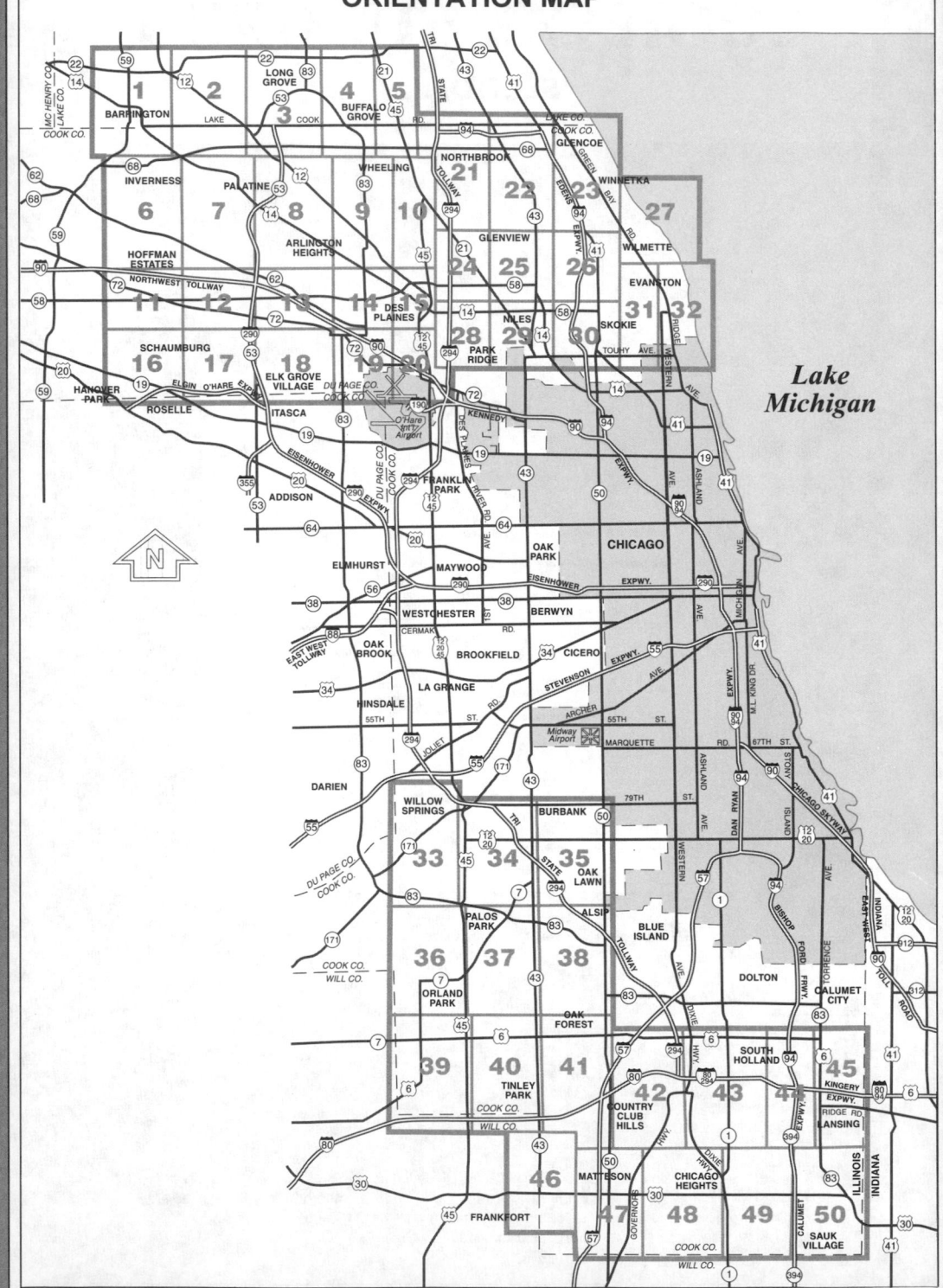

# SECTION 2
## ORIENTATION MAP

*Lake Michigan*

N

© BY CSC

**NORTH BARRINGTON**

**LAKE ZURICH**

**DEER PARK**

**CUBA MARSH FOREST PRESERVE**

**BARRINGTON**

**BARRINGTON HILLS**

**DEER PARK**

**INVERNESS**

Blumore Country Club

Honey Lake

Lake Zurich

Kuechmann Park

Paulus Park

The Barn Recreation Office

Village Wildlife Refuge

Village Hall

Village Hall

Lafferty Park

Braemar Park

Braemar Park

Columbian Lake

Stillwater Lake

Jewel Lagoon

Lake Louise

High School Lagoon

Langendorf Park

Barrington High School

St. Ann Cem.

Lake Shore

Baker Lake

Thunderbird Country Club

FOREST PRESERVE

Hawthorne Lake

Stephanie Lake

Ron Beese Park

Deer Lake

1. Commonwealth Ct.
2. Hampton Park
3. Marlborough Rd.
4. Churchill Ct.
5. Covington Dr.
6. Fairfax Ct.
7. Spruce
8. Magnolia Rd.
9. Pine
10. Sycamore
11. Willow

SIGNAL HILL RD.

LAKE ZURICH-HIGHWOOD RD.

CUBA TOWNSHIP

ELA TOWNSHIP

NORTHWEST HWY.

Chicago & Northwestern

LAKE CO.

COOK CO.

CONTINUED IN SEC. 5, PAGE 4 AND SEC. 6, PAGE 29

CONTINUED ON PAGE 2

.5 MILE

© BY CSC

V  W  X  A

3  4  5

CONTINUED IN SEC. 6, PAGES 30 AND 31

**LAKE ZURICH**

Oak Ridge Marsh Nature Park
North Athletic May Field Whitney Sch.
Lake Zurich Jr. H.S.
St. Francis de Sales Sch.

A. Ramblewood Ct.
B. Red Bridge Ct.
C. Burr Oak Ct.
D. Meadowbrook Ct.

Rose Rd.
LAKE ZURICH HWY.

Kemper Lakes Golf Course

23000 N

Lions Park

Library

Old Mill Grove Park

Knox Park

Bristol Trails Park

22500 N

1. Margate Ct.
2. Stanton Ct.
3. Century Ct.
4. Timberwood
5. Sussex Ct.
6. Newgate Ct.
7. Buckingham Ct.
8. Greystone Ln.
9. Ravenswood Ct.
10. Brookfield Ct.

**LONG GROVE**

Sarah Adams Sch. Richard Staples Youth Sports Complex
Sandlewood Park

Chestnut Corners Pk.

11. Buffalo Creek Dr.
12. Apache Ct.
13. Huntington Ct.
14. Huntington Dr.
15. Pheasant Ridge Ct.
16. Warwick Ct.
17. Thorndale Ct.
18. Broadway Ct.
19. Thornridge Dr.
20. Whitehall Ct.
21. Stratford Ct.

**KILDEER**

22000 N

Warwick Pk.

Sparrow Thornridge Pk.

A. Cromwell Ct.
B. Newberry Ct.
C. Rush Ct.
D. Wilkes Ln.
E. Lexington Ln.
F. Bushron Ct.
G. Orrington Ct.
M. Garland Ct.

Quail Run Pk.
Foxfire

21500 N

RAND RD.

**CUBA**

Countryside W. Soccer Field

Countryside West Park

21000 N

**DEER PARK**

Lake Farmington

**QUENTINS CORNERS**

Quentin Sch. Shefley Rd.

Weatherstone Ct.

20500 N

LONG GROVE RD.

20000 N

**ELA TOWNSHIP**

**PALATINE TOWNSHIP**

Hillcrest Rd.

Woodland Public

1. Rosalie Ln.
2. Brentwood

**BARRINGTON WOODS**

W. Center Rd.
W. Rosiland Dr.
W. Fallkirk Pl.

**PALATINE**

**PALATINE**

**DEER GROVE**

Deer Grove Lake

Bike Trail

**DEER GROVE FOREST PRESERVE**

Camp Reinberg

1. Arthur Ave.
2. Gatewood Ave.
3. Denton Ave.
4. Dresden Ave.
5. Dartmoor Ave.
6. Broadmoor Ct.

**FOREST PRESERVE**

**DUNDEE** RD.

**COOK CO.**

CONTINUED ON PAGE 1
CONTINUED ON PAGE 3
CONTINUED ON PAGE 7

.5 MILE

© BY CSC

CONTINUED IN SEC. 6, PAGE 32

Kemper Lakes Golf Course

LAKE ZURICH

Royal Melbourne Golf Course

LAKE ZURICH HWY.

McHENRY HWY.

KILDEER

TWIN ORCHARD COUNTRY CLUB

Tandy Park

Private Nature Preserve

LONG GROVE-APTAKISIC RD.

CUBA RD.

LONG GROVE

KILDEER

Spring Valley

Kildeer Sch.
Village Hall

F.D. COFFIN
Bob-O-Link
Wild-wood

TWP. TOWNSHIP

ROBERT PARKER

BREESE RD.

Children's Park

Hillcrest Country Club

Pottawatomie Ct.

Meadowlark Dr.

Knopf Cem.

CONTINUED ON PAGE 2

CONTINUED ON PAGE 4

BUFFALO CREEK FOREST PRESERVE

BUFFALO GROVE

Lexington Park

ELA TOWNSHIP

VERNON

ELA VERNON

LAKE CO.
COOK CO.

PALATINE TWP.

TOWNSHIP LAKE-COOK RD.

PALATINE

Whispering Oaks

ARLINGTON HEIGHTS

ARLINGTON HEIGHTS

Nichols Golf Course

Creekside Pk.
Lake Terramere Park

A. Wainright Ct.
B. Almond Ct.
C. Bradley Ct.
D. Queensbury Ct.
E. Queensbury Cir.
F. Williamsburg Dr.
G. Dogwood Ct.
H. Heather Ln.
I. Hancock Dr.
J. Heritage Ct.
K. Lexington Dr.
L. Jamestown Dr.
M. N. Cambridge Ct.
N. S. Cambridge Ct.

1. Pleasant Tr. Ct.
2. Mallard Ct.
3. Pheasant Tr. Ln.
Partridge Ct.

1. White Sands Dr.
2. Shannon Bay
3. Hudson Bay
4. Clear Creek Dr.
5. Canterbury Dr.
6. Canterbury Ln.
7. Wind River Dr.
8. Donegal Bay
9. Cascade Bay
10. Rainbow Bay
11. Waterford Bay
12. Vermilion Ln.
13. Olive Branch Ct.
14. Whispering Springs
15. Shadow Lake Ter.
16. White Water Ln.
17. Conway Bay
18. Isle Royale Cir

Nichols

DUNDEE

Northwest Deer Grove S.C.

Buffalo Grove

Boeger Dr.

Plaza Verde

.5 MILE

CONTINUED ON PAGE 8

© BY CSC

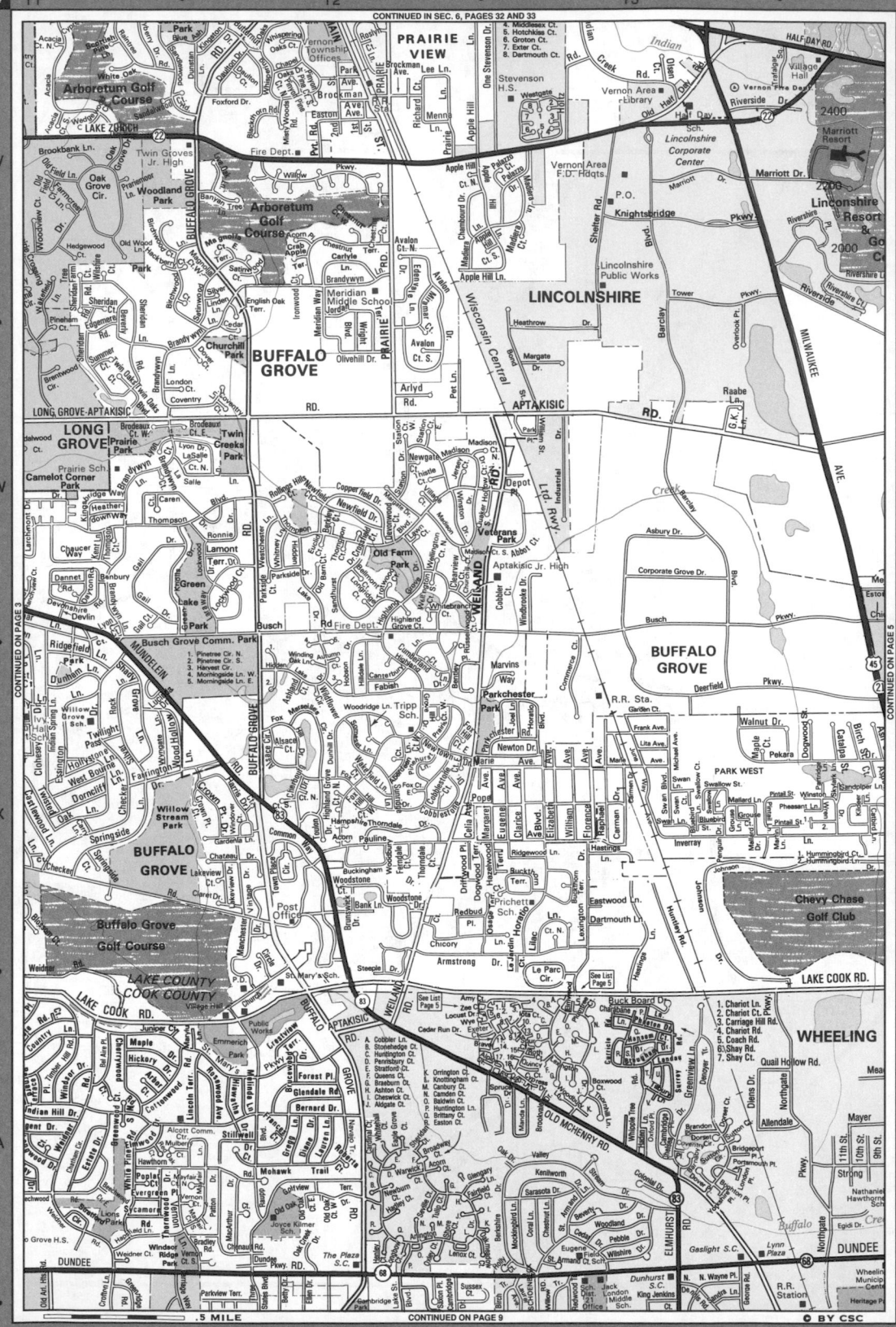

CONTINUED IN SEC. 6, PAGES 32 AND 33

CONTINUED ON PAGE 9

CONTINUED ON PAGE 3

CONTINUED ON PAGE 5

© BY CSC

.5 MILE

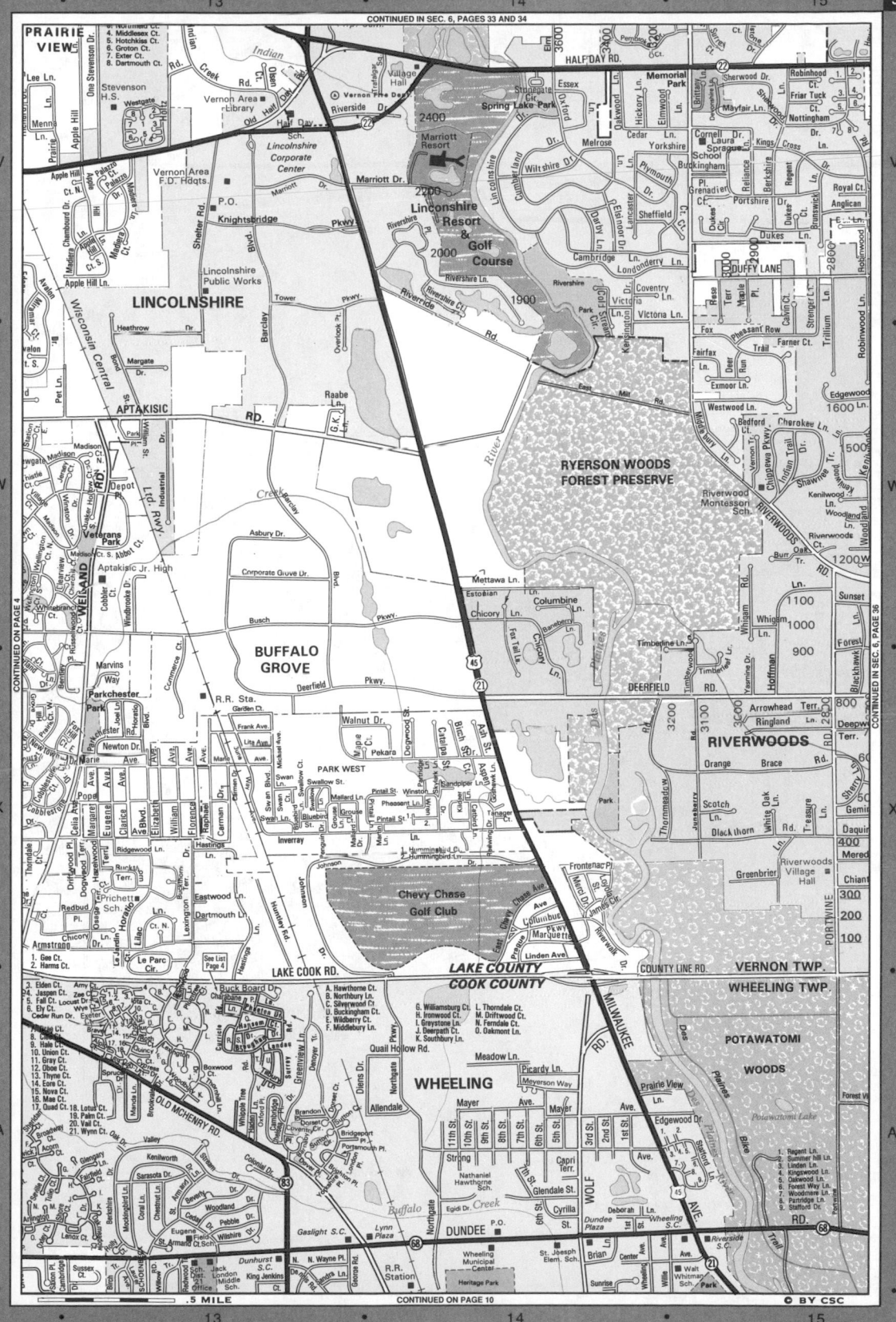

CONTINUED ON PAGE 1

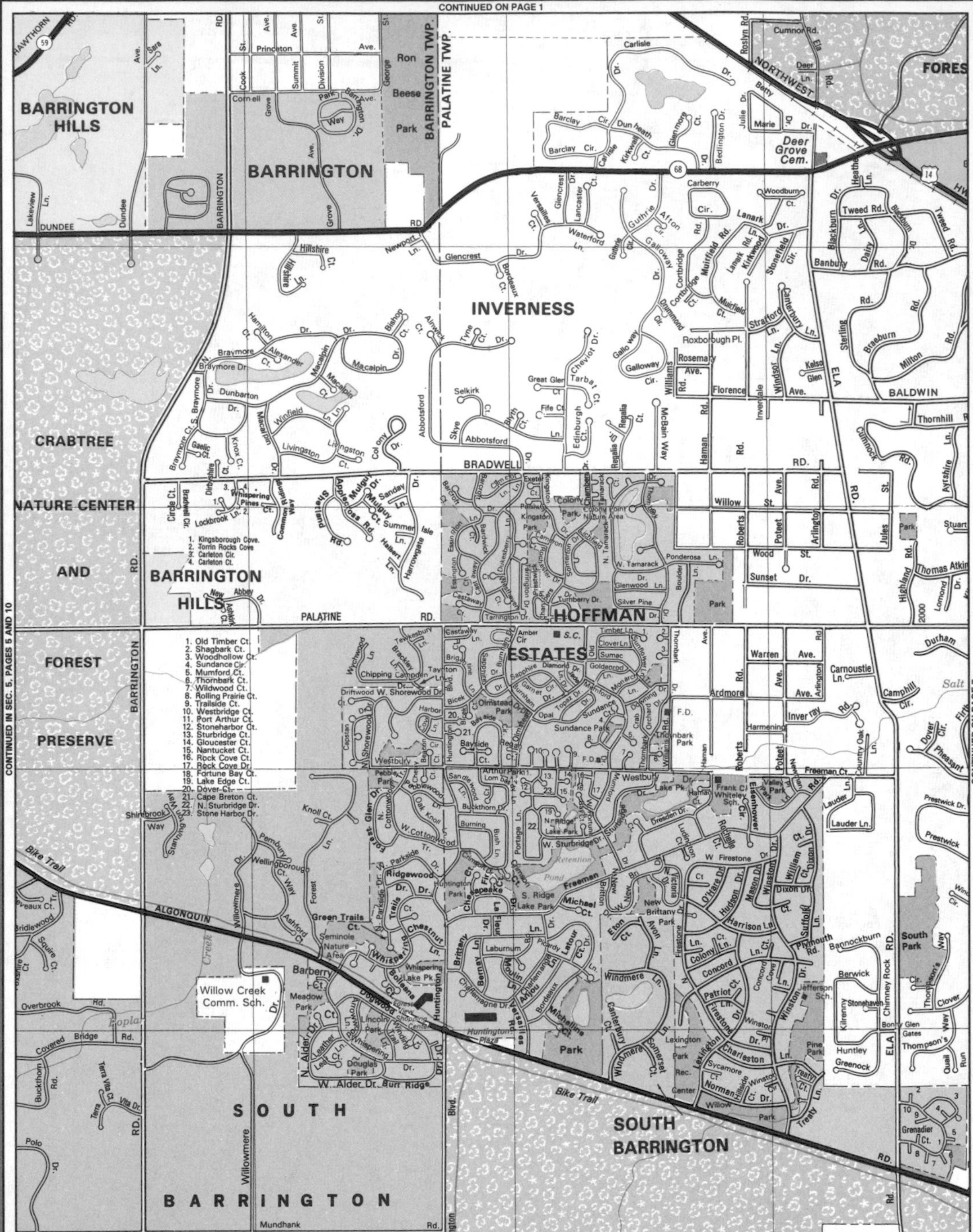

BARRINGTON HILLS

BARRINGTON

PALATINE TWP.

NORTHWEST

Deer Grove Cem.

FOREST

INVERNESS

CRABTREE

NATURE CENTER

AND

BARRINGTON HILLS

FOREST

PRESERVE

1. Kingsborough Cove.
2. Torrin Rocks Cove.
3. Carleton Cir.
4. Carleton Ct.

1. Old Timber Ct.
2. Shagbark Ct.
3. Woodhollow Ct.
4. Sundance Ct.
5. Mumford Ct.
6. Thornbark Ct.
7. Wildwood Ct.
8. Rolling Prairie Ct.
9. Trailside Ct.
10. Westbridge Ct.
11. Port Arthur Ct.
12. Stoneharbor Ct.
13. Sturbridge Ct.
14. Gloucester Ct.
15. Nantucket Ct.
16. Rock Cove Ct.
17. Rock Cove Dr.
18. Fortune Bay Ct.
19. Lake Edge Ct.
20. Dover Ct.
21. Cape Breton Ct.
22. N. Sturbridge Ct.
23. Stone Harbor Dr.

BRADWELL

HOFFMAN ESTATES

ALGONQUIN

Willow Creek Comm. Sch.

Green Trails

Bike Trail

SOUTH BARRINGTON

SOUTH

BARRINGTON

PAUL DOUGLAS

FOREST PRESERVE

HOFFMAN ESTATES

Lakewood Blvd.

Mundhank Rd.

FOREST

CONTINUED IN SEC. 5, PAGES 5 AND 10

CONTINUED ON PAGE 7

.5 MILE

© BY CSC

CONTINUED ON PAGE 2

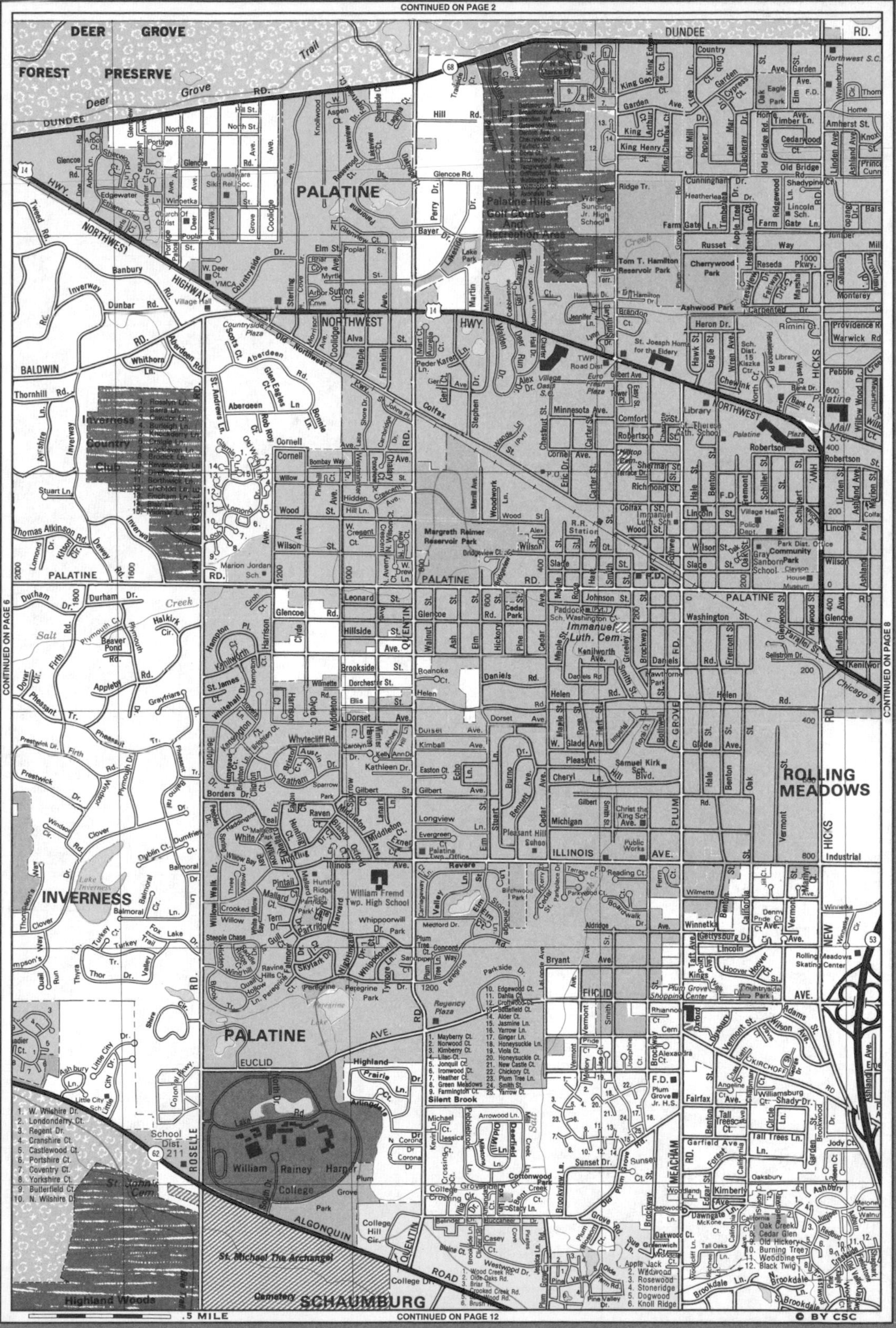

CONTINUED ON PAGE 6

CONTINUED ON PAGE 8

CONTINUED ON PAGE 12

# DEER GROVE FOREST PRESERVE

**PALATINE**

**NORTHWEST HWY.**

**BALDWIN**

**INVERNESS COUNTRY CLUB**

**INVERNESS**

**PALATINE**

**ROLLING MEADOWS**

**SCHAUMBURG**

**William Rainey Harper College**

**William Fremd Twp. High School**

DUNDEE RD.

.5 MILE

© BY CSC

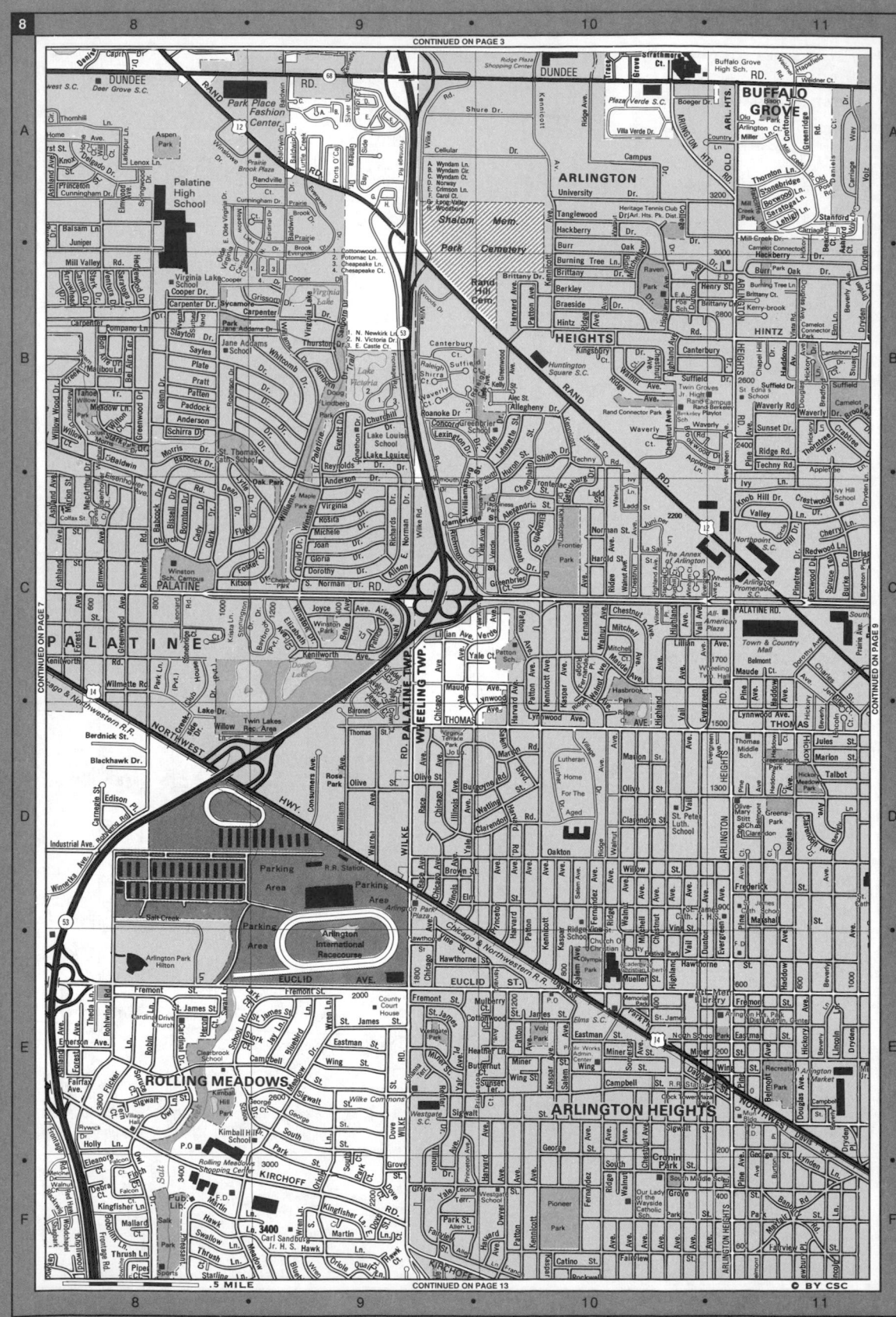

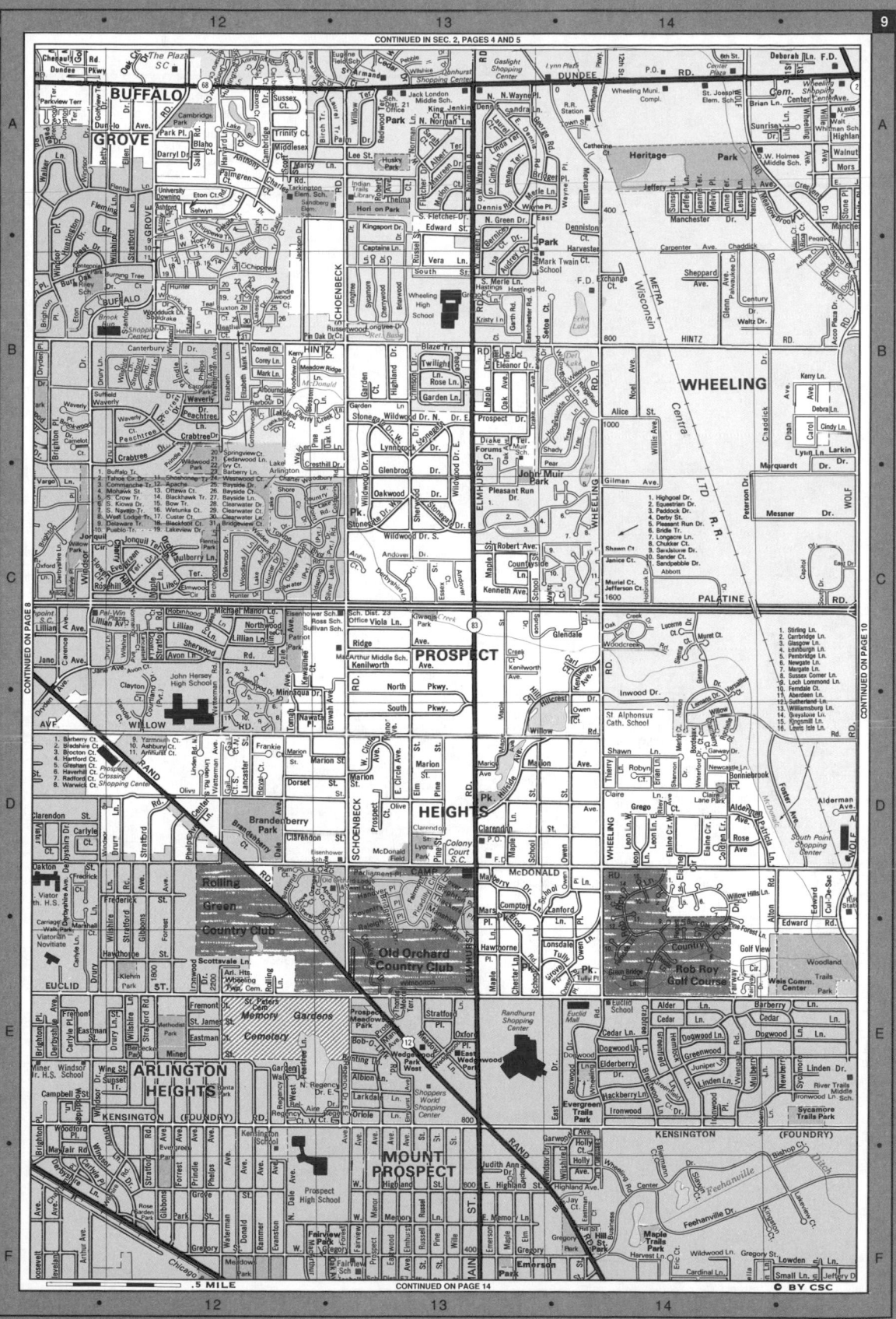

CONTINUED ON PAGE 8

CONTINUED ON PAGE 10

© BY CSC

.5 MILE

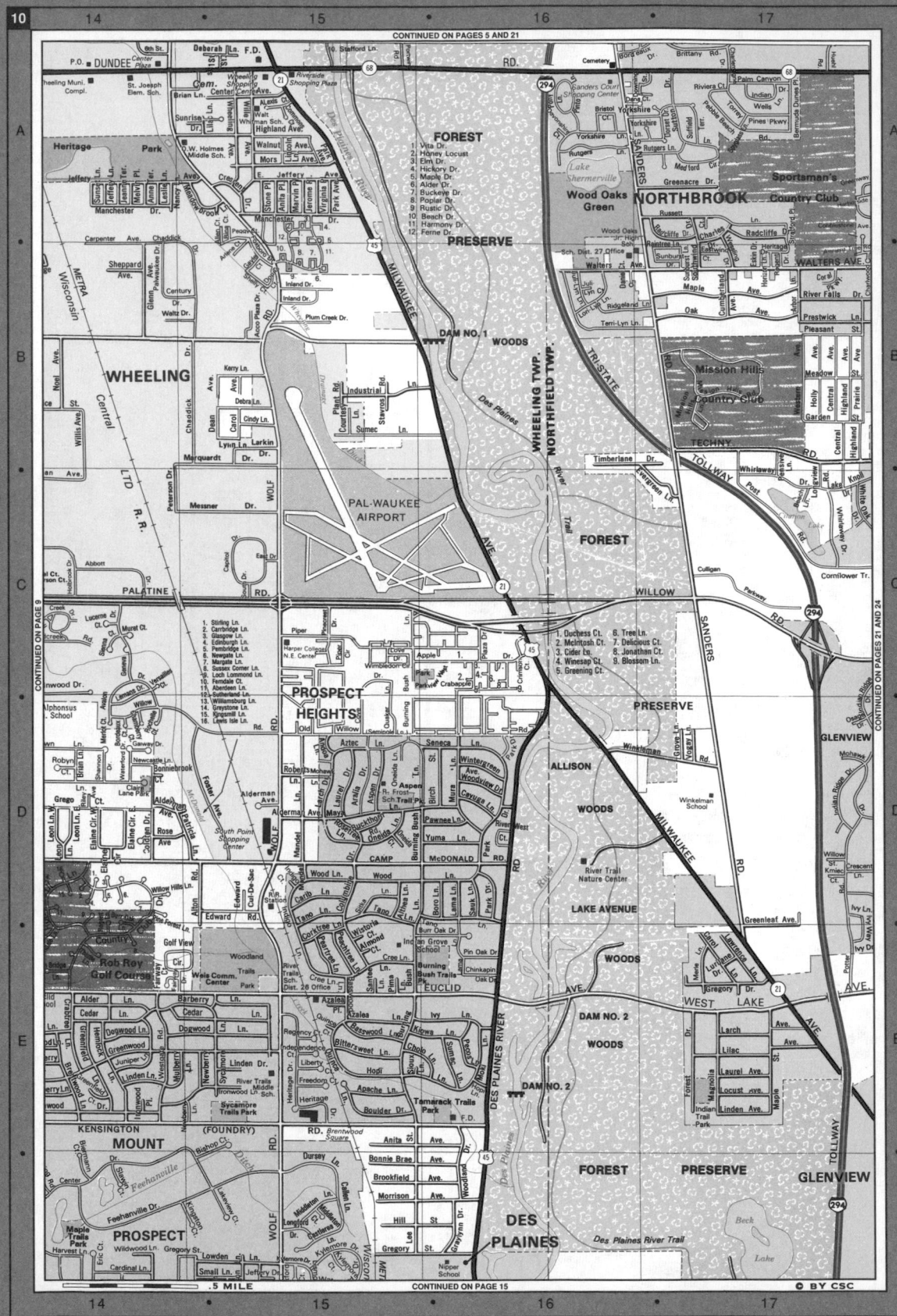

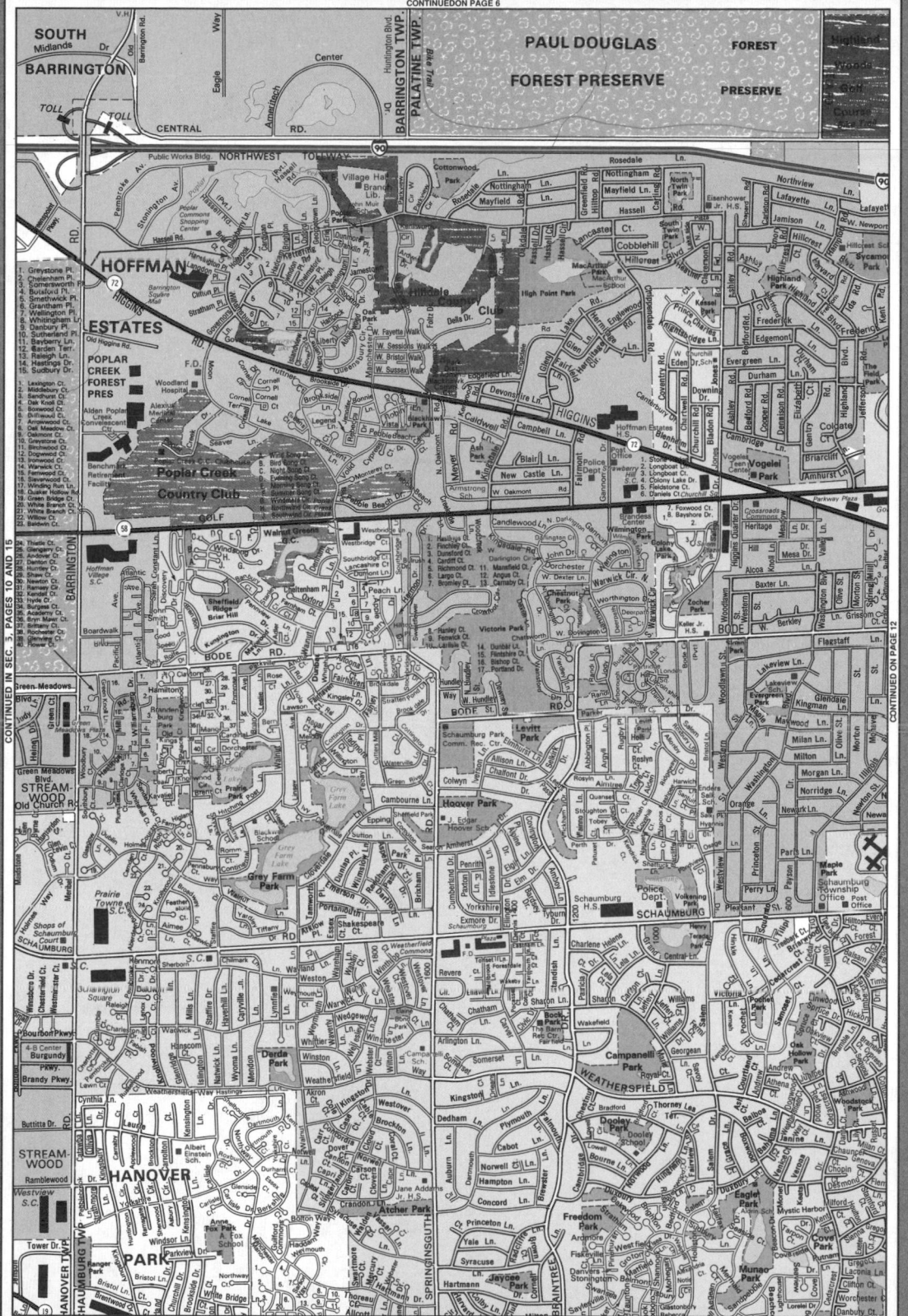

CONTINUED ON PAGE 6

CONTINUED IN SEC. 5, PAGES 10 AND 15

CONTINUED ON PAGE 12

CONTINUED ON PAGE 16

© BY CSC

CONTINUED ON PAGE 7

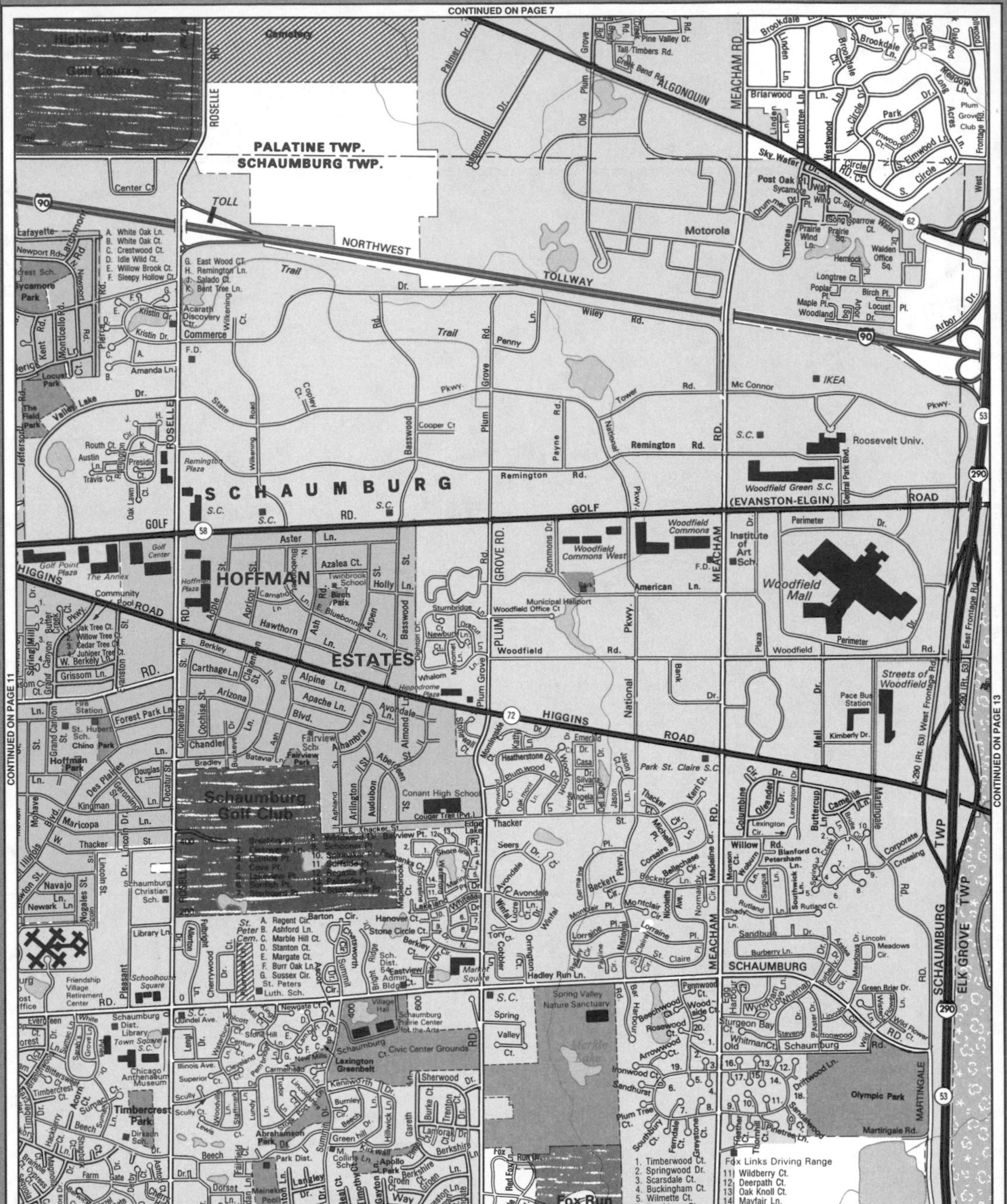

PALATINE TWP.
SCHAUMBURG TWP.

NORTHWEST TOLLWAY

MOTOROLA

IKEA

Roosevelt Univ.

Woodfield Green S.C.
(EVANSTON-ELGIN)

Institute of Art Sch.

SCHAUMBURG

Woodfield Commons

Woodfield Commons West

Woodfield Mall

HOFFMAN

ESTATES

HIGGINS ROAD

GOLF ROAD

Schaumburg Golf Club

Conant High School

Schaumburg Christian Sch.

Friendship Village Retirement Center

Timbercrest Park

SCHAUMBURG

Spring Valley Nature Sanctuary

Olympic Park

Martingale Rd.

Fox Run Golf Links

ELK GROVE VILLAGE

Woodland Meadows Park

Fox Links Driving Range

1. Timberwood Ct.
2. Springwood Dr.
3. Scarsdale Ct.
4. Buckingham Ct.
5. Wilmette Ct.
6. Northbury Ct.
7. Oak Meadow Ct.
8. Woodbury Ct.
9. Maplewood Ct.
10. Wildberry Ct.
11. Deerpath Ct.
12. Oak Knoll Ct.
13. Mayfair Ln.
14. Elmwood Ln.
15. Hawthorne Ct.
16. Middlebury Ct.
17. Seven Pines Rd.
18. Williamsburg Dr.
19. Brookton Dr.

CONTINUED ON PAGE 11
CONTINUED ON PAGE 13

.5 MILE

© BY CSC

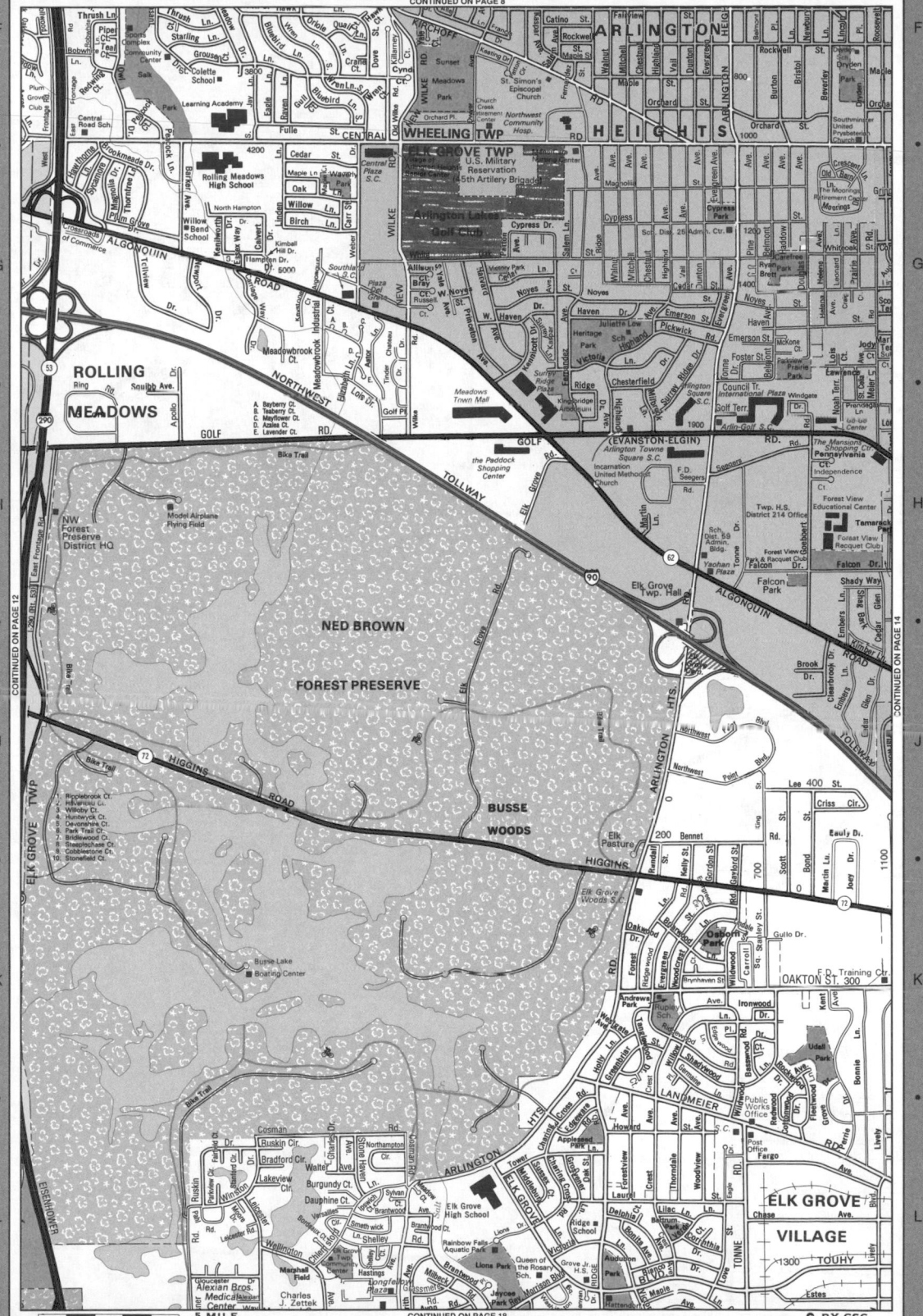

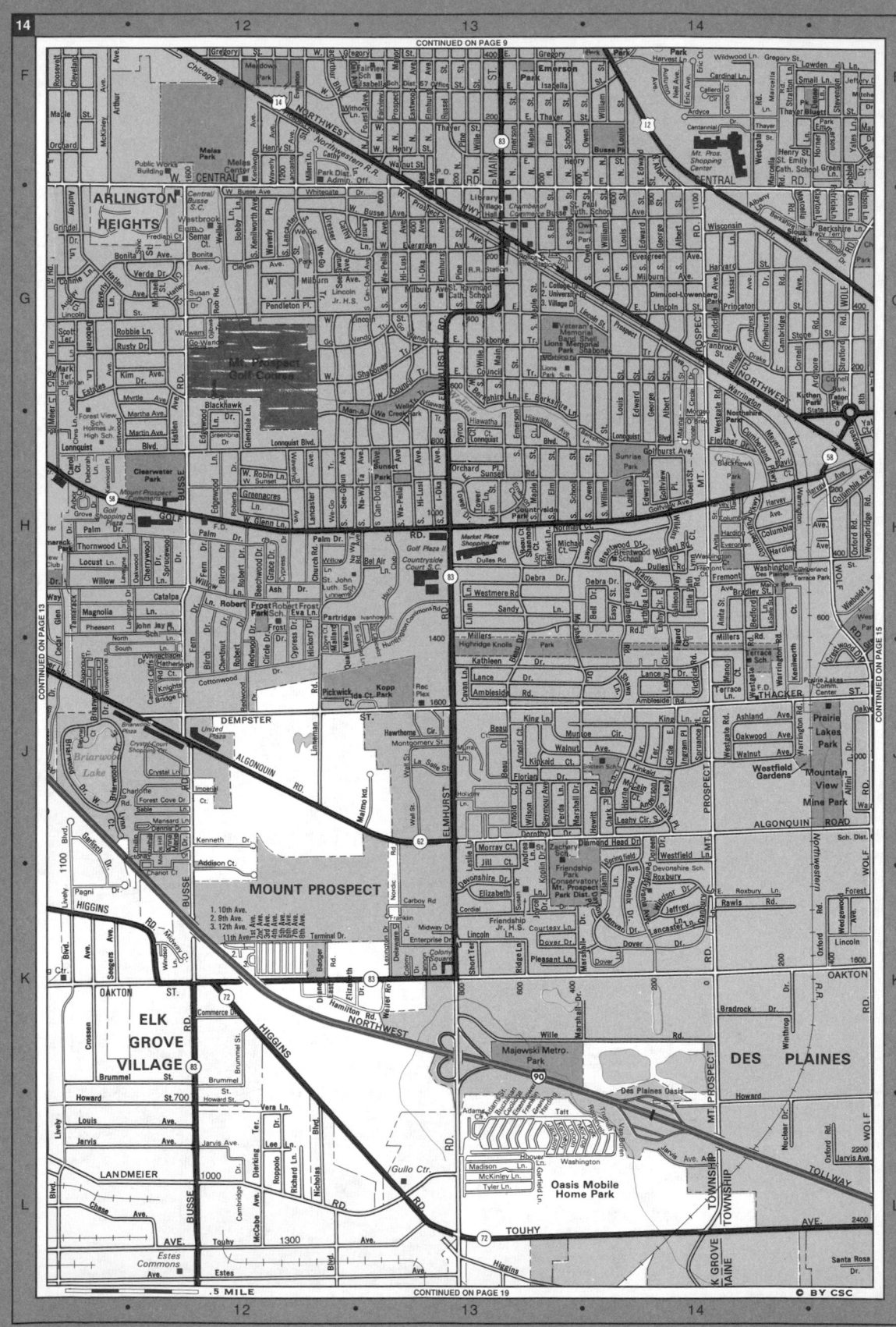

CONTINUED ON PAGE 9
CONTINUED ON PAGE 13
CONTINUED ON PAGE 15
CONTINUED ON PAGE 19

**ARLINGTON HEIGHTS**

**MOUNT PROSPECT**

**ELK GROVE VILLAGE**

**DES PLAINES**

.5 MILE

© BY CSC

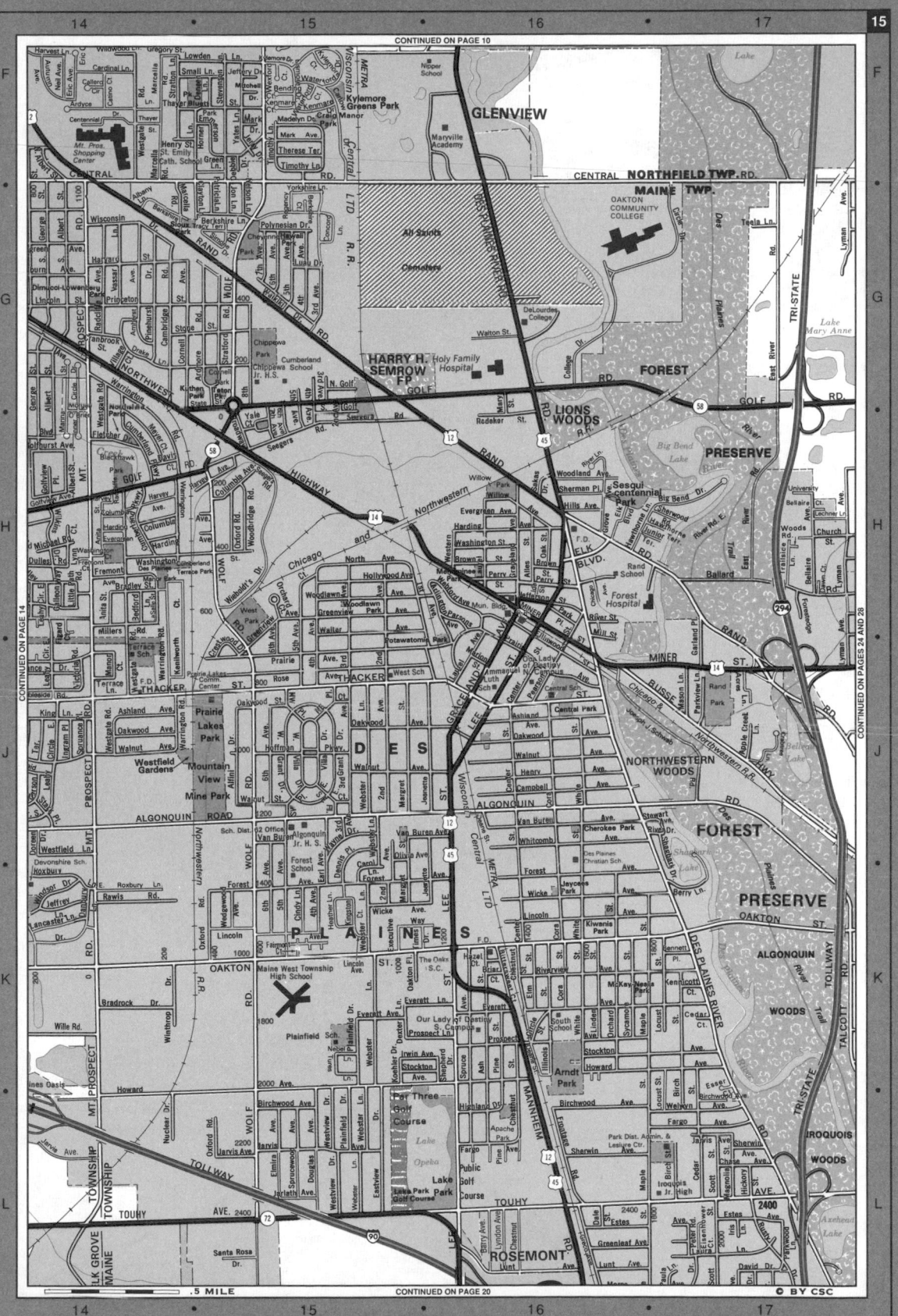

CONTINUED ON PAGE 11

POPLAR CREEK FOREST PRES

1. Lexington Ct.
2. Middlebury Ct.
3. Sandhurst Ct.
4. Oak Knoll Ct.
5. Boxwood Ct.
6. Driftwood Ct.
7. Amplewood Ct.
8. Oak Meadow St.
9. Oakmont Ct.
10. Greystone Ct.
11. Richwood Ct.
12. Dogwood Ct.
13. Ironwood Ct.
14. Warwick Ct.
15. Fernwood Ct.
16. Silverwood Ct.
17. Winding Run Ln.
18. Quaker Hollow Rd.
19. Green Bridge Ct.
20. White Branch Ct.
21. Willow Ct.
22. Baldwin Ct.

HOFFMAN ESTATES

Woodland Hospital

Alexian Medical Center

Poplar Creek C.C. Clubhouse

Poplar Creek Country Club

Benchmark Retirement Facility

Walnut Green G.C.

Hoffman Village S.C.

BARRINGTON

BODE RD.

Green Meadows Blvd

STREAMWOOD

Old Church Rd.

Grey Farm Lake

Gray Farm Park

Prairie Towne S.C.

Shops of Schaumburg Court SCHAUMBURG

Levitt Park

Schaumburg Park Comm. Rec. Ctr.

Hoover Park

J. Edgar Hoover Sch.

Schaumburg H.S.

Police Dept.

SCHAUMBURG

Maple Park Schaumburg Township Office Post Office

Campanelli Park

Oak Hollow Park

Darda Park

WEATHERSFIELD

STREAMWOOD

Westview S.C.

Tower Dr.

Albert Einstein Sch.

Anne Fox Rd. A. Fox School

Ranger Park

Atcher Park

Dooley Park

Dooley School

Freedom Park

Eagle Park

Cove Park

Munao Park

Seafarer

WISE

HANOVER PARK

George Georgian Memorial Baseball Fields

Hanover Park Water Reclamation Plant

Hanover Highland School

Hanover Square

Edgebrook Park

Liberty Park

Tradeworks Shopping Center

Hanover Park Commuter Station

Countryside

WISE

Valley View Park

Park Plaza

ELGIN O'HARE EXPWY.

SCHAUMBURG

IRVING PARK

Alexian Field (Schaumburg Flyers)

St. John's Sch.

St. John's Cemetery

Schaumburg Commuter Rail Facility

Schaumburg Regional Airport

Future Site of Sch. P.D. Hockey Rink

SCHAUMBURG TWP
BLOOMINGDALE TWP

R.R. Station

Soo Line

MSD Basin

LAKE ST.

.5 MILE

CONTINUED IN SEC. 3, PAGES 2 AND 3

CONTINUED IN SEC. 5, PAGES 11 AND 15

CONTINUED ON PAGE 17

© BY CSC

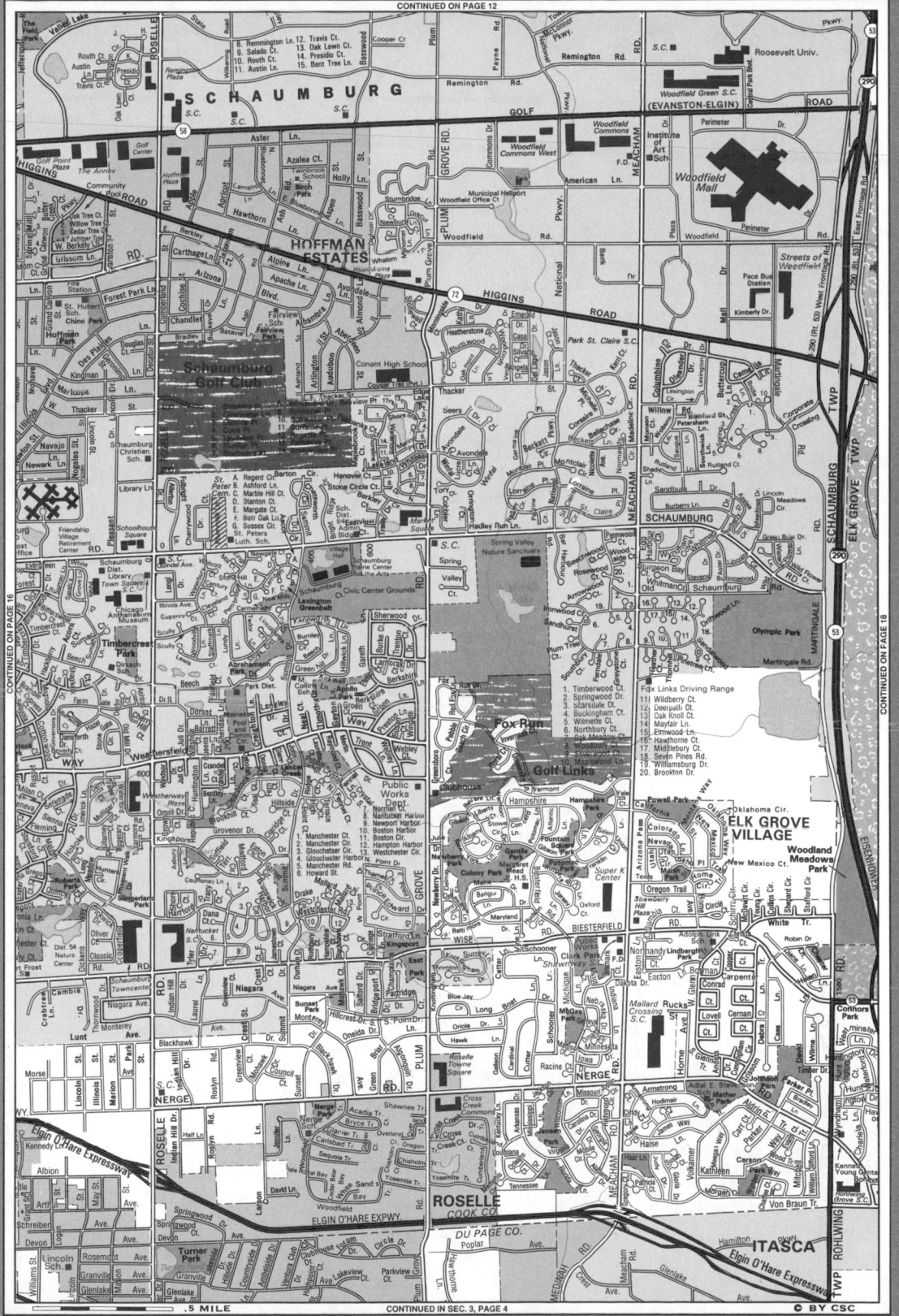

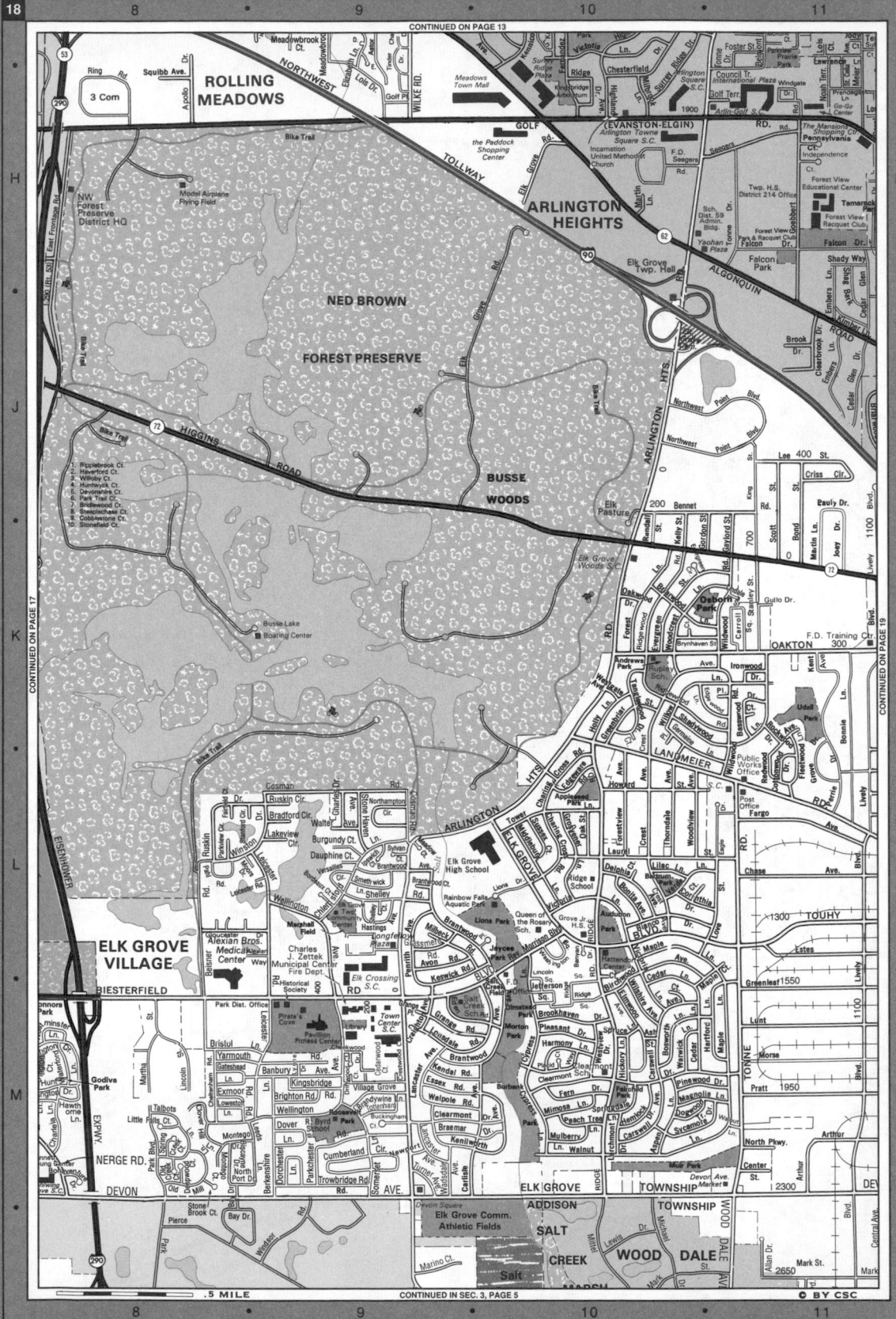

CONTINUED ON PAGE 13

ROLLING
MEADOWS

3 Com

ARLINGTON
HEIGHTS

NED BROWN

FOREST PRESERVE

BUSSE
WOODS

1. Rippleбrook Ct.
2. Haverford Ct.
3. Wilkby Ct.
4. Huntwyck Ct.
5. Devonshire Ct.
6. Park Trail Ct.
7. Bridlewood Ct.
8. Steeplechase Ct.
9. Cobblestone Ct.
10. Stonefield Ct.

Elk
Pasture

Busse Lake
Boating Center

Osborn
Park

OAKTON

ELK GROVE
VILLAGE

ELK GROVE    TOWNSHIP

BIESTERFIELD

Godiva
Park

NERGE RD.

DEVON

Elk Grove Comm.
Athletic Fields

ELK GROVE    TOWNSHIP

ADDISON

SALT

CREEK

WOOD    DALE

CONTINUED ON PAGE 17

CONTINUED ON PAGE 19

.5 MILE

CONTINUED IN SEC. 3, PAGE 5

© BY CSC

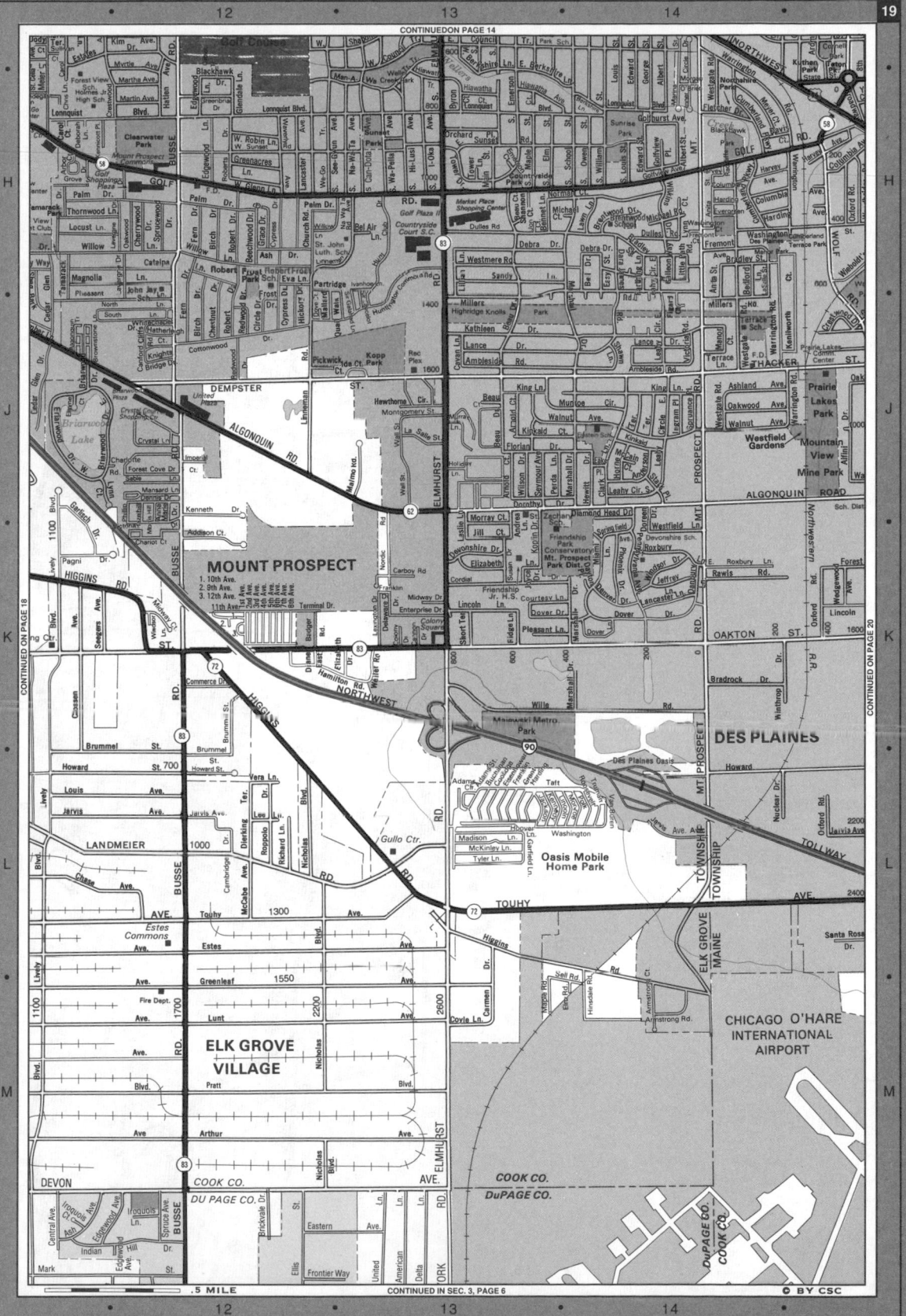

CONTINUED ON PAGE 18

CONTINUED ON PAGE 20

MOUNT PROSPECT

1. 10th Ave.
2. 9th Ave.
3. 12th Ave.
4. 11th Ave.

DES PLAINES

ELK GROVE
VILLAGE

CHICAGO O'HARE
INTERNATIONAL
AIRPORT

Oasis Mobile
Home Park

COOK CO.
DU PAGE CO.

COOK CO.
DuPAGE CO.

DuPAGE CO.
COOK CO.

.5 MILE

© BY CSC

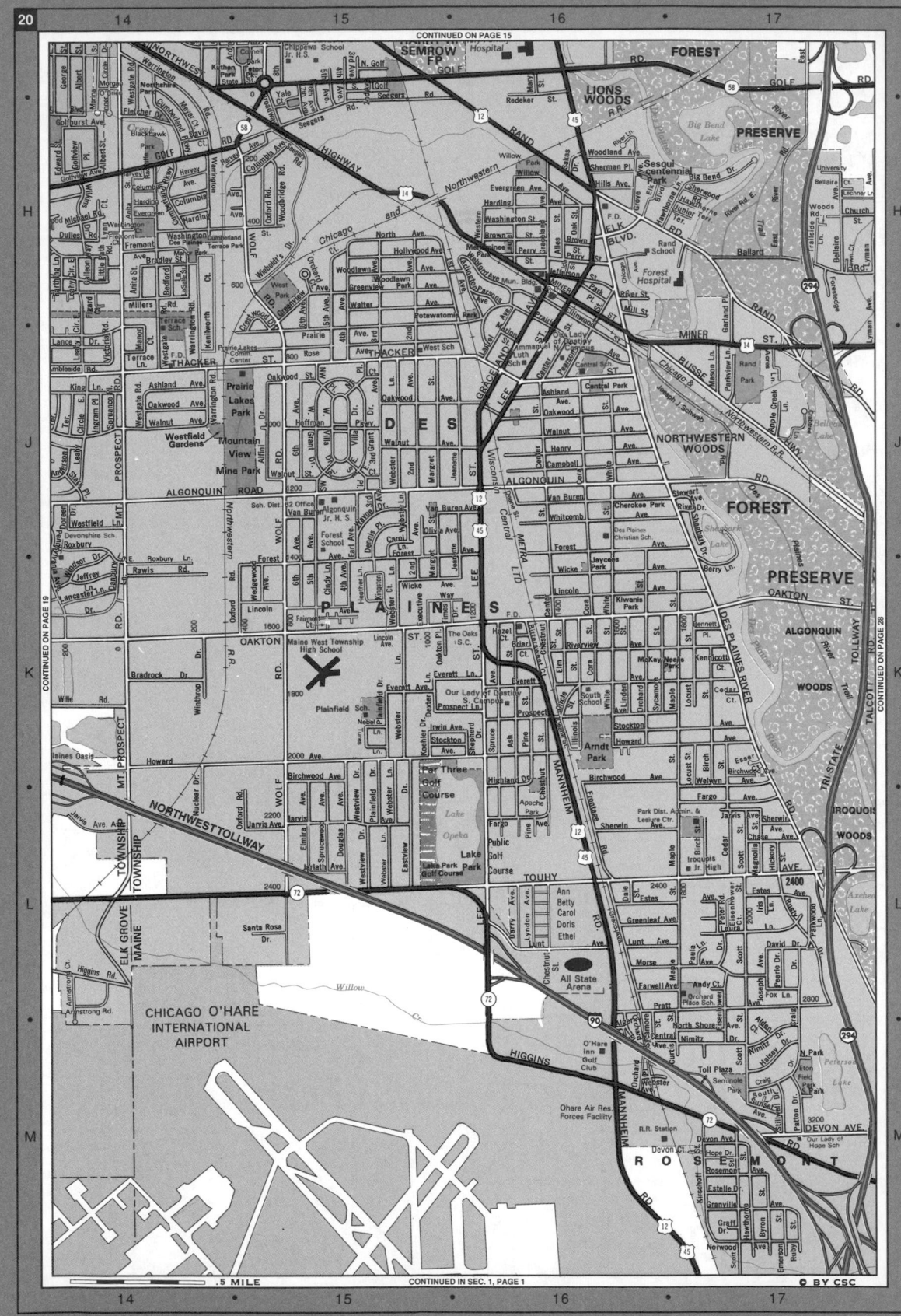

CONTINUED ON PAGE 15

CONTINUED ON PAGE 19

CONTINUED ON PAGE 28

.5 MILE

© BY CSC

CONTINUED IN SEC. 6, PAGES 36 AND 37

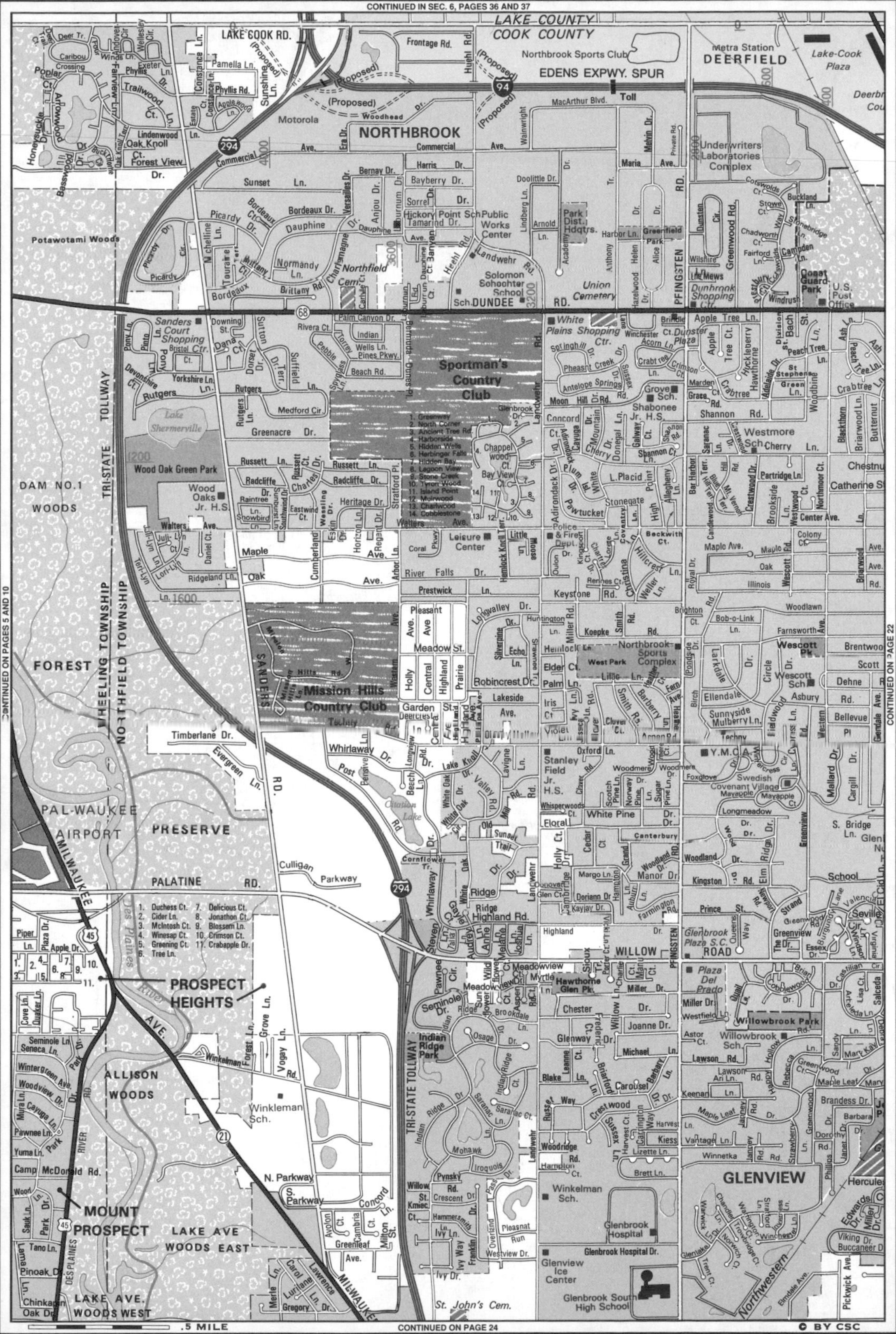

LAKE COUNTY
COOK COUNTY

LAKE COOK RD.

Northbrook Sports Club

EDENS EXPWY. SPUR

Metra Station
DEERFIELD

Lake-Cook Plaza

EDENS EXPWY. SPUR

Toll

MacArthur Blvd.

Underwriters Laboratories Complex

NORTHBROOK

Motorola

Public Works Center

Solomon Schechter School

DUNDEE RD.

Union Cemetery

Coast Guard Park

U.S. Post Office

Potawatomi Woods

Sportman's Country Club

White Plains Shopping Ctr.

Sanders Court Shopping Ctr.

Wood Oak Green Park

Glenbrook North H.S.

Wood Oaks Jr. H.S.

Westmore Sch.

DAM NO.1 WOODS

Shermerville

Leisure Center

Police & Fire Dept.

Northbrook Sports Complex

West Park

Wescott Sch.

FOREST

Mission Hills Country Club

Stanley Field Jr. H.S.

Y.M.C.A.

Swedish Covenant Village

PAL-WAUKEE AIRPORT

PRESERVE

PALATINE RD.

TRI-STATE TOLLWAY

Glenbrook Plaza S.C.

WILLOW ROAD

PROSPECT HEIGHTS

Glenbrook Plaza

Plaza Del Prado

Willowbrook Park

Willowbrook Sch.

ALLISON WOODS

Winkleman Sch.

Indian Ridge Park

Hawthorne Glen Pk.

GLENVIEW

MOUNT PROSPECT

LAKE AVE. WOODS EAST

Winkleman Sch.

Glenbrook Hospital

Glenview Ice Center

LAKE AVE. WOODS WEST

St. John's Cem.

Glenview Hospital Dr.

Glenbrook South High School

CONTINUED ON PAGE 24

CONTINUED ON PAGES 5 AND 10

CONTINUED ON PAGE 22

.5 MILE

© BY CSC

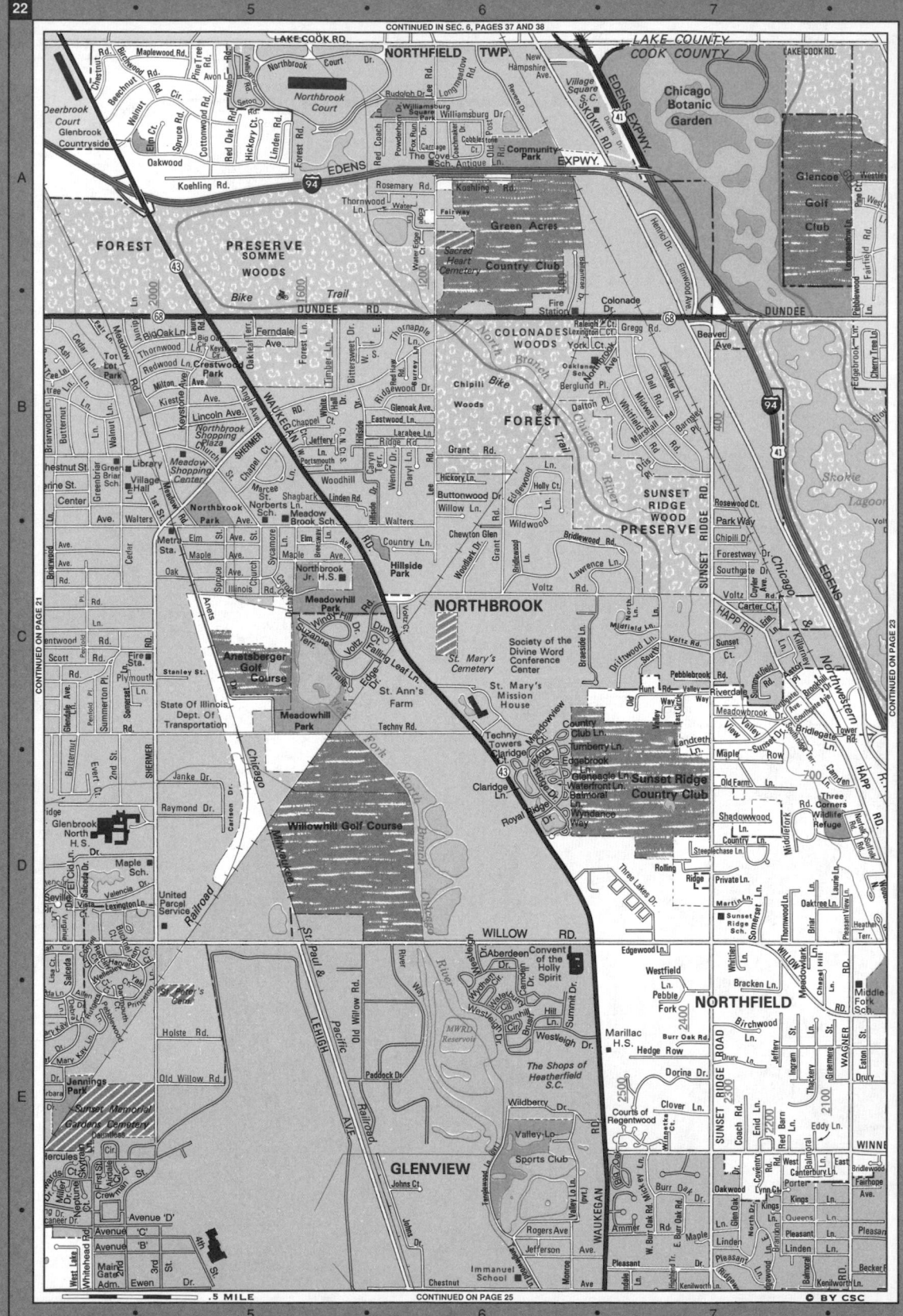

CONTINUED ON PAGE 22

CONTINUED ON PAGE 27

© BY CSC

.5 MILE

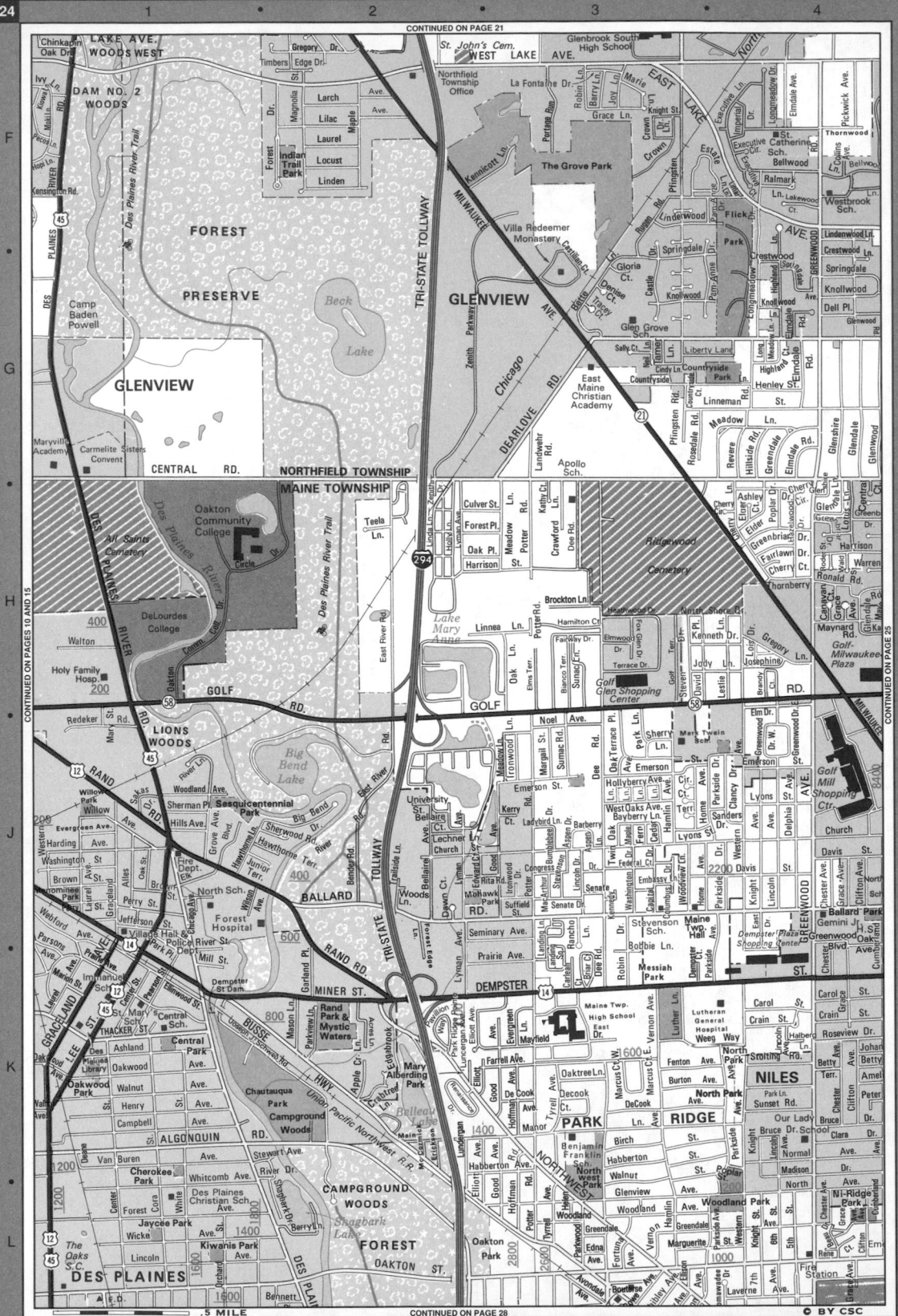

CONTINUED ON PAGE 21

CONTINUED ON PAGES 10 AND 15

CONTINUED ON PAGE 25

CONTINUED ON PAGE 28

.5 MILE

© BY CSC

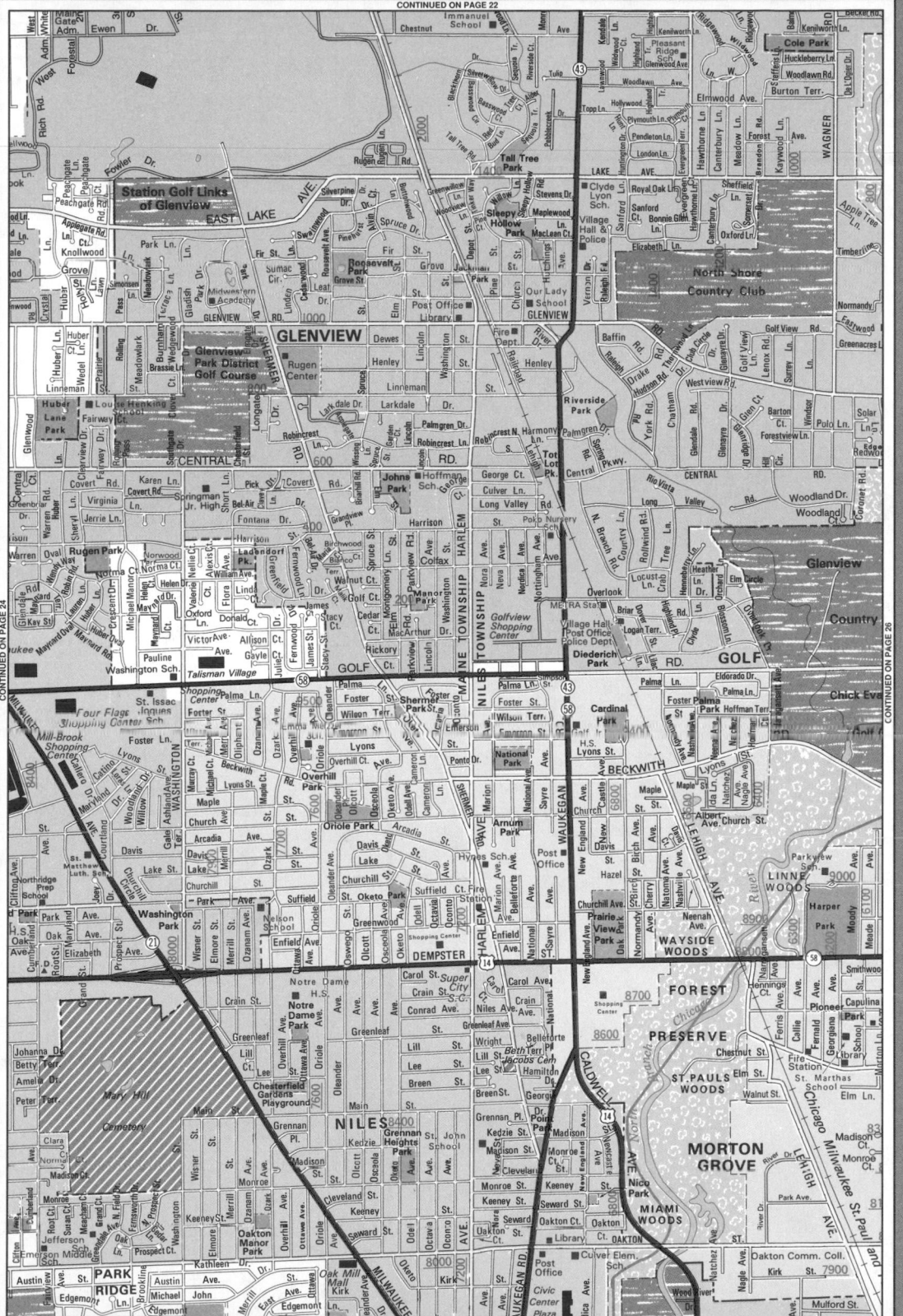

CONTINUED ON PAGE 22

CONTINUED ON PAGE 24

CONTINUED ON PAGE 26

CONTINUED ON PAGE 29

.5 MILE

© BY CSC

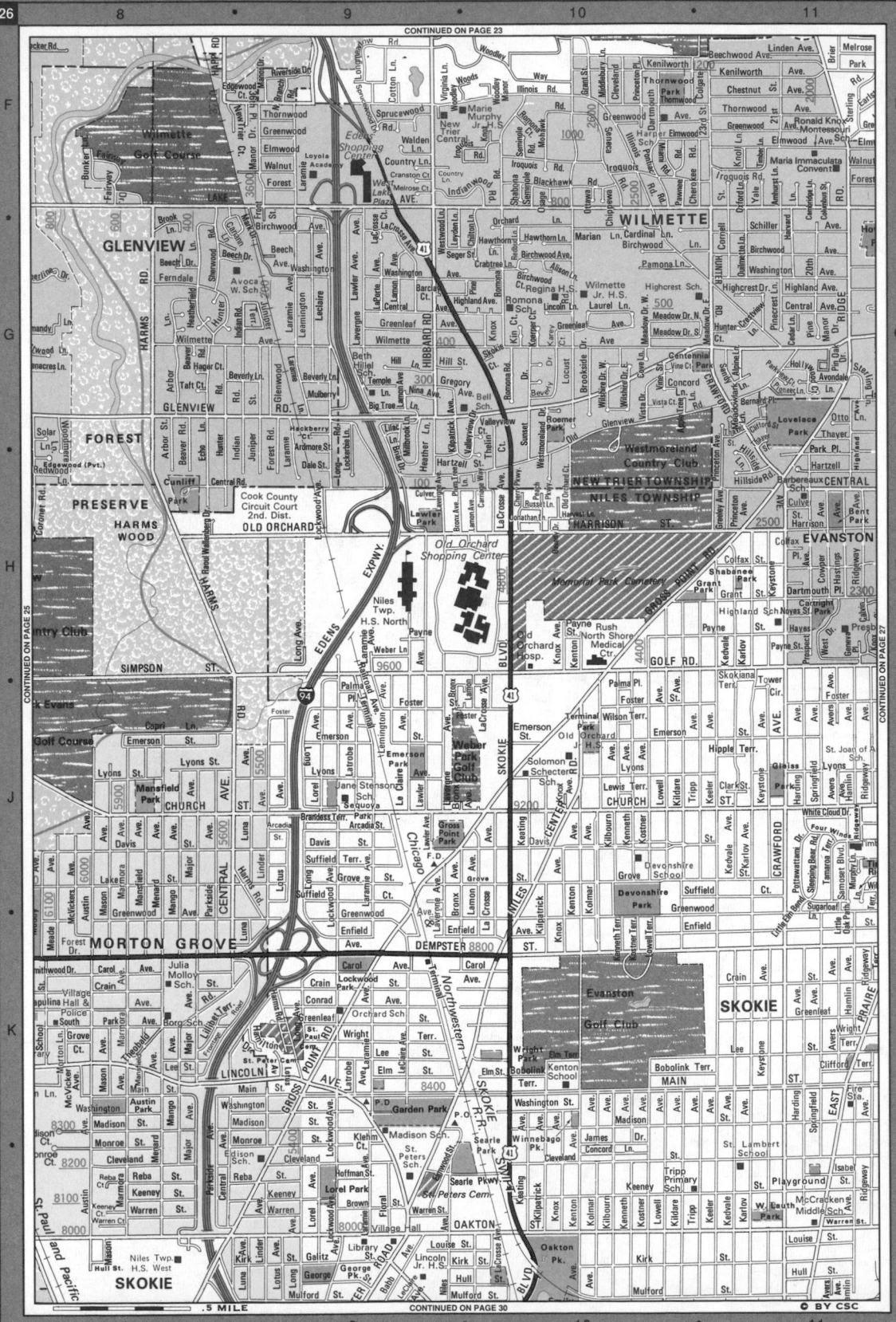

CONTINUED ON PAGE 23

CONTINUED ON PAGE 25

CONTINUED ON PAGE 27

CONTINUED ON PAGE 30

.5 MILE

© BY CSC

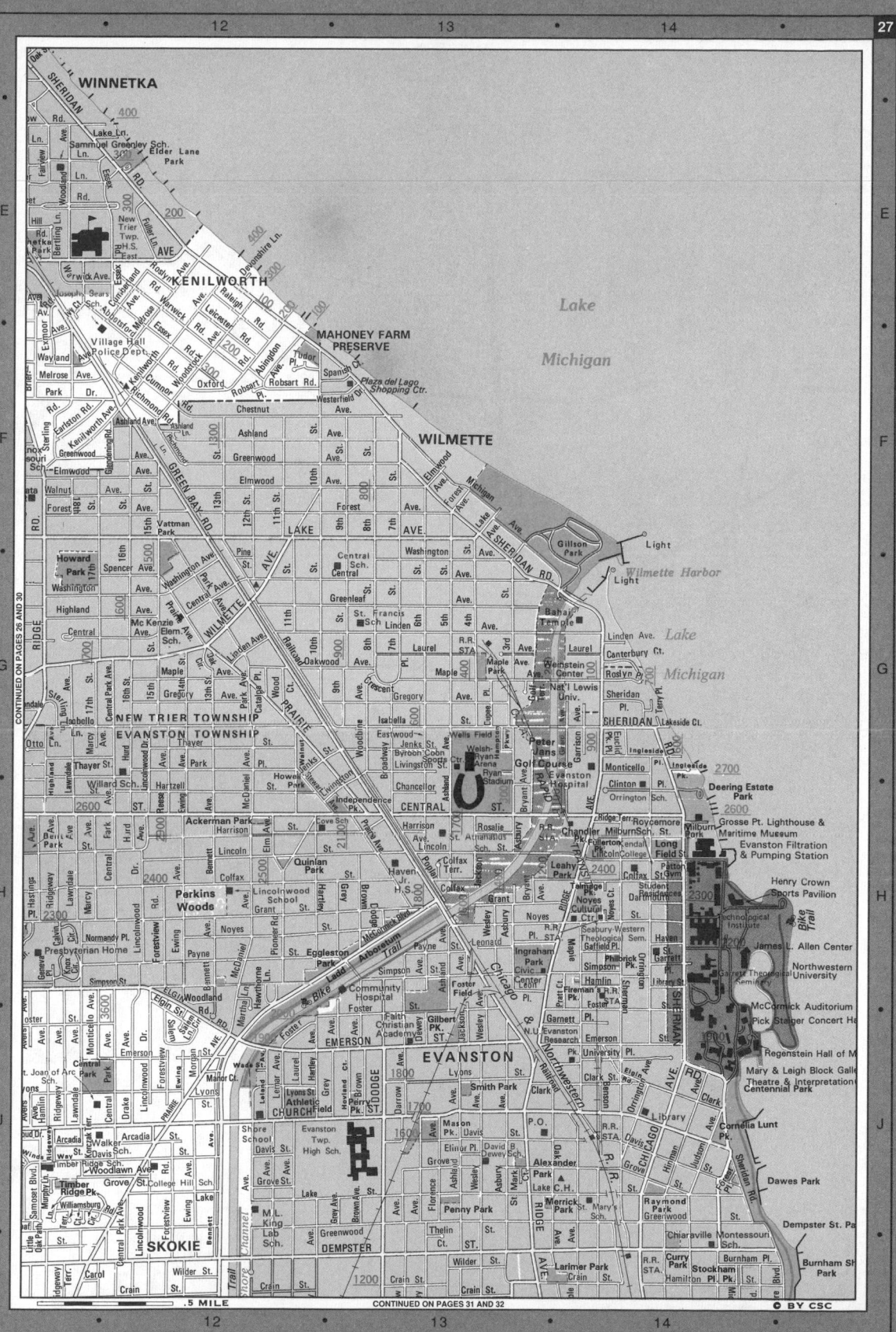

CONTINUED ON PAGES 31 AND 32

CONTINUED ON PAGES 26 AND 30

© BY CSC

.5 MILE

CONTINUED ON PAGE 24

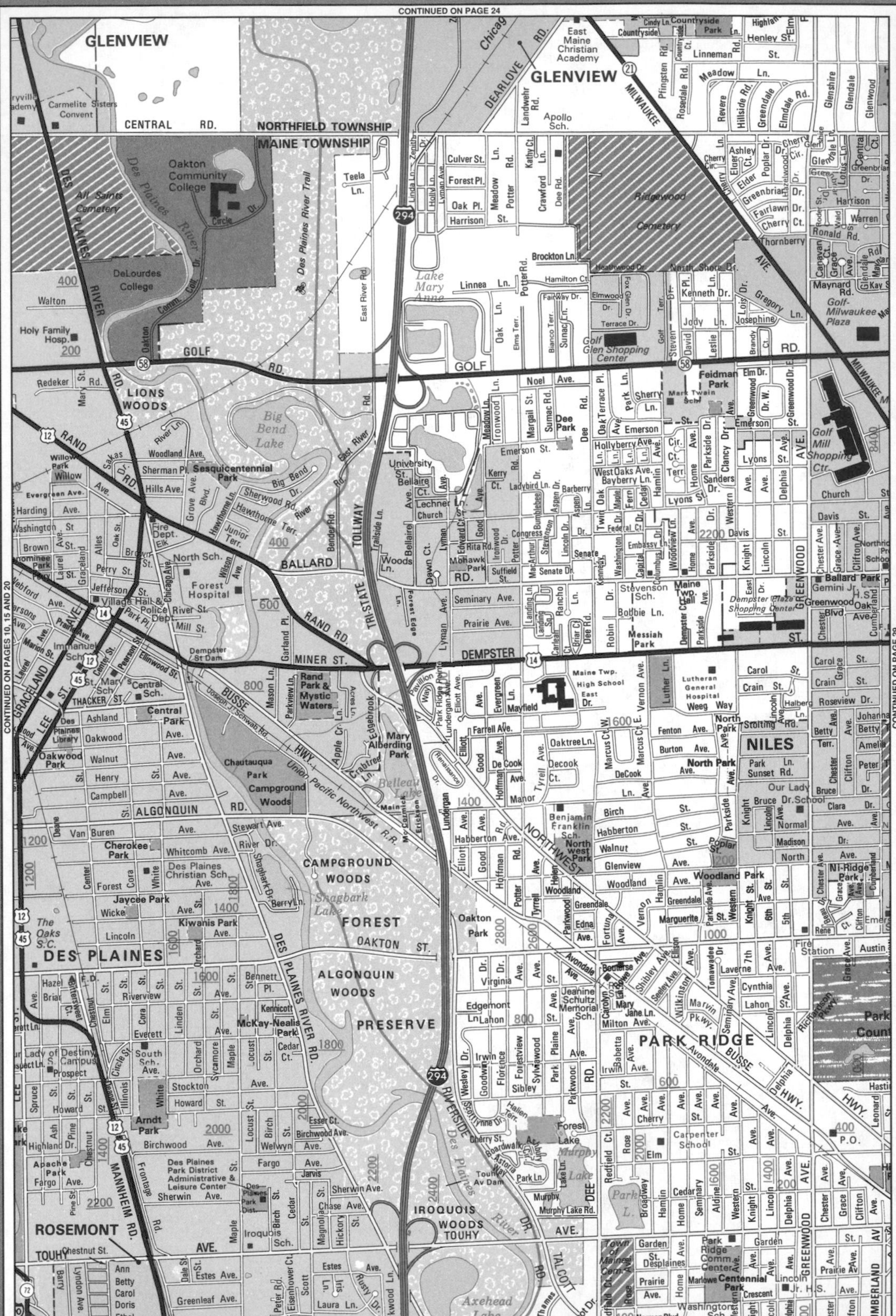

GLENVIEW

GLENVIEW

CENTRAL RD.

NORTHFIELD TOWNSHIP

MAINE TOWNSHIP

East Maine Christian Academy

Carmelite Sisters Convent

Oakton Community College

DeLourdes College

All Saints Cemetery

Holy Family Hosp.

Ridgewood Cemetery

Golf Glen Shopping Center

Golf-Milwaukee Plaza

GOLF RD.

GOLF

Golf Mill Shopping Ctr.

LIONS WOODS

Big Bend Lake

Sesquicentennial Park

Feidman Park

Dee Park

BALLARD RD.

Forest Hospital

Ballard Park

Maine Twp. Hall

Messiah Park

Dempster Plaza Shopping Center

Greenwood

MINER ST.

DEMPSTER

Maine Twp. High School East

Lutheran General Hospital

NILES

Rand Park & Mystic Waters

Mary Alberding Park

Our Lady School

Benjamin Franklin Sch.

North West Park

CAMPGROUND WOODS

FOREST

OAKTON ST.

ALGONQUIN WOODS

PRESERVE

Stagbark Lake

Cherokee Park

Jaycee Park

Kiwanis Park

DES PLAINES

The Oaks S.C.

Chautauqua Park Campground Woods

NI-Ridge Park

PARK RIDGE

Jeanine Schultz Memorial Sch.

McKay-Nealis Park

Fire Station

Park County

Apache Park

Des Plaines Park District Administrative & Leisure Center

Arndt Park

Forest Lake

Murphy Lake

Park L.

Carpenter School

ROSEMONT

IROQUOIS WOODS TOUHY

Axehead Lake

Park Maines Community Center

Marlowe Centennial Jr. H.S.

Washington Sch.

.5 MILE

© BY CSC

CONTINUED ON PAGES 10, 15 AND 20

CONTINUED ON PAGE 29

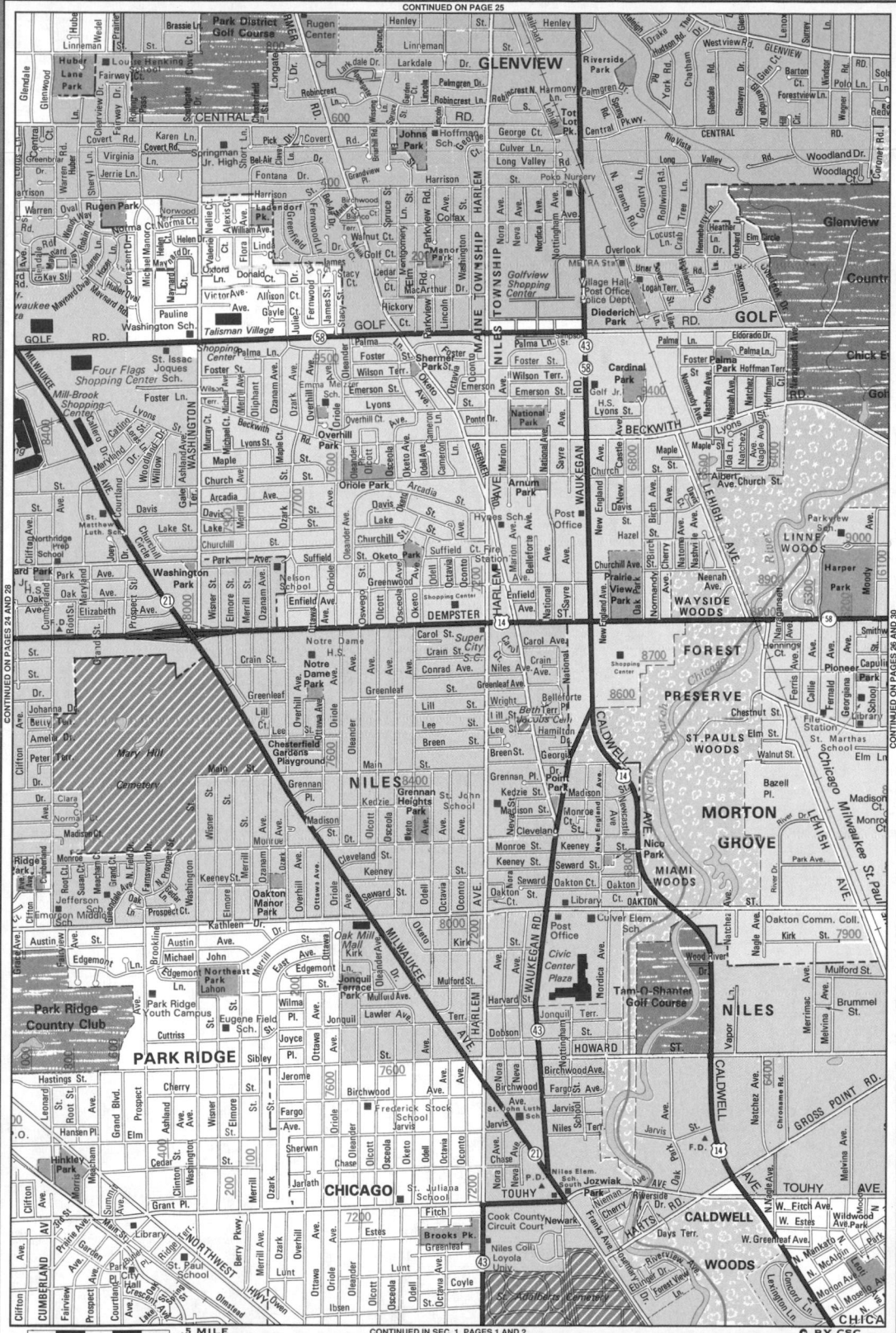

CONTINUED ON PAGE 26

CONTINUED ON PAGES 25 AND 29

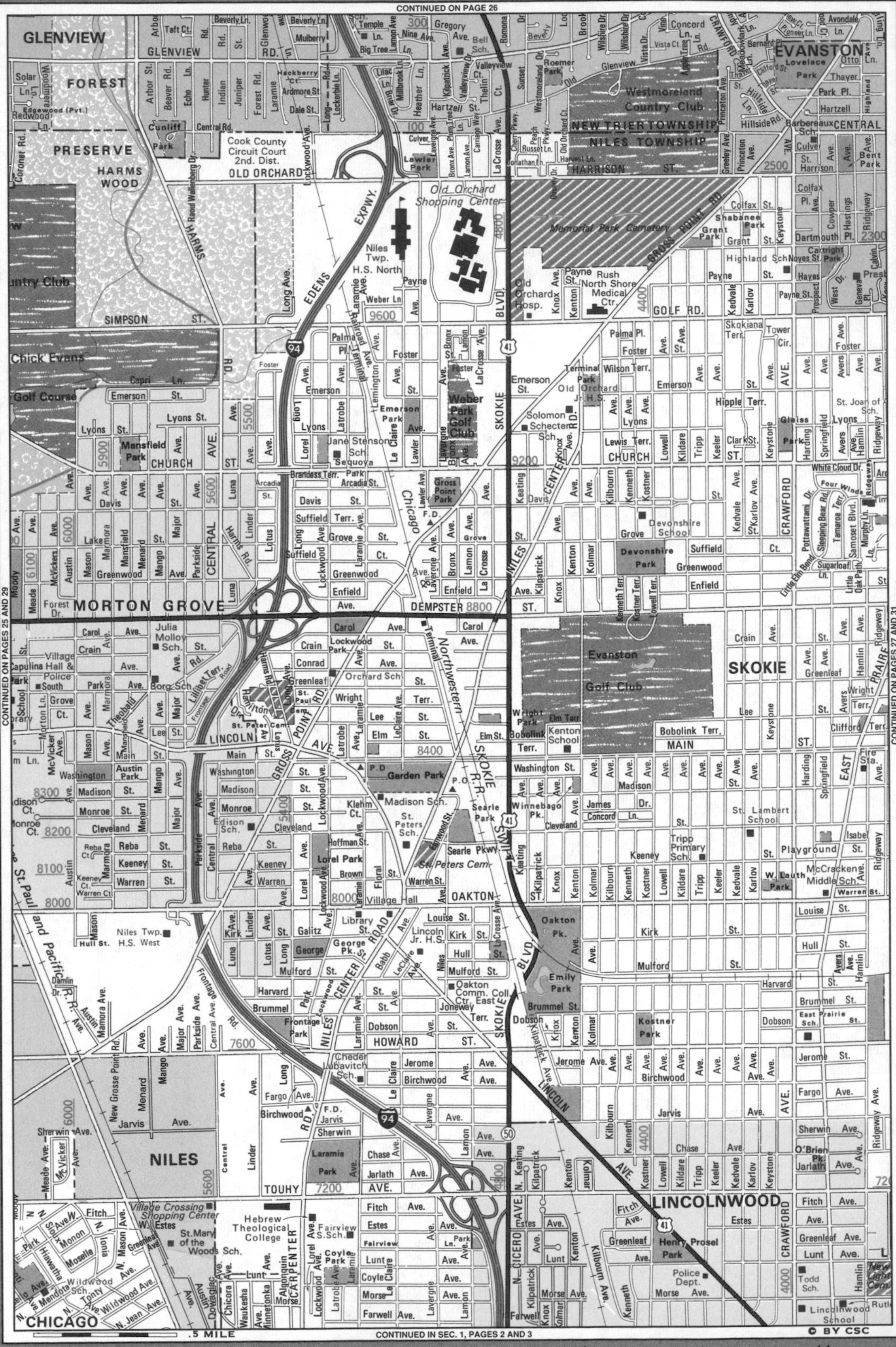


CONTINUED ON PAGES 27 AND 31

CONTINUED IN SEC. 1, PAGES 2 AND 3

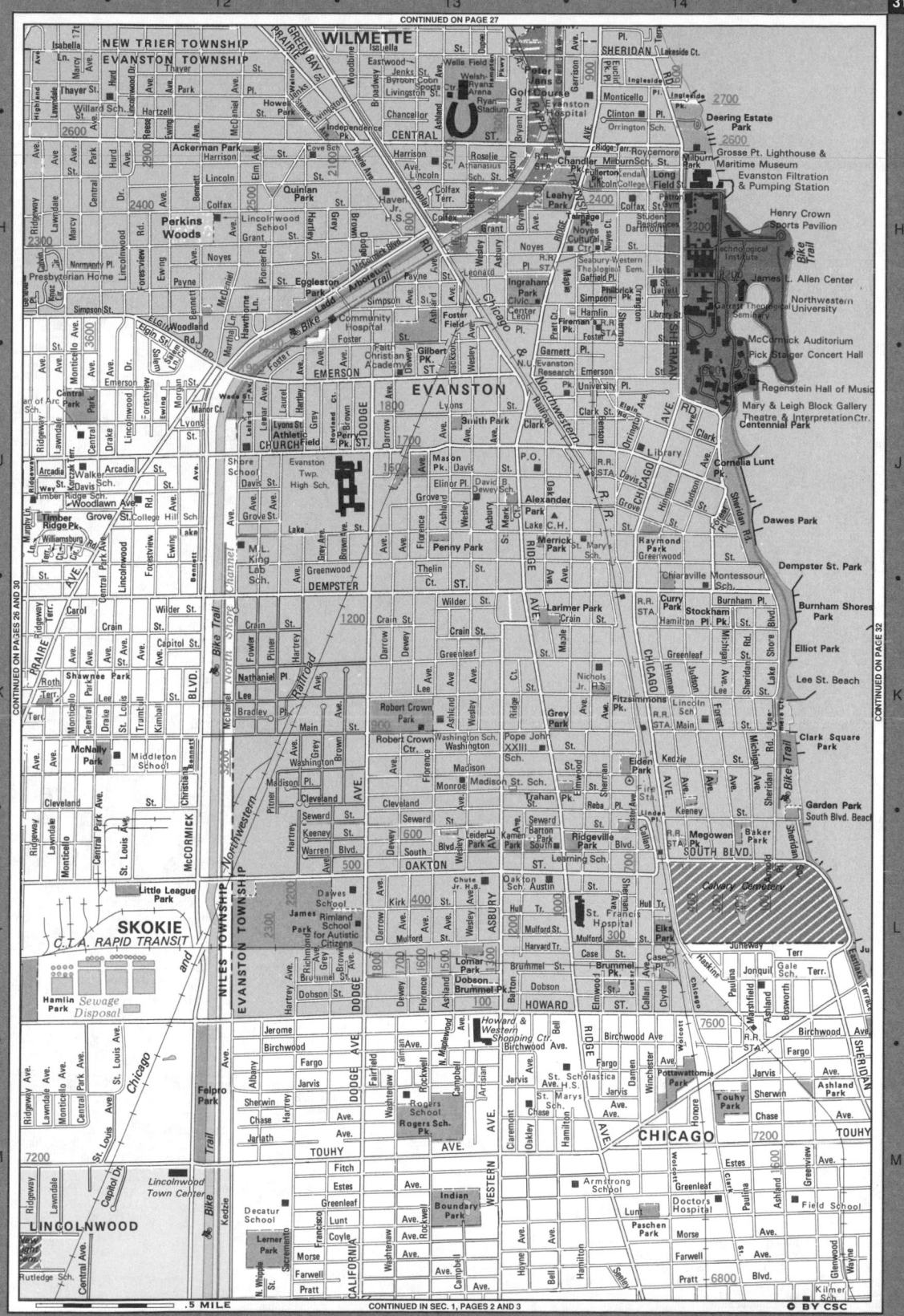

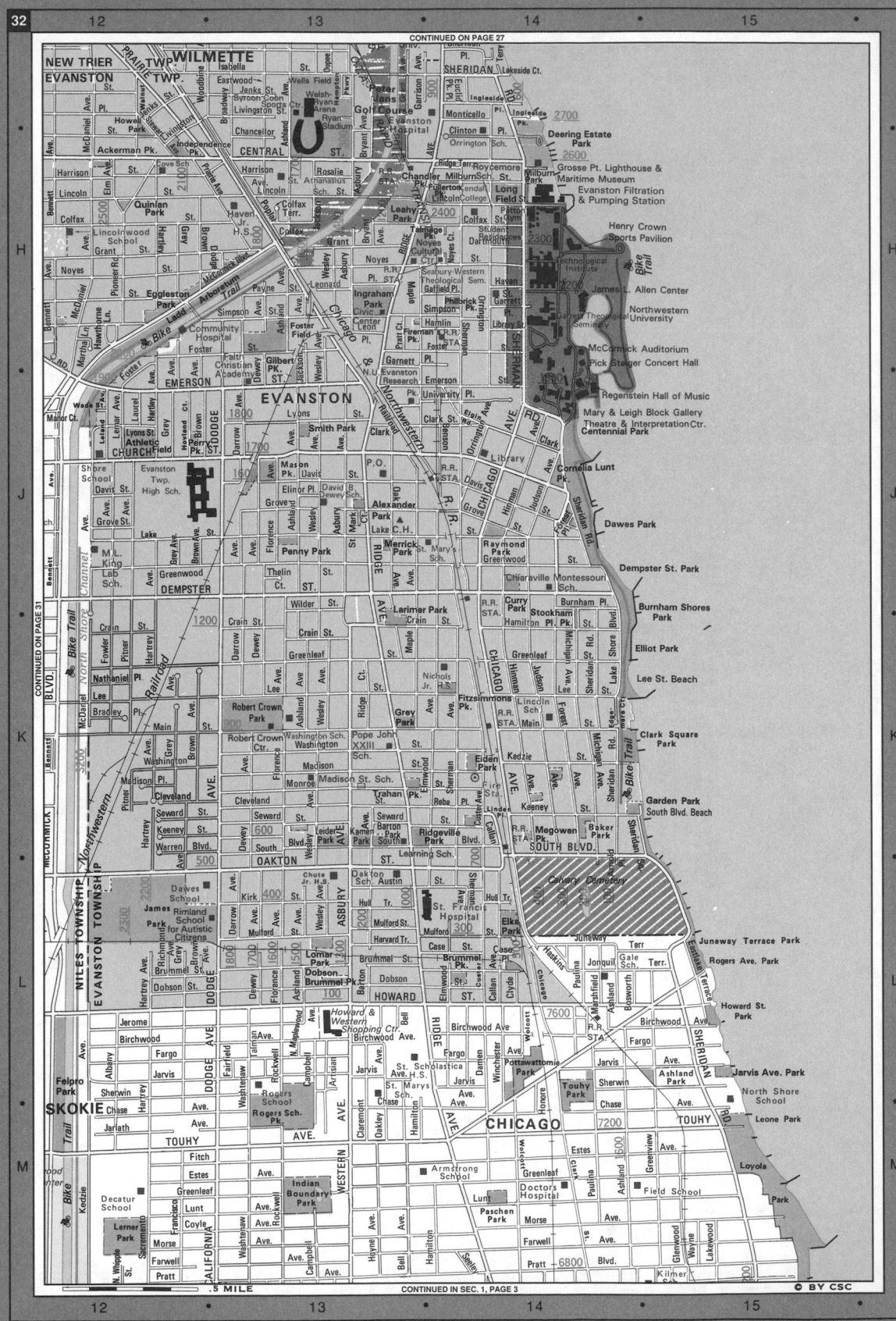

CONTINUED ON PAGE 27

CONTINUED ON PAGE 31

CONTINUED IN SEC. 1, PAGE 3

.5 MILE

© BY CSC

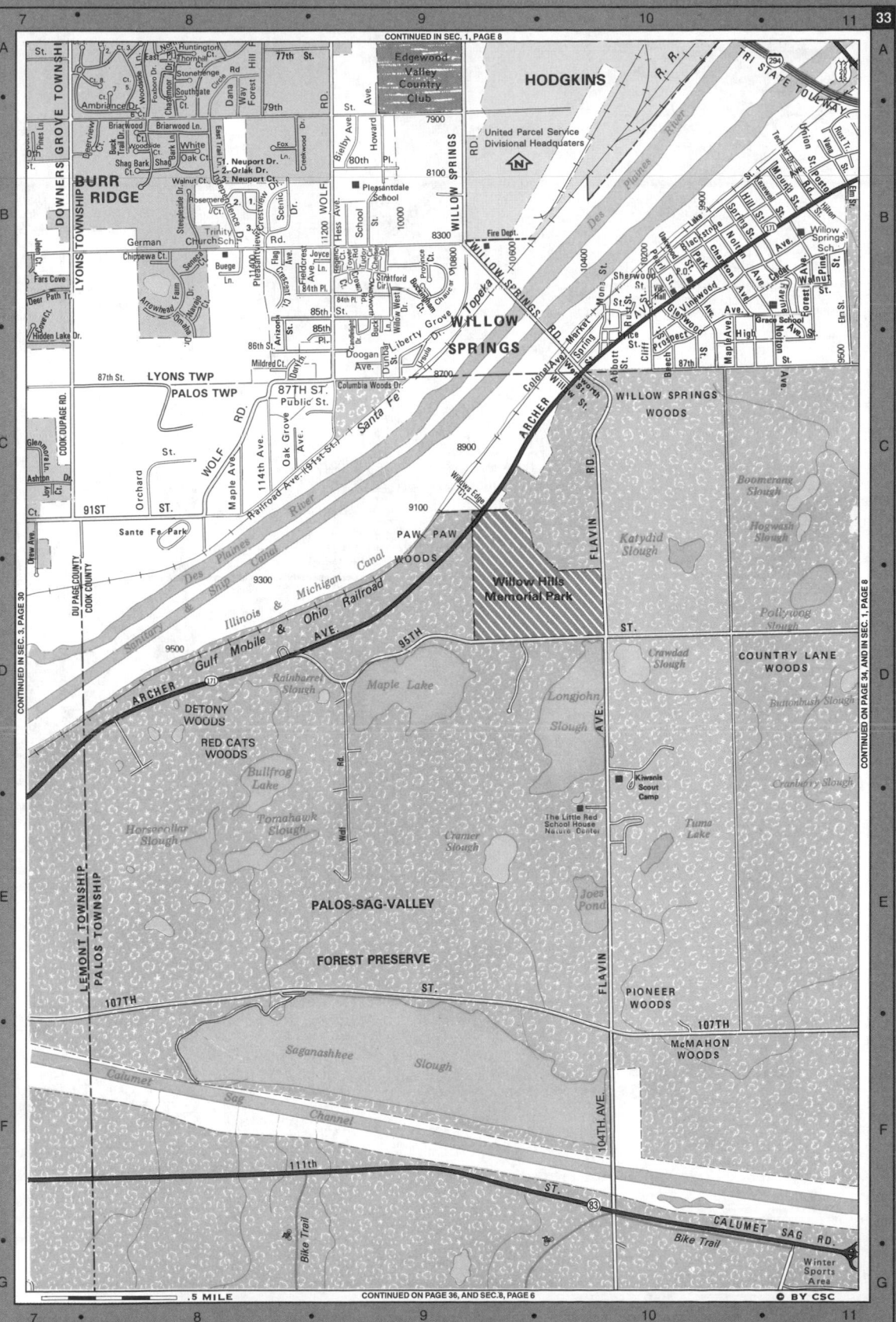

**33**

HODGKINS

United Parcel Service
Divisional Headquaters

BURR
RIDGE

DOWNERS GROVE TOWNSHIP

LYONS TOWNSHIP

Edgewood
Valley
Country
Club

Pleasantdale
School

1. Neuport Dr.
2. Orlak Dr.
3. Neuport Ct.

WILLOW SPRINGS RD.

Fire Dept.

WILLOW
SPRINGS

LYONS TWP

PALOS TWP

87TH ST.
Public St.

Santa Fe

Columbia Woods Dr.

ARCHER

WILLOW SPRINGS
WOODS

Grace School

FLAVIN

Boomerang
Slough

Hogwash
Slough

Santa Fe Park

PAW PAW
WOODS

Willow Hills
Memorial Park

Katydid
Slough

Pollywog
Slough

ST.

Des Plaines & Ship Canal

Sanitary

Illinois & Michigan Canal

Gulf Mobile & Ohio Railroad

Crawdad
Slough

COUNTRY LANE
WOODS

Buttonbush Slough

ARCHER

95TH

DETONY
WOODS

Rainbarrel
Slough

Maple Lake

Longjohn
Slough

RED CATS
WOODS

Bullfrog
Lake

Kiwanis
Scout
Camp

Cranberry Slough

Horsecollar
Slough

Tomahawk
Slough

The Little Red
School House
Nature Center

Cramer
Slough

Tuma
Lake

PALOS-SAG-VALLEY

Joes
Pond

FLAVIN

FOREST PRESERVE

PIONEER
WOODS

107TH

ST.

107TH

McMAHON
WOODS

104TH AVE.

LEMONT TOWNSHIP
PALOS TOWNSHIP

Saganashkee
Slough

Calumet
Sag
Channel

111th
ST.

CALUMET SAG RD.

Bike Trail

Bike Trail

Winter
Sports
Area

.5 MILE

CONTINUED IN SEC. 3, PAGE 30

CONTINUED ON PAGE 34, AND IN SEC. 1, PAGE 8

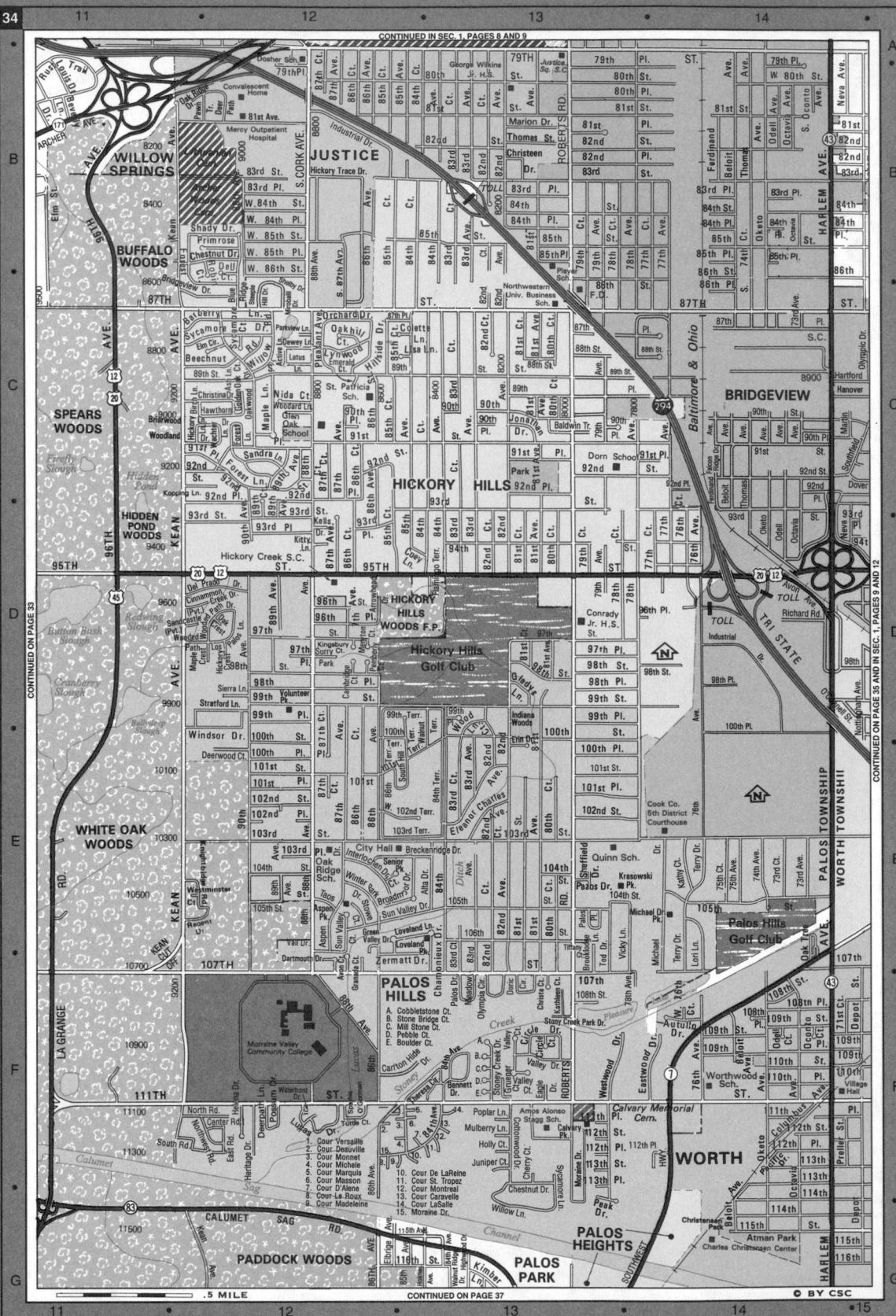

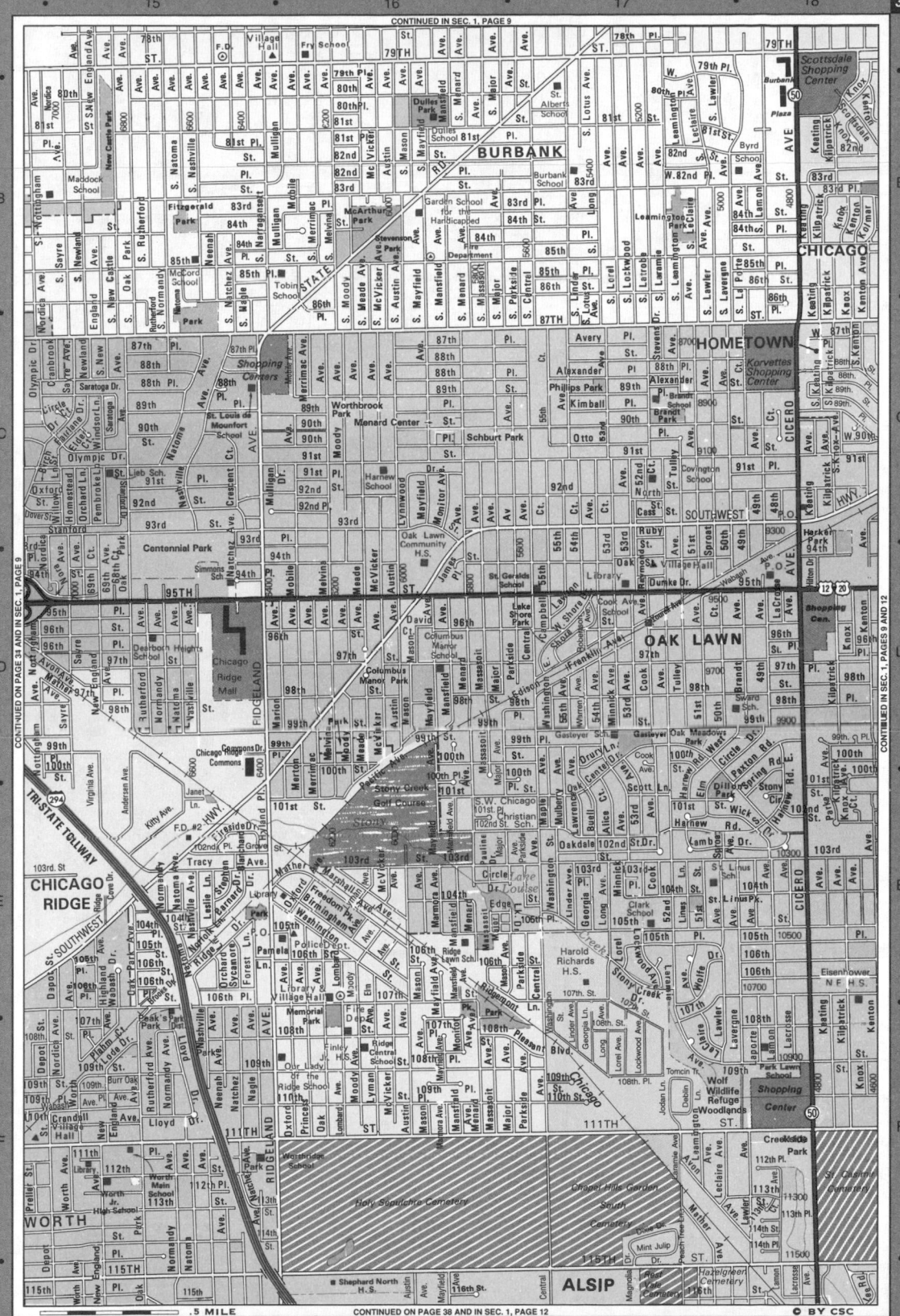

CONTINUED IN SEC. 1, PAGE 9

CONTINUED ON PAGE 31 AND IN SEC. 1, PAGE 9

CONTINUED IN SEC. 1, PAGES 9 AND 12

CONTINUED ON PAGE 38 AND IN SEC. 1, PAGE 12

BURBANK

CHICAGO

HOMETOWN

CICERO

SOUTHWEST

OAK LAWN

CHICAGO
RIDGE

WORTH

ALSIP

TRI-STATE TOLLWAY

.5 MILE

© BY CSC

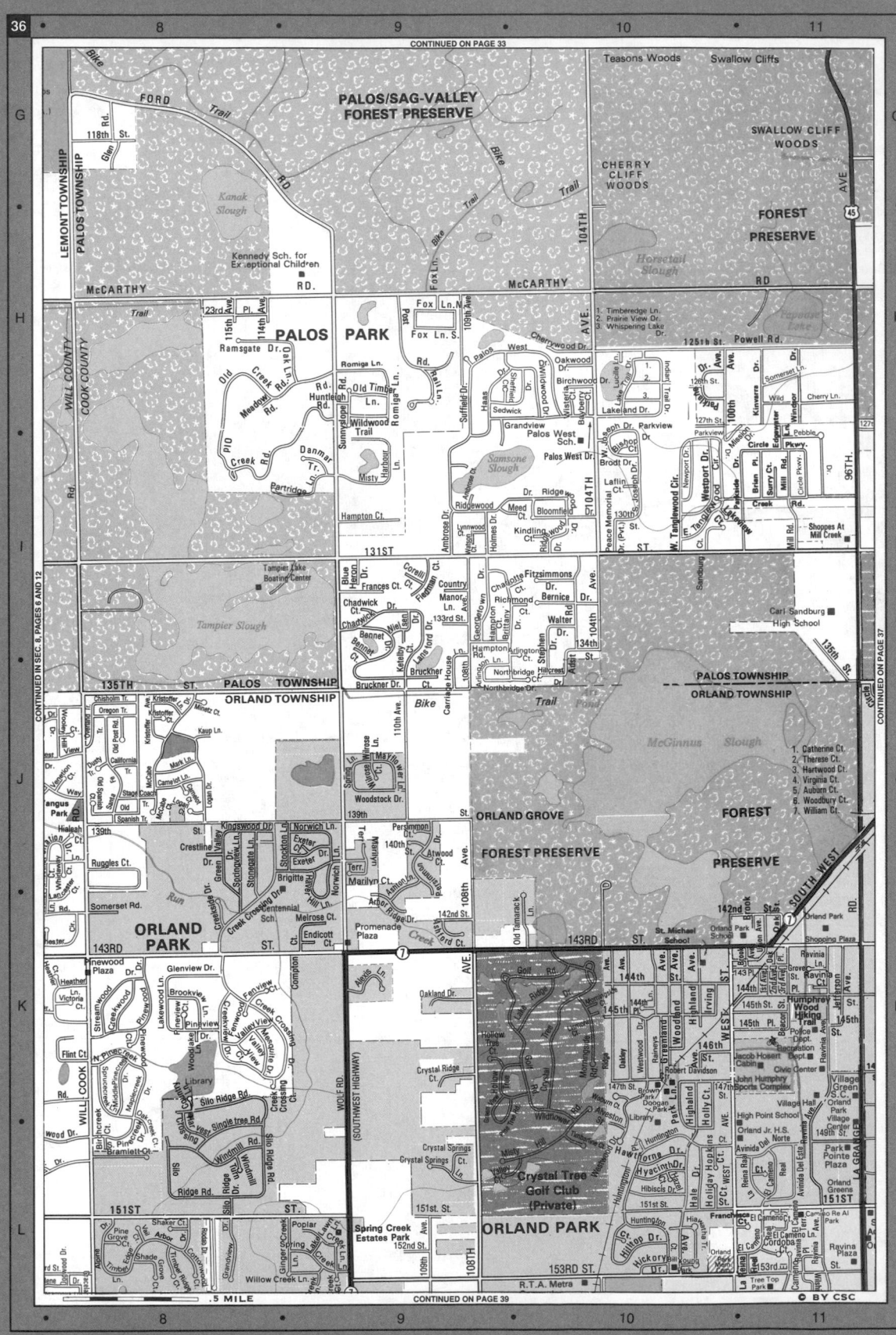

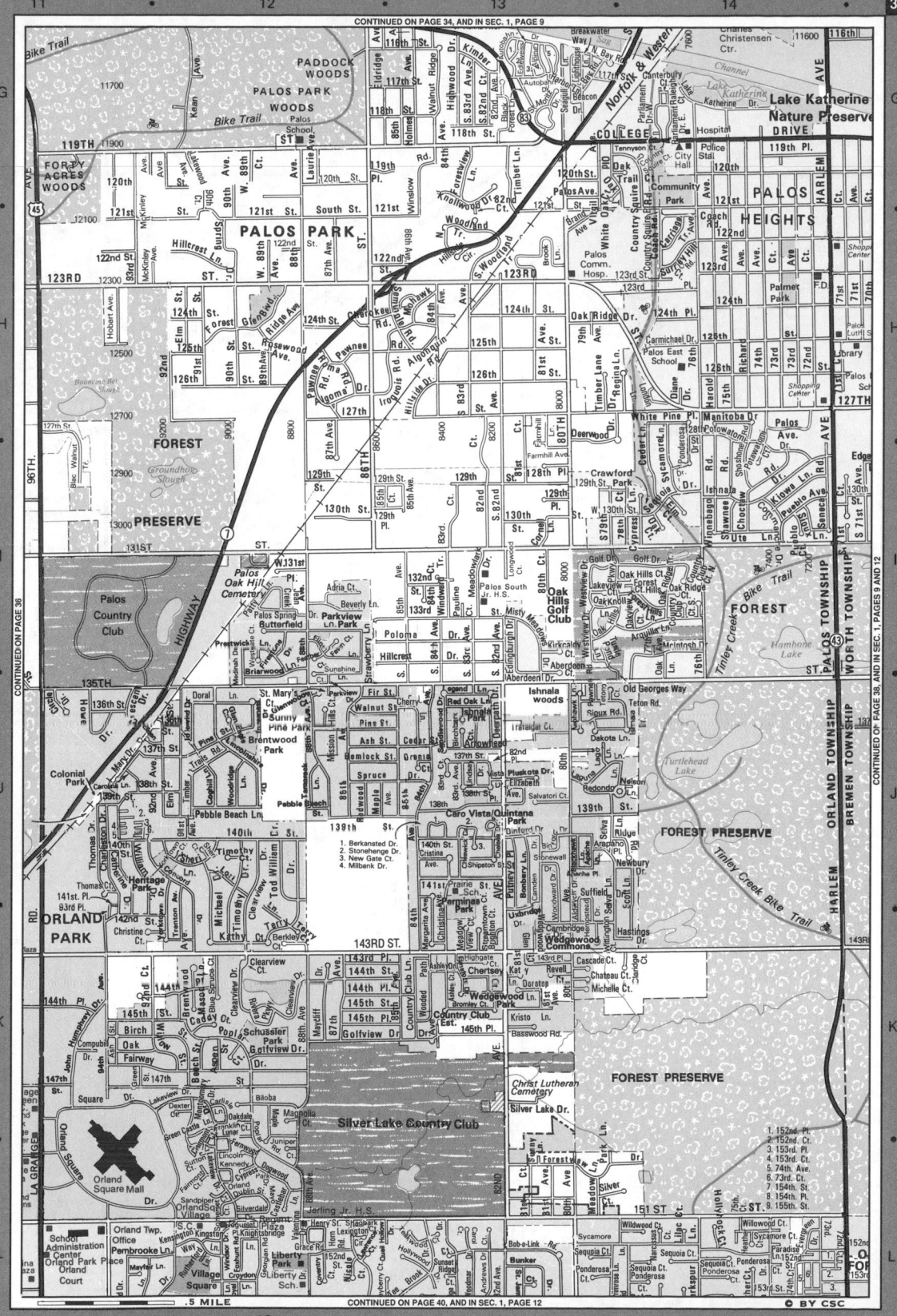

CONTINUED ON PAGE 34, AND IN SEC. 1, PAGE 9

CONTINUED ON PAGE 36

CONTINUED ON PAGE 38, AND IN SEC. 1, PAGES 9 AND 12

CONTINUED ON PAGE 40, AND IN SEC. 1, PAGE 12

.5 MILE

© BY CSC

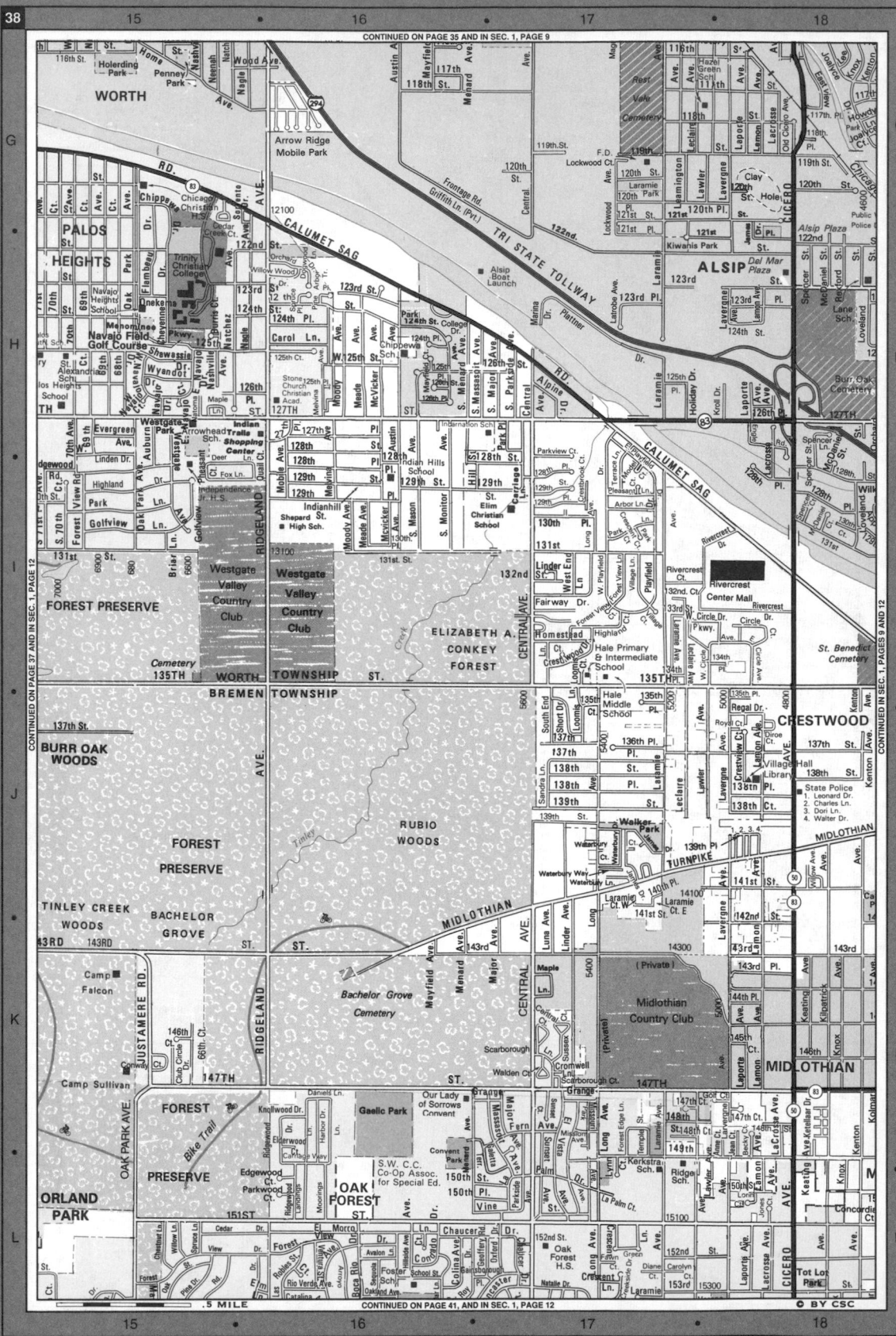

CONTINUED ON PAGE 36

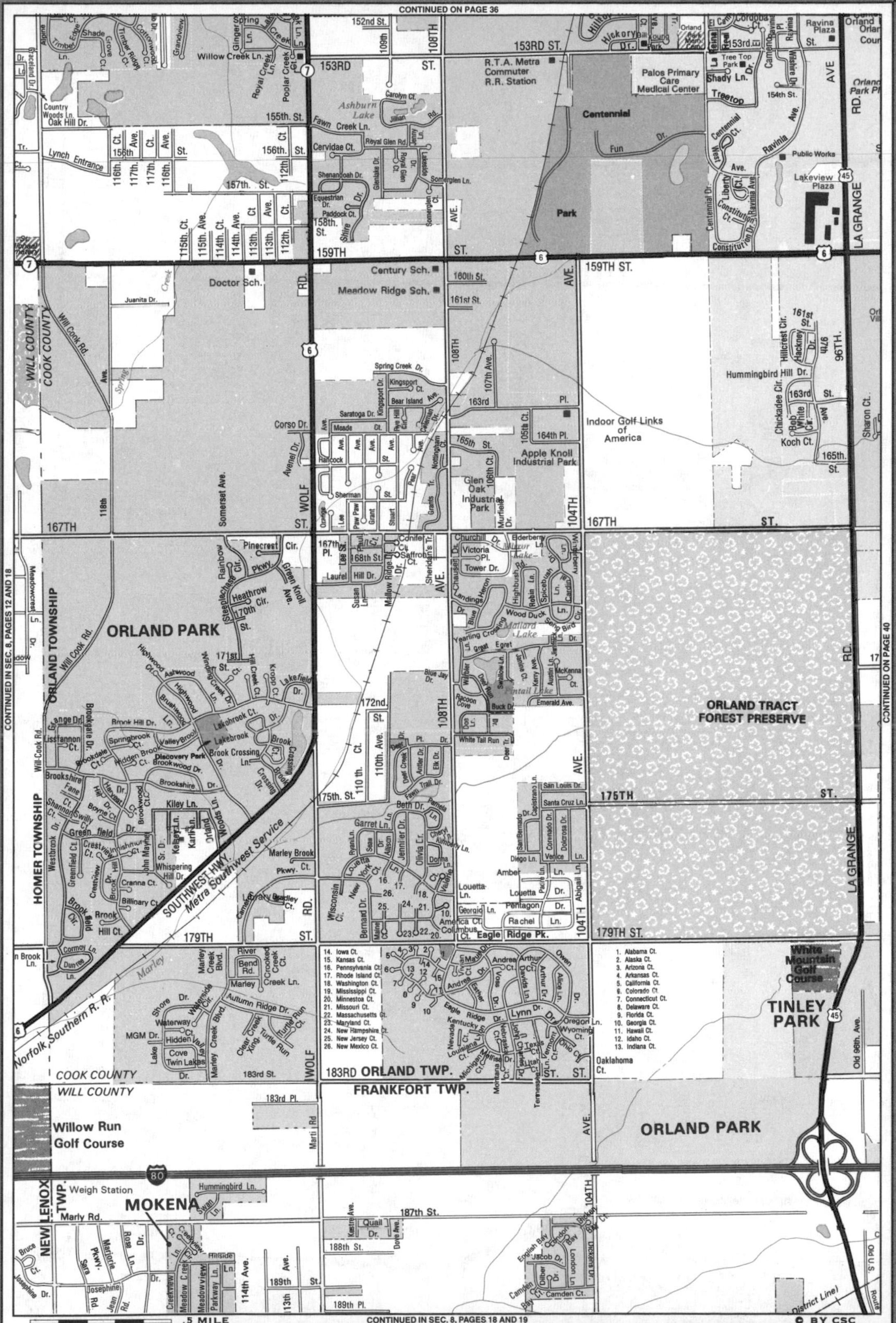

ORLAND PARK

ORLAND TOWNSHIP

HOMER TOWNSHIP

CONTINUED IN SEC. 8, PAGES 12 AND 18

ORLAND TRACT FOREST PRESERVE

TINLEY PARK

White Mountain Golf Course

Willow Run Golf Course

MOKENA

NEW LENOX TWP.

COOK COUNTY
WILL COUNTY

ORLAND TWP.
FRANKFORT TWP.

ORLAND PARK

CONTINUED ON PAGE 40

Pa) Primary Care Medical Center

R.T.A. Metra Commuter R.R. Station

Centennial Park

Lakeview Plaza

Indoor Golf Links of America

Apple Knoll Industrial Park

Glen Oak Industrial Park

LA GRANGE

Weigh Station

14. Iowa Ct.
15. Kansas Ct.
16. Pennsylvania Ct.
17. Rhode Island Ct.
18. Washington Ct.
19. Mississippi Ct.
20. Minnesota Ct.
21. Missouri Ct.
22. Massachusetts Ct.
23. Maryland Ct.
24. New Hampshire Ct.
25. New Jersey Ct.
26. New Mexico Ct.

1. Alabama Ct.
2. Alaska Ct.
3. Arizona Ct.
4. Arkansas Ct.
5. California Ct.
6. Colorado Ct.
7. Connecticut Ct.
8. Delaware Ct.
9. Florida Ct.
10. Georgia Ct.
11. Hawaii Ct.
12. Idaho Ct.
13. Indiana Ct.

.5 MILE

CONTINUED IN SEC. 8, PAGES 18 AND 19

© BY CSC

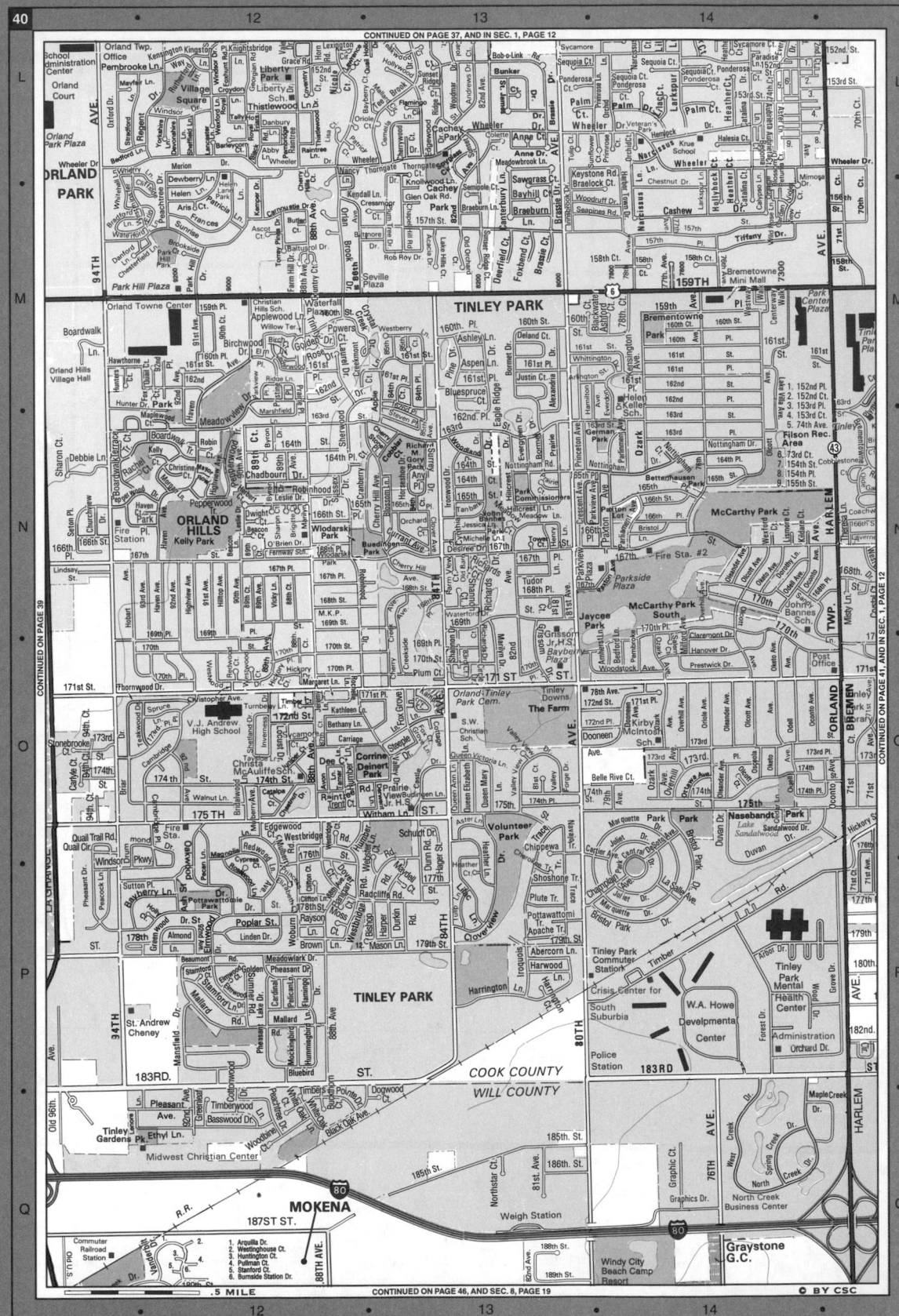

CONTINUED ON PAGE 37, AND IN SEC. 1, PAGE 12

CONTINUED ON PAGE 39

CONTINUED ON PAGE 41, AND IN SEC. 1, PAGE 12

CONTINUED ON PAGE 46, AND SEC. 8, PAGE 19

ORLAND PARK

TINLEY PARK

ORLAND HILLS

MOKENA

COOK COUNTY
WILL COUNTY

Graystone G.C.

.5 MILE

© BY CSC

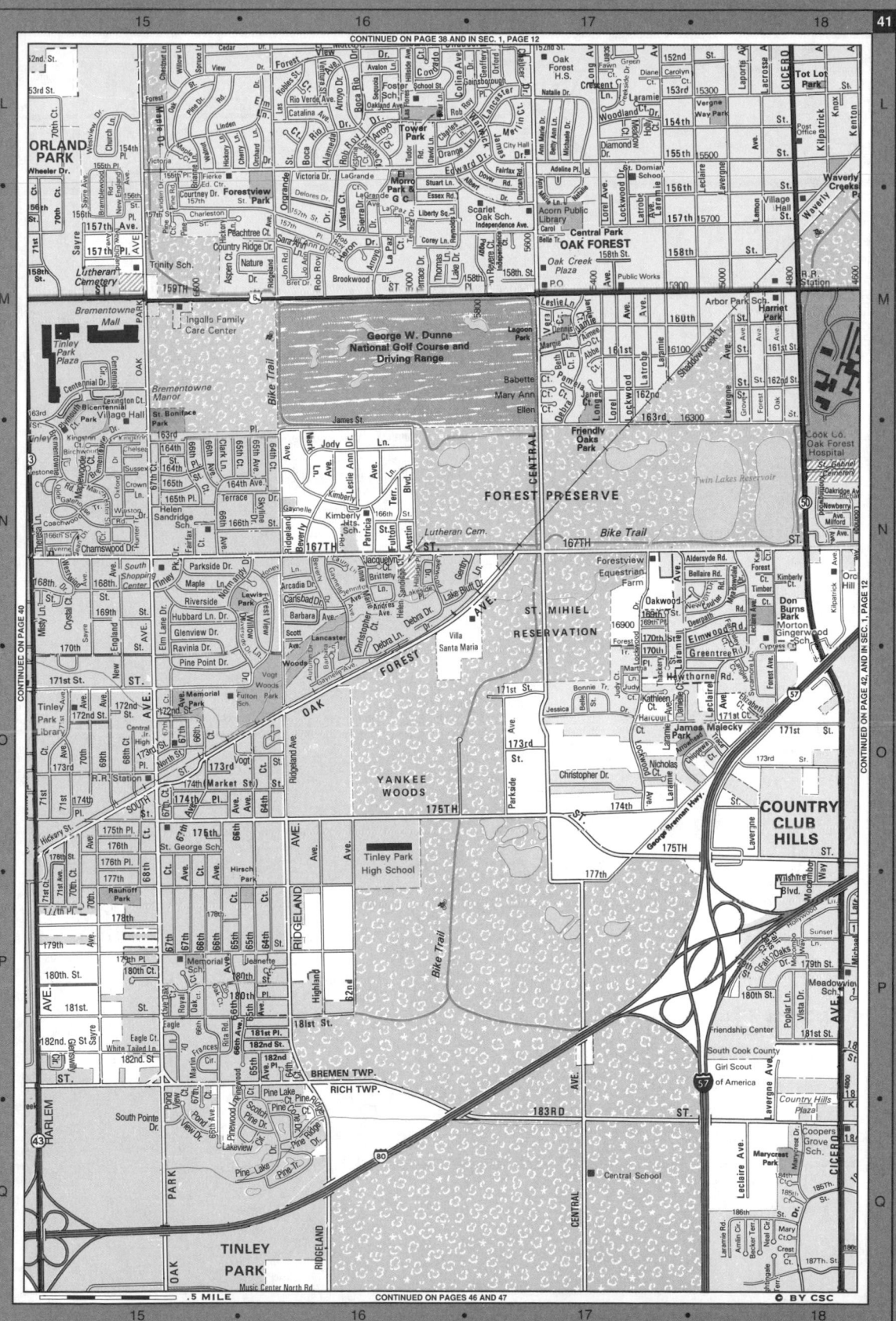

CONTINUED ON PAGE 38 AND IN SEC. 1, PAGE 12

ORLAND PARK

OAK FOREST

George W. Dunne National Golf Course and Driving Range

Brementowne Mall

Tinley Park Plaza

FOREST PRESERVE

ST. MIHIEL RESERVATION

YANKEE WOODS

Tinley Park High School

COUNTRY CLUB HILLS

TINLEY PARK

CONTINUED ON PAGE 40

CONTINUED ON PAGE 42, AND IN SEC. 1, PAGE 12

.5 MILE

CONTINUED ON PAGES 46 AND 47

© BY CSC

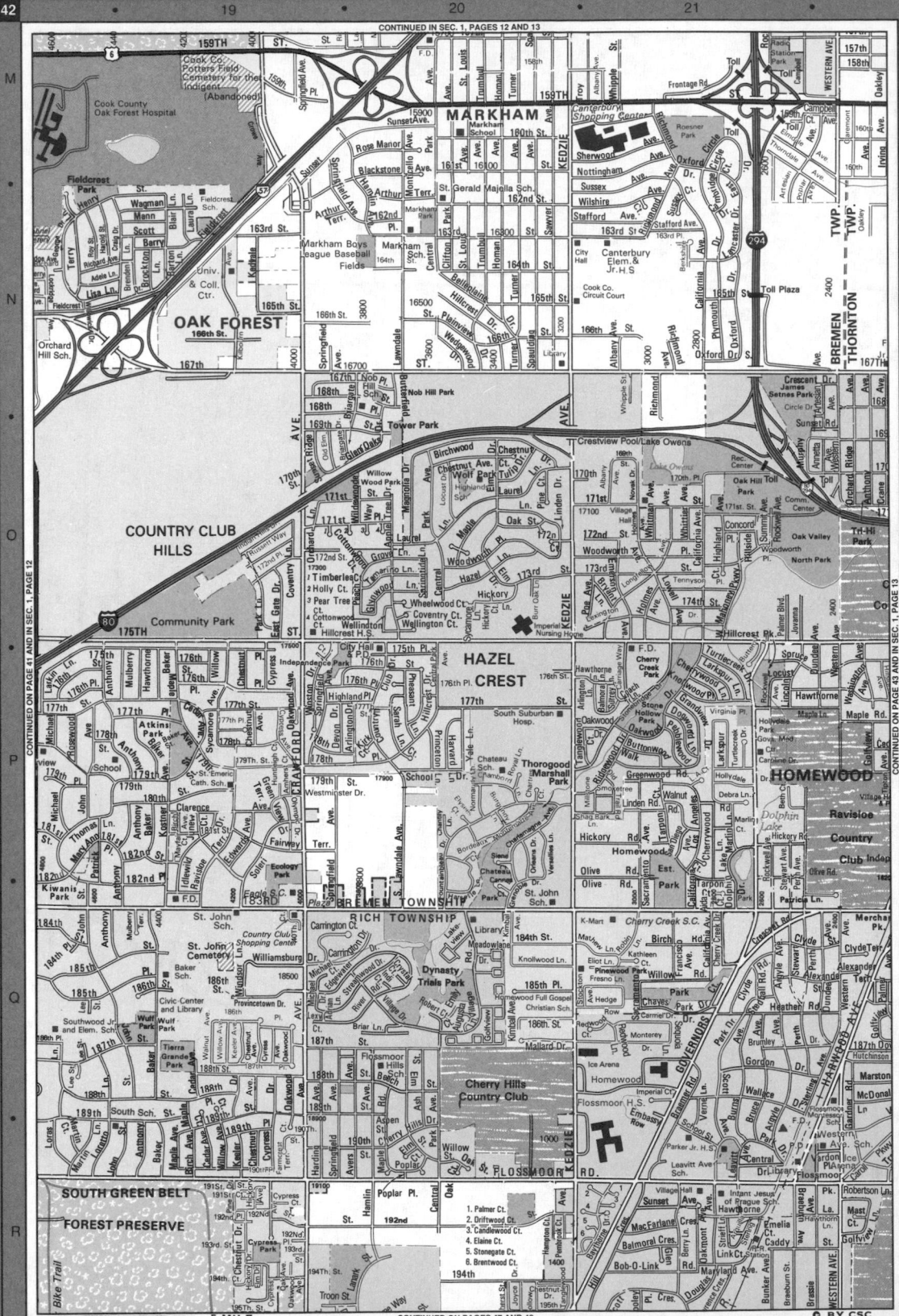

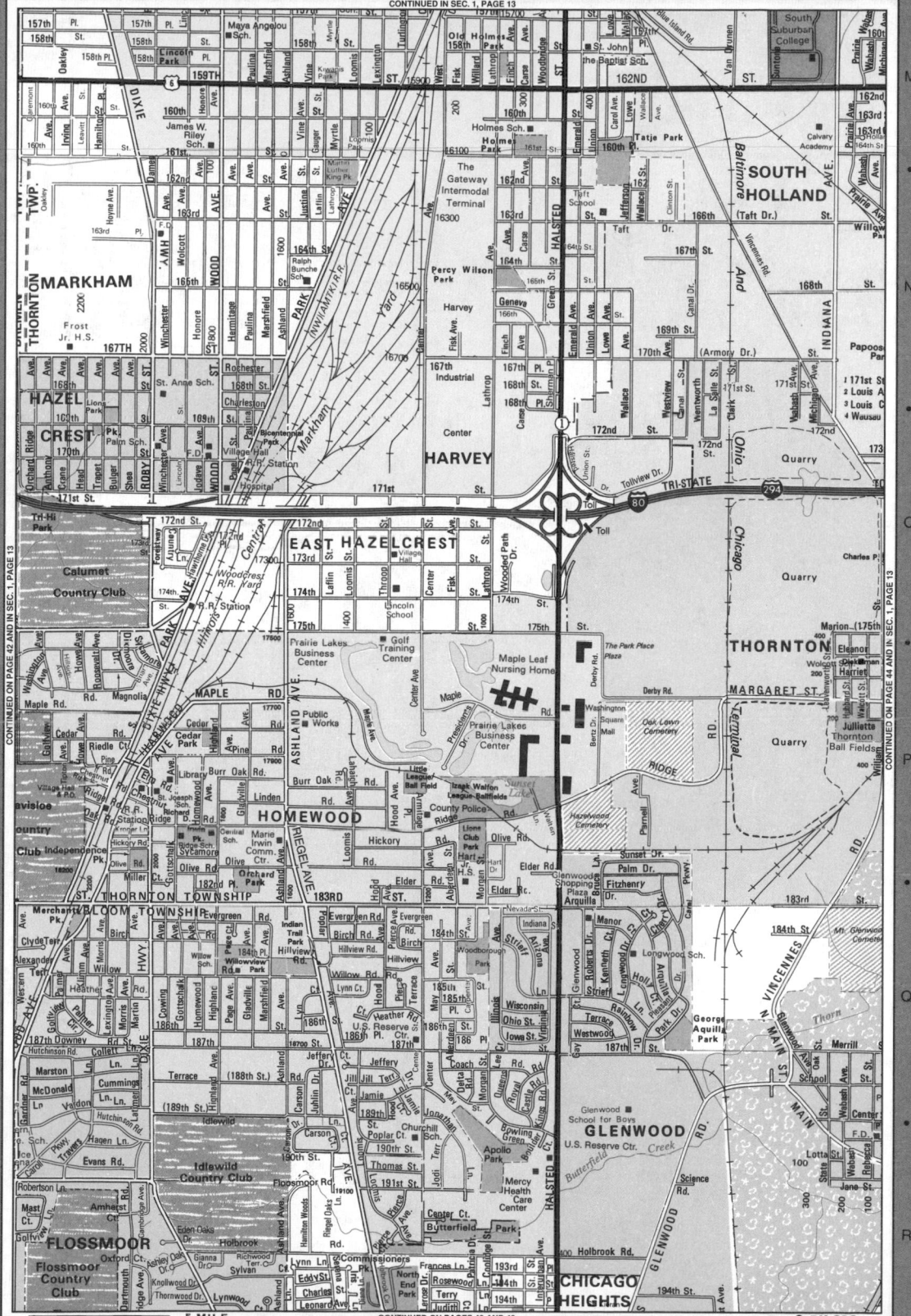

CONTINUED IN SEC. 1, PAGE 13

MARKHAM

THORNTON TWP.

HAZEL CREST

HARVEY

EAST HAZELCREST

SOUTH HOLLAND

THORNTON

HOMEWOOD

THORNTON TOWNSHIP

BLOOM TOWNSHIP

GLENWOOD

FLOSSMOOR

CHICAGO HEIGHTS

Flossmoor Country Club

Calumet Country Club

Idlewild Country Club

CONTINUED ON PAGE 42 AND IN SEC. 1, PAGE 13

CONTINUED ON PAGE 44 AND IN SEC. 1, PAGE 13

CONTINUED ON PAGES 48 AND 49

© BY CSC

.5 MILE

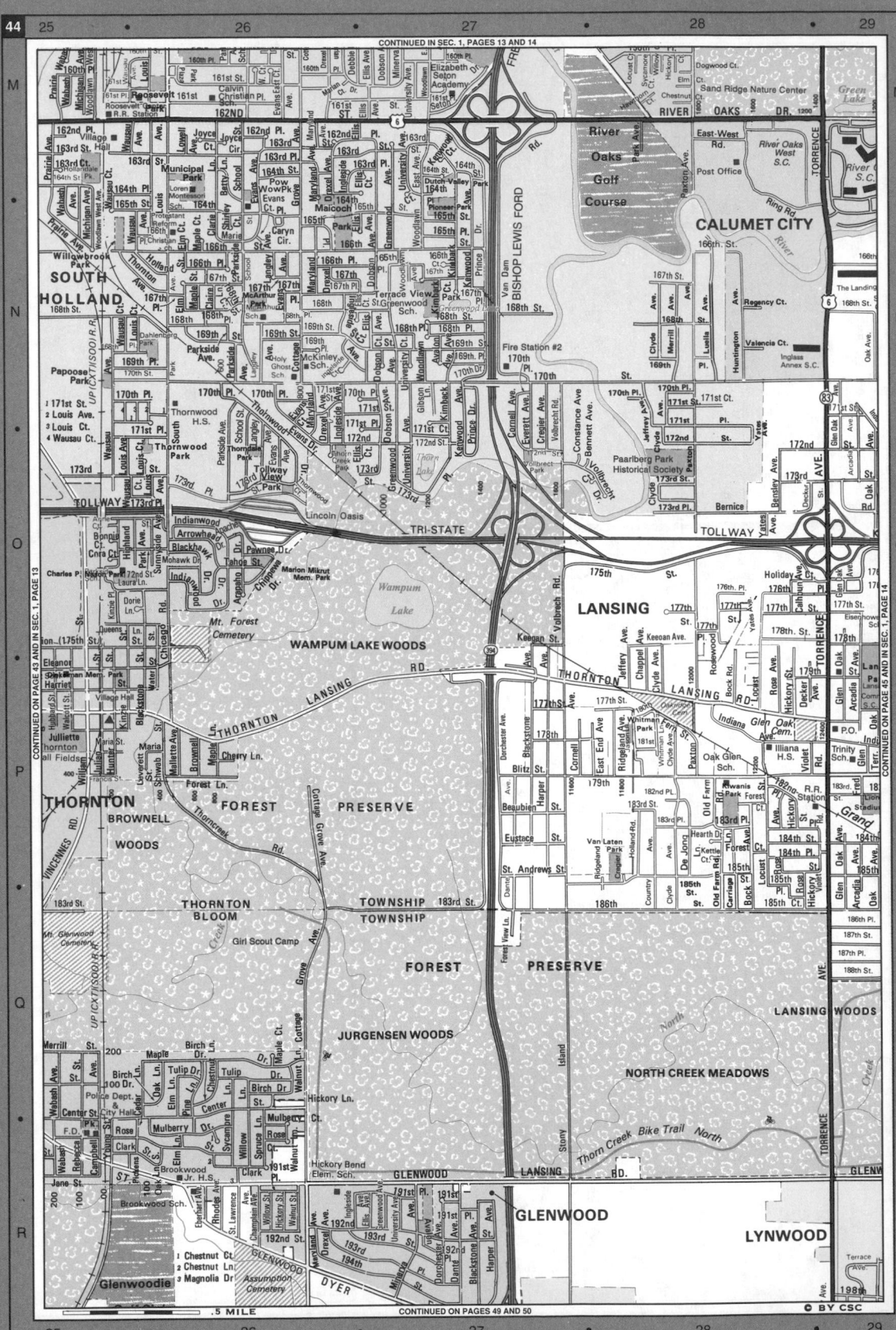

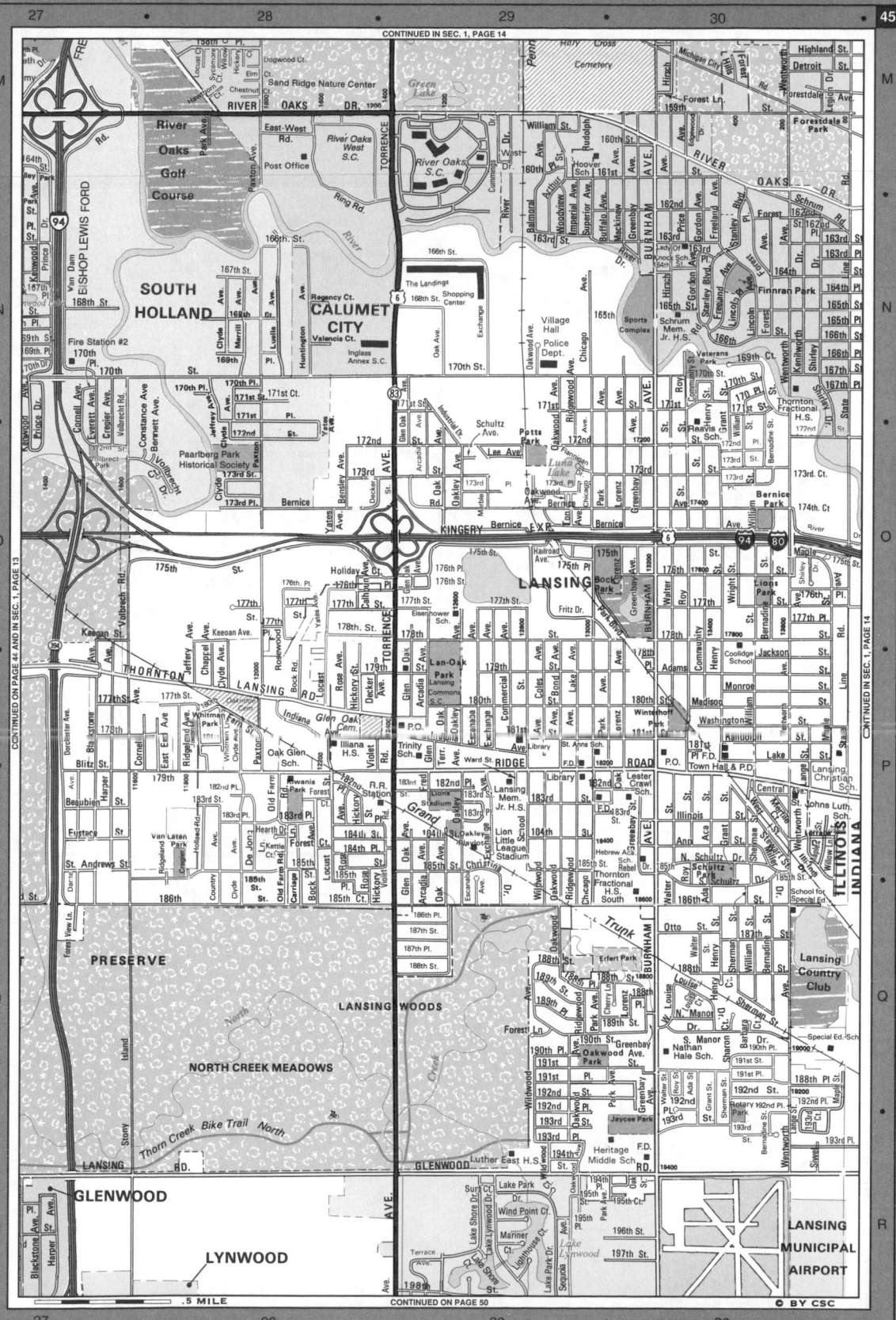

CONTINUED IN SEC. 1, PAGE 14

CONTINUED ON PAGE 44 AND IN SEC. 1, PAGE 13

CONTINUED IN SEC. 1, PAGE 14

CONTINUED ON PAGE 50

© BY CSC

.5 MILE

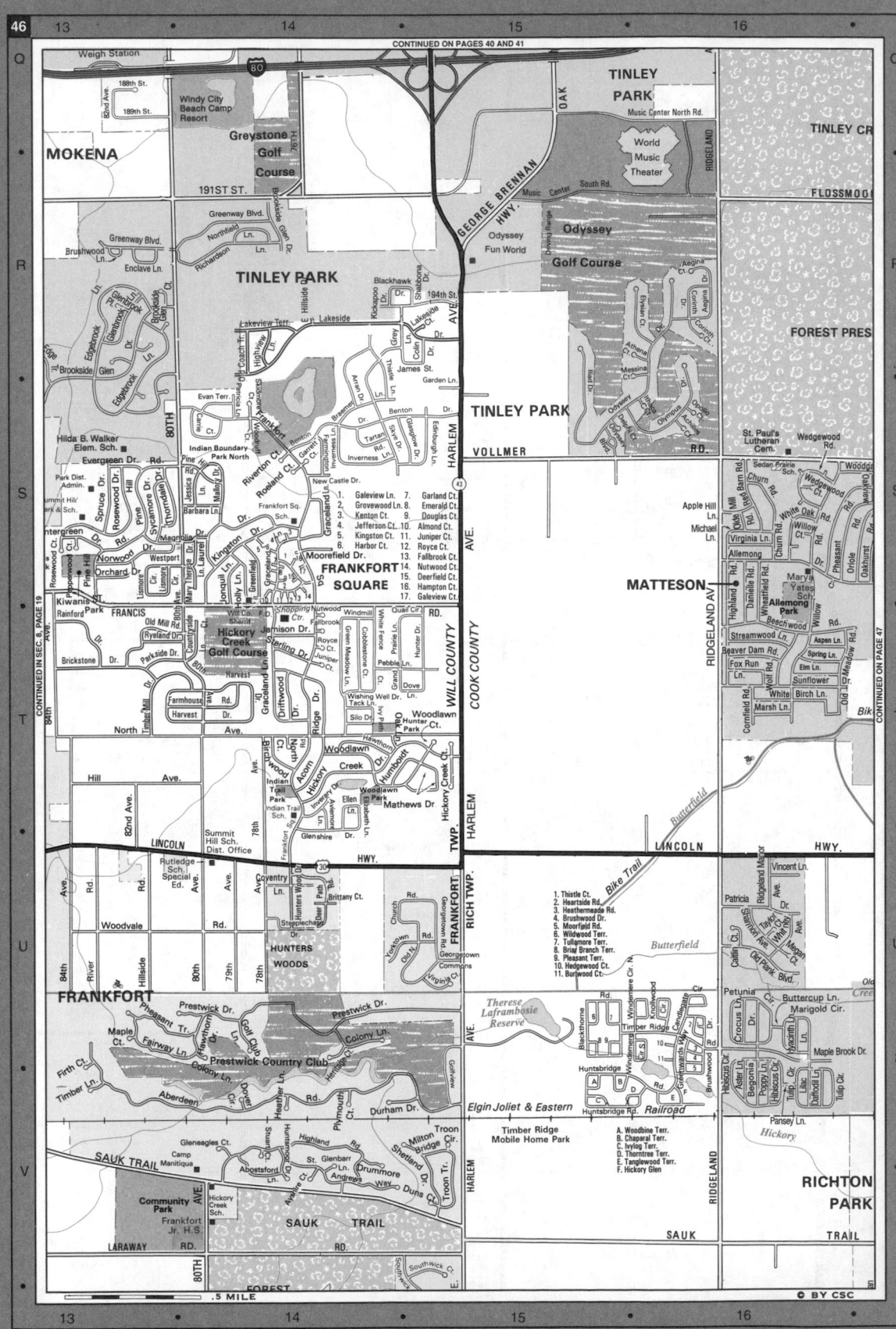

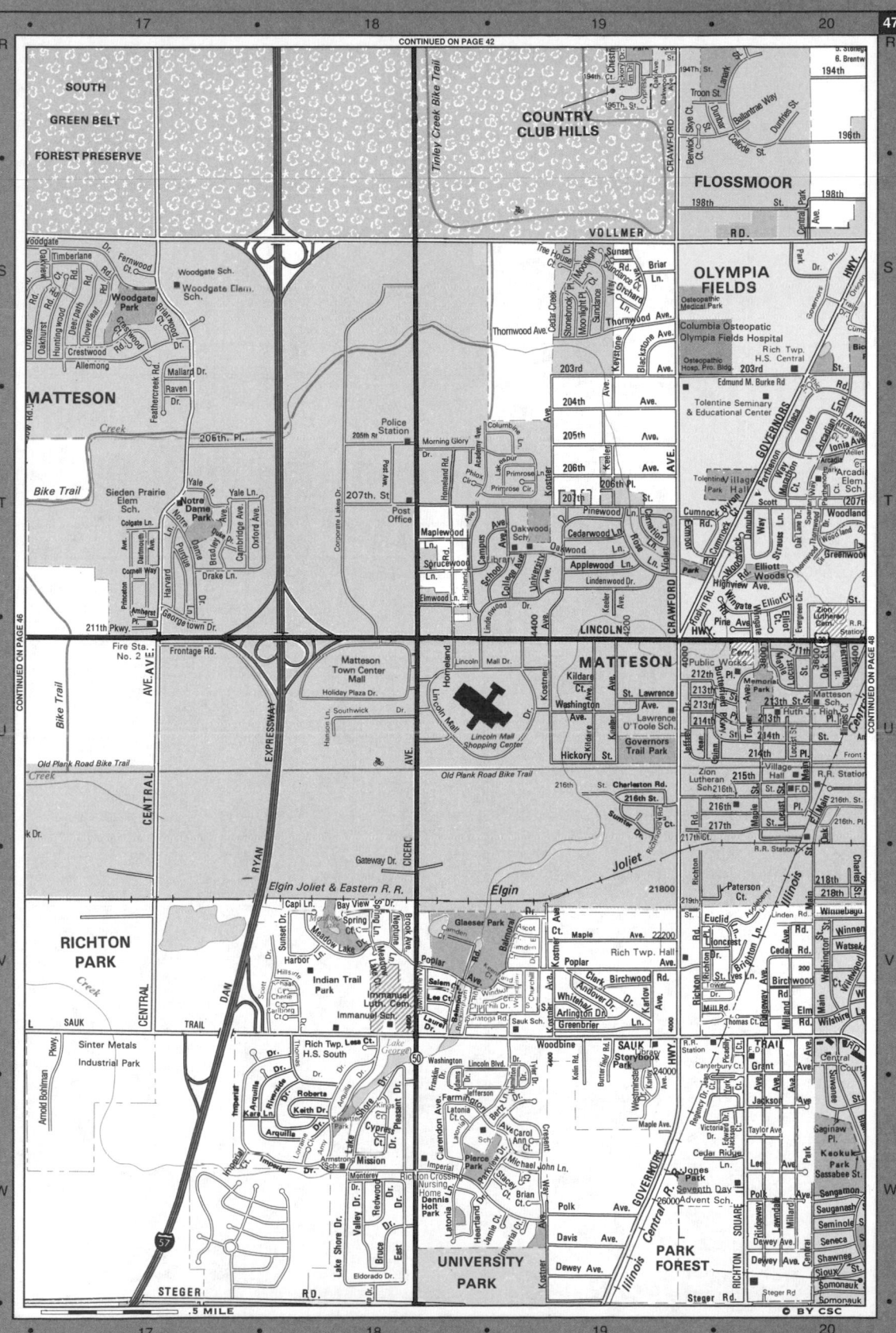

CONTINUED ON PAGE 42

CONTINUED ON PAGE 46

CONTINUED ON PAGE 48

© BY CSC

.5 MILE

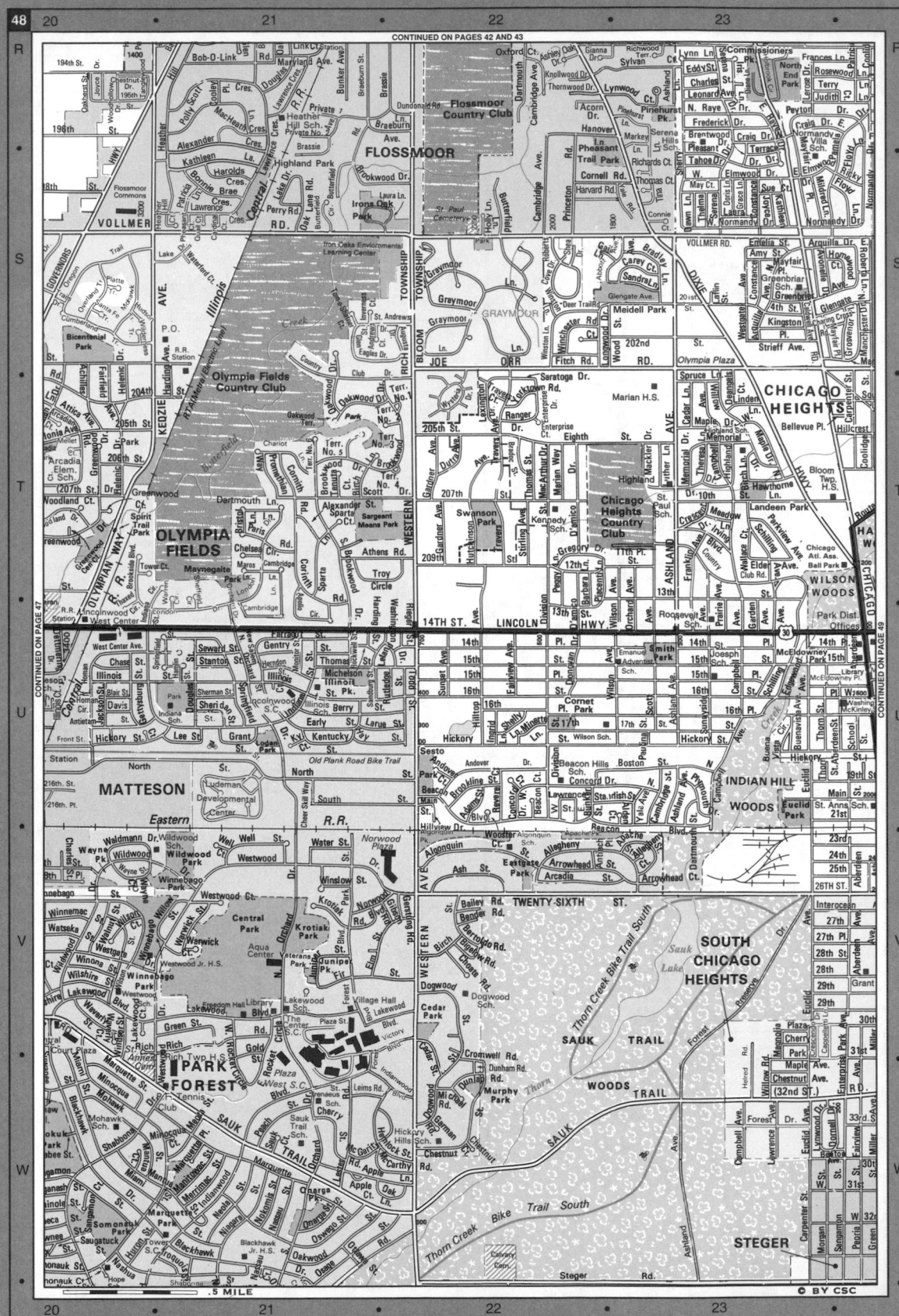

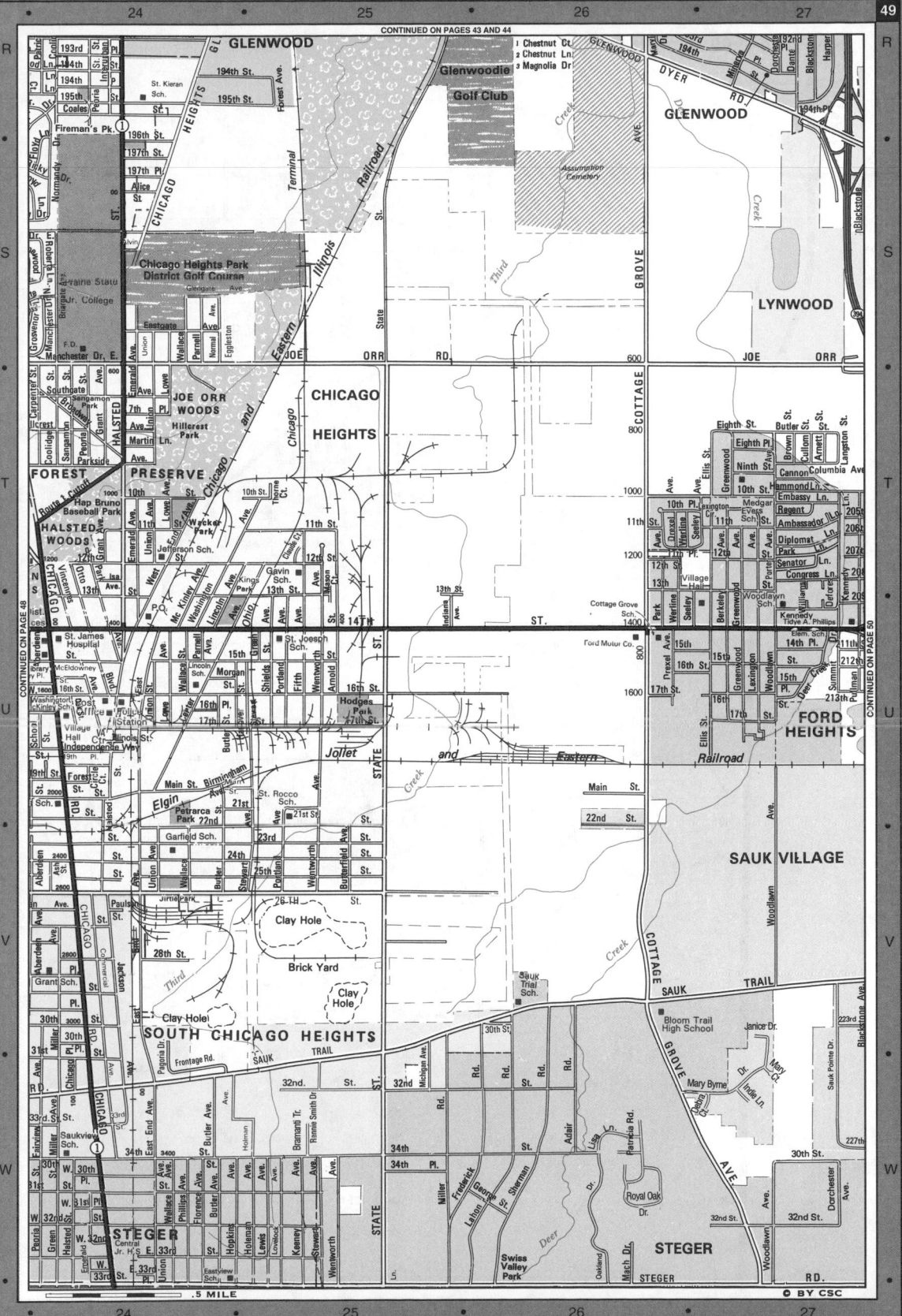

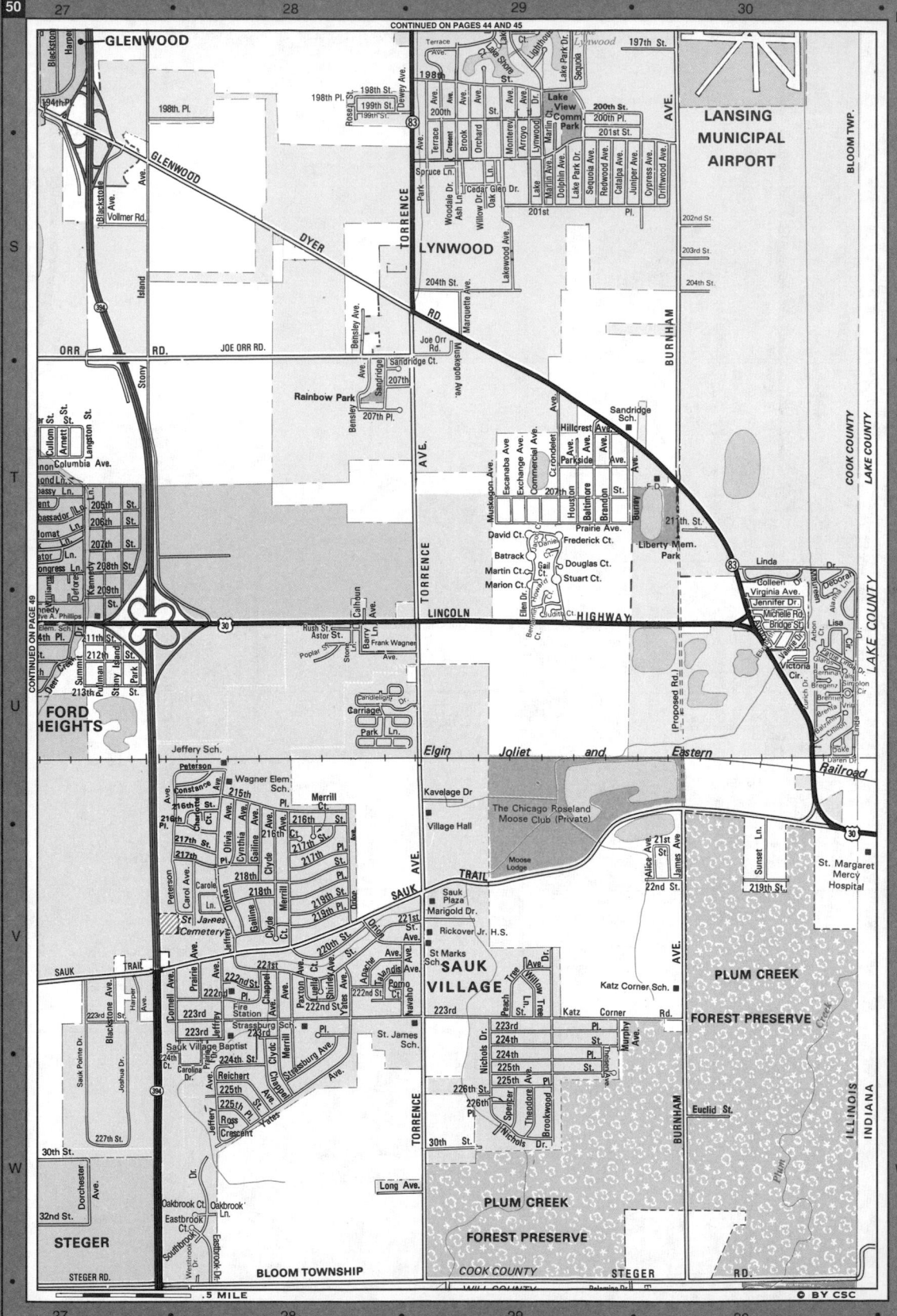

# INDEX TO SUBURBAN COOK COUNTY

## ARLINGTON HEIGHTS

Pages 3,8,9,13,14

### STREETS

Alec St. . . . . Pg.8 . . . . B9
Alexandria St. Pg.8 . . . C10
Algonquin Rd. Pg.13 . . . H11
Allegheny Dr. Pg.8 . . . . B10
Allen Ln. . . . . Pg.8 . . . . F9
Allison Ct. . . Pg.13 . . . G9
Amhurst Ct. . . Pg.9 . . . D12
Appletree Ln. . Pg.8 . . . B11
Arlington Heights Rd.
. . . . . . . . . Pg.8,13 A-H11
Arthur Ave. . . Pg.14 . . . F11
Ashbury Ct. . . Pg.9 . . . D12
Ashford Ln. . . Pg.3 . . . A11
Avon Ct. . . . Pg.9 . . . C12
Avon Ln. . . . Pg.9 . . . C12
Banbury Rd. . Pg.8 . . . F11
Barberry Ct. . Pg.9 . . . D12
Bayside Dr. . . Pg.3 . . . A10
Bel Aire Dr. . . Pg.9 . . . E12
Belmont Ave. . Pg.8,13
Belmont Ct. . . Pg.8 . . . D-G11
Berkley Dr. . . Pg.8 . . . C11
Best Dr. . . . . Pg.8 . . . B10
Betty Dr. . . . . Pg.8 . . . B12
Beverly Ave. . Pg.8 . . . A12
Beverly Ln. . . Pg.8 . . . C-F11
Birchwood Ln. Pg.13 C-F11
Bloomington Ave.
. . . . . . . . . Pg.3 . . . A10
Boeger Dr. . . Pg.8 . . . A10
Bradford Dr. . Pg.8 . . . B11
Bradshire Ct. . Pg.9 . . . D12
Braeside Dr. . Pg.8 . . . B10
Brampton Ln. . Pg.3 . . . A11
Brandenberry Ct.
. . . . . . . . . Pg.9 . . . D12
Bray Ct. . . . . Pg.13 . . . G9
Briar Ln. . . . . Pg.8 . . . C11
Brighton Pl. . . Pg.9 . . . D-C11
Bristol Ln. . . . Pg.13 . . . F11
Brittany Dr. . . Pg.8 . . . B10
Brittany Dr. . . Pg.8 . . . B10
Brocton Ct. . . Pg.9 . . . D12
Brook Dr. . . . Pg.13 . . . A11
Brookwood Dr. Pg.8 . . B10-11
Brown St. . . . Pg.8 . . . D9
Buffalo Grove Rd.
. . . . . . . . . Pg.9 . . . A-C12
Burgoyne Rd. . Pg.9 . . . D10
Burke Dr. . . . Pg.8 . . . C11
Burkitt Pl. . . . Pg.3 . . . A11
Burning Tree Ct.
. . . . . . . . . Pg.9 . . . B12
Burning Tree Ln.
. . . . . . . . . Pg.8 . B10,11
Burr Oak Dr. . Pg.8 . . . A10
Burton Ct. . . . Pg.13 . . . F11
Butternut Ct. . Pg.8 . . . E10
Cambridge Rd. Pg.8 . C9,E10
Camelot Ct. . . Pg.8 . . . B11
Campbell St. . Pg.8,9 E10-12
Campus Dr. . . Pg.8 . . . A10
Canterbury Ct. Pg.8 . . . B11
Canterbury Dr. Pg.8 . B10-12
Carlyle Ln. . . Pg.9 . . . D12
Carlyle Ln. . . Pg.9 . . . E11
Carlyle Pl. . . . Pg.9 . . . F12
Carriage Way Dr.
. . . . . . . . . Pg.8 . . . A11
Catino St. . . . Pg.8 . . . F10
Cedar Glenn Dr.
. . . . . . . . . Pg.13 . . . J11
Cedar Ln. . . . Pg.13 . . . G10
Cedar St. . . . Pg.13 . . . G10
Cellular Blvd. . Pg.8 . . . A9
Central St. . . . Pg.13 F9-11
Champlain St. . Pg.8 . . . B10
Chapel Hill Dr. Pg.8 . . . B11
Charles St. . . Pg.8 . . . C11
Charter Point Dr. (Pvt.)
. . . . . . . . . Pg.9 . . . C12
Chatham Pl. . . Pg.8 . . . F11
Cherry Hill Dr. Pg.9 . . . C12
Cherry Ln. . . . Pg.8 . . . C11
Chesterfield Dr.
. . . . . . . . . Pg.13 . . . G10
Chestnut Ave. Pg.8,13 B-G10
Chicago Ave. . Pg.8 . . . D9
Circle Hill Dr. . Pg.8 . . . C11
Clarence Ave. . Pg.8 . . . C11
Clarendon Ave. Pg.8 . . . C11
Clarendon Dr. . Pg.8 . . . D11
Clarendon Rd. Pg.8 . . . D11
Clarendon St. . Pg.8 . . . D10
Clayton Ct. . . Pg.9 . . . E11
Clearbrook Dr. Pg.13 . . . J11
Cleveland Ave. Pg.9,14 . F11
Coldspring Dr. (Pvt.)
. . . . . . . . . Pg.9 . . . C13
College Dr. . . Pg.8 . . . A10
Concord Dr. . . Pg.8 . . . B9
Cottonwood Ct.
. . . . . . . . . Pg.8 . . . C10
Council Tr. . . . Pg.13 . . . H11
Country Lake Rd.
. . . . . . . . . Pg.9 . . . C13
Country Ln. . . Pg.8 . . . A11

Courtland Dr. (Pvt.)
. . . . . . . . . Pg.9 . . . C12
Crabtree Dr. . Pg.8,9 B11-12
Crane St. . . . Pg.3 . . . A10
Crescent Ln. . Pg.13 . . . G11
Crestwood Dr. Pg.8 . . . C11
Cypress Dr. . . Pg.13 . . . G10
Cypress St. . . Pg.13 . . . G11
Dale Ave. . . . Pg.9 . C-D12
Daniels Ct. . . Pg.8 . . . A11
Davis St. . . . Pg.8 . E10-11
Derbyshire Ave.
. . . . . . . . . Pg.9 . . . E11
Derbyshire Dr. Pg.9 . . A,B-G10
Derbyshire Ln. Pg.9 . . . C,F11
Donald Ave. . . Pg.9 . . . F12
Dorothy Ave. . Pg.8 . . . C11
Douglas Ave. . Pg.13
. . . . . . . . . . . . . B,D,E,G11
Dover Ct. . . . Pg.9 . . . C12
Dover Ln. . . . Pg.9 . . . C12
Drury Ln. . . . Pg.9 . B-E12
Dryden Ave. . . Pg.8 . C,E11
Dryden Ct. . . Pg.9 . . . B11
Dryden Ln. . . Pg.11 . . C11
Dryden Pl. . . Pg.8,13 A-F11
Dundee Rd. . . Pg.8 . . . A11
Dunhill Ct. . . Pg.8 . . . C10
Dunton Ave. . . Pg.8,13
. . . . . . . . . . . . . B,D,G-10
Dwyer Ave. . . Pg.8 . . . F10
Eastman Ave. . Pg.8 . . . F10
Eastman Ct. . . Pg.9 . . . E12
Eastman St. . . Pg.9 . . . E12
Fastwood Dr. . Pg.8 . . . C11
Elizabeth Dr. . Pg.8 . . . C10
Elizabeth Ln. . Pg.9 . . . B12
Elk Grove Rd. Pg.13 . . H10
Ellen Dr. . . . . Pg.9 . . . A12
Elm Ln. . . . . Pg.8 . . . E11
Elm St. . . . . Pg.9 . . . D9
Elmwood Cir. . Pg.9 . . . C12
Embers Ln. . . Pg.13 . . H11
Emerson St. . Pg.13 . . G10
Eton Dr. . . . . Pg.9 . . . B12
Euclid St. . . . Pg.8 . . . C11
Evanston Ave. Pg.8 . . . F10
Evergreen Ave. Pg.8,13 B-G11
Evergreen Terr. Pg.9 . . . C12
Fairview St. . . Pg.8 . . . D10
Falcon Dr. . . Pg.9 . . . C12
Fernandez Ave. Pg.8,13 C-G10
Fernandez Pl. . Pg.8 . . . F10
Fernandez St. . Pg.13 . . F10
Fleming Dr. . . Pg.9 . . . A12
Flentie Ln. . . . Pg.9 . . . A12
Flower Circle . Pg.9 . . . C12
Forrest Ave. . . Pg.9 . D-F12
Forrest Dr. . . Pg.8 . . . B12
Forrest Ln. . . Pg.8 . . . B12
Foster St. . . . Pg.13 . . G11
Foxdale Ln. . . Pg.3 . . . A11
Francis Ct. . . Pg.9 . . . F10
Frederick Ct. . Pg.9 . . . D11
Frederick St. . Pg.9 . . . D11
Fremont Ct. . . Pg.9 . . . E12
Fremont St. . . Pg.8 . E9-11
Frontenac St. . Pg.9 . . . G11
Garden Walk . Pg.8 . . . E12
George St. . . Pg.8 . E10-11
Gettysburg Dr. Pg.9 . . . C12
Gibbons Ave. . Pg.9 . D-F12
Goebbert Rd. . Pg.13 . . H11
Golf (Evanston-Elgin Rd.)
. . . . . . . . . Pg.13 . . . H10
Golf Terr. . . . Pg13 . . . H11
Greenbrier Ct. Pg.8 . . . C10
Greenwood Ave.
. . . . . . . . . Pg.8 . . . B9
Gregory St. . . Pg.8 . . . D10
Greshan Ct. . . Pg.9 . . . D12
Grove St. . . . Pg.8 . F9-12
Hackberry Dr. Pg.8 . . . A10
Haddow Ave. . Pg.8,13 B-G11
Haddow Ct. . . Pg.8 . . . B11
Happfield Dr. . Pg.3 . . . A11
Harold St. . . . Pg.8 . . . C10
Hartford Ct. . . Pg.9 . . . C12
Harvard Ave. . Pg.8,13

Harvard Rd. . Pg.13
. . . . . . . . . . . . . F9,B-G10
Haven Dr. . . . Pg.13 . . . G10
Haverhill Ct. . Pg.9 . . . D12
Hawkes St. . . Pg.3 . . . A10
Hawthorne St. Pg.8 . . . E9
Heather Ln. . . Pg.8 . . . B10
Henry St. . . . Pg.8 . . . B10
Hickory Ave. . Pg.8 . D-E11
Hickory Ln. . . Pg.8 . . . C11
Highland Ave. Pg.3,8
. . . . . . . . . . . . . A11,B-H10
Hintz Rd. . . . Pg.8 . B10-12
Hunter Dr. . . Pg.9 . . . C12
Huntington Dr. Pg.9 . . . C12
Huron St. . . . Pg.8 . . . B10
Illinois Ave. . . Pg.8 . . . C10
Illinois Dr. . . . Pg.8 . . . E9
Independence Ct.
. . . . . . . . . . . . . A11,B-H10
Ironwood Dr. . Pg.13 . . H11
Ivy Ln. . . . . Pg.13 . . . G11
Jade Ave. . . . Pg.8 . . . B9
James Ct. . . . Pg.8 . . . B10
Jane Ave. . . . Pg.9 . . . C12

Jennifer Ct. . . Pg.8 . . . D11
Jo Ln. . . . . Pg.8 . . . D9
Johanna Terr. Pg.8 . . . E9
Jonquil Cir. . . Pg.9 . . . C12
Jonquil Terr. . Pg.9 . . . C12
Jules St. . . . Pg.8 . . . D11
Juniper Ln. . . Pg.8 . . . C10
Kaspar Ave. . Pg.8,13 C-G10
Keating Dr. . . Pg.13 . . F10
Kelly St. . . . Pg.8 . . . B9
Kendal Ct. . . Pg.9 . . . D12
Kennicott Ave. Pg.3,8,13
. . . . . . . . . . . . . D-F9,G10
Kennicott Dr. . Pg.13 . . G10
Kensington (Foundry Rd.)
. . . . . . . . . Pg.9 . . . E12
Kerry-Brook Ct. Pg.8 . . B11
Kimber Ln. . . Pg.13 . . . J11
Kingsbury Dr. Pg.8 . . . B10
Kingsbury Dr. Pg.8 . . . B10
Kingsley Dr. . Pg.9 . . . A11
Kirchoff Rd. . . Pg.13 . . F10
Knob Hill Dr. . Pg.8 . . . C11
La Salle St. . . Pg.8 . . . C10
Ladd St. . . . Pg.8 . . . C10
Lafayette St. . Pg.8 . . . B10
Lake Arlington Dr.
. . . . . . . . . Pg.9 . . . C12
Lake Shore Cir. Pg.9 . . C12
Lake-Cook Rd. Pg.3 . . . A10
Lancaster . . . Pg.9 . . . C12
Lawrence Ln. . Pg.13 . . G11
Leona Terr. . . Pg.8 . . . F9
Lexington Dr. . Pg.8 . . . B9
Lilac Terr. . . . Pg.8 . . . C12
Lillian Ave. . . Pg.9 . . . C12
Lillian Ln. . . . Pg.9 . . . C12
Lincoln Ct. . . Pg.8 . . . D11
Lincoln Ln. . . Pg.8 . . . E11
Luther Dr. . . . Pg.8 . . . D10
Lynden Ln. . . Pg.8 . . . F11
Lynnwood Ave. Pg.8 . . . G10
Magnolia St. . Pg.13 . . G10
Mallard Dr. . . Pg.3 . . . A10
Maple Ln. . . . Pg.9 . . . C12
Maple St. . . . Pg.13 . . F10
Marion Rd. . . Pg.8 . . . D10
Marion St. . . Pg.8 . D10-11
Marshall Ct. . Pg.9 . . . E12
Marshall St. . Pg.8 . . . D11
Martin Ln. . . . Pg.9 . . . H10
Maude Ave. . . Pg.8 . . . E11
Mayfair Rd. . . Pg.8,9 F11-12
McKinley Ave. Pg.9,14 . F11
McKone Ct. . . Pg.13 . . G11
Meade Ln. . . . Pg.3 . . . A10
Meier Rd. . . . Pg.8 . . . H11
Michael Manor Ln.
. . . . . . . . . . . . . B9
Milida . . . . . Pg.8 . . . C11
Millbrook Ln. . Pg.3 . . . H10
Miller St. . . . Pg.8 . . . D11
Mitchell Ave. . Pg.8,13
. . . . . . . . . . . . . B,D-G10
Mitchell Dr. . . Pg.8 . C-G10
Mitchell St. . . Pg.3 . . . A11
Moorings Dr. . Pg.13 . . G11
Mueller St. . . Pg.8 . . . E10
Mulberry Ct. . Pg.8 . . . E10
Mulberry Dr. . Pg.9 . . . C12
New Wilke Rd. Pg.13 . F,G9
Newbury Pl. . . Pg.9 . . . F11
Newport Ct. . . Pg.3 . . . A10
Newport Ln. . . Pg.3 . . . A10
Nichols Rd. . . Pg.9 . . . A10
Norman St. . . Pg.8 . . . C10
Normandy Ct. . Pg.9 . . . C12
Northwest Hwy. Pg.8 . . . E11
Northwest Tollway
. . . . . . . . . Pg.13 . . . J11
Northwood Ct. Pg.9 . . . C12
Noyes St. . . . Pg.13 . . G10
Noyes St. W. . Pg.13 . . . G9
Oakton St. . . Pg.9 . . . D11
Oakwood Dr. . Pg.9 . . . C12
Old Arlington Hts. Rd.
. . . . . . . . . Pg.8 . . . A10
Old Barn Ln. . Pg.13 . . G11
Olive St. . . . Pg.8 . . . D10
Orchard Ct. . . Pg.13 . . . F9
Orchard St. . . Pg.13 . . F11
Orchid Ln. . . Pg.9 . . . C12
Oxford Ln. . . Pg.8 . . . C11
Page Rd. . . . Pg.9 . . . A12
Palatine Rd. . Pg.8 . . . C11
Park Pl. . . . . Pg.8 . . . B11
Park St. . . . . Pg.8 . F9-12
Parkview . . . Pg.13 . . G11
Partridge Ct. . Pg.8 . . . A11
Partridge Ln. . Pg.3 . . . A10
Patton Ave. . . Pg.8 . . C-F10
Patton Cir. . . Pg.8 . . . F10
Peachtree Dr. Pg.9 . . . B12
Peachtree Ln. Pg.9 . . . B12
Peartree Ln. . Pg.9 . . . E12
Pennsylvania Ct.
. . . . . . . . . . . . . H11
Pheasant Trail Ct.
. . . . . . . . . Pg.13 . . . J11
Pheasant Trail Dr.
. . . . . . . . . Pg.13 . . . J11
Pheasant Trail Ln.
. . . . . . . . . Pg.3 . . . A10

Phelps Ave. . . Pg.9 . . . B12
Pickwick Rd. . Pg.13 . . G10
Pin Oak Dr. . . Pg.3 . . . A11
Pine Ave. . . . Pg.8,13 B-G11
Pine Ct. . . . . Pg.8 . . . B11
Pinetree Dr. . . Pg.8 . . . C11
Plymouth Dr. . Pg.8 . . . C9
Plymouth St. . Pg.8 . . . B9
Portsmith Ln. . Pg.8 . . . C11
Prairie Ave. . . Pg.8 . . . C11
Princeton Ave. Pg.8,13
. . . . . . . . . . . . . D-F9,G10
Princeton Ct. . Pg.8 . . . G11
Prindle Ave. . . Pg.9 . . B-F12
Proctor Ct. . . Pg.3 . . . A11
Quail Ct. . . . Pg.3 . . . A10
Race Ave. . . . Pg.8 . . . D9
Radford Ct. . . Pg.9 . . . D12
Raleigh Ct. . . Pg.8 . . . B9
Raleigh St. . . Pg.8 . . . B9
Rammer Ave. . Pg.9 . . . F12
Rand Rd. . . . Pg.8,9
. . . . . . . . . . . . . B10,D12
Redwood Ln. . Pg.8 . . . C11
Regency Ct. . Pg.8 . . . E13
Regency Dr. . Pg.8 . . . E13
Reuter Dr. . . . Pg.8 . . . B12
Richmond St. . Pg.8 . . . C9
Ridge Ave. . . Pg.3,8
. . . . . . . . . . . . . A11,A-G10
Ridge Ct. . . . Pg.8 . . . A12
Ridge Dr. . . . Pg.13 . . H10
Ridge Pl. . . . Pg.8 . . . C10
Ridge Rd. . . . Pg.8 . . . B9
Roanoke Dr. . Pg.8 . . . B9
Robinhood Ln. Pg.9 . . . C12
Rockwell St. . Pg.13 . . F11
Rolling Ln. . . Pg.9 . . . C12
Roosevelt Ave. Pg.9,14 . F11
Rosehill Dr. . . Pg.9 . . . C12
Russell Ct. . . Pg.13 . . . G9
Russetwood Dr. Pg.9 . . . C12
Salem Ave. . . Pg.8,13 E-F10
Salem Blvd. . . Pg.8 . . . A10
Salem Dr. . . . Pg.3 . . . A10
Salem Pl. . . . Pg.13 . . G10
Schaefer Rd. . Pg.3 . . . A10
Scottsvale Ln. Pg.9 . . . E12
Seegers Rd. . Pg.13 . . H11
Shady Way . . Pg.13 . . H11
Shag Bark . . Pg.13 . . H11
Shenandoah Cir.
. . . . . . . . . Pg.8 . . . C10
Shenandoah Dr. Pg.8 . . . C10
Sherwood Rd. Pg.9 . . . C12
Shiloh Dr. . . . Pg.8 . . . B10
Shirra Ct. . . . Pg.8 . . . B9
Shure Dr. . . . Pg.8 . . . A9
Sigwalt St. . . Pg.8 . . . E9
Silver Lake Rd. Pg.9 . . . C13
Somerset Ave. Pg.8 . . . E10
Spruce Terr. . Pg.8 . . . C11
St. James Pl. . Pg.8 . . . B9
St. James St. . Pg.8 . E10-12
Stanford . . . . Pg.9 . . . B12
Stanton Ct. . . Pg.8 . . . C10
Stillwater Rd. (Pvt.)
. . . . . . . . . Pg.9 . . . C12
Stratford Dr. . Pg.9 . . . A12
Stratford Ln. . Pg.9 . . . A12
Stratford Rd. . Pg.9 . . . C12
Stuart Dr. . . . Pg.8 . . . B11
Suffield Ct. . . Pg.8 . . . A9
Suffield Dr. . . Pg.8,9 R10-12
Sunset Terr. . Pg.8,9 E10-12
Surrey Ln. . . Pg.13 . . G10
Surrey Park Ln. Pg.13 . . . G9
Surrey Ridge Dr.
. . . . . . . . . Pg.13 . . . G10
Talbot St. . . . Pg.8 . . . D11
Tanglewood Dr. Pg.8 . B10-11
Terramere Ave. Pg.3 . . . A11
Thomas Ave. . Pg.8 . . . D11
Thorntree Terr. Pg.8 . . . B11
Thurston Pl. . Pg.3 . . . A10
Tonne Dr. . . . Pg.13 . . G11
Towne Blvd. . . Pg.9 . . . C12
University Dr. . Pg.8 . . . A11
Vail Ave. . . . Pg.8,13 C-G10
Valley Ln. . . . Pg.8 . . . C11
Vargo Ln. . . . Pg.9 C11-12
Ventura Dr. . . Pg.3 . . . A11
Verde Ave. . . Pg.8 . . . C10
Verde Dr. . . . Pg.8 . . . C10
Viator Ct. . . . Pg.9 . . . D11
Victoria Ln. . . Pg.13 . . G10
Village Dr. . . . Pg.8 . . . D10
Vine St. . . . . Pg.8 . D9-10
Vista Rd. . . . Pg.8 . . . B11
Volz Dr., E. . . Pg.9 . . . A11
Volz Dr., W. . . Pg.9 . . . A11
Walden Ln. . . Pg.9 . . . C12
Walker Ln., E. Pg.9 . . . A11
Walker Ln., W. Pg.9 . . . A11
Walnut Ave. . . Pg.3,8,13
. . . . . . . . . . . . . A11,B-G10
Walnut Dr. . . Pg.8 . . . A12
Warwick Dr. . . Pg.9 . . . D12

Waterman Ave. Pg.8 . B,D-F12
Watling St. . . Pg.8 . . . D10
Waverly Ct. . . Pg.8 . . B9-10
Waverly Ln. . . Pg.8,9 D11-12
Waverly Pl. . . Pg.9 . . . B12
Waverly Rd. . . Pg.8 . . . A10
West Haven Dr. Pg.13 . . G10
Weston Dr. . . Pg.3 . . . A10
Wheeler St. . . Pg.8 . . . C11
White Oak St. . Pg.13 . . G10
Whitehall Dr. . Pg.3 . . . A10
Whiting Ln. . . Pg.3 . . . A10
Wilke Rd. . . . Pg.8 . . . A-D9
Williamsburg St.
. . . . . . . . . Pg.8 . . . C9
Willow Rd. . . . Pg.9 . . . D12
Willow St. . . . Pg.9 . . . D10
Wilshire Ave. . Pg.9 . . . C12
Wilshire Ln. . . Pg.9 . . A-E12
Wilshire Rd. . Pg.9 . . . F12
Wilson Pl. . . . Pg.9 . . . C11
Windgate Dr. . Pg.13 . . H11
Windsor Dr. . . Pg.9 . . A-F12
Wing St. . . . . Pg.8,9 E11-12
Winham Ct. . . Pg.8 . . . C10
Woodbury Dr. Pg.9 . . . C13
Woodford Pl. . Pg.9 . . . E11
Woodland Ln. Pg.9 . . . E11
Woodridge Ln. Pg.9 . . . E11
Woods Dr. . . . Pg.8 . . . B9
Yale Ave. . . . Pg.8 . . C-F9
Yale Ave. S. . Pg.13 . . . G9
Yale Ct. . . . . Pg.13 . . . F9
Yarmouth Ct. . Pg.9 . . . D12

### CEMETERIES

Arl. Hts. Wheeling Twp. Cem.
. . . . . . . . . Pg.9 . . . E12
Memory Gardens Cem.
. . . . . . . . . Pg.9 . . . E12
Rand Hill Cem. Pg.8 . . . B10
Shalom Mem. Pk. Cem.
. . . . . . . . . Pg.8 . . . A9
St. Peters Cem. Pg.9 . . . E12

### GOLF COURSES

Arlington Lakes Golf Club
. . . . . . . . . Pg.13 . . . G9
Nichol Knoll G.C.
. . . . . . . . . Pg.3 . . . Z10
Rolling Green C.C.
. . . . . . . . . Pg.9 . . . D12

### PARKS

Arlington Hts. Pk. Dist.
Admin. Ctr. . Pg.8 . . . E11
Banta Park . . Pg.9 . . . E12
Berbecker Park Pg.9 . . . E12
Brandenberry Park
. . . . . . . . . Pg.9 . . . D12
Camelot Connector Park
. . . . . . . . . Pg.8 . . . B11
Camelot Park Pg.8 . . . B11
Carefree Park Pg.13 . . G11
Carousel Park Pg.9 . . . B12
Carriage Walk Park
. . . . . . . . . Pg.8 . . . A11
Centennial Park Pg.8 . . . B11
Clock Tower Plaza Park
. . . . . . . . . Pg.8 . . . E11
Creekside Park Pg.9 . . . F10
Cronin Park . . Pg.8 . . . F10
Cypress Park . Pg.13 . . G11
Dryden Park . Pg.13 . . F11
Evergreen Park Pg.9 . . . C12
Falcon Park . . Pg.13 . . H11
Festival Park . Pg.8 . . . E10
Flentie Park . . Pg.9 . . . C12
Forest View Pk. & Racquet
Club . . . . Pg.13 . . . H11
Frontier Park . Pg.13 . . H11
Green Slopes Park
. . . . . . . . . Pg.9 . . . C12
Greenbrier Park Pg.8 . . . B10
Greens Park . . Pg.13 . . G11
Happiness Park Pg.8 . . . C11
Hasbrook Park Pg.13 . . G11
Heritage Park . Pg.13 . . G11
Heritage Tennis Club
. . . . . . . . . Pg.13 . . . G11
Hickory Meadows Park
. . . . . . . . . Pg.8 . . . B11
Kingsbridge Arboretum
. . . . . . . . . Pg.13 . . . H10
Klehm Park . . Pg.9 . . . C12
Lake Arlington Pg.9 . . . C12
Lake Terramere Park
. . . . . . . . . Pg.3 . . . A11
Memorial Park Pg.8 . . . E10
Methodist Park Pg.9 . . . F12
North School Park
. . . . . . . . . Pg.8 . . . E11
Olympic Park . Pg.9 . . . C12
Patriot Park . . Pg.9 . . . C12
Pioneer Park . Pg.9 . . . F10
Prairie Park . . Pg.13 . . G11
Rand Connector Park
. . . . . . . . . Pg.9 . . . C12
Rand-Berkley Playlot
. . . . . . . . . Pg.8 . . . B10
Raven Park . . Pg.9 . . . B12
Recreation Park Pg.8 . . . E11
Rose Garden Park
. . . . . . . . . Pg.9 . . . F12

Sunset Meadows Park
. . . . . . . . . Pg.13 . . . F9
Victory Park . . Pg.13 . . G10
Virginia Terr. Park
. . . . . . . . . Pg.8 . . . D9
Volz Park . . . Pg.8 . . . E10
Westgate Park Pg.8 . . . E9
Wildwood Park Pg.8 . . . B11
Willow Park . . Pg.8 . . . C11

### SCHOOLS

Academy of Christian
Liberty . . . Pg.8 . . . E10
Berkeley Sch. Pg.8 . . . B10
Dryden Sch. . Pg.13 . . F11
Greenbrier Sch. Pg.8 . . . B10
Ivy Hill Sch. . . Pg.8 . . . C11
John Hersey H.S.
. . . . . . . . . Pg.9 . . . C12
Juliette Low Sch.
. . . . . . . . . Pg.13 . . . G10
Kensington Sch.
. . . . . . . . . Pg.9 . . . F12
Miner Jr. H.S. Pg.8 . . . D11
Olive-Mary Stitt Sch.
. . . . . . . . . Pg.8 . . . D11
Our Lady of Wayside Cath.
Sch. . . . . Pg.8 . . . F10
Patton Sch. . . Pg.8 . . . F10
Poe Sch. . . . Pg.8 . . . B10
Rand Campus Pg.8 . . . B11
Ridge Sch. . . Pg.13 . . G10
Riley Sch. . . . Pg.9 . . . F12
Sch. Dist. 25 Admin. Bldg.
. . . . . . . . . Pg.8 . . . C11
Sch. Dist. 59 Admin. Bldg.
. . . . . . . . . Pg.13 . . . H11
South Jr. H.S. Pg.8 . . . F10
St. Edna's Cath. Sch.
. . . . . . . . . Pg.8 . . . C10
St. James Cath. Jr. H.S.
. . . . . . . . . Pg.8 . . . D11
St. James Cath. Sch.
. . . . . . . . . Pg.8 . . . D11
St. Peter's Luth. Sch.
. . . . . . . . . Pg.8 . . . D10
St. Viator Cath. H.S.
. . . . . . . . . Pg.8 . . . D10
Thomas Middle Sch.
. . . . . . . . . Pg.8 . . . B10
Twin Groves Jr. H.S.
. . . . . . . . . Pg.8 . . . B10
Westgate Sch. Pg.8 . . . E10
Windsor Sch. Pg.8 . . . F10

### SHOPPING CENTERS

All-American Plaza
. . . . . . . . . Pg.8 . . . C11
Arlin-Golf S.C. Pg.13 . . H11
Arlington Market
. . . . . . . . . Pg.8 . . . E11
Arlington Park Plaza
. . . . . . . . . Pg.13 . . . H10
Arlington Promenade
. . . . . . . . . Pg.8 . . . B8
Arlington Square S.C.
. . . . . . . . . Pg.13 . . . H10
Brook Run S.C. Pg.8 . . . B11
Central Plaza . Pg.13 . . . G9
Central/Busse S.C.
. . . . . . . . . Pg.13 . . . G12
Elms S.C. . . . Pg.8 . . . E10
Huntington Sq. Pg.8 . . . B10
Internstional Plaza
. . . . . . . . . Pg.13 . . . H11
Mansions S.C. Pg.13 . . H11
Northpoint S.C. Pg.8 . . . E11
Pal-Win Plaza Pg.9 . . . C12
Plaza Del Grato Pg.13 . . . G9
Ridge Plaza . . Pg.3 . . . A10
Southpoint S.C. Pg.8 . . . C11
Surrey Ridge S.C.
. . . . . . . . . Pg.13 . . . H10
Terramere S.C. Pg.3 . . . A11
The Annex of Arlington
. . . . . . . . . Pg.8 . . . C10
Town & Country Mall
. . . . . . . . . Pg.8 . . . C11
Westgate S.C. Pg.8 . . . E9
Yaohan Plaza Pg.13 . . . H11

### MISCELLANEOUS

Arlington International
Racecourse . Pg.8 . . . E8
Arlington Mem. Library
. . . . . . . . . Pg.8 . . . E11
Church Creek Retirement
Center . . . Pg.9 . . . C12
Commerce Point Industrial
Park . . . . Pg.3 . . . Z10
Fire Dept. . . . Pg.8 . . . E11
Lutheran Home for the Aged
. . . . . . . . . Pg.8 . . . D10
Manor Care Nursing Home
. . . . . . . . . Pg.13 . . . G10
Moorings Retirement Center
. . . . . . . . . Pg.13 . . . G11
Municipal Bldg. Pg.8 . . . E10
Northwest Comm. Hosp.
. . . . . . . . . Pg.13 . . . F10
Post Office . . Pg.8 . . . E10
Public Works . Pg.8 . . . E10

Railroad Station Pg.8 . . . E10
U.S. Military Reservation
. . . . . . . . . Pg.13 . . . G10
Viatorian Novitiate
. . . . . . . . . Pg.9 . . . D11
Village of Arlington Heights
Senior Center Pg.13 . . . G9
Wheeling Township Hall
. . . . . . . . . Pg.8 . . . C11

## BARRINGTON

Page 1
(Portions within Lake County,
for additional listings, see
Sections 5 and 6)

### STREETS

Applebee St. . . . . . . . . . X4
Balmoral St. . . . . . . . . . A5
Barrington Pt. . . . . . . . . A4
Bellingham St. . . . . . . . . A5
Bent Bridge Ln. . . . . . . . X4
Berry Rd. . . . . . . . . . . . X4
Beverly Rd. . . . . . . . . . . X5
Birch . . . . . . . . . . . . . . A4
Birchwood Dr. . . . . . . . . A4
Braeside Pl. . . . . . . . . . A4
Bristol Dr. . . . . . . . . . . A4
Bryant Ave. . . . . . . . . . X4
Burr Oak Ln. . . . . . . . . . X5
Carl Ave. . . . . . . . . . . . X4
Castle Ct. . . . . . . . . . . . A4
Center Ct. . . . . . . . . . . . X5
Chateaux Bourne . . . . . . A5
Chestnut St. . . . . . . . . . X4
Church Hill Ct. . . . . . . . . X4
Coldspring Rd. . . . . . . . . X5
Commonwealth Ct. . . . . . A4
Concord Ct. . . . . . . . . . A4
Concord Ln. . . . . . . . . . A4
Concord Pl. . . . . . . . . . . A4
Cook St. . . . . . . . . . . A,X4
Coolidge Ave. . . . . . . . . X4
Cornell Ave. . . . . . . . . . B4
County Dr. . . . . . . . . . . A4
Covington . . . . . . . . . . . A4
Cumnor Ave. . . . . . . . . . X3
Division St. . . . . . . . . . . A4
Drury Ln. . . . . . . . . . . . A4
Dundee Ave. . . . . . . . . . A4
Dundee Rd. . . . . . . . . . . B4
Dunstan Ave. . . . . . . . . . A4
Ela St. . . . . . . . . . . . . . X4
Elm Ave. . . . . . . . . . . . X4
Elm Park Ave. . . . . . . . . X4
Exmoor Ave. . . . . . . . . . X4
Fairfax Ct. . . . . . . . . . . . X4
Forest Dr. . . . . . . . . . . . A3
Fox Hunt Trail . . . . . . . . X5
Foxglove Ln. . . . . . . . . . X5
Franklin St. . . . . . . . . . . A4
Bartield St. . . . . . . . . . . X4
George St. . . . . . . . . . A,B4
George Towne Ln. . . . . . X4
Glendale Ave. . . . . . . . A,X4
Grant St. . . . . . . . . . . . X4
Grove Ave. . . . . . . . . . A,B4
Hager Ave. . . . . . . . . . . A3
Harriet Ln. . . . . . . . . . . A4
Harrison St. . . . . . . . . . X4
Hart Rd. . . . . . . . . . . . . X3
Hawthorne Rd. . . . . . . . . A4
Heath Ct. . . . . . . . . . . A,C5
Highland Ave. . . . . . . . . A4
Highland Ct. . . . . . . . . . A4
Hillcrest Ave. . . . . . . . . . A4
Hillside Ave. . . . . . . . . . A4
Hillside Ave. Ext. . . . . . . A3
Hilltop Ave. . . . . . . . . . . X5
Home Ave. . . . . . . . . . . X3
Hough St. . . . . . . . . . . A,X4
Illinois St. . . . . . . . . . . . A4
Indian Way . . . . . . . . . . X5
James St. . . . . . . . . . . . X4
June Terr. . . . . . . . . . . . A4
Kainer Ave. . . . . . . . . . . A4
Kings Row . . . . . . . . . . . A5
Lageshulte St. . . . . . . . . A3
Lake Shore Ct. . . . . . . . . X5
Lake Shore Dr. . . . . . . . . X5
Lake Shore Dr., S. . . . . . X5
Lake St. . . . . . . . . . . . . X4
Lake Zurich Rd. . . . . . . . X4
Lakeview Ln. . . . . . . . . . A1
Laverne St. . . . . . . . . . . X3
Liberty St. . . . . . . . . . . . X4
Lill St. . . . . . . . . . . . . . X4
Lincoln Ave. . . . . . . . . . A4
Linden Ave. . . . . . . . . . . A4
Lions Pkwy. . . . . . . . . . . X4
Magnolia Rd. . . . . . . . . . X4
Main St. . . . . . . . . . . . A3,4
Maple . . . . . . . . . . . . . . A4
Marlborough Rd. . . . . . . . A4
Martin Ct. . . . . . . . . . . . A4
Meadow Ln. . . . . . . . . . . A4
Meadow Way . . . . . . . . . X5
Monument Ave. . . . . . . . . A4
New Bridge Ct. . . . . . . . . X4
New Hart Rd. . . . . . . . . . A3
North Ave. . . . . . . . . . . . X4
North St. . . . . . . . . . . . . X3
Northwest Hwy. . . . . . . . X3

52

BARRINGTON · · · · · · · · · · · · · · · · · · · · · · · · · · · · · · · · · · · · · · · · · · · · · · · · · · · · · · · · · BUFFALO GROVE

Oak Rd. . . . . . . . . . . . . . X4
Oak Ridge Cir. . . . . . . . . A5
Oak Ridge Rd. . . . . . . . . A5
Old Creek Ct. . . . . . . . . . X4
Old Mill Ct. . . . . . . . . . . . A5
Old Mill Rd. . . . . . . . . . . A5
Orchard Dr. . . . . . . . . . . A3
Oxbow Ln. . . . . . . . . . . . X5
Park Ave. . . . . . . . . . . . . A4
Park Barrington Dr. . . . . A2
Park Barrington Way . . . A2
Park Ln. . . . . . . . . . . . . . X4
Park N. . . . . . . . . . . . . . . X4
Paul Cir. . . . . . . . . . . . . . X4
Pine . . . . . . . . . . . . . . . . X4
Ponderosa Ct. . . . . . . . . X5
Prairie Ave. . . . . . . . . . . A4
Prospect Ave. . . . . . . . . X4
Providence Rd. . . . . . . . X4
Pump St. . . . . . . . . . . . . X4
Queens Cove . . . . . . . . . X4
Railroad St. . . . . . . . . . . X4
Raymond Ave. . . . . . . . . X3
Red Barn Ln. . . . . . . . . . A5
Redwood Ct. . . . . . . . . . X4
Roslyn Rd. . . . . . . . . . . . X3
Roslyn Rd., W. . . . . . . . X3
Russell St. . . . . . . . . . . A3-4
Scott Ave. . . . . . . . . . . . X3
Shady Ln. . . . . . . . . . . . . X5
Sharon Dr. . . . . . . . . . . . X5
Shore Ct., N. & S. . . . . . X5
Shorley Dr. . . . . . . . . . . . A4
Skyline Dr. . . . . . . . . . . . A4
South St. . . . . . . . . . . . . A5
Spring St. . . . . . . . . . . . . X5
Spruce . . . . . . . . . . . . . . A4
Station St. . . . . . . . . . . . A4
Stillwater Ln. . . . . . . . . . A4
Sturtz St. . . . . . . . . . . . . A4
Summit St. . . . . . . . . . . . A4
Sunny Ln. . . . . . . . . . . . . X4
Sunny Rd. . . . . . . . . . . . A3
Sunset Rd. . . . . . . . . . . . A3
Surrey Ln. . . . . . . . . . . . X4
Sycamore . . . . . . . . . . . X4
Tall Trees Cir. . . . . . . . . X5
Tall Trees Dr. . . . . . . . . . X5
The Point . . . . . . . . . . . . X4
Tower Ln. . . . . . . . . . . . . X4
Tower Rd. . . . . . . . . . . . . A4
Tudor Dr. . . . . . . . . . . . . A5
Valencia Ave. . . . . . . . . X4
Valley Ct., N. . . . . . . . . . X5
Valley Rd. . . . . . . . . . . . X5
Valley Rd., N. . . . . . . . . X5
Vernon . . . . . . . . . . . . . . X4
Victoria Ave. . . . . . . . . . X4
Walnut . . . . . . . . . . . . . . A4
Walton St. . . . . . . . . . . . A4
Warwick Ave. . . . . . . . . A4
Washington St. . . . . . . . X4
Waverly Rd. . . . . . . . . . . A4
Werton Rd., W. . . . . . . . X3
Wesley . . . . . . . . . . . . . . X3
Western Ave. . . . . . . . . . X3
Westwood Dr. . . . . . . . . A3
White Oak Ct. . . . . . . . . X5
Whitney Dr. . . . . . . . . . . X4
Willow . . . . . . . . . . . . . . X4
Wisconsin Ave. . . . . . . . A5
Woodside Ln. . . . . . . . . A5
Wool St. . . . . . . . . . . . . . A4
Wyngate Dr. . . . . . . . . . A5
13th St. . . . . . . . . . . . . . X3

**CEMETERIES**
Evergreen Cemetery . . . . A3
St. Anne Cemetery . . . . . A4

**PARKS**
Bosworth Field . . . . . . . . X4
Hampton Park . . . . . . . . X4
Langendorf Park (Northside
  Park) . . . . . . . . . . . . . X4
Northside Park . . . . . . . . X4
Playground . . . . . . . . . . . X4
Ron Beese Park . . . . . . . X4
Williamsburg Park . . . . . X4

**SCHOOLS**
Barrington H.S. . . . . . . . X3
Grove Sch. . . . . . . . . . . . A4
Hough Sch. . . . . . . . . . . A4
Middle Sch. . . . . . . . . . . X5
Roslyn Sch. . . . . . . . . . . X4
St. Ann Sch. . . . . . . . . . X4

**MISCELLANEOUS**
Barrington Camp Ground . A4
Library . . . . . . . . . . . . . . A4
Village Hall . . . . . . . . . . A4

**BARRINGTON
HILLS**
Page 1,6
(Portions within Lake and Kane
County, for additional listings,
see Sections 5 and 6)
**STREETS**
Dundee Ave. . . . Pg.6 . . . A1
Dundee Ln. . . . Pg.1 . . . . A4
Hart Rd. . . . Pg.6 . . . . . . X3
Hawthorne Pg.1 . . . . . . . A3

Lakeview Ln. . Pg.6 . . . . A1
Otis Rd. . . . . Pg.1 . . . . . A3
Sara Ln. . . . Pg.6 . . . . . A1

**BARRINGTON
TOWNSHIP**
Pages 1,6
(For additional listings,
see Section 5)
**STREETS**
Algonquin Rd. Pg.6 . . . . D1
Barrington Rd. Pg.6 . . . . A1
Cook St. . . . . Pg.1 . . . . . A4
Division St. . . . Pg.1 . . . . A4
George St. . . . Pg.1 . . . . A4
Grove Ave. . . . Pg.1 . . . . A4
Harvard Ave. . Pg.1 . . . . A4
Palatine Rd. . Pg.6 . . . C1,2
Princeton Ave. Pg.1 . . . . A4
Summit Ave. . . Pg.1 . . . . A4
Willowmere Dr. Pg.6 . . . . D1
Yale Ave. . . . Pg.1 . . . . . A4

**SCHOOLS**
Willow Creek Comm. Sch.
. . . . . . . . . . . Pg.6 . . . . D2

**BLOOM
TOWNSHIP**
Pages 43-45,48-50
**STREETS**
Alice Ave. . . . Pg.50 . . . V30
Arnett St. . . . Pg.49 . . . T27
Ashland Ave. . Pg.48 . . . W22
Audry . . . . . . Pg.50 . . . U30
Baltimore Ave. Pg.50 . . . T29
Batrack . . . . . Pg.50 . . . T29
Benjamin Ct. . Pg.50 . . . U29
Bensley Ave. . Pg.50 . . . S28
Blackstone Ave. Pg.50 . . S27
Brandon Ave. . Pg.50 . . . T29
Bridge . . . . . . Pg.50 . . . U30
Brown St. . . . Pg.49 . . . U29
Burley Ave. . . Pg.49 . . . T29
Burnham Ave. Pg.45,50 W30
Butler St. . . . Pg.49 . . . T27
Calhoun Ave. . Pg.50 . . . U28
Calumet Expy. Pg.50 . . . W27
Candlelight . . Pg.50 . . . U28
Carondellet Ave.

Carriage . . . . Pg.50 . . . U28
Coales St. . . . Pg.49 . . . R24
Collom St. . . . Pg.49 . . . T27
Columbia Ave. Pg.49 . . . T27
Commercial Ave.

Coolidge St. . . Pg.43 . . . R24
Cottage Grove Ave.

. . . . . . . . . . Pg.44,49 V26
Daniel Ct. . . . Pg.50 . . . T29
Daren Dr. . . . Pg.50 . . . U30
David Ct. . . . Pg.50 . . . T29
Division St. . . Pg.42 . . . T22
Douglas Ct. . . Pg.50 . . . T29
Dutra Ave. . . . Pg.48 . . . V24
East End . . . . Pg.49 . . . T29
Eighth St. . . . Pg.50 . . . T27
Elizabeth . . . Pg.50 . . . U30
Ellen Dr. . . . . Pg.50 . . . U29
Ellis St. . . . . Pg.49 . . . T27
Escanaba Ave. Pg.50 . . . T29
Euclid St. . . . Pg.50 . . . W30
Exchange Ave. Pg.50 . . . T29
Forest Ln. . . . Pg.44 . . . Q27
Frederick Ct. . Pg.50 . . . T29
Gail Ct. . . . . Pg.50 . . . T29
Gardner Ave. . Pg.48 . . . T22
Glenwood Dyer Rd.
. . . . . . . . . . Pg.50 . . . R26
Glenwood-Lansing Rd.
. . . . . . . . Pg.44,45 R27
Halsted . . . . . Pg.43 . . . R24
Hammond Ln. Pg.49 . . . T27
Hillcrest Ave. . Pg.50 . . . T29
Holbrook Rd. . Pg.43 . . . R24
Houston Ave. . Pg.50 . . . T29
Howard Ct. . . Pg.50 . . . U29
Hutchinson Ave.

Indiana Ave. . Pg.48 . . . U25
Interurban Ave. Pg.43 . . . R24
Jacob Ct. . . . Pg.50 . . . T29
James Ave. . . Pg.50 . . . V30
Jennifer Dr. . . Pg.50 . . . U30
Joe Orr Rd. . . Pg.49 . . . S27
Judith Ct. . . . Pg.50 . . . T29
Katz Corner Rd. Pg.50 . . V29
Langston St. . Pg.49 . . . T27
Lincoln Hwy. . Pg.50 . . . W29
Long Ave. . . . Pg.50 . . . W29
Marion Ct. . . . Pg.49 . . . Q25
Martin Ct. . . . Pg.50 . . . T29
Michelle . . . . Pg.50 . . . U30
Michigan Ave. Pg.50 . . . W25
Muskegon Ave. Pg.50 . . . T29
Park . . . . . . . Pg.50 . . . U27
Park Ln. . . . . Pg.50 . . . T29
Parkside Ave. Pg.50 . . . T29
Prairie Ave. . . Pg.50 . . . T29
Pullman St. . . Pg.49 . . . U27

Rhodes . . . . . Pg.44 . . . R26
Sauk Trail Rd. Pg.49 . . . W22
St. Lawrence Pg.44 . . . R26
State St. . . . . Pg.50 . . . W22
Steger Rd. . . . Pg.49 . . . W22
Stirling Ave. . Pg.48 . . . T22
Stoney Island Ave.

. . . . . . . . . . . . Pg.44,50
. . . . . . . . . . . . . . . . S,U27
Stuart Ct. . . . Pg.50 . . . T29
Summit Dr. . . Pg.49 . . . U27
Sunset Ln. . . Pg.50 . . . V30
Torrence Ave. Pg.50 . . . W29
Travers Ave. . Pg.48 . . . T22
Valerie Dr. . . Pg.50 . . . U30
Vincinnes Rd. Pg.43 . . . Q25
Vollmer Rd. . . Pg.48 . . . S20
Vollmer St. . . Pg.50 . . . T22
Wentworth Ave. Pg.45,49

. . . . . . . . . . . . . . R30,W25
Western Ave. . Pg.48 . . . T29
Woodlawn Ave. Pg.49 . . . W27
10th St. . . . . Pg.27 . . . T27
13th St. . . . . Pg.49 . . . T25
14th St. . . . . Pg.49 . . . U25
16th St. . . . . Pg.49 . . . U25
21st St. . . . . Pg.50 . . . V30
22nd St. . . . Pg.49,50 V30
26th St. . . . . Pg.48 . . . V22
28th St. . . . . Pg.49 . . . V24
30th St. . . . . Pg.50 . . . W24
32nd St. . . . . Pg.49 . . . W25
34th St. . . . . Pg.49 . . . W25
184th St. . . . Pg.43,45 Q25
186th St. . . . Pg.44 . . . Q28
193rd Pl. . . . Pg.43 . . . R24
194th St. . . Pg.49,50 R24
194th St. . . . Pg.44 . . . R24
195th St. . . . Pg.49 . . . R24
196th St. . . . Pg.49 . . . R24
205th St. . . . Pg.48 . . . T22
207th St. . . Pg.48,50 T22
209th St. . . . Pg.48 . . . T22
211th St. . . . Pg.49 . . . U27
212th St. . . . Pg.49 . . . U27
213th St. . . . Pg.49 . . . U27
219th St. . . . Pg.50 . . . V30
223rd St. . . . Pg.50 . . . V29

**CEMETERIES**
Assumption Cemetery
. . . . . . . . . . Pg.49 . . . S26
Calvery Cemetery
. . . . . . . . . . Pg.48 . . . W22
Mt. Glenwood Cemetery
. . . . . . . . . . Pg.44 . . . Q25

**FOREST PRESERVES**
Jurgensen Woods

Lansing Woods Pg.44 . . . Q29
North Creek Meadows
. . . . . . . . . . Pg.44 . . . Q28
Plum Creek F.P. Pg.50 . . W29
Sauk Trail Woods
. . . . . . . . . . Pg.48 . . . V22

**GOLF COURSES**
Glenwood Country Club
. . . . . . . . . . Pg.49 . . . R26
Idlewild Country Club
. . . . . . . . . . Pg.43 . . . R23

**SCHOOLS**
Katz Corner Sch.
. . . . . . . . . . Pg.50 . . . V30
Sandridge Sch. Pg.50 . . . T30

**MISCELLANEOUS**
Girl Scout Camp
. . . . . . . . . . Pg.44 . . . Q26

**BREMEN
TOWNSHIP**
Pages 38,41,42
(For additional listings,
see Section 1)
**STREETS**
Anne Ct. . . . . Pg.38 . . . K18
Artesian Ave. Pg.41 . . . M21
Austin Blvd. . Pg.41 . . . N16
Bachelor Grove Rd.

. . . . . . . . . . Pg.38 . . . J15
Beverly Ave. . Pg.41 . . . N16
Central Ave. . Pg.38,41 K17
Elmdale . . . . Pg.42 . . . M21
Fairway Terr. . Pg.42 . . . P19
Forest Ave. . . Pg.41 . . . O18
Fulton Terr. . . Pg.41 . . . N16
Gaynelle Rd. . Pg.41 . . . N16
George Brennan Hwy.

. . . . . . . . . . Pg.41 . . . O17
Golf Ct. . . . . Pg.38 . . . K18
Harlem Ave. . Pg.40 . . . P15
Highland Ave. Pg.41 . . . P16
Jean Ct. . . . . Pg.38 . . . K18
Jody Ln. . . . . Pg.41 . . . N16
Justamere Rd. Pg.38 . . . K15
Kedvale . . . . Pg.41 . . . N19
Kenneth Ave. Pg.38 . . . L18
Kilbourne Ave. Pg.41 . . . N16
Kilpatrick . . . Pg.41 . . . N18
Kimberly Ln. . Pg.41 . . . N16
LaCrosse . . . Pg.38 . . . K18
Lamon Ave. . Pg.38 . . . J18

Laramie Ave. . Pg.41 . . J,O17
Lavergne Ave. Pg.38,41
. . . . . . . . . . . . . . . J,O,P18
Lawndale Ave., S.
. . . . . . . . . . Pg.42 . . . P20
Leclaire Ave. . Pg.38,41 J17
Leslie Ann Dr. Pg.41 . . . N16
Linder Ave. . . Pg.38,41 K17
Lockwood . . . Pg.41 . . . O17
Long Ave. . . . Pg.38 . . . J17
Luna Ave. . . . Pg.38 . . . K17
Major Ave. . . Pg.38 . . . K17
Mark Ln. . . . . Pg.41 . . . N16
Mayfield Ave. Pg.38 . . . K16
Menard Ave. . Pg.38 . . . K16
Midlothian Turnpike
. . . . . . . . . . Pg.38 . . . J16
New England Ave.

. . . . . . . . . . Pg.41 . . . M15
Oak Forest Ave. Pg.41 . . N16
Oak Park Ave. Pg.41 . . . P15
Parkside Ave. Pg.41 . . . O17
Patricia Ave. . Pg.41 . . . N16
Poplar . . . . . Pg.42 . . . M21
Ridgeland Ave. Pg.38,41 K16
Sayre Ave. S. Pg.41 . . M,P15
Springfield Ave. Pg.42 . . . P19
Thorndale . . . Pg.42 . . . M21
Waverly Ave. . Pg.41 . . . L18
62nd Ave. . . . Pg.41 . . . P16
135th . . . . . . Pg.38 . . . I17
136th Pl. . . . Pg.38 . . . J17
137th St. . . . Pg.38 . . . J15
139th St. . . . Pg.38 . . . J17
141st St. . . . Pg.38 . . . J18
142nd St. . . . Pg.38 . . . J18
143rd . . . . . . Pg.38 . . . K20
143rd St. . . . Pg.38 . . . J18
147th St. . . . Pg.38 . . . J18
148th St. . . . Pg.38 . . J,K18
149th St. . . . Pg.38 . . . J18
151st St. . . . Pg.38 . . . L21
152nd St. . . . Pg.38 . . . L18
153rd St. . . . Pg.40 . . . L15
157th Ave. . . Pg.41 . . . M15
157th Pl. . . . Pg.41 . . P,M15
159th Ct. . . . Pg.42 . . . M21
162nd St. . . . Pg.42 . . . N21
163rd St. . . . Pg.42 . . . N19
166th St. . . . Pg.41 . . . N16
167th St. . . . Pg.41 . . N16,18
171st St. . . . Pg.41 . . O17,18
173rd St. . . . Pg.41 . . O17,18
174th St. . . . Pg.41 . . . O17
175th St. . . . Pg.41 . . . O17
177th St. . . . Pg.41

. . . . . . . . . . . O17,P16,20
178th St. . . . Pg.41 . . . P15
179th St. . . . Pg.41,42

. . . . . . . . . . . . P15,16,19
180th St. . . . Pg.41 . . . P15
181st St. . . . Pg.41 . . . P15
182nd St. . . . Pg.41 . . . P15
183rd St. . . . Pg.41 P15,16

**CEMETERIES**
Bachelor Grove Cemetery
. . . . . . . . . . Pg.38 . . . K15
County Cemetery
. . . . . . . . . . Pg.42 . . . M19
Lutheran Cemetery
. . . . . . . . . . Pg.41 . . . M15
St. Gabriel Cemetery
. . . . . . . . . . Pg.41 . . . N18

**FOREST PRESERVES**
Bachelor Grove Pg.38 . . . J15
Burr Oak Woods

. . . . . . . . . . Pg.38 . . . J15
Rubio Woods Pg.38 . . . J16
Tinley Creek Woods

. . . . . . . . . . Pg.38 . . . J15
Yankee Woods Pg.41 . . . O16

**GOLF COURSES**
Midlothian C.C. Pg.38 . . . K17

**SCHOOLS**
Kimberly Heights Sch.
. . . . . . . . . . Pg.41 . . . N16
Orchard Hill Sch.
. . . . . . . . . . Pg.41 . . . N18
Trinity Sch. . . Pg.41 . . . M15

**MISCELLANEOUS**
Camp Falcon . Pg.38 . . . K15
Camp Sullivan Pg.38 . . . K15
Oak Forest Infirmary

. . . . . . . . . . Pg.41 . . . M18
South Cook Girl Scouts of
America . . . Pg.41 . . . P18
Villa Santa Maria

. . . . . . . . . . Pg.41 . . . L15
Walter Fierke Educ. Center

**BUFFALO GROVE**
Pages 3,4,8,9
(Portions within Lake County, for
additional lsitings,
see Section 6)
**STREETS**
Aberdeen Ln. . Pg.4 . . . X12
Acacia Ct., N. Pg.4 . . . V11
Acacia Ct., S. Pg.4 . . . V11

Acacia Terr. . . Pg.4 . . . V11
Acorn Ct. . . . Pg.4 . . . X12
Acorn Pl. . . . Pg.4 . . . V12
Alden Ln. . . . Pg.3 . . . X11
Amherst Ct. . . Pg.3 . . . X11
Anderson Ln. . Pg.3 . . . X11
Anthony Ct. . . Pg.9 . . . A12
Anthony Rd. . . Pg.9 . . . B12
Arbor Ct. . . . Pg.4 . . . X12
Arbor Gate Ln. Pg.9 . . . A11
Arlington Hts. Rd.

. . . . . . . . . . Pg.3 . . . A-X11
Armstrong Dr. Pg.4 . . . X12
Asbury Dr. . . . Pg.4 . . . W13
Ashford Ct. . . Pg.4 . . . X11
Aspen Ct. . . . Pg.3 . . . X11
Aspen Dr. . . . Pg.3 . . . X11
Aspen Pl. . . . Pg.3 . . . X11
Auburn Ln. . . Pg.4 . . . X11
Autumn Ct. . . Pg.4 . . . X12
Banberry . . . Pg.4 . . . W11
Banyon Tree Ln.

. . . . . . . . . . Pg.4 . . . V12
Barclay Blvd. . Pg.4 . . . W13
Beacon Ct. . . Pg.9 . . . B11
Bedford Ct. . . Pg.3 . . . X10
Beechwood Ct., E.

. . . . . . . . . . Pg.4 . . . A11
Beechwood Ct., W.

. . . . . . . . . . Pg.3 . . . A11
Beechwood Rd. Pg.3 . . . A11
Bel Aire Ct. . . Pg.3 . . . A11
Bel Aire Dr. . . Pg.3 . . . A11
Bellmont Ct. . Pg.4 . . . W30
Belmar Ct. . . Pg.3 . . . X11
Belmar Ln. . . Pg.3 . . . X11
Bentley Pl. . . Pg.3 . . . X12
Berkley Ct. . . Pg.4 . . . W12
Bernard Ct., W. Pg.3 . . . A11
Bernard Dr. . . Pg.4 . . A11-12
Betty Dr. . . . . Pg.4 . . . X12
Birchwood Ct. Pg.3 . . . A12
Birchwood Ln. Pg.4 . . . V12
Blackthorn Dr. Pg.3 . . . V12
Blaho Ct. . . . Pg.4 . . . A12
Blue Ash Ct. . Pg.3 . . . X12
Bourdeaux Ct., E. & W.

. . . . . . . . . . Pg.4 . . . W11
Boxwood Ln. . Pg.3 . . . B11
Brandywyn Ct. Pg.4 . . . W12
Brandywyn Ln. Pg.4 . . . W12
Brentwood Terr.

. . . . . . . . . . Pg.4 . . . W11
Bristol Ln. . . . Pg.3 . . . X11
Brucewood Ct. Pg.4 . . . A12
Buckingham Ln.

. . . . . . . . . . Pg.4 . . . X12
Buckthorn Ct. Pg.4 . . . X13
Buckthorn Terr. Pg.4 . . . X12
Buffalo Grove Rd.

. . . . . . . . . . Pg.4 . . . X12
Bunescu Ln. . Pg.3 . . . X11
Burgess Ct. . . Pg.3 . . . X11
Burnt Ember Ct.

. . . . . . . . . . Pg.3 . . . X11
Burnt Ember Ln.

. . . . . . . . . . Pg.3 . . . X11
Busch Pkwy. . Pg.4 . . . X13
Busch Rd. . . . Pg.4 . . . X12
Cambridge Dr. Pg.9 . . . B12
Camden Ct. . . Pg.3 . . . X11
Cameron Way Pg.4 . . . A11
Canterbury Ln. Pg.4 . . . X12
Caren Ct. . . . Pg.4 . . . W12
Caren Dr. . . . Pg.4 . . . W12
Carlton Pl. . . Pg.3 . . . X11
Carman Dr. . . Pg.4 . . . X13
Carriage Way Dr.

Cary Ln. . . . . Pg.4 . . . X11
Castlewood Ln. Pg.4 . . . X11
Cedar St. . . . Pg.4 . . . X11
Chapel Oaks Dr. Pg.3 . . . V12
Charles Ct. . . Pg.3 . . . B12
Chase Ct. . . . Pg.4 . . . X11
Chatham Cir. . Pg.4 . . . X11
Chaucer Way . Pg.4 . . . W11
Checker Dr. . . Pg.4 . . . X11
Chenault Rd. . Pg.4 . . . A12
Cherrywood Rd.

. . . . . . . . . . Pg.4 . . . A11
Chestnut Ct., E. & W.

. . . . . . . . . . Pg.4 . . . V12
Chestnut Terr. Pg.4 . . . V12
Chevy Chase Ave. E.

. . . . . . . . . . Pg.5 . . . X14
Chicory Ct. . . Pg.3 . . . X11
Chicory Ln. . . Pg.3 . . . X11
Churchill Ct. . Pg.3 . . . W13
Circle Dr. . . . Pg.4 . . . X12
Clearwater Ct. Pg.4 . . . W13
Clohesey Dr. . Pg.3 . . . X11
Cloverdale . . Pg.3 . . . X11
Cobblestone Ln.

. . . . . . . . . . Pg.4 . . . X12
Cocoawood Cir. Pg.3 . . . X13
Commerce Ct. Pg.4 . . . X13
Cooper Ct. . . Pg.3 . . . X11
Copperwood Dr.

. . . . . . . . . . Pg.4 . . . W12
Corporate Grove Dr.

Cottonwood Rd.

. . . . . . . . . . Pg.4 . . A11-12

Country Ln. . . Pg.3 . . . A11
Court 'N.' . . . Pg.4 . . . X13
Courtland Dr. . Pg.3 . . . W11
Coventry Ct. . Pg.3 . . . W12
Coventry Ln. . Pg.3 . . . W12
Covington Terr. Pg.3 . . . X11
Crab Apple Terr.

Crestview Terr. Pg.4 . . . A12
Crofton Ln. . . Pg.8 . . . B11
Crossfield Ct. . Pg.4 . . . W11
Crown Point Dr.

. . . . . . . . . . Pg.4 . . . X12
Cumberland Ln.

. . . . . . . . . . Pg.4 . . . X13
Dannet Ct. . . Pg.3 . . . X11
Dannet Rd. . . Pg.4 . . . W11
Darryl Dr. . . . Pg.9 . . . A12
Dartmouth Ln. Pg.4 . . . X13
Daulton Ct. . . Pg.3 . . . X11
Daulton Dr. . . Pg.3 . . . X12
Dayton Rd. . . Pg.4 . . . X11
Deerfield Pkwy. Pg.4 . . . X13
Depot Pl. . . . Pg.9 . . . W11
Devonshire Rd. Pg.4 . . . W11
Devonwood Ct. Pg.4 . . . W12
Diane Dr. . . . Pg.4 . . P W11-14
Dogwood Terr. Pg.3 . . . A12
Dorncliff Ln. . Pg.4 . . . X11
Dover Ct. . . . Pg.3 . . . A12
Dover Dr. . . . Pg.3 . . . A11
Downing Rd. . Pg.4 . . . X12
Driftwood Pl. . Pg.4 . . . X12
Dun-lo Ave. . . Pg.3 . . . A12
Dundee Pkwy. Pg.4 . . . A12
Dundee Rd. . . Pg.4 . . . A12
Dunham Ln. . Pg.4 . . . X11
Dunhill Dr. . . Pg.3 . . . V12
Dunston Ln. . Pg.3 . . . V12
Eastwood Ln. Pg.4 . . . X13
Ellen Dr. . . . . Pg.4 . . . A12
Elmwood Dr. . Pg.4 . . . A11
English Oak Terr.

. . . . . . . . . . Pg.4 . . . W12
Essington Ln. . Pg.4 . . . A11
Estate Dr. . . . Pg.4 . . . X12
Eton Ct. . . . . Pg.4 . . . W12
Euclid Ct. . . . Pg.4 . . . W12
Evergreen Pl. . Pg.3 . . . X11
Fabish Dr. . . . Pg.4 . . . X12
Fairfax Ln. . . Pg.4 . . . A12
Farnsworth Ln. Pg.3 . . . W11
Farrington Dr. Pg.4 . . . X11
Ferndale Ct. . Pg.4 . . . X12
Forest Pl. . . . Pg.4 . . . A12
Forest Way Dr. Pg.3 . . . X11
Fox Ct., E. & W.

. . . . . . . . . . Pg.4 . . . A12
Fox Hill Dr. . . Pg.4 . . . X12
Fox Tail Ct. . . Pg.5 . . . X14
Foxford Dr. . . Pg.3 . . . V12
Frances Ct. . . Pg.4 . . . X12
Franklin Ln. . Pg.3 . . . X11
Fremont Way . Pg.3 . . . W-X11
Gail Dr. . . . . Pg.4 . . . W11
Garden Ct. . . Pg.3 . . . X11
Gardenia Ln. . Pg.4 . . . X12
Glendale Rd. . Pg.4 . . . A12
Golfview Terr. Pg.4 . . . A12
Green Knolls Dr.

. . . . . . . . . . Pg.4 . . . W-X12
Greenbridge Rd.

. . . . . . . . . . Pg.8 . . . B11
Greenwood Ct., N. & S.

. . . . . . . . . . Pg.4 . . . W11
Gregg Ln. . . . Pg.4 . . . A11
Grove Cir. . . . Pg.4 . . . A11
Grove Dr. . . . Pg.4 . . . A11
Hackberry Ct. Pg.3 . . . V12
Hampshire Ln. Pg.4 . . . X11
Happsfield Ln. Pg.4 . . . X11
Harris Dr. . . . Pg.4 . . . X12
Harvard Ln. . . Pg.3 . . . X11
Harvest Cir. . . Pg.4 . . . X12
Hastings Ln. . Pg.4 . . . X13
Hawthorn Rd. Pg.4 . . A11-12
Hazelwood Terr.

Heatherwood Way

Hiawatha Dr. . Pg.4 . . . X12
Hickory Dr. . . Pg.4 . . . X11
Hidden Lake Dr.

Highland Grove Ct., N.

Highland Grove Dr.

Hill Ct., E. & W. Pg.4 . . X12
Hilldale Ln. . . Pg.4 . . . X12
Hobson Dr. . . Pg.4 . . . A12
Hollystone Ln. Pg.4 . . . X12
Horatio Blvd. . Pg.4 . . . X12
Indian Hill Dr. Pg.4 . . . A11
Indian Spring Ln.

Kingston Dr. . Pg.3 . . . V12
Kirkwood Dr. . Pg.4 . . . X12
Knight Hill Ct. Pg.3 . . . X11
Knollwood Dr. Pg.3 . . . W11
La Salle Ct., N. Pg.4 . . . W12
La Salle Ln. . . Pg.4 . . . X11
Lake Cook Rd. Pg.3,4 A11,12
Lake St. . . . . Pg.9 . . . A12
Lamont Ter. . . Pg.4 . . . W12
Landcaster Ct. Pg.4 . . . A12
Larchmont Dr. Pg.4 . . . W11
Larraway Dr. . Pg.4 . . . A12
Lauren Ln. . . Pg.4 . . . A12
Le Parc Cir. . . Pg.3 . . . X11
Lee Ct. . . . . Pg.3 . . . A11
Lehigh Ln. . . Pg.4 . . . A11
Lexington Dr. . Pg.4 . . . X13
Lilac Ln. . . . . Pg.4 . . . X13
Lincoln Terr. . Pg.4 . . . X13
Linden Ave. . . Pg.5 . . . X14
Live Oak Ln. . Pg.4 . . . W12
Lockwood Ct. Pg.4 . . . W12
Lockwood Dr. Pg.4 . . . W12
Logsdon Ln. . Pg.3 . . . W11
London Ct. . . Pg.3 . . . W12
Long Grove Aptaksic Rd.

. . . . . . . . . . Pg.4 P W11-14
Long Ridge Ct. Pg.4 . . . A11
Longwood Ct. Pg.3 . . . A11
Longwood Dr. Pg.3 . . . A11
Lyon Ct. . . . . Pg.4 . . . X11
Lyon Dr. . . . . Pg.4 . . . X12
MacArthur Ct. Pg.4 . . . A12
MacArthur Dr. Pg.4 . . . A12
Madison Dr. . Pg.4 . . . W13
Madison Ct. . Pg.4 . . . W12
Magnolia Ct. . Pg.3

Magnolia Ct., E.

. . . . . . . . . . Pg.4 . . . V12
Magnolia Ct., W.

. . . . . . . . . . Pg.3
Maple Dr. . . . Pg.4 . . . A11
Margate Dr. . . Pg.4 . . . A11
Marie Ave. . . Pg.4 . . . X13
Marylu Ln. . . Pg.4 . . . A12
Mayfair Ct., N. & S.

. . . . . . . . . . Pg.4 . . . A11
Mayfair Ln. . . Pg.4 . . . A11
Melinda Ln. . . Pg.4 . . . A12
Middlesex Ct. Pg.9 . . . A12
Millcreek Dr. . Pg.4 . . . A12
Miller Ln. . . . Pg.8 . . . B11
Milwaukee Ave. Pg.5 . . . X14
Misty Woods . Pg.3 . . . X11
Mohawk Ct. . Pg.4 . . . A12
Mohawk Trail . Pg.4 . . . A12
Morningside Ln., E. & W.

. . . . . . . . . . Pg.3 . . . X11
Mulberry Ct. . Pg.4 . . . X11
Mundelein Rd. Pg.4 . . . X11
Navajo Trail . . Pg.4 . . . A12
New Dover . . Pg.3 . . . A12
Newfield Dr. . Pg.4 . . . W12
Newport Ct. . Pg.3 . . . X11
Newtown Ct. . Pg.4 . . . X13
Newtown Dr. . Pg.4 . . . X13
Oak Creek Dr. Pg.3 . . . A12
Old Arlington Ct.

Old Arlington Hts. Rd.

. . . . . . . . . . Pg.4 . . . A11
Old Oak Ct., E. & W.

Old Oak Dr. . . Pg.4 . . . A12
Old Post Rd. . Pg.4 . . . A11
Osage Terr. . . Pg.4 . . . X12
Oxford Dr. . . Pg.3 . . . W11
Palmgren Ct. . Pg.4

Park Ln. . . . . Pg.3 . . . X11
Park Pl. . . . . Pg.4 . . . X11
Parker Ln. . . Pg.3 . . . X11
Parkside Dr. . Pg.4 . . . W12
Parkview Terr. Pg.4 . . . X11
Patton Dr. . . Pg.4 . . . X12
Pauline Ave. . Pg.4 . . . X13
Penny Ln. . . . Pg.3 . . . X11
Pinehurst Ln. Pg.4 . . . X11
Pinetree Cir., N. & S.

. . . . . . . . . . Pg.3 . . . X11
Pinyon Ct. . . Pg.3 . . . V12
Plum Grove Cir. Pg.3 . . . X11
Poplar Ct. . . . Pg.3 . . . X11
Prairie Ln. . . Pg.3 . . . X11
Providence Ln. Pg.4 . . . X11
Quaker Hollow Ct., N. & S.

Rachel Ln. . . Pg.3 . . A10
Radcliffe Rd. . Pg.4 . . . X13
Ranchview Ct. Pg.3 . . . X11
Raphael Ave. . Pg.4 . . . X13
Raupp Blvd. . Pg.4 . . . A12
Red Oak Ct. . Pg.4 . . . X12
Redbud Pl. . . Pg.4 . . . X12
Regent Ct., E. & W.

Regent Dr. . . Pg.3 . . . A11
Ridgefield Ln. Pg.4 . . . X13
Ridgewood Ln. Pg.4 . . . X13
Rivershire Ln. Pg.5 . . . V14
Roberta Ct. . . Pg.4 . . . A12
Ronnie Dr. . . Pg.4 . . . X11
Rose Blvd. . . Pg.3 . . A10
Rose Ct., W. . Pg.3 . . . A11

Rosewood Ave. Pg.4 .... A12
Russellwood Ct. .......... Pg.4 ... W13
Salk Rd. ..... Pg.9 .... A12
Sandalwood Ct. Pg.4 .... V12
Sandalwood Rd. .......... Pg.4 .... V12
Sandhurst Dr. Pg.4 ... W12
Saratoga Ln. . Pg.8 .... A11
Satinwood Ct. Pg.4 .... V12
Satinwood Terr. .......... Pg.4 ... W12
Saxon Ct. .... Pg.9 .... A12
Saybrook Ln. . Pg.3 .... X11
Scottish Pine Ln. .......... Pg.4 ... V11
Selwyn Ln. .. Pg.9 .... A12
Shady Grove Ln. .......... Pg.4 .... X11
Shambliss Ct. Pg.3 .... X11
Shambliss Ln. Pg.3 .... X11
Silver Linden Ln. .......... Pg.4 ... W12
Silver Rock Ln. Pg.4 .... X11
Someset Ln. . Pg.4 .... X12
Springside Ct. Pg.4 .... X11
Springside Ln. Pg.4 .... X11
St. Mary's Pkwy. .......... Pg.4 .... A12
Stanford Ln. . Pg.8 .... A11
Station Ct., E. & W. .......... Pg.4 ... W12
Station Dr. ... Pg.4 ... W12
Steeple Dr. ... Pg.4 .... X12
Stillwell Dr. .. Pg.4 .... A12
Stonebridge .. Pg.8 .... A11
Stonegate Ct. . Pg.3 .... A11
Stonegate Rd. Pg.3 .... A11
Strathmore Ct. Pg.3 .... A11
Sunridge Ln. . Pg.4 .... X12
Sussex Ct. ... Pg.9 .... A12
Sycamore Rd. Pg.4 .... A11
Teakwood Cir. Pg.4 .... X13
Terrace Pl. ... Pg.3 .... A11
Thistle Ct. ... Pg.4 ... W12
Thompson Blvd. .......... Pg.4 ... W11
Thompson Ct. Pg.4 ... W12
Thorndale Ct. Pg.4 .... X12
Thorndale Dr. Pg.3 .... X12
Thornton Ln. . Pg.8 .... A11
Thornwood Rd. Pg.4 .... A12
Three States Blvd. .......... Pg.9 .... A11
Timber Hill Rd. Pg.4 .... A11
Trace Dr. .... Pg.3 .... A11
Trinity Ct. ... Pg.9 .... A12
Trotwood Ct. . Pg.4 ... W12
Twilight Pass . Pg.4 .... X11
Twisted Oak Ln. Pg.3,4 .. A11
University Dr. Pg.9 .... A12
Vernon Ct., N. & S. .......... Pg.4 .... A11
Vernon Ln. .. Pg.4 .... A11
Villa Verde Dr. Pg.8 .... A11
Village Ct. ... Pg.4 ... W12
Wakefield Ln. . Pg.4 .... X13
Wedgewood Ct. Pg.4 .... V11
Weidner Ct. .. Pg.4 .... A11
Weidner Rd. . Pg.4 .... A11
Weiland Rd. .. Pg.4 .. A-X12
Wellington Ct., N. & S. .......... Pg.4 ... W12
Westbourne Ln. Pg.4 .... X11
Westchester Ln. Pg.4 ... W12
Wheeling Ave. Pg.4 .... X13
Whispering Oaks Ct. .......... Pg.4 .... V12
Whispering Oaks Dr. .......... Pg.4 .... V12
White Oak ... Pg.4 .... V11
White Pine Rd. Pg.4 .... A11
Whitebranch Ct. Pg.4 .... X12
Whitehall Ct. . Pg.3 .... A11
Whitehall Pl. . Pg.3 .... A11
Whitney Ln. .. Pg.4 ... W12
Wildflower Ct. Pg.4 .... X12
Willow Pkwy. . Pg.4 .... V12
Windbrooke Dr. Pg.4 .... X13
Winding Oak Ln. .......... Pg.4 .... X12
Windover Ct. . Pg.4 .... X12
Windsor Dr. .. Pg.4 .... A11
Windwood Ct. Pg.4 .... X12
Wood Hollow Ln. .......... Pg.4 .... X12
Woodbury Ln. Pg.4 .... X12
Woodridge Ln. Pg.4 .... X12
Wyngate Ln. . Pg.4 .... X12

**CEMETERIES**
Knopf Cemetery .......... Pg.3 .... X11
St. Mary's Cem. Pg. .... A12

**FOREST PRESERVES**
Buffalo Grove Forest Preserve .......... Pg.3 . A10,11

**GOLF COURSES**
Buffalo Grove G.C. .......... Pg.4 .... X11
Chevy Chase C.C. .......... Pg.5 .... X14

**PARKS**
Bicentennial Park .......... Pg.3 ... W11
Bison Park ... Pg.3 .... A11
Cambridge Park .......... Pg.9 .... A12
Emmerich Park Pg.4 .... A12
Kingsbridge Park .......... Pg.3 ... W11
Lions Park ... Pg.4 .... A11
Longfellow Park .......... Pg.3 .... A11
Mill Creek Park Pg.4 .... A11
Willow Stream Park .......... Pg.4 .... X12
Windsor Ridge Park .......... Pg. .... A12

**SCHOOLS**
Buffalo Grove H.S. .......... Pg.3 .... A11
Cooper Jr. H.S. Pg.3 .... A11
Ivy Hall Sch. . Pg.4 .... X11
Joyce Kilmer Sch. .......... Pg.4 .... A12
Longfellow Sch. .......... Pg.3 .... A11
St. Mary's Sch. Pg.4 .... A12
Willow Grove Sch. .......... Pg.4 .... X11

**SHOPPING CENTERS**
Plaza Verde S.C. .......... Pg.4 .... A10
The Plaza .... Pg.4 .... A12

**MISCELLANEOUS**
Alcott Community Center .......... Pg.4 .... A12
Police Dept. .. Pg.4 .... A12

### CHICAGO

Pages 29-32
(For additional listings, see Section 1)

**STREETS**
Albany ...... Pg.31 ... L12
Algonquin .... Pg.30 ... M9
Artisian ..... Pg.31 ... L13
Ashland ..... Pg.31 . L,M14
Bell Ave. .... Pg.31 . L,M13
Birchwood Ave. Pg.29,31 .......... M5,6,12-15
Bosworth .... Pg.31 ... L14
Caldwell Ave. . Pg.29 ... M7
California .... Pg.31 .. M13
Campbell .... Pg.31 . L,M13
Carpenter Rd. Pg.30 ... M9
Chase Ave. ... Pg.29,31 .......... M5,6,12-15
Chicora Ave. . Pg.30 ... M9
Claremont ... Pg.31 .. M12
Clark St. ..... Pg.31 . L,M14
Coyle Ave. ... Pg.29,31 .......... M6,12
Damen ...... Pg.31 ... L14
Dodge Ave. .. Pg.31 ... L13
Eastlake Terr. . Pg.31 ... L15
Estes Ave. ... Pg.29-31 .......... M6,7,12-15
Fairfield ..... Pg.31 ... L13
Fargo Ave. ... Pg.29,31 .......... L12-15,M5
Farwell Ave. .. Pg.31 M12-15
Fitch ....... Pg.29-31 .......... M6-8,12
Francisco .... Pg.31 .. M12
Glenwood .... Pg.31 .. M15
Greenleaf .... Pg.29-31 .......... M6-8,12-15
Greenview ... Pg.31 .. M15
Hamilton ..... Pg.31 . L,M14
Harlem Ave. .. Pg.29 ... M6
Hartley ...... Pg.31 ... L12
Haskins ..... Pg.31 ... L14
Hiawatha Ave. Pg.30 ... M8
Howard St. .. Pg.31 L12-15
Hoyne Ave. .. Pg.31 .. M13
Ibsen St. .... Pg.29 .. M5,6
Ionia, N. .... Pg.30 ... M8
Jarlath Ave. .. Pg.29,31 .......... L12,M5
Jarvis Ave. ... Pg.29,31 .......... L12-15,M6
Jean Ave., N. . Pg.30 ... M8
Jerome ..... Pg.29,31 .......... L12,M5
Jonquil Terr. . Pg.31 ... L14
Juneway Terr. Pg.31 ... L14
Kedzie Ave. .. Pg.31 . L,M12
Lakewood .... Pg.31 .. M15
Lehigh Ave. .. Pg.30 ... M8
Leoti Ave. ... Pg.29 ... M8
Lunt ....... Pg.29-31 .......... L12-15,M5,6,9
Mankato, N. .. Pg.29 ... M7
Maplewood Ave., N. .......... Pg.31 ... L13
Marshfield ... Pg.31 ... L14
Mason Ave., N. Pg.30 ... M8
McAlpin, N. .. Pg.29 ... M7
Mendota, N. .. Pg.30 ... M8
Merrill Ave. .. Pg.29 ... M5
Milwaukee Ave. Pg.29 ... M6
Monon Ave., N. Pg.29,30 M8
Moody ...... Pg.29 ... M8
Morse Ave. .. Pg.30,31 .......... M9,12-15
Moselle Ave, N. Pg.29,30 M8
Nagle Ave., N. Pg.29 ... M7
Oakley Ave. .. Pg.31 .. M13
Oconto Ave. .. Pg.29 ... M6
Octavia Ave. .. Pg.29 ... M6
Odell Ave. ... Pg.29 ... M6
Oketo ...... Pg.29 ... M6
Olcott Ave. ... Pg.29 ... M6
Oleander Ave. Pg.29 ... M5
Oriole Ave. ... Pg.29 ... M5
Osceola Ave. . Pg.29 ... M6
Ottawa Ave. .. Pg.29 ... M5
Overhill Ave. . Pg.29 ... M5
Ozark St. .... Pg.29 ... M5
Park Ave. .... Pg.30 ... M8
Paulina ..... Pg.31 . L,M14
Pratt Ave. ... Pg.31 .. M12
Pratt Blvd. ... Pg.31 .. M14
Ridge Ave. ... Pg.31 . L,M14
Rockwell .... Pg.31 . L,M13
Seeley ...... Pg.31 .. M14
Sibley St. .... Pg.29 .. M5,6
Sheridan Rd. . Pg.31 . L,M15
Sherwin ..... Pg.29,31 .......... M5,12-15
Souix, N. .... Pg.30 ... M8
State Rte. 21 . Pg.29 ... M6
State Rte. 43 . Pg.29 ... M6
Talman ..... Pg.31 ... L13
Tonty Ave., N. Pg.30 ... M8
Touhy Ave. .. Pg.29,31 .......... M6,7,12-15
Washtenaw .. Pg.31 . L,M13
Wayne ...... Pg.31 .. M15
Western Ave. . Pg.31 . L,M13
Wildwood Ave. Pg.30 ... M8
Winchester .. Pg.31 ... L13
Wolcott ..... Pg.31 . L,M14

**PARKS**
Ashland Park . Pg.31 ... L15
Brooks Park .. Pg.29 ... M6
Howard St. Park .......... Pg.31 ... L15
Indian Boundary Park .......... Pg.31 .. M13
Jarvis Ave. Park .......... Pg.31 ... L15
Juneway Terr. Park .......... Pg.31 ... L15
Leona Park .. Pg.31 .. M15
Lerner Park .. Pg.31 .. M13
Loyola Park .. Pg.31 .. M15
Paschen Park . Pg.31 .. M14
Pottawattomie Park .......... Pg.31 .. M14
Rogers Ave. Park .......... Pg.31 ... L15
Touhy Park .. Pg.31 ... L14
Wildwood Park Pg.30 ... M8

**SCHOOLS**
Armstrong Sch. Pg.31 .. M14
Decatur Sch. . Pg.31 .. M12
Field Sch. ... Pg.31 .. M15
Frederick Stock Sch. .......... Pg.29 ... M6
Gale Sch. .... Pg.31 ... L14
North Shore Sch. .......... Pg.31 .. M15
Rogers Sch. . Pg.31 ... L13
St. Juliana Sch. Pg.29 ... M6
St. Mary's Sch. Pg.31 ... L13
St. Scholastica H.S. .......... Pg.31 ... L14
Wildwood Sch. Pg.30 ... M8

**SHOPPING CENTERS**
Howard & Western S.C. .......... Pg.31 ... L13

**MISCELLANEOUS**
Doctor's Hospital .......... Pg.31 .. M14
R.R. Station .. Pg.31 ... L14

### CHICAGO HEIGHTS

Pages 48,49

**STREETS**
Abbott Ave. .......... S23
Aberdeen St. .......... U24
Adams St. .......... U22
Alden Ct. .......... U23
Alice St. .......... R24
Alvin Pl. .......... S24
Amy St. .......... S23
Andover Ct. .......... U22
Andover Dr. .......... U22
Arnold St. .......... U25
Arquilla Ave., N. .......... S23
Arquilla Dr., E. .......... S23
Ash St. .......... V24
Ashland Ave. .......... R23
Ashland Ln. .......... R23
Avonelle Dr. .......... S23
Barbara Ln. .......... T22
Beacon Blvd. .......... U22
Beacon Ct. .......... U22
Bellevue Pl. .......... T24
Birch Ln. .......... T23
Birmingham Ave. .......... U24
Boston St., N. .......... U23
Bradley Ln. .......... S23
Bradoc St. .......... T22
Brentwood Dr. .......... R23
Briargate Ave. .......... S24
Broadway .......... T24
Brookline St. .......... U22
Buena Vista Ave. .......... U23
Buena Vista Cir. .......... U23
Bunker St. .......... U22
Butler St. .......... U24
Butterfield Ave. .......... V25
Caldwell Ave. .......... S23
Cambridge St. .......... U23
Campbell Ave. .......... T23
Carey Ct. .......... S23
Carpenter St. .......... T24
Cedar Ln. .......... T23
Center Ave. .......... U24
Charing Cross Rd. .......... S23
Charles St. .......... R23
Chicago Heights-Glenwood Rd. .......... R24
Chicago Rd. .......... R23
Circle Ct. .......... U24
Claude Ct. .......... T24
Coales St. .......... R24
Commercial Ave. .......... S24
Concord Ct. .......... U22
Concord Dr. .......... U22
Constance .......... S23
Coolidge St. .......... R,T24
Cottage Grove Ave. .......... T26
Country Club Rd. .......... T23
Cove Dr. .......... S22
Craig Dr., E. & W. .......... R23
Crescent Dr. .......... T23
D'Amico Dr. .......... T22
Dartmouth Dr. .......... U23
Dawn Ln. .......... S23
Deangels Ct. .......... S23
Deer Trail Rd. .......... S22
Diane Ln. .......... R23
Division St. .......... T22
Dixie Hwy. .......... S23
Donovan Dr. .......... U22
Doris Ln. .......... S23
Dutra Ave. .......... T22
East End Ave. .......... U24
Eastgate Ave. .......... S24
Eddy St. .......... R23
Edgewood Ave. .......... U23
Eggleston Ave. .......... S24
Eighth St. .......... T23
Elder Ave. .......... T23
Elmwood Dr., E & W .......... S23
Emelia St. .......... S23
Emerald Ave. .......... S24
Enterprise Ct. .......... T22
Enterprise Dr. .......... T22
Euclid Ave. .......... U23
Fairview Ave. .......... U22
Fifth Ave. .......... U25
Fitch Rd. .......... S22
Flossmoor Rd. .......... R23
Floyd Ln. .......... S24
Forest Ave. .......... U24
Frances Ln. .......... R23
Franklin Ave. .......... T23
Frederick Dr. .......... R23
Gail Ln. .......... S23
Garden Ave. .......... U23
Glengate Ave. .......... S23,24
Glengate, W. .......... S23
Grace Ln. .......... S23
Grant Ave. .......... T24
Green St. .......... U25
Greenbrier Ave. .......... S23
Gregory Dr. .......... T22
Grosvenor Pl. .......... S24
Halsted St. .......... R24
Hamilton Woods .......... R23
Hanover St. .......... U24
Hawthorne Ln. .......... T23
Hickory St. .......... U22
Highland Dr. .......... T23
Hillcrest Ave. .......... T24
Hilltop Ave. .......... U22
Hillview Dr. .......... U22
Holbrook Cir. .......... R23
Holbrook Rd. .......... R23
Homewood Ct. .......... S24
Hutchinson Ave. .......... T22
Illinois St. .......... U24
Independence Way .......... U24
Ingrid Ln. .......... U22
Iris Ln. .......... R23
Irving Blvd. .......... S23
Isa Ave. .......... T24
Joe Orr Rd. .......... S23
Joyce Ln. .......... S23
Judith Ln. .......... R24
Kathleen Ln. .......... S23
Kingston Pl. .......... S23
Laflin St. .......... S23
Laura .......... S23
Lawrence St. .......... U22
Leonard Ave. .......... R23
Lerose Dr. .......... R23
Lexington Dr. .......... R23
Lincoln Ave. .......... T24
Lincoln Hwy. .......... U22
Linden Ln. .......... T23
Longwood Ct. .......... S22
Longwood Dr. .......... S22
Lowe Ave. .......... S24
Luther Ln. .......... T23
Lynn Ln. .......... R23
MacArthur Dr. .......... T22
Mackler Dr. .......... T23
Main St. .......... U22
Manchester Dr., E & N .......... S24
Maple Dr., N & W .......... T23
Marian Way .......... T22
Martin Ln. .......... T24
Mason Ct. .......... T25
May Ct. .......... S23
Mayfair Pl. .......... S23
McEldowney Pl. .......... U24
McKinley Ave. .......... T24
Meadow Ln. .......... T23
Memorial Dr. .......... U24
Mildred Ln. .......... S23
Minette Ln. .......... U22
Morgan St. .......... U24
Normal Ave. .......... S24
Normandy Dr. .......... S23
Normandy Dr., E & W .......... S24
Oak St. .......... U24
Orchard Ave. .......... U23
Otto Blvd. .......... T24
Pamela Dr. .......... R24
Park Ave. .......... T24
Parkside Ave. .......... T24
Parkview Ave. .......... T23
Parnell Ave. .......... S24
Patricia Dr. .......... R24
Paulina St. .......... U23
Peggy Ln. .......... T22
Peoria St. .......... R,T24
Peyton Dr. .......... R23
Piacenti Ln. .......... T22
Pleasant Dr. .......... S23
Plymouth Dr. .......... U23
Plymouth St. .......... U23
Portland Ave. .......... U25
Prairie Ave. .......... U23
Ranger Dr. .......... T22
Raye Dr. .......... R23
Revere Ct. .......... U22
Ricky Dr. .......... S24
Roberta Ln. .......... S24
Roberts .......... S22
Rosewood Ln. .......... R23
Route 1 Cutoff .......... T24
Sandra Ln. .......... S23
Sangamon St. .......... T24
Saratoga Dr. .......... T22
Sauk Tr. .......... W24
Schilling Ave. .......... T23
School St. .......... U24
Scott Ave. .......... U25
Serena Dr. .......... R23
Shea Dr. .......... S22
Shelly Ln. .......... U22
Sherry Ln. .......... S23
Shields Ave. .......... U25
Southgate Ave. .......... T24
Spruce Ln. .......... T23
Standish St. .......... U23
State St. .......... S25
Stewart Ave. .......... U25
Stirling Ave. .......... T22
Strieff Ave. .......... S23
Sue Ct. .......... S23
Sunnyside Ave. .......... U23
Sunset Ave. .......... U22
Tahoe Dr. .......... S23
Terrace Dr. .......... S23
Terry Ct. .......... R23
Terry Ln. .......... R23
Thelma Ln. .......... S23
Theresa Ln. .......... T23
Thomas St. .......... T22
Thorn St. .......... U23
Thorne Ct. .......... T25
Travers Ave. .......... T22
Travers Ct. .......... T22
Union Ave. .......... S24
Union St. .......... S24
Vincennes Ave. .......... T24
Vollmer Rd. .......... S23
Wallace Ct. .......... T23
Wallace St. .......... U24
Washington Ave. .......... T24
Wentworth Ave. .......... U25
West End Ave. .......... T24
Western Ave. .......... T22
Westgate Ave. .......... S23
Willow Dr. .......... T23
Wilson Ave. .......... U23
Winchester Rd. .......... S22
Winston Ln. .......... S22
Wood St. .......... S22
Wooster Ct. .......... U22
Yale Ave. .......... U23
Yorktown Rd. .......... T22
4th St. .......... S23
7th Pl. .......... T24
8th St. .......... T22
10th St. .......... T25
11th Pl. .......... T23
11th St. .......... T25
12th St. .......... T25
13th St. .......... U22,T25
14th Pl. .......... U22
14th St. .......... U22
15th Pl. .......... U22
15th St. .......... U22
16th Pl. .......... U22
16th St. .......... U22
17th St. .......... U24
19th Pl. .......... U24
19th St. .......... U24
21st St. .......... U24
22nd St. .......... U24
23rd St. .......... V25
24th St. .......... V25
25th St. .......... V25
26th St. .......... V24
28th St. .......... V24
193rd Pl. .......... R24
195th St. .......... R24
196th St. .......... R24
197th Pl. .......... R24
197th St. .......... R24
201st St. .......... S23
202nd St. .......... S23
205th St. .......... T22
209th St. .......... T22

**FOREST PRESERVES**
Halsted Woods .......... T24
Indian Hill Woods .......... U23
Joe Orr Woods .......... T24
Wilson Woods .......... T24

**GOLF COURSES**
Chicago Heights C.C. .......... T23
Chicago Heights Pk. Dist. G.C. .......... S24

**PARKS**
Chicago Hts. Athletic Ball Pk. .......... T24
Commissioners Park .......... R23
Cornet Park .......... U22
Euclid Park .......... U23
Fireman's Park .......... S24
Hap Bruno Baseball Park .......... T24
Hillcrest Park .......... T24
Hodges Park .......... U25
Jirtle Park .......... V24
King Park .......... U24
Landeen Park .......... T23
McEldowney Park .......... U23
Meidell Park .......... S23
North End Park .......... R23
Petrarca Park .......... U24
Sangamon Park .......... T24
Sesto Park .......... U22
Smith Park .......... U23
Swanson Park .......... T22
Wacker Park .......... T24

**SCHOOLS**
Beacon Hills Sch. .......... U22
Bloom Twp. H.S. .......... T23
Emanuel Adventis Sch. .......... U23
Garfield Sch. .......... V24
Gavin Sch. .......... T25
Greenbriar Sch. .......... S23
Highland Sch. .......... T23
Jefferson Sch. .......... T24
Kennedy Sch. .......... T22
Lincoln Sch. .......... U24
Marian H.S. .......... T23
Normandy Villa Sch. .......... S23
Prairie St. Jr. College .......... S24
Roosevelt Sch. .......... U23
Serena Hills Sch. .......... R23
St. Agnes Sch. .......... U24
St. Anns Sch. .......... U24
St. Josephs Sch. .......... U23,25
St. Kieran Sch. .......... R24
St. Pauls Sch. .......... T23
St. Rocco Sch. .......... U25
Washington McKinley Sch. .......... U24
Wilson Sch. .......... U22

**SHOPPING CENTERS**
Olympia Plaza .......... S23

**MISCELLANEOUS**
City Hall & Police Dept. .......... U24
Fire Dept. .......... S24
Library .......... U24
Post Office .......... U24
St. James Hosp. .......... U24

### CHICAGO RIDGE

Page 34,35

**STREETS**
Anderson Ave. .......... E15
Austin Ave. .......... F16
Barnard Dr. .......... E15
Birmingham St. .......... E16
Blanchard .......... E15
Central Ave. .......... F16
Donna Ave. .......... D15
Fireside Dr. .......... E15
Forest Ln. .......... E15
Grove St. .......... E15
Hyland Pl. .......... E15
Janet Ln. .......... E15
Kitty Ave. .......... E15
Klein Ave. .......... E15
Leslie Ln. .......... E15
Lombard Ave. .......... E16
Lyman Ave. .......... E,F16
Major Ave. .......... F16
Mansfield Ave. .......... F16
Marshall Ave. .......... E16
Mason Ave. .......... E,F16
Massasoit Ave. .......... F16
Mather Ave. .......... D15,E16
Mayfield Ave. .......... E16
McVicker Ave. .......... E,F16
Meade Ave. .......... E16
Melvina .......... F16
Menard Ave. .......... E,F16
Monitor Ave. .......... E16
Moody Ave. .......... E,F16
Mormora .......... F16
Nashville Ave. .......... D,E15
Natoma Ave. .......... D,E15
New England Ave. .......... D15
Norfolk Ln. .......... E15
Normandy Ave. .......... D,E15
Nottingham Ave. .......... D14
O'Connell St. .......... D14
Oak Ave. .......... F16
Oak Park Ave. .......... D,E15
Orchard Ln. .......... E15
Oxford Ave. .......... E,F16
Pacific Ave. .......... D16
Pamela Ln. .......... E15
Parkside Ave. .......... E17,F16
Pleasant Blvd. .......... F17
Princess Ave. .......... F16
Ridge Dr. .......... E15
Ridgeland Ave. .......... F16
Ridgemont Ln. .......... E16
Sayre .......... D15
Southwest Hwy. .......... E15
Stephen Dr. .......... E15
Sycamore .......... E15
Tracy Ave. .......... E15
Tri-State Tollway .......... D14
Washington St. .......... E16
97th Pl. .......... D15
98th St. .......... D14,15
99th Pl. .......... D14
99th St. .......... D14-16
100th St. .......... D15
101st St. .......... E16
103rd St. .......... E16
104th Pl. .......... E15
104th St. .......... E15
105th St. .......... E15,16
106th Pl. .......... E15
106th St. .......... E15,16
107th Pl. .......... E16
107th St. .......... E16
108th Pl. .......... F16
108th St. .......... F16
109th Pl. .......... F16
110th St. .......... F16
111th St. .......... F16

**PARKS**
Memorial Park .......... E16

**SCHOOLS**
Finley Jr. H.S. .......... F16
Our Lady of the Ridge Sch. F16
Ridge Central Sch. .......... F16
Ridge Lawn Sch. .......... E16

**SHOPPING CENTERS**
Chicago Ridge Commons D15
Chicago Ridge Mall .......... D15

**MISCELLANEOUS**
Fire Department .......... E16
Police Department .......... E16
Village Hall & Library .......... E16

### COUNTRY CLUB HILLS

Page 41,42

**STREETS**
Amherst Ct. .......... P19
Amlin Cir. .......... Q18
Anthony .......... P,Q19,R19
Apple Tree Dr. .......... Q20
Arlington Dr. .......... P20
Baker Ave. .......... P-R19
Baker St. .......... P19
Becker Terr. .......... Q18
Birch Ave. .......... P,R19
Briargate .......... N20
Butterfield .......... N20
Cedar Ave. .......... P-R19
Cedar Ct. .......... R19
Central Park Ave. .......... P20
Chestnut Ave. .......... P-R19
Chestnut Dr. .......... R19
Cicero Ave. .......... Q18
Clarence Ave. .......... P19
Cottonwood Ct. .......... Q19
Country Club Dr. .......... P20
Coventry Ln. .......... Q19
Crawford Ave. .......... P19
Crest Ct. .......... Q18
Cypress Ave. .......... P,Q19
Cypress Ct. .......... R19
Cypress Dr. .......... R19
Devon Dr. .......... P19
East Gate Dr. .......... Q19
Edwards Ave. .......... P19
Elm Dr. .......... R19
Fairway Terr. .......... P19

Farmcrest Terr. R19
Glen Oaks O20
Green View Terr. P19
Harvard Ln. P20
Hawthorne P19
Hickory Ave. R19
Hickory Dr. R19
Highland Pl. P20
Hillcrest Dr. P20
Holly Ct. O19
Hollywood Ln. P18
Huntleigh Ct. P19
Idlewild Dr. P19
Indian Hill Dr. O19
John Ave. P18
John St. Q18,R19
Junew Ct. P19
Keeler Ave. Q19
Keeler Dr. R19
Kirk Ct. P20
Kostner Ave. P19
Laramie Rd. Q18
Larkin Ln. P18
Laurel Ln. O20
Lavergne Ave. O,P18
Lee St. Q18
Loras Ln. R19
Loretto Ln. R19
Maple Ave. P-R19
Martin Ct. R18
Martin Ln. R18
Mary Ann Ln. P18
Mary Ct. Q18
Marycrest Dr. Q18
Mayfair Ct. P19
Michael Ave. P18
Mocombo Way P18
Mulberry P19
Mulberry Terr. Q19
Neal Cir. Q18
Nightingale Ter. Q18
Oak Ave. R19
Oakwood Ave. P-R19
Oakwood Ct. R19
Old Elm O19
Olympic Dr. P19
Orchard Ln. O19
Park Ln. O19
Patrick P18
Pear Tree Ct. O19
Pheasant Ln. P20
Pine Dr. R19
Princeton Ln. P20
Provincetown Dr. Q19
Ravisloe Terr. P19
Rosewood P18
Russett Way O19
Sarah Ct. P20
Sarah Ln. P20
School Dr. P20
Soleri Dr. P19
Springfield Ave. P19
Sunset Ln. P18
Sunset Ridge O19
Sycamore Ave. P19
Thomas Ln. P18
Timberlea Ct. O19
Walnut Ave. Q19
Wildwoode Way O20
Williamsburg Dr. Q19
Willow Ave. P-R19
Willow Ct. Q19
Wilshire Blvd. P18
Windsor Ln. Q19
Winston Ct. O19
Winston Dr. P19
Yale Ln. R20
40th Ct. Q19
167th Pl. N19
167th St. N19
168th Pl. N19
168th St. N19
169th St. O19
171st Pl. O19
171st St. O19
172nd Pl. O19
172nd St. O19
173rd St. O18
175th Pl. O20,P18
175th St. O19
176th Pl. P18-20
176th St. P18-20
177th Pl. P19
177th St. P18-20
178th Pl. P19
178th St. P18,19
179th Pl. P18
179th St. P19
180th St. P19
181st Pl. P18
181st St. P18,19
182nd Pl. P19
182nd St. P19
184th Ct. Q18
184th Pl. Q18
184th St. Q18
185th Ct. Q18
185th Pl. Q18
185th St. Q18
186th Pl. Q18,19
186th St. Q19
187th Pl. Q19
187th St. Q18,19
188th Pl. Q19
188th St. Q18,19
189th Pl. R19
189th St. Q18,19
190th Pl. R19
190th St. R19
191st Ct. R19
191st St. R19
192nd Pl. R19
192nd St. R19
193rd St. R19
194th Ct. R19
194th St. R19
195th St. R19

**CEMETERIES**
St. John Cemetery Q19

**PARKS**
Atkins Park P19
Community Park O19
Cypress Park R19
Ecology Park P18
Independence Park P19
Kiwanis Park Q18
Marycrest Park Q19
Nob Hill Park O20
Tierra Grande Park Q19
Willow Wood Park O20
Wulf Park Q19

**SCHOOLS**
Baker Sch. Q19
Cooper Grove Sch. Q18
Hillcrest H.S. O19
Knob Hill Sch. N20
Meadowview Sch. P18
South Sch. Q19
Southwood Jr. H.S. Q18
St. Emeric Cath. Sch. P19
St. John Sch. Q19

**SHOPPING CENTERS**
Country Club Hills Shopping Plaza P18
Country Club S.C. Q19

**MISCELLANEOUS**
City Hall & Police Dept. O20
Civic Center & Library Q19
Fire Department Q19
Friendship Center P18

## DEER PARK

Pages 1,2
Lake County
(For additional listings, see Section 6)

**STREETS**
Amherst Ln. Pg.1 X6
Bobwhite Ln. Pg.2 X6
Bramble Ln. Pg.2 X7
Briargate Ln. Pg.2 X7
Cardinal Ct. Pg.2 X6
Cheshire Ct. Pg.2 X7
Circle Dr. Pg.2 X7
Clover Ln. Pg.2 X6
Corners Dr. Pg.2 X6
Court Lagrov Pg.2 X7
Court Touraine Pg.2 X7
Covington Dr. Pg.2 X7
Creek Wood Dr. Pg.2 A8
Deer Lake Dr. Pg.2 X6
Deer Valley Rd. Pg.2 W6
Deerchase Rd. Pg.1 X6
Dogwood Ct. Pg.2 X7
Doncaster Cir. Pg.2 X7
Dover Ct. Pg.2 X7
Edgeview Ct. Pg.2 X6
Fairview Dr. Pg.2 X6
Ferndale Rd. Pg.2 X6
Fox Chase Rd. Pg.2 X6
Glengarry Cir. Pg.1 X6
Glenhurst Rd. Pg.2 X6
Heather Ln. Pg.2 X7
Hollington Ln. Pg.2 X7
Juniper Ct. Pg.2 X6
Juniper Ln. Pg.2 X6
Lake View Ct. Pg.2 X6
Lake-Cook Rd. Pg.2 X7
Landmark Ln. Pg.2 X7
Laurel Dr. Pg.2 X6
Lea Rd. Pg.2 X6
Lois Ln. Pg.1 X6
Lone Pine Pg.1 X6
Long Grove Rd. Pg.2 X5
Madach Ct. Pg.2 X7
Mallard Ct. Pg.2 X6
Mariel Ct. Pg.2 X6
Meadow Ct. Pg.1 X6
Meadow Ln. Pg.1 X6
Newcastle Ct. Pg.2 X7
Oak Ridge Ln. Pg.2 X6
Park Hill Dr. Pg.2 X6
Pheasant Tr. Pg.2 X6
Pleasant Hill Rd. Pg.2 X6
Primrose Ct. Pg.2 X6
Public Rd. Pg.2 A7
Quail Ct. Pg.2 X6
Rand Rd. Pg.2 X7
Rue Chamonix Pg.2 X7
Rue Orleanais Pg.2 X7
Rue Touraine Pg.2 X7
Shady Ln. Pg.2 X6
Shoreham Ct. Pg.2 X7
Sunset Ridge Rd. Pg.2 X6
Sunshine Ln. Pg.2 X7
Surrey Ct. Pg.2 X7
Swallow Ct. Pg.2 X6
Teal Ct. Pg.2 X6
Thornbury Ct. Pg.2 X7
Thornhill Ct. Pg.2 X6
Wagon Ct. Pg.2 X7
Wallingford Ave. Pg.2 X7
Wehrheim Rd. Pg.2 X6
Wheel Ct. Pg.2 X7
Wicker Dr. Pg.2 X7
Wildrose Dr. Pg.2 X6
Willow Ct. Pg.2 X7
Woodberry Ct. Pg.2 X6
Woodberry Rd. Pg.2 X6

## DEERFIELD

Pages 21,22
(Portions within Lake County, see Section 6)

**STREETS**
Edens Expwy. Spur Pg.21 A2-4
Huehl Rd. Pg.21 A2
Lake Cook Rd. Pg.21 A2-4
Pfingsten Rd. Pg.21 A3
Tri State Tollway Pg.21 A2
Waukegan Rd. Pg.22 A4

**SHOPPING CENTERS**
Deerbrook Court Pg.21 A4
Lake Cook Plaza Pg.21 A4

**MISCELLANEOUS**
Northbrook Sports Club Pg.21 A3

## DES PLAINES

Pages 14,15,19,20,28,29

**STREETS**
Acres Ln. Pg.15 J17
Albany Ln. Pg.15 G14
Alden Ct. Pg.20 M17
Alfini Dr. Pg.15 J15
Alger Pg.20 M16
Algonquin Rd. Pg.15 J16
Alles St. Pg.15 H16
Ambleside Rd. Pg.14 J13,14
Amherst Ave. Pg.14 G14
Anderson Ter. Pg.19 J14
Andrea Ln. Pg.14 J13
Andy Ct. Pg.15 L17
Anita St. Pg.15 H14
Apple Creek Ln. Pg.15 J17
Ardmore Rd. Pg.15 G15
Arlington Ave. Pg.15 H16
Armstrong Ct. Pg.19 M14
Armstrong Rd. Pg.19 M14
Arnold Ct. Pg.19 J13
Ash St. Pg.15 K16
Ashland Ave. Pg.14,15 J14-16
Ballard Rd. Pg.15 H17
Beau Ct. Pg.14 J13
Beau Dr. Pg.14 J13
Bedford Ln. Pg.14 H14
Bell Dr. Pg.14 H14
Bellaire Ave. Pg.15 H17
Bellaire Ct. Pg.28 J2
Bender Rd. Pg.15,20 H17
Bending Ct. Pg.15 F15
Bennett Ln. Pg.14 H13
Bennett Pl. Pg.15 K17
Berkshire Ct. Pg.15 G15
Berkshire Ln. Pg.15 G15
Berry Ln. Pg.15 K17
Big Bend Dr. Pg.15 H17
Birch St. Pg.15 L17
Birchwood Ave. Pg.15 L17
Bittersweet Ct. Pg.24 L1
Bradley St. Pg.14 H14
Bradrock Dr. Pg.14 K14
Brentwood Dr. Pg.14 H14
Briar Ct. Pg.15 K16
Broadway Pg.15 H15
Brown St. Pg.15 H16
Busse Hwy. Pg.15 J17
Cambridge Rd. Pg.14 G14
Campbell Ave. Pg.15 J16
Carlow Dr. Pg.15 F15
Carol Ln. Pg.15 K15
Cavan Ln. Pg.14 J13
Cedar Ct. Pg.15 K17
Cedar St. Pg.15 L17
Center St. Pg.15 J16
Central Ave. Pg.20 M16
Central Rd. Pg.14 G13
Chase Ave. Pg.15 L17
Chestnut St. Pg.15 K-L16
Chicago Ave. Pg.24 J1
Church St. Pg.15 H17
Cindy Ln. Pg.15 K15
Circle Dr. Pg.15 G17
Circle St. Pg.15 K16
Clark Ln. Pg.19 J14
Clayton Ln. Pg.15 G15
College Dr. Pg.15 G16
Columbia Ave. Pg.15 H14-15
Concord Ln. Pg.15 G15
Cora St. Pg.15 K16
Cordial Dr. Pg.14 K13
Cornell Ave. Pg.14 G14
Courtesy Ln. Pg.14 K13
Crabtree Ln. Pg.15 J17
Craig Dr. Pg.20 M17
Cranbrook St. Pg.14 G14
Crestwood Dr. Pg.15 J15
Cumberland Pkwy. Pg.14 H14
Curtis St. Pg.20 M17
Dale St. Pg.15 L16
Danbury Ln. Pg.14 K14
Dara James Rd. Pg.14 H14
David Dr. Pg.20 L17
Davis Ct. Pg.14 H14
Dawn Ct. Pg.15 H17
Dayton Pl. Pg.14 K13
Deane St. Pg.15 J-K16
Debra Dr. Pg.14 H13
Dempster St. Pg.15 J17
Dennis Pl. Pg.15 K15
Denver Dr. Pg.14 K14
Des Plaines River Rd. Pg.15 K17
Devon Ave. Pg.20 M17
Devonshire Dr. Pg.14 K13
Dexter Ln. Pg.15 K15
Diamond Head Dr. Pg.14 J13-14
Doreen Dr. Pg.14 J14
Dorothy Dr. Pg.14 J13
Douglas Ave. Pg.15 L15
Dover Dr. Pg.14 K13-14
Dover Ln. Pg.14 K14
Drake Ln. Pg.14 G14
Dulles Rd. Pg.14 H14
Eaker Pl. Pg.19 J14
Earl Ave. Pg.15 K15
East Grant Dr. Pg.15 J15
East River Rd. Pg.15 H17
East Villa Dr. Pg.15 J15
Eastview Dr. Pg.15 L15
Easy St. Pg.14 H14
Edward Ct. Pg.28 J2
Eisenhower Ct. Pg.15 L17
Eisenhower Dr. Pg.20 M17
Elizabeth Ln. Pg.14 K13
Elk Blvd. Pg.15 H16
Ellinwood St. Pg.15 J16
Elm St. Pg.15 K16
Elmhurst Rd. Pg.14 K13
Elmira Ave. Pg.15 L15
Emerson St. Pg.28 J3
Esser Ct. Pg.15 K17
Estes Ave. Pg.15 L17
Everett Ave. Pg.15 K16
Everett Ln. Pg.15 K16
Evergreen Ave. Pg.15 H14,16
Executive Way Pg.15 K15
Fairmont Ct. Pg.20 K15
Farewell Ave. Pg.20 L16
Fargo Ave. Pg.15 L16-17
Farthing Ln. Pg.14 H14
Figard Ct. Pg.14 H14
Fletcher Dr. Pg.14 H14
Florian Dr. Pg.14 J13
Forest Ave. Pg.15 K15
Forest Edge Ln. Pg.15 H17
Fox Ln. Pg.20 M17
Fremont Ave. Pg.14 H14
Fremont Ct. Pg.15 H14
Frontage Rd. Pg.15 L16
Galleon Way Pg.14 H14
Garland Pl. Pg.15 J17
Golf Rd. Pg.15 G16
Good Ave. Pg.24 J2
Graceland Ave. Pg.15 H16
Grant Dr., E. & W. Pg.15 J15
Greco Ave. Pg.15 L16
Greenleaf Ave. Pg.15 L16
Greenview Ave. Pg.15 H15
Gregory St. Pg.10 F15
Grove Ave. Pg.15 H16
Halsey Dr. Pg.20 M17
Harding Ave. Pg.14,15 H14,16
Harvard St. Pg.14 G14
Harvey Ave. Pg.14,15 H14,15
Hawthorne Ln. Pg.15 H17
Hawthorne Terr. Pg.15 H17
Hazel Ct. Pg.15 K16
Heather Ln. Pg.15 J15
Henry Ave. Pg.15 J16
Hewitt Dr. Pg.14 J14
Hickory St. Pg.15 L17
Higgins Rd. Pg.20 M16
Highland Dr. Pg.15 L16
Hills Ave. Pg.15 H16
Hoffman Pkwy. Pg.15 J15
Holiday Ln. Pg.19 J13
Hollywood Ave. Pg.15 H15
Horne Terr. Pg.19 J14
Howard Ave. Pg.15 K16,L14
Ida St. Pg.15 H16
Illinois St. Pg.15 K16
Ingram Pl. Pg.19 J14
Inner Circle Dr. Pg.15 H14
Iris Ln. Pg.15 L17
Ironwood Dr. Pg.24 J2
Irwin Ave. Pg.15 K15
Jarlath Ave. Pg.15 L15
Jarvis Ave. Pg.15 L15-17
Jeanette St. Pg.15 J16
Jefferson St. Pg.15 H16
Jeffrey Ln. Pg.14 K14
Jill Ct. Pg.14 J13
Jon Ct. Pg.14 H13
Jon Ln. Pg.15 G15
Joseph Ave. Pg.20 L17
Joseph J. Schwab Rd. Pg.15,20 J17
Joyce Dr. Pg.14 K13
Junior Terr. Pg.15 H17
Kathleen Dr. Pg.14 J13
Kenilworth Ct. Pg.14 J14
Kenmare Ct. Pg.15 F15
Kenmare Dr. Pg.15 F15
Kennicott Ct. Pg.15 K17
Kerry Ct. Pg.24 J3
Kincaid Ct. Pg.14 J13,14
King Ln. Pg.19 J13,14
Kingston Ct. Pg.15 K15
Koehler Dr. Pg.15 K15
Koplin Dr. Pg.14 K13
Kylemore Ct. Pg.15 F15
Kylemore Dr. Pg.15 F15
LaSalle St. Pg.19 H14
Lancaster Ln. Pg.14 K14
Lance Dr. Pg.14 J14
Laura Ln. Pg.15 L17
Laurel Ave. Pg.15 J-H16
Lawn Ln. Pg.14 H14
Leahy Circle, E. & S. Pg.19 J14
Lechner Ln. Pg.15 H17
Lee St. Pg.15 K16
Leslie Ln. Pg.14 J13
Lillian Ln. Pg.14 H13
Lincoln Ave. Pg.15 K15,16
Lincoln Ln. Pg.14 K13
Linden St. Pg.15 K16
Lismore Dr. Pg.15 F15
Little Path Rd. Pg.14 H14
Locust St. Pg.15 K17
Luau Dr. Pg.15 G15
Lunt Ave. Pg.15 L16
Lyman Ave. Pg.15 H-J17
Lynn Ct. Pg.14 H14
Madelyn Dr. Pg.15 F15
Magnolia St. Pg.15 L17
Mannheim Rd. Pg.15 L16
Manor Ct. Pg.14 J14
Maple St. Pg.15,20 K-L17
Marcella Rd. Pg.14 G14
Margaret St. Pg.15,20 J,K15
Marina St. Pg.15 H14
Marion St. Pg.15 J16
Mark Ave. Pg.15 F15
Marshall Dr. Pg.14 H-K14
Mary St. Pg.15 H16
Mason Ln. Pg.15 J17
McCain Ct. Pg.14,19 J14
Meyer Ct. Pg.14 H14
Miami Ln. Pg.14 K14
Michael Ct. Pg.14 H13
Michael Rd. Pg.14 H14
Mill St. Pg.15 H16
Millers Rd. Pg.14 H14
Miner St. Pg.15 H16
Mitchell Ln. Pg.15 F15
Morgan-O'Brien Pg.15 H14
Morray Ct. Pg.14 J13
Morse Ave. Pg.20 L16
Mt. Prospect Rd. Pg.14 J14
Munroe Cir. Pg.14,19 J13,14
Murray Ln. Pg.14 J13
Nebel N. Pg.15 K15
Nelson Ln. Pg.15 G15
Nimitz Dr. Pg.20 M17
Norman Ct. Pg.14 H13
North Ave. Pg.15 H15
North Golf Pg.15 G15
North Shore Ave. Pg.20 M17
Northeast Ct. Pg.15 J15
Northeast Pl. Pg.15 J15
Northwest Hwy. Pg.15 H15
Northwest Pl. Pg.15 J15
Northwest Tollway Pg.15 L15
Nuclear Dr. Pg.14 L14
Oak St. Pg.15 H16
Oakton St. Pg.15 K15
Oakwood Ave. Pg.14,15 J14-16
Oakwood St. Pg.15 J15
Olivia Ave. Pg.15 K15
Orchard Ct. Pg.15 H15
Orchard Pl. Pg.20 M16
Orchard St. Pg.15 K16
Oxford Rd. Pg.15 H,K-L15
Park Pl. Pg.15 H16
Park, N. Pg.20 M17
Park, S. Pg.20 M17
Parkview Ln. Pg.15 J17
Parkwood Ln. Pg.15 L17
Parsons Ave. Pg.15 H16
Patricia Ln. Pg.15 G15
Patton Dr. Pg.20 M17
Paula Ln. Pg.20 L17
Pearle Dr. Pg.20 L17
Pearson St. Pg.15 J16
Pennsylvania Ave. Pg.14 K14
Perda Ln. Pg.14 J13
Perry St. Pg.15 H16
Peter Rd. Pg.15 L17
Phoenix Dr. Pg.14 K14
Pine St. Pg.15 K16
Pinehurst Dr. Pg.14 G14
Plainfield Dr. Pg.15 K15
Pleasant Ln. Pg.14 K13
Polynesian Dr. Pg.15 G15
Potter Rd. Pg.28 J3
Prairie Ave. Pg.15 J15-16
Pratt Ave. Pg.20 M17
Princeton St. Pg.14 G14
Prospect Ave. Pg.15 K16
Prospect Ln. Pg.15 K16
Radcliffe Ave. Pg.14,15 G,H14
Railroad Ave. Pg.15 L16
Rand Rd. Pg.15 G15
Rawls Rd. Pg.14 K14
Redeker Rd. Pg.15 H16
Regency Pg.15 G15
Ridge Ln. Pg.14 K13
Rita Rd. Pg.28 J2
River Dr. Pg.15 J17
River Ln. Pg.15 H16
River St. Pg.15 H16
Riverview Ave. Pg.15 K16
Rose Ave. Pg.15 J15
Roxbury Ln. Pg.14 K14
Roxbury Ln., E. Pg.15 K14
Rusty Dr. Pg.15 L17
Sakas Dr. Pg.15 H16
Sandy Ln. Pg.14 H13
Santa Rosa Dr. Pg.15 L15
Scott St. Pg.20 L-M17
Seegers Rd. Pg.15 H15
Seminary Ave. Pg.24 J2
Seymour Ave. Pg.14 J13
Shagbark Dr. Pg.15 J17
Shannon Ct. Pg.14 H13
Shawn Ln. Pg.14 J14
Shepherd Dr. Pg.15 K16
Sherman Pl. Pg.15 H16
Sherwin Ave. Pg.15 K16-17
Sherwood Rd. Pg.15 H17
Short Terr. Pg.14 K13
Simone Dr. Pg.15 G15
Small Ln. Pg.15 F15
South Golf Pg.15 H15
Southeast Ct. Pg.15 J15
Southeast Pl. Pg.15 J15
Southwest Pl. Pg.15 J15
Springfield Ave. Pg.14 J14
Spruance Pl. Pg.14,19 J14
Spruce Ave. Pg.15 K16
Sprucewood Ave. Pg.15 L15
Stark Pl. Pg.14,19 J14
State St. Pg.15 G15
Stewart Ave. Pg.15 J17
Stillwell Dr. Pg.20 M17
Stockton Ave. Pg.15 K16
Stone St. Pg.15 G15
Stratford Rd. Pg.15 G15
Suffield St. Pg.24 J2
Sunset Ave. Pg.20 M17
Susan Dr. Pg.14 K13
Sycamore St. Pg.15,20 K-M16
Teela Ln. Pg.15 G17
Terrace Ln. Pg.14 J14
Thacker St. Pg.15 J15
Therese Terr. Pg.15 F15
Times Dr. Pg.15 K16
Timothy Ln. Pg.15 F15
Touhy Ave. Pg.15 L16
Tracy Terr. Pg.15 G15
Trailside Ln. Pg.15 H17
Tri-State Tollway Pg.15 K17
Tures Ln. Pg.15 K15
University Ln. Pg.15 H17
University St. Pg.15 H17
Van Buren Ave. Pg.15 J15-16
Vassar Ln. Pg.14 G14
Victoria Rd. Pg.14 J14
Villa Dr., E. Pg.15 J15
Villa Dr., W. Pg.15 J15
Village Ct. Pg.14 G14
Waikiki Dr. Pg.15 G15
Walnut Ave. Pg.15,19 J14,15
Walnut St. Pg.15 J15
Walter Ave. Pg.15 H15
Walton St. Pg.15 G16
Warrington Rd. Pg.14 G-J14
Washington Ave. Pg.14 H14
Washington Ct. Pg.15 H14
Washington St. Pg.15 H16
Waterford Ct. Pg.15 F15
Waterford Dr. Pg.15 F15
Wayne Dr. Pg.15 J15
Webford Ave. Pg.15 H16
Webster Ave. Pg.20 M16
Webster Ln. Pg.15 J-L15
Wedgewood Ave. Pg.15 K15
Welwyn Ave. Pg.15 L17
West Grant Dr. Pg.15 J15
West Villa Dr. Pg.15 J15
Western Pg.15 H16
Westfield Ln. Pg.14 J14
Westgate Rd. Pg.15 G-J14
Westmere Rd. Pg.14 H13,14
Westview Dr. Pg.15 L15
Wexford Ct. Pg.15 F15
Whitcomb Ave. Pg.15 J16
White St. Pg.15 K16
Wicke Ave. Pg.15 K16
Wiebolдt's Dr. Pg.15 H15
Wilkins Dr. Pg.14 H14
Wille Rd. Pg.14 K13
Willow Ave. Pg.15 H16
Wilson Ave. Pg.24 J1
Wilson Dr. Pg.14 J13
Windsor Dr. Pg.14 K14
Winthrop Dr. Pg.14 K14
Wisconsin Dr. Pg.14 G14
Wolf Rd. Pg.15 K15
Woodbridge Rd. Pg.15 H15
Woodland Ave. Pg.15 H16
Woodlawn Ave. Pg.15 H15
Woods Ln. Pg.15 H17
Yale Ct. Pg.15 H15
Yorkshire Ln. Pg.15 G15
1st Pg.15 H16
2nd Ave. Pg.15 H-K15
3rd Ave. Pg.15 G-J15
4th Ave. Pg.15 G-K15
5th Ave. Pg.15 G-K15
5th Ct. Pg.15 H15
6th Ave. Pg.15 G-J15
7th Ave. Pg.15 G15
8th Ave. Pg.15 G15

**CEMETERIES**
All Saints Cem. Pg.15 G16

**FOREST PRESERVES**
Lions Woods Pg.24 J1

**PARKS**
Apache Park Pg.15 L16
Arndt Park Pg.15 K16
Blackhawk Park Pg.14 H14
Central Park Pg.24 K1
Chautauqua Park Pg.28 K2
Cherokee Park Pg.24 L1
Cheyenne Park Pg.15 G15
Chino Park Pg.14 J14
Chippewa Park Pg.15 G15
Cornell Park Pg.15 G15
Craig Manor Park Pg.15 F15
Cumberland Terr. Park Pg.15 H15
Des Plaines Park Dist. Pg.15 L17
Dimucci-Lowenberg Park Pg.15 G14
Eton Field Pg.20 M17
Hawaii Park Pg.15 G15
Highridge Knolls Park Pg.14 J13
Jaycee Park Pg.24 L1
Kiwanis Park Pg.24 L1
Kutchen Park Pg.15 G15
Kylemore Greens Park Pg.15 F15
Lake Park Pg.28 M1
Majewski Metro Park Pg.14 K13
McKay-Nealis Park Pg.24 L2
Menominee Park Pg.24 J1
Mountain View Mine Pg.20 J15
Northshire Park Pg.15 H14
Oakwood Park Pg.24 K1
Potawatomie Park Pg.15 H16
Prairie Lakes Park Pg.15 J15
Rand Park & Mystic Waters Pg.15 J17
Seminole Park Pg.20 M17
Sesquicentennial Park Pg.15 H16
Sioux Park Pg.15 G15
Teton Park Pg.15 G15
Tomahawk Park Pg.14 H14
West Park Pg.15 H15
Westfield Gardens Pg.15 J14
Willow Park Pg.15 H16
Woodlawn Park Pg.15 H15

**SCHOOLS**
Algonquin Jr. H.S. Pg.15 J15
Brentwood Sch. Pg.14 H14
Central Sch. Pg.15 J16

Chippewa Jr. H.S. ... Pg.15 ... G15
Cumberland Sch. ... Pg.15 ... G15
DeLourdes College ... Pg.15 ... G16
Des Plaines Christian Sch. ... Pg.15 ... K16
Devonshire Sch. ... Pg.14 ... K14
Einstein Sch. ... Pg.14 ... J14
Forest Sch. ... Pg.15 ... K15
Friendship Jr. H.S. ... Pg.14 ... K13
High Ridge Knoll Sch. ... Pg.14 ... H14
Immanuel Lutheran Sch. ... Pg.15 ... J16
Iroquois Sch. ... Pg.15 ... L17
Maine West Township H.S. ... Pg.15 ... K15
Maryville Academy ... Pg.15 ... F16
Nipper Sch. ... Pg.15 ... F16
North Sch. ... Pg.15 ... H16
Oakton Comm. College ... Pg.15 ... G16
Orchard Place Sch. ... Pg.20 ... M17
Our Lady of Destiny N. Campus ... Pg.20 ... J16
Our Lady of Destiny S. Campus ... Pg.20 ... K16
Plainfield Sch. ... Pg.15 ... K15
Sch. Dist. 62 Office ... Pg.15 ... J16
South Sch. ... Pg.15 ... K16
St. Zachary Catholic Sch. ... Pg.14 ... J13
Terrace Sch. ... Pg.14 ... J14
Willows Academy ... Pg.15 ... J15

**SHOPPING CENTERS**

Market Place S.C. ... Pg.14 ... H13
The Oaks ... Pg.15 ... K16

**MISCELLANEOUS**

Carmelite Sisters Convent ... Pg.28 ... H1
Des Plaines Library ... Pg.15 ... J16
Des Plaines River Trail ... Pg.15 ... G17
Fire Dept. ... Pg.24 ... L1
Forest Hospital ... Pg.15 ... H17
Holy Family Hospital ... Pg.15 ... G16
Park District Admin. and Lesiure Center ... Pg.15 ... L17
Police Dept. ... Pg.24 ... K1
Post Office ... Pg.15 ... K15
Prairie Lakes Comm. Center ... Pg.15 ... J15
Railroad Station ... Pg.15 ... H15
Village Hall ... Pg.24 ... K1

## EAST HAZEL CREST

Page 43

**STREETS**

Ashland Ave. ... P23
Center St. ... O23
Country Ln. ... O22
Dixie Hwy. ... P22
Fisk Ave. ... O23
Forestway Dr. ... O22
Halsted St. ... N24
Hawthorne Dr. ... O22
Laflin St. ... O23
Lathrop St. ... O24
Loomis St. ... O23
Park Ave. ... O22
Throop St. ... O23
Wooded Path Dr. ... O24
171st St. ... O23
172nd Pl. ... O23
172nd St. ... O22,23
173rd St. ... O23
174th St. ... O22,23
175th St. ... O19,23

**SCHOOLS**

Lincoln Sch. ... O23

**MISCELLANEOUS**

R.R. Station ... O22
Village Hall ... O23

## ELA TOWNSHIP

Pages 1-3
Lake County
(For additional listings, see Section 6)

**STREETS**

Buckeye Rd. ... X6
Dorothy Ln. ... X9
Hazel Crest Rd. ... X8
Lake-Cook Rd. ... A10
Old Hicks Rd. ... X9
Plum Pl. ... X6
Plum Rd. ... X8
Rand Ct. ... X8
Rand Rd. ... X8
Redwing Pl. ... X6
Shirley Rd. ... X8

**MISCELLANEOUS**

U.S. Military Reservation ... X8

## ELK GROVE TOWNSHIP

Pages 13,14,18,19

**STREETS**

Aker Pl. ... Pg.19 ... J14
Anderson Terr. ... Pg.19 ... J14
Arnold Ct. ... Pg.19 ... J13
Blackhawk Dr. ... Pg.19 ... H12
Brian Ln. ... Pg.18 ... K11
Briarwood Dr., E. & W. ... Pg.19 ... J11
Busse Rd. ... Pg.19 ... J12
Central Ave. ... Pg.13 ... G11
Clark Ln. ... Pg.19 ... J14
Council Tr. ... Pg.13 ... G11
Crest Ave. ... Pg.18 ... K13
David St. ... Pg.18 ... K11
Dempster St. ... Pg.19 ... J12
Denise St. ... Pg.18 ... K11
Diane East ... Pg.19 ... K12
Edgewood Ln. ... Pg.19 ... H12
Elane Ct. ... Pg.19 ... J11
Elizabeth Dr. ... Pg.19 ... K13
Elm Rd. ... Pg.19 ... L13
Emerson St. ... Pg.13 ... G11
Forest View Ave. ... Pg.18 ... L10
Foster St. ... Pg.13 ... G11
Glendale Ln. ... Pg.19 ... H12
Greenbriar Dr. ... Pg.19 ... H12
Hamilton Rd. ... Pg.19 ... K13
Hayen St. ... Pg.13 ... G11
Hickory Ave. ... Pg.13 ... G11
Higgins Rd. ... Pg.19 ... K12
Hinsdale Rd. ... Pg.19 ... L13
Horne Terr. ... Pg.19 ... J14
Howard St. ... Pg.18 ... L10
Imperial Ct. ... Pg.19 ... J12
Ingram Pl. ... Pg.19 ... J14
Kenneth Dr. ... Pg.19 ... J12
King Ln. ... Pg.19 J13-14
King St. ... Pg.18 ... K11
Kinkaid Ct. ... Pg.19 ... J13
Laurel St. ... Pg.18 ... L10
Leahy Cir., E. & S. ... Pg.19 ... J14
Lee Ln. ... Pg.19 ... L12
Lela St. ... Pg.19 ... L13
Lincoln St. ... Pg.18 ... M8
Linneman Rd. ... Pg.19 ... J12
Lund Rd. ... Pg.19 ... L13
Malmo Rd. ... Pg.19 ... J12
Maple Rd. ... Pg.19 ... L13
Martha St. ... Pg.18 ... M8
McCain Ct. ... Pg.19 ... J14
Meyer Ave. ... Pg.19 ... H12
Munroe Cir. ... Pg.19 ... J14
Northwest Point Rd. ... Pg.13 J10,11
Northwest Tollway ... Pg.19 ... K13
Oakton St. ... Pg.19 ... K13
Prairie Ave. ... Pg.13 ... G11
Prospect Rd. ... Pg.19 ... J14
Richard Ln. ... Pg.19 ... L12
Roppolo Dr. ... Pg.19 ... L12
Sell Rd. ... Pg.19 ... L13
Spruance Pl. ... Pg.19 ... J14
Stark Pl. ... Pg.19 ... J14
Sunset Rd., W. ... Pg.19 ... H12
Susan Lane ... Pg.14 ... G12
Thorndale ... Pg.18 ... L10
Tina Ln. ... Pg.18 ... K11
Tonne Dr. ... Pg.13 ... G11
Touhy Ave. ... Pg.19 ... L13
Vera Ln. ... Pg.19 ... L12
Walnut Ave. ... Pg.19 ... J14
Weiler Rd. ... Pg.19 ... K13
Woodview Ave. ... Pg.18 ... L10
1st Ave. ... Pg.14 ... K12
2nd Ave. ... Pg.14 ... K12
3rd Ave. ... Pg.14 ... K12
4th Ave. ... Pg.14 ... K12
5th Ave. ... Pg.14 ... K12
6th Ave. ... Pg.14 ... K12
7th Ave. ... Pg.14 ... K12
8th Ave. ... Pg.14 ... K12
9th Ave. ... Pg.14 ... K12
10th Ave. ... Pg.14 ... K12
11th Ave. ... Pg.14 ... K12
12th Ave. ... Pg.14 ... K12

**FOREST PRESERVES**

Busse Lake Boating Center ... Pg.13 ... K9
Busse Woods ... Pg.18 ... J10
Model Airplane Flying Field ... Pg.13 ... H8
Ned Brown Forest Preserve ... Pg.18 ... J9

**PARKS**

Carefree Park ... Pg.13 ... G11
Prairie Park ... Pg.13 ... G11

**SCHOOLS**

Einstein Sch. ... Pg.19 ... J14

## ELK GROVE VILLAGE

Pages 17-19
(Portions within DuPage County, for additional listings, see Section 3)

**STREETS**

Alabama Dr. ... Pg.17 ... M6
Albany Ct. ... Pg.17 ... L6
Aldrin Tr. ... Pg.17 ... M7
Alexian Way ... Pg.18 ... L9
Allan Dr. ... Pg.18 ... N11
American Ln. ... Pg.19 ... M13
Anders Dr. ... Pg.17 ... M7
Arizona Pass ... Pg.17 ... L7
Arkansas Dr. ... Pg.17 ... M6
Arlington Heights Rd. ... Pg.18 ... L9
Armstrong Ct. ... Pg.17 ... M7
Armstrong Ln. ... Pg.17 ... M7
Arthur Ave. ... Pg.19 ... M12
Ash St. ... Pg.18 ... M10
Aspen Ln. ... Pg.18 ... M10
Atlantic Ln. ... Pg.17 ... L6
Avon Rd. ... Pg.18 ... L9
Baltimore Dr. ... Pg.17 ... L6
Banbury Ave. ... Pg.18 ... M9
Bangor Ln. ... Pg.17 ... L6
Banyan Dr. ... Pg.18 ... L10
Basswood Ct. ... Pg.18 ... K11
Basswood Dr. ... Pg.18 ... K11
Bay Dr. ... Pg.17 ... M8
Beisner Rd. ... Pg.18 ... L8
Bennett Rd. ... Pg.18 ... J10
Berkenshire Ln. ... Pg.18 ... M9
Bianco Dr. ... Pg.18 ... L10
Biesterfield Rd. ... Pg.17,18 ... L7,M8
Birchwood Ave. ... Pg.18 ... L10
Biscayne Dr. ... Pg.18 ... M8
Bismark Ct. ... Pg.17 ... L7
Blue Jay Cir. ... Pg.17 ... L6
Boardwalk St. ... Pg.13 ... L9
Bonaventure Dr. ... Pg.18 ... M8
Bond St. ... Pg.18 ... J11
Bonita Ave. ... Pg.18 ... L10
Bonnie Ln. ... Pg.18 ... K11
Bordeaux Ct. ... Pg.13 ... L9
Borman Ct. ... Pg.17 ... L7
Bosworth Ln. ... Pg.18 ... M10
Bradford Cr. ... Pg.18 ... L9
Bradley Ln. ... Pg.17 ... M7
Braemar Dr. ... Pg.18 ... M9
Brandywine Ln. ... Pg.18 ... M9
Brantwood Ave. ... Pg.18 ... L9
Brantwood Ct. ... Pg.18 ... L9
Brantwood Pl. ... Pg.18 ... L9
Briarwood Ln. ... Pg.18 ... K10
Brickvale Dr. ... Pg.19 ... M12
Brighton Rd. ... Pg.18 ... M9
Bristol Ln. ... Pg.18 ... M8
Brookhaven Dr. ... Pg.18 ... M10
Brown Cir. ... Pg.17 ... L6
Brummel St. ... Pg.19 ... K11
Brynhaven Ct. ... Pg.18 ... K10
Brynhaven St. ... Pg.18 ... K10
Buckingham Ct. ... Pg.18 ... M9
Burgundy Ct. ... Pg.13 ... L9
Busse Rd. ... Pg.19 ... L12
California St. ... Pg.17 ... L7
Cambridge Dr. ... Pg.19 ... L12
Cardinal Ln. ... Pg.17 ... M6
Carl Blvd. ... Pg.18 ... N11
Carlisle Ave. ... Pg.18 ... M9
Carmen Dr. ... Pg.19 ... L13
Carolina Dr. ... Pg.17 ... M7
Carpenter Ct. ... Pg.17 ... L7
Carr Ct. ... Pg.17 ... M7
Carroll Sq. ... Pg.18 ... K11
Carswell Ave. ... Pg.18 ... M10
Cass Ln. ... Pg.17 ... L7
Cedar Ln. ... Pg.18 ... L10
Cedarwood Ct. ... Pg.18 ... M9
Center St. ... Pg.18 ... M11
Cernan Ct. ... Pg.17 ... L7
Chaffee Ct. ... Pg.17 ... M7
Charing Cross ... Pg.18 ... L10
Charlela Ln. ... Pg.17 ... M8
Charles Dr. ... Pg.18 ... L9
Chase Ave. ... Pg.18 ... L11
Cheekwood Ct. ... Pg.18 ... M9
Cheekwood Dr. ... Pg.18 ... M9
Chelmsford Ln. ... Pg.18 ... L9
Cheltenham Rd. ... Pg.18 ... M8
Chester Ln. ... Pg.17 ... L7
Christa Ct. ... Pg.17 ... L7
Cindy Ln. ... Pg.17 ... M7
Circle Ct. ... Pg.17 ... L7
Clearmont Dr. ... Pg.18 ... M10
Clifford, William Ln. ... Pg.17 ... M7
Clover Hill Ct. ... Pg.18 ... M8
Clover Hill Ln. ... Pg.18 ... M8
Collins Cir. ... Pg.17 ... L7
Colorado Ln. ... Pg.17 ... L7
Columbia Ct. ... Pg.17 ... L7
Columbia Ct. ... Pg.17 ... L7
Commerce Dr. ... Pg.19 ... K12
Concord Ln. ... Pg.17 ... L6
Conrad Ct. ... Pg.17 ... L7
Cooper Ct. ... Pg.17 ... L7
Corrinthia Ct. ... Pg.18 ... L10
Corrinthia Dr. ... Pg.18 ... L10
Cosman Rd. ... Pg.18 ... K9
Cottonwood Dr. ... Pg.18 ... K11
Coyle Ln. ... Pg.19 ... M13
Creighton Ave. ... Pg.18 ... M9
Crest Ave. ... Pg.18 ... L10
Crestwood Ct. ... Pg.18 ... M9
Criss Cir. ... Pg.18 ... J11
Crossen Ave. ... Pg.19 ... K11
Cumberland Cir. ... Pg.18 ... M9
Cunningham Cir. ... Pg.17 ... M7
Cutter Ln. ... Pg.17 ... M6
Cypress Ln. ... Pg.18 ... M10
Dakota Dr. ... Pg.17 ... M7
Dauphine Ct. ... Pg.18 ... L9
David Ln. ... Pg.17 ... M7
Debra Ln. ... Pg.17 ... M7
Deep Wood Ct. ... Pg.18 ... M8
Delaware Ln. ... Pg.17 ... L6
Delmar Ct. ... Pg.12 ... L6
Delphia Ave. ... Pg.18 ... L10
Delphia Ct. ... Pg.18 ... L10
Delta Ln. ... Pg.19 ... M13
Devon Ave. ... Pg.19 ... M11
Diane Ln. ... Pg.17 ... L7
Dierking Terr. ... Pg.19 ... L12
Dogwood Tr. ... Pg.18 ... M10
Doral Ct. ... Pg.12 ... L6
Dorchester Ln. ... Pg.18 ... M9
Dover Ln. ... Pg.18 ... M9
Driftwood Ct. ... Pg.18 ... M9
Dupont Ct. ... Pg.12 ... L6
Eagle Dr. ... Pg.18 ... L11
Eastern Ave. ... Pg.19 ... M13
Easton Ln. ... Pg.17 ... M7
Eden Rd. ... Pg.18 ... M9
Edgeware Rd. ... Pg.18 ... K10
Edgewood Ln. ... Pg.18 ... K10
Elk Grove Blvd. ... Pg.18 ... L10
Elmwood Ln. ... Pg.18 ... M10
Essex Rd. ... Pg.18 ... M9
Estes Ave. ... Pg.18 ... L11
Evans Ct. ... Pg.17 ... M7
Evergreen Cir. ... Pg.13 ... K10
Evergreen St. ... Pg.18 ... K10
Exmoor Rd. ... Pg.18 ... M8
Fairfield Cir. ... Pg.18 ... L8
Fargo Ave. ... Pg.18 ... L11
Fern Dr. ... Pg.18 ... M10
Fleetwood Ln. ... Pg.18 ... K11
Florida Ln. ... Pg.17 ... M6
Forest Ln. ... Pg.18 ... K10
Fox Run Dr. ... Pg.17 ... K6
Franklin Ln. ... Pg.17 ... L7
Galleon Ln. ... Pg.17 ... M6
Garlisch Dr. ... Pg.18 ... J11
Gateshead Ln. ... Pg.18 ... M8
Gaylord St. ... Pg.18 ... J11
Geneva Cir. ... Pg.17 ... L6
Georgia Dr. ... Pg.17 ... M6
Germaine Ln. ... Pg.18 ... K10
Germaine Pl. ... Pg.18 ... K10
Gibson Dr. ... Pg.17 ... L6
Glenn Tr., S. & W. ... Pg.17 ... M7
Gloria Dr. ... Pg.17 ... M7
Gloucester Dr. ... Pg.18 ... L8
Gordon St. ... Pg.18 ... J11
Grange Pl. ... Pg.18 ... M9
Grange Rd. ... Pg.18 ... M9
Grassmere Rd. ... Pg.18 ... L9
Greenbriar St. ... Pg.18 ... K10
Greenleaf Ave. ... Pg.19 ... L12
Greensboro Ct. ... Pg.12 ... K6
Gregory Ct. ... Pg.17 ... M7
Grissom Tr. ... Pg.17 ... M7
Grosvener Ct. ... Pg.18 ... L10
Grosvener Ln. ... Pg.18 ... L10
Grove Dr. ... Pg.18 ... L11
Gullo Ave. ... Pg.18 ... K11
Haar Ln. ... Pg.17 ... M7
Haise Ct. ... Pg.17 ... M7
Haise Ln. ... Pg.17 ... M7
Hampshire Ln. ... Pg.17 ... K6
Harmony Ln. ... Pg.18 ... M10
Hartford Ln. ... Pg.18 ... M11
Hastings Ave. ... Pg.18 ... L9
Hawk Ln. ... Pg.17 ... M6
Hawthorne Ln. ... Pg.18 ... M8
Helen Ln. ... Pg.17 ... L7
Hemlock Dr. ... Pg.18 ... M10
Hickory Ln. ... Pg.18 ... M10
Higgins Rd. ... Pg.18 ... K10
Hodlmair Ct. ... Pg.17 ... M7
Hodlmair Ln. ... Pg.17 ... M7
Holly Ln. ... Pg.18 ... K10
Home Ave. ... Pg.17 ... L-M7
Home Cir. ... Pg.17 ... L7
Howard St. ... Pg.18,19 L11
Hudson Ct. ... Pg.17 ... L6
Huntington Ct. ... Pg.18 ... M8
Huntington Dr. ... Pg.18 ... M8
Idaho Pl. ... Pg.17 ... L7
Indiana Ln. ... Pg.17 ... L7
Inverness Ct. ... Pg.17 ... K6
Iowa Dr. ... Pg.17 ... M6
Ipswich Ct. ... Pg.18 ... L9
Ironwood Dr. ... Pg.18 ... K11
Jackson Cir. ... Pg.17 ... M6
James Ct. ... Pg.17 ... M7
James Way ... Pg.17 ... M7
Jarvis Ave. ... Pg.19 ... L11
Jefferson Sq. ... Pg.18 ... L10
Jersey Ln. ... Pg.17 ... L6
Joey Ln. ... Pg.18 ... K11
Joplin Cir. ... Pg.17 ... M7
Judy Dr. ... Pg.17 ... M7
Julie Dr. ... Pg.17 ... L6
Katherine Way ... Pg.19 ... N11
Kathleen Way ... Pg.17 ... M7
Kelly St. ... Pg.18 ... J10
Kendal Rd. ... Pg.18 ... M9
Kenilworth Ave. ... Pg.18 ... M9
Kennedy, J.F. Blvd. ... Pg.18 ... L9
Kent Ave. ... Pg.18 ... K11
Kentucky Ln. ... Pg.17 ... M6
Keswick Rd. ... Pg.18 ... L9
King St. ... Pg.18 ... J11
Kingsbridge Rd. ... Pg.18 ... M9
Lakeview Ct. ... Pg.18 ... L9
Lancaster Ave. ... Pg.18 ... M9
Landmeier Rd. ... Pg.18 ... L10
Larchmont Dr. ... Pg.18 ... M10
Laurel St. ... Pg.18 ... L10
Lee St. ... Pg.18 ... J11
Leeds Ln. ... Pg.18 ... M8
Leicester Rd. ... Pg.18 ... L-M9
Liberty Ct. ... Pg.17 ... L6
Lilac Ln. ... Pg.18 ... L10
Lincoln Sq. ... Pg.18 ... L10
Lindale St. ... Pg.18 ... K11
Lions Dr. ... Pg.13 ... L10
Little Falls Ct. ... Pg.18 ... M8
Lively Blvd. ... Pg.19. J-L11
Long Boat Dr. ... Pg.17 ... L6
Lonsdale Rd. ... Pg.18 ... M9
Louis Ave. ... Pg.19 ... K11
Louisiana Dr. ... Pg.17 ... M6
Love St. ... Pg.18 ... L11
Lovell Ct. ... Pg.17 ... L7
Lowestoft Ln. ... Pg.18 ... M8
Lunt Ave. ... Pg.19 ... L12
Lynne Dr. ... Pg.18 ... M9
Madison Ct. ... Pg.17 ... M6
Magnolia Ln. ... Pg.18 ... M10
Maine Dr. ... Pg.17 ... L6
Maple Ct. ... Pg.18 ... L11
Maple Ln. ... Pg.18 ... L10
Mark St. ... Pg.18 ... N11
Martha St. ... Pg.18 ... M8
Martin Ln. ... Pg.18 ... J11
Maryland Dr. ... Pg.17 ... L6
McCabe Ave. ... Pg.19 ... L12
McDevitt Cir. ... Pg.17 ... L7
Meacham Rd. ... Pg.17 ... L7
Meadow Ct. ... Pg.18 ... L9
Meegan Way ... Pg.17 ... M7
Memphis Cir. ... Pg.17 ... L6
Michigan Ln. ... Pg.17 ... L6
Middlebury Ln. ... Pg.18 ... L10
Midway Ct. ... Pg.14 ... K12
Milbeck Ave. ... Pg.18 ... L9
Mimosa Ln. ... Pg.18 ... M10
Minnesota Dr. ... Pg.17 ... M7
Minot Ct. ... Pg.17 ... L7
Mississippi Ln. ... Pg.17 ... M6
Missouri Dr. ... Pg.17 ... M6
Mitchell Tr. ... Pg.17 ... M7
Mobile Cir. ... Pg.17 ... M6
Montana Way ... Pg.17 ... L7
Montego Ct. ... Pg.18 ... M8
Montego Dr. ... Pg.18 ... M8
Moore Dr. ... Pg.18 ... L9
Morgan Dr. ... Pg.17 ... M7
Morse Ave. ... Pg.18 ... M11
Mulberry Ln. ... Pg.18 ... M10
Nebraska Dr. ... Pg.17 ... L7
Nerge Rd. ... Pg.17 ... M7
Nevada Ln. ... Pg.17 ... L7
New Mexico Ct. ... Pg.12 ... L7
New Mexico Tr. ... Pg.17 ... L7
New York Ln. ... Pg.17 ... L6
Newberry Dr. ... Pg.17 ... L6
Newport Ave. ... Pg.18 ... M9
Nicholas Blvd. ... Pg.19 ... M12
Normandy Ct. ... Pg.17 ... M7
North Pkwy. ... Pg.18 ... M11
North Port Dr. ... Pg.18 ... M8
Northampton Cir. ... Pg.18 ... L9
Northwest Point Blvd. ... Pg.18 ... J10
Northwest Tollway ... Pg.18 ... J11
Oak St. ... Pg.18 ... L10
Oakton St. ... Pg.18 ... K11
Oakwood Dr. ... Pg.18 ... K10
Oklahoma Cir. ... Pg.17 ... K7
Oklahoma Way ... Pg.17 ... L7
Old Creek Ct. ... Pg.18 ... M8
Old Mill Ln. ... Pg.18 ... M8
Omaha Cir. ... Pg.17 ... L7
Oregon Trail ... Pg.17 ... L7
Oriole Dr. ... Pg.17 ... M6
Orleans Ct. ... Pg.17 ... M6
Oxford Cir. ... Pg.17 ... L7
Pagni Dr. ... Pg.19 ... J11
Pahl Rd. ... Pg.18 ... L8
Pan Am Blvd. ... Pg.19 ... N13
Park Blvd. ... Pg.18 ... M8
Parkchester Rd. ... Pg.18 ... M9
Parker Pl. ... Pg.17 ... M7
Parkview Cr. ... Pg.18 ... L8
Patricia Ct. ... Pg.17 ... M7
Pauly Dr. ... Pg.18 ... J11
Peach Tree Ln. ... Pg.18 ... M10
Pebble Beach Cir. ... Pg.12 ... K6
Penrith Ave. ... Pg.18 ... L9
Perrie Dr. ... Pg.18 ... K11
Pinewood Dr. ... Pg.18 ... M10
Placid Ct. ... Pg.18 ... M10
Placid Way ... Pg.18 ... M10
Pleasant Dr. ... Pg.18 ... L10
Potomac Ln. ... Pg.17 ... L6
Pratt Blvd. ... Pg.19 ... M12
Racine Cir. ... Pg.17 ... M6
Randall St. ... Pg.18 ... K10
Red Fox Ln. ... Pg.17 ... K6
Redwood Ave. ... Pg.18 ... K11
Rev. Morrison Blvd. ... Pg.10 ... L10
Revere Ln. ... Pg.17 ... K6
Richmond Ct. ... Pg.17 ... M7
Ridge Ave. ... Pg.18 ... L10
Ridge Ct. ... Pg.18 ... L10
Ridge Sq. ... Pg.18 ... L10
Ridgewood Rd. ... Pg.18 ... K10
Robin Dr. ... Pg.17 ... L7
Rockwood Dr. ... Pg.18 ... K11
Rohlwing Rd. ... Pg.17 ... M7
Roosa Ln. ... Pg.17 ... M7
Roppolo Dr. ... Pg.19 ... L12
Ruskin Cr. ... Pg.18 ... L9
Ruskin Dr. ... Pg.18 ... L8
Rutgers Ln. ... Pg.17 ... L6
Salem Ct. ... Pg.17 ... L7
Schirra Cir. ... Pg.17 ... L7
Schooner Ln. ... Pg.17 ... L6
Scott St. ... Pg.18 ... J11
Seegers Ave. ... Pg.19 ... K11
Shadywood Ln. ... Pg.18 ... K10
Shelley Ct. ... Pg.18 ... L9
Shelley Rd. ... Pg.18 ... L9
Shepard Cir. ... Pg.17 ... L7
Smethwick Ln. ... Pg.18 ... L9
Somerset Ln. ... Pg.18 ... M9
South Glen Tr. ... Pg.17 ... M7
Spring Creek Ct. ... Pg.18 ... M8
Springdale Ln. ... Pg.18 ... M10
Spruce Ln. ... Pg.18 ... L10
Stafford Cir. ... Pg.17 ... L7
Stanford Cir. ... Pg.18 ... L8
Stanley St. ... Pg.13 ... K11
Stone Brook Ct. ... Pg.18 ... M8
Stone Haven Ave. ... Pg.18 ... L9
Stowe Cir. ... Pg.17 ... L6
Susan Ct. ... Pg.17 ... M7
Sussex Ct. ... Pg.18 ... L10
Sycamore Dr. ... Pg.18 ... M10
Sylvan Ct. ... Pg.13 ... L9
Talbots Ln. ... Pg.18 ... M8
Tanglewood Ct. ... Pg.13 ... K10
Tanglewood Dr. ... Pg.18 ... K10
Tennessee Ln. ... Pg.17 ... M6
Texas St. ... Pg.17 ... L7
Thorndale Ave. ... Pg.18 ... N10
Thorndale Rd. ... Pg.18 ... L10
Timber Dr. ... Pg.17 ... M7
Tonne Rd. ... Pg.18 ... M11
Tottenham Ln. ... Pg.18 ... M9
Touhy Ave. ... Pg.18 ... L11
Tower Ln. ... Pg.18 ... L10
Trowbridge Rd. ... Pg.18 ... M9
Turner Ave. ... Pg.18 ... M9
Union Cir. ... Pg.17 ... L7
United Ln. ... Pg.19 ... M13
University Ln. ... Pg.17 ... K6
Utah Cir. ... Pg.17 ... L7
Utah St. ... Pg.17 ... L7
Verde Ln. ... Pg.18 ... L10
Vermont Dr. ... Pg.17 ... K6
Vernon Cir. ... Pg.17 ... L6
Versailles Cir. ... Pg.18 ... L9
Victoria Ln. ... Pg.18 ... L10
Village Grove Dr. ... Pg.18 ... M9
Vine Ln. ... Pg.17 ... L6
Virginia Dr. ... Pg.17 ... M6
Volkamer Tr. ... Pg.17 ... M7
Von Braun Tr. ... Pg.17 ... M7
Walnut Ln. ... Pg.18 ... M10
Walpole Rd. ... Pg.18 ... M9
Walter Ave. ... Pg.18 ... L9
Warwick Ln. ... Pg.18 ... M10
Wasdale Ave. ... Pg.18 ... M9
Washington Sq. ... Pg.18 ... L10
Waterford Ln. ... Pg.18 ... M8
Wellington Ave. ... Pg.18 ... L9
West Glen Tr. ... Pg.17 ... L7
Westgate Ave. ... Pg.18 ... K10
Westminister Ln. ... Pg.18 ... L8
Westview Dr. ... Pg.18 ... M10
White Tr. ... Pg.17 ... L7
Wildwood Pl. ... Pg.18 ... K11
Wildwood Rd. ... Pg.18 ... K11
Willow Ln. ... Pg.18 ... L10
Wilma Ln. ... Pg.17 ... M7
Wilshire Ave. ... Pg.18 ... L10
Windsor Ln. ... Pg.19 ... K12
Winston Dr. ... Pg.18 ... L8
Wisconsin Ln. ... Pg.17 ... M6
Wise Rd. ... Pg.17 ... L6
Wood Tr. ... Pg.17 ... M7
Woodcrest Ln. ... Pg.18 ... K10
Worden Way ... Pg.17 ... M7
Wyndham Ln. ... Pg.18 ... M8
Yale Ct. ... Pg.17 ... K7
Yarmouth Rd. ... Pg.18 ... M8
York Rd. ... Pg.19 ... M13
Young Cir. ... Pg.17 ... L7

**CEMETERIES**

Elk Grove Cem. ... Pg.18 ... H11

**PARKS**

Appleseed Park ... Pg.18 ... L10
Audubon Park ... Pg.18 ... L10
Bartum Park ... Pg.18 ... L10
Burbank Park ... Pg.18 ... M10
Carson Park ... Pg.17 ... M7
Clark Park ... Pg.17 ... L6
Colony Park ... Pg.17 ... L6
Connor Park ... Pg.17 ... M6
Disney Park ... Pg.17 ... L9
Fairchild Park ... Pg.18 ... M10
Fountain Square Park ... Pg.17 ... L6
Gentile Park ... Pg.17 ... L6
Godiva Park ... Pg.18 ... M8
Hampshire Park ... Pg.17 ... K7
Jaycee Park ... Pg.18 ... L10
Jensen Park ... Pg.17 ... M6
Johnson Park ... Pg.17 ... M7
Lindbergh Park ... Pg.17 ... L7
Lions Park ... Pg.18 ... L10
Marsh Park ... Pg.17 ... L7
Mather Park ... Pg.17 ... M7
McGee Park ... Pg.17 ... L6
Morton Park ... Pg.18 ... M10
Muir Park ... Pg.18 ... M11
Newberry Park ... Pg.17 ... L6
Olmstead Park ... Pg.18 ... L10
Osborn Park ... Pg.18 ... K11
Park District Athletic Field ... Pg.17. N9,10
Potomac Park ... Pg.17 ... L6
Powell Park ... Pg.17 ... K7
Roosevelt Park ... Pg.17 ... M9
Udall Park ... Pg.18 ... K11
Woodland Meadows Park ... Pg.17 ... L8

**SCHOOLS**

Adlai E. Stevenson Sch. ... Pg.17 ... M7
Adolph Link Sch. ... Pg.17 ... L7
Byrd Sch. ... Pg.18 ... M9
Clearmont Sch. ... Pg.18 ... M10
Elk Grove H.S. ... Pg.18 ... L9
Grove Jr. H.S. ... Pg.18 ... L10
Margaret Mead Jr. H.S. ... Pg.17 ... L6
Queen of Rosary Sch. ... Pg.18 ... L10
Ridge Sch. ... Pg.18 ... L10
Rupley Sch. ... Pg.18 ... K10
Salt Creek Sch. ... Pg.18 ... L9

**SHOPPING CENTERS**

Devon Ave. Market ... Pg.18 ... M11
Devon Square ... Pg.18 ... M9
Elk Crossing S.C. ... Pg.18 ... L9
Elk Grove Woods S.C. ... Pg.18 ... K10
Estes Commons ... Pg.19 ... L12
Gullo Center ... Pg.19 ... L13
Longfellow Plaza ... Pg.18 ... L9
Mallard Crossing ... Pg.17 ... L7
Shawnway S.C. ... Pg.17 ... L7
Strawberry Hill S.C. ... Pg.17 ... L7
Super K Center ... Pg.17 ... L7
Town Center S.C. ... Pg.18 ... L9

**MISCELLANEOUS**

Alexian Bros. Hosp. ... Pg.18 ... L8
Elk Grove Park Dist. Office ... Pg.18 ... L9
Fire Departments ... Pg.17-19 ... K11,L7,9,12
Fire Dept. Office ... Pg.18 ... L10
Fire Dept. Training Center ... Pg.19 ... K4
Hattendorf Center ... Pg.18 ... L10
Historical Society ... Pg.18 ... L9
Kenneth Young Center ... Pg.17 ... M8
Library ... Pg.18 ... L9
Municipal Center ... Pg.18 ... L9
Pavillon Fitness Center ... Pg.18 ... L9

Pirate's Cove . Pg.18 ... L9
Post Office ... Pg.18 ... K11
Public Works Office ... Pg.17 ... K11
Rainbow Falls Aquatic Center ... Pg.18 ... L10

## EVANSTON

Pages 27,30,31

### STREETS

Arnold Pl. ... Pg.31 ... L14
Asbury Ave. ... Pg.27,31 ... H-L13
Ashland Ave. . Pg.27,31 ... H-L13
Austin St. ... Pg.31 ... L13
Barton Ave. ... Pg.31 ... L13
Bennett Ave. . Pg.27 ... H12
Benson ... Pg.27 ... J14
Bernard Pl. ... Pg.30 ... G11
Bradley Pl. ... Pg.31 ... K12
Broadway ... Pg.27 ... G13
Brown Ave. . Pg.27,31 ... H-L13
Brummel St. . Pg.31 L12-13
Bryant Ave. .. Pg.27 ... H13
Burnham Pl. . Pg.27 ... K14
Callan Ave. ... Pg.31 ... L14
Calvin Cir. ... Pg.27,30,31 ... H11
Case Pl. ... Pg.31 ... L14
Case St. ... Pg.31 ... L14
Central Park Ave. ... Pg.27 ... H11
Central St. ... Pg.27,30 ... H11,13
Chancellor ... Pg.27 ... H13
Chicago Ave. . Pg.27,31 ... J,K14
Church St. ... Pg.27 ... J12
Clark St. ... Pg.27 J13-14
Cleveland St. . Pg.31 K12-13
Clifford St. ... Pg.30 ... G11
Clinton Pl. ... Pg.27 ... H14
Clyde ... Pg.31 ... L14
Colfax Pl. ... Pg.30 ... H11
Colfax St. ... Pg.27 H12-14
Colfax Terr. .. Pg.27 ... H13
Cowper Ave. . Pg.30 ... H11
Crain St. ... Pg.27 K12-14
Crawford Ave. Pg.30 ... G11
Culver St. ... Pg.30 ... H11
Custer Ave. .. Pg.31 ... L14
Darrow Ave. ... Pg.27,31 ... J-L13
Dartmouth ... Pg.27 ... H14
Dartmouth Pl. Pg.30 ... H11
Davis St. ... Pg.27 J12-14
Dempster St. . Pg.27 ... K12
Dewey Ave. . Pg.27,31 ... J-L13
Dobson St. ... Pg.31 L12-13
Dodge ... Pg.27 ... H13
Dodge Ave. . Pg.27,31 ... J-L13
Eastwood ... Pg.27 ... G13
Edgemere Ct. . Pg.31 ... K14
Elgin Rd. ... Pg.27 ... H-J12,J14
Elinor Pl. ... Pg.27 ... J13
Elm Ave. ... Pg.27 ... H12
Elmwood Ave. Pg.31 ... K14
Emerson St. . Pg.27 J13-14
Euclid Park Pl. Pg.27 ... G14
Ewing Ave. .. Pg.27 ... H12
Florence Ave. . Pg.27,31 ... J-L13
Forest Ave. .. Pg.31 ... K14
Forest Pl. ... Pg.27,31 J14
Forestview Rd. Pg.27 ... H12
Foster St. ... Pg.27,31 ... J12-14
Fowler ... Pg.31 ... K12
Gaffield Pl. ... Pg.27 ... H14
Garnett Pl. ... Pg.27 J13-14
Garrison Ave. . Pg.27 ... G14
Geneva Pl. ... Pg.27 ... H11
Girard Ave. .. Pg.27 ... G13
Grant St. ... Pg.27 H12,13
Greeley Ave. ... Pg.30 ... H11
Greenleaf St. . Pg.31 K13-14
Greenwood St. Pg.27 J12-14
Grey Ave. ... Pg.31 . H-K12
Grove St. ... Pg.27 J12-14
Hamilton St. . Pg.27 ... K14
Hamlin ... Pg.27 ... H14
Hampton Pkwy. Pg.27 ... G13
Harrison Ave. . Pg.27 ... H13
Harrison St. .. Pg.27,30 ... H11-12
Hartley Ave. .. Pg.31 . H-L12
Hartrey Ave. .. Pg.31 . H-L12
Hartzell St. ... Pg.30,31 ... H11-12
Harvard Tr. .. Pg.31 ... L13
Hastings Ave. Pg.30 ... H11
Haven St. ... Pg.27 ... H14
Hawthorne Ln. Pg.27 ... H12
Hayes ... Pg.30 ... H11
Highland Ave. Pg.30 ... H11
Hillside Ln. .. Pg.30 ... H11
Hillside Rd. .. Pg.30 ... H11
Hinman Ave. . Pg.31 . J-K14
Hovland Ct. .. Pg.27 ... J13
Howard St. .. Pg.31 ... L13
Hull Tr. ... Pg.31 L13-14
Hurd Ave. ... Pg.27 ... H12
Ingleside Park Pl. ... Pg.27 ... G14
Jackson ... Pg.27 . H-J13
Jenks St. ... Pg.27 G12-13
Judson Ave. . Pg.31 . J-K14
Kedzie St. ... Pg.31 ... K14
Keeney St. ... Pg.31 L12-14
Kirk St. ... Pg.31 ... L13
Knox Cir. ... Pg.30,31 H11
Lake Shore Blvd. ... Pg.31 ... K14
Lake St. ... Pg.27 J12-13
Lakeside Ct. .. Pg.27 ... G14
Laurel ... Pg.27 ... J12
Lawndale Ave. Pg.27 ... H11
Lee St. ... Pg.31 K12-14
Leland Ave. .. Pg.27 ... J12
Lemar Ave. .. Pg.27 ... J12
Leon Pl. ... Pg.27 ... H13
Leonard Pl. .. Pg.27 ... H13
Library St. ... Pg.27 ... H14
Lincoln St. ... Pg.27 H12-14
Lincolnwood Dr. ... Pg.27 ... H12
Linden Pl. ... Pg.31 ... L14
Livingston St. Pg.27 ... G13
Lyons St. ... Pg.27 J12-13
Madison Pl. .. Pg.31 ... K12
Madison St. .. Pg.31 ... K13
Main St. ... Pg.31 K12-14
Maple Ave. ... Pg.31 . H-K14
Marcy Ave. ... Pg.27 . G-H11
Martha Ln. ... Pg.27 ... H12
McCormick Blvd. ... Pg.27 ... H12
McDaniel Ave. Pg.27 . G-K12
Meadowlark Ln. Pg.27 ... G11
Michigan Ave. Pg.31 ... K14
Milburn St. .. Pg.31 ... H14
Monroe St. .. Pg.31 ... K13
Monticello ... Pg.27 ... G14
Mulford St. .. Pg.31 L13-14
Nathaniel Pl. . Pg.31 ... K12
Normandy Pl. Pg.27 ... H11
Noyes Ct. ... Pg.27 ... H14
Noyes St. ... Pg.30 H11-13
Oak Ave. ... Pg.27 ... J14
Oakton St. ... Pg.31 ... L13
Orrington Ave. Pg.27 . H-J14
Otto Ln. ... Pg.30 ... G11
Park Pl. ... Pg.30 ... G12
Payne St. ... Pg.30 H11-13
Pioneer Rd. .. Pg.27 ... H12
Pitner Ave. ... Pg.31 ... K12
Poplar ... Pg.27 ... H13
Prairie Ave. .. Pg.27 . G,H12
Pratt Ct. ... Pg.27 ... H14
Princeton Ave. Pg.30 ... G11
Prospect Ave. Pg.30 ... H11
Railroad ... Pg.31 ... J13
Reba Pl. ... Pg.31 ... K14
Reese Ave. ... Pg.27 ... H12
Richmond Ave. Pg.31 ... L12
Ridge Ave. ... Pg.27 . H-J14
Ridge Ct. ... Pg.31 ... K13
Ridge Terr. .. Pg.31 ... H14
Ridgeway Ave. Pg.30 ... H11
Rosalie ... Pg.27 ... H13
Roslyn Pl. ... Pg.27 ... G14
Seward St. ... Pg.31 L12-13
Sheridan Pl. .. Pg.27 ... G14
Sheridan Rd. . Pg.31 . G-K14
Sheridan Sq. . Pg.31 ... L15
Sherman Ave. Pg.31 ... K14
Simpson St. . Pg.27 ... H13
South Blvd. .. Pg.31 L13-14
St. Mark Ct. .. Pg.31 ... J13
Stewart Ave. . Pg.27 ... G12
Terry Pl. ... Pg.27 ... G14
Thayer St. ... Pg.30 G11-12
Thelin Ct. ... Pg.27 ... J13
University Pl. . Pg.27 ... J14
Wade St. ... Pg.27 ... J12
Walnut ... Pg.27 ... G12
Warren Blvd. . Pg.31 ... L12
Washington St. Pg.31 K12,13
Wesley Ave. .. Pg.31 . H-L13
West Dr. ... Pg.30 ... H11
Wilder St. ... Pg.27 ... K13
Woodbine ... Pg.27 ... G13
Woodland Rd. Pg.27 ... H12

### CEMETERIES

Calvary Cem. . Pg.31 ... L14

### FOREST PRESERVES

Perkins Woods Pg.31 ... H12

### GOLF COURSES

Peter Jan's G.C. Pg.31 ... H13

### HOSPITALS

Community Hosp. ... Pg.27 ... H12
Evanston Hosp. Pg.27 ... G14
St. Francis Hosp. ... Pg.31 ... L14

### PARKS

Ackerman Park Pg.31 ... H12
Alexander Park Pg.31 ... J13
Athletic Field . Pg.27 ... J12
Baker Park ... Pg.31 ... L14
Barton Park ... Pg.31 ... L13
Bent Park ... Pg.30 ... H11
Brummel Park Pg.31 ... L13
Burnham Shores Park ... Pg.31 ... K15
Cartright Park Pg.30 ... H11
Centennial Park Pg.31 ... J14
Chandler Park Pg.31 ... H14
Clark Square Park ... Pg.31 ... K15
Cornelia Lunt Park ... Pg.31 ... J14
Curry Park ... Pg.27 ... K14
Dawes Park .. Pg.31 ... J14
Deering Estate Park ... Pg.31 ... H14
Dempster St. Park ... Pg.31 ... K14
Dobson Brummel Park ... Pg.31 ... L13
Eggleston Park Pg.31 ... H12
Eiden Park ... Pg.31 ... K14
Elks Park ... Pg.31 ... L14
Elliott Park ... Pg.31 ... K15
Fireman's Park Pg.27 ... H14
Fitzsimmons Park ... Pg.31 ... K14
Foster Field .. Pg.27 ... H13
Fullerton Park Pg.27 ... H14
Garden Park .. Pg.31 ... L13
Gilbert Park .. Pg.27 ... J13
Grey Park ... Pg.31 ... K13
Howell Park .. Pg.17 ... G12
Independence Park ... Pg.27 ... H12
Ingraham Park Pg.31 ... H13
James Park .. Pg.31 ... L12
Kamen Park .. Pg.31 ... L13
Larimer Park . Pg.31 ... L14
Leahy Park .. Pg.31 ... H13
Leider Park .. Pg.31 ... H13
Lomar Park .. Pg.31 ... L13
Lovelace Park Pg.30 ... H11
Mason Park .. Pg.27 ... J13
Megowen Park Pg.31 ... L13
Merrick Park . Pg.31 ... J13
Milburn Park . Pg.31 ... H14
Penny Park .. Pg.31 ... J13
Philbrick Park Pg.27 ... H14
Quinlan Park . Pg.31 ... H12
Raymond Park Pg.27 ... J14
Ridgeville Park Pg.31 ... L14
Robert Crown Park ... Pg.31 ... K13
Smith Park .. Pg.31 ... J13
Stockholm Pl. Park ... Pg.27 ... K14
Talmage Park . Pg.27 ... H14
Trahan Park .. Pg.31 ... K14

### SCHOOLS

Barbereaux Sch. ... Pg.26 ... H11
Chiaravalle Montessori Sch. ... Pg.31 ... K14
Chute Jr. H.S. Pg.31 ... L13
Cove Sch. ... Pg.27 ... H13
David B. Dewey Sch. ... Pg.27 ... J13
Dawes Sch. .. Pg.31 ... L13
Evanston Twp. H.S. ... Pg.27 ... J12
Faith Christian Academy ... Pg.31 ... J13
Haven Jr. H.S. Pg.27 ... H13
Kendall College Pg.27 ... H14
King Lab Sch. Pg.27 ... H13
Learning Sch. Pg.31 ... L13
Lincoln Sch. . Pg.31 ... K14
Lincolnwood Sch. ... Pg.27 ... H12
Madison Street Sch. ... Pg.31 ... K13
Nichols Sch. . Pg.31 ... K14
Northwestern University ... Pg.27 ... H14
Oakton Sch. .. Pg.31 ... L13
Orrington Sch. Pg.27 ... H14
Pope John XXIII Sch. ... Pg.31 ... K14
Rimland Sch. for Autistic Citizens ... Pg.31 ... L13
Roycemore Sch. ... Pg.27 ... H14
Shore Sch. .. Pg.27 ... J12
Skiles Jr. H.S. Pg.27 ... J12
St. Athanasius Sch. ... Pg.27 ... H13
St. Mary's Sch. Pg.27 ... J14
Washington Sch. ... Pg.31 ... K13
Willard Sch. .. Pg.27 ... H12

### MISCELLANEOUS

Byron Coon Sports Ctr. ... Pg.27 ... G13
Fire Station .. Pg.31 ... K14
Grosse Pt. Lighthouse & Maritime Museum ... Pg.27 ... H14
Henry Crown Sports Pavilion ... Pg.27 ... H14
James L. Allen Center ... Pg.27 ... H14
Ladd Arboretum ... Pg.27 ... H13
Lee St. Beach Pg.31 ... K15
Library ... Pg.31 ... J14
Mary & Leigh Black Gallery ... Pg.27 ... H14
McCormick Auditorium ... Pg.27 ... H14
N.U. Evanston Research Park ... Pg.27 ... J14
Noyes Cultural Ctr. ... Pg.31 ... H14
Patton Gym .. Pg.27 ... H14
Pick Staiger Concert Hall ... Pg.27 ... H14
Post Office ... Pg.31 ... J13
Presbyterian Home for the Aged Pg.27 ... H11
Regenstein Hall of Music ... Pg.27 ... H14
Robert Crown Center ... Pg.31 ... K13
Ryan Stadium Pg.27 ... H13
Seabury Western Theological Seminary .. Pg.27 ... H14
South Blvd. Beach ... Pg.31 ... L15
Student Residences ... Pg.27 ... H14
Theater & Interpretation Center ... Pg.27 ... H14
Wells Field ... Pg.27 ... G13
Welsh-Ryan Arena ... Pg.27 ... G13

## FLOSSMOOR

Pages 42,43,48

### STREETS

Acorn Dr. ... Pg.48 ... R22
Alexander Crescent ... Pg.48 ... R21
Amherst Ct. .. Pg.43 ... R22
Argyle Ave. .. Pg.42 ... Q21
Arquilla ... Pg.42 ... R21
Ash St. ... Pg.42 ... Q20
Ashland Ave. . Pg.43 ... R23
Ashland Ln. .. Pg.48 ... R23
Ashley Oak Dr. Pg.43 ... R22
Aspen St. ... Pg.42 ... Q20
Avers Ave. ... Pg.42 ... R20
Ballantrae Way Pg.47 ... R20
Balmoral Crescent ... Pg.42 ... R21
Balmoral Glen Pg.42 ... R21
Baythorne Dr. Pg.42 ... R21
Beech St. ... Pg.42 ... Q20
Berry Rd. ... Pg.42 ... R21
Berwick Ct. .. Pg.47 ... R20
Bob-O-Link Rd. Pg.48 ... R21
Bonnie Brae Crescent ... Pg.48 ... S21
Braeburn Ave. Pg.42,48 ... R21,22
Braeburn St. . Pg.48 ... R21
Braemer Rd. . Pg.42 ... Q21
Brassie Ave. .. Pg.42,48 ... R22,S21
Brentwood Ct. Pg.42 ... R20
Brookwood Dr. Pg.48 ... S21
Bruce Ave. ... Pg.42 ... Q21
Brumley Dr. .. Pg.42 ... Q21
Bunker Ave. .. Pg.42,48 R21
Burns Ave. ... Pg.42 ... Q21
Butterfield Cir. Pg.48 ... S21
Butterfield Ln. Pg.48 ... S22
Butterfield Rd. Pg.48 ... S21
Caddy St. ... Pg.42 ... R21
Cambridge Ave. Pg.43,48 ... R,S22
Candlewood Ct. Pg.42 ... R20
Cardinal Ct. .. Pg.48 ... S21
Carmel Dr. ... Pg.48 ... Q21
Caroll Pkwy. . Pg.43 ... R22
Central Dr. ... Pg.42 ... R21
Central Park Ave. ... Pg.42. R,S20
Cherry Hills Dr. Pg.42 ... R20
Chestnut Dr. . Pg.48 ... R20
Collett Ln. ... Pg.43 ... Q22
Connie Ct. ... Pg.48 ... S23
Cooley Pl. ... Pg.48 ... R21
Cornell Rd. .. Pg.48 ... S22
Crawford Ave. Pg.42 ... R19
Cullade St. ... Pg.47 ... R20
Cummings Ln. Pg.43 ... Q22
Dartmouth Rd. Pg.48 ... R22
Dixie Hwy. ... Pg.43 ... Q22,S23
Douglas Ave. . Pg.42 ... R21
Driftwood Ct. . Pg.42 ... R20
Dunbar St. ... Pg.47 ... R20
Dundonald Ln. Pg.48 ... R22
Dunfries St. .. Pg.47 ... R20
Eden Oaks Dr. Pg.43 ... R22
Elaine Ct. ... Pg.42 ... R20
Elm Ct. ... Pg.42 ... R20
Elm St. ... Pg.42 ... Q20
Embassy Row Pg.42 ... Q21
Emelia Ct. ... Pg.42 ... R21
Evans Rd. ... Pg.43 ... R22
Flossmoor Rd. Pg.42,43 R20
Gardner Rd. .. Pg.43 ... Q22
Gianna Dr. ... Pg.43 ... R22
Golfview Ln. . Pg.42 ... R22
Gordon Dr. .. Pg.42 ... Q21
Governors Hwy. Pg.42 ... Q21
Hagen Ln. ... Pg.43 ... R22
Hamlin Ave. .. Pg.42 ... R20
Hampton Ct. . Pg.42 ... R20
Hanover Ln. .. Pg.48 ... R22
Harding Ave. . Pg.42 ... R19
Harold's Crescent ... Pg.48 ... S21
Harvard ... Pg.48 ... S22
Harwood Ave. Pg.42 ... Q22
Hawthorne Ln. Pg.42 ... R21
Heather Hill Crescent ... Pg.48 ... R21
Heather Hill Ct. Pg.48 ... S21
Heather Rd. .. Pg.42 ... Q21
Holbrook Rd. . Pg.43 ... R23
Holly Ln. ... Pg.48 ... S22
Hutchinson Rd. Pg.43 ... Q22
Imperial Ct. .. Pg.42 ... Q21
Joyce Dr. ... Pg.48 ... R20
Kathleen Ln. . Pg.48 ... S21
Kedzie Ave. .. Pg.42 ... R20
Knollwood Dr. Pg.48 ... R22
Lake Dr. ... Pg.48 ... S21
Lanark St. ... Pg.47 ... R20
Latimer Ln. .. Pg.43 ... Q22
Laura Ln. ... Pg.48 ... S21
Laurel Ave. .. Pg.48 ... R22
Lawrence Crescent ... Pg.48. R,S21
Leavitt Ave. .. Pg.42 ... R21
Link Ct. ... Pg.42 ... R21
Lynwood Ct. . Pg.48 ... R23
MacFarlane Crescent ... Pg.42 ... R21
MacHeath Crescent ... Pg.48 ... R21
Maple Rd. ... Pg.42 ... R20
Markey Ln. .. Pg.48 ... R23
Marston Ln. .. Pg.43 ... Q22
Maryland Ave. Pg.42 ... R21
Mast Ct. ... Pg.43 ... R22
McDonald Ln. Pg.43 ... Q22
Monterey Dr. . Pg.48 ... Q21
Oak Ct. ... Pg.42 ... R20
Oak Lane Rd. . Pg.48 ... S21
Oak St. ... Pg.42 ... R20
Oakherst St. . Pg.48 ... R20
Oakmont Ave. Pg.42 ... R21
Oxford Ct. ... Pg.48 ... R22
Palmer Ct. ... Pg.42 ... R20
Park Dr. ... Pg.42. Q,R21
Patricia Ln. .. Pg.48 ... S21
Perry Rd. ... Pg.48 ... S21
Perth ... Pg.42 ... Q21
Pheasant Ct. . Pg.48 ... S21
Pinehurst ... Pg.48 ... R23
Polly Ln. ... Pg.48 ... R21
Poplar ... Pg.42 ... R20
Poplar Pl. ... Pg.42 ... R20
Princeton Rd. Pg.48 ... S22
Quail Ct. ... Pg.48 ... S21
Redwood Ct. . Pg.48 ... Q21
Redwood Ln. . Pg.48 ... Q21
Richards Ct. . Pg.48 ... S23
Richwood Terr. Pg.48 ... R23
Robertson Ln. Pg.42 ... R22
School St. ... Pg.42 ... R21
Scott Ave. ... Pg.42 ... Q21
Scott Cres. ... Pg.48 ... R21
Sequoia Ln. .. Pg.48 ... Q21
Skye Ct. ... Pg.47 ... R20
Springfield Ave. Pg.42 ... R19
Sterling Ave. . Pg.42. Q,R21
Stonegate ... Pg.48 ... R20
Stonegate Ct. Pg.42 ... R21
Strieff Ln. ... Pg.42 ... R21
Sunset Ave. .. Pg.42 ... R21
Sylvan Ct. ... Pg.48 ... R23
Tanglewood Dr. Pg.42 ... R20
Thomas Ct. .. Pg.48 ... S23
Thornwood Dr. Pg.48 ... R22
Tina Ln. ... Pg.48 ... S23
Travers Ln. .. Pg.43 ... R22
Troon St. ... Pg.47 ... R20
Vardon Ln. .. Pg.43 ... Q22
Vardon Pl. ... Pg.42 ... R22
Verne Ln. ... Pg.42 ... Q21
Vollmar Rd. .. Pg.48 ... S20
Wallace Dr. .. Pg.42 ... Q21
Western Ave. . Pg.48 ... T22
Willow St. ... Pg.42 ... R20
Woodhollow Dr. ... Pg.42 ... R20
Yale Rd. ... Pg.48 ... S23
187th St. ... Pg.43 Q19,22
188th St. ... Pg.42 ... Q19
189th St. ... Pg.42 ... Q19
190th St. ... Pg.42 ... R20
192nd St. ... Pg.42 ... R20
194th St. ... Pg.48 ... R20
195th St. ... Pg.48 ... R20
196th St. ... Pg.42 ... R20
198th St. ... Pg.48 ... S20

### CEMETERIES

St. Paul Cemetery ... Pg.48 ... S22

### GOLF COURSES

Cherry Hill Country Club ... Pg.42 ... Q20
Flossmoor Country Club ... Pg.48 ... R22
Pinehurst Park Pg.48 ... R23

### PARKS

Flossmoor Park ... Pg.42 ... R22
Highland Park Pg.48 ... S21
Iron Oak Park Pg.48 ... S21
Pheasant Trail Park ... Pg.48 ... S22

### SCHOOLS

Flossmoor Hills Sch. ... Pg.42 ... Q20
Flossmoor Montessori Sch. ... Pg.42 ... Q22
Heather Hill Sch. ... Pg.48 ... R21
Homewood Flossmoor H.S. ... Pg.42 ... Q21
Infant Jesus of Prague Sch. ... Pg.42 ... R21
Leavitt Ave. Sch. ... Pg.42 ... R21
Parker Jr. H.S. Pg.42 ... R21
Western Avenue Sch. ... Pg.42 ... R22

### SHOPPING CENTERS

Flossmoor Commons ... Pg.48 ... S20

### MISCELLANEOUS

Fire Dept. ... Pg.42 ... Q21
Ice Arena ... Pg.48 ... Q21,R22
Library ... Pg.42 ... R21
Police Dept. . Pg.42 ... R21
R.R. Station .. Pg.42 ... R21
Village Hall ... Pg.48 ... R21

## FORD HEIGHTS

Pages 49,50

### STREETS

Ambassador Ln. ... T27
Berkeley Ave. ... T27
Calumet Expwy. ... R,T27
Cannon Ln. ... T27
Columbia Ave. ... T27
Congress Ln. ... T27
Cottage Grove Ave. ... T26
Deer Creek Dr. ... U27
Defores ... T27
Diplomat Ln. ... T27
Drexel Ave. ... T26
Eighth Pl. ... T27
Eighth St. ... T27
Ellis St. ... T27
Embassy Ln. ... T27
Greenwood Ave. ... T27
Hammond Ln. ... T27
Hickory St. ... R26
Kennedy Ln. ... T27
Lexington Ave. ... T27
Lexington Cir. ... T27
Lincoln Hwy. ... U27
Ninth St. ... T27
Park Ave. ... T26
Park Ln. ... T27
Park St. ... T27
Porter Ave. ... T27
Pullman ... T27
Regent ... T27
Seeley Ave. ... T27
Senator Ln. ... T27
State Route 394 ... T27
Stoney Island ... T27
Stony Island Ave. ... T27
Summit Dr. ... U27
Torrence Ave. ... T28
U.S. Route 30 ... U27
Vincennes Rd. ... Q25
Werline ... T26
Williams ... T27
Willow St. ... R26
Woodlawn Ave. ... T27
10th Pl. ... T26
10th St. ... T27
11th Pl. ... T26
11th St. ... T27
12th St. ... T27
13th St. ... T26
14th Pl. ... U27
14th St. ... U27
15th Pl. ... U27
16th St. ... U26
15th St. ... U26
17th St. ... U26
205th St. ... T27
206th St. ... T27
207th St. ... T27
208th St. ... T27
209th St. ... T27

### CEMETERIES

Mt. Glenwood Cemetery . Q25

### FOREST PRESERVES

Jurgensen Woods ... Q26

### GOLF COURSES

Glenwoodie Golf Course . R25

### SCHOOLS

Cottage Grove Sch. ... U26
Medgar Evers Sch. ... T27
Tideye A. Phillips Elem. Sch. ... U27
Woodlawn Sch. ... U27

### MISCELLANEOUS

Fire Department ... R25
Police Department ... R25
Village Hall ... U27

## FRANKFORT

Page 46
Will County
(For additional listings, see Section 8)

### STREETS

Abbottsford Ln. ... V14
Aberdeen Rd. ... V13
Ascot Ln. ... U12
Ayshire Ct. ... V14
Bramble Dr. ... U12
Bristol Ct. ... U12
Brittany Ct. ... U14
Brown Dr. ... U12
Burgundy Dr. ... U12
Chadwick Ct. ... U12
Colin Dr. ... S14
Colony Ln. ... U14
Coventry Ln. ... U14
Deer Path Rd. ... U14
Dover Ct. ... V14
Drummore Ln. ... V14
Duns Ct. ... V15
Durham Dr. ... V14
Fairway Ln. ... U13
Firth Ct. ... V13
Georgetown Rd. ... U15
Ginger Ln. ... U12
Glen Eagles Ct. ... V14
Glenbar Ln. ... V14
Golf Club Ln. ... U14
Grey Ln. ... S14
Hawthorn Dr. ... U14
Heather Ln. ... V14
Heritage Ct. ... V14
Highland Rd. ... V14
Hunter Woods Dr. ... U14
Huntsmore Dr. ... V14
James St. ... S14
Lakeside Ct. ... S14
Laraway Rd. ... V13
Maple Ct. ... U13
Milton Bridge ... V15
Old N. Church Rd. ... U14
Pheasant Trail ... U13
Plymouth Ct. ... V14
Prestwick Dr. ... U14
Shetland Dr. ... V15
St. Andrews Way ... V14
Steeplechase Dr. ... U14
Stuart Ct. ... V14
Timber Ln. ... V13
Troon Cir. ... V15
Troon Tr. ... V15
Virginia Ct. ... U15
Yorktown Rd. ... U15
80th Ave. ... V14
84th Ave. ... U13

### GOLF COURSES

Prestwick C.C. ... U14

### SCHOOLS

Hickory Creek Sch. ... V14

### MISCELLANEOUS

Camp Manitoqua ... V14

## FRANKFORT TOWNSHIP

Pages 39,40,46
Will County
(For additional listings, see Section 8)

### STREETS

Acorn Ridge Dr. ... Pg.46 ... T14
Almond Ct. .. Pg.46 ... S15
Arran Dr. ... Pg.46 ... S14
Avimore Ln. .. Pg.46 ... T14
Barbara Ln. .. Pg.46 ... S14
Benton Dr. ... Pg.46 ... S14
Birchwood Ln. Pg.46 ... T14
Braemer Ln. . Pg.46 ... S14
Brickstone Dr. Pg.46 ... T13
Bruce Ct. ... Pg.39 ... Q8
Carrie Ct. ... Pg.46 ... S14
Cobblestone Ct. Pg.46 ... T14
Countryside Ct. Pg.46 ... T14
Countryside Ln. Pg.46 ... T14
Deerfield Ct. . Pg.46 ... S15
Douglas Ct. .. Pg.46 ... S15
Dove Ln. ... Pg.46 ... T14
Driftwood Dr. . Pg.46 ... T14
Edinburgh Ln. Pg.46 ... S15
Elizabeth Ln. . Pg.46 ... T14

Ellen Ln. . . . . Pg.46 . . T14
Emerald Ct. . . Pg.46 . . S15
Ethyl Ln. . . . . Pg.46 . . Q12
Evan Terrace . Pg.46 . . S14
Evergreen Dr. . Pg.46 . . S13
Fallbrook Ct. . . Pg.46 . . T14
Farmhouse Rd. Pg.46 . . T14
Farmington Ln. Pg.46 . . T14
Frankfort Sq. Rd.
                 Pg.46 . . S14
Gailview Ct. . . Pg.46 . . S15
Gailview Ln. . . Pg.46 . . S14
Garland Ct. . . . Pg.46 . . S15
Garrett Ct. . . . Pg.46 . . S14
Glasgow Dr. . . Pg.46 . . S15
Graceland Ln. . Pg.46 . . S14
Green Meadow Ln.
                 Pg.46 . . T14
Greenfield . . . Pg.46 . . S14
Grovewood Ln. Pg.46 . . T13
Hampton Ct. . . Pg.46 . . S15
Harbor Ct. . . . Pg.46 . . T14
Harlem Ave. . . Pg.46 . . S15
Harvest Dr. . . . Pg.46 . . T14
Hawthorn . . . . Pg.46 . . T14
Hickory Creek Ct.
                 Pg.46 . . T15
Hickory Creek Dr.
                 Pg.46 . . T14
Highview Ln. . . Pg.46 . . R14
Hill Ave. . . . . . Pg.46 . . T13
Hillside Dr. . . . Pg.46 . . R14
Hillside Rd. . . . Pg.46 . . U13
Holly Ln. . . . . . Pg.46 . . S14
Humboldt Ct. . Pg.46 . . T14
Hunter Dr. . . . . Pg.46 . . T15
Inverary Dr. . . . Pg.46 . . T14
Inverness Ln. . Pg.46 . . S14
Jamison Dr. . . . Pg.46 . . T14
Jean Rd. . . . . . Pg.39 . . Q8
Jefferson Ct. . . Pg.46 . . S14
Jessica Ln. . . . Pg.46 . . S14
Jonquil Ln. . . . Pg.46 . . S14
Josephine Dr. . Pg.39 . . Q8
Juniper Ct. . . . Pg.46 . . G15
Kenton Ct. . . . Pg.46 . . S14
Kingston Ct. . . Pg.46 . . S14
Kingston Dr. . . Pg.46 . . S14
Lakeside Dr. . . Pg.46 . . R14
Lakeview Terr. . Pg.46 . . R14
Laraway Rd. . . Pg.46 . . V13
Laurel Dr. . . . . Pg.46 . . S14
Lenore Ln. . . . Pg.46 . . Q12
Lismore Cir . . Pg.46 . . S13
Magnolia Dr. . . Pg.46 . . S14
Majoire Pkwy. . Pg.39 . . Q8
Malorie Dr. . . . Pg.39 . . Q8
Marly Rd. . . . . Pg.39 . . Q8
Marti Rd. . . . . . Pg.39 . . Q8
Mary Therese Ln.
Matthew Dr. . . Pg.46 . . T14
Moorefield Ln. . Pg.46 . . S14
New Castle Dr. Pg.46 . . S14
North Ave. . . . Pg.46 . . T13
North Ct. . . . . . Pg.46 . . T14
Norwood Dr. . . Pg.46 . . S13
Nutwood Ct. . . Pg.46 . . T14
Oak Ln. . . . . . . Pg.46 . . T14
Old Coach Tr. . Pg.46 . . R14
Old Mill Rd. . . . Pg.46 . . T13
Orchard Dr. . . . Pg.46 . . S13
Parkside Dr. . . Pg.46 . . T13
Patricia Ln. . . . Pg.46 . . S14
Pepperwood Ct. Pg.46 . . S13
Pine Hill Rd. . . Pg.46 . . S13
Pleasant Ave. . Pg.46 . . Q12
Quail Cir. . . . . Pg.46 . . T14
Rainford Dr. . . Pg.46 . . T13
River Rd. . . . . . Pg.46 . . U13
Riverton Ct. . . Pg.46 . . S14
Roeland Ct. . . . Pg.46 . . S14
Rose Ln. . . . . . Pg.39 . . Q8
Rosewood Ct. . Pg.46 . . S13
Rosewood Dr. . Pg.46 . . S13
Royce Ct. . . . . Pg.46 . . S15
Ryeland Dr. . . . Pg.46 . . T13
Sara Rd. . . . . . Pg.39 . . Q8
Silo Dr. . . . . . . Pg.46 . . T14
Skidmore Ct. . . Pg.46 . . S14
Skye Dr. . . . . . Pg.46 . . S14
Spruce Dr. . . . Pg.46 . . S13
St. Francis Rd. Pg.46 . . S14
Sterling Dr. . . . Pg.46 . . T14
Sycamore Dr. . Pg.46 . . S13
Tack Ln. . . . . . Pg.46 . . T14
Tartan Rd. . . . . Pg.46 . . S14
Thistle Ln. . . . . Pg.46 . . R14
Thorndale Dr. . Pg.46 . . S13
Westport Dr. . . Pg.46 . . S14
Whitefence Ct. Pg.46 . . T14
Windmill Dr. . . Pg.46 . . T14
Wishing Well Dr.
Woodlawn Dr. . Pg.46 . . T14
Woodruff Ct. . . Pg.46 . . S14
Woodvale Rd. . Pg.46 . . U13
78th Ave. . . . . Pg.46 . . T14
79th Ave. . . . . Pg.46 . . U14
80th Ave. . . . . Pg.46 . . S13
82nd Ave. . . . . Pg.46 . . T13
84th Ave. . . . . Pg.46 . . U13
88th Ave. . . . . Pg.40 . . Q12

104th Ave. . . . Pg.39 . . Q10
113th Ave. . . . Pg.39 . . Q9
114th Ave. . . . Pg.39 . . Q9
183rd St. . . . . Pg.40 . . Q13
185th St. . . . . Pg.40 . . Q13
187th St. . . . . Pg.46 . . Q12
188th St. . . . . Pg.39 . . Q9
189th St. . . . . Pg.39 . . Q9
196th St. . . . . Pg.46 . . R14

**GOLF COURSES**
Hickory Creek G.C.
                 Pg.46 . . T14

**PARKS**
Hunter Park . . Pg.46 . . T15
Indian Boundary Park North
Indian Boundary Park South
Kiwanis Park . Pg.46 . . T13
Woodlawn Park Pg.46 . . T14

**SCHOOLS**
Ann Rutledge Sch. for Special
   Education . . Pg.46 . . U14
Frankfort Sq. Sch.
                 Pg.46 . . S14
Indian Trail Sch.
                 Pg.46 . . T14
Summit Hill Jr. H.S.
                 Pg.46 . . S13

**MISCELLANEOUS**
Summit Hill Sch. Dist. Office
                 Pg.46 . . U14
Will Co. Sheriff Pg.46 . . T14

**GLENCOE**
Pages 22,23
**STREETS**
Adams . . . . . . . . . . . . . . . B9
Apple Tree Ln. . . . . . . . . . B8
Aspen Ln. . . . . . . . . . . . . A9
Beach Rd. . . . . . . . . . . . . B8
Birch . . . . . . . . . . . . . . . . B8
Bluff . . . . . . . . . . . . . . B,C9
Bluff Rd. . . . . . . . . . . . . . A8
Brentwood Dr. . . . . . . . . C9
Briar Ln. . . . . . . . . . . . . . C9
Brookside . . . . . . . . . . . . C9
Brookside Ln. . . . . . . . . . C9
Carol Ln. . . . . . . . . . . . . B9
Cedar Ln. . . . . . . . . . . . . B9
Cherry Tree Ln. . . . . . . . B8
Chestnut Ln. . . . . . . . . . . B8
Clover Ln. . . . . . . . . . . . . B8
Country Ln. . . . . . . . . . . C9
County Line Rd. . . . . . . . A7
Dell Pl. . . . . . . . . . . . . . B10
Dennis Ln. . . . . . . . . . . . B9
Drexel Ave. . . . . . . . . . . C9
Dundee Rd. . . . . . . . . . . B7
Eastwood Rd. . . . . . . . . . A8
Edgebrook Ln. . . . . . . . . A8
Elder Ct. . . . . . . . . . . . . B8
Elm Ct. . . . . . . . . . . . . . . A9
Elm Pl. . . . . . . . . . . . . . . A9
Elm Ridge Dr. . . . . . . . . A8
Estate Dr. . . . . . . . . . . . . A9
Euclid Ave. . . . . . . . . . . . C9
Fairfield Rd. . . . . . . . . . . A9
Fairview Rd. . . . . . . . . . B10
Forest . . . . . . . . . . . . . . . A9
Forest Way . . . . . . . . . . B8
Franklin Rd. . . . . . . . . . . A9
Glade Rd. . . . . . . . . . . . . A9
Glencoe Rd. . . . . . . . . . . B9
Glenwood Ave. . . . . . . . C10
Green Bay Rd. . . A8,9,C10
Greenleaf Ave. . . . . . . . . B9
Greenwood . . . . . . . . B-C9
Grove . . . . . . . . . . . . . B,C9
Harbor . . . . . . . . . . . . . . B9
Hawthorne . . . . . . . . . . . B9
Hazel . . . . . . . . . . . . . . . A9
Hillcrest Dr. . . . . . . . . . . A9
Hogarth Ln. . . . . . . . . . . A9
Hohfelder Rd. . . . . . . . . . A8
Ida Pl. . . . . . . . . . . . . . . B9
Ivy Ln. . . . . . . . . . . . . . . A9
Jackson Rd. . . . . . . . . . . A8
Jefferson . . . . . . . . . . . . B9
Julia Ct. . . . . . . . . . . . . . B8
Knollwood Ln. . . . . . . . . A9
Lake . . . . . . . . . . . . . . . . C9
Lakeside Terr. . . . . . . . B10
Lakewood Dr. . . . . . . . . . A9
Lapier . . . . . . . . . . . . . . B10
Lincoln Dr. . . . . . . . . A9-B8
Linda Ln. . . . . . . . . . . . . A8
Linden Ave. . . . . . . . . . . C9
Longmeadow Ln. . . . . . . A9
Longwood Rd. . . . . . . . . A9
Madison Ave. . . . . . . . . . C9
Maple Hill Rd. . . . . . . . . A9
Maple Ln. . . . . . . . . . . . . A9
Mary . . . . . . . . . . . . . . . C10
Mayfair Ln. . . . . . . . . . . . A8
Meadow Rd. . . . . . . . . . . A9
Milton . . . . . . . . . . . . . . . B8
Monroe . . . . . . . . . . . . . . C9
Montgomery . . . . . . . . . B10
Mortimer Rd. . . . . . . . . . B9

N-S St. . . . . . . . . . . . . . . B9
Northwood Dr. . . . . . . . . A8
Oak Dr. . . . . . . . . . . . . . B8
Oak Ridge Dr. . . . . . . . . A8
Oak Terr. . . . . . . . . . . . . A9
Oakdale . . . . . . . . . . . . . C9
Old Elm Ln. . . . . . . . . . . A8
Old Elm Pl. . . . . . . . . . . . A8
Orchard Ln. . . . . . . . . . . A8
Palos Rd. . . . . . . . . . . . B10
Park . . . . . . . . . . . . . . . . B9
Park Pl. . . . . . . . . . . . . . A8
Peach Tree Ln. . . . . . . . . B8
Pebblewood Ln. . . . . . . . B8
Pine Ct. . . . . . . . . . . . . . A8
Pinewood Ln. . . . . . . . . . A8
Prairie St. . . . . . . . . . . . B8
Ravine Glade . . . . . . . . B10
Redwood Ln. . . . . . . . . . C9
Robin Ln. . . . . . . . . . . . . C9
Rockgate Ln. . . . . . . . . . A9
Rolling Ln. . . . . . . . . . . . A8
Scott Ave. . . . . . . . . . . C10
Scott Ln. . . . . . . . . . . . C10
Sheridan Rd. . . . . . . . . . B9
Skokie Ln., N. & S. . . . . C9
Skokie Ridge Dr. . . . . . . B8
Skokie Ridge Rd. . . . . . . A8
South Ave. . . . . . . . . . . . B9
South Ln. . . . . . . . . . . . . B9
Stonegate Terr. . . . . . . . B8
Strawberry Hill . . . . . . . . B8
Sunrise Cir. . . . . . . . . . B10
Sunset Ln. . . . . . . . . . . . A8
Surfside Pl. . . . . . . . . . B10
Sycamore Ln. . . . . . . . . B8
Sylvan Rd. . . . . . . . . . . . A9
Temple Ct. . . . . . . . . . . . B8
Terrace Ct. . . . . . . . . . . . A8
Thornapple Ln. . . . . . . . . A9
Timber Ln. . . . . . . . . . . . A9
Tudor Ct. . . . . . . . . . . . . B9
Valley Rd. . . . . . . . . . . . . B8
Vernon Ave. . . . . . . . . B-C9
Village Ct. . . . . . . . . . . . D9
Walden Crescent . . . . . . A9
Washington . . . . . . . . . . B9
Washington Pl. . . . . . . . . B8
Wentworth . . . . . . . . . . C10
Westley Rd. . . . . . . . . . . A8
Westwood Ln. . . . . . . . . A8
Whitebridge Hill . . . . . . C10
Willow Tree Ln. . . . . . . . B8
Wingate Terr. . . . . . . . . . B8
Woodlawn Ave. . . . . . C9-10
Woodridge Ln. . . . . . . . . B8

**FOREST PRESERVES**
Chicago Botanical Garden . A7
**GOLF COURSES**
Glencoe G.C. . . . . . . . . . A7
Lake Shore C.C. . . . . . . A9
Skokie C.C. . . . . . . . . . . C8
**PARKS**
Glencoe Park . . . . . . . . B10
Watts Park . . . . . . . . . . . C9
**SCHOOLS**
Central Sch. . . . . . . . . . . B9
North Sch. . . . . . . . . . . . C9
West Sch. . . . . . . . . . . . . B8
**MISCELLANEOUS**
Post Office . . . . . . . . . . . B9
Village Hall . . . . . . . . . . . B9

**GLENVIEW**
Pages 21,22,24-26
**STREETS**
Aberdeen Dr. . Pg.22 . . E6
Adm. Whitehead Rd.
                 Pg.25 . . F4
Airdale Ct. . . . Pg.22 . . E4
Alder Pl. . . . . . Pg.25 . . F6
Alvin Ct. . . . . . Pg.25 . . G6
Ammer Rd. . . . Pg.22 . . F7
Apple Gate . . . Pg.25 . . H5
Apple Tree Ln. Pg.25 . . G8
Arbor Ln. . . . . Pg.26 . . G8
Arbor St. . . . . . Pg.25 . . G7
Ardmore St. . . Pg.26 . . G9
Ari Ln. . . . . . . . Pg.21 . . E4
Aspen Ct. . . . . Pg.22 . . F7
Astor Ct. . . . . . Pg.25 . . F7
Avenue 'B' . . . Pg.25 . . F5
Avenue 'C' . . . Pg.25 . . F5
Avenue 'D' . . . Pg.25 . . F5
Avolon Ct. . . . Pg.21 . . E2
Baffin Rd. . . . . Pg.25 . . G7
Balmoral . . . . . Pg.22 . . F7
Barbara Dr. . . Pg.21 . . E4
Barbary Ln. . . . Pg.21 . . E3
Barry Ln. . . . . . Pg.25 . . F3
Barton Ct. . . . . Pg.25 . . F5
Basswood Cir. Pg.25 . . F6
Basswood Ct. . Pg.25 . . F6
Beaver Rd. . . . Pg.26 . . G8
Becker Rd. . . . Pg.22 . . E8
Beech Dr. . . . . Pg.26 . . G8,9
Beir Dr. . . . . . . Pg.21 . . E4
Bel Air Dr. . . . . Pg.25 . . H5
Bellwood Ln. . Pg.24 . . F4

Bette Ln. . . . . . Pg.24 . . G3
Beverly Ln. . . . Pg.26 . . G9
Bianco Terr. . . Pg.25 . . H5
Big Oak . . . . . Pg.22 . . E6
Birchwood Ct. Pg.25 . . F5
Blackthorn Dr. Pg.25 . . F6
Blake Ln. . . . . Pg.21 . . E3
Bonnie Glen Ln.
                 Pg.25 . . G7
Branch Rd., N. Pg.25 . . H7
Brandless Dr. . Pg.21 . . E4
Brandon Rd. . . Pg.22,25 . F7
Brassie Ln. . . . Pg.25 . . G5
Breh Ln. . . . . . Pg.21 . . E3
Briarford . . . . . Pg.25 . . F4
Briarhill Rd. . . Pg.25 . . H6
Brook Ln. . . . . Pg.25 . . G8
Brookdale Ln. . Pg.21 . . D3
Brush Hill Ln. . Pg.22 . . E6
Buccaneer Dr. Pg.22 . . F4
Bucknell Ln. . . Pg.26 . . D5
Burnham Ct. . . Pg.25 . . G5
Burr Oak Dr. . . Pg.22 . . E7
Burr Oak Dr., E. & W.
                 Pg.22 . . E7
Burton Terr. . . Pg.25 . . F7
Buttonwood Ln.
                 Pg.25 . . G6
Cambria Ct. . . Pg.21 . . E4
Camden Dr. . . Pg.22 . . E6
Canterbury St. Pg.25 . . G7
Cariann Ln. . . . Pg.26 . . G8
Carol Ln. . . . . Pg.24 . . F2
Carousel Dr. . . Pg.25 . . E3
Carpington . . . Pg.21 . . E4
Castilian Ct. . . Pg.25 . . H8
Castle Dr. . . . . Pg.24 . . G3
Cedar Ct. . . . . Pg.25 . . H6
Cedarwood Ln. Pg.25 . . G6
Central Ct. . . . Pg.24 . . H4
Central Rd. . . . Pg.25,26 H5-8
Chandler Ln. . . Pg.21 . . F4
Chatham Dr. . . Pg.25 . . G7
Chester Dr. . . . Pg.21 . . D3
Chesterfield St. Pg.25 . . I15
Chestnut Ave. Pg.25 . . F6
Church St. . . . . Pg.25 . . H6
Cindy Ln. . . . . Pg.21 . . G3
Clavey Ln. . . . Pg.25 . . H5
Clearview Dr. . Pg.25 . . H4
Clover Ct. . . . . Pg.25 . . G6
Club Circle Dr. Pg.25 . . G7
Colfax Ave. . . . Pg.25 . . H6
Collins Ave . . . Pg.25 . . F4
Concord Ln. . . Pg.21 . . G4
Cornell Ct. . . . Pg.25 . . D5
Coronet Rd. . . Pg.25 . . H4
Country Ln. . . . Pg.25 . . H7
Countryside Ct. Pg.24 . . G3
Countryside Ln. Pg.24 . . G3
Covert Rd. . . . Pg.25 . . H5
Crain Ln. . . . . . Pg.26 . . G9
Crescent . . . . . Pg.21 . . E2
Crestwood Ct. Pg.21 . . E3
Crestwood Dr. Pg.21 . . E4
Crestwood Ln. Pg.24 . . G4
Crewman Dr. . Pg.22 . . F4
Crown Ln. . . . . Pg.25 . . F3
Crystal . . . . . . Pg.25 . . H6
Culver Ln. . . . . Pg.25 . . H6
Dale St. . . . . . Pg.26 . . H9
Dartmouth Ct. Pg.25 . . D5
Dauntless Cir. Pg.22 . . F4
De L'Ogier Dr. Pg.25 . . F8
Dearlove Rd. . Pg.24 . . G3-4
Dell Pl. . . . . . . Pg.24 . . G4
Denise Ct. . . . Pg.24 . . G3
Depot St. . . . . Pg.25 . . G6
Dewes St. . . . . Pg.25 . . G6
Dorothy Rd. . . Pg.21 . . E4
Drake Rd. . . . . Pg.25 . . G7
Dunhill Cir. . . . Pg.22 . . E6
East Lake St. . Pg.24 . . F3-4
Eastwood Ln. . Pg.25 . . G8
Echo Ln. . . . . . Pg.26 . . G9
Edgewood (Pvt)
                 Pg.26 . . H8
Edwards Dr. . . Pg.25 . . E4
Elizabeth Ln. . Pg.25 . . G7
Elm St. . . . . . . Pg.25 . . G-H6
Elmdale Ave. . Pg.21 . . D4
Elmdale Rd. . . Pg.24 . . G4
Elmgate Dr. . . Pg.25 . . G5
Elmwood Ave. Pg.25 . . F7
Estate Ln. . . . . Pg.21 . . E4
Evanston/Elgin Rd. (Golf Rd.)
                 Pg.25 . . H6
Evergreen Ln. . Pg.25 . . F7
Evergreen Terr. Pg.25 . . F7
Executive Ct. . Pg.24 . . F4
Executive Ln. . Pg.24 . . F4
Fairhope Ave. Pg.22 . . E8
Fairway Ct. . . . Pg.25 . . G5
Fairway Dr. . . . Pg.25 . . H4
Ferndale Rd. . Pg.26 . . G9
Fir St. . . . . . . . Pg.25 . . G5-6
First St. . . . . . . Pg.25 . . G6
Fontana Dr. . . Pg.25 . . H5
Forest . . . . . . . Pg.25 . . F4
Forest Dr. . . . . Pg.24 . . F2
Forest Rd. . . . . Pg.26 . . G9

Forestal . . . . . Pg.25 . . F4
Forestview Ln. Pg.25 . . H7
Fowler Dr. . . . . Pg.25 . . F5
Franklin Ln. . . Pg.21 . . E2
Frederick Ct. . Pg.21 . . E3
Garden Ct. . . . Pg.25 . . G6
George Ct. . . . Pg.25 . . H6
Gladish Ln. . . . Pg.25 . . G5
Glen Ct. . . . . . Pg.25 . . G7
Glen Oak Dr. . Pg.25 . . F7
Glenayre Dr. . Pg.25 . . G,H7
Glenbrook Hospital Dr.
                 Pg.25 . . E3
Glendale Rd. . Pg.25 . . H7
Glenlake Dr. . . Pg.21 . . F4
Glenridge Dr. . Pg.25 . . H7
Glenview Rd. . Pg.25,26 G5-7
Glenway Dr. . . Pg.21 . . E3
Glenwood . . . . Pg.25,26
                                 F7,G9
Glonwood Rd. Pg.25 . . G4
Gloria Ct. . . . . Pg.24 . . G3
Golf Ct. . . . . . . Pg.25 . . H6
Golf Rd. . . . . . Pg.25 . . H6
Golf View Ln. . Pg.25 . . G7
Golf View Rd. . Pg.25 . . G7
Grace Ln. . . . . Pg.24 . . F3
Grandview Pl. . Pg.25 . . H5-6
Green Willow Ln.
                 Pg.25 . . F6
Greenacres Ln. Pg.25 . . G8
Greenbrier Dr. Pg.24 . . H4
Greenfield Dr. . Pg.25 . . H5
Greenwood Ct. Pg.21 . . E4
Greenwood Rd. Pg.21 . . E4
Gregory Dr. . . Pg.21 . . E4
Gregory Ln. . . Pg.24 . . H4
Grove St. . . . . Pg.25 . . G6
Hackberry Ct. . Pg.26 . . G9
Hager Ct. . . . . Pg.25 . . G5
Hammersmith Ln.
                 Pg.21 . . E3
Hampton Ct. . . Pg.21 . . E3
Happy Hollow Rd.
                 Pg.21 . . E4
Mary Kay Ln. . Pg.25 . . F7
Harlem Ave. . . Pg.25 . . H6
Harmony Ln. . Pg.25 . . H6
Harrison St. . . Pg.25 . . H5-6
Harvard Ct. . . Pg.25 . . D5
Harvest Ct. . . . Pg.25 . . E3
Harvest Ln. . . . Pg.25 . . E3
Hawthorne Ln. Pg.25 . . G6
Heather (Pvt). Pg.25 . . H7
Heatherfield Ln Pg.26 . . G8
Henley St. . . . . Pg.25 . . H7
Hennemerry Ln. Pg.24 . . G4
Hercules Ct. . . Pg.22 . . E4
Hickory Ct. . . . Pg.25 . . F8
Highland Ave. . Pg.24 . . G4
Highland Tr. . . Pg.25 . . E3
Hill Cir. . . . . . . Pg.25 . . H7
Hollywood . . . Pg.26 . . G7
Holste Rd. . . . . Pg.22 . . E5
Huber Ct. . . . . Pg.25 . . E4
Huber Ln. . . . . Pg.25 . . H4
Huckelberry Ln. Pg.25 . . G8
Hudson Rd. . . Pg.25 . . G7
Hunt Ln. . . . . . Pg.25 . . F7
Hunter Rd. . . . Pg.26 . . G8
Huntington Dr. Pg.25 . . F7
Hutchings Ave. Pg.25 . . G6
Imperial Dr. . . Pg.24 . . F4
Indian Rd. . . . . Pg.26 . . G9
Indian Ridge Dr.Pg.25 . . F8
Indian Ridge Dr.
                 Pg.21 . . E2
Inverness Ln. . Pg.21 . . E4
Iroquois Dr. . . Pg.25 . . F3
Ivy Dr. . . . . . . . Pg.21 . . F2
Ivy Ln. . . . . . . . Pg.25 . . F2
Ivy Way . . . . . Pg.21 . . F2
Janny Rd. . . . . Pg.21 . . E4
Jefferson Ave. Pg.22 . . F6
Jerrie Ln. . . . . Pg.25 . . H4
Joanne Dr. . . . Pg.21 . . D3
Johns Ct. . . . . Pg.22 . . E6
Johns Dr. . . . . Pg.22 . . E6
Joy Ln. . . . . . . Pg.25 . . G7
Juniper St. . . . Pg.26 . . G9
Juniper Terr. . . Pg.26 . . G9
Karen Ln. . . . . Pg.25 . . H5
Kaywood Ln. . Pg.25 . . F8
Keenan Ln. . . . Pg.21 . . E4
Kendale Ln. . . Pg.25 . . F7
Kenilworth Ln. Pg.25 . . F7
Kennicott Ln. . Pg.24 . . F3
Kiess . . . . . . . Pg.21 . . E4
Kings Ln. . . . . Pg.22 . . F7
Kinker Way . . Pg.25 . . F6
Kmiec Ct. . . . . Pg.21 . . E4
Knight . . . . . . . Pg.25 . . F3
Knollwood Ct. Pg.24 . . G3
LaFontaine Ct. Pg.25 . . F7
Lake Ave. . . . . Pg.25 . . F3
Lake St., E. . . Pg.24 . . F3
Lakewood Ct. Pg.24 . . F4
Landreth Ln. . . Pg.22 . . C7
Laramie Ln. . . Pg.26 . . G9
Larch Ave. . . . Pg.25 . . F6
Larkdale Ct. . . Pg.25 . . G6
Laurel Ave. . . . Pg.25 . . F2

Lawnwood Terr.
                 Pg.25 . . F7
Lawrence . . . . Pg.24 . . F7
Lawson Rd. . . Pg.21 . . E4
Leaf Dr. . . . . . Pg.25 . . G2
Leanne Ct. . . . Pg.21 . . E3
Lehigh . . . . . . Pg.25 . . H6
Lenox Rd. . . . . Pg.25 . . G7
Lexington Ln. . Pg.25 . . D4
Liberty Ln. . . . Pg.24 . . F2
Lilac Ave. . . . . Pg.24 . . F2
Limar Ln. . . . . Pg.24 . . F2
Lincoln Ave. . . Pg.25 . . F-H6
Linden . . . . . . Pg.25 . . G5
Linden Dr. . . . Pg.24 . . G5
Linden Ln. . . . Pg.22 . . F7
Lindenwood Ln.
                 Pg.25 . . G3
Linneman St. . Pg.25 . . F6
Lizette Ln. . . . Pg.21 . . E3
Locust Ave. . . Pg.24 . . F2
Locust Ln. . . . Pg.25 . . H7
Golf C. . . . . . . Pg.25 . . H6
Golf Rd. . . . . . Pg.25 . . H6
London Ln. . . . Pg.25 . . F7
Long Acre Ln. Pg.26 . . G9
Long Valley Rd. Pg.25 . . H6-7
Longate Dr. . . Pg.25 . . G5
Longmeadow Dr.
                 Pg.24 . . F4
Lori Dr. . . . . . . Pg.22 . . E4
Lotus Ln. . . . . Pg.24 . . H4
Lurilane . . . . . Pg.24 . . G3
MacArthur Dr. Pg.25 . . H6
MacLean Ct. . Pg.25 . . G2
Magnolia . . . . Pg.24 . . F2
Malik Ct. . . . . Pg.25 . . H5
Maple Leaf Dr. Pg.21 . . E4
Maple Ln. . . . . Pg.21 . . E4
Maple St. . . . . Pg.25 . . F2
Maplewood Ln. Pg.25 . . G6
Maria Ln. . . . . Pg.25 . . H5
Maria Ct. . . . . Pg.25 . . H5
Mark Dr. . . . . . Pg.26 . . G9
Mary Ct. . . . . . Pg.21 . . E4
Mary Ln. . . . . . Pg.25 . . H5
Meadow Ln. . . Pg.25 . . F7
Meadowlark . . Pg.25 . . G5
Meadowview Ct.
                 Pg.21 . . D3
Meadowview Dr.
                 Pg.21 . . D3
Merle Ln. . . . . Pg.24 . . F2
Michael Ln. . . Pg.21 . . E3
Mickey Ln. . . . Pg.22 . . F7
Miller Dr . . . . . Pg.21 . . D3
Miller Dr. . . . . Pg.22 . . E4
Milwaukee Ave. Pg.24 . . F3
Mohawk Ln. . . Pg.21 . . E2
Monroe . . . . . Pg.22 . . E6
Montgomery Ln.
                 Pg.25 . . H6
Mulberry . . . . Pg.26 . . G9
Myrtis Ln. . . . . Pg.21 . . E3
Neil Ln. . . . . . . Pg.24 . . G3
Neptune Dr. . . Pg.22 . . E4
Neva Ave. . . . Pg.26 . . G9
Nora Ave. . . . . Pg.25 . . H6
Nordica Ave. . Pg.26 . . G9
Norma Ct. . . . Pg.25 . . H5
North Dr.(Pvt) Pg.22 . . E-F7
Norwich Ct. . . Pg.21 . . F4
Norwood Terr. Pg.25 . . H5
Nottingham Ave.
                 Pg.25 . . H6
O'Hare Dr. . . . Pg.22 . . E4
Oakwood . . . . Pg.25 . . E3
Old Willow Rd. Pg.25 . . D5
Osage Dr. . . . Pg.21 . . E2
Overlook Dr. . . Pg.25 . . H7
Oxford Ln. . . . Pg.25 . . F7
Paddock Dr. . . Pg.22 . . F4
Palmgren Dr. . Pg.25 . . G6-7
Pam-Anne Dr. Pg.24 . . G4
Park Dr. . . . . . Pg.25 . . G5
Parkview Ln. . Pg.25 . . H6
Pawnee Ln. . . Pg.21 . . D2
Pebble Creek Dr.
                 Pg.25 . . F6
Pebble Dr. . . . Pg.25 . . F6
Pebblewood . . Pg.25
                 Pg.22 . . D5
Pendleton Ln. Pg.25 . . D5
Penn Ct. . . . . . Pg.25 . . D5
Pfingsten . . . . Pg.25 . . F7
Pfingsten Rd. . Pg.21 . . E3
Phillips Dr. . . . Pg.21 . . E4
Pick Dr. . . . . . Pg.25 . . H5
Pine Ct. . . . . . Pg.25 . . G-H6
Pine Dr. . . . . . Pg.25 . . F6
Pinehurst Dr. . Pg.25 . . G5-6
Pleasant Dr. . Pg.22 . . F7
Pleasant Ln. . Pg.22 . . F7
Plymouth Ct. . Pg.25 . . F7
Plymouth Ln. . Pg.25 . . F7
Polo Ln. . . . . . Pg.25 . . F6
Portage Run . Pg.24 . . F3
Porter Ct. . . . . Pg.25 . . D5
Potter Rd. . . . . Pg.25 . . F7
Prairie St. . . . . Pg.25 . . F6
Princeton Ln. . Pg.25 . . D5
Pynsky Rd. . . . Pg.21 . . E2

Queens Ln. . . Pg.22 . . F7
Radcliff Ct. . . . Pg.25 . . D5
Railroad . . . . . Pg.25 . . G6
Raleigh Dr. . . . Pg.25 . . G7
Raleigh Rd. . . Pg.25 . . G7
Ralmark Ln. . . Pg.24 . . F4
Rebecca Ln. . . Pg.21 . . E4
Red Bud Ln. . . Pg.25 . . F6
Redwood Ln. . Pg.26 . . H8
Rich Rd. . . . . . Pg.25 . . F4
Ridgewood Ln., E. & W.
                 Pg.25 . . F7
Rio Vista (Pvt) Pg.25 . . H7
River Dr. . . . . . Pg.25 . . G6
River Way . . . . Pg.22 . . E6
Riverside Ct. . Pg.21 . . E3
Robin Ln. . . . . Pg.24 . . F3
Robincrest Ln. Pg.25 . . H5,6
Robincrest Ln., N. & S.
                 Pg.25 . . H6
Rogers Ave. . . Pg.22 . . F6
Rolling Pass . . Pg.25 . . G5
Rollwind Rd. . . Pg.25 . . H7
Ronald Rd. . . . Pg.24 . . H4
Roosevelt Ave. Pg.25 . . G5
Royal Oak Ln. Pg.25 . . F6
Rugen Ln. . . . . Pg.25 . . F6
Rugen Rd. . . . Pg.25 . . F3,6
Russet Way . . Pg.21 . . E3
Rutgers Ct. . . . Pg.22 . . D5
Sally Ct. . . . . . Pg.24 . . G3
Sandy Ln. . . . . Pg.21 . . E4
Sanford Ct. . . Pg.25 . . G2
Sanford Ln. . . Pg.25 . . F-G7
Saranac Ct. . . Pg.21 . . E3
Saranac Ln. . . Pg.21 . . E3
Seminole Dr. . Pg.21 . . D2
Sequoia Trail . Pg.25 . . F6
Sheffield Ln. . Pg.25 . . G7
Shermer Rd. . . Pg.25 . . G6
Sherwood Rd. Pg.26 . . G8
Sheryl Ln. . . . . Pg.25 . . H4
Short Ln. . . . . Pg.25 . . H5
Silver Willow Dr.
                 Pg.25 . . F6
Silverpine Dr. . Pg.25 . . G5
Simonson . . . . Pg.25 . . G5
Sioux Tr. . . . . . Pg.21 . . D3
Skytrain Ln. . . Pg.22 . . E4
Sleepy Hollow Rd.
                 Pg.25 . . G6
Solar Ln. . . . . Pg.25 . . G3
Somerset Dr. . Pg.25 . . G7
Southgate Dr. Pg.25 . . H5
Spring Rd. . . . Pg.25 . . H7
Springdale Ave. Pg.24 . . G4
Spruce Dr. . . . Pg.25 . . G6
Spruce St. . . . Pg.25 . . G-H6
Steffens Ln. . . Pg.25 . . F7
Stevens Dr. . . Pg.25 . . F6
Stratford Ln. . Pg.21 . . F4
Strawberry . . . Pg.21 . . F4
Sumac Cir. . . . Pg.25 . . G5
Summit Dr. . . . Pg.22 . . E6
Sunflower Ct. . Pg.21 . . D3
Sunset Ridge Rd.
                 Pg.25 . . E7
Surrey Ln. . . . Pg.25 . . H7
Sussex Ln. . . . Pg.21 . . E3
Swainwood Dr. Pg.25 . . G5
Taft Ct. . . . . . . Pg.26 . . G8
Tall Tree Rd. . . Pg.25 . . H5
Tamer Ln. . . . . Pg.24 . . G3
Tanglewood Ln.
                 Pg.22 . . F6
Terrace Ln. . . Pg.25 . . G5
Thornberry . . . Pg.24 . . H4
Thornwood Ln. Pg.25 . . G7
Timberline Dr. Pg.25 . . G8
Timbers Edge . Pg.25 . . G2
Tinker Way . . . Pg.26 . . G6
Topp Ln. . . . . . Pg.25 . . E3
Tracy Ct. . . . . Pg.24 . . G3
Trent Ct. . . . . . Pg.21 . . F4
Tri-State Tollway
                 Pg.21 . . E2
Trowbridge Ln. Pg.25 . . F4
Tulip Tree Ln. . Pg.25 . . F6
Valley Lo Ln.(Pvt)
                 Pg.22 . . E6
Vantage Ln. . . Pg.21 . . E3
Vernon Dr. . . . Pg.25 . . G7
Viking Dr. . . . . Pg.25 . . H5
Virginia Ln. . . Pg.25 . . F8
Wagner Rd. . . Pg.25 . . F7
Walnut Ct. . . . Pg.25 . . H5-6
Warren Ct. . . . Pg.24 . . H4
Warren Rd. . . . Pg.25 . . H4
Warrington Dr. Pg.21 . . F4
Warwick . . . . . Pg.21 . . F4
Washington St. Pg.25 . . G-H6
Waterbury Cir. Pg.21 . . E2
Waukegan Rd. Pg.22,25 F-K6
Wedgewood Ct. Pg.25 . . G5
Wedgewood Dr.
                 Pg.25 . . G5
Wellesley Ct. . Pg.25 . . D5
West Lake Ave. Pg.24 . . F2-4
Westfield Ln. . Pg.21 . . E3
Westleigh Dr. . Pg.25 . . E6
Westview Rd. . Pg.25 . . G2
Wildberry Ct. . Pg.22 . . E6
Wildflower Ct. Pg.21 . . D3

## GLENVIEW

Wildwood ... Pg.25 ... F7
Willow ... Pg.21 ... E3
Willow Ln. .. Pg.25 ... G6
Wilmette Ave. Pg.25 ... G8
Winchester Ln. Pg.21 ... F4
Windsor Rd. .. Pg.25 ... G7
Winnetka Ave. Pg.21 ... K4
Wissing Ln. .. Pg.25 ... H6
Woodland Dr. Pg.25 ... P8
Woodlawn Ave. Pg.25 ... F7
Woodlawn Rd. Pg.25 ... F7
Woodmere Ln. Pg.25 ... G8
Woodridge Rd. Pg.21 ... E3
Woodview Ln. Pg.25 ... G6
Wyndham Cir. Pg.22 ... E6
Yale Ct. .... Pg.25 ... D5
York Rd. .... Pg.25 ... F5
Zenith Pkwy. . Pg.24 ... G2
2nd St. .... Pg.22 ... E4
3rd St. .... Pg.25 ... F5
4th St. .... Pg.25 ... F5

### CEMETERIES
Sunset Mem. Gdns. Cem.
.......... Pg.22 .... E4

### GOLF COURSES
Glenview Pk. G.C.
.......... Pg.25 ... G5
North Shore C.C.
.......... Pg.25 ... G7
Northwestern G.C.
.......... Pg.26 .... J8
Station Golf Links of
Glenview .. Pg.25 ... G5
Valley-Lo Sports Club
.......... Pg.22 ... E6

### PARKS
Cole Park ... Pg.25 ... F7
Country Lane Park
.......... Pg.24 .... G3
Countryside Park
.......... Pg.24 .... G3
Cunliff Park . Pg.26 ... H8
Flick Park ... Pg.24 .... F3
Hawthorne Glen Park
.......... Pg.21 .... D3
Huber Lane Park
.......... Pg.25 .... G4
Indian Trail Park
.......... Pg.24 .... F2
Jackman Park Pg.25 ... G6
Jennings Park Pg.21,22 . E4
John's Park .. Pg.25 ... H6
Manor Park .. Pg.25 ... H6
Riverside Park Pg.25 ... H6
Roosevelt Park Pg.25 ... G5
Rugen Park .. Pg.25 ... H4
Sleepy Hollow Park
.......... Pg.25 ... G6
Tall Tree Park Pg.25 ... F6
The Grove Park Pg.24 ... F3
Tot Lot Park . Pg.25 ... H6
Willowbrook Park
.......... Pg.21 .... E4

### SCHOOLS
Avoca W. Sch. Pg.26 ... G9
Clyde Lyons Sch.
.......... Pg.25 .... G7
Glen Grove Sch.
.......... Pg.24 .... G3
Glenbrook South H.S.
.......... Pg.21 .... F3
Hoffman Sch. Pg.25 ... H6
Immanuel Sch. Pg.22 ... F6
Louise Henking Sch.
.......... Pg.25 .... G4
Midwestern Academy
.......... Pg.25 ... G5
Our Lady Sch. Pg.25 ... G6
Pleasant Ridge Sch.
.......... Pg.25 .... F7
Poko Nursery Sch.
.......... Pg.25 ... H6
Springman Jr. H.S.
.......... Pg.25 ... H5
Westbrook Sch. Pg.24 ... F4
Willowbrook Elem. Sch.
.......... Pg.24 .... E4
Winkleman Sch. Pg.21 ... E3

### SHOPPING CENTERS
Golfview S.C. . Pg.25 ... H6
Plaza del Prado Pg.21 ... D3
The Shops of Heatherfield
S.C. ..... Pg.22 ... E6

### MISCELLANEOUS
Convent of the Holy Spirit
.......... Pg.22 .... D6
Fire Department
.......... Pg.25 ... G6
Glenbrook Hospital
.......... Pg.21 .... E3
Glenview Ice Center
.......... Pg.21 .... F3
Library .... Pg.25 ... G6
Post Office .. Pg.25 ... G6
Rugen Center Pg.25 ... G5
Village Hall / Police Dept.
.......... Pg.25 ... G7

## GLENWOOD
Pages 43,44,49

### STREETS
Arizona Ave. . Pg.43 ... Q24
Arquilla Dr. .. Pg.43 ... Q24
Avalon .... Pg.44 ... R27
Birch Dr. ... Pg.44 ... Q26
Blackstone Ave. Pg.44 ... R27
Bruce Ln. .. Pg.43 ... P24
Campbell Ave. Pg.44 ... R25
Carol Pkwy. . Pg.43 ... Q24
Cedar Ln. .. Pg.43 ... Q26
Center St. .. Pg.44 ... Q25
Champlain .. Pg.44 ... R26
Cherry Dr. .. Pg.43 ... Q24
Chestnut Ct. . Pg.43 ... Q26
Chestnut Ln. Pg.44 ... Q26
Chicago Heights-Glenwood
Rd. .... Pg.43,49 R24
Clark St. ... Pg.44 ... R26
Cottage Grove Ave.
.......... Pg.44 ... Q26
Dante Ave. .. Pg.44,49 R27
Dorchester Ave. Pg.44 ... R27
Drexel Ave. . Pg.44 ... R26
Eberhart ... Pg.44 ... R26
Ellis ..... Pg.44 ... R27
Elm Ln. ... Pg.44 ... Q26
Fitzhenry Dr. Pg.43 ... Q24
Forest Ave. . Pg.44 ... R25
Gay Ct. .... Pg.43 ... Q24
Glenwood Ave. Pg.43 ... Q25
Glenwood Dyer Rd.
.......... Pg.44 ... R25
Glenwood Lansing Rd.
.......... Pg.44 ... R27
Greenwood . Pg.43 ... R27
Halsted St. .. Pg.44 ... R24
Harper Ave. . Pg.44 ... R27
Hickory Ln. . Pg.44 ... Q26
Holbrook Rd. . Pg.43 ... R24
Holly Ct. ... Pg.43 ... Q24
Illinois Ave. . Pg.44 ... Q24
Indiana .... Pg.43 ... Q24
Ingleside Ave. Pg.44 ... R26
Iowa St. ... Pg.43 ... Q24
Jane St. ... Pg.43 ... R25
Kenneth Ct. . Pg.43 ... Q24
Lee Ct. .... Pg.43 ... Q24
Longwood Ct. Pg.43 ... Q24
Longwood Dr. Pg.43 ... Q24
Lotta St. ... Pg.43 ... R25
Magnolia Ave. Pg.44 ... Q26
Main St. ... Pg.43 ... R25
Main, N. ... Pg.43 ... R25
Maple Ct. ... Pg.44 ... Q26
Maple Dr. ... Pg.44 ... Q26
Maryland Ave. Pg.44 ... R26
Merrill St. ... Pg.43 ... Q24
Minerva Ave. . Pg.44 ... R27
Mulberry Ct. . Pg.44 ... R26
Mulberry Dr. . Pg.44 ... R26
Nevada St. . Pg.44 ... R26
Oak Lane, S. . Pg.44 ... R26
Oak Ln. ... Pg.43 ... Q25
Oak St. .... Pg.43 ... Q24
Ohio St. ... Pg.43 ... Q24
Palm Dr. ... Pg.44 ... P24
Park Dr. ... Pg.44 ... R25
Pickens ... Pg.44 ... R25
Pine Ln. ... Pg.44 ... Q26
Pleasant Dr. . Pg.43 ... Q24
Rainbow Dr. . Pg.43 ... Q24
Rebecca St. . Pg.44 ... R25
Rhodes .... Pg.44 ... R26
Roberts Dr. . Pg.43 ... Q24
Rose Ct. ... Pg.44 ... R26
Rose St. ... Pg.44 ... R26
School St. .. Pg.43 ... R24
Science Rd. . Pg.44 ... R24
Spruce Ln. .. Pg.44 ... R26
St. Lawrence Pg.44 ... R26
State St. ... Pg.43 ... R25
Strieff Ln. .. Pg.43 ... Q24
Sunset Dr. .. Pg.43 ... P24
Sycamore Ln. Pg.44 ... R26
Terrace .... Pg.43 ... Q24
Tulip Dr. ... Pg.44 ... Q26
University .. Pg.44 ... R27
Virginia Ave. . Pg.43 ... Q24
Wabash Ave. . Pg.43 ... R25
Walnut Ln. .. Pg.43 ... Q26
Westwood .. Pg.43 ... Q24
Willow Ln. .. Pg.44 ... R26
Wisconsin .. Pg.43 ... Q24
Young St. .. Pg.44 ... R25
187th St. ... Pg.43 ... Q24
191st Pl. ... Pg.44 ... R26
192nd Pl. ... Pg.44 ... R27
192nd St. ... Pg.44 ... R26
193rd Pl. ... Pg.44 ... R27
193rd St. ... Pg.44 ... R27
194th Pl. ... Pg.49 ... R27
194th St. ... Pg.43,44
.......... R24,27
195th St. ... Pg.49 ... R24

### PARKS
George Aquilla Park
.......... Pg.43 ... Q24

### SCHOOLS
Brookwood Jr. H.S.
.......... Pg.44 ... R26
Brookwood Sch.
.......... Pg.44 ... R26
Glenwood Sch. for Boys
.......... Pg.43 ... Q24
Hickory Bend Elem. Sch.
.......... Pg.44 ... R26
Longwood Sch. Pg.43 ... Q24

### SHOPPING CENTERS
Glenwood Shopping Plaza
.......... Pg.43 ... Q24

### MISCELLANEOUS
City Hall ... Pg.44 ... R25

## GOLF
Page 25

### STREETS
Blossom Ln. ........... H7
Briar Rd. ............. H7
Clyde Ln. ............. H7
Dover St. ............. H7
Elm Cir. .............. H7
Highland Pl. ........... H7
Lilac Ln. .............. H7
Logan Terr. ........... H7
Orchard Ln. ........... H7
Overlook Dr. .......... H7

### GOLF COURSES
Glenview C.C. .......... H8

### PARKS
Diederich Park ......... H7

### MISCELLANEOUS
Metra Station .......... H7
Police Department ...... H7
Post Office ............ H7
Village Hall ........... H7

## HANOVER PARK
Page 16
(Portions within DuPage
County,for additional lsitings,
see Sections 3 and 5)

### STREETS
Adams St. ............. M2
Apple Tree St. ......... M1
Applewood Ct. ......... L1
Asbury Cir. ............ L1
Barrington Rd. ......... M1
Berkshire Dr. ......... L1-2
Birch Ave. ............. M1
Bolton Way ........... M1
Brentwood Ct. ......... L1
Briar Ln. .............. L1
Briarwood Ave. ........ L1
Briarwood St. ......... M1
Bristol Cir. ............ L1
Bristol Dr. ............ L1
Bristol Ln. ............ L1
Brockton Ct. ........... M1
Brookside Dr. .......... L1
Canterbury Dr. ........ M1
Carlisle Ct. ............ L1
Carlisle Dr. ............ L1
Carnaby Ct. ........... L1
Carrolton Ct. .......... L1
Catawba Ln. ........... L1
Churchill Dr. ........... L1
Countryside Dr. ...... M1-2
Coventy Dr. ........... L1
Crescent Way ......... M1
Cumberland Dr. ........ L1
Cynthia Ln. ............ L1
Cypress Ave. .......... M1
Dartmouth Ct. ......... L1
Dartmouth Ln. ....... L1-2
Deerpath Ln. .......... M1
Durham Ct. ............ L2
Edgebrook Ln. ......... M1
Essex Ct. .............. L1
Evergreen ............. M1
Fairhaven Dr. .......... M2
Filmore Ave. ........... M1
Forest Glen Ave. ....... L1
Glenside Ct. ........... L1
Glenwood Ln. .......... M2
Grant Cir. .............. L1
Greenwood Ave. ....... M1
Guilford Commons ...... L2
Haddam Way ........... M1
Hanover St. ............ M1
Harrison St. ........... M1
Hartman Dr. ........... L2
Hasting Ln. ........... L1-2
Hawthorn Ln. .......... M1
Hearth St. ............. M1
Highland St. ........... M1
Hillcrest Ave. .......... M1
Huntington Cir. ........ L1
Indian Hill Ave. ........ M1
Irving Park Rd. ......... L1
Jackson St. ............ M2
Jenson Blvd. ........... L1
Kensington Ln. ......... L1
Kent Ct. ............... L1
Kingsbury Dr. .......... L1
Kingsbury Ln. .......... L1
Laurel Ave. ............ M1

Laurie Dr. ............. L1
Lexington Cir. .......... M1
Lexington Pk. .......... L2
Linden Ave. ............ M1
Longmeadow Ct. ....... M1
Madison St. ............ M1
Manchester Manor ...... L2
Maple Ave. ............. M1
Maplewood Ave. ........ M1
Meadowbrook Ln. ....... M1
Nantucket Cove ......... L2
Northway Ct. ........... L1
Northway Dr. ......... L-M1
Oakwood Ave. .......... M1
Old Mill Ln. ............ M1
Olde Salem Cir. ......... M2
Olde Salem Ln. ......... L2
Olivia Ln. .............. L1
Orchard Ln. ............ M2
Oxford ................ L1
Park Ave. .............. M1
Parkview Dr. ........... L1
Peach Tree ............ L1
Pebblebrook Ln. ........ L1
Pine Tree .............. M1
Polk St. ............... M2
Poplar Ave. ............ M1
Princeton Cir. .......... L1
Ramblewood Dr. ........ L1
Ramsgate Cir. .......... L1
Redwood ............... M1
Rocton Way ............ L2
Rosewood St. .......... M1
Roxbury Ct. ............ L1
Sarson Way ............ M1
Shelbourne Ct. ........ L1-2
Sherwood Dr. .......... L1
Somerset Cir. .......... M1
Spruce Ave. ........... M1
Stratford Ln. ........... L1
Strathmore Ln. ......... L1
Sycamore ............. M1
Taft Cir. ............... M1
Tanglewood Ave. ....... M1
Taylor St. ............. M2
Tower Dr. .............. L1
Truman St. ............ M2
Valley View Rd. ......... M1
Walnut Ave. ............ M1
Washington St. ........ M1
Waterford Dr. .......... M2
Wedgewood Dr. ........ M1
Westchester Dr. ...... M1-2
Weymouth Cir. ......... L2
White Bridge Ln. ....... L1
White Bridge Ln. ....... L1
Wilson St. ............. M2
Windsor Ln. ............ L1
Wise ................. M2
Yorkshire Ct. .......... L1
Yorkshire Dr. ......... L1-2

### PARKS
Anne Fox Park .......... L1
Edgebrook Park ........ M1
George Georgan Memorial
Baseball Fields ....... M1
Liberty Park ........... M1
MSD Basin ............. M1
Ranger Park ........... L1

### SCHOOLS
A. Fox Sch. ............ L1
Albert Einstein Sch. ..... M1
Hanover Highland Sch. .. M1

### SHOPPING CENTERS
Hanover Square ........ M1
Tradewinds S.C. ........ L1

### MISCELLANEOUS
Hanover Park Water
Reclamation Plant ..... M1

## HARVEY
Page 43
(For additional listings,
see Section 1)

### STREETS
Ashland .............. M23
Carol Ave. ............ M24
Carse Ave. ............ N24
Center Ave. ........... N23
Clinton St. ............ N24
Dixie Hwy. ............ M22
Emerald Ave. .......... M24
Finch Ave. ............ N24
Fisk Ave. ............. N23
Gauger St. ............ M23
Geneva ............... N24
Green St. ............. M24
Halsted St. ......... M-O24
Hermitage Ave. ........ M22
Honore Ave. ........... M22
Jefferson ............. N24
Lathrop Ave. .......... M24
Lexington ............ M23
Loomis ............... M23
Lowe Ave. ............ N24
Marshfield ............ M23
Myrtle ............... N24
Park Ave. ............. M23
Paulina .............. M23
Sherman Pl. .......... N24

Taft Dr. .............. N24
Union Ave. ............ N24
Vine Ave. ............. M23
Wallace Ave. .......... N24
Wallace St. ........... N24
Wood Ave. ............ N24
159th St. ........... M23-24
160th Pl. ........... M23-24
160th St. ........... M23-24
161st St. ............. M24
162nd St. ............ N24
163rd St. ............. N24
164th St. ............. N24
165th St. ............. N24
166th St. ............. N23
167th Pl. ............. N24
167th St. ............. N24
168th Pl. ............. N24
168th St. ............. N24
171st St. ............. O23

### PARKS
Holmes Park .......... M24
Loomis Park .......... M23
Percy Wilson Park ..... N23
Tatje Park ............ M24

### SCHOOLS
Holmes Sch. .......... M24
James W. Riley Sch. .... M22
Taft Sch. ............. N24

### MISCELLANEOUS
Harvey Industrail Center . N23
The Gateway International
Terminal ............ N23

## HAZEL CREST
Pages 42,43

### STREETS
Adrian Ln. ............ Q19
Albany Ave. ........... O21
Annetta .............. N22
Annetta Ave. .......... O22
Anthony Ave. .......... O22
Arlington Pl. .......... P21
Artesian .............. N,O22
Artesian Ave. ......... N22
Augusta Ln. ........... O20
Balmoral Ln. .......... P21
Birchwood ............ O20
Bordeaux Ct. .......... P20
Briar Ln. ............. O20
Bryant Ln. ............ O21
Bulger Ave. ........... O20
Burgundy Ct. .......... P20
Burr Oak Ln. .......... O20
Butternut ............. O21
Buttonwood Walk ...... P21
California Ave. ........ O20
Cannes Ct. ............ P20
Carriage Way ......... P21
Carrington Ct. ........ Q20
Carrington Dr. ........ Q20
Central Park Ave. ...... O20
Chambord ............ P20
Chantilly Ln. .......... O20
Charlemagne Ave. ..... P20
Charleston ............ N23
Charters Ct. .......... O20
Cherry Creek Dr. ...... O21
Cherrywood Ln. ....... O20
Chestnut Ave. ......... O20
Chestnut Ct. .......... O20
Circle Dr. ............. P21
Coach Ln. ............ P21
Concord Pl. ........... O21
Cottonwood Ct. ....... O20
Coventry Ct. .......... O20
Crane Ave. ............ O22
Crawford Ct. .......... P19
Crescent Dr. .......... N21
Crystal Ct. ............ P20
Dogwood Ln. .......... P21
Edgewater Dr. ........ Q19
Elm Dr. ............... O20
Emerson Ave. ......... O21
Emily Ct. ............. O20
Eylsees Ct. ........... O20
Fountainbleau Dr. ..... P20
Glynwood Ln. ......... O20
Golfview Dr. .......... Q20
Grandview Dr. ......... O20
Grenoble Ct. .......... P20
Harseile Ln. .......... O20
Hawthorne Ln. ........ P21
Hazel Ln. ............. O20
Head Ave. ............ O22
Hickory Ct. ........... O20
Hickory Ln. ........... O20
Highland Ave. ........ O21
Highland Ct. .......... O21
Hillside .............. O21
Holmes Ave. .......... O21
Indi Ct. .............. O20
Jodave Ave. .......... O22
Jovanna .............. O21
Kedzie Ave. ........... O20
Knollwood Ct. ......... P21
Lakeview Dr. .......... Q20
Larkspur Ln. .......... O20
Laurel Ln. ............ O20
Lawndale Ave., S. ..... P20
Lexington Dr. ......... O21

Lexy Ct. .............. Q19
Lincoln Ave. .......... O22
Linden Dr. ............ O20
Locust Dr. ............ O20
Longfellow Ave. ....... O21
Lowell Ave. ........... O21
Magnolia Dr. .......... O20
Mahoney Pkwy.,W. ..... O21
Maple Ln. ............. O20
Meadow Dr. ........... Q20
Michael Ct. ........... Q19
Michael Dr. ........... Q19
Millstone Rd. ......... P21
Montmarte Ave. ....... P20
Murphy ............... P20
Normandy Ln. ......... P20
Novak Dr. ............ O21
Oak St. ............... O20
Oakwood Dr. .......... P21
Old Trail Rd. .......... P21
Orchard Ridge Ave. .... O22
Orleans Dr. ........... P20
Page St. .............. O23
Palmer Blvd. .......... O20
Park Ave. ............. N23
Paulina .............. O23
Peach Grove Ln. ....... O20
Pebblewood .......... P21
Pine Ct. ............. O20
Poe Ave. ............. O21
Recreation Ct. ........ O21
Ridgewood Dr. ........ P21
River Rd. ............. Q20
Robert Ct. ............ Q20
Roby St. .............. O22
Rochester Ave. ........ N23
Rockwell Ave. ......... O21
Royale Ln. ............ P20
Seine Ct. ............. P21
Shagbark Ln. .......... P21
Shea Ave. ............. O22
Smoketree ........... P21
Springfield Ave. ....... P20
Springtide Ln. ......... O20
Spruce ............... O21
Stonebridge Dr. ....... P21
Streamwood Dr. ....... Q20
Summit Ave. .......... O21
Sunset Rd. ............ P20
Surrey Ln. ............ P21
Sycamore Ln. ......... O20
Tamarino Ln. .......... O20
Tanglewood Ct. ....... P21
Tennyson Pl. .......... O21
Trapet Ave. ........... O22
Tulip Dr. ............. O20
Turtlecreek Dr. ....... P21
Versailles Ln. ......... P20
Village Dr. ............ Q20
Village Rd. ........... O20
Wellington ........... O20
Wellington Ct. ........ O20
Western .............. O22
Wheelwood Ct. ........ N21
Whipple St. ........... N21
Whitman Ave. ......... O21
Whittier Ave. ......... O21
Winchester Ave. ....... O22
Wood St. ............. O22
Woodworth Pl. ....... O20,21

### GOLF COURSES
Calumet C.C. .......... O22

### PARKS
Bicentennial Park ...... O23
Chateaux Park ........ P20
Cherry Creek Park ..... P21
Dynasty Trails Park .... Q20
Hillcrest Park ......... O21
James Setnes Park ..... N21
Lions Park ............ O22
Oak Hill Park .......... O21
Oak Valley North Park .. O21
Stone Hollow Park ..... P21
Thorogood Marshall Park P20
Tri Hi Park ............ O22
Wolf Park ............. P19

### SCHOOLS
Chataux Sch. .......... P20
Highland Sch. ......... O20
Palm Sch. ............ O22
St. Anne Sch. ......... N22
St. John Sch. ......... O20

### SHOPPING CENTERS
Eagle S.C. ............ P19

### MISCELLANEOUS
Community Center ..... O21
Crestview Pool/Lake Owens
.................... O21
Fire Department ..... O21,22
Hazel Crest Hospital .... O23
Imperial Nursing Home . O20
Library ............... Q20
R.R. Station ........... O23
South Suburban Hospital P20
Village Hall ......... O21,23

## HICKORY HILLS
Page 34

### STREETS
Active Ln. ............ C12
Ash Ln. .............. C12
Baldwin Trail .......... C13
Barberry Ln. .......... C12
Beechnut Rd. ......... C12
Birch Ln. ............. C12
Blue Ridge ........... C12
Briarwood ............ C12
Chestnut Dr. .......... B12
Christina Dr. .......... C12
Coey Ln. ............. D13
Colette Ln. ........... C12
Dell Ct. ............... B12
Elm Dr. .............. C12
Emerald Ave. ......... C12
Flamingo Terr. ........ D13
Forest ............... B11
Forest Ln. ............ C12
Forest Ln. East ....... C12
Golden Oak Ct. ....... C12
Hawthorn Dr. ......... C12
Hickory Ln. ........... C12
Hillside Dr. ........... C12
Jonathan Dr. ......... C13
Kean Ave. ............ C11
Kells Dr. ............. D12
Kitty Ln. ............. C12
Kopping Ln. .......... C12
Lisa Ln. .............. C12
Lynwood ............. C12
Meadowview Dr. ....... C11
Nida Ct. .............. C12
Oak Hill Ct. .......... C12
Oakwood ............. C12
Orchard Dr. .......... C12
Pleasant Ave. ......... C12
Primrose Ln. .......... B12
Robin Ct. ............ B12
Sandra Ln. ........... C12
Shady Dr. ............ B12
Sycamore Ct. ......... C12
Sycamore Dr. ......... C12
Wachter Ln. .......... C12
Willow Rd. ........... C12
Woodard Ln. ......... C12
Woodland ............ C12
76th Ct. ............. D14
76th Ct. ............. C12
77th Ave. ............ D14
77th Ct. ............. D13
78th St. ............. D13
79th Ave. ............ D13
79th St. ............. D13
79th Ct. ............. C12
80th Ave. (Roberts Rd.) . D13
80th Ct. ............. D13
81st Ave. ............ D13
81st Ct. ............. D13
82nd Ave. ............ D13
82nd Ct. ............. D13
83rd Ave. ............ D13
83rd Ct. ............. D13
84th Ave. ............ D13
84th Ct. ............. D13
85th Ave. ............ D13
85th Ct. ............. D13
85th St. .............. B13
86th Ct. ............. D12
86th Pl. ............. D12
86th Pl. ............. C13
87th Ave. ............ D13
87th St. ........... C12,13
88th Ave. ............ D13
88th Ct. ............. D13
88th St. ............. C13
89th Ave. ............ D12
89th Ct. ............. C13
89th St. ............. D13
90th Ave. ............ D12
90th Ct. ............. C13
90th St. ........... D12,13
91st Ave. ......... C12,14
91st St. ............. C12
92nd Pl. ........... C12,13
92nd St. ........... C12,13
93rd Pl. ............. D12
93rd St. .......... D12,C13
94th St. ............. D13
95th St. ............. D12
96th Pl. ............. D14
97th Pl. ............. D13
97th St. ............. D13
98th Pl. ............. D13

## HICKORY HILLS


98th St. ........... D13,14
99th St. .............. D13

### FOREST PRESERVES
Hickory Hills Woods .... D12

### GOLF COURSES
Hickory Hills G.C. ....... D13

### SCHOOLS
Conrady Jr. H.S. ........ D13
Dorn Sch. ............ C13
Glen Oak Sch. ......... C12
St. Patricia Sch. ......... C12

### SHOPPING CENTERS
Hickory Creek S.C. ...... D12


## HOFFMAN ESTATES

Pages 6,11,12
(For additional listings, see Section 5)


### STREETS
Abbey Wood Dr. .......... Pg.11 .... G2
Aberdeen St. . Pg.12 .... J6
Alcoa Ln. .... Pg.11 .... H4
Alder Ct. .... Pg.6 ..... E2
Alder Dr., N. & W. .......... Pg.6 ..... E2
Algonquin Rd. (Rte. 62) .......... Pg.7 ..... F5
Alhambra Ln. Pg.12 .... J5
Almond Ln. .. Pg.12 .... J6
Alpine Ln. ... Pg.12 .... H5
Amber Cir. ... Pg.6 ..... C3
Ameritech Center Dr. (Pvt.) .......... Pg.11 .... F2
Amherst Ln. . Pg.11 .... H4
Anjou Ln. ... Pg.6 ..... D3
Apache Ln. .. Pg.12 .... H5
Apple St. ... Pg.12 .... H5
Apricot St. .. Pg.12 .... H5
Arizona Blvd. . Pg.12 .... H5
Arlington St. . Pg.12 .... J5
Arrowwood Ln. Pg.6 ..... D2
Ascot Ct. .... Pg.11 .... J3
Ash Rd. ..... Pg.12 .... J5
Ashland St. .. Pg.12 .... J5
Ashley Ct. ... Pg.11 .... G4
Ashley Rd. .. Pg.11 .... G4
Aspen St. .... Pg.12 .... H5
Aster Ln. .... Pg.12 .... H5
Atlantic Ave. .. Pg.11 .... J1
Audubon St. . Pg.12 .... J5
Avondale Ln. . Pg.12 .... H6
Azalea Ln. ... Pg.12 .... H5
Barberry Ct. .. Pg.6 ..... D2
Barcroft Ct. .. Pg.6 ..... B2
Barcroft Dr. .. Pg.6 ..... B2
Bardwick Ct. . Pg.6 ..... C3
Barrington Rd. Pg.11 .... H1
Basswood St. Pg.12 .... H6
Batavia Ln. ... Pg.12 .... J5
Baxter Ln. ... Pg.11 .... H4
Bayberry Ln. . Pg.11 .... F1
Bayside Cir. .. Pg.6 ..... D1
Bayside Ct., E. Pg.6 ..... D2
Beacon Ct. ... Pg.6 ..... C2
Bedford Rd. .. Pg.11 .... G4
Berkley Ln., E. Pg.12 .... H5
Berkley Ln., W. Pg.11 .... H4
Bernay Ln. ... Pg.6 ..... D2
Bicek Ct. .... Pg.6 ..... C2
Bicek Dr. .... Pg.6 ..... C2
Blackberry Ln. Pg.11 .... G1
Blair Ln. ..... Pg.11 .... H3
Bluebonnet Ln., E. & N. .......... Pg.12 .... H5
Boardwalk Blvd. Pg.11 .... H1
Bode Cir.(Pvt) Pg.11 .... J3
Bode Rd. .... Pg.11 .... H4
Bolleana Ct. . Pg.6 ..... D2
Bonnie Ln. ... Pg.11 .... H2
Bordeaux Dr. . Pg.6 ..... D3
Botsford Pl. .. Pg.11 .... F1
Boulder Ln. .. Pg.6 ..... C3
Bradley Ln. .. Pg.12 .... J5
Bradwell Rd. . Pg.6 ..... B2
Briar Ct. .... Pg.11 .... G1
Briarcliff Ln. .. Pg.11 .... H4
Brigantine Ct. Pg.6 ..... C2
Brigantine Ln. Pg.6 ..... C2
Brighton Pl. .. Pg.11 .... G2
Bristol Walk .. Pg.11 .... G2
Brittany Ln. .. Pg.6 ..... D2
Brookside Dr. Pg.11 .... H2
Brookside Ln. Pg.11 .... H2
Buckeye Dr. .. Pg.12 .... J5
Buckingham Ct. Pg.11 .... J3
Buckthorn Dr. Pg.6 ..... D2
Bulrush Dr. .. Pg.11 .... H2
Burnham Dr. . Pg.6 ..... C3
Burning Bush Ln. .......... Pg.6 ..... D2
Burr Ridge Dr. Pg.6 ..... E2
Buttercreek Ct. Pg.12 .... H4
Butterfield Ct. Pg.6 ..... E4
Caldwell Ln. .. Pg.11 .... H2
Cambridge Ln. Pg.11 .... H4
Camelot Ln. .. Pg.6 ..... B2
Cameron Ct. . Pg.6 ..... C3
Candlewood Ln. .......... Pg.11 .... H3
Cape Breton Ct. Pg.6 ..... D2
Capstan Dr. .. Pg.6 ..... C2
Cardigan Pl. .. Pg.11 .... G2
Carleton Rd. . Pg.11 .... G4
Carling Rd. .. Pg.11 .... G3
Carmel Ct. ... Pg.11 .... H2
Carnation Ln. Pg.11 .... H5
Carthage Ln. . Pg.12 .... H5
Castaway Ct. . Pg.6 ..... C2
Castaway Ln. . Pg.6 ..... C2
Castlewood Ct. Pg.6 ..... E4
Cedar Tree Ct. Pg.12 .... H4
Central Rd. .. Pg.11 .... F1
Chambers Dr. Pg.6 ..... B3
Chandler Ln. . Pg.12 .... J5
Charlemagne Dr., N. .......... Pg.6 ..... D3
Charlemagne Dr., W. .......... Pg.6 ..... D2
Charleston Ln. Pg.6 ..... E3
Chatsworth Ln. Pg.11 .... J3
Chelmsford Pl. Pg.11 .... G2
Cheltenham Pl. Pg.11 .... G1
Cherry Ct. ... Pg.6 ..... D2
Chesapeake Ct. Pg.6 ..... D2
Chesapeake Dr. Pg.6 ..... D2
Chestnut Ln. . Pg.6 ..... D2
Chippendale Rd. .......... Pg.11 .... G3
Claremont Rd. Pg.11 .... G3
Clarendon St. Pg.12 .... H5
Claridge Cir. . Pg.11 .... J3
Clifton Pl. ... Pg.11 .... G1
Clover Ln. ... Pg.6 ..... C3
Cobblehill Ct. . Pg.11 .... G3
Cochise St. .. Pg.12 .... J5
Colgate Ct. ... Pg.11 .... H4
Colony Ln. ... Pg.6 ..... D3
Concord Cove Pg.6 ..... D3
Concord Ln. . Pg.6 ..... D3
Cooper Rd. .. Pg.11 .... H4
Cornell Cir. .. Pg.11 .... H1
Cornell Ct. ... Pg.11 .... H2
Cornell Dr. ... Pg.11 .... H1
Cornell Pl. ... Pg.11 .... H1
Cornell Terr. . Pg.11 .... H1
Cottonwood Tr., N. & W. .......... Pg.6 ..... D2
Cougar Trail (Pvt.) .......... Pg.12 .... J6
Cove Ln. ..... Pg.6 ..... C2
Coventry Ct. . Pg.6 ..... F4
Crab Orchard Dr. .......... Pg.6 ..... C3
Cranshire Ct. . Pg.6 ..... E4
Creekside Dr. . Pg.11 .... H2
Crescent Ln. . Pg.11 .... H2
Crimson Ct. .. Pg.6 ..... D3
Crimson Dr. .. Pg.6 ..... D2
Crowfoot Cir., N. .......... Pg.11 .... H2
Cumberland St. Pg.12 .... J5
Cypress Ct. .. Pg.11 .... H2
Danbury Pl. .. Pg.11 .... F1
Darien Ct. ... Pg.11 .... J3
Darlington Cir., N. .......... Pg.11 .... H3
Darlington Ct. Pg.11 .... H3
Decatur St. .. Pg.12 .... J5
Deerpath Ct. . Pg.11 .... H3
Deerpath Ln. . Pg.11 .... H3
Della Dr. .... Pg.11 .... G2
Dennison Rd. Pg.11 .... H4
Des Plaines Ln. Pg.12 .... J4
Devonshire Ln. Pg.11 .... G3
Dexter Ln., N. & W. .......... Pg.11 .... H3
Diamond Dr. . Pg.6 ..... C3
Dixon Ct. .... Pg.6 ..... D4
Dixon Dr. .... Pg.6 ..... D4
Dogwood Dr. . Pg.6 ..... D2
Dorchester Ln. Pg.11 .... H3
Douglas Ct. .. Pg.12 .... J5
Dover Ct. .... Pg.6 ..... D2
Dovington Ct. Pg.11 .... H3
Dovington Dr., N. .......... Pg.11 .... H3
Dovington Dr., W. .......... Pg.11 .... J3
Downey St. .. Pg.11 .... J3
Downing Dr. . Pg.6 ..... C3
Dresden Ct. .. Pg.6 ..... D3
Dresden Dr. .. Pg.6 ..... D3
Driftwood Ct. . Pg.6 ..... C2
Dukesberry Ln. Pg.6 ..... C3
Dunmore Pl. . Pg.11 .... G2
Durham Ct. .. Pg.11 .... G4
Durham Ln. .. Pg.11 .... G4
Eagle Way ... Pg.11 .... F1
Edgefield Ln. . Pg.11 .... G2
Edgemont Ln. Pg.11 .... G4
Eisenhower Cir. Pg.6 ..... D3
Elizabeth Ct. . Pg.11 .... H4
Emory Rd. ... Pg.11 .... G4
Englewood Rd. Pg.11 .... G3
Erie Ln. ..... Pg.11 .... G2
Essington Ct. . Pg.6 ..... C2
Essington Ln. Pg.6 ..... C2
Evanston St. . Pg.12 .... H4
Evergreen Ln. Pg.11 .... G4
Exeter Ct. .... Pg.6 ..... B3
Fairfield Ln. .. Pg.11 .... G3
Fairmont Rd. . Pg.11 .... H3
Fairway Ct. ... Pg.11 .... G2-3
Fayette Walk . Pg.11 .... G2
Fir Ct. ...... Pg.6 ..... D2
Firestone Dr., N. & W. .......... Pg.6 ..... D3
Firestone Ln., N. .......... Pg.6 ..... D3
Flagstaff Ln. .. Pg.11 .... J4
Foltz Dr. ..... Pg.11 .... G2
Forest Glen Dr. Pg.6 ..... D2
Forest Park Ln. Pg.12 .... J5
Fortune Bay Ct. Pg.6 ..... D2
Franklin Pl. .. Pg.11 .... G2
Frederick Ln. . Pg.11 .... G4
Freeman Rd. . Pg.6 ..... D3
Fremont Rd. . Pg.11 .... G4
Gannon Ct. .. Pg.11 .... H3
Gannon Dr. .. Pg.11 .... H3
Garden Terr. . Pg.11 .... F1
Garnet Cir. .. Pg.6 ..... C3
Gentry Rd. ... Pg.11 .... H4
Georgetown Ln. .......... Pg.11 .... G2
Geronimo St. . Pg.12 .... G4
Glen Lake Rd. Pg.11 .... G3
Glen Ln. ..... Pg.11 .... G3
Glendale Ln. . Pg.11 .... J4
Glenwood Ln. Pg.6 ..... C3
Gloucester Ct. Pg.6 ..... D2
Goldenrod Ln. Pg.6 ..... C3
Golf Rd. (Rte. 58) .......... Pg.11 .... H1
Governors Ln. Pg.11 .... G1
Grand Canyon Pkwy. .......... Pg.12 .... H4
Grand Canyon St. .......... Pg.12 .... J4
Grantham Pl. . Pg.11 .... F1
Greenfield Rd. Pg.11 .... G3
Greens Ct. ... Pg.11 .... H2
Greenspoint Pkwy. .......... Pg.11 .... G1
Greystone Pl. . Pg.11 .... F1
Grissom Ln. . Pg.12 .... H4
Haddam Pl. .. Pg.11 .... G2
Haman Ave. .. Pg.6 ..... C3
Haman Ct. ... Pg.6 ..... D3
Hampton Rd. . Pg.11 .... G4
Hancock Dr. . Pg.11 .... G2
Harbor Cir. .. Pg.6 ..... C2
Harrison Ln. . Pg.6 ..... D3
Hartford Ct. . Pg.11 .... G4
Harvard Ln. .. Pg.11 .... G4
Harwinton Pl. Pg.11 .... G1
Hassell Cir. .. Pg.11 .... G3
Hassell Ct. ... Pg.11 .... G3
Hassell Dr. ... Pg.11 .... G3
Hassell Pl. ... Pg.11 .... G3
Hassell Rd. .. Pg.11 .. G1-3
Hastings Dr. . Pg.11 .... F1
Hawthorn Ln. Pg.12 .... H5
Heather Ln. .. Pg.11 .... G3
Heritage Dr. . Pg.11 .... H4
Hermitage Cir. Pg.11 .... G3
Hermitage Ln. Pg.11 .... G3
Higgins Quarter Dr. .......... Pg.11 .... H4
Higgins Rd. (Rte. 72) .......... Pg.11 .... G2
Highland Blvd. Pg.11 .... G4
Hill Dr. ...... Pg.11 .... H4
Hillcrest Blvd. Pg.11 .... G3
Hillcrest Ct. . Pg.11 .... G4
Hillside Ct. .. Pg.6 ..... E3
Hilltop Rd. .. Pg.11 .... G3
Holbrook Ln. . Pg.11 .... G1
Holly Ln. .... Pg.12 .... H5
Hudson Dr. .. Pg.6 ..... D3
Hundley St., N. & W. .......... Pg.11 .... J2
Hundley Way . Pg.11 .... J2
Huntington Blvd. .......... Pg.11 .... G2
Huttner Ct. .. Pg.11 .... G2
Ida Rd. ..... Pg.11 .... G4
Illinois Blvd. . Pg.11 .... J4
Islandview Ct. Pg.11 .... G2
Jamestown Cir. Pg.11 .... G2
Jamison Ln. . Pg.11 .... G4
Jefferson Rd. . Pg.11 .... G4
Jennifer Ln. . Pg.11 .... H2
Jody Ln. .... Pg.11 .... J3
John Dr. .... Pg.11 .... H3
Jones Rd. ... Pg.11 .... G4
Juniper Tree Ct. Pg.12 .... H4
Kenilworth Cir. Pg.11 .... G2
Kensington Ln. Pg.11 .... G2
Kent Rd. .... Pg.11 .... G4
Kenwood Rd. Pg.11 .... G2
Kettering Rd. . Pg.11 .... G2
Kingston Dr. . Pg.11 .... C3
Knoll Ln. .... Pg.11 .... H4
Laburnum Rd. Pg.6 ..... D2
Lafayette Ln. . Pg.11 .... G4
Lafleur Ln. ... Pg.6 ..... D2
Lake Edge Ct. Pg.6 ..... D2
Lakeside Plaza, N. & W. .......... Pg.11 .... G3
Lakeview Ln. . Pg.11 .... J4
Lakewood Blvd. .......... Pg.11 .. F1-2
Lancaster Ct. . Pg.11 .... G3
Langdon Pl. . Pg.11 .... G1
Larchmont Rd. Pg.12 .... G4
Latour Ct. ... Pg.6 ..... D3
Leatherleaf Ct. Pg.6 ..... E2
Leatherleaf Ln. Pg.6 ..... E1
Legend Ln. ... Pg.11 .... H2
Lexington Dr. Pg.6 ..... E3
Liberty Pl. ... Pg.11 .... G2
Lichfield Dr. .. Pg.6 ..... C3
Lincoln St. ... Pg.12 .... J4
Lincolnshire Ln. Pg.11 .... J3
Lombardy Ln. Pg.6 ..... D3
London Sq. .. Pg.11 .... J3
Londonderry Ct. .......... Pg.6 ..... E4
Ludington Ct. Pg.6 ..... D3
Manchester Dr. Pg.11 .... G2
Maple Ln. ... Pg.11 .... J4
Maricopa Ln. . Pg.12 .... J4
Marquette Ln. Pg.11 .... G2
Mason Dr. ... Pg.6 ..... D3
Mayfield Ln. .. Pg.11 .... G3
Maywood Ln. Pg.11 .... J4
McCormack Dr. Pg.11 .... G2
Meadow Ln. . Pg.11 .... H4
Mesa Dr. .... Pg.11 .... H4
Meyer Rd. ... Pg.11 .... H2
Michael Ct. .. Pg.6 ..... D3
Michelline Ct. . Pg.6 ..... D3
Milan Ln. .... Pg.11 .... J4
Milton Ln. ... Pg.11 .... J4
Mohave St. .. Pg.11 .... J4
Monarch Ln. . Pg.6 ..... C3
Monterey Ct. . Pg.11 .... H2
Monticello Rd. Pg.12 .... G4
Moon Lake Blvd. .......... Pg.11 .. H1-2
Morgan Ln. .. Pg.11 .... J4
Morton St. ... Pg.11 .. J-H4
Moulin Ln. ... Pg.6 ..... D3
Mumford Ct. . Pg.6 ..... D2
Mumford Dr. . Pg.6 ..... D3
Nantucket Ct. . Pg.6 ..... D2
Navajo Ln. ... Pg.12 .... J4
New Britton Dr., N. & W. .......... Pg.6 ..... D3
Newark Ln. .. Pg.11 .... J4
Newcastle Ln. Pg.11 .... H3
Newman Pl. .. Pg.6 ..... D4
Newport Rd., N. .......... Pg.12 .... G4
Newport Rd., W. .......... Pg.11 .... G4
Newton St. ... Pg.11 .... J4
Nogales St. .. Pg.12 .... J4
Norman Dr. .. Pg.6 ..... E3
Norridge Ln. . Pg.11 .... J4
Northview Ln. Pg.11 .... G4
Nottingham Ln. Pg.11 .... G3
O'Hare Dr. ... Pg.6 ..... D3
Oak Knoll Ln. . Pg.6 ..... D2
Oak Tree Ct. . Pg.12 .... H4
Oakdale Rd. . Pg.11 .... G3
Oakmont Rd., N. .......... Pg.11 .... H2
Oakmont Rd., W. .......... Pg.11 .... H3
Old Barrington Rd. .......... Pg.11 .... F1
Old Higgins Rd. Pg.11 .... G1
Old Timber Ct. Pg.6 ..... C3
Old Timber Ln. Pg.6 ..... C3
Olive St. .... Pg.11 .. J-H4
Olmstead Dr. . Pg.6 ..... C3
Opal Dr. ..... Pg.6 ..... C3
Orange Ln. .. Pg.11 .... J4
Osage Ln. ... Pg.11 .... J4
Oxford Ln. ... Pg.11 .... G2
Pacific Ave. .. Pg.11 .... J1
Paisley Ct. ... Pg.6 ..... B2
Paris Ln. .... Pg.11 .... J4
Park Ln. ..... Pg.6 ..... D3
Parkside Dr., N. & W. .......... Pg.6 ..... D2
Parkview Cir., E.& W. .......... Pg.11 .... G2
Partridge Hill Dr. .......... Pg.11 .... J3
Patriot Ln. ... Pg.6 ..... D3
Payson Dr. .. Pg.11 .... J4
Pebble Beach Ct. .......... Pg.11 .... H2
Pebble Beach Dr. .......... Pg.11 .... H2
Pebblewood Ln. .......... Pg.6 ..... D2
Pembroke Ave. Pg.11 .... G1
Perry Ln. .... Pg.11 .... K4
Picardy Ln. .. Pg.6 ..... D3
Pierce Rd. ... Pg.12 .... G4
Pleasant St. . Pg.11 .... K4
Plum Grove Rd. Pg.12 .... J6
Plymouth Rd. Pg.6 ..... D3
Ponderosa Ln. Pg.6 ..... C3
Poplar Creek Dr. .......... Pg.11 .... H1
Port Arthur Ct. Pg.6 ..... D2
Portage Ln. .. Pg.6 ..... D3
Portshire Ct. . Pg.6 ..... E4
Prestwick Pl. . Pg.6 ..... C3
Princeton St. . Pg.11 .... J4
Queensbury Cir. .......... Pg.11 .... G2
Raleigh Ln. .. Pg.11 .... F1
Raleigh Pl. ... Pg.11 .... G2
Randi Ln. .... Pg.11 .... J3
Rebecca Dr. .. Pg.11 .... H2
Regan Ct. ... Pg.6 ..... C3
Regent Dr. ... Pg.6 ..... E4
Ridgewood Ln. Pg.6 ..... D2
Robin Cir. ... Pg.11 .... H2
Robin Ln. ... Pg.11 .... H2
Rochester Dr. Pg.11 .... C3
Rock Cove Ct. Pg.6 ..... D2
Rock Cove Dr. Pg.6 ..... D2
Rolling Prairie Ct. .......... Pg.6 ..... D2
Rosedale Ln. . Pg.11 .... G3
Sandlewood Ln. .......... Pg.6 ..... D2
Sapphire Dr., N. .......... Pg.6 .... C2-3
Sessions Walk Pg.11 .... G2
Shagbark Ct. . Pg.6 ..... C3
Shepard Rd. . Pg.11 .... G4
Shoe Factory Rd. .......... Pg.11 .... G1
Shorewood Ct. Pg.6 ..... C2
Shorewood Dr., N. & W. .......... Pg.6 ..... C2
Silver Pine Dr. Pg.6 ..... C3
Smethwick Ln. Pg.11 .... F1
Somersworth Pl. .......... Pg.11 .... F1
Somerton Dr. Pg.6 ..... C3
Spring Mill Dr. Pg.11 .... H4
Stockton Dr. . Pg.11 .... G2
Stoneharbor Ct. .......... Pg.6 ..... D2
Stoneharbor Dr., N. .......... Pg.6 ..... D1
Stonington Ave. .......... Pg.11 .... G1
Stratham Pl. . Pg.11 .... G1
Sturbridge Ct. Pg.6 ..... D2
Sturbridge Dr., N. & W. .......... Pg.6 ..... D3
Sudbury Dr. . Pg.11 .... F1
Suffolk Ln. ... Pg.6 ..... D4
Sumac Tr. ... Pg.6 ..... C3
Sundance Ct. . Pg.6 ..... C3
Sunflower Ln. Pg.6 ..... C3
Sussex Walk . Pg.11 .... G2
Sutherland Pl. Pg.11 .... F1
Sweetflower Dr. Pg.11 .... H2
Swindon Pl. .. Pg.11 .... H1
Sycamore Ct. . Pg.6 ..... E3
Tamarack Ct. . Pg.6 ..... B3
Tamarack Dr., W. .......... Pg.6 ..... C3
Tarrington Dr. Pg.6 ..... C2
Thacker St., E. Pg.12 .... J5
Thacker St., W. Pg.12 .... J1
Thornbark Ct. Pg.6 ..... C1
Thornbark Dr. Pg.6 ..... C3
Topaz Dr. .... Pg.6 ..... C3
Trailside Ct. .. Pg.6 ..... C3
Treaty Ln. ... Pg.6 ..... E3
Turnberry Dr. Pg.6 ..... C3
Valley Ln. .... Pg.12 .... H4
Versailles Rd. . Pg.6 ..... D3
Victoria Dr. .. Pg.6 ..... D3
Victoria Dr., N. Pg.6 ..... D3
Vista Ln. .... Pg.11 .... H2
Volid Dr. .... Pg.11 .... H2
Wainsford Dr. Pg.11 .... J3
Warington Ln. Pg.11 .... H2
Warwick Cir., N. & W. .......... Pg.11 .... H3
Washington Blvd. .......... Pg.11 .. J3-4
Wellington Pl. Pg.11 .... F1
Westbridge Ct. Pg.6 ..... C3
Westbury Dr. . Pg.6 ..... C2
Western St. .. Pg.11 .... J3
Westhaven Ct. Pg.6 ..... C3
Westview St. . Pg.11 .... J4
Whispering Trails Ct. .......... Pg.6 ..... D2
Whispering Trails Dr. .......... Pg.6 ..... E2
Whitingham Ln. .......... Pg.11 .... F1
Wildwood Ct. . Pg.6 ..... C3
William Ct. ... Pg.6 ..... D4
Williams Rd. . Pg.6 ..... C3
Williamsburg Dr. .......... Pg.11 .... G1
Willow Tree Ct. Pg.12 .... H4
Wilmington Ln. Pg.11 .... H3
Wilshire Dr., N. & W. .......... Pg.6 ..... E4
Winding Trail Ln. .......... Pg.6 ..... E2
Winston Cir. . Pg.6 ..... E3
Winston Dr. . Pg.6 ..... D3
Winston Ln. . Pg.6 ..... E3
Winston Pl. .. Pg.6 ..... E3
Woodcreek Ln. Pg.11 .... H2
Woodhollow Ct. .......... Pg.6 ..... C3
Woodlawn St. Pg.11 .. H,J4
Worthington Dr. .......... Pg.11 .... H2
Yardley Ln. .. Pg.11 .... J3
Yorkshire Ct. . Pg.6 ..... E4

### GOLF COURSES
Highland Woods G.C. .......... Pg.11,12 F4
Hilldale C.C. . Pg.11 .... G2
Poplar Creek C.C. .......... Pg.11 .... H1

### PARKS
Ash Park .... Pg.11 .... H3
Birch Park ... Pg.17 .... H5
Blackhawk Park Pg.16 .... H2
Chestnut Park Pg.3 ..... H3
Chino Park .. Pg.12 .... J4
Cottonwood Park .......... Pg.11 .... F2
Douglas Park . Pg.6 ..... E2
Evergreen Park Pg.11 .... J4
Fairview Park . Pg.17 .... J5
Field Park, The Pg.11 .... G4
High Point Park Pg.11 .... G3
Highland Park Pg.11 .... G4
Hoffman Park Pg.17 .... J4
Lincoln Park . Pg.6 ..... D2
Locust Park . Pg.12 .... G4
Maple Park .. Pg.16 .... J4
Meadow Park . Pg.6 ..... D2
North Twin Park .......... Pg.11 .... G3
Oak Park .... Pg.11 .... G2
Pebble Park .. Pg.6 ..... D2
Pine Park .... Pg.6 ..... E4
Poplar Park .. Pg.11 .... G2
Seminole Nature Area .......... Pg.6 ..... D2
Sloan Park ... Pg.11 .... J4
South Twin Park .......... Pg.11 .... G3
Sycamore Park Pg.11 .... G4
Valley Park .. Pg.6 ..... D4
Victoria Park . Pg.11 .... J3
Vogelei Park . Pg.11 .... H4
Whispering Lake Park .......... Pg.6 ..... D2
Willow Park .. Pg.6 ..... E3

### SCHOOLS
Armstrong Sch. Pg.11 .... H2
Conant H.S. .. Pg.12 .... J6
Eisenhower Jr. H.S. .......... Pg.11 .... G3
Enders Salk Sch. .......... Pg.11 .... J3
Fairview Sch. . Pg.12 .... J5
Hillcrest Sch. . Pg.11 .... G4
Hoffman Estates H.S. .......... Pg.11 .... H3
Lakeview Sch. Pg.11 .... J4
MacArthur Sch. Pg.11 .... G3
Muir Sch. .... Pg.11 .... G2
St. Hubert Sch. Pg.12 .... J4
Twinbrook Sch. Pg.12 .... H5

### SHOPPING CENTERS
Barrington Square Mall .......... Pg.11 .... G1
Brandess West S.C. .......... Pg.11 .... H3
Crossroads Commons .......... Pg.12 .... H4
Forest View S.C. .......... Pg.6 ..... D2
Golf Center .. Pg.12 .... H5
Hoffman Plaza Pg.12 .... H5
Hoffman Village S.C. .......... Pg.11 .... H1
Huntington Plaza .......... Pg.6 ..... D2
Poplar Commons S.C. .......... Pg.11 .... G1
Poplar Creek Plaza .......... Pg.11 .... H2
Strawberry Hill S.C. .......... Pg.11 .... H3

### MISCELLANEOUS
Community Pool .......... Pg.11 .... H4
Fire Stations . Pg.6 ..... C3
Hoffman Estates Park Dist. Admin. Office Pg.11 .... H2
Hoffman Estates Police Dept. .......... Pg.11 .... H3
Hoffman Estates Public Works Ctr. ..... Pg.11 .... G1
Hoffman Estates Village Hall .......... Pg.11 .... H3
Library, Hoffman Estates .......... Pg.11 .... G2
Library, Schaumburg Twp. .......... Pg.11 .... G2
Poplar Creek C.C. Clubhouse .......... Pg.11 .... H1
Post Office, Hoffman Estates .......... Pg.11 .... H3
Schaumburg Township Office .......... Pg.11 .... K4
St. Alexius Hoffman Estates Medical Center .......... Pg.11 .... H2
Vogelei Teen Center .......... Pg.11 .... H3
Woodland Hosp. .......... Pg.11 .... G1


## HOMEWOOD

Pages 42,43


### STREETS
Aberdeen St. ......... P,Q23
Aida Ct. ............. Q21
Alexander St. ......... Q22
Alexander Terr. ........ Q22
Argyle Ave. ........... Q21
Armitage Pl. ........... P23
Ashland Ave. ........ P,Q23
Bertz Dr. ............. P24
Beth Ct. .............. P21
Birch Rd. ........... Q21-23
Boulder Ct. ............ R24
Bowling Green .......... R24
Briar Ave. ............. P22
Burr Oak Rd. ........... P23
California Ave. ....... P,Q21
Caroline Dr. ........... P21
Carpenter Ave. ......... Q24
Carson Ct. ............. R23
Carson Dr. ........... Q,R23
Castle Rd. ............. Q24
Cedar Rd. ............. P22
Center Ave. ............ P23
Center Ct. ............. R23
Center St. ............. Q23
Chayes Park Ct. ........ Q21
Chayes Park Dr. ........ Q21
Cherrycreek Dr. ........ Q21
Cherrywood Ln. ......... P21
Chestnut Rd. ........... P22
Chicago Rd. ............ P23
Clyde Rd. ............. Q21
Clyde St. .............. Q21
Clyde Terr. ............ Q22
Coach Rd. ............. Q24
Cowing Ave. ........... Q22
Crescent Rd. ........... Q21
Debra Ln. ............. P21
Delta Rd. ............. Q24
Dixie Hwy. .......... P,Q22
Dixmoor Dr. ........... P22
Dolphin Lake Dr. ....... P21
Downey Rd. ........... Q22
Dundee Ave. ......... P,Q22
Elder Rd. ....... P23,P,Q24
Eliot Ln. .............. Q21
Elm Rd. .............. P22
Evergreen Rd. .......... Q23
Francisco Ave. ......... Q21
Fresno Ln. ............ Q21
Gladville Ave. ........ P,Q23
Golfview Ave. ........ P,Q22
Gottshalk Ave. ....... P,Q22
Governors Hwy. ........ Q21
Greenwood Rd. ......... P21
Halsted St. ............ R24
Hart Dr. .............. P24
Harwood Ave. .......... P22
Hawthorne Rd. ......... P22
Heather Ct. ............ Q23
Heather Rd. ......... Q21-23
Hedgerow Ln. .......... Q21
Hickory Rd. ......... P21-23
Highland Ave. ........ P,Q22
Hillside Ave. ........... P22
Hillview Rd. ........... Q23
Holbrook Rd. ........... R23
Hollydale Dr. ........... P21
Homewood Ave. ...... P,Q22
Hood Ave. .......... P,Q23
Howe Ave. ............ P22
Idlewild Ln. ........... Q22
Jamie Ct. ............. Q23
Jamie Ln. ............. Q23
Jeffery Ct. ............ Q23
Jeffery Dr. ............ Q23
Jill Ct. ............... Q23
Jill Terr. .............. Q23
Jodi Terr. ............. R23
Jonathan Ln. .......... Q23
Juhlin Dr. ............. Q23
Kathleen Ct. ........... Q21
Kedzie Ave. ........... R20
Kimball Ave. ........... Q20
Kings Rd. ............. Q24
Klimm Ave. ............ Q22
Knollwood Ln. ......... Q20
Kroner Ln. ............ P22
Lahaigh Rd. ........... P23
Larkspur Ln. ........... P21
Lexington Ave. ......... Q22
Lincoln ............... P21
Linden Rd. .......... P21,23
Locust ................ P21
Loomis Ave. ......... P,R23
Los Angeles Ave. ....... P21
Los Angeles Ct. ........ P21
Lynn Ct. .............. Q23
Magnolia Rd. .......... P22
Mallard Dr. ............ Q20
Maple Ave. ............ P24
Maple Ln. ............. P22
Maple Rd. ............. P22
Marlin Ct. ............. P21
Marlin Ln. ............. P21
Marshfield Ave. ........ Q23
Martin Ave. ............ Q22
Mathew Ln. ............ Q21
May Ave. .............. Q23
May St. ............... Q23

Miller Ct. P22
Morgan St. P,Q24
Morris Ave. Q22
Oak Rd. P22
Olive Rd. P21-24
Page Ave. Q23
Page Ct. Q23
Palmer Ave. Q22
Palmer Cir. Q22
Patricia Ln. Q21
Perth Ave. P21
Pierce Ave. Q,R23
Pierce Ct. R23
Pierce Terr. Q23
Pine Rd. P22,23
Poplar Ave. Q23
Poplar Ct. R23
Presidents Dr. P24
Queens Q24
Ridge Rd. P22,23
Riedle Ct. P22
Riegel Ave. P23
Riegel Oaks Ln. R23
Riegle Ct. Q23
Robin Ln. Q21
Rockwell Ave. P21
Roosevelt Ave. P22
Royal Rd. Q24
Sacramento Q21
Sacramento Ave. P21
San Diego Ave. P21
Spruce P21
Stedhall Rd. Q21
Stewart Ave. P,Q21
Stockton Ave. Q21
Sycamore Dr. P22
Tarpon Ct. P21
Terrace Rd. Q22
Thomas St. R23
Tipton Ave. P22
Turtlecreek Dr. P21
Virginia Pl. P21
Walnut Rd. P21
Walton Ln. P24
Washington Ave. P22
Western Ave. P,Q22
Willow Rd. Q21,22,23
174th St. Q25
175th St. Q24
182nd Pl. Q22
183rd St. Q23
184th Pl. Q23
184th St. Q20,23
185th Pl. Q20,23
185th St. Q23
186th Pl. Q23,24
186th St. Q22,23
186th St. Q20
187th St. Q22,23
188th St. Q23
189th St. Q22,23
190th St. R23
191st St. R23

### CEMETERIES
Hazelwood Cemetery P24

### GOLF COURSES
Idlewild Country Club R23
Ravisloe Country Club P22

### PARKS
Apollo Park R24
Butterfield Park R24
Cedar Park P22
Hollydale Park P21
Homewood Estates Park P21
Independence Park P22
Indian Trail Park Q23
Izaak Walton League Ballfields P24
Lions Club Park P24
Little League Ballfields P23
Merchants Park Q22
Orchard Park P23
Richard D. Irwin Park P22
Willowview Park Q23
Woodborough Park Q24

### SCHOOLS
Central Sch. P23
Churchill Sch. R23
Full Gospel Christian Sch. Q20
Hart Jr. H.S. P24
Ridge Sch. P22
St. Joseph Sch. P22
Willow Sch. Q22

### SHOPPING CENTERS
Cherry Creek S.C. Q21
Park Place Plaza Q24
Washington Park Plaza P24
Washington Square Mall P24

### MISCELLANEOUS
County Police P23
Golf Training Center P23
Governors Med. Center P21
Maple Leaf Nursing Home P24
Marie Irwin Comm. Center P23
Mercy Health Care Center R24
Prairie Lakes Business Center P23
Public Works P23
R.R. Station P22
Village Hall & Police Dept. P22

## INVERNESS
Pages 6,7

### STREETS
Abbotsford Dr. B2
Aberdeen Ln. B5
Aberdeen Rd. B5
Afton Cir. A3
Alexander Ct. B2
Alnwick B2
Appleby Rd. C4
Applecross Rd. C2
Ardmore Ave. C3
Arlington Rd. B,C4
Ashkirk Ct. C1
Ayrshire Ln. B4
Balmoral Cir. D5
Balmoral Dr. D5
Balmoral Ln. D5
Banbury Rd. B4
Bannockburn D4
Barclay Cir. A3
Barra Ln. B5
Beaver Pond Rd. C4
Bedlington Dr. A3
Berwick D4
Betty Dr. A3
Bishop Ct. B2
Blackburn Dr. A4
Blair Ln. C4
Blyth Ct. B2
Bonnie Ln. B5
Bonny Glen Gates D4
Bordeaux Ct. B2
Borthwick Ln. C4
Bradwell Ave. B2-3
Bradwell Cir. C1
Braeburn Rd. B4
Braymore Ct. B1
Braymore Dr., N. & S. B1
Brodick Ln. B5
Burleigh Ln. B5
Camphill Cir. C4
Canterbury Ln. B3
Carberry Cir. A3
Carleton Cir. C1
Carleton Ct. C1
Carlisle Dr. A3
Carnoustie Ln. C4
Cawdor Ln. B5
Cheviot Dr. B3
Chimmey Rock D4
Clover Dr. D4
Colonial Pkwy. E5
Colony Dr. B2
Common Ridings Way B2
Cornell Ave. B5
Country Oak Ln. C4
Courtbridge Ct. B3
Courtbridge Rd. B3
Craigie Ln. B5
Crichton Ln. C4
Cumnock Rd. B4
Day Ct. C5
Dewey Rd. C4
Diary Ln. B4
Dirbyshire Ct. B1
Direlton Ln. B5
Dover Cir. C4
Drummond Cir. B3
Dublin Ct. D5
Dumfries Ct. D5
Dunbar Rd. B5
Dunbarton Dr. B1
Dundee Rd. A4
Dunheath Cir. A3
Dunheath Dr. A3
Durham Dr. C4
Edinburgh Ct. B3
Ela Rd. B-D4
Fife Ct. B3
Fincharn Ln. C4
Firth Rd. D4
Florence Ave. B3
Fox Tr. D5
Gaelic Ct. B1
Galloway Cir. B3
Galloway Dr. B3
Glamis Ln. B5
Glen Eagles Ct. B5
Glencrest Dr. B2,A3
Glenmore Ct. A3
Grayfriars Ln. C5
Great Glen Ct. B3
Greenrock D4
Guthrie Cir. A3
Guthrie Dr. A3
Halbert Ln. C2
Halkirk Dr. C5
Haman Ave. B3
Hamilton Ct. B2
Harmening C3
Harrow Gate Dr. C2
Heather Ln. A4
Highland Rd. C4
Hillshire Ct. B2
Hillshire Ln. B2
Huntly D4
Inverray Rd. C4
Inverway Rd. B4-5
Jules St. C4
Julie Dr. A3
Kelso Glen B4
Kilrenny D4
Kingsborough Cove C1
Kirkwall Ct. A3
Kirkwood Dr. B3
Kitson Cir. C4
Knockderry Ln. B5
Knox Ct. B2
Lamond Dr. C4
Lancaster Ct. A3
Lauder Ln. D4
Livingston Ct. B2
Livingston Ln. B2
Loch Lomond Dr. C5
Lochleven Ln. B5
Lockbrook Ln. C1
Macalpin Cir. B2
Macalpin Ct. B2
Macalpin Dr. B2
Marie Dr. A3
McBain Way B3
Midmar Ln. C4
Milton Rd. B4
Muirfield Rd. B3
Mulgay Ct. C2
Mulgay Dr. C2
New Abbey Dr. C1
Newport Ln. B2
Northwest Hwy. A4
Oldwick Ln. B5
Palatine Rd. C4
Pheasant Tr. C4
Plymouth Ct. C4
Plymouth Rd. C-D5
Poteet Ave. C3
Prestwick Dr. D4
Quail Run D4
Ravenscraig Ln. B,C5
Regalia Ct. B3
Regalia Dr. B3
Rob Roy Ct. B5
Roberts Rd. C3
Roselle Rd. C-E5
Rosemary Ave. B3
Rosslyn Ln. B5
Rozborough Pl. B4
Sanday Ln. B2
Scotts Ct. B5
Selkirk B2
Shetland Rd. C2
Shire Cir. E5
Skye Ln. B2
St. Andrews Ln. B5
Sterling Rd. B4
Stonefield Cir. B3
Stonehaven D4
Stratford Ln. B3
Stuart Ln. B4
Summer Isle Ln. C2
Sunset Dr. C4
Tarbat Ct. B3
Thomas Atkinson Rd. C4
Thompson's Way D4
Thor Dr. E5
Thornhill Rd. B4
Thyra Ln. E4
Torrin Rocks Cove C1
Turkey Ct. E4
Turkey Tr. E5
Tweed Rd. A4
Tyne Ct. B2
Valley Lake Dr. E5
Warren Ave. C4
Waterford Ln. A3
Whispering Pines Ct. B1
Whithorn Ln. B5
Williams Rd. B3
Willow St. B3
Windsor Cir. D4
Windsor Dr. D4
Windsor Ln. B3
Windsor Rd. D4
Winfield Ln. B2
Wood St. C3
Woodburn Ct. A4

### CEMETERIES
Cady Cemetery A4
Deer Grove Cemetery A4

### GOLF COURSES
Inverness Golf Club B5

### PARKS
South Park D4

### MISCELLANEOUS
Village Hall B5

## JUSTICE
Page 34

### STREETS
Christeen Dr. B13
Deer Path B12
Hickory Trace Dr. B12
Kean Ave. B11
Marion St. B13
Oak Ridge Dr. B12
Pawn Tr. B12
Thomas St. B13
78th Ct. B13
79th Ave. B13
79th Ct. B13
79th Pl. B12
80th Ave. B13
80th St. B13
81st Ave. B12,13
81st St. B13
82nd Ave. B13
82nd Ct. B13
82nd St. B13
83rd Ave. B13
83rd Ct. B13
83rd Pl. B12,13
83rd St. B12
84th Ave. B13
84th Ct. B12
84th Pl. B13
84th Pl., W. B12
84th St. B13
84th St., W. B12
85th Ave. B12
85th Ct. B12
85th Pl. B13
85th Pl., W. B12
85th St. B13
85th St., W. B12
86th Ave. B12
86th Ct. B12
86th St. C13
86th St., W. B12
87th Ave. B12
87th Ave., S. B12
87th Ct. B12
87th St. C12
88th Ave., S. B12
90th Ave. B12

### CEMETERIES
Archer Woods Cemetery B12
Lithuanian Cemetery B12

### SCHOOLS
Dosher Sch. B12
George Wilkins Jr. H.S. B13
Player Sch. B13

### MISCELLANEOUS
Convalescent Home B12
Fire Department C13

## KENILWORTH
Pages 23,27

### STREETS
Abbotsford Rd. Pg.27 F12
Abingdon Ave. Pg.27 F12
Brier Pg.23 F11
Cumberland Ave. Pg.27 E12
Cummings Ave. Pg.23 E11
Cumnor Rd. Pg.27 E11,F12
Devonshire Ln. Pg.27 E12
Earlston Rd. Pg.27 F11
Essex Rd. Pg.27 F12
Exmoor Rd. Pg.27 F11
Greenwood Ave. Pg.27 F11
Ivy Ct. Pg.27 E11
Kenilworth Ave. Pg.27 E-F12
Kent Rd. Pg.23 F11
Leicester Rd. Pg.27 E12
McLean Ave. Pg.23 E11
Melrose Ave. Pg.27 E12,F11
Oxford Rd. Pg.27 F12
Park Dr. Pg.27 F11
Raleigh Rd. Pg.27 E12
Richmond Rd. Pg.27 F12
Robsart Pl. Pg.27 F12
Robsart Rd. Pg.27 F12
Roger Ave. Pg.23 F11
Roslyn Rd. Pg.27 E12
Sheridan Rd. Pg.27 E11-12
Sterling Rd. Pg.27 F11
Tudor Pl. Pg.27 F12
Warwick Rd. Pg.27 E12
Wayland Ave. Pg.27 F11
Woodstock Ave. Pg.27 F12

### SCHOOLS
Joesph Sears Sch. Pg.27 E11

### MISCELLANEOUS
Police Dept. Pg.27 F12
Village Hall Pg.27 F12

## KILDEER
Pages 2,3
Lake County
(For additional listings, see Section 6)

### STREETS
Abbey Ct. W7
Acorn Ct. W8
Amberley Dr. X8
Amy Ln. V8
Andover Rd. W8
Barbara Ct. W8
Barkley Ct. W7
Boschome Cir., N. W8
Boschome Cir., S. X8
Boschome Dr. X8
Boschome, N. W8
Boschome, S. X8
Brandon Rd. W8
Bridal Tr. W8
Buffalo Run X8
Burning Tree Ct. W7
Cambridge Dr. W7
Chadwick Ct. V8
Chartwell Dr. X8
Chestnut Ridge Rd. W7
Circle Bay Rd. X7
Clayton Ct. V8
Cliffside Dr. X8
Concorde Ct. X7
Cuba Rd. W8
Dallas Ct. W8
Dorothea Ct. W9
Elder Ct. W7
Eleanor Ln. V8
Exeter Rd. W9
Foxtail Dr. W8
Green Wood Dr. W8
Grove Dr. X8
Hampton Rd. W8
Hanaford Ct. X7
Hawthorn Ln. W7
Heather Ct. X8
Hickory Hill Dr. W8
Hidden Valley Rd. X7
Highwood Rd. X7
Hilandale Ct. V8
Hilandale Rd. V8
Honey Ridge Ct. W8
Hopewell Ct. W8
Kerwick Ln. X8
Kirkley Dr. X8
Krueger Rd. V8
Lake Zurich Rd. V8
Laurel Ln. W8
Lexington Ln. X8
Linden Ln. X8
Little Pond Rd. X7
Long Meadow Dr. X8
Maple Ct. W7
Marcy Ln. W8
Meadows Ct. X8
Middleton Dr. W9
Newberry Ct. V9
Oak Knoll Ct. X8
Oak Trail X8
Pine Grove Ct. W8
Pine Lake Cir. X7
Pine Lake Ct. X7
Plumwood Dr. X8
Providence Dr. V8
Quentin Rd. V7
Rand Rd. X8
Rebecca Ln. V8
Richmond Ct. W8
Ruth Ct. V8
Salem Lake Dr. V9
Scott Ct. X8
Sherley Rd. X8
South Rd. V8
Stoneybrook Ct. W7
Thornridge Dr. W7
Timberidge Ct. W8
Timberleaf Ln. W7
Tree Rd. X7
Valley Rd. X8
Vermont Ct. W8
Weatherstone Ct. X8
Weatherstone Rd. X8
White Pine Rd. X7
Willow Dr. X8
Wooded Ridge Dr. X7
York Ct. X8
Yorkshire Dr. V9

## LANSING
Page 45

### STREETS
Ada St. P,Q30
Adams St. P30
Ann St. P30
Arcadia Ave. O,P29
Barbara Ct. Q30
Bensley Ave. O28
Bernadine St. O,Q,R30
Bernice Ave. O29,30
Bernice Rd. O28,29
Blackstone Ave. P27
Bock Ave. P28
Bond Ave. P29
Burnham Ave. O,Q30
Calhoun Ave. O28
Carriage Ln. P28
Central P30
Cherry Q29
Chicago Ave. N-P29
Christina Dr. P29
Clyde Ave. P28
Coles Ave. P29
Commercial Ave. P29
Community St. N,O30
Country Ave. P28
Cregier P28
DeJong Ln. P28
Decker Ave. O,P28
Decker St. O28
Dorchester Ave. P27
Escanaba Ave. O29
Exchange Ave. N,P29
Flannigan Dr. O29
Forest Ct. P28
Forest View Ln. Q29
Fred St. P29
Fritz Dr. O29
Glen Oak Ave. O,P29
Glen Terr. P29
Grant St. N,P,Q30
Greenbay Ave. O,Q30
Greenbay St. P30
Harper Ave. P27
Hearth Dr. P28
Henry Ct. Q30
Henry St. N,O,Q30
Hickory St. P28
Holiday Ct. O28
Holland Rd. P28
Illi-Indi Dr. P30
Illinois St. P30
Indiana Ave. P28,29
Industrial Dr. N29
Jackson St. O30
Jason Ln. P28
Jeffery Ave. P28
Keegan Ave. O28
Keegan St. O27
Kettle Ct. P28
Kingery Expressway O29
Lake Ave. P29
Lake St. P30
Lange St. R,P30
Lee Ave. O29
Locust St. P28
Lorenz Ave. O-Q30
Louise Ct. Q30
Louise Dr. Q30
Madison St. P30
Manor Dr., N & S Q30
Maple Ave. O30
Maple St. P,Q30
Marble Ave. O29
Mertile Ct. P30
Miller Dr. P30
Monroe St. P30
Oak Ave. N-P29,P30
Oak St. R30
Oakley Ave. O,P29
Oakwood Ave. N-Q29
Old Farm Rd. P28
Otto St. Q30
Park Ave. O-R29,Q30
Park Blvd. O29
Railroad Ave. O29
Randolph St. P30
Rebel Dr. P30
Ridge Rd. P29
Ridgeland P28
Ridgewood Ave. N,P,Q29
River Dr. O30
Rose Ave. P28
Rosewood Dr. O28
Roy St. N-Q30
School St. P29
Schultz Ave. O29
Schultz Dr., N & S P30
Sharon Ct. Q30
Sherman St. P,Q30
Shirley Dr. O30
Siwel R30
State Line Rd. P30
Stewart St. P30
Terrace Dr. P30
Thornton Lansing Rd. P28
Ton Ave. O29
Torrence Ave. O29
Violet Rd. P28
Volbrech Rd. O27
Walter St. O,Q30
Ward St. P29
Washington St. P30
Wentworth Ave. P30
West St. P30
Whitman Ln. P28
Wildwood Ave. P-R29
William St. N-Q30
Willow Ln. P30
Wright St. O30
Yates Ave. O28
166th St. N29
168th St. N29
169th Ct. N30
170th Pl. N30
170th St. N29,30
171st St. N29,30
172nd Pl. O30
172nd St. (Elizabeth Ave.) O28,30
173rd Ct. O30
173rd Pl. O28-30
173rd St. O28,30
174th Ct. O30
175th Pl. O29
175th St. O30
176th Pl. O28,29
176th St. O29,30
177th Pl. O28,30
177th St. O28-30,P27,28
178th Ct. P28
178th St. O28-30,P27
179th St. P28,29
180th St. P28,29
181st Pl. P30
181st St. P28,29
182nd Pl. P28,29
182nd St. P29
183rd Pl. P28,29
183rd St. P28,29
184th Pl. P28
184th St. P28,29
185th Ct. Q28
185th Pl. P28
185th St. P28-30
186th Pl. Q29
186th St. Q28
187th Pl. Q29
187th St. Q29,30
188th Pl. Q29
188th St. Q29,30
189th Pl. Q29,30
189th St. Q29,30
190th Pl. Q29,30
190th St. Q29
191st Pl. Q29,30
191st St. Q29
192nd Pl. Q29,30
192nd St. Q29,30
193rd Ct. R30
193rd Pl. R29,30
193rd St. R29,30
194th Pl. R30
194th St. R29
195th Ct. R30

### CEMETERIES
Glen Oak Cemetery P28

### GOLF COURSES
Lansing C.C. Q30

### PARKS
Bernice Park O30
Bock Park O29
Erfert Park Q30
Jaycee Park R30
Kiwanis Park P28
Lan-Oak Park P29
Lions Park O30
Oakley Playlot Q29
Oakwood Park Q29
Potts Park O29
Rotary Park Q30
Schultz Park P30
Van Laten Park P28
Veterans Park N30
Whitman Park P28
Winterhoff Park P30

### SCHOOLS
Coolidge Sch. O30
Eisenhower Sch. O29
Hebrew Acad. Sch. P30
Heritage Middle Sch. R29
Illiana H.S. P28
Lansing Christian Sch. P30
Lansing Memorial Jr. H.S. P29
Lester Crawl Sch. P30
Luther East H.S. R29
Nathan Hale Sch. Q30
Oak Glen Sch. P28
Reavis Sch. O30
Special Ed. Sch. Q30
St. Anns Sch. P29
St. John's Luth Sch. P30
Thornton Fractional South H.S. Q30
Trinity Sch. P29

### SHOPPING CENTERS
Landings S.C. N20
Lansing Commons P29

### MISCELLANEOUS
Fire Department P29,30,R30
Lansing Municipal Airport R30
Library P29
Lions Little League Stadium P29
Post Office P29,30
R.R. Station P28
Sports Complex N30
Village Hall & Police Dept. N29

## LEMONT
See Sections 3 and 8 for complete listings

## LONG GROVE
Page 3
Lake County
(For additional listings, see Section 6)

### STREETS
Andrew Ct. X10
Antietam Dr. X10
Arlington Heights Rd. X11
Bayberry Ln. X9
Bernay Ln. X11
Bordeaux Ln. X11
Bridgewater Ct. X10
Brittany Ct. X11
Brittany Ln. X11
Brookside Ln. X10
Calvary Ct. X9
Carriage Ct. X10
Checker Rd. X9-10
Chickamauga Ln. X10
Coach Rd. X9
Country Club X10
Countryside Ln. X10
Cumberland Cir. X9
Dawn Ct. X10
Dorothy Ln. X9
Edgewood Ln. X10

## LONG GROVE

Federal Ct. . . . . . . . . . X9
Holly Ct. . . . . . . . . . . X10
Juniper Ln. . . . . . . . . X9
Knoll Ct. . . . . . . . . . . X9
Knoll Dr. . . . . . . . . . . X9
Lake Cook Rd. . . . . . . X9
Lexington Dr. . . . . . . . X9
Lincoln Ave. . . . . . . . . X10
Long Grove Rd. . . . . . . X9
Manasas Ct. . . . . . . . . X10
Manasas Ln. . . . . . . . . X10
Meadowlark Dr. . . . . . . X10
Oak Hill Ln. . . . . . . . . X9
Old Hicks Rd. . . . . . . . X9
Picardy Ct. . . . . . . . . . X11
Picardy Ln. . . . . . . . . . X11
Popp Ln. . . . . . . . . . . X10
Pottawatomie Ct. . . . . . X10
Roanoke Ct. . . . . . . . . X10
Shaeffer Rd. . . . . . . . . X10
Shenandoah Ln. . . . . . X10
Sheridan Ct. . . . . . . . . X10
Sumter Dr. . . . . . . . . . X10
Tanager Way . . . . . . . . X10
Union St. . . . . . . . . . . X10
Walnut Ln. . . . . . . . . . X9
Willow Valley Rd. . . . . . X9
Woodland Ln. . . . . . . . X9

## LYNWOOD
Pages 45,50
### STREETS
Aianna Ln. . . . Pg.50 . . T30
Arbon Dr. . . . . Pg.50 . . U30
Arroyo Ave. . . . Pg.50 . . S29
Ash Ln. . . . . . Pg.50 . . S29
Balzano . . . . . Pg.50 . . U30
Bensely Ave. . . Pg.50 . . T28
Bergenz . . . . . Pg.50 . . U30
Bernina . . . . . Pg.50 . . U30
Brenner . . . . . Pg.50 . . U30
Brenta . . . . . . Pg.50 . . U30
Brook Ave. . . . Pg.50 . . S29
Burnham Ave. . . Pg.50 . . S30
Carondelet Ave. Pg.50 . . S29
Catalpa Ave. . . Pg.50 . . S29
Cedar Glen Dr. . Pg.50 . . U30
Chillon . . . . . . Pg.50 . . U30
Colleen Dr. . . . Pg.50 . . T30
Crescent Ave. . Pg.50 . . S29
Cypress Ave. . . Pg.50 . . S30
Deborah . . . . . Pg.50 . . T30
Dewey Ave. . . . Pg.50 . . R28
Dolphin Ave. . . Pg.50 . . S29
Driftwood Ave. . Pg.50 . . S30
Duke . . . . . . . Pg.50 . . U30
Glarus . . . . . . Pg.50 . . U30
Glenwood Dyer Rd.
. . . . . . . . . . Pg.50 . . S28
Glenwood Rd. . . Pg.45 . . R29
Joe Orr Rd. . . . Pg.50 . . S27
Juniper Ave. . . Pg.50 . . S30
Lake Lynwood Dr.
. . . . . . . . . . Pg.45 . . S29
Lake Park Ct. . . Pg.45 . . R29
Lake Shore Ct. . Pg.45,50 S29
Lake Shore Ct. . Pg.45 . . R29
Lake Shore Ave. Pg.45 . . R29
Lakewood Ave. Pg.50 . . S29
Lighthouse Ct. . Pg.50 . . R29
Linda Dr. . . . . Pg.50 . . T30
Lisa Cir. . . . . . Pg.50 . . U30
Mariner Ct. . . . Pg.50 . . S29
Marlin Ave. . . . Pg.50 . . S29
Marquette Ave. . Pg.50 . . S29
Maureen Ct. . . Pg.50 . . T30
Merlin Ct. . . . . Pg.50 . . S29
Monterey Ave. . Pg.50 . . S29
Muskegan Ave. Pg.50 . . S29
Oak Ln. . . . . . Pg.50 . . S29
Oakwood Ave. . Pg.50 . . S29
Orchard Ave. . . Pg.50 . . S29
Park Ave. . . . . Pg.50 . . S29
Pattie . . . . . . . Pg.50 . . U30
Redwood Ave. . Pg.50 . . S29
Rose St. . . . . . Pg.50 . . R28
Sandridge Ct. . Pg.50 . . T28
Sandridge Rd. . Pg.50 . . T28
Sequoia Ave. . . Pg.45 . . R29
Simplon Cir. . . Pg.50 . . U30
Spruce Ln. . . . Pg.50 . . U30
Stoney Island Ave.
. . . . . . . . . . Pg.45 . . S27
Surf Ct. . . . . . Pg.45 . . R29
Terrace Ave. . . Pg.50 . . S29
Torrence Ave. . Pg.50 . . S29
Vals . . . . . . . . Pg.50 . . U30
Victoria Cir. . . . Pg.45 . . R29
Vollmer St. . . . Pg.45 . . S27
Vrin . . . . . . . . Pg.50 . . U30
Willow Dr. . . . . Pg.50 . . S29
Wind Point Ct. . Pg.50 . . S29
Woodale Dr. . . Pg.50 . . U30
Zurich Dr. . . . . Pg.50 . . U30
195th Pl. . . . . Pg.45 . . R30
196th St. . . . . Pg.45 . . R30
197th St. . . . . Pg.50 . . R30
198th Pl. . . . . Pg.45 . . R28
198th St. . . . . Pg.50 . . R28
199th St. . . . . Pg.50 . . R28
200th Pl. . . . . Pg.45 . . R29
200th St. . . . . Pg.50 . . R29

201st St. . . . . Pg.50 . . S29
201st St. . . . . Pg.50 . . S29
202nd St. . . . . Pg.50 . . S30
203rd St. . . . . Pg.50 . . S30
204th St. . . . . Pg.50 . . S29,30
207th Pl. . . . . Pg.50 . . T28
207th St. . . . . Pg.50 . . T30
208th St. . . . . Pg.50 . . T30
### PARKS
Lake View Comm. Park
. . . . . . . . . . Pg.50
Liberty Memorial Park
. . . . . . . . . . Pg.50 . . R29
Rainbow Park . . Pg.50 . . T30
Rainbow Park . . Pg.50 . . T28
### SCHOOLS
Sandridge Sch. Pg.50 . . T30
### MISCELLANEOUS
Fire Department Pg.50 . . T30

## LYONS TOWNSHIP
Page 33,34
(For additional listings,
see Section 1)
### STREETS
Bielby Ave. . . . . . . . . . B9
Both Pl. . . . . . . . . . . . B9
Buege Ln. . . . . . . . . . . B8
Cook-DuPage Rd. . . . . . C7
German Church Rd. . . . . B8
Hess Ave. . . . . . . . . . . B9
Howard Ave. . . . . . . . . B9
Pleasantview . . . . . . . . B9
79th St. . . . . . . . . . . . B8
80th Pl. . . . . . . . . . . . B9
87th St. . . . . . . . . . . . C8
### FOREST PRESERVES
Buffalo Woods . . . . . . . B11
### GOLF COURSES
Edgewood Valley C.C. . . A9
### SCHOOLS
Pleasantdale Sch. . . . . . B9

## MAINE TOWNSHIP
Pages 24,25
### STREETS
Alexis Ct. . . . . . . . . . . H5
Allison Dr. . . . . . . . . . . H4
Ashley Dr. . . . . . . . . . . H4
Aspen Dr. . . . . . . . . . . J3
Aspen Ln. . . . . . . . . . . J3
Ballard Rd. . . . . . . . . . J3
Barberry Ln. . . . . . . . . J3
Bianco Terr. . . . . . . . . . H3
Bobbie Ln. . . . . . . . . . K3
Brandy Ct. . . . . . . . . . H4
Briar Ct. . . . . . . . . . . . H4
Briarwood Ln. . . . . . . . H5
Bumblebee Dr. . . . . . . J3
Capital Dr. . . . . . . . . . J3
Carleah Ct. . . . . . . . . . K3
Cedar Ln. . . . . . . . . . . J3
Central Rd. . . . . . . . . . H4
Cherry Cir. . . . . . . . . . H4
Cherry Ct. . . . . . . . . . . H4
Cherry Ln. . . . . . . . . . J4
Chester Ave. . . . . . . . . J4
Clancy Dr. . . . . . . . . . J4
Columbus Dr. . . . . . . . J3
Congress Dr. . . . . . . . . J3
Crawford Ln. . . . . . . . . H3
Crescent Dr. . . . . . . . . J3
Culver St. . . . . . . . . . . H2
David Pl. . . . . . . . . . . . J3
Davis St. . . . . . . . . . . J4
Dee Rd. . . . . . . . . . . . J-K3
Delphia Ave. . . . . . . . . J4
Dempster St. . . . . . . . . J3
Donald Ct. . . . . . . . . . H5
Donald Terr. . . . . . . . . H5
East Dr. . . . . . . . . . . . J4
East River Rd. . . . . . . . H4
Elder Ct. . . . . . . . . . . . H4
Elder Ln. . . . . . . . . . . . H4
Elm Dr. . . . . . . . . . . . J4
Elms Terr. . . . . . . . . . . H4
Elmwood Dr. . . . . . . . . H3
Embassy Ln. . . . . . . . . J3
Emerson St. . . . . . . . . J3-4
Fairlawn Dr. . . . . . . . . H4
Fairway Dr. . . . . . . . . . H3
Federal Ct. . . . . . . . . . K3
Fern Ln. . . . . . . . . . . . J3
Fernwood Dr. . . . . . . . H5
Flora Ave. . . . . . . . . . . H5
Forest Pl. . . . . . . . . . . J5
Foster St. . . . . . . . . . . J5
Gayle Ct. . . . . . . . . . . H4
Glendale Ln. . . . . . . . . H4
Glenshire . . . . . . . . . . H4
Golf Rd. . . . . . . . . . . . J3
Greenbriar Dr. . . . . . . . H4
Greenwood Ave. . . . . . . H-K4
Greenwood Dr. (E & W) . J4
Gregory Ln. . . . . . . . . . H4
Hamilton Ct. . . . . . . . . H3
Hamlin Ave. . . . . . . . . H3
Harrison St. . . . . . . . . H2-4

Hazelwood Dr. . . . . . . . H4
Heathwood Dr. . . . . . . . H3
Helen Ct. . . . . . . . . . . H5
Helen Dr. . . . . . . . . . . H5
Holly Ln. . . . . . . . . . . . H2
Hollyberry Ave. . . . . . . J3
Home Ave. . . . . . . . . . J3
Home Cir. . . . . . . . . . . J3
Home Ct. . . . . . . . . . . J3
Home Terr. . . . . . . . . . J3
Ironwood Ln. . . . . . . . . J3
James Ct. . . . . . . . . . . H5
James St. . . . . . . . . . . H5
Jody Ln. . . . . . . . . . . . H5
Josephine Ln. . . . . . . . H4
Julie Dr. . . . . . . . . . . . H5
Kathy Ct. . . . . . . . . . . H3
Kennedy . . . . . . . . . . . J3
Kenneth Ct. . . . . . . . . H3
Knight Ave. . . . . . . . . . J4
Ladybird Ln. . . . . . . . . J3
Landing Ln. . . . . . . . . . J3
Landing Sq. . . . . . . . . . J3
Leslie Ln. . . . . . . . . . . J4
Lincoln Ave. . . . . . . . . J4
Lincoln Dr. . . . . . . . . . J3
Linda Ct. . . . . . . . . . . H5
Linda Ln. . . . . . . . . . . H2
Linnea Ln. . . . . . . . . . . H3
Lois Dr. . . . . . . . . . . . H4
Lyman Ave. . . . . . . . . . H2
Lyons St. . . . . . . . . . . J3-4
MacArthur . . . . . . . . . . J3
Maple Ln. . . . . . . . . . . J3
Margail St. . . . . . . . . . J3
Maynard Ct. . . . . . . . . H4
Maynard Dr. . . . . . . . . H4
Meadow Ln. . . . . . . . . H3
Michael Manor . . . . . . . H5
Milwaukee Ave. . . . . . . H4
Nellie Ct. . . . . . . . . . . H5
Noel Ave. . . . . . . . . . . J3
Norma Ct. . . . . . . . . . . H5
North Shore Dr. . . . . . . H3
Oak Ave. . . . . . . . . . . J3
Oak Ln. . . . . . . . . . . . H5
Oak Pl. . . . . . . . . . . . . H2
Oxford Ln. . . . . . . . . . . H5
Park Ln. . . . . . . . . . . . J3
Parkside Dr. . . . . . . . . J3
Pauline Ave. . . . . . . . . H5
Poplar Dr. . . . . . . . . . . H4
Potter Rd. . . . . . . . . . . H-J3
Rancho Ln. . . . . . . . . . J-K3
Reding Cir. . . . . . . . . . H3
River Rd., E. . . . . . . . . H2
Robin Dr. . . . . . . . . . . K3
Roder St. . . . . . . . . . . H4
Ronald Rd. . . . . . . . . . H4
Sanders Dr. . . . . . . . . J4
Senate Dr. . . . . . . . . . J3
Sherry Ln. . . . . . . . . . J3
Stacy Ct. . . . . . . . . . . H5
Stacy St. . . . . . . . . . . H5
Steven Dr. . . . . . . . . . J3
Stevenson Dr. . . . . . . . J3
Sumac Ln. . . . . . . . . . H3
Sumac Rd. . . . . . . . . . J3
Teela Ln. . . . . . . . . . . H2
Terrace Pl. . . . . . . . . . J3
Thornberry . . . . . . . . . H4
Tri-State Tollway . . . . . . J2
Twin Oak Ln. . . . . . . . . J3
Valerie Ct. . . . . . . . . . H5
Victor Ave. . . . . . . . . . H5
Wald St. . . . . . . . . . . . H4
Washington Dr. . . . . . . J3
West Oaks Ave. . . . . . . H3
Western Ave. . . . . . . . . H-J4
William Ave. . . . . . . . . H5
Zenith Dr. . . . . . . . . . . H2
### CEMETERIES
Ridgewood Cemetery . . H3-4
### PARKS
Dee Park . . . . . . . . . . . J3
Ladendorf Park . . . . . . . H5
### SCHOOLS
Apollo School . . . . . . . . H3
Stevenson Sch. . . . . . . J3
Washington Sch. . . . . . . H5
### SHOPPING CENTERS
Talisman Village S.C. . . J5

## MATTESON
Pages 46-48
### STREETS
Allemong Dr. . Pg.46 . . S16
Amherst Pl. . . Pg.47 . . U17
Apple Hill Ln. . Pg.46 . . S16
Applewood Ln. Pg.47 . . T19
Aspen Ln. . . . Pg.46 . . T16
Aster Ln. . . . . Pg.46 . . V16
Basswood Rd. Pg.47 . . S17
Beachwood Ct. Pg.47 . . T17
Beachwood Rd. Pg.47 T16,17
Beaver Dam Rd.
. . . . . . . . . . Pg.46 . . T16
Begonia Ln. . . Pg.46 . . V16
Bradley Ave. . Pg.47 . . T17
Briarwood Ct. Pg.47 . . S17

Bridgewood Ct. Pg.47 . . S17
Bridgewood Rd.
. . . . . . . . . . Pg.47 . . T17
Buttercup Ln. . Pg.46 . . U16
Butterfield Pkwy.
. . . . . . . . . . Pg.47 . . U20
Caitlin Ct. . . . Pg.46 . . U16
Cambridge Ave. Pg.47 . . T17
Campus Ave. . Pg.47 . . T19
Carnation Ln. . Pg.47 . . T19
Cedar Creek Dr. Pg.47 . . S19
Cedarwood Ln. Pg.47 . . T19
Central Ave. . . Pg.47 . . T19
Charles St. . . Pg.47 . . V20
Charleston Rd. Pg.47 . . T19
Church Rd. . . Pg.46 . . S16
Churn Rd. . . . Pg.46 . . S16
Cicero Ave. . . Pg.47 . . V18
Cloverleaf Rd. Pg.47 . . S17
Colgate Ln. . . Pg.47 . . T17
College Ave. . Pg.47 . . T19
Columbine Ln. Pg.47 . . T19
Cornell Way . . Pg.47 . . T17
Cornfield Rd. . Pg.46 . . T16
Corporate Lakes Dr.
. . . . . . . . . . Pg.47 . . T18
Crawford Ave. Pg.47 . . T19
Crestwood Ct. Pg.47 . . S17
Crestwood Rd. Pg.47 . . S17
Crows Ln. . . . Pg.46 . . U16
Daffodil Ln. . . Pg.46 . . V16
Dan Ryan Expwy.
. . . . . . . . . . . . . . . S16,17
Danielle Rd. . Pg.46 . . S16
Dartmouth Ave. Pg.47 . . T17
Deerpath Rd. . Pg.47 . . T17
Dettmering Dr. Pg.47 . . U20
Drake Ln. . . . Pg.47 . . T17
Duke Dr. . . . . Pg.47 . . T17
Elm Ct. . . . . . Pg.46 . . T18
Elmwood Ln. . Pg.47 . . T18
Fernwood Ct. . Pg.47 . . S17
Fox Run Ln. . . Pg.47 . . T16
Front St. . . . . Pg.47 . . U20
Gateway Dr. . Pg.47 . . V18
Georgetown Dr. Pg.47 . . U17
Goldenrod Cir. Pg.47 . . T16
Hanson Ln. . . Pg.47 . . T18
Harvard Ln. . . Pg.47 . . T17
Hibiscus Cir. . Pg.46 . . V16
Hickory St. . . Pg.47 . . V16
Highland Ave. Pg.47 . . T16
Highland Rd. . Pg.46 . . T16
Holiday Plaza Dr.
. . . . . . . . . . Pg.47 . . U18
Homan Ave. . Pg.47 . . U20
Homeland Ave. Pg.47 . . T18
Huntingwood Rd.
. . . . . . . . . . Pg.47 . . S17
Hyacinth Ln. . Pg.46 . . U16
Illinois Ct. . . . Pg.47 . . U20
Jean . . . . . . . Pg.47 . . U20
Jeffrey Dr. . . . Pg.47 . . U17
Keeler Ave. . . Pg.47 . T,U19
Kildare Ave. . Pg.47 . U19,20
Kildare Ct. . . Pg.47 . . U20
Kostner Ave. . Pg.47 . T,U19
Lakespur . . . Pg.47 . . T19
Lilac Ln. . . . . Pg.46 . . V16
Lincoln Hwy . Pg.47 . . U19
Lincoln Mall Dr. Pg.47 . . U18
Lindenwood Dr.
. . . . . . . . . . Pg.47 . . T19
Locust St. . . . Pg.47 . . U20
Main St. . . . . Pg.47 . U,V20
Main St., E. . . Pg.47 . . U20
Maple Brook Dr.
. . . . . . . . . . Pg.46 . . U16
Maple St. . . . Pg.47 . . V16
Marigold Cir. . Pg.46 . . U16
Marsh Ln. . . . Pg.47 . . U16
Megan Ct. . . Pg.46 . . U16
Moonlight Ln. . Pg.47 . . S19
Moonlight Pl. . Pg.47 . . S19
Morning Glory Dr.
. . . . . . . . . . Pg.46 . . T18
North St. . . . . Pg.48 . . U20
Notre Dame Dr. Pg.47 . . T17
Oak St. . . . . . Pg.47 . . U20
Oakhurst Rd. . Pg.47 . . S17
Oakview Rd. . Pg.47 . . S17
Old Creek Ln. Pg.46 . . T16
Old Farm Rd. . Pg.46 . . T16
Old Meadow Dr.
. . . . . . . . . . Pg.46 . . T16
Old Mill Rd. . . Pg.46 . . S16
Old Plank Blvd. Pg.46 . . U16
Olde Mill Rd. . Pg.46 . . S16
Oriole Rd. . . . Pg.47 . . S17
Oxford Ave. . . Pg.47 . . T17
Pansy Ln. . . . Pg.46 . . V16
Partridge Ave. Pg.47 . . T17
Paterson Ct. . Pg.47 . . V20
Patricia Dr. . . Pg.46 . . U16
Petunia Cir. . . Pg.46 . . U16
Pheasant Rd. Pg.47 . . S16
Phlox Ct. . . . Pg.47 . . T18
Pinewood Ln. Pg.47 . . T19
Poppy Ln. . . . Pg.46 . . V16
Post Ave. . . . Pg.47 . . T18
Primrose Ln. . Pg.47 . . V16
Primrose Ln. . Pg.47 . . T19

Princeton Ave. Pg.47 . . T17
Purdue Ln. . . Pg.47 . . T17
Quail Run Rd. Pg.46 . . T16
Quinn . . . . . . Pg.47 . . U20
Red Barn Rd. . Pg.47 . . S16
Richmond Ct. Pg.47 . . U19
Richmond Rd. Pg.47 . . U19
Richton Rd. . . Pg.47 . . V19
Ridgeland . . . Pg.47 . . R16
Ridgeland Manor Ln.
. . . . . . . . . . Pg.47 . . T19
Rose Ln. . . . Pg.47 . . T19
School Ave. . . Pg.47 . . T19
Shannon Ave. Pg.47 . . T19
Southwick Dr. Pg.47 . . U18
Spring Ln. . . . Pg.46 . . T16
Sprucewood Ln.
. . . . . . . . . . Pg.47 . . T19
St. Lawrence Ave.
. . . . . . . . . . Pg.47 . . U19
Stonebrook Pl. Pg.47 . . S19
Streamwood Rd.
. . . . . . . . . . Pg.46 . . T16
Sumter Dr. . . Pg.47 . . S19
Sundance Ct. Pg.47 . . S19
Sundance Way Pg.47 . . S19
Sunflower Dr. Pg.47 . . S16
Taylor Ct. . . . Pg.46 . . U16
Thornwood Ave.
. . . . . . . . . . Pg.47 . . S19
Timberlane Dr. Pg.46,47
. . . . . . . . . . . . . . . S16,17
Tower Ave. . . Pg.47 . . U20
Treehouse Ct. Pg.47 . . S19
Tulip Cir. . . . . Pg.46 . . V16
University Ave. Pg.47 . . T19
Vincent Ln. . . Pg.47 . . T19
Violet Ln. . . . Pg.47 . . T19
Virginia Ln. . . Pg.46 . . S16
Vollmer Rd. . . Pg.47 . . S15
Washington Ave.
. . . . . . . . . . Pg.47 . . T19
Wedgewood Ct. Pg.46 . . S16
Wedgewood Rd.
. . . . . . . . . . Pg.46 . . T16
Wheatfield Rd. Pg.46 . . S16
White Birch Ln. Pg.46 . . T16
White Oaks Rd. Pg.46 . . S16
Whitney Ave. . Pg.46 . . S16
Willow Ct. . . . Pg.46 . . S16
Willow Rd. . . . Pg.46 . . S16
Wolf Rd. . . . . Pg.46 . . T16
Woodgate Dr. Pg.47 . . S17
Yale Ln. . . . . Pg.47 . . T17
205th Pl. . . . . Pg.47 . . T18
205th St. . . . . Pg.47 . . T18
206th Pl. . . . . Pg.47 . . T17
207th St. . . . . Pg.47 . . T19
211th Pkwy. . . Pg.47 . . T17
211th St. . . . . Pg.47 . . U20
212th Pl. . . . . Pg.47 . . U19
213th Pl. . . . . Pg.47 . U19,20
214th Pl. . . . . Pg.47 . U19,20
214th St. . . . . Pg.47 . . U20
215th St. . . . . Pg.47 . . U20
216th Pl. . . . . Pg.47 . U19,20
216th St. . . . . Pg.47 . U19,20
217th St. . . . . Pg.47 . . V20
218th Pl. . . . . Pg.47 . . V20
218th St. . . . . Pg.47 . . V20
219th St. . . . . Pg.47 . . V19
### CEMETERIES
St. Paul's Lutheran Cemetery
. . . . . . . . . . Pg.46 . . S16
### PARKS
Allemong Park Pg.46 . . T16
Memorial Park Pg.47 . . U20
Notre Dame Park
. . . . . . . . . . Pg.47 . . T17
Oakwood Park Pg.47 . . T19
Woodgate Park Pg.47 . . S17
### SCHOOLS
Hurth Jr. H.S. Pg.47 . . U20
Marya Yates Sch.
. . . . . . . . . . Pg.46 . . S16
Matteson Sch. Pg.47 . . T18
Oakwood Sch. Pg.47 . . T19
Sieden Prairie Sch.
. . . . . . . . . . Pg.47 . . T17
St. Lawrence O'Toole Sch.
. . . . . . . . . . Pg.47 . . U19
Woodgate Sch. Pg.47 . . S17
Zion Lutheran Sch.
. . . . . . . . . . Pg.47 . . U19
### SHOPPING CENTERS
Lincoln Mall . Pg.47 . . U18
Matteson Town Center Mall
. . . . . . . . . . Pg.47 . . U18
### MISCELLANEOUS
Fire Station #2 Pg.47 . . U17
Old Plank Road Bike Trail
. . . . . . . . . . Pg.47
Police Station Pg.47 . . T18
Post Office . . Pg.47 . . T18
Public Works . Pg.47 . . U20
R.R. Station . Pg.47 . U,V20
Village Hall . . Pg.47 . . U20

## MOKENA
Pages 40,46
Will County
(For additional listings,
see Section 8)
Arquilla Dr. . . Pg.40 . . Q12
Burnside Station Dr.
. . . . . . . . . . Pg.40 . . Q12
Huntington Dr. Pg.40 . . Q12
Pullman Ct. . . Pg.40 . . Q12
Stanford Ct. . Pg.40 . . Q12
Vanderbilt Dr. Pg.40 . . Q12
Westinghouse Ct.
. . . . . . . . . . Pg.40 . . Q12
82nd Ave. . . Pg.46 . . Q13
188th St. . . . Pg.46 . . Q13
189th St. . . . Pg.40 . . Q13
189th St. . . . Pg.40 . . Q12
### PARKS
Tinley Gardens Park
. . . . . . . . . . Pg.47 . . Q12

## MORTON GROVE
Pages 29,30
### STREETS
Albert Ave. . . Pg.29 . . J7
Arcadia St. . . Pg.29 . . J5-6
Austin Ave. . . Pg.30 . . J-L8
Beckwith Rd. . Pg.29 . . J5-7
Belleforte Ave. Pg.29 . . J6
Birch Ave. . . . Pg.29 . . J7
Caldwell Ave. Pg.29 . . K,L7
Callie Ave. . . Pg.29 . . K7
Cameron Ln. . Pg.29 . . J6
Capri Ln. . . . Pg.30 . . J8
Capulina Ave. Pg.29,30 K7-8
Carol Ave. . . Pg.29 . . J6
Central Ave. . Pg.30 . . K-L8
Cherry Ave. . Pg.29 . . J7
Chestnut St. . Pg.29 . . J6
Church St. . . Pg.29,30 J5-8
Churchill St. . Pg.29 . . J6-7
Cleveland St. Pg.30 . . L8
Crain St. . . . Pg.29 . . K8
Davis Ct. . . . Pg.29 . . J7
Davis St. . . . Pg.29,30 J5-8
Dempster St. Pg.29 . . J6
Edens Expwy. Pg.29 . . K8-L9
Eldorado Dr. . Pg.29 . . J7
Elm Ln. . . . . Pg.30 . . J-L8
Elm St. . . . . Pg.29 . . J7
Emerson St. . Pg.29,30 J6-8
Enfield Ave. . Pg.29 . . K5-6
Fernald Ave. . Pg.29 . . J7
Ferris Ave. . . Pg.29 . . K7
Forest Dr. . . Pg.30 . . J8
Foster St. . . . Pg.29 . . J7
Frontage Rd. . Pg.30 . . K8
Georgiana Ave. Pg.29 . . J8
Golf Rd. . . . . Pg.29 . . J5-7
Greenwood Ave.
. . . . . . . . . . Pg.29,30
. . . . . . . . . . . . . . . K6,J8
Gross Point Rd.
. . . . . . . . . . Pg.30 . . K9
Grove Ct. . . . Pg.30 . . K9
Harlem Ave. . Pg.29 . . J6
Harms Rd. . . Pg.30 . . H8,J9
Hazel St. . . . Pg.29 . . J7
Hennings Ct. Pg.29 . . J7
Hoffman Ct. . Pg.29 . . J7
Hoffman Terr. Pg.29 . . J7
Ida Ln. . . . . . Pg.29 . . J7
Keeney Ct. . . Pg.30 . . L8
Keeney St. . . Pg.30 . . L8-9
Kirk St. . . . . Pg.30 . . L9
Lake St. . . . . Pg.29,30 J5-8
Lee St. . . . . . Pg.29 . . K8
Lehigh Ave. . Pg.29 . . J-L7
Lillibet Terr. . Pg.29 . . K8
Lincoln Ave. . Pg.29 . . K9
Linder Ave. . . Pg.30 . . L8
Long Ave. . . Pg.30 . . L9
Lotus Ave. . . Pg.30 . . L9
Luna Ave. . . Pg.30 . . K8
Lyons St. . . . Pg.29,30 J5-8
Madison Ct. . Pg.30 . . K8
Madison St. . Pg.30 . . K8-9
Main St. . . . . Pg.30 . . K8
Major St. . . . Pg.29 . . J-K8
Mango Ave. . Pg.30 . . K8
Mansfield Ave. Pg.30 . . J8
Maple Ave. . . Pg.29 . . J7
Maple Ct. . . . Pg.29 . . J5
Maple St. . . . Pg.29 . . J6
Marion Ave. . Pg.30 . . J-L8
Marmora Ave. Pg.30 . . J-L8
Mason Ave. . Pg.30 . . J-L8
McVickers Ave. Pg.30 . . J-L8
Meade Ave. . Pg.30 . . J-L8
Menard Ave. . Pg.30 . . K8
Merrill Ave. . . Pg.29 . . J5
Michael Ave. Pg.29 . . J5
Michael Ct. . Pg.29 . . J5
Monroe Ct. . Pg.30 . . K8
Monroe St. . . Pg.30 . . K8-9
Moody Ave. . Pg.30 . . K8
Morton Ln. . . Pg.30 . . L9
Mulford St. . . Pg.30 . . L9
Murray Ct. . . Pg.30 . . L9
Nagle Ave. . . Pg.29 . . J-L7

Narragansett Ave.
. . . . . . . . . . Pg.29 . . J7
Nashville Ave. Pg.29 . . J7
Natchez Ave. Pg.29 . . J-L7
National Ave. Pg.29 . . J-K6
Natoma Ave. Pg.29 . . J7
Neenah Ave. Pg.29 . . J,K7
New Castle Ave. Pg.29 . . J7
New England Ave.
. . . . . . . . . . Pg.29 . . J-K7
Normandy Ave. Pg.29 . . K7
Oak Park . . . Pg.29 . . K7
Oakton St. . . Pg.30 . . L7
Oconto Ave. . Pg.29 . . J-K6
Octavia . . . . Pg.29 . . J-K6
Odell Ave. . . Pg.29 . . J-K6
Oketo Ave. . . Pg.29 . . J6
Olcott . . . . . Pg.29 . . J-K6
Oleander Ave. Pg.29 . . K5
Oleander Pl. . Pg.29 . . J5
Oliphant Ave. Pg.29 . . J5
Oriole Ave. . . Pg.29 . . J5
Osceola Ave. Pg.29 . . J6
Oswego St. . Pg.29 . . K6
Ottawa Ave. . Pg.29 . . K5
Overhill Ct. . . Pg.29 . . J5
Ozanam Ave. Pg.29 . . J5
Ozark Ave. . . Pg.29 . . J5
Ozark St. . . . Pg.29 . . J5
Palma Ln. . . Pg.29 . . J5-7
Park Ave. . . . Pg.29 . . L7
Park Ave., S. Pg.30 . . K8
Parkside Ave. Pg.30 . . H-L8
Ponto Dr. . . . Pg.29 . . J6
Prospect . . . Pg.29 . . J-K6
Reba Ct. . . . Pg.30 . . L8
Reba St. . . . Pg.30 . . L8-9
River Dr. . . . Pg.29 . . J-K6
Sayre Ave. . . Pg.29 . . J6
School St. . . Pg.30 . . K8
Shermer Rd. . Pg.29 . . J6
Simpson St. . Pg.30 . . K8
Smithwood Dr. Pg.29 . . K7
South Park Ave. Pg.30 . . K8
Suffield Ct. . . Pg.29 . . J5
Suffield St. . . Pg.29 . . J5
Theobald Rd. Pg.30 . . K8
Warren Ct. . . Pg.30 . . L8
Warren St. . . Pg.30 . . L8-9
Washington . Pg.30 . . K8
Waukegan Rd. Pg.29 . . J5
Wilson Terr. . Pg.29 . . J5-6
104 Ln. . . . . Pg.29 . . J7
### PARKS
Arnum Park . . Pg.29 . . J6
Austin Park . . Pg.30 . . K8
Cardinal Park Pg.29 . . J7
Harper Park . Pg.29,30 K7-8
Mansfield Park Pg.30 . . J8
National Park Pg.29 . . J8
Oketo Park . . Pg.29 . . J6
Oriole Park . . Pg.29 . . J5
Overhill Park Pg.29 . . J5
Palma Ln. Park Pg.29 . . J7
Pioneer Park Pg.30 . . K8
Prairie View Park
. . . . . . . . . . Pg.29 . . K7
Shermer Park Pg.29 . . J6
### SCHOOLS
Blanche Borg Sch.
. . . . . . . . . . Pg.30 . . K8
Edison Sch. . Pg.30 . . L9
Emma Melzzer Sch.
. . . . . . . . . . Pg.29 . . J6
Golf Jr. H.S. . Pg.29 . . J6
Hynes Sch. . Pg.29 . . J6
Julia Molloy Sch.
. . . . . . . . . . Pg.30 . . K8
Parkview Sch. Pg.29 . . J7
St. Marthas Sch.
. . . . . . . . . . Pg.30 . . K8
### MISCELLANEOUS
Fire Stations Pg.29 . J6,K7
Library . . . . . Pg.30 . . K8
Police Department
. . . . . . . . . . Pg.30 . . K8
Post Office . . Pg.29 . . J6
Village Hall . . Pg.30 . . K8

## MOUNT PROSPECT
Pages 9,10,13-15
### STREETS
Addison Ct. . . Pg.14 . . J12
Albert St. . . . Pg.14 . F,G14
Albion Ln. . . Pg.9 . . F13
Algonquin Rd. Pg.14 . . J12
Algonquin Tr. Pg.14 . . J11
Almond Ct. . . Pg.10 . . E15
Althea Ln. . . Pg.10 . . D15
Andoa Ln. . . Pg.10 . . D13
Ann-Marie Dr. Pg.14 . . J12
Apache Ln. . . Pg.10 . . E15
Apple Ct. . . . Pg.9 . . D13
Apricot Ct. . . Pg.9 . . D13
Araila Dr. . . . Pg.10 . . D15
Arbor Ct. . . . Pg.14 . . H11
Ardyce Ln. . . Pg.14,15 F14
Arthur Ave. . . Pg.14 . . F11
Ash Ln. . . . . Pg.14 . . H12

Aspen Dr. . . . Pg.10 . . D15
Audrey Ct. . . Pg.14 . . G11
Audrey Ln. . . Pg.14 . . G11
Autumn Ave. . Pg.14 . . E15
Azalea Ln. . . Pg.10 . . E15
Azalea Pl. . . . Pg.10 . . D15
Aztec Ln. . . Pg.10 . . D15
Badger Rd. . . Pg.14 . . E15
Barberry Ln. . Pg.9 . . E14
Basswood Ln. Pg.10 . . E15
Beechwood Ln. Pg.14 . . H12
Bel Aire Ln. . . Pg.14 . . H13
Berkshire Ln. . Pg.14 . . G13
Beverly Ln. . . Pg.14 . . G11
Biermann Ct. . Pg.9 . . F14
Birch Dr. . . Pg.14 . . H12
Birch St. . . Pg.10 . . D15
Bishop Ct. . . Pg.14 . . F14
Bittersweet Ln. Pg.10 . . E15
Blackhawk Dr. Pg.14 . . H12
Blue Jay Ct. . . Pg.9 . . F14
Bob-O-Link Rd. Pg.9 . . E13
Bobby Ln. . . Pg.14 . . G12
Bonita Ave. . . Pg.9 . . G12
Boro Ln. . . Pg.10 . . D16
Boulder Dr. . . Pg.9 . . E14
Boxwood Dr. . Pg.9 . . E14
Brentwood Dr. Pg.9 . . E14
Briarwood Dr. . Pg.14 . . J11
Bridgeport Dr. . Pg.9 . . D13
Brighton Pl. . . Pg.9 . . D13
Brownstone Ln. Pg.14 . . J11
Buckthorn Rd. . Pg.10 . . E15
Bunting Ln. . . Pg.10 . . E13
Burning Bush Ln.
. . . . . . . . Pg.10 . . E15
Burr Oak Dr. . . Pg.10 . . E16
Business Center Dr.
. . . . . . . . Pg.14 . . F14
Busse Ave. . . Pg.14 . . G13
Busse Rd. . . Pg.9 . . G12
Butternut Ln. . Pg.9 . D12,13
Byron Ct. . . Pg.14 . . H13
Callero Cir. . . Pg.14 . . F14
Camp McDonald Rd.
. . . . . . Pg.10 . . D15,16
Can-Dota Ave., S.
. . . . . . . . Pg.14 . . H,G13
Candota Ave. . Pg.14 . . G13
Canford Cliffs Rd.
. . . . . . . . Pg.14 . . J12
Cannon Dr. . . Pg.14 . . K13
Carboy Rd. . . Pg.14 . . K13
Cardinal Ln. . . Pg.14 . . F14
Carib Ln. . . Pg.10 . . D15
Carol Ct. . . Pg.14 . . H11
Carol Ln. . . Pg.14 . . G11
Catalpa Ln. . . Pg.14 . . H12
Cathy Ln. . . Pg.14 . . G13
Catino Ct. . . Pg.14 . . F14
Cayuga Ln. . . Pg.10 . . D16
Cedar Ln. . . Pg.9 . E14,15
Centennial Dr. . Pg.14 . . F14
Central Rd. . . Pg.14 . . F14
Chariot Ct. . . Pg.14 . . J12
Charlotte Rd. . . Pg.9 . . J11
Cherrywood Dr. Pg.14 . . H12
Chestnut Dr. . . Pg.14 . . H12
Chinkapin Oak Pg.10 . . E15
Cholo Ln. . . Pg.10 . . E15
Chris Ln. . . Pg.14 . . H11
Church Rd. . . Pg.14 . . H12
Circle Dr. . . Pg.14 . . J12
Cleven Ave. . . Pg.14 . . G12
Clove Ct. . . Pg.9 . . D12
College Dr. . . Pg.14 . . G13
Colony Dr. . . Pg.14 . . K13
Columbine Dr. . Pg.10 . . D15
Connie Ln. . . Pg.14 . . E15
Corktree Ln. . . Pg.10 . . E15
Cottonwood Dr. Pg.14 . . J12
Council Tr. . . Pg.14 . . G13
Coventry Pl. . . Pg.9 . . D13
Crabtree Ln. . . Pg.9 . . E14
Craig Ct. . . Pg.13 . . G11
Cree Ln. . . Pg.10 . . E15
Creekside . . . Pg.9 . . E14
Crestwood Ave. Pg.14 . . G11
Crystal Ln. . . Pg.14 . . J12
Cypress Dr. . . Pg.14 . . H12
Dale Ave. . . Pg.9 . . F12
Debbie Dr. . . Pg.14 . . F15
Deborah Ct. . . Pg.14 . . F15
Deborah Ln. . . Pg.14 . . G,H11
Delaware Dr. . . Pg.14 . . K13
Dempster St. . . Pg.14 . . J12
Deneen Ln. . . Pg.14 . . F15
Dennis Dr. . . Pg.14 . . J12
Des Plaines River Rd.
. . . . . . . . Pg.10 . . E16
Dogwood Ln. . Pg.9 . . E14
Douglas Ave. . . Pg.13 . . G11
Dove Ct. . . Pg.14 . . J12
Dover Pl. . . Pg.9 . . D13
Dresser Dr. . . Pg.14 . . F14
East Dr. . . Pg.14 . . E14
Eastman Ct. . . Pg.14 . . E14
Eastman Dr. . . Pg.14 . . E14
Eastwood Ave. . Pg.14 . . G11
Edgewood Ln. . Pg.14 . . H12
Edward St. . . Pg.14 . . F14
Elayne Ct. . . Pg.14 . . J11
Elderberry Dr. . Pg.9 . . E14

Elm St. . . . . Pg.14 . . F-H13
Elmhurst Ave. . Pg.14 . . F13
Elmhurst Rd. . . Pg.9,14 E-J13
Emerson Dr. . . Pg.14 . . H13
Emerson St. . . Pg.14 . . H13
Emmerson Ln. . Pg.14 . . F15
Enterprise Dr. . Pg.14 . . K13
Eric Ave. . . Pg.14 . . F14
Eric Ct. . . Pg.14 . . F14
Estates Dr. . . Pg.14 . . G11
Euclid Ave. . . Pg.10 . . E16
Eva Ln. . . Pg.14 . . H12
Evanston Ave. . Pg.14 . . F12
Evergreen Ave. . Pg.14 . . G13
Fairmont . . . Pg.9 . . D13
Fairview Ave. . . Pg.14 . . F13
Feehanville Dr. . Pg.9 . . E14
Fern Dr. . . Pg.14 . . H12
Forest Ave. . . Pg.9 . . F13
Forest Cove Dr. Pg.14 . . J12
Franklin Dr. . . Pg.9 . . E14
Frediana Ct. . . Pg.14 . . G12
Freedom Ct. . . Pg.10 . . E15
Frost Dr. . . Pg.14 . . H12
Garwood Ave. . Pg.9 . . E14
George St. . . Pg.14 . . G14
Glendale Ln. . . Pg.14 . . H12
Glenn Ln. . . Pg.14 . . H12
Go-Wan-Do Tr. Pg.14 . G12,13
Golf (Evanston-Elgin) Rd.
. . . . . . Pg.14 H13-14
Golfhurst Ave. . Pg.14 . . H14
Golfview Ave. . . Pg.14 . . H14
Golfview Pl. . . Pg.14 . . H14
Grace Dr. . . Pg.14 . . H12
Green Ln. . . Pg.14 . . F15
Greenacres Ln. . Pg.14 . . H12
Greenbriar Dr. . Pg.14 . . J12
Greenfield Ct. . Pg.9 . . E14
Greenfield Ln. . Pg.9 . . E14
Greenwood Dr. . Pg.14 . . E14
Gregory St. . . Pg.9 . . F13
Grindle Dr. . . Pg.14 . . G11
Grove Dr. . . Pg.14 . . H11
Hackberry Ln. . Pg.9 . . E14
Hanover Pl. . . Pg.9 . . D13
Harvest Ln. . . Pg.14 . . F14
Hatherleigh Ct. . Pg.14 . . J12
Hatlen Ave. . . Pg.14 . . G11
Hatlen Ct. . . Pg.14 . . G11
Haven St. . . Pg.14 . . G11
Hawthorne Cir. . Pg.14 . . H12
Hazelhill . . . Pg.14 . . J12
Helena Ave. . . Pg.13,14 . G13
Hemlock Ln. . . Pg.9 . . E14
Henry St. . . Pg.14 . . F14
Heritage Dr. . . Pg.14 . . H11
Hi-Lusi Ave. . . Pg.14 . . G13
Hiawatha Ave. . Pg.14 . . H13
Hiawatha Tr. . . Pg.14 . . H13
Hickory Dr. . . Pg.14 . . F14
Highland Ave. . Pg.9 . . F14
Highland St. . . Pg.14 . . F14
Hill St. . . Pg.14 . . F14
Holly Ave. . . Pg.14 . . E14
Holly Ct. . . Pg.14 . . E14
Hopi Ln. . . Pg.10 . . E15
Horner Ln. . . Pg.14 . . F15
Hunt Club Dr. . Pg.14 . . H13
Huntington Commons Dr.
. . . . . . . . Pg.14 . . H13
I-Oka Ave. . . Pg.14 . . G13
Imperial Ct. . . Pg.14 . . J12
Independence Ct.
. . . . . . . . Pg.14 . . E15
Indigo Ct. . . Pg.10 . . E15
Indigo Dr. . . Pg.10 . . D,E15
Ironwood Dr. . . Pg.10 . . E15
Ironwood Pl. . . Pg.10 . . E14
Isabella St. . . Pg.14 . . F14
Ivanhoe Ln. . . Pg.14 . . H13
Ivy Ln. . . Pg.14 . . G12
Jeffery Dr. . . Pg.15 . . F15
Jerry Dr. . . Pg.14 . . F15
Jody Ct. . . Pg.13 . . G11
Judith Ann Dr. . Pg.9 . . F13
Juniper Dr. . . Pg.14 . . E14
Kenilworth Ave. Pg.14 . . F12
Kenneth Dr. . . Pg.14 F-H12
Kennicott Pl. . . Pg.14 . . G11
Kensington Rd. . Pg.9 E12-15
Kim Ave. . . Pg.10 . . E16
Kingston Ct. . . Pg.9 F14,15
Kiowa Ln. . . Pg.10 . . E16
Knights Bridge Dr.
. . . . . . . . Pg.14 . . J12
La Salle St. . . Pg.14 . . J13
Lakeview Ct. . . Pg.9 . . F15
Lama Ln. . . Pg.10 . . E16
Lams Ct. . . Pg.14 . . H12
Lancaster Ave. . Pg.14 F-H12
Lancaster St. . . Pg.14 . . F13
Larch Dr. . . Pg.10 . . D15
Larkdale Ln. . . Pg.9 . . E14
Laurel Dr. . . Pg.14 . . H12
Lavergne Dr. . . Pg.14 . . H15
Lawrence Ln. . Pg.13 . . G11
Leonard Ln. . . Pg.9 . . D13
Lexington Dr. . . Pg.14 . . K13
Liberty Ct. . . Pg.10 . . E15
Lincoln St. . . Pg.14 . . G13

Linden Ln. . . Pg.9 . . E14
Linneman Rd. . Pg.14 . . H13
Locust Ln. . . Pg.14 . . H11
Lois Ct. . . Pg.13 . . G11
Lonnquist Blvd. Pg.14 . . H12
Louis St. . . Pg.14 . . F14
Lowden Ln. . . Pg.14 . . F15
Lynn Ct. . . Pg.14 . . J11
MacArthur Blvd.
. . . . . . . . Pg.14 . . G11
Magnolia Ln. . . Pg.14 . . H11
Main St. . . Pg.14 . . F,G13
Mallard . . . Pg.14 . . J13
Malmo Rd. . . Pg.14 . . G13
Man-A-Wa Tr. . Pg.14 . . G13
Mandel Ln. . . Pg.10 . . D15
Mansard Ct. . . Pg.14 . . J12
Manshire Pl. . . Pg.9 . . D13
Maple Ct. . . Pg.9 . . F13
Maple St. . . Pg.14 . . F13
Marcella Rd. . . Pg.14 . . F14
Marina Dr. . . Pg.14 . . G14
Mark Dr. . . Pg.15 . . F15
Mark Terr. . . Pg.14 . . G11
Martha Ave. . . Pg.14 . . G11
Martin Ave. . . Pg.14 . . G12
Maya Ln. . . Pg.10 . . D15
Meadow Ln. . . Pg.9 . E13,14
Meier Rd. . . Pg.13 . . G11
Memory Ln. . . Pg.9 . . F13
Michael St. . . Pg.14 . . F14
Midway Dr. . . Pg.14 . . K13
Milburn Ave. . . Pg.14 . . F12
Millers Ln. . . Pg.14 . . F12
Mitchell Dr. . . Pg.15 . . F15
Moehling Dr. . . Pg.14 . . G13
Mohawk Ln. . . Pg.10 . . E15
Moki Ln. . . Pg.10 . . E16
Montgomery St.
. . . . . . . . Pg.14 . . J13
Morris Hill . . . Pg.14 . . J12
Mt. Prospect Rd.
. . . . . . . . Pg.14 . . G14
Mulberry Ln. . . Pg.9 . . E14
Murray Ln. . . Pg.10 . . D16
Myrtle Ave. . . Pg.14 . . G13
Na-Wa-Ta Ave. Pg.14 . . H13
Neil Ave. . . Pg.15 . . F15
Newberry Ln. . Pg.10 . . E15
Noan Terr. . . Pg.13 . . H11
Nordic Rd. . . Pg.14 . . K13
North Ln. . . Pg.14 . . J11,12
Northwest Hwy. Pg.14 . . F13
Nutmeg Ct. . . Pg.9 . . D,E13
Oak Ave. . . Pg.14 . . F13
Oakton St. . . Pg.14 . . K13
Oakwood Dr. . . Pg.14 . . H12
Ojibwa Tr. . . Pg.14 . . G12
Oneida Ct. . . Pg.10 . . D15
Oneida Ln. . . Pg.10 . . D15
Orange Ct. . . Pg.9 . . D13
Orchard Pl. . . Pg.14 . . H13
Oriole Ln. . . Pg.9 . . E14
Owen St. . . Pg.14 . . F14
Oxford Pl. . . Pg.9 . . D13
Palm Dr. . . Pg.14 . . H12
Park Dr. . . Pg.10 . . D16
Parliament Pl. . Pg.9 . . D13
Partridge . . . Pg.14 . . F14
Pawnee Ln. . . Pg.10 . . D16
Peachtree Ln. . Pg.10 . . E15
Peartree Ln. . . Pg.14 . . E15
Pecos Ln. . . Pg.10 . . D15
Pendleton Pl. . Pg.14 . . G12
Persimmon Ln. Pg.9 D12,13
Pheasant Ln. . . Pg.9 . . J11
Phillip . . . Pg.14 . . J12
Picadilly Cir. . . Pg.9 . . D13
Pickwick Ct. . . Pg.14 . . J12
Pima Ln. . . Pg.10 . . E15
Pin Oak Dr. . . Pg.10 . . E15
Pine St. . . Pg.14 . . F,G13
Plum Ct. . . Pg.9 . . D12
Prairie Ave. . . Pg.9 . . G11
Prendergast Ln. Pg.13 . . H11
Prospect Ave. . Pg.14
. . . . . . . . . . F12,G13
Prospect Manor Ave.
. . . . . . Pg.9,14 E,F13
Quail Walk . . Pg.14 . . J11
Quince Ct. . . Pg.10 . . E15
Quince Ln. . . Pg.10 . . E15
Raleigh Pl. . . Pg.9 . . D13
Rand Rd. . . Pg.14 . . E13
Redwood Dr. . . Pg.14 . . J12
Regency Ct. . . Pg.10 . . E15
Ridge Ave. . . Pg.14 . . F13
River Rd. . . Pg.14 . . E16
Rob Rd. . . Pg.10 . . D16
Robbie Ln. . . Pg.14 . . G12
Robert Dr. . . Pg.14 . . F14
Robin Ln. . . Pg.14 . . H12
Rosetree Ln. . . Pg.10 . . D15
Russel St. . . Pg.14 . . F13
Rusty Dr. . . Pg.14 . . J12
Sable Ln. . . Pg.9 . . J11
Santee Ln. . . Pg.10 . . E15
Sauk Ln. . . Pg.10 . . D16
Schoenbeck Rd.
. . . . . . . . Pg.9 . . D13
Scott Terr. . . Pg.14 . . G11
See-Gwun Ave. Pg.14 . . H13

Semar Ct. . . Pg.14 . . G12
Seminole Ln. . Pg.10 . . D15
Seneca Ln. . . Pg.10 . . D16
Shabonee Tr. . Pg.14 G13-14
Sioux Ln. . . Pg.14 . . G12
Sir Galahad Ln. Pg.14 . . J13
Sir Lancelot . . Pg.14 . . J13
Sitka Ln. . . Pg.10 . . D15
Sivic St. . . Pg.14 . . G12
Slawin Ct. . . Pg.9 . . F14
Small Ln. . . Pg.9,10 . F15
South Ln. . . Pg.14 J11,12
Sprucewood Dr.
. . . . . . . . Pg.14 . . H12
St. Celia St. . . Pg.13 . . H11
Stevenson Ln. . Pg.14 . . F15
Stratford Pl. . . Pg.9 . . E13
Stratton Ln. . . Pg.14 . . F14
Sullivan Ct. . . Pg.14 . . G11
Sumac Ln. . . Pg.10 . . E16
Sunset Rd. . . Pg.14 . . G12
Susan Dr. . . Pg.14 . . G12
Sycamore Ln. . Pg.14 . . H11
Tamarack Dr. . Pg.14 . . H11
Tano Ln. . . Pg.10 . . D15
Terminal Dr. . . Pg.14 . . K12
Thackery Pl. . . Pg.9 . . D13
Thayer St. . . Pg.14 . . F13
Thomas Moore Terr.
. . . . . . . . Pg.9 . . G13
Thornwood Ln. Pg.14 . . H11
Tower Dr. . . Pg.14 . . H13
Tower Ln. . . Pg.14 . . H13
University Dr. . Pg.14 . . G13
Verde Dr. . . Pg.14 . . J12
Verde Dr. . . Pg.14 . . J12
Victoria Dr. . . Pg.14 . . J12
Village Dr. . . Pg.14 . . J12
Wa Pella Ave. . Pg.14 . . G13
Wall St. . . Pg.14 . . J13
Walnut St. . . Pg.14 . . F13
Waverly Ln. . . Pg.14 . . H12
Waverly Ln. . . Pg.14 . . H12
Waverly Pl. . . Pg.14 . . G12
We-Go Tr. . . Pg.14 . G,H12
Wedgewood Ln.
. . . . . . . . Pg.9 . . E13
Weller Ln. . . Pg.14 . . G12
Westgate Rd. . Pg.14 . . F14
Wheeling Rd. . Pg.9 . . F14
White Chapel Dr.
. . . . . . . . Pg.10 . . E15
White Oak St. . Pg.13 . . G11
Whitegate Dr. . Pg.14 . . G13
Wigwam . . . Pg.14 . . G12
Wildwood Ln. . Pg.14 . . F14
Wille St. . . Pg.14 . . F13
William St. . . Pg.14 . . F13
Willow Ln. . . Pg.14 . . H12
Wilshire Dr. . . Pg.14 . . G13
Wimbolton Dr. . Pg.9 . . E13
Windsor Tr. . . Pg.14 . . E13
Wintergreen Ave.
. . . . . . . . Pg.10 . . D16
Wistoria St. . . Pg.14 . . F13
Withorn Ln. . . Pg.14 . . F12
Wolf Rd. . . Pg.14 . . F15
Wood Ln. . . Pg.10 . . D15
Woodview Dr. . Pg.10 . . D16
Yarmouth Pl. . Pg.10 . . F15
Yates Ln. . . Pg.14 . . F15
Yuma Ln. . . Pg.10 . . D16

**GOLF COURSES**
Mount Prospect Park
Country Club Pg.14 . . G12
Old Orchard C.C.
. . . . . . . . Pg.9 . . D13
Old Orchard Lodge & Swim
Club . . . Pg.9 D12,13
Rob Roy C.C. Pg.9 . . D14

**PARKS**
Aspen Trail Park
. . . . . . . . Pg.10 . . D15
Bluett Park . . Pg.15 . . F15
Burning Bush Trails Park
. . . . . . . . Pg.10 . . E16
Busse Park . . Pg.14 . . G13
Clearwater Park Pg.14 . . H12
Countryside Park
. . . . . . . . Pg.14 . . H13
East Wedgewood Park
. . . . . . . . Pg.9 . . E13
Emerson Park . Pg.14 . . F13
Evergreen Trails Park
. . . . . . . . Pg.9 . . E14
Fairview Park . Pg.14 . . F13
Gregory Park . Pg.9 . . F14
Hill Street Park Pg.14 . . F14
Kopp Park . . Pg.14 . . J13
Lions Mem. Park
. . . . . . . . Pg.14 . . G13
Maple Trails Park
. . . . . . . . Pg.9 . . F14
Meadows Park Pg.14 . . F12
Melas Center . Pg.14 . . F12
Melas Park . . Pg.14 . . F12
Oak Ave. Park Pg.10 . . D15
Owen Park . . Pg.14 . . F14
Parkview Park . Pg.10 . . D15
Prospect Meadows Park
. . . . . . . . Pg.9 . . E13
Rec Plex . . . Pg.14 . . J13

Robert Frost Park
. . . . . . . . Pg.14 . . H12
Sunrise Park . Pg.14 . . H14
Sunset Park . . Pg.14 . . H13
Sycamore Trails Park
. . . . . . . . Pg.10 . . E15
Tamarack Park Pg.14 . . H11
Tamarack Trails Park
. . . . . . . . Pg.10 . . E15
We-Go Park . . Pg.14 . . G12
Weiss Community Center
. . . . . . . . Pg.10 . . E15
Weller Creek . Pg.14 . . H13
West Wedgewood Park
. . . . . . . . Pg.9 . . E13
Westbrook Park Pg.14 . . G12
Woodland Trails Park
. . . . . . . . Pg.9 . . E15

**SCHOOLS**
Busse Sch. . . Pg.14 . . F14
Dempster Jr. H.S.
. . . . . . . . Pg.14 . . J13
Euclid Sch. . . Pg.14 . . E15
Fairview Sch. . Pg.9 . . F13
Forest View Sch.
. . . . . . . . Pg.14 . . H11
Frost Sch. . . Pg.14 . . D15
Gregory Sch. . Pg.14 . . F14
Holmes Jr. H.S. Pg.14 . . H11
Indian Grove Sch.
. . . . . . . . Pg.14 . . E15
John Jay Sch. . Pg.14 . . H12
Lincoln Jr. H.S. Pg.14 . . G12
Lions Park Sch. Pg.14 . . G13
Parkview Sch. . Pg.14 . . E15
Prospect H.S. . Pg.9 . . F12
River Trails Middle Sch.
. . . . . . . . Pg.14 . . E15
River Trails Sch. Dist. 26
Office . . . Pg.10 . . E15
Robert Frost Sch.
. . . . . . . . Pg.14 . . H12
Sch. Dist. 57 Office
. . . . . . . . Pg.14 . . F13
Shadrach Bond Sch.
. . . . . . . . Pg.10 . . E15
St. Emily Cath. Sch.
. . . . . . . . Pg.14 . . G12
St. John Luth. Sch.
. . . . . . . . Pg.14 . . H13
St. Paul Luth. Sch.
. . . . . . . . Pg.14 . . G13
St. Raymond Cath. Sch.
. . . . . . . . Pg.14 . . G13
Sunset Park Sch.
. . . . . . . . Pg.14 . . H13
Westbrook Sch. Pg.14 . . G12

**SHOPPING CENTERS**
Brentwood Square
. . . . . . . . Pg.10 . . E15
Briarwood Plaza
. . . . . . . . Pg.14 . . J12
Colony Court . Pg.9 . . D13
Colony Square Pg.14 . . K13
Countryside Court
. . . . . . . . Pg.14 . . H13
Crystal Court . Pg.14 . . J12
Euclid Mall . . Pg.9 . . E14
Golf Plaza II . . Pg.14 . . H13
Golf Shopping Plaza
. . . . . . . . Pg.14 . . H12
Mt. Prospect Commons
. . . . . . . . Pg.14 . . H12
Mt. Prospect Plaza
. . . . . . . . Pg.14 . . F14
Randhurst S.C. Pg.14 . . E13
Shoppers World S.C.
. . . . . . . . Pg.14 . . K13
United Plaza . Pg.14 . . J12

**MISCELLANEOUS**
Chamber of Commerce
. . . . . . . . Pg.14 . . G13
Fire Department
. . . . . . . . Pg.10 . . E16
Library . . . Pg.14 . . G13
Police & Fire Station
. . . . . . . . Pg.14 . . G13
Post Office . . Pg.14 . . F13
R.R. Station . . Pg.14 . . G13
Rec Plex . . . Pg.14 . . J13
Village Hall . . Pg.14 . . G13

**NEW TRIER TOWNSHIP**
Pages 23,26
STREETS
Cotton Ln. . . Pg.26 . . F9
Illinois Rd. . . Pg.26 F9,F10
Indian Hill Rd. . Pg.23 . . E11
Locust Ln. . . Pg.23 . . F10
Longmeadow Rd.
. . . . . . . . Pg.26 . . F9
Oxford Ln. . . Pg.23 . . E10
Porter . . . Pg.23 . . E10
Washington . . Pg.23 . . E10
Woodley Manor
. . . . . . . . Pg.26 . . F10
Woodley Way . Pg.26 . . F10
Woodley Woods
. . . . . . . . Pg.26 . . F9

**FOREST PRESERVES**
Turnbull Woods
. . . . . . . . Pg.23 . . A8

**NILES**
Pages 28-30
(For additional listings,
see Section 1)
STREETS
Amelia Dr. . . Pg.29 . . K4
Ashland Ave. . Pg.29 . . J4
Austin Ave. . . Pg.30 . . M8
Belleforte Pl. . Pg.29 . . K6
Betty Terr. . . Pg.29 . . K4
Birchwood Ave. Pg.29 . . M6
Breen St. . . Pg.29 . . K6
Bruce Dr. . . Pg.29 . . L4
Brummel . . . Pg.29 . . L8
Caldwell Ave. . Pg.29 . . M7
Callero Dr. . . Pg.29 . . J4
Canavan Ct. . Pg.28 . . J4
Carol Ave. . . Pg.29 . . K6
Carol Ct. . . Pg.29 . . K6
Carol St. . . Pg.28,29 K4,6
Catino . . . Pg.29 . . J4
Cedar Ln. . . Pg.25 . . L5
Chase . . . Pg.29 . . M6
Cherry . . . Pg.29 . . M7
Chester Ave. . Pg.28 . . J4
Chroname Rd. Pg.29 . . M7
Church St. . . Pg.29 . . J4-5
Churchill Ave. . Pg.25 . . J5
Churchill Cir. . Pg.25 . . J5
Clara Ct. . . Pg.29 . . L4
Clara Dr. . . Pg.29 . . L4
Cleveland St. . Pg.29 . . L5-6
Clifton Ave. . . Pg.29 . . J-K4
Concord Ln. . Pg.29 . M-N7
Conrad Ave. . Pg.29 . . K6
Courtland Dr. . Pg.29 . . L4
Crain Ave. . . Pg.29 . . K4-6
Crain St. . . Pg.28 . . K4-6
Cumberland Ave.
. . . . . . . . Pg.29 . . L6
Davis St. . . Pg.28 . . J4-5
Days Terr. . . Pg.29 . . M7
Dempster St. . Pg.29 . . K6
Dobson St. . . Pg.29 . . L6
Dowagiac Ave. Pg.30 . . M8
Ebinger Dr. . . Pg.29 . M-N7
Elizabeth Ave. Pg.29 . . K4
Elmore St. . . Pg.29 . . K-L5
Elmwood Dr. . Pg.28 . . J3
Emerson St. . Pg.28 . . J4
Fargo Ave. . . Pg.29 . . M6
Farnsworth Dr. Pg.29 . . L5
Field Dr., N. . . Pg.25 . . J5
Forest View Ln. Pg.29 . . M7
Foster Ln. . . Pg.29 . . J5
Fox Glen Dr. . Pg.28 . . J3
Franks Ave. . Pg.29 . . J4
Gale Ter. . . Pg.29 . . J5
Georgia Dr. . Pg.29 . . K6
Glendale Rd. . Pg.29 . . H4
Golf Terrace . Pg.28 . . J3
Golf(Evanston-Elgin Rd.)
. . . . . . . . Pg.29 . . K4
Grace Ave. . . Pg.29 . . K4
Grand Ct. . . Pg.29 . . K4
Grand St. . . Pg.29 . . K4
Greendale Ave. Pg.29 . . L4-5
Greenleaf Ave. Pg.29 . . L4
Greenleaf St. . Pg.29 . . K5,6
Greenwood Ave.
. . . . . . . . Pg.28 . . J-K4
Greenwood Blvd.
. . . . . . . . Pg.29 . . K4
Grennan Pl. . Pg.29 . . K5-6
Gross Point Rd. Pg.29 . . M7
Hamilton Dr. . Pg.29 . . K6
Harlem Ave. . Pg.29 . . M7
Harts Rd. . . Pg.29 . . M7
Harvard St. . . Pg.29 . . L6
Heathwood Dr. Pg.28 . . H3
Howard St. . . Pg.29 . M6-8
Huber Ln. . . Pg.29 . . H4
Huber Oval . . Pg.25 . . H4
Jarvis Ave. . . Pg.30 . . M8
Jarvis St. . . Pg.29 . M6-7
Joey Dr. . . Pg.29 . . J4
Johanna Dr. . Pg.29 . . K4
Jonquil Ter. . . Pg.29 . . L5-6
Kay St. . . Pg.29 . . M6
Kedzie St. . . Pg.29 . . K4
Keeney St. . . Pg.29 . . L5-7
Kirk Dr. . . Pg.29 . . L6
Kirk St. . . Pg.29 . . L6
Knight . . . Pg.28 . . J5
Lake St. . . Pg.29 . . J5
Lauren Ln. . . Pg.29 . . H4
Lawler Ave. . . Pg.29 . . K5-6
Lee St. . . Pg.29 . . K5-6
Lexington Ln. . Pg.29 . M-N7
Lill Ct. . . Pg.29 . . K5
Lill St. . . Pg.29 . . K5
Lincoln Ave. . Pg.24 . . K4
Loras Dr. . . Pg.29 . . L4
Lyons St. . . Pg.29 . . L5
Madison Ct. . Pg.29 . . L4
Madison Dr. . Pg.28 . . L4
Madison St. . Pg.29 . . L5-7
Main St. . . Pg.29 . . K5-6

Maryland St. . Pg.29 . . J-K4
Maynard Oval . Pg.25 . . H4
Maynard Rd. . Pg.29 . . H4
Maynard Ter. . Pg.29 . . H4
Meacham Ct. . Pg.29 . . L4
Melvina Ave. . Pg.29 L7,M8
Menard Ave. . Pg.30 . . M8
Merrill St. . . Pg.29 K5,L5
Merrimac Ave. Pg.29 . . L7
Milwaukee Ave. Pg.29 J4,L6
Monroe Ct. . . Pg.29 . . L6
Monroe St. . . Pg.29 . . L4-6
Mulford Ave. . Pg.29 . . L6-8
Mulford St. . . Pg.29 . . L6-8
Natchez Ave. . Pg.29 . . M7
National . . . Pg.29 . . K6
Neva St. . . Pg.29 . . L6
New England Ave.
. . . . . . . . Pg.29 . . K-L6
Newark . . . Pg.29 . . M6
Newcastle Ave. Pg.29 . . L7
Nieman Ave. . Pg.29 . . M7
Niles Ave. . . Pg.29 . . K6
Niles Terr. . . Pg.29 . . M6
Nora Ave. . . Pg.29 . . M6
Nordica Ave. . Pg.29 . . L7
Norma Ct. . . Pg.29 . . H5
Normal Ave. . Pg.28 . . L4
Normal Ct. . . Pg.29 . . L4
Normal St. . . Pg.28 . . L4
North Ave. . . Pg.29 . . L4
Nottingham . . Pg.29 . L-M6
Oak Ave. . . Pg.28 . . K4
Oak Ln. . . Pg.29 . . L5
Oak Park Ave. Pg.29 . . M7
Oakton Ct. . . Pg.29 . . L6-7
Oakton St. . . Pg.29 . . L6
Oconto Ave. . Pg.29 . . L6
Octavia Ave. . Pg.29 . . L6
Odell Ave. . . Pg.29 . . L6
Oketo Ave. . . Pg.29 . . K-L6
Olcott Ave. . . Pg.29 . . L6
Oleander Ave. Pg.29 K5,L6
Oriole Ave. . . Pg.29 . . K-L5
Osceola Ave. . Pg.29 . . L6
Ottawa Ave. . Pg.29 . . K-L5
Oval . . . Pg.29 . . H4
Overhill Ave. . Pg.29 . . K-L5
Ozanam Ave. . Pg.29 . . L5
Ozark Ave. . . Pg.29 . . L5
Park Ave. . . Pg.28 . . K4
Park Ln. . . Pg.24 . . K4
Peter Ter. . . Pg.29 . . L5
Prospect Ave. . Pg.29 . . L5
Prospect Ct. . Pg.29 . . L5
Prospect St. . Pg.29 . . L5
Prospect St., N. Pg.29 . . L5
Riverside Dr. . Pg.29 . . M7
Riverview Ave. Pg.29 . . M7
Robin Rd. . . Pg.29 . . H4
Root Ct. . . Pg.29 . . L4
Root St. . . Pg.29 . . L4
Rosemary Dr. . Pg.29 . . M7
Roseview Dr. . Pg.28 . . H4
School St. . . Pg.29 . . M6
Seward St. . . Pg.29 . . L5
Shermer Rd. . Pg.29 . J-L6
Sibley St. . . Pg.29 . M5-6
Stolting Rd. . . Pg.29 . . L6
Sunset Rd. . . Pg.28 . . L4
Susan Ct. . . Pg.29 . . L4
Terrace Dr. . . Pg.28 . . J3
Washington Ave.
. . . . . . . . Pg.29 . . J5
Washington St. Pg.29 . . L5
Waukegan Rd. Pg.29 . . L6
Wendy Way . . Pg.29 . . H4
Western Ave. . Pg.24 . . C4
Willow . . . Pg.29 . . J5
Wisner St. . . Pg.29 . K-L5
Wood River Dr. Pg.29 . . L7
Woodland Dr. . Pg.29 . . J5
Wright Ter. . . Pg.29 . . L5

**CEMETERIES**
Beth Jacobs Cemetery
. . . . . . . . Pg.29 . . K6
Mary Hill Cemetery
. . . . . . . . Pg.29 . . K5
St. Adalberts Cemetery
. . . . . . . . Pg.29 . . N6

**FOREST PRESERVES**
Caldwell Woods
. . . . . . . . Pg.29 . . K7

**GOLF COURSES**
Chick Evans G.C.
. . . . . . . . Pg.30 . . J8
Tam-O-Shanter G.C.
. . . . . . . . Pg.29 . . L7

**PARKS**
Ballard Park . Pg.29 . . J4
Chesterfield Gdns.
Playground . Pg.29 . . J4
Feldman Park . Pg.28 . . J4
Greenleaf Park Pg.29 . . K6
Grennan Hts. Park
. . . . . . . . Pg.29 . . L6
Jonquil Terr. Park
. . . . . . . . Pg.29 . . L5
Jozwiak Park . Pg.29 . . M6
Notre Dame Park
. . . . . . . . Pg.29 . . K5

## NILES

Oakton Manor Park
.......... Pg.29..... L5
Point Park ...... Pg.29.... K6
Regent Park .... Pg.29.... H5
Washington Park
.......... Pg.29.... K5

**SCHOOLS**

Culver Elem. Sch.
.......... Pg.29.... L7
Emerson Middle Sch.
.......... Pg.29.... L4
Gemini Jr. H.S. Pg.28.. K4
Jefferson Sch. Pg.29.... L4
Mark Twain Sch.
.......... Pg.28.... J3
Nelson Sch. .... Pg.29.... K5
Niles College/Loyola University
.......... Pg.29.... M6
Niles Elem. Sch. S.
.......... Pg.29.... M6
Northridge Prep Sch.
.......... Pg.28.... H3
Notre Dame H.S.
.......... Pg.29.... K5
Our Lady Sch. Pg.28.... L4
St. Issac Joques Sch.
.......... Pg.29.... J5
St. John Luth. Sch.
.......... Pg.29.... M6
St. John Sch. .. Pg.29.... K6
St. Mary of the Woods Sch.
.......... Pg.30.... M8
St. Matthew Luth. Sch.
.......... Pg.29.... J4
Wildwood Sch. Pg.30.... M8

**SHOPPING CENTERS**

Dempster Plaza S.C.
.......... Pg.28.... K4
Four Flags S.C. Pg.29.... J4
Golf Glen S.C. Pg.28.... J3
Golf Mill S.C. .. Pg.28.... J4
Golf-Milwaukee Plaza
.......... Pg.20.... H4
Mill-Brook S.C. Pg.29.... H5
Oak Mill Mall .. Pg.29.... J4
Super City S.C. Pg.29.... K6
Village Crossing S.C.
.......... Pg.30.... M8

**MISCELLANEOUS**

Civic Center Plaza
.......... Pg.29.... L6
Fire Dept. .... Pg.28,29
.......... K4,M7
Library ...... Pg.25.... L6
Police Department
.......... Pg.29.... M6
Post Office ... Pg.25.... L6

## NILES TOWNSHIP

Pages 25,26

**STREETS**

Golf Rd. .......... H6-10
McVicker Ave. ...... M8
Meade Ave. ........ H6
Sherwin Ave. ...... H6
Waukegan Rd. ...... H6

**FOREST PRESERVES**

Harms Woods .......... H8
Linne Woods ........ J7-8
Miami Woods ........ L7
St. Pauls Woods ...... K7
Wayside Woods ...... K7

## NORTHBROOK

Pages 10,21,22

**STREETS**

Academy Ln. . Pg.21.... A3
Acorn Ln. .... Pg.21.... B3
Adelaide Dr. .. Pg.21.... B4
Adirondack Dr. Pg.21.... B3
Alice Rd. .... Pg.21.... B3
Alleghany .... Pg.21.... B3
Allen Dr. .... Pg.22.... E4
Ancient Tree . Pg.21... B2-3
Andover Cir. . Pg.21.... A1
Anets Dr. .... Pg.22.... C5
Angle Ave. ... Pg.22.... B5
Anjou Dr. .... Pg.21.... D2
Anne Ln. .... Pg.21.... D2
Antelope Sprs. Rd.
Anthony Trail . Pg.21.... A3
Antique Ln. .. Pg.22.... A6
Apple Tree Ct. .... B4
Apple Tree Ln. Pg.21.. B3-4
Applewood Ln. Pg.21.... A1
Arbeleda Ln. . Pg.21.... E4
Arbor Ln. .... Pg.21.... C2
Arnold Ln. ... Pg.21.... A3
Arrowwood Dr. Pg.21.... A1
Asbury Rd. ... Pg.21.... C4
Ash Ln. ...... Pg.21.... B4
Aspen Rd. ... Pg.21.... C3
Astor Pl. ..... Pg.22.... C5
Auburn Ln. .. Pg.21.... D3
Audrey Ln. ... Pg.21.... D2
Avon Ln. ..... Pg.22.... A5
Avon Rd. ..... Pg.22.... A5
Bach St. ...... Pg.21.... B4
Ballantrae Dr. . Pg.21... A,B6

Balmoral Ln. . Pg.22.... D6
Banyan Dr. ... Pg.21.... A2
Bar Harbor Terr.
.......... Pg.21.... B3
Barberry ....
Barnsley Pl. .. Pg.22.... B7
Basswood Dr. . Pg.21.... A1
Bay View Ct. . Pg.21.... B3
Bayberry Dr. . Pg.21.... A1
Beaver Ave. .. Pg.22.... B7
Beckwith Ct. . Pg.21.... B1
Bellevue Pl. .. Pg.21.... C4
Berglund Pl. . Pg.21.... C4
Bernay Dr. ... Pg.21.... A2
Big Oak Cir. .. Pg.22.... B5
Big Oak Ln. .. Pg.22.... B5
Birch Rd. .... Pg.21.... C3
Bittersweet Dr., E., W. & S.
Blackthorn .. Pg.21.... R4
Blue Hill .... Pg.21.... B4
Bob-O-Link Ln. Pg.21.... C4
Bordeaux Dr. . Pg.21.... C4
Bordeaux Dr. . Pg.21.... A2
Braeside Ln. . Pg.22.... A5
Breesway Ln. . Pg.22.... C5
Brentwood Rd. Pg.21.... A4
Brian Dr. .... Pg.21.... D4
Briarwood Ln. Pg.21.... B4
Bridge Ln., S. Pg.21.... D4
Bridlewood Ln. Pg.21.... C6
Bridlewood Rd. Pg.22.... C6
Brighton Ct. .. Pg.21.... C3
Brindle Ct. ... Pg.21.... B3
Bristol Ct. .... Pg.21.... B1
Brittany Ct. ... Pg.21.... A2
Brittany Rd. .. Pg.21.... A2
Brookside Ln. . Pg.21.... B4
Buckland Ln. . Pg.21.... D4
Buckthorne Cir. Pg.21.... A1
Burgundy Ln. . Pg.21.... C4
Burmuda Dunes Pl.
Buttornut Ln. . Pg.21... B-D4
Buttonwood Dr. Pg.22.... B6
Cambridge Dr. Pg.21.... D3
Campden Ln. . Pg.21.... A4
Candlewood Hill Rd.
.......... Pg.21.... B5
Canterbury Ct. Pg.21.... D3
Cargill Dr. .... Pg.21.... C4
Caribou Crossing
.......... Pg.21.... A1
Carlson Dr. ... Pg.22.... D5
Carlyle Ct. ... Pg.21.... A2
Carol Ct. ..... Pg.22.... B5
Carriage Ln. .. Pg.21.... A6
Carter Ct. .... Pg.22.... C7
Caryn Ter. ... Pg.22.... B6
Castilian Cir. . Pg.21... D-E4
Catherine St. . Pg.21.... B3
Cayuga Dr. ... Pg.21.... B3
Cedar Ct. .... Pg.22.... D3
Cedar Ln. .... Pg.21.... C4
Center Ave. .. Pg.21.... C4
Chadworth Ct. Pg.21.... A4
Chapel Ct. ... Pg.21.... C4
Chapel Dr. ... Pg.22.... C4
Chappelwood Ct.
.......... Pg.21.... B3
Charlemagne Dr.
.......... Pg.21.... A2
Charles Dr. ... Pg.21.... A2
Charlwood ... Pg.21.... B2
Chartries .... Pg.21.... C3
Cherry Ln. ... Pg.21... B3-4
Chesapeake Ln. Pg.21... B-A4
Chestnut St. .. Pg.21.... B4
Chewton Glen . Pg.22.... B5
Chipiti Dr. .... Pg.22.... C7
Christiana Ln. . Pg.21.... A1
Church St. ... Pg.22... B,C5
Claridge Ct. .. Pg.21.... A3
Claridge Ln. .. Pg.22.... D6
Clover Ct. .... Pg.21.... C3
Clover Rd. .... Pg.21.... C3
Coachmaker Dr.
Cobblestone .. Pg.22.... A6
Cobblestone Ct.
Cobblewood Dr.
.......... Pg.21.... D4
Colonade Dr. . Pg.22.... B6
Colony Ct. .... Pg.21.... C4
Commercial Ave.
Concord Ct. .. Pg.21.... A2
Constance Ln. Pg.21.... A1
Coral Pkwy. .. Pg.21.... C2
Cornflower Tr. Pg.21.... D2
Cotswolds Ct. Pg.21.... A4
Cotswolds Way Pg.21.... A4
Country Club Ln.
Country Ln. .. Pg.22.... C6
Coventry Ln. . Pg.21.... B3
Crabtree Ln. . Pg.21.... B3
Crestwood Dr. Pg.21.... B4
Crimson Ct. .. Pg.21.... B3
Cuyler Ave. .. Pg.22.... C7
Cypress Ln. .. Pg.21.... C4
Dalton Pl. .... Pg.21.... B7

Dana Ct. ..... Pg.21.... B1
Daniel Ct. .... Pg.21.... C1
Daryl Ln. .... Pg.22.... B6
Dauphine .... Pg.21.... A2
Debra Ln. .... Pg.22.... E4
Deer Trail .... Pg.21.... A1
Deer Trail Ct. . Pg.21.... A1
Dehne Rd. .... Pg.21.... A4
Dell Rd. ...... Pg.22.... B7
Dennis Dr. ... Pg.21.... A4
Devonshire Ct. Pg.21.... B1
Division St. ... Pg.21.... B4
Donegal Ln. .. Pg.21.... B3
Donovan Glen Ct.
Doolittle Dr. .. Pg.21.... A3
Doriann Dr. .. Pg.21.... D3
Dorset Dr. .... Pg.21.... B2
Downing St. .. Pg.21.... B2
Driftwood Ln. Pg.22.... C7
Dundee Rd. .. Pg.21.. B2-6
Dunhill Ct. ... Pg.22.... C5
Dunston Cir. . Pg.21.... A3
Eastwind Ct. . Pg.21.... B2
Eastwood Ln. Pg.22.... B6
Echo Ln. ..... Pg.21.... C3
Edens Expwy. Spur
.......... Pg.21.... B2
Edgebrook Ln. Pg.22.... C6
Edgewood Ln. Pg.22.... B2
El Cid Ln. .... Pg.22.... D4
Elder Ct. ..... Pg.21.... C3
Ellendale Dr. . Pg.21.... C4
Elm Ave. ..... Pg.22.... C5
Elm Ridge Dr. Pg.21.... A1
Era Dr. ....... Pg.21.... A2
Eric Ln. ...... Pg.22.... C7
Eskine Dr. ... Pg.21.... D4
Essex Dr. .... Pg.21.... D4
Estate Ct. .... Pg.21.... A1
Euclid Ave. .. Pg.22.. A6,B7
Evert Ct. ..... Pg.21.... A2
Exeter Ln. ... Pg.21.... A1
Fair Ln. ...... Pg.22.... B4
Fairford Ln. .. Pg.21.... A4
Fairview Ln. .. Pg.21.... A1
Fairway ...... Pg.21.... A6
Falling Leaf Ln. Pg.22.... C5
Farmington Rd. Pg.21.... D3
Farnsworth Ln. Pg.21.... C4
Fern Ave. .... Pg.21.... C3
Ferndale Ave. . Pg.22.... B5
Fieldwood Dr. Pg.21.... A2
Floral Dr. .... Pg.21.... C1
Forest Ln. .... Pg.22.... B5
Forest View Dr. Pg.21.... C1
Forestway Dr. Pg.22.... C7
Four Winds Ln.
.......... Pg.21.... A1
Fox Run Dr. .. Pg.22.... A6
Foxglove Rd. . Pg.21.... A4
Galway Ct. ... Pg.21.... B3
Gayle Ct. ..... Pg.21.... D2
Glenbrook Dr. Pg.21.... B3
Glendale Ave. . Pg.21.... D4
Gleneagle Ln. Pg.22.... A6
Glenoak Ave. . Pg.22.... B6
Grace Rd. .... Pg.21.... B3
Grand ....... Pg.21.... D3
Grant Rd. .... Pg.22.. B,C4
Greenacre Dr. Pg.21.... C2
Greenbriar Ln. Pg.22.... B4
Greenview Rd. Pg.21.... D4
Greenway ... Pg.21.... B2
Greenwood Rd. Pg.21.. A,E4
Gregg Rd. .... Pg.22.... C7
Hampton Ln. . Pg.21.... D3
Happ Rd. ..... Pg.22.... C7
Harbinger Falls Pg.21.... A1
Harbor Ln. ... Pg.22.... B4
Harborside ... Pg.21.... A2
Harris Dr. .... Pg.21.... A2
Hawthorne Ln. Pg.21.. A,B4
Hazelwood Ln. Pg.21.... A3
Heather Ct. .. Pg.21.... C3
Heather Ln. .. Pg.21.... C3
Helen Dr. .... Pg.21.... A3
Hemlock Knoll Terr.
Hemlock Ln. .. Pg.21.... C3
Henrici Dr. ... Pg.22.... A7
Heritage Dr. .. Pg.21.... B4
Hickory Ln. .. Pg.22.... B6
Hidden Bay .. Pg.21.... B2
Hidden Wells . Pg.21.... B2
High Point ... Pg.21.... B3
Highland Dr. . Pg.21.... C3
Hill Rd. ....... Pg.21.... B4
Hillcrest Ln. .. Pg.21.... B4
Hillside Dr. .. Pg.22.... B5,6
Holly Ave. ... Pg.21.... B5
Holly Ct. ..... Pg.21.... C2
Holste Rd. .... Pg.22.... E5
Honeysuckle Dr.
.......... Pg.21.... A1
Horizon Ln. .. Pg.21.... B2
Huckleberry Ln. Pg.21.... B4
Huehl Rd. .... Pg.21.... A2
Huntington Ln. Pg.21.... C3
Illinois Rd. ... Pg.21.. C4-5
Indian Wells Ln.
Iris Ct. ...... Pg.21.... C3

Island Point .. Pg.21.... B2
Ivy Ln. ...... Pg.21.... C3
Janke Dr. .... Pg.22.... D5
Jeffrey Ct., N., S & W.
Jeffrey Ln. ... Pg.21.... B5
Jessica Ln. ... Pg.21.... C3
Juli-Lyn Ct. .. Pg.21.... C1
Juli-Lyn Ln. .. Pg.21.... C1
Juniper Ln. ... Pg.21.... B4
Kayjay Dr. ... Pg.21.... D3
Keystone Ln. . Pg.22.... B5
Keystone Cir. . Pg.22.... B5
Keystone Rd. . Pg.21.... C3
Kiest Ave. .... Pg.22.... B5
Killarney Ln. .. Pg.22.... C7
Kingsport Ct. . Pg.21.... A3
Kingston Rd. . Pg.21.... D3
Koehling Rd. . Pg.21.... B2
Koepke Rd. ... Pg.21.... C3
Laburnum Dr. Pg.21.... B1
Lagoon View Dr.
.......... Pg.21.... B2
Lake Knoll Dr. Pg.21.... C2
Lake Knoll Rd. Pg.21.... C2
Lake Placid Ln. Pg.21.... B3
Lake-Cook Rd. Pg.21.... A2
Lakeside .... Pg.21.... B2
Landwehr Rd. Pg.21.. A-D3
Lane Winchester
.......... Pg.21.... B3
Larabee Ln. .. Pg.22.... B6
Larkdale Rd. . Pg.21.... B2
Laurel Rd. .... Pg.22.... B5
Lavigne Ln. .. Pg.21.... D4
Lawrence Ln. . Pg.22.... A5
Lee Rd. ...... Pg.22.. A-B6
Lexington ... Pg.22.... B6
Lilac Ln. ..... Pg.21.... B2
Lincoln Ave. . Pg.21.... B5
Lindberg Ln. . Pg.21.... A3
Linden Ave. .. Pg.21.... A7
Linden Rd. ... Pg.22.... B5
Lindenwood Ln.
.......... Pg.21.... A1
Lisa Ct. ...... Pg.21.... D4
Little Moose Ln.
.......... Pg.21.... C3
Longaker Rd. . Pg.21.... D3
Longmeadow Dr.
.......... Pg.21... D3-4
Longmeadow Rd.
.......... Pg.22.... A6
Longvalley Dr. Pg.21.... C3
Longview Rd. . Pg.21.... C2
Lorete Ln. .... Pg.21.... B2
Lori-Lyn Ln. .. Pg.21.... C1
MacArthur Blvd.Pg.21.... A3
Mallard Dr. ... Pg.21.... D4
Manor Dr. ... Pg.21.... A1
Maple Ave. .. Pg.21.. C4-5
Maple Hill Rd. Pg.22.... A7
Marcee Ln. ... Pg.21.... B2
Marden Ct. ... Pg.21.... B3
Margo Ln. .... Pg.21.... D4
Maria Ave. ... Pg.21.... A3
Marshall Rd. . Pg.22.... B4
Mayapple Ct. . Pg.21.... D4
Mayapple Ln. Pg.21.... D4
Meadow Rd. . Pg.22.... B5
Meadowview Ct.
Medford Cir. . Pg.22.... C6
Melvin Dr. .... Pg.21.... A3
Micheline ... Pg.21.... A1
Midfield Ln. .. Pg.22.... C7
Midway Rd. .. Pg.21.... D3
Mill Rd. ...... Pg.21.... D3
Miller Rd. .... Pg.22.... A6
Milton Ave. .. Pg.22.... B5
Milton Dr. .... Pg.22.... A7
Mission Hills Ln.
.......... Pg.21.... R2
Mission Hills Rd., W.
.......... Pg.21.... B3
Moon Hill Rd. Pg.21.... B3
Mountain Dr. . Pg.21.... B2
Mt. Vernon Ter. Pg.21.... B4
Muirwood ... Pg.22.... C5
Mulberry Ln. . Pg.21.... C4
Newport Rd. . Pg.21.... D4
Normandy Ln. Pg.21.... A2
North Corner . Pg.21.... B2
North Ln. .... Pg.22.... C7
Northbrook Ave.
.......... Pg.22.... B7
Northmoor Ct. Pg.21.... B4
Northwood .. Pg.22.... A7
Norway Pine Ln.
.......... Pg.21.... D3
Oak Ave. ..... Pg.21.. C4-5
Oak Knoll Ct. . Pg.21.... A1
Oak Knoll Ter. Pg.21.... A1
Oak Leaf Ter. . Pg.22.... B5
Old Mill Ln. .. Pg.21.... D3
Old Mill Rd. .. Pg.21.... D3
Old Post Rd. . Pg.22.... A6
Old Willow Rd. Pg.22.... E5
Orchard .... Pg.22.... B5
Otis Pl. ...... Pg.21.... B7
Oxford Ln. ... Pg.21.... C3
Palm Canyon Dr.
.......... Pg.21.... B2

Palm Ln. ..... Pg.21.... C3
Pamella Ln. .. Pg.21.... A1
Park Way .... Pg.22.... B7
Partridge Ln. . Pg.21.... B4
Pawtucket ... Pg.21.... B3
Peach Tree Ln. Pg.21.... B4
Pebble Beach Rd.
.......... Pg.21.... B2
Pebblebrook Rd.
.......... Pg.22.... C7
Penfold Pl. ... Pg.21.... A3
Pfingsten Rd. . Pg.21.... A3
Pheasant Creek Dr.
.......... Pg.21.... B3
Phillips Ave. .. Pg.21.... C3
Phyllis Dr. .... Pg.21.... A1
Phyllis Rd. .... Pg.21.... A1
Picardy Cir. .. Pg.21.. A,B1
Picardy Dr. .. Pg.21.... A1
Pine Ln. ...... Pg.21.... D3
Pinto Ln. ..... Pg.21.... B1
Pleasant St. .. Pg.21.... C2
Plum Is. Dr. .. Pg.21.... B3
Plymouth Ln. . Pg.22.... C4
Pondside Dr. . Pg.21.... C3
Pony Ln. ..... Pg.21.... B1
Poplar Ct. .... Pg.21.... A1
Portsmouth Ct. Pg.22.... B5
Post Rd. ..... Pg.21.... D2
Powderhorn Dr.
.......... Pg.21.... A6
Prairie ...... Pg.21.... C2
Prestbury Ct. . Pg.21.... A4
Prestwick Ln. . Pg.21.... C2
Prince St. .... Pg.21.... D4
Private Rd. ... Pg.21.... D4
Quail Ln. ..... Pg.21.... D4
Queens Way . Pg.21.... D4
Radcliffe Dr. . Pg.21.... B2
Raintree Ln. .. Pg.21.... B2
Raleigh Ct. ... Pg.22.. B6-7
Raymond Dr. . Pg.21.... C3
Red Coach Ln. Pg.22.... A6
Red Haw Rd. . Pg.22.... B5
Redwood Ln. . Pg.21.... B5
Regent Dr. ... Pg.21.... A2
Rennes Ct. ... Pg.21.... C3
Revere Dr. ... Pg.21.... A2
Ridge Dr. .... Pg.21.... D3
Ridgeland Ct. Pg.21.... C1
Ridgewood Dr. Pg.22.... B6
Ring Rd. ..... Pg.22.... A5
River Falls Dr. Pg.21.. C2-3
Riviera Dr. ... Pg.21.... B2
Robincrest Dr. Pg.21.... C3
Rosemary Rd. Pg.22.... A6
Rosewood Ct. Pg.22.... B7
Royal Dr. ..... Pg.21.... C3
Royal Ridge Dr Pg.22.... B3
Rudolph Dr. .. Pg.22.... A6
Russett Ct. ... Pg.21.... B2
Russett Ln. ... Pg.21.... B2
Rutgers Ln. .. Pg.21.... B1
Salceda Dr. .. Pg.21.... D4
Sanders Rd. .. Pg.21.... C2
Saranac Ln. .. Pg.21.... B3
School Dr. .... Pg.21.... C4
Scotch Pine Ln. Pg.21.... D3
Scott Rd. ..... Pg.21.... C4
Seton Rd. .... Pg.22.... A5
Seville Circle . Pg.21.... A2
Shagbark Ln. . Pg.22.... B5
Shannon Ct. .. Pg.21.... B3
Shannon Rd. . Pg.21.. B3-4
Shawnee Trail Pg.21.... C2
Shermer Rd. . Pg.21.... D5
Silverpine Dr. Pg.21.... B3
Skokie Rd. .. Pg.22.... A6
Sleepy Hollow Pg.21.... C3
Smith Rd. .... Pg.21.... C3
Snowbird Ln. . Pg.21.... B2
Somerset Ln. . Pg.22.... D6
Sorrol Dr. .... Pg.21.... C2
South Ln. .... Pg.22.... C7
Southgate Dr. Pg.21.... B2
Southwind Dr. Pg.21.... B2
Springhill Dr. . Pg.21.... B3
Spruce St. ... Pg.22.... C5
Spyglass Ln. . Pg.21.... B2
St. Stephens Green
.......... Pg.21.... B4
Stanley St. ... Pg.22.... C5
Steven Ln. ... Pg.21.... D2
Stone Creek .. Pg.21.... B2
Stonebridge Ln.
.......... Pg.21.... A4
Stonegate ... Pg.22.... B3
Stowe St. .... Pg.21.... A4
Stratford Pl. .. Pg.21.... B2
Suffield Terr. . Pg.21.... B2
Sugar Pine Ln. Pg.21.... D3
Summerfield Rd.
.......... Pg.22.... C7
Summerton Pl. Pg.22.... C4
Sunburst Ln. . Pg.21.... B2
Sunnyside Circle
.......... Pg.21.... C4
Sunset Ct. ... Pg.22.... C7
Sunset Ln. ... Pg.21.. A1-2
Sunset Ridge Rd.
.......... Pg.22.. B,C7

Sunset Tr. .... Pg.21.... D3
Sunshine Ln. . Pg.21.... A2
Surrey Ln. .... Pg.22.... B6
Sussex Dr. ... Pg.21.... B3
Sutton Dr. ... Pg.21.... B2
Suzanne Terr. Pg.22.... C5
Sycamore Ln. Pg.21.... C5
Talia Ln. ..... Pg.21.... D2
Tamarind Ln. Pg.21.... A2
Techny Rd. ... Pg.21.. C2-5
Terri-Lyn Ct. . Pg.21.... C1
Terri-Lyn Rd. . Pg.21.... C1
The Mews .... Pg.21.... A3
The Strand ... Pg.21.... D4
Thornapple Ln. Pg.22.... B6
Thornwood Ln. Pg.22. A6,B5
Timber Ln. ... Pg.22.... C5
Torrey Pines Pkwy.
.......... Pg.21.... B2
Toulon Dr. ... Pg.21.... C3
Touraine Ter . Pg.21.... A1
Trails Edge Dr. Pg.22.... C5
Trailwood Ct. Pg.21.... A1
Trailwood Ln. Pg.21.... A1
Tri-State Tollway
.......... Pg.21.... B1
Turnberry Ln. Pg.22.... C6
Tyron Woods . Pg.21.... B2
Valencia Dr. .. Pg.21-22. D4
Valley Rd. .... Pg.21.... D3
Vermont Ave. Pg.22.... A6
Versailles Dr. . Pg.21.... A2
Vicki Ln. ..... Pg.21.... D3
Violet Ln. .... Pg.21.... C3
Virginia Ln. .. Pg.21.... D4
Vista Ct. ..... Pg.22.... C6
Voltz Ct. ..... Pg.22.... C6
Voltz Rd. ..... Pg.21.. C6-7
Wainwright .. Pg.21.... A3
Walnut Ln. ... Pg.21.... B2
Walters Ave. . Pg.21-22. B2-6
Wateredge Ct. Pg.22.... A6
Wateredge Ln. Pg.22.... A6
Waterfront Ln. Pg.22.... D6
Waukegan Rd. Pg.21.... B5
Weller Ln. .... Pg.21.... C3
Wellesley Cir. Pg.21.... A1
Wellington Rd. Pg.22.... A5
Wendy Dr. ... Pg.21.... D2
Wessling Dr. . Pg.21.... B2
Westcott Rd. . Pg.21.... C4
Western Ave. . Pg.21.. C2-4
Westwood Ct. Pg.21.... B4
Whirlaway Dr. Pg.21.... D2
Whirlaway Ct. Pg.21.... C2
Whisperwoods Ct.
.......... Pg.21.... D3
White Dr. .... Pg.21.... B3
White Hall Dr. Pg.22.... B5
White Oak Cir. Pg.21.... D2
White Oak Dr. Pg.21.... D2
White Pine Dr. Pg.21.... D3
Whitefield Rd. Pg.22.... B7
Wildwood Ln. Pg.22.... B6
Williamsburg Dr.
.......... Pg.22.... A6
Willow Ln. ... Pg.21.... B6
Willow Rd. ... Pg.21.... D3
Wilshire Ln. .. Pg.21.... A3
Windrush Ln. . Pg.21.... B4
Windsor Lane Pg.21.... B3
Windy Hill Dr. Pg.22.... C5
Wintercress Cir. Pg.21.... C4
Wood Dr. .... Pg.21.... B4
Woodbine Ln. Pg.21.... B4
Woodhead Dr. Pg.21.... A2
Woodland Dr. Pg.21... D3-4
Wndrhll Dr. .. Pg.22.... B5
Woodland Dr. Pg.21.... D3
Woodlark Dr. Pg.21.... C3
Woodlawn Rd. Pg.21.... C4
Woodmere Dr. Pg.21.... D3
Woodmere Dr. Pg.21.... D3
Wyndance Way Pg.22.... D6
York Ct. ..... Pg.22.. B6-7
Yorkshire Ln. Pg.21.... B1
1st St. ....... Pg.22.... B5
2nd St. ...... Pg.22.... D4

**PARKS**

Coast Guard Park
.......... Pg.21.... A3
Colonades Woods
.......... Pg.22.... B6
Community Park
.......... Pg.22.... A6
Crestwood Park Pg.22.... B5
Greenfield Park Pg.21.... A3
Hillside Park . Pg.22.... C6
Meadowhill Park
.......... Pg.22.... C5
Northbrook Park
.......... Pg.21.... B5
Tot Lot Park .. Pg.22.... B4
Wescott Park . Pg.21.... C4
West Park .... Pg.21.... C3
Williamsburg Park
.......... Pg.22.... A6
Wood Oak Green Park
.......... Pg.21.... B1

**SCHOOLS**

Glenbrook North H.S.
.......... Pg.21.... D5
Green Briar Sch.
.......... Pg.22.... B4
Grove Sch. .. Pg.21.... B3
Hickory Point Sch.
.......... Pg.21.... A2
Maple Sch. .. Pg.22.... D4
Meadow Brook Sch.
.......... Pg.22.... B5
Northbrook Jr. H.S.
.......... Pg.22.... C5
Oaklane Sch. . Pg.22.... B6
Sch. Dist. 27 Office
.......... Pg.10.... B16
Shabonee Jr. H.S.
.......... Pg.21.... B3
Solomon Schecter Sch.
.......... Pg.22.... A6
Solomon Schecter Sch.
.......... Pg.22.... A6
St. Norberts Sch.
.......... Pg.22.... B5
Stanley Field Jr. H.S.
.......... Pg.21.... D3
The Cove School
.......... Pg.22.... A6
Westcott Sch. Pg.21.... C4
Westmoor Sch. Pg.21.... C4
Wood Oaks Jr. H.S.
.......... Pg.21.... B1

**SHOPPING CENTERS**

Dunnbrook S.C.
.......... Pg.21.... A3
Dunster Plaza Pg.21.... B3
Meadow Shopping Plaza
.......... Pg.22.... B5
Northbrook Court
.......... Pg.21.... A5
Northbrook Shopping Plaza
.......... Pg.22.... B5
Sanders Court S.C.
.......... Pg.21.... B1
Village Square S.C.
.......... Pg.22.... A6
White Plains S.C.
.......... Pg.21.... B3

**MISCELLANEOUS**

Fire Station .. Pg.21.. B6,C5
Leisure Center Pg.21.... C2
Library ...... Pg.21.... B4
Metra Station . Pg.22.... C5
Park Dist. Hdqtrs.
.......... Pg.21.... A3
Police/Fire Department
.......... Pg.21.... C3
Post Office ... Pg.21.... B4
Society of the Divine Word
Conference Ctr.
.......... Pg.22.... C6
Sports Complex
.......... Pg.21.... C3
St. Mary's Mission House
.......... Pg.22.... C6
Swedish Covenant Village
.......... Pg.21.... D4
United Parcel Service
.......... Pg.22.... D5
Village Hall .. Pg.21.... B5
YMCA ...... Pg.21.... C3

## NORTHFIELD

Pages 22,23

**STREETS**

Abbott Ct. .......... E8
Alice Pl. .......... E8
Arbor Ln. .......... E8
Ash .......... D8
Avon Ave. .......... E7
Birchwood Ln.(Pvt.) E7
Bosworth Ln. .......... E8
Bracken Ln. .......... D7
Briar Ln. .......... D7
Bridlegate Ln. .......... E7
Bridlewood Ln. .......... E8
Bristol Ave. .......... E8
Bristol Rd. .......... E8
Bristol St. .......... E8
Brookhill Dr. .......... C7

Burr Oak Rd. E7
Camden Ln. D8
Canterbury Ln. (E&W) E7
Central Rd. E8
Chapel Hill Ln. D7
Cherry D8
Churchill St. E8
Clover Ln. E7
Coach Rd. E7
Country Ln. D7
Coventry Rd. E7
Crooked Creek E8
Dickens Rd. E8
Dickens St. E8
Dorina Dr. E7
Drury Ln.(Pvt.) E7-8
Earl Dr. D8
East Valley Cir. Way C7
Eaton St. E8
Eddy Ln. E7
Edens Expwy. C8
Edens Ln. D8
Edgewood Ln. D7
Elder St. E9
Elm D8
Enid Ln. E7
Graemere St. E7
Grove Dr. E8
Happ Rd. D-E8
Harbor Ln. E8
Harding Rd. E8
Hawthorne D8
Heather Ter. D8
Hedge Row E7
Hickory D8
Hickory Ln. E7
Holder Ln. E8
Ingram St. E7
Jeffery St. E8
Lagoon Dr. E9
Lagoon Ln. E9
Landreth Ln. D-F,G3
Latrobe Ave. E9
Laurie Ln. D8
Linder Ave. E9
Lockwood Ave. E9
Maple Row D7
Maple St. E8
Martin Ln. D7
Meadowbrook Dr. C7
Meadowview Ln. E9
Meadowview Rd. F9
Meadowwood Ln. E8
Middlefork Rd. D7
Mt. Pleasant St. E9
Norfolk Rd. D8
Northfield Rd. E8
Northgate Ave. C7
Oak D8
Oak Tree Ln. D7
Old Farm Ln. D7
Old Hunt Rd. C7
Old Willow Rd. D7
Orchard Ln. E8
Pebble Fork E7
Pine St. D8
Pleasant View Ln. D8
Red Barn Ln. E7
Riverdale C7
Riverside Dr. E8
Robinhood Ln. E8
Somerset Ln. D7
South Ridge Ter. C7
Southgate Ave. C7
Southgate Terr. C7
Steeplechase Ln. D7
Steifel Ln. E8
Sterling Ln. D8
Stockton Dr. E8
Suffolk Rd. D8
Sunset Rd. E9
Sunset Ridge Rd. E7
Thackery Ln. E7
Thornwood Ln. D7
Three Lakes Dr. D7
Tower Rd. C8
Valley View C7
Valley Way C7
Wagner Rd. E8
Walnut E8
Westfield Ln. D7
Whittier Ln. D7
Willow Rd. E8
Willow Rd.(Old) D7
Willow Ter. E8
Willow View Terr. E8
Winfield Cir. F9
Winfield Dr. E9
Winnetka Ct. E7
Winnetka Rd. E8
Woodland Ln. (N&S) D8

**PARKS**
Clarkson Park E8
Northfield Park E8
Three Corners Wildlife Refuge D8
Willow Park E8

**SCHOOLS**
Christian Heritage Academy D7
Middle Fork Sch. D8
New Trier H.S. West E9
St. Phillips Sch. D8
Sunset Ridge D7

**SHOPPING CENTERS**
Northfield Square E8

## NORTHFIELD TOWNSHIP

Pages 21-25

**STREETS**
Anets Dr. Pg.22 C5
Applegate Ct. Pg.25 G4
Beach Ln. Pg.21 D2
Beechnut Rd. Pg.22 A4
Birchwood Pg.22 A4
Castillian Ct. Pg.24 G3
Central Ave. Pg.21 C2
Central Rd. Pg.24 H1-2
Charlie Ct. Pg.21 D3
Chestnut Ave. Pg.25 F6
Chestnut Rd. Pg.22 A4
Constance Ln. Pg.21 A1
Cottonwood Rd. Pg.22 A5
Countryside Ln. Pg.24 G3
Culligan Pkwy. Pg.21 D2
Cumberland Ave. Pg.21 C2
Dearlove Rd. Pg.24 G3
Dundee Rd. Pg.21 B1
East Lake St. Pg.24 G4-5
Elm Ct. Pg.22 A5
Elmdale Rd. Pg.24 F-H4
Enterprise Pg.22 F4
Evergreen Ln. Pg.21 C1
Ewen Pg.25 F4
Forest Ln. Pg.21 E2
Forest Rd. Pg.22 A5
Forestview Rd. Pg.21 A1
Garden St. Pg.21 C2
Gayle Ct. Pg.21 D2
Glendale Pg.24 G4
Glenshire Pg.21 G4
Glenview Rd. Pg.24 G4
Glenwood Ln. Pg.25 G4
Greenleaf Pg.21 E2
Greenwood Rd. Pg.24 G4
Grove Ln. Pg.21 E2,G3-4
Halsey Pg.22 F5
Henley St. Pg.24 G4
Hickory Ct. Pg.22 A5
Highland Ave. Pg.21 C2
Highland Ct. Pg.24 G4
Highland Rd. Pg.21 D3
Hillside Rd. Pg.24 G4
Holly Ave. Pg.21 C2
Holly Ct. Pg.21 D3
Holly Ln. Pg.25 G4
Huber Ln. Pg.25 G4
Huehl Rd. Pg.21 A2
Johns Dr. Pg.22 F6
Joshua Ln. Pg.21 D3
Kennicott Ln. Pg.24 F2
Knollwood Pg.24 G3-5
Koehling Rd. Pg.22 A5
Lee Rd. Pg.22 A6
Lehigh Ave. Pg.22 E5
Linden Rd. Pg.22 A5
Linneman St. Pg.24 G3-4
Long Meadow Ln. Pg.24 G3
Longmeadow Dr. Pg.24 F-G4
Longview Rd. Pg.21 C2
Maple Ave. Pg.21 C2,F2
Maplewood Rd. Pg.22 A5
McCain Pg.24 F4
Meadow Ln. Pg.24 G4
Meadow St. Pg.21 C2
Melane Ln. Pg.21 D3
Milton St. Pg.21 E2
Milwaukee Ave. Pg.21 D1,F2
Nimitz Pg.22 F5
Oak Ave. Pg.21 C2
Oakwood Pg.22 A5
Overland Pass Pg.21 E3
Palatine Rd. Pg.21 D1-2
Pamela Ln. Pg.21 A1
Parkway, N. Pg.21 E2
Parkway, S. Pg.21 E2
Peachgate Rd. Pg.25 G4
Pensive Ln. Pg.21 D2
Pfingsten Rd. Pg.24 F-G3
Phyllis Rd. Pg.21 A1
Pickwick Ave. Pg.21 F4
Pine Tree Rd. Pg.22 A5
Pleasant Pg.21 C2
Pleasant Run Pg.22 E3
Post Rd. Pg.21 D2
Prairie Pg.21 C2
Prairie Lawn Rd. Pg.25 G4
Red Oak Rd. Pg.22 A5
Revere Rd. Pg.24 G4
Richard West Dr. Pg.25 F4
Rolling Ridge Pg.22 D7
Rosedale Rd. Pg.24 G3
Sable Pg.25 F4
Sanders Rd. Pg.21 C2
Shermer Rd. Pg.22 D5
Shilt Pg.22 F4
Southridge Terr. Pg.22 C7
Spruce Rd. Pg.22 A5
Steeplechase Ln. Pg.22 D7
Sunset Dr. Pg.22 C7
Sunset Ln. Pg.21 A1-2
Sunset Ridge Rd. Pg.22 C7
Sunset Trail Pg.21 D2
Sunshine Ln. Pg.21 A2
Techny Rd. Pg.21 C2-5
Thornwood Pg.24 F4
Timberlane Dr. Pg.21 C1
Tri-State Tollway Pg.21 B1,E2
Vogay Ln. Pg.21 E2
Walnut Cir. Pg.22 A5
Washburn Pg.24 F5
Waukegan Rd. Pg.22 A4
Wedel Ln. Pg.25 G4
West Lake Terr. Pg.24 F4
Western Pg.21 C2
Westview Dr. Pg.21 F3
Whirlaway Dr. Pg.21 D2
White Oak Dr. Pg.21 D2
Willow Rd. Pg.21 D3,6
Wilton Pg.21 E2
Winkelman Rd. Pg.21 E1
Woodridge Pg.21 E3

**CEMETERIES**
St. John's Cemetery Pg.21 F2

**FOREST PRESERVES**
Allison Woods Pg.21 E1
Camp Pine Woods Pg.24 F1
Colonades Woods Pg.22 B6
Lake Avenue Woods East Pg.21 E1
Lake Avenue Woods West Pg.21 F1
Potowatomie Woods Pg.21 A1
Somme Woods Pg.22 A5
Sunset Ridge Woods Pg.22 B7

**GOLF COURSES**
Green Acres C.C. Pg.22 A6
Mission Hills G.C. Pg.21 C2
Sunset Ridge C.C. Pg.22 D7

**PARKS**
Country Lane Park Pg.24 G3-4
Countryside Park Pg.24 G3-4
Flick Park Pg.24 F-G4
Garden Park Pg.24 G4
Huber Lane Park Pg.25 G4

**SCHOOLS**
East Main Christian Academy Pg.24 G3
St. Catherine Sch. Pg.24 F4
Villa Redeemer Monastery Pg.24 G3

**MISCELLANEOUS**
Camp Pine Pg.24 F1

## OAK FOREST

Pages 38,41,42

**STREETS**
Abbe Ct. Pg.41 M17
Adele Pg.42 N18
Adeline Pl. Pg.41 L17
Aimee Ln. Pg.41 M17
Alameda Ave. Pg.41 L16
Albert Dr. Pg.41 L17
Aldersyde Dr. Pg.41 N19
Ann Marie Dr. Pg.41 L17
Ann Marie Ln. Pg.41 M17
Anne Ct. Pg.38 K18
Arrowhead Trace Pg.41 O18
Arroyo Ct. Pg.41 L15
Arroyo Dr. Pg.41 L,M16
Aspen Ct. Pg.41 M16
Avalon Pg.38 L16
Babette Ct. Pg.41 M17
Barry Ln. Pg.42 N19
Barton Ln. Pg.42 N19
Bellaire Rd. Pg.41 N19
Belle St. Pg.41 O17
Beth Ct. Pg.41 M17
Betty Ann Ln. Pg.41 L17
Blair Ln. Pg.42 N19
Boca Rio Dr. Pg.41 L16
Bonnie Tr. Pg.41 O17
Bramblewood Rd. Pg.41 M15
Brendon Ln. Pg.42 N19
Bret Dr. Pg.41 M16
Brianne Ln. Pg.41 L15
Briar Ln. Pg.41 L16
Brockton Ln. Pg.42 N19
Brookwood Dr. Pg.41 M16
Carol Belle Tr. Pg.41 M17
Carolyn Ct. Pg.38 L17
Carriage Way Pg.38 L16
Catalina Ave. Pg.41 L16
Cedar Pg.38 L15
Central Ave. Pg.38 N19
Central Ct. Pg.38 K17
Charles Pg.41 L16
Charleston St. Pg.41 M15
Chaucer Dr. Pg.38 L16
Cherry Ln. Pg.41 L16
Chestnut Ln. Pg.38 L15
Chippewa Ct. Pg.41 O18
Christopher Dr. Pg.41 O17
Church Pg.41 L15
Cicero Ave. Pg.41 L18
Club Circle Dr. Pg.38 K15
Colina Ave. Pg.41 L16
Concha Ct. Pg.41 L16
Condado Pg.38 L16
Conway Ct. Pg.38 K15
Corey Ln. Pg.41 M16
Coulter Rd. Pg.41 N18
Country Ridge Dr. Pg.41 M16
Courtney Ln. Pg.41 M15
Craig Dr. Pg.42 N19
Creekside Dr. Pg.41 L17
Crescent Ln. Pg.38 L17
Cromwell Ln. Pg.38 K17
Crowe Ave. Pg.42 M19
Cypress Ct. Pg.41 O18
Danielle Ct. Pg.41 O17
Daniels Ln. Pg.38 K16
David Ln. Pg.41 L16
Debra Dr. Pg.41 M17
Deerpath Rd. Pg.41 N18
Dennis Ct. Pg.41 M17
Diamond Dr. Pg.41 L17
Diane Ct. Pg.38 L17
Dolores St. Pg.41 M16
Dover Rd. Pg.41 L17
Duncan Rd. Pg.41 M17
Edgewood Ct. Pg.38 L16
Edward Dr. Pg.41 L16
El Morro Ln. Pg.38 L16
El Vista Ave. Pg.38 K17
Elderwood Ct. Pg.38 K16
Elizabeth Ct. Pg.41 O18
Ellen Ct. Pg.41 M17
Elm Ln. Pg.41 L16
Elmwood Rd. Pg.41 N18
Essex Rd. Pg.41 M16
Fairfax Rd. Pg.41 L17
Farmsley Ct. Pg.41 N18
Fawn Ct. Pg.41 L17
Fern Pg.38 K17
Fieldcrest Ln. Pg.42 N18
Forest Ave. Pg.41 M18
Forest Ct. Pg.41 N,O18
Forest Edge Ln. Pg.38 K17
Forest Tr. Pg.41 N17
Forest View Dr. Pg.38 L16
Gainsborough Pl. Pg.41 L17
Galetta Terr. Pg.38 K17
Geoffrey Rd. Pg.38 L17
George Dr. Pg.42 N18
Grange Ave. Pg.38 K17
Green Ln. Pg.38 L17
Greentree Rd. Pg.41 O18
Grove Ave. Pg.41 M18
Harbor Dr. Pg.38 K16
Harcourt Ct. Pg.41 O17
Harold St. Pg.42 N18
Harriet Creek Dr. Pg.41 M18
Hawthorne Pg.41 O17
Henry Pg.42 N18
Heron Dr. Pg.41 M16
Hickory Ln. Pg.41 L,M15
Hillside Ave. Pg.38 L16
Hillside Ct. Pg.41 L16
Holly Ct. Pg.41 L17
Independence Ave. Pg.41 M17
Independence Ct. Pg.41 M17
James Dr. Pg.41 L17
Jamie Ct. Pg.41 M17
Janet Ct. Pg.41 M17
Jean Ct. Pg.38 K18
Jessica Dr. Pg.41 O17
Jill Ann Ln. Pg.41 M16
Joann Pg.41 M16
Jon Rd. Pg.41 M16
Jones Ct. Pg.38 L16
Judy Ct. Pg.41 O17
Kara Ct. Pg.41 M16
Kathleen Ct. Pg.41 O17
Kenton Ave. Pg.41 L18
Kilbourne Pg.42L18,N19
Kilpatrick Ave. Pg.41 L,N18
Kimberly Ct. Pg.41 N18
Knollwood Dr. Pg.38 K16
Knox Pg.41 L18
La Grande Ave. Pg.41 M16
La Grande Ct. Pg.41 L16
La Grange Ave. Pg.41 M16
La Palm Ct. Pg.38 L17
La Palm Dr. Pg.38 L17
La Paz Ct. Pg.41 M16
La Paz Dr. Pg.41 M16
La Porte Ave. Pg.38 L18
Lacrosse Ave. Pg.38 L18
Lake Dr. Pg.41 M16
Lamon Pg.41 L,M18
Lancaster Dr. Pg.41 L17
Landings Ln. Pg.38 L16
Langley Ct. Pg.41 O18
Laramie Ave. Pg.41 M,O17
Laramie Ct. Pg.41 L17
Las Flores Ave. Pg.41 L16
Las Robles Pg.38 L16
Latrobe Ave. Pg.41 M17
Laura Ln. Pg.42 N19
Lavergne Ave. Pg.41 L,M18
Leclaire Ave. Pg.41 L,N18
Leslie Ln. Pg.41 M17
Liberty Sq. Pg.41 M16
Linden Dr. Pg.41 L16,M15
Lisa Ln. Pg.42 N18
Lockwood Ave. Pg.41 O17
Lockwood Dr. Pg.41 O17
Long Ave. Pg.41 K,M17
Lorel Ave. Pg.41 M17
Lorin Ct. Pg.38 L18
Lynne Ct Pg.38 L17
Major Ave. Pg.38 K17
Mann Pg.42 N19
Maple Ct. Pg.41 L15
Maple Dr. Pg.41 L15
Margie Ln. Pg.41 M17
Martha Ln. Pg.41 O17
Mary Ann Ct. Pg.41 M17
Massasoit Ave. Pg.38 K17
Meadow Ct. Pg.41 L17
Meadowdale Dr. Pg.41 N18
Menard Ave. Pg.38 L17
Merlin Ct. Pg.41 L17
Michaele Dr. Pg.41 L17
Mission Ave. Pg.38 K17
Moorings Ln. Pg.38 L16
Natalie Dr. Pg.41 L17
Nature Dr. Pg.41 M16
New England Ave. Pg.41 M15
Newport Dr. Pg.41 N18
Nicholas Ct. Pg.41 O17
Oak Ave. Pg.41 M18
Oak St. Pg.41 L15
Oakland Ave. Pg.38 L16
Oakwood Pg.41 N17
Orange Ln. Pg.41 L16
Orchard Ln. Pg.41 L16
Orogrande Ct. Pg.41 L16
Orogrande St. Pg.41 L16
Oxford Dr. Pg.38 L17
Pamela Ct. Pg.41 M17
Park Ave. Pg.38 K17
Parkside Ave. Pg.38 L17
Parkwood Ct. Pg.38 L16
Peachtree Ct. Pg.41 M16
Peggy Ln. Pg.41 M17
Pine Ct. Pg.41 M15
Pine Dr. Pg.41 L15
Pine Rd. Pg.41 M15
Revere Ct. Pg.41 M17
Reynolds Dr. Pg.41 M16
Richard Ave. Pg.42 N18
Ridgeland Ave. Pg.38 M16
Ridgewood Dr. Pg.38 K,L16
Rio Verde Ave. Pg.38 L16
Rob Roy Ct. Pg.41 M16
Rob Roy Dr. Pg.41 L,M16
Roy St. Pg.42 N18
Sara Ann Ln. Pg.41 M16
Sayre Ave. Pg.41 M15
Scarborough Ct. Pg.38 K17
Scarborough Ln. Pg.38 K17
School Ln. Pg.38 L16
Scott Pg.42 N19
Sequoia St. Pg.38 L16
Shaddow Creek Dr. Pg.41 M18
Sierra Dr. Pg.41 M16
Spruce Ln. Pg.38 L15
Stuart Ln. Pg.41 L16
Sunset Ave. Pg.30 K17
Sunset Ct. Pg.38 K17
Sussex Ct. Pg.38 K17
Sycamore Ln. Pg.41 O18
Temple Dr. Pg.38 K17
Terrace Dr. Pg.41 M16
Terry Ln. Pg.42 N18
Thackery St. Pg.41 O17
Thomas Ln. Pg.41 M16
Timber Ct. Pg.41 N18
Tudor Rd. Pg.41 L16
Ventura St. Pg.38 L16
Vera Ct. Pg.41 M17
Victoria Ct. Pg.41 L16
Victoria Dr. Pg.41 L15,16
Vine St. Pg.38 L17
Vista Ct. Pg.41 M16
Wagman Pg.42 N19
Walden Ct. Pg.38 K17
Walnut Rd. Pg.41 L15
Warwick Pg.41 L17
Waverly Ave. Pg.41 M18
Westview Dr. Pg.41 L15
Willow Ln. Pg.38 L15
Willowwick Pg.42 N18
Woodland Dr. Pg.41 L17
66th Ct. Pg.38 K15
70th Ct. Pg.40 L15
146th Ct. Pg.38 K15
148th St. Pg.38 K17
150th Pl. Pg.38 L16
150th St. Pg.38 L16,18
151st St. Pg.38 L16
152nd St. Pg.38 L17,18
153rd St. Pg.38 L15,17
154th Pl. Pg.41 L15
154th St. Pg.41 L17
155th Pl. Pg.41 L15
155th St. Pg.41 L17
156th Pl. Pg.41 M15
156th St. Pg.41 L17,M15
157th Ave. Pg.41 M15
157th Pl. Pg.41 M16
157th St. Pg.41 M15-17
158th Pl. Pg.41 M16
158th St. Pg.41 M17
159th St. Pg.41 M15
160th St. Pg.41 M17,18
161st St. Pg.41 M17,18
162nd St. Pg.41 M18
163rd St. Pg.41 M17
165th St. Pg.42 N19
166th St. Pg.42 N19
167th St. Pg.41 N18,19
169th Pl. Pg.41 N17
169th St. Pg.41 N17
170th Pl. Pg.41 O17
170th St. Pg.41 N17

**CEMETERIES**
Cook County Potters Field Cemetery Pg.42 M19
St. Gabriel Cem. Pg.41 N18

**FOREST PRESERVES**
Midlothian Meadows Pg.41 M19

**GOLF COURSES**
El Morro Park and Golf Course Pg.41 L16
George Dunn G.C. Pg.41 M16

**PARKS**
Central Park Pg.41 M17
Chicago Gaelic Park Pg.38 K16
Convent Park Pg.38 K16
Don Burns Park Pg.42 N18
Fieldcrest Park Pg.42 N18
Forestview Park Pg.41 L16
Friendly Oaks Park Pg.41 M17
James Malecky Park Pg.41 O17
Lagoon Park Pg.41 M17
Tower Park Pg.41 L16
Vergne Way Park Pg.41 L18

**SCHOOLS**
Arbor Park Sch. Pg.41 M18
Fieldcrest Sch. Pg.42 N19
Forest Ridge Sch. Pg.38 L17
Foster Sch. Pg.41 L16
Gingerwood Sch. Pg.41 N18
Jack Hills Sch. Pg.38 L16
Kerkstra Sch. Pg.38 L17
Oak Forest H.S. Pg.38 L17
Orchard Hill Sch. Pg.41 N18
S.W. Case Sch. Pg.38 L16
Scarlet Oak Sch. Pg.41 M17
St. Damon Sch. Pg.41 L17
Walter Fierke Ed. Ctr. Pg.41 L15

**SHOPPING CENTERS**
Oak Creek Plaza Pg.41 M17

**MISCELLANEOUS**
Acorn Public Library Pg.41 M17
City Hall Pg.41 L17
Commuter R.R. Station Pg.41 M18
Forest View Equestrian Farm Pg.41 N17
Oak Forest Hospital Pg.42 M18
Our Lady of Sorrows Convent Pg.38 K16
Post Office Pg.41 L18,M17
Public Works Pg.41 M17
Southwest Co Op Assoc. for Special Education Pg.38 L16
St. Mihiel Reservation Pg.41 N17

## OAK LAWN

Page 34,35
(For additional listings, see Section 1)

**STREETS**
Alexander Pl. C17
Alice Ct. E17
Austin Ave. C,D16
Avery Pl. C17
Avon Ave. D15
Buell Ave. E17
Campbell D17
Cass St. C17
Central Ave. C-E17
Cicero Ave. C-F18
Cook Ave. D17
Crescent Ct. C15
Deblin Ln. F17
Dixie Dr. F17
Drury Ln. D17
Dumke Dr. D17
Edison D17
Elm Circle Dr. E17
Franklin Ave. D17
Georgia E17
Harlem Ave. D14
Harnew Rd. E17
James Pl. C16
Jordan Ln. F17
Kimball Pl. C17
Lacrosse Ave. D,F18
Lamb Dr. E17
Lamon Ave. E,F18
Laporte Ave. E,F18
Lavergne Ave. E,F18
Lawler Ave. E,F18
Lawrence Ct. E17
Leclaire Ave. F18
Linder Ave. E17
Linus Ln. E18
Lockwood Ave. E17
Long Ave. E17
Lorel E17
Lynwood Dr. C16
Magnolia Dr. F17
Major Ave. C-E16
Mansfield Ave. C-E16
Maple Ave. E17
Marion Ave. D16
Marmora Ave. E16
Mason D16
Massasoit Ave. C-E16
Mayfield Ave. C,D16
McVicker Ave. C,D16
Meade Ave. C,D16
Melvina Ave. C,D16
Menard Ave. C-E16
Merrimac Ave. C,D16
Merton Ave. D16
Minnick Ave. D,E17
Mint Julip Dr. F17
Mobile Ave. C,D16
Monitor Ave. C16
Moody Ave. C,D16
Mulberry Ave. E17
Mulligan Dr. C16
Nashville Ave. C,D15
Natchez Ave. C15
Natoma Ave. C,D15
Neva D15
New England Ave., S. C,D15
Newland Ave. C,D15
Nora Ave. D15
Nordica D15
Normandy Ave. D15
North St. C17
Nottingham Ave. D15
Oak Center Dr. E17
Oak Park Ave. C,D15
Oak St. D17
Oakdale Dr. E17
Otto Pl. C17
Parkside Ave. C-E17
Pauline Dr. E17
Paxton Rd. D18
Peach Tree Ln. F17
Raymond Ave. D17
Ridgeland Ave. C,D15
Robertson Ave. D17
Ruby St. C17
Rutherford Ave. D15
Sayre Ave. C,D15
Scott Ln. E17
Shore Dr., E. & W. D17
Spring Rd. E18
Sproat Ave. E17
Stevens Dr. C17
Stony Circle E18
Stony Creek Dr. E17
Tomcin Dr. F17
Tulley Ave. C,D17
Wabash Ave. D17
Warren Ave. D17
Washington St. D,E17
Wick Dr. E17
Yourell Ave. D17
48th Ct. C18
49th Ave. C-D18
49th Ct. C-D18
50th Ave. C,D17
50th Ct. D17
51st Ave. C-E17

52nd Ave. C-E17
52nd Ct. C17
53rd Ave. C-E17
53rd Ct. C17
54th Ave. C-E17
54th Ct. C17
55th Ave. D17
55th Ct. C17
68th Ct. D15
69th Ave. D15
69th Ct. D15
87th Pl. C15,16
87th St. C15,16
88th Pl. C15-17
88th St. C16-17
89th Pl. C15-16
90th Pl. C16
90th St. C15,17
91st Pl. C15-16
91st Ct. C15-17
92nd Pl. C16
92nd St. C15-17
93rd Pl. C15
93rd St. C15-16
94th Pl. D15
94th St. D15-17
95th Pl. D15
95th St. D15-17
96th Pl. D15,18
96th St. D15-18
97th Pl. D18
97th St. D15-17
98th Pl D15-17
98th St. D15-17
99th Pl. D15,17
99th St. D15-17
100th Pl. D16
100th St. D16-17
101st Pl. E16
101st St. E15-16
102nd St. E16
103rd St. E16-17
104th St. E16-17
105th Pl. E16
105th St. E16-17
106th Pl. E17
106th St. E17
107th Pl. F17
107th St. F17
108th Pl. F17
108th St. F17
109th St. F17
110th St. F17
111th St. F16-17
157th St. F17

### FOREST PRESERVES
Wolf Wildlife Refuge Wetlands F17

### PARKS
Centennial Park D15
Columbus Manor Park D16
Dillon Park E17
Gasteyer Oak Meadows Park D17
Lake Shore Park D17
Menard Center C16
Phillips Park C17
Schburt Park C16
St. Linus Park E17
Worthbrook Park C16

### SCHOOLS
Brandt Sch. C17
Clark Sch. E16
Columbus Manor Sch. D16
Cook Ave. Sch. D17
Covington Sch. C17
Dearborn Heights Sch. D15
Eisenhower NE H.S. E18
Gasteyer Sch. D17
Harnew Sch. C16
Oak Lawn Comm. H.S. D16
Park Lawn Sch. F18
Richards H.S. Campus Bldg. E17
SW Shicago Christian Sch. D17
Simmons Sch. D15
St. Geralds Sch. D17
St. Linus Sch. E17
St. Louis de Mounfort Sch. C15
Sward Sch. D17

### SHOPPING CENTERS
E. J. Korvettes S.C. D17

### MISCELLANEOUS
Library C17
Post Office D18
Village Hall D17

## OLYMPIA FIELDS
Pages 47,48

### STREETS
Achilles Ave. T20
Alexander St. T21
Apollo Cir. U21
Arcadian Ct. T20
Arcadian Dr. T20
Athens Rd. T21
Attica Rd. T20
Augusta Dr. S22
Birch Ln. T21
Bristol Ln. T21
Brookside Blvd. T20
Brookwood Dr T21
Brookwood Dr., S. T21
Byron Ct. T20
Cambridge Ln. U21
Chariot Ln. T21
Chelsea Cir. T21
Corinth Rd. T21
Country Club Dr. S21
Crawford Ave. T19
Cumberland Tr. S20
Cumnock Rd. T19
Danube Way T20
Dartmouth Ln. T21
Doria Ln. T20
Edmund M. Burke Rd. T20
Elliot Ct. T20
Evergreen Cir. U20
Exmoor Rd. T19
Fairfield Ave T20
Glen Eagles Dr. S21
Governors Dr. S20
Governors Hwy. T20
Graymoor Ln. S22
Greenwood Center Ct. T20
Greenwood Ct. T20
Greenwood Dr. T20
Harding Ave. T21
Harding St. U21
Helenic Dr. T20
Highview Ave. T20
Hudson Tr. S20
Indiana Cir. T20
Inverness Ct. S21
Ionia Ave. T20
Ithaca Ct. T20
Ithaca Rd. T20
Joe Orr Rd. S22
Kedzie Ave. T21
Lake Dr. S21
Leland U22
Lincoln Hwy. U21
London Dr. U21
Marathon Ct. T20
Maros Ln. T21
Mellet Ct. T20
Mohawk Tr. S20
Oak Lane Dr. T20
Oakwood Dr. T21
Oakwood Terr. T21
Olympian Way T20
Orchard Dr. U21
Oregon Tr. S20
Overland Tr. S20
Paris Rd. T21
Park Dr. S20
Parthenon Ct. T20
Parthenon Way T20
Pine Ave. U20
Platte Tr. S20
Promethian Way T21
Rieger St. U22
Rockwell U21
Roslyn Rd. T19
Sante Fe Tr. S20
Scott Dr. T20,22
Sheffield Cir. T21
Sparta Ct. T21
Sparta Ln. T21
Spartan Way T20
St. Andrews Ct. S21
St. Andrews Dr. S21
Strauss Ln. T20
Tam-O-Shanter Ct. S21
Tenuta Ct. T21
Terr. No. 1 T22
Terr. No. 2 T22
Terr. No. 3 T22
Terr. No. 4 T22
Terr. No. 5 T21
Terr. No. 6 T21
Thaxed Cir. U20
Thomas St. U21
Thornwood Cir. T20
Thornwood Dr. T20
Tower Ct. T20
Trails Dr. S20
Troy Cir. T21
Vollmer Rd. S20
Warren Cir. T21
Washington Dr. U22
Waterford Ct. S21
Western Ave. T22
Wilderness Tr. S20
Wingate Rd. T,U20
Woodland Ct. T20
Woodland Dr. T20
Woodstock Rd. T20
Wysteria Dr. T22
203rd St. S20
204th St. T20
205th St. T20
206th St. T20
207th T20

### FOREST PRESERVES
Elliott Woods T20

### GOLF COURSES
Olympia Fields Country Club T21

### PARKS
Bicentennial Park S20
Maynegaite Park U21
Means Park T21
Spirit Trail Park T21
Tolentine Park T20

### SCHOOLS
Arcadia Sch. T20
Rich Twp. H.S. Central S20

### MISCELLANEOUS
Columbia Osteopathic Olympic Fields Hospital S20
Iron Oaks Enviornmental Learning Ctr. S22
Osteopathic Medical Park S19
Post Office S21
R.R. Station S21,U20
Tolentine Seminary & Educational Center T20
Village Hall T20

## ORLAND HILLS
Page 40

### STREETS
Beacon Ct. N12
Beacon Ln. N12
Birch Ct. M12
Birchwood Dr. M12
Boardwalk Tr. N11
Brigitte Ct. N12
Cedarwood M12
Chadbourne Dr. N12
Christine Ct. N12
Christopher Ave O12
Dwight Ct. N12
Elm Pl. M12
Fox Ct. M12
Haven Ave. M,N12
Haven Ct. N12
Hawthorn M11
Herbert Ct. N12
Hickory Ct. O12
Hickory Dr. O12
Highview Ave. N12
Hilltop Ave. N12
Hunter Ct. M11
Hunter Dr. M11
Kelly Ct. N12
La Grange Rd. N11
Leslie Dr. N12
Lindsey St. N11
Maplewood Ct. N12
Marilyn Ct. N12
Marshfield N12
Meadowview N12
Morgan Ln. N12
O'Brien Dr. N12
Parkview Pl. M12
Pepperwood Dr. N12
Prairie Pl. M12
Pristine Pl. M12
Quail Ct. M12
Rachel Ct. M12
Redwood Ct. O12
Ridge Ln. M12
Robin Ct. N12
Sharon Ct. N12
Terrace Ct. M12
U.S. Route 6 M12
Vicky Ln. N12
Westwood Ct. O12
Westwood Dr. O12
Willow Terr. M12
88th Ave. O12
88th Ct. N,O12
89th Ave. N,O12
09th Ct. N12
90th Ave. N12
90th Ct. M12
91st Ave. M,N12
92nd Ave. M,N12
92nd Pl. M12
93rd Ave. N12
94th Ave. P11
159th Pl. M12
159th St. M14
160th Pl. M12
161st St. M12
162nd St. M12
167th Pl. N12
167th St. N12
169th Pl. N12
169th St. N12
170th Pl. O12
170th St. O12
171st St. O13

### PARKS
Kelly Park N12

### SCHOOLS
Christian Hills Sch. M12

### SHOPPING CENTERS
Orland Towne Center M11

### MISCELLANEOUS
Fire Station N11
Village Hall N11

## ORLAND PARK
Pages 36,37,39-41

### STREETS
Abby Ln. Pg.40 L12
Abigail Ln. Pg.39 P10
Acacia Dr. Pg.40 M13
Adria Ct. Pg.37 I12
Alabama Ct. Pg.39 P10
Alaska Ct. Pg.39 P10
Aldwych Dr. Pg.37 J13
Alexis Ln. Pg.12 K9
Alice Ln. Pg.39 P10
Allison Ln. Pg.39 O9
Alpine Dr. Pg.36 L8
Alveston St. Pg.36 K10
Amber Ln. Pg.39 P10
America Ct. Pg.39 P10
Andrea Ct. Pg.39 P10
Andrea Dr. Pg.39 P9
Anne Ct. Pg.40 L13
Anne Dr. Pg.40 L13
Antler Dr. Pg.12 O9
Apache Ln. Pg.37 J13
Apache Pl. Pg.37 J13
Arapaho Pl. Pg.37 J13
Arbor Dr. Pg.30 L0
Arbor Ridge Dr. Pg.36 K9
Aris Ct Pg.40 M12
Arizona Ct. Pg.39 P10
Arkansas Ct. Pg.39 P10
Arrowhead Ct. Pg.37 J13
Arrowhead Ln. Pg.37 J13
Arthur Ct. Pg.39 P10
Arthur Dr. Pg.39 P10
Ascot Ct. Pg.40 M12
Ash St. Pg.37 J12,K11
Ashford Ct. Pg.36 K9
Ashley Ct. Pg.37 K13
Ashley Dr. Pg.37 K13
Ashton Ln. Pg.36 J9
Ashwood Ln. Pg.39 O8
Aspen St. Pg.37 K12
Aster Ln. Pg.40 L14
Atwood Ct. Pg.36 J9
Aubrieta Ct. Pg.40 L14
Aubrieta Ln. Pg.40 L14
Auburn Ct. Pg.37 J11
Austin Ln. Pg.12 O10
Autumn Ridge Dr. Pg.39 P9
Avalon Ct. Pg.37 J13
Avenel Dr. Pg.12 N9
Avenida Del Este Pg.36 L11
Avenida Del Notre Pg.36 L11
Baltusrol Dr. Pg.40 M12
Barleycorn Ct. Pg.40 L12
Basswood Rd. Pg.37 K13
Bayberry Ct. Pg.40 L13
Bayhill Ct. Pg.40 M13
Beacon Ave. Pg.36 K11
Bear Island Ave. Pg.39 N9
Bedford Ln. Pg.40 L11
Beech St. Pg.37 K12
Begonia Ct. Pg.40 L14
Berkhansted Ct. Pg.37 J13
Berkley Ct. Pg.37 K12
Bernard Dr. Pg.39 P9
Beth Dr. Pg.39 O9
Beverly Ln. Pg.37 I12
Billinary Ct. Pg.39 P8
Biloba Pg.37 K12
Biltmore Dr. Pg.40 M13
Binford Dr. Pg.37 J13
Birch St. Pg.37 K11
Birchbark Ct. Pg.37 J13
Black Friars Rd. Pg.40 L12
Blackhawk Ln. Pg.37 J13
Blarney Ct. Pg.39 N9
Blue Heron Dr. Pg.39 O9
Blue Jay Dr. Pg.39 N9
Blue Spruce Ct. Pg.37 K12
Boardwalk Ln. Pg.36 M11
Bob White Cir. Pg.36 N11
Bob-O-Link Ct. Pg.37 L13
Bob-O-Link Rd. Pg.37 L13
Bonbury Ln. Pg.37 J13
Boyne Ct. Pg.39 O8
Bradford Ln. Pg.40 M12
Bradley Ct. Pg.39 P9
Braeburn Ln. Pg.40 M13
Braelock Ct. Pg.40 M13
Bramlett Ct. Pg.36 L8
Brassie Ct. Pg.40 M13
Brassie Dr. Pg.40 L,M13
Brentwood Ave. Pg.37 K12
Briarwood Ln. Pg.37 I12
Brighton Ct. Pg.37 K13
Brigitte Terr. Pg.36 J9
Bromley St. Pg.37 K13
Brook Ave. Pg.36 K11
Brook Crossing Ct. Pg.39 O9
Brook Crossing Dr. Pg.39 O9
Brook Crossing Ln. Pg.39 O9
Brook Hill Ct. Pg.39 P8
Brook Hill Dr. Pg.39 O8
Brookdale Ct. Pg.39 O8
Brookfield Cir. Pg.39 P8
Brookgate Dr. Pg.39 O8
Brookshire Dr. Pg.39 O8
Brookside Ct. Pg.40 M12
Brookwood Ct. Pg.39 O8
Brookwood Dr. Pg.39 O8
Brushwood Ln. Pg.39 O8
Buck Dr. Pg.39 O10
Bunker Dr. Pg.40 L13
Butler Ct. Pg.40 M12
Butterfield Ln. Pg.37 I12
Byron Dr. Pg.40 N12
Caddy Ct. Pg.37 K12
California Ct. Pg.39 P10
Calypso Ln. Pg.40 M14
Cambridge Dr. Pg.37 K14
Camden Dr. Pg.37 J13
Camelia Ln. Pg.40 L13
Cameron Pkwy. Pg.39 P9
Canterbury Ln. Pg.40 M13
Capistrano Ln. Pg.12 O10
Cardinal Dr. Pg.39 N10
Carlisle Ln. Pg.37 K12
Carnousite Dr. Pg.40 M12
Carol Ct. Pg.37 L13
Carolina Ln. Pg.37 J11
Carolyn Ct. Pg.39 I9
Cascade Ct. Pg.37 K13
Cashew Dr. Pg.40 M14
Castlebar Ln. Pg.37 L12
Catalina Ct. Pg.40 M14
Catalina Dr. Pg.40 L14
Catherine Ct. Pg.36 J11
Catherine Dr. Pg.37 J11
Cedar St. Pg.37 J13
Centennial Ct. Pg.39 M11
Centennial Dr. Pg.39 M11
Cervidae Ct. Pg.12 M9
Chapel Hill Rd. Pg.40 M13
Charleston Dr. Pg.37 J11
Chateau Ct. Pg.37 K13
Chaucer Dr. Pg.39 N9
Chelsea Dr. Pg.37 J13
Cherry Hills Ct. Pg.40 L12
Cherry Ln. Pg.40 J13
Cherrywood Ct. Pg.40 L13
Chertsey Ct. Pg.37 K13
Cheryl Ln. Pg.39 O9
Chesterfield Ln. Pg.40 M12
Chestnut Dr. Pg.40 M14
Cheswick Dr. Pg.37 J13
Chickadee Cir. Pg.36 N11
Christine Ct. Pg.37 K11
Churchill Dr. Pg.39 N9
Churchview Dr. Pg.40 N11
Clairmont Ct. Pg.37 L12
Claridge Ct. Pg.37 K14
Clear Creek X'ing Pg.39 P9
Clearview Ct. Pg.37 J12
Clearview Dr. Pg.37 K12
Cliffside Ln. Pg.40 M12
Coghill Ln. Pg.37 J12
Coleman Dr. Pg.39 N9
Colette Ct. Pg.40 L13
Colorado Ct. Pg.39 P10
Columbus Ct. Pg.39 P9
Compubill Dr. Pg.37 K11
Concord Dr. Pg.37 J12
Conifer Ct. Pg.39 N9
Conmoy Ln. Pg.39 P8
Connecticut Ct. Pg.39 P10
Constitution Ct. Pg.39 M11
Constitution Dr. Pg.39 M11
Cordoba Ct. Pg.36 L11
Coronado Dr. Pg.12 O10
Corso Dr. Pg.12 N9
Cottonwood Ct. Pg.36 L8
Country Club Ln. Pg.37 K13
Country Ct. Pg.40 M12
County Ln. Pg.36 K8
Coventry Ct. Pg.37 I12
Cranna Ct. Pg.39 P8
Creek Crossing Dr. Pg.36 J,K8
Creekside Dr. Pg.36 J8
Cressmoor Ct. Pg.40 M13
Crestline Dr. Pg.36 J8
Crestview Ct. Pg.39 P8
Crestview Dr. Pg.39 P8
Crestwood Dr. Pg.36 J8
Cristina Ave. Pg.37 J,K13
Crooked Creek Ct. Pg.39 P9
Croydon Ln. Pg.40 L12
Crystal Creek Dr. Pg.40 M12
Crystal Ridge Ct. Pg.36 K9
Crystal Springs Ct. Pg.36 L9
Crystal Springs Ln. Pg.36 L9
Crystal Tree Dr. Pg.36 K10
Cypress Ct. Pg.37 L12
Dakota Ln. Pg.37 J13
Danbury Ln. Pg.40 L12
Danford Ln. Pg.40 M12
Davids Ln. Pg.39 P10
Debbie Ln. Pg.36 N11
Deer Creek Dr. Pg.12 O9
Deer Point Dr. Pg.12 O9
Deer Run Dr. Pg.39 O9
Deer Trial Pg.39 O10
Deerfield Ct. Pg.40 M13
Deerpath Dr. Pg.37 J13
Delaware Ct. Pg.39 P10
Devonshire Ln. Pg.40 L12
Dewberry Ln. Pg.40 L12
Dexter Ct. Pg.37 K12
Diego Ln. Pg.12 P10
Doe Ln. Pg.39 O9
Dogwood Ave. Pg.37 L12
Dolorosa Dr. Pg.12 O10
Donna Ln. Pg.39 O9
Doorstep Ln. Pg.37 K13
Doral Ln. Pg.37 J12
Dublin St. Pg.37 L12
Dunree Ln. Pg.39 P8
Eagle Ridge Dr. Pg.39 P9
Edgewood Dr. Pg.40 L13
Eileen Ct. Pg.37 J11
El Cameno Ct. Pg.36 L11
El Cameno Ln. Pg.36 L11
El Cameno Terr. Pg.36 L11
El Camino Re'Al Pg.36 L11
Elderberry Ln. Pg.39 N10
Elizabeth Ave. Pg.37 J13
Elk Dr. Pg.12 O9
Elm St. Pg.37 J12
Emerald Ave. Pg.12 O10
Equestrian Dr. Pg.39 M9
Erin Ln. Pg.40 M12
Esther Dr. Pg.39 P9
Evergreen Dr. Pg.37 L14
Eynsford Dr. Pg.37 K13
Fairmont Ct. Pg.37 L12
Fairway Dr. Pg.37 K11
Fane Ct. Pg.39 O8
Farm Hill Dr. Pg.40 M12
Fawn Creek Ln. Pg.12 M9
Fawn Ct. Pg.37 I12
Fawn Trail Dr. Pg.12 O9
Feather Ct. Pg.37 I12
Fernwood Ct. Pg.37 L12
Fir St. Pg.37 J12
Firestone Dr. Pg.37 I12
First Ave. Pg.36 K11
Flamingo Cir. Pg.40 L13
Flint Ln. Pg.37 I12
Florida Ct. Pg.39 P10
Forestview Dr. Pg.37 L13
Foxbend Ct. Pg.40 M13
Frances Ln. Pg.40 M12
Franchesca Ct. Pg.36 L10
Franklin Ct. Pg.37 K12
Fun Dr. Pg.39 M10
Garden View Ct. Pg.40 M14
Garret Ln. Pg.39 P9
Georgia Ct. Pg.39 P10
Ginger Creek Ln. Pg.36 L8
Glen Eagle Ct. Pg.37 J12
Glen Oak Rd. Pg.40 M13
Glenlake Dr. Pg.39 M9
Glenwoody Ct. Pg.37 J12
Golden Rose Dr. Pg.36 M12
Golf Rd. Pg.36 K10
Golfview Dr. Pg.37 K12
Grace Rd. Pg.37 L12
Grandview Dr. Pg.36 L8
Grange Dr. Pg.39 O8
Grants Tr. Pg.39 N9
Great Egret Dr. Pg.39 O9
Green Knoll Ave. Pg.39 N8
Green St. Pg.37 K11
Green View Rd. Pg.36 K9
Greencastle Ln. Pg.37 K12
Greenfield Ct. Pg.39 O8
Greenfield Dr. Pg.39 O8
Greenland Ave. Pg.36 K10
Greenvalley Dr. Pg.36 J8
Hackney Dr. Pg.39 N11
Hale Dr. Pg.36 L10
Halesia Ct. Pg.40 L14
Harbor Town Dr. Pg.40 M14
Harlem Ave. Pg.40 M15
Hartwood Ct. Pg.37 J11
Harvest Crossing Pg.36 L8
Harvest Hill Ct. Pg.39 O8
Harvest Hill Dr. Pg.39 O8
Hastings Dr. Pg.37 J13
Hawaii Ct. Pg.39 P10
Hawthorne Dr. Pg.36 L10
Hazel Ct. Pg.36 L10
Heather Ct. Pg.40 L14
Heathrow Cir. Pg.39 N8
Helen Ln. Pg.40 M12
Hemlock Dr. Pg.40 J12,L14
Hempstead Dr. Pg.37 K13
Henry St. Pg.37 L12
Hiawatha Tr. Pg.36 L10
Hibiscus Dr. Pg.36 L10
Hickory Dr. Pg.36 L10
Hidden Brook Ct. Pg.39 O8
Hidden Valley Cove Pg.39 P8
Highbush Rd. Pg.39 N10
Highgate Ct. Pg.37 K13
Highland Ave. Pg.36 K10
Highwood Ct. Pg.39 O8
Highwood Dr. Pg.39 O8
Hill Creek Ct. Pg.39 O9
Hillcrest Cir. Pg.39 M11
Hilltop Ct. Pg.36 L10
Hilltop Dr. Pg.36 L10
Holiday Ct. Pg.36 L10
Hollow Tree Ct. Pg.36 K9
Hollow Tree Rd. Pg.36 K9
Holly Ct. Pg.36 K10
Hollyhock Ct. Pg.37 L,M14
Hollywood Dr. Pg.40 L13
Hopkins Ct. Pg.36 L10
Hughuelet Pl. Pg.37 L12
Hummingbird Dr. Pg.39 N11
Huntington Ct. Pg.36 L10
Huntington Pl. Pg.36 L10
Hyacinth Dr. Pg.36 L10
Idaho Ct. Pg.39 P10
Idlewild Dr. Pg.37 J12
Illinois Ct. Pg.39 P10
Indiana Ct. Pg.39 P10
Innishmor Ct. Pg.39 P8
Innsbrook Dr. Pg.40 M13
Interstate 80 Pg.40 O11
Inverness Dr. Pg.37 J12
Iowa Ct. Pg.39 P9
Irving Ave. Pg.36 K10
Ishnala Dr. Pg.37 J14
Janine Ct. Pg.12 O10
Jean Creek Dr. Pg.37 I12
Jefferson Ave. Pg.36 K11
Jennifer Dr. Pg.39 O9
Jillian Rd. Pg.39 L9
Jimmick Ln. Pg.12 O10
John Charles Dr. Pg.39 P10
John Humphrey Dr. Pg.37 K11
John Mayher Sr. Dr. Pg.39 P8
Juniper Ct. Pg.37 L12
Kansas Ct. Pg.39 P9
Karli Ln. Pg.39 O8
Kathy Ct. Pg.37 K12,13
Katy Ln. Pg.37 K13
Kelsey Ln. Pg.39 O8
Kemper Dr. Pg.40 M12
Kendall Ln. Pg.40 M12
Kennedy Ct. Pg.37 L12
Kensington Way Pg.37 L12
Kentucky Ct. Pg.39 P9
Kerry Ave. Pg.12 O10
Keystone Rd. Pg.40 M13
Kiley Ln. Pg.39 O8
Kimberly Ln. Pg.39 O9
Kingsport Ct. Pg.12 N9
Kingsport Rd. Pg.39 N9
Kingston Ln. Pg.37 L12
Kingswood Dr. Pg.36 J8
Knightsbridge Ln. Pg.37 L12
Knollwood Ln. Pg.40 M13
Koch Ct. Pg.36 N11
Kristo Ln. Pg.37 K13
Kropp Ct. Pg.39 O9
La Grange Rd. (96th Ave.) Pg.36 L11
La Reina Ct. Pg.36 L11
La Reina Real Pg.36 L11
Lago Ln. Pg.37 J13
Laguna Ln. Pg.37 J13
Lake Hills Ct. Pg.40 M13
Lake Lawn Ln. Pg.36 L9
Lake Ridge Rd. Pg.36 K10
Lake Shore Dr. Pg.39 P8
Lakebrook Ct. Pg.39 O9
Lakebrook Dr. Pg.39 O9
Lakefield Dr. Pg.39 O9
Lakeside Dr. Pg.39 M9
Lakeview Dr. Pg.37 K,L12
Lancaster Ln. Pg.40 L12
Landings Dr. Pg.40 N9
Larkspur Ln. Pg.40 L,M14
Laurel Dr. Pg.40 M12
Laurel Hill Dr. Pg.39 N9
Lawrence Ct. Pg.37 L12
Lee St. Pg.39 N9
Legend Ln. Pg.37 J13
Lennan Brook Ln. Pg.39 P8
Lexington Cir. Pg.37 L12
Lilac Ct. Pg.37 L14
Lincoln Ct. Pg.37 L12
Lincolnshire Dr. Pg.37 J12
Lindsay Dr. Pg.37 J13
Lisa Ct. Pg.40 L12
Lismore Ct. Pg.36 K10
Lissfannon Ct. Pg.39 O8
Lori Ln. Pg.37 J12
Louetta Dr. Pg.39 P10
Louetta Ln. Pg.39 P9
Louisiana Ct. Pg.39 P9
Lunar Pg.37 K12
Lynn Dr. Pg.39 P9
M.G.M. Dr. Pg.39 P8
Magnolia Ct. Pg.37 K12
Maine Ct. Pg.39 O9
Mallard Cir. Pg.40 L13
Mallow Ridge Dr. Pg.39 N9
Maple Ave. Pg.37 J12
Margarita Ave. Pg.37 K13
Marilyn Ct. Pg.36 J9

## ORLAND PARK

Marilyn Terr. . Pg.36 . . . . J9
Marley Brook Ct.
. . . . . . . . . . Pg.39 . . . P9
Marley Creek Blvd.
. . . . . . . . . . Pg.39 . . . P8
Marley Creek Ln.
. . . . . . . . . . Pg.39 . . . P9
Mary Dr. . . Pg.37 . . J11
Maryland Ct. . Pg.39 . . . O9
Mason Ln. . . Pg.37 . . K12
Massachusetts Ct.
. . . . . . . . . . Pg.39 . . . O9
Maue Dr. . . Pg.39 . . . P9
Maycliff Dr. . Pg.37 . . K12
Mayfair Ln. . Pg.37 . . L11
Mayo Dr. . . Pg.37 . . L12
McKenna Ct. . Pg.12 . . L10
Meade St. . . Pg.39 . . . N9
Meadow Ln. . Pg.37 . . L13
Meadowbrook Ln.
. . . . . . . . . . Pg.40 . . L13
Meadowview Ct.
. . . . . . . . . . Pg.37 . . K13
Medinah Dr. . Pg.37 . . I12
Mellisa Dr. . . Pg.39 . . P10
Merion Dr. . . Pg.40 . . L12
Michael Dr. . Pg.37 . . K12
Michelle Ct. . Pg.37 . . K13
Michigan Ct. . Pg.39 . . . P9
Millbank Dr. . Pg.37 . . J12
Mimosa Dr. . Pg.40 . . L14
Minnesota Ct. . Pg.39 . . . O9
Mission Hill Ct. . Pg.39 . . . O9
Mississippi Ct. . Pg.39 . . . O9
Missouri Ct. . Pg.39 . . . O9
Misty Hill Rd. . Pg.36 . . M10
Mohawk Ln. . Pg.37 . . J13
Montana Ct. . Pg.39 . . P10
Montgomery Dr.
. . . . . . . . . . Pg.37 . . K12
Morningside Ct.
. . . . . . . . . . Pg.36 . . K10
Morningside Rd.
. . . . . . . . . . Pg.36 . . K10
Muirfield Dr. . Pg.39 . . N10
Nancy Ln. . . Pg.40 . . L12
Narcissus Ct. . Pg.40 . . L14
Narcissus Ln. . Pg.40 . L,M14
Nebraska Ct. . Pg.39 . . P10
Nelson Ln. . . Pg.37 . . J14
Nevada Ct. . . Pg.39 . . . P9
New Hampshire Ct.
. . . . . . . . . . Pg.39 . . . O9
New Jersey Ct. . Pg.39 . . . O9
New Mexico Ct. . Pg.39 . . . O9
New York Ct. . Pg.39 . . . O9
Newbury Dr. . Pg.37 . . J13
Newgate Ct. . Pg.37 . . J12
Nicole Ct. . . Pg.37 . . L12
Nottingham Ct. . Pg.39 . . . N9
O'Brien Dr. . . Pg.40 . . M14
Oak Pl. . . . Pg.36 . . K11
Oak St. . . . Pg.36 . . K11
Oakdale Ct. . Pg.37 . . K12
Oakland Dr. . Pg.36 . . . K9
Oakley Ave. . Pg.36 . . K10
Ohio Ct. . . . Pg.39 . . P10
Oklahoma Ct. . Pg.39 . . P10
Old Orchard Ct. Pg.40 . . M13
Old Tamarack Ln.
. . . . . . . . . . Pg.36 . . K10
Olivia Dr. . . Pg.39 . . . O9
Orange Ave. . Pg.39 . . . N9
Orange Blossom Dr.
. . . . . . . . . . Pg.40 . . M14
Orchid Ct. . . Pg.40 . . L14
Orchid Ln. . . Pg.40 . . L14
Oregon Ln. . . Pg.39 . . P10
Orenia Ct. . . Pg.37 . . J13
Oriole Ct. . . Pg.40 . . L12
Orlan Brook Dr. Pg.40 . . M12
Orland Ct. . . Pg.37 . . L12
Orland Square Dr.
. . . . . . . . . . Pg.37 . . L11
Orland Woods Ln.
. . . . . . . . . . Pg.39 . . O,P8
Owen Dr. . . Pg.39 . . P10
Oxford Ct. . . Pg.40 . . L11
Paddock Ct. . Pg.39 . . . M9
Padre Ln. . . Pg.12 . . P10
Palm Ct. . . Pg.40 L13,14
Palm Dr. . . . Pg.40 . . L14
Palos Spring Dr.
. . . . . . . . . . Pg.37 . . I12
Pamela Ln. . . Pg.39 . . . O9
Paradise Ln. . Pg.37 . . L14
Park Hill Dr. . Pg.40 . . M12
Park Ln. . . . Pg.36 . . K10
Parkview Dr. . Pg.37 . . J12
Patricia Ln. . . Pg.40 . . M12
Patrick Ct. . . Pg.40 . . L12
Patty Ln. . . . Pg.37 . . I12
Paul Ct. . . . Pg.39 . . . N9
Pawnee Rd. . . Pg.37 . . J13
Peachtree Ct. . Pg.40 . . M12
Pebble Beach Ln.
. . . . . . . . . . Pg.37 . . J12
Pebble Beach St.
. . . . . . . . . . Pg.37 . . J12
Pembridge Rd. . Pg.40 . . L12
Pembrooke Ln. . Pg.37 . . L11
Pennsylvania Ct.
. . . . . . . . . . Pg.39 . . . O9

Pentagon Dr. . Pg.39 . . P10
Pepperwood Ave.
. . . . . . . . . . Pg.40 . . N12
Persimmon Ct. Pg.36 . . . J9
Persimmon Dr. Pg.36 . . . J9
Petunia Ct. . . Pg.40 . . L14
Pine Grove Ct. Pg.36 . . . L8
Pine St. . . . Pg.37 . . J12
Pine Tree Rd. . Pg.36 . . . J9
Pinecrest Cir. . Pg.39 . . . N8
Plum Tree Dr. . Pg.40 . . M13
Pluskota Dr. . Pg.37 . . J13
Ponderosa Ct. Pg.37 L13,14
Poplar Creek Ct.
. . . . . . . . . . Pg.39 . . . O9
Poplar Creek Ln.
. . . . . . . . . . Pg.36 . . . L9
Poplar Ct. . . Pg.37 . . K12
Poplar Rd. . . Pg.37 . . K12
Powers Ct. . . Pg.36 . . M12
Prestwick Ln. . Pg.37 . . I12
Primrose Ct. . Pg.40 . . L14
Primrose Ln. . Pg.40 . . L14
Putney Pl. . . Pg.37 . . K13
Quail Hollow Dr.
. . . . . . . . . . Pg.37 . . L13
Raccoon Curve Pg.39 . . . O9
Racheal Ln. . Pg.39 . . P10
Rainbow Cir. . Pg.39 . . . N8
Raintree Dr. . Pg.40 . . L12
Raintree Ln. . Pg.40 . . L12
Raneys Ln. . . Pg.36 . . L12
Ravinia Ave. . Pg.36 . L,M11
Ravinia Ln. . . Pg.36 . . K11
Ravinia Pl. . . Pg.39 . . L11
Red Oak Ln. . Pg.37 . . J13
Redondo Ln. . Pg.40 . . L12
Redwood Dr. . Pg.37 . . J12
Regent Ct. . . Pg.40 . . L12
Revell Ct. . . Pg.37 . . K13
Rhode Island Ct.
. . . . . . . . . . Pg.39 . . . O9
Ridge Ave. . . Pg.36 . . K10
River Bend Rd. Pg.39 . . . P9
Riviera Pkwy. . Pg.39 . . . P9
Rob Roy Dr. . Pg.40 . . M13
Robin Ln. . . Pg.39 N10,12
Robinhood Dr. Pg.40 . . N12
Rodao Dr. . . Pg.36 . . L12
Royal Creek Ln. Pg.39 . . . L9
Royal Foxhunt Rd.
. . . . . . . . . . Pg.39 . . . P9
Royal Georgian Rd.
. . . . . . . . . . Pg.40 . . L12
Royal Glen Ct. Pg.39 . . . M9
Royal Glen Rd. Pg.39 . . . M9
Rutherford Ln. Pg.37 . . L12
Ryan Ln. . . . Pg.39 . . . P9
Ryehill Ct. . . Pg.39 . . . N9
Saffron Ct. . . Pg.39 . . . N9
Salvatori Ct. . Pg.37 . . J13
San Bernado Dr.
. . . . . . . . . . Pg.12 . . O10
San Louis Dr. . Pg.12 . . O10
Sandlewood Dr.
. . . . . . . . . . Pg.37 . . J13
Sandpiper Ct. . Pg.37 . . L12
Santa Cruz Ln. Pg.12 . . O10
Saratoga Dr. . Pg.37 . . L12
Sawgrass Ct. . Pg.40 . . L13
Scott Ln. . . . Pg.37 . . K12
Sean Dr. . . . Pg.39 . . . P9
Seapines Rd. . Pg.40 . . M14
Second Ave. . Pg.36 . . K11
Selva Ln. . . Pg.37 L13,14
Seminole Ct. . Pg.40 . . M13
Sequoia Ct. . Pg.37 L13,14
Seton Pl. . . . Pg.40 . . N11
Shade Cove Ct. Pg.36 . . L9
Shady Ln. . . Pg.37 . . L11
Shagbark Ct. . Pg.37 . . L12
Shaker Ct. . . Pg.36 . . L8
Shannon Ct. . Pg.39 . . O9
Sharon Ct. . . Pg.36 . . N11
Sheffield Ln. . Pg.40 . . L12
Shenandoah Dr.
. . . . . . . . . . Pg.39 . . . M9
Sheri Ct. . . . Pg.37 . . J12
Sheri Ln. . . . Pg.37 . . J12
Sheridan's Ir. . Pg.39 . . . N9
Sherwood Dr. . Pg.40 . . M13
Shipston St. . Pg.37 . . L11
Shire Dr. . . . Pg.39 . . . M9
Silo Ridge Dr. . Pg.36 . . L8
Silo Ridge Rd., E. W. & S.
. . . . . . . . . . Pg.36 . . . L8
Silo Ridge Rd., N.
. . . . . . . . . . Pg.36 . . . K8
Silverdale Dr. . Pg.37 . . L11
Singletree Rd. . Pg.36 . . L8
Sioux Ct. . . . Pg.37 . . J13
Somerglen Ct. Pg.39 . . . M9
Somerglen Ln. Pg.39 . . . M9
Somerset Ave. Pg.39 . . . N8
Somerset Ct. . Pg.39 . . . N8
Song Bird Cir. . Pg.39 . . O10
Southwest Hwy. Pg.36 . . . P7
Spicebush Ln. . Pg.39 . . N10
Spring Creek Dr.
. . . . . . . . . . Pg.12 . . N9
Spring Creek Ln.
. . . . . . . . . . Pg.36 . . . L9

Springbrook Ct.
. . . . . . . . . . Pg.39 . . . O8
Springview Ln. Pg.36 . . . J8
Spruce Dr. . . Pg.37 . . J12
Spyglass Cir. . Pg.40 . . L13
St. Andrews Ct. Pg.40 . . L13
St. Andrews St. Pg.40 . . L13
St. James Ct. . Pg.40 . . L13
St. James Dr. . Pg.40 . . L13
St. Mary's Cir. Pg.37 . . J12
Steeplechase Pkwy.
. . . . . . . . . . Pg.39 . . . O8
Stonegate Ln. . Pg.36 . . J8
Stonehenge Dr. Pg.37 . . J13
Stonewall Dr. . Pg.37 . . J13
Stradford Ln. . Pg.40 . . L11
Strawberry Ln. Pg.37 . . I12
Streamstown Ct.
. . . . . . . . . . Pg.37 . . K13
Suffield Dr. . . Pg.37 . . J13
Sunflower Ct. . Pg.40 . . L14
Sunny Ln. . . Pg.37 . . L12
Sunrise Ln. . . Pg.40 . . M12
Sunset Ridge Ct.
. . . . . . . . . . Pg.40 . . L13
Sunset Ridge Dr.
. . . . . . . . . . Pg.40 . . L13
Sunshine Ct. . Pg.37 . . I12
Sunshine Ln. . Pg.37 . . I12
Susan Ln. . . Pg.39 . . . N9
Sussex Dr. . . Pg.40 . . L12
Sutton Ct. . . Pg.40 . . L12
Swallow Ln. . Pg.39 . . O10
Swilly Ct. . . . Pg.39 . . . O8
Sycamore Ct. . Pg.37 . . L14
Sycamore Dr. . Pg.37 . . L13
Tally Ho Ln. . Pg.40 . . L12
Tamarack Ln. . Pg.37 . . J12
Teakwood Ct. . Pg.37 . . L13
Tee Brook Dr. . Pg.40 . . L13
Tennessee Ln. . Pg.39 . . P10
Terry Ct. . . . Pg.37 . . K12
Terry Dr. . . . Pg.37 . . J13
Teton Ct. . . . Pg.37 . . J13
Teton Rd. . . . Pg.39 . . J13
Texas Ct. . . . Pg.39 . . P10
Therese Ct. . . Pg.37 . . J11
Third Ave. . . Pg.36 . . K11
Thistlewood Dr. Pg.40 . . L12
Thistlewood Ln.
. . . . . . . . . . Pg.40 . . L12
Thomas Ct. . . Pg.37 . . J11
Thomas Dr. . . Pg.37 . . J11
Thorngate Ct. . Pg.37 . . L13
Thorngate Dr. . Pg.40 . . L13
Tiffany Dr. . . Pg.40 . . M14
Timber Edge Ln.
. . . . . . . . . . Pg.36 . . . L8
Timber Ridge Ct.
. . . . . . . . . . Pg.36 . . . L8
Timber Trails Rd.
. . . . . . . . . . Pg.36 . . . L8
Timberline Ct. Pg.36 . . L10
Timothy Ct. . . Pg.37 . . J12
Timothy Dr. . . Pg.37 . . J12
Tod William Dr. Pg.37 . . J12
Torrey Pines Dr.
. . . . . . . . . . Pg.40 . . M12
Tower Dr. . . Pg.39 . . N10
Trafalgar Ct. . Pg.37 . . J13
Treetop Dr. . . Pg.39 . . . N9
Trenton Ct. . . Pg.37 . . K12
Trinity Dr. . . Pg.36 . . M12
Tulip Ct. . . . Pg.40 L13,14
Turtle Run Dr. . Pg.39 . . . P9
Turtle Run Ct. . Pg.39 . . . P9
Twin Lakes Dr. Pg.39 . . . P8
Union Ave. . . Pg.36 . . K11
Utah Ct. . . . Pg.39 . . P10
Uxbridge Dr. . Pg.37 . . K13
Vail Ct. . . . . Pg.36 . . . L8
Valentina Dr. . Pg.37 . . L12
Valerie Ln. . . Pg.39 . . . O9
Valley Brook Dr. Pg.39 . . . O8
Valley Ct. . . Pg.36 . . L9
Venice Ln. . . Pg.12 . . P10
Vermont Ct. . Pg.39 . . J11,13
Victoria Pl. . . Pg.39 . . N10
Villa Ct. . . . Pg.37 . . J13
Violet Ct. . . . Pg.40 . . M14
Virginia Ct. . . Pg.37 . . J11
Vista Dr. . . . Pg.37 . . J13
Vivian Ct. . . Pg.39 . . . P9
Voss Dr. . . . Pg.39 . . P10
Walnut St. . . Pg.37 . . J12
Warbler Ln. . Pg.39 . . . O9
Washington St. Pg.39 . . . O9
Waterford Ln. . Pg.40 . . M11
Waterside Cir. . Pg.39 . . . P8
Waterway Ct. . Pg.39 . . . P8
Wedgewood Glen Dr.
. . . . . . . . . . Pg.37 . . K13
West Ave. . . Pg.36
. . . . . . . . . . Pg.36 . L10,M11
Westbrook Dr. . Pg.39 . . . O8
Westgate Ct. . Pg.37 . . I12
Westminster Dr. Pg.40 . . M12
Westwood Dr. . Pg.36 . K,L10
Wexford Ln. . Pg.37,40 L14
Wheeler Dr. . . Pg.40 . . L14
Wherry Ln. . . Pg.40 . . L11
Whispering Hill Dr.
. . . . . . . . . . Pg.39 . . . P8

White Tail Run Pg.39 . . O10
Whitehall Ln. . Pg.40 . . M11
Wild Rose Ln. . Pg.40 . . M14
Wildflower Rd. . Pg.36 . . K10
Will-Cook Rd. . Pg.36 . . . L8
William Ct. . . Pg.36 . . J11
William Dr. . . Pg.37 . . J11
Willow Creek Ln.
. . . . . . . . . . Pg.36 . . . L8
Willow St. . . Pg.37 . . K12
Willowood Ct. . Pg.40 . . L14
Wilshire Dr. . . Pg.39 . . L11
Winding Creek Ct.
. . . . . . . . . . Pg.39 . . . O8
Winding Creek Dr.
. . . . . . . . . . Pg.39 . . . O8
Windmill Rd. . Pg.36 . . . L8
Windmill Turn . Pg.36 . . . L8
Windsor Dr. . Pg.37 . . L12
Winterberry Ln. Pg.39 . . N10
Wisconsin Ct. . Pg.39 . . . P8
Wittington Ct. . Pg.37 . . K13
Woburn Ct. . . Pg.36 . . K10
Wolf Rd. . . . Pg.39 . . . N9
Wood Duck Ln. Pg.39 . . O10
Woodbury Dr. . Pg.37 . . J11
Wooded Path Ln.
. . . . . . . . . . Pg.37 . . K13
Woodland Ave. Pg.36 . . K10
Woodmar Dr. . Pg.40 . . L13
Woodridge Ln. Pg.37 . . J12
Woodruff Dr. . Pg.40 . . M13
Woodward Dr. Pg.37 . . J13
Wyoming Ct. . Pg.39 . . P10
Yearling Crossing
. . . . . . . . . . Pg.39 . . . O9
Yorkshire Ln. . Pg.40 . . L12
Yorktown Ct. . Pg.37 . . J12
Yorktown Dr. . Pg.37 . . J12
70th Ct. . . . Pg.41 M14,15
71st Ct. . . . Pg.41 M14,15
72nd Ct. . . . Pg.40 . . L14
73rd Ave. . . Pg.40 . . L14
73rd Ct. . . . Pg.40 . . L14
74th Ct. . . . Pg.40 . . L14
75th Ct. . . . Pg.37 . . J11
76th Ave. . . Pg.40 . . L14
77th Ct. . . . Pg.40 . . L14
78th Ave. . . Pg.40 . . L14
80th Ave. . . Pg.37
. . . . . . . . . . Pg.37 . . J12,K,L13
81st Ave. . . Pg.37 . K,L13
81st Pl. . . . Pg.37 . . K,L13
82nd Ct. . . . Pg.37 . . L,M13
82nd Pl. . . . Pg.37 . . J13
83rd Ave. . . Pg.37 . . J13
83rd Ct. . . . Pg.37 . . J13
84th Ave. . . Pg.37 . J,K13
85th Ave. . . Pg.37 . J,K13
86th Ave. . . Pg.37 J,M12
87th Ave. . . Pg.37 . . K11
88th Ave. . . Pg.37,40
. . . . . . . . . . Pg.37 . I,K,M12
89th Ct. . . . Pg.40 . K,N12
89th Ct. . . . Pg.40 . . M12
90th Ave. . . Pg.40 . . N12
91st Ave. . . Pg.37 . . J11
92nd Ct. . . . Pg.37 . . K11
93rd Pl. . . . Pg.37 . . K11
94th Ave. . . Pg.37,40
96th Ave. . . Pg.39 . . . O9
97th Ave. . . Pg.39 . . . O9
104th Ave. . . Pg.39 . . P10
105th Ct. . . . Pg.39 . . N10
106th Ct. . . . Pg.39 . . N10
107th Ave. . . Pg.39 . . N10
108th Ave. . . Pg.36 . . L,P9
110th Ave., S. . Pg.39 . . . O9
111th Ave. . . Pg.36 . . . N8
135th St. . . . Pg.37 . . J12
136th St. . . . Pg.39 . . . O9
138th Pl. . . . Pg.37 . . J12,13
138th Pl. . . . Pg.37 . . J11,13
139th St. . . . Pg.37 J11-13
141st Pl. . . . Pg.37 J11-13
141st Pl. . . . Pg.40 . . M14
141st St. . . . Pg.37 . . J12
142nd St. . . . Pg.36 . . K11
143rd Pl. . . . Pg.37 K12,13
143rd Pl. . . . Pg.37 . . K8
144th Pl. . . . Pg.37 . . J12
144th St. . . . Pg.36 K10,12
145th Ct. . . . Pg.36 . . K12
145th Pl. . . . Pg.36 . . K12
145th St. . . . Pg.36 K10-12
147th St. . . . Pg.36 . . K11
149th Ct. . . . Pg.36 . . L11
149th St. . . . Pg.36 . . L11
151st St. . . . Pg.36 . L8,11
152nd Pl. . . . Pg.37 . . L14
152nd St. . . . Pg.37
. . . . . . . . . . Pg.37 . L12,14,15
153rd Ct. . . . Pg.36 . . L11
153rd St. . . . Pg.37,40 L14
153rd St. . . . Pg.40
154th Pl. . . . Pg.37 . L9,11,14
154th St. . . . Pg.39 L11,14

155th St. . . . Pg.40 . . L14
156th St. . . . Pg.40 . . M15
157th Pl. . . . Pg.40 . . M14
157th St. . . . Pg.40 . . M13
158th Ct. . . . Pg.37 . . M14
158th St. . . . Pg.40 . . M15
159th St. . . . Pg.39,40 M9
160th St. . . . Pg.39 . . . M9
161st Pl. . . . Pg.40 . . M12
161st St. . . . Pg.39 M9,11
162nd St. . . . Pg.40 . . M12
163rd Pl. . . . Pg.39 . . . N9
163rd St. . . . Pg.39 N11,12
164th Ct. . . . Pg.40 N10,12
164th St. . . . Pg.40 . . N12
165th Pl. . . . Pg.39 . . . N9
165th St. . . . Pg.39 . . . N9
166th Pl. . . . Pg.36,40
. . . . . . . . . . Pg.37 . . N11,12
166th St. . . . Pg.40 N11,12
167th Pl. . . . Pg.39,40
167th St. . . . Pg.37 . . . N9,12
167th Ct. . . . Pg.39,40 N10
168th St. . . . Pg.39,40
. . . . . . . . . . Pg.37 . . N9,12
169th St. . . . Pg.40 . . N12
170th Pl. . . . Pg.40 . . O12
170th St. . . . Pg.39,40
. . . . . . . . . . Pg.37 . . . O8,12
171st St. . . . Pg.39,40
. . . . . . . . . . Pg.37 . . . O8,12
175th St. . . . Pg.39 . . . O9
179th St. . . . Pg.39 . . P8,11
183rd St. . . . Pg.39 . . . P9

### CEMETERIES
Christ Lutheran
Cemetery . . Pg.37 . . K13
Orland Park Mem.
Cemetery . . Pg.36 . . L10
Palos Oak Hill Cemetery
. . . . . . . . . . Pg.37 . . I12

### FOREST PRESERVES
Orland Tract Forest Preserve
. . . . . . . . . . Pg.39 . . O10

### GOLF COURSES
Crystal Tree G.C. (Private)
. . . . . . . . . . Pg.36 . . L10
Indoor Golflinks of America
. . . . . . . . . . Pg.39 . . N10
Silver Lake Country Club
. . . . . . . . . . Pg.37 . . K13
White Mountain G.C.
. . . . . . . . . . Pg.40 . . P11

### PARKS
Bill Young Park Pg.36 . . L10
Brentwood Park
. . . . . . . . . . Pg.37 . . J12
Brown Park . . Pg.40 . . L12
Cachey Park. . Pg.40 . . L13
Cameno Re Al Park
. . . . . . . . . . Pg.37 . . J12
Caro Vista Park Pg.37 . . J13
Centennial Park Pg.39 . . L10
Colonial Park . Pg.39 . . J11
Community Park
. . . . . . . . . . Pg.39 . . M10
Country Club Estates
. . . . . . . . . . Pg.37 . . K13
Country Club Estates Park
. . . . . . . . . . Pg.37 . . K13
Discovery Park Pg.39 . . . O8
Dogwood Park Pg.37 . . L12
Doogan Park . Pg.36 . . K10
Eagle Ridge Park
. . . . . . . . . . Pg.39 . . . P9
Helen Lane Park
. . . . . . . . . . Pg.40 . . M12
Heritage Park . Pg.37 . . J12
Humphrey Wood Hiking Trail
. . . . . . . . . . Pg.36 . . K11
Ishnala Park . Pg.37 . . J13
Ishnala Woods Pg.37 . . J13
Jacob Hostert Cabin
. . . . . . . . . . Pg.36 . . K11
Liberty Park . . Pg.40 . . L12
Park Hill . . . Pg.40 . . M12
Parkview Park . Pg.37 . . J12
Porminas Park Pg.37 . . J13
Schussler Park Pg.37 . . K12
Spring Creek Estates Park
. . . . . . . . . . Pg.37 . . . L9
Sunny Pine Park
. . . . . . . . . . Pg.37 . . J12
Tree Top Park . Pg.39 . . L11
Veteran's Park Pg.40 . . L14
Wedgewood Commons
. . . . . . . . . . Pg.37 . . K13
Wedgewood Park
. . . . . . . . . . Pg.37 . . K13

### SCHOOLS
Centennial Sch. Pg.36 . . K8
Center School Pg.37 . . L11
Century Sch. . Pg.39 . . . M9
Doctor Sch. . . Pg.39 . . . N9
Fernway Elem. Sch.
. . . . . . . . . . Pg.40 . . N12
High Point Sch. Pg.36 . . K11
Jerling Jr. H.S. Pg.37 . . L11
Kruse School . Pg.40 . . L14
Liberty Sch. . . Pg.37 . . L12

Meadow Ridge Sch.
. . . . . . . . . . Pg.39 . . . M9
Orland Center Sch.
. . . . . . . . . . Pg.37 . . L11
Orland Park Jr. H.S.
. . . . . . . . . . Pg.36 . . L11
Orland Park Sch.
. . . . . . . . . . Pg.39 . . . M9
Prairie Sch. . . Pg.37 . . J13
School District 135/230
Admin. Bldg. Pg.36 . . K10
St. Michael Sch.
. . . . . . . . . . Pg.36 . . K10
Sunrise Center Pg.37 . . L11

### SHOPPING CENTERS
Lakeview Plaza Pg.39 . . M11
Orland Greens Pg.36 . . L11
Orland Park Place
. . . . . . . . . . Pg.39 . . L11
Orland Square Mall
. . . . . . . . . . Pg.39 . K,L11
Orland Square S.C.
. . . . . . . . . . Pg.37 . . L11
Park Hill Plaza Pg.40 . . M12
Park Pointe Plaza
. . . . . . . . . . Pg.37 . . L11
Promenade Plaza
. . . . . . . . . . Pg.36 . . . K9
Ravinia Plaza . Pg.36 . . L11
Seville Plaza . Pg.40 . . M13
Village Green S.C.
. . . . . . . . . . Pg.36 . . K11
Waterfall Plaza Pg.40 . . K11

### MISCELLANEOUS
Antique Row . Pg.36 . . K11
Appleknoll Industrial Park
. . . . . . . . . . Pg.39 . . N10
Civic Center . . Pg.36 . . K11
Fire Station . . Pg.39
. . . . . . . K12,11,13,P9
Glen Oak Industrial Park
. . . . . . . . . . Pg.39 . . . N9
Humphrey Woods Hiking
Trail . . . . . . Pg.36 . . K11
Jacob Hostert Cabin
. . . . . . . . . . Pg.36 . . K11
John Humphrey Complex
. . . . . . . . . . Pg.36 . . K11
Library . . . . Pg.36 . . L10
Metra Commuter Station
. . . . . . . . . . Pg.39
. . . . . . . . . L11,L10,P8
Orland Township Office
. . . . . . . . . . Pg.39 . . L10
Palos Primary Care Med. Ctr.
. . . . . . . . . . Pg.39 . . L10
Police Department
. . . . . . . . . . Pg.36 . . K11
Post Office . . Pg.37 . . L11
Public Works . Pg.36 . . M11
Recreation Dept.
. . . . . . . . . . Pg.36,39 L,O9
Robert Davidson Center
. . . . . . . . . . Pg.36 . . K10
Village Center . Pg.36 . . K11
Village Hall . . Pg.36 . . K11

## ORLAND TOWNSHIP

Pages 36,37,39,40

### STREETS
Arapaho Pl. . . Pg.37 . . J13
Aster Ln. . . . Pg.40 . . L14
Bernard Dr. . . Pg.39 . . . P9
Birchcreek Ct. Pg.36 . . . L8
Brighton Ct. . . Pg.37 . . L13
Brookview Ln. . Pg.36 . . . K8
California Tr. . Pg.36 . . . J8
Camelot Dr. . Pg.36 . . . J8
Camelot Ln. . . Pg.36 . . . J8
Chisholm Tr. . Pg.36 . . . J8
Circle Dr. . . . Pg.37 . . J11
Creek Crossing Ct.
. . . . . . . . . . Pg.36 . . . K8
Creekview Dr. . Pg.36 . . . K8
Creekwood Dr. Pg.36 . . . K8
Crescent Dr. . Pg.37 . . J13
Dusty Tr. . . . Pg.36 . . . J0
Fenview Ct. . . Pg.36 . . . J8
Fernwood Ct. . Pg.36 . . . K8
Forestview Dr. Pg.37 . . J13
Fun Dr. . . . Pg.39 . . M10
Glenview Dr. . Pg.36 . . . K8
Grant Ave. . . Pg.39 . . . N9
Hancock St. . . Pg.39 . . . N9
Harlem Ave. . Pg.40 . . . N9
Howe Dr. . . . Pg.37 . . J12
Juanita Dr. . . Pg.39 . . . M8
Kaup Ln. . . . Pg.36 . . . J8
Kristoffer Ct. . Pg.36 . . . J8
Kristoffer Ln. . Pg.36 . . . J8
Lakewood Ln. Pg.36 . . . K8
Lee Ave. . . . Pg.39 . . . N9
Logan Ct. . . . Pg.40 . . . N9
Logan St. . . . Pg.40 . . . N9
Lynch Entrance Pg.39 . . . M8
Mark Ln. . . . Pg.36 . . . K8
Maplecreek Dr. Pg.39 . . . M8
McCabe Ct. . . Pg.39 . . . N9
McCabe Dr. . . Pg.39 . . . N9
Meade St. . . . Pg.39 . . . N9

Meadow Ln. . Pg.37 . . L13
Mesquite Dr. . Pg.36 . . . K8
Middle Pinecreek Dr.
. . . . . . . . . . Pg.36 . . . K8
Minetz Ct. . . Pg.36 . . . J8
N. Pinewood Dr.
. . . . . . . . . . Pg.36 . . . J8
Natchez Tr. . . Pg.36 . . . L8
Oak Creek Dr. Pg.36 . . . L8
Oak Hill Dr. . Pg.39 . . . L8
Old Post Rd. . Pg.36 . . . J8
Old Spanish Ct. Pg.36 . . . N8
Old Spanish Tr. Pg.36 . . . N8
Orange Ave. . Pg.39 . . . N9
Oregon Tr. . . Pg.36 . . . J8
Overland Tr. . Pg.36 . . . J8
Park Ln. . . . Pg.37 . . L13
Park Pl. . . . Pg.36 . . N11
Paw Paw Ave. Pg.39 . . . N9
Pear Ave. . . Pg.39 . . . N9
Pinecreek Dr., N.
. . . . . . . . . . Pg.36 . . . J8
Pinecreek Dr., S.
. . . . . . . . . . Pg.36 . . . K8
Pineview Cir. . Pg.36 . . . L8
Pineview Ct. . Pg.36 . . . K8
Pineview Dr. . Pg.36 . . . L8
Pinewood Ct. . Pg.36 . . J,K8
Pinewood Dr., N.
. . . . . . . . . . Pg.36 . . J,K8
Ruggles Ct. . . Pg.36 . . . J8
Santa Fe Tr. . Pg.36 . . . J8
Selva Ln. . . . Pg.37 . . J13
Sherman St. . Pg.39 . . . N9
Silver Ct. . . . Pg.37 . . L13
Silver Lake Dr. Pg.37 . . K13
Southwest Hwy.
. . . . . . . . . . Pg.36 J11,P8
Sprucecreek Ln.
. . . . . . . . . . Pg.36 . . . K8
Stagecoach Rd. Pg.36 . . . J8
Streamwood Dr.
. . . . . . . . . . Pg.36 . . . K8
Stuart Ave. . . Pg.39 . . . N9
Touchstone Pl. Pg.36 . . N10
Valley View Ct. Pg.36 . . . K8
Wolf Rd. . . . Pg.39 . . . N9
Woodlake Ln. . Pg.36 . . . K8
74th Ct. . . . Pg.40 . . L14
77th Ave. . . Pg.40 . . M14
80th Ave. . . Pg.37 . J,O13
81st Ave. . . Pg.37 . . K13
81st Ct. . . . Pg.37 . . K13
82nd Ave. . . Pg.37 . . K13
84th Ave. . . Pg.37 . . K13
92nd Ct. . . . Pg.37 . . K11
94th Ave. . . Pg.40 K,M11
94th Ct. . . . Pg.40 . . O11
96th Ave. . . Pg.40 . . O11
102nd Ave. . . Pg.39 . . O10
104th St. . . . Pg.36 . . . N9
108th Ave. . . Pg.36 . . J,N9
109th Ave. . . Pg.36 . . . L9
110th Ave. . . Pg.36,39 J,O9
110th Ct. . . . Pg.39 . . . O9
112th Ct. . . . Pg.39 . . . M9
113th Ave. . . Pg.39 . . . M9
113th Ct. . . . Pg.39 . . . M9
114th Ave. . . Pg.39 . . . M8
114th Ct. . . . Pg.39 . . . M8
115th Ave. . . Pg.39 . . . M8
115th Ct. . . . Pg.39 . . . M8
116th Ave. . . Pg.39 . . . M8
117th Ave. . . Pg.39 . . . M8
117th Ct. . . . Pg.39 . . . M8
118th Ave. . . Pg.36,37,39
. . . . . . . . . . Pg.36 . . . N8
135th St. . . . Pg.36 . . 8,11
136th St. . . . Pg.37 . . J11
139th St. . . . Pg.38 . . J8,12
143rd St. . . . Pg.36,37
. . . . . . . . . . Pg.37 . . K8,12
145th Pl. . . . Pg.37 . . K13
145th St. . . . Pg.37 . . K11
151st St. . . . Pg.36,37
. . . . . . . . . . Pg.37 . . L8,13
152nd St. . . . Pg.36 . . . L9
153rd St. . . . Pg.40 . . L9
155th St. . . . Pg.36 . . . L9
156th St. . . . Pg.39 . . . M8
157th St. . . . Pg.39 . M8,13
158th St. . . . Pg.39 . . . M9
159th St. . . . Pg.39,40 . . N9
167th Pl. . . . Pg.39,40 . . N8
167th St. . . . Pg.39,40 . . N8
169th St. . . . Pg.39 . . N10
171st St. . . . Pg.39 . O9,10
172nd St. . . . Pg.39 . . . O9
175th St. . . . Pg.39,40
. . . . . . . . . . Pg.37 . . . O9,10
179th St. . . . Pg.39,40 . . P8
183rd St. . . . Pg.39,40 P11

### FOREST PRESERVES
Orland Grove Forest Preserve
. . . . . . . . . . Pg.39 . . . J9

### GOLF COURSES
Silver Lake Country Club
. . . . . . . . . . Pg.37 . . K13

### SHOPPING CENTERS
Pinewood Plaza Pg.36 . . K8

# PALATINE

## PALATINE
Pages 3,7,8

### STREETS

| Street | Pg | Grid |
|---|---|---|
| Abbey Hill Ln. | Pg.7 | D6 |
| Aldridge Ave. | Pg.7 | D6 |
| Alex Ct. | Pg.7 | C6 |
| Allison Dr. | Pg.8 | C9 |
| Almond Ct. | Pg.8 | A9 |
| Alva St. | Pg.7 | B5,6 |
| Amherst St. | Pg.7 | A7 |
| Anderson Dr. | Pg.8 | B8-9 |
| Apple Tree Dr. | Pg.7 | A7 |
| Arbor Ct. | Pg.7 | A4 |
| Arbor Ln. | Pg.7 | A4 |
| Arlene Ave. | Pg.7 | C9 |
| Arrowhead Dr. | Pg.8 | B8 |
| Ash St. | Pg.7 | C6 |
| Ashland Ave. | Pg.8 | C8 |
| Auburn Woods Ct. | | |
|  | Pg.7 | B6 |
| Auburn Woods Dr. | | |
|  | Pg.7 | B6 |
| Aurelia Ct. | Pg.7 | B6 |
| Austin Ln. | Pg.7 | D5 |
| Avondale Dr., W. | | |
|  | Pg.7 | A7 |
| Azalea Ln. | Pg.8 | A9 |
| Babcock Dr. | Pg.8 | C8 |
| Baldwin Ln. | Pg.8 | A9 |
| Baldwin Rd. | Pg.7 | B6-9 |
| Balsam Ln. | Pg.8 | A8 |
| Bank Ct. | Pg.7 | B7 |
| Darberry Ln. | Pg.8 | A9 |
| Baronet Ln. | Pg.8 | D9 |
| Barrington Woods Rd. | | |
|  | Pg.8 | A8 |
| Baybrook Dr. | Pg.8 | C9 |
| Bedford Dr., W. | Pg.7 | D5 |
| Bel Aire Terr. | Pg.8 | B8 |
| Belle Ave. | Pg.7 | C6 |
| Bennett Ave. | Pg.8 | D6 |
| Benton St. | Pg.7 | D7 |
| Big Oaks Rd. | Pg.8 | A8 |
| Birchwood Ave. | Pg.7 | A6 |
| Bishop Ct. | Pg.7 | D5 |
| Bissell Dr. | Pg.8 | C8 |
| Boardwalk Ct. | Pg.7 | D6 |
| Boardwalk Dr. | Pg.7 | D6 |
| Bombay Way | Pg.7 | C6 |
| Bon Aire Dr. | Pg.8 | B8 |
| Borders Ct. | Pg.7 | D5 |
| Bothwell St. | Pg.7 | C7 |
| Boynton Dr. | Pg.7 | C8 |
| Bradley Ct. | Pg.8 | A9 |
| Brandon Ct.(Pvt.) | | |
|  | Pg.7 | B7 |
| Bridgeview St. | Pg.7 | C6 |
| Bridgeview St. | Pg.7 | C6 |
| Brighton Ct. | Pg.7 | D5 |
| Brighton Ln. | Pg.7 | D5 |
| Bristol Ct. | Pg.7 | D5 |
| Broadmoor Ave. | | |
|  | Pg.7 | A6 |
| Brockway St. | Pg.7 | C7 |
| Bryant Ave. | Pg.7 | E6 |
| Burno Dr. | Pg.7 | C6 |
| Cady Dr. | Pg.8 | C8 |
| California St. | Pg.7 | D7 |
| Cambridge Dr., N. | | |
|  | Pg.7 | B6 |
| Candlelit Ln. | Pg.8 | A9 |
| Cardinal Ct. | Pg.8 | A9 |
| Cardinal Dr., N. | Pg.8 | A9 |
| Carlton Ave. | Pg.7 | E6 |
| Carmel Dr. | Pg.8 | B8 |
| Carriageway Ln. | | |
|  | Pg.7 | D6 |
| Carol Ct. | Pg.7 | D6 |
| Carolyn Dr. | Pg.7 | D6 |
| Carpenter Dr. | Pg.7 | B7-9 |
| Carriage Rd. | Pg.8 | A9 |
| Carriageway Ct. | Pg.7 | D6 |
| Carriageway Ln. | | |
|  | Pg.7 | D6 |
| Carter St. | Pg.7 | B6 |
| Castle Ct. | Pg.8 | A9 |
| Castle Ct., E. | Pg.8 | B9 |
| Cavalry Ct. | Pg.8 | A9 |
| Cedar Ave. | Pg.7 | D6 |
| Cedar St. | Pg.7 | D6 |
| Cedarwood Ct. | Pg.7 | A7 |
| Center Rd. | Pg.7 | A7 |
| Center Rd., W. | Pg.8 | A8 |
| Chalary Ct. | Pg.7 | C6 |
| Charlotte St. | Pg.7 | B7 |
| Charter Hall Dr. | Pg.7 | B6 |
| Chatham Dr. | Pg.7 | D5 |
| Cherrywood Dr. | Pg.7 | A6 |
| Cheryl Ln. | Pg.7 | D6 |
| Chesapeake Ct. | Pg.8 | B9 |
| Chesapeake Ln. | Pg.8 | B9 |
| Chestnut St. | Pg.7 | B7 |
| Chewink St. | Pg.7 | B7 |
| Church | Pg.8 | C6 |
| Churchill Dr. | Pg.7 | B9 |
| Citadel Ct. | Pg.7 | A7 |
| Clark Dr. | Pg.8 | C8 |
| Clearwater Ct. | Pg.8 | A9 |
| Clinton Ct. | Pg.7 | D5 |
| Club House Dr. | Pg.8 | C5 |
| Clyde Ave. | Pg.7 | D5 |
| Clyde St. | Pg.7 | C5 |

| Street | Pg | Grid |
|---|---|---|
| Coach Rd. | Pg.8 | A9 |
| Cobblestone Ct. | | |
|  | Pg.7 | B6 |
| Colfax St. | Pg.8 | C8 |
| Comfort St. | Pg.7 | B7 |
| Concord Way | Pg.7 | E6 |
| Consumers Ave. | | |
|  | Pg.8 | D9 |
| Coolidge Ave. | Pg.7 | B5 |
| Cooper. Dr. | Pg.8 | B8 |
| Cornell Ave. | Pg.7 | B6 |
| Cottonwood | Pg.8 | B9 |
| Country Club Ct. | | |
|  | Pg.2 | A-B8 |
| Countryside Dr. | Pg.7 | B5 |
| Cove Dr., N. | Pg.7 | B5 |
| Creekside Dr. | Pg.8 | D8 |
| Creekwood Dr. | Pg.8 | A8 |
| Crescent Ct. | Pg.7 | A7 |
| Crestview Dr. | Pg.7 | B7 |
| Crimson Ln. | Pg.8 | A9 |
| Crooked Willow Ln. | | |
|  | Pg.7 | D6 |
| Crown Ct. | Pg.8 | A9 |
| Cunningham Dr. | | |
|  | Pg.7 | A7,8 |
| Cypress Ln. | Pg.7 | A10 |
| Dartmoor Ave. | Pg.7 | A6 |
| David Dr. | Pg.7 | C6 |
| Dean Dr. | Pg.7 | C8 |
| Deer Ave. | Pg.7 | A5 |
| Deer Ct., W. | Pg.7 | AB5 |
| Deer Run Dr. | Pg.7 | A5 |
| Del Mar Dr. | Pg.7 | A7 |
| Delgado Dr. | Pg.7 | C6-7 |
| Denton Ave. | Pg.7 | A6 |
| Dogwood Ln. | Pg.8 | A9 |
| Doral Ct. | Pg.8 | A9 |
| Dorothy Ct. | Pg.8 | C9 |
| Dorset Ave. | Pg.7 | D5 |
| Dresden Ave. | Pg.7 | A7 |
| Driftwood Ave. | Pg.7 | A7 |
| Drovers Ln. | Pg.7 | C5 |
| Dundee Quarter | Pg.8 | A9 |
| Eagle St. | Pg.7 | B7 |
| Earls Ct. | Pg.7 | A5 |
| Easton Ct. | Pg.7 | A5 |
| Easy St. | Pg.7 | D5 |
| Eaton Ct. | Pg.7 | D5 |
| Echo Ln. | Pg.7 | D6 |
| Edgewater Ct. | Pg.7 | A5 |
| Edgewater Ln. | Pg.7 | A5 |
| Eisenhower Ave. | | |
|  | Pg.8 | B8 |
| Eliabeth Ct. | Pg.8 | C9 |
| Elizabeth Ave. | Pg.8 | C9 |
| Ellis St. | Pg.7 | C6 |
| Elm Ct. | Pg.7 | D6 |
| Elm St. | Pg.7 | C6 |
| Elmwood Ave. | Pg.7 | A,C8 |
| Erie Dr. | Pg.7 | B6 |
| Ethans Glen Dr. | Pg.7 | A5 |
| Euclid Ave. | Pg.7 | C6 |
| Everett St. | Pg.8 | B9 |
| Evergreen Dr. | Pg.7 | C6 |
| Exner Ct. | Pg.7 | D6 |
| Fairfield Ct. | Pg.8 | A9 |
| Fairway Ct. | Pg.7 | B7 |
| Fairway Dr. | Pg.7 | B7 |
| Falkirk Pl. | Pg.8 | A8 |
| Falmore Dr. | Pg.7 | D5 |
| Fawn Ln., E. | Pg.8 | A9 |
| First Bank Dr. | Pg.7 | B7 |
| Flake Dr. | Pg.8 | C8 |
| Forest Ave. | Pg.8 | C8 |
| Forest Ct. | Pg.8 | C7 |
| Forest Knoll Dr. | Pg.8 | A9 |
| Forest View Ct. | Pg.8 | A9 |
| Fosket Dr. | Pg.8 | C8 |
| Foxglove Ln. | Pg.8 | A9 |
| Franklin Ave. | Pg.7 | B6 |
| Fremont St. | Pg.7 | B8 |
| Frontage Rd. | Pg.8 | B9 |
| Garden Ave. | Pg.7 | D6 |
| Gatewood Ave. | Pg.7 | A6 |
| Geri Ave. | Pg.7 | D5 |
| Geri Ct. | Pg.7 | D5 |
| Gilbert Ave. | Pg.7 | B7,D6 |
| Gilbert Rd. | Pg.7 | D6 |
| Glade Ave. | Pg.7 | B7 |
| Glencoe Rd. | Pg.7 | C6 |
| Glencoe St. | Pg.7 | C7 |
| Glenn Dr. | Pg.7 | A8 |
| Glenwood St. | Pg.7 | C7 |
| Gloria Dr. | Pg.7 | C6 |
| Golf Course Dr. | Pg.7 | B6 |
| Golfview Terr. | Pg.7 | C7 |
| Greeley St. | Pg.7 | C7 |
| Greenbrier Ln. | Pg.8 | A9 |
| Greenwood Ave. | | |
|  | Pg.8 | B8 |
| Grissom Dr. | Pg.8 | C8 |
| Gull Ct. | Pg.7 | D5 |
| Haddington Ct. | Pg.7 | B6 |
| Hale St. | Pg.7 | B7 |
| Hamilton Dr. | Pg.7 | A5 |
| Hamilton Ln. | Pg.7 | B6 |
| Hampton Ct. | Pg.7 | D5 |
| Hampton Pl. | Pg.7 | C5 |
| Hancock Ave. | Pg.7 | E5 |
| Harmstead Ct. | Pg.7 | D5 |

| Street | Pg | Grid |
|---|---|---|
| Harrison Ave. | Pg.7 | C5 |
| Harrison St. | Pg.7 | C6 |
| Hart St. | Pg.7 | C6 |
| Harvard Ct. | Pg.7 | D5 |
| Harvard St. | Pg.7 | D5 |
| Hawk St. | Pg.7 | B7 |
| Heather Ln. | Pg.8 | A9 |
| Heatherlea Dr. | Pg.7 | A,B7 |
| Hedgewood Dr. | Pg.8 | B8 |
| Helen Rd. | Pg.7 | C6-7 |
| Heritage Cir. | Pg.8 | A-9 |
| Heron Dr. | Pg.7 | B7 |
| Hickory St. | Pg.7 | C6 |
| Hicks Pl. | Pg.7 | C7 |
| Hicks Rd. | Pg.7 | B7 |
| Hidden Brook Tr. | | |
|  | Pg.7 | E5 |
| Hill Ave. | Pg.7 | B5 |
| Hillcrest Rd. | Pg.7 | A7 |
| Hillside St. | Pg.7 | C6 |
| Home Ave. | Pg.7 | A7 |
| Home Ct. | Pg.8 | A8 |
| Hunting Ct. | Pg.7 | D5 |
| Hunting Dr. | Pg.7 | D5 |
| Illinois Ave. | Pg.7 | D6 |
| Imperial Ct. | Pg.7 | D7 |
| Inverarry | Pg.3 | A10 |
| Jack Pine Dr. | Pg.7 | A5 |
| Jamestown Dr. | Pg.7 | A9 |
| Jane Addams Dr. | | |
|  | Pg.7 | B8 |
| Jennifer Ln. | Pg.7 | B6 |
| Jewel Ct. | Pg.7 | D9 |
| Joan Dr. | Pg.7 | A6 |
| Johnson St. | Pg.7 | C6-7 |
| Jonathan Dr. | Pg.7 | B8 |
| Joyce Ave. | Pg.8 | C9 |
| Juniper Dr. | Pg.8 | A8 |
| Karen Ln. | Pg.7 | B6 |
| Kathleen Dr. | Pg.7 | B6 |
| Kelly Ann Dr. | Pg.7 | D6 |
| Kenilworth Ave. | Pg.7 | C5-9 |
| Kenilworth St. | Pg.7 | C8 |
| Kennedy Dr. | Pg.3 | A10 |
| Kensington Ct. | Pg.7 | D5 |
| Kerry Ct. | Pg.7 | D6 |
| Kerwood St. | Pg.7 | C7 |
| Kimball Ave. | Pg.7 | C6 |
| King Arthur | Pg.7 | A7 |
| King Charles Ct. | Pg.7 | A7 |
| King Edward Ct. | | |
|  | Pg.7 | A7 |
| King George Ct. | Pg.7 | A7 |
| King Henry Ct. | Pg.7 | A7 |
| Kings Row (Pvt.) | | |
|  | Pg.7 | A9 |
| Kitson Dr. | Pg.8 | C8 |
| Knollwood Dr. | Pg.8 | A9 |
| Knox St. | Pg.8 | A8 |
| Krista Ct. | Pg.8 | C9 |
| Krista Ln. | Pg.8 | C8 |
| LaLonda Ave. | Pg.7 | E8 |
| Laguna Ct. | Pg.7 | A5 |
| Lake Dr. | Pg.8 | D8 |
| Lake Louis Dr. | Pg.8 | B9 |
| Lake Rd. | Pg.7 | E5 |
| Lakeshore Dr., N. | | |
|  | Pg.7 | B6 |
| Lakeview Ct. | Pg.7 | A5 |
| Lakeview Dr. | Pg.7 | A5 |
| Lanark Ln. | Pg.7 | D5 |
| Lancelot Ln. | Pg.8 | A9 |
| Lenox Ln. | Pg.8 | A8 |
| Leonard Rd. | Pg.8 | C8 |
| Leonard St. | Pg.7 | C6 |
| Lexington Dr. | Pg.8 | A9 |
| Lincoln St. | Pg.7 | C7 |
| Linden Ave. | Pg.8 | C8 |
| Linden St. | Pg.8 | C8 |
| Long Valley | Pg.8 | A9 |
| Longview Ln. | Pg.7 | D6 |
| Lynn Dr. | Pg.7 | B8 |
| Lytle Dr. | Pg.7 | B8 |
| MacArthur Dr. | Pg.8 | B8 |
| Malibu Ln. | Pg.8 | A9 |
| Mallard Ct. | Pg.7 | D5 |
| Mallard Dr. | Pg.7 | D5 |
| Maple Ave. | Pg.7 | B7 |
| Maple St. | Pg.7 | C6 |
| Marion St. | Pg.8 | C8 |
| Marsha Dr. | Pg.7 | B7 |
| Marshall Ct. | Pg.8 | A9 |
| Mart Ct. | Pg.7 | B6 |
| Meadow Lake Dr., E. | | |
|  | Pg.8 | A8,9 |
| Meadow Ln. | Pg.8 | A9 |
| Medford Dr. | Pg.7 | A7 |
| Merrill Ave. | Pg.7 | C6 |
| Michelle Dr. | Pg.7 | C6 |
| Michigan Ave. | Pg.7 | D5 |
| Middleton Ave. | Pg.7 | D5 |
| Middleton St. | Pg.7 | D5 |
| Mill Valley Rd. | Pg.8 | A8 |
| Minafred Dr. | Pg.8 | C8 |
| Minnesota Ave. | Pg.7 | B6 |
| Monterey Rd. | Pg.8 | B7 |
| Morris Dr. | Pg.7 | A7 |
| Morrison Ave. | Pg.7 | B5 |
| Mozart St. | Pg.7 | C6 |
| Mulligan Ct. | Pg.7 | D5 |
| Newkirk Ln., N. | Pg.8 | B9 |
| Nightingale Dr. | Pg.7 | E5 |
| Norman Dr. | Pg.8 | C9 |

| Street | Pg | Grid |
|---|---|---|
| North Ct. | Pg.7 | B7 |
| North St. | Pg.7 | E5 |
| North St. | Pg.7 | B7 |
| Northumberland Pass | | |
|  | Pg.8 | A8 |
| Northwest Hwy. | Pg.7 | C7 |
| Norway | Pg.7 | A9 |
| Oak Ct. | Pg.7 | C7 |
| Oak Ridge Ct. | Pg.7 | A5 |
| Oak St. | Pg.7 | C7 |
| Old Bridge Rd. | Pg.7 | A5 |
| Old Hicks Rd. | Pg.7 | A7 |
| Old Mill Dr. | Pg.7 | A7 |
| Olde Virginia Ct. | | |
|  | Pg.8 | A8 |
| Olde Virginia Dr., E. | | |
|  | Pg.8 | A8 |
| Olive St. | Pg.8 | D9 |
| Oxford St. | Pg.7 | D7 |
| Paddock Dr. | Pg.7 | D6 |
| Palatine Rd. | Pg.7 | C6-7 |
| Palos Ave. | Pg.7 | A5 |
| Panorama Dr. | Pg.7 | A5 |
| Parallel St. | Pg.7 | C7 |
| Park Ave. | Pg.7 | C8 |
| Park St. | Pg.7 | C8 |
| Parkplace Dr. | Pg.7 | A6 |
| Parkwood Ct. | Pg.7 | D6 |
| Partridge Ct. | Pg.7 | D5 |
| Partridge Dr. | Pg.7 | D5 |
| Patricia Ct. | Pg.7 | D5 |
| Patricia Ln. | Pg.7 | D5 |
| Patten Rd. | Pg.8 | C9 |
| Pebble Creek Rd. | | |
|  | Pg.8 | B8 |
| Pebbles Dr. | Pg.7 | D5 |
| Peder Ln. | Pg.7 | B6 |
| Pendleton Ct. | Pg.7 | A6 |
| Pepper Tree Dr. | Pg.7 | E5 |
| Peregrine Ct. | Pg.7 | E5 |
| Peregrine Dr. | Pg.7 | E5 |
| Pine St. | Pg.7 | C6 |
| Pinehill Ct. | Pg.7 | A6 |
| Pineview Dr. | Pg.7 | C6 |
| Pintail Ct. | Pg.7 | D5 |
| Plate Dr. | Pg.8 | C8 |
| Pleasant Hill Blvd. | | |
|  | Pg.8 | B8 |
| Plum Grove Rd. | Pg.7 | C-D7 |
| Plum Tree Ct. | Pg.7 | E6 |
| Pompano Ln. | Pg.8 | A9 |
| Poplar St. | Pg.7 | A5 |
| Ports O' Call | Pg.8 | A9 |
| Potomac Ln. | Pg.8 | D9 |
| Prairie Brook Dr. | | |
|  | Pg.7 | A9 |
| Pratt Dr. | Pg.8 | B8 |
| Providence Rd. | Pg.8 | A9 |
| Public St. | Pg.7 | A7 |
| Quail Hollow Ln. | | |
|  | Pg.7 | E5 |
| Queens Ln. | Pg.3 | A9 |
| Queensbury Cir. | | |
|  | Pg.7 | E6 |
| Queensbury Ln. | | |
|  | Pg.7 | A9 |
| Quinten Rd. | Pg.7 | C6 |
| Randville Dr. | Pg.7 | B6 |
| Raven Ct. | Pg.7 | D5 |
| Ravine Hills Ct. | Pg.7 | A5 |
| Reading Ct. | Pg.7 | D6 |
| Renaissance Pl. | Pg.7 | B7 |
| Reseda Pkwy. | Pg.7 | A9 |
| Revere Ln. | Pg.7 | E5 |
| Reynolds Dr. | Pg.8 | B9 |
| Richards Dr. | Pg.7 | C9 |
| Richmond St. | Pg.7 | C7 |
| Ridge Tr. | Pg.7 | A6 |
| Rimini Ct. | Pg.7 | B7 |
| Roanoke Ct. | Pg.7 | A7 |
| Robertson Dr. | Pg.7 | B7 |
| Robinson Dr. | Pg.8 | B7 |
| Rohlwing Rd. | Pg.8 | C8 |
| Rose St. | Pg.7 | D7 |
| Roselle Rd. | Pg.7 | E5 |
| Rosewood Ct. | Pg.7 | A5 |
| Rosiland Dr. | Pg.7 | A7 |
| Rosita Dr. | Pg.8 | C9 |
| Royal Ct. | Pg.7 | D7 |
| Ruhl Rd. | Pg.7 | B7 |
| Run Away Bay | Pg.8 | A9 |
| Russet Way | Pg.7 | B7 |
| Saddle Ridge Ct. | | |
|  | Pg.7 | E5 |
| Salem Ct. | Pg.8 | B8 |
| Sanborn Dr. | Pg.8 | C8 |
| Sandpiper St. | Pg.7 | B7 |
| Saratoga Dr. | Pg.7 | B7 |
| Sayles Dr. | Pg.8 | B8 |
| Schiller St. | Pg.7 | C6 |
| Schirra Dr. | Pg.8 | C8 |
| Schubert St. | Pg.7 | A5 |
| Sellstrom Dr. | Pg.7 | C6,D7 |
| Shady Ln. | Pg.8 | A8 |
| Shadypine Ct. | Pg.7 | A7 |
| Sherman St. | Pg.7 | B7 |
| Sherwood Ct. | Pg.8 | A9 |
| Sherwood Dr. | Pg.7 | A7 |
| Shoreside Ct. | Pg.7 | A6 |
| Silver Ln. | Pg.8 | A9 |
| Skylark Ct. | Pg.7 | E5 |
| Skylark Dr. | Pg.7 | E5 |
| Slade St. | Pg.7 | C6-7 |

| Street | Pg | Grid |
|---|---|---|
| Slayton Dr. | Pg.8 | B8 |
| Smith Rd. | Pg.7 | B7 |
| Smith St. | Pg.7 | C7 |
| South Dr. | Pg.7 | F5 |
| Sparrow Ct. | Pg.7 | D5 |
| Spring Willow Bay | | |
|  | Pg.7 | A9 |
| Springwood Dr. | Pg.7 | A8 |
| Spruce Ln. | Pg.8 | A9 |
| St. James Ct. | Pg.7 | C5 |
| St. John's Pl. | Pg.7 | B8 |
| Stark Dr. | Pg.8 | C8 |
| Steeple Chase Ln. | | |
|  | Pg.7 | D5 |
| Stephen Dr. | Pg.7 | B6 |
| Sterling Ave. | Pg.7 | A5 |
| Stonebridge Ct. | Pg.8 | C7 |
| Stonegate Ln. | Pg.7 | D6 |
| Stuart Ln. | Pg.7 | D6 |
| Sunset Rd. | Pg.7 | A7 |
| Sutherland St. | Pg.8 | B8 |
| Suthers Ln. | Pg.7 | A7 |
| Sutton Ct. | Pg.7 | B5 |
| Tahoe Tr. | Pg.8 | B8 |
| Tanglewood Ave. | | |
|  | Pg.7 | A6 |
| Teal Ct. | Pg.7 | D5 |
| Tern Dr. | Pg.7 | D5 |
| Terrace Ct. | Pg.7 | B7 |
| Terrace Dr. | Pg.7 | B7 |
| Thackeray Dr. | Pg.7 | A7 |
| Thomas Ave. | Pg.7 | D9 |
| Thornhill Ln. | Pg.8 | A8 |
| Three Willows Ct. | | |
|  | Pg.7 | B9 |
| Thurston Dr. | Pg.7 | B9 |
| Timber Ln. | Pg.7 | A7 |
| Timberlea | Pg.7 | A7 |
| Topango Dr. | Pg.8 | A-B8 |
| Tower Ct. | Pg.7 | A6 |
| Tower Pl. | Pg.7 | B7 |
| Trailside Ct. | Pg.7 | A6 |
| Turtle Creek | Pg.7 | A6 |
| Tymore | Pg.7 | E6 |
| Valley Ln. | Pg.7 | D6 |
| Valor Ct. | Pg.7 | D9 |
| Ventura Ave. | Pg.8 | B8 |
| Vermont Ave. | Pg.7 | D6 |
| Vermont St. | Pg.7 | D7 |
| Victoria Dr., N. | Pg.8 | B9 |
| Virginia Dr. | Pg.8 | C9 |
| Virginia Lake Ct. | | |
|  | Pg.8 | B9 |
| Wainright Ct. | Pg.8 | A9 |
| Walden Dr. | Pg.7 | B6 |
| Walnut St. | Pg.7 | C6 |
| Wanda Ln.(Pvt.) | | |
|  | Pg.7 | B6 |
| Warren Ave. | Pg.8 | D9 |
| Warwick Rd. | Pg.7 | B9 |
| Washington St. | Pg.7 | C7 |
| Waterbury Cir. | Pg.7 | A7 |
| Wellington Ct. | Pg.7 | A7 |
| Wellington Dr., N. | | |
|  | Pg.7 | A7 |
| Wente | Pg.8 | B8 |
| West Ct. | Pg.7 | B7 |
| Westminster Dr. | Pg.7 | C6 |
| Westmoreland Dr. | | |
|  | Pg.7 | A9 |
| Whippoorwill Ln. | | |
|  | Pg.7 | E5 |
| Whispering Ct. | Pg.8 | A9 |
| Whispering Oaks | | |
|  | Pg.7 | A9 |
| Whitcomb Dr. | Pg.8 | B9 |
| White Willow Bay | | |
|  | Pg.7 | D5 |
| Whitehall Dr. | Pg.7 | C5 |
| Whytecliff Rd. | Pg.7 | D5 |
| Wilke Rd. | Pg.7 | D9 |
| Will Ct. | Pg.7 | D6 |
| Williams Ave. | Pg.7 | D9 |
| Williams Dr. | Pg.7 | B,C9 |
| Williamsburg Dr. | | |
|  | Pg.7 | A9 |
| Willow Ct. | Pg.7 | B8 |
| Willow Ln. | Pg.8 | B8 |
| Willow Walk Dr. | Pg.7 | D5 |
| Willow Wood Dr. | | |
|  | Pg.7 | B8 |
| Wilmette Ave. | Pg.7 | C7 |
| Wilmette St. | Pg.7 | C8 |
| Wilshire Ct. | Pg.7 | A6 |
| Wilson Ct. | Pg.7 | C6 |
| Wilson Dr. | Pg.7 | C6 |
| Wilton Ct. | Pg.7 | B8 |
| Windmill Dr. | Pg.7 | E5 |
| Winnetka St. | Pg.7 | A5 |
| Winslowe Dr. | Pg.8 | A8 |
| Winston Dr. | Pg.7 | C9 |
| Wood St. | Pg.7 | D7 |
| Woodbury Dr. | Pg.7 | A6 |
| Woodland St. | Pg.7 | D7 |
| Woodwork Ln. | Pg.7 | C6 |
| Wren Ave. | Pg.7 | B7 |
| Yale Ct. | Pg.7 | B8 |

### CEMETERIES
| Hilltop Cem. | Pg.7 | B7 |
| Immanuel Lutheran Cem. | Pg.7 | C6 |

### GOLF COURSES
| Palatine Hills G.C. & Rec. Area | Pg.7 | A6 |

### PARKS
| Ashwood Park | Pg.7 | D9 |
| Aspen Park | Pg.8 | A8 |
| Birchwood Park | Pg.7 | D6 |
| Cedar Park | Pg.7 | |
| Cherrywood Park | Pg.7 | B7 |
| Community Park | Pg.7 | C7 |
| Doug Lindberg Park | Pg.8 | B9 |
| Locust Park | Pg.8 | D8 |
| Mallard Park | Pg.8 | D5 |
| Maple Park | Pg.8 | C9 |
| Margreth Riemer Park | Pg.7 | C6 |
| Oak Park | Pg.8 | A9 |
| Osage Park | Pg.8 | A9 |
| Partridge Park | Pg.7 | D5 |
| Peregrine Park | Pg.7 | E6 |
| Sparrow Park | Pg.7 | D5 |
| Sycamore Park | Pg.8 | B8 |
| Tom T. Hamilton Park | Pg.7 | B7 |
| Whippoorwill Park | Pg.7 | |
| Willow Park | Pg.8 | B8 |
| Winston Park | Pg.8 | C9 |

### SCHOOLS
| Christ the King Sch. | Pg.7 | D7 |
| Frank C. Whitley Sch. | Pg.7 | D3 |
| Gray Sanborn Sch. | Pg.7 | |
| Hunting Ridge Sch. | Pg.7 | D5 |
| Immanuel Lutheran Sch. | Pg.7 | C7 |
| Jane Addams Sch. | Pg.8 | B8 |
| Lake Louise Sch. | Pg.8 | B9 |
| Marion Jorden Sch. | Pg.7 | C5 |
| Paddock Sch. | Pg.7 | C6 |
| Palatine H.S. | Pg.8 | A8 |
| Palatine Hills Jr. H.S. | Pg.7 | B6 |
| Pleasant Hills Sch. | Pg.7 | D6 |
| Samuel Kirk Sch. | Pg.7 | D7 |
| Sch. Dist 15 Kiszka Center | Pg.7 | |
| School Dist. 211 | Pg.7 | E5 |
| St. Therese Cath. Sch. | Pg.7 | B7 |
| St. Thomas Cath. Sch. | Pg.8 | B8 |
| Virginia Lake Sch. | Pg.8 | B8 |
| William Fremd Twp. H.S. | Pg.7 | D6 |
| William Rainey Harper College | Pg.7 | E5 |
| Winston Campus | Pg.8 | C8 |

### SHOPPING CENTERS
| Countryside Plaza | Pg.7 | B5 |
| Deer Grove S.C. | Pg.8 | A8 |
| Euro Fresh Plaza | Pg.7 | B7 |
| Northwest S.C. | Pg.7 | A7 |
| Palatine Mall S.C. | | |
| Palatine Plaza | Pg.7 | B7 |
| Park Place Fashion Center | | |
| Prairie Brook Plaza | | |
| Regency Plaza | Pg.7 | E6 |
| Village Oasis S.C. | Pg.7 | B6 |

### MISCELLANEOUS
| Fire Departments | Pg.8 | A8,D7 |
| Library | Pg.7 | B3-4 |
| Palatine Township Office | Pg.7 | D6 |
| Palatine Trail | Pg.7 | A6-B9 |
| Park Dist. Office | Pg.7 | A9 |
| Police Dept. | Pg.7 | C7 |
| Public Works | Pg.7 | D7 |
| St. Joseph's Cath. Home for the Elderly | Pg.7 | B7 |
| Township Road Dist. | | |
| Village Hall | Pg.7 | C7 |

## PALATINE TOWNSHIP
Pages 1-3,6-8,11,12

### STREETS

| Street | Pg | Grid |
|---|---|---|
| Abbeywood Dr. | Pg.3 | A9 |
| Abbotsford Dr. | Pg.6 | B2 |
| Aldridge Ave. | Pg.7 | D6 |
| Almond Ct. | Pg.3 | A9 |
| Almwick | Pg.6 | B2 |
| Alva St. | Pg.7 | B5 |
| Anna Ct. | Pg.2 | A6 |
| Apple Tree Ct. | Pg.7 | A7 |
| Arbor Cove | Pg.7 | B5 |
| Ardmore Ave. | Pg.6 | C3 |
| Arlington Heights Rd. | | |
|  | Pg.3 | A11 |
| Arlington Ln. | Pg.1 | A5 |
| Ashbury Ln. | Pg.7 | E4 |
| Ashland Ave. | Pg.7 | A7 |
| Aster Ave. | Pg.3 | A9 |
| Baldwin Ct. | Pg.8 | A9 |
| Baldwin Ln. | Pg.8 | A9 |
| Baldwin Rd. | Pg.3 | A-B9 |
| Baldwin Way | Pg.3 | A9 |
| Bayer Dr. | Pg.7 | A5 |
| Bayer Rd. | Pg.7 | A6 |
| Bayside Dr. | Pg.3 | A10 |
| Beaumont Ln. | Pg.3 | A9 |
| Bedford Ln. | Pg.3 | A10 |
| Benton St. | Pg.7 | E7 |
| Bloomington Ave. | | |
|  | Pg.3 | A10 |
| Bombay Way | Pg.7 | B5 |
| Bon Hill Dr. | Pg.3 | A9 |
| Bradley Ct. | Pg.3 | A9 |
| Bradwell Ave. | Pg.6 | B3 |
| Brentwood Dr. | Pg.2 | A8 |
| Briar Cove | Pg.7 | B5 |
| Briar Pl. | Pg.1 | A5 |
| Briar Wood Ln. | Pg.1 | F7 |
| Brookdale Ln. | Pg.1 | F7 |
| Brookdale Ln. | Pg.7 | F7 |
| Brookside St. | Pg.7 | C5 |
| Bryant Ave. | Pg.7 | E6 |
| California St. | Pg.7 | E7 |
| Cambridge Ct., N. & S. | | |
|  | Pg.3 | A9 |
| Canterbury Ln. | Pg.3 | A10,B3 |
| Canterbury Tr. | Pg.3 | A10 |
| Capri Dr. | Pg.3 | A9 |
| Carol Ct. | Pg.3 | A9 |
| Carriage Ln. | Pg.3 | A9 |
| Carriage Ln.(Pvt.) | | |
|  | Pg.3 | A9 |
| Cascade Bay | Pg.3 | A10 |
| Chesapeake Ln. | Pg.8 | B8 |
| Circle Dr. | Pg.1 | F7 |
| Circle Ln. | Pg.7 | F7 |
| Clear Creek Bay | Pg.3 | A10 |
| Clyde Ave. | Pg.7 | C5 |
| Colson Ct. | Pg.7 | E7 |
| Colonial Pkwy. | Pg.7 | E8 |
| Conway Bay | Pg.3 | A10 |
| Coolidge Ave. | Pg.7 | B5 |
| Cottonwood Way | | |
|  | Pg.8 | B8 |
| Cove Dr., N. | Pg.7 | B5 |
| Crescent Ave. | Pg.7 | C6 |
| Crestwood Ln. | Pg.7 | F7 |
| Crimson Ln. | Pg.3 | A9 |
| Crooked Creek Tr. | | |
|  | Pg.2 | A6 |
| Crystal Ln. | Pg.3 | A10 |
| Cumnor Rd. | Pg.3 | A4 |
| Cunningham Dr. | | |
|  | Pg.7 | A8 |
| Dee Ln. | Pg.7 | A8 |
| Deer Ave. | Pg.7 | A5 |
| Deer Ln. | Pg.6 | A5 |
| Deerpath Rd. | Pg.2 | A6 |
| Denise Dr. | Pg.7 | A9 |
| Diane Dr. | Pg.2 | A6 |
| Doe Rd. | Pg.7 | A4 |
| Donegal Bay | Pg.3 | A10 |
| Dorchester St. | Pg.7 | C6 |
| Dundee Rd. | Pg.2 | A8-11 |
| Dupont Ave. | Pg.7 | E6 |
| Edgebrook Dr. | Pg.3 | A9 |
| Ela Rd. | Pg.1 | A-F4 |
| Ellis St. | Pg.7 | C6 |
| Elmwood Ln. | Pg.7 | F7 |
| Emerson Ave. | Pg.7 | E6 |
| Enlund Dr. | Pg.3 | A9 |
| Euclid Ave. | Pg.7 | E6 |
| Evergreen Dr. | Pg.8 | A9 |
| Fairfax Ave. | Pg.7 | E7-8 |
| Farm Gate Ln. | Pg.7 | A7 |
| Fern Ct. | Pg.7 | D7 |
| Florence Ave. | Pg.6 | B3-4 |
| Forest Ln. | Pg.7 | E7 |
| Foxwood Ln. | Pg.2 | A6 |
| Frances Ln. | Pg.1 | A5-6 |
| Franklin Ave. | Pg.7 | B6 |
| Frost Rd. | Pg.6 | F4 |
| Galena Ave. | Pg.3 | A10 |
| Galesburg Ave. | Pg.3 | A10 |
| Garden Ct. | Pg.7 | A7 |
| Garden St. | Pg.7 | E7 |
| Gardenia Ln. | Pg.3 | A9 |
| Garfield Ave. | Pg.7 | E7 |
| Gary Dr. | Pg.7 | B6 |

Geneva Dr. . . . . Pg.8 . . . . A9
Geri Ave. . . . . . . Pg.7 . . . . B6
Geri Ct. . . . . . . . Pg.7 . . . . B6
Ginger Cr. Cir. . . Pg.3 . . . . A10
Ginger Cr. Dr. . . Pg.3 . . . . A10
Glavin Ct. . . . . . Pg.3 . . . . A9
Glencoe Rd. . . . Pg.7 . . A5-6,C5
Goodwin Dr. . . . Pg.3 . . . . A10
Grace Ln. . . . . . Pg.1 . . . . A5
Greenwich Ct. . . Pg.7 . . . . F7
Grove Ln. . . . . . Pg.2 . . . . A6
Guthrie Ct. . . . . Pg.6 . . . . A3
Haig Ct. . . . . . . . Pg.3 . . . . A9
Haman Rd. . . . . Pg.6 . . . . C3
Harrison Ave. . . Pg.7 . . . . C5
Hawk Dr. . . . . . Pg.1 . . . . A5
Hawthorne Dr. . Pg.1 . . . . A5
Heatherlea Dr. . Pg.7 . . . . A7
Helen Rd. . . . . . Pg.7 . . . . C6
Heritage Dr. . . . Pg.3 . . . . A9
Hickory Ln. . . . . Pg.7 . . . . F4
Hicks Rd. . . . . . Pg.3 . . . . A9
Hidden Creek Dr.
. . . . . . . . . . . . Pg.3 . . . . A10
Hidden Hill Ln. . Pg.7 . . . . C6
Hidden Oaks Dr.
. . . . . . . . . . . . Pg.2 . . . . A6
Hill Rd. . . . . . . . Pg.7 . . . . A6
Hill St. . . . . . . . Pg.7 . . . . A5
Hillcrest Ct. . . . Pg.1 . . . . A5
Hillcrest Dr. . . . Pg.1 . . . . A5
Hillcrest Terr. . . Pg.1 . . . . A5
Hillside Ave. . . . Pg.7 . . . . C5
Hillside St. . . . . Pg.7 . . . . C5
Holly Way . . . . . Pg.3 . . . . A9
Howe Terr. . . . . Pg.1 . . . . A5
Hudson Bay . . . Pg.3 . . . . A10
Illinois Ave. . . . Pg.7 . . . . D6-7
Inverarry Dr. . . . Pg.3 . . . . A10
Irene Dr. . . . . . . Pg.2 . . . . A8
Iris Dr. . . . . . . . Pg.3 . . . . A9
Isle Royal Cir. . . Pg.3 . . . . A10
Ivy Pl. . . . . . . . . Pg.3 . . . . A9
Jarvis Ct. . . . . . Pg.3 . . . . A9
Jennifer Ln. . . . Pg.3 . . . . A10
Joan Dr. . . . . . . Pg.1 . . . . A6
Jody Ct. . . . . . . Pg.7 . . . . E7
Karen Ln. . . . . . Pg.7 . . . . B6
Kelly Ann Dr. . . Pg.7 . . . . D6
Kenilworth Ave. Pg.7 . . . . C5
Kennedy Dr. . . . Pg.3 . . . . A10
Kevin Ct. . . . . . . Pg.3 . . . . A9
Kimberly Ave. . . Pg.7 . . . . F7
Knollwood . . . . Pg.8 . . . . F8
Knoxboro Ln. . . Pg.2 . . . . A6
LaLonde Ct. . . . Pg.2 . . . . E6
Lake Cook Rd. . Pg.3 . . . . X9
Lakeside Dr. . . . Pg.7 . . . . A6
Laurel Dr. . . . . . Pg.3 . . . . A9
Lee Ct. . . . . . . . Pg.3 . . . . A9
Lenwood Dr. . . . Pg.2 . . . . A8
Leonard St. . . . . Pg.7 . . . . C5
Lilac Dr. . . . . . . Pg.3 . . . . A9
Lilac Pl. . . . . . . . Pg.3 . . . . A9
Lily Ln. . . . . . . . Pg.3 . . . . A9
Linden Ave. . . . Pg.7 . . . . A7
Linden Ln. . . . . Pg.1 . . . . A7
Linder Ln. . . . . . Pg.1 . . . . A5
Little City Dr. . . Pg.7 . . . . F7
Long Acres Ln. . Pg.1 . . . . F8
Long Grove Rd.
. . . . . . . . . . . . Pg.3 . . . . A9
Long Valley . . . Pg.8 . . . . A9
Lorelei Dr. . . . . Pg.1 . . . . A5
Louise Ln. . . . . Pg.2 . . A-B7
Lynda Dr. . . . . . Pg.3 . . . . A9
Mallard Ln. . . . . Pg.3 . . . . A10
Maple Ave. . . . . Pg.7 . . . . B5
Marshall Ct. . . . Pg.3 . . . . A9
Martin Dr. . . . . . Pg.7 . . . . B6
Meadow Ln. . . . Pg.1 . . . . F8
Merrill Ave. . . . . Pg.7 . . . . C6
Middleton Ave. . Pg.7 . . . . C5
Morrison Ave. . . Pg.7 . . . . B5
Mudhank Rd. . . Pg.6 . . . . C1
Myrtle St. . . . . . Pg.7 . . . . B5
Nantucket Ln. . . Pg.2 . . . . A6
New Haven Ave. Pg.3 . . . . A9
Newport Sq. . . . Pg.3 . . . . A10
Nichols Rd. . . . . Pg.3 . . A9,10
North St. . . . . . Pg.7 . . . . A5
Norway . . . . . . Pg.8 . . . . A9
Oak Brook Cir. . Pg.3 . . . . A10
Oak Ct. . . . . . . . Pg.1 . . . . A5
Oaksbury Ln. . . Pg.7 . . . . E7
Oakwood . . . . . Pg.1 . . . . F8
Old Northwest Hwy.
. . . . . . . . . . . . Pg.7 . . . . B5
Olde Virginia Dr.
. . . . . . . . . . . . Pg.8 . . . . A8
Palm Dr. . . . . . . Pg.2 . . . . A6
Palmer Ln. . . . . Pg.3 . . . . A10
Palos Ave. . . . . Pg.7 . . . . A5
Park Ave. . . . . . Pg.7 . . . . A5
Park Dr. . . . . . . Pg.1 . . . . A5
Perry Dr. . . . . . Pg.7 . . . . A6
Pheasant Ln. . . Pg.1 . . . . A5
Pheasant Tr. . . . Pg.3 . . . . A10
Pinehill Ct. . . . . Pg.7 . . . . C5
Plum Grove Rd. Pg.7 . . . . F7
Pondview Dr. . . Pg.7 . . . . B6
Poplar St. . . . . . Pg.7 . . . . A5
Portage Ave. . . Pg.7 . . . . A5

Portsmith Ln. . . Pg.3 . . . . A10
Poteet Ave. . . . Pg.6 . . . . C3
Potomac Ln. . . . Pg.8 . . . . A8
Princeton St. . . Pg.8 . . . . A8
Prospect Dr. . . . Pg.1 . . . . A5
Quail Ct. . . . . . . Pg.3 . . . . A10
Quentin Rd. . . . Pg.2 . . . . A7
Rainbow Bay . . Pg.3 . . . . H15
Rand Rd. . . . . . Pg.3 . . A8-9
Randall Ln. . . . . Pg.3 . . . . A9
Randville Dr. . . . Pg.8 . . . . A8
Ridgewood Ln. Pg.7 . . . . A7
Roberts Rd. . . . Pg.6 . . . . C3
Rosalie Ln. . . . . Pg.3 . . . . A9
Rose Ave. . . . . . Pg.3 . . . . A9
Roslyn Rd. . . . . Pg.1 . . . . A5
Roth Ave. . . . . . Pg.1 . . . . A5
Run Away Bay . Pg.8 . . . . A9
Schaefer Rd. . . Pg.3 . . . . A10
Shadow Lake Terr.
. . . . . . . . . . . . Pg.3 . . . . A10
Shagbark Ct. . . Pg.1 . . . . A5
Shannon Bay . . Pg.3 . . . . A10
Silver Ln. . . . . . Pg.8 . . . . A8
Silver Strand Cir.
. . . . . . . . . . . . Pg.3 . . . . A10
Smith St. . . . . . Pg.7 . . . . E7
Spring Ridge Dr.
. . . . . . . . . . . . Pg.3 . . . . A10
Stephen Dr. . . . Pg.7 . . . . B6
Sterling Ave. . . Pg.7 . . . . B5
Stillwater Ct. . . Pg.1 . . . . A6
Tall Trees Ln. . . Pg.1 . . . . A6
Thorntree Ln. . . Pg.1 . . . . F7
Timberlea Dr. . . Pg.7 . . . . A7
Trail Ridge St. . Pg.3 . . . . A10
Tulip Way . . . . . Pg.3 . . . . A9
Tyne Ct. . . . . . . Pg.6 . . . . B2
Vermillion Ln. . . Pg.3 . . . . A10
Vermont St. . . . Pg.7 . . . . D7
Wainwright Ct. . Pg.3 . . . . A10
Warren Ave. . . . Pg.6 . . . . C3
Waterford Bay . Pg.3 . . . . A10
Weatherstone Rd.
. . . . . . . . . . . . Pg.1 . . . . A6
Wedgewood Dr.
. . . . . . . . . . . . Pg.2 . . . . A6
Westminster Dr.
. . . . . . . . . . . . Pg.7 . . . . B6
Westmoreland Ct.
. . . . . . . . . . . . Pg.3 . . . . A9
Westwood Ln. . Pg.2 . . . . A8
Whispering Ct. Pg.3 . . . . A9
Whispering Oak Ln.
. . . . . . . . . . . . Pg.2 . . . . A6
Whispering Oaks Dr.
. . . . . . . . . . . . Pg.3 . . . . A9
Whispering Sprs. Cir.
. . . . . . . . . . . . Pg.3 . . . . A10
White Gate Ct. Pg.1 . . . . A6
White Sand Bay Pg.3 . . . . A10
White Water Ln.
. . . . . . . . . . . . Pg.3 . . . . A10
Wildwood Ct. . Pg.7 . . . . F7
Wilke Rd. . . . . . Pg.3 . . . . A9
Williamsburg Ct.
. . . . . . . . . . . . Pg.7 . . . . E7
Willow St. . . . . Pg.6 . . C3-5
Wilmette Rd. . . Pg.7 . . . . C5
Wilson St. . . . . Pg.7 . . . . C5
Wind River Terr.
. . . . . . . . . . . . Pg.3 . . . . A10
Winnetka Ave. . Pg.7 . . . . D7
Winnetka St. . . Pg.7 . . . . A5
Winter Haven Ct.
. . . . . . . . . . . . Pg.7 . . . . D6
Wood St. . . . . . Pg.7 . . . . A5
Woodbury . . . . Pg.8 . . . . A9
Woodcliff Ln. . . Pg.7 . . . . A7
Wyndam Cir. . . Pg.8 . . . . A9
Wyndam Ct. . . Pg.8 . . . . A9
Zinnia Ln. . . . . Pg.3 . . . . A9

**CEMETERIES**
St. John's Cemetery
. . . . . . . . . . . . Pg.7 . . E-F5
St. Michael the Archangel
Cemetery . . Pg.7 . . . . F5

**FOREST PRESERVES**
Barrington Woods
. . . . . . . . . . . . Pg.2 . . . . A8
Deer Grove Forest Preserve
. . . . . . . . . . . . Pg.2 . . A6-9
Paul Douglas Forest Preserve
. . . . . . . . . . . . Pg.6 . . E2-4

**GOLF COURSES**
Highland Woods G.C.
. . . . . . . . . . . . Pg.1 . . . . F4

**PARKS**
Lake Park . . Pg.7 . . . . B6

**SCHOOLS**
Lincoln Sch. . Pg.7 . . . . A7
Little City Sch. Pg.7 . . . . A4

**MISCELLANEOUS**
Camp Reinberg Pg.2 . . . . A7

## PALOS HEIGHTS
Pages 37,38

**STREETS**
Aberdeen Ct. . . . . . . . I13
Aberdeen Ln. . . . . . . . I13
Arquilla Dr. . . . . . . . . I14
Auburn . . . . . . . . . . . . H15
Bachelor Grove Rd. . . J15
Bay Rd. . . . . . . . . . . . . G13
Beacon Dr. . . . . . . . . . G13
Brand Ave. . . . . . . . . . H13
Breakwater Way . . . . . G13
Briar Ln. . . . . . . . . . . . I15
Burris Ct. . . . . . . . . . . H15
Canterbury Ct. . . . . . . G14
Carmichael . . . . . . . . . H14
Carol Ln. . . . . . . . . . . . H16
Carriage Tr. . . . . . . . . H14
Cedar Creek Dr. . . . . . G15
Cedar Ln. . . . . . . . . . . I14
Cheyenne Dr. . . . . . . . H15
Chippewa Dr. . . . . . . . G15
Choctaw Rd. . . . . . . . . I14
Coach Rd. . . . . . . . . . . H14
College Dr. Rd. . . . . . . G14
Comanche Dr. . . . . . . . I14
Country Club Ct. . . . . . I14
Country Squire Ct., N. . I14
Country Squire Pl. . . . . H13
Country Squire Rd. . . . . I14
Cypress Ln. . . . . . . . . . I14
Deer Ln. . . . . . . . . . . . I15
Diane Dr. . . . . . . . . . . H14
Dogwood Ln. . . . . . . . H16
Edgewood Dr. . . . . . . . I15
Elm Ct. . . . . . . . . . . . . I14
Evergreen Ave. . . . . . . H15
Flambeau Dr. . . . . . . . I15
Forest Hill Ct. . . . . . . . I14
Forest Hill Dr. . . . . . . . I14
Forest View Rd. . . . . . . I15
Fox Ln. . . . . . . . . . . . . I15
Golf Oak Dr. . . . . . . . . I14
Golfview Ln. . . . . . . . . I15
Harbor Ln. . . . . . . . . . G13
Harlem Ave. . . . . . . . . G14
Harold Ave. . . . . . . . . . H14
Highland Dr. . . . . . . . . I14
Ishnala Dr. . . . . . . . . . I15
Justamere Rd. . . . . . . . K15
Kiowa Ln. . . . . . . . . . . I14
Kirkaldy Ct. . . . . . . . . . I13
Lake Katherine Dr. . . . . G14
Lakeview Ct. . . . . . . . . I13
Lighthouse Ln. . . . . . . G13
Linden Ave., W. . . . . . . H15
London Ln. . . . . . . . . . H14
MacIntosh Dr. . . . . . . . I14
Manitoba Dr. . . . . . . . . H15
Maple Ln. . . . . . . . . . . H15
Melvina Ave. . . . . . . . . H16
Menominee Pkwy. . . . . H15
Misty Meadow Dr. . . . . I13
Nagle Ave. . . . . . . . . . H15
Nashville Ave. . . . . . . . H15
Natchez Ave. . . . . . . . . H15
Natoma . . . . . . . . . . . . H15
Navajo Ct., E & W . . . . H15
Navajo Dr., E & W . . . . H15
Oak Ct. . . . . . . . . . . . . I14
Oak Hills Pkwy. . . . . . . I13
Oak Ln. . . . . . . . . . . . . I14
Oak Park Ave. . . . . . . . H,I15
Oak Ridge Dr. . . . . . . . I14
Oak Ridge Tr. . . . . . . . . I14
Oak Trail Ct. . . . . . . . . G13
Old Georges Ct. . . . . . . I13
Old Oak Tr. . . . . . . . . . G13
Onekema Dr. . . . . . . . . H15
Orchard Dr. . . . . . . . . . H16
Palos Ave. . . . . . . . . . . H14
Park Ln. . . . . . . . . . . . . I15
Parliament Dr., E & W . . I14
Pheasant . . . . . . . . . . I15
Pine Arbor Pl. . . . . . . . H16
Pine Arbor Tr. . . . . . . . H16
Pine Pl. . . . . . . . . . . . . H16
Ponderosa Dr. . . . . . . . I14
Ponderosa Ln. . . . . . . . H14
Potawatomi Ct. . . . . . . H14
Potawatomi Dr. . . . . . . H14
Pueblo Ave. . . . . . . . . I14
Pueblo Ct. . . . . . . . . . . I14
Quail . . . . . . . . . . . . . . I15
Raleigh Ct. . . . . . . . . . G14
Richard Ave. . . . . . . . . H14
Ridgeland Ave. . . . . . . K16
Seagull Ln. . . . . . . . . . G13
Seneca Rd. . . . . . . . . . I14
Sequoia Dr. . . . . . . . . I14
Shawassie Dr. . . . . . . . H15
Shawnee Rd. . . . . . . . . I14
Shoshone Rd. . . . . . . . I14
Sioux Ln. . . . . . . . . . . I14
Sorrento Dr. . . . . . . . . G15
Spruce Pl. . . . . . . . . . . H16
Surrey Hill Ct. . . . . . . . H14
Surrey Hill Rd. . . . . . . H14
Sycamore Ln. . . . . . . . G14
Tennyson Ct. . . . . . . . . G14

Turtle Pond Ln. . . . . . . I13
Ute Ln. . . . . . . . . . . . . I14
Virgil Ave. . . . . . . . . . . G13
West Gate Ave. . . . . . . H15
Westview Dr. . . . . . . . . I13
White Oak Ct. . . . . . . . G13
White Pine Pl. . . . . . . . H14
Willow Wood Dr. . . . . . H16
Winnebago Rd. . . . . . . I14
Worth St. (135th St.) . . I15
Wyandot Dr. . . . . . . . . I14

**CEMETERIES**
Bachelor Grove Cemetery K16

**FOREST PRESERVES**
Bachelor Grove . . . . . . J15
Burr Oak Woods . . . . . J15
Elizabeth A. Conkey F.P. . I16
Rubio Woods . . . . . . . . J15
Tinley Creek Woods . . . J15

**GOLF COURSES**
Oak Hills Golf Course . . H15
Oak Hills Golf Course . . I14
Westgate Valley C.C. . . . I15

**PARKS**
Crawford Park . . . . . . . . I14
Palmer Park . . . . . . . . . G14
Westgate Park . . . . . . . H15

**SCHOOLS**
Arrowhead Sch. . . . . . . H15
Chicago Christian H.S. . G15
Independence Jr. H.S. . . I15
Navajo Hts. Sch. . . . . . H15
Palos East Sch. . . . . . . H15
Palos Heights Sch. . . . . H15
Palos Lutheran Sch. . . . H15
Palos South Jr. H.S. . . . I13
St. Alexander Sch. . . . . H15
Stone Church Christian
Acad. . . . . . . . . . . . . H16
Trinity Christian College . H15

**SHOPPING CENTERS**
Indian Trails S.C. . . . . . H15
Shopping District . . . . . H14

**MISCELLANEOUS**
Campos Falcon & Sullivan . K15
City Hall . . . . . . . . . . . . H15
Fire Department . . . . . . H14
Hospital . . . . . . . . . . . . G14
Library . . . . . . . . . . . . . H14
Palos Community Hosp. . H13
Police Station . . . . . . . . G14

## PALOS HILLS
Page 34

**STREETS**
Alta Dr. . . . . . . . . . . . . E13
Arrowhead Dr. . . . . . . . D12
Aspen Dr. . . . . . . . . . . E12
Avon Ct. . . . . . . . . . . . F12
Bennett Dr. . . . . . . . . . F12
Boulder Ct. . . . . . . . . . E13
Breckenridge Dr. . . . . . E13
Broadmoor Dr. . . . . . . . E13
Brook Lodge Ln. . . . . . . E13
Cambridge Ct. . . . . . . . D12
Carlton Ct. . . . . . . . . . . F12

Catherine Dr. . . . . . . . . F13
Center Rd. . . . . . . . . . . F12
Chamonieux Ct. . . . . . . E13
Charles Ave. . . . . . . . . . E13
Cherry Ct. . . . . . . . . . . . F13
Chestnut Dr. . . . . . . . . F13
Christa Ct. . . . . . . . . . . E13
Cinnamon Creek Dr. . . . D12
Circle Ct. . . . . . . . . . . . F13
Circle Ct. . . . . . . . . . . . F13
Circle Dr. . . . . . . . . . . . F13
Cobblestone Ct. . . . . . . E13
Cork Rd. . . . . . . . . . . . . D12
Cottonwood Dr. . . . . . . F13
Cour Caravelle . . . . . . . F12
Cour D'Alene . . . . . . . . E13
Cour De LaReine . . . . . F12
Cour Deauville . . . . . . . F12
Cour LaSalle . . . . . . . . F12
Cour LeRoux . . . . . . . . F13
Cour Madeleine . . . . . . F12
Cour Marquis . . . . . . . . F12
Cour Masson . . . . . . . . G12
Cour Michele . . . . . . . . E13
Cour Monnet . . . . . . . . F12
Cour Montreal . . . . . . . E12
Cour St. Tropez . . . . . . D12,13
Cour Versaille . . . . . . . . F12
Dartmouth Rd. . . . . . . . E12
Deerpath Ln. . . . . . . . . F13
Del Prado Ln. . . . . . . . . D12
Doric Cir. . . . . . . . . . . . E13
East Rd. . . . . . . . . . . . . F12
Eastwood Dr. . . . . . . . . F14
Eleanor Ave. . . . . . . . . E13
Erin Dr. . . . . . . . . . . . . D13
Gladys Ln. . . . . . . . . . . D13
Granada Ct. . . . . . . . . . E12
Green Valley Dr. . . . . . . E12
Gruener Ct. . . . . . . . . . F13
Harlem Ave. . . . . . . . . . G14
Helena Dr. . . . . . . . . . . E12
Heritage Dr. . . . . . . . . . E12
Hickory Crest Ct. . . . . . F13
Holly Ct. . . . . . . . . . . . . F13
Interlochen Ct. . . . . . . . E12
Interlochen Dr. . . . . . . . E12
Juniper Ct. . . . . . . . . . . F13
Kathy Ct. . . . . . . . . . . . E14
Kean Ave. . . . . . . . . . . F13
Kingsbury Ct. . . . . . . . . D12
Lori Ln. . . . . . . . . . . . . E13
Los Palos Ln. . . . . . . . . D12
Loveland Ln. . . . . . . . . E12
Lucas Dr. . . . . . . . . . . . F12
Maple Crest Ct . . . . . . . D12
Meadow Ln. . . . . . . . . . F13
Meryton Ct. . . . . . . . . . D12
Michael Dr. . . . . . . . . . E14
Mill Stone Ct. . . . . . . . . F12
Moraine Dr. . . . . . . . . . F13
Mulberry Ln. . . . . . . . . . F13
North Rd. . . . . . . . . . . . F12
Northwest Rd. . . . . . . . F12
O'Gorman . . . . . . . . . . F12
Oak Crest Ct. . . . . . . . . D12
Oconto Ct. . . . . . . . F13,14
Olympia Cir. . . . . . . . . . F13
Palos Dr. . . . . . . . . . . . F13
Palos Rd. . . . . . . . . . . . F13
Peak Dr. . . . . . . . . . . . . F13
Pebble Ct. . . . . . . . . . . F12
Pemberly Ct. . . . . . . . . D12
Poplar Ln. . . . . . . . . . . F12
Possum Dr. . . . . . . . . . F12
Roberta Rd. . . . . . . . . . F13
Sheffield Dr. . . . . . . . . . E13
Sierra Ln. . . . . . . . . . . . D12
South Hill . . . . . . . . . . . E12
South Rd. . . . . . . . . . . . H12
Southwest Hwy. . . . . . . F14
Spathis . . . . . . . . . . . . . F12
Stone Bridge Ct. . . . . . . F12
Stoney Creek Dr. . . . . . F13
Stowe Ct. . . . . . . . . . . . F12
Stratford Ln. . . . . . . . . . D12
Sun Valley Ct. . . . . . . . . F12
Sun Valley Dr. . . . . . . . . F12
Surry Park . . . . . . . . . . . D12
Sycamore Ln. . . . . . . . . F13
Taos . . . . . . . . . . . . . . . E12
Terry Dr. . . . . . . . . . . . . E14
Theresa Cir. . . . . . . . . . F13
Tod Dr. . . . . . . . . . . . . . E13
Tuttle Ct. . . . . . . . . . . . F12
Vail Dr. . . . . . . . . . . . . . D13
Valley Dr. . . . . . . . . . . . F13
Valley Rd. . . . . . . . . . . . F13
Vicky Ln. . . . . . . . . . . . E13
Walnut Terr. . . . . . . . . . I11
Westwood Dr. . . . . . . . F13
Willow . . . . . . . . . . . . . F13
Windsor Dr. . . . . . . . . . D12
Winter Park Dr. . . . . . . . E12
Wood Ln. . . . . . . . . . . . D13
Wooded Path Dr. . . . . . D12
Zermatt Dr. . . . . . . . . . E13
73rd Ave. . . . . . . . . . . . E14
73rd Ct. . . . . . . . . . . . . E14
74th Ave. . . . . . . . . . . . E14
75th Ave. . . . . . . . . . . . E14
75th Ct. . . . . . . . . . . . . E14
76th Ave. . . . . . . . . . E,F14
78th Ave. . . . . . . . . . . . F14

80th (Roberts Rd.) Ave. . D13
80th Ct. . . . . . . . . . . . . E13
81st Ave. . . . . . . . . . . . D13
81st Ct. . . . . . . . . . . . . D13
81st St. . . . . . . . . . . . . E13
82nd Ave. . . . . . . . . . . . D13
83rd Ave. . . . . . . . . . . . E13
83rd Ct. . . . . . . . . . . . . E13
84th Ave. . . . . . . . . . E,F13
84th Terr. . . . . . . . . . . . E13
85th Ave. . . . . . . . . . . . F13
86th Ave. . . . . . . . . . E,F12
86th Ct. . . . . . . . . . . . . F12
86th St. . . . . . . . . . . . . F12
86th Terr. . . . . . . . . . . . F12
87th Ave. . . . . . . . . . . . E12
87th Ct. . . . . . . . . . . . D,E12
88th Ave. . . . . . . . . . . . F12
89th Ave. . . . . . . . . . . . D12
90th Ave. . . . . . . . . . . . E12
96th Pl. . . . . . . . . . . . . D12
96th St. . . . . . . . . . . . . D12
97th Ave. . . . . . . . . . . . D12
97th Pl. . . . . . . . . . . . . D12
97th St. . . . . . . . . . . D12,13
98th St. . . . . . . . . . . D12,13
99th Pl. . . . . . . . . . . D12,13
99th St. . . . . . . . . . . . . D12
99th Terr. . . . . . . . . . . . D12
100th Pl. . . . . . . . . . D13,E12
100th St. . . . . . . . . . D12,13
100th Terr. . . . . . . . . . . D12
101st Pl. . . . . . . . . . E12,13
101st St. . . . . . . . . . E12,13
101st Terr. . . . . . . . . . . E12
102nd Pl. . . . . . . . . . . . E12
102nd St. . . . . . . . . . E12,13
102nd Terr., W. . . . . . . . E12
103rd Pl. . . . . . . . . . . . . E12
103rd St. . . . . . . . . . . . E12
103rd Terr. . . . . . . . . . . E12
104th Pl. . . . . . . . . . E12,13
104th St. . . . . . . . . . . . E12
105th St. . . . . . . . . . E12-14
106th St. . . . . . . . . . . . E13
107th St. . . . . . . . . . . . E14
108th St. . . . . . . . . . . . F13
111th Pl. . . . . . . . . . . . . F13
111th St. . . . . . . . . . . . F11
112th Pl. . . . . . . . . . . . . F13
112th St. . . . . . . . . . . . F13
113th Pl. . . . . . . . . . . . . F13
113th St. . . . . . . . . . . . F13

**CEMETERIES**
Calvary Mem. Cemetery . . F13

**GOLF COURSES**
Palos Hills G.C. . . . . . . E14

**PARKS**
Aspen Park . . . . . . . . . E12
Atman Park . . . . . . . . . G14
Calvary Park . . . . . . . . . F13
Holerding Park . . . . . . . G15
Indiana Woods . . . . . . . D13
Krasowski Park . . . . . . . E13
Loveland Park . . . . . . . . E12
Michael Dr. Park . . . . . . E14
Penny Park . . . . . . . . . . G15
Senior Park . . . . . . . . . . E12
Smile Park . . . . . . . . . . F15
Stanick Park . . . . . . . . . F15
Volunteer Park . . . . . . . D12

**SCHOOLS**
Amos Alonzo Stagg H.S. . F12
Moraine Valley Comm.
College . . . . . . . . . . . F12
Oak Ridge Sch. . . . . . . F12
Quinn Sch. . . . . . . . . . . E13
Worth Main Sch. . . . . . . F15

**MISCELLANEOUS**
Charles Christianson Center
. . . . . . . . . . . . . . . . G14
City Hall . . . . . . . . . . . . E13
Fire Department . . . . . . E13
Village Hall . . . . . . . . . . F12

## PALOS PARK
Pages 34,36,37

**STREETS**
Algoma Dr. . . . . . . . . . H12
Algonquin Rd. . . . . . . . H13
Alpine Ave. . . . . . . . . . I13
Autobahn Dr. . . . . . . . . H13
Black Forest Ln. . . . . . . G13
Black Walnut Tr. . . . . . . I11
Brand Ave. . . . . . . . . . . H13
Brook Ln. . . . . . . . . . . . H13
Calumet Sag Rd. . . . . . G11
Cherokee Rd. . . . . . . . . H13
Commons Dr. . . . . . . . . H13
Danmar Tr. . . . . . . . . . . H9
Deer Ct. . . . . . . . . . . . . H13
Edelweiss Dr. . . . . . . . . H13
Edgewater Ln. . . . . . . . H11
Eldridge Ave. . . . . . . . . H12
Elm St. . . . . . . . . . . . . . H12
Forest Glen Blvd. . . . . . H12
Forestview Ln. . . . . . . . H12
Fox Ln., N. & S. . . . . . . H9

Highwood Dr. . . . . . . . G13
Hillcrest Ln. . . . . . . . . . H12
Hillside Cir. . . . . . . . . . H13
Hillside Dr. . . . . . . . . . H13
Hobart Ave. . . . . . . . . . H11
Holmes Ave. . . . . . . . . G13
Huntleigh Rd. . . . . . . . H9
Iroquois Rd. . . . . . . . . . H13
Kean Ave. . . . . . . . . . . G12
Kimber Ln. . . . . . . . . . . G13
Kinvarra Dr. . . . . . . . . . H11
Knollwood Dr. . . . . . . . G13
Lakewood Ave. . . . . . . G12
Laurie Ave. . . . . . . . . . G12
McCarthy Rd. . . . . . . . . H8
McKinley Ave. . . . . . . . H11
Meadow Rd. . . . . . . . . . H8
Mill Rd. . . . . . . . . . . . . I11
Mission Dr. . . . . . . . . . H10
Mohawk Rd. . . . . . . . . . H13
Oak Ln. . . . . . . . . . . . . H13
Oak Ridge Dr. . . . . . . . H13
Old Creek Rd. . . . . . . . . H8
Old Prague Path . . . . . . G13
Old Timber Ln. . . . . . . . H9
Palos Ave. . . . . . . . . . . G13
Parklane Dr. . . . . . . . . . H10
Partridge Ln. . . . . . . . . H8
Pawnee Rd. . . . . . . . . . H12
Post Rd. . . . . . . . . . . . . H9
Rail Ln. . . . . . . . . . . . . . H9
Ramsgate Dr. . . . . . . . . H8
Regina Ln. . . . . . . . . . . H13
Ridge Ave. . . . . . . . . . . H12
Roberts Rd. . . . . . . . . . G12
Roma Rd. . . . . . . . . . . . H12
Romiga Ln. . . . . . . . . . . H9
Rosewood Ave. . . . . . . H12
Seminole Rd. . . . . . . . . H13
Somerset Ln. . . . . . . . . H11
South St. . . . . . . . . . . . G12
Spring Dr. . . . . . . . . . . H13
St. Moritz Dr. . . . . . . . . G13
Sunnyslope Rd. . . . . . . H9
Timber Ln. . . . . . . . G,H13
Vienna Ave. . . . . . . . . . G13
Walnut Ridge . . . . . . . . I13
Wild Cherry Ln. . . . . . . H11
Wildwood Tr. . . . . . . . . H9
Windsor Dr. . . . . . . . . . H11
Winslow Rd. . . . . . . . . . G13
Wolf Rd. . . . . . . . . . . . . K9
Woodland Trail, N & S . . H13
79th Ave. . . . . . . . . . . . H13
80th Ave. . . . . . . . . . . . H13
81st Ave. . . . . . . . . . . . H13
81st Ct. . . . . . . . . . . . . I13
82nd Ave., S. . . . . . . . . G13
82nd Ct. . . . . . . . . . . . . G13
82nd Ct., S. . . . . . . . . . G13
83rd Ave., S. . . . . . . . G,H13
84th Ave. . . . . . . . . . . . G13
85th Ave. . . . . . . . . . . . H13
86th Ave. . . . . . . . . . G12,H13
87th Ave. . . . . . . . . . . . H12
88th Ave. . . . . . . . . . . . H13
89th Ave. . . . . . . . . . . . H11
89th Ave., W. . . . . . . . . H13
89th Ct., W. . . . . . . . . . G12
90th Ave. . . . . . . . . . . . G13
90th Ct. . . . . . . . . . . G,H12
91st Ave. . . . . . . . . . . . G13
92nd Ave. . . . . . . . . . . H12
93rd Ave. . . . . . . . . . . . H11
94th Ave. . . . . . . . . . . . G13
100th Ave. . . . . . . . . . . H10
108th Ave. . . . . . . . . . . H9
109th Ave. . . . . . . . . . . H9
114th Ave. . . . . . . . . . . H9
115th Ave. . . . . . . . . G13,H8
116th St. . . . . . . . . . . . G13
117th St. . . . . . . . . . . . G13
118th St. . . . . . . . . . . . G12
119th Pl. . . . . . . . . . . . . G12
119th St. . . . . . . . . . . . G13
120th St. . . . . . . . . . G11-13
121st St. . . . . . . . G11,12,H13
122nd St. . . . . . . . . . H11,12
123rd Pl. . . . . . . . . . . . . H8
123rd St. . . . . . . . . . . . H11
124th St. . . . . . . . . . . H12,13
125th St. . . . . . . . . . . H12,13
126th St. . . . . . . . H10,12,13
127th St. . . . . . . . . . . H10-12
128th St. . . . . . . . . . . . I13
129th St. . . . . . . . . . . . I13
131st St. . . . . . . . . . . . . I11

**CEMETERIES**
Palos Oak Hill Cemetery . . I12

**FOREST PRESERVES**
Forty Acres Woods . . . . G11
Paddock Woods . . . . . . G12
Palos Park Woods . . . . . G12
Swallow Cliff Woods . . . G11
Swallow Cliffs . . . . . . . . G10

**SCHOOLS**
Palos School . . . . . . . . G12

**MISCELLANEOUS**
Library . . . . . . . . . . . . . H12
Village Hall . . . . . . . . . . H12
Winter Sports Area . . . . G11

## PALOS TOWNSHIP

Pages 33,34,36,37

**STREETS**

Adist Rd. .... Pg.36 ... I10
Ambrose Ct. . Pg.36 .... I9
Ambrose Dr. . Pg.36 .... I9
Arlington Ct. . Pg.36 ... I10
Bayberry Ct. . Pg.36 ... H10
Bennet Ct. ... Pg.36 .... I9
Bennet Dr. ... Pg.36 .... I9
Bernice Dr. .. Pg.36 ... I10
Birchwood Dr. Pg.36 ... H10
Bishop Ct. ... Pg.36 ... I10
Bloomfield Dr. Pg.36 ... I10
Blue Heron Dr. Pg.36 .... I9
Brian Pl. .... Pg.36 ... I11
Brittany Dr. .. Pg.36 .... I9
Brodt Dr. .... Pg.36 ... I10
Bruckner Ct. . Pg.36 .... J9
Bruckner Dr. . Pg.36 .... J9
Calumet Sag Rd.
.......... Pg.34 ... F10
Carriage House Ln.
.......... Pg.36 .... J9
Chadwick Ct. . Pg.36 .... I9
Chadwick Dr. . Pg.36 .... I9
Charlotte Ct. . Pg.36 .... I9
Cherrywood Dr. Pg.36 ... H10
Circle Pkwy. .. Pg.36 ... I11
Corelli Ct. .... Pg.36 .... I9
Cornell Ln. .. Pg.37 ... I13
Country Manor Ln.
.......... Pg.36 .... I9
Creek Rd. .... Pg.36 ... I11
Deerwood Dr. Pg.37 ... H13
Edgewater Ln. Pg.36 ... H11
Elridge Ave. .. Pg.37 ... G12
Farmhill Ave. . Pg.37 ... I13
Farmhill Ln. .. Pg.37 ... H13
Fiedman Ct. .. Pg.36 .... I9
Fitzsimmons Dr.
.......... Pg.36 ... I10
Flavin Rd. .... Pg.33 ... C10
Ford Rd. .... Pg.36 ... G8
Frances Ct. .. Pg.36 .... I9
Georgetown Dr.
.......... Pg.36 .... I9
Glen Rd. .... Pg.36 .... G8
Grandview ... Pg.36 ... H10
Haas Dr. .... Pg.36 .... H9
Hampton Ct. . Pg.36 .... I9
Hampton Rd. . Pg.36 .... I9
Hillcrest Dr. .. Pg.36 I13,J10
Holmes Ave. . Pg.37 ... G13
Holmes Dr. .. Pg.36 .... I9
Indian Trail Dr. Pg.36 ... H10
Joseph Dr., W. Pg.36 ... H10
Kean Ave. .... Pg.37 ... G12
Ketelby Ct. .... Pg.36 .... I9
Kilbilly Ct. .... Pg.36 ... I10
Laflin Ct. .... Pg.36 ... I10
Lake Trail Dr. . Pg.36 ... H10
Lakeland Dr. . Pg.36 ... H10
Lakeview Ct. . Pg.36 ... I10
Lansford Dr. . Pg.36 .... J9
Longwood Ct. Pg.37 ... I13
Lucille Ln. ... Pg.36 ... H10
Lynnwood Ct. Pg.36 .... I9
Maple Ave. .... Pg.33 ... C8
McCarthy Rd. Pg.36 ... H8
Meadowlark Dr. Pg.37 ... I13
Meed Ct. .... Pg.36 .... I9
Mill Rd. ..... Pg.36 ... I11
Mission Dr. .. Pg.36 ... H10
Newport Dr. .. Pg.36 ... I10
Nielsen Ct. ... Pg.36 .... I9
Northbridge Ct. Pg.36 .... J9
Northbridge Dr. Pg.36 .... J9
Oak Grove ... Pg.33 ... C8
Oakwood Dr. . Pg.36 ... H10
Paloma Dr. .. Pg.37 ... I13
Palos West Dr. Pg.36 ... H9
Parkside Dr. .. Pg.36 ... I10
Parkview Dr. . Pg.36 ... H10
Pauline Ct. ... Pg.37 ... I13
Peace Memorial Dr. (Pvt.)
.......... Pg.36 ... I10
Pebble Dr. ... Pg.36 ... H11
Poloma Dr. .. Pg.37 ... I13
Powell Rd. ... Pg.36 ... H10
Prairie View Dr. Pg.36 ... H10
Public St. .... Pg.33 .... C9
Railroad Ave. (91st St.)
.......... Pg.33 .... C8
Richmond Ct. Pg.36 .... I9
Ridgewood Dr. Pg.36 ... I10
Sandburg Ct. . Pg.36 ... I10
Sedwick Dr. .. Pg.36 .... H9
Sheffield Ct. .. Pg.36 .... H9
Southwest Hwy. Pg.37 ... I12
St. Joseph Dr. Pg.36 ... I10
Stephen Dr. .. Pg.36 ... I10
Suffield Dr. .............. G3
Surrey Ct. ... Pg.36 ... I11
Tanglewood Cir., E. & W.
.......... Pg.36 ... I10
Tanglewood Ct. Pg.36 ... I10
Timber Edge Ln.
.......... Pg.36 ... H10
Walter Dr. ... Pg.36 ... I10
Watson Ct. ... Pg.36 .... I9
Westport Dr. . Pg.36 ... I10
Whispering Lake Dr.
.......... Pg.36 ... H10
Wildwood Dr. Pg.36 ... H10
Will-Cook Rd. Pg.36 .... K8
Windward Tr. Pg.37 ... I13
Wisteria Ct. .. Pg.36 ... H10
Wolf Rd. .... Pg.36 .... I9
76th Ave. .... Pg.37 ... I14
80th Ave. (Roberts Rd.)
.......... Pg.37 ... H13
80th Ct. ..... Pg.37 ... I13
81st Ct. ..... Pg.37 ... I13
82nd Ave., S. Pg.37 ... I13
82nd Ct. .... Pg.37 ... I13
83rd Ave., S. . Pg.37 ... I13
83rd Ct. .... Pg.37 ... I13
84th Ave., S. . Pg.37 ... I13
84th Ct. .... Pg.37 ... I13
84th St. .... Pg.37 ... I13
85th Ave. .... Pg.37 ... I13
85th Ct. .... Pg.37 ... I12
86th St. .... Pg.37 ... I12
87th Ave. .... Pg.37 ... H12
88th Ave. .... Pg.37 ... I12
92nd St. .... Pg.37 ... H12
95th St. .... Pg.33 ... D9
96th Ave. .... Pg.34 ... I11
104th Ave. ... Pg.36 .. F,I10
107th St. .... Pg.33 ... E8
108th Ave. ... Pg.36 ... I,J9
111th St. .... Pg.33,34F8,11
114th Ave. .... Pg.33 ... C8
116th Ct. .... Pg.37 ... G13
117th St. .... Pg.37 ... G13
118th St. .... Pg.36 ... G8
119th St. .... Pg.37 ... G11
125th St. .... Pg.36 ... H10
127th St. .... Pg.37 H11,12
128th Pl. .... Pg.37 ... I13
129th Pl. .... Pg.37 . I12,13
129th St. .... Pg.37 . I12,13
130th St. .... Pg.36
.............. I10,12,13
131st Pl., W. . Pg.37 ... I12
131st St. .... Pg.36 .... I9
132nd St. .... Pg.37 ... I13
133rd St. .... Pg.37 .. I9,13
134th St. .... Pg.36 ... I10
135th St. .... Pg.36 .... J9

**CEMETERIES**

Willow Hills Memorial Park
.......... Pg.33 .... D9

**FOREST PRESERVES**

Cherry Cliff Woods
.......... Pg.36 ... G10
Country Lane Woods
.......... Pg.33 ... D11
Delony Woods Pg.33 .... D8
Forty Acres Woods
.......... Pg.37 ... G11
Hidden Pond Woods
.......... Pg.33 ... D11
McMahon Woods
.......... Pg.33 ... F10
Paddock Woods
.......... Pg.37 ... G12
Palos Park Woods
.......... Pg.37 ... G12
Paw Paw Woods
.......... Pg.33 .... C9
Pioneer Woods Pg.33 ... E10
Red Cats Woods
.......... Pg.33 .... D8
Spears Woods Pg.33 ... C11
Swallow Cliff Woods
.......... Pg.36 ... G10
Teasons Woods
.......... Pg.36 ... G10
White Oak Woods
.......... Pg.33 ... E11
Willow Springs Woods
.......... Pg.33 ... C10

**GOLF COURSES**

Oak Hill G.C. . Pg.37 ... I14
Palos C.C. ... Pg.37 ... I11

**SCHOOLS**

Carl Sandburg H.S.
.......... Pg.36 ... I11
Kennedy Sch. for Exceptional
Children ... Pg.36 ... H9
Palos Sch. ... Pg.37 ... G12
Palos South Jr. H.S.
.......... Pg.37 ... I13
Palos West Sch. Pg.36 ... H10

**MISCELLANEOUS**

Kiwanis Scout Camp
.......... Pg.33 ... D10
Little Red School House
.......... Pg.33 ... E10
Winter Sports Area
.......... Pg.33 ... G11

## PARK FOREST

Pages 47,48

**STREETS**

Algonquin St. ........ V22
Allegheny Ct. ........ V23
Allegheny St. ........ V23
Antietam St. ........ U22
Antioch Pl. ........ V22
Apache St. ........ V23
Apple Ct. ........ W21
Apple Ln. ........ W21
Arbor Tr. ........ X22
Arcadia St. ........ V22
Arrowhead Ct. ........ V23
Arrowhead St. ........ V22
Ash St. ........ V22
Bailey Rd. ........ V22
Bay View Dr. ........ V17
Bender Rd. ........ V22
Berry St. ........ U21
Bertoldo Rd. ........ V22
Bigelow Rd. ........ V22
Birch St. ........ V22
Blackhawk Dr. ........ W20
Blair St. ........ U20
Brook Ave. ........ V17
Cedar St. ........ W22
Central Park Ave. ........ W20
Chase St. ........ U20
Cheer Skill Way ........ U21
Cherry St. ........ W21
Chestnut Ct. ........ W22
Chestnut St. ........ W22
Choate Rd. ........ V22
Cromwell Rd. ........ W22
Davis St. ........ U20
Dogwood St. ........ W22
Douglas St. ........ U21
Dunham Rd. ........ W22
Dunlap Rd. ........ W22
Early St ........ U21
Elm St. ........ V21
Farragut St. ........ U21
Fir St. ........ V21
Forest Blvd. ........ V21
Garman Rd. ........ W22
Gentry St. ........ U21
Gerstung Rd. ........ V22
Gettysburg St. ........ U20
Gibson Rd. ........ V22
Gold St. ........ V21
Grant St. ........ U21
Green St. ........ V21
Hamlin St. ........ U21
Hay St. ........ U21
Hemlock St. ........ W22
Herndon St. ........ U21
Hickory Ct. ........ U20
Hickory St. ........ U20
Homan Ave. ........ U20
Homan Cir. ........ U20
Huron St. ........ W20
Illinois Ct. ........ U21
Illinois St. ........ U21
Indiana St. ........ U21
Iroquois St. ........ W21
Jackson St. ........ U20
Juniper St. ........ V21
Kentucky Ct. ........ U21
Kentucky St. ........ U21
Krotiak Rd. ........ V21
Lakewood Blvd. ........ V21
Lakewood Ct. ........ V20
Larue St. ........ U21
Lee St. ........ U21
Leims Rd. ........ W21
Lester Rd. ........ W21
Manitowac St. ........ W21
Mantua Ct. ........ W20
Mantua St. ........ W21
Marquette Pl. ........ W21
Marquette St. ........ W20
McCarthy Rd. ........ W22
McGarity Rd. ........ W21
Meadow Lake Ct. ........ V17
Meadow Lake Dr. ........ V17
Meota St. ........ W21
Merrimac St. ........ W21
Miami St. ........ W20
Michael Rd. ........ W22
Minocqua Ct. ........ W21
Minocqua St. ........ W20
Mohawk St. ........ W20
Monee Rd. ........ W20
Monitor St. ........ U21
Nashua St. ........ W20
Nassau Ct. ........ W21
Nassau St. ........ W21
Neloa St. ........ W21
Neptune Ln. ........ V17
New Salem St. ........ U21
Niagara St. ........ W21
Nokomis St. ........ W21
North St. ........ U21
Norwood Blvd. ........ V21
Oak Ln. ........ W22
Oakwood St. ........ W21
Onarga St. ........ W21
Orchard Dr. ........ X21
Orchard Dr., N. ........ V21
Orchard Dr., S. ........ W21
Osage St. ........ W21
Oswego St. ........ W21
Ottawa St. ........ W21
Park St. ........ V21
Peach St. ........ W21
Plaza St. ........ V21
Rich Ct. ........ V20
Rich Rd. ........ V21
Rocket Cir., E. & W. ........ W21
Ruthledge St. ........ U22
Saginaw Pl. ........ W20
Sandburg St. ........ U21
Sangamon Ct. ........ W20
Sangamon St. ........ W20
Sassabee St. ........ W20
Sauganash St. ........ W20
Saugatuck St. ........ W20
Sauk Ct. ........ W21
Sauk Trail ........ W21
Seminole St. ........ W20
Seneca St. ........ W20
Seward St. ........ U21
Shabonna Dr. ........ W20
Shawnee St. ........ W20
Sheridan St. ........ U21
Sherman St. ........ U21
Sioux St. ........ W20
Somonauk Ct. ........ W20
Somonauk St. ........ W20
South St. ........ U21
Spring Ln. ........ V17
Springfield St. ........ U21
Stanton St. ........ U21
Stuenkel Rd. ........ X20
Suwanee St. ........ W20
Sycamore Rd. ........ X22
Thomas St. ........ U21
Todd St. ........ U22
Topeka St. ........ X20
Victory Blvd. ........ V22
Waldmann Dr. ........ V20
Walnut St. ........ V20
Warwick Ct. ........ V21
Warwick St. ........ V21
Washington Ct. ........ V20
Washington St. ........ V20
Water St. ........ V21
Watseka St. ........ V20
Waverly Ct. ........ V20
Waverly St. ........ V20
Wayne Ct. ........ V20
Wayne St. ........ V20
Well Ct. ........ V21
Well St. ........ V21
Western Ave. ........ V,X22
Westgate Dr. ........ V20
Westwood Ct. ........ V21
Westwood Dr. ........ W21
Wildwood Dr. ........ V20
Willow St. ........ V21
Wilshire St. ........ V20
Wilson Ct. ........ V20
Wilson St. ........ V20
Windsor St. ........ V20
Winnebago St. ........ V20
Winnemac St. ........ V20
Winona St. ........ V20
Winslow St. ........ V21

**CEMETERY**

Calvary Cemetery ........ W22
St. Annes Cemetery ........ W20

**PARKS**

Algonquin Park ........ V22
Apache Park ........ V22
Cedar Park ........ V22
Central Park ........ V21
Eastgate Park ........ V22
Illinois Park ........ U21
Indiana Park ........ U21
Juniper Park ........ V21
Keokuk Park ........ W20
Krotiak Park ........ V21
Logan Park ........ U21
Marquette Park ........ W21
Murphy Park ........ W22
Onarga Park ........ W20
Somonauk Park ........ W20
Veterans Park ........ V21
Wayne Park ........ V20
Wildwood Park ........ V21
Winnebago Park ........ V21

**SCHOOLS**

Algonquin Sch. ........ V22
Blackhawk Jr. H.S. ........ W21
Dogwood Sch. ........ V22
Hickory Hills Sch. ........ W22
Hope Sch. ........ W20
Illinois Sch. ........ U21
Indiana Sch. ........ U21
Lakewood Sch. ........ V21
Mohawk Sch. ........ W20
Rich Twp. H.S. East ........ W21
Sauk Trail Sch. ........ W21
St. Irenaeus Sch. ........ W21
Westwood Jr. H.S. ........ V21
Westwood Sch. ........ V20
Wildwood Sch. ........ V21

**SHOPPING CENTERS**

Central Court Plaza ........ V20
Lincolnwood S.C. ........ U21
Lincolnwood West S.C. ........ U20
Norwood Plaza ........ V22
Plaza West S.C. ........ W21
The Center S.C. ........ V21
Tower S.C. ........ W21

**MISCELLANEOUS**

Aqua Center ........ V21
Freedom Hall ........ V21
Library ........ V21
Ludeman Mental Rehab.
Center ........ U21
Park Forest Tennis Club ... W21
Thorn Creek Woods Nature
Center ........ X20
Village Hall ........ V21

## PARK RIDGE

Pages 28,29
(For additional listings,
see Section 1)

**STREETS**

Aldine Ave. ........ M4
Ascot Dr. ........ N3
Ashbury Cir. ........ M3
Ashland Ave. ........ K3,M5
Astoria Way ........ M3
Austin Ave. ........ L5
Austin St. ........ L4
Avondale Ave. ........ M3-4
Babetta Ave. ........ M3
Beau Dr. ........ L4
Bender Rd. ........ J2
Berry Pkwy. ........ M5
Birch St. ........ L3
Boardwalk ........ M3
Bouterse ........ L3
Broadway Ave. ........ M3
Brockton Ln. ........ H3
Brookline Ave. ........ L5
Burton Ave. ........ K3
Busse Hwy. ........ M4
Butler Pl. ........ N4
Carol St. ........ K4
Carolyn Ln. ........ M3
Cedar St. ........ M3-5
Cherry St. ........ M3-5
Chester Ave. ........ L-N4
Clifton Ave. ........ L-N4
Clinton St. ........ M5
Courtland Ave. ........ N4
Crain St. ........ K4
Crescent Ave. ........ M4-5
Cumberland Ave. ........ L-N4
Cuttriss St. ........ L5
Cynthia St. ........ L4
Davis St. ........ J4
DeCook Ave. ........ L3
DeCook Ct. ........ K3
Dee Rd. ........ M3
Delphia Ave. ........ L-M4
Dempster Ct. ........ K3
Des Plaines ........ M3
East Ave. ........ L5
Edgemont Ln. ........ L4-5
Edna Ave. ........ L3
Elliott Ave. ........ K-L2
Ellison ........ L3
Elm St. ........ M3-5
Elmore St. ........ M5
Evergreen Ln. ........ K3
Fairview Ave. ........ L-N4
Farrell Ave. ........ K3
Florence Dr. ........ M3
Forest Lake ........ M3
Forestview Ave. ........ M3
Fortuna Ave. ........ M3
Garden Park ........ N4
Garden St. ........ M3-4
Glenview Ave. ........ L3
Good Ave. ........ K-L3
Goodwin Dr. ........ M3
Grace Ave. ........ L-M4
Grand Blvd. ........ M4
Grant Pl. ........ M5
Greendale Ave. ........ L3
Greenwood Ave. ........ M-N4
Habberton Ave. ........ L2-3
Habberton St. ........ L3
Halberg Ln. ........ K4
Halien Terr. ........ M3
Hamlin Ave. ........ L-M3
Hansen Pl. ........ M4
Hastings St. ........ M4
Helen Ave. ........ L3
Hoffman Ave. ........ K-L3
Hoffman Rd. ........ L3
Home Ave. ........ K-N3
Irwin Ave. ........ M3
Jonquil ........ L5
Joyce Pl. ........ M5
Kathleen Dr. ........ L5
Knight Ave. ........ L-N4
Knight St. ........ L4
Lahon St. ........ M3-5
Lake ........ N5
Laverne Ave. ........ L4
Leonard St. ........ M4
Lincoln Ave. ........ K,M-N4
Lundergram Ave. ........ K-L2
Luther Ln. ........ K3
Main St. ........ M4
Manor Ln. ........ L3
Marcus Ct., E. & W. ........ K3
Marguerite St. ........ L3
Marlowe ........ M3
Marvin Pkwy. ........ M3
Mary Jane Ln. ........ M3
Mayfield Dr. ........ K3
Meacham Ave. ........ M4
Merrill Ave. ........ M5
Merrill St. ........ L-M5
Michael John Dr. ........ L5
Milton Ave. ........ M3
Morris ........ M4
Murphy Lake Ln. ........ M3
Murphy Lake Rd. ........ M3
Norman Blvd. ........ M3
Northwest Hwy. ........ L3,M5
Oak St. ........ N5
Oaktree Ln. ........ K3
Olmstead ........ N5
Oriole Ave. ........ L-M5
Ottawa Ave. ........ L-M5
Ozark St. ........ M5
Park Ln. ........ M3
Park Pl. ........ M4
Park Plaine Ave. ........ M3
Park Ridge Pointe ........ K2
Parkside Ave. ........ K-L4
Parkside Dr. ........ K4
Parkwood Ave. ........ L-M3
Pavilion Way ........ K2
Poplar St. ........ L3
Potter Rd. ........ L3
Prairie Ave. ........ M3-4
Prospect Ave. ........ L-M5,N4
Rand Rd. ........ L3
Redfield Ct. ........ M-N4
Renaissance Dr. ........ L2
Rene Ct. ........ L4
Richardson Pkwy. ........ M4
Ridge Terr. ........ M5
Riverside Dr. ........ L2
Root St. ........ M4
Rose Ave. ........ M-N4
Rowe Ave. ........ L3
Saloman Ln. ........ K3
Scottylynne Dr. ........ M3
Seeley Ave. ........ L3
Seminary Ave. ........ M-N3
Shibley Ave. ........ L3
Sibley St. ........ M3-5
Spring St. ........ N5
Summit Ave. ........ M4
Sylviawood Ave. ........ M3
Talcott Rd. ........ L-M2
Thames ........ N3
Tomawadee Dr. ........ L3
Touhy Ave. ........ M2-3
Tyrell Ave. ........ L3
Vernon Ave. ........ K-L3
Virginia St ........ L3
Walnut St. ........ L3
Washington Ave. ........ M5
Weeg Way ........ K3
Wesley Dr. ........ M2
Western Ave. ........ L-N4
Wilkinson Ave. ........ L3
Wilma Pl. ........ L5
Wisner St. ........ M5
Woodland Ave. ........ L3
Woodview Ln. ........ K3
3rd St ........ M4
5th St. ........ L4
6th St. ........ L4
7th St. ........ L4

**CEMETERIES**

Town of Maine Cemetery .. N3

**GOLF COURSES**

Park Ridge C.C. ........ L4

**PARKS**

Centennial Park ........ M3
Hinkley Park ........ M4
Maine Park ........ M3
Mary Alderding Park ........ K2
Messiah Park ........ K3
Ni-Ridge Park ........ L4
North Park ........ K4
Northeast Park ........ L5
Northwest Park ........ L3
Oakton Park ........ L3
Woodland Park ........ L3

**SCHOOLS**

Benjamin Franklin Sch. ... L3
Carpenter Sch. ........ M3
Eugene Field Sch. ........ L5
Jeanine Schultz Mem. Sch. L3
Lincoln Sch. ........ N4
Maine Twp. H.S. East .... K3
St. Pauls Sch. ........ M5
Washington Sch. ........ N4

**MISCELLANEOUS**

City Hall ........ F5
Fire Station ........ L4
Lutheran General Hospital . K3
Maine Township Hall ........ K3
Park Ridge Community Center
........ M4
Park Ridge Youth Campus L5
Post Office ........ M4

## PROSPECT HEIGHTS

Pages 9,10

**STREETS**

Aberdeen Ln. ........ C15
Alderman Ave. ........ D14-15
Alton Rd. ........ D-E14
Andover Ct. ........ C13
Andover Dr. ........ C13
Anne Ct. ........ C13
Apple Dr. ........ C16
Blossom Ln. ........ C16
Blossom Ln. ........ B12
Bonniebrook Ct. ........ D14
Bonniebrook Dr. ........ D14
Brian Ln. ........ D14
Brook Rd. ........ D13
Burning Bush Ln. ........ C13
Burr Oak Ln. ........ C15
Camp McDonald Rd. . D13-15
Carl Ct. ........ C14
Carrbridge Ln. ........ D14
Center Ln. ........ D12
Cherry Creek Ln. ........ B12
Chester Ln. ........ E13
Cider Ln. ........ C16
Circle Ave. ........ D13
Claire Ln. ........ D14
Clarendon St. ........ D12-13
Coldren Dr. ........ D14
Compton Ln. ........ D13
Country Club Dr. ........ D,E14
Countryside Ln. ........ C13
Cove Dr. ........ C-D15
Crabapple Dr. ........ C16
Creek Ct. ........ C13
Crest Hill Dr. ........ B13
Crimson Ct. ........ C16
Delicious Ct. ........ C16
Derbyshire Ct. ........ C13
Derbyshire Ln. ........ C13
Dorset St. ........ D12-13
Drake Ave. ........ B13
Drake Terr. ........ B13
Drury Ln. ........ D12
Duchess Ct. ........ C16
Edinburgh Ln. ........ D14
Edward Cul De Sac ........ D15
Edward Rd. ........ E14
Elaine Cir. ........ D14
Eleanor Dr. ........ B13
Elmhurst Rd. ........ B-E13
Essex St. ........ C13
Etowah Ave. ........ D13
Euclid Ave. ........ E14-15
Fairway Ct. ........ E14
Fairway Dr. ........ E14
Ferndale Ct. ........ C15
Ferndale Ln. ........ C15
Forrest Ave. ........ D12
Frankie Ct. ........ D1
Gail Ct., N. & S. ........ D12
Galway Dr. ........ D14
Garden Ct. ........ B13
Garden Ln. ........ C13
Glasgow Ln. ........ D14
Glenbrook Dr. ........ B13
Glendale Dr. ........ C14
Golfview Cir. ........ E14
Green Bridge Ln. ........ C15
Greening Ct. ........ C16
Grego Ct. ........ D14
Greystone Ln. ........ D15
Grove Pl. ........ E14
Hawthorne Pl. ........ E13
Highland Dr. ........ B13
Hill Ct. ........ D13
Hillcrest Dr. ........ D13-14
Hillside Ave. ........ D13
Hintz Rd. ........ B13
Jonathan Ct. ........ C16
Kenilworth Ave. ........ C13-14
Kenneth Ave. ........ C13
Kerry Ct. ........ B12,13
Kewaunee Ct. ........ C13
Kingsmill Ln. ........ D15
Lancaster St. ........ D12
Lanford Ln. ........ D14
Leon Ln. ........ D14
Lewis Isle Ln. ........ D15
Linden Rd., N. & S. ........ D12
Loch Lommond Ln. ........ C15
Lonsdale Ln. ........ D13-14
Love Dr. ........ C15
Lynnbrook Dr. ........ B13
Mandel Ln. ........ D15
Manor Ave. ........ D13
Maple Ave. ........ D13
Maple Ln. ........ B,D13
Maple St. ........ C13
Marberry Dr. ........ D13
Margate Ln. ........ C15
Marion Ave. ........ D13-14
Marion St. ........ D12
Mars Pl. ........ D13
McIntosh Ct. ........ C16
Meadow Ridge Ln. ........ B12,13
Milwaukee Ave. ........ D16-17
Minnaqua Dr. ........ C12-13
Mohawk Ln. ........ D15
Nawata Pl. ........ D12
Newcastle Ln. ........ D14
Newgate Ln. ........ D14
North Pkwy. ........ D13
Oak Ave. ........ B13
Oakwood Dr. ........ C13
Old Willow Rd. ........ D15
Olive Ave. ........ D12-14
Olive St. ........ D12,13
Owen Ct. ........ D14
Owen Pl. ........ D-E14
Owen St. ........ D14

Palatine Rd. C12-13
Parkview West C16
Patricia Ln. D14
Pembridge Ln. D14
Phelps Ave. D12
Pin Oak B13
Pine Forest Ln. C15
Pine St. D13
Pinecrest Dr. C15
Piper Cir. C15
Piper Ln. C15
Plaza Dr. C16
Prospect Ct. D13
Prospect Dr. B13
Quaker Ln. C-D15
Rand Rd. D12
Regent Ln. C15
Ridge Ave. C13
Riley Ave. D14
Rob Roy Ln. D,E14
Robert Ave. C13
Roberts Ln. D15
Robyn Ct. D14
Rose Ave. D14
Royal Ct. C13
Schoenbeck Rd. B,D13
School Ln. E13
School St. C-D13
Seminole Ln. D16
Shannon Dr. D14
Shawn Ln. D14
Sherwood Dr. B,C13
South Pkwy. D13
Spruce Dr. C13,14
Stirling Ln. D14
Stonegate Dr. B,C13
Stratford Rd. D12
Sussex Corner Ln. C15
Sutherland Ln. C15
Thierry Ln. D14
Thistle Ln. C15
Tomah Ave. C-D12
Tree Ln. C16
Tully Pl. E13-14
Viola Ln. C13
Walden Ln. B12
Waltz Ct. C14
Waterford Dr. D14
Waterman Ave. D12
Wheeling Rd. D14
Wildwood Dr. B,C13
Williamsburg Ln. D15
Willow Hills Ln. C15
Willow Rd. D13
Wimbledon Cir. C15
Winesap Ct. C16
Wolf Rd. C-D15
Woodview Dr. B12

### GOLF COURSES
Rob Roy G.C. E14

### PARKS
Claire Ln. Park D14
John Muir Park C14
Kiwanis Park C13
Lyons Park D13
McDonald Field D13
Tully Park E14

### SCHOOLS
Eisenhower Sch. C12
Harper Coll. N.E. Center C15
MacArthur Jr. H.S. B13
Muir Sch. B13
Ross Sch. C13
Sch. Dist. 23 Office C13
St. Alphonsus Cath. Sch. D14
Sullivan Sch. C13

### SHOPPING CENTERS
Prospect Crossing S.C. D12

### MISCELLANEOUS
Fire Department D13
Post Office D13
Railroad Station E15

## RICH TOWNSHIP
Pages 41,42,46-48

### STREETS
Birchwood Ln. Pg.47 T18
Blackstone Ave. Pg.47 S19
Blackthorne Rd. Pg.46 U15
Briar Branch Terr. Pg.46 U15
Briar Ln. Pg.47 S19
Brushwood Dr. Pg.46 U,V15
Burlwood Ct. Pg.46 V15
Candlegate Cir. Pg.46 U16
Central Ave. Pg.41 U17
Central Park Ave. Pg.42 R,S20
Chaparal Terr. Pg.46 V16
Cicero Ave. Pg.47 V18
Crawford Ave. Pg.42 R,T19
Dan Ryan Expwy. Pg.47 V17
Davis Ave. Pg.47 W19
Dewey Ave. Pg.47 W19
Elmwood Ln. Pg.47 T18
Flossmoor Rd. Pg.42 R20
Governors Hwy. Pg.47 Q21,W19
Greenwards Way Pg.46 V16
Hamlin Ave. Pg.42 R20
Harlem Ave. Pg.47 S15
Heartside Rd. Pg.46 U15
Heathermeade Rd. Pg.46 U15
Hedgewood Ct. Pg.46 V15
Hickory Glen Pg.46 V16
Homeland Rd. Pg.47 T18
Huntsbridge Rd. Pg.46 V15
Ivylog Terr. Pg.46 V16
Kedzie Ave. Pg.42 T21
Keeler Ave. Pg.47 T19
Keystone Ave. Pg.47 S19
Knollwood Cir. Pg.46 U16
Kostner Ave. Pg.47 T,V,W19
Leclaire Ave. Pg.47 Q18
Lincoln Hwy. Pg.41 U16
Maple Ave. Pg.46,47 V19
Maplewood Ln. Pg.47 T18
Moorfield Rd. Pg.46 U15
Oak Park Ave. Pg.41 Q15
Orchard Ln. Pg.47 S19
Pleasant Terr. Pg.46 V15
Polk Ave. Pg.47 W19
Poplar Ave. Pg.47 V19
Richton Sq. Pg.47 W20
Ridgeland Ave. Pg.41 V16
Sauk Tr. Pg.46,47 V16
Sprucewood Ln. Pg.47 T18
Steger Rd. Pg.47 W17
Sunset Rd. Pg.47 S19
Tanglewood Terr. Pg.46 V16
Thistle Ct. Pg.46 U15
Thorntree Terr. Pg.46 V16
Thornwood Ave. Pg.47 S19
Timber Ridge Rd. Pg.46 U16
Tullamore Terr. Pg.46 U15
Vollmer Rd. Pg.46,47 S19
Wildwood Terr. Pg.46 U15
Windmere Cir., N & S Pg.46 U15
Woodbine Terr. Pg.46 V16
66th Ave. Pg.41 Q15
183rd St. Pg.41 Q17
192nd St. Pg.42 R20
194th St. Pg.42 R20
196th St. Pg.47 R20
198th St. Pg.47 S20
203rd Ave. Pg.47 S19
204th Ave. Pg.47 T19
205th Ave. Pg.47 T19
206th Ave. Pg.47 T19
207th St. Pg.47 T19

### FOREST PRESERVES
South Greenbelt F.P. Pg.47 Q16

### SCHOOLS
Central Sch. Pg.41 Q17
Sedan Prairie Sch. Pg.46 S16

### MISCELLANEOUS
Old Plank Rd. Bike Trail Pg.47 U17

## RICHTON PARK
Page 47

### STREETS
Adams Dr. W18
Amy Dr. W18
Andover Dr. V19
Appleberry Ln. V20
Arlington Dr. V19
Arnold Bohlman Pkwy. W17
Arquilla Dr. W18
Ascot Ct. V19
Balmoral Dr. V19
Bay View Dr. V18
Belmont Rd. V18
Birchwood Rd. V19,20
Bretz Dr. W19
Brian Ct. W19
Brighton Ln. V20
Brook Ave. V18
Bruce Dr. W18
Butterfield Dr. V19
Cambridge Ln. T21
Camden Ct. V18,19
Canterbury Ct. V19
Capi Ln. V18
Carlborg Ct. V18
Carol Ann Ct. W19
Cedar Rd. V20
Cedar Ridge Ln. W20
Central Park Ave. W20
Cherie Ct. V18
Churchill Dr., E. V19
Churchill Dr., S. V18
Cicero Ave. V18
Clarendon Ave. W18
Clark Dr. V19
Coachway Ln. V19
Crescent Way W19
Cypress Ct. W18
Davis Ave. W20
Dewey Ave. W20
East Dr. W18
Edward Dr. W19
Elm Rd. V20
Euclid Ln. V20
Farmington Ave. W18
Franklin Dr. W18
Governors Hwy. W19
Grant Ave. V20
Greenbrier Ln. V19
Hamilton Dr. W19
Harbor Ln. V18
Hawthorne Way V18
Heartland Dr. W18
Hillside Dr. V18
Imperial Ct. East W19
Imperial Ct. West W19
Imperial Dr. W19
Jackson Ave. W20
Jackson Ct. V20
Jean Ct. W19
Jefferson St. W18
Kara Ln. W17
Karlov Ave. V19
Keenhand Ct. V19
Keith Dr. W18
Kings Ct. W18
Kostner Ave. V19
Lake Shore Dr. W18
Latonia Ct. W18
Latonia Ln. W18
Laurel Dr. V18
Lawndale Ave. W20
Lee Ave. W20
Lee Ct. V18
Lesa Ct. V18
Lincoln Blvd. W19
Linden Rd. V20
Lioncrest Dr. V19
Lorraine Ct. V19
Madison W18
Maple Ave. V19
Meadow Lake Ct. V18
Meadow Lake Dr. V18
Michael John Ct. W19
Michael John Ln. W19
Mill Rd. V19
Millard Ave. V20
Mission Dr. W18
Monroe W18
Monterey Dr. W18
Neptune Ln. V18
Parkview Ct. W19
Parkview Dr. W19
Picadilly Ct. V20
Pleasant Dr. W18
Polk Ave. W20
Poplar Ave. V18
Redwood Dr. W18
Regency Dr. W19
Richton Pl. V19
Richton Rd. V19
Richton Sq. W20
Ridgeway Ave. V,W20
Riverside Dr. W18
Roberta Ln. W18
Rockingham Rd. V18
Salem Ct. V18
Saratoga Rd. V18
Sauk Trail Rd. V19
Schaat Ct. V18
Scott Dr. V18
Spring Ct. V18
Spring Ln. V18
St. Ives Ln. V20
Steger Rd. W20
Sunset Dr. V18
Taylor Ave. W20
Thomas Ct. V20
Thomas Dr. V18
Tower Dr. V19
Tyler Dr. W19
Valley Dr. W18
Victoria Dr. W19
Washington Ct. W19
Washington Dr. W19
Westminster Dr. W19
Whitehall V19
Windsor Ct. V19
Woodbine Rd. V19
York Ct. W20

### CEMETERIES
Immanuel Lutheran Cem. V18
Zion Lutheran Cemetery U20

### PARKS
Dennis Holt Park W18
Glaeser Park W19
Indian Trail Park V18
Jones Park W19
Klawitter Park W18
Pierce Park W18
Spirit Trail Park T20
Storybook Park W19

### SCHOOLS
Armstrong Sch. W18
Immanuel Sch. W18
Rich Twp. H.S. South V18
Richton Sq. Sch. W20
Sauk Sch. V19

### MISCELLANEOUS
Fire Department V20
Library V19
Osteopathic Hosp. Professional Bldg. T19
R.R. Station V19
Rich Twp. Hall V19
Richton Crossing Nursing Home V18
Sinter Metals Industrial Park W17

## ROLLING MEADOWS
Pages 7,8,12,13

### STREETS
Adams St. Pg.7 E7
Alder Ct. Pg.7 E6
Alexandria Ct. Pg.7 E7
Algonquin Pkwy. Pg.13 G9
Algonquin Rd. Pg.13 G8
Amanda Ct. Pg.7 F6
Angeline Ct. Pg.7 E7
Apollo Ave. Pg.13 H8
Apple Jack Rd. Pg.7 D6
Arbor Dr. Pg.12 G8
Arlingdale Ct. Pg.7 E5
Arlingdale Dr. Pg.7 E5
Arrowwood Ln. Pg.7 E6
Ashbury Pg.7 F7
Ashland Ave. Pg.8 E8
Astor Ln. Pg.13 G9
Auburn Pg.7 F7
Azalea Ct. Pg.13 H9
Barker Ave. Pg.13 G8
Bayberry Ct. Pg.13 H9
Bent Creek Ct. Pg.7 F6
Berdnick St. Pg.8 D8
Birch Ln. Pg.13 G9
Blackhawk Dr. Pg.8 D8
Blacktwig Rd. Pg.7 F8
Bluebird Ln. Pg.8 E9
Bluebird Ln., S. Pg.13 F9
Bobolink Ln. Pg.8 F8
Bobwhite Ln. Pg.13 F8
Brockway St. Pg.7 E7
Brookmeade Dr. Pg.13 G8
Brookview Ln. Pg.7 F6
Brookwood Dr. Pg.7 E7
Bryant Ave. Pg.8 E8
Burning Trees Rd. Pg.7 D6
Butterfield Ct. Pg.7 E6
California Ave. Pg.7 F7
California Ct. Pg.7 F7
Calvert Dr. Pg.13 G9
Campbell St. Pg.8 E9
Cardinal Dr. Pg.8 E8
Carnegie St. Pg.8 D8
Carr St. Pg.13 G9
Carriage Way Dr. Pg.13 G9
Castle Ct. Pg.7 E6
Cedar Glen Rd. Pg.7 D7
Cedar St. Pg.13 G9
Central Rd. Pg.13 F8,9
Chas Dr. Pg.7 E7
Chateau Dr. Pg.13 H9
Chicory Ct. Pg.7 E6
College Crossing Pg.7 F6
Corona Dr., N. & S. Pg.7 E6
Crane Ct. Pg.13 F9
Creekside Dr. Pg.7 D7,F7-8
Crestwood Ln. Pg.7 D7
Croftwood Ct. Pg.7 E6
Crossing Ct. Pg.7 E6
Crossroads of Commerce Pg.13 G8
Cyndi Ct. Pg.13 F9
Dahlia Ct. Pg.7 E6
Davis Ct. Pg.7 E7
Dawngate Ct. Pg.7 F7
Debra Ct. Pg.7 F8
Deepwood Ln. Pg.7 F7
Deerfield Ln. Pg.7 E6
Denny Ct. Pg.7 D7
Dogwood Rd. Pg.7 D6
Dove Ct. Pg.8 F9
Dove St. Pg.8 E-F9
Duxbury Pg.7 E7
Eagle Ln. Pg.13 F9
East Frontage Rd. Pg.13 F8
Eastman St. Pg.8 E9
Edgewood Ct. Pg.7 E6
Edison Pl. Pg.8 D8
Eleanore Ct. Pg.8 F8
Elizabeth Ln. Pg.13 G9
Elk Grove Rd. Pg.13 H10
Emerson Ave. Pg.8 E8
Essex Way Pg.13 G9
Euclid Ave. Pg.7 E7
Fairfax Ave. Pg.8 E8
Falcon Ct. Pg.8 F8
Falcon Dr. Pg.8 F8
Farmington Ct. Pg.7 E6
Fieldstone Rd. Pg.7 D7
Finch Ct. Pg.8 F8
Flicker Ln. Pg.8 E8
Forest Ave. Pg.8 E8
Fox Ln. Pg.7 F6
Fremont St. Pg.8 E8-9
Fulle St. Pg.13 F9
George Ct. Pg.8 E9
George St. Pg.8 E9
Gettysburg Dr. Pg.7 D7
Ginger Ct. Pg.7 E6
Golf Pl. Pg.13 H9
Green Meadow Ct. Pg.7 E6
Greenwich Ct. Pg.7 F7
Grouse Ct. Pg.13 F8
Grouse Ln. Pg.13 F8
Grove Rd. Pg.7 F7
Grove St. Pg.8 F9
Groveside Ln. Pg.7 F6
Gull Ct. Pg.13 F9
Hampton Dr., N. & S. Pg.13 G9
Hawk Ct. Pg.8 F9
Hawk Ln. Pg.8 F8-9
Hawthorne Ln. Pg.13 G8
Heather Ct. Pg.7 E6
Heron Ct. Pg.8 E8
Hicks Rd. Pg.7 D7
Highland Dr. Pg.7 E5
Holly Ln. Pg.8 E8
Honeysuckle Ct. Pg.7 E6
Honeysuckle Ln. Pg.7 E6
Hoover Ct. Pg.7 E7
Hoover St. Pg.7 E7
Industrial Ave. Pg.7 D8
Ironwood Ct. Pg.7 E6
Jasmine Ln. Pg.7 E6
Jay Ln. Pg.8 E9
Jay Ln., S. Pg.13 F9
Jessica Ct. Pg.7 E6
Jill Ct. Pg.7 D7
Jonquil Ct. Pg.7 E6
Josephine Ct. Pg.7 E7
Juniper Rd. Pg.7 D6
Keith Ct. Pg.7 E7
Kenilworth Dr. Pg.13 G8
Kevin Ln. Pg.7 E6
Keystone Ct. Pg.13 G9
Killarney Ct. Pg.8,13 F9
Kimball Hill Dr. Pg.13 G9
Kimberly Ct. Pg.7 E6
Kingfisher Ln. Pg.8 F8
Kingfisher Ln., E. Pg.8 F9
Kings Walk Dr. Pg.7 E7
Kirchoff Rd. Pg.7 E7,F9
Knoll Ridge Dr. Pg.7 D6
Lark Ct. Pg.8 E8
Lavender Ct. Pg.13 H9
Lilac Ct. Pg.7 E6
Lincoln Ave. Pg.7 D7
Linden Ln. Pg.13 G9
Lisa Ct. Pg.7 E6
Lois Dr. Pg.13 H9
Magnolia Dr. Pg.13 G8
Mallard Ct. Pg.8 F8
Mallory Pg.7 F6
Maple Ct. Pg.13 G9
Maple Ln. Pg.13 G9
Marilyn Ct. Pg.7 D7
Martin Ct. Pg.8 F8-9
Martin Ln. Pg.8 F9
Mayberry Ct. Pg.7 E6
Mayflower Ct. Pg.13 H9
McKone Ct. Pg.7 F7
Meacham Rd. Pg.7 F7
Meadow Dr. Pg.8 E9
Meadowbrook Ct. Pg.13 G9
Meadowbrook Industrial Ct. Pg.13 G9
Melone Dr. Pg.7 F8
Michael Ct. Pg.7 E6
Mill Creek Ln. Pg.7 E6
Millstone Ln. Pg.7 E6
Moraine Pg.13 H9
New Castle Ct. Pg.7 E6
Newport Dr. Pg.13 G8
Norwood Ct. Pg.7 E6
Oak Ln. Pg.13 G9
Oaksbury Ct. Pg.7 F7
Oakwood Ct. Pg.7 E7
Old Creek Rd. Pg.7 D7
Old Hickory Rd. Pg.7 D7
Old Mill Ln. Pg.7 E6
Old Plum Grove Rd. Pg.7 F6
Old Valley Rd. Pg.7 F7
Old Wilke Rd. Pg.13 F9
Oriole Ln. Pg.8 E-F9
Owl Dr. Pg.8 F8
Owl Ln. Pg.8 E8
Oxford Pg.7 E7
Oxford Rd. Pg.7 F7
Park Ct. Pg.8 E9
Park St. Pg.8 F9
Peacock Ct. Pg.13 F8
Peacock Ln. Pg.13 G8
Pebblebrook Ln. Pg.7 E6
Pheasant Dr. Pg.8 F8
Pine Valley Pg.7 D7
Piper Ct. Pg.13 F8
Plum Blossom Ct. Pg.7 F6
Plum Grove Dr. Pg.13 G9
Plum Tree Ln. Pg.7 E6
Polk Ave. Pg.7 E7
Prairie Ln. Pg.7 E5-6
Pride Ct. Pg.7 D7
Quail Ct. Pg.13 F9
Quail Ln. Pg.13 F9
Quinten Rd. Pg.7 C6
Raven Ln. Pg.13 F9
Red Haw Rd. Pg.8 F8
Redbud Rd. Pg.7 D6
Redwing Ct. Pg.13 F8
Rhiannon Ct. Pg.7 E7
Richnee Ln. Pg.7 F7
Robin Ln. Pg.8 E8
Rohlwing Rd. Pg.8 E8
Rosewood Dr. Pg.7 D6
Rywick Dr. Pg.8 E8
Salt Creek Dr. Pg.8 D8
Salt Creek Ln. Pg.8 D8
School Dr. Pg.8 E8
Shady Ct. Pg.7 F7
Shagbark Rd. Pg.7 F8
Sigwalt St. Pg.8 E8-9
Silent Brook Ln. Pg.7 E6
Smith St. Pg.7 E6
South Ct. Pg.8 E9
South St. Pg.8 E9
Spruce Ct. Pg.8 E8
Squibb Ave. Pg.13 G8
St. James St. Pg.8 E8-9
Stacy Ln. Pg.7 E7
Starling Ln. Pg.13 F8
Stoneridge Rd. Pg.7 D6
Stork Ct. Pg.8 E8
Sunset Dr. Pg.6 C3
Swallow Ln. Pg.8 F8
Swan Ln. Pg.8 E8
Sycamore Dr. Pg.13 G8
Taft Ave. Pg.7 E7
Tall Oaks Ln. Pg.7 F7
Tall Trees Ct. Pg.7 E7
Teaberry Ct. Pg.13 H9
Teal Ct. Pg.13 F8
Tern Ct. Pg.8 E8
Theda Ln. Pg.8 E8
Thorntree Ln. Pg.13 G8
Thrush Ct. Pg.8 F8
Thrush Ln. Pg.8 F8
Tinder Pg.13 H9
Tollview Dr. Pg.13 G8
Vermont Ave. Pg.7 E6
Vermont St. Pg.7 E7
Villa Cir. Dr. Pg.7 F6
Viola Ct. Pg.7 E6
Walnut Ct. Pg.7 F8
West Frontage Rd. Pg.13 F8
Wildwood Dr. Pg.7 D6
Wilke Rd. Pg.13 G9
Willow Ln. Pg.13 G9
Wilson Ave. Pg.7 E7
Wing St. Pg.8 E9
Winnetka Cir. Pg.7 D7
Winnetka Rd. Pg.7,8 D7,8
Woodbine Rd. Pg.7 F7
Woodcliff Ct. Pg.7 F7
Woodcliff Ln. Pg.7 F7
Woodland Ct. Pg.7 F7
Woods Chapel Rd. Pg.8 F8
Wren Ct. Pg.13 F9
Wren Ln. Pg.13 E9
Wren Ln. S. Pg.8 F9
Yarrow Ct. Pg.7 E6
Yarrow Ln. Pg.7 E6

### GOLF COURSES
Plum Grove Country Club Pg.13 F8

### PARKS
Countryside Park Pg.7 E6
Creekside Woods Pg.7 F7
Kimball Hill Park Pg.8 E8
Salk Park Pg.8 F8
Waverly Park Pg.13 G9

### SCHOOLS
Carl Sandburg Jr. H.S. Pg.8 F9
Central Road Sch. Pg.13 F8
Kimball Hill Sch. Pg.8 E8
Learning Academy Pg.13 F8
Plum Grove Jr. H.S. Pg.7 E7
Rolling Meadows H.S. Pg.13 G8
St. Collette Sch. Pg.13 F8
Willow Bend Sch. Pg.13 G8

### SHOPPING CENTERS
Meadows Town Mall Pg.13 H10
Paddock S.C. Pg.13 H10
Plum Grove S.C. Pg.7 E7
Rolling Meadows S.C. Pg.8 F8
Southland S.C. Pg.13 G9

### MISCELLANEOUS
Community Center Pg.13 F8
County Court House Pg.8 E9
Fire Department Pg.7,8 E7,F8
Rolling Meadows Skating Center Pg.7 E8
Sports Complex Pg.8 F8
Village Hall Pg.8 E8

## ROSELLE
Page 17
(Portions within DuPage County, for additional listings, see Section 3)

### STREETS
Acadia Bay M6
Acadia Ct. M6
Acadia Tr. M6
Albion Ave. M6
Arthur Ave. M6
Bryce Tr. M6
Candle Lyte Ct. M4
Canterbury Ct. M6
Carlsbad Tr. M6
Cedar Bear Bay M5
Chisolm Ct. M6
Chisolm Tr. M6
Club House Dr. M6
Conway Bay M6
Cross Creek Ct. M6
Cross Creek Dr., N. & W. M6
Cumberland Ct. M6
Cumberland Tr. M6
David Ln. M5
Glacier Bay M6
Glacier Ct. M6
Glacier Tr. M6
Indian Hill Dr. M5
Jennifer Ln. M5
Kennedy Ct. M4
Larson Ln. M5
Logan St. M4
May St. M6
Medinah Rd. M6
Nerge Rd. M6
Oregon Tr. M6
Overland Ct. M6
Overland Tr. M6
Roslyn Rd. M5
Schrieber Ave. M6
Shadow Lake Bay M6
Shawnee Tr. M6
Springwood Ct. M5
Springwood Dr. M5
Washington St. M4
Williams St. M4
Yosemite Ct. M6
Yosemite Tr. M6

### PARKS
Nerge Park M5

### SCHOOLS
Nerge Sch. M5

### SHOPPING CENTERS
Cross Creek Commons M6
Roselle Towne Square M6

## ROSEMONT
Page 20
(For additional listings, see Section 1)

### STREETS
Ann L16
Barry Ave. L16
Betty L16
Carol L16
Devon Ave. M17
Doris L16
Ethel L16
Lunt Ave. M16
Lyndon Ave. L16
Mannheim Rd. L16

### GOLF COURSES
O'Hare Inn G.C. M16

### MISCELLANEOUS
Allstate Arena (Horizon) M16
O'Hare Air Res. Forces Facility M16
Railroad Station M17

## SAUK VILLAGE
Pages 49,50

### STREETS
Apache Ave. Pg.50 V28
Astor St. Pg.50 U28
Barry Ln. Pg.50 U28
Blackstone Ave. Pg.50 V27
Brookwood Dr. Pg.50 W29
Burnham Ave. Pg.50 W30
Calhoun Ave. Pg.50 U28
Calumet Expwy. Pg.50 U27
Carol Ave. Pg.50 V28

# SAUK VILLAGE

Carol Ln. ... Pg.50 ... V28
Carolina Dr. .. Pg.50 .. W27
Chappel .... Pg.50 ... U28
Charlotte Ct. .. Pg.50 ... U28
Clyde Ave. .. Pg.50 ... U28
Clyde Ct. .... Pg.50 ... U28
Constance .. Pg.50 ... U28
Cottage Grove Ave.
........... Pg.49 .. V26
Cynthia Ave. . Pg.50 .. V27
Debra Ct. ... Pg.49 .. W27
East Brook Pl. . Pg.50 .. W28
Eastbrook Ct. . Pg.50 .. W28
Frank Wagner Ave.
........... Pg.50 .. U28
Gailine Ave. .. Pg.50 .. V28
Harper Ave. .. Pg.50 .. W27
Indie Ln. .... Pg.49 .. W27
Janice Dr. ... Pg.49 ... V27
Jeffrey Ave. .. Pg.50 ... V27
Joshua Dr. .. Pg.50 ... V27
Kalveage Dr. . Pg.50 .. U29
Katz Corner Rd Pg.50 ... V29
Lincoln Hwy. . Pg.50 ... U28
Long Ave. ... Pg.50 ... U28
Luella Ct. ... Pg.50 ... V28
Main St. .... Pg.50 ... U26
Marigold Dr. . Pg.50 ... V29
Mary Byrne Dr. Pg.49 ... W27
Mary Ct. .... Pg.49 ... W27
Merrill Ave. .. Pg.50 ... V28
Merrill Ct. ... Pg.50 ... V28
Murphy Ave. . Pg.50 ... V29
Navaho Ave. . Pg.50 ... V20
Nichols Dr. .. Pg.50 ... W28
Oakbrook Ct. . Pg.50 .. W28
Oakbrook Ln. . Pg.50 .. W28
Olivia Ave. ... Pg.50 .. W28
Orion Ln. .... Pg.50 .. V28
Paxton Ave. . Pg.50 ... V29
Peach Tree Ave. Pg.50 ... V29
Peterson Ave. Pg.50 ... U28
Pomo Ct. ... Pg.50 ... U28
Poplar St. ... Pg.50 ... U28
Prairie Ave. .. Pg.50 ... U28
Prairie Dr. ... Pg.50 ... W27
Reichert Ave. . Pg.50 ... W28
Ross Crescent Pg.50 ... W28
Rush St. .... Pg.50 ... U28
Sauk Pointe Dr. Pg.50 ... V28
Sauk Trail ... Pg.49-50 .. V27
Shirley Ave. .. Pg.50 ... W28
Southbrook Dr. Pg.50 ... W28
Spencer .... Pg.50 .. W29
State Route 394 Pg.50 ... V27
Steger Rd. ... Pg.50 ... W28
Stone Ln. ... Pg.50 ... W28
Strassburg Ave. Pg.50 ... W28
Talandis Ave. . Pg.50 ... V29
Theisen Ave. . Pg.50 .. W29
Theodore Ave. Pg.50 ... V29
Torrence Ave. . Pg.50 ... V29
U.S. Route 30 . Pg.50 ... V28
Westbrook Dr. . Pg.50 ... W28
Willow Tree Ln. Pg.50 ... W28
Woodlawn Ave. Pg.50 ... V27
Yates Ave. ... Pg.50 ... V28
22nd St. .... Pg.50 ... U28
30th St. .... Pg.50 .. W29
215th Pl .... Pg.50 ... V27
216th Ct. .... Pg.50 ... U28
216th Pl. .... Pg.50 ... U28
216th Pl. .... Pg.50 ... U28
216th St. .... Pg.50 ... U28
217th Pl. .... Pg.50 ... U28
217th Pl. .... Pg.50 ... V28
218th Pl. .... Pg.50 ... U28
218th St. .... Pg.50 ... V28
219th Pl. .... Pg.50 ... U28
219th St. .... Pg.50 ... U28
220th St. .... Pg.50 ... U28
221st St. .... Pg.50 ... U28
222nd Pl. .... Pg.50 ... U28
222nd St. .... Pg.50 ... U28
223rd Pl. .... Pg.50 ... U28
223rd St. .... Pg.50 ... U28
224th Pl. .... Pg.50 ... W27
224th Pl. .... Pg.50 ... U28
224th St. .... Pg.50 ... V27
225th Pl. .... Pg.50 ... U28
225th Pl. .... Pg.50 ... U28
225th St. .... Pg.50 ... U28
226th St. .... Pg.50 ... W28
226th St. .... Pg.50 ... U28
227th St. .... Pg.50 .. W28

## CEMETERIES

St. James Cem. Pg.50 ... U28

## FOREST PRESERVES

Plum Creek F.P. Pg.50 .. W29

## SCHOOLS

Cornell Sch. .. Pg.50 ... V28
Jeffery Sch. .. Pg.50 ... V28
Rickover Jr. H.S.
........... Pg.50 ... V29
Sauk Village Baptist Sch.
........... Pg.50 ... V29
St. James Sch. Pg.50 ... V29
St. Mark's Sch. Pg.50 ... V29
Strassburg Sch.
........... Pg.50 ... V28
Wagner Elem. Sch.
........... Pg.50 ... U28

## SHOPPING CENTERS

Sauk Plaza .. Pg.50 ... V29

## MISCELLANEOUS

Fire Station .. Pg.50 ... U29
Moose Lodge . Pg.50 ... U29
Village Hall .. Pg.50 ... U29

# SCHAUMBURG

Pages 7,11,12,16,17

## STREETS

Abbington Pl. . Pg.16 ... J3
Aberdeen Ct. . Pg.11,16 .. J1
Academy Ct. . Pg.11 ... K1
Acorn Ct. .... Pg.17 ... K4
Adler Ct. .... Pg.16 ... F6
Aegean Dr. .. Pg.16 ... L3
Aimee Ln. ... Pg.11 ... K1
Aimtree Pl. .. Pg.16 ... J3
Akron Ct. .... Pg.16 ... K2
Albany Ct. ... Pg.16 ... M2
Albion Ave. .. Pg.16 ... M3
Alden Ln. .... Pg.16 ... J3
Alder Ct. .... Pg.16 ... K4
Alexandria Ct. Pg.11 ... L3
Algonquin Rd. Pg.12 ... F6
Allcott Ct. ... Pg.16 ... L2
Allerton Dr. .. Pg.17 ... J5
Allison Ln. ... Pg.16 ... J3
Allonby Ln. .. Pg.16 ... J3
Alpine Dr. ... Pg.16 ... J3
Altoona Ct. .. Pg.16 ... J4
Amanda Ln. . Pg.12 ... G5
Amboy Ln. .. Pg.16 ... K3
American Ln. . Pg.17 .. H6-7
Amherst Dr. .. Pg.16 ... J2
Andover Ct. .. Pg.11,16 H,J1
Andrew Ct. .. Pg.16 ... K4
Andrew Ln. .. Pg.16 ... K4
Andria Ct. ... Pg.16 ... L2
Angela Ct. ... Pg.12 ... J6
Angus Ct. ... Pg.16 ... K4
Apple Dr. .... Pg.16 ... H2
Arbor Dr. .... Pg.12 ... G2
Arbor Sq. .... Pg.12 ... G7
Ardmore Ct. . Pg.16 ... L2
Argyll Ln. .... Pg.16 ... J3
Arklow Pl. ... Pg.16 ... K2
Arleen Ct. ... Pg.16 ... L2
Arlington Ln. . Pg.11 ... K1
Arrowwood Ct. Pg.17 ... K7
Arthur Ave. .. Pg.16 ... M4
Asbury Ln. ... Pg.17 ... L6
Ascot Ct. .... Pg.12,17 .. J6
Ash Ct. ..... Pg.16 ... H1
Ashcroft Ln. .. Pg.17 ... J5
Ashley Ln. ... Pg.16 ... J3
Ashton Ct. ... Pg.12 ... K5
Ashwood Ct. . Pg.16 ... K4
Ashwood Dr. . Pg.16 ... K4
Aspen Ct. ... Pg.16 ... K2
Aspen Dr. ... Pg.12 ... G6
Aster Ct. .... Pg.12 ... K7
Athena Ct. ... Pg.16 ... L3
Attleboro Ct. . Pg.16 ... L3
Auburn Ct. ... Pg.11 ... L2
Auburn Ln. ... Pg.16 ... L2
Austin Ln. ... Pg.12 ... J7
Autumn Ave. . Pg.16 ... M2
Avon Ct. .... Pg.16 ... M2
Avondale Ct. . Pg.12 ... L2
Avondale Ln. . Pg.12 ... L2
Azelea Cir. ... Pg.12 ... J7
Bahama Ct. .. Pg.16 ... L4
Bahama Ln. .. Pg.16 ... L4
Balboa Ct. ... Pg.16 ... L4
Baldwin Ct. .. Pg.11,16 .. H1
Balsam Ct. ... Pg.16 ... L4
Bank Dr. .... Pg.17 .. H17
Bar Harbor .. Pg.17 ... K7
Barcliff Ct. ... Pg.16 ... L3
Barcliff Ln. ... Pg.16 ... L3
Bardsey Dr. .. Pg.16 ... K3
Barkwood Rd. Pg.12 ... F6
Barnaby Ct. .. Pg.16 ... L5
Barnaby Ln. .. Pg.12 ... K5
Barrett Ln. ... Pg.17 ... K5
Barton Cir. ... Pg.12,17 .. J6
Basswood Rd. Pg.12 ... G6
Bates Ct. .... Pg.16 ... L4
Bates Ln. .... Pg.16 ... L2
Bay Dr. ..... Pg.7 ... F6
Bayshore Ct. . Pg.16 ... H3
Bayview Pt. .. Pg.12 ... K4
Beachcomber Pg.16 ... L4
Beacon Dr. .. Pg.16 ... L4
Beckett Cir. .. Pg.12 ... J6
Beckett Ln. .. Pg.12,17 J6,7
Bedford Ct. .. Pg.16 ... L3
Beech Ct. ... Pg.17 ... K4
Beech Dr. ... Pg.17 ... K5
Beechwood Ct. Pg.12,17 .. J6
Bellechase Dr. Pg.12 ... J7
Belmont .... Pg.16 ... L3
Bent Tree Ln. . Pg.12 ... G5
Bentley Ln. .. Pg.17 ... L5
Berkley Ct. ... Pg.17 ... K6
Berkshire Ct. . Pg.17 ... K6
Berkshire Ln. . Pg.16 ... L2
Berry Ct. .... Pg.16 ... L3
Berwick Ct. .. Pg.12 ... K4
Beverly Ln. .. Pg.12 ... K4
Birch Pl. .... Pg.12 ... G7
Bird Song ... Pg.16 ... H1
Bishop Ct. ... Pg.16 ... J2
Bittersweet Ct. Pg.17 ... K4
Blackhawk .. Pg.17 ... L5
Bladon Rd. .. Pg.16 ... H3
Blaine Ct. ... Pg.12 ... F6
Blanford Ct. .. Pg.17 ... J7
Blenheim Dr. . Pg.16 ... H3
Bode Rd. .... Pg.16 ... J1
Boston Cir. ... Pg.12 ... L5
Boston Harbor Pg.17 ... M5
Bourne Ln. ... Pg.16 ... L3
Boxwood Dr. . Pg.16 ... L4
Bradford Ct. .. Pg.11 ... L3
Bradford Ln. . Pg.16 ... L3
Braintree Dr. . Pg.16 ... F6
Bramble Ct. .. Pg.11 ... K4
Bramble Ln. .. Pg.16 ... K4
Branchwood Dr.
Breakers Pt. . Pg.16 ... J6
Brendon Dr. . Pg.16 .. H-J1
Brent Ct. .... Pg.16 ... J1
Brentwood Ct. Pg.16 ... L3
Brewster Ln. . Pg.16 ... L3
Brian Ave. ... Pg.16 ... F6
Briar Hill Dr. .. Pg.16 .. J1-2
Briarwood Ct. Pg.16 ... K4
Bridgeport Ct. Pg.17 ... L5
Bridgeview Pl. Pg.16 ... J6
Bridle Ln. .... Pg.12 ... J2
Bridlewood Ct. Pg.13 ... J8
Bright Ridge Dr.
Brighton Ct. .. Pg.12,17 .. J5
Bristol Ln. ... Pg.11 ... J3
Brittany Ct. .. Pg.16 ... H1
Brixham Pl. .. Pg.16 ... K2
Broadway Ln. Pg.11 ... K1
Brockton Ln. . Pg.16 ... L2
Bromley Ct. .. Pg.16 ... L2
Brookdale Dr. Pg.17 ... J2
Brookhill Ct. .. Pg.17 ... L5
Brookstone Ct. Pg.17 ... K7
Brown Ct. ... Pg.16 ... L3
Brunswick Ct. Pg.12 ... L5
Brunswick Harbor
........... Pg.17 ... L5
Brush Rd. ... Pg.16 ... F6
Bryn Mawr Ct. Pg.11 ... K1
Buccaneer Dr. Pg.7 ... F6
Buckingham Ct. Pg.17 ... K7
Burberry Cir. . Pg.17 ... K7
Durberry Ln. . Pg.17 ... L7
Burgess Ct. .. Pg.16 ... H1
Burke Ct. .... Pg.17 ... K6
Burnley Cir. .. Pg.17 ... K5
Burr Oak Ln. . Pg.17 ... K5
Buttercup Ln. Pg.17 ... J7
Buttonwood Cir.
Cable Ln. .... Pg.16 ... K2
Cabot Ln. .... Pg.16 ... K2
Cambia Dr. .. Pg.17 ... L4
Cambourne Ln. Pg.16 ... J2
Cambridge Dr. Pg.16 ... K3
Camden Ct. .. Pg.11 ... J1
Camellia Ln. . Pg.17 ... J7
Cannon Ct. .. Pg.16 ... L2
Canterbury Rd. Pg.16 ... H3
Cape Ln. .... Pg.16 ... L2
Capitol Ct. ... Pg.16 ... L2
Capri Ln. .... Pg.16 ... L2
Captains Cove Pg.7 ... F6
Cardiff Ct. ... Pg.16 ... H2
Cardinal Ct. .. Pg.16 ... J1
Carlisle Ct. ... Pg.16 ... J2
Carlton Ct. ... Pg.16 ... K3
Carlton Ln. ... Pg.11 ... K3
Carmelhead .. Pg.17 ... K5
Carnaby Ct. .. Pg.16 ... J2
Carolina Ct. .. Pg.16 ... M2
Caron Ct. .... Pg.16 ... L2
Carr Ct. ..... Pg.16 ... L2
Carriage Cir. . Pg.17 ... L5
Carriage Ln. .. Pg.17 ... L5
Carryville Ln. . Pg.16 ... K1
Carson Ct. ... Pg.16 ... L2
Carver Ln. ... Pg.16 ... K3
Casa Dr. .... Pg.17 ... J6
Case Ct. ..... Pg.16 ... L2
Cedar Ct. .... Pg.16 ... K4
Cedarcrest Dr. Pg.16 ... L4
Center Ct. ... Pg.16 ... G4
Central Park Blvd.
Century Ct. .. Pg.12 ... H7
Chalfont Ct. .. Pg.16 ... J3
Champlaine Ct. Pg.17 ... L5
Charlene Ln. . Pg.16 ... L4
Charleston Ct. Pg.11 ... K1
Charleston Dr. Pg.11 ... K1
Charlotte Ct. . Pg.16 ... K1
Chartwell Rd. Pg.16 ... H3
Chatham Ct. . Pg.16 ... K2
Chatham Ln. . Pg.16 ... K2
Chatsworth Ct. Pg.12,17 .. J6
Chaucer Ct. .. Pg.16 ... K5
Chelsea Ct. .. Pg.16 .. L3
Chelsea Ln. .. Pg.16 .. L3
Cheltenham Ct. Pg.16 ... H2
Cherry Dr. ... Pg.16 ... J2
Cherry Hill Ct. Pg.16 ... K4
Cherrywood Dr. Pg.12 ... J6
Chesapeake Ln. Pg.16 ... M2
Chestnut Ct. . Pg.16 ... K3
Cheswick Ct. . Pg.11,16 .. J1
Chilmark Ct. . Pg.16 ... L3
Chilmark Ln. . Pg.16 ... K1
Chopin Ct. ... Pg.16 ... K2
Churchill Rd. . Pg.16 ... H3
Civic Dr. ..... Pg.16 ... K3
Clarendon Springs
........... Pg.16 ... J2
Claridge Ct. .. Pg.17 ... L6
Classic Rd. .. Pg.17 ... L4
Clayton Cir. .. Pg.16 ... J1
Clearbrook Ct. Pg.16 ... L5
Clearwater Ln. Pg.17 ... J6
Cleveland Ct. Pg.16 ... K2
Clifton Ct. ... Pg.16 ... L4
Clipper Dr. ... Pg.7 ... F6
Cloud Ct. .... Pg.16 ... L2
Clover Ln. ... Pg.16 ... L2
Cloverdale Ct. Pg.16 ... J2
Cloverdale Ln. Pg.16 ... J2
Cobbler Ln. .. Pg.12 ... J6
Cobblestone Ct. Pg.13 ... J8
Colby Ln. .... Pg.16 ... L2
Cole Ct. ..... Pg.16 ... K2
College Dr. .. Pg.7 ... F6
College Hill Cir. Pg.7 ... F5
Colony Lake Dr. Pg.16 ... H3
Columbia Ct. . Pg.11 ... K1
Columbine Ct. Pg.17 ... J7
Columbine Dr. Pg.17 ... J7
Columbus Dr. Pg.7 ... F6
Colwyn Dr. .. Pg.16 ... J2
Commadore Ct. Pg.16 ... M2
Commadore Ln.
........... Pg.16 ... M2
Commerce Dr. Pg.12 ... J5
Commons Ct. Pg.17 ... H6
Compton Ln. . Pg.16 ... L2
Concord Ln. . Pg.16 ... L3
Concordia ... Pg.17 ... L5
Continental Ln. Pg.16 ... J2
Cooper Ct. ... Pg.12 ... G6
Copley Ct. ... Pg.16 ... L2
Copperfield Ln. Pg.17 ... L6
Coral Ct. .... Pg.16 ... L2
Cornell Ln. ... Pg.16 ... I3
Corporate Crossing
Corsaire Ct. .. Pg.12 ... J7
Cottington Ct. Pg.16 ... J2
Cottington Ln. Pg.16 ... J2
Cottonwood Ct. Pg.12 ... K4
Cottonwood Ln.
........... Pg.17 ... K4
Cotuit Ct. .... Pg.16 ... K3
Country Club Ln.
Countryside Dr. Pg.16 ... L2
County Farm Ln.
........... Pg.11,16 .. H1
Courtenay Ln. Pg.17 ... K6
Courtland Ct. . Pg.16 ... L4
Cove Point .. Pg.17 ... J6
Covehill Ct. .. Pg.16 ... J3
Coventry Rd. . Pg.16 ... G3
Coveside Ln. . Pg.16 ... L4
Covinton Pl. .. Pg.17 ... H2
Crabtree Ln. . Pg.17 ... M4
Cranbrook Ct. Pg.16 ... M3
Cranbrook Dr. Pg.16 ... M3
Crandell Ct. .. Pg.17 ... L5
Crandell Ln. .. Pg.17 ... L5
Crandon I Ln. Pg.16 ... L4
Creek Bend Rd. Pg.12 ... F6
Creekside Dr. Pg.17 ... L4
Creighton Ln. Pg.17 ... L5
Crest Ct., E. .. Pg.17 ... M5
Crest St. ..... Pg.17 ... M5
Crestwood Dr. Pg.12 ... G5
Crooked Creek Rd.
Crown Ct. ... Pg.12 ... F6
Crystal Ct., N. & S.
Cumberland Dr. Pg.16 ... K2
Cutters Mill Ct. Pg.16 ... J2
Cutters Mill Ln. Pg.16 ... J2
Cypress Ct. .. Pg.16 ... K4
Dana Ct. .... Pg.17 ... M5
Danbury Ct. .. Pg.16 ... L4
Daniels Ct. ... Pg.16 ... H3
Dansford Dr. . Pg.12 ... L4
Dante Ct. .... Pg.16 ... K2
Danvers Ct. .. Pg.16 ... L3
Dartmouth Ct. Pg.16 ... K2
Dartmouth Ln. Pg.16 ... K2
Deborah Ct. . Pg.16 ... L5
Dedham Ln. . Pg.16 ... K2
Deerfield Ct. . Pg.16 ... L3
Deerpath Ct. . Pg.17 ... K7
Del Lago Dr. . Pg.16 ... H3
Denham Pl. .. Pg.16 ... H2
Dennis Ct. ... Pg.16 ... L3
Denton Ct. ... Pg.11 ... K1
Derby Ct. .... Pg.12 ... L5
Derry Ct. .... Pg.17 ... L4
Desmond Dr. Pg.16 ... L4
Devonshire Dr. Pg.13 ... J8
Dickens Way . Pg.17 ... L4
Dighton Ln. .. Pg.17 ... H6
Discovery Dr. . Pg.16 ... H1
Dixie Ct. ..... Pg.16 ... M2
Dogwood Ct. . Pg.16 ... K4
Donna Ct. ... Pg.17 ... L5
Dorchester Ct. Pg.16 ... J1
Dorset Ln. ... Pg.17 ... K5
Dover Ct. .... Pg.16 ... L2
Downing Dr. . Pg.16 ... H3
Dracut Ln. ... Pg.17 ... H6
Drake Cir. ... Pg.12 ... L5
Driftwood Ln. Pg.17 ... K7
Drummer Dr. Pg.12 ... G7
Dublin Ln. ... Pg.11,16 .. H1
Dumont Ln. .. Pg.16 ... H2
Dunbar Ct. ... Pg.16 ... J2
Dunlap Pl. ... Pg.16 ... L3
Dunsford Ct. . Pg.16 ... H2
Durham Ct. .. Pg.16 ... L3
Duxbury Ln. . Pg.16 ... L3
E. Point Dr. ... Pg.16 ... L3
Eagle Ct. .... Pg.16 ... J1
East Wood Ct. Pg.12 ... G5
Eastham Ct. . Pg.16 ... K3
Eastham Ln. . Pg.16 ... K3
Eastview St. .. Pg.16 ... J6
Eaton Ct. .... Pg.17 ... L6
Ebbtide Pt. ... Pg.16 ... J6
Eden Dr. .... Pg.16 ... G3
Edgelake Pt. . Pg.16 ... J6
Elgin Ln. ..... Pg.16 ... J3
Ellington Dr. .. Pg.16 ... K3
Ellisville Ln. ... Pg.16 ... J3
Elm Dr. ..... Pg.16 ... K3
Elmhurst Ln. . Pg.16 ... L2
Elmont Ct. ... Pg.16 ... L2
Elmwood Ln. Pg.17 ... K7
Emerald Dr. .. Pg.17 ... J6
Emerson Dr. . Pg.16 ... J2
Epping Pl. ... Pg.16 ... J2
Essex Ct. .... Pg.16 ... K2
Estes Ave. ... Pg.16 ... M3
Estes Ct. .... Pg.16 ... M3
Evening Song Ln.
........... Pg.16 ... H1
Evergreen Ct. Pg.17 ... K4
Exeter Ct. .... Pg.17 ... L4
Exmore Dr. .. Pg.16 ... K3
Fabish Ct. ... Pg.11,16 .. K1
Fairbanks Ct. . Pg.16 ... J6
Fairfield Ct. ... Pg.16 ... K5
Fairhaven Ct. . Pg.16 ... J2
Fairhaven Ln. Pg.16 ... J2
Fairlane Ct. ... Pg.16 ... J2
Fairlane Dr. .. Pg.16 .. L-M2
Fairview Cir. .. Pg.11 ... L3
Fairview Ln. .. Pg.16 ... L3
Falmouth Ln. . Pg.16 ... K3
Farm Gate Dr. Pg.17 ... K4
Farnham Ct. . Pg.16 ... K2
Featherstone Ct.
........... Pg.16 ... J2
Fennel Ct. ... Pg.17 ... K6
Fennel Ln. ... Pg.17 ... K6
Fenwick Ct. .. Pg.16 ... J3
Fenz Rd. .... Pg.16 ... M2
Fermi Ct. .... Pg.16 ... K4
Fern Ct. ..... Pg.17 ... K6
Ferndale Ct. .. Pg.16 ... J3
Fieldstone Ct. Pg.16 ... L3
Finchley Ct. .. Pg.16 ... H2
Fiskeville Ln. . Pg.16 ... L3
Fleming Ln. .. Pg.17 ... L4
Flintshire Dr. . Pg.16 ... J2
Flower Ct. .... Pg.16 ... J1
Forest Ct. .... Pg.17 ... L4
Forest Ln. .... Pg.16 ... L4
Forestdale Ct. Pg.16 ... K2
Foxboro Ct. .. Pg.16 ... L3
Foxboro St. .. Pg.16 ... L3
Foxwood Ct. . Pg.16 ... H3
Fulbright Ln. .. Pg.16 ... J5
Gallery Ct. ... Pg.7 ... F6
Gareth Ln. ... Pg.17 ... K6
Garnet Cir. ... Pg.17 ... J6
Gary Ave. .... Pg.16 ... K2
Gary Ct. ..... Pg.16 ... M2
Gastonbury Cir. Pg.16 ... L3
Gayton Ln. ... Pg.17 ... K5
Geneva Ct. .. Pg.16 ... L2
Georgean Ln. Pg.16 ... K2
Georgia Ct. .. Pg.16 ... M2
Glasgow Ct. . Pg.11,16 .. H1
Glasgow Ln. . Pg.16 ... H1
Glastonbury Ln.
Glen Byron Ct. Pg.11 ... J3
Glengarry Ct. Pg.11,16 .. J1
Glenn Ct. .... Pg.17 ... K5
Glenridge Ln. Pg.16 ... K5
Glenview Ct. . Pg.11 ... L3
Glouchester Cir.
Glouchester Harbor
........... Pg.17 ... M5
Golf (Evanston- Elgin) Rd.
........... Pg.16 ... H6
Good Speed Ln.
Governors Dr. Pg.16 ... J1
Grace Ct. .... Pg.16 ... L3
Grace Ln. .... Pg.16 ... L3
Grand Central Ln.
........... Pg.16 ... K3
Green Briar Dr. Pg.12 ... K7
Green Bridge Ct.
........... Pg.11,16 .. H1
Greenhill Ln. . Pg.17 ... K5
Greenview Ct. Pg.17 ... L5
Gregory Ct. .. Pg.16 ... L4
Gregory Ln. .. Pg.16 ... L4
Greystone Ct. Pg.17 ... K7
Groen Ct. .... Pg.16 ... K6
Groen Ln. .... Pg.17 ... K6
Grove Ave. ... Pg.16 ... M2
Grovenor Dr. . Pg.17 ... L6
Hackberry Ct. Pg.17 ... K4
Hadley Run Ln. Pg.12 ... J6
Halifax Ct. ... Pg.16 ... L3
Hamilton Cir. . Pg.11 ... J1
Hamilton Pl. .. Pg.11 ... J1
Hammond Dr. Pg.12 ... F6
Hampshire Ct. Pg.17 ... L5
Hampton Harbor
........... Pg.17 ... M5
Hampton Ln. . Pg.16 ... J2
Hanley Ct. ... Pg.16 ... H2
Hanover Ct. .. Pg.12 ... J6
Hanscom Ct. . Pg.16 ... K1
Harbour Ct. .. Pg.16 ... M2
Harmon Dr. .. Pg.16 ... K2
Hartford Ct. .. Pg.17 ... L4
Hartford Dr. .. Pg.17 ... L3
Hartley Rd. .. Pg.12 ... H7
Hartmann Dr. Pg.16 ... L2
Harvard Ct. .. Pg.16 ... L2
Harvard Ln. .. Pg.16 ... L2
Harwich Ln. .. Pg.16 ... J3
Hastings Ct. .. Pg.16 ... K4
Haverford Ct. Pg.13 ... J8
Haverhill Ln. . Pg.16 ... L3
Hawthorne Ct. Pg.17 ... K7
Heather Ct. .. Pg.17 ... K7
Heatherstone Ct.
Heatherstone Dr.
........... Pg.12,17 .. J6
Helene Ln. ... Pg.16 ... K3
Hemlock Pl. .. Pg.12 ... G7
Heron Ave. ... Pg.16 ... M2
Heron Ct. .... Pg.16 ... M2
Hickory Ct. ... Pg.17 ... K4
Hickory Ln. .. Pg.16 ... K4
Higgins Rd. .. Pg.16 ... J7
High Pl. ..... Pg.17 ... K6
Highland Ct. . Pg.11,16 .. H1
Hillcrest Blvd. Pg.12 ... G4
Hillcrest Dr., S. Pg.17 ... M6
Hillside Ct. ... Pg.17 ... L5
Hilltop Ct. .... Pg.16 ... K4
Hilton Dr. .... Pg.16 ... K4
Hillwick Ln. ... Pg.17 ... K5
Hingham Ct. . Pg.11 ... L3
Hingham Ln. . Pg.16 ... L3
Hinkle Ct. .... Pg.17 ... K4
Hinkle Ln. .... Pg.11,16 .. K4
Hitching Post Ln.
Holli Ct. ..... Pg.16 ... J2
Holliston Ct. .. Pg.16 ... J3
Holliston Dr. .. Pg.16 ... J3
Holmes Way . Pg.16 ... J1
Holyoke Ct. .. Pg.17 ... L4
Houlton Ct. .. Pg.16 ... L4
Howard St. .. Pg.17 ... M5
Hunterdon Ct. Pg.11 ... J1
Hunters Cir. .. Pg.17 ... L4
Hunters Crescent
Huntington Ct. Pg.17 ... L5
Huntley Ct. .. Pg.16 ... H1
Huntwyck Ct. Pg.13 ... J8
Hyannis Ct. .. Pg.12 ... J6
Hyde Ct. ..... Pg.11 ... K1
Idle Wild Ct. .. Pg.12 ... G5
Idleston Ln. .. Pg.16 ... K4
Illinois Ave. .. Pg.17 ... K5
Indian Hill Dr. Pg.16 ... M5
Ironwood Ct. . Pg.17 ... K6
Irving Park Rd. Pg.16 ... M3
Islington Ln. .. Pg.16 ... J2
Iverson Ct. ... Pg.16 ... J2
Iverson Ln. ... Pg.16 ... J2
Ivy Ct. ...... Pg.17 ... L4
James Ct. ... Pg.16 ... J2
Jamestown Ct. Pg.17 ... L5
Janine Ln. ... Pg.16 ... L4
Jason Ct. .... Pg.16 ... H1
Jason Ct. .... Pg.16 ... H1
Jeffery Ct. ... Pg.16 ... K3
Jeffery Ln. ... Pg.16 ... K3
Jessica Ct. ... Pg.16 ... F6
John Ct. ..... Pg.17 ... K5
John Rolfe Dr. Pg.16 ... K5
John Smith Dr. Pg.16 ... K5
Jones Rd. .... Pg.16 ... G3
Juli Ct. ...... Pg.16 ... L3
Juli Dr. ...... Pg.16 ... L3
Juniper Ln. ... Pg.16 ... K4
Kathy Dr. .... Pg.17 ... L6
Kavalier Ct. .. Pg.16 ... L3
Keats Ct. ..... Pg.16 ... K5
Kemah Ct. ... Pg.16 ... K4
Kemah Ln. ... Pg.16 ... K4
Kendall Ct. ... Pg.11 ... K1
Kendrick Ct. .. Pg.12 ... J3
Kenilworth Dr. Pg.17 ... K5
Kenmore Ct. . Pg.11,16 .. K1
Kensington Dr. Pg.16 ... J1
Kent Ct. ..... Pg.16 ... L4
Kerri Ct. ..... Pg.12 ... J6
Killarney Ct. .. Pg.16 ... L4
Kimberly Dr. . Pg.17 ... J7
Kings Mill Ct. . Pg.17 ... K5
Kingsbury Dr. Pg.11 ... L1
Kingsley Dr. .. Pg.12 ... J2
Kingsport Dr. Pg.17 ... L6
Kingston Ct. . Pg.11 ... K2
Kingston Ln. . Pg.16 ... K2
Kirkwall Ln. .. Pg.17 ... K5
Knights Bridge Ln.
........... Pg.11 ... G3
Knollwood Dr. Pg.16 .. H-K1
Knollwood Dr. Pg.16 .. H-K1
Knottingham Ct.
Knottingham Dr.
........... Pg.17 ... L6
Kristen Cir. ... Pg.12 ... G5
Kristen Dr. ... Pg.12 ... G5
Laconia Ln. .. Pg.16 ... L4
Lakeland Dr. . Pg.17 ... J6
Lakeview Pt. . Pg.17 ... J6
Lambert Ct. .. Pg.17 ... K5
Lamorak Ct. .. Pg.16 ... K6
Lamorak Ln. . Pg.16 ... K6
Lancshire Ct. . Pg.16 ... H2
Langley Dr. .. Pg.17 ... K5
Largo Ct. .... Pg.16 ... L2
Lauder Ln. ... Pg.16 ... L6
Laurel Ln. .... Pg.17 ... M5
Laurette Ln. .. Pg.17 ... K5
Lawn Ct. ..... Pg.11,16 .. K1
Lawson Rd. .. Pg.16 ... J2
Lear Ct. ..... Pg.17 ... J1
Leeds Pass .. Pg.16 ... J3
Lela Ct. ..... Pg.16 ... K3
Lengl Dr. ..... Pg.16 ... K3
Lela Ln. ..... Pg.16 ... K3
Lenox Ct. .... Pg.11,16 .. K1
Leslie Ln. .... Pg.16 ... J2
Lewis Ct. ..... Pg.17 ... K5
Lexington Cir. Pg.12 ... J7
Lexington Dr. Pg.17 ... J7
Liberty Ct. ... Pg.16 ... J1
Library Ln. ... Pg.17 ... J4
Lighthouse ... Pg.16 ... L6
Lilac Ct. ..... Pg.16 ... M2
Lily Ct. ...... Pg.16 ... L4
Limerick Ln. .. Pg.17 ... L4
Lincoln Meadows Cir.
Lincoln Meadows Dr.
........... Pg.12 ... J7
Lincoln St. ... Pg.17 ... J4
Lincolnshire Ct. Pg.12 ... K5
Linden Ln. ... Pg.12 ... F7
Linsey Ave. .. Pg.16 ... J2
Linton Ct. .... Pg.16 ... M2
Linwood Ln. . Pg.16 ... L4
Lippitt Ct. .... Pg.16 ... L3
Locust Dr. ... Pg.12 ... G7
Long Island Dr. Pg.17 ... L5
Long Meadow Dr.
Longboat Dr. . Pg.16 ... H3
Longboat Ln. . Pg.16 ... H3
Longtree Ct. . Pg.12 ... G7
Lorelei Dr. ... Pg.16 ... J2
Lorraine Pl. .. Pg.12 ... J7
Lowell Cir. ... Pg.11 ... L3
Lowell Ln. .... Pg.16 ... L3
Lucre Ct. ..... Pg.12 ... J6
Lundy Ln. .... Pg.17 ... K5
Lunt Ave. .... Pg.16 .. M3-4
Lynnfield Ln. . Pg.16 ... K2
Madeline Ct. . Pg.16 ... J1
Magnolia Ct. . Pg.11 ... J1
Maidstone Ct. Pg.11 ... J1
Malden Ct. ... Pg.17 ... L4
Mall Dr. ..... Pg.17 ... K5
Mallard Ct. ... Pg.12 ... L5
Mallard Dr. ... Pg.12 ... L5
Manchester Cir. Pg.16 ... L3
Manchester Ct. Pg.16 ... L3
Manchester Dr. Pg.16 ... L3
Manchester Rd. Pg.12 ... L6
Manomet Ct. . Pg.12,17 .. H6
Manomet Ln. Pg.16 ... H6
Manor Ct. .... Pg.16 ... J1
Mansfield Ct. . Pg.16 ... J2
Maple Pl. .... Pg.12 ... G7
Maplewood Ct. Pg.17 ... K7
Marble Hill Ct. Pg.17 ... J5
Margate Ct. .. Pg.16 ... K5
Marie Ln. .... Pg.16 ... K3
Mariner Pt. ... Pg.16 ... J6
Martingale Rd. Pg.17 ... J7
Mashpee Ln. Pg.16 ... J3
Matfield Ct. .. Pg.16 ... L3
Mayfair Ln. ... Pg.16 ... K7
Maywood Ln. Pg.16 ... L2
McConnor Pkwy.
Meacham Rd. Pg.16 ... J7
Medford Cir. . Pg.17 ... L6

Melody Ct. Pg.16 J2
Mendon Ln. Pg.16 K2
Mercury Ct. Pg.16 L2
Mercury Dr. Pg.16 M2
Merlin Dr. Pg.17 K6
Mermaid Ct. Pg.16 L4
Michelle Cir. Pg.12 J7
Michelle Pl. Pg.12 J7
Middlebury Ct. Pg.17 K7
Milan Ct. Pg.16 L4
Milford Ct. Pg.16 L4
Millbrook Ct. Pg.16 K2
Millbrook Ln. Pg.16 K3
Mills Ln. Pg.16 K1
Milton Ln. Pg.16 L3
Mirage Ln. Pg.11 J1
Mitchell Blvd. Pg.16 M4
Mohawk Ct. Pg.17 L-M5
Mohegan Ln. Pg.16 L3
Monet Ct. Pg.16 L4
Monson Ct. Pg.7 J7
Montclair Cir. Pg.12 J6
Montclair Pl. Pg.12 J6
Monterey Ave. Pg.17 M5
Moon Raker Dr. Pg.7 F6
Mora Ct. Pg.16 M2
Morning Song Ct. Pg.16 H1
Morningside Ct. Pg.12 J6
Morningside Dr. Pg.12 J6
Morse Ave. Pg.16 M3-4
Mullinger Ct. Pg.17 L4
Mystic Harbor Ln. Pg.16 L4
Nantucket Har. Pg.17 M5
National Pkwy. Pg.12 H6
Natwick Ln. Pg.16 K1
Nauset Pg.16 K3
Neal Ct. Pg.17 K5
New Mills Ct. Pg.17 K5
Newbury Ct. Pg.12,17 H6
Newbury Ln. Pg.12,17 H6
Newgate Ct. Pg.17 K5
Newport Harbor Pg.16 M5
Newton Ct. Pg.11 K1
Niagara Ave. Pg.17 L5
Nicolette Ave. Pg.12 J7
Night Song Ct. Pg.16 H1
Norman Ct. Pg.17 M5
Normandy Cir. Pg.12 J7
Northbury Ct. Pg.17 K6
Northwest Tollway Pg.12 G5-6
Northwind Cir. Pg.11 H2
Norwell Ct. Pg.16 L2
Norwell Ln. Pg.16 L2
Norwood Ln. Pg.16 L3
Notis Ct. Pg.11 L3
Oak Creek Ln. Pg.17 K4
Oak Knoll Ct. Pg.17 K7
Oak Lawn Ct. Pg.12 G5
Oak Meadow Ct. Pg.17 K7
Oakmont Ln. Pg.12,17 J6
Oakview Ct. Pg.16 K4
Oakwood Ct. Pg.16 L3
Ocean Dr. Pg.17 L5
Odlum Dr. Pg.11 J1
Old Barn Rd. Pg.17 K5
Old Bridge Pg.17 K5
Old Kings Ct. Pg.16 J1
Old Mill Dr. Pg.17 K5
Old Plum Grove Rd. Pg.7 F6
Old Schaumburg Rd. Pg.12 K7
Oleander Dr. Pg.17 J7
Oliver Ct. Pg.17 L4
Omni Dr. Pg.12 L5
Onyx Pg.16 J1
Onyx Ct. Pg.16 J1
Orchard Ct. Pg.16 M2
Orleans Ln. Pg.16 K3
Orrington Ct. Pg.12 J6
Osage Ln. Pg.16 J3
Oxford Ct. Pg.16 H2
Oxhill Ct. Pg.16 J1
Palace Ct. Pg.16 J1
Palisades Pt. Pg.17 J6
Palmer Dr. Pg.12 F6
Park Dr. Pg.16 J2
Park Trail Ct. Pg.13 J8
Parker Ct. Pg.16 J3
Parker Dr. Pg.16 J3
Parkville Rd. Pg.16 J2
Partridge Dr. Pg.17 L5
Patricia Ct. Pg.16 K3
Patricia Dr. Pg.16 K3
Patuxet Ct. Pg.16 J3
Pauline Cir. Pg.12 J6
Paxton Ln. Pg.16 K2
Payne Rd. Pg.17 H6
Peach Ln. Pg.16 H2
Pebble Ct. Pg.17 K6
Pembridge Ln. Pg.17 K5
Pembroke Ct. Pg.11 K1
Pembroke Dr. Pg.11,16 K1
Pennsbury Ct. Pg.11,16 J1
Pennview Ln. Pg.16 H1
Pennwood Ct. Pg.12,17 K6
Penny Ln. Pg.12 G6
Penrith Pl. Pg.16 J2
Peppertree Pg.17 K4
Perimeter Dr. Pg.12 H7
Persimmon Ct. Pg.16 M2
Perth Dr. Pg.16 J3
Petersham Ln. Pg.17 J7
Pheasant Walk Dr. Pg.17 L5
Pickwick Dr. Pg.17 L4
Pine Valley Dr. Pg.7 F6
Pinehurst Ln. Pg.16 L3
Pinetree Ln. Pg.17 K7
Pirates Cove Pg.7 F6
Plaza Dr. Pg.17 H7
Pleasant Dr. Pg.17 K4
Plum Grove Rd. Pg.17 J6
Plum Tree Ct. Pg.17 K6
Plumrose Ct. Pg.12 J5
Plumrose Ln. Pg.12 J5
Plumwood Ct. Pg.12,17 J6
Plumwood Dr. Pg.12,17 J6
Plymouth Ln. Pg.16 L3
Pocasset Ct. Pg.16 K2
Pochet Ct. Pg.16 K4
Pochet Ln. Pg.16 K4
Point Dr., N., S., E. & W. Pg.17 L6
Pondview Ct. Pg.16 K3
Poplar Pl. Pg.12 G7
Port Way Pg.7 F6
Portland Dr. Pg.16 J2
Portsmouth Ln. Pg.16 K2
Post Oak Pl. Pg.12 G7
Prairie Sq. Pg.12 G7
Prairie Wind Ln. Pg.12 G7
Pratt Ave., N. & S. Pg.16 M3
Presidio Ct. Pg.12 G5
Preston Dr. Pg.16 J3
Preston Ln. Pg.17 K6
Primrose Ln. Pg.16 J1
Prince Charles Ct. Pg.11 G3
Prince Charles Ln. Pg.11 G3
Prince Edward Cir. Pg.17 L5
Prince Edward Dr. Pg.17 L6
Princeton Ct. Pg.16 L2
Princeton Ln. Pg.16 L2
Putnam Ln. Pg.16 L4
Quanset Ct. Pg.16 J3
Queens Ct. Pg.17 K5
Quincy Ct. Pg.17 L4
Quindel Ave. Pg.17 K5
Quonset Ct. Pg.16 J3
Radcliffe Ln. Pg.16 L3
Radley Cir. Pg.12 J6
Raleigh Ct. Pg.11 K1
Ramsey Cir. Pg.16 H1
Raymond Ct. Pg.17 K5
Rebecca Ct. Pg.16 L3
Redwood Ln. Pg.16 K4
Reedham Pass Pg.16 K2
Reflections Way Pg.11 J1
Regal Ct. Pg.16 J2
Regatta Ct. Pg.12 J6
Regatta Pt. Pg.17 J6
Regency Ct. Pg.16 M3
Regency Dr. Pg.16 M3
Regent Cir. Pg.17 J5
Regent Cir. Ln. Pg.17 H5
Remington Ln. Pg.12 G5
Remington Rd. Pg.17 H6
Republic Ct. Pg.12 L5
Revere Cir. Pg.16 K2
Richard Ct. Pg.17 K5
Richmond Ct. Pg.16 H2
Ridge Ct. Pg.17 K6
Ridgeway Ct. Pg.16 J3
Ripplebrook Ct. Pg.13 J8
Rob Roy Ct. Pg.11,16 H1
Rochester Ct. Pg.11 K1
Rockne Ct. Pg.16 J1
Rodenburg Rd. Pg.16 M3
Romm Ct. Pg.16 J1
Rose Ct. Pg.16 J2
Roselle Rd. Pg.17 L5
Rosewood Ct. Pg.12,17 K6
Roslyn Ct. Pg.16 J3
Roslyn Ln. Pg.16 J3
Roslyn Rd. Pg.17 M5
Rothbury Ct. Pg.17 L5
Routh Ct. Pg.12 G5
Roxbury Ln. Pg.16 J3
Royal Ct. Pg.16 K3
Rugby Pl. Pg.16 J3
Ruskin Ct. Pg.16 L3
Ruskin Ln. Pg.16 L3
Russelwood Ct. Pg.11,16 K1
Russet Ct. Pg.17 L4
Rutland Ln. Pg.17 J7
Sagamore Ct. Pg.16 J3
Sagamore Dr. Pg.16 J3
Salado Ct. Pg.12 G5
Salem Ct. Pg.16 K3
Salem Dr. Pg.16 H-L3
Salford Dr. Pg.17 L6
Samoset Ct. Pg.16 K4
Samoset Ln. Pg.16 K4
Sandalwood Ct. Pg.17 K7
Sandburg Dr. Pg.12 J7
Sandhurst Ct. Pg.17 K6
Sandpebble Dr. Pg.16 L4
Santuit Ct. Pg.16 J3
Sarah Constant Ln. Pg.16 H1
Sarah's Grove Ln. Pg.12 K4
Saugus Ln. Pg.17 J7
Savannah Ln. Pg.16 M2
Savoy Ct. Pg.16 K3
Saylesville Ln. Pg.16 L3
Scarsdale Ct. Pg.17 K7
Schaumburg Ct. Pg.17 K5
Schaumburg Rd. Pg.16 K3
Schooner Pt. Pg.17 L4
Scully Ct. Pg.12 K5
Scully Dr. Pg.17 K5
Seafarer Dr. Pg.16 L4
Seaside Ct. Pg.16 L3
Seaton Ln. Pg.11 J2
Seaview Ct. Pg.16 L4
Seers Ct. Pg.12 J6
Seers Dr. Pg.12 J6
Selkirk Dr. Pg.16 J3
Sequoia Ct. Pg.16 K4
Serenade Ct. Pg.17 L4
Seven Pines Rd. Pg.17 K7
Seville Ct. Pg.16 M2
Shady Ln. Pg.12 J7
Shagbark Ct. Pg.17 K4
Shakespeare Ct. Pg.16 K2
Shannock Cir. Pg.16 L3
Shannock Ln. Pg.16 L3
Sharon Ln. Pg.16 K3
Shattuck Ct. Pg.16 K3
Shattuck Ln. Pg.16 K3
Shaw Ct. Pg.16 H1
Sheffield Ridge Pg.16 H1
Shell Ct. Pg.16 L4
Sherborn Ln. Pg.16 K1
Sheridan Ln. Pg.17 K5
Sherwood Dr. Pg.17 K6
Shore Ct. Pg.17 M5
Shore Dr. Pg.17 M5
Shoreline Cir. Pg.17 J6
Sienna Ct. Pg.17 L4
Silhouette Pl. Pg.11 J1
Silvana Ct. Pg.16 J6
Silverwood Ct. Pg.17 K7
Sky Water Dr. Pg.12 F7
Skyvue Ln. Pg.16 J1
Sleepy Hollow Ct. Pg.12 G5
Slingerland Dr. Pg.16 L2
Somerset Ct. Pg.16 K7
Somerset Ln. Pg.16 K3
Song Sparrow Ct. Pg.12 G7
Southbridge Ct. Pg.11 H2
Southbridge Ln. Pg.11 H2
Southbury Ct. Pg.17 K6
Southwick Ln. Pg.17 J7
Southwind Cir. Pg.11 H2
Spinnaker Pt. Pg.17 J6
Spring Cove Dr. Pg.16 L4
Spring South Rd. Pg.16 M2
Spring Valley Ct. Pg.12,17 K6
Springinsguth Rd. Pg.16 L2
Spruce Ct. Pg.16 K4
Spruce Dr. Pg.16 K4
Squanto Ct. Pg.16 K4
St. Claire Cir. Pg.12 J6
St. Claire Pl. Pg.12 J7
Staffire Ln. Pg.16 K1
Staffmark Ln. Pg.17 K5
Stamford Ct. Pg.16 L4
Standish Ln. Pg.16 K3
Stanley Ct. Pg.16 H2
Stanton Ct. Pg.17 J5
Starboard Pt. Pg.17 J6
State Pkwy. Pg.12 J5
Steeplechase Ct. Pg.13 J8
Stevens Dr. Pg.12 K7
Stirling Ln. Pg.11,16 H1
Stock Port Ln. Pg.17 K5
Stockbridge Ct. Pg.16 J2
Stone Circle Ct. Pg.12 J6
Stone Gate Cir. Pg.17 K5
Stone Hedge Pg.16 H3
Stone Hill Ln. Pg.17 K5
Stonefield Ct. Pg.13 J8
Stonewall Ct. Pg.17 J6
Stonington Ct. Pg.16 L3
Stormy Ct. Pg.16 M2
Stoughton Ct. Pg.16 J3
Stratford Ln. Pg.17 L6
Stratham Ct. Pg.16 L3
Stratton Pond Ln. Pg.16 J2
Sturnbridge Ct. Pg.12,17 H6
Sturnbridge Ln. Pg.17 H6
Sudbury Ct. Pg.16 L3
Sue Ln. Pg.7 F7
Suffield Terr. Pg.17 L6
Sumac Ct. Pg.17 K4
Sumac Ln. Pg.17 K4
Summer Song Ct. Pg.16 H1
Summit Ct. Pg.17 K5
Summit Dr. Pg.17 M5
Sunfish Pt. Pg.17 J6
Superior Ct. Pg.12 K5
Surfside Pt. Pg.17 J6
Surrey Ln. Pg.17 L6
Susan Ct. Pg.17 K6
Sussex Cir. Pg.17 K5
Sutton Ln. Pg.16 J2
Swansea Ct. Pg.16 L3
Swartmore Ct. Pg.16 L2
Sycamore Pl. Pg.17 G7
Syracuse Ln. Pg.16 L2
Tadmore Ct. Pg.16 J2
Tall Timbers Rd. Pg.12 F6
Tamworth Pl. Pg.16 K2
Tarpon Ct. Pg.16 L4
Taunton Ct. Pg.16 L3
Teal Ct. Pg.17 K6
Tebay Pl. Pg.16 J2
Terrace Ct. Pg.17 K6
Thacker St. Pg.17 J6
Thames Cir. Pg.17 L5
Thames Dr. Pg.17 L5
Thistle Ct. Pg.11,16 J1
Thoreau Ct. Pg.16 L2
Thoreau Ln. Pg.12 G7
Thorney Lea Terr. Pg.16 K3
Thornhill Ct. Pg.17 K7
Thornton Ct. Pg.17 L5
Thornwood Dr. Pg.17 M4
Ticknor Ct. Pg.16 M2
Tiffany Dr. Pg.16 K1
Tilipi Ct. Pg.16 K4
Tilipi Ln. Pg.16 K4
Timbercrest Ct. Pg.16 K4
Timbercrest Dr. Pg.16 K4
Timberwood Ct. Pg.12,17 K6
Timothy Ct. Pg.17 K5
Tipperary Ct. Pg.17 L5
Tisbury Ct. Pg.16 L3
Tisbury Ln. Pg.16 L3
Tiverton Ct. Pg.16 L3
Tobey Ct. Pg.16 J3
Tonset Pg.16 K2
Tory Ct. Pg.12 J6
Tower Rd. Pg.12 G6-7
Tracy Ct. Pg.17 M5
Trails Dr. Pg.12 J6
Tralee Ct. Pg.17 L4
Travis Ct. Pg.12 G5
Treebark Ct. Pg.11 K4
Treebark Dr. Pg.16 K4
Trent Ln. Pg.17 K6
Trenton Ct. Pg.17 K6
Truro Ct. Pg.16 J3
Tudor Lane Pg.17 K5
Tulip Ct. Pg.11,16 K1
Tullarmore Ct. Pg.17 L5
Tyburn Dr. Pg.16 K3
Tyler Dr. Pg.17 M5
Vado Ct. Pg.16 M2
Valley Lake Dr. Pg.12 G4
Valley View Dr. Pg.16 M2
Vassar Ct. Pg.16 L2
Vassar Ln. Pg.16 L2
Venice Ct. Pg.16 L4
Verona Pl. Pg.16 L4
Victoria Ln. Pg.16 K3
Viola Ct. Pg.16 J2
Vista Ct. Pg.16 M2
Waban Ct. Pg.16 K2
Waban Ln. Pg.16 K2
Wainno Ln. Pg.16 J3
Wakeby Pg.16 K2
Wakefield Ln. Pg.16 K3
Walden Ct. Pg.16 L2
Walnut Ln. Pg.16 H-L2
Walpole Ln. Pg.16 K3
Wapoos Ct. Pg.16 J3
Wareham Ln. Pg.16 K2
Warwick Ct. Pg.16 K2
Warwick Ln. Pg.16 K1-2
Waterbury Ln. Pg.12 K5
Waterford Dr. Pg.17 J6
Waterford Rd. Pg.17 L5
Waverley Ln. Pg.16 K2
Wax Wing Ct. Pg.12 G7
Wayland Ct. Pg.12 G7
Wayland Ln. Pg.16 K2
Weathersfield Way Pg.16,17 K2-5
Webley Ct. Pg.17 K6
Webley Ln. Pg.17 K6
Webster Ct. Pg.16 K2
Webster Ln. Pg.16 K-L2
Wedgewood Ln. Pg.16 K2
Wellesley Ln. Pg.16 K2
Westbridge Ct. Pg.11 H2
Westbridge Ln. Pg.11 H2
Westchester Cir. Pg.12 L5
Westchester Dr. Pg.16 M2
Westchester Rd. Pg.17 L5
Westfield Ln. Pg.16 L3
Weston Pg.16 K2
Westover Ct. Pg.16 K2
Westover Ln. Pg.16 K-M2
Weyers Ct. Pg.16 M2
Weymouth Ct. Pg.16 K2
Weymouth Ln. Pg.11 K2
Whalom Ln. Pg.17 H6
Whidah Ct. Pg.16 J3
White Branch Ct., N. & S. Pg.16 H1
White Oak Ct. Pg.12 G5
White Oak Ln. Pg.12 G5
White Pines Dr. Pg.12 K4
Whitehall Ct. Pg.16 J2
Whitesail Dr. Pg.17 J6
Whitman Ct. Pg.12 K7
Whitman Dr. Pg.12 K7
Whittier Ln. Pg.16 K2
Wianno Ln. Pg.16 J3
Wickham Dr. Pg.16 J3
Wild Flower Ct. Pg.12 K7
Wild Flower Ln. Pg.12 K7
Wildberry Ct. Pg.17 K7
Wiley Rd. Pg.12 G6
Wilkening Ct. Pg.12 G5
Williams Ct. Pg.16 K3
Williams Dr. Pg.16 K3
Williamsburg Dr. Pg.17 K7
Willington Dr. Pg.16 J2
Willow Brook Ct. Pg.12 G5
Willow Ct. Pg.11,16 H1
Willow Rd. Pg.17 J7
Willowby Ct. Pg.13 J8
Wilmette Ct. Pg.17 K7
Wilmslow Ln. Pg.16 J2
Wilton Ln. Pg.16 K2
Wiltshire Ct. Pg.17 K5
Winchester Ct. Pg.16 K2
Winchester Ln. Pg.16 K2
Wind Mill Pg.17 K4
Wind Song Ct. Pg.16 H1
Wind Song Dr. Pg.16 H1
Windemere Cir. Pg.11 H2
Windsor Dr. Pg.17 L5
Windward Dr. Pg.17 J6
Wingate Dr. Pg.17 K6
Winston Ln. Pg.16 K2
Winthrop Ct. Pg.16 K2
Winthrop Ln. Pg.16 K2
Wise Rd. Pg.16 L4
Wisteria Ln. Pg.12 K7
Withaeger Dr. Pg.17 H5
Woburn Ln. Pg.17 J7
Wolcott Ct. Pg.12 K5
Woodbury Ct. Pg.17 K7
Woodcroft Ln. Pg.12,17 J6
Woodfield Dr. Pg.12 H7
Woodfield Office Ct. Pg.17 H6
Woodfield Rd. Pg.17 H6-7
Woodland Dr. Pg.12 G7
Woodside Ct. Pg.12,17 K6
Woodville Ln. Pg.17 K5
Woonsocket Ct. Pg.16 L3
Worcester Ct. Pg.16 L4
Wright Blvd. Pg.16 M3
Wyoma Ln. Pg.16 K1
Yale Ln. Pg.16 L2
Yardley Ln. Pg.16 K1
Yarmouth Pg.16 K3
Yorkshire Pg.16 K2

### AIRPORTS
Municipal Helistop Pg.12 H6
Schaumburg Regional Airport Pg.16 M3

### CEMETERIES
St. Peter's Cemetery Pg.17 J5

### GOLF COURSES
Schaumburg Golf Club Pg.12 J5
Walnut Greens G.C. Pg.11 H2

### PARKS
Abrahamson Park Pg.17 K5
Apollo Park Pg.17 K5
Atcher Park Pg.16 L2
Bock Park Pg.16 K3
Brandenburg Park Pg.16 J1
Campanelli Park Pg.16 K3
Colony Lake Park Pg.16 H3
Cove Park Pg.16 L4
Derda Park Pg.16 K2
Dooley Park Pg.16 L3
Eagle Park Pg.16 L4
Fairview Park Pg.17 J5
Falk Park Pg.16 L3
Freedom Park Pg.16 L3
Grey Farm Park Pg.16 K2
Henry Tereda Park Pg.16 K3
Hilltop Park Pg.16 J2
Hoover Park Pg.16 J2
Jaycee Park Pg.16 L3
Kessel Park Pg.11 G3
Kingsport East Park Pg.17 L6
Lancer Creek Park Pg.17 L5
Levitt Park Pg.16 L3
Munao Park Pg.16 L4
Oak Hollow Park Pg.16 K4
Pochet Park Pg.16 K4
Prairie Park Pg.16 J2
Roberts Park Pg.16 L4
Slingerland Park Pg.17 L5
Sunset Park Pg.17 M5
The Field Park Pg.16 H4
Timbercrest Park Pg.17 K5
Vogelei Park Pg.16 H4
Woodstock Park Pg.16 K4
Zocher Park Pg.16 H3

### SCHOOLS
Acarath Discovery Center Pg.12 G5
Addams Jr. H.S. Pg.16 L2
Aldrin Sch. Pg.16 L4
Blackwell Sch. Pg.16 J2
Campanelli Sch. Pg.16 K2
Churchill Sch. Pg.11 G3
Collins Sch. Pg.17 K5
Dirkson Sch. Pg.17 K5
Dooley Sch. Pg.16 L3
Enders Salk Sch. Pg.16 J3
Frost Jr. H.S. Pg.17 L4
Hale Sch. Pg.16 L3
J. Edgar Hoover Sch. Pg.16 J2
Keller Jr. H.S. Pg.16 H3
Roosevelt University Pg.12 G7
Schaumburg Christian Sch. Pg.12 J5
Schaumburg H.S. Pg.11 K3
St. Peter's Luth. Sch. Pg.17 K5

### SHOPPING CENTERS
Annex S.C. Pg.16 H4
Higgins Golf S.C. Pg.16 H4
Park St. Claire S.C. Pg.12 J7
Poplar Creek South Plaza Pg.16 H2
Prairie Towne S.C. Pg.16 K1
Schaumburg Rd. Shopping Plaza Pg.16 K2
Shopping Plaza Pg.17 H5
Shops of Schaumburg Court Pg.11 K1
Streets of Woodfield S.C. Pg.12 J7
Town Square S.C. Pg.17 K5
Weatherway Shopping Plaza Pg.17 L5
Wiseway Plaza Pg.16 M2
Woodfield Commons S.C. Pg.17 H7
Woodfield Commons West Pg.12 H6
Woodfield Green S.C. Pg.12 H7
Woodfield Mall Pg.17 H7

### MISCELLANEOUS
Alexian Baseball Stadium (Schaumburg Flyers) M2
Chicago Antheneum Museum Pg.16 K4
Dist. 54 Administration Bldg. Pg.17 K6
Dist. 54 Nature Center Pg.17 L4
Fire Department Pg.12 G5
Meineke Pool & Comm. Center Pg.12 K5
Meinke Park District Administration Pg.17 K5
Pace Bus Station Pg.12 J7
Post Office Pg.16 K4
Schaumburg Community Recreation Center Pg.16 J2
Schaumburg Police Dept. Pg.16 K3
Schaumburg Township Bldg. Pg.16 K4
The Barn Rec. Center Pg. K3

## SCHAUMBURG TOWNSHIP
Pages 12,16,17

### STREETS
Albion Ave. Pg.17 M4
Algonquin Dr. Pg.17 M6
Blackhawk Dr. Pg.17 M5
Circle Ct. Pg.12 G7
Circle Dr., S. Pg.12 G7
Council Ct. Pg.17 M5
Crest Ave. Pg.16 M2
Crest St. Pg.17 M5
Devon Pg.17 M5
Elmwood Ln., N. & S. Pg.12 G7
Grant St. Pg.17 M4
Green Briar Ln. Pg.17 M6
Greenview Ct. Pg.17 M5
Half Ln. Pg.17 M5
Higgins Rd. Pg.12 J6
Hillcrest Dr. Pg.17 M5
Illinois St. Pg.17 M4
Indian Hill Dr. Pg.17 M5
Irving Park Rd. Pg.16 M3
Lang Ave. Pg.16 M3
Larson Ln. Pg.17 M5
Lincoln St. Pg.17 M4
Logan St. Pg.17 M4
Marion Pg.17 M4
Meadows Ln. Pg.16 M2
Mohawk Dr. Pg.17 M5
Monterey Ave. Pg.17 M5
Morse Ave. Pg.17 M4
Nerge Rd. Pg.16 M3
North Shore Ave. Pg.17 M4
Oneida Dr. Pg.17 M6
Park Ave. Pg.16 M3
Park St. Pg.17 M5
Parkview Dr. Pg.16 M3
Pleasant Dr. Pg.16 M2
Pratt Blvd. Pg.17 M4
Rodenburg Rd. Pg.16 M3
Roselle Rd. Pg.17 M5
Roslyn Rd. Pg.17 M5
Rucks St. Pg.17 M7
Schaumburg Rd. Pg.12 K7
Seward St. Pg.17 M4
Springinsguth Rd. Pg.16 M2
Summit Dr. Pg.17 M5
Sunset Dr. Pg.17 M5
Valley View Dr. Pg.16 M2

### CEMETERIES
St. John's Cemetery Pg.16 M3

### SCHOOLS
St. John's Sch. Pg.16 M3

### SHOPPING CENTERS
Park Plaza Pg.16 L2

## SKOKIE
Pages 30,31
(For additional listings, see Section 1)

### STREETS
Arcadia St. J9-12
Avers Ave. J-K11
Babb Ave. L9
Bennett Ave. J-K12
Beverly Dr. H10
Birchwood Ave. M9-11
Bobolink Terr. K10
Brandess Terr. J9
Bronx Ave. H-J9
Brown St. L9
Brummel St. L9-11
Capitol St. K12
Carol Ave. K9-11
Carpenter Rd. M9
Central Ave. H8,L-M8
Central Park Ave. J-M11
Chase Ave. M9
Cherry Pkwy. H10
Christiana K12
Church St. J10
Clark St. J11
Cleveland St. L9-12
Clifford Terr. K11
Colfax Pl. H9
Colfax St. H9-11
Concord Ln. K10
Conrad Ave. K9
Coyle Ave. M9
Crain St. K9-12
Crawford Ave. J-11
Culver H9
Dartmouth Pl. H9
Davis St. J9-12
Dempster St. K9
Dobson St. L9-11
Drake Ave. J-K12
East Prairie Ave. K11
Edens Expwy. H9
Elgin Rd. H-J12
Elgin St. H12
Elm St. K9
Elm Terr. K10
Elmwood St. L9

Emerson St. . . . . . . . J9,J10-12
Enfield Ave. . . . . . . . . . . K9-11
Estes Ave. . . . . . . . . . . . . M9
Ewing Ave. . . . . . . . . . . . J12
Fairview Ln. . . . . . . . . . . . M9
Fargo Ave. . . . . . . . . . M9-11
Farwell Ave. . . . . . . . . . . M9
Fitch Ave. . . . . . . . . . . . . M9
Floral . . . . . . . . . . . . . . . L9
Forestview Rd. . . . . . . . . . L9
Foster St. . . . . . . . . . . J9-11
Four Winds Way . . . . . . . J11
Galitz St. . . . . . . . . . . . . . L9
George St. . . . . . . . . . . . . L9
Golf Rd. . . . . . . . . . . . . . H10
Grant St. . . . . . . . . . . . H9-11
Greenleaf St. . . . . . . . . K9-11
Greenwood Ave. . . . . . . J9-12
Gross Point Rd. . . . . . H10,K9
Grove St. . . . . . . . . . . J9-10
Hamilton Dr. . . . . . . . . . . K9
Hamlin Ave. . . . . . . . . . J-L11
Harding Ave. . . . . . . . . J-K11
Harms Rd. . . . . . . . . . . . . K9
Harrison St. . . . . . . . . . . H10
Harvard St. . . . . . . . . . L9-11
Harvest Ln. . . . . . . . . . . H10
Hipple Terr. . . . . . . . . . . . J11
Hoffman St. . . . . . . . . . . . L9
Howard St. . . . . . . . . . . . L9
Hull St. . . . . . . . . . . L8-9-11
Isabel . . . . . . . . . . . . . . L11
James St. . . . . . . . . . . . K10
Jarlath Ave. . . . . . . . . . . M0
Jarvis Ave. . . . . . . . . . M9-11
Jerome Ave. . . . . . . . . . M11
Jerome St. . . . . . . . . . . M11
Jonathan Ln. . . . . . . . . . H10
Joneway Terr. . . . . . . . . . L9
Karlov Ave. . . . . . . . . . H-L11
Keating Ave. . . . . . . . . J-L10
Kedvale Ave. . . . . . . . . H-L11
Keeler Ave. . . . . . . . . . H-L11
Keeney St. . . . . . . . . . . . L10
Kenneth Ave. . . . . . . . . . K10
Kenneth Terr. . . . . . . . . . K10
Kenton Ave. . . . . . . . . . H-L10
Keystone Ave. . . . . . . . H-K11
Kilbourn Ave. . . . . . . . . J-L10
Kildare Ave. . . . . . . . . . . K10
Kilpatrick Ave. . . . . . . . J-M10
Kimball Ave. . . . . . . . . . K12
Kirk St. . . . . . . . . . . . L9-10
Klehm Ct. . . . . . . . . . . . . K9
Knox Ave. . . . . . . . . . . H-L10
Kolmar Ave. . . . . . . . . . J-L10
Korczak Terr. . . . . . . . . . J11
Kostner Ave. . . . . . . . . J-L10
Kostner Terr. . . . . . . . . . K10
LaCrosse Ave. . . . . . . . H-L10
Lake . . . . . . . . . . . . . . . J12
Lamon Ave. . . . . . . . . . H-M10
Laramie Ave. . . . . . . . . H-L11
Latrobe Ave. . . . . . . . . H-M9
Lavergne Ave. . . . . . . . . J-M9
Lawler . . . . . . . . . . . . . . J9
Lawndale Ave. . . . . . . . J-M11
Le Claire Ave. . . . . . . . J,K-M9
Lee St. . . . . . . . . . . . K9-12
Lemington Ave. . . . . . . . . J9
Lewis Terr. . . . . . . . . . . . L9
Lincoln Ave. . . . . . . . . . . K9
Lincoln St. . . . . . . . . . . M10
Lincolnwood Dr. . . . . . . . J12
Linder Ave. . . . . . . . . . . . M9
Little Elm Bend . . . . . . . . K11
Little Oak Path . . . . . . . . K11
Lockwood Ave. . . . . . . . H-M9
Lorel Ave. . . . . . . . . . . J,L-M9
Lotus Ave. . . . . . . . . . . . H-J9
Louise St. . . . . . . . . . . L9-11
Lowell Ave. . . . . . . . . . J-L10
Lowell Terr. . . . . . . . . . . K10
Lunt Ave. . . . . . . . . . . . . M9
Lyons Ave. . . . . . . . . . . J9-12
Lyons St. . . . . . . . . . . . . J12
Madison St. . . . . . . . . . K9-10
Main St. . . . . . . . . . . . . K10
Major Ave. . . . . . . . . . . . H-L8
Mamora Ave. . . . . . . . . . L8
Mango Ave. . . . . . . . . . . L8
Manor Ct. . . . . . . . . . . . . L9
Mason . . . . . . . . . . . . . . L8
McCormick Blvd. . . . . . . K-L12
McDaniel Ave. . . . . . . . . K12
Menard Ave. . . . . . . . . . L-M8
Monroe St. . . . . . . . . . . M9
Monticello Ave. . . . . . . . J-M11
Morgan . . . . . . . . . . . . . J12
Morse Ave. . . . . . . . . . . M9
Mulford St. . . . . . . . . . . L9-10
Murphy Ln. . . . . . . . . . . J11
New Gross Point Rd. . . . . . L8
Niles Ave. . . . . . . . . . . . L9
Niles Center Rd. . . . . . . J10,L9
Oakton St. . . . . . . . . . . L9-10
Old Orchard . . . . . . . . . . H9
Old Orchard Ct. . . . . . . . H10
Palma Pl. . . . . . . . . . . J9,H10
Park Ave. . . . . . . . . . . . . M9
Parkside Ave. . . . . . . . . . K9
Payne St. . . . . . . . . . . H9-11

Peach Pkwy. . . . . . . . . . H10
Pottawattami Dr. . . . . . . . J11
Prairie Ave., E. . . . . . J-M11,12
Railroad Ave. . . . . . . . . H-J9
Raoul Wallenberg Dr. . . . . H8
Ridgeway Ave. . . . . . . . J-M11
Ridgeway Terr. . . . . . . . . K11
Roth Terr. . . . . . . . . . . . K11
Russet Ln. . . . . . . . . . . H10
Salem Cir. . . . . . . . . . . . J12
Salem Ln. . . . . . . . . . . . J12
Samoset Blvd. . . . . . . . . J11
Searle Pkwy. . . . . . . . . . L9
Sherwin Ave. . . . . . . . . . M9
Skokiana Terr. . . . . . . . . H11
Skokie Blvd. . . . . . . . . J-L10
Sleeping Bear Rd. . . . . . . J11
Springfield Ave. . . . . . . J-K11
St. Louis Ave. . . . . . . . K-M12
Suffield Ct. . . . . . . . . . J9-11
Suffield Dr. . . . . . . . . . . . J9
Sugarloaf Ln. . . . . . . . . . J11
Tamaroa Terr. . . . . . . . . J11
Terminal . . . . . . . . . . . J-K9
Touhy Ave. . . . . . . . . . . M9
Tower Cir. . . . . . . . . . . . H11
Tripp Ave. . . . . . . . . . . J-L10
Trumbull Ave. . . . . . . . . K12
Warren St. . . . . . . . . . . . L11
Washington St. . . . . . . . . K10
Weber Ln. . . . . . . . . . . . H9
White Cloud Dr. . . . . . . . . J11
Wilder St. . . . . . . . . . . . K12
Williamsburg Cir. . . . . . . . J11
Williamsburg Ln. . . . . . . . J11
Williamsburg Rd. . . . . . . . J11
Williamsburg Terr. . . . . . . J11
Wilson Terr. . . . . . . . . . . J10
Woodlawn Ave. . . . . . . . . J11
Wright Terr. . . . . . . . . . K9-11

**CEMETERIES**

Memorial Park . . . . . . . . H10
St. Paul Cemetery . . . . . . K9
St. Peters Cemetery . . . K,L9

**GOLF COURSES**

Evanston G.C. . . . . . . . . K10
Weber Park G.C. . . . . . . . J10

**PARKS**

Central Park . . . . . . . . . J11
Coyle Park . . . . . . . . . . M9
Devonshire Park . . . . . . . J10
Emerson Park . . . . . . . . J9
Emily Park . . . . . . . . . . L10
Frontage Park . . . . . . . . L9
Garden Park . . . . . . . . . K9
George Park . . . . . . . . . L9
Gleiss Park . . . . . . . . . . J11
Grant Park . . . . . . . . . . H11
Gross Point Park . . . . . . . J9
Hamlin Park . . . . . . . . . L11
Kostner Park . . . . . . . . . L10
Laramie Park . . . . . . . . . M9
Lawler Park . . . . . . . . . . H9
Little League Park . . . . . . L12
Lockwood Park . . . . . . . . K9
Lorel Park . . . . . . . . . . . L9
McNally Park . . . . . . . . . K12
Oakton Park . . . . . . . . . L10
Searle Park . . . . . . . . . . K10
Sequoya Park . . . . . . . . J9
Shabanee Park . . . . . . . H11
Shawnee Park . . . . . . . . K11
Terminal Park . . . . . . . . J10
Timber Ridge Park . . . . . . J11
Weber Park . . . . . . . . J9-10
West Lauth Park . . . . . . . L11
Winnebago Park . . . . . . . K10
Wright Park . . . . . . . . . . K10

**SCHOOLS**

Cheder Lubavitch Sch. . . . M9
College Hill Sch. . . . . . . . J12
Devonshire Sch. . . . . . . . J10
East Prairie Sch. . . . . . . . L11
Fairview S. Sch. . . . . . . . M9
Hebrew Theological College
. . . . . . . . . . . . . . . . . M9
Highland Sch. . . . . . . . . H11
Joan Stensen Sch. . . . . . . J9
Kenton Sch. . . . . . . . . . K10
Lincoln Jr. H.S. . . . . . . . . L9
Madison Sch. . . . . . . . . K9
McCracken Middle Sch. . . . L11
Middleton Sch. . . . . . . . K12
Niles Twp. H.S. North . . . . H9
Niles Twp. H.S. West . . . . L8
Oakton Comm. College Center
East . . . . . . . . . . . . . J-M10
Old Orchard Jr. H.S. . . . . . J10
Orchard Sch. . . . . . . . . . K9
Solomon Schechter Day Sch.
. . . . . . . . . . . . . . . . . J10
St. Joan of Arc Sch. . . . . . J11
St. Lambert Sch. . . . . . . . K11
St. Peters Sch. . . . . . . . . L9
Timber Ridge Sch. . . . . . . J11
Tripp Primary Sch. . . . . . . L10
Walker Sch. . . . . . . . . . . J12

**SHOPPING CENTERS**

Old Orchard S.C. . . . . . . H10

**MISCELLANEOUS**

Fire Departments . . K11,J,M9
Library . . . . . . . . . . . . . L9
Police Department . . . . . . K9
Post Office . . . . . . . . . . K9
Rush North Shore Med. Ctr.
. . . . . . . . . . . . . . . . . H10
Village Hall . . . . . . . . . . . L9

**SOUTH BARRINGTON**

Pages 6,11
(For additional listings,
see Section 5)

**STREETS**

Algonquin Rd. . . . . Pg.6 . . . D1
Avon Ln. . . . . . Pg.6 . . . D3
Barrington Rd. . . Pg.6 . . . D1
Brackley . . . . . . Pg.6 . . . C2
Bridlewood Dr. . . Pg.6 . . . D1
Buckthorn Rd. . . Pg.6 . . . D1
Canterbury Ct. . . Pg.6 . . . E3
Chipping Campden
. . . . . . . . . Pg.6 . . . C2
Corey Dr. . . . . . Pg.6 . . . F1
Covered Bridge Rd.
. . . . . . . . . Pg.6 . . . E1
Deveaux Ct. . . . Pg.6 . . . E1
Eton Ct. . . . . . . Pg.6 . . . D3
Forest Ln. . . . . Pg.6 . . . D2
Huntington Blvd.
. . . . . . . . . Pg.6 . . . E2
Knoll Ct. . . . . . Pg.6 . . . D2
McGlashen Ln. . Pg.6 . . . F1
Mohawk Ct. . . . Pg.6 . . . E2
Mohawk Dr. . . . Pg.6 . . . E2
Mundhank Rd. . Pg.6 . . . E1
Old Barrington Rd.
. . . . . . . . . Pg.11 . . F1
Overbrook Rd. . Pg.6 . . . E1
Palatine Rd. . . Pg.6 . . . C-1
Pembury Way . . Pg.6 . . . E1
Polo Dr. . . . . . Pg.6 . . . E1
Red Hill Ln. . . . Pg.6 . . . E2
Rose Blvd. . . . Pg.6 . . . F1
Shirebrook Way Pg.6 . . . E1
Somerset Ct. . . Pg.6 . . . E3
Squire Ct. . . . . Pg.6 . . . D1
Stannington Way
. . . . . . . . . Pg.6 . . . D1
Sunburst Locust Dr.
. . . . . . . . . Pg.11 . . F1
Taynton Ln. . . . Pg.6 . . . C2
Tennis Club Ln. Pg.6 . . . F1
Terra Vita Ct. . . Pg.6 . . . E1
Terra Vita Dr. . . Pg.6 . . . E1
Tewkesbury Ln. Pg.6 . . . C2
Wescott Dr. . . . Pg.6 . . . F1
Willowmere Dr. Pg.6 . . . D1
Windmere Ln. . . Pg.6 . . . D3
Wychwood Ln. . Pg.6 . . . C2

**MISCELLANEOUS**

Village Hall . . . Pg.11 . . F1

**SOUTH CHICAGO HEIGHTS**

Pages 48,49

**STREETS**

Aberdeen Ave. . . . . . . . . V24
Benton Ave. . . . . . . . . . W25
Bramanti Tr. . . . . . . . . . W25
Butler Ave. . . . . . . . . . . W25
Campbell Ave. . . . . . . . . W23
Cappelletti Ln. . . . . . . . . V23
Cherry Ln. . . . . . . . . . . V23
Chestnut Ave. . . . . . . . . W24
Chicago Pl. . . . . . . . . . . W24
Chicago Rd. . . . . . . . . . V24
Commercial Ave. . . . . . . . V24
Crescent Dr. . . . . . . . . . V23
Dixie Hwy. . . . . . . . . . . W24
Dornell Dr. . . . . . . . . . . V24
East End Ave. . . . . . . . . V24
Enterprise Pk. Ave. . . . . . V24
Euclid Ave. . . . . . . . . . . V23
Fairview Ave. . . . . . . . . . W24
Forest Dr. . . . . . . . . . . . W23
Forest Preserve Dr. . . . . . W23
Helred Rd. . . . . . . . . . . W23
Holeman Ave. . . . . . . . . W23
Intercoean Ave. . . . . . . . V24
Jackson Ave. . . . . . . . . . V24
Lawrence Ave. . . . . . . . . W23
Lynwood Dr. . . . . . . . . . W23
Magnolia . . . . . . . . . . . V23
Maple Ave. . . . . . . . . . . W23
Michigan Ave. . . . . . . . . W25
Miller Ave. . . . . . . . . . . W24
Miller Rd. . . . . . . . . . . . W25
Pagoria Dr. . . . . . . . . . . W23
Park Terr. . . . . . . . . . . . W23
Paulsen St. . . . . . . . . . . V24
Plaza St. . . . . . . . . . . . V23
Rennie Smith Dr. . . . . . . . W24
Sauk Trail Rd. (32nd St.) . . W24
State St. . . . . . . . . . . . . W23
Willow Rd. . . . . . . . . . . W23
27th St. . . . . . . . . . . . . V24
28th St. . . . . . . . . . . . . W24
28th St. . . . . . . . . . . . . V24

29th Pl. . . . . . . . . . . . . V24
29th St. . . . . . . . . . . . . V24
30th Pl. . . . . . . . . . . . . V24
30th St. . . . . . . . . . V24,26
31st St. . . . . . . . . . . . . W24
32nd St. . . . . . . . . . . . . W23
33rd St. . . . . . . . . . . . . W24
34th St. . . . . . . . . . . . . W24

**SCHOOLS**

Grant Sch. . . . . . . . . . . V24
Saukview Sch. . . . . . . . . W24

**SOUTH HOLLAND**

Pages 43-44
(For additional listings,
see Section 1)

**STREETS**

Armory Dr. . . . Pg.43 . . N24
Avalon Ave. . . . Pg.44 . . N27
Bennet Ave. . . Pg.44 . . O27
Bernice Rd. . . . Pg.44 . . O28
Betty Ln. . . . . . Pg.44 . . M26
Bishop Ford Freeway
. . . . . . . . . Pg.44 . . N27
Canal St. . . . . Pg.43 . . N24
Caryn Cir. . . . . Pg.44 . . N26
Claire Ln. . . . . Pg.44 . . N26
Clyde . . . . . . . Pg.44 . . N,O28
Constance Ave. Pg.44 . . N27
Cornell Ave. . . . Pg.44 . . N27
Cottage Grove Ave.
. . . . . . . . . . . . . . . M26
Court Terr. . . . Pg.44 . . N26
Cregier Ave. . . Pg.44 . . N27
Dante Dr. . . . . Pg.44 . . M26
DeYoung Grove Pg.44 . . M25
Debbie Ln. . . . Pg.44 . . N26
Dobson Ave. . . Pg.44 . . N27
Drexel Ave. . . . Pg.44 . . N27
Ellis . . . . . . . . Pg.44 . . N26
Ellis Ave. . . . . Pg.44 . . N27
Ellis Ct. . . . . . Pg.44 . . M-O26
Elm Ct. . . . . . . Pg.44 . . N26
Elm St. . . . . . . Pg.44 . . N26
Evans Ave. . . . Pg.44 . . N27
Evans Ct. . . . . Pg.44 . . M,N26
Everett Ave. . . . Pg.44 . . N27
Gibson Ln. . . . Pg.44 . . N27
Grant St. . . . . Pg.44 . . N24
Greenwood Ave.
. . . . . . . . . Pg.44 . . N,O27
Greenwood Dr. Pg.44 . . N26
Halsted St. . . . Pg.43 . . O24
Holland Ave. . . Pg.44 . . M26
Indiana Ave. . . Pg.44 . . N25
Ingleside . . . . . Pg.44 . . M26
Ingleside Ave. . Pg.44 . . N26
Ingleside Ct. . . Pg.44 . . M26
Joyce Cir. . . . . Pg.44 . . M26
Joyce Ct. . . . . Pg.44 . . M26
Kenwood Ave. . Pg.44 . . N27
Kenwood Ct. . . Pg.44 . . N27
Kimbark . . . . . Pg.44 . . N27
Kimbark Ave. . . Pg.44 . . N27
Langley Ave. . . Pg.44 . . N27
Louis Ave. . . . . Pg.44
. . . . . . . . . M,O26,N,O25
Lowell Ave. . . . Pg.44 . . N26
Luella Ave. . . . Pg.44 . . N28
Maple Ct. . . . . Pg.44 . . M26
Maple St. . . . . Pg.44 . . M26
Marian Ct. . . . Pg.44 . . M26
Marian Dr. . . . Pg.44 . . M26
Marie . . . . . . . Pg.44 . . M26
Maryland Ave. . Pg.44 . . M,N25
Merrill . . . . . . . Pg.44 . . N20
Michigan Ave. . Pg.44 . . M,N25
Minerva . . . . . Pg.44 . . M27
Parkside Ave. . Pg.44 . . M,O26
Parkside Ct. . . Pg.44 . . N26
Paxton Ave. . . Pg.44 . . N27
Prairie Ave. . . Pg.44 . . M,N25
Prince Dr. . . . . Pg.44 . . N27
Riverside Dr. . . Pg.44 . . M26
Riverview St. . . Pg.44 . . M26
Roosevelt Ctr. . Pg.44 . . M26
School St. . . . Pg.44 . . M-O26
Seton Dr. . . . . Pg.44 . . M26
Shirley Ct. . . . Pg.44 . . N26
South Park Ave. Pg.44 . . M26
State St. . . . . . Pg.44 . . N25
Suntone Rd. . . Pg.44 . . M25
Taft Dr. . . . . . . Pg.44 . . N26
Thornton Ave. . Pg.44 . . N26
Thornton-Blue Island Rd.
. . . . . . . . . . . . . . . M24
Thornwood Ct. Pg.44 . . O26
Thornwood Dr. Pg.44 . . O26
Tollview Dr. . . . Pg.43 . . O24
Union Ave. . . . Pg.43 . . N24
Union St. . . . . Pg.43 . . O24
University Ave. Pg.44 . . M,O27
University Ct. . . Pg.44 . . N27
VanDam Rd. . . Pg.44 . . N27
Vandrunen . . . Pg.44 . . M25
Vincennes Rd. Pg.43-44
. . . . . . . . . M24,N25
Volbrecht Ave. Pg.44 . . N27
Volbrecht St. . . Pg.44 . . N27
Wabash Ave. . Pg.44 . . M25
Wallace Ave. . . Pg.43 . . N24

Wausau Ave. . . Pg.44
. . . . . . . . . M,O25,N26
Wausau Ct. . . Pg.44 . M-O25
Westview Ave. . Pg.43 . . N24
Woodlawn Ave. Pg.44 . . N27
Woodlawn Ave., E.
. . . . . . . . . Pg.44 . . N27
Yates Ave. . . . Pg.44 . . N28
160th Pl. . . . . Pg.44 M25-27
160th St. . . . . Pg.44 . . M26
161st Ct., E. & W.
. . . . . . . . . Pg.44 . . M25
161st Pl. . . . . Pg.44 M25,27
161st St. . . . . Pg.44 . . M26
162nd Pl. . . . . Pg.44 M25,26
162nd St. . . . . Pg.44 M25,26
163rd Ct. . . . . Pg.44 . . N26
163rd Pl. . . . . Pg.44 . . M26
163rd St. . . . . Pg.44 M26,27
164th Ct. . . . . Pg.44 . . N26
164th Pl. . . . . Pg.44
. . . . . . . . . M25,27,N26
164th St. . . . . Pg.44 M25-27
165th Pl. . . . . Pg.44 N26,27
165th St. . . . . Pg.44
. . . . . . . . . M25,N27
166th Ct. . . . . Pg.44 . . N26
166th Pl. . . . . Pg.44 . . N26
166th St. . . . . Pg.44
. . . . . . . . . N25,26,28
167th Pl. . . . . Pg.44 N26,27
167th St. . . . . Pg.43-44
. . . . . . . . . N24,26-28,O24
168th Pl. . . . . Pg.44 N25-27
168th St. . . . . Pg.44 N25-28
169th Pl. . . . . Pg.44 N26,28
169th St. . . . . Pg.43-44
. . . . . . . . . N24,26-27
170th Ct. . . . . Pg.44 . . N26
170th Pl. . . . . Pg.44 . . N26
170th St. . . . . Pg.43-44
. . . . . . . . . N24,26,27
171st Ct. . . . . Pg.44 . . N26
171st Pl. . . . . Pg.44 . . N26
1/1st St. . . . . Pg.44 N25-28
172nd St. . . . . Pg.44 . . O26,27
173rd Pl. . . . . Pg.44 . . O26-28
173rd St. . . . . Pg.44
. . . . . . . . . O25,27,28

**PARKS**

Arrowhead Park
. . . . . . . . . Pg.44 . . N26
Dahlenberg Park
. . . . . . . . . Pg.44 . . N26
Dutch Valley Park
. . . . . . . . . Pg.44 . . M27
Hollendale Park Pg.44 . . M25
Little Calumet Park
. . . . . . . . . Pg.44 . . N26
Maicoch Park . Pg.44 . . N26
McArthur Park . Pg.44 . . N26
Municipal Park Pg.44 . . M26
Pacesetter Park Pg.44 . . N24
Papoose Park . Pg.44 . . N25
Pioneer Park . . Pg.44 . . M26
Pow Wow Park Pg.44 . . M26
Roosevelt Park Pg.44 . . N26
Terraceview Park
. . . . . . . . . Pg.44 . . N25

**SCHOOLS**

Calvary Academy
. . . . . . . . . Pg.44 . . M25
Calvin Christian Sch.
. . . . . . . . . Pg.44 . . M26
Eisenhower Sch.
. . . . . . . . . Pg.44 . . M27
Elizabeth Seton H.S.
. . . . . . . . . Pg.44 . . M26
Greenwood Sch.
. . . . . . . . . Pg.44 . . N27
Holy Ghost Sch.
. . . . . . . . . Pg.44 . . N26
Loren Montessori Sch.
. . . . . . . . . Pg.44 . . N26
McArthur Sch. . Pg.44 . . N26
McKinley Sch. . Pg.44 . . N26
Protestant Reform Christian
Sch. . . . . . . Pg.44 . . N26
South Suburban College
. . . . . . . . . Pg.44 . . N25
Thornwood H.S.
. . . . . . . . . Pg.44 . . O25

**MISCELLANEOUS**

Fire Station #2 Pg.44 . . N27
Paarlberg Park Historical
Society . . . . Pg.44 . . N25
R.R. Station . . . Pg.44 . . O28
Village Hall . . . Pg.44 . . M25

**STEGER**

Pages 48,49

**STREETS**

Adair Rd. . . . . . . . . . . . W26
Butler Ave. . . . . . . . . . . W24
Calumet Expy. . . . . . . . . W27
Carpenter St. . . . . . . . . . W23
Chicago Rd. . . . . . . . . . . W24
Cottage Grove Ave. . . . . . W26
Dixie Hwy. . . . . . . . . . . . W24
Dorchester Ave. . . . . . . . W27
Emerald Ave. . . . . . . . . . W24
Florence Ave. . . . . . . . . . W24
George St. . . . . . . . . . . . W24
Green St. . . . . . . . . . . . . W24
Halsted St. . . . . . . . . . . . W25
Holeman Ave. . . . . . . . . . W26
Hopkins Ave. . . . . . . . . . W24
Keeney Ave. . . . . . . . . . . W26
Lahon Rd. . . . . . . . . . . . W26
Lewis Ave. . . . . . . . . . . . W26
Lisa Ln. . . . . . . . . . . . . . W25
Lovelock Ave. . . . . . . . . . W26
Mach Dr. . . . . . . . . . . . . W26
Michigan Ave. . . . . . . . . . W25
Miller Rd. . . . . . . . . . . . . W25
Morgan St. . . . . . . . . . . . W23
Oakland Dr. . . . . . . . . . . W26
Patricia Rd. . . . . . . . . . . W26
Peoria St. . . . . . . . . . . . W24
Phillips Ave. . . . . . . . . . . W26
Royal Oak Dr. . . . . . . . . . W26
Sangamon St. . . . . . . . . . W24
Sherman Rd. . . . . . . . . . W26
State St. . . . . . . . . . . . . W26
Steger Rd. . . . . . . . . . . . W25
Stewart . . . . . . . . . . . . . W24
Union Ave. . . . . . . . . . . . W24
Wallace Ave. . . . . . . . . . W25
Wentworth Ave. . . . . . . . . W24
Woodlawn Ave. . . . . . . . . W27
30th Pl., E & W . . . . . . . . W27
30th St. . . . . . . . . . . . . . W27
31st Pl., E & W . . . . . . . . W24
31st St., E & W . . . . . . . . W24
32nd Pl., E . . . . . . . . W24,27
32nd St. . . . . . . . . . . . . . W24
33rd Pl., E . . . . . . . . . . . W25
33rd St., E & W . . . . . . . . W25
34th Pl. . . . . . . . . . . . . . W25
34th St. . . . . . . . . . . . . . W25

**SCHOOLS**

Bloom Trail H.S. . . . . . . . V26
Central Jr. H.S. . . . . . . . . W24
East View Sch. . . . . . . . . W24
Sauk Trail Sch. . . . . . . . . V26

**STREAMWOOD**

Page 16
(For additional listings,
see Section 5)

**STREETS**

Arrowwood Ln. . . . . . . . . H1
Barrington Rd. . . . . . . . . J1
Bode Rd., E. . . . . . . . . . J1
Boxwood Ct. . . . . . . . . . H1
Claridge Ct. . . . . . . . . . . H1
Driftwood Ct. . . . . . . . . . H1
Fernwood Ct. . . . . . . . . . H1
Green Knoll Ln. . . . . . . . . H1
Greystone Ct. . . . . . . . . . H1
Hastings Mill Rd. . . . . . . . J1
Ironwood Ct. . . . . . . . . . H1
Lexington Ct. . . . . . . . . . H1
Middlebury Ct. . . . . . . . . H1
Oak Knoll Ct. . . . . . . . . . H1
Oak Meadow Ct. . . . . . . . H1
Oakmont Ct. . . . . . . . . . H1
Plum Tree Ct. . . . . . . . . . H1
Quaker Hollow Ct. . . . . . . H1
Sandalwood Ct. . . . . . . . H1
Sandhurst Ct. . . . . . . . . . H1
Southbury Ct. . . . . . . . . . H1
Warwick Ct. . . . . . . . . . . H1
Whitehall Ct. . . . . . . . . . H1
Williamsburg Dr. . . . . . . . J1
Winding Run Ln. . . . . . . . J1
Woodbury Ct. . . . . . . . . . J1

**SHOPPING CENTERS**

4B Center . . . . . . . . . . . K1
Green Meadow Plaza . . . . J1
Wetview S.C. . . . . . . . . . L1

**THORNTON**

Pages 43,44

**STREETS**

Anne Ct. . . . Pg.44 . . O25
Apache St. . . Pg.44 . . O26
Arapaho Dr. . Pg.44 . . O26
Arrowhead . . Pg.44 . . O26
Blackhawk Dr. Pg.44 . . O26
Blackstone St. Pg.44 . . O25
Bonnie Dr. . . Pg.44 . . P26
Brown Derby Rd.

Chicago Rd. . . Pg.44 . . O26
Chippewa Dr. . Pg.44 . . O26
Clark St. . . . . Pg.43 . . N25
Cora Ct. . . . . Pg.44 . . O25
Derby Rd. . . . Pg.43 . . P24
Dorie Ln. . . . Pg.44 . . O26
Eleanor St. . . Pg.44 . . P25
Forest Ln. . . . Pg.44 . . P26
Francis St. . . Pg.44 . . P25
Harriet St. . . . Pg.44 . . P25
Highland . . . . Pg.44 . . P25
Hubbard St. . . Pg.43 . . P25
Hunter St. . . . Pg.44 . . O25
Indiana Ave. . Pg.43 . . O25
Indianwood Dr. Pg.44 . . O26
Julian St. . . . Pg.44 . . P25
Julliette St. . . Pg.44 . . P25
Kinzie Pl. . . . Pg.44 . . O25
Kinzie St. . . . Pg.44 . . O25
La Salle St. . . Pg.43 . . N25
Laura Ln. . . . Pg.44 . . O25
Leavenworth St.
. . . . . . . . . Pg.43 . . P25
Leverett St. . . Pg.44 . . P26
Mallette Ave. . Pg.44 . . P26
Maple Ln. . . . Pg.44 . . P26
Margaret St. . Pg.43,44
. . . . . . . . . P24,25
Maria . . . . . . Pg.44 P25,26
Marion St. (175th St.)
. . . . . . . . . Pg.43 . . O25
Michigan Ave. Pg.43 . . N25
Mohawk . . . . Pg.44 . . O26
Park Ave. . . . Pg.44 . . P24
Parnell Ave. . Pg.44 . . P24
Pawnee Dr. . . Pg.44 . . O26
Queens Ln. . . Pg.44 . . O25
Ridge Rd. . . . Pg.43 . . P24
Schwab St. . . Pg.44 . . O25
Sunnyside Ave. Pg.44 . . O26
Tahoe St. . . . Pg.44 . . O26
Thorncreek Rd. Pg.44 . . O26
William St. . . Pg.44 . . P25
Wolcott St. . . Pg.44 . . P25
170th (Armory Dr.)
. . . . . . . . . Pg.43 . . N25
171st St. . . . Pg.43 N25,O26
172nd St. . . . Pg.44 . . O25
175th St. . . . Pg.44 . . O25
183rd St. . . . Pg.43 . . O25

**CEMETERIES**

Mt. Forest Cemetery
. . . . . . . . . Pg.44 . . O26
Oak Lawn Cemetery
. . . . . . . . . Pg.43 . . O24

**FOREST PRESERVES**

Brownell Woods
. . . . . . . . . Pg.44 . . P26
Wampum Lake Woods F.P.
. . . . . . . . . Pg.44 . . O26
Charles P. Nason Park
. . . . . . . . . Pg.44 . . O26
Diekelman Memorial Park
. . . . . . . . . Pg.44 . . O26
Marion Mikrut Memorial Park
. . . . . . . . . Pg.44 . . O26

**SCHOOLS**

Parkside Sch. . . . . Pg.44 . . O25
Wolcott Sch. . . . . Pg.43 . . P25

**MISCELLANEOUS**

Thornton Ball Fields
. . . . . . . . . Pg.43 . . P25
Village Hall . . Pg.44 . . P25

**THORNTON TOWNSHIP**

Pages 42-45

**STREETS**

Artesian Ave. . Pg.42 . . M21
Beaubien St. . Pg.44 . . P27
Blackstone Ave. Pg.44 . . P27
Blitz St. . . . . . Pg.44 . . P27
Bock Rd. . . . . Pg.44 . . P28
Calumet Expwy. Pg.45 . . P27
Campbell Ave. Pg.41 . . M21
Chappel Ave. . Pg.44 . M,P28
Claremont St. Pg.43 . . M22
Clyde Ave. . . Pg.44 . . L,P28
Cornell Ave. . Pg.44 . . P27
Cottage Grove Ave.
. . . . . . . . . Pg.44 . . P26
Dante . . . . . . Pg.44 . . P27
Dixie Hwy. . . . Pg.43 . . M22
East End Ave. Pg.44 . . L,P24
Elmdale Ave. . Pg.42 . . M21
Eustace St. . . Pg.44 . . P27
Fern St. . . . . Pg.44 . . P28
Forest Hills . . Pg.45 . . M30
Forest Ln. . . . Pg.45 . . Q27
Greenwood Ave.
. . . . . . . . . Pg.44 . . M27

## THORNTON

Hamilton Pl. ... Pg.43 ... M22
Harper Ave. ... Pg.44 ... P27
Indiana Ave. ... Pg.44 ... P28
Irving ... Pg.43 ... M22
Jeffery Ave. ... Pg.44 ... L28
Keegan St. ... Pg.44 O27,28
Leavitt St. ... Pg.43 ... M22
Locust ... Pg.44 ... P28
Oakley Ave. ... Pg.43 ... M22
Paxton ... Pg.44 M,P28
Poplar Ave. ... Pg.42 ... M21
Ridgeland Ave. Pg.44 ... P28
River Oaks Dr. Pg.44 ... M28
Rosewood ... Pg.44 ... O28
St. Andrews St. Pg.44 ... P27
Stony Island Ave. ... Pg.44 ... P27
Thorncreek Rd. Pg.44 ... P26
Thorndale Ave. Pg.42 ... M21
Thornton Lansing Rd. ... Pg.44 ... P28
Volbrecht Rd. Pg.44 ... P27
Wentworth Ave. Pg.45 ... M30
Whitman Ln. ... Pg.45 ... P28
159th Ct. ... Pg.42 ... M22
159th St. ... Pg.43 ... M22
160th Pl. ... Pg.43 ... M22
160th St. ... Pg.43 ... M22
161st St. ... Pg.43 ... M22
162nd St. ... Pg.42 ... M21
177th Pl. ... Pg.44 ... O28
177th St. ... Pg.44 O28,P27
178th St. ... Pg.44 ... P27
179th St. ... Pg.44 ... P28
183rd St. ... Pg.44 ... Q27
186th St. ... Pg.44 ... Q27

### CEMETERIES

Oakridge Cem. Pg.44 ... P28

### FOREST PRESERVES

Jurgensen Woods ... Pg.44 ... Q27

### GOLF COURSES

Calumet C.C. ... Pg.43 ... O22

## TINLEY PARK

Pages 40,41,46
(For additional listings, see Section 8)

### STREETS

Abercorn Ln. ... Pg.40 ... P13
Achilles Ct. ... Pg.46 ... S16
Aegina Ct. ... Pg.46 ... R16
Aegina Dr. ... Pg.46 ... R16
Alexandria Dr. Pg.40 ... M13
Almond Ln. ... Pg.40 ... P12
Amherst Ln. ... Pg.40 ... O14
Andres Ave. ... Pg.41 ... N16
Anne Marie Ave. ... Pg.41 ... N16
Anvil Pl. ... Pg.40 ... N13
Apache Trail ... Pg.40 ... P13
Apollo Ct. ... Pg.46 ... S16
Apple Ln. ... Pg.40 ... M13
Arcadia Dr. ... Pg.41 ... N16
Arlington St. ... Pg.40 ... M13
Ash St. ... Pg.40 ... P12
Ashford Ct. ... Pg.40 ... M14
Ashley Ln. ... Pg.40 ... M13
Aspen Ln. ... Pg.40 ... M13
Aster Ln. ... Pg.40 ... O13
Athenia Ct. ... Pg.46 ... R16
Autumn Dr. ... Pg.41 ... O16
Avon Ln. ... Pg.40 ... O12
Barbara Ave. ... Pg.41 ... N16
Barbara Ln. ... Pg.41 ... O16
Basswood Dr. Pg.41 ... Q12
Bayberry Ln. ... Pg.40 ... P11
Beaumont Rd. Pg.40 ... P12
Bedford Ln. ... Pg.40 ... O14
Belle Rive Ct. ... Pg.40 ... O14
Berrybrook Ct. Pg.41 ... R13
Bethany Ln. ... Pg.40 ... O12
Beverly Ave. ... Pg.41 ... N16
Birchwoode Ct. Pg.41 ... N15
Bishop Rd. ... Pg.40 ... P13
Black Oak Ave. Pg.40 ... Q12
Blackhawk Dr. Pg.46 ... R15
Blackwater Ct. Pg.40 ... M13
Blossom Ln. ... Pg.40 ... N13
Blue Spruce Ct. Pg.40 ... M13
Bluebird Dr. ... Pg.40 ... P12
Bormet Dr. ... Pg.40 M,N13
Brementowne Dr. ... Pg.41 ... N15
Brementowne Rd. ... Pg.41 ... N15
Briar Dr. ... Pg.40 ... O11
Bridlewood Ln. Pg.40 ... O12
Bristol Ln. ... Pg.40 ... N14
Bristol Park Dr. Pg.40 ... P14
Brittney Ln. ... Pg.41 ... N16
Brookpoint Ct. Pg.41 ... R13
Brookside Glen Ct. ... Pg.41 ... R13
Brookside Glen Dr. ... Pg.46 ... R14
Brown Ln. ... Pg.40 ... P12
Brushwood Ln. Pg.41 ... R13
Buckthorn Ct. Pg.40 ... Q12
Budingen Ln. Pg.40 ... O13
Cambridge Pl. Pg.40 ... O12
Cardinal Ln. ... Pg.40 ... P12
Carlsbad Dr. ... Pg.41 ... N16
Carlyle Ct. ... Pg.40 ... O11
Carriage Ln. ... Pg.40 ... O13
Cartier Ave. ... Pg.40 ... P14
Caryle Ct. ... Pg.40 ... O11
Catalpa Ct. ... Pg.40 ... O12
Caxton Ct. ... Pg.40 ... P13
Cedar Ln. ... Pg.40 ... O14
Centennial Cir. Pg.41 ... M15
Centennial Dr. Pg.41 ... M15
Centerway Walk Pg.40 ... M14
Champlain Ave. Pg.40 ... P14
Charnswood Ct. ... Pg.41 ... N15
Charnswood Dr. ... Pg.41 ... N15
Chelsea Dr. ... Pg.41 ... N15
Cherokee Trail Pg.40 ... O13
Cherry Creek Ave. ... Pg.40 ... O13
Cherry Hill Ave. Pg.40 ... N13
Cherry Stone Pl. ... Pg.40 ... N13
Chestnut Dr. ... Pg.40 ... O12
Chippewa Trail Pg.40 ... O13
Christopher Ct. Pg.41 ... N16
Circle Dr. ... Pg.40 ... O13
Claremont Dr. Pg.40 ... N14
Clark Ln. ... Pg.41 ... N15
Clifton Ct. ... Pg.40 ... P12
Clifton Ln. ... Pg.40 ... P12
Clover Ave. ... Pg.40 ... N13
Cloverview Dr. Pg.40 ... P13
Coachwood Tr. Pg.41 ... N15
Cobbler Ct. ... Pg.40 ... N13
Cobblestone Ct. Pg.41 ... N15
Corinth Ct. ... Pg.46 ... R16
Corinth Dr. ... Pg.46 ... R16
Cottage Ct. ... Pg.40 ... O13
Cottonwood Dr. Pg.40 ... Q12
Cranberry Ct. ... Pg.40 ... N12
Creekmont Ct. Pg.40 ... M12
Creekside Ave. Pg.40 ... O13
Crescent Ave. ... Pg.40 ... N13
Crown Ln. ... Pg.41 ... N15
Crystal Ct. ... Pg.41 ... N15
Current Ave. ... Pg.40 ... N13
Cynthia Ct. ... Pg.40 ... N13
Cypress Ct. ... Pg.40 ... O12
De Soto Ave. ... Pg.40 ... P14
Debra Ave. ... Pg.41 ... O16
Debra Dr. ... Pg.41 ... O16
Debra Ln. ... Pg.41 ... N16
Dee Ct. ... Pg.40 ... O12
Deland Ct. ... Pg.40 ... M13
Delphi Ct. ... Pg.46 ... S15
Derwent Ln. ... Pg.40 ... O13
Desiree Dr. ... Pg.40 ... N13
Dogwood Ct. ... Pg.40 ... Q12
Dooneen Ave. Pg.40 ... O14
Dorothy Ln. ... Pg.40 ... N14
Dover Ct. ... Pg.40 ... P13
Drummond Dr. Pg.40 ... O11
Dunn Rd. ... Pg.40 ... O13
Durkin Rd. ... Pg.40 ... P13
Duvan Dr. ... Pg.40 ... O14
Eagle Ct. ... Pg.41 ... P15
Eagle Dr. ... Pg.41 ... P15
Eagle Ridge Dr. Pg.40 ... M13
Edgebrook Ln. Pg.41 ... R13
Edgewood Ct. Pg.40 ... O12
Elm Lane ... Pg.41 ... N15
Elmwood Ct. ... Pg.40 ... P12
Elmwood Dr. ... Pg.40 ... P12
Elysian Dr. ... Pg.46 ... R16
Enclave Ln. ... Pg.41 ... R13
Everdon Dr. ... Pg.40 ... M14
Evergreen Dr. Pg.40 ... N13
Fairfax Ct. ... Pg.41 ... N15
Farmview Ct. ... Pg.40 ... N13
Flamingo Dr. ... Pg.40 ... P12
Flanigan Ct. ... Pg.40 ... P12
Forestview Dr. Pg.41 ... N16
Fox Grove Ln. Pg.40 ... O13
Funsbury Ct. ... Pg.40 ... P12
Gaynelle Rd. ... Pg.41 ... N16
Gentry Ln. ... Pg.41 ... N16
George Brennan Hwy. ... Pg.46 ... R15
Glenbrook Ln. Pg.41 ... R13
Glenbrook Pl. Pg.41 ... R13
Glenshire Ct. ... Pg.41 ... R13
Glenswilly Cir. Pg.41 ... P15
Glenview Dr. ... Pg.41 ... N15
Golden Pheasant Dr. ... Pg.40 ... P12
Graphics Dr. ... Pg.40 ... Q14
Greenleaf Ct. ... Pg.40 ... Q12
Greenway Blvd. Pg.46 ... R14
Greenwood Dr. Pg.40 ... P12
Grissom Dr. ... Pg.40 ... O13
Hager St. ... Pg.40 ... O13
Hamilton Lakes Dr. ... Pg.40 ... M13
Hanover Dr. ... Pg.40 ... O14
Harlem Ave. ... Pg.41. N,P15
Harper Rd. ... Pg.40 ... P13
Harrington Ct. Pg.40 ... P13
Harrington Ln. Pg.40 ... P13
Harwood Ln. ... Pg.40 ... P13
Heather Ct. ... Pg.40 ... P13
Heather Ln. ... Pg.40 ... O13
Helen Sandidge Ct. ... Pg.41 ... N16
Henry Ln. ... Pg.40 ... N13
Hickory St. ... Pg.41 ... O15
Highland Ave. Pg.41 ... P16
Hillcrest Dr. ... Pg.40 ... N13
Hillcrest Ln. ... Pg.40 ... N13
Hillside Pl. ... Pg.41 ... N16
Holly Ct. ... Pg.40 ... P12
Honey Ln. ... Pg.41 ... N16
Horseshoe Dr. Pg.40 ... N13
Hubbard Ln. ... Pg.41 ... N15
Humber Ln. ... Pg.40 ... O12
Hummingbird Ln. ... Pg.40 ... P12
Hunter Tr. ... Pg.41 ... N15
Iliad Dr. ... Pg.46 ... S15
Interstate 80 ... Pg.40 ... Q14
Inverness Dr. ... Pg.40 ... O12
Ironwood Dr. ... Pg.40 ... N13
Iroquois Trace Pg.40 ... P13
Ithaca Ct. ... Pg.46 ... S16
Jacquelyn Ct. ... Pg.41 ... N16
Jean Ln. ... Pg.41 ... N15
Jeannette Ct. ... Pg.41 ... P16
Jennifer Ave. ... Pg.41 ... N16
Jeremy Ln. ... Pg.40 ... O12
Jessica Ln. ... Pg.40 ... N13
Joliet Dr. ... Pg.40 ... P14
Juniper Ct. ... Pg.40 ... O12
Justin Ct. ... Pg.40 ... M13
Kamp Ct. ... Pg.40 ... O13
Kathleen Ln. ... Pg.40 ... O12
Kensington Ave. ... Pg.40 ... M14
Kickapoo Dr. ... Pg.46 ... R15
Kildare Ct. ... Pg.40 ... N14
Kingston Ct. ... Pg.41 ... N15
Kingston Rd. ... Pg.41 ... N15
La Grange Rd. Pg.40 ... O11
LaSalle Ave. ... Pg.40 ... P14
Lake Bluff Dr. ... Pg.41 ... N16
Lake Villa Ave. Pg.40 ... M14
Lakeside Pl. ... Pg.41 ... N16,R14
Lakeview Cir. ... Pg.41 ... Q16
Lakeview Terr. Pg.46 ... R14
Lakewood Dr. ... Pg.41 ... N16
Laura Ln. ... Pg.41 ... N16
Laverne Ln. ... Pg.41 ... N15
Lexington Ct. ... Pg.41 ... M15
Lilac Ln. ... Pg.40 ... P13
Linden Dr. ... Pg.40 ... P12
Lismore Ct. ... Pg.40 ... N14
Live Oak Ct. ... Pg.41 ... P15
Locust Ave. ... Pg.40 ... O12
Magnolia Ln. ... Pg.40 ... O12
Mallard Rd. ... Pg.40 ... P12
Manchester St. Pg.41 ... N15
Mannheim Rd. Pg.40 ... P11
Mansfield Dr. ... Pg.40 ... P12
Maple Creek Dr. Pg.40 ... Q14
Maple Ln. ... Pg.41 ... N15
Maplewood Ct. Pg.41 ... N15
Margaret Ln. ... Pg.40 ... O12
Marilyn Dr. ... Pg.40 ... O13
Market St. ... Pg.41 ... O16
Marquette Dr. Pg.40 ... P14
Martin Frances Cir. ... Pg.41 ... P15
Mason Ln. ... Pg.40 ... P13
Maydell Ct. ... Pg.40 ... P13
Meadow Ct. ... Pg.40 ... N13
Meadow Edge Tr. ... Pg.41 ... R13
Meadow Ln. ... Pg.40 ... N13
Meadowlark Dr. Pg.40 ... P12
Messina Ct. ... Pg.46 ... R16
Michelle Ln. ... Pg.40 ... N13
Milford Ave. ... Pg.40 ... O14
Misty Ln. ... Pg.41 ... N15
Mockingbird Ln. ... Pg.40 ... P12
Moss Ct. ... Pg.40 ... P12
Mulberry Ave. Pg.40 ... O12
Music Center North Rd. ... Pg.41 ... Q16
Music Center South Rd. ... Pg.46 ... R16
Navajo Trace ... Pg.40 ... O13
New England Ave. ... Pg.41 ... N15
Normandy Dr. Pg.41 ... N16
North Creek Dr. Pg.40 ... Q14
North St. ... Pg.41 ... O15
North Star Ct. Pg.40 ... Q13
Northfield Ln. Pg.46 ... R14
Northstar Ct. ... Pg.40 ... Q13
Nottingham Ct. Pg.40 ... N14
Nottingham Dr. Pg.40 ... N14
Nottingham Rd. Pg.40 ... N13
Oak Forest Ave. Pg.41 ... O16
Oak Park Ave. Pg.41 ... M15
Oakwood Dr. ... Pg.40 ... O12
Oconto Ave. ... Pg.40,41 ... N,O14,O16
Odell Ave. ... Pg.40. N,O14
Odyssey Blvd. Pg.46 ... S15
Odyssey Dr. ... Pg.46 ... S15
Oketo Ave. ... Pg.40. N,O14
Olcott Ave. ... Pg.40. N,O14
Olcott Ct. ... Pg.40 ... O14
Old 96th Ave. Pg.40 ... P11
Old Barn Ct. ... Pg.40 ... N13
Olde Gatehouse Rd. ... Pg.41 ... N15
Oleander Ave. Pg.40. N,O14
Olympus Dr. ... Pg.46 ... S16
Orchard Ct. ... Pg.40 ... N13
Orchard Dr. ... Pg.40 ... P14
Oriole Ave. ... Pg.40 ... O14
Osceola Ave. ... Pg.40 ... O14
Ottawa Ave. ... Pg.40 ... O14
Overhill Ave. ... Pg.40. N,O14
Oxford Dr. ... Pg.41 ... N15
Ozark Ave. ... Pg.40. N,O14
Park Central Dr. Pg.40 ... P14
Parkside Dr. ... Pg.41 ... N15
Parkview Ave. Pg.40 ... N13
Parkview Plaza Pg.40 ... N13
Parliament Ave. Pg.40 ... N14
Paxton Ave. ... Pg.40 ... N14
Peachtree Dr. ... Pg.40 ... Q12
Peacock Ln. ... Pg.40 ... P11
Pecan Ln. ... Pg.40 ... P12
Pelican Ln. ... Pg.40 ... P12
Pembroke Ave. Pg.40 ... O14
Pheasant Dr. ... Pg.40 ... P11
Pheasant Lake Dr. ... Pg.40 ... P12
Pin Oak Ct. ... Pg.41 ... P15
Pine Cone Dr. Pg.41 ... Q15
Pine Dr. ... Pg.40 ... M13
Pine Lake Ct. ... Pg.41 ... Q16
Pine Lake Dr. ... Pg.41 ... Q16
Pine Point Dr. Pg.41 ... O15
Pine Ridge Ct. Pg.41 ... Q16
Pine Ridge Dr. Pg.41 ... Q16
Pine Trail ... Pg.41 ... Q16
Pine Wood Ct. Pg.41 ... P15
Pine Wood Ln. Pg.41 ... O15
Piute Trail ... Pg.40 ... P13
Plum Ct. ... Pg.40 ... O13
Plymouth Ct. ... Pg.41 ... M15
Pond View Ct. Pg.41 ... Q15
Pond View Dr. Pg.41 ... Q15
Poplar St. ... Pg.40 ... P12
Pottawattomi Trail ... Pg.40 ... P13
Prairie Ct. ... Pg.40 ... N13
Prairie Dr. ... Pg.40 ... N13
Prestwick Dr. ... Pg.40 ... O14
Princess Elizabeth Ct. ... Pg.40 ... P12
Princeton Ave. Pg.40 ... N13
Quail Cir. ... Pg.40 ... O11
Quail Tr. ... Pg.40 ... O11
Quail Trail Rd. Pg.40 ... O11
Queen Ann Ln. Pg.40 ... P13
Queen Elizabeth Ln. ... Pg.40 ... O13
Queen Mary Ln. Pg.40 ... O13
Queen Victoria Ln. ... Pg.40 ... O13
Radcliffe Rd. ... Pg.40 ... P13
Raintree Rd. ... Pg.40 ... O12
Ravina Dr. ... Pg.41 ... O15
Rayson Ln. ... Pg.40 ... P12
Redwood Ct. ... Pg.40 ... P14
Redwood Ln. ... Pg.40 ... O12
Richards Ct. ... Pg.40 ... N13
Richards Dr. ... Pg.40. N,O13
Richardson Ln. Pg.46 ... R14
Ridgeland Ave. Pg.41,46 ... N,P,R16
Ridgemont Rd. Pg.41 ... P15
Rita Rd. ... Pg.41 ... P15
Riverside Dr. ... Pg.41 N15,16
Rochelle Ln. ... Pg.40 ... O12
Rosewood Ln. Pg.40 ... P12
Rossmore Rd. Pg.40 ... P13
Royal Oak Ct. ... Pg.41 ... P15
Salem Ct. ... Pg.40 ... O14
Sandalwood Dr. Pg.40 ... O14
Sandy Ln. ... Pg.40 ... N14
Sayre Ave. ... Pg.41. N,P15
Schuldt Dr. ... Pg.40 ... P13
Scotch Pine Dr. Pg.46 ... R16
Scott Ct. ... Pg.41 ... N16
Shabbona Dr. Pg.46 ... R14
Shannon Ct. ... Pg.40 ... N13
Shannon Dr. ... Pg.40 ... O13
Shetland Dr. ... Pg.40 ... O12
Shoshone Trail Pg.40 ... P13
Silverside Dr. ... Pg.41 ... R13
Skyline Dr. ... Pg.41 ... N16
South Pointe Dr. ... Pg.41 ... Q15
South St. ... Pg.41,46 ... O,R15
Spring Creek Dr. ... Pg.40 ... Q14
Spruce Ln. ... Pg.40 ... O12
Stamford Ct. ... Pg.40 ... P12
Stamford Ln. ... Pg.40 ... P12
Steeple Dr. ... Pg.40 ... O13
Steven Pl. ... Pg.40 ... N13
Stonebroke Ct. Pg.40 ... O11
Sumner Rd. ... Pg.40 ... P12
Surrey Dr. ... Pg.40 ... N13
Sussex Rd. ... Pg.41 ... N15
Sutton Pl. ... Pg.40 ... P11
Sycamore Ct. ... Pg.40 ... O12
Tamar Ln. ... Pg.40 ... O12
Tanbark Dr. ... Pg.40 ... N13
Tayside Ln. ... Pg.40 ... O12
Teakwood Dr. Pg.40 ... O11
Terrace Dr. ... Pg.41 ... N15
Theresa Ln. ... Pg.41 ... N15
Thornwood Dr. Pg.40 ... O11
Timber Ct. ... Pg.40 ... O12
Timber Pointe Dr. ... Pg.40 ... Q12
Timber Rd.(Pvt.) ... Pg.40 ... P14
Timbers Point Dr. West ... Pg.40 ... Q12
Timberwood Ln. ... Pg.40 ... Q12
Tinley Park Dr. Pg.41 ... N15
Tinley Park Rd. Pg.46 ... R13
Tower Ct. ... Pg.40 ... N13
Trent Ct. ... Pg.40 ... O12
Tudor Ln. ... Pg.40 ... N13
Tulip Ln. ... Pg.40 ... P13
Turnberry Ln. Pg.40 ... O12
Valley Dr. ... Pg.40 ... O13
Valley Forge Dr. Pg.40 ... O13
Valley View Ct. Pg.40 ... O13
Valley View Dr. Pg.40 ... O13
Vogt St. ... Pg.41 ... O16
Vollmer Rd. ... Pg.46 ... S15
Walnut Ln. ... Pg.40 ... O12
Waterford Dr. Pg.40 ... N13
Webster Ct. ... Pg.40 ... P13
West Creek Dr. Pg.40 ... Q14
Westberry Ln. Pg.40 ... M13
Westridge Ct. ... Pg.40 ... O12
Westridge Rd. Pg.40 ... P13
Westway Walk Pg.40 ... M14
Westwind Dr. ... Pg.41 ... N15
Wexford Ct. ... Pg.40 ... N14
White Oak Ct. ... Pg.40 ... Q12
White Oak Ln. Pg.40 ... Q12
White Tailed Ln. ... Pg.41 ... P15
Whittington Dr. Pg.40 ... M13
Willow Ln. ... Pg.41 ... N16
Windsor Pkwy. Pg.40 ... O12
Winston Dr. ... Pg.41 ... N15
Witham Ct. ... Pg.40 ... O13
Woburn Rd. ... Pg.40 ... P12
Woodbine Ct. Pg.40 ... Q12
Woodland Dr. Pg.40 ... N13
Woodstock Ave. ... Pg.40 ... O14
62nd Ave. ... Pg.41 ... P16
64th Ct. ... Pg.41. N-P16
65th Ave. ... Pg.41. N,P16
65th Ct. ... Pg.41. N,P15
66th Ave. ... Pg.41. N-P15
66th Ct. ... Pg.41. N-P15
67th Ave. ... Pg.41 O16,P15
67th Ct. ... Pg.41. N-Q15
68th Ct. ... Pg.41. O,P15
69th Ave. ... Pg.41 ... O15
70th Ave. ... Pg.41. O,P15
70th Ct. ... Pg.41 ... P15
71st Ave. ... Pg.41. O,P15
71st Ct. ... Pg.41. O,P15
76th Ave. ... Pg.40. N,Q14
78th Ave. ... Pg.40 ... M14
79th Ave. ... Pg.40 ... O14
80th Ave. ... Pg.40,46 ... M,S13
81st Ave. ... Pg.40. N,Q13
81st Ct. ... Pg.40. N,O13
82nd Ave. ... Pg.40 ... O13
83rd Ct. ... Pg.40 ... O13
84th Ave. ... Pg.40 ... N13
84th Ct. ... Pg.40 M,N13
84th Pl. ... Pg.40 ... M13
85th Ave. ... Pg.40 M,N13
85th Ct. ... Pg.40 ... M13
87th Ct. ... Pg.40 ... O12
88th Ave. ... Pg.40 O,P,S12
92nd Ave. ... Pg.40. O,P12
94th Ave. ... Pg.40 ... P11
94th Ct. ... Pg.40 ... O11
159th Pl. ... Pg.40 ... M14
159th St. ... Pg.40 ... M14
160th Ct. ... Pg.40 ... M14
160th Pl. ... Pg.40 M13,14
160th St. ... Pg.40 M13,14
161st Pl. ... Pg.40 M13,14
161st St. ... Pg.40 M13,14
162nd Pl. ... Pg.40 ... M14,N13
162nd St. ... Pg.40 ... M14
163rd Pl. ... Pg.40 N14,15
163rd St. ... Pg.40 ... N13,14,M15
164th Ave. ... Pg.41 ... N16
164th Ct. ... Pg.40 ... N13
164th Pl. ... Pg.40 N14,15
164th St. ... Pg.40 N13,15
165th Pl. ... Pg.40 N13-15
165th St. ... Pg.40 N13-15
166th Pl. ... Pg.40 N13,14
166th St. ... Pg.40 N14,16
167th Pl. ... Pg.40 ... N13
167th St. ... Pg.40 ... N13
168th Pl. ... Pg.40 N13,15
168th St. ... Pg.40,41 ... N13,15
169th Pl. ... Pg.40 ... O13
169th St. ... Pg.40 N13,15
170th Pl. ... Pg.40 ... N14,O13
170th St. ... Pg.40 ... N14,O13,15
171st Pl. ... Pg.40 ... O13
171st St. ... Pg.41 ... O15
172nd Pl. ... Pg.40 ... O14
172nd St. ... Pg.40 O12,15
173rd Pl. ... Pg.40 ... O12,14,15
173rd St. ... Pg.40 ... O11,14,15
174th Pl. ... Pg.40 O13-15
174th St. ... Pg.40 O11-15
175th Pl. ... Pg.40 O14,15
175th St. ... Pg.40 ... O12,13,16
176th Pl. ... Pg.41 ... O15
176th St. ... Pg.40 ... P12,O15
177th Pl. ... Pg.41 ... P15
177th St. ... Pg.41 ... P15
178th St. ... Pg.40 ... P11,12,15
179th Pl. ... Pg.41 ... P15
179th St. ... Pg.40,41 ... P10,15
180th Ct. ... Pg.41 ... P15
180th Pl. ... Pg.41 ... P16
180th St. ... Pg.41 ... P15
181st Pl. ... Pg.41 ... P16
181st St. ... Pg.41 ... P15
182nd Pl. ... Pg.41 ... P16
182nd St. ... Pg.41 P15,16
183rd St. ... Pg.40 P11,14
185th St. ... Pg.40 ... Q13
186th St. ... Pg.40 ... Q13
194th St. ... Pg.46 ... R15
196th St. ... Pg.46 ... R14

### CEMETERIES

Lutheran Cemetery ... Pg.41 ... M15
Orland/Tinley Park Cem. ... Pg.40 ... O13

### GOLF COURSES

Greystone Golf Course ... Pg.40 ... Q14
Odyssey G.C. ... Pg.46 ... R15

### PARKS

Bettenhausen Park ... Pg.40 ... N14
Bicentennial Park ... Pg.41 ... M15
Brementowne Park ... Pg.40 ... M14
Buedingen Park ... Pg.40 ... N13
Commissioners Park ... Pg.40 ... N13
Corrine Deinert Park ... Pg.40 ... O13
Filson Rec. Area ... Pg.40 ... N14
German Park ... Pg.40 ... N14
Hirsch Park ... Pg.41 ... P16
Jaycee Park ... Pg.40 ... N13
John Bannes Park ... Pg.40 ... N13
Lancaster Woods ... Pg.41 ... N16
Lewis Park ... Pg.41 ... N16
McCarthy Park Pg.40 ... N14
Memorial Park Pg.40 N14,O16
Nasebandt Park Pg.40 ... O14
Paxton Lot ... Pg.40 ... N14
Pottawattomie Park ... Pg.40 ... P12
Rauhoff Park ... Pg.41 ... P15
Richard M. Gory Park ... Pg.40 ... N13
St. Boniface Park ... Pg.41 ... N15
Sundale Park ... Pg.40 ... O14
The Farm ... Pg.40 ... O13
Vogt Woods ... Pg.41 ... O16
Volunteer Park Pg.41 ... O13

### SCHOOLS

Central Jr. High Pg.41 ... O15
Christa McAuliffe Sch. ... Pg.40 ... O12
Fulton Sch. ... Pg.41 ... O16
Helen Sandidge Sch. ... Pg.41 ... N15
Hellen Keller Sch. ... Pg.40 ... M14
Hilda B. Walker Elem. Sch. ... Pg.46 ... S13
John Bannes Sch. ... Pg.40 ... N14
Kirby McIntosh Sch. ... Pg.40 ... O14
Memorial Sch. Pg.41 ... P15
Prairie View Jr. H.S. ... Pg.40 ... O13
S.W. Christian Sch. ... Pg.40 ... O13
St. George Sch. Pg.41 ... O15
Tinley Park H.S. ... Pg.41 ... O16
V.J. Andrew H.S. ... Pg.40 ... O12
Virgil Grissom Jr. High ... Pg.40 ... O13

### SHOPPING CENTERS

Bayberry Plaza Pg.40 ... O13
Brementowne Mall ... Pg.41 ... M15
Brementowne Manor ... Pg.41 ... N15
Brementowne Mini Mall ... Pg.40 ... M14
Park Center Plaza ... Pg.40 ... M14
Parkside Plaza Pg.40 ... N14
South S.C. ... Pg.41 ... N15
Tinley Court ... Pg.41 ... N15
Tinley Downs S.C. ... Pg.40 ... O13
Tinley Park S.C. Pg.41 ... M15

### MISCELLANEOUS

Commuter Station ... Pg.40 ... P13
Crisis Center for South Suburbia ... Pg.40 ... P14
Fire Station ... Pg.40 ... N14
Ingalls Family Care Center ... Pg.41 ... M15
Midwest Christian Center ... Pg.40 ... Q12
Northcreek Business Center ... Pg.40 ... Q14
Police Dept. ... Pg.40 ... P14
Post Office ... Pg.41 ... O15
Public Works ... Pg.40 ... P14
R.R. Station ... Pg.41 ... O15
The New World Music Theater ... Pg.46 ... R16
Tinley Downs ... Pg.40 ... O14
Tinley Park Library ... Pg.40 ... O15
Tinley Park Mental Health Center ... Pg.40 ... P14
Village Hall ... Pg.41 ... M15
Weigh Station Pg.40 ... Q13
William A. Howe Developmental Center ... Pg.40 ... P14
Windy City Beach Camp Resort ... Pg.40 ... Q14

## VERNON TOWNSHIP

Page 5
Lake County
(For additional listings, see Section 6)

### STREETS

Arlington Heights Rd. ... X11
Ash St. ... X14
Aspen Ct. ... X14
Birch St. ... X14
Bluebird Ln. ... X13
Bluebird St. ... X13
Carmen Dr. ... X13
Catalpa St. ... X14
Catbird Ln. ... X14
Celia Ave. ... X12
Checker Rd. ... X10
Chevy Chase Ave., E. ... X14
Clarice Ave. ... X13
Columbus Pkwy ... X14
Dogwood St. ... X14
Driftwood Pl. ... X12
East Chevy Chase Ave. ... X14
Elizabeth Ave. ... X13
Eugene Ave. ... X13
Florence Ave. ... X13
Frank Ave. ... X13
Frontenac ... X14
Garden Ct. ... X13
Goshawk Ln. ... X14
Grouse Ct. ... X13
Grouse Ln. ... X13
Horatio Blvd. ... X13
Hummingbird Ct. ... X14
Hummingbird Ln. ... X14
Inverray Ln. ... X14
James Cir. ... X14
Juneway Ave. ... X13
Kildeer Ln. ... X14
Lake-Cook Rd. ... X10
Linden Ave. ... X13
Lita ... X13
Long Beach Dr. ... X14
Loyola Ave. ... X14
Mallard Dr. ... X13
Mallard Ln. ... X13
Maple Ct. ... X13
Margaret Ave. ... X13
Marie Ave. ... X13
Marquette Pl. ... X14
Martin Ln. ... X14
Mercier Ave. ... X13
Milwaukee Ave. ... A14
Partridrge Ln. ... X14
Pauline Ave. ... X12
Pekara Dr. ... X14
Penguin Dr. ... X13
Pheasant Ln. ... X14
Pintail Ln. ... X14
Pintail St. ... X12
Pope Blvd. ... X13
Pope Blvd., W. ... X13
Raphael Ave. ... X13
Redwing Dr. ... X14

Sandpiper Ln. .......... X10
Schaeffer Rd. .......... X14
Skylark Ln. .......... X14
Swallow Ct. .......... X13
Swallow Ln. .......... X13
Swallow St. .......... X13
Swan Blvd. .......... X13
Swan Ct. .......... X13
Swan Ln. .......... X13
Tanager Ct. .......... X14
Walnut Dr. .......... X13
William Ave. .......... X13
Winston Dr. .......... X14
Wren Ln. .......... X14

## WHEELING

Pages 4,5,9,10

**STREETS**

Abbott Dr. ... Pg.9 .... C14
Acco Plaza Dr. Pg.9 .... B15
Acorn Ct. .... Pg.4 .... A12
Albert Terr. .. Pg.9 .... A13
Alder Dr. .... Pg.10 ... B14
Alderman Ave. Pg.9 .... D15
Aldgate Ct. ... Pg.4 .... A12
Alexis Ct. .... Pg.10 ... A15
Alice St. ..... Pg.9 .... B14
Allen Ct. ..... Pg.10 ... B15
Allendale Dr. . Pg.4 .... A13
Alpine Ct. .... Pg.4 .... A12
Amy Ct. ..... Pg.4 .... A12
Anita Pl. ..... Pg.10 ... A15
Anne Terr. ... Pg.9 .... A14
Anthony Rd. . Pg.9 . A12-13
Apache ..... Pg.9 .... B11
Arlene Ct. .... Pg.10 ... B15
Arlington Dr. . Pg.4 .... A12
Arrow Tr. .... Pg.9 .... B12
Ash Ln. ..... Pg.9 .... C12
Ashford Cir. .. Pg.9 .... A12
Ashton Ct. ... Pg.4 .... A12
Auborndale Ct. Pg.9 .... B12
Audrey Ct. ... Pg.9 .... B13
Avalon Dr. ... Pg.10 ... D14
Baldwin Ct. .. Pg.4 .... A12
Barberry Ln. . Pg.9 .... B13
Barnaby Pl. .. Pg.5 .... A13
Bayside Ct. .. Pg.9 .... C12
Bayside Dr. .. Pg.9 .... C12
Bayside Ln. .. Pg.9 .... C12
Beech Dr. .... Pg.10 ... B14
Berkshire Dr. . Pg.5 .... A13
Bernice Ct. ... Pg.9 .... A13
Beverly Dr. ... Pg.5 .... A13
Bina Ct. ..... Pg.10 ... A15
Birch Tr. .... Pg.9 .... A13
Blackfoot Ct. . Pg.9 .... B11
Blackhawk Tr. Pg.9 .... B11
Blaze Tr. .... Pg.9 .... B13
Bordeaux Ct. . Pg.10 ... D14
Bow Tr. ..... Pg.9 .... B12
Boxwood Ct. . Pg.4 .... A12
Braeburn Ct. . Pg.4 .... A12
Brandon Pl. .. Pg.4 .... A13
Braver Ct. ... Pg.4 .... A12
Brian Ln. .... Pg.9 .... A15
Briarwood Dr. Pg.9 .... B13
Bridgeport Pl. Pg.5 .... A13
Bridget Pl. ... Pg.9 .... A14
Bridgeview Ct. Pg.9 .... B13
Bridle Tr. .... Pg.9 .... C14
Brighton Pl. .. Pg.5 .... A13
Bristol Ct. ... Pg.9 .... B12
Brittany Ct. .. Pg.9 .... A12
Broadway Ct. . Pg.4 .... A12
Brookvale Dr. . Pg. ..... A13
Brougham Dr. Pg.5 .... A13
Buckboard Dr. Pg.4 .... A13
Buckeye Dr. .. Pg.10 ... B14
Buckingham Ct. Pg.5 .... A13
Buffalo Grove Rd.
.......... Pg.9 .. A,B12
Buffalo Tr. ... Pg.9 .... B11
Buxton Ct. ... Pg.9 .... B12
Cambridge Pl. Pg.5 .... A13
Camden Ct. .. Pg.4 .... A12
Canbury Ct. .. Pg.4 .... A12
Candlewood Ct. Pg.9 .... C12
Capitol Dr. ... Pg.9 .... C15
Capri Terr. ... Pg.5 .... A14
Captains Ln. . Pg.9 .... B13
Cardinal Ct. .. Pg.4 .... A12
Carpenter Ave. Pg.9 .... B14
Carriage Hill Rd.
.......... Pg.5 .... A13
Catherine Ct. . Pg.9 .... A14
Cedar Dr. .... Pg.9 .... A13
Cedar Run Dr. Pg.4 .... A12
Cedarwood Ln. Pg.9 .... B13
Center Ave. .. Pg.9 .... A15
Century Dr. .. Pg.9 .... B15
Chaddick Dr. . Pg.9 .... B15
Chamberry Ct. Pg.10 ... D14
Charabanc Ln. Pg.4 .... A13
Chariot Ct. ... Pg.5 .... A13
Chariot Ln. ... Pg.5 .... A13
Chariot Rd. ... Pg.5 .... A13
Chelsea Dr. .. Pg.5 .... A13
Cherrywood Dr. Pg.9 .... B13
Chestnut Ln. . Pg.5 .... A13
Cheswick Ct. . Pg.4 .... A12
Chippewa Tr. . Pg.9 .... B12
Chukker Ct. .. Pg.9 .... C14
Cindy Ln. .... Pg.9 .... A13
Clearwater Ct. Pg.9 .... B13
Clearwater Dr. Pg.9 .... B13
Clearwater Ln. Pg.9 .... B13
Cleo Ct. ..... Pg.5 .... A13
Coach Rd. ... Pg.5 .... A13
Cobbler Ln. .. Pg.4 .... A12
Colonial Dr. .. Pg.5 .... A13
Commanche Tr. Pg.9 .... B11
Commons Ct. Pg.10 ... A15
Coral Ln. .... Pg.5 .... A13
Corey Ln. .... Pg.9 .... B12
Cornell Ave. .. Pg.9 .... B12
Cottonwood Ct. Pg.9 .... B12
Courtesy Ln. . Pg.10 ... B15
Coventry Pl. .. Pg.5 .... A13
Creekside Ct. . Pg.9 .... B12
Crescent Dr. .. Pg.9 .... A15
Crimson Dr. .. Pg.9 .... B13
Crow Tr., S. .. Pg.9 .... C12
Curricle Rd. .. Pg.4 .... A13
Custer Ct. ... Pg.9 .... B11
Cypress Dr. .. Pg.4 .... A12
Cyrilla St. ... Pg.5 .... A14
Dakota Tr. ... Pg.9 .... A13
Dean Ave. ... Pg.9 .... B15
Deborah Ln. . Pg.5 .... A14
Debra Ln. ... Pg.9 .... B15
Deerpath Ct. . Pg.5 .... A13
Delaware Tr. . Pg.9 .... B11
Dennis Rd. ... Pg.9 .... A13
Denniston Ct. Pg.9 .... A14
Denoyer Tr. .. Pg.5 .... A13
Derby St. .... Pg.9 .... C14
Diens Dr. .... Pg.4 .... A13
Donna Ct. ... Pg.9 .... B15
Dorset Cir. ... Pg.4 .... A13
Dorset Ct. ... Pg.4 .... A13
Dover Pl. .... Pg.5 .... A13
Drae Ct. ..... Pg.5 .... A13
Driftwood Ct. . Pg.5 .... A13
Dundee Rd. .. Pg.5 .... A14
E. Jeffrey Ave. Pg.10 ... A15
Eagle Grove Ct. Pg.4 .... A12
East Dr. ..... Pg.9 .... B13
Eastchester Rd. Pg.9 .... B14
Easton Ct. ... Pg.4 .... A12
Edgewood Dr. Pg.5 .... A13
Edward St. ... Pg.9 .... B13
Egidi Dr. .... Pg.5 .... A14
Elden Ct. .... Pg.5 .... A13
Elizabeth Ct. . Pg.9 .... B12
Elizabeth Ln. . Pg.9 .... B12
Elm Dr. ..... Pg.10 ... B14
Elmhurst Rd. . Pg.9 .. B-C13
Elmwood Ln. . Pg.4 .... A12
Ely Ct. ...... Pg.5 .... A13
Equestrian Dr. Pg.9 .... C14
Exchange Ct. . Pg.9 .... B14
Exeter Ct. ... Pg.4 .... A12
Fairfield Ct. .. Pg.4 .... A12
Fairview Dr. .. Pg.5 .... A13
Fairway View Dr.
.......... Pg.5 .... A13
Fall Ct. ..... Pg.5 .... A13
Ferndale Ct. .. Pg.5 .... A13
Ferne Dr. .... Pg.10 ... B14
Fletcher Dr. .. Pg.9 .... A13
Fore Ct. ..... Pg.4 .... A12
Forest Way Ln. Pg.5 .... A15
Forums Ct. ... Pg.9 .... B14
Foster Ave. .. Pg.9 .... D15
Foxboro Dr. .. Pg.9 .... B15
Garden Ln. ... Pg.9 .... B13
Garth Rd. .... Pg.9 .... B14
Gayle Ct. .... Pg.10 ... B15
Gee Ct. ..... Pg.5 .... A13
Geneva Dr. ... Pg.10 ... C14
George Rd. ... Pg.9 .... A14
Gilman Ave. .. Pg.9 .... C14
Glendale St. . Pg.5 .... A14
Glengary Ct. . Pg.4 .... A12
Glengary Ln. . Pg.4 .... A13
Glenn Ave. ... Pg.9 .... B14
Gray Ct. ..... Pg.5 .... A13
Green Dr. .... Pg.5 .... A13
Gregor Ln. ... Pg.9 .... B13
Greystone Ln. Pg.5 .... A13
Haben Ln. ... Pg.4 .... A13
Hadley Ct. ... Pg.4 .... A12
Hale Ct. ..... Pg.5 .... A13
Hansom Ct. .. Pg.5 .... A13
Hansom Dr. .. Pg.4 .... A13
Harbour Ct. .. Pg.9 .... B12
Harbour Dr. .. Pg.9 .... B13
Harmony Dr. . Pg.10 ... B14
Harms Ct. ... Pg.5 .... A13
Harvester Ct. . Pg.9 .... B14
Hastings Ct. . Pg.9 .... B13
Hastings Rd. . Pg.9 .... B14
Hawthorne Ct. Pg.5 .... A13
Henley Ct. ... Pg.4 .... A12
Hickory Dr. .. Pg.10 ... B14
Highgoal Dr. . Pg.9 .... C14
Highland Ave. Pg.10 ... A15
Hintz Ln. .... Pg.9 .... B12
Hintz Rd. .... Pg.9 .... B15
Holbrook Dr. . Pg.9 .... C14
Holly Ct. .... Pg.5 .... A13
Honey Locust Dr.
.......... Pg.10 B14-15
Honeysuckle Dr.
.......... Pg.9 .... B14
Hopi Tr. .... Pg.9 .... B12
Hunter Dr. ... Pg.9 .... B12
Huntington Ct. Pg.4 .... A12
Huntington Ln. Pg.9 .... A12
Inwood Dr. ... Pg.9 .... C14
Iota Ct. ..... Pg.4 .... A12
Ironwood Ct. . Pg.5 .... A13
Irvine Ct. .... Pg.9 .... A12
Isa Dr. ...... Pg.9 .... B13
Ivy Ct. ...... Pg.9 .... B13
Jackson Dr. .. Pg.9 .... B12
Janice Ct. ... Pg.9 .... C14
Jaspen Ct. ... Pg.5 .... A13
Jeanne Terr. . Pg.9 .... A14
Jefferson Ct. . Pg.9 .... C14
Jeffery Ave. .. Pg.9 .... A14
Jeffery Ln. ... Pg.9 .... A14
Jenkins Ct. ... Pg.9 .... A13
Jerome Pl. ... Pg.10 ... A15
Kenilworth Dr. Pg.5 .... A13
Kerry Ln. .... Pg.9 .... B15
King Ct. ..... Pg.9 .... A13
Kingsport Dr. . Pg.9 .... B13
Kingswood Ln. Pg.5 .... A15
Kiowa Dr., S. . Pg.9 .... C12
Knottingham Ct.
.......... Pg.4 .... A12
Kristy Ln. .... Pg.9 .... B13
Laguna Ct. ... Pg.9 .... B12
Lake-Cook Rd. Pg.5 .... A14
Lakeland Ct. . Pg.9 .... B12
Lakeside Dr. . Pg.9 .... B12
Lakeview Dr. . Pg.9 .... B11
Landau ..... Pg.5 .... A13
Larkin Dr. ... Pg.9 .... B15
Laurel Ct. ... Pg.9 .... A13
Laurel Tr. ... Pg.9 .... A13
Lee St. ..... Pg.9 .... A13
Lemans Dr. .. Pg.10 ... C14
Lenox Ct. .... Pg.4 .... A13
Leslie Ln. .... Pg.9 .... A14
Lexington Dr. Pg.4 .... A12
Lilac Ln. .... Pg.9 .... A15
Lincoln Rd. .. Pg.10 ... A15
Linda Terr. .. Pg.9 .... A13
Linden Ln. ... Pg.5 .... A15
Locust Dr. ... Pg.4 .... A12
London Pl. ... Pg.5 .... A13
Longacre Ln. . Pg.9 .... C14
Longbow Ct. . Pg.9 .... A12
Longtree Dr. . Pg.9 .... B13
Lotus Ct. .... Pg.5 .... A13
Lucerne Ct. .. Pg.10 ... C14
Lynn Ln. .... Pg.9 .... B15
Mae Ct. ..... Pg.5 .... A13
Mallard Ln. .. Pg.9 .... B12
Manchester Dr. Pg.10 A14-15
Manda Dr. ... Pg.4 .... A13
Manda Ln. ... Pg.5 .... A13
Maple Dr. .... Pg.10 ... B14
Marcy Ln. ... Pg.9 .... A13
Marion Ct. ... Pg.9 .... A13
Mark Ln. .... Pg.9 .... B12
Marquardt Dr. Pg.9,10 . B15
Marvin Pl. ... Pg.10 ... A15
Maureen Dr. . Pg.9 .... A13
Mayer Ave. .. Pg.5 .... A14
Meadow Ln. .. Pg.5 .... A14
Meadowbrook Ln.
.......... Pg.9 .... A15
Melvin Pl. ... Pg.9 .... A14
Mercantile Ct. Pg.9 .... A14
Merle Ln. .... Pg.9 .... A14
Merlot Ct. ... Pg.10 ... D14
Messner Dr. .. Pg.9 .... B15
Meyerson Way Pg.5 .... A14
Middlebury Ln. Pg.5 .... A13
Milwaukee Ave. Pg.10 ... A15
Mockingbird Ln.
.......... Pg.5 .... A13
Mohawk St. .. Pg.9 .... B11
Mors Ave. ... Pg.10 ... A15
Muret Ct. .... Pg.10 ... C14
Muriel Ct. ... Pg.9 .... C14
Nancy Ln. ... Pg.9 .... A14
Navajo Tr., S. . Pg.9 .... C12
Newburn Ct. . Pg.4 .... A12
Noel Ave. .... Pg.9 .... B14
Norman Ln. .. Pg.5 .... A13
Northbury Ln. Pg.5 .... A13
Northgate Pkwy.
.......... Pg.4 .... A14
Nottingham Ct. Pg.9 .... A12
Nova Ct. ..... Pg.5 .... A13
Oak Creek Dr. Pg.9 .... C14
Oak Dr. ..... Pg.5 .... A13
Oakmeadow Ct. Pg.4 .... A13
Oakmont Ln. . Pg.5 .... A13
Oakwood Ln. . Pg.5 .... A15
Oboe Ct. .... Pg.5 .... A13
Old McHenry Rd.
.......... Pg.4 .... A13
Orrington Ct. . Pg.4 .... A12
Osage Tr. .... Pg.9 .... B13
Ottawa Ct. ... Pg.9 .... B11
Oxford Pl. ... Pg.5 .... A13
Oxley Ct. .... Pg.9 .... A12
Pacific Ct. .... Pg.9 .... B13
Paddock Dr. . Pg.9 .... C14
Palatine Rd. .. Pg.9 .... C14
Palm Dr. .... Pg.9 .... A13
Palwaukee Dr. Pg.9 .... B14
Pam Ct. ..... Pg.5 .... A13
Park Ave. .... Pg.10 ... A15
Partridge Ln. . Pg.5 .... A15
Peace Dr. .... Pg.9 .... B13
Pear Tree Ln. . Pg.9 .... B14
Pebble Dr. ... Pg.5 .... A13
Peggy Ct. .... Pg.9 .... B15
Pensbury Ct. . Pg.4 .... A12
Peterson Dr. . Pg.9 .... C14
Phaeton Dr. .. Pg.5 .... A13
Pleasant Run Dr.
.......... Pg.9 .... C14
Plumtree Ct. . Pg.4 .... A12
Poplar Dr. ... Pg.10 ... B14
Portsmouth Pl. Pg.5 .... A13
Prairie View Ln. Pg.5 .... A14
Pueblo Tr. ... Pg.9 .... B11
Quad Ct. .... Pg.5 .... A13
Quail Hollow Rd.
.......... Pg.4 .... A13
Queens Ct. ... Pg.4 .... A12
Quincy Ct. ... Pg.4 .... A12
Railroad Ave. . Pg.9 .... A14
Redwood Terr. Pg.9 .... A13
Reef Ct. ..... Pg.9 .... B13
Regent Ln. ... Pg.5 .... A15
Renee Terr. .. Pg.9 .... A13
Ridgefield Ln. Pg.9 .... B14
Robert Ave. .. Pg.9 .... A13
Rochelle Ct. .. Pg.10 ... D14
Rose Ln. .... Pg.9 .... B13
Roth Ct. ..... Pg.4 .... A12
Russetwood Ct. Pg.9 .... B13
Rustic Dr. ... Pg.10 ... B14
Salvington Pl. Pg.9 .... A12
Sander Ct. ... Pg.9 .... C14
Sandpebble Dr. Pg.9 .... C14
Sandra Ln. ... Pg.9 .... C14
Sandstone Dr. Pg.9 .... C14
Sarah Ct. .... Pg.9 .... A13
Sarasota Dr. . Pg.5 .... A13
Scanlon Dr. .. Pg.5 .... A13
Schoenbeck Rd.
.......... Pg.9 .... B13
Scott St. .... Pg.9 .... A12
Seton Ct. .... Pg.9 .... B14
Seville Ct. ... Pg.4 .... A12
Shadow Bend Dr.
.......... Pg.5 .... A15
Shady Tree Ln. Pg.9 .... B14
Shawn Ct. ... Pg.9 .... C14
Shay Ct. ..... Pg.5 .... A13
Shay Rd. .... Pg.5 .... A13
Sheldrake Dr. . Pg.9 .... B12
Shelly Ct. .... Pg.10 ... B15
Sheppard Ave. Pg.9 .... B14
Sheridan Ct. . Pg.4 .... A12
Shore Ct. .... Pg.4 .... A12
Shoshone Tr. . Pg.9 .... B11
Sienna Ct. ... Pg.10 ... C14
Silverwood Ct. Pg.5 .... A13
South Dr. .... Pg.9 .... B13
Southbury Ln. Pg.5 .... A13
Springview Ct. Pg.9 .... B11
Spruce Dr. ... Pg.4,5 A12-13
Spur Ct. ..... Pg.4 .... A12
St. Armand Ct. Pg.5 .... A13
St. Armand Ln. Pg.5 .... A13
Stafford Dr. .. Pg.5 .... A15
Stafford Ln. .. Pg.5 .... A15
Stone Pl. .... Pg.9 .... A15
Stonehedge Ct. Pg.4 .... A12
Stratford Ct. .. Pg.4 .... A12
Strong Ave. .. Pg.5 .... A14
Sumac Ln. ... Pg.10 ... B15
Summer Hill Ln.
.......... Pg.5 .... A15
Sunrise Dr. .. Pg.9 .... A15
Sunset Ln. ... Pg.9 .... A14
Surf Ct. ..... Pg.9 .... B12
Surrey Rd. ... Pg.5 .... A13
Sutton Cir. ... Pg.4 .... A13
Sutton Ct. ... Pg.4 .... A13
Sycamore Ln. Pg.9 .... B13
Tahoe Cir. Dr. Pg.9 .... B11
Tanglewood Dr. Pg.9 .... B14
Teal Ln. ..... Pg.9 .... B12
Thelma Ct. ... Pg.5 .... A13
Thorndale Ct. Pg.5 .... A13
Thornhill Ln. . Pg.4 .... A12
Thyne Ct. .... Pg.5 .... A13
Tide Ct. ..... Pg.9 .... B13
Tilbury Ln. ... Pg.5 .... A13
Town St. .... Pg.9 .... A14
Tulip Ct. ..... Pg.4 .... A12
Twilight Ln. .. Pg.9 .... B13
Union Ct. .... Pg.5 .... A13
Vail Ct. ..... Pg.5 .... A13
Valley Stream Dr.
.......... Pg.5 .... A13
Vera Ln. .... Pg.9 .... B13
Versailles Ct. . Pg.10 ... C14
Virginia Pl. ... Pg.10 ... A15
Vita Dr. ..... Pg.10 ... B14
Walnut Ave. .. Pg.10 ... A15
Waltz Dr. .... Pg.9 .... B15
Warwick Ct. .. Pg.4 .... A12
Wayne Pl. ... Pg.9 .... A14
Weeping Willow Dr.
.......... Pg.9 .... B14
Weiland Rd. .. Pg.4 .. A-X12
West Lodge Tr. Pg.9 .... B11
Westwood Ct. Pg.9 .... B13
Wetumka Ct. . Pg.9 .... C12
Wheeling Ave. Pg.9 .... A15
Wheeling Rd. . Pg.9 .. B-C14
Whipple Tree Rd.
.......... Pg.5 .... A13
Whitehall Ct. . Pg.4 .... A12
Widgeon Dr. . Pg.9 .... B12
Wildberry Ct. . Pg.5 .... A13
Wille Ave. .... Pg.9 .... A15
Williamsburg Ct.
.......... Pg.5 .... A13
Willis Ave. ... Pg.9 .... B14
Willow Rd. ... Pg.9 .... D15
Willow Terr. .. Pg.9 .... A13
Willowbrook Dr.
.......... Pg.9 .... B14
Wilshire Dr. .. Pg.9 .... A13
Wolf Rd. .... Pg.10
.......... A14,D15
Woodbury Ln. Pg.4 .... A12
Woodcreek Rd. Pg.9 .... C14
Woodduck Dr. Pg.9 .... B12
Woodduck Ln. Pg.9 .... B12
Woodland Dr. Pg.5 .... A13
Woodmere Ln. Pg.5 .... A15
Wye Ct. ..... Pg.4 .... A12
Wynn Ct. .... Pg.5 .... A13
Yorkshire Pl. . Pg.5 .... A13
Zee Ct. ..... Pg.4 .... A12
1st St. ...... Pg.5 .... A14
2nd St. ..... Pg.5 .... A14
3rd St. ...... Pg.5 .... A14
6th St. ...... Pg.5 .... A14
6th St. ...... Pg.5 .... A14
7th St. ...... Pg.5 .... A14
8th St. ...... Pg.5 .... A14
9th St. ...... Pg.5 .... A14
10th St. ..... Pg.5 .... A14
11th St. ..... Pg.5 .... A14
12th St. ..... Pg.5 .... A14

**PARKS**

Chamber Park Pg.5 .... A15
Childerly Park Pg.4 .... A13
Heritage Park . Pg.9 .... A14
Horizon Park . Pg.9 .... A13
Husky Park .. Pg.9 .... A13

**SCHOOLS**

Cooper Middle Sch.
.......... Pg.3 .... A11
Eugene Field Sch.
.......... Pg.5 .... A13
Jack London Middle Sch.
.......... Pg.9 .... A13
Mark Twain Sch.
.......... Pg.9 .... B14
Nathaniel Hawthorne Sch.
.......... Pg.5 .... A14
O.W. Holmes Middle Sch.
.......... Pg.9 .... A15
Sandburg Elem. Sch.
.......... Pg.9 .... A13
Sch. Dist. 21 Office
.......... Pg.9 .... A13
St. Joesph Elem. Sch.
.......... Pg.10 ... A14
Tarkington Elem. Sch.
.......... Pg.5 .... A13
Walt Whitman Sch.
.......... Pg.10 ... A15
Wheeling H.S. Pg.9 .... B13

**SHOPPING CENTERS**

Center Plaza . Pg.5 .... A14
Dundee Plaza . Pg.5 .... A14
Dunhurst S.C. Pg.9 .... A13
Gaslight S.C. . Pg.5 .... A13
Lexington Plaza Pg.5 .... A13
Riverside S.C. Pg.10 ... A15
South Point S.C.
.......... Pg.10 ... D15
Wheeling S.C. Pg.10 ... A15

**MISCELLANEOUS**

Des Plaines River Trail
.......... Pg.10 ... B15
Fire Dept. .... Pg.9 .... B14
Indian Trails Library
.......... Pg.9 .... A13
Pal-Waukee Airport
.......... Pg.10 ... C15
Post Office ... Pg.9 .... A14
Railroad Station
.......... Pg.10 ... A14
Wheeling Municipal Complex
.......... Pg.9 .... A14

## WHEELING TOWNSHIP

Pages 3-5,8-10,13

**STREETS**

Anita Ave. ... Pg.10 E15-16
Apple Dr. .... Pg.21 .... D1
Bonnie Brae Ave.
.......... Pg.10 F15-16
Brookfield Ave. Pg.10 F15-16
Camp McDonald Rd.
.......... Pg.21 .... E1
Carol Ave. ... Pg.10 ... B15
Cayuga Ln. .. Pg.21 .... E1
Chicago Ave. . Pg.8 .... C9
Chinkapin Oak Dr.
.......... Pg.24 .... F1
Cider ....... Pg.21 .... D1
Cindy Ln. .... Pg.9 .... B15
Cove Ln. .... Pg.21 .... D1
Crab Apple Dr. Pg.21 .... D1
Crimson .... Pg.21 .... D1
Dean Ave. ... Pg.10 ... B15
Debra Ln. ... Pg.10 ... B15
Des Plaines River Rd.
.......... Pg.10 ... E16
Dundee Rd. .. Pg.4 . A11-12
Edward St. ... Pg.8,9
.......... A13,B10
Forest View Dr. Pg.21 .... A1
Graylynn Dr. . Pg.10 ... F16
Gregory St. .. Pg.10 F15-16
Hill St. ...... Pg.10 F15-16
Industrial Ln. . Pg.10 ... B15
Inland Dr. ... Pg.10 ... B15
Ivy Ln. ..... Pg.24 .... F1
Jackson Dr. .. Pg.9 .... B13
Johnathon ... Pg.21 .... D1
Lama Ln. .... Pg.21 .... F1
Lee St. ..... Pg.10 ... F15
Lillian Ave. ... Pg.8,9 C9,C11
Lynwood Ave. Pg.8 .... D13
Maude Ave. .. Pg.8 .... C9
McIntosh Ct. . Pg.21 .... D1
Milwaukee Ave. Pg.21 .... D1
Moki Ln. .... Pg.24 .... F1
Morrison Ave. Pg.10 F15-16
Mura Ln. .... Pg.21 .... E1
Park Dr. ..... Pg.21 .... E1
Pinoak Dr. ... Pg.21 .... F1
Piper Dr. .... Pg.21 .... D1
Plant Rd. .... Pg.10 ... B15
Plum Creek Dr. Pg.10 ... B15
Portwine Rd. . Pg.5 .... A15
Quaker Ln. ... Pg.21 .... E1
Rolling Ln. ... Pg.9 .... E12
Russell St. ... Pg.9 .... B13
Sauk Ln. .... Pg.21 .... E1
Seminole Ln. . Pg.21 .... E1
Seneca Ln. .. Pg.21 .... E1
South St. .... Pg.9 .... B13
Stavros Rd. .. Pg.10 ... B15
Thomas Ave. . Pg.8 .... D9
Tree ....... Pg.21 .... D1
Vera Ln. .... Pg.9 .... B13
Verde Ave. ... Pg.8 . C9-10
Wilkie Rd. ... Pg.13 .... F9
Winesap .... Pg.21 .... D1
Wintergreen .. Pg.21 .... E1
Wolf Rd. .... Pg.5,10
.......... A14,B15
Woodland Dr. Pg.10 ... F16
Woodview Dr. Pg.21 .... E1
Yale Ave. .... Pg.8 .... C9
Yale Ct. ..... Pg.8 .... C9
Yuma ....... Pg.21 .... E1

**FOREST PRESERVES**

Allison Woods Pg.10 ... D16
Lake Ave. Woods
.......... Pg.10 ... E16
Potawatomi Woods
.......... Pg.5 .... A15

## WILLOW SPRINGS

Pages 33,34
(Portions within DuPage County, for additional Isitings, see Sections 1 & 3)

**STREETS**

Abbott St. .......... C10
Archer Ave. .......... C9
Arizona Tr. .......... C8
Beech St. .......... C10
Beverly Ln. .......... B11
Blackstone Ave. .......... B10
Buck Ln. .......... B9
Buckingham Ct. .......... B9
Candlelight Dr., E. & W. .. B9
Cedar St. .......... B11
Charlton Ave. .......... B10
Chaucer Dr. .......... B9
Chelsea Ln. .......... B9
Cliff St. .......... C10
Colonel Ave. .......... C10
Columbia Woods Dr. ..... C9
Crescent Ct. .......... B8
Crestview Dr. .......... B8
Crown Cir. .......... B9
Doogan Ave. .......... C9
Dunbar St. .......... C9
Elm St. .......... B11
Fieldcrest Ave. .......... B8
Flag Ave. .......... B8
Forest Ave. .......... B11
German Church Rd. ..... B8
Glenwood St. .......... B10
Hess Ave. .......... B9
High St. .......... C10
Hill St. .......... B10
Hilton St. .......... B11
Independence Dr. ....... B8
Kazewell St. .......... B11
Lake Ave. .......... B10
Lake St. .......... B11
Liberty Grove Dr. ...... C9
Louis Dr. .......... B11
Maple Ave. .......... C10
Market St. .......... C10
Mona St. .......... B10
Mound St. .......... B11
Nolton Ave. .......... B10
Nueport Ct. .......... B8
Nueport Dr. .......... B8
Oakwood Ave. .......... B10
Orchard St. .......... C8
Park St. .......... B10
Pearl St. .......... B10
Pine St. .......... B11
Pleasantview .......... B8
Poston Rd. .......... B11
Price St. .......... C10
Prospect Ave. .......... C10
Province Ct. .......... B9
Rainford .......... C8
Ravine Ave. .......... B11
Regency Ct. .......... B9
Reserve Dr. .......... C8
Ridge Ct. .......... C8
Rosemere Ct. .......... B8
Rust St. .......... B10
Rust Trail .......... B11
Santa Fe Ct. .......... C8
Santa Fe Ln. .......... C8
Scenic Dr. .......... B8
School St. .......... B9
Sherwood St. .......... B10
Spring St. .......... B,C10
Stratford Dr. .......... B9
Tower Rd. .......... B9
Tri-State Tollway ....... A10
Tudor Cir. .......... B0
Union St. .......... B11
Ursala Dr. .......... C9
Vana Dr. .......... B11
Vinewood Ave. .......... B10
Wadsworth Rd. .......... B9
Walnut St. .......... B11
Westport Ln. .......... B8
Willow Edge Ct. .......... C9
Willow Ridge Dr. ........ C8
Willow Springs Rd. ...... B9
Willow West Dr. ........ B9
Winding Ct. .......... C8
Winding Trails Dr. ...... C8
Wolf Rd. .......... B9
84th Pl. .......... B8
85th St. .......... B8
86th St. .......... C8
87th St. .......... C10
91st St. .......... C8

**SCHOOLS**

Grace Sch. .......... B11
Willow Springs Sch. ..... B11

**MISCELLANEOUS**

Fire Department .......... B9
Post Office .......... D10
Village Hall .......... B10

## WILMETTE

Pages 26,27

**STREETS**

Alison Ln. .......... G10
Alpine Ln. .......... G11
Amhurst Ln. .......... F11
Apple Tree Ln. .......... G10
Ashland Ave. .......... F12
Avondale Ln. .......... G11
Barclay Ct. .......... G9
Beech Ave. .......... G9
Beechwood Ave. ........ F11
Beverly Dr. .......... G10
Big Tree Ln. .......... G9
Birchwood Ave. ....... G9-11
Birchwood Ct. .......... G10
Birchwood Ln. .......... G10
Blackhawk Rd. .......... F10
Briar Dr. .......... G9
Brookside Dr. .......... G10
Bunker Ln. .......... F8
Cambridge Ln. .......... F11
Canterbury Ct. .......... G14
Cardinal Ln. .......... G10
Carriage Way .......... H10
Catalpa Pl. .......... G12
Cedar Ln. .......... G11
Central Ave. ....... G9,11-13
Central Park Ave. ....... G12
Cherokee Rd. .......... F11
Chestnut Ave. ....... F11-12
Chilton Ln. .......... G10
Chippewa .......... F10
Cleveland .......... F10
Colgate .......... F11
Columbus St. .......... F11
Concord Ln. .......... G10
Cornell St. .......... F-G11
Country Ln. .......... F9
Cove Ln. .......... G10
Crabtree Ln. .......... G10
Cranston Ct. .......... F9
Crescent Pl. .......... G13
Crestview Ln. .......... G11
Dartmouth .......... F10
Dupee Pl. .......... G13
Edgewood Ct. .......... F9
Elmwood .......... F9-10
Elmwood Ave. ....... F11-13
Fairway Dr. .......... F8

## WILMETTE

Forest ... F9
Forest Ave. ... F11-13
Glendening Rd. ... F12
Glenview Rd. ... G8-9
Golf Terr. ... G13
Grant St. ... G13
Green Bay Rd. ... F12
Greenleaf Ave. ... G9,10,12,13
Greenwood Ave. ... F9-12
Gregory Ave. ... G9,12-13
Hartzell St. ... H9
Harvard Ln. ... F,G11
Hawthorn Ln. ... G10
Heather Ln. ... G9
Hibbard St. ... G9
Highcrest Dr. ... G11
Highland Ave. ... G9-12
Hill Ln. ... G9
Hill St. ... G9
Hollywood Ct. ... G11
Hunter Ct. ... G11
Hunter Rd. ... G11
Illinois Rd. ... F10
Indianwood Rd. ... F10
Iroquois Rd. ... F10-11
Isabella Ln. ... G11
Isabella St. ... G13
Karey Ct. ... G10
Kenilworth Ave. ... F10-11
Kilpatrick Ave. ... G9
Kin Ct. ... G10
Knoll Ln. ... F11
Knox ... F-G10
Koerper Ct. ... G10
La Crosse Ave. ... G9
La Crosse Ct. ... G9
LaPorte Ave. ... G9
Lake Ave. ... F9-13
Lamon Ave. ... G9
Laramie Ave. ... F-G9
Laurel Ave. ... G13-14
Laurel Ln. ... G10
Lavergne Ave. ... G9
Lawler Ave. ... G9
Lawndale Ave. ... G11
Leamington ... G9
Leclaire Ave. ... G9
Leyden Ln. ... G9
Lilac Ln. ... G9
Lincoln Ln. ... G9
Linden Ave. ... F11,G12-14
Lockerbie Ln. ... G9-12
Locust Rd. ... G10
Manor Dr. ... G9
Maple Ave. ... G12-13
Marian Ln. ... G10
Meadow Dr., N., S., E. & W. ... G10
Melrose Ct. ... F9
Miami Rd. ... F10
Michigan Ave. ... F13
Middlebury Ln. ... F10
Millbrook Ln. ... G9
Mohawk Rd. ... F10
New Trier Ct. ... F9
Nina Ave. ... G9
North Branch Rd. ... F9
Oak Cir. ... G12
Oakwood Ave. ... G12
Old Glenview Rd. ... G9-11
Orchard Ln. ... F10
Osage ... F10
Ottawa ... F10
Ouilmette Ln. ... G11
Oxford Ln. ... F11
Pamona Ln. ... G10
Park Ave. ... G12

Parkview Ct. ... G11
Pawnee Rd. ... F10
Pine ... G10
Pine Manor Dr. ... G11
Pinecrest Ln. ... G11
Pioneer Ln. ... G11
Plum Tree Ln. ... H9
Pontiac Rd. ... F10
Prairie Ave. ... G12
Princeton Pl. ... F10
Railroad ... G10
Redbud Ln. ... G10
Richmond Ln. ... F12
Ridge Rd. ... F,G11
Riverside Dr. ... F10
Romona Ct. ... F9
Romona Rd. ... F,G10
Sandy Ln. ... G11
Schiller Ave. ... G11
Seger St. ... G9
Seminole Rd. ... F10
Seneca Rd. ... F10
Shabona ... G10
Sheridan Rd. ... F13
Skokie Blvd. ... H-J10
Skokie Ct. ... G10
Spanish Ct. ... G10
Spencer Ave. ... G12
Sprucewood Ln. ... F9
Sprucewood Rd. ... F9
Sterling Ln. ... G10
Sunset Dr. ... G9
Temple Ln. ... G9
Thelin Ct. ... G10
Thornwood ... F9
Thornwood Ave. ... F11
Timber Ln. ... F11
Valley View Dr. ... G10
Valleyview Ct. ... G10
Vine Ct. ... G10
Vine St. ... G10
Virginia Ln. ... F9
Vista Ct. ... G10
Vista Dr. ... G10
Walden ... F9
Walnut ... F9
Walnut Ave. ... F11
Washington Ave. ... G9-12
Westerfield Dr. ... F12
Westmoreland Dr. ... G10
Westwood Ln. ... G9
Wilmette Ave. ... G9-12
Wilshire Dr., E. & W. ... G10
Wood Ct. ... G12
Yale St. ... F11
3rd St. ... G13
4th St. ... G13
5th St. ... G13
6th St. ... F12,G13
7th St. ... F-G13
8th St. ... F-G13
9th St. ... F-G13
10th St. ... F12
11th St. ... F-G12
12th St. ... F12
13th St. ... F-G12
14th St. ... G12
15th St. ... F,G12
16th St. ... F,G12
17th St. ... G11
18th St. ... F11
20th St. ... G11
23rd St. ... F11
36th Pl. ... F9

**GOLF COURSES**
Westmoreland C.C. ... G10
Wilmette G.C. ... F8

**PARKS**
Centennial Park ... G11
Gillson Park ... F14
Howard Park ... G11
Maple Ave. Park ... G13
Roemer Park ... G10
Thornwood Park ... F10
Vattman Park ... F12

**SCHOOLS**
Avoco Jr. H.S. East ... F9
Bell Sch. ... G10
Beth Hillel Sch. ... G9
Central Sch. ... G13
Harper Sch. ... F10
Highcrest Sch. ... G10
Howard Sch. ... G11
Locust Jr. H.S. ... G10
Logan Sch. ... F12
Loyola Academy ... F9
Marie Murray Jr. H.S. ... F10
McKenzie Sch. ... G12
National College ... G14
National Lewis University ... G14
Regina H.S. ... G10
Romona Sch. ... G10
Ronald Knox Montessori Sch. ... F11
St. Francis Sch. ... G13

**SHOPPING CENTERS**
Edens S.C. ... F9
Plaza del Lago S.C. ... F13

**MISCELLANEOUS**
Bahai Temple ... G14
Mahoney Farm Preserve ... F12
Maria Immaculata Convent ... F11
Weinstein Center ... G14

## WINNETKA

Pages 23,27
**STREETS**
Alles Rd. ... Pg.23 ... E10
Apple Tree Rd. ... Pg.23 ... E10
Arbor Viate ... Pg.23 ... D11
Ardsley Rd. ... Pg.23 ... D10
Asbury Ave. ... Pg.23 ... C9
Asbury Ct. ... Pg.23 ... C9
Ash St. ... Pg.23 D10-11
Auburn Rd. ... Pg.23 ... C-E9
Bell Ln. ... Pg.23 ... C9
Berkeley ... Pg.23 ... D10
Bertling Ln. ... Pg.23 ... E11
Birch St. ... Pg.23 ... D10
Blackthorn Rd. ... Pg.23 ... D10
Boal Pkwy. ... Pg.23 ... D9
Briar Ln. ... Pg.23 ... D11
Broadmeadow Rd. ... Pg.23 ... E10
Bryant Ave. ... Pg.23 ... D11
Burr ... Pg.23 ... D10
Cedar ... Pg.23 ... C9
Chatfield Rd. ... Pg.23 ... C10
Cherry St. ... Pg.23 D10-11
Chestnut ... Pg.23 ... D-E10
Church Rd. ... Pg.23 ... C9
Crescent Ln. ... Pg.23,27 ... C10,E11
De Windt Rd. ... Pg.23 ... C10
Dinsmore Rd. ... Pg.23 ... D10
Edgewood Ln. ... Pg.23 ... C9
Elder Ln. ... Pg.23 ... C10
Eldorado St. ... Pg.23 ... D10
Essex Rd. ... Pg.23 ... E12
Evergreen Ln. ... Pg.23 ... E10
Fairview ... Pg.23 ... E11

Fisher Ln. ... Pg.23 ... C10
Forest ... Pg.23 ... E11
Forest Glen Dr., N., S., E. & W. ... Pg.23 ... C9
Forest Way ... Pg.23 ... D9
Foxdale Ave. ... Pg.23 ... D10
Fuller Ln. ... Pg.27 ... E12
Gage ... Pg.23 ... C10
Garland Ave. ... Pg.23 ... E11
Glen Oak Dr. ... Pg.23 ... E10
Glendale Ave. ... Pg.23 D-E10
Golf Rd. ... Pg.23 ... E11
Gordon Terr. ... Pg.23 ... C10
Green Bay Rd. ... Pg.23 ... D11
Greenwood ... Pg.23 ... C9
Grove ... Pg.23 ... C9
Hackberry Ln. ... Pg.23 ... D10
Hamptondale ... Pg.23 ... D10
Hawthorne Ln. ... Pg.23 ... E11
Hazel Ln. ... Pg.23 ... D9
Heather Ln. ... Pg.23 ... E11
Hibbard St. ... Pg.23 ... D9
Hickory Ln. ... Pg.23 ... C9
Higginson Ln. ... Pg.23 ... E10
High St. ... Pg.23 ... E11
Hill Rd. ... Pg.23 ... E11
Hill Terr. ... Pg.23 ... E11
Holly Ln. ... Pg.23 ... D9
Hoyt Ln. ... Pg.23 ... D11
Hubbard Pl. ... Pg.23 ... C10
Humboldt ... Pg.23 ... C10
Indian Hill Rd. ... Pg.23 ... E11
Kent Rd. ... Pg.23 ... D9
Lake Ln. ... Pg.27 ... E11
Lamson Dr. ... Pg.23 ... C10
Laurel ... Pg.23 ... D10
Lincoln Ave. ... Pg.23 D10-11
Linden ... Pg.23 ... D10
Lindenwood ... Pg.23 ... E10
Lloyd Pl. ... Pg.23 ... D10
Locust ... Pg.23 D-E10
Maple ... Pg.23 ... D11
Meadow Ln. ... Pg.23 ... E10
Meadow Rd. ... Pg.23 ... E11
Merrill St. ... Pg.23 ... C10
Mt. Pleasant ... Pg.23 E9,10
Myrtle ... Pg.23 ... E11
Oak ... Pg.23 D10-11
Oakley ... Pg.23 ... C10
Orchard Ln. ... Pg.23 ... E11
Park Ln. ... Pg.23 ... D10
Pelham Rd. ... Pg.23 ... D10
Pine Ln. ... Pg.23 ... D10
Pine St. ... Pg.23 D10-11
Pine Tree Ln. ... Pg.23 ... C9
Plum Tree Ln. ... Pg.23 ... C9
Poplar ... Pg.23 ... E11
Prospect Ave. ... Pg.23 ... C10
Provident Ave. ... Pg.23 ... D10
Ravine Rd. ... Pg.23 ... D10
Ridge Rd. ... Pg.23 ... E11
Rosewood Ave. ... Pg.23 ... D10
Scott Ave. ... Pg.23 ... C9
Sheridan Rd. ... Pg.23,27
Spring Ln. ... Pg.23 ... C10
Spruce ... Pg.23 D10-11
Starr Rd. ... Pg.23 ... D10
Sumac Ln. ... Pg.23 ... D9
Summit ... Pg.23 ... D10
Sunset Rd. ... Pg.23 E10-11
Sunview Ln. ... Pg.23 ... D9
Taylorsport Ln. ... Pg.23 ... C10
Thorn Tree Ln. ... Pg.23 ... E10
Tower Manor Dr. ... Pg.23 ... C10
Tower Rd. ... Pg.23 ... C10

Trapp Ln. ... Pg.23 ... D9
Vernon Ave. ... Pg.23 ... C9
Vine ... Pg.23 ... D10
Walden Rd. ... Pg.23 ... D10
Walnut St. ... Pg.23 ... E11
Warwick Ave. ... Pg.27 ... E11
Westmoor Rd. ... Pg.23 ... D10
Westmoor Trail ... Pg.23 ... D9
Westview ... Pg.23 ... E9
White Oak Ln. ... Pg.23 ... E10
Whitebridge Ln. ... Pg.23 ... D9
Willow Rd. ... Pg.23 E10-11
Wilson Ave. ... Pg.23 ... E11
Winnetka Ave. ... Pg.23 E10-11
Winnetka Mews ... Pg.23 ... C9
Woodland Ave. ... Pg.27 ... E11

**GOLF COURSES**
Indian Hill G.C. ... Pg.23 ... E10
Winnetka G.C. ... Pg.23 ... D9

**PARKS**
Crow Island Park ... Pg.23 ... E10
Dwyer Park ... Pg.23 ... D10
Edgewood Park Pg.23 ... C9
Elder Lane Park Pg.27 ... E12
Lake Front Park Pg.23 ... D11
Lloyd Park ... Pg.23 ... D11
Tower Rd. Park Pg.23 ... C11
Village Green Park ... Pg.23 ... C10
W. Elm St. Park Pg.23 ... D10
Winnetka Park ... Pg.23 ... E11

**SCHOOLS**
Crow Island Sch. ... Pg.23 ... E10
Hubbard Woods Sch. ... Pg.23 ... D10
New Trier H.S. East Campus ... Pg.27 ... E12
North Shore County Day Sch. ... Pg.23 ... C10
Sacred Heart Sch. ... Pg.23 ... C10
Sammuel Greenley Sch. ... Pg.27 ... E11
School of Saints Faith, Hope & Charity ... Pg.23 ... D10
Skokie School Pg.23 ... D10
Washburn Jr. H.S. ... Pg.23 ... D9

**MISCELLANEOUS**
Community House ... Pg.23 ... D11
Fire Department Pg.23 ... D11
Ice Arena ... Pg.23 ... D9
Library ... Pg.23 ... D11
Police Department ... Pg.23 ... D11
Post Office ... Pg.23 ... C10
Tennis Neilsen Center ... Pg.23 ... D9
Village Hall ... Pg.23 ... D11

## WORTH

Pages 34,35,38
**STREETS**
Autullo Dr. ... Pg.34 ... F14
Beloit Ave. ... Pg.34 F,G14
Columbus Ave. ... Pg.34 ... F14
Crandall Ave. ... Pg.35 ... F15
Depot St. ... Pg.34 ... F15
Harlem Ave. ... Pg.34 ... G14
Highland Ave. ... Pg.35 ... E15
Home Ave. ... Pg.38 ... G15

Lloyd Dr. ... Pg.35 ... F15
Lode Dr. ... Pg.35 ... E15
Nagle Ave. ... Pg.35,38 ... F,G15
Nashville Ave. ... Pg.34 ... G15
Natchez Ave. ... Pg.34,38 ... F,G15
Natoma Ave. ... Pg.35 ... F15
Neenah Ave. ... Pg.35,38 ... F,G15
New England Ave. ... Pg.35 F,G15
Nordica Ave. ... Pg.35 ... F15
Normandy Ave. ... Pg.35 ... F15
Oak Park Ave. ... Pg.35 ... E15
Oak Tree ... Pg.34 ... E14
Oconto Ct. ... Pg.34 ... F14
Octavia Ave. ... Pg.34 ... F14
Odell Pl. ... Pg.34 ... F14
Oketo Ave. ... Pg.34 ... F14
Pacific Dr. ... Pg.34 ... F14
Plahm Ct. ... Pg.34 ... F14
Preller St. ... Pg.34 ... F14
Ridgeland Ave. ... Pg.35,38 F16
Rutherford Ave. ... Pg.35 ... F15
Southwest Hwy. ... Pg.35 ... E15
Wabash St. ... Pg.35 ... E15
Wood Ave. ... Pg.38 ... G15
Worth Ave. ... Pg.35 F,G15
71st St. ... Pg.34 ... F14
76th Ave. ... Pg.34 ... F14
76th Ct., W. ... Pg.34 ... F14
105th Pl. ... Pg.35 ... E15
106th Pl. ... Pg.35 ... E15
107th Pl. ... Pg.35 ... E15
107th St. ... Pg.34 ... E14
108th Pl. ... Pg.34 ... E14
108th St. ... Pg.34 ... E14
109th Pl. ... Pg.34 F14,15
110th Pl. ... Pg.34 ... F14
110th St. ... Pg.34 ... F14
111th Pl. ... Pg.34,35 ... F14,15
111th St. ... Pg.34,35 F15
112th Pl. ... Pg.34,35 ... F14,15
112th St. ... Pg.34,35 ... F14,15
113th Pl. ... Pg.34,35 F14
113th St. ... Pg.34,35 ... F14,15
114th Pl. ... Pg.34,35 F14
114th St. ... Pg.34,35 ... F14,15
115th Pl. ... Pg.34,35 G14
115th St. ... Pg.34,35 F14
116th St. ... Pg.34,38 ... G14,15

**PARKS**
Atman Park ... Pg.34 ... G14
Christensen Park ... Pg.34 ... F14
Holersing Park Pg.38 ... G15
Peak's Park ... Pg.35 ... F15
Penney Park ... Pg.38 ... I16

**SCHOOLS**
Libra Sch. ... Pg.34 ... F14
Worth Jr. H.S. ... Pg.35 ... F15
Worth Main Sch. ... Pg.35 ... F15
Worthridge Sch. ... Pg.35 ... F16
Worthwood Sch. ... Pg.34 ... F14

## WORTH TOWNSHIP

**MISCELLANEOUS**
Charles Christensen Center ... Pg.34 ... G14
Library ... Pg.35 ... F15
Library ... Pg.35 ... F15
Park District ... Pg.35 ... E15
Village Hall ... Pg.35 ... E15

## WORTH TOWNSHIP

Page 35,38
(For additional listings, see Section 1)
**STREETS**
Austin Ave. ... Pg.38 ... H16
Calumet Sag Rd. ... Pg.38 ... H16
Central Ave. ... Pg.38 ... H17
Circle Ave., W. ... Pg.38 ... I17
Le Claire Ave. ... Pg.38 ... I17
Major Ave., S. ... Pg.38 ... H17
Mason Ave., S. ... Pg.38 ... I16
Massasoit Ave., S.
McVicker Ave. ... Pg.38 ... H,I16
Meade Ave. ... Pg.38 ... H,I16
Melvina Ave. ... Pg.38 ... I16
Menard Ave., S. ... Pg.38 ... H16
Mobile Ave. ... Pg.38 ... I17
Monitor Ave., S. ... Pg.38 ... I16
Moody Ave. ... Pg.38 ... H16
Parkside Ave., S. ... Pg.38 ... H17
Ridgeland ... Pg.38 G16,19
123rd St. ... Pg.38 ... H16
124th St. ... Pg.38 ... H16
125th St., W. ... Pg.38 ... H16
126th St. ... Pg.38 H17,20
127th Pl. ... Pg.38 ... H16
127th St. ... Pg.38 ... H16
128th Pl. ... Pg.38 ... H16
129th Pl. ... Pg.38 ... H16
129th St. ... Pg.38 ... H16
130th Pl. ... Pg.38 ... I20
130th St. ... Pg.38 ... H16
131st St. ... Pg.38 ... I20
135th St. ... Pg.38 ... I16
174th Pl. ... Pg.38 ... I18

**CEMETERIES**
Burr Oak Cem. ... Pg.38 ... H18
Chapel Hills Garden South Cem. ... Pg.38 ... F17
Hazelgreen Cem. ... Pg.35 ... G17
Holy Sepulchre Cemetery ... Pg.35 ... F15
Rest Vale Cem. ... Pg.38 ... F17
St. Casimir Cem. ... Pg.35 ... F19

**FOREST PRESERVES**
Elizabeth A. Conkey F.P. ... Pg.38 ... I16

**GOLF CLUBS**
Westgate Valley C.C. ... Pg.38 ... I15

**SCHOOLS**
Chippewa Sch. ... Pg.38 ... H16
Indian Hills Sch. ... Pg.38 ... I16
Shepard H.S. ... Pg.38 ... I16

# DU PAGE COUNTY
## SECTION 3

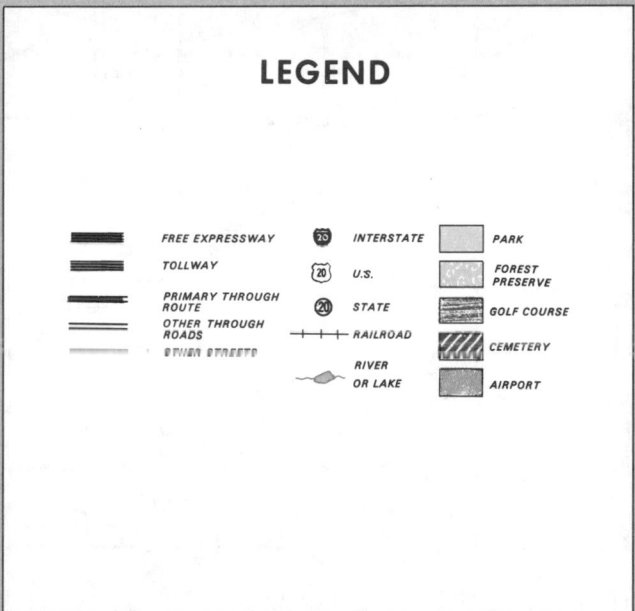

## LEGEND

| | | | |
|---|---|---|---|
| FREE EXPRESSWAY | INTERSTATE | PARK | |
| TOLLWAY | U.S. | FOREST PRESERVE | |
| PRIMARY THROUGH ROUTE | STATE | GOLF COURSE | |
| OTHER THROUGH ROADS | RAILROAD | CEMETERY | |
| OTHER STREETS | RIVER OR LAKE | AIRPORT | |

**TURN PAGE FOR ORIENTATION MAP**

# SECTION 3
## ORIENTATION MAP

Information on this page is to be used for general reference only.
For definitive listings of all information, see index at end of this section.

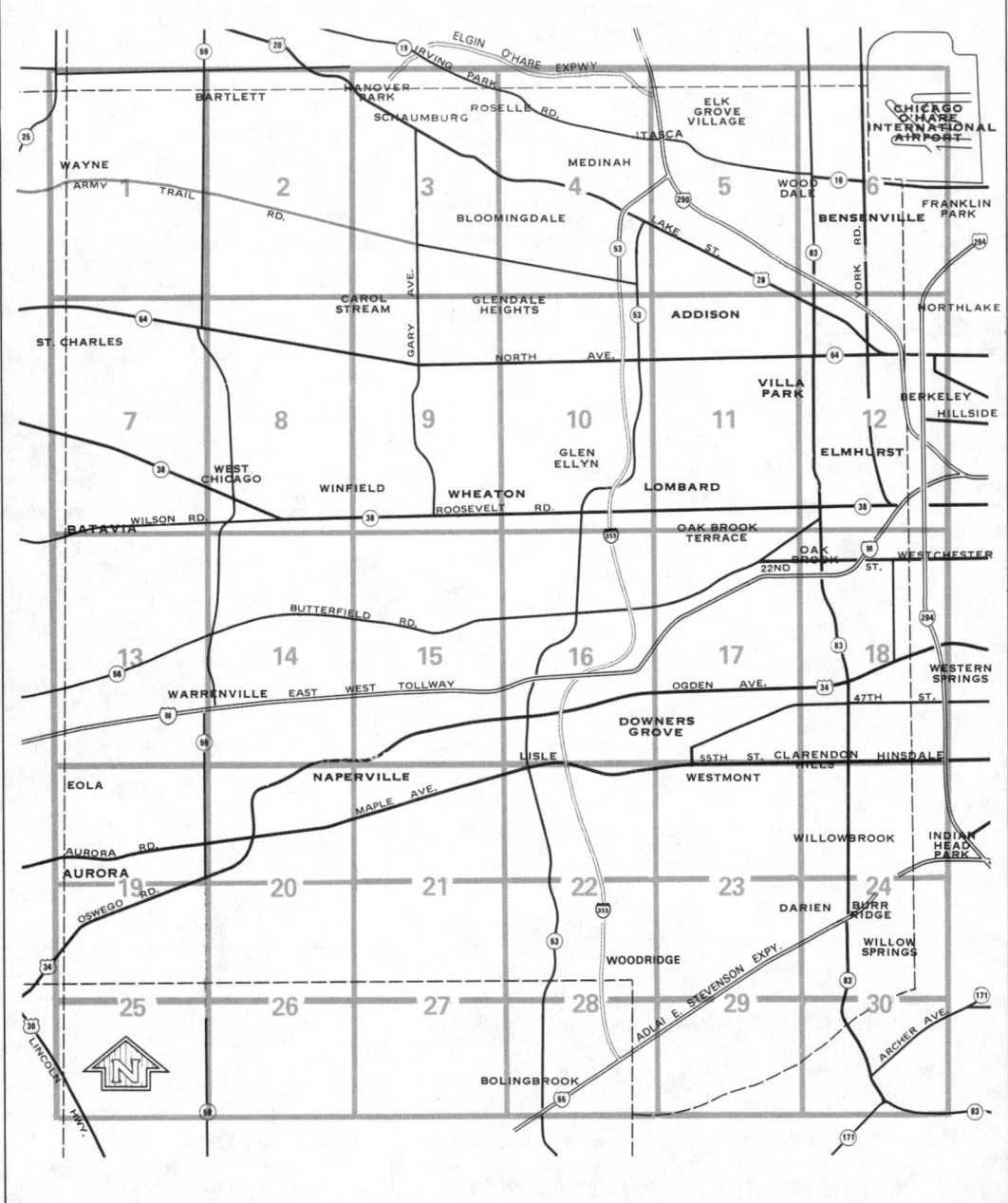

© BY CSC

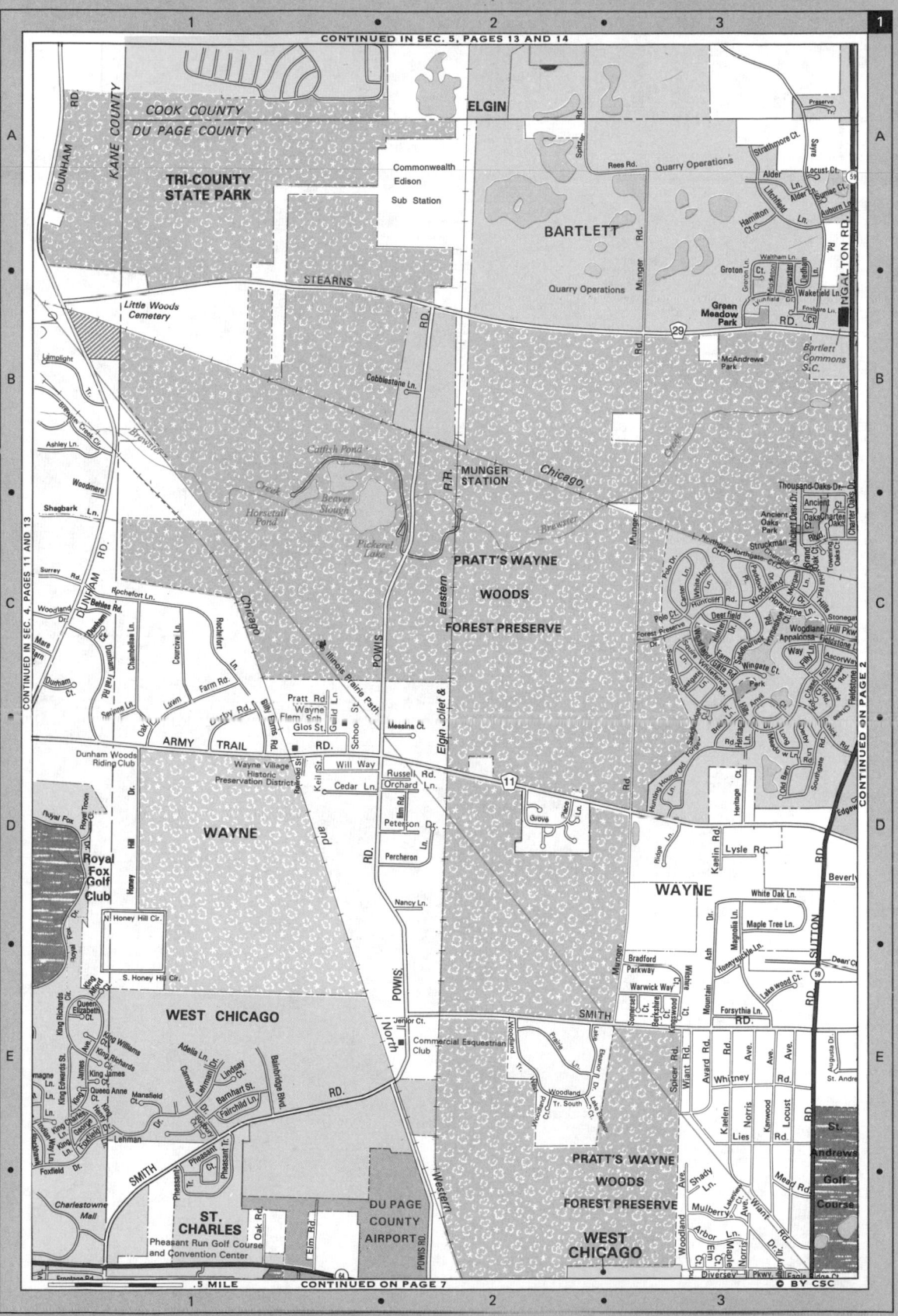

ELGIN

COOK COUNTY
DU PAGE COUNTY

TRI-COUNTY
STATE PARK

Commonwealth
Edison
Sub Station

BARTLETT

Quarry Operations

Quarry Operations

Green
Meadow
Park

McAndrews
Park

Bartlett
Commons
S.C.

STEARNS

Little Woods
Cemetery

Lamplight
Tr.

Ashley Ln.

Woodmere

Shagbark Ln.

Cobblestone Ln.

Catfish Pond

Creek

Beaver
Slough

Horsetail
Pond

Pickerel
Lake

MUNGER
STATION

Chicago,

Thousand Oaks Dr.

Ancient
Oaks
Park

PRATT'S WAYNE

WOODS

FOREST PRESERVE

Woodland

Surrey Rd.

Woodland
Dr.

Mara
Fern

Dunham
Ct.

Rochefort Ln.

Battles Rd.

Chambella Ln.

Courcive Ln.

Farm Rd.

Oak

Lawn

Pratt Rd.
Wayne
Elem Sch
Glos St.

Schoo

Messina Ct.

Polo

Forest Preserve

Deer field

Woodland
Appaloosa
Way

Hill Pkwy

Park

Wingate Ct.

ARMY        TRAIL

RD.

Dunham Woods
Riding Club

Wayne Village
Historic
Preservation District

Will Way

Cedar Ln.

Russell  Rd.

Orchard Ln.

Elm Rd.

Grove

Heritage

WAYNE

Peterson
Dr.

Percheron
Ln.

Ridge

Kaelin Rd.

Lysle Rd.

WAYNE

Beverly

Royal Fox

Royal Troon

Royal Fox
Golf
Club

Hill

Honey

N. Honey Hill Cir.

S. Honey Hill Cir.

Nancy Ln.

White Oak Ln.

Maple Tree Ln.

Magnolia Ct.

Ash

Bradford
Parkway

Warwick Way

Honeysuckle Ln.

Mountain

Lakewood Ct.

Dean Ct.

WEST CHICAGO

Adelia Ln.

Lindsay
Dr.

Mansfield
Dr.

Barnhart St.

Fairchild Ln.

Junior Ct.

Commercial Esquestrian
Club

SMITH

Forsythia Ln.

RD.

Charmagne
Ln.

King
Edwards
Ct.

James
Ave.

King Richards
Ct.

King Williams
Ave.

Camden

King James
Ct.

Queen Anne
Ct.

George

Rotting

Woodland
Tr. South

Spicer Rd.

Wiant Rd.

Whitney

Avard Rd.

Ave.

Ave.

Ave.

Augusta Dr.

St. Andre

King Richards
Ct.

Queen
Elizabeth
Ct.

King Charles
Ct.

Lehman

Foxfield
Dr.

SMITH

Pheasant
Tr.

Pheasant Ct.

Charlestowne
Mall

ST.
CHARLES

Pheasant Run Golf Course
and Convention Center

DU PAGE
COUNTY
AIRPORT

Oak Rd.

Elm Rd.

POWIS RD.

Western

Kaelen

Norris

Kenwood

Locust

Lies

Rd.

PRATT'S WAYNE

WOODS

FOREST PRESERVE

WEST
CHICAGO

Shady
Ln.

Mulberry

Arbor

Woodland

Mead Rd.

Norris

Diversey

Pkwy.

Eagle Ridge Ln.

St.
Andrews
Golf
Course

© BY CSC

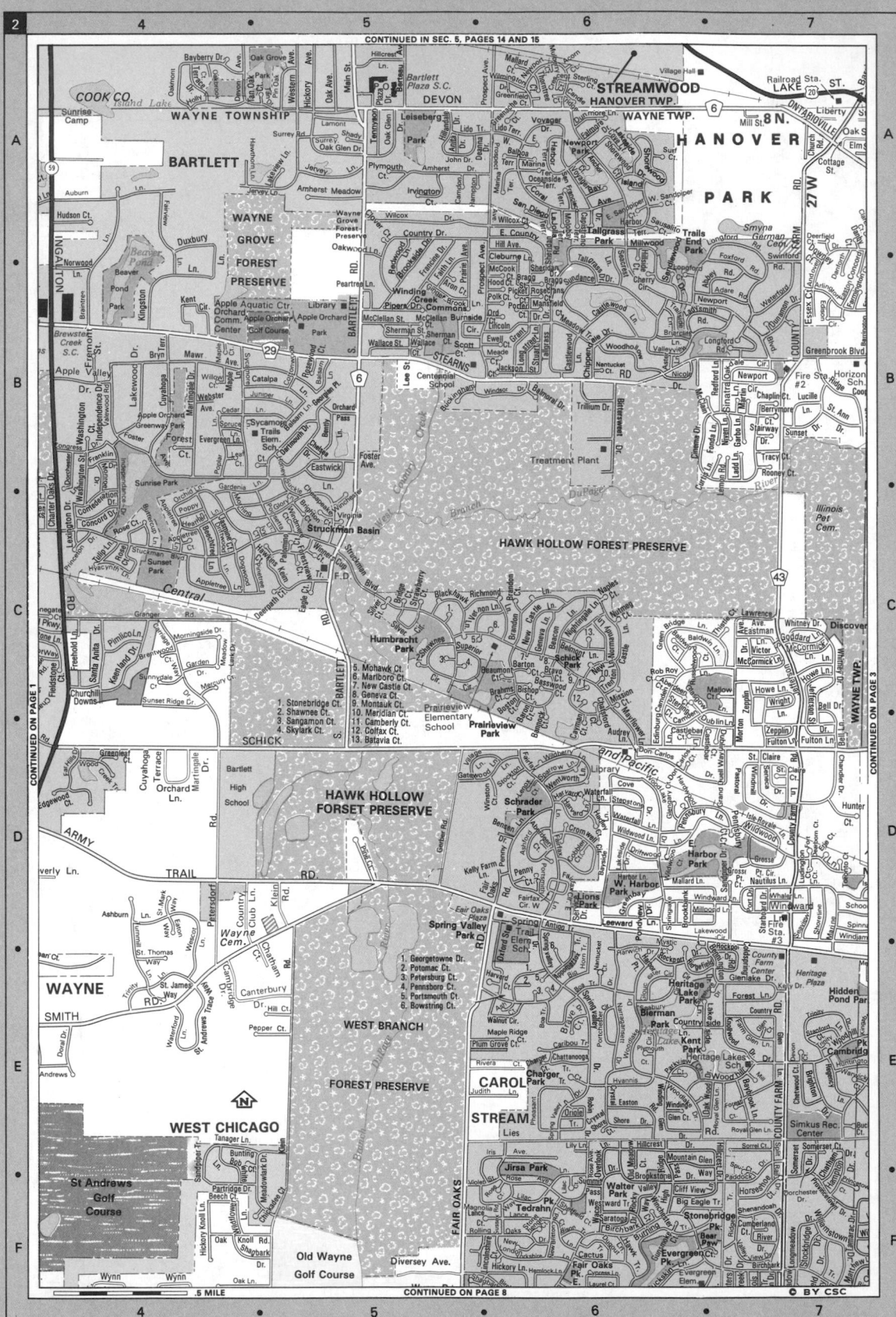

CONTINUED IN SEC. 5, PAGES 14 AND 15

CONTINUED ON PAGE 1

CONTINUED ON PAGE 3

CONTINUED ON PAGE 8

© BY CSC

.5 MILE

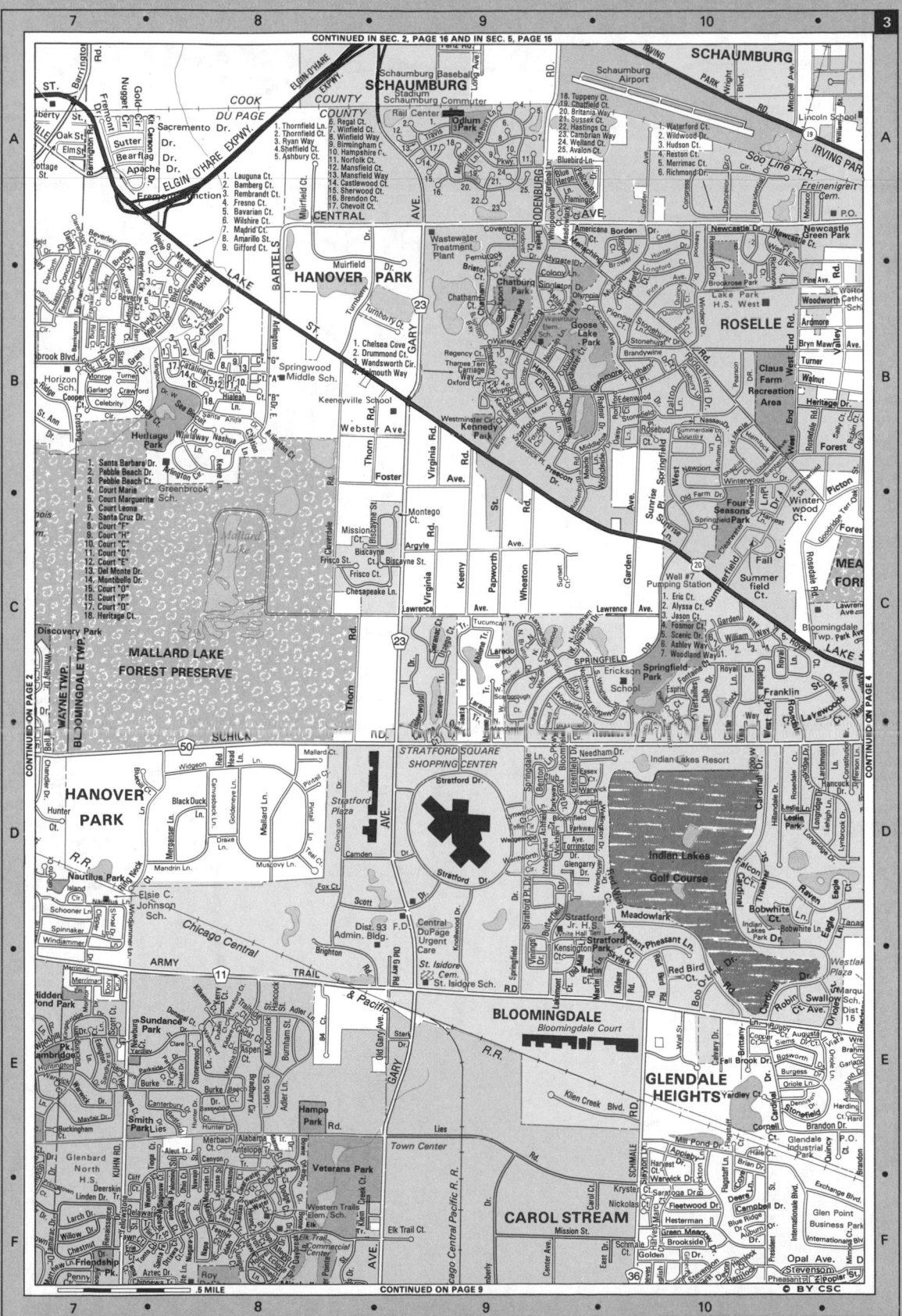

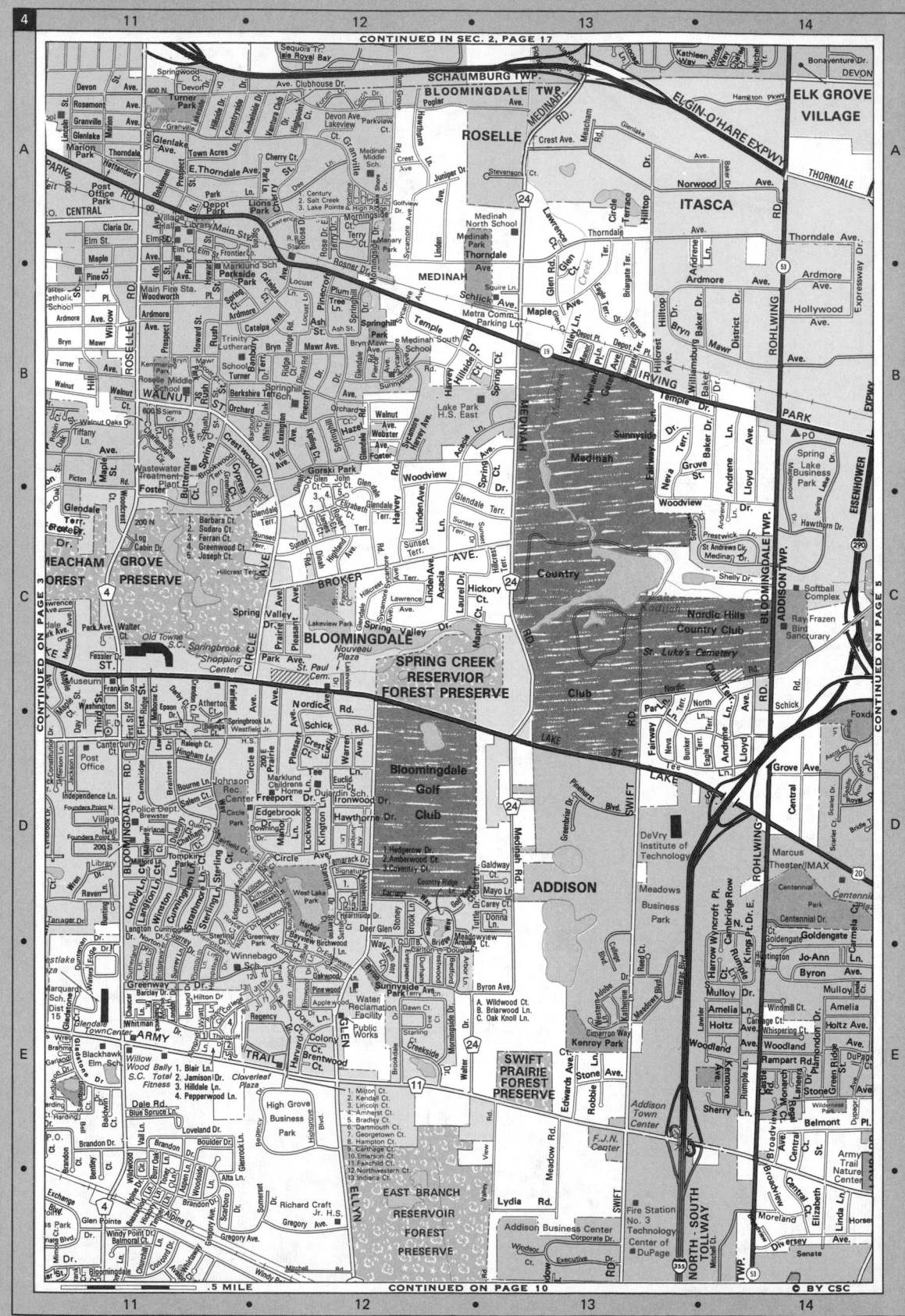

.5 MILE

© BY CSC

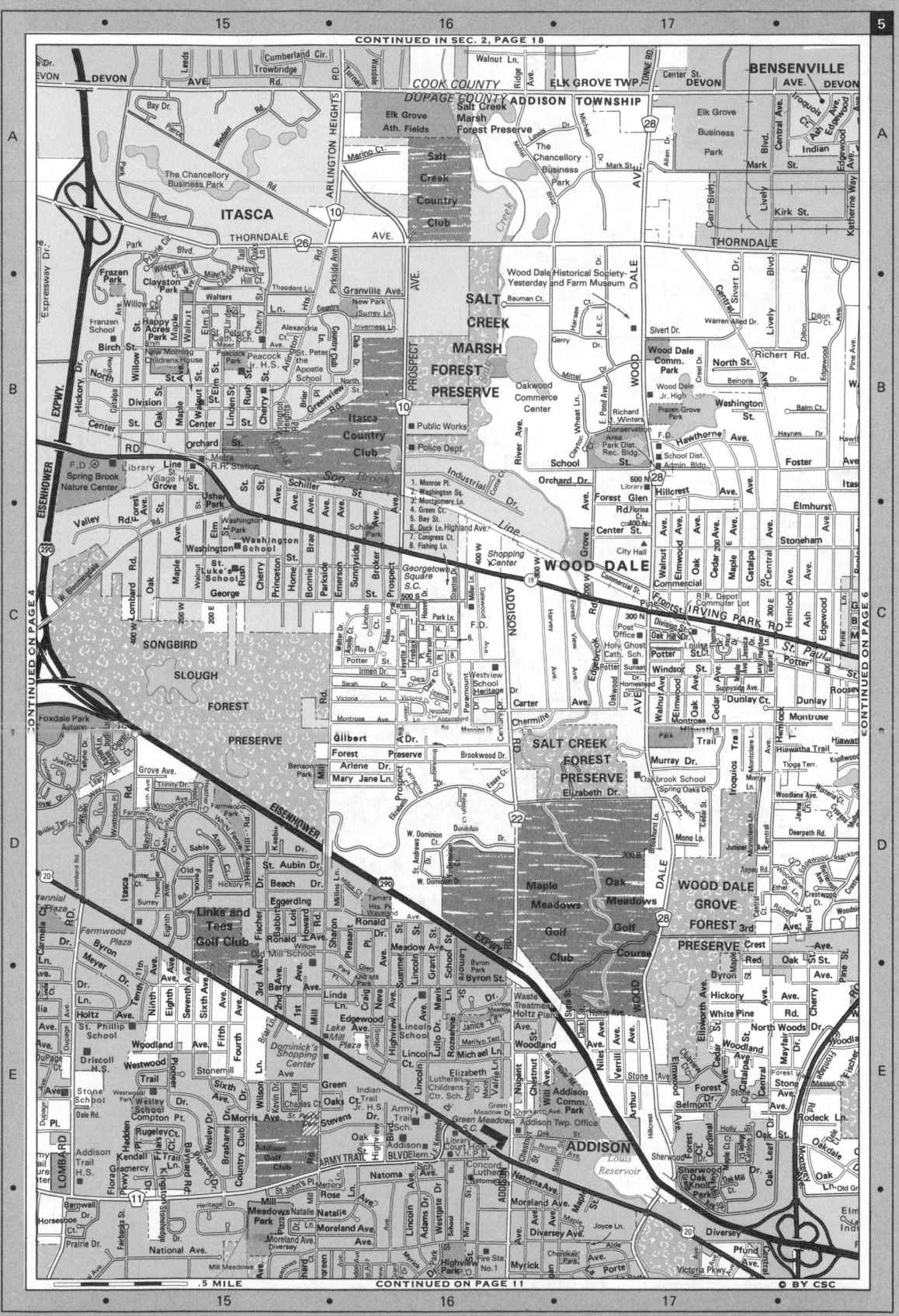

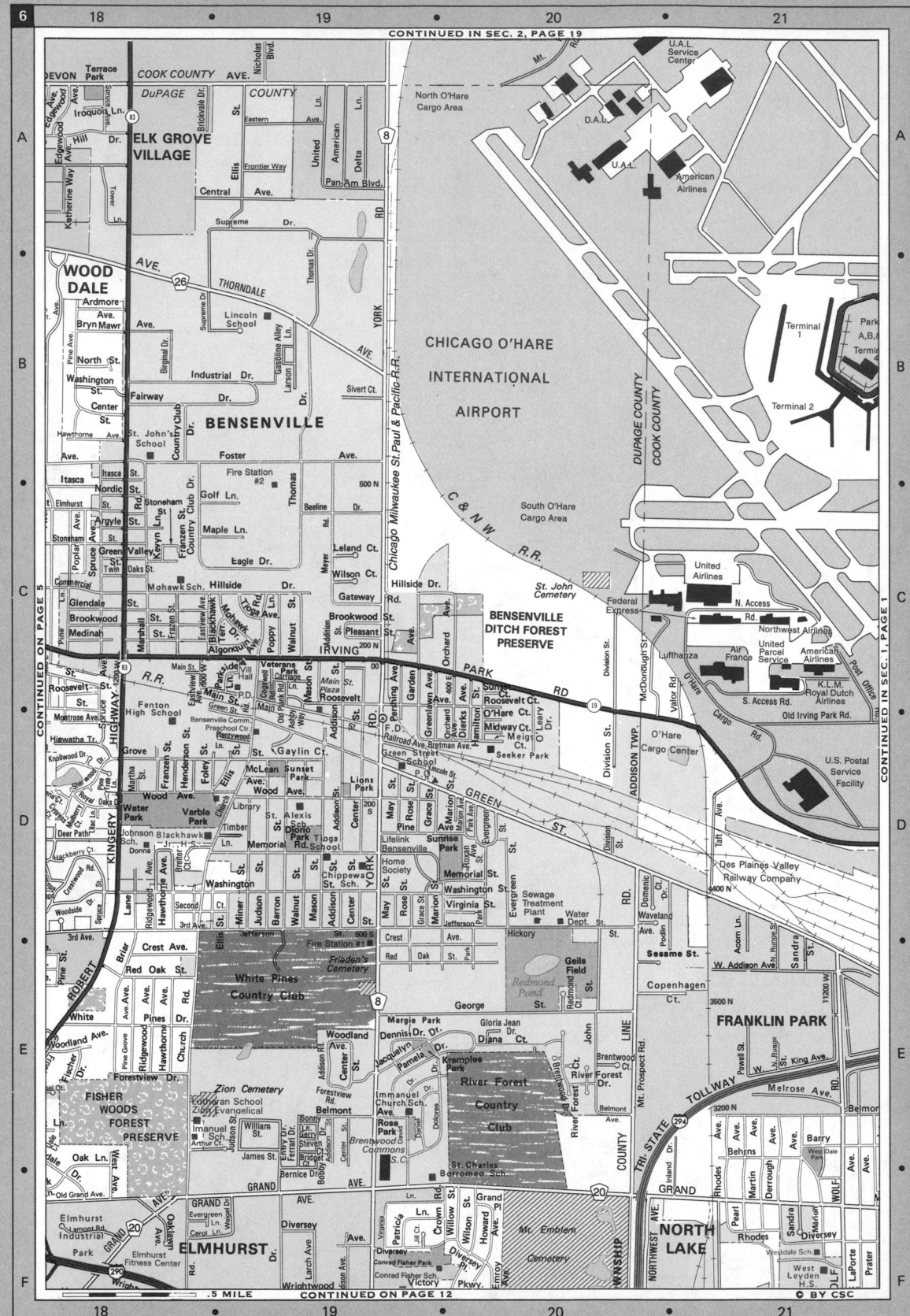

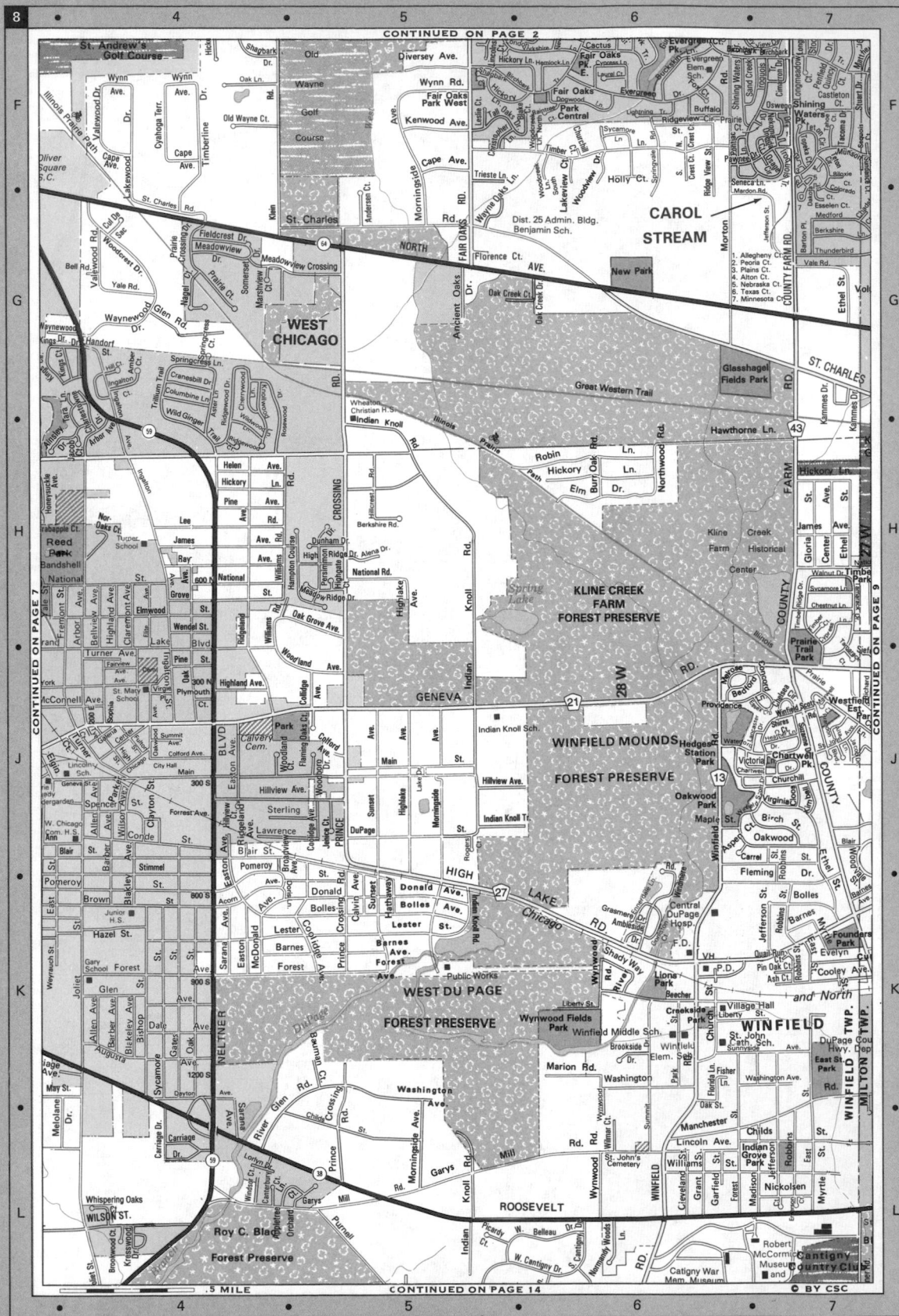

CONTINUED ON PAGE 7
CONTINUED ON PAGE 9

CAROL STREAM

1. Allegheny Ct.
2. Peoria Ct.
3. Plains Ct.
4. Alton Ct.
5. Nebraska Ct.
6. Texas Ct.
7. Minnesota Ct.

WEST CHICAGO

St. Andrew's Golf Course

KLINE CREEK FARM FOREST PRESERVE

WINFIELD MOUNDS FOREST PRESERVE

WEST DU PAGE FOREST PRESERVE

WINFIELD

Roy C. Black Forest Preserve

Cantigny Country Club

Robert McCormick Museum

ROOSEVELT

.5 MILE

© BY CSC

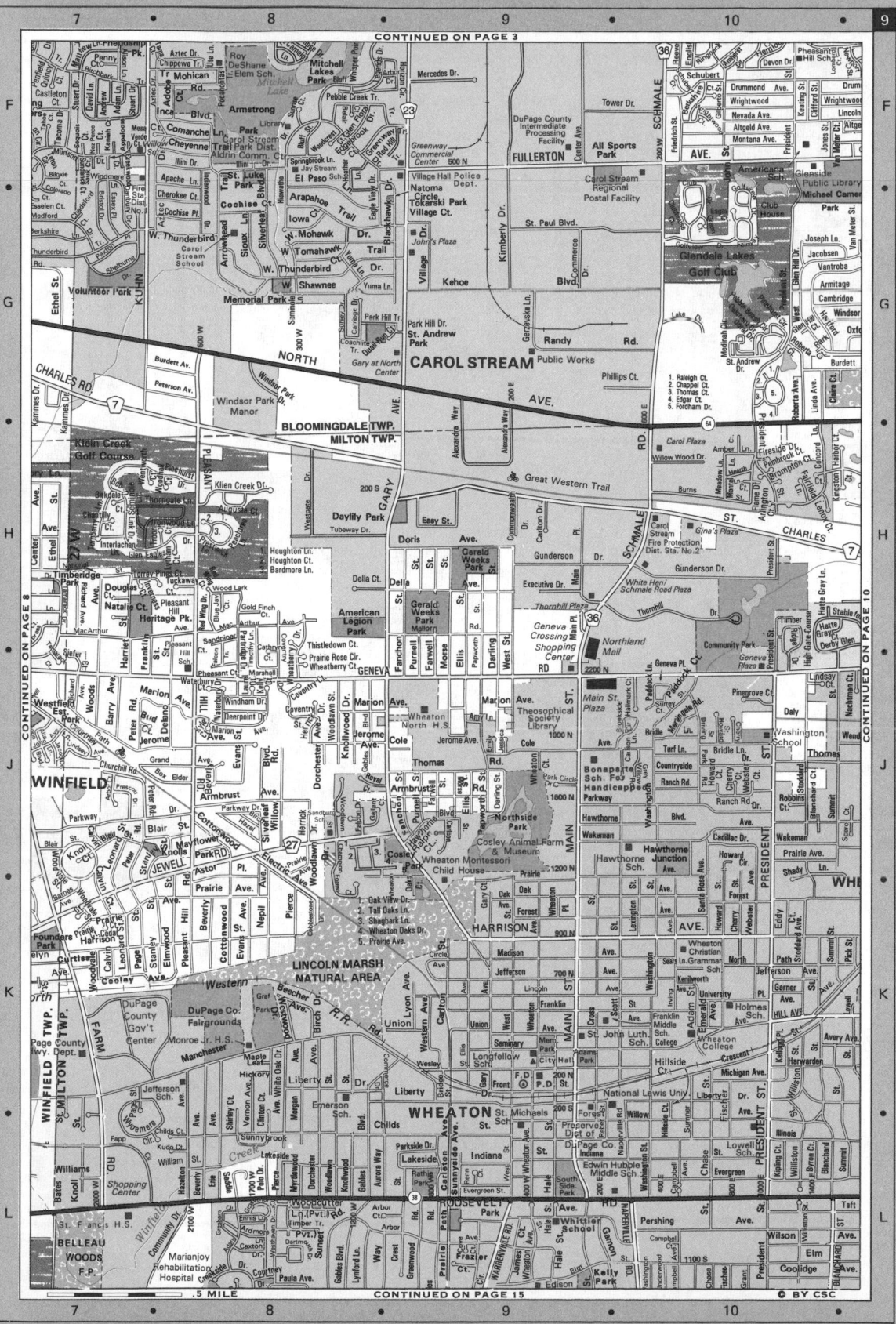

CONTINUED ON PAGE 8

CONTINUED ON PAGE 10

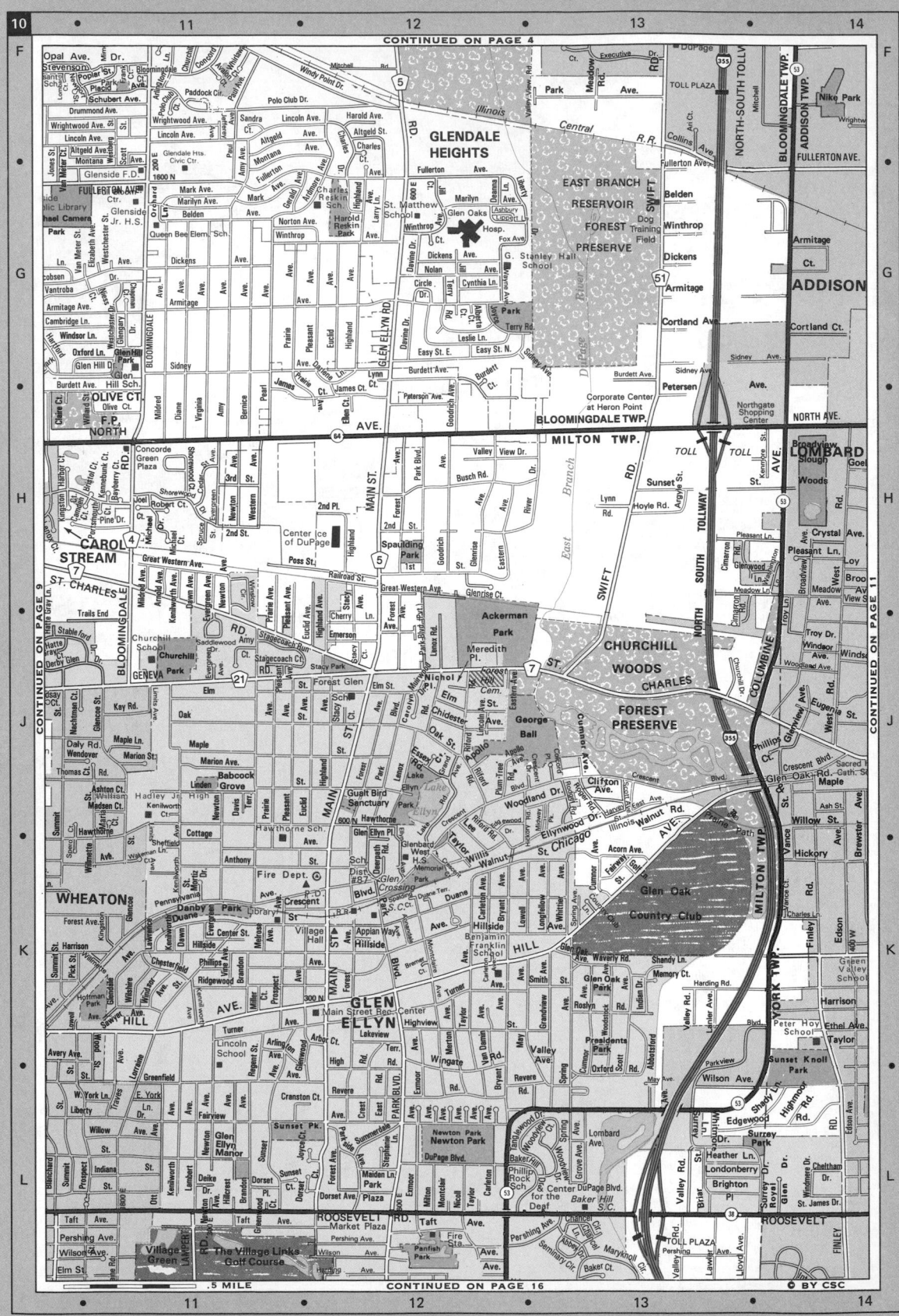

CONTINUED ON PAGE 4
CONTINUED ON PAGE 9
CONTINUED ON PAGE 11
CONTINUED ON PAGE 16

GLENDALE
HEIGHTS

EAST BRANCH
RESERVOIR
FOREST
PRESERVE

Dog
Training
Field

ADDISON

Northgate
Shopping
Center

BLOOMINGDALE TWP.
MILTON TWP.

Corporate Center
at Heron Point

LOMBARD

Broadview
Slough
Woods

CAROL
STREAM

Center Ice
of DuPage

Spaulding
Park

Ackerman
Park

CHURCHILL
WOODS

FOREST
PRESERVE

CHARLES

Churchill
Park

GENEVA

Gault Bird
Sanctuary

George
Ball

Glen Oak
Country Club

WHEATON

GLEN
ELLYN

HILL

Green
Valley
School

Newton Park
Newton Park
DuPage Blvd.

Phillip
Rock Park
for the
Deaf

Center of DuPage Blvd.

Peter Hoy
School

Sunset Knoll
Park

ROOSEVELT RD.
ROOSEVELT

Village
Green

The Village Links
Golf Course

Panfish
Park

TOLL PLAZA

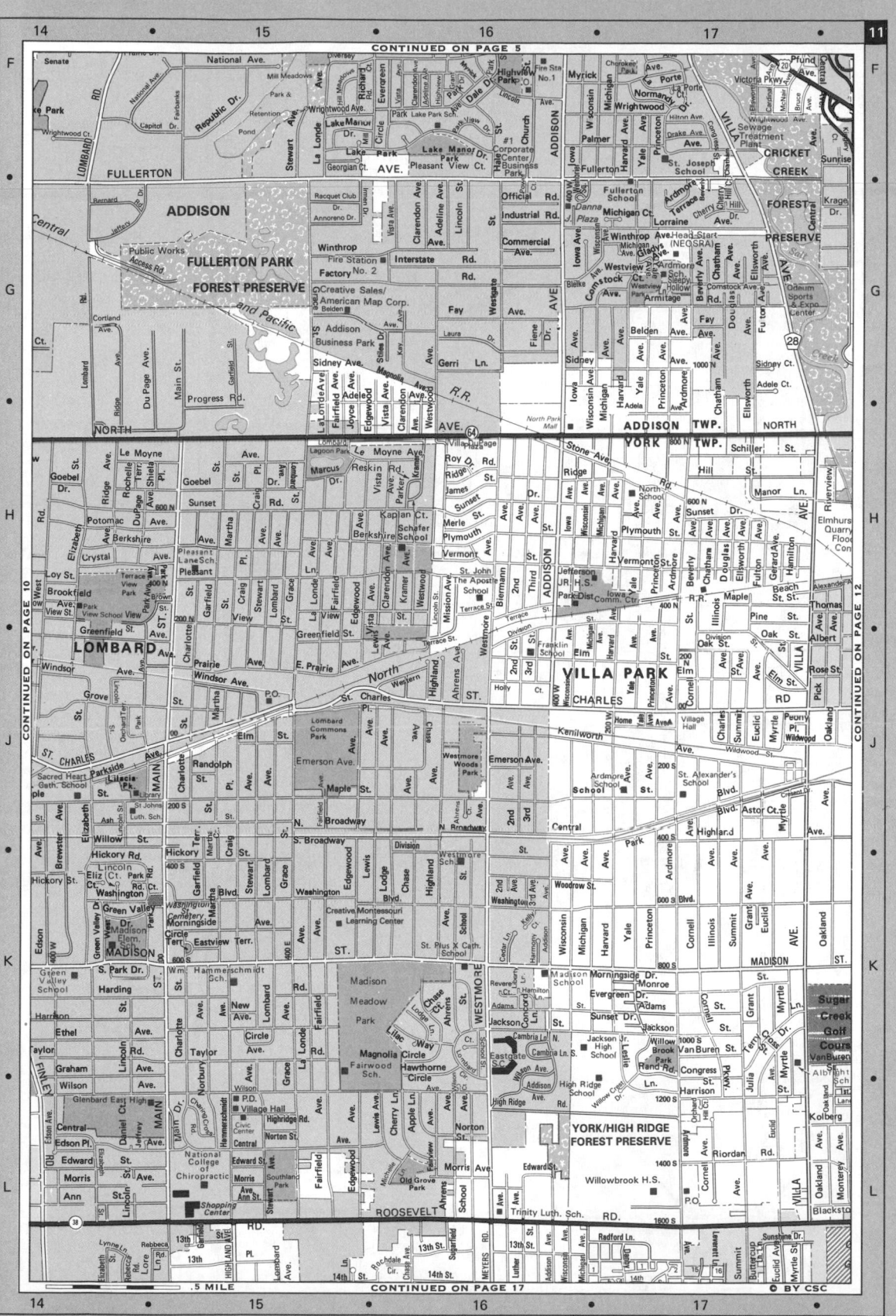

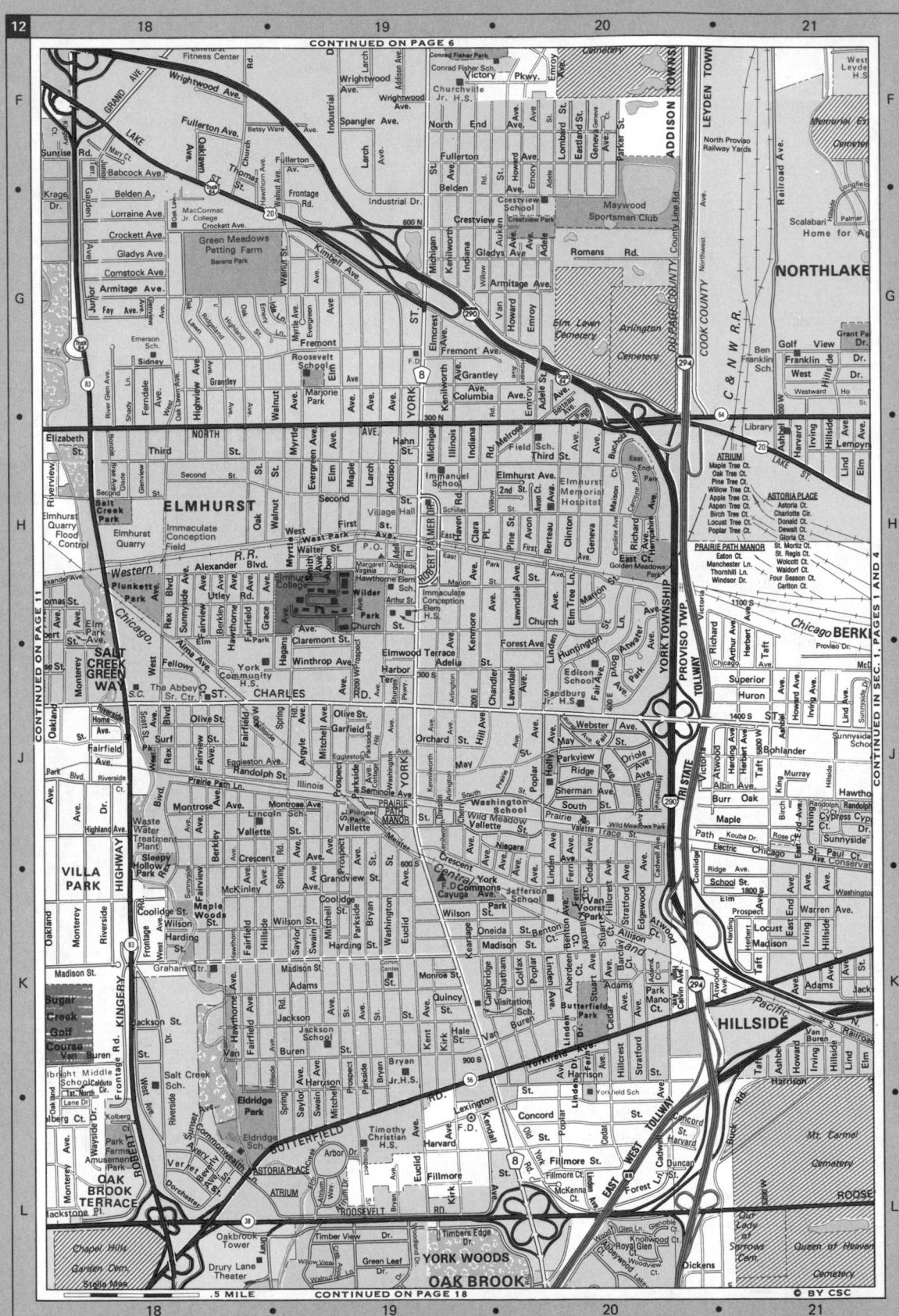

CONTINUED ON PAGE 6
CONTINUED ON PAGE 18
CONTINUED ON PAGE 11
CONTINUED IN SEC. 1, PAGES 1 AND 4

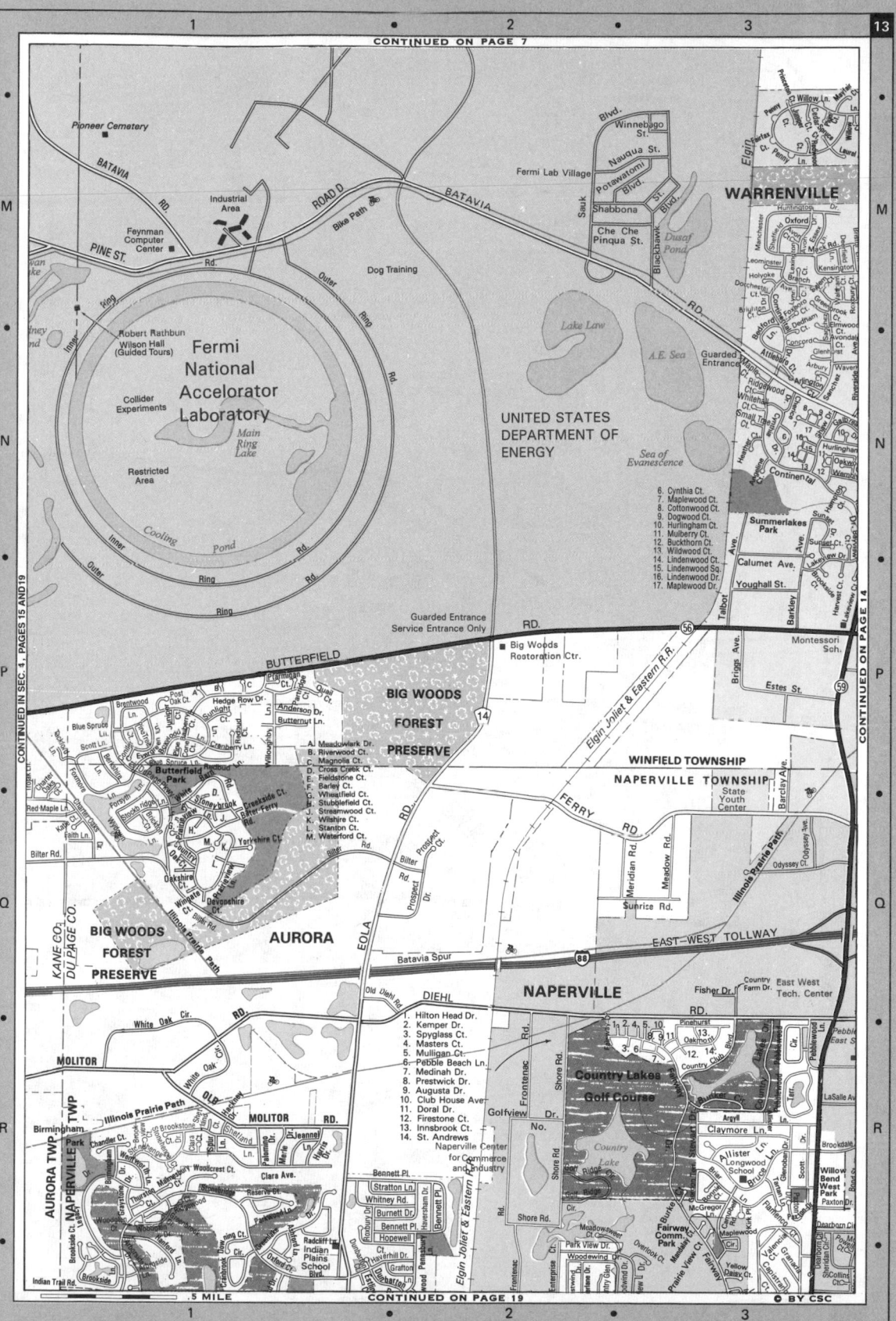

CONTINUED ON PAGE 7

BATAVIA RD.

Pioneer Cemetery

PINE ST.

Industrial Area

Feynman Computer Center

ROAD D

BATAVIA

Bike Path

RD.

Fermi Lab Village

Blvd.

Winnebago St.

Nauqua St.

Potawatomi Blvd.

Shabbona

Che Che Pinqua St.

Dusaf Pond

Blackhawk

Sauk

Blvd.

Elgin

Fairfax

Ct.

Peony

Willow Ln.

WARRENVILLE

Robert Rathbun Wilson Hall (Guided Tours)

Fermi National Accelerator Laboratory

Collider Experiments

Main Ring Lake

Lake Law

A.E. Sea

Guarded Entrance

UNITED STATES DEPARTMENT OF ENERGY

Sea of Evanescence

Restricted Area

Cooling Pond

Inner Ring

Outer Ring Rd.

6. Cynthia Ct.
7. Maplewood Ct.
8. Cottonwood Ct.
9. Dogwood Ct.
10. Hurlingham Ct.
11. Mulberry Ct.
12. Buckthorn Ct.
13. Wildwood Ct.
14. Lindenwood Ct.
15. Lindenwood Sq.
16. Lindenwood Dr.
17. Maplewood Dr.

Summerlakes Park

Calumet Ave.

Youghall St.

Continental

Ring Rd.

Guarded Entrance Service Entrance Only

RD.

Big Woods Restoration Ctr.

Talbot

56

BUTTERFIELD

BIG WOODS

FOREST

PRESERVE

Quail

Hedge Row Dr.

Anderson Ct.
Butternut Ln.

14

Briggs Ave.

Estes St.

Montessori Sch.

59

Brentwood Ln.

Blue Spruce Ln.

Scott Ln.

A. Meadowlark Dr.
B. Riverwood Ct.
C. Magnolia Ct.
D. Cross Creek Ct.
E. Fieldstone Ct.
F. Barley Ct.
G. Wheatfield Ct.
H. Stubblefield Ct.
J. Streamwood Ct.
K. Wilshire Ct.
L. Stanton Ct.
M. Waterford Ct.

Butterfield Park

Stoneybrook

Creekside Ct.

Yorkshire Ct.

Illinois Prairie Path

RD.

Ferry

WINFIELD TOWNSHIP

NAPERVILLE TOWNSHIP

State Youth Center

Elgin Joliet & Eastern R.R.

Meridian Rd.

Meadow Rd.

Barclay Ave.

Odyssey Ct.

Red Maple Ln.

Bilter Rd.

Oakshire

Wingate Ct.

Devonshire

Illinois Prairie Path

BIG WOODS

FOREST

PRESERVE

AURORA

EOLA

Bilter Rd.

Prospect Dr.

Sunrise Rd.

EAST-WEST TOLLWAY

88

KANE CO.

DU PAGE CO.

Batavia Spur

Old Diehl Rd.

DIEHL

NAPERVILLE

Fisher Dr.

Country Farm Dr.

East West Tech. Center

White Oak Cir.

MOLITOR

White Oak Cir.

OLD

MOLITOR

RD.

Illinois Prairie Path

Birmingham

1. Hilton Head Dr.
2. Kemper Dr.
3. Spyglass Ct.
4. Masters Ct.
5. Mulligan Ct.
6. Pebble Beach Ln.
7. Medinah Dr.
8. Prestwick Dr.
9. Augusta Dr.
10. Club House Ave.
11. Doral Dr.
12. Firestone Ct.
13. Innsbrook Ct.
14. St. Andrews

Golfview Dr.

Frontenac Rd.

Shore Rd.

RD.

Oakmont

Pinehurst

Country Club Blvd.

Country Lakes Golf Course

13.

Pebble East

AURORA TWP

NAPERVILLE TWP

Chandler Ct.

Clara Ave.

Woodcrest Ct.

Naperville Center for Commerce and Industry

Bennett Pl.

Stratton Ln.
Whitney Rd.
Burnett Dr.
Bennett Dr.
Hopewell
Haverhill Dr.
Grafton

Elgin Joliet & Eastern

Frontenac Rd.

Shore Rd.

Country Lake

Argyll

Allister School

Longwood

Claymore Ln.

Brookdale

Willow Bend West Park

Paxton Ct.

Radcliff Ln.

Indian Plains School Blvd.

Indian Trail Rd.

Brookside

McGregor Ln.

Fairway Comm. Park

Yellow Daisy Ct.

.5 MILE

© BY CSC

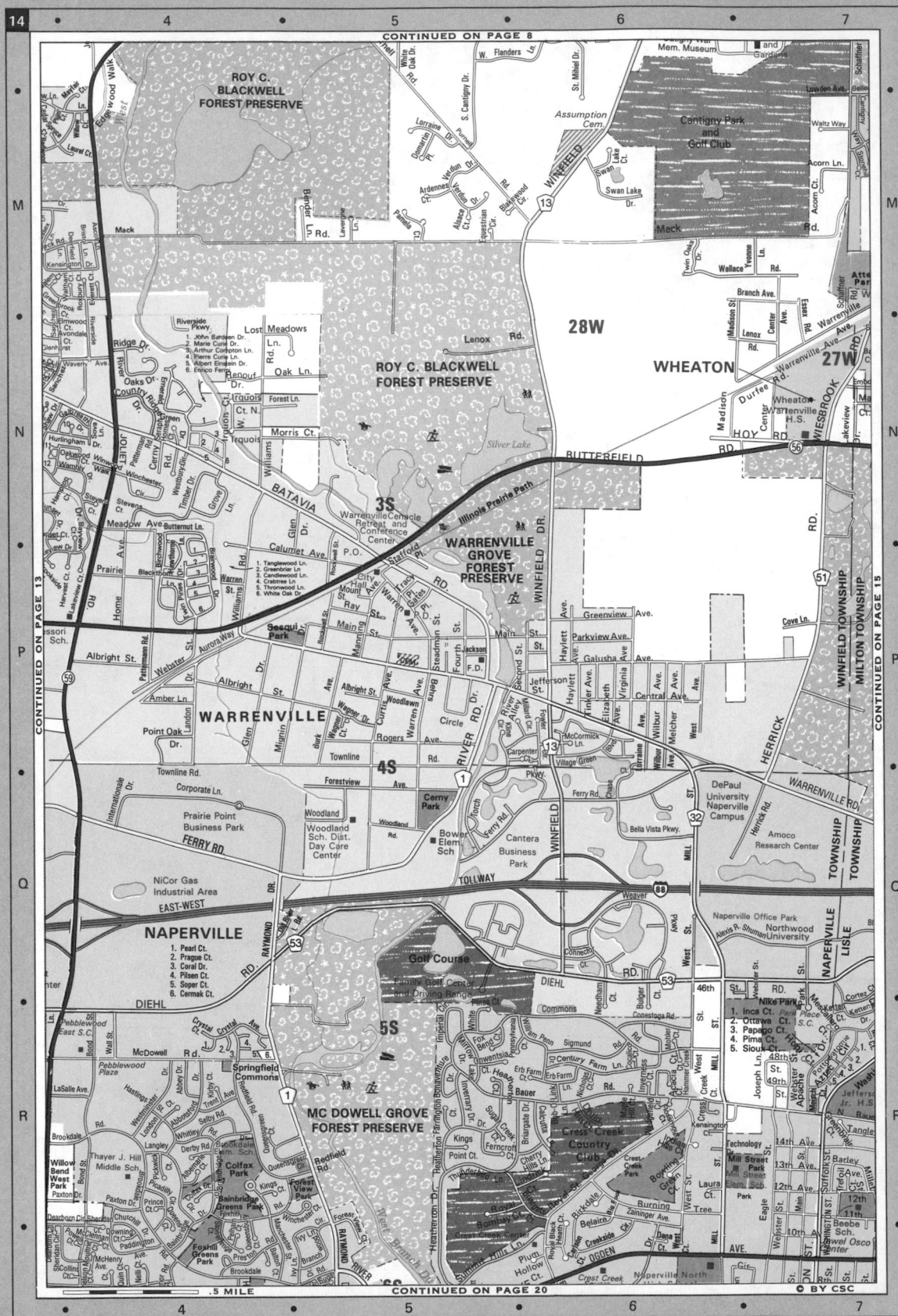

CONTINUED ON PAGE 8

CONTINUED ON PAGE 13

CONTINUED ON PAGE 15

.5 MILE

© BY CSC

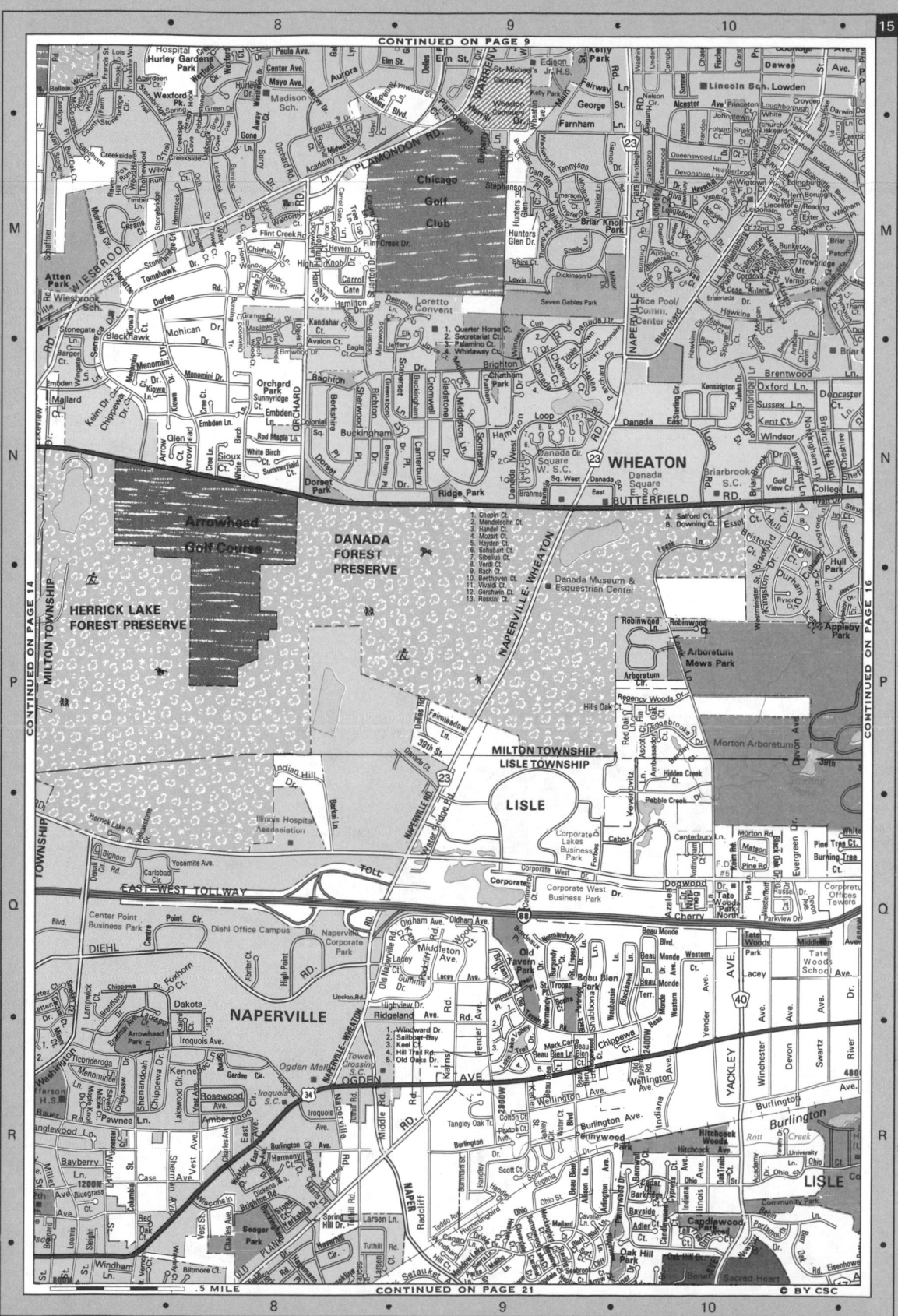
CONTINUED ON PAGE 9
CONTINUED ON PAGE 14
CONTINUED ON PAGE 16
CONTINUED ON PAGE 21

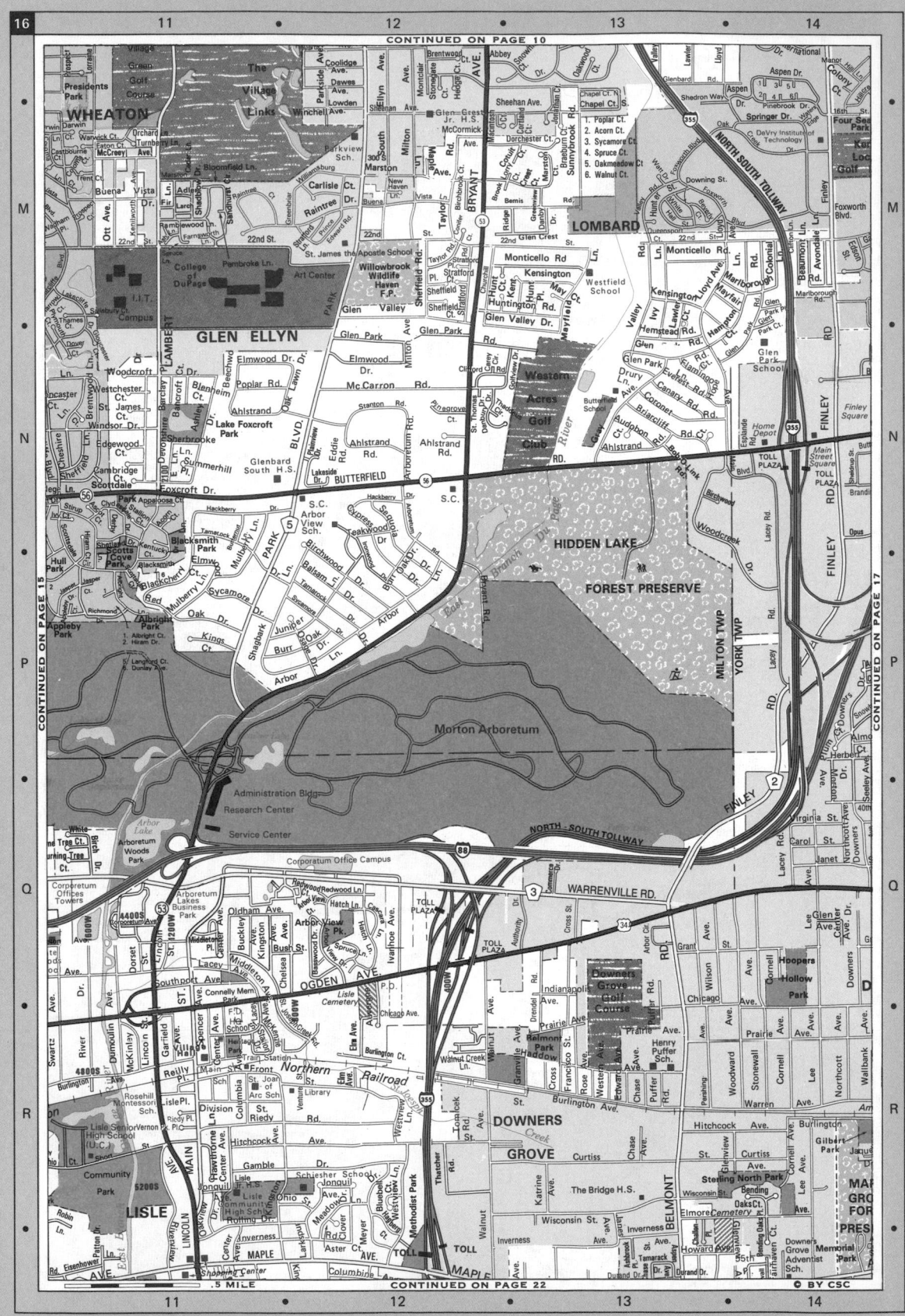

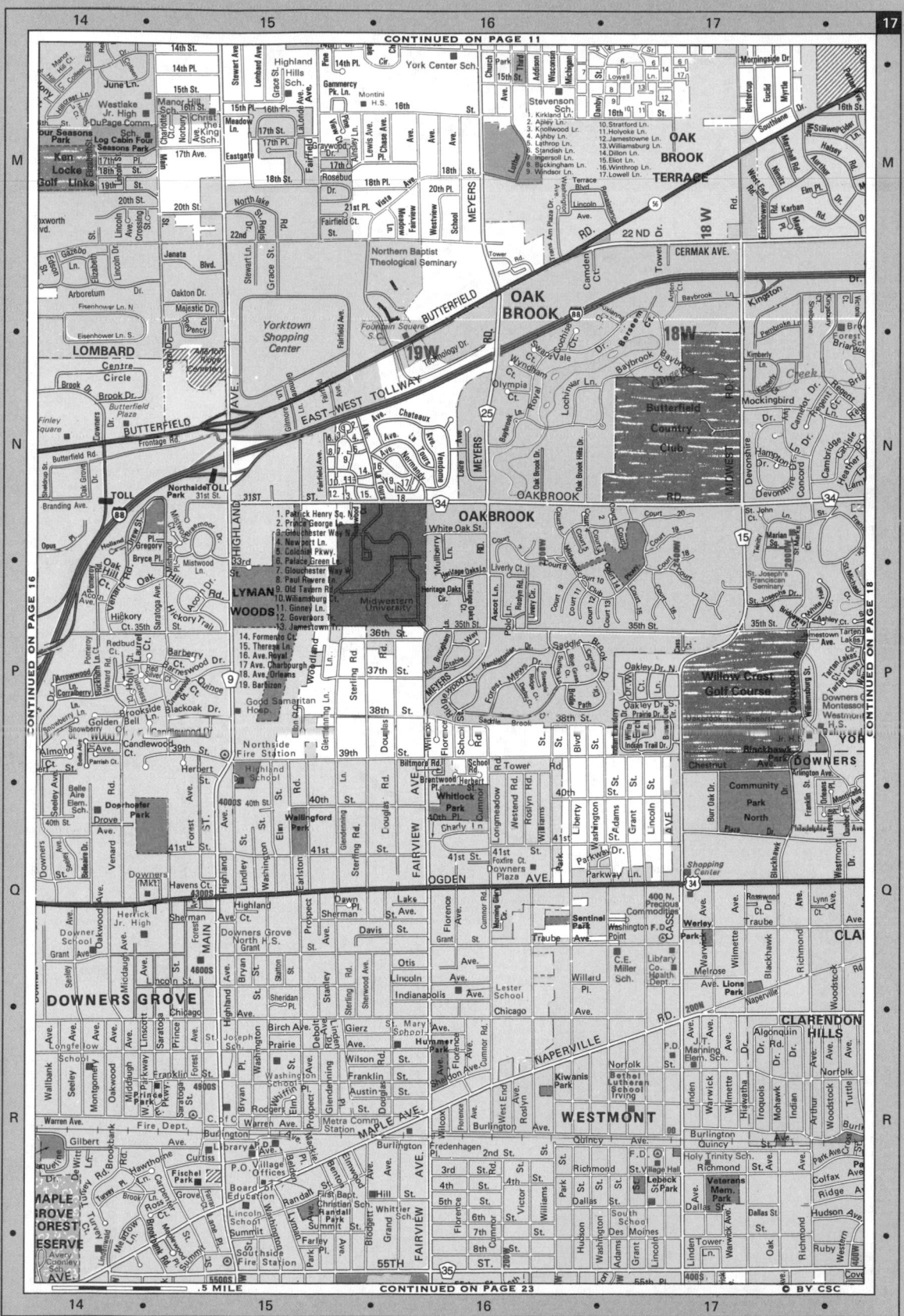

CONTINUED ON PAGE 11

CONTINUED ON PAGE 16

CONTINUED ON PAGE 18

CONTINUED ON PAGE 23

© BY CSC

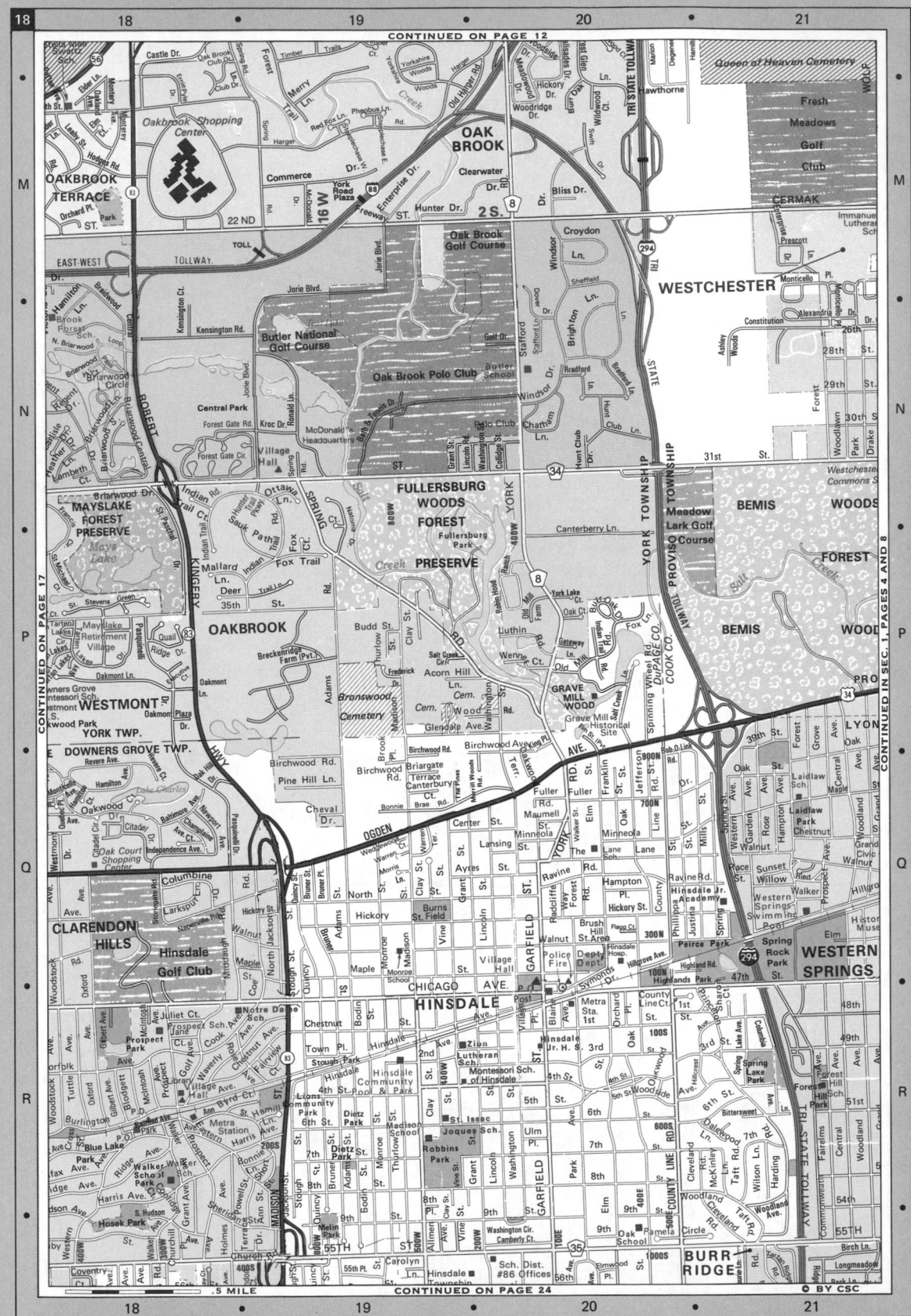

CONTINUED ON PAGE 12

OAKBROOK
TERRACE

Oakbrook Shopping Center

OAK BROOK

Oak Brook Golf Course

WESTCHESTER

Queen of Heaven Cemetery

Fresh Meadows Golf Club

CERMAK

Butler National Golf Course

Oak Brook Polo Club

MAYSLAKE FOREST PRESERVE

FULLERSBURG WOODS FOREST PRESERVE

Fullersburg Park

BEMIS WOODS

BEMIS WOODS

OAKBROOK

Branswood Cemetery

GRAVE MILL WOOD

Grave Mill Salt Creek Historical Site

WESTMONT

YORK TWP.

DOWNERS GROVE TWP.

OGDEN

Lake Charles

CLARENDON HILLS

Hinsdale Golf Club

HINSDALE

CHICAGO AVE.

WESTERN SPRINGS

Spring Rock Park

Village Hall

Police Fire Dept.

Peirce Park

Prospect Park

Lions Community Park

Hinsdale Community Pool & Park

Robbins Park

Hosek Park

BURR RIDGE

CONTINUED ON PAGE 24

CONTINUED ON PAGE 17

CONTINUED IN SEC. 1, PAGES 4 AND 8

.5 MILE

© BY CSC

CONTINUED ON PAGE 13

CONTINUED ON PAGE 25

.5 MILE

© BY CSC

CONTINUED ON PAGE 14

NAPERVILLE

AURORA

CONTINUED ON PAGE 19

CONTINUED ON PAGE 21

Naper Aero
Private Airfield

9S

SPRINGBROOK

PRAIRIE

FOREST

PRESERVE

28W

Springbrook
Golf
Course

DUPAGE COUNTY
WILL COUNTY

10S

87TH

27W

NAPERVILLE TOWNSHIP

WHEATLAND TWP.

LISLE TWP.

.5 MILE

CONTINUED ON PAGE 26

© BY CSC

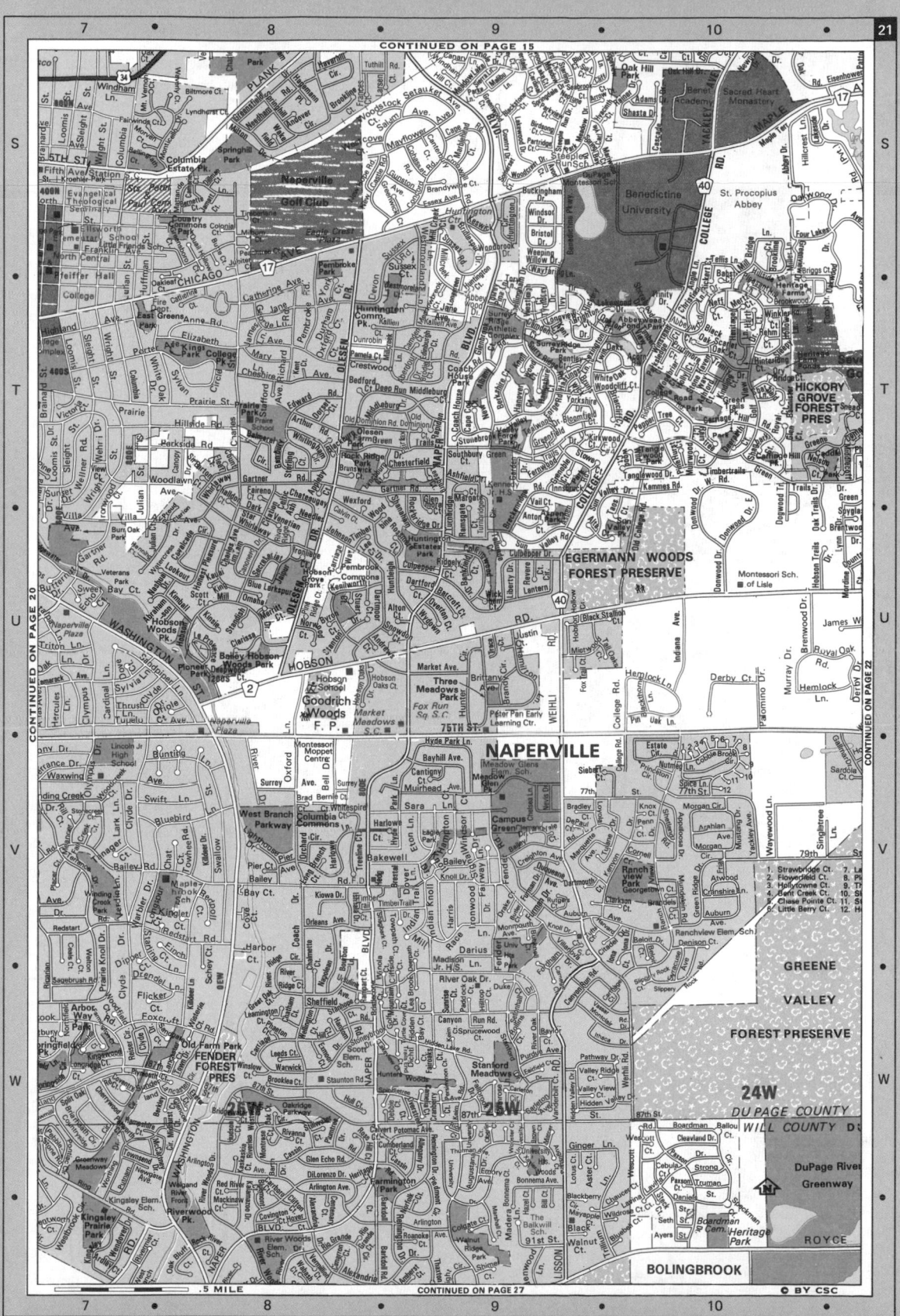

CONTINUED ON PAGE 15

NAPERVILLE

EGERMANN WOODS
FOREST PRESERVE

HICKORY
GROVE
FOREST
PRES

GREENE

VALLEY

FOREST PRESERVE

24W

DU PAGE COUNTY
WILL COUNTY

DuPage River
Greenway

BOLINGBROOK

CONTINUED ON PAGE 20

CONTINUED ON PAGE 22

CONTINUED ON PAGE 27

.5 MILE

© BY CSC

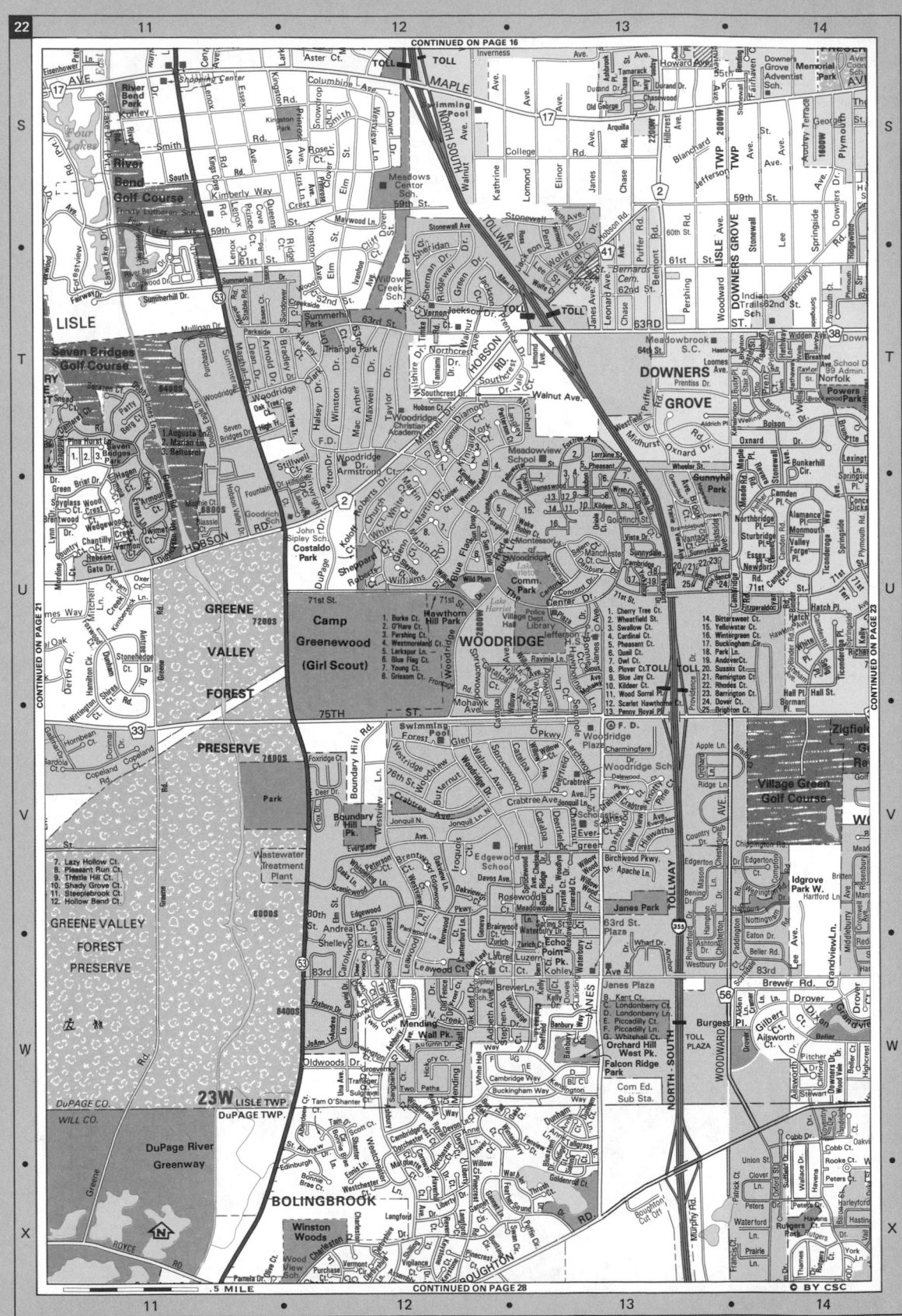

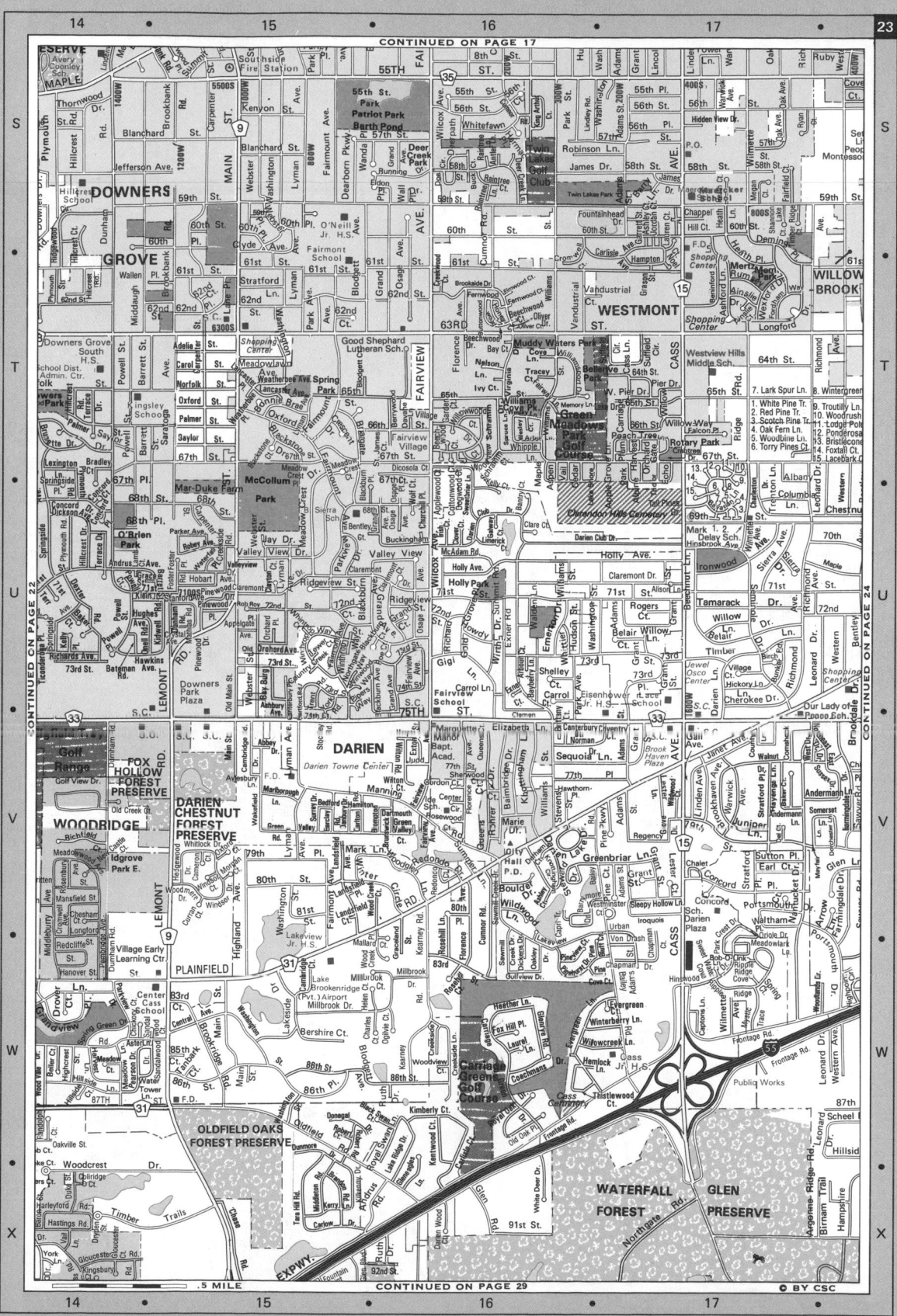

CONTINUED ON PAGE 17

CONTINUED ON PAGE 29

CONTINUED ON PAGE 22

CONTINUED ON PAGE 24

.5 MILE

© BY CSC

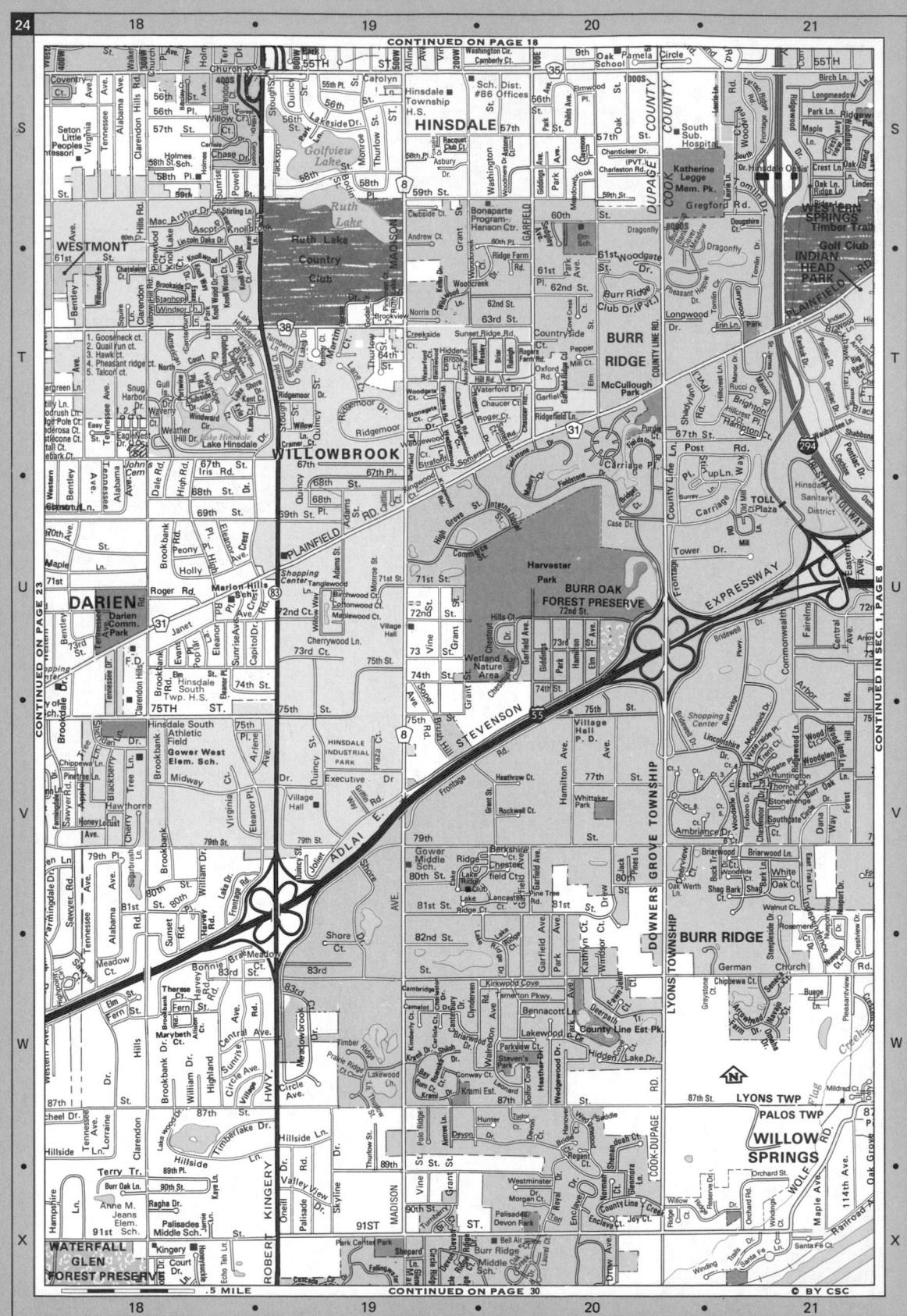

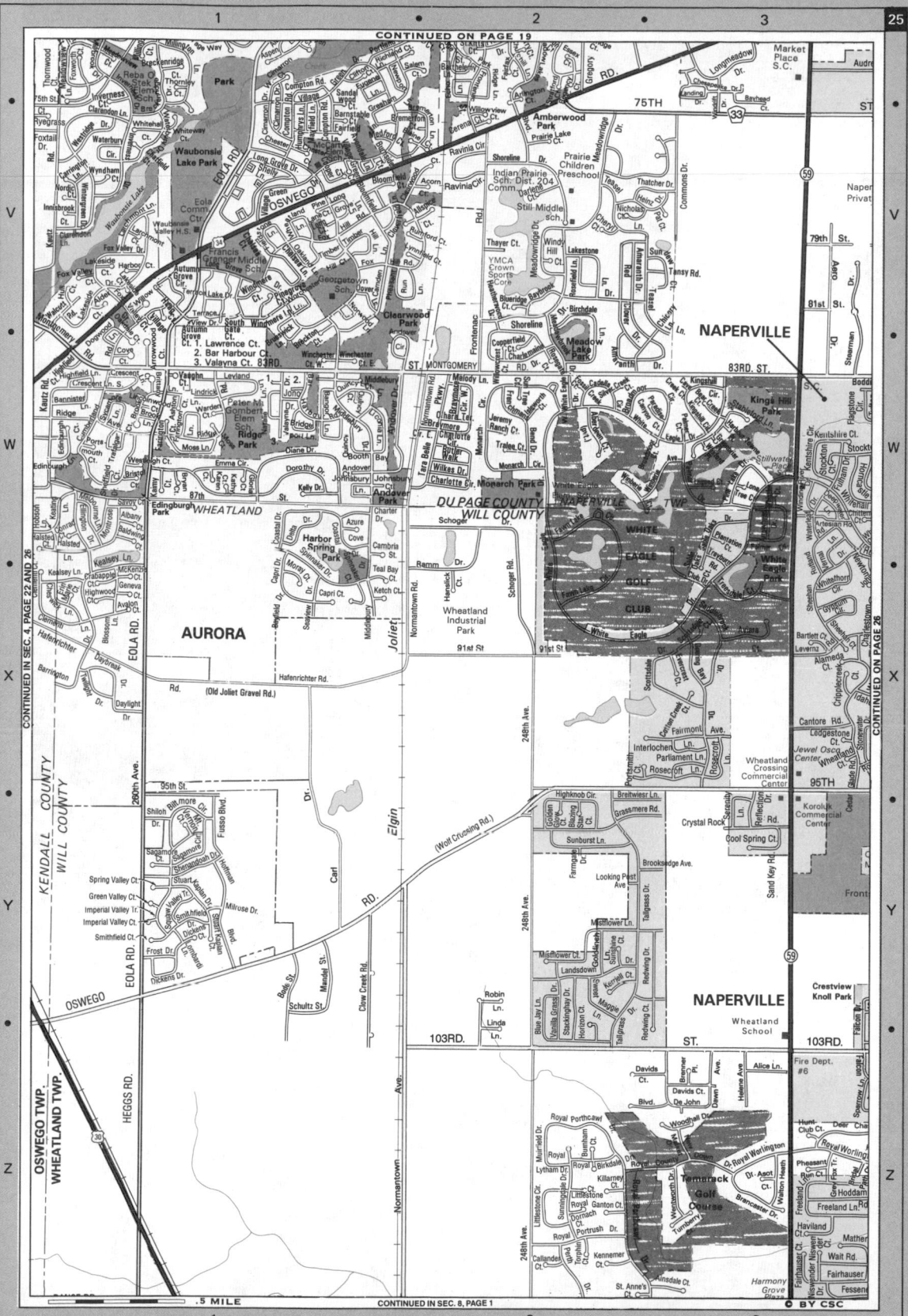

CONTINUED ON PAGE 19

CONTINUED IN SEC. 4, PAGE 22 AND 26

CONTINUED ON PAGE 26

CONTINUED IN SEC. 8, PAGE 1

© BY CSC

.5 MILE

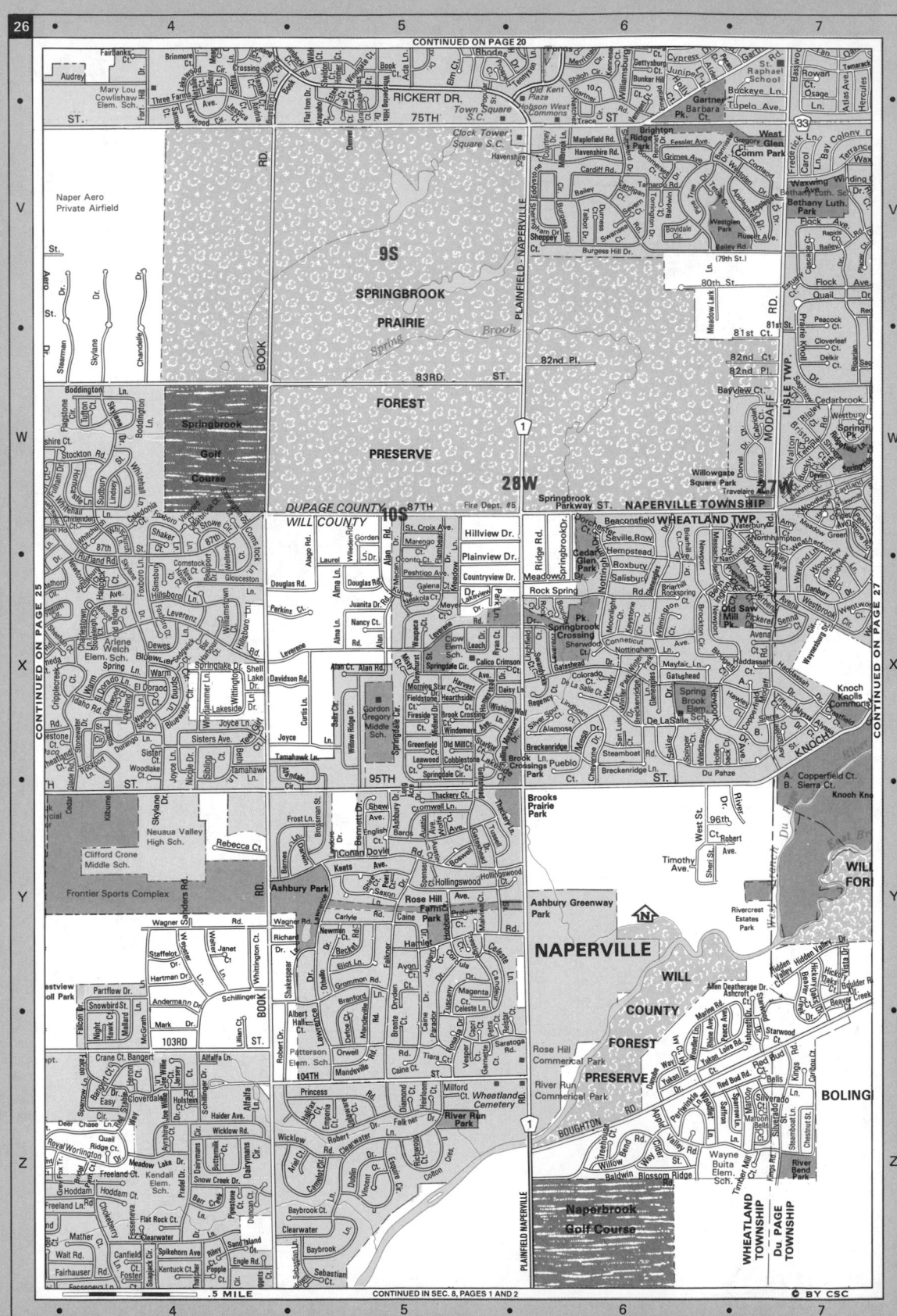

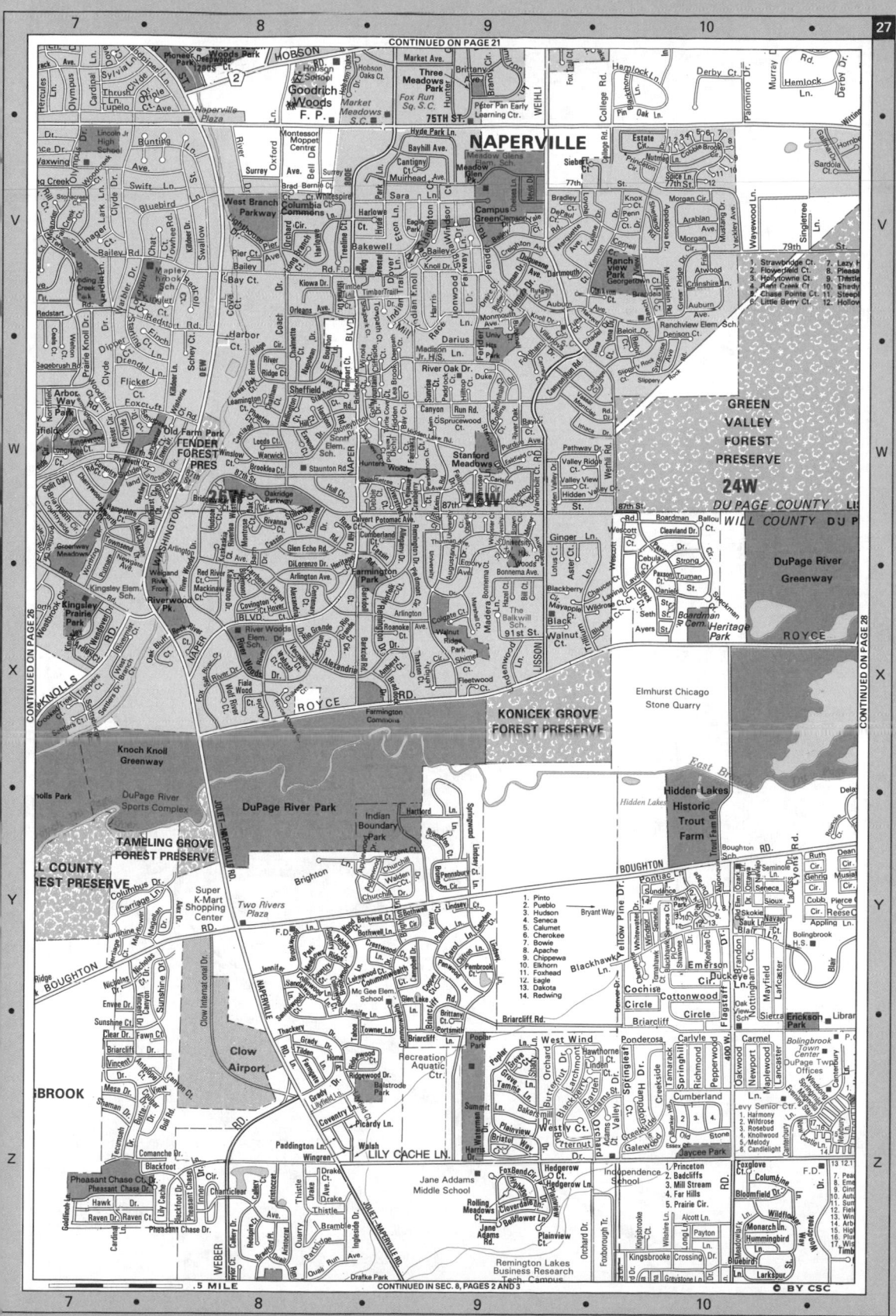

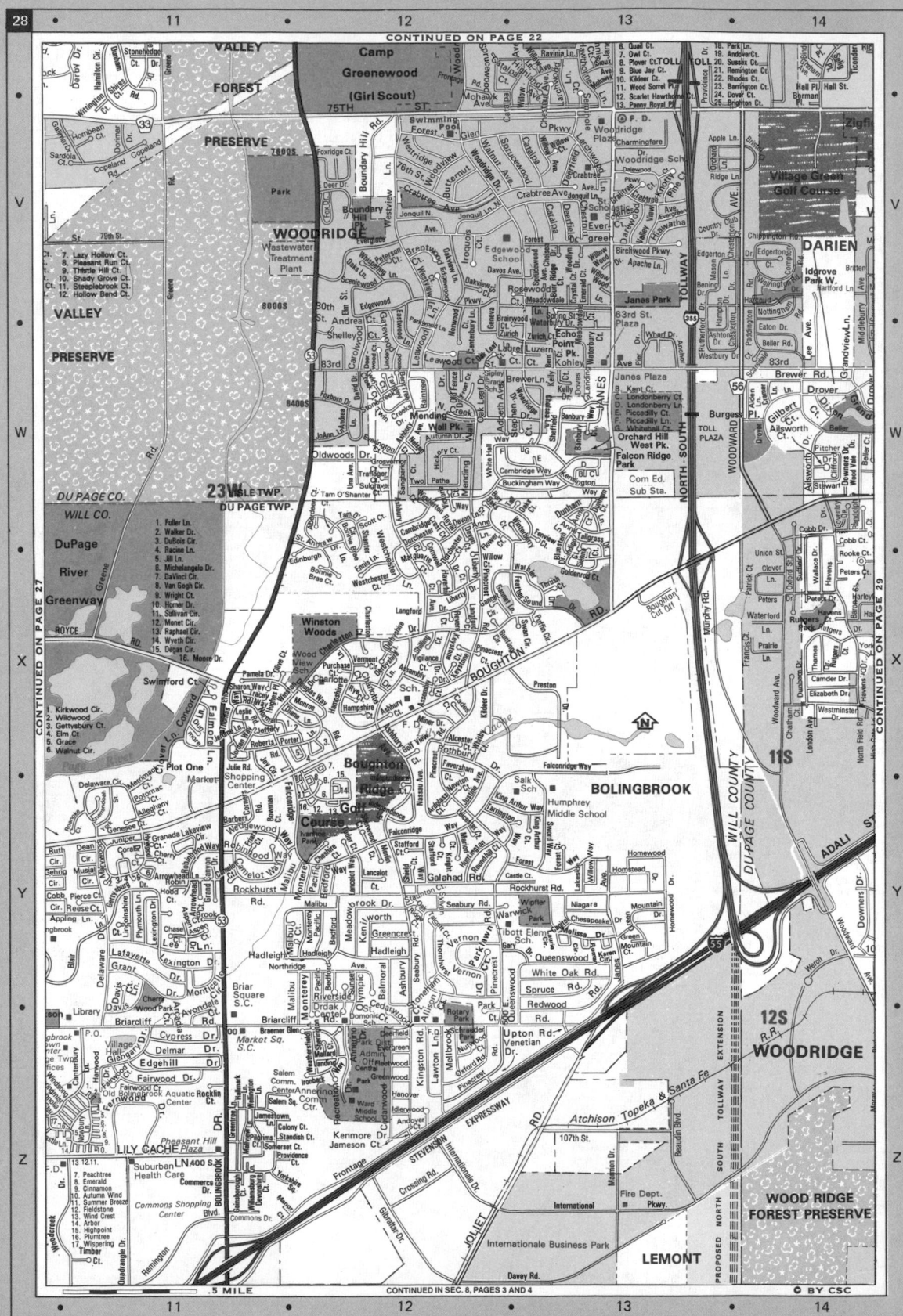

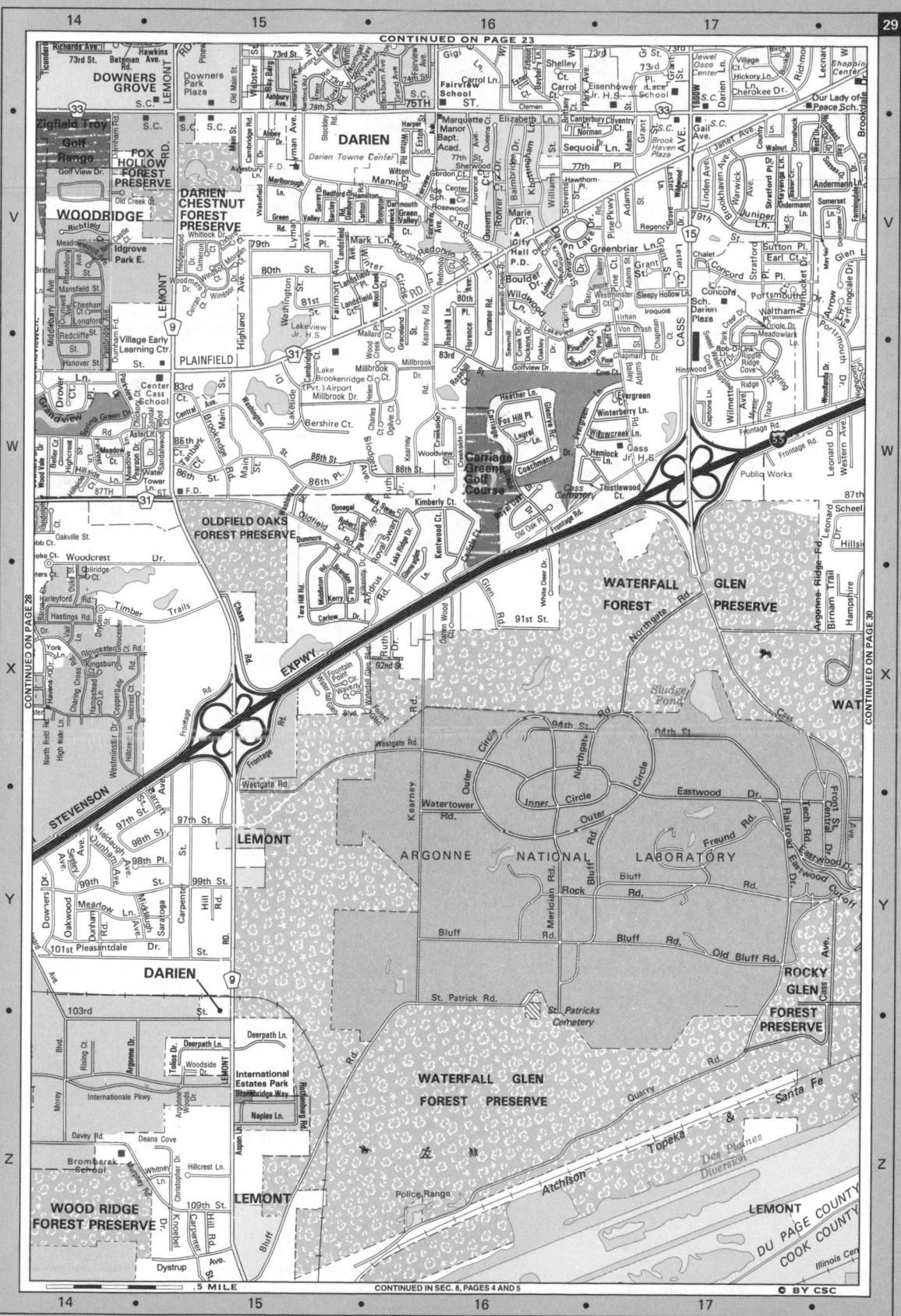

CONTINUED ON PAGE 23

CONTINUED ON PAGE 28

CONTINUED ON PAGE 30

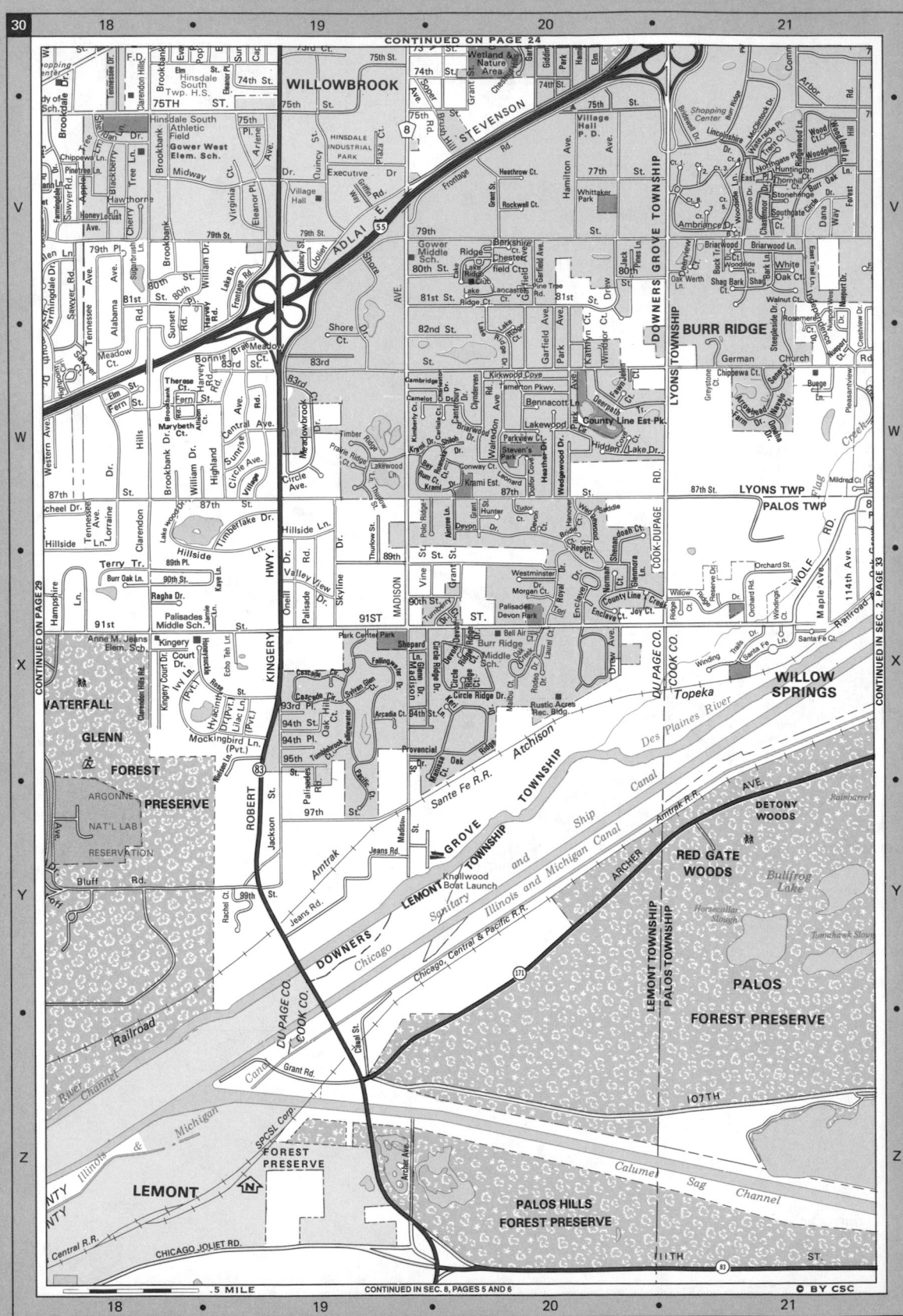

CONTINUED ON PAGE 24

CONTINUED ON PAGE 29

CONTINUED IN SEC. 2, PAGE 33

WILLOWBROOK

STEVENSON

BURR RIDGE

LYONS TOWNSHIP

DOWNERS GROVE TOWNSHIP

LYONS TWP

PALOS TWP

WILLOW SPRINGS

WATERFALL GLENN

FOREST PRESERVE

ARGONNE NAT'L LAB RESERVATION

LEMONT

DETONY WOODS

RED GATE WOODS

PALOS FOREST PRESERVE

PALOS HILLS FOREST PRESERVE

.5 MILE

© BY CSC

# INDEX TO DU PAGE COUNTY

## ADDISON
Pages 4,5,10-12

### STREETS
Adams Dr. ... Pg.5 ... F16
Addison Rd. ... Pg.11 ... F16
Adeline Ave. ... Pg.11 ... F,G16
Adobe Dr. ... Pg.4 ... E13
Alden Dr. ... Pg.5 ... F17
Amelia Ln. ... Pg.4 ... E14
Amoreno Dr. ... Pg.11 ... G15
Anvil Ct. ... Pg.5 ... D14
Ardmore Terr. ... Pg.11 ... G17
Ari Ct. ... Pg.10 ... F13
Armitage Ct. ... Pg.10 ... G14
Army Trail Blvd. ... Pg.5 ... E16
Ascot Pl. ... Pg.5 ... D15
Ashley Ln. ... Pg.5 ... D15
Ashwood Ct. ... Pg.5 ... D14
Aspen Way ... Pg.5 ... D14
Autumn Tr. ... Pg.5 ... D15
Babbitt Ave. ... Pg.5 ... D15
Darbara Ct. ... Pg.4 ... E14
Barnwall Dr. ... Pg.5 ... D14
Baybrook Ct. ... Pg.5 ... E15
Baynard Dr. ... Pg.5 ... E15
Beach Dr. ... Pg.5 ... E15
Belden Ave. ... Pg.11 ... G16
Belmont Ave. ... Pg.5 ... E17
Bernard Dr. ... Pg.11 ... G14
Beverly Ave. ... Pg.5 ... G17
Blelke Ave. ... Pg.11 ... G16
Brashares Dr. ... Pg.5 ... E15
Briar Hill Ct. ... Pg.5 ... D14
Bridle Terr. ... Pg.5 ... D14
Broadview Ave. ... Pg.5 ... F14
Byron Ave. ... Pg.4,5 ... D14
Cambridge Row ... Pg.4 ... E14
Capital Dr. ... Pg.11 ... F14,15
Cardinal Ave. ... Pg.5,11 ... E17
Carmela Ct. ... Pg.4 ... D14
Carolan Pkwy. ... Pg.11 ... G17
Carriage Ct. ... Pg.4 ... E14
Castle Rd. ... Pg.4 ... E14
Catalpa Ct. ... Pg.5 ... E17
Centennial Dr. ... Pg.4 ... D14
Central Ave. ... Pg.11 ... F16
Charles Ct. ... Pg.11 ... G17
Chatham Ave. ... Pg.11 ... G17
Cherry Hill Dr. ... Pg.11 ... G17
Church St. ... Pg.11 ... F16
Cimarron Way ... Pg.4 ... E13
Circle Dr. ... Pg.11 ... F16
Clarendon Ave. ... Pg.11 ... F,G16
Clark St. ... Pg.5 ... E17
Clover Ct. ... Pg.5 ... D15
Clubview Ct. ... Pg.4 ... E13
College Blvd. ... Pg.4 ... E13
Collins Ave. ... Pg.10 ... F13
Commercial Ave. ... Pg.11 ... G16
Compton Pl. ... Pg.5 ... E15
Comstock Ave. ... Pg.11 ... G16
Congress Dr. ... Pg.11 ... F14
Corporate Dr. ... Pg.4 ... F13
Cortland Ave. ... Pg.11 ... G14
Cortland Ct. ... Pg.10 ... G14
Country Club Dr. ... Pg.6 ... E16
Craig Pl. ... Pg.5 ... E16
Dale Dr. ... Pg.11 ... F16
Dale Rd. ... Pg.5 ... E15
Denise Ct. ... Pg.5 ... E16
Diversey Ave. ... Pg.5 ... F15
Douglas Ave. ... Pg.11 ... G17
Drake Ave. ... Pg.11 ... F17
DuPage Ave. ... Pg.4,5 ... E14
Edgewood Ave. ... Pg.5 ... E16
Eggerding Dr. ... Pg.5 ... D15
Elizabeth ... Pg.5 ... E16
Ellsworth Ave. ... Pg.11 ... G17
Elm St. ... Pg.10 ... F13
Evergreen Ave. ... Pg.11 ... F15
Executive Dr. ... Pg.4 ... F13
Factory Rd. ... Pg.11 ... G15
Fairbanks Dr. ... Pg.11 ... F15
Farmwood Dr. ... Pg.5 ... D15
Fay Ave. ... Pg.11,12 ... G16,18
Fiene Dr. ... Pg.11 ... G16
Fischer Ave. ... Pg.5 ... D15
Flora Pkwy. ... Pg.5 ... F15
Forest Dr. ... Pg.5 ... E17
Forest Dr. ... Pg.5 ... E17
Foxtale Dr. ... Pg.5 ... D14
Frairs Ct. ... Pg.5 ... D14
Frontage Rd. ... Pg.11 ... H14
Fullerton Ave. ... Pg.11 ... F17
Georgian Ct. ... Pg.5 ... D15
Gerri Ln. ... Pg.11 ... G16
Gladys Ave. ... Pg.11,12 ... G17
Goldengate Ct. ... Pg.4 ... D14
Goldengate Dr. ... Pg.4 ... D14
Grace St. ... Pg.11 ... G15
Gramercy Ln. ... Pg.5 ... E15
Grand Ave. ... Pg.11 ... F17
Grant Dr. ... Pg.11 ... F16
Grant St. ... Pg.5 ... E16
Green Meadow Dr. ... Pg.5 ... E16
Green Oaks Ct. ... Pg.5 ... E16
Green Ridge St. ... Pg.4 ... E14
Greenbriar Dr. ... Pg.4 ... D13
Grove Ave. ... Pg.5 ... D15
Hadden Ct. ... Pg.5 ... E16
Hale St. ... Pg.11 ... F16
Harrow Ct. ... Pg.5 ... D14
Harvard Ave. ... Pg.11 ... F17
Heather Ct. ... Pg.5 ... D15
Heritage Dr. ... Pg.5 ... D15
Hickory Pl. ... Pg.5 ... D15
Hickory St. ... Pg.5 ... D15
Hickory Trail Ln. Pg.5 ... D15

Highview Ave. ... Pg.5,11 ... E,F16
Highview Blvd. ... Pg.5 ... E16
Hill Meadows Ln. ... Pg.11 ... F15
Hilton Ave. ... Pg.11 ... F17
Holly Ct. ... Pg.5 ... E17
Holtz Ave. ... Pg.4,5 ... E14,16
Honey Hill Rd. ... Pg.5 ... D15
Horseshoe Ct. ... Pg.5 ... F14
Howard Rd. ... Pg.5 ... D15
Hunter Ct. ... Pg.5 ... D15
Huntington Rd. ... Pg.4 ... E14
Industrial Rd. ... Pg.11 ... G16
Interstate Rd. ... Pg.11 ... G16
Iowa Ave. ... Pg.11 ... F16
Irmen Dr. ... Pg.11 ... F15
Itasca Rd. ... Pg.5 ... D15
J.F. Kennedy Dr. Pg.5 ... F16
Jamey Ct. ... Pg.11 ... G17
Janice Ln. ... Pg.5 ... D15
Jeffrey Dr. ... Pg.11 ... G14
Joseph Ln. ... Pg.5 ... D15
Joyce Ln. ... Pg.5 ... F17
Justin Ct. ... Pg.5 ... D14
Katherine Ln. ... Pg.4 ... E13
Kay Ave. ... Pg.11 ... G16
Keebie Ct. ... Pg.5 ... D15
Kendall Tr. ... Pg.4 ... E14
Kenmore Ave. ... Pg.4 ... E14
Kennedy Dr. ... Pg.5 ... E16
Kingery Ct. ... Pg.11 ... F18
Kings Point Dr., N. & E. ... Pg.5
Kings Point Dr., S. ... Pg.4 ... E13
Kings Point Dr., W. ... Pg.4 ... E13
Kingston Dr. ... Pg.5 ... D15
Krage Dr. ... Pg.11,12 ... G18
La Londe Ave. ... Pg.11 ... F15
La Porte Ct. ... Pg.11 ... F17
Lake Manor Dr. Pg.11 ... F15
Lake Park Dr. ... Pg.11 ... F15
Lake St. ... Pg.5 ... E16
Laneers Dr. ... Pg.4 ... E14
Laura Dr. ... Pg.11 ... G16
Lawler Ave. ... Pg.4 ... E14
Lemore St. ... Pg.5 ... E16
Lilac Ln. ... Pg.5 ... D14
Lincoln Ave. ... Pg.5 ... E16
Lincoln Ct. ... Pg.5 ... E16
Lincoln St. ... Pg.5,11 ... D,G16
Linda C. ... Pg.4,5 ... E14
Linda Ln. ... Pg.5 ... E14
Lois Ave. ... Pg.5 ... E16
Lombard Rd. ... Pg.5 ... D-G14
Lorraine Ave. ... Pg.11 ... G17
Lullo Dr. ... Pg.5 ... E16
Macie Ct. ... Pg.5 ... E16
Maple Ct. ... Pg.5 ... E17
Maple St. ... Pg.5 ... F17
Mare Barn Ln. ... Pg.5 ... E16
Marilyn Terr. ... Pg.5 ... E16
Mavis Ln. ... Pg.5 ... E16
May St. ... Pg.5 ... D16
Meadow Ave. ... Pg.5 ... E16
Meadows Blvd. ... Pg.4 ... E13
Memory Ln. ... Pg.5 ... F15
Meyer Dr. ... Pg.4 ... E14
Michael Ln. ... Pg.5 ... D14
Michigan Ave. ... Pg.11 ... F16
Michigan Ct. ... Pg.11 ... F16
Mill Rd. ... Pg.5 ... E15,F16
Millns Ct. ... Pg.5 ... D17
Millns Ln. ... Pg.5 ... D16
Mitchell Ct. ... Pg.10 ... F14
Mitton Ave. ... Pg.11 ... F17
Monarch Ln. ... Pg.4 ... E14
Moreland Ave. ... Pg.5 ... F16
Morris Ave. ... Pg.5 ... D15
Mullins Ct. ... Pg.5 ... D16
Mullins Ln. ... Pg.5 ... D16
Mulloy Dr. ... Pg.4 ... E14
Myrick Ave. ... Pg.5 ... F16
Natalie Ln. ... Pg.5 ... D15
National Ave. ... Pg.5 ... F14,15
Natoma Ave. ... Pg.5 ... E16
Neva Ave. ... Pg.5 ... E16
Nike Rd. ... Pg.10 ... G13
Ninth Ave. ... Pg.5 ... D15
Norman Ct. ... Pg.4 ... E14
Northway Dr. ... Pg.11 ... F17
North Ave. ... Pg.5 ... E16
Oak Ct. ... Pg.5 ... E17
Oak Leaf Dr. ... Pg.5 ... E17
Oak Mill Ct. ... Pg.5 ... E17
Oak Mill St. ... Pg.5 ... E17
Oak St. ... Pg.5 ... E16,17
Official Rd. ... Pg.5 ... F14
Old Fence ... Pg.5 ... D15
Orchard Pl. ... Pg.10 ... G14
Overkamp Ave. ... Pg.5 ... E16
Page Ave. ... Pg.4 ... E14
Palmer Ave. ... Pg.11 ... F16
Park Ave. ... Pg.11 ... F16
Park Pl. ... Pg.11 ... F14
Park St. ... Pg.11 ... F16
Parkview Dr. ... Pg.11 ... F16
Pinehurst Blvd. ... Pg.4 ... D13
Pioneer Dr. ... Pg.5 ... E14
Plamondon Dr. ... Pg.4 ... D13
Plaza Dr. ... Pg.5 ... F15
Pleasant Dr. ... Pg.5 ... D16
Pleasant View Ct.

Republic Dr. ... Pg.11 ... F15
Richard Ct. ... Pg.11 ... F15
River Dr. West ... Pg.5 ... E17
Rohlwing Rd. ... Pg.4 ... D14
Ronald Ave. ... Pg.5 ... D15
Ronald Dr. ... Pg.5 ... D16
Rose Ave. ... Pg.5 ... E16
Rosebud Ln. ... Pg.5 ... D15
Royal Dr. ... Pg.4,5 ... D14
Rozeanne Ct. ... Pg.5 ... E16
Rozeanne Dr. ... Pg.5 ... E16
Rugeley Ct. ... Pg.5 ... E15
Rumple Ln. ... Pg.4 ... E14
Sable Ct. ... Pg.5 ... D14
Saddle Row ... Pg.5 ... D14
Scarlet Ct. ... Pg.4 ... D14
Scarlet Dr. ... Pg.4 ... D14
School St. ... Pg.5 ... F16
Senate Dr. ... Pg.4 ... E14
Sharon Dr. ... Pg.5 ... D16
Sherry Ln. ... Pg.4 ... D14
Sherwood Dr. ... Pg.5 ... E16
Sidney Ave. ... Pg.10 ... G14
Sleepy Hollow Ln.
Squire Ln. ... Pg.4 ... E14
St. Aubin Dr. ... Pg.5 ... D15
St. John's Pl. ... Pg.5 ... D15
State St. ... Pg.5 ... E17
Stevens Dr. ... Pg.5 ... E16
Stewart Ave. ... Pg.11 ... F15
Stiles Ave. ... Pg.5 ... G15
Stone Ct. ... Pg.5 ... E17
Stonehedge Ct. ... Pg.5 ... D15
Stonemill Ave. ... Pg.4,5 ... E14,16
Summer St. ... Pg.5 ... E16
Sunrise Dr. ... Pg.5 ... F18
Sunset Dr. ... Pg.5 ... E14
Surrey Rd. ... Pg.5 ... D15
Swift Rd. ... Pg.4 ... D13
Tallyho Ct. ... Pg.5 ... D14
Tallyho Dr. ... Pg.5 ... D14
Tamarac Blvd. ... Pg.4 ... E13
Tenth Ave. ... Pg.5 ... E15
Thatcher ... Pg.5 ... D15
Trinity Dr. ... Pg.5 ... D15
Valerie Ln. ... Pg.5 ... E16
Victoria Dr. ... Pg.4 ... E13
Victoria Pkwy. ... Pg.5 ... E17
Villa Ave. ... Pg.11 ... F17
Vista Ave. ... Pg.11 ... F,G16
Vista Dr. ... Pg.11 ... F16
Waveland Ave. ... Pg.5 ... D16
Weinbrier Sq. ... Pg.11 ... F15
Wesley Dr. ... Pg.5 ... E15
Western Ln. ... Pg.4 ... E13
Westgate Dr. ... Pg.5 ... F16
Westgate St. ... Pg.11 ... G16
Westridge Pl ... Pg.5 ... D15
Westview Ct. ... Pg.11 ... G17
Westwood Ave. ... Pg.11 ... G16
Westwood Trail ... Pg.5 ... E15
Whispering Ct. ... Pg.4 ... E14
White Fence Ln. ... Pg.5 ... D15
Willow Glen ... Pg.5 ... E15
Wilxen Ln ... Pg.5 ... E14
Windmill Ct. ... Pg.4 ... E14
Windsor Ct. ... Pg.4 ... F13
Winthrop Ave. ... Pg.11 ... G15,17
Wisconsin Ave. ... Pg.11 ... F16
Wood Ave. ... Pg.5 ... D15
Woodland Ave. ... Pg.5 ... E16
Wrightwood Ave.

### CEMETERIES
St. Paul's Cem. ... Pg.5 ... E15

### FOREST PRESERVES
Fullerton Park F.P.

### GOLF COURSES
Addison Golf Club ... Pg.5 ... E15
Links and Tees Golf Club ... U15

### PARKS
Addison Community Park ... Pg.5 ... E17
Centennial Park ... Pg.4 ... D14
Cherokee Park ... Pg.11 ... F17
Highview Park ... Pg.5 ... F16
Lake Manor Park ... Pg.11 ... F16
Mill Meadows Park
Nike Park ... Pg.11 ... F14
Old Wall Park ... Pg.5 ... F16
Sherwood Oak Knoll Park ... Pg.5 ... E17
Westview Park ... Pg.11 ... G17
Westwood Park ... Pg.5 ... E14
Wilderness Park Pg.5 ... E14

### SCHOOLS
Addison Sch. ... Pg.5 ... E17
Addison Trail H.S. ... Pg.11 ... F14
Ardmore Sch. ... Pg.11 ... G17
Army Trail Sch. ... Pg.5 ... E16
Concord/Lutheran Sch.
Driscoll H.S. ... Pg.5 ... E16
Fullerton Sch. ... Pg.11 ... F17
Indian Trail Jr. H.S. ... Pg.5 ... E16
Lake Park Sch. ... Pg.11 ... F16
Lincoln Sch. ... Pg.5 ... E16
Lutheran Childrens Ctr. Sch. ... Pg.5 ... E16
Oak Sch. ... Pg.5 ... E16
Old Mill Sch. ... Pg.5 ... D15
St. Joseph Sch. ... Pg.11 ... F17
St. Phillip Sch. ... Pg.5 ... E15
Technology Center of DuPage ... Pg.4 ... F13
Wesley Sch. ... Pg.5 ... E15

### SHOPPING CENTERS
Addison Town Center ... Pg.4 ... E13
Centennial Plaza Pg.4 ... D14
Danna J Plaza ... Pg.11 ... G16
Farmwood Plaza Pg.5 ... D14
Green Meadows Shopping Center ... Pg.5 ... E16
Lake Mill Plaza ... Pg.5 ... E15

### MISCELLANEOUS
American Map Corporation ... Pg.11 ... G15
Army Trail Nature Center ... Pg.4 ... E14
Courthouse ... Pg.5 ... E16
Fire Station #2 ... Pg.11 ... G15
Fire Station #3 ... Pg.4 ... F13
Library ... Pg.5 ... E16
Police Dept. ... Pg.5 ... E16
Village Hall ... Pg.5 ... E16

## ADDISON TOWNSHIP
Pages 4-6,10-12

### STREETS
Addison Ave. ... Pg.5 ... D15
Adele Ave. ... Pg.11 ... G15
Allen Dr. ... Pg.5 ... A17
Ann Ct. ... Pg.5 ... E16
Ardmore Ave. ... Pg.6 ... B18
Arlington Hts. Rd. ... Pg.5 ... A16
Armitage Rd. ... Pg.11 ... G17
Army Trail Rd. ... Pg.4 ... E13
Arthur Ave. ... Pg.11 ... F17
Barry Ave. ... Pg.5 ... B18
Beinoris Dr. ... Pg.5 ... B18
Belmont Ave. ... Pg.6 ... C20
Belmont Pl. ... Pg.4,5 ... E14
Beverly Ave. ... Pg.11 ... F17
Bloomingdale Rd. ... Pg.5 ... C14
Briar Ln. ... Pg.6 ... D18
Broadview Ave. ... Pg.4 ... F14
Brookhurst Ln. ... Pg.5 ... D17
Bruce Ave. ... Pg.11 ... H17
Bryn Mawr ... Pg.6 ... B18
Byron Ave. ... Pg.4,5 ... E14,17
Byron St. ... Pg.5 ... E16
Cardinal St. ... Pg.11 ... F17
Carolan Pkwy. ... Pg.11 ... F17
Catalpa St. ... Pg.5 ... E17
Cedar St. ... Pg.5 ... E17
Center St. ... Pg.4 ... E14
Central Ave. ... Pg.5,6,11
Central Ct. ... Pg.4,5 ... F14
Central Rd. ... Pg.11 ... G14
Chatham Ave. ... Pg.11 ... G17
Cherry St. ... Pg.5 ... E18
Chestnut St. ... Pg.5 ... E16
Church Rd. ... Pg.6 ... E18
Church St. ... Pg.6 ... D18
Clarendon Ave. ... Pg.11 ... G16
Clark St. ... Pg.11 ... G17
Comstock Ave. ... Pg.11 ... G17
County Line Rd. ... Pg.6 ... E20
Creel Dr. ... Pg.5 ... B18
Crest Ave. ... Pg.6 ... D18
Crown Rd. ... Pg.6 ... F19
Dale Ct. ... Pg.5 ... D18
Death Path Rd. ... Pg.6 ... D18
Devon Ave. ... Pg.4 ... A14
Diversey Pl. ... Pg.6 ... C19
Douglas Ave. ... Pg.11 ... F17
Dunlay ... Pg.6 ... C18
Dupage Ave. ... Pg.4 ... E14
Eastland St. ... Pg.6 ... E20
Edgewood Ave. ... Pg.11 ... G15
Edward St. ... Pg.6 ... D18
Eighth Ave. ... Pg.5 ... D15
Elizabeth St. ... Pg.4 ... F14
Ellis St. ... Pg.6 ... A,D19
Ellsworth Ave. ... Pg.5,11 ... E,F17
Elmhurst St. ... Pg.5,6 ... E18
Elmwood Ave. ... Pg.5 ... E17
Emroy Ave. ... Pg.12 ... F20
Ethel Ln. ... Pg.5 ... E18
Evergreen St. ... Pg.6 ... E20
Fairfield Ave. ... Pg.11 ... G15
Fay Ave. ... Pg.11 ... F17
Fischer Dr. ... Pg.5 ... E18
Foresteview Dr. ... Pg.6 ... B18
Foresteview Rd. ... Pg.6 ... B18
Foster Ave. ... Pg.5,6 ... B18
Fourth Ave. ... Pg.5 ... D15
Franzen St. ... Pg.6 ... E18
Fullerton Ave. ... Pg.11 ... F14
Fulton Ave. ... Pg.11 ... G17
George St. ... Pg.5,6 ... C15,E18
Grace St. ... Pg.11 ... G15
Grand Ave. ... Pg.6 ... F18
Grand Pl. ... Pg.6 ... F20
Grove Ave. ... Pg.4,5
... D14,15,18
Hawthorne Ave. ... Pg.5,6 B17,E18
Henderson St. ... Pg.6 ... D18
Hickory Ave. ... Pg.5 ... E17
Highview Blvd. ... Pg.5 ... E17
Hillcrest Ave. ... Pg.5 ... E18
Hillside Dr. ... Pg.6 ... C19
Holtze Ave. ... Pg.5 ... E17
Howard Ave. ... Pg.6 ... F20
Irving Ave. ... Pg.5,6 ... D15
Irving Park Rd. ... Pg.6 ... G19
Itasca Rd. ... Pg.5 ... C14
Jefferson St. ... Pg.6 ... B17
Jill Ct. ... Pg.6 ... F19,E,F20
Jo Ct. ... Pg.4 ... E14
Jo-Ann Ln. ... Pg.4 ... E14
John St. ... Pg.6 ... E20
Joyce Ave. ... Pg.11 ... F15
Kingston Dr. ... Pg.5 ... F15
LaLonde Ave. ... Pg.11 ... G15
Lemore St. ... Pg.5 ... E16
Linda Ln. ... Pg.4 ... F14
Line Rd. ... Pg.6 ... F20
Lombard Rd. ... Pg.5 ... F14
Magnolia Ave. ... Pg.11 ... G16
Marino Ct. ... Pg.5 ... A16
Massell Ct. ... Pg.5 ... E18
Mayfair Dr. ... Pg.5,11 ... E18
McNair ... Pg.11 ... F17
Mill Rd. ... Pg.5 ... D,E15
Millns Ct. ... Pg.5 ... D16
Millns Dr. ... Pg.5 ... D17
Mono Ln. ... Pg.5 ... E18
Monterey Ave. ... Pg.5 ... E18
Montrose Ave. ... Pg.6 ... D18
Moreland ... Pg.4 ... F14
Niles Ave. ... Pg.5 ... E17
North Ave. ... Pg.11 ... G14
North St. ... Pg.5,6 ... B17
North Woods Dr. Pg.6 ... E18
Nugent ... Pg.5 ... E16
Oak Ln. ... Pg.5,6 ... E18
Oak St. ... Pg.5 ... E18
Oakdale Dr. ... Pg.5,6 ... E18
Old Grand Ave. ... Pg.5 ... E18
Overkamp Ave. ... Pg.5 ... E16
Park St. ... Pg.6 ... E20
Parker St. ... Pg.6 ... E18
Patricia Ln. ... Pg.6 ... F19
Pfund Ave. ... Pg.11 ... F17
Pierce Rd. ... Pg.5 ... A15
Pine Ave. ... Pg.5 ... B18
Pine Grove Ave. ... Pg.5 ... E18
Pine St. ... Pg.5,6 ... B18
Pine Tree Ln. ... Pg.6 ... B18
Poplar Ave. ... Pg.6 ... C18
Potter St. ... Pg.6 ... E18
Ralph St. ... Pg.6 ... D18
Red Oak St. ... Pg.5,6 ... E17
Ridge Ave. ... Pg.5 ... A16
Ridgewood Ave. ... Pg.6 ... D18
Riverview ... Pg.11 ... H17
Robert Kingery Hwy. ... Pg.6 ... D18
Robert Ln. ... Pg.6 ... D18
Rodeck Ln. ... Pg.6 ... D18
Rohlwing Rd. ... Pg.4 ... D14
Roosevelt Rd. ... Pg.5 ... F18
Route 83 ... Pg.6 ... D18
Schick Rd. ... Pg.5 ... C15
Sidney Ave. ... Pg.11 ... G15
Spring Oaks Dr. Pg.5 ... D18
Spruce Ave. ... Pg.5 ... D18
St. Aubin Dr. ... Pg.5 ... D15
State St. ... Pg.5 ... E17
Stone Ave. ... Pg.5 ... E15,18
Sunset Dr. ... Pg.5 ... F17
Thorndale Ave. ... Pg.5 ... A15,17
Tioga Tr. ... Pg.5 ... E18
Verrill Ave. ... Pg.5 ... E17
Victory Pkwy. ... Pg.12 ... F20
Villa Ave. ... Pg.5 ... F19
Virginia Ln. ... Pg.5 ... E18
Vista Ave. ... Pg.11 ... G16
Vista Dr. ... Pg.11,12 ... F18
Walnut Ave. ... Pg.5 ... D17
Washington St. ... Pg.5
... B17,B,D18
Waveland Ave. ... Pg.5 ... E16
West Ave. ... Pg.6 ... D18
West River Rd. ... Pg.5 ... E17
White Pine Rd. ... Pg.5 ... E17
White Pines Dr. ... Pg.6 ... C18
Will Ave. ... Pg.5 ... E16
Willow St. ... Pg.6 ... E20
Wilson St. ... Pg.6 ... E20
Winthrop Ave. ... Pg.12 ... G18
Wood Ave. ... Pg.5 ... D15,18
Wood Dale Ave. ... Pg.5 ... A,E,F17
Woodland Ave. ... Pg.5 ... E15,18
Woodside Ln. ... Pg.5 ... D18
Wrightwood Ave. ... Pg.13 ... F20
1st Ave. ... Pg.5 ... E15
2nd Ave. ... Pg.5 ... D15
2nd Pl. ... Pg.5 ... E15
3rd Ave. ... Pg.5 ... D17,E15
5th Ave. ... Pg.5 ... D15
6th Ave. ... Pg.5 ... D15
7th Ave. ... Pg.5 ... D15
9th Ave. ... Pg.5 ... D17

### FOREST PRESERVES
Fisher Woods Forest Preserve ... Pg.6 ... E18
Salt Creek Marsh F.P. ... Pg.5 ... A,B16
Wood Dale Grove F.P. ... Pg.6 ... D17

### GOLF COURSES
Links & Tees Golf Club ... Pg.5 ... D15
Maple Meadows G.C. ... Pg.5 ... D17
Oak Meadows Golf Club ... Pg.5 ... D17
Salt Creek C.C. ... Pg.5 ... A16

### PARKS
Elk Grove Athletic Fields ... Pg.5 ... A16
Farmwood Park Pg.5 ... D15
Frazen Grove Park ... Pg.5 ... B17
Green Meadow Park ... Pg.5 ... E16
Tamara Heights Park ... Pg.5 ... D16
Wooddale Grove Park ... Pg.5 ... D17

### SCHOOLS
Blackhawk Jr. H.S. ... Pg.6 ... D18
Campus Dr. ... Pg.11 ... T2
Head Start (NEDSRA) ... Pg.11 ... G17
Immanuel Sch. ... Pg.5 ... E14
Stone Sch. ... Pg.5 ... E14
W.A. Johnson Sch. ... Pg.6 ... D18

## AURORA
Pages 13,19
(For additional listings, see Section 4)

### STREETS
Aberdeen Ct. ... Pg.19 ... W2
Acorn Ct. ... Pg.19
Adamsway Dr. ... Pg.19 ... W1
Albany Ct. ... Pg.19 ... W1
Alder Ct. ... Pg.19 ... U1
Alderwood Ln. ... Pg.19 ... U1
All Spice Ct. ... Pg.19 ... W3
Amarath Dr. ... Pg.19 ... T1
Amli Ct. ... Pg.19 ... T1
Amli Dr. ... Pg.19 ... T1
Amli Ln. ... Pg.19 ... T1
Anderson Dr. ... Pg.13 ... P1
Andover Cir. ... Pg.19 ... W2
Andover Ct. ... Pg.10 ... W1
Andover Dr. ... Pg.19 ... W1
Angela Ln. ... Pg.19 ... U1
Anton Dr. ... Pg.19 ... U1
Arborside Ct. ... Pg.19 ... S1
Arborside Ln. ... Pg.19 ... S1
Argent Ln. ... Pg.19 ... U3
Arrowhead Ct. ... Pg.19 ... W1
Arrowwood Ct. ... Pg.19 ... W1
Asbury Dr. ... Pg.19 ... T1
Asbury Ln. ... Pg.19 ... T1
Ascot Ln. ... Pg.19 ... U1
Ashbrook Ct. ... Pg.19 ... U1
Ashford Ln. ... Pg.13,19 ... S1
Ashton Ct. ... Pg.19 ... W1
Ashton Dr. ... Pg.19 ... W1
Aspen Ct. ... Pg.19 ... U1
Aspen Ln. ... Pg.19 ... U1
Aster Ct. ... Pg.19 ... U2
Aurora Ave. ... Pg.19 ... T4
Autumn Grove Cir. ... Pg.19 ... W2
Autumn Lake Dr. Pg.19 ... U1
Avalon Ct. ... Pg.25 ... X1
Avondale Ln. ... Pg.19 ... V1
Azure Cove ... Pg.19 ... W1
Baldwing Ct. ... Pg.19 ... W1
Bangor Ln. ... Pg.19 ... W1
Bannister Ln. ... Pg.19 ... V1
Bar Harbor Ct. ... Pg.19 ... W1
Bar Harbor Rd. ... Pg.19 ... W1
Barberry Ct. ... Pg.13 ... P1
Barclay Ave. ... Pg.13 ... Q1
Barley Ct. ... Pg.19 ... V1
Barnstable Ct. ... Pg.19 ... V1
Barrington Ln. ... Pg.25 ... X1
Baybrook Dr. ... Pg.19 ... W1
Bayfield Dr. ... Pg.25 ... V1
Bayview Ct. ... Pg.19 ... V3
Bear Creek Ct. ... Pg.19 ... W1
Beaumont Ct. ... Pg.19 ... U1
Benjamin Franklin Ct. ... Pg.19 ... U2
Bennett Pl. ... Pg.19 ... U2
Berkshire Ln. ... Pg.13 ... P1
Betsy Ross Ct. ... Pg.19 ... U2
Birder Ferry Rd. ... Pg.13 ... U1
Bilmore Ct. ... Pg.25 ... Y1
Birchdale Ln. ... Pg.19 ... W1
Birmingham Dr. ... Pg.19 ... W1
Biscay Ct. ... Pg.19 ... V1
Blaine Ct. ... Pg.19 ... V1
Bloomfield Ct. ... Pg.19 ... V1
Blossom Ln. ... Pg.25 ... X1
Blue Spruce Ln. Pg.13 ... P1
Blueridge Ct. ... Pg.19 ... V1
Booth Bay Ln. ... Pg.19 ... W1
Boxwood Ln. ... Pg.13 ... Q3
Braymore Cir. E. Pg.19 ... W2
Brayton Ln. ... Pg.19 ... W1
Breckenridge Ct. Pg.19 ... W1
Breckenridge Ln. Pg.19 ... W1
Bremerton Ct. ... Pg.19 ... V2
Bremerton Ln. ... Pg.19 ... V2
Brentwood Ln. ... Pg.13,19 ... Q-V1
Brickton Ct. ... Pg.13 ... Q1
Bridgeport Ln. ... Pg.19 ... W1
Bridle Path Ln. ... Pg.13 ... R1
Brighton Dr. ... Pg.19 ... R1
Brittany Ct. ... Pg.19 ... W1
Broadmoor Cir. ... Pg.19 ... W3
Broadmoor Ln. ... Pg.19 ... W3

Brockton Ct. ... Pg.19 ... W1
Brook Ct. ... Pg.19 ... W1
Brook Ln. ... Pg.19 ... W1
Brooklyn Dr. ... Pg.19 ... T1
Brookshire Ct. ... Pg.19 ... U1
Brookside Ct. ... Pg.19 ... S1
Brookside Ln. ... Pg.19 ... S1
Brunswick Ln. ... Pg.19 ... W1
Bryan Ct. ... Pg.19 ... W1
Bunker Hill Cir. ... Pg.19 ... U2
Burnett Dr. ... Pg.19 ... R2
Burnham Ct. ... Pg.19 ... S1
Burnside Ct. ... Pg.19 ... V1
Butterfield Rd. ... Pg.13 ... P2
Butternut Ln. ... Pg.13 ... P1
Butterwalk ... Pg.19 ... W2
Cadella Cir. ... Pg.19 ... W1
Cambria St. ... Pg.25 ... W1
Camden Ln. ... Pg.19 ... U1
Cammeron Dr. ... Pg.19 ... U1
Campus Dr. ... Pg.19 ... T2
Candlewood Ct. ... Pg.19 ... R2
Cane Garden Cir. Pg.10 ... U2
Capri Ct. ... Pg.25 ... X1
Carriage Ct. ... Pg.19 ... U1
Carriage Way ... Pg.19 ... U1
Carrington Ln. ... Pg.19 ... V1
Casey Ct. ... Pg.19 ... T1
Castlewood Ct. ... Pg.19 ... V1
Cerena Ct. ... Pg.19 ... V2
Chadwick St. ... Pg.19 ... S1
Chandler Ct. ... Pg.19 ... R1
Charlemaine Dr. ... Pg.19 ... W2
Charlotte Ct. ... Pg.19 ... W2
Charter Dr. ... Pg.25 ... W1
Charter Oaks Ct. Pg.13 ... U1
Charter Oaks Dr. Pg.13 ... U1
Chasewood Ct. ... Pg.19 ... S1
Chatfield Ct. ... Pg.19 ... V1
Chelsea Ln. ... Pg.19 ... V1
Cheryl Ct. ... Pg.19 ... V2
Chesapeake Dr. ... Pg.19 ... U3
Cheshire Dr. ... Pg.19 ... U1
Chester Ct. ... Pg.19 ... V1
Cheswick Ln. ... Pg.25 ... X1
Chicory Ln. ... Pg.19 ... W3
Churchill Ln. ... Pg.19 ... U2
Cimarron Dr., E. & W. ... Pg.19 ... V1
Clara Ave. ... Pg.13 ... R1
Clardon Ln. ... Pg.19 ... V1
Claremont Ct. ... Pg.19 ... T2
Clarendon Ln. ... Pg.19 ... V1
Clearwood Ct. ... Pg.19 ... V2
Clementi Ct. ... Pg.25 ... X1
Clementi Ln. ... Pg.25 ... X1
Clifton Ct. ... Pg.19 ... U1
Cloverfield Ln. ... Pg.19 ... U1
Coastal Dr. ... Pg.25 ... W1
Commerce St. ... Pg.19 ... T2
Commons Dr. ... Pg.19 ... T2,V3
Compton Rd. ... Pg.19 ... V1
Conifer Ct. ... Pg.13 ... P1
Conrad Ct. ... Pg.19 ... V1
Cooper Ct. ... Pg.19 ... V1
Copperfield Ct. ... Pg.19 ... W2
Corvallis Ct., N. Pg.19 ... V1
Corvallis Ct., S. Pg.19 ... V1
Country Oaks Ct. Pg.13 ... U1
County Line Rd. ... Pg.19 ... T1
Courtland Pl. ... Pg.19 ... S1
Cove Ct. ... Pg.19 ... W1
Coventry Ct. ... Pg.19 ... U1
Crabapple Ct ... Pg.25 ... X1
Cranberry Ln. ... Pg.13 ... P1
Cranbrook Ct. ... Pg.19 ... S1
Creekside Ct. ... Pg.19 ... T1
Crescent Ln., S. Pg.19 ... W1
Crestview Dr. ... Pg.19 ... T1
Cross Creek Ct. ... Pg.13 ... Q1
Cumberland Dr. ... Pg.19 ... V1
Cumberland Rd. ... Pg.19 ... V1
Danhaven Ct. ... Pg.19 ... V1
Darlene Ct. ... Pg.19 ... V2
Daybreak Dr. ... Pg.25 ... X1
Daylight Dr. ... Pg.19 ... X1
Delta Dr. ... Pg.25 ... X1
Devonshire Ct. ... Pg.13 ... Q1
Diane Dr. ... Pg.19 ... R1
Dickens Ct. ... Pg.19 ... Y1
Dickens Dr. ... Pg.19 ... Y1
Dogwood Ln. ... Pg.19 ... U1
Doncaster Dr. ... Pg.19 ... U1
Dorothy Dr. ... Pg.19 ... V1
Dorsett Ct. ... Pg.19 ... U2
Dover Ln. ... Pg.19 ... V1
Downing Ct. ... Pg.19 ... R1
Driftwood Ln. ... Pg.19 ... U2
DuPage Park Way ... Pg.13 ... P1
Dunbarton Dr. ... Pg.19 ... P2
Dunbarton Rd. ... Pg.19 ... S2
East-West Tollway ... Pg.13 ... Q3
Echo Ln. ... Pg.19 ... V2
Edinburgh Ct. ... Pg.19 ... W1
Edinburgh Ln. ... Pg.19 ... W1
Ellington Dr. ... Pg.19 ... W1
Elmgate Dr. ... Pg.19 ... W1
Emma Cir. ... Pg.19 ... W1
Enterprise St. ... Pg.19 ... T2
Enterprize Ct. ... Pg.19 ... T2
Eola Rd. ... Pg.13,19 ... Q-V1
Erin Marie Ct. ... Pg.25 ... X1
Essex Ct. ... Pg.19 ... T1
Estling Ct. ... Pg.19 ... R2
Eugene Ln. ... Pg.19 ... V1
Evergreen Ln. ... Pg.19 ... U2
Exchange Ave. ... Pg.19 ... T2
Exchange Ct. ... Pg.19 ... T2

Executive Dr. Pg.19 U3
Fairfax Ct. Pg.19 U2
Fairfield Ln. Pg.19 V1
Fairmont Ct. Pg.19 U2
Faith Ln. Pg.13 Q1
Farington Ct. Pg.19 W1
Farington Ln. Pg.19 W1
Ferry Rd. Pg.13 Q2
Fieldstone Ct. Pg.13 Q1
Fieldstone Ln. Pg.19 V1
Flanders Ct. Pg.19 S1
Forest Dr. Pg.19 U1
Forestview Ct. Pg.19 U1
Forestview Ln. Pg.19 U1
Forsyth Ln. Pg.13 Q1
Fossil Creek Ct. Pg.19 W2
Fox Hill Rd. Pg.19 V1
Fox River Rd. Pg.19 V1
Fox Valley Center Dr.
Pg.19 U3
Fox Valley Ct. Pg.19 V1
Fox Valley Dr. Pg.19 V1
Foxmore Ln. Pg.13 P1
Foxtail Dr. Pg.19 V1
Foxworth Ct. Pg.19 U1
Frenchman's Bend Dr.
Pg.19 W2
Frontenac Ct. Pg.19 U2
Frontenac Rd. Pg.19 V2
Frontenac St. Pg.19 U2
Gabrielle Ct. Pg.19 T2
Geneva Ct. Pg.25 X1
Glenford Dr. Pg.19 T1
Gloria Ct. Pg.19 W1
Goldenwood Ct. Pg.19 U1
Goldenwood Dr. Pg.19 U1
Grafton Ln. Pg.19 R2
Graystone Dr. Pg.19 R1
Green Valley Ct. Pg.25 Y1
Greenam Ln. Pg.19 V1
Greenbriar Pl. Pg.19 W3
Greenbrook Dr. Pg.13 R1
Greenlake Dr. Pg.13,19 S1
Gregory St. Pg.19 U2
Gresham Ln. Pg.19 U1
Haag Ct. Pg.19 W1
Hackney Dr. Pg.13 R1
Half Moon Cir. Pg.19 V2
Halsted Ct. Pg.19 W1
Halsted Ln. Pg.19 W1
Hanford Rd. Pg.13 S1
Harbor Ct. Pg.19 V1
Harbour Towne Pl.
Pg.19 W3
Harris Dr. Pg.13 R1
Hartstone Dr. Pg.19 T1
Harvest Ct. Pg.19 U1
Haverhill Dr. Pg.19 R2
Haversham Dr. Pg.19 R2
Healthway Dr. Pg.19 U3
Heather Glen Dr. Pg.19 U2
Heatherwood Dr. Pg.19 W2
Hedge Row Dr. Pg.13 P1
Heggs Rd. Pg.19 W1
Heinz Dr. Pg.19 V3
Hidden Pond Cir. Pg.19 U1
Highfield Ct. Pg.19 W1
Highfield Ln. Pg.19 W1
Highwood Ct. Pg.25 X1
Hobson Ln. Pg.19 W1
Hoffman Blvd. Pg.25 Y1
Hopewell Ct. Pg.19 R2
Horseshoe Ct. Pg.13 R1
Hull Ct. Pg.19 V1
Humphrys Ln. Pg.19 V1
Imperial Ct. Pg.25 Y1
Imperial Valley Tr.
Pg.25 Y1
Innisbrook Ct. Pg.19 V1
Inverness Ct. Pg.19 U,V1
Inverness Dr. Pg.19 U,V1
Isleworth Ct. Pg.19 W2
Jasmine Ct. Pg.19 U2
Jason Ct. Pg.19 U1
Jeannel Ln. Pg.13 R1
Jeremy Ranch Ct.
Pg.19 W2
John Hancock Ct.
Pg.19 U2
Johnsbury Ct. Pg.19 W1
Johnsbury Ln. Pg.19 W1
Jono Dr. Pg.19 W1
Jonquil Ct. Pg.19 U2
Juniper Ct. Pg.13 P,Q1
Kaimy Ct. Pg.19 W1
Karen Ct. Pg.19 W1
Kathy Ct. Pg.19 W1
Katie Ct. Pg.13 Q1
Kautz Rd. Pg.13,19
U,V1,W2
Kealsey Ln. Pg.25 X1
Keating Ln. Pg.19 W1
Kelly Dr. Pg.19 W1
Kendridge Ln. Pg.19 T1
Kenyon Ct. Pg.19 S1
Kenyon Ln. Pg.19 S1
Ketch Ct. Pg.25 X1
Kimberly Ct. Pg.19 U2
Kingshill Cir. Pg.19 W3
Kirkwood Ln. Pg.19 U2
Knightsbridge Ct.
Pg.19 U3
Lakeridge Ct. Pg.19 S1
Lakeside Ct. Pg.19 V1
Lakeside Dr. Pg.19 V1
Lakestone Ln. Pg.19 V2
Lakeview Ct. Pg.19 V1
Landing Dr. Pg.19 U3
Langburgh Ct. Pg.19 S1
Larchmont Ct. Pg.19 V1
Larchmont Ln. Pg.19 V1
Lawrence Ct. Pg.19 W1
Legacy Dr. Pg.19 R1
Legend Ct. Pg.19 W3
Leyland Ln. Pg.19 W1
Liberty St. Pg.19 T1-2
Liconia Ln. Pg.19 W1
Lincolnwood Ct. Pg.19 W1
Lindrick Ct. Pg.19 W1
Lindrick Ln. Pg.19 W1
Lombardi Ln. Pg.25 Y1
Lone Tree Ct. Pg.19 W3
Long Ct. Pg.19 V1
Long Grove Dr. Pg.19 V1
Long Grove Ln. Pg.19 V1
Longmeadow Dr.
Pg.19 U3
Looking Glass Ct.
Pg.19 T1
Lynnfield Ct. Pg.19 V2
Magnolia Ct. Pg.13 P1
Malmesbury Ct. Pg.19 R1
Mapleside Ct. PG.19 U1
Mapleside Ln. Pg.19 U1
Mayfair Dr. Pg.19 U2
Mayfair Ln. Pg.19 U2
Mayfield Ln. Pg.19 V1
McCoy Dr. Pg.19 U3
McKenzie Ct. Pg.25 X1
Meadow Lakes Blvd.
Pg.19 U2
Meadow Rd. Pg.13 Q3
Meadowbrook Dr.
Pg.19 W2
Meadowlark Dr. Pg.13 P1
Meadowridge Dr.
Pg.19 V2
Meadowview Ln. Pg.19 U1
Medford Ct. Pg.19 V1
Melbourne Ln. Pg.19 W1
Melody Ln. Pg.19 W2
Meridian Lake Dr.
Pg.19 T3
Meridian Pkwy. Pg.19 T2
Meridian Rd. Pg.13 Q3
Merle Dr. Pg.13 R1
Merriam Dr. Pg.19 U3
Michael Jordan Dr.
Pg.19 T3
Middlebury Ct. Pg.19 W1
Middlebury Dr. Pg.19 W1
Millbrook Dr. Pg.19 U1
Millington Ct. Pg.19 U1
Millington Ln. Pg.19 U1
Milrose Dr. Pg.25 Y1
Molitor Rd. Pg.13 R1
Monarch Cir. Pg.19 W2
Monmouth Ct. Pg.19 U2
Montclare Ct. Pg.19 U1
Montrose Dr. Pg.19 W1
Moray Dr. Pg.25 X1
Moss Ct. Pg.19 W1
Moss Ln. Pg.19 W1
Mt. Vernon Ct. Pg.25 Y1
Natalie Ln. Pg.19 W1
New York St. Pg.19 T2
Newport Ln. Pg.19 U1
Nicholas Ct. Pg.19 V3
Nordic Ct. Pg.19 V1
Norfolk Ct. Pg.19 U1
Normandy Ct. Pg.19 U2
Normantown Rd. Pg.19 W2
Norwalk Ct. Pg.19 S1
Norwood Ln. Pg.19 V1
O'Brien Rd. Pg.19 T1
O'hara Ter. Pg.19 W2
Oakdale Ct. Pg.19 W1
Oakhurst Dr. Pg.19 U1
Oakland Ln. Pg.19 V1
Oakshire Ct. Pg.13 Q1
Old Diehl Rd. Pg.13 R2
Old Eloa Rd. Pg.19 S1
Old Molitor Rd. Pg.13 R1
Oswego Rd. Pg.19 U3
Oxford Ct. Pg.13,19 S1
Palmer Ct. Pg.19 W3
Palmer Dr. Pg.19 W3
Palomino Dr Pg.13 R1
Panorama Ct. Pg.19 T1
Paradise Canyon Ct.
Pg.19 W3
Park Hill Cir. Pg.19 T1
Park Ridge Ct. Pg.19 U2
Park Ridge Ln. Pg.19 U2
Parkwood Ln. Pg.13,19 R1
Partridge Ct. Pg.13 P1
Pat Ct. Pg.19 V3
Patrick Henry Ct. Pg.19 U2
Paul Revere Ct. Pg.19 U2
Pennsburg Ln. Pg.19 R2
Peppertree Ln. Pg.19 U2
Persimmon Ct. Pg.19 U2
Pheasant Run Ln.
Pg.19 V2
Pine Cone Ct. Pg.13 P1
Pine Lake Ct. Pg.19 W3
Pine Lane Ct. Pg.19 V1
Pine Tree Ct. Pg.13 P1
Pinecrest Ct. Pg.13 P1
Pinegrove Ct. Pg.19 W1
Plymouth Ct. Pg.19 U2
Port Royal Pg.19 V2
Portland Ct. Pg.19 U2
Portland Ln. Pg.19 U1
Portsmouth Ct. Pg.19 W1
Poss Rd. Pg.13,19 S1
Post Oak Ct. Pg.13 P1
Prairie Lake Ct. Pg.19 V2
Prairieview Ln. Pg.13 Q1
Preston Ct. Pg.13 Q1
Primrose Ct. Pg.19 T2
Princeton Ave. Pg.19 U2
Prospect Ct. Pg.13 Q2
Prospect Dr. Pg.13 Q2
Ptarmigan Ct. Pg.13 P1
Quail Ct. Pg.13 P1
Quaker Hill Ct. Pg.19 U2
Quincy Ct. Pg.19 W1
Quincy Ln. Pg.19 W1
Radcliff Ln. Pg.13,19 R1
Radford Dr. Pg.19 S1
Raintree Ln. Pg.19 U2
Raintree Rd. Pg.19 U3
Ravinia Cir. Pg.19 V2
Red Clover Dr. Pg.19 W3
Red Maple Ln. Pg.13 Q1
Redbud Ct. Pg.13 P1
Redbud Ln. Pg.13 P1
Reddington Dr. Pg.19 S1
Reflections Dr. Pg.19 T1
Regency Ct. Pg.19 U2
Reid Pl. Pg.13,19 S1
Reserve Ct. Pg.13,19 R1
Richland Ct. Pg.19 U1
Richmond Ct. Pg.19 U1
Richmond Ln. Pg.19 U1
Ridge Ave. Pg.19 W1
Ridgewood Ct. Pg.13 R1
Riverwood Ct. Pg.13 P1
Rosefield Ln. Pg.19 V2
Rosegate Ct. Pg.19 W2
Roxbury Dr. Pg.19 S2
Rte. 34 Pg.19 V1
Rte. 56 Pg.13 P3
Rte. 59 Pg.19 V3
Rumford Ct. Pg.19 V2
Russo Blvd. Pg.25 Y1
Ryegrass Ct. Pg.19 V1
Sagamore Cir. Pg.25 Y1
Sagamore Ct. Pg.25 Y1
Salem Ct. Pg.19 U1
Sandalwood Ct. Pg.19 V1
Sandpebble Pg.19 U2
Sandpiper Ct. Pg.19 U2
Sandpiper Ln. Pg.19 U2
Sandstone Ct. Pg.19 S1
Saratoga Dr. Pg.19 T1
Savoy Ct. Pg.19 W1
Scheffer Rd. Pg.19 S1
Scott Ln. Pg.13 P1
Seaview Dr. Pg.25 X1
Shadybrook Ln. Pg.19 U2
Sheffield Ct. Pg.19 W1
Shelly Ln. Pg.19 U1
Shenandoah Dr. Pg.25 Y1
Shiloh Dr. Pg.25 Y1
Shoreline Dr. Pg.19 V1
Silver Creek Ct. Pg.19 W2
Smithfield Ct. Pg.25 Y1
Smithfield Dr. Pg.25 Y1
Sommerset Ct. Pg.19 U2
South Rd. Pg.13 Q1
Southgate Ct. Pg.19 V1
Sparrow Ct. Pg.19 U2
Spinnaker Ct. Pg.25 X1
Spinnaker Dr. Pg.25 X1
Spring Shore Dr. Pg.19 U2
Spring Valley Ct. Pg.25 Y1
Springlake Ln. Pg.19 U2
Spur Ln. Pg.13 R1
Squaw Valley Tr. Pg.25 Y1
St. Annes Ct. Pg.19 U2
St. Barthelamy Ln.
Pg.19 U2
St. Croix Ct. Pg.19 U2
St. Kitts Ct. Pg.19 U2
Stableford Ln. Pg.19 W3
Stanton Ct. Pg.13 Q1
Stockbridge Ln. Pg.13 Q1
Stockton Ct. Pg.19 S1
Stockton Ln. Pg.19 S1
Stonebridge Blvd.
Pg.13,19 R1
Stonybrook Ln. Pg.13 Q1
Stratford Ct. Pg.19 V2
Stratton Ln. Pg.19 R2
Streamwood Ct. Pg.13 Q1
Stuart Kaplan Ct.
Pg.25 Y1
Stuart Kaplan Dr.
Pg.25 Y1
Stubblefield Ct. Pg.13 Q1
Sundew Ct. Pg.19 W3
Sunlight Ct. Pg.13 P1
Sunrise Rd. Pg.13 Q1
Suntree Ct. Pg.19 W2
Sussex Ave. Pg.19 T2
Sutton Ln. Pg.19 S1
Sycamore Ln. Pg.19 W1
Tackford Ln. Pg.13 P1
Tansy Rd. Pg.19 W3
Tara Belle Parkway
Pg.19 W2
Teal Bay Pg.25 X1
Teasel Ln. Pg.19 W3
Terrace Lake Dr. Pg.19 V1
Terrace View Dr. Pg.19 V1
Thatcher Dr. Pg.19 V3
Thayer Ct. Pg.19 V2
Thomas Jefferson Ct.
Pg.19 U2
Thomas Paine Ct.
Pg.19 U2
Thornley Ct. Pg.19 U1
Thornwood Ct. Pg.19 V1
Thurston Ct. Pg.19 R1
Timber Hill Ct. Pg.19 V1
Timber Hill Ln. Pg.19 V1
Trade St. Pg.19 U3
Trafalgar Ct. Pg.19 W1
Trafalgar Ln. Pg.19 W1
Tralee's Ct. Pg.19 W2
Tremont Ave. Pg.19 T1
Trenton Ct. Pg.19 U2
Trojak Ln. Pg.13 Q1
Twilight Dr. Pg.25 X1
Valayna Ct. Pg.19 W1
Valayna Dr. Pg.19 W1
Valley Forge Ct. Pg.19 U2
Valleyview Ct. Pg.19 T1
Vaughn Rd. Pg.19 T1,U1
Venuti Dr. Pg.19 U3
Village Ct. Pg.19 W1
Village Green Ct. Pg.19 V1
Village Green Dr. Pg.19 U1,V1
Walcott Rd. Pg.19 V1
Warden Ct. Pg.19 W1
Water Edge Cir. Pg.19 U1
Waterbury Cir. Pg.19 V1
Waterbury Dr. Pg.19 V1
Waterford Ct. Pg.13 Q1
Waterside Ct. Pg.19 S1
Waterside Dr. Pg.19 S1
Waverly Ct. Pg.19 S1
Weather Glen Dr. Pg.19 U1
Weber Rd. Pg.19 T1
Wedgefield Ct. Pg.19 S1
Welch Dr. Pg.19 U1
Wentworth Ln. Pg.19 R1
Westbrook Dr. Pg.19 U3
Westhampton Ct.
Pg.19 U2
Westleigh Ct. Pg.19 W1
Westmoor Ct. Pg.19 U1
Westridge Dr. Pg.19 V1
Wexford Pl. Pg.19 W3
Wheatfield Ct. Pg.13 Q1
Wheatland Ln. Pg.19 V1
Whistler Ct. Pg.19 W3
White Barn Rd. Pg.13 Q1
White Eagle Dr. Pg.19 W2-3
White Eagle Dr., W.
Pg.19 W2
White Oak Cir. Pg.13 R1
Whitehall Ct. Pg.19 V1
Whiteway Ct. Pg.19 V1
Whitney Rd. Pg.19 R2
Wild Meadow Ln.
Pg.19 U1
Wildberry Ct. Pg.19 U2
Wilkes Dr. Pg.19 W2
Willoughby Ln. Pg.13 P1
Willow Ct. Pg.19 V1
Willowcrest Ct. Pg.19 W2
Willowview Ct. Pg.19 V2
Willowview Ln. Pg.19 V2
Wilshire Ct. Pg.13 Q1
Winberie Ave. Pg.19 W3
Winberie Ct. Pg.19 W3
Winchester Ct. Pg.19 W1
Windmere Ct. Pg.19 V1
Windmere Ln. Pg.19 V1
Windrift Dr. Pg.19 V3
Windstream Ct. Pg.19 T2
Windy Hill Ct. Pg.19 V2
Wingate Ct. Pg.13 Q1
Wolverine Dr. Pg.19 T1
Woodcrest Ct. Pg.19 R1
Woodglen Ct. Pg.13 R1
Woodglen Dr. Pg.13 R1
Woodview Ct. Pg.19 T1
Worchester Ln. Pg.19 V1
Wright Ct. Pg.19 U1
Wydown Ln. Pg.13 Q1
Wyndham Ct. Pg.19 V1
Wyndham Ln. Pg.19 V1
Yorkshire Ct. Pg.13 Q1
Yorktown Ct. Pg.19 U2
4th St. Pg.19 S1
5th St. Pg.19 S1
75th St. Pg.19 V1
83rd St.(Montgomery Rd.)
Pg.19 W1
87th St. Pg.19 W1
95th St. Pg.25 Y1

**FOREST PRESERVES**
Big Woods Pg.13 P2
Illinois Prairie Path
Pg.13 R,Q1

**GOLF COURSES**
Michael Jordan Golf Center
Pg.19 T3
Stonebridge G.C.
Pg.13 S1
White Eagle G.C.
Pg.25 W3

**PARKS**
Amberwood Park
Pg.19 V2
Andover Park Pg.25 V1
Birmingham Park
Pg.13 R1
Butterfield Park Pg.13 P1
Clearwood Park Pg.19 U1
Edingburgh Park
Pg.19 W1
Frontenak Park Pg.19 U2
Harbor Spring Park
Pg.25 W1
Kings Hill Park Pg.19 W3
Meadow Lake Park
Pg.25 V2
Monarch Park Pg.19 W2
Parks Pg.19 S,U1
Ridge Park Pg.19 W1
Spring Lake Park
Pg.19 V1
Waubonsie Lake Park
Pg.19 V1
Willow Lake Park
Pg.19 U1

**SCHOOLS**
Francis Granger Middle Sch.
Pg.11 V1
Georgetown Elem. Sch.
Pg.19 V1
Indian Plains Sch.
Pg.19 S1
Indian Prairie Dist. 204
Pg.11 V2
McCarty Elem. Sch.
Pg.19 V1
Peter Gombert Elem. Sch.
Pg.11 W1
Reba Steck Elem. Sch.
Pg.11 V1
Still Middle Sch. Pg.19 V2
Waubonsie Sch. Pg.19 T1
Waubonsie Valley H.S.
Pg.19 V1

**SHOPPING CENTERS**
Fox Valley Center
Pg.19 U3
Market Place Shopping Center
Pg.19 U3
Yorkshire Plaza Pg.19 T3

**MISCELLANEOUS**
Eola Comm Ctr. Pg.19 V1
Fermi Nat'l Lab Pg.13 N1
Oakhurst North Sports Core
Pg.19 T1
YMCA Crown Sports Core
Pg.19 V2

## BARTLETT

Pages 1,2
(For additional listings, see Section 5)

**STREETS**
Abbey Rd. Pg.2 B6
Aberdeen Ct. Pg.2 D6
Acorn Ct. Pg.2 A6
Adare Rd. Pg.2 B6
Alder Ln. Pg.1 A3
Amherst Dr. Pg.2 A5
Amherst Meadow
Pg.2 A5
Anchor Ct. Pg.2 A6
Ancient Oaks Ct. Pg.1 B3
Ancient Oaks Dr. Pg.1 C3
Anita Dr. Pg.2 A5
Anvil Ct. Pg.1 C3
Appaloosa Way Pg.1 C3
Apple Orchard Dr.
Pg.2 B5
Apple Valley Dr. Pg.2 B4
Appletree Ct. Pg.2 C4
Appletree Ln. Pg.2 C4
Arbor St. Pg.2 B5
Aron Ct. Pg.2 B5
Ascot Way Pg.2 C4
Ashford Cir. Pg.2 D6
Ashford Ln. Pg.2 D6
Aster Ln. Pg.2 B6
Auburn Ln. Pg.1,2 A4
Balboa Terr. Pg.2 A6
Balmoral Dr. Pg.2 B6
Balsam Ln. Pg.2 B5
Bannock Ct. Pg.2 D6
Baron Ct. Pg.2 D6
Bartlett Rd., S. Pg.2 B5
Barton Ct. Pg.2 C6
Basswood Ct. Pg.2 D6
Batavia Ct. Pg.2 C5
Bay Ct. Pg.2 A6
Bayberry Dr. Pg.2 A4
Beacon Ln. Pg.2 C6
Beaumont Cir. Pg.2 C6
Beaumont Ct. Pg.2 C6
Beechtree Ln. Pg.2 C4
Bentley Ln. Pg.2 B5
Berteau Ave. Pg.2 A5
Bishop Ct. Pg.2 C6
Bittersweet Pg.2 B6
Blackhawk Ln. Pg.2 C5
Boston Ct. Pg.2 D6
Bragg Ct. Pg.2 A6
Brahms Ct. Pg.2 D6
Braintree Ln. Pg.2 B4
Branden Ct. Pg.2 C6
Branden Ln. Pg.2 C6
Bravo Ct. Pg.2 C6
Brewster Pg.1 B3
Briarcliff Ln. Pg.2 B6
Bridge Ct. Pg.2 C5
Bridle Ln. Pg.1 D3
Brighton Ct. Pg.2 C5
Brookside Dr. Pg.2 B5
Bryn Mawr Ave. Pg.2 B4
Buckingham Pg.2 B5
Burnside Cir. Pg.2 B5
Buttercup Ln. Pg.2 C4
Camberly Ct. Pg.2 C5
Camdon Cir. Pg.2 A4
Candleridge Ct. Pg.2 A6
Canter Ln. Pg.1 C3
Capistrano Terr. Pg.2 A6
Castlewood Dr. Pg.2 B6
Catalpa Ln. Pg.1 B5
Cedar Ln. Pg.2 B4
Charter Oaks Ct. Pg.1 B3
Charter Oaks Dr. Pg.2 B4
Chatsford Ct. Pg.2 C5
Cherry Cir. Pg.2 B6
Chesapeake Ct. Pg.2 C5
Chippendale Dr. Pg.2 B6
Churchill Ct. Pg.1 C3
Churchill Downs Pg.2 C4
Churchill Rd. Pg.1 C3
Circle Ct. Pg.2 B5
Cleburne Ln. Pg.2 A6
Clover Ct. Pg.2 A5
Cobbler Ct. Pg.2 D6
Cobblestone Ln. Pg.1 B2
Colfax Ct. Pg.2 C5
Columbia Ct. Pg.2 C5
Concord Dr. Pg.2 C4
Confederation Dr.
Pg.2 C4
Congress Dr. Pg.2 B4
Coral Ave. Pg.2 A6
Cottonwood Ln. Pg.2 B6
Country Dr. Pg.2 A5
County Farm Rd. Pg.2 B7
Cove Ct. Pg.2 A6
Crescent Ct. Pg.2 A6
Cromwell Cir. Pg.2 D6
Crystal Pg.2 A6
Cuyahoga Terr. Pg.2 B4
Daffodil Ln. Pg.2 C5
Dartmouth Ct. Pg.2 B5
Dartmouth Dr. Pg.2 B5
Deanna Dr. Pg.2 A5
Dedham Ln. Pg.1 B3
Deerfield Ln. Pg.1 C3
Deerpath Ct. Pg.2 C5
Derby Ln. Pg.1 D3
Devon Ave. Pg.2 A5
Dogwood Ln. Pg.2 C4
Dorchester Ln. Pg.2 B4
Driftwood Ln. Pg.2 C4
Dunamon Dr. Pg.2 B7
Dunmore Ln. Pg.2 A6
Duxbury Cir. Pg.2 A4
Duxbury Ln. Pg.2 A4
Eagle Ct. Pg.2 C5
Eastgate Ln. Pg.1 C3
Eastwick Ln. Pg.2 B5
Edgewood Pg.2 D4
Estate Ln. Pg.1 D3
Evergreen Ln. Pg.2 B4
Ewell Ct. Pg.2 B6
Fairfax Cir., E. & W.
Pg.2 D6
Fairfax Ln. Pg.2 D6
Fairview Ln. Pg.2 A4
Faith Ln. Pg.2 B5
Falmore Dr. Pg.2 A6
Far Hills Dr. Pg.2 D4
Farm Gate Rd. Pg.1 C3
Fieldstone Ct. Pg.2 C4
Fieldstone Ln. Pg.2 C4
Filly Ln. Pg.1 C3
Forest Ave. Pg.2 B4
Forest Ct. Pg.2 B4
Forest Preserve Dr.
Pg.1 C3
Forestview Ct. Pg.2 C5
Foster Ave. Pg.2 B4
Four Oaks Rd. Pg.2 D6
Fox Chase Rd. Pg.1 C3
Foxboro Ln. Pg.1 B3
Foxford Rd. Pg.2 B6
Francine Dr. Pg.2 B5
Franklin Dr. Pg.2 B4
Freehold Ln. Pg.2 C4
Fremont St. Pg.2 B4
Garden St. Pg.2 B5
Gardenia Ln. Pg.2 B4
Gatewood Ln. Pg.2 D6
Geneva Ct. Pg.2 C5
Georgian Pl. Pg.2 B5
Gerber Rd. Pg.2 D5
Ginger Brook Ln. Pg.2 B5
Gloria Pg.2 B5
Grand Oak Ct. Pg.1 C3
Granger Rd. Pg.2 C4
Grant Pg.2 B6
Greenache Ct. Pg.2 A6
Greenfield Ct. Pg.2 A6
Greenleaf Ct. Pg.2 D4
Groton Ct. Pg.1 B3
Groton Ln. Pg.1 B3
Hadley Ct. Pg.2 D6
Hamilton Ct. Pg.1 A3
Hampton Cir. Pg.2 A5
Harbor Terr. Pg.2 A6
Harvard Ct. Pg.2 D6
Harvard Ln. Pg.2 D6
Hawkins Ct. Pg.2 C5
Hawthorne Ave. Pg.2 A4
Heather Ln. Pg.2 C4
Heritage Ln. Pg.1 D3
Hickory Ave. Pg.2 A5
Hill Ln. Pg.2 A5
Hillandale Dr. Pg.2 A5
Hillcrest Ln. Pg.2 A5
Hillside Ave. Pg.2 A5
Hillside Ct. Pg.2 A6
Holly Dr. Pg.2 A4
Honeysuckle Ln. Pg.2 C5
Hood Ct. Pg.2 B6
Horseshoe Ct. Pg.1 C3
Horseshoe Ln. Pg.1 C3
Hudson Ct. Pg.2 A4
Humbracht Rd. Pg.2 C5
Huntcliff Rd. Pg.2 C5
Hunter Dr. Pg.2 C3
Hunting Hound Ln.
Pg.2 D3
Hyacynth Ln. Pg.2 C4
Independence Dr.
Pg.2 C4
Ingalton Rd. Pg.2 A4
Irvington Ct. Pg.2 A5
Island Ct. Pg.2 A6
Ivy Ct. Pg.2 C4
Ivy Ln. Pg.2 C5
Jackson Ct. Pg.2 B5
Jackson St. Pg.2 B5
Jasmine Ct. Pg.2 C4
Jervey Ln. Pg.2 A5
John Dr. Pg.2 A5
Juniper Ln. Pg.2 C4
Kaelin Rd. Pg.2 D3
Keenland Dr. Pg.2 C4
Keim Tr. Pg.2 C5
Kelly Farm Ln. Pg.2 D6
Kent Cir. Pg.2 B4
Kingston Ln. Pg.2 B4
LaJolla Ct. Pg.2 A6
Ladysmith Pg.2 B6
Lake Eleanor Dr. Pg.1 E2
Lakeside Dr. Pg.2 A6
Lakeview Ln. Pg.2 A5
Lakewood Dr. Pg.2 B4
Lamont Pkwy. Pg.2 A5
Lark Dr. Pg.2 C4
Leaf Ct. Pg.2 B4
Lee St. Pg.2 B5
Lenox Ct. Pg.2 D6
Lexington Dr. Pg.2 C4
Lido Terr., E. & W.
Pg.2 A6
Lido Tr. Pg.2 A6
Lincoln Dr. Pg.2 B6
Litchfield Ln. Pg.1 A3
Locust Ct. Pg.1 A3
Long Rd. Pg.1 D3
Longford Ct. Pg.2 B6
Longford Rd. Pg.2 B6
Longstreet Ct. Pg.2 B6
Lynnfield Ln. Pg.1 B3
Lysle Rd. Pg.1 D3
Main St. Pg.2 A5
Mallard Ct. Pg.2 A6
Mansfield Ct. Pg.2 B6
Maple Ct. Pg.2 B4
Maple Ln. Pg.2 B4
Marina Ct. Pg.2 A6
Marina Terr., E. Pg.2 A6
Marlboro Ct. Pg.2 C5
Martingale Dr. Pg.2 B4
Mayflower Pg.2 C6
McCellan St. Pg.2 B5
McClellan St. Pg.2 B5
McCook Ct. Pg.2 B6
Meade Ct. Pg.2 B6
Meadow Ln. Pg.1 D3
Meridian Ct. Pg.2 C5
Middleton Pg.1 B3
Millwood Dr. Pg.2 A6
Mohawk Ct. Pg.2 C5
Molobay Ct. Pg.2 A6
Monroe Dr. Pg.2 B4
Montauk Ct. Pg.2 C5
Morgan Ln. Pg.1 C3
Morning Glory Ln.
Pg.2 C4
Mulberry Ct. Pg.2 A6
Munger Rd. Pg.1 A3
Nantucket Ct. Pg.2 B6
New Castle Ct. Pg.2 C5
New Castle Ln. Pg.2 C6
Newport Blvd. Pg.2 A6,B7
Newport Ct. Pg.2 A6
Newport Ln. Pg.2 A6
Nicole Pg.2 B6
Northgate Ct. Pg.1 C3
Northgate Dr. Pg.1 C3
Norwood Ln. Pg.2 A4
Oak Ave. Pg.2 A5
Oak Glen Dr. Pg.2 A5
Oakbrook Ct. Pg.2 A4
Oakmont Dr. Pg.2 A4
Oakwood Ln. Pg.2 A5
Oceanside Terr. Pg.2 A6
Old Barn Pg.1 D3
Old Forge Pg.1 D3
Orchards Pass Pg.2 B5
Orchid Ln. Pg.2 B4
Ord Ct. Pg.2 B6
Paddock Pl. Pg.1 C3
Palamino Ct. Pg.2 C5
Park Way Pg.1 C3
Peartree Ln. Pg.2 B5
Penny Ct. Pg.2 D6
Penny Ln. Pg.2 D6
Percheron Ln. Pg.1 D2
Pickett Ct. Pg.2 B6
Pimlico Ln. Pg.2 C4
Pin Oak Dr. Pg.2 A5
Pinetree Ln. Pg.2 C4
Pipers Dr. Pg.2 B5
Plaza Dr. Pg.2 A5
Plymouth Ct. Pg.2 A5
Poinsetta Ln. Pg.2 C4
Polk Ct. Pg.2 B6
Polo Ct. Pg.1 C3
Polo Dr. Pg.1 C3
Poplar Ln. Pg.2 B4
Poppy Ct. Pg.2 C4
Poppy Ln. Pg.2 C4
Porter Ct. Pg.2 B6
Portsmith Ct. Pg.2 D6
Powis Rd. Pg.1 C2
Prairie Ave. Pg.2 B5
Preserve Tr. Pg.1 A3
Princeton Dr. Pg.2 C4
Prospect Ave. Pg.2 A5
Richmond Ln. Pg.2 C6
Ridge Ln. Pg.1 D3
Rose Ct. Pg.2 C4
Rose Ln. Pg.2 C4
Rosecrans Ct. Pg.2 B6
Rosewood Ct. Pg.2 A5
Saddlebrook Rd. Pg.1 C3
Saddleridge Ct. Pg.1 D3
Saddleridge Pl. Pg.1 C3
San Diego Pl. Pg.2 A6
San Francisco Terr.
Pg.2 A6
Sandalwood Ct. Pg.2 B6
Sandpiper Ct., E. & W.
Pg.2 A6
Sangamon Ct. Pg.2 C5
Santa Anita Dr. Pg.2 C4
Sausalito Ct. Pg.2 A6
Sayre Rd. Pg.1 B3
Schick Rd. Pg.1 D3
Scott Ct. Pg.2 B5
Seacrest Ln. Pg.2 A6
Service Dr. Pg.2 D6
Shady Ln. Pg.2 A5
Shawnee Cir. Pg.2 C5
Shawnee Ct. Pg.2 C5
Sheridan Dr. Pg.2 A6
Sherman Ct. Pg.2 B5
Sherman St. Pg.2 B5
Shorewood Ct. Pg.2 A6
Shorewood Dr. Pg.2 A6
Silver Cir. Pg.2 C5
Silver Ct. Pg.2 C5
Skylark Ct. Pg.2 C5
Southgate Rd. Pg.1 D3
Sparrow Ln. Pg.2 D6
Spitzer Rees Rd. Pg.1 A2
Spruce Ln. Pg.2 B4
Squire Ln. Pg.1 C3
Stearns Rd. Pg.1,2 B1,5
Stockton Ct. Pg.2 D6
Stonebridge Ct. Pg.2 C5
Stonegate Ct. Pg.1 C5
Strathmore Ct. Pg.1 A3
Strawberry Ct. Pg.1 C5
Struckman Blvd. Pg.1 C3
Stuart Ln. Pg.2 B6
Sumac Ct. Pg.1 A3
Sundance Dr. Pg.2 B6
Superior Cir. Pg.1 C5
Surf Ct. Pg.2 A6
Surrey Rd. Pg.2 A4
Sycamore Ln. Pg.2 B4

Tallgrass Dr. Pg.2 B6
Tanoak Ct. Pg.2 A4
Tennyson Rd. Pg.2 A5
Terrace Dr. Pg.2 A4
Thorntree Ct. Pg.2 A6
Thousand Oaks Ct. Pg.1 B3
Thousand Oaks Dr. Pg.1 B3
Towering Oaks Ct. Pg.1 C3
Trailside Ln. Pg.2 B6
Trillium Dr. Pg.2 B6
Tulip Ln. Pg.2 C4
Valewood Rd. Pg.2 B4
Valleyview Pg.2 B6
Vernon Ln. Pg.2 C6
Village Ln. Pg.2 D6
Virginia Ct. Pg.2 C5
Voyager Dr. Pg.2 A6
Wakefield Ln. Pg.1 B3
Wallace Ct. Pg.2 B5
Wallace St. Pg.2 B5
Waltham Ln. Pg.1 A3
Washington Ct. Pg.2 B4
Washington St. Pg.2 B4
Waterford Pg.2 B6
Webster Ave Pg.2 B4
Wentworth Ln. Pg.2 D6
Western Ave. Pg.2 A5
White Horse Ln. Pg.1 C3
Whitefence Rd. Pg.1 C3
Wilcox Ct. Pg.2 A6
Wilcox Dr. Pg.2 A5
Wildberry Ln. Pg.2 D6
Willow Ct. Pg.2 B4
Wilmington Dr. Pg.2 A6
Winchester Pg.2 C5
Windmere Ct. Pg.2 C5
Windsor Dr. Pg.2 B6
Winford Pg.2 B6
Wingate Ct. Pg.1 C3
Winners Cup Ct. Pg.2 C5
Winston Ct. Pg.2 D6
Wood Creek Tr. Pg.2 D4
Woodbine Cir. Pg.1 C3
Woodhollow Ln. Pg.2 B6
Woodland Hills Dr. Pg.1 C3
Woodland Hills Pkwy. Pg.1 C3
Woodside Ln Pg.2 D6

### CEMETERIES
Smyna German Cemetery Pg.2 A7

### FOREST PRESERVES
Pratts Wayne Woods Pg.1 B1
Tri-County State Park Pg.1 A1
Wayne Grove Pg.2 A4

### GOLF COURSES
Apple Orchard G.C. Pg.2 B4

### PARKS
Apple Orchard Pk. Pg.2 D6
[illegible] Pg.[illegible] B1
Canter Park Pg.1 C3
Leiseberg Park Pg.2 A5
McAndrews Park Pg.1 B3
Oak Grove Park Pg.2 A4
Prairieview Park Pg.2 C6
Schick Park Pg.2 C6
Schrader Park Pg.2 C5
Struckman Basin Pg.2 C4
Sunrise Park Pg.2 C4
Sunset Park Pg.2 C4
Tallgrass Park Pg.2 A6
Trails End Park Pg.2 A6
Winding Creek Commons Pg.2 B5

### SCHOOLS
Bartlett H.S. Pg.2 D4

### SHOPPING CENTERS
Bartlett Commons S.C. Pg.1 B3
Bartlett Plaza S.C. Pg.2 A5
Brewster Creek S.C. Pg.2 B3

### MISCELLANEOUS
Apple Orchard Comm. Center Pg.2 B4
Aquatic Center Pg.2 B5
Commonwealth Edison Substation Pg.1 A2
Fire Dept. Pg.2 C5
Post Office Pg.2 A5
Sunrise Camp Pg.2 A4
Treatment Plant Pg.2 B6

## BENSENVILLE
Pages 5,6
Portions within Cook County

### STREETS
Addison St. Pg.6 D,E19
Algonquin Ave. Pg.6 C19
Argyle St. Pg.6 C18
Arthur Ct. Pg.6 E18
Ash Ave. Pg.5 A18
Ashbury Ln. Pg.6 C19
Barron St. Pg.6 D19
Beeline Dr. Pg.6 C19
Belmont Ave. Pg.6 E19
Bernice Dr. Pg.6 E19
Blackhawk Terr. Pg.6 C19
Bobby Dr. Pg.6 E19
Brentwood Ct. Pg.6 E20
Brentwood Dr. Pg.6 E20
Bretman Ave. Pg.6 D20
Briar Ln. Pg.6 D18
Bridget Ct. Pg.6 E19
Briginal St. Pg.6 B18
Brookwood St. Pg.6 C18,19
Bryn Mawr Ave. Pg.6 B18
Busse Rd. Pg.6 M12
Carriage Ln. Pg.6 C19
Center St. Pg.6 D,E19
Central Ave. Pg.5 A19
Church Rd. Pg.6 C19
Cogswell Rd. Pg.6 C19
Country Club Dr. Pg.6 B,C18
County Line Rd. Pg.6 E20
Crest Ave. Pg.6 D19
Daniel Dr. Pg.6 E19
David Dr. Pg.6 E19
Dennis Dr. Pg.6 E19
Devon Ave. Pg.6 A19
Diana Ct. Pg.6 E20
Dierks St. Pg.6 D20
Division St. Pg.6 D20
Dolores Dr. Pg.6 E19
Domenic Ct Pg.6 D20
Donna Ln. Pg.6 D18
Eagle Dr. Pg.6 C19
Eastern Ave. Pg.6 A19
Eastview Ave. Pg.6 C18
Edgewood Ave. Pg.6 A18
Ellis St. Pg.6 A,D19
Elmhurst St. Pg.6 C18
Entry Dr. Pg.6 E19
Evergreen St. Pg.6 D20
Fairway Dr. Pg.6 B18,19
Ferrari Dr. Pg.6 E19
Foley St. Pg.6 D18
Forestview Rd. Pg.6 E19
Foster Ave. Pg.6 B19
Franzen St Pg.6 D18
Frontage Rd. Pg.6 E18
Frontier Way Pg.6 A19
Garden Ave. Pg.6 C19
Gasoline Alley Pg.6 B19
Gateway Rd. Pg.6 C19
Gaylin Ct. Pg.6 D19
George St. Pg.6 E20
Gerry Steven Ct. Pg.6 E19
Glendale St. Pg.6 C18
Gloria Jean Dr. Pg.6 E20
Golf Ln. Pg.6 C19
Grace St. Pg.6 D19
Grand Ave. Pg.6 F18
Green St. Pg.6 D19
Green Valley St. Pg.6 C18
Greenlawn Ave. Pg.6 D19
Grove St. Pg.6 D18
Hamilton St. Pg.6 C20
Hawthorne Ave. Pg.6 B18
Henderson St. Pg.6 D18
Hickory St. Pg.6 D20
Hillside Dr. Pg.6 C18,19
Indian Hill Dr. Pg.5,6 A18
Industrial Dr. Pg.6 B18
Iroquois Ct. Pg.5 A18
Iroquois Ln. Pg.6 A18
Irving Park Rd. Pg.6 C19
Itasca St. Pg.6 B18
Jacquelyn Dr. Pg.6 E19
James St. Pg.6 F19
Jefferson St Pg.6 D20
John St. Pg.6 E20
Judson St. Pg.6 D,E19
Kevyn Ln. Pg.6 C18
Kingery Hwy. Pg.6 C,D18
Larson Ln. Pg.6 B19
Leland Ct. Pg.6 C19
Lincoln St. Pg.6 D19
Main St. Pg.6 C18
Maple Ln. Pg.6 C19
Marion Ct Pg.6 D20
Marion St. Pg.6 D19
Mark St. Pg.6 A18
Marshall Rd. Pg.6 C18
Martha St. Pg.6 D18
Mason St. Pg.6 C19
May St. Pg.6 D19
McLean Ave. Pg.6 D19
Medinah St. Pg.6 C18
Meigs Ct. Pg.6 D20
Memorial Rd. Pg.6 D19
Memorial St. Pg.6 D20
Meyer Rd. Pg.6 C19
Midway Ct. Pg.6 D20
Miner St. Pg.6 D19
Mohawk Dr. Pg.6 C19
Nordic St. Pg.6 B18
O'Hare Ct. Pg.6 C20
O'Leary Dr. Pg.6 D20
Old Plank Rd. Pg.6 C19
Orchard Ave. Pg.6 C,D20
Pamela Dr. Pg.6 E19
Park St. Pg.6 D20
Parkside Ln. Pg.6 C19
Pershing Ave. Pg.6 C19
Pine Ave. Pg.6 D19
Pine Ln. Pg.6 C18
Pleasant St. Pg.6 C19
Plentywood Ln. Pg.6 C19
Podlin Dr. Pg.6 D21
Poplar Ave. Pg.6 C18
Poppy Ln. Pg.6 C19
Railroad Ave. Pg.6 D20
Red Oak St. Pg.6 D19
Redmond Ct. Pg.6 E20
Ridgewood Ave. Pg.6 D18
River Forest Ct. Pg.6 E20
River Forest Dr. Pg.6 E20
Roosevelt Ave. Pg.6 C19
Roosevelt Ct. Pg.6 C20
Rose St. Pg.6 D19
Roxan Ave. Pg.6 D20
Second Ct. Pg.6 D18
Sesame St. Pg.6 C18
Sivert Ct. Pg.6 B19
Sonny Ln. Pg.6 E19
Spruce Ave. Pg.6 A,C18
Stoneham St. Pg.6 C18
Sunset Ct. Pg.6 C20
Supreme Dr. Pg.6 A19,B18
Thomas Dr. Pg.6 B19
Thorndale Ave. Pg.6 A18
Timber Ln. Pg.6 D19
Tioga Ave. Pg.6 C19
Tower Ln. Pg.6 A18
Twin Oaks St. Pg.6 C18
Virginia St. Pg.6 D20
Walnut St. Pg.6 C,D19
Washington St. Pg.6 D19,20
Waveland Ave. Pg.6 D21
William St. Pg.6 E19
Wilson Ct. Pg.6 C19
Wood Ave. Pg.6 D19
Woodland Ave. Pg.6 E19
York Rd. Pg.6 D19

### CEMETERIES
Frieden's Cemetery Pg.6 E19
Zion Cemetery Pg.6 E19

### FOREST PRESERVES
Bensenville Ditch F.P. Pg.6 D20

### GOLF COURSES
White Pines Country Club Pg.6 E19

### PARKS
Diorio Park Pg.6 D19
Geils Field Pg.6 E20
Kremples Park Pg.6 E19
Lions Park Pg.6 D19
Margie Park Pg.6 E19
Rose Park Pg.6 E19
Seeker Park Pg.6 D20
Sunrise Park Pg.6 D19
Sunset Park Pg.6 D19
Terrace Park Pg.6 A18
Varble Park Pg.6 D18
Veterans Park Pg.6 D19
Water Park Pg.6 D18

### SCHOOLS
Bensenville Comm. Pre-School Pg.6 D19
Blackhawk Jr. H.S. Pg.6 D18
Chippewa Sch. Pg.6 D19
Fenton H.S. Pg.6 C18
Green Street Sch. Pg.6 D19
Immanuel Church Sch. Pg.6 E19
Lincoln Sch. Pg.6 B19
Mohawk Sch. Pg.6 C18
St. Alexis Sch. Pg.6 D19
St. Charles Borromeo Sch. Pg.6 E19
St. John's Sch. Pg.6 B18
Tioga Sch. Pg.6 D19
W. A. Johnson Sch. Pg.6 D18
Zion Ev. Lutheran Sch. Pg.6 E19

### SHOPPING CENTERS
Brentwood Commons S.C. Pg.6 E19
Main St. Plaza Pg.6 D19

### MISCELLANEOUS
Fire Station #1 Pg.6 D19
Fire Station #2 Pg.6 B19
Library Pg.6 D18
Lifelink Bensenville Home Society Pg.6 D19
Police Department Pg.6 D19
Sewage Treatment Plant Pg.6 E19
Village Hall Pg.6 C19
Water Department Pg.6 E19

## BLOOMINGDALE
Pages 3,4

### STREETS
Acorn Ln. E12
Alsace Ct. D10
Alyssa Ct. C10
Amberwood Ct. D12
Amherst Ct. E12
Applewood Ln. E12
Arbor Ln. E12
Army Trail Rd. E8
Arquilla Ct. E12
Ashfield Ct. D9
Ashley Way C10
Atherton Ct. D11
Bayview Ct. E12
Bedford Ln. E12
Benton Ln. D9
Biarritz Ct. D10
Billings Ct. D11
Birchwood Ln. E12
Biscayne Ct. C8
Biscayne St. C8
Bloomfield Cir. D9
Bloomfield Pkwy. D9
Bloomingdale Rd. D11
Bob-O-Link Dr. E10
Bobwhite Ct. D10
Bobwhite Ln. D10
Bourne Ln. D11
Bradley Ct. E12
Braintree Dr. D11
Brentwood Ct. E12
Brewster Ct. D11
Briarwood Ln. E12
Bridgewater Ln. E11
Brighton Rd. E8
Bristol Ct. C9
Bristol Dr., N. C9
Broker Rd. C12
Brookdale Dr. E12
Bunting Ln. D11
Butterfield Dr. D9
Byron Ave. E12
Calvary Dr. E10
Cambridge Ln. D11
Camden Dr. D8
Canterbury Ct. D11
Cardinal Dr. D10
Carlton Dr. E12
Carriage Way D12
Carthage Ct. E12
Castle Rock Ln. C10
Cayuga Ct. D9
Chambord Ct. D10
Chatham Ct. D11
Chelsea St. C10
Chesapeake Ln. C8
Circle Ave. D12
Clare Ln. D13
Clearbrook Ln. D12
Clubhouse Ln. D9
College Dr. E12
Collin Cir. D9
Colony Ct. E12
Colony Green Dr. E12
Constitution Dr. E12
Country Club Ln. C10
Country Ridge Ln. D12
Coventry Ct. D12
Covington Dr. D8
Crandon Ct. D11
Creekside Dr. E12
Crest Ct. D12
Crestwood Ln. E12
Cunningham Dr. E11
Cunningham Ln. D11
Darby Ct. D11
Dartmouth Ct. E12
Dawn Ct. E12
Day St. D11
Dee Ct. D11
Deer-Glen Way D12
Dijon Ct. C10
Donna Ln. D12
Douglas Dr. E12
Dover Ct. E12
Downing Dr. D12
Driftwood Ln. D12
Durham Ln. E12
Duxbury Ct. D11
Eagle Ct. D11
Eagle Ln. D11
Edgebrook Dr. D12
Edgewater Ct. D11
Edgewater Dr. E12
Elmwood Ln. E12
Emerson Ct. F12
Epson Dr. E11
Eric Ct. C10
Esprit Ct. C10
Essex Ct. D9
Euclid Ave. D12
Euclid Ct. D12
Evergreen Ln. E12
Fairchild Ct. F12
Fairfield Ct. D11
Fairfield Way D11
Fairlane Ct. D11
Falcon St. D10
Fernwood Ln. C9
Fessler Dr. C11
First St. D11
Fontaine Ct. C10
Fosmor Ct. C10
Founders Point N. D11
Founders Point S. D11
Fox Ct. D8
Franklin St. C10,11
Freeport Dr. D12
Fremont Ct. E12
Frisco Ct. C8
Frisco St. C8
Galdway Ct. D13
Garden Way D12
Gary Ave. F9
Georgetown Ct. F12
Glen Ellyn Rd. E12
Glen Ridge Ct. D12
Glendale Terrace C11
Glengarry Dr. D12
Glenwood Dr. C9
Greenfield Dr. D9
Hampshire Ct., N. C9
Hampshire Dr., W. C9
Hampton Ct. E12
Hancock Dr. D11
Harbor Ct. E12
Harvard Ln. D12
Hawthorne Dr. D12
Hearthside Dr. D12
Hedgerow Dr. D12
Hempstead Dr. E11
Hempstead Ln. E11
Hillandale Dr. D10
Hingham Ln. D11
Independence Ln. D11
Indiana Ct. F12
Ironwood Dr. D12
Ivy Ln. D12
Jackson Ln. D11
Jason Ct. D12
Jefferson Ln. D11
Juniper Ln. D12
Kendall Ct. E12
Kensington Ct. E9
Kildeer Rd. E10
Kingston Ln. D12
Klein Creek Blvd. E9
Knollwood Dr. D9
Lake St. C11
Lakemont Ct. E9
Lakeshore Ln. D12
Lakeview Ct. D12
Lakeview Dr. C12
Lakeview Ln. D12
Lakewoods Ct. C11
Langton Ct. D11
Langton Dr. E11
Langton Ln. D11
Larchmont Ln. D11
Lawford Ct. D11
Lawrence Ave. C10,11
Lehigh Ln. D11
Leslie Ln. D10
Lincoln Ct. E12
Lockwood Ln. D12
Log Cabin Dr. C11
Longridge Dr. D11
Loraine Cir. D10
Lynbrook Dr. D11
Lynwood Ct. D9
Lynwood Ln. D9
Manchester Ln., N. C9
Manor Ln. D12
Maple Ave. C11
Maple Ct. C11
Martin Ct. E9
Martin Ln. F10
Mayo Ln. D13
Meadowlark Rd. D10
Meadowview Ct. E12
Medinah Rd. D13
Melborne Ct. D11
Millcreek Ln. D12
Millford Ct. D11
Millford Ln. D11
Milton Ct. E12
Mission Ct. C9
Montego Ct. C9
Morningside Dr. E12
Needham Dr. D9
Nordic Rd. C12
North Ln. B13
Northwestern Ct. F12
Northwoods Ln. C9
Norton Dr. E11
Norton Ln. E11
Oak Knoll Ln. D12
Oak St. C11
Oakwood Ln. E12
Old Gary Rd. E9
Old Mill Ln. E9
Oneida Ct. D9
Orchard Ln. C9
Oriole St. E11
Otsego Ct. C9
Oxford Ct. D11
Oxford Ln. D11
Park Ave. C11,12
Parkway Ave. D9
Pebblecreek Dr. D12
Pheasant Ct. E10
Pheasant Ln. E10
Pinewood Ln. E12
Pleasant Ave. C,D12
Plymouth Ln. E12
Prairie Ave. C,D12
Quincy St. D11
Radcliffe Ct. D9
Raleigh Ct. D11
Raven Ln. D10
Red Bird Ct. E10
Red Bird Rd. E10
Red Wing Ct. D10
Regency Dr. E12
Ridge St. C11
Ridgewood Dr. C9
Robin Ct. E10
Rosedale Ct. D10
Royal Ct. C10
Royal Ln. C10
Royce Ct. E11
Royce Dr. E11
Salem Ct. D11
Saranac Ct. C9
Scarborough Ct., W. C9
Scenic Dr. C10
Schick Rd. D12
Scott Dr. D9
Seneca Tr. C9
Sheffield Dr., W. C10
Sherwood Ct., W. C9
Signature Dr. E10
Skylark Dr. E10
Spring Ct. D12
Spring Valley Dr. C12
Springbrook Ln. D11
Springdale Ln. D9
Springfield Dr. C10
St. Francis Ct. C12
Stanyon Ct. E11
Stanyon Dr. D12
Starling Ct. E12
Sterling Ct. D11
Sterling Dr. E11
Sterling Ln. D11
Stoney Brook Ln. E12
Stratford Dr. D9
Stratford Pl. Dr. D9
Strathmore Ct. D11
Strathmore Ln. D11
Surrey Dr. E11
Surrey Ln. E11
Sutherland Ln. E11
Sutton Ct. D12
Swallow Ave. E10
Tamarack Dr. D12
Tanager Dr. E10
Tee Ln. D12
Terry Ln. E12
Third St. C11
Thrasher St. D10
Torrington Dr. D9
Versailles Ct. C10
Villa Way D10
Vinings Dr. D9
Walter Ct. C11
Warren Ave. D12
Warwick Ln. D9
Washington St. C11
Wedgefield Ln. D9
Wedgewood Cir. D9
Wellington Dr. D10
Wendover Dr. D9
Wentworth Cir. D9
West Rd. D10
White Hall Terr. E10
Wickham Ave. D9
Wildwood Ct. E12
William Way C10
Willow Bridge Way E12
Willow Ln. D12
Windham Ln., N. C9
Windham Ln., S. C10
Windsor Cir., N. C9
Windsor Dr., W. C9
Winston Ln. D11
Woodland Way C10
Woodside Dr. C9
Wren Dr. D11

### CEMETERIES
St. Isidore Cemetery E9
St. Paul Cemetery C12

### FOREST PRESERVES
Meacham Grove C11
Spring Creek Reservoir F.P. C12
Swift Prairie F.P. E13

### GOLF COURSES
Bloomingdale G.C. D12
Indian Lakes Golf Course D10
Indian Lakes Resort D10

### PARKS
Circle Park D11
Indian Lakes Park D10
Lakeview Park C12
Leslie Park D10
Springfield Park C10
Stratford Park D9
Sunnyside Park E12
Tompkins Park D11
Westlake Park D12

### SCHOOLS
Dist. 93 Admin Bldg. D9
DuJardin School D12
Erickson School C9
St. Isidore Sch. E9
Stratford Jr. H.S. D9
Westfield Jr. H.S. D11
Winnebago Sch. E11

### SHOPPING CENTERS
Bloomingdale Court E10
Old Towne S.C. C11
Springbrook S.C. C11
Stratford Plaza D8
Stratford Square D9

### MISCELLANEOUS
Bloomingdale Twp. Offices C11
Indian Lakes Resort D10
Library D11
Marklund Children's Home D12
Police Dept. D11
Post Office D11
Public Works E12
Village Hall D11
Water Reclamation Facility F12
Well #7 Pumping station C10

## BLOOMINGDALE TOWNSHIP
Pages 3,4,9,10

### STREETS
Abilene Trail Pg.3 C9
Acacia Ln. Pg.4 C12
Alma Ave. Pg.10 G13
Almond Ln. Pg.4 E11
Amy Ave. Pg.10 G11
Andrene Ln. Pg.4 A,B,D14
Andrews Ct. Pg.3 A9
Andrews Dr. Pg.3 A9
Ardmore Ave. Pg.3 B10
Argyle Ave. Pg.3 C9
Argyle St. Pg.10 G13
Armitage Ave. Pg.10 G13
Army Trail Rd. Pg.3 D,E8,E11
Atherton Ct. Pg.4 C11
Baker Dr. Pg.4 A,B14
Barbara Ct. Pg.4 C11
Bartels Rd. Pg.3 B8
Belden Ave. Pg.10 G13
Bernice Ave Pg.10 G11
Berwick Ct. Pg.3 A8
Black Duck Ln. Pg.3 D7
Blair Ln. Pg.4 E11
Bloomingdale Rd. Pg.4,10 D,G11
Bluebill Ct. Pg.3 D8
Briargate Terr. Pg.4 B13
Broker Ave. Pg.4 C12
Bryn Mawr Ave. Pg.3,4 B10,11
Bunker Terr. Pg.4 D13
Burdett Ave. Pg.9,10 G8,11-13
Byron Ave. Pg.4 E13
Canvasback Ln. Pg.3 D8
Carey Dr. Pg.4 E13
Central Ave. Pg.3 A9
Circle Terr. Pg.4 A13
Clarie Ct. Pg.9,10 G10
Cloverdale Rd. Pg.3 C8
Club Terr. Pg.4 C14
Collins Ave. Pg.10 F13
Cortland Ave. Pg.10 G13
Creekwood Ct. Pg.9 F7
Crest Ave. Pg.4 A13
Dale Rd. Pg.4 E11
Deerskin Terr. Pg.3 F7
Depot Pl. Pg.4 B13
Devon Ave. Pg.4 A11
Diane Ave. Pg.10 G11
Dickens Ave. Pg.10 G11,13
Dinah Ct. Pg.4 C11
Dinah Rd. Pg.4 C12
Drake Ln. Pg.3 D8
Eagle Ave. Pg.4 A13
Eagle Terr. Pg.4 B13
Edwards Ave. Pg.4 E13
Elizabeth Ct. Pg.4 C11
Elm St. Pg.10 G12
Ethel St. Pg.9 G7
Euclid Ave. Pg.10 G12
Fairway Ln. Pg.4 B,D13
Ferrari Ct. Pg.4 C11
Forest Ave. Pg.3 B11
Forest Dr. Pg.3,4 C11
Foster Ave. Pg.3,4 B9,12
Fullerton Ave. Pg.9 G9
Garden Ave. Pg.3 C10
Gary Ave. Pg.3 E9
Gates Ave. Pg.4 B13
Glen Ct. Pg.4 A13,C11
Glen Ellyn Rd. Pg.4 E12
Glen Rd. Pg.4 B13
Glendale Rd. Pg.4 B,C12
Glendale Terr. Pg.4 C13
Goldeneye Ln. Pg.3 D8
Goodrich Ave Pg.10 G12
Goodridge Terr. Pg.3 C11
Greenwood Ave. Pg.4 C11
Grove St. Pg.4 B13
Harvey Ave. Pg.4 B12
Harvey Rd. Pg.4 B12
Hawthorne Pg.4 A12
Helen St. Pg.10 G13
Hickory Ct. Pg.4 C13
Highland Ave. Pg.4,10 C,G12
Hill St. Pg.4 B11
Hillcrest Terr. Pg.4 C12,13
Hilldale Ln. Pg.4 E11
Hillside Ct. Pg.4 B12
Horncliff Dr. Pg.4 E11
Irving Park Rd Pg.4 B13
James Ct. Pg.4 C11
Jamison Dr. Pg.4 E11
John Ct. Pg.4 C11
Joseph Ct. Pg.4 C11
Juniper Dr. Pg.4 A12
Keeny Rd. Pg.3 C9
Kenmore St. Pg.10 G14
Kuhn Rd. Pg.3,9 E,G7
Lake St. Pg.3 B8,D13
Laramie Tr. Pg.3 C9
Laredo Tr. Pg.3 C9
Laurel Dr. Pg.4 C12
Lawler Ave. Pg.10 G14
Lawrence Ave. Pg.3,4 C9,12
Lawrence Ct. Pg.4 A13
Lies Rd. Pg.3 E,F8
Lincoln St. Pg.4 A11
Linda Ave. Pg.9 G,H10
Linden Ave. Pg.4 A,C12
Lloyd Ave. Pg.4,10 B,D,G14
Lydia Rd. Pg.4 F13
Magnolia Ave. Pg.10 F14
Mallard Ct. Pg.3 D8
Mallard Ln. Pg.3 D8
Mandarin Ln. Pg.3 D8
Manor Ln. Pg.4 B13
Maple Ave. Pg.3,4 B11,13
Maple Ct. Pg.4 C13
McWalter Ln. Pg.4 F13
Meacham Rd Pg.4 A12
Meadow Rd. Pg.10 F13
Medinah Rd. Pg.4 B,D13
Mensching Rd. Pg.3 B10
Merganser Ln. Pg.3 D8
Mesa Verde Ct. Pg.9 F7
Mildred Ave. Pg.10 G11
Murfield Dr. Pg.3 A8
Muscovy Ln. Pg.3 D8
Neva Terr. Pg.4 B13
Newland Pl Pg.4 B13
Nordic Rd. Pg.4 C13
North Ave. Pg.9,10 G8,11
Oak St. Pg.3,4 B11
Olive St. Pg.10 G11
Papworth St. Pg.3 C9
Par Ln. Pg.4 C13
Park Ave. Pg.10 F13
Payson Cir. Pg.4 E11
Pearl Ave. Pg.10 F13
Pearson Dr. Pg.3 B10
Petersen Ave. Pg.9,10 G8,13
Picton Rd. Pg.3 B11
Pintail Ct. Pg.3 D8
Pintail Ln. Pg.3 D8
Pleasant Ave. Pg.10 G12
Poplar Ave. Pg.4 A12
Prairie Ave. Pg.10 G11
Red Head Ln. Pg.3 D8
Ring Neck Ct. Pg.3 D7
Ring Neck Ln. Pg.3 D8
Robbie Ln. Pg.4 E13
Robert Ct. Pg.4 C11
Roberta Ave. Pg.9 G10
Rodenburg Rd. Pg.3 A9
Rosedale Ave. Pg.3 C10
Santa Fe Trail Pg.3 C9
Sauk Ct. Pg.9 F7
Schick Rd. Pg.3 D8,9
Schlick Ave. Pg.4 B13
Schmale Rd. Pg.9 E10
Shelley Dr. Pg.4 C14
Sidney Ave. Pg.10 G,G12
Sodaro Ct. Pg.4 C11
Spring Ct. Pg.4 B13
Spring Valley Dr. Pg.4 C12
Springwood Ct. Pg.3 A11
Springwood Dr. Pg.3 A11
Squire Ln. Pg.4 B13
St. Charles Rd. Pg.9 G8
St. Francis Ct. Pg.4 C12
Stone Ave. Pg.4 E13
Sunnyside Dr. Pg.4 B13
Sunset Ct. Pg.3 C9
Sunset Dr. Pg.4 C13
Sunset Terr. Pg.4 C12
Swift Rd. Pg.4 D,G13
Sycamore Ave. Pg.4 A,B,C12

Teal Ct. Pg.3 D8
Tee Ln. Pg.4 D13
Temple Dr. Pg.4 B12,13
Terrace Ct. Pg.4 B13
Thorn Rd. Pg.3 B,C8
Thorndale Ave. Pg.4 A13
Tucumcari Tr. Pg.3 C9
Turnberry Loop Pg.3 A8
Turner Ave. Pg.3,4 B10,11
Tuttle Dr. Pg.4 E13
Valley Ln. Pg.4 B13
Valley Rd. Pg.3 B11
Valley View Rd. Pg.4 F13
Virginia Ave. Pg.10 G11
Virginia Rd. Pg.3 B,C9
Walnut Ave. Pg.3,4 B11,12
Walter Dr. Pg.4 E13
Webster Ave. Pg.3,4 B9,12
West End Rd. Pg.3 B10
Wheaton Rd. Pg.3 C9
Widgeon Ln. Pg.3 D8
Willard St. Pg.10 G11
William St. Pg.3 A11
Willow St. Pg.4 B11
Winthrop Pg.10 G13
Woodview Dr. Pg.4 C13,B12
Woodworth Pl. Pg.3 B11
Wyatt Ln. Pg.4 E11
84th Ct. Pg.3 E8

**CEMETERIES**
St. Luke's Cem. Pg.4 C13

**FOREST PRESERVES**
E. Branch Res. Forest Preserve Pg.4,10 G13
Mallard Lake Forest Preserve Pg.3 C8

**GOLF COURSES**
Medinah C.C. Pg.4 C13
Nordic Hills C.C. Pg.4 C14

**PARKS**
Medinah Park Pg.4 A13

**SCHOOLS**
Benjamin Sch. Pg.8 G6
Dist. 25 Admin Bldg. Pg.8 G6
Medinah North Sch. Pg.4 A13

## BOLINGBROOK

Pages 26,27,28
(For additional listings, see Section 8)

**STREETS**
Aberdeen Ct. Pg.28 W12
Adams Ct. Pg.27 Z10
Adams St. Pg.27 Z9
Alcester Cir. Pg.28 X13
Alcester Ct. Pg.28 X12
Alcott Ln. Pg.27 Z10
Algonquin Cir. Pg.27 Y10
Alleghany Ct. Pg.28 Y11
Allen Deatherage Dr. Pg.26 Y7
Allison Ct. Pg.28 X12
Andover Ct. Pg.28 Z12
Anne Ct. Pg.28 W13
Anne Ln. Pg.28 W12,13
Annerino Dr. Pg.28 Z12
Antelope Ct. Pg.27 Z7
Apache Pg.27 Y10
Apple Valley Rd. Pg.27 Z7
Applewood Ct. Pg.27 Y8
Applewood Dr. Pg.27 Y8
Appling Ln. Pg.28 Y11
Arbor Pg.28 Z11
Arcadia Ct. Pg.28 Z11
Ardglass Ct. Pg.28 Y12
Aristocrat Pg.27 Z8
Arrowhead Ct. Pg.28 Y11
Arrowhead Ln. Pg.28 Y11
Ashbury Ave. Pg.28 X,Y12
Ashbury Ct. Pg.28 W13
Ashcroft Ct. Pg.26 Z6
Ashcroft Dr. Pg.26 Z6
Aspen Ct. Pg.28 Y11,Y,Z10
Aspen Dr. Pg.28 Y11
Assembly Ct. Pg.28 W13
Assembly Dr. Pg.28 X12
Autumn Wind Pg.28 Z11
Avondale Ct. Pg.28 Z11
Ayers St. Pg.27 X10
Bakersmill Dr. Pg.27 Z9
Baldwin Way Pg.27 Z7
Ballou Ct. Pg.27 W10
Balmoral Pg.28 Y12
Banbury Ct. Pg.28 W13
Banbury Way Pg.28 W13
Barbers Corners Rd. Pg.28 X11
Barnwood Dr. Pg.27 Y8
Beaconridge Dr. Pg.28 Z11
Beaver Creek Ct. Pg.26 Y7
Beaver Creek Dr. Pg.26 Y7
Bedford Pg.28 Y12
Beech Dr. Pg.27 Z9
Bellflower Ln. Pg.27 Z9
Bent Tree Ct. Pg.28 W12
Blackberry Pg.27 Z9
Blackfoot Dr. Pg.27 Z8
Blackhawk Ln. Pg.27 Y9
Blair Ln. Pg.27 Y10
Bloomfield Dr. Pg.27 Z10
Blosson Ridge Rd. Pg.27 Z7
Bluebird Ln. Pg.27 Z10
Boardman Cir. Pg.27 W10
Bolingbrook Dr. Pg.28 Z11
Bonnie Brae Ct. Pg.28 X12
Bonnie Brae Ln. Pg.28 W12
Bothwell Cir. Pg.27 Y9
Bothwell Ct. Pg.27 Y9
Bothwell Ln. Pg.27 Y9
Boughton Rd. Pg.27 Y9
Boulder Ridge Ct. Pg.26 Y7
Boulder Ridge Dr. Pg.26 Y7
Bowie Pg.27 Y10
Bowmans Ct. Pg.28 Y11,12
Bradford Pl. Pg.27 Z8
Braemer Glenn Ct. Pg.28 Z12
Bramble Pg.27 Z8
Brandon Ct. Pg.27 Y10
Briarcliff Dr. Pg.27 Z7
Briarcliff Rd. Pg.27 Z9-12
Brighton Ln. Pg.27 Y8
Bristol Ct. Pg.27 Z9
Bristol Way Pg.27 Z9
Brittany Ct. Pg.27 Z9
Brompton Cir. Pg.27 Y9
Brompton Ct. Pg.27 Y9
Brook Ct. Pg.28 Y11
Brookwood Ln. Pg.27 Y8
Buckeye Ln. Pg.27 Y10
Buckingham Way Pg.28 W12,X13
Buli Ln. Pg.27 Z8
Bunker Hill Pg.27 Z10
Bunting Cir. Pg.28 X12
Burr Oaks Ct. Pg.28 W13
Butte View Pg.27 Z7
Butternut Dr. Pg.27 Z9
Cades Ct. Pg.28 X12,13
Callery Ct. Pg.27 Z8
Callery Dr. Pg.27 Z8
Calumet Pg.27 Y10
Cambridge Way Pg.28 W13
Camden Ct. Pg.27 Y9
Camelot Way Pg.28 Y11
Campbell Dr. Pg.27 Y9
Candlelight Pg.28 Z11
Canterbury Pg.28 Z11
Canyon Ct. Pg.27 Z8
Canyon Rd. Pg.27 Y7
Capitol Dr. Pg.28 Y13
Cardinal Ln. Pg.27 Z7
Caribou Ct. Pg.26 Z7
Carmel Pg.27 Z10
Carol Ln. Pg.27 Y9
Carriage Ln. Pg.27 Y7
Caryle Pg.28 Z11
Castle Ct. Pg.28 X13
Castle Ln. Pg.27 Z10,11
Cebula Ct. Pg.27 X10
Cedarwood Pg.28 Z12
Cedarwood Ct. Pg.28 Z12
Chantileer Ave. Pg.27 Z8
Charlestown Pg.28 X12
Charlotte Ct. Pg.28 X12,W13
Charlotte Dr. Pg.28 W13
Chase Ct. Pg.28 Y11
Chelsea Ln. Pg.28 W13
Cherokee Rd. Pg.27 Y10
Cherry Ct. Pg.28 Y11
Chesapeake Dr. Pg.28 Y13
Cheshire Ct. Pg.28 Y12
Chestnut Ct. Pg.27 Z10
Chestnut Dr. Pg.27 Z10
Chestnut St. Pg.26 Z7
Cheyenne Ct. Pg.27 X,Y10
Chippewa Ct. Pg.27 Y10
Churchill Dr. Pg.27 Z8
Cider St. Pg.27 Z7
Cinnamon Pg.28 Z11
Clear Dr. Pg.27 Z7
Cleveland Dr. Pg.27 W10
Clifton Ln. Pg.27 Y9
Clover Ln. Pg.28 X11
Clow International Dr. Pg.27 Y8
Cobb Cir. Pg.27 Y10
Cochise Cir. Pg.27 Y10
Collinwood Ct. Pg.27 Y8
Collinwood Ln. Pg.27 Y8
Colony Ct. Pg.28 Z11
Columbine Ln. Pg.27 Z10
Columbus Dr. Pg.27 Y7
Comanche Dr. Pg.27 Z7
Commerce Dr. Pg.28 Z11
Commonwealth Ct. Pg.27 Y9
Commonwealth Dr. Pg.27 Y9
Concord Ln. Pg.28 X11
Copper Ct. Pg.27 Y9
Coral Ct. Pg.28 Y11
Cornwall Ct. Pg.28 X13
Cottonwood Cir. Pg.27 Y10
Cougar Rd. Pg.27 Z7
Country Ct. Pg.27 Y8
Country Ridge Pg.27 Y8
Coventry Ln. Pg.27 Y8
Creekside Pg.27 Z10
Crestwood Ct. Pg.27 Y9
Crestwood Ln. Pg.27 Y8
Crossing Rd. Pg.28 Z12
Cumberland Ln. Pg.27 Z10
Cypress Dr. Pg.28 Z11
Da Vinci Cir. Pg.28 X11
Dakota Pg.27 Y10
Daniels St. Pg.27 X10
Danube Way Pg.26 Z6
Davis Ct. Pg.28 Y11
Davis Ln. Pg.28 Y11
Dean Cir. Pg.28 Y11
Deerfield Pg.28 Z12
Degas Cir. Pg.28 X11
Delaware Cir. Pg.28 Y11
Delaware Dr. Pg.28 Y11
Delmar Dr. Pg.28 Z11
Denver Dr. Pg.27 Y,Z10
Derbyshire Ct. Pg.28 X12,W13
Derbyshire Ln. Pg.28 X12
Devon Ct. Pg.28 W13
Devon Ln. Pg.28 W12
Devonshire Ct. Pg.28 Z11
Diane Ln. Pg.28 W11
Dorchester Ct. Pg.28 X13
Dorchester Ln. Pg.28 X13
Douglas Way Pg.28 W11
Drake Ave. Pg.27 Z8
Drake Ct. Pg.27 Z8
Du Bois Cir. Pg.28 W11
Du Page Dr. Pg.27 Y10
Dunham Ct. Pg.28 W13
Dunham Ln. Pg.28 W13
Eagle Ct. Pg.27 Y10
Edgehill Dr. Pg.28 Z11
Edinburgh Ct. Pg.28 X12
Elkhorn Ct. Pg.27 Y10
Elm Ct. Pg.28 X11
Emerald Pg.28 Z11
Emerson Cir. Pg.27 Y10
Ennis Ct. Pg.28 W11
Ennis Ln. Pg.28 X12
Envee Dr. Pg.27 Y7
Eric Way Pg.28 X11
Essex Ct. Pg.27 Z10
Evergreen Pg.28 Z12
Everington Ct. Pg.28 W12
Fairgate Ln. Pg.27 Z8
Fairwood Ct. Pg.28 Z11
Fairwood Dr. Pg.28 Z11
Falcon Ridge Way Pg.28 X13,Y12
Falmore Ln. Pg.28 X11
Far Hills Pg.27 Z10
Farmgate Ln. Pg.27 Z8
Faversham Ct. Pg.28 Y13
Feather Sound Dr. Pg.28 X13
Fenview Ct. Pg.28 X13
Fernwood Dr. Pg.28 Z11
Fieldstone Pg.28 Z11
Flagstaff Dr. Pg.27 Y10
Fleetwood Pg.28 Z12
Forest Ct. Pg.28 Y13
Forest Way Pg.28 Y13
Fox Bend Cir. Pg.27 Z9
Foxglove Ct. Pg.27 Z10
Foxhead Ct. Pg.27 Y10
Frontage Rd. Pg.28 Z12
Fuller Rd. Pg.28 W11
Gainsborough Ln. Pg.28 Z11
Galahad Rd. Pg.28 Y12
Galewood Pg.27 Z10
Gannet Cir. Pg.28 X12
Gannet Ln. Pg.28 X12
Garden Pg.27 Z9
Gary Dr. Pg.28 Y12
Gehrig Cir. Pg.27 Y10
Genesee Ct. Pg.28 Y11
Gettysburg Dr. Pg.28 Z11
Gibraltar Dr. Pg.28 Z12
Glen Lake Ln. Pg.27 Y9
Glengary Dr. Pg.28 Z11
Goldfinch Ln. Pg.27 Z7
Grace Pg.28 Z11
Grady Dr. Pg.27 Z8
Granada Ct. Pg.28 Y11
Grand Canyon Dr. Pg.28 Y11
Grant Dr. Pg.28 Y11
Green Mt. Ct. Pg.28 Y13
Green Mt. Dr. Pg.28 Y13
Greencrest Pg.28 Y12
Greentree Ct. Pg.28 Z11
Greentree Ln. Pg.28 Z11
Greenwood Pg.28 Z12
Grosvenor Ct. Pg.28 W12
Grove Ct. Pg.27 Z9
Grove Ln. Pg.27 Z9
Hadleigh Pg.28 Y12
Hallmark Ln. Pg.27 Z10
Hampdon Ct. Pg.27 Z10
Hampshire Cir. Pg.28 X11,W13
Hampshire Ct. Pg.28 W13
Hampshire Ln. Pg.28 X12
Hanover Pg.28 Z12
Harmony Pg.28 Z11
Harris Dr. Pg.27 Z9
Hartford Ln. Pg.27 Y9
Harwood Dr. Pg.28 Z11
Haverhill Ct. Pg.28 W13
Hawk Dr. Pg.27 Z7
Hawthorne Ct. Pg.27 Z9
Hedgerow Ct. Pg.27 Z9
Hedgerow Ln. Pg.27 Z9
Heritage Ct. Pg.27 Y7
Hickory Oaks Ct. Pg.26 Y7
Hickory Oaks Dr. Pg.26 Y7
Hidden Valley Ct. Pg.26 Y7
Hidden Valley Dr. Pg.26 Y7
Highknob Pg.27 Z9
Highpoint Pg.28 Z11
Home Pl. Pg.27 Z8
Homer Dr. Pg.28 X11
Homestead Dr. Pg.28 Y13
Homewood Dr. Pg.28 Y13
Hood Ct. Pg.28 Y11
Hudson Dr. Pg.27 Y9
Hughes Pg.28 W11
Hummingbrid Ln. Pg.27 Z10
Huntington Way Pg.28 X11
Hywood Dr. Pg.28 Y11
Idlerwood Pg.28 Z12
Independence Ct. Pg.28 Y12
Ingleside Dr. Pg.27 Z8
Inner Cir. Pg.27 Z8
Internationale Dr. Pg.28 Z12
Ironbark Way Pg.28 Z12
Ivy Ct. Pg.26 Z6
Ivy Ln. Pg.26 Z6
Jameson Ct. Pg.28 Z12
Jamestown Ln. Pg.28 Z11
Jane Adams Rd. Pg.27 Z9
Janes Pg.28 Y13
Jeffery Ln. Pg.28 X11
Jennifer Ln. Pg.27 Y8
Jerome Ln. Pg.28 X11
Jill Ln. Pg.28 X11
Joliet-Naperville Rd. Pg.27 Z9
Jordon Way Pg.28 X11
Julie Rd. Pg.28 X11
Juniper Pg.28 Y11
Karen Cir. Pg.28 X11
Kedvale Ct. Pg.27 Y10
Kenilworth Pg.28 Y12
Kenmore Dr. Pg.28 Z12
Kensington Way Pg.22 W13
Kent Ct. Pg.28 W13
Keystone Ct. Pg.28 X13
Keystone Dr. Pg.28 X13
Kildeer Dr. Pg.28 X12
King Arthur Ct. Pg.28 X,Y13
King Arthur Way Pg.28 Y13
Kings Dr. Pg.27 Z7
Kings Rd. Pg.26 Z7
Kingston Rd. Pg.28 Z12
Kirkwood Cir. Pg.28 X11
Knight Ct. Pg.28 X13
Knollwood Pg.28 Z11
La Crosse Pg.27 Y10
Lafayette Dr. Pg.28 Y11
Lakeside Pg.28 Y13
Lakeview Cir. Pg.28 Y11
Lakewood Ct. Pg.27 Y8
Lancaster Pg.27 Y,Z10
Lancelot Ct. Pg.28 Y12
Lancelot Way Pg.28 Y12
Langford Ct. Pg.28 X13
Langford Dr. Pg.28 X12
Larchmont Pg.27 Z9
Larkspur St. Pg.27 Z10
Laurie Cir. Pg.28 Y13
Lavina Ct. Pg.27 X10
Lavina Dr. Pg.27 X10
Lawton Ln. Pg.28 Z12
Lee Ln. Pg.28 Y11
Leicester Ct. Pg.28 Y13
Leslie Ln. Pg.28 X11
Lexington Dr. Pg.28 Y13
Liberty Pg.28 X12
Liberty Ct. Pg.28 X13
Lily Cache Ln. Pg.27 Z9,10
Lilyfield Ct. Pg.27 Z8
Lilyfield Ln. Pg.27 Z8
Lincolnshire Pg.28 Y11
Linden Ct. Pg.27 Z9
Lindsey Ct. Pg.27 Y9
Lindsey Ln. Pg.27 Y9
Loire Rd. Pg.26 Z6
Londonberry Ct. Pg.28 W13
Londonberry Ln. Pg.28 W13
Long Ln. Pg.28 Z10
Lotus Dr. Pg.27 Y10
Lyons Rd. Pg.27 Y10
Magellen Dr. Pg.27 Y7,8
Malibu Pg.28 Y,Z12
Malibu Ct. Pg.28 Y12
Mallard Ct. Pg.28 X13
Mallard Landing Pg.28 Z12
Mallview Ln. Pg.28 Z11
Manor Ct. Pg.28 Z11
Maplewood Pg.27 Z10
Marine Rd. Pg.26 Z6
Maroon Bells Ct. Pg.27 Z7
Maroon Bells Ln. Pg.27 Z7
Marquette Ct. Pg.28 X13
Marywood Pg.28 Y11
Mayfield Pg.27 Y10
Mayflower Ln. Pg.27 Y7
Meadowbrook Dr. Pg.28 Y12
Meadowlark Ln. Pg.27 Z10
Melissa Dr. Pg.28 Y13
Mellbrook Pg.28 Z12
Melody Pg.28 Z11
Merlin Ct. Pg.28 Y12
Merrill Ct. Pg.27 Y8
Merrimack Ct. Pg.28 Y11
Mesa Dr. Pg.27 Z7
Michelangelo Dr. Pg.28 X11
Mill Stream Pg.27 Z10
Miner Ct. Pg.28 X12
Miner Dr. Pg.28 Y13
Monarch Ln. Pg.27 Z10
Monet Cir. Pg.28 X11
Monroe Rd. Pg.28 W11
Monterey Pg.28 Y12
Monticello Cir. Pg.28 Y11
Moore Dr. Pg.28 X11
Murphy Rd. Pg.28 Z14
Musial Cir. Pg.28 Y11
Naperville Rd. Pg.27 Y,Z8
Nausau Ave. Pg.28 Y12
Navajo Pg.27 Y10
Navajo Ct. Pg.27 Y10
Nelson Ct. Pg.28 W12
Newbury Ln. Pg.28 Z11
Newcastle Ln. Pg.28 Z11
Newport Pg.27 Z10
Newton Ct. Pg.28 Y12
Niagara Pg.28 Y13
Nicholas Ct. Pg.27 Y7
Nicholas Dr. Pg.27 Y7
Norman Pg.28 W11
Norman Way Pg.28 W11
Northridge Ave. Pg.28 Y12
Nottingham Pg.27 Y10
Nutwood Ct. Pg.28 Z12
Oak Ridge Ct. Pg.28 Y12
Oakwood Pg.27 Z10
Old Elm Pg.27 Y10
Old Stone Pg.27 Z10
Olive Ct. Pg.28 X11
Olympic Pg.28 Y12
Orchard Dr. Pg.27 Z9
Ottawa Pg.27 Y10
Oxford Rd. Pg.28 Z12
Ozark Pg.27 Y10
Pacific Pg.28 Y12
Paddington Ln. Pg.27 Y8
Pamela Way Pg.28 X11
Park Ct. Pg.28 Z12
Park Meadows Pg.27 Y8
Parklawn Ct. Pg.28 Y12
Partridge Pg.27 Z8
Paxson Ct. Pg.27 X10
Paxson Dr. Pg.27 X10
Payton Ln. Pg.27 Z10
Peace Ave. Pg.26 Z6
Peachtree Pg.28 Z11
Pebble Ct. Pg.27 Y8
Pembrook Ct. Pg.27 Y9
Pennsbury Ct. Pg.27 Y9
Penny Ct. Pg.27 Y9
Penny Ln. Pg.27 Y9
Penwood Ln. Pg.27 Y9
Pepperwood Pg.27 Z10
Perwinkle Ln. Pg.27 Z7
Pheasant Chase Ct. Pg.27 Z7
Pheasant Chase Dr. Pg.27 Z8
Pheasant Run Pg.28 X13,Z12
Picardy Ln. Pg.27 Y8
Piccadilly Ct. Pg.28 W13
Piccadilly Ln. Pg.28 W13
Pierce Ct. Pg.28 Y11
Pilgrims Ct. Pg.28 Z11
Pinecrest Ct. Pg.28 X13
Pinecrest Rd. Pg.28 X-Z12
Pinto Dr. Pg.27 Y10
Plainview Ct. Pg.27 Z9
Plainview Dr. Pg.27 Z9
Plot One Pg.28 X11
Plumtree Pg.28 Z11
Plymouth Ln. Pg.28 Y11
Ponderosa Pg.27 Z10
Pontiac Ln. Pg.27 Y10
Poplar Ln. Pg.27 Z9
Porter Ln. Pg.28 W12
Portsmith Ln. Pg.27 Z9
Potomac Ct. Pg.28 Y11
Prairie Cir. Pg.27 Z10
Preston Dr. Pg.28 X13
Prestwick Ct. Pg.28 W12
Princeton Pg.27 Z10
Providence Ct. Pg.28 Z11
Pueblo Dr. Pg.27 Y9
Puffin Cir. Pg.28 X13
Quadrangle Dr. Pg.28 Z11
Quail Run Pg.27 Z8
Quarry Pg.27 Z8
Queenswood Pg.28 Y13
Racine Ln. Pg.28 X11
Radcliff Pg.27 Z10
Raintree Pg.28 W12
Raphael Cir. Pg.28 X11
Raven Ct. Pg.27 Z7
Raven Dr. Pg.27 Z7
Recreation Dr. Pg.28 Z12
Red Bud Ct. Pg.26 Z6
Red Bud Rd. Pg.26 Z6
Redspire Ct. Pg.27 Z8
Redwing Ct. Pg.27 Y9
Redwood Rd. Pg.28 Y13
Regent Ct. Pg.27 Y9
Remington Lake Dr. Pg.27 Z9
Revere Ct. Pg.28 X13
Rhine Ave. Pg.26 Z6
Richmond Pg.27 Z10
Ridgewood Ct. Pg.27 Z8
Ridgewood Dr. Pg.27 Z8
Riverside St. Pg.28 Y12
Roanoke Ct. Pg.28 Y11
Roberts Rd. Pg.28 X11
Robin Hood Way Pg.28 Y11
Rockhurst Rd. Pg.28 Y11,12
Rocklin Ct. Pg.27 Z10
Rolling Meadows Ct. Pg.27 Z9
Roman Cir. Pg.28 Y13
Rosebud Pg.28 Z11
Rothbury Dr. Pg.28 X12
Round Hill Ct. Pg.28 Y13
Royal Crest Pg.28 W12
Rye Ct. Pg.28 X13
Saffron Ln. Pg.26 Z6
Salem Square Pg.28 Z11
Sandlewood Ct. Pg.27 Y8
Sandlewood Ln. Pg.27 Y8
Sauk Pg.27 Y10
Schmidt Rd. Pg.27 Z10
Scotts Ct. Pg.28 W12
Seabury Rd. Pg.28 Y12
Seminole Pg.27 Y10
Seneca Pg.27 Y10
Seneca Ct. Pg.27 Y10
Seth St. Pg.27 X10
Shaman Dr. Pg.27 Z7
Sharon Way Pg.28 X11
Sheffield Ln. Pg.28 W13
Shenandoah Pg.28 Y11
Sherington Ct. Pg.28 Z12
Sherwood Ct. Pg.28 Y12
Shield Ct. Pg.28 Y12
Shilling Ct. Pg.28 X13
Sierra Pg.27 Y10
Silverado Ct. Pg.27 Z7
Silverado St. Pg.27 Z7
Sioux Pg.27 Y10
Skokie Pg.27 Y10
Somerset Ct. Pg.28 Z11
Sparrow Ln. Pg.26 Z6
Speckman Ct. Pg.27 X10
Springhill Pg.27 Z10
Springleaf Dr. Pg.27 Z10
Springwood Way Pg.27 Y9
Spruce Rd. Pg.28 Y13
St. Andrews Dr. Pg.28 W12
Stafford Ct. Pg.28 Y12
Stafford Way Pg.28 Y12
Standish Ct. Pg.28 Z11
Staunton Ct. Pg.28 Y12
Steamboat Ln. Pg.26 Z7
Steck Ct. Pg.27 X10
Stonecreek Pg.28 W12
Stonegate Ct. Pg.27 Y8
Stoneham Ct. Pg.28 Y12,13
Strong Pg.27 X10
Sulgrave Ct. Pg.28 W12
Sullivan Cir. Pg.28 X11
Summer Breeze Pg.28 Z11
Summit Ln. Pg.27 Z9
Sundance Pg.27 Y10
Sunflower Ct. Pg.28 X12
Sunset Pg.28 Y12
Sunshine Ct. Pg.27 Y7
Sunshine Dr. Pg.27 Y7
Sussex Ln. Pg.28 W13
Swan Cir. Pg.28 X13
Swimford Ct. Pg.28 X11
Sword Way Pg.28 Y13
Sylvan Pg.28 Y12
Tahoe St. Pg.27 Z8
Talcott Ct. Pg.28 Y12
Tall Oaks Ct. Pg.28 W13
Tam O'Shanter Pg.28 W12
Tamarack Pg.27 Z10
Tamms Ln. Pg.27 Z9
Tangley Pg.28 W12
Taylor Ct. Pg.27 Z8
Tecumseh Dr. Pg.27 Z7
Thackery Dr. Pg.27 Z8
Thistle Pg.27 Z8
Thomas Rd. Pg.28 X11
Thornhurst Rd. Pg.28 Y12
Tilden Ln. Pg.27 Z8
Timber Ct. Pg.28 Z11
Timber Mill Ct. Pg.26 Z6
Tolios Dr. Pg.28 Z15
Tomahawk Cir. Pg.27 Y10
Totem Pl. Pg.27 Y9
Towner Ln. Pg.27 Z8
Tracy Way Pg.28 X11
Trafalgar Ct. Pg.28 W12
Tree Ct. Pg.28 W11
Treehouse Ct. Pg.27 Z7
Trout Farm Rd. Pg.27 X10
Truman St. Pg.27 X10
Tudor Ct. Pg.28 Y12
Turtle Dr. Pg.27 Y7
Twin Creek Ct. Pg.28 W12
Twin Creek Dr. Pg.28 W12
Upton Rd. Pg.28 Z13
Valley Dr. Pg.27 Z10
Van Gogh Cir. Pg.28 X11
Venetian Dr. Pg.28 Z12
Vermont Cir. Pg.28 X13
Vernon Dr. Pg.28 Y12
Victoria Ct. Pg.28 W12
Vigilance Ct. Pg.28 X13
Vincent Dr. Pg.27 Y7
Vista Dr. Pg.27 Y7
Walden Ct. Pg.27 Y8
Walker Dr. Pg.28 W11
Walnut Cir. Pg.28 X11
Walsh Pg.27 Y8
Warwick Ct. Pg.28 Y12
Waterman Dr. Pg.27 Z9
Weathersfield Way Pg.28 Z12
Weber Rd. Pg.27 Z8
Wedgewood Way Pg.28 Y11
Wellington Ln. Pg.28 Z11
Wescott Ct. Pg.27 W10
Wescott Rd. Pg.27 W10
West Wind Pg.27 Z9
Westchester Ct. Pg.28 X12
Westchester Ln. Pg.28 X13
Westly Ct. Pg.27 Z9
Whispering Pg.28 Z11
Whitby Ct. Pg.28 Y13
White Oak Rd. Pg.28 Y13
Whitehall Ct. Pg.28 W13
Whitehall Way Pg.28 W12
Whitewater Dr. Pg.27 Y10
Wildflower Way Pg.27 Z10
Wildrose Pg.28 Z11
Wildwood Pg.28 X11
Williams Rd. Pg.27 Z8
Williamsburg Ln. Pg.28 Z11
Willow Bend Rd. Pg.27 Z7
Willow Ct. Pg.28 X13
Willoway Pg.28 Y13
Wilshire Ln. Pg.27 Z10
Wimbledon Ct. Pg.28 W12
Winchester Pg.28 Z12
Wind Crest Pg.28 Z11
Windsor Ave. Pg.28 Y12
Windsor Dr. Pg.27 Y10
Wingren Pg.27 Y8
Winston Ct. Pg.28 X11
Winston Dr. Pg.28 X11
Winterberry Ct. Pg.28 X13
Wobbler Dr. Pg.28 X13
Wood Ct. Pg.27 Y8
Woodlet Ln. Pg.26 Z6
Wright Ct. Pg.28 X11
Wyeth Cir. Pg.28 X11
Yellow Pine Rd. Pg.27 Y10
York St. Pg.28 Y11
Yorkshire Ln. Pg.28 Z11
Yukon Dr. Pg.26 Z6
107th St. Pg.27 Z9

**CEMETERIES**
Boardman Cemetery Pg.27 X10

**GOLF COURSES**
Boughton Ridge G.C. Pg.28 Y12

**PARKS**
Balstrode Park Pg.27 Z8
Cherry Park Pg.28 Y,Z11
Cherry Wood Park Pg.28 Y11
Du Page River Greenway Pg.27 X10
Erickson Park Pg.27 Y10
Heritage Park Pg.27 X10
Indian Boundary Park Pg.27 Y9
Ivanhoe Park Pg.28 Y12
Jaycee Park Pg.27 Z10
Poplar Park Pg.27 Z9
Recreation Park Pg.28 Z12
River Bend Park Pg.27 Z7
Rotary Park Pg.28 Z12
Schraeder Park Pg.28 Z12
Two Rivers Plaza Pg.27 Y8
Winston Wood Pg.28 X12
Wipfler Park Pg.28 Y13

**SCHOOLS**
Bolingbrook H.S. Pg.27 Y10
Boughton Sch. Pg.27 Y10
Humphrey Middle Sch. Pg.28 Y13
Independence Sch. Pg.27 Z10
Jane Addams Middle Sch. Pg.27 Z9
McGee Elem. Sch. Pg.27 Y8
Oak View Sch. Pg.27 Y10
Salk Sch. Pg.28 Y13
St. Dominic Sch. Pg.28 Z12
Tibott Elem. Sch. Pg.28 Y12
Ward Middle Sch. Pg.28 Z12
Wayne Buita Elem. Sch. Pg.27 Z7
Wood View Sch. Pg.28 X12

**SHOPPING CENTERS**
Commons S.C. Pg.28 Z11
Market Square S.C. Pg.28 Z11
Pheasant Hill Plaza Pg.28 Z11
Shopping Centers Pg.27 Y10,11,Z13

**MISCELLANEOUS**
Annerino Comm. Center Pg.28 Z12
Bolingbrook Aquatic Center Pg.28 Z11
Bolingbrook Town Center Pg.28 Z11
Clow Airport Pg.27 Z8
Drdak Center Pg.28 Z12
DuPage Township Office Pg.27 Z10
Fire Department Pg.28 Z12
Hidden Lakes Historic Trout Farm Pg.27 X10
Levy Senior Ctr. Pg.28 Z11
Library Pg.28 Z11
Recreation Aquatic Center Pg.27 Z9
Remington Lakes Bus. Res. Tech. Campus Pg.27 Z9
Salem Comm. Center Pg.28 Z11
Suburban Health Care Pg.28 Z11
Village Hall/Police Dept. Pg.28 Y11

## BURR RIDGE

Pages 24,30
(For additional listings, see Section 1)

**STREETS**
Aintree Ln. Pg.24 W19
Ambriance Dr. Pg.24 V20
Andrew Ct. Pg.24 S19
Arbor Pg.24 U21
Arcadia Ct. Pg.30 X19
Arrowhead Farm Dr. Pg.24 W20
Bark Ln. Pg.24 V21
Bay Rum Ct. Pg.24 W19
Bel-Air Ct. Pg.30 X20
Bennacott Ln. Pg.24 W20
Berkshire Ct. Pg.24 V20
Briarwood Ct. Pg.24 U21
Briarwood Dr. Pg.24 W19
Briarwood Ln. Pg.24 V21
Bridewell Dr. Pg.24 U,V21
Bridget Ct. Pg.24 U20
Bridle Ct. Pg.24 W20
Brighton Pl. Pg.24 T21
Buck Tr. Pg.24 V21
Burr Oak Ln. Pg.24 V21
Burr Ridge Club Dr. Pg.24 T20
Burr Ridge Pkwy. Pg.24 V21
Buttercup Bank Pg.24 S20
Cambridge Dr. Pg.24 W19
Camelot Dr. Pg.24 W19
Canterbury Dr. Pg.24 W19
Carlisle Ct. Pg.24 W19
Carriage Pl. Pg.24 T20
Carriage Way Pg.24 T21
Cascade Cir. Pg.30 X19
Case Dr. Pg.24 U20
Central Ave. Pg.24 U21
Charleston Dr. Pg.24 W19
Chasemoor Dr. Pg.24 V21
Chesterfield Ct. Pg.24 V20
Chestnut Hills Ct. Pg.24 U20
Chestnut Hills Dr. Pg.24 U20
Chippewa Ct. Pg.24 W20
Circle Rd. Pg.24 U21
Circle Ridge Dr. Pg.30 X19
Clover Pg.24 S20

Clubside Ct. . . Pg.24 . . . S19
Clyndervan Rd. Pg.24 . . W19
Commerce St. Pg.24 . . . U20
Commonwealth Pg.24 . . . U21
Conway Ct. . . Pg.24 . . W19
Cook-DuPage Rd.
. . . . . . . . . Pg.24 . . W20
Countryside Ct. Pg.24 . . . T20
County Line Creek
. . . . . . . . . . Pg.30 . . . X20
County Line Dr. Pg.24 . . . V20
County Line Ln. Pg.24 . . . U20
County Line Rd. Pg.24 . . . U20
Cove Creek Ct. Pg.24 . . . T20
Cove Ct. . . . . . Pg.24 . . W20
Creekwood Dr. Pg.24 . . . V21
Ct.1 . . . . . . . . Pg.24 . . . V20
Ct.2 . . . . . . . . Pg.24 . . . V20
Ct.3 . . . . . . . . Pg.24 . . . V21
Ct.4 . . . . . . . . Pg.24 . . . V21
Ct.5 . . . . . . . . Pg.24 . . . V21
Ct.6 . . . . . . . . Pg.24 . . . V21
Ct.7 . . . . . . . . Pg.24 . . . V21
Ct.8 . . . . . . . . Pg.24 . . . V20
Dana Way . . . Pg.24 . . . U21
Deer Path Tr. . Pg.24 . . W20
Deerview Ct. . Pg.24 . . . V21
Devon Ct. . . . . Pg.24 . . W20
Devon Dr. . . . Pg.24 . . W19
Devon Ridge Dr. Pg.30 . . X19
Dolfor Cove . . Pg.24 . . W20
Dougshire Ct. . Pg.24 . . . S21
Dragonfly . . . . Pg.24 . . . S20
Drew Ave. . . . Pg.30 . V,X20
East Pl. . . . . . Pg.24 . . . V21
East Trail Ln. . Pg.24 . . . U21
Elm Ave. . . . . Pg.24 . . . U20
Elm St. . . . . . Pg.24 . . . T20
Enclave Ct. . . Pg.30 . . . X20
Enclave Dr. . . Pg.30 . . . X20
Erin Ln. . . . . . Pg.24 . . . T21
Fairelms . . . . . Pg.24 . . . U21
Falling Water Dr. Pg.30 . . . X19
Fawn Ct. . . . . Pg.24 . . W20
Fieldstone Dr. Pg.24 . . . T20
Forest Hill Rd. Pg.24 . . . U21
Fox Ln. . . . . . Pg.24 . . . V21
Foxborough Dr. Pg.24 . . . V21
Frontage Rd. . Pg.24 . U,V20
Frontage Rd. . Pg.24 . . . V20
Garfield Ave. . Pg.24 . U-W20
Garywood Dr. Pg.24 . . . T21
German Church Rd.
. . . . . . . . . Pg.24 . . W21
Giddings Ave. Pg.24 . . . U20
Glen Dr. . . . . . Pg.30 . . X19
Glenmora Ct. . Pg.24 . . . X20
Grant St. . . . . Pg.24 S,U-W20
Gregford Rd. . Pg.24 . . . S21
Greystone Ct. . Pg.24 . . W19
Hamilton Ave. Pg.24 . . . V20
Hampton Ct. . Pg.24 . . . T21
Hanover Ct. . . Pg.24 . . W20
Heather Dr. . . Pg.24 . . W20
Heathrow Ct. . Pg.24 . . . V20
Hidden Lake Dr. Pg.24 . . W20
High Grove Blvd. Pg.24 . . . U19
Hillcrest Ct. . . Pg.24 . . . T21
Hillcrest Ln. . . Pg.24 . . . T21
Hunter Ct. . . . Pg.24 . . W20
Huntington Ct. Pg.24 . . . V21
International St. Pg.24 . . . T20
Jack Pines Ln. Pg.24 . . . U20
Jelen Ct. . . . . Pg.24 . . W20
Joy Ct. . . . . . Pg.24 . . . X20
Kathryn Ct. . . Pg.24 . . W20
Keller Dr. . . . . Pg.24 . . . T19
Keri Ln. . . . . . Pg.30 . . . X19
Kimberly Ct. . . Pg.24 . . W19
Kirkwood Cove Pg.24 . . W20
Kraml Estate . Pg.24 . . W19
Kraml Dr. . . . . Pg.24 . . W19
Lake Ridge Ct. Pg.24 . . W20
Lake Ridge Dr. Pg.24 . . W20
Lakewood Cir. Pg.24 . . W20
Lakewood Ln. Pg.24 . . W19
Lancaster Ct. . Pg.24 . . . V20
Laurel Oak Ct. Pg.24 . . . X20
Laurie Ct. . . . . Pg.24 . . . S21
Laurie Ln. . . . . Pg.24 . . . S21
Leonard Ln. . . Pg.24 . . W20
Lincolnshire Dr. Pg.24 . . . U21
Longwood Dr. Pg.24 . . . T20
Madison Ave. . Pg.30 . . . X19
Malibu Ct. . . . Pg.30 . . . X20
Mallory Ct. . . . Pg.24 . . . U20
Manor Dr. . . . . Pg.24 . . . T21
Marissa Ct. . . Pg.30 . . . X19
McClintock Dr. Pg.24 . . . V21
Meadow . . . . . Pg.24 . . . S20
Meadowbrook Dr.
. . . . . . . . . Pg.24 . . W19
Morgan Ct. . . Pg.30 . . . X20
Navajo Ct. . . . Pg.24 . . W20
Norman Ct. . . Pg.30 . . . X20
Norris Dr. . . . . Pg.24 . . . T19
Northgate Pl. . Pg.24 . . . V21
Oak Creek Dr. Pg.30 . . . X20
Oak Ridge Dr. Pg.30 . . . X19
Oak Werth Ln. Pg.24 . . . V20
Old Mill Ct. . . Pg.24 . . . U21
Old Mill Ln. . . Pg.24 . . . U21
Old Surrey Rd. Pg.24 . . . S19
Omaha Dr. . . . Pg.24 . . W20
Pacific Ct. . . . Pg.24 . . . Y19
Park Ave. . . . . Pg.24 . . T,W20
Parkview Ct. . . Pg.24 . . W19
Parkview Pl. . . Pg.24 . . W20
Pepper Mill Ct. Pg.24 . . . T20
Pheasant Hollow Dr.
. . . . . . . . . Pg.24 . . . T20
Pine Tree Rd. . Pg.24 . . . V20
Polo Ridge . . . Pg.24 . . W19
Post Rd. . . . . . Pg.24 . . . T20
Prairie Ridge Ct. Pg.24 . . W19
Provincial Dr. . Pg.30 . . . X19
Purdie Ct. . . . Pg.24 . . . T20
Quincy St. . . . Pg.24 . . . S19
Regent Ct. . . . Pg.30 . . . X20
Ridge Farm Rd. Pg.24 . . . T20
Ridgepoint Dr. Pg.24 . . W20
Ridgewood Ln. Pg.24 . . . V21
Roanoke Ct. . . Pg.24 . . W19
Rockwell Ct. . . Pg.24 . . . V20
Rodeo Dr. . . . Pg.30 . . . X20
Rosemere Ct. . Pg.24 . . . V21
Royal Dr. . . . . Pg.30 . . . X20
Rucci Ct. . . . . Pg.24 . . . T21
Saddle Ct. . . . Pg.24 . . W20
Sedgley Ave. . Pg.24 . . . S20
Seneca Ct. . . . Pg.24 . . W20
Shadylane Rd. Pg.24 . . . T20
Shag Bark Ct. Pg.24 . . . U21
Shag Bark Ln. Pg.24 . . . V21
Shenandoah Ct. Pg.24 . . W20
Shepard Ln. . . Pg.30 . . . X19
Shiloh Ct. . . . Pg.24 . . W19
Shore Ct. . . . . Pg.24 . . W19
Shore Dr. . . . . Pg.24 . . . V19
Southgate Ct. . Pg.24 . . . V21
St. James Ct. . Pg.24 . . . T21
Steeplechase Dr. Pg.24 . . W20
Steepleside Dr. Pg.24 . . . V21
Stirrup Ln. . . . Pg.24 . . . T21
Stirrup Pl. . . . Pg.24 . . . T20
Stonehenge Ct. Pg.24 . . . V21
Surrey La. . . . Pg.24 . . . U20
Sylvan Glen Ct. Pg.30 . . . X19
Tamerton Pkwy. Pg.24 . . W20
Tartan Ridge Rd. Pg.24 . . . S21
Thornhill Ct. . . Pg.24 . . . V21
Thurlow St. . . Pg.24 . . W19
Timber Ridge Ln.
. . . . . . . . . Pg.24 . . W19
Tomlin Cir. . . . Pg.24 . . . T21
Tomlin Dr. . . . Pg.24 . . . T21
Tori Ct. . . . . . Pg.30 . . . X20
Tower Dr. . . . . Pg.24 . . . U20
Trent Ct. . . . . Pg.24 . . . V21
Tudor Ct. . . . . Pg.24 . . W20
Turnberry Ct. . Pg.30 . . . X19
Walnut Ct. . . . Pg.24 . . . V21
Walredon Ave. Pg.24 . . W20
Waterside Pl. . Pg.24 . . . V21
Wedgewood Dr. Pg.24 . . W20
Westminster Dr. Pg.24 . . . X20
White Oak Ct. . Pg.24 . . . V21
Wildwood Ln. . Pg.24 . . . T19
Windsor Ct. . . Pg.24 . . W20
Wolf Rd. . . . . . Pg.24 . . . U21
Wood Ct. . . . . Pg.24 . . . V21
Woodcreek Ct. Pg.24 . . S,T19
Woodcreek Dr. Pg.24 . . . T20
Woodgate Dr. . Pg.24 . . . T20
Woodglen . . . . Pg.24 . . . V21
Woodside Ct. . Pg.24 . . . V21
Woodside Ln. . Pg.24 . . . V21
Woodview Rd. Pg.24 . . . S21
60th Pl. . . . . . Pg.24 . . . S20
60th St. . . . . . Pg.24 . . . S20
61st Pl. . . . . . Pg.24 . . . T20
61st St. . . . . . Pg.24 . . . T20
62nd St. . . . . . Pg.24 . . . T20
63rd St. . . . . . Pg.24 . . . T20
67th St. . . . . . Pg.24 . . . T20
71st St. . . . . . Pg.24 . . . U19
72nd St. . . . . . Pg.24 . . . U20
73rd St. . . . . . Pg.24 . . . U20
74th St. . . . . . Pg.24 . . . U21
75th St. . . . . . Pg.24 . . . V20
77th St. . . . . . Pg.24 . . . V20
79th St. . . . . . Pg.24 . . . V19
80th St. . . . . . Pg.24 . . . V20
81st St. . . . . . Pg.24 . . . V20
83rd Ct. . . . . . Pg.24 . . W19
83rd St. . . . . . Pg.24 . . W19
87th St. . . . . . Pg.24 . . W20
90th St. . . . . . Pg.30 . . . X19
94th . . . . . . . . Pg.30 . . . X19

**FOREST PRESERVES**

Burr Oak Forest Preserve
. . . . . . . . . Pg.24 . . . U20

**PARKS**

County Line Estate Park
. . . . . . . . . Pg.24 . . W20
Garywood Park Pg.24 . . . T21
Harvester Park Pg.24 . . . U20
Lake Ridge Club Pg.24 . . . V19
Lakewood Park Pg.24 . . W20
McCullough Park
. . . . . . . . . Pg.24 . . . T20
Palisades/Devon Park
. . . . . . . . . Pg.30 . . . X20
Park Center Park
. . . . . . . . . Pg.30 . . . X19
Rustic Acres Rec. Bldg.
. . . . . . . . . Pg.30 . . . X20
Stevens Park . Pg.24 . . W20
Whittaker Park Pg.24 . . . V20

**SCHOOLS**

Burr Ridge Middle Sch.
. . . . . . . . . Pg.30 . . . X20
Elm Sch. . . . . Pg.24 . . . S20
Gower Middle School
. . . . . . . . . Pg.24 . . . V19
Pleasant Dale Sch.
. . . . . . . . . Pg.24 . . . U21

**MISCELLANEOUS**

Bonaparte Program-Hanson Center . . . . Pg.24 . . . S20
Village Hall . . Pg.24 . . . V20
Public Works . Pg.9 . . . . G9

## CAROL STREAM

Pages 2,3,8,9

**STREETS**

Adam Ln. . . . . Pg.9 . . . . . F7
Adler Ln. . . . . Pg.3 . . . . . E8
Adobe Ct. . . . . Pg.9 . . . . . F8
Alabama Tr. . . Pg.3 . . . . . E8
Alamo Ct. . . . . Pg.3 . . . . . F8
Aleut Trail . . . Pg.3 . . . . . E8
Alexandra Way Pg.9 . . . . . G9
Alison Ln. . . . . Pg.3 . . . . . F7
Allegheny Ct. . Pg.8 . . . . . F7
Allegro Ln. . . . Pg.3 . . . . . F8
Alton Ct. . . . . . Pg.8 . . . . . G7
Amber Ct. . . . . Pg.9 . . . . H10
Amber Ln. . . . . Pg.9 . . . . H10
Andrew Ln. . . . Pg.9 . . . . . F7
Antelope Tr. . . Pg.3 . . . . . E8
Antigo Tr. . . . . Pg.2 . . . . . D6
Apache Ln. . . . Pg.9 . . . . . G8
Appaloosa Tr. . Pg.9 . . . . . F7
Appomattox Tr. Pg.2 . . . . . E6
Arapahoe Trail Pg.9 . . . . . G8
Arbor Dr. . . . . Pg.9 . . . . . F9
Army Trail Rd. Pg.3 . . . . . D8
Arrowhead Trail Pg.9 . . . . . F8
Ash Ct. . . . . . . Pg.2 . . . . . E6
Aspen Ct. . . . . Pg.3 . . . . . E8
Aztec Dr. . . . . Pg.3 . . . . . F7
Barton Pl. . . . . Pg.8 . . . . . G7
Basswood Ct. . Pg.3 . . . . . E8
Baybrook Ln. . Pg.2 . . . . . E7
Bear Paw Ct. . Pg.2 . . . . . F6
Bedford Dr. . . . Pg.3 . . . . . E8
Beech Ct. . . . . Pg.3 . . . . . E8
Belair Ct. . . . . Pg.9 . . . . . F8
Bennington Dr. Pg.2 . . . . . E6
Berkshire Ln. . Pg.2 . . . . . G7
Big Eagle Tr. . Pg.2 . . . . . F6
Big Horn Tr. . . Pg.2 . . . . . E6
Biloxie Ct. . . . Pg.8,9 . . . . F7
Birchbark Tr. . Pg.2 . . . . . F7
Bison Tr. . . . . Pg.2 . . . . . F6
Blackhawk Dr. Pg.9 . . . . . G9
Blake Ct. . . . . Pg.8 . . . . . F5
Bluff St. . . . . . Pg.9 . . . . . F8
Boa Tr. . . . . . . Pg.2 . . . . . E6
Boone Dr. . . . . Pg.3 . . . . . F8
Bowie Dr. . . . . Pg.3 . . . . E,F8
Bowstring Ct. . Pg.2 . . . . . E5
Bradbury Cir. . Pg.3 . . . . . E8
Brave Ct. . . . . Pg.2 . . . . . E6
Brighton Dr. . . Pg.2 . . . . . F6
Bristol Dr. . . . . Pg.9 . . . . . F7
Brompton Ct. . Pg.9 . . . . H10
Brookstone Dr. Pg.2 . . . . . E7
Buckingham Ct. Pg.3 . . . . . E7
Buckingham Dr. Pg.3 . . . . . E7
Buckskin Ln. . . Pg.2 . . . . . F6
Buffalo Cir. . . . Pg.8 . . . . . F6
Burke Dr. . . . . Pg.3 . . . . . E8
Burnham St. . . Pg.3 . . . . . E8
Burning Tr. . . . Pg.2 . . . . . F6
Burns St. . . . . Pg.9 . . . . H10
Cactus Tr. . . . Pg.2 . . . . . F6
Camelot Ln. . . Pg.3 . . . . . E8
Canterbury Ct. Pg.2 . . . . . F5
Canterbury Dr. Pg.3 . . . . . E8
Canyon Trail . . Pg.3 . . . . . E8
Caribou Tr. . . . Pg.2 . . . . . E6
Carlton Dr. . . . Pg.9 . . . . . H9
Carol Ct. . . . . . Pg.3 . . . . . F9
Carriage Ln. . . Pg.9 . . . . . G8
Carson Dr. . . . Pg.3 . . . . . F8
Castleton Ct. . Pg.8 . . . . . F7
Cedar Ct. . . . . Pg.3 . . . . . E8
Center Ave. . . Pg.3,9 . . . . F8
Chadsford Ct. . Pg.9 . . . . . F7
Chalet Dr. . . . . Pg.3 . . . . . E8
Charger Ct. . . . Pg.2 . . . . . E6
Chatham Dr. . . Pg.2 . . . . . F7
Chattanooga Tr. Pg.2 . . . . . F6
Cherokee Ct. . . Pg.9 . . . . . G8
Chestnut Dr. . . Pg.3 . . . . . E8
Chetwood Ct. . Pg.2 . . . . . E7
Cheyenne Tr. . Pg.9 . . . . . F8
Chippewa Tr. . Pg.9 . . . . . F7
Christopher Ln. Pg.8 . . . . . F5
Cimarron Dr. . . Pg.8 . . . . . F7
Clare Ct. . . . . . Pg.3 . . . . . E8
Clearwater Ct. Pg.3 . . . . . F7
Cliff Ct. . . . . . . Pg.3 . . . . . F8
Cliff View Ln. . Pg.2 . . . . . F6
Coachlite Tr. . . Pg.9 . . . . . G8
Cochise Ct. . . . Pg.9 . . . . . G8
Cochise Pl. . . . Pg.9 . . . . . G8
Coldspring Rd. Pg.2 . . . . . E7
Colorado Ct. . . Pg.8,9 . . . . G7
Columbia Ct. . . Pg.3 . . . . . F8
Comanche Ln. . Pg.9 . . . . . F8
Commerce Dr. . Pg.9 . . . . . G9
Commonwealth Dr.
. . . . . . . . . . Pg.9 . . . . . H9
Concord Ct. . . . Pg.9 . . . . H10
Concord Ln. . . . Pg.9 . . . . H10
Country Glen Ln. Pg.2 . . . . . E7
Countryside Ln. Pg.2 . . . . . E6
County Farm Rd. Pg.2 . . . . . F7
Creekwood Ct. Pg.9 . . . . . F7
Crystal Shore Ct.
. . . . . . . . . . Pg.2 . . . . . E6
Crystal Shore Dr.
. . . . . . . . . . Pg.2 . . . . . E6
Cumberland Ct. Pg.2 . . . . . F7
Cypress Ln. . . . Pg.2 . . . . . F6
Dakota Ct. . . . . Pg.8 . . . . . G7
Danbury Dr. . . . Pg.9 . . . . . F7
Dancing Water Ct.
. . . . . . . . . . Pg.3 . . . . . F8
David Ln. . . . . . Pg.9 . . . . . F7
Daybreak Ln. . . Pg.3 . . . . . F8
Dearborn Cir. . Pg.3 . . . . . F8
Deskin Tr. . . . . Pg.3 . . . . . F8
Delaware Tr. . . Pg.3 . . . . . F7
Della Ct. . . . . . Pg.9 . . . . . H8
Devon Ct. . . . . Pg.2 . . . . . E7
Dodge Ct. . . . . Pg.3 . . . . . F8
Dogwood Ln. . . Pg.8 . . . . . F6
Donegal Ct. . . . Pg.3 . . . . . E8
Dorchester Dr. Pg.2 . . . . . E7
Doris Ave. . . . . Pg.9 . . . . . H9
Dublin Ct. . . . . Pg.3 . . . . . E8
Dugout Tr. . . . . Pg.2 . . . . . F6
Eagle View Dr. Pg.9 . . . . . G8
East Ave. . . . . Pg.3 . . . . F10
East Dr. . . . . . Pg.3 . . . . . F9
Easton Dr. . . . . Pg.2 . . . . . E6
Easy St. . . . . . Pg.9 . . . . . H9
Eclipse Dr. . . . Pg.3 . . . . . F8
Edgebrook Ct. . Pg.9 . . . . . F8
Edington Ct. . . Pg.3 . . . . . E7
Edington Ln. . . Pg.3 . . . . . E7
El Paso Ln. . . . Pg.9 . . . . . G8
Elk Trail . . . . . Pg.3 . . . . . F8
Elk Trail Ct. . . Pg.3 . . . . . F9
Erie Ct. . . . . . . Pg.3 . . . . . F8
Esselen Ct. . . . Pg.9 . . . . . G7
Essex Pl. . . . . . Pg.9 . . . . . F7
Evergreen Dr. . Pg.8 . . . . . F6
Executive Dr. . Pg.9 . . . . . H9
Fair Oaks Rd. . Pg.2 . . . . . F5
Fairfield Ln. . . Pg.9 . . . . H10
Farm Glen Ln. . Pg.2 . . . . . E7
Fawn Ct. . . . . . Pg.3 . . . . . F7
Feather Ct. . . . Pg.3 . . . . . F8
Fireside Dr. . . . Pg.9 . . . . H10
Flame Ct. . . . . Pg.9 . . . . H10
Flame Dr. . . . . Pg.9 . . . . H10
Flint Tr. . . . . . Pg.3 . . . . . F8
Forest Ct. . . . . Pg.2 . . . . . E7
Forest Ln. . . . . Pg.2 . . . . . E7
Fox Ct. . . . . . . Pg.8 . . . . . F6
Fullerton Ave. . Pg.9 . . . . . F9
Gary Ave. . . . . Pg.9 . . . . . G9
Geneva Rd. . . . Pg.9 . . . . J10
Georgetown Dr. Pg.2 . . . . . E5
Gerzevske Ln. Pg.9 . . . . . G9
Glen Ct. . . . . . Pg.2 . . . . . E7
Glen Flora Dr. . Pg.9 . . . . . F8
Glenlake Dr. . . Pg.2 . . . . . E7
Gloucester Cir. Pg.2 . . . . . E6
Greenway Tr. . Pg.9 . . . . . F9
Gundersen Dr. Pg.9 . . . . . H9
Gunsmoke Ct. . Pg.2,8 . . . . F6
Hampton Dr. . . Pg.2 . . . . . F7
Hancock St. . . Pg.3 . . . . . E8
Harbor Pt. . . . . Pg.2 . . . . . E6
Harvard Ct. . . . Pg.2 . . . . . E6
Harwich Dr. . . . Pg.2 . . . . . E6
Hawk Ln. . . . . . Pg.2 . . . . . F6
Hearth Ln. . . . . Pg.9 . . . . . F7
Heather Ln. . . . Pg.9 . . . . . F8
Hemlock Ln. . . Pg.2,8 . . . . F6
Hiawatha Dr. . . Pg.9 . . . . . G8
Hickory Ln. . . . Pg.2 . . . . . F6
High Ridge Pass Pg.2 . . . . . F6
Hillcrest Dr. . . . Pg.2 . . . . . E6
Hoover Dr. . . . . Pg.3 . . . . . F8
Hopi Ct. . . . . . . Pg.3 . . . . . F8
Horizon Cir. . . . Pg.9 . . . . . F9
Horseshoe Ct. . Pg.2 . . . . . F7
Hunter Dr. . . . . Pg.3 . . . . . E8
Huntington Ct. . Pg.3 . . . . . E8
Huntington Dr. . Pg.3 . . . . . E7
Huron Ct. . . . . . Pg.3 . . . . . F8
Hyannis Cir. . . . Pg.2 . . . . . E6
Idaho St. . . . . . Pg.3 . . . . . F8
Illini Dr. . . . . . . Pg.9 . . . . . F8
Inca Blvd. . . . . Pg.9 . . . . . F8
Indianwood Dr. Pg.9 . . . . . F7
Iowa Ct. . . . . . . Pg.9 . . . . . G8
Iris Ave. . . . . . . Pg.2 . . . . . F6
Ironhawk Ct. . . Pg.3 . . . . . F8
Iroquois Tr. . . . Pg.9 . . . . . F7
Juniper Ct. . . . . Pg.2 . . . . . F6
Kalamazoo Ct. . Pg.3 . . . . . E8
Kamiah Ct. . . . . Pg.9 . . . . . F7
Kansas St. . . . . Pg.3 . . . . . F8
Kehoe Blvd. . . . Pg.9 . . . . . G9
Kelly Dr. . . . . . . Pg.2 . . . . . F7
Kerry Ct. . . . . . Pg.3 . . . . . E8
Kildare Ct. . . . . Pg.3 . . . . . E8
Kilkenny Ct. . . . Pg.3 . . . . . E8
Kimberly Dr. . . . Pg.9 . . . . . G9
Kingsbridge Dr. Pg.3 . . . . . E7
Klein Creek Ct. Pg.3 . . . . . F8
Knollwood Dr. . Pg.2 . . . . . E7
Kuhn Rd. . . . . . Pg.9 . . . . . F7
Lacrosse St. . . Pg.3 . . . . . E8
Laguna Ct. . . . . Pg.3 . . . . . F8
Lakeshore Dr. . Pg.2 . . . . . E7
Lakeside Ln. . . Pg.2 . . . . . E6
Lakewood Cir. . Pg.2 . . . . . E6
Lance Ct. . . . . . Pg.3 . . . . . E8
Lance Ln. . . . . . Pg.2 . . . . . F6
Larch Dr. . . . . . Pg.3 . . . . . F7
Laurel Ct. . . . . Pg.8 . . . . . F6
Legends Dr. . . . Pg.9 . . . . . F8
Leslie Ct. . . . . . Pg.8 . . . . . F5
Lies Rd. . . . . . . Pg.3 . . . . . E8
Lightning Tr. . . Pg.8 . . . . . F6
Lilac Ct. . . . . . . Pg.8 . . . . . F6
Lilac Ln. . . . . . . Pg.2 . . . . . F6
Lily Ln. . . . . . . . Pg.2 . . . . . E6
Lincolnshire Ct. Pg.2 . . . . . F5
Linden Dr. . . . . Pg.3 . . . . . F7
Longmeadow Ct.
. . . . . . . . . . Pg.8 . . . . . F7
Longmeadow Dr.
. . . . . . . . . . Pg.2 . . . . . F6
Magnolia Way . Pg.2 . . . . . F6
Main Pl. . . . . . . Pg.9 . . . . . H9
Malibu Ct. . . . . Pg.3 . . . . . F8
Mantle Ln. (Meadow Ln.)
. . . . . . . . . . Pg.9 . . . . H10
Maple Ridge Ct. Pg.2 . . . . . E5
Matthew Ln. . . . Pg.9 . . . . . F7
Mayfair Dr. . . . . Pg.3 . . . . . E8
McCormick St. . Pg.3 . . . . . E8
Meadow Ln. (Mantle Ln.)
. . . . . . . . . . Pg.9 . . . . H10
Medford Dr. . . . Pg.8 . . . . . G7
Merbach Ct. . . . Pg.3 . . . . . E8
Merbach Dr. . . . Pg.3 . . . . . E8
Mercedes Dr. . . Pg.9 . . . . . F9
Mesa Verde Ct. Pg.9 . . . . . F7
Mill Ct. . . . . . . . Pg.2 . . . . . E7
Minnesota Ct. . Pg.8 . . . . . G7
Mission St. . . . . Pg.3 . . . . . F9
Moccasin Ct. . . Pg.3 . . . . . E8
Mohawk Dr., W. Pg.9 . . . . . G8
Mohican Rd. . . . Pg.9 . . . . . F8
Monitor Dr. . . . . Pg.3 . . . . . E7
Morton Rd. . . . . Pg.8 . . . . . G7
Mountain Glen Way
. . . . . . . . . . Pg.2 . . . . . E6
Munson Dr. . . . . Pg.8,9 . . . . F7
Mystic Ct. . . . . . Pg.2 . . . . . E6
Nantucket Ct. . . Pg.2 . . . . . E6
Napa St. . . . . . . Pg.3 . . . . . F8
Narragansett Dr. Pg.2 . . . . . E6
Natoma Circle . Pg.9 . . . . . G9
Navaho Dr. . . . . Pg.9 . . . . G10
Nebraska Ct. . . Pg.8 . . . . . G7
Nekoma Dr. . . . Pg.8 . . . . . F7
New Britton Rd. Pg.2 . . . . . F6
New London Ct. Pg.2 . . . . . F6
Newburg Ct. . . . Pg.3 . . . . . E7
Nez Perce Ct. . . Pg.9 . . . . . F7
Niagara St. . . . . Pg.3 . . . . . E8
North Ave. . . . . Pg.9 . . . . . G8
Oak Wood Dr. . . Pg.2 . . . . . E6
Ohio Ct. . . . . . . Pg.3 . . . . . F8
Old Gary Ave. . . Pg.3 . . . . . E9
Old Meadow Ct. Pg.2 . . . . . E6
Omaha Ct. . . . . Pg.3 . . . . . F8
Oneida Ct. . . . . Pg.8 . . . . . F7
Oriole Tr. . . . . . Pg.2 . . . . . E6
Osage Cir. . . . . Pg.8 . . . . . F7
Oswego Dr. . . . . Pg.8 . . . . . F7
Ottawa Ct. . . . . Pg.3 . . . . . F8
Overlook Ln. . . . Pg.2 . . . . . E6
Oxford St. . . . . . Pg.2 . . . . . E6
Paddock Dr. . . . Pg.2 . . . . . F7
Palomino St. . . . Pg.3 . . . . . F8
Papoose Ct. . . . Pg.3 . . . . . F8
Park Hill Dr. . . . Pg.9 . . . . . G9
Park Hill Tr. . . . Pg.9 . . . . . G8
Parkside Ct. . . . Pg.3 . . . . . E8
Parkside Dr. . . . Pg.3 . . . . . E8
Parkview Cir. . . Pg.2 . . . . . E6
Parkview Ct. . . . Pg.2 . . . . . E6
Pawnee Dr. . . . . Pg.8 . . . . . F7
Paxton Pl. . . . . . Pg.9 . . . . . G7
Pebble Creek Tr. Pg.9 . . . . . F8
Pembrook Ct. . . Pg.9 . . . . H10
Penfield Dr. . . . Pg.8 . . . . . F7
Pennsboro Ct. . . Pg.2 . . . . . E5
Pennsbury Ct. . . Pg.9 . . . . H10
Penny Ct. . . . . . Pg.2 . . . . . D6
Peoria Ct. . . . . . Pg.8 . . . . . G7
Petersburg Ct. . Pg.2 . . . . . E5
Pheasant Tr. . . . Pg.2 . . . . . E6
Phillips Ct. . . . . Pg.3 . . . . . F8
Plains Ct. . . . . . Pg.8 . . . . . G7
Plum Grove Ct. . Pg.2 . . . . . E6
Plymouth Ct. . . . Pg.2 . . . . . E6
Pocahontas Tr. . Pg.9 . . . . . F7
Pontiac Ln. . . . . Pg.8 . . . . . F7
Portchester Cir. Pg.2 . . . . . E6
Portsmouth Ct. . Pg.2 . . . . . E5
Potomac Ct. . . . Pg.2 . . . . . E6
Prairie Ct. . . . . . Pg.8 . . . . . F7
President St. . . Pg.9 . . . . . F7
Princetown Ct. . Pg.2,3 . . . . F7
Provincetown Dr.
. . . . . . . . . . Pg.2 . . . . . F7
Quail Run Ct. . . Pg.9 . . . . . G8
Quincy Ct. . . . . . Pg.8 . . . . . F7
Raintree Ct. . . . Pg.8 . . . . . F6
Randy Rd. . . . . . Pg.8 . . . . . G8
Red Hill Tr. . . . . Pg.3 . . . . . F9
Regency Ln. . . . Pg.2 . . . . . E7
Renaissance Dr. Pg.3 . . . . . F7
Ridge Tr. . . . . . . Pg.2 . . . . . F7
Ridgefield Cir. . Pg.2 . . . . . E6
River Dr. . . . . . . Pg.2 . . . . . F7
Robin Dr. . . . . . Pg.2 . . . . . E6
Rockport Dr. . . . Pg.2 . . . . . E6
Rocky Valley Way
. . . . . . . . . . Pg.2 . . . . . F6
Rolling Oaks Dr. Pg.2 . . . . . F5
Rose Ave. . . . . . Pg.2 . . . . . F6
Rose Ct. . . . . . . Pg.2 . . . . . F6
Royal Glen Ln. . Pg.2 . . . . . E7
Saginaw Ct. . . . Pg.3 . . . . . F8
Sand Creek Dr. . Pg.8 . . . . . F7
Sandhurst Ct. . . Pg.3 . . . . . F7
Sandhurst Ln. . . Pg.3 . . . . . E7
Santa Fe Ct. . . . Pg.3 . . . . . F8
Saratoga Dr. . . . Pg.2 . . . . . F6
Sauk Ct. . . . . . . Pg.9 . . . . . F7
Schmale Rd. . . . Pg.9 . . . . H10
Scott Ct. . . . . . . Pg.3 . . . . . E7
Seabury Cir. . . . Pg.2 . . . . . E6
Seminole Ln. . . . Pg.9 . . . . . G8
Seneca Ln. . . . . Pg.8 . . . . . F7
Sequoia Ct. . . . . Pg.8,9 . . . . F7
Shagbark Ct. . . . Pg.8 . . . . . F5
Shawnee Dr. . . . Pg.9 . . . . . G8
Sheffield Ct. . . . Pg.2 . . . . . F6
Shelburne Dr. . . Pg.9 . . . . . F7
Shenandoah Dr. Pg.2 . . . . . F7
Shining Water Dr.
. . . . . . . . . . Pg.8 . . . . . F7
Silverleaf Blvd. . Pg.9 . . . . . G8
Sioux Ln. . . . . . Pg.9 . . . . . G8
Somerset Ct. . . . Pg.2 . . . . . E7
Somerset Dr. . . . Pg.2 . . . . . F7
Sorrel Ct. . . . . . Pg.2 . . . . . E7
Split Rail Dr. . . . Pg.2 . . . . . F7
Spring Vale Rd. Pg.8 . . . . . F6
Spring Valley Ct. Pg.2 . . . . . E6
Spring Valley Dr. Pg.2 . . . . . E6
Springbrook Ln. Pg.9 . . . . . F8
Springwood Ct. Pg.9 . . . . H10
St. Charles Rd. . Pg.9 . . . . . H9
St. Paul Blvd. . . Pg.9 . . . . . G9
Stanford Ln. . . . Pg.2 . . . . . E7
Stark Dr. . . . . . . Pg.3 . . . . . E8
Stockbridge Dr. Pg.8 . . . . . F7
Stonehenge Ct. Pg.2 . . . . . F6
Stonewood Cir. Pg.3 . . . . . E8
Stuart Dr. . . . . . Pg.9 . . . . . F7
Summit Pass . . . Pg.2 . . . . . F6
Sundance Ct. . . Pg.8,9 . . . . F7
Sunrise Ct. . . . . Pg.9 . . . . . F8
Surrey Dr. . . . . . Pg.9 . . . . . G8
Sussex Rd. . . . . Pg.2 . . . . . F6
Tacoma Dr. . . . . Pg.8 . . . . . F7
Tahoe Ct. . . . . . Pg.9 . . . . . F7
Tall Oaks Dr. . . . Pg.8 . . . . . F5
Tama Ct. . . . . . . Pg.9 . . . . . F8
Tamarac Dr. . . . Pg.3 . . . . . F7
Teton Cir. . . . . . Pg.8,9 . . . . F7
Texas Ct. . . . . . Pg.8 . . . . . G7
Thornhill Dr. . . . Pg.9 . . . . H10
Thunderbird Tr., W.
. . . . . . . . . . Pg.9 . . . . . G8
Timber Ridge Dr.
. . . . . . . . . . Pg.9 . . . . . F7
Tioga Ct. . . . . . Pg.3 . . . . . E8
Tomahawk Ct., W.
. . . . . . . . . . Pg.9 . . . . . G8
Tonto Ct. . . . . . Pg.3 . . . . . F7
Topeka Ct. . . . . Pg.8 . . . . . F7
Tower Dr. . . . . . Pg.9 . . . . F10
Trailside Ct. . . . Pg.3 . . . . . E8
Trinity Ct. . . . . . Pg.2 . . . . . E7
Trinity Dr. . . . . . Pg.2 . . . . . E7
Tubeway Dr. . . . Pg.9 . . . . . H8
Ute Ln. . . . . . . . Pg.9 . . . . . F7
Vale Rd. . . . . . . Pg.8 . . . . . G7
Valley View Dr. . Pg.2 . . . . . F7
Village Ct. . . . . . Pg.9 . . . . . G9
Village Dr. . . . . Pg.9 . . . . . G9
Violet St. . . . . . Pg.2 . . . . . F5
Wabash St. . . . . Pg.3 . . . . . F8
Waco Dr. . . . . . Pg.2 . . . . . F6
Walnut Cir. . . . . Pg.2 . . . . . E6
Wampum Ct. . . . Pg.3 . . . . . F8
Warwick Ct. . . . Pg.2 . . . . . E7
Warwick Dr. . . . Pg.3 . . . . . E7
Waterford Ct. . . Pg.3 . . . . . E8
Westgate Dr. . . . Pg.9 . . . . . H8
Westward Tr. . . . Pg.2 . . . . . F6
Wexford Ct. . . . . Pg.3 . . . . . E8
Whisper Pointe . Pg.9 . . . . . F8
Williamstown Dr.
. . . . . . . . . . Pg.2 . . . . . F7
Willow Dr. . . . . . Pg.3 . . . . . F7
Willow Wood Dr. Pg.9 . . . . H10
Winchester Ct. . Pg.2 . . . . . F6
Windemere Ln. . Pg.9 . . . . . F7
Winding Glen Dr. Pg.2 . . . . . E6
Windsor Park Dr.
. . . . . . . . . . Pg.9 . . . . . G8
Woodcrest Ct. . . Pg.9 . . . . . F8
Woodhill Dr. . . . Pg.2 . . . . . E7
Woodlake Dr. . . Pg.2 . . . . . E6
Yardley Dr. . . . . Pg.3 . . . . . E8
Yellowstone St. Pg.3 . . . . . F7
Yorkshire Ln. . . Pg.2 . . . . . F6
Yuma Ln. . . . . . Pg.9 . . . . . G8

**PARKS**

All Sports Park Pg.9 . . . . . F9
Armstrong Park Pg.9 . . . . . F8
Bierman Park . . Pg.2 . . . . . E6
Cambridge Park Pg.2 . . . . . E7
Charger Park . . Pg.2 . . . . . E6
Community Park
. . . . . . . . . . Pg.9 . . . . H10
Daylily Park . . . Pg.9 . . . . . H9
Evergreen Park . Pg.2 . . . . . F6
Fair Oaks Park Central
. . . . . . . . . . Pg.8 . . . . . F6
Fair Oaks Park East
. . . . . . . . . . Pg.8 . . . . . F6
Fair Oaks Park West
. . . . . . . . . . Pg.8 . . . . . F5
Friendship Park Pg.3 . . . . . F7
Gerald Weeks Park
. . . . . . . . . . Pg.9 . . . . . H9
Hampe Park . . . Pg.3 . . . . . E8
Heritage Lake Park
. . . . . . . . . . Pg.2 . . . . . E6
Jirsa Park . . . . . Pg.2 . . . . . E6
Kent Park . . . . . Pg.2 . . . . . E7
Memorial Park . . Pg.9 . . . . . G8
Mitchell Lakes Park
. . . . . . . . . . Pg.9 . . . . . F8
New Park . . . . . Pg.8 . . . . . G6
Shining Waters Park
. . . . . . . . . . Pg.8 . . . . . F7
Simkus Rec. Center
. . . . . . . . . . Pg.2 . . . . . E7
Smith Park . . . . Pg.3 . . . . . E8
Spring Valley Park
. . . . . . . . . . Pg.2 . . . . . E6
St. Andrew Park Pg.9 . . . . . G8
St. Luke Park . . Pg.9 . . . . . F8
Stonebridge Park
. . . . . . . . . . Pg.2 . . . . . E7
Sundance Park . Pg.3 . . . . . E8
Tedrahn Park . . Pg.2 . . . . . E7
Tokarski Park . . Pg.9 . . . . . F9
Veterans Park . . Pg.3 . . . . . E9
Volunteer Park . Pg.9 . . . . . G7
Walter Park . . . . Pg.2 . . . . . F6

**SCHOOLS**

Carol Stream Sch.
. . . . . . . . . . Pg.9 . . . . . G8
Dist. 93 Admin. Bldg.
. . . . . . . . . . Pg.3 . . . . . E8
Evergreen Sch. . Pg.8 . . . . . F6
Glenbard North H.S.
. . . . . . . . . . Pg.3 . . . . . E7
Heritage Lakes Sch.
. . . . . . . . . . Pg.2 . . . . . E7
Jay Stream Sch. Pg.9 . . . . . F8
Roy DeShane Jr. H.S.
. . . . . . . . . . Pg.9 . . . . . F8
Spring Trail Sch. Pg.2 . . . . . E6
St. Lukes Sch. . Pg.9 . . . . . G8
Western Trails Sch.
. . . . . . . . . . Pg.3 . . . . . F8

**SHOPPING CENTERS**

Carol Plaza . . . . Pg.9 . . . . H10
County Farm Center
. . . . . . . . . . Pg.2 . . . . . E7
Elk Trail Commercial Ctr.
. . . . . . . . . . Pg.3 . . . . . F8
Fair Oaks Plaza Pg.2 . . . . . D6
Gary at North Center
. . . . . . . . . . Pg.9 . . . . . G8
Geneva Crossing S.C.
. . . . . . . . . . Pg.9 . . . . . H9
Geneva Plaza . . Pg.9 . . . . H10
Gina's Plaza . . . Pg.9 . . . . H10
Greenway Commercial Ctr.
. . . . . . . . . . Pg.9 . . . . . F9
Heritage Plaza . Pg.2 . . . . . E7
John's Plaza . . . Pg.9 . . . . . G9
Northland Mall . . Pg.9 . . . . . J9
Thornhill Plaza . Pg.9 . . . . . H9
White Hen / Schmale Rd. Plaza . . . . Pg.9 . . . . H10
Willow Square . . Pg.9 . . . . . F7

**MISCELLANEOUS**

Carol Stream Regional Postal Facility . . . . Pg.9 . . . . F10
Central Du Page Urgent Care
. . . . . . . . . . Pg.3 . . . . . E9
DuPage Intermediate Processing Facility . . . . Pg.9 . . . . . F9
Fire Station #1 . Pg.9 . . . . . F7
Fire Station #2 . Pg.9 . . . . H10
Great Western Trail
. . . . . . . . . . Pg.9 . . . . . H9
Library . . . . . . . Pg.9 . . . . . F9
Police Dept. . . . Pg.9 . . . . . F9
Village Hall . . . . Pg.9 . . . . . F9

## CHICAGO

COOK COUNTY

**STREETS**

Bessie Coleman Dr. . . . . . . A21
Mt. Prospect Rd. . . . . . . . . A20
N. Access Rd. . . . . . . . . . . C20
O'Hare Cargo Rd. . . . . . . . . C20
Old Irving Park Rd. . . . . . . C20
Post Office Rd. . . . . . . . . . C20
S. Access Rd. . . . . . . . . . . C20

**CEMETERIES**

St. John Cemetery . . . . . . . C20

**MISCELLANEOUS**

Air France . . . . . . . . . . . . C20
Airport Transit System (Monorail) . . . . . . . . . A21
American Airlines . . . . . . A,C20
C.T.A. Station Rapid Transit B21
Delta Airlines (DAL) . . . . . . A20
Federal Express . . . . . . . . . C20
KLM Royal Dutch Airlines . . C20
Luftanza . . . . . . . . . . . . . . C20
North O'Hare Cargo Area . . A20
Northwest Airlines . . . . . . . C20
Parking Lot A,B & C . . . . . B21
Parking Lot D . . . . . . . . . . B21
South O'Hare Cargo Area . . C20
Terminal 1 . . . . . . . . . . . . . B21
Terminal 2 . . . . . . . . . . . . . B21
Terminal 3 . . . . . . . . . . . . . B21
Terminal 4 . . . . . . . . . . . . . B21
Terminal 5 (International Terminal) . . . . . . . . . . . B21
U.S. Air Force . . . . . . . . . . A21
U.S. Postal Service Facility C20
United Airlines . . . . . . . . . C20
United Airlines Service Center (UAL) . . . . . . . . . . . . . A20
United Parcel Service . . . . . C20

## CLARENDON HILLS

Pages 17,18,24

**STREETS**

Algonquin Rd. . Pg.17 . . . R17
Ann Ct. . . . . . . Pg.18 . . . R18
Ann St. . . . . . . Pg.18 . . R,S18
Arthur Ave. . . . Pg.17 . . . R18
Barclay Ct. . . . Pg.24 . . . S18
Blodgett . . . . . Pg.18 . . . R18
Blue Lake Park Pg.18 . . . R18
Bonnie Ln. . . . Pg.18 . . . R18
Burlington Ave. Pg.18 . . . R18
Byrd Ct. . . . . . Pg.18 . . . R18
Carlisle Dr. . . . Pg.24 . . . S18
Chase Dr. . . . . Pg.24 . . . S18
Chestnut Ave. . Pg.18 . . . R19
Chicago Ave. . . Pg.18 . . . R18
Church Rd. . . . Pg.18 . . . S18
Churchill Pl. . . Pg.18 . . . S18
Claredon Ct. . . Pg.24 . . . S18
Coe Rd. . . . . . Pg.18 . . . Q18
Colfax Ave. . . . Pg.17 . . . R18
Columbine Dr. . Pg.18 . . . Q18
Concord . . . . . Pg.24 . . . S18
Coolidge Ct. . . Pg.18 . . . R18
Coventry Ct. . . Pg.24 . . . S18
Cross St. . . . . Pg.18 . . . R18
Eastern . . . . . Pg.18 . . . R18
Fairview Ct. . . Pg.18 . . . R19
Forest Hills Dr. Pg.24 . . . S18
Gilbert . . . . . . Pg.18 . . . R18
Golf Ave. . . . . Pg.18 . . . R18
Grant Ave. . . . Pg.18 . . . R18
Hamill Ln. . . . . Pg.18 . . . R19
Harris Ave. . . . Pg.18 . . . R18
Hiawatha Dr. . . Pg.18 . . . R17
Hickory St. . . . Pg.18 . . . Q18
Holmes Ave. . . Pg.18 . . . S18
Hudson Ave. . . Pg.17 . . . R18
Indian Dr. . . . . Pg.17 . . . R17
Iroquois Dr. . . . Pg.17 . . . R17
Jackson St., N. Pg.18 . . . Q19
Jane Ct. . . . . . Pg.18 . . . R18
Jane Rd. . . . . . Pg.18 . . . R18
Juliet Ct. . . . . . Pg.18 . . . R18
Larkspur Ln. . . Pg.18 . . . Q18
Lynn Ct. . . . . . Pg.17 . . . Q17
McIntosh . . . . . Pg.18 . . . R18
Metra Station . . Pg.18 . . . R18
Middaugh Rd. . . Pg.18 . . . Q18
Mohawk Dr. . . . Pg.17 . . . R17
Naperville Rd. . Pg.18 . . . Q18
Norfolk Ave. . . . Pg.18 . . . R18
Oxford Ave. . . . Pg.18 . . . R18

# CLAREDON HILLS


Park Ave. Pg.17 R18
Powell St. Pg.18 R18
Prospect Ave. Pg.18 R18
Railroad Ave. Pg.18 R18
Ridge Ave. Pg.17 R18
Ridge St. Pg.18 R18
Rose Ave. Pg.18 R18
Ruby St. Pg.17 S18
Sheridan St. Pg.18 R18
Short St. Pg.18 R18
Stonegate Rd. Pg.18 Q18
Terrace Dr. Pg.18 S18
Tuttle Ave. Pg.18 R18
Walker Pg.18 S18
Walnut Pg.18 Q18
Waverly Ave. Pg.18 R18
Western Ave. Pg.18 S18
Willow Cr. Ct. Pg.24 S18
Woodstock Ave. Pg.17 Q18
55th St. Pg.18 S18

**GOLF COURSES**
Hinsdale G.C. Pg.18 Q18

**PARKS**
Hosek Park Pg.18 R18
Lions Community Park Pg.18 R19
Prospect Park Pg.18 R18
Walker School Park Pg.18 R18

**SCHOOLS**
Notre Dame Sch. Pg.18 R18
Prospect Sch. Pg.18 R18
Walker Sch. Pg.18 R18

**MISCELLANEOUS**
Police Dept. Pg.18 R18
Post Office Pg.18 R18
Village Hall Pg.18 R18


## DARIEN

Pages 22-24

**STREETS**


Abbey Dr. Pg.23 V15
Adams St. Pg.23 V17
Ailsworth Ct. Pg.22 W14
Alabama Ave. Pg.23 U,V18
Albany Ln. Pg.23 T17
Alden Ln. Pg.22 W14
Alison Ln. Pg.22 U17
Andermann Ln. Pg.23 V17
Arbour Ct. Pg.23 U16
Arrow Ln. Pg.23 V18
Ashley Ct. Pg.23 V16
Aylesbury Ln. Pg.23 V15
Bailey Rd. Pg.23 W17
Bailey Rd. Pg.29 V16
Baker Ct. Pg.23 V17
Bantry Ct. Pg.23 T16
Barclay Rd. Pg.23 V15
Barrymore Dr. Pg.23 V16
Bavarian Ln. Pg.23 U17
Bayberry Ln. Pg.23 U16
Bayview Ln. Pg.23 W16
Bedford Ln. Pg.23 V15
Beechnut Ln. Pg.23 U17
Belair Dr. Pg.23 U17
Bentley Ave. Pg.24 U18
Birch Ct. Pg.23 U17
Black Swan Ct. Pg.23 W16
Bob-O-Link Ln. Pg.23 W17
Boulder Dr. Pg.23 V16
Bradon Rd. Pg.23 X15
Brewer Rd. Pg.22 W14
Bristlecone Ct. Pg.23 T18
Brittany Ct. Pg.23 V16
Brompton Dr. Pg.23 V16
Brook Haven Plaza Pg.29 V17
Brookbank Rd. Pg.24 U18
Brookdale Dr. Pg.24 U18
Brookhaven Ave. Pg.23 V17
Brunswick Rd. Pg.23 V16
Bunker Rd. Pg.23 U17
Cambridge Rd. Pg.23 V15
Cameron Ct. Pg.29 V15
Canterbury Ct. Pg.23 V16
Capitol Dr. Pg.24 U18
Capri Tr. Pg.29 V16
Captons Ln. Pg.23 W17
Carlow Dr. Pg.23 X15
Carlton Rd. Pg.23 V15
Carriage Green Dr. Pg.23 W16
Carrol Ct. Pg.23 U16
Carrol Ln. Pg.23 U16
Cass Ave. Pg.23 W17
Center Cir. Pg.23 V16
Chalet Pg.23 V17
Chapman Ct. Pg.29 W17
Chapman Dr. Pg.29 W17
Charleston Dr. Pg.23 U17
Chase Rd. Pg.23 X15
Cherokee Dr. Pg.23 U17
Chestnut Ln. Pg.23 U18
Chickory Ct. Pg.29 X15
Chippewa Ln. Pg.24 V17
Clare Ct. Pg.22 U16
Claremont Dr. Pg.23 U17
Clarendon Hills Rd. Pg.24 T,U18
Clemens Rd. Pg.23 V16
Clifford Pg.22 W14
Clover Ct. Pg.23 U16
Coachmans Dr. Pg.23 W16
Columbia Ln. Pg.23 U17
Comshock Pg.23 V17
Country Ln. Pg.23 V17
Coventry Ct. Pg.23 V16
Cramer Ln. Pg.22 W14
Creekside Ct. Pg.23 W16
Creekside Ln. Pg.23 W16
Crest Rd. Pg.24 U18
Curran Ct. Pg.29 V15
Dale Rd. Pg.24 U18
Danbury Dr. Pg.23 V15
Darien Club Dr. Pg.23 U16
Darien Lake Dr. Pg.23 V16
Darien Ln. Pg.23 U17
Darien Wood Ct. Pg.29 X15
Dartmouth Ln. Pg.23 V16
Del Ct. Pg.23 V17
Dickens Cir. Pg.23 W16
Discosola Ct. Pg.22 T16
Dixon Ct. Pg.22 W14
Donegal Dr. Pg.23 W15
Dorchester Ln. Pg.23 V18
Downers Dr. Pg.23 W14
Drover Ct. Pg.22 W14
Dunmore Dr. Pg.23 W15
Durham Ct. Pg.23 V16
Eagles Nest Dr. Pg.24 T18
Easy St. Pg.24 T18
Eleanor Pl. Pg.24 U18
Elm St. Pg.23 U18
Emerson Dr. Pg.23 U16
Evans Pl. Pg.24 U18
Evergreen Ln. Pg.23 W16
Exner Ct. Pg.23 V16
Exner Rd. Pg.23 U16
Exton St. Pg.23 V16
Fairview Ave. Pg.23 V16
Falcon Ct. Pg.24 T18
Farmingdale Dr. Pg.24 V18
Florence Ave. Pg.23 V16
Forest Glen Pg.29 X15
Fountain Point Cir. Pg.29 X15
Fox Hill Pl. Pg.23 W16
Foxtail Ct. Pg.23 T18
Gail Ave. Pg.23 V17
Galway Ct. Pg.23 U16
Gigi Ln. Pg.23 U16
Gilbert Ct. Pg.22 W14
Glen Ln. Pg.23 V17
Gleneagles Ln. Pg.23 X16
Glenery Rd. Pg.23 W16
Gold Grove Pl. Pg.23 U16
Golfview Dr. Pg.23 W16
Gooseneck Ct. Pg.24 T18
Gordon Ct. Pg.23 V16
Grandview Ln. Pg.22 W14
Grant St. Pg.23 V17
Green Valley Ct. Pg.23 V16
Green Valley Rd. Pg.23 V15
Greenbriar Ln. Pg.23 V17
Grove Dr. Pg.23 V17
Hamilton Ln. Pg.23 V15
Harper Pg.23 V16
Hawk Ct. Pg.24 T18
Hawthorne Pl. Pg.23 V16
Hayenga Ln. Pg.23 V17
Heather Ln. Pg.23 W16
Hedgewood Dr. Pg.29 V15
Hemlock Ln. Pg.23 W16
Hickory Ln. Pg.23 U17
High Rd. Pg.24 U18
Highpoint Cir. Pg.24 W18
Hinsbrook Ave. Pg.23 U17
Hinswood Dr. Pg.23 W17
Holly Ave. Pg.24 U16,18
Honey Locust Ln. Pg.23 V18
Iris Rd. Pg.23 T18
Irish Ct. Pg.23 U16
Ironwood Ave. Pg.23 U17
Iroquois Ln. Pg.23 V17
Janet Ave. Pg.24 U18,V17
Joliet Rd. Pg.23 W16,17
Judd St. Pg.23 V16
Juniper Ln. Pg.23 V17
Kelly Ct. Pg.23 X15
Kentwood Ct. Pg.23 W16
Kerry Ln. Pg.23 X15
Kimberly Ct. Pg.23 W16
Knottingham Cir. Pg.23 V16
Lacebark Ct. Pg.23 T18
Lake Ridge Pg.23 W16
Lakeview Dr. Pg.23 V16
Lark Spur Ln. Pg.23 T17
Laurel Ln. Pg.23 W16
Leonard Dr. Pg.23 U18
Lester Ct. Pg.23 V17
Lester Ln. Pg.23 V17
Limerick Ct. Pg.23 U16
Linden Ave. Pg.23 V17
Lodge Pole Ct. Pg.23 T18
Lyman Ave. Pg.23 V15
Main St. Pg.23 V15
Manning Rd. Pg.23 V16
Maple Ln. Pg.24 U18
Marlborough Ln. Pg.23 V15
Mayfair Ln. Pg.23 V17
McAdam Rd. Pg.23 U16
Meadow Ct. Pg.23 W14
Meadowlark Ln. Pg.23 W17
Middleton Rd. Pg.23 X15
Morgan Ct. Pg.29 V15
Mystic Trace Pg.23 W17
Norman Ct. Pg.23 V16
Norman Dr. Pg.23 V16
Oak Fern Ln. Pg.23 T17
Oakley Dr. Pg.23 W16
Old Oak Dr. Pg.23 W16
Oldfield Rd. Pg.23 W15
Oriole Ct. Pg.23 V17
Oxford Ct. Pg.29 V15
Park Ave. Pg.23 U16
Parkcrest Dr. Pg.23 W17
Peony Pl. Pg.23 U18
Pheasant Ridge Ct. Pg.24 T18
Pine Bluff Ct. Pg.23 W17
Pine Cove Ct. Pg.23 W17
Pine Ct. Pg.23 V17
Pine Pkwy. Pg.23 V17
Pine Tree Ln. Pg.23 V18
Pinehurst Dr. Pg.23 W16
Pineview Ct. Pg.23 W16
Pitcher Dr. Pg.22 W14
Plainfield Rd. Pg.23 V17
Ponderosa Ct. Pg.23 T18
Poplar Ln. Pg.24 U18,19
Portsmouth Dr. Pg.23 W18
Quail Run Ct. Pg.24 T18
Queens Ct. Pg.23 V16
Red Pine Tr. Pg.23 T17
Redondo Ct. Pg.29 Z16
Redondo Dr. Pg.23 V16
Regency Pg.23 V17
Richard Pg.23 U16
Richmond Ave. Pg.23 T,U17
Ridge Rd. Pg.23 T17
Ripple Ridge Pg.23 W17
Ripple Ridge Cove Pg.23 W17
Robert Ct. Pg.23 W15
Robert Rd. Pg.23 W15
Roger Rd. Pg.24 U18
Rosewood Ct. Pg.23 V16
Royal Oak Dr. Pg.23 W16
Royal Swan Ln. Pg.23 W16
Sandalwood Ct. Pg.29 X15
Sandalwood Dr. Pg.29 X15
Sawmill Creek Dr. Pg.23 W16
Sawyer Ct. Pg.24 W18
Sawyer Rd. Pg.24 V18
Scotch Pine Tr. Pg.23 T17
Seminole Dr. Pg.23 U17
Sequoia Ln. Pg.23 V16
Shelley Ct. Pg.23 U16
Sierra Ave. Pg.23 U17
Sierra Dr. Pg.23 U17
Sleepy Hollow Ln. Pg.23 V17
Spring Ct. Pg.23 W17
Stevens St. Pg.23 V16
Stewart Dr. Pg.23 V16
Stratford Pl. Pg.23 V17
Summit Rd. Pg.23 U16
Sunrise Ave. Pg.24 U18
Surrey Dr. Pg.23 V15
Sweet Water Cove Pg.23 W17
Sweetbriar Ln. Pg.23 U16
Tall Pines Dr. Pg.23 U17
Tamarack Dr. Pg.23 U17
Tara Hill Rd. Pg.23 X15
Tennessee Ave. Pg.24 T,U18
Tennessee Dr. Pg.23 U18
Thistlewood Ct. Pg.23 W16
Timber Ln. Pg.23 U17
Torry Pines Ct. Pg.23 T17
Trenton Ln. Pg.23 U17
Troutilly Ln. Pg.23 T18
Urban Pg.29 W17
Village Ct. Pg.23 U17
Von Dash Pg.29 W17
Wakefield Dr. Pg.23 V15
Walden Ln. Pg.23 U16
Walnut Dr. Pg.23 V17
Warwick Ave. Pg.23 V17
Waterfall Glen Blvd. Pg.29 X15
Waverly Ct. Pg.29 X15
Western Ave. Pg.23 U18
Westminster Ct. Pg.23 V17
White Pine Tr. Pg.23 T17
Whitlock Dr. Pg.29 V15
Whittier Pg.23 U16
Wilcox Ave. Pg.23 U16
Wildwood Ct. Pg.23 V17
Wildwood Ln. Pg.23 V16
William Dr. Pg.23 U18
Willow Ln. Pg.23 U17
Willowcreek Pg.23 W16,17
Wilmette Ave. Pg.23 U,W17
Wilton Ct. Pg.23 V16
Wilton Rd. Pg.23 V16
Windsor Ct. Pg.29 V15
Windsor Dr. Pg.29 V15
Winterberry Pg.23 W16
Wintergreen Ln. Pg.23 T18
Wirth Dr. Pg.23 U16
Wood Vale Dr. Pg.23 W14
Woodbine Ln. Pg.23 T17
Woodlands Dr. Pg.23 W17
Woodmere Dr. Pg.29 V15
Woodrush Ln. Pg.23 T18
Woodview Ct. Pg.23 W16
67th St. Pg.24 T17,18
68th St. Pg.24 U18
69th St. Pg.24 U17,18
70th Pl. Pg.23 U17
70th St. Pg.24 U18
71st St. Pg.24 U16,17
72nd St. Pg.23 U16,18
73rd Ct. Pg.23 U16
73rd St. Pg.23 U16-18
74th St. Pg.24 U18
75th St. Pg.23 V18
77th Pl. Pg.23 V17
79th St. Pg.23 V17,18
83rd St. Pg.22 W14

**CEMETERIES**
Cass Cemetery Pg.23 W16
St. John's Cemetery Pg.24 T18

**FOREST PRESERVES**
Darien Chestnut F.P. Pg.23 V15
Oldfield Oaks Forest Preserve Pg.29 X15

**GOLF COURSES**
Carriage Greens G.C. Pg.23 W16

**PARKS**
Darien Comm. Pk. Pg.23 U18
Holly Park Pg.23 U16

**SCHOOLS** Pg.23
Cass Jr. H.S. Pg.23 W17
Concord Sch. Pg.23 V17
Eisenhower Jr. High Pg.23 V16
Elizabeth Ide Sch. Pg.23 V15
Fairview Sch. Pg.23 U16
Hinsbrook Sch. Pg.23 U17
Hinsdale S. Twp. H.S. Pg.24 U18
Lace Sch. Pg.23 U17
Marion Hills Sch. Pg.24 U18
Mark Delay Sch. Pg.23 T17
Marquette Manor Baptist Academy Pg.23 V16
Our Lady of Peace Sch. Pg.23 V17
St. Mary's Sch. Pg.23 V17

**SHOPPING CENTERS**
Darien Plaza Pg.23 W17
Shopping Ctr. Pg.23 U18,V15,17

**MISCELLANEOUS**
City Hall Pg.23 V16
Fire Dept. Pg.24 V16
Hinsbrook Rec. Club Pg.23 U17
Public Works Pg.29 X15


## DOWNERS GROVE

Pages 16,17,22,23

**STREETS**


Acorn Ave. Pg.17 P14
Acorn Dr. Pg.17 P15
Alamance Pl. Pg.22 U14
Aldrich Pl. Pg.22 T13
Almond Ct. Pg.17 P14
Andrus Ave. Pg.23 U15
Applegate Ave. Pg.23 U15
Applewood Ct. Pg.23 T16
Arbor Cir. Pg.16 Q13
Arguilla Dr. Pg.22 S13
Arrowwood Ln. Pg.17 P14
Ashbrook Pl. Pg.22 S13
Ashbury Ave. Pg.23,29 U15
Aspen Ave. Pg.22 S13
Aubrey Terr. Pg.22 S14
Austin St. Pg.17 R15
Authority Dr. Pg.16 Q13
Baimbridge Dr. Pg.23 V16
Baker Ct. Pg.22,23 U14
Banburry Rd. Pg.22 T14
Barberry Ct. Pg.17 P15
Barclay Ct. Pg.22 T14
Barneswood Dr. Pg.17 P15
Barrett St. Pg.23 T14
Bateman Rd. Pg.23 U14
Bates Pl. Pg.22 T14
Bayburg Rd. Pg.23 U15
Belden Ave. Pg.17 R15
Belle Aire Dr. Pg.17 P,Q14
Belle Aire Ln. Pg.17 Q14
Belmont Rd. Pg.16,22 R-T13
Bending Oaks Ct. Pg.16 R14
Bending Oaks Pl. Pg.16 R14
Bentley Ct. Pg.23 U16
Benton Ave. Pg.17 R15
Berrywood Ln. Pg.23 T16
Biltmore Rd. Pg.17 Q16
Binder Rd. Pg.22 U14
Birch Ave. Pg.17 R15
Birchwood Pl. Pg.16 N13
Black Oak Dr. Pg.17 P15
Blackburn Ave. Pg.23 U16
Blackburn Ct. Pg.23 U16
Blackburn Pl. Pg.23 U16
Blackstone Ct. Pg.23 T15
Blackstone Dr. Pg.23 T15
Blanchard St. Pg.22,23 S14
Blodgett Ave. Pg.17,23 R16,T15
Blodgett Ct. Pg.23 T15
Bolson Dr. Pg.22,23 T14
Bonnie Brae Dr. Pg.23 T15
Borman Pl. Pg.22,28 U14
Boundary Rd. Pg.22 T14
Bradely Ct. Pg.23 T14
Braemoor Dr. Pg.17 N15
Branding Ave. Pg.17 N14
Breasted Ave. Pg.22 T14
Brentwood Pl. Pg.17 Q16
Briargate Dr. Pg.23 T15
Brighton St. Pg.22 T14
Brook Dr. Pg.17 N14
Brook Ln. Pg.17 R15
Brookbank Rd. Pg.17 R14,T15
Brookside Ln. Pg.17 P14
Brookwood Dr. Pg.22 T14
Brunette Dr. Pg.23 T14
Bryan Pl. Pg.17 R15
Bryan St. Pg.17 Q15
Bryant Rd. Pg.16 P12
Bryce Pl. Pg.17 N14
Buckingham Pl. Pg.23 U16
Buckthorn Ln. Pg.17 P14
Bunkerhill Cir. Pg.22 U14
Bunning Dr. Pg.23 S16
Burlington Ave. Pg.16,17 R13,15
Bush Pl. Pg.22 R14
Butterfield Rd. Pg.17 N14
Cambridge Rd. Pg.22 U14
Camden Ct. Pg.22 U14
Camden Pl. Pg.22 U14
Camden Rd. Pg.22 U14
Candlewood Ct. Pg.17 P15
Candlewood Dr. Pg.17 P15
Canterbury Pl. Pg.23 U15
Carol St. Pg.16 Q14
Carpenter St. Pg.17,23 R,S,U15
Centre Cir. Pg.17 N14
Challen Pl. Pg.16 R13
Chase Ave. Pg.16 R13
Chase Rd. Pg.22 S13
Chicago Ave. Pg.16,17 R13,16
Churchill Ct. Pg.23 U15
Claremont Ct. Pg.23 U16
Claremont Dr. Pg.23 U15
Clayton Ct. Pg.23 U15
Clyde Ave. Pg.23 S15
College Rd. Pg.22 S12
Commerce Dr. Pg.16 Q13
Concord Ct. Pg.23 U14
Concord Dr. Pg.23 U14
Concord Pl. Pg.23 U14
Coralberry Ln. Pg.17 P14
Cornell Ave. Pg.16 Q,R14
Cottonwood Ct. Pg.23 T16
Country Creek Way Pg.23 U15
Creek Wood Ct. Pg.17 P15
Creekside Rd. Pg.23 U15
Crescent Dr. Pg.23 T15
Cross St. Pg.16 Q13
Crystal Ave. Pg.23 U15
Cumnor Rd. Pg.23 S16
Curtiss St. Pg.16 R13
Davane Ct. Pg.23 T16
Davane Ln. Pg.23 T16
Davis St. Pg.17 Q15
Dawn Pl. Pg.17 Q15
De Witt Ln. Pg.17 R14
Dearborn Pkwy. Pg.23 S15
Debolt Ave. Pg.17 R15
Deerpath Lm. Pg.23 S16
Devereux Rd. Pg.22 U14
Dexter Rd. Pg.22 U14
Dickson Ave. Pg.23 U14
Dillon Ct. Pg.22 P15
Dillon Ct. Pg.17 P15
Dogwood Ct. Pg.23 T16
Douglas Rd. Pg.17 R,Q16
Downers Dr. Pg.17 N14
Drendel Rd. Pg.16 Q13
Drew St. Pg.17 N14
Drove Ave. Pg.17 Q14
Dunham Rd. Pg.23 S,U14,U15
Durand Ct. Pg.22 S13
Durand Dr. Pg.22 S13
Dutchess Ct. Pg.17 P14
Earlston Rd. Pg.17 Q15
Edward Ave. Pg.16 R13
Eldon Pl. Pg.23 S16
Elizabeth Ln. Pg.23 V16
Elm St. Pg.17 Q,R15
Elmore Ave. Pg.16 R13
Elmwood Ave. Pg.17 R15
Esplanade Rd. Pg.16 N14
Esplanade Rd. Pg.16 N14
Essex Pl. Pg.22 U14
Fairhaven Ct. Pg.16,22 S14
Fairmount Ave. Pg.23 S,T15
Fairview Ave. Pg.17,23 Q-U16
Farley Pl. Pg.17 S15
Farrar Ct. Pg.17 R15
Finley Rd. Pg.16 P14
Florence Ave. Pg.17,23 Q,V16
Forest Ave. Pg.17 Q15
Foster Pl. Pg.23 U15
Foster Rd. Pg.23 U15
Foxfire Ct. Pg.17 Q16
Francisco St. Pg.16 R13
Franklin St. Pg.17 R15
Frontage Rd. Pg.17 N14
Garden Ct. Pg.23 T16
George St. Pg.17 S14
Gierz Ave. Pg.17 R15
Gilbert Ave. Pg.17 R14
Glen Ave. Pg.16 Q14
Glendenning Rd. Pg.17 Q,R15
Glenview Ave. Pg.16 R13
Golden Bell Ct. Pg.17 P14
Grace Ct. Pg.23 U15
Graham Ave. Pg.22,28 U14
Grand Ave. Pg.17,23 R,S,U16
Grand Ct. Pg.23 U16
Grand St. Pg.17 Q14
Grant Ave. Pg.16,17 Q13,16
Grant Ave. Pg.17 Q14
Granville Ave. Pg.16 R13
Gregory Pl. Pg.17 N15
Grove St. Pg.17 R15
Haddow Ave. Pg.22 R13
Hall Pl. Pg.22,28 U14
Hall St. Pg.22,28 U14
Harmarc Pl. Pg.23 S16
Hartford Rd. Pg.23 U15
Hastings Ave. Pg.22 T13
Hatch Pl. Pg.22 U14
Hatch St. Pg.22 U14
Hathaway Ln. Pg.22 T14
Havens Ct. Pg.17 Q15
Hawkins Ave. Pg.23 U14
Hawthorne Ln. Pg.17 R14
Herbert St. Pg.17 P15
Hickory Ct. Pg.17 P14
Hickory Tr. Pg.17 P15
Highland Ave. Pg.17 R15
Highland Ct. Pg.17 Q15
Hill St. Pg.17 R16
Hillcrest Ct. Pg.23 T14
Hillcrest Dr. Pg.23 U14
Hillcrest Rd. Pg.22,23 S,T14
Hitchcock Ave. Pg.16 R13
Hobart Ave. Pg.23 U15
Hobson Rd. Pg.22 S13
Holland Pl. Pg.17 N14
Holly Ct. Pg.17 P14
Howard Ave. Pg.16 S13
Hughes Ave. Pg.23 U14
Indianapolis Ave. Pg.17 Q16
Interstate 355 Pg.16 M14
Interstate 88 Pg.16 N15
Inverness Ave. Pg.16 S13
Jacqueline Dr. Pg.17 R14
Janes Ave. Pg.16,22 S,T13
Janet St. Pg.16 Q14
Jay Dr. Pg.23 U15
Jefferson Ave. Pg.22,23 S14
Katrine Ave. Pg.16 R13
Kelly Pl. Pg.22,23 U14
Kensington Pl. Pg.22 T14
Kenyon St. Pg.23 S15
Kidwell Rd. Pg.23 U15
Klein Ave. Pg.23 U15
Knottingham Ln. Pg.23 V16
Lacey Rd. Pg.16 P14
Lake Ave. Pg.17 Q16
Lamb Ct. Pg.23 U14
Lancaster Ave. Pg.23 T15
Lancaster Pl. Pg.23 T15
Lane Pl. Pg.17,23 R,T15
Laurel Ct. Pg.17 P15
Lee Ave. Pg.16,17 R14
Lemont Rd. Pg.23 U15
Leonard Ave. Pg.22 T13
Lexington Ln. Pg.22 T14
Lincoln Ave. Pg.17 Q16
Linden Pl. Pg.17 R15
Lindenwald Pg.17 R14
Lindley St. Pg.17 Q15
Linscott Ave. Pg.17 R15
Longmeadow Rd. Pg.17 Q16
Loomes Ave. Pg.22 T14
Lyman Ave. Pg.17,23 R,S,U15
Mackie Pl. Pg.17 R15
Main Blvd. Pg.16 N14
Main St. Pg.17,23 P,Q,S15
Manning Rd. Pg.23 V16
Maple Ave. Pg.16,17 R16,S11
Maplewood Pl. Pg.23 S14,15
Marie Dr. Pg.23 V16
Matthais Rd. Pg.23 V15
McIntyre Rd. Pg.17 Q12
Meade Pl. Pg.22 T14
Meade Rd. Pg.22 U14
Meadow Crest Ct. Pg.23 U15
Meadow Crest Dr. Pg.23 U15
Meadow Crest Pl. Pg.23 U15
Meadow Ln. Pg.17 S14
Middaugh Ave. Pg.23 S14
Middaugh Ct. Pg.23 S14
Middaugh St. Pg.23 S14
Midhurst Rd. Pg.22 T13
Mistwood Ct. Pg.17 N15
Mistwood Ln. Pg.17 N15
Mistwood Pl. Pg.17 N15
Monmouth Pl. Pg.22 U14
Montgomery Ave. Pg.17 R14
Morton Ave. Pg.16 Q14
Nash St. Pg.22 T14
Newport Rd. Pg.22 U14
Norfolk St. Pg.22,23 T14
Northbridge Pl. Pg.22 U14
Northcott Ave. Pg.16 Q,R14
Northgate Way Pg.23 U15
O'Neill Rd. Pg.23 U14
Oak Grove Dr. Pg.17 N14
Oak Hill Ct. Pg.17 P14
Oak Hill Rd. Pg.17 P15
Oakwood Ave. Pg.17 R14
Ogden Ave. Pg.17 Q16
Old George Way Pg.22 S13
Old Main St. Pg.23 U15
Old Orchard Ave. Pg.23 U15
Opus Pl. Pg.17 N14
Orchard Pl. Pg.23 U15
Osage Ave. Pg.23 T16
Osage Pl. Pg.23 U16
Otis Ave. Pg.17 Q16
Otto Pl. Pg.22 T14
Oxford Ct. Pg.23 T15
Oxnard Dr. Pg.22 T13
Palmer St. Pg.22,23 T14
Park Ave. Pg.17,23 S,T15
Parker Ave. Pg.23 U15
Parkview Dr. Pg.23 U15
Parkway Dr. Pg.17 R15
Parrish Ct. Pg.17 P14
Penner Ave. Pg.22 U14
Penner Pl. Pg.22 U14
Pershing Ave. Pg.16 R13
Pinewood Dr. Pg.23 U15
Pinewood Pl. Pg.23 U15
Pipers Way Pg.23 U15
Plainfield Rd. Pg.23 V16
Plum Ct. Pg.16 P14
Plymouth Ct. Pg.22 T14
Plymouth Rd. Pg.22,23 U14
Plymouth St. Pg.23 T14
Pomeroy Ct. Pg.17 P14
Pomeroy Rd. Pg.17 P14
Powell Ct. Pg.23 U14
Powell Pl. Pg.23 U14
Powell St. Pg.23 T,U14
Prairie Ave. Pg.16,17 R13-15
Prentiss Ct. Pg.22 T14
Prentiss Dr. Pg.22 T13
Prideham St. Pg.22 T14
Prince St. Pg.17 R15
Prospect Ave. Pg.17 R15
Puffer Rd. Pg.16,22 R,T13
Queens Ct. Pg.23 V16
Quince Ct. Pg.17 P15
Randall St. Pg.17 R15
Red Silver Ct. Pg.17 P15
Redbud Ct. Pg.17 P14
Revere Rd. Pg.22 U14
Richards Ave. Pg.23 U16
Ridgeview St. Pg.23 U15
Ridgewood Cir. Pg.23 T14
Rob Roy Pl. Pg.23 U15
Robey Ave. Pg.23 U15
Roe Ct. Pg.23 U16
Rogers St. Pg.17 R15
Rohrer Dr. Pg.23 V16
Rosewood Pl. Pg.17 N15
Roslyn Rd. Pg.17 Q16
Ross Ct. Pg.17 R15
Running Dr. Pg.23 S16
Saint James Ct. Pg.23 T16
Saratoga Ave. Pg.23 T15
Saratoga St. Pg.17 R15
Saylor St. Pg.23 T14
Scheldrup St. Pg.17 N14
School Rd. Pg.17 P15
Seeley Ave. Pg.17 Q14
Selig Pl. Pg.22 U14
Shady Ln. Pg.17 Q16
Sheldon Ave. Pg.17 R16
Sheridan Pl. Pg.17 Q15
Sherman Rd. Pg.17 Q15
Sherman St. Pg.17 Q15
Sherwood Ave. Pg.17 Q16
Sherwood Ct. Pg.23 V16
Snowberry Ct. Pg.17 P14
Snowberry Ct. Pg.17 P14
Snowberry Ln. Pg.17 P14
Springside Ave. Pg.22 T,U14
Springside Pl. Pg.22 T14
St. James Ct. Pg.23 T16
Stair Pl. Pg.22 T14
Stair St. Pg.22 T14
Stanford Ave. Pg.23 U15
Stanley Ave. Pg.17 Q15
Statton St. Pg.17 Q15
Sterling Rd. Pg.17 Q15
Stockley Rd. Pg.23 U15
Stonewall Ave. Pg.16,22 R-T14
Stratford Ln. Pg.23 T15
Sturbridge Pl. Pg.22 U14
Summit St. Pg.17,23 S15
Tamarack Dr. Pg.22 S13
Taylor St. Pg.22 T14
Terrace Dr. Pg.23 T,U14
Thatcher Rd. Pg.16 R12
Thornwood Dr. Pg.23 S14
Ticonderoga Pl. Pg.22 U14
Ticonderoga Rd. Pg.22,28 U14
Tower Ct. Pg.23 U16
Tower Rd. Pg.17 P16
Traube Ave. Pg.17 Q16
Trent Rd. Pg.23 U16
Turvey Ct. Pg.17 R14
Turvey Rd. Pg.17 R14
Valley Forge Pl. Pg.22 U14
Valley View Dr. Pg.23 U15,16
Venard Rd. Pg.17 P,Q14
Victor St. Pg.17 R16
Village Dr. Pg.23 T16
Virginia St. Pg.16 Q14
Wall Pl. Pg.17,23 S16
Wallbank Ave. Pg.17 R14
Wallen Pl. Pg.23 T15
Walnut Ave. Pg.16,22 S12
Wanda Pl. Pg.17,23 S15
Warren Ave. Pg.16 R14
Warrenville Rd. Pg.16 Q13
Washington St. Pg.17 Q-T15
Waterfall Pl. Pg.23 U15
Weatherbee Ave. Pg.23 T15
Weatherbee Pl. Pg.23 T15
Webster Pl. Pg.23 S15
Webster St. Pg.23 S,U15
Wellington Pl. Pg.22 T14
Wells St. Pg.22 T14
Westend Rd. Pg.17 Q16
Westfield Dr. Pg.22 T13
Whidden Ave. Pg.22 T14
Whiffin Pl. Pg.17 R15
White Pl. Pg.22 U14
Whitefawn Tr. Pg.23 S16
Wilcox Ave. Pg.23 R,S16
Willard Pl. Pg.23 U14
Williams St. Pg.17,23 R,Q,V16
Willowood Ct. Pg.23 T16
Wilson Ave. Pg.16 Q13
Wilson St. Pg.17 R15
Windsor Ct. Pg.22 T13
Winthrop Ct. Pg.23 U15
Winthrop Way Pg.23 U15
Winwood Way Pg.23 U15
Wisconsin St. Pg.16 R13
Wolf Pl. Pg.23 U16
Wood Ave. Pg.17 P14
Woodcreek Dr. Pg.16 N13
Woodland Ln. Pg.17 P15
Woods Ave. Pg.17 P15
Woodview Ct. Pg.23 T16
Woodward Ave. Pg.16 R13
York Rd. Pg.23 U15
2nd St. Pg.17 R16
3rd St. Pg.17 R16
4th St. Pg.17 R16
5th St. Pg.17 R16
6th St. Pg.17 R16
7th St. Pg.17 S16
8th St. Pg.17,23 S16
31st St. Pg.17 N15
35th St. Pg.17 P14
36th St. Pg.17 P16
39th St. Pg.17 P15
40th Pl. Pg.23 Q14,16
40th St. Pg.17 Q15
41st St. Pg.17 Q15,16
55th Pl. Pg.16 S14
55th St. Pg.17,23 S16
56th Ct. Pg.23 S16
56th St. Pg.23 S16
57th St. Pg.23 S16
59th Pl. Pg.23 S15
59th St. Pg.23 S15
60th Pl. Pg.23 S15
60th St. Pg.23 S15
61st St. Pg.23 T15
62nd Ct. Pg.23 T15
62nd Pl. Pg.23 T15
62nd St. Pg.22,23 T13,15

## DOWNERS GROVE

63rd St. Pg.22,23 T13,14
64th St. Pg.22 T13
65th St. Pg.23 T15
66th St. Pg.23 T16
67th Ct. Pg.23 T16
67th Pl. Pg.23 U14
67th St. Pg.23 T15
68th Pl. Pg.23 U14
68th St. Pg.23 U14,15
71st St. Pg.22,23 U15
71st Ter. Pg.22 U14
72nd Ct. Pg.23 U15
72nd St. Pg.23 U15
73rd St. Pg.23 U14,16
74th St. Pg.23 U16
75th St. Pg.23 V16
77th St. Pg.23 V16

**CEMETERIES**
Main St. Cem. Pg.17 R15

**FOREST PRESERVES**
Maple Grove Pg.16,17 R,S14

**GOLF COURSES**
Downers Grove G.C. Pg.16 R13
Western Acres G.C. Pg.16 N13

**PARKS**
Belmont Park Pg.16 R12
Coopers Hollow Pk. Pg.16 Q14
Doerhoefer Park Pg.17 Q14
Fischel Park Pg.17 R15
Gilbert Park Pg.16 R14
Hummer Park Pg.17 R16
Lyman Woods Pg.17 P15
Mar-Duke Farm Pg.23 U15
McCollum Park Pg.23 U15
Memorial Park Pg.16 S14
Northside Park Pg.17 N15
Northwest Park Pg.16 R14
O'Brien Park Pg.23 W14
Patriot Park Pg.23 S16
Powers Park Pg.23 T14
Prince Park Pg.17 R15
Randall Park Pg.17 R15
Spring Park Pg.23 T15
Sterling N. Park Pg.16 R14
Wallingford Park Pg.17 Q15
Whitlock Park Pg.17 P16

**SCHOOLS**
Agnes Hefty Sch. Pg.16 R13
Avery Coonley Sch. Pg.17,23 S14
Belle Aire Sch. Pg.17 Q14
Board of Education Pg.17 R15
Downer Sch. Pg.17 Q14
Downers Grove Adventist Sch. Pg.17 S14
Downers Grove Comm. H.S. Pg.17 Q15
Downers Grove North H.S. Pg.17 Q15
Downers Grove South H.S. Pg.23 T14
El Sierra Sch. Pg.23 U15
Fairmount Sch. Pg.23 S15
First Baptist Christian Sch. Pg.17 R15
Geo. Williams College Pg.17 P15
George William College Ed. Center Pg.17 N14
Good Shepard Lutheran Sch. Pg.20 T10
Henry Puffer Sch. Pg.16 R13
Herrick Jr. High Pg.17 Q14
Highland Sch. Pg.17 Q15
Hillcrest Sch. Pg.23 S14
Indian Trails Sch. Pg.23 T14
Kingsley Sch. Pg.23 T14
Lester Sch. Pg.17 Q16
Lincoln Sch. Pg.17 R15
Longfellow Sch. Pg.17 R14
Midwestern University Pg.17 P16
O'Neill Jr. H.S. Pg.23 S15
Puffer Sch. Pg.16 R13
School Dist. 99 Admin. Ctr. Pg.22 T14
St. Joseph Sch. Pg.17 R15
St. Marys Sch. Pg.17 R15
The Bridge H.S. Pg.16 R13
Washington Sch. Pg.17 R15
Whittier Sch. Pg.17 R16

**SHOPPING CENTERS**
Butterfield Plaza Pg.17 N14
Downer's Park Plaza Pg.23 V15
Downers Market Pg.17 Q14
Downers Plaza Shopping Center Pg.17 Q16
Home Depot Pg.16 N14
Main Street Square Pg.16 N14
Meadowbrook S.C. Pg.17 T13
Shopping Centers Pg.17,22,23 N14,15,U15

**MISCELLANEOUS**
Chamber of Commerce Pg.17 R15
Fairview Village Pg.23 T16
Fire Dept. Pg.17 R15
Good Samaritan Hospital Pg.17 P14
Library Pg.17 R15
Northside Fire Sta. Pg.17 P15
Pool Assn. of Downers Grove Pg.23 S15
Southside Fire Sta. Pg.17 S15
Village Offices Pg.17 R15

## DOWNERS GROVE TOWNSHIP

Pages 16,17,22-24,28-30

**STREETS**
Adams St. Pg.17,23 Q,U17
Adelia St. Pg.23 T15
Adlai E. Stevenson Expwy. Pg.29,30 V19,Y14
Ailsworth Ct. Pg.22 W14
Ailsworth Dr. Pg.28 W14
Alabama Ave. Pg.24,30 S,V,W18
Alden Ln. Pg.22 W14
Allison Ct. Pg.30 W18
Andrus Rd. Pg.29 X16
Applegate Ave. Pg.23 U15
Argonne Ridge Rd. Pg.29 X17
Ashley Rd. Pg.16 W13
Aster Ln. Pg.29 W15
Bailey Rd. Pg.29 V17
Baimbridge Dr. Pg.29 V16
Barrett St. Pg.29 Y15
Bellair Ct. Pg.23 U17
Beller Ct. Pg.28,29 W14
Beller Dr. Pg.28 W14
Belmont Rd. Pg.22 S13
Bentley Ave. Pg.24 T18
Birnam Trail Pg.29 X18
Blackburn Pl. Pg.23 U16
Blodgett Ave. Pg.23,27 T,W15
Bluff Rd. Pg.29,30 Y16,18,Z15
Bodin St. Pg.24 S19
Bonnie Brae Pg.30 W18
Boundary Rd. Pg.22 T14
Brewer Ln. Pg.28 W14
Brewer Rd. Pg.28 W14
Brookbank Dr. Pg.30 W,V18
Brookbank Rd. Pg.30 W18
Brookridge Rd. Pg.29 W15
Brookview Ct. Pg.24 T19
Bruner St. Pg.24 S19
Brush Hill Rd. Pg.24,30 V19
Burgess Pl. Pg.28 W14
Burr Oak Ln. Pg.30 X18
Cambridge Ct. Pg.29 V15
Camden Dr. Pg.22,28 X14
Carol St. Pg.23 T15
Carpenter St. Pg.23,29 T,Y,Z15
Cass Ave. Pg.23,29 W,X17
Center Ave. Pg.16 Q14
Central Ave. Pg.29,30 W15,18
Central Dr. Pg.29 Y17,18
Charles Ct. Pg.29 W15
Chatelane Ct. Pg.24 T18
Chicago Ave. Pg.17 R16
Christopher Dr. Pg.29 Z15
Circle Ave. Pg.30 W18
Claremont Ave. Pg.23 U17
Clarendon Hills Rd. Pg.24,30 S,W18
Clifford Dr. Pg.28 W14
Clover Dr. Pg.29 W15
Cobb Dr. Pg.22,28 W14
Cobb St. Pg.22,28 W14
Concord Pl. Pg.29 V17
Country Creek Way Pg.23,29 U15
County Line Rd. Pg.24,30 W20
Coventry Ct. Pg.24 S18
Coventry Dr. Pg.22,28 W14
Cumnor Rd. Pg.17 S,W16
Davey Rd. Pg.28,29 Z14
Deans Cove Pg.29 Z15
Deerpath Ln. Pg.29 Z15
Dixon Ct. Pg.28 W14
Downers Dr. Pg.17,22,23 S-Y14
Drew Ave. Pg.30 X20
Drover Ct. Pg.28,29 W14
Drover Ln. Pg.28 W14
Dunham Dr. Pg.22,28 X14
Dunham Rd. Pg.23,29 U,V,Y14
Dystrup Ave. Pg.29 Z15
Earl Ct. Pg.29 V17
Eastwood Cutoff Pg.29 Y18
Eastwood Dr. Pg.29 Y18
Echo Ten Ln. (Pvt.) Pg.30 X18
Edgewood Dr. Pg.29 V14
Elizabeth Dr. Pg.22,28 X14
Elizabeth Ln. Pg.23,29 V16
Elm Ave. Pg.24 U20
Elm St. Pg.24,30 W18
Elmore Ave. Pg.16 R14
Executive Dr. Pg.24,30 V19
Fairmont Ave. Pg.23,29 T-V15
Fairview Ave. Pg.23 T16
Fern St. Pg.30 W18
Finley Rd. Pg.16 Q14
Florence Ave. Pg.23,29 T-W16
Freund Rd. Pg.29 Y17
Front St. Pg.29 Y18
Frontage Rd. Pg.23,30 V19,W16
Garfield Pg.24,30 V20
Giddings Ave. Pg.24,30 S,U20
Gigi Ln. Pg.23,29 U16
Gilbert Ct. Pg.28 W14
Glen Ave. Pg.16 Q14
Glen Rd. Pg.29 X16
Glenn Dr. Pg.30 X19
Godair Cir. Pg.24 T19
Godair Dr. Pg.24 T19
Gold Grove Pl. Pg.23 U16
Graceland St. Pg.23 V16
Grand Ave. Pg.23 U16
Grandview Ln. Pg.28 W14
Grandview Pl. Pg.29 W14
Grant Ave. Pg.16 Q14
Grant St. Pg.12,17,24 Q,U17,S,U19
Hampshire Ln. Pg.29 X18
Harvest Ln. Pg.29 W14
Harvest Pl. Pg.29 W14
Harvey Rd. Pg.30 W18
Havens Ct. Pg.22,28 X14
Havens Dr. Pg.22 W14
Helen Ct. Pg.29 W15
Herbert St. Pg.17 Q16
Hidden View Dr. Pg.23 S17
Highcrest St. Pg.29 W14
Highland Ave. Pg.29 W15
Highland Rd. Pg.30 W18
Highpoint Cir. Pg.30 W18
Hill Rd. Pg.29 Y,Z15
Hillcrest Ln. Pg.29 Z15
Hillside Ct. Pg.29 W14
Hillside Dr. Pg.24 S19
Hillside Ln. Pg.29,30 W14,18
Holly Ave. Pg.23 U17
Holmes Ave. Pg.24 S18
Honeysuckle Rose Ln.(Pvt.) Pg.30 X18
Howdy Ln. Pg.23 U16
Hudson St. Pg.23 U16
Hyacinth Dr.(Pvt) Pg.30 X18
Inner Circle Pg.29 Y16
Ivy Ln.(Pvt) Pg.30 X16
Jackson Pg.24 S19
Jackson St. Pg.30 Y19
Jamie Ln. Pg.24 X18
Jeans Rd. Pg.30 X,Y19
Joliet Rd. Pg.29 W17
Kaye Ln. Pg.30 X18
Kearney Rd. Pg.23,29 W-Y16
Kingery Court Dr. Pg.30 X18
Kings Ct. Pg.29 V17
Knob Hill Dr. Pg.28 W14
Knoebel Dr. Pg.29 Z15
Knottingham Ln. Pg.29 V16
Lake Dr. Pg.30 V18
Lakeside Dr. Pg.24,29 S19,W15
Lakewood Dr. Pg.30 W18
Landsfield Ave. Pg.29 V15
Landsfield Ct. Pg.29 V15
Landsfield Pl. Pg.29 V15
Lee Ave. Pg.16,22,28 S,W14
Lemont Rd. Pg.23,29 V,Z15
Leonard Dr. Pg.29 W18
Liberty Blvd. Pg.17 Q16
Lilac Ln.(Pvt) Pg.30 X18
Lincoln St. Pg.17 Q17
London Ave. Pg.28 X14
Lorraine Dr. Pg.30 W18
Lyman Ave. Pg.23,29 U,V15
Madison St. Pg.24,30 T,W19
Main St. Pg.23,29 U,W15
Mallard Ct. Pg.29 Z15
Manning Rd. Pg.29 V16
Marie Dr. Pg.29 V16
Mark Ln. Pg.29 V15
Marybeth Ct. Pg.30 W18
Meadow Ct. Pg.29,30 W14,18
Meadow Ln. Pg.29 W,Y14
Meadowbrook Dr. Pg.30 W19
Meadowlark Ln. Pg.23 W17
Meadowlawn Ave. Pg.23 T15
Meridian Rd. Pg.29 Y16
Middaugh Ave. Pg.29 Y14
Millbrook Dr. Pg.29 W16
Millbrook Dr. Pg.29 W15
Mockingbird Ln. (Pvt) Pg.30 X18
Monroe St. Pg.24 S19
Murphy Rd. Pg.28 X,Z14
Nantucket Dr. Pg.29 V17
Nelson Ln Pg.30 X18
Norfolk St. Pg.23 T15
Northgate Rd. Pg.29 X17
Oak Hill Ct. Pg.30 X19
Oakville Pg.22 W14
Oakwood Ave. Pg.29 Y14
Ogilvie Ct. Pg.29 W16
Old Bluff Rd. Pg.29 Y17
Old Orchard Ave. Pg.23 U15
Oldfield Rd. Pg.29 W15
Oneill Dr. Pg.30 X19
Orchard Pl. Pg.23 U15
Orchard Rd. Pg.28,29 Y14
Osage Ave. Pg.23 U16
Outer Cir. Pg.29 Y16
Oxford St. Pg.23 T15
Palisades Rd. Pg.30 X19
Palmer St. Pg.23 T15
Park Ln. Pg.24 S19
Park St. Pg.17,24 Q16,U20
Parkview Dr. Pg.29 W14
Parkway Dr. Pg.17 Q16,17
Pearson Dr. Pg.29 W14
Peters Ct. Pg.22,28 X14
Peters Dr. Pg.22,28 X14
Pinecrest Ct. Pg.24 T19
Pipers Way Pg.23,29 U15
Pitcher Dr. Pg.22,28 U,W14
Plainfield Rd. Pg.28 U19,V15
Plaza Ct. Pg.24,30 V19
Pleasantdale Dr. Pg.29 Y14
Portsmouth Ct. Pg.29 V17
Portsmouth Dr. Pg.29 V17
Powell Pg.24 S18
Quarry Rd. Pg.29 Z17
Quarter Pg.30 X18
Queens Ct. Pg.29 V16
Quincy Ct. Pg.24 T19
Quincy St. Pg.24,30 S19
Ragha Dr. Pg.30 X18
Railroad Dr. Pg.29 Y17
Redondo Ct. Pg.29 V16
Redondo Dr. Pg.29 V16
Richmond Ave. Pg.23 T17
Ridge Rd. Pg.23 T17
Robert Kingery Hwy. Pg.24,30 X19,Y18
Rock Rd. Pg.29 Y16
Rogers Ct. Pg.23 U17
Rohrer Dr. Pg.29 V16
Rooke Ct. Pg.22,28 X14
Rosehill Ct. Pg.29 W16
Rosehill Ln Pg.29 W16
Rutgers Ct. Pg.22,28 X14
Rutgers Dr. Pg.22,28 X14
Ruth Dr. Pg.29 W,X16
Ruth Lake Ct. Pg.24 T19
Saratoga Ave. Pg.23,29 Y15
Saylor St. Pg.23 T15
Scheel Dr. Pg.29 W18
Seeley Ave. Pg.29 Y14
Shephard Ln. Pg.30 X19
Sherman Ave. Pg.22 S14
Sherwood Ct. Pg.23 V16
Skyline Dr. Pg.30 X19
Soper Ave. Pg.24,30 U19
Spring Green Dr. Pg.29 W14
Springside Ave. Pg.22,23,29 U14
St. Patrick Rd. Pg.29 Y16
Stonewall Ave. Pg.16,22 S13
Stough St. Pg.24 S19
Stratford Pl. Pg.29 V17
Suffield Dr. Pg.22,28 X14
Summer Ln. Pg.29 V16
Summit Rd. Pg.23 U16
Sunrise Ave. Pg.24,30 S,W18
Sunset Rd. Pg.30 W18
Sutton Pl. Pg.29 V17
Tanbark Ct. Pg.29 W15
Tech Rd. Pg.29 Y17
Tennessee Ave. Pg.24,30 S,W18
Terry Tr. Pg.30 X18
Thames Ave. Pg.22,28 X14
Therese Ct. Pg.30 W18
Thurlow St. Pg.24 S,T19
Timber Trails Pg.29 X14
Timberlake Dr. Pg.30 W18
Tower Ct. Pg.23 U15
Traube Ave. Pg.22 U16
Tumblebrook Ct. Pg.28 X19
Valley View Dr. Pg.30 X19
Village Rd. Pg.30 W18
Vine St. Pg.24,30 U,X19
Virginia Ave. Pg.24 S18
Wallace Dr. Pg.22,28 X14
Waltham Pl. Pg.29 V17
Washington Pl. Pg.29 W15
Washington St. Pg.17,23,29 Q,U17,V,W15
Water Tower Ln. Pg.29 W14
Water Tower Rd. Pg.29 W15
Webster St. Pg.23,29 U15
Western Ave. Pg.23,24 T,W18
Westgate Rd. Pg.29 Y15
Westminster Dr. Pg.28 X14
White Deer Dr. Pg.23 X16
Whitney Ln. Pg.29 Z15
William Dr. Pg.30 V,W18
Williams St. Pg.17,23 R,U,V16
Willow Ln. Pg.23 U17
Wilmette Ave. Pg.23,29 S,W17
Winter Circle Pg.29 V15
Winthrop Ct. Pg.23,29 U15
Winthrop Way Pg.23,29 U15
Wirth Dr. Pg.23 U16
Wolf Pl. Pg.23 U16
Wood Creek Pl. Pg.29 Z15
Woodcreek Ct. Pg.23 V16
Woodcrest Dr. Pg.28,29 X14
Woodglen Ln. Pg.29 V16
Woodward Ave. Pg.22 X14
York Ln. Pg.28 X14
39th St. Pg.17 P16
40th St. Pg.17 Q16
41st St. Pg.17 Q16
55th Pl. Pg.16,22 S19,20
56th Pl. Pg.24 S19
56th St. Pg.23,24 S18-20
57th St. Pg.24 S18,20
58th Pl. Pg.24 S18,19
58th St. Pg.23,24 S18,19
59th St. Pg.23,24 S14,18,19
60th Ct. Pg.24 S18
60th St. Pg.23,24 S16,17,20
61st St. Pg.23,24 T16,18
62nd St. Pg.23 T14
63rd St. Pg.23 T17
64th St. Pg.24 T19
65th St. Pg.23 T17
66th St. Pg.23 T16
67th Ct. Pg.23 T16
67th Pl. Pg.24 T19
67th St. Pg.23 T15
68th Pl. Pg.24 U19
68th St. Pg.24 T19
69th St. Pg.24 U19
71st St. Pg.23,24 U15,17,19
72nd Ct. Pg.24 U19
72nd St. Pg.23,24 U19,20
73rd Ct. Pg.24 U19
73rd Pl. Pg.23,29 U17
73rd St. Pg.23,24 U15,19
74th St. Pg.28,30 U19
75th St. Pg.23,24 V14,19
79th Pl. Pg.29,30 V15,18
79th St. Pg.30 V18
80th Pl. Pg.30 V16,18
80th St. Pg.29,30 V15,18,19
81st St. Pg.29,30 V15,18
82nd St. Pg.30 V19
83rd Ct. Pg.29,30 W15,19
83rd St. Pg.28,29 W14,16,18
85th Ct. Pg.29 W15
86th Pl. Pg.29 W15
86th St. Pg.29 W15
87th St. Pg.29 W14,18
89th Pl. Pg.30 X18
89th St. Pg.30 X18,19
90th St. Pg.30 X18,19
91st St. Pg.23,29,30 X16-19
92nd St. Pg.29 X16
93rd Pl. Pg.30 X19
94th Pl. Pg.30 X19
94th St. Pg.29,30 X17,19
95th St. Pg.30 X19
97th St. Pg.29,30 Y14,19
98th Pl. Pg.29 Y14
98th St. Pg.29 Y14
99th St. Pg.29 Y14
101st St. Pg.29 Y14
103rd St. Pg.29 Z14
109th St. Pg.29 Z15

**CEMETERIES**
Clarendon Hills Cem. Pg.23 U16
St. Patricks Cem. Pg.29 Y16

**FOREST PRESERVES**
Waterfall Glen Foerst Preserve Pg.29,30 X17,18,Z16

**SCHOOLS**
Anne M. Jeans Elem. Sch. Pg.30 X18
Bromberek Sch. Pg.29 Z14
Center Cass Sch. Pg.29 W15
Gower Middle Sch. Pg.24 V19
Holmes Sch. Pg.24 S18
Indian Trail Sch. Pg.22 T14
Lakeview Jr. H.S. Pg.29 W15
Maercker Jr. H.S. Pg.23 T17
Palisades Middle Sch. Pg.30 X18
Seton Little Peoples Montessori Sch. Pg.24 S18
Sierra Sch. Pg.30 W21
Village Early Learning Center Pg.23 W15

**SHOPPING CENTERS**
Shopping Center Pg.23 T17

**MISCELLANEOUS**
Argonne National Laboratory Reservation Pg.29 Y16,17
Fire Dept. Pg.23 W15
Knollwood Boat Launch Pg.30 Y19
Lake Brookenridge Airport Pg.23 W15
Village Hall Pg.24 U19

## DU PAGE TOWNSHIP

(WILL COUNTY)
Pages 26-28
(For additional listings, see Section 8)

**STREETS**
Bolingbrook Rd. Z11
Boughton Rd. Y7
Frontage Rd. Z12
Greene Rd. X11
Joliet Rd. Z13
Joliet-Naperville Rd. Y8
Knolls Rd. X7
Lily Cache Ln. Z9
Lindsey Ln. Y9
Marimon Dr. Z13
Remington Blvd. Z11
Royce Rd. X11
Schmidt Rd. Z10
Weber Rd. Z8
107th St. Z13

**PARKS**
DuPage River Park X8
Knock Knolls Commons X7
Winston Woods X12

## ELK GROVE VILLAGE

Pages 5,6
(For additional listings, see Section 2)

**STREETS**
Allen Dr. Pg.5 A17
American Ln. Pg.6 A19
Arlington Hts. Rd. Pg.5 A16
Brickvale Pg.6 A18
Carl Blvd. Pg.5 A17
Center St. Pg.5 A17
Central Ave. Pg.5 A18
Cumberland Cir. Pg.5 A15
Delta Ln. Pg.6 A19
Devon Ave. Pg.5 A17
Eastern Ave. Pg.6 A19
Katherine Way Ave. Pg.5,6 A18
Kirk St. Pg.5 A19
Leeds Pg.5 A15
Lively Blvd Pg.5 A17
Mark St. Pg.5 A17
Meacham Rd. Pg.4 A13
Nicholas Blvd. Pg.6 A19
Pam-Am Blvd. Pg.6 A19
Parkchester Pg.6 A19
Thorndale Ave. Pg.5 A17
Tonne Rd. Pg.5 A17
Trowbridge Cir. Pg.5 A15
Turner Pg.5 A15
United Ln. Pg.6 A19
Wasdale Pg.5 A16
York Rd. Pg.6 B19

**MISCELLANEOUS**
Elk Grove Business Park Pg.5 A17

## ELMHURST

Pages 6,11,12

**STREETS**
Aberdeen Ct. Pg.12 K20
Adams Ct. Pg.12 K20
Adams St. Pg.12 K19
Addison Ave. Pg.6,12 D,F,H19
Adelaide Pg.12 H19
Adele St. Pg.12 G20
Adelia St. Pg.12 J19
Adell Pl. Pg.12 H19
Albert St. Pg.11 H17
Alexander Ave. Pg.12 H18
Alexander Blvd. Pg.12 H18
Allison St. Pg.12 K20
Alma Ave. Pg.12 H18
Apple Tree Ct. Pg.12 H21,L18
Arbor Dr. Pg.12 L19
Argyle Ave. Pg.12 J19
Arlington Ave. Pg.12 J19
Armitage Ave. Pg.12 G18-20
Arthur St. Pg.12 H19
Aspen Tree Ct. Pg.12 H21,L18
Astoria Ct. Pg.12 H21,L18
Atrium Dr. Pg.12 L19
Atrium Way Pg.12 L19
Atwater Ave. Pg.12 H20
Atwood Ct. Pg.12 K20
Avery St. Pg.12 L18
Avon Ct. Pg.12 H20
Avon Rd. Pg.12 H20
Babcock Ave. Pg.12 F18
Barclay Ct. Pg.12 K20
Belden Ave. Pg.12 F18
Benton Ave. Pg.12 K20
Benton Ct. Pg.12 K20
Berkley Ave. Pg.12 H18
Berteau Ave. Pg.12 G,H20
Betsey Ware Ave. Pg.12 F18
Beverly Ave. Pg.12 L18
Birch Tree Ct. Pg.12 H21,L18
Bonnie Brae Pg.12 H18
Boyd Ave. Pg.12 J20
Bryan St. Pg.12 K19
Bucholz Ct. Pg.12 H20
Butterfield Rd. Pg.12 L19
Caldwell Ave. Pg.12 J20
Cambridge Ave. Pg.12 K19
Carlton Ct. Pg.12 H21,L18
Carol Ln. Pg.6 F18
Caroline Ave. Pg.12 H20
Cayuga Ave. Pg.12 K19
Cedar Ave. Pg.12 K20
Chandler Ave. Pg.12 H-J19
Charles Pg.12 H19
Charlotte Cir. Pg.12 H21,L18
Chatham Ave. Pg.12 K19
Cherry St. Pg.12 J19
Church Rd. Pg.12 F18
Church St. Pg.12 H19,20
Clara Pl. Pg.12 H19
Claremont St. Pg.12 H19
Clayton St. Pg.12 L18
Clinton Ave. Pg.12 H20
Colfax Ave. Pg.12 K20
Columbia Ave. Pg.12 G19
Commonwealth Ln. Pg.12 L18
Comstock Ave. Pg.12 G18
Coolidge St. Pg.12 K18,19
Cottage Hill Ave. Pg.12 J19
Crescent Ave. Pg.12 J18,19
Crestview Ave. Pg.12 G19
Crockett Ave. Pg.12 G18
Dewalt Ct. Pg.12 H21,L18
Diversey Ave. Pg.6 F19
Division St. Pg.12 J19
Donald Ct. Pg.12 H21,L18
Dorchester Ave. Pg.12 L18
DuPage Pg.12 G20
East Ct. Pg.12 H20
East First St. Pg.12 H19
East Park Ave. Pg.12 H19
Eastland St. Pg.12 F20
Eaton Ct. Pg.12 H21,J19
Edgewood Ave. Pg.12 K20
Eggleston Ave. Pg.12 J18,19
Elizabeth St. Pg.12 H18
Elm Ave. Pg.12 G19
Elm Creek Ln. Pg.12 L19
Elm Park Ave. Pg.12 H18,19
Elm Tree Ln. Pg.12 H20
Elmcrest Ave. Pg.12 G19
Elmhurst Ave. Pg.12 H20
Elmwood Terr. Pg.12 J19
Emery Ln. Pg.12 G18
Emroy Ave. Pg.12 G,H20
Euclid Ave. Pg.12 K19
Evergreen Ave. Pg.12 G19
Evergreen Ln. Pg.6 F18
Fair Ave. Pg.12 J20
Fairfield Ave. Pg.12 H,K18
Fairlane Ave. Pg.12 H20
Fay Ave. Pg.12 G18
Fellows Ct. Pg.12 J18
Fern Ave. Pg.12 K20
Fern Ct. Pg.12 K20
Ferndale Ave. Pg.12 G18
Forest Ave. Pg.12 H20
Four Seasons Ct. Pg.12 H21,L18
Fremont Ave. Pg.12 G19
Fullerton Ave. Pg.12 F18,19
Garden Ave. Pg.12 G18
Garfield Pg.12 J19
Geneva Ave. Pg.12 F,H20
Geneva Ct. Pg.12 F20
Glade Ave. Pg.12 H18
Gladys Ave. Pg.12 G18,19
Glenview Ave. Pg.12 H18
Gloria Ct. Pg.12 H21,L18
Grace Ave. Pg.12 H18
Grand Ave. Pg.6,12 F18
Grandview St. Pg.12 J20,K19
Grantley Ave. Pg.12 G18
Hagans Ave. Pg.12 J19
Hahn St. Pg.12 H19
Hale St. Pg.12 K19
Hampshire Ave. Pg.12 J,H20
Harbor Terr. Pg.12 J19
Harding St. Pg.12 K18,19
Harrison St. Pg.12 K18,20
Haven Rd. Pg.12 H19
Hawthorne Ave. Pg.12 F-K18
High Ave. Pg.12 K20
Highland Ave. Pg.12 G18
Hill Ave. Pg.12 J19
Hillcrest Ave. Pg.12 K20
Hillside Ave. Pg.12 K18
Holly Ave. Pg.12 J20
Howard Ave. Pg.12 G20
Huntington Ln. Pg.12 H20
Ida Ln. Pg.12 G18
Illinois Pg.12 H19
Indiana Pg.12 G19
Industrial Dr. Pg.6,12 F19
Jackson St. Pg.12 K18
Jill Ct. Pg.6 F19
Junior Terr. Pg.12 F18
Kearsage Ave. Pg.12 K19
Kenilworth Ave. Pg.12 G,J19
Kenmore Ave. Pg.12 H19
Kent Ave. Pg.12 K19
Killarney Ct Pg.12 K20
Kimbell Ave. Pg.12 G19
Kirk Ave. Pg.12 K19
Lamont Rd. Pg.6 F18
Larch Ave. Pg.12 F,H19
Laurel Ave. Pg.12 J20
Lawndale Ave. Pg.12 H20
Lexington Ave. Pg.12 L19,20
Linden Ave. Pg.12 H,K20
Linden Dr. Pg.12 K20
Locust Tree Ct. Pg.12 H21,L18
Lombard St. Pg.12 F20
Lorraine Ave. Pg.12 G18
Madison St. Pg.12 K19
Maison Ct. Pg.12 H20
Manchester Ln. Pg.12 H21,J19
Maple Ave. Pg.12 G,H19
Maple Tree Ct. Pg.12 H21,L18
Margaret Pg.12 H19
Marion St. Pg.12 H20
Mary Ct. Pg.12 F18
Mason Ct. Pg.12 H20
May St. Pg.12 J19
McKinley Ave. Pg.12 K18
McKinley St. Pg.12 J20
Meister Ave. Pg.12 J19
Melrose Ave. Pg.12 H20
Michigan St. Pg.12 F,G19
Mission Ct. Pg.12 H20
Mitchell Ave. Pg.12 J19
Monroe St. Pg.12 K18,19
Monterey Ave. Pg.12 J18
Myrtle Ave. Pg.12 G,H19
Nelson St. Pg.12 L18
Niagara Ave. Pg.12 J19
North Ave. Pg.12 G18
North End Ave. Pg.12 F19
Oak Lawn Ave. Pg.6,12 F,G18
Oak St. Pg.12 G,H18
Oak Tree Ct. Pg.12 H21,L18
Oakland Ave. Pg.12 J18
Old York Rd. Pg.12 L20
Olive St. Pg.12 J18
Oneida St. Pg.12 K19
Orchard St. Pg.12 J19
Oriole Ave. Pg.12 J20
Park Ave. Pg.12 H19,20
Park Manor Ct. Pg.12 K20
Parker St. Pg.12 F20
Parkside Ave. Pg.12 J,L19
Parkside Pl. Pg.12 J19
Parkview Ave. Pg.12 J20
Pick Ave. Pg.11 J17
Pine St. Pg.12 H20
Pine Tree Ct. Pg.12 H21,L18
Poplar Ave. Pg.12 J20
Poplar Tree Ct. Pg.12 H21,L18
Prairie Ave. Pg.12 J20
Prairie Path Ln. Pg.12 J18,19

**ELMHURST**

Prospect Ave. . . . Pg.12 . . H-L19
Quincy St. . . . . . Pg.12 . . . K19
Railway St. . . . . . Pg.12 . . . J18
Randolph St. . . . . Pg.12 . . . J18
Rex Blvd. . . . . . . Pg.12 . . H,J18
Richard Ave. . . . . Pg.12 . . . H20
Ridge Ave. . . . . . Pg.12 . . . J20
Ridgeland Ave. . . . Pg.12 . . . G18
River Glen Ave. . . Pg.12 . . G,H18
Riverside Dr. . . . . Pg.12 . . . L18
Robert Palmer Dr.
. . . . . . . . . . . . . Pg.12 . . . H19
Romans Rd. . . . . Pg.12 . . . G20
Rose St. . . . . . . . Pg.11 . . . J19
Saylor Ave. . . . . . Pg.12 . . K,L19
Schiller St. . . . . . Pg.12 . . . H19
Scott St. . . . . . . . Pg.12 . . . J18
Second St. . . . . . Pg.12 . . . H20
Seminole Ave. . . . Pg.12 . . . K19
Shady Ln. . . . . . . Pg.12 . . G,H18
Sherman Ave. . . . Pg.12 . . . J20
Sidney Ave. . . . . . Pg.12 . . . G18
Smith Ave. . . . . . Pg.12 . . . H19
South St. . . . . . . . Pg.12 . . . J20
Spangler Ave. . . . Pg.12 . . . F19
Spring Rd. . . . . . . Pg.12 . . . K19
St. Charles Rd. . . . Pg.12 . . . J18
St. Moritz Ct. . . . . Pg.12 . . H21,L18
St. Regis Ct. . . . . Pg.12 . . H21,L18
Stratford Ave. . . . Pg.12 . . . J,K20
Stuart Ave. . . . . . Pg.12 . . . K20
Stuart Ct. . . . . . . Pg.12 . . . K20
Sturges Pkwy. . . . Pg.12 . . . J19
Sunnyside Ave. . . Pg.12 . . H,J18
Sunrise Rd. . . . . . Pg.12 . . . F18
Sunset Ave. . . . . . Pg.12 . . . L18
Surf St. . . . . . . . . Pg.12 . . . J18
Swain Ave. . . . . . Pg.12 . . K,L19
Third St. . . . . . . . Pg.12 . . . H20
Thomas St. . . . . . Pg.11 . . . F18
Thornhill St. . . . . . Pg.12 . . H21,J19
Utley Rd. . . . . . . . Pg.12 . . . H18
Vallette St. . . . . . Pg.12 . . . J18
Van Auken St. . . . Pg.12 . . . G20
Van Buren St. . . . . Pg.12 . . . K19
Verret St. . . . . . . Pg.12 . . . L18
Virginia St. . . . . . Pg.12 . . . H19
Waldorf Ct. . . . . . Pg.12 . . H21,L18
Walnut St. . . . . . . Pg.12 . . F,H18
Walter St. . . . . . . Pg.12 . . . H18
Washington St. . . . Pg.12 . . . J19
Webster Ave. . . . . Pg.12 . . . J20
Weigel Dr. . . . . . . Pg.12 . . . F19
West Ave. . . . . . . Pg.12 . . G,J18
West First St. . . . . Pg.12 . . . H19
West Park Ave. . . . Pg.12 . . . H19
Willow Rd. . . . . . . Pg.12 . . G,H19
Willow Tree Ct. . . . Pg.12 . . H21,L18
Wilson St. . . . . . . Pg.12 . . K18,19
Windsor Dr. . . . . . Pg.12 . . H21,J19
Winthrop Ave. . . . Pg.12 . . . J19
Wolcott Ct. . . . . . Pg.12 . . H21,L18
Wrightwood Ave.
. . . . . . . . . . . . . Pg.12 . F18,19
York St. . . . . . . . . Pg.12 . . . J19
Yorkfield Ave. . . . . Pg.12 . . . K20

**CEMETERIES**
Arlington Cem. . . . Pg.12 . . . G20
Elm Lawn Cem. . . Pg.12 . . . G19
Mt. Emblem Cem.
. . . . . . . . . Pg.6,12 . . . F20
St. Mary's Cem. . . Pg.12 . . . H19

**FOREST PRESERVES**
Salt Creek Parkway
. . . . . . . . . . . . . Pg.12 . . H,J18

**PARKS**
Berens Park . . . . . Pg.12 . . . G18
Butterfield Park . . Pg.12 . . . K20
Conrad Fisher Park
. . . . . . . . . . . . . Pg.6 . . . F19
Crestview Park . . . Pg.12 . . . H20
East End Park . . . . Pg.12 . . . H20
Eldridge Park . . . . Pg.12 . . . L18
Elmhurst Park . . . Pg.12 . . . H20
Golden Meadows Park
Cranston Ct. . . . . Pg.12
Maple Trail Woods Park
. . . . . . . . . . . . . Pg.12 . . . K18
Marjorie Davis Park
. . . . . . . . . . . . . Pg.12 . . . G19
Marjorie Park . . . . Pg.12 . . . J19
Pioneer Park . . . . Pg.12 . . . H18
Plunkett Park . . . . Pg.12 . . . H18
Salt Creek Park . . Pg.12 . . . H18
Sleepy Hollow Park
. . . . . . . . . . . . . Pg.12 . . . J18
Van Voorst Park Pg.12 . . . K20
Washington Park
. . . . . . . . . . . . . Pg.12 . . . J20
Wild Meadows Park
. . . . . . . . . . . . . Pg.12 . . . J20
Wilder Park . . . . . Pg.12 . . . H19
York Commons Park
. . . . . . . . . . . . . Pg.12 . . . K19

**SCHOOLS**
Bryan Jr. H.S. . . . Pg.12 . . . K19
Churchville Jr. H.S.
. . . . . . . . . . . . . Pg.6 . . . F19
Conrad Fisher Sch.
. . . . . . . . . . . . . Pg.6 . . . F19
Cornille Sch. . . . . Pg.12 . . . G18
Crestview Sch. . . . Pg.12 . . . H20
Edison Sch. . . . . . Pg.12 . . . K19
Eldridge Sch. . . . . Pg.12 . . . K18
Elmhurst College
. . . . . . . . . . . . . Pg.12 . . . H19
Emerson Sch. . . . Pg.12 . . . J19
Field Sch. . . . . . . Pg.12 . . . H20
Hawthorne Sch. . . Pg.12 . . . J20
Immaculate Conception Elem.
. . . . . . . . . . . . . Pg.12 . . . H19
Immaculate Conception H.S.
. . . . . . . . . . . . . Pg.12 . . . H19
Immanuel Sch. . . Pg.12 . . . H19

Jackson Sch. . . . . Pg.12 . . . K19
Jefferson Sch. . . . Pg.12 . . . K20
Lincoln Sch. . . . . Pg.12 . . . J19
MacCormac Jr. Coll.
Madison Sch. . . . . Pg.12 . . . G18
Mary Queen of Heaven Sch.
Roosevelt Sch. . . . Pg.12 . . . G19
Salt Creek Sch. . . Pg.12 . . . K18
Sandburg Jr. H.S.
. . . . . . . . . . . . . . . . . . . J20
Timothy Christian H.S.
. . . . . . . . . . . . . Pg.12 . . . L19
Visitation Sch. . . . Pg.12 . . . L19
Washington Sch.
. . . . . . . . . . . . . . . . . . . J19
York Community H.S.
. . . . . . . . . . . . . Pg.12 . . . J18
Yorkfield Sch. . . . Pg.12 . . . K20

**MISCELLANEOUS**
Community Center
. . . . . . . . . . . . . . . . . . . K19
Elmhurst Industrial Park
Elmhurst Memorial Hospital
. . . . . . . . . . . . . . . . . . . F18
Fire Dept. . . . . . . Pg.12 . . . H20
Graham Ctr. . . . . Pg.12 . . . G19
Green Meadows Petting Farm
Maywood Sportsman Club
Post Office . . . . . Pg.12 . . . G20
The Abbey Sr. Ctr.
Village Hall . . . . . Pg.12 . . . H19

**FLOWERFIELD**
Page 10 . . . K13
For listings see Milton & York
Twps.

**GLEN ELLYN**
Pages 10,16
**STREETS**
Abbey Dr. . . . . Pg.10,16 . . L13
Abbotsford Ct. . . . Pg.10 . . . K13
Adler Ln. . . . . . . . Pg.16 . . . M11
Amy Ct. . . . . . . . . Pg.16 . . . J11
Annandale Ave. . . Pg.10 . . . K12
Anthony St. . . . . . Pg.16 . . . K12
Apollo Ave. . . . . . Pg.10 . . . K12
Appian Way . . . . . Pg.10 . . . K12
Arbor Ct. . . . . . . . Pg.16 . . . K13
Arlingdale Cir. . . . Pg.10 . . . L13
Arlington Ave. . . . Pg.10 . . . K11
Ash Ln. . . . . . . . . Pg.16 . . . M11
Baker Ct. . . . . . . . Pg.10 . . . J12
Baker Hill Dr. . . . . Pg.10 . . . K11
Bloomfield Ct. . . . Pg.16 . . . M11
Braeburn Ct. . . . . Pg.16 . . . K11
Brandon Ave. . . . . Pg.10 . . . K11
Bremer Ct. . . . . . . Pg.16 . . . M11
Brentwood Ct. . . . Pg.16 . . . M12
Briar St. . . . . . . . . Pg.16 . . H,J,L11
Brighton Pl. . . . . . Pg.16 . . . L13
Bryant Ave. . . . . . Pg.10 . . . K13
Buena Vista Dr. . . Pg.16 . . . K12
Carleton Ave. . . . . Pg.10 . . . K12
Carlisle Ct. . . . . . Pg.16 . . . M11
Carolyn Dr. . . . . . Pg.10 . . . L12
Cedar Ln. . . . . . . Pg.16 . . . M11
Center St. . . . . . . Pg.10 . . . K11
Chancel Cir. . . . . . Pg.10 . . . L13
Chancel Ln. . . . . . Pg.10 . . . L13
Chapel Ct. N. . . . . Pg.10 . . . M13
Chapel Ct. S. . . . . Pg.10 . . . M13
Cheltham Dr. . . . . Pg.10 . . . L14
Chesterfield Ave. Pg.10 . . . K11
Chickester Ave. . . Pg.10 . . . K11
Colcord Pl. . . . . . . Pg.10 . . . J13
College Rd. . . . . . Pg.16 . . M11,12
Concord Pl. . . . . . Pg.10 . . . J11
Coolidge Ave. . . . Pg.10 . . . J11
Cottage Ave. . . . . Pg.10 . . . J11
Cranston Ct. . . . . Pg.16 . . . J12
Crescent Blvd. . . . Pg.10 . . J,K12
Crescent Ct. . . . . Pg.10 . . . J12
Crescent Dr. . . . . Pg.10 . . . J13
Crest Rd. . . . . . . . Pg.10 . . . L12
Cumnor Ave. . . . . Pg.10 . . . K13
Dale . . . . . . . . . . Pg.10 . . . J12
Davis Ave. . . . . . . Pg.16 . . . M11
Davis Terrace . . . . Pg.16 . . . K12
Dawes Ave. . . . . . Pg.16 . . . K12
Dawn Ave. . . . . . . Pg.10 . . . L12
Deerpath Rd. . . . . Pg.10 . . . L12
Delcke Dr. . . . . . . Pg.10 . . . L11
Dell Ave. . . . . . . . Pg.10 . . . L12
Dorset Ct. . . . . . . Pg.10 . . . L12
Dorset St. . . . . . . Pg.10 . . . L12
Du Page Blvd. . . . Pg.10 . . . K11
Duane St. . . . . . . Pg.10 . . . K11
Duane Terr. . . . . . Pg.10 . . . L12
East Rd. . . . . . . . . Pg.10 . . . L12
Eastern Ave. . . . . Pg.10 . . . J12
Edgewood Dr. . . . Pg.10 . . . J12
Ellen Ave. . . . . . . Pg.10 . . . L11
Ellyn Ct. . . . . . . . Pg.16 . . . K11
Ellynwood Dr. . . . Pg.16 . . . J11
Elm St. . . . . . . . . . Pg.10 . . . J11
Essex Ct. . . . . . . . Pg.10 . . . L13
Essex Rd. . . . . . . Pg.10 . . . L13
Euclid Ave. . . . . . Pg.10 . . . J11
Evergreen . . . . . . Pg.16 . . . K11
Exmoor Ave. . . . . Pg.16 . . . K11
Fairview Ave. . . . . Pg.10 . . L11,12
Farnsworth Ln. . . . Pg.16 . . . M11
Fir Ct. . . . . . . . . . Pg.16 . . . M11
Fir Ln. . . . . . . . . . Pg.16 . . . M11
Florence . . . . . . . Pg.16 . . . L13
Forest Ave. . . . . . Pg.10 . . . J11
Geneva Rd. . . . . . Pg.10 . . . J11
Glen Ellyn Pl. . . . Pg.10 . . . J12

Glen Haven Ave. Pg.16 . . . M12
Glen Oak Ave. . . . Pg.10 . . . K13
Glen Park Rd. . . . Pg.10 . . . N14
Glenbard Rd. . . . . Pg.16 . . L12,13
Glenwood Ave. . . . Pg.10 . . . K12
Grand Ave. . . . . . Pg.10 . . . K12
Grandview Ave. . . Pg.10 . . . K13
Greenbrier . . . . . . Pg.16 . . . M12
Greenfield Ave. . . Pg.16 . . . K11
Greenwood Ave. Pg.10 . . . L11
Greenwood St. . . . Pg.10 . . . L11
Grove Ave. . . . . . . Pg.10 . . . L13
Harding Ave. . . . . Pg.10 . . . J13
Harding Rd. . . . . . Pg.10 . . . K13
Hawthorne St. . . . Pg.10 . . . J12
Heather Ln. . . . . . Pg.10 . . . L11
Hedge Ct. . . . . . . Pg.16 . . . L12
Hickory Rd. . . . . . Pg.10 . . . J13
High Rd. . . . . . . . Pg.10 . . . J12
Highland Ave. . . . Pg.10 . . . K12
Highview Ave. . . . Pg.10 . . . K12
Hill Ave. . . . . . . . . Pg.10 . . . K12
Hillcrest Ave. . . . . Pg.10 . . . L11
Hillside Ave. . . . . Pg.10 . . . K11
Illinois St. . . . . . . Pg.10 . . . L11
Indian Dr. . . . . . . Pg.10 . . . K13
Jonathan Ct. . . . . Pg.16 . . . L13
Joyce Ct. . . . . . . . Pg.10 . . . L12
Kenilworth Ave. . . Pg.10 . . . K11
Kenilworth Ct. . . . Pg.10 . . . J11
Lake Rd. . . . . . . . Pg.10 . . . J12
Lakeview Terr. . . . Pg.16 . . . K12
Lambert Rd. . . . . Pg.10 . . . L11
Larch Ln. . . . . . . . Pg.16 . . . M11
Lawrence . . . . . . . Pg.16 . . . K12
Lee St. . . . . . . . . . Pg.10 . . . J12
Lenox Rd. . . . . . . Pg.10 . . . L12
Limits Ave. . . . . . Pg.10 . . . J11
Lincoln Ave. . . . . Pg.10 . . . J11
Linden St. . . . . . . Pg.10 . . . L13
Lombard Ave. . . . Pg.10 . . . L13
Londonderry Ln. . . Pg.10 . . . L13
Longfellow Ave. . . Pg.10 . . . K13
Lorraine St. . . . . . Pg.10 . . . L11
Lowden Ave. . . . . Pg.16 . . . M11
Lowell Ave. . . . . . Pg.16 . . . K13
Macintosh Ct. . . . Pg.16 . . . M12
Maiden Ln. . . . . . Pg.10 . . . J12
Main St. . . . . . . . . Pg.10 . . . J12
Maple St. . . . . . . . Pg.16 . . . J11
Marion Ct. . . . . . . Pg.10 . . . J11
Marion St. . . . . . . Pg.10 . . . J11
Marston Ave. . . . . Pg.16 . . M11,12
Mary Knoll Cir. . . . Pg.10 . . . L13
May Ave. . . . . . . . Pg.16 . . . K13
Melrose Ave. . . . . Pg.16 . . . K13
Memory Ct. . . . . . Pg.16 . . . K13
Meredith Pl. . . . . . Pg.10 . . . L13
Merton Ave. . . . . . Pg.16 . . . K13
Midway Pl. . . . . . . Pg.10 . . . J11
Miller Ct. . . . . . . . Pg.10 . . . K11
Milton Ave. . . . . . Pg.16 . . . M12
Montclair Ave. . . . Pg.16 . . . K12
Muirwood Ave. . . Pg.16 . . . M12
Muirwood Dr. . . . . Pg.16 . . . M12
New Haven Ln. . . . Pg.16 . . . M12
Newton Ave. . . . . Pg.10 . . H,J,L11
Nichol Pl. . . . . . . . Pg.10 . . . L11
Nicoll Ave. . . . . . . Pg.10 . . . L12
Nicoll Way . . . . . . Pg.10 . . . L12
Oak St. . . . . . . . . Pg.10 . . . J11
Oakwood Ct. . . . . Pg.10 . . . L13
Old Bond Ct. . . . . Pg.10 . . . L14
Orchard St. . . . . . Pg.16 . . . M11
Ott Ave. . . . . . . . . Pg.10 . . . L11
Oxford Rd. . . . . . . Pg.10 . . . L13
Park Blvd. . . . . . . Pg.10 . . J,L12
Park Row . . . . . . . Pg.10 . . . L13
Parkside Ave. . . . Pg.10 . . . L12
Pembroke Ln. . . . Pg.16 . . . M11
Pennsylvania Ave.
. . . . . . . . . . . . . Pg.10 . . . K11
Pershing Ave. . . . Pg.10 . . . K11
Phillips Ave. . . . . . Pg.10 . . . K11
Pleasant Ave. . . . Pg.10 . . . J11
Plum Tree Rd. . . . Pg.10 . . . J11
Prairie Ave. . . . . . Pg.10 . . . J11
Prince Edward Rd.
. . . . . . . . . . . . . Pg.16 . . . M12
Prospect Ave. . . . Pg.10 . . . K12
Raintree Ct. . . . . . Pg.16 . . . M11
Raintree Dr. . . . . . Pg.16 . . . M12
Ramblewood Ln.
. . . . . . . . . . . . . Pg.16 . . . M11
Regent St. . . . . . . Pg.10 . . . M11
Revere Rd. . . . . . . Pg.10 . . . L12
Ridgewood Ave. . . Pg.16 . . . K11
Riford Rd. . . . . . . . Pg.10 . . . L12
Riverside Ave. . . . Pg.10 . . . L13
Rodger Rd. . . . . . Pg.10 . . . J13
Roosevelt Rd. . . . . Pg.10 . . . L12
Roslyn Rd. . . . . . . Pg.10 . . . K13
Royal Glen Dr. . . . Pg.10 . . . L13
Saddlewood Dr. . . Pg.10 . . . M11
Sandhurst . . . . . . Pg.16 . . . M11
Sawyer Ave. . . . . Pg.10 . . . K11
Scott Ave. . . . . . . Pg.10 . . . L13
Seminary Cir. . . . Pg.10 . . . L13
Shadeblow Ln. . . . Pg.16 . . . M11
Shady Ln. . . . . . . Pg.16 . . . K13
Sheehan Ave. . . . Pg.10 . . . K12
Sheffield Ln. . . . . Pg.10 . . . K11
Sheldrup St. . . . . Pg.16 . . . N14
Smith St. . . . . . . . Pg.16 . . . L13
Snowhill Ct. . . . . . Pg.16 . . . L13
South Ellyn Ave. Pg.16 . . . M12
Spaulding Ct. . . . Pg.10 . . . K11
Spring Ave. . . . . . Pg.10 . . . K12
Spruce Ln. . . . . . . Pg.16 . . . L11
St. James Dr. . . . . Pg.16 . . . L14
St. Moritz Dr. . . . . Pg.10 . . . J12
Stacy Ct. . . . . . . . Pg.16 . . . J12
Stafford Ln. . . . . . Pg.16 . . . M11
Stagecoach Dr. . . Pg.16 . . J11,12
Stagecoach Run Pg.16 . . J11,12
Stephanie Ln. . . . Pg.16 . . . M11
Stewart Ave. . . . . Pg.10 . . . K12

Stongate Ct. . . . . Pg.16 . . . L12
Stratford Ln. . . . . Pg.16 . . . M12
Summerdale Ave.
Sunset Ave. . . . . . Pg.10 . . . L11
Sunset Ct. . . . . . . Pg.10 . . . L11
Surrey Dr. . . . . . . Pg.10 . . . L13
Sylvan Ave. . . . . . Pg.10 . . . L13
Sylvan Ct. . . . . . . Pg.10 . . . J12
Taft Ave. . . . . . . . Pg.10 . . . K11
Tanglewood Dr. . . Pg.10 . . . L11
Taylor Ave. . . . . . Pg.10 . . . K12
Thompson Ave. . . Pg.10 . . . J13
Traves Ave. . . . . . Pg.10 . . . L11
Turnberry Ln. . . . . Pg.10 . . . M11
Turner Ave. . . . . . Pg.10 . . . K11
Valley Ave. . . . . . Pg.10 . . . L12
Van Damin Ave. . . Pg.10 . . . L11
Vine Ave. . . . . . . . Pg.10 . . . K11
Walnut St. . . . . . . Pg.10 . . . K12
Waverly Rd. . . . . . Pg.16 . . . M11
Western Ave. . . . . Pg.10 . . . J11
Whittier Ave. . . . . Pg.10 . . . K13
Williamston Rd.
. . . . . . . . . . . . . Pg.16 . . . M12
Willis St. . . . . . . . Pg.10 . . . M12
Wilson Ave. . . . . . Pg.10 . . . L12
Wilson Ct. . . . . . . Pg.10 . . . L12
Winchell Way . . . Pg.16 . . . L14
Windermere Dr. . . Pg.10 . . . L14
Windsor Ave. . . . . Pg.16 . . . N11
Wingate Rd. . . . . . Pg.16 . . . M12
Woodcroft Dr. . . . Pg.16 . . . N11
Woodland Dr. . . . Pg.10 . . . J13
Woodstock Ave. . . Pg.16 . . . K12
Woodview Ct. . . . Pg.10 . . . L13
Woodview Dr. . . . . Pg.10 . . . L13

**CEMETERIES**
Forest Hill Cem. Pg.10 . . . J12

**FOREST PRESERVES**
Willowbrook Wildlife Haven
. . . . . . . . . . . . . Pg.16 . . . M12

**GOLF COURSES**
Glen Oak C.C. . . . Pg.10 . . . K13
The Village Green
. . . . . . . . . . . . . Pg.16 . . . L11
The Village Links
. . . . . . . . . . . . . Pg.10,16 L,M11

**PARKS**
Ackerman Pk. . . . Pg.10 . . . H12
Babcock Grove . . Pg.10 . . . J11
Churchill Pk. . . . . Pg.10 . . . J11
Danby Park . . . . . Pg.10 . . . K11
Foxcroft Park . . . . Pg.16 . . . N11
George Ball Pk. . . Pg.10 . . . J13
Glen Ellyn Manor
. . . . . . . . . . . . . . . . . . . L11
Lake Ellyn Pk. . . . Pg.10 . . . K12
Gualt Bird Sanct. Pg.10 . . . J12
Newton Park . . . . Pg.10 . . . L12
Panfish Park . . . . Pg.10 . . . L12
Presidents Pk. . . . Pg.10 . . . K13
South Park . . . . . Pg.10 . . . L12
Stacy Park . . . . . . Pg.10 . . . J12
Sunset Park . . . . . Pg.10 . . . L12
Surrey Park . . . . . Pg.10 . . . L14

**SCHOOLS**
Benjamin Franklin Sch.
. . . . . . . . . . . . . Pg.10 . . . K12
Churchill Sch. . . . Pg.10 . . . J11
College of DuPage
. . . . . . . . . . . . . Pg.16 . . . M11
Forest Glen Sch. Pg.10 . . . L13
Glen Crest Jr. H.S.
. . . . . . . . . . . . . Pg.16 . . . M12
Glenbard West H.S.
. . . . . . . . . . . . . Pg.10 . . . K12
Hawthorne Sch. . . Pg.10 . . . J11
Ill. Inst. of Tech. Pg.16 . . . M11
Lewis College of Law
. . . . . . . . . . . . . Pg.16 . . . L13
Lincoln Sch. . . . . Pg.10 . . . L11
Parkview Sch. . . . Pg.10 . . . L12
Phillip Rock Sch. & Center for
the Deaf . . . . . . Pg.10 . . . L12

**SHOPPING CENTERS**
Baker Hill S.C. . . . Pg.10 . . . L13
Glen Crossing S.C.
. . . . . . . . . . . . . Pg.10 . . . L11
Market Plaza . . . . Pg.10 . . . L12
Village Plaza . . . . Pg.10 . . . J11

**MISCELLANEOUS**
DuPage Co. Forest Preserve
Admin. Offices
. . . . . . . . . . . . . Pg.10 . . . K11
Fire Dept. . . . . . . Pg.10 . . . K13
Library . . . . . . . . Pg.10 . . . K11
Main St. Rec. Ctr.
Police Dept. . . . . . Pg.10 . . . K12
Village Hall . . . . . Pg.10 . . . K12

**GLENDALE HEIGHTS**
Pages 3,4,9,10
**STREETS**
Alberta Ct. . . . . . Pg.10 . . . G12
Almond Ln. . . . . . Pg.4 . . . E11
Alpine Dr. E. . . . . . Pg.4 . . . E11
Alta Ln. . . . . . . . . Pg.4 . . . F11
Altgeld Ave. . . . Pg.9,10 F10,11
Altgeld St. . . . . . . Pg.10 . . . F10
Amhurst Cir. . . . . . Pg.9 . . . F10
Amy Ave. . . . . . . . Pg.4 . . . F10
Appleby Dr. . . . . . Pg.3 . . . E10
Ardmore Ave. . . . Pg.10 . . . G12
Arlington Ln. . . . . Pg.4 . . . F11
Armitage Ave. . . Pg.9,10 G10,11
Army Trail Rd. . . . Pg.4 . . . E11
Ashbury Ln. . . . . . Pg.10 . . . G11
Aspen Ln. . . . . . . Pg.4 . . E,F11

Auburn Dr. . . . . . Pg.3 . . . F10
Audubon Dr. . . . . Pg.4 . . . E11
Augusta Ct. . . . . . Pg.3 . . . E10
Avalon Ct. . . . . . . Pg.10 . . . F11
Baldwin Ct. . . . . . Pg.4 . . . E11
Barclay Dr. . . . . . Pg.4 . . . E11
Basswood Ln. . . . Pg.4 . . . E11
Bayberry Dr. . . . . Pg.3 . . . H11
Belden Ave. . . . . . Pg.10 . . . G11
Bell Ln. . . . . . . . . Pg.4 . . . E11
Bentley Ct. . . . . . Pg.4 . . . E11
Berkshire Ct. . . . . Pg.9 . . . F10
Berkshire St. . . . . Pg.9 . . . F10
Bernice Ave. . . . . Pg.10 . . . G11
Blair Ln. . . . . . . . Pg.4 . . . E11
Bloomingdale Ct.
. . . . . . . . . . . . . Pg.10 . . . F11
Bloomingdale Rd.
Blue Ridge Dr. . . Pg.3 . . . F10
Blue Spruce Ln. Pg.4 . . . E11
Bosworth Ct. . . . . Pg.3 . . . E10
Boulder Dr. . . . . . Pg.4 . . . E11
Brahms Ct. . . . . . Pg.3 . . . E11
Brandon Ct. . . . . Pg.4 . . . E11
Brandon Dr. N. . . Pg.4 . . . E11
Brandon Dr. S. . . Pg.4 . . . E11
Brian Dr. . . . . . . . Pg.3 . . . E11
Bristol Ct. . . . . . . Pg.10 . . . H11
Brittany Ln. . . . . . Pg.3 . . . E11
Brockton Ln. . . . . Pg.4 . . . F10
Brookside Dr. . . . . Pg.3 . . . F10
Burdett Ct. . . . . . Pg.10 . . . G12
Burdett Ct. . . . . . Pg.10 . . . G12
Burgess Dr. . . . . . Pg.3 . . . F10
Burr Oak Ln. . . . . Pg.4 . . . E11
Cambridge Ln. . . Pg.10 . . . G11
Camden Ct. . . . . . Pg.10 . . . H11
Campbell Dr. . . . . Pg.4 . . . E10
Cardinal Dr. . . . . . Pg.3 . . . E10
Cedar St. . . . . . . . Pg.10 . . . H11
Chadwick Ln. . . . Pg.4 . . . E11
Chapman Ct. . . . . Pg.10 . . . G11
Chappel Ct. . . . . . Pg.9 . . . G10
Charles Ct. . . . . . Pg.10 . . . F12
Charles St. . . . . . Pg.10 . . . F11
Charles St. . . . . . Pg.9 . . . G10
Chaucer Ln. . . . . Pg.4 . . . E11
Chippendale . . . . Pg.3 . . . E11
Churchill Ln. . . . . Pg.4 . . . F11
Circle Dr. . . . . . . . Pg.10 . . . G12
Clifford St. . . . . . Pg.9 . . . F10
Club Dr. . . . . . . . Pg.9 . . . G10
Clubhouse Ct. . . . Pg.9 . . . G10
College Dr. . . . . . Pg.4 . . . E11
Concord Dr. . . . . . Pg.4 . . . E11
Copper Ct. . . . . . . Pg.3 . . . E10
Cornell Ct. . . . . . . Pg.3 . . . E11
Cove Ln. . . . . . . . Pg.4 . . . F10
Cynthia Ln. . . . . . Pg.4 . . . E11
Cypress Ct. . . . . . Pg.4 . . . E11
Dale Rd. . . . . . . . Pg.4 . . . F11
Darlene Ln. . . . . . Pg.10 . . . G12
Davine Dr. . . . . . . Pg.10 . . . G12
Deanna Ln. . . . . . Pg.10 . . . G11
Deere Ln. . . . . . . Pg.3 . . . F10
Dennison Dr. . . . . Pg.3 . . . F10
Devon Ave. . . . . Pg.3,9 . . . F10
Dickens Ave. . . . . Pg.10 . . . G12
Doral Dr. . . . . . . . Pg.3 . . . F10
Drummond Ave. Pg.9 . . . F10
Dunteman Dr. . . . Pg.4 . . . F11
Eagle Ct. . . . . . . . Pg.9 . . . G10
East Lake Ridge Dr.
. . . . . . . . . . . . . Pg.4 . . . E11
Easy St. E. . . . . . Pg.10 . . . G12
Easy St. N. . . . . . Pg.10 . . . G12
Edgar Ct. . . . . . . Pg.9 . . . G10
Elizabeth Ave. . . . Pg.10 . . . G11
English Dr. . . . . Pg.3,9 . . . F10
Evergreen Ave. . . Pg.10 . . . G11
Exchange Blvd. . . Pg.4 . . . F11
Fairway Dr. . . . . . Pg.9 . . . G10
Fall Brook Dr. . . . Pg.3 . . . E10
Flagstaff Ct. . . . . Pg.3 . . . E10
Flagstaff Ln. . . . . Pg.3 . . . E10
Fleetwood Dr. . . . Pg.3 . . . F10
Fordham Ct. . . . . Pg.9 . . . G10
Fox Ave. . . . . . . . Pg.10 . . . G12
Frank Ct. . . . . Pg.4,10 . . . F10
Friedrich St. . . . . Pg.9 . . . F10
Fullerton Ave. . . . Pg.10 . . . G11
Garland Ct. . . . . . Pg.4 . . . E11
Gerald Ave. . . . . . Pg.10 . . . G11
Gilberto St. . . . . . Pg.9 . . . F10
Gladstone Ct. . . . Pg.4 . . . E11
Gladstone Dr. . . . Pg.4 . . . E11
Glen Ellyn Rd. . . . Pg.4 . . . E12
Glen Hill Ct. . . . . Pg.10 . . . H11
Glen Hill West Ct.
. . . . . . . . . . . . . . . . . . . H11
Glen Pointe Dr. . . Pg.9 . . . F11
Glengary Dr. . . . . Pg.10 . . . G11
Glenrock Ln. . . . . Pg.4 . . . E11
Golden Dr. . . . . . Pg.3 . . . F10
Golfview Dr. . . . . Pg.9 . . . G10
Green Ct. . . . . . . Pg.9 . . . G10
Green Meadows Dr.
. . . . . . . . . . . . . Pg.3 . . . E10
Gregory Ave. . . . . Pg.4 . . . F12
Hale Ct. . . . . . . . Pg.10 . . . H11
Harbor Ct. . . . . . . Pg.10 . . . H11
Harding St. . . . . . Pg.3 . . . E11
Harding Dr. . . . . . Pg.9 . . . F10
Harold Ave. . . . . . Pg.10 . . . G12
Hartford Dr. . . . . Pg.9,10 . . E12
Harvest Ln. . . . . . Pg.4 . . . E11
Harvest St. . . . . . Pg.4 . . . E11
Hemlock Ln. . . . . Pg.4 . . . E11
Hemlock Dr. . . . . Pg.3 . . . F10
Hesterman Dr. . . . Pg.3 . . . E10
Hickory Ln. . . . . . Pg.4 . . . E11
Highcrewe Blvd. . Pg.4 . . E12
Highland Ave. . . . Pg.10 . . . G11
Hilldale Ln. . . . . . Pg.4 . . . E11
Hilton Dr. . . . . . . Pg.4 . . . E11
Jacobsen Ave. . . Pg.9,10 . . G10
James Ct. . . . . . . Pg.10 . . . G12

Jamison Dr. . . . . Pg.4 . . . E11
Jeffery Ave. . . . . . Pg.10 . . . F11
Jill Ct. . . . . . . . . . Pg.10 . . . G12
Joel Ct. . . . . . . . . Pg.10 . . . G12
John St. . . . . . . . Pg.9 . . . F10
Jones St. . . . . . Pg.9,10 . . F10
Joseph Ln. . . . . Pg.9,10 . . G10
Joyce Ave. . . . . . Pg.4 . . . F10
Keating St. . . . . . Pg.9 . . . F10
Kennebunk Ct. . . Pg.4 . . . E10
Kingston Ct. . . . . Pg.10 . . . H11
Krysten Ct. . . . . . Pg.3 . . . E10
Lake Dr. . . . . . . . Pg.9 . . . G10
Lake Ridge Dr. . . Pg.4 . . . E11
Larry Ln. . . . . . . . Pg.10 . . . G12
Leslie Ln. . . . . . . Pg.10 . . . G12
Liberty Dr. . . . . . . Pg.10 . . . G12
Lincoln Ave. . . . . Pg.10 . . . G11
Lippert Ln. . . . . . Pg.10 . . . G12
Lombard Ct. . . . . Pg.3 . . . F11
London Dr. . . . . . Pg.4 . . . E11
Loveland Dr. . . . . Pg.4 . . . E11
Lynn Ct. . . . . . . . Pg.10 . . . G12
Main St. . . . . . . . Pg.10 . . . H12
Marci Ct. . . . . . . . Pg.4 . . . F11
Marilyn Ave. . . . . Pg.10 . . G11,12
Mark Ave. . . . . . . Pg.10 . . . G11
Medinah Cir. . . . . Pg.9 . . . G10
Michael Ct. . . . . . Pg.10 . . . H11
Mill Pond Dr. . . . . Pg.3 . . . E10
Mimosa Ct. . . . . . Pg.3 . . . E10
Mitchell Rd. . . . . . Pg.10 . . . F12
Montana Ave. . . . Pg.9,10 . . F10
Morse Ln. . . . . . . Pg.4 . . . E11
Nevada Ave. . . . . Pg.9 . . . F10
Newport St. . . . . . Pg.9 . . . F11
Nickolas Ct. . . . . Pg.10 . . . G12
Niess Ct. . . . . . . Pg.10 . . . G12
Nolan Ave. . . . . . Pg.10 . . . G12
North Ave. . . . . . . Pg.10 . . . H11
Norton Ave. . . . . . Pg.10 . . . G11
Oakmont Dr. . . . . Pg.9 . . . G10
Opal Ave. . . . . . Pg.3,10 . . F10
Oriole Ln. . . . . . . Pg.3 . . . E10
Oxford Ln. . . . . . Pg.10 . . . G11
Paddock Ct. . . . . Pg.9 . . . G10
Paul Ave. . . . . . . Pg.10 . . . G10
Payson Ct. . . . . . Pg.4 . . . E11
Pearl Ave. . . . . . . Pg.10 . . . G11
Pebble Beach Cir.
. . . . . . . . . . . . . Pg.9 . . . G10
Pepperwood Ln. Pg.4 . . . E11
Peterson Ave. . . . Pg.10 . . . G11
Pinehurst Cir. . . . Pg.9 . . . G10
Placid Ave. . . . . . Pg.10 . . . G11
Pleasant Ave. . . . Pg.10 . . . G11
Polo Club Ct. . . . Pg.9 . . . G10
Polo Club Dr. . . . Pg.9 . . . G10
Poplar St. . . . . . . Pg.10 . . . H11
Portsmouth Ct. . . Pg.4 . . . E11
Prairie Ave. . . . . . Pg.10 . . . G12
President St. . . . . Pg.9 . . . F10
Quincy Ct. . . . . Pg.2,3 . . . E10
Raleigh Ct. . . . . . Pg.9 . . . G10
Reeves Dr. . . . . . Pg.3,9 . . . F10
Regency Dr. . . . . Pg.4 . . . E12
Ringneck Dr. . . . . Pg.9 . . . F10
Robert Ct. . . . . . . Pg.10 . . . H11
Roberta Ave. . . . . Pg.10 . . . G11
Roland Dr. E. . . . . Pg.4 . . . F11
Roland Dr. N. . . . . Pg.4 . . . F11
Roland Ct. . . . . . Pg.4 . . . F11
Rugby Ct. . . . . . . Pg.3 . . . E10
Sandburg Ct. . . . Pg.4 . . . E11
Sandra Ct. . . . . . Pg.10 . . . F11
Saratoga Dr. . . . . Pg.3 . . . F10
Scarboro Dr. . . . . Pg.4 . . . F11
Schmale Ct. . . . . Pg.3 . . . E10
Schmale Rd. . . . . Pg.9,10 . . F10
Schubert Ave. . . . Pg.9,10 . . F10
Schubert Ct. . . . . Pg.4 . . . F10
Scott St. . . . . . . . Pg.10 . . . F11
Shorewood Ct. . . Pg.10 . . . H11
Shorewood Dr. . . Pg.10 . . . H11
Sidney Ave. . . . . . Pg.10 . . . G12
Siems Dr. . . . . . . Pg.3 . . . E10
Slayton Ln. . . . . . Pg.3 . . . E10
Somerset Dr. . . . . Pg.4 . . . F11
Spruce St. . . . . . Pg.10 . . . H11
Standren Dr. . . . . Pg.4 . . . E11
Stevenson Dr. . . Pg.3,10 . . F10
Stonefield Dr. . . . Pg.3 . . . F10
Terry Rd. . . . . . . . Pg.10 . . . G12
Thomas Ct. . . . . . Pg.9 . . . G10
Thorncliff Dr. . . . . Pg.4 . . . F11
Timber Ln. . . . . . Pg.4 . . . E11
Towner Ln. . . . . . Pg.4 . . . F11
Vail Ln. . . . . . . . . Pg.4 . . . E11
Van Meter Ct. . . . Pg.9 . . F,G11
Van Meter St. . . . Pg.9 . . . F10
Vantroba Dr. . . . . Pg.9,10 G10,11
Vista Ct. . . . . . . . Pg.3 . . . E11
Wall St. . . . . . . . . Pg.9 . . . F10
Warwick Dr. . . . . Pg.4 . . . F11
Waters Edge Dr. Pg.4 . . . E11
Wayne Ave. . . . . . Pg.3 . . . F10
Westburg St. . . . . Pg.9 . . . F10
Westchester Dr. Pg.4 . . . E11
Whirlaway Ct. . . . Pg.4 . . . F11
Whitman Dr. . . . . Pg.4 . . . E11
Wildwood Ct. . . . Pg.4 . . E,F11
Windsor Ln. . . . . Pg.4 . . . E11
Windy Pt. Dr. . . Pg.4,10 F11,12
Winthrop Ave. . . . Pg.10 . . . G12
Winthrop Ct. . . . . Pg.10 . . . G12
Woodside Ln. . . . Pg.4 . . . F11
Wren Ct. . . . . . . . Pg.2 . . . E10
Wrightwood Ave.
. . . . . . . . . . . . . Pg.9,10 . . F10
Wrightwood Ct. . . Pg.9 . . . G10
Wyatt Ln. . . . . . . Pg.10 . . . G11
Yardley Ln. . . . . . Pg.4 . . . E11

**FOREST PRESERVES**
East Branch F.P. Pg.4,10 . . F12

**GOLF COURSES**
Glendale Lakes G.C.
. . . . . . . . . . . . . Pg.10 . . . G10

**PARKS**
Gladstone Park Pg.4 . . . E11
Glen Hill Park . . . Pg.10 . . . G11
Harold Reskin Pk.
. . . . . . . . . . . . . Pg.10 . . . G12
Michael Camera Park
. . . . . . . . . . . . . Pg.9 . . . G10
Nazos Park . . . . . Pg.10 . . . G13

**SCHOOLS**
Americana Sch. Pg.9 . . . F10
Charles Reskin Sch.
. . . . . . . . . . . . . Pg.10 . . . G12
G. Stanley Hall Sch.
. . . . . . . . . . . . . Pg.10 . . . G12
Glen Hill Sch. . . . Pg.10 . . . G11
Glenside Jr. H.S.
. . . . . . . . . . . . . Pg.10 . . . G11
Marquardt Sch. Dist. 15
. . . . . . . . . . . . . Pg.4 . . . E12
Queen Bee Sch. Pg.10 . . . G11
Richard Craft Jr. H.S.
. . . . . . . . . . . . . Pg.4 . . . F12
St. Matthew Sch.
. . . . . . . . . . . . . Pg.10 . . . G12

**SHOPPING CENTERS**
Cloverleaf Plaza Pg.4 . . . E12
Concorde Green Plaza
. . . . . . . . . . . . . Pg.10 . . . H11
Full Bloom Center
. . . . . . . . . . . . . Pg.10 . . . G11
Glendale Town Center
. . . . . . . . . . . . . Pg.4 . . . E11
Westlake Plaza Pg.4 . . . E11
Willow Wood S.C.
. . . . . . . . . . . . . Pg.4 . . . E11

**MISCELLANEOUS**
Chicago Health Club
. . . . . . . . . . . . . Pg.3 . . . E11
Glenside F.D. . . . Pg.10 . . . G11
Glenside Public Library
. . . . . . . . . . . . . Pg.9 . . . G11
Post Office . . . . . Pg.9 . . . E11
Village Hall . . . . . Pg.10 . . . G11

**HANOVER PARK**
Pages 2,3
(For additional listings,
see Sections 2 and 5)
**STREETS**
Aberdeen Ct. . . . . . . . . . . . . C6
Alpine Ct. . . . . . . . . . . . . . . A8
Amarillo St. . . . . . . . . . . . . B8
Andover Dr. E. . . . . . . . . . . B7
Andover Dr. W. . . . . . . . . . . B7
Apache Dr. . . . . . . . . . . . . . A7
Arbor Ave. . . . . . . . . . . . . . A7
Argyle Rd. . . . . . . . . . . . . . B8
Arlington Ct. . . . . . . . . . . . B8
Arlington Dr. . . . . . . . . . . . B8
Arlington Dr. . . . . . . . . . . . B8
Arlington Dr. East . . . . . . . B7
Arlington Dr. West . . . . . . . B7
Audrey Ln. . . . . . . . . . . . . . D6
Baldwin Ct. . . . . . . . . . . . . C6
Baldwin Ln. . . . . . . . . . . . . A8
Bamberg Ct. . . . . . . . . . . . A8
Barr Ct. . . . . . . . . . . . . . . . B8
Barrington Rd. . . . . . . . . . . A7
Barrymore Ct. . . . . . . . . . . B7
Bavarian Ct. . . . . . . . . . . . A8
Bayside Dr. . . . . . . . . . . . . D6
Bearflag Dr. . . . . . . . . . . . . B7
Bedford Ct. . . . . . . . . . . . . B7
Bell Dr. . . . . . . . . . . . . . . . C7
Bell Ln. . . . . . . . . . . . . . . . C7
Belle Isle Dr. . . . . . . . . . . . D7
Beverley Cir. . . . . . . . . . . . B7
Beverley Dr. . . . . . . . . . . . B7
Bradley Ct. . . . . . . . . . . . . B7
Brookbank Dr. . . . . . . . . . . D6
Camden Ln. . . . . . . . . . . . . C6
Carson Dr. . . . . . . . . . . . . . A8
Castlebar Ct. . . . . . . . . . . . D6
Castlebar Ln. . . . . . . . . . . . D6
Catalina Dr. . . . . . . . . . . . . B8
Celebrity Cir. E. . . . . . . . . . B8
Celebrity Cir. W . . . . . . . . . B8
Center Ave. . . . . . . . . . . . . A7
Chandler Dr. . . . . . . . . . . . D7
Chaplin Ct. . . . . . . . . . . . . B7
Charleston Ct. . . . . . . . . . . B7
Chatsworth Ct. . . . . . . . . . . B7
Chelsea Ct. . . . . . . . . . . . . B5
Church Rd. . . . . . . . . . . . . A7
Cinema Dr. E. . . . . . . . . . . B7
Citation Ln. . . . . . . . . . . . . B8
Clarendon Ct. . . . . . . . . . . D7
Clipper Dr. . . . . . . . . . . . . D7
Concord Ct. . . . . . . . . . . . . C7
Cooper Ct. . . . . . . . . . . . . . B8
Cottage St. . . . . . . . . . . . . A7
County Farm Rd. . . . . . . . . A7
Court "A" . . . . . . . . . . . . . . B8
Court "B" . . . . . . . . . . . . . . B8
Court "C" . . . . . . . . . . . . . . B8
Court "D" . . . . . . . . . . . . . . B8
Court "E" . . . . . . . . . . . . . . B8
Court "F" . . . . . . . . . . . . . . B8
Court "G" . . . . . . . . . . . . . . B8
Court "H" . . . . . . . . . . . . . . B8
Court "N" . . . . . . . . . . . . . . B8
Court "O" . . . . . . . . . . . . . . B8
Court "P" . . . . . . . . . . . . . . B8
Court "R" . . . . . . . . . . . . . . B8
Court Leona . . . . . . . . . . . . B8
Court Marguerite . . . . . . . . B8
Court Maria . . . . . . . . . . . . B8
Cove Dr. . . . . . . . . . . . . . . . D6
Crawford Ln. . . . . . . . . . . . B7
Crosby Ct. . . . . . . . . . . . . . B7

39
HANOVER PARK
LISLE

Curtis Ln. B7
Danby Ct. A7
Dansforth Ct. A7
De Forest Ln. C7
Dearborn Ct. D7
Deerfield Ct. A7
Del Monte Dr. C8
Don Carlos Ct. D6
Don Carlos Dr. D6
Dory Circle E8
Downey Ct. B7
Driftwood Ln. D6
Du Pont Dr. D7
Dublin Ln. D6
Dupont Dr. D7
Eastman Ln. D7
Easton B7
Edinburg Ln. D6
Edison Cir. B7
Elgin-O'Hare Expwy. A7
Elm Ave. A7
Elm St. D7
Erie Ct. D7
Essex Ct. B7
Farmington Hills Cir. D7
Farnham Ct. B7
Farrell Ave. A7
Fonda Ln. D7
Franklin Ct. B7
Fremont Dr. A7
Fremont Junction A7
Fresno Ct. A8
Ft. Dearborn Ct. D7
Fulton Ln. C7
Gable Ct. B7
Galgow Ct. C6
Garbo Ln. B7
Gardner Ct. B7
Garland Ln. B7
Gifford Ct. B8
Glengary Ct. D6
Goddard Ln. C7
Gold Cir. A7
Grand Blanc Ct. D7
Grand Blanc Ln. D7
Grand Duell Way C7
Grant Ct. B7
Green Bridle Ln. C6
Greenbay Dr. D6
Greenbrook Blvd. B8
Greenbrook Ct. B8
Gross Isle Ct. D7
Grosse Pointe Cir. D7
Grosse Pointe Ct. D7
Hamtrank Ct. D7
Harbor Ln. D6
Hardwood Ct. D6
Hardy Dr. B7
Heritage Ct. C8
Hileah Ln. B8
Howe Ln. C7
Hunter Ln. D7
Island Cir. D7
Isle Royal Ln. D7
Jefferson St. C,D7
Keene Ln. B8
Kit Carson Dr. A7
Ladd Ln. B7
Laguna Ct. A8
Lake St. A7
Lakeside Dr. D6
Lawrence Ave. C7
Leeward Ln. D6
Lemon Rd. B7
Liberty St. D7
Lucille Ln. B7
Maclain Ln. B6
Madera St. A8
Madrid Ct. A8
Mallard Ln. D6
Mallow Ct. D6
Maple Ave. A7
Marine Dr. D7
Martin Ln. B7
McCormick Ln. C7
Medera St. B8
Merrimac Ln. E8
Mill Ct. A7
Millpond Ln. D6
Monitor Dr. E7
Monroe Ln. B7
Monterey Dr. B8
Montibello Dr. C8
Morton Ave. C7
Nashua Ln. B8
Nautilus Ln. D7
Newport Cir. D7
Niven Ln. B7
Nugget Cir. A7
Oak St. D7
Oakdale Cir. B7
Ontarioville Rd. A7
Pastoral Ln. D7
Pebble Beach Ct. B8
Pebble Beach Dr. B8
Pennsbury Ct. D7
Pennsbury Ln. D6
Pondview Dr. D6
Port Dr. D7
Presque Isle Ct. D7
Prestwick Ct. B9
Redford Ln. B7
Rembrandt Ct. A8
Ridge Crossing B7
Ring Ct. B7
Rob Roy Ln. C6
Rooney Ct. B7
Russelwood Ct. C6
Sacremento Dr. A7
Sandpiper Ln. D7
Santa Anita Dr. B8
Santa Barbara Dr. B8
Santa Cruz Dr. B8
Schooner Ln. D7
Sea Biscuit Ct. B8
Seaview Dr. D7
Seneca Dr. D7
Shoal Dr. D7
Shoreline Dr. D7
Sinatra Ln. B7
Spinnaker Ln. D7
Springlake Dr. D6
St. Ann Dr. B7
St. Clair Ln. D7
St. Claire Ct. D7
Stairway Dr. B7
Star Dr. B7
Starboard Dr. D7
Stepstone Ln. D6
Sterling Ct. C6
Sunset Dr. B7
Sutter Dr. A7
Thistle Ct. C7
Tiburon Ct. B8
Tiburon Dr. B8
Tracy Ct. B7
Troon Ct. B8
Turnberry Ct. B9
Turnberry Dr. B8
Turnberry Loop A8
Turner Ln. B7
Unit Ct. D7
Victor Ln. C7
Waterfall Ln. D6
Whaler Ln. D7
Whirlaway Ln. B8
Whitney Dr. C7
Wildwood Ct. D6
Wildwood Ln. D6
Wilshire Ct. A8
Windjammer Ln. D7
Windmill Dr. D7
Windsor Ct. D7
Windward Ln. D6,7
Woodlake Dr. D6
Wright Ln. C7
Wyandotte Ct. B8
Zeppelin Dr. C,D7

**CEMETERIES**

Illinois Pet Cemetery C7

**PARKS**

Discovery Park C7
East Hampton Park D6
Heritage Park B8
Hidden Pond Park E7
Lions Park D6
Nautilus Park D7
Newport Park A6
West Hampton Park D6

**SCHOOLS**

Elsie C. Johnson Sch. D7
Greenbrook Sch. B8
Horizon Sch. B7
Springwood Middle H.S. B8

**MISCELLANEOUS**

Fire Station #2 B7
Fire Station #3 D7
Railroad Station A7

## HINSDALE

Portions within Cook County
Pages 18,24

**STREETS**

Adams St. Pg.18 Q,R19
Allmen Ave. Pg.18 S19
Ashbury Dr. Pg.24 S19
Astony Ct. Pg.24 S20
Ayres St. Pg.18 Q19
Birchwood Ave. Pg.18 P19
Bittersweet Ln. Pg.18 R21
Blaine Ave. Pg.18 R20
Bobolink Dr. Pg.18 P20
Bodin St. Pg.18 R19
Bonnie Brae Rd. Pg.18 Q19
Briargate Terr. Pg.18 Q19
Brook Pl. Pg.18 Q19
Bruner Pl. Pg.18 Q19
Bruner St. Pg.18 Q,R19
Burr Oak Dr. Pg.18 P20
Camberley Ct. Pg.18,24 S20
Cambridge Ct. (Pvt.) Pg.24 S19
Canterbury Ct. Pg.18 Q19
Carolyn Ln. Pg.18,24 S19
Center St. Pg.18 Q19
Chanticleer Ln. Pg.24 S20
Charleston Rd. Pg.24 S20
Chestnut St. Pg.18 R19
Chicago Ave. Pg.18 R19
Childs Ave. Pg.24 S20
Clay St. Pg.18 P-R19
Claymoor Pg.24 S20
Cleveland Rd. Pg.18 R,S20
Columbia Ave. Pg.18 R21
County Line Ct. Pg.18 Q20
County Line Rd. Pg.18 Q20
Dalewood Ln. Pg.18 R21
Elm St. Pg.18 Q,R20
Elmwood Pl. Pg.24 S20
Flagg Ct. Pg.18 Q20
Forest Rd. Pg.18 Q20
Fox Ln. Pg.18 P20
Foxgate Dr. Pg.24 S19
Franklin St. Pg.18 Q20
Fuller Dr. Pg.18 Q20
Fuller Rd. Pg.18 Q20
Garfield Ave. Pg.18 Q20
Giddings Ave. Pg.24 S20
Grant St. Pg.18 Q,R19
Hampton Pl. Pg.18 Q20
Harding Rd. Pg.18 R21
Hawthorne Cir. Pg.18 P20
Hickory St. Pg.18 Q19
Highland Pg.18 Q20
Hillcrest Ave. Pg.18 R20
Hillgrove Ave. Pg.18 Q20
Hinsdale Ave. Pg.18 R19
Indian Trail Pg.18 P20
Jackson St. Pg.18 R19
Jefferson St. Pg.18 Q20
Justina St. Pg.18 Q20
King Pl. Pg.18 P20
Lansing St. Pg.18 Q20
Lincoln St. Pg.18 Q,R19
Madison St. Pg.18,24 Q,S19
Maple St. Pg.18 Q19
Maumell St. Pg.18 Q20
McKinley Ln. Pg.18 R20
Meadowbrook Ln. Pg.24 S20
Merrill Woods Rd. Pg.18 Q19
Mills St. Pg.18 Q20
Minneola St. Pg.18 Q20
Monroe St. Pg.18 Q,R19
Morris Ln. Pg.18 Q19
North St. Pg.18 Q19
Oak St. Pg.18,24 Q-S20
Oakwood Terr. Pg.18 Q20
Ogden Ave. Pg.18 Q19
Old Mill Rd. Pg.18 P20
Orchard Pl. Pg.18 R20
Pamela Cir. Pg.18,24 S20
Park Ave. Pg.18,24 R,S20
Phillippa St. Pg.18 Q20
Post Dr. Pg.18 Q20
Princeton Pg.18 R20
Quincy St. Pg.18 R,Q19
Racket Club Ct. Pg.24 S19
Radcliffe Way Pg.18 Q20
Ravine Rd. Pg.18 Q20
Salt Creek Ln. Pg.18 P20
Sharron Ct. Pg.18 R21
Spinning Wheel Rd. Pg.18 P20
Spring St. Pg.18 Q21
Springlake Ave. Pg.18 R21
Stough St. Pg.18 Q19
Symonds Dr. Pg.18 Q20
Taft Rd. Pg.18 R,S21
The Lane Pg.18 Q20
The Pines Pg.18 Q19
Thurlow St. Pg.18 R19
Town Pl. Pg.18 R19
Ulm Pl. Pg.18 R19
Village Pl. Pg.18 R20
Vine St. Pg.18 Q-S19
Walker Rd. Pg.18 Q20
Walnut St. Pg.18 Q19,20
Warren Ct. Pg.18 Q19
Warren Terr. Pg.18 Q19
Washington Cir. Pg.18 S20
Washington St. Pg.18,24 R20,S19,20
Wedgewood Ct. Pg.18 Q19
Wilson Ln. Pg.18 R21
Woodland Pg.18 R20
Woodmere Dr. Pg.24 S20
Woodside Ave. Pg.18 R20
York Rd. Pg.18 Q20
1st St. Pg.18 R20
2nd St. Pg.18 R19
3rd Ave. Pg.18 R20
3rd St. Pg.18 R20
4th St. Pg.18 R19,20
5th Ave. Pg.18 R20
5th St. Pg.18 R20
6th Ave. Pg.18 R20
6th St. Pg.18 R19,20
7th Ave. Pg.18 R20
7th St. Pg.18 R20,21
8th Ave. Pg.18 R20
8th Pl. Pg.18 R19
8th St. Pg.18 R20
9th Ave. Pg.18 S20
9th Ct. Pg.18 S20
9th St. Pg.18,24 S19,20
55th St. Pg.18,24 S19
56th Pl. Pg.24 S20
56th St. Pg.24 S20
57th St. Pg.24 S20
58th Pl. Pg.24 S19
58th St. Pg.24 S20
59th St. Pg.24 S19,20

**GOLF COURSES**

Ruth Lake C.C. Pg.24 S19

**PARKS**

Brush Hill Area Pg.18 Q20
Dietz Park Pg.18 R19
Highlands Park Pg.18 Q20
Melin Park Pg.18 R19
Pierce Park Pg.18 Q20
Robbins Park Pg.18 R19
Spring Lake Park Pg.18 R21
Stough Park Pg.18 R19

**SCHOOLS**

Hinsdale Central H.S. Pg.24 S19
Hinsdale Jr. Academy Pg.18 Q20
Hinsdale Jr. H.S. Pg.18 R20
Lane Sch. Pg.18 Q20
Madison Sch. Pg.18 R19
Monroe Sch. Pg.18 Q19
Montessori Sch. of Hinsdale Pg.18 R19
Oak Sch. Pg.18,24 S20
School District #86 Offices Pg.24 S20
St. Isaac Joques Sch. Pg.18 R19
Zion Lutheran Sch. Pg.18 R19

**MISCELLANEOUS**

Burns Field Pg.18 Q19
Hinsdale Community Pool and Park Pg.18 R19
Hinsdale Hosp. Pg.18 Q20
Sanitarium Pg.18 Q20
South Suburban Hospital Pg.24 S20
Village Hall Pg.18 Q19

## ITASCA

Pages 4,5

**STREETS**

Alexandria Ct. B15
Andrene Ln. A13
Ardmore Ave. B14
Arlington Heights Rd. A16,B15
Arlington Rd. B15
Baker Dr. A,B14
Bay Dr. A15
Birch St. B14
Bloomingdale Rd. W. C14,15
Bonnie Brae Ave. C15
Briar Pl. B15
Broker Ave. C16
Bryn Mawr Ave. B13-15
Catalpa Ave. B15
Center St. B14,15
Cherry St. B15
Circle Terrace A13
Cotte Ct. B16
Country Club Dr. B16
Country Club Ln. B15
Crest Ave. A13
Devon Ave. A14-17
District Dr. B14
Division St. B15
Elgin-O'Hare Expwy. A14
Elm St. B,C15
Emerson Ave. C16
Expressway Dr. B14
Forest Ave. C15
Frontage Rd. A15
George St. C15
Glenlake Ave. A13
Granville Ave. B16
Greenview Rd. B15
Grove St. B15
Hamilton Pkwy A14
Hawthorn Dr. C14
Hickory Dr. B14
Highland Ave. A13
Highland Ave. C16
Hillcrest Ave. B13
Hilltop Dr. A,B13
Hollywood Ave. B14
Home Ave. C15
Inverness Ln. B16
Irving Park Rd. B13,15,C16
Itasca Industrial Dr. B16
Linden St. B15
Line St. B15
Lombard Rd. C15
Maple Ave. B,C15
Maplewood Dr. B14
Marino Ct. A16
Meacham Rd. A13
Medina Dr. C14
Medinah Rd. A13
Millers Crossing A15
No. Port Dr. A15
North Cir. B14
North St. B14,16
Norwood Ave. A14
Oak St. B,C15
Orchard St. B15
Park Blvd. A14
Parkside Ave. B,C16
Pierce Rd. A15
Prestwick Ln. C14
Princeton Ave. C15
Prospect Ave. C16
Rohlwing Rd. B14
Rush St. B,C15
Schiller St. B15
Shelley Dr. C14
Spring Lake Dr. B,C14
Spyglass Ct. C14
St. Andrews Cir. C14
Sunnyside Ave. C16
Surrey Ln. B16
Theodore Ln. B15
Thorndale Ave. A13,15
Valley Rd. C14
Walnut St. B,C15
Walters B15
Washington St. C15
Williamsburg Dr. B14
Willow St. B15
Windsor Rd. A15

**CEMETERIES**

St. Luke's Cemetery C13

**GOLF COURSES**

Itasca Country Club B16
Medinah Country club B13
Nordic Hills Country Club C14
Salt Creek Country Club A16

**PARKS**

Clayston Park B15
Frazen Park B15
Happy Acres Park B15
New Park B16
Peacock Park B15
Schiller Park C16
Springbrook Nature Center B14
Usher Park B15
Washington Park C15

**SCHOOLS**

Chicago College of Osteopathic Medicine A15
Franzen Sch. B14
Itasca Jr. H.S. B15
St. Luke's Sch. C15
St. Peter's Catholic Sch. B15
Washington Sch. C15

**MISCELLANEOUS**

Fire Department B14
Hamilton Lakes A15
Library B15
Post Office B14
Village Hall B15

## LEMONT TOWNSHIP

Pages 29,30
(For additional listings, see Section 8)

**STREETS**

Archer Ave. Y20
Canal St. Z19
Chicago & Joliet Rd. Z18
Grant Rd. Z19
Tri-State Rd. Y19
107th St. Z20
111th St. Z19

**GOLF COURSES**

Cog Hill Country Club Z18

## LISLE

Pages 15,16,21,22

**STREETS**

Abbey Dr. Pg.21 S10
Abbeywood Dr. Pg.21 T10
Academy Dr. Pg.15 R10
Acorn Hill Pg.21 T9
Adams Dr. Pg.21 S10
Adler Ct. Pg.15 R10
Alta Ct. Pg.21 U9
Ambassador Ct. Pg.15 P10
Angle Ln. Pg.21 S10
Anton Ct. Pg.21 U9
Arbor View Ct. Pg.16 Q12
Arbor View Dr. Pg.16 Q12
Arlington Ave. Pg.15 R10
Arlington Pl. Pg.15 R10
Ascot Ct. Pg.15 P10
Ashford Ct. Pg.21 T10
Ashley Cir. Pg.15 R9
Aspen Rd. Pg.21 U9
Aster Ct. Pg.16 S12
Auvergne Ave. Pg.16 R12
Auvergne Ct. Pg.16 R12
Azalea Pg.15 Q10
Babst Ct. Pg.20 T11
Bannister Ct. Pg.20 T10
Barclay Ct. Pg.15 P10
Barkdoll Rd. Pg.21 T9
Barkridge Ct. Pg.15 R10
Barnwall Ct. Pg.15 R10
Basswood Dr. Pg.16 Q12
Bayside Ct. Pg.15 R10
Beau Bien Ct. Pg.15 R9
Beau Bien Ln., E. & W. Pg.15 R9
Beau Monde Blvd. Pg.15 Q9
Beau Monde Dr. Pg.15 R10
Beau Monde Ln. Pg.15 Q10
Beau Monde Terr. Pg.15 Q10
Beechwood Ct. Pg.21 T10
Benedictine Pkwy. Pg.21 S0
Bentley Ln. Ct. Pg.21 T9
Berkshire Ct. Pg.21 T9
Black Oak Ct. Pg.21 T10
Black Partridge Ln. Pg.15 R9
Blackhawk Ln. Pg.15 R10
Bloomfield Dr. Pg.21 T0
Bluebell Ct. Pg.16 R12
Bonita Cir. Pg.16 Q9
Bordeaux Pl. Pg.15 Q9
Breckenbridge Pg.21 U9
Briarcliff Ct. Pg.21 T9
Bridge Ln. Pg.21 S10
Briggs Ct. Pg.15 S10
Brigton Ct. Pg.21 T9
Bristol Dr. Pg.21 S9
Brittany Dr. Pg.15 Q9
Brookline Ct. Pg.21 S9
Brookwood Rd. Pg.21 T10
Brunswick Ct. Pg.21 T9
Buckingham Dr. Pg.21 S9
Buckley Ave. Pg.16 Q11
Burgundy Ct. Pg.15 Q9
Burnham St. Pg.15 R9
Burlington Ave. Pg.15 R10
Burlington Ct. Pg.16 R12
Burning Tree Ct. Pg.15 R10
Burr Oak Rd. Pg.15,21 S10
Bush St. Pg.16 Q12
Cabot Dr. Pg.15 Q9
Camden Ct. Pg.21 T9
Candlewood Ct. Pg.15 R10
Canterbury Ln. Pg.15 Q10
Cape Cod Ct. Pg.21 T9
Carl Dr. Pg.15 Q10
Carriage Hill Rd. Pg.21 T10
Carriage Rd. Pg.21 T10
Cascade Dr. Pg.15,21 S10
Cascara Ln. Pg.16 Q12
Cedar Ct. Pg.15 R11
Center Ave. Pg.16 Q-S11
Chateau Pl. Pg.15 Q9
Chatfield Ln. Pg.21 T10
Chatham Pl. Pg.15 Q9
Chelsea Ave. Pg.16 Q11
Cherry Pg.15 Q10
Chicago Ave. Pg.16 R12
Chippewa Ct. Pg.15 R10
Christian Ln. Pg.20 T10
Clover Dr. Pg.16 S12
Coach House Rd. Pg.21 T9
College Rd. Pg.21 T9
Colton Ct. Pg.15 R9
Columbia Ave. Pg.16 R11
Commerce Ct. Pg.15 Q9
Concord Pl. Pg.15 Q9
Corporate West Dr. Pg.15 Q9
Corporetum Ave. Pg.16 Q11
Cypress Ct. Pg.15 R10
Deerpath Ct. Pg.21 T10
Devon Ave. Pg.15 R10
Division St. Pg.16 R11
Dixon Dr. Pg.15 S10
Dogwood Pg.15 Q10
Donwood Trails Dr. Pg.21 T10
Dorset St. Pg.16 Q11
Driftwood Ct. Pg.15 R10
Dry Bridge Ct. Pg.20 T10
Dumoulin Ave. Pg.16 R11
Edgebrooke Dr. Pg.15 P10
Eisenhower Ln. Pg.15 S10
Elm Ave. Pg.16 R12
Elm St. Pg.16 R12
Fairway Dr. Pg.21 T11
Fernwood Dr. Pg.21 T9
Forbes Dr. Pg.15 Q9
Forestview Rd. Pg.21 S11
Four Lakes Ave. Pg.21 S11
Front St. Pg.16 R11
Gamble Dr. Pg.16 R11
Garden Dr. Pg.21 T9
Garfield Ave. Pg.16 R11
Glenbrook Ct. Pg.21 T9
Golfview Dr. Pg.21 T10
Green Trails Dr. Pg.21 T9,10
Greenfield Dr. Pg.21 T9
Grenoble Ct. Pg.21 T9
Hagberg Ct. Pg.22 S12
Hampshire Ct. Pg.21 T9
Handley Ct. Pg.15 R9
Handley Dr. Pg.15 R9
Hanover Ct. Pg.21 T9
Harth Ct. Pg.21 T10
Hasting Pg.21 T9
Hatch Ln. Pg.16 Q12
Hawthorne Ln. Pg.16 R11
Heritage Ct. Pg.15 R10
Heritage Ln. Pg.21 T10
Hertz Ct. Pg.21 T11
Hickory Dr. Pg.21 T9
Hidden Creek Ct. Pg.15 P10
Hidden Creek Dr. Pg.15 P10
Hill Dr. Pg.15 R10
Hill Trail Rd. Pg.15 R8
Hillside Ln. Pg.21 S10
Hinterlong Ct. Pg.20 T10
Hitchcock Ave. Pg.16 R10
Holly Ct. Pg.21 T10
Huntington Cir. Pg.21 T9
Illinois Ave. Pg.15 R10
Indiana Ave. Pg.15 R10
Innsbruck Ct. Pg.21 T9
Inverness Rd. Pg.16 S11
Ironwood Dr. Pg.22 S11
Ivanhoe Ave. Pg.16 Q12
Ivy Dr. Pg.21 T9
Jonquil Ave. Pg.16 R11,12
Keel Ct. Pg.15 R8
Keim Rd. Pg.15 Q10
Keller St. Pg.15 R9
Kent Ct. Pg.21 T9
Keswick Ln. Pg.21 S9
Kindling Ct. Pg.21 T10
Kingston Ave. Pg.16,22 Q,R,S11
Kirkwood Ct. Pg.21 T9
Knollwood Ct. Pg.21 T9
Lacey Ave. Pg.15,16 Q10,11
Lake Trail Dr. Pg.15 R9
Lake Valley Dr. Pg.15 R8
Lakeshore Dr. Pg.22 S11
Lakeside Dr. Pg.21 S11
Lakewood Ct. Pg.21 T9
Larkspur Pg.16 S12
Lexington Rd. Pg.21 T9
Lincoln Ave. Pg.16 R11
Lincoln St. Pg.16 Q,R11
Linden Ct. Pg.21 T10
Lisle Pl. Pg.16 R11
Longview Dr. Pg.21 T9
Longwood Dr. Pg.22 S11
Lundy Ln. Pg.21 T10
Main St. Pg.16 Q11
Maple Ave. Pg.16,21 S10,11
Maple Terr. Pg.21 S10
Mark Carre Pg.15 R9
McKenzie Station Dr. Pg.16 R11
McKinley Ave. Pg.16 R11
Meadow Ln. Pg.16 R12
Mertz Ct. Pg.21 T10
Methodist Park Pg.22 S12
Meyer Dr. Pg.16 S12
Middleton Ave. Pg.15,16 Q10,11
Mill Bridge Ln. Pg.21 S10
Miller Ln. Pg.21 S10
Morton Rd. Pg.15 Q10
Muirwood Ct. Pg.21 T10
Neff Ct. Pg.21 T10
New Albany Rd. Pg.21 T9
Newport Dr. Pg.15 S10
Normandy Dr. Pg.15 Q9
Nottingham Ct. Pg.15 Q10
Nutmeg Pg.15 Q10
Oak Hill Dr. Pg.15 R10
Oak Trails Ct. Pg.21 R10
Oakton Ct. Pg.21 T9
Oakview Dr. Pg.16 S11
Ogden Ave. Pg.15,16 R9,10,12
Ohio Ct. Pg.15 R10
Ohio St. Pg.15 R10
Old Oaks Dr. Pg.15 R8
Old Tavern Rd. Pg.15 R9
Oldham Ave. Pg.16 Q11
Oldham St. Pg.15 Q9
Ory Bridge Ct. Pg.21 T10
Parke Ln. Pg.15 S8
Parksledge Ct. Pg.21 T10
Parkview Dr. Pg.15 Q10
Patton Dr. Pg.22,28 S10
Paxton Ct. Pg.15 R9
Pebble Creek Ct. Pg.15 Q10
Pebblewood Dr. Pg.15 P10
Pennywood Dr. Pg.15 R10
Peppertree Ct. Pg.21 T10
Pine Ln. Pg.15 Q10
Pine Rd. Pg.15 Q10
Pine Tree Ct. Pg.15 Q10
Pinehurst Ct. Pg.21 T10
Pleasant Hill Ln. Pg.20 T10
Portsmouth Dr. Pg.15 S10
Prutimore Ct. Pg.21 T10
Raintree Ct. Pg.21 T10
Ranier Dr. Pg.21 S10
Redwood Ct. Pg.16 Q12
Redwood Ln. Pg.16 Q12
Regency Woods Dr. Pg.15 P10
Rehm Ct. Pg.21 T10
Reidy Rd. Pg.16 R11
Reilly Pl. Pg.16 R11
Rickert Ct. Pg.20 T10
Ridgewood Rd. Pg.21 T10
Riedy Pl. Pg.16 R11
River Bend Dr. Pg.22 S11
River Rd. Pg.15,16 R11
Riverview Dr. Pg.16 S11
Robin Ln. Pg.15,16 R,S10
Rolling Dr. Pg.16 S11
Royal Glen Ct. Pg.21 T10
Rue Beauchamp Pg.15 R9
Rue Beavoir Cir. Pg.15 Q9
Ruebienvenu Pg.15 R9
Russel Dr. Pg.15 Q10
Sail Boat Bay Pg.15 R8
Scarlet Oak Ct. Pg.21 T10
Scott Cir. Pg.15 R9
Scott Ct. Pg.15 R9
Shabbona Ln. Pg.15 R9
Shagbark Ct. Pg.21 T10
Shagbark Rd. Pg.21 T10
Shasta Dr. Pg.15,21 S10
Shellingham Pg.21 T9
Shire Pg.21 T9
Shorewood Ct. Pg.21 T10
Short St. Pg.16 R11
Sierra Ln. Pg.15 S8
Sleepy Hollow Ln. Pg.21 T10
Southbury Ct. Pg.21 T9
Southport Ave. Pg.16 Q11
Spencer Ave. Pg.16 R11
Spruce Ln. Pg.16 Q12
St. Joesph Creek Rd. Pg.16 R11
St. Tropez Ln. Pg.15 Q9
Stone Brook Ct. Pg.21 T9
Stone Haven Way Pg.21 T10
Stowe Ct. Pg.21 T9
Sun Valley Ct. Pg.21 U9
Sun Valley Rd. Pg.21 U9
Sunnydale Ln. Pg.21 T10
Surry Ridge Rd. Pg.21 T9
Swartz Ave. Pg.15,16 R10
Tall Tree Ct. Pg.15 R10
Tanglewood Dr. Pg.21 T10
Tangley Oak Tr. Pg.15 R9
Taos Ct. Pg.21 U10
Tealwood Dr. Pg.21 T9
Tellis Ln. Pg.21 S10
Telluride Ct. Pg.21 U9
Timber Trails Rd. Pg.21 T10
Timberview Pg.21 T10
Timothy Ln. Pg.21 T11
Torrey Pines Ln. Pg.21 T9
Tory Ln. Pg.21 T9
Trinity Dr. Pg.21 T10
Trowbridge Way Pg.20 T10
Twin Oak Ln. Pg.21 T9
Tyrnbury Dr. Pg.21 T9
University Ln. Pg.15 R9
Vail Ct. Pg.21 U9
Valley Forge Rd. Pg.21 T9
Varsity Dr. Pg.15 R9
Venture St. Pg.16 R12
Vernon Pk. Pl. Pg.16 R11
Walnut Creek Ln. Pg.16 R12
Warrenville Rd. Pg.15,16 Q9,12
Water Bridge Rd. Pg.15 Q8
Water Ct. Pg.15 R9
Waubansie Ln. Pg.15 R10
Wayfairing Ln. Pg.21 T9
Wedgewood Ct. Pg.15 R9
Weeping Willow Dr. Pg.21 S9
Wellington Ct. Pg.15 R10
West Ave. Pg.16 R12
Westerhoff Dr. Pg.15 Q10
Western Ave. Pg.15 Q,R10
Western Ct. Pg.15 Q10
Western Ln. Pg.16 R12
Westleigh Pg.21 T9
Westview Ln. Pg.16 R12
White Birch Dr. Pg.15 Q10
White Oak Ln. Pg.21 T9
Wildwood Ct. Pg.21 T10
Winchester Ave. Pg.15 R10
Windsor Dr. Pg.21 S9
Windward Dr. Pg.15 R8
Wingate Dr. Pg.15 S10
Winkler Ct. Pg.21 T10
Winstead Ct. Pg.20 T10
Wisconsin St. Pg.15 R10
Woodbriar Ct. Pg.21 T10
Woodcliff Ct. Pg.21 T9
Yackley Ave. Pg.15,21 R,S10
Yender Ave. Pg.15 R10
Yorkshire Dr. Pg.21 T9
Yovonovitz Ln. Pg.15 Q10

**CEMETERIES**

Lisle Cemetery Pg.16 Q12

**GOLF COURSES**

River Bend Golf Course Pg.21 S11

**PARKS**

Abbeywood Pond Park Pg.21 T10

## LISLE

Arbor View Park Pg.16 Q12
Arboretum Woods Park Pg.16 Q11
Aspen Park Pg.21 U9
Beau Bien Pk. Pg.15 Q9
Candlewood Park Pg.15 R10
Carriage Hills Park Pg.21 T10
Coach House Pk. Pg.21 T9
College Road Park Pg.21 T10
Community Park Pg.15,16 R10,11
Connelly Memorial Park Pg.16 Q11
Green Trails Park Pg.21 T10
Heritage Commons Pg.16 R11
Heritage Farms Park Pg.21 T10
Hitchcock Woods Pg.15 R10
Kingston Park Pg.22 S12
Oak Hill South Park Pg.21 S10
Old Tavern Road Park Pg.15 Q9
Pennywood Park Pg.15 R10
River Road Park Pg.21 S11
Sun Valley Park Pg.21 U9
Surrey Ridge Athletic Complex Pg.21 T9
Surrey Ridge Park Pg.21 T9
Tanglewood Park Pg.21 T10
Tate Woods Park Pg.15 Q10
Tate Woods Park North Pg.15 Q10
Valley Forge Park Pg.21 T9

### SCHOOLS

Benet Academy Pg.21 S10
Kennedy Jr. H.S. Pg.21 U9
Lisle Jr. H.S. Pg.16 R11
Lisle Senior H.S. Pg.16 R11
Main St. Sch. Pg.16 R11
Rosehill Montessori Sch. Pg.16 R11
Sacred Heart Monastery Pg.21 S10
Schiesher Sch. Pg.16 R12
St. Joan of Arc Sch. Pg.16 R11
Tate Woods Sch. Pg.16 Q10

### SHOPPING CENTERS

Shopping Center Pg.16,22 S11

### MISCELLANEOUS

Arboretum Lakes Business Park Pg.16 Q11
Corporate Lakes Business Park Pg.15 Q9
Corporate West Business Park Pg.15 Q9
Corporetum Office Campus Pg.16 Q11
Corporetum Office Towers Pg.16 Q11
Fire Dept. #4 Pg.21 T10
Fire Dept. #5 Pg.15 Q10
Fire Dept. HQ Pg.16 R11
Library Pg.16 R11
Post Office Pg.16 Q12
St. Procopius Abbey Pg.21 S10
Train Station Pg.16 R11
Village Hall Pg.16 R11

## LISLE TOWNSHIP

Pages 15,16,21,22

### STREETS

Abbey Dr. Pg.21 S10
Aintree Dr. Pg.22 U11
Allison Ln. Pg.15 R9
Andrews Ct. Pg.21 U8
Arlington Ave. Pg.15 R10
Arrow Ct. Pg.15,21 S9
Auble Dr. Pg.21 T,U10
Augusta Ln. Pg.22 T11
Auvergne Ave. Pg.16 R12
Avon Ct. Pg.21 S9
Azalea Dr. Pg.15 Q10
Balmoral Cir. Pg.21 T8
Baltusrol Ln. Pg.22 T11
Basswood Dr. Pg.16 Q12
Bauer Rd. Pg.15 R7
Beau Bien Blvd. Pg.15 R9
Bell Dr. Pg.21 V8
Belmont Rd. Pg.16,22 S13
Bernett Cir. Pg.21 S8
Bernie Ct. Pg.21 V8
Biltmore Ct. Pg.15 S8
Birdsong Ct. Pg.21 S9
Blackstone Ct. Pg.21 S9
Blackthorne Ln. Pg.21 U9
Blanchard St. Pg.22 S13
Bluff Ct. Pg.15,21 S9
Bluff Ln. Pg.15 S9
Boundary Hill Rd. Pg.22 V12
Brandywine Ct. Pg.21 S9
Brentwood Dr. Pg.22 U11
Bridgeview Ln. Pg.21 S9
Bridlespur Dr. Pg.21 S9
Brookline Ct. Pg.21 S8
Brookwood Rd. Pg.21 T10
Burlington Ave. Pg.15 R7-9
Buttonwood Ct. Pg.15 S9
Canary Ct. Pg.21 S9
Canterbury Ct. Pg.21 S9
Cape Rd. Pg.21 S9
Cardinal Ct. Pg.15 S9
Carlyle Ct. Pg.21 S9
Carriage Way Dr. Pg.21 U8
Cascara Ln. Pg.16 Q12
Case St. Pg.15 R7
Cavalier Pg.15 R9
Cavalier Ln. Pg.15 R9
Chantilly Ct. Pg.22 U11
Charles Ave. Pg.15 S8
Charles St. Pg.21 T8
Chase Ave. Pg.22 S13
Chase Rd. Pg.22 T13
Cliff Ct. Pg.15,21 S9
Clover Dr. Pg.22 S12
Cloverdale Ct. Pg.15 S9
Cohasset Rd. Pg.21 S9
College Rd. Pg.21,22 S13,T,U10
Columbia St. Pg.15 R7
Columbine Ave. Pg.22 S12
Concord Rd. Pg.21 S9
Cornwall Rd. Pg.21 S9
Country Ct. Pg.22 U11
Country Dr. Pg.21 S9
Cove Ln. Pg.15 P7
Creek Ct. Pg.22 U11
Creek Dr. Pg.22 U11
Crest Ln. Pg.22 S12
Cross Pg.16 R13
Derby Ct. Pg.21 U10
Derby Dr. Pg.22 U11
Devon Ave. Pg.15 Q10
Dognood Dr., W. Pg.15 Q10
Dogwood Tr. Pg.21 T10
Donwood Dr., E. Pg.21 U10
Dorset St. Pg.16 Q11
Dover Dr. Pg.22 S12
Dover Ln. Pg.21 V9
Dover St. Pg.22 S12
Drendall Rd. Pg.16 R13
DuPage Dr. Pg.22 U12
East Ave. Pg.15 R8
East Lake Dr. (Pvt) Pg.22 S11
East-West Tollway Pg.15,16 Q7,13
Edward Ave. Pg.16 R13
Elinor Ave. Pg.22 S13
Elm St. Pg.16,22 R,S,T12
Elmore Ave. Pg.16,22 R13
Essex Ave. Pg.21,22 S9,11
Essex Ct. Pg.22 T11
Essex Rd. Pg.22 T11
Eugenia Dr. Pg.15 R9
Evergreen Dr. Pg.15 Q10
Faganel Dr. Pg.15 Q10
Fairway Dr. (Pvt) Pg.22 T11
Fender Ave. Pg.15 R9
Fender Rd. Pg.15 V9
Finley Rd. Pg.16 Q13
Forestview Rd.(Pvt) Pg.21,22 T11
Four Lakes Ave.(Pvt.) Pg.22 S11
Foxwood Ct. Pg.22 U11
Francisco St. Pg.16 R13
Gartner Rd. Pg.21 T8
Glenview Ave. Pg.16 Q13
Granville Ave. Pg.16 R13
Green Briar Dr. Pg.22 U11
Green Trails Rd. Pg.21 T10
Greene Rd. Pg.22 U11
Greenview Dr. Pg.21 S10
Greenwich Ct. Pg.21 S9
Greenwood Ct. Pg.21 S9
Gunston Ave. Pg.21 S9
Haddow Ave. Pg.16 R13
Hamilton Ct. Pg.22 U11
Heather Ct. Pg.15,21 R10,S9
Hemlock Ln. Pg.21 U10
Henning Ct. Pg.21 U7
High Tr. Pg.22 T11
Highview Dr. Pg.15 Q9
Hillcrest Ave. Pg.22 S13
Hillcrest Ln.(Pvt) Pg.21 S10
Hills Oak Ln. Pg.15 P10
Hillside Rd. Pg.21 T8
Hitchcock Ave. Pg.15 R10
Hitchcock St. Pg.16 R12
Hobson Rd. Pg.21,22 T11,12,U9
Hobson Trails Dr. Pg.21 U10
Howard Ave. Pg.16,22 S13
Hummingbird Ct. Pg.21 S9
Huntington Ct. Pg.21 T9
Hyacinth Ct. Pg.21 S9
Illinois Ave. Pg.15 R10
Indian Hill Dr. Pg.15 P8,Q11
Indiana Ave. Pg.15,21 U10
Indianapolis Ave. Pg.16 Q13
Iris Ln. Pg.22 S12
Ironwood Dr. Pg.21 U7
Ivanhoe Ave. Pg.16,22 Q,T12
James Way Pg.21,22 U10
Jane Ave. Pg.21 T9
Janes Ave. Pg.22 S13
Jefferson Ave. Pg.22 S13
Johnson Dr. Pg.21 U8
Julian St. Pg.21 U7
Kammes Dr. Pg.21 T10
Kane Ct. Pg.15 Q9
Karns Rd. Pg.15 R9
Kathrine Ave. Pg.22 S13
Keller St. Pg.15 R9
Kenilworth Cir. Pg.21 U8
Keswick Ln. Pg.15 S9
Kimberly Way Pg.22 S11
Kimberwick Ln. Pg.22 U11
Kings Cove Pg.22 S11
Kingston Ave. Pg.22 S12
Kohley Ave. Pg.22 W13
Kohley Rd. Pg.22 S11
Lacey Ave. Pg.15 Q9
Lacey Ct. Pg.15 Q9
Lakeside Dr. (Pvt) Pg.21 S10
Lakewood Dr. Pg.21 S9
Lenox Ct. Pg.22 T11
Lenox Rd. Pg.22 S11
Leonard Ave. Pg.22 T13
Lincoln St. Pg.16 Q11
Linda Ln. Pg.15 Q8
Lomond Ave. Pg.22 S13
Longreen Rd. Pg.21 T9
Lynn Dr. Pg.21,22 U11
Malibu Ct. Pg.21 S9
Malibu Ln. Pg.21 S9
Mallard Ln. Pg.15 S9
Maple Ave. Pg.15,16 S11,13
Maple Terr.(Pvt) Pg.21,22 S11
Marblehead Ct. Pg.21 S9
Marion Way Pg.22 T11
Mariwood Ct. Pg.21 S9
Matson Ln. Pg.15 Q9
Mayflower Ave. Pg.21 S9
Maywood Ln. Pg.22 S11
McIntrye Rd. Pg.16 Q12
Meadow Lake Ct. Pg.15 S9
Meadow Lake Dr. Pg.15,21 S9
Meadowbrook Ct. Pg.21 T9
Meissch Ct. Pg.15 R7
Meyer Rd. Pg.22 T11
Middle Rd. Pg.15 R8
Middleton Ave. Pg.15 Q9,1C
Millcreek Ct. Pg.21 S9
Millcreek Ln. Pg.21 S9
Milton Dr. Pg.21 S8
Mitchell Ln. Pg.22 U11
Mockingbird Ct. Pg.15 S9
Moraine Ct. Pg.22 U11
Murray Dr. Pg.21 U10
Naper Blvd. Pg.21 S9
Naper Ct. Pg.15 R8
Naperville Rd. Pg.15 R8
Neptune Ct. Pg.21 S9
New Castle Rd. Pg.21 S8
New Hope Rd. Pg.21 S8
Northcrest Dr. Pg.22 T12
Norwood Ave. Pg.21 U8
Nutmeg Ln. Pg.15 Q10
Oak Trails Dr. Pg.21 T10
Oaktree Tr. Pg.22 T12
Oakwood Dr. (Pvt) Pg.21 S10
Ogden Ave. Pg.15,16 Q12,R8
Ohio St. Pg.15 R9,10
Old College Rd. Pg.21 U10
Old Naperville Rd. Pg.15 Q8
Old Plank Rd. Pg.15,21 S8
Oldham Ave. Pg.15,16 Q9,11
Oldwoods Dr. Pg.22 W12
Olympia Ct. Pg.22 T11
Oriole Ln. Pg.15 S9
Oxer Ct. Pg.22 U11
Oxford Ln. Pg.21 V8
Palomino Dr. Pg.21 U10
Pana Ln. Pg.21 S9
Park Meadow Dr. Pg.21 S9
Parke Ln. Pg.21 S9
Parkside Rd. Pg.21 T8
Parkview Ct. Pg.21 S9
Partridge Ct. Pg.21 S9
Pelham Ct. Pg.22 U11
Pershing Rd. Pg.22 T13
Pin Oak Ct. Pg.15 P10
Pin Oak Ln. Pg.21 V10
Pinehurst Ln. Pg.22 T11
Prairie Ave. Pg.16 R13
Prentice Dr. Pg.22 T13
Primrose Ave. Pg.22 S12
Prince Ct. Pg.22 S11
Puffer Rd. Pg.16,22 Q,T13
Queens Cove Pg.22 S11
Radcliff Rd. Pg.15 Q,R9
Railroad S. Pg.16 R12
Red Oak Ln. Pg.15 P10
Redwood Ln. Pg.16 Q12
Ridge Ct. Pg.22 S12
Ridgeland Ave. Pg.15 Q8
Ridgeview Rd. Pg.21 S9
River Dr. Pg.21 V8
River Rd. Pg.22 S11
Riverview Dr. Pg.22 S11
Rose Ave. Pg.16 R13
Rose Ct. Pg.22 S12
Royal Oak Rd. Pg.21 U10
Salem Ave. Pg.21 S9
Seabrook Ct. Pg.21 S9
Setauket Ave. Pg.21 S9
Sherman Ave. Pg.15 R8
Shires Ct. Pg.22 U11
Sierra Ln. Pg.21 S9
Singletree Ln. Pg.21 V10
Smith Rd. Pg.22 S11
Snowdon Ct. Pg.21 U9
Snowdrop Ln. Pg.22 S12
Somerset Ct. Pg.21 S9
South Rd. Pg.22 S11
Southcrest Dr. Pg.22 T12
Spring Bay Dr. Pg.21 S9
Springdale Dr. Pg.21 S9
Spyglass Ct. Pg.22 U11
Stable Rd. Pg.22 T11
Stanton Dr. Pg.21 U8
Starling Ct. Pg.15 S9
State Hwy. 53 Pg.16,22 Q,T,W11
Steeple Run Dr. Pg.21 S9
Stonehedge Ct. Pg.22 U11
Summerhill Dr. Pg.22 T11
Summit Dr. Pg.15 Q9
Sundowner Rd. Pg.22 T12
Surf Ct. Pg.21 S9
Surrey Ave. Pg.21 V8
Surrey Ct. Pg.21 V8
Sussex Rd. Pg.21 S9
Tamiami Dr. Pg.22 T12
Teddo Ave. Pg.15,21 R,S9
Timke Rd. Pg.22 T12
Tuthill Rd. Pg.15,21 S8
Una Ave. Pg.22 W12
Vale Ct. Pg.22 T13
Vernon Ct. Pg.22 T12
Vest Ave. Pg.15 R8
Vest St. Pg.15 R8
Villa Ave. Pg.21 U7
Walnut Ave. Pg.16,22 R,T12
Warrenville Rd. Pg.15,16 Q12
Washington St. Pg.15 R7
Watercress Dr. Pg.21 U7
Wavewood Ln. Pg.21 V10
Wedgewood Ct. Pg.22 U11
Wehrli Rd. Pg.21 W9
Wellington Ave. Pg.15 R9
Western Ave. Pg.16 R13
Westove Ct. Pg.21 S9
Westview Ln. Pg.16,22 R,S12
Wilshire Dr. Pg.22 T12
Windham Hill Ct. Pg.21 S9
Wisconsin St. Pg.15,16 R8,13
Wittington Ct. Pg.22 U11
Wood Ct. Pg.15,22 Q9,T12
Woodbrook Dr. Pg.21 S9
Woodcrest Ct. Pg.22 U11
Woodcrest Dr. Pg.21 S9
Woodlawn Ave. Pg.21 T7
Woodstock Ct. Pg.21 S9
11th Ave. Pg.15 R7
39th St. Pg.15,16 P11
55th Pl. Pg.16,22 S14
59th St. Pg.22 S11-12
61st St. Pg.22 T11,13
62nd St. Pg.22 T12,13
63rd St. Pg.22 T13
75th St. Pg.21,22 V9,12
77th St. Pg.21 V10
79th St. Pg.21,22 V10-11

### CEMETERIES

Oakhill Cem. Pg.16 R13

### FOREST PRESERVES

Green Valley F.P. Pg.21,22 U,V11
Hickory Grove F.P. Pg.21 T10

### PARKS

Morton Arboretum Pg.16 P12

### SCHOOLS

Benedictine University Pg.21 S10
Du Page Montessori Sch. Pg.15 S9
Hobson Sch. Pg.21 U8
Meadows Sch. Pg.22 S12
Montessori Moppet Ctr. Pg.21 V8
Montessori Sch. of Lisle Pg.21 U10
Steeple Run Elem. Sch. Pg.21 S9
Trinity Lutheran Sch. Pg.22 S11

### SHOPPING CENTERS

Shopping Center Pg.22 S11

### MISCELLANEOUS

Camp Greenwood Pg.22 U12
Camp Seager Pg.15,21 S8
Swimming Pool Pg.16,22 S12

## LOMBARD

Pages 10,11,16,17

### STREETS

Acorn Ct. Pg.16 M14
Adams St. Pg.11 K16
Addison Ave. Pg.11 K16
Ahrens Ave. Pg.11 J,K16
Ahrens Ct. Pg.11 J16
Ainsley Ln. Pg.17 M15
Ann St. Pg.11 L14
Apple Ln. Pg.11 L16
Arboretum Dr. Pg.17 M14
Ash St. Pg.10,11 J14
Aspen Dr. Pg.16 L14
Babcocks Grove Ave. Pg.11 H14
Berkshire Ave. Pg.11 H14
Beverly Ct. Pg.16 M13
Brewster Ave. Pg.10,11 J14
Broadview Ave. Pg.10 H14
Broadway N. Pg.11 J15
Broadway S. Pg.11 J15
Brookfield Ave. Pg.11 H14
Brown St. Pg.11 H14
Cambria Ln. (N & S) Pg.11 K16
Cedar Ln. Pg.11 K16
Central Ave. Pg.11 L14
Charing Cross Rd. Pg.11 L15
Charles Ln. Pg.11 K14
Charlotte Ct. Pg.17 M15
Charlotte St. Pg.11 J,K15
Chase Ave. Pg.11 J,K16
Chase Ct. Pg.11 K16
Chase Ln. Pg.11 K16
Cherry Ln. Pg.10 L16
Cimarron Rd. Pg.10 J13
Circle Ave. Pg.11 K15
Circle Terrace Pg.11 K15
Clarendon Ave. Pg.11 H16
Colleen Dr. Pg.17 M14
Colony Ct. Pg.16 L14
Columbine Ave. Pg.10 J14
Concord Ln. Pg.11 K16
Cortland Ave. Pg.11 G14
Craig Pl. Pg.11 H15
Crescent Blvd. Pg.10 J14
Crossing St. Pg.17 M14
Crystal Ave. Pg.10,11 H14
Daniel Ct. Pg.11 L14
Division St. Pg.11 J16
Downing St. Pg.16 M13
Du Page Ave. Pg.11 G,H14
Eastview Terr. Pg.11 K15
Edgewood Ave. Pg.11 H15
Edson Ave. Pg.11 K14
Edson Pl. Pg.10,11 L14
Edson St. Pg.17 M14
Edward St. Pg.11 L14
Eisenhower Ln., N. & S. Pg.17 M14
Elizabeth Ct. Pg.11 K14
Elizabeth St. Pg.11 H-M14
Elm St. Pg.11 J15
Emerson Ave. Pg.11 J16
Ethel Ave. Pg.10,11 K14
Eugenia St. Pg.10,11 J14
Faifield Ct. Pg.17 M15
Fairfield Ave. Pg.11 L15
Fairview Ave. Pg.11 I15
Finley Rd. Pg.10,16 K,M14
Foxworth Blvd. Pg.16 M13
Garfield St. Pg.11 G15
Garfield Terr. Pg.11 J15
Gazebo Ln. Pg.17 M14
Gilmore Ln. Pg.17 N15
Glen Oak Rd. Pg.10 J14
Glenmore Ct. Pg.21 T9
Glenview Dr. Pg.10 J14
Goebel Dr. Pg.11 H14,15
Grace Ave. Pg.11 K15
Grace St. Pg.11,17H,M15
Graham Ave. Pg.11 K14
Graywood Dr. Pg.17 M15
Green Valley Dr. Pg.11 K14
Green Valley Dr. W. Pg.11 K14
Greenfield Ave. Pg.11 H14
Greenfield St. Pg.11 H15
Grove Ln. Pg.11 H14
Grove St. Pg.11 J14
Hamilton Ln. Pg.11 K16
Hammerschmidt Ave. Pg.11 L15
Harding Rd. Pg.11 K14
Harmony Ln. Pg.11 K16
Harrison Rd. Pg.10,11 K14
Hawthorne Cir. Pg.11 K16
Hickory Rd. Pg.11 K14
Hickory St. Pg.11 K15
High Ridge Rd. Pg.11 L15,16
Highland Ave. Pg.11,17 J-M15
Hillcrest Ct. Pg.17 M14
Hillcrest Ln. Pg.17 M14
Hunter St. Pg.16 M13
International Dr. Pg.10 L14
Jackson St. Pg.11 K16
Janata Blvd. Pg.17 M15
Jeffrey Ct. Pg.11 L14
Joyce Ave. Pg.11 H15
Julie Ln. Pg.17 L14
June Ln. Pg.17 M14
Kaplan Ct. Pg.11 H16
Kelly Ct. Pg.11 K16
Kramer Ave. Pg.11 H16
LaLonde Ave. Pg.11 H,K15
Le Moyne Ave. Pg.11 H14
Lewis Ave. Pg.11 H,L15
Liberty Ln. Pg.11 K16
Lilac Way Pg.11 K16
Lincoln Ave. Pg.11 J14
Lincoln Ct. Pg.11 K14
Lincoln Dr. Pg.17 M14
Lincoln St. Pg.11 J,K14
Lloyd Ave. Pg.16 M13
Lloyd Ave. Pg.16 M14
Lodge Ave. Pg.11 J15
Lodge Ln. Pg.11 K16
Lombard Ave. Pg.11 H15
Lombard Cir. Pg.11 K15
Lombard Ct. Pg.11 K16
Lore Ln. Pg.11 L14
Loy St. Pg.10,11 H14
Lynne Ln. Pg.11 L14
Madison St. Pg.11 K15
Magnolia Circle Pg.11 K16
Main Dr. Pg.11 L15
Main St. Pg.11,17 J,L,M15
Majestic Dr. Pg.17 M15
Manor Hill Ct. Pg.17 L14
Manor Hill Ln. Pg.16 L14
Maple St. Pg.10,11 J14
Marcus Dr. Pg.11 H15
Marion Ave. Pg.11 K15
Martha Ct. Pg.11 J15
Martha St. Pg.11 H15
Meadow Ave. Pg.10 J14
Michelle Ln. Pg.11 L16
Morningside Ave. Pg.11 K15
Morris Ave. Pg.11 L14
New Ave. Pg.11 K15
Norbury Ave. Pg.11 L15
North Ave. Pg.11 H14,15
Northlake Rd. Pg.17 M15
Norton St. Pg.11 L16
Oak Creek Dr. Pg.16 M14
Oak Meadow Ct. Pg.16 M14
Oakton Dr. Pg.17 M15
Orchard Terr. Pg.11 J14
Park Ave. Pg.11 H14
Park Dr. S. Pg.11 K14
Park Rd. Pg.11 K14
Park Rd. Ct. Pg.11 K14
Parker Pg.11 H16
Parkside Ave. Pg.11 J14
Parkview Blvd. Pg.11 K13,14
Phillips Ct. Pg.10 J14
Pinebrook Dr. Pg.16 M14
Pleasant Ln. Pg.10,11 H14,15
Poplar Ct. Pg.16 L14
Potomac Ave. Pg.11 H14
Prairie Ave. Pg.11 J15
Prairie Ave. E. Pg.11 J15
Progress Rd. Pg.11 G15
Queensport Ct. Pg.16 M13
Randolph St. Pg.11 J15
Rebecca Rd. Pg.11 L14
Regency Dr. Pg.17 M15
Reskin Rd. Pg.11 H16
Revere Ct. Pg.11 K16
Ridge Ave. Pg.11 G,H14
Rochelle Terr. Pg.11 H14
Roosevelt Rd. Pg.10 L14
Rosebud Dr. Pg.17 M15
Royal Dr. Pg.17 M15
School Ave. Pg.11 K16
School Ct. Pg.11 K16
School St. Pg.11 K16
Shedron Way Pg.16 M13
Shiela Pl. Pg.11 H14
Springer Dr. Pg.16 M14
Spruce Ct. Pg.16 M14
St. Charles Pl. Pg.11 J15
St. Charles Rd. Pg.11 J14
St. Regis Dr. Pg.17 M15
Stewart Ave. Pg.11 H15
Stewart Ln. Pg.17 M15
Sunset Rd. Pg.11 H15
Sycamore Ct. Pg.16 L14
Taylor Rd. Pg.10,11 K14,15
Technology Dr. Pg.17 N16
Troy Dr. Pg.10 H14
Troy Ln. Pg.10 H14
Valley Rd. Pg.16 M13
Vance Ct. Pg.10 K14
Vance St. Pg.11 J14
View Ave. Pg.11 K15
View St. Pg.10,11 H15,J14
Vista Ave. Pg.11 H15
Walnut Ct. Pg.16 M14
Washington Blvd. Pg.11 K14
Waters Edge Pg.16 M14
Watt Dr. Pg.16 M13
West Rd. Pg.10,11 H,J14
Western Pg.11 J16
Westmore Ave. Pg.11 K16
Westwood Ave. Pg.11 H,J16
Whitehall St. Pg.16 M13
Willow St. Pg.10,11 J14
Wilson Ave. Pg.11 K16,L14
Wilson Ct. Pg.11 K16
Windsor Ave. Pg.11 J14
Woodland Ave. Pg.10 J14
Woodrow Ave. Pg.11 J16
2nd St. Pg.11 J16
3rd St. Pg.11 J16
13th St. Pg.11 L15
16th Pl. Pg.10 J14
16th St. Pg.17 M14
17th Ave. Pg.17 M15
17th Pl. Pg.17 M15
17th Pl. Pg.17 M15
17th St. Pg.17 M15
18th St. Pg.17 M14
19th St. Pg.17 M14
20th St. Pg.17 M14

### CEMETERIES

Washington St. Cemetery Pg.11 K15

### FOREST PRESERVES

Broadview Slough Woods Pg.10 H14
Churchill Preserve Pg.10 J13

### GOLF COURSES

Glen Briar Golf Club Pg.16 N13
Glen Oak C.C. Pg.10 K13
Ken Locke Golf Links Pg.16,17 M14

### PARKS

Four Seasons Park Pg.16,17 M14
Lagoon Park Pg.11 H15
Lilacia Park Pg.10 J14
Log Cabin Four Seasons Park Pg.17 M14
Lombard Common Park Pg.11 J15
Lombard Lagoon Park Pg.11 H15
Madison Meadow Park Pg.11 K15
Old Grove Park Pg.11 L16
Sunset Knoll Park Pg.10 K14
Terrace View Park Pg.11 H14
Westmore Woods Park Pg.16 J16

### SCHOOLS

DeVry Institute of Technology Pg.17 M14
Edgewood Sch. Pg.11 K15
Fairwood Sch. Pg.11 K15
Glenbard East H.S. Pg.11 K14
Green Valley Sch. Pg.11 K14
Lincoln Sch. Pg.11 J14
Madison Sch. Pg.11 K14
Manor Hill Sch. Pg.17 M15
National College of Chiropractic Pg.11 L15
Northern Baptist Theological Seminary Pg.17 M15
Park View Sch. Pg.11 H14
Peter Hoy Sch. Pg.10 K14
Pleasant Lane Sch. Pg.11 H15
Sacred Heart Catholic Sch. Pg.11 J14
Schaefer Sch. Pg.11 H16
St. John's Lutheran Sch. Pg.11 J14
St. Pius X Catholic Sch. Pg.11 K16
W. Suburban Sch. for Retarded Children Pg.11 K16
Westlake Jr. H.S. Pg.17 M14
Westmore Sch. Pg.11 J16
Wm. Hammerschmidt Sch. Pg.11 K15

### SHOPPING CENTERS

Eastgate Shopping Center Pg.11 K16
Fountain Square S.C. Pg.17 N16
Northgate S.C. Pg.10 H13
Shopping Center Pg.11 L15
Yorktown Shopping Center Pg.17 N15

### MISCELLANEOUS

Lombard Sewer Treatment Plant Pg.16 M13
Northern Theological Seminary Pg.17 M15
Police Station Pg.11 L15
Post Office Pg.11 J15
Village Hall Pg.11 L15

## MEDINAH

Page 4...B12
For listings see Bloomingdale Twp.

## MILTON TOWNSHIP

Pages 9,10,15,16

### STREETS

Acorn Ave. Pg.10 K13
Ahlstrand Rd. Pg.16 N12,13
Apache Dr. Pg.15 M8
Arbor Ln. Pg.16 P11,12
Arboretum Rd. Pg.16 N12
Argyle St. Pg.10 H13
Armburst Ave. Pg.9 J8
Armburst Rd. Pg.9 J9
Arnold Ave. Pg.10 H11
Arrow Glen Ct. Pg.15 N8
Arrowhead Dr. Pg.15 M8
Ashley Dr. Pg.16 N11
Astor Pl. Pg.9 K8
Audobon Ct. Pg.16 N13
Audobon Rd. Pg.16 N13
Avalon Ct. Pg.15 M8
Avondale Ln. Pg.16 M14
Balsam Dr. Pg.16 P12
Bancroft Ct. Pg.16 N11
Barclay Pl. Pg.16 N11
Barry Ave. Pg.9 J7
Bayberry Ln. Pg.15 M9
Beaumont Ln. Pg.16 M14
Beechwood Ct. Pg.15 N8
Beechwood Ln. Pg.16 N11
Bemis Rd. Pg.16 M13
Beverly St. Pg.9 J8
Big Horn Ct. Pg.15 M8
Big Horn Dr. Pg.15 M8
Birch Pg.9 J8
Birchbrook Ct. Pg.16 M12
Birchwood Dr. Pg.16 P12
Blackcherry Ln. Pg.16 P11
Blackhawk Dr. Pg.15 N7
Blanchard St. Pg.15 M10
Blenheim Ct. Pg.16 N11
Bloomingdale Rd. Pg.10 J11
Blue Jay Ct. Pg.9 H8
Bob-O-Link Rd. Pg.16 N13
Box Elder Ave. Pg.9 J7
Briarcliff Ct. Pg.16 N13
Briarcliff Rd. Pg.16 N13
Brighton Dr. Pg.15 M9
Broadview Ave. Pg.8 J5
Brook Ct. Pg.16 M13
Bryant Ave. Pg.10,16 J,M12
Bryant Rd. Pg.16 P12
Bud Ct. Pg.9 J7
Buena Vista Dr. Pg.16 M11,12
Burdett Ct. Pg.10 G12
Burning Trail Pg.15 M,N8
Burr Oak Dr. Pg.16 P12
Busch Rd. Pg.10 H12
Butterfield Rd. Pg.15,16 N10,11
Calvin Pg.9 K7
Cambridge Ct. Pg.16 N11
Canary Rd. Pg.16 N13
Carey Cir. Pg.16 N12
Carrol Gate Pg.15 M8
Cathryn Ct. Pg.9 J8
Caxton Ct. Pg.9 L8
Cedar Ct. Pg.9 K7
Cherry Ln. Pg.10 J12
Cherry St. Pg.10 K13
Chieftan Ln. Pg.9 M8
Chippewa Dr. Pg.15 N7
Churchill Dr. Pg.10 J13
Churchill Ln. Pg.16 M12
Clayford Ct. Pg.16 N12
Clifford Rd. Pg.16 N12
Clifton Ave. Pg.10 J13
Clifton Ln. Pg.16 M14
Cole Ave. Pg.9 J9

## MILTON TOWNSHIP

Colonial Dr. Pg.15 N8
Comner Ave. Pg.10 J13
Conifer Ct. Pg.16 M12
Cooley Ave. Pg.9 K7
Coronet Rd. Pg.16 N13
Cottonwood Pg.9 J8
Cotuit Ct. Pg.16 M13
Country Club Ln. Pg.15 M8
County Farm Rd. Pg.9 J,K7
Courtenay Dr. Pg.9 L8
Coventry Ct. Pg.9 J8
Coventry Dr. Pg.9 J8
Coventry St. Pg.9 J8
Cree Ct. Pg.15 N8
Cree Ln. Pg.15 N8
Creekside Dr. Pg.9 L8
Crescent Blvd. Pg.10 J13
Crest Ct. Pg.16 M13
Cumnor Ave. Pg.10 K13
Curtiss Pg.9 K7
Cypress Dr. Pg.16 N12
Daly Dr. Pg.9 J10
Danbury Dr. Pg.16 N12
Danby Dr. Pg.16 M13
Darling St. Pg.9 H,J9
Davis Ave. Pg.16 M11
Davis Ct. Pg.15 N8
Dawn Ave. Pg.10 H11
Deerpath Ln. Pg.15 M9
Deerpoint Dr. Pg.9 J8
Delano St. Pg.9 J7
Della Ave. Pg.9 H9
Delles Rd. Pg.15 P9
Derby Glen Dr. Pg.9 H10
Devon Ave. Pg.16 P10
Devonshire Ln. Pg.16 N11
Dorchester Ave. Pg.9 J8
Dorchester Ct. Pg.16 M13
Doris Ave. Pg.9 H9
Douglas Ct. Pg.9 H7
Drury Ln. Pg.16 N13
Durfee Rd. Pg.15 M7
East Ave. Pg.10 J13
Eastern Ave. Pg.10 H12
Eddie Rd. Pg.16 N12
Edgewood Ct. Pg.16 N11
Edgewood Rd. Pg.10 L13
Electric Ave. Pg.9 K8
Elk Ct. Pg.15 M9
Ellis St. Pg.9 H9
Ellynwood Dr. Pg.10 J13
Elmwood Dr. Pg.15,16 N8,11,12
Elmwood St. Pg.9 K8
Embden Ln. Pg.14,15 N7
Emerson Ave. Pg.10 J12
Ethel Ave. Pg.10 H12
Evans Ave. Pg.9 K8
Evans St. Pg.9 J8
Everest Rd. Pg.16 N13
Evergreen Ave. Pg.10 H,J11
Fairmeadow Ln. Pg.15 P9
Fairway St. Pg.10 K13
Falcon Tr. Pg.9 J8
Fanchon St. Pg.9 J,H9
Farwell St. Pg.9 H9
Flamingo Ct. Pg.16 N13
Flamingo Ln. Pg.16 N13
Flint Creek Dr. Pg.15 M8
Flint Creek Rd. Pg.15 M8
Foothill Dr. Pg.15 M8
Forest Ave. Pg.10 H12
Foxcroft Dr. Pg.16 N11
Franchon St. Pg.9 H9
Franklin St. Pg.9 J7
Front St. Pg.10 H12
Gables Blvd. Pg.9 J8
Gary Ave. Pg.9,16 H9,N13
Geneva Rd. Pg.9,10 J8,11
Glen Crest Dr. Pg.16 M13
Glen Park Ct. Pg.16 M14
Glen Park Pl. Pg.16 M14
Glen Park Rd. Pg.16 N12,13
Glen Valley Dr. Pg.16 M,N12,N13
Glenbard Rd. Pg.16 L13
Glenn Ave. Pg.16 N14
Glenrise Ave. Pg.10 H12
Glenrise Ct. Pg.10 H12
Gold Finch Ct. Pg.9 H8
Golf Ave. Pg.10 K13
Golf Ln. Pg.10 K13
Golfview Dr. Pg.16 N12,13
Goodrich Ave. Pg.10 J12
Grand Ave. Pg.9 J7
Grange Ct. Pg.15 N8
Grange St. Pg.15 N8
Gray Ave. Pg.16 N13
Great Western Ave. Pg.10 H11,12
Greenview Dr. Pg.16 M13
Grove Ln. Pg.10 H13
Hackberry Dr. Pg.16 N11
Hamilton Ct. Pg.15 M8
Hamilton Dr. Pg.15 M8
Harriet St. Pg.9 J7
Harrison St. Pg.9 K7
Harvest St. Pg.10 J13
Harvey St. Pg.10 J13
Hatte Gray Ct. Pg.9 H10
Hatte Gray Ln. Pg.9 H10
Hawthorne Ln. Pg.15 M9
Hazel Ln. Pg.9 J8
Hedge Ct. Pg.16 L12
Hemstead Rd. Pg.16 N13
Herrick Dr. Pg.9 J8
Hevern Dr. Pg.15 M8
High Gate Course Pg.9 H10
High Knob Dr. Pg.9 M8
Highland Ave. Pg.10 H12
Hill Ave. Pg.10 K13
Hiram Dr. Pg.9,16 J8,P10
Hope Pg.16 N13
Hoyle Rd. Pg.10 H13
Hunt Ct. Pg.16 M13
Hunt Pl. Pg.16 M13
Huntington Rd. Pg.16 M13
Ironwood Dr. Pg.16 M13
Ironwood Ln. Pg.10 M8
Ivy Ln. Pg.16 M,N13
Jeffery Ct. Pg.15 M9
Jerome Ave. Pg.9 J7,9
Joyce Ct. Pg.15 M9
Juniper Ln. Pg.16 P12
Keim Dr. Pg.15 N7
Kelly Ct. Pg.9 J8
Kenilworth Ave. Pg.10,16 H,M11
Kenmore St. Pg.10 H14
Kensington Rd. Pg.16 M,N13
Kent Pg.16 M13
Kilkenny Ct. Pg.9 L8
Kings Ct. Pg.16 P11
Kiowa Ct. Pg.15 N7
Kiowa Dr. Pg.15 N7
Kiowa Ln. Pg.15 N7
Knollwood Dr. Pg.9 J8
Kyle Ct. Pg.9 J8
Lakeside Dr. Pg.16 N12
Lakeview Dr. Pg.14,15 N7
Lakewood Ln. Pg.15 M8
Lambert Rd. Pg.16 M,N11
Langford Dr. Pg.15 N10
Lanier Ave. Pg.10 K13
Laurel Ct. Pg.9 J8
Lawler Ave. Pg.10,16 L13
Lawler Ct. Pg.16 M13
Lawler Ln. Pg.16 N13
Leask Ln. Pg.15 P10
Lenox Rd. Pg.10 J12
Leonard St. Pg.9 K7
Lloyd Ave. Pg.10,16 L14,M,N13
Lloyd Ct. Pg.15 M8
Loretto Ln.(Pvt.) Pg.15 M7,N8
Lorry Ct. Pg.16 M13
Lynn Rd. Pg.10 H13
Lyon Ave. Pg.9 K9
MacArthur Ave. Pg.9 H7
Madison Ave. Pg.10 K13
Main St. Pg.9,10 H10,12
Mallard Ct. Pg.14,15 N7
Manor Pg.10 H11
Maple Ln. Pg.16 M12
Maplewood Dr. Pg.15 N8
Marion Ave. Pg.9 J8
Marlborough Rd. Pg.16 M14
Marshall Pg.9 J8
Marston Ave. Pg.16 M12
Marston Ct. Pg.16 M13
Marywood Cir. Pg.9 M9
May Ct. Pg.16 M13
Mayfair Ln. Pg.16 M13
Mayfield Ln. Pg.16 M13
Mayflower Pg.9 J8
McCarron Rd. Pg.16 N12
McCormick Ave. Pg.16 M12
McCreey Ave. Pg.16 M11
Meadow Ln. Pg.10 H13
Mellor Rd. Pg.9 H,J9
Menomini Ct. Pg.15 N7
Menomini Dr. Pg.15 N7
Menomini Ln. Pg.15 N7
Merrill Dr. Pg.15 M9
Mildred Ave. Pg.10 H11
Milton Ave. Pg.16 N12
Mohican Dr. Pg.15 M,N8
Montclair Ave. Pg.16 L12
Monticello Rd. Pg.16 M13
Morse St. Pg.9 H9
Mulberry Ln. Pg.16 P11
Naperville Rd. Pg.15 M10
Naperville-Wheaton Rd. Pg.15 P9
Natalie Ct. Pg.9 H7
National St. Pg.9 H7
Nepil Ave. Pg.9 K8
Newton Ave. Pg.10 H11
North Ave. Pg.9,10 G7,J14
Oak Lawn Dr. Pg.16 N12
Oakwood Ct. Pg.15 N8
Orchard Rd. Pg.15 M,N8
Osage Dr. Pg.16 P12
Ott Ave. Pg.16 M11
Page St. Pg.9 K7
Papworth St. Pg.9 H,J9
Park Blvd. (Pvt.) Pg.10 H12
Parkway Dr. Pg.9 J7
Partridge Dr. Pg.9 J8
Paxton Pl. Pg.9 G7
Pershing Ave. Pg.10 L13
Peter Rd. Pg.9 J7
Pheasant Ct. Pg.9 J8
Picadilly Pg.15 M8
Pierce Pg.9 K8
Pine Dr. Pg.10 H11
Pinegrove Ct. Pg.16 N12
Plainview Dr. Pg.16 N12
Plamondon Rd. Pg.15 M8
Pleasant Ave. Pg.10 H11
Pleasant Hill Rd. Pg.9 J8
Pleasant Ln. Pg.10 H13
Polo Dr. Pg.9 L8
Poplar Rd. Pg.16 N11
Poss St. Pg.10 H11,12
Prairie Ave. Pg.9,10 H11,12,J8
President St. Pg.9 H10
Purnell St. Pg.9 H9
Railroad St. Pg.10 H12
Red Maple Ln. Pg.15 N8
Red Oak Dr. Pg.16 P11
Red Wing Ct. Pg.9 H8
Red Wing Dr. Pg.9 H8
Redwood Ct. Pg.15 N8
Richard Ave. Pg.9 H-J7
Richmond Dr. Pg.16 P11
Ridge Rd. Pg.16 M13
Riford Rd. Pg.10 L13
River Dr. Pg.10 H13
Riverside Ave. Pg.10 L13
Roger Rd. Pg.10 J13
Roosevelt Rd. Pg.9,10 L9,12
Saddle Rd. Pg.9 L8
Sandpiper Ct. Pg.9 H8
Schaeffer Rd. Pg.14 M7
Schmale Rd. Pg.9 H10
Scott Ave. Pg.10 J13
Scottsdale Ct. Pg.16 P11
Seneca Dr. Pg.15 M,N7
Sequoia Dr. Pg.16 N12
Shagbark Ln. Pg.16 P11
Sheehan Ave. Pg.16 M12
Sheffield Ct. Pg.16 M12
Sheffield Pl. Pg.16 M12
Sheffield Rd. Pg.16 M12
Shelburne Dr. Pg.9 G7
Sherbrooke Ln. Pg.16 N11
Siefer Ct. Pg.9 J7
Silverleaf Blvd. Pg.9 J8
Sioux Ct. Pg.15 N8
Spring Ave. Pg.10 K13
St. Charles Rd. Pg.9,10 H8,10
St. James Ct. Pg.16 N11
St. Thomas Dr. Pg.16 N12
Stableford Dr. Pg.9 H10
Stacy Ave. Pg.10 H12
Stacy Ct. Pg.10 J12
Stanley St. Pg.9 K7
Stanton Rd. Pg.16 N12
State Hwy 53 Pg.12 M9
Stevenson Pl. Pg.15 M9
Stoddard Pg.9 J10
Stonegate Ct. Pg.16 L12
Stratford Ct. Pg.16 M12
Stratford Pl. Pg.16 M12
Stratford Rd. Pg.16 M12
Stuarton Dr. Pg.15 M8
Summerfield Ct. Pg.15 N8
Summerhill Pl. Pg.16 N11
Sunnybrook Rd. Pg.16 M13
Sunnyridge Ct. Pg.15 N8
Sunset Ave. Pg.10 H13
Sunset St. Pg.10 H13
Swift Rd. Pg.10 H13
Sycamore Dr. Pg.16 P11
Sycamore Ln. Pg.16 P12
Tamarack Dr. Pg.16 N11,P12
Taylor Rd. Pg.16 M12
Teakwood Dr. Pg.16 N12
Terrace Dr. Pg.16 N12
Thaddeus Cir. Pg.16 N12
Thomas Rd. Pg.9 J8
Timothy Ln. Pg.9 J8
Tomahawk Dr. Pg.15 M7
Towpath Ct. Pg.15 M8
Trails End Pg.10 J10
Tree Top Ln. Pg.15 M8
Valley Ave. Pg.10 K13
Valley Rd. Pg.10,16 L,N13
Valley View Dr. Pg.10 H12
Walnut Rd. Pg.10 J13
Walz Way Pg.14 M7
Warrenville Ave. Pg.15 M8
Washington Ln. Pg.10 H14
Waterbury Ct. Pg.9 J8
Waterbury Dr. Pg.9 J8
Wenona Ln. Pg.15 M8
West St. Pg.9 H9
Westchester Ct. Pg.16 N11
Western Ave. Pg.10 H11
Westmore Ln. Pg.15 N8
White Birch Ct. Pg.15 N8
White Birch Ln. Pg.15 N8
Whitmore Ln. Pg.10 L13
Wiesbrook Rd. Pg.15 M7
Willow Rd. Pg.9 J8
Wilson Ave. Pg.10 L13
Wilson Rd. Pg.10 L13
Windham Dr. Pg.9 J8
Windsor Dr. Pg.16 N11
Winslow Cir. Pg.10 H11
Wood Lark Dr. Pg.9 H8
Woodcroft Dr. Pg.16 N11
Woodlawn Dr. Pg.9 J8
Woods Ave. Pg.9 J7
Woodvale Ct. Pg.9 K7
1st St. Pg.10 H12
2nd Pl. Pg.10 H12
2nd St. Pg.10 H11,12
3rd St. Pg.10 H11,12
22nd St. Pg.16 M11,12
39th St. Pg.15 P9

### CEMETERIES
Assumption Cem. Pg.14 M6

### FOREST PRESERVES
Belleau Woods Pg.14 M7
Churchill Woods Pg.10 J13
Herrick Lake Forest Preserve Pg.15 P7
Hidden Lake Forest Preserve Pg.16 P13

### GOLF COURSES
Arrowhead G.C. Pg.15 N8
Western Acres Golf Club Pg.16 N13

### PARKS
American Legion Park Pg.9 H8
Gerald Weeks Pk. Pg.9 H9
Morton Arboretum Pg.16 P12
Pleasant Hill/Heritage Park Pg.9 H8
Spaulding Park Pg.10 H12

### SCHOOLS
Arbor View Sch. Pg.16 N11
Butterfield Sch. Pg.16 N13
Churchill Sch. Pg.9 J9
Glenbard South H.S. Pg.16 N11
Pleasant Hill Sch. Pg.9 J8
Sandburg Sch. Pg.9 J8
Stepping Stone Child Dev. Ctr. Pg.10 H12
Westfield Sch. Pg.16 M13
Wiesbrook Sch. Pg.15 M7

### SHOPPING CENTERS
Shopping Center Pg.16 N12

### MISCELLANEOUS
Center Ice of DuPage Pg.10 H12
Glen Ellyn Heights Sewer Treatment Plant Pg.10 J13

## NAPERVILLE

Pages 13-15,19-21,25-27

### STREETS
Abbotsford Dr. Pg.14 R4
Abby Dr. Pg.14 R4
Aberdour Dr. Pg.21 T9
Abrahamson Ct. Pg.21 U8
Abriter Ct. Pg.15 Q8
Acacia Ct. Pg.14 R6
Ada Ct. Pg.20 U5
Ada Ln. Pg.20 U5
Alameda Ct. Pg.25 X3
Alamosa Dr. Pg.26 X6
Alan Ct. Pg.26 X5
Alan Rd. Pg.26 X5
Alandale Cir. Pg.26 X5
Albermarle Ct. Pg.14 R4
Albert Hall Ct. Pg.26 Z5
Alder Ln. Pg.20 U6
Alexandria Dr. Pg.21 X8,9
Alexis R. Shuman Blvd. Pg.14 Q7
Alfalfa Ln. Pg.26 Z4
Allegany Dr. Pg.21 W8
Almond Ct. Pg.20 T5
Alton Ct. Pg.21 U9
Alyssa Ct. Pg.26 X7
Alyssa Dr. Pg.26 X7
Ambassador Dr. Pg.20 T4
Amberwood Cir. Pg.15 R8
Ambleside Cir. Pg.20 U5
Ames Ct. Pg.20 U5
Amherst Ct. Pg.27 X9
Amy Ct. Pg.20 W7
Andover Ct. Pg.21 S8
Andrews Ct. Pg.21 U8
Andria Ct. Pg.20 U4
Anne Rd. Pg.21 T8
Anthony Ct. Pg.20 S4
Antietam Ct. Pg.20 U6
Apache Dr. Pg.14 R7
Appaloosa Dr. Pg.21 V10
Apple River Dr. Pg.21 X8
Appleby Ct. Pg.21 T8
Applegate Ct. Pg.20 V7
Applegate Dr. Pg.20 V6
Appomattox Cir. Pg.20 U6
Arabian Ave. Pg.21 V10
Arapaho Ct. Pg.20 U5
Arcadia Cir. Pg.20 U4
Ardley Ct. Pg.26 X7
Ardmore Dr. Pg.20 U5
Ariel Ct. Pg.26 Z4
Arlington Ave. Pg.21 W8
Arrowhead Dr. Pg.19 W3
Artesian Rd. Pg.25 W3
Arthur Rd. Pg.21 T8
Ashbury Dr. Pg.26 Y5
Ashfield Rd. Pg.21 T9
Ashton Ln. Pg.20 U5
Ashtonlee Ct. Pg.26 X7
Aspen Ct. Pg.20 U6
Aster Ct. Pg.21 W9
Atlanta Ct. Pg.20 U6
Atlas Ln. Pg.20,21 U7
Atwood Cir. Pg.21 V10
Auburn Ave. Pg.21 V10
Audrey Rd. Pg.20 U4
Augusta Dr. Pg.13 R2
Augustana Ct. Pg.21 W9
Augustana Dr. Pg.27 X9
Aurora Ave. Pg.20 T4,6
Austin Ave. Pg.26 Y5
Austin Ct. Pg.26 Y5
Avena Cir. Pg.26 X7
Avena Ct. Pg.26 X7
Aviara Ct. Pg.25 X2
Avon Ct. Pg.26 Y5
Ayrshire Ct. Pg.26 Z4
Ayssa Ct. Pg.27 X7
Azalea Ct. Pg.20 U4
Aztec Cir. Pg.14 R7
Bailey Rd. Pg.20,21,27 V6-9
Bainbridge Dr. Pg.14 R4
Bakewell Ln. Pg.21,27 X8
Baldwin Ct. Pg.20 V6
Baldwin Dr. Pg.20 V6
Balmoral Cir. Pg.21 T8
Balton Ct. Pg.20 S4
Banbury Cir. Pg.21 T8
Bangert Ct. Pg.26 Z4
Bangert Ln. Pg.26 Z4
Bankfield Ct. Pg.21 U9
Bannister Dr. Pg.20 V6
Banyon Ct. Pg.20 U5
Bar Harbour Ct. Pg.26 X4
Barbara Ct. Pg.20 V6
Barcroft Ct. Pg.21 U9
Bards Ave. Pg.26 Y5
Barkdoll Ct. Pg.21 W9
Barkdoll Rd. Pg.27 X8
Barkei Rd. Pg.15 Q8
Barley Ave. Pg.14 R7
Barnes Ln. Pg.26 Y4
Barr Creek Ln. Pg.26 Z4
Barth Dr. Pg.27 W8
Bartlett Ct. Pg.25 X3
Basswood Dr. Pg.20 U7
Bauer Rd. Pg.14 R6
Bauer Rd. N. Pg.15 R7
Bay Colony Dr. Pg.20 V7
Bay Ct. Pg.21,27 V8
Bayberry Ln. Pg.15 R7
Baybrook Ct. Pg.26 Z4
Baybrook Ln. Pg.26 Z5
Bayhill Ave. Pg.21 V8
Baylor Ct. Pg.21 W9
Bayview Ave. Pg.20 W6
Beaconsfield Dr. Pg.20 W6
Beaumont Ln. Pg.20 U4
Beauport Dr. Pg.26 X4
Beaver Ct. Pg.20 S5
Beaver Dr. Pg.20 S5
Becket Rd. Pg.26 Y5
Bedford Ct. Pg.21 U6
Beech Ct. Pg.20 T5
Belaire Ct. Pg.14 S6
Bellingrath Ct. Pg.21 S8
Beloit Ct. Pg.21 W10
Beloit Dr. Pg.21 V10
Benedetti Dr. Pg.20 S6
Bennett Dr. Pg.26 Y5
Bennington Ct. Pg.20 X6
Bent Creek Ct. Pg.21,27 V10
Benton Ave Pg.20,21 S6,8
Berkley Ct. Pg.21 W7
Bernette Ct. Pg.21 S8
Bornio Ct. Pg.21,27 V0
Beth Ln. Pg.26 X4
Big Foot Ln. Pg.14 R6
Big Horn Rd. Pg.15 Q7
Bighorn Rd. Pg.14 Q7
Bill Ct. Pg.21 X9
Biltmore Ct. Pg.21 S8
Birchwood Dr. Pg.20 S,T5
Birkdale Ct. Pg.14 R6
Black Stallion Ct. Pg.21 U9
Black Stallion Dr. Pg.21 U9
Black Walnut Ct. Pg.21,27 X9
Blackberry Cir. Pg.21,27 X9
Blackburn Ct. Pg.21 T8
Blackhawk Ct. Pg.15 R6
Blackhawk Ln. Pg.15 R7
Blakely Ln. Pg.20 U4
Blazing Star Ct. Pg.25 Y2
Blodgett Ct. Pg.26 X6
Blossom Ct. Pg.20 U4
Blue Jay Ln. Pg.25 Y2
Blue Larkspur Ln. Pg.21 U8
Bluebell Ct. Pg.21,27 X10
Bluebird Ln. Pg.21,27 V7
Bluegrass Ct. Pg.15 R7
Bluemont Ct. Pg.27 X8
Bluewater Cir. Pg.26 X4
Bob-O-Link Ct. Pg.14 R6
Boddington Ln. Pg.20 W4
Bonaventure Dr. Pg.14 R5
Bond St. Pg.14 R4
Boneset Ct. Pg.20 U4
Bonnema Ave. Pg.21 X9
Bonnema Ct. Pg.21 X9
Bonnema Rd. Pg.21 W9
Book Ct. Pg.20 U5
Bordeaux Cir. Pg.20 U4
Boswell Ln. Pg.26 Y5
Boulder Ct. Pg.21 X6
Bourbon Ln. Pg.21,27 W8
Bovidale Cir. Pg.20 V6
Bowling Green Ct. Pg.14 R6
Brad Ct. Pg.21,27 V8
Braddock Dr. Pg.27 X8
Bradley Ct. Pg.21 V9
Braemar Ave. Pg.15 Q7
Brainard St. Pg.15,20,21 S,T7
Branchwood Cir. Pg.15 S5
Brandeis Ct. Pg.21,27 V10
Brandy Cir. Pg.21 U9
Branford Ln. Pg.26 Y5
Breckenridge Ln. Pg.26 X6
Breitwieser Ln. Pg.25 Y3
Brentford Dr. Pg.15 R7
Brestal Ct. Pg.21 V8
Briar Rose Ct. Pg.20 X6
Briarheath Ln. Pg.21,25 W7
Briarhill Ct. Pg.20 W6
Briarhill Dr. Pg.20 W6
Briarwood Dr. Pg.20 T5
Bridgewater Ct. Pg.21 W8
Bridlespur Dr. Pg.21 S9
Briergate Dr. Pg.14 R5
Brighton Rd. Pg.15 R8
Brinmore Ct. Pg.20 U4
Bristlecone Ct. Pg.21 W8
Bristol Ct. Pg.20 W7
Brittany Ave. Pg.21 Q9
Brocks End Ct. Pg.20 U5
Brockton Cir. Pg.26 X6
Brodie Ct. Pg.21 T9
Brom Dr. Pg.20 T6
Bronte Ct. Pg.26 Z5
Brook Crossing Ct. Pg.26 X5
Brook Ln. Pg.20 T5
Brookdale Rd. Pg.14 S4
Brooklea Ct. Pg.21,27 W8
Brookline Ct. Pg.15 S8
Brooksedge Ave. Pg.25 Y3
Brookshire Ct. Pg.20 S4
Brossman St. Pg.26 Y5
Brown Ct. Pg.21 W9
Bruno Ct. Pg.20 S4
Brunswick Ct. Pg.21 T8
Brush Hill Cir. Pg.20 S5
Buckeye Dr. Pg.20 U6
Buckingham Dr. Pg.15 R8
Buckley Ct. Pg.20 W7
Bucknell Ct. Pg.21 W9
Buell Dr. Pg.20 T5
Bull Run Ct. Pg.20 U6
Bunker Cir. Pg.13 R3
Bunker Hill Ct. Pg.20 U6
Bunting Ln. Pg.21,27 V7
Burgess Hill Rd. Pg.20 V6
Burke Ct. Pg.13,19 R3
Burning Tree Ln. Pg.14 R6
Burr Oak Ct. Pg.20 T5
Butler Ct. Pg.21,27 V10
Butte Ct. Pg.21 S8
Buttermilk Ct. Pg.26 Z4
Butternut Dr. Pg.21 U7
Buttonwood Cir. Pg.20 U5
Byron Ct. Pg.21 U8
Cabriolet Ct. Pg.20 W7
Cactus Dr. Pg.15 R7
Cahdwicke Cir. Pg.20 U4
Caine Ct. Pg.26 Z5
Caine Dr. Pg.26 Z5
Calcutta Ln. Pg.14 R6
Caledonia Ct. Pg.26 W4
Calico Ave. Pg.26 X5
Calvert Ct. Pg.21 W8
Calvin Ct. Pg.21 U8
Camarie Ct. Pg.21 S8
Cambridge Ln. Pg.21,27 V9
Camden Ct. Pg.21 T9
Camelot Cir. Pg.26 Z5
Campbell Dr. Pg.13 R3
Candeur Dr. Pg.26 Y6
Candlenut Dr. Pg.20 S5
Canfield Ct. Pg.26 Z4
Canonero Dr. Pg.21 U8
Canopy Dr. Pg.21 T8
Cantigny Ct. Pg.21,27 V9
Cantore Rd. Pg.25 X3
Canyon Run Rd. Pg.21,27 W9
Capri Ct. Pg.26 Z5
Caraway Ct. Pg.20 U4
Cardiff Rd. Pg.20 V6
Cardigan Ct. Pg.20 V6
Cardinal Ln. Pg.21,27 U7
Carleton Ave. Pg.21 W9
Carleton Cir. Pg.21 W9
Carlsbad Cir. Pg.14 Q7
Carlson Ct. Pg.14,20 S6
Carlyle Rd. Pg.26 Y5
Carmel Ct. Pg.20 S6
Carnegie Ct. Pg.21 W9
Carol Ln. Pg.20 V7
Carrboro Ct. Pg.27 X8
Carriage Ct. Pg.20 T6
Carriage Hill Rd. Pg.21,27 W8
Carrolwood Rd. Pg.20 U4
Carthage Ct. Pg.21 W10
Cascade Ct. Pg.20 V7
Cassin Rd. Pg.21,27 W8
Castilleja Ct. Pg.20 U5
Catalpa Ln. Pg.20 U7
Catherine Ave. Pg.21 T8
Catherine Ct. Pg.21 T8
Cavalcade Cir. Pg.21 U8
Ceals Ct. Pg.20 W7
Cedar Glade Rd. Pg.25 X3
Cedarbrook Rd. Pg.20 W7
Celeste Ln. Pg.26 Y,Z5
Celtic Ash Ct. Pg.21 U8
Centenary Ct. Pg.27 X8
Center St. Pg.20 S7
Central Park Ct. Pg.20 S7
Central Park Rd. Pg.20 S7
Centre Pt. Cir. Pg.15 Q8
Century Farms Ln. Pg.14 R6
Cermak Ct. Pg.14 Q4
Chalet Rd. Pg.20 S5
Challdon Ct. Pg.21 U8
Chalmette Ct. Pg.21,27 W8
Chamberlain Ln. Pg.20 U5
Champagne Ct. Pg.15 R8
Chancellor Ct. Pg.20 U6
Chang Ct. Pg.20 U4
Charles Ave. Pg.21 T8
Charles St. Pg.21 T8
Charlestowne Ln. Pg.26 X4
Chase Pointe Ct. Pg.21,27 V10
Chat Ct. Pg.21,27 V7
Chateaugay Ave. Pg.21 U8
Chatham Ct. Pg.21,27 W8
Chattanooga Ct. Pg.20 U6
Chaucer Ct. Pg.27 X10
Chelsea Ln. Pg.21 V9
Chepstow Ct. Pg.20 U5
Cherry Blossom Lane Pg.20 U6
Cherry Hills Ln. Pg.14 R5
Cherrywood Cir. Pg.21 W7
Cheshire Ave. Pg.21 T8
Chesterfield Ave. Pg.21 T9
Chestnut Ridge Dr. Pg.20 S5
Cheyenne Dr. Pg.26 X6
Chicago Ave. Pg.20 T7
Chickasaw Dr. Pg.15 R7
Chicory Ct. Pg.20 U5
Chilvers Ct. Pg.27 X8
Chippewa Dr. Pg.15 R8
Chittenden Ct. Pg.26 W4
Chokeberry Dr. Pg.26 Z4
Christie Ct. Pg.26 Y5
Churchill Dr. Pg.14 R4
Cimarron Ct. Pg.27 X8
Citadel Dr. Pg.21,27 V9,10
Citation Dr. Pg.21 U8
Claremont Dr. Pg.20 T5
Clarissa Ct. Pg.21 U8
Clarkson Ct. Pg.21,27 V9
Clearbrook Ct. Pg.26 W4
Clearwater Dr. Pg.26 Z5
Clearwater Ln. Pg.26 Z4
Clemson Dr. Pg.21,27 V9
Cliffside Ct. Pg.21,27 W9
Clifton Ct. Pg.21 X8
Cloverdale Rd. Pg.26 Z4
Cloverleaf Ct. Pg.20 W7
Clovetree Ct. Pg.20 U5
Club Dr. Pg.25 X3
Club House Ave. Pg.13 R3
Clyde Dr. Pg.21,27 U,V,W7
Coach Dr. Pg.21,27 W8
Cobblebrook Ln. Pg.21,27 V10
Cobblestone Ct. Pg.26 X5
Cocalico Ct. Pg.20 R6
Cocalico Dr. Pg.14 R6
Cody Ct. Pg.20 T6
Colfax Ct. Pg.14 R4
Colgate Ct. Pg.27 X9
College Rd. Pg.21 U9
Collingwood Dr. Pg.21 U9
Collins Ct. Pg.20 S3
Colonial Ct. Pg.21 S8
Colorado Ct. Pg.26 X6
Colton Cres. Pg.26 Z5
Columbia St. Pg.21 R-T7
Commons Rd. Pg.14 R6
Comstock Ct. Pg.26 X4
Comstock Ln. Pg.26 X4
Conan Doyle Rd. Pg.26 Y5
Concert Ln. Pg.20 S7
Conestoga Rd. Pg.20 R6
Connecticut Ave. Pg.26 X6
Connecticut Dr. Pg.26 X6
Continental Ave. Pg.25 S3
Cool Spring Ct. Pg.25 Y3
Cool Springs Ct. Pg.25 Y3
Copperfield Ct. Pg.26 X6,7
Copperfield Dr. Pg.26 X7
Coral Dr. Pg.14 R4
Corday Dr. Pg.20 U4
Corday Ln. Pg.20 U4
Cordula Cir. Pg.26 Y5
Cornell Ct. Pg.21,27 V10
Corporate Ln. Pg.14 Q4
Cortez Ct. Pg.15 Q7
Cortland Dr. Pg.20 V7
Cottage Ave. Pg.20 S6
Cotton Creek Ct. Pg.25 X3
Cottonwood Ln. Pg.20 T5
Count Fleet Ct. Pg.21 T8
Country Club Blvd. Pg.13 R3
Country Farm Dr. Pg.13 Q3
Country Glen St. Pg.13 S2
Country Lakes Dr. Pg.13,19 R3
Countryside Cir. Pg.21,27 W7
Court Pl. Pg.20 S7
Courtland Dr. Pg.20 V7
Courtney Dr. Pg.20 V5
Cove Ct. Pg.21,27 V8
Coventry Ct. Pg.21,27 W7
Covington Ct. Pg.27 X8
Crab Apple Ct. Pg.20 S5
Cranberry Ct. Pg.27 W9
Crane Ct. Pg.26 Z4
Cranshire Ln. Pg.21 V10
Creekside Cir. Pg.14 S6
Creighton Ave. Pg.21,27 V9
Cress Creek Ct. Pg.14 R6
Crestfield Ct. Pg.26 X7
Crestwood Ct. Pg.21 T8
Crimson Ct. Pg.20 X5
Cripple Creek Ct. Pg.25 X3
Cromwell Ln. Pg.26 Y5
Crooked Tree Ct. Pg.26 X7
Crossing Ct. Pg.20 U4
Crossing Ln. Pg.20 U4
Crystal Ave. Pg.14 R4
Crystal Ct. Pg.14 R4
Crystal Rock Rd. Pg.25 Y3
Culpepper Dr. Pg.21 U9
Cumberland Ct. Pg.21,27 X,W8
Cypress Dr. Pg.20 U6
Daggets Ct. Pg.26 Z4
Dairymans Cir. Pg.26 Z4
Daisy Ln. Pg.26 X5
Dakota Cir. Pg.15 Q8
Dana Ct. Pg.14 S6
Danada Ct. Pg.15 Q9
Danbury Dr. Pg.20 V7
Darius Ln. Pg.21,27 V9
Dark Star Rd. Pg.21 U8
Dartford Ct. Pg.21 U9
Dartmoor Ct. Pg.21 U8
Dartmouth Ct. Pg.21,27 V9
Darwin St. Pg.26 Y5
De LaSalle Ave. Pg.26 X6
De LaSalle Ct. Pg.26 X6
DeFoe Ct. Pg.26 Z5
DePaul Ct. Pg.21,27 V9
Dearborn Cir. Pg.20 S4
Dearborn Ct. Pg.20 S4
Debbie Ct. Pg.27 W8
Deep Run Rd. Pg.21 T8
Deep Water Ln. Pg.25 W3
Deepwood Ct. Pg.21 U8
Deering Bay Dr. Pg.25 X2
Deerpath Ct. Pg.21,27 W9
Delaware Ct. Pg.26 Z5
Delkir Ct. Pg.20 W7
Denali Cir. Pg.14 Q7
Denison Rd. Pg.21 W10
Denver Ct. Pg.20 U5
Derby Ct. Pg.14 R4
Devlin Ct. Pg.20 W7
Devon Ln. Pg.21 T8
Devonshire Ct. Pg.20 T6
Dewes Ln. Pg.26 X4
Dewhurst St. Pg.26 X5
DiLorezno Dr. Pg.21 W8
Diamond Ct. Pg.26 Z5
Diane Ln. Pg.20 U7
Dichtl Ct. Pg.21,27 W9
Dickens Ave. Pg.15 R8
Diehl Rd. Pg.15 Q8
Dillman Ct. Pg.21 S8
Dipper Ct. Pg.21,27 W7
Dockside Ct. Pg.22 T6
Donelson Ct. Pg.20 S4
Doral Dr. Pg.19 R3
Dorchester Ct. Pg.20 W6
Dorset Ct. Pg.21 T8
Dorval Dr. Pg.20 W6
Douglas Ave. Pg.20 S6
Dove Ct. Pg.21 U7
Dover Ln. Pg.27 V9
Downing Ct. Pg.14 R4

Drake Ct. . . . . Pg.21,27 . . V9
Drendel Ln. . . . Pg.21,27 . . W7
Druid Hills Ct. . . Pg.14 . . . . R6
Dryden Ct. . . . . Pg.26 . . . . Y5
Du Pahze St. . . . Pg.26 . . . X6,7
Dublin Dr. . . . . Pg.26 . . . . Z4
Duke Ct. . . . . . Pg.21,27 . . W9
Duncan Ct. . . . . Pg.26 . . . . Z4
Dunrobin Rd. . . . Pg.21 . . . . T9
Duquesne Ave. . . Pg.21 . . . . V9
Durango Ln. . . . Pg.26 . . . . Z4
Durham Ct. . . . . Pg.21 . . . . T8
Durness Ct. . . . Pg.20 . . . . V6
Eagle St. . . . . . Pg.14,20 R7,S6
East Ave. . . . . . Pg.15 . . . . R8
East-West Tollway
. . . . . . . . . Pg.14,15,04,7,8
Eastland Ct. . . . Pg.20 . . . . W7
Easy Cir. . . . . . Pg.26 . . . . Z4
Eddystone Ct. . . Pg.20 . . . . V6
Edgewater Ct. . . Pg.21 . . . . T9
Edinburgh Ct. . . Pg.21 . . . . T9
Edward Rd. . . . Pg.21 . . . . T8
El Dorado Ct. . . Pg.26 . . . . X4
El Dorado Ln. . . Pg.26 . . . . X4
Elderberry Ct. . . Pg.20 . . . . S6
Eliot Ln. . . . . . Pg.26 . . . . Y5
Elizabeth Ave. . . Pg.21 . . . . T8
Ellsworth St. . . . Pg.20 . . . . W7
Elm Ct. . . . . . . Pg.20 . . . . U5
Elm St. . . . . . . Pg.20 . . . . U5
Elmwood Dr. . . . Pg.26 . . . . U6
Emerald Dr. . . . Pg.20 . . . . U6
Emerson Ln. . . . Pg.21 . . . . S8
Emory Ave. . . . Pg.27 . . . . X9
Emporia Ct. . . . Pg.26 . . . . Z5
Encina Cir. . . . . Pg.20 . . . . T5
Engle Rd. . . . . Pg.26 . . . . Z4
English Ct. . . . . Pg.26 . . . . Y5
Enterprise Ct. . . Pg.19 . . . . S2
Erb Farm Ct. . . . Pg.21 . . . . R6
Erb Farm Ln. . . . Pg.21 . . . . R6
Esquire Cir. . . . Pg.21 . . . . Z5
Estate Cir. . . . . Pg.21 . . . V10
Estes Ct. . . . . . Pg.20 . . . . U5
Estuary Ct. . . . Pg.20 . . . . U5
Eton Ln. . . . . . Pg.21,27 . . V9
Evercrest Ct. . . . Pg.25 . . . . X3
Evergreen Ave. . Pg.20 . . . . T5
Ewing St. . . . . Pg.20 . . . . T6
Exmoor Ct. . . . Pg.21,27 . . W8
Exeter Ct. . . . . Pg.20 . . . . W8
Fair Oak Ct. . . . Pg.19 . . . . W9
Fair Oak Rd. . . . Pg.21,27 . . W8
Fairbanks Ct. . . . Pg.20 . . . . U4
Faireno Ct. . . . . Pg.21 . . . . T8
Fairfax Dr. . . . . Pg.21 . . . . T9
Fairfield Ct. . . . Pg.21,27 . . W8
Fairhauser Ct. . . Pg.25 . . . . Z3
Fairmont Ave. . . Pg.25 . . . . Z3
Fairway Dr. . . . Pg.13,19 . . R3
Fairway Ln. . . . . Pg.21,27 . . V9
Fairwinds Ct. . . Pg.21 . . . . S8
Falcon Ct. . . . . Pg.26 . . . . Z4
Falkner Dr. . . . . Pg.26 . . . Y,Z5
Fall Brook Dr. . . Pg.21 . . . . V10
Fallcreek Ct. . . . Pg.21 . . . . V9
Farington Ct. . . . Pg.14 . . . . R5
Farm Gate Dr. . . Pg.25 . . . . Z3
Farmington Ct. . Pg.21,27 . . W7
Fawn Lake Ct. . . Pg.26 . . . . X2
Feldott Ln. . . . . Pg.19 . . . . T4
Fender Rd. . . . . Pg.21 . . . . V9
Ferncroft Ct. . . . Pg.14 . . . . R6
Fernwood Dr. . . Pg.20 . . . . U6
Ferry Rd. . . . . . Pg.14 . . . . Q4
Fesseneva Ct. . . Pg.26 . . . . Z4
Fesseneva Ln. . . Pg.26 . . . . Z4
Fessler Ave. . . . Pg.20 . . . . V6
Fiala Woods Ct. . Pg.27 . . . . X8
Field Ct. . . . . . Pg.21 . . . . U8
Fieldcrest Dr. . . Pg.20 . . . . U4
Fieldstone Ct. . . Pg.26 . . . . X5
Finch Ct. . . . . . Pg.21,27 . . W7
Fir Ct. . . . . . . . Pg.20 . . . . U5
Fireside Ct. . . . Pg.20 . . . . X5
Firestone Ct. . . . Pg.13 . . . . R3
Fisher Dr. . . . . Pg.13 . . . . Q3
Flagstone Cir. . . Pg.20 . . . . W4
Flambeau Dr. . . Pg.26 . . . W,X5
Flat Iron Dr. . . . Pg.20 . . . . U5
Flat Rock Ct. . . . Pg.26 . . . . X4
Fleetwood Ct. . . Pg.27 . . . . X9
Flicker Ct. . . . . Pg.21,27 . . W7
Flock Ave. . . . . Pg.20 . . . . V7
Flossmoor Ct. . . Pg.14 . . . . R6
Flowerfield Ct. . . Pg.21,27 . V10
Fordham Ct. . . . Pg.21,27 V9,10
Forest Ave. . . . Pg.20 . . . . S6
Forest View Ct. . Pg.14 . . . . R5
Fort Hill Dr. . . . Pg.20 . . . T,U4
Foster Ct. . . . . Pg.26 . . . . Z4
Fox Bend Ct. . . . Pg.14 . . . . R6
Fox Trail Ct. . . . Pg.21 . . . . V9
Foxboro Ct. . . . Pg.26 . . . . W4
Foxboro Ln. . . . Pg.26 . . . . W4
Foxcroft Dr. . . . Pg.21,27 . . W7
Foxhill Rd. . . . . Pg.14 . . . . R5
Foxhorn Ct. . . . Pg.15 . . . . Q8
Frances Ct. . . . Pg.21 . . . . R8
Franklin Ave. . . Pg.20,21 . S6,7
Frederick Ln. . . . Pg.21,27 . . V9
Fredericksburg Ct
. . . . . . . . Pg.20,21 . . . U6
Freeland Cir. . . . Pg.20 . . . . Z3
Freeland Ct. . . . Pg.26 . . . . Z3
Fremont St. . . . Pg.20 . . . . V6
Fresno Ct. . . . . Pg.20 . . . . T5
Friar Ln. . . . . . Pg.26 . . . . X4
Frontenac Ct. . . Pg.13 . . . . R2
Frost Ln. . . . . . Pg.20 . . . . Y4
Fulham Dr. . . . . Pg.26 . . . . W3
Furman Dr. . . . Pg.21,27 V9,10
Galena Ct. . . . . Pg.26 . . . . X5
Garden Ct. . . . . Pg.21 . . . . U5
Gardenside Dr. . Pg.21 . . . . U5

Garnette Ct. . . . Pg.26 . . . . Z5
Garth Ct. . . . . . Pg.20 . . . . W7
Gartner Rd. . . . Pg.20,21 U6,7
Gateshead Dr. . . Pg.26 . . . . X6
George Ln. . . . . Pg.21 . . . . T8
Georgetown Ct. . Pg.21,27 . V10
Georgia Ct. . . . Pg.20 . . . . T5
Gettysburg Ct. . Pg.20 . . . . U6
Ginger Ln. . . . . Pg.21 . . . . W9
Glacier Park Ave.Pg.20 . . . . T3
Glencoe Ct. . . . Pg.21 . . . . W8
Gleneagles Ct. . Pg.26 . . . . X6
Gleneagles Dr. . Pg.26 . . . . X6
Glenecho Rd. . . Pg.21 . . . . W8
Glenmore Ct. . . Pg.21 . . . . T9
Gloucester Ln. . Pg.26 . . . . X4
Golden Glow Ct. Pg.25 . . . . Y2
Golden Larch Ct. Pg.20 . . . . T7
Golden Oaks Ct. Pg.25 . . . . Y2
Goldenrod Dr. . . Pg.20 . . . . T5
Golf Dr. . . . . . . Pg.21,27 . . W8
Golf Ridge Cir. . Pg.25 . . . . R2
Golfview Rd. . . . Pg.13 . . . . R2
Gowdey Rd. . . . Pg.19 . . . . S3
Grand Lake Ct. . Pg.20 . . . . U5
Grassmere Rd. . Pg.25 . . . . Y2
Great Oak Ct. . . Pg.21 . . . . W8
Green Trails Dr. . Pg.21 . . . . U7
Green Valley Dr. Pg.20 . . . . S5
Greenbriar Ct. . Pg.14 . . . . R7
Greene Ridge Dr.Pg.21 . . . . V10
Greenfield Ct. . . Pg.26 . . . . X5
Greensboro Ct. . Pg.21 . . . . S8
Greensfield Dr. . Pg.15,21 . . S8
Gregory Ct. . . . Pg.20 . . . . V6
Grey Fox Tr. . . . Pg.25 . . . . Z3
Grimes Ave. . . . Pg.20 . . . . W8
Grommon Rd. . . Pg.26 . . . . Y5
Gypsum Cir. . . . Pg.26 . . . . W4
Haddassah Ct. . Pg.20 . . . . T5
Haddassah Dr. . Pg.20 . . . . S8
Hagemann Pl. . . Pg.15 . . . . S7
Haider Ave. . . . Pg.26 . . . . Z4
Halifax Ct. . . . . Pg.21 . . . . W8
Hamilton Ln. . . . Pg.21 . . . . U9
Hamlet Rd. . . . . Pg.20 . . . . U9
Hammer Creek Ct.
. . . . . . . . . . . . Pg.20 . . . . R6
Hampshire Ct. . . Pg.14 . . . . W8
Hampton Ct. . . . Pg.20,21,27
. . . . . . . . . . . . . . . V9,X7
Hancock Ct. . . . Pg.26 . . . . X4
Hannah Ct. . . . Pg.20 . . . . U4
Hanover Ct. . . . Pg.20 . . . . W7
Hansom Ct. . . . Pg.21 . . . . W8
Harbor Ct. . . . . Pg.21,27 . . W8
Harlowe Ct. . . . Pg.21,27 . . V8
Harlowe Ln. . . . Pg.21,27 . . V8
Harmony Ct. . . . Pg.15 . . . . R8
Harris Ln. . . . . Pg.21 . . . . U7
Hartford Ct. . . . Pg.26 . . . . Z4
Harvard Ave. . . Pg.21 . . . . V9
Harvest Ct. . . . Pg.20 . . . . U9
Hastings Ct. . . . Pg.14 . . . . R4
Havenshire Ct. . Pg.14 . . . . R4
Havenshire Rd. . Pg.14 . . . . R4
Haverhill Cir. . . Pg.15,21 . . S8
Haviland Ct. . . . Pg.25 . . . . Z3
Hawley Ct. . . . . Pg.26 . . . . X4
Hawthorn Dr. . . Pg.21 . . . . U8
Hayle Ct. . . . . . Pg.20 . . . . U4
Hazel Ct. . . . . . Pg.21 . . . . V8
Hazelwood Dr. . Pg.20 . . . . U6
Hearthside Ct. . . Pg.20 . . . . X5
Heather Ct. . . . Pg.21,27 . . W9
Heatherton Ct. . Pg.14 . . . . R5
Heatherton Dr. . Pg.14 . . . . R5
Heathrow Ln. . . Pg.20 . . . . U5
Hedg Ct. . . . . . Pg.21 . . . . V8
Heirloom Ct. . . . Pg.26 . . . . Z5
Hemlock Ln. . . . Pg.21 . . . . V8
Hempstead Ave. Pg.20 . . . . W6
Henning Ct. . . . Pg.20,21,27 U7
Hercules Ln. . . . Pg.21,27,27 U7
Heritage Ct. . . . Pg.14 . . . . S6
Heritage Hills (Pvt.)
. . . . . . . . . . . . Pg.20 . . . . S5
Heron Ct. . . . . Pg.26 . . . . Z4
Herrick Lake Ct. Pg.14 . . . . Q7
Herrick Rd. . . . Pg.14 . . . . Q7
Hickory Ln. . . . Pg.20 . . . . U4
Hidden Bay Ct. . Pg.21,27 T6,7
Hidden Lake Rd. Pg.21,27 . . W8
Hidden Spring Rd.
. . . . . . . . . . . . Pg.20 . . . . S5
Hidden Valley Dr.
. . . . . . . . . . . . Pg.21 . . . . V8
High Grove Ln. . Pg.20 . . . S3,4
High Point Dr. . . Pg.15 . . . . U7
Highknob Cir. . . Pg.25 . . . . Y2
Highland Ave. . . Pg.20 . . . . U6
Hill St. . . . . . . . Pg.21 . . . . T7
Hillsboro Ln. . . . Pg.26 . . . . X4
Hillside Rd. . . . Pg.20,21 T6,7
Hilltop Ct. . . . . Pg.21,27 . . W9
Hilton Head Dr. . Pg.26 . . . . X6
Hinderlong Ln. . Pg.21 . . . . W8
Hobbes Dr. . . . Pg.26 . . . . Y5
Hobson Hollow Dr.
. . . . . . . . . . . . Pg.21 . . . . U9
Hobson Oaks Ct. Pg.21 . . . . U8
Hobson Oaks Dr.Pg.21 . . . . U8
Hobson Rd. . . . Pg.21,27 U8,9
Hoddam Ct. . . . Pg.26 . . . . Z4
Hoddam Rd. . . . Pg.26 . . . . Z4
Hollenback Dr. . Pg.26 . . . . X6
Hollingswood Av.
. . . . . . . . . . . . Pg.15 . . . . Y5
Hollingswood Ct.Pg.26 . . . . Y5
Hollow Bend Ct. Pg.21,27 . V10
Holly Ct. . . . . . Pg.26 . . . . U6
Hollytowne Ct. . Pg.21,27 . V10
Holstein Ct. . . . Pg.20 . . . . V7
Homer Ct. . . . . Pg.20 . . . . U5

Homestead Dr. . Pg.26 . . . . X5
Honest Pleasure Ct.
. . . . . . . . . . . . Pg.20 . . . . U8
Honeyberry Ct. . Pg.20 . . . . S5
Honeysuckle Dr. Pg.20 . . . . T5
Hopi Ct. . . . . . Pg.14 . . . . R7
Horizon Ct. . . . Pg.25 . . . . Y2
Horncastle Ln. . Pg.26 . . . . W3
Hoyer Ct. . . . . Pg.27 . . . . X8
Hudson Ct. . . . Pg.21 . . . . W8
Hulham St. . . . . Pg.21 . . . . T7
Hull Ct. . . . . . . Pg.21,27 . . W8
Hunter Cir. . . . Pg.21 . . . . U9
Huntington Dr. . Pg.21 . . . . U9
Huntleigh Dr. . . Pg.21 . . . . T8
Hyde Park Ln. . . Pg.21,27 . . W8
Idaho Ct. . . . . . Pg.26 . . . . X4
Imperial Cir. . . . Pg.14 . . . . R5
Inca Ct. . . . . . Pg.14,15 . . R7
Indian Hills Ct. . Pg.14 . . . . R6
Indian Knoll Rd. Pg.21,27 . . V9
Indian Trail Dr. . Pg.21,27 . . V9
Industrial Dr. . . Pg.19 . . . . S3
Inland Cir. . . . . Pg.13,19 . . S3
Interlochen Ln. . Pg.27 . . . . X9
Internationale Dr.
. . . . . . . . . . . . Pg.14 . . . . Q4
Inverness Ct. . . Pg.14 . . . . R6
Inverrary Dr. . . Pg.14 . . . . R5
Iona Ct. . . . . . Pg.21 . . . W10
Iona Dr. . . . . . Pg.21 . . . W10
Iron Liege Ct. . . Pg.20 . . . . U8
Ironwood Ct. . . Pg.21 . . . . U7
Ironwood Dr. . . Pg.21 . . . . U7
Iroquois Ave. . . Pg.15 . . . . R8
Ishnala Dr. . . . Pg.21 . . . . V8
Ithaca Dr. . . . . Pg.21 . . . . W9
Ivy Ln. . . . . . . Pg.19 . . . . T3
Jackson Ave. . . Pg.20 . . . . T6
Jaipur St. . . . . Pg.20 . . . . S8
Jamatt Ct. . . . . Pg.21 . . . . S8
Jane Ave. . . . . Pg.21 . . . . T8
Jasmine Ct. . . . Pg.20 . . . . U5
Jefferson Ave. . Pg.20 . . . T5,6
Jersey Ct. . . . . Pg.26 . . . . Z4
Jessica Ct. . . . Pg.20 . . . . U4
Joan Ct. . . . . . Pg.20 . . . . U4
Joe Willie Ct. . . Pg.26 . . . . Z4
Joe Willie Dr. . . Pg.26 . . . . Z4
John Friend Dr. . Pg.21 . . . . W9
Johnsburg Ct. . Pg.26 . . . . X4
Johnson Dr. . . . Pg.21 . . . . U8
Joliet Rd. . . . . Pg.14 . . . . V9
Jonester Ct. . . . Pg.15 . . . . R7
Jonquil Ct. . . . Pg.20 . . . . U5
Joshua Ct. . . . Pg.20 . . . . T5
Joyce Ln. . . . . Pg.26 . . . . X4
Jubilant Ct. . . . Pg.20 . . . . Y5
Julian Ct. . . . . Pg.21 . . . . U7
Julian St. . . . . Pg.21 . . . . T7
Juniper Dr. . . . Pg.20 . . . . U5
Jupiter Ct. . . . . Pg.21 . . . . S8
Justin Ct. . . . . Pg.21 . . . . U9
Kaimi Ct. . . . . Pg.15 . . . . Q9
Kalamazoo Ct. . Pg.27 . . . . X8
Kallien Ave. . . . Pg.21 . . . . T9
Kallien Ct. . . . . Pg.21 . . . . T9
Kaskaskia Ct. . . Pg.15 . . . . R7
Kathy Ct. . . . . Pg.20 . . . . U5
Kauai King Ct. . Pg.20 . . . . U8
Keats Ave. . . . Pg.26 . . . . Y5
Keim Ct. . . . . . Pg.21 . . . . W9
Keim Rd. . . . . Pg.21 . . . . W9
Kemper Ct. . . . Pg.13 . . . . R2
Kendridge Ct. . . Pg.19 . . . . T1
Kenilworth Ct. . Pg.14 . . . . R5
Kenmare Ct. . . Pg.26 . . . . X6
Kennesaw Ct. . Pg.26 . . . . W3
Kensington Ct. . Pg.14 . . . . R6
Kent Ct. . . . . . Pg.21 . . . . U7
Kentshire Ct. . . Pg.26 . . . . W3
Kentshire Ln. . . Pg.26 . . . . W3
Kentuck Ct. . . . Pg.26 . . . . Z4
Kenyon Dr. . . . Pg.21,27 . . U7
Kerin Ct. . . . . Pg.14 . . . . S6
Kernell Ct. . . . Pg.25 . . . . Y2
Ketten Ct. . . . . Pg.14 . . . . R7
Ketten Dr. . . . . Pg.14,15 Q,R7
Keystone Ct. . . Pg.26 . . . . X6
Kilburne Ln. . . Pg.26 . . . . X4
Kildeer Dr. . . . Pg.21,27 . . U8
Kimball Ct. . . . Pg.21 . . . . U8
Kinglet Ct. . . . Pg.20 . . . . U8
Kings Ct. . . . . Pg.14 . . . . R6
Kings Point Ct. . Pg.14 . . . . R5
Kingsley Dr. . . Pg.27 . . . . X8
Kingswood Ct. . Pg.21,27 . . W7
Kinsie Ct. . . . . Pg.21 . . . . U8
Kinston Ct. . . . Pg.20 . . . . U6
Kiowa Dr. . . . . Pg.14 . . . . R7
Kirby Ct. . . . . . Pg.14 . . . . R4
Knoch Knolls Rd.
. . . . . . . . . . . . Pg.27 . . . . W7
Knoll Dr. . . . . . Pg.21,27 . . V9
Knox Ct. . . . . . Pg.21,27 . . U9
Kubek Rd. . . . Pg.26 . . . . X5
LaFox Ave. . . . Pg.19 . . . . U3
LaSalle Ave. . . Pg.14,19 R3,4
Laird St. . . . . . Pg.20 . . . . S6
Lakeside Ct. . . Pg.21 . . . . W8
Lakeside Dr. . . Pg.21 . . . . W8
Lakeview Ct. . . Pg.26 . . . . W3
Lakeview Dr. . . Pg.26 . . . . W3
Lakewood Cir. . Pg.21 . . . . U8
Lamont Ct. . . . Pg.20 . . . . U4
Lampwick Ct. . . Pg.20 . . . . U7
Lancaster Cir. . Pg.27 . . . . W8
Lancaster St. . . Pg.21 . . . . U7
Landore Dr. . . . Pg.26 . . . . X5
Landsdown Dr. . Pg.25 . . . . Y2
Langley Dr. . . . Pg.14 . . . . R4
Lantern Ct. . . . Pg.21 . . . . U9
Larchmont Ct. . Pg.26 . . . . V7
Lark Ln. . . . . . Pg.21,27 . . V7
Larkspur Ct. . . Pg.15 . . . . Q7

Larsen Ct. . . . . Pg.15 . . . . R8
Larsen Ln. . . . . Pg.15 . . . . R8
Laura Ct. . . . . Pg.14 . . . . R4
Laurel Ln. . . . . Pg.20 . . . . U7
Laureli Cir. . . . Pg.20 . . . . S5
Lawrence Dr. . . Pg.26 . . . . V5
Lazy Hollow Ct. Pg.21,27 . V10
Le Provence Ct. Pg.21 . . . . U8
Lea Brook Ct. . . Pg.21,27 . . W9
Leach Dr. . . . . Pg.20 . . . . V6
Leamington Ct. . Pg.21,27 . . W8
Leawood Ct. . . Pg.21 . . . . R8
Ledgestone Ct. . Pg.25 . . . . X3
Leeds Ct. . . . . Pg.21,27 . . W8
Leesburg Ct. . . Pg.21 . . . . T9
Lehigh Dr. . . . . Pg.27 . . . . X9
Lemmon Dr. . . . Pg.26 . . . . X7
Leverenz Dr. . . Pg.26 . . . X5,6
Lexington Ln. . . Pg.20 . . . . U4
Liberty Dr. . . . . Pg.21 . . . . U3
Lighthouse Dr. . Pg.21 . . . . U6
Lilac Ln. . . . . . Pg.20 . . . . U6
Lincoln Rd. . . . Pg.15 . . . . Q7
Linden Ct. . . . . Pg.20 . . . . U5
Linden Dr. . . . . Pg.20 . . . . U5
Lindholm Ct. . . Pg.27 . . . . X9
Lindrick Ct. . . . Pg.14 . . . . R5
Lindsay Dr. . . . Pg.26 . . . . W4
Lindsey Ln. . . . Pg.26 . . . . W4
Lindsey Ct. . . . Pg.20 . . . . S4
Lisson Rd. . . . . Pg.21,27 W,X9
Litchfield Ct. . . Pg.26 . . . . X6
Little Berry Ct. . Pg.21,27 . V10
Livingston Ct. . . Pg.20 . . . . U4
Lockwood Cir. . Pg.15 . . . . R7
Locust Ct. . . . . Pg.20 . . . . S5
Lois Ann Ln. . . Pg.21 . . . . U9
Lombardy Ln. . . Pg.20 . . . . U5
Lona Ct. . . . . . Pg.21,27 W10
London Ct. . . . Pg.14 . . . . R4
Long Acre Dr. . . Pg.26 . . . . Y5
Long Branch Ct. Pg.21 . . . . S8
Longleaf Dr. . . . Pg.20 . . . . S5
Longridge Ct. . . Pg.21,27 . . W7
Longspur Ct. . . Pg.21,27 . . V7
Lonsdale Ave. . Pg.20 . . . . U4
Lonsdale Dr. . . Pg.20 . . . . U4
Look Out . . . . Pg.21 . . . . U8
Looking Post Ave.
. . . . . . . . . . . . Pg.25 . . . . Y2
Loomis St. . . . . Pg.15,21 R-T7
Lotus Ct. . . . . Pg.21 . . . . W9
Loveland Ct. . . Pg.26 . . . . X4
Lowell Ln. . . . . Pg.20 . . . . U4
Loyola Dr. . . . . Pg.21,27 . . V9
Lynchburg Ct. . Pg.21 . . . . T9
Lyndhurst Ct. . . Pg.21 . . . . X8
Mackinaw Ct. . . Pg.27 . . . . X8
Madera Ln. . . . Pg.21 . . . . T5
Magenta Ct. . . Pg.26 . . . . X4
Magnolia Ln. . . Pg.20 . . . . U5
Main St. . . . . . Pg.20 . . . S,T7
Mallard Ln. . . . Pg.26 . . . . Z4
Mallory Ct. . . . Pg.20 . . . . U4
Malvina Ct. . . . Pg.26 . . . . Y5
Manassas Ct. . Pg.20 . . . . U6
Manchester St. . Pg.14 . . . . R4
Mandalay Ct. . . Pg.13 . . . . R3
Mandeville Rd. . Pg.26 . . . . Z5
Manydown Ct. . Pg.26 . . . . Z5
Maple Ave. . . . Pg.20,21 T6,8
Maple Hills Ct. . Pg.14 . . . . R6
Maple Knoll Dr. Pg.15 . . . . R7
Maple St. . . . . Pg.20 . . . . T7
Maplefield Rd. . Pg.20 . . . . V6
Maplewood Cir. Pg.13 . . . . R3
Marengo Ct. . . Pg.14 . . . . W5
Margate Ct. . . . Pg.20 . . . . T9
Marigold Ct. . . Pg.20 . . . . U5
Mark Ct. . . . . Pg.21 . . . . R8
Market Ave. . . Pg.21 . . . . U9
Marls Ct. . . . . Pg.15 . . . . R8
Marquette Ave. Pg.21,27 . . V9
Marshall Ct. . . . Pg.27 . . . . X9
Martin Ave. . . . Pg.21 . . . . T6
Mary Ln. . . . . Pg.21 . . . . T8
Marydown Ct. . Pg.26 . . . . Z4
Massachusetts Ct
. . . . . . . . . . . . Pg.21 . . . . V9
Masters Ct. . . . Pg.13 . . . . R3
Mather Ct. . . . Pg.25 . . . . Z3
Mather Dr. . . . Pg.25 . . . . Z3
Mattande Ln. . . Pg.18 . . . . S4
Matthew Ct. . . Pg.21 . . . . U9
Mayapple Ct. . . Pg.20 . . . . S5
Mayfair Ln. . . . Pg.26 . . . . X4
McCartney Dr. . Pg.21 . . . . W7
McClennan Ct. . Pg.20 . . . . S4
McDowell Rd. . Pg.14 . . . . R4
McHenry Ave. . Pg.20 . . . . U6
Meadow Dr. . . Pg.20 . . . . X5
Meadow Green Dr.
. . . . . . . . . . . . Pg.20 . . . . W7
Meadow Lake Dr.
. . . . . . . . . . . . Pg.26 . . . . Z4
Meadow Ln. . . Pg.26 . . . W,X5
Meadowland Dr.Pg.20 . . . . U5
Meagan Ct. . . . Pg.14 . . . . U7
Meander Dr. . . Pg.21 . . . . W7
Mecan Dr. . . . Pg.26 . . . . X4
Medinah Dr. . . Pg.13 . . . . R3
Meisch Ct. . . . Pg.26 . . . . Z4
Meisinger Ln. . . Pg.20 . . . . S4
Melody Ln. . . . Pg.21 . . . . T7
Menominee Ln. Pg.15 . . . . R7
Mercer Ct. . . . Pg.21 . . . . U6
Merion Ct. . . . Pg.13 . . . . R3
Merrimac Ct. . . Pg.20 . . . . U6
Merritt Ave. . . Pg.21 . . . . U5
Mesa Dr. . . . . Pg.26 . . . . X6
Mescalnero Ct. Pg.14 . . . . R6
Michigan Ave. . Pg.13 . . . . T9
Middle Rd. . . . Pg.20 . . . . T8
Middleburg Ct. . Pg.21 . . . . T8
Middleburg Rd. . Pg.21 . . . . T8

Midhurst Ct. . . . Pg.21 . . . . W7
Midland Dr. . . . Pg.26 . . . . X5
Mike Ct. . . . . . Pg.20 . . . . S4
Milburn Ct. . . . Pg.21 . . . . S8
Milford Ct. . . . . Pg.26 . . . . Z5
Mill Race Ln. . . Pg.21,27 . . V9
Mill St. . . . . . . Pg.14,20 T6
Millbrook Ln. . . Pg.20 . . . . V6
Millcreek Ln. . . Pg.21 . . . . T9
Millet St. . . . . Pg.14 . . . . R7
Milton Dr. . . . . Pg.21 . . . . S8
Mirror Lake Dr. Pg.14 . . . . R5
Mistflower Ct. . Pg.25 . . . . V2
Mistflower Ln. . Pg.26 . . . . Y2
Mistwood Dr. . Pg.21 . . . . U9
Misty Ct. . . . . Pg.20 . . . . X5
Mobile Ct. . . . Pg.20 . . . . U6
Modaff Rd. . . . Pg.26 . . . W,X7
Mohler Ct. . . . Pg.20 . . . . R6
Monmouth Ave. Pg.21,27 . . V9
Montclair Dr. . . Pg.21 . . . . V7
Monterey Ct. . . Pg.20 . . . . S6
Montgomery Ct. Pg.20 . . . . U5
Monticello Dr. . Pg.21 . . . . S7
Montrose Ct. . . Pg.21 . . . . V9
Moonlight Ct. . . Pg.26 . . . . X6
Moonridge Rd. . Pg.20 . . . . S5
Morgan Cir. . . . Pg.21 . . . V10
Morningside Dr. Pg.20 . . . . U7
Morningstar Ct. . Pg.20 . . . . X5
Mortonsberry Dr.
. . . . . . . . . . . . Pg.20 . . . . X5
Morven Ct. . . . Pg.21 . . . . S8
Moultrie St. . . . Pg.20 . . . . S4
Mountain Ct. . . Pg.20 . . . . W9
Mt. Vernon Ct. . Pg.15,21 . . S7
Muirhead Ave. . Pg.21 . . . V10
Mulberry Ct. . . Pg.20 . . . . T5
Mulligan Dr. . . Pg.13 . . . . Q3
Mundelein Rd. . Pg.21 . . . V10
Murdstone Dr. . Pg.15 . . . . R8
Mustang Dr. . . Pg.21 . . . . V8
Naner Blvd. . . . Pg.21 T,U,X9
Naperville Rd. . Pg.15 . . . . R8
Napolean Dr. . . Pg.21,27 . X,W8
Nashua Dr. . . . Pg.21 . . . . U8
Nashville Ct. . . Pg.20 . . . . U8
Natalie Ct. . . . Pg.20 . . . . U4
Natchez Trace Cir.
. . . . . . . . . . . . Pg.20 . . . . U6
Navarone Dr. . . Pg.26 . . . . Z4
Needham Rd. . . Pg.15,21 . . S8
Needles Ct. . . . Pg.21 . . . . U8
Nelli Ct. . . . . . Pg.20 . . . . U4
Neskola Ct. . . . Pg.26 . . . . X5
Nevis Dr. . . . . Pg.21 . . . . U9
New Haven Ct. Pg.26 . . . . X4
New Haven Dr. Pg.26 . . . . X4
Newgate Ave. . Pg.21 . . . . W7
Newman Ct. . . Pg.26 . . . . Z4
Newport Ct. . . Pg.20 . . . WX6
Newton Ave. . . Pg.26 . . . . Z4
Nicholas Ct. . . Pg.20 . . . . R6
Nicole Dr. . . . . Pg.26 . . . . Z4
Night Hawk Ct. Pg.26 . . . . Z5
Niswender Ct. . Pg.25 . . . . Z3
Niswender Dr. . Pg.25 . . . . Z3
Norfolk Ct. . . . Pg.21,27 W8,9
North Aurora Rd.Pg.20 . . . . S4
North Ave. . . . Pg.20,21 S7,8
Northampton Dr. Pg.26 . . . . W4
Northfield Ct. . . Pg.27 . . . . W4
Northwich Ct. . . Pg.26 . . . . W3
Norwood Ct. . . Pg.21 . . . . V9
Notre Dame Dr. Pg.20 . . . . U7
Nottingham Dr. Pg.14 . . . . R5
Nottingham Ln. Pg.26 . . . . W5
Nutmeg Ln. . . . Pg.21 . . . V10
Oak Bluff Ct. . . Pg.27 . . . . X8
Oak Ct. . . . . . Pg.21 . . W8,X9
Oakhurst Ct. . . Pg.21 . . . . U5
Oakhurst Dr. . . Pg.21 . . . . U5
Oakleaf Ct. . . . Pg.21 . . . . W8
Oakton Ln. . . . Pg.20 . . . . U5
Oakwood Dr. . . Pg.21 . . . . U7
Oberlin Ct. . . . Pg.20 . . . . U6
Oconto Dr. . . . Pg.21 . . . . U9
Odyssey Ave. . Pg.25 . . . . Q3
Odyssey Dr. . . Pg.13 . . . . Q3
Ogden Ave. . . Pg.14,15,20
. . . . . . . . . R8,S5,6
Okolona Ct. . . . Pg.14 . . . . R6
Old Bridge Ln. . Pg.26 . . . . X4
Old Dominion Ct.Pg.21 . . . . T9
Old Mill Ct. . . . Pg.20 . . . . T9
Old Naperville Rd.
. . . . . . . . . . . . Pg.15 . . . . Q9
Olesen Dr. . . . Pg.26 . . . . Z4
Olympus Dr. . . Pg.21,27 . V10
Omaha Ct. . . . Pg.20 . . . . U6
Ontario Ave. . . Pg.20 . . . . U4
Onwentsia Ct. . Pg.14 . . . . R6
Orchard Ct. . . . Pg.21 . . . . V9
Orchid Ct. . . . Pg.20 . . . . U7
Oriole Ct. . . . . Pg.21 . . . . U7
Orleans Ave. . . Pg.21 . . . . V9
Orwell Rd. . . . Pg.26 . . . . Z5
Osage Ln. . . . Pg.20 . . . . U7
Osler Dr. (Pvt.) . Pg.20 . . . . W7
Oswego Rd. . . Pg.21 . . . . U8
Othello Ct. . . . Pg.14 . . . . R6
Ottawa Ct. . . . Pg.21 . . . . U8
Overlook Ct. . . Pg.14 . . . . R7
Overstreet Dr. . Pg.26 . . . . X4
Overton St. . . . Pg.20 . . . . U4
Oxford Ct. . . . Pg.21 . . . . U8
Oxford Ln. . . . Pg.21 . . . . U8
Pacific Dr. . . . . Pg.26 . . . . X6
Paddington Ave. Pg.14 . . . . R6
Paddock Ct. . . Pg.21 . . . . V8
Page Ct. . . . . Pg.20 . . . . T6
Pakeside Rd. . . Pg.21 . . . . U8
Palm Ct. . . . . Pg.20 . . . . U5
Palmer Cir. . . . Pg.13 . . . . W3
Palmer Dr. . . . Pg.13 . . . . W3
Palmetto St. . . Pg.20 . . . . U5

Pamela Ct . . . . Pg.21 . . . . T8
Papago Ct. . . . Pg.14 . . . . R7
Parador Dr. . . . Pg.26 . . . Y,Z5
Park St. . . . . . Pg.14 . . . . Q7
Parkfield Ct. . . Pg.20 . . . . U8
Parkside Rd. . . Pg.21 . . . . T8
Parkway Dr. . . Pg.20 . . . . S6
Parliament Ln. . Pg.25 . . . . X3
Partlow Dr. . . . Pg.26 . . . . Z4
Pas Ct. . . . . . Pg.20 . . . . S4
Pathway Dr. . . Pg.21 . . . . W9
Paxton Dr. . . . Pg.14 . . . . R4
Peach Tree Ct. . Pg.21 . . . . S8
Peacock Ct. . . Pg.20 . . . . V7
Pearl Ct. (Pvt.) . Pg.14 . . . . R7
Pearson Ct. . . Pg.21 . . . . S6
Pebble Beach Ct.Pg.13 . . . . R3
Pebblestone Rd. Pg.20 . . . . U8
Pebblewood Ln. Pg.13 . . . . R3
Pecan Ct. . . . . Pg.20 . . . . U6
Pelham Ct. . . . Pg.14 . . . . R4
Pembroke Rd. . Pg.21 . . . . T8
Pena Dr. . . . . Pg.27 . . . V10
Pennsylvania Ct.Pg.14 . . . . R6
Pepperdine Dr. . Pg.20 . . . . S5
Pepperidge Rd. Pg.20 . . . . S5
Periwinkle Ct. . Pg.20 . . . . U4
Periwinkle Ln. . Pg.20 . . . . U4
Persimmon Ct. . Pg.21 . . . . W9
Peshtigo Ave. . Pg.20 . . . . X5
Petra Ct. . . . . Pg.26 . . . . Z5
Petterson Ct. . . Pg.20 . . . . X8
Petworth Dr. . . Pg.21 . . . . W7
Phaeton Ct. . . Pg.21 . . . . W8
Pheasant Run Ct.
. . . . . . . . . . . . Pg.21 . . . V10
Piccadilly Cir. . . Pg.14 . . . . R4
Pickerel Ct. . . . Pg.26 . . . . X7
Pickwick Ct. . . Pg.14 . . . . R4
Pier Ave. . . . . Pg.21 . . . . V8
Pier Ct. . . . . . Pg.21 . . . . V8
Pilsen Ct. (Pvt.) Pg.14 . . . . R7
Pima Ct. . . . . Pg.14 . . . . R7
Pimpernel Ct. . . Pg.20 . . . . U4
Pine Cir. . . . . . Pg.20 . . . . T7
Pine Ridge Ct. . Pg.21 . . . . U8
Pinetree Dr. . . Pg.20 . . . . W9
Piper Ave. . . . Pg.27 . . . . W7
Pipestone Ct. . Pg.26 . . . . Z4
Placer Ct. . . . . Pg.20 . . . . V7
Plainfield Naperville Rd.
. . . . . . . . . . . . Pg.20 . . . . V5
Plank Rd. . . . . Pg.15 . . . . R8
Plantation Ct. . Pg.19 . . . . W3
Pleasant Run Ct.Pg.21,27 . V10
Plum Hollow Ct. Pg.14,20 . . S6
Plum Tree Dr. . Pg.27 . . . W,X8
Plymouth Ct. . . Pg.21 . . . . W7
Poet Ct. . . . . . Pg.26 . . . . Y5
Pomeroen St. . Pg.20 . . . . U4
Pomona Ct. . . Pg.20 . . . . X5
Pontiac Cir. . . . Pg.20 . . . . W7
Poplar St. . . . . Pg.20 . . . . W9
Popple Ct. . . . Pg.26 . . . . Z4
Porter Ave. . . . Pg.20,21 T6,7
Portsmith Ct. . . Pg.25 . . . . X3
Potomac Ave. . Pg.27 . . . . X9
Pottawatomie Ct.
. . . . . . . . . . . . Pg.20 . . . . U6
Powell Ct. . . . Pg.14 . . . . R7
Pradel Dr. . . . Pg.26 . . . . Z4
Prague Ct. . . . Pg.21 . . . . T8
Prairie Ave. . . Pg.20 . . . . U6
Prairie Knoll Dr. Pg.20 . . . . U5
Prairie View Ct. Pg.13,19 . . S3
Prelude Ct. . . . Pg.26 . . . . Y5
Prescott Ct. . . Pg.20 . . . . U6
Prestige Ct. . . . Pg.26 . . . . Y5
Preston Rd. . . . Pg.21 . . . . U7
Prestwick Dr. . . Pg.14 . . . . R3
Primrose Ln. . . Pg.21 . . . . U8
Prince Ct. . . . . Pg.14 . . . . R4
Princess Cir. . . Pg.26 . . . . U6
Princeton Cir. . Pg.21 . . . . V10
Prospect Ct. . . Pg.20 . . . . U9
Proud Clarion Ct.Pg.21 . . . . U8
Providence Ct. . Pg.21 . . . . X6
Pueblo Ct. . . . Pg.26 . . . . X6
Purdue Ave. . . Pg.21 . . . . V9
Putnam Ct. . . . Pg.14 . . . . R7
Quail Court Ct. Pg.20 . . . . V7
Quail Hollow Ct. Pg.14 . . . . R5
Queens Ct. . . . Pg.14 . . . . R4
Queensbury Ct. Pg.14 . . . . R4
Queensgreen Cir.
. . . . . . . . . . . . Pg.14 . . . . R4
Queensgreen Dr.Pg.14 . . . . R4
Quin Ct. . . . . . Pg.20 . . . . U6
Quincy Ave. . . Pg.21 . . . . T9
Railway Dr. . . . Pg.25 . . . . X3
Raintree Dr. . . Pg.20 . . . . U4
Rampart Ct. . . Pg.27 . . . . X9
Ramsgate Ct. . Pg.26 . . . . W4
Ranch View Ct. Pg.21,27 . . W7
Rapidan Ct. . . Pg.27 . . . . X9
Rapids Ct. . . . Pg.20 . . . . V8
Raymond Dr. . . Pg.14 . . . . Q4
Red Oak Ct. . . Pg.20 . . . . U5
Red River Ct. . Pg.20 . . . . V8
Red Stable Way Pg.26 . . . . Y4
Redbud Ct. . . . Pg.20 . . . . T7
Redfield Rd. . . Pg.14 . . . . R4
Redpoll Ct. . . . Pg.21 . . . . W9
Redstart Rd. . . Pg.21 . . . . W9
Redwing Ct. . . Pg.14 . . . . R4
Redwing Dr. . . Pg.20 . . . . U8
Reflection Ct. . Pg.25 . . . . Y2
Regency Ct. . . Pg.26 . . . . Z5
Relstar Ct. . . . Pg.26 . . . . Z5
Remington Dr. . Pg.20 . . . . W9
Rennet Dr. . . . Pg.26 . . . . Z5
Revere Ct. . . . Pg.14 . . . . R4
Rhodes Ln. . . . Pg.20 . . . . S4
Rice Ct. . . . . . Pg.20 . . . . U9
Richard Rd. . . . Pg.21 . . . . T8

Richmond Ct. . . Pg.20 . . . . U6
Richwood Ct. . . Pg.26 . . . . Z5
Rickert Dr. . . . Pg.20 . . . . U4
Ridgefield Ln. . . Pg.26 . . . . W7
Ridgeland Ave. . Pg.15 . . . . Q8
Ridgely Ct. . . . Pg.21 . . . . U9
Rieser Ct. . . . Pg.26 . . . . Z5
Riley Ct. . . . . Pg.26 . . . . Z4
Rill Ct. . . . . . . Pg.21 . . . . U7
Ring Rd. . . . . Pg.20,21 W,X7
Rio Grande Ct. . Pg.21 . . . . X8
Rio Grande Dr. . Pg.21 . . . . X8
Ripley Ct. . . . . Pg.20 . . . . W7
Riva Ridge Ct. . Pg.21 . . . . U8
Rivanna Ct. . . Pg.27 . . . . X8
River Bend Rd. Pg.20 . . . . T6
River Bluff Cir. . Pg.26 . . . . Z5
River Front Cir. . Pg.20 . . . . T6
River Oak Dr. . Pg.27 . . . . W9
River Rd. . . . . Pg.20 . . . . U5
River Ridge Cir. Pg.21 . . . . W8
River Ridge Dr. Pg.21 . . . . W8
River Woods Dr.Pg.21 . . . . W8
Riverlea Dr. . . Pg.21 . . . . W8
Rivermist Ct. . . Pg.21 . . . . X7
Riverview Dr. . . Pg.27 . . . . T7
Roanoke Ct. . . Pg.20 . . . . U4
Robin Dr. . . . . Pg.26 . . . . Z5
Robin Hill Ct. . . Pg.20 . . . . U6
Robin Hill Dr. . . Pg.20 . . . . U6
Rock Ct. . . . . Pg.20 . . . . V8
Rock River Ct. . Pg.20 . . . . X8
Rock Spring Ct. Pg.26 . . . . X6
Rock Spring Rd. Pg.26 . . . . X6
Rockbridge Dr. Pg.21 . . . . T9
Rockport Ct. . . Pg.20 . . . . X6
Rockspring Ct. . Pg.26 . . . . X6
Rocky Glen Dr. Pg.20 . . . . U5
Rolling Meadows Dr.
. . . . . . . . . . . . Pg.26 . . . . X5
Rollins Ct. . . . Pg.21 . . . . W9
Rosada Dr. . . . Pg.26 . . . . Z5
Rose Hill Ct. . . Pg.21 . . . . W8
Rose Ln. . . . . Pg.20 . . . . U6
Rosecroft Ln. . . Pg.25 . . . . U5
Rosemere Ct. . Pg.21 . . . . U9
Rosewood Ave. Pg.15 . . . . R8
Rowan Ct. . . . Pg.20 . . . . U7
Roxbury Dr. . . Pg.20 . . . . W6
Royal Blackheath Ct.
. . . . . . . . . . . . Pg.14 . . . . R5
Royal Bombay Ct.
. . . . . . . . . . . . Pg.14 . . . . R5
Royal St. George Dr.
. . . . . . . . . . . . Pg.20 . . . . S6
Royce Rd. . . . Pg.26 . . . . X8
Royce Woods Ct.
. . . . . . . . . . . . Pg.27 . . . . X8
Russet Ave. . . Pg.20 . . . . V6
Rutgers Ct. . . . Pg.21 . . . . V9
Rutland Rd. . . Pg.26 . . . . X4
Ryan Ct. . . . . Pg.26 . . . . X5
Saber Ct. . . . . Pg.20 . . . . W9
Sable Oaks Ct. Pg.21 . . . . X3
Sable Oaks Dr. Pg.25 . . . . X3
Saddlebrook Ct. Pg.25 . . . . X2
Sagebrush Rd. . Pg.20,21 . . W7
Saginaw Ct. . . Pg.20 . . . . U6
Salisbury Dr. . . Pg.26 . . . . W4
Salix Cir. . . . . Pg.26 . . . . Z4
Salt River Ct. . Pg.21 . . . . X8
Samstag Ct. . . Pg.15 . . . . R7
Samuel Ct. . . . Pg.21 . . . . U4
San Luis Ct. . . Pg.26 . . . . Z4
Sanctuary Ln. . Pg.20 . . . . U5
Sand Island Ct. Pg.26 . . . . Z4
Sand Key Rd. . Pg.25 . . . . Y3
Sandalwood Dr. Pg.20 . . . . U6
Sandgate Ct. . . Pg.21,27 . . W7
Sandpiper Ln. . Pg.27 . . . . U7
Santa Fe Dr. . . Pg.21 . . . . S3
Santa Maria Dr. Pg.25 . . . . T7
Sara Ln. . . . . Pg.21 . . . . U9
Saranell Ave. . Pg.20 . . . . U5
Saratoga Rd. . Pg.26 . . . . X4
Savannah Cir. . Pg.20 . . . . U6
Saw Mill Rd. . . Pg.20 . . . . W7
Saxon Ln. . . . Pg.20 . . . . V5
Schey Ct. . . . . Pg.26 . . . . W7
Schillinger Ct. . Pg.26 . . . . Z5
School St. . . . . Pg.20 . . . . S7
Schumacher Ln. Pg.21 . . . . U4
Scott Ct. . . . . Pg.21 . . . . U8
Scottsbridge Rd.Pg.26 . . . . X7
Scottsdale Ct. . Pg.25 . . . . X3
Scottsdale Ct. . Pg.25 . . . . X3
Sebastian Ct. . Pg.26 . . . . Z4
Sebastian Dr. . Pg.26 . . . . Z4
Secretariat Ct. . Pg.20 . . . . U8
Sedgewick Ct. . Pg.26 . . . . X4
Seiler Dr. . . . . Pg.26 . . . . X5
Selma Ln. . . . Pg.20 . . . . U4
Senna Ct. . . . Pg.26 . . . . X7
Sequoia Ct. . . Pg.20 . . . . U5
Sequoia Rd. . . Pg.20 . . . . U5
Serenity Ln. . . Pg.25 . . . . Y3
Seton Hall Ct. . Pg.21 . . . . V9
Settlers Ct. . . . Pg.26 . . . . X7
Settlers Dr. . . . Pg.26 . . . . X7
Severn Ct. . . . Pg.26 . . . . W4
Seville Ct. . . . Pg.26 . . . . X6
Shady Grove Ct.Pg.21 . . . V10
Shagbark Ct. . Pg.21 . . . . U8
Shaker Ct. . . . Pg.26 . . . . W4
Shakespeare Ln.Pg.26 . . . . Y5
Shanahan Ct. . Pg.21 . . . . T9
Shandrew Dr. . Pg.21 . . . . U4
Shaw Ave. . . . Pg.20 . . . . U5
Sheehan Dr. . . Pg.26 . . . . Z5
Sheehan Dr. . . Pg.26 . . . . Z5
Sheffield Rd. . . Pg.27 . . . . W8
Sheldon Ct. . . Pg.26 . . . . Z5
Shell Lake Dr. . Pg.26 . . . . X4
Shenandoah Ln. Pg.15 . . . . R7
Shepherd Dr. . . Pg.21 . . . . S8
Sheppey Ct. . . Pg.20 . . . . V6

# NAPERVILLE

Sheridan Cir. . Pg.14 . . . . R4
Sheridan Ln. . Pg.14 . . . . R4
Sheringham Dr. Pg.20 . . . V6
Sherman Ave. . Pg.18 . . . R8
Sherwood Ct. . Pg.20 . . . N6
Shetland Rd. . Pg.21 . . . V10
Shiloh Ct. . . . Pg.20 . . . U6
Shimer Ct. . . . Pg.27 . . . X9
Shire Ct. . . . . Pg.26 . . . Y5
Shome Ct. . . . Pg.20 . . . V7
Shore Rd. . . . Pg.13 . . . R2
Sibling Ct. . . . Pg.26 . . . X4
Siebert Ct. . . . Pg.21 . . . V10
Sierra Ave. . . . Pg.26 . . . X4
Sierra Ct. . . . . Pg.26 . . . X7
Sigmund Rd. . Pg.20 . . . R6
Signal Dr. . . . Pg.21 . . . V9
Silver Maple Ct. Pg.15 . . . R7
Silver Spur Ct. Pg.26 . . . X6
Simsbury Ct. . Pg.26 . . . X4
Singletree Ln. . Pg.27 . . . V10
Sioux Ct. . . . . Pg.14 . . . R7
Sir Barton Ct. . Pg.21 . . . T8
Sisters Ave. . . Pg.26 . . . X4
Sixtons Ct. . . . Pg.26 . . . X4
Skylane Dr. . . Pg.20 . . . W4
Sleight St. . . . Pg.15,21 . S,T7
Slippery Rock Ct.
 . . . . . . . . . . Pg.21 . . . W10
Slippery Rock Rd.
 . . . . . . . . . . Pg.21 . . . W10
Small Ct. . . . . Pg.20 . . . S4
Smokey Ct. . . Pg.15 . . . Q7
Snap Jack Ct. . Pg.21 . . . V8
Snow Creek Rd. Pg.26 . . . Z4
Snowbird Ln. . Pg.26 . . . Z4
Snowdon Ct. . Pg.20 . . . U8
Somerset Ct. . Pg.20 . . . V6
Soper Ct. . . . . Pg.20 . . . U6
Spalding Dr. (Pvt.)
 . . . . . . . . . . Pg.26 . . . T7
Spenser Ct. . . Pg.27 . . . Y5
Spice Cir. . . . . Pg.21 . . . V10
Spikehorn Ave. Pg.21 . . . W8
Spindletree Ave. Pg.21 . . W8
Spinner Ct. . . . Pg.26 . . . X6
Split Oak Rd. . Pg.27 . . . W7
Spring Ave. . . Pg.20 . . . S6
Spring Garden Cir.
 . . . . . . . . . . Pg.15 . . . R4
Springbrook Dr. Pg.20 . . W6
Springbrook Pkwy.
Springdale Ct. . Pg.20 . . . X5
Springhill Ct. . Pg.21 . . . T8
Springhill Dr. . Pg.15 . . . S8
Springside Ct. . Pg.27 . . . W7
Springwood Dr. Pg.20 . . . U7
Spruce Dr. . . . Pg.21 . . . U6
Sprucewood Ct. Pg.27 . . . W9
St. Albans Cir. . Pg.26 . . . X4
St. Croix Ave. . Pg.20 . . . W5
Stacie Ct. . . . . Pg.13 . . . S4
Stackinghay Dr. Pg.25 . . . Y2
Stafford Ave. . Pg.21 . . . T8
Standish Ct. . . Pg.21 . . . U8
Stanford Dr. . . Pg.27 . . . W9
Stanhope Ct. . Pg.27 . . . W8
Stanton Dr. . . Pg.21 . . . T8
Starling Ln. . . . Pg.27 . . . W7
Starlite Ct. . . . Pg.26 . . . X5
Stauffer Dr. . . . Pg.20 . . . S5
Staunton Rd. . Pg.21 . . . T8
Steamboat Ave. Pg.26 . . . X6
Steeplebrook Ct. Pg.21 . . W9
Steinbeck Ct. . Pg.20 . . . U6
Sterling Ct. . . . Pg.21 . . . T8
Stevens St. . . . Pg.20 . . . T6
Stillwater Ct. . . Pg.27 . . . W8
Stockton Ct. . . Pg.21 . . . W9
Stockton Rd. . Pg.26 . . . W9
Stone Ct. . . . . Pg.15 . . . R8
Stonecreek Dr. . Pg.21 . . . V7
Stonegate Rd. . Pg.20 . . . V6
Stonehenge Ct. Pg.14 . . . R4
Stoneleigh Dr. . Pg.20 . . . W4
Stonewater Dr. Pg.26 . . . W4
Stoney Brook Ct. Pg.21,27 . W9
Stonington Ct. . Pg.26 . . . W4
Stoos Ln. . . . . Pg.20 . . . U7
Stowe Cir. . . . Pg.26 . . . W4
Stratford Ct. . . Pg.20 . . . T5
Strawbridge Ct. Pg.21 . . . V10
Stuart Ct. . . . . Pg.21 . . . U8
Sudbury St. . . Pg.26 . . . W4
Suffolk St. . . . Pg.14 . . . R7
Sugar Creek Ct. Pg.14 . . . R5
Sugar Ct. . . . . Pg.20 . . . S5
Summerset Ct. . Pg.20 . . . V6
Summit Hills Ln. Pg.14,20 . S5
Sumter Ct. . . . Pg.20 . . . V6
Sunburst Ln. . . Pg.25 . . . Y2
Sunderland Ct. . Pg.21 . . . W7
Sunnybrook Ct. Pg.14,20 . S,T5
Sunrise Ct. . . . Pg.21 . . . W9
Sunset Dr. . . . Pg.20,21 . T9
Sunshine Ct. . . Pg.25 . . . Y2
Superior Ct. . . Pg.13 . . . S4
Surrey Ct. . . . Pg.21,27 . V7
Sussex Ct. . . . Pg.21 . . . S9
Sussex Rd. . . . Pg.21 . . . S9
Swallow St. . . . Pg.21,27 . V8
Swandyke Ct. . Pg.26 . . . X6
Swansea Ct. . . Pg.20 . . . U8
Sweet Bay Ct. . Pg.20 . . . U7
Sweet Maggie Ln.
 . . . . . . . . . . Pg.25 . . . Y2
Swift Ln. . . . . Pg.21 . . . V7
Sycamore Dr. . Pg.20 . . . V6
Sylvan Circle . Pg.14 . . . R5
Sylvia Ln. . . . . Pg.20 . . . U6
Syracuse Ave. . Pg.21 . . . W10
Talbot Ct. . . . . Pg.20 . . . V6
Tall Oaks Ct. . . Pg.21 . . . T8
Tallgrass Dr. . . Pg.25 . . . Y3
Tamahawk Ln. . Pg.26 . . . X4
Tamarack Ave. Pg.20 . . . U7

Tamarou Rd. . Pg.20 . . . V6
Tan Oak Ln. . . Pg.20 . . . U7
Tanager Ct. . . Pg.21 . . . V7
Tandom Ct. . . Pg.27 . . . W9
Tanglewood Ln. Pg.15 . . . R7
Tappingo Dr. . Pg.20 . . . U4
Teakwood Ct. . Pg.20 . . . U5
Technology Dr. Pg.14 . . . R6
Tee Girl Ct. . . . Pg.26 . . . X4
Templar Ct. . . Pg.20 . . . W7
Tennyson Ln. . Pg.20 . . . U7
Terrance Dr. . . Pg.21 . . . V7
Terri Ct. . . . . . Pg.21 . . . V7
Testa Dr. . . . . Pg.20 . . . T5
Teton Ct. . . . . Pg.21 . . . V6
Thackery Ct. . . Pg.26 . . . Y5
Thackery Ln. . . Pg.26 . . . Y5
Thatcher Dr. . . Pg.26 . . . Z4
Thaxton Ct. . . Pg.27 . . . X9
Thistle Hill Ct. . Pg.21 . . . V10
Thornapple Rd. Pg.20 . . . U6
Thornhill Ct. . . Pg.27 . . . W7
Thornwood Dr. Pg.20 . . . T7
Three Farms Ave.
 . . . . . . . . . . Pg.20 . . . U4
Thrush Ln. . . . Pg.21 . . . U7
Thunderbird Ln. Pg.14 . . . H5
Thurman Ave. Pg.21 . . . W9
Tiara Ct. . . . . . Pg.26 . . . Z5
Ticonderoga Ln. Pg.15 . . . R7
Tiffany Ct. . . . Pg.21 . . . X7
Tim Tam Cir. . . Pg.21 . . . U8
Timber Ln. . . . Pg.21 . . . U8
Timber Trail Ct. Pg.21 . . . V8
Timber Trail Dr. Pg.21 . . . V8
Timberlane Ct. Pg.21 . . . S8
Torrington Dr. . Pg.20 . . . V6
Towhee Ln. . . Pg.21 . . . U5
Town Dr. . . . . Pg.27 . . . W8
Townsend Cir. . Pg.21 . . . V8
Trails End Ct. . . Pg.21 . . . V8
Trappers Ct. . . Pg.26 . . . X7
Travelaire Ave. Pg.21 . . . W6
Treeline Ct. . . . Pg.21 . . . V8
Treesdale Ct. . Pg.26 . . . X2
Trefoil Ct. . . . . Pg.14 . . . R4
Trent Ave. . . . Pg.14 . . . R4
Treyburn Rd. . Pg.25 . . . W,X3
Trillium Ln. . . . Pg.21 . . . X9
Triton Ln. . . . . Pg.21 . . . U7
Tudor Dr. . . . . Pg.20 . . . U4
Tufton Ct. . . . . Pg.20 . . . W4
Tufts Ct. . . . . . Pg.21 . . . U8
Tulane Dr. . . . Pg.21 . . . V9
Tulip Ln. . . . . . Pg.20 . . . U6
Turnbridge Dr. . Pg.20,21 . U7
Turtle Cove Ct. Pg.27 . . . W8
Tussell St. . . . Pg.26 . . . Y12
Tuthill Rd. . . . Pg.15 . . . S8
Union Ct. . . . . Pg.13,19 . R3
University Dr. . Pg.21 . . . W9
University Ct. . . Pg.27 . . . W9
Ursuline Ave. . Pg.27 . . . W8
Vail Ct. . . . . . . Pg.20 . . . W6
Valley Dr. . . . . Pg.20 . . . S5
Valley Ridge Ct Pg.21 . . . W9
Valley View Ct. . Pg.14 . . . R4
Van Buren Ave. Pg.20 . . . S6
Vanderbilt Ct. . Pg.21 . . . V7
Vanilla Grass Dr. Pg.25 . . . Y2
Vassar Dr. . . . Pg.21 . . . V7
Venetian Ct. . . Pg.21 . . . V7
Ventura Ct. . . Pg.20 . . . T5
Verbena Ct. . . Pg.26 . . . X7
Vermilion Ct. . . Pg.21 . . . V7
Vermillion Ln. . Pg.21 . . . U8
Vermont Ct. . . Pg.20 . . . U6
Vernal Ln. . . . . Pg.20 . . . X6
Versailles Ave. . Pg.20 . . . U4
Vesper Ct. . . . Pg.20 . . . U4
Vest St. . . . . . Pg.15 . . . R8
Vicksburg Ct. . Pg.20 . . . U6
Victoria Ct. . . . Pg.21 . . . T7
Villa Ave. . . . . Pg.21 . . . U7
Village Green Rd.
 . . . . . . . . . . Pg.20 . . . T6
Villanova Dr. . . Pg.21 . . . V9
Vincent Ct. . . . Pg.21 . . . V7
Vineyard Ct. . . Pg.20 . . . W4
Violet Cir. . . . . Pg.20 . . . U4
Virginia Ct. . . . Pg.20 . . . U6
Wabash St. . . . Pg.21 . . . X8
Wait Rd. . . . . Pg.25 . . . Z3
Wakefield Ct. . Pg.21 . . . S8
Walcott Dr. . . . Pg.20 . . . V6
Walton Ct. . . . Pg.20 . . . U7
Warbler Dr. . . . Pg.21 . . . V7
Warm Springs Ct.
 . . . . . . . . . . Pg.26 . . . X4
Warrenville Rd. Pg.14,15 . Q7
Warwick Dr. . . Pg.21 . . . T7
Washington St. Pg.14,21

Wehrli Dr. . . . Pg.21 . . T7,W10
Wellesley Ct. . . Pg.26 . . . X4
Wellington Ct. . Pg.27 . . . W8
Wellner Rd. . . Pg.21 . . . T7
Welton Ct. . . . Pg.21 . . . V7
Wendover Dr. . Pg.21 . . . X7
Wenmouth Ct. . Pg.20 . . . X6
Wentworth Ct. . Pg.20 . . . X7
Werhli Rd. . . . Pg.21 . . . W10
Wesley Ave. . . Pg.26 . . . X7
West Branch Ct. Pg.21 . . . X7
West Ct. . . . . Pg.14 . . . S6
West St. . . . . Pg.14,20
 . . . . . . . . . . . . . . . . R,S,U6
Westbrook Dr. . Pg.20 . . . W7
Westbury Ct. . Pg.20 . . . W7
Westglen Dr. . Pg.21 . . . V6
Westminster Dr. Pg.14 . . . R4
Westmoreland Ct.
 . . . . . . . . . . Pg.21 . . . T9
Westmoreland Dr.
 . . . . . . . . . . Pg.21 . . . S9
Weston Ridge Dr.
 . . . . . . . . . . Pg.13 . . . S3
Wexford Ct. . . Pg.21 . . . X8
Wexford Ct. . . Pg.21 . . . U7
Wheatland Ct. . Pg.25 . . . X3
Whirlaway Ave. Pg.21 . . . U8
Whispering Hills Ct.
 . . . . . . . . . . Pg.20 . . . S5
Whispering Hills Dr.
 . . . . . . . . . . Pg.21 . . . U5
Whispering Hills Rd.
 . . . . . . . . . . Pg.20 . . . S5
White Eagle Dr. Pg.26 . . . X2
White Pines Ct. Pg.14 . . . R5
Whitebark Ct. . Pg.20 . . . U5
Whitechurch Ct. Pg.26 . . . W4
Whitechurch Ln. Pg.26 . . . W4
Whitehall Ln. . Pg.26 . . . W3
Whitehorn Ct. . Pg.20 . . . W3
Whitehorn Dr. . Pg.27 . . . V8
Whitethorn Ct. Pg.26 . . . W4
Whitewater Ln. Pg.20 . . . U5
Whitingham Ct. Pg.21 . . . T8
Whitley Rd. . . Pg.14 . . . R4
Wickfield Ct. . . Pg.15 . . . R7
Wickham Ct. . . Pg.21 . . . U9
Wild Cherry Rd. Pg.20 . . . T5
Wild Rose Ct. . Pg.21,27 . X10
Wilder Ct. . . . Pg.20 . . . U5
Wildflower Ct. . Pg.20 . . . U4
Wildflower Ct. . Pg.20 . . . U4
Willard Ct. . . . Pg.20 . . . U4
Willcrest Rd. . . Pg.20 . . . T5
William Penn Dr. Pg.20 . . . R6
Williamsburg Dr. Pg.20 . . U6
Williamstown Ct. Pg.26 . . W4
Willow Rd. . . . Pg.20 . . . T7
Willow Ridge Dr. Pg.26 . . . X6
Willoway Dr. . . Pg.20 . . . T6
Wilmington Ct. Pg.26 . . . X6
Wilshire Dr. . . . Pg.20 . . . T5
Wilson Ave. . . Pg.20 . . . S6
Winchester Ave. Pg.14 . . . R4
Windemere Ave. Pg.26 . . . X5
Windgate Ct. . . Pg.20 . . . U6
Windham Ln. . . Pg.15,21 . S7
Winding Creek Dr.
 . . . . . . . . . . Pg.21 . . . V7
Winding River Dr.
 . . . . . . . . . . Pg.25 . . . W3
Windridge Ct. . Pg.20 . . . U5
Windrush Ct. . . Pg.20 . . . S4
Windward Ct. . Pg.20 . . . S4
Windward St. . Pg.20 . . . S4
Winola Ct. . . . Pg.14 . . . W8
Winslow Ct. . . Pg.27 . . . W8
Winter Park Ct. Pg.20 . . . X6
Winter Park Dr. Pg.20 . . . X6
Wintergreen Ln. Pg.20 . . . U4
Wishing Well Ln. Pg.26 . . . X5
Wisteria Ct. . . . Pg.21 . . . X7
Wolf River Ct. . Pg.27 . . . X8
Wolfe Ct. . . . . Pg.21 . . . Y5
Woodbine Ct. . Pg.14 . . . R4
Woodchuck Ln. Pg.20 . . . S5
Woodcreek Dr. Pg.21 . . . V7
Woodfield Ct. . Pg.27 . . . W7
Woodlake Ct. . Pg.26 . . . X4
Woodland Dr. . Pg.20 . . . U5
Woodlawn Ave. Pg.21 . . . T8
Woodview Ln. . Pg.20 . . . W7
Woodview I n . . Pg.20 . . . W7
Woodwind Dr. Pg.25 . . . S3
Wooster Dr. . . Pg.21 . . . W9
Worthing Dr. . . Pg.21 . . . W7
Wright St. . . . Pg.15,21 . S,T7
Wydown Ct. . . Pg.20 . . . U4
Xavier Ct. . . . . Pg.21 . . . V10
Yackley Ave. . . Pg.21 . . . V7
Yale Ct. . . . . . Pg.21 . . . V9
Yellow Daisy Ct. Pg.13,19 . S3
Yellowstone Dr. Pg.20 . . . Q8
York Ct. . . . . . Pg.21 . . . T8
Yorkshire Dr. . . Pg.15 . . . R8
Yosemite Ave. Pg.15 . . . S8
Zaninger Ave. Pg.14 . . . R4
Zephyr Rd. . . Pg.25 . . . S3
Zinnia Ct. . . . Pg.20,21 . U7,8

87th St. . . . . . Pg.27 . . . W7
91st St. . . . . . Pg.27 . . . X9
95th St. . . . . . Pg.26 . . . Y6
104th St. . . . . Pg.26 . . . Z4,5

CEMETERIES
Cemetery . . . . Pg.20 . . . T6
St. Peter and Paul Cemetery
 . . . . . . . . . . Pg.21 . . . S7
Wheatland Cemetery
 . . . . . . . . . . Pg.25 . . . Z5

FOREST PRESERVES
Egermann Woods
 . . . . . . . . . . Pg.21 . . . U9
Fender Forest Preserve
 . . . . . . . . . . Pg.20 . . . W8
Goodrich Woods Forest Pres.
Konicek Grove Forest Preserve
 . . . . . . . . . . Pg.21 . . . X9
Spring Brook Prairie Preserve
 . . . . . . . . . . Pg.21 . . V,W4-6
Tameling Grove Forest Preserve
 . . . . . . . . . . Pg.21 . . . Y8

GOLF COURSES
Country Lakes G.C.
 . . . . . . . . . . Pg.13 . . . R2
Cress Creek C.C. Pg.14 . . . R6
Naperville C.C. Pg.21 . . . S8

PARKS
Arbor Way Pk. Pg.21 . . . W7
Ashbury Greenway Park
 . . . . . . . . . . Pg.25 . . . Y3
Ashbury Park Pg.25 . . . Y4
Bailey Hobson Woods Park
 . . . . . . . . . . Pg.21 . . . U8
Bethany Lutheran Pk
 . . . . . . . . . . Pg.20 . . . V7
Brighton Ridge Pk
 . . . . . . . . . . Pg.21 . . . V6
Brooks Prairie Park
 . . . . . . . . . . Pg.25 . . . Y3
Burlington Square Pk. Pg.20 . S6
Campus Green Pg.21 . . . T8
Cedar Glen Park Pg.26 . . . X6
Central Park . Pg.20 . . . S7
Columbia Commons
 . . . . . . . . . . Pg.21 . . . U8
Crestview Knoll Park
 . . . . . . . . . . Pg.20 . . . V7
DuPage River Sports Complex
 . . . . . . . . . . Pg.21 . . . X7
Fox Hill Park . Pg.20 . . . U6
Gartner Park . Pg.21 . . . U6
Hobson Ponds Pg.21 . . . U8
Hobson Woods Park
 . . . . . . . . . . Pg.21 . . . U9
Kings Park . . . Pg.21 . . . T8
Kingsley Prairie Park
 . . . . . . . . . . Pg.21 . . . X7
Knoch Knoll Greenway
 . . . . . . . . . . Pg.21 . . . X7
Knoch Park . . Pg.20 . . . U7
Knoch Knolls Park
 . . . . . . . . . . Pg.21 . . . X7
Lincoln Park . Pg.20 . . . T7
Little League Field
 . . . . . . . . . . Pg.21 . . . T6
Meadow Glen Park
 . . . . . . . . . . Pg.21 . . . V6
Miledji Square Park
 . . . . . . . . . . Pg.20 . . . S6
Mill Street Park Pg.14 . . . R7
Night Crawler Park
 . . . . . . . . . . Pg.21 . . . T6
Nike Park . . . Pg.15 . . . R7
Old Farm Park Pg.21 . . . W8
Old Saw Mill Pk. Pg.26 . . . W4
Olesen Farm Park
 . . . . . . . . . . Pg.21 . . . T8
Pembrooke Commons
 . . . . . . . . . . Pg.21 . . . U8
Pioneer Park . Pg.20 . . . T7
Ranchview Park Pg.21 . . . V10
River Run Park Pg.27 . . . Z5
Riverwoods Pk. Pg.27 . . . X8
Rock Ridge Park Pg.21 . . . X7
Rose Hill Farm Park
 . . . . . . . . . . Pg.26 . . . Y5
Sportsman Park Pg.20 . . . T6
Springbrook Crossing Pk.
 . . . . . . . . . . Pg.20 . . . X6
Springbrook Parkway
 . . . . . . . . . . Pg.20 . . . W6
Springfield Park Pg.21 . . . W7
Stanford Meadows
 . . . . . . . . . . Pg.21 . . . W9
West Branch Parkway
 . . . . . . . . . . Pg.21 . . . U8
West Glen Commons Park
 . . . . . . . . . . Pg.26 . . . U6
White Eagle Park
 . . . . . . . . . . Pg.25 . . . X3
Willow Park . Pg.20,21 . U7
Willowgate Square Park
 . . . . . . . . . . Pg.26 . . . W6
95th St. Pk. . Pg.26 . . . Y4

SCHOOLS
Arlene Welch Elem. Sch.
 . . . . . . . . . . Pg.20 . . . X4
Beebe Sch. . . Pg.14 . . . R7
Bethany Lutheran Sch.
 . . . . . . . . . . Pg.20 . . . V7
Brookdale Elem. Sch.
 . . . . . . . . . . Pg.21 . . . R4
Calvary Christian Sch.
 . . . . . . . . . . Pg.20 . . . T6
Clifford Crone Middle Sch.
 . . . . . . . . . . Pg.26 . . . X5
Clow Elem. Sch. Pg.26 . . . X4
DePaul University Naperville Campus . . . Pg.15 . . . Q7
Ellsworth Elem. Sch.
 . . . . . . . . . . Pg.20 . . . S7

Elmwood Elem. Sch.
 . . . . . . . . . . Pg.20 . . . U7
Evangelical Theological Seminary . . . Pg.20 . . . S7
Gordon Gregory Middle Sch.
 . . . . . . . . . . Pg.26 . . . X5
Highland Elem. Sch.
 . . . . . . . . . . Pg.20 . . . T7
Jefferson Jr. H.S.
 . . . . . . . . . . Pg.14,15 . R7
Kendall Elem. Sch.
 . . . . . . . . . . Pg.25 . . . Z3
Kingsley Elem. Sch.
 . . . . . . . . . . Pg.21 . . . X7
Lincoln Jr. H.S. Pg.21,27 . X7
Little Friends Sch.
 . . . . . . . . . . Pg.21 . . . S7
Madison Jr. H.S. Pg.21 . . . W4
Maplebrook Sch.
 . . . . . . . . . . Pg.21,27 . V8
Mary Lou Cowlishaw Elem. Sch.
 . . . . . . . . . . Pg.20 . . . U4
May Watts Elem. Sch.
 . . . . . . . . . . Pg.20 . . . U5
Meadow Glens Elem. Sch.
 . . . . . . . . . . Pg.21 . . . V9
Mill Street Elem. Sch.
 . . . . . . . . . . Pg.14 . . . R6
Naper Elementary
 . . . . . . . . . . Pg.20 . . . S6
Naperville Central H.S.
 . . . . . . . . . . Pg.20 . . . T6
Naperville North H.S.
 . . . . . . . . . . Pg.15 . . . R7
Neuqua Valley High Sch.
 . . . . . . . . . . Pg.26 . . . Y4
North Central College
 . . . . . . . . . . Pg.20 . . . S7
North Central College Sports Complex . . . Pg.20 . . . T7
Northwood University
 . . . . . . . . . . Pg.14 . . . Q7
Patterson Elem. Sch.
 . . . . . . . . . . Pg.26 . . . Z4
Peter Pan Early Learning Ctr.
 . . . . . . . . . . Pg.21 . . . T8
Prairie Sch. . . Pg.21 . . . T8
Ranch View Elem. Sch.
 . . . . . . . . . . Pg.21 . . . V10
River Woods Elem. Sch.
 . . . . . . . . . . Pg.27 . . . X8
Riverview Elem. Sch.
 . . . . . . . . . . Pg.21 . . . V10
Sch. Dist. 203 Admin. Office
 . . . . . . . . . . Pg.20 . . . T6
Scott Elem. Sch. Pg.21 . . . W8
Spring Brook Elem. Sch.
 . . . . . . . . . . Pg.20 . . . W5
St. Peter & Paul Sch.
 . . . . . . . . . . Pg.20 . . . S7
St. Raphael Sch. Pg.26 . . . X5
Thayer J. Hill Middle Sch.
 . . . . . . . . . . Pg.14 . . . R4
The Balkwill Sch.
 . . . . . . . . . . Pg.21 . . . T8
Washington Jr. H.S.
 . . . . . . . . . . Pg.20 . . . T7

SHOPPING CENTERS
Clock Tower Square S.C.
 . . . . . . . . . . Pg.20 . . . V5
Crest Creek Center
 . . . . . . . . . . Pg.20 . . . S6
Crest Creek Square S.C.
 . . . . . . . . . . Pg.14 . . . R6
Eagle Crest Plaza
 . . . . . . . . . . Pg.21 . . . V9
Fifth Ave. Sta. Shopping Center
 . . . . . . . . . . Pg.20 . . . U5
Fox River Commons
 . . . . . . . . . . Pg.20 . . . U5
Fox Run Sq. S.C.
 . . . . . . . . . . Pg.21 . . . U9
Heritage Square S.C.
 . . . . . . . . . . Pg.20 . . . T4
Hobson West Commons
 . . . . . . . . . . Pg.21 . . . T8
Iroquois S.C. . Pg.15 . . . R8
Jefferson Square S.C.
 . . . . . . . . . . Pg.20 . . . T6
Jewel Osco Center
 . . . . . . . . . . Pg.20,26 . T,W4
Manor S.C. . . Pg.20 . . . S5
Market Meadows S.C.
 . . . . . . . . . . Pg.20 . . . T3
Naper Meet S.C. Pg.19 . . . T3
Naperville Plaza Pg.20 . . . S7
Ogden Mall . . Pg.15 . . . R8
Old Kent Plaza Pg.20 . . . V7
Park Place S.C. Pg.20 . . . T4
Pebblewood East S.C.
 . . . . . . . . . . Pg.21 . . . T8
Pebblewood Plaza
 . . . . . . . . . . Pg.13 . . . T3
River North S.C. Pg.20 . . . T4
Shopping Centers
 . . . . . . . . . . Pg.15,19,20
 . . . . . . . . . . . . . . R8,U3,7
Stillwater Place S.C.
 . . . . . . . . . . Pg.26 . . . W4
Tower Crossing S.C.
 . . . . . . . . . . Pg.21 . . . T8
Town Square S.C.
 . . . . . . . . . . Pg.20 . . . S6
West Ridge S.C.
 . . . . . . . . . . Pg.21 . . . T3
Westridge Court S.C.
 . . . . . . . . . . Pg.14

MISCELLANEOUS
Amoco Research Center
 . . . . . . . . . . Pg.20 . . . T6
Burlington Northern Industrial Park . . . Pg.20 . . . U7
Carol Acres Commercial Park
 . . . . . . . . . . Pg.20 . . . S7
Center Point Business Park
 . . . . . . . . . . Pg.14 . . . Q7

# NAPERVILLE TOWNSHIP

Civic Center . . Pg.20 . . . T7
Commuter R.R. Sta.
 . . . . . . . . . . Pg.20 . . . S7
Diehl Office Campus
 . . . . . . . . . . Pg.15 . . . Q8
East West Tech. Center
 . . . . . . . . . . Pg.25 . . . Q3
Edward Hosp. Pg.20 . . . T6
F.D. #2 . . . . . Pg.21 . . . V8
Fire Dept. . . . Pg.21 . . . T8
Fire Dept. #5 . Pg.20 . . . W5
Fire Dept. #6 . Pg.25 . . . Z3
Frontier Sports Complex
 . . . . . . . . . . Pg.25 . . . Y3-4
High Grove Business Park
 . . . . . . . . . . Pg.20 . . . T4
Illinois Hospital Association
 . . . . . . . . . . Pg.15 . . . Q8
Illinois Prairie Path
 . . . . . . . . . . Pg.13 . . . Q3
Koroluk Commercial Center
 . . . . . . . . . . Pg.25 . . . Y3
Merner Field House
 . . . . . . . . . . Pg.20 . . . S7
Municipal Center Pg.20 . . . T7
Naperville Center for Commerce and Industry Pg.25 . . . Y2
Naperville Corporate Park
 . . . . . . . . . . Pg.15 . . . Q8
Naperville Office Park
 . . . . . . . . . . Pg.14 . . . Q7
Nichols Library Pg.20 . . . T7
Pfeiffer Hall . Pg.20 . . . T7
Prairie Point Business Park
 . . . . . . . . . . Pg.14 . . . Q7
River Run Commercial Park
 . . . . . . . . . . Pg.25 . . . Z5
Riverbrook Center
 . . . . . . . . . . Pg.20 . . . S7
Rose Hill Commercial Park
 . . . . . . . . . . Pg.26 . . . Z5
Scout Reservation
 . . . . . . . . . . Pg.26 . . . Z4
Weston Ridge Industrial Park
 . . . . . . . . . . Pg.25 . . . S3
Wheatland Crossing Commercial Center . . . Pg.20 . . . T6
Youth Center . Pg.20 . . . T6

## NAPERVILLE TOWNSHIP
Pages 13,14,19,20
STREETS
Aero Dr. . . . . Pg.19 . . . V3
Allister Ln. . . . Pg.19 . . . R3
Arbor Dr. . . . . Pg.20 . . . U2
Argyll Ln. . . . . Pg.19 . . . R2
Audrey Rd. . . Pg.19 . . . R2
Aurora Ave. . . Pg.19,20 . T2,4,6
Aurora Rd. N. Pg.19 . . . S3,6
Barclay Ave. . . Pg.19 . . . Q2,3
Bauer Rd. . . . Pg.14 . . . R3
Berry Ct. . . . . Pg.20 . . . Q1
Bilter Rd. . . . . Pg.19 . . . Q1
Bob-O-Link Ln. Pg.14 . . . R5
Bond St. . . . . Pg.14 . . . S4
Bonnie Ct. . . . Pg.19 . . . T4
Book Rd. . . . . Pg.20 . . . T4
Briar Ln. . . . . Pg.14,19 . R3
Byerum St. . . Pg.14 . . . R6
Campbell Dr. Pg.19 . . . R3
Capistrano Ct. Pg.19 . . . R3
Cermak Dr. . . Pg.14 . . . R4
Champagne Ct. Pg.15 . . . R9
Chandelle Dr. Pg.20 . . . W4
Claymore Ln. Pg.14 . . . R3
Clover Ct. . . . Pg.20 . . . T3
Collins Ct. . . . Pg.19 . . . S3
Country Club Blvd
 . . . . . . . . . . Pg.13 . . . R3
Country Glen Dr. Pg.19 . . . S2
Country Lakes Dr.
 . . . . . . . . . . Pg.13 . . . R3
Dearborn Ln. Pg.14 . . . R3
Diehl Rd. . . . . Pg.15 . . . Q2
Dockside Ct. . Pg.21 . . . Q2
Donelson Ct. . Pg.14 . . . R3
Doral Dr. . . . . Pg.19 . . . R3
East West Tollway
 . . . . . . . . . . Pg.14,19 . Q3
Eastwind Dr. Pg.14 . . . R3
Elderberry Cir. Pg.19 . . . R3
Eola Rd. . . . . Pg.19 . . . Q,T1
Ewing St. . . . Pg.14 . . . R6
Fairview Dr. . . Pg.14 . . . R3
Ferry Rd. . . . . Pg.14,19 . Q2,5
Firestone Dr. . Pg.19 . . . R3
Flamenco Ct. Pg.14,19 . R3
Forest Dr. . . . Pg.19 . . . U1
Fort Hill Dr. . . Pg.19 . . . R3
Frontenac Dr. Pg.19 . . . V2
Glenoban Dr. Pg.20 . . . W5
Golfview Dr. N. & S.
Gordon Terr. Pg.19 . . . R2
Granada Ct. . Pg.19 . . . R3
Green Acres Dr. Pg.20 . . . U6
Harmony Ct. . Pg.15 . . . R9
Hinterlong Ln. Pg.14 . . . R3
Huntington Ct. Pg.19 . . . S9
Innisbrook Dr. Pg.19 . . . R3
Joseph Ln. . . Pg.14 . . . R7
Kautz Rd. . . . Pg.19 . . . R3
Ketten Ct. . . . Pg.19 . . . R2
Kirk Pl. . . . . . Pg.19 . . . R3
Lakewood Cir. Pg.15 . . . R8
Lampwick Ct. Pg.19 . . . R3
Lancer Dr. . . . Pg.14 . . . R3
Landing Rd. . . Pg.21 . . . R3
Larkspur Ct. . Pg.15 . . . R3
Lawn Meadow Ln.
 . . . . . . . . . . Pg.19 . . . R3
Liberty St. . . . Pg.19 . . . T5
Martin Ave. . . Pg.20 . . . T5
McDowell Rd. Pg.14 . . . R4
McGregor Ln. Pg.19 . . . R3

Meadow Lark Ln.
 . . . . . . . . . . Pg.20 . . . V6
Meadow Rd. Pg.19 . . . Q3
Meadowsweet Ct.
 . . . . . . . . . . Pg.25 . . . S2
Medinah Dr. . Pg.13 . . . R3
Meridian Rd. Pg.19 . . . Q3
Mill St. . . . . . Pg.14 . . . R6
Molitor Rd. . . Pg.19 . . . R1
Montgomery Rd. Pg.20 . . V1,W3
Moultrie Ct. . . Pg.14 . . . S4
New York St. Pg.19 . . . T1
North Ln. . . . Pg.20 . . . T6
Oakmont Dr. Pg.19 . . . R3
Ogden Ave. . . Pg.20 . . . S5
Osler Dr. . . . . Pg.19 . . . R3
Oswego Rd. . . Pg.20 . . . T,U5
Park View Dr. Pg.25 . . . S2
Paxton Ct. . . . Pg.19 . . . R3
Pearson St. . . Pg.14 . . . R6
Pebble Beach Ct. Pg.19 . . . R3
Pebblewood Ct. Pg.13 . . . R3
Pebblewood Ln. Pg.19 . . . R3
Pebblewood Terr.
 . . . . . . . . . . Pg.13 . . . R3
Pilsen Ct. . . . Pg.14 . . . R4
Pinehurst Dr. Pg.13 . . . R3
Plainfield-Naperville Rd.
 . . . . . . . . . . Pg.20 . . . U6
Poss Rd. . . . . Pg.19 . . . S1
Powell Ct. . . . Pg.14 . . . R3
Prague Ct. . . . Pg.19 . . . R4
Queensgreen Ct. Pg.14 . . . R3
Reid Pl. . . . . . Pg.14 . . . S1
Rigi Rd. . . . . Pg.19 . . . Q3
River Bend Rd. Pg.21 . . . T6
River Rd. . . . . Pg.14 . . . R5
Riverfront Dr. Pg.21 . . . T6
Scots Dr. . . . . Pg.19 . . . R3
Sheffer Rd. . . Pg.19 . . . S3
Sheridan Cir. Pg.19 . . . S3
Shore Rd. . . . Pg.19 . . . R2
Shore Rd. . . . Pg.14 . . . R3
Skylane Dr. . . Pg.21 . . . W4
Soper Ct. . . . Pg.14 . . . R4
South Ln. . . . Pg.20 . . . U6
Spyglass Ct. . Pg.19 . . . R3
St. Andrews Ct. Pg.19 . . . R3
State Hwy. 59 Pg.14,19 . P,S3
Stearman Dr. Pg.19 . . . W4
Stewart Dr. . . Pg.19 . . . R2
Sugar Creek Ct. Pg.19 . . . R5
Sunrise Ave. . Pg.19 . . . R3
Surrey Ct. . . . Pg.19 . . . R3
Tartan Ln. . . . Pg.19 . . . R3
Technology Dr. Pg.14 . . . T5
Thorn Apple Rd. Pg.20 . . . T5
Timber Ln. . . . Pg.19 . . . R3
Valencia Ct. . . Pg.19 . . . R3
Vista Circle . . Pg.19 . . . R3
Webster St. . . Pg.14 . . . R7
West St. . . . . Pg.19 . . . R6
Weston Ridge Dr.
Westwind Dr. Pg.19 . . . S3
Whispering Winds Dr.
 . . . . . . . . . . Pg.19 . . . S2
Whistler Ct. . . Pg.19 . . . W3
Whitespire Ct. Pg.19 . . . V8
Wild Cherry Rd. Pg.19 . . . T6
Willoway Dr. Pg.20 . . . T6
Winberie Ave. Pg.25 . . . W3
Winberie Ct. . Pg.25 . . . W3
Woodwind Dr. Pg.19 . . . R2
4th St. . . . . . Pg.19 . . . S1
7th St. . . . . . Pg.19 . . . S3
13th Ave. S.W. (75th St.)
 . . . . . . . . . . Pg.20 . . . V6
47th St. . . . . Pg.19 . . . S6
48th St. . . . . Pg.14 . . . R6,7
49th St. . . . . Pg.14 . . . R6,7
75th St. . . . . Pg.19,20 . V3,4
79th St. . . . . Pg.20 . . . V6
80th St. . . . . Pg.20 . . . V6
81st St. . . . . Pg.20 . . . V6
82nd Ct. . . . . Pg.20 . . . W6
82nd St. . . . . Pg.20 . . . W6
83rd St. . . . . Pg.19,20 . W1-5
87th St. . . . . Pg.20 . . . W1,5

CEMETERIES
Naperville Cem. Pg.20 . . . T6

FOREST PRESERVES
McDowell Grove F.P.
 . . . . . . . . . . Pg.14 . . . R5

GOLF COURSES
Country Lakes G.C.
 . . . . . . . . . . Pg.19 . . . R3
Naperville Park District G.C.
 . . . . . . . . . . Pg.20 . . . W5

PARKS
Broeker Park . Pg.20 . . . T6
Burlington Square Pk.
 . . . . . . . . . . Pg.21 . . . S7
Colfax Park . . Pg.14 . . . R4
College Park . Pg.21 . . . T8
Columbia Estate Pk.
 . . . . . . . . . . Pg.21 . . . S8
Country Commons Park
 . . . . . . . . . . Pg.21 . . . S8
Country Lakes Park
 . . . . . . . . . . Pg.19 . . . R3
Fairway Comm. Park
 . . . . . . . . . . Pg.19 . . . S3
Huntington Commons Park
 . . . . . . . . . . Pg.19 . . . U9
Three Meadows Park
 . . . . . . . . . . Pg.21 . . . U9
West Greens Pk. Pg.20 . . . S6
Willow Bend West Park
 . . . . . . . . . . Pg.25 . . . R3

**SCHOOLS**
Indian Plains Sch. Pg.14 R3
Longwood Sch. Pg.19 R3
Waubonsie Sch. Pg.19 T1

**SHOPPING CENTERS**
Fox Valley S.C. Pg.19 U3
Ogden Mall Pg.15 R8

**MISCELLANEOUS**
Naper Aero Private Airfield Pg.19 V3

## OAK BROOK
Pages 12,17,18

**STREETS**
Abbywood Ct. Pg.12 L20
Acorn Hill Ln. Pg.18 P19
Adams St. Pg.18 P19
Arden Ct. Pg.17 M17
Ascot Ln. Pg.17 P16
Ashley Ct. Pg.18 P18
Avenue Lorie Pg.17 N16
Bath & Tennis Dr. Pg.18 N19
Baybrook Ct. Pg.17 N17
Baybrook Ln. Pg.17 N17
Bernwood Ln. Pg.17 N16
Berseem Ct. Pg.17 M17
Birchwood Rd. Pg.18 Q19
Bliss Dr. Pg.18 M20
Blue Grass Ct. Pg.17 P16
Bradford Ln. Pg.18 N20
Breckenridge Farm Pg.18 P19
Briarwood Ave. Pg.18 N18
Briarwood Central Pg.18 N18
Briarwood Cir. Pg.18 N18
Briarwood Ct. Pg.18 N18
Briarwood Dr. Pg.18 N18
Briarwood Ln. Pg.18 N18
Briarwood Loop Pg.18 N18
Briarwood N. Pg.18 N18
Briarwood Pass Pg.18 N18
Briarwood S. Pg.18 N18
Bridal Path Pg.17 P16
Bridge Way Ct. Pg.17 P17
Brighton Ln. Pg.18 N20
Brougham Ln. Pg.17 P16
Budd St. Pg.18 P19
Burr Oak Ct. Pg.18 M20
Cambridge Dr. Pg.17 N18
Camden Ct. Pg.17 M17
Camelot Dr. Pg.17 N17
Canterberry Ln. Pg.18 N20
Carlisle Dr. Pg.17 N18
Carriage Ct. Pg.17 P16
Cass Ct. Pg.17 P17
Castle Dr. Pg.18 M18
Cermak Rd. Pg.18 M20
Charleton Ln. Pg.17 N17
Chatham In. Pg.18 N20
Cheval Dr. Pg.18 Q19
Clearwater Dr. Pg.18 M19
Club Dr. Pg.12 L,M18
Cochise Ct. Pg.17 N16
Commerce Dr. Pg.18 M19
Concord Dr. Pg.17 N17
Coolidge St. Pg.18 N20
Court #1-20 Pg.17 P17
Crab Apple Pg.12 L19
Croydon Ln. Pg.18 M20
Deer Trail Ln. Pg.18 P18
Derby Ct. Pg.17 P16
Devonshire Dr. Pg.17 N17
Dover Dr. Pg.18 N20
East West Tollway Pg.17 M16,K20
Enterprise Dr. Pg.18 M19
Ernie Pyle Dr. Pg.18 L18
Ferndale Rd. Pg.18 P20
Forest Gate Cir. Pg.18 N18
Forest Gate Rd. Pg.18 N18
Forest Glen Ln. Pg.12,18 L,M20
Forest Mews Dr. Pg.17 P16
Forest Trail Pg.18 L19
Fox Ct. Pg.18 P19
Fox Trail Pg.18 P19
Foxianna Ct. Pg.17 N17
Frederick Dr. Pg.18 P19
Freeway Pg.18 M19
Gateway Ln. Pg.18 P20
Glendale Ave. Pg.18 P19
Glenoble Ct. Pg.12 L20
Golf Dr. Pg.18 N20
Grant St. Pg.18 N19
Green Leaf Dr. Pg.12 L19
Hambletonian Dr. Pg.17 P16
Hamilton Ln. Pg.18 N18
Hampton Dr. Pg.17 N17
Harger Rd. Pg.18 M19
Heather Ln. Pg.18 N18
Heritage Oaks Cir. Pg.17 P16
Heritage Oaks Ct. Pg.17 P16
Heritage Oaks Ln. Pg.17 P16
Hickory Dr. Pg.18 M20
Hunt Club Ln. Pg.18 N20
Hunter Dr. Pg.18 M19
Hunter Trail Pkwy. Pg.18 N19
Indian Trail Ct. Pg.18 N18
Indian Trail Rd. Pg.18 N,P18
Ivy Ln. Pg.17 N17
Jorie Blvd. Pg.18 M19
Kendall Ave. Pg.18 L19
Kenilworth Ave. Pg.18 M18
Kensington Ct. Pg.18 N18
Kensington Rd. Pg.18 N18
Kent Ave. Pg.18 L19
Kimberly Cir. Pg.17 N17
Kimberly Ln. Pg.17 N17
Kingsbury Ct. Pg.17 M17
Kingston Dr. Pg.17 M17
Knollwood Ct. Pg.12 L20
Kroc Dr. Pg.18 N19
La Salle Pg.18 L19
Lakewood Ct. Pg.12 L20
Lambeth Ct. Pg.18 N18
Lincoln Rd. Pg.18 N19
Livery Cir. Pg.17 P16
Livery Ct. Pg.17 P16
Lochinvar Ln. Pg.17 N16
Lorie Ave. Pg.17 N16
Luthin Rd. Pg.18 P20
Madison St. Pg.18 P19
Mallard Ln. Pg.18 P18
Marian Sq. Pg.17 N17
McDonald's Dr. Pg.18 M19
Meadowood Dr. Pg.18 L20
Menard Pg.12 L19
Merry Ln. Pg.18 M19
Meyers Rd. Pg.17 N16
Midwest Club Pkwy. Pg.17 P16
Midwest Rd. Pg.17 M17
Mockingbird Ln. Pg.17 N17
Mulberry Ln. Pg.17 P16
Natoma Ct. Pg.18 P19
Natoma Dr. Pg.18 P19
Niagra St. Pg.18 P19
Oak Brook Club Dr. Pg.18 M18
Oak Ct. Pg.18 P20
Oakbrook Dr. Pg.17 N16
Oakbrook Hills Dr. Pg.17 N16
Old Harger Rd. Pg.18 M19
Olympia Ct. Pg.17 N16
Ottawa Ln. Pg.18 P19
Palisades Dr. Pg.18 L20
Pembroke Ln. Pg.17 N17
Pheobus Ln. Pg.18 M19
Pine Hill Ln. Pg.18 Q19
Polo Ln. Pg.17 P16
Public Park Pg.17 M17
Radford Ln. Pg.18 L17
Red Fox Ln. Pg.18 M19
Red Stable Way Pg.17 P16
Regent Ct. Pg.17 N18
Regent Dr. Pg.17,18 N18
Ridge Ct. Pg.17 P16
Ridgewood Pg.12 L20
Ridgewood Ct. Pg.17 P16
Robert Kingery Hwy. Pg.18 N18
Robinhood Ranch Pg.18 P20
Ronald Ln. Pg.18 N19
Rose Ct. Pg.18 M18
Rose St. Pg.18 L,M18
Roslyn Rd. Pg.17 P16
Royal Glen Ct. Pg.12 L20
Royal Vale Dr. Pg.17 N16
Saddle Brook Dr. Pg.17 P16
Salt Cr. Cir. Pg.18 P19
Sauk Path Pg.18 P19
Sheffield Ln. Pg.18 N20
Shelburne Dr. Pg.17 M17
Spring Rd. Pg.18 N19
St. Francis Cir. Pg.17,18 N,P18
St. Johns Ct. Pg.17 N17
St. Josephs Dr. Pg.17 P17
St. Marks Ct. Pg.17 N17
St. Michaels Ct. Pg.17,18 P18
St. Paschal Dr. Pg.18 P18
Stable Brook Ct. Pg.17 P16
Stafford Ln. Pg.18 N20
Steeple Ridge Ct. Pg.17 P16
Steeplechase East Pg.18 M19
Steeplechase West Pg.18 M19
Suffolk Ln. Pg.17 P16
Surrey Dr. Pg.18 N18
Swaps Ct. Pg.17 N16
Swift Dr. Pg.18 M20
Tarten Lakes Cir. Pg.18 P18
Tarten Lakes Village Dr. Pg.18 P18
Thurlow St. Pg.18 P19
Timber Ct. Pg.12 L19
Timber Trail Dr. Pg.18 M19
Timber View Dr. Pg.12 L19
Timbers Edge Dr. Pg.12 L19
Tower Dr. Pg.17 M17
Trinity Ln. Pg.17 N17
Twin Oaks Dr. Pg.12 L19
Victoria Ct. Pg.17 M18
Walnut Ln. Pg.12 L19
Washington St. Pg.18 N,P20
Wennes Rd. Pg.18 P20
White Oak Ln. Pg.17 N16
Whitehall Dr. Pg.18 P18
Wildwood Ct. Pg.18 M20
Willow View Pg.12 L19
Windsor Dr. Pg.18 N20
Wood Ave. Pg.18 P19
Wood Glen Ln. Pg.12 L20
Woodland Dr. Pg.12 L19
Woodridge Dr. Pg.18 M20
Woodside Dr. Pg.12 L20
Woodview Ct. Pg.12 L20
Wyndham Ct. Pg.17 N16
York Lake Ct. Pg.18 P20
York Rd. Pg.18 M20
Yorkshire Dr. Pg.18 M19
Yorkshire Woods Pg.18 M19
15th St. Pg.18 L18
16th St. Pg.18 M18
22nd St. Pg.18 M19
31st St. Pg.18 N19
35th St. Pg.17,18 P16,18
38th St. Pg.17 P16

**CEMETERIES**
Bronswood Cem. Pg.18 P19
Cemetery Pg.18 P19

**FOREST PRESERVES**
Fullersburg Woods Forest Preserve Pg.18 P19
Grave Mill Woods Pg.18 P20
Mayslake Forest Preserve Pg.18 P18
York Woods Forest Preserve Pg.18 L19

**GOLF COURSES**
Butler National Golf Club Pg.18 N19
Butterfield C.C. Pg.17 N17
Executive Golf Course Pg.18 M20
Midwest Golf Club Pg.17 N17
Oak Brook Golf Course Pg.18 N20

**PARKS**
Central Park Pg.18 N18

**SCHOOLS**
Brook Forest Sch. Pg.18 N18
Butler Sch. Pg.18 N20
St. Joseph's Franciscan Seminary Pg.17 N17
St. Paschal Sch. Pg.18 P18

**SHOPPING CENTERS**
Oakbrook S.C. Pg.18 M18

**MISCELLANEOUS**
Grave Mill Historical Site Pg.18 P20
International Sports Core Pg.18 N19
Mayslake Retirement Village Pg.18 P18
Oak Brook Sports Core Pg.18 N19
Oak Brook Polo Club Pg.18 M19
Village Hall Pg.18 N19

## OAKBROOK TERRACE
Pages 11,12,17,18

**STREETS**
Buttercup Ln. Pg.17 M17
Butterfield Rd. Pg.17 M16
Cermak Rd. Pg.17 M17
Drury Ln. Pg.12 L18
Eisenhower Rd. Pg.17 M17
Elder Ln. Pg.17,18 M18
Elm Ct. Pg.18 M18
Elm Pl. Pg.17 M17
Halsey Rd. Pg.17 M17
Hodges Rd. Pg.18 M18
Karban Rd. Pg.17 M17
Kolberg Ct. Pg.12 L18
Leahy St. Pg.18 M18
Lincoln Ave. Pg.17 M16
MacArthur Dr. Pg.17 M17
Maple Pl. Pg.17 M17
Marshall Rd. Pg.17 M17
Michael Rd. Pg.17 M17
Monterey Ave. Pg.18 M18
Nimitz Rd. Pg.17 M17
Oakland Ave. Pg.18 M18
Orchard Pl. Pg.18 M18
Patton Ave. Pg.18 M18
Public Park Pg.17 M18
Renaissance Pg.17 M17
Stillwell Rd. Pg.17 M17
Summit Ave. Pg.11 L17
Terrace Blvd. Pg.17 M16
Trans Am Plaza Dr. Pg.17 M16
Wainwright St. Pg.18 M18
Washington Ave. Pg.17 M16
West End Rd. Pg.17 M17
16th St. Pg.17,18 M18
22nd St. Pg.17 M17

**CEMETERIES**
Chapel Hill Garden Cemetery Pg.11,17 L18

**PARKS**
Public Park Pg.18 M18

**SCHOOLS**
Stella Mae Swartz Sch. Pg.18 L18
Drury Lane Theater Pg.12 L18
Park Farms Amusement Park Pg.12 L18

## PALOS TOWNSHIP
(COOK COUNTY)

**MISCELLANEOUS**
Sante Fe Speedway Pg.24 X21
Park Dist. Admin. Offices Pg.28 Z12

## ROSELLE
Pages 3,4
(For additional listings, see Section 2)

**STREETS**
Acacia Ln. Pg.4 B12
Ambleside Dr. Pg.4 A12
Andover Dr. Pg.3 A9
Ardmore Ave. Pg.4 B12
Asbury Ln., E. & W. Pg.3 A9
Ash St. Pg.4 B12
Ashley Ct. Pg.3 B9
Autumn Dr. Pg.3 B10
Avalon Ct. Pg.3 A9
Avebury Ct. Pg.3 B10
Avebury Ln. Pg.3 B10
Banbury Terrace Pg.4 B12
Berkshire Terrace Pg.4 B11
Berwick Pl. Pg.3 B9
Birch Ct. Pg.4 B12
Birmingham Ct. Pg.3 A9
Blue Heron Ln. Pg.3 A9
Bluebird Ln. Pg.3 A9
Bokelman St. Pg.4 A11
Borden Ct. Pg.3 A10
Borden Dr. Pg.3 A10
Brandywine Dr. Pg.3 B10
Brendon Ct. Pg.3 A9
Brentwood Ct. Pg.3 B10
Briarwood Ln. Pg.3 B9
Brighton Bay Pg.3 B9
Bristol Ct. Pg.3 B9
Brittania Way Pg.3 A9
Brookside Dr. Pg.3 A10
Brookwood Terr. Pg.4 B11
Brower Dr. Pg.3 A10
Bryn Mawr Ave. Pg.4 B11
Butternut Ct. Pg.4 B11
Calaro Ct. Pg.4 B11
Cambrian Way Pg.3 A9
Canterbury Tr. Pg.4 A12
Cardinal Ln. Pg.3 A9
Carnoustie Ct. Pg.3 B9
Carriage Way Pg.3 B9
Case Dr. Pg.3 A10
Castlewood Ct. Pg.3 A9
Catalpa Ave. Pg.4 B12
Catalpa Ct. Pg.4 B12
Catino Ct. Pg.4 B11
Central Ave. Pg.4 A11
Century Dr. Pg.4 A12
Chancellor Dr. Pg.3 A10
Charlemagne Cir. Pg.4 B11
Chatfield Ct. Pg.3 A9
Chatham Pg.3 B9
Chatham Ct. Pg.3 A9
Chelsea Cove Pg.3 B9
Cherry Ct. Pg.4 A12
Cherry St. Pg.4 A12
Chevoit Ct. Pg.3 A9
Circle Dr. Pg.4 A12
Claria Dr. Pg.4 A11
Clearwater Pg.3 C10
Colony Ln. Pg.3 B9
Congress Cir. Pg.3 A10
Country Ln. Pg.3 B10
Countryside Dr. Pg.4 A11
Coventry Ct. Pg.3 A9
Crest Ave. Pg.4 A12
Crestwood Dr. Pg.4 B11
Cypress Ct. Pg.4 B11
Daisy Ln. Pg.3 B10
Dalton Ln. Pg.3 B10
Darby Ln. Pg.3 B9
Dee Ln. Pg.4 A12
Deeke Ct. Pg.3 B9
Devon Ave. Pg.4 A11
Dinah Rd. Pg.4 B12
Dorchester Ct. Pg.3 B9
Dover Ct. Pg.3 B9
Dover Dr. Pg.3 B9
Downing St. Pg.3 B9
Drummond Ct. Pg.3 B9
Edenwood Dr. Pg.3 B10
Elgin O'Hare Expwy. Pg.4 A11
Elm Ct. Pg.4 B12
Elm St. Pg.4 A11
Exeter Ct. Pg.3 A9
Fall Cir. Pg.3 C10
Falmouth Way Pg.3 B9
Flamingo Dr. Pg.3 A9
Fordham Pl. Pg.3 B10
Forest Ave. Pg.4 B11
Forum Dr. Pg.4 A12
Foxdale Ct. Pg.3 B9
Frontier Ln. Pg.4 A11
Garden Ave. Pg.3 B10
Glendale Rd. Pg.4 B12
Glendale Terr. Pg.4 C11
Gleneagle Ct. Pg.3 A9
Glenlake Ave. Pg.4 A11
Glenmore Pl. Pg.3 B10
Golfview Dr. Pg.4 A12
Granville Ave. Pg.4 A11,12
Greenwood Ct. Pg.4 B11
Hampshire Ct. Pg.3 A9
Hampton Ln. Pg.3 B9
Hamstead Ct. Pg.3 B9
Harvest Ln. Pg.3 C10
Harvest Pl. Pg.3 B10
Harvey Ave. Pg.4 B12
Hastings Ct. Pg.3 A9
Hattendorf Pg.4 A11
Hawthorne Ln. Pg.4 A12
Hazel Pg.4 B12
Hemlock Pg.3 B10
Heritage Dr. Pg.3 B10
High Ridge Rd. Pg.4 A12
Highpoint Ct. Pg.4 A12
Hillside Ct. Pg.4 B12
Hillside Dr. Pg.4 A11
Howard St. Pg.4 B11
Hudson Ct. Pg.3 B10
Hunter Dr. Pg.3 A10
Hygate Dr. Pg.3 A9
Irving Park Rd. Pg.4 A11
Isle Royal Bay Pg.4 A12
Kensington Ct. Pg.3 B9
Kingston Ct. Pg.3 B9
Kipling Ct. Pg.4 B12
Lake Point Dr. Pg.4 A12
Lake Shore Dr. Pg.4 A12
Lake St. Pg.3 B8
Lakeside Dr. Pg.4 A11
Lakeview Ct. Pg.4 A12
Lawrence Ave. Pg.4 A12
Leawood Dr. Pg.3 A10
Lexington Ave. Pg.4 B12
Lincoln St. Pg.4 A11
Locust Ln. Pg.4 B12
Longford Ct. Pg.3 B10
Longford Dr. Pg.3 A10
Main St. Pg.4 A11
Mansfield Ct. Pg.3 A9
Mansfield Way Pg.3 A9
Maple Ave. Pg.4 A11
Maple St. Pg.4 B11
Marion St. Pg.4 A11
Meade Ln. Pg.3 B10
Meadowlark Ct. Pg.3 A9
Mensching Rd. Pg.3 A9
Merriford Ln. Pg.3 A9
Merrimac Ct. Pg.3 B10
Middleton Dr. Pg.3 B9
Milford Ct. Pg.3 B10
Monaco Dr. Pg.3 A10
Morningside Ct. Pg.4 A12
Morningside Dr. Pg.4 A12
Muirfield Ct. Pg.3 A9
Mulford Ln. Pg.3 B9
Nairn Ct. Pg.3 A9
Nassau Dr. Pg.3 B10
Newcastle Ct. Pg.3 A10
Newcastle Dr. Pg.3 A10
Newport Pg.3 B10
Norfolk Ct. Pg.3 A9
Norman Ln. Pg.3 B9
Northampton Ln. Pg.3 B9
Oak St. Pg.4 C11
Old Farm Dr. Pg.3 C10
Olympia Ct. Pg.3 B9
Orchard Ct. Pg.4 B12
Orchard Terrace Pg.4 B11
Oxford Cir. Pg.3 B9
Oxford Pl. Pg.3 B9
Park Ln. Pg.4 A11,12
Park St. Pg.4 A,B11
Parkview Ct. Pg.4 A12
Pelican Bay Pg.3 A9
Pembrook Cir. Pg.3 B9
Pierce Ave. Pg.4 B12
Pine Ave. Pg.3 B10,11
Pinecroft Dr. Pg.4 B12
Pioneer Ct. Pg.3 B10
Plum Grove Rd. Pg.4 A12
Plumtree Ln. Pg.4 B12
Poplar Ave. Pg.4 A12
Portwine Rd. Pg.4 A12
Prescott Dr. Pg.3 B9
Presidential Dr. Pg.3 A10
Prospect St. Pg.4 B11
Quincy Ct. Pg.3 B10
Quincy Dr. Pg.3 B10
Radnor Dr. Pg.3 B10
Red Maple Ln. Pg.3 B10
Regal Ct. Pg.3 A9
Regency Ct. Pg.3 B9
Reston Ct. Pg.3 B10
Richmond Dr. Pg.3 A10
Ridge Ct. Pg.4 B12
Ridge Rd. Pg.4 B12
Ridgefield Dr. Pg.3 B10
Robin Ct. Pg.4 B11
Rodenburg Rd. Pg.3 A,B9
Romford Ct. Pg.3 B10
Rose Dr. Pg.4 A12
Rosebud Ct. Pg.3 B10
Rosedale Rd. Pg.4 B11
Roselle Rd. Pg.4 A11
Rosemont Ave. Pg.4 A11
Rosewood Dr. Pg.3 A10
Rosner Dr. Pg.4 A12
Royce Ln. Pg.3 B10
Rush St. Pg.4 B11
Ryan Way Pg.3 A9
Sally Ct. Pg.4 B11
Salt Creek Pg.4 A12
Scott Ct. Pg.4 B11
Sequoia Tr. Pg.4 A12
Shagbark Ave. Pg.3 B10
Shagbark Ct. Pg.3 B10
Sheffield Ct. Pg.3 A9
Sherwood Ct. Pg.3 A9
Siems Cir. Pg.4 B11
Singleton Dr. Pg.3 B9
Spring Ct. Pg.4 B11
Spring St. Pg.4 A12,B11
Springfield Ct. Pg.3 C10
Springfield Dr. Pg.3 B10
Springhill Dr. Pg.4 B12
Stafford Dr. Pg.3 B9
Stevenson Ct. Pg.4 A13
Stockport Ct. Pg.3 B9
Stonefield Pl. Pg.3 B10
Stonehurst Dr. Pg.3 B10
Stonehurst Ln. Pg.3 B10
Summerdale Ln. Pg.3 B10
Summerfield Ct. Pg.3 C10
Summerfield Dr. Pg.3 C10
Sunnyside Rd. Pg.4 B12
Sunrise Ln. Pg.3 C10
Sunrise Pl. Pg.3 C10
Sussex Ct. Pg.3 A9
Sycamore Pg.4 B12
Terry Ct. Pg.4 A12
Terry Dr. Pg.4 A12
Thames Terr. Pg.3 A9
Thorndale Ave. Pg.4 A11
Thornfield Ct. Pg.3 A9
Thornfield Ln. Pg.3 A9
Tiffany Ln. Pg.4 B11
Town Acres Ln. Pg.4 A11
Travis Pkwy. Pg.3 A9
Tuppeny Ct. Pg.3 A9
Turner Ave. Pg.4 B11
Ventura Club Dr. Pg.4 A12
Walnut Ct. Pg.4 B11
Walnut Oaks Dr. Pg.4 B11
Walnut St. Pg.4 B11
Walter Dr. Pg.4 A11
Wandsworth Cir. Pg.3 B9
Waterbury Ln. Pg.3 B9
Waterford Ct. Pg.3 B10
West End Rd. Pg.3 A10
Westminster Cir. Pg.3 B9
Whipporwill Ct. Pg.3 A9
White Oak Dr. Pg.4 B12
White Sands Bay Pg.4 A12
Wildwood Dr. Pg.3 B10
Willow St. Pg.4 B11
Windsor Dr. Pg.3 B10
Winfield Ct. Pg.3 A9
Winfield Way Pg.3 A9
Winterwood Ct. Pg.3 C10
Winterwood Dr. Pg.3 C10
Woodfield Tr. Pg.4 A12
Woodside Dr. Pg.3 B9
Woodworth Pl. Pg.4 B11
York Pg.4 B12
4th Ave. Pg.4 A11

**CEMETERIES**
Freinenigreit Cemetery Pg.4 A11

**PARKS**
Brookstone Park Pg.4 B11
Chatburg Park Pg.3 B9
Depot Park Pg.4 A11
Glenlake Park Pg.4 A11
Goose Lake Park Pg.3 B9
Gorski Park Pg.4 B12
Kemmering Park Pg.4 A12
Kennedy Park Pg.3 B9
Lions Park Pg.4 A12
Marion Park Pg.4 A11
Newcastle Green Park Pg.3 A10
Oldum Park Pg.3 A9
Pine Park Pg.4 B11
Post Office Park Pg.4 A11
Springhill Park Pg.4 B12
Thorndale Park Pg.4 A11
Turner Park Pg.4 A11

**SCHOOLS**
Lake Park H.S. East Pg.4 B13
Lake Park H.S. West Pg.3 B10
Lincoln Sch. Pg.4 A11
Marklund Learning Ctr. Pg.4 A11
Medinah Middle Sch. Pg.4 A12
Medinah South School Pg.4 B12
Roselle Middle Sch. Pg.4 B11
Springhill Sch. Pg.4 B12
St. Walter Catholic Sch. Pg.4 A,B11
Trinity Lutheran Sch. Pg.4 B11
Waterbury Elem. Sch. Pg.3 B9

**MISCELLANEOUS**
Claus Farm Recreation Area Pg.3 B10
Fire Department Pg.4 A11
Metra Comm. Parking Lot Pg.4 B13
Post Office Pg.4 A11
Railroad Station Pg.4 A12
Village Hall Pg.4 A11
Wastewater Treatment Plant Pg.4 B11

## VILLA PARK
Pages 11,12

**STREETS**
Adams St. Pg.11 K17
Addison Ave. Pg.11 H16
Adele Ave. Pg.11 G16
Adele Ct. Pg.11 G17
Ardmore Ave. Pg.11 H17
Armitage Rd. Pg.11 G17
Astor Ct. Pg.11 J17
Beach St. Pg.11 H17
Belden Ave. Pg.11 G17
Beverly Ave. Pg.11 H17
Biermann Ave. Pg.11 H16
Blackstone Pl. Pg.11 L17
Brandywine Pg.11 L17
Calduto Cir. Pg.12 K18
Central Blvd. Pg.11 J16
Charles Ave. Pg.11 J17
Charles Ct. Pg.11 H16
Chatham Ave. Pg.11 G17
Congress St. Pg.11 K17
Coolidge St. Pg.11 K18
Cornell Ave. Pg.11 J,K17
Cornell Pkwy. Pg.11 K17
Cornell St. Pg.11 J17
Crescent Dr. Pg.11 J17
Cross St. Pg.11 K17
Division St. Pg.11 H16
Douglas Ave. Pg.11 H17
Edward St. Pg.11 L16
Elizabeth St. Pg.11 H18
Ellsworth Ave. Pg.11 G17
Elm Park Ave. Pg.11 H18
Elm St. Pg.11 J16-17
Euclid Ave. Pg.11 J,L17
Evergreen Dr. Pg.11 K17
Fairfield Ave. Pg.12 J18
Fay Ave. Pg.11 G17
Frank St. Pg.11 K17
Frontage Ct. Pg.11 L18
Frontage Rd. Pg.12 K18
Fulton Ave. Pg.11 G17
Gerard Ave. Pg.11 H17
Grant Ave. Pg.11 K17
Great Western Blvd. Pg.11 J17
Green Briar Rd. Pg.11 G18
Hamilton Pg.11 H17
Harding St. Pg.11 K18
Harrison St. Pg.11 L17
Harvard Ave. Pg.11 H17
High Ridge Rd. Pg.11 L16
Highland Ave. Pg.11 J17,18
Hill St. Pg.11 H17
Holly Ct. Pg.11 J16
Home Ave. Pg.12 J17
Hugo Ct. Pg.11 H16
Illinois Ave. Pg.11 H,J17
Iowa Ave. Pg.11 G,H16
Jackson St. Pg.11 K17
James St. Pg.11 H16
Julia Dr. Pg.11 K,L17
Kenilworth Ave. Pg.11 J16,17
Kolberg Ct. Pg.11 L17
Lane Dr. Pg.12 K18
Leslie Ln. Pg.11 K17
Lincoln Ave. Pg.11 H16
Madison St. Pg.11 K18
Main St. Pg.11 J17
Manor Ln. Pg.11 H17
Maple St. Pg.11 H17
Merle St. Pg.11 H16
Michigan Ave. Pg.11 G,K16
Mission Ave. Pg.11 H16
Monroe St. Pg.11 K17
Monterey Ave. Pg.12 K18
Morningside Dr. Pg.11 K17
Myrtle Pg.11 J,K17
New St. Pg.11 J17
North Ave. Pg.11 H18
Oak Ct. Pg.11 J17
Oak St. Pg.11 J17
Oakland Ave. Pg.11 K17
Orchard Hill Ct. Pg.11 L17
Park Blvd. Pg.11 J17
Peony Pl. Pg.11 J17
Pick Ave. Pg.11 J17
Pine St. Pg.11 H17
Plymouth St. Pg.11 H16
Princeton Ave. Pg.11 G,K17
Railroad Ave. Pg.11 H17
Rand Rd. Pg.11 K17
Ridge Rd. Pg.11 H16,17
Riordan Rd. Pg.11 L17
Riverside Ct. Pg.12 J18
Riverside Dr. Pg.12 J,K18
Riverview Pg.11 H18
Robert Kingery Hwy. Pg.11 K18
Rose St. Pg.11 L17
Roy Dr. Pg.11 H16
Schiller St. Pg.11 H17
School St. Pg.11 J16
Sidney Ave. Pg.11 G17
Sidney Ct. Pg.11 G17
St. Charles Rd. Pg.11 J17
Stone Ave. Pg.11 H16
Stone Rd. Pg.11 H16
Summit Ave. Pg.11 J17
Sunset Dr. Pg.11 H16-17
Terrace Ave. Pg.11 H16
Terrace St. Pg.11 H16,17
Terry Ln. Pg.11 K17
Third Ave. Pg.11 H16
Thomas Pg.11 H18
Van Buren St. Pg.12 K17
Vermont St. Pg.11 H16
Villa Park Ave. Pg.11 H17
Washington Blvd. Pg.11 K17
Wayside Dr. Pg.12 L18
West Ave. Pg.11 K18
Westmore Ave. Pg.11 H,J16
Wildwood St. Pg.11 J17
Willow Crest Dr. Pg.11 K17
Wilson St. Pg.11 K18
Wisconsin Ave. Pg.11 G,L16
Woodlane Path Pg.11 G18
Woodrow St. Pg.11 J,K16
Yale Ave. Pg.11 G,K17
1st N. Pg.12 K18
1st St., W. Pg.11 H16
2nd Ave. Pg.11 H,J16
2nd St. Pg.11 H16
3rd Ave. Pg.11 J16
3rd St. Pg.11 H16
3rd St.Ct. Pg.11 H17

**FOREST PRESERVES**
York/High Ridge F.P. Pg.11 L17

**GOLF COURSES**
Sugar Creek G.C. Pg.12 K18

**PARKS**
Willow Brook Park K17

**SCHOOLS**
Albright Middle Sch. Pg.11 K17
Ardmore Sch. Pg.11 J17
Franklin Sch. Pg.11 J16
High Ridge Sch. Pg.11 K16
Iowa Sch. Pg.11 H16
Jackson Jr. H.S. Pg.11 H16
Jefferson Jr. High Pg.11 H16
Lincoln Sch. Pg.11 H17
Madison Sch. Pg.11 K16
North Sch. Pg.11 H17
Salt Creek Sch. Pg.11 K18
St. Alexander's Sch. Pg.11 J17
St. John The Apostle Sch. Pg.11 H16
Washington Sch. Pg.11 J18
Willow Brook H.S. Pg.11 L17

**SHOPPING CENTERS**
North Park Mall Pg.11 G16

## VILLA PARK

### MISCELLANEOUS
Iowa Comm. Center Pg.11 H17
Odeum Sports & Expo Center Pg.11 G17
Village Hall Pg.11 J17

## WARRENVILLE
Pages 13,14

### STREETS
Albert Einstein Dr. Pg.14 N4
Albright St. Pg.14 P4,5
Ambassador Ct. Pg.14 P10
Amber Ln. Pg.14 P4
Angeline Ct. Pg.14 N3
Arbury Ct. Pg.13 M3
Arlington Ct. Pg.13 M3
Arthur Compton Ln. Pg.14 N4
Ascot Ct. Pg.14 P10
Ascot Ln. Pg.14 M4
Attleboro Ct. Pg.14 N3
Aurora Way Pg.14 P4
Avon Ct. Pg.13 M3
Avon Dr. Pg.13 M3
Avondale Ct. Pg.14 N3
Barclay Ct. Pg.14 P10
Barkley Ave. Pg.14 P3
Batavia-Warrenville Rd. Pg.14 N4
Bayview Ct. Pg.14 N4
Bedford Ln. Pg.13 M3
Behrs Circle Dr. Pg.14 P5
Bella Vista Pkwy. Pg.14 Q6
Birchwood Dr. Pg.14 P4
Blackthorn Ln. Pg.14 P4
Branch Ave. Pg.13 M3
Branch Dr. Pg.13 M3,4
Briarwood Dr. Pg.14 P4
Briggs Ave. Pg.14 P3
Brighton Ct. Pg.13 M3
Bristol Ln. Pg.14 M4
Brookside Ct. Pg.14 P3
Buckthorn Ct. Pg.14 N3
Bulger Ct. Pg.14 Q6
Burr Ave. Pg.14 P5
Butterfield Rd. Pg.14 P4
Butternut Ln. Pg.14 N4
Butternut Sq. Pg.14 N3
Calumet Ave. Pg.14 P3
Candlewood Ln. Pg.14 P4
Carpenter Ct. Pg.14 P5
Cedar Ct. Pg.13 M3
Central Ave. Pg.14 P6
Cerny Rd. Pg.14 N4
Chase Ct. Pg.14 P6
Cherice Dr. Pg.14 N3
Chestnut Ct. Pg.14 N3
Christopher Ct. Pg.14 N4
Circle Dr. Pg.14 P5
Commons Rd. Pg.14 R6
Concord Ct. Pg.14 N3
Connector Ct. Pg.14 Q6
Continental Dr. Pg.13 M3
Cottonwood Ct. Pg.14 N3
Country Ridge Dr. Pg.14 N4
Crabtree Ln. Pg.14 P4
Curtis Ave. Pg.14 P5
Cynthia Dr. Pg.14 N3
Danbury Dr. Pg.14 N3
David Dr. Pg.14 N3
Dedham Ct. Pg.13 M3
Deerfield Ln. Pg.14 M4
Denise Dr. Pg.14 N4
Diehl Rd. Pg.14 Q5,6
Dogwood Ct. Pg.14 N3
Dorchester Ct. Pg.13 M3
Edgebrook Dr. Pg.14 P10
Elizabeth Ave. Pg.14 P6
Elmwood Ct. Pg.13 M3
Emerald Green Dr. Pg.14 N4
Enrico Fermi Dr. Pg.14 N4
Essex Ln. Pg.13 M3
Estes St. Pg.14 P3
Everett Ct. Pg.14 M4
Fairfax Ct. Pg.13 M3
Ferry Rd. Pg.14 Q5
Forest St. Pg.14 L6
Forestview Ave. Pg.14 Q5
Forestview Dr. Pg.14 M4
Fourth St. Pg.14 P5
Fowler Cir. Pg.14 P6
Foxboro Ct. Pg.13 M3
Galbreath Dr. Pg.14 P4
Galusha Ave. Pg.14 P6
Gates Pl. Pg.14 P5
Glen Dr. Pg.14 N,P4
Glenhurst Ct. Pg.14 N3
Greenbriar Ln. Pg.14 P4
Greenbrook Ct. Pg.13 M3
Greenview Ave. Pg.14 P6
Grove Ln. Pg.14 N4
Hampton Ct. Pg.14 N3
Hampton Dr. Pg.14 N3
Hampton Ln. Pg.14 N4
Harvest Ct. Pg.14 P3
Hawthorne Ln. Pg.14 N4
Haylett Ave. Pg.14 P6
Heather Ct. Pg.14 N3
Herrick Rd. Pg.14 P6
Holyoke Ct. Pg.13 M3
Home Ave. Pg.14 P4
Huntington Dr. Pg.13 M3
Hurlingham Ct. Pg.14 N3
Iroquois Ct. N., S. & W. Pg.14 N4
Ivy Ct. Pg.14 N11
Jackson St. Pg.14 P5
Jefferson St. Pg.14 P6
John Bardeen Dr. Pg.14 N4
Joliet Rd. Pg.14 N4
Juniper Ct. Pg.13 M3
Kensington Dr. Pg.13 M3
Kline Cir. Pg.14 P5
Lakeview Ct. Pg.14 P4
Lakeview Dr. Pg.14 P3
Landon Dr. Pg.14 P4
Laurel Ct. Pg.14 M4
Leominster Ct. Pg.13 M3
Lexington Ct. Pg.13 M3
Lindenwood Ct. Pg.14 N3
Lindenwood Dr. Pg.14 N3
Lindenwood Sq. Pg.14 N3
Lorraine Ave. Pg.14 Q6
Lynn Ct. Pg.13 M3
Mack Rd. Pg.13 M3,4
Main St. Pg.14 P5
Manchester Ln. Pg.13 M3
Manning Ave. Pg.14 P5
Maple Ct. Pg.14 N3
Maplewood Ct. Pg.14 N3
Maplewood Dr. Pg.14 N3
Marie Curie Ln. Pg.14 N4
Mayfair Ct. Pg.14 M4
McCormick Ln. Pg.14 P6
Meadow Ave. Pg.14 N4
Melcher Ave. Pg.14 P6
Mignin Dr. Pg.14 P4
Mill St. Pg.14 R6
Millard Cir. Pg.14 P5
Mount St. Pg.14 P5
Mulberry Ct. Pg.14 N3
Needham Ct. Pg.14 Q6
Oakwood Ct. Pg.14 N3
Oxford Dr. Pg.13 M3
Parkview Ave. Pg.14 P6
Patterman Rd. Pg.14 N,P4
Paul Pl. Pg.14 N4
Pedham Ct. Pg.13 M3
Penny Ln. Pg.13 M3
Pierre Curie Ln. Pg.14 N4
Plum Ct. Pg.13 M3
Point Oak Dr. Pg.14 P4
Prairie Pg.14 P4
Princeton Ct. Pg.14 L3
Ray St. Pg.14 P5
Redwood Ct. Pg.13 M3
Renout Dr. Pg.14 N4
Ridge Dr. Pg.14 N4
Ridgewood Ct. Pg.14 N3
Ridgewood Dr. Pg.14 P6
River Alley Pg.14 P5
River Oaks Dr. Pg.14 N4
River Rd. Pg.14 P5
Riverside Ave. Pg.14 N4
Riverside Pkwy. Pg.14 N4
Riverview Dr. Pg.14 P5
Rockwell St. Pg.14 P5
Rogers Ave. Pg.14 P5
Roxbury Ct. Pg.14 M4
Salem Ct. Pg.13 M3
Sanchez Pg.14 N3
Second St. Pg.14 P5
Seraph Homes Ct. Pg.14 N4
Shaw Dr. Pg.14 N3
Small Trees Ct. Pg.14 N3
Sova Ln. Pg.14 N3
Spruce Ct. Pg.13 M3
Stafford Pl. Pg.14 P5
Steadman St. Pg.14 P5
Stevens Ct. Pg.14 N4
Sunset Ct. Pg.14 N3
Sunset Dr. Pg.14 N3
Talbot Ave. Pg.14 P3
Tanglewood Ln. Pg.14 P4
Thornwood Ln. Pg.14 P4
Timber Dr. Pg.14 P4
Tinker Ave. Pg.14 P6
Torch Pkwy. Pg.14 Q5
Townline Rd. Pg.14 P4
Tracy Pl. Pg.14 P5
Twin Pines Dr. Pg.14 P4
Village Green Blvd. Pg.14 P6
Virginia Ave. Pg.14 P6
Wagner Ct. Pg.14 P5
Wagner Dr. Pg.14 P5
Waltham Ct. Pg.14 M4
Warren Ave. Pg.14 P5
Warren St. Pg.14 P5
Warrenville Rd. Pg.14 Q7
Waverly Ave. Pg.14 N4
Weaver Pkwy. Pg.14 Q6
Webster St. Pg.14 P4
Wembly Dr. Pg.14 N3
West Ave. Pg.14 P6
Westbury Cir. Pg.14 N4
White Oak Dr. Pg.14 P4
Whitehall Ct. Pg.14 N3
Wilbur Ave. Pg.14 Q6
Wildwood Ct. Pg.14 N3
Williams Ct. Pg.14 P4
Williams Rd. Pg.14 P4
Willow Ct. Pg.14 M4
Willow Ln. Pg.13 M3
Winchester Cir. Pg.14 N4
Winfield Dr. Pg.14 P6
Winwood Walk Pg.14 N4
Woodland Ave. Pg.14 Q5
Woodlawn Pg.14 P5
Youghall St. Pg.14 P3

### CEMETERIES
Warrenville Cemetery Pg.14 P5

### FOREST PRESERVES
Illinois Prairie Path Pg.14 N5
Warrenville Grove Pg.14 P5

### GOLF COURSES
Family Golf Center and Driving Range Pg.14 Q5

### PARKS
Cerny Park Pg.14 Q5
Sesqui Park Pg.14 N3
Summerlakes Park Pg.14 N3

### SCHOOLS
Holmes Sch. Pg.14 P5
Johnson Sch. Pg.14 N3
Montessori Sch. Pg.14 P3
Woodland Sch. Pg.14 Q5
Cantera Business Park Pg.14 Q5
Warrenville Cenacle Retreat & Confernece Ctr. Pg.14 N5
Woodland Sch. Dist. Day Care Ctr. Pg.14 Q5

## WAYNE
Page 1
(For additional listings, see Section 4)

### STREETS
Army Trail Rd. D1
Ashley Ln. B1
Behles Rd. C1
Berkshire Ct. E3
Billy Burns Rd. C1
Bradford Pkwy. E3
Brewster Creek Cir. B1
Cedar Ln. D1
Chambellan Ave. C1
Courcival Ln. C1
Dean Ct. E3
Derby Rd. D1
Dunham Cir. C1
Dunham Ct. C1
Dunham Rd. C1
Dunham Trail Rd. C1
Elm St. D2
Grove Place Ln. D2
Guild Ln. D1
Heritage Ct. D3
Honey Hill Cir., N. D1
Honey Hill Cir., S. E1
Honey Hill Dr. D1
Kaelin Rd. D3
Keil St. D1
Kingswood Ct. E3
Lake Eleanor Ct. E2
Lake Eleanor Dr. E2
Lamplight Trail B1
Lysle Rd. D3
Mare Barn Rd. C1
Messina Ct. D2
Munger Rd. E3
Nancy Ln. D2
Oak Lawn Farm Rd. C1
Orchard Ln. D2
Percheron Ln. D2
Peterson Dr. D2
Powis Rd. C1
Pratt Rd. C1
Railroad St. D1
Ridge Ln. D3
Rochefort Ln. C1
Russell Rd. D2
School St. D1
Serinne Ln. C1
Shagbark Ln. F11
Smith Rd. E2
Somerset Ct. E3
Surrey Rd. C1
Warwick Way E3
Will Way D1
Wilshire Ct. E3
Woodland Ct. E2
Woodland Dr. C1
Woodland Trail S. E2
Woodland Trail W. E2

### FOREST PRESERVES
Pratts Wayne Forest Preserve C2

### SCHOOLS
Wayne Sch. D1

### MISCELLANEOUS
Dunham Woods Riding Club E1
Illinois Prairie Path C1
Wayne Village Historic Preservation District D1

## WAYNE TOWNSHIP
Pages 1,2,7,8

### STREETS
Ancient Oaks Dr. Pg.8 G5
Anderson Rd. Pg.2 F5
Arbor Ln. Pg.1 F3
Army Trail Rd. Pg.1,2 D2,4,7
Ashburn Ln. Pg.2 D4
Augusta Dr. Pg.1 E3
Avard Rd. Pg.1 E3
Barnes Ave. Pg.7 K3
Bartlett Rd. Pg.2 B,C5
Barton Pl. Pg.8 G7
Beech Ct. Pg.2 F4
Berkshire Ln. Pg.8 G7
Brentwood Ct. Pg.2 C4
Burnside Cir. Pg.2 B5
Byron Ave. Pg.2 E4
Cambridge Dr. Pg.2 E4
Canterbury Dr. Pg.2 E5
Cape Ave. Pg.8 F4,5
Carriage Way Dr. Pg.2 C4
Chatham Ct. Pg.2 E5
Churchill Ct. Pg.8 F6
Country Club Ln. Pg.2 D4
County Farm Rd. Pg.8 G7
Crest Ct. Pg.8 F6
Cul' de Sac Pg.8 G4
Curahoag Ave. Pg.8 F4
Cuyahoga Terrace Pg.2 D4
Dell Rd. Pg.8 G4
Devon Ave. Pg.2 A6
Diversey Ave. Pg.2,8 F5
Diversey Pkwy. Pg.1,7 F3
Doral Dr. Pg.2 E4
Eaton Way Pg.2 D4
Elm Ct. Pg.1 F3
Elm Rd. Pg.1 F1
Elm St. Pg.2 A7
Ennis Ln. Pg.9 L8
Ethel St. Pg.8 G7
Ewell Ct. Pg.2 B5
Fair Oaks Rd. Pg.2,8 F,G5
Florence Ct. Pg.8 G5
Garden Dr. Pg.2 C4
Gerber Rd. Pg.2 F6
Glen Rd. Pg.8 G4
Granger Rd. Pg.2 C4
Gresham Cir. Pg.9 L8
Grosvenor Cir. Pg.9 L8
Hawthorne Ln. Pg.7 H2
Heritage Ln. Pg.2 D7
Hickory Knoll Ln. Pg.2 F4
Hill Ct. Pg.2 E5
Holly Ct. Pg.8 F6
Indian Knoll Rd. Pg.8 G5
Ingalton Rd. Pg.1,2 B4,E3
Jefferson St. Pg.8 C,G7
Jenlor Ct. Pg.1 E2
Judith Ln. Pg.8 E6
Kaelin Rd. Pg.1 D,E3
Kammes Dr. Pg.8 G7
Kautz Rd. Pg.7 H1
Keil St. Pg.7 F1
Kenwood Ave. Pg.1,8 E3,F5
Klein Rd. Pg.2,8 E4,G5
Lake Eleanor Ct. Pg.1 E2
Lake Eleanor Dr. Pg.1 E2
Lakeview Ct. Pg.1,8 F3,F6
Lakeview Dr. Pg.8 F4
Lakewood Dr. Pg.8 F4
Liberty St. Pg.2 A7
Lies Rd. Pg.1,2 E3,6
Lincoln Dr. Pg.2 B5
Locust Ave. Pg.1 E3
Lysle Rd. Pg.1 D3
Maple Ct. Pg.1 F3
Mardon Rd. Pg.8 G7
Martingale Dr. Pg.2 D4
Mead Rd. Pg.1 F3
Meade Ct. Pg.2 B5
Meadowlark Dr. Pg.2 C4
Medford Dr. Pg.8 G7
Mercury Ct. Pg.2 C4
Morningside Ave. Pg.8 G5
Morningside Dr. Pg.2 C4
Morton Rd. Pg.8 G6
Mulberry Dr. Pg.1 F3
Munger Rd. Pg.1 C3
Norris Ave. Pg.1 E3
North Ave. Pg.7 F2
Oak Creek Ct. Pg.8 G6
Oak Creek Dr. Pg.8 G6
Oak Knoll Rd. Pg.2 F4
Oak Ln. Pg.8 F4
Oak Rd. Pg.1 F1
Oak St. Pg.2 A7
Old St. Charles Rd. Pg.8 G4
Old Wayne Ct. Pg.8 F5
Ontarioville Rd. Pg.2 A7
Orchard Ln. Pg.2 D4
Pepper Ct. Pg.2 E5
Petersdorf Rd. Pg.2 D4
Pine Ct. Pg.2 F6
Powis Rd. Pg.1 C1,G2
Prairie Ln. Pg.1 E2
Prospect Ave. Pg.2 B5
Roque Rd. Pg.7 G2
Ridge Ln. Pg.1 D3
Ridgeview St. Pg.8 F6
Riviera Ct. Pg.2 E5
Sayer Rd. Pg.1 B3
Schick Rd. Pg.2 D5
Scott Ct. Pg.2 B5
Shady Ln. Pg.1 E3
Shagbark Dr. Pg.2 F4
Smith Rd. Pg.1 E1,2
Spicer Rd. Pg.1 E3
Springvale Rd. Pg.8 F6
St. Andrews Ln. Pg.2 E4
St. Andrews Trace Pg.2 E4
St. Charles Rd. Pg.8 G5,7
St. James Way Pg.2 E4
St. Mark Way Pg.2 D4
St. Thomas Way Pg.2 E4
Stearns Rd. Pg.1 B1,5
Sunnydale Dr. Pg.2 C4
Sunset Ridge Dr. Pg.2 C4
Sutton Rd. Pg.1 D3
Sycamore St. Pg.8 F6
Timber Ln. Pg.8 F6
Timberline Dr. Pg.8 F4
Trieste Ln. Pg.8 F,G5
Trinity Ln. Pg.2 E4
Turnmill Ln. Pg.2 E4
Vale Rd. Pg.8 G7
Valewood Rd. Pg.8 G4
Waterford Ln. Pg.2 E4
Wayne Oaks Ln. Pg.8 G5
Waynewood Dr. Pg.8 G4
Wescot Ln. Pg.2 E4
Whitney Rd. Pg.1 E3
Wiant Rd. Pg.1 E3
Wildflower Ln. Pg.2 F4
Woodcreek Ln., N. & S. Pg.8 F6
Woodcrest Dr. Pg.8 G4
Woodland Ave. Pg.1,7 G3
Woodland Ct. Pg.1 E2
Woodland Tr., S. & W. Pg.1 E2
Woods Ct. Pg.1,2 D4
Woodview Dr. Pg.8 F6
Wynn Ave. Pg.2,8 F4
Yale Rd. Pg.8 G4

### AIRPORT
DuPage County Airport Pg.7 G1

### CEMETERIES
Manor Cemetery Pg.8 G6
Wayne Cemetery Pg.2 D4

### FOREST PRESERVES
Hawk Hollow F.P. Pg.2 C6
Illinois Prairie Path Pg.1 D2
Pratts Wayne Woods Pg.1 B1
West Branch F.P. Pg.2 E5

### GOLF COURSES
Old Wayne G.C. Pg.2,8 F5
St. Andrews G.C. Pg.1,2,8 F4

### PARKS
Morton Park Pg.8 G6

### SCHOOLS
Benjamin Sch. Pg.8 G6
Dist. 25 Administration Bldg. Pg.8 G6
Wheaton Christian H.S. Pg.8 G5
Commercial Equestrian Club Pg.1 E2

## WEST CHICAGO
Pages 7,8

### STREETS
Acorn Hill Ln. Pg.7 G3
Adelia Ln. Pg.1 E1
Ainsley Dr. Pg.8 G4
Allen Ave. Pg.8 J4
Amber Ct. Pg.8 G4
Ann St. Pg.7 J3
Applegate Ave. Pg.7 H3
Appletree Ln. Pg.8 L5
Arapaho Dr. Pg.7 F3
Arbor Ave. Pg.8 H4
Arthur Dr. Pg.7 G2
Aster Ln. Pg.8 G4
Atlantic Dr. Pg.7 G3
Augusta Ave. Pg.8 K4
Aurora St. Pg.7 J3
Avard Ave. Pg.7 J3
Bainbridge Blvd. Pg.1 E1
Barber Ave. Pg.8 J4
Barnes Ave. Pg.7 K3
Barnhart St. Pg.1 E1
Bayberry Ct. Pg.7 H3
Bell Rd. Pg.8 G4
Bellview Ave. Pg.8 H4
Bishop St. Pg.8 K4
Blackhawk Dr. Pg.7 G2
Blair St. Pg.7 J3
Blakely St. Pg.8 J,K4
Bobwhite Ln. Pg.8 G4
Brentwood Ct. Pg.7 K3
Brentwood Dr. Pg.7 K3
Brookwood Ct. Pg.8 L4
Brown St. Pg.8 K4
Bunting Ct. Pg.8 G4
Camden Dr. Pg.1 E1
Canterbury Ct. Pg.8 L4
Carolina Dr. Pg.7 G3
Carriage Ave. Pg.8 K4
Carriage Dr. Pg.8 L4
Center Pg.8 J4
Charles Ct. Pg.7 J2
Charlestowne Dr. Pg.8 H4
Cherokee Dr. Pg.7 F3
Cherry Blossom Ct. Pg.7 H3
Cherrywood Ln. Pg.8 G4
Chicago Pg.8 J4
Chickadee Ct. Pg.8 F5
Church St. Pg.7 J3
Clara St. Pg.7 J3
Claremont Ave. Pg.8 H4
Clayton St. Pg.8 J4
Colford Ave. Pg.8 J4
Columbine Ln. Pg.8 G4
Commerce Dr. Pg.7 K2
Conde St. Pg.8 J5
Coolidge Ave. Pg.8 J5
Crab Apple Ct. Pg.8 H4
Cranesbill Dr. Pg.8 G4
Crestview Ln. Pg.7 G3
Crossing Rd. Pg.8 H5
Crown Ct. Pg.7 F2
Cul de Sac Pg.8 G4
Dale Ave. Pg.8 K4
Dayton Ave. Pg.8 K4
Dayton St. Pg.8 K4
Downs Dr. Pg.7 J2
Dunham Dr. Pg.8 H5
East St. Pg.7 K3
Easton Ave. Pg.8 J4
Elgin Pg.7 J3
Elite Ave. Pg.8 H4
Elizabeth St. Pg.8 K4
Elliot Ave. Pg.7 J3
Elmwood Ave. Pg.8 H4
Elmwood St. Pg.7 K2
Fabyan Pkwy. Pg.7 K1
Factory St. Pg.7 K3
Fairbank Ct. Pg.7 J3
Fairchild Ln. Pg.1 E1
Fairview Ave. Pg.8 J4
Fenton Ln. Pg.7 J2
Fieldcrest Dr. Pg.8 H5
Flaming Oaks Ct. Pg.8 J5
Forest Ave. Pg.8 K,J4
Foxfield Dr. Pg.1 E1
Fremont St. Pg.8 H4
Fulton St. Pg.8 J4
Galena Pg.8 J4
Garden St. Pg.8 K4
Gates St. Pg.8 K4
Gavin Ct. Pg.7 G3
Geneva St. Pg.8 J4
George St. Pg.7 J3
Glen Ave. Pg.8 K4
Glen Rd. Pg.8 G4
Grand Lake Blvd. Pg.8 H4
Green Meadow Ct. Pg.7 G3
Grove Ave. Pg.8 H4
Hampton Course Pg.8 H4
Handorf St. Pg.8 G4
Harrison St. Pg.7 J3
Harvester Rd. Pg.7 G2
Hawthorne Ln. Pg.7 H2
Hazel St. Pg.8 K4
Helena Dr. Pg.7 J2
High Ridge Dr. Pg.8 H4
High St. Pg.8 J4
Highgate Ct. Pg.8 H4
Highland Ave. Pg.8 H,J4
Hill Ct. Pg.8 G4
Hillview Ave. Pg.8 J4
Hillview Ct. Pg.8 J4
Honeysuckle Ave. Pg.8 H4
Howard Dr. Pg.7 G1
Indianwood Dr. Pg.7 F3
Industrial Dr. Pg.7 H2
Ingalton Ave. Pg.8 G4
Ingalton Ct. Pg.8 G4
Ingalton Rd. Pg.7 F3
Ingalton St. Pg.8 J4
International Dr. Pg.7 G1
Jacob Pg.8 G4
Jenice Ct. Pg.8 J5
Joliet St. Pg.8 K4
Kenwood Ave. Pg.7 K3
Kings Cir. Pg.7 G3,4
Kings Ct. Pg.7 G3,4
Knollwood Ln. Pg.8 G4
Kress Rd. Pg.7 J1
Lake Blvd. Pg.8 H4
Lake Side Dr. Pg.8 G4
Lawrence Pg.8 J4
Lehman Dr. Pg.1 E1
Lester St. Pg.7 K3
Lincoln Ave. Pg.7 K3
Lindsay Ct. Pg.1 E1
Long Oak Dr. Pg.7 H3
Longest Dr. Pg.7 J1
Lorlyn Dr. Pg.8 L4
Lyman Ave. Pg.7 K3
Main St. Pg.8 J4
Mansfield Ct. Pg.7 G3
Marcella Ln. Pg.7 G3
Marshview Ct. Pg.8 G4
McChesney Rd. Pg.7 K1
McConnell Ave. Pg.8 J4
Meadow Ridge Dr. Pg.8 H4
Meadowlark Dr. Pg.8 F5
Meadowview Crossing Pg.8 G5
Meadowview Dr. Pg.8 G4
Mellington Ave. Pg.7 J2
Milo Ct. Pg.7 J3
Mulberry Dr. Pg.7 F3
Nagel Ct. Pg.8 G4
Natalie Dr. Pg.7 G3
National St. Pg.8 H4
Neltnor Blvd. Pg.8 K4
Nickolson Ave. Pg.8 J5
Nor-Oaks Ct. Pg.8 H4
Norris St. Pg.7 J3
North Rd. Pg.7 F2
Northwest Ave. Pg.7 G2
Nuclear Dr. Pg.7 G2
Oak Ave. Pg.8 J4
Oak St. Pg.8 K4
Oakwood Ave. Pg.8 J4
Orchard Ct. Pg.8 L5
Parker Ave. Pg.8 J4
Parkside Ave. Pg.7 K3
Partridge Dr. Pg.8 F4
Peachtree Ln. Pg.7 H3,4
Pear St. Pg.7 J3
Pearl St. Pg.7 J3
Persimmon Dr. Pg.8 H4
Pilsen Rd. Pg.7 H3
Pine St. Pg.8 J4
Plumtree Ln. Pg.8 H4
Plymouth Ct. Pg.8 J4
Pomeroy St. Pg.8 J4
Powis Ct. Pg.7 F2
Powis Rd. Pg.7 G2
Prairie Crossing Dr. Pg.8 G4
Prairie Ln. Pg.8 G4
Prince Crossing Rd. Pg.8 H4
Ray Ave. Pg.7 H3
Ridgewood Ct. Pg.8 H4
Ridgewood Dr. Pg.8 H4
Roosevelt Rd. Pg.7 K2
Rosewood Dr. Pg.8 G5
Sandpiper Tr. Pg.8 G4
Sarana Ave. Pg.8 K4
Seanor Ave. Pg.8 H4
Sherman St. Pg.7 K3
Somerset Dr. Pg.8 G4
Sophia St. Pg.8 J4
Spencer St. Pg.8 J4
Springcress Ct. Pg.8 G4
Springcress Ln. Pg.8 G4
St. Andrews Ct. Pg.7 F3
St. Charles Rd. Pg.8 G5
Sterling Pg.8 J4
Stimmel St. Pg.7 J3
Sudbury Ct. Pg.7 G3
Summit Ave. Pg.8 J4
Sycamore Ave. Pg.8 K4
Tanager Ln. Pg.8 G4
Thomas Dr. Pg.7 G3
Town Rd. Pg.7 K3
Trillium Tr. Pg.8 G4
Turner Ave. Pg.8 H4
Turner Ct. Pg.8 H4
Tye Ct. Pg.8 J4
Valewood Rd. Pg.8 G4
Vine St. Pg.7 J3
Washington St. Pg.8 J4
Waynewood Dr. Pg.8 G4
Wegner Dr. Pg.7 J2
Wendal St. Pg.8 H4
Western Dr. Pg.7 H1,2
Weyrauch St. Pg.7 K3
Whispering Oaks Ct. Pg.8 L4
Wild Ginger Tr. Pg.8 G4
Wildwood Ln. Pg.8 G4
Williams Rd. Pg.8 H4
Willow Creek Pg.7 G3
Wilson Ave. Pg.8 J4
Windsor Ct. Pg.8 L4
Winston Dr. Pg.7 H3
Winston St. Pg.7 G3
Wood St. Pg.7 K3
Woodboro Dr. Pg.8 J5
Woodcrest Dr. Pg.8 G4
Woodland Ave. Pg.7 G3
Woodland Ct. Pg.8 J5
Woodside Ct. Pg.7 G3
Woodside Dr. Pg.7 H3
Yale Dr. Pg.8 G4
Yale St. Pg.8 G,H4
York Ave. Pg.8 J4

### CEMETERIES
Calvary Cemetery Pg.8 J4
Glen Oak Cemetery Pg.7 H3

### FOREST PRESERVES
West Chicago Prairie Pg.7 H2,3
Pheasant Run Golf Course Pg.7 F1
Pheasant Run Resort and Convention Center Pg.7 F1

### PARKS
Reed Park Pg.7 H3

### SCHOOLS
Carrie Roundy Kindergarten Pg.7 J3
Christ the King Seminary Pg.7 F3
Gary Sch. Pg.8 K4
Junior High Sch. Pg.8 K4
Lincoln Sch. Pg.7 J3
McAuley Sch. Pg.7 J1
Pioneer Sch. Pg.7 K3
St. Marys Sch. Pg.8 J4
Trinity Lutheran Sch. Pg.7 J3
Turner Sch. Pg.8 H4
West Chicago Community H.S. Pg.7 J3

### MISCELLANEOUS
City Hall Pg.8 J4

## WESTCHESTER
COOK COUNTY
Page 18

### STREETS
Burton Cir. N21
Burton Ct. N21
Constitution Dr. N21
Summerdale St. N21

### SHOPPING CENTERS
Westchester Commons S.C. N21

### MISCELLANEOUS
West Manor Nursing Home N21

## WESTMONT
Pages 17,18,23

### STREETS
Adams St. Pg.17,23 S17
Ainslie Ct. Pg.23 T17
Ainslie Dr. Pg.23 T17
Alpine Pg.23 T17
Antler Ct. Pg.23 S16
Antler Ln. Pg.23 S16
Apple Grove Ln. Pg.23 T17
Arbor Ln. Pg.23 T16
Arlington Ave. Pg.17 P18
Ashford Ln. Pg.23 T17
Ashley Ct. Pg.23 S17
Aspen Pg.23 T16
Baltimore Ave. Pg.18 Q18
Barry Ln. Pg.23 S17
Bay Ct. Pg.23 T16
Beechwood Ct. Pg.23 T16
Beechwood Dr. Pg.23 T16
Beninford Ln. Pg.23 T17
Blackhawk Dr. Pg.17 Q17
Boundary Dr. Pg.17 P17
Brookside Dr. Pg.23 T16
Buck Ct. Pg.23 S16
Burlington Ave. Pg.17 R16,17
Burr Oak Dr. Pg.17 Q17
Buttonwood Dr. Pg.23 T16
Carlisle Ave. Pg.23 T17
Carlisle Ct. Pg.23 S16
Carriage Ln. Pg.23 T16
Cass Ave. Pg.17,23 Q,T17
Cass Ln. W. Pg.23 T16
Champlaine Ave. Pg.18 Q18
Champlaine Ct. Pg.18 Q18
Chappel Hill Ct. Pg.23 S17
Chestnut Ave. Pg.17 P17
Chicago Ave. Pg.17 R16
Citadel Cir. Pg.18 Q18
Citadel Dr. Pg.18 Q18
Cove Ln. Pg.23 T16
Crabtree Dr. Pg.23 T17
Creekwood Ct. Pg.23 T16
Cromwell Ct. Pg.23 S16
Cumnor Rd. Pg.23 S16
Dallas St. Pg.17 R16

## WESTMONT

Deer Creek Ln. . Pg.23 . . . S16
Deming Pl. . . Pg.23 . . . S17
Des Moines St. Pg.17 . . . S17
Doe Circle . . . Pg.23 . . . S16
Echo . . . Pg.23 . . . T17
Elmwood Ct. . Pg.23 . . . T16
Executive Ct. . Pg.18 . . . P18
Fairfield Ct. . . Pg.23 . . . S17
Fairway Ln. . . Pg.23 . . . T16
Falcon Pl. . . Pg.23 . . . T16
Fernwood Ct. . Pg.23 . . . T16
Fernwood Dr. . Pg.23 . . . T16
Florence Ave. . Pg.23 . . . T16
Fordham Way . Pg.23 . . . T16
Fountain Head Dr.
. . . . . Pg.23 . . . S17
Franklin St. . . Pg.17 . . . Q17
Garrett St. . . Pg.23 . . . T17
Gate . . . Pg.17 . . . S17
Grant St. . . Pg.17 . . . S17
Grayson St. . . Pg.17 . . . S17
Hamilton Ave. . Pg.18 . . . Q18
Hamilton Ct. . Pg.18 . . . Q18
Hampton Ave. . Pg.23 . . . T17
Harvest . . . Pg.23 . . . T17
Heath Ct. . . Pg.23 . . . S17
Heath Ln. . . Pg.23 . . . S17
Heath Pl. . . Pg.23 . . . S17
Honeywood Dr. Pg.23 . . . T16
Hudson St. . . Pg.17,23 . S16
Independence Ave.
. . . . . Pg.18 . . . Q18
Indian Trail Ln. . Pg.17 . . . P17
Irving . . . Pg.23 . . . T17
Ivy Ct. . . . Pg.23 . . . T16
James Dr. . . Pg.23 . S16,17
Jamestown Ave. Pg.17 . . . P17
Jordan Ct. . . Pg.23 . . . T16
King Arthur Ct. Pg.23 . . . S17
Lafayette Ln. . Pg.17 . . . Q17
Lake Dr. . . . Pg.23 . . . T16
Lake Shore . . Pg.23 . . . S16
Laurel Ct. . . Pg.23 . . . S17
Lincoln St. . . Pg.17 . . . S17
Linden Ave. . . Pg.17 . R,S17
Lindley Rd. . . Pg.23 . . . S16
Longford Dr. . Pg.23 . . . T17
Maple . . . Pg.23 . . . T16
Maple Ave. . . Pg.17 . . . Q17
Megan Ct. . . Pg.23 . . . S17
Melrose Ave. . Pg.17 . . . Q17
Memory Ct. . . Pg.23 . . . T16
Monfore Ave. . Pg.23 . . . T16
Monticello Ave. Pg.18 . . . Q18
Morning Glory Cir.
. . . . . Pg.17 . . . Q16
Naperville Rd. . Pg.17 . . . R16
Nelson Ln. . . Pg.18 . . . Q18
Newport . . . Pg.23 . . . S17
Noel Ct. . . . Pg.23 . . . S17
Norfolk St. . . Pg.17 . . . R17
Oak Ave. . . . Pg.17 . . . R17
Oakhill Ln. . . Pg.18 . . . P18
Oakley Ct. . . Pg.17 . . . P17
Oakley Dr. . . Pg.17 . . . P17
Oakley Ln. . . Pg.17 . . . P17
Oakmont Dr. . Pg.18 . . . P18
Oakmont Ln. . Pg.18 . . . P18
Oakmont Plaza Dr.
. . . . . Pg.18 . . . P18
Oakwood Ct. . Pg.17,18
Oakwood Dr. . Pg.17,18
. . . . . P17,O18
Ogden Ave. . . Pg.17 . . . Q17
Oliver Ct. . . . Pg.17 . . . Q17
Orchard . . . Pg.17 . . . T17
Orleans Pl. . . Pg.17 . . . Q17
Park . . . Pg.23 . . . T17
Park St. . . . Pg.17,23 R,S16
Parkway Dr. . Pg.23 . . . T17
Pasquinelli Dr. . Pg.18 . . . Q18
Peachtree Ln. . Pg.23 . . . T17
Pear Tree Ln. . Pg.23 . . . T17
Philadelphia . . Pg.17 . . . Q17
Pier Dr. . . . Pg.23 . . . T16
Pier Dr. W. . . Pg.23 . . . T16
Plaza Dr. . . . Pg.17 . . . Q17
Plum . . . Pg.17 . . . P17
Prairie Dr. . . Pg.17 . . . P17
Quail Ridge Dr. Pg.18 . . . P18
Quebec Pl. . . Pg.17,18
. . . . . Q17,18
Quincy Ave. . . Pg.17 . . . R16
Quincy St. . . Pg.17 . . . R17
Raintree Ct. . . Pg.23 . . . S16
Raintree Ln. . . Pg.23 . . . S16
Revere Ave. . . Pg.18 . . . Q18
Revere Ct. . . Pg.18 . . . Q18
Richmond Ave. Pg.17 . . . Q17
Richmond St. . Pg.17 . . . R17
Robinson Ln. . Pg.23 . . . S16
Rosewood Ct. . Pg.17 . . . Q17
Roslyn Rd. . . Pg.17 . . . R16
Rumsey Pl. . . Pg.23 . . . S17
Ryan Ct. . . . Pg.23 . . . S17
Schramm St. . Pg.23 . . . S17
Schramm Dr. . Pg.23 . . . S17
Shannon Lake Ct.
. . . . . Pg.23 . . . S17
Sherburne Dr. . Pg.18 . . . N17
Spicewood Ct. Pg.23 . . . S16
Spruce Ln. . . Pg.23 . . . T16
Stonegate Rd. . Pg.18 . . . Q18
Suffield Ct. . . Pg.23 . . . T17
Tartan Lakes Cir. Pg.18 . . . P18
Tartan Lakes Ln. Pg.18 . . . P18
Tartan Lakes Way
. . . . . Pg.18 . . . P18
Timber Ridge Ct. Pg.23 . . S17
Tower Ln. . . . Pg.17 . . . S17
Tracey Ct. . . . Pg.23 . . . T16
Traube Ave. . . Pg.17 . Q16,17
Tudor . . . Pg.23 . . . T16
Vail . . . Pg.23 . . . T16
Vandustrial St. . Pg.18 . . . Q18
Virginia Dr. . . Pg.23 . . . T16
Warwick Ave. . Pg.17 . . Q,S17

Washington Point
. . . . . Pg.17 . . . Q17
Washington St. Pg.17,23 . S17
Wesley Ct. . . Pg.17 . . . T16
Wesley Ln. . . Pg.23 . . . T16
West End Ave. . Pg.17 . . . R16
Westmont Dr. . Pg.17,18 . S18
Wexford Dr. . . Pg.17 . . . Q17
Whipple Ln. . . Pg.23 . . . T16
White Birch Ln. Pg.17 . . . P17
Willard Pl. . . Pg.17 . . . Q16
Williams St. . . Pg.17 . . . S17
Williamsburg St. Pg.17 . . . P17
Willow Oak Dr. Pg.17 . . . Q17
Willow Way . . Pg.23 . . . T17
Wilmette Ave. . Pg.17,23 Q,S17
39th St. . . . Pg.17 . . . T17
55th Pl. . . . Pg.23 . . . S17
55th St. . . . Pg.17,23 . S17
56th Pl. . . . Pg.23 . . . S17
56th St. . . . Pg.23 . . . S17
57th St. . . . Pg.23 . . . S17
58th St. . . . Pg.23 . . . S17
59th St. . . . Pg.23 . . . S17
60th St. . . . Pg.23 . . . T16
63rd St. . . . Pg.23 . . . T16
64th St. . . . Pg.23 . . . T16
65th St. . . . Pg.23 . . . T16
66th St. . . . Pg.23 . . . T16
68th St. . . . Pg.23 . . . T17

### CEMETERIES
Clarendon Hills Cemetery
. . . . . Pg.23 . . . U16

### GOLF COURSES
Easy Aces G.C. Pg.23 . . . S17
Green Meadows Park G.C.
. . . . . Pg.23 . . . T16
Oakbrook Hills Golf Course
. . . . . Pg.17 . . . P17
Twin Lakes G.C. Pg.23 . . . S16

### PARKS
Bellerive Park . Pg.23 . . . T16
Blackhawk Park Pg.17 . . . P17
Community Park North
. . . . . Pg.17 . . . Q17
Deer Creek Pk. Pg.23 . . . S17
Kiwanis Park . Pg.17 . . . Q16
Lebeck Park . . Pg.17 . . . Q17
Lions Park . . Pg.17 . . . Q17
Memorial Park . Pg.17 . . . Q17
Mertz Mem. Park
. . . . . Pg.23 . . . T16
Muddy Waters Pk.
. . . . . Pg.23 . . . S16
Oakwood Park . Pg.18 . . . P18
Rotary Pk. . . Pg.17 . . . S17
Sentinal Park . Pg.17 . . . Q16
Werley Park . . Pg.17 . . . Q17
Williams Cove Pk.
. . . . . Pg.23 . . . T16

### SCHOOLS
Bethel Lutheran Sch.
. . . . . Pg.17 . . . R17
C.E. Miller Sch. Pg.17 . . . R17
Central Sch. . . Pg.17 . . . S17
Downers Grove Montessori Sch.
. . . . . Pg.17 . . . R17
Holy Trinity Sch. Pg.17 . . . R17
J.T. Manning Elem. Sch.
. . . . . Pg.23 . . . S17
Maercker Sch. . Pg.23 . . . S17
Oakwood H.S. . Pg.17 . . . P18
Precious Commodities
. . . . . Pg.17 . . . Q17
Southside Sch. Pg.17 . . . R17
Westmont H.S. Pg.17 . . . T18
Westmont Jr. H.S.
. . . . . Pg.17 . . . P17
Westview Hills Middle Sch.
. . . . . Pg.17 . . . P17

### SHOPPING CENTERS
Oak Court S.C. Pg.18 . . . Q18
Shopping Centers
. . . . . Pg.17,23 Q,T17

### MISCELLANEOUS
County Health Dept.
. . . . . Pg.17 . . . Q17
Fire Dept. . . . Pg.17 . Q,R17
Library . . . Pg.17 . . . Q16
Oakbrook Hills Resort
. . . . . Pg.17 . . . P17
Police Dept. . . Pg.17 . . . S17
Post Office . . Pg.17 . . . S17
Village Hall . . Pg.17 . . . R17

## WHEATLAND TOWNSHIP
(WILL COUNTY)
Page 25,26
### STREETS
Ainsdale Ct. . . Pg.25 . . . Z3
Alago Rd. . . . Pg.26 . . . W5
Alice Ln. . . . Pg.26 . . . W5
Alma Ln. . . . Pg.26 . . . W5
Andermann Dr. Pg.26 . . . Z4
Ascot Ct. . . . Pg.25 . . . Z3
Birkdale Dr. . . Pg.25 . . . Z2
Blvd. de John . Pg.25 . . . Y3,4
Bode St. . . . Pg.25 . . . Z1
Book Rd. . . . Pg.26 . . W,Z4
Brancaster Dr. Pg.26 . . . Z4
Brenner Pl. . . Pg.25 . . . Z4
Bridle Path Ct. Pg.26 . . . Z4
Burnham Ct. . Pg.25 . . . Z2
Callander Ct. . Pg.26 . . . Z4
Carl Dr. . . . Pg.25 . . X,Y1
Clow Creek Rd. Pg.26 . . . W5
Club Dr. . . . Pg.25 . . . X3
Countryview Dr. Pg.26 . . . W5
Curtis Ln. . . . Pg.26 . . . X4
Davids Dr. . . Pg.25 . . . Z3

Davidson Rd. . Pg.26 . . . X4
Dawn Ave. . . Pg.25 . . . Z3
Deer Chase Ln. Pg.25 . . . Z3
Douglas Rd. . . Pg.26 . . . W5
Ganton Ct. . . Pg.25 . . . Z2
Gordon Ct. . . Pg.20 . . . W5
Grey Fox Tr. . . Pg.26 . . . Z2
Hafenrichter Rd. Pg.25 . . X1,2
Hanslik Ct. . . Pg.25 . . . X2
Hartman Dr. . Pg.26 . . . Z4
Heggs Rd. . . Pg.26 . . X,Z1
Helene Ave. . . Pg.25 . . . Z3
Hillview Dr. . . Pg.26 . . . W5
Hunt Club Ct. . Pg.25 . . . Z3
Joyce Ln. . . . Pg.26 . . . X4
Juanita Dr. . . Pg.26 . . . Z3
Kennemer Ct. Pg.25 . . . Z2
Killarney Ct. . . Pg.25 . . . Z2
Lakeside . . . Pg.26 . . . X4
Lakeview Dr. . Pg.26 . . . X5
Laurel Dr. . . Pg.26 . . . X5
Lillian Ct. . . . Pg.26 . . . Z4
Linda Ln. . . . Pg.25 . . . Z2
Littlestone Cir. Pg.26 . . . Z2
Littlestone Ct. Pg.26 . . . Z2
Mark Dr. . . . Pg.26 . . . Z4
Mayre Ave. . . Pg.25 . . . Z4
McGrath Ln. . Pg.26 . . . Z4
Meadow Dr. . Pg.26 . . . X4
Meadow Lake Dr.
. . . . . Pg.26 . . . X5
Muirfield St. . . Pg.26 . . . X5
Nancy Ct. . . . Pg.26 . . . X5
New Market Dr. Pg.25 . . . Z3
Normantown Rd. Pg.26 . . W,X2
Old Joliet Gravel Rd.
. . . . . Pg.26 . . . X4
Oswego (Wolf's Crossing Rd.)
. . . . . Pg.25 . . . Y1,2
Oswego Rd. . . Pg.25 . . . Y1,2
Park Ln. . . . Pg.26 . . . Z4
Perkins Ct. . . Pg.26 . . . Z4
Perth Ln. . . . Pg.25 . . . Z2
Pheasant Run Ct.
. . . . . Pg.25 . . . Z3
Plainfield-Naperville Rd.
. . . . . Pg.26 . . . W5
Plainview Dr. . Pg.26 . . . W5
Port Marnock Ct. Pg.26 . . . Z4
Quail Ridge Ct. Pg.26 . . . Z4
Ramm Dr. . . Pg.26 . . . Z4
Rebecca Ct. . . Pg.26 . . . Y4
Red Stable Way Pg.26 . . . Z4
Richard Dr. . . Pg.26 . . . Z4
Ridge Rd. . . . Pg.26 . . . X6
River Dr. . . . Pg.26 . . . Y6
River Rd. . . . Pg.26 . . . Y6
Robert Ave. . . Pg.26 . . . Y6
Robert Dr. . . Pg.26 . . . Y6
Robin Ln. . . . Pg.26 . . . Y2
Royal Birkdale Dr.
. . . . . Pg.25 . . . Z2
Royal County Down Dr.
. . . . . Pg.25 . . . Z3
Royal Dornach Ct.
. . . . . Pg.25 . . . Z3
Royal Lytham Dr.
. . . . . Pg.25 . . . Z3
Royal Porthcrawl Dr.
. . . . . Pg.25 . . . Z3
Royal Portrush Dr.
. . . . . Pg.25 . . . Z2
Royal Worthington Dr.
. . . . . Pg.25 . . . Z2
Ruff St. . . . Pg.25 . . . Z1
Sanders Rd. . . Pg.26 . . . Z4
Schoger Dr. . . Pg.26 . . . W2
Schoger Rd. . . Pg.26 . . . X2
Shell Lake Dr. . Pg.26 . . . X4
Sheri St. . . . Pg.25 . . . Z1
Springbrook Dr. Pg.26 . . . X6
Springlake Dr. Pg.26 . . . X6
St. Annes Ct. . Pg.25 . . . Z2
Staffeldt Dr. . . Pg.25 . . . Z4
Sunningdale Dr. Pg.26 . . . Z4
Sunridge Dr. . Pg.26 . . . Y2
Timothy Ave. . Pg.25 . . . Y6
Torphin Ct. . . Pg.25 . . . Z3
Torphin Hill Ct. Pg.25 . . . Z3
Wagner Rd. . . Pg.26 . . . Y4
Walter Ln. . . Pg.25 . . . Y4
Walton Heath Dr. Pg.25 . . . Y4
Webster Ln. . . Pg.26 . . . Z4
Wentworth Dr. Pg.26 . . . Z3
West Ln. . . . Pg.26 . . . W5
White Eagle Dr. Pg.25 . . X2,3
Whittington Ln. Pg.26 . . . Y4
Wileden Rd. . . Pg.26 . . . W5
Winchester Dr., E. & W.
. . . . . Pg.25 . . . W1
Windjammer Ct. Pg.26 . . . X4
Wolf's Crossing Rd.
. . . . . Pg.25 . . . Y1
Woodhall Dr. . Pg.25 . . . Z3
Worlington Dr. Pg.25 . . . Z3
75th St. . . . Pg.19 . . . V3
80th St. . . . Pg.20 . . . V6
81st St. . . . Pg.19 . . . V3
87th St. . . . Pg.25 . . . W5
91st St. . . . Pg.25 . . X2,3
95th St. . . . Pg.25 . . Y3,4
96th Ct. . . . Pg.26 . . . Y4
103rd St. . . . Pg.25 . . . V2
104th St. . . . Pg.25,26 Z2-4
248th St. . . . Pg.25 . . . V2
260th Ave. . . Pg.25 . . X,Z1

### GOLF COURSES
White Eagle G.C. Pg.25 . . . W3

### SCHOOLS
White Eagle Elem. Sch.
. . . . . Pg.25 . . . W2

### MISCELLANEOUS
Wheatland Industrial Park
. . . . . Pg.25 . . . X2

## WHEATON
### STREETS
Pages 9,10,14-16
Aberdeen Ct. . Pg.15 . . . L7
Academy Ln. . Pg.15 . . . M8
Acorn Ct. . . . Pg.16 . . . N11
Adam St. . . . Pg.9 . . . K10
Adare Dr. . . . Pg.9 . . . L8
Albright Ct. . . Pg.16 . . . P11
Albright Ln. . . Pg.16 . . . P11
Alcester Ave. . Pg.15 . . . M10
Alieden Ct. . . Pg.15 . . . L8
Apollo Ct. . . . Pg.15 . . . M10
Appaloosa Ct. E. & W.
. . . . . Pg.16 . . . N11
Appleby Ct. . . Pg.15 . . . P9
Appleby Dr. . . Pg.15 . . . P10
Arabian Ct. . . Pg.15 . . . M10
Arbor Ave. . . Pg.9 . . . L8
Arbor Ct. . . . Pg.9 . . . L8
Arbor Pl. . . . Pg.9 . . . L8
Arboretum Ct. Pg.15 . . . M10
Ardmore Ln. . Pg.9 . . . L8
Armhrust Rd. . Pg.9 . . . J9
Ascot Ct. . . . Pg.16 . . . M10
Ashburn Ct. . . Pg.15 . . . M10
Ashford Ct. . . Pg.15 . . . M10
Ashton Ct. . . Pg.10 . . . J11
Aurora Way . . Pg.15 . . . L9
Austin Ct. . . . Pg.15 . . . N10
Avalon Ct. . . Pg.15 . . . M8
Avery Ave. . . Pg.9,10 . K10
Bach Ct. . . . Pg.15 . . . P9
Barger Ct. . . Pg.15 . . . N7
Bates St. . . . Pg.9 . . . L7
Beecher Ave. . Pg.15 . . . K8
Beechwood Ct. Pg.15 . . . N8
Beethoven Ct. Pg.15 . . . P9
Belleau Woods Ct.
. . . . . Pg.15 . . . L6
Belleau Woods Dr.
. . . . . Pg.15 . . . L6
Belter Dr. . . . Pg.15 . . M,N9
Berkshire Dr. . Pg.15 . . . N8
Beverly Ave. . Pg.9 . . . L8
Birch Dr. . . . Pg.9 . . . K8
Blackburn . . . Pg.15 . . . M10
Blacksmith Dr. Pg.16 . . . P11
Blanchard Ct. Pg.15 . . . M9
Blanchard Dr. Pg.9 . . . J10
Blanchard St. . Pg.9,15 . K,N10
Bluegrass Cir. . Pg.15 . . . M10
Borough Ct. . . Pg.15 . . . P10
Bradford Ct. . Pg.15 . . . M8
Brahms Ct. . . Pg.15 . . . N9
Brandon Dr. . Pg.15 . . . L9
Brentwood Ct. Pg.16 . . . N11
Brentwood Ln. Pg.15,16
. . . . . N10,11
Briar Patch . . Pg.15,16 . N10
Briarbrook Dr. Pg.15 . . . N10
Briarcliffe Blvd. Pg.15,16 M,N10
Briarcove . . . Pg.15 . . . M8
Bridge St. . . . Pg.9 . . . J10
Bridle Ln. . . . Pg.9 . . . L8
Brighton Dr. . Pg.15 . . N7,9
Bristol Ct. . . . Pg.15 . . . L9
Brittany Ct. . . Pg.15 . . . M10
Brookside Circle Pg.9 . . . J10
Browning Ct. . Pg.15 . . . M9
Buckingham Dr. Pg.15 . . N8,9
Buena Vista Dr. Pg.15 . . . M8
Bunker Hill . . Pg.15 . . . N10
Burnham Pl. . Pg.15 . . . N8
Burning Ct. . . Pg.15 . . . M8
Burning Trail . Pg.15 . . . M8
Burr Oak Ct. . Pg.15 . . . N9
Butterfield Rd. Pg.15 . . . N9
Byron Ct. . . . Pg.9 . . . L10
Cadet Ct. . . . Pg.14 . . . M8
Cadillac Dr. . . Pg.9 . . . L10
Cambridge Ln. Pg.15 . . . N10
Cambridge Ln. Pg.15 . . . N10
Camden Pl. . . Pg.15 . . . M9
Campbell Ave. Pg.9 . . . L10
Campbell Ct. . Pg.9 . . . L10
Campbell St. . Pg.9 . . . L10
Canada Dr. . . Pg.15 . . . N9
Cannon Ct. . . Pg.15 . . . M10
Canterbury Pl. Pg.15 . . . N9
Cantigny Way . Pg.15 . . . M7
Carlson Ln. . . Pg.9 . . . J8
Carlton Ave. . Pg.9 . . . J9
Carlton St. . . Pg.9 . . . K9
Casa Solana Dr. Pg.15 . . . M10
Castbourne Ct. Pg.16 . . . M11
Castlewood Dr. Pg.9 . . . L10
Cavalier Ct. . . Pg.15 . . . N10
Caxton Dr. . . Pg.9 . . . L8
Cedar Ct. . . . Pg.15 . . . M8
Center Ave. . . Pg.9 . . . K9
Cesario Cir. . . Pg.9 . . . M7
Challenger Ct. Pg.15 . . . N10
Champion Forest Ct.
. . . . . Pg.14 . . . J8
Charlotte Ct. . Pg.15 . . . M7
Chase St. . . . Pg.9,15 . L10
Chatham Dr. . Pg.15 . . . N10
Chelsea Ct. . . Pg.15 . . . M8
Cherry Ct. . . Pg.9 . . . J10
Cherry St. . . Pg.9 . . . K10
Cheshire Ln. . Pg.15,16 . N11
Childs Ct. . . . Pg.15 . . . L8
Childs St. . . . Pg.9 . . . L8
Chopin Ct. . . Pg.15 . . . P9
Christina Cir. . Pg.15 . . . M10
Christina Ct. . Pg.15 . . . M10
Circle Ave. . . Pg.9 . . . K9
Citation Cir. . . Pg.15 . . . M10
Clinton Ct. . . Pg.9 . . . L8
Clydesdale Dr. Pg.16 . . . N11
Cole Ave. . . . Pg.9 . . . J9
College Ave. . Pg.9,15 . K,N10

Coloma Ct. . . Pg.16 . . . M11
Coloma Pl. . . Pg.15,16 . M11
Colonial Sq. . . Pg.14 . . . M8
Commerce Dr. Pg.9 . . . K9
Community Dr. Pg.9 . . . L7
Coolidge Ave. . Pg.9,15 . L10
Cordova Ct. . . Pg.15 . . . M10
Countryside Dr. Pg.9 . . . J10
County Farm Ct. Pg.15 . . . M6
County Farm Rd. Pg.9 . . . L7
Courtney Dr. . Pg.15 . . . L8
Cove Ct. . . . Pg.9 . . . M8
Creekside Cove Pg.15 . . . M7
Creekside Dr. Pg.9,15 . L,M8
Crescent St. . Pg.9 . . . K10
Crest St. . . . Pg.9 . . . L9
Cromwell Ct. . Pg.14 . . . M9
Cross St. . . . Pg.9 . . . K9
Croydon Ct. . Pg.15 . . . M10
Culham Ct. . . Pg.15 . . . P10
Daly Rd. . . . Pg.15 . . . N9
Danada Dr. . . Pg.15 . . . M9
Danada E. Loop Rd.
. . . . . Pg.15 . . . N9
Danada Sq. E. Pg.15 . . . N9
Danada Sq. W. Pg.15 . . . M9
Danada W. Loop Rd.
. . . . . Pg.15 . . . M9
Darling St. . . Pg.15 . . . J9
Dartmouth Dr. Pg.9 . . . L8
Darwin Ct. . . Pg.15 . . . M10
Darwin Ln. . . Pg.15 . . . M10
Davis Ct. . . . Pg.15 . . . M10
Dawes Ave. . . Pg.15 . . . L10
Deerpath . . . Pg.16 . . . N10
Delles Rd. . . Pg.15 . . . L9
Derby Ct. . . . Pg.16 . . . N11
Devonshire Dr. Pg.15 . . . M8
Dickinson Dr. Pg.15 . . . N8
Doncaster Ct. Pg.15 . . . N10
Dorchester Ave. Pg.9 . . . K,L8
Dorsett Dr. . . Pg.15 . . . K9
Dover Ct. . . . Pg.16 . . . N11
Dover Ct. . . . Pg.16 . . . N11
Downing Ct. . Pg.15 . . . N10
Driving Park Rd. Pg.15 . . . L9
Dundee Dr. . . Pg.15 . . . L8
Dunlay Ave. . Pg.16 . . . P11
Durham Dr. . Pg.15 . . . N10
Eagle Ct. . . . Pg.15 . . . N8
Eaton Ct. . . . Pg.15 . . . M10
Eddy Ct. . . . Pg.15 . . . K10
Edinburgh Ct. Pg.15 . . . N10
Ellis Ave. . . . Pg.9 . . . K9
Elm St. . . . Pg.9,15 . K,N10
Elmwood Dr. . Pg.9 . . . L9
Embden Ln. . . Pg.14,15 . N7
Emerald Ave. . Pg.9 . . . K10
Emerson Ct. . Pg.15 . . . M9
Emily . . . Pg.9 . . . L8
Ennis Ln. . . . Pg.15 . . . L8
Ensenada Dr. . Pg.15 . . . M10
Erie Ave. . . . Pg.9 . . . L8
Essel Ct. . . . Pg.15 . . . N10
Evergreen St. . Pg.9 . . . L,N10
Exeter . . . Pg.15 . . . N10
Faganel Ct. . . Pg.15 . . . M10
Fairway Ln. . . Pg.15 . . . M7
Falcon Dr. . . Pg.14 . . . J8
Falson Ct. . . Pg.15 . . . M10
Fanchon St. . Pg.9 . . . L9
Fapp Cir. . . . Pg.9 . . . L7
Farnham Ln. . Pg.15 . . . N9
Farragut Ct. . Pg.15 . . . M10
Farwell St. . . Pg.9 . . . J9
Fischer St. . . Pg.9,15 . L10
Fitzer Rd. . . . Pg.15 . . . N8
Folkstone Ct. . Pg.15 . . . M10
Folsom Ct. . . Pg.15 . . . M10
Foothill Ct. . . Pg.15 . . . M8
Foothill Dr. . . Pg.15 . . . M8
Forest Ave. . . Pg.9,10 . K9,10
Fox Run . . . Pg.15 . . . M7
Franklin St. . . Pg.9 . . . L10
Frazier Ct. . . Pg.9 . . . L9
Friar's Ct. . . . Pg.15 . . . N10
Gables Blvd. . Pg.9,15 . L8
Gainsboro Ct. Pg.15 . . . N10
Gallant Ct. . . Pg.14 . . . J8
Gamon Rd. . . Pg.9,15 . L,M8
Garner Ave. . . Pg.9 . . . K10
Gary Ave. . . . Pg.9 . . . K9
Gary Ct. . . . Pg.9 . . . J9
Gary St. . . . Pg.9 . . . K9
Geneva Pl. . . Pg.9 . . . J10
Gershwin Ct. . Pg.15 . . . P9
Gladstone Dr. Pg.15 . . . N9
Glencoe St. . . Pg.10 . . . J10
Glendale Ave. . Pg.15 . . . K11
Glouchester Ct. Pg.16 . . . N11
Golden Pond Ln. Pg.16 . . . N8
Golf Circle . . Pg.15 . . . M8
Golf Ln. . . . Pg.15 . . . M8
Golf View Dr. . Pg.15 . . . M8
Gone Away Ct. Pg.16 . . . N10
Gone Away Ln. Pg.15 . . . M8
Gorton Ln. . . Pg.15 . . . M10
Grange Ct. . . Pg.15 . . . M10
Grant St. . . . Pg.9,15 . L10
Greensboro Dr. Pg.15 . . . N10
Greenwood Rd. Pg.15 . . . P10
Gresham Cir. . Pg.9 . . . L8
Grey Willow Rd. Pg.15 . . . M8
Grosvenor Cir. Pg.15 . . . N10
Groton Ct. . . Pg.9 . . . L10
Hailshaw Ct. . Pg.15 . . . M10
Hale St. . . . Pg.9 . . . L10
Hampton Dr. . Pg.9 . . . L9
Handel Ct. . . Pg.15 . . . P9
Harrison Ave. . Pg.9 . . . K10
Harrow Ct. . . Pg.15 . . . K10
Harwarden Dr. Pg.15 . . . K10
Haverhill Dr. . Pg.15 . . . M7

Hawkins Cir. . Pg.15 . . . M10
Hawkins Dr. . Pg.15 . . . N9
Hawthorne Blvd. Pg.9,10 . J9,10
Hawthorne St. Pg.9,10 . J9,11
Hayden Ct. . . Pg.15 . . . P9
Hazelton Ave. Pg.9 . . . L8
Heatherbrook Ct. Pg.15 . . . M10
Heathrow Ct. . Pg.15 . . . M10
Helen Ct. . . . Pg.15 . . . N10
Hemstock Ave. Pg.15 . . . M8
Heritage Lake . Pg.15 . . . M10
Hertford Ct. . . Pg.15 . . . M10
Hickory Ln. . . Pg.9 . . . K8
Hidden Ct. . . Pg.15 . . . M8
Hillside Ct. . . Pg.9 . . . K10
Hiram Ct. . . . Pg.16 . . . N10
Hiram Dr. . . . Pg.15 . . . P10
Howard Circle Pg.15 . . . P10
Howard St. . . Pg.9 . . . K10
Hull Dr. . . . Pg.15 . . . N8
Hunters Glen Ct. Pg.15 . . . M9
Hunters Glen Dr. Pg.15 . . . M9
Huntleigh Ct. . Pg.15 . . . N10
Huntleigh Dr. Pg.15 . . . M10
Hurly Dr. . . . Pg.15 . . . L8
Hyatt Dr. . . . Pg.16 . . . N10
Illinois St. . . . Pg.9,10 . L10,11
Indiana St. . . Pg.9,10 . L9,11
Irving Ave. . . Pg.9 . . . K10
Ivy Ct. . . . Pg.16 . . . P11
Jahns Dr. . . . Pg.15 . . . N10
James Ct. . . . Pg.9 . . . L9
Jasper Ct. . . . Pg.16 . . . N10
Jasper Dr. . . Pg.15 . . . N10
Jefferson Ave. Pg.9 . . . K8,9
Jeffery Ct. . . Pg.15 . . . N10
Jerome Ave. . Pg.9 . . . J10
Jessica . . . Pg.15 . . . M10
Johnstown . . Pg.15 . . . N10
Joyce Ct. . . . Pg.15 . . . N9
Kandahar Ct. . Pg.15 . . . M8
Karlsroga Ave. Pg.9 . . . K9
Kay Rd. . . . Pg.10 . . . J11
Kelle Ct. . . . Pg.15 . . . P10
Kellogg Pl. . . Pg.15 . . . M8
Kenilworth Ave. Pg.9 . . . K10
Kensington Cir. Pg.15 . . . N10
Kent Ct. . . . Pg.15 . . . L9
Kentucky Ct. . Pg.16 . . . N11
Kikenny Ct. . . Pg.15 . . . L8
Kilkenny Dr. . Pg.15 . . . L8
Kingsbury . . . Pg.15 . . . J9
Kingston Dr. . Pg.15 . . . P10
Kingston St. . Pg.10 . . . K11
Kipling Ct. . . Pg.9 . . . L10
Knapp Ct. . . Pg.15 . . . M8
Knoll St. . . . Pg.9 . . . L7
Knollwood St. Pg.9 . . . L7
Kudo Ct. . . . Pg.15 . . . M9
La Palma Ct. . Pg.15 . . . M10
Lakecliff Dr. . Pg.16 . . . M11
Lakeside Dr. . Pg.9 . . . L8
Lakeview Dr. . Pg.15 . . . N10
Lancaster Ln. . Pg.15 . . . N10
Landford Ct. . Pg.16 . . . N10
Landford Ln. . Pg.16 . . . P11
Langford Ct. . Pg.15 . . . N9
Leafbrook Cove Pg.15 . . . M7
Leafbrook Ln. Pg.15 . . . M7
Leask Ln. . . . Pg.15 . . . M10
Leeds Ct. . . . Pg.15 . . . P10
Leicester Ct. . Pg.15 . . . N10
Lewis Ln. . . . Pg.15 . . . M9
Lexington St. . Pg.10 . . . K11
Leytonstone Dr. Pg.15 . . . M10
Leytonstone Dr. Pg.15 . . . M10
Liberty Dr. . . Pg.9,10 . K9,L11
Lincoln Ave. . Pg.9 . . . L10
Lindsay Ct. . . Pg.15 . . . M10
Liskeard Ct. . Pg.15 . . . N9
Lloyd Ct. . . . Pg.15 . . . M8
Lois Ln. . . . Pg.15 . . . L7
Longfellow Ct. Pg.15 . . . M9
Longfellow Dr. Pg.15 . . . N8
Lorraine Rd. . Pg.16 . . . L11
Loughborough Pg.15 . . . L10
Lowden Ave. . Pg.15 . . . K10
Lowell Ave. . . Pg.10 . . . K10
Lucky Debonaire Ct.
. . . . . Pg.15 . . . N9
Lyford Ct. . . Pg.9,15 . L10
Lynwood St. . Pg.9 . . . L9
Lyon Ave. . . Pg.9 . . . K9
Madera Dr. . . Pg.15 . . . M10
Madison Ave. Pg.9 . . K8,9
Madsen Ct. . . Pg.10 . . . K11
Main Pl. . . . Pg.9 . . . L9
Main St. . . . Pg.9 . . J,M9
Mallard Ct. . . Pg.14,15 . N7
Manchester Rd. Pg.10 . . . K10
Maple Leaf . . Pg.15 . . . M8
Maple Ln. . . Pg.15 . . . J11
Maplewood Dr. Pg.15 . . . N8
Marcey Dr. . . Pg.15 . . . N8
Maria Ct. . . . Pg.15 . . . M10
Marion St. . . Pg.10 . . . J11
Martingale Rd. Pg.9 . . . L10
Marywood Ct. Pg.16 . . . N10
Mayo Ave. . . Pg.15 . . . L8
McCormick Pl. Pg.15 . . . M11
McCreey Ave. Pg.15 . . . M11
Meadow Cir. . Pg.15 . . . N8
Meadow Pl. . . Pg.15 . . . P9
Medinah Ct. . Pg.15 . . . N8
Mendelsohn Ct. Pg.15 . . . P9
Merdian Ct. . . Pg.15 . . . M9
Michigan Ave. Pg.9 . . . K10
Middleton Ct. Pg.15 . . . M10
Middleton Dr. Pg.15 . . . N8
Midwest Ln. . Pg.15 . . . M10
Milton Ln. . . Pg.15 . . . K10
Monticello Ln. Pg.15 . . . M10
Morgan Ave. . Pg.9 . . . J9
Morgan Ct. . . Pg.15 . . . M10
Morse St. . . . Pg.15 . . . J9
Mozrt Ct. . . . Pg.15 . . . P9
Mt. Vernon Ct. Pg.15 . . . M7
Muirfield Cir. . Pg.15 . . . M7

Mustang Ct. . Pg.15 . . . M9
Myrtlewood . . Pg.9 . . . L8
Nachtman Ct. Pg.14 . . . J11
Naperville Rd. Pg.9 . . L,M10
Nelson Circle . Pg.15 . . . M10
Newbury Ln. . Pg.15 . . . M10
North Path . . Pg.10 . . . K11
Nottingham Ln. Pg.15 . . . N10
Oak Ave. . . . Pg.9 . . . K9
Oak Knolls St. Pg.9 . . . K8
Oak View Dr. . Pg.9 . . . K9
Oakwood Ct. . Pg.15 . . . M8
Orchard Rd. . Pg.15 . . . M8
Orth St. . . . Pg.15 . . . M8
Ott Ave. . . . Pg.10,16 . L11
Oxford Ln. . . Pg.15 . . . N10
Paddock Ct. . Pg.9 . . . J10
Paddock Ln. . Pg.9 . . . J10
Page St. . . . Pg.9 . . . L7
Palamino Ct. . Pg.15 . . . N8
Papworth St. . Pg.9 . . . J9
Park Ave. . . . Pg.9 . . . L9
Park Circle Dr. Pg.9 . . . J9
Parkside Dr. . Pg.9 . . . L9
Parkway Dr. . Pg.9,15 . L8
Paula Ave. . . Pg.15 . . . L8
Pebblestone Cove
. . . . . Pg.15 . . . M8
Pebblestone Dr. Pg.15 . . . M8
Pembroke Ln. Pg.15 . . . M10
Penny Ln. . . Pg.15 . . . N9
Pershing Ave. Pg.9 . . . L10
Pick St. . . . Pg.9,10 . K11
Pierce Ave. . . Pg.9 . . . L8
Pin Oak Ct. . Pg.15 . . . N9
Pinegrove Ct. Pg.9 . . . J10
Pinto Ct. . . . Pg.15 . . . N8
Plamondon Ct. Pg.15 . . . M8
Plamondon Rd. Pg.15 . . . M8
Plymouth Ct. . Pg.16 . . . M11
Prairie Ave. . . Pg.9,10 . K9,10
Prairie Path . . Pg.9 . . . L8
President St. . Pg.9,15 . K,L10
Princeton Ct. . Pg.15 . . . L8
Promenade Ln. Pg.15 . . . M8
Prospect Ave. Pg.10 . . . L10
Prospect Ct. . Pg.16 . . . M11
Prospect St. . Pg.10,15,16
. . . . . L11
Purnell St. . . Pg.9 . . . L9
Quarter Horse Ct.
. . . . . Pg.15 . . . N9
Queenswood Ct. Pg.15 . . . M10
Queenswood Ln. Pg.15 . . . M10
Raleigh Ct. . . Pg.15 . . . M9
Ralph Ct. . . . Pg.9 . . . J9
Ranch Rd. . . Pg.10 . . . J10
Raven Hill . . Pg.15 . . . M7
Reading Ct. . . Pg.15 . . . N10
Reber St. . . . Pg.9 . . . J9
Redwood Ct. . Pg.15 . . . N8
Renn Ct. . . . Pg.9 . . . L9
Rhodes Ct. . . Pg.15 . . . N10
Richmond Dr. Pg.16 . . . P11
Richton Dr. . . Pg.15 . . . N10
Riva Ct. . . . Pg.15 . . . M10
Robbins Ct. . Pg.10 . . . K10
Robinwood Ct. Pg.15 . . . P10
Robinwood Ln. Pg.15 . . . P10
Romeo Ct. . . Pg.10 . . . J11
Roosevelt Rd. Pg.9 . . . L9
Rosebud Ct. . Pg.15 . . . M10
Rossini Ct. . . Pg.15 . . . P9
Royal Ct. . . . Pg.9 . . . J8
Ryson Ct. . . Pg.15 . . . N9
Salford Ct. . . Pg.15 . . . N10
Salisbury Ct. . Pg.16 . . . M11
Sandhurst Ct. Pg.15 . . . N8
Sandy Hook . Pg.15 . . . M8
Santa Rosa Ave. Pg.9 . . . K10
Schaeffer Rd. Pg.14 . . . N7
Schaffner Rd. Pg.15 . . . L,M7
Schillerstrom Ct. Pg.15 . M,N10
Schubert Ct. . Pg.15 . . . P9
Scott St. . . . Pg.9 . . . K9
Scottsdale Ct. Pg.16 . . . N11
Scottsdale Dr. Pg.15,16
. . . . . N10,11
Sears Ln. . . . Pg.15 . . . N9
Secretariat Ct. Pg.15 . . . M9
Seminary Ave. Pg.9 . . . K9
Seneca Dr. . . Pg.15 . . . M10
Shady Ln. . . Pg.9 . . J,K10
Shagbark Ln. . Pg.9 . . . K9
Sheffield Ln. . Pg.15 . . . N10
Sheldon Ct. . Pg.15 . . . M10
Shelley Ln. . . Pg.15 . . . N10
Sherwin Ave. . Pg.9 . . . K10
Sherwin Ct. . Pg.15 . . . M10
Sherwood Pl. Pg.15 . . . N10
Shetland Dr. . Pg.16 . . . N11
Shire Ct. . . . Pg.16 . . . N11
Shirley Ct. . . Pg.9 . . . L8
Sibelius Ct. . . Pg.15 . . . P9
Sjogren Ct. . . Pg.15 . . . M10
Somerset Ave. Pg.15 . . . L9
Somerset Ln. . Pg.15 . . . L9
Southampton Ct. Pg.15 . . . M10
Spero Ct. . . . Pg.15 . . . M10
Spring Green Dr. Pg.15 . . . M8
St. Francis Ct. Pg.16 . . . N11
Stallion Ct. . . Pg.16 . . . N11
Stephenson Pl. Pg.15 . . . M9
Stewart Ave. . Pg.9 . . . K10
Stillwell Ct. . . Pg.15 . . . M,N9
Stirrup Ln. . . Pg.16 . . . N11
Stoddard Ave. Pg.15 . . . K10
Stonebridge Cir. Pg.15 . . . M7
Stonebridge Ln. Pg.15 . . . M7
Stonebridge Trail
. . . . . Pg.15 . . . M7
Stonegate Ln. Pg.15 . . . M6
Stonehill Ct. . Pg.15 . . . N8
Summit St. . . Pg.9,10,J,K,L10
Sumner St. . . Pg.15 . . . L10

## WHEATON

Sunderland Ct. . . Pg.15 . . M10
Sunnybrook . . Pg.9 . . . K8
Sunnyside Ave . Pg.9 . . . L9
Sunset Rd. . . . Pg.9 . . . L8
Surrey Ct. . . . Pg.9 . . . J10
Surrey Rd. . . . Pg.9 . . . J10
Surrey St. . . . Pg.9 . . . J10
Surry Dr. . . . Pg.15 . . M8
Sussex Ln. . . . Pg.15 . . N10
Sussex Rd. . . . Pg.9 . . . J10
Taft Ave. . . . Pg.9 . . . L10
Tall Oaks Ln. . . Pg.9 . . . L8
Tennyson Dr. . Pg.15 . . M9
Thames . . . . Pg.16 . . M11
Thomas Rd. . . Pg.9,10 . J9,10
Thompson Dr. . Pg.15 . . M9
Thornwood . . . Pg.15 . . M7
Tiger Tr. . . . . Pg.9 . . . L8
Timber Ln. . . . Pg.15 . . M7
Timber Tr. . . . Pg.9 . . . L8
Tow Path Ct. . . Pg.15 . . M8
Traves Ave. . . Pg.10 . . K11
Tree Top Ln. . . Pg.15 . . L8
Trent Ct. . . . Pg.16 . . M11
Triple Crown Ct. Pg.15 . . N9
Trotter Ct. . . . Pg.15 . . M9
Trowbridge Ct . Pg.15 . . M10
Turf Ln. . . . . Pg.15 . . J10
Underwood . . . Pg.15 . . L10
Union Ave. . . . Pg.9 . . . K9
University Pl. . . Pg.9 . . . K10
Vail Ct. . . . . Pg.14 . . M10
Valley Forge Ct. Pg.15 . . M10
Venetian Cir . . Pg.15 . . M10
Verdi Ct. . . . Pg.15 . . P9
Vernon St. . . . Pg.9 . . . L8
Vivaldi Ct. . . . Pg.15 . . P9
Wadham Ct. . . Pg.15,16 M10
Wadham Pl. . . Pg.15 . . M10
Wadsworth St. . Pg.15 . . M9
Wakeman Ave. Pg.9,10 . K10
Wakeman St. . Pg.14 . . J11
Waldorth St. . . Pg.15 . . M8
Wales Dr. . . . Pg.15 . . M10
Walnut Ct. . . . Pg.15 . . M8
Warrenville Ave. Pg.14 . . N7
Warrenville Rd. Pg.9,15 . L,M9
Warwick Ct. . . Pg.16 . . M11
Washington St. . Pg.9 . . . J,K10
Water Tower Ct. Pg.15 . . M7
Webster Ave. . Pg.9 . . . K10
Webster Ct. . . Pg.9 . . . K9
Wendover Ct. . Pg.14 . . J11
Wesley St. . . . Pg.15 . . K9
West St. . . . . Pg.9 . . . K9
Westchester Ct. Pg.16 . . N11
Western Ave. . Pg.9 . . . K9
Westhaven Dr. . Pg.9 . . . L8
Westminster Dr. Pg.15 . . P10
Westwood Dr. . Pg.9 . . . K8
Wexford Cir. . . Pg.9 . . . L8
Wextord Lt. . . Pg.15 . . L8
Wheaton Ave. . Pg.9,15 . K-L9
Wheaton Ct. . . Pg.9 . . . K9
Wheaton Oaks Ct.
. . . . . . . . . Pg.9 . . . K9
Wheaton Oaks Dr.
. . . . . . . . . Pg.9 . . . K9
Whirlaway St. . Pg.15 . . N9
White Oak Dr. . Pg.9 . . . K8
Whitman Ln. . . Pg.15 . . M9
Whittier Ln. . . Pg.15 . . M9
Wiesbrook Rd. . Pg.14 . . N7
Wigtown Ct. . . Pg.15 . . M10
Williams St. . . Pg.15 . . L7
Williams St. . . Pg.9 . . . L8
Williamsburg Ct. Pg.15 . . M10
Williston St. . . Pg.9 . . . K9
Willow Ave. . . Pg.9,10 .
. . . . . . . . . K,L10,L11
Willow Run . . . Pg.15 . . M7
Wilmette Ln. . . Pg.10 . . J10
Wilmette St. . . Pg.10 . . K11
Wilshire . . . . Pg.10 . . K11
Wilson Ave. . . Pg.9,10 . L10
Windemere Ct. Pg.9 . . . L7
Windsor Dr. . . Pg.15,16 N8,11
Wingate Ln. . . Pg.15 . . N7
Winners Cup Cir. Pg.15 . . M9
Winners Cup Dr. Pg.15 . . N9
Winners Cup Pl. Pg.15 . . N9
Wood Haven . . Pg.15 . . M7
Wood St. . . . Pg.10 . . K11
Woodcutter Ln. Pg.9 . . . L9
Woodlawn St. . Pg.9 . . . J-L8
York Ln., E. & W.
. . . . . . . . . Pg.10 . . L11
Yorkshire Woods Ct.
. . . . . . . . . Pg.15 . . L7
22nd St. . . . . Pg.15,16
. . . . . . . . . M10,11

### CEMETERIES
Wheaton Cemetery
. . . . . . . . . Pg.15 . . M9

### FOREST PRESERVES
Belleau Woods Forest Preserve
. . . . . . . . Pg.9,15 . L7
Danada Forest Preserve
. . . . . . . . Pg.15 . . P8
Lincoln Marsh Natural Area
. . . . . . . . Pg.9 . . . K8

### GOLF COURSES
Chicago Golf Club
. . . . . . . . Pg.15 . . M9

### PARKS
Adams Park . . Pg.9 . . . K9
Albright Park . Pg.15 . . P11
Appelby Park . Pg.15 . . P10
Arboretum Mews Park
. . . . . . . . Pg.15 . . P10
Atten Park . . Pg.15 . . M7
Blacksmith Park Pg.15 . . P11

---

Briarknoll Park Pg.15 . . M10
Chatham Park . Pg.15 . . N9
Cosley Park . . Pg.9 . . . N9
Dorset Park . . Pg.15 . . N8
Graf Park . . . Pg.9 . . . K8
Hoffman Park . Pg.10 . . K11
Hull Park . . . Pg.15 . . P10
Hurley Gardens Park
. . . . . . . . Pg.15 . . L8
Kelly Park . . . Pg.15 . . L8
Memorial Park . Pg.9 . . . K9
North Path Park Pg.10 . . K10,11
Northside Park Pg.9 . . . J9
Orchard Park . Pg.15 . . N8
Presidents Park Pg.16 . . M11
Rathje Park . . Pg.15 . . L9
Ridge Park . . Pg.15 . . N9
Scott Cove Park Pg.16 . . N,P11
Scotts Cove . . Pg.15 . . P11
Scottsdale Park Pg.9 . . . P10
Seven Gables Park
. . . . . . . . Pg.15 . . M9
Wexford Park . Pg.15 . . L8

### SCHOOLS
Bonaparte School for the
Handicapped Pg.12 . . M10
Briar Glen Elem. Sch.
. . . . . . . . Pg.15 . . M10
Edison Jr. H.S. Pg.15 . . L9
Emerson Sch. . Pg.9 . . . K8
Franklin Jr. H.S. Pg.9 . . . K9
Hawthorne Sch. Pg.9 . . . J10
Holmes Sch. . Pg.9 . . . K10
Jefferson Sch. Pg.9 . . . K8
Lincoln Sch. . . Pg.9 . . . L8
Longfellow Sch. Pg.9 . . . K9
Lowell Sch. . . Pg.9 . . . L10
Madison Sch. . Pg.15 . . M8
Monroe Jr. H.S. Pg.9 . . . K9
National Louis University
. . . . . . . . Pg.9 . . . L9
St. Francis H.S. Pg.9 . . . L7
St. John Lutheran Sch.
. . . . . . . . Pg.9 . . . K8
St. Michael's Sch.
. . . . . . . . Pg.9 . . . L9
Washington Sch. Pg.9 . . . J10
Wheaton College Pg.9 . . . K10
Wheaton North H.S.
. . . . . . . . Pg.9 . . . K10
Wheaton-Warrenville H.S.
. . . . . . . . Pg.15 . . N7
Wheaton-Warrenville Middle
Sch. . . . . . Pg.15 . . N7
Whittier Sch. . Pg.15 . . M7
Wiesbrook Sch. Pg.15 . . M7
William Hadley Jr. H.S.
. . . . . . . . Pg.9 . . . J11

### SHOPPING CENTERS
Brierbrook Shopping Center
. . . . . . . . Pg.15 . . N9
Danada Square E. Shopping
Center . . . . Pg.15 . . P9
Main St. Plaza Pg.9 . . . J9
Town Sqaure . Pg.15 . . N10

### MISCELLANEOUS
City Hall . . . . Pg.9 . . . K9
Cosley Animal Farm &
Museum . . . Pg.9 . . . J9
Danada Museum & Equestrian
Ctr. . . . . . Pg.15 . . P9
DuPage County Fairgrounds
. . . . . . . . Pg.9 . . . K9
DuPage County Government
Center . . . . Pg.9 . . . K7
DuPage County Hwy. Dept.
. . . . . . . . Pg.9 . . . K7
Fire Dept. . . . Pg.9 . . . K,L9
Loretto Convent Pg.15 . . M9
Marianjoy Rehabilitation Hosp.
. . . . . . . . Pg.9 . . . L9
Police Dept. . Pg.9 . . . L9
Rice/Pool Community Center
. . . . . . . . Pg.9 . . . K9
Theosophical Society Library
. . . . . . . . Pg.9 . . . J9

### WILLOW SPRINGS
Page 30
Portions within Cook County

### STREETS
Orchard St. . . Pg.9 . . . X21
Reserve Dr . . . . . . . . X21
Ridge Ct. . . . . . . . . . X21
Santa Fe Ct. . . . . . . . X21
Santa Fe Ln. . . . . . . . X21
Willow Ridge Dr. . . . . . X21
Winding Trails Dr. . . . . X21
Windings Ct. . . . . . . . X21
75th St. . . . . . . . . . . V22

### WILLOWBROOK
Page 24
STREETS
Adams St. . . . . . . . . . U19
American . . . . . . . . . T18
Apple Tree Ln. . . . . . . V18
Arlene Ave. . . . . . . . . V19
Ascot Ln. . . . . . . . . . S18
Bentley Ave. . . . . . . . T18
Bentwood Ln. . . . . . . . T19
Birchwood Ct. . . . . . . V18
Blackberry Ln. . . . . . . V18
Breton Lakes Dr. . . . . . P17
Briar Rd. . . . . . . . . . T20
Brookbank Rd. . . . . . . V18
Brookside . . . . . . . . . T18
Caitlin Ct. . . . . . . . . U19
Cambridge Rd. . . . . . . T19
Canterbury Ln. . . . . . . T18
Chatelaine Ct. . . . . . . T18
Chaucer Ct. . . . . . . . . T20
Chaucer Rd. . . . . . . . . T20

---

Cherry Tree Ln. . . . . . . V18
Cherrywood Ln. . . . . . . U19
Clubhouse Cir. . . . . . . T18
Clubhouse Dr. . . . . . . . T18
Cottonwood Ct. . . . . . . U19
Cramer Ct. . . . . . . . . T19
Creekside Ct. . . . . . . . T19
Eleanor Pl. . . . . . . . . V19
Emerald Ct. . . . . . . . . P17
Essex Ct. . . . . . . . . . T18
Executive Dr. . . . . . . . V19
Frontage Rd. . . . . . . . V19
Garfield Ridge . . . . . . T20
Griffin Way . . . . . . . . P17
Gull Ln. Dr. . . . . . . . . T18
Hawthorne Ln. . . . . . . V18
Hiddenbrook Ln. . . . . . T19
Highridge Rd. . . . . . . . T18
Hill Rd. . . . . . . . . . . T20
Hill Rd. . . . . . . . . . . T20
Honey Locust Ln. . . . . . V18
Joliet Rd. . . . . . . . . . T18
Kane Ct. . . . . . . . . . . T18
Kent Ct. . . . . . . . . . . T10
Kingwood Ct. . . . . . . . T19
Kingwood Rd. . . . . . . . V19
Knoll Lake Ct. . . . . . . . T19
Knoll Valley Ct. . . . . . . T18
Knoll Way Ave. . . . . . . T18
Knoll Wick Ct. . . . . . . . T18
Knoll Wick Rd. . . . . . . T18
Knollbrook Ln. . . . . . . . S18
Knollwood Ct. . . . . . . . T18
Knollwood Dr. . . . . . . . T19
Knollwood Rd. . . . . . . . T18
Kyle Ct. . . . . . . . . . . T18
Lake Hinsdale Rd. . . . . . T18
Lake Park Ln. . . . . . . . T18
Lakeshore Dr. . . . . . . . T18
Lakeview Ct. . . . . . . . . T18
Lane Ct. . . . . . . . . . . T19
Lincoln Oaks Dr. . . . . . . S18
Locust Ln. . . . . . . . . . V18
MacArthur Dr. . . . . . . . S18
Maplewood Ct. . . . . . . U19
Martin Ct. . . . . . . . . . T19
Meadow Ln. . . . . . . . . T19
Midway Dr. . . . . . . . . V18
Monroe St. . . . . . . . . . P17
North Court Dr. . . . . . . I18
Oxford Rd. . . . . . . . . . T20
Pinewood Ct. . . . . . . . T18
Plainfield Rd. . . . . . . . U19
Plaza Ct. . . . . . . . . . . V19
Portwine Rd. . . . . . . . . T18
Quincy St. . . . . . . . . . T19
Raleigh Rd. . . . . . . . . T20
Ridgefield Ln. . . . . . . . T19
Ridgemoor Ct. . . . . . . . T18
Ridgemoor Dr. . . . . . . . T19
Rodgers Ct. . . . . . . . . T20
Rodgers Dr. . . . . . . . . T19
Rogers Farm Rd. . . . . . . T19
Sheffield Ln. . . . . . . . . T19
Sheridan Dr. . . . . . . . . V18
Snug Harbor Dr. . . . . . . T20
Somerset Ct. . . . . . . . . T20
Somerset Rd. . . . . . . . . T20
Squire Ln. . . . . . . . . . T18
Stanhope . . . . . . . . . . T18
Stewart . . . . . . . . . . . S18
Stirling Ln. . . . . . . . . . S18
Stonegate Ct. . . . . . . . T19
Stough St. . . . . . . . . . T19
Stratford Ln. . . . . . . . . V19
Sugar Bush Ln. . . . . . . . V18
Sunset Ridge Rd. . . . . . . T20
Sussex Ct. . . . . . . . . . T18
Tanglewood Ln. . . . . . . T19
Tennessee Dr. . . . . . . . U18
Tremont . . . . . . . . . . . T20
Turnberry Ln. . . . . . . . . P17
Virginia Ct. . . . . . . . . . V18
Waterford Ct. . . . . . . . . T19
Waterford Rd. . . . . . . . . T20
Waverly St. . . . . . . . . . T18
Weather Hill Dr. . . . . . . . T18
Wedgewood Ct. . . . . . . . T19
Wedgewood Ln. . . . . . . . T19
Wesley Rd. . . . . . . . . . T20
Willow Hill Rd. . . . . . . . T19
Willow Ln. . . . . . . . . . . T19
Willow Way . . . . . . . . . T19
Willowood Ln. . . . . . . . . T18
Windsor Ln. . . . . . . . . . V19
Windward Cir. . . . . . . . . I18
Wingate Rd. . . . . . . . . . T19
Woodgate Ct. . . . . . . . . T18
60th Ct. . . . . . . . . . . . T18
63rd St. . . . . . . . . . . . V19
67th . . . . . . . . . . . . . T19
67th Pl. . . . . . . . . . . . U19
68th St. . . . . . . . . . . . U19
68th St. . . . . . . . . . . . U19
69th St. . . . . . . . . . . . U19
71st St. . . . . . . . . . . . P17
72nd Ct. . . . . . . . . . . . U19
73rd Ct. . . . . . . . . . . . U19
75th Ct. . . . . . . . . . . . V18
75th St. . . . . . . . . . . . U18
79th St. . . . . . . . . . . . V18

### GOLF COURSES
Ruth Lake Country Club . . . S19

### SCHOOLS
Gower West . . . . . . . . . V18
Marion Hills Seminary . . . . S18

### SHOPPING CENTERS
Shopping Center . . . . . . . U19

### MISCELLANEOUS
Hinsdale So. Athletic Field . . V18

---

## WINFIELD
Pages 8,9
STREETS
Alena Dr. . . . . . . . . . . H5
Alta Ln . . . . . . . . . . . J7
Ambleside Dr. . . . . . . . . K6
Arbor Ct. . . . . . . . . . . J7
Ash Ct. . . . . . . . . . . . K6
Aspen Ct. . . . . . . . . . . J6
Bardmore Ln. . . . . . . . . H7
Barnes Ave. . . . . . . . . . K7
Bedford . . . . . . . . . . . K6
Beecher Ave. . . . . . . . . K6
Birch St. . . . . . . . . . . J7
Birkdale Ct. . . . . . . . . . H7
Blair St. . . . . . . . . . . . J7,8
Bob-O-Link Dr. . . . . . . . K7
Bolles . . . . . . . . . . . . K7
Brandon Blvd. . . . . . . . . K6
Brookside Dr. . . . . . . . . K6
Calvin Ct. . . . . . . . . . . J7
Carrell St. . . . . . . . . . . J7
Chantilly Ct. . . . . . . . . . H7
Charlwell Dr. . . . . . . . . J6
Chelsea Cir. . . . . . . . . . J7
Chestnut Ln. . . . . . . . . H7
Childs St. . . . . . . . . . . L7
Church St. . . . . . . . . . . K6
Churchill Rd. . . . . . . . . J7
Cleveland St. . . . . . . . . L6
Cloos . . . . . . . . . . . . J7
Concord . . . . . . . . . . . J7
Cooley Ave. . . . . . . . . . K6
Courtney Ln. . . . . . . . . J7
Coventry Ct. . . . . . . . . H7
Coventry St. . . . . . . . . . H7
Cypress Ln. . . . . . . . . . J7
East St. . . . . . . . . . . . K7
Emerson Ct. . . . . . . . . . L7
Ennerdale Ln. . . . . . . . . K6
Essex Ln. . . . . . . . . . . J7
Ethel St. . . . . . . . . . . . J,J7
Evelyn . . . . . . . . . . . . K7
Fischer Ln. . . . . . . . . . K6
Fleming Dr. . . . . . . . . . K7
Florida Ln. . . . . . . . . . K6
Garfield St. . . . . . . . . . J6
Glen Eagles Dr. . . . . . . . J6
Grant St . . . . . . . . . . . L6
Grasmere Dr. . . . . . . . . K6
Heather Ln. . . . . . . . . . J7
Houghton Ct. . . . . . . . . H7
Interlachen Ln. . . . . . . . J7
Inverness Ct. . . . . . . . . J7
Jacob Dr. . . . . . . . . . . J7
Jefferson St. . . . . . . . . . K7
Jewell Rd. . . . . . . . . . . K6
Kimball . . . . . . . . . . . J7
Knoll Ct. . . . . . . . . . . . J7
Lancaster Dr. . . . . . . . . J7
Leonard St. . . . . . . . . . K7
Liberty St. . . . . . . . . . . K6
Lincoln Ave. . . . . . . . . L6
Lindsey Ave. . . . . . . . . K6
Lytham Ct. . . . . . . . . . H7
Madison . . . . . . . . . . . L7
Manchester Rd. . . . . . . . L6
Maple St. . . . . . . . . . . J6
Maxwell Ct. . . . . . . . . . J7
Melrose . . . . . . . . . . . J7
Myrtle St. . . . . . . . . . . K,L7
Nickolsen . . . . . . . . . . L7
Normandy Woods Ln. . . . . L6
Oak . . . . . . . . . . . . . L6
Oakwood . . . . . . . . . . J7
Park St. . . . . . . . . . . . K6
Parkway Dr. . . . . . . . . . H7
Peachtree Ln. . . . . . . . . J7
Peter Rd. . . . . . . . . . . J7
Peter St. . . . . . . . . . . . J7
Pin Oak Ct. . . . . . . . . . K6
Pinehurst Dr. . . . . . . . . J7
Prairie Rose Cir. . . . . . . . H7
Prescott Dr. . . . . . . . . . J7
Prestwick Ln. . . . . . . . . H7
Providence Ln. . . . . . . . J6
Quail Run Ct. . . . . . . . . K6
River . . . . . . . . . . . . K6
Robbins Ave. . . . . . . . . K6
Shady Way . . . . . . . . . K6
Shires Ct. . . . . . . . . . . J7
St. John Ave. . . . . . . . . J7
Stanley St. . . . . . . . . . . K6
Summit Dr. . . . . . . . . . L6
Sunnyside Ave . . . . . . . . K6
Suzanne Ct. . . . . . . . . . J7
Sycamore Ln. . . . . . . . . H7
Tamarack Ct. . . . . . . . . H7
Tamarack Ln. . . . . . . . . H7
Thistledown Ct. . . . . . . . H7
Timber Ct. . . . . . . . . . . J7
Timber Ridge Dr. . . . . . . H7
Torrey Pines Ct. . . . . . . . H7
Tuckaway Ct. . . . . . . . . H7
Turnberry Ln. . . . . . . . . H7
Victoria Ln. . . . . . . . . . J6
Virginia . . . . . . . . . . . J7
Walnut St. . . . . . . . . . . K6
Washington Ave. . . . . . . K6
Waterford Dr. . . . . . . . . H7
Wentworth Ct. . . . . . . . . H7
Wheatberry Ct. . . . . . . . H7
Wheatberry Dr. . . . . . . . H7
Wheaton Rd. . . . . . . . . J6
Whittield Way . . . . . . . . K6
Williams St. . . . . . . . . . L6
Wilmar Ct. . . . . . . . . . . L6
Windmere Rd. . . . . . . . . K6
Winfield Rd. . . . . . . . . . K6
Winfield Scott Rd. . . . . . . H7
Woodhall Ct. . . . . . . . . . H7
Woodvale . . . . . . . . . . J7
Wynwood Way . . . . . . . . L6

### CEMETERIES
St. John's Cemetery . . . . . L6

---

## FOREST PRESERVES
Winfield Mounds . . . . . . . J6

### GOLF COURSES
Klein Creek Golf Course . . . H7

### PARKS
Chartwell Park . . . . . . . . J7
Creekside Pk. . . . . . . . . K6
East St. Pk. . . . . . . . . . K7
Founders Park . . . . . . . . K7
Glasshagels Fields Park . . . . G7
Hedges Station Park . . . . . J7
Indian Grove Park . . . . . . L7
Knolls Park . . . . . . . . . J8
Lions Pk. . . . . . . . . . . K7
Oakwood Park . . . . . . . . J7
Prairie Trail Park . . . . . . . H7
Timberidge Park . . . . . . . H7
Winfield Est. Park . . . . . . J7
Wynwood Fields Park . . . . . K6

### SCHOOLS
St. John Catholic Sch. . . . . K7
Winfield Elem. Sch. . . . . . K6
Winfield Middle Sch. . . . . . K6

### MISCELLANEOUS
Central DuPage Hospital . . . K6
Fire Department . . . . . . . K6
Police Department . . . . . . K6
Village Hall . . . . . . . . . . K6

### WINFIELD TOWNSHIP
Pages 7,8,13,14
STREETS
Acorn Ave. . . Pg.8 . . . K5
Acorn Ct . . . Pg.14 . . M7
Acorn Ln. . . Pg.14 . . M7
Alena Dr. . . . Pg.8 . . . H5
Alsace Ct. . . . Pg.14 . . M5
Anderson Dr. . Pg.13 . . P1
Ardennes Ct. . Pg.14 . . M5
Averill-Barton Rd.
. . . . . . . . . Pg.7 . . . K1
Barnes Ave. . Pg.7,8 . . K3,4
Batavia Rd. . . Pg.13 . . L1,M2
Bauman Ct. . . Pg.8 . . . K5
Belleau Dr. . . Pg.8 . . . L5
Belleau Dr. W. Pg.8 . . . L6
Bender Ln. . . Pg.14 . . M5
Berkshire Rd. . Pg.8 . . . H5
Blackhawk Blvd. Pg.13 . . M3
Blair St. . . . . Pg.8 . . . J4
Blakewood Ct. Pg.14 . . M5
Bolles Ave. . . Pg.8 . . . L5
Branch Ave. . Pg.14 . . M4,7
Burr Oak Rd. . Pg.8 . . . H5
Butterfield Dr. Pg.13,14 N6,P2
Butternut Ln. . Pg.8 . . . P1
Calvin Ave. . . Pg.8 . . . J7
Cantigny Dr. S. Pg.14 . . M5
Cantigny Dr. W. Pg.8 . . . L6
Center Ave. . . Pg.8,14 . H,N7
Charles Ave. . Pg.8 . . . K4
Che Che Pinqua St.
. . . . . . . . . Pg.13 . . M2
Childs St. . . . Pg.8 . . . L5
Circle Dr. . . . Pg.7 . . . L3
Colford Ave. . Pg.8 . . . J5
Conston Ct. . . Pg.8 . . . K6
Connolly Ct. . Pg.14 . . M5
Coolidge Ave. . Pg.14 . . K5
County Farm Rd. Pg.8 . . . H,J7
Cove Ln. . . . Pg.14 . . P7
Domartin Pl. . Pg.8 . . . M5
Donald Ave. . Pg.8 . . . M5
Doris Ln. . . . Pg.8 . . . K6
DuPage St. . . Pg.8 . . . J5
Durfee Rd. . . Pg.14 . . N7
Easton . . . . . Pg.8 . . . K4
Edgewood Walk Pg.8 . . . M4
Elm Dr. . . . . Pg.8 . . . H6
Elmwood St. . Pg.7 . . . H1
Eola Rd. . . . Pg.13 . . M2
Equestrian Ct. Pg.14 . . M5
Essex Rd. . . . Pg.14 . . N7
Ethel St. . . . Pg.8 . . . H7
Fabyan Pkwy. . Pg.7 . . . K1
Flanders Ln. W. Pg.14 . . M5
Forest Ave. . . Pg.7 . . . K3
Forestview Dr. . Pg.14 . . M4
Galusha Ave. . Pg.14 . . P6
Garys Mill Rd. . Pg.8 . . . L5
Geneva Rd. . . Pg.7,8 . . J3,5
Gloria St. . . . Pg.8 . . . H7
Grove St. . . . Pg.8 . . . H4
Gunness Dr. . Pg.7 . . . L3
Hathaway . . . Pg.8 . . . K5
Hawthorne Ln. Pg.7,8 . . H2,7
Hazel St. . . . Pg.7 . . . K3
Helen Ave. . . Pg.8 . . . H4
Herrick Rd. . . Pg.14 . . P7
Hickory Ln. . . Pg.8 . . . H,4,7
Highlake Ave. . Pg.8 . . . H5
Hill Crest Rd. . Pg.8 . . . H5
Hillview Rd. . . Pg.8 . . . J4,5
Howard Ave. . Pg.8 . . . K4
Hoy Rd. . . . . Pg.14 . . M5
Indian Knoll Rd. Pg.8 . . . H5
Indian Knoll Trail
. . . . . . . . . Pg.8 . . . J5
Inner Ring Rd. Pg.13 . . M,P1
James Ave. . . Pg.8 . . . H,4,7
Joliet Rd. . . . Pg.14 . . M,N4
Joy Rd. . . . . Pg.7 . . . L3
Kautz Rd. . . . Pg.7 . . . H1
Kress Rd. . . . Pg.7 . . . H1
Lake Ave. . . . Pg.8 . . . J5
Lane Rd. . . . Pg.7 . . . H3
Lavergne Ln. . Pg.14 . . M5
Lee Rd. . . . . Pg.7,8 . . H2,4
Lenox Rd. . . . Pg.14 . . N5,7
Lester St. . . . Pg.7,8 . . K3,4
Liberty Dr. . . Pg.8 . . . K6
Lorraine Ct. . . Pg.14 . . M5

---

## WOOD DALE
Lost Meadow Ln.
. . . . . . . . . Pg.14 . . M4
Lowden Ave. . Pg.14 . . M7
Mac Queen Dr. Pg.7 . . . H2
Mack Rd. . . . Pg.14 . . M5
Madison St. . . Pg.14 . . N6
Main St. . . . . Pg.8 . . . K6
Marion Rd. . . Pg.8 . . . K6
May St. . . . . Pg.7 . . . K3
McChesney Rd. Pg.7 . . . K1
McDonald Ave. Pg.8 . . . K4
Melolane Dr. . Pg.7,8 . . L3
Morningside Ave.
. . . . . . . . . Pg.8 . . . J,L5
Morris Ct. . . . Pg.14 . . N4
National Rd. . Pg.8 . . . H5
National St. . . Pg.8 . . . H4,7
Neltner Blvd. . Pg.8 . . . K4
Nequa St. . . . Pg.13 . . M3
Northwood Rd. Pg.8 . . . H6
Oak Grove Ave. Pg.8 . . . H5
Oak Ln. . . . . Pg.14 . . M4
Old Farm Ln. . Pg.8 . . . H6
Outer Ring Rd. Pg.13 . . M,P1
Pamela Ct. . . Pg.14 . . N4
Pearl Rd. . . . Pg.7 . . . K3
Picardy Ct. . . Pg.8 . . . L5
Pilsen Rd. . . . Pg.7 . . . H2
Pine Ave. . . . Pg.8 . . . H4
Pine St. . . . . Pg.13 . . M1
Pomeroy . . . Pg.8 . . . J4
Potawatomi Blvd.
. . . . . . . . . Pg.13 . . M3
Prince Crossing Rd.
. . . . . . . . . Pg.8 . . . H,L5
Purnell Rd. . . Pg.14 . . L5
Ray Ave. . . . Pg.8 . . . H4
Renouf Dr. . . Pg.14 . . N4
Richton Ave. . Pg.8 . . . K4
Rigi Rd. . . . . Pg.8 . . . J4
River Glen Rd. Pg.8 . . . L6
Road "D" . . . Pg.13 . . M1
Road "L" . . . Pg.13 . . M1
Robin Ln. . . . Pg.8 . . . K6
Rogers Ct. . . Pg.8 . . . J5
Roosevelt Rd. . Pg.8 . . . K3
Sarana Ave. . . Pg.8 . . . K4
Sauk Blvd. . . Pg.13 . . M2
Schaefer Rd. . Pg.14 . . N6
Shabonna St. . Pg.13 . . M2
Cherman Ct. . Pg.7 . . . K3
St. Mihiel Dr. . Pg.14 . . M5
State Hwy. 38 Pg.7,8 . . J1,L5
Sunset Ave. . . Pg.8 . . . J5
Swan Lake Ct. Pg.14 . . M5
Swan Lake Dr. Pg.14 . . M5
Twin Oaks Dr. Pg.8 . . . H6
Verdun Dr. . . Pg.14 . . P6
Virginia Ave. . Pg.14 . . M5
Wallace Rd. . . Pg.8 . . . J5
Walz Way . . . Pg.14 . . M7
Warrenville Ave. Pg.14 . . N7
Washington Ave. Pg.8 . . . K4
White Oak Dr. Pg.14 . . L5
Williams Rd. . Pg.8,14 . M,M4
Willoughby Ln. Pg.13 . . P1
Wilson Rd. . . Pg.7 . . . L1
Wilson St. . . . Pg.8 . . . L4
Winfield Rd. . . Pg.8,14 . J,M6
Winnebago St. Pg.13 . . M3
Woodland Ave. Pg.8 . . . M5
Wynwood Rd. . Pg.8 . . . J6
Yvonne Ln. . . Pg.14 . . M7

### CEMETERIES
Assumption Cem.
. . . . . . . . . Pg.14 . . M6
Pioneer Cemetery
. . . . . . . . . Pg.13 . . M1

### FOREST PRESERVES
Roy C. Blackwell Forest
Preserve . . . Pg.14 . . M,N5
Spring Lake Forest Preserve
. . . . . . . . . Pg.8 . . . H6
Timber Ridge Forest Preserve
. . . . . . . . . Pg.14 . . H6
West DuPage Park
. . . . . . . . . Pg.8 . . . J6,K5

### GOLF COURSES
Cantigny Park & Golf Club
. . . . . . . . . Pg.14 . . N6

### MISCELLANEOUS
Big Woods Restoration Center
. . . . . . . . . Pg.13 . . P2
Cantigny War Memorial
Museum . . . Pg.8 . . . L7
Fermilab Village Pg.7,13 . . K2
Feynmon Computing Ctr.
. . . . . . . . . Pg.13 . . M1
Illinois Prairie Path
. . . . . . . . . Pg.8 . . . J7
Industrial Area . Pg.13 . . M1
Kline Creek Farm Historical Ctr.
. . . . . . . . . Pg.8 . . . H6
National Accelerator Laboratory
. . . . . . . . . Pg.7,13 . . K2
Robert McCormick Museum &
Gardens . . . Pg.8 . . . L6
Science Education Center
. . . . . . . . . Pg.8 . . . L6
Wilson Hall . . Pg.13 . . M1

### WOOD DALE
Pages 5,6
STREETS
A.E.C. Dr. . . . Pg.5 . . . B17
Abbotsford Rd. Pg.5 . . . C16
Addison Rd. . . Pg.5 . . . D18
Allen Dr. . . . Pg.5 . . . A17
Apollo Ct. Dr. . Pg.5 . . . C16
Arlene Dr. . . . Pg.5 . . . D16
Ash Ave. . . . Pg.5,6 . . C18
Aspen Rd. . . . Pg.5 . . . D17
Balm Ct. . . . Pg.5 . . . B18

---

Bauman Ct. . . Pg.5 . . . B16
Bay St. . . . . Pg.5 . . . C16
Beinoris Dr. . . Pg.5 . . . B17
Brookhurst Ln. Pg.5 . . . D17
Brookwood Dr. Pg.5 . . . D16
Brookwood Pl. Pg.5 . . . D16
Butternut Ave. Pg.6 . . . C18
Carter Ave. . . Pg.5 . . . C16
Catalpa Ave. . Pg.5 . . . C16
Catherine Ct. . Pg.5 . . . D16
Cedar Ct. . . . Pg.5 . . . C18
Cedar St. . . . Pg.5 . . . D17
Central Ave. . Pg.5 . . . C17
Central Ct. . . Pg.5 . . . D17
Century Dr. . . Pg.5 . . . C16
Charmille Ln. . Pg.5 . . . C16
Clare Ct. . . . Pg.5 . . . C16
Clayton Ct. . . Pg.5 . . . B17
Commercial St. Pg.5,6 . . C17
Congress Ct. . Pg.5 . . . C16
Creel Dr. . . . Pg.5 . . . B17
Crestwood Ct. Pg.5 . . . D18
Crestwood Rd. Pg.5,6 . . D18
Cypress Ct. . . Pg.5 . . . D18
Dalewood Ave. Pg.5 . . . C16
Deerpath Rd. . Pg.5 . . . C18
Devon Ave. . . Pg.5 . . . A18
Dillon Ct. . . . Pg.5 . . . B18
Dillon Dr. . . . Pg.5 . . . B18
Division St. . . Pg.5 . . . C17
Dominion Ct., E. & W.
. . . . . . . . . Pg.5 . . . D16
Dominion Dr. . Pg.5 . . . D16
Dominion Dr., W.
. . . . . . . . . Pg.5 . . . D16
Duck Ln. . . . Pg.5 . . . C16
Dunlay Ct. . . Pg.5 . . . C17
Dunlay St. . . Pg.5 . . . C18
Edgebrook Rd. Pg.5 . . . C17
Edgewood Ave. Pg.5 . . . B-D18
Elizabeth Ct. . Pg.5 . . . D17
Elizabeth Dr. . Pg.5 . . . D16
Elmhurst St. . Pg.5,6 . . C18
Elmwood Ave. Pg.5 . . . B18
Essex Ct. . . . Pg.5 . . . D16
Ethel Ln. . . . Pg.5 . . . D17
Fishing Ln. . . Pg.5 . . . C16
Florina Ct. . . Pg.5 . . . C17
Forest Glen Rd. Pg.5 . . . C17
Forest Preserve Dr.
. . . . . . . . . Pg.5 . . . D16
Forest View Ave. Pg.5 . . . C17
Foster Ave. . . Pg.5 . . . B18
Frederick Pl. . Pg.5 . . . C16
Front St. . . . Pg.5 . . . C17
Gerry Dr. . . . Pg.5 . . . B17
Gilbert Dr. . . Pg.5 . . . D16
Greene Ct. . . Pg.5 . . . C16
Grey Ct. . . . Pg.5 . . . C16
Grey St. . . . Pg.5 . . . C15
Grove Ave. . . Pg.5 . . . C16
Hackberry Ct. Pg.6 . . . D18
Hansen Ct. . . Pg.5 . . . B17
Harvey Ave. . Pg.5 . . . C16
Haynes Dr. . . Pg.5 . . . B18
Heather Ln. . . Pg.5 . . . C17
Hemlock Ave. Pg.5 . . . C16
Heritage Dr. . Pg.5,6 . . D16,17
Hiawatha Trail Pg.5 . . . C16
Homestead Dr. Pg.5 . . . C16
Hoover Dr. . . Pg.5 . . . C16
Irman Dr. . . . Pg.5 . . . D17
Iroquois Tr. . . Pg.5 . . . C17
Irving Park Rd Pg.5 . . . C17
Itasca St. . . . Pg.5,6 . . B18
Janis Ln. . . . Pg.5 . . . C16
Jason Ln. . . . Pg.5 . . . C16
Jeanne Ct. . . Pg.5 . . . C16
Jefferorn Pl . . Pg.5 . . . C16
Jennifer Ct. . . Pg.5 . . . C16
Jessica Dr. . . Pg.5 . . . C16
Juliann Dr. . . Pg.5 . . . C16
Juniper Ave. . Pg.5 . . . C16
Knollwood Dr. Pg.5 . . . D18
Lafayette St. . Pg.5 . . .
Lewis Dr. . . . Pg.5 . . . A16
Lilac Ln. . . . Pg.5 . . . D18
Lincoln Ct. . . Pg.5 . . . C16
Lively Blvd. . . Pg.5 . . . B18
Louise Ct. . . Pg.5 . . . C16
Manning Dr. . Pg.5 . . . C16
Maple Ave. . . Pg.5 . . . C16
Mark St. . . . Pg.5 . . . A17
Mary Jane Ln. Pg.5 . . . C16
Michael Dr. . . Pg.5 . . . A17
Mill Rd. . . . . Pg.5 . . . C16
Miller Ln. . . . Pg.5 . . . C16
Mittel Blvd. . . Pg.5 . . . A16
Mittel Dr. . . . Pg.5 . . . A16
Monroe Ct. . . Pg.5 . . . D17
Montclare Ln. . Pg.5 . . . C16
Montgomery Ln. Pg.5 . . . B16
Montrose Ave. Pg.6 . . . C18,D16
Mulberry Ct. . Pg.6 . . . D18
Murray Ct. . . Pg.5 . . . C16
Murray Ln. . . Pg.5 . . . C16
North St. . . . Pg.5 . . . B17
Oak Ave. . . . Pg.5 . . . C17
Oakwood Dr. . Pg.5 . . . C17
Orchard Dr. . . Pg.5 . . . C16
Paramount Dr. Pg.5 . . . B18
Pine Tree Ln. . Pg.6 . . . D18
Pond Ave., E. . Pg.5 . . . B17
Potter St. . . . Pg.5 . . . C16,17
Prospect Ave. . Pg.5 . . . B17
Raleigh Ct. . . Pg.5 . . . D16
Richert Rd. . . Pg.5 . . . B18
River Ave. . . Pg.5 . . . B16
Robert Kingery Hwy.
. . . . . . . . . Pg.5 . . .
Robert Ln. . . Pg.5 . . . D18
Robin Ln. . . . Pg.5 . . . D18
Roosevelt Ct. . Pg.5 . . . B18
Roosevelt St. . Pg.5,6 . . C18
Roy Dr. . . . . Pg.5 . . . C16
Royal Ct. . . . Pg.5 . . . D18

## WOOD DALE


Royal Oaks Dr. Pg.6 .... D18
Sarah Dr. .... Pg.5 .... C16
School St. ... Pg.5 .... B17
Sherwood Dr. Pg.6 .... D18
Sivert Dr. .... Pg.5 .... B17
Spring Oaks Dr. Pg.5 .... D17
Spruce Ave. .. Pg.6 .... C18
Spruce St. ... Pg.6 .... D18
St. Andrews Dr. Pg.5 .... D16
Station Ave. .. Pg.5 .... C16
Stoneham ... Pg.5,6 ... C18
Sunnyside Ave. Pg.5 .... C17
Sunset Dr. ... Pg.5 .... C17
Thomas Dr. .. Pg.5 .... C17
Tosca Dr. .... Pg.5 .... C17
Victoria Dr. .. Pg.5 .... C16
Victoria Ln. .. Pg.5 .... C16
Walnut Ave. .. Pg.5 .... C17
Warren Allen Dr. Pg.5 .... B17
Warren Ct. ... Pg.5 .... C16
Washington Sq. Pg.5 .... C16
Welter Dr. ... Pg.5 .... C16
Wheat Ln. ... Pg.5 .... B17
Windsor St. .. Pg.5 .... C17
Wisteria Ct. .. Pg.5 .... D18
Wood Dale Ave. Pg.5 .... B17
Wood Lane .. Pg.5 .... D17
Woodbine Dr. Pg.5 .... D18
Woodlane Ave. Pg.5 .... D18
Woodside Dr. . Pg.6 .... D18

**FOREST PRESERVES**
Richard Winters Conservation
Area ..... Pg.5 .... B17
Salt Creek F.P. Pg.5 .... D17

**GOLF COURSES**
Brookwood C.C. Pg.5 .... D16
Dominion C.C. Pg.5 .... D17
Elmhurst C.C. Pg.5 .... D16

**PARKS**
Benson Park . Pg.5 .... D15
Wood Dale Community Park
......... Pg.5 .... B17

**SCHOOLS**
Highland Sch. Pg.5 .... B17
Holy Ghost Catholic Sch.
......... Pg.5 .... C17
Oakbrook Sch. Pg.5 .... D17
Westview Sch. Pg.5 .... C16
Wood Dale Jr. H.S.
......... Pg.5 .... B17

**SHOPPING CENTERS**
Georgetown Square S.C. ... C16
Shopping Center ........ C16

**MISCELLANEOUS**
City Hall ..... Pg.5 .... C17
Fire Department Pg.5 .... B17
Library ...... Pg.5 .... B17
Oakwood Commerce Center
......... Pg.5 .... B16
Park District Recreation Building
.......... Pg.5 .... B17
Post Office ... Pg.5 .... B17
Railroad Station Pg.5 .... C17
School District Administration
Bldg. ..... Pg.5 .... B17
The Chancellory Business Park
......... Pg.5 .... A16


## WOODRIDGE


Page 22,23,28,29
(For additional listings, see Section 8)

**STREETS**
Adbeth Ave. .. Pg.22 .. W12
Alden Ln. .... Pg.22 .. W14
Allan Dr. .... Pg.22 ... T13
Anchor Dr. ... Pg.22 .. W13
Andover Ct. .. Pg.22 ... U13
Andrea Ct. ... Pg.22 ... V12
Andrea Ln. ... Pg.22 .. W12
Apache Ln. .. Pg.22 ... V13
Apple Ln. .... Pg.22 ... V13
Argonne Dr. .. Pg.28 ... Z14
Argonne Woods Dr.
......... Pg.29 ... Z15
Armour Ct. ... Pg.22 ... U11
Armstrong Ct. Pg.22 ... T12
Arnold Dr. ... Pg.22 ... T11
Ashbury Ave. . Pg.22 .. W12
Ashton Dr. ... Pg.23 ... V14
Aspen Ln. ... Pg.28 ... Z15
Audobon Ave. Pg.22 ... U13
Audobon Ct. . Pg.22 ... U14
Autumn Dr. .. Pg.22 .. W12
Baron St. .... Pg.29 ... X14
Barrington Ct. Pg.22 ... U13
Beaudin Blvd. Pg.28 ... Z13
Beller Rd. .... Pg.22 .. W14
Bening Dr. ... Pg.23 ... V14
Bern Ct. ..... Pg.22 .. W13
Biassie Ct. ... Pg.22 ... T11
Birchwood Pkwy.
......... Pg.22 ... V13
Bittersweet Ct. Pg.22 ... U13
Blue Flag Ct. . Pg.22 ... U12
Blue Jay Ct. .. Pg.22 ... U14
Bobby Jones Ln. Pg.22 ... T11
Bonnie Ct. ... Pg.22 ... U13
Boughton Cut Off
......... Pg.28 ... X13
Bradley ..... Pg.22 ... T12
Bramblebush Ct. Pg.22 ... U13
Brentwood Ct. Pg.22 ... V12
Brewer Ln. ... Pg.22 .. W12
Briarwood Ct. Pg.22 .. W13
Brighton Ct. .. Pg.22 ... U13
Bristol Ct. ... Pg.22 ... V14
Britten St. ... Pg.23 ... V14
Brook Ct. .... Pg.22 ... U13
Brunswick Cir. Pg.22 ... U13
Buckingham Cir. Pg.22 ... U13
Burke Ct. .... Pg.22 ... U12
Burr Ridge Ct. Pg.22 ... V13
Butternut .... Pg.22 ... V12
Cambridge ... Pg.22 ... U13
Canterbury Ln. Pg.22 .. W12
Cardinal Ave. . Pg.22 ... U14
Cardinal Ct. .. Pg.22 ... U13
Carlton Dr. ... Pg.22 ... U13
Carolwood Ln. Pg.22 .. W12
Carpenter Ct. . Pg.22 ... T12
Catalina Ct. .. Pg.22 ... U13
Catalpa Ave. . Pg.22 . U,V13
Catalpa Ct. ... Pg.22 ... U12
Charing Cross Rd.
......... Pg.28 ... X14
Charmingfare Dr. Pg.22 ... V13
Chatham Ct. .. Pg.28 ... X14
Chelsea Dr. .. Pg.22 ... V13
Chelsea Ln. .. Pg.22 .. W12
Cherry Tree Ct. Pg.22 ... U13
Cherry Tree Ln. Pg.22 ... U13
Chesham Ct. . Pg.22 ... V14
Chesterton Ct. Pg.23 ... V14
Chesterton Dr. Pg.23 ... V14
Chestnut Ave. Pg.22 . U,V13
Chic Evans Ln. Pg.22 ... U11
Chippington Rd. Pg.28 ... V14
Church Ct. ... Pg.22 ... U12
Clarendon Ct. . Pg.22 .. W12
Clark Dr. .... Pg.22 ... T12
Clover Ln. ... Pg.28 ... X14
Coliridge Ct. .. Pg.29 ... X14
Concord Dr. .. Pg.22 ... U13
Cooper Ct. ... Pg.22 ... U12
Copeland Ct. . Pg.22 ... V11
Copeland Rd. . Pg.22 ... V11
Coppergate Rd. Pg.29 ... X14
Country Club Dr. Pg.22 ... V13
Crabtree Ave. . Pg.22 V12,13
Crabtree Ct. .. Pg.22 ... V13
Cramer Ln. .. Pg.22 .. W14
Creek Dr. N. .. Pg.22 .. W12
Creekside Ct. . Pg.22 ... T12
Cromwell Ave. Pg.23 ... V14
Crown Point St. Pg.22 ... U13
Crystal Ct. ... Pg.22 ... V13
Dalewood Ct. . Pg.22 ... V13
Dalewood Pkwy. Pg.22 ... V13
Danbury Dr. .. Pg.22 ... U13
Davey Rd. ... Pg.28 ... Z14
Davos Ave. .. Pg.22 ... V12
Dean Dr. .... Pg.22 ... T11
Deer Dr. ..... Pg.22 ... V12
Deerfield .... Pg.22 ... V13
Deerpath Ln. . Pg.28 ... Z15
Deerwood Ct. . Pg.22 .. W12
Demaret Ct. .. Pg.22 ... T11
Diamond Ct. . Pg.22 ... T12
Didrikson Dr. . Pg.22 ... U11
Dorimar Dr. .. Pg.22 ... V11
Double Eagle Dr. Pg.22 ... T11
Dove Ave. ... Pg.22 ... U13
Dover Ct. .... Pg.22 ... U13
Dryden St. ... Pg.29 ... X14
Duke St. ..... Pg.29 ... X14
Dunham Rd. . Pg.22 .. W14
Eastgate Ct. .. Pg.22 ... T13
Eastside Ave. . Pg.22 ... U13
Eastwood Ln. . Pg.22 .. W12
Edgerton Dr. . Pg.23 ... V14
Edgewood Cir. Pg.22 ... V12
Edgewood Ct. Pg.22 ... V12
Edgewood Pkwy.
......... Pg.22 ... V12
Elm St. ..... Pg.22 ... V12
Emerald Dr. .. Pg.22 ... V13
Essex Ct. .... Pg.22 ... T11
Essex Rd. ... Pg.22 ... T11
Everglade Ave. Pg.22 ... V12
Evergreen Ln. Pg.22 ... V13
Fairfield ..... Pg.22 ... S13
Fairmont .... Pg.22 ... S13
Fitzgerald .... Pg.22 ... U14
Forest Dr. ... Pg.22 ... V13
Forest Glen Pkwy.
......... Pg.22 ... V12
Fountain Dr. .. Pg.22 ... T11
Fox Dr. ...... Pg.22 ... V12
Fox Tree Ave. . Pg.22 U13,14
Foxboro Dr. .. Pg.22 .. W12
Foxglove St. . Pg.22 ... U12
Foxridge Ct. .. Pg.22 ... V12
Francis Ct. ... Pg.29 ... X14
Frost Ct. ..... Pg.22 .. W12
Gallmar Dr. .. Pg.22 ... V11
Gatewood ... Pg.22 .. W12
Geneva St. ... Pg.22 ... V12
Glen Ct. ..... Pg.22 ... U12
Glouchester Ct. Pg.29 ... X14
Goldfinch Ct. . Pg.22 ... U13
Goldfinch St. . Pg.22 U13,14
Golf View Dr. . Pg.22 ... V14
Green Dr. .... Pg.22 ... T12
Greene Rd. .. Pg.22 ... U11
Greenleaf St. . Pg.22 ... U13
Grissom Ct. .. Pg.22 ... U12
Hagen ...... Pg.22 ... T11
Halsey Ct. ... Pg.22 ... T12
Halsey Dr. ... Pg.22 ... T12
Hampton Dr. . Pg.23 ... V14
Hanover St. .. Pg.23 ... V14
Harleyford Rd. Pg.29 ... X14
Hartford Ln. .. Pg.22 ... V14
Harvest Ave. . Pg.22 ... U13
Hastings Rd. . Pg.29 ... X14
Hawthorne Ln. Pg.22 ... U13
Hiawatha .... Pg.22 ... V13
Hickory Ct. ... Pg.22 .. W12
High Gate Ln. . Pg.28 ... X14
High Tr. ..... Pg.22 ... T11
Highland Ave. Pg.22 ... V12
Hillcrest Ct. .. Pg.29 ... X14
Hillcrest Ln. .. Pg.29 ... X14
Hillside Ct. ... Pg.22 ... T11
Hobson Ct. .. Pg.22 ... T12
Hobson Rd. .. Pg.22 ... U11
Hobson Valley Dr.
......... Pg.22 ... U11
Hornbean Ct. . Pg.22 ... V11
Internationale Pkwy.
......... Pg.28 Z13-15
Iroquois Ct. .. Pg.22 ... V12
Jackson Ct. .. Pg.22 ... T12
Jackson Dr. .. Pg.22 T12,13
Jameswood Dr. Pg.22 ... U13
Janes Ave. ... Pg.22 ... U13
Janes Ct. .... Pg.22 ... V13
Janes Pl. .... Pg.22 .. W13
Janes Rd. ... Pg.22 ... V13
JoAnn Ln. ... Pg.22 .. W12
Jonquil Ln. .. Pg.22 ... V12
Jonquil Ln. N. Pg.22 ... V12
Juneberry Ave. Pg.22 ... U12
Kelly Ct. ..... Pg.22 .. W13
Kelly Dr. ..... Pg.22 .. W13
Kildeer Ct. ... Pg.22 ... U13
Kildeer St. ... Pg.22 ... U13
Kimball Ct. ... Pg.22 ... U12
Kincaid ..... Pg.22 ... T12
King Ct. ..... Pg.22 ... T12
Knob Hill Dr. . Pg.22 .. W14
Knotty Pine .. Pg.22 ... V13
Kohley Ave. .. Pg.22 .. W13
Koloff Ct. .... Pg.22 ... U12
Lakeview Ct. . Pg.22 ... T11
Langley Ct. .. Pg.22 ... T13
Larchwood Ln. Pg.22 . U,V13
Larkspur Ln. . Pg.22 ... U12
Laurel Ave. .. Pg.22 ... V13
Lavos Ave. ... Pg.22 ... V12
Leawood Ct. . Pg.22 .. W12
Leawood Ln. . Pg.22 .. W12
Lee St. ...... Pg.22 ... T13
Lemont Rd. .. Pg.28 ... Z15
Lindenwood Ln. Pg.22 ... U13
Locust Ct. N. . Pg.22 ... V13
London Ave. . Pg.28 ... X14
Longford St. . Pg.23 ... V14
Lorraine Ct. .. Pg.22 ... T13
Luzern Ct. ... Pg.22 .. W13
MacArthur Dr. Pg.22 ... T12
Manchester Ct. Pg.22 ... U13
Mansfield St. . Pg.22 ... V14
Marmon Dr. .. Pg.28 ... Z13
Marshall Dr. .. Pg.22 ... T11
Martin Ct. ... Pg.22 ... U12
Martin Dr. ... Pg.22 ... U12
Mashie Ct. ... Pg.22 ... T11
Mason Ln. ... Pg.23 ... V14
Maxwell Dr. .. Pg.22 ... T12
Meadowdale Ct. Pg.22 ... U13
Meadowdale Ln. Pg.22 ... V13
Meadowwood Ave.
......... Pg.23 ... V14
Mending Wall Dr.
......... Pg.22 .. W12
Meyer Rd. ... Pg.22 ... T11
Middlebury Ave. Pg.22 ... V14
Middlecott ... Pg.22 ... T11
Mitchell Dr. .. Pg.22 T12,13
Mohawk Ave. . Pg.22 ... U12
Morey Blvd. .. Pg.28 ... X14
Mourning Dove Ct.
......... Pg.22 ... W13
Mulligan Dr. .. Pg.22 ... T11
Naples Ln. ... Pg.28 ... Z15
Nelson Ct. ... Pg.22 .. W12
New Castle Ct. Pg.23 ... V14
Newport Dr. .. Pg.22 ... U13
North Field Rd. Pg.28 ... X14
Northgate Ct. . Pg.22 ... S13
Norwood Ct. . Pg.22 .. W12
O'Hare Ct. ... Pg.22 ... U12
Oak Leaf Ct. .. Pg.22 .. W12
Oak Leaf Dr. .. Pg.22 .. W12
Oak Tree Ct. .. Pg.22 ... T11
Oak Tree Tr. .. Pg.22 ... T11
Oakleaf Ct. ... Pg.22 .. W12
Oakview Ct. .. Pg.22 ... V12
Oakview Ln. .. Pg.22 ... V12
Old Creek Ct. . Pg.23 ... V14
Old Fence Dr. . Pg.22 .. W12
Olympia Ct. .. Pg.22 ... T11
Orchard Ln. .. Pg.22 ... V13
Oriole Ct. .... Pg.22 ... U14
Ouimet Ct. ... Pg.22 ... U11
Owl Ct. ...... Pg.22 ... U13
Oxford St. ... Pg.28 ... X14
Park Ln. ..... Pg.22 ... U13
Parklane Dr. .. Pg.22 ... U13
Parkside Dr. .. Pg.22 ... T11
Parkwood Ln. Pg.22 .. W12
Patrick Ct. ... Pg.28 ... X14
Patterson Ct. . Pg.22 ... U12
Patton Dr. ... Pg.22 ... U12
Patty Berg Ct. Pg.22 ... T11
Pembridge Ave. Pg.23 ... V14
Penny Royal Pl. Pg.22 ... U13
Perry ....... Pg.22 ... S13
Pershing Ct. .. Pg.22 ... U12
Peters Dr. ... Pg.28 ... X14
Peterson Ct. .. Pg.22 ... V12
Pheasant Ct. . Pg.22 ... U13
Piers Dr. .... Pg.22 .. W13
Plaza Dr. .... Pg.22 ... U13
Plover Ct. .... Pg.22 ... U14
Prairie Ln. ... Pg.29 ... X14
Prairie View Ave. Pg.22 ... U13
Providence Dr. Pg.22 ... U13
Purchase Dr. . Pg.22 ... T11
Quail Ct. ..... Pg.22 ... U14
Quimet Ct. ... Pg.22 ... V11
Randolph Ct. . Pg.29 .. W14
Ravinia Ln ... Pg.22 ... U13
Red Bud Ln. . Pg.22 ... U13
Redcliffe St. .. Pg.23 ... V14
Redwing Dr. .. Pg.22 ... U13
Remington Ct. Pg.22 ... U13
Rhodes Ct. ... Pg.22 ... U13
Richfield Ct. .. Pg.23 ... V14
Ridge Ln. .... Pg.22 ... V13
Ridgeway Dr. . Pg.22 ... T12
Rising Ct. .... Pg.29 ... Z14
Roberts Ct. .. Pg.22 ... U12
Roberts Dr. .. Pg.22 ... U12
Rosenbury Ave. Pg.23 ... V14
Rosewood Ct. Pg.22 ... V13
Ross Dr. .... Pg.22 ... S13
Rothenburg Rd. Pg.28 ... Z15
Rutgers Dr. .. Pg.28 ... X14
Rutherford Dr. Pg.23 ... V14
Ryan Rd. .... Pg.22 ... U14
Salem Ct. .... Pg.22 ... U13
Sanbark Ct. .. Pg.22 .. W12
Sarazen Ct. .. Pg.22 ... T11
Sardola Ct. ... Pg.22 ... V11
Scarlet Hawthorne Ct.
......... Pg.22 ... U13
Scarsdale Ct. . Pg.22 .. W14
Scenicwood Ln. Pg.22 ... V12
Seminole Ct. . Pg.22 ... U13
Seven Bridges Dr.
......... Pg.22 ... T11
Shagbark Ct. . Pg.22 .. W12
Shagbark St. . Pg.22 .. W12
Shelley Ct. ... Pg.22 .. W12
Sheppard Ct. . Pg.22 ... U12
Sheridan .... Pg.22 ... T12
Sherman Dr. . Pg.22 ... T12
Sioux Ave. ... Pg.22 ... U13
Slayton Ct. ... Pg.22 ... U12
Snead Ct. .... Pg.22 ... T11
Southcrest Dr. Pg.22 ... T12
Spring St. ... Pg.22 ... V13
Sprucewood . Pg.22 U12,V13
Stable Rd. ... Pg.22 ... T11
Stephen Ct. .. Pg.22 .. W12
Stillwell Ct. .. Pg.22 ... T12
Stonebridge Way
......... Pg.28 ... Z15
Stonewall Ave. Pg.22 S12,13
Sumac ...... Pg.22 ... U13
Summerhill Dr. Pg.22 ... T11
Sundowner Rd. Pg.22 ... T11
Sundrop Ave. . Pg.22 ... U12
Sundrop Ct. .. Pg.22 ... U12
Sunnydale St. Pg.22 ... U13
Sussex Ct. ... Pg.22 ... U13
Sussex Ln. .. Pg.22 .. W13
Swallow Ct. .. Pg.22 ... U13
Taylor Dr. .... Pg.22 ... T12
The Center Dr. Pg.22 ... U13
Timke Rd. ... Pg.22 ... T12
Tolios Dr. .... Pg.28 ... Z15
Two Paths ... Pg.22 .. W12
Tyler Ct. ..... Pg.22 ... T12
Tyler Dr. .... Pg.22 ... T12
Union St. .... Pg.28 ... X14
Vail Ct. ...... Pg.28 ... X14
Vail Ln. ..... Pg.29 ... X14
Valley View .. Pg.22 ... V13
Vantage Ct. .. Pg.22 ... U13
Vantage St. .. Pg.22 ... U13
Vardon Ct. ... Pg.22 ... U11
Vernon Ct. ... Pg.22 ... T12
Vista Dr. .... Pg.22 ... U13
Wainwight Dr. Pg.22 ... U12
Wake Robin Ct. Pg.22 ... U13
Wall Dr. ..... Pg.22 .. W12
Walnut Ave. .. Pg.22 ... T13
Waterbury Ct. Pg.22 ... U13
Waterbury Dr. Pg.22 ... V13
Waterford Ln. Pg.29 ... X14
Werch Dr. ... Pg.28 ... X14
Westbury Dr. . Pg.23 ... V14
Westgate Ct. . Pg.22 ... T13
Westmoreland Ct.
......... Pg.22 ... U12
Westmoreland Dr.
......... Pg.22 ... U12
Westridge ... Pg.22 ... V12
Westview Ln. . Pg.22 ... V12
Wharf Dr. .... Pg.22 .. W13
Wheatfield St. Pg.22 ... U13
Wheeler St. .. Pg.22 ... T13
Whispering Oaks Ct.
......... Pg.22 ... V12
Whispering Oaks Ln.
......... Pg.22 ... V12
White Ct. .... Pg.22 ... U12
White Dr. .... Pg.22 ... U12
Whitehall Way Pg.22 ... W2
Wild Plum Dr. Pg.22 ... U12
Williams Ct. .. Pg.22 ... U12
Williams Dr. .. Pg.22 ... U12
Willow Ave. .. Pg.22 ... V13
Willow Ln. ... Pg.22 ... U13
Willow Wood Dr. Pg.22 ... V13
Winston Dr. .. Pg.22 ... T12
Wintergreen Ct. Pg.22 ... U13
Wolfe Ct. .... Pg.22 ... T13
Wolfe Dr. .... Pg.22 ... S13
Wood Ct. .... Pg.22 ... T12
Wood Sorrel Ct. Pg.22 ... U13
Wood Sorrel Pl. Pg.22 ... U13
Woodlyn Dr. . Pg.22 ... V13
Woodridge Dr. Pg.22 . T,V12
Woodside Dr. . Pg.29 ... Z15
Woodview ... Pg.22 ... V12
Woodward Ave. Pg.22 ... V14
Wren Ct. .... Pg.22 ... U14
Yellow Star Ct. Pg.22 ... U13
Yellow Star St. Pg.22 ... U13
York Ct. ..... Pg.22 ... T12
Yorkshire .... Pg.22 ... U13
Young Ct. ... Pg.22 ... U12
Zurich Ct. .... Pg.22 .. W13
Zurich Ln. ... Pg.22 ... V12
63rd Ct. ..... Pg.22 ... T12
63rd St. ..... Pg.22 ... T12
71st St. ..... Pg.22 U12,13
75th St. ..... Pg.22 ... V12
76th St. ..... Pg.22 ... V12
80th St. ..... Pg.22 ... V12
83rd St. ..... Pg.22 .. W12
107th St. .... Pg.28 ... Z13
107th St. .... Pg.28 ... Z13

**CEMETERIES**
St. Bernard's Cemetery
......... Pg.22 ... T13

**FOREST PRESERVES**
Fox Hollow F.P. Pg.23 ... V14
Hickory Grove F.P.
......... Pg.21 ... T10
Woodridge F.P. Pg.28 ... Z14

**GOLF COURSES**
Seven Bridges G.C.
......... Pg.22 ... T11
Village Greens Golf Course
......... Pg.22 ... V14
Zigfield Troy Golf Range
......... Pg.22 ... V14

**PARKS**
Boundary Hill Pk.
......... Pg.22 ... V12
Caddle Park .. Pg.22 ... T10
Castaldo Park Pg.22 ... U12
Echo Point Park Pg.22 .. W13
Falcon Ridge Park
......... Pg.22 .. W13
Hawthorn Hill Pk.
......... Pg.22 ... U12
Idgrove Park E. Pg.23 ... V14
Idgrove Park W. Pg.22 ... V14
International Estate Park
......... Pg.29 ... Z15
Janes Park ... Pg.22 ... V13
Mending Wall Park
......... Pg.22 .. W12
Orchard Hill West Park
......... Pg.22 .. W13
Park ........ Pg.22 ... T12
Rutgers Park . Pg.28 ... X14
Seven Bridges Park
......... Pg.22 ... T11
Summerhill Park Pg.22 ... T13
Sunnyhill Park Pg.22 ... U13
Triangle Park . Pg.22 ... T12

**SCHOOLS**
Edgewood Sch. Pg.22 ... V12
Goodrich Sch . Pg.22 ... U11
Jefferson Jr. H.S.
......... Pg.22 ... U13
John L. Sipley Sch.
......... Pg.22 ... T11
Meadowview Sch.
......... Pg.22 ... T13
Montessori of Woodridge
......... Pg.22 ... U13
Sipley Grade Sch.
......... Pg.22 .. W12
St. Scholastic Sch.
......... Pg.22 ... V13
Willow Creek Sch.
......... Pg.22 ... T12
Woodridge Christian Academy
......... Pg.22 ... T12
Woodridge Sch. Pg.22 ... V13
63rd St. Plaza Pg.22 .. W13

**SHOPPING CENTERS**
Shopping Center Pg.23 ... V14
Woodridge Plaza Pg.22 ... V13

**MISCELLANEOUS**
Fire Dept. .... Pg.22,28 U,Z13
Internationale Business Park
......... Pg.28 ... Z13
Police Dept. .. Pg.22 ... U13
Swimming Pool Pg.22 . T,V12
Village Hall .. Pg.22 ... V14


## YORK TOWNSHIP


Pages 10-12,16-18

**STREETS**
Addison Ave. . Pg.17 .. M16
Addison St. .. Pg.11 ... L16
Ahrens Ave. .. Pg.11 ... L16
Ann St. ..... Pg.11 ... L15
Apley Ln. .... Pg.17 .. M16
Ardmore Ave. Pg.17 .. M17
Ashby Ln. ... Pg.17 .. M16
Avenue Barbizon Pg.17 ... N16
Avenue Chateau, N. & E.
......... Pg.17 ... N16
Avenue Cherbourg
......... Pg.17 ... N16
Avenue La Tours Pg.17 ... N16
Avenue Normandy
......... Pg.16 ... N16
Avenue Orleans Pg.17 ... N16
Avenue Royal . Pg.17 ... N16
Avenue Verdome Pg.17 ... N16
Avondale Ln. . Pg.16 .. M14
Barbara Ln. .. Pg.17 ... N15
Beaumont Ln. Pg.16 .. M14
Bryan St. .... Pg.12 ... L19
Buckingham Ln. Pg.17 .. M16
Buttercup Ln. . Pg.17 .. M17
Butterfield Rd. Pg.12,17
............... L19,N14
Cadwell Ave. . Pg.12 ... L20
Central Ave. .. Pg.11 ... L15
Charlotte Ln. . Pg.17 ... P15
Chase Ave. .. Pg.11,17 L,M16
Church Ave. .. Pg.11 ... L16
Cimarron Rd. . Pg.10 ... H13
Clara Ct. ..... Pg.17 ... N15
Clifton Ln. ... Pg.16 .. M14
Colonial Ln. .. Pg.16 .. M14
Concord St. .. Pg.12 ... L20
Cornell Ave. .. Pg.11 ... L17
Danby St. .... Pg.17 .. M17
Dickens ..... Pg.12 ... L20
Dillon Ln. .... Pg.17 .. M17
Douglas Rd. .. Pg.17 ... P16
Duncan St. ... Pg.12 ... L20
East West Tollway
......... Pg.17 ... N15
Eastgate ..... Pg.17 .. M15
Edgewood Ave. Pg.11 ... L15
Edgewood Rd. Pg.10 ... L14
Edward St. ... Pg.11 L15,16
Eliot Ln. ..... Pg.17 .. M17
Euclid Ave. .. Pg.11,12,17
............... L19,M17
Fairfield Ave. . Pg.11,17
............... L,M,N15
Fairview Ave. . Pg.17 . M,Q16
Fillmore Ct. .. Pg.12 ... L20
Fillmore St. .. Pg.12 ... L19
Finley Rd. ... Pg.16 . M,P14
Florence ..... Pg.17 ... P16
Forest Ln. ... Pg.12 ... L20
Ginger Brook Dr. Pg.17 ... P15
Ginny Ln. .... Pg.17 ... P15
Glen Ln. ..... Pg.17 ... L20
Glen Park Ct. . Pg.16 .. M14
Glen Park Pl .. Pg.16 .. M14
Glen Park Rd. Pg.16 .. M14
Glendenning Rd. Pg.17 ... P15
Glenwood Ln. Pg.10 ... H13
Gloria Ln. .... Pg.17 ... N15
Grace St. .... Pg.11,17 L,M15
Grammercy Pk. Ln.
......... Pg.17 .. M15
Hampton Ln. . Pg.16 .. M14
Harvard St. .. Pg.12 ... L19
Herbert St. ... Pg.17 ... P16
Highland Ave. Pg.17 .. M15
Highmoor Rd. Pg.10 ... L14
Highridge Rd. Pg.11 L15,16
Hill St. ...... Pg.17 ... H17
Holyoke Ln. .. Pg.17 .. M17
Ingersoll Ln. . Pg.17 .. M16
Ingrid Ln. .... Pg.17 ... N15
Jamestowne Ln. Pg.17 .. M17
Karen Dr. .... Pg.17 ... N15
Kendall Ave. . Pg.12 ... L19
Kirk Ave. .... Pg.12 ... L19
Kirkland Ln. .. Pg.17 .. M16
Knollwood Ln. Pg.17 .. M16
Lacey Rd. ... Pg.16 ... P14
Lathrop Ln. .. Pg.17 .. M16
Lewis Ave. ... Pg.17 .. M15
Lexington St. . Pg.12 ... L19
Liberty Blvd. . Pg.17 ... Q16
Linden Ave. .. Pg.12 ... L20
Lombard Ave. Pg.17 ... L15
Lowell Ln. ... Pg.17 .. M17
Luther Ave. .. Pg.11,17 L,M16
Main St. ..... Pg.17 .. M15
Manor Ln. ... Pg.11 ... H17
Margaret Ln. . Pg.17 ... P15
Marlborough Rd. Pg.16 .. M14
Marys Ln. ... Pg.17 .. M15
Mayfair Pl. ... Pg.16 .. M14
McKenna Ct. . Pg.12 ... L20
Meadow Ln. . Pg.17 .. M16
Meyers Rd. .. Pg.17 .. M16
Michigan Ave. Pg.11,17 L,M16
Morningside Dr. Pg.17 ... L17
Morris Ave. .. Pg.11 L15,16
Myrtle Ave. .. Pg.11,17 . L17
Old York Rd. . Pg.12 ... L20
Park St. ..... Pg.17 ... Q16
Pine Ln. ..... Pg.17 ... L15
Pine View St. . Pg.17 .. M15
Poplar Ave. .. Pg.12 ... L20
Prospect St. .. Pg.12 ... L19
Riorden Rd. .. Pg.11 ... L17
Riverview .... Pg.11 ... H18
Rochdale Circle Pg.14 ... L16
Roosevelt Rd. Pg.10 L14,15
School Ave. .. Pg.11,17 L,M16
School St. ... Pg.17 ... P16
Shady Ln. ... Pg.10 ... L14
Southlane Dr. . Pg.17 .. M17
Spring Ave. .. Pg.12 ... L18
Standish Ln. . Pg.17 .. M16
Sterling Rd. .. Pg.17 ... P15
Stewart Ave. . Pg.11 ... L15
Stratford Ln. . Pg.17 .. M17
Sugarfield Ct. . Pg.11 ... L16
Summit Ave. . Pg.11 ... L17
Sunshine Dr. . Pg.11 ... L17
Theresa Ln. .. Pg.17 ... P15
Third St. .... Pg.11 ... L16
Vista Ave. ... Pg.17 .. M16
Vivian Ln. ... Pg.17 ... P15
Washington .. Pg.17 ... Q16
Westview Ave. Pg.17 .. M16
Wilcox ...... Pg.17 ... P16
Williamsburg Ln. Pg.17 .. M17
Windsor Ln. .. Pg.17 .. M17
Winthrop Ln. . Pg.17 .. M17
Wisconsin Ave. Pg.11 ... L16
Woodland Dr. Pg.12 ... L19
Woodland St. . Pg.17 ... P15
13th Pl. ..... Pg.11 ... L15
13th St. ..... Pg.11 L15,16
14th Pl. ..... Pg.17 ... L15
14th St. ..... Pg.11,17
............... L15,17
15th Pl. ..... Pg.17 .. M15
15th St. ..... Pg.17 M15,16
16th St. ..... Pg.17 .. M16
17th Pl. ..... Pg.17 .. M16
17th St. ..... Pg.17 .. M15
18th Pl. ..... Pg.17 .. M15
18th St. ..... Pg.17 .. M15
20th Pl. ..... Pg.17 .. M16
20th Pl. ..... Pg.17 .. M16
20th St. ..... Pg.17 M14,15
21st Pl. ..... Pg.17 .. M15
22nd St. ..... Pg.16,17 M15
31st St. ..... Pg.17 ... N15
36th St. ..... Pg.17 ... P16
37th St. ..... Pg.17 ... P16
38th St. ..... Pg.17 ... P16
39th St. ..... Pg.17 ... P16
40th St. ..... Pg.17 ... Q16
41st St. ..... Pg.17 ... Q16

**SCHOOLS**
Bethany Theological Seminary
......... Pg.17 .. M16
Christ the King Sch.
......... Pg.17 .. M15
Highland Hills Sch.
......... Pg.17 .. M15
Montini H.S. . Pg.17 .. M15
Nat'l Coll. of Education
......... Pg.17 .. M14
Northern Theological Seminary
......... Pg.17 .. M16
Stevenson Sch. Pg.11 .. M16
York Center Sch. Pg.11 ... L16

**MISCELLANEOUS**
Fire Dept. .... Pg.18 ... L19

# KANE COUNTY

## SECTION 4

## LEGEND

| | | |
|---|---|---|
| PARKS | TOLL FREE **90** | INTERSTATE HIGHWAYS |
| FOREST PRESERVES | **20** | U.S. HIGHWAYS |
| GOLF COURSES | **58** | STATE HIGHWAYS |
| CEMETERIES | **1** | COUNTY HIGHWAYS & OTHER PRIMARY ROADS |
| AIRPORTS & POINTS OF INTEREST | | OTHER ROADS |
| RIVERS OR LAKES | | OTHER STREETS |
| | | RAILROADS |

**TURN PAGE FOR ORIENTATION MAP**

# SECTION 4
## ORIENTATION MAP

Information on this page is to be used for general reference only.
For definitive listings of all information, see index at the end of this section.

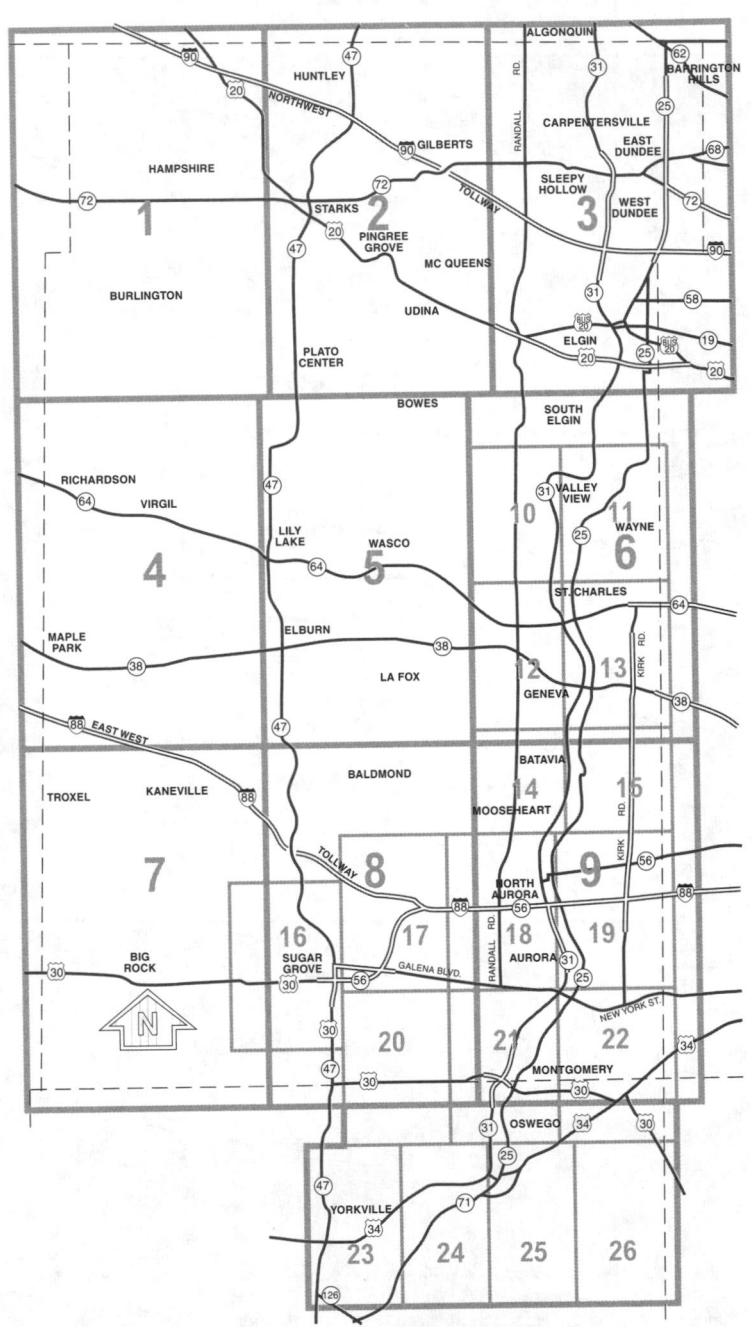

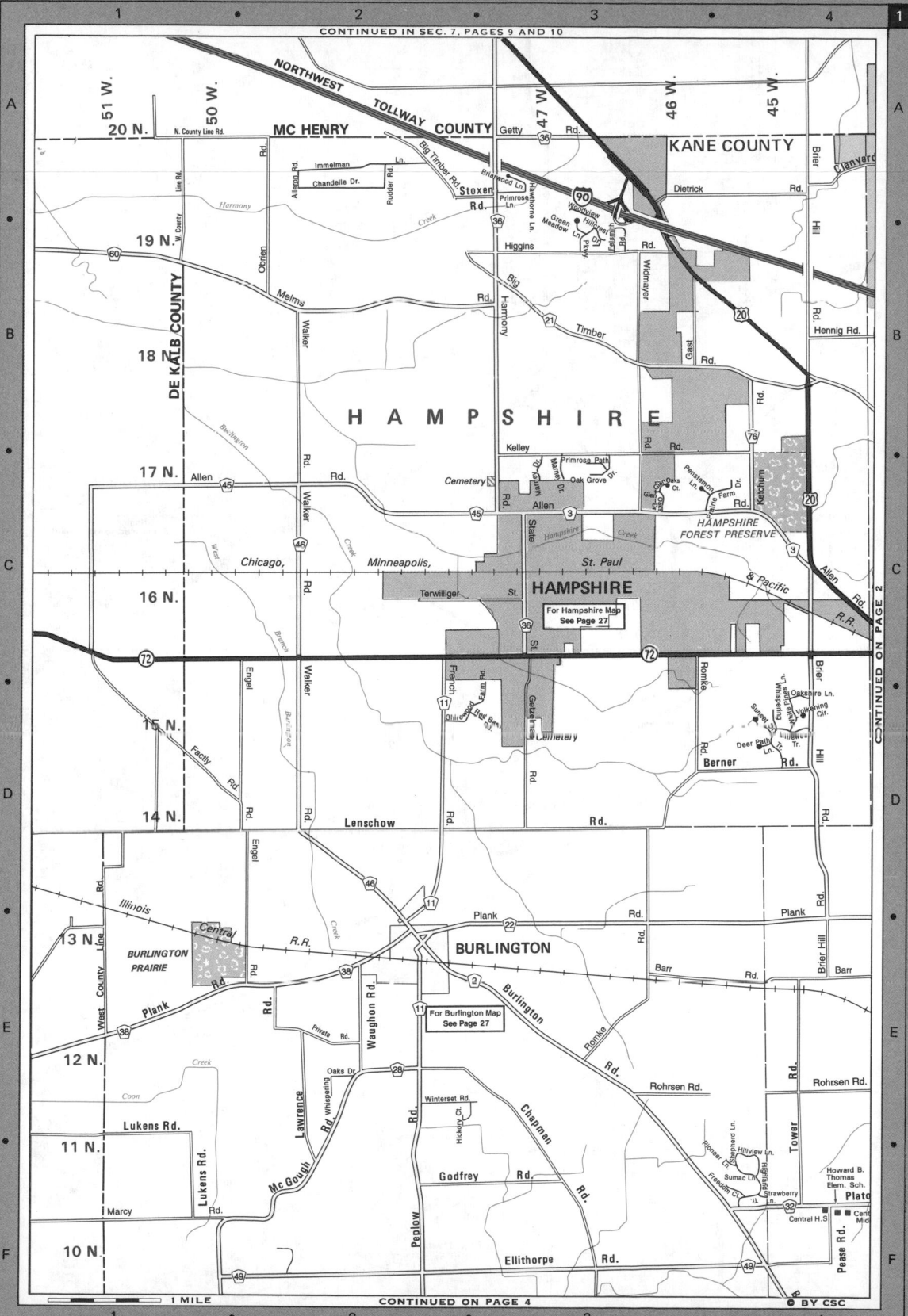

CONTINUED IN SEC. 7, PAGES 9 AND 10

NORTHWEST TOLLWAY

51 W.

50 W.

47 W.

46 W.

45 W.

20 N.

N. County Line Rd.

MC HENRY COUNTY

Getty Rd.

36

KANE COUNTY

Brier

Clanyard

Immelman Rd.

Chandelle Dr.

Big Timber Rd.

Stoxen

Rd.

Briarwood Ln.

Hawthorne Ln.

Primrose Ln.

36

Woodview

Hillcrest Dr.

Fox Pkwy.

90

Green Meadow Ln.

Dietrick

Rd.

Allison Rd.

Rudder Rd.

W. County Line Rd.

Walker

Melms

80

19 N.

Harmony

Creek

Higgins

Rd.

Big

Harmony

Widmayer

Rd.

20

DE KALB COUNTY

18 N.

Rd.

Walker

21

Timber

Gast

Rd.

Rd.

Hennig Rd.

H A M P S H I R E

76

17 N.

Allen

45

Walker

Rd.

Rd.

Kelley

Cemetery

Marnes Dr.

Primrose Path

Oak Grove Dr.

Allen

Rd.

45

3

Glen

Oaks Ct.

Penstemon Ln.

Farm Dr.

Rd.

Ketchum

20

HAMPSHIRE FOREST PRESERVE

3

Burlington

West

Creek

Chicago,

Minneapolis,

St. Paul

& Pacific

Allen Rd.

R.R.

16 N.

Rd.

Rd.

Terwilliger

St.

HAMPSHIRE

Hampshire Creek

For Hampshire Map See Page 27

72

Engel

Walker

Rd.

36

St.

72

Romke

Brier

15 N.

Facility

Rd.

Burlington

Branch

11

French

Getzelms

Red Barn

Olde

Cemetery

Berner

Surrey

Deer Path Ln.

Oakshire Ln.

Vollmering Cir.

Rd.

Hill

Rd.

14 N.

Engel

Rd.

Rd.

Lenschow

Rd.

Rd.

Rd.

Rd.

46

11

Plank

22

Plank

Rd.

Plank

Rd.

13 N.

West County Line

Illinois

Central

R.R.

38

BURLINGTON

2

Burlington

Barr

Rd.

Brier Hill Rd.

Barr

BURLINGTON PRAIRIE

Rd.

For Burlington Map See Page 27

11

Romke

Rd.

Plank

38

12 N.

Creek

Private

Waughon Rd.

Rd.

26

Winterset Rd.

Hickory Ct.

Rohrsen Rd.

Tower

Rd.

Rohrsen Rd.

Coon

Lawrence

Rd.

Whispering

Chapman

Rd.

11 N.

Lukens Rd.

Lukens Rd.

Oaks Dr.

Godfrey

Rd.

Pioneer Ln.

Shepherd Ln.

Hillview Ln.

Sumac Ln.

Freedom Ct.

Strawberry Ln.

Howard B. Thomas Elem. Sch.

Plato

Central H.S.

Central Mid.

Mc Gough

Rd.

32

Pease Rd.

Marcy

Rd.

Peplow

Rd.

10 N.

49

Ellithorpe

Rd.

49

1 MILE

CONTINUED ON PAGE 4

© BY CSC

CONTINUED IN SEC. 7, PAGES 10 AND 11

44 W.    43 W.    42 W.    41 W.    40 W.    39 W.    38 W.

Kreutzer   Rd.

Brier   Clanyard   Rd.   Hill   Rd.

Eakin Creek

Chicago Northwestern R.R.

Huntley   Rd.

Square Barn Rd.

Boyer   Rd.

30

Powers   Rd.

Freeman

Hennig   Rd.

**R U T L A N D**

Charles Ln.

Darby Ct.

Darby Ln.

Cheryl Ct.

Karen Ct.

Carriage Way

Freeman

Apache Ln.

ED MEAGHER FOREST PRESERVE

Galligan   Rd.

FREEMAN KAME FOREST PRESERVE

Spring Creek Rd.

Hidden Hills

BINNIE FOREST PRESERVE

CARP

6

**HUNTLEY**

Big   Timber   Rd.

21

Sandwald

Manning Rd.

52

NORTHWEST

Powers   Rd.

Binnie Rd.

Binnie Lakes Tr.

Oak Knoll Tr.

Randa Golf Cl

HAMPSHIRE FOREST PRESERVE

20

3

Allen   Rd.

Reinking

RUTLAND FOREST PRESERVE

Big   Timber   Rd.

90   Tollway

Tower Hill Rd.

Koppie

6

Tyler Creek

Tollview Tr.

Windmill

Windmill Ct.

Park St.

Errol Dr.

Center Ct.

East St.

Sola Dr.

**GILBERTS**

Higgins

1. Arrowhea
2. Sleeping B
3. Red Hawk
4. Running F
5. Running D
6. Shining M

1

cific

Pacific   R.R.

Tyler   Cr.

**STARKS**

72

Settlers Grove Rd.

Old Stage Rd.

Triple Oaks   Farm Rd.

Farm View Ln.

Red Leaf Rd.

Harper

Homestead Dr.

Maplehurst Ln.

Atchinson Ct.

Pheasant Field Ln.

Guthrie Ct.

21

7

Industrial   Dr.

59

NOR

Josh

Kathleen

Pamela

Suza

Debor

Mason

1. Kilkenny Ct.
2. Kildare St.
3. Welch St.
4. Kerry Ct.
5. Tipperary St.
6. Hennessy Ct.
7. Mason Rd.

CONTINUED ON PAGE 1

Oakshire Ln.

Walkening Cir.

Littlewoods Tr.

Berner

Brier   Hill

Thurnau   Rd.

47

Chicago,   Minneapolis

Reinking

Highland   Ave.

Damisch   Rd.

McCornack

Big   Timber   Ave.

Olive Dr.

Gang   Rd.

Timber   Ridge   Rd.

Pleasant Dr.

BURNRIDGE FOREST PRESERVE

21

CONTINUED ON PAGE 3

**PINGREE GROVE**

20

Mansfield Dr.

Store St.

Railroad St.

Jackson St.

Oak

Grove   Prairie

St.

Limerick Ln.

47

St. Paul &

Highland

Abilene Tr.

Cody Ct.

Chisolm

High Chaparral

Pacific

Polo Dr.

R.R.

For Pingree Grove Map See Page 27

Plank   Rd.

22

Robin Ln.

Hummingbird St.

Barr

Meadowlark Ct.

Marshall Rd.

**MC QUEENS**

Coombs

47

Elmer Ct.

Brier   Hill   Rd.

Barr   Rd.

Switzer   Rd.

79

Plank

22   Rd.

**UDINA**

20

33

Orchard

Old Barn Rd.

Oxwind Rd.

**P L A T O**

Illinois

Tower   Rd.

Rohrsen Rd.

Rohrsen

Central

Muirhead   Rd.

Fitchie

Cliff Dr.

Romeo Dr.

Verona Dr.

Rd.

Raleigh Dr.

Stratford Ln.

Burgess Dr.

Jaguar Ct.

York

N

Plato   Rd.

Chicago St.

R.R.

Russell

Rambli Rose Ln.

Wiggins

Lakes Dr.

Crestview Ln.

Pass

Grove

FITCHIE CREEK FOREST PRESERVE

Nesler

South   Water   Rd.

Wakesburg Dr.

Oxford

Newport Ct.

Otter

Bo

Howard B. Thomas Elem. Sch.

32

Strawberry Rd.

**PLATO CENTER**

33

Rippburger

Plato Center Elem. Sch.

32

Lakeview Ct.

Tributary Ct.

Chippewa

Pass

Long View Ln.

Crossing

**Plato**

Central H.S.

Central Middle Sch.

Pease   Rd.

Kendall   Rd.

47

Dittman   Rd.

51

Muirhead

Greenfield Rd.

1. Highbank Ct.
2. Current Ct.
3. Tributary Ct.
4. Channel Ct.
5. Bending Ln.

Meadow

Whitetail

**BOWES**

17

Heatherington Pl.

Lori Ln.

Hogan

Nesler

Hopi

1. Koshare Cir.
2. Wokomis Cir.
3. Thunder Gap
4. Park Path
5. Trails End
6. N. Leland Ct.
7. S. Leland Ct.

Ellithrope Rd.

**Bowes**

Ln.

CONTINUED ON PAGE 5

1 MILE

© BY CSC

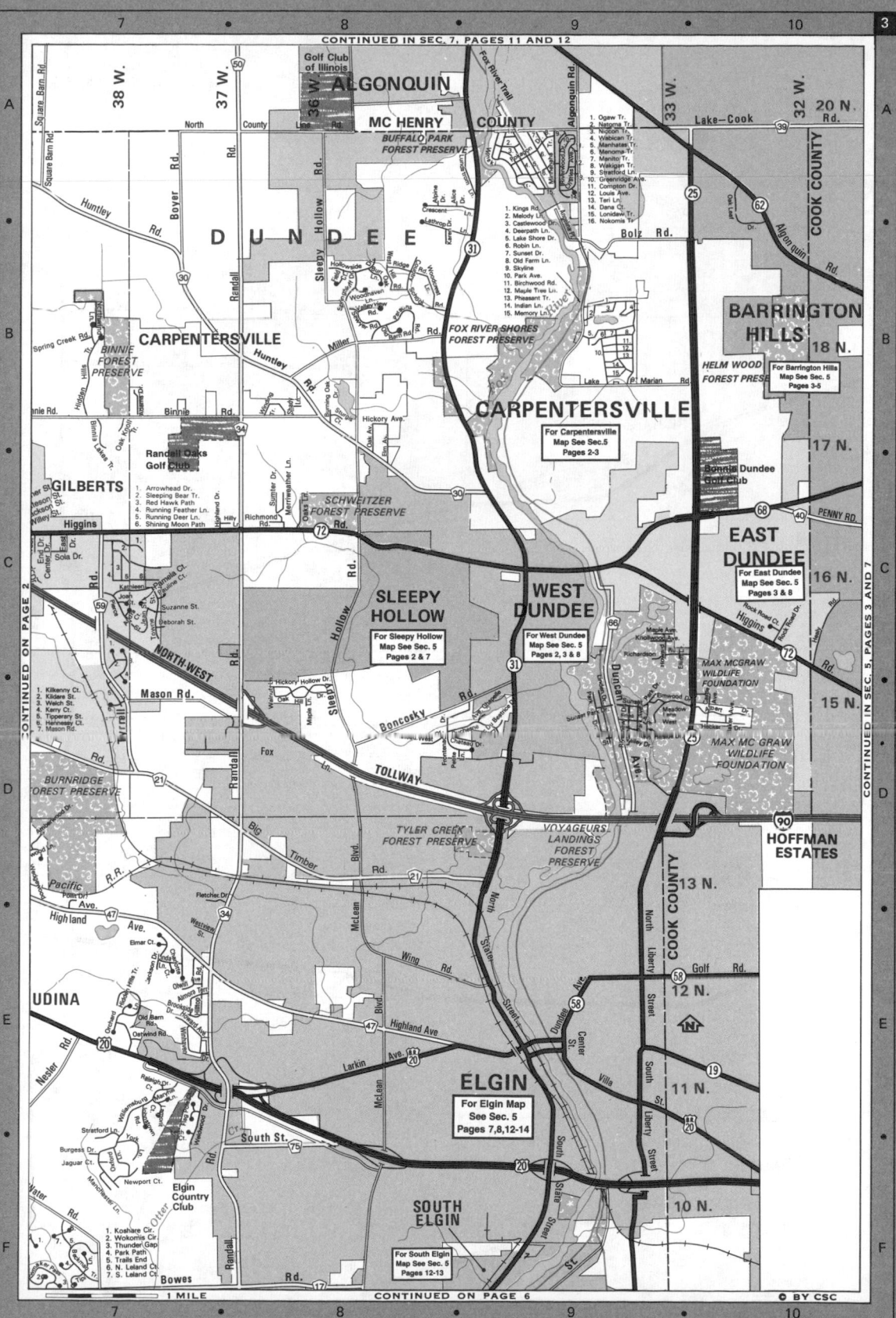

CONTINUED IN SEC. 7, PAGES 11 AND 12

ALGONQUIN

MC HENRY COUNTY

BUFFALO PARK
FOREST PRESERVE

Golf Club
of Illinois

BARRINGTON
HILLS

D U N D E E

CARPENTERSVILLE

BINNIE
FOREST
PRESERVE

FOX RIVER SHORES
FOREST PRESERVE

HELM WOOD
FOREST PRESE

For Barrington Hills
Map See Sec. 5
Pages 3-5

CARPENTERSVILLE

For Carpentersville
Map See Sec. 5
Pages 2-3

Bonnie Dundee
Golf Club

GILBERTS

Randall Oaks
Golf Club

1. Arrowhead Dr.
2. Sleeping Bear Tr.
3. Red Hawk Path
4. Running Feather Ln.
5. Running Deer Ln.
6. Shining Moon Path

SCHWEITZER
FOREST PRESERVE

EAST
DUNDEE

For East Dundee
Map See Sec. 5
Pages 3 & 8

SLEEPY
HOLLOW

For Sleepy Hollow
Map See Sec. 5
Pages 2 & 7

WEST
DUNDEE

For West Dundee
Map See Sec. 5
Pages 2, 3 & 8

MAX MCGRAW
WILDLIFE
FOUNDATION

1. Kilkenny Ct.
2. Kildare St.
3. Welch St.
4. Kerry Ct.
5. Tipperary St.
6. Hennessy Ct.
7. Mason Rd.

Mason Rd.

NORTH-WEST

Boncosky

MAX MC GRAW
WILDLIFE
FOUNDATION

BURNRIDGE
FOREST PRESERVE

Pacific

TOLLWAY

TYLER CREEK
FOREST PRESERVE

VOYAGEURS
LANDINGS
FOREST
PRESERVE

HOFFMAN
ESTATES

UDINA

ELGIN

For Elgin Map
See Sec. 5
Pages 7,8,12-14

Elgin
Country
Club

1. Koshare Cir.
2. Wokomis Cir.
3. Thunder Gap
4. Park Path
5. Trails End
6. N. Leland Ct.
7. S. Leland Ct.

SOUTH
ELGIN

For South Elgin
Map See Sec. 5
Pages 12-13

COOK COUNTY

1. Kings Rd.
2. Melody Ln.
3. Castlewood Dr.
4. Deerpath Ln.
5. Lake Shore Dr.
6. Robin Ln.
7. Sunset Dr.
8. Old Farm Ln.
9. Skyline
10. Park Ave.
11. Birchwood Rd.
12. Maple Tree Ln.
13. Pheasant Tr.
14. Indian Ln.
15. Memory Ln.

1. Ogaw Tr.
2. Natoma Tr.
3. Niotion Tr.
4. Wabican Tr.
5. Manhatas Tr.
6. Menoma Tr.
7. Manitoi Tr.
8. Wakigan Tr.
9. Stratford Ln.
10. Greenridge Ave.
11. Compton Dr.
12. Louis Ave.
13. Teri Ln.
14. Dana Ct.
15. Lonidaw Tr.
16. Nokomis Tr.

1 MILE

CONTINUED ON PAGE 6

© BY CSC

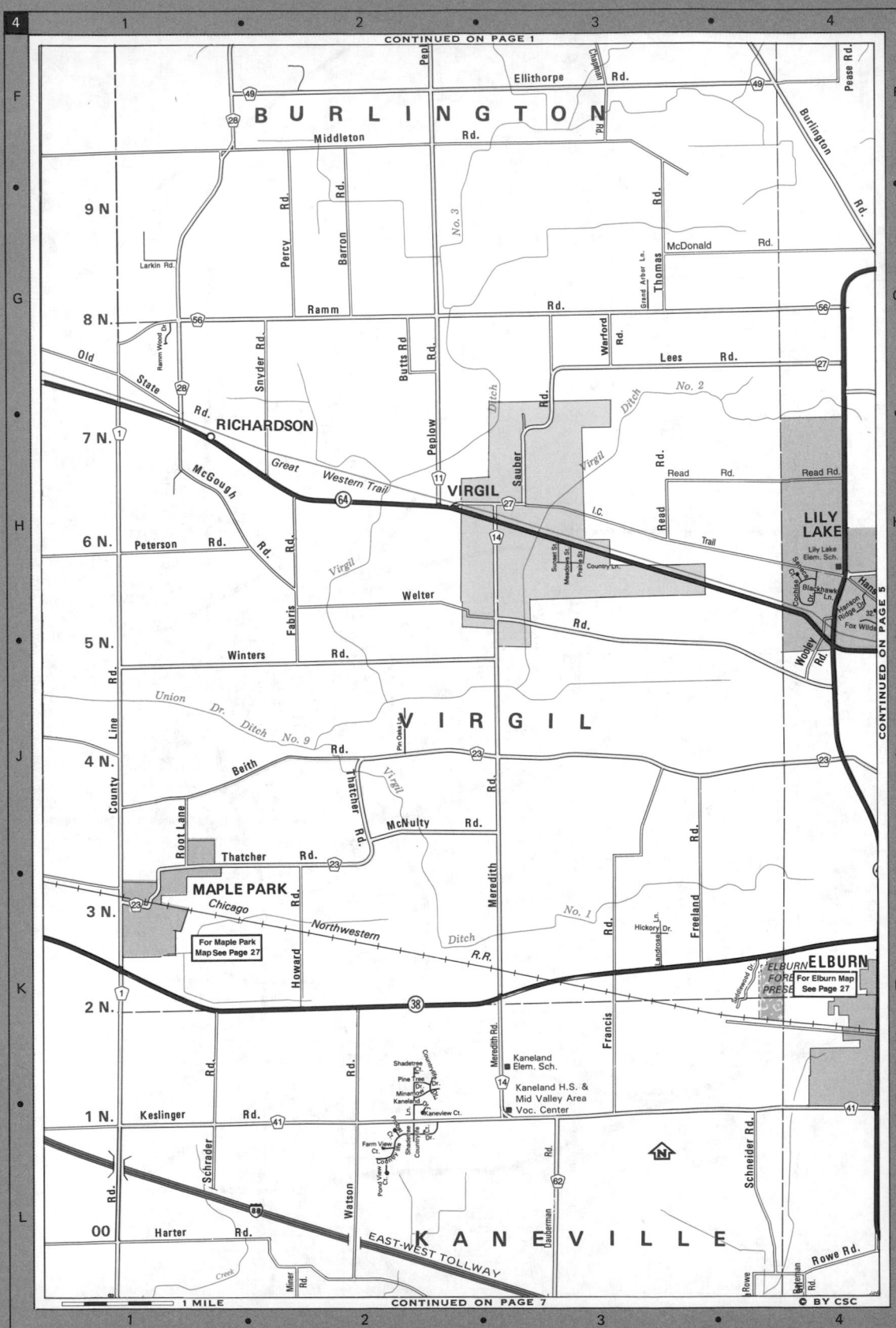

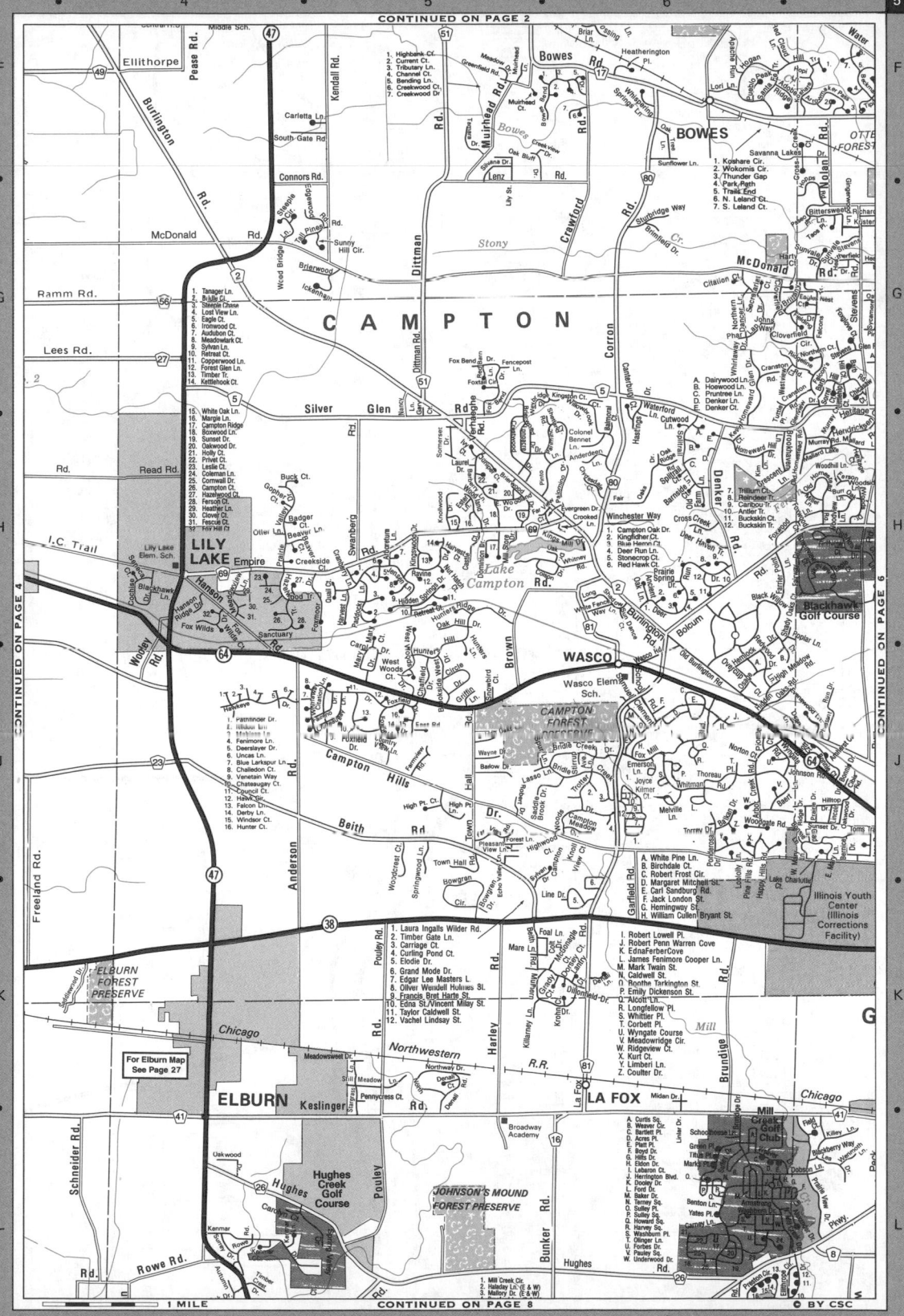

CONTINUED ON PAGE 4

CONTINUED ON PAGE 6

© BY CSC

1 MILE

For Elburn Map
See Page 27

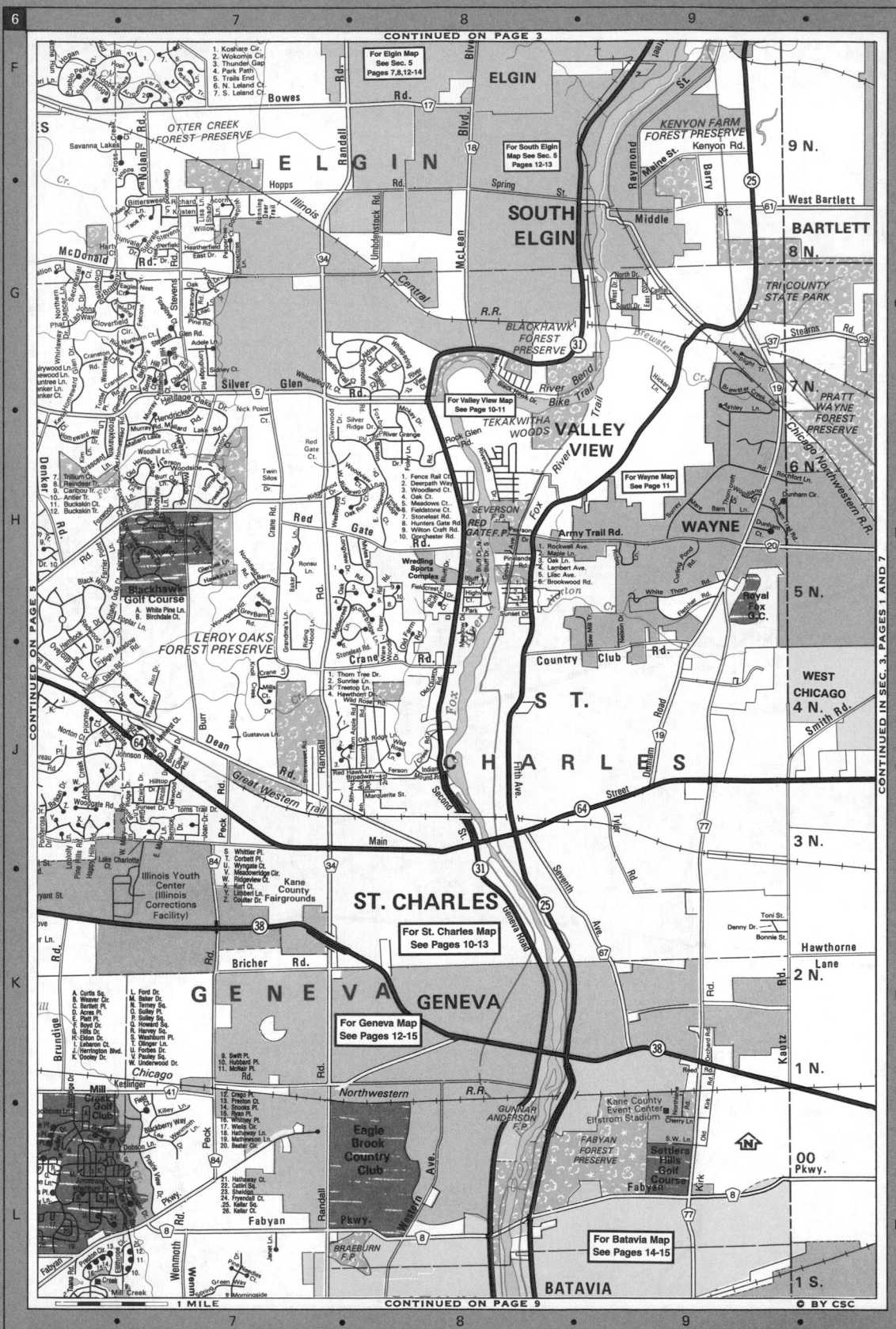

CONTINUED ON PAGE 3

1. Koshare Cir.
2. Wokomis Cir.
3. Thunder Gap
4. Park Path
5. Trails End
6. N. Leland Ct.
7. S. Leland Ct.

For Elgin Map
See Sec. 5
Pages 7,8,12-14

For South Elgin
Map See Sec. 5
Pages 12-13

ELGIN

Bowes

OTTER CREEK
FOREST PRESERVE

KENYON FARM
FOREST PRESERVE
Kenyon Rd.

Savanna Lakes

ELGIN

Hopps

SOUTH
ELGIN

West Bartlett

BARTLETT
8 N.

9 N.

McDonald

TRI-COUNTY
STATE PARK

G

Silver Glen

R.R.

BLACKHAWK
FOREST
PRESERVE

PRATT
WAYNE
FOREST
PRESERVE

7 N.

6 N.

For Valley View Map
See Page 10-11

TEKAKWITHA
WOODS

VALLEY
VIEW

For Wayne Map
See Page 11

Red
Gate

7. Trillium Ct.
8. Reindeer T.
9. Caribou Tr.
10. Antler Tr.
11. Buckskin Ct.
12. Buckskin Tr.

1. Fence Rail Ct.
2. Deerpath Way
3. Woodland Ct.
4. Oak Ct.
5. Meadows Ct.
6. Fieldstone Ct.
7. Stoneleaf Way
8. Hunters Gate Rd.
9. Wilton Craft Rd.
10. Dorchester Rd.

SEVERSON
RED GATE F.P.

Army Trail Rd.

WAYNE

H

Wredling
Sports
Complex

1. Rockwell Ave.
2. Maple Ln.
3. Oak Ln.
4. Lambert Ave.
5. Lilac Ave.
6. Brookwood Rd.

5 N.

Royal
Fox
G.C.

BLACKHAWK
GOLF COURSE
A. White Pine Ln.
B. Birchdale Ct.

LEROY OAKS
FOREST
PRESERVE

Crane

ST.

Country Club

WEST
CHICAGO
4 N.

1. Thorn Tree Dr.
2. Sunrise Ct.
3. Treetop Ln.
4. Hawthorn Dr.
   Wild Rose

J

64

Great Western Trail

CHARLES

Fifth Ave.

3 N.

Main

St.

64

77

31

25

67

S. Whittier Pl.
T. Corbett Pl.
U. Wyngate Ct.
V. Meadowridge Cir.
W. Ridgeview Ct.
X. Kurl Ct.
Y. Limberl Ln.
Z. Coulter Dr.

Illinois Youth
Center
(Illinois
Corrections
Facility)

Kane
County
Fairgrounds

ST. CHARLES

For St. Charles Map
See Pages 10-13

Hawthorne
Lane

2 N.

84

38

Bricher Rd.

GENEVA

GENEVA

A. Curtis Sq.
B. Weaver Cir.
C. Bartlett Pl.
D. Acres Pl.
E. Platt Pl.
F. Boyd Dr.
G. Hills Dr.
H. Eldon Dr.
I. Lebaron Ct.
J. Herrington Blvd.
K. Dooley Dr.

L. Ford Dr.
M. Baker Dr.
N. Terney Ln.
O. Sulley Pl.
P. Sulley Sq.
Q. Howard Sq.
R. Harvey Sq.
S. Washburn Pl.
T. Olinger Ln.
U. Forbes Dr.
V. Pauley Sq.
W. Underwood Dr.

9. Swift Pl.
10. Hubbard Pl.
11. McNair Pl.

For Geneva Map
See Pages 12-15

Chicago

41

1 N.

Northwestern

R.R.

00
Pkwy.

12. Crego Pl.
13. Preston Ct.
14. Snooks Pl.
15. Hunt Pl.
16. Whitney Pl.
17. Wells Cir.
18. Hathaway Ln.
19. Mathewson Ln.
20. Bealer Dr.

Mill
Creek Golf
Club

Eagle
Brook
Country
Club

GUNNAR
ANDERSON
F.P.

Kane County
Event Center
Elfstrom Stadium

FABYAN
FOREST
PRESERVE

Settlers
Hills
Golf
Course

21. Hathaway Ct.
22. Catlel Sq.
23. Sheldon
24. Fryendall Ct.
25. Kellar Sq.
26. Kellar Pl.

Fabyan

Fabyan

Pkwy.

BRAEBURN
F.P.

For Batavia Map
See Pages 14-15

84

38

77

8

BATAVIA

1 MILE

© BY CSC

CONTINUED ON PAGE 4

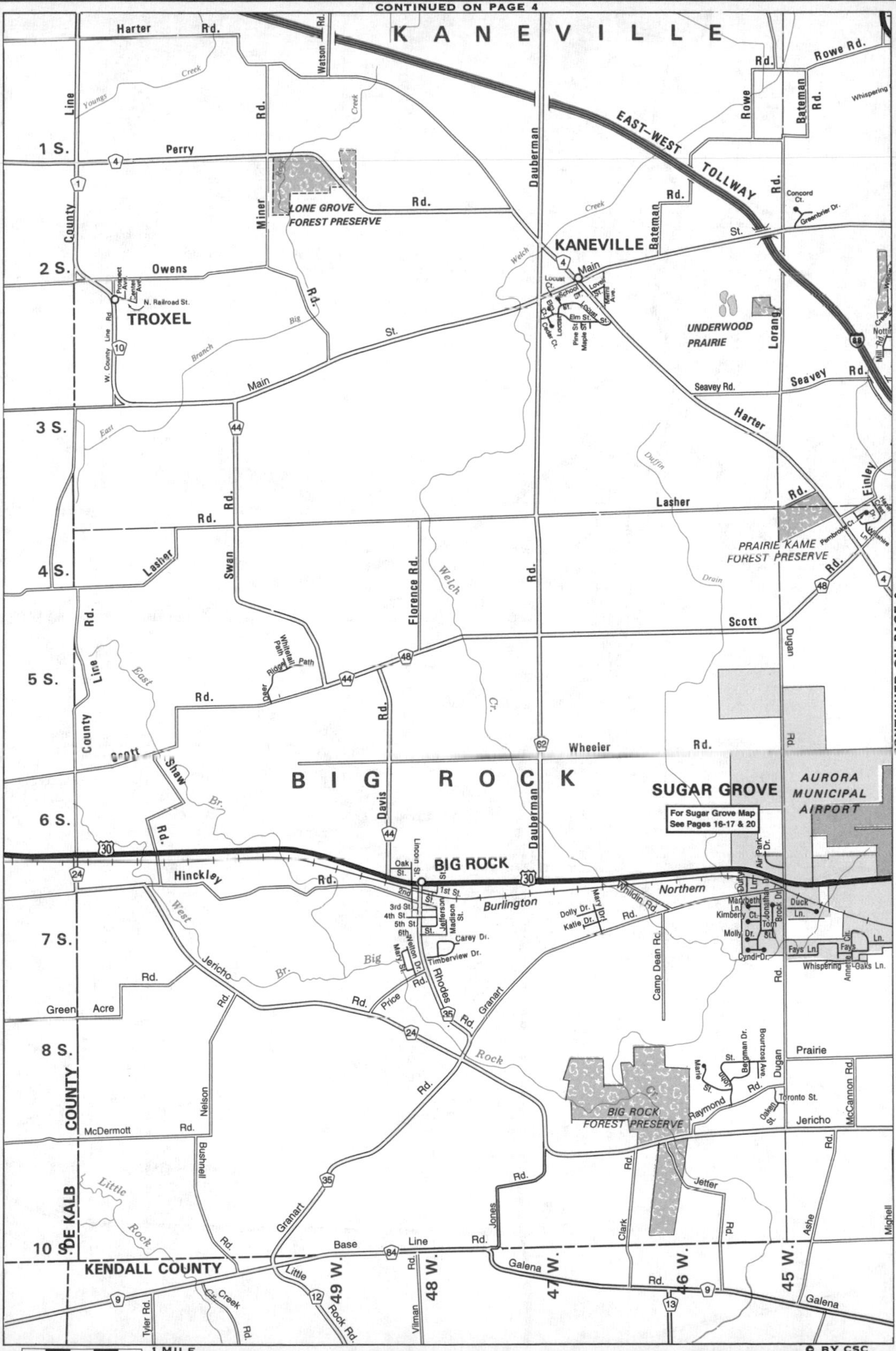

K A N E V I L L E

Harter Rd.

L

1 S.
Perry

Line
Young's Creek

Watson Rd.

Creek

LONE GROVE
FOREST PRESERVE

Miner Rd.

Rowe Rd.

Rowe Rd.

Bateman Rd.

Whispering

Dauberman Rd.

EAST–WEST TOLLWAY

Creek

Rd.

Concord Ct.

Greenbriar Dr.

KANEVILLE

Bateman St.

Loranv

Rd.

County

County Line Rd.

2 S.
Owens

N. Railroad St.

TROXEL

Big

Branch

Main St.

Welch

Main

Locust

School

Elm St.

Pine St.

Maple St.

UNDERWOOD
PRAIRIE

Seavey Rd.

Seavey Rd.

M

Mill Rd.

Nettle

3 S.
East

44

Duffin

Harter

N

Lasher

Swan Rd.

Rd.

Florence Rd.

Welch

Rd.

PRAIRIE KAME
FOREST PRESERVE

Finley

Rd.

48

4 S.
Lasher

Scott

Drain

Dugan

O

Line Rd.

County

East

Deer

Whitetail Path

Bloom Path

44

48

Cr.

62

Wheeler Rd.

Rd.

AURORA
MUNICIPAL
AIRPORT

5 S.

Scott

Shaw Br.

B I G   R O C K

Davis

44

Dauberman

SUGAR GROVE

For Sugar Grove Map
See Pages 16-17 & 20

6 S.
Rd.

30

Hinckley Rd.

BIG ROCK

Oak St.

Lincoln St.

2nd

1st St.

30

Northern

Thielin Rd.

Air Park

Duck Ln.

P

West Br.

24

3rd St.
4th St.
5th St.
6th

Jefferson

Madison St.

Burlington

Dolly Dr.

Katie Dr.

Kimberly Ct.

Molly

Cyndi Dr.

Fays Ln.

Whispering Oaks Ln.

7 S.
Rd.
Green Acre

Jericho Rd.

Big

Br.

Price Rd.

Rhodes Rd.

Carey Dr.

Timberview Dr.

Granart

Camp Dean Rd.

Dugan

Prairie

DE KALB COUNTY

8 S.

Nelson

Bushnell

McDermott Rd.

35

24

Rd.

Rock

BIG ROCK
FOREST PRESERVE

Marie

Bugman Dr.

Raymond

Jetter

Toronto St.

McCannon Rd.

Jericho

Q

10

Little Rock

Granart

Rock Rd.

84

49 W.

48 W.

Base
Line

Vilman Rd.

47 W.

Jones

Galena

Clark

46 W.

Rd.

Galena

45 W.

Mighell

KENDALL COUNTY

9

Tyler Rd.

12

13

9

1 MILE

© BY CSC

CONTINUED ON PAGE 8

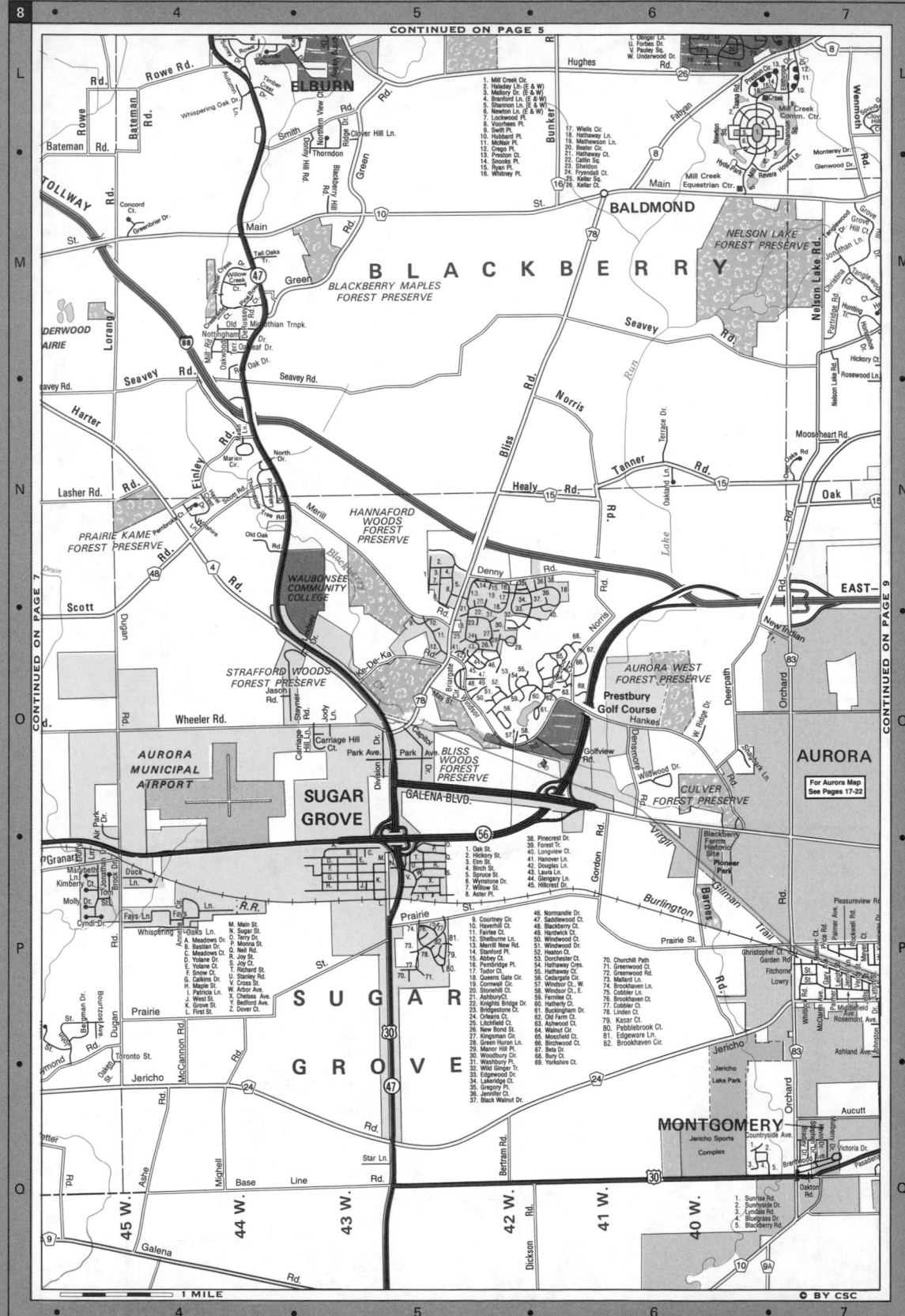

CONTINUED ON PAGE 6

L

**BATAVIA**

For Batavia Map
See Pages 14-15

1 S.

Fabyan PKWY.

BRAEBURN F.P.

Wenmoth

McKee St.

Wilson St.

A Wilson St.

FERMI
NATIONAL
ACCELERATOR
LABORATORY

2 S.

M

**B A T A V I A**

NELSON LAKE
FOREST PRESERVE

1. Mill Creek Cir.
2. Halsday Ln. (E & W)
3. Mallory Dr. (E & W)
4. Stanford Ln. (E & W)
5. Shannon Ln. (E & W)
6. Newlen Ln. (E & W)
7. Larkspur Pl.
8. Voorhees Pl.
9. Swift Pl.
10. Hubbard Pl.
11. McNeil Pl.
12. Clegg Pl.

13. Preston Ct.
14. Snooks Pl.
15. Ryan Pl.
16. Whitney Pl.
17. Wells Cir.
18. Hathaway Ln.
19. Mathewson Ln.
20. Beater Cir.

DU PAGE COUNTY

3 S.

Morton Ln.

Walnut St.

Pine St.

Illinois Prairie

Seavey Rd.

GLENWOOD PARK F.P.

LES ARDENS F.P.

Banbury

MOOSEHEART

Orchard Rd.

Mooseheart Rd.

4

N

**NORTH AURORA**

For North Aurora Map
See Pages 18-19

Oak St.

Tanner Rd.

EAST-WEST TOLLWAY

**MARY WOOD**

5 S.

O

**LOVE DALE**

**AURORA**

For Aurora Map
See Pages 17-22

Indian Trail Rd.

Old Indian Trail

6 S.

Randall Rd.

Galena Blvd.

7 S.

West Galena Blvd.

OAKHURST
FOREST PRESERVE

Farnsworth Ave.

York St.

P

Aurora Country Club

**MONTGOMERY**

**A U R O R A**

**SCRAPER-MOECHERVILLE**

8 S.

9 S.

Ashland Ave.

Fox River

Montgomery Rd.

Virgil Gilman Trail

83rd St.

10 S.

Q

For Montgomery Map
See Pages 21-22

**KENDALL COUNTY**

WILL CO.

**OSWEGO**

1. Sunrise Rd.
2. Sunnyside Dr.
3. Lyndale Rd.
4. Bluegrass Dr.
5. Blackberry Dr.

Countryside Ave.

1 MILE

© BY CSC

CONTINUED ON PAGE 8

CONTINUED IN SEC. 3, PAGE 19

7    8    9

CONTINUED IN SEC. 5, PAGES 11 AND 12

K · L · M · N

ELGIN TOWNSHIP
ST. CHARLES TOWNSHIP

SOUTH ELGIN

McLEAN BLVD.

BLACKHAWK
FOREST PRESERVE

SILVER GLEN

VALLEY
VIEW

FERSON CREEK
FOREST PRESERVE

CONTINUED ON PAGE 6

CONTINUED ON PAGE 11

KANE
COUNTY
FOREST
PRESERVE

PRIMROSE FARM
PARK

Blackhawk Golf Course

St. Charles
Athletic Field

FOX
RIVER
BLUFF W
FOREST
PRESERV

Wredling
Middle Sch.

Wredling
Sports
Complex

KANE CO.
FOREST PRESERVE

Ferson
Creek
Fen
Nature
Preserve

Norris
Nature

LEROY OAKS
FOREST PRESERVE

DEAN ST.

.5 MILE

CONTINUED ON PAGE 12

K · L · M · N

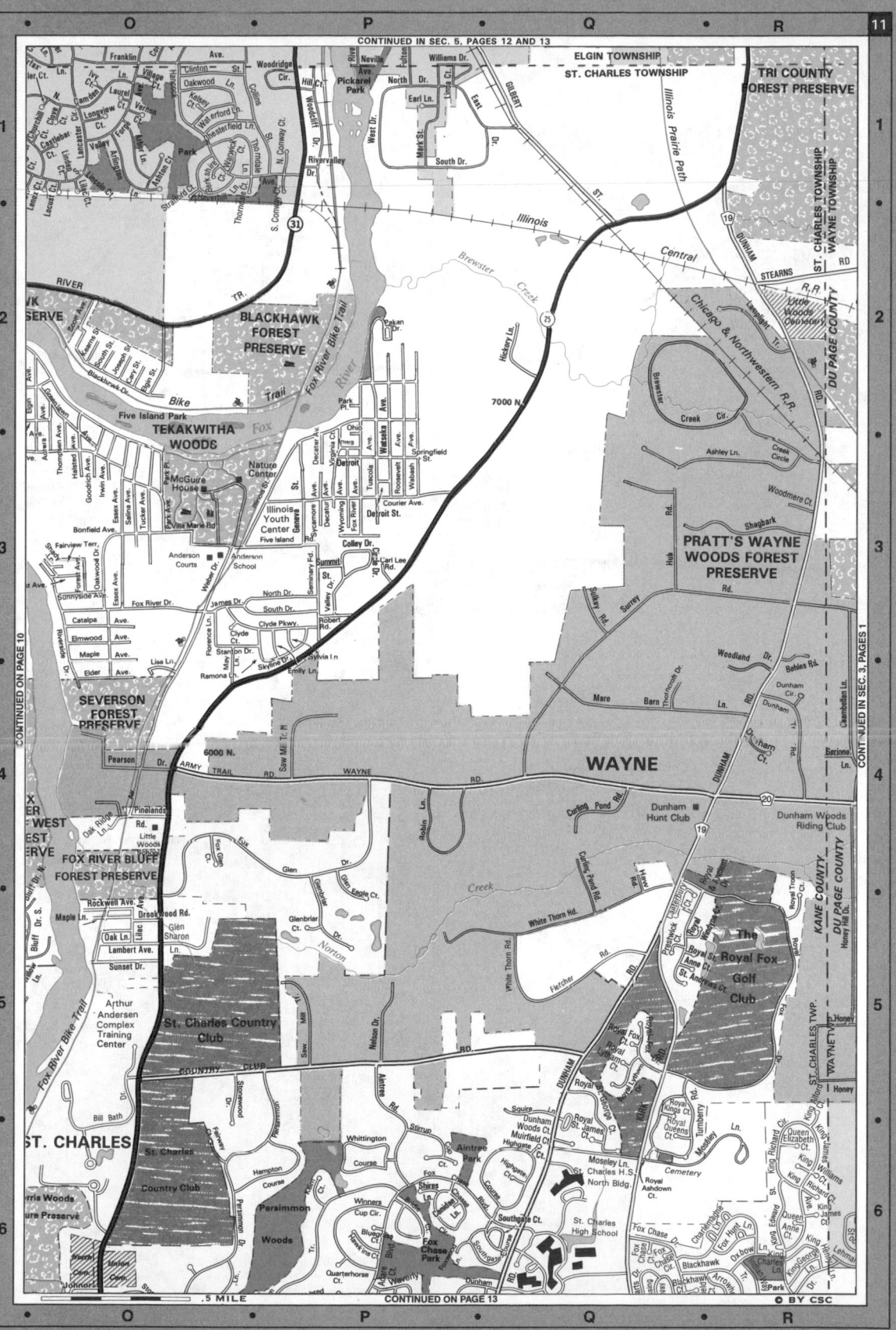

CONTINUED IN SEC. 5, PAGES 12 AND 13

ELGIN TOWNSHIP
ST. CHARLES TOWNSHIP

TRI COUNTY
FOREST PRESERVE

Illinois Prairie Path

BLACKHAWK
FOREST
PRESERVE

Brewster Creek

Chicago & Northwestern R.R.

STEARNS RD.

DU PAGE COUNTY

ST. CHARLES TOWNSHIP
WAYNE TOWNSHIP

Five Island Park

TEKAKWITHA
WOODS

Fox

Nature
Center

McGuire
House

Illinois Youth
Center
Five Island

Villa Marie Rd.

7000 N.

Creek Cir.

Ashley Ln.

Creek
Circle

Woodmere Ct.

Shagbark

PRATT'S WAYNE
WOODS FOREST
PRESERVE

Hub Rd.

Surrey

Woodland Dr.

Behlies Rd.

CONTINUED ON PAGE 10

SEVERSON
FOREST
PRESERVE

6000 N.

WAYNE

DUNHAM

WAYNE

CONTINUED IN SEC. 3, PAGES 1

FOX RIVER BLUFF
FOREST PRESERVE

Dunham
Hunt Club

Dunham Woods
Riding Club

KANE COUNTY
DU PAGE COUNTY

Fox River Bike Trail

Arthur
Andersen
Complex
Training
Center

St. Charles Country
Club

White Thorn Rd.

The
Royal Fox
Golf
Club

ST. CHARLES TWP.
WAYNE TWP.

ST. CHARLES

St. Charles
Country Club

Aintree
Park

St. Charles H.S.
North Bldg

Fox Chase

St. Charles
High School

CONTINUED ON PAGE 13

© BY CSC

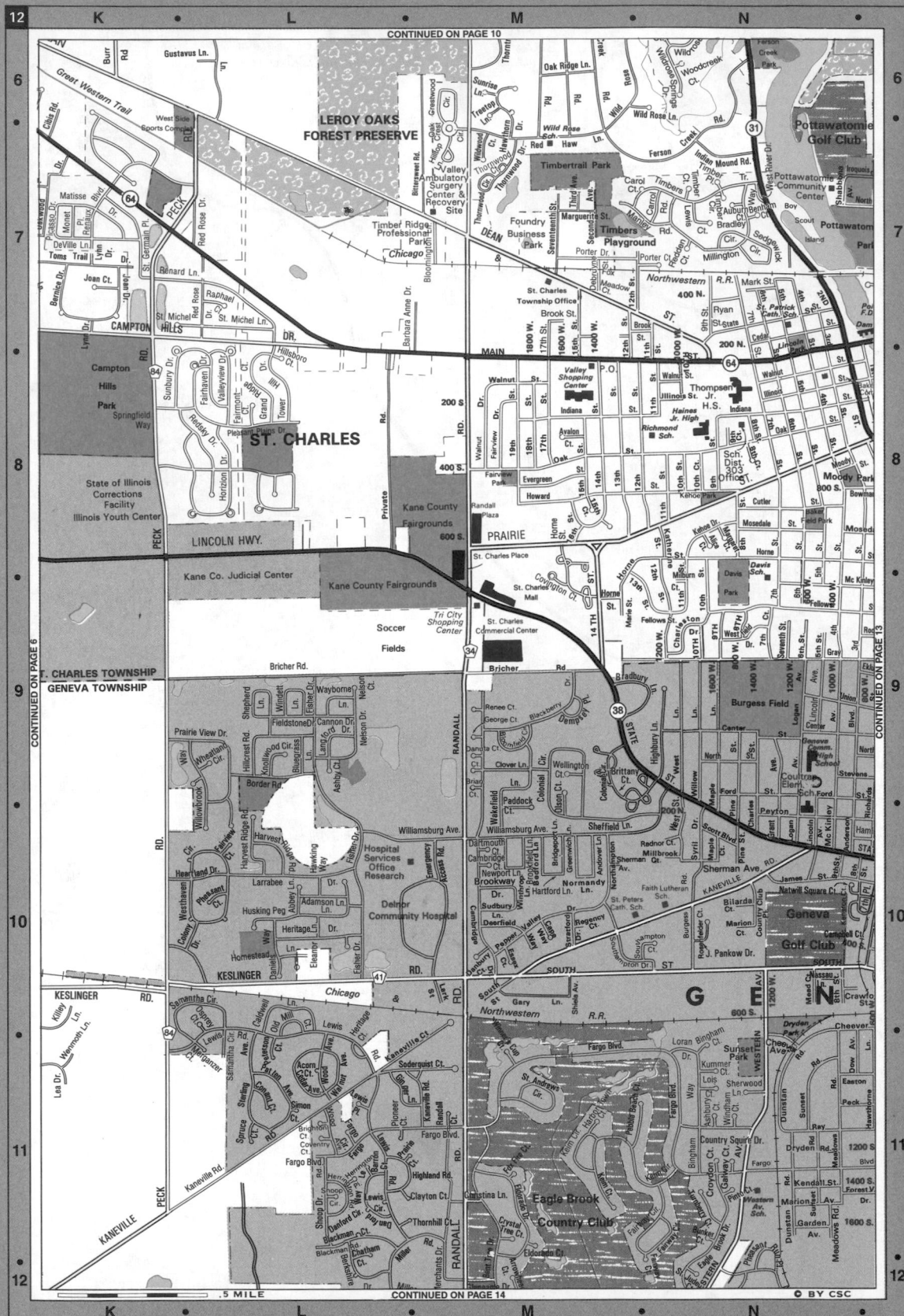
CONTINUED ON PAGE 10
CONTINUED ON PAGE 6
CONTINUED ON PAGE 13
CONTINUED ON PAGE 14

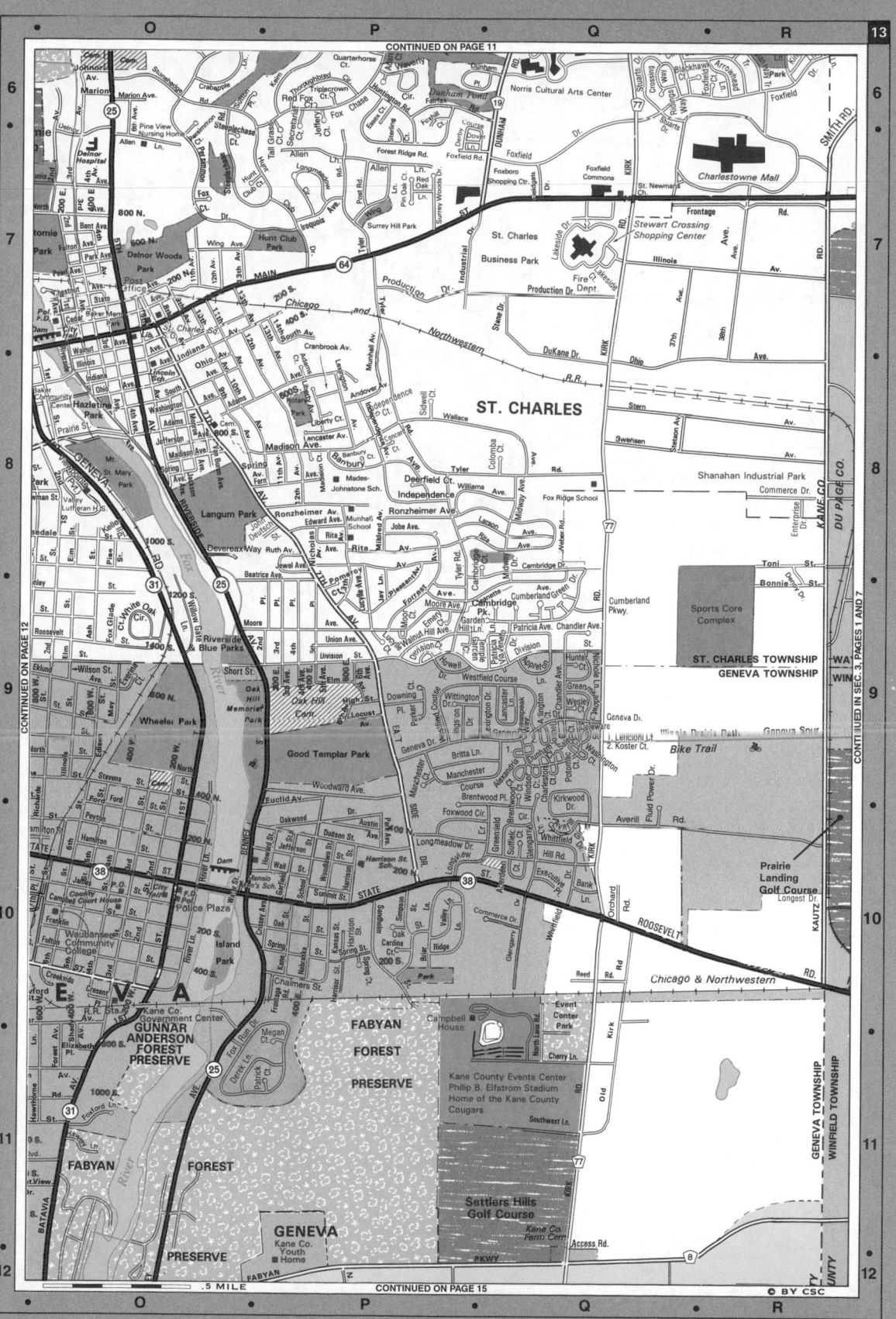

CONTINUED ON PAGE 11

CONTINUED ON PAGE 12

CONTINUED ON PAGE 15

**ST. CHARLES**

Charlestowne Mall

Stewart Crossing Shopping Center

St. Charles Business Park

Foxboro Shopping Ctr.

Foxfield Commons

Norris Cultural Arts Center

Shanahan Industrial Park

Sports Core Complex

ST. CHARLES TOWNSHIP
GENEVA TOWNSHIP

Prairie Landing Golf Course

Bike Trail

Good Templar Park

GUNNAR ANDERSON FOREST PRESERVE

FABYAN FOREST PRESERVE

FABYAN FOREST PRESERVE

GENEVA
Kane Co. Youth Home

Kane County Events Center
Philip B. Elfstrom Stadium
Home of the Kane County Cougars

Event Center Park

Campbell House

Settlers Hills Golf Course

GENEVA TOWNSHIP
WINFIELD TOWNSHIP

KANE CO.
DU PAGE CO.

.5 MILE

© BY CSC

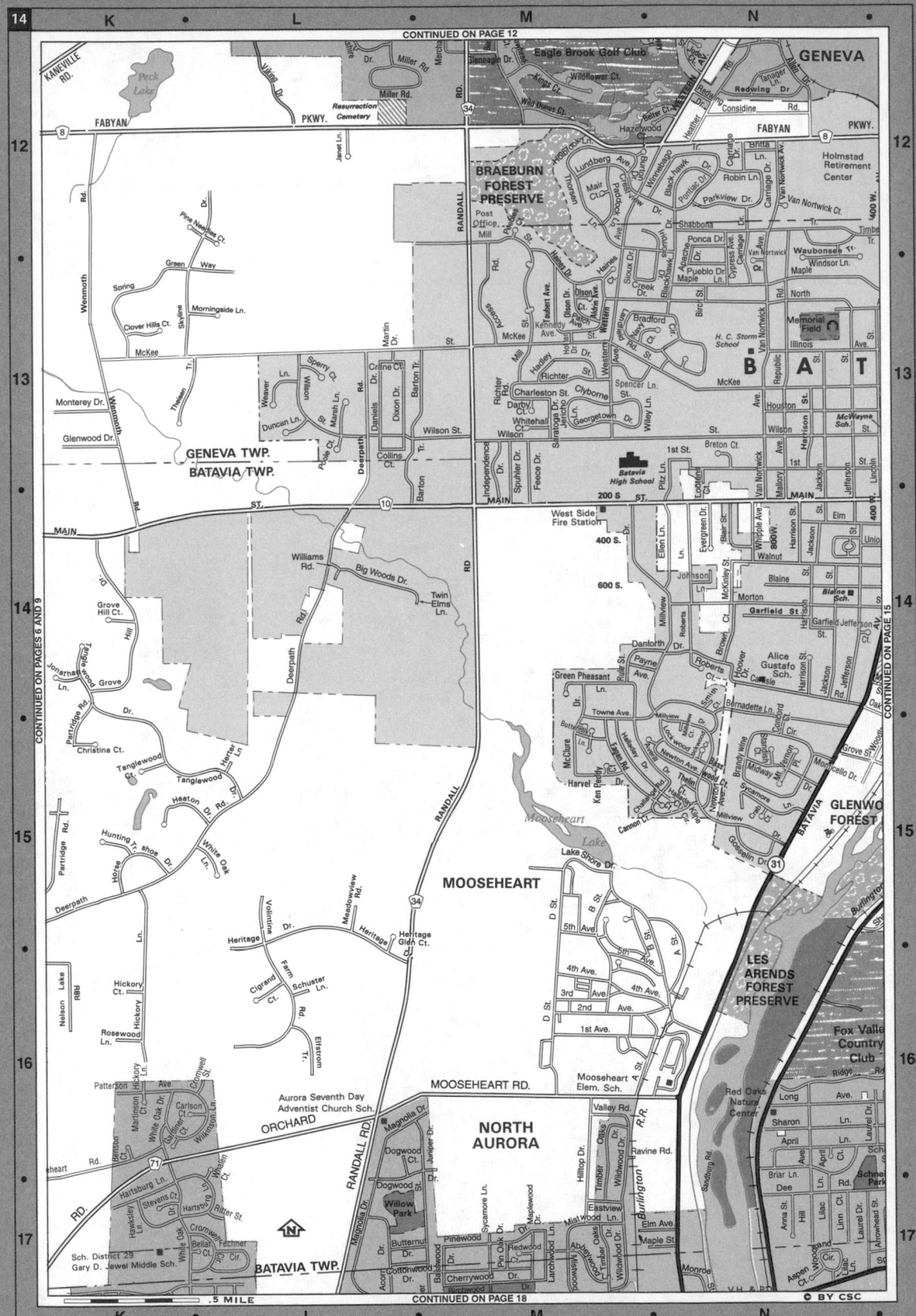

CONTINUED ON PAGE 12

GENEVA

Eagle Brook Golf Club

KANEVILLE RD.

Peck Lake

Resurrection Cemetery

FABYAN PKWY.

FABYAN PKWY.

Holmstad Retirement Center

BRAEBURN FOREST PRESERVE

Post Office, Mill

Memorial Field

H. C. Storm School

Illinois

B A T

McKee

Batavia High School

GENEVA TWP.
BATAVIA TWP.

West Side Fire Station

MAIN

Williams Rd.

Big Woods Dr.

Twin Elms Ln.

Batavia High School

200 S

400 S.

600 S.

CONTINUED ON PAGES 6 AND 9

CONTINUED ON PAGE 15

Green Pheasant Ln.

Grove Hill Ct.

Tanglewood

Heaton

Hunting Horse Dr.

White Oak

Mooseheart Lake

GLENWOOD FOREST

BATAVIA

MOOSEHEART

Lake Shore Dr.

Deerpath

Volintine

Heritage

Heritage Dr.

Heritage Glen Ct.

LES ARENDS FOREST PRESERVE

Fox Valley Country Club

Nelson Lake

Hickory Ct.

Rosewood Ln.

Mooseheart Elem. Sch.

MOOSEHEART RD.

Aurora Seventh Day Adventist Church Sch.

ORCHARD

NORTH AURORA

Valley Rd.

Red Oaks Nature Center

Patterson

Cromwell St.

Willow Park

Sch. District 29
Gary D. Jewel Middle School

BATAVIA TWP.

RANDALL RD.

.5 MILE

CONTINUED ON PAGE 18

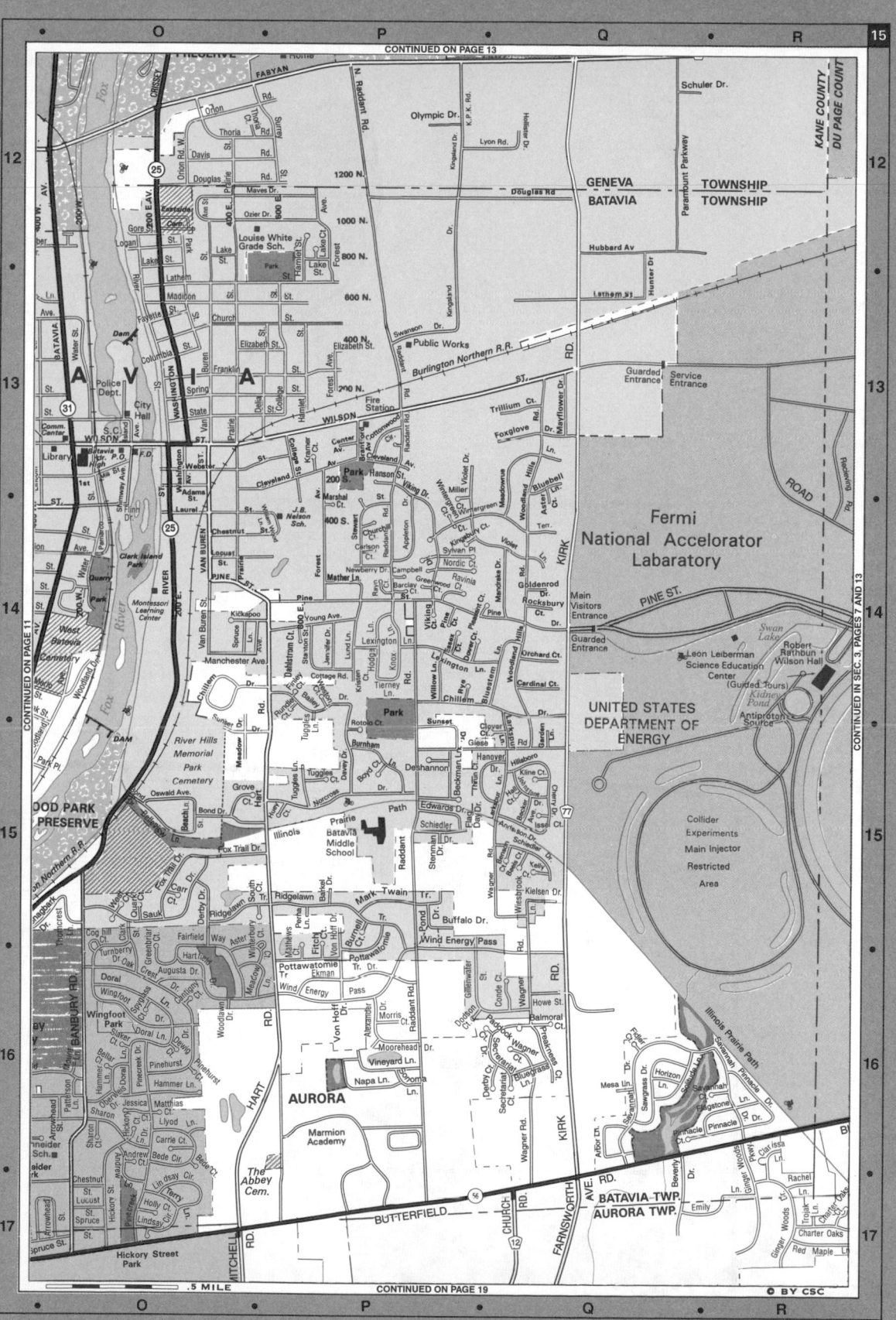

CONTINUED ON PAGE 11

CONTINUED IN SEC. 3, PAGES 7 AND 13

Fermi
National Accelorator
Laboratory

UNITED STATES
DEPARTMENT OF
ENERGY

Collider
Experiments
Main Injector
Restricted
Area

AURORA

Marmion
Academy

© BY CSC

.5 MILE

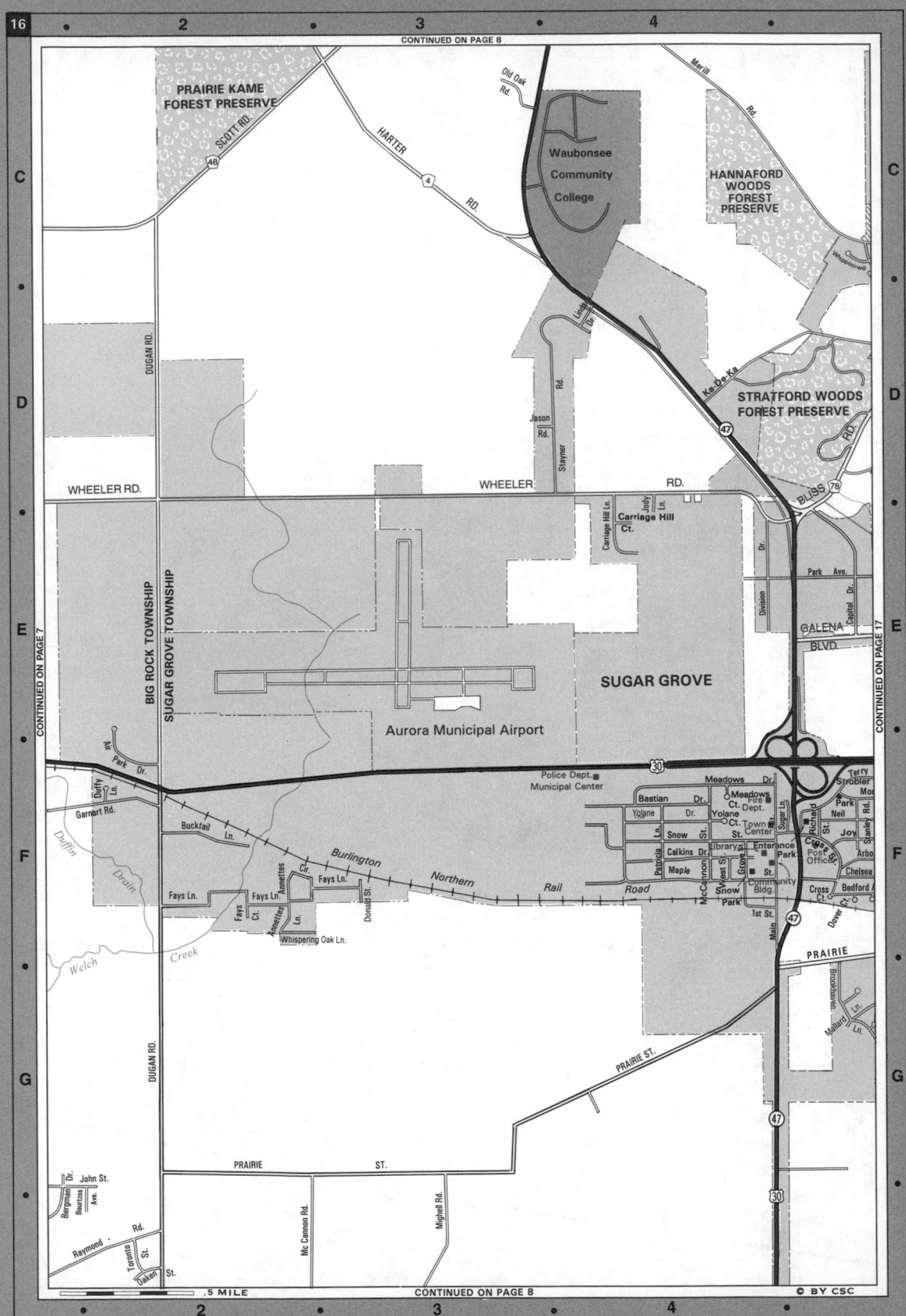

CONTINUED ON PAGE 8

PRAIRIE KAME
FOREST PRESERVE

Old Oak
Rd.

Merill

HARTER

SCOTT RD.

48

4

RD.

Waubonsee
Community
College

HANNAFORD
WOODS
FOREST
PRESERVE

Whippoorwill

DUGAN RD.

Lindsey
Dr.

Steyner
Rd.

Jason
Rd.

Ka-De-Ka

STRATFORD WOODS
FOREST PRESERVE

47

BLISS
RD.

78

WHEELER RD.

WHEELER

RD.

Carriage Hill Ln.

Jody Ln.

Carriage Hill
Ct.

BIG ROCK TOWNSHIP

SUGAR GROVE TOWNSHIP

Park Ave.

Division Dr.

Capitol Dr.

GALENA
BLVD.

CONTINUED ON PAGE 7

CONTINUED ON PAGE 17

SUGAR GROVE

Aurora Municipal Airport

Av Park Dr.

Duffy Ln.

Garnart Rd.

Bucktail Ln.

30

Police Dept.
Municipal Center

Meadows Dr.

Bastian Dr.

Yolane Dr.

Meadows
Ct.

Fire Dept.

Yolane
Ct.

Town
Center

Sugar Ln.

Terry

Strubler
Mo

Park

Neil

Richmond

Joy

St.

Stanley Rd.

Burlington

Fays Ln.

Cir.

Fays Ln.

Annettes

Northern

Rail

Road

Snow St.

Calkins Dr.

Patricia

Maple

Library

McCannon

West St.

Snow
Park

Grove Ln.

Entrance
Park

Community
Bldg.

Cross
Ct.

Post
Office

Arbo

Chelsea

Bedford A

Duffin
Drain

Fays Ln.

Fays
Ct.

Annettes
Ln.

Donald St.

Whispering Oak Ln.

1st St.

47

Main

Dover Ct.

Welch

Creek

PRAIRIE

Brookmeadow

Mallard
Ln.

DUGAN RD.

PRAIRIE ST.

47

Bergman Dr.

John St.

Bourtzos
Ave.

PRAIRIE

ST.

Mc Cannon Rd.

Mighell Rd.

30

Raymond

Rd.

Toronto
St.

Daken St.

.5 MILE

CONTINUED ON PAGE 8

© BY CSC

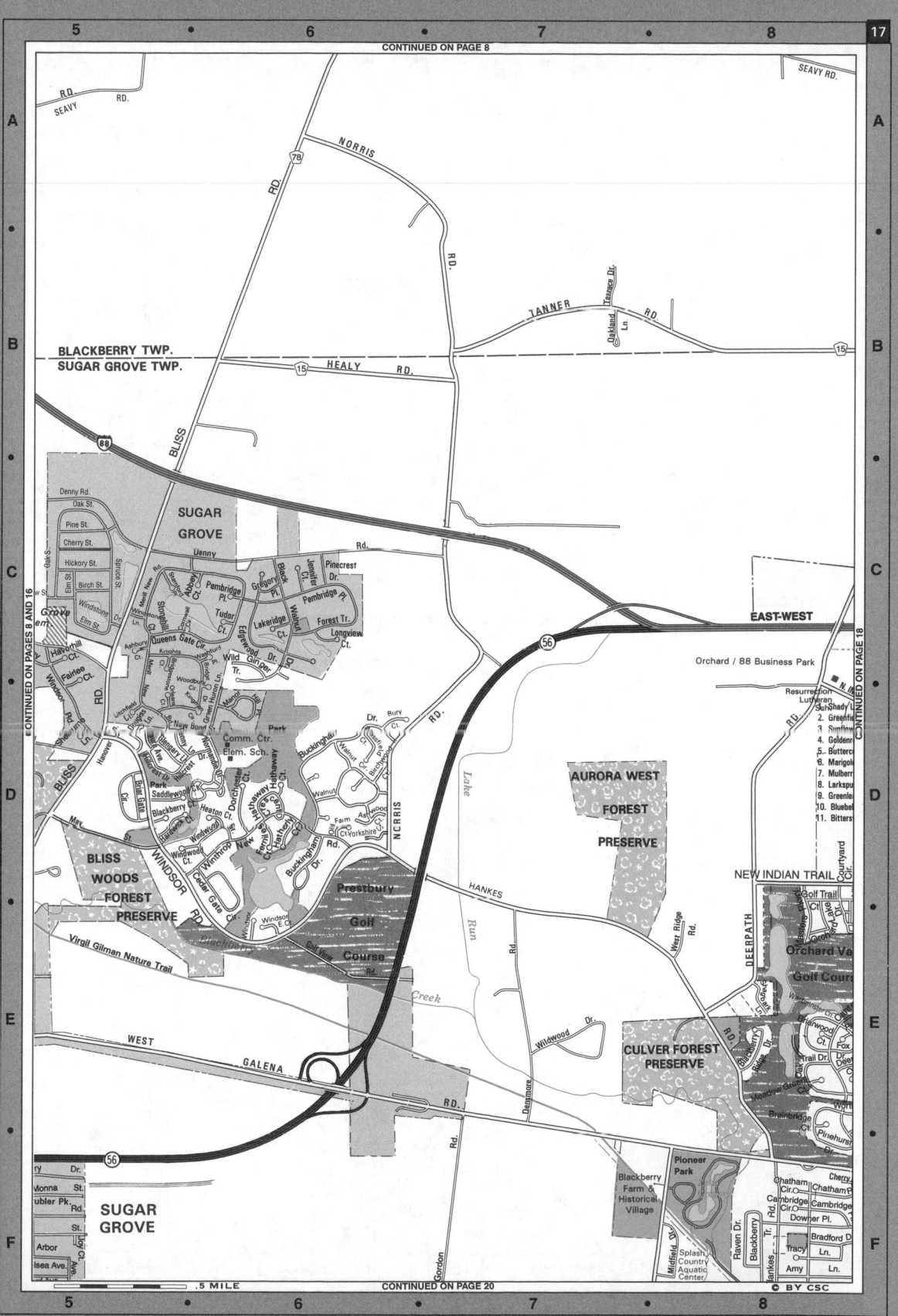

CONTINUED ON PAGE 8

SEAVY RD.

RD.
SEAVY RD.

A

NORRIS

78
RD.

RD.

TANNER

Testate Dr.

Oakland Ln.

15

B
BLACKBERRY TWP.
SUGAR GROVE TWP.

15    HEALY    RD.

88

BLISS

Denny Rd.

Oak St.

Pine St.

SUGAR
GROVE

Cherry St.

Hickory St.

Denny

Elm St.

Birch St.

Oak St.

Rd.

Rd.

C

Windstone

Grove
Elm St.

CONTINUED ON PAGES 8 AND 16

Jennifer
Dr.

Pinecrest
Dr.

Black

Gregory

Pembridge
Pl.

Abbey

Springhill

Moot New

Pembridge Pl.

EAST-WEST

Haverhill
Ct.

Fairlee
Ct.

Windstone
Elm St.

Tudor
Ct.

Lakeridge
Ct.

Walnut

Forest Tr.

Longview
Ct.

56

Orchard / 88 Business Park

Resurrection
Lutheran

Sch. Shady L.

2. Greenfi

Windsor Rd.

Shering

Bliss

Aanbury

Queens Gate Cir.

Knights

Wild
Tr.

Ginger

3. Sunflow

4. Golden

5. Butterc

6. Marigol

CONTINUED ON PAGE 18

CONTINUED ON PAGE 18

Woodbu
Ct.

Knolls

Mana

Bury
Ct.

Dr.

7. Mulberr

8. Larkspu

9. Greenle

Comm. Ctr.
Elem. Sch.

Dorchester Ct.

Park

Buckingha

Walnut

Buckinghall
Dr.

Birchwood

10. Bluebel

11. Bitters

N.

D
BLISS

May

Hanover

Bent Ave.

West Dr.

Park
Saddlewh

Hathaway

Bend Gate

Blackberry Dr.

Heaton Ct.

Cente

Canterb

Farm
Ct.

Ash

Yorkshire

Walnut

Farm
Rd.

AURORA WEST
FOREST
PRESERVE

NEW INDIAN TRAIL

Golf Trail

Courtyard

WINDSOR

Windwood
Ct.

Winthrop

Buckingham
Dr.

Cedar Gate Ctr.

New

DEERPATH

Orchard Va

Golf Cours

BLISS
WOODS
FOREST
PRESERVE

Windsor
E.O.

Prestbury

HANKES

West Ridge
Rd.

E
Virgil Gilman Nature Trail

Golf

Golfview
Rd.

Course

Run

Culfwood
Ct.

Fox

Trail Dr.

Dr. Dee

CULVER FOREST
PRESERVE

Meadow Green
Ct.

Brainbridge

WEST

Creek

Wildwood
Dr.

Ct.

Worl

Pinehurst
Dr.

GALENA

RD.

Denmore

Cherry

56

Dr.

Monna    St.

Tubler Pk.    Rd.

St.

SUGAR
GROVE

Arbor

Isea Ave.

Gordon

Blackberry
Farm &
Historical
Village

Pioneer
Park

Midfield St.

Splash
Country
Aquatic
Center

Raven Dr.

Blackberry
Tr.

Chatham
Cir.

Cambridge
Cir.

Tracy
Ln.

Amy
Ln.

Chatham P

Cambridge

Downer Pl.

Bradford D

.5 MILE

CONTINUED ON PAGE 20

© BY CSC

5    6    7    8

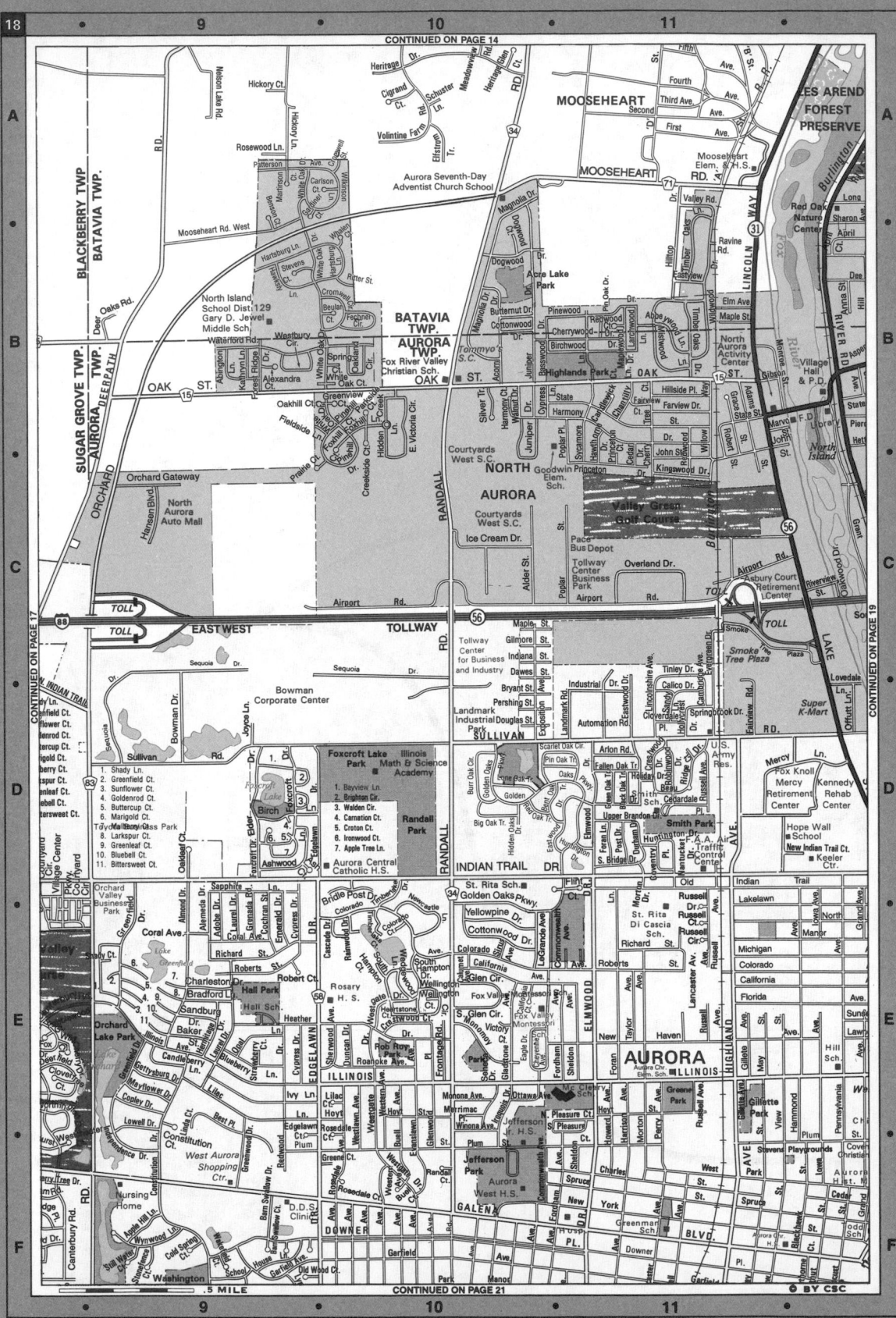

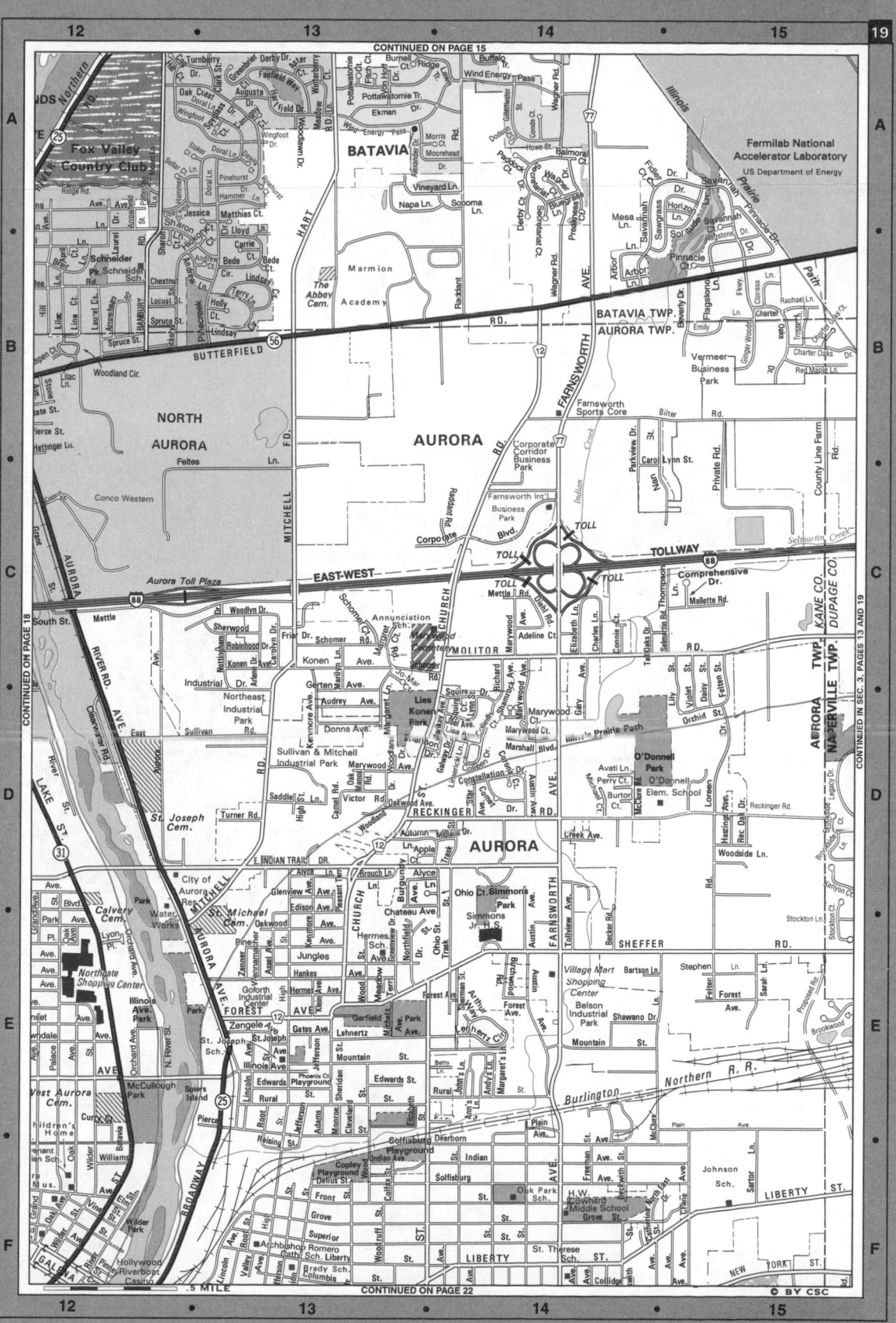

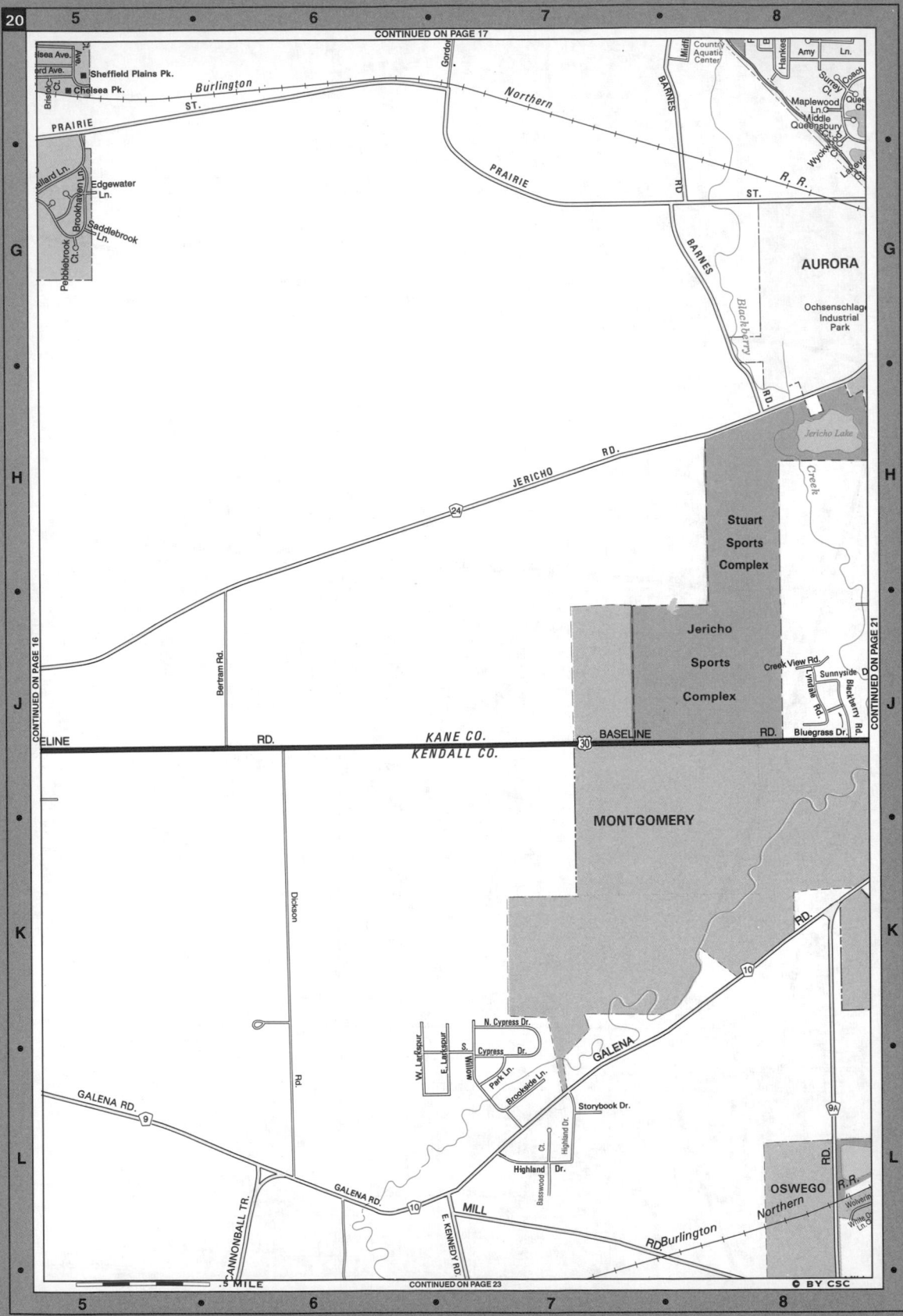

CONTINUED ON PAGE 17

Sheffield Plains Pk.
Chelsea Pk.

Burlington ST.

PRAIRIE

Northern

PRAIRIE

Edgewater Ln.

Saddlebrook Ln.

Pebblebrook Ct.

Brookhaven Ln.

Mallard Ln.

Bristol Ct.

Chelsea Ave.

Gordon

Barnes

RD.

ST.

Barnes

Blackberry

RD.

Country Aquatic Center

Maplewood Ln.
Middle Queensbury

Wyckwood Dr.

Surrey Ln.

Amy Ln.

Coach

Hankes

Lakeview

R. R.

Middle

Quail Ct.

**AURORA**

Ochsenschlager Industrial Park

Jericho Lake

JERICHO RD.

24

Bertram Rd.

**Stuart Sports Complex**

**Jericho Sports Complex**

Creek

Creek View Rd.

Sunnyside Dr.

Lyndale Rd.

Blackberry Rd.

Bluegrass Dr.

CONTINUED ON PAGE 16

CONTINUED ON PAGE 21

ELINE RD.

KANE CO.
KENDALL CO.

BASELINE RD.

30

**MONTGOMERY**

Dickson Rd.

RD.

10

GALENA RD.
9

W. Larkspur
E. Larkspur

S. Willow

N. Cypress Dr.
Cypress Dr.
Park Ln.
Brookside Ln.

GALENA

Storybook Dr.

Highland Dr.

Highland Dr.

Basswood Ln.

Ct.

GALENA RD.
10

MILL

E. Kennedy Rd.

RD. Burlington

Northern

R. R.

**OSWEGO**

9A

RD.

Wolverine

White Oak

.5 MILE

CONTINUED ON PAGE 23

© BY CSC

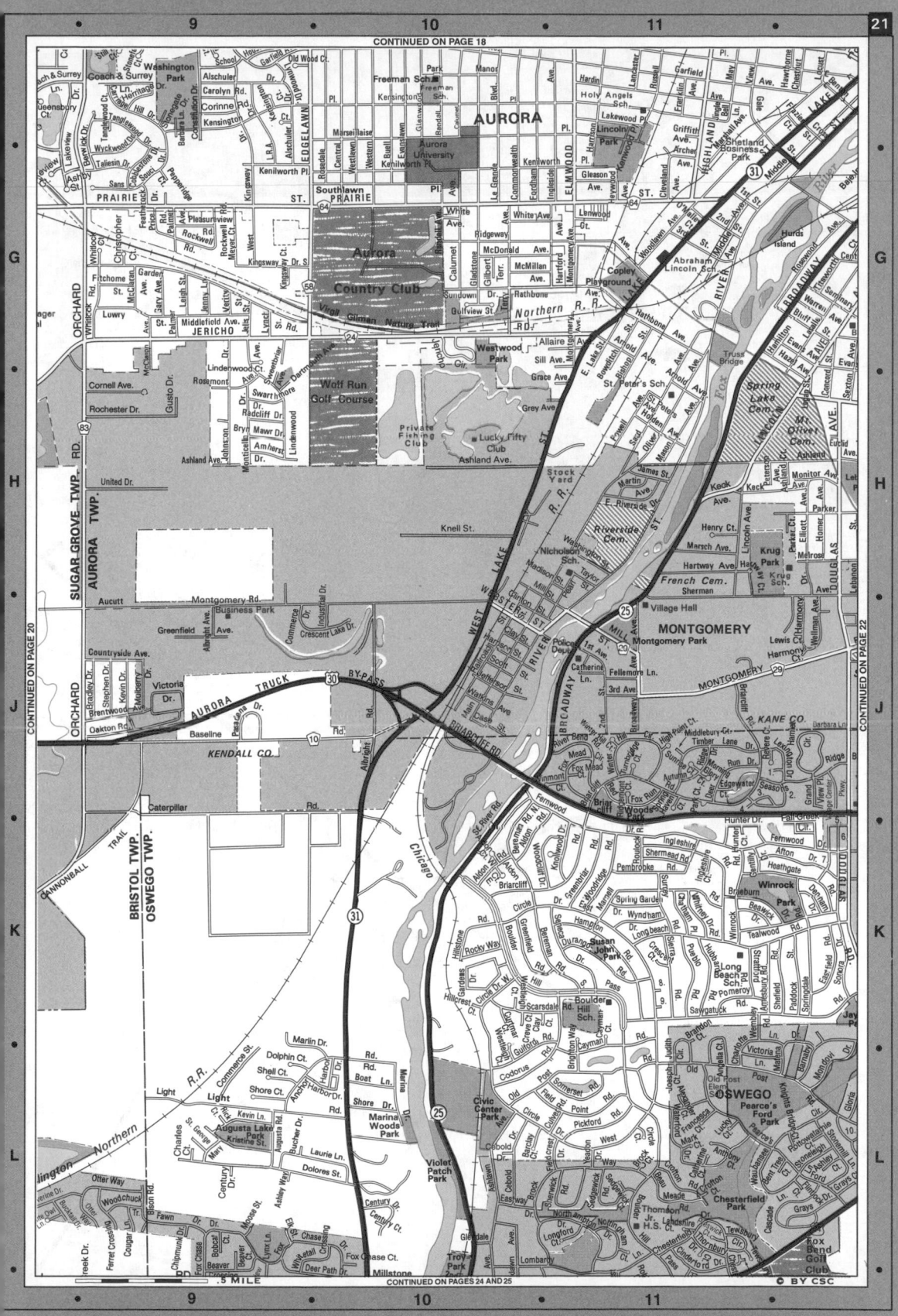
CONTINUED ON PAGE 18
CONTINUED ON PAGE 20
CONTINUED ON PAGE 22
CONTINUED ON PAGES 24 AND 25
© BY CSC

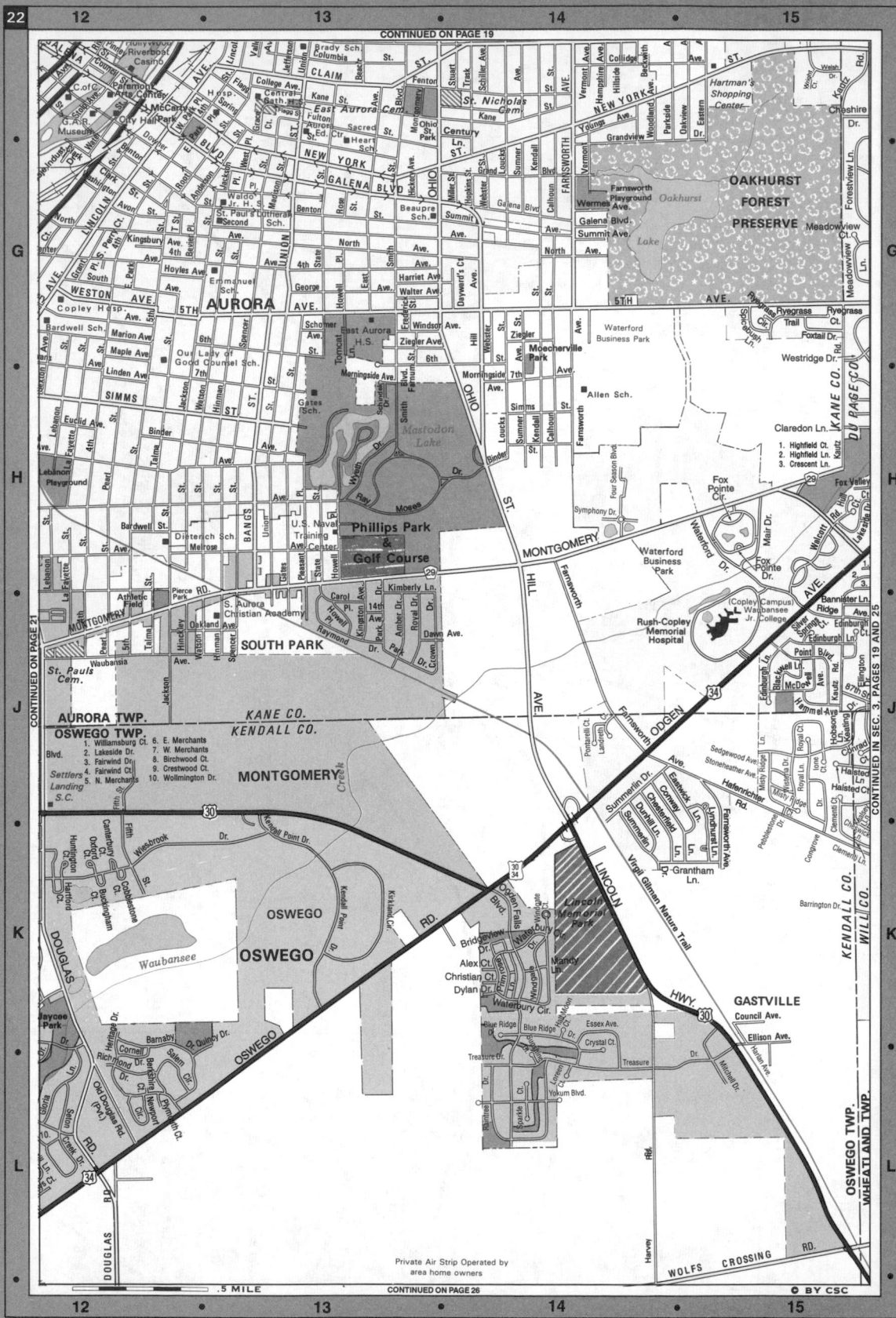

CONTINUED ON PAGE 19

CONTINUED ON PAGE 21

CONTINUED IN SEC. 3, PAGES 19 AND 25

CONTINUED ON PAGE 26

.5 MILE

© BY CSC

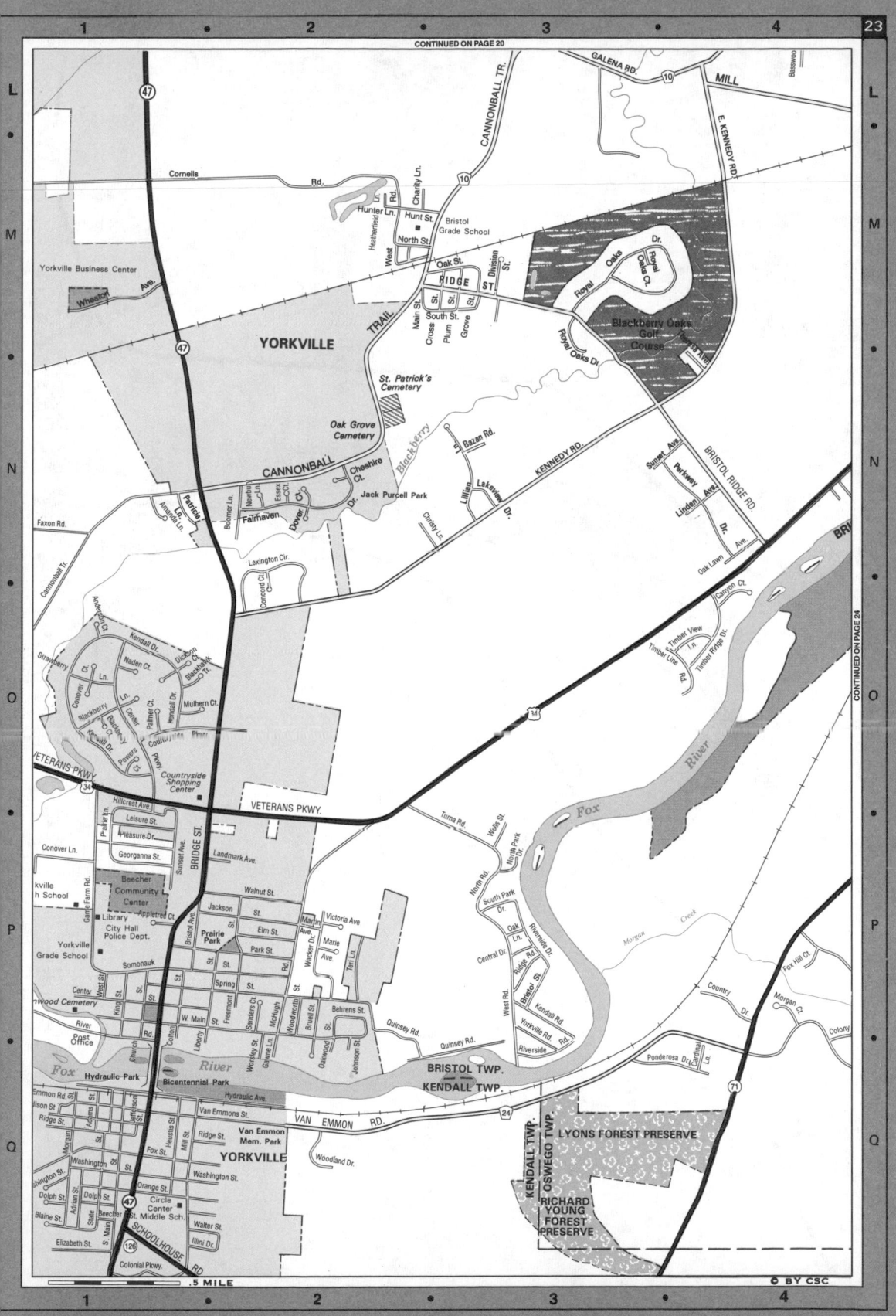

CONTINUED ON PAGE 20

CONTINUED ON PAGE 24

L

M

N

O

P

Q

1    2    3    4

GALENA RD.

CANNONBALL TR.

MILL

E. KENNEDY RD.

Corneils   Rd.

Hunter Ln.   Charity Ln.

Heatherfield Ln.   Hunt St.

West   North St.

Bristol Grade School

Oak St.

RIDGE   Division   ST.

Main St.   Cross St.   Plum St.   South St.   Grove

Royal Oaks   Dr.

Royal Oaks Ct.

YORKVILLE

Blackberry Oaks Golf Course

St. Patrick's Cemetery

Oak Grove Cemetery

Blackberry

Royal Oaks Dr.

CANNONBALL

Cheshire Ct.

Jack Purcell Park

KENNEDY RD.

Bazan Rd.

Lillian   Lakeview Dr.

Christy Ln.

BRISTOL RIDGE RD.

Sunset Ave.

Parkway

Linden Ave.

Oak Lawn   Ave.

Faxon Rd.

Patricia

Amber Ln.

Bloomer Ln.

Newbury

Essex Ct.

Dover Ct.

Fairhaven

Cannonball Tr.

Lexington Cir.

Concord Ct.

Anderson

Kendall Dr.

Strawberry

Cooper Ct.

Blackberry

Naden Ct.

Dickson

Blackhawk Tr.

Palmer Ct.

Mulhern Ct.

Conover Ct.   Carolyn Ct.

Kendall Dr.

Powers Ct.

Kaywood Dr.

Coulter

Phelps

Canyon Ct.

Timber View

Timber Line Rd.

Timber Ridge Dr.

Fox   River

VETERANS PKWY.

Countryside Shopping Center

VETERANS PKWY.

Hillcrest Ave.

Leisure St.

Pleasure Dr.

Georganna St.

BRIDGE ST.

Landmark Ave.

Tuma Rd.

Wells St.

Fox

Norra Park Dr.

Conover Ln.

Beecher Community Center

Yorkville High School

Garde Farm Rd.

Library

City Hall

Police Dept.

Appleton Ct.

Jackson St.

Walnut St.

Victoria Ave.

North Rd.

South Park Dr.

Morgan   Creek

Prairie Park

Bristol Ave.

Elm St.

Park St.

Marie Ave.

Marjon

Wacker Dr.

Terri Ln.

Lincoln Ln.

Central Dr.

Riverside Dr.

Ridge St.

Morgan Ln.

Fox Hill Ct.

Yorkville Grade School

Somonauk

Spring St.

Center

West St.

King St.

W. Main St.

Freemont

Sanders Ct.

Wooley Ln.

McHugh

Woodworth

Brant St.

Behrens St.

West Rd.

Bristol Rd.

Kendall Rd.

Country   Dr.

Morgan Ct.

Colony

Linwood Cemetery

River

Post Office

Church

Colton

Liberty

Galena Ln.

Oakwood St.

Johnston St.

Quinsey Rd.

Yorkville Rd.

Riverside Rd.

Ponderosa Dr.

Central

BRISTOL TWP.

KENDALL TWP.

71

Fox   River

Hydraulic Park

Bicentennial Park

Hydraulic Ave.

VAN EMMON RD.

24

KENDALL TWP.

OSWEGO TWP.

LYONS FOREST PRESERVE

Emmon Rd. E.

Madison St.

Ridge St.

Adams St.

Jefferson St.

Van Emmons St.

Heustis St.

Ridge St.

Mill St.

Fox St.

Van Emmon Mem. Park

Woodland Dr.

YORKVILLE

Morgan St.

Washington St.

Washington St.

RICHARD YOUNG FOREST PRESERVE

Washington St.

Orange St.

Dolph St.

Adrian St.

Dolph St.

State St.

Beecher St.

47

Circle Center St. Middle Sch.

Blaine St.

Main St.

Walter St.

Elizabeth St.

Illini Dr.

126

SCHOOLHOUSE RD.

Colonial Pkwy.

47

Yorkville Business Center

Wheaton Ave.

.5 MILE

© BY CSC

1    2    3    4

CONTINUED ON PAGES 21 AND 22

CONTINUED ON PAGE 24

CONTINUED ON PAGE 26

OSWEGO TWP.

NA-AU-SAY TWP.

© BY CSC

.5 MILE

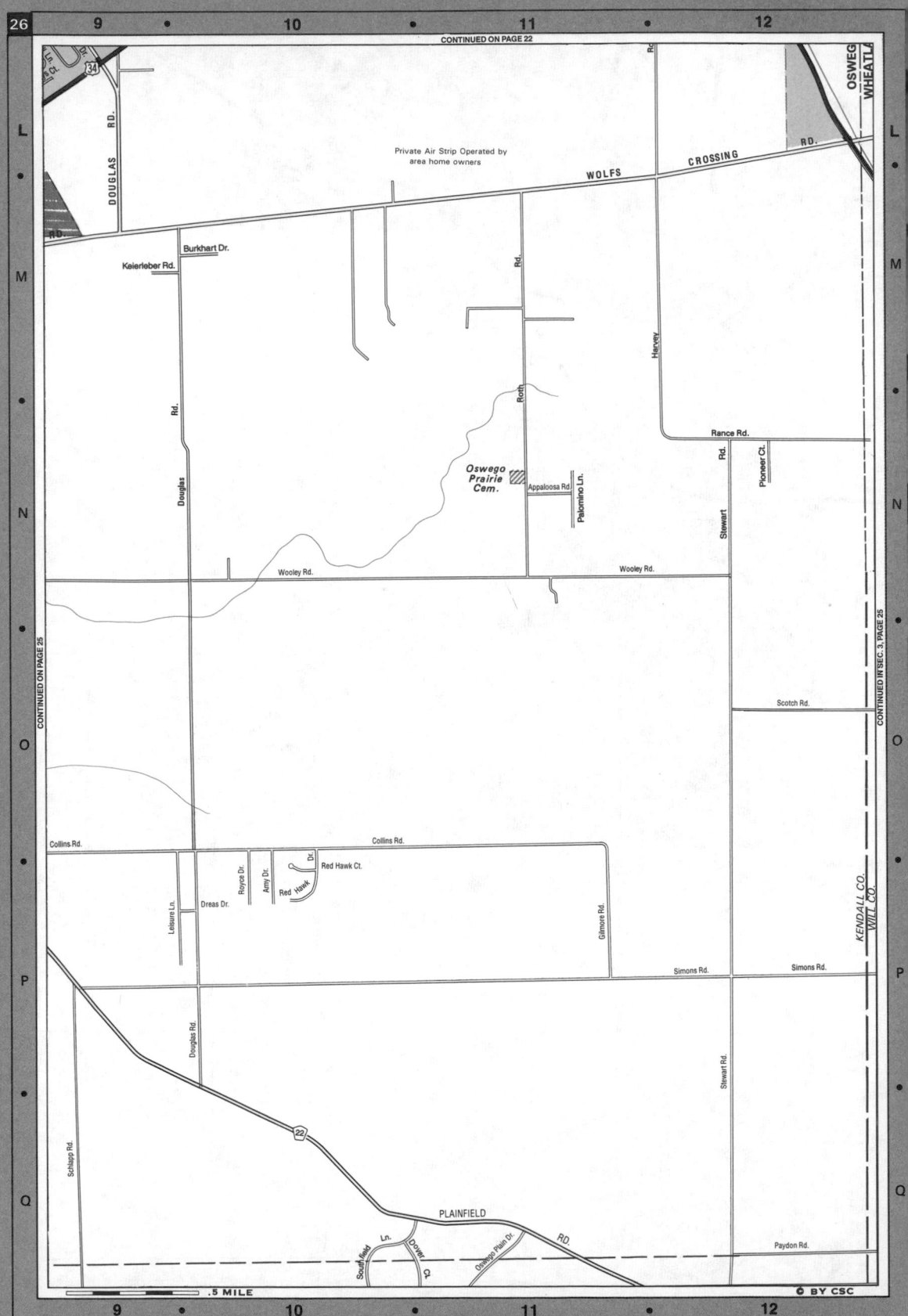

CONTINUED ON PAGE 22

Private Air Strip Operated by
area home owners

WOLFS CROSSING

OSWEG
WHEATL

RD.

DOUGLAS RD.

Burkhart Dr.

Keierleber Rd.

Rd.

Harvey

Douglas Rd.

Roth

Oswego
Prairie
Cem.

Appaloosa Rd.

Palomino Ln.

Rance Rd.

Rd.

Stewart

Pioneer Ct.

Wooley Rd.

Wooley Rd.

CONTINUED ON PAGE 25

CONTINUED IN SEC. 3, PAGE 25

Scotch Rd.

Collins Rd.

Collins Rd.

Leisure Ln.

Dreas Dr.

Royce Dr.

Amy Dr.

Red Hawk Dr.

Red Hawk Ct.

Gilmore Rd.

KENDALL CO.
WILL CO.

Douglas Rd.

Simons Rd.

Simons Rd.

Stewart Rd.

22

Schlapp Rd.

PLAINFIELD

Southfield Ln.

Dover Ct.

Oswego Plain Dr.

RD.

Paydon Rd.

.5 MILE

© BY CSC

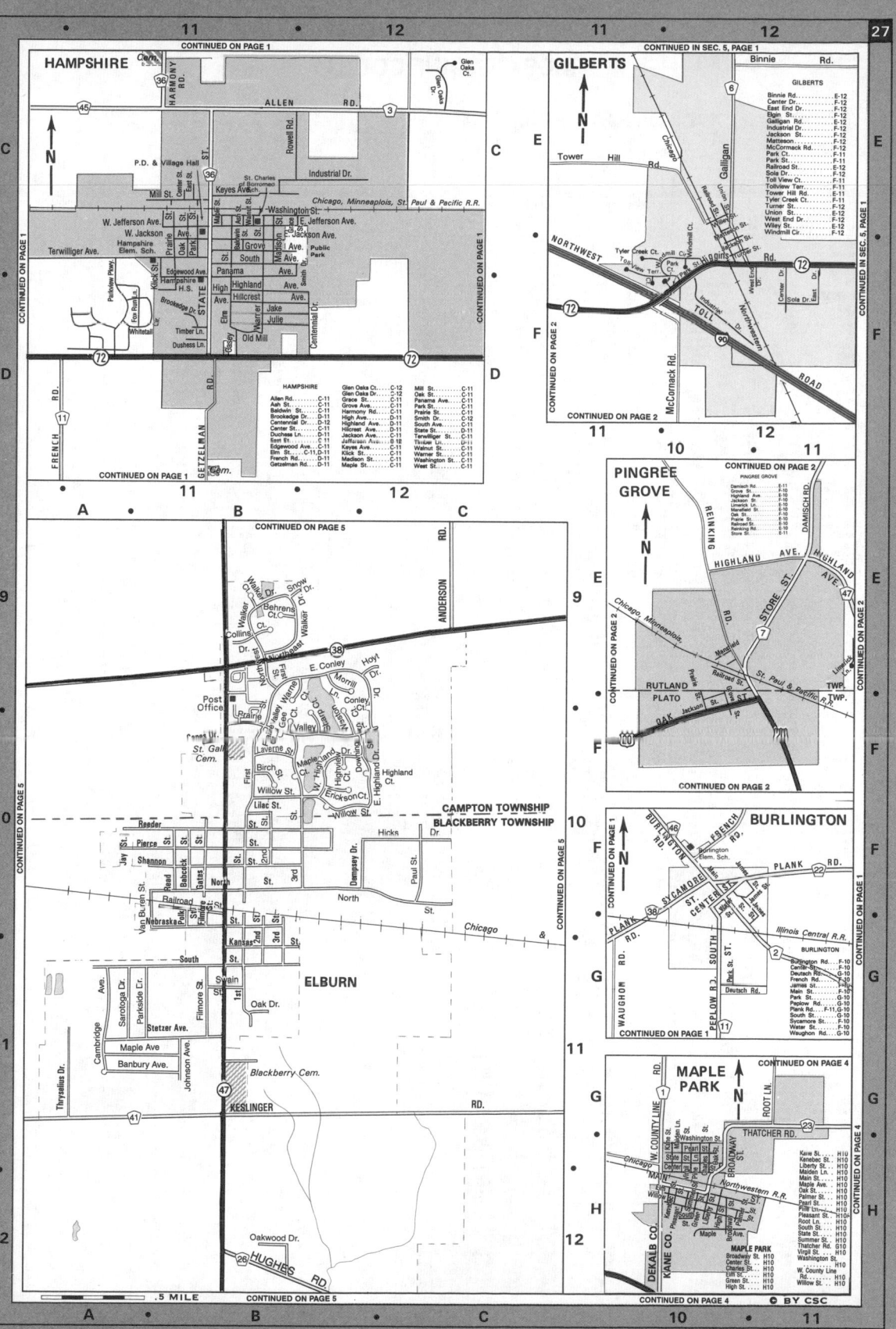

CONTINUED ON PAGE 1

# HAMPSHIRE

CONTINUED ON PAGE 1

| HAMPSHIRE | | |
|---|---|---|
| Allen Rd. | C-11 | Glen Oaks Ct. ... C-12 | Mill St. ... C-11 |
| Ash St. | C-11 | Glen Oaks Dr. ... C-12 | Oak St. ... C-11 |
| Baldwin St. | C-11 | Grace St. ... C-11 | Panama Ave. ... C-11 |
| Brookedge Dr. | C-11 | Grove Ave. ... C-11 | Park St. ... C-11 |
| Centennial Dr. | C-12 | Harmony Rd. ... C-11 | Prairie St. ... C-11 |
| Center St. | C-11 | High Ave. ... C-11 | Smith Dr. ... C-12 |
| Duchess Ln. | D-11 | Highland Ave. ... D-11 | South Ave. ... C-11 |
| Eent St. | C-11 | Hillcrest Ave. ... D-11 | State St. ... C-11 |
| Edgewood Ave. | D-11 | Jackson Ave. ... C-11 | Terwilliger St. ... C-11 |
| Elm St. | C-11, D-11 | Jefferson Ave. ... D-12 | Tinker Ln. ... C-11 |
| French Rd. | D-11 | Keyes Ave. ... C-11 | Walnut St. ... C-11 |
| Getzelman Rd. | D-11 | Klick St. ... C-11 | Warner St. ... C-11 |
| | | Madison St. ... C-11 | Washington St. ... C-11 |
| | | Maple St. ... C-11 | West St. ... C-11 |

# GILBERTS

CONTINUED IN SEC. 5, PAGE 1

| GILBERTS | |
|---|---|
| Binnie Rd. | E-12 |
| Center Dr. | E-12 |
| East End Dr. | F-12 |
| Elgin St. | F-12 |
| Galligan Rd. | E-12 |
| Industrial Dr. | F-12 |
| Jackson St. | F-12 |
| Matteson | F-12 |
| McCormack Rd. | F-12 |
| Park Ct. | F-11 |
| Park St. | F-11 |
| Railroad St. | E-12 |
| Sola Dr. | F-12 |
| Toll View Ct. | F-11 |
| Tollview Terr. | F-11 |
| Tower Hill Rd. | E-11 |
| Tyler Creek Ct. | F-11 |
| Turner St. | F-12 |
| Union St. | F-12 |
| West End Dr. | E-12 |
| Wiley St. | E-12 |
| Windmill Cir. | F-12 |

CONTINUED ON PAGE 2

# PINGREE GROVE

CONTINUED ON PAGE 2

| PINGREE GROVE | |
|---|---|
| Damisch Rd. | F-10 |
| Grove St. | F-10 |
| Highland Ave. | E-10 |
| Jackson St. | E-10 |
| Limerick Ln. | E-10 |
| Mansfield St. | E-10 |
| Oak St. | E-10 |
| Prairie St. | E-10 |
| Railroad St. | E-10 |
| Reinking Rd. | E-10 |
| Store St. | E-10 |

CONTINUED ON PAGE 2

CONTINUED ON PAGE 5

# ELBURN

CAMPTON TOWNSHIP
BLACKBERRY TOWNSHIP

CONTINUED ON PAGE 5

# BURLINGTON

CONTINUED ON PAGE 1

| BURLINGTON | |
|---|---|
| Burlington Rd. | F-10 |
| Center St. | G-10 |
| Deutsch Rd. | G-10 |
| French Rd. | F-10 |
| James St. | F-10 |
| Main St. | F-10 |
| Park St. | G-10 |
| Peplow Rd. | G-10 |
| Plank Rd. | F-11, G-10 |
| South St. | G-10 |
| Sycamore St. | F-10 |
| Water St. | F-10 |
| Waughon Rd. | G-10 |

CONTINUED ON PAGE 1

# MAPLE PARK

CONTINUED ON PAGE 4

| MAPLE PARK | |
|---|---|
| Kane St. | H-10 |
| Kenebec St. | H-10 |
| Liberty St. | H-10 |
| Maiden Ln. | H-10 |
| Main St. | H-10 |
| Maple Ave. | H-10 |
| Oak St. | H-10 |
| Palmer St. | H-10 |
| Pearl St. | H-10 |
| Pine Ln. | H-10 |
| Pleasant St. | H-10 |
| Root Ln. | H-10 |
| State St. | H-10 |
| Summer St. | H-10 |
| Thatcher Rd. | G-10 |
| Virgil St. | H-10 |
| Washington St. | H-10 |
| W. County Line | H-10 |
| Willett St. | H-10 |
| Willow St. | H-10 |
| Broadway St. | H-10 |
| Center St. | H-10 |
| Charles St. | H-10 |
| Elm St. | H-10 |
| Green St. | H-10 |
| High St. | H-10 |

DEKALB CO.
KANE CO.

CONTINUED ON PAGE 4

.5 MILE

CONTINUED ON PAGE 5

© BY CSC

# INDEX TO KANE COUNTY

## ALGONQUIN
Page 3
(Portions within McHenry County; for additional listings, see Sections 5 & 7)

**STREETS**
Algonquin Rd. .......... A9
Charles Ave. ........... A9
Compton Dr. ........... A9
County Line Rd. ....... A8
Dana Ct. .............. A9
Greenridge Ave. ....... A9
Hillside Ct. ........... A8
Lonidaw Trail ......... A9
Minnehaha Tr. ......... A9
Riverwood Dr. ......... A9
Sleepy Hollow Rd. ..... A8
Stratford Ln. .......... A9
Teri Ln. .............. A9

## AURORA
Pages 8,9,15,17-22
(Portions within DuPage County for additional listings, see Section 3)

**STREETS**
Adams ....... Pg.18 .... E13
Adobe Dr. .... Pg.18 .... E9
Alclaire Ave. . Pg.21 .... G10
Almeda Dr. ... Pg.18 .... E9
Almond Dr. ... Pg.18 .... E9
Alschuler Ct. . Pg.21 .... F9
Alschuler Dr. . Pg.21 .... F9
Alyce Ln. ..... Pg.19 .... D13
Amy Ln. ...... Pg.20 .... F8
Anderson St. .. Pg.22 .... G12
Apple Ct. ..... Pg.19 .... D13
Apple Hill Ln. . Pg.18 .... E9
Apple Tree Ln. Pg.18 .... D10
Arbor Ln. .... Pg.15,19
.................... B14,Q16
Archer Ave. ... Pg.21 .... G11
Arlene Dr. .... Pg.19 .... C13
Arlon Rd. ..... Pg.18 .... D11
Arnold Ave. ... Pg.21 .... G11
Arthur Way ... Pg.19 .... E14
Ash Ct. ....... Pg.18 .... D10
Ashby St. ..... Pg.20 .... F8
Ashland Ave. .. Pg.21 .... F9
Ashland Ct. ... Pg.21 .... H12
Ashwood Ln. .. Pg.18 .... D9
Assel Ave. .... Pg.19 .... E13
Aurora Ave. ... Pg.19 .... D13
Aurora Ave. Ln. Pg.19 .... D12
Austin Ave. ... Pg.19 .... D,E14
Autumn Ln. ... Pg.19 .... D13
Avati Ln. ..... Pg.19 .... D14
Avon St. ...... Pg.22 .... G12
Bainbridge Ct. Pg.14 .... E8
Baje Industrial Dr.
.................... B14,Q16
Baker St. ..... Pg.18 .... D9
Balmoral Ct. .. Pg.19 .... A14
Bangs St. ..... Pg.22 .... H13
Bannister Ln. . Pg.21 .... F9
Barbara Ln. ... Pg.21 .... F9
Bardwell St. .. Pg.22 .... G12
Barn Swallow Ct.
.................... Pg.18 .... F9
Barn Swallow Dr.
.................... Pg.18 .... F9
Barnes Rd. .... Pg.20 .... F8
Barrington Dr. . Pg.21 .... K15
Batavia St. .... Pg.19 .... F12
Beach St. ..... Pg.19,22 . F13
Bean Ridge Dr. Pg.18 .... D11
Beau Ridge Dr. Pg.18 .... D11
Becker Rd. .... Pg.19 .... E14
Beckwith St. .. Pg.19 .... F14
Bent Oak Trail Pg.18 .... D10
Benton St. .... Pg.22 .... G12,13
Berwyck Dr. ... Pg.21 .... G9
Best Place .... Pg.18 .... E9
Betty Ln. ..... Pg.19 .... E14
Bevier Pl. ..... Pg.22 .... G12
Big Oak Trail .. Pg.18 .... D10
Bilter Rd. ..... Pg.19 .... E15
Binder Ave. ... Pg.22 .... G12
Birch Ln. ..... Pg.18 .... D9
Birchwood Rd. Pg.19 .... E14
Bishop St. .... Pg.21 .... G11
Bittersweet Ct. Pg.18 .... D9
Black Oak Tr. . Pg.18 .... D11
Blackberry Ridge Dr.
Blackberry Tr. . Pg.17 .... F8
Blackhawk St. Pg.18 .... F12
Blackwell Ct. .. Pg.22 .... J15
Bluebell Ct. ... Pg.18 .... D9
Blueberry Ln. . Pg.18 .... D9
Bluegrass Ln. . Pg.15 .... Q16
Bluff St. ...... Pg.21 .... G12
Bowditch St. .. Pg.21 .... G11
Bowman Dr. ... Pg.18 .... D9
Bradford Dr. .. Pg.17 .... F8
Bradford Dr. .. Pg.17 .... F8
Bradford Ln. .. Pg.18 .... F9
Briarwood Ct. Pg.15 .... Q16
Bridge Dr. S. .. Pg.19 .... F11
Bridle Post Dr. Pg.18 .... E10
Brighton Cir. .. Pg.18 .... D9
Broadway ..... Pg.19,21 F12
Brookside Ct. . Pg.19 .... D15
Brookside Ln. . Pg.19 .... D15
Brookwood Dr. Pg.19 .... E15
Brouch Ln. .... Pg.19 .... D13
Buell Ave. .... Pg.18,21 E-G10
Buell Ct. ...... Pg.18 .... F10
Burgundy Ave. Pg.19 .... D13
Burr Oak Cir. .. Pg.18 .... D10
Burton St. .... Pg.19 .... D14
Buttercup Ct. . Pg.18 .... D9
Butterfield Rd. Pg.19 .... B13
Calhoun St. ... Pg.22 .... J15
Calico Dr. ..... Pg.18 .... D11
California Ave. Pg.18 . D11
California Ct. .. Pg.21 .... F10
Calumet Ave. Pg.21 .... F10
Cambridge Ave. Pg.18 .... D11
Cambridge Cir. Pg.17 .... F8
Cambridge Rd. Pg.17 .... F8

Candleberry Ln. Pg.18 .... E9
Canterbury Rd. Pg.18 .... E,F8
Carnation Ct. . Pg.18 .... D10
Carolyn Rd. ... Pg.21 .... F9
Carriage Hill Dr. Pg.21 .... F9
Cascade Dr. .. Pg.18 .... E10
Catherine St. . Pg.18 .... E11
Cedar St. ..... Pg.18,19 . F12
Cedardale Pl. . Pg.18 .... D11
Center Ave. ... Pg.21,22 . G12
Central Ave. .. Pg.21 .... G10
Century Ln. ... Pg.22 .... G14
Charles St. .... Pg.18 .... F11
Charleston Dr. Pg.18 .... D9
Charter Oaks Ct. Pg.15,19
Charter Oaks Ln. Pg.15,19
.................... B15,R17
Chateau Ave. . Pg.19 .... E13
Chatham Cir. .. Pg.17 .... F8
Chatham Rd. .. Pg.17 .... F8
Cherry Tree Dr. Pg.17,18 . F8
Chesterfield Ln. Pg.18 .... F12
Chestnut St. .. Pg.18 .... F12
Cheswick Ln. .. Pg.22 .... J15
Cheyenne Ave. Pg.18 .... E10
Christopher Ct. Pg.21 .... G9
Church Rd. .... Pg.19 .... F11
Church St. .... Pg.19 .... F13
Claim St. ..... Pg.22 .... G12
Clarissa Ln. .. Pg.15,19
.................... B15,R17
Clark St. ...... Pg.22 .... G12
Clement Ct. ... Pg.21 .... F10
Clementi Ln. .. Pg.22 .... J15
Cleveland Ave. Pg.21 .... G11
Cleveland St. . Pg.19 .... E13
Cloverdale Pl. . Pg.18 .... D11
Clovertree Ct. Pg.18 .... E8
Coach & Surrey Ln.
Cobblestone Dr. Pg.21 .... G9
Cochran St. ... Pg.18 .... E9
Cold Spring Dr. Pg.18 .... F9
Colfax St. ..... Pg.19 .... F13
Colleen Ct. .... Pg.19 .... D14
Colleen Dr. .... Pg.19 .... D14
College Ave. .. Pg.22 .... F13
Colorado Ave. Pg.18 . E10,11
Colorado Ct. .. Pg.18 .... E10
Columbia St. . Pg.22 .... F13
Comet Dr. ..... Pg.19 .... D9
Commonwealth Ave.
.................... Pg.18,21 E,G10
Comprehensive Dr.
Concord St. ... Pg.19 .... C15
Congrove Dr. . Pg.22 .... H12
Constellation Dr. Pg.19 .... D14
Constitution Dr. Pg.18 .... F9
Conway Ln. ... Pg.22 .... K14
Coolidge Ave. Pg.22 .... F14
Copley Dr. .... Pg.18 .... E9
Coral Ave. .... Pg.18 .... E9
Corinne Rd. ... Pg.21 .... F9
Corona Ct. .... Pg.19 .... D14
Corporate Blvd. Pg.19 .... N
Council St. .... Pg.22 .... F12
Courtyard Cir. Pg.17,18 . D8
Coventry Pl. ... Pg.18 .... E9
Creek Ave. .... Pg.19 .... D14
Crescent Ln. .. Pg.22 .... J15
Crestwood Ct. Pg.18 .... E10
Crestwood Dr. Pg.18 .... D11
Cross St. ...... Pg.21 .... F12
Croton Ct. .... Pg.19 .... D10
Curry Ct. ...... Pg.19 .... E12
Cypress Dr. ... Pg.18 .... E9
Daisy St. ...... Pg.19 .... F15
Dayward's St. . Pg.22 .... G14
Dearborn Ave. Pg.19 .... F14
Deerfield Dr. .. Pg.19 .... E8
Deerpath Rd. . Pg.17 .... E8
Delius St. ..... Pg.19 .... F13
Derby Ct. ..... Pg.19 .... A14
Donna Ave. ... Pg.19 .... D13
Douglas Ave. . Pg.21 .... H12
Downer Pl. .... Pg.17,18,22
Duncan Dr. ... Pg.18 .... D9
Dunhill Ln. .... Pg.22 .... K14
Durham Dr. ... Pg.18 .... D11
Eagle Dr. ..... Pg.18 .... D11
East Ave. ..... Pg.22 .... G13
East Indian Trail Pg.19 .... D13
East Sullivan Rd.
East-West Tollway
.................... Pg.18,19 C9,15
Eastern Ave. .. Pg.22 .... F15
Eastwick Ct. .. Pg.22 .... G14
Eastwood Dr. . Pg.18 .... D11
Edgelawn Ct. . Pg.18 .... E8
Edgelawn Dr. . Pg.18,21 D,F9
Edinburgh Ct. Pg.22 .... J15
Edinburgh Ln. Pg.22 .... J15
Edison Ave. ... Pg.19 .... D13
Edwards St. .. Pg.19 .... D15
Elder Dr. ...... Pg.18 .... D9
Elizabeth St. .. Pg.19 .... E13
Elliott Ave. .... Pg.21 .... H12
Elm St. ....... Pg.19 .... F12
Elmwood Dr. . Pg.18,21 D,G11
Emerald Dr. .. Pg.18 .... E9
Emily Ln. ..... Pg.15,19
Euclid Ave. ... Pg.22 .... H12
Evans Ave. .... Pg.22 .... G12
Evanslawn Ave. Pg.18,21 F,G10
Evergreen Dr. Pg.18 .... D11
Fallen Oak Tr. . Pg.18 .... D11
Farnsworth Ave. Pg.18 . E,G14
Farnum St. .... Pg.22 .... J15
Feathercck Dr. Pg.21 .... G10
Felten St. ..... Pg.19 .... D15
Fenton St. .... Pg.22 .... F13
Fidler Ct. ..... Pg.15,19
Flagg St. ...... Pg.22 .... G12
Flagstone Dr. . Pg.19 .... A15
Flagstone Ln. . Pg.15,19
.................... B15,R16

Florida Ave. ... Pg.18 .... E11
Foran Ln. ..... Pg.18 .... D,E11
Fordham Ave. Pg.18,21 E,G10
Forest Ave. ... Pg.19 .... E13
Four Season Blvd.
.................... Pg.22 .... H14
Fox Dr. ....... Pg.17,18 . E8
Fox Pointe Ct. Pg.21 .... H15
Fox Pointe Dr. Pg.21 .... H15
Fox Valley Ct. . Pg.21 .... H15
Foxcroft Dr. ... Pg.18 .... D9
Foxtail Dr. .... Pg.22 .... G15
Franklin Ave. . Pg.21 .... F11
Frazier Ct. .... Pg.21 .... F12
Frederick St. .. Pg.21 .... F12
Fromage Rd. .. Pg.18 .... E10
Fulton St. ..... Pg.22 .... F13
Gale St. ...... Pg.21 .... F11
Galena Blvd. .. Pg.18,22
.................... F10,12,G13
Galway Dr. .... Pg.19 .... D14
Garfield Ave. .. Pg.18,21 F9,11
Gates Ave. .... Pg.18 .... E13
Gates St. ..... Pg.22 .... H13
George Ave. .. Pg.22 .... G13
Gettysburg Dr. Pg.18 .... E9
Gillette Ave. .. Pg.18 .... E11
Ginger Woods Dr.
Ginger Woods Pkwy.
.................... Pg.15,19
.................... B15,R17
Gladstone Ave. Pg.18,21 E,G10
Gladstone Terr. Pg.18 .... E10
Gleason Ave. .. Pg.21 .... F10
Glen Cir. ..... Pg.19 .... D13
Glenview Ave. Pg.19 .... D13
Glenwood Ave. Pg.18,21 . F10
Glenwood Pl. . Pg.18 .... E10
Golden Oaks Pkwy.
Goldenrod Ct. Pg.18 .... D9
Golf Trail Ct. .. Pg.18 .... D8
Grace Ave. .... Pg.21 .... F11
Grace Ct. ..... Pg.22 .... F13
Grand Ave. .... Pg.18,19 E,F12
Grand Blvd. ... Pg.22 .... G14
Grandview Dr. Pg.21 .... F14
Grant Pl. ...... Pg.22 .... G12
Grantham Ln. . Pg.21 .... K14
Green Leaf Ct. Pg.18 .... D9
Green Oak Tr. Pg.18 .... D11
Greenfield Ct. Pg.18 .... D9
Greenfield Ct. Pg.18 .... D9
Greenfield Dr. Pg.18 .... D9
Greenvale Dr. Pg.19 .... E13
Greenwood Dr. Pg.18 .... F9
Grenada Rd. .. Pg.18 .... F9
Griffith Ave. ... Pg.21 .... F11
Grove St. ..... Pg.19 .... F13
Hamilton Ave. Pg.21 .... G11
Hammond Ave. Pg.22 .... J15
Hampshire Ave. Pg.22 .... F14
Hankes Ave. .. Pg.19 .... E13
Hankes Rd. ... Pg.17 .... D7
Hardin Ave. ... Pg.21 .... F11
Harmon Ave. . Pg.22 .... G13
Harrison Ave. Pg.18,21 E,F11
Hart Rd. ...... Pg.19 .... A13
Hartford Ave. Pg.21 .... G11
Hawthorne Ct. Pg.22 .... H11
Hazel Ave. .... Pg.18 .... D8,9
Heartstone Ct. Pg.18 .... E10
Heritage Dr. .. Pg.21 .... F11
Hermes Ave. . Pg.19 .... E13
Hermitage Dr. Pg.18 .... E9
Heywood Ave. Pg.21 .... G11
Hickory Ave. .. Pg.22 .... G13
Hidden Oaks Ln. Pg.18 .... D10
High St. ...... Pg.19 .... E,F13
Highfield Ct. .. Pg.22 .... J15
Highfield Ln. .. Pg.22 .... J15
Highland Ave. Pg.18,21 E,G11
Hill Ct. ....... Pg.22 .... G14
Hill Dr. ....... Pg.22 .... H15
Hillside Ave. .. Pg.18 .... E9
Hinkley Ave. .. Pg.22 .... H-J12
Hinman St. ... Pg.22 .... F13
Holden Ave. .. Pg.21 .... H11
Holiday Dr. ... Pg.18 .... D11
Hollycrest Dr. Pg.18 .... E11
Homer Ave. ... Pg.22 .... G14
Hopkins St. ... Pg.22 .... G14
Horizon Ln. ... Pg.15,19
.................... A15,Q16
Howard Ave. .. Pg.18 .... E11
Howell Pl. ..... Pg.22 .... G,H13
Hoyles Ave. ... Pg.22 .... J15
Hoyt St. ...... Pg.18 .... E10,11
Huntington Dr. Pg.18 .... D11
Illinois Ave. ... Pg.18,19 E9,13
Independence Dr.
.................... Pg.18 .... F11
Indian Ave. ... Pg.19 . F13,14
Indian Trail Dr. Pg.17-19 D8,10
Industrial Dr. . Pg.18 .... D11
Ingelside Ave. Pg.21 .... F11
Interstate 88 . Pg.19 .... C15
Ione Ct. ...... Pg.22 .... G15
Ione Dr. ...... Pg.22 .... G15
Iowa Ave. ..... Pg.18 . E,F12
Ironwood Ct. Pg.18 .... D9
Iroquois Dr. ... Pg.18 .... E9
Ivy Ln. ....... Pg.18 .... E9
Jackson Pl. ... Pg.22 .... G13
Jackson St. ... Pg.22 .... G12
Jefferson St. .. Pg.19,22 E,F13
Jericho Ct. .... Pg.21 .... G10
Jericho Rd. ... Pg.21 .... G9
Jingle Bell Ln. Pg.21 .... G9
Joel Ave. ..... Pg.18 .... E13
Joyce Ln. ..... Pg.18 .... D9
Jungles Ave. .. Pg.19 .... E13
Kane St. ...... Pg.22 . F13,14
Kautz Rd. ..... Pg.19 .... H-J15
Kealsey Ln. ... Pg.21 .... H11
Keck Ave. ..... Pg.21 .... G11
Kendall St. ... Pg.22 .... G14
Kenilworth Pl. Pg.21 .... G14
Kenmore Ave. Pg.19 .... D,E13

Kensington Ct. Pg.21 .... F9
Kensington Pl. Pg.21 .... F9,10
Kenwood Pl. .. Pg.21 .... F11
Kenyon Ct. .... Pg.19 .... D15
Kingsbury Ave. Pg.22 .... G12
Kingsway Dr. S. Pg.21 .... F9
Klein Ave. ..... Pg.19 .... E13
Konen Ave. ... Pg.19 .... C13
L.R.A. Rd. .... Pg.21 .... F9
LaFayette St. . Pg.22 .... H12
Lake St. ...... Pg.21 . F12,G11
Lake View Dr. Pg.20 .... F8
Lakelawn Blvd. Pg.18 .... D11
Lakeview Dr. .. Pg.20 .... F8
Lakeview Dr. .. Pg.18,21
.................... D10,F8
Lakewood Pl. . Pg.21 .... H11
Lancaster Ave. Pg.18,21 E,F11
Landmark Rd. Pg.18 .... D11
Landreth Ct. .. Pg.22 .... J14
Larkspur Ct. .. Pg.18 .... D9
Lasalle St. .... Pg.21 .... E13
Laurel Dr. ..... Pg.18 .... E9
Lawndale Ave. Pg.18,19 . E12
LeGrande Ave. Pg.18 .... E10
LeGrande Blvd. Pg.21 .... G10
Lebanon St. .. Pg.22 .... H12
Legacy Dr. .... Pg.19 .... D15
Lehnertz Ave. Pg.21 .... F14
Lehnertz Cir. .. Pg.19 .... E14
Lenwood Ct. . Pg.21 .... G11
Liberty St. .... Pg.19 . F13,14
Lilac Ct. ...... Pg.18 .... D15
Lilac Ln. ...... Pg.18 .... D15
Lily St. ....... Pg.19 .... D15
Limerick Ln. .. Pg.19 .... D14
Lincoln Ave. .. Pg.19,22
.................... E,F13,G12
Lincolnshire Ave.
.................... Pg.18 .... D11
Linda Ct. ..... Pg.18 .... D11
Linda Ln. ..... Pg.19 .... C14
Linden Ave. ... Pg.22 .... G13
Loden St. ..... Pg.18 .... E13
Locust St. .... Pg.18,21 . F12
Logan St. ..... Pg.21 .... H12
Lone Oak Trail Pg.18 .... D10
Loreen Dr. .... Pg.19 .... D15
Loucks St. .... Pg.22 .... G14
Lowell Dr. .... Pg.18 .... E9
Lyndhurst Ln. Pg.20 .... F8
Lynn St. ...... Pg.19 .... D14
Lynwood Dr. .. Pg.21 .... F10
Lyon Pl. ...... Pg.19 .... E12
Madison St. .. Pg.22 .... H15
Maher Dr. ..... Pg.22 .... H15
Mallette Rd. .. Pg.19 .... D9
Manchester Way
.................... Pg.17 .... F8
Manor Pl. ..... Pg.18,19 . F12
Maple Ave. ... Pg.22 .... G12
Maplewood Ln. Pg.20 .... F8
Margaret Ln. . Pg.19 .... D13
Marigold Ct. .. Pg.18 .... D9
Marikay Ave. . Pg.19 .... D14
Marion Ave. .. Pg.22 .... G12
Marseillaise Pl. Pg.21 .... F10
Marshall Ave. Pg.21 .... F11
Marshall Blvd. Pg.19 .... D14
Marshall St. .. Pg.21 .... F11
Marywood Ave. Pg.19 .... D14
Marywood Ct. Pg.19 .... D14
Mason Ct. .... Pg.21 .... H11
Masters Pkwy. Pg.17 . D8,9
May St. ....... Pg.18,21 E,F11
Mayflower Dr. Pg.18 .... E9
Mc Clure Rd. . Pg.19 .... D14
McCarty Ct. .. Pg.21 .... F11
McClure Ln. .. Pg.19 .... E14
McClure Rd. .. Pg.19 .... D14
McDowell Ave. Pg.22 .... J15
Meadow Terr. Pg.18 .... E13
Meadowgreen Dr.
.................... Pg.17 .... E8
Melrose Ave. . Pg.21 . H12,13
Mercy Ln. .... Pg.18 .... D12
Merrimac Rd. Pg.15 .... Q16
Mesa Ln. ..... Pg.19 .... A14
Mettel Rd. .... Pg.19 .... D14
Michael Ct. ... Pg.19 .... D14
Michels Ave. . Pg.18 .... E13
Michigan Ave. Pg.18,19 . E12
Middle Ave. ... Pg.21 .... G11
Middle Queensbury Ct.
Midfield Dr. ... Pg.20 .... F8
Midlane Dr. ... Pg.17 .... F8
Miller St. ..... Pg.22 .... F13
Misty Ridge Ct. Pg.22 .... J15
Misty Ridge Ln. Pg.22 .... J15
Mitchell Rd. .. Pg.19 .... D13
Molitor Rd. ... Pg.19 .... C14
Monitor Ave. .. Pg.21 .... H12
Monomoy St. . Pg.18 .... D13
Monona St. ... Pg.18 .... D13
Monroe St. ... Pg.19 .... D14
Montgomery Ave.
.................... Pg.21 .... G11
Montgomery Rd. Pg.22 H15,J12
Montgomery St. Pg.21 . H11
Morningside Dr.
Morton Ave. .. Pg.18 .... E13
Morton Dr. .... Pg.21 .... F11
Mountain St. . Pg.21 . E13,14
Mulberry Ct. .. Pg.18 .... D9
Nan St. ....... Pg.19 .... C14
Nantucket Dr. Pg.18 .... D11
Napa Ln. ..... Pg.19 .... D13
New Haven Ave. Pg.18 .... E11
New Indian Tr. Ct.
New Indian Trail Dr.
New York St. . Pg.18,22
.................... F11,14,G13
Newcastle Ln. Pg.21 .... F9
North Ct. ..... Pg.22 . G12,13
North East Dr. Pg.19 .... D14
North Park Ave. Pg.18,19 . E12

Northeast Industrial
.................... Pg.19 .... D13
Northfield Ct. . Pg.19 .... C13
Nottingham Dr. Pg.19 .... C13
O'Malley Ct. .. Pg.21 .... G11
Oak Ave. ...... Pg.19 . E,F12
Oak Trails Dr. Pg.17 .... E8
Oaklview Ave. Pg.22 .... F15
Oakwood Ave. Pg.19 .... E14
Ogden Ave. ... Pg.21 .... G11
Ogden Ave. ... Pg.21 . J14,15
Ohio Ct. ...... Pg.19 .... D14
Ohio St. ...... Pg.19,22 E,H14
Old Indian Trail Rd.
Old Wood Ct. Pg.18 .... F9
Oliver Ave. .... Pg.21 .... H11
Opal Ln. ...... Pg.18 .... E9
Orchard Ave. . Pg.19 .... E12
Orchard Lake Dr. Pg.19 .... D7
Orchard Rd. .. Pg.18,21 D,G8
Orchid St. .... Pg.19 .... D15
Ottawa Ave. .. Pg.19 .... E13
Paddock Ct. .. Pg.19 .... A14
Palace St. ..... Pg.18 .... E12
Park Manor .. Pg.21 .... F10
Park Pl. ...... Pg.22 .... F12
Park.E. ....... Pg.22 .... G12
Parker Ave. ... Pg.21 .... H12
Parkside Ave. Pg.22 .... F14
Parkview Dr. .. Pg.19 .... B14
Pearl St. ...... Pg.22 .... G12
Pebblestone Dr. Pg.22 .... J15
Pebblewood Ct. Pg.17,18 . E8
Pennsylvania Ave.
.................... Pg.18 .... E12
Pepperidge Ct. Pg.21 .... G10
Perry Ave. .... Pg.18 .... E11
Perry Ct. S. .. Pg.19,22
.................... D14,G12
Peterson Ave. Pg.22 .... H11
Phoenix Ct. ... Pg.19 .... E13
Pierce St. ..... Pg.19 .... E13
Pin Oak Trail . Pg.18 .... D10
Pine Ave. ..... Pg.19 .... F14
Pinehurst Dr. . Pg.17 .... E8
Pinnacle Ct. .. Pg.15,19
Pinnacle Dr. .. Pg.15,19
.................... A15,R16
Pinney St. .... Pg.19 .... F12
Plain Ave. ..... Pg.19 .... E14
Pleasant Pl. .. Pg.22 .... H13
Pleasant Terr. Pg.19 .... E14
Pleasure Ct. .. Pg.18 .... E11
Plum St. ...... Pg.18 . F10,12
Pointe Blvd. .. Pg.22 .... J15
Pond Ave. .... Pg.18 .... E11
Pontarelli Dr. . Pg.22 .... J14
Post Dr. ...... Pg.18 .... D11
Powell Ave. ... Pg.21 .... H11
Prairie St. .... Pg.21 .... G9
Preakness Ct. Pg.19 .... A14
Preakness Dr. Pg.19 .... A14
Proposed Rd. . Pg.19 .... E15
Queensbury Ct. N.
Rachel Ln. .... Pg.20 .... G8
.................... B15,R17
Raddant Rd. .. Pg.19 .... Q16
Rainwood Dr. Pg.18 .... E10
Randall Ave. .. Pg.21 .... G10
Randall Cir. ... Pg.19 .... D14
Randall Rd. ... Pg.18,21 D,F10
Rathbone Ave. Pg.21 G10,11
Raven Dr. ..... Pg.17 .... F8
Ray Moses Dr. Pg.22 .... H13
Reckinger Rd. Pg.19 .... D14
Red Maple Ln. Pg.15,19
.................... B15,R17
Red Oak Tr. .. Pg.19 .... D10
Redwood Dr. . Pg.19 .... D14
Reising St. .... Pg.19 .... F13
Richard St. ... Pg.18 . E9,11
Ridge Ave. .... Pg.22 .... H15
Ridgeway Ave. Pg.21 .... G10
River Rd. ..... Pg.19 .... C12
River St. ...... Pg.19,21
.................... F12,G11
Roanoke Ave. Pg.18 .... E10
Robert Ct. .... Pg.18 .... E9
Roberts St. ... Pg.18 . E9,11
Robinhood Dr. Pg.19 .... C13
Robinwood Dr. Pg.18 .... D11
Root St. ...... Pg.19,22
.................... E,F13,G12
Rose St. ...... Pg.22 .... G12
Rosedale Ave. Pg.18 . F13
Rosedale Ct. . Pg.18 .... F13
Rosewood Ave. Pg.21 .... G12
Royal Ct. ..... Pg.22 .... J15
Royal Ln. ..... Pg.22 .... J15
Rural St. ..... Pg.19 .... E13
Russel Ct. .... Pg.21 .... E11
Russell Ave. .. Pg.18,21
Russell Ct. .... Pg.18
.................... D,E,F11
Russell Cir. ... Pg.18 .... E11
Russell Dr. ... Pg.18 .... E11
Ryegrass Cir. . Pg.21 .... G9
Ryegrass St. . Pg.21 .... G9
Ryegrass Tr. .. Pg.21 .... G9
San Souci Dr. Pg.21 .... G9
Sandburg Dr. Pg.18 .... E10
Sandy Ln. .... Pg.18 .... E10
Sapphire Ln. Pg.18 .... D9
Sarah Ln. .... Pg.15,19
Savannah Ct. Pg.15 .... Q16
.................... A15,R16
Savannah Dr. Pg.15,19
.................... A14,Q16
Sawgrass Dr. Pg.15,19
.................... A14,Q16
Scarlet Oak Cir. Pg.18 .... D10
Schiller Ave. .. Pg.22 .... F14
Schindel Dr. .. Pg.22 .... G14
Schomer Ave. Pg.18,21 . E12
School House Ln.
Second Ave. .. Pg.22 .... G13
Secretariat Ct. Pg.19 .... Q16
Secretariat Dr. Pg.15,19 . Q16

Sedgewood Ave. Pg.22 .... J15
Selmartin Rd. Pg.19 .... C15
Seminary Ave. Pg.21 .... G12
Seneca Dr. ... Pg.18 .... E10
Sequoia Dr. .. Pg.18 . C9,10
Serendipity Dr. Pg.22 .... H14
Sexton Ave. .. Pg.21 .... H12
Shady Ct. ..... Pg.18 .... E9
Shady Ln. ..... Pg.18 .... D9
Shagbark Ln. Pg.17 .... E8
Shamrock Ave. Pg.19 .... D14
Shannon Dr. . Pg.19 .... D14
Shawano Dr. Pg.19 .... E14
Sheffer Rd. ... Pg.19 .... E14
Sheldon Ave. Pg.18 .... E11
Sheridan St. .. Pg.19 .... E13
Sherman St. .. Pg.19 .... E14
Sherwood Ave. Pg.18 .... E11
Sherwood Dr. Pg.19 .... C13
Sill Ave. ...... Pg.21 .... G10
Silver Springs Ct.
.................... Pg.22 .... J15
Silvis Rd. ..... Pg.18 .... D11
Simms St. .... Pg.22 .... H12
Sirus Ave. .... Pg.18 .... E13
Smith Blvd. ... Pg.18 .... H13
Smith St. ..... Pg.22 .... G12
Solfsburg Ave. Pg.19 .... E13
Solitude Ln. .. Pg.15,19
.................... A15,Q16
Sonoma Ln. .. Pg.15 .... P16
South Ave. .... Pg.22 .... G12
South Hampton Ct.
South Hampton Dr.
.................... Pg.18 .... E10
Southlawn Pl. Pg.21 .... G10
Spencer St. ... Pg.22 .... F13
Spicebush Ln. Pg.22 .... J15
Spring St. ..... Pg.22 .... F13
Springbrook Dr. Pg.18 .... D11
Spruce Ave. .. Pg.18 .... F11
Spruce St. .... Pg.18 .... F11
Squire Ct. ..... Pg.19 .... D14
Squire Dr. ..... Pg.19 .... D14
St. Joseph Ave. Pg.19 .... E13
Stanton Rd. .. Pg.19 .... H11
Star Ave. ..... Pg.19 .... E13
State St. ...... Pg.22 .... G13
Still Water Ct. Pg.18 .... F9
Stockton Ct. .. Pg.19 .... D15
Stockton Ln. .. Pg.19 .... D15
Stolp Ave. .... Pg.22 .... F12
Stone Ave. .... Pg.18 .... E11
Stonefence Ct. Pg.18 .... F9
Stonegate Dr. Pg.21 .... F9
Stoneheather Ave.
Strawberry Ct. Pg.18 .... D9
Stuart Ave. ... Pg.22 .... F14
Sullivan Rd. .. Pg.18 . D9,10
Summerlin Dr. Pg.22 .... K14
Summit Ave. .. Pg.22 .... G13
Sumner Ave. .. Pg.21 .... F10
Sunflower Ct. Pg.18 .... D9
Sunset Ave. .. Pg.18,19 . F12
Superior St. .. Pg.19 .... F13
Surrey Ct. .... Pg.17 .... G8
Symphony Dr. Pg.22 .... F13
T St. ......... Pg.22 .... G14
Taleisin Dr. ... Pg.21 .... G11
Tall Oaks Dr. Pg.19 .... D14
Talma St. ..... Pg.22 .... H12
Tanglewood Ct. Pg.19 .... F9
Tanglewood Dr. Pg.21 .... F9
Taylor Ave. ... Pg.18 .... E13
Terry Ave. .... Pg.21 .... G10
Terry Tr. ...... Pg.21 .... G10
Thompson Ln. Pg.19 .... C14
Timberlake Ct. Pg.18 .... D10
Timberlake Dr. Pg.18 .... D10
Tinley Dr. ..... Pg.18 .... C11
Tinsworth Dr. Pg.21 .... G10
Tollview Ave. .. Pg.19 .... E14
Tomcat Ln. ... Pg.22 .... G13
Tracy Ln. ..... Pg.17 .... F8
Trask St. ..... Pg.19,22 D,F14
Trojak Ln. .... Pg.15,19
.................... B15,R17
Turner Rd. .... Pg.19 .... D13
Union St. ..... Pg.22 . F,H13
Upper Brandon Dr.
.................... Pg.18 .... D11
Vermont Ave. Pg.22 .... F13
Vernon Ave. .. Pg.19 .... C13
View St. ...... Pg.18,21 E,F11
Village Center Pkwy.
Vine St. ...... Pg.19 .... F12
Vineyard Ln. . Pg.15 .... P16
Violet St. ..... Pg.19 .... D15
Wagner Ct. ... Pg.15 .... Q16
Wagner Rd. ... Pg.15 .... Q16
Wakefield Ct. Pg.18 .... F11
Walcott Rd. ... Pg.22 .... F15
Walden Cir. ... Pg.18 .... E10
Walter Ave. ... Pg.22 .... G13
Warren Ave. .. Pg.21 .... G12
Washington St. Pg.19 .... E13
Water St. ..... Pg.21 .... G12
Watson St. ... Pg.22 .... H12
Webster St. .. Pg.22 .... F13
Wedgewood Ln. Pg.18 .... E10
Wellington Cir. Pg.18 .... E10
Wellington Ln. Pg.18 .... E10
Welsh Dr. .... Pg.22 .... F15
Wennamacher Ave.
Wermes Ave. . Pg.22 .... H14
West Park Ave. Pg.18 .... E11
West Pl. ...... Pg.22 .... G13
Westchester Dr. Pg.18 .... E11
Western Ave. Pg.18 . E,G10
Westgate Dr. . Pg.18 .... E11
Westlawn Av. Pg.18,21 E,G10
Westminster Dr. Pg.17 .... E8
Weston Ave. .. Pg.22 .... G12
Westwood Dr. Pg.18 .... E10
White Ave. ... Pg.21 .... G10
Wild Cherry Ct. Pg.20 .... E8
Wilder St. .... Pg.19 .... F12

Williams St. .. Pg.19 .... F12
Windfield Dr. . Pg.21 .... F9
Windsor Ave. . Pg.22 .... G13
Winfield Dr. ... Pg.21 .... F9
Winona Ave. .. Pg.18 .... E10
Wisteria Dr. ... Pg.22 .... J15
Wood St. ..... Pg.19,22 E,F13
Woodland Ave. Pg.22 .... F14
Woodlawn Ave. Pg.21 .... G11
Woodlyn Dr. .. Pg.19 .... C13
Woodruff St. . Pg.19 .... D13
Worthington Dr. Pg.18 .... E8
Wright Ct. .... Pg.22 .... F15
Wyckwood Ct. Pg.20 .... F8
Wyckwood Dr. Pg.21 .... G9
Wyeth Dr. .... Pg.22 .... H13
Wynwood Ln. Pg.18 .... F9
Yorkshire Ct. . Pg.17 .... D7
Youngs Ave. . Pg.22 .... F14
Zengele Ave. . Pg.19 .... E14
Zenner St. .... Pg.19 .... E13
Ziegler ....... Pg.22 .... G11
1st St. ....... Pg.21 .... G11
2nd St. ...... Pg.21 .... G11
3rd St. ....... Pg.21 .... G11
4th Ave. ..... Pg.22 . G12,13
4th St. ....... Pg.22 . G,H12
5th Ave. ..... Pg.22 .... G12
5th St. ....... Pg.22 .... G,J12
6th St. ....... Pg.22 . G12,13
7th St. ....... Pg.18 . H12,13
75th St. ...... Pg.22 .... G11

## CEMETERIES
Calvary Cem. Pg.19 .. D,E12
East Aurora Cem.
.................... Pg.22 .... F13
Marywood Cem. Pg.21 .. H12
Mt. Olivet Cem. Pg.21 .. H12
Spring Lake Cem.
.................... Pg.21 .... H11
St. Joseph's Cem.
.................... Pg.22 .... D12
St. Michael Cem.
.................... Pg.22 .... F14
St. Nicholas Cem.
The Abbey Cem. Pg.15 .. P16
West Aurora Cem.
.................... Pg.19 .... E12

## FOREST PRESERVES
Oakhurst F.P. Pg.22 .... G15

## GOLF COURSES
Aurora C.C. ... Pg.21 .... G10
Orchard Valley Golf Course
Phillips Park and Golf Course
.................... Pg.22 .... H15
Wolf Run Golf Course
.................... Pg.21 .... H10

## PARKS
Beau Bridge Park
.................... Pg.18 .... D11
Copley Playground
.................... Pg.21 .... G11
Farnsworth Playground
.................... Pg.22 .... G14
Foxcroft Lake Park
.................... Pg.18 .... D9
Garfield Park . Pg.18 .... E13
Gillette Park .. Pg.18 .... E11
Greene Park .. Pg.18 .... E11
Hall Park ..... Pg.18 .... E9
Hurds Island Park
.................... Pg.21 .... G12
Illinois Ave. Park
.................... Pg.19 .... E12
Jefferson Park Pg.18 .... E10
Jericho Sports Complex
.................... Pg.20 .... J8
Lebanon Playground
.................... Pg.22 .... H12
Lies Konen Park Pg.19 .. D13
Lincoln Park .. Pg.21 .... F11
McCarthy Park Pg.22 .... F13
McCullough Park
.................... Pg.19 .... E12
O'Donnell Park Pg.19 .. D14
Ohio St. Park Pg.22 .... F13
Orchard Lake Park
.................... Pg.18 .... E9
Philips Park .. Pg.22 .... H13
Pigeon Hill Playground
.................... Pg.19 .... E13
Pioneer Park . Pg.17 .... F9
Randall Park . Pg.18 .... D10
Rob Roy Park Pg.18 .... D10
Simmons Park Pg.19 .... D14
Smith Park ... Pg.18 .... D11
Solfsburg Playground
.................... Pg.19 .... E13
Spiers Island Park
Stevens Playground
.................... Pg.18 .... F11
Stuart Sports Complex
.................... Pg.20 .... H8
Tracy Park ... Pg.17 .... F8
Vermeer Business Park
.................... Pg.18 .... B15
Washington Park
.................... Pg.18 .... E13
Westwood Park Pg.21 .. G10
Wilder Park .. Pg.19 .... F12

## SCHOOLS
Abraham Lincoln Sch.
.................... Pg.22 .... H14
Allen Sch. .... Pg.22 .... H14
Annunciation Sch.
.................... Pg.19 .... C13
Arch Bishop Romero Catholic
.................... Pg.19 .... F13
Aurora Central H.S.
.................... Pg.19 .... F14
Aurora Chr. H.S. Pg.18 .. F11
Aurora Christian Elem. Sch.
.................... Pg.18 .... E11
Aurora Ed. Ctr. Pg.22 .... G12
Aurora University
.................... Pg.21 .... G10

# AURORA

## AURORA TOWNSHIP
Pages 9,18,19,21,22

### STREETS

## BALDMOND
Page 8 ... M6

## BARRINGTON HILLS
Page 3 ... B10
(Portions within Cook, Lake & McHenry Counties, for additional listings, see Sections 2,5,6, and 7)

## BARTLETT
(Portions within DuPage County, for additional listings, see Sections 3 & 5)

## BATAVIA
Pages 6,9,14,15,19

### STREETS

## BATAVIA TOWNSHIP
Pages 8,9,14,15,18,19

### STREETS

## BIG ROCK
Page 7 ... O2

## BIG ROCK TOWNSHIP
Page 7

### STREETS

## BLACKBERRY TOWNSHIP
Pages 5,8,17

### STREETS

Catlin Sq. .... Pg.8 ..... M6
Clover Hill Ln. . Pg.8 ..... L5
Concord Ct. .... Pg.8 ..... M4
Creekside Ct. . Pg.8 ..... M4
Crego Pl. ..... Pg.8 ..... M5
Curtis Sq. .... Pg.5 ..... L6
DeRussey Rd. . Pg.8 ..... M4
Denali Ct. .... Pg.5 ..... K5
Denali Rd. .... Pg.5 ..... K5
Dobson Ln. .... Pg.5 ..... L7
Donny Hill Rd. Pg.8 ..... M5
Dooley Dr. .... Pg.5 ..... L6
East-West Tollway .......... Pg.8 ..... M4
Eldon Dr. ..... Pg.5 ..... L6
Ellithorpe Cir. . Pg.8 ..... M7
Fabyan Pkwy. . Pg.8 ..... L6
Field Ct. ..... Pg.5 ..... L7
Finley Rd. .... Pg.8 ..... N4
Forbes Dr. .... Pg.5 ..... L6
Ford Dr. ..... Pg.5 ..... L6
Fryendall Ct. .. Pg.8 ..... M6
Green Pl. ..... Pg.5 ..... L7
Green Rd. .... Pg.8 ..... M5
Greenbrier Dr. . Pg.8 ..... M4
Haladay Ln. ... Pg.8 ..... M5
Harley Rd. .... Pg.5 ..... K5
Harvey Sq. ... Pg.5 ..... L6
Hathaway Ct. . Pg.8 ..... M6
Hathaway Ln. . Pg.8 ..... M6
Hazelcrest Dr. . Pg.8 ..... N4
Healy Rd. .... Pg.8 ..... N6
Herrington Blvd. Pg.5 ..... L6
Herrington Dr. . Pg.5 ..... L6
Hilts Dr. ..... Pg.5 ..... L6
Howard Sq. ... Pg.5 ..... L6
Hubbard Pl. ... Pg.8 ..... M5
Hughes Rd. ... Pg.5,8 .. L7,9
Hyde Park .... Pg.8 ..... M7
Kellar Ct. .... Pg.8 ..... M6
Kellar Sq. .... Pg.8 ..... M6
Kenmar Ct. ... Pg.5 ..... L4
Kenmar Dr. ... Pg.5 ..... L4
Kenmar Ln. ... Pg.5 ..... L4
Keslinger Rd. . Pg.5 ..... K5
Killarney Ln. .. Pg.5 ..... K6
Krohn Ct. .... Pg.5 ..... K6
La Fox Rd. ... Pg.5 ..... K6
Lakewood Dr. . Pg.8 ..... N4
Lasher Rd. ... Pg.8 ..... N4
Lebaron Ct. ... Pg.5 ..... L6
Linlar Dr. .... Pg.5 ..... K6
Lockwood Pl. . Pg.8 ..... M5
Lorang Rd. ... Pg.8 ..... M4
Maian Ln. .... Pg.8 ..... N4
Main St. ..... Pg.8 ... M7-9
Mallory Dr. ... Pg.8 ..... M5
Marian Cir. ... Pg.8 ..... N4
Marks Pl. .... Pg.5 ..... L7
Mathewson Ln. Pg.8 ..... M6
McKinley St. .. Pg.9 ..... M8
McNair Pl. .... Pg.8 ..... M5
Meadowsweet Dr. .......... Pg.5 ..... K5
Midan Dr. .... Pg.5 ..... K6
Mill Creek Cir. . Pg.8 ..... M5
Mill Creek Dr., N. .......... Pg.5 ..... L6
Mill Creek Dr., S. .......... Pg.8 ..... M7
Mill Rd. ...... Pg.8 ..... M4
Mulhern Dr. ... Pg.5 ..... K6
Newton Ln. ... Pg.8 ..... M5
Newton Sq. ... Pg.8 ..... M7
Norris Rd. .... Pg.8,17 A6,N6
North Dr. .... Pg.8 ..... N4
North Rd. .... Pg.5 ..... K5
Northern View Ct. .......... Pg.8 ..... L5
Northway Dr. . Pg.5 ..... K5
Nottingham Tr. Pg.8 ..... M4
Oakland Ln. .. Pg.8,17 B7,N6
Oakleaf Dr. ... Pg.8 ..... M4
Oakwood Dr. .. Pg.5 ..... L4
Oakwood Terr. Pg.8 ..... M4
Old Midlothian Tpk. .......... Pg.8 ..... M4
Olinger Ln. ... Pg.5 ..... L6
Pauley Sq. ... Pg.5 ..... L6
Pennycress Ct. Pg.5 ..... K5
Pine Row Ct. .. Pg.8 ..... M4
Platt Pl. ..... Pg.5 ..... L6
Pouley Rd. ... Pg.5 ..... L5
Prairie View Dr. Pg.5 ..... L6
Preston Cir. ... Pg.8 ..... M7
Preston Ct. ... Pg.8 ..... M5
Red Oak Dr. .. Pg.8 ..... M4
Revere House Ln. .......... Pg.8 ..... M7
Rowe Rd. .... Pg.5,8 .... L4
Ryan Pl. ..... Pg.8 ..... M5
Seavey Rd. ... Pg.8,17 ............... A5,M4-6
Shannon Ln. .. Pg.8 ..... M5
Shannon Sq. .. Pg.8 ..... M7
Sheldon ...... Pg.8 ..... M6
Smith Rd. .... Pg.8 ..... L5
Snooks Pl. ... Pg.8 ..... M5
Stargrass Ln. . Pg.5 ..... K5
State Rte. 47 .. Pg.8 ..... M4
Still Meadows Ln. .......... Pg.5 ..... K5
Sulley Dr. .... Pg.5 ..... L6
Sulley Pl. .... Pg.5 ..... L6
Sulley Sq. .... Pg.5 ..... L6
Surrey Dr. .... Pg.5,8 .... L4
Swift Pl. ..... Pg.8 ..... M5
Taana Rd. .... Pg.8 ..... L6
Tall Oaks Tr. .. Pg.8 ..... M4
Tanner Rd. ... Pg.8,17 B7,N6
Terney Ln. .... Pg.5 ..... L6
Terney Sq. ... Pg.5 ..... L6
Terrace Dr. ... Pg.8,17 B7,N6
Thornapple Tree Rd. .......... Pg.8 ..... N4
Thorndon Ridge Dr. .......... Pg.8 ..... L5
Timber Crest Dr. Pg.5,8 .... L4
Titus Pl. ..... Pg.5 ..... L7
Underwood Dr. Pg.5 ..... L6
Voorhees Pl. .. Pg.8 ..... M5
Washburn Dr. . Pg.5 ..... L6
Washburn Pl. . Pg.5 ..... L6
Weaver Cir. ... Pg.5 ..... L6
Weaver Ln. ... Pg.5 ..... L7
Whitney Pl. ... Pg.8 ..... M5
Wielis Cir. .... Pg.8 ..... M6
Willow Creek Ct. Pg.8 ..... M4
Willow Creek Dr. Pg.8 ..... M4
Yates Pl. ..... Pg.5 ..... L7

**FOREST PRESERVES**

Blackberry Maples Forest Preserve ... Pg.8 ..... M5
Johnsons Mound Forest Preserve ... Pg.5 ..... L5
Nelson Lake Forest Preserve .......... Pg.8 ..... M7

**GOLF COURSES**

Mill Creek Golf Course .......... Pg.5 ..... L6

**SCHOOLS**

Broadway Academy .......... Pg.5 ..... L5

**MISCELLANEOUS**

Mill Creek Comm. Ctr. .......... Pg.8 ..... M7
Mill Creek Equestrian Ctr. .......... Pg.8 ..... M7

## BOWES

Page 5...F6

## BRISTOL TOWNSHIP

(Kendall County)
Pages 20,21,23,24

**STREETS**

Amanda Ln. .. Pg.23 ..... N4
Anna Marie Ln. Pg.24 .... M7
Arbor Ln. .... Pg.24 ..... N8
Baseline Rd. .. Pg.20 ... J5-8
Basswood Ct. . Pg.20 ..... L7
Bayberry Dr. .. Pg.24 .... M9
Bazan Rd. .... Pg.23 ..... N6
Bentson St. ... Pg.24 .... M9
Bristol Ct. .... Pg.24 ..... N8
Bristol Ridge Rd. .......... Pg.23 ..... N6
Bristol St. .... Pg.23 ..... Q6
Brookside Ln. . Pg.20 ..... L6
Brookwood Ct. Pg.20 ..... L7
Budlong Crossing Dr. .......... Pg.24 ..... N7
Cannonball Tr. Pg.20,23 L6,N4
Canyon Ct. ... Pg.23 ..... O6
Center Dr. .... Pg.24 ..... N8
Central Dr. ... Pg.23 ..... P6
Charity Ln. ... Pg.23 ..... M5
Charles St. ... Pg.24 ..... N7
Christy Ln. ... Pg.23 ..... N5
Clark Rd. ..... Pg.24 .. M,N8
Concord Ct. ... Pg.23 ..... O5
Conover Ln. .. Pg.23 ..... P4
Cornelis Rd. .. Pg.23 ... M4,5
Cross St. ..... Pg.23 ..... M5
Cypress Dr., N. & S. .......... Pg.20 ..... L7
David Ct. ..... Pg.24 .... M7
Dickson Rd. .. Pg.20 ... K,L6
Division St. ... Pg.23 .... M6
Edythe St. .... Pg.24 ..... N7
Faxon Rd. .... Pg.23 ..... N4
Forest Ct. .... Pg.24 ..... N8
Galena Rd. ... Pg.20 ............... K7,8,L5,6
Game Farm Rd. Pg.23 ..... P4
Georganna St. . Pg.23 ..... P4
Grove St. ..... Pg.23 ..... M6
Heatherfield Ln. Pg.23 ..... M5
Hickory Ln. ... Pg.24 ..... N8
Highland Dr. .. Pg.20 ..... L7
Hunt St. ..... Pg.23 ..... M5
Hunter Ln. .... Pg.23 ..... M5
Kendall Rd. ... Pg.23 ..... P6
Kennedy Rd. .. Pg.23 ..... M6
Kennedy Rd., E. Pg.20 ..... L7
Lakespur E. & W. .......... Pg.20 ..... L7
Lakeview Dr. .. Pg.23 ..... N6
Lewis St. ..... Pg.24 ..... M7
Lexington Cir. . Pg.23 ..... O5
Lillian Ln. .... Pg.23 ..... N6
Linden Ave. ... Pg.23 ..... N6
Lyncliff Dr. ... Pg.24 ..... N7
Main St. ..... Pg.23 ..... M5
Marie Ave. ... Pg.23 ..... P5
Martin Ave. ... Pg.23 ..... P5
McHugh Rd. .. Pg.23 ..... P4
Mill Rd. ...... Pg.20,24 ............... L7,M9
North Park Dr. . Pg.23 ..... P6
North Rd. .... Pg.23 ..... P6
North St. ..... Pg.23 ..... M5
Oak Lawn Ave. Pg.23 ..... N7
Oak Ln. ...... Pg.23 ..... P6
Oak St. ...... Pg.23 ..... M5
Oakhill Dr. .... Pg.24 ..... N8
Orchard Rd. .. Pg.24 ..... M8
Osage Ct. .... Pg.24 ..... M8
Park Ln. ..... Pg.20 ..... L6
Parkway Dr. .. Pg.23 ..... N6
Patricia Ln. ... Pg.23 ..... N4
Pleasant View Dr. .......... Pg.24 ..... N8
Pleasure Dr. .. Pg.23 ..... P4
Plum St. ..... Pg.23 ..... M5
Prairie Ln. .... Pg.23 ..... P4
Quinsey Rd. .. Pg.23 ..... P6
Richard Dr. ... Pg.24 ..... M7
Ridge Rd. .... Pg.23 ..... P6
Ridge St. ..... Pg.23 ..... M5
River Rd. ..... Pg.23 ..... P4
River Wood Ct. Pg.24 ..... N7
River Wood Dr. Pg.24 ..... N7
River Wood Ln. Pg.24 ..... N8
Riverside Dr. .. Pg.23 ..... P6
Riverside Rd. . Pg.23 ..... P6
Riverview Dr. .. Pg.24 ..... N8
Royal Oaks Ct. Pg.23 ..... M6
Royal Oaks Dr. Pg.23 ..... M6
South Park Dr. Pg.23 ..... P6
South St. ..... Pg.23 ..... M5
Spring St. .... Pg.23 ..... P5
Spruce Ct. .... Pg.24 ..... M9
State Rte. 47 .. Pg.23 ... L-P4
Storybook Dr. . Pg.20 ..... L7
Sunset Ave. ... Pg.23 ..... P4
Sunset Ave. ... Pg.23 ..... N6
Theresa Ave. .. Pg.23 ..... M7
Timber Line Rd. Pg.23 ..... O6
Timber Ridge Dr. .......... Pg.23 ..... O6
Timber View Ln. Pg.23 ..... O6
Tuma Rd. .... Pg.23 ..... P6
U.S. Rte. 30 .. Pg.20 ... J5-8
U.S. Rte. 34 .. Pg.23 .. N8,O6
Veterans Pkwy. Pg.23 ..... P4
Victoria Ave. .. Pg.23 ..... P5
Wacker Dr. ... Pg.23 ..... P5
Walnut Creek Ln. .......... Pg.24 ..... N9
Wells St. ..... Pg.23 ..... P6
West Rd. ..... Pg.23 ..... P6
Willow Ln. .... Pg.20 ..... L6
Yorkville Rd. .. Pg.23 ..... P6

**CEMETERIES**

Oak Grove Cemetery .......... Pg.23 ..... N5
St. Patrick's Cemetery .......... Pg.23 ..... N5

**GOLF COURSES**

Blackberry Oaks Golf Course .......... Pg.23 .... M6

**PARKS**

Bristol Grade School .......... Pg.23 .... M5

## BURLINGTON

Pages 1,23

**STREETS**

Burlington Rd. Pg.23 .... F10
Center St. .... Pg.23 .... F10
Deutsch Rd. .. Pg.23 .... G10
French Rd. ... Pg.23 .... F10
James St. .... Pg.23 .... F10
Main St. ..... Pg.23 .... F10
Park St. ..... Pg.23 .... G10
Peplow Rd. ... Pg.23 .... G10
Plank Rd. .... Pg.23 F11,G10
South St. .... Pg.23 .... G10
Sycamore St. . Pg.23 .... F10
Water St. ..... Pg.23 .... F10
Waughon Rd. . Pg.23 .... G10

**SCHOOLS**

Burlington Elem. Sch. .......... Pg.23 .... F10

## BURLINGTON TOWNSHIP

Pages 1,4

**STREETS**

Barr Rd. ..... Pg.1 ...... E4
Barron Rd. ... Pg.4 ...... G2
Burlington Rd. Pg.1 ...... E3
Chapman Rd. . Pg.1 ...... E3
County Line Rd. Pg.1 ...... E1
Ellithorpe Rd. . Pg.1,4 .... F3
Engel Rd. .... Pg.1 ...... D2
Freedom Ln. .. Pg.1 ...... F4
Godfrey Rd. .. Pg.1 .... F2,3
Grand Arbor Ln. Pg.4 ...... G3
Hickory Ct. ... Pg.1 ...... E2
Highland Tr. .. Pg.1 ...... F4
Highview Ln. .. Pg.1 ...... F4
Hillview Ln. ... Pg.1 ...... F4
Larkin Rd. .... Pg.1 ...... G1
Lawrence Rd. . Pg.1 ...... E2
Lenschow Rd. . Pg.1 ...... D2
Lukens Rd. ... Pg.1 .... E,F1
Marcy Rd. .... Pg.1 ...... F1
McDonald Rd. . Pg.4 ...... G4
McGough Rd. . Pg.1,4 .. F-G1
Middleton Rd. . Pg.4 ...... F2
Peplow Rd. ... Pg.1 ...... F2
Percy Rd. .... Pg.4 ...... G2
Pioneer Ln. ... Pg.1 ...... F4
Plank Rd. .... Pg.1 .... E1-4
Plato Rd. ..... Pg.1 ...... F4
Ramm Rd. .... Pg.4 .... G2,3
Rohrsen Rd. .. Pg.1 ...... E4
Romke Rd. ... Pg.1 ...... E3
Shepherd Ln. . Pg.1 ...... F4
Strawberry Ln. Pg.1 ...... F4
Sumac Ln. ... Pg.1 ...... F4
Thomas Rd. .. Pg.4 ...... G3
Waughon Rd. . Pg.1 ...... E2
Whispering Oaks Dr. .......... Pg.1 ...... E2
Winterset Rd. . Pg.1 ...... E2

**FOREST PRESERVES**

Burlington Priarie .......... Pg.1 ...... E1

## CAMPTON TOWNSHIP

Page 5
(For additional listings, see Section 5)

**STREETS**

Aberdeen Ln.
Alcott Ln. ............... K6
Ancient Oak Ln. ........... H6
Anderson Rd. ............. J4
Antler Tr. ................ H6
Arber Creek Rd. ........... J6
Arboretum Ln. ............ G4
Arrowhead Dr. ............ J5
Audubon ................. G4
Badger Ct. ............... H4
Baert Ln. ................ J7
Balkan Dr. ............... J6
Balmoral Ct. .............. H6
Barberry Ln. .............. H5
Barlow Dr. ............... J5
Barnside Ct. .............. G6
Beaver Ct. ............... H4
Beaver Ln. ............... H4
Beith Rd. ............... J,K5
Birchdale Ct. .............. H6
Black Willow Dr. ........... H6
Blackhawk Ln. ............. H4
Blue Heron Ct. ............ H6
Blue Larkspur Ln. .......... J4
Bolcum Rd. ............... H6
Bonnie Ct. ................ J7
Boothe Tarkington St. ....... K6
Bowgren Cir. .............. K5
Bowgren Dr. .............. K5
Boxwood Ln. .............. G4
Bridal Creek Dr. ........... J6
Bridle Ct. ................ G4
Brierwood Dr. ............. H5
Brittany Ct. ............... G7
Brookhaven Ln. ............ H6
Brookside Dr. ............. J5
Brown Rd. ................ J5
Brundige Rd. .............. K6
Buck Ct. ................. H4
Buckskin Ct. .............. H6
Buckskin Trail ............. H6
Burlington Rd. ............. H6
Campton Ct. .............. H5
Campton Hills Dr. .......... J5
Campton Meadow Dr. ....... J6
Campton Oak Dr. .......... H6
Campton Ridge Dr. ......... G4
Campton Woods Dr. ........ J6
Canterbury Ct. ............ G6
Caribou Tr. ............... H6
Carl Sandberg Rd. ......... J6
Carol Dr. ................. H5
Carriage Ct. ............... J6
Castle Dr. ................ H4
Chaffield Dr. .............. J5
Challedon Ct. .............. J4
Chateaugay Ct. ............ J4
Chateaugay Ln. ............ J5
Circle Dr. ................. J5
Citation Ln. ............... J5
Clemens Course ........... J6
Clover Ct. ................ H5
Cloverfield Cir. ............ G6
Cloverfield Dr. ............ G7
Clydesdale Ct. ............. H6
Cochise Dr. ............... H4
Coleman Ct. .............. H5
Colonel Bennet Ln. ......... H5
Colson Dr. ................ H6
Colt Dr. .................. K6
Copperwood Ln. ........... H4
Corbett Pl. ................ K6
Corron Rd. ................ G6
Corrway Dr. ............... H5
Coulter Dr. ................ K6
Coulter Ln. ................ J6
Council Ct. ................ J4
Country View Ln. ........... J5
Cranberry Ln. .............. G4
Cranston Rd. .............. G6
Creekside Ct. .............. H5
Crescent Ln. ............... H6
Crestwood Dr. ............. H5
Crooked Ln. ............... H6
Crosscreek Ln. ............ H6
Curling Pond Ct. ........... J6
Cutwood Ln. .............. G6
Dairyherd Ln. ............. G6
Dean Ln. .................. J7
Dean St. .................. H6
Deer Run Dr. .............. H6
Deer Run Ln. .............. H6
Deerhaven Tr. ............. H6
Deerslayer Dr. ............. J4
Denali Ln. ................. K6
Denker Ct. ................ G6
Denker Ln. ................ G6
Denker Rd. ................ H6
Derby Ln. ................. J4
Dillonfield Dr. .............. K6
Dittman Rd. ............... G5
Dominion Dr. .............. G4
Dorsey Ct. ................ K6
Eagle Ct. ................. H4
East Rd. .................. J5
Echo Valley Ln. ............ J5
Edgar Lee Master Ln. ....... J6
Edna St. .................. K5
EdnaFerber Cove .......... J6
Elodie Dr. ................. J6
Emerson Ln. ............... J6
Emily Dickinson St. ......... K6
Empire Rd. ................ H4
Esther Ln. ................ G4
Evergreen Dr. ............. H6
Fair Oaks Dr. .............. H6
Faireno Dr. ................ J5
Falcon Ln. ................ J4
Far View Ct. ............... H6
Far View Rd. .............. J5
Farmview Rd. .............. J5
Farrier Point Ln. ........... H6
Fencepost Ln. ............. G5
Fenimore Ln. .............. J4
Ferson Ct. ................ H5
Fescue Ct. ................ H5
Fielding Ct. ............... G7
Foal Ln. .................. K6
Forest Glen Ln. ............ H4
Forest Ln. ................ J5
Fox Bend Dr. .............. G5
Fox Hill Ct. ............... H5
Fox Mill Blvd. ............. J6
Fox Wilds Ct. .............. H4
Foxfield Dr. ............... J5
Foxmoor Dr. ............... H5
Foxtail Cir. ................ G5
Foxwilds Dr. ............... H4
Francis Bret Hart St. ........ J6
Garfield Rd. ............... K6
Gary Ct. .................. G5
Golden Oaks Ln. ........... J5
Gopher Ct. ................ H5
Grady Ct. ................. K6
Grand Monde Dr. ........... J6
Griffin Ln. ................. J5
Hanson Rd. ............... H4
Hanson Ridge Dr. .......... H4
Happy Hills Rd. ............ J6
Harley Rd. ................ K5
Harvest Ct. ............... H4
Harvest Ln. ............... G4
Hastings Dr. ............... H6
Hawk Cir. ................. J4
Hawkeye Dr. ............... J4
Hazelwood Tr. ............. H5
Heather Ln. ............... H4
Hemingway St. ............. J6
Hemlock Dr. ............... H6
Henricksen Rd. ............ H7
Heritage Oaks Dr. .......... H7
Hidden Oaks Rd. ........... J7
Hidden Springs Dr. ......... H5
High Meadow Rd. .......... J6
High Point Ct. ............. J5
High Point Ln. ............. J5
Highwood Ct. .............. K6
Hill Dr. ................... H6
Hilltop Dr. ................ J6
Hoeweed Ln. .............. G6
Holly Ct. ................. H4
Homeward Glen Dr. ......... G6
Homeward Hills Dr. ......... H6
Howard ................... J5
Hunter Ct. ................ J4
Hunters Hill Dr. ............ H5
Hunters Ln. .............. H,J5
Hunters Ridge ............. H5
Ironwood Ct. .............. H4
Ivy Ct. ................... H5
Jack London St. ............ J6
James Fenimore Cooper Ln. . J6
Jensen Ln. ................ H5
Johns Way ................ G6
Johnson Rd. ............... J7
Juniper Ct. ................ H5
Kettlehook Ct. ............. H4
Kevin Ct. ................. H6
Kildeer Ln. ................ J4
Kilmer St. ................. J6
Kim Ln. ................... H6
Kingfisher Ct. .............. H6
Kings Mill Dr. .............. H6
Kingston Ct. ............... G6
Kingswood Dr. ............. H4
Knoll View Ct. ............. J6
Knollwood Dr. ............. H5
Kurt Ct. .................. J6
La Fox Rd. ................ J6
Lantry Ct. ................. K6
Lasso Ln. ................. J6
Laura Ingalls Wilder Rd. ..... K6
Laurel Dr. ................ H4
Lees Rd. .................. G4
Leslie Ct. ................. H5
Limberi Ln. ................ J6
Line Dr. ................... J6
Loblolly Ln. ................ J6
Long Shadow Ln. .......... H6
Longacre Dr. .............. H5
Longfellow Pl. .............. K6
Loretta Dr. ................ J6
Lost View Ln. .............. G4
Mare Ln. .................. K6
Margaret Mitchell St. ........ J6
Margie Ln. ................ H4
Mark Twain St. ............. K6
Mary Ct. .................. H5
Mary Dr. ................. H,J5
McGonagle Ct. ............. K6
Meadowlark Ct. ............ H4
Meadowridge Cir. .......... J6
Meadowview Ln. ........... H4
Melville Ln. ................ J6
Mill Stone Dr. ............. G4
Millstead Pl. ............... J6
Mohican Ln. ............... J4
Mulhern Dr. ............... K6
Nancy Ln. ................. G5
Northern Dancer Ln. ........ G6
Norton Ct. ................ J6
Nut Hatch Ct. ............. H4
Oak Dr. .................. H6
Oak Hill Dr. ............... H5
Oak Ridge Rd. ............. H6
Oakwood Dr. .............. H4
Old Burlington Rd. ......... J6
Old Farm Ln. .............. G6
Oliver Wendell Holmes St. .. K6
Osage Dr. ................. J6
Otter Ln. ................. H4
Overcup Ct. ............... J6
Paddock Ln. ............... H5
Palomino Dr. .............. H6
Pathfinder Dr. ............. J4
Phar Lap Dr. .............. G6
Pine Hills Rd. .............. J6
Pine Ln. .................. H6
Pinto Ln. ................. H6
Pioneer Ct. ................ J6
Pleasant View Ln. .......... J5
Ponderosa Dr. ............. J6
Poplar Ln. ................ H7
Pouley Rd. ................ K5
Prairie Spring Dr. .......... H6
Prairie Valley Dr. ........... H4
Prairie View Dr. ............ H5
Privet Ct. ................. H4
Prunetree Ln. ............. G6
Quail Ct. ................. G4
Ravine Dr. ................ H5
Read Rd. ................. H4
Red Barn Ln. .............. G5
Red Hawk Ct. .............. H6
Redwood Ln. .............. H6
Reindeer Trail ............. H6
Retreat Ct. ................ H4
Ridgeview Ct. .............. J6
Robert Dr. ................ J5
Robert Frost Cir. ........... J6
Robert Lowell Pl. ........... J6
Robert Penn Warren Cove .. J6
Saddle Brook Dr. ........... J6
Seneca Ct. ................ H4
Seneca Tr. ................ H4
Shady Oaks Ct. ............ H7
Shetland Rd. .............. H6
Silver Glen Rd. ............ G5
Snowbird Ct. .............. J5
Splitrail Ct. ............... G6
Splitrail Ln. ............... H6
Springwood Ln. ............ J5
Spur Ln. .................. J6
State Rte. 38 .............. K5
State Rte. 47 .............. J4
State Rte. 64 .............. J4
Steeple Chase ............. G4
Stirrup Ave. ............... J6
Stonecrop Ct. ............. H6
Stringwood Ln. ............ J5
Sun Dance Ct. ............. H6
Sunset Dr. ................ G4
Swanberg Rd. ............. H5
Sylvan Dr. ................ J6
Sylvan Ln. ................ H4
Tanager Ct. ............... H4
Taylor Caldwell St. ......... K6
Thoreau Ln. ............... J6
Timber Trail ............... H4
Timbergate Ln. ............ J6
Torrey Dr. ................ J6
Town Hall Rd. ............. J5
Trillium Ct. ................ H6
Trotter Ln. ................ J6
Turtle Pl. ................. H6
Uncas Ln. ................. J4
Vachel Lindsay St. ......... K6
Venetian Way .............. J4
Verhaeghe Rd. ............. H5
Vincent Milay St. ........... J6
Wasco Rd. ................ J6
Waterford Ln. .............. G6
Wayne Dr. ................ J5
West Woods Ct. ............ J5
West Woods Dr. ............ J5
Westview Ct. .............. G7
Weybridge Dr. ............. G5
Whirlaway Dr. ............. J5
White Fence Way .......... H6
White Oak Ln. ............. H5
White Pine Ln. ............ H6
Whitman Rd. .............. J6
Whitney Rd. ............... H6
Whittier Pl. ............... K6
William Cullen Bryant St. .... J6
Willowbrook Ct. ............ G6
Willowbrook Dr. ............ G6
Winchester Way ............ H6
Windsor Ct. ............... J4
Woodland Dr. .............. H5
Wooley Rd. ............... J4
Wyngate Ct. ............... J7
Wyngate Rd. .............. J7

**FOREST PRESERVES**

Campton Forest Preserve ... J5

**SCHOOLS**

Wasco Elem Sch. .......... J6

**MISCELLANEOUS**

Kane Co. Div. of Transportation ...................... G5

## CARPENTERSVILLE

Page 3...B9
(For full listings, see Section 5)

## DUNDEE TOWNSHIP

Page 3
(For additional listings, see Section 5)

**STREETS**

Adams Dr. ................ B7
Albert Dr. ................ D10
Algonquin Rd. ............. A9
Alice Dr. ................. A8
Alpine Dr. ................ A8
Angelina Pl. ............... B9
Avenue Chapelle ........... D9
Baker Ave. ............... D10
Big Timber Rd. ............ D7
Binnie Rd. ................ B7
Birchwood Rd. ............. B9
Bolz Rd. .................. B9
Boncosky Rd. .............. D8
Boyer Rd. ................. A7
Burning Oak Dr. ........... B8
Burr Oak Ln. .............. B8
Castle Ave. ............... D10
Castlewood Dr. ............ B9
Chateau Dr. ............. D8,9
Country School Rd. ........ B8
County Line Rd. ........... A8
Covey St. ................. D9
Crescent Ln. .............. A8
Deerpath Ln. .............. B9
Duchesne Dr. ............ D8,9
Duncan Ave. .............. C9
Elliot Dr. ................. C9
Elm Ave. ................. B8
Elmwood Dr. .............. D9
Field Ct. .................. B8
Fountain Valley Dr. ........ D9
Fox Lane .................. D8
Fries Ave. ................. D9
Frontenac Dr. ............. D9
Hecker Dr. ............... D10
Hickory Ave. .............. B8
Hickory Hollow Dr. ......... D8
Highland Dr. ............... C7
Hillside Dr. ................ D9
Hilly Ln. .................. C7
Hollowside Dr. ............. B8
Howard Ave. .............. C9
Huntley Rd. ............... B8
Indian Ln. ................. B9
Karen Dr. ................. B8
Kings Rd. ................ A,B9
Knollwood Ave. ............ C9
Lac DuBeatrice Dr. ......... D9
Lake Cook Rd. ............ A10
Lake Marian Rd. ........... B9
Lake Shore Dr. ............ B9
Lathrop Ln. ............... A8
Linden Dr. ................ D9
Louis Ave. ................ A9
Lunstrom Ln. .............. A9
Manhatas Tr. .............. A9
Manito Tr. ................ A9
Maple Ave. ................ C9
Maple Ln. ................. D8
Maple Tree Ln. ............ B9
Mason Rd. ................ D7
Meadow Ln. W. ............ D9
Melody Ln. .............. A,B9
Memory Ln. ............... B9
Menoma Trail .............. A9
Merriweather Ln. ........... C8
Miller Rd. ................. B8
Minnehaha Trail ............ A9
Natoma Trail .............. A9
Niccon Trail ............... A9
Nokomis Tr. ............... A9
Northwest Tollway .......... C7
Oak Ave. .................. B8
Oak Hill Dr. ............... D8
Oaks Ln. ................. C8
Ogaw Trail ................ A9
Old Barn Rd. .............. B8
Old Farm Ln. .............. B9
Park Ave. ................. B9
Park Dr. .................. D9
Parsons Rd. ............... B8
Petite Ln. ................. D8
Pheasant Tr. .............. B9
Pokagon Tr. ............... A9
Randall Rd. ............. B,D8
Richardson Rd. ............ C9
Richmond Rd. ............. C8
Ridge Rd. ................. B8
River Ridge Dr. ............ D9
Riverview Dr. .............. D9
Robert Ave. ............... C9
Robin Ln. ................. B9
Sawyer Rd. ............... B8
Shady Ln. ................. B8
Skyline ................... B9
Sleepy Hollow Rd. ....... B,D8
Spring Bluff Dr. ............ B8
State Rte. 25 ............. A10
State Rte. 31 .............. B9
State Rte. 62 ............. A10
State Rte. 68 ............. C10
State Rte. 72 .............. C8
Sturgis Ct. ................ B8
Sumter Dr. ................ C8
Sunset Dr. ................ B9
Sunset Park Dr. ............ D9
Tyrrell Rd. ................ D7
Valley View Rd. ............ B8
Wabican Trail ............. A9
Wakigan Trail ............. A9
Walnut Ln. ................ D8
West Hill Rd. .............. B8
Winaki Trail ............... A9
Winding Tr. ............... B8
Woodcrest Ln. ............. B8
Woodhaven Ln. ............ B8

**FOREST PRESERVES**

Buffalo Park Forest Preserve A9
Fox River Shores Forest Preserve .............. B9
Helm Wood Forest Preserve B10
Max McGraw Wildlife Foundation ............. C9
Schweitzer Forest Preserve . B8

## EAST DUNDEE

Page 3...C10
(For full listings, see Section 5)

## ELBURN

Pages 5,23

**STREETS**

Babcock St. .. Pg.23 .... B10
Banbury Ave. . Pg.23 .. A,B11
Behrens Ct. ... Pg.23 ..... B9
Birch St. ..... Pg.23 .... B10
Cambridge Ave. Pg.23 .... A11
Capes Dr. .... Pg.23 .... B10
Collins Ct. .... Pg.23 ..... B9
Collins Dr. .... Pg.23 ..... B9
Conley Ct. .... Pg.23 ..... B9
Conley Dr., E. . Pg.23 ..... B9
Dempsey Dr. .. Pg.23 .... B10
Downing St. .. Pg.23 .... B10
Erickson Ct. .. Pg.23 .... B10
Filmore St. ... Pg.23 . B10-11
First St. ...... Pg.23 ..... B9
Gates St. ..... Pg.23 .... B10
Gee Ct. ...... Pg.23 .... B10
Hicks Dr. ..... Pg.23 .... C10
Highland Ct. .. Pg.23 .... B10
Highland Dr., E. Pg.23 .. B,C10
Highview Ct. .. Pg.23 .... B10
Hoyt Dr. ..... Pg.23 ..... C9
Jay St. ....... Pg.23 .... A10
Johnson Ave. . Pg.23 .... B11
Johnson St. .. Pg.23 .... B10
Kansas St. ... Pg.23 .... B11
Keslinger Rd. . Pg.23 .... B11
Laverne St. ... Pg.23 .... B10
Lilac St. ...... Pg.23 .... B10
Main St. ..... Pg.23 .... B11
Maple Ave. ... Pg.23 .. A,B11
Maple Ct. .... Pg.23 .... B10
Merril Ln. .... Pg.23 ..... B9
Morrill Ln. .... Pg.23 .... G12
Nebraska St. .. Pg.23 .... B10
North St. ..... Pg.23 .... B10
Northeast Walker Dr. .......... Pg.23 ..... B9
Northwest Walker Dr. .......... Pg.23 ..... B9
Oak St. ...... Pg.23 .... B11
Parkside Dr. .. Pg.23 .... A11
Paul St. ..... Pg.23 .... C10
Pierce St. .... Pg.23 .... B10
Prairie Valley Ct. Pg.23 .... B10
Prairie Valley St. Pg.23 .... B10
Railroad St. ... Pg.23 .... B10
Read St. ..... Pg.23 .... B10
Reeder St. ... Pg.23 .... B10
Saratoga Dr. .. Pg.23 .... A11
Shannon St. .. Pg.23 .... B10
Sharp Ct. .... Pg.23 .... B10
Snow ........ Pg.23 ..... B9
Snow Dr. ..... Pg.23 ..... B9
South St. .... Pg.23 .... B11
State Rte. 38 .. Pg.23 ..... B9
State Rte. 47 .. Pg.23 .... B11
Stetzer Ave. .. Pg.23 .... B11
Swain St. .... Pg.23 .... B11
Thryselius Dr. . Pg.23 .... A11
Van Buren St. . Pg.23 .... B10
Walker Dr. .... Pg.23 ..... B9
Warne Ct. .... Pg.23 ..... B9
Weston Ct. ... Pg.23 .... B10
Willow St. .... Pg.23 .... B10
1st St. ...... Pg.23 . B10-11
2nd St. ...... Pg.23 . B10-11
3rd St. ...... Pg.23 . B10-11

**CEMETERIES**

Blackberry Cem. Pg.23 .... B11
St. Gall Cemetery .......... Pg.23 .... B10

**GOLF COURSES**

Hughes Creek Golf Course .......... Pg.5 ...... K4

**MISCELLANEOUS**

Post Office ... Pg.23 .... B10

## ELGIN

(For full listings, see Section 5)

## ELGIN TOWNSHIP

Pages 2,3,6
(For additional listings, see Section 5)

**STREETS**

Acorn Ln. .... Pg.6 ...... G7
Almora Terr. .. Pg.3 ...... E7
Amberwood Dr. Pg.2,3 .... D7
Arrowmaker Pass .......... Pg.2,6 .... F7
Barry ........ Pg.6 ...... F9
Beckman Tr. .. Pg.2,3,6 .. F7
Big Timber Rd. Pg.3 ...... D7
Bittersweet Ln. Pg.6 ...... G7
Bowes Rd. ... Pg.3,6 .... F7
Brindlewood Ln. Pg.2,3 .... D7

Brookside Dr. . . Pg.3 . . . . E7
Center St. . . . . Pg.3 . . . . . E9
Charlotte Ct. . . Pg.2,3 . . . E7
Cross Creek Ct. . Pg.2,3 . . . E7
Dundee Ave. . . . Pg.3 . . . . . E9
Elmar Ct. . . . . Pg.2,3 . . . E7
Flag Pole Ct. . . Pg.3 . . . . E9
Fox Ln. . . . . . Pg.3 . . . . . D8
Gingerwood Ln. . Pg.6 . . . . . G7
Heatherfield Dr. . Pg.6 . . . . G7
Hidden Hills Tr. . Pg.2,3 . . . E7
Highland Ave. . . Pg.3 . . . . . E8
Hilltop Ct. . . . . Pg.2 . . . . E7
Hogan Hill . . . . Pg.2,6 . . . F7
Holmes Rd. . . . Pg.3 . . . . . D8
Hopi . . . . . . . Pg.2,6 . . . F7
Hopps Rd. . . . . Pg.6 . . . . . G7
Howard Ave. . . . Pg.6 . . . . . G7
Jackson Dr. . . . Pg.2,3 . . . E7
Johnstown Rd. . . Pg.6 . . . . . F9
Kenyon Rd. . . . Pg.6 . . . . . F9
Koshare Cir. . . . Pg.2,3,6 . . F7
Koshare Tr. . . . Pg.6 . . . . . F7
Kristen Dr. . . . Pg.6 . . . . . G7
Lamont Ct. . . . Pg.2,3 . . . E7
Larkin Ave. . . . Pg.6 . . . . . F7
Leith Ct. . . . . . Pg.6 . . . . F7
Leland Ct. . . . . Pg.6 . . . . F7
Liberty St. . . . . Pg.3 . . . . E7
Linda Ln. . . . . Pg.3 . . . . . E7
Lisa Ln. . . . . . Pg.6 . . . . . G7
Main St. . . . . . Pg.6 . . . . . F9
Maryhill Ln. . . . Pg.2,3 . . . E7
McDonald Rd. . . Pg.6 . . . . . G6
McLean Blvd. . . . Pg.3,6 . . . F,G8
Middle St. . . . . Pg.6 . . . . . G9
Nesler Rd. . . . . Pg.3 . . . . . E7
Nokomis Ln. . . . Pg.2,3,6 . . F7
Nolan Rd. . . . . Pg.6 . . . . . F7
Northwest Toll Rd.
. . . . . . . . . Pg.3 . . . . . D8
Oatwind Rd. . . . Pg.2,3 . . . E7
Old Barn Rd. . . . Pg.2,3 . . . E7
Olwin Ave. . . . . Pg.6 . . . . F7
Orchard Ct. . . . Pg.2 . . . . . F7
Oxford Ln. . . . . Pg.2 . . . . . F7
Park Path . . . . Pg.2,3,6 . . F7
Pasec Pl. . . . . Pg.6 . . . . . F7
Peppertree Ct. . . Pg.6 . . . . G7
Peppertree Dr. . . Pg.6 . . . . G7
Pollitt Dr. . . . . Pg.2,3 . . D,E7
Raleigh Ct. . . . Pg.2,3 . . . E7
Randall Rd. . . . Pg.3,6 . . . F7,8
Raymond Dr. . . . Pg.3,6 . . . F9
Richard Dr. . . . Pg.6 . . . . . G7
Ridgewood Ln. . . Pg.2 . . . . D7
Running Deer Trail
. . . . . . . . . Pg.6 . . . . . F7
Savanna Lakes Dr.
. . . . . . . . . Pg.6 . . . . . F7
South St. . . . . . Pg.3 . . . . . F8
State Rte. 25 . . . Pg.6 . . . . E7
State Rte. 58 . . . Pg.3 . . . . E9
State St. . . . . . Pg.3 . . . . D,F9
Stevens Ln. . . . Pg.2 . . . . . E7
Stevens Rd. . . . Pg.2 . . . . . E7
Stratford Ln. . . . Pg.2 . . . . E7
Summit St. . . . . Pg.3 . . . . . E9
Sunvale Ct. . . . Pg.3 . . . . . E7
Sunvale Dr. . . . Pg.3 . . . . . E7
Taos Pl. . . . . . Pg.6 . . . . . F7
Thunder Gap . . . Pg.2,3,6 . . F7
Tina Tr. . . . . . Pg.3 . . . . . E7
Tipi Ln. . . . . . Pg.2,3,6 . . F7
Trails End . . . . Pg.6 . . . . . F7
U.S. Bus. Rte. 20
. . . . . . . . . Pg.3 . . . . . E9-10
U.S. Hwy. 20 . . . Pg.3 . . . . E8-9
Umdenstock Rd. . Pg.6 . . . . G8
Villa St. . . . . . Pg.3 . . . . . E9
Water Rd., S. . . Pg.2,3,6 . . F7
Wedgewood Dr. . Pg.2 . . . . . D7
Weldwood Dr. . . Pg.2 . . . . . E7
West Bartlett Rd. . Pg.6 . . . . G9
Westview Rd. . . . Pg.3 . . . . . F7
Wildemere Dr. . . Pg.3 . . . . . E7
Wildwood Dr. . . Pg.6 . . . . . G7
Williamsburg Dr. . Pg.2,3 . . . E7
Willow Ln. . . . . Pg.6 . . . . . G7
Win-Haven Dr. . . Pg.6 . . . . F9
Wing Rd. . . . . . Pg.3 . . . . . E8
Wokomis Cir. . . Pg.2,6 . . . F7
York Ln. . . . . . Pg.3 . . . . . E7

FOREST PRESERVES
Burnridge F.P. . . Pg.3 . . . . . D7
Otter Creek Forest Preserve
. . . . . . . . . Pg.6 . . . . . G7
Tyler Creek Forest Preserve
. . . . . . . . . Pg.3 . . . . . D9
Voyageurs Landings Forest
Preserve . . . . Pg.3 . . . . . D9

GENEVA
Pages 6,12-15
STREETS
Aberdeen Ct. . . . Pg.13 . . . . Q10
Access Rd. . . . . Pg.13 . . . . Q11
Acorn Ct. . . . . . Pg.12 . . . . L11
Adamson Ln. . . . Pg.12 . . . . L10
Alexandria Ct. . . Pg.13 . . . . Q10
Allen Dr. . . . . . Pg.12 . . . . N12
Anderson Blvd. . . Pg.12 . . . . M10
Andover Ln. . . . Pg.12 . . . . Q10
Appleton Ln. . . . Pg.13 . . . . Q9
Arlington Ct. . . . Pg.13 . . . . Q9
Arrowhead Ct. . . Pg.14 . . . . M12
Ashbury Ct. . . . Pg.12 . . . . N11
Ashby Ct. . . . . . Pg.13 . . . . L9
Austin Ave. . . . . Pg.13 . . . . P10
Averhill Ct. . . . . Pg.13 . . . . Q9
Averill Cir. . . . . Pg.13 . . . . Q9
Bank Ln. . . . . . Pg.13 . . . . Q10
Batavia Ave. . . . Pg.13 . . . . O11
Bedford Ln. . . . Pg.14 . . . . N12
Belter Ct. . . . . . Pg.14 . . . . N12
Bennett St. . . . . Pg.13 . . . . O9,10
Bent Tree Dr. . . . Pg.14 . . . . M11
Berkshire Dr. . . . Pg.14 . . . . L12
Biarda Ct. . . . . Pg.12 . . . . N10
Bingham Ct. . . . Pg.13 . . . . M11
Bingham Way . . . Pg.13 . . . . M11
Blackberry Ln. . . Pg.12 . . . . M9
Blackman Ct. . . . Pg.13 . . . . L11
Blackman Rd. . . . Pg.12 . . . . L11
Bloomfield Cir. . . Pg.12 . . . . M9
Bluegrass Ln. . . . Pg.12 . . . . L9

Border Rd. . . . . Pg.12 . . . . L9
Bradbury Ln. . . . Pg.12 . . . . N9
Brentwood Ct. . . Pg.13 . . . . Q9
Brentwood Pl. . . Pg.13 . . . . Q9
Brian Ct. . . . . . Pg.12 . . . . M9
Briar Ln. . . . . . Pg.12 . . . . P10
Bridgeport Ln. . . Pg.12 . . . . M10
Brigham Ct. . . . Pg.12 . . . . N11
Brigham Way . . . Pg.12 . . . . N11
Brighton Ct. . . . Pg.12 . . . . L11
Britta Ln. . . . . . Pg.13 . . . . P9
Brittany Ct. . . . . Pg.12 . . . . M9
Brookfield Ln. . . Pg.12 . . . . . . . . . . . . . M,N10,11
Brookway Dr. . . . Pg.12 . . . . M10
Bunker Ct. . . . . Pg.12 . . . . N11
Burgess Rd. . . . Pg.12 . . . . N10
Caldwell Ln. . . . Pg.12 . . . . L10
Cambridge Ct. . . Pg.12 . . . . M10
Cambridge Dr. . . Pg.12 . . . . M10
Campbell Ct. . . . Pg.12 . . . . N10
Campbell Ct. . . . Pg.13 . . . . O10
Cannon Dr. . . . . Pg.12 . . . . L9
Cape Way . . . . . Pg.12 . . . . M10
Cardine Ct. . . . . Pg.13 . . . . P10
Cedar Ave. . . . . Pg.12 . . . . L11
Center St. . . . . . Pg.12 . . . . N9
Chalmers St . . . Pg.13 . . . . P10
Chandler Ave. . . Pg.13 . . . . Q9
Charles St. . . . . Pg.12 . . . . N10
Charleston Ct. . . Pg.13 . . . . Q9
Chatham Ct. . . . Pg.12 . . . . L11
Cheever Ave. . . . Pg.12 . . . . L11
Chesapeake Way
. . . . . . . . . Pg.13 . . . . Q9
Christina Ln. . . . Pg.12 . . . . M11
Clayton Ct. . . . . Pg.13 . . . . JK12
Clover Ct. . . . . . Pg.12 . . . . M9
Clover Ln. . . . . Pg.12 . . . . M9
Colonial Cir. . . . Pg.12 . . . . M9
Colony Dr. . . . . Pg.12 . . . . L10
Commerce Dr. . . Pg.13 . . . . Q10
Conant Ct. . . . . Pg.13 . . . . O11
Country Club Pl. . Pg.12 . . . . N10
Country Squire Dr.
. . . . . . . . . Pg.12 . . . . N11
Coventry Ct. . . . Pg.12 . . . . L11
Crawford St. . . . Pg.12 . . . . N10
Creekside Dr. . . . Pg.13 . . . . O10
Crescent Pl. . . . Pg.13 . . . . O10
Crissey Ave. . . . Pg.13 O11,P10
Croydon Ct. . . . Pg.12 . . . . N11
Crystal Tree Ct. . Pg.13 . . . . M11
Danbury Ct. . . . Pg.12 . . . . M10
Danford Ct. . . . . Pg.12 . . . . L11
Danford Way . . . Pg.12 . . . . L11
Daniels Way . . . Pg.13 . . . . M11
Danuta Ct. . . . . Pg.12 . . . . M9
Dartmouth Ct. . . Pg.12 . . . . M10
Deerfield Way . . . Pg.12 . . . . M11
Delaware Ct. . . . Pg.13 . . . . Q9
Dempsey Ln. . . . Pg.12 . . . . M9
Derek Ln. . . . . . Pg.12 . . . . P11
Division St. . . . . Pg.13 . . . . P9
Dodson St. . . . . Pg.13 . . . . O10
Dow Ave . . . . . Pg.12 . . . . N11
Downing Pl. . . . Pg.13 . . . . P9
Dryden Rd. . . . . Pg.13 . . . . N11
Dunham Ct. . . . Pg.12 . . . . Q9
Dunstan Rd. . . . Pg.12 . . . . N11
Eagle Brook Dr. . Pg.12 . . . . N11
East Side Dr. . . . Pg.13 . . . . P9
Easton Ave. . . . Pg.12 . . . . N11
Edison St. . . . . . Pg.13 . . . . O9
Eklund St. . . . . Pg.13 . . . . O9
Eldorado Dr. . . . Pg.12 . . . . M10
Eleanor Ln. . . . . Pg.12 . . . . L11
Elizabeth Pl. . . . Pg.13 . . . . O11
Elm Ave. . . . . . Pg.13 . . . . P9
Emergency Access Rd.
Essex Ct. . . . . . Pg.12 . . . . M10
Euclid Ave. . . . . Pg.13 . . . . P10
Evernia Ct. . . . . Pg.12 . . . . O9
Executive Pl. . . . Pg.13 . . . . Q10
Fahayan Pkwy. . . Pg.12 . N,P12
Fairview Ct. . . . . Pg.12 . . . . L11
Fairway Ct. . . . . Pg.12 . . . . M10
Fairway Ln. . . . . Pg.12 . . . . M11
Fargo Blvd. . . . . Pg.12 . . . . M11
Fargo Cir. . . . . . Pg.12 . . . . L11
Fieldstone Dr. . . Pg.12 . . . . L9
Fisher Dr. . . . . . Pg.12 . . . . L9
Fluid Power Dr. . Pg.13 . . . . Q11
Ford St. . . . . . . Pg.12 . N9,O10
Forest Ave. . . . . Pg.13 . . . . O11
Forest View Dr. . Pg.13 . . . . N11
Fox Fire Ct. . . . Pg.13 . . . . N11
Fox Run Dr. . . . Pg.13 . . . . P11
Foxford Ln. . . . . Pg.12 . . . . M10
Foxwood Cir. . . . Pg.12 . . . . P10
Franklin St. . . . . Pg.13 . . . . O10
Frontage Rd. . . . Pg.12 . . . . P10
Fulton St. . . . . . Pg.13 . . . . O10
Galway Ct. . . . . Pg.12 . . . . N11
Garden Ave. . . . Pg.12 . . . . N11
Garfield Ct. . . . . Pg.13 . . . . P10
Gary Ln. . . . . . Pg.12 . . . . M10
Geneva Dr. . . . . Pg.12 . . . . P9
Ginger Ln. . . . . Pg.12 . . . . L11
Gleneagle Dr. . . Pg.14 . . . . M12
Glengarry Dr. . . Pg.12 . . . . Q10
Grant St. . . . . . Pg.13 . . . . O10
Gray St. . . . . . . Pg.12 . . . . N9
Greenfield Cir. . . Pg.13 . . . . Q10
Greenmeadow Ln.
. . . . . . . . . Pg.13 . . . . Q9
Greenwich Ln. . . Pg.12 . . . . M10
Hamilton St. . . . Pg.13 . . . . O10
Harrison St. . . . Pg.13 . . . . P10
Hartford Ln. . . . Pg.12 . . . . M10
Harves Ridge Rd.
. . . . . . . . . Pg.12 . . . . L10
Hawkins Way . . . Pg.12 . . . . L10
Hawley Ln. . . . . Pg.12 . . . . L9
Hawthorne Ln. . . Pg.13 . . . . O11
Heartland Dr. . . . Pg.12 . . . . L10
Heather Rd. . . . Pg.14 . . . . N12
Heritage Ct. . . . Pg.12 . . . . L10
Heritage Ln. . . . Pg.12 . . . . L10
Herrington Pl. . . Pg.12 . . . . M10
Herrington Rd. . . Pg.12 . . . . L11
High St. . . . . . . Pg.12 . . . . P9
Highbury Ln. . . . Pg.12 . . . . N9
Highland Ave. . . Pg.12 . . . . N10
Hillcrest Ave. . . . Pg.12 . . . . L9

Homestead Ln. . . Pg.12 . . . . L10
Howard St. . . . . Pg.13 . . . . P10
Howell Dr. . . . . Pg.13 . . . . P10
Husking Peg Ln. . Pg.12 . . . . L9
Illinois St. . . . . . Pg.13 . . . . O9
J. Pankow Dr. . . Pg.13 . . . . P10
James St. . . . . . Pg.13 . . . . O10
Jefferson St. . . . Pg.13 . . . . P10
Joshel Ct. . . . . . Pg.13 . . . . P10
Kane St. . . . . . . Pg.13 . . . . P10
Kaneville Ave. . . Pg.13 . . . . P9
Kaneville Rd. . . . Pg.12
Kansas St. . . . . Pg.13 . . . . P10
Keim Cir. . . . . . Pg.12 . . . . M11
Keim Ct. . . . . . Pg.12 . . . . M11
Kendall St. . . . . Pg.13 . . . . N11
Kenston Ct. . . . . Pg.13 . . . . N10
Keslinger Rd. . . . Pg.12 . . . . L9
Kings Ct. . . . . . Pg.14 . . . . M12
Kingston Dr. . . . Pg.12 . . . . L11
Kirk Rd. . . . . . . Pg.12 . . . . Q9
Kirkwood Dr. . . . Pg.13 . . . . Q9
Knollwood Ct. . . Pg.12 . . . . N10
Koster Ct. . . . . . Pg.13 . . . . Q9
Kummer Ct. . . . . Pg.12 . . . . N11
Lake Ct. . . . . . . Pg.12 . . . . L11
Lancaster Ln. . . . Pg.12 . . . . Q10
Langford Dr. . . . Pg.13 . . . . L9
Larrabee Dr. . . . Pg.12 . . . . L10
Le Baron Ct. . . . Pg.12 . . . . L11
Lencioni Ct. . . . Pg.12 . . . . Q9
Lewis Cir. . . . . . Pg.12 . . . . L11
Lewis Pl. . . . . . Pg.13 . . . . L11
Lewis Rd. . . . . . Pg.12 . . . . L11
Lexington Dr. . . . Pg.13 . . . . Q9
Lincoln Ave. . . . Pg.12 . . N9,10
Locust Ave. . . . . Pg.12 . . . . M9
Logan Ave. . . . . Pg.12 . . N9,10
Lois Ct. . . . . . . Pg.12 . . . . Q9
Longmeadow Dr.
. . . . . . . . . Pg.13 . . . . Q9
Longview Dr. . . . Pg.12 . . . . P10
Lorenz Ct. . . . . Pg.12 . . . . Q10
Manchester Course
Manchester Dr. . Pg.13 . . . . O10
Maple Ln. . . . . . Pg.12 . . . . N10
Marion Ave. . . . Pg.13 . . . . N11
Marion Ct. . . . . Pg.12 . . . . N10
May St. . . . . . . Pg.13 . . . . O9
McKinley Ave . . Pg.12 . . . . N10
Mead Ct. . . . . . Pg.12 . . . . N10
Meadows Rd. . . Pg.12 . . . . N11
Megan Ct. . . . . Pg.14 . . . . M12
Merchants Dr. . . Pg.13 . . . . P11
Merganza Ct. . . . Pg.12 . . . . L11
Millbrook Ct. . . . Pg.12 . . . . L9
Miller Rd. . . . . . Pg.12 . . . . L11
Nassau Ln. . . . . Pg.12 . . . . L10
Natwill Square Ct.
Nebraska St. . . . Pg.13 . . . . P10
Nelson Dr. . . . . Pg.12 . . . . L12
Newport Ln. . . . Pg.12 . . . . M10
Normandy Ln. . . Pg.12 . . . . O9
North St. . . . . . Pg.13 . . . . O9
Northampton Dr. Pg.12 . . . . M10
Oak Ct. . . . . . . Pg.12 . . . . P10
Oak St. . . . . . . Pg.12 . . . . P10
Oakwood Dr. . . . Pg.12 . . . . L9
Old Mill Ln. . . . . Pg.12 . . . . L10
Osprey Ct. . . . . Pg.12 . . . . L11
Paddock Ct. . . . Pg.12 . . . . M9
Park Ave. . . . . . Pg.12 . . . . P10
Parker Ct. . . . . . Pg.12 . . . . P9
Patrick Ct. . . . . Pg.13 . . . . P11
Patten Ave. . . . . Pg.12 . . . . N11
Pebble Beach Ct.
Peck Rd. . . . . . Pg.12 . . . . M11
Pepper Valley Dr.
Peterson Dr. . . . Pg.12 . . . . M10
Peyton St. . . . . Pg.13 . . . . P10
Pheasant Ct. . . . Pg.12 . . . . O10
Pheasant Run Pl.
Pine St. . . . . . . Pg.14 . . . . N12
Pinto Ct. . . . . . Pg.12 . . . . N10
Pioneer Ct. . . . . Pg.12 . . . . M11
Potomac Ct. . . . Pg.12 . . . . M11
Prairie View Dr. . Pg.13 . . . . L9
Randall Ct. . . . . Pg.12 . . . . N10
Randall Ln. . . . . Pg.12 . . . . N10
Ray St. . . . . . . Pg.13 . . . . O11
Redwing Dr. . . . Pg.14 . . . . N12
Regency Ct. . . . Pg.12 . . . . M9
Renee Ct. . . . . . Pg.12 . . . . M9
Richards St. . . . Pg.13 . . . . O10
Ridge Ln. . . . . . Pg.13 . . . . P10
River Ln. . . . . . Pg.13 . . . . O10
Rosenfelder Ct. . Pg.12 . . . . N10
Rosewood Ln. . . Pg.12 . . . . L9
Samantha Ct. . . Pg.12 . . . . L11
Sandholm St. . . Pg.13 . . . . P10
School St. . . . . . Pg.13 . . . . P10
Scott Blvd. . . . . Pg.13 . . . . P11
Shady Ave. . . . . Pg.13 . . . . O11
Sheffield Ln. . . . Pg.12 . . . . M10
Sheila Ave. . . . . Pg.12 . . . . N11
Sheperd Ln. . . . Pg.12 . . . . L9
Sherman Ave. . . Pg.13 . . . . L9
Sherwood Ln. . . Pg.12 . . . . M10
Shoop Cir. . . . . Pg.13 . . . . O11
Shoop Ct. . . . . . Pg.13 . . . . O11
Short St. . . . . . Pg.13 . . . . P9
Simon Ct. . . . . . Pg.12 . . . . L11
Simpson St. . . . Pg.13 . . . . P10
Southerquist Ct. . Pg.12 . . . . M10
South St. . . . . . Pg.12 . M,N10
Southampton Ct.
Southampton Dr.
. . . . . . . . . Pg.12 . . . . M10
Spring Ct. . . . . . Pg.13 . . . . P10
Spring St. . . . . . Pg.13 . . . . P10
Spruce Ct. . . . . Pg.13 . . . . L11
St. Andrews Cir. . Pg.12 . . . . N9
St. Jude Ct. . . . Pg.12 . . . . L11
State St. . . . . . . Pg.13 . . . . O10

Sterling Ave. . . . Pg.12 . . . . L11
Stevens St. . . . . Pg.13 . . . . O9
Stratfrod Dr. . . . Pg.12 . . . . N10
Sudbury Ln. . . . Pg.12 . . . . M10
Suffield Ct. . . . . Pg.13 . . . . Q10
Summit St. . . . . Pg.12 . . . . P10
Sunset Rd. . . . . Pg.12 . . . . N11
Syril Dr. . . . . . . Pg.12 . . . . N12
Tanager Ln. . . . Pg.14 . . . . N12
Thornhill Ct. . . . Pg.12 . . . . M11
Turnberry Ct. . . Pg.12 . . . . N11
Union St. . . . . . Pg.13 . . . . N9
Valley Ln. . . . . . Pg.13 . . . . Q10
Viking Dr. . . . . . Pg.14 . . . . L12
Wakefield Ln. . . Pg.12 . . . . M9
Wall St. . . . . . . Pg.12 . . . . P10
Walnut Ave. . . . Pg.12 . . . . L11
Washington St. . Pg.13 . . . . Q9
Water St. . . . . . Pg.13 . . . . O10
Waybourne Ln. . Pg.12 . . . . L9
Wellington St. . . Pg.12 . . . . M9
West Ln. . . . . . Pg.12 . . . . N9
Western Ave. . . . Pg.12 . . . . N11
Westfield Course
Westhaven Cir. . Pg.12 . . . . Q10
Wheatland Cir. . Pg.12 . . . . L9
Whitfield Dr. . . . Pg.13 . . . . Q10
Whittington St. . Pg.13 . . . . L9
Wild Dunes Ct. . Pg.14 . . . . M12
Wildflower Ct. . . Pg.14 . . . . M12
Williamsburg Ln.
. . . . . . . . . Pg.12 . . . . M10
Willow Ln. . . . . Pg.12 . . . . N9
Willowbrook Way
. . . . . . . . . Pg.12 . . . . L9
Wilson St. . . . . . Pg.13 . . . . O9
Windett Ln. . . . . Pg.13 . . . . L9
Windham Ct. . . . Pg.12 . . . . N11
Windsor Dr. . . . Pg.12 . . . . Q9
Winner's Cup Ct. Pg.12 . . . . M11
Winthrop Ln. . . . Pg.12 . . . . M10
Wood Ave. . . . . Pg.12 . . . . L11
Woodlawn St. . . Pg.13 . . . . P10
Woodward Ave. . Pg.12 . . . . P9
1st St. . . . . . . . Pg.13 . . . . O10
2nd St. . . . . . . Pg.13 . . . . O10
3rd Ave. . . . . . . Pg.13 . . . . P9
3rd St. . . . . . . . Pg.13 . . . . O10
4th Ave. . . . . . . Pg.13 . . . . P9
4th St. . . . . . . . Pg.13 . . . . O10
5th Ave. . . . . . . Pg.13 . . . . P9
5th St. . . . . . . . Pg.13 . . . . N10
6th Ave. . . . . . . Pg.13 . . . . P9
6th St. . . . . . . . Pg.13 . . . . N10
7th St. . . . . . . . Pg.13 . . . . N10
8th St. . . . . . . . Pg.13 . . . . N10
9th St. . . . . . . . Pg.13 . . . . N10

CEMETERIES
Oak Hill Cem. . . Pg.13 . . . . P9

FOREST PRESERVES
Fabyan F.P. . . . . Pg.12 . . . . O11
Gunnar Anderson F.P.

GOLF COURSES
Eagle Brook C.C. Pg.12 . . . . M11
Geneva G.C. . . . Pg.12 . . . . N10
Settlers Hills G.C.
. . . . . . . . . Pg.15 . . . . G11

PARKS
Burgess Field . . Pg.12 . . . . N11
Droves Park . . . Pg.12 . . . . N10
Good Templar Park
. . . . . . . . . Pg.13 . . . . P9
Island Park . . . . Pg.13 . . . . O10
Oak Hill Mem. Park
. . . . . . . . . Pg.13 . . . . P9
Sunset Park . . . Pg.12 . . . . N11
Wheeler Park . . Pg.12 . . . . O9

SCHOOLS
Coultrap Elem. Sch.
Faith Lutheran Sch.
. . . . . . . . . Pg.12 . . . . M10
Geneva Comm. H.S.
. . . . . . . . . Pg.12 . . . . N9
Harrison St. Sch.
Mansio Mens Sch.
St. Peter Cath. Sch.
Western Ave. Sch.
Waubansee Community
College . . . . Pg.13 . . . . N11

MISCELLANEOUS
City Hall . . . . . . Pg.13 . . . . O10
County Courthouse
County Home . . Pg.12 . . . . P11
Delnor Community Hosp.
. . . . . . . . . Pg.12 . . . . M10
Elfstrom Stadium (Kane County
Cougars) . . . Pg.12 . . . . Q11
Kane Co. Government Center
. . . . . . . . . Pg.13 . . . . O10
Kane County Event Center
Kane County Youth Home
Police Dept. . . . Pg.12 . . . . P12
Post Office . . . . Pg.13 . . . . O10
R.R. Station . . . Pg.13 . . . . O10

GENEVA TOWNSHIP
Pages 6,9,12-15
STREETS
Access Rd. . . . . Pg.15 . . . . Q11
Blackberry Way . Pg.6 . . . . . L7
Bricher Rd. . . . . Pg.12 . . . . M9
Cherry Ln. . . . . Pg.15 . . . . Q11
Clover Hills Dr. . Pg.14 . . . . K13
Considine Rd. . . Pg.14 . . . . N12
Deerpath Rd. . . Pg.14 . . . . L11
Fabyan Pkwy. . . Pg.14,15
. . . . . . . . . . . . . . . . K,L,Q12
Glenwood Dr. . . Pg.14 . . . . K13
Heather Rd. . . . Pg.14 . . . . N12
Janet Ln. . . . . . Pg.14 . . . . L12
Kautz Rd. . . . . . Pg.15 . . . . Q11
Keslinger Rd. . . Pg.12 . . . . M11

Killey Ln. . . . . . Pg.12 . . . . K10
Kirk Rd. . . . . . . Pg.15 . . . . Q11
Lea Dr. . . . . . . Pg.6 . . . . . L7
McKee St. . . . . Pg.14 . K,L13
Monterey Dr. . . Pg.14 . . . . K13
Morningside Ln. Pg.14 . . . . K13
North Lane Rd. . Pg.15 . . . . Q11
Old Kirk Rd. . . . Pg.13 . . . . Q11
Orchard Rd. . . . Pg.13 . . . . Q10
Peck Rd. . . . . . Pg.12 . K10-11
Pine Needles Ct. Pg.14 . . . . L12
Randall Rd. . . . . Pg.13 . . . . M9
Reed Rd. . . . . . Pg.14 . . . . L12
Roosevelt Rd. . . Pg.13 . . . . O11
Skyline Dr. . . . . Pg.14 . . . . K13
Southwest Ln. . . Pg.13 . . . . Q11
Spring Green Way
Theisen Tr. . . . . Pg.9 . . . . . U7
Viking Dr. . . . . Pg.14 . . . . L12
Wenmoth Ln. . . Pg.14 . . . . K11
Western Ave. . . Pg.14 . . . . N12

CEMETERIES
Kane Co. Farm Cem.
Resurrection Cem.
. . . . . . . . . Pg.14 . . . . I 12

GOLF COURSES
Settlers Hills Golf Course

PARKS
Event Center Park

MISCELLANEOUS
Campbell House Pg.13 . . . . Q11
Elfstrom Stadium (Kane County
Cougars) . . . Pg.15 . . . . Q12
Kane Co. Event Ctr.
. . . . . . . . . Pg.13 . . . . Q11

HAMPSHIRE
TOWNSHIP
Page 1
STREETS
Aileron Ave. . . . Pg.1 . . . . . C7
Allen Rd. . . . . . Pg.1 . . . . . C2,4
Berner Rd. . . . . Pg.1 . . . . . D4
Big Timber Rd. . Pg.1 . . . . . B-D4
Briarwood Ln. . . Pg.1 . . . . . V3
Brier Hill Rd. . . . Pg.1 . . . . . B-D4
Cemetery . . . . . Pg.1 . . . . . B,C3
Chandelle Dr. . . Pg.1 . . . . . C4
Clanyard Rd. . . Pg.1 . . . . . A1
County Line Rd. Pg.1 . . . . . A3
Deer Path Ln. . . Pg.1 . . . . . C4
Dietrich Rd. . . . Pg.1 . . . . . A1
Engel Rd. . . . . . Pg.1 . . . . . D2
Factly Rd. . . . . . Pg.1 . . . . . D2
Felsmith Rd. . . . Pg.1 . . . . . B3
Fox Run Ln. . . . Pg.23 . . . . C11
French Rd. . . . . Pg.1 . . . . . B3
Getty Rd. . . . . . Pg.1 . . . . . B3
Getzelman Rd. . Pg.1 . . . . . D3
Glen Oaks Ct. . . Pg.1 . . . . . B3
Glen Oaks Dr. . . Pg.1 . . . . . C3
Green Meadow Ln.
. . . . . . . . . Pg.1 . . . . . B3
Harmony Hd. . . Pg.1 . . . . . A1
Hawthorne Ln. . Pg.1 . . . . . A3
Hennig Rd. . . . Pg.1 . . . . . B4
Higgins Rd. . . . Pg.1 . . . . . B3
Immelman Ct. . Pg.1 . . . . . C4
Kelley Rd. . . . . Pg.1 . . . . . A3
Ketchum Rd. . . Pg.1 . . . . . C4
Lenschow Rd. . . Pg.1 . . . . . C4
Littlewoods Tr. . Pg.1 . . . . . B3
Marney Dr. . . . . Pg.1 . . . . . C4
Melms Rd. . . . . Pg.1 . . . . . C2,3
Northwest Tollway (I-90)
. . . . . . . . . Pg.1 . . . . . A2
Oak Grove Dr. . Pg.1 . . . . . C3
Obrien Rd. . . . . Pg.1 . . . . . B2
Raceview Pkwy. Pg.23 . . . . C11
Penstemon Ln. . Pg.1 . . . . . C3
Prairie Farm Dr. Pg.1 . . . . . A3
Primrose Ln. . . . Pg.1 . . . . . A3
Primrose Path . . Pg.1 . . . . . A3
Red Barn Rd. . . Pg.1 . . . . . D2
Romke Rd. . . . . Pg.1 . . . . . C4
Rudder Rd. . . . . Pg.1 . . . . . A2
Shirewood Farm Rd.
. . . . . . . . . Pg.1 . . . . . A2
State Rte. 72 . . . Pg.1 . . . . . C2
Suzanne St. . . . Pg.1 . . . . . C2
Tipperary St. . . . Pg.1 . . . . . C2
Tollview Dr. . . . Pg.3,23 C6,F11
Tollview Terr. . . Pg.3,23 C6,F11
Tower Hill Rd. . . Pg.3,23 C6,F11
Towne Ct. . . . . Pg.3 . . . . . C7
Towne St. . . . . Pg.3 . . . . . C7
Turner St. . . . . Pg.3,23 C7,F12
Tyler Creek Ct. . Pg.23 . . . . F11
Tyler Creek Dr. . Pg.3 . . . . . C6
Union St. . . . . . Pg.3,23 C7,F12
Welch St. . . . . . Pg.3 . . . . . D7
West End Dr. . . Pg.3,23 C7,F12
White Feather Ln.
. . . . . . . . . Pg.1 . . . . . B3
Willey St. . . . . . Pg.3,23 C7,F12
Windmill Ct. . . . Pg.3,23 C6,F12
Windmill Pl. . . . Pg.3,23 . . . C6

HAMPSHIRE
Pages 1,23
MISCELLANEOUS
Allen Rd. . . . . . Pg.23 . . . . C11
Ash St. . . . . . . . Pg.23 . . . . C11
Baldwin St. . . . . Pg.23 . . . . C11
Brookedge Dr. . Pg.23 . . . . C11
Centennial Dr. . Pg.23 . . . . C12
Center . . . . . . . Pg.23 . . . . C11
Duchess Ln. . . . Pg.23 . . . . D11
East St. . . . . . . Pg.23 . . . . C11
Edgewood Ave. Pg.23 . . . . C11
Edgewood Ct. . Pg.23 . . . . C11
Elm St. . . . . . . Pg.23 . . C,D11
French Rd. . . . . Pg.23 . . . . D11
Getzelman Rd. . Pg.23 . . . . D11
Grace St. . . . . . Pg.23 . . . . C11
Grove St. . . . . . Pg.23 . . . . C11
Harmony Rd. . . Pg.23 . . . . D11
High Ave. . . . . . Pg.23 . . . . D11
Highland Ave. . Pg.23 . . . . D11
Hillcrest Ave. . . Pg.23 . . . . C11
Industrial Dr. . . Pg.23 . . . . C12

Jackson Ave. Pg.23 . . . . C12
Jefferson Ave. E.
Jefferson St. . . . Pg.23 . . . . C12
Keyes Ave. . . . . Pg.23 . . . . C11
Klick St. . . . . . . Pg.23 . . . . C11
Madison . . . . . Pg.23 . . . . C11
Meyer St. . . . . . Pg.23 . . . . D11
Meyer St. . . . . . Pg.23 . . . . C11
Mill St. . . . . . . Pg.23 . . . . C11
Oak St. . . . . . . Pg.23 . . . . C11
Panama St. . . . Pg.23 . . . . D11
Park Ave. . . . . . Pg.23 . . . . C11
Park St. . . . . . . Pg.23 . . . . C11
Prairie St. . . . . Pg.23 . . . . C12
Rowell Rd. . . . . Pg.23 . . . . C12
Smith Dr. . . . . . Pg.23 . . . . D11
South Ave. . . . . Pg.23 . . . . C11
State St. . . . . . Pg.23 . . . . D11
Terwilliger St. . . Pg.23 . . . . D11
Timber Ln. . . . . Pg.23 . . . . C11
Walnut St. . . . . Pg.23 . . . . D11
Warner St. . . . . Pg.23 . . . . C11
Washington St. Pg.23 . . . . C11
West St. . . . . . Pg.23 . . . . C11

SCHOOLS
Hampshire Elem. Sch.
Hampshire H.S. Pg.23 . . . . D11
St. Charles of Borromeo Sch.

MISCELLANEOUS
Police Dept. & Village Hall
. . . . . . . . . Pg.23 . . . . C11

KENDALL
TOWNSHIP
Pages 23,24
STREETS
Van Emmon Rd. Pg.23 . . . . Q2,3
Woodland Dr. . . Pg.23 . . . . Q2

FOREST PRESERVES
Lyons F.P. . . . . Pg.23 . . . . Q6
Richard Young F.P.
. . . . . . . . . Pg.23 . . . . Q6

LAFOX
Page 5 . . . . . . . . . K6

LILY LAKE
Page 5
STREETS
Blackhawk Ln. . . . . . . . . . . H4
Campton Ct. . . . . . . . . . . . H4
Clover Ct. . . . . . . . . . . . . H4
Cochise Ct. . . . . . . . . . . . H4
Coleman Ln. . . . . . . . . . . . H4
Cornwall Dr. . . . . . . . . . . . H4
Ferson Ct. . . . . . . . . . . . . H4
Fescue Ct. . . . . . . . . . . . . H4
Fox Hills Ct. . . . . . . . . . . . H4
Fox Wilds Ct. . . . . . . . . . . H4
Fox Wilds Dr. . . . . . . . . . . H4
Foxmoor Dr. . . . . . . . . . . . H4
Hanson Rd. . . . . . . . . . . . . H5
Hannon Ridge Dr.
. . . . . . . . . . . . . . . . . . H4
Hazelwood Ct. . . . . . . . . . . H4
Hazelwood Trail . . . . . . . . . H4
Leslie Ct. . . . . . . . . . . . . . H4
Meadowview Ln. . . . . . . . . . H4
Read Rd. . . . . . . . . . . . . . H4
Sanctuary Trail . . . . . . . . . . H4
Seneca Ct. . . . . . . . . . . . . H4

SCHOOLS
Lily Lake Elem. Sch. . . . . . . H4

MAPLE PARK
Pages 4,23
STREETS
Broadway St. . . Pg.23 . . . . H10
Center St. . . . . Pg.23 . . . . H10
Charles St. . . . . Pg.23 . . . . H10
County Line Rd. W.
Elm St. . . . . . . Pg.23 . . . . H10
Green . . . . . . . Pg.23 . . . . H10
High St. . . . . . . Pg.23 . . . . H10
Kane St. . . . . . Pg.23 . . . . H10
Kenebec St. . . . Pg.23 . . . . H10
Liberty St. . . . . Pg.23 . . . . H10
Maiden Ln. . . . . Pg.23 . . . . G10
Main St. . . . . . Pg.23 . . . . G10
Maple Ave. . . . Pg.23 . . . . H10
Mulberry St. . . Pg.23 . . . . H10
Oak St. . . . . . . Pg.23 . . . . H10
Palmer St. . . . . Pg.23 . . . . H10
Pearl St. . . . . . Pg.23 . . . . H10
Pine Ln. . . . . . Pg.23 . . . . H10
Pleasant St. . . . Pg.23 . . . . H10
Root Ln. . . . . . Pg.23 . . . . G11
South St. . . . . . Pg.23 . . . . H10
State St. . . . . . Pg.23 . . . . H10
Summer St. . . . Pg.23 . . . . H10
Thatcher Rd. . . Pg.23 . . . . G11
Virgil St. . . . . . Pg.23 . . . . H10
Washington St. Pg.23 . . . . H10
Willow St. . . . . Pg.23 . . . . H10

MARYWOOD
Page 9 . . . . . . . . . N9

MC QUEENS
Page 2 . . . E6

MONTGOMERY
(Portions within Kendall County)
Pages 9,21,22
STREETS
Albright Ave. . . Pg.21 . . . . J9
Albright Rd. . . . Pg.21 . . . . J9
Amber Dr. . . . . Pg.21 . . . . J9
Ashland Ave. . . Pg.21 . . . . H10
Ashland Ct. . . . Pg.21 . . . . L10
Aucutt Rd. . . . . Pg.21 . . . . J9
Autumn Ridge Dr.
. . . . . . . . . Pg.21 . . . . J11

## MONTGOMERY

Bangs St. Pg.21 H13
Barbara Ln. Pg.22 J12
Base Line Rd. Pg.21 J9
Brentwood Ave. Pg.21 J9
Briarcliff Rd. Pg.21 J11
Broadway Ave. Pg.21 J11
Cannonball Trail Pg.21 K8
Carol Pl. Pg.21 J13
Case St. Pg.21 J10
Catherine Ln. Pg.21 J11
Cayman Rd. Pg.21 L11
Cebold Dr. Pg.21 L10
Circle Ct. Pg.21 L11
Clay St. Pg.21 J10
Clinton St. Pg.21 J10
Commerce Dr. Pg.21 J9
Cornell Ave. Pg.21 H9
Countryside Ave. Pg.21 J9
Crescent Lake Dr. Pg.21 J9
Crown St. Pg.21 J13
Dawn Ave. Pg.21 J13
Deer Run Dr. Pg.21 J11
Douglas Ave. Pg.21 H12
Edgewater Ct. Pg.21 J11
Fairwind Ct. Pg.21 J11
Fairwind Dr. Pg.21 J11
Fallcreek Cir. Pg.21 J11
Fellemore Ln. Pg.21 J11
Fifth St. Pg.22 K12
Fox Mead Cir. Pg.21 J11
Fox Mead Ct. Pg.21 J10
Galena Rd. Pg.21 K8
Gates St. Pg.21 H13
Grand View Pl. Pg.21 J11
Greenfield Ave. Pg.21 J9
Grey Ave. Pg.21 H10
Gusto Dr. Pg.21 H9
Hamlet Cir. Pg.21 J12
Harmony Ct. Pg.21 J12
Harmony Dr. Pg.21 J12
Harrison St. Pg.21 J10
Hartway Ct. Pg.21 H11
Hartway Dr. Pg.21 H11
Henry Ct. Pg.21 H11
High Point Ct. Pg.21 J11
Hinkley St. Pg.21 J12
Hinman St. Pg.21 J13
Howell Pl. Pg.21 J13
Hunter Ct. Pg.21 J11
Hunter Dr. Pg.21 J11
Industrial Dr. Pg.21 J9
Jackson St. Pg.21 J12
James St. Pg.21 H11
Jefferson St. Pg.21 J10
Jericho Rd. Pg.21 G9
Keck Ave. Pg.21 H11
Kimberly Ln. Pg.21 H13
Kingston Ave. Pg.21 J13
Knell St. Pg.21 H10
LaFayette St. Pg.21 J12
Lakeside Dr. Pg.21 J11
Lebanon St. Pg.22 H12
Lewis Ct. Pg.21 J12
Lewis St. Pg.21 J12
Lexington Dr. Pg.21 J12
Lincoln Ave. Pg.21 H11
Madison St. Pg.21 H10
Main St. Pg.21 J10
Marsch Ave. Pg.21 H11
Martin Ave. Pg.21 H11
McClaran Ave. Pg.21 G9
Meadowlane Ct. Pg.21 J9
Melrose Ave. Pg.21,22 H12
Mill St. Pg.21 J11
Montgomery Rd. Pg.21 J11
Morning Glory Ct. Pg.21 J11
Mulberry Dr. Pg.21 J9
Oakland Ave. Pg.21 J13
Oakton Rd. Pg.21 J9
Orchard Rd. Pg.21 J9
Park Ct. Pg.21 J11
Park Dr. Pg.21 J13
Parker Ct. Pg.21 H12
Pearl St. Pg.21 J11
Pleasant St. Pg.21 H13
Railroad St. Pg.21 J10
Raymond Dr. Pg.21 J13
Red Fox Run Pg.21 J11
Revere Ct. Pg.21 J11
Ridgemont Ct. Pg.21 J11
River Bend Rd. Pg.21 J11
River St. Pg.21 J10
Riverside Dr.,E. Pg.21 H11
Rochester Dr. Pg.21 H9
Royal Dr. Pg.21 J13
Rte. 30 Pg.21 J10
Scott St. Pg.21 J10
Seasons Ridge Blvd. Pg.21 J12
Sherman Ave. Pg.21 H11
Spencer St. Pg.21 J13
Spring Haven Ct. Pg.21 J11
Sunrise Ct. Pg.21 J11
Talma St. Pg.21 J12
Taylor St. Pg.21 H11
Timber Lane Dr. Pg.21 J11
Turnbridge Ct. Pg.21 J11
Union St. Pg.21 H13
Victoria Dr. Pg.21 J9
Village Center Pkwy. Pg.22 J12
Washington St. Pg.21 H11
Watkins St. Pg.21 J10
Watson St. Pg.21 J12
Waubansia Ave. Pg.21 J12
Webster St. Pg.21 J10
Wellman Ave. Pg.21 J12
West Lake St. Pg.21 J10
Williamsburg Ct. Pg.21 J11
Windmere Ct. Pg.21 J11
Winmont Ct. Pg.21 J10
Winter Hill Cir. Pg.21 J11
Winter Hill Ct. Pg.21 J11
1st Ave. Pg.21 J11
2nd St. Pg.21 J11
3rd Ave. Pg.21 J11
4th St. Pg.21 J12
5th St. Pg.21 J12
14th Ave. Pg.21 J13

**CEMETERIES**
French Cem. Pg.21 H11
Riverside Cem. Pg.21 H11
St. Pauls Cem. Pg.21 J12

**PARKS**
Briarcliff Woods Park Pg.21 J11
Crestwood Park Pg.21 G10
Krug Park Pg.21 H11
Montgomery Park Pg.21 J11
Pierce Park Pg.21 J12

**SCHOOLS**
Krug Sch. Pg.21 H12
Nicholson Sch. Pg.21 H11
S. Aurora Schristian Academy Pg.21 J13

**SHOPPING CENTERS**
Settlers Landing S.C. Pg.21 J12

**MISCELLANEOUS**
Jericho Sports Complex Pg.21 J8
Lucky Fifty Club Pg.21 H10
Montgomery Business Pk. Pg.21 J9
Police Department Pg.21 J10
Stock Yard Pg.21 H11
Stuart Sports Complex Pg.21 H8
Village Hall Pg.21 J11

## MOOSEHEART

Pages 9,14

**STREETS**
A St. Pg.14 M16
B St. Pg.14 M15
D St. Pg.14 M15,16
Lake Shore Dr. Pg.14 M15
1st Ave. Pg.14 M16
2nd Ave. Pg.14 M16
3rd Ave. Pg.14 M16
4th Ave. Pg.14 M16
5th Ave. Pg.14 M15

**SCHOOLS**
Mooseheart Elem. & H.S. Pg.14 N16

## NA-AH-SAY TOWNSHIP

(Kendall County)
Pages 24-26

**STREETS**
Abbeyfeale Dr. Pg.24 Q9
Chippewa Dr. Pg.25 Q10
Dover Ct. Pg.26 Q14
Grove Rd. Pg.25 Q11
Oswego Plain Dr. Pg.26 Q14
Paydon Rd. Pg.26 Q15
Schlapp Rd. Pg.25 Q12
Southfield Ln. Pg.26 Q13
Stewart Rd. Pg.26 Q15

**MISCELLANEOUS**
Waish-Kee-Shaw Reservation Pg.25 Q10

## NORTH AURORA

Pages 9,14,15,18,19

**STREETS**
Abbeywood Ln. Pg.18 B11
Abington Ln. Pg.18 B9
Acorn Dr. Pg.18 B10
Adams St. Pg.18 B11
Airport Rd. Pg.18 C10,11
Alder St. Pg.18 C10
Alexandra Ct. Pg.18 B9
Andrew Ct. Pg.15,19 B12,O16
Andrew Ct. Pg.19 A13
Andrew Ln. Pg.15 O16
Anna St. Pg.18 B11
April Ct. Pg.14,19 B12,N16
April Ln. Pg.14 N16
Arrowhead St. Pg.14 N16
Aspen Ct. Pg.14 L16
Aster Ct. Pg.15 O16
Augusta Dr. Pg.15 O16
Aurora Ave. Pg.19 C12
Banbury Rd. Pg.15 O16,17
Basswood Dr. Pg.18 B10
Bede Cir. Pg.15 O16
Bede Ct. Pg.15 O16
Bellar Ct. Pg.14 K17
Benson Ct. Pg.14,18 A9,K16
Beular Ct. Pg.18 B9
Birchwood Dr. Pg.18 B11
Briar Ln. Pg.14 N16
Butterfield Rd. Pg.19 B13
Butternut Dr. Pg.18 B10
Candlewick Ct. Pg.18 B11
Cantigny Ct. Pg.19 A13
Carlson Ct. Pg.14,18 A9,K16
Carrie Ct. Pg.15 O16
Cedar Dr. Pg.18 C11
Chantilly Ln. Pg.18 B11
Cherry Tree Ct. Pg.18 B11
Cherrywood Dr. Pg.18 B11
Chestnut St. Pg.19 B12
Clark St. Pg.15 O16
Clearwater Rd. Pg.19 D12
Cog Hill Ct. Pg.15 O16
Conco St. Pg.19 C12
Conco Western Pg.19 C12
Constitution Ct. Pg.18 F9
Cottonwood Dr. Pg.18 B10
Creekside Ct. Pg.18 B10
Cromwell Cir. Pg.14,18 B9,K17
Cromwell St. Pg.14,18 A9,K16
Cypress Ln. Pg.18 B10
Dee Rd. Pg.19 B12
Derby Dr. Pg.19 A13
Dewig Ct. Pg.15 O16
Dogwood Ct. Pg.14 L16
Dogwood Dr. Pg.18 B10
Doral Ln. Pg.15 O16
Eastview Pg.18 B11
Elm Ave. Pg.18 B11
Fairfield Way Pg.15 O16
Fairview Ct. Pg.18 B11
Fairview Dr. Pg.18 B11
Fairview Rd. Pg.18 D11
Fechner Cir. Pg.14,18 B9,K17
Feltes Ln. Pg.19 B13
Fieldside Ln. Pg.18 B9
Flint Ct. Pg.18 E11
Forest Ridge Dr. Pg.18 B9
Foxhill Ct. Pg.18 B10
Foxhill Ln. Pg.18 B10
Gardiner Ct. Pg.14,18 A9,K16
Gibson Pg.18 B11
Grace St. Pg.18 B11
Grant St. Pg.19 C12
Greenbriar Ct. Pg.15,19 A13,O15
Greenview Ct. Pg.18 B10
Hammer Ln. Pg.15 O16
Hansen Blvd. Pg.18 C9
Harmony Ct. Pg.18 B10
Harmony Dr. Pg.18 B11
Hart Rd. Pg.19 A13
Hartfield Dr. Pg.15 O16
Hartsburg Ln. Pg.14,18 B9,K17
Hawksley Ln. Pg.14 K17
Hawksly Ln. Pg.18 B9
Hawthorne Dr. Pg.18 C11
Hettinger Ln. Pg.19 C12
Hickory Ct. Pg.15 O16
Hickory Ln. Pg.14 K16
Hickory St. Pg.19 B12
Hidden Creek Ln. Pg.18 B10
Hill Ave. Pg.14 N16,17
Hillside Pl. Pg.18 B11
Hilltop Dr. Pg.18 B11
Holly Ct. Pg.19 B13
Ice Cream Dr. Pg.18 C10
Jessica Ct. Pg.19 A13
John St. Pg.18 C11
Juniper Dr. Pg.18 B10
Kathryn Ln. Pg.18 B9
Kingswood Dr. Pg.18 C11
Larchwood Ln. Pg.18 B11
Laurel Dr. Pg.19 B12
Lilac Ln. Pg.19 B12
Lindsay Cir. Pg.19 B13
Linn Ct. Pg.19 B12
Lloyd Ln. Pg.15 O16
Locust St. Pg.19 B12
Long Ave. Pg.14 N16
Lovedale Ln. Pg.19 D12
Magnolia Dr. Pg.14 L16
Maple St. Pg.18 B11
Maplewood Dr. Pg.18 B11
Martinson Ct. Pg.14,18 A9,K16
Marvo St. Pg.18 B11
Matthias Ct. Pg.15 O16
Meadow Ln. Pg.15 O16
Mistwood Ln. Pg.18 B11
Mitchell Rd. Pg.19 C13
Monroe St. Pg.18 B11
Mooseheart Rd., W. Pg.14 K16
Mount Ln. Pg.15,19 A12,O16
Oak Crest Dr. Pg.15 O16
Oak St. Pg.19 B11
Oakhill Ct. Pg.18 B9
Oakland Cir. Pg.18 B10
Oakwood Dr. Pg.18 C12
Oberweis Dr. Pg.15,19 A13,O16
Offutt Ln. Pg.18 D12
Orchard Gateway Pg.18 C9
Orchard Rd. Pg.18 C9
Overland Dr. Pg.18 C11
Parkside Ct. Pg.18 B10
Patterson Ave. Pg.14,18 A9,K16
Patterson Ln. Pg.15,19 A12,O16
Pierce St. Pg.19 B12
Pin Oak Dr. Pg.18 B11
Pinecreek Dr. Pg.15,19 B12,O17
Pinehill Ct. Pg.18 B10
Pinehill Dr. Pg.18 B10
Pinehurst Ct. Pg.14,15 N-O16
Pinehurst Dr. Pg.15 O16
Pinewood Dr. Pg.18 B11
Poplar Pl. Pg.18 C11
Poplar St. Pg.18 C11
Prairie Ct. Pg.18 C9
Princeton Ct. Pg.18 C11
Princeton Dr. Pg.18 C11
Randall Rd. Pg.18 C10
Ravine Rd. Pg.14 M16
Redwood Ct. Pg.18 B11
Ridge Rd. Pg.15,19 A12,O16
Ritter St. Pg.14,18 B9,K17
River Rd. Pg.19 A,B12
Riverview St. Pg.19 C12
Robert St. Pg.18 B11
Sellar Ct. Pg.19 A13
Sharon Ct. Pg.15 O16
Sharon Ln. Pg.14,19 B12,N16
Silver Tr. Pg.18 B10
Slaker Pg.19 A13
Slaker Ct. Pg.15 O16
South St. Pg.19 C12
Spring Ct. Pg.18 B10
Spruce St. Pg.15 O16
Spyglass Ct. Pg.15 O16
State St. Pg.18 B11
Stevens Ct. Pg.14,18 B9,K17
Stone Ave. Pg.19 B12
Sullivan Rd. Pg.18 D10
Sycamore Ln. Pg.18 C11
Terry Ln. Pg.19 B13
Timber Oaks Dr. Pg.18 B11
Timber Oaks Ln. Pg.14 M16,17
Turnberry Dr. Pg.15 O16
Valley Rd. Pg.18 A11
Victoria Cir., E. Pg.18 B10
Walnut Dr. Pg.18 B10
Waterford Rd. Pg.18 B9
Westbury Cir. Pg.18 B9
Westgate Dr. Pg.18 F10
Whalen Ct. Pg.14,18 B9,K17
White Oak Ct. Pg.18 B10
White Oak Dr. Pg.14,18 B10,K16
Wildwood Dr. Pg.18 B11
Wilkinson Ln. Pg.14,18 A9,K16
Willow Way Pg.18 B11
Wingfoot Dr. Pg.15 O16
Winterberry Ct. Pg.15 O16
Woodland Cir. Pg.14 L16
Woodlawn Dr. Pg.15 O16
Yellow Pine Dr. Pg.18 E10

**FOREST PRESERVES**
Les Arends F.P. Pg.14 N16

**GOLF COURSES**
Fox Valley C.C. Pg.15 N,O16
Valley Green G.C. Pg.18 C11

**PARKS**
Green Field Park Pg.18 B10
Hickory Street Park Pg.15 O17
Highlands Park Pg.18 B11
North Island Pg.18 B12
Schnieder Park Pg.19 B12
Willow Park Pg.18 B10
Wingfoot Park Pg.15 O16

**SCHOOLS**
Aurora Central Catholic H.S. Pg.18 D10
Gary D. Jewel Middle Sch. Pg.14 K17
Goodwill Sch. Pg.18 B10
Schneider Sch. Pg.15 O16
School Dist. 129 Pg.14 K17

**SHOPPING CENTERS**
Courtyards West S.C. Pg.18 C10
North Aurora Auto Mall Pg.18 C9
Smoke Tree Plaza Pg.18 C11
Super K-Mart Pg.19 C12
Tommy's S.C. Pg.18 B10

**MISCELLANEOUS**
Asbury Court Retirement Center Pg.18 C11
Aurora Toll Plaza Pg.19 C12
Bowman Corporate Center Pg.18 D9
Fire Dept. Pg.18 B12
Landmark Industrial Park Pg.18 C10
Library Pg.18 B12
North Aurora Activity Center Pg.18 B11
Pace Bus Depot Pg.18 C11
Red Oaks Nature Center Pg.14 N16
Tollway Center Business Park Pg.18 C11
Village Hall/Police Department Pg.19 B12

## OSWEGO

(Kendall County)
Pages 21,22,24,25

**STREETS**
Adams St. Pg.25 M10
Alex Ct. Pg.22 K14
Alexander Ct. Pg.21 L11
Angella Ct. Pg.21 L11
Anthony Ct. Pg.21 L11
Arbor Ct. Pg.24 M8
Arbor Ln. Pg.24 M8
Arrowhead Ln. Pg.24 M8
Ash Grove Ln. Pg.24 M9
Ashland St. Pg.25 M10
Ashlawn Ave. Pg.21 L10
Ashley Ct. Pg.21 L12
Avenue 'A' Pg.25 N10
Badger Ct. Pg.24 M9
Badger Ln. Pg.24 M9
Barnaby Dr. Pg.22 L12
Bayberry Dr. Pg.24 M9
Beau Meade Rd. Pg.21 L11
Beaver Crossing Pg.21 L9
Beaver Ct. Pg.21 L9
Bednarick Ct. Pg.25 M10
Bell Ct. Pg.25 M11
Bent Tree Ct. Pg.21 L11
Benton St. Pg.25 M10
Berkshire Ct. Pg.22 L12
Bison Rd. Pg.21 L9
Blossom Ct. Pg.25 O10
Blossom Ln. Pg.25 O10
Blue Ridge Ct. Pg.22 K14
Blue Ridge Dr. Pg.22 K14
Bobcat Ct. Pg.21 L9
Boulder Hill Pass Pg.21 L11
Brandon Ct. Pg.21 L11
Briar Cliff Rd. Pg.22 K12
Briarwood Ln. Pg.25 N10
Bridgeview Dr. Pg.22 K14
Brock Ct. Pg.21 L11
Brock Way Pg.21 L11
Buckingham Ct. Pg.21 K11
Bucktail Dr. Pg.21 L9
Burr Oak Dr. Pg.24 M9
Calumet Pg.25 N10
Canterbury Ct. Pg.21 K11
Carnation Dr. Pg.25 O10
Carriage Ct. Pg.25 N10
Cascade Ct. Pg.24 M9
Cascade Ln. Pg.21 L11
Catherine Ct. Pg.21 L11
Cebold Dr. Pg.21 L10
Charlotte Ln. Pg.21 L11
Chesterfield Dr. Pg.21 L11
Chicago Rd. Pg.25 M11
Chipmunk Dr. Pg.21 L9
Christian Ct. Pg.22 K14
Churchill Ct. Pg.25 N10
Churchill Ln. Pg.25 N10
Cinderford Dr. Pg.21 L11
Clearwater Ct. Pg.24 M9
Clearwater Ln. Pg.24 M9
Cobblestone Ct. Pg.21 K11
Coolidge Dr. Pg.24 M9
Cornell Dr. Pg.22 L12
Cougar Ln. Pg.21 L9
Coventry Ct. Pg.24 M9
Coyote Ct. Pg.24 M9
Creekside Ct. Pg.25 N10
Crofton Ct. Pg.21 L11
Crofton Rd. Pg.21 L11
Crystal Ct. Pg.22 L14
Deer Path Ct. Pg.21 L9
Deer Path Dr. Pg.21 M9
Della Ln. Pg.25 M11
Derby Ct. Pg.25 N10
Dorchester Ct. Pg.25 N10
Douglas Rd. Pg.22 K12
Dylan Dr. Pg.22 K14
East Way Dr. Pg.21 L10
Edgewater Ct. Pg.24 M9
Eisenhower Dr. Pg.24 M9
Elk St. Pg.21 L9
Elmwood Dr. Pg.25 M10
Essex Ave. Pg.22 L14
Etsinger Ct. Pg.24 M9
Evergreen Ct. Pg.25 M10
Faro Ct. Pg.25 M10
Fawn Dr. Pg.21 L9
Fernwood Rd. Pg.22 K12
Ferret Crossing Pg.21 L9
Fieldcrest Dr. Pg.21 L11
Fifth St. Pg.22 K12
Flintlock Ct. Pg.21 L12
Forest Ave. Pg.25 N10
Forest St. Pg.25 N10
Fox Chase Ct. Pg.21 L10
Fox Chase Dr. Pg.21 L9
Francesca Ct. Pg.21 L11
Franklin St. Pg.25 N10
Garfield St. Pg.25 M11
Gates Creek Dr. Pg.24 M8
Glendale Pg.25 M10
Gloria Ln. Pg.22 L12
Grant St. Pg.25 M11
Gray's Ct. Pg.22 L12
Gray's Dr. Pg.21 L11
Greenview Ct. Pg.24 M9
Greenview Ln. Pg.24 M9
Grove Rd. Pg.25 N10
Half Moon Ct. Pg.22 K14
Harrison St. Pg.25 M10
Hartford Ct. Pg.21 K11
Hartland Ct. Pg.25 N10
Heritage Dr. Pg.22 L12
Hickory St. Pg.25 N10
Highland Ct. Pg.25 N10
Highview Ct. Pg.24 M9
Hintlock Ct. Pg.21 L12
Hoover Dr. Pg.24 M9
Huntington Ct. Pg.21 K11
Iris Ct. Pg.24 N9
Jackson Pl. Pg.25 M10
Jackson St. Pg.25 M10
Jay St. Pg.25 M10
Jefferson St. Pg.25 M10
Joesph Ct. Pg.21 L11
Judith Cir. Pg.21 L11
Judson St. Pg.25 N10
Kendall Point Dr. Pg.22 K13
Kentwood Dr. Pg.21 L10
Kirkland Cir. Pg.22 K13
Knights Bridge Ct. Pg.22 L12
Lake Ct. Pg.24 M9
Lakelawn Ave. Pg.25 M10
Lakeview Ct. Pg.25 N10
Lakeview Dr. Pg.25 N10
Landshire Ct. Pg.21 L11
Lattice Dr. Pg.24 N9
Lincoln Hwy. Pg.22 K14
Locust St. Pg.25 N10
Lombardy Ln. Pg.21 L11
Long Meadow Dr. Pg.25 N10
Longford Ct. Pg.21 L11
Loreen Ct. Pg.22 L14
Lucky Ct. Pg.21 L11
Lynx Ln. Pg.21 L9
Madison Ct. Pg.24 N9
Madison St. Pg.25 M10
Main St. Pg.25 N10
Mandy Ln. Pg.22 K14
Mark Ct. Pg.21 L11
Matena Dr. Pg.21 L11
Merchants Pg.21 K9
Mill Race Ct. Pg.21 L12
Mill Rd. Pg.24 M9
Millstream Ln. Pg.24 M9
Mitchell Dr. Pg.22 L14
Mondovi Dr. Pg.22 L12
Monroe St. Pg.25 N10
Moose St. Pg.21 L9
Newport Cir. Pg.22 L12
North St. Pg.25 M10
Northampton Dr. Pg.21 L11
Northgate Cir. Pg.25 N10
Northgate Dr. Pg.25 N10
Norway Pl. Pg.24 M8
Nottingham Ct. Pg.21 L11
Nottingham Dr. Pg.21 L11
Oak Lawn Ave. Pg.21 L11
Oakwood Ct. Pg.25 M11
Oakwood Dr. Pg.25 M11
Ogden Falls Blvd. Pg.22 K14
Old Douglas Rd. Pg.22 L12
Old Post Rd. Pg.21 L11
Orchard Rd. Pg.20 K,L8
Oswego Rd. Pg.22 K13
Otter Way Pg.21 L9
Oxford Ct. Pg.21 K11
Paradise Pkwy. Pg.24 N9
Park St. Pg.25 M10
Parkland Ct. Pg.24 M9
Parkside Ct. Pg.25 N10
Parkside Dr. Pg.25 N10
Parkview Ct. Pg.25 N10
Partridge Sq. Pg.25 M11
Pearce's Ford Pg.22 L12
Penn Ct. Pg.25 M10
Persimmon Ln. Pg.24 N9
Peund Ct. Pg.25 M10
Pinehurst Ln. Pg.25 O10
Plainfield Rd. Pg.25 N10
Plymouth Ct. Pg.22 L12
Polk St. Pg.25 M10
Ponds Ct. Pg.24 M9
Poplar Ct. Pg.25 O10
Pottowatamie Ct. Pg.22 L12
Prairieview Ct. Pg.25 N10
Prairieview Dr. Pg.25 N10
Presidential Blvd. Pg.24 M9
Prestwick Ct. Pg.21 L11
Preswick Ct. Pg.21 L11
Primrose Ln. Pg.22 K14
Quincy Dr. Pg.22 L12
Raintree Dr. Pg.22 L14
Reagan Dr. Pg.24 M9
Richmond Dr. Pg.22 L12
River Run Blvd. Pg.24 M9
River Run Ct. Pg.24 M9
River Wood Ct. Pg.24 N8
River Wood Dr. Pg.24 N8
River Wood Ln. Pg.24 N8
Riverwood Ln. Pg.24 M9
Robert Rd. Pg.25 M11
Robinhood Cir. Pg.25 M11
Robinhood Dr. Pg.25 M11
Roosevelt Dr. Pg.24 M9
Rosebush Ln. Pg.25 O10
Rte. 25 Pg.21 L10
Rte. 30 Pg.22 K12
Rte. 31 Pg.25 M10
Rte. 34 Pg.22 K13
Saddlebrook Ct. Pg.25 O10
Salem Cir. Pg.22 L12
Saratoga Ct. Pg.25 O10
Sedgewick Ct. Pg.21 L11
Sedgewick Rd. Pg.21 L11
Seton Creek Dr. Pg.22 L12
Sherwick Rd. Pg.21 L11
Sherwood Dr. Pg.25 M11
Sparkle Ct. Pg.22 L14
Stone Gate Dr. Pg.25 M10
Stone Hill Rd. Pg.25 M11
Stone Rd. Pg.25 M11
Stoneleigh Ln. Pg.21 L12
Stonemill Ln. Pg.21 L12
Sunshine Ct. Pg.22 L14
Taft Dr. Pg.24 M9
Taft Dr. Pg.24 M9
Terrace Ct. Pg.25 O10
Terrace Ln. Pg.25 O10
Tewksburg Cir. Pg.21 L11
Tewksburg Ct. Pg.21 L11
Thornbury Ct. Pg.21 L11
Thornbury Dr. Pg.21 L11
Treasure Dr. Pg.22 L14
Tyler St. Pg.25 M10
Van Buren Pg.25 M10
Victoria Ln. Pg.21 L11
Village Green Pg.22 K14
Washington St. Pg.24 M9
Waterbury Cir. Pg.22 K14
Waterford Dr. Pg.21 L11
Waubaness Cir. Pg.21 L12
Waubaness Cir. Ct. Pg.25 L12
Waubaness Ct. Pg.21 L11
Wembley Rd. Pg.21 L11
West End Ct. Pg.24 N9
White Ln. Pg.25 M11
White Owl Ln. Pg.21 L9
Whitetail Crossing Pg.21 L9
Whitewater Ln. Pg.24 M9
Wildwood St. Pg.25 M11
Willowwood Dr. Pg.24 M9
Wilmette Pg.25 N11
Wilson Pl. Pg.25 N10
Windcrest Dr. Pg.25 M11
Windgate Ct. Pg.22 K14
Wolf's Crossing Rd. Pg.22,25 L15,M11
Wollmington Dr. Pg.22 L12
Wolverine Dr. Pg.21 L9
Woodchuck Tr. Pg.21 L9
Wooley Rd. Pg.25 N11
Yokum Blvd. Pg.22 L14
1st St. Pg.25 M10
2nd St. Pg.25 M10
3rd St. Pg.25 M10

**CEMETERIES**
Lincoln Mem. Park Pg.22 K14
Pearce Cem. Pg.25 M11

**GOLF COURSES**
Fox Bend G.C. Pg.22 M11

**PARKS**
Chesterfield Park Pg.21 L11
Civic Center Park Pg.21 L10
Heritage Park Pg.25 M10
Hudson Crossing Park Pg.24 M9
Jaycee Park Pg.22 L12
Pearce's Ford Park Pg.21 L11
Prairie Point Center Park Pg.25 N10
Prairieview Park Pg.25 N10
Stonegate Park Pg.25 M10
Troy Park Pg.21 L10
Village Green Park Pg.25 M10
Violet Patch Park Pg.21 L10

**SCHOOLS**
East View Elem. Sch. Pg.25 M11
Old Post Elem. Sch. Pg.21 L11
Oswego Senior H.S. Pg.25 M11
Thompson Jr. H.S. Pg.21 L21
Traughter Jr. H.S. Pg.25 N10

**MISCELLANEOUS**
Library Pg.25 M10
Post Office Pg.25 M10

## OSWEGO TOWNSHIP

(Kendall County)
Pages 21,22

**STREETS**
Abbeyfeale Dr. Pg.24 Q9
Afton Dr. Pg.21 K12
Aldon Ct. Pg.21 K11
Aldon Rd. Pg.21 K10
Amesbury Rd. Pg.21 K11
Amy Dr. Pg.26 P13
Anchor Rd. Pg.21 L10
Appaloosa Rd. Pg.26 N14
Ashley Way Pg.21 L10
Augusta Rd. Pg.21 L9
Barclay Ct. Pg.21 K10
Beauwick Dr. Pg.21 K11
Bentson St. Pg.21 M9
Bereman Rd., N. Pg.21 K11
Birchwood Ct. Pg.21 K11
Blackhart Dr. Pg.22 L12
Boat Ln. Pg.21 L10
Boulder Hill Pass Pg.21 K10
Braeburn Dr. Pg.21 K11
Breman Rd. Pg.21 K10
Briarcliff Dr. Pg.21 K11
Briarcliff Rd. Pg.21 K10
Brighton Way Pg.21 K11
Buell Rd. Pg.24 O8
Burkhart Dr. Pg.26 M13
Butcher Dr. Pg.21 L10
Cardinal Ln. Pg.23 P7
Caterpillar Rd. Pg.21 K9
Cayman Ct. Pg.21 K11
Cayman Dr. Pg.21 K10
Cebold Dr. Pg.21 L9
Century Ct. Pg.21 L10
Century Dr. Pg.21 L10
Charles Ct. Pg.21 L9
Chatham Pl. Pg.21 K11
Cherry Dr. Pg.24 N9
Chippewa Dr. Pg.24 Q9
Circle Dr. Pg.21 K10
Clay Ct. Pg.21 K10
Codorus Rd. Pg.21 K10
Collins Rd. Pg.25 O12-14
Colony Ct. Pg.24 P7
Commerce Pg.21 L9
Council Ave. Pg.22 K15
Country Dr. Pg.23 P7
Country Rd. Pg.24 P8
Crescent Ct. Pg.21 K11
Crestview Dr. Pg.25 Q10
Crestwood Ct. Pg.21 K11
Creve Ct. Pg.21 K10
Culver Rd. Pg.21 K10
Curtmar Ct. Pg.21 K10
Denham Dr. Pg.21 K11
Dolores St. Pg.21 L9
Doplhin Ct. Pg.21 L9
Douglas Rd. Pg.21 K-P12
Douglas St. Pg.24 N9
Dover Ct. Pg.26 Q13
Dreas Dr. Pg.26 P12
Durango Rd. Pg.21 K10
Eagle Ln. Pg.24 Q9
Eastfield Rd. Pg.21 K12
Ellison Ave. Pg.22 K15
Farm Ct. Pg.24 P7
Fernwood Rd. Pg.21 K11
Field Point Rd. Pg.21 K10
Fieldcrest Dr. Pg.21 K10
Fox Hill Ct. Pg.24 P7
Gardens Dr. Pg.21 K10
Gentilly Dr. Pg.21 K12
Gilmore Rd. Pg.26 P14
Greenbriar Rd. Pg.21 K11
Greenfield Rd. Pg.21 K10
Grove Rd. Pg.25 O12
Gullgord Rd. Pg.21 K10
Hafenrichter Rd. Pg.22 J15
Half Hollow Ct. Pg.25 Q10
Half Round Rd. Pg.25 Q10
Hampton Rd. Pg.21 K10
Harbor Dr. Pg.21 L9
Harlan Ave. Pg.22 L15
Harvey Rd. Pg.22,26 L14,M15
Heathgate Rd. Pg.21 K11
Hill Stone Rd. Pg.21 K10
Hillcrest Ct. Pg.21 K10
Hillstone Rd. Pg.21 K10
Hubbard Rd. Pg.21 K11
Ingelside Ct. Pg.21 K11
Ingelside Rd. Pg.21 K11
Ingleshire Ct. Pg.21 K11
Ingleshire Rd. Pg.21 K11
Keierleber Rd. Pg.26 M13
Kevin Ln. Pg.21 L9
Knollwood Dr. Pg.21 K11
Kristine St. Pg.21 L9
Laurie Ln. Pg.21 L9
Leisure Ln. Pg.26 P12
Light Rd. Pg.21 L9
Lincoln Hwy. Pg.22 L14
Longbeach Rd. Pg.21 K11
Longmeadow Ln. Pg.25 Q10
Marina Dr. Pg.21 L10
Marlin Dr. Pg.21 K9
Marnell Rd. Pg.21 K11
Martin Dr. Pg.21 L10
Mary Pg.21 L9
Minkler Rd. Pg.24 O-Q8
Mo-Ah-Way Path Pg.25 Q10
Morgan Creek Ct. Pg.25 Q10
Morgan Ct. Pg.24 P7
Oak Creek Dr. Pg.24 P7
Old Post Rd. Pg.21 K10
Old Reservation Rd. Pg.25 Q10
Osage Ct. Pg.24 M9
Oswego Plain Dr. Pg.26 Q14
Oswego Rd. Pg.22 L12
Ottawa Ct. Pg.24 Q9
Palomino Ln. Pg.24 N8
Park Dr. Pg.21 K11
Paydon Rd. Pg.26 Q15
Pembrook Rd. Pg.21 K11
Pickford Rd. Pg.21 K11
Pioneer Ct. Pg.26 N15
Plainfield Rd. Pg.25,26 Q11,14
Pleasant View Dr. Pg.24 N9
Pomeroy Rd. Pg.21 K11
Ponderosa Dr. Pg.23 P7
Prairie Crossing Pg.24 Q10
Pueblo Rd. Pg.21 K11

# ST. CHARLES

Valley S.C. ... Pg.12 .... M8

**MISCELLANEOUS**
Arthur Anderson Complex
... Pg.13 ..... Q7
Baker Comm. Ctr.
... Pg.13 ..... O8
City Hall ... Pg.13 ..... O7
Delnor Hosp. ... Pg.13 ..... O7
Foundry Business Park
... Pg.12 ..... M7
Illinois Youth Center
... Pg.12 ..... K8
Kane Co. Judical Ctr.
... Pg.12 ..... L9
Kane County Fairgrounds
... Pg.13 ..... O7
Library ... Pg.13 ..... O7
Norris Sports Complex &
Cultural Arts Ctr.
... Pg.12 ..... Q6
Pheasant Run Resort &
Convention Center
... Pg.13 ..... R7
Pine View Nursing Home
... Pg.13 ..... O7
Police Dept. ... Pg.13 ..... O7
Post Office ... Pg.12 ..... N7
Pottawatomie Comm. Ctr.
... Pg.12 ..... N7
Shanahan Industrial Park
... Pg.13 ..... R8
Sports Core Complex
... Pg.13 ..... R9
St. Charles Business Pk.
... Pg.13 ..... Q7
St. Charles Commercial Ctr.
... Pg.12 ..... M9
St. Charles Twp. Office
... Pg.12 ..... M8
Timber Ridge Prof. Park
... Pg.12 ..... M7
Valley Ambulatory Surgery Ctr.
& Recovery Sit
... Pg.12 ..... M7

# ST. CHARLES TOWNSHIP
Pages 6,10-13

**STREETS**
Adele Ln. ... Pg.10 ..... K2
Aldrea Ct. ... Pg.10 ..... M2
Amherst Ct. ... Pg.6 ..... J6
Army Trail Rd. ... Pg.6 ..... H8
Aurora Ave. ... Pg.11 ..... O3
Babson Ln. ... Pg.10 ..... L6
Baker Ln. ... Pg.10 ..... L5
Barb Hill Ct. ... Pg.6 ..... G7
Barb Hill Rd. ... Pg.10 ..... K2
Barton Dr. ... Pg.10 ..... N6
Bernice Dr. ... Pg.12 ..... K7
Bittersweet Rd. ... Pg.12 ..... M7
Bluestem Ct. ... Pg.10 ..... K2
Bluff Dr. ... Pg.11 ..... O5
Bolcum Rd. ... Pg.10 ..... K4
Bonfield Ave. ... Pg.11 ..... O3
Bonnie Ct. ... Pg.6 ..... J7
Bonnie Ln. ... Pg.11 ..... O3
Bonnie St. ... Pg.11 ..... O3
Bricher Rd. ... Pg.12 ..... L9
Bristol Ct. ... Pg.6 ..... G8
Bristol Rd. ... Pg.10 ..... N2
Brookwood Rd. ... Pg.11 ..... O5
Burr Oak Ln. ... Pg.10 ..... K3
Burr Rd. ... Pg.10 ..... K3,5
Burnside Ln. ... Pg.11 ..... O3
Campton Hills Dr.
... Pg.12 ..... K7
Carl Lee Rd. ... Pg.11 ..... P3
Cary St. ... Pg.11 ..... O2
Catalpa Ave. ... Pg.11 ..... O3
Cedar Rock Ave. ... Pg.11 ..... O3
Chambellan Ln. ... Pg.11 ..... R4
Chickasaw Ct. ... Pg.10 ..... A2
Cibis Rd. ... Pg.12 ..... K7
Circle Dr. ... Pg.11 ..... P3
Cloverfield Dr. ... Pg.10 ..... K1
Clubhouse Ct. ... Pg.6 ..... H7
Clyde Ct. ... Pg.11 ..... O3
Clyde Pkwy. ... Pg.11 ..... P3
Colley Dr. ... Pg.11 ..... P3
Columbine East ... Pg.10 ..... K1
Columbine West
... Pg.6 ..... G6
Country Club Rd.
... Pg.11 ..... P5
Courier Ave. ... Pg.11 ..... P3
Crane Ln. ... Pg.10 ..... L6
Crane Rd. ... Pg.10 ..... M5
Cranston Rd. ... Pg.13 ..... G7
Creekside Dr. ... Pg.10 ..... L3
Creekview Ln. ... Pg.10 ..... K4
Dean Rd. ... Pg.12 ..... M6,7
Decatur Ave. ... Pg.11 ..... P3
Deerpath Way ... Pg.10 ..... M5
Denny Dr. ... Pg.13 ..... R8
Detroit St. ... Pg.11 ..... P3
Dogwood Ln. ... Pg.11 ..... O3
Dorchester Rd. ... Pg.10 ..... N5
Dover Hill Rd. ... Pg.10 ..... N4
Dunham Rd. ... Pg.11 ..... Q5
Eagle Ct. ... Pg.6 ..... H7
Eagles Nest Ct. ... Pg.6 ..... G7
East Dr. ... Pg.11 ..... P1
Elder Ave. ... Pg.11 ..... O4
Elgin St. ... Pg.11 ..... O5
Elliott Ct. ... Pg.6 ..... J6
Elmwood Ave. ... Pg.11 ..... O4
Emily Ln. ... Pg.11 ..... P4
Essex Ave. ... Pg.11 ..... P3
Evenswood Ln. ... Pg.6 ..... J7
Fairview Ter. ... Pg.11 ..... O3
Fairway Dr. ... Pg.6 ..... H7
Falcon's Ct. ... Pg.6 ..... G7
Fence Rail Ct. ... Pg.10 ..... M5
Ferson Creek Rd.
... Pg.12 ..... M6
Ferson Woods Dr.
... Pg.10 ..... K3
Fieldcrest Dr. ... Pg.10 ..... N5
Fielding Ct. ... Pg.6 ..... G7

Fieldstone Ct. ... Pg.10 ..... M5
Five Island Rd. ... Pg.11 ..... P3
Fletcher Rd. ... Pg.11 ..... Q5
Florence Ln. ... Pg.11 ..... O3
Foley Ln. ... Pg.11 ..... P3
Forest Ave. ... Pg.11 ..... O3
Fox Bluff Ct. ... Pg.10 ..... N5
Fox Bluff Dr. ... Pg.10 ..... N5
Fox River Ave. ... Pg.11 ..... P3
Fox River Dr. ... Pg.11 ..... P3
Foxborough Rd. ... Pg.10 ..... O3
Foxglove Ct. ... Pg.10 ..... K2
Foxwood Ln. ... Pg.6 ..... H7
Geneva St. ... Pg.11 ..... O3
Gilbert St. ... Pg.11 ..... Q2
Glad Ln. ... Pg.6 ..... J7
Glencoak Ln. ... Pg.10 ..... K4
Glenview Dr. ... Pg.11 ..... O3
Glenwood Dr. ... Pg.10 ..... M3
Golfview Ct. ... Pg.6 ..... H7
Goodrich Ave. ... Pg.11 ..... O3
Grandmaw's Ln. ... Pg.10 ..... L,M5
Greenlawn Ave. ... Pg.11 ..... O2
Greenview Ct. ... Pg.6 ..... J7
Grey Barn Rd. ... Pg.10 ..... L5
Grove Ave. ... Pg.11 ..... O3
Gustavus Ln. ... Pg.10 ..... L6
Halsted Ave. ... Pg.11 ..... O3
Hampton Dr. ... Pg.10 ..... M2
Hawkins Ln. ... Pg.10 ..... K5
Hawthorn Dr. ... Pg.12 ..... M6
Hendricksen Ct. ... Pg.10 ..... K3
Hendricksen Rd. ... Pg.10 ..... K3
Heritage Ct. ... Pg.10 ..... K3
Hickory Ln. ... Pg.13 ..... G9
Highview Ct. ... Pg.10 ..... N5
Hill Ct. ... Pg.11 ..... P1
Hillcrest Ave. ... Pg.11 ..... O3
Hillside Dr. ... Pg.10 ..... N5
Hilltop Dr. ... Pg.6 ..... J7
Hunters Gate Rd.
... Pg.10 ..... M5
Illinois St. ... Pg.11 ..... P3
Indian Mound Rd.
... Pg.12 ..... N7
Iowa St. ... Pg.11 ..... P3
Irvin Ave. ... Pg.11 ..... N2
Irwin Ave. ... Pg.11 ..... N2
Jackson Ave. ... Pg.11 ..... N2
James Dr. ... Pg.11 ..... P3
Joan Ct. ... Pg.12 ..... K7
Joan Dr. ... Pg.12 ..... K7
Joseph St. ... Pg.11 ..... O2
Kane Ave. ... Pg.11 ..... O3
Kearns St. ... Pg.11 ..... O2
Kimberly Dr. ... Pg.10 ..... M2
Knoll Creek Dr. ... Pg.10 ..... L6
Ladue Ct. ... Pg.12 ..... J2
Lake Charlotte Ct.
... Pg.6 ..... J7
Lakeview Circle ... Pg.10 ..... K4
Lambert Ave. ... Pg.11 ..... O3
Leola Ln. ... Pg.11 ..... L4
Lilac Ave. ... Pg.11 ..... O3
Lilac Ln. ... Pg.10 ..... K1
Lincoln Dr. ... Pg.6 ..... J7
Line Dr. ... Pg.6 ..... J6
Lisa Ln. ... Pg.11 ..... O3
Littlehip Ct. ... Pg.6 ..... J7
Longridge Rd. ... Pg.10 ..... K2
Longview Dr. ... Pg.10 ..... M4
Lookout Ln. ... Pg.6 ..... H7
Lynn Dr. ... Pg.12 ..... K7
Main St. ... Pg.13 ..... Q7
Mallard Lake Rd.
... Pg.10 ..... H7
Maple Ave. ... Pg.10,11 N2,O3
Maple Ct. ... Pg.10 ..... L5
Maple Ln. ... Pg.11 ..... O5
Marguerite St. ... Pg.12 ..... M7
Mary Ln. ... Pg.6 ..... J7
May Ln. ... Pg.11 ..... O3
McDonald Rd. ... Pg.10 ..... L1
McKay Dr. ... Pg.10 ..... M5
McLean Blvd. ... Pg.10 ..... N1
Meadow Dr. ... Pg.10 ..... N4
Meadows Ct. ... Pg.10 ..... M4
Michael Ct. ... Pg.10 ..... M2
Middle Creek Ln.
... Pg.10 ..... M5
Miller Ln. ... Pg.6 ..... J7
Mills Ct. ... Pg.11 ..... O2
Moseley Ln. ... Pg.11 ..... P3
Murray Ct. ... Pg.6 ..... H7
Murray Rd. ... Pg.6 ..... H7
Myles Rd. ... Pg.10 ..... M4
North Dr. ... Pg.11 ..... P3
Northern Ct. ... Pg.6 ..... J7
Northfield Rd. ... Pg.11 ..... O4
Oak Ct. ... Pg.10 ..... M5
Oak Dr. ... Pg.10 ..... K4
Oak Ln. ... Pg.11 ..... O5
Oak Rd. ... Pg.11 ..... O5
Oak Ridge Ln. ... Pg.12 ..... M6
Oak Run Ct. ... Pg.10 ..... M4
Oakwood Dr. ... Pg.11,12 O3,K7
Ohio St. ... Pg.11 ..... P2
Old Farm Rd. ... Pg.10 ..... N5
Old Homestead Rd.
... Pg.6 ..... H7
Old Quarry Rd. ... Pg.10 ..... N6
Orchard Rd. ... Pg.6 ..... G7
Pakan Dr. ... Pg.11 ..... P2
Park Ave. ... Pg.10,11 N2,O3
Park Ln. ... Pg.10 ..... N3,5
Park Pl. ... Pg.10,11 O3,P2
Pearson Dr. ... Pg.6 ..... H8
Peck Rd. ... Pg.12 ..... H7
Pheasant Run Dr.
... Pg.6 ..... J7
Pine Rd. ... Pg.10 ..... K3
Pinelands Rd. ... Pg.11 ..... O4
Plymouth Ct. ... Pg.6,10 G8,M2
Prairie Dr. ... Pg.12 ..... J7
Promontory Ct. ... Pg.10 ..... L3
Ramona Ln. ... Pg.11 ..... O3
Randall Rd. ... Pg.10 ..... M3
Red Gate Ct. ... Pg.10 ..... M3
Red Gate Rd. ... Pg.10 ..... L-N4
Red Haw Ln. ... Pg.12 ..... M7

Ridge Dr. ... Pg.6 ..... J7
Ridge Line Rd. ... Pg.6 ..... G7
Ridgewood Ct. ... Pg.10 ..... M3-4
Ridgewood Dr. ... Pg.10 ..... M4
Riding Hood Ln. ... Pg.10 ..... M5
River Dr. ... Pg.11 ..... O3
River Grange Dr. ... Pg.6 ..... H8
River Grange Rd.
... Pg.10 ..... N3
Riverside Dr. ... Pg.10,11 N2,O3
Rivervalley Dr. ... Pg.11 ..... P3
Robert Rd. ... Pg.11 ..... F7,P3
Rockwell Ave. ... Pg.11 ..... O5
Ronsu Ln. ... Pg.10 ..... L4
Roosevelt Ave. ... Pg.11 ..... P3
Rose Ave. ... Pg.10 ..... N3
Salina Ave. ... Pg.11 ..... O3
Scott Ave. ... Pg.11 ..... O2
Seminary Rd. ... Pg.11 ..... P3
Shady Ln. ... Pg.11 ..... O3
Sidney Ct. ... Pg.10 ..... N2
Silver Glen Ct. ... Pg.10 ..... N2
Silver Glen Rd. ... Pg.10 ..... L2
Silver Ridge Dr. ... Pg.10 ..... M3
Skyline Dr. ... Pg.11 ..... P3
Smith Rd. ... Pg.6 ..... J7
Sorrell Ct. ... Pg.6 ..... G7
South Ct. ... Pg.11 ..... P1
South Ln. ... Pg.11 ..... N4
South Ln. ... Pg.11 ..... O2
Springfield St. ... Pg.11 ..... P3
Stanton Dr. ... Pg.11 ..... O3
State Rte. 25 ... Pg.11 ..... O2
State Rte. 31 ... Pg.10 ..... N2
State Rte. 38 ... Pg.12 ..... K8
State Rte. 64 ... Pg.6 ..... J7,9
Stearns Rd. ... Pg.11 ..... R2
Stevens Glen Rd.
... Pg.6 ..... G7
Stevens Rd. ... Pg.10 ..... K2
Stonebridge Ln. ... Pg.10 ..... M5
Stoneleaf Rd. ... Pg.10 ..... M5
Summit St. ... Pg.11 ..... O3
Sunnyside Ave. ... Pg.11 ..... O3
Sunrise Ln. ... Pg.10 ..... M6
Sunset Dr. ... Pg.11 ..... M5
Sycamore Ave. ... Pg.11 ..... P3
Sycamore Rd. ... Pg.11 ..... K1
Sylvia Ln. ... Pg.11 ..... P3
Thompson Ave. ... Pg.11 ..... O3
Thorn Apple Rd. Pg.10 ..... M6
Thorn Tree Dr. ... Pg.10 ..... M6
Thornly Rd. ... Pg.10 ..... M6
Timber Ridge Ct. Pg.10 ..... M4
Toms Trail Dr. ... Pg.12 ..... M7
Toni St. ... Pg.13 ..... R8
Treetop Ln. ... Pg.12 ..... M7
Tucker Ave. ... Pg.11 ..... O3
Tuscola Ave. ... Pg.11 ..... P3
Twin Silos Dr. ... Pg.12 ..... M7
Valley Dr. ... Pg.11 ..... O3
Villa Marie Rd. ... Pg.11 ..... P3
Virginia Ct. ... Pg.11 ..... P3
Wabash Ave. ... Pg.11 ..... P3
Ware Woods Dr. Pg.10 ..... M5
Watseka Ave. ... Pg.11 ..... P3
Weber Dr. ... Pg.11 ..... O3
West Dr. ... Pg.11 ..... P1
Westwood Ln. ... Pg.10 ..... M4
Whispering Tr. ... Pg.10 G8,M2
Whispering Tr. Ct.
... Pg.6,10 G8,M2
Whispering Willow Rd.
... Pg.10 ..... K1
White Thorn Rd. Pg.11 ..... Q5
Wild Rose Ln. ... Pg.12 ..... N6
Wild Rose Rd. ... Pg.12 ..... N6
Willow Ln. ... Pg.10 ..... N3
Wilton Croft Rd. Pg.10 ..... M5
Winsdor Dr. ... Pg.11 ..... M2
Woodgate Rd. ... Pg.10 ..... K5
Woodhill Ln. ... Pg.11 ..... O3
Woodland Ct. ... Pg.10 ..... M5
Woodside Ln. ... Pg.10 ..... K3
Woodview Ct. ... Pg.10 ..... M3
Woodview Ln. ... Pg.10 ..... K3
Wyoming Ave. ... Pg.11 ..... P3
17th St. ... Pg.12 ..... M7

**CEMETERIES**
Little Woods Cemetery
... Pg.11 ..... R2
Prairie Cemetery Pg.10 ..... L3

**FOREST PRESERVES**
Blackhawk F.P. ... Pg.10 ..... N2
Ferson Creek Fen
... Pg.10 ..... M4

**GOLF COURSES**
Blackhawk G.C. Pg.10 ..... N4

**PARKS**
St. Charles Athletic Fields
... Pg.10 ..... L4
Vasa Park ... Pg.10 ..... J1

**SCHOOLS**
Anderson Sch. ... Pg.11 ..... O3
Ferson Creek Sch.
... Pg.10 ..... K4
Little Woods Sch.
... Pg.11 ..... O3
Wild Rose Sch. Pg.12 ..... M7

**MISCELLANEOUS**
Fox River Bike Trail
... Pg.11 ..... P3
Illinois Youth Center
... Pg.11 ..... P3
McGuire House Pg.10 ..... M4
River Bend Bike Trail
... Pg.10 ..... L,M3
Tekakwitha Woods Nature
Center ... Pg.11 ..... M4

# STARKS
Page 2 ....C5

# SUGAR GROVE
Pages 8,16,17,20

**STREETS**
Abbey Ct. ... Pg.8,16 ... C,P5
Air Park Dr. ... Pg.16 ..... F2,P4
Annette Ct. ... Pg.16 ..... F2
Annettes Ln. ... Pg.16 ..... F2
Arbor Ave. ... Pg.16 ..... F4
Ashbury Ct. ... Pg.8,17 ... C,P5
Aster Pl. ... Pg.8 ..... P5
Bastian Dr. ... Pg.16 ..... F4
Bedford Ave. ... Pg.16 ..... F4
Birch St. ... Pg.8,17 ... D,P5
Black Walnut Dr. Pg.8,16 C6,G5
Bliss Rd. ... Pg.8,16 ... D,O5
Bridgestone Ct. Pg.8,16 ... D,P5
Bristol Ct. ... Pg.20 ..... F5
Brock Dr. ... Pg.8 ..... P4
Brookhaven Ln. Pg.20 ..... G5
Calkins Dr. ... Pg.16 ..... E,O5
Capitol Dr. ... Pg.8,16 ... E,O5
Cardinal Crest Dr.
... Pg.17 ..... D5
Carriage Hill Ct. Pg.8,16 E4,O5
Carriage Hill Ln. Pg.8,16 E4,O5
Chelsea Ave. ... Pg.16 ..... F4
Cherry St. ... Pg.17 ..... C5
Cornwall Cir. ... Pg.8,17 ... C5
Courtney Cir. ... Pg.8,16 ... C,P6
Cross Ct. ... Pg.16 ..... F5
Cross St. ... Pg.16 ..... F4
Cyndi Dr. ... Pg.8 ..... P4
Denny Rd. ... Pg.8,17 C6,N5
Densmore Rd. ... Pg.16 ..... F4
Division Dr. ... Pg.8,16 E4,O5
Donald St. ... Pg.16 ..... F3
Dover Ct. ... Pg.16 ..... F5
Duffy Ln. ... Pg.8,16 ... D2,P4
Dugan Rd. ... Pg.8,16 ... D2,P4
Edgewater Ln. ... Pg.20 ..... G5
Edgewood Dr. ... Pg.8,17 C6,G5
Elm St. ... Pg.8,17 ... C,P5
Fairlee Ct. ... Pg.8,17 ... C,P5
Fay's Ln. ... Pg.17 ..... F2
Fays Ct. ... Pg.16 ..... F2
First St. ... Pg.16 ..... F4
Forest Tr. ... Pg.17 ..... C6
Forest Tr. ... Pg.8 ..... O6
Galena Blvd. ... Pg.8 ..... O4
Garnart Rd. ... Pg.16 ..... F4
Good View Rd. ... Pg.17 ..... E6
Green Huron Ln. Pg.8,17 D6,P5
Gregory Pl. ... Pg.8,17 C6,G5
Grove St. ... Pg.16 ..... F4
Hampshire Dr. ... Pg.17 ..... C6
Haverhill Ct. ... Pg.8,17 ... C,P5
Interstate 88 ... Pg.8 ..... N6
Jason Rd. ... Pg.8,16 D3,O5
Jennifer Ct. ... Pg.8,17 ... C,P5
Jericho Rd. ... Pg.8 ..... Q5
Jody Ln. ... Pg.8,16 D4,O5
Jonathon Dr. ... Pg.8 ..... P4
Joy Ct. ... Pg.17 ..... F5
Ke-De-Ka Rd. ... Pg.8,16 D4,O5
Kimberly Ct. ... Pg.8 ..... P4
Kingsman Ct. ... Pg.8,17 D6,P5
Knights Bridge Dr.
... Pg.8,17 ... C,P5
Lakeridge Ct. ... Pg.8,17 C6,G5
Lindsay Dr. ... Pg.8,16 D4,O5
Litchfield Ct. ... Pg.8,17 ... C,P5
Longview Ct. ... Pg.8,17 C6,G5
Main St. ... Pg.16 ..... F4
Mallard Ln. ... Pg.20 ..... F5
Manor Hill Pl. ... Pg.8,17 D6,P5
Maple St. ... Pg.16 ..... F4
Marybeth Ln. ... Pg.8 ..... P4
McCannon St. ... Pg.16 ..... F4
Meadowlark Run
... Pg.17 ..... D5
Meadows Ct. ... Pg.16 ..... F4
Meadows Dr. ... Pg.16 ..... F4
Merrill New Rd. Pg.8,17 ... C,P5
Merrill Rd. ... Pg.8,16 C4,O5
Molly Dr. ... Pg.8 ..... P4
Monna St. ... Pg.16 ..... F4
Neil Rd. ... Pg.16 ..... F4
New Bond St. ... Pg.8,17 D6,P5
Orleans St. ... Pg.8,17 ... C,P5
Park Ave. ... Pg.8,17 . E,O5
Patricia Ln. ... Pg.16 ..... F4
Pebblebrook Ct. Pg.17 ..... G5
Pembridge Pl. ... Pg.8,17 C6,P5
Pine St. ... Pg.17 ..... C5
Pinecrest Dr. ... Pg.8,17 . C,O6
Queens Gate Cir. Pg.8,20 . F,P5
Richard St. ... Pg.16 ..... F4
Saddlebrook Ln. Pg.20 ..... G5
Shelburne Ln. ... Pg.8,17 D2,P5
Snow Ct. ... Pg.8,17 ... C,P5
Snow St. ... Pg.16 ..... F4
Spruce St. ... Pg.8,17 ... C,P5
Stamford Pl. ... Pg.8 ..... P5
Stamford Rd. ... Pg.8 ..... P5
Stanley Rd. ... Pg.16 ..... F4
State Rte 47 ... Pg.16 ..... F4
State Rte 56 ... Pg.8 ..... P5
Stayner Rd. ... Pg.8,16 D4,O5
Stonehill Cir. ... Pg.17 ..... C5
Stonewall Ct. ... Pg.8 ..... P5
Sugar Ln. ... Pg.17 ..... F5
Sugar St. ... Pg.16 ..... F4
Terry Dr. ... Pg.16 ..... F4
Tom St. ... Pg.8 ..... P4
Tudor Ct. ... Pg.8,17 C6,P5
US Rte 30 ... Pg.8 ..... P5
Washford Pl. ... Pg.8,17 C6,P5
West Galena Rd. Pg.17 ..... E5
West St. ... Pg.16 ..... F4
Wild Ginger Tr. Pg.8,16 D,O4
Whippoorwill Way
... Pg.17 ..... C5
Whispering Oaks Ln.
... Pg.8,16 F2,P4
Wild Ginger Tr. ... Pg.8 ..... P5
Willow St. ... Pg.8,17 ... C,P5

Windstone Dr. ... Pg.17 ..... C5
Windstone Ln. ... Pg.17 ..... C5
Woodbury Ct. ... Pg.8,17 D6,P5
Woodthrush Dr. Pg.17 ..... D5
Wynstone Dr. ... Pg.8 ..... P5
Yolane Ct. ... Pg.16 ..... F4
Yolane Dr. ... Pg.16 ..... F4
1st St. ... Pg.16 ..... F4

**CEMETERIES**
Sugar Grove Cem.
... Pg.17 ..... D5

**FOREST PRESERVES**
Bliss Wood Forest Preserve
... Pg.8,17 ... D,O5
Hannaford Woods Forest
Preserve ... Pg.16 ..... C4

**GOLF COURSES**
Prestbury Golf Course
... Pg.17 ..... E6

**PARKS**
Chelsea Park ... Pg.20 ..... F5
Park ... Pg.17 ..... D6
Sheffield Plains Park
... Pg.20 ..... F5

**SCHOOLS**
Elementary Sch. Pg.17 ..... D6
Waubonsee Comm. College
... Pg.8,16 C4,N5

**MISCELLANEOUS**
Aurora Municipal Airport
... Pg.16 ..... F3
Community Ctr. ... Pg.16 ..... F3
Municipal Center Pg.16 ..... F3

# SUGAR GROVE TOWNSHIP
Pages 8,16-18,20,21

**STREETS**
Alderley Dr. ... Pg.8 ..... P5
Ashe Rd. ... Pg.8,16 ... E4
Ashwood Ct. ... Pg.8,17 . D,P6
Barnes Rd. ... Pg.20 ..... F8
Bertram Rd. ... Pg.20 ..... J6
Beta Dr. ... Pg.8 ..... P4
Birchwood Ct. ... Pg.8,17 . D,P6
Black Walnut Dr. Pg.20 ..... L6
Blackberry Ct. ... Pg.8,17 D5,P6
Blackberry Rd. ... Pg.20 ..... J8
Bliss Rd. ... Pg.20 ..... J8
Bluegrass Dr. ... Pg.20 ..... J8
Briar Gate Ct. ... Pg.8,17 ... D5
Brookhaven Cir. Pg.8 ..... O6
Brookhaven Ln. Pg.8 ..... P6
Buckingham Dr. Pg.8,17 . D,P6
Bury Ct. ... Pg.8 ..... P6
Capitol Dr. ... Pg.16 ..... E,O5
Cedar Gate Ct. ... Pg.8 ..... P6
Cedargate Cir. ... Pg.8 ..... P6
Churchill Path ... Pg.8 ..... P6
Cobbler Ct. ... Pg.8 ..... P6
Cobbler Ln. ... Pg.8 ..... P6
Creek View Rd. Pg.20 ..... J8
Deerpath Rd. ... Pg.17 ..... D,E8
Denny Rd. ... Pg.17 ..... C6
Densmore Rd. ... Pg.17 ..... E7
Dorchester Ct. ... Pg.8,17 D,P6
Douglas Ln. ... Pg.8,17 D5,P6
Dugan Rd. ... Pg.16 ..... G2
East-West Tollway
... Pg.17 ..... O6
Edgeware Ln. ... Pg.8 ..... P6
Fernlee Ct. ... Pg.8,17 D5,P6
Glengary Ln. ... Pg.8,17 D5,P6
Golf View Rd. ... Pg.8 ..... P6
Gordon Rd. ... Pg.17 ..... F7
Greenwood Ct. Pg.8 ..... P6
Greenwood Rd. Pg.8 ..... P6
Hanes Rd. ... Pg.17 ..... D6
Hanover Ln. ... Pg.8,17 D5,P6
Hardwick Ct. ... Pg.8,17 D5,P6
Harter Rd. ... Pg.16 ..... C3
Hathaway Crescent
... Pg.8,17 . D,P6
Hathaway St. ... Pg.8,17 D5,P6
Hatherly Ct. ... Pg.8,17 D5,P6
Hazelcrest Dr. ... Pg.8 ..... N4
Healey Rd. ... Pg.17 ..... B6
Heaton Ct. ... Pg.8,17 D5,P6
Hillcrest Dr. ... Pg.8,17 D5,P6
Jericho Rd. ... Pg.20 ..... H7
Ka-De-Ka Rd. ... Pg.16 ..... D4
Kasar Ct. ... Pg.8 ..... O6
Laura Ave. ... Pg.17 ..... O5
Laura Ln. ... Pg.8 ..... P6
Linden Ct. ... Pg.8 ..... P6
Lyndale Rd. ... Pg.20 ..... J8
Mallard Ln. ... Pg.8 ..... P6
Massfield Ct. ... Pg.17 ..... D6
May St. ... Pg.17 ..... D5
McCannon Rd. Pg.16 ..... H2
Merill Rd. ... Pg.17 ..... C5
Merrill New Rd. Pg.17 ..... D5
Midfield Dr. ... Pg.17 ..... D5
Mossfield Ct. ... Pg.8 ..... P6
New Indian Trail Dr.
... Pg.18 ..... D8
Normandie Dr. ... Pg.8,17 . D,P6
Old Farm Ct. ... Pg.8,17 D5,P6
Old Oak Rd. ... Pg.16 ..... C3
Patton Dr. ... Pg.18 ..... D8
Pebblebrook Ct. Pg.8 ..... N4
Pembroke Ct. ... Pg.8 ..... P6
Penny Ln. ... Pg.17 ..... D5
Prairie St. ... Pg.20 ..... G7,8
Ridge Dr., W. ... Pg.17 ..... D5
Saddlewood Dr. Pg.8,17 D5,P6
Scott Rd. ... Pg.16 ..... D3
Shagbark Ln. ... Pg.17 ..... E8
Star Ln. ... Pg.8 ..... Q5
State Rte. 47 ... Pg.17 ..... C8
State Rte. 56 ... Pg.17 ..... F4
Sunnyside Dr. ... Pg.20 ..... J8
Tanner Rd. ... Pg.17 ..... B7
Thornapple Tree Rd.
... Pg.8 ..... N4
U.S. Hwy. 30 ... Pg.8 ..... Q6

Walnut Cir. ... Pg.8,17 . D,P6
West Galena Rd. Pg.17 ..... E5
Whispering Oaks W.
... Pg.16 ..... F2
Wild Ginger Tr. ... Pg.17 ..... C6
Wildwood Dr. ... Pg.17 ..... C7
Wiltshire Ln. ... Pg.8 ..... N4
Windsor Ct. E. Pg.8,17 . E,P6
Windsor Ct., W. Pg.8,17 . E,P6
Windsor Rd. ... Pg.17 ..... D6
Winwood Ct. ... Pg.8,17 D5,P6
Winwood Dr. ... Pg.8,17 D5,P6
Winthrop New Rd.
... Pg.17 ..... D6
Yorkshire Cir. ... Pg.8 ..... P6

**FOREST PRESERVES**
Aurora West F.P.
... Pg.17 ..... D7
Bliss Woods F.P.
... Pg.17 ..... D7
Culver F.P. ... Pg.8,17 E7,O6
Hannaford Woods F.P.
... Pg.16 ..... C4
Prairie Kame F.P.
... Pg.16 ..... C2

**GOLF COURSES**
Prestbury Golf Course
... Pg.8 ..... O6

**SCHOOLS**
Resurrection Lutheran Sch.
... Pg.17 ..... C8
Waubonsee Comm. College
... Pg.16 ..... C4

**MISCELLANEOUS**
Jericho Sports Complex
... Pg.20 ..... J8
Orchard/88 Business Park
... Pg.17 ..... C8
Virgil Gilman Nature Trail
... Pg.17 ..... E5

# TROXEL
Page 7...M1

# UDINA
Page 2...E7

# VALLEY VIEW
Page 6...H8

# VIRGIL
Page 4

**STREETS**
Country Ln. ..... H3
Meadows St. ..... H3
Meredith Rd. ..... H3
Prairie St. ..... H3
Sauber Rd. ..... H3
State Route 64 ..... H3
Sunset St. ..... H3
Welter Rd. ..... H3

# VIRGIL TOWNSHIP
Page 4

**STREETS**
Beith Rd. ..... J1
Butts Rd. ..... J2
Country Line Rd. ..... J1
Fabris Rd. ..... H2
Francis Rd. ..... K3
Freeland Rd. ..... K3
I.C. Trail ..... K3
Lees Rd. ..... K3
McGough Rd. ..... H1
McNulty Rd. ..... J2
Meredith Rd. ..... K4
Old State Rd. ..... G1
Peplow Rd. ..... H2
Pin Oaks Ln. ..... J2
Ramm Rd. ..... G2
Ramm Wood Dr. ..... G1
Read Rd. ..... N4
Root Lane ..... J3
Saddlewood Dr. ..... K4
Sauber Rd. ..... H3
Snyder Rd. ..... G2
State Rte. 38 ..... K2
State Rte. 64 ..... H3
Thatcher Rd. ..... J2
Warford Rd. ..... H2
Welter Rd. ..... H2
Winters Rd. ..... J2

**FOREST PRESERVES**
Elburn Forest Preserve ... K4

# WASCO
Page 5...J6

# WAYNE
Pages 6,11
(Portions within DuPage County
for additional listings,
see Sections 3 & 5)

**STREETS**
Army Trail Rd. ... Pg.11 ..... O4
Ashley Ln. ... Pg.11 ..... O4
Behles Rd. ... Pg.11 ..... R3
Brewster Creek Cir.
... Pg.11 ..... Q2
Country Club Rd.
... Pg.11 ..... O4
Dunham Ct. ... Pg.11 ..... R4
Dunham Ct. ... Pg.11 ..... R4
Dunham Ln. ... Pg.11 ..... R4
Dunham Rd. ... Pg.11 ..... R4
Fletcher Rd. ... Pg.11 ..... Q5
Haw Rd. ... Pg.11 ..... O4
Honey Hill Ct. ... Pg.11 ..... R5
Hub Rd. ... Pg.11 ..... O4
Lamplight Tr. ... Pg.11 ..... P4
Mare Barn Ln. ... Pg.11 ..... P4
Nelson Dr. ... Pg.11 ..... P5
Pearson Dr. ... Pg.11 ..... O4
Robin Ln. ... Pg.11 ..... P4

Saw Mill Tr. ... Pg.11 ..... P5
Serinne Ln. ... Pg.11 ..... R4
Shagbark Ln. ... Pg.11 ..... R3
Sulkey Rd. ... Pg.11 ..... Q3
Surrey Rd. ... Pg.11 ..... O3
Thorncroft Dr. ... Pg.11 ..... O4
Wayne Rd. ... Pg.11 ..... R3
White Thorn Rd. Pg.11 ..... Q5
Woodland Dr. ... Pg.10 ..... M5
Woodland Dr. ... Pg.11 ..... R3
Woodmere ... Pg.11 ..... R3
Woodmere Ct. ... Pg.11 ..... R3

**MISCELLANEOUS**
Dunham Hunt Club
... Pg.11 ..... Q4
Dunham Woods Riding Club
... Pg.11 ..... R4

# WEST DUNDEE
Page 3. C9
(For full listings, see Section 5)

# YORKVILLE
(Kendall County)
Page 23

**STREETS**
Adams St. ..... Q5
Adrian St. ..... O4
Anderson Ct. ..... O4
Appletree Ct. ..... P4
Beecher St. ..... O2
Behrens St. ..... O4
Blackberry Ct. ..... O4
Blackberry Ln. ..... O4
Blackhawk Tr. ..... O4
Blaine St. ..... Q2
Boomer Ln. ..... N5
Bridge St. ..... O4
Bristol Ave. ..... P4
Bruell St. ..... P4
Cannonball Tr. ..... N5
Center Pkwy. ..... O4
Center St. ..... P4
Cheshire Ct. ..... N5
Church St. ..... P4
Colonial Pkwy. ..... Q2
Colton St. ..... P4
Conover Ct. ..... O4
Countryside Pkwy. ..... O4
Dickson Ct. ..... O4
Dolph St. ..... Q5
Dover Ct. ..... N5
Elizabeth St. ..... Q2
Elm St. ..... P5
Essex Ct. ..... N5
Fairhaven Dr. ..... N5
Fox St. ..... P4
Freemont St. ..... O4
Game Farm Rd. ..... P4
Gawne Ln. ..... P4
Heustis St. ..... Q5
Hillcrest Ave. ..... P4
Hydraulic Ave. ..... P4
Illini Dr. ..... Q4
Jackson St. ..... P4
Jefferson St. ..... P4
Johnson St. ..... P4
Kendall Dr. ..... O4
Kennedy Rd. ..... N5
King St. ..... P4
Landmark Ave. ..... P4
Leisure St. ..... P4
Liberty St. ..... P4
Madison St. ..... Q4
Main St., S. & W. ..... Q5
Martin Ave. ..... P4
McHugh Rd. ..... P4
Mill St. ..... O5
Morgan St. ..... O5
Mulhern Ct. ..... P4
Naden Ct. ..... O4
Newbury Ln. ..... N5
Oakwood St. ..... P4
Orange St. ..... O5
Palmer Ct. ..... O4
Park St. ..... P4
Powers Ct. ..... O4
Ridge St. ..... P4
River Rd. ..... P4
Sanders Ct. ..... P4
Schoolhouse Rd. ..... O2
Somonauk St. ..... P4
Spring St. ..... P4
State St. ..... Q5
Strawberry Ln. ..... P4
Sunset Ave. ..... P4
Teri Ln. ..... N5
U.S. Rte. 34 ..... Q4,5
Van Emmons Rd. ..... P5
Veterans Pkwy. ..... P5
Walnut St. ..... P4
Washington St. ..... O5
West St. ..... P4
Wheaton Ave. ..... M4
Woodworth St. ..... M4
Worsley St. ..... P4

**CEMETERIES**
Elmwood Cemetery ..... P4

**PARKS**
Bicentennial Park ..... Q5
Hydraulic Park ..... Q4
Jack Purcell Park ..... N5
Prairie Park ..... P5
Van Emmon Mem. Park ... Q5

**SCHOOLS**
Circle Center Middle Sch. .. Q4
Yorkville Grade School ..... P4
Yorkville High School ..... P4

**SHOPPING CENTERS**
Countryside Shopping Center O5

**MISCELLANEOUS**
Beecher Community Center .. P4
City Hall ..... P4
Library ..... P4
Police Dept. ..... P4
Post Office ..... P4
Yorkville Business Center .. M4

# ELGIN AND VICINITY

## SECTION 5

## LEGEND

 INTERSTATE HIGHWAY

 U.S. HIGHWAY

 STATE HIGHWAY

———————— OTHER PRIMARY THRU ROADS

———————— ALL OTHER ROADS

+++++++ RAILROAD

• SCHOOL

FIRE STATION

■ POINTS OF INTEREST

 FOREST PRESERVE

 PARK

 GOLF COURSE

 CEMETERY

 INSTITUTIONAL

RIVER OR LAKE

**TURN PAGE FOR ORIENTATION MAP**

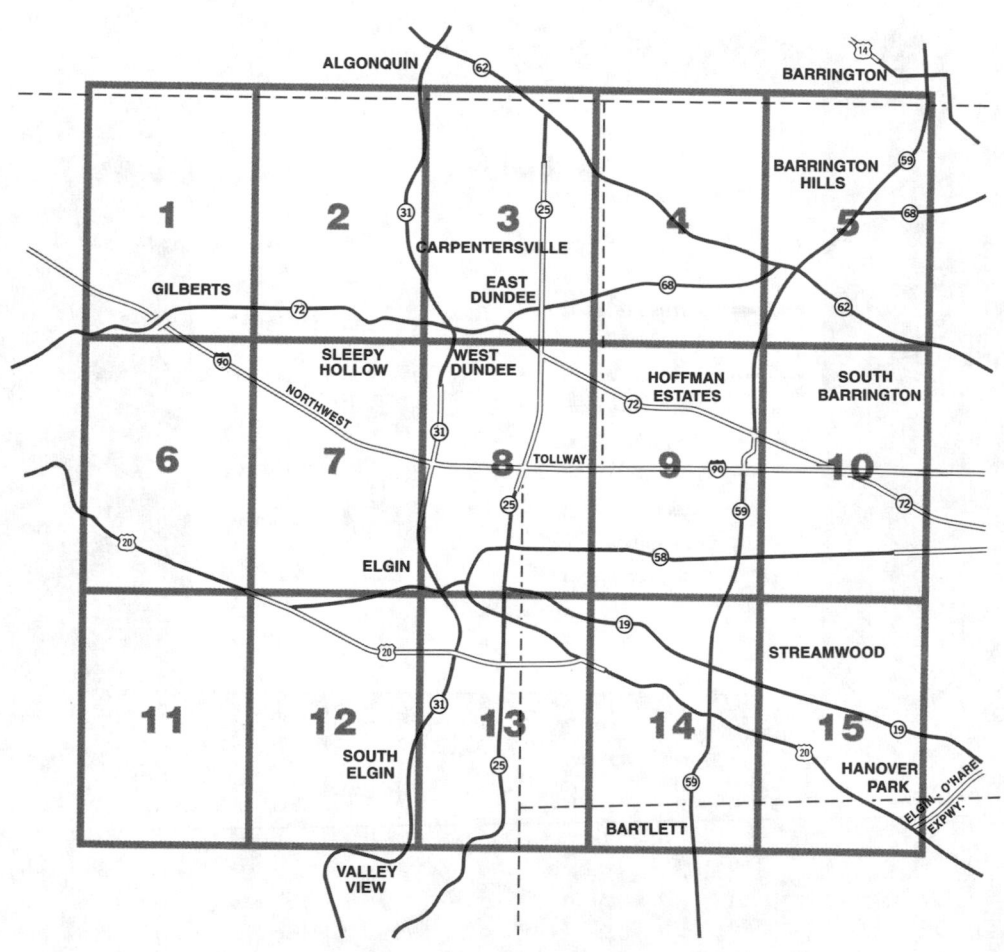

# SECTION 5
## ORIENTATION MAP

Information on this page is to be used for general reference only.
For definitive listings of all information, see index at end of this section.

ALGONQUIN

BARRINGTON

BARRINGTON
HILLS

1    2    3    4    5

CARPENTERSVILLE

EAST
DUNDEE

GILBERTS

SLEEPY
HOLLOW

WEST
DUNDEE

HOFFMAN
ESTATES

SOUTH
BARRINGTON

NORTHWEST

6    7    8    9    10

TOLLWAY

ELGIN

STREAMWOOD

11    12    13    14    15

SOUTH
ELGIN

HANOVER
PARK

ELGIN - O'HARE
EXPWY.

BARTLETT

VALLEY
VIEW

II

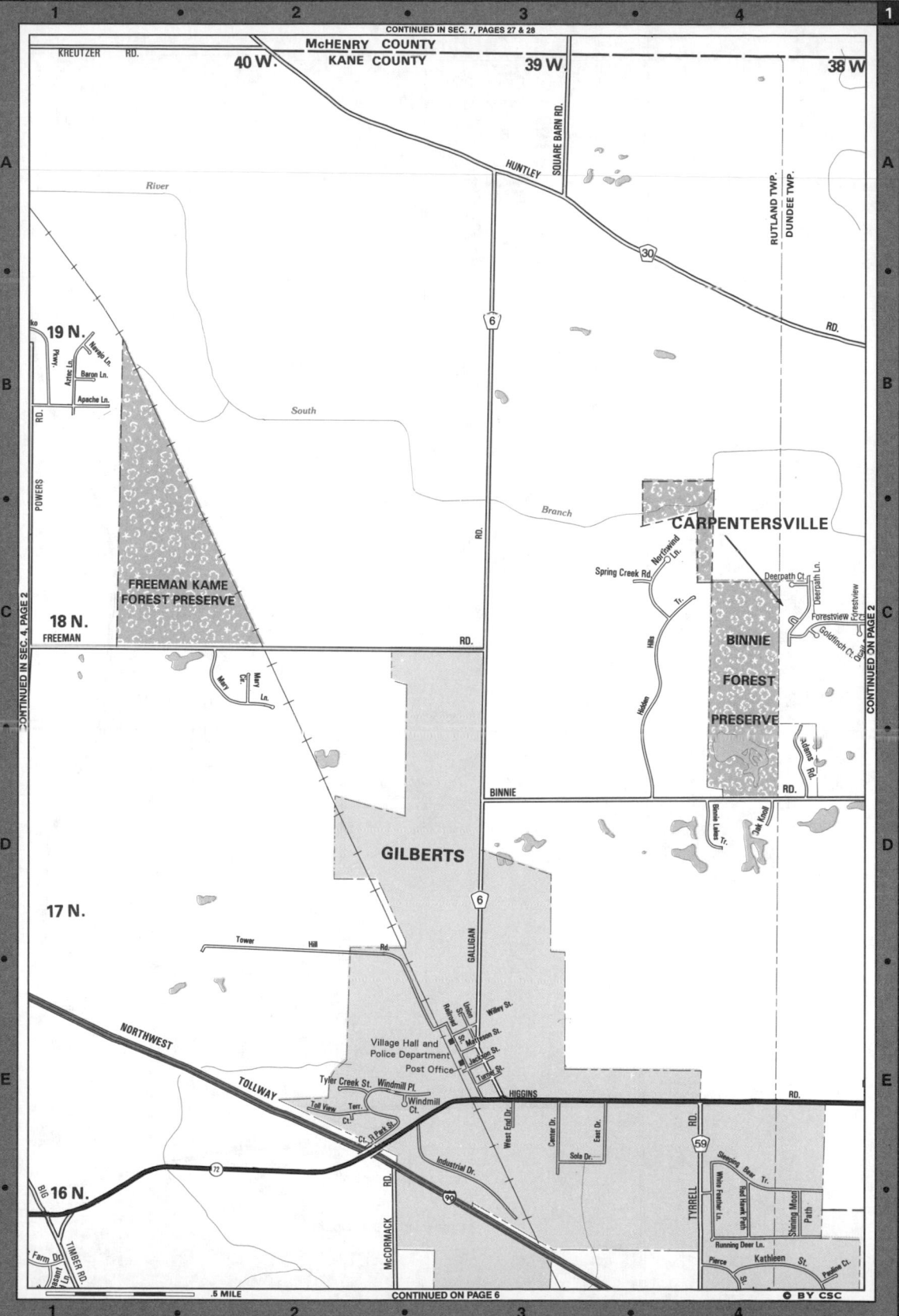

CONTINUED IN SEC. 7, PAGES 27 & 28

McHENRY COUNTY
KANE COUNTY

KREUTZER RD.

40 W.

39 W.

38 W.

HUNTLEY

SQUARE BARN RD.

RUTLAND TWP.
DUNDEE TWP.

A

River

30

RD.

19 N.

B

South

CONTINUED IN SEC. 4, PAGE 2

POWERS

Branch

CARPENTERSVILLE

Spring Creek Rd.

Northwind Ln.

Deerpath Ct.

Deerpath Ln.

Forestview

C

Forestview Ct.

FREEMAN KAME
FOREST PRESERVE

Goldfinch Ct.

18 N.

FREEMAN

RD.

Hills

Hidden

BINNIE

FOREST

PRESERVE

CONTINUED ON PAGE 2

Mary Ct.

Mary Ln.

Adams Rd.

BINNIE

Binnie Lakes Tr.

Oak Knoll

D

GILBERTS

17 N.

Tower

Hill

Rd.

GALLIGAN

6

NORTHWEST

E

Willey St.

Union St.

Railroad St.

Matteson St.

Jessie St.

Tyler Creek St.

Windmill Pl.

Village Hall and
Police Department

Post Office

Turner St.

West End Dr.

Center Dr.

East Dr.

RD.

TOLLWAY

Toll View
Terr.

Ct.

St. Paul St.

Windmill
Ct.

HIGGINS

Sola Dr.

59

TYRELL

Sleeping Bear Tr.

White Feather Ln.

Shining Moon
Path

16 N.

BIG

TIMBER RD.

72

McCORMACK

RD.

90

Industrial Dr.

Running Deer Ln.

Pierce St.

Kathleen St.

Pauline Ct.

Farm Dr.

.5 MILE

CONTINUED ON PAGE 6

© BY CSC

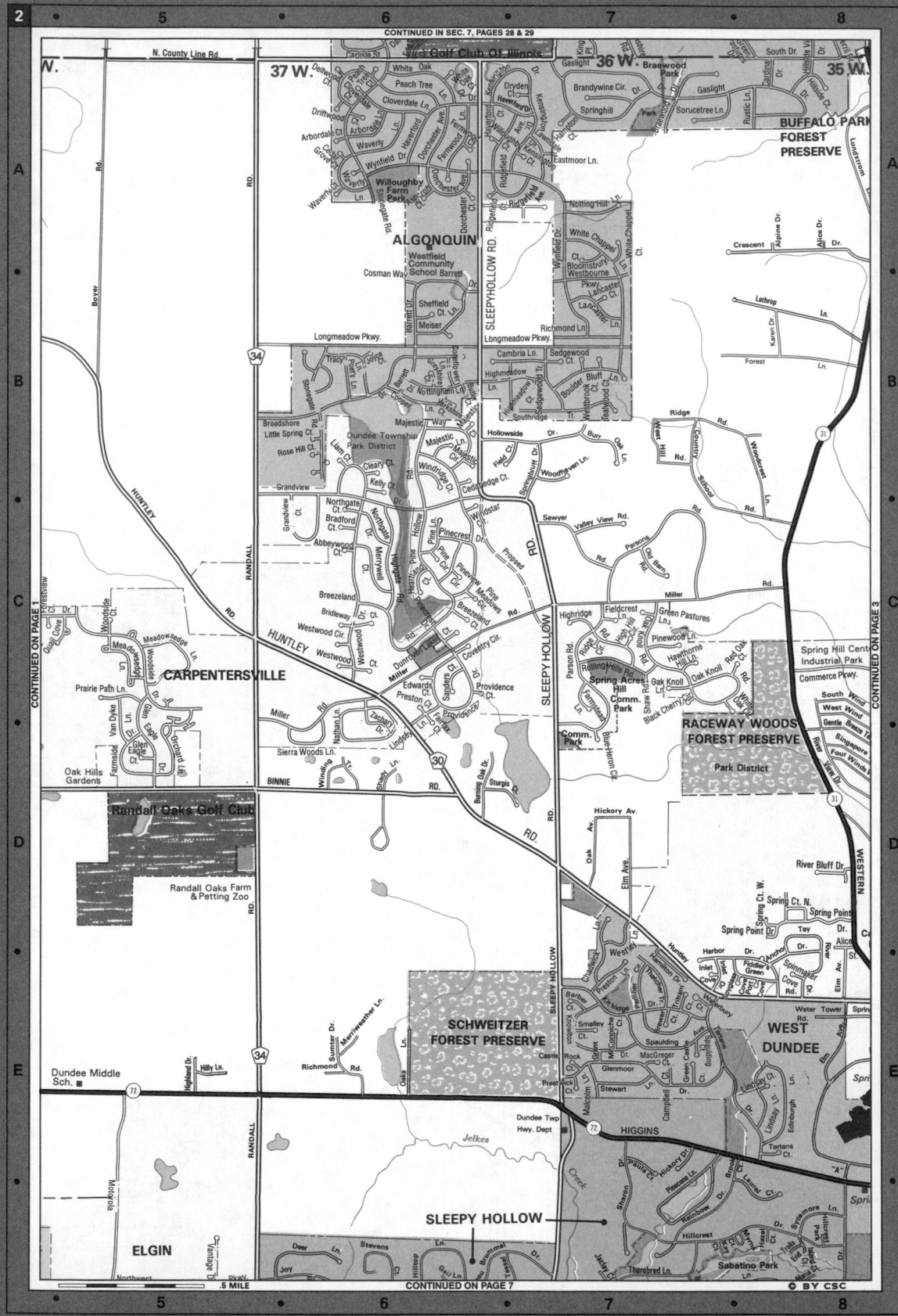

CONTINUED IN SEC. 7, PAGES 28 & 29

Golf Club Of Illinois

37 W. 36 W. Braewood Park 35 W.

Gaslight

**BUFFALO PARK FOREST PRESERVE**

N. County Line Rd.

White Oak

Peach Tree

Cloverdale Ln.

Brandywine Cir.

Springhill

Gaslight

Sorucetree Ln.

Rustic Ln.

South Dr.

Driftwood

Arbordale Ln.

Waverly

Wynfield Dr.

Willoughby Farm Park

Dryden Ct.

Crescent

Alpine Dr.

Alice Dr.

Dr.

Eastmoor Ln.

Notting Hill

Lathrop Ln.

Karen Ct.

A

**ALGONQUIN**

Westfield Community School Barrett

Cosman Way

Sheffield

Meiser

Longmeadow Pkwy.

White Chappel

Bloomsbury Westbourne Pkwy. Lancaster

Richmond Ln.

Forest Ln.

Ridge Rd.

B

Broadshore

Little Spring Ct.

Rose Hill Ct.

Dundee Township Park District

Grandview

Majestic Way

Cambria Ln.

Sedgewood Ct.

Highmeadow Ln.

Southridge Tr.

Hollowside

Boulder Ct.

Bluff Ct.

Burr

Woodhaven Ln.

Woodcrest Rd.

West Hill

Country Rd.

Redford Rd.

**CARPENTERSVILLE**

Oak Hills Gardens

Prairie Path Ln.

Van Dyke

Glen Eagle

Woodside

Meadowsedge Ln.

HUNTLEY RD.

Northgate Ct.

Bradford Ct.

Abbeywood Ct.

Merrywell

Breezeland

Bridleway Dr.

Westwood Cir.

Westwood

Edwards

Preston

Sanders

Coventry Cir.

Providence Ct.

Providence

Sierra Woods Ln.

Windridge Ct.

Pinecrest

Heartland Pines

Pine Ln.

Pine Hollow

Pinewye

Pine Meadows

Dunrobin Lake

Miller

Wildstar Ct.

Prospect

Cedaredge Ln.

Springbluff Rd.

Sawyer

Valley View Rd.

Parsons Rd.

Oak Barn Rd.

Miller Rd.

Highridge

Fieldcrest

Green Pastures

Pinewood Ln.

Hawthorne Dr.

Oak Knoll

Red Oak

Spring Acres Hill Comm. Park

Black Cherry Ct.

Blue Heron Ct.

Shaw Rd.

Comm. Park

**RACEWAY WOODS FOREST PRESERVE**

Park District

Spring Hill Cent. Industrial Park

Commerce Pkwy.

South Wind

West Wind

Gentle Breeze Ter.

Singapore

Four Winds

C

Randall Oaks Golf Club

Randall Oaks Farm & Petting Zoo

Hickory Av.

Oak Av.

Elm Ave.

River Bluff Dr.

Spring Ct. W.

Spring Ct. N.

Spring Point

Dr.

Alice St.

D

SLEEPY HOLLOW RD.

**SCHWEITZER FOREST PRESERVE**

Dundee Middle Sch.

Highland Dr.

Hilly Ln.

Richmond Rd.

Sumter Dr.

Meriweather Ln.

Oaks Ln.

Prestwick Ln.

Castle Rock

Spaulding

MacGregor Dr.

Glenmoor

Stewart Dr.

Huntley

Hamilton Dr.

Harbor

Inlet

Cove

Fiddler Green

Spinnaker

Cove Rd.

Water Tower Rd.

**WEST DUNDEE**

Lindsay Ln.

Edinburgh

Tartans Ct.

E

Dundee Twp. Hwy. Dept.

HIGGINS

"A"

**SLEEPY HOLLOW**

**ELGIN**

Jelkes Creek

Deer Ln.

Stevens Ln.

Joy

Hillcrest

Therobred Ln.

Sabatino Park

Hillcrest Dr.

Sycamore Dr.

Laurel Dr.

Rainbow

CONTINUED ON PAGE 1

CONTINUED ON PAGE 3

.5 MILE

CONTINUED ON PAGE 7

© BY CSC

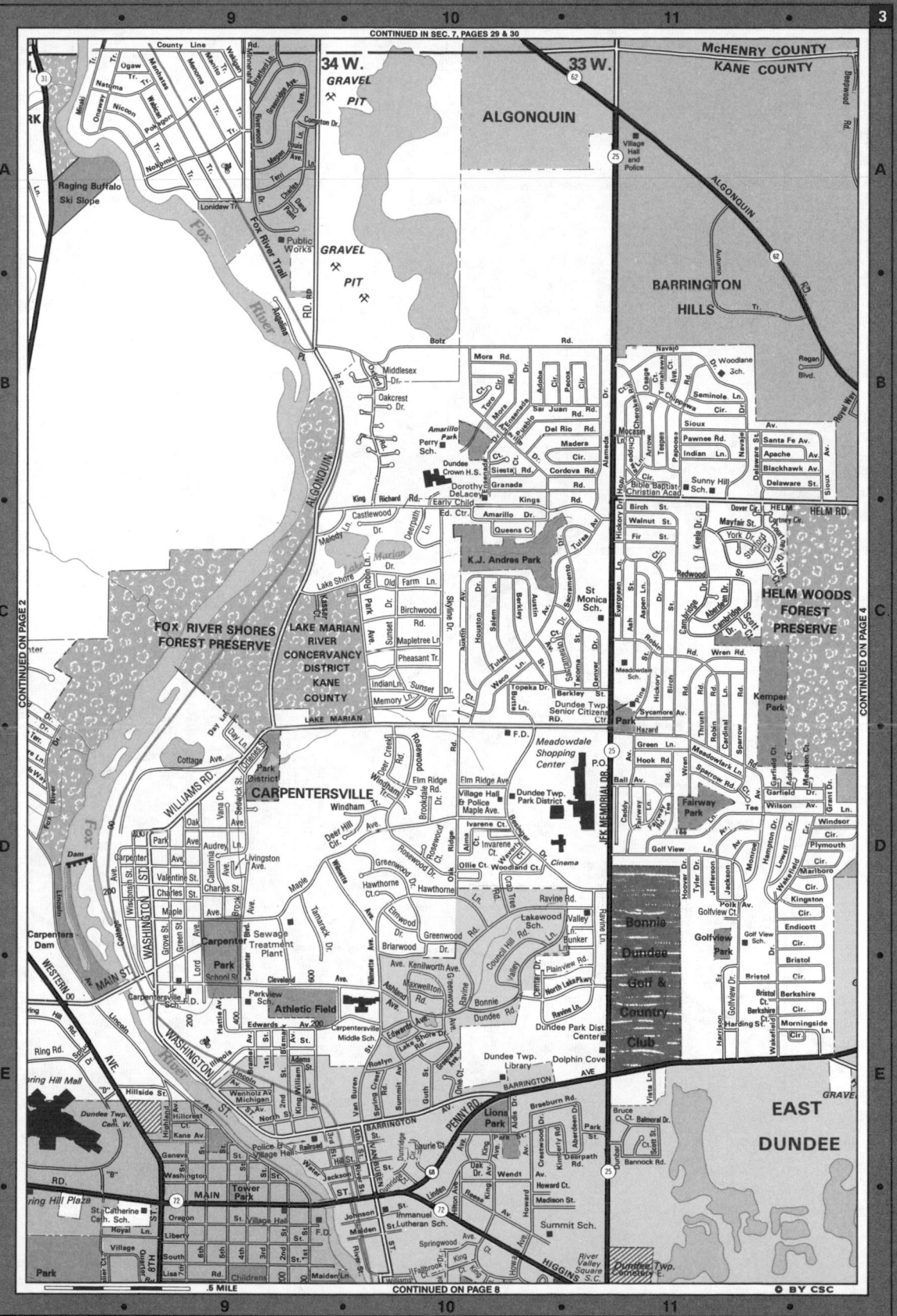

**ALGONQUIN**

McHENRY COUNTY
KANE COUNTY

BARRINGTON
HILLS

34 W.
*GRAVEL
PIT*

33 W.

Village
Hall and
Police

*GRAVEL
PIT*

Raging Buffalo
Ski Slope

Public
Works

Fox River Trail

HELM WOODS
FOREST
PRESERVE

FOX RIVER SHORES
FOREST PRESERVE

LAKE MARIAN
RIVER
CONCERVANCY
DISTRICT
KANE
COUNTY

K.J. Andres Park

Kemper
Park

Meadowdale
Shopping
Center

CARPENTERSVILLE

Dundee Twp.
Park District

Fairway
Park

Bonnie
Dundee
Golf &
Country
Club

Golfview
Park

Carpenter
Park

Sewage
Treatment
Plant

Athletic Field

Lions
Park

EAST
DUNDEE

CONTINUED ON PAGE 2

CONTINUED ON PAGE 4

.5 MILE

© BY CSC

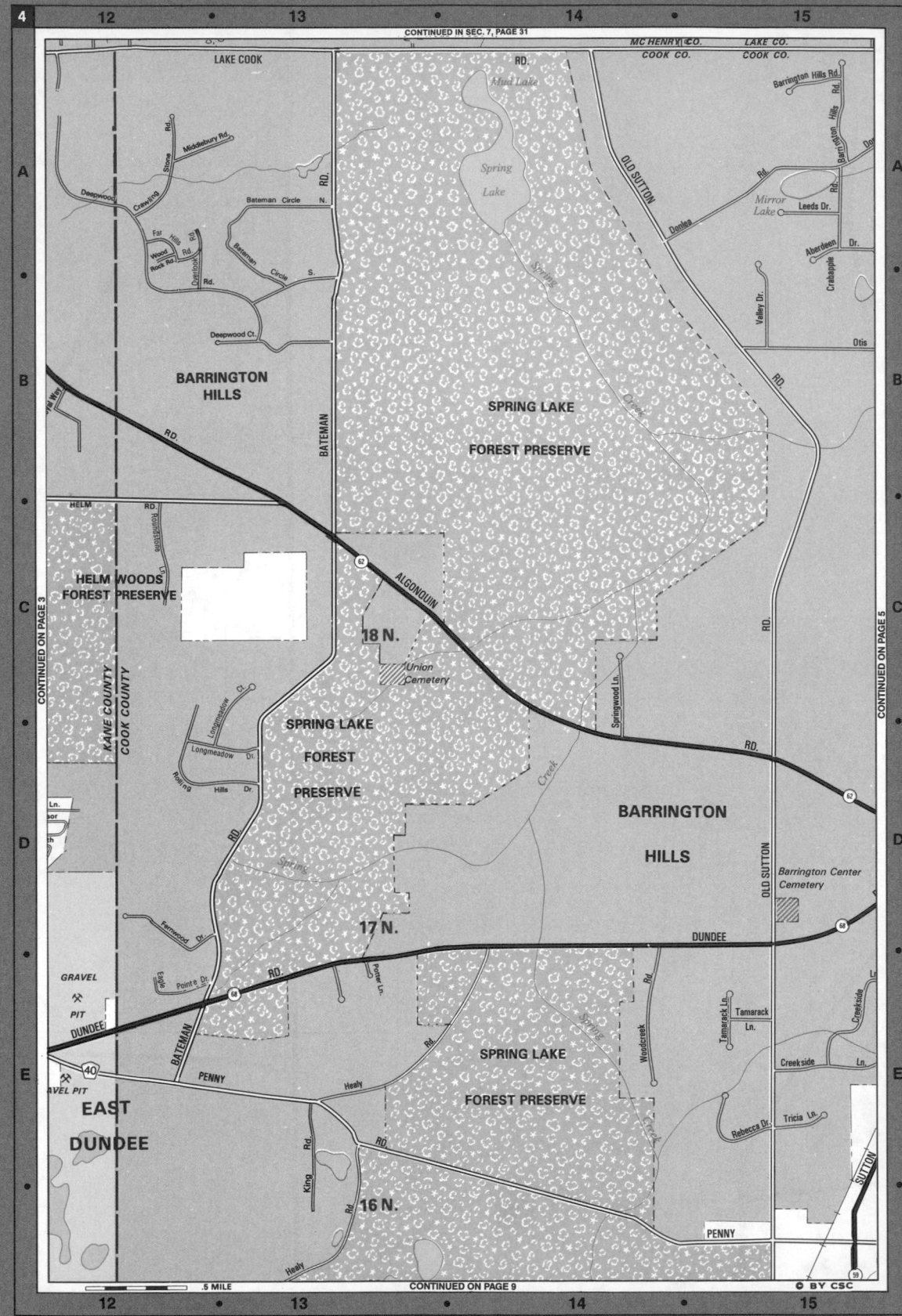

CONTINUED IN SEC. 7, PAGE 31

MC HENRY CO.   LAKE CO.

COOK CO.   COOK CO.

Mud Lake

RD.

Barrington Hills Rd.

Barrington Hills Rd.

LAKE COOK

Middlebury Rd.

Crossing

Stone

Deepwood

Far Hills

Wood Rock Rd.

Overbrook

Rd.

Bateman Circle  N.

Bateman Circle  S.

Deepwood Ct.

Spring Lake

OLD SUTTON

Mirror Lake

Donlea

Leeds Dr.

Aberdeen  Dr.

Crabapple

Valley Dr.

Otis

**BARRINGTON HILLS**

BATEMAN

Spring Creek

**SPRING LAKE**

**FOREST PRESERVE**

RD.

CONTINUED ON PAGE 3

KANE COUNTY

COOK COUNTY

HELM

RD.

Foundation

**HELM WOODS FOREST PRESERVE**

62

ALGONQUIN

**18 N.**

Union Cemetery

Longmeadow Ct.

Longmeadow Dr.

Rolling Hills Dr.

**SPRING LAKE**

**FOREST**

**PRESERVE**

RD.

Spring

Springwood Ln.

RD.

Creek

**BARRINGTON**

**HILLS**

62

RD.

OLD SUTTON

Barrington Center Cemetery

68

CONTINUED ON PAGE 5

Windsor Ln.

**17 N.**

Fernwood Dr.

Eagle

Pointe Dr.

68

Potter Ln.

DUNDEE

Spring Creek

DUNDEE

Woodcreek Rd.

Tamarack Ln.

Tamarack Ln.

Creekside Ln.

*GRAVEL PIT*

DUNDEE

40

*GRAVEL PIT*

BATEMAN

PENNY

Healy

RD.

RD.

**SPRING LAKE**

Creek

Creekside Ln.

Rebecca Dr.

Tricia Ln.

**EAST**

**DUNDEE**

King Rd.

RD.

**FOREST PRESERVE**

SUTTON

59

**16 N.**

Healy Rd.

PENNY

.5 MILE

© BY CSC

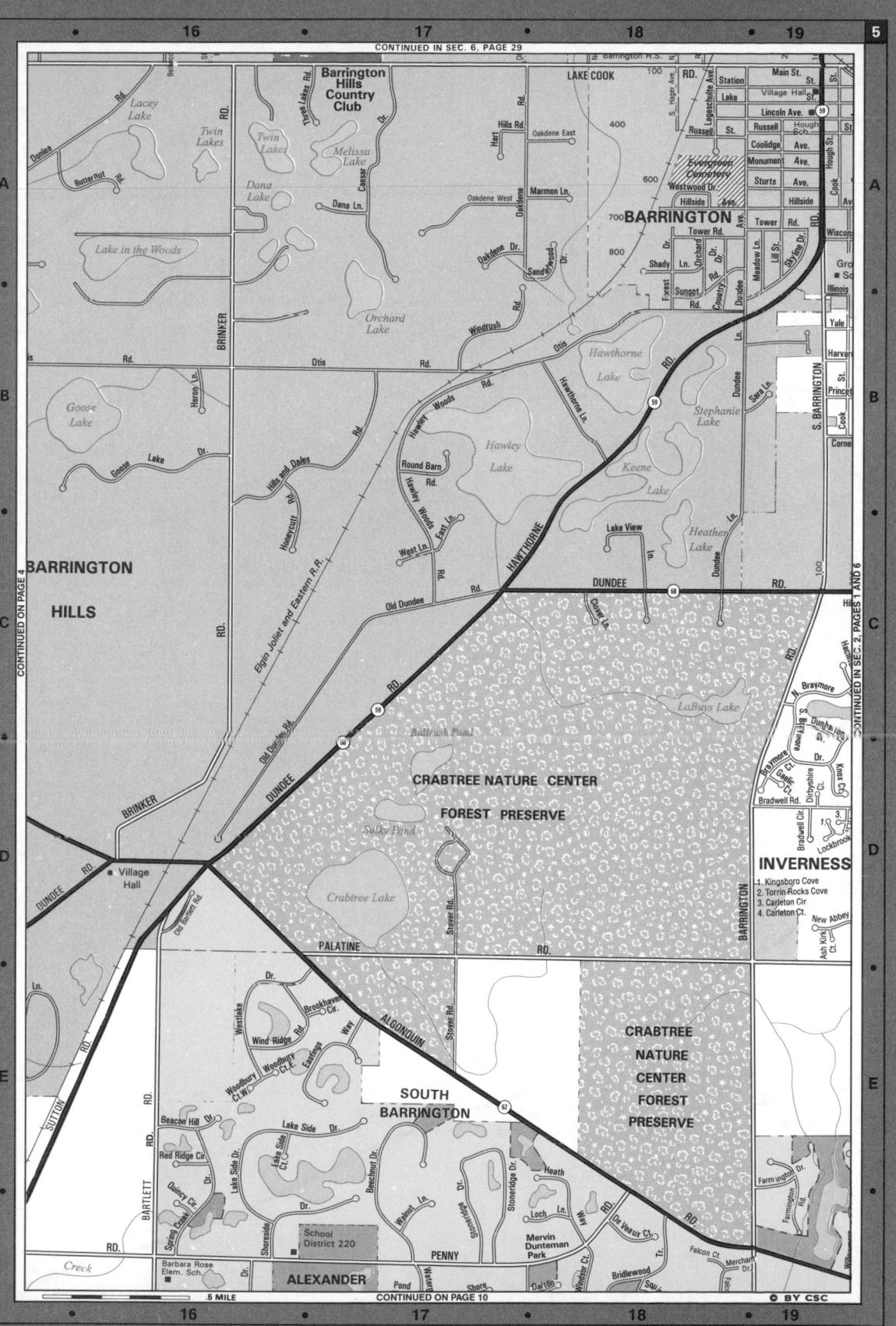

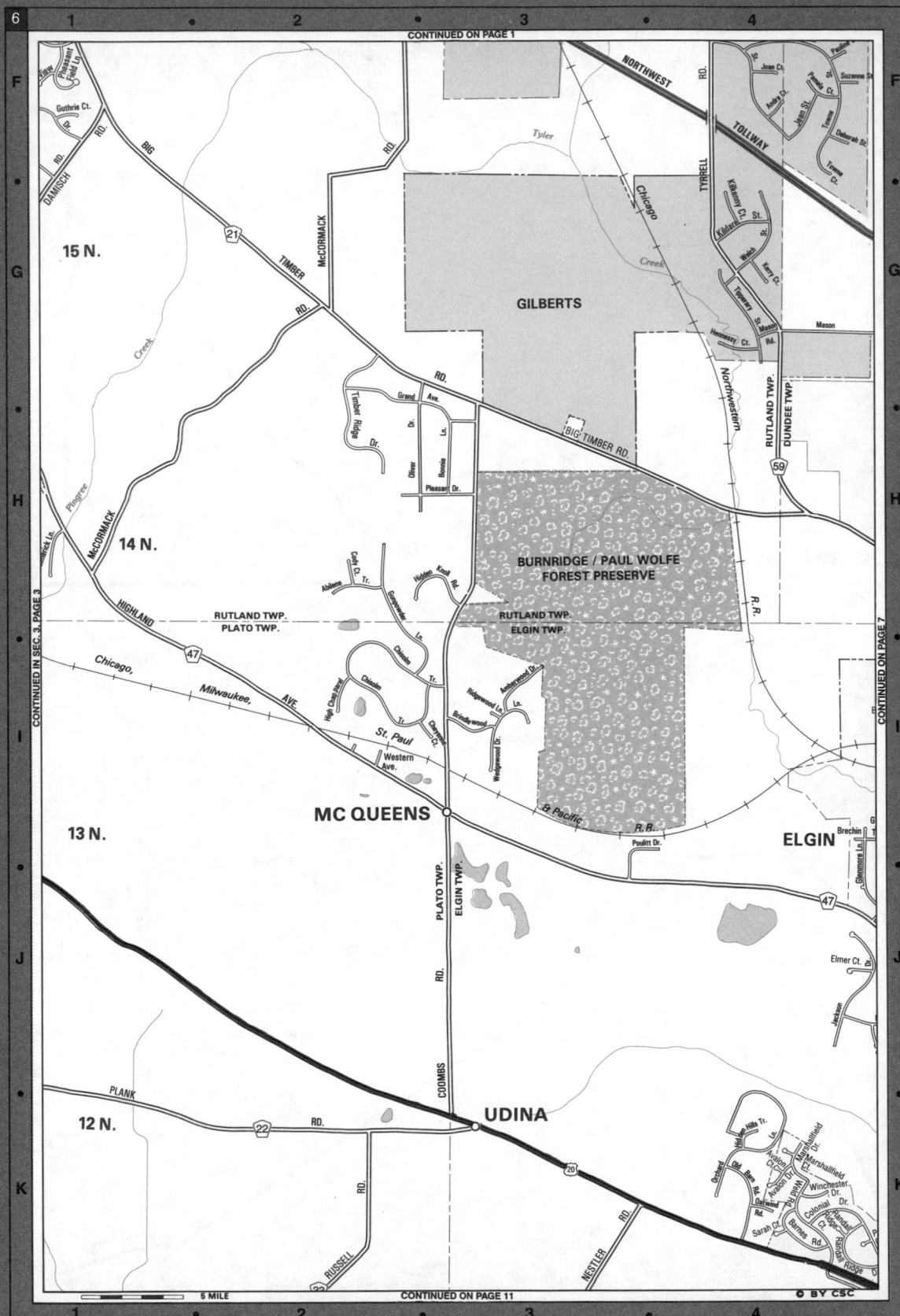

CONTINUED ON PAGE 1

NORTHWEST RD.

TOLLWAY

F

Joan Ct.
Guthrie Ct.
Joan St.
Suzanne St.
Deborah St.
Tawny Ct.

DAMISCH RD.

BIG TIMBER McCORMACK RD.

Tyler

Chicago

TYRRELL

15 N.

21

G

GILBERTS

Killarny Ct.
K'Kildare St.
Kerry Ct.
Welch St.
Tipperary St.
Hennessy Ct.
Mason Rd.
Mason

RUTLAND TWP.
DUNDEE TWP.

Creek

Northwestern

59

RD.

Grand Ave.

Timber Ridge Dr.

Oliver Dr.
Bonnie Ln.
Pleasant Dr.

BIG TIMBER RD.

Creek

H

McCORMACK

Pingree

14 N.

Cody Ct.
Abilene Tr.
Edgewater
Holden Knoll Rd.

BURNRIDGE / PAUL WOLFE
FOREST PRESERVE

R.R.

HIGHLAND

RUTLAND TWP.
PLATO TWP.

RUTLAND TWP.
ELGIN TWP.

CONTINUED IN SEC. 3, PAGE 3

CONTINUED ON PAGE 7

Chicago,

47

Milwaukee, AVE.

High Chaparral

Chisolm
Ln.

Chisolm Tr.

Chisolm
Ct.

Amherwood Dr.

I

St. Paul

Chaparral

Brindlewood

Ridgewood Ln.

Wedgewood Dr.

Western Ave.

MC QUEENS

B. Pacific

R.R.

ELGIN

Brechin

Glenmore Ln.

13 N.

Poulitt Dr.

47

PLATO TWP.
ELGIN TWP.

J

Elmer Ct. Ln.

Jackson

COOMBS RD.

PLANK

Highland Hills Tr.

22 RD.

UDINA

Marshallfield Dr.

12 N.

20

Orchard Old Barn Rd.
Avalon Ct.
Delrand Rd.
Avalon Dr.

Winchester Dr.

Colonial Dr.

Randall Ridge

K

RUSSELL RD.

NESTLER RD.

Saran Ct.
Barnes Rd.
Randall Ridge

22

5 MILE

© BY CSC

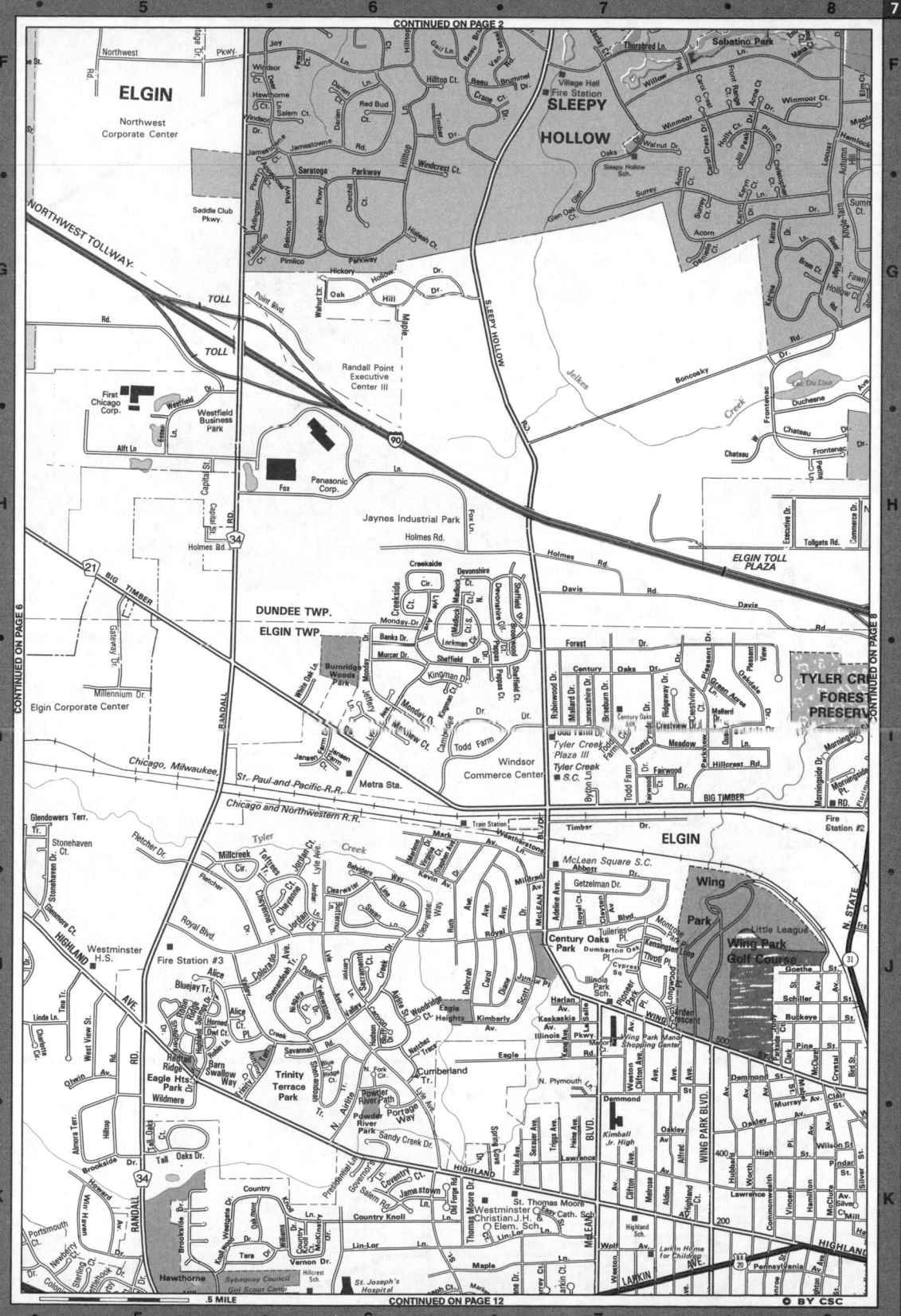

CONTINUED ON PAGE 2

ELGIN

Northwest
Corporate Center

SLEEPY
HOLLOW

CONTINUED ON PAGE 6

CONTINUED ON PAGE 8

DUNDEE TWP.
ELGIN TWP.

TYLER CREEK
FOREST
PRESERVE

ELGIN

CONTINUED ON PAGE 12

.5 MILE

© BY CSC

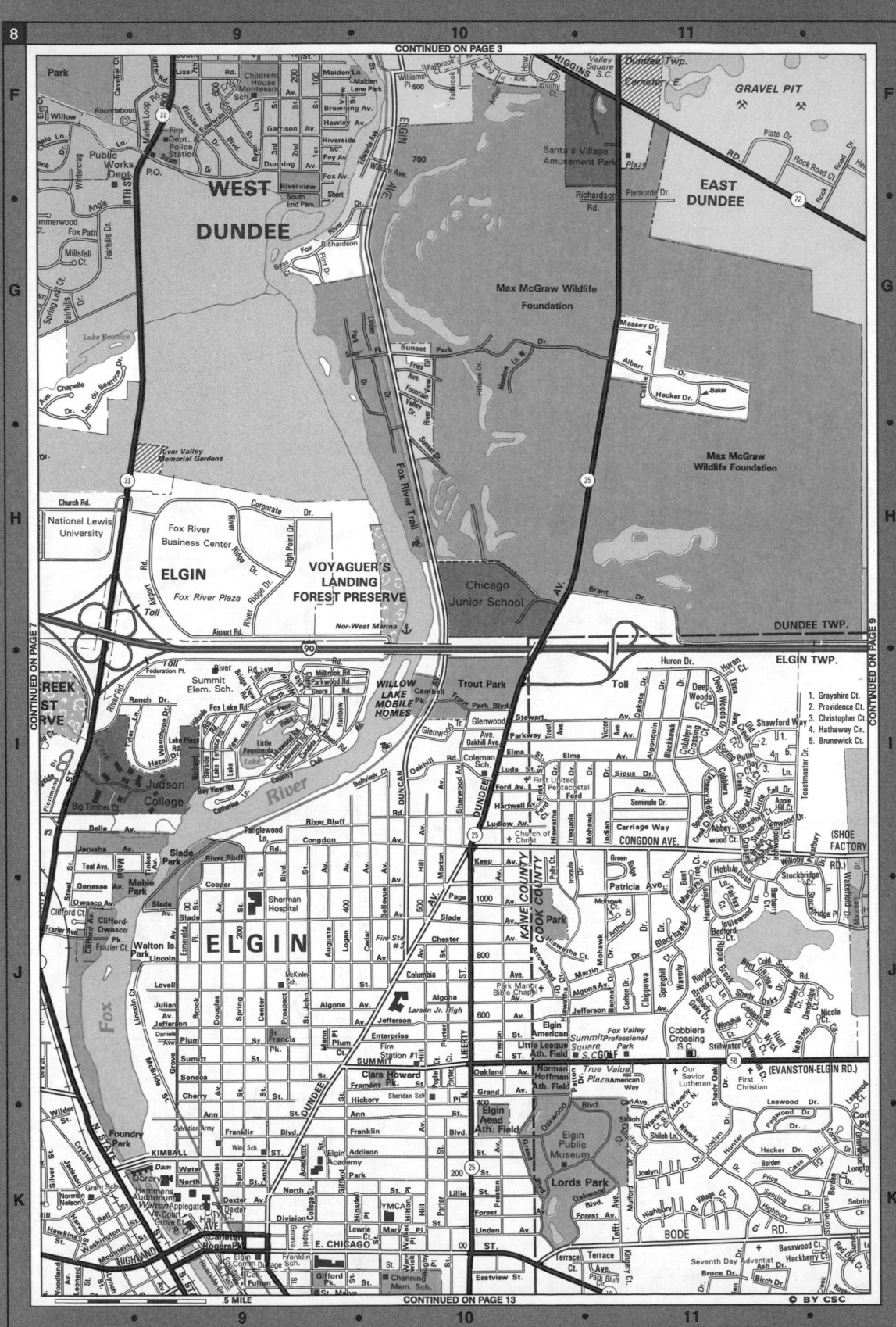

CONTINUED ON PAGE 7

CONTINUED ON PAGE 9

WEST DUNDEE

EAST DUNDEE

GRAVEL PIT

Max McGraw Wildlife Foundation

Max McGraw Wildlife Foundation

ELGIN

VOYAGUER'S LANDING FOREST PRESERVE

National Lewis University

Fox River Business Center

ELGIN

Chicago Junior School

DUNDEE TWP.

ELGIN TWP.

1. Grayshire Ct.
2. Providence Ct.
3. Christopher Ct.
4. Hathaway Cir.
5. Brunswick Ct.

Trout Park

WILLOW LAKE MOBILE HOMES

Judson College

Sherman Hospital

Lords Park

Elgin Public Museum

BODE

.5 MILE

© BY CSC

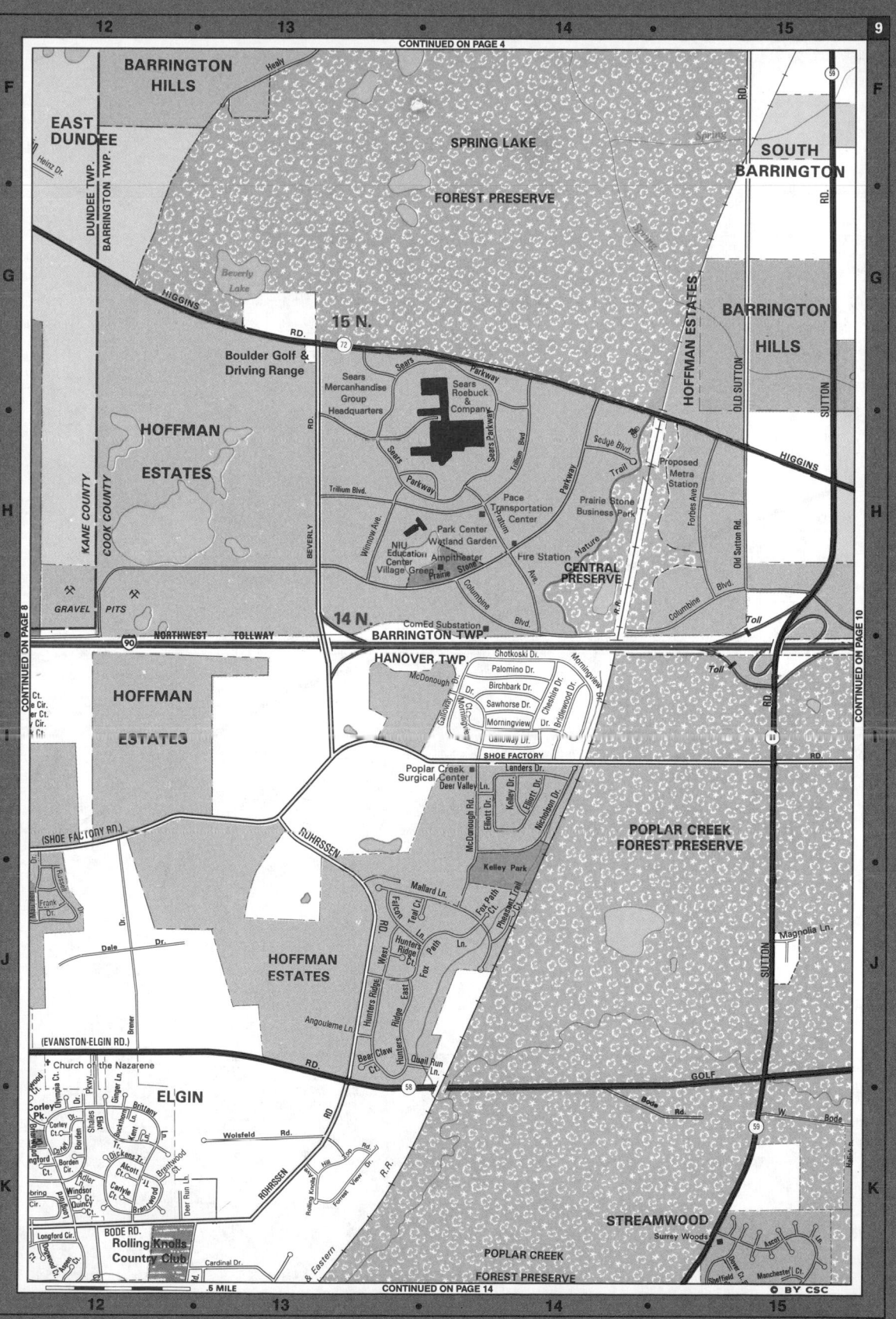

CONTINUED ON PAGE 4

F

BARRINGTON
HILLS

EAST
DUNDEE

Heinz Dr.

SPRING LAKE

FOREST PRESERVE

SOUTH
BARRINGTON

G

Beverly
Lake

HIGGINS

RD.

15 N.

Boulder Golf &
Driving Range

HOFFMAN

ESTATES

HOFFMAN ESTATES

BARRINGTON

HILLS

OLD SUTTON

SUTTON

HIGGINS

Sears Parkway

Sears
Roebuck &
Company

Sears Mercanhandise
Group
Headquarters

Sears Parkway

Tatum Blvd.

Sedge Blvd.

Trail

Parkway

Proposed
Metra
Station

Forbes Ave.

Old Sutton Rd.

H

KANE COUNTY
COOK COUNTY

BEVERLY   RD.

Sears   Parkway

Trillium Blvd.

Willow Ave.

Tatum

Pace
Transportation
Center

Prairie Stone
Business Park

NIU
Education
Center
Village Green

Park Center
Wetland Garden
Amphitheater

Prairie   Stone

Fire Station

Nature

CENTRAL
PRESERVE

Columbine

Ave.

Blvd.

Columbine   Blvd.

GRAVEL
PITS

14 N.

ComEd Substation

BARRINGTON TWP.

Toll

CONTINUED ON PAGE 8

CONTINUED ON PAGE 10

I-90   NORTHWEST   TOLLWAY

HANOVER TWP.

HOFFMAN

ESTATES

McDonough Dr.

Galloway Dr.

Chotkoski Dr.
Palomino Dr.
Birchbark Dr.
Sawhorse Dr.
Morningview Dr.
Galloway Dr.

Morningview Dr.

Cheshire Dr.
Bridlewood Dr.

Toll

Poplar Creek
Surgical Center
Deer Valley

SHOE FACTORY

Landers Dr.

Kelley Dr.

Elliott Dr.

Elliott Dr.

Nicholson Dr.

POPLAR CREEK
FOREST PRESERVE

(SHOE FACTORY RD.)

RUHRSSEN

McDonough Rd.

Kelley Park

Magnolia Ln.

J

Dr.

Frank   Dr.

Dale   Dr.

Breer

Breer

HOFFMAN
ESTATES

Angouleme Ln.

Mallard Ln.

West   CR.

Hunters Ridge Ln.

Teal Ct.

Falcon Ct.

Hunters
Ridge Ct.

Ridge   East

Fox Path

For. Path

Fox   Ln.

Pheasant Trail

SUTTON

(EVANSTON-ELGIN RD.)

Church of the Nazarene

ELGIN

Wolsfeld   Rd.

Corley
Pk.

Olympia Ct.

Brittany

Kent

Shales

Borden

Alcott   Tr.

Dickens Tr.

Windsor   Ct.

Carlyle   Ct.

Brentwood

Quincy

Bear
Claw
Ct.

Quail Run
Ln.

Hunters
Ridge

RD.

58

GOLF

Bode   Rd.

59

W   Bode

K

Longford Cir.

BODE RD.
Rolling Knolls
Country Club

Cardinal Dr.

ROHRSSEN   RD.

Rolling Knolls

Forest View

R.R.

& Eastern   R.R.

POPLAR CREEK

FOREST PRESERVE

STREAMWOOD

Surrey Woods

Ascot

Sheffield

Manchester   Ct.

.5 MILE

CONTINUED ON PAGE 14

© BY CSC

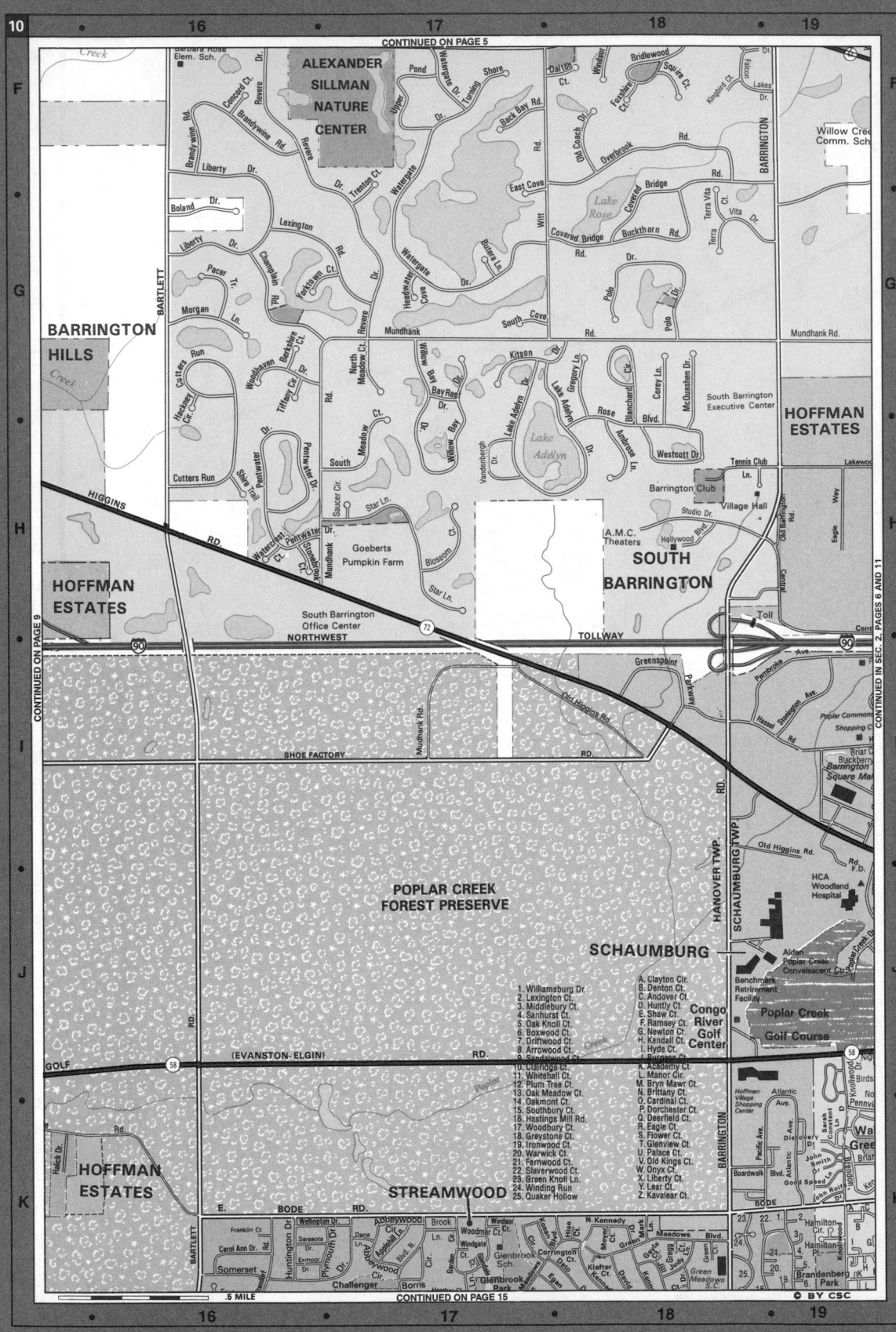

CONTINUED ON PAGE 5

ALEXANDER
SILLMAN
NATURE
CENTER

Barbara Rose
Elem. Sch.

Willow Creek
Comm. Sch.

BARRINGTON
HILLS

Creek

Lake
Rose

Covered Bridge

South Barrington
Executive Center

HOFFMAN
ESTATES

Lake
Adelyn

Goeberts
Pumpkin Farm

Barrington Club

Tennis Club
Village Hall

A.M.C.
Theaters

SOUTH
BARRINGTON

HOFFMAN
ESTATES

South Barrington
Office Center

Toll

CONTINUED ON PAGE 9

NORTHWEST

TOLLWAY

Greenspoint

SHOE FACTORY

Briar Ct.
Blackberry
Barrington
Square Mall

POPLAR CREEK
FOREST PRESERVE

Old Higgins Rd.

HCA
Woodland
Hospital

SCHAUMBURG

Alden
Poplar Creek
Convalescent Cr.

Benchmark
Retirement
Facility

Poplar Creek

Congo
River
Golf
Center

Poplar Creek
Golf Course

1. Williamsburg Dr.
2. Lexington Ct.
3. Middlebury Ct.
4. Sanhurst Ct.
5. Oak Knoll Ct.
6. Boxwood Ct.
7. Driftwood Ct.
8. Arrowood Ct.
9. Sandalwood Ct.
10. Carriage Ct.
11. Whitehall Ct.
12. Plum Tree Ct.
13. Oak Meadow Ct.
14. Oakmont Ct.
15. Southbury Ct.
16. Hastings Mill Rd.
17. Woodbury Ct.
18. Greystone Ct.
19. Ironwood Ct.
20. Warwick Ct.
21. Fernwood Ct.
22. Slaverwood Ct.
23. Green Knoll Ln.
24. Winding Run
25. Quaker Hollow

A. Clayton Cir.
B. Denton Ct.
C. Andover Ct.
D. Huntly Ct.
E. Shaw Ct.
F. Ramsey Ct.
G. Newton Ct.
H. Kendall Ct.
I. Hyde Ct.
J. Burgess Ct.
K. Academy Ct.
L. Manor Cir.
M. Bryn Mawr Ct.
N. Brittany Ct.
O. Cardinal Ct.
P. Dorchester Ct.
Q. Deerfield Ct.
R. Eagle Ct.
S. Flower Ct.
T. Glenview Ct.
U. Palace Ct.
V. Old Kings Ct.
W. Onyx Ct.
X. Liberty Ct.
Y. Lear Ct.
Z. Kavalear Ct.

Hoffman
Village
Shopping
Center

HOFFMAN
ESTATES

GOLF

(EVANSTON-ELGIN)

STREAMWOOD

Somerset

Glenbrook
Sch.

Glenbrook
Park

Green
Meadows
S.C.

Brandenberg
Park

.5 MILE

© BY CSC

CONTINUED ON PAGE 12

CONTINUED IN SEC. 4, PAGES 2 AND 5

**FITCHIE CREEK FOREST PRESERVE**

**OTTER CREEK FOREST PRESERVE**

**Elgin Country Club**

**BOWES**

11 N.

8 N.

L

M

N

O

P

Fitchie

RUSSELL

33

Cliff Dr.

Romeo Cir.

Juliet Dr.

Capulet Ct.

Cir.

Romeo

Central Dr.

Swinden Dr.

WATER

RD.

Weld Rd.

Raleigh Ct.

Mayhill Ln.

Johnston

Williamsburg Dr.

Stratford Ln.

York

Williamsburg Dr.

Burgess Dr.

Jaguar Ct.

Oxford Ln.

Newport Ct.

Williamsburg

Manchester Ln.

NESTLER

W. Lori Ln.

Lori Ln.

BOWES

17 RD.

Springhill

Waldenburg Ln.

Bowes

Oak Tree Ln.

Sunflower Ln.

CORRON RD.

Way

Sturbridge

Greenfield Ct.

Red Cloud Ln.

Hogan Hill

Hopi Ln.

Kershaw Cir.

S. Legend Ct.

N. Legend Ct.

Trails End

Tipi Tr.

Beckman

Beckman

Park Path

WATER RD.

Tipi Tr.

Santa Fe Tr.

Adobe Ridge

Kershaw

Arrowwater

Nelonis Ln.

Pass

Thunder Gap

Fitchie

BOWES 17

Creek

Savanna Creek Ct.

Savanna Lakes Dr.

Savanna Lakes Ct.

Cross

Kopp

NOLAN RD.

HOPPS RD.

Chicago Central and Pacific R.R.

Creek

Otter

Creek

Stony

Creek

McDONALD

PLATO TWP.

ELGIN TWP.

Bittersweet Ln.

Passe Pl.

Tans Pl.

Gingerwood Ln.

Kristen

Stevens Ln.

Richard Dr.

Acorn Ln.

Wildwood Dr.

Lisa

Shady

Running Deer Tr.

Willow Ln.

Sunvale Ct.

Sunvale Dr.

Heatherfield Dr.

Heatherfield East Dr.

STEVENS

RD.

Peppertree Ln.

Oakview Way

Courtland Way

Thornwood Way

Ellington Ct.

Ellington Ct.

Oak Ln.

Oak Dr.

Lilac Ln.

Dogwood Ln.

Sycamore Rd.

Otter

ST. CH

Oak Ln.

Way

Laurel View Ct.

Sterling Ct.

Laura Way

Lake Ridge

Persimmon Dr.

Landsbrook Dr.

Kaleland Way

Ashton

Countryside

Ascot Ln.

Citation Ct.

Harry Ct.

Screwpost Ct.

Cloverfield

Brittany Ct.

Eagles Nest Ct.

Big Red Oak West Ave

Yaupon Ct.

Columbine East Dr.

Columbine Tr.

Cloverfield

Cloverfield Dr.

Pine Rd.

RD.

Whitney Dr.

Northam

Pfair Ln.

Dance Ln.

Johnsway

Chapel Field

Fielding Ct.

Falcons Ct.

Oak Dr.

Pine Rd.

Foxglove Ct.

Glen Rd.

Steven Glen Rd.

Wagontire

Ridge Ln.

Northern Ct.

RD.

PLATO TWP.
CAMPTON TWP.

.5 MILE

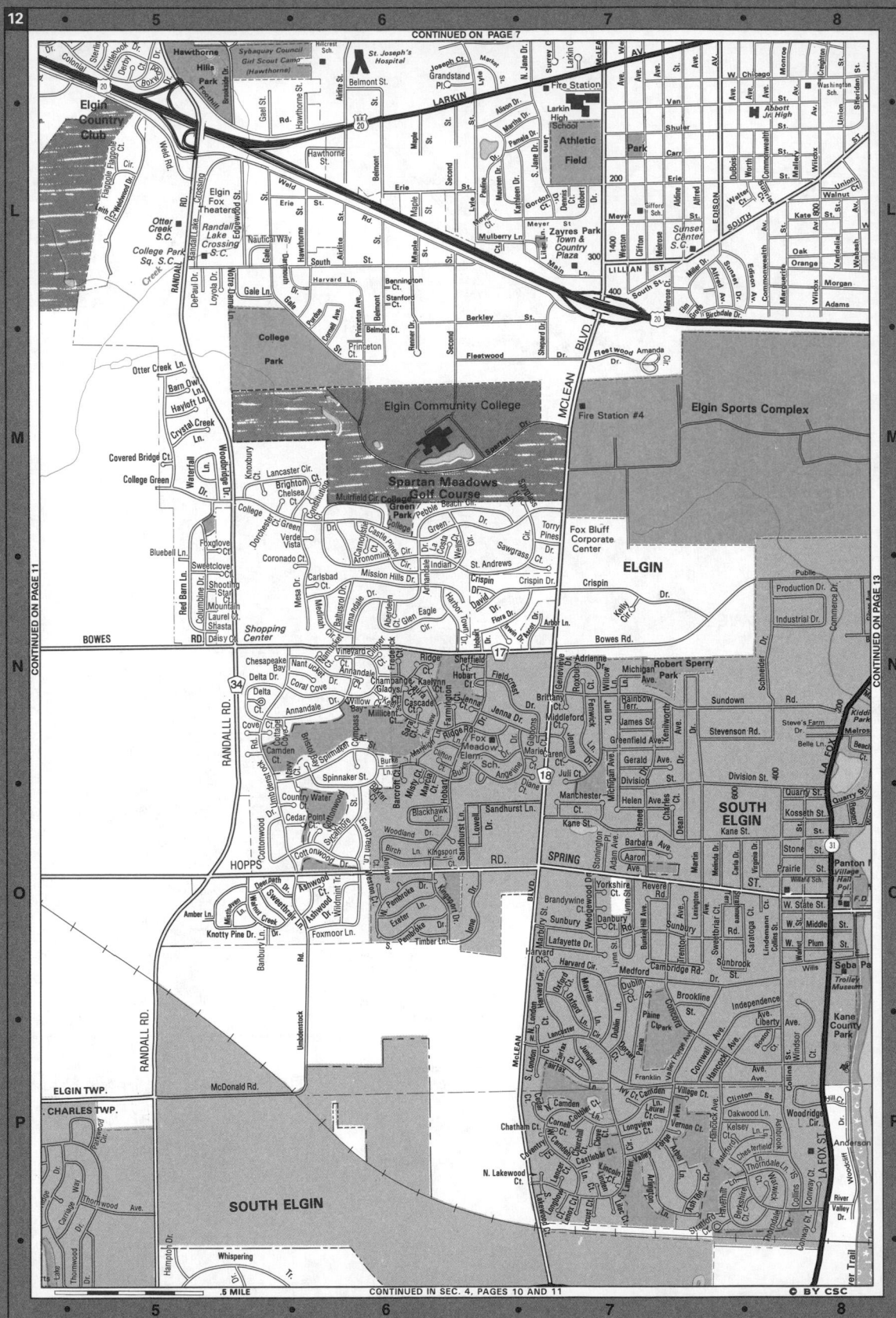

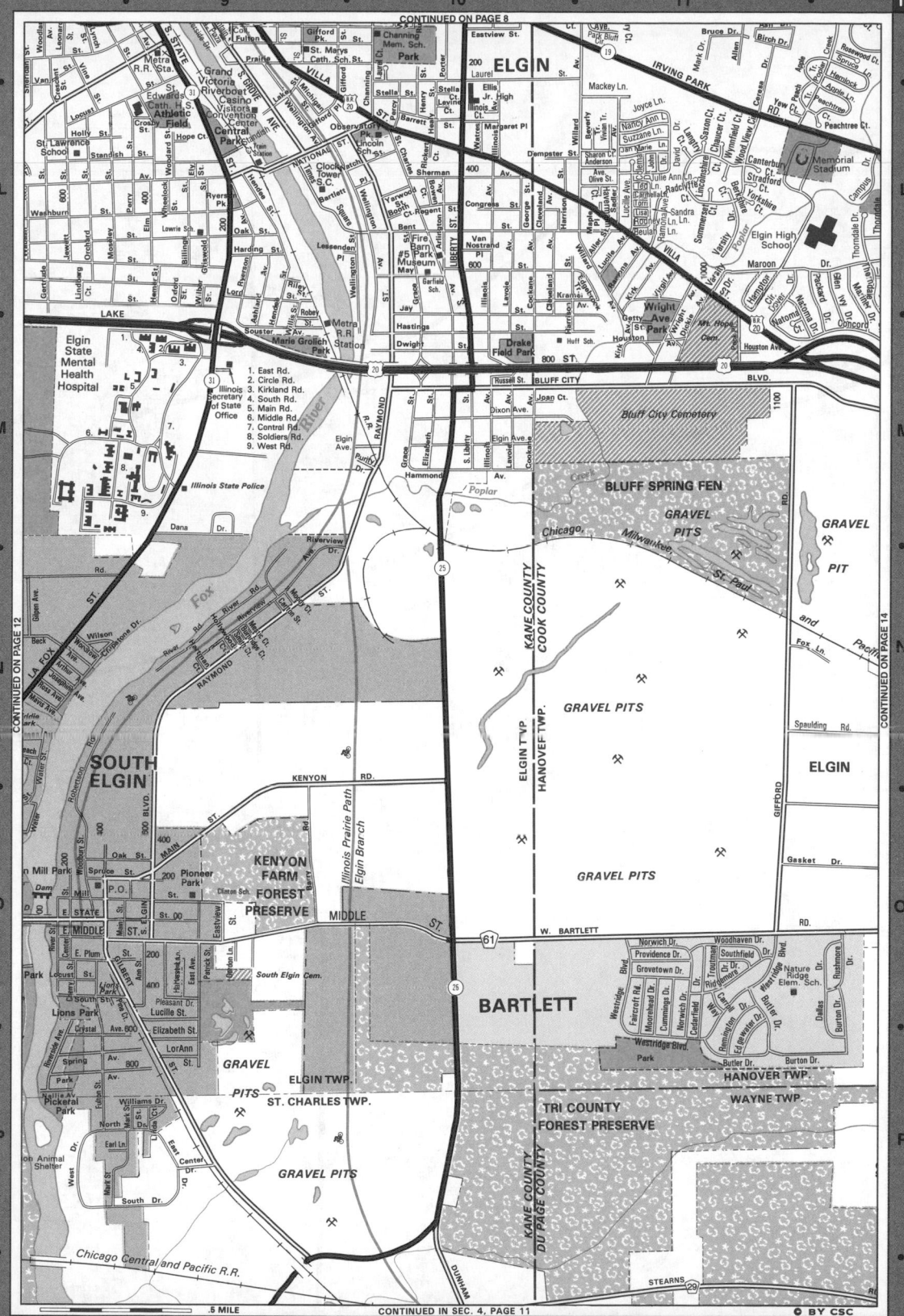

CONTINUED ON PAGE 8

ELGIN

CONTINUED ON PAGE 12

CONTINUED ON PAGE 14

Elgin
State
Mental
Health
Hospital

Illinois State Police

1. East Rd.
2. Circle Rd.
3. Kirkland Rd.
4. South Rd.
5. Main Rd.
6. Middle Rd.
7. Central Rd.
8. Soldiers Rd.
9. West Rd.

Illinois
Secretary
of State
Office

BLUFF SPRING FEN

GRAVEL
PITS

GRAVEL
PIT

SOUTH
ELGIN

GRAVEL PITS

ELGIN

GRAVEL PITS

KENYON
FARM
FOREST
PRESERVE

BARTLETT

GRAVEL
PITS

TRI COUNTY
FOREST PRESERVE

GRAVEL PITS

Chicago Central and Pacific R.R.

.5 MILE

CONTINUED IN SEC. 4, PAGE 11

© BY CSC

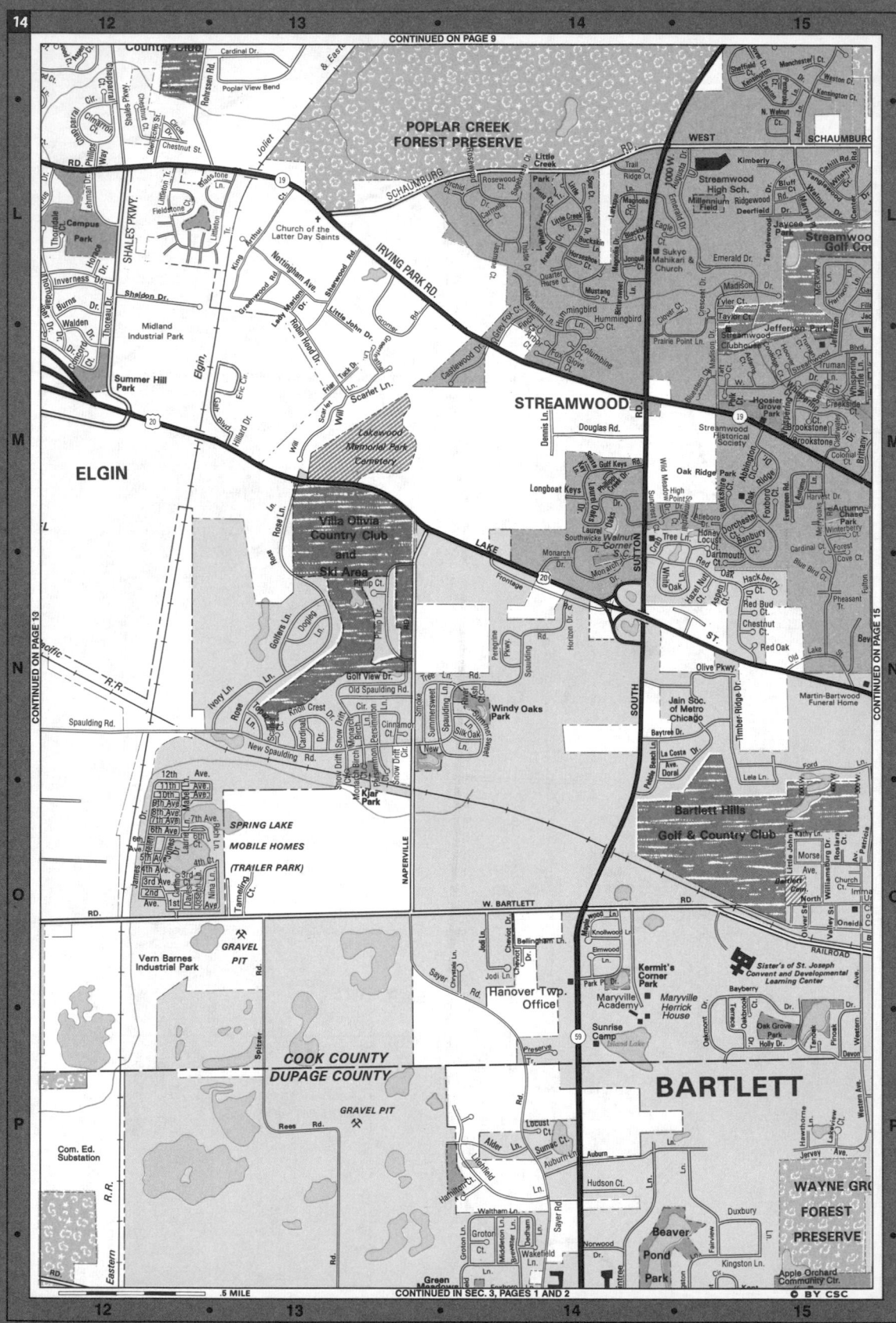

CONTINUED ON PAGE 9

CONTINUED ON PAGE 13

CONTINUED ON PAGE 15

CONTINUED IN SEC. 3, PAGES 1 AND 2

POPLAR CREEK
FOREST PRESERVE

WEST SCHAUMBURG

SCHAUMBURG

Streamwood High Sch.

IRVING PARK RD.

Church of the Latter Day Saints

STREAMWOOD

Streamwood Golf Course

ELGIN

Midland Industrial Park

Summer Hill Park

Campus Park

Lakewood Memorial Park Cemetery

Villa Olivia Country Club and Ski Area

Longboat Keys

Oak Ridge Park

Streamwood Historical Society

Windy Oaks Park

Jain Soc. of Metro Chicago

Martin-Bartwood Funeral Home

Spring Lake MOBILE HOMES (TRAILER PARK)

Kief Park

Bartlett Hills Golf & Country Club

Vern Barnes Industrial Park

GRAVEL PIT

Hanover Twp. Office

Kermit's Corner Park

Maryville Academy

Maryville Herrick House

Sister's of St. Joseph Convent and Developmental Learning Center

Oak Grove Park

Com. Ed. Substation

COOK COUNTY
DUPAGE COUNTY

GRAVEL PIT

BARTLETT

Sunrise Camp

Beaver Pond Park

WAYNE GROVE FOREST PRESERVE

Apple Orchard Community Ctr.

.5 MILE

© BY CSC

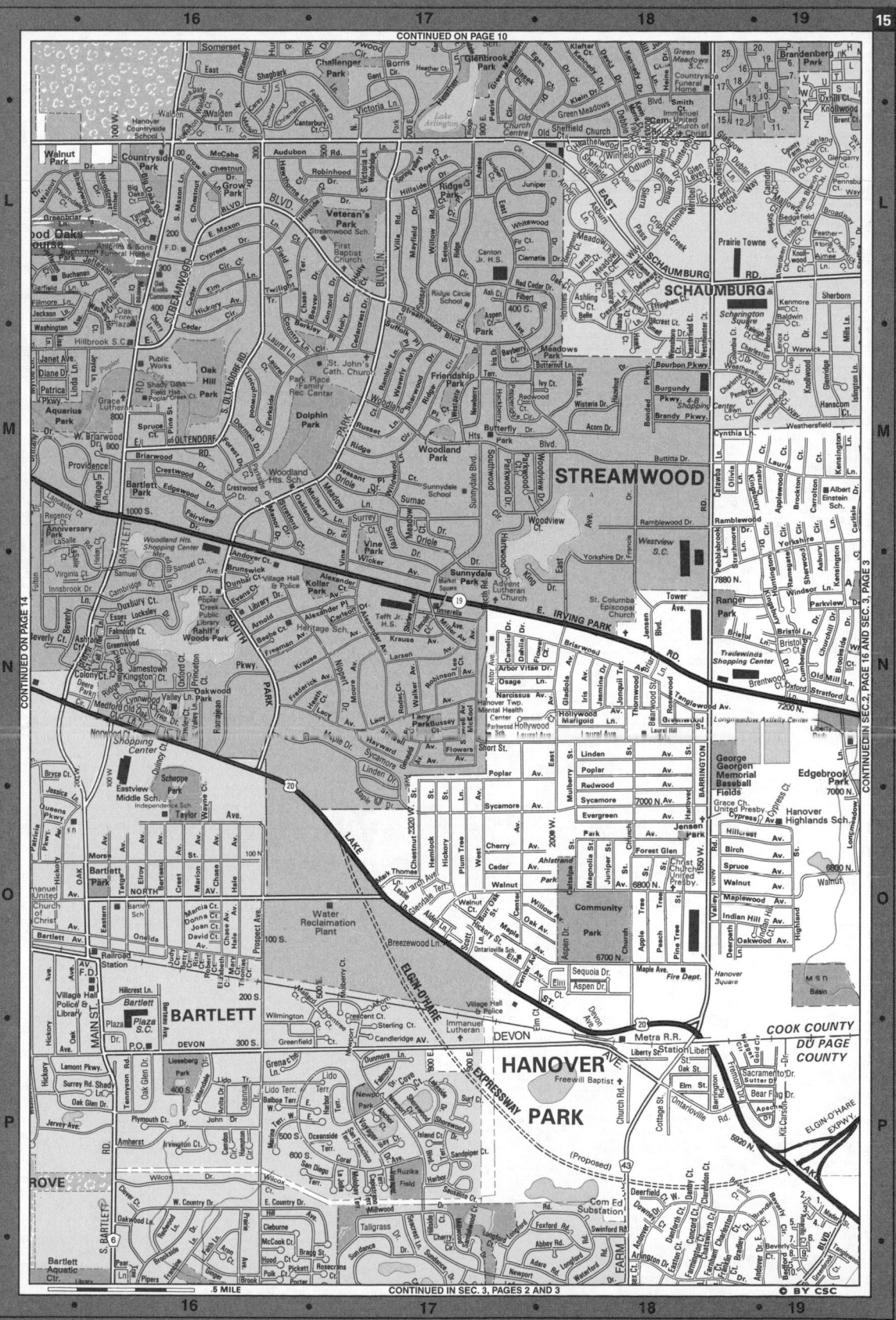

CONTINUED ON PAGE 10

CONTINUED ON PAGE 14

CONTINUED IN SEC. 2, PAGE 16 AND SEC. 3, PAGE 3

CONTINUED IN SEC. 2, PAGE 16 AND SEC. 3, PAGE 3

STREAMWOOD

SCHAUMBURG

BARTLETT

HANOVER PARK

COOK COUNTY
DU PAGE COUNTY

.5 MILE

© BY CSC

# INDEX TO ELGIN AND VICINITY

## ALGONQUIN

(For additional listings, see Section 7)
Pages 2,3

### STREETS

| | |
|---|---|
| Algonquin Rd. | A9 |
| Angelica Pl. | B9 |
| Arbordale Ct. | A6 |
| Arbordale Ln. | A6 |
| Ashcroft Ct. | A6 |
| Barrett Dr. | A7 |
| Bloomstory Ct. | B7 |
| Boulder Bluff Ln. | B7 |
| Braewood Dr. | A7 |
| Brandywine Cir. | A7 |
| Broadshore Dr. | B6 |
| Butler Ct. | B6 |
| Cambria Ln. | B7 |
| Cardinal Dr. | A8 |
| Carlisle St. | A6 |
| Cedar Grove Ct. | A6 |
| Charles Dr. | A9 |
| Cloverdale Ct. | A6 |
| Cloverdale Ln. | A6 |
| Compton Dr. | A9 |
| Coneflower Ln. | B6 |
| Cooper Ln. | B6 |
| Cosman Way | B6 |
| County Line Rd. | A6,7 |
| Dana Pt. | A9 |
| Dellwood Dr. | A6 |
| Dorchester Ave. | A6 |
| Dorchester Ct. | A6 |
| Driftwood Dr. | A6 |
| Dryden Ct. | A7 |
| Eastmoor Ln. | A7 |
| Fernwood Ct. | A6 |
| Fernwood Ln. | A6 |
| Gaslight Dr. | A7,8 |
| Greenridge Ave. | A9 |
| Greyshire Dr. | B6 |
| Hampton Ct. | A7 |
| Haverford Ct. | A6 |
| Haverford Ln. | A6 |
| Highmeadow Dr. | B7 |
| Highmeadow Ln. | B7 |
| Hillside Dr. | A8 |
| Hillside Ln. | A8 |
| Joyce Ct. | B6 |
| Kensington Ct. | A7 |
| Kensington Dr. | A6 |
| Lancaster Ct. | B7 |
| Lancaster Ln. | B7 |
| Lawndale Dr. | A7 |
| Little Spring Ct. | B6 |
| Longmeadow Pkwy. | B6,7 |
| Lonidaw Tr. | A9 |
| Louis Ave. | A9 |
| Megan Ave. | A9 |
| Meiser Ln. | B6 |
| Notting Hill Rd. | A7 |
| Nottingham Ln. | B6 |
| Peach Tree Ct. | A6 |
| Peach Tree Ln. | A6 |
| Poet's Ln. | B6 |
| Randall Rd. | B5 |
| Richmond Ln. | A9 |
| Ridgefield Ave. | A7 |
| Ridgefield Ct. | A6 |
| Riverwood Dr. | A9 |
| Rose Hill Ct. | B6 |
| Rustic Ln. | A8 |
| Sedgewood Ct. | B7 |
| Sedgewood Tr. | B7 |
| Sheffield Ct. | B6 |
| Sleepy Hollow Rd. | B6 |
| Southridge Tr. | B7 |
| Springhill Dr. | A7 |
| Spruce Tree Ln. | A7 |
| Stonegate Ln. | B6 |
| Stonegate Rd. | B6 |
| Stratford Ln. | A9 |
| Tealwood Ct. | B7 |
| Terri Ln. | A9 |
| Tracy Ln. | B6 |
| Waverly Ct. | A6 |
| Waverly Ln. | A6 |
| Westbourne Pkwy. | A7 |
| Westbrook Ct. | A7 |
| White Chapel Ct. | A7 |
| White Chapel Dr. | A7 |
| White Oak Ct. | A6 |
| White Oak Dr. | A6 |
| Willoughby Ct. | A7 |
| Wynnfield Dr. | A6 |
| Yorkshire Dr. | B6 |

### GOLF COURSES

| | |
|---|---|
| Golf Club of Illinois | A6,7 |

### PARKS

| | |
|---|---|
| Braewood Park | A7 |
| Willoughby Farm Park | A6 |

### SCHOOLS

| | |
|---|---|
| Westfield Community School | A6 |

### MISCELLANEOUS

| | |
|---|---|
| Fox River Trail | A9 |
| Public Works | A8 |

## BARRINGTON

(For additional listings, see Sections 2 and 6)
Page 5

### STREETS

| | |
|---|---|
| Barrington Rd. | A19 |

| | |
|---|---|
| Cook St. | A19 |
| Coolidge Ave. | A19 |
| Cornell Ave. | B19 |
| Dundee Ave. | A19 |
| Forest Dr. | A19 |
| Grove Ave. | A19 |
| Hager Ave., S. | A18 |
| Hillside Ave. | A18 |
| Hough St. | A19 |
| Illinois Ave. | A19 |
| Lageschulte Ave. | A18 |
| Lake Cook Rd. | A18 |
| Lake St. | A18 |
| Lill St. | A18 |
| Lincoln Ave. | A18 |
| Main St. | A19 |
| Meadow Ln. | A19 |
| Monument Ave. | A18 |
| Orchard Dr. | A19 |
| Otis Rd. | A19 |
| Russel St. | A19 |
| Shady Ln. | A18 |
| Skyline Dr. | A19 |
| Station St. | A18 |
| Sturts Ave. | A18 |
| Sunset Rd. | A19 |
| Tower Rd. | A18 |
| Westwood Dr. | A18 |
| Wisconsin Ave. | A19 |

### CEMETERIES

| | |
|---|---|
| Evergreen Cemetery | A18 |

### SCHOOLS

| | |
|---|---|
| Barrington H.S. | A18 |
| Hough Sch. | A19 |
| Grove Sch. | A19 |

### MISCELLANEOUS

| | |
|---|---|
| Village Hall | A19 |

## BARRINGTON HILLS

(For additional listings, see Sections 2, 6 and 7)
Pages 3-5,9

### STREETS

| | |
|---|---|
| Aberdeen Dr. | Pg.4 ... A15 |
| Algonquin Rd. | Pg.4 A11,C13 |
| Autumn Tr. | Pg.3 ... A11 |
| Barrington Hills Rd. | |
| | Pg.4 ... A15 |
| Barrington Rd. | Pg.5 ... B19 |
| Bateman Cir., N. & S. | |
| | Pg.4 ... A13 |
| Bateman Rd. | Pg.4 ... B13 |
| Bellwood | Pg.5 ... A16 |
| Brinker Rd. | Pg.5 .. B-D16 |
| Butternut Rd. | Pg.4 ... A15 |
| Caesar Dr. | Pg.5 ... A17 |
| Clover Ln. | Pg.5 ... C18 |
| Crabapple Rd. | Pg.4 ... A15 |
| Crawling Stone Rd. | |
| | Pg.4 ... A12 |
| Creekside Ln. | Pg.4 ... E15 |
| Dana Ln. | Pg.5 ... A17 |
| Deepwood Ct. | Pg.4 ... A15 |
| Deepwood Rd. | Pg.4 .. A,B12 |
| Donalea Rd. | Pg.4 ... A15 |
| Dundee Ln. | Pg.5 ... C18 |
| Dundee Rd. | Pg.4 D16,E12 |
| Eagle Pointe Dr. | Pg.4 ... E12 |
| East Ln. | Pg.5 ... C17 |
| Far Hills Rd. | Pg.4 ... A17 |
| Fernwood Dr. | Pg.4 ... D12 |
| Goose Lake Dr. | Pg.5 ... B16 |
| Hart Hill Rd. | Pg.5 ... A17 |
| Hawley Woods Rd. | |
| | Pg.5 ... B17 |
| Hawthorne Ln. | Pg.5 ... B18 |
| Hawthorne Rd. | Pg.5 ... C17 |
| Healy Rd. | Pg.4 .. E,F13 |
| Helm Rd. | Pg.4 ... C12 |
| Heron Ln. | Pg.5 ... B16 |
| Hills and Dale Rd. | Pg.5 ... B16 |
| Honey Cut Rd. | Pg.5 ... C16 |
| Lake View Ln. | Pg.5 ... B18 |
| Lake-Cook Rd. | Pg.5 ... A16 |
| Leeds Dr. | Pg.4 ... A15 |
| Longmeadow Dr. | Pg.4 ... D12 |
| Longmeadow Dr. | Pg.4 ... D12 |
| Marmon Ln. | Pg.4 ... A18 |
| Middlebury Rd. | Pg.4 ... A12 |
| Oakdene Ct. | Pg.4 ... A18 |
| Oakdene East | Pg.4 ... A18 |
| Oakdene Rd. | Pg.4 ... A18 |
| Oakdene West | Pg.4 ... A18 |
| Old Dundee Rd. | Pg.5 ... D16 |
| Old Sutton Rd. | Pg.4 A14,D15 |
| Otis Rd. | Pg.4 . B15,18 |
| Overlook Rd. | Pg.4 ... A12 |
| Palatine Rd. | Pg.5 ... D17 |
| Penny Rd. | Pg.4 ... C12 |
| Potter Ln. | Pg.4 ... E13 |
| Rebecca Dr. | Pg.4 ... E15 |
| Regan Blvd. | Pg.3 ... B12 |
| Ridge Rd. | Pg.4 ... A12 |
| Rolling Hills Dr. | Pg.4 ... D12 |
| Round Barn Rd. | Pg.5 ... B17 |
| Roundstone Ln. | Pg.4 ... A12 |
| Royal Way | Pg.5 ... B12 |
| Sandalwood Dr. | Pg.5 ... A19 |
| Sara Ln. | Pg.5 ... B19 |
| Springwood Lon. | Pg.4 ... C14 |
| Tamarack Ln. | Pg.4 ... A15 |
| Three Lakes Rd. | Pg.5 ... A17 |
| Tricia Ln. | Pg.4 ... E15 |

| | |
|---|---|
| Valley Dr. | Pg.4 ... B15 |
| West Ln. | Pg.5 ... C17 |
| Windrush Rd. | Pg.5 ... B17 |
| Wood Rock Rd. | Pg.4 ... A12 |
| Woodcreek Rd. | Pg.4 ... E14 |

### CEMETERIES

| | |
|---|---|
| Barrington Center Cemetery | |
| | Pg.4 ... D15 |
| Union Cemetery | Pg.4 ... C13 |

### FOREST PRESERVES

| | |
|---|---|
| Helms Woods Forest Preserve | |
| | Pg.3 . C11,12 |
| Spring Lake Forest Preserve | |
| | Pg.4 ... B14 |

### GOLF COURSES

| | |
|---|---|
| Barrington Hills Country Club | |
| | Pg.5 ... A17 |

### MISCELLANEOUS

| | |
|---|---|
| Crabtree Nature Center | |
| | Pg.5 ... D17 |
| Village Hall | Pg.5 ... D16 |

## BARRINGTON TOWNSHIP

Page 4,5,9,10

### STREETS

| | |
|---|---|
| Barrington Rd. | Pg.5 ... B19 |
| Bartlett Rd. | Pg.10 ... G16 |
| Boland Dr. | Pg.10 ... G16 |
| Higgins Rd. | Pg.10 ... H16 |
| Stover Rd. | Pg.5 ... E17 |
| Sutton Rd. | Pg.5 ... E15 |

## BARTLETT

(For additional listings, see Section 3)
Pages 13-15

### STREETS

| | |
|---|---|
| Acorn Ct. | Pg.15 ... P17 |
| Adare Rd. | Pg.15 ... P18 |
| Alda Ln. | Pg.14 ... P14 |
| Amhurst Dr. | Pg.15 ... P15 |
| Anchor Ct. | Pg.15 ... P17 |
| Anita Dr. | Pg.15 ... P16 |
| Aspen Ct. | Pg.14 ... N15 |
| Auburn Ln. | Pg.14 ... P14 |
| Balboa Terr. | Pg.15 ... N15 |
| Bartlett Ave. | Pg.15 ... O15 |
| Bartlett Rd. E. | Pg.15 ... N16 |
| Bartlett Rd. | Pg.15 ... O16 |
| Bartlett Rd. W. | Pg.14 ... O14 |
| Bay St. | Pg.15 ... P17 |
| Bayberry Dr. | Pg.14 ... O15 |
| Baytree Dr. | Pg.14 ... N14 |
| Bellingham Ln. | Pg.14 ... O14 |
| Berteau Ave. | Pg.15 . O,P16 |
| Betty Ct. | Pg.15 ... O16 |
| Bryce Ct. | Pg.15 ... N15 |
| Camdon Ct. | Pg.15 ... P16 |
| Candleridge Ct. | Pg.15 ... P17 |
| Capistrano Terr. | Pg.15 ... P17 |
| Cardinal Dr. | Pg.14 ... N13 |
| Carlino Dr. | Pg.14 ... O12 |
| Chase Ave. | Pg.15 ... O15 |
| Chestnut Ct. | Pg.14 ... N15 |
| Cheviot Dr. | Pg.14 ... O14 |
| Chrystals Ln. | Pg.14 ... O13 |
| Church Ct. | Pg.15 ... O15 |
| Cleburne | Pg.15 ... P16 |
| Clover Ct. | Pg.15 ... P16 |
| Coral Ave. | Pg.15 ... P17 |
| Costa Ave. | Pg.14 ... N14 |
| Country Dr., E. | Pg.15 ... P16 |
| Country Dr., W. | Pg.15 ... P16 |
| Cove Ct. | Pg.15 ... P17 |
| Crab Tree Ln. | Pg.14 ... N14 |
| Crescent Ct. | Pg.15 ... P17 |
| Crest Ave. | Pg.15 ... O16 |
| Cutlass Ave. | Pg.15 ... N15 |
| David Ct. | Pg.15 ... O16 |
| Davies | Pg.14 ... O12 |
| Deanne Dr. | Pg.15 ... P16 |
| Devon Ave. | Pg.15 ... P15 |
| Dogleg Ln. | Pg.14 ... N13 |
| Donna Ct. | Pg.15 ... O16 |
| Doral Dr. | Pg.14 ... N14 |
| Dunmore Ln. | Pg.15 ... P17 |
| Duxbury Ln. | Pg.14 ... P15 |
| Eastern Ave. | Pg.15 ... O16 |
| Elizabeth Ct. | Pg.15 ... O16 |
| Elmwood Ln. | Pg.14 ... O14 |
| Elroy Ave. | Pg.15 ... O16 |
| Falmore Dr. | Pg.15 ... P17 |
| Ford Ln. | Pg.15 ... N15 |
| Frontage Rd. | Pg.14 ... N14 |
| Golfers Ln. | Pg.14 ... N13 |
| Greenfield Ct. | Pg.15 ... P16 |
| Groton Ct. | Pg.14 ... Q14 |
| Hackberry Ln. | Pg.14 ... N15 |
| Hale Ave. | Pg.15 ... O16 |
| Hampton Cir. | Pg.15 ... P16 |
| Harbor Terr. | Pg.15 ... P17 |
| Hawthorne Ln. | Pg.14 ... P15 |
| Hazel Nut Ct. | Pg.14 ... N15 |
| Helen Dr. | Pg.15 ... O12 |
| Hill Ave. | Pg.15 ... P16 |
| Hillandale Dr. | Pg.15 ... O16 |
| Hillcrest Ln. | Pg.15 ... O16 |
| Holly Dr. | Pg.14 ... P15 |
| Honey Locust Ln. | Pg.15 . M15 |
| Horizon Dr. | Pg.14 ... N14 |
| Hudson Ct. | Pg.15 ... P14 |
| Irvington Ct. | Pg.14 ... P16 |

| | |
|---|---|
| Island Ct. | Pg.15 ... P17 |
| Ivory Ln. | Pg.14 ... N13 |
| James Dr. | Pg.14 ... O12 |
| Jervey Ln. | Pg.14 ... P15 |
| Jessica Ln. | Pg.15 ... O16 |
| Joan Ct. | Pg.15 ... O16 |
| Jodi Ln. | Pg.14 ... O14 |
| John Dr. | Pg.15 ... O12 |
| Joseph Dr. | Pg.14 ... O12 |
| Judy Ct. | Pg.15 ... O16 |
| Kathy Ln. | Pg.14 ... O15 |
| Knoll Crest Dr. | Pg.14 ... O14 |
| Knollwood Ln. | Pg.14 ... O14 |
| La Jolla Terr. | Pg.15 ... P16 |
| Lake St. | Pg.14 ... N14 |
| Lakeside Ct. | Pg.15 ... P17 |
| Lakeview Ct. | Pg.14 ... P15 |
| Lamont St. | Pg.15 ... P16 |
| Laurie Ln. | Pg.14 ... O12 |
| Lela Ln. | Pg.15 ... O16 |
| Lido Terr. | Pg.15 ... P16 |
| Little John Ct. | Pg.15 ... O15 |
| Locust Ct. | Pg.14 ... O14 |
| Longford Rd. | Pg.15 P17,18 |
| Mabel Ln. | Pg.15 ... P16 |
| Main St. | Pg.15 ... P16 |
| Mallard Ct. | Pg.14 ... N14 |
| Maplewood Ln. | Pg.14 ... N14 |
| Marcia Ct. | Pg.15 ... O16 |
| Mary Ct. | Pg.15 ... O16 |
| Millwood Dr. | Pg.15 ... P17 |
| Molobay Terr. | Pg.15 ... P17 |
| Morse Ave. | Pg.15 O15,16 |
| Morse Ave. | Pg.14 ... O15 |
| Mulberry Ct. | Pg.15 ... O16 |
| Naperville Rd. | Pg.14 ... O13 |
| New Spaulding Rd. | |
| | Pg.14 ... N13 |
| Newport Ln. | Pg.15 ... P17 |
| North Ave. | Pg.15 O15,16 |
| Oak Ave. | Pg.15 . O,P15 |
| Oak Glen Dr. | Pg.15 ... P15 |
| Oakbrook Ct. | Pg.14 ... P15 |
| Oakmont Dr. | Pg.15 ... P15 |
| Oakwood Ln. | Pg.15 ... P16 |
| Oceanside Dr. | Pg.15 ... P17 |
| Old Lake St. | Pg.14 ... N15 |
| Old Spaulding Rd. | Pg.14 ... N13 |
| Olive Pkwy. | Pg.14 ... O15 |
| Oliver St. | Pg.15 ... O15 |
| Oneida Ave. | Pg.15 ... O16 |
| Park Place Dr. | Pg.14 ... O14 |
| Patricia Pkwy. | Pg.15 ... O15 |
| Pebble Beach Ln. | Pg.15 .. O16 |
| Peregrine Pkwy. | Pg.14 ... N13 |
| Philip Ct. | Pg.14 ... N13 |
| Phillip Dr. | Pg.14 ... N13 |
| Pinoak Dr. | Pg.15 ... O16 |
| Plaza Dr. | Pg.15 ... P16 |
| Plymouth Ct. | Pg.15 ... P14 |
| Preserve Tr. | Pg.14 ... P14 |
| Prospect Ave. | Pg.14 ... O14 |
| Queens Pkwy. | Pg.15 ... O15 |
| Red Bud Ct. | Pg.14 ... N15 |
| Red Oak Dr. | Pg.14 ... N15 |
| Redwood Ln. | Pg.15 ... P16 |
| Rees Rd. | Pg.14 ... P13 |
| Rich Ln. | Pg.14 ... O12 |
| Ridge Ln. | Pg.14 .. M13 |
| Rita Ct. | Pg.15 ... O15 |
| River Ash Ct. | Pg.14 ... N14 |
| Robert Ln. | Pg.15 ... O16 |
| Rose Ln. | Pg.15 ... O16 |
| Roslara Ct. | Pg.15 ... O15 |
| San Diego Terr. | Pg.15 ... P17 |
| Sandpiper Ct. | Pg.15 ... P16 |
| Sausalito Ct. | Pg.15 ... P17 |
| Scarlett Ct. | Pg.14 ... N13 |
| Shady Ln. | Pg.15 ... P16 |
| Shorewood Ct. | Pg.15 ... P17 |
| Spaulding Rd. | Pg.14 ... N14 |
| Spitzer Rd. | Pg.14 ... O13 |
| Sterling Ct. | Pg.15 ... P17 |
| Sumac Ct. | Pg.14 ... N15 |
| Surf Ct. | Pg.15 ... P17 |
| Surrey Rd. | Pg.15 ... P15 |
| Tanoak | Pg.14 ... P15 |
| Tatge Ave. | Pg.15 ... O16 |
| Taylor Ave. | Pg.15 ... O16 |
| Tennyson Rd. | Pg.14 ... O14 |
| Terrace Dr. | Pg.15 ... P17 |
| Thomas Ct. | Pg.15 ... P17 |
| Thorntree St. | Pg.15 ... P17 |
| Timberidge Dr. | Pg.15 ... O16 |
| Topaz Ln. | Pg.14 ... N13 |
| Valley St. | Pg.15 ... O15 |
| Voyager Terr. | Pg.15 ... P17 |
| Wakefield Ln. | Pg.14 ... Q14 |
| Waltham Ln. | Pg.14 ... N14 |
| Wayne Ct. | Pg.15 ... O16 |
| Western Ave. | Pg.14 ... O15 |
| White Oak Ln. | Pg.14 ... N14 |
| Williamsburg Dr. | Pg.15 ... P17 |
| Wilmington Ct. | Pg.15 ... P17 |
| Wilmington Dr. | Pg.15 ... P17 |
| 1st Ave. | Pg.14 ... O12 |
| 2nd Ave. | Pg.15 ... O12 |
| 3rd Ave. | Pg.14 ... O12 |
| 4th Ave. | Pg.14 ... O12 |
| 5th Ave. | Pg.14 ... O12 |
| 6th Ave. | Pg.15 ... O12 |
| 7th Ave. | Pg.14 ... O12 |
| 8th Ave. | Pg.14 ... O12 |
| 9th Ave. | Pg.14 ... O12 |

| | |
|---|---|
| 10th Ave. | Pg.14 ... O12 |
| 11th Ave. | Pg.14 ... O12 |
| 12th Ave. | Pg.14 ... O12 |

### CEMETERIES

| | |
|---|---|
| Bartlett Cem. | Pg.14 ... O15 |

### FOREST PRESERVES

| | |
|---|---|
| Wayne Grove Forest Preserve | |
| | Pg.14 ... P15 |

### GOLF COURSES

| | |
|---|---|
| Bartlett Hills Golf & Country Club | Pg.15 ... P15 |
| Villa Olivia C.C. & Ski Area | |
| | Pg.14 . M,N13 |

### PARKS

| | |
|---|---|
| Bartlett Park | Pg.15 ... O16 |
| Kjar Park | Pg.14 ... N13 |
| Leiseberg Park | Pg.15 ... P16 |
| Newport Park | Pg.15 ... P17 |
| Oak Grove Park | Pg.14 ... P15 |
| Park | Pg.13 ... P11 |
| Ruzika Field | Pg.15 ... P17 |
| Schoppe Park | Pg.15 ... N16 |

### SCHOOLS

| | |
|---|---|
| Bartlett Sch. | Pg.15 ... O16 |
| East View Middle Sch. | |
| | Pg.15 ... N16 |
| Independence Sch. | |
| | Pg.15 ... O16 |
| Maryville Herrick House | |
| | Pg.14 ... O14 |
| Nature Ridge Elem. Sch. | |
| | Pg.13 ... O11 |

### SHOPPING CENTERS

| | |
|---|---|
| Bartlett Plaza S.C. | Pg.15 ... P16 |
| Brewster Creek S.C. | |
| | Pg.14 ... P14 |
| Walnut Corners S.C. | |
| | Pg.14 .. M14 |

### MISCELLANEOUS

| | |
|---|---|
| Apple Orchard Community Ctr. | |
| | Pg.15 ... P16 |
| Bartlett Aquatic Center | |
| | Pg.15 ... Q15 |
| Fire Department | Pg.15 ... O16 |
| Hanover Township Office | |
| | Pg.14 ... O14 |
| Maryville Academy | |
| | Pg.14 ... P14 |
| Public Library | Pg.14 ... P14 |
| Railroad Station | Pg.15 ... P16 |
| Village Hall & Police Dept. | |
| | Pg.15 ... O16 |

## BOWES

Page 11..N2

## CAMPTON TOWNSHIP

(For additional listings, see Section 4)
Page 11

### STREETS

| | |
|---|---|
| Brittany Ct. | P3 |
| Cloverfield Cir. | P2 |
| Cloverfield Dr. | P2 |
| Fielding Ct. | P3 |
| Johnsway | P2 |
| Northern Dancer Ln. | P2 |
| Phar Lap Dr. | P2 |
| Whirlway Dr. | P2 |

## CARPENTERSVILLE

Pages 1-3

### STREETS

| | |
|---|---|
| Abbeywood Ct. | Pg.2 ... C6 |
| Aberdeen Dr. | Pg.3 ... C11 |
| Adams Ct. | Pg.3 ... D12 |
| Adobe Cir. | Pg.3 ... B10 |
| Alameda Dr. | Pg.3 ... B11 |
| Algonquin Rd. | Pg.3 ... C9 |
| Alice St. | Pg.2 ... E8 |
| Allison | Pg.3 ... E8 |
| Alma Ct. | Pg.3 ... B10 |
| Amarillo Ct. | Pg.3 ... B10 |
| Amarillo Dr. | Pg.3 ... C10 |
| Anchor Dr. | Pg.2 ... E8 |
| Apache Ave. | Pg.3 ... B11 |
| Arlington Dr. | Pg.3 ... B11 |
| Arrow St. | Pg.3 ... B11 |
| Ash St. | Pg.3 ... C11 |
| Aspen Ln. | Pg.2 ... C6 |
| Audrey Ln. | Pg.3 ... D9 |
| Austin Ave. | Pg.3 ... D12 |
| Ball Ave. | Pg.3 ... E8 |
| Barrington Ave. | Pg.3 .. E11 |
| Berkley St. | Pg.3 . C10,11 |
| Berkshire Cir. | Pg.3 ... E12 |
| Berkshire Ct. | Pg.3 ... E11 |
| Besinger Dr. | Pg.3 ... B10 |
| Binnie Rd. | Pg.2 ... D5 |
| Birch St. | Pg.3 ... C11 |
| Birchwood Rd. | Pg.3 ... C10 |
| Bismark Ave. | Pg.3 ... B11 |
| Black Cherry Cir. | Pg.2 ... D7 |
| Blackhawk Ave. | Pg.3 ... B11 |
| Blue Heron Cir. | Pg.2 ... E8 |
| Bolz Rd. | Pg.3 ... E9 |
| Bradford Ct. | Pg.2 ... C6 |
| Bramer Ave. | Pg.3 ... E9 |
| Breezeland Ct. | Pg.2 ... C6 |

| | |
|---|---|
| Breezeland Rd. | Pg.2 ... C6 |
| Briarwood Ave. | Pg.3 ... D10 |
| Bridleway Ct. | Pg.2 ... C6 |
| Bristol Ct. | Pg.3 ... E12 |
| Bristol Ct. | Pg.3 ... E11 |
| Brook St. | Pg.3 ... D9 |
| Brookdale Dr. | Pg.3 ... D10 |
| Bunker Ln. | Pg.2 ... C6 |
| Butte Ln. | Pg.3 ... C10 |
| Caddy Ave. | Pg.3 ... D11 |
| California Ave. | Pg.3 ... D9 |
| Cardinal Ln. | Pg.3 ... B11 |
| Carpenter Ave. | Pg.3 ... D9 |
| Carpenter Blvd. | Pg.3 ... E9 |
| Cedarledge Ct. | Pg.2 ... C6 |
| Center Dr. | Pg.3 ... E10 |
| Charles St. | Pg.3 ... D9 |
| Cherokee Ct. | Pg.3 ... B11 |
| Cherokee Rd. | Pg.3 ... B11 |
| Chippewa Cir. | Pg.3 ... B11 |
| Cleary Ct. | Pg.2 ... B6 |
| Cleveland Ave. | Pg.3 ... E9 |
| Commerce Pkwy. | Pg.2 ... C8 |
| Cordova Rd. | Pg.3 ... B11 |
| Cottage Ave. | Pg.3 ... D8 |
| Country School Rd. | |
| | Pg.2 ... B7 |
| Courtney Ct. | Pg.3 ... C11 |
| Courtney Dr. | Pg.3 ... C11 |
| Coventry Cir. | Pg.2 ... C6 |
| Crab Tree Dr. | Pg.3 ... D10 |
| D St. | Pg.3 ... D11 |
| Day Ln. | Pg.3 ... D9 |
| Deer Creek Rd. | Pg.3 ... B10 |
| Deer Hill Cir. | Pg.3 ... D9 |
| Deerpath Ct. | Pg.1 ... C4 |
| Deerpath Ln. | Pg.1 ... C4 |
| Del Rio Rd. | Pg.3 ... B10 |
| Delaware St. | Pg.3 . B,C11 |
| Denver Dr. | Pg.3 ... C11 |
| Dover Cir. | Pg.3 ... C11 |
| Dunroven Lakes Cir. | |
| | Pg.2 ... C6 |
| Edwards Ave. | Pg.3 ... E9 |
| Edwards Ct. | Pg.2 ... C6 |
| Elm Ave. | Pg.1 ... C3 |
| Elm Ridge Rd. | Pg.3 ... D10 |
| Elmwood Dr. | Pg.3 ... D10 |
| Endicott Cir. | Pg.3 ... B10 |
| Ensenada Ct. | Pg.3 ... B10 |
| Ensenada Dr. | Pg.3 B10,11 |
| Evergreen Ln. | Pg.3 ... C11 |
| Fairfax Ct. | Pg.2 ... D6 |
| Fairway Ln. | Pg.3 ... D11 |
| Fairway Rd. | Pg.3 ... D11 |
| Farmside Dr. | Pg.2 ... D5 |
| Farmstead Ln. | Pg.2 ... C7 |
| Fiddler's Green | Pg.2 ... C7 |
| Fieldcrest Ln. | Pg.2 ... C7 |
| Fir St. | Pg.3 ... C11 |
| Forestview Dr. | Pg.1 ... C4 |
| Forestview Ct. | Pg.2 ... C5 |
| Four Winds Way | Pg.2,3 .. D8 |
| Fox River Dr. | Pg.3 ... D8 |
| Garfield Ct. | Pg.3 ... D11 |
| Garfield Dr. | Pg.3 ... D11 |
| Gentle Breeze Terr. | |
| | Pg.2 ... D8 |
| Glen Eagle Cir. | Pg.2 ... D5 |
| Glen Eagle Dr. | Pg.2 ... D5 |
| Goethe St. | Pg.3 ... D8 |
| Goldfinch Ct. | Pg.1 ... C4 |
| Golfview Ct. | Pg.3 ... D11 |
| Golfview Dr. | Pg.3 ... D11 |
| Granada Rd. | Pg.3 ... B10 |
| Grandview Ct. | Pg.2 ... C6 |
| Grandview Dr. | Pg.2 ... C6 |
| Grant Dr. | Pg.3 ... D12 |
| Green Ln. | Pg.3 ... D11 |
| Green Pastures Ln. | |
| | Pg.2 ... C7 |
| Green St. | Pg.3 ... E9 |
| Greenwood Ave. | Pg.3 ... D10 |
| Greenwood Ct. | Pg.3 ... D10 |
| Grove St. | Pg.3 ... D9 |
| Hampton Dr. | Pg.3 ... D11 |
| Harbor Dr. | Pg.2 ... E8 |
| Harding St. | Pg.3 ... E11 |
| Harrison St. | Pg.3 ... E11 |
| Hattie Ave. | Pg.3 ... C10 |
| Hawthorne Cir. | Pg.3 ... D10 |
| Hawthorne Ln. | |

| | |
|---|---|
| | Pg.2 ... C7 |
| Hawthorne Ln. | Pg.3 ... D10 |
| Hazard Rd. | Pg.3 ... D11 |
| Heartland Cir. | Pg.2 ... C6 |
| Hickory Ct. | Pg.3 ... C11 |
| Hickory Dr. | Pg.3 ... C11 |
| High Hill Cir. | Pg.2 ... C6 |
| Highgate Rd. | Pg.2 ... C6 |
| Highridge Rd. | Pg.2 ... C7 |
| Hillside St. | Pg.3 ... D9 |
| Hook Rd. | Pg.3 ... D10 |
| Hoover Dr. | Pg.3 ... D12 |
| Hopi Ln. | Pg.3 ... B11 |
| Houston Dr. | Pg.3 ... C10 |
| Huntley Rd. | Pg.2 .. D6,E8 |
| Illinois St. | Pg.3 ... D8 |
| Indian Ln. | Pg.3 B11,C10 |
| Inlet Cove | Pg.2 ... D8 |
| Inlet Dr. | Pg.2 ... D8 |
| Ivarene Ct. | Pg.2 ... D8 |
| JFK Memorial Dr. | Pg.3 ... E9 |
| Jackson Ave. | Pg.3 ... D12 |
| Jefferson Ave. | Pg.3 ... C11 |
| Keele Dr. | Pg.3 ... C11 |

| | |
|---|---|
| Kelly Ct. | Pg.2 ... C6 |
| Kings Rd. | Pg.3 ... C10 |
| Kingston Cir. | Pg.3 ... D12 |
| Lake Marian Rd. | Pg.3 ... C9 |
| Lake Shore Dr. | Pg.3 ... C10 |
| Lexington Dr. | Pg.3 ... D10 |
| Liam Ct. | Pg.2 ... B6 |
| Lincoln Ave. | Pg.3 . D,E8 |
| Lindsey Ln. | Pg.2 ... D6 |
| Livingston Ave. | Pg.3 ... D9 |
| Lord St. | Pg.3 ... E9 |
| Lowell Dr. | Pg.3 ... D11 |
| Madera Cir. | Pg.3 ... B11 |
| Madison St. | Pg.3 ... D12 |
| Main St. | Pg.3 ... E8 |
| Majestic Cir. | Pg.2 ... B6 |
| Majestic Ct. | Pg.2 ... B6 |
| Majestic Ln. | Pg.2 ... B6 |
| Majestic Way | Pg.2 ... B6 |
| Maple Ave. | Pg.3 . D9,10 |
| Maple Ln. | Pg.2 ... D6 |
| Marlboro Cir. | Pg.3 ... D12 |
| Mayfair St. | Pg.3 ... C11 |
| Meadowdale Dr. | Pg.3 ... D10 |
| Meadowlark Ln. | Pg.3 ... D11 |
| Meadowsedge Ln. | |
| | Pg.3 ... D10 |
| Merrywell Ct. | Pg.2 ... C6 |
| Middlesex Dr. | Pg.3 ... B10 |
| Miller Rd. | Pg.2 ... C7 |
| Mocasin Ln. | Pg.3 ... B11 |
| Monroe Ave. | Pg.3 ... D11 |
| Monticello Dr. | Pg.3 ... B10 |
| Mora Rd. | Pg.3 ... B10 |
| Morningside Cir. | Pg.3 ... E12 |
| Morningside Ln. | Pg.3 ... E12 |
| Nathan Ln. | Pg.2 ... C6 |
| Navajo Dr. | Pg.3 ... B11 |
| North Lake Pkwy. | Pg.3 ... C10 |
| Northgate Ct. | Pg.2 ... C6 |
| Northgate Dr. | Pg.2 ... C6 |
| Oak Ave. | Pg.3 ... D9 |
| Oak Knoll Ln. | Pg.2 ... C7 |
| Oak Knoll Rd. | Pg.2 ... C7 |
| Oak Ridge Rd. | Pg.3 ... D10 |
| Oakcrest Dr. | Pg.3 ... B10 |
| Ollie Ct. | Pg.3 ... D10 |
| Orchard Ln. | Pg.3 ... D8 |
| Orleans St. | Pg.3 ... D9 |
| Osage Ct. | Pg.3 ... B11 |
| Oxford Rd. | Pg.3 ... C10 |
| Papoose Rd. | Pg.3 ... B11 |
| Park Ave. | Pg.3 ... D9 |
| Parsons Rd. | Pg.2 ... C7 |
| Pawnee Rd. | Pg.3 ... B11 |
| Pecos Cir. | Pg.3 ... B11 |
| Pine Cir. | Pg.2 ... C6 |
| Pine Hollow Rd. | Pg.2 ... C6 |
| Pine Ln. | Pg.2 ... C6 |
| Pine Meadows Cir. | |
| | Pg.2 ... C6 |
| Pine St. | Pg.3 ... C11 |
| Pinecrest Dr. | Pg.2 ... C6 |
| Pineview Cir. | Pg.2 ... C6 |
| Pinewood Ln. | Pg.2 ... C7 |
| Plainview Rd. | Pg.3 ... E10 |
| Plymouth Cir. | Pg.3 ... D12 |
| Polk Ave. | Pg.3 ... D11 |
| Port Cove | Pg.2 ... E8 |
| Prairie Path Ln. | Pg.2 ... C5 |
| Preston Ct. | Pg.2 ... D6 |
| Providence Ct. | Pg.2 ... C6 |
| Providence Dr. | Pg.2 ... C6 |
| Pueblo Rd. | Pg.3 ... B10 |
| Quail Cove | Pg.2 ... C5 |
| Queens Ct. | Pg.3 ... C10 |
| Randall Rd. | Pg.2 ... C5 |
| Ravine Ln. | Pg.3 D10,E11 |
| Red Oak Ct. | Pg.2 ... C7 |
| Redwood St. | Pg.3 ... C11 |
| Ridge Cir. | Pg.2 ... C7 |
| Ridge Rd. | Pg.2 ... B7 |
| Ring Rd. | Pg.3 ... D8 |
| River Bluff Dr. | Pg.3 ... D8 |
| River View Dr. | Pg.2 ... D8 |
| Robin Rd. | Pg.3 . D,E11 |
| Rolling Hills Rd. | Pg.2 ... C7 |
| Rosewood Dr. | Pg.3 ... D10 |
| Rosewood Dr. | Pg.3 ... D10 |
| Sacramento Ct. | Pg.3 ... C10 |
| Sacramento Dr. | Pg.3 ... C11 |
| Salem Ln. | Pg.3 ... C10 |
| San Juan Rd. | Pg.3 ... B10 |
| Sanders Ct. | Pg.2 ... C6 |
| Santa Fe Ave. | Pg.3 ... B11 |
| Saratoga Dr. | Pg.3 ... C11 |
| Scott Ct. | Pg.3 ... C11 |
| Sedgewick St. | Pg.3 ... C11 |
| Seminole Ln. | Pg.3 ... B11 |
| Shaw Rd. | Pg.2 ... C7 |
| Sierra Woods Ln. | Pg.2 ... D6 |
| Siesta Ct. | Pg.3 ... B10 |
| Siesta Rd. | Pg.3 ... B10 |
| Singapore Ln. | Pg.2 ... C7 |
| Sioux Ave. | Pg.3 . B11,12 |
| Sleepy Hollow Rd. | |
| | Pg.2 ... C6 |
| South Wind Dr. | Pg.2 ... C6 |
| Sparrow Ct. | Pg.3 ... D11 |
| Sparrow Rd. | Pg.3 ... D11 |
| Spinmaker Cove | Pg.2 ... D8 |
| Spring Ct., N. | Pg.2 ... D8 |
| Spring Ct., W. | Pg.2 ... D8 |
| Spring Hill Rd. | Pg.2,3 .. D8 |
| Spring Point Dr. | Pg.2 ... D8 |
| Spruce Dr. | Pg.3 ... E8 |

Spyglass Cove ... Pg.2 ... E8
Stanford Dr. ... Pg.2 ... C11
State Rte. 25 ... Pg.3 ... D11
State Rte. 31 ... Pg.2 ... D8
State Rte. 68 ... Pg.3 ... E11
Stuart ... Pg.3 ... B10
Sycamore Ave. ... Pg.3 ... C11
Tacoma St. ... Pg.3 ... C11
Tamarac Dr. ... Pg.3 ... E10
Tay River Dr. ... Pg.2 ... D8
Tee Ln. ... Pg.3 ... D11
Tee Rd. ... Pg.3 ... D11
Tepee Ave. ... Pg.3 ... B11
Thrush Rd. ... Pg.3 ... B11
Tomahawk Ct. ... Pg.3 ... B11
Topeka Dr. ... Pg.3 ... C10
Toro Cir. ... Pg.3 ... B10
Tulsa Ave. ... Pg.3 ... C10
Tulsa Ct. ... Pg.3 ... C10
Tyler Dr. ... Pg.3 ... D11
Valentine St. ... Pg.3 ... D9
Van Dyke Ln. ... Pg.7 ... D5
Vana St. ... Pg.3 ... D9
Vista Ln. ... Pg.3 ... F11
Waco Ln. ... Pg.3 ... C10
Wakefield Dr. ... Pg.3 ... C11
Walnut St. ... Pg.3 ... C11
Washington St. ... Pg.3 ... E9
Waverly Ct. ... Pg.3 ... D10
West Hill Rd. ... Pg.2 ... B7
West Wind Dr. ... Pg.2 ... C8
Western Ave. ... Pg.2,3 ... C8
Westwood Cir. ... Pg.2 ... C6
Westwood Ct. ... Pg.2 ... C6
Westwood Dr. ... Pg.2 ... C6
White Oak Dr. ... Pg.2 ... C8
William St. ... Pg.3 ... D9
Wilmette Ave. ... Pg.3 ... D10
Wilson Ave. ... Pg.3 ... D9
Windham Tr. ... Pg.3 ... D9
Windridge Ct. ... Pg.2 ... C6
Windsor Cir. ... Pg.3 ... D12
Windstar Cir. ... Pg.2 ... C6
Wisconsin St. ... Pg.3 ... D9
Woodcrest Ln. ... Pg.3 ... D10
Woodland Dr. ... Pg.3 ... D10
Woodside Ct. ... Pg.2 ... C5
Woodside Dr. ... Pg.2 ... C5
Wren Rd. ... Pg.3 ... C,D11
York Ct. ... Pg.3 ... A9
York Dr. ... Pg.3 ... A9
Zachary Ct. ... Pg.2 ... D6
1st St. ... Pg.3 ... D11

**FOREST PRESERVES**

Fox River Shores Forest
Preserve ... Pg.3 ... B10
Raceway Woods Forest
Preserve ... Pg.2 ... C8

**GOLF COURSES**

Bonnie Dundee Golf & C.C.
... Pg.3 ... D11

**PARKS**

Amarillo Park ... Pg.3 ... E9
Athletic Fields ... Pg.3 ... E9
Carpenter Park ... Pg.3 ... D9
Comm. Park ... Pg.2 ... C7
Fairway Park ... Pg.3 ... E10
Golfview Park ... Pg.3 ... E10
K. J. Andres Park Pg.3 ... C11
Kemper Park ... Pg.3 ... C11
Oak Hills Gardens Pg.2 ... D6
Spring Acres Hill Comm. Park
... Pg.2 ... C7

**SCHOOLS**

Carpentersville Middle Sch.
... Pg.3 ... E10
Carpentersville Sch.
... Pg.3 ... E9
Dundee Crown H.S.
... Pg.3 ... D11
Golf View Sch. ... Pg.3 ... D11
Lakewood Jr. H.S.
... Pg.3 ... D11
Meadowdale Sch. Pg.3 ... C11
Parkview Sch. ... Pg.3 ... E9
Perry Sch. ... Pg.3 ... B10
St. Monica Sch. ... Pg.3 ... C11
Sunny Hill Sch. ... Pg.3 ... B11
Woodlane Sch. ... Pg.3 ... B11

**SHOPPING CENTERS**

Meadowdale S.C. Pg.3 ... D10
Spring Hill Mall ... Pg.2,3 ... E8

**MISCELLANEOUS**

Bible Bapt. Christian Acad.
... Pg.3 ... C8
Carpentersville Dam
... Pg.3 ... C8
DeLacey Early Child Ed. Ctr.
... Pg.3 ... C10
Dolphins Cove ... Pg.3 ... A9
Dundee Park District Center
... Pg.3 ... E11
Dundee Township Library
... Pg.3 ... E11
Dundee Twp. Park Dist.
... Pg.3 ... D11
Dundee Twp. Sr. Citizens Ctr.
... Pg.3 ... D11
Fire Department Pg.3 ... E9
Fire Station ... Pg.3 ... E9
Post Office ... Pg.3 ... D10
Randall Oaks Farm & Petting
Zoo ... Pg.2 ... D5
Spring Hill Center Industrial
Park ... Pg.2 ... C8
Village Hall & Police Dept.
... Pg.3 ... D10

**DUNDEE TOWNSHIP**
Pages 1-3,6-8

**STREETS**

Albert Dr. ... Pg.8 ... G11
Algonquin Rd. ... Pg.3 ... C9
Alice Dr. ... Pg.2 ... A8
Alpine Dr. ... Pg.3 ... A8
Angelina Pl. ... Pg.3 ... B9
Baker ... Pg.8 ... G11
Bass Ct. ... Pg.8 ... G9
Binnie Rd. ... Pg.2 ... D5
Birchwood Rd. ... Pg.3 ... C10
Bolz Rd. ... Pg.3 ... B10
Boncosky Rd. ... Pg.7 ... C7
Boyer Rd. ... Pg.2 ... B5
Burning Oak Dr. ... Pg.2 ... D6
Burr Oak Ln. ... Pg.2 ... B7
Castle Ave. ... Pg.8 ... G11
Castlewood Dr. ... Pg.3 ... A9
Chapelle ... Pg.8 ... G8
Country Line Rd. ... Pg.3 ... A9
Country School Rd.
... Pg.2 ... B7
Crescent Dr. ... Pg.2 ... A8
Deerpath Ln. ... Pg.3 ... C10
Duchesnne Dr. ... Pg.2 ... A8
Dundee Ave. (Route 25)
... Pg.8 ... G10
Elm Ave. ... Pg.2 ... B8
Field Ct. ... Pg.2 ... B7
Forest Ln. ... Pg.2 ... B8
Fox River Dr. ... Pg.8 ... G11
Frontenac Dr. ... Pg.7 ... G8
Hecker Dr. ... Pg.8 ... G11
Hickory Ave. ... Pg.2 ... D7
Hickory Hill Dr. ... Pg.2 ... E5
Highland Dr. ... Pg.2 ... E5
Hillside Dr. ... Pg.8 ... G10
Hilly Ln. ... Pg.2 ... E5
Hollowside Dr. ... Pg.2 ... B7
Indian Ln. ... Pg.3 ... C10
Karen Dr. ... Pg.2 ... A8
Kasser Ct. ... Pg.3 ... C9
King Richard Rd. ... Pg.3 ... C10
Lac Du Beatrice Dr.
... Pg.8 ... G8
Lake Marian Rd. ... Pg.8 ... G11
Lake Shore Dr. ... Pg.3 ... C10
Lathrop Ln. ... Pg.2 ... B8
Linden Dr. ... Pg.2 ... A8
Lonidaw Tr. ... Pg.3 ... A9
Lundstrom Ln. ... Pg.3 ... A8
Manhatas Tr. ... Pg.3 ... A9
Manito Tr. ... Pg.3 ... A9
Mapletree Ln. ... Pg.3 ... C10
Mason Rd. ... Pg.6 ... G5
Massey Dr. ... Pg.8 ... G11
Meadow Ln., W. Pg.2 ... A10
Melody Ln. ... Pg.3 ... C10
Memory Ln. ... Pg.3 ... C10
Menoma Tr. ... Pg.3 ... A9
Merriweather Ln. Pg.2 ... E6
Miller Rd. ... Pg.2 ... C7,8
Minaki Tr. ... Pg.3 ... A8
Motorola Rd. ... Pg.2 ... E5
N. County Line Rd.
... Pg.7 ... G5
Natoma Tr. ... Pg.3 ... A8
Niccon Tr. ... Pg.3 ... A9
Nokomis Tr. ... Pg.3 ... A9
Northwest Tollway (I-90)
... Pg.7 ... G5
Oak Ave. ... Pg.3 ... A9
Oak Hollow Dr. ... Pg.7 ... G6
Onaway Tr. ... Pg.3 ... A9
Ogaw Tr. ... Pg.3 ... A9
Old Barn Rd. ... Pg.2 ... C7
Old Farm Ln. ... Pg.3 ... C10
Onaway Tr. ... Pg.3 ... A9
Park Dr. ... Pg.8 ... G9
Parsons Rd. ... Pg.2 ... C7
Pheasant Tr. ... Pg.3 ... C10
Pokagon Tr. ... Pg.3 ... A9
Randall Rd. ... Pg.2 ... C,E5
Richardson Rd. ... Pg.8 ... G10
Richmond Rd. ... Pg.2 ... B7
Ridge Rd. ... Pg.2 ... D7
River View Dr. ... Pg.8 ... G10
Riverwood Rd. ... Pg.3 ... A9
Robin Ln. ... Pg.3 ... C10
Sawyer Rd. ... Pg.2 ... C7
Shady Ln. ... Pg.2 ... C9
Skyline Dr. ... Pg.3 ... C10
Sleepy Hollow Rd.
... Pg.2,7,B6,E,G7
Springbluff Dr. ... Pg.2 ... B7
Sturgis Ct. ... Pg.2 ... E6
Sumter Dr. ... Pg.2 ... E6
Sunset Dr. ... Pg.3 ... A9
Sunset Park Dr. ... Pg.8 ... G10
Valley View Rd. ... Pg.8 ... G11
Wabican Tr. ... Pg.3 ... A9
Wakigan Tr. ... Pg.3 ... A9
Walnut Ln. ... Pg.7 ... G6
West Hill Rd. ... Pg.2 ... B7
Winding Tr. ... Pg.2 ... B8
Woodcrest Ln. ... Pg.3 ... B8
Woodhaven Ln. ... Pg.2 ... B7

**CEMETERIES**

Dundee Twp. Cem. E.
... Pg.3 ... F11
Dundee Twp. Cem. W.
... Pg.3 ... E9
River Valley Memorial Gardens
... Pg.3 ... E9

**FOREST PRESERVES**

Buffalo Park F.P. Pg.2 ... A8
Fox River Shores F.P.
... Pg.3 ... C9

Lake Marian River Concervancy
District ... Pg.3 ... C10
Max McGraw Wildlife
Foundation ... Pg.8 ... G10
Raceway Woods F.P.
... Pg.2 ... D8
Schweiter Forest Preserve
... Pg.2 ... E6
Voyagers Landing F.P.
... Pg.8 ... H10

**GOLF COURSES**

Randall Oaks C.C. Pg.2 ... D5

**PARKS**

Raging Buffalo Ski Slope
... Pg.3 ... A8

**SCHOOLS**

Dundee Middle Sch.
... Pg.2 ... E5
St. Catherine Cath. Sch. ... Pg.3
... E9

**MISCELLANEOUS**

Nor-West Marina Pg.8 ... H10
Randall Oaks Farm & Petting
Zoo ... Pg.2 ... D5
Santa's Village Amusement
Park ... Pg.8 ... E11

**EAST DUNDEE**
Pages 3,4,8

**STREETS**

Aberdeen Dr. ... Pg.3 ... E11
Adams St. ... Pg.3 ... E9
Aldis Dr. ... Pg.3 ... E10
Arthur Ln. ... Pg.8 ... F10
Ashland Rd. ... Pg.3 ... E11
Balmoral Ct. ... Pg.3 ... E11
Balmoral Dr. ... Pg.3 ... E11
Bannock Rd. ... Pg.3 ... E11
Barrington Ave. ... Pg.3 ... E10
Braeburn Rd. ... Pg.3 ... E10
Bramer Ave. ... Pg.3 ... F11
Bruce Ct. ... Pg.3 ... E11
Center Dr. ... Pg.3 ... E10
Council Hill Rd. ... Pg.3 ... D10
Crab Tree Ct. ... Pg.3 ... D10
Crestwood Dr. ... Pg.3 ... E10
Dawn Ct. ... Pg.3 ... E11
Deerpath Rd. ... Pg.3 ... E11
Dunbar Ct. ... Pg.3 ... E11
Dundee Rd. ... Pg.3 ... E10
Dunridge Cir. ... Pg.3 ... F10
Dunridge Dr. ... Pg.3 ... F10
Edwards Ave. ... Pg.3 ... F10
Elgin Ave. ... Pg.3 ... F10
Fallbrook Ct. ... Pg.3 ... F10
Fallbrook Dr. ... Pg.3 ... F10
Fountain Valley Dr.
... Pg.8 ... G10
Fries Ave. ... Pg.8 ... G10
Greenwood Ave. ... Pg.3 ... G10
Greenwood Dr. ... Pg.3 ... D10
Guth St. ... Pg.3 ... E10
Hawthorne Ln. ... Pg.3 ... F11
Heinz Dr. ... Pg.8 ... F12
Higgins Rd. ... Pg.8 ... F10
Hill St. ... Pg.3 ... E10
Hilton Ave. ... Pg.8 ... F10
Howard Ave. ... Pg.3 ... F10
Howard Ct. ... Pg.3 ... F10
Jackson St. ... Pg.3 ... E9
Johnson St. ... Pg.3 ... E10
Kenilworth Ave. ... Pg.3 ... D10
Kimberly Rd. ... Pg.3 ... E10
Klay Ave. ... Pg.7 ... F10
King Ct. ... Pg.8 ... F10
King William St. ... Pg.3 ... E10
Lake Shore Dr. ... Pg.3 ... E10
Lincoln Ave. ... Pg.3 ... E10
Linder Ave. ... Pg.3 ... E10
Madison St. ... Pg.3 ... F7
Maiden St. ... Pg.3 ... F9
Main St. ... Pg.3 ... F9
Maxwellton Rd. ... Pg.3 ... E10
Michigan Ave. ... Pg.3 ... F9
North Lake Pkwy. Pg.8 ... F10
North St. ... Pg.3 ... F10
Oak Dr. ... Pg.3 ... F10
Park St. ... Pg.3 ... E10,11
Penny Rd. ... Pg.3,4,5
... Pg.8 ... E10,12,F17
Piemonte Dr. ... Pg.8 ... E11
Plate Dr. ... Pg.3 ... F11
Railroad St. ... Pg.3 ... E9
Ravine Rd. ... Pg.3 ... D,E10
Reese Ave. ... Pg.3 ... F11
River St. ... Pg.3 ... E,F10
Rock Road Ct. ... Pg.8 ... F12
Rock Road Dr. ... Pg.8 ... F12
Roslyn Rd. ... Pg.3 ... E11
Scott St. ... Pg.3 ... E11
South St. ... Pg.3 ... F10
Spring Crest Rd. ... Pg.8 ... E10
Spring Green Rd. ... Pg.8 ... E10
Springwood Ave. ... Pg.8 ... E10
Springwood Ct. ... Pg.8 ... E10
Summit Ave. ... Pg.8 ... E10
Timothy Ct. ... Pg.8 ... E10
Valley Ln. ... Pg.12 ... N5
Van Buren St. ... Pg.3 ... E9
Washington St. ... Pg.3 ... E9
Water St. ... Pg.3 ... E9
Wendt Ave. ... Pg.3 ... E9
Wendolz Ave. ... Pg.3 ... E9
Williams Ct. ... Pg.8 ... F10
Williams Pl. ... Pg.8 ... F10
Wilmette Ave. ... Pg.3 ... E9
1st St. ... Pg.3 ... E10
2nd St. ... Pg.3 ... E10
3rd St. ... Pg.3 ... E10
4th St. ... Pg.3 ... E10

**CEMETERIES**

Dundee Twp. Cemetery East
... Pg.3 ... F11

**PARKS**

Lions Park ... Pg.3 ... E10
Max McGraw Wildlife
Foundation ... Pg.8 ... G11

**SCHOOLS**

Immanuel Lutheran Sch.
... Pg.3 ... F10
Summit Sch. ... Pg.8 ... F11

**SHOPPING CENTERS**

River Valley Square S.C.
... Pg.3 ... F11

**MISCELLANEOUS**

Dundee Twp. Library
... Pg.3 ... E10
Fire Department Pg.3 ... E9
Frontier Museum Pg.8 ... G11
Santa's Village Amusement
Park ... Pg.8 ... E11
Village Hall & Police Dept.
... Pg.3 ... E9

**ELGIN**
Pages 6-9,12-14

**STREETS**

Abbeywood Ct. ... Pg.8 ... I11
Abbott Dr. ... Pg.7 ... J7
Academy Pl. ... Pg.8 ... K9
Adams St. ... Pg.12 ... L8
Addison St. ... Pg.8 ... K10
Adeline Ave. ... Pg.7 ... J7
Adler Ln. ... Pg.9 ... K12
Airlite St. ... Pg.7 ... K6
Airport Rd. ... Pg.8 ... H9
Alcott Ct. ... Pg.9 ... K12
Alder Ln. ... Pg.9 ... K12
Aldine St. ... Pg.7 ... J,K7
Alfred Ave. ... Pg.7 ... K,L7
Alft Dr. ... Pg.12 ... O5
Algona Ave. ... Pg.8 ... J9,I10
Algonquin Dr. ... Pg.8 ... I11
Alice Ct. ... Pg.7 ... J5
Alice Pl. ... Pg.7 ... J5
Alison Dr. ... Pg.12 ... L12
Allen Dr. ... Pg.13 ... L12
Aller St. ... Pg.13 ... L11
Amanda Cir. ... Pg.12 ... M7
Amber Ln. ... Pg.12 ... L12
American Way ... Pg.8 ... J11
Anderson Ave. ... Pg.7 ... J6
Ann St. ... Pg.8 ... K9
Annandale Ave. ... Pg.12 ... N6
Annandale Ct. ... Pg.12 ... N6
Apple Hill Ct. ... Pg.8 ... I11
Apple Ln. ... Pg.13 ... L11
Arlington Ave. ... Pg.13 ... L10
Aronomink Cir. ... Pg.12 ... M6
Arrowhead Dr. ... Pg.8 ... J10
Arthur Dr. ... Pg.8 ... J11
Ash Ln. ... Pg.8 ... K11
Ashland Ave. ... Pg.13 ... M9
Ashwood Ct. ... Pg.12 ... O6
Ashwood Dr. ... Pg.12 ... O6
Aspen Ct. ... Pg.9 ... K12
Augusta Ave. ... Pg.7 ... J9
Autumn Ct. ... Pg.7 ... J5
Avalon Ct. ... Pg.7 ... K4
Avalon Dr. ... Pg.7 ... K4
Ball St. ... Pg.8 ... K8
Ballustrol Dr. ... Pg.12 ... M6
Danbury Ln. ... Pg.12 ... O6
Banks Dr. ... Pg.7 ... I6
Barberry Ct. ... Pg.8 ... J11
Barn Owl Ln. ... Pg.12 ... M5
Barn Swallow Way
... Pg.7 ... J6
Barnes Rd. ... Pg.5 ... K4
Barrett St. ... Pg.13 ... L10
Bartlett Pl. ... Pg.13 ... L9
Baxter Ct. ... Pg.12 ... N6
Bayside Rd. ... Pg.8 ... I9
Bayview Rd. ... Pg.8 ... I9
Bedford Ct. ... Pg.8 ... J11
Behr Ave. ... Pg.8 ... J8
Bellevue Ave. ... Pg.8 ... J10
Belmont St. ... Pg.12 ... L6
Belvidere Line Dr. Pg.7 ... J6
Bennet Dr. ... Pg.8 ... J11
Bennington Ct. ... Pg.12 ... L6
Bent Ridge Ln. ... Pg.8 ... J11
Bent St. ... Pg.13 ... L10
Bent Tree Ct. ... Pg.8 ... J11
Berkley St. ... Pg.12 ... L6
Berkshire Ct. ... Pg.8 ... J11
Beulah Ln. ... Pg.13 ... L11
Big Timber Ct. ... Pg.8 ... I6
Big Timber Rd. ... Pg.7 ... I6
Billings St. ... Pg.13 ... L9
Birch Dr. ... Pg.8 ... K11
Birchdale Dr. ... Pg.12 ... L7
Bird St. ... Pg.7 ... J8
Blackhawk Dr. ... Pg.8 ... I,J11
Blue Ridge Dr. ... Pg.7 ... J6
Bluebell Ln. ... Pg.12 ... N5
Bluff City Blvd. ... Pg.13 ... M10
Booth Ct. ... Pg.13 ... L10
Borden Cir. ... Pg.8 ... J9
Borden Dr. ... Pg.8 ... J9
Bowen Ct. ... Pg.13 ... L12
Bowes Rd. ... Pg.12 ... M6
Boxwood Dr. ... Pg.12 ... K5
Bradford Ct. ... Pg.8 ... I9
Braeburn Dr. ... Pg.7 ... J5
Brant Dr. ... Pg.8 ... H11

Brechin Tr. ... Pg.7 ... I5
Brentwood Ct. ... Pg.9 ... K12
Brentwood Tr. ... Pg.8 ... K12
Briarwood Ct. ... Pg.8 ... K12
Brighton Ct. ... Pg.12 ... M6
Bristol Bay ... Pg.12 ... N6
Brittany Tr. ... Pg.9 ... K12
Brook St. ... Pg.8 ... J9
Brookwood Ct. ... Pg.7 ... I7
Bruce Dr. ... Pg.8 ... K11
Buckeye St. ... Pg.7 ... J8
Burns Dr. ... Pg.14 ... L12
Butler Bay Ct. ... Pg.8 ... I11
Butternut Ln. ... Pg.7 ... J6
Byron Ln. ... Pg.7 ... I7
Cambridge Dr. ... Pg.7 ... I6
Camden Ct. ... Pg.12 ... N5
Campus Dr. ... Pg.13 ... L12
Candida Rd. ... Pg.8 ... I9
Candlewood Rd. ... Pg.8 ... I9
Canyon Ln. ... Pg.7 ... J6
Capital St. ... Pg.7 ... J5
Carl Ave. ... Pg.8 ... K11
Carlsbad Ct. ... Pg.12 ... N6
Carlton Dr. ... Pg.8 ... J11
Carlyle Ct. ... Pg.9 ... K12
Carmella Ln. ... Pg.13 ... L11
Carnoustie Dr. ... Pg.12 ... M6
Carol Ave. ... Pg.7 ... J6
Carr St. ... Pg.12 ... L7
Carriage Way ... Pg.8 ... I11
Case Dr. ... Pg.8 ... K11
Castle Pines Cir. ... Pg.12 ... M6
Catherine Ln. ... Pg.12 ... I9
Cedar Ave. ... Pg.8 ... J10
Cedar Point Ct. ... Pg.12 ... L6
Center St. ... Pg.8 ... J,K9
Century Oaks Dr. Pg.7 ... I7
Ceresa Dr. ... Pg.13 ... L11
Channing St. ... Pg.13 ... L11
Chaparral Ct. ... Pg.14 ... L12
Chaparral Ct. ... Pg.14 ... L12
Chapel St. ... Pg.8 ... K9
Chaucer Ct. ... Pg.13 ... L11
Chelsea Ct. ... Pg.12 ... M6
Cherry St. ... Pg.8 ... J9
Chesapeake Bay Pg.12 ... N6
Chester Ave. ... Pg.8 ... J10
Chestnut Ct. ... Pg.14 ... L12
Chestnut St. ... Pg.14 ... L12
Cheyenne Ct. ... Pg.7 ... J6
Cheyenne Ln. ... Pg.7 ... J6
Chicago St. ... Pg.8 ... J9
Chicago St., W. ... Pg.12 ... K8
Chippewa Dr. ... Pg.8 ... J11
Church Rd. ... Pg.8 ... H8
Cimarron Ct. ... Pg.14 ... L12
Circle Dr. ... Pg.12 ... L12
Clair St. ... Pg.7 ... K8
Clark St. ... Pg.7 ... J8
Clayton Ave. ... Pg.7 ... J6
Clearwater Way Pg.7 ... J5
Cleveland Ave. ... Pg.13 ... L10
Clifford Ave. ... Pg.8 ... J11
Clifford Ct. ... Pg.7 ... J8
Clifton Ave. ... Pg.7 ... J,L7
Clipper Ct. ... Pg.12 ... N6
Clover Hill Ct. ... Pg.8 ... I11
Clover Hill Ln. ... Pg.8 ... I11
Cobblers Crossing
... Pg.8 ... I11
Cobblers Crossing Ct.
... Pg.8 ... I11
Cobblestone Dr. ... Pg.8 ... J11
Cold Spring Rd. ... Pg.8 ... J11
Coleman Dr. ... Pg.13 ... L11
College Green Dr. Pg.12 ... M5,6
College St. ... Pg.8 ... K9
Colonial Dr. ... Pg.8 ... K10
Colorado Ave. ... Pg.7 ... J6
Columbia Ave. ... Pg.13 ... M9
Columbine Dr. ... Pg.12 ... N5
Commerce Dr. ... Pg.7 ... H8
Commonwealth Ave.
... Pg.8 ... K,L8
Compass Pt. ... Pg.12 ... N6
Concord Ct. ... Pg.14 ... M12
Concord Dr. ... Pg.13 ... M12
Congdon Ave. ... Pg.8 ... I9
Congress St. ... Pg.13 ... L10
Constitution Ct. ... Pg.12 ... M6
Cookane Ave. ... Pg.13 ... L,M10
Cooper Ave. ... Pg.8 ... J9
Coral Cove ... Pg.7 ... J5
Corley Ct. ... Pg.9 ... K12
Corley Dr. ... Pg.9 ... K12
Cornell Ave. ... Pg.12 ... M6
Coronado Ct. ... Pg.14 ... L12
Corporate Dr. ... Pg.7 ... H9
Cottage Cove ... Pg.7 ... J5
Cottonwood Ct. ... Pg.12 ... O6
Cottonwood Dr. ... Pg.12 ... O6
Country Club Rd. Pg.8 ... I9
Country Knoll Ct. Pg.7 ... K6
Country Knoll Ln. Pg.7 ... K6
Country Water Ct. Pg.12 ... O6
Countryside Dr. ... Pg.7 ... J7
Cove Ct. ... Pg.7 ... J5
Coventry Ct. ... Pg.7 ... H6
Covered Bridge Ct.
... Pg.12 ... M5
Covered Bridge Dr.
... Pg.12 ... M5
Creekside Cir. ... Pg.7 ... K6
Creekside Ct. ... Pg.7 ... K6
Creighton Ave. ... Pg.8 ... K9
Crescent St. ... Pg.7 ... J8
Crestview Ave. ... Pg.7 ... I7
Crestview Dr. ... Pg.7 ... I7
Crispin Dr. ... Pg.12 ... N7
Crosby St. ... Pg.7 ... J8

Crystal Ave. ... Pg.8 ... K8
Crystal Creek Ln. Pg.12 ... M5
Cumberland Ct. ... Pg.7 ... J6
Cypress Sq. ... Pg.7 ... J7
Dakota Dr. ... Pg.8 ... I11
Dale Dr ... Pg.9 ... J12
Dandridge Ct. ... Pg.8 ... J12
Daniels Ave. ... Pg.8 ... J9
Dartmouth Dr. ... Pg.12 ... L6
David Dr. ... Pg.13 ... L11
Davis Rd. ... Pg.7 ... H7,8
DePaul Dr. ... Pg.12 ... L5
Deborah Ave. ... Pg.7 ... J8
Deep Woods Ct. ... Pg.8 ... I11
Deep Woods Dr. ... Pg.8 ... I11
Deer Run Ln. ... Pg.8 ... K13
Deer Woods Dr. ... Pg.8 ... I11
Deerpath Dr. ... Pg.12 ... O5
Delta Ct. ... Pg.12 ... N5
Delta Dr. ... Pg.12 ... N5
Demmond St. ... Pg.7 ... J8
Dempster St. ... Pg.13 ... L12
Dennis Ct. ... Pg.12 ... L7
Derby Dr. ... Pg.12 ... K5
Devonshire Cir. ... Pg.7 ... H6
Devonshire Dr. ... Pg.7 ... H6
Dexter Ave. ... Pg.8 ... K9
Dexter Ct. ... Pg.8 ... K9
Diane Ave. ... Pg.7 ... J7
Dickens Tr. ... Pg.9 ... K12
Dickie Ave. ... Pg.13 ... M11
Division St. ... Pg.8 ... K8
Dixon Ave. ... Pg.13 ... M10
Dogwood Ct. ... Pg.9 ... K12
Dorchester Dr. ... Pg.12 ... M6
Douglas Ave. ... Pg.8 ... J,K9
Dover Dr. ... Pg.13 ... L11
Du Bois Ave ... Pg.12 ... L7
Du Page St. ... Pg.8 ... K9
Dumbarton Oak ... Pg.7 ... J7
Duncan Ave. ... Pg.8 ... I10
Dundee Ave. ... Pg.8 ... K9,I10
Dwight St. ... Pg.13 ... M10
Eagle Rd. ... Pg.8 ... J7
Easy St. ... Pg.7 ... K7
Edgebrook Tr. ... Pg.13 ... L10
Edison Ave. ... Pg.12 ... L7
Elgin Ave. ... Pg.13 ... M10
Elizabeth St. ... Pg.13 ... M10
Elm Grove Ct. ... Pg.12 ... L7
Elm St. ... Pg.13 ... L9
Elma Ave. ... Pg.8 ... I11
Elma Dr. ... Pg.8 ... I11
Elma St. ... Pg.8 ... I10
Ely St. ... Pg.13 ... L9
Enterprise St. ... Pg.8 ... K9
Eric Dr. ... Pg.13 ... M13
Eric St. ... Pg.8 ... J7
Esmeralda Dr. ... Pg.8 ... J9
Essex Ln. ... Pg.7 ... H5
Executive Dr. ... Pg.7 ... H8
Fairfax Ct. ... Pg.8 ... J11
Fairwood Ct. ... Pg.8 ... I11
Fairwood Dr. ... Pg.7 ... I7
Federation Pl. ... Pg.8 ... I11
Fitzsimme Ct. ... Pg.8 ... I11
First St. ... Pg.8 ... I10
Flag Pole Cir. ... Pg.12 ... L5
Flag Pole Ct. ... Pg.12 ... L5
Fleetwood Dr. ... Pg.12 ... M6,7
Fletcher Dr. ... Pg.7 ... J7
Flora Dr. ... Pg.12 ... K7
Florimond Dr. ... Pg.8 ... J8
Foothill Rd. ... Pg.12 ... K5
Ford Ave. ... Pg.8 ... I10
Ford Ct. ... Pg.8 ... I10
Forest Ave. ... Pg.8 ... K10
Forest Dr. ... Pg.7 ... I6
Fork Cir., N. ... Pg.7 ... J6
Fountain Sq. Plaza
... Pg.8 ... K9
Fox Ln. ... Pg.12 ... N6
Foxglove Ct. ... Pg.12 ... N5
Foxmoor Ln. ... Pg.12 ... N5
Franklin Blvd. ... Pg.8 ... K9
Frazier Ave. ... Pg.8 ... J8
Frazier Ct. ... Pg.7 ... J8
Fremont St. ... Pg.12 ... J10
Fulton St. ... Pg.8 ... K9
Gale Ln. ... Pg.10 ... L5
Galt Blvd. ... Pg.14 ... M13
Garden Crescent Ct.
... Pg.12 ... M5
Gasket Dr. ... Pg.13 ... O11
Gateway Dr. ... Pg.7 ... I5
Genesee Ave. ... Pg.8 ... K9
Geneva St. ... Pg.8 ... J9
George St. ... Pg.13 ... L10
Gertrude St. ... Pg.12 ... L6
Getty St. ... Pg.13 ... M11
Getzelman Dr. ... Pg.7 ... I8
Gifford Pl. ... Pg.13 ... L9
Gifford St. ... Pg.13 ... O11
Gifford St. ... Pg.8 ... K9
Ginger Ln. ... Pg.12 ... O5
Gladstone Ln. ... Pg.14 ... L13
Glen Ivy Dr. ... Pg.7 ... J6
Glendowers Terr. Pg.7 ... I5
Gleneagle Ct. ... Pg.12 ... N6
Glenmore Ct. ... Pg.7 ... J5
Glenmore I. ... Pg.6 ... J4
Glenwood Ave. ... Pg.8 ... I10
Glenwood Tr. ... Pg.12 ... O5
Goethe St. ... Pg.12 ... L6
Golf (Evanston- Elgin) Rd.
... Pg.8 ... G,J10
Gordon Ct. ... Pg.12 ... L7
Governors Ln. ... Pg.7 ... K6

Grace St. ... Pg.13 ... L10
Grand Ave. ... Pg.13 ... J10
Grand Blvd. ... Pg.8 ... K10
Grandstand Pl. ... Pg.12 ... K6
Green Acres Ln. ... Pg.7 ... I7
Green Ridge Cir. ... Pg.7 ... J11
Griswold St. ... Pg.13 ... L9
Grove Ave. ... Pg.8 ... K9
Grove Ct. ... Pg.8 ... K9
Hamilton Ave. ... Pg.7 ... J8
Hammond Ave. ... Pg.13 ... M10
Hampshire Ln. ... Pg.8 ... J11
Harbor Town Dr. ... Pg.12 ... N6
Harlan Ave. ... Pg.7 ... I8
Harlan Ave. ... Pg.7 ... J7
Hartley Ct. ... Pg.8 ... J11
Hartwell Ave. ... Pg.8 ... I10
Harvey St. ... Pg.8 ... K8
Haverman Ct. ... Pg.12 ... L11
Hawkins St. ... Pg.8 ... K8
Hawthorne St. ... Pg.12 ... L6
Hayloft Ln. ... Pg.12 ... M5
Hazel Dr. ... Pg.8 ... I9
Heald Ln. ... Pg.13 ... L10
Hecker Ct. ... Pg.8 ... K11
Hecker Dr. ... Pg.8 ... K11
Heine Ave. ... Pg.7 ... K7
Hemlock Ln. ... Pg.13 ... L12
Hendee St. ... Pg.13 ... L9
Henry St. ... Pg.13 ... L10
Hiawatha Ct. ... Pg.8 ... J10
Hiawatha Dr. ... Pg.8 ... I,J10
Hickory Pl. ... Pg.8 ... J11
High Point Dr. ... Pg.8 ... H9
Highbury Ct. ... Pg.8 ... K11
Highbury Dr. ... Pg.8 ... K11
Highland Ave. ... Pg.7 ... J5,K6,8
Highland Dr. ... Pg.7 ... K7
Hill Ave. ... Pg.8 ... J,K10
Hillcrest Rd. ... Pg.7 ... I8
Hillside Rd. ... Pg.7 ... I8
Hilton Pl. ... Pg.8 ... K10
Hinsdell Pl. ... Pg.8 ... K10
Hobart Dr. ... Pg.12 ... N6
Hobble Bush Ln. Pg.8 ... J11
Holly St. ... Pg.13 ... L8
Holmes Rd. ... Pg.7 ... H6,7
Homer St. ... Pg.13 ... L11
Hope Ct. ... Pg.9 ... L9
Horace Dr. ... Pg.14 ... L12
Horned Owl Ct. ... Pg.7 ... J5
Houston Ave. ... Pg.13 ... L11
Howard Ave. ... Pg.7 ... K5
Hoxie Ave. ... Pg.7 ... K7
Hubbard Ave. ... Pg.7 ... J7
Hudson Bluff Dr. Pg.7 ... J4
Hunter Dr. ... Pg.8 ... K11
Huntwyck Ct. ... Pg.8 ... J11
Huron Ct. ... Pg.8 ... J8
Huron Dr. ... Pg.8 ... I11
Illinois Ave. ... Pg.13 ... L,M10
Illinois Pkwy. ... Pg.7 ... J7
Indian Dr. ... Pg.8 ... I11
Indian Wells Cir. Pg.12 ... M6
Inglewood Ln. ... Pg.8 ... J11
Inverness Dr. ... Pg.14 ... L12
Ironhood Dr. ... Pg.8 ... I11
Ironwood Dr. ... Pg.8 ... I11
Iroquois Dr. ... Pg.8 ... I11
Irving Park Rd. ... Pg.13
... Pg.7 ... K11,M12
Jackson St. ... Pg.13 ... K8
Jamestown Ln. ... Pg.7 ... K6
Jan Marie Ln. ... Pg.13 ... L11
Jane Dr. ... Pg.12 ... K,L7
Jansen Farm Ct. Pg.7 ... I6
Jansen Farm Dr. Pg.7 ... I6
Jay St. ... Pg.13 ... M10
Jefferson Ave. ... Pg.8 ... J9,10
Jeffery Ln. ... Pg.7 ... J6
Jerusha Ave. ... Pg.8 ... I8
Jewett St. ... Pg.13 ... L8
Joan Ct. ... Pg.13 ... M10
John Dr. ... Pg.13 ... L11
Jordan Cir. ... Pg.7 ... J6
Jordan Ct. ... Pg.7 ... I6
Jordan Ln. ... Pg.7 ... J6
Joseph Ct. ... Pg.12 ... K6
Joslyn Dr. ... Pg.8 ... K11
Joyce Ln. ... Pg.13 ... L11
Judy Ct. ... Pg.7 ... J8
Julian Ave. ... Pg.8 ... J9
Julie Ann Ln. ... Pg.13 ... L11
Junior Pl. ... Pg.12 ... J7
Kane Ave. ... Pg.7 ... J7
Kaskaskia Ave. ... Pg.7 ... J7
Kate St. ... Pg.12 ... L8
Kathleen Dr. ... Pg.12 ... L7
Keel's Ct. ... Pg.12 ... M6
Keep Ave. ... Pg.8 ... J8
Kelly Cir. ... Pg.12 ... N7
Kenneth Cir. ... Pg.8 ... J11
Kensington Loop Pg.7 ... J11
Kent Ln. ... Pg.9 ... K12
Kettlehook Dr. ... Pg.12 ... K5
Kevin Ave. ... Pg.7 ... J7
Kimball St. ... Pg.8 ... K9
Kimberly Ave. ... Pg.7 ... J8
Kingman Ct. ... Pg.7 ... I6
Kingman Dr. ... Pg.7 ... I6
Kirk Ave. ... Pg.13 ... L,M11
Knollwood Dr. ... Pg.7 ... J6
Knotty Pine Dr. ... Pg.12 ... O5
Knoxbury Ct. ... Pg.12 ... M6
Kramer Ave. ... Pg.13 ... L12
LaCosta Ln. ... Pg.12 ... N6
LaSalle Ave. ... Pg.13 ... L9
Lake St. (US Rte. 20)
... Pg.13 ... M8
Lake Ter. Rd. ... Pg.8 ... I9

Lake View Rd. Pg.8 I9
Lakewood Rd. Pg.8 I9
Lancaster Cir. Pg.12 N5
Langtry Ct. Pg.13 L11
Larkin Ave. Pg.12 L6
Larkin Ct. Pg.12 K7
Laurel Ct. Pg.13 L10
Laurel St. Pg.13 L10
Lavoie Ave. Pg.13 L,M10
Lawrence Ave. Pg.7 K7,8
Leawood Ct. Pg.8 K12
Leawood Dr. Pg.8 K11,12
Lehman Dr. Pg.13 L12
Leith Ct. Pg.12 L5
Lennoxshire Dr. Pg.7 I7
Leonard St. Pg.8 K8
Lessenden Pl. Pg.13 L9
Levine Ct. Pg.13 L10
Liberty St., N. Pg.8 K,M10
Liberty St., S. Pg.13 M10
Lilac Ln. Pg.12 L7
Lillian St. Pg.12 L7
Lillie St. Pg.8 K10
Lin-Lor Ct. Pg.7 K6
Lin-Lor Ln. Pg.7 K6,7
Lincoln Ave. Pg.8 J9
Lincoln Ct. Pg.8 J9
Lincolnshire Ct. Pg.13 L11
Lindberg Ct. Pg.13 L8
Linden Ave. Pg.8 K10
Lisa Ln. Pg.13 L11
Little Falls Dr. Pg.8 I11
Little Peninsula Rd. Pg.8 I9
Littleton Tr. Pg.14 L12
Lockman Cir. Pg.7 I6
Locust St. Pg.13 L8
Logan Ave. Pg.8 J9
Longford Cir. Pg.9 K12
Longford Ct. Pg.9 K12
Longford Dr. Pg.9 K12
Longwood Pl. Pg.7 J7
Lord St. Pg.13 L9
Lovell St. Pg.8 J9
Loyola Dr. Pg.12 L5
Lucille Ave. Pg.13 L11
Lucille Dr. Pg.13 L11
Luda St. Pg.8 I10
Ludlow Ave. Pg.8 I10
Ludlow Pl. Pg.13 M11
Lyle Ave. Pg.7 I,P6
Lyle St. Pg.12 K,L6
Lynch St. Pg.8 K8
Mackey Ln. Pg.13 L11
Madlock Ct., N. & S. Pg.7 H6
Main Ln. Pg.12 L7
Mallard Dr. Pg.7 I7
Mallery Ave. Pg.12 L8
Mann Pl. Pg.8 J9
Manor Ct. Pg.7 J7
Maple Ln. Pg.7 K6
Maple Pl. Pg.13 L11
Maple St. Pg.12 L6
Marbilynn Dr. Pg.8 J11
Margaret Pl. Pg.13 L10
Marguerite St. Pg.12 L8
Mariner Dr. Pg.13 L12
Mark Ave. Pg.7 I6
Mark Dr. Pg.13 K11
Market St. Pg.12 K6
Marlene Dr. Pg.7 I6
Maroon Dr. Pg.13 L11,12
Marshfield Ct. Pg.6 K4
Marshfield Dr. Pg.6 K4
Martha Dr. Pg.12 L7
Martin Dr. Pg.8 J11
Mary Pl. Pg.8 K10
Maryhill Ln. Pg.12 L5
Matthew Ct. Pg.7 I6
Maureen Dr. Pg.12 L7
May St. Pg.13 L10
McBride St. Pg.8 J9
McClure Ave. Pg.7 J,K8
McKinstry Dr. Pg.7 K6
McLean Blvd. Pg.7 J,K,M7
Meadow Ln. Pg.7 I7
Medinah Cir. Pg.12 N6
Melbrooke Rd. Pg.8 I9
Melrose Ave. Pg.7 K,L7
Melrose Ct. Pg.12 L7
Mesa Dr. Pg.12 N6
Meyer St. Pg.12 L7
Michigan St. Pg.13 L9
Mildred Ave. Pg.7 J7
Mill St. Pg.7 K8
Millcreek Cir. Pg.7 J6
Millennium Dr. Pg.7 I5
Miller Dr. Pg.12 L7
Mission Hills Dr. Pg.12 M,N6
Mohawk Dr. Pg.8 I,J11
Monday Dr. Pg.7 H,I6
Monroe St. Pg.12 K8
Monterey Ct. Pg.12 N6
Montrose Park Pl. Pg.7 J7
Moreti Dr. Pg.12 O6
Morgan St. Pg.12 L8
Morningside Ct. Pg.7 I8
Morningside Dr. Pg.7 I8
Morningside Pt. Pg.7 I8
Morton Ave. Pg.8 I10
Moseley St. Pg.13 L8
Motorola Rd. Pg.2 E5
Mountain Laurel Ct. Pg.12 N5
Mountain St. Pg.8 K8
Muirfield Cir. Pg.12 M6
Mulberry Ct. Pg.12 L7
Mulberry Ln. Pg.12 L7
Mulford Ct. Pg.8 K11
Mulford Dr. Pg.8 K11
Murcer Dr. Pg.7 I6
Murray Ave. Pg.7 K8
Nancy Ann Ln. Pg.13 L11
Nantucket Ct. Pg.12 N6
Nantucket Dr. Pg.12 N6
Natchez Trace Pg.7 J6
National St. Pg.13 L9
Natoma Ct. Pg.13 L11
Natoma Dr. Pg.13 L11
Nautical Way Pg.12 L5
Navy Ct. Pg.12 N6
Newberry Ct. Pg.6 K4
Niagara Ct. Pg.7 J6
Nicola Dr. Pg.8 J12
Norman Nelson Pg.8 K12
North Shore Rd. Pg.8 I9
North St. Pg.8 K9
Northwest Pkwy. Pg.7 F5
Northwest Tollway Pg.8 I11
Notre Dame Ln. Pg.12 L5
Oak St. Pg.12 L8
Oakdale Ave. Pg.8 I10
Oakdale Dr. Pg.7 I8
Oakhill Rd. Pg.8 I10
Oakland Ave. Pg.8 J10
Oakwood Blvd. Pg.8 K11
Old Forge Rd. Pg.7 K6
Olive St. Pg.13 L11
Olympia Ct. Pg.9 K12
Orange St. Pg.12 L8
Orchard St. Pg.13 L8
Otter Creek Ln. Pg.12 M5
Owasco Ave. Pg.8 J8
Oxford St. Pg.13 L9
Page Ave. Pg.8 J10
Palmer Circle Pg.12 M7
Pamela Dr. Pg.12 L7
Pappas Ct. Pg.7 I6
Pappas Dr. Pg.7 I6
Park Ln. Pg.8 I9
Park St. Pg.8 K10
Parkside St. Pg.7 J8
Parkview Dr. Pg.7 I7
Parkway Ave. Pg.8 I10
Parkwood Rd. Pg.8 I9
Patricia Ave. Pg.8 J11
Patton Dr. Pg.8 J10
Pauline Dr. Pg.12 L6
Peach Tree Ct. Pg.13 L11
Peach Tree Ln. Pg.13 L11
Pebble Beach Cir. Pg.12 M6,7
Pegwood Dr. Pg.8 K11
Pennsylvania Ave. Pg.7 K8
Percy St. Pg.13 L10
Perry St. Pg.13 L9
Philips Way Pg.14 L12
Pindar St. Pg.7 K8
Pine St. Pg.7 J8
Pinehurst Dr. Pg.12 N6
Pioneer Park Pl. Pg.7 J7
Pleasant Dr. Pg.7 I7
Pleasant View Dr. Pg.7 I8
Plum Ct. Pg.8 J9
Plum St. Pg.8 J9
Plymouth Ln., N. Pg.7 J7
Point Blvd. Pg.7 G6
Polly Ct. Pg.8 J10
Poplar Creek Dr. Pg.13 L11
Poplar Ct. Pg.8 J10
Portage Way Pg.7 J6
Porter St. Pg.8 J,K10
Portsmouth Ct. Pg.6 K4
Potomac Pl. Pg.7 J6
Powder River Path Pg.7 J6
Prairie St. Pg.13 K9
Presidential Ln. Pg.7 K6
Prestbury Dr. Pg.8 I11
Preston Ave. Pg.8 J,K10
Price Dr. Pg.8 K11
Princeton Ave. Pg.12 M6
Princeton Ct. Pg.12 M6
Prospect Blvd. Pg.8 J9
Purdue Ln. Pg.12 L5
Purify Dr. Pg.13 M10
Quakerhill Ct. Pg.8 J11
Quincy Ct. Pg.9 K12
Radclyffe Ct. Pg.13 L11
Raleigh Ct. Pg.12 L5
Ramona Ave. Pg.13 L11
Ranch Dr. Pg.8 I9
Randall Lake Crossing Pg.12 L5
Randall Rd. Pg.7 I,K,L5
Randall Ridge Ct. Pg.6 K4
Randall Ridge Dr. Pg.6 K4
Raymond St. Pg.13 M10
Red Barn Ln. Pg.12 M5
Red Oak Ct. Pg.8 K12
Red Tail Ridge Pg.7 J6
Regent St. Pg.13 L10
Renner Dr. Pg.12 M6
Rickert Ct. Pg.13 L10
Ridge Ln. Pg.14 M13
Ridgeway Dr. Pg.7 I7
Riley St. Pg.13 L9
Ripple Brook Ct. Pg.13 J11
Ripple Brook Ln. Pg.8 J11
River Bluff Rd. Pg.8 I9
River Rd. W. Pg.8 I9
River Ridge Rd. Pg.8 H9
Riverside Dr. Pg.8 K9
Robert Dr. Pg.12 L7
Robey St. Pg.13 M9
Robin Ridge Pg.7 J6
Robinwood Dr. Pg.7 I7
Rodney Ln. Pg.13 L11
Rosewood Ct. Pg.13 K12
Royal Blvd. Pg.7 J6
Royal Ct. Pg.7 J7
Rugby Pl. Pg.8 K10
Russell St. Pg.13 M10
Ruth Dr. Pg.7 J6
Ryerson Ave. Pg.13 L9
Sacramento Ct. Pg.7 J6
Sadler Ave. Pg.13 L11
Salem Rd. Pg.7 K6
Sandra Ln. Pg.13 L11
Sandy Creek Dr. Pg.7 K6
Sarah Ct. Pg.6 K4
Savannah Rd. Pg.7 J6
Sawgrass Ct. Pg.12 M7
Saxon Ct. Pg.13 L11
Schiller St. Pg.7 J8
Scott Dr. Pg.7 J7
Sebring Dr. Pg.8 K11
Second St. Pg.12 L,M6
Seminole Dr. Pg.8 I11
Seneca St. Pg.8 J9
Sexauer Ave. Pg.7 K7
Shady Oaks Ct. Pg.8 J11
Shady Oaks Dr. Pg.8 J11
Shagbark Dr. Pg.7 J5
Sharon Ct. Pg.13 L11
Sharon Dr. Pg.8 I9
Shasta Daisy Ct. Pg.12 N5
Sheffield Ct. Pg.7 I7
Sheffield Dr. Pg.7 H7
Sheldon Dr. Pg.14 L12
Shenandoah Tr. Pg.7 J5
Shepard Dr. Pg.12 M7
Sheridan St. Pg.12 L8
Sherman Ave. Pg.13 L10
Sherwood Ave. Pg.8 I10
Shiloh Ct. Pg.8 K11
Shiloh Ln. Pg.8 K11
Shoe Factory Rd. Pg.8 I11
Shooting Star Ct. Pg.12 N5
Shuler St. Pg.12 L7
Silver Ct. Pg.7 K8
Silver St. Pg.7 K8
Sioux Dr. Pg.8 I11
Slade Ave. Pg.8 J10
Sleepy Hollow Rd. Pg.7 I7
Sommerfield Ct. Pg.13 L11
Souster Ave. Pg.13 M9
South St. Pg.12 L6,7
Spartan Dr. Pg.12 M6
Spaulding Rd. Pg.13 N12
Spinnaker St. Pg.12 N6
Spring Cove Dr. Pg.7 K6
Spring Creek Ct. Pg.7 J5
Spring Creek Dr. Pg.8 I11
Spring St. Pg.8 J,K9
Springhill Ct. Pg.8 J11
Spruce Ln. Pg.13 K12
Spyglass Hill Ct. Pg.12 M7
St. Andrews Cir. Pg.12 N6
St. Charles Ave. Pg.13 L10
St. John St. Pg.8 J9
Standish Ct. Pg.13 L9
Standish St. Pg.13 L8
Stanford Ct. Pg.12 L6
State St., N. Pg.8 J,K8
State St., S. Pg.13 K9
Steel St. Pg.8 J8
Stella Ct. Pg.13 L10
Stella St. Pg.13 L10
Stephen Ave. Pg.7 J6
Sterling Ct. Pg.7 K5
Stewart Ave. Pg.8 I10
Stillwater Rd. Pg.8 J11
Stockbridge Ct. Pg.8 J11
Stockbridge Pl. Pg.8 J11
Stonebridge Ct. Pg.8 I11
Stonehaven Ct. Pg.7 I5
Stonehaven Dr. Pg.7 J5
Stonehurst Dr. Pg.8 K12
Sumac Ln. Pg.8 K12
Summit St. Pg.8 J9
Sunrise Ct. Pg.12 L8
Sunset Dr. Pg.12 L7
Surrey Dr. Pg.12 K7
Suzzanne Ln. Pg.13 L11
Swan Ln. Pg.7 J6
Sweetbriar Ln. Pg.12 O6
Sweetclover Ct. Pg.12 N5
Tanney Ridge Rd. Pg.8 I11
Tara Dr. Pg.7 K5
Teal Ave. Pg.8 I9
Ted Ln. Pg.13 L11
Tefft Ave. Pg.8 K11
Terrace Ave. Pg.8 K11
Terrace Ct. Pg.8 K10
Thomas Moore Dr. Pg.7 K6
Thoreau Dr. Pg.14 L12
Thorndale Ct. Pg.14 L12
Thorndale Dr. Pg.14 L12
Thunderbird Pg.12 N7
Timber Dr. Pg.7 I7
Tina Tr. Pg.7 J5
Tinker Ave. Pg.8 I9
Tivoli Pl. Pg.7 J7
Toastmaster Dr. Pg.8 I11
Todd Farm Ct. Pg.7 I7
Todd Farm Dr. Pg.7 I7
Toftress Tr. Pg.7 J6
Toll Gate Rd. Pg.7 H8
Torrey Pines Dr. Pg.12 M7
Torri Ln. Pg.13 L11
Tower Ct. Pg.13 L9
Triggs Ave. Pg.7 K7
Trinity Terr. Pg.7 J6
Trout Park Blvd. Pg.8 I10
Tuileries Pl. Pg.7 J7
Tyler Ln. Pg.8 I8
Tyrrell Rd. Pg.6 H4
Umbdenstock Rd. Pg.12 O5
Union Ct. Pg.12 L8
Union St. Pg.12 L8
Valley Creek Dr. Pg.7 J5
Van Nostrand Pl. Pg.13 L10
Van St. Pg.12 L7,8
Vandalia St. Pg.12 L8
Vantage Dr. Pg.2 F5
Varsity Dr. Pg.13 L11
Verde Vista Ct. Pg.12 N6
Vernon Dr. Pg.7 K6
Victor Ave. Pg.8 I11
Villa St. Pg.13 L11
Vincent Pl. Pg.7 K8
Vine St. Pg.13 K8
Vineyard Ct. Pg.12 N6
Virgil Ave. Pg.13 L11
Virginia Ct. Pg.7 I6
Vivian Tr. Pg.13 L11
Wabash Ave. Pg.12 L8
Wakefield Dr. Pg.8 J11
Walden Dr. Pg.14 M12
Walker Pl. Pg.8 K10
Walnut Ave. Pg.12 L8
Walnut Creek Dr. Pg.12 O5
Walter Ct. Pg.12 L8
Warwick Pl. Pg.8 K10
Washburn St. Pg.12 L8
Washington St. Pg.7 K8
Watch St. Pg.13 L9
Water St. Pg.7 K9
Waterfall Ln. Pg.12 M5
Watres Ave. Pg.13 L10
Watson Ave. Pg.12 L7
Wauchope Dr. Pg.8 I9
Waverly Ct., N. & S. Pg.8 K11
Waverly Dr. Pg.8 J,K11
Weatherstone Ln. Pg.7 I7
Weld Rd. Pg.6 K4
Weldwood Dr. Pg.12 L5
Wellington Ave. Pg.13 L10
Wellington St. Pg.13 L9
Westfield Dr. Pg.7 H5
Westhaven Ln. Pg.12 O5
Weston Ave. Pg.7 J-L7
Wheelock St. Pg.13 L9
Wilber St. Pg.13 L9
Wilcox Ave. Pg.12 L8
Wilder St. Pg.8 K8
Willard Ave. Pg.13 L10
Williams Dr. Pg.7 K6
Williamsburg Dr. Pg.12 L5
Willis St. Pg.13 M9
Willoby Ln. Pg.8 J11
Willow Bay Pg.12 N6
Willow Lake Rd. Pg.8 I9
Wilson St. Pg.7 K8
Win Haven Dr. Pg.7 K5
Winchester Dr. Pg.6 K4
Windsor Ct. Pg.9 K12
Wing Park Blvd. Pg.7 K7
Wing St. Pg.7 J7
Wolf Ave. Pg.7 K7
Woodard St. Pg.13 L9
Woodbridge Dr. Pg.12 M5
Woodhill Ct. Pg.8 J11
Woodland Ave. Pg.8 K8
Woodridge Ct. Pg.7 J6
Worth Ave. Pg.12 K,L8
Wright Ave. Pg.13 M11
Wynnfield Ct. Pg.13 L11
Yarwood St. Pg.13 L10
Yellowstone Dr. Pg.7 J6
Yew Ct. Pg.13 L11

### CEMETERIES
Bluff City Cem. Pg.13 M11
Lakewood Memorial Park Cemetery Pg.14 M13
Mt. Hope Cem. Pg.13 L11
River Valley Memorial Gardens Pg.8 H9

### FOREST PRESERVES
Bluff Spring Fen Pg.13 M11
Tyler Creek Forest Preserve Pg.7 I8

### GOLF COURSES
Elgin Country Club Pg.12 L5
Rolling Knolls Country Club Pg.9 K12
Spartan Meadows Golf Courses Pg.12 M6
Wing Park Golf Course Pg.7 J8

### PARKS
Burnridge Woods Park Pg.7 I6
Campus Park Pg.14 L12
Carleton Rogers Park Pg.8 K9
Central Park Pg.13 L9
Century Oaks Park Pg.7 J7
Clara Howard Park Pg.8 J10
Clifford-Owasco Park Pg.8 J8
College Green Park Pg.12 M6
College Park Pg.12 M5
Corley Park Pg.9 K12
Drake Field Park Pg.13 M10
Eagle Heights Park Pg.7 J6
Foundry Park Pg.8 K8
Gifford Park Pg.8 K9
Hawthorne Hills Park Pg.12 K5
Illinois Park Sch. Pg.7 J7
Jaynes Industrial Park Pg.7 H6
Little League Pg.7 J8
Lords Park Pg.8 K10
Mable Park Pg.8 J8-9
Marie Grolich Park Pg.13 M9
Observatory Park Pg.13 L10
Powder River Park Pg.7 J6
Slade Park Pg.8 I9
St. Francis Park Pg.8 J9
Summer Hill Park Pg.14 M12
Trinity Terrace Park Pg.7 J6
Trout Park Pg.8 I10
Walton Is. Park Pg.8 J9
Wing Park Pg.7 J7
Wright Ave. Park Pg.13 L11
Zayres Park Pg.12 L7

### SCHOOLS
Abbott Jr. H.S. Pg.12 L8
Century Oaks Sch. Pg.7 I7
Channing Mem.Sch. Pg.8 K10
Coleman Sch. Pg.8 I10
Elgin Academy Pg.8 K9
Elgin Community College Pg.8,12 K9,M6
Elgin H.S. Pg.13 L11
Ellis Jr. H.S. Pg.13 L10
Franklin Sch. Pg.8 K9
Garfield Sch. Pg.13 L10
Gifford Sch. Pg.12 L7
Grant Sch. Pg.8 K8
Highland Sch. Pg.7 K7
Hillcrest Sch. Pg.7 K6
Huff Sch. Pg.13 M10
Judson College Pg.8 I9
Kimball Jr. H.S. Pg.7 K7
Larkin H.S. Pg.12 L7
Larsen Jr. H.S. Pg.8 J10
Lincoln Sch. Pg.13 L10
Lowrie Sch. Pg.13 L9
McKinley Sch. Pg.8 J9
National Lewis University Pg.8 H8
Sheridan Sch. Pg.8 J10
St. Edwards Cath. H.S. Pg.13 L9
St. Lawrence Sch. Pg.13 L8
St. Mary's Cath. Sch. Pg.13 K9
St. Thomas Moore Cath. Sch. Pg.7 K7
Summit Elem. Sch. Pg.8 I9
Washington Sch. Pg.12 K8
Westminster Christian J.H. & Elem. Sch. Pg.7 K7
Westminster H.S. Pg.7 J5
Wing Sch. Pg.8 K9

### SHOPPING CENTERS
Clock Tower S.C. Pg.12 L9
Cobblers Crossing S.C. Pg.8 J11
College Park Square S.C. Pg.12 L5
Fox River Plaza Pg.8 H9
McLean Square S.C. Pg.7 J7
Otter Creek S.C. Pg.12 L5
Randall Lake Crossing S.C. Pg.12 L5
Shopping Center Pg.12 N6
Summit Square S.C. Pg.8 J10
Sunset Center S.C. Pg.12 L7
Town & Country Plaza Pg.12 L7
True Value Plaza Pg.8 J11
Tyler Creek Plaza III Pg.7 I7
Tyler Creek S.C. Pg.7 I7
Wing Park Manor S.C. Pg.7 J7

### MISCELLANEOUS
Appelate Court Pg.8 K9
City Hall Pg.8 K9
Elgin Corporate Center Pg.7 I5
Elgin Fox Theaters Pg.12 L5
Elgin Little League Fld. Pg.8 J10
Elgin Public Museum Pg.8 K10
Elgin Sports Complex Pg.12 M8
Elgin State Hospital Pg.13 M8
Fire Barn #5 Park Museum Pg.13 L10
Fire Station #1 Pg.8 J10
Fire Station #2 Pg.7 I8
Fire Station #3 Pg.7 J5
Fire Station #4 Pg.12 M7
First Chicago Corp. Pg.7 G5
Fox Bluff Corporate Center Pg.12 M7
Fox Valley Professional Park Pg.8 J11
Grand Victoria Riverboat Casino Pg.13 L9
Hemmens Auditorium Pg.8 K9
Illinois Sec. of State Office Pg.13 M9
Illinois State Police Pg.13 M9
Library Pg.8 K9
Memorial Stadium Pg.13 L11
Metra R.R. Stations Pg.7,13 I6,M9
Midland Industrial Park Pg.14 L12
Norman Hoffman Athletic Fields Pg.8 J10
Northwest Corporate Center Pg.7 F5
Panasonic Corp. Pg.7 H6
Post Office Pg.8 K9
Randall Point Executive Center III Pg.7 G6
Sherman Hospital Pg.8 J9
St. Joseph's Hospital Pg.12 K6
Sybaquay Council Girl Scout Camp Pg.7 K5
Vern Barnes Industrial Park Pg.14 O12
Westfield Business Park Pg.7 H5
Windsor Commerce Center Pg.7 I6
YMCA Pg.8 K10

## ELGIN TOWNSHIP
Pages 6-8,11-13

### STREETS
Acorn Ln. Pg.11 O4
Airlite St. Pg.12 L6
Almora Terr. Pg.7 K5
Amberwood Dr. Pg.6 I3
Arrowmaker Pass Pg.11 N3
Barry Rd. Pg.13 O9
Beckman Tr. Pg.11 M3
Belmont St. Pg.12 L6
Bittersweet Ln. Pg.11 O3
Bowes Rd. Pg.11 N4
Brindlewood Ln. Pg.6 I3
Brookside Dr. Pg.7 K5
Burgess Dr. Pg.11 L4
Center Dr. Pg.13 P9
Charlotte Ct. Pg.7 J5
Crispin Dr. Pg.12 N7
Cross Creek Ct. Pg.11 N3
David Dr. Pg.12 N6
Eagle Rd. Pg.7 J7
Elmar Ct. Pg.6 J4
Erie St. Pg.12 L6
Flagpole Ct. Pg.12 L5
Fletcher Dr. Pg.7 I5
Flora Dr. Pg.12 N7
Frontage Rd. Pg.7 K5,L6
Gale St. Pg.12 L5
Gingerwood Ln. Pg.11 O3
Gordon Ln. Pg.13 O9
Hawthorne St. Pg.12 L6
Heatherfield Dr. Pg.11 P3
Heatherfield East Dr. Pg.11 P4
Hidden Hills Tr. Pg.6 K4
Highland Ave. Pg.7 J5
Hill Ct. Pg.12 P8
Hilltop Rd. Pg.7 J,K5
Hobart Dr. Pg.12 N6
Hopi Tr. Pg.11 M3
Hopps Rd. Pg.11 O3-6
Howard Ave. Pg.7 K5
Hoxie Ave. Pg.7 K7
Irwin Dr. Pg.12 N7
Jackson Dr. Pg.6 J4
Jaguar Ct. Pg.11 L4
Johnstown Rd. Pg.12 L5
Kenyon Rd. Pg.13 N9
Kingsman Ct. Pg.12 P6
Koshare Cir. Pg.11 M3
Koshare Tr. Pg.11 N3
Kristen Dr. Pg.11 O3
Lamont Ct. Pg.12 L5
Leith Ct. Pg.12 L5
Leland Ct., N. & S. Pg.11 M3
Linda Ln. Pg.7 J5
Lisa Ln. Pg.11 O4
Manchester Ln. Pg.11 M4
Maple St. Pg.12 L6
Maryhill Ln. Pg.12 L5
McDonald Rd. Pg.12 P5
McLean Blvd. Pg.12 P7
Middle St., E. Pg.13 O10
Nestler Rd. W. Pg.6 K3
Newport Ct. Pg.11 L4
Nokomis Ln. Pg.11 N3
Nolan Rd. Pg.11 N,O3
Northwest Tollway Pg.7 H7
Oatwind Rd. Pg.6 K4
Old Barn Rd. Pg.6 K4
Olwin Ave. Pg.7 J5
Orchard Ln. Pg.6 K4
Oxford Ln. Pg.2 F7
Park Path Pg.11 N3
Pasec Pl. Pg.11 O3
Peppertree Ct. Pg.11 P4
Peppertree Ln. Pg.11 P4
Poulitt Dr. Pg.6 I3
Raleigh Ct. Pg.12 L5
Randall Rd. Pg.7,12 I,M5
Richard Dr. Pg.11 O3
Ridgewood Ln. Pg.6 I3
River Valley Dr. Pg.12 P8
Running Deer Tr. Pg.11 O4
Sandhurst Ln. Pg.12 O6
Savanna Lakes Ct. Pg.11 N3
Savanna Lakes Dr. Pg.11 N3
Shady Ln. Pg.11 O4
South St. Pg.12 L5
State Rte. 25 Pg.13 N10
Stevens Ln. Pg.11 P3
Sunvale Ct. Pg.11 P3
Sunvale Dr. Pg.11 P3
Taos Pl. Pg.11 O3
Thunder Gap Pg.11 N3
Tina Tr. Pg.7 J5
Tipi Ln. Pg.11 N3
Trails End Pg.11 M3
Umdenstock Rd. Pg.12 P6
Water Rd. Pg.11 M3,N4
Wedgewood Dr. Pg.6 I3
Weld Rd. Pg.12 L6
Weldwood Dr. Pg.12 L5
West River Rd. Pg.8 I9
West View St. Pg.7 J5
Wildwood Dr. Pg.11 O4
Williamsburg Dr. Pg.12 L5
Willow Ln. Pg.11 O4
Win Haven Dr. Pg.7 K5
Windmere Dr. Pg.7 K5
Woodcliff Dr. Pg.12 P8
York Ln. Pg.3 F7

### FOREST PRESERVES
Otter Creek Forest Preserve Pg.11 N4

## GILBERTS
Pages 1,6

### STREETS
Andra Ct. Pg.6 F4
Big Timber Rd. Pg.6 H3
Center Dr. Pg.1 E3
Deborah St. Pg.6 F4
East Dr. Pg.1 E3
Freeman Rd. Pg.1 C3
Galligan Rd. Pg.1 D3
Hennessy Ct. Pg.6 G4
Higgins Rd. Pg.1 E3
Industrial Dr. Pg.1 E3
Jackson St. Pg.1 E3
Jean St. Pg.6 F4
Joan Ct. Pg.6 F4
Kathleen St. Pg.1 F4
Kerry Ct. Pg.6 G4
Kildare St. Pg.6 G4
Kilkenny Ct. Pg.6 G4
Mason Rd. Pg.6 G4
Matteson St. Pg.1 E3
McCormack Rd. Pg.1 F2
Northwest Toll Rd. Pg.1 E1
Pamela St. Pg.6 F4
Park Ct. Pg.1 E2
Park St. Pg.1 E2
Pauline Ct. Pg.1 F4
Pierce St. Pg.1 F4
Railroad St. Pg.1 E3
Red Hawk Path Pg.1 E4
Running Deer Ln. Pg.1 F4
Shining Moon Path Pg.1 F4
Sleeping Bear Tr. Pg.1 E4
Sola Dr. Pg.1 E3
Suzanne St. Pg.6 F4
Tipperary St. Pg.6 G4
Tollview Ct. Pg.1 E2
Tollview Terr. Pg.1 E2
Tower Hill Rd. Pg.1 D2
Towne Ct. Pg.6 F4
Towne St. Pg.6 F4
Turner St. Pg.1 E3
Tyler Creek Ct. Pg.1 E2
Tyrrell Rd. Pg.1 F4
Union St. Pg.1 E3
Welch St. Pg.6 G4
West End Dr. Pg.1 E3
White Feather Ln. Pg.1 E4
Willey St. Pg.1 E3
Windmill Ct. Pg.1 E2
Windmill Pl. Pg.1 E2

### MISCELLANEOUS
Post Office Pg.1 E3
Village Hall & Police Dept. Pg.1 E3

## HANOVER PARK
(For additional listings, see Sections 2 and 3)
Page 15

### STREETS
Alden Ln. O17
Apple Tree St. O18
Arbor Vitae Dr. N17
Argyle Rd. P18
Arlington Ct. Q19
Aspen Ln. O18
Astor Ave. N17
Barrington Rd. P18
Bartels Rd. P10
Bear Flag Dr. P18
Birch Ave. O18
Brairwood Ave. N18
Breezewood Ln. O17
Brentwood Ct. N19
Briar Ln. N18
Briarwood St. N18
Bristol Ct. N19
Bristol Ln. N18
Burr Oak St. O17
Camelia Dr. N17
Catalpa St. O18

# HANOVER PARK

Catawba Ln. . . . . . . . . M18
Cedar Ave. . . . . . . . . . O17
Center Ave. . . . . . . . . O17
Cherry Ave. . . . . . . . . O17
Chestnut St. . . . . . . . . O17
Church St. . . . . . . . O,Q18
Clarendon Ct. . . . . . . . P18
Cottage St. . . . . . . . . P18
County Farm Rd. . . . . . R17
Curtis Ln. . . . . . . . . . R17
Cynthia Ln. . . . . . . . . M18
Cypress Ave. . . . . . . . O18
Cypress Ct. . . . . . . . . O19
Dahlia Dr. . . . . . . . . . N17
Dandy Ct. . . . . . . . . . P18
Danforth Ct. . . . . . . . . P18
Deerfield Ct. . . . . . . . . P18
Deerpath Ln. . . . . . . . . P16
Devon Ave. . . . . . . . . P16
Downey Ct. . . . . . . . . P18
East Ave. . . . . . . . . . N18
Elm Ave. . . . . . . . . . O17
Elm Ct. . . . . . . . . . . O18
Elm St. . . . . . . . . . . O18
Evergreen Ave. . . . . . . O18
Fluwei Ct. . . . . . . . . . N10
Forest Glen . . . . . . . . O18
Fremont Dr. . . . . . . . . P18
Fremont Ct. . . . . . . . . P18
Gladiola Ave. . . . . . . . O17
Glendale Terr. . . . . . . . O17
Gold Cir. . . . . . . . . . O18
Greenwood St. . . . . . . . O18
Hanover Ave. . . . . . . . O18
Hemlock St. . . . . . . . . O17
Hickory Ave. . . . . . . . O17
Hillcrest Ave. . . . . . . . O18
Hollywood Ave. . . . . . . N18
Hollywood Ct. . . . . . . . N18
Huntington Cir. . . . . . . N19
Indian Hill Ave. . . . . . . O18
Indian Hill Ct. . . . . . . . O19
Iris Ave. . . . . . . . . . N19
Irving Park Rd. . . . . . . N18
Jasmine Dr. . . . . . . . . N18
Jonquil Terr. . . . . . . . O18
Juniper St. . . . . . . . . O18
Larch Ave. . . . . . . . . O17
Laurel Ave. . . . . . . . . N18
Lemon Ln. . . . . . . . . O17
Liberty St. (Ontarioville) . . P18
Linden Ave. . . . . . . . . N18
Magnolia Ave. . . . . . . . O18
Maple Ave. . . . . . . O17,18
Maplewood Ave. . . . . . . O18
Marigold Ln. . . . . . . . . N18
Mark Thomas Ln. . . . . . O18
Mulberry St. . . . . . . . . O18
Narcissus Ave. . . . . . . . N17
Nugget Cir. . . . . . . . . P18
Oak Ave. . . . . . . . . . O18
Oak St. (Ontarioville) . . . . P18
Oakwood Ave. . . . . . . . O18
Olivia Ln. . . . . . . . . . M18
Ontarioville Rd. (Ontarioville)P18
Osage Ln. . . . . . . . . . N17
Oak Ave. . . . . . . . . . O18
Peach Tree St. . . . . . . . O18
Pebblebrook . . . . . . . . M18
Pine Tree St. . . . . . . . . O17
Plum Tree Ln. . . . . . . . O17
Poplar Ave. . . . . . . . . O18
Ramblewood Dr. . . . . . . M18
Redwood Ave. . . . . . . . O18
Rosewood . . . . . . . . . N18
Sacramento Dr. . . . . . . O18
Scott Ln. . . . . . . . . . U1/
Sequoia Dr. . . . . . . . . O18
Short St. . . . . . . . . . N17
Spruce Ave. . . . . . . . . O18
Strathmore Ln. . . . . . . . N18
Sutter Dr. . . . . . . . . . P18
Sycamore Ave. . . . . . . . O18
Tanglewood Ave. . . . . . . N18
Thornwood St. . . . . . . . N18
Tower Dr. . . . . . . . . . N18
Valley View Rd. . . . . . . . N18
Walnut Ave. . . . . . . O17,18
Walnut Ct. . . . . . . . . . O17
West Ave. . . . . . . . . . O17
Willow Ave . . . . . . . . . O18

## PARKS

Community Park . . . . . . . O18
Geo. Georgen Mem. Baseball
  Fields . . . . . . . . . . N18
Ranger Park . . . . . . . . . N18

## SCHOOLS

Laurel Hill Sch. . . . . . . . N18
Ontarioville Sch. . . . . . . O17
Parkwood Sch. . . . . . . . N17

## SHOPPING CENTERS

Hanover Square . . . . . . . O18
Tradewinds S.C. . . . . . . . N18

## MISCELLANEOUS

ComEd Substation . . . . . . P18
Hanover Twp. Mental Health
  Ctr. . . . . . . . . . . . N17
Railroad Station . . . . . . . N18
Village Hall & Police Dept. . . O17

# HANOVER TOWNSHIP

Pages 8-10,13-14

## STREETS

Barrington Rd. . . . Pg.10 . . . K18
Bartlett Rd. . . . . Pg.10 . . . I16
Bartlett Rd. W. . . Pg.13 . . . O11
Berner Dr. . . . . . Pg.9 . . . J12

---

Beverly Rd. . . . . Pg.9 . . . I13
Birchbark Dr. . . . Pg.9 . . . I14
Bode Rd. . . . . . Pg.9, K16,18
Bridlewood Dr. . . Pg.9 . . . I14
Castlewood Dr. . . Pg.14 . . . M14
Cheshire Dr. . . . Pg.9 . . . I14
Chestnut St. . . . Pg.14 . . . L12
Chevoit Ln. . . . . Pg.14 . . . O14
Circle Dr. . . . . . Pg.14 . . . L12
Dale Dr. . . . . . Pg.9 . . . J12
Dennis Ln. . . . . Pg.14 . . . M14
Douglas Rd. . . . Pg.14 . . . M14
Forrest View Dr. . . Pg.9 . . . K13
Friar Tuck Dr. . . Pg.14 . . . M13
Galloway Dr. . . . Pg.9 . . . I14
Gifford Rd. . . . . Pg.13 . . . O11
Glen Echo St. . . Pg.14 . . . L12
Golf Rd. (Evanston- Elgin)
. . . . . . . . . . . . . Pg.9,10
Golfview Dr. . . . Pg.14 . . . N13
Greenwood Rd. . . Pg.14 . . . L13
Gromer Rd. . . . . Pg.14 . . . M13
Higgins Rd. . . . . Pg.10 . . . I18
Hill Top Rd. . . . . Pg.9 . . . K13
Ill. Rte. 10 (Irving Pk. Rd.)
Ill. Rte. 20 (Lake St.)
. . . . . . . . . . . . . Pg.14 . . . N14
Ill. Rte. 59 (Sutton Rd.)
. . . . . . . . . . . . . Pg.9 . . . I15
Irving Park Rd. (Rte.19)
. . . . . . . . . . . . . Pg.14 . . . N14
King Arthur . . . Pg.14 . . . L13
Lady Marion Dr. . Pg.14 . . . L13
Lake St. . . . . . Pg.14 . . . M14
Little John Dr. . . Pg.14 . . . L13
Magnolia Ln. . . . Pg.9 . . . J15
McDonough Dr. . . Pg.9 . . . I14
Morningview Ct. . . Pg.9 . . . I14
Morningview Dr. . . Pg.9 . . . I14
Mudhank Rd. . . . Pg.10 . . . I17
Naperville Rd. . . Pg.14 . . . O13
Northwest Tollway (I-90)
. . . . . . . . . . . Pg.9,10,I12-16
Nottingham Ln. . . Pg.14 . . . L13
Old Higgins Rd. . . Pg.10 . . . I18
Old Lake St. . . . Pg.14 . . . N15
Palomino Ln. . . . Pg.9 . . . I14
Robin Hood Dr. . . Pg.14 . . . M13
Rohrssen Rd. . . . Pg.9 . . . J13
Rolling Knolls Ave.
. . . . . . . . . . . . . Pg.9 . . . K13
Sawhorse Dr. . . . Pg.9 . . . I14
Sayer Rd. . . . . Pg.14 . . . O14
Schaumburg Rd. . . Pg.9,10
. . . . . . . . . . . . . . . L14-19
Sherwood Ln. . . Pg.14 . . . L13
Shoe Factory Rd. . Pg.9 . . . I14,16
Shotkoski Dr. . . Pg.8 . . . I14
Tameling Ct. . . . Pg.14 . . . L13
Will Scarlet Ln. . . Pg.14 . . . M13
Wolsfeld Rd. . . . Pg.9 . . . K13

## CEMETERIES

Lakewood Memorial Park
Cemetery . . . . Pg.14 . . . N18

## FOREST PRESERVES

Poplar Creek Forest Preserve
. . . . . . . . . . . Pg.10 . . . I16

## GOLF COURSES

Rolling Knolls Golf Club
Villa Olivia Golf & Country Club
. . . . . . . . . . . Pg.14 . . . M13

## MISCELLANEOUS

Maywood Park Training Track

# HOFFMAN ESTATES

(For additional listings,
see Section 2)
Pages 9,10

## STREETS

Angouleme Ln. . . Pg.9 . . . J13
Atlantic Ave. . . . Pg.10 . . . H19
Barrington Rd. . . Pg.10 . . . J18
Bear Claw Ct. . . Pg.9 . . . H13
Beverly Rd. . . . Pg.9 . . . H13
Blackberry Ln. . . Pg.10 . . . H19
Boardwalk Blvd. . . Pg.10 . . . H19
Bode Rd. . . . . Pg.10 . . . K19
Central Rd. . . . Pg.10 . . . H19
Columbine Blvd. . Pg.9 . . . H15
Eagle Way . . . . Pg.10 . . . H19
Falcon Ln. . . . . Pg.9 . . . H15
Forbes Ct. . . . . Pg.9 . . . H15
Fox Path Ct. . . . Pg.9 . . . J13
Fox Path Ln. . . . Pg.9 . . . J13
Frank Dr. . . . . Pg.9 . . . J12
Golf Rd. (Evanston-Elgin)
. . . . . . . . . . . Pg.9 . . . J15-19
Hassell Rd. . . . Pg.10 . . . J18
Higgins Rd. . . . Pg.9,10
. . . . . . . . . . . . . . G12,I19
Hunters Ridge Ct. Pg.9 . . . J13
Hunters Ridge, E. & W.
Mallard Ln. . . . Pg.9 . . . J13
Maureen Dr. . . . Pg.9 . . . J12
Old Barrington Rd.
. . . . . . . . . . . Pg.10 . . . H19
Old Higgins Rd. . Pg.10 . . . I18,19
Old South Rd. . . Pg.10 . . . H19
Pacific Ave. . . . Pg.10 . . . K19
Pembroke Ave. . . Pg.10 . . . K19
Pheasant Trail Ct. Pg.9 . . . J13

---

Poplar Creek Dr. . Pg.10 . . . J19
Prairie Stone Pkwy.
. . . . . . . . . . . Pg.9 . . . H14
Pratum Ave. . . . Pg.9 . . . H14
Quail Run Ct. . . Pg.9 . . . H14
Rohrssen Rd. . . . Pg.9 . . . J13
Russell Dr. . . . . Pg.9 . . . J12
Sears Pkwy. . . . Pg.9 . . . H14
Sedge Blvd. . . . Pg.9 . . . H14
Shoe Factory Rd. . Pg.9 . . . H14
Stonington Ave. . . Pg.10 . . . I19
Teal Ct. . . . . . Pg.9 . . . J13
Trillium Blvd. . . . Pg.9 . . . H13
Winnow Ave. . . . Pg.9 . . . H13

## FOREST PRESERVES

Poplar Creek Forest Preserve
. . . . . . . . . . . Pg.10 . . . J18

## GOLF COURSES

Boulder Golf & Driving Range
Poplar Creek G.C. Pg.10 . . . J19

## PARKS

Kelley Park . . . . Pg.9 . . . J14
Park Center . . . Pg.9 . . . H14
Village Green . . . Pg.9 . . . H14

## SCHOOLS

NIU Education Ctr.
. . . . . . . . . . . Pg.9 . . . H13

## SHOPPING CENTERS

Barrington Sq. S.C.
Hoffman Village S.C.
. . . . . . . . . . . Pg.10 . . . K18

## MISCELLANEOUS

Amphitheater . . . Pg.9 . . . H14
Benchmark-Alden Retirement
  Facility . . . . Pg.10 . . . J18
Humana Hosp. . . Pg.10 . . . J18
Pace Transportation Center
Poplar Creek Surgical Center
Sears Roebuck & Company H.Q.
. . . . . . . . . . . Pg.9 . . . H13

# INVERNESS

(For additional listings,
see Section 2)
Page 5

## STREETS

Ash Kirk Ct. . . . . . . . D19
Barrington Rd. . . . . . . C19
Bradwell Rd. . . . . . . . D19
Braymore Ct. . . . . . . . D19
Braymore Dr. . . . . . . . D19
Dundarton Dr. . . . . . . . C19
Gaelic Ct. . . . . . . . . D19
Hamilton Ct. . . . . . . . D19
Knox Ct. . . . . . . . . . D19
New Abbey Dr. . . . . . . D19
Palatine Rd. . . . . . . . C19

# MO QUEENS

Page 6...I3

# PLATO TOWNSHIP

(For additional listings,
see Section 4)
Pages 6,11

## STREETS

Adohe Ridge . . . Pg.11 . . . N2
Apache Run . . . Pg.11 . . . M2
Binnfield Dr. . . . Pg.11 . . . N1
Bowes Rd. . . . . Pg.11 . . . N1
Capulet Cir. . . . Pg.11 . . . L2
Central Dr. . . . . Pg.11 . . . L2
Cheyenne Ct. . . Pg.6 . . . I3
Chisholm Tr. . . . Pg.6 . . . I2
Citation Ct. . . . Pg.11 . . . K2
Cliff Dr. . . . . . Pg.11 . . . K2
Coombs Rd. . . . Pg.6 . . . I2
Corron Rd. . . . . Pg.11 . . . O1
Harty Ct. . . . . Pg.11 . . . P2
High Chapparel . Pg.6 . . . I2
Highland Ave. . . Pg.11 . . . L2
Ilogan Hill Trail . . Pg.11 . . . M2
Juliet Dr. . . . . Pg.11 . . . L2
Lori Ln. . . . . . Pg.11 . . . N2
Lori Ln. W. . . . Pg.11 . . . N2
McDonald Rd. . . Pg.11 . . . P1
Nestler Rd. . . . Pg.11 . . . O1
Oak Tree Ln. . . Pg.6 . . . K2
Plank Rd. . . . . Pg.6 . . . K2
Pueblo Peak . . . Pg.11 . . . M2
Red Cloud Ln. . . Pg.11 . . . M2
Romeo Cir. . . . Pg.11 . . . L2
Romeo Dr. . . . . Pg.11 . . . L2
Russell Rd. . . . Pg.11 . . . K2
Saindon Dr. . . . Pg.11 . . . L2
Santa Fe Tr. . . . Pg.11 . . . N2
Secretariat Ct. . . Pg.11 . . . K2
Sturbridge Way . . Pg.11 . . . O1
Sunflower Ln. . . Pg.11 . . . N2
Switzer Rd. . . . Pg.6 . . . I2
Verona Dr. . . . . Pg.11 . . . L2
Water Rd. . . . . Pg.11 . . . M2
Western Ave. . . Pg.6 . . . I2
Whispering Springs Ln.
. . . . . . . . . . . Pg.11 . . . N1

## FOREST PRESERVES

Fitchie Creek Forest Preserve
. . . . . . . . . . . Pg.11 . . . M2

---

# RUTLAND TOWNSHIP

(For additional listings,
see Section 1)
Pages 1,6

## STREETS

Abilene Tr. . . . Pg.6 . . . H2
Apache Ln. . . . Pg.1 . . . B1
Aztec Ln. . . . . Pg.1 . . . B1
Balko Parkway . . Pg.1 . . . B1
Baron Ln. . . . . Pg.1 . . . B1
Big Timber Rd. . . Pg.6 . . . G2
Binnie Lakes Tr. . Pg.1 . . . D4
Binnie Rd. . . . . Pg.1 . . . D3
Bonnie Lane . . . Pg.6 . . . H3
Cody Ct. . . . . Pg.6 . . . H2
Damisch Rd. . . . Pg.1 . . . G1
Freeman Rd. . . . Pg.1 . . . C1
Gary Ln. . . . . Pg.1 . . . B1
Grand Ave. . . . Pg.6 . . . G2
Gunpowder Ln. . . Pg.6 . . . H2
Guthrie Ct. . . . Pg.6 . . . F1
Hidden Hills Trail Pg.1 . . . C4
Hidden Knoll Rd. Pg.6 . . . H3
Highland Ave. . . Pg.1 . . . H1
Huntley Rd. . . . Pg.1 . . . A3,B4
Mary Cir. . . . . Pg.1 . . . C2
Mary Ln. . . . . Pg.1 . . . C2
McCormack Rd. . . Pg.6 . . . G2
Navajo Ln. . . . Pg.1 . . . B1
Northwind Lane . . Pg.1 . . . D4
Oak Knoll . . . . Pg.1 . . . D4
Oliver Dr. . . . . Pg.1 . . . H2
Pheasant Field Ln.
. . . . . . . . . . . Pg.6 . . . F1
Pleasant Dr. . . . Pg.6 . . . H3
Powers Rd. . . . Pg.1 . . . C1
Spring Creek Rd. . Pg.1 . . . C4
Square Barn Rd. . Pg.1 . . . A3
Timber Ridge Dr. Pg.6 . . . H2

## FOREST PRESERVES

Binnie F.P. . . . . Pg.1 . . . C4
Burnidge/Paul Wolfe F.P.
. . . . . . . . . . . Pg.6 . . . H3
Freeman Kame Forest Preserve
. . . . . . . . . . . Pg.1 . . . C2
Meagher F.P. . . Pg.1 . . . B1

# SCHAUMBURG

(For additional listings,
see Section 2)
Page 10,15

## STREETS

Adams Ct. . . . Pg.15 . . . L18
Amber Ln. . . . Pg.15 . . . L19
Andover Ct. . . . Pg.10 . . . J18
Ashburn Ct. . . . Pg.15 . . . L18
Ashling Ct. . . . Pg.15 . . . L18
Barrington Rd. . . Pg.15 . . . L18
Beechmont Ct. . . Pg.15 . . . L18
Belle Ln. . . . . Pg.15 . . . M18
Broadway Ln. . . Pg.15 . . . L19
Burgess Ct. . . . Pg.10 . . . J18
Charleston Dr. . . Pg.15 . . . M10
Charlotte Ct. . . Pg.15 . . . L18
Chesterfield Ct. . Pg.15 . . . M18
Cheswick Ct. . . Pg.15 . . . L18
Columbia Ct. . . Pg.15 . . . L18
Crescent Ln. . . Pg.15 . . . M19
Delaware Ct. . . Pg.15 . . . L18
Dorshire Ct. . . Pg.15 . . . L18
Dublin Ln. . . . Pg.15 . . . L18
Effingham Ct. . . Pg.15 . . . L18
Fallbrook Ct. . . Pg.15 . . . I19
Featherstone Ct. . Pg.15 . . . L19
Fernwood Ct. . . Pg.15 . . . M18
Fremont Ct. . . . Pg.15 . . . M18
Gilcrest Ct. . . . Pg.15 . . . L18
Glasgow Ct. . . Pg.15 . . . L18
Glasgow Ln. . . Pg.15 . . . L18
Glen Byron Ct. . Pg.15 . . . L18
Glen Leven Ct. . Pg.15 . . . L18
Glengarry Ct. . . Pg.15 . . . L18
Green Bridge Ct. Pg.15 . . . L18
Green Knoll Ln. . Pg.15 . . . L18
Hamilton Cir. . . Pg.15 . . . L18
Hamilton Pl. . . . Pg.10 . . . K19
Hanson Ct. . . . Pg.15 . . . M19
Hawk Ct. . . . . Pg.15 . . . L18
Heatherwood Dr. . Pg.15 . . . L18
Holmes Way . . Pg.15 . . . M18
Hunterdon Ct. . . Pg.15 . . . L18
Island Ct. . . . . Pg.15 . . . M18
Larch Ct. . . . . Pg.15 . . . M18
Maidstone Ct. . . Pg.15 . . . L18
Meadow Lane Ct. Pg.15 . . . L18
Meadow Ln. . . . Pg.15 . . . L18
Meribel Ct. . . . Pg.15 . . . L18
Odlum Ct. . . . Pg.15 . . . L18
Odlum Dr. . . . . Pg.15 . . . L18
Old Church Rd. . Pg.15 . . . L18
Pembroke Ct. . . Pg.15 . . . M18
Raleigh Ct. . . . Pg.15 . . . M18
Schaumburg Rd. . Pg.15 . . . L18
Sheffield Dr. . . Pg.10 . . . L18
Small Dr. . . . . Pg.15 . . . M18
Weathersfield Way
. . . . . . . . . . . . Pg.15 . . . M19
Westminister Ct. . Pg.15 . . . M18
Winfield Ct. . . . Pg.15 . . . L18
Winnsboro Ct. . . Pg.15 . . . M18

# SLEEPY HOLLOW

Pages 2,7,8

## STREETS

Acorn Ct. . . . . Pg.7 . . . G7
Acorn Ln. . . . . Pg.7 . . . G7,8
Appaloosa Ct. . . Pg.7 . . . F6

---

Arabian Pwy . . . Pg.7 . . . G6
Arlington Pwky. . . Pg.7 . . . G6
Beau Brummel Dr.
. . . . . . . . . . . Pg.7 . . . G6
Belmont Pwy . . . Pg.7 . . . G8
Brom Ct. . . . . Pg.7 . . . G8
Brook Ct. . . . . Pg.2 . . . E8
Bull Frog . . . . Pg.7 . . . F8
Carol Crest Ct. . . Pg.7 . . . F7
Christopher Ct. . . Pg.7 . . . F8
Churchill Pwy . . . Pg.7 . . . G7
Crane Ct. . . . . Pg.7 . . . F6
Crane Dr. . . . . Pg.7 . . . F6
Danielle Ct. . . . Pg.7 . . . G7
Darien Ct. . . . . Pg.7 . . . F7
Darien Ln. . . . . Pg.7 . . . F7
Deer Ln. . . . . Pg.2 . . . E7
Elm Ct. . . . . . Pg.8 . . . F8
Fawn Ct. . . . . Pg.7 . . . F6
Front Range Ct. . Pg.7 . . . F6
Gail Ln. . . . . . Pg.7 . . . F6
Glen Oak Ct. . . Pg.7 . . . G7
Glen Oak Dr. . . Pg.7 . . . G8
Hawthorne Ct. . . Pg.7 . . . F8
Hazel Ct. . . . . Pg.7 . . . F8
Hemlock Ct. . . . Pg.7 . . . F8
Hialeah Ct. . . . Pg.7 . . . G6
Hickory Dr. . . . Pg.2 . . . E7
Higgins Rd. . . . Pg.7 . . . F6
Hillcrest Ct. . . . Pg.2 . . . E7
Hillcrest Park . . . Pg.2 . . . E8
Hilltop Ct. . . . . Pg.7 . . . F8
Hilltop East . . . Pg.7 . . . G6
Hilltop Ln. . . . . Pg.7 . . . F8
Holly Ct. . . . . Pg.7 . . . F8
Island Ct. . . . . Pg.2 . . . F8
Jaclay Ct. . . . . Pg.7 . . . F8
Jamestowne Ct. . Pg.7 . . . F6
Jamestowne Ln. . Pg.7 . . . F6
Jill Peak Dr. . . . Pg.7 . . . F8
Joy Ln. . . . . . Pg.7 . . . F8
Karyn Ct. . . . . Pg.7 . . . G8
Karyn Dr. . . . . Pg.7 . . . G8
Katrina Ct. . . . Pg.7 . . . F7
Katrina Ln. . . . Pg.7 . . . F7
Kay Ct. . . . . . Pg.7 . . . F7
Laurel Ct. . . . . Pg.7 . . . F6
Locust Dr. . . . . Pg.7 . . . F6
Maple Ln. . . . . Pg.8 . . . F8
Maria Ct. . . . . Pg.7 . . . F6
Mason Rd. . . . . Pg.7 . . . G5
Myrna Ct. . . . . Pg.7 . . . F8
Palimino Ct. . . . Pg.7 . . . G6
Paula Ct. . . . . Pg.2 . . . E8
Pimlico Pwy . . . Pg.7 . . . G6
Pinecone Ln. . . Pg.2 . . . F7
Plum Ct. . . . . Pg.7 . . . F8
Rainbow Dr. . . . Pg.2 . . . E7
Red Bud Cir. . . Pg.7 . . . F8
River Ridge Rd. . Pg.7 . . . G8
Tewkesbury Ln. . Pg.7 . . . F8
Tiffany Cir. . . . Pg.7 . . . F6
Trenton Ct. . . . Pg.7 . . . F7
Turning Shore . . Pg.7 . . . F7
Upper Pond . . . Pg.7 . . . F7
Vanderberg Dr. . . Pg.7 . . . F8
Walnut Ln. . . . Pg.7 . . . F8
Watercrest Ct. . . Pg.7 . . . G6
Westlake Dr. . . Pg.7 . . . F8
Willow Bay Dr. . . Pg.7 . . . F8
Wind Ridge Rd. . Pg.7 . . . F8
Windsor Ct. . . . Pg.7 . . . F8
Witt Rd. . . . . Pg.7 . . . F8
Woodbury Ct. . . Pg.7 . . . G6

## PARKS

Sabatino Park . . Pg.7 . . . F8

## SCHOOLS

Sleepy Hollow Sch.

## MISCELLLANEOUS

Fire Station . . . Pg.7 . . . F7
Village Hall . . . Pg.7 . . . F7

# SOUTH BARRINGTON

(For additional listings,
see Section 2)
Pages 5,10

## STREETS

Algonquin Rd. . . Pg.5 . . . E17
Back Bay Rd. . . Pg.10 . . . F17
Barrington Rd. . . Pg.10 . . . H18
Bartlett Rd. . . . Pg.5 . . . E-G16
Bay Reef Dr. . . . Pg.10 . . . G17
Beachnut Dr. . . . Pg.5 . . . E17
Beacon Hill Dr. . . Pg.5 . . . F16
Berkshire Ct. . . . Pg.10 . . . G18
Blanchard Cir. . . Pg.10 . . . G18
Blossom Ct. . . . Pg.10 . . . H17
Brandywine Rd. . . Pg.10 . . . F18
Bridlewood Tr. . . Pg.5 . . . F18
Brookhaven Cir. . Pg.5 . . . E17
Buckthorn Rd. . . Pg.10 . . . G18
Butera Ct. . . . Pg.10 . . . H18
Campoen Dr. . . . Pg.5 . . . E19
Central Rd. . . . Pg.5 . . . E16
Champlain Ct. . . Pg.10 . . . G16
Chipping Dr. . . Pg.5 . . . E18
Concord Ct. . . . Pg.10 . . . F16
Corey Ln. . . . . Pg.10 . . . G18

---

Covered Bridge Rd.
. . . . . . . . . . . Pg.10 . . . G18
Cutters Run . . . Pg.10 . . . H16
Dalton Ct. . . . . Pg.10 . . . F18
De Veaux Ct. . . Pg.5 . . . F18
East Cove . . . . Pg.10 . . . F17
Eastings Way . . . Pg.5 . . . E17
Foxshire Ct. . . . Pg.10 . . . G18
Gregory Ln. . . . Pg.10 . . . G18
Hackney Cir. . . . Pg.10 . . . G18
Headwater Cove . Pg.10 . . . G17
Heath Way . . . Pg.5 . . . E18
Higgins Rd. . . . Pg.10 . . . H16
Kitson Dr. . . . . Pg.5 . . . E18
Lake Adalyn Dr. . Pg.10 . . . G18
Lakeside Ct. . . . Pg.5 . . . E16
Lakeside Dr. . . . Pg.5 . . . E16
Lexington Rd. . . . Pg.10 . . . G16
Liberty Dr. . . . . Pg.5 . . . E18
Loch Ln. . . . . Pg.5 . . . F18
McQuashen Dr. . . Pg.10 . . . H18
Midlands Dr. . . . Pg.10 . . . H18
Mohawk Ct. . . . Pg.5 . . . E17
Mohawk Dr. . . . Pg.5 . . . E16
Morgan Ln. . . . Pg.10 . . . G16
Mundhank Rd. . . Pg.10 . . . G,H17
North Meadow Ct.Pg.10 . . . G17
Northwest Tollway
. . . . . . . . . . . Pg.10 . . . H17
Old Barrington Rd.
. . . . . . . . . . . Pg.10 . . . H18
Old Coach Dr. . . Pg.10 . . . H18
Old Sutton Rd. . . Pg.9 . . . F15
Overbrook Rd. . . Pg.10 . . . G18
Pacer Tr. . . . . Pg.10 . . . G16
Palatine Rd. . . . Pg.5 . . . E17
Penny Rd. . . . . Pg.5 . . . F17
Pentwater Dr. . . Pg.10 . . . G16
Polo Dr. . . . . . Pg.5 . . . E16
Quincy Ct. . . . . Pg.5 . . . F16
Red Ridge Cir. . . Pg.5 . . . E16
Revere Dr. . . . . Pg.10 F16,G17
Rose Blvd. . . . Pg.10 . . . G18
Saucer Cir. . . . Pg.10 . . . H17
Shire Trail . . . . Pg.10 . . . F18
Shirebrook Way . Pg.5 . . . E19
Shoreside Dr. . . Pg.5 . . . E16
South Cove . . . Pg.10 . . . G17
South Meadow Ct
. . . . . . . . . . . Pg.10 . . . H17
Spring Creek Dr. . Pg.5 . . . E19
Squire Ct. . . . . Pg.10 . . . F18
Stannington Way . Pg.5 . . . E19
Star Ln. . . . . . Pg.10 . . . H17
Stoneridge Dr. . . Pg.5 . . . F17
Sutton Rd. . . . . Pg.5 . . . H15
Taynton Ln. . . . Pg.5 . . . E19
Tennis Club Dr. . . Pg.10 . . . H18
Terra Vita Ct . . . Pg.10 . . . G18
Terra Vita Dr. . . Pg.10 . . . G18
Tiffany Cir. . . . Pg.10 . . . G18
Trenton Ct. . . . Pg.10 . . . F17
Turning Shore . . Pg.10 . . . F17
Upper Pond . . . Pg.10 . . . F17
Vanderberg Dr. . . Pg.10 . . . H17
Walnut Ln. . . . Pg.5 . . . E19
Watergate Dr. . . Pg.10 F,G17
Westlake Dr. . . Pg.5 . . . E19
Gilbert St. . . . . Pg.10 . . . G18
Gilpin Ave. . . . Pg.5 . . . N6
Gladys Ct. . . . Pg.5 . . . N6
Greenfield Ave. . . Pg.5 . . . N7
Hancock Ave. . . Pg.5 . . . N7
Hartman Ct. . . . Pg.5 . . . N9
Harvard Ct. . . . Pg.5 . . . O7
Harvard Ct. . . . Pg.5 . . . O7
Harvest Ln. . . . Pg.5 . . . O9
Haverhill Ct. . . . Pg.5 . . . P7
Helen Ave. . . . Pg.5 . . . O7
Hobart Ct. . . . Pg.5 . . . N6
Hobart Dr. . . . Pg.5 . . . N6
Hollywood Ct. . . Pg.5 . . . N9
Hopps Rd. . . . Pg.5 . . . O6
Independence Ave. . Pg.5 . . . O8
Industrial Dr. . . Pg.5 . . . N8
Ione Dr. . . . . Pg.5 . . . O8
Ivy Ct. . . . . . Pg.5 . . . N8
James St. . . . . Pg.5 . . . N6
Jenna Dr. . . . . Pg.5 . . . N6
Josephine Ave. . . Pg.5 . . . N8
Juli Ct. . . . . . Pg.5 . . . N8
Juli Dr. . . . . . Pg.5 . . . O8
Juniper Ln. . . . Pg.5 . . . P7
Kaelynn Ct. . . . Pg.5 . . . N8
Kane St. . . . . Pg.5 . . . O7
Kateland Way . . Pg.5 . . . P4
Kelsey Ct. . . . Pg.5 . . . P7
Kenilworth Ave. . Pg.5 . . . N7
Kingsport Ct. . . Pg.5 . . . O6
Kingsport Dr. . . Pg.5 . . . O7
Kossuth St. . . . Pg.5 . . . O8
La Fox St. . . . Pg.5 . . . N8

## PARKS

Gey Day Farm . . Pg.10 . . . G19
Marvin Dunteman Park

## SCHOOLS

School District 220
. . . . . . . . . . . Pg.5 . . . D19

## MISCELLANEOUS

Alexander Sillman Nature
  Center . . . . Pg.10 . . . F17
Barrington Club . Pg.10 . . . H18
Crabtree Nature Preserve
Goeberts Pumpkin Farm
. . . . . . . . . . . Pg.10 . . . H17
South Barrington Office Center
. . . . . . . . . . . Pg.10 . . . H17

# SOUTH ELGIN

(For additional listings,
see Section 4)
Page 12,13

## STREETS

Aaron Ave. . . . . . . . . O7
Adam Ave. . . . . . . . . P4
Adrienne Dr. . . . . . . . N7
Andover Ct. . . . . . . . O6
Angeline Dr. . . . . . . . N6-7
Ann St. . . . . . . . . . O9
Arbor Ln. . . . . . . . . P7
Arlington Ln. . . . . . . . P7
Arthur Ave. . . . . . . . N8
Ascot Ln. . . . . . . . . P4
Ashton Ct. . . . . . . . . P7
Ashton Ln. . . . . . . . . N4
Barbara Ave. . . . . . . . P7
Barcroft Ct. . . . . . . . N6
Beach Ct. . . . . . . . . N8
Beck Ave. . . . . . . . . N8
Belle Ln. . . . . . . . . N8

---

# SOUTH ELGIN

Berkshire Ct. . . . . . . . P8
Birch Ln. . . . . . . . . O6
Blackhawk Cir. . . . . . . O6
Boston Ct. . . . . . . . . P8
Brandywine Ct. . . . . . . P7
Brittany Ct. . . . . . . . N7
Brookline St. . . . . . . . O7
Brookside Dr. . . . . . . . P4
Bunker Hill Ave. . . . . . O7
Burke Dr. . . . . . . . . N6-7
Burnidge Rd. . . . . . . . N9
Cambridge Rd. . . . . . . O7
Camden Ln., N. & W. . . . P7
Caren Ct. . . . . . . . . O7
Carla Dr. . . . . . . . . O7
Carlton St. . . . . . . . . N9
Carriage Way . . . . . . . P5
Cascade Ct. . . . . . . . N6
Castlebar Ct. . . . . . . . P7
Cedar Ct. . . . . . . . . P7
Center St. . . . . . . . . O8
Champange Ln. . . . . . . N6
Charles Ct. . . . . . . . . O7
Chatham Ct. . . . . . . . P7
Cherry St. . . . . . . . . O8
Chesterfield Ct. . . . . . . N8
Chipstone Dr. . . . . . . . N8
Churchill Ct. . . . . . . . P7
Clifton Ct. . . . . . . . . N6
Clinton St. . . . . . . . P7,8
Clove Ct. . . . . . . . . P7
Cobbler Ct. . . . . . . . P7
Collins St. . . . . . . . . P8
Commerce Dr. . . . . . . N8
Concord Ave. . . . . . . . N7
Conway Ct. . . . . . . . P8
Cornell Ct. . . . . . . . . P7
Cornwall Ave. . . . . . . . P7
Countryside Ln. . . . . . . P4
Courtland Way . . . . . . O4
Coventry Ct. . . . . . . . P7
Crystal Ave. . . . . . . . P8
Danbury Ct. . . . . . . . O7
Dean Dr. . . . . . . . . O7
Diane Ct. . . . . . . . . N7
Division St. . . . . . . . . O8
Dorset Ct. . . . . . . . . P7
Dublin Ct. . . . . . . . . O7
Dublin Ln. . . . . . . . . O7
Earl Ln. . . . . . . . . . P4
East Ave. . . . . . . . . O9
East Dr. . . . . . . . . . P9
Eastview St. . . . . . . . O8
Elgin Blvd., S. . . . . . . P9
Elizabeth St. . . . . . . . P9
Exeter Dr. . . . . . . . . O6
Exeter Ln. . . . . . . . . P7
Fairfax Ct. . . . . . . . . P7
Fairfax Ln. . . . . . . . . P7
Fairview Ln. . . . . . . . N6
Farmington Ct. . . . . . . N6
Fenwick Ln. . . . . . . . N7
Fieldcrest Dr. . . . . . . . N6
Franklin Ave. . . . . . . . N7
Frederick Ct. . . . . . . . N7
Fulton Dr. . . . . . . . . P8
Genevieve Dr. . . . . . . N7
George Ave. . . . . . . . P7
Gibbons Ct. . . . . . . . N7

Lincoln Ct. P7
Linda Ct. P9
Lindemann Ct. O8
Linden Ct. P7
Locust Ct. P7
Locust St. O8
London Ct., N. & S. P7
Longbow Ct. P7
Longview Ct. P7
Lor-Ann St. P9
Lowell Dr. O6
Lucille St. O9
Lynn St., E. & W. O7
Main St. O9
Manchester Ct.Rd. O7
Marbury St. O7
Marcia Ct. N6
Marie Ct. N7
Mark St. P8
Marleigh Ln. N6
Martin Dr. O7
Mavis Ave. N8
Mayfair Ln. O7
McDonald Rd. P5
McLean Blvd. P7
Medford Dr. O7
Melinda Dr. O7
Melrose Ave. N8
Mestic Ct. N9
Michigan Ave. N7
Middle St., E. O9
Middle St., W. O8
Middleford Ct. N7
Mill St. O8
Millicent Ct. N6
Misty Ct. N6
Moody Ct. N9
Nellie Ave. P8
North Dr. P8
Oak Ln. P4
Oak St. O8
Oakview Ct. O4
Oakwood Ln. P8
Oxford Ct. O7
Oxford Ln. O7
Paine St. P7
Park Ave. P8
Parkwood Cir. P5
Patrick St. O9
Pembroke Dr., N. & S. O6
Persimmon Ln. P4
Pine Ct. O8
Pleasant Dr. O9
Plum St., E. & W. O8
Prairie St. O8
Production Dr. N8
Public Rd. N8
Quarry St. O8
Rainbow Terr. N7
Raymond St. N9
Regent St. O8
Renee Dr. O7
Revere Rd. O7
Ridge Ct. N6
Ridge Rd. N6
River Rd. N9
River St. O8
Riverside Ave. P8
Riverview Dr. N9
Robertson Rd. N8
Ross Ave. N8
Roxbury Ct. N7
Sandhurst Ln. O6
Sara Ct. N6
Saratoga Ct. N6
Schneider Dr. N8
Sheffield Ct. N6
Smith Ct. N9
South Dr. P9
Spring Ave. P8
Spring St. O7
Spruce St. O8
State St., E. O8
State St., W. O8
Sterling Ct. P4
Steve's Farm Dr. N8
Stevenson Rd. N8
Stone St. O8
Stonington Pl. O7
Stratford Ct. P7
Strathmore Terr. O7
Sunbrook St. O7
Sunbury Rd. O7
Sundown Rd. N7
Sweetbriar Ct. O7
Terrace Ln. P4
Thorndale Ct. P8
Thorndale Ln. P8
Thornwood Dr. P5
Thornwood Way P5
Timber Ln. O6
Trenton Ave. O7
Valley Forge Ave. P7
Vernon Ct. P7
Village Ct. P7
Virginia Dr. O8
Walnut St. O8
Warwick Ct. P8
Water St. O8
Waterford Ln. P8
Waters Edge Dr. P4
Waterside Dr. P4
Wedgewood Dr. O7
West Dr. P8
Weston Ct. O6
Williams Dr. P9
Willow Ln. N7
Wills St. O8
Wilson Ave. N8
Windsor Ct. P8
Woodbury St. O8
Woodland Dr. O6
Woodridge Cir. P8
Woodrow Ave. N8
Yorkshire Ct. O7

#### FOREST PRESERVES
Kenyon Farm Forest Preserve O9

#### PARKS
Conservation Area P4
Kane County Park P8
Lions Park O8
Panton Mill Park O8
Pickeral Park P8
Robert Sperry Park N7
Seba Park O8

#### SCHOOLS
Clinton Sch. O9
Fox Meadow Elem. Sch. N7
Pioneer Sch. O8
Willard Sch. O8

#### MISCELLANEOUS
Fire Department O8
Post Office O8
Trolley Museum O8
Village Hall and Police O8

## ST. CHARLES TOWNSHIP
(For additional listings, see Section 4)
Pages 11-13

#### STREETS
Big Axe Rd. Pg.11 P3
Cloverfield Dr. Pg.11 P3
Columbine East Pg.11 P3
Columbine West Pg.11 P3
Crane Rd. Pg.11 P4
Dogwood Ln. Pg.11 P4
Eagles Nest Ct. Pg.11 P3
East Dr. Pg.13 P9
Falcons Tr. Pg.11 P3
Foxglove Ct. Pg.11 Q3
Hill Ct. Pg.12 P8
Lilac Ln. Pg.11 P4
Oak Dr. Pg.11 P3
Pine Rd. Pg.11 P3
Red Bay Ct. Pg.11 P3
River Valley Dr. Pg.12 P8
South Dr. Pg.13 P9
Stevens Glen Rd. Pg.11 Q3
Wagontire Rd. Pg.11 Q3
Woodcliff Dr. Pg.12 P8
Yaupon Ct. Pg.11 P3

## STREAMWOOD
Pages 9,10,14,15

#### STREETS
Abbeywood Cir. Pg.10 K17
Abbington Ct. Pg.14 M15
Acorn Dr. Pg.15 M18
Adams Ct. Pg.14 M15
Alexander Ave. Pg.15 N17
Alexander Ct. Pg.15 N17
Alexander Pl. Pg.15 N17
Andover Ct. Pg.15 N16
Apple Hill Ln. Pg.10 K17
Arabian Ct. Pg.14 L14
Arbor Ct. Pg.14 L14
Arbor Dr. Pg.14 M14
Arnold Ave. Pg.15 N16
Arrowwood Ct. Pg.10,15 K19
Arthur Ct. Pg.15 L16
Ascot Ln. Pg.9 K15
Ash Ct. Pg.15 L17
Ashton Ct. Pg.15 N16
Aspen Ct. Pg.15 L17
Attleboro Dr. Pg.14 M15
Audubon Rd. Pg.15 L16
Augusta Dr. Pg.14 L15
Autumn Ln. Pg.14 M15
Azalea Cir. Pg.15 L17
Banbury Ct. Pg.14 M15
Barrington Rd. Pg.15 M18
Bartlett Rd. Pg.15 N16
Bayberry Ct. Pg.15 L17
Beaver Dr. Pg.15 L17
Beebe Ct. Pg.15 N16
Berkley Pl. Pg.15 M17
Berkshire Ct. Pg.14 M15
Beverly Ct. Pg.15 N15
Beverly Ln. Pg.15 N15
Big Oaks Ct. Pg.15 L16
Big Oaks Rd. Pg.15 L16
Bittersweet Ln. Pg.14 L14
Blackberry Ct. Pg.14 L14
Bluestem Ct. Pg.14 L15
Blue Bird Ct. Pg.14 M14
Bluff Ct. Pg.14 L15
Bode Rd., E. Pg.10 K16
Bonded Pkwy. Pg.10 K18
Borris Cir. Pg.10 K17
Bourbon Pkwy. Pg.14 M14
Boxwood Ct. Pg.10 K19
Brandy Pkwy. Pg.15 M18
Briarwood Dr. Pg.15 M16
Briarwood Dr., W. Pg.15 M16
Bristol Ct. Pg.15 N16
Brittany Dr. Pg.14 M15
Brook Ln. Pg.10 K17
Brookstone Ct. Pg.14 M15
Brookstone Dr. Pg.14 M15
Brunswick Ct. Pg.15 N16
Buchanan Ln. Pg.15 L15
Buckskin Ln. Pg.14 L14
Burgundy Pkwy. Pg.15 M18
Bussey Ct. Pg.15 N17
Butternut Ln. Pg.15 M18
Buttitta Dr. Pg.15 M18
Cahill Rd. Pg.14 L15
Cambridge Ave. Pg.15 N16
Canterbury Ct. Pg.15 L17
Canton Ln. Pg.14 K15
Cardinal Ct. Pg.14 M14
Carey Ln. Pg.15 L16
Carlson Dr. Pg.15 N17
Carmella Ct. Pg.14 L14
Carol Ann Dr. Pg.10 K16
Castlewood Dr. Pg.14 M14
Cedar Cir. Pg.15 L16
Cedar Circle Ct. Pg.15 L16
Cedarcrest Dr. Pg.15 M17
Center Rd. Pg.14 L15
Chase Ct. Pg.15 L16
Chase Terr. Pg.15 L16
Chaucer Ln. Pg.15 L16
Cherry Ln. Pg.15 M16
Chestnut Dr., E. Pg.15 L16
Chestnut Dr., S. Pg.15 L16
Chrisman Dr. Pg.15 L16
Clairidge Ct. Pg.15 K19
Clearwater Ct. Pg.14 M15
Clematis Dr. Pg.15 L17
Clover Ct. Pg.14 L15
Club Tree Dr. Pg.15 N16
Colonial Ct. Pg.14 M15
Colony Ct. Pg.15 N16
Columbine Ct. Pg.14 M14
Concord Dr. Pg.15 L17
Coolidge Ct. Pg.14 M15
Corrington Ct. Pg.10 K18
Country Ln. Pg.15 M16
Creekside Ct. Pg.14 M15
Crescent Ct. Pg.14 L15
Crestwood Ct. Pg.15 M16
Crestwood Dr. Pg.15 M16
Cypress Dr. Pg.15 L16
Dana Ln. Pg.10 K17
Dartmouth Ct. Pg.14 M15
Dato Ct. Pg.15 K18
Dato Dr. Pg.10 K18
David Dr. Pg.15 N15
Debbie Ln. Pg.15 L18
Deerfield Dr. Pg.14 L15
Diane Dr. Pg.15 M15
Dorchester Ct. Pg.14 M15
Dorman Dr. Pg.15 M16
Dover Ct. Pg.9 K15
Driftwood Ct. Pg.15 K19
Dunbar Ct. Pg.15 N16
Duxbury Ct. Pg.15 N16
Eagle Ct. Pg.14 L14
East Ave. Pg.15 L,M17
Edgewood Ln. Pg.15 M16
Egan Ct. Pg.15 K18
Egan Dr. Pg.15 K18
Eliasek Ct. Pg.15 K17
Elm Ln. Pg.15 L16
Emerald Dr. Pg.14 L15
Essex Ct. Pg.15 N16
Evans Ct. Pg.15 N16
Evergreen Rd. Pg.14 M15
Exmoor Dr. Pg.10 K16
Fairview Dr. Pg.15 M16
Fallstone Dr. Pg.15 L17
Falmouth Ct. Pg.15 N16
Fernwood Ct. Pg.10 K18
Field Ln. Pg.15 L16
Filbert Dr. Pg.15 L17
Fillmore Ln. Pg.15 L15
Finch Ct. Pg.14 M14
Fir Ct. Pg.15 L17
Flowers Ave. Pg.15 N17
Forest Cove Ct. Pg.14 M14
Forest Dr. Pg.15 M16
Foxboro Ct. Pg.14 M15
Foxglove Ct. Pg.14 M14
Francis Dr. Pg.15 M18
Franklin Ct. Pg.10 K16
Frederick Ave. Pg.15 N17
Freeman Ave. Pg.15 N16
Fulton Dr. Pg.14 M15
Gant Cir. Pg.15 K17
Garden Cir. Pg.10 K17
Garfield Ln. Pg.15 L15
Gayle Ct. Pg.10 K18
Genualdi Ave. Pg.15 N17
Glendale Ct. Pg.10 K17
Green Ct. Pg.10 K18
Green Knoll Ln. Pg.10 K18
Green Meadows Blvd. Pg.10 K18
Greenbriar Ln. Pg.15 L15
Greenwood Ct. Pg.15 N16
Gregg Ct. Pg.10 K18
Grey Fox Ct. Pg.14 L14
Greystone Ct. Pg.15 K18
Grow Ln. Pg.15 L16
Gulf Keys Rd. Pg.14 M14
Hackberry Dr. Pg.15 M17
Hampton Ct. Pg.15 N16
Harrison Ln. Pg.14 L15
Hartwood Dr. Pg.15 M17
Harvest Dr. Pg.14 M15
Hastings Mill Rd. Pg.15 K18
Haverton Ct. Pg.15 L16
Hawthorne Ln. Pg.15 L16
Hayward Ave. Pg.15 N17
Hazelnut Dr. Pg.15 M18
Heath Ct. Pg.15 N17
Heather Ct. Pg.15 K17
Heather Ln. Pg.15 K17
Hecht Rd. Pg.15 N17
Heine Ct. Pg.15 K18
Heine Dr. Pg.15 K18
Helen Ct. Pg.15 M16
Heritage Ln. Pg.15 M16
Hickory Ave. Pg.15 L16
High Point Dr. Pg.14 M15
Hillside Ct. Pg.15 L17
Hillside Dr. Pg.15 L17
Hise Ct. Pg.10 K18
Holly Ct. Pg.15 L17
Holly Dr. Pg.15 M17
Hoover Ct. Pg.14 M15
Horseshoe Ct. Pg.14 L14
Hummingbird Ct. Pg.14 M14
Hummingbird Ln. Pg.14 M14
Huntington Dr. Pg.10 K16
Innsbrook Dr. Pg.15 N15
Iris Dr. Pg.15 M17
Ironwood Ct. Pg.10 K19
Irving Park Rd., E. Pg.15 N18
Irving Park Rd., W. Pg.14 M14
Ivy Ct. Pg.15 M18
Jackson Ln. Pg.15 L15
Jamestown Ct. Pg.15 N16
Janet Ave. Pg.15 M15
Jasmine Ct. Pg.14 L14
Jefferson Ct. Pg.15 L15
Jefferson Ln. Pg.15 L15
Jill Ln. Pg.10 K18
Jonquil Ct. Pg.14 L14
Joyce Ln. Pg.15 M16
Judy Ln. Pg.10 K18
Juniper Cir. Pg.15 L17
Juniper Ct. Pg.15 L17
Kennedy Dr. Pg.15 K18
Kennedy Dr., N. Pg.10 K18
Kensington Ct. Pg.14 K15
Kensington Dr. Pg.14 K15
Kevin Morris Ct. Pg.15 L18
Kimberly Ln. Pg.14 L15
King Dr. Pg.15 N18
Kingston Ct. Pg.15 N16
Klafter Ct. Pg.10 K18
Klein Dr. Pg.15 L18
Kosan Cir. Pg.10 K17
Krause Ave. Pg.15 N16
La Salle Ct. Pg.15 M15
La Salle Rd. Pg.15 M15
Lacy Ave. Pg.15 N17
Lake St. Pg.15 O17
Lancaster Ct. Pg.15 M15
Larkspur Ln. Pg.14 L14
Larsen Ave. Pg.15 N17
Laurel Ct. Pg.15 M16
Laurel Ln. Pg.15 M16
Laurel Oaks Dr. Pg.14 M14
Lee Ct. Pg.15 N17
Lexington Ct. Pg.10 K17
Library Dr. Pg.15 N16
Lincoln Ct. Pg.15 N17
Lincolnwood Dr. Pg.15 M16
Linda Ln. Pg.15 M15
Linden Dr. Pg.15 O17
Lisa Ln. Pg.15 M15
Little Creek Ct. Pg.14 L14
Little Creek Dr. Pg.14 L14
Locksley Dr. Pg.15 N16
Longboat Key Ln. Pg.14 M14
Lynnwood Ct. Pg.15 N16
Madison Dr. Pg.14 M15
Magnolia Ct. Pg.14 L14
Magnolia Dr. Pg.14 L14
Manchester Ct. Pg.9 K15
Manor Dr. Pg.15 M16
Maple Dr. Pg.15 N17
Marion Ln. Pg.15 L16
Mark Ln. Pg.10 K18
Marryat Pl. Pg.14 L15
Maxon Ln., E. Pg.15 L16
Maxon Ln., S. Pg.15 L16
Mayfield Dr. Pg.15 L17
McCabe Dr. Pg.15 L16
McKinley Ln. Pg.14 L15
McKool Ave. Pg.15 N17
Meadow Ct. Pg.15 M17
Meadow Ln. Pg.15 M17
Medford Ct. Pg.15 N16
Merideth Ln. Pg.15 N16
Merryoaks Rd. Pg.14 M15
Meyer Ct. Pg.10 K18
Middlebury Ct. Pg.10 K19
Miller Ave. Pg.15 N17
Monarch Dr. Pg.14 N14
Monroe Ct. Pg.15 L16
Moore Ave. Pg.15 N17
Mulberry Ln. Pg.15 M17
Mustang Ct. Pg.14 L14
Myrtle Ln. Pg.14 M15
Newberry Dr. Pg.15 M17
Nippert Dr. Pg.15 N16
Norwood Ct. Pg.15 N16
Oak Knoll Ct. Pg.10 K19
Oak Meadow Ct. Pg.15 L18
Oak Ridge Dr. Pg.14 M15
Oakland Dr. Pg.15 M17
Oakmont Ct. Pg.15 L18
Old Church Rd. Pg.15 L18
Old Oak Ct. Pg.15 N16
Old Oak Ln. Pg.15 N16
Oltendorf Ct. Pg.15 M16
Oltendorf Ct. Pg.15 M16
Oltendorf Rd., E. Pg.15 M16
Oltendorf Rd., N. Pg.15 L16
Oltendorf Rd., S. Pg.15 M16
Orchid Ct. Pg.14 L13
Oriole Dr. Pg.15 M17
Oxford Ct. Pg.15 N16
Park Ave. Pg.15 N16
Park Blvd., N. Pg.15 M17
Park Blvd., S. Pg.15 M17
Parkside Cir. Pg.15 M16
Parkside Ct. Pg.15 M16
Parkwood Ct. Pg.15 M17
Parkwood Dr. Pg.15 M17
Patricia Pkwy. Pg.15 M15
Pembroke Ct. PG.14 L15
Pepperidge Cir. Pg.15 M17
Petrie Cir. Pg.15 L17
Pheasant Tr. Pg.15 L13
Phillippi Cr. Dr. Pg.14 M14
Pine St., E. & S. Pg.15 M16
Pinto Ct. Pg.14 L14
Pleasant Pl. Pg.15 M17
Plum Tree Ct. Pg.15 L16
Plymouth Dr. Pg.10 K16
Polk Ct. Pg.14 M15
Poplar Creek Ct. Pg.15 M16
Post Ct. Pg.15 L17
Post Ln. Pg.15 L17
Prairie Point Ln. Pg.14 M15
Princeton Ct. Pg.15 N16
Prospect Ave. Pg.15 O16
Providence Ln. Pg.15 M16
Quaker Hollow Ct. Pg.10 K18
Quarter Horse Ct. Pg.14 L14
Quincy Ct. Pg.15 N16
Rambler Ln. Pg.15 M17
Rambler Pl. Pg.15 M17
Ramblewood Dr. Pg.15 M18
Red Cedar Dr. Pg.15 L17,18
Redwood Ct. Pg.15 M17
Regency Ct. Pg.15 M15
Ridge Cir. Pg.15 M17
Ridge Ct., N. Pg.15 L17
Ridge Pl. Pg.15 M17
Ridgewood Rd. Pg.14 L15
Robinhood Ct. Pg.15 L17
Robinhood Dr. Pg.15 L17
Robinson Ave. Pg.15 N17
Roder Ct. Pg.15 N17
Rosewood Ct. Pg.14 L14
Rosewood Dr. Pg.14 L14
Roma Jean Pkwy. Pg.15 N16
Rowley Ct. Pg.15 N16
Russet Ln. Pg.15 M17
Sagebrush Ct. Pg.14 L14
Samuel Ct. Pg.14 L14
Samuel Dr. Pg.15 N16
Sandalwood Ct. Pg.15 K19
Sandhurst Ct. Pg.10 K19
Sarasota Dr. Pg.10 K16
Schaumburg Rd., E. Pg.15 L18
Schaumburg Rd., W. Pg.15 L15
Seneca Ct. Pg.14 M15
Seton Ct. Pg.15 L17
Seton Pl. Pg.15 L17
Shadywood Ln. Pg.15 L15
Shagbark Ln., E. Pg.15 K17
Sheffield Ct. Pg.14 K15
Sherwood Dr. Pg.15 M17
Shirley Ave. Pg.15 N17
Short St. Pg.15 N17
Siesta Key Ln. Pg.14 M14
Slaverwood Ct. Pg.10 K18
Smith Ct. Pg.15 L18
Somerset Dr. Pg.10 K16
Southbury Ct. Pg.15 L19
Southwicke Dr. Pg.14 N14
Southwood Cir. Pg.15 M17
Spring Valley Ln. Pg.15 L17
Spruce Ct. Pg.15 M16
Spur Ct. Pg.14 L14
Stonegate Ln. Pg.15 K16
Stowell Ave. Pg.15 N17
Stowell Pl. Pg.15 N17
Stratford Cir. Pg.15 M16
Stratford Ct. Pg.15 M16
Streamwood Blvd., E. Pg.15 L16
Streamwood Blvd., W. Pg.14 M15
Suffolk Ct. Pg.15 M17
Suffolk Pl. Pg.15 M17
Sumac Dr. Pg.15 M17
Summerhill Ct. Pg.14 M14
Suncrest Ct. Pg.14 M15
Sunnydale Blvd. Pg.15 M17
Sunset Cir. Pg.15 L17
Surrey Ct. Pg.15 M17
Surrey Dr. Pg.15 M17
Sutton Rd., N. Pg.14 L,M14
Sutton Rd., S. Pg.14 M14
Sycamore Ave. Pg.15 N17
Taft Ct. Pg.14 M15
Tall Tree Rd. Pg.15 N16
Tanglewood Dr. Pg.14 L15
Taylor Ct. Pg.14 L15
Teak Ln. Pg.15 M18
Thistle Ct. Pg.14 M14
Thorndale Ct. Pg.15 L15
Timber Tr. Pg.15 L16
Timber Trail Ct. Pg.15 L16
Tinnerella Ave. Pg.15 N17
Trail Ridge Ct. Pg.14 L14
Truman Ct. Pg.14 M15
Truman Ln. Pg.14 M15
Twilight Tr. Pg.15 L16
Tyler Ct. Pg.14 L15
Valley Ln. E. Pg.15 N16
Valley Ln. S. Pg.15 N16
Victoria Ln., N. Pg.15 L17
Victoria Ln., S. Pg.15 L17
Villa Rd. Pg.15 L17
Vine St. Pg.15 N17
Virginia Ct. Pg.15 N15
Walden Ct. Pg.15 N16
Walden Tr. Pg.15 N16
Walker Ave. Pg.15 N17
Walnut Ct., N. Pg.14 L15
Walnut Dr. Pg.14 L15
Warwick Ct. Pg.10 K18
Washington Ave. Pg.15 M15
Washington Ct. Pg.15 L16
Waverly Ave. Pg.15 M17
Wellington Dr. Pg.10 K16
Westgate Ct. Pg.15 M17
Westgate Terr. Pg.15 M17
Weston Ct. Pg.14 K15
Whispering Ct. Pg.14 M15
Whispering Dr. Pg.14 M15
White Fence Tr. Pg.14 L14
White Hall Ct. Pg.15 L19
Whitewood Dr. Pg.15 L17
Wicker Ave. Pg.15 N17
Wild Meadow Dr. Pg.14 M14
Wild Rose Ct. Pg.14 N15
Wildflower Way Pg.14 M14
Wildwood Ct. Pg.15 M17
Wildwood Ln. Pg.15 M17
Williamsburg Dr. Pg.10 K19
Willow Ct. Pg.15 L17
Willow Rd. Pg.15 L17
Wilshire Ct. Pg.14 L15
Windgate Ct. Pg.10 K17
Winding Run Ln. Pg.10 K18
Windsor Ct. Pg.10 K17
Winterberry Ct. Pg.14 N15
Wisteria Dr. Pg.15 M18
Woodbury Ct. Pg.15 K18
Woodcrest Cir. Pg.15 L16
Woodland Hts. Blvd. Pg.15 M17
Woodmar Ct. Pg.10 K17
Woodridge Ln. Pg.15 L17
Woodview Ct. Pg.15 M17
Woodview Dr. Pg.15 M18
Yorkshire Dr. Pg.15 N18

#### GOLF COURSES
Streamwood Oaks G.C. Pg.14 L15

#### PARKS
Anniversary Park Pg.14 M15
Aquarius Park Pg.15 M15
Autumn Chase Park Pg.14 M15
Bartlett Park Pg.15 M16
Buchanan Park Pg.15 L15
Butterfly Park Pg.15 M18
Challenger Park Pg.15 K17
Countryside Park Pg.15 L16
Dolphin Park Pg.15 M16
Friendship Park Pg.15 M17
Glenbrook Park Pg.10 K17
Grow Park Pg.15 L16
Hoosier Grove Park Pg.14 M15
Jaycee Park Pg.14 L15
Jefferson Park Pg.14 M15
Kiddie Corner Park Pg.15 N17
Kollar Park Pg.15 N17
Lacy Park Pg.15 N17
Little Creek Park Pg.14 L14
Meadows Park Pg.15 M18
Millenium Field Pg.14 L15
Oak Hill Park Pg.15 M16
Oak Ridge Pg.14 M15
Oakwood Park Pg.15 N16
Rahlf's Woods Park Pg.15 N16
Ridge Park Pg.15 L17
Sherwood Forest Park Pg.15 N16
Sunnydale Park Pg.15 N17
Surrey Woods Park Pg.9 K15
Veteran's Park Pg.15 L17
Vine Park Pg.15 M17
Walnut Park Pg.15 L15
Woodland Park Pg.15 M17

#### SCHOOLS
Canton Jr. H.S. Pg.15 L17
Glenbrook Sch. Pg.10 K17
Hanover Countryside Sch. Pg.15 L16
Heritage Sch. Pg.15 N16
Oakhill Sch. Pg.15 M16
Ridge Circle Sch. Pg.15 L17
Streamwood H.S. Pg.14 L15
Streamwood Sch. Pg.15 L17
Sunnydale Sch. Pg.15 M17
Tefft Jr. H.S. Pg.15 N17
Woodland Hts. Sch. Pg.15 M16

#### SHOPPING CENTERS
Green Meadows S.C. Pg.10 K18
Hillbrook S.C. Pg.15 L16
Market Square Pg.15 N17
Oak Forest Plaza Pg.15 L16
Oak Knolls Commons Pg.15 L16
Westview S.C. Pg.15 M18
Woodland Hts. S.C. Pg.15 N16

#### MISCELLANEOUS
Fire Dept. Pg.15 L,N16,L18
Park Place Family Rec. Ctr. Pg.15 M17
Public Works Pg.15 M16
Streamwood Historical Society Pg.14 M15
Village Hall & Police Dept. Pg.15 N16

## UDINA
Page 6...K3

## WEST DUNDEE
Pages 2,3,8

#### STREETS
A St. Pg.2 E8
Angle Tarn Pg.8 G8
Autumn Hill Pg.8 G8
B St. Pg.3 E8
Barber Ct. Pg.2 E7
Bass Ct. Pg.8 G9
Brewer Ct. Pg.2 E7
Browning Ave. Pg.8 F9
Campbell Ct. Pg.2 E7
Castle Ct. Pg.2 E7
Castle Rock Ct. Pg.2 E7
Cavalier Ct. Pg.8 F8
Chadwick Ln. Pg.2 E7
Dunning Ave Pg.8 F9
Edinburgh Ln. Pg.2 E8
Edwards Ave. Pg.8 F9
Eichler Dr. Pg.8 F9
Fawn Hollow Ct. Pg.8 G8
Fay Ave. Pg.8 F9
Flint Dr. Pg.8 G9
Fox Ave. Pg.8 F9
Fox Path Pg.8 G8
Garrison Ave. Pg.8 F9
Geneva St. Pg.3 E9
Glenmoor Dr. Pg.2 E7
Grant St. Pg.2 E7
Green Castle Ct. Pg.2 E7
Green Ct. Pg.2 E7
Hamilton Dr. Pg.2 E7
Hawley Ave. Pg.8 F9
Highland Ave. Pg.3 E9
Hillcrest Ct. Pg.3 E9
Kane Ave. Pg.3 E9
Kittridge Dr. Pg.2 E7
Knowlton Dr. Pg.2 E7
Liberty St. Pg.3 F9
Lincoln Ave. Pg.3 E9
Lindsay Ct. Pg.2 E8
Lindsay Ln. Pg.2 E8
Lisa Rd. Pg.3 F9
Mac Gregor Ct. Pg.2 E7
Maiden Ln. Pg.8 F9
Main St. Pg.3 E9
Malcolm Ln. Pg.2 E7
Market Loop Pl. Pg.8 F9
McConniche Ct. Pg.2 E7
Millsfell Ct. Pg.8 G8
Oregon St. Pg.3 E9
Pember Cir. Pg.2 E7
Preston Ave. Pg.2 E7
Prestwick Ct. Pg.2 E7
Richardson Pg.8 G9
Riverside Ave. Pg.8 F9
Riverview St. Pg.8 F9
Roundabout Pg.8 F8
Royal Ln. Pg.3 F9
Ryan Ln. Pg.3 F9
Short St. Pg.8 F9
Smalley Ct. Pg.2 E7
South St. Pg.3 F9
Spaulding Ave. Pg.2 E7
Spring Hill Ring Rd. Pg.3 E8
Spring Leaf Ct. Pg.8 G8
Sterling Ct. Pg.2 E8
Stewart Ln. Pg.2 E7
Strom Dr. Pg.8 F9
Summerwood Ct. Pg.8 G8
Tartans Ct. Pg.2 E8
Tartans Dr. Pg.2 E8
Thatcher Tr. Pg.2 E7
Tritram Ct. Pg.2 E8
View St. Pg.3 F9
Village Quarter Rd. Pg.3 F9
Washington St. Pg.3 E9
Water Tower Rd. Pg.2 E8
Waterbury Ct. Pg.2 E7
Western Ave. Pg.3 E9
Westley Ln. Pg.2 E7
Wintercrag Pg.8 G8
1st St. Pg.3 F9
2nd St. Pg.3 F9
3rd St. Pg.3 F9
4th St. Pg.3 F9
5th Ct. Pg.8 F9
5th St. Pg.3 F9
6th St. Pg.3 F9
7th St. Pg.3 F9
8th St. Pg.3 F9

#### CEMETERIES
Dundee Twp. Cemetery West Pg.3 E8

#### PARKS
Tower Park Pg.3 E9

#### SCHOOLS
Childrens House Mont. Sch. Pg.8 F9
St. Catherine's Sch. Pg.3 F9

#### SHOPPING CENTERS
Spring Hill Plaza Pg.3 E8

#### MISCELLANEOUS
Fire Department Pg.3 F9
Public Library Pg.3 E9
Village Hall & Police Dept. Pg.5 F9

# LAKE COUNTY

## SECTION 6

## LEGEND

| | |
|---|---|
| ═══ FREE EXPRESSWAY | 🛡 INTERSTATE |
| ▬▬▬ MULTI-LANE DIVIDED | 70 U.S. |
| ▬▬▬ PRIMARY THROUGH ROUTE | 70 STATE |
| ═══ OTHER THRU ROADS | ▢ PARK |
| ─── OTHER STREETS | ▢ FOREST PRESERVE |
| +++++ RAILROAD | ▨ GOLF COURSE |
| RIVER OR LAKE | ▨ CEMETERY |
| | ▮ AIRPORT |

**TURN PAGE FOR ORIENTATION MAP**

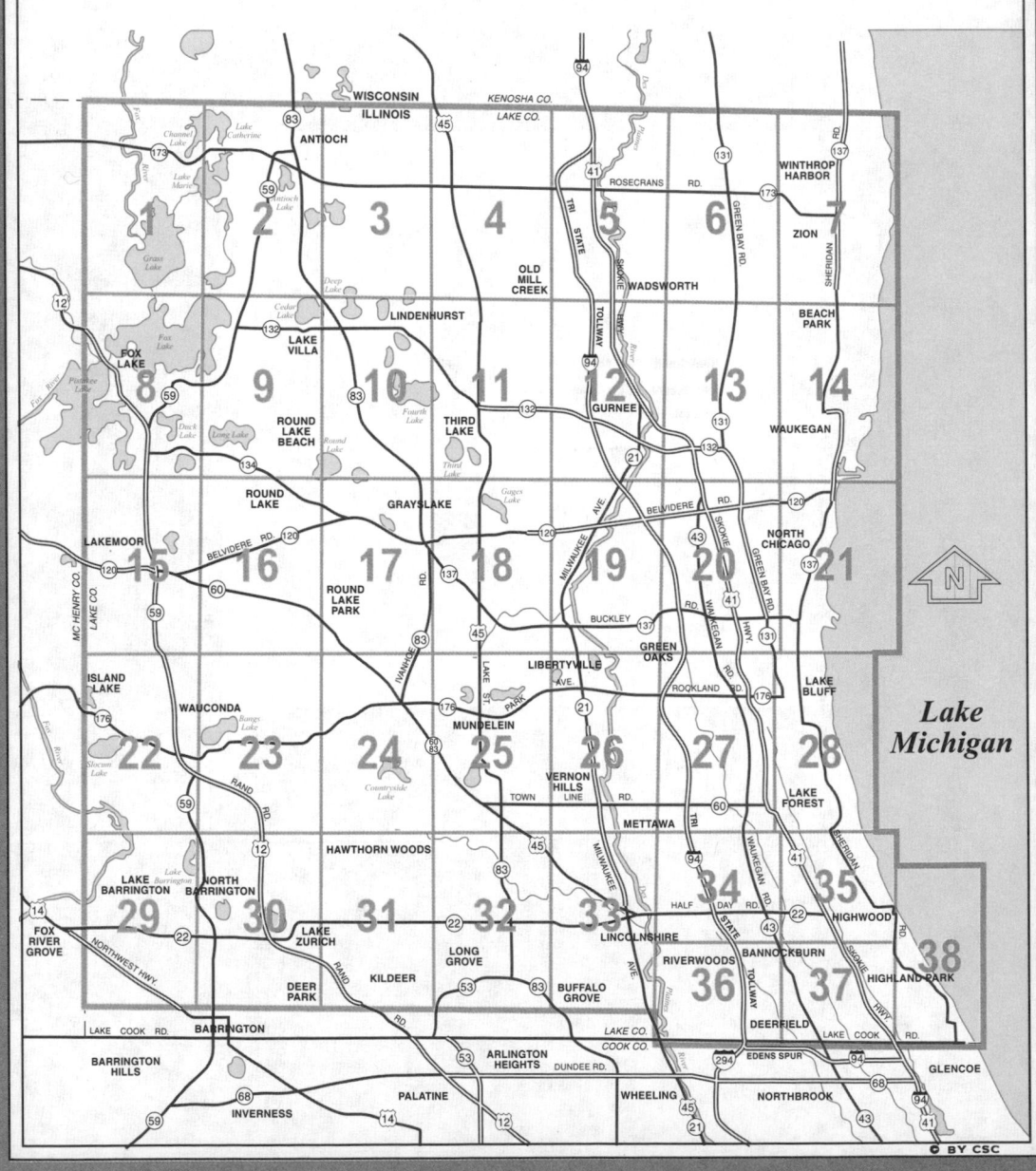

# SECTION 6
## ORIENTATION MAP

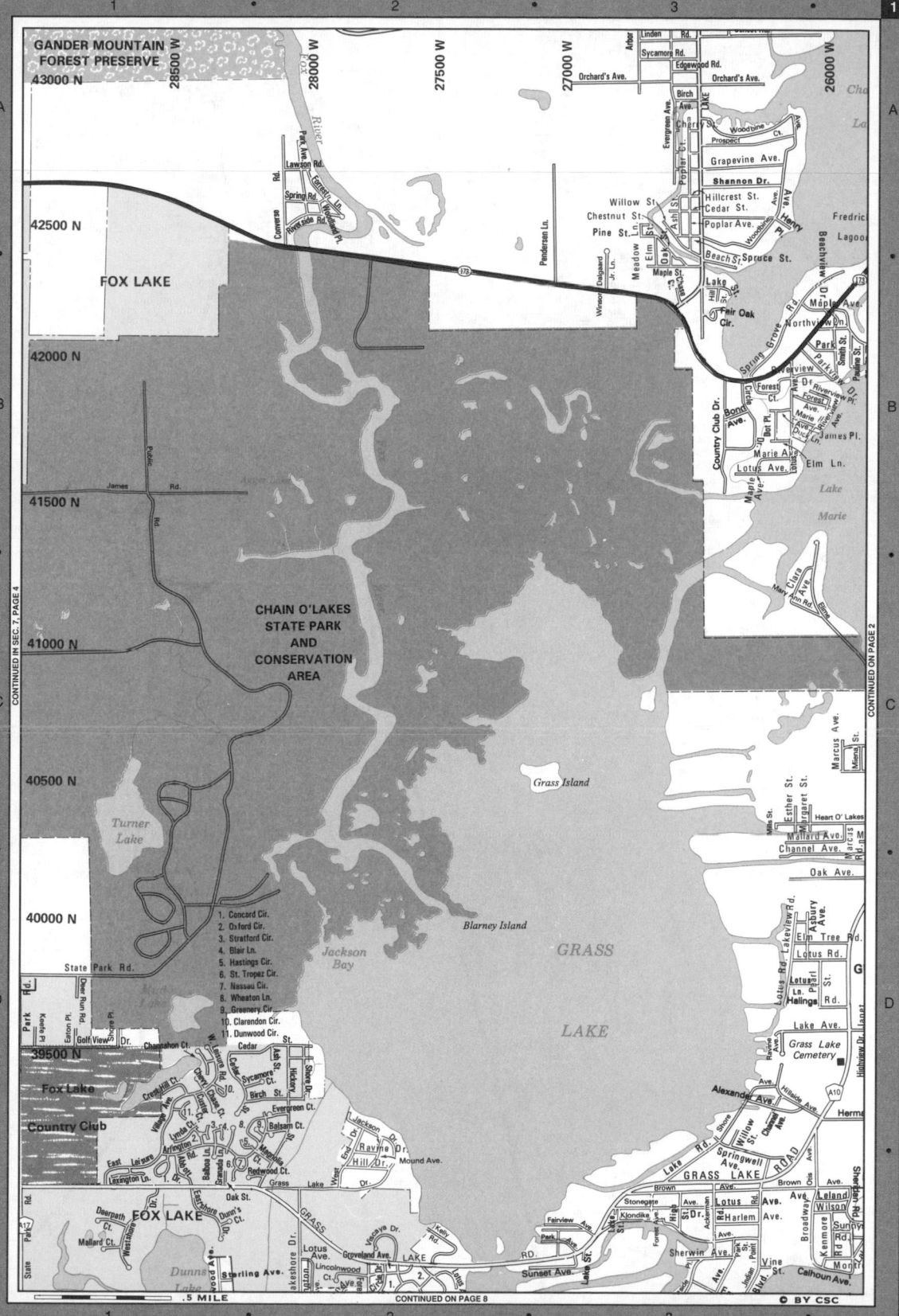

GANDER MOUNTAIN
FOREST PRESERVE
43000 N

28500 W
28000 W
27500 W
27000 W
26000 W

Linden Rd.
Arbor
Sycamore Rd.
Orchard Ave.
Edgewood Rd.
Orchard's Ave.

Cha
La

A

42500 N

FOX LAKE

Park Ave.
Lawson Rd.
Forest Rd.
Woodland Pl.
Spring Rd.
Ridge Rd.
Converse Rd.
Riverside Ave.

Birch
Ave.
Evergreen Ave.
Woodbine Ct.
Prospect
Grapevine Ave.
Shannon Dr.
Willow St.
Hillcrest St.
Chestnut St.
Cedar St.
Pine St.
Poplar Ave.
Elm
Beach St.
Spruce St.
Meadow

Fredric
Lagoo

Ln.
Pendersen Ln.

Maple St.
Wineeo
Jr. Ln.
Dalgaard

Lake
St.

Fair Oak
Cir.
Maple Ave.
Northview Dr.

42000 N

Spring Grove Rd.
Park

Riverview Pl.
Smith St.
Pauline St.

Country Club Dr.
Bond
Ave.
Creba
Ct.
Forest
Ct.
Maria
Di
Riverview Pl.
Forest
Boi Pl.
Pick Ln.
James Pl.

B

41500 N

James
Public
Rd.
Rd.

Marie Ave.
Lotus Ave.
Maple
Ave.
Elm Ln.

Lake
Marie

CHAIN O'LAKES
STATE PARK
AND
CONSERVATION
AREA

Clara
Ave.
Mary
Ann Rd.
Elm

41000 N

Marcus Ave.
Miena St.

C

40500 N

Grass Island

Turner
Lake

Mills St.
Esther St.
Margaret St.
Heart O' Lakes
Mallard Ave.
Channel Ave.

Marcis
St.
Marcis
Rd.
M

Oak Ave.

40000 N

1. Concord Cir.
2. Oxford Cir.
3. Stratford Cir.
4. Blair Ln.
5. Hastings Cir.
6. St. Tropez Cir.
7. Nassau Cir.
8. Wheaton Ln.
9. Greenery Cir.
10. Clarendon Cir.
11. Dunwood Cir.

Blarney Island

Jackson
Bay

GRASS

Lakeview Rd.
Elm Tree Rd.
Asbury
Ave.
Lotus Rd.
Pearl St.
Lotus
Ln.
Halings
Lake Ave.

G

State Park Rd.

LAKE

Grass Lake
Cemetery

D

39500 N

Deer Run Rd.
Park
Rd.
Keele Rd.
Eaton Pl.
Golf View
Dr.
Channahon Ct.
Cedar
Ash St.
Hickory
Shore Dr.

Ravine
Highway Dr.
Janet
A10

Fox Lake

Creek Hill Ct.
Cherry
Sycamore Ct.
Birch Ct.
Evergreen Ct.
Balsam Ct.

Alexander Ave.
Hillside
Ave.
Herma

Country Club

Lynda Ln.
Village Ave.
Arlington
Balboa Ln.
Zaranda
Magnolia
Redwood Ct.

Jackson
Ravine Dr.
Hill Dr.
Mound Ave.

Lake Rd.
Shore
Willow
Springwell
Ave.
Channel
Ave.
Brown
GRASS LAKE
ROAD
Sheridan Rd.

East
Leisure
Lexington Ln.
Oak St.
Grass
West
End
Lake
Dr.

Stonegate
Brown
Fairview
Klondike
Hippo
St.
Auburn
Lotus
Harlem
Ave.
Ave.
Leland
Wilson
Broadway
Ave.
Sunny
Kenmore
Rd.
Mor

Mallard Ct.
Dearpath Rd.
Westshore Dr.
Dunn's
Ct.
Oak St.
FOX LAKE
Dunn's
Vesava Dr.
Kelly
Park
Sunset Ave.
Lake St.
Sherwin Ave.
Forest
Park
Vine
St.
Blvd.
Caihoun Ave.

Dunns
Lake
Sterling Ave.
Lotus
Ave.
Lincolnwood Ave.
Lakeshore Dr.
Groveland Ave.
GRASS
LAKE
RD.

State
Pistakee

© BY CSC

CONTINUED IN SEC 7, PAGE 4

CONTINUED ON PAGE 2

CONTINUED ON PAGE 8

.5 MILE

1    2    3

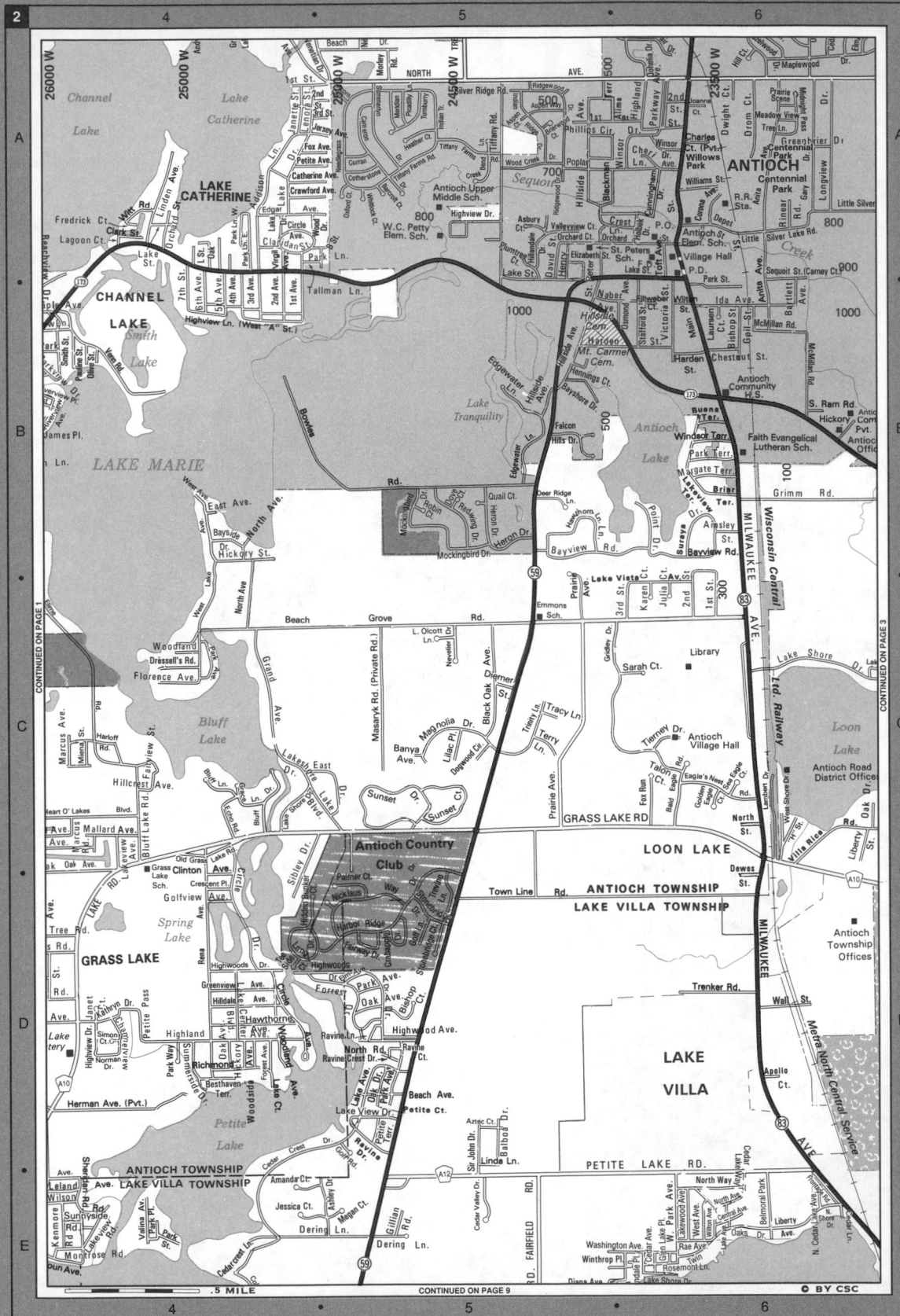

CONTINUED ON PAGE 1
CONTINUED ON PAGE 3
CONTINUED ON PAGE 9

.5 MILE

© BY CSC

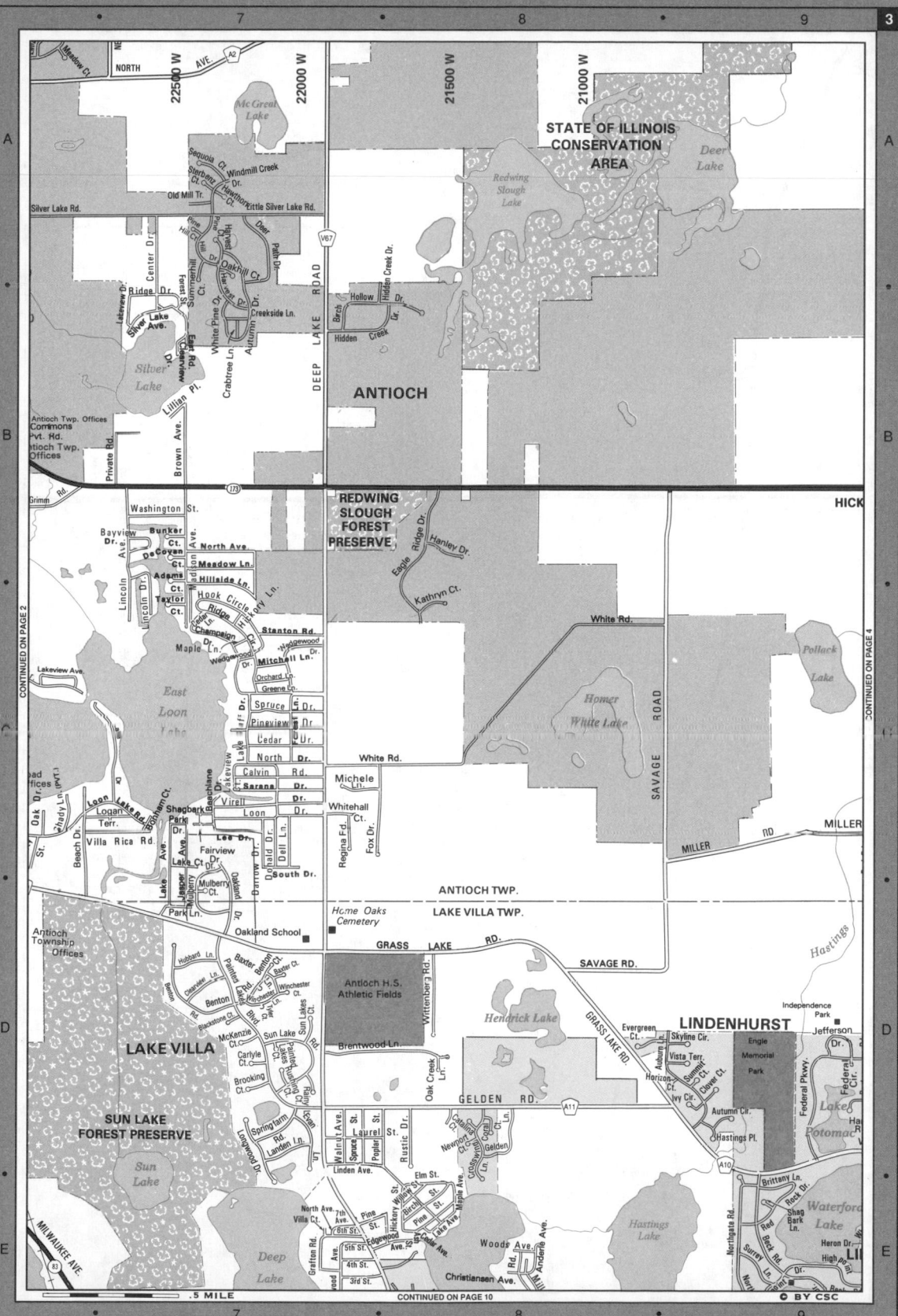

CONTINUED ON PAGE 2

CONTINUED ON PAGE 4

CONTINUED ON PAGE 10

STATE OF ILLINOIS
CONSERVATION
AREA

ANTIOCH

REDWING
SLOUGH
FOREST
PRESERVE

LAKE VILLA

SUN LAKE
FOREST PRESERVE

LINDENHURST

Antioch H.S.
Athletic Fields

Home Oaks
Cemetery

Antioch Township
Offices

ANTIOCH TWP.
LAKE VILLA TWP.

.5 MILE

© BY CSC

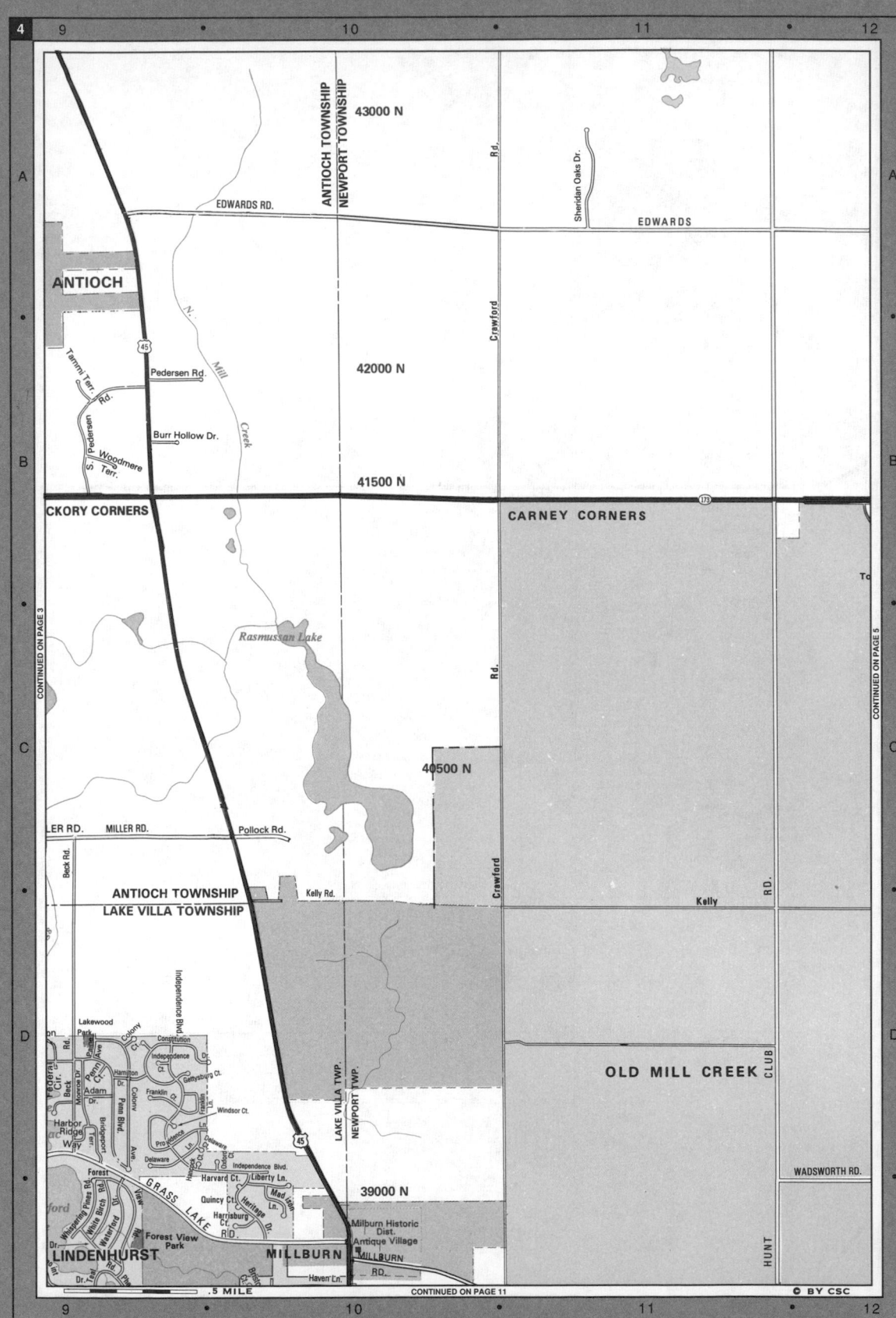

A

43000 N

ANTIOCH TOWNSHIP
NEWPORT TOWNSHIP

EDWARDS RD.

Sheridan Oaks Dr.

EDWARDS

ANTIOCH

Rd.

Crawford

45

Tammi Terr.

Pedersen Rd.

42000 N

N. Mill Creek

Rd.

S. Pedersen

Burr Hollow Dr.

Woodmere Terr.

B

41500 N

CKORY CORNERS

173

CARNEY CORNERS

CONTINUED ON PAGE 3

Rasmussan Lake

Rd.

CONTINUED ON PAGE 5

To

C

40500 N

LER RD.   MILLER RD.

Pollock Rd.

Beck Rd.

Crawford

ANTIOCH TOWNSHIP
LAKE VILLA TOWNSHIP

Kelly Rd.

Kelly

RD.

OLD MILL CREEK

CLUB

Lakewood Park

Colony

Independence Blvd

Constitution

Federal Cir.

Beck Rd.

Monroe Dr.

Penn Ave.

Adam Dr.

Independence Dr.

Gettysburg Ct.

Hamilton

Colony Ave.

Franklin

Windsor Ct.

Harbor Ridge Way

Bridgeport

Providence

Delaware

LAKE VILLA TWP.
NEWPORT TWP.

45

WADSWORTH RD.

Forest

Harvard Ct.

Liberty Ln.

Independence Blvd.

39000 N

HUNT

Whispering Pines Rd.

White Birch

Waterford

Quincy Ct

Heritage Dr.

Harrisburg Ct.

Mad Isla

Forest View Park

LINDENHURST

GRASS LAKE RD.

MILLBURN

Milburn Historic Dist.
Antique Village

MILLBURN RD.

Haven Ln.

Dr. Teal Dr

Brigh

.5 MILE

CONTINUED ON PAGE 11

© BY CSC

9     10     11     12

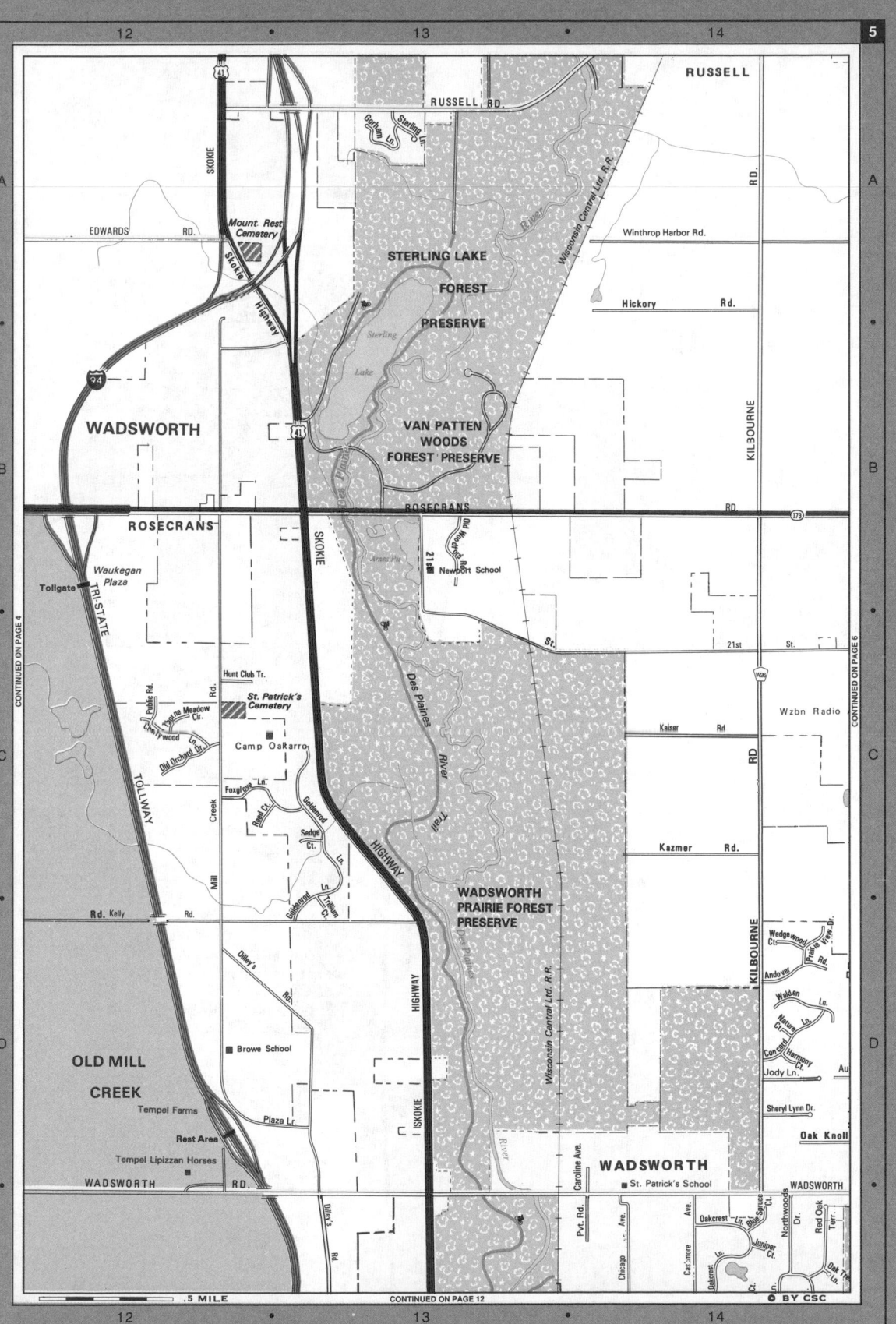

# RUSSELL

RUSSELL RD.

**STERLING LAKE**

**FOREST**

**PRESERVE**

EDWARDS RD.

Mount Rest Cemetery

Gerham Ln.

Sterling Ln.

Winthrop Harbor Rd.

Hickory Rd.

Sterling Lake

**VAN PATTEN WOODS FOREST PRESERVE**

**WADSWORTH**

KILBOURNE

ROSECRANS RD.

**ROSECRANS**

SKOKIE

Waukegan Plaza

Tollgate

Newport School

21st St.

21st St.

Wzbn Radio

Hunt Club Tr.

**St. Patrick's Cemetery**

Kaiser Rd

Cherrywood Ln.

Public Rd.

Pine Meadow Cir.

Old Orchard Dr.

Camp Oakarro

Kazmer Rd.

Foxglove Ln.

Reed Ct.

Goldenrod

Sedge Ct.

**Des Plaines River**

Ln.

Trillium Ln.

Goldenrod Ct.

**WADSWORTH PRAIRIE FOREST PRESERVE**

KILBOURNE RD

Wedgewood Ct.

Prairie View Dr.

Rd. Kelly Rd.

Creek

Mill

Dilley's Rd.

Andover

Walden Ln.

Natural Ct.

Concord Ct.

Harmony

Jody Ln.

Au

**Browe School**

Sheryl Lynn Dr.

**OLD MILL**

**CREEK**

Tempel Farms

Plaza Lr.

Oak Knoll

Rest Area

Tempel Lipizzan Horses

**WADSWORTH**

**St. Patrick's School**

WADSWORTH

WADSWORTH RD.

Caroline Ave.

Pvt. Rd.

Chicago Ave.

Cat'more Ave.

Oakcrest Ln.

Northwoods

Red Oak Terr.

Juniper Ct.

Square Ct.

Oak Tr.

Oakcrest

Ct.

© BY CSC

CONTINUED ON PAGE 4

CONTINUED ON PAGE 6

CONTINUED ON PAGE 12

.5 MILE

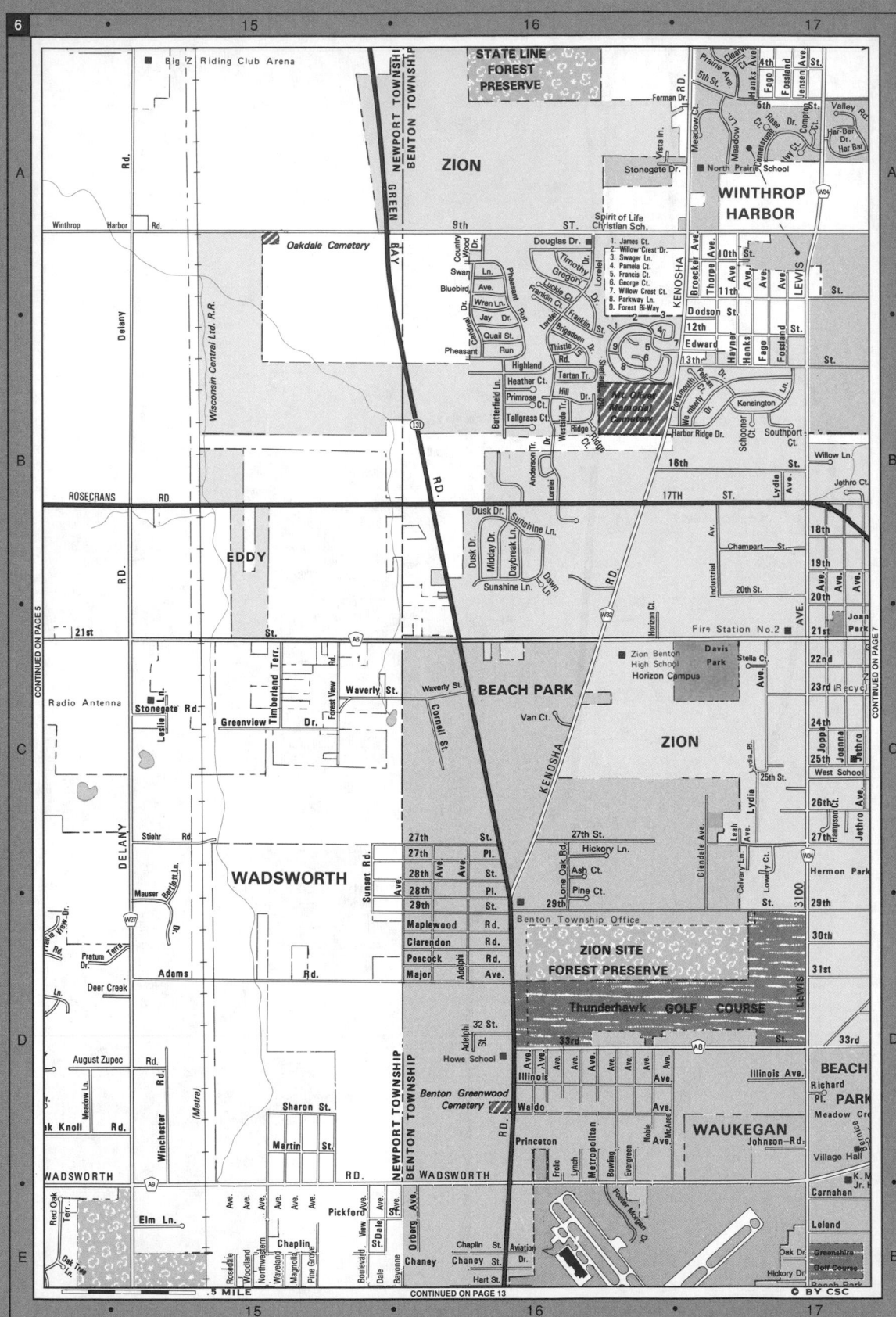

CONTINUED ON PAGE 5

CONTINUED ON PAGE 7

CONTINUED ON PAGE 13

© BY CSC

.5 MILE

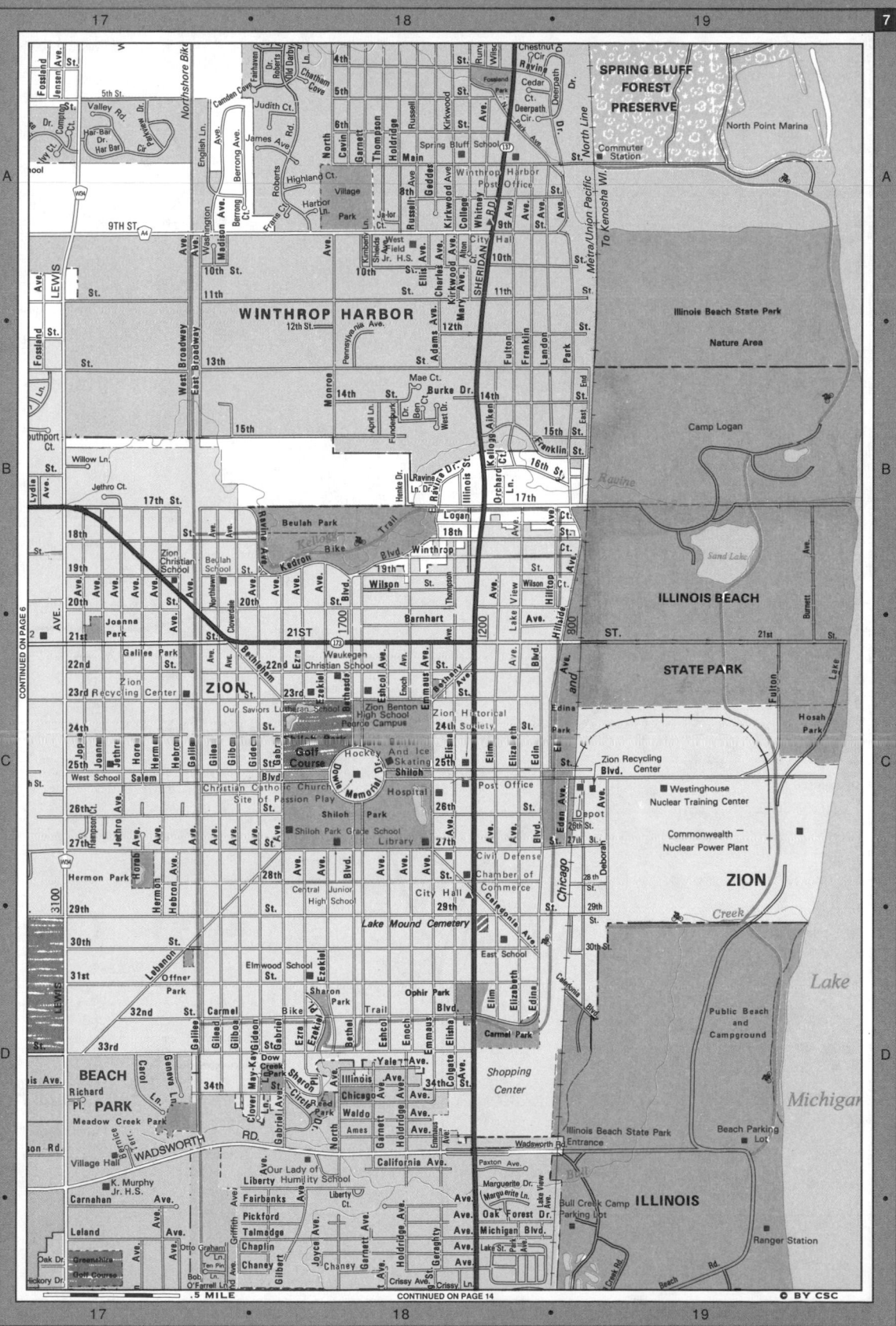

CONTINUED ON PAGE 1

# FOX LAKE
38500 N

1. Hillandale Dr.
2. Woodland Ave.

CONTINUED IN SEC. 7, PAGE 4

ANTIOCH TOWNSHIP
GRANT TOWNSHIP

ANTIOCH TOWNSHIP
LAKE VILLA TOWNSHIP

GRANT TOWNSHIP

Crab Apple Island

Nippersink Lake

FOX LAKE

37500 N

Metra

1. Lakewood Ave.
2. Troy St.
3. Oak St.
4. Hillside Ave.

Mineola Bay

Lippincott Ln.

37000 N

Hilltop Ave.

400

200

00

200

400

600

Grand

Lakeland Shopping Center

Arlington Rd.
Covington
Fairfax
Tremont

36500 N

36000 N

PISTAKEE LAKE

800

Regional Sewage

Treatment Plant

FOX LAKE

GRAND AVE.

ROLLINS ROAD

Deer Haven Park

Lincoln Ave.
Garfield

Library

Grant H.S.

Pleasant Rd.
Wind Mill Rd.

Cooney Island Rd.

CONTINUED ON PAGE 9

Meyers Bay

1000

Crestview
Frazier Ct.
Wildwood

Longwood

Duck Lake

35500 N

INGLESIDE

Chris Larkin Rd.

Cherry Ln.
Willow Rd.
Rabbit Run

INGLESIDE

King's Lake

1. White Rabbit Tr.
2. Great Bear Tr.
3. Snowshoe Tr.
4. Paupukkeewis Tr.
5. Mishenamua Tr.

Laughing Water

35000 N

Redhead Lake

Hollow Way

White Tail Ln.

Big Hollow Elem. Sch.

Edward Ave.

Wooster

34500 N

Pistakee Bog
Nature Preserve

Lake of the Hollows

Brandenburg Lake

Shopping Center

Big Hollow Middle Sch.

BIG HOLLOW RD.

Wooster Ln.

Wooster Lake

Wooster Lake

Volo Bog
Nature Preserve

O'Kelly Ln.

Burkhart Ln.

Sunnybrook

.5 MILE

© BY CSC

4 · 5 · 6

E

**Columbia Bay**

Columbia Bay Rd.
Buena Ln.
Sunset Ln.
N. Columbia Bay Dr.

ANTIOCH TOWNSHIP
LAKE VILLA TOWNSHIP

59

FAIRFIELD RD.

Winthrop Pl.
Rosemont Ln.
Diana Ave.
Rose Ln.
Cedar Lake
Lake Shore Dr.

Cedar Island

**Cedar Lake**

**LAKE COUNTY FOREST PRESERVE**

800

Cleveland
Sherwood Village Hall
Oak Knoll Dr.
Burnett
Laurie
Walden St.

GRAND AVE. 132

Academy Dr.
Entrance Dr.
St. Theresa Trauma Center
Gavin North Sch.

**Lake Villa Park**

1. Waterbury Ct.
2. Chelsea Cir.
Coventry Cove

Oakwood Ave.

Lehmann St.
Chesney
Glade Dr.
Obermeier
Marshfield Rd.
Raska Ln.
Bald
Eagle Rd.

**FOX LAKE HILLS**

**GRANT WOODS FOREST PRESERVE**

Big Oak Dr.
Saxony Haigl
Alpine Ct.
Cherokee Ln.
Apache Tr.
Apache Tr.

Amber Ln.
Majestic Ln.
Majestic Ln.
Grace Ln.

**LAKE VILLA**

CEDAR LAKE RD.

Eagle

Northwind Dr.
Winddance Ct.
Meadowview
Southwind
Overlook Ct.
Summit
Breeze

Creek

F

GRANT TOWNSHIP
LAKE VILLA TOWNSHIP

Arcade Dr. N.
Arcade Dr.
Wacker Dr.
Newberry
Nayside Pl.
Fairview Dr.
Carson Dr.
Woodland Terr.
Timber
Lincoln

**Stanton Bay**

Bay Shore Rd.
Lakeview St.
Lakeview Ln.

MONAVILLE RD. A18

Fox Lake Cemetery

Old Monaville Rd.

**MONAVILLE**

MONAVILLE RD.

Calvary Christian Sch.

Appleton Ct.
Wiltshire Ln.
Waverly Dr.
Northwood Tr.
Greenview Ln.
Pathway Dr.
Beverly

Redhead Ct.
Tall Grass

G

CONTINUED ON PAGE 8

Hickory St.
Oak St.
Brodie Dr.

**Hickory Knoll Golf Club**

GRANT TOWNSHIP

Albert Ave.
Fox Tr.
Westmoor Ave.
Eastmoor Ave.
Morey Ln.

FAIRFIELD RD.

Northwood Tr.

V63

1. Sauk Ct.
2. Fruitwood
3. Apache
4. Comanche
5. Willow Ridge
6. Red Wood
7. Woodside Dr.
8. Yvonne Ct.

CONTINUED ON PAGE 10

St. Dads Sch.
Shandon Dr.
Falcon Ct.
Clara Dr.
Marquette Dr.
Ave.

**GRANT WOODS FOREST PRESERVE**

Crabtree
Cedarwood Ln.
Caine Rd.
Blackcherry Ln.

V61

Eagle Ct.
South Ave.
1600
Hazelwood

**Shag Bark Nature Preserve**

**Shag Bark Park**

Navajo St.
Ottawa Dr.
Cheyenne
Iroquois Tr.
Chippewa Tr.
Seminole Ct.
Mohican

Circuit Ct.

500

Country Walk
Sunrise
Honeysuckle Ln.
Lindsay Dr.
Karen Ln.
Spicewood

Laneville Dr.
Greenleaf Ave.
1. Greenleaf Ave.
2. Franklin Ave.
3. Sunnyside Ave.
High Point Rd.

**LAKE VILLA TOWNSHIP**
**AVON TOWNSHIP**

Indian Hill Elem. Sch.

**ROUND LAKE HEIGHTS**

Mohawk
Cedarwood Ln.
Normandie
Cedarwood

Mary Ct.
Christopher
Nicole Ln.
Carl Ct.

Wilma Park

Hawthorne Dr.
Orchard
Wabash Ave.

Turkey Run Dr.

Eagle Creek

1000 Eagle Creek
Fire Sta. No. 2

ROLLINS ROAD

BLVD.
Clinton
Hillside
Lake Shore

Warrior Dr.
Flintwood Ct.
Pontiac
Arrowhead Dr.
Timber Ln.

Summit
V.H.
P.D.

Geneva Terr.

**ROUND LAKE BEACH**

H

WILSON RD.

Oak Ct.
Hickory Ct.
Benjamin
Laurel Ave.
Hillside Ave.
Bay View Ave.
Marion
Linden

**Long Lake**

1. Bergan St.
2. Muskego Ave.
3. Rock Island St.
4. Madison
5. Decora Ave.
6. Racine Ave.
7. Anderson
8. Oak St.

Forest Ave.
Hillside Ave.
Summit
Poplar
Hickory

Lake Ave.
Oak St.
Brorson Ave.

Greenview
Golfview Pk.
Morningside
Woodridge
Maple Dr.
Walnut

Golfview
Laurel Ln.
Highland
Orchard

Juneway
Channel
Pheasant Ct.

Fairview Park
Juniper

CEDAR LAKE RD.

K

Larkin

Gavin South Sch.

Graham Ct.

V58

**ROUND LAKE**

Catherine
Lake

Hilltop Dr.
Sunset Terr.
Venetian

Oden
Olaf
Oak Ln.
Peterson

Fretheim Ave.

**LONG LAKE**

R.R. Station

134

Main St.

LONG LAKE RD.

Mud Creek

FAIRFIELD

N.A.S.A. Cir.
Antares
Tyler Dr.
Prairie Grass

Mayfield
Corona Ct.
Buena Vista Ct.

**Ellis Park**

Southview

Idlewild Park

Roundlake H.S.
High School
S.C.

Park Rd.

N. Rosedale Dr.
S. Rosedale
Bernice
Petite St.
Ridge

Beach View Park
Ferndale
Beachview
Glanwood Dr.
Woodland Dr.

© BY CSC

.5 MILE

4 · 5 · 6

CONTINUED ON PAGE 3

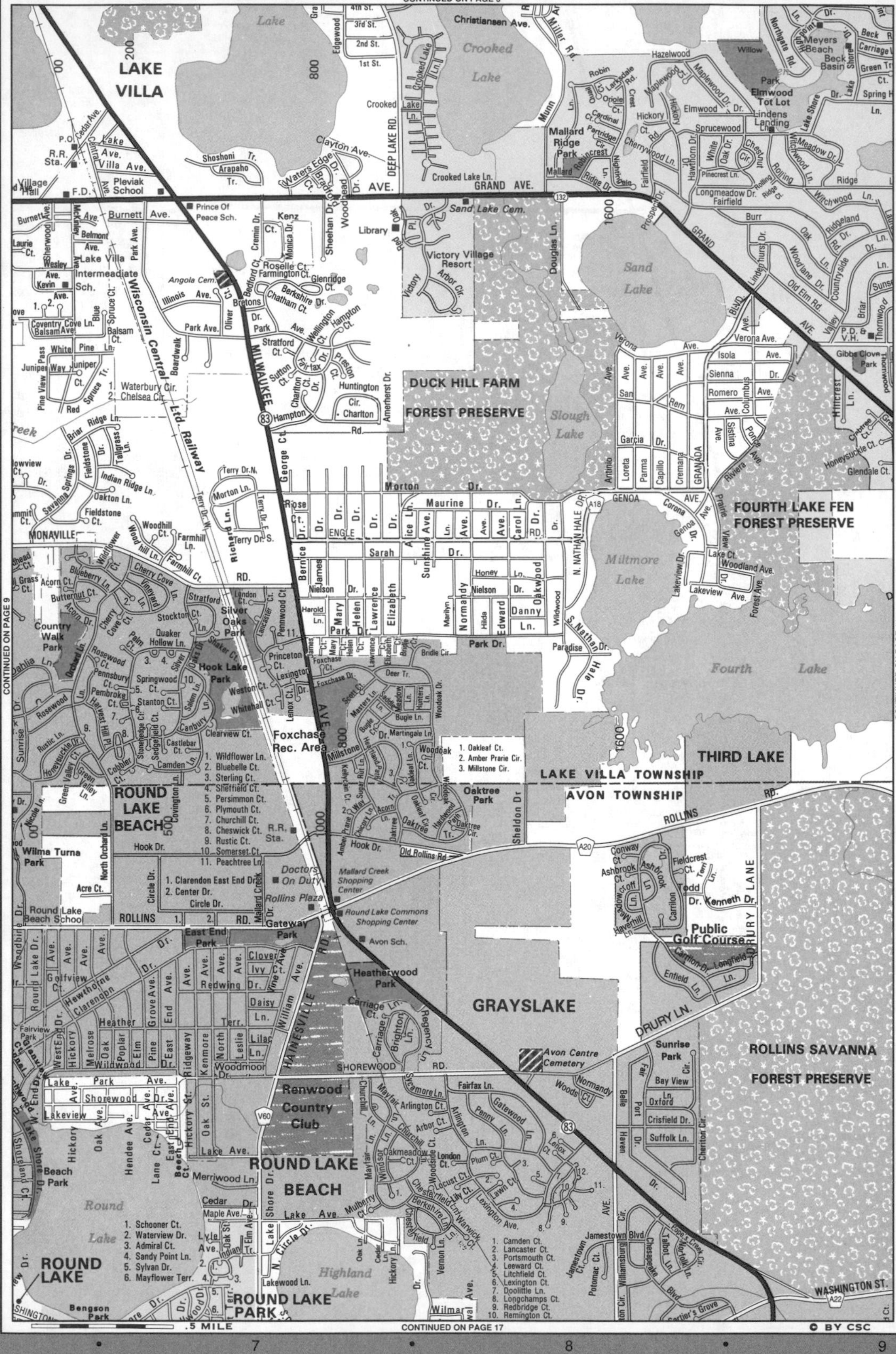

LAKE VILLA

DUCK HILL FARM FOREST PRESERVE

FOURTH LAKE FEN FOREST PRESERVE

Sand Lake

Slough Lake

Miltmore Lake

Fourth Lake

THIRD LAKE

LAKE VILLA TOWNSHIP
AVON TOWNSHIP

ROUND LAKE BEACH

Foxchase Rec. Area

GRAYSLAKE

ROLLINS SAVANNA FOREST PRESERVE

Renwood Country Club

ROUND LAKE BEACH

ROUND LAKE

ROUND LAKE PARK

Public Golf Course

CONTINUED ON PAGE 9

CONTINUED ON PAGE 11

CONTINUED ON PAGE 17

© BY CSC

.5 MILE

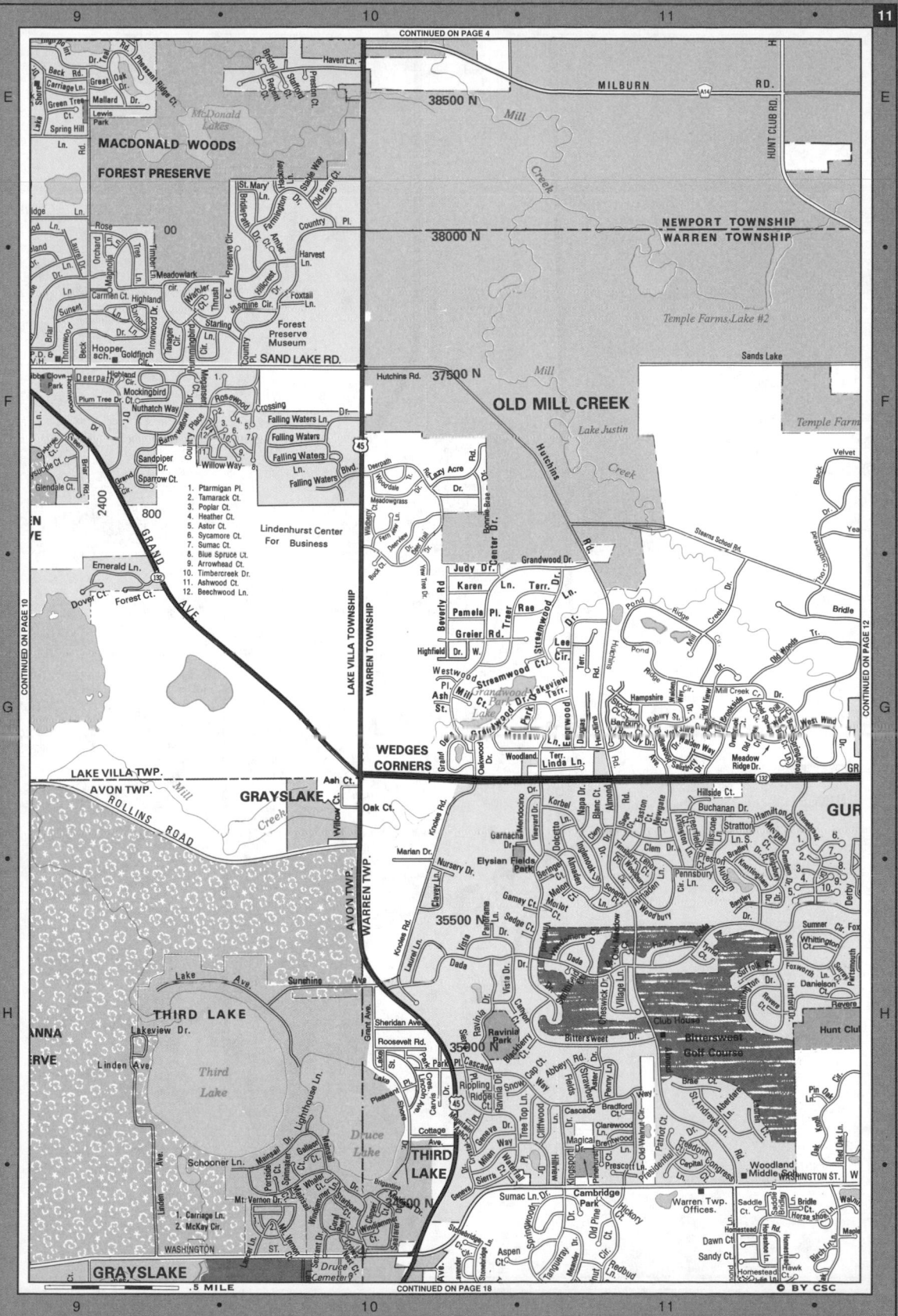

CONTINUED ON PAGE 4

CONTINUED ON PAGE 10

CONTINUED ON PAGE 12

CONTINUED ON PAGE 18

© BY CSC

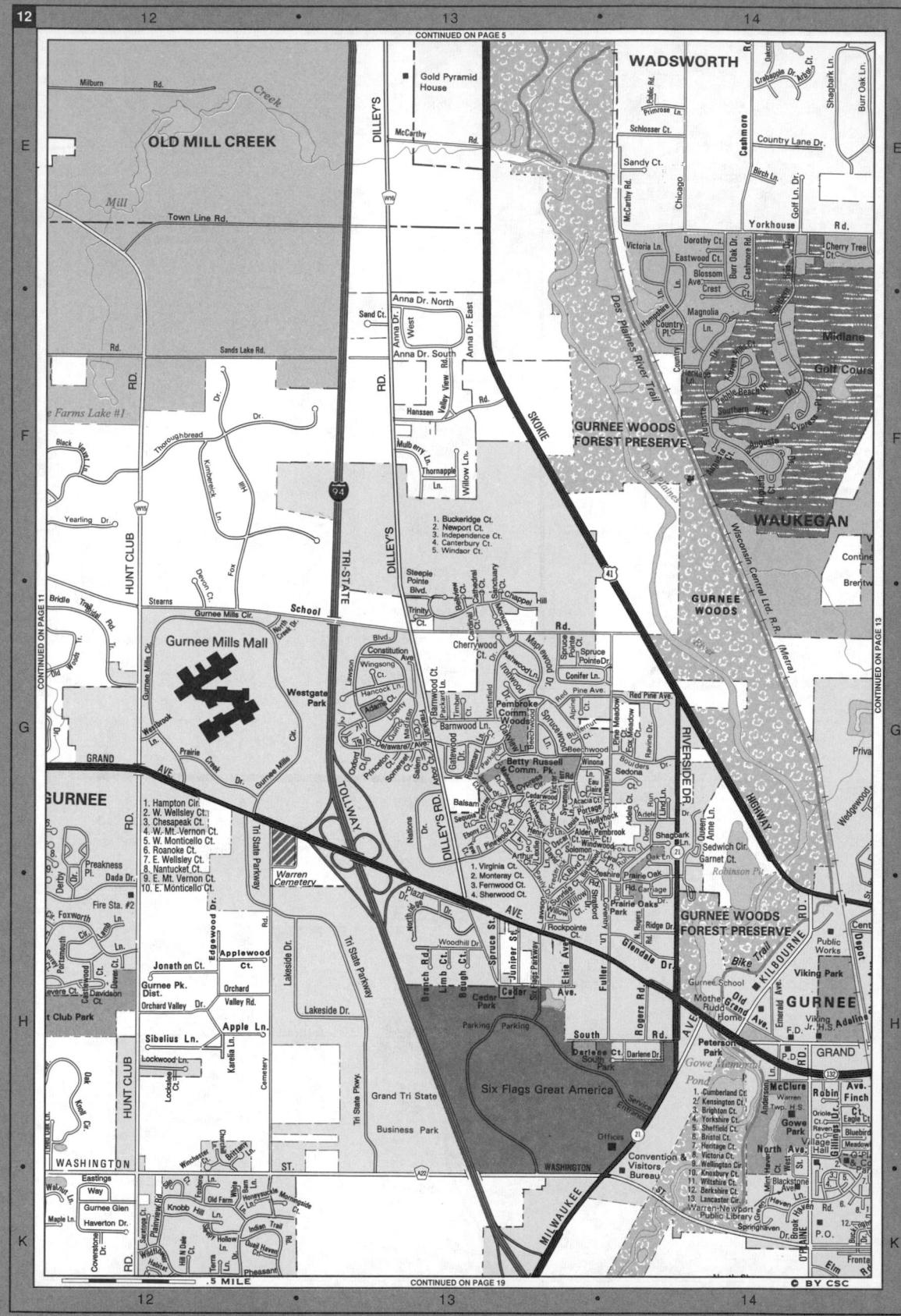

CONTINUED ON PAGE 5

**WADSWORTH**

**OLD MILL CREEK**

Milburn Rd.

Gold Pyramid House

McCarthy Rd.

Town Line Rd.

Primrose Ln.
Schlosser Ct.
Sandy Ct.
Chicago
Yorkhouse Rd.
Cherry Tree Ct.
Dorothy Ct.
Eastwood Ct.
Blossom
Crest
Magnolia

Sands Lake Rd.

Sand Ct.
Anna Dr. North
Anna Dr. West
Anna Dr. East
Anna Dr. South

Valley View Rd.
Hanssen

**Midlane Golf Course**

Farms Lake #1

Black Walnut

Kimberwick Ln.

Thoroughbred Dr.

Yearling Dr.

Devon Ct.
Fox

Bridle Trail Rd.

Stearns

Mulberry Ln.
Thornapple
Willow Ln.

**GURNEE WOODS FOREST PRESERVE**

**WAUKEGAN**

1. Buckeridge Ct.
2. Newport Ct.
3. Independence Ct.
4. Canterbury Ct.
5. Windsor Ct.

Steeple Pointe Blvd.

Chappel Hill

**GURNEE WOODS**

School

Gurnee Mills Cir.

**Gurnee Mills Mall**

Westgate Park

Prairie Creek

**GRAND AVE.**

**GURNEE**

1. Hampton Cir.
2. W. Wellsley Ct.
3. Chesapeak Ct.
4. W. Mt. Vernon Ct.
5. W. Monticello Ct.
6. Roanoke Ct.
7. E. Wellsley Ct.
8. Nantucket Ct.
9. E. Mt. Vernon Ct.
10. E. Monticello Ct.

Preakness Pl.
Dada Dr.
Derby
Foxworth
Portsmouth
Cantwood
Davidson
Dawe Ct.

Fire Sta. #2

Cherrywood
Constitution Ave.
Wingsong
Lawson
Hancock Ln.
Adams
Delaware
Princeton
Salem
Aroor

Barnwood Ct.
Packard Ln.
Westfield

Pine Ave.
Conifer Ln.
Red Pine Ave.

Maplewood Ln.
Spruce
Spruce Pointe Dr.

Pembroke Comm. Woods

Betty Russell Comm. Pk.

Balsam

1. Virginia Ct.
2. Monterey Ct.
3. Fernwood Ct.
4. Sherwood Ct.

Windwood
Shagbark
Oak Ln.

Garnet Ct.
Sedwich Cir.
Queen Anne Ln.

Prairie Oak
Prairie Oaks Park

Rockpointe

**GURNEE WOODS FOREST PRESERVE**

Gurnee School

Mother Rudd Home

Public Works

Viking Park

**GURNEE**

Adaline
GRAND

**Hunt Club Park**

Jonathon Ct.
Edgewood Ct.
Applewood Ct.

Gurnee Pk. Dist.
Orchard Valley Dr.

Sibelius Ln.
Lockwood Ln.
Apple Ln.
Karelia Ln.

Lakeside Dr.

Lakeside Dr.

Branch Rd.
Limb Ct.
Bough Ct.

Cedar Park

Woodhill Ln.

Spruce St.
Juniper St.
Cedar Ave.

Elsie Ave.
Fuller

Glendale Dr.

Rogers Rd.

Ridge Dr.

Bike Trail

Kilbourne

Emerald Ave.

**Six Flags Great America**

Darlene Ct.
Darlene Dr.

South Park

Peterson Park

Gowe Memorial Pond

McClure

Robin Ave. Finch Ct.
Eagle Ct.
Oriole
Raven
Bluebird
Gowe Park

Anderson
Warren Twp. H.S.

North Ave.

Village Hall

**WASHINGTON**

Eastings Way

Gurnee Glen

Haverton Dr.

Walnut Ln.
Maple Ln.

Coverstone Rd.

Wildlife Ln.
Hill & Dale Ln.
Hollow Ln.
Pheasant

Indian Trail
Quail Haven
Tern

Knobb Hill
Old Farm
Honeysuckle Ct.
Morningside Ct.

1. Cumberland Ct.
2. Kensington Ct.
3. Brighton Ct.
4. Yorkshire Ct.
5. Sheffield Ct.
6. Bristol Ct.
7. Heritage Ct.
8. Victoria Ct.
9. Wellington Cir.
10. Knoxbury Ct.
11. Wiltshire Ct.
12. Berkshire Ct.
13. Lancaster Ct.

Convention & Visitors Bureau

Warren-Newport Public Library

Springhaven

Blackstone Ave.

P.O.

Elm Fronta

WASHINGTON ST.

MILWAUKEE AVE.

CONTINUED ON PAGE 19

.5 MILE

© BY CSC

CONTINUED ON PAGE 11

CONTINUED ON PAGE 13

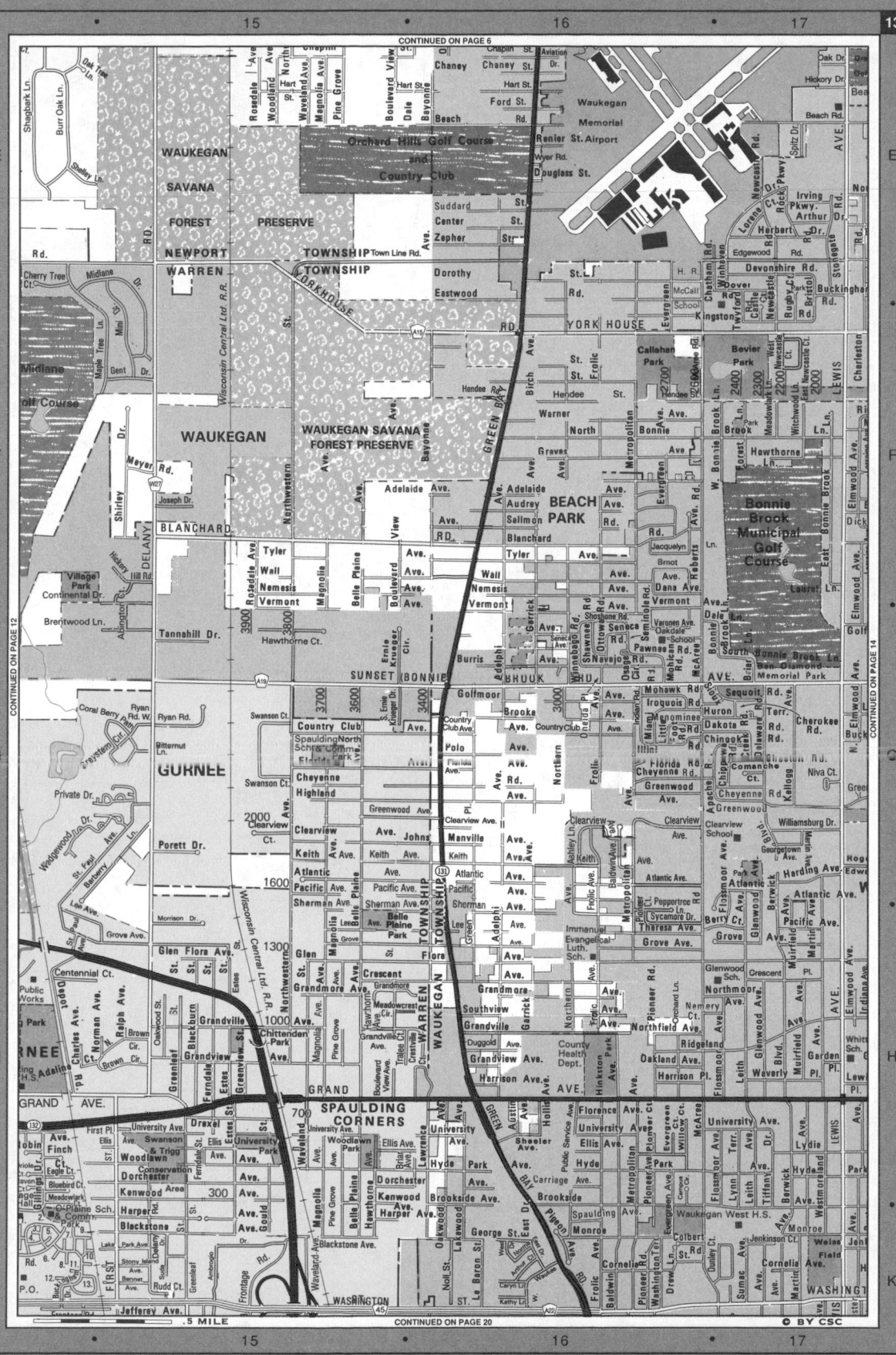

CONTINUED ON PAGE 6

CONTINUED ON PAGE 12

CONTINUED ON PAGE 14

© BY CSC

.5 MILE

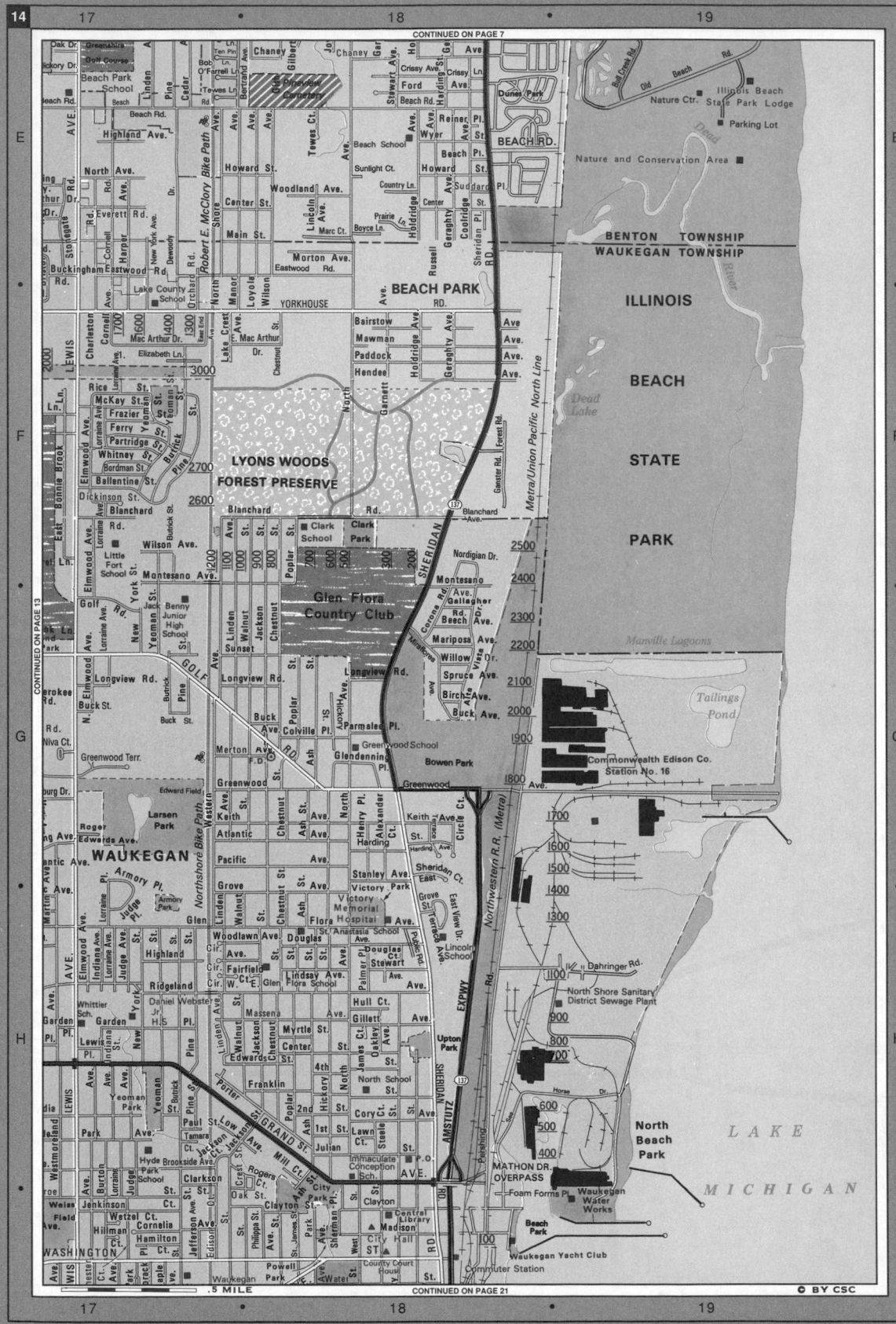

CONTINUED ON PAGE 7
CONTINUED ON PAGE 13
CONTINUED ON PAGE 21

© BY CSC

CONTINUED ON PAGE 8

K

O'Kelly Ln.
Harrigan Rd.
Champion RD.

59
12

Carol Ln.
Racker Dr.
Single Ct.
Camp Horner Rd.
Brandenburg
Stone Ct.
Rd.
Dolores
Christa Ct.
Bellevue

Pistakee Bog
Nature Preserve

34000 N

Tamarack

VOLO
BOG
STATE
NATURAL
AREA

Creek Ct.
Christa Dr.
Oak Dr.
NIPPERSINK RD.

Stockholm Dr.

33500 N

BRANDENBURG

Tamarack View

Volo Bog
Nature Preserve

Grant
Cemetery

Kelly Ln.

Stanton Rd.
Molidor

WILSON RD.

Trail

Portside
Beacon
Bay

SULLIVAN LAKE RD.

Leviwaite Rd.

ROUND
LAKE

L

MC HENRY COUNTY.
LAKE CO.

MC HENRY TOWNSHIP
GRANT TOWNSHIP

Sullivan
Lake

1. Stowaway Bay
2. Rusty Scupper
3. Neptune Cove
4. Hornblower
5. Sinker Bay
6. Fishook
7. Captain's Love
8. Oyster Bay
9. Leaward

Fish
Lake

32500 N

LAKEMOOR

Blacksmith

Wagon

Spring Creek

Wagon Trail Ct.

Concrete Dr.

Saw mill

Carriage Way

Honeysuckle Ct.

S. Lake Shore Dr.

Sullivan Lake Blvd.

32000 N

Valley View Dr.

Sunset Dr.

Morningside Dr.

Wagner Rd.

Highland Dr.

RD.

County
Banquet Hall

120

VOLO

FOX RD.

VOLO RD.

LAKE RD.

GRANT TOWNSHIP
WAUCONDA TOWNSHIP

FISH LAKE RD.

120

M

CONTINUED IN SEC. 7, PAGES 4 AND 8

CONTINUED ON PAGE 16

LAKEMOOR

60

FISHER RD.

V47

DARRELL RD.

V76

GILMER RD.

59
12

RD.

SINGING
FOREST P

N

FISHER RD.

VOLO

Monahan Lake

27000 W

CALLAHAN RD.

GILMER
RD.

DOWELL RD.

DARRELL RD.

29000 W. NUNDA TWP.
WAUCONDA TWP.

28000 W

NEVILLE RD.

DARRELL RD.

CASE RD.

27000 W

Monahan Lake

SINGING HILLS
FOREST PRESERVE

RD.

P

.5 MILE

CONTINUED ON PAGE 22

© BY CSC

CONTINUED ON PAGE 9

**ROUND LAKE**

Mud Lake

Heron Rookery
Protection Area

Tyler Ct.
Ross Ave.
Harts Woods Park

3. Moon River Dr.
4. Lem Dr.
5. Houston Ct.
6. Kitty Hawk Dr.
7. Apollo Ct.
8. Nasa Cir.

Prairie Grass
Nature Center
& Museum
Library

Red Oak
Havenwood Cir.
Finch Ct.
Red Oak Dr.
Prairie
Prairie

Colombus Dr.
Havenwood Dr.
HeronView
Lily Ln.
Marigold Ln.
Blue Heron Ct.
Havenwood Ct.

**Fairfield Park**

Jubilee Park

Metra R.R. Sta.

Old Farm Rd.
Deerwood Ct.
Haywood Ct.
Briarwood Ct.
Haywood Cir.
Harts Park

Viking Park

Capri Ct.

Round Lake S.C.

**NIPPERSINK**

Park District

Public Utility Bldg.

Round Lake Village Elem. Sch.

St. Joseph Sch.
Ravine Ave.

W.J. Murphy Elem.

Davis St.

Park Ave.

1000

Squaw

Forest Ave.

Wildspring

1500

2. Primrose
3. 4.
500
5.
6. Holly Ct.
8.
9.
7. Willow
11.
12. 10.
13.
Sweet Clover
Wildspring Rd.

Blackthorn Ct.

Boxwood Ct.
Dogwood Ct.

**WILSON RD.**

Leviwate Rd.

**GRANT TOWNSHIP**
**AVON TOWNSHIP**

Valley

Valley View Dr.

Main Dam

High Point Rd.

**FAIRFIELD RD.**

**Country Lake Resort**

Fort Hill Cemetery

**Recreational Vehicle Park**

**CEDAR LAKE RD.**

Curran Rd.

1. Buckthorn Ln.
2. Osage Ct.
3. Thistle Ct.
4. Basswood Ct.
5. Applegate Ct.
6. Tanglewood Ct.
7. Wildrose Ct.
8. Hackberry Ct.
9. Clearview Cir.
10. Arrowhead Ct.
11. Sagebrush Cir.
12. Honey Ct.
13. Quail Hollow Ct.

120

**WILSON RD.**

CONTINUED ON PAGE 15

**BELVIDERE RD.**

120

**GRANT TWP.**
**WAUCONDA TWP.**

**AVON TWP.**
**FREMONT TWP.**

Town Line Rd.

BACON RD.

CONTINUED ON PAGE 17

V58

V61

BACON

Meadow Ln.

60

FAIRFIELD RD.

Cherokee Tr.
Blackhawk Tr.
Manor Hill Rd.

BACON RD.

Fremont Ave.

**WAUCONDA TOWNSHIP**
**FREMONT TOWNSHIP**

GING HILLS
EST PRESERVE

Chardon

Chardon Ln.
Imperial Ct.

26000 W
GILMER RD.

25500 W

25000 W

24500 W

24000 W

23500 W

GARLAND RD.

GOSSELL

GILMER

Gossell Rd.

.5 MILE

© BY CSC

CONTINUED ON PAGE 10

7   8   9

**ROUND LAKE PARK**

**HAINESVILLE**

**GRAYSLAKE**

**AVON TOWNSHIP**

**FREMONT TOWNSHIP**

**CAMPBELL AIRPORT**

**ROUND LAKE PARK**

**PETERSON**

WASHINGTON

Bengson Park

St. Paul Luth. Sch.

W.J. Murphy Elem. Sch.

Jean Hein Pk.

Cranberry Lake

Washington Tennis Courts

Avon Twp. Offices & Rec. Area

Avon Baseball Complex

Parrot Park

American Legion Hall

Parkview Ct.

Manor Lake

Rock Hall

Cartier's Grove

Central Park

Grayslake Middle Sch.

F.O. Police Dept.
Village Hall

Library

Post Office

Jaycee Park

Grayslake Outdoor Theatre

St. Gilbert School

Grayslake H.S.

Hillside Ave.

Lakeview School

Grays Lake

Metra Commuter Train Station

Metra Milwaukee District North Line

BELVIDERE

Hainesville Sch.

Town Line Rd.

Northshore Gun Club

Lake Churchill

Bluegrass Ct.

Esquestrian Dr.

Winchester Rd.

PETERSON RD.

ALLEGHANY RD.

BARRON BLVD.

IVANHOE RD.

Squaw Creek

1. Mac Gillis Dr.
2. Bison Dr.
3. Jorgensen Ct.
4. Barbara Ct.
5. Cedar Mount Rd.
6. Model Ct.
7. Timber Creek Dr.
8. Center Dr.
9. Porter Dr.

1. Buck Dr.
2. Kathrine Dr.
3. Christine Ln.
4. Fawn Ln.
5. Deer Run Dr.

1. Langley Ct.
2. Banbury D
3. Braymore
4. W. Cambri
5. Attenborou

1. Banbury D
2. Braymore
3. W. Cambri
4. Attenborou

6. Doolittle Dr.
7. Longchamps Ct.
8. Redbridge Ct.
9. Remington Ct.
10. Keeneland Ct.
12. Stockton Dr.

23000 W   22500 W   22000 W   21500 W   21000 W   20500 W

.5 MILE

CONTINUED ON PAGE 24

CONTINUED ON PAGE 16

CONTINUED ON PAGE 18

© BY CSC

7   8   9

K   K
L   L
M   M
N   N
P   P

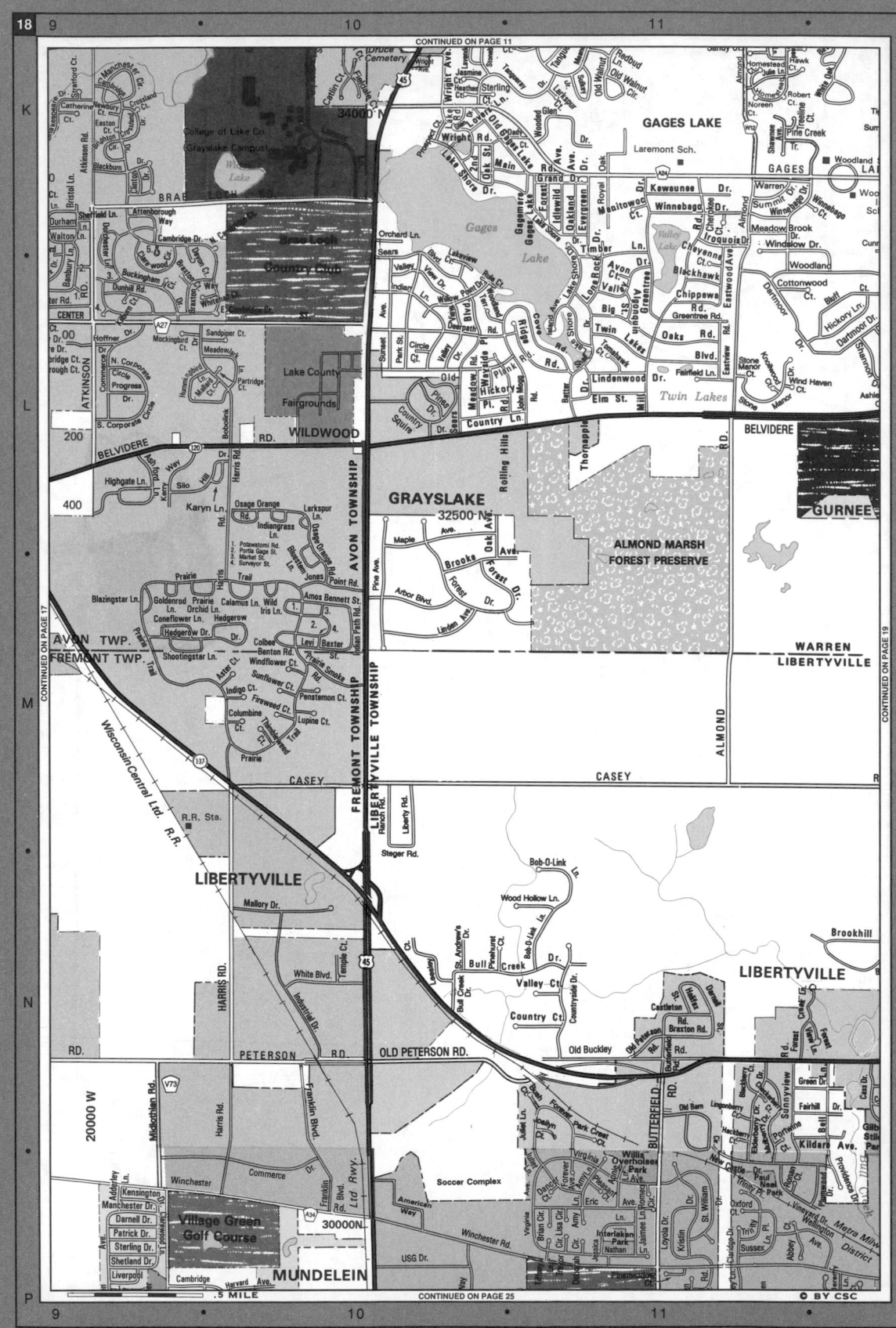

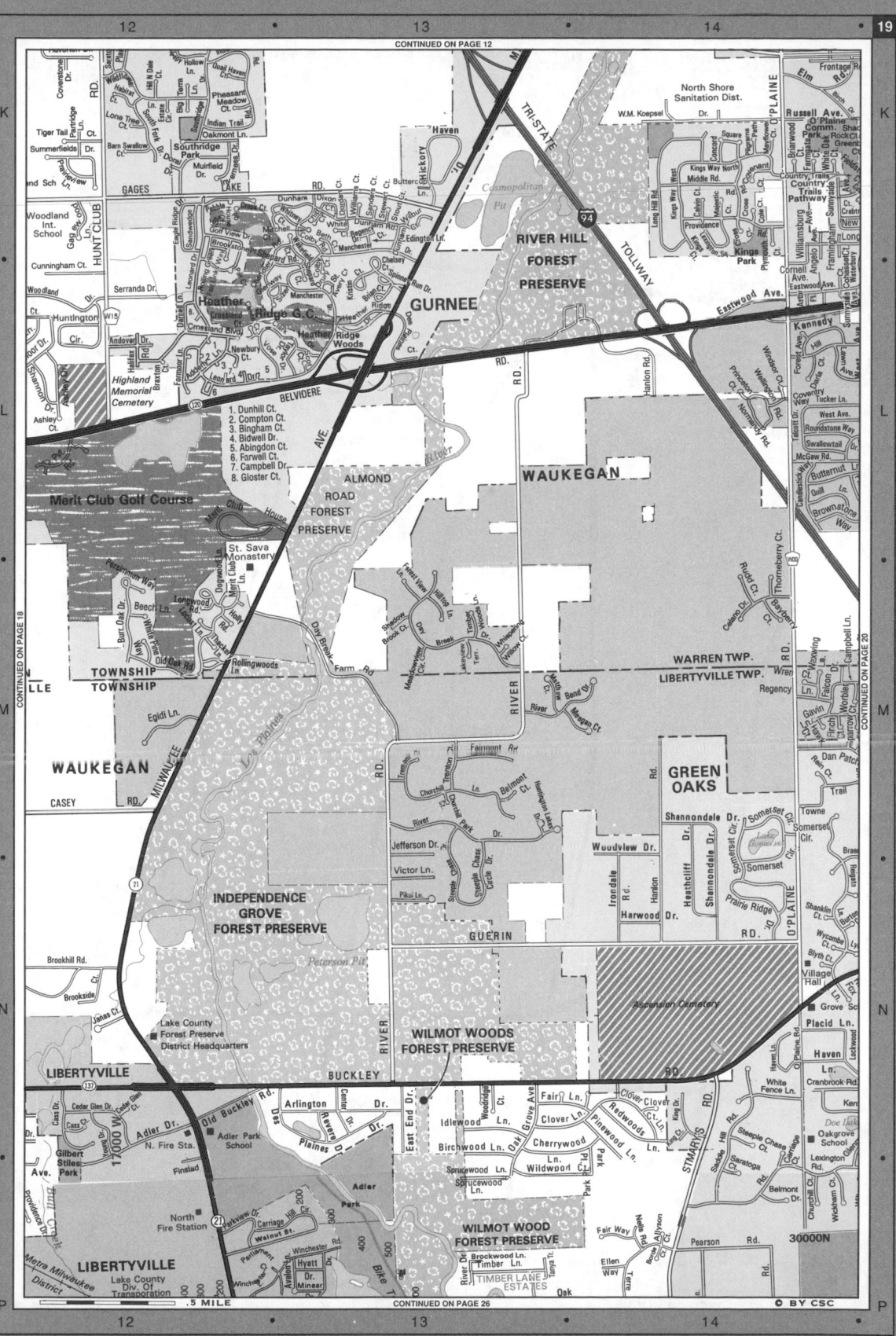

CONTINUED ON PAGE 12

CONTINUED ON PAGE 18

CONTINUED ON PAGE 20

CONTINUED ON PAGE 26

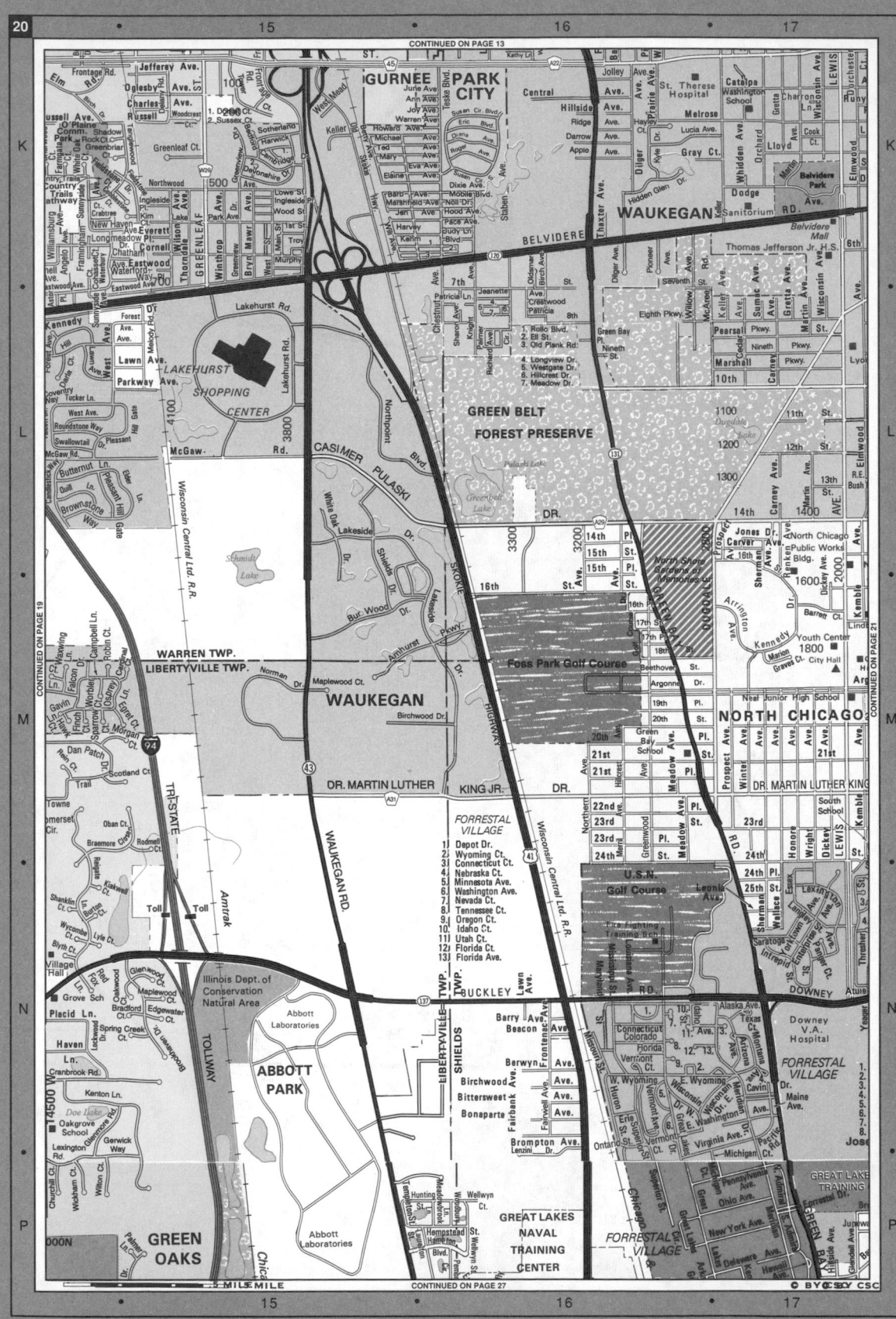

CONTINUED ON PAGE 13

CONTINUED ON PAGE 19

CONTINUED ON PAGE 21

CONTINUED ON PAGE 27

GURNEE PARK CITY

WAUKEGAN

LAKEHURST SHOPPING CENTER

GREEN BELT FOREST PRESERVE

WARREN TWP.
LIBERTYVILLE TWP.

WAUKEGAN

NORTH CHICAGO

DR. MARTIN LUTHER KING JR. DR.

DR. MARTIN LUTHER KING

FORRESTAL VILLAGE

1) Depot Dr.
2) Wyoming Ct.
3) Connecticut Ct.
4) Nebraska Ct.
5) Minnesota Ct.
6) Washington Ave.
7) Nevada Ct.
8) Tennessee Ct.
9) Oregon Ct.
10) Idaho Ct.
11) Utah Ct.
12) Florida Ct.
13) Florids Ave.

Foss Park Golf Course

U.S.N. Golf Course

Fire Fighting Training Sch.

Illinois Dept. of Conservation Natural Area

Abbott Laboratories

ABBOTT PARK

Abbott Laboratories

FORRESTAL VILLAGE

Downey V.A. Hospital

GREAT LAKES NAVAL TRAINING CENTER

GREEN OAKS

GREAT LAKES TRAINING

TOLLWAY

TRI-STATE

© BY CSC

.5 MILE MILE

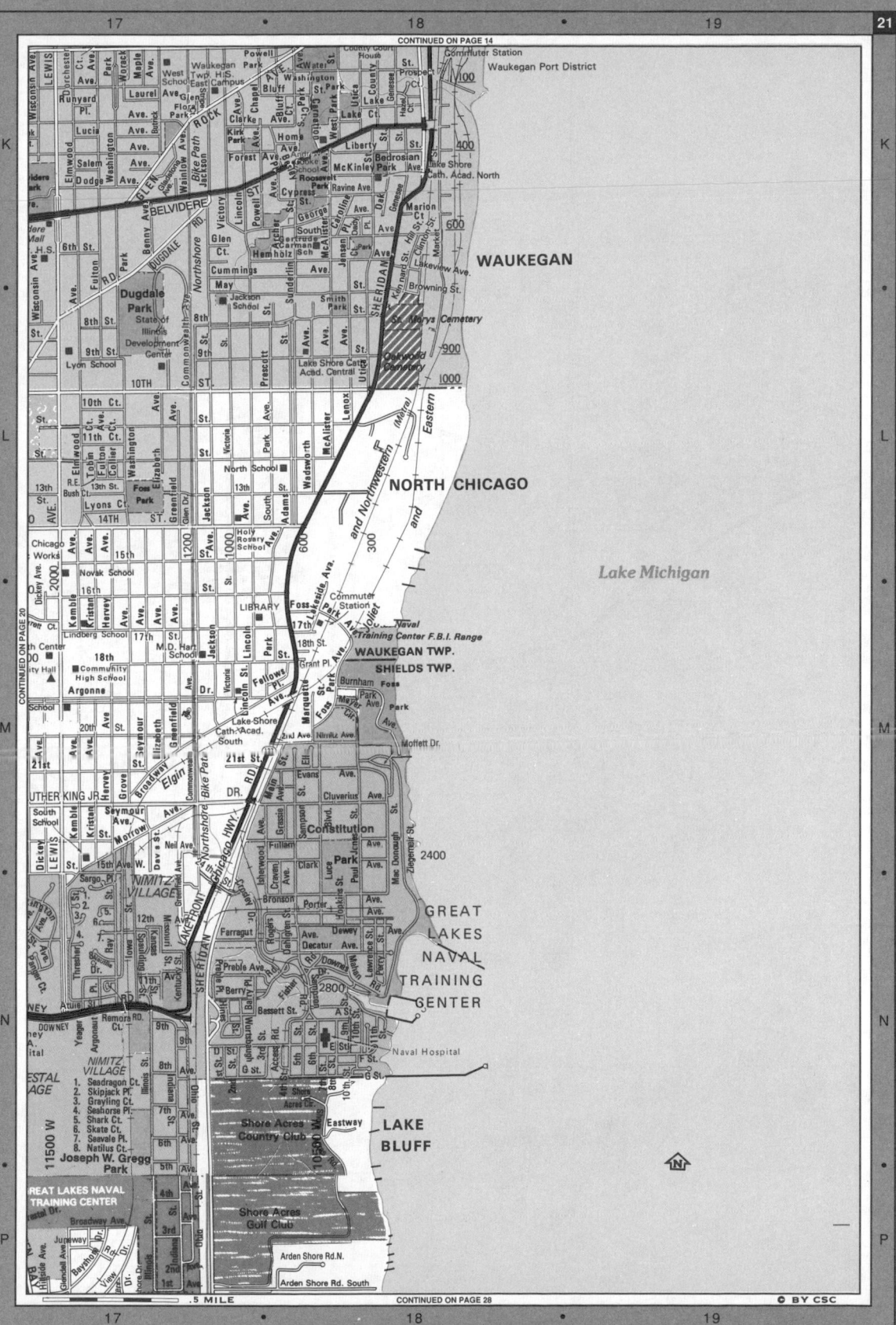

CONTINUED ON PAGE 14

WAUKEGAN

NORTH CHICAGO

*Lake Michigan*

WAUKEGAN TWP.
SHIELDS TWP.

GREAT
LAKES
NAVAL
TRAINING
CENTER

LAKE
BLUFF

NIMITZ
VILLAGE

Joseph W. Gregg
Park

GREAT LAKES NAVAL
TRAINING CENTER

NIMITZ VILLAGE
1. Seadragon Ct.
2. Skipjack Pl.
3. Grayling Ct.
4. Seahorse Pl.
5. Shark Ct.
6. Skate Ct.
7. Seevale Pl.
8. Natilus Ct.

Shore Acres
Country Club

Shore Acres
Golf Club

Arden Shore Rd. N.
Arden Shore Rd. South

.5 MILE

CONTINUED ON PAGE 28

© BY CSC

CONTINUED ON PAGE 20

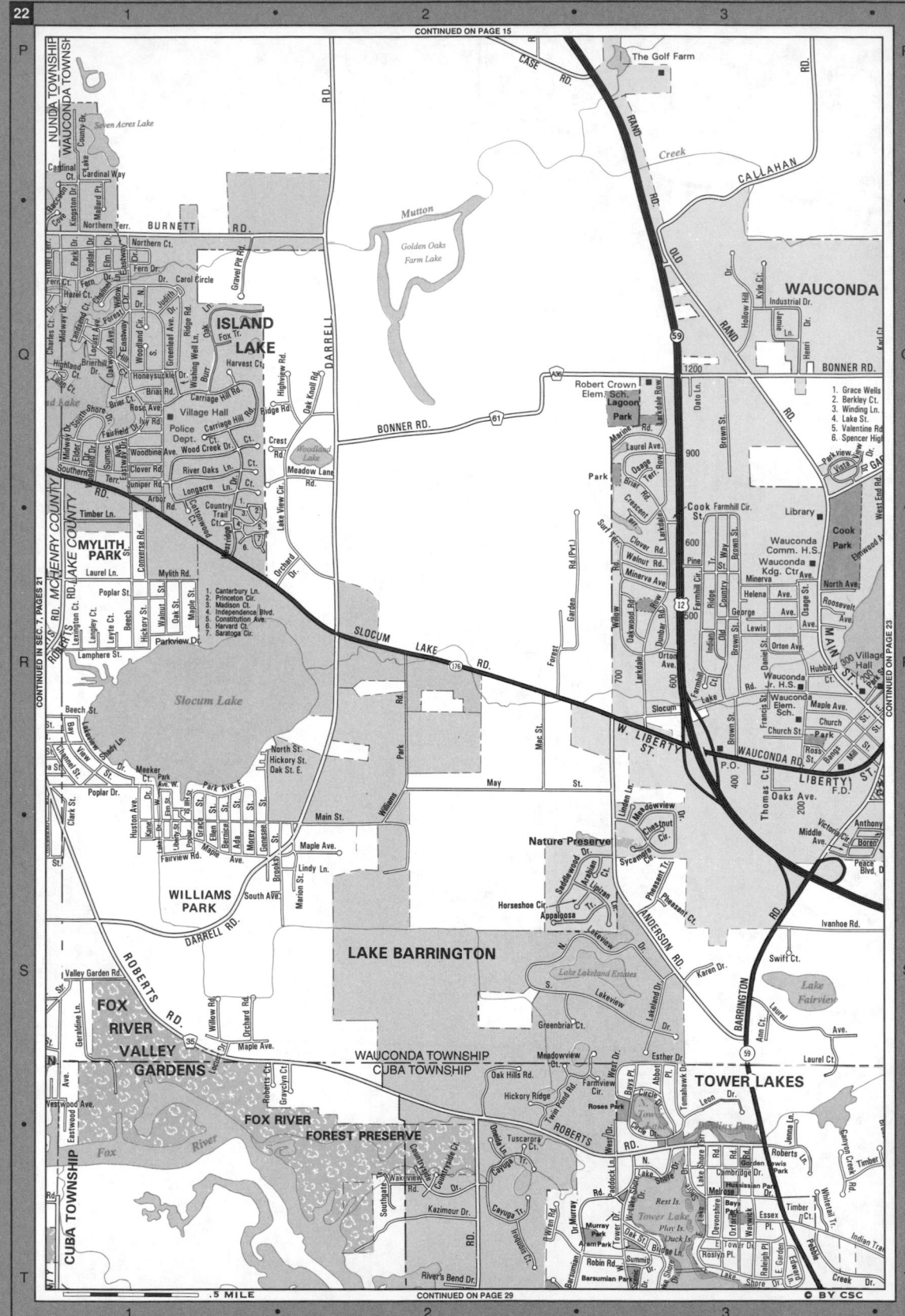

CONTINUED ON PAGE 15

P

Q

R

S

T

**ISLAND LAKE**

**WAUCONDA**

1. Grace Wells
2. Berkley Ct.
3. Winding Ln.
4. Lake St.
5. Valentine Rd.
6. Spencer High

**MYLITH PARK**

1. Canterbury Ln.
2. Princeton Cir.
3. Madison Ct.
4. Independence Blvd.
5. Constitution Ave.
6. Harvard Ct.
7. Saratoga Cir.

**Slocum Lake**

**WILLIAMS PARK**

Nature Preserve

**LAKE BARRINGTON**

**FOX RIVER VALLEY GARDENS**

WAUCONDA TOWNSHIP
CUBA TOWNSHIP

**TOWER LAKES**

**CUBA TOWNSHIP**

**FOX RIVER FOREST PRESERVE**

.5 MILE

© BY CSC

CONTINUED IN SEC. 7, PAGES 21

CONTINUED ON PAGE 23

CONTINUED ON PAGE 16

P 4 5 6 P

**WAUCONDA**

Wauconda Industrial Park

Lake Napa Suwe

Baker Lake #1

Lake Fairfield

Mud Lake

GARLAND RD.
GOSSELL RD.
WAUCONDA FREMONT T
FAIRFIELD RD.
GILMER RD.
ERHART RD.

Robin Ct.
Marilyn Meadow
Virginia Ln.
Timothy Tr.
Virginia
Sunset Ct.
Baker Ln.
Russell
Lake Fairfield Rd.

Wade St.
Gardner Rd.
Madison Ave.
Washington Ave.
Monroe Ave.
Harrison
Macintosh
Jonathan
Cortland
Cortland Terr.
Baldwin Ln.

1. Grace Wells Dr.
2. Berkley Dr.
3. Winding Lane Ave.
4. Lake St.
5. Valentine Rd.
6. Spencer-Highland Rd.

BONNER RD.
BONNER RD.

Lake Pkwy.
Grant Pl.
Pershing Dr.
Sheridan
Jackson
Harrison
Garfield
Van Buren
Summit Ave.
Jessica
Erica Dr.
Wauconda Ave.
Pleasant View Ave.

Pamela Ct.
Nancy Ct.
North Shore Ct.
Jack Hill Dr.
Oak Shore
Oakdale Ave.
Edgewater Pkwy.
North
Madison Ave.
Monroe
Adams
Jackson
Park Pl.
Ridge
Shore Dr.

West End Rd.
Elmwood Ave.
Myrtle
Ash St.
Bluff St.
Hickory Ln.
Lake
Ct.
Cook St.
Pleasant View Ave.
Cary Plaza
Lindy's Landing

Cook Park

Bangs Lake

Wauconda Bog

Four Winds Golf Course

Lake County Museum

WAUCONDA RD.

Marina St.
Marina
Sunnyside Rd.
Foster Rd.
Grand Blvd.
Highland Ave.
Woodland

Country Lane Ct.
Oak
Bluff Ct.
South St.
Edgewater
Lake Shore Dr.
Park
Clearview
Brett
Crestview
Delpa Dr.
Washington
Washington Cir.

Village Hall
Cook St.
Lotus St.
Main St.
Mill St.

Illinois Nature Preserve & National Natural Landmark

Sky Hill Rd.
High St.
Ridge
Alma
Lakeview
Wilson
Werden Dr.
Hammond

Wauconda Geol. Oaks Ave.
Kent Ave.
Anthony Dr.
Naples Ave.
Peace Blvd.
Delo Dr.

Kimball
High St.
Ridge
Alvina Ave.
Taylor Ct.

Banana Lake
Taylor Lake
Heron Lake
Davis Lake
Schreiber Lake

Winter Sports Area

IVANHOE RD.
SCHWERMAN RD.
FAIRFIELD RD.

Hillside Ave.
Hermosa Ave.
Tamarack Rd.
Oak
Greenview Dr.
Ivanhoe Rd.
York Rd.
Ivanhoe Ct.
Barnswallow Ln.
Schwerman Rd.
Horizon Spur
Pond Shore Dr.

LAKEWOOD FOREST PRESERVE

WAUCONDA TOWNSHIP
FREMONT TOWNSHIP

RAND RD.
BROWN RD.

Acorn Lake
Beaver Lake

LAKE CORNERS

MILTON RD.

Lake Shore Ct.
E. Lake Shore Dr.
Hill Ave.
Meadow Ln.
Blakely Pkwy.
Blakely
E. Lake Shore Dr.

Timber Lake
Lakeview Pkwy.
W. Lake Shore Dr.

CUBA TWP.
ELA TWP.

Anna Ct.
Ravine Ln.
August Ln.
Marsh
Steen

FREMONT TOWNSHIP
ELA TOWNSHIP

Winding Branch Rd.
Bent Tree Ct.
Pheasant Run
Ford Hunt Tr.
Fox Hunt Cir.
Biltmore
Mongarts

Brierwood Estates Park
Paddock Ct.
Derby Dr.
Furlong Dr.
North Trail
Steeplechase

Bridlewoods Park
Equestrian Way
Westwind Ct.

Sanford Creek Dr.
Broken Bow Pass
Timber Lake
Oak Creek Cir.
Wheel
Wagon
Knollwood
North Oaks
Oakwood
Wildwood
Greenwood

Indian Trails Rd.
Tara Dr.
Stonehenge Dr.

**TOWER LAKES**

**NORTH BARRINGTON**

Wynstone Golf Club

Candlewood Dr.
Wynstone
Lakeside Dr.
Clarington
Rose Ave.
Valentine Ave.
OLD MCHENRY RD.

© BY CSC

CONTINUED ON PAGE 22
CONTINUED ON PAGE 24
CONTINUED ON PAGE 30

.5 MILE

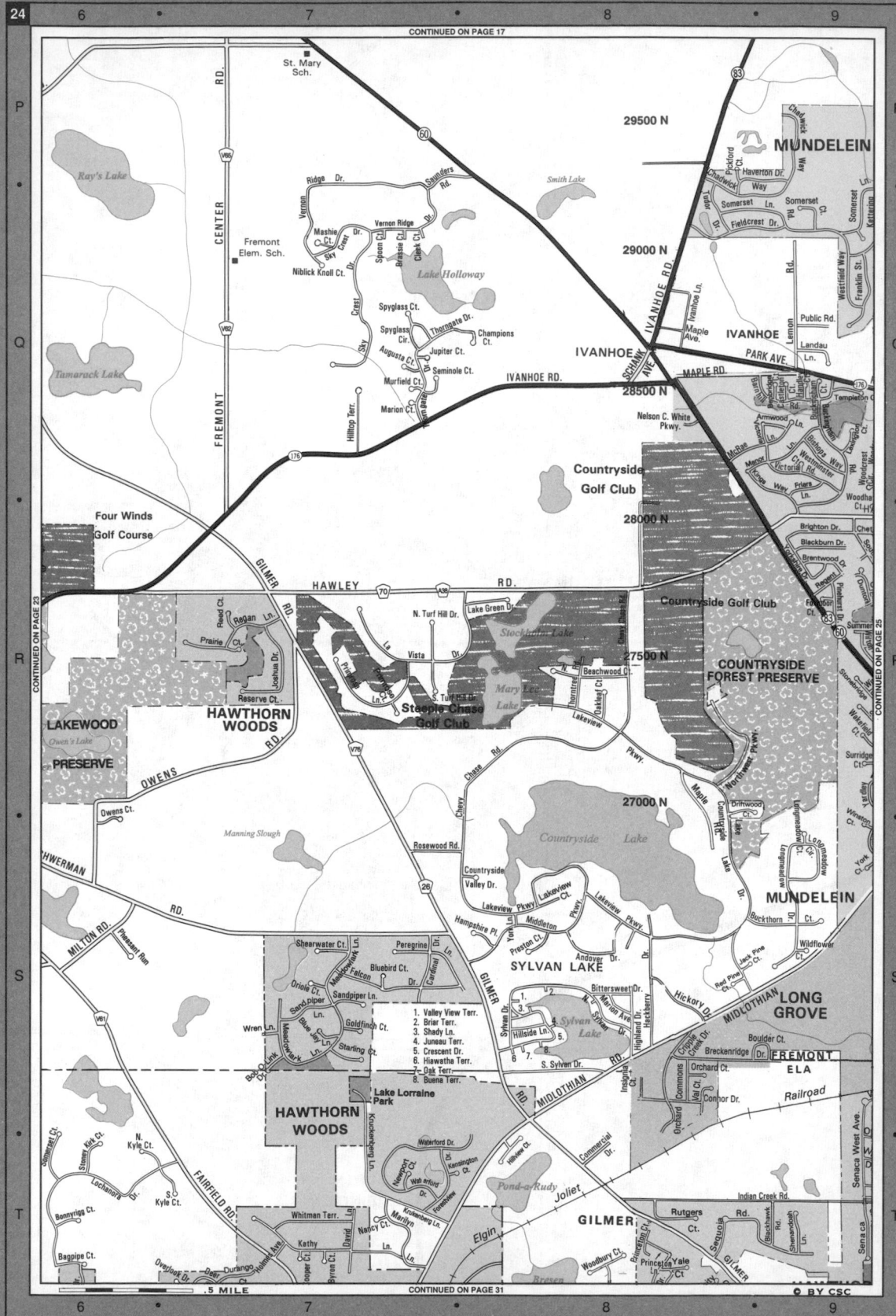

P

Ray's Lake

St. Mary Sch.

29500 N

MUNDELEIN

Chadwick Ct.

Pickford Ct.
Haverton Dr.
Chadwick Way
Somerset
Somerset Ln.
Ketterling

CENTER RD.

Ridge Dr.
Vernon
Vernon Ridge
Saunders Rd.

Fremont Elem. Sch.

Mashie Ct.
Sky Crest
Brassie Cir.
Cleek Ct.
Niblick Knoll Ct.

Lake Holloway

29000 N

Tudor Rd.
Fieldcrest Dr.

Rd.

Westfield Way
Franklin St.

Smith Lake

Public Rd.

IVANHOE

Maple Ave.

Landau Ln.

Q

Tamarack Lake

FREMONT

Spyglass Ct.
Spyglass Cir.
Thorngate Dr.
Champions Ct.
Augusta Ct.
Jupiter Ct.
Seminole Ct.
Murfield Ct.
Marion Ct.
Hilltop Terr.

Crest
Sky

176

IVANHOE

IVANHOE RD.

28500 N

Nelson C. White Pkwy.

Schank Ave.
Maple Rd.
PARK AVE.

176

Templeton Ct.

Armwood
McRae
Menor
Victorial Rd.
Friars Ln.
Westminster

Countryside Golf Club

28000 N

Brighton Dr.
Blackburn Dr.
Brentwood

Four Winds Golf Course

GILMER RD.

HAWLEY 70 A36 RD.

Regent
Pinehurst Dr.

Countryside Golf Club

83 60

R

CONTINUED ON PAGE 23

Reed Ct.
Regan Ln.
Prairie Ct.
Joshua Dr.
Reserve Ct.

N. Turf Hill Dr.
La Vista Dr.
Prairie
S. Turf Hill Dr.

Lake Green Dr.

Stockholm Lake

27500 N

Beachwood Ct.

Oakleaf Ct.
Lakeview

COUNTRYSIDE FOREST PRESERVE

CONTINUED ON PAGE 25

HAWTHORN WOODS

Staeple Chase Golf Club

Mary Lee Lake

Thorntree

LAKEWOOD PRESERVE

Owen's Lake

OWENS RD.

Owens Ct.

Manning Slough

Chase Rd.

27000 N

Countryside Lake

Maple
Countryside Lake Dr.
Northwest Pkwy.

Driftwood Ct.

MUNDELEIN

SHWERMAN RD.

MILTON RD.

Pleasant Run

Rosewood Rd.

26

Countryside Valley Dr.

Lakeview Pkwy.
Middleton
Preston Ct.

Longmeadow
mt Prasubury

York Ct.

Buckthorn Ct.
Wildflower

S

Shearwater Ct.
Peregrine Dr.
Bluebird Ct.
Cardinal
Oriole Ct.
Sandpiper Ln.
Falcon
Meadowlark

Hampshire Pl.

SYLVAN LAKE

Andover Dr.

Bittersweet Dr.
Marion Ave.
Highland Dr.

Hickory Dr.

Red Pine Ct.
Jack Pine

MIDLOTHIAN

LONG GROVE

Wren Ct.
Sandpiper Ln.
Goldfinch Ct.
Starling Ln.
Blue Jay Ln.
Meadowlark

1. Valley View Terr.
2. Briar Terr.
3. Shady Ln.
4. Juneau Terr.
5. Crescent Dr.
6. Hiawatha Terr.
7. Oak Terr.
8. Buena Terr.

Sylvan Dr.
Hillside Dr.
Sylvan Lake
S. Sylvan Dr.

Cripple Crest Ct.
Breckenridge Dr.
Boulder Ct.

FREMONT ELA

HAWTHORN WOODS

Lake Lorraine Park

Orchard Commons
Val Ct.
Connor Dr.

Orchard Ct.

Railroad

Indian Creek Rd.

T

Somerset Ct.
N. Kyle Ct.
Stacey
Lochanora
S. Kyle Ct.

Bennyriga Ct.

Bagpipe Ct.

FAIRFIELD RD.

Whitman Terr.
Kathy Ln.
David Ct.
Nancy Ct.
Marilyn Ln.

Waterford
Newport Ct.
Kensington Dr.
Forestone

Joliet
Elgin

Pond-a-Rudy

GILMER

Rutgers Ct.
Sequoia Ct.
Blackburn Rd.
Shawnee

Senaca West Ave.

Woodbury Ct.
Princeton Ct.
Yale Ct.

GILMER

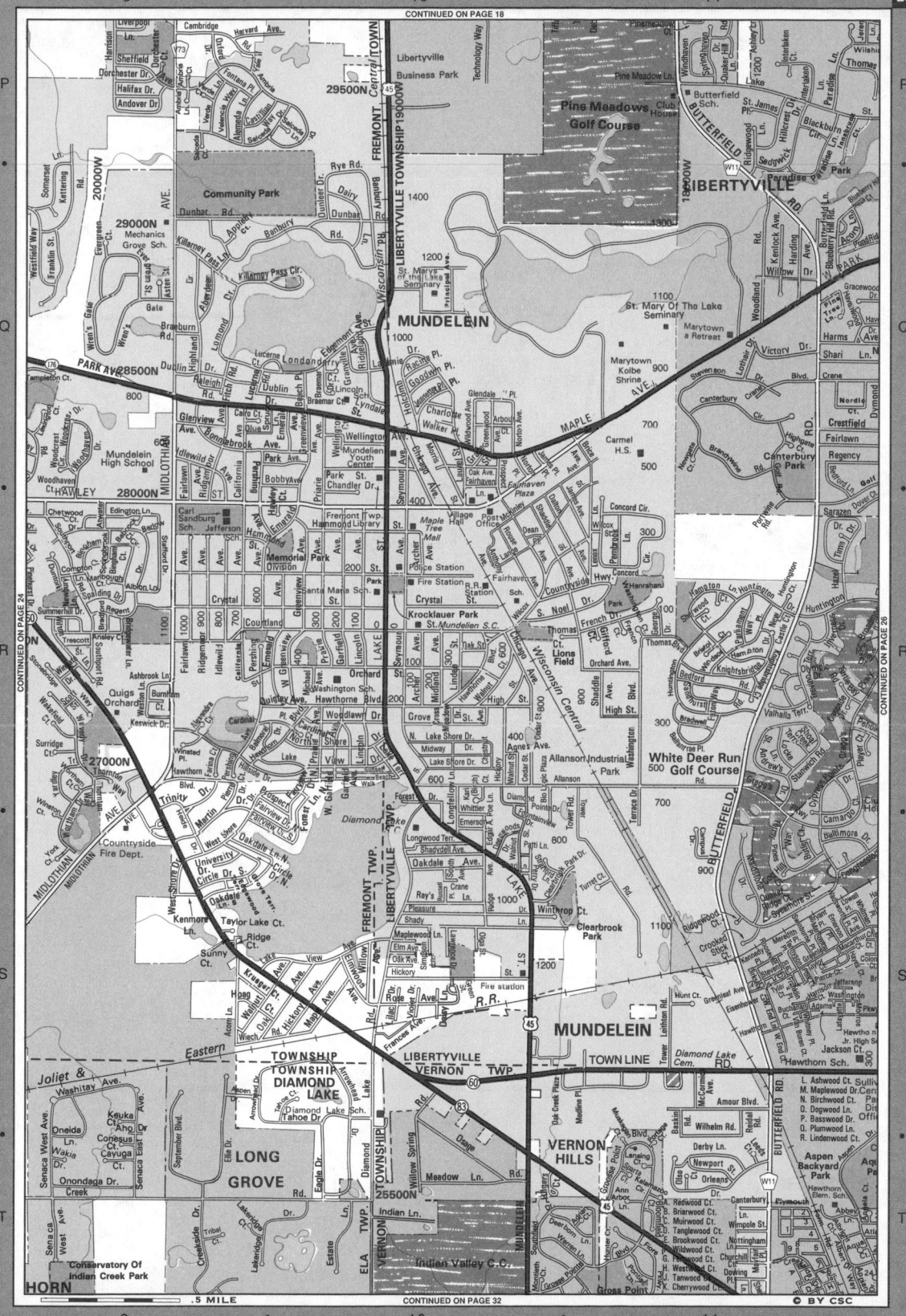

CONTINUED ON PAGE 18

CONTINUED ON PAGE 24

CONTINUED ON PAGE 26

© BY CSC

.5 MILE

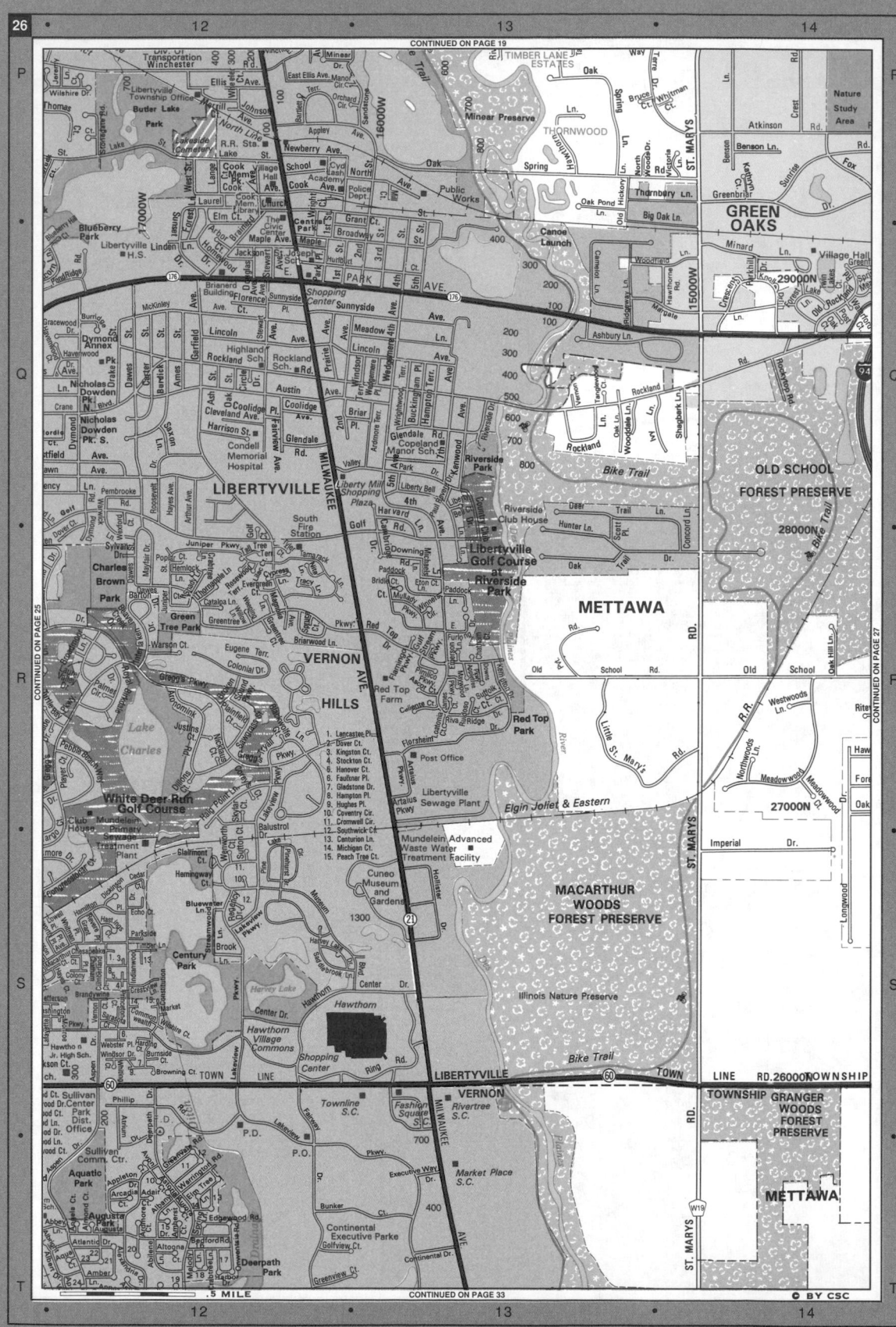

CONTINUED ON PAGE 19

CONTINUED ON PAGE 25

CONTINUED ON PAGE 27

CONTINUED ON PAGE 33

.5 MILE

© BY CSC

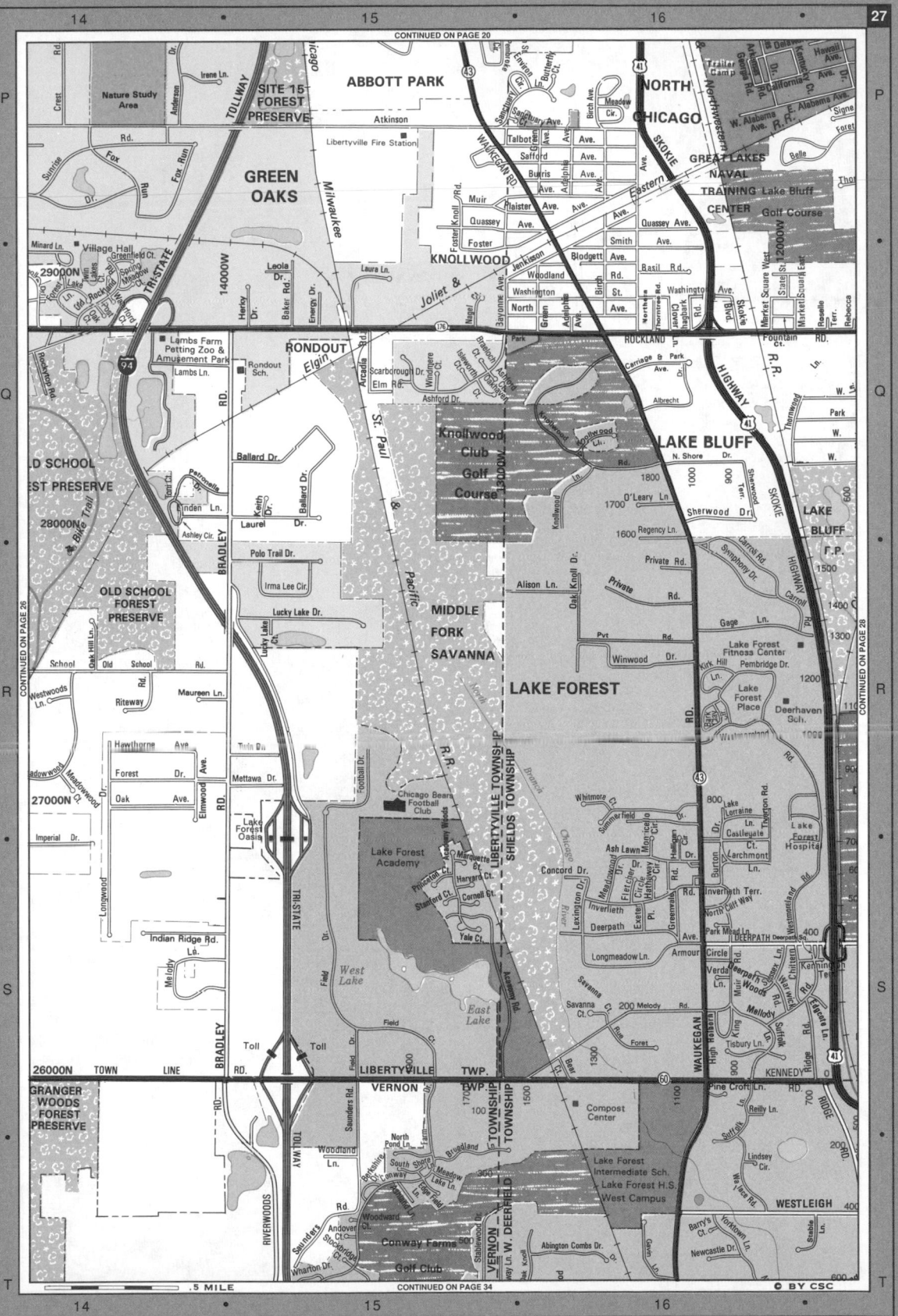

14     15     16

P

ABBOTT PARK

Nature Study
Area

SITE 15
FOREST
PRESERVE
Atkinson

NORTH
CHICAGO

Trailer
Camp

Libertyville Fire Station

GREEN
OAKS

GREAT
LAKES
NAVAL
TRAINING
CENTER

Lake Bluff
Golf Course

Talbot Ave.

Safford Ave.

Burris Ave.

Muir Ave.

Quassey Ave.

Foster Ave.

KNOLLWOOD

Quassey Ave.

Smith Ave.

Blodgett Ave.

Basil Rd.

Woodland Rd.

Washington Ave.

North Ave.

Village Hall

29000N

Joliet &

Q

Lambs Farm Petting Zoo & Amusement Park

RONDOUT

Elgin

Rondout Sch.

Arcadia

Scarborough Ct.

Elm Rd.

Ashford Dr.

Windmere

Knollwood
Club
Golf
Course

ROCKLAND

LAKE BLUFF

Carriage & Park

Albrecht

LAKE
BLUFF
F.P.

OLD SCHOOL
FOREST PRESERVE

Ballard Dr.

Ballard Dr.

Keith Dr.

Laurel Dr.

1800

1700

O'Leary Ln.

Sherwood Dr.

28000N

Polo Trail Dr.

Irma Lee Cir.

Lucky Lake Dr.

MIDDLE
FORK
SAVANNA

1600

Regency Dr.

Private Rd.

LAKE FOREST

Alison Ln.

Oak Knoll Dr.

Private Rd.

Gage Ln.

1500

1400

1300

OLD SCHOOL
FOREST
PRESERVE

R

School Rd.

Old School Rd.

Riteway

Maureen Ln.

27000N

Imperial Dr.

Hawthorne Ave.

Forest Dr.

Oak Ave.

Mettawa Dr.

Lake Forest Oasis

Winwood Dr.

Lake Forest
Fitness Center

Pembridge Dr.

Lake Forest
Place

Deerhaven Sch.

1200

1100

1000

Indian Ridge Rd.

Melody Ln.

Chicago Bears
Football Club

Lake Forest
Academy

Princeton Ct.

Marquette Ct.

Harvard Ct.

Cornell St.

Stamford Ct.

Yale Ct.

Whitmore

Summerfield

Ash Lawn

Concord Dr.

Monticello Ct.

Lorraine

Castlegate Ct.

Larchmont Ln.

800

Lake Forest
Hospital

S

West
Lake

East
Lake

Field

Inverlieth

Deerpath

Longmeadow Ln.

Laxington Ln.

Meadow

Exeter Pl.

Greenwood Ave.

Inverleith Terr.

North Calf Way

Park Mead Ln.

Armour Circle

Verda Ln.

Woods

DEERPATH

400

26000N TOWN LINE

BRADLEY RD.

Toll

Toll

LIBERTYVILLE TWP.

VERNON TWP.

North Pond Ln.

Saunders Rd.

Berkshire Ln.

South Shore Meadow

Conway

Woodland Ln.

Savanna Ct.

200 Melody

Forest

Tisbury Ln.

KENNEDY

Pine Croft Ln.

Reilly Ln.

Lindsey Cir.

WESTLEIGH

T

GRANGER
WOODS
FOREST
PRESERVE

RIVERWOODS

Woodward Ct.

Andover Ct.

Stockbridge Ct.

Wharton Ct.

Conway Farms
Golf Club

Stablewood

Abington Combs Dr.

Compost
Center

Lake Forest
Intermediate Sch.
Lake Forest H.S.
West Campus

Barry's Ct.

Newcastle Dr.

Yorktown Ln.

14     15     16

CONTINUED ON PAGE 26

CONTINUED ON PAGE 28

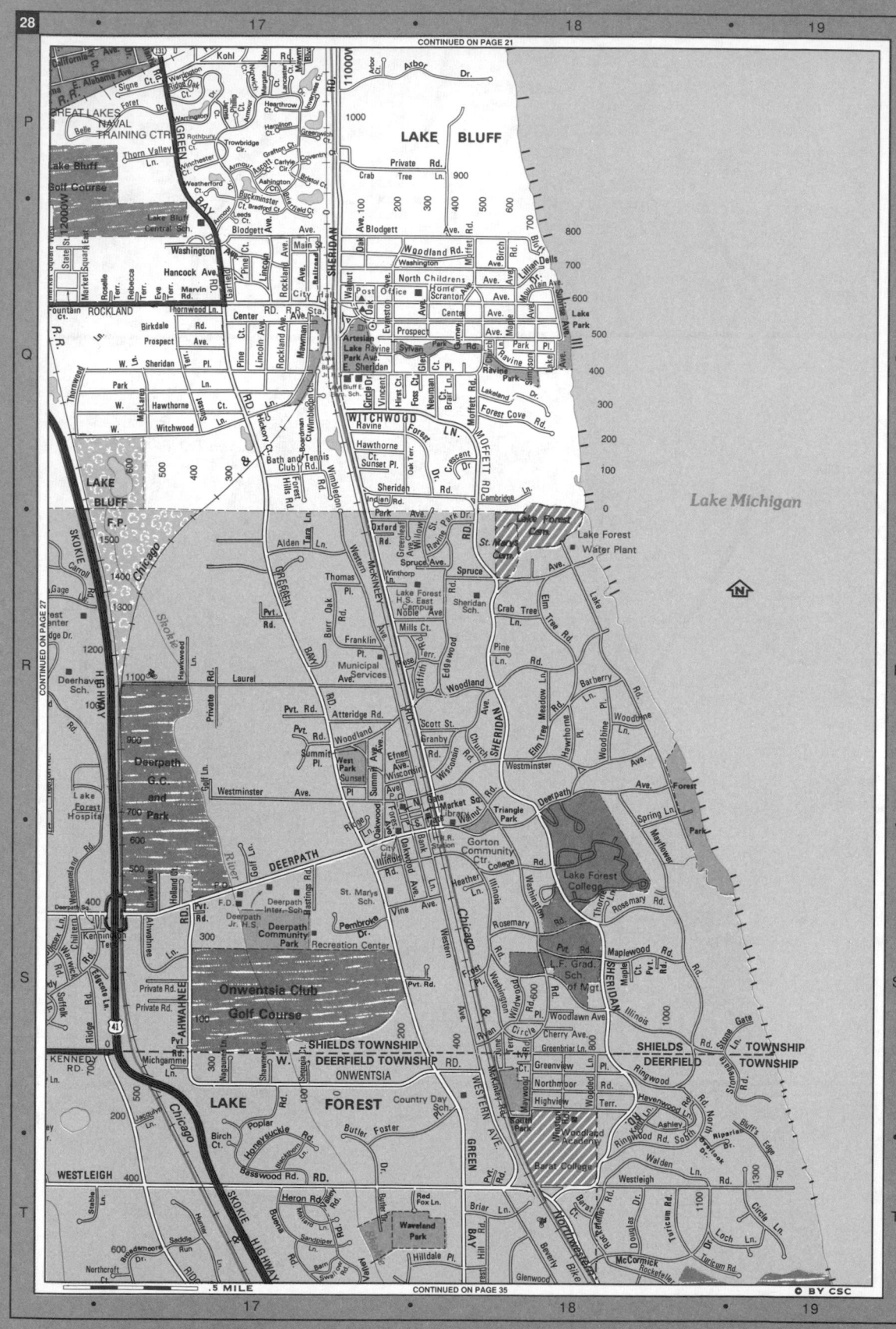

CONTINUED ON PAGE 21

LAKE BLUFF

Lake Michigan

CONTINUED ON PAGE 27

.5 MILE

CONTINUED ON PAGE 35

© BY CSC

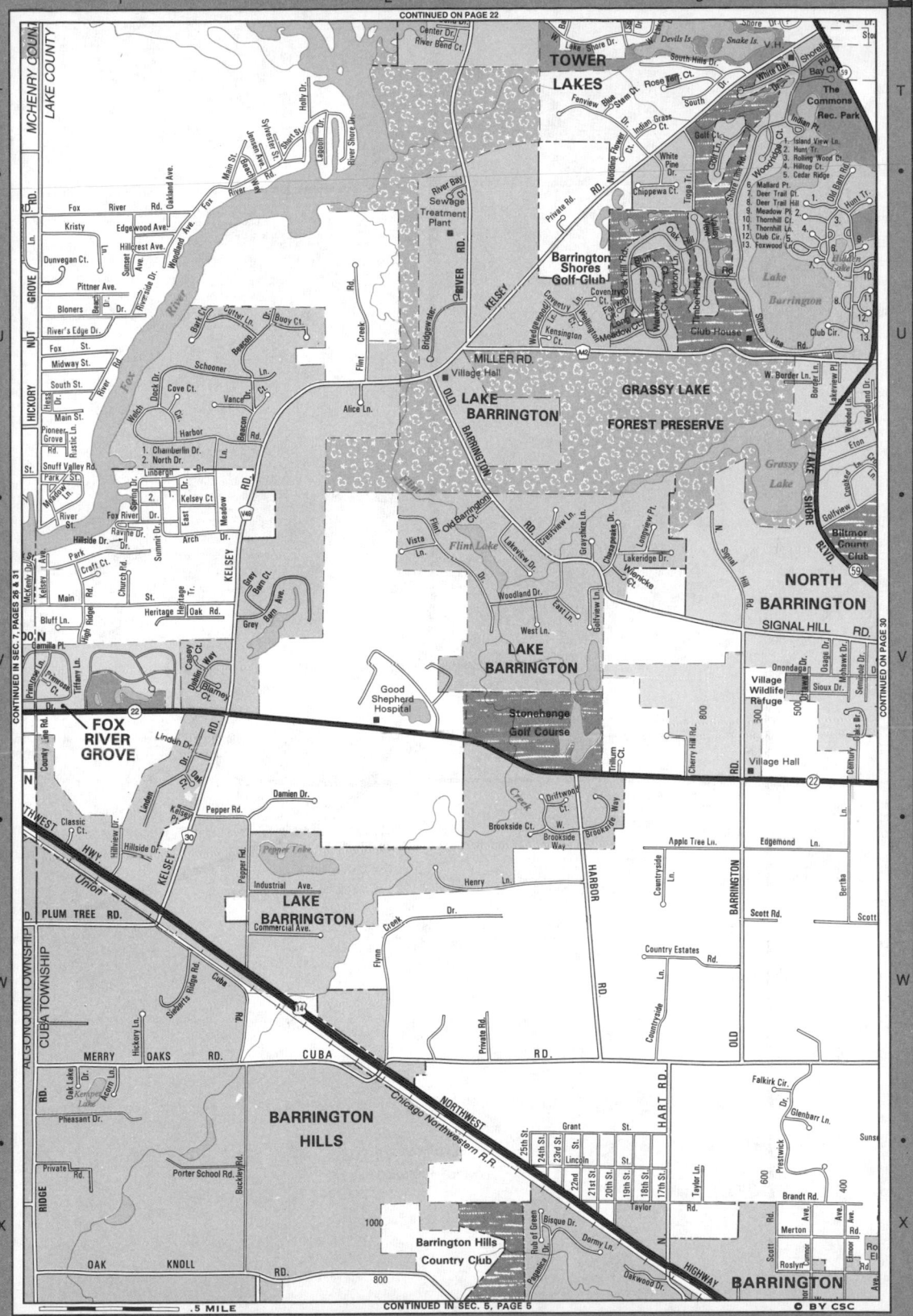

CONTINUED ON PAGE 22

TOWER
LAKES

The Commons
Rec. Park

1. Island View Ln.
2. Hunt Tr.
3. Rolling Wood Ct.
4. Meadow Pl.
5. Cedar Ridge
6. Mallard Pt.
7. Deer Trail Ct.
8. Deer Trail Hill
9. Meadow Pl.
10. Thornhill Ct.
11. Thornhill Ln.
12. Club Cir.
13. Foxwood Ct.

Barrington Shores
Golf Club

Club House

GRASSY LAKE

FOREST PRESERVE

Grassy
Lake

Biltmor
Country
Club

MILLER RD.
Village Hall

OLD
BARRINGTON

LAKE
BARRINGTON

NORTH
BARRINGTON

SIGNAL HILL

Village
Wildlife
Refuge

LAKE
BARRINGTON

Stonehenge
Golf Course

Good
Shepherd
Hospital

FOX
RIVER
GROVE

Village Hall

LAKE
BARRINGTON

BARRINGTON
HILLS

Barrington Hills
Country Club

BARRINGTON

CONTINUED IN SEC. 7, PAGES 26 & 31
CONTINUED ON PAGE 30
CONTINUED IN SEC. 5, PAGE 5

.5 MILE

© BY CSC

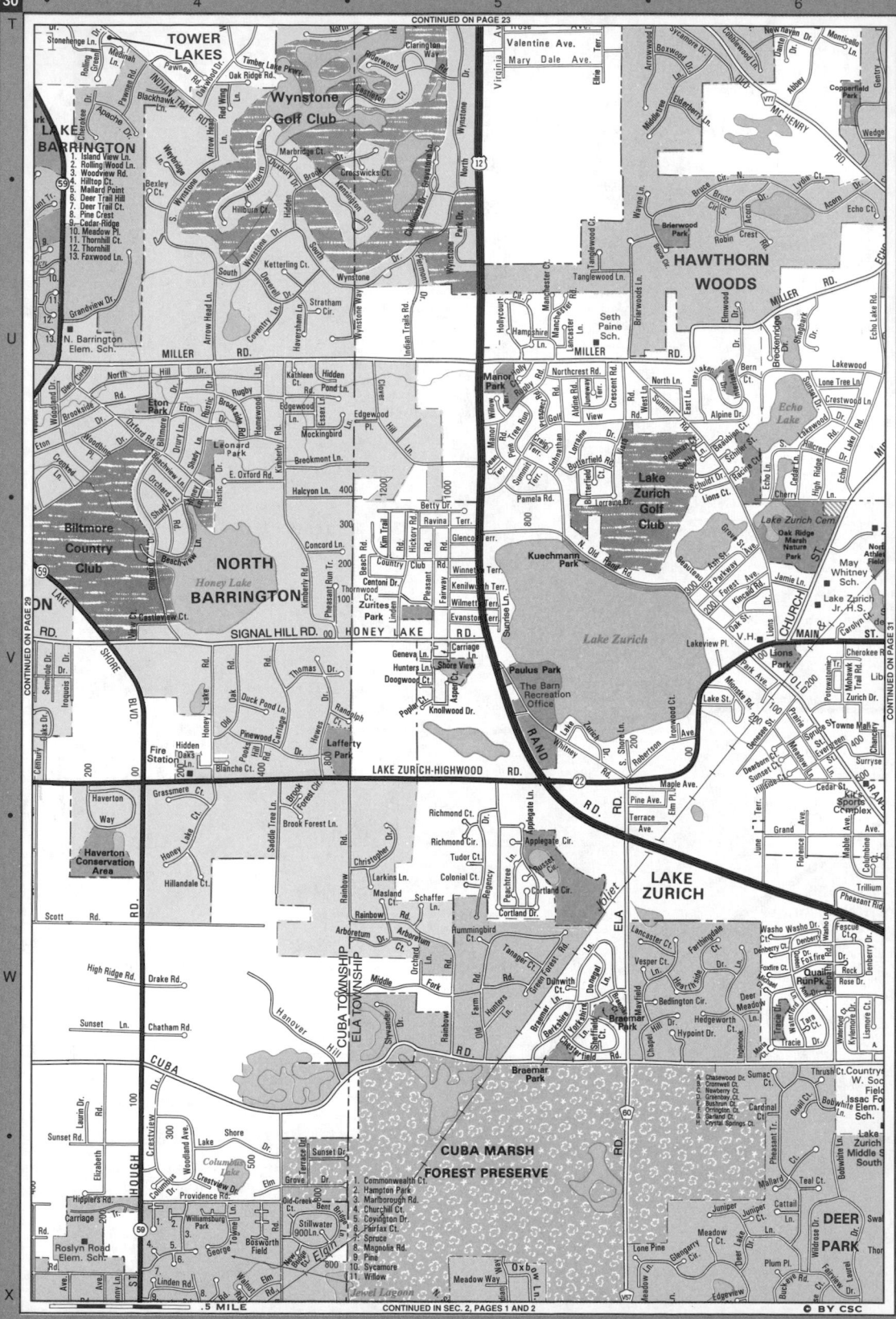

CONTINUED ON PAGE 23

TOWER LAKES

Wynstone Golf Club

LAKE BARRINGTON
1. Island View Ln.
2. Rolling Wood Ln.
3. Woodview Rd.
4. Hilltop Ct.
5. Mallard Point
6. Deer Trail Hill
7. Deer Trail Ct.
8. Pine Crest
9. Cedar Ridge
10. Meadow Pl.
11. Thornhill Ct.
12. Thornhill
13. Foxwood Ln.

13. N. Barrington Elem. Sch.

HAWTHORN WOODS

MILLER       RD.

Echo Lake

Biltmore Country Club

NORTH BARRINGTON

Honey Lake

Lake Zurich Golf Club

Kuechmann Park

Lake Zurich Cem.

SIGNAL HILL RD.      HONEY LAKE      RD.

Lake Zurich

Paulus Park
The Barn Recreation Office

Haverton Way

Haverton Conservation Area

LAKE ZURICH-HIGHWOOD      RD.

LAKE ZURICH

CUBA TOWNSHIP
ELA TOWNSHIP

Braemar Park

CUBA MARSH FOREST PRESERVE

1. Commonwealth Ct.
2. Hampton Park
3. Marlborough Rd.
4. Churchill Ct.
5. Covington Dr.
6. Fairfax Ct.
7. Spruce
8. Magnolia Rd.
9. Pine
10. Sycamore
11. Willow

Columbus Lake

Roslyn Road Elem. Sch.

DEER PARK

A. Chasewood Dr.
B. Cromwell Ct.
C. Newberry Ct.
D. Greenbay Ct.
E. Buckhorn Ct.
F. Orrington Ct.
G. Garland Ct.
H. Crystal Springs Ct.

W. Soc. Field
Issac Fo Elem. Sch.

Lake Zurich Middle S South

Jewel Lagoon      Meadow Way      Oxbow

.5 MILE

© BY CSC

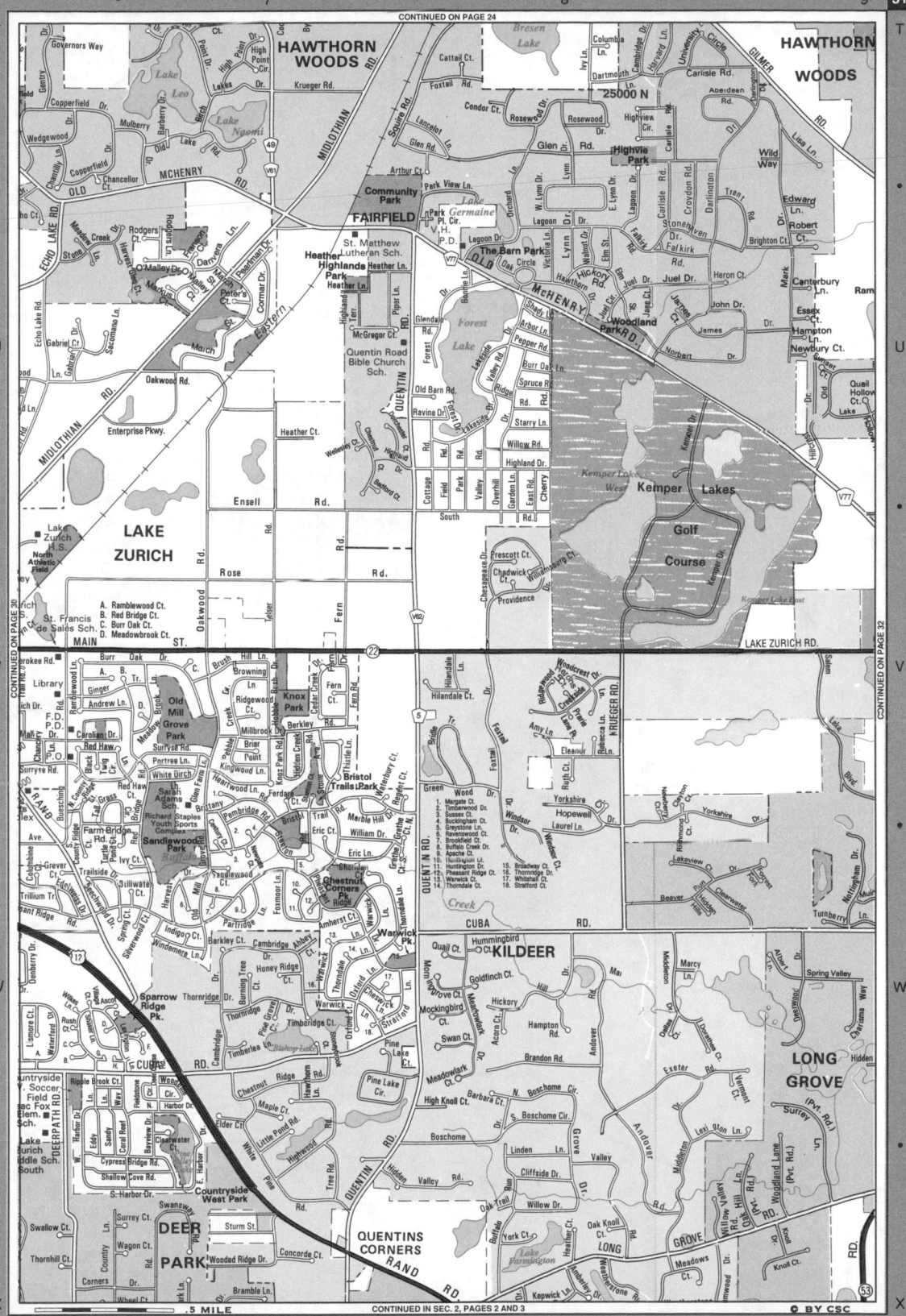

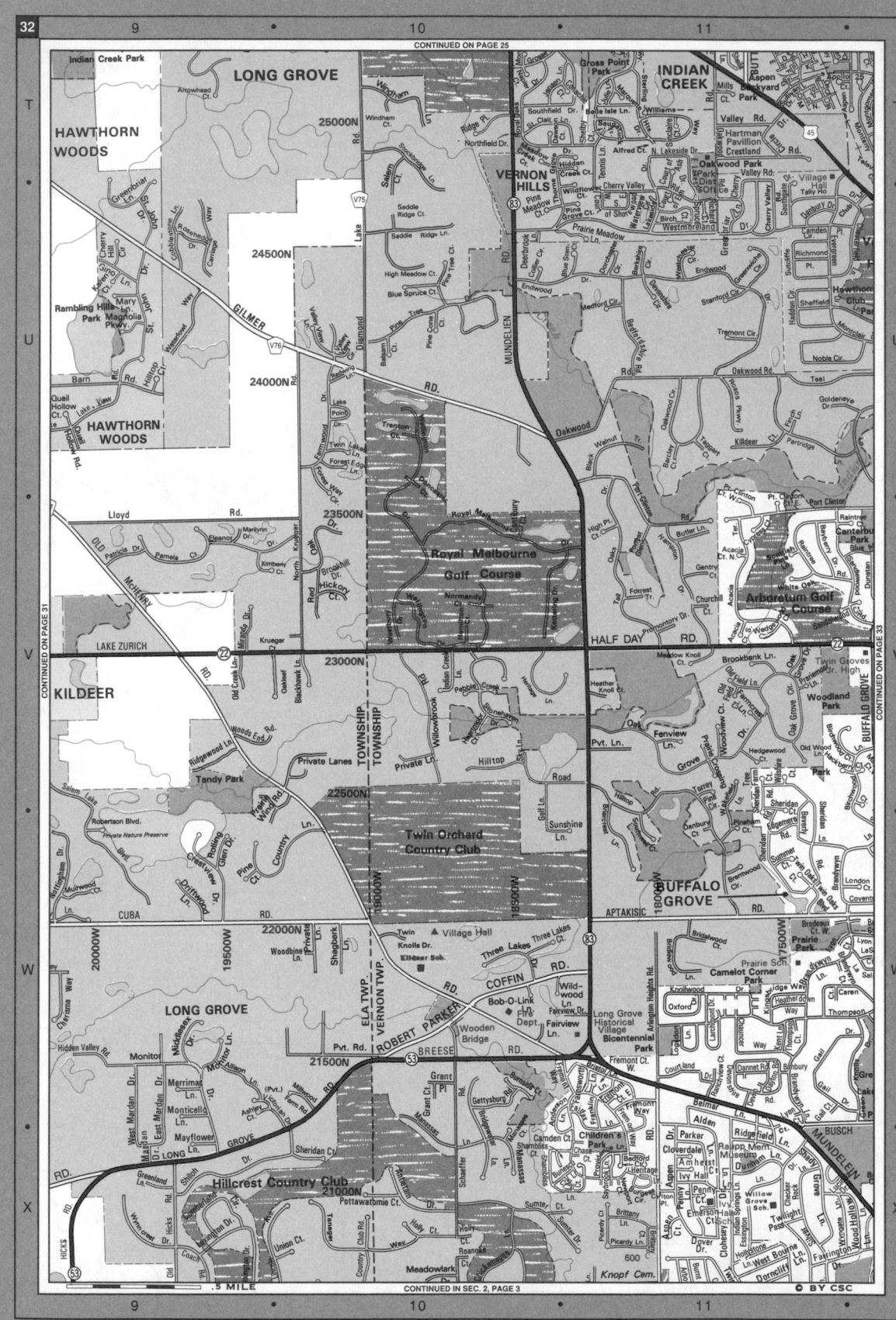

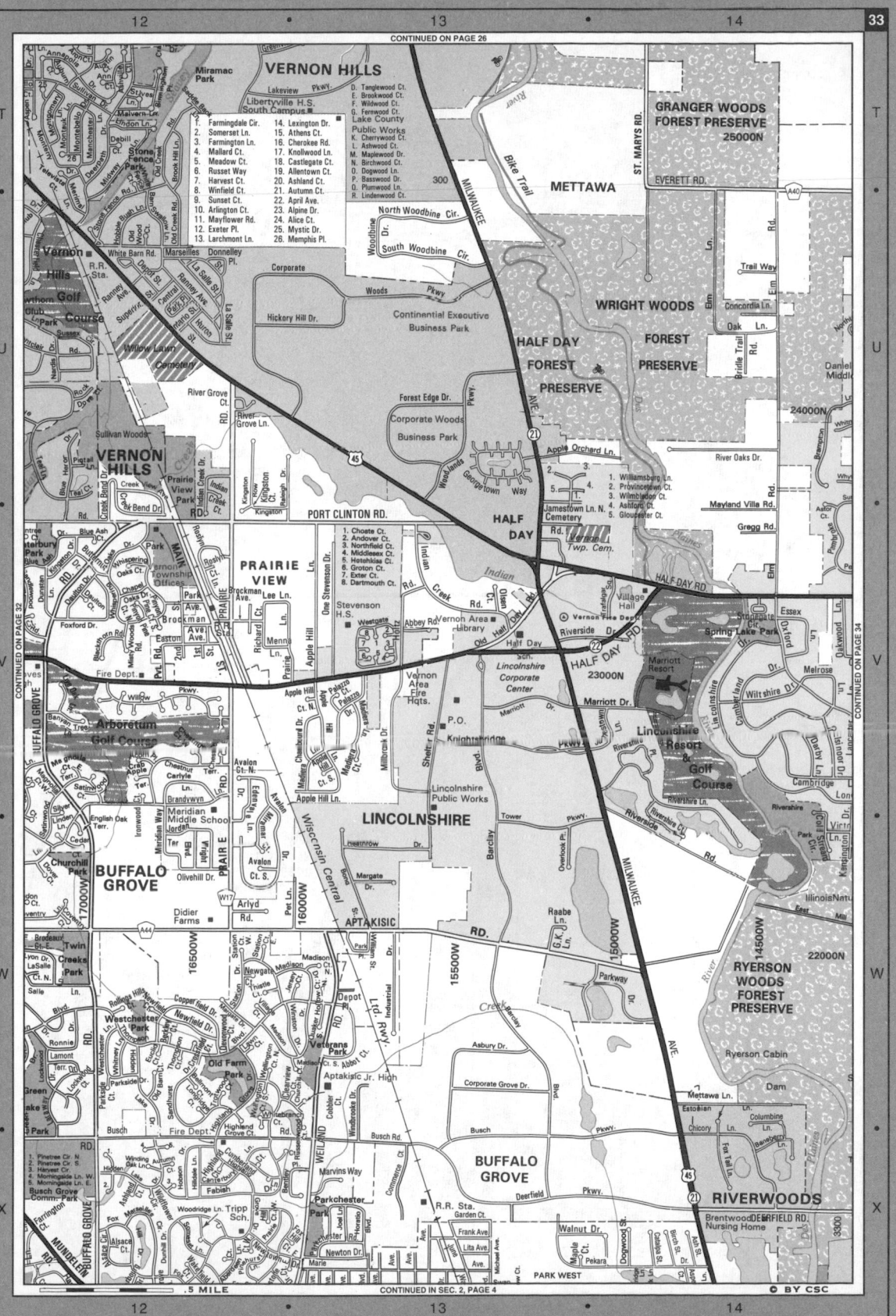

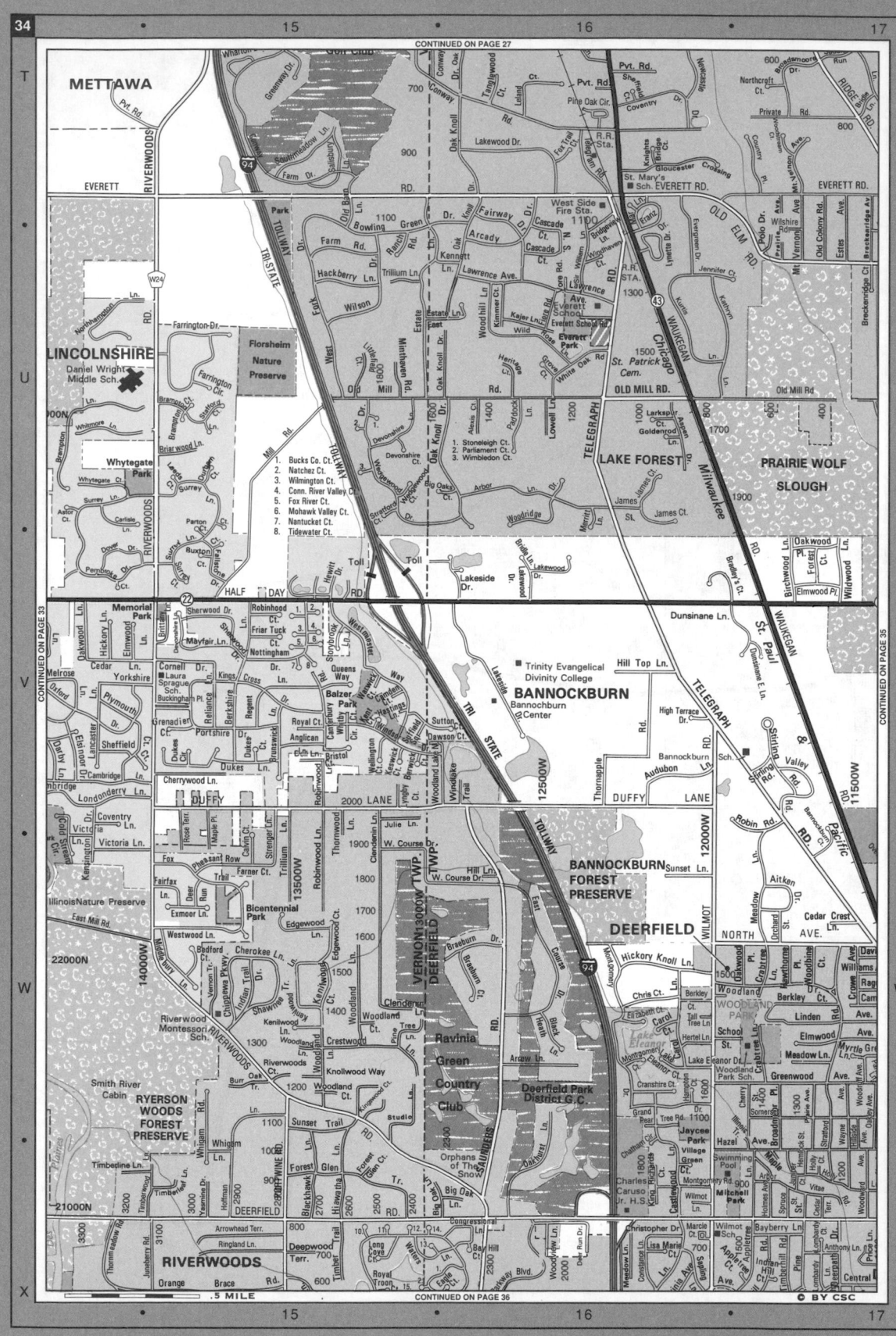

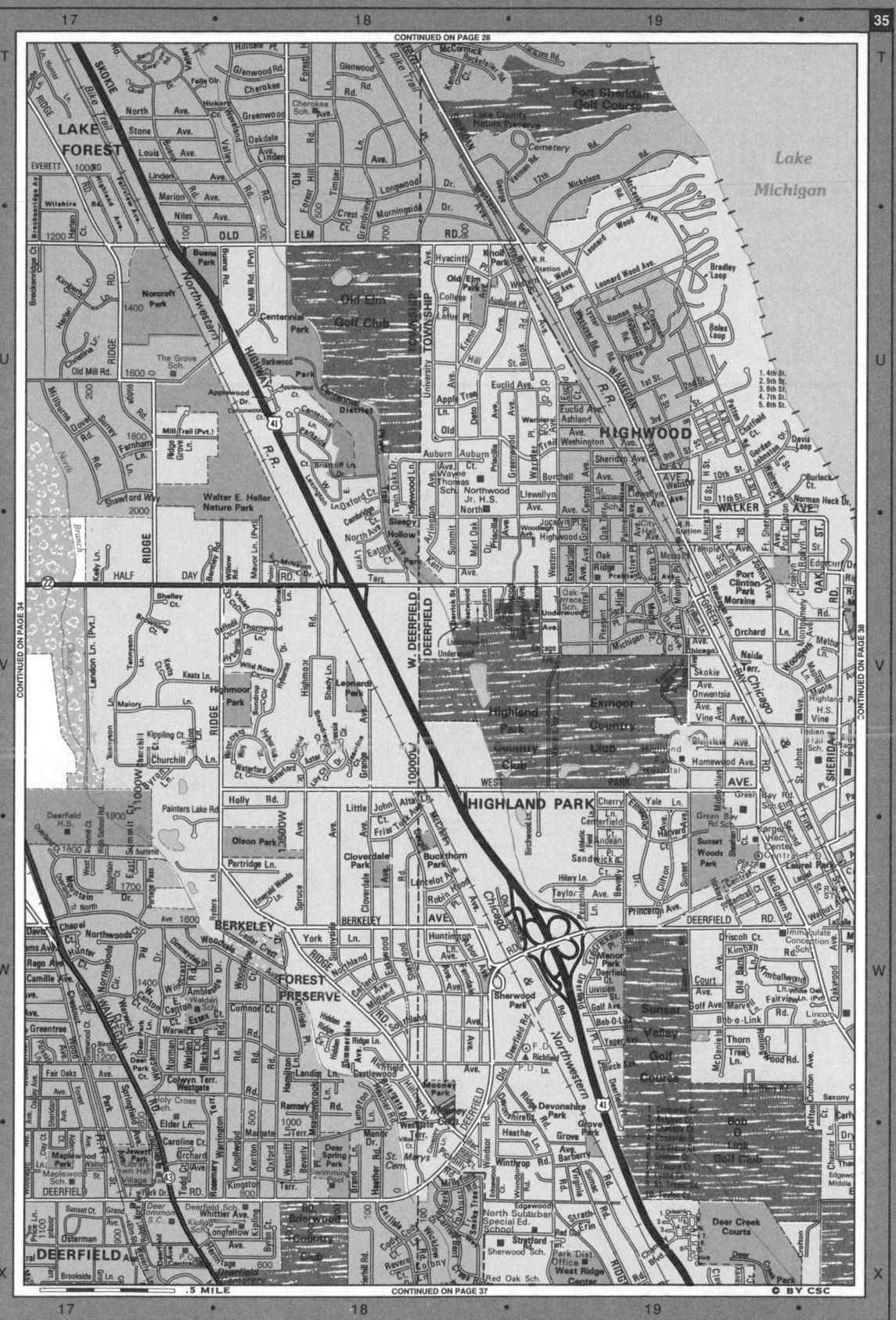

CONTINUED ON PAGE 28

CONTINUED ON PAGE 34

CONTINUED ON PAGE 38

Lake
Michigan

LAKE
FOREST

HIGHWOOD

WALKER

W. DEERFIELD
DEERFIELD

Highland
Park
Country
Club

Exmoor
Country
Club

HIGHLAND PARK

DEERFIELD RD.

FOREST
PRESERVE

Sunset
Valley
Golf
Course

DEERFIELD

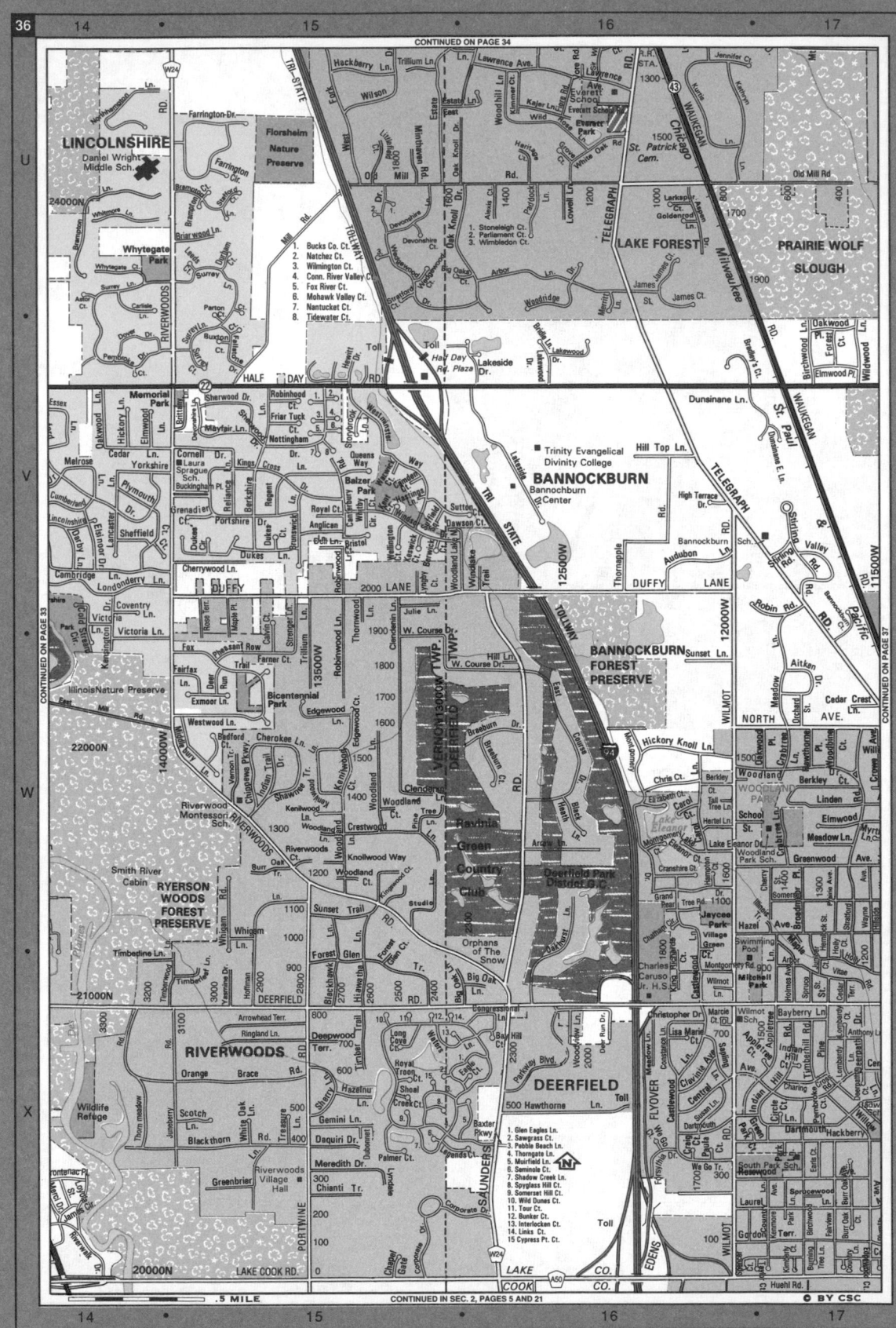

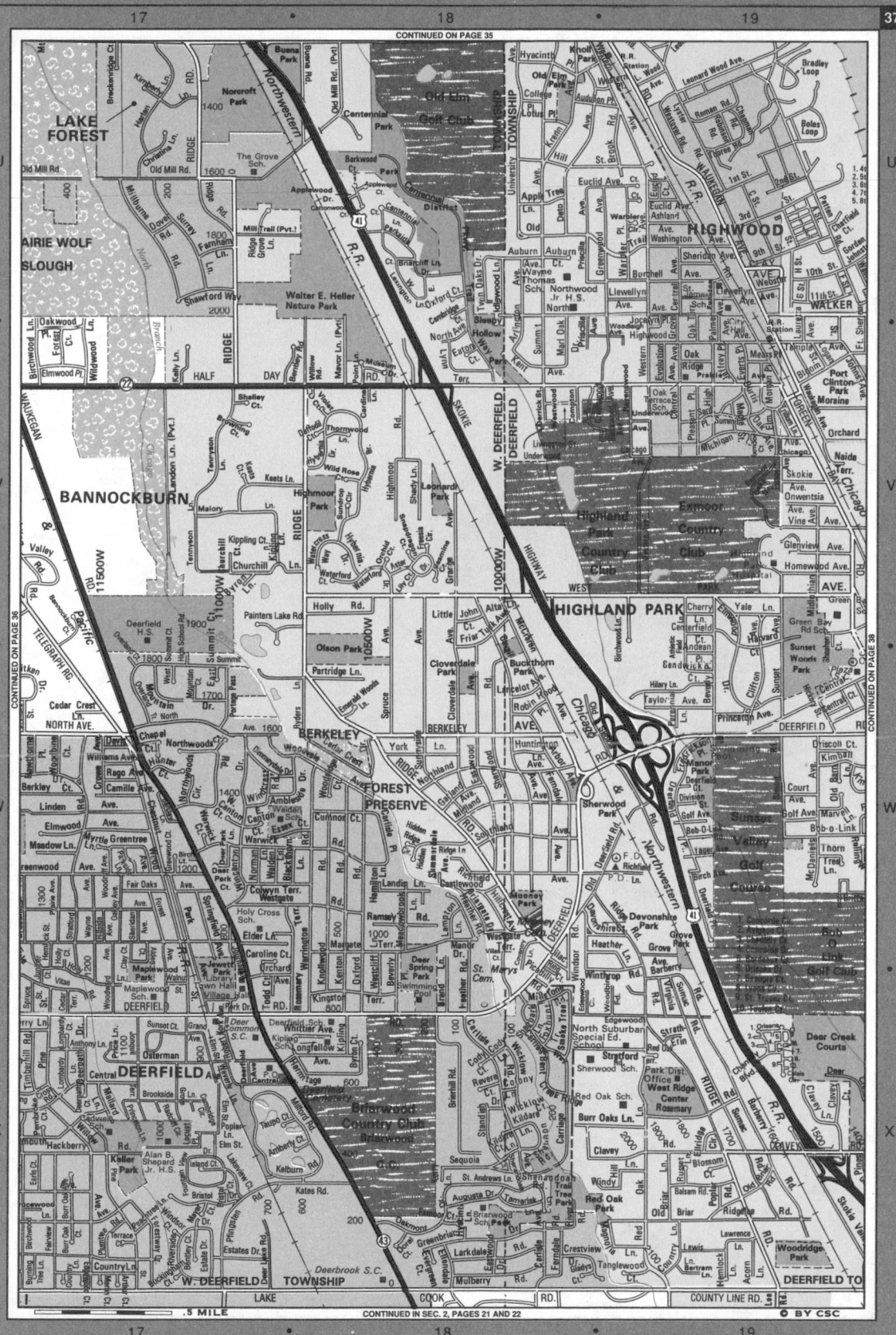

CONTINUED ON PAGE 35

CONTINUED ON PAGE 36

CONTINUED ON PAGE 38

© BY CSC

.5 MILE

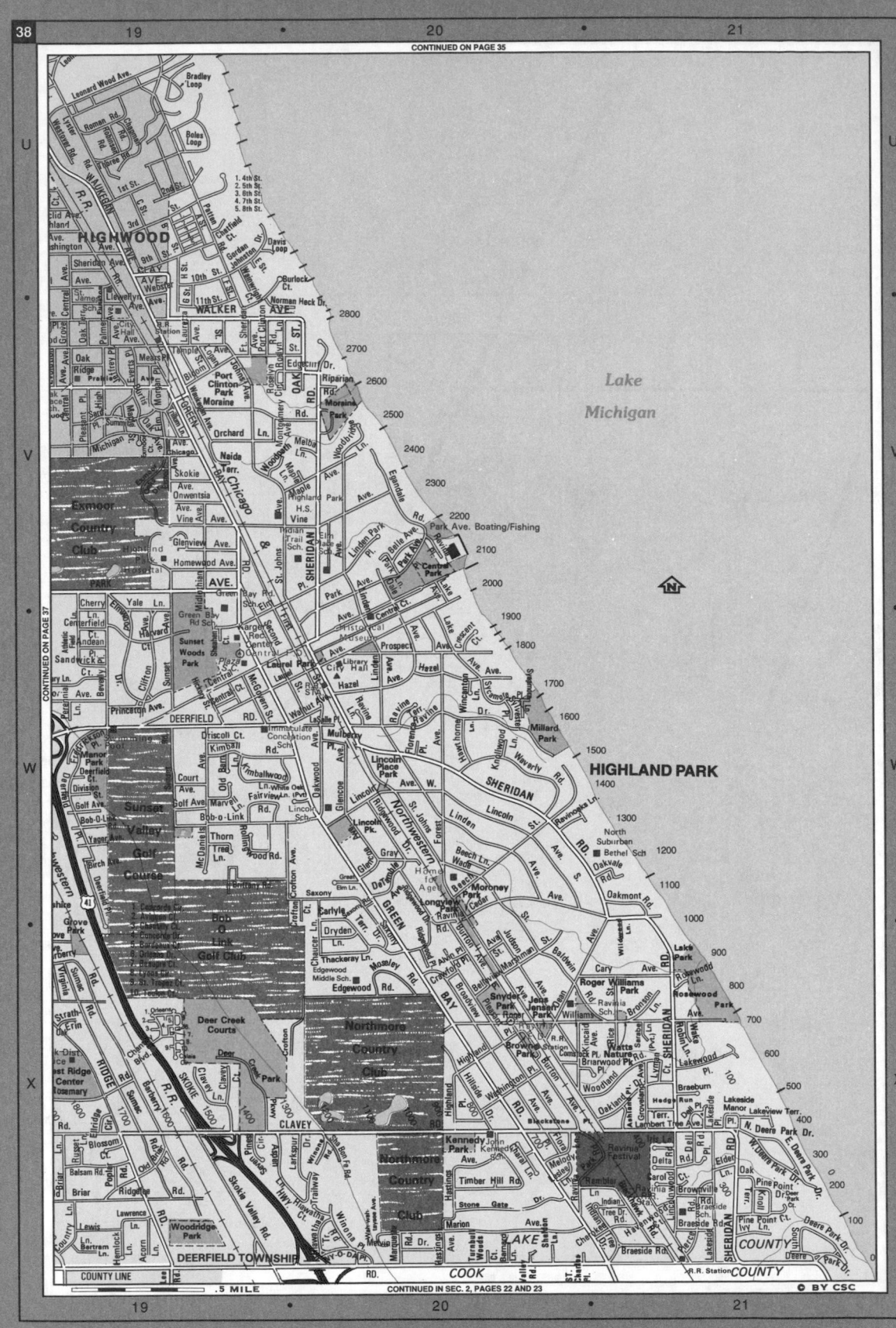

*Lake*

*Michigan*

HIGHWOOD

1. 4th St.
2. 5th St.
3. 6th St.
4. 7th St.
5. 8th St.

WALKER   AVE.

2800

2700

2600

2500

2400

2300

2200

Park Ave. Boating/Fishing

2100

Central Park

2000

1900

1800

1700

1600

1500

HIGHLAND PARK

1400

SHERIDAN

1300

North Suburban

1200

1100

1000

900

800

700

600

500

400

300

200

100

CONTINUED ON PAGE 37

Exmoor Country Club

DEERFIELD   RD.

Sunset Valley Golf Course

41

Northmoor Country Club

Northmoore Country Club

DEERFIELD TOWNSHIP
COUNTY LINE
.5 MILE
CONTINUED IN SEC. 2, PAGES 22 AND 23
COOK   COUNTY
R.R. Station
© BY CSC

19  •  20  •  21

# INDEX TO LAKE COUNTY

Princeton Ave. Pg.6 D16
Reiner Pl. Pg.14 E18
Reiner St. Pg.14 E18
Richard Pl. Pg.6 D17
Russell Ave. Pg.14 E18
Ruth Ave. Pg.13 E16
Sallmon Rd. Pg.13 F16
Sheridan Pl. Pg.14 E18
Sheridan Rd. Pg.14 E18
Spitz Dr. Pg.13 E17
Stewart Ave. Pg.14 E18
Stratton Ave. Pg.14 E18
Suddard Pl. Pg.14 E18
Suddard St. Pg.13 E18
Sunlight Ct. Pg.14 E18
Talmadge Ave. Pg.14 E18
Tewes Ct. Pg.14 E18
Van Ct. Pg.6 C16
Vercoe Ave. Pg.13 F16
Wadsworth Rd. Pg.7 D18
Waldo Ave. Pg.6,7 D16-18
Warner Ave. Pg.13 F16
Waverly St. Pg.6 C16
Wilson Ave. Pg.14 F18
Woodland Ave. Pg.14 E18
Wyer Rd. Pg.13 E16
Wyer St. Pg.13 E16
Yale Ave. Pg.7 D18
York House Rd. Pg.13 F16
Zephyr St. Pg.13 E16
21st St. Pg.6 C16
27th Pl. Pg.6 C16
27th St. Pg.6 C16
28th Pl. Pg.6 D16
28th St. Pg.6 C16
29th St. Pg.6 D16
30th St. Pg.6 D16
31st St. Pg.6 D16
32nd St. Pg.6 D16
33rd St. Pg.6 D16

**CEMETERIES**
Benton Greenwood Cemetery Pg.6 D16
Pineview Cemetery Pg.14 E18

**FOREST PRESERVES**
Lyons Woods F.P. Pg.14 F18
Zion Site F.P. Pg.6 D16

**GOLF COURSES**
Greenshire Golf Course Pg.7,14 E17
Orchard Hills Golf Course & C.C. Pg.13 E16

**PARKS**
Reed Park Pg.6 E16
Callahan Park Pg.13 F16

**SCHOOLS**
Beach Park Sch. Pg.14 E18
Howe Sch. Pg.6 E16
K. Murphy Jr. H.S. Pg.7 E16
Our Lady of Humility Sch Pg.7 D18

**MISCELLANEOUS**
Benton Township Office Pg.6 D16

## BENTON TOWNSHIP
Pages 6,7,13,14

**STREETS**
Bayonne Ave. Pg.6 D16
Berrong Ave. Pg.7 A17
Berrong Ct. Pg.7 A17
Bull Creek Rd. Pg.7 E19
Burnett Ave. Pg.7 B,C19
East Ravine Dr. Pg.7 B18
Edward Pg.6 B17
Elizabeth Pg.7 B18
Emanuel Ave. Pg.6 E16
English Ln. Pg.7 A17
Fago Ave. Pg.6 A-B17
Forman Dr. Pg.6 A-B17
Fossland Ave. Pg.6,7 A-B17
Fulton Ave. Pg.7 C19
Hanks Ave. Pg.6 A-B17
Hayner Ave. Pg.6 B17
Henke Dr. Pg.7 B18
Illinois St. Pg.7 B18
Kellogg Ct. Pg.7 B18
Kenosha Rd. Pg.6 B16
Logan Ct. Pg.7 B18-19
Old Beach Rd. Pg.7 E19
Orchard Ln. Pg.7 B18
Ravine Dr. Pg.7 B18
Ravine Lane Dr. Pg.7 B18
Strong Ave. Pg.7 C19
Suddard Pl. Pg.14 E18
Thorpe Ave. Pg.6 A17
3rd St. Pg.6 A17
4th St. Pg.6 A17
5th St. Pg.6,7 A17
9th St. Pg.6 A16
10th St. Pg.6 A17
11th St. Pg.6 A17
12th St. Pg.6 B17
13th St. Pg.6 B16
16th St. Pg.7 B19
17th St. Pg.7 B18
18th St. Pg.7 B18-19
19th St. Pg.7 B18-19
21st St. Pg.7 C19

**CEMETERIES**
Mt. Oliver Mem Pk. Cemetery Pg.6 B16

**GOLF COURSES**
Orchard Hill G.C. & C.C. Pg.13 E16

**PARKS**
Dunes Park Pg.14 E18
Illinois Beach State Pk. Pg.7,14 D-E19

**MISCELLANEOUS**
Benton Township Office Pg.6 D16
North Point Marina Pg.7 A19

## BUFFALO GROVE
Pages 32,33
(For additional listings, see Section 2)

**STREETS**
Aberdeen Ct. X12
Aberdeen Ln. X12
Acacia Ct., N. & S. V11
Acacia Terr. V11
Acorn Pl. V12
Alsace Cir. X12
Alsace Ct. X12
Apple Hill Ct. N. & S. V13
Apple Hill Ln. V13
Appletree Ct. X11
Aptakisic Rd. W11-14
Arlington Hts. Rd. W11
Asbury Dr. W13
Ashland Ct. X12
Auburn Ln. X11
Avalon Ct., N. & S. W12
Avalon Dr. W12
Bank Ln. X12
Banyon Tree Ln. V12
Baybury X12
Bedford Ct. X11
Berkley Ct. W12
Beverly Ln. W11
Blackthorn Rd. V12
Blossom Ct. X11
Blue Ash Dr. V12
Brandywyn Ct. W12
Brandywyn Ln. W12
Bristol Ln. W11
Brockman Ave. X13
Brodeaux Ct., W W11
Brunswick Dr. X12
Bunescu Ct. X11
Busch Pkwy. X13
Camden Ct. W12
Carlyle Ln. V12
Carton Ave. W13
Cedar Ct. X12
Cedar St. X12
Chambourd Dr. V13
Chateau Dr. X12
Checker Ct. X11
Cherbourg Ct., N. & S. X12
Cherbourg Dr. X12
Chestnut Ct. W. V12
Chestnut Terr. V12
Church Rd. X12
Churchill Ct. W13
Circle Ct. X12
Claret Dr. X12
Clearview Ct. W12
Cobbler Ct. W12
Cobblestone Ct. X12
Cobblestone Dr. X12
Commerce Ct. X13
Common Way X12
Cooperfield Dr. W12
Courtland Dr. W11
Crab Apple Terr. V12
Crossfield Ct. W12
Crown Point Ct. X12
Crown Point Dr. X12
Cumberland Ct. X12
Cumberland Ln. X12
Cypress Ct. V11
Daulton Dr. X12
Deerfield Pkwy. X13
Depot Pl. W13
Devlin W12
Driftwood Pl. X12
Edenvale Dr. W12
Edgemere Rd. W11
Emerson Ct. X12
Estonian Ln. V12
Euclid Ct. W12
Fabish Dr. X12
Fairfax Ln. X11
Farrington Ct. X12
Ferndale Ct. X12
Fox Ct., E & W X12
Fox Hill Ct., E & W X13
Fremont Ct., E. & W. W11
Fremont Way X12
Frontenac Pl. X14
Gail Ct. W12
Gail Dr. W12
Green Knolls Dr. W12
Hackberry Ct. V12
Harris Ct. X12
Harvest Cir. X12
Heritage Ln. X11
Highland Ct. X12
Highland Grove Ct., N. X12
Highland Grove Dr. X12
Hill Dr. X12
Hilldale Ln. X12
Horatio Blvd. X12
Huntley Rd. X13
Indian Spring Ln. X12
Ironwood Ct. X12
James Cir. X14
Jersey Ct. W12
Joel Ln. X12
Johnson Dr. X13
Jordan Terr. W12
Kent Ln. W11
LaSalle Ct., N. W12
LaSalle Ln. W12
Lakeview Ct. X12
Lakeview Dr. X12
Lamont Ter. W12
Laraway Dr. W12
Lawn Ct. W12
Le Jardin Ct. X12
Live Oak Ln. V12
Lockwood Ct. W12
Lockwood Dr. W12
Longridge Ct. W12
Loyola St. X14
Lucinda Dr. X11
Lyon Ct. W12
Lyon Dr. W12
Madiera Ct. V13
Madiera Ln. V13
Magnolia Ct., E. & W. V12
Main St. V12
Manchester Dr. X12
Margate Dr. W12
Marseilles Cir. X12
Marvins Way X13
Merci Dr. X14
Meridian Way W12
Millbrook Dr. X13
Miramar Ct. W12
Miramar Ln. W12
Misty Woods Rd. V12
Morningside Ln., E & W V12
Mundelein Rd. X11-12
Newfield Ct. W12
Newgate Ct. W11
Newton Dr. X13
Newtown Ct., E. X12
Newtown Ct., W. X12
Newtown Dr. X12
Old Barn Ct. W12
Olivehill Dr. W12
Palazzo Ct. V13
Palazzo Dr. V13
Parchester Rd. X13
Park Ave. V12
Parkchester Rd. X13
Parkside Ct. W12
Parkside Dr. W12
Penny Ct. X11
Pinetree Cir., N & S X12
Pinyon Pine Ct., N. V12
Port Clinton Ct., E. & W. V11
Port Clinton Rd. V11
Prague Ave. X14
Prairie Rd. W,V12
Quaker Hollow Ct., N & S W13
Raintree Ct. V12
Raintree Rd. V11
Ranchview Ct. W11
Riverwalk Dr. X14
Rolling Hills Ct. W12
Ronnie Dr. W12
Roslyn Ct. V12
Roslyn Ln. T13
Russellwood Ct. W13
Sandalwood Ct. V12
Sandalwood Rd. V12
Sandhurst Dr. W12
Satinwood Ct., N. V12
Satinwood Terr. W12
Scottish Pine Ln. V12
Sheridan Ct. W11
Sheridan Rd. W11
Silver Rock Ln. X11
Somerset Ln. V12
Spring Ln. X11
Station Ct., E & W W12
Summer Ct. W11
Sunridge Ln. X12
Thistle Ct. W12
Thompson Blvd. W12
Thompson Ct. W12
Thornapple Ct. X12
Thorndale Ct. X14
Timber Hill Rd. X12
Toulon Dr. X12
Town Place Cir. X12
Tree Farm Ct. W11
Twilight Pass X12
Twin Oaks Blvd. W11
Twin Oaks Ct. W11
Twisted Oak Ln. X11
Village Ct. W12
Vintage Dr. X12
Wakefield Ct. X12
Wakefield Ln. X12
Wedgewood Ct. V11
Weidner Rd. X12
Weiland Rd. W12
Wellington Ct., N & S W12
Westchester Ln. W12
White Oak V11
Whitney Ln. W12
Wildflower Cir. X12
Wilshire Ct. W11
Winding Oak Ln. X12
Windwood Ct. W12
Winston Dr. W12
Woodstone Ct. X12
Woodstone Dr. X12
Wright Blvd. W12
2nd St. V12

**CEMETERIES**
St. Mary's Cem. X12

**GOLF COURSES**
Arboretum G.C. V11

**PARKS**
Bicentennial Park W11
Buffalo Creek Nature Preserve X11
Busch Grove Comm. Pk. X12
Camelot Corner Park W11
Canterbury Park V12
Children's Park X11
Churchill Park W12
Green Lake Park W12
Lexington Park X12
Old Farm Park W12
Parkchester Park X13
Prairie Park W11
Twin Creeks Park W12
Veterans Park W12
Westchester Park W12
Willow Stream Pk. X12
Woodland Park V12

**SCHOOLS**
Aptakisic Jr. H.S. W13
Ivy Hall Sch. X11
Prairie Sch. W11
Prichett Sch. X13
St. Mary's Sch. X12
Tripp Sch. X12
Twin Groves Jr. H.S. V12
Meridian Middle School W12

**MISCELLANEOUS**
Fire Depts. X,V12
Police Dept. X12
Post Office X12
R.R. Station X13
Raupp Mem. Museum X12
Village Hall X12

## CARNEY CORNERS
Page 4...B11

## CEDAR LAKE
Page 9...E6

## CHANNEL LAKE
Pages 1,2...B4
(For listings, see Antioch Township)

## CUBA TOWNSHIP
Pages 22,23,29,30
(For additional listings, see Section 2)

**STREETS**
Apple Tree Ln. Pg.29 W3
Arch Dr. Pg.29 U1
Barrington Rd. Pg.22 T3
Beach Dr. Pg.29 U1
Beach Way Pg.29 T2
Bertha Ln. Pg.29 W3
Blanch Ct. Pg.30 V4
Bloners Dr. Pg.29 U1
Bluff Ln. Pg.29 V1
Border Rd. Pg.30 W,X4
Brisbane Dr. Pg.29 U1
Broken Bow Pass Pg.23 T4
Buckley Rd. Pg.29 X1
Canyon Creek Rd. Pg.22 T3
Chamberlin Dr. Pg.29 U1
Chatham Rd. Pg.30 W4
Church Rd. Pg.29 V1
Columbus Dr. Pg.30 X4
Country Estates Rd. Pg.29 W3
Countryside Ln. Pg.29 W3
Craft Ct. Pg.29 V1
Crestview Dr. Pg.30 X4
Cuba Rd. Pg.29 W2
Damien Dr. Pg.29 V2
Drake Rd. Pg.30 W4
Dunvegan Ct. Pg.29 U1
East Dr. Pg.29 V1
Edgemond Ln. Pg.29 W3
Edgewood Ave. Pg.29 U1
Elizabeth Rd. Pg.30 W,X4
Fairview Pg.30 X4
Falkirk Cir. Pg.29 W3
Flint Creek Dr. Pg.29 W2
Flint Creek Rd. Pg.29 U2
Fox River Dr. Pg.29 T2,U-V1
Fox River Rd. Pg.29 U1
Fox St. Pg.29 U1
Glenbarr Ln. Pg.29 X3
Grant St. Pg.29 X3
Grayclyn Ct. Pg.22 S2
Greenwood Ln. Pg.23 T4
Hanover Hill Pg.30 W4
Harbor Rd. Pg.29 W3
Hart Rd. Pg.29 W3
Henry Rd. Pg.29 V2
Heritage Oaks Pg.29 V1
Heritage Tr. Pg.29 V1
Hess Dr. Pg.29 U1
Hickory Nut Grove Rd. Pg.29 U1
High Ridge Rd. Pg.29,30 U-V1,W4
Highland Rd. Pg.29 X3
Hillcrest Ave. Pg.29 U1
Hipplers Rd. Pg.30 X4
Holly Dr. Pg.30 T2
Hough Rd. Pg.30 X4
Indian Trails Rd. Pg.30 T4
Jensen Ave. Pg.29 T2
Kelsey Ave. Pg.29 V1
Kelsey Ct. Pg.29 V1
Kelsey Pt. Pg.29 W1
Kelsey Rd. Pg.29 U3
Knollwood Dr. Pg.23 T4
Kraft Rd. Pg.23 T4
Kristy Ln. Pg.29 U1
Lagoon Dr. Pg.29 T2
Lake Shore Dr. Pg.23,30 T,X4
Lakeview Pkwy. Pg.23 S4
Laurin Dr. Pg.30 W4
Linbergh Dr. Pg.29 U1
Lincoln St. Pg.29 X3
Main St. Pg.29 T-V1
Meadow Ln. Pg.29 V1
Meadow Ln., S. Pg.29 U1
Merton Rd. Pg.29 X3
Midway St. Pg.29 U1
North Dr. Pg.29 V1
Northwest Hwy. Pg.29 W2
Oak Creek Cir. Pg.23 T4
Oak Knoll Rd. Pg.29 X2
Oakland Ave. Pg.29 U1
Oakridge Rd. Pg.23 T4
Oaks Ct., N. Pg.23 T4
Oakwood Dr., E. & W. Pg.23,30 T4
Old Barrington Rd. Pg.29 W3
Park Dr. Pg.29 V1
Park St. Pg.29 U1
Pepper Rd. Pg.29 W1
Pioneer Grove Rd. Pg.29 U1
Pittner Ave. Pg.29 U1
Prestwick Dr. Pg.29 X3
Providence Rd. Pg.30 X4
Ravine Dr. Pg.29 V1
Ridge Rd. Pg.29 W1
River Rd. Pg.29 U1
River Shore Dr. Pg.29 T2
River St. Pg.29 V1
River's Edge Dr. Pg.29 U1
Riverside Dr. Pg.29 U1
Roberts Rd. Pg.22 S2
Rustic Ln. Pg.29 U1
Short St. Pg.29 T2
Snuff Valley Rd. Pg.29 U1
South St. Pg.29 U1
Southgate Tr. Pg.22 T2
Spring Dr. Pg.29 U1
Summit Dr. Pg.29 V1
Sunset Dr. Pg.29 U1
Sunset Ln. Pg.29 U1
Sunset Rd. Pg.30 X4
Sylvester St. Pg.29 T2
Tara Dr. Pg.23 T4
Taylor Ln. Pg.29 X3
Taylor Rd. Pg.29 X3
Timber Lake Pkwy. Pg.30 T4
Timber Lake Rd. Pg.23 T4
Trillium Ct. Pg.29 V3
Wagon Wheel Ct. Pg.23 T4
Whitetail Tr. Pg.22,23 T3
Wildwood Dr. Pg.23 T4
17th St. Pg.29 X3
18th St. Pg.29 X3
19th St. Pg.29 X3
20th St. Pg.29 X3
21st St. Pg.29 X3
22nd St. Pg.29 X3
23rd St. Pg.29 X3
24th St. Pg.29 X2
25th St. Pg.29 X2

**FOREST PRESERVES**
Fox River F.P. Pg.22 T1,2
Grassy Lake F.P. Pg.29 U3

**GOLF COURSES**
Barrington Hills C.C. Pg.29 X2

**MISCELLANEOUS**
Good Shepherd Hospital Pg.29 V2

## DEEP LAKE
Page 3...E6-7

## DEER PARK
Pages 30,31
(For additional listings, see Section 2)

**STREETS**
Bedlington Ct. W6
Cardinal Ct. W6
Chapel Hill Dr. W6
Country Ln. X6
Cuba Rd. W6
Deer Lake Dr. X6
Deer Meadow Ln. W6
Deerpath Rd. X6
Edgeview Ct. X6
Ela Rd. X5
Essex Ct. W5
Fairview Dr. X6
Farthingdale Ct. W6
Glengarry Cir. X6
Green Forest Rd. W5
Hampton Ct. W5
Hanover Hill W4
Harrow Way X7
Hearthside Ct. W6
Hedgeworth Ct. W6
Hilltop Dr. W6
Hummingbird Ct. W5
Hunters Ln. W5
Huntington Rd. X7
Hypoint Dr. W6
Inglenook Ln. W6
Juniper Ct. X6
Juniper Ln. X6
Lancaster Ct. W6
Laurel Dr. X6
Lone Pine Ct. X6
Mallard Ct. X6
Mayfield Ln. W6
Meadow Ct. X6
Meadow Ln. X6
Old Farm Rd. W5
Pheasant Trail W6
Rainbow Rd. W5
Slyvander Dr. W5
Sumac Ct. W6
Sunset Dr. X4
Swansway Rd. X7
Tanager Ct. W5
Teal Ct. X6
Terrace Dr. X4
Thrush Ct. W6
Vesper Ct. W6
Wildrose Dr. X6

**FOREST PRESERVES**
Cuba Marsh F.P. W6

## DEERFIELD
Pages 36,37
(For additional listings, see Section 2)

**STREETS**
Alden Ct. X17
Amberly Ct. X18
Ambleside Dr. W17
Anthony Ln. X17
Appletree Ct. X17
Appletree Ln. X17
Arbor Vitae Rd. X17
Arthur Ct. X17
Augusta Dr. X17
Barclay Ln. W17
Bayberry Ln. X17
Bent Creek Ridge X18
Bentley Ct. X17
Berkley Ct. W16-17
Beverly Pl. X18
Birch Ct. W17
Birchwood Ave. X17
Blackthorn Ln. W18
Brand Ln. X18
Briarhill Rd. X18
Broadmoor Pl. X17
Brookside Ln. X17
Buckingham Ct. X17
Burning Tree Ln. X17
Burr Oak Ave. X17
Burr Oak Ct. X17
Byron Ct. X18
Cambridge Cir. X16
Camille Ave. W17
Canton Ct., E. & W. W17
Carlisle Ave. X18
Carlisle Pl. W18
Carol Ct. W16
Carol Ln. W16
Caroline Ct. X16
Carriage Way X18
Castlewood Ln. X16
Cedar Terr. X17
Central Ave. X18
Chapel Ct. W17
Charing Cross Rd. X17
Chatham Cir. X16
Cherry St. X18
Chestnut St. W,X17
Christopher Dr. X16
Circle Ct. X16
Clavinia Ave. X16
Clay Ct. X17
Cody Ct. X18
Cody Ln. X18
Colony Ln. X18
Colwyn Terr. W18
Constance Ln. X16
Country Ct. X17
Country Ln. X17
County Line Rd. X16
Crabtree Ln. X17
Craig Ct. X17
Cranshire Ct. W16
Crestview Dr. X18
Cross Rd. X17
Crowe Ave. W17
Cumnor Ct. W18
Dartmouth X16-17
Davis W17
Deer Lake Dr. X17
Deer Park Ct. W17
Deer Park Ln. W17
Deer Run Dr. X16
Deerfield Ave. X17
Deerfield Rd. X17
Deerpath Ct. X16
Deerpath Dr. X18
Dimmeyway Dr. W17
Doral Ct. X18
Earls Ct. X17
Eastwood Dr. X18
Elder Ln. X17
Elizabeth Ct. W16
Ellendale X18
Elm St. X17
Elmwood Ave. W17
Essex Ct. W17
Estate Dr. X17
Evergreen Ct. X16
Exmoor Ct. X18
Fair Oaks Ave. W17
Fairview Ave. X17
Ferndale Rd. X18
Forest Ave. X17
Forestway Dr. X17
Forsythia X16
Fountain View Dr. X17
Foxhunt Tr. X18
Franken Ave. X17
Gordon Terr. X16
Grand Ave. X17
Grand Dr. W16
Green Park Ct. X18
Greenbriar Dr. X18
Greentree W17
Greenwood Ave. X17
Greenwood Ct. W17
Grove X17
Hackberry Rd. X17
Hamilton Ln. W18
Hampton Ct. W16
Hawthorne Ln. X16
Hawthorne Pl. W17
Hazel Ave. X16,17
Heather Rd. W,X18
Hemlock St. X17
Hermitage Dr. X18
Hertel Ln. W16
High School Rd. W17
Hillside Ave. X17
Hoffman Ln. X17
Holly Ct. X17
Holly Ln. X17
Holmes Ave. X17
Huehl Rd. X17
Hunter Ct. W17
Hyacinth Ln. X18
Illinois Tr. W17
Indian Hill Ct. X17
Indian Hill Rd. X16
Island Ct. X17
Jonquil Terr. X17
Juniper Ct. X17
Kates Rd. X18
Kelburn Rd. X18
Kenmore Ave. X17
Kenton Rd. W,X18
Kerry Ln. X18
Kildare Ct. X18
Kildare Ln. X16
Kimberly Ct. X17
King Richard Ct. X16
Kingston Terr. W,X18
Kipling Pl. X18
Knollwood Rd. W,X18
Lake Eleanor Dr. W16
Lakeview Ct. X17
Lampton Ln. X18
Landis Ln. W18
Larkdale Rd. X18
Laurel Ave. X16
Linden Ave. W17
Lisa Marie Ct. X16
Locust Pl. X17
Lombardy Ct. X17
Lombardy Ln. X17
Longfellow Ave. X18
Mallard Ln. X16
Manor Dr. X18
Maple X17
Marcie Ct. X16
Margate Terr. X18
Martha Ct. X17
Meadow Ln. X18
Meadowbrook Ln. X18
Merlin Ct. X17
Milford Rd. X18
Millstone Rd. X18
Montgomery Ct. W16
Montgomery Dr. W16
Montgomery Rd. X16
Mountain Ct. W17
Mountain Dr. W17
Mulberry Rd. X18
Myrtle Ln. X17
Norman Ln. W17
North Ave. X17
Northwoods Cir. W17
Northwoods Rd. W17
Oakley Ave. W17
Oakmont Dr. X17
Oakwood Pl. W17
Orchard Ave. X17
Osterman Ave. X17
Osterman Pl. X17
Overland Ct. W17
Overland Tr. W17
Oxford Rd. W,X18
Park Ave. X17
Park Dr. X17
Parkside Ln. W17
Parkway Blvd. X16
Paula Ct. X16
Peach Tree Ln. X17
Pear Tree Rd. W16
Pembroke Ct. X17
Petersen Ln. X17
Pfingsten Rd. X16
Pine St. X17
Plum Tree Rd. X17
Poplar Ln. X18
Portage Pass X18
Prairie Ave. X17
Price Ln. X17
Princeton Ln. X17
Private Rd. X18
Radcliff Cir. X16
Rago Ave. W17
Ramsey Rd. X18
Revere Ct. X18
River Rd. X18
Riverside Dr. X17
Robert York Ave. X17
Rosemary Terr. X18
Rosewood Ave. X17
Sapling Ln. X16
School St. W16
Sequoia Ln. X17
Shagbark Ln. X18
Shannon Rd. X16
Shenandoah Ct. X18
Shenandoah Rd. X18
Sheridan Ave. X17
Smoke Tree X18
Somerset Ave. W17
Springfield Ave. W,X17
Spruce St. X17
Sprucewood X17
St. Andrews X18
Standish Dr. X18
Stratford Rd. W,X17
Summit Ct., E. & W. W17
Summit Dr. W17
Sunset Ct. X17
Susan Ln. X16
Tall Tree Ln. W16
Tamarisk Ln. X18
Taupo Ct. X17
Terrace Ct. X17
Timberhill Rd. X17
Todd Ct. X17
Village Green Ct. X16
Walden Ln. W17
Walnut St. X17
Warrington Rd. W,X18
Warwick Ct. W17
Warwick Rd. W17,18
Waukegan Rd. W17
Waverly Ln. X17
Wayne Ave. X17
We-Go Ct. X16
We-Go Trail X16
Westcliff Ln. X18
Westgate Rd. W17,18
Whittier Ave. X18
Wicklow Ct. X18
Wicklow Rd. X18
Williams Ave. W17
Willow Ave. X17
Wilmot Ln. W16
Wilmot Rd. X16
Wincanton Dr. W17
Windcrest Rd. W17
Windsor Ct. X17
Wood Ave. W17
Woodbine Ct. W17
Woodland Dr. X16,17
Woodridge Ct. W18
Woodruff Ave. W17
Woodvale Ave. W18
Woodview Ln. X16
Woodward Ave. X17

**CEMETERIES**
Deerfield Cem. X17
St. Mary's Cem. X18

**GOLF COURSES**
Briarwood C.C. X18
Deerfield Park Dist. G.C. W16

**PARKS**
Deer Spring Park X18
Jewett Park X17
Keller Park X17
Mitchell Park X16

**SCHOOLS**
Alan B. Shepard Jr. H.S. X17
Briarwood Sch. X18
Cadwell Sch. X17
Charles Caruso Jr. H.S. X16
Deerfield H.S. W17
Deerfield Sch. X18
Holy Cross Sch. W17
Kipling Sch. X18
Maplewood Sch. X17
South Park Sch. X17
Walden Sch. W17
Wilmot Sch. X16
Woodland Park Sch. W17

**SHOPPING CENTERS**
Deerbrook S.C. X18
Deerfield Commons X17
Deerfield S.C. X17

**MISCELLANEOUS**
Library X17
Swimming Pool X16,18
Village and Town Hall X17

## DEERFIELD TOWNSHIP
Pages 35,37,38

## DIAMOND LAKE
Page 25...S10

## EDDY
Page 6...B15

## ELA TOWNSHIP
Pages 23-25,30-32
(For additional listings, see Section 2)

**STREETS**
Anna Ct. Pg.23 S5
Arbor Ln. Pg.31 U8
Arrowhead Dr. Pg.25 T10
Aspen Dr. Pg.25 S10
August Ln. Pg.23 S5
Bagpipe Ct. Pg.23 T6
Bonnie Ln. Pg.31 U8
Bonnyrigg Ct. Pg.26 T6
Briggs Rd. Pg.31 U6
Burr Oak Ln. Pg.31 U8
Camel Ct. Pg.31 U6
Cattail Ln. Pg.30 X6
Cedar Ave. Pg.30 U6
Cherry Ln. Pg.30 U6
Cherry Rd. Pg.31 U8
Clover Hill Ln. Pg.31 U5
Columbia Ln. Pg.31 T8
Commercial Dr. Pg.24 T8
Cottage Rd. Pg.31 U8
Crestwood Ln. Pg.30 U6
Cuba Rd. Pg.30,32 W6,9
Danvera Ln. Pg.31 U7
Dartmouth Ln. Pg.31 T8
Deerpath Rd. Pg.30 W6
Eagle Dr. Pg.25 T10
East Ln. Pg.31 U8
East Rd. Pg.31 U8
Echo Lake Rd. Pg.30,31 U6
Echo Ln. Pg.30 U6
Edgewood Pl. Pg.30 U5
Eleanor Ln. Pg.31 V8
Ellrie Terr. Pg.30 T5
Fern Rd. Pg.31 V7
Field Rd. Pg.24,31 S7,U8
Florence Ave. Pg.30 W6
Forest Dr. Pg.31 U8
Forest Rd. Pg.31 U8
Gabriel Dr. Pg.31 U6
Garden Ln. Pg.31 U8
Gilmer Rd. Pg.24,32 T8,U10
Glendale Rd. Pg.31 U8
Golfview Rd. Pg.30 U5
Grand Ave. Pg.30 W6
Hazel Crest Rd. Pg.2 X8
Hicks Rd. Pg.31 X9
High Ridge Rd. Pg.30 U6
Highland Dr. Pg.31 U8
Hillcrest Dr. Pg.31 U9
Hillcrest Dr., S. Pg.31 U6
Hillview Ct. Pg.31 T8
Indian Creek Rd. Pg.24,25 T8,9
Indian Trail Rd. Pg.30 U5
Ivy Ln. Pg.31 T8
Kathy Ln. Pg.24 T7
Kruckenberg Rd. Pg.24 T7
Krueger Rd. Pg.31 T7
Kyle Ct., N. Pg.24 T6
Kyle Ct., S. Pg.24 T7
Lake Zurich Rd. Pg.31 V8
Lakeside Dr. Pg.31 U8
Lakewood Dr. Pg.30 U6
Lakewood Ln., N. Pg.30 U6
Lisa Ln. Pg.31 T9
Lloyd Rd. Pg.32 U9
Lochanora Dr. Pg.23,24 T6
Lone Tree Ln. Pg.30 U6
Mable Ave. Pg.30 W6
March St. Pg.31 U7
Marilyn Ln. Pg.24 T7

## ELA TOWNSHIP

Mary Dale Ave. ... Pg.30 ... T5
Middle Fork Rd. ... Pg.30 ... W5
Midlothian Rd. ... Pg.31 ... U6
Miller Rd. ... Pg.31 ... U5
Milton Rd. ... Pg.23 ... S5
Nancy Ct. ... Pg.31 ... T7
North Ln. ... Pg.30 ... U6
Oakwood Rd., N. ... Pg.31 ... U7
Old Hicks Rd. ... Pg.32 ... X9
Old McHenry Rd. ... Pg.23,30 ... T5-6
Orchard Ln. ... Pg.30 ... W5
Overhill Dr. ... Pg.31 ... U8
Park Rd. ... Pg.31 ... U8
Pepper Rd. ... Pg.31 ... U8
Plum Pl. ... Pg.30 ... W6
Quentin Rd. ... Pg.31 ... V7
Rainbow Rd. ... Pg.30 ... W5
Ravine Dr. ... Pg.31 ... U8
Ridge Rd. ... Pg.31 ... U8
Rose Ave. ... Pg.23 ... T5
Rose Rd. ... Pg.31 ... V7
Sacomano Ln. ... Pg.31 ... U8
Shady Ln. ... Pg.31 ... U8
Shagbark Ct. ... Pg.23 ... U6
Somerset Ct. ... Pg.23 ... T6
South Rd. ... Pg.31 ... V8
Spruce Rd. ... Pg.31 ... U8
Starry Ln. ... Pg.31 ... U8
Stoney Kirk Ct. ... Pg.24 ... T6
Strum St. ... Pg.31 ... X7
Summit Dr. ... Pg.30 ... U6
Sunset Dr. ... Pg.30 ... U6
Sylvan Rd., S. ... Pg.24 ... U6
Tahoe Ct. ... Pg.25 ... T10
Tahoe Dr. ... Pg.25 ... T10
Telser Rd. ... Pg.31 ... V7
Valentine Ave. ... Pg.30 ... T5
Valley Rd. ... Pg.31 ... U8
Virginia Ave. ... Pg.30 ... T5
West Ln. ... Pg.30 ... U5
Willow Rd. ... Pg.31 ... U8
Woodbury Ct. ... Pg.24 ... T8

PARKS
Ela Twp. Soccer Field ... Pg.31 ... U6

SCHOOLS
St. Matthew Lutheran Sch. ... Pg.30 ... U7

SHOPPING CENTERS
Oakwood Commons Plaza ... Pg.31 ... V7

## FAIRFIELD
Page 31...U7

## FOX LAKE
Pages 1,8
STREETS
Abbot Dr. ... Pg.1 ... E2
Adams Ct. ... Pg.8 ... G3
Amundsen St. ... Pg.8 ... F2
Arlington Rd. ... Pg.1,8 ... D,G1
Arthur Ave. ... Pg.8 ... F2
Ash St. ... Pg.1 ... D2
Atwater Pkwy. ... Pg.1 ... D2
Balboa Ln. ... Pg.8 ... G2
Balsam Ct. ... Pg.1 ... D2
Bay Rd. ... Pg.8 ... G2
Benjamin Ave. ... Pg.8 ... E1
Birch St. ... Pg.1 ... D2
Blair Ln. ... Pg.1 ... D2
Boulder Pl. ... Pg.8 ... G1
Castle Rd. ... Pg.8 ... F1
Cathryn St. ... Pg.8 ... F2
Cedar Ave. ... Pg.8 ... G2
Cedar St. ... Pg.1 ... D2
Center St. ... Pg.8 ... G3
Channahan Dr. ... Pg.1 ... D2
Cherry Chase Ct. ... Pg.1 ... D1
Christopher Way ... Pg.1 ... D1
Clarendon Ct. ... Pg.1 ... D2
Columbia Ave. ... Pg.8 ... G1
Commercial Ave. ... Pg.8 ... G2
Concord Ct. ... Pg.1 ... D2
Cora Ave. ... Pg.8 ... F2
Covington Rd. ... Pg.8 ... G1
Crest Hill Ct. ... Pg.1 ... D1
Crestview Dr. ... Pg.8 ... G2
Cross St. ... Pg.1 ... 0E
Custer Ct. ... Pg.1 ... D2
Deerpath Ct. ... Pg.1 ... D2
Devlin Rd. ... Pg.8 ... G2
Dewey St. ... Pg.8 ... E1
Dunn's Ln. ... Pg.1 ... E2
Dunn's Pl. ... Pg.1 ... D1
Eagle Point Rd. ... Pg.8 ... G2
Eastshore Dr. ... Pg.1 ... D2
Edison Ct. ... Pg.8 ... F2
Elm Ave. ... Pg.8 ... G2
Elm St. ... Pg.1 ... D2
Ernest Ave. ... Pg.8 ... F2
Evergreen Ct. ... Pg.1 ... D2
Fairfax Rd. ... Pg.8 ... G1
Fern Pl. ... Pg.8 ... F3
Forest Ave. ... Pg.8 ... F3
Forest Rd. ... Pg.1 ... E2
Fortress Ct. ... Pg.8 ... F1
Fortress Dr. ... Pg.8 ... F2
Fossil Dr. ... Pg.1 ... G3
Frazier Ct. ... Pg.8 ... G2
Garfield Ave. ... Pg.8 ... F3
Glen Ave. ... Pg.1 ... F2
Glenview Ave. ... Pg.1 ... G2
Glenview Pl. ... Pg.1 ... G2
Golfview Dr. ... Pg.1 ... D1
Grace ... Pg.8 ... G2
Granada Ln. ... Pg.1 ... D2
Grand Ave. ... Pg.8 ... G2-3
Grass Lake Rd. ... Pg.1 ... D1
Greenery Ct. ... Pg.1 ... D2
Greenwood Ave. ... Pg.1 ... D2
Harding Ave. ... Pg.8 ... F2
Haskel St. ... Pg.8 ... G3
Hastings Cir. ... Pg.1 ... D2
Hawthorne Ln. ... Pg.1 ... D2
Hazel ... Pg.8 ... F3
Helens Ct. ... Pg.8 ... F3
Hickory Ave. ... Pg.8 ... G2
Highland Ave. ... Pg.8 ... F2
Highview Ave. ... Pg.8 ... G2
Hill Rd. ... Pg.1 ... D2
Hillcrest Ave. ... Pg.8 ... G2
Hillcrest Rd. ... Pg.8 ... H2
Hilldale Rd. ... Pg.8 ... G2
Hillside Ave. ... Pg.8 ... G2
Hillside Rd. ... Pg.8 ... H2
Hilltop Ave. ... Pg.1,8 ... E-F2
Holiday Trail, N. ... Pg.8 ... E1
Holly Ave., N. ... Pg.8 ... F2
Holly Ave., S. ... Pg.8 ... G2
Honing St. ... Pg.8 ... G3
Hooks Ct. ... Pg.8 ... F1
Howard Ave. ... Pg.8 ... F2
Industrial Ave. ... Pg.8 ... G2
Jack Frost Ln. ... Pg.8 ... G2
Jackson Dr. ... Pg.1 ... D2
Jefferson St. ... Pg.8 ... G2
Jefferson St. ... Pg.8 ... G3
Judson St. ... Pg.1 ... E1
Keystone ... Pg.8 ... G3
Kings Rd. ... Pg.8 ... G3
Kingston Blvd. ... Pg.8 ... G3
Knollwood Dr. ... Pg.8 ... G3
Lagoon ... Pg.8 ... G3
Lake Ave., N. ... Pg.8 ... G3
Lake Ave., S. ... Pg.8 ... G3
Lakeland Ave. ... Pg.8 ... G1
Lakeline Rd. ... Pg.8 ... G1
Lakeshore Dr. ... Pg.1,8 ... E2
Lakeside ... Pg.8 ... G2
Lakeside Rd. ... Pg.8 ... G3
Lakeview Ave. ... Pg.8 ... F2
Lakewood Ave. ... Pg.8 ... F2
Leisure Rd., E. ... Pg.1 ... D1
Leisure Rd., W. ... Pg.1 ... D1
Leisure Village Ave. ... Pg.1 ... D1
Lexington Ln. ... Pg.1 ... D1
Lincoln Ave. ... Pg.8 ... G3
Linden ... Pg.8 ... G2
Lindy Ln. ... Pg.8 ... G2
Lippincott Ln. ... Pg.8 ... H3
Lippincott Rd. ... Pg.8 ... H3
Livingston St. ... Pg.8 ... F1
Longwood Dr. ... Pg.8 ... R5
Lotus Ave. ... Pg.1 ... C2
Lynda Cir. ... Pg.1 ... D2
Madison Ave. ... Pg.8 ... G2
Magnolia Ct. ... Pg.1 ... D2
Mallard Ct. ... Pg.1 ... D2
Manor Ave. ... Pg.8 ... G2
Maple Ave. ... Pg.8 ... G2
Marine Dr. ... Pg.8 ... F2
Marvin St. ... Pg.8 ... F2
Mastodon Dr. ... Pg.8 ... G3
Matts Rd. ... Pg.8 ... G2
Maud Ave. ... Pg.8 ... F2
McHenry Rd. ... Pg.8 ... F1
McKinley St. ... Pg.8 ... E1
Meade Ct. ... Pg.8 ... G3
Medinah ... Pg.8 ... F1
Mineola Rd. ... Pg.8 ... F2
Monterrey Terr. ... Pg.8 ... F1
Muriel Rd. ... Pg.8 ... E1
Nassau Ct. ... Pg.1 ... D2
Nippersink Blvd. ... Pg.8 ... G2
Nippersink St. ... Pg.8 ... G2
North Ave. ... Pg.8 ... F2
North Way ... Pg.1 ... D1
Oak Ave. ... Pg.8 ... G2
Oak Ct. ... Pg.8 ... G3
Oak St. ... Pg.1,8 ... D,F2
Orchard Pl. ... Pg.8 ... G3
Oxford Cir. ... Pg.1 ... D2
Park Ave. ... Pg.8 ... G2
Park Ln. ... Pg.8 ... G2
Park Ln. ... Pg.8 ... G3
Pistakee Lake Rd. ... Pg.8 ... G2
Pistakee Pkwy. ... Pg.8 ... G2
Precision Ave. ... Pg.8 ... G2
Randrich Rd. ... Pg.8 ... F4
Redwood Ct. ... Pg.1 ... D2
Ridgeland Ave. ... Pg.8 ... G2
Riverside Island Dr. ... Pg.8 ... F1
Riverview Ave. ... Pg.8 ... F1
Rollins Rd. ... Pg.8 ... G2
Rose Ave. ... Pg.8 ... G2
Rushmore Rd. ... Pg.8 ... F3
Rushmore Rd., N. ... Pg.8 ... G2
Sayton Rd. ... Pg.8 ... G2
Scenic Ln. ... Pg.8 ... G2
Scenic Rd. ... Pg.8 ... G2
Shady Ln. ... Pg.8 ... G2
Shore Dr. ... Pg.1,8 ... G2
Sildam Ave. ... Pg.8 ... G2
Clolilen Ln. ... Pg.8 ... G2
South St. ... Pg.8 ... F2
Spring Dr. ... Pg.8 ... G3
Spruce St. ... Pg.8 ... G2
St. James St. ... Pg.8 ... G3
St. Tropez Ct. ... Pg.1 ... D2
Stanton Point ... Pg.8 ... G2
State Park Rd. ... Pg.1 ... D1
Stratford Cir. ... Pg.1 ... D2
Sycamore Ct. ... Pg.1 ... D2
Tremont Rd. ... Pg.8 ... G1
Trout Ave. ... Pg.8 ... G2
Troy St. ... Pg.8 ... F3
Tweed Rd. ... Pg.8 ... G3
Union ... Pg.8 ... G3
Venice ... Pg.1 ... D1,2
Village Ave. ... Pg.1 ... D1,2
Viscaya Dr. ... Pg.1 ... D2
Waltonia Terr. ... Pg.8 ... F3
Waltonian Ave. ... Pg.8 ... G2
Washington Ave. ... Pg.1,8 ... G2
West End Ave. ... Pg.8 ... G2
Westshore Dr. ... Pg.1 ... D2
Wheaton Ln. ... Pg.1 ... D2
White Tail Ln. ... Pg.8 ... H3
Whitten St. ... Pg.8 ... F2
Wildwood Dr. ... Pg.8 ... H3
Woodland Ave. ... Pg.8 ... G2
Woodstock St. ... Pg.8 ... G3
Woodstock St. ... Pg.8 ... G3
York St. ... Pg.8 ... G3

GOLF COURSES
Fox Lake C.C. ... Pg.1 ... D1

PARKS
Deer Haven Park ... Pg.8 ... G3

SCHOOLS
Forest Elem. Sch. ... Pg.8 ... F2
Grant H.S. ... Pg.8 ... G2
Stanton Sch. ... Pg.8 ... G3

SHOPPING CENTERS
Lakeland Shopping Plaza ... Pg.8 ... G2

MISCELLANEOUS
Library ... Pg.8 ... G3
Regional Sewage Treatment Plant ... Pg.8 ... H3
Village Hall ... Pg.8 ... G3

## FOX LAKE HILLS
Page 9...F4

## FOX RIVER GROVE
(For additional listings, see Section 7)
Page 29
STREETS
Camilla Pl. ... V1
Primrose Ct. ... V1
Primrose Ln. ... V1
Southgate Tr. ... T2
Tiffany Ln. ... V1
Victoria Ln. ... V1

## FOX RIVER VALLEY GARDENS
Page 22
(For additional listings, see Section 7)
STREETS
Eastwood Ave. ... S1
Roberts Rd. ... S1
Valley Garden Rd. ... S1

## FREMONT TOWNSHIP
Pages 16-18,23-25
STREETS
Alleghany Rd. ... Pg.17 ... M8
Andover Ct. ... Pg.24 ... S8
Augusta Ct. ... Pg.24 ... S8
Bacon Rd. ... Pg.16 ... N5
Baker Ln. ... Pg.23 ... P5
Barnswallow Ln. ... Pg.23 ... S5
Beachwood Ct., N. ... Pg.24 ... R8
Bittersweet Dr. ... Pg.24 ... S8
Blackhawk Tr. ... Pg.16 ... N5
Brassie Ct. ... Pg.24 ... Q7
Briar Terr. ... Pg.24 ... S7,8
Buckthorn Ct. ... Pg.24 ... S7
Buena Terr. ... Pg.24 ... S7
Cambridge Rd. ... Pg.25 ... P9
Cardinal Ct. ... Pg.23 ... Q5
Casey Rd. ... Pg.18 ... M10
Champions Ct. ... Pg.24 ... Q8
Chardon Ln. ... Pg.24 ... N5
Chardon Rd. ... Pg.16 ... N5
Cherokee Tr. ... Pg.24 ... R8
Chevy Chase Rd. ... Pg.24 ... R8
Circle Dr., N. ... Pg.25 ... S10
Circle Dr., S. ... Pg.25 ... S10
Cleek Ct. ... Pg.24 ... Q7
Countryside Lake Dr. ... Pg.24 ... S8
Countryside Valley Dr. ... Pg.24 ... S8
Crescent Dr., N., S. & E. ... Pg.24 ... S8
Daisy Ln. ... Pg.24 ... S8
Driftwood Dr. ... Pg.24 ... R8
Edgewood Terr. ... Pg.25 ... S10
Elmwood Ave. ... Pg.25 ... S9
Ernst Rd. ... Pg.23 ... P6
Fairfield Rd. ... Pg.18,25 ... N-Q5
Fairview Dr. ... Pg.25 ... R10
Fairview Dr., N. ... Pg.25 ... S10
Forest Ln., N. ... Pg.25 ... R10
Forest Ln., S. ... Pg.25 ... R-S10
Frances Ave. ... Pg.25 ... S10
Fremont Ave. ... Pg.16 ... N6
Fremont Center Rd. ... Pg.24 ... Q7
Gilmer Rd. ... Pg.16,23,24 ... P5-6,Q6,S8
Greenleaf Rd. ... Pg.25 ... S8
Grove Terr. ... Pg.25 ... S10
Hackberry Dr. ... Pg.24 ... S8
Hampshire Pl. ... Pg.24 ... S7,8
Harris Rd. ... Pg.18 ... M10
Harvard Ave. ... Pg.18,25 ... P9,10
Hawley Rd. ... Pg.24,25 ... Q9,R7
Heide Dr. ... Pg.25 ... R9
Hiawatha Terr. ... Pg.25 ... S10
Hickory Ln. ... Pg.25 ... S10
Hickory Rd. ... Pg.24 ... S8
Highland Dr. ... Pg.24 ... S8
Hillside Ln. ... Pg.25 ... S8
Hilltop Terr. ... Pg.25 ... S8
Hoag Ct. ... Pg.25 ... S9
Horizon Spur ... Pg.23 ... S6
Imperial Ct. ... Pg.16 ... N5
Iride Dr. ... Pg.25 ... R8
Ivanhoe Ct. ... Pg.23 ... R5
Ivanhoe Rd. ... Pg.17,23,24 ... N9,R7,S5
Jack Pine Ct. ... Pg.24 ... S8
Juneau Terr. ... Pg.24 ... S8
Jupiter Ct. ... Pg.24 ... S8
Kenmore Ln. ... Pg.24 ... S8
Krueger Ct. ... Pg.25 ... S10
La Vista Dr. ... Pg.24 ... R7,8
Lake Fairfield Rd. ... Pg.23 ... Q5
Lake Green Dr. ... Pg.24 ... R7
Lake View Ave. ... Pg.25 ... S10
Lakeview Ct. ... Pg.25 ... S7
Lakeview Dr. ... Pg.25 ... R-S8
Landau Ln. ... Pg.24 ... S7
Lemon Rd. ... Pg.24 ... O9
Lilac Ln. ... Pg.25 ... S10
Longmeadow Ct. ... Pg.24 ... S8
Longmeadow Dr. ... Pg.24 ... S9
Longmeadow Dr. ... Pg.24 ... S9
Manor Hill Rd. ... Pg.16 ... N5
Maple Ave. ... Pg.24,25 ... Q8,S10
Maple Rd. ... Pg.24 ... Q-R8
Maple Terr. ... Pg.24 ... S7
Marion Ave. ... Pg.25 ... S7
Marion Ct. ... Pg.24 ... Q7
Martin Dr. ... Pg.25 ... S9
Mashie Ct. ... Pg.24 ... Q7
Meadow Ln. ... Pg.16 ... M5
Middleton Pkwy. ... Pg.25 ... S7,8
Midlothian Rd. ... Pg.24,25 ... N5,P,Q9
Milton Rd. ... Pg.23,24 ... S5-6
Murifield Ct. ... Pg.24 ... S7
Niblick Knoll Ct. ... Pg.24 ... Q8
Northwest Pkwy. ... Pg.24 ... S7
Oak Ct. ... Pg.25 ... S10
Oak Terr. ... Pg.24 ... S7
Oakdale Ln., N. & S. ... Pg.24 ... S7
Oakdale Ln., N. & S. ... Pg.25 ... S10
Oakleaf Dr. ... Pg.24 ... S8
Old Oak Dr. ... Pg.25 ... S8
Owens Ct. ... Pg.24 ... S6
Owens Rd. ... Pg.24 ... R7
Oxford Dr. ... Pg.25 ... S8
Park Ave. ... Pg.24 ... Q8
Peterson Rd. ... Pg.17,18 ... N7-10
Pheasant Run ... Pg.24 ... S6
Pierre Dr. ... Pg.25 ... S10
Pond Shore Rd. ... Pg.23 ... S6
Preston Ct. ... Pg.24 ... S8
Primrose Ct. ... Pg.24 ... R7
Primrose Ln. ... Pg.24 ... R8
Prospect ... Pg.25 ... R10
Public Rd. ... Pg.24 ... Q9
Rand Rd. ... Pg.23 ... S5
Red Pine Ct. ... Pg.24 ... S8
Ridge Ct. ... Pg.25 ... S9
Rose Ave. ... Pg.25 ... S10
Rosewood Rd. ... Pg.24 ... S8
Russel Ln. ... Pg.23 ... P5
Saunders Rd. ... Pg.24 ... Q7
Schank Ave. ... Pg.24 ... S7
Schwerman Rd. ... Pg.23,24 ... S6-7
Seminole Ct. ... Pg.24 ... R7
Shady Ln. ... Pg.24 ... S7
Sky Crest Dr. ... Pg.24 ... S8
Spoon Ct. ... Pg.24 ... Q7
Spring Ct. ... Pg.23 ... Q5
Spyglass Ct. ... Pg.24 ... Q7
Spyglass Dr. ... Pg.24 ... Q7
Sunny Ct. ... Pg.25 ... S9
Sunnyside Dr. ... Pg.25 ... S8
Sylvan Dr., N. & S. ... Pg.24 ... S8
Taylor Lake Ct. ... Pg.25 ... S8
Thorngate Dr. ... Pg.24 ... R8
Thorntree Rd. ... Pg.24 ... R8
Trinity Dr. ... Pg.25 ... R9
Turf Hill Dr., N. & S. ... Pg.24 ... R7
University Dr. ... Pg.26 ... C10
Valley View Terr. ... Pg.25 ... S8
Vernon Ridge Dr. ... Pg.24 ... Q7
Violet Ln. ... Pg.25 ... S10
Walnut Ave. ... Pg.25 ... S10
Wauconda Rd. ... Pg.23 ... R5
West Ln. ... Pg.25 ... S10
West Shore Dr. ... Pg.25 ... S9
Wild Flower Terr. ... Pg.24 ... S7
Wildflower Ct. ... Pg.24 ... S9
Willow Ave. ... Pg.25 ... S7
Winchester Rd. ... Pg.17 ... P9
York Ln. ... Pg.24 ... S8

AIRPORTS
Cambell Airport ... Pg.17 ... M7

FOREST PRESERVES
Countryside F.P. ... Pg.24 ... R8-9
Lakewood F.P. ... Pg.23 ... R5

GOLF COURSES
Countryside G.C. ... Pg.24 ... S8
Four Wind G.C. ... Pg.23 ... R6
Steeple Chase Golf Club ... Pg.24 ... R7,8

SCHOOLS
Fremont Elem. Sch. ... Pg.24 ... Q7

MISCELLANEOUS
Countryside F.P. ... Pg.24 ... S9
Northshore Gun Club ... Pg.17 ... M7
Winter Sports Area ... Pg.23 ... R6

## GAGES LAKE
Page 18...K10-11

## GILMER
Page 24...T8

## GRANT TOWNSHIP
Pages 8,9,15,16
STREETS
Anchorage Ln. ... Pg.8 ... H2
Anderson ... Pg.9 ... H4
Andrew Ct. ... Pg.9 ... H4
Ash Ct. ... Pg.9 ... H3
Augustana Ave. ... Pg.9 ... H3
Bayview Ave. ... Pg.9 ... H4
Bayview Dr. ... Pg.8 ... H2
Bellevue Pl. ... Pg.8,15 ... K3
Belvidere Rd. ... Pg.16 ... M4
Benjamin Ave. ... Pg.9 ... H4
Bergan St. ... Pg.9 ... H4
Beverly Dr. ... Pg.8 ... H2
Big Hollow Rd. ... Pg.9 ... G5
Black Cherry Ln. ... Pg.9 ... H5
Blackhawk Ave. ... Pg.8 ... H2
Bonesh Pl. ... Pg.9 ... H4
Brandenburg Rd. ... Pg.15 ... K1-3
Broadway ... Pg.9 ... H4
Brodie Dr. ... Pg.9 ... H4
Burkhart Ln. ... Pg.8 ... H2
Caine Rd. ... Pg.15 ... K3
Camp Horner Rd. ... Pg.15 ... K3
Carol Ln. ... Pg.8,15 ... K3
Catherine St. ... Pg.9 ... H4
Cedarwood Ln. ... Pg.15 ... K3
Central ... Pg.9 ... H4
Champion Rd. ... Pg.15 ... K2
Channel Dr. ... Pg.8,9 ... H1,G4
Chicago Ave. ... Pg.9 ... H4
Chris Larkin Rd. ... Pg.9 ... H5
Christa Dr. ... Pg.9 ... H4
Clara Dr. ... Pg.9 ... G4
Clarendon ... Pg.9 ... H4
Converse Ln. ... Pg.9 ... K4
Cooney Island Rd. ... Pg.9 ... G5
Crabtree Ln. ... Pg.9 ... H4
Creek Ct. ... Pg.15 ... K3
David Ct. ... Pg.9 ... G4
Decora Ave. ... Pg.9 ... H4
Delores Ct. ... Pg.15 ... K3
Dewey Ave. ... Pg.9 ... H4
Donald Ct. ... Pg.9 ... H4
East End Ave. ... Pg.9 ... H4
Edgewater Ln. ... Pg.8 ... H2
Edward Ave. ... Pg.9 ... H4
Elm Ave. ... Pg.9 ... G4
Elm St. ... Pg.8 ... H3
Elmwood Ave. ... Pg.9 ... H4
Everett Ave. ... Pg.9 ... H4
Faith Ct. ... Pg.8 ... H2
Falcon Dr. ... Pg.9 ... H4
Fischer Ln. ... Pg.15 ... K3
Fish Lake Rd. ... Pg.15 ... L,M3
Forest Ave. ... Pg.8 ... H3
Fox Lake Rd. ... Pg.15 ... M2
Francis Ave. ... Pg.8 ... H3
Frank Ct. ... Pg.9 ... H4
Franklin Ave. ... Pg.9 ... H4
Fretheim Ave. ... Pg.9 ... H4
Gerberding Ave. ... Pg.9 ... H4
Glen Ayre St. ... Pg.9 ... H4
Grace Ln. ... Pg.8 ... H2
Graham Ct. ... Pg.9 ... H4
Grand Ave. ... Pg.9 ... H4
Great Bear Tr. ... Pg.9 ... H5
Great Heart Ln. ... Pg.9 ... H4
Greenleaf Ave. ... Pg.9 ... H4
Grove Ave. ... Pg.9 ... H5
Hartigan Rd. ... Pg.8,15 ... K2
Hawthorne Ln. ... Pg.9 ... G4
Hazelwood Dr. ... Pg.9 ... G5
Helen Ct. ... Pg.8 ... H2
Helendale Rd. ... Pg.8 ... H3
Hiawatha Tr. ... Pg.8 ... H1
Hickory Ave. ... Pg.9 ... H4
Hickory Ct. ... Pg.8,9 ... F,G4,K3
Hickory St. ... Pg.8,9 ... G3-4
High Point Rd. ... Pg.8 ... H3
Highpoint Ave. ... Pg.8 ... H3
Hilldale Dr. ... Pg.8 ... H3
Hillside ... Pg.9 ... H4
Hilltop Rd. ... Pg.8 ... H3
Hillwood Ave. ... Pg.8 ... H3
Holman Ave. ... Pg.8 ... H3
Hudson Ave. ... Pg.8 ... H3
Hunt Ave. ... Pg.8 ... H4
Indian Ln. ... Pg.8,9 ... H4
Ingleside Ave. ... Pg.9 ... H4
Ingleside Rd. ... Pg.8 ... F3
Iola Ave. ... Pg.9 ... H4
Iroquois Tr. ... Pg.9 ... H5
Jackson Ave. ... Pg.9 ... H4
James ... Pg.9 ... H4
James Ct. ... Pg.8 ... G3
Jennette Ct. ... Pg.8 ... F1
Jennette Pl. ... Pg.8 ... F1
Karen Ct. ... Pg.8 ... H3
Kelly Ln. ... Pg.15 ... L3
Kendall Ave. ... Pg.8 ... E1
Kerwin Ln. ... Pg.9 ... H4
Knollwood Dr. ... Pg.8 ... H3
Lake Ave. ... Pg.9 ... H4
Lake Dr. ... Pg.9 ... H4
Lake Mathews Tr. ... Pg.8,9 ... G4,H3
Lake Shore Dr. ... Pg.8 ... H3
Lake Shore Woods Dr. ... Pg.8 ... H3
Lake St. ... Pg.8 ... H3
Lake Vista Terr. ... Pg.8 ... F1
Lakeview ... Pg.9 ... H4
Lakeview Ave. ... Pg.8,9 ... H4
Laneville Dr. ... Pg.8 ... H3
Lannon Ln. ... Pg.9 ... H4
Laughing Water Tr. ... Pg.8 ... H1
Laurel Ave. ... Pg.9 ... H4
Lee Ct. ... Pg.8 ... H2
Leonard Ave. ... Pg.8 ... H3
Leviwaite ... Pg.15 ... L4
Lincoln Ct. ... Pg.9 ... H4
Linder Ave. ... Pg.9 ... H4
Linder Rd. ... Pg.9 ... H4
Long Ave. ... Pg.9 ... H4
Long Beach Dr. ... Pg.9 ... H4
Long Lake Rd. ... Pg.8,9 ... H2-5
Longwood Dr. ... Pg.9 ... H4
Louise Pl. ... Pg.9 ... H4
Lovers Tr. ... Pg.8 ... H1
Lowood Ave. ... Pg.9 ... H4
Luana Ln. ... Pg.9 ... H4
Luby Ct. ... Pg.8 ... H2
Madison St. ... Pg.9 ... H4
Mall Rd. ... Pg.8 ... H3
Malmquist Dr. ... Pg.8 ... H2
Manitoba Tr. ... Pg.9 ... H4
Maple Ave. ... Pg.9 ... H4
Maple Rd. ... Pg.8 ... G3
Margie Pl. ... Pg.9 ... H4
Marian Ave. ... Pg.9 ... H4
Marie Ln. ... Pg.8 ... H3
Marino Dr. ... Pg.9 ... G4
Marion Ct. ... Pg.8 ... H3
Marvin Ln. ... Pg.8 ... H3
Mary Ct. ... Pg.9 ... G4
Mattalina Ct. ... Pg.8 ... H3
McHenry Rd. ... Pg.8 ... H3
Meadow Ln. ... Pg.8 ... H3
Michael Rd. ... Pg.8 ... H3
Milwaukee Ave. ... Pg.8 ... M10
Mishenauma Tr. ... Pg.9 ... H4
Mitchell Ct. ... Pg.9 ... G4
Minkirkr Rd. ... Pg.1 ... L3
Monaville Rd. ... Pg.9 ... H4
Moody St. ... Pg.9 ... H4
Moraine Dr. ... Pg.8 ... H2
Mudjekeemis Tr. ... Pg.8 ... H1
Muskego Ave. ... Pg.9 ... H4
Myrtle Ln. ... Pg.9 ... H4
Navajo Tr. ... Pg.8 ... H1
Nippersink Ave. ... Pg.8,15 ... H2,3,K1
Nokomis ... Pg.8 ... H1
Nora Pl. ... Pg.9 ... H4
North St. ... Pg.9 ... H4
O'Kelly Ln. ... Pg.8,15 ... K2
Oak Ave. ... Pg.9 ... H4
Oak Cir. ... Pg.15 ... L3
Oak Ln. ... Pg.9 ... H4
Oak St. ... Pg.9 ... H4
Oakland Dr. ... Pg.9 ... H4
Oakside St. ... Pg.9 ... H4
Oakwood Ave. ... Pg.9 ... H4
Oden Ave. ... Pg.9 ... H4
Old Grand Ave. ... Pg.9 ... H4
Old Monaville Rd. ... Pg.9 ... H4
Olive Ct. ... Pg.9 ... H4
Orchard Ave. ... Pg.9 ... H4
Park Ave. ... Pg.9 ... H4
Park Dr. ... Pg.8 ... H2
Patricia Ln. ... Pg.8 ... H2
Paupukkeuis Tr. ... Pg.8 ... H1
Petersen Ave. ... Pg.9 ... H4
Pheasant Rd. ... Pg.8 ... H3
Poik St. ... Pg.9 ... H4
Poplar Ave. ... Pg.9 ... H4
Rabbit Hill Ln. ... Pg.9 ... H5
Racine Ave. ... Pg.9 ... H4
Rand Hill Dr. ... Pg.8 ... H2
Randrich Rd. ... Pg.8 ... F4
Ravine Ln. ... Pg.8 ... H2
Ridge Ave. ... Pg.9 ... H4
Ridge St. ... Pg.8,9 ... G4,K3
Robin Rd. ... Pg.9 ... H4
Rock Island St. ... Pg.9 ... H4
Rollins Rd. ... Pg.8 ... F4
Roseland Ct. ... Pg.9 ... H4
Rosewood Dr. ... Pg.8 ... H3
Sequoia Tr. ... Pg.8 ... H1
Sheridan Dr. ... Pg.9 ... H4
Shore Rd. ... Pg.8 ... F3
Single Oak Ct. ... Pg.8 ... K3
Snowshoe Tr. ... Pg.8 ... H1
South Ave. ... Pg.9 ... F1
South St. ... Pg.8 ... H1-2
South St. ... Pg.8 ... G3
Square Rd. ... Pg.8 ... G3
St. Olaf Ave. ... Pg.9 ... H4
Stanley Rd. ... Pg.8 ... K2
Stanton Bay Rd. ... Pg.8 ... F1
Stanton Ct. ... Pg.15 ... L3
Stockholm Dr. ... Pg.15 ... L3
Stone Ct. ... Pg.15 ... K3
Stoughton ... Pg.9 ... H4
Sullivan Lake Rd. ... Pg.15 ... L2
Sunnybrook Rd. ... Pg.8 ... H3
Sunnyside ... Pg.9 ... H4
Sunset Dr. ... Pg.8 ... H3
Sunset Terr. ... Pg.8 ... H3
Sunshine Ln. ... Pg.8 ... K3
Tamarack Dr. ... Pg.9 ... H4
Tami Ln. ... Pg.9 ... H4
Tara Ct. ... Pg.9 ... H4
Terrace Ln. ... Pg.8 ... F1
Tree Top Rd. ... Pg.8 ... H1
Tyrone Pl. ... Pg.9 ... H4
Valley Rd. ... Pg.8 ... H3
Van Buren St. ... Pg.9 ... H4
Venetian Dr. ... Pg.9 ... H4
Vincent Ct. ... Pg.9 ... G4
Wally Ct. ... Pg.8 ... H3
Ward Ln. ... Pg.9 ... H4
Waterside Ln. ... Pg.8 ... H3
Watson Ave. ... Pg.9 ... H4
Watts Ave. ... Pg.9 ... H4
Wenonah Tr. ... Pg.8 ... H1
Wesley Rd. ... Pg.8 ... G3
West Lake Ave. ... Pg.8 ... F1
West Lake Vista Terr. ... Pg.8 ... F1

CEMETERIES
Grant Cemetery ... Pg.15 ... L3

FOREST PRESERVES
Grant F.P. ... Pg.9 ... G4
Grant Woods F.P. ... Pg.9 ... F5
Pistakee Bog Nature Preserve ... Pg.15 ... K1
Volo Bog State Nature Area ... Pg.15 ... K1,2

GOLF COURSES
Hickory Knoll G.C. ... Pg.9 ... F4

SCHOOLS
Big Hollow Elem. Sch. ... Pg.9 ... H4
Big Hollow Middle Sch. ... Pg.9 ... H4
Gavin Central Elem. Sch. ... Pg.8,9 ... G4
Gavin South Elem. Sch. ... Pg.9 ... H4
St. Bede Sch. ... Pg.9 ... H4

## GRAYSLAKE
Pages 10,17,18
STREETS
Allegheny Ln. ... Pg.17 ... L8
Allen Ave. ... Pg.17 ... L8
Allen St. ... Pg.17 ... L8
Allison Ct. ... Pg.17 ... L8
Alta Dr. ... Pg.17 ... L8
Amos Bennett St. ... Pg.18 ... L8
Arlington Ct. ... Pg.10 ... H8
Arlington Ln. ... Pg.10 ... H8
Aster Ct. ... Pg.18 ... M10
Atkinson Rd. ... Pg.17 ... K8,9
Attenborough Way ... Pg.17 ... K9
Augusta St. ... Pg.17 ... L8
Banbury Ct. ... Pg.17 ... L9
Barron Blvd. ... Pg.17 ... L8
Bay View Ln. ... Pg.10 ... H8
Behm Dr. ... Pg.17 ... K9
Belle Ct. ... Pg.17 ... L8
Belle Haven Pl. ... Pg.17 ... K9
Belvidere Rd. ... Pg.18 ... L9,10
Berkshire Ln. ... Pg.17 ... K9
Berry Ave. ... Pg.17 ... L8
Blackburn Dr. ... Pg.17 ... K9
Blazingstar Ln. ... Pg.18 ... M9
Bluestem Ln. ... Pg.18 ... M9
Bluff Ave. ... Pg.17 ... K10
Bobolink Dr. ... Pg.18 ... L8
Bonnie Brae Ave. ... Pg.17 ... L8
Brae Loch Rd. ... Pg.18 ... K10
Braxton Ct. ... Pg.17 ... K8
Braxton Way ... Pg.17 ... L9,10
Braymore Dr. ... Pg.17 ... K9
Briargate Dr. ... Pg.17 ... H3-4
Brighton Cir. ... Pg.17 ... L8
Brighton Ct. ... Pg.17 ... L8
Brittain Ave. ... Pg.17 ... L8
Brittany Square E. ... Pg.17 ... L8
Brookstone Ct. ... Pg.17 ... K9
Buckingham Ct. ... Pg.17 ... L8
Buckingham Dr. ... Pg.17 ... L8
Burr Oak Ct. ... Pg.17 ... L9
Burton St. ... Pg.17 ... L8
Calamus Ln. ... Pg.18 ... M10
Cambridge C. W. ... Pg.17 ... K9
Cambridge Ln., N. & S. ... Pg.17 ... K9
Carriage Ln. ... Pg.17 ... K,L9
Cartier's Grove Ct. ... Pg.18 ... K8,9
Catherine Ct. ... Pg.17 ... K9
Cecelia St. ... Pg.17 ... L8
Cedar Ln. ... Pg.17 ... L8
Center St. ... Pg.17 ... L8
Chard Ct. ... Pg.17 ... L10
Cheriton Cir. ... Pg.10 ... H8
Chesapeake Blvd. ... Pg.17 ... K8,9
Chesterfield Ln. ... Pg.17 ... K9
Christy Ct. ... Pg.17 ... L8
Churchill Ln. ... Pg.17 ... H7
Clinton Dr. ... Pg.17 ... L8
Colbee Benton Rd. ... Pg.18 ... M10
Columbine Ct. ... Pg.18 ... M9
Coneflower Ln. ... Pg.18 ... M9
Corporate Cir., N. & S. ... Pg.18 ... L9
Country Squire Rd. ... Pg.18 ... L10
Cristfield Dr. ... Pg.10 ... H8
Cross Arm Ct. ... Pg.17 ... K9
Crossland Ct. ... Pg.17 ... K9
Crossland Dr. ... Pg.17 ... K9
Dawn Cir. ... Pg.17 ... K8
Deep Woods Ct. ... Pg.17 ... K8
Devon Ct. ... Pg.17 ... K,L9
Doolittle Ct. ... Pg.17 ... K8
Dorchester Ln. ... Pg.17 ... K,L9
Dove Ct. ... Pg.17 ... K9
Drury Ln. ... Pg.17 ... K9
Dunhill Rd. ... Pg.17 ... L9
Durnam Ln. ... Pg.17 ... K9
East St. ... Pg.17 ... L8
Easton Ct. ... Pg.17 ... L10
Fair Port Dr. ... Pg.10 ... H8
Fairfax Ln. ... Pg.17 ... K8
Fireweed Ct. ... Pg.18 ... M10
Flanders Ln. ... Pg.17 ... K8
Galway Ct. ... Pg.17 ... L9
Garfield Blvd. ... Pg.17 ... M9
Gatewood Ln. ... Pg.17 ... L8
George St. ... Pg.17 ... L8
Getchell Ave. ... Pg.17 ... L8
Glen St. ... Pg.17 ... L8
Goldenrod Ln. ... Pg.18 ... M9
Gray Ct. ... Pg.17 ... L8
Hamelitz Ct. ... Pg.17 ... L8
Hampshire Ln. ... Pg.17 ... L9
Harding St. ... Pg.17 ... K8
Harris Rd. ... Pg.18 ... L10
Harvey Ave. ... Pg.17 ... K8
Waterside Ln. ... Pg.17 ... K8
Hawley Ct. ... Pg.17 ... L8
Hawley St. ... Pg.17 ... L8
Heather Ave. ... Pg.17 ... K8
Hedgerow Dr. ... Pg.18 ... M9
Hickory St. ... Pg.17 ... L8
Highland Ct. ... Pg.17 ... K8
Highland Rd. ... Pg.17 ... K8
Hillside Ave. ... Pg.17 ... L8
Hummingbird Ct. ... Pg.18 ... M9
Indian Path Rd. ... Pg.18 ... M10
Indiangrass Ln. ... Pg.18 ... L10
Indigo Ct. ... Pg.18 ... M10
Iron Horse Ct. ... Pg.17 ... L9
Jackson Blvd. ... Pg.10 ... K8,9
Jamestown Blvd. ... Pg.10 ... K8,9
Jamestown Ct. ... Pg.10 ... K8,9
Jeffrey Ave. ... Pg.17 ... L8
Jennifer Ln. ... Pg.17 ... K8
Jones Point Rd. ... Pg.18 ... M10
Junilor Ave. ... Pg.17 ... L8
Karyn Ln. ... Pg.18 ... L10
Keeneland Ct. ... Pg.18 ... L9
Kelly Ave. ... Pg.17 ... L8
Kenilworth ... Pg.17 ... L8
Kerry Way ... Pg.17 ... L9
Kilburn Ct. ... Pg.17 ... L8
Kildare Ct. ... Pg.17 ... L9
Killarney Ct. ... Pg.17 ... L9
Lake Ave. ... Pg.17 ... L8
Lancaster Dr. ... Pg.10 ... H8
Lancer Dr. ... Pg.11 ... K10
Landon Ct. ... Pg.17 ... L8
Langley Ln. ... Pg.17 ... K8
Larkspur Ln. ... Pg.18 ... L10
Laurel Terr. ... Pg.17 ... K9
Lawn Ct. ... Pg.18 ... L9
Lawrence Ave. ... Pg.17 ... L8
Leeward Ct. ... Pg.17 ... K8
Lenox Ct. ... Pg.17 ... L9
Lexington Ct. ... Pg.10 ... H8
Lexington Ct. ... Pg.10 ... H8
Lily Ct. ... Pg.18 ... M9
Lincoln Ave. ... Pg.17 ... L8
Linden Ct. ... Pg.10 ... H8
Lindsey Ave. ... Pg.17 ... L8
Litchfield Ct. ... Pg.17 ... L9
Locust Ct. ... Pg.17 ... L8
London Ct. ... Pg.17 ... L8
Longchamps Ct. ... Pg.18 ... L9
Lupine Ct. ... Pg.18 ... M9
Mallard Ct. ... Pg.17 ... L9
Manchester Cir. ... Pg.17 ... L9
Manor ... Pg.17 ... K8
Market St. ... Pg.18 ... L10
May St. ... Pg.17 ... L8
Mayfair Ln. ... Pg.17 ... K8
McKay Cir. ... Pg.11 ... K10
McKinley Ave. ... Pg.17 ... L8
McMillan St. ... Pg.17 ... L8
Meadowlark Ln. ... Pg.17 ... L8
Merrill Ln. ... Pg.17 ... L9
Mitchell Dr. ... Pg.17 ... L8
Mockingbird Ct. ... Pg.18 ... M9
Mt. Vernon Ct. ... Pg.11 ... K10
Mt. Vernon Dr. ... Pg.11 ... K10
Mulberry Ln. ... Pg.17 ... L9
Mulrany Pl. ... Pg.17 ... L8
Neville Dr. ... Pg.17 ... L8
Newberry Ln. ... Pg.18 ... H8
Newbury Ct. ... Pg.17 ... L8
Norfolk Ln. ... Pg.17 ... K8,9
Normandy Ln. ... Pg.17 ... K8
Oak Ct. ... Pg.17 ... L8
Oakmeadow Dr. ... Pg.17 ... H7
Oakwood Dr. ... Pg.17 ... L8
Old Center St. ... Pg.17 ... L8
Oriole Ct. ... Pg.18 ... L8
Osage Orange Rd. ... Pg.17 ... L10
Oxford Ct. ... Pg.17 ... L8
Park Pl. ... Pg.17 ... L8
Park Pl. ... Pg.17 ... L8
Partridge Ct. ... Pg.17 ... L9
Paul St. ... Pg.17 ... L8
Penny Ln. ... Pg.17 ... K8
Penton Ct. ... Pg.18 ... M10
Pheasant Ct. ... Pg.17 ... L8
Pierce Ct. ... Pg.17 ... L8
Pines Dr. ... Pg.17 ... L8
Plum Ct. ... Pg.17 ... L8
Pope's Creek Ln. ... Pg.17 ... K8,9
Portsmouth Ct. ... Pg.17 ... K8
Potomac Ct. ... Pg.17 ... K8,9
Potowatomi Rd. ... Pg.18 ... L10
Prairie Orchid Ln. ... Pg.18 ... M9
Prairie Smoke Rd. ... Pg.18 ... M10
Prairie Trail ... Pg.18 ... M10
Prairieview Ave. ... Pg.17 ... K8
Proctor St. ... Pg.17 ... L9

Quail Creek Dr. Pg.17 K9
Quist Ct. Pg.17 L8
Railroad Ave. Pg.17 L8
Reagans Pl. Pg.17 M9
Redbridge Ct. Pg.17 K8
Remington Ct. Pg.17 K8
Robin Ct. Pg.17 K9
Rock Hall Cir. Pg.17 K8,9
Rock Hall Ct. Pg.17 K8,9
Roosevelt Ct. Pg.17 M9
Sandpiper Ct. Pg.18 L9
School St. Pg.17 L8
Seymour Ave. Pg.17 L8
Shakespheare Ct. Pg.17 K9
Shefield Ln. Pg.18 K9
Shootingstar Ln. Pg.18 M9
Shorewood Rd. Pg.10 H8
Signal Ln. Pg.17 L9
Silo Hill Dr. Pg.17 L9
Siwiha Dr. Pg.17 L8
Slusser St. Pg.17 L8
Stockton Dr. Pg.17 K8
Stratford Ct. Pg.17 K9
Stuart St., S. Pg.17 K8
Suffolk Ln. Pg.10 H8
Summerset Dr. Pg.17 L8
Sunflower Ct. Pg.18 M10
Surveyor St. Pg.18 L10
Swan Dr. Pg.17 K9
Sycamore Ln. Pg.10 H8
Talbot Ln. Pg.10 K8,9
Tempest Way Pg.17 K9
Thimblewood Ct. Pg.18 M10
Tylerton Cir. Pg.17 K8,9
Vernon Ln. Pg.10 H8
Warren Ln. Pg.17 L8
Warwick Ct. Pg.10 H8
Washington Blvd. Pg.17 L9
Webb Pg.17 L9
Wellington Ct. Pg.17 K8
West Shore Dr. Pg.17 L8
West Trail Ct. Pg.17 K8
Westerfield Pl. Pg.17 L9
White St. Pg.17 L8
Whitehall Ct. Pg.18 L10
Whitney St. Pg.17 L8
Wicks St. Pg.17 L8
Wild Iris Ln. Pg.18 M10
Wildberry Ct. Pg.10 H8
Williamsburg Cir. Pg.10 K8,9
Willow Cir. Pg.10 H8
Willowby Ct. Pg.17 K8
Windflower Ct. Pg.18 M10
Windsor Ln. Pg.10 H7
Woodland Dr. Pg.17 L8
Woodside Pg.10 H8
York Dr. Pg.17 L9
Yorkshire Ct. Pg.17 L9
Ziegler Dr. Pg.17 K9
1st St. Pg.17 K8
2nd St. Pg.17 K8

**CEMETERIES**
Avon Center Cem. Pg.10 H8

**PARKS**
Central Park Pg.17 K8
Jaycee Park Pg.17 L8
Jones Island Pg.17 L8

**SCHOOLS**
College of Lake Co. Pg.18 K10
Grayslake H.S. Pg.17 K8
Grayslake Middle Sch. Pg.17 K9
Lakeview Sch. Pg.17 L8
St. Gilberts Sch. Pg.17 L8
Woodview Sch. Pg.17 L8

**MISCELLANEOUS**
Lake Co. Fairgrounds Pg.18 L10
Library Pg.17 L8
Metra Commuter Train Station Pg.17 L8
Police Dept. Pg.17 L8
Post Office Pg.17 L8
Village Hall Pg.17 L8

## GREAT LAKES NAVAL TRAINING CENTER

Pages 20,21,27

**STREETS**
A St. Pg.21 N18
Access Rd. Pg.20 N16
Admiral N. Pg.20 P17
Admiral S. Pg.20 P17
Alabama Ave., E. Pg.20 P16-17
Alabama Ave., W. Pg.20 P16
Alaska Ave. Pg.20 N16
Argonaut Pl. Pg.21 N17
Arizona Ave. Pg.20 N17
Arkansas Rd. Pg.20 P16
Atlantic Rd. Pg.28 P17
Atuie St. Pg.21 N17
Barry Pl. Pg.21 N18
Bassett St. Pg.21 N18
Berry Rd. Pg.21 N18
Broadway Ave. Pg.20 P17
Bronson Ave. Pg.21 N18
Burnham Ave. Pg.21 M18
California Ave. Pg.20 P16-17
Cavin Dr. Pg.20 N16
Clark Ave. Pg.21 M18
Cluverius Ave. Pg.21 M18
Colorado W. Pg.20 N16
Connecticut Pg.20 N16
Connecticut Ct. Pg.20 M16
Craven Ave. Pg.21 M18
Crosley Dr. Pg.21 N18
D St. Pg.21 N18
Dahlgren St. Pg.21 N18
Decatur Ave. Pg.21 N18
Delaware Ave. Pg.20 P16-17
Depot Dr. Pg.20 M16
Dewey Ave. Pg.21 N18
Downes Dr. Pg.21 N18
Downey Rd. Pg.20 N17
E St. Pg.21 N18
Ellis Pg.21 M18
Enterprise Ave. Pg.20 N17
Erie Ct. Pg.20 N16
Essex Pg.20 N17
Evans Ave. Pg.21 M18
F St. Pg.21 N18
Fairway Ave. Pg.20 N16
Farragut Ave. Pg.21 N18
Fisher Rd. Pg.21 N18
Florida Ave. Pg.20 N16
Florida Ct. Pg.20 N16
Florida W. Pg.20 N16
Forrestal Dr. Pg.20 P17
Fullam Ave. Pg.21 M18
G St. Pg.21 N18
Georgia Rd. Pg.20 P16
Grassie Ave. Pg.21 M18
Grayling Ct. Pg.21 N17
Great Lakes Cir. Pg.20 P16
Great Lakes Dr. Pg.20 P16
Green Bay Rd. Pg.20 P17
Greenview Ave. Pg.20 N16
Hawaii Ave. Pg.20 P17
Hilldale Ave. Pg.20 N16
Hines St. Pg.21 N18
Hopkins St. Pg.21 N18
Huron St. Pg.20 N16
Idaho Ct. Pg.20 N16
Idaho St. Pg.20 N16
Illinois St. Pg.21 N-P17
Indiana St. Pg.21 N-P17
Intrepid St. Pg.20 N17
Iowa St. Pg.21 N17
Isherwood Ave. Pg.21 M18
Kansas St. Pg.21 N17
Kentucky St. Pg.21 N17
Knollwood Ave. Pg.20 N16
Lake Front Hwy. Pg.21 M17
Lakes Dr. Pg.20 N16
Langley St. Pg.20 N17
Lawrence St. Pg.21 N18
Leonia Ave. Pg.20 N16
Lexington Ave. Pg.20 N17
Louisiana Ave. Pg.20 N16
Luce Blvd. Pg.21 M18
MacDonough Pg.21 M18
Mahan Rd. Pg.21 N18
Main St. Pg.21 M18
Maine Ave. Pg.20 N17
Maryland St. Pg.20 N16
Meridian Pg.20 P17
Meyer Cir. Pg.21 M18
Michigan Ct. Pg.20 N17,P16
Minnesota Ave. Pg.20 N16
Mississippi St. Pg.20 N16
Missouri St. Pg.20,21 N16,17
Moffett Dr. Pg.21 M18
Montana Ave. Pg.20 N17
N.Y. Ave. Pg.20 P16-17
Nautilus Ct. Pg.21 N17
Nebraska Ct. Pg.20 M16
Nevada Ct. Pg.20 N16
Nimitz Ave. Pg.21 M18
Ohio Ave. Pg.20 P16-17
Ohio St. Pg.21 N-P17
Ontario Ave. Pg.20 N16
Oregon Ct. Pg.20 N16
Pacific Rd. Pg.20 N17
Panger Ct. Pg.20 N17
Park Ave. Pg.21 M18
Paul Jones St. Pg.21 M18
Pennsylvania Ave. Pg.20 P16-17
Perry St. Pg.21 N18
Porter Ave. Pg.21 N18
Preble Ave. Pg.21 N18
Preble Pl. Pg.21 N17
Ray St. Pg.21 N17
Remora Ct. Pg.21 N17
Rogers Ave. Pg.21 N18
Sampson Rd. Pg.21 N18
Samspon St. Pg.21 M,N18
Saratoga St. Pg.20 N17
Sargo Pl. Pg.21 M17
Seadragon Ct. Pg.21 N17
Seahorse Pl. Pg.21 N17
Seavale Pl. Pg.21 N17
Shark Ct. Pg.21 N17
Sheridan Rd. Pg.21 N17
Skate Ct. Pg.21 N17
Skipjack Pl. Pg.21 N17
Spaulding St. Pg.21 N17
Superior St. Pg.20 P16
Tennessee Ct. Pg.20 N16
Texas Ct. Pg.20 N17
Thresher St. Pg.21 N17
Utah Ct. Pg.20 N16
Vermont Ave. Pg.21 N16
Vermont Ct., N. & S. Pg.20 N16
Virginia Ave. Pg.20 N16
Washington Ave., E. Pg.20 N16
West Lawn Ave. Pg.20 N16
Wisconsin Dr., E. & W. Pg.20 N16
Wurtsbaugh Pg.21 N18
Wyoming Ct. Pg.20 N16
Wyoming, E. & W. Pg.20 N16
Yeager Dr. Pg.21 N17
Yorktown Ave. Pg.20 N17
Ziegemeir St. Pg.21 N18
1st St. Pg.21 N17
2nd St. Pg.21 N18
3rd St. Pg.21 N18
4th St. Pg.21 N18
5th Ave. Pg.21 N17
5th St. Pg.21 N18
6th Ave. Pg.21 N17
6th St. Pg.21 N18
7th Ave. Pg.21 N17
7th St. Pg.21 N18
8th Ave. Pg.21 N17
8th St. Pg.21 N18
9th Ave. Pg.21 N17
9th St. Pg.21 N18
10th Ave. Pg.21 N17
10th St. Pg.21 N18
11th Ave. Pg.21 N17
11th St. Pg.21 N18
12th Ave. Pg.21 N17
15th Ave. West Pg.21 M17
24th Pl. Pg.20 N16
25th Pl. Pg.20 N16
25th St. Pg.20 N16
26th St. Pg.20 N16

**GOLF COURSES**
U.S.N. Golf Course Pg.20 N16

**PARKS**
Constitution Park Pg.21 M18
Joseph W. Gregg Park Pg.21 N17

**MISCELLANEOUS**
Downey V.A. Hospital Pg.20 N17
Fire Fighter Training Center Sch. Pg.20 N16
Naval Hosp. Pg.21 N18
U.S. Naval Trianing Center F.B.I. Range Pg.21 M18

## GREEN OAKS

Pages 19,20,26,27

**STREETS**
Ashford Ct. Pg.27 Q15
Ashford Dr. Pg.27 Q15
Ashley Cir. Pg.27 Q14
Atkinson Rd. Pg.26,27 P14
Belmont Dr. Pg.19 P14
Benson Ln. Pg.26 P14
Benson Rd. Pg.19,26 P14
Berwick Way Pg.19,20 N,P14
Bishop Ct. Pg.2 D5
Blyth Ct. Pg.20 M14
Bradford Ct. Pg.20 N15
Braeloch Ct. Pg.27 Q15
Braemore Close Pg.20 M15
Brookhaven Dr. Pg.20 N15
Buckley Rd. Pg.19 N13
Burton Ct. Pg.20 M14
Carriage Ct. Pg.19 P14
Churchill Ct. Pg.19 P14
Cranbrook Rd. Pg.19,20 N14
Crescent Knoll Dr. Pg.26 Q14
Crest Rd. Pg.26 P14
Dan Patch Dr. Pg.20 M14
Edgewater Ct. Pg.20 N15
Forest Lake Ln. Pg.27 Q14
Fox Run Pg.27 P14
Gerwick Way Pg.26 P14
Glenmore Rd. Pg.19,26 P14
Glenwood Ct. Pg.20 N15
Greenbriar Dr. Pg.26 P14
Greenbriar Ln. Pg.26 P14
Greenfield Ct. Pg.27 Q14
Guerin Rd. Pg.19 N13
Hanlon Rd. Pg.19 N14
Harwood Dr. Pg.19 N14
Haven Ln. Pg.19 N14
Hawthorne Rd. Pg.26 Q14
Heathercliff Dr. Pg.19 N14
Irma Lee Cir. Pg.27 R15
Irondale Rd. Pg.19 N14
Isleworth Ct. Pg.27 Q15
Jefferson Dr. Pg.19 N13
Kathryn Ct. Pg.26 P14
Kenton Ln. Pg.19,20 N14
King Ct. Pg.19 N14
King Dr. Pg.19 N14
Kirkwell Ct. Pg.19 N15
Lambs Ln. Pg.27 Q14
Lexington Rd. Pg.19 N14
Lockwood Dr. Pg.20 N15
Longwood Dr. Pg.19,20 N14
Lyle Ct. Pg.20 M14
Maplewood Ct. Pg.20 N15
Margate Ln. Pg.26 Q14
Minard Ln. Pg.26 Q14
Morgan Ct. Pg.20 M15
O'Plaine Rd. Pg.19 N14
Oakhaven Ct. Pg.27 Q15
Oakwood Ct. Pg.20 N15
Oban Ct. Pg.20 M15
Old Rockland Rd. Pg.27 Q14
Parkhill Dr. Pg.26 Q14
Pearson Rd. Pg.19 P14
Placid Ln. Pg.19,20 N14
Post Oak Ct. Pg.27 Q14
Prairie Ridge Dr. Pg.19 N14
Red Fox Ln. Pg.20 N14
Reigate Ln. Pg.20 M14
Rein Ct. Pg.19 N14
Rockytop Rd. Pg.26 Q14
Rodmell Ct. Pg.20 M14
Saddle Hill Rd. Pg.19 N-P14
Saratoga Ct. Pg.19 P14
Scarborough Dr. Pg.27 Q15
Scotland Ct. Pg.20 M15
Shanklin Ct. Pg.20 M14
Shannondale Dr. Pg.19 M14
Somerset Cir. Pg.19 N14
Spring Creek Ct. Pg.20 N15
Spring Meadow Ct. Pg.27 Q14
St. Marys Rd. Pg.19 N14
Steeplechase Ct. Pg.19 N14
Sunrise Rd. Pg.26 P14
Towne Trail Pg.19 M14
Tri State Tollway Pg.20 N15
Twin Lakes Ct. Pg.27 Q14
Waterford Ct. Pg.27 Q14
White Fence Ln. Pg.19 N14
Wickham Ct. Pg.20 P14
Wickham Dr. Pg.20 N,P15
Wilton Ct. Pg.20 P14
Wilton Ln. Pg.20 P14
Windmere Ct. Pg.27 Q15
Woodfield Ln. Pg.26 Q14
Woodview Dr. Pg.19 M14
Wycome Ct. Pg.20 M14

**CEMETERIES**
Ascension Cem. Pg.19 N14

**FOREST PRESERVES**
Site 15 F.P. Pg.27 P15

**SCHOOLS**
Oak Grove Sch. Pg.19 N14

**MISCELLANEOUS**
Lamb's Farm Petting Zoo & Amusement Park Pg.27 Q14
Nature Study Area Pg.27 P14
Village Hall Pg.27 Q14

## GURNEE

Pages 11-13,19,20

**STREETS**
Abbey Rd. Pg.11 G,H11
Aberdare Ln. Pg.11 H11
Abingdon Ct. Pg.19 L12
Acacia Ct. Pg.12 G13
Acorn Ct. Pg.12 G13
Adaline Ct. Pg.13 H14
Adams Ct. Pg.12 G13
Adderly Ln. Pg.19 L12
Adele Ct. Pg.12 G14
Alder Ct. Pg.12 G13
Almaden Ln. Pg.11 H11
Almond Rd. Pg.11 H11
Alpine Ct. Pg.12 G13
Ambrogio Dr. Pg.13 K15
Anderson Ln. Pg.12 H14
Andover Dr. Pg.19 L12
Angelo Ave. Pg.19 K14
Arbor Ct. Pg.12 G13
Arlington Ln. Pg.11 G11
Arthur Ct. Pg.12 G13
Ashwood Ln. Pg.12 G13
Aster Dr. Pg.11 H10
Astor Pl. Pg.19 L14
Atlantic Ave. Pg.13 G15
Auburn Ct. Pg.11 G,H11
Avery Ct. Pg.19 L13
Balsam Ct. Pg.12 G13
Barberry Ln. Pg.13 G15
Barn Swallow Ct. Pg.19 K12
Barnwood Ct. Pg.12 G13
Barnwood Dr. Pg.12 G13
Bay Pl. Pg.13 G16
Beech Ln. Pg.19 M12
Beechwood Ave. Pg.12 G13
Belle Plaine Ave. Pg.13 H15
Bellview Ct. Pg.12 G13
Belvidere Ave. Pg.19 L12
Bennett Ave. Pg.13 K15
Bennington Dr. Pg.11 H11
Bentley Dr. Pg.11 H11
Beringer Ct. Pg.11 H11
Berkshire Ct. Pg.12 K14
Beth Ct. Pg.19 K13
Bidwell Ct. Pg.19 L12
Big Terra Ln. Pg.19 K12
Bingham Ct. Pg.19 L12
Birch Dr. Pg.19 K14
Birchwood Ln. Pg.12 G13
Bitternut Ln. Pg.13 G15
Bittersweet Dr. Pg.11 H10
Blackberry Ct. Pg.11 H10
Blackburn St. Pg.13 H15
Blackstone Ave. Pg.12,13 H14,K15
Blanc Ct. Pg.11 G11
Bluebird Ct. Pg.12,13 H14
Bough Rd. Pg.12 H13
Boulders Dr. Pg.12 G14
Boulevard View Ave. Pg.13 H15
Bradford Ct. Pg.11 H11
Bradley Dr. Pg.11 G11
Branch Rd. Pg.12 H13
Braxton Ct. Pg.19 L12
Brea Ct. Pg.11 H11
Brentwood Ln. Pg.11 H11
Brian Ct. Pg.19 L13
Briar Ave. Pg.13 H15
Briarwood Ct. Pg.19 K14
Bridle Trail Rd. Pg.12 G12
Brighton Ct. Pg.12 H14
Bristol Ct. Pg.12 K14
Brittany Ln. Pg.12 H12
Brook Haven Rd. Pg.12 K14
Brookstone Pl. Pg.19 K12
Brown Cir. (N&S) Pg.13 H15
Brown Pl. Pg.13 H14
Buchanan Dr. Pg.11 G11
Buckeridge Ct. Pg.12 G13
Buckingham Dr. Pg.13 K14
Burr Oak Dr. Pg.19 M12
Buttercup Ln. Pg.19 K13
Butternut Ct. Pg.12 G13
Calvin Ct. Pg.19 K14
Camden Dr. Pg.11 H11
Campbell Dr. Pg.19 L12
Canterbury Ct. Pg.12 G13
Canyon Ct. Pg.11 H10
Capitol Ln. Pg.11 H11
Cardinal Ct. Pg.12 G13
Carol Ln. Pg.12 G13
Carriage Dr. Pg.12 H14
Cascade Way Pg.11 H10
Castlewood Ct. Pg.12 H12
Cathedral Ct. Pg.12 G13
Cedar Ave. Pg.12 H13
Cedarwood Ct. Pg.12 G13
Cemetery Rd. Pg.12 H12
Centennial Ct. Pg.13 H14
Chandler Rd. Pg.19 K12
Chapel Hill Pg.12 G13
Charles Ave. Pg.13,20 H14,K15
Chase Ct. Pg.19 L12
Chatham Ave. Pg.19 K14
Chelsey Ct. Pg.19 K13
Cherrywood Ct. Pg.12 G13
Chesapeake Ct. Pg.11,12 G11,H12
Cheshire Rd. Pg.12 G14
Cheswick Dr. Pg.11 H11
Cheyenne Rd. Pg.13 G15
Chip Ct. Pg.19 K13
Churchill Ln. Pg.12 H12
Clarewood Dr. Pg.11 H11
Clark Dr. Pg.19 L13
Clavey Ln. Pg.11 H10
Clearview Ave. Pg.13 G15
Clearview Ct. Pg.13 G15
Clem Dr. Pg.11 G11
Cliffwood Ln. Pg.11 H11
Club House Ct. Pg.19 K12
Cobblestone Ct. Pg.20 K14
Cohasset Ct. Pg.19 K14
Colby Ct. Pg.19 K13
Colby Rd. Pg.19 K13
Cole Ct. Pg.19 K14
Compton Ct. Pg.19 L12
Concord Sq. Pg.19 K14
Congress Ct. Pg.11 H11
Conifer Ln. Pg.12 G13
Constitution Ave. Pg.12 G13
Coral Berry Path Pg.13 G15
Cornell Ave. Pg.19 K14
Country Club Ave. Pg.13 G15
Country Tr. Pg.19 K14
Covenant Ct. Pg.19 K14
Coventry Ln. Pg.12 H14
Crabtree Ct. Pg.20 K14
Crescent Ave. Pg.13 H15
Crestville Ct. Pg.13 H15
Cross Ct. Pg.19 K14
Cross Rd. Pg.19 K14
Crossland Blvd. Pg.19 L12
Crossland Ct. Pg.19 L12
Crystal Pl. Pg.11 H10
Cumberland Ct. Pg.12 K14
Cypress Cir. Pg.12 G13
Dada Dr. Pg.11 H11-12
Danielson Ct. Pg.11 H12
Darlene Ct. Pg.12 H14
Darlene Dr. Pg.12 H14
Darnell Ln. Pg.19 L12
David Ct. Pg.12 G13
Davidson Ct. Pg.12 H12
Deer Run Pg.12 G14
Delany Rd. Pg.20 K15
Delaware Ave. Pg.12 G13
Depot Rd. Pg.12 H14
Derby Dr. Pg.11 G,H11
Des Plaines Ct. Pg.19 L13
Dilley's Rd. Pg.12 H13
Dixon Ct. Pg.19 K13
Dogwood Ln. Pg.19 M12
Dolcetto Ln. Pg.11 G11
Doral Dr. Pg.19 K12
Dorchester Ave. Pg.13 H15
Dordan Ct. Pg.19 K13
Dover Ct. Pg.12 H12
Drexel Ave. Pg.13 H15
Drury St. Pg.19 K13
Dunham Rd. Pg.19 K13
Dunhill Ct. Pg.19 L12
Eagle Ct. Pg.13 H14
Eagle Ridge Dr. Pg.19 K12
Easton Ct. Pg.11 G11
Eastwood Ave. Pg.19 L14
Eau Claire Ct. Pg.12 G13
Ebony Ct. Pg.12 G13
Edington Ln. Pg.19 K13
Ellis Ave. Pg.13 H15
Elm Rd. Pg.19 K14
Elsie Ave. Pg.12 H13
Emerald Ave. Pg.12 H14
Estate Cir. Pg.12 K12
Estes St. Pg.13 H15
Fair Links Way Pg.19 K12
Farmgate Ct. Pg.20 K14
Farwell Ct. Pg.19 L12
Ferndale St. Pg.13 H15
Fernwood Ct. Pg.12 G13
Fieldstone Ct. Pg.20 K14
Fieldstone Dr. Pg.20 K14
Finch Ct. Pg.12 H14
First Pl. Pg.13 H15
First St. Pg.13 K15
Florida Ave. Pg.13 G15
Formoor Ln. Pg.19 L12
Fox Ln. Pg.12 G14
Fox Meadow Ct. Pg.12 G14
Foxboro Ln. Pg.19 K12
Foxworth Ln. Pg.12 H12
Framingham Ct. Pg.19 K14
Franklin Ct. Pg.12 G13
Frederick Ct. Pg.12 H13
Freedom Ct. Pg.11 H11
Frontage Rd. Pg.20 K15
Fuller Rd. Pg.12 H14
Gages Lake Rd. Pg.19 K12
Gamay Ct. Pg.11 H10
Garnacha Dr. Pg.11 G10
Garnet Ct. Pg.12 G14
Gatewood Dr. Pg.12 G13
Geneva Dr. Pg.11 H10
George Ct. Pg.12 G13
Gillings Dr. Pg.12 H14
Glen Flora Ave. Pg.13 H15
Glen Way Pg.19 L12
Glendale Dr. Pg.12 H14
Gloster Ct. Pg.19 L12
Golf View Dr. Pg.19 K12
Gould St. Pg.13 K15
Grand Ave. Pg.12,13 H14,15
Grandmore Ave. Pg.13 H15
Grandview Ave. Pg.13 H15
Grandville Ave. Pg.13 H15
Green Haven Ln. Pg.12 K14
Greenbriar Ct. Pg.20 K14
Greenfield Ct. Pg.11 G,H11
Greenleaf St. Pg.13 H15
Greenview St. Pg.13 H15
Greenwood Ave. Pg.13 G15
Greystem Cir. Pg.13 G15
Grove Ave. Pg.13 H15
Gurnee Mills Cir., E. & W. Pg.12 G12
Habitat Ct. Pg.19 K12
Hadley Cir. Pg.11 H11
Halifax Rd. Pg.19 L12
Hamilton Dr. Pg.11 G11
Hampton Cir. Pg.12 G12
Hancock Ln. Pg.12 G13
Harper Ave. Pg.13 H15
Hartford Dr. Pg.11 H11
Hawthorne Ave. Pg.13 H15
Hazelwood Ct. Pg.12 G13
Heather Ridge Dr. Pg.19 L13
Henry Ct. Pg.12 G13
Heritage Ct. Pg.13 K14
Hickory Haven Dr. Pg.19 K13
Highland Ave. Pg.13 G15
Hill N' Dale Ct. Pg.12 K12
Hillside Ct. Pg.11 G11
Hillview Dr. Pg.11 H10
Holly Rd. Pg.19 M12
Hollyhock Ct. Pg.12 G13
Honeysuckle Ct. Pg.12 K12
Independence Ct. Pg.12 G13
Indian Trail Rd. Pg.19 K12
Ingelbrook Ln. Pg.11 G11
Inverness Dr. Pg.19 K12
Ironwood Ct. Pg.12 G13
Jeffery Ave. Pg.20 K15
Johns Manville Ave. Pg.13 G16
Joshua Ct. Pg.12 G13
Juniper St. Pg.12 H13
Keith Ave. Pg.13 G15
Kensington Ct. Pg.12 H14
Kenwood Ave. Pg.13 H15
Kilbourne Rd. Pg.12 H14
Kim Ct. Pg.20 K15
Kings Ct. Pg.19 K14
Kings Way, N. & W. Pg.19 K14
Kingsbury Ct. Pg.11 H11
Kingsport Dr. Pg.11 G,H11
Knobb Hill Ln. Pg.12 K12
Knottingham Dr. Pg.11 H11
Knowles Rd. Pg.11 G10
Knoxbury Ct. Pg.12 K15
Korbel Dr. Pg.11 G11
Kristin Ct. Pg.19 L13
Lake Park Ave. Pg.13 K15
Lakeside Dr. Pg.12 H12
Lamb Ln. Pg.12 H12
Lancaster Cir. Pg.13 K15
Laurel Ln. Pg.11 H10
Lauren Ct. Pg.11 H11
Lawrence Ave. Pg.13 H16
Lawson Blvd. Pg.12 G,H13
Lee Ave. Pg.13 H15
Lenox Ct. Pg.11 H11
Leonard Dr. Pg.19 K12,L13
Lexington Sq., E. & W. Pg.19 K14
Lexlie Ln. Pg.12 G13
Liberty Ln. Pg.12 G13
Lind Ln. Pg.12 G14
Lockeslee Ct. Pg.12 H12
Lockwood Ln. Pg.12 H12
Locust Ln. Pg.19 M12
Lone Tree Ct. Pg.19 K12
Long Hill Rd. Pg.19 K14
Longmeadow Dr. Pg.19 K14
Longwood Ln. Pg.19 M12
Louis Ct. Pg.12 G13
Madison Ave. Pg.12 G13
Magical Dr. Pg.11 G,H11
Magnolia Ave. Pg.13 H15
Mahogany Ct. Pg.12 G13
Majestic Ct. Pg.19 K14
Manchester Dr. Pg.19 K13
Maplewood Dr. Pg.12 G13
Mayflower Ct. Pg.19 K14
McClure Ave. Pg.12 H14
Meadowcrest Cir. Pg.13 H15
Meadowlark Ct. Pg.13 H14
Melon Ct. Pg.11 H11
Mendocino Dr. Pg.11 G10
Merit Club Ln. Pg.19 M12
Merlot Ct. Pg.11 H11
Middle Rd. Pg.19 K14
Milan Way Pg.11 H10
Millstone Ln. Pg.11 G,H11
Milwaukee Ave. Pg.12 K14
Mint Haven Ct. Pg.12 K14
Mitchell Ct. Pg.19 K13
Monterey Ct. Pg.12 G13
Monticello Ct., E. & W. Pg.12 H12
Monument Ct. Pg.12 G13
Morgan Ct. Pg.11 G11
Morningside Ct. Pg.12 K12
Morrison Dr. Pg.13 G15
Mountain Ash Ct. Pg.11 H10
Mt. Vernon Ct., E. & W. Pg.12 H12
Muirfield Dr. Pg.19 K12
Nantucket Ct. Pg.12 G12
Napa Dr. Pg.11 G11
Nations Dr. Pg.12 G13
New Haven Ave. Pg.19 K14
Newbury Ct. Pg.19 L12
Newgate Ct. Pg.11 G11
Newport Ct. Pg.12 G13
Norfolk Ct. Pg.12 G13
Norman Ave. Pg.12,13 H15
North Ave. Pg.12 H14
North Creek Dr. Pg.12 G12
Northridge Dr. Pg.12 H13
Northwestern Ave. Pg.13 H15
Nursery Dr. Pg.11 H10
O'Plaine Rd. Pg.12,19 H,K14
Oak Ln. Pg.12 G14
Oak Meadow Ct. Pg.11 G,H11
Oakmont Ln. Pg.19 K12
Oakview Ln. Pg.12 G13
Oakwood St. Pg.13 H15
Oglesby Ave. Pg.20 K15
Old Farm Ln. Pg.12 K12
Old Grand Ave. Pg.12 H14
Old Oak Rd. Pg.19 M12
Old Walnut Clr. Pg.11 H11
Oriole Ct. Pg.12 H14
Oscar Ct. Pg.12 G13
Oxford Ct. Pg.12 G13
Pacific Ave. Pg.13 G15
Packard Ln. Pg.12 G13
Panorama Ln. Pg.11 H10
Par Ct. Pg.19 L12
Parkside Ct. Pg.12 G13
Patriot Ct. Pg.11 H11
Pauly Dr. Pg.12 H13
Pebble Creek Ct. Pg.19 K12
Pembrook Ct. Pg.12 G13
Pennsbury Ln. Pg.11 G,H11
Penny Ln. Pg.11 H11
Persimmon Way Pg.19 M12
Pheasant Meadow Ct. Pg.19 K12
Pilgrims Path Pg.19 K14
Pine Grove St. Pg.13 H15
Pine Meadow Ct. Pg.12 G14
Pinehurst Ct. Pg.11 H11
Pinetree Dr. Pg.12 G13
Pinewood Rd. Pg.12 G13
Plainview Rd. Pg.12 K12
Plaza Dr. Pg.12 H13
Plymouth Ct. Pg.19 K14
Porett Dr. Pg.13 G15
Portage Ln. Pg.12 G13
Portsmouth Cir. Pg.12 H12
Prairie Creek Dr. Pg.12 G12
Prairie Oak Rd. Pg.12 H14
Preakness Pl. Pg.11 G,H11
Prescott Ln. Pg.11 H11
Presidential Dr. Pg.11 H11
Preston Ct. Pg.11 G,H11
Princeton Ct. Pg.12 G13
Private Dr. Pg.12 G14
Private Rd. Pg.19 L12
Providence Rd. Pg.19 K14
Quail Haven Ct. Pg.19 K12
Queen Anne Ln. Pg.12 G14
Quincy Ct. Pg.12 G13
Ralph Ave. Pg.13 H15
Raven Ct. Pg.12 H14
Ravine Dr. Pg.12 G14
Ravinia Dr. Pg.11 H10
Red Pine Ave. Pg.12 G13
Regency Ct. Pg.19 K13
Regency Dr. Pg.19 K13
Revere Ct. Pg.11 H11
Ridge Dr. Pg.12 H14
Rippling Ridge Ct. Pg.11 H10
Riverside Dr. Pg.12 G14
Roanoke Ct. Pg.12 G12
Robin Ct. Pg.12 H14
Rockpointe Ct. Pg.12 H13
Rogers Rd. Pg.12 H14
Rolling Green St. Pg.19 K12
Rollingwoods Ln. Pg.19 M12
Rosemary Ln. Pg.12 G13
Rudd Ct. Pg.20 K15
Russell Ave. Pg.19,20 K14-15
Ryan Rd. Pg.13 G15
Ryan Rd., W. Pg.13 G15
Sage Ct. Pg.11 G11
Salem Ct. Pg.12 G13
Sanctuary Ct. Pg.12 G13
Sanders Ct. Pg.19 K13
Sandwedge Pl. Pg.19 K12
Saratoga Ct. Pg.19 K12
Scot Ct. Pg.19 L13
Sedge Ct. Pg.11 H10
Sedona Ct. Pg.12 G14
Sedwich Cir. Pg.12 G14
Sequoia Ct. Pg.12 G13
Serranda Dr. Pg.19 K12
Shadow Rock Ct. Pg.20 K14
Shagbark Ln. Pg.12 G14
Sheffield Ct. Pg.12 H14
Shepard Ct. Pg.19 K13
Shepard Rd. Pg.19 K13
Sherman Ave. Pg.13 H15
Sherwood Ct. Pg.12 G13
Sierra Pl. Pg.11 H10
Silo Ct. Pg.12 K12
Six Flags Pkwy. Pg.12 H13
Sizer Rd. Pg.19 L13
Skokie Highway Pg.12 G14
Sleepy Hollow Ln. Pg.19 K12
Smithfield Ct. Pg.11 G,H11
Snow Cap Ct. Pg.11 H11
Solomon Ct. Pg.12 G13
Somerset Ct. Pg.12 G13
Sonoma Ct. Pg.11 H11
South Fork Dr. Pg.19 K12
South Rd. Pg.12 H14
South Ridge Dr. Pg.19 K12
Spinney Run Dr. Pg.19 K13
Springhaven Dr. Pg.12 K14
Spruce Pointe Ct. Pg.12 G13
Spruce Pointe Dr. Pg.12 G13
Spruce St. Pg.12 H13
Sprucewood Ln. Pg.12 G13
St. Andrews Ln. Pg.11 H11
St. Paul Ave. Pg.13 G14
State Rte. 132 Pg.12 G11-H14
State Rte. 45 Pg.11 H10
Stearns School Rd. Pg.12 G12-13
Steeple Pointe Blvd. Pg.12 G13
Stewart Ct. Pg.19 K13
Stonebrook Dr. Pg.11 G11
Stony Island Ave. Pg.13 K15
Stout Ct. Pg.19 K13
Stratford Dr. Pg.12 H13
Stratton Ln., S. Pg.11 G11
Strawberry Fields Pg.11 G,H11
Suda Dr. Pg.13 K15
Suffolk Ct. Pg.11 H11
Sumner Cir. Pg.11 H11
Sunnyside Ave. Pg.19 K14
Sunrise Ln. Pg.12 H13
Surrey Ct. Pg.12 H12
Swanson Ct. Pg.13 G15
Sycamore Ln. Pg.12 G13
Tanglewood Rd. Pg.20 K14
Taylor Dr. Pg.19 L13
Thackery Ln. Pg.19 M12
Timber Ct. Pg.12 G13
Timsbury Ct. Pg.11 G11
Tower Ct. Pg.20 K15
Tralee Ct. Pg.12 H15
Tree Top Ln. Pg.11 H11
Tri State Pkwy. Pg.12 H13
Tri State Tollway Pg.12 G14
Trinity Ct. Pg.12 G13
Tronwood Dr. Pg.12 G13
Tyme Ct. Pg.11 H11
U.S. Rte. 41 Pg.12 G14
U.S. Rte. 45 Pg.12 G12
University Ave. Pg.13 H15
Victor Terr. Pg.12 G13
Victoria Ct. Pg.12 K14
Village Ln. Pg.11 H11
Vineyard Dr. Pg.11 G10
Virginia Ct. Pg.12 G13
Vista Dr. Pg.11 H10
Vose Dr. Pg.19 L19
Wakefield Ct. Pg.19 K13
Washington St. Pg.12,13 K14
Waterbury Ave. Pg.19 K14
Waterfall Ct. Pg.11 H10
Waterford Way Pg.19 K14
Wausau Ln. Pg.12 G14
Waveland Ave. Pg.20 K15
Waveland St. Pg.13 H15
Wedgewood Dr. Pg.12 G14
Wellington Cir. Pg.13 K14
West St. Pg.12 H14
Westbrook Ln. Pg.12 G12
Westfield Dr. Pg.12 G13
White Barn Ln. Pg.19 K12
White Ct. Pg.19 K13
White Oak Ct. Pg.19,20 K14
White Pine Way Pg.19 M12
Whitney Ct. Pg.19 K13
Whittington Ct. Pg.11 H11
Wilbur Ct. Pg.19 K13
Wildflower Dr. Pg.19 K12
Williams Ct. Pg.19 K13
Williamsburg Ave. Pg.19 K14
Willow Ct. Pg.12 H13
Willow Ln. Pg.12 H13
Wiltshire Ct. Pg.13 K14
Winchester Ct. Pg.12 H12
Windemere Cir. Pg.11 H11
Windsong Ct. Pg.12 G13
Windsor Ct. Pg.12 G13
Windwood Ct. Pg.12 G13
Winona Ln. Pg.12 G13
Woodbury Cir. Pg.11 H11
Woodcrest Ct. Pg.20 K15
Woodhill Dr. Pg.12 H13
Woodlawn Ave. Pg.13 H15
Yew Ct. Pg.12 G13
Yorkshire Ct. Pg.12 H14

**FOREST PRESERVES**
Gurnee Woods Pg.12 G14
River Hill F.P. Pg.19 K13

**GOLF COURSES**
Bittersweet Golf Course Pg.11 H11
Heather Ridge G.C. Pg.19 L12
Merit Club Golf Course Pg.19 L12

**PARKS**
Betty Russell Comm. Park Pg.12 G13
Cambridge Park Pg.12 H11
Cedar Park Pg.12 H13
Chittenden Park Pg.12 H15
Country Trails Pathway Pg.20 K14
Elysian Fields Park Pg.11 G11
Gowe Park Pg.12 H14
Heather Ridge Woods Pg.19 L13
Hunt Club Park Pg.12 H12
Kings Park Pg.19 K14
O'Plaine Comm. Park Pg.19 K15
Pembroke Comm. Woods Pg.12 G13
Prairie Oaks Park Pg.12 G14
Ravinia Park Pg.11 H10
Russell Comm. Park Pg.19 K14
Shaw Park Pg.13 G14
South Park Pg.12 H13
South Ridge Park Pg.19 K12
Swanson & Trigg Conservation Pg.13 H15
University Park Pg.13 H15
Viking Park Pg.12 H14
Westgate Park Pg.12 G13
Woodlawn Park Pg.13 H15

**SCHOOLS**
Gurnee Sch. Pg.12 H14
O'Plaine Sch. Pg.13 K14
Spaulding North Sch. Pg.13 G15
Viking Jr. H.S. Pg.12 H14
Warren Township H.S. Pg.12 H14
Woodland Middle Sch. Pg.12 H12

**SHOPPING CENTERS**
Gurnee Mills Mall Pg.12 G12

**MISCELLANEOUS**
Fire Dept. Pg.12 H14
Fire Station #2 Pg.11 G,H11

## GURNEE

Grand Tri-State Business Park ... Pg.12 ... H13
Gurnee Industrial Park ... Pg.13 ... G15
Gurnee Park Dist. ... Pg.12 ... H12
Merit Club House ... Pg.19 ... L12
Mother Rudd Home ... Pg.19 ... H14
North Shore Sanitation Dist. ... Pg.12 ... K14
Police Dept. ... Pg.12 ... K14
Post Office ... Pg.19 ... H14
Public Works ... Pg.12 ... K14
Six Flags Great America Theme Park ... Pg.12 ... H13
Village Hall ... Pg.12 ... K14
Warren Newport Library ... Pg.12 ... K14

## HAINESVILLE
Page 17

**STREETS**
Antioch St. ... L7
Aspen Cir. ... K7
Belvidere Rd. ... L7
Big Horn Dr. ... K7
Brittany Ln. ... K8
Buck Dr. ... K8
Caribou Dr. ... L7
Center Dr. ... L7
Christine Ln. ... K8
Deer Crossing Dr. ... K7
Deer Lake Dr. ... K7
Deer Run Dr. ... K8
Deerpoint Dr. ... K8
Deerview Dr. ... K8
Devoe St. ... L7
Elk Ct. ... K7
Emerson Ln. ... K8
Fawn Ln. ... L7
Gage St. ... L7
Hainesville Rd. ... L7
Hall Ct. ... L7
Heritage Tr. ... L7
Hunters Way ... K7
Katherine Dr. ... K8
Lisle Dr. ... L7
Littleton Tr. ... L7
Misty Hill Ln. ... L7
North St. ... L7
Sanctuary Ct. ... K7
White Tail Dr. ... K7

**SCHOOLS**
Hainesville Sch. ... L7

**MISCELLANEOUS**
Avon Township Offices ... K7
Village Hall ... L7

## HALF DAY
Page 33...V13

## HAWTHORN WOODS
Pages 23,24,30-32

**STREETS**
Aberdeen Rd. ... Pg.31 ... T8
Acorn Dr. ... Pg.30 ... U6
Aho Dr. ... Pg.25 ... T9
Albert Cir. ... Pg.31 ... U8
Arrowwonnt Dr ... Pg.30 ... T6
Arthur Ct. ... Pg.31 ... T8
Bagpipe Ct. ... Pg.24 ... T6
Barberry Dr. ... Pg.31 ... T7
Bedford Ct. ... Pg.31 ... U7
Bent Tree Dr. ... Pg.25 ... S5
Bixtone Ln. ... Pg.23 ... T5
Blackhawk Rd. ... Pg.31 ... U8
Blue Jay Ln. ... Pg.24 ... S7
Bluebird Ct. ... Pg.30 ... S7
Bob 'O' Link Dr. ... Pg.31 ... S7
Boxwood Dr. ... Pg.30 ... T6
Briarwoods Ln. ... Pg.30 ... U5
Bridle Path ... Pg.23 ... S6
Brighton Ct. ... Pg.31 ... U9
Bruce Cir., N. ... Pg.31 ... T6
Bruce Cir., S. ... Pg.30 ... U6
Byron Ct. ... Pg.31 ... T8
Cambridge Dr. ... Pg.31 ... T8
Canterbury Ln. ... Pg.31 ... U8
Cardinal Dr. ... Pg.24 ... S7
Carlisle Rd. ... Pg.31 ... T9
Cattail Ct. ... Pg.24 ... T7
Cayuga Ct. ... Pg.25 ... T9
Chancellor Ct. ... Pg.23 ... T6
Chantilly Ln. ... Pg.23 ... T6
Cherry Hill Dr. ... Pg.32 ... U8
Chestnut Ct. ... Pg.31 ... U8
Circle Dr. ... Pg.31 ... U8
Cobblewood Ln. ... Pg.31 ... T8
Condor Ct. ... Pg.31 ... T8
Conesco Ct. ... Pg.25 ... T9
Cooper Ct. ... Pg.24 ... T9
Copperfield Dr. ... Pg.31 ... T6
Croydon Rd. ... Pg.31 ... U8
Darlington Dr. ... Pg.31 ... T8
Dartmouth Ln. ... Pg.31 ... T8
David Ln. ... Pg.24 ... T7
Deer Point Dr. ... Pg.31 ... T7
Derby Ln. ... Pg.24 ... T7
Dorchester Dr. ... Pg.31 ... S6
Dorset Cir. ... Pg.23 ... T6
Durango Ct. ... Pg.31 ... T7
Echo Ct. ... Pg.31 ... U6
Echo Lake Rd. ... Pg.31 ... U6
Edward Ln. ... Pg.31 ... U5
Elderberry Ln. ... Pg.30 ... T6
Elm St. ... Pg.31 ... U6
Elmwood Dr. ... Pg.30 ... U6
Equestrian Way ... Pg.23 ... S6
Essex Ct. ... Pg.31 ... T7
Fairfield Rd. ... Pg.31 ... T7
Falcon Dr. ... Pg.24 ... T7
Falkirk Rd. ... Pg.31 ... T7
Forestview Dr. ... Pg.23 ... T7
Fox Hunt Ct. ... Pg.23 ... S5
Fox Hunt Tr. ... Pg.23 ... S5
Foxtail Rd. ... Pg.31 ... S6
Furlong Dr. ... Pg.23 ... T6
Gentry Dr. ... Pg.23 ... T6
Gilmer Rd. ... Pg.31 ... U8
Gino Ln. ... Pg.32 ... U9
Glen Rd. ... Pg.31 ... U8
Goldfinch Ct. ... Pg.24 ... S7
Governors Way ... Pg.23 ... S6
Greenbriar Ln. ... Pg.32 ... T9
Hampton Ln. ... Pg.31 ... T8
Harvard Ln. ... Pg.31 ... T8
Hawley Rd. ... Pg.24 ... R7
Hawthorn Dr. ... Pg.31 ... U8
Heather Ln. ... Pg.31 ... T8
Heron Ct. ... Pg.24 ... T7
Hickory Rd. ... Pg.31 ... U8
High Point Ct. ... Pg.31 ... T7
High Point Dr. ... Pg.31 ... T7
Highland Terr. ... Pg.31 ... U7
Highview Cir. ... Pg.31 ... T8
Hillcrest Dr. ... Pg.31 ... U8
Hilltop Ct. ... Pg.31 ... T8
Holmes Ave. ... Pg.24 ... T7
Indian Creek Rd. ... Pg.31 ... T8
Iver Point Ct. ... Pg.31 ... T7
James Ct. ... Pg.31 ... T7
James Dr. ... Pg.31 ... U8
Jamie Ln. ... Pg.31 ... U8
Jane Ct. ... Pg.31 ... U8
John Dr. ... Pg.31 ... U8
Joshua Dr. ... Pg.31 ... R7
Juel Cir. ... Pg.31 ... U8
Juel Dr. ... Pg.31 ... U8
Karen Ct. ... Pg.32 ... U9
Kathy Ln. ... Pg.24 ... T7
Kensington Dr. ... Pg.31 ... U8
Keuka Ct. ... Pg.25 ... T9
Kruckenberg Rd. ... Pg.24 ... T7
Kruger Rd. ... Pg.31 ... T7
Lagoon Dr. ... Pg.31 ... U8
Lake View Rd. ... Pg.31 ... U8
Lanceiot Ln. ... Pg.31 ... T7
Lisa Ln. ... Pg.31 ... U5
Lydia Ct. ... Pg.30 ... T6
Lynn Dr., E. & W. ... Pg.31 ... U8
Magnolia Pkwy ... Pg.32 ... U9
Mark Dr. ... Pg.31 ... U8
Mary Ln. ... Pg.32 ... U9
McGregor Ct. ... Pg.31 ... U7
Meadowlark Dr. ... Pg.24 ... S7
Meadowlark Ln. ... Pg.31 ... S7
Middletree Ln. ... Pg.30 ... T6
Midlothian Rd. ... Pg.31 ... U7
Milbrook Dr. ... Pg.31 ... U8
Milton Rd. ... Pg.23 ... S5
Moorgate Tr. ... Pg.23 ... T5-6
Mulberry Dr. ... Pg.31 ... U8
Newbury Ct. ... Pg.31 ... U9
Newhaven Dr. ... Pg.23 ... T6
Newport Dr. ... Pg.31 ... T7
North Trail ... Pg.23 ... S6
Oak Ln. ... Pg.31 ... U8
Old Barn Rd. ... Pg.31,32 ... U9
Old Lake Rd. ... Pg.31 ... T7
Old McHenry Rd. ... Pg.31 ... T7,U8
Oneida Ln. ... Pg.25 ... T9
Onondaga Dr. ... Pg.25 ... T9
Orchard Ln. ... Pg.31 ... U8
Oriole Ct. ... Pg.24 ... S7
Overlook Dr. ... Pg.31 ... T7
Paddock Ct. ... Pg.31 ... U8
Park Pl. Dr. ... Pg.31 ... U8
Park View Ln. ... Pg.31 ... U8
Peregrine Ln. ... Pg.24 ... S7
Pheasant Run ... Pg.23 ... S5
Piper Ln. ... Pg.24 ... T7
Prairie Ct. ... Pg.31 ... R7
Princeton Ct. ... Pg.24 ... T8
Princeton Ln. ... Pg.24 ... T8
Quail Hollow Ct. ... Pg.31 ... U9
Quail Hollow Rd. ... Pg.31 ... U9
Quentin Rd. ... Pg.31 ... V7
Redwood Ln. ... Pg.23 ... T6
Reed Ct. ... Pg.24 ... R7
Regan Ln. ... Pg.31 ... R7
Reserve Ct. ... Pg.31 ... R7
Robert Ct. ... Pg.31 ... U8
Robin Crest Rd. ... Pg.30 ... U6
Rosewood Dr. ... Pg.24 ... T6
Rutgers Ct. ... Pg.31 ... T8
Sandpiper Ln. ... Pg.24 ... S7
Schwerman Rd. ... Pg.24 ... S7
Seneca E. Ave. ... Pg.25 ... T9
Seneca W. Ave. ... Pg.25 ... T9
Sequoia Rd ... Pg.24 ... T8
Shearwater Ct. ... Pg.24 ... S7
Sheridan Ln. ... Pg.24 ... T7
Squire Rd. ... Pg.31 ... T7
St. John Dr. ... Pg.32 ... U9
Starling Ct. ... Pg.31 ... S7
Steeplechase Dr. ... Pg.23 ... S6
Stonehaven Dr. ... Pg.31 ... S7
Sunset Rd. ... Pg.30 ... U6
Sycamore Dr. ... Pg.24 ... S7
Tanglewood Dr. ... Pg.30 ... U5
Tanglewood Ln. ... Pg.30 ... U5
Thornfield Ln. ... Pg.23 ... S5
Trent Rd. ... Pg.31 ... U8
University Cir. ... Pg.31 ... T8 ... X19,20
Victoria Ln. ... Pg.31 ... U8
Wakia Ct. ... Pg.25 ... T9
Wareham Dr. ... Pg.31 ... T8
Washiray Ave. ... Pg.25 ... S9
Waterford Dr. ... Pg.31 ... T7
Wayne Ln. ... Pg.31 ... U5
Wedgewood Dr. ... Pg.31 ... T8
Wellesley Ct. ... Pg.31 ... U7
Westwind Ct. ... Pg.24 ... T6
Whitman Terr. ... Pg.24 ... T7
Wild Way ... Pg.31 ... T7
Winding Branch Rd. ... Pg.23 ... S5
Wooded Ln. ... Pg.25 ... S6
Wren Ln. ... Pg.31 ... T7
Yale Ct. ... Pg.31 ... T8

**GOLF COURSES**
Kemper Lakes G.C. ... Pg.31 ... U8

**PARKS**
Bridlewoods Park ... Pg.23 ... S5
Brierwood Estate Park ... Pg.23 ... T6
Brierwood Park ... Pg.30 ... U6
Community Park ... Pg.24 ... T7
Conservatory of Indian Creek Park ... Pg.24 ... T9
Copperfield Pk. ... Pg.30 ... T6
Heather Highlands Park ... Pg.31 ... U7
Highview Park ... Pg.31 ... U7
Lake Lorraine Park ... Pg.31 ... U7
Rambling Hills Park ... Pg.31 ... U9
The Barn Park ... Pg.31 ... U8
Woodland Park ... Pg.31 ... U8

**SCHOOLS**
Quentin Road Bible Church Sch. ... Pg.31 ... U8
Seth Paine Sch. ... Pg.31 ... U5
St. Matthew Lutheran Sch.

## HIGHLAND PARK
Pages 37,38

**STREETS**
A St. ... Pg.37 ... U19
Acorn Ln. ... Pg.37 ... X19
Alta Ln. ... Pg.37 ... V18
Alvin Pl. ... Pg.38 ... X20
Andean Pl. ... Pg.38 ... W19
Apple Tree Ln. ... Pg.37 ... U18
Applewood Ct. ... Pg.37 ... U18
Applewood Dr. ... Pg.37 ... U18
Arbor Ave. ... Pg.37 ... U19
Arlington Ave. ... Pg.37 ... U18
Ashland Pl. ... Pg.38 ... X21
Aspen Ln. ... Pg.37 ... X19
Aster Ct. ... Pg.37 ... X19
Athletic Field Ln. ... Pg.37 ... V19
Auburn Ave. ... Pg.37 ... U18
Auburn Ct. ... Pg.37 ... U18
Audubon Pl. ... Pg.37 ... U18
Avignon Ct. ... Pg.38 ... X20
B St. ... Pg.37 ... U19
Baldwin Rd. ... Pg.38 ... X20
Balsam Rd. ... Pg.37 ... X19
Barberry Rd. ... Pg.37 ... X19
Barkwood Ct. ... Pg.37 ... X19
Barnard Ln. ... Pg.38 ... X20
Beaupre Ct. ... Pg.37 ... X19
Beech Ln. ... Pg.38 ... W20
Beech St. ... Pg.38 ... W20
Belle Ave. ... Pg.38 ... V20
Bellevue Pl. ... Pg.37 ... V17
Bentley Rd. ... Pg.37 ... X19
Berkeley Rd ... Pg.37 ... W18
Bertram Ln. ... Pg.37 ... X19
Beverly Pl. ... Pg.37 ... W19
Birch Ave. ... Pg.37 ... W19
Birch Ln. ... Pg.37 ... W19
Birchwood Ave. ... Pg.37 ... W19
Birchwood Dr. ... Pg.37 ... U18
Blackhawk Rd. ... Pg.38 ... X21
Blackstone Pl. ... Pg.38 ... X20
Blackwood Ave. ... Pg.37 ... W19
Blossom St. ... Pg.37 ... X19
Blossom Ct. ... Pg.37 ... X19
Bob-O-Link Rd. ... Pg.37 ... W19
Boles Loop ... Pg.35 ... U19
Bordeaux Ct. ... Pg.38 ... X20
Bowstock ... Pg.38 ... X20
Boxer Ct. ... Pg.37 ... V18
Bradley Loop ... Pg.35 ... U19
Braeburn St. ... Pg.38 ... X21
Braeside Rd. ... Pg.38 ... W18
Briar Ln. ... Pg.37 ... X19
Briarcliff Ln. ... Pg.37 ... U18
Briargate Dr. ... Pg.37 ... W19
Briarwood Pl. ... Pg.38 ... X21
Brittany Rd. ... Pg.37 ... W18
Broadview Ave. ... Pg.38 ... X20
Bronson Ln. ... Pg.38 ... X21
Browning Ct. ... Pg.37 ... V17
Brownville Rd. ... Pg.38 ... X21
Buena Rd. ... Pg.37 ... V18
Burchell Ave. ... Pg.37 ... V19
Burlock Ct. ... Pg.37 ... V18
Burr Oaks Ln. ... Pg.37 ... X19
Burton Ave. ... Pg.38 ... X20
Calais Dr. ... Pg.37 ... V17
Calais Dr. ... Pg.37 ... V17
Cambridge Ct. ... Pg.37 ... V18
Cardinal Ln. ... Pg.37 ... X19
Carlyle Terr. ... Pg.38 ... X20
Carol Ct. ... Pg.38 ... X21
Cary Ave. ... Pg.38 ... X21
Castlewood Rd. ... Pg.37 ... W19
Cavell Ave. ... Pg.37 ... V18
Cedar Ave. ... Pg.38 ... W20
Cedar Crest Dr. ... Pg.37 ... W18
Centennial Ct. ... Pg.37 ... U18
Centennial Ln. ... Pg.37 ... U18
Centennial Pkwy. ... Pg.37 ... U18
Central Ct. ... Pg.37 ... W19
Central Ave. ... Pg.38 ... V20
Central Ct. ... Pg.38 ... X20
Chantilly Blvd. ... Pg.37 ... V19
Chantilly Ct. ... Pg.37 ... V19
Chatfield Ct. ... Pg.38 ... X20
Chaucer Ln. ... Pg.38 ... X20
Cherokee Rd. ... Pg.38 ... X21
Cherry Ln. ... Pg.37 ... V19
Chicago Ave. ... Pg.37 ... V19
Churchill St. ... Pg.37 ... V19
Churchill Ln. ... Pg.37 ... V17
Clavey Ln. ... Pg.37 ... V19
Clavey Ln. ... Pg.37 ... V19
Clavey Rd. ... Pg.37,38 ... X19,20
Clifton Ave. ... Pg.37 ... W19
Cloverdale Ave. ... Pg.37 ... W19
College Pl. ... Pg.37 ... U18
Compton Ave. ... Pg.37 ... V18
Comstock Dr. ... Pg.38 ... X21
Concorde Cir. ... Pg.37 ... V19
Concorde Dr. ... Pg.37 ... V19
Cottonwood Ct. ... Pg.37 ... X19
Country Ln. ... Pg.37 ... X19
Coventry Ln. ... Pg.37 ... W19
Crawford Pl. ... Pg.38 ... X20
Crescent Ct. ... Pg.38 ... X20
Crofton Ave. ... Pg.38 ... W,X20
Crofton Ct. ... Pg.38 ... X20
Daffodil Ct. ... Pg.37 ... X19
Dale Ave. ... Pg.37 ... V20
Dato Ave. ... Pg.37 ... V20
Davis Loop ... Pg.35 ... U19
De Tamble Ave. ... Pg.38 ... W20
Dean Ave. ... Pg.38 ... W20
Deel Pl. ... Pg.38 ... X21
Deer Creek Pkwy. ... Pg.37 ... W19
Deere Park Ct. ... Pg.38 ... X21
Deere Park Dr., E. ... Pg.37 ... W19
Deere Park Dr., N., S. & W. ... Pg.37 ... W19
Deerfield Ct. ... Pg.37 ... W19
Deerfield Ln. ... Pg.37 ... W19
Deerfield Pl. ... Pg.37 ... W19
Deerfield Rd. ... Pg.37,38 ... X18,W19
Dell Rd. ... Pg.37 ... W19
Della Rd. ... Pg.38 ... X19
Derrick St. ... Pg.37 ... V18
Devonshire Dr. ... Pg.37 ... W19
Division St. ... Pg.37 ... V19
Driscoll Ct. ... Pg.37 ... V19
Dryden Ln. ... Pg.38 ... X20
E St. ... Pg.37 ... U19
Eastwood Ave. ... Pg.37 ... V18
Eaton Ct. ... Pg.37 ... X19
Edgecliff Dr. ... Pg.37 ... V20
Edgewood Ct. ... Pg.37 ... X19
Edgewood Rd. ... Pg.37,38 ... X19,20
Egandale Rd. ... Pg.38 ... X20
Elder Ln. ... Pg.38 ... X21
Ellridge Cir. ... Pg.37 ... X19
Elm Pl. ... Pg.37 ... V19
Elmwood Dr. ... Pg.37 ... W19
Euclid Ct. ... Pg.37 ... U18
Euclid Ave. ... Pg.37 ... U18
Exmoor Ave. ... Pg.37 ... U19
Exmoor Oaks Dr. ... Pg.37 ... U19
Fairview Rd. ... Pg.37 ... W19
Ferndale Ave. ... Pg.37 ... W18
First St. ... Pg.38 ... W20
Florence Pl. ... Pg.38 ... W20
Forest Ave. ... Pg.38 ... W20
Fredrickson Pl. ... Pg.37 ... W19
Freesia Cir. ... Pg.37 ... X19
Friar Tuck Ave. ... Pg.37 ... X19
Ft. Sheridan Ave. ... Pg.37 ... V19
G St. ... Pg.37 ... U19
Garland Ave. ... Pg.37 ... V19
George Bell Rd. ... Pg.35 ... U19
Glencoe Ave. ... Pg.38 ... W20
Glenview Ave. ... Pg.38 ... V19
Golf Ave. ... Pg.37 ... V19
Gordon Johnston Loop
Grange Ave. ... Pg.37 ... U18
Gray Ave. ... Pg.38 ... W20
Great Elm Ln. ... Pg.37 ... X19
Green Bay Rd. ... Pg.37 ... U,V19
Greenwood Ave. ... Pg.37 ... U19
Grove Ave. ... Pg.37 ... X19
Groveland Ave ... Pg.38 ... W20
H St. ... Pg.37 ... U19
Half Day Rd. ... Pg.37 ... V17
Halsted Ln. ... Pg.38 ... W19
Harvard Ct. ... Pg.37 ... W19
Hastings Ave. ... Pg.38 ... X20
Havenwood Ct. ... Pg.38 ... X20
Hawthorne Ln. ... Pg.38 ... X20
Hawthorne St. ... Pg.37 ... X19
Hazel Ave. ... Pg.38 ... W20
Heather Ln. ... Pg.37 ... X19
Hedge Run Terr. ... Pg.38 ... X21
Hemlock Ln. ... Pg.37 ... X19
Hiawatha Ct. ... Pg.38 ... X20
Hickory Ln. ... Pg.37 ... X19
Hidden Ridge Cir. ... Pg.38 ... W18
Hidden Ridge Ln. ... Pg.38 ... X18
Highland Pl. ... Pg.38 ... W20
Highmoor Rd. ... Pg.37 ... W19
Hilary Ln. ... Pg.37 ... W19
Hill St. ... Pg.37 ... V19
Hillcrest Ave. ... Pg.38 ... W18
Hitchcock St. ... Pg.37 ... W19
Holly Rd. ... Pg.37 ... V18
Homewood Ave. ... Pg.37 ... W19
Huntington Ln. ... Pg.38 ... W18
Hyacinth Pl. ... Pg.37 ... X19
Hybernia Dr. ... Pg.37 ... X19
Idlewood Ln. ... Pg.37 ... U18
Indian Tree Dr. ... Pg.38 ... X21
Iris Ln. ... Pg.37 ... X19
Ivy Ln. ... Pg.37 ... X19
Jasmine Ct. ... Pg.37 ... X19
Johns Ave. ... Pg.37 ... V19
Judson Ave. ... Pg.38 ... V20
Keats Ct. ... Pg.38 ... X20
Keats Ln. ... Pg.37 ... V17
Kelly Ln. ... Pg.37 ... V17
Kent Ave. ... Pg.37 ... V19
Kimball Rd. ... Pg.38 ... W18
Kimballwood Ln. ... Pg.37 ... W19
Kincaid Ave. ... Pg.38 ... X21
Kipling Ct. ... Pg.37 ... V17
Kipling Ln. ... Pg.37 ... V17
Knollwood Ln. ... Pg.38 ... X20
Krenn Ave. ... Pg.37 ... V19
Lake Ave. ... Pg.38 ... V,W20
Lake Spur Dr. ... Pg.38 ... W20,X21
Lakeside Manor Pl. ... Pg.38 ... X21
Lakeside Pl. ... Pg.38 ... X21
Lakespur Dr. ... Pg.37 ... W19
Lakeview ... Pg.37 ... V18
Lakeview Terr. ... Pg.38 ... X21
Lakewood Pl. ... Pg.38 ... X21
Lambert Tree Ave. ... Pg.37 ... W18
Lancelot Ave. ... Pg.37 ... V18
Landon Ln. (Pvt) ... Pg.37 ... V19
Laurel Ave. ... Pg.38 ... X20
Lauretta Pl. ... Pg.37 ... V19
Lawrence Ln. ... Pg.37 ... W19
Leonard Wood Ave. ... Pg.37 ... V19
Leslee Ln. ... Pg.38 ... X20
Lewis Ln. ... Pg.37 ... X19
Lexington St. ... Pg.38 ... V20
Lexington Ln. ... Pg.37 ... V18
Lily Ct. ... Pg.37 ... X19
Lily Ct. ... Pg.38 ... X20
Lincoln Ave. ... Pg.38 ... W20
Lincoln Ave., W. ... Pg.38 ... W20
Lincolnwood Rd. ... Pg.37 ... W19
Linden Ave. ... Pg.38 ... W20
Linden Park Pl. ... Pg.37 ... V19
Little John Ct. ... Pg.37 ... X19
Livingston St. ... Pg.38 ... V20
Llewellyn Ave. ... Pg.37 ... V19
Lorraine Cir. ... Pg.37 ... X19
Lotus Pl. ... Pg.37 ... X19
Lyman Ct. ... Pg.38 ... X20
Lyman Terr. ... Pg.38 ... X20
Lyons Cir. ... Pg.37 ... X19
Magnolia Ln. ... Pg.37 ... X19
Malory Ln. ... Pg.37 ... X19
Maple Ave. ... Pg.38 ... W20
Maple Ln. ... Pg.38 ... W20
Maplewood Rd. ... Pg.37 ... W19
Marl Oak Dr. ... Pg.37 ... X19
Marguerite Rd. ... Pg.38 ... W18
Marshman St. ... Pg.38 ... W18
Marvell Ln. ... Pg.38 ... X20
Mavor Ln. (Pvt.) ... Pg.37 ... W19
McCaskey Rd. ... Pg.38 ... X20
McCraren Rd. ... Pg.37 ... V19
McDaniels Ave. ... Pg.37 ... V19
McGovern St. ... Pg.38 ... W18
McKibben Rd. ... Pg.38 ... X18
Melba Ln. ... Pg.38 ... X20
Melody Ln. ... Pg.38 ... W20
Melvin Dr. ... Pg.38 ... X21
Midland Ave. ... Pg.38 ... W20
Midlothian Ave. ... Pg.37 ... V17
Mill Trail (Pvt.) ... Pg.37 ... W18
Montgomery Ave. ... Pg.38 ... V20
Moraine Rd. ... Pg.37 ... W18
Moseley Rd. ... Pg.38 ... W20
Mulberry Dr. ... Pg.37 ... X19
Museum Dr. ... Pg.37 ... V19
Naida Terr. ... Pg.38 ... X20
Norman Heck Rd. ... Pg.37 ... U19
North Ave. ... Pg.37 ... V18
Northland Ave. ... Pg.37 ... W18
Ny-O-Da Pl. ... Pg.38 ... X20
Oak Knoll Terr. ... Pg.38 ... X21
Oak St. ... Pg.38 ... W20
Oakland Dr. ... Pg.38 ... X21
Oakmont Rd. ... Pg.38 ... W21
Oakvale Rd. ... Pg.38 ... W21
Oakwood Ave. ... Pg.38 ... W20
Old Barn Ln. ... Pg.37 ... W19
Old Deerfield Rd. ... Pg.37 ... W19
Old Briar Rd. ... Pg.37 ... X19
Old Skokie Rd. ... Pg.37 ... V19
Old Trail ... Pg.37 ... X19
Onwentsia Ave. ... Pg.37 ... V19
Orchard Ln. ... Pg.37 ... X19
Orchard Ct. ... Pg.37 ... X19
Orleans Dr. ... Pg.37 ... X19
Oxford Ct. ... Pg.37 ... X19
Park Ave. ... Pg.38 ... V20
Park Ln. ... Pg.38 ... X20
Parkside Dr. ... Pg.37 ... W18
Partridge Ln. ... Pg.37 ... W18
Patten Rd. ... Pg.37 ... X19
Perennial Ln. ... Pg.37 ... X19
Picadilly Rd. ... Pg.37 ... W19
Pierce Rd. ... Pg.38 ... X21
Pine Point Ct. ... Pg.37 ... X19
Pine Point Ln. ... Pg.37 ... X19
Pleasant Ave ... Pg.38 ... V20
Point Ln. ... Pg.37 ... V18
Poplar Rd. ... Pg.37 ... X19
Port Clinton Rd. ... Pg.37 ... X19
Princeton Ave. ... Pg.37 ... W19
Priscilla Ave. ... Pg.37 ... U18
Prospect Ave. ... Pg.38 ... W20
Rambler Ln. ... Pg.38 ... X21
Ravenswood Ave. ... Pg.38 ... X21
Ravine Dr. ... Pg.36 ... W20
Ravine Ct. ... Pg.38 ... X20
Ravine Pl. ... Pg.37 ... V19
Ravine Terr. ... Pg.37 ... V20
Ravinia Park Rd. ... Pg.38 ... W20
Ravinia Rd. ... Pg.38 ... W20
Red Oak Ln. ... Pg.37 ... X19
Rice St. ... Pg.38 ... W20
Richfield Ave. ... Pg.37 ... V19
Ridge Ave. N. ... Pg.37 ... W18
Ridge Grove Ln. ... Pg.37 ... X19
Ridge Rd. ... Pg.37,38 ... V17,W,X19
Ridgelea Rd. ... Pg.38 ... X21
Ridgewood Dr. ... Pg.38 ... W,X20
Ring Ct. ... Pg.37 ... V18
Riparian Rd. ... Pg.38 ... X20
Robin Hood Pl. ... Pg.37 ... W18
Roger Williams Ave. ... Pg.38 ... X20
Rollingwood Rd. ... Pg.37 ... W19
Rosemary Rd. ... Pg.37 ... V18
Rosewood Ln. ... Pg.37 ... W19
Roslyn Cir. ... Pg.37 ... V17
Roslyn Ln. ... Pg.37 ... V17
Russet Ln. ... Pg.37 ... V18
Ryders Ln. ... Pg.37 ... X19
Sandwick Ct. ... Pg.37 ... X19
Sandy Ln. ... Pg.37 ... V17
Sarabel Ln. ... Pg.38 ... X21
Saxony Dr. ... Pg.38 ... W,X20
Saxony Rd. ... Pg.38 ... X20
Second St. ... Pg.37 ... V19
Seven Pines Cir. ... Pg.37 ... X19
Sha Bon Fe Rd. ... Pg.37 ... X19
Sheldon Ln. ... Pg.38 ... W18
Shelly Ct. ... Pg.37 ... V17
Sheridan Ct. ... Pg.37 ... W19
Sheridan Rd. ... Pg.37 ... W19
Sherwood Rd. ... Pg.37 ... X19
Skokie Ave. ... Pg.38 ... X20
Skokie Valley Rd. ... Pg.37 ... V18
Snapdragon Ct. ... Pg.37 ... X19
Southland Ave. ... Pg.37 ... W18
Spruce Ave. ... Pg.37 ... X19
St. Charles Pl. ... Pg.38 ... W18
St. Johns Ave. ... Pg.38 ... V,W20
St. Tropez Ct. ... Pg.38 ... X20
Stonegate Dr. ... Pg.37 ... X19
Stratford Rd. ... Pg.37 ... X19
Strath-Erin ... Pg.37 ... X19
Sumac Rd. ... Pg.37 ... X19
Summerdale Ave. ... Pg.38 ... X20
Summit Ave. ... Pg.37 ... V19
Sundrop Ct. ... Pg.37 ... X19
Sunnyside Ave. ... Pg.38 ... V20
Sunset Ave. ... Pg.37 ... V19
Sunset Rd. ... Pg.38 ... W20
Sycamore Pl. ... Pg.38 ... X20
Sylvester Pl. ... Pg.37 ... V19
Tanglewood Ct. ... Pg.38 ... X20
Taylor Ave. ... Pg.37 ... V19
Temple Ave. ... Pg.37 ... V17
Tennyson Ln. ... Pg.38 ... X20
Thackery Dr. ... Pg.38 ... X21
Thornwood Ln. ... Pg.37 ... X19
Timber Hill Rd. ... Pg.37 ... X19
Trail Way ... Pg.37 ... U18
Trailway ... Pg.37 ... X19
Turnbull Woods Ct. ... Pg.37 ... X19
Turnstile Ln. ... Pg.37 ... X19
Twin Oaks Dr. ... Pg.37 ... X19
U.S. Highway 41 ... Pg.37 ... U18,W19
Underwood Ave. ... Pg.38 ... V20
University Ave. ... Pg.38 ... U18
Valley Rd. ... Pg.37 ... X19
Villas Ct. ... Pg.37 ... V19
Vine Ave. ... Pg.37 ... V19,20
Violet Ct. ... Pg.37 ... X19
Virginia Rd. ... Pg.37 ... X19
Wah-wahtaysee Ave. ... Pg.37 ... W19
Wainwright Ct. ... Pg.38 ... W18
Wake Robin Ln. ... Pg.38 ... X18
Walker Ave. ... Pg.37 ... V19
Walnut St. ... Pg.38 ... W20
Warbler Cir. ... Pg.37 ... X19
Warbler Ln. ... Pg.37 ... X19
Warbler Pl. ... Pg.37 ... X19
Washington Pl. ... Pg.38 ... W18
Watercrest Way ... Pg.37 ... V19
Waterford Ct. ... Pg.37 ... V19
Waveland Ave. ... Pg.38 ... W20
Webster Ave. ... Pg.37 ... V19
West Park Ave. ... Pg.37 ... V18,19
Western Ave. ... Pg.37 ... V19
Western Pl. ... Pg.37 ... V19
Westgate Terr. ... Pg.38 ... X20
Westwood Ct. ... Pg.37 ... V18
White Oak Ln. ... Pg.38 ... W20
Wild Rose Ct. ... Pg.37 ... V18
Wildwood Ln. ... Pg.38 ... X21
Wincanton Ln. ... Pg.38 ... W20
Windsor Rd. ... Pg.37 ... X18
Windy Hill Ln. ... Pg.37 ... X19
Winona Rd. ... Pg.38 ... W20
Winthrop Rd. ... Pg.37 ... X18
Wintruth Ln. ... Pg.37 ... X18
Woodbine Ln. ... Pg.37 ... X19
Woodbine Pl. ... Pg.38 ... X19
Woodland Rd. ... Pg.38 ... V20
Woodleigh Av. ... Pg.37 ... V19
Woodpath ... Pg.37 ... X19
Yager Ave. ... Pg.37 ... W19
Yale Ln. ... Pg.37 ... X19
York Ln. ... Pg.37 ... W18
2nd St. ... Pg.37 ... V19
3rd St. ... Pg.37 ... V19
4th ... Pg.37 ... V19
5th ... Pg.37 ... V19
6th ... Pg.37 ... V19
7th ... Pg.37 ... V19
8th ... Pg.37 ... V19
9th ... Pg.37 ... V19
10th St. ... Pg.37 ... V19
11th St. ... Pg.37 ... V19

**CEMETERIES**
Mooney Cem. ... Pg.37 ... X18

**FOREST PRESERVES**
Berkeley F.P. ... Pg.37 ... W17

**GOLF COURSES**
Bob-O-Link G.C. ... Pg.37 ... X19
Exmoor C.C. ... Pg.37 ... U19
Highland Park C.C. ... Pg.37 ... V19
Northmoor C.C. ... Pg.38 ... X20
Old Elm G.C. ... Pg.37 ... U18
Sunset Valley G.C. ... Pg.37 ... V19

**PARKS**
Arthur Olson Pk. ... Pg.37 ... W18
Brown Park ... Pg.38 ... X20
Buckthorn Park ... Pg.38 ... W18
Buena Park ... Pg.37 ... V18
Centennial Park ... Pg.37 ... U18
Central Park ... Pg.38 ... V20
Cloverdale Park ... Pg.37 ... W19
Deer Creek Courts ... Pg.37 ... X19
Devonshire Park ... Pg.37 ... W19
Fort Clinton Pk. ... Pg.38 ... X20
Grove Park ... Pg.37 ... W19
Highmoor Park ... Pg.37 ... W19
Jens Jensen Park ... Pg.38 ... X20
John F. Kennedy Pk. ... Pg.38 ... X20
Knoll Park ... Pg.38 ... U18
Lake Park ... Pg.38 ... X21
Larry Fink Mem. Pk. ... Pg.37 ... X19
Laurel Park ... Pg.38 ... X20
Leonardi Park ... Pg.37 ... V18
Lincoln Place Park ... Pg.38 ... W20
Longview Park ... Pg.37 ... V18
Manor Park ... Pg.38 ... X18
Millard Park ... Pg.38 ... W20
Moraine Park ... Pg.38 ... V20
Old Elm Pk. ... Pg.37 ... U18
Olson Park ... Pg.37 ... W19
Park District Pk. ... Pg.37 ... U18,X19
Port Clinton Park ... Pg.38 ... X20
Ravinia Park Rd. ... Pg.37 ... V19
Ravinia Festival Park
Red Oak Park ... Pg.37 ... X19
Roger Williams Park
Rosewood Park ... Pg.38
Sleepy Hollow Park ... Pg.37 ... V18
Snyder Park ... Pg.38 ... X20
Sunset Woods Pk. ... Pg.37 ... V19
Walter E. Heller Nature Pk. ... Pg.37
West Ridge Center ... Pg.37 ... X21

**SCHOOLS**
Braeside Sch. ... Pg.38 ... X21
Edgewood Middle Sch. ... Pg.38 ... W20
Elm Place Sch. ... Pg.38 ... W20
Green Bay Rd. Sch. ... Pg.37 ... W19
Highland Park H.S. ... Pg.37 ... W19
Immaculate Conception Sch. ... Pg.37 ... V19
Indian Trail Sch. ... Pg.38 ... X20
John Kennedy Sch. ... Pg.38 ... X20
Lincoln Sch. ... Pg.37 ... V19
North Sub. Bethel Sch. ... Pg.38 ... W21
North Suburban Special Ed. School ... Pg.37 ... X19
Northwood Jr. H.S. ... Pg.37 ... V19
Ravina Sch. ... Pg.38 ... X20
Red Oak Sch. ... Pg.37 ... X19
Sherwood Sch. ... Pg.37 ... X19
Wayne Thomas Sch. ... Pg.37 ... U18

**SHOPPING CENTERS**
Plaza S.C. ... Pg.38 ... W19

**MISCELLANEOUS**
City Hall ... Pg.38 ... W20
Fire & Police Dept. ... Pg.37 ... V19
Highland Park Hosp. ... Pg.38
Historical Museum ... Pg.38 ... V19
Home for the Aged ... Pg.37 ... V19
Karger Recreation Center ... Pg.38
Library ... Pg.38 ... W20
Park District Office ... Pg.37 ... X19
R.R. Stations ... Pg.38 ... X20,21
Swimming Pool ... Pg.38 ... X19
Village Hall & Police Dept. ... Pg.31 ... U18

## HIGHWOOD
Page 35

**STREETS**
Ashland Ave. ... U19
Burchell Ave. ... V19
Burtis Ave. ... V19
Central Ave. ... U,V19
Chapman Rd. ... U19
Chicago Ave. ... V19
Clay St. ... V19
Euclid Ave. ... V19
Everts Pl. ... V19
Evolution Ln. ... V19
Exmoor Ct. ... V19
Funston Ave. ... V19
Green Bay Rd. ... U19
Grove ... V19
Half Day Rd. ... U19
High St. ... V19
Highwood Ave. ... V19
Jeffery Pl. ... V19
Jocelyn Pl. ... V19
Llewellyn Ave. ... V19
Lyster Rd. ... V19
Maple St. ... V19
Mears Pl. ... V19
Michigan Ave. ... V19
Morgan Pl. ... V19
Oak Ave. ... V19
Oak Ridge Ave. ... V19
Oak Terr. ... V19
Palmer Ave. ... V19
Pleasant Pl. ... V19
Robinson Rd. ... V19
Roman Rd. ... V19
Sard Pl. ... V19
Sheridan Ave. ... V19
Summit Ave. ... V19
Thoree Rd. ... V19
Washington Ave. ... V19
Waukegan Ave. ... U19
Webster Ave. ... V19
Western Ave. ... V19
Westover Rd. ... U19
Wrendale ... V19
1st St. ... U19
2nd St. ... U19
3rd St. ... U19
9th St. ... U19

**SCHOOLS**
Oak Terrace Sch. ... V19
St. James Sch. ... V19

**MISCELLANEOUS**
City Hall ... U19
R.R. Stations ... U,V19

## INDIAN CREEK
Pages 25,32

**STREETS**
Circle Dr. ... Pg.32 ... T11
Crestland Rd. ... Pg.32 ... T11
Oakwood Rd. ... Pg.32 ... T11
U.S. Route 45 ... Pg.32 ... T11
Valley Rd. ... Pg.32 ... T11

## INGLESIDE
Page 8...H3

## ISLAND LAKE
Page 22
(For additional listings, see Section 7)

**STREETS**
Arbor Rd. ... Q1
Bassler St. ... Q1
Briar Rd. ... Q1
Brier Ct. ... Q1
Brierhill Dr. ... Q1
Burnett Rd., C ... Q1
Burr Oak Ln. ... Q1
Canterbury Ln. ... Q2
Cardinal Cove ... P1
Cardinal Way ... P1
Carol Circle ... Q1
Carriage Hill Ct. ... Q1
Carriage Hill Rd. ... Q1
Channel Dr. ... Q1
Clover Rd. ... Q1
Constitution Ave. ... Q1
Cottonwood Ct. ... Q1
Country Trail Ct. ... Q1
Countryside Ct. ... Q1
Dorothy Ct. ... Q1
Eastway Dr., N. & S. ... Q1
Elder Dr. ... Q1
Elm Ct. ... Q1
Elm Dr. ... Q1
Ethel Terr. ... Q1
Fairfield Dr. ... Q1
Fern Ct. ... Q1
Fern Dr. ... Q1
Forest Dr. ... Q1
Fox Tr. ... Q1
Greenleaf Ave. ... Q1
Harvard Ct. ... R2
Harvest Ct. ... Q1
Hazel Ct. ... Q1
Highland Ct. ... Q1
Hill Ct. ... R1
Honeysuckle Ln. ... R2
Independence Blvd. ... R2
Ivy Rd. ... Q1
Janet Dr. ... Q1
Judith Dr. ... Q1
Juniper Rd. ... Q1
Kingston Dr. ... Q1
Landsend Ct. ... Q1
Les Cir. Dr. ... Q1
Lilian Ct. ... Q1
Locust Ave. ... Q1
Longacre Ct. ... Q1
Longacre Ln. ... Q1
Madison Ct. ... R2
Mallard Pl. ... Q1
Marion Ct. ... Q1
Midway Dr. ... Q1
Northern Ct. ... Q1
Northern Ter. ... Q1
Oakwood Ave. ... Q1
Park Dr. ... Q1
Poplar Dr. ... Q1
Princeton Ct. ... Q2
Raccoon Cove ... Q1
Ridge Rd. ... Q1
River Oaks St. ... Q1
River Oaks Ln. ... Q1
Rose Ave. ... Q1
Saratoga Cir. ... Q1
Slocum Lake Rd. ... R2
South Shore Dr. ... Q1
Southern Terr. ... Q1
Southhampton Dr. ... R1
Sumac Ave. ... Q1
Timber Ln. ... Q1
Timber Trail ... R1
Westridge Dr. ... Q1
Wishing Well Ln. ... Q1
Wood Creek Dr. ... Q1
Woodbine Ave. ... Q1
Woodland Cir., N. & S. ... Q1
Woodland Dr. ... Q1

**MISCELLANEOUS**
Village Hall & Police Dept. ... Q1

## IVANHOE
Page 24...Q8-9

## KILDEER
Page 31
(For additional listings, see Section 2)

**STREETS**
Abbey Ct. ... W7
Acorn Ct. ... W8
Amberley Dr. ... X8
Amy Ln. ... V8
Andover Rd. ... W8
Barbara Ct. ... W8
Barkley Ct. ... W7
Boschome Dr. ... X8
Brandon Rd. ... W8
Bridle Tr. ... V8
Buffalo Run ... X8
Burning Tree Ct. ... W7
Cambridge Dr. ... W7
Chadwick Ct. ... V8
Chartwell Dr. ... X8
Chesapeake Dr. ... U8
Chestnut Ridge Rd. ... W7
Circle Bay Rd. ... X7
Circle Dr. ... Q17
Clayton Ct. ... V8
Cliffside Dr. ... X8
Concorde Ct. ... X7
Cuba Rd. ... W8
Dallas Ct. ... W8
Dorothea Ct. ... W8
Elder Ct. ... W7
Eleanor Ln. ... V8
Exeter Rd. ... W8
Foxtail Dr. ... V8
Goldfinch Ct. ... W8
Green Wood Dr. ... V8
Grove Dr. ... X8
Hampton Rd. ... W8
Hanaford Ct. ... X7
Hawthorne Ln. ... W7
Heather Ct. ... X8
Herons Ct. ... V8
Hickory Hill Dr. ... W8
Hidden Valley Rd. ... X7
Highwood Rd. ... X7
Hilandale Ct. ... V8
Hilandale Ln. ... V8
Honey Ridge Ct. ... W7
Hopewell Ct. ... W8
Hummingbird Ct. ... W8
Kepwick Ln. ... X8
Kirkley Dr. ... X8
Krueger Rd. ... W8
Lake Zurich Rd. ... W8
Laurel Ln. ... W8
Lexington Ln. ... X8
Linden Ln. ... X8
Little Pond Rd. ... X7
Long Meadow Dr. ... X8
Maple Ct. ... W7
Marcy Ln. ... W8
Meadowlark Ct. ... W8
Meadowlark Dr. ... W8
Meadows Ct. ... X8
Middleton Dr. ... W,X8
Mockingbird Ct. ... W8
Morninggrove Ct. ... W8
Newberry Ct. ... V8
Oak Knoll Ct. ... X8
Oak Trail ... X8
Pine Grove Ct. ... W7
Pine Lake Cir. ... X7
Pine Lake Ct. ... X7
Plumwood Dr. ... X8
Prescott Ct. ... U8
Providence Dr. ... V8
Quail Ct. ... W8
Quentin Rd. ... V7
Rand Rd. ... X8
Rebecca Ln. ... V8
Richmond Ct. ... W8
Ruth Ct. ... V8
Salem Lake Dr. ... V9
Sherley Rd. ... X8
South Rd. ... V8
Stoneybrook Ct. ... W7
Swan Ct. ... W8
Thornridge Dr. ... W7
Timberidge Ct. ... W7
Timberlea Ln. ... W7
Tree Rd. ... X7
Valley Rd. ... X8
Vermont Ct. ... W8
Weatherstone Ct. ... X8
Weatherstone Rd. ... X8
White Pine Rd. ... X7
Williamsburg Ct. ... U8
Willow Dr. ... X8
Wooded Ridge Dr. ... X7
York Ct. ... X8
Yorkshire Dr. ... V,W8

## LAKE BARRINGTON
Pages 22,29,30

**STREETS**
Alice Ln. ... Pg.29 ... U2
Apache Dr. ... Pg.30 ... T4
Apache Path ... Pg.29 ... T3
Arburdour Ct. ... Pg.30 ... T5
Averill Ct. ... Pg.30 ... T5
Bark Ct. ... Pg.29 ... U1
Barrington Rd. ... Pg.29 ... U2
Bay Ct. ... Pg.29 ... T3
Beacon Ct. ... Pg.29 ... U2
Beacon Dr. ... Pg.29 ... U2
Blackhawk Ln. ... Pg.30 ... T4
Blarney Ct. ... Pg.29 ... V1
Bluff Ct. ... Pg.29 ... U3
Bridgewater Ct. ... Pg.29 ... U2
Brookside Ct. ... Pg.29 ... W3
Brookside Way ... Pg.29 ... W3
Buoy Ct. ... Pg.29 ... U2
Casey Ct. ... Pg.29 ... V1
Cayuga Tr. ... Pg.22 ... T2
Cedar Ridge ... Pg.30 ... U4
Center Dr. ... Pg.29 ... T2
Cherokee Dr. ... Pg.30 ... T4
Chesapeake Dr. ... Pg.29 ... V3
Chippewa Ct. ... Pg.29 ... U3
Classic Ct. ... Pg.29 ... W1
Club Cir. ... Pg.30 ... U4
Commercial Ave. ... Pg.29 ... W2
Countryside Ct. ... Pg.22 ... T2
Countryside Dr. ... Pg.22 ... T2
Cove Ct. ... Pg.29 ... U1
Coventry Ct. ... Pg.29 ... U3
Coventry Ln. ... Pg.29 ... U3
Creek Dr. ... Pg.30 ... T4
Crestview Ln. ... Pg.29 ... V2
Cutter Ln. ... Pg.29 ... U1
Deer Trail Ct. ... Pg.29 ... U3
Deer Trail Hill ... Pg.29 ... U3
Dock Dr. ... Pg.29 ... U1
Driftwood Ct. ... Pg.29 ... V2,W3
Dublin Way ... Pg.29 ... V1
East Ln. ... Pg.29 ... V3
Fairview Ct. ... Pg.22 ... S3
Fairway Cir. ... Pg.29 ... U3
Farmview Cir. ... Pg.22 ... S3
Flint Dr. ... Pg.29 ... V2
Flynn Creek Dr. ... Pg.29 ... W2
Foxwood Ln. ... Pg.30 ... U4
Golf Ct. ... Pg.29 ... V3
Golf Ln. ... Pg.29 ... U3
Golfview Ln. ... Pg.29 ... U3
Grandview Dr. ... Pg.30 ... U4
Grayshire Ln. ... Pg.29 ... U3
Greenbriar Ct. ... Pg.22 ... S2
Hallbrath Ct. ... Pg.30 ... T5
Harbor Rd. ... Pg.29 ... U1
Henry Ln. ... Pg.29 ... W2
Hickory Ln. ... Pg.29 ... U3
Hickory Ridge ... Pg.22 ... S2
Hillside Dr. ... Pg.29 ... W1
Hilltop Ct. ... Pg.29 ... U3
Hillview Dr. ... Pg.29 ... W1
Hunt Tr. ... Pg.30 ... U4
Indian Pt. ... Pg.22 ... T3
Indian Trails Rd. ... Pg.22 ... T3
Industrial Ave. ... Pg.29 ... W2
Iroquois Ct. ... Pg.22 ... T2
Island View Ln. ... Pg.29 ... U3
Kazimour Dr. ... Pg.22 ... T2
Kelsey Rd. ... Pg.29 ... U2,V1
Kensington Ct. ... Pg.29 ... U3
Lakeland Dr. ... Pg.29 ... S3
Lakeridge Dr. ... Pg.29 ... V3
Lakeview Dr. ... Pg.29 ... V2
Lakeview Dr., N. & S.
... Pg.22 ... S3
Lakeview Rd. ... Pg.22 ... T2
Linden Dr. ... Pg.29 ... V1
Long Meadow Ct. ... Pg.29 ... U3
Longview Pt. ... Pg.29 ... U3
Mallard Pt. ... Pg.29 ... U3
Meadow Ct. ... Pg.22 ... S3
Meadow Pl. ... Pg.30 ... U4
Medinah Ln. ... Pg.30 ... T4
Miller Rd. ... Pg.29 ... U3
Northwest Hwy.(US 14)
... Pg.29 ... W1
Oak Ct. ... Pg.29 ... V1
Oak Hills Rd. ... Pg.22 ... S2
Old Barn Rd. ... Pg.29 ... U3
Old Barrington Ct. ... Pg.29 ... V2
Old Barrington Rd. ... Pg.29 ... U2
Oneida Ln. ... Pg.22 ... T2
Pawnee Rd. ... Pg.30 ... T4
Pebble Creek Dr. ... Pg.30 ... T4
Pepper Rd. ... Pg.29 ... W2
Pine Cest ... Pg.29 ... U3
River Bay Ct. ... Pg.29 ... U2
River Bend Ct. ... Pg.29 ... U2
River Rd. ... Pg.29 ... U2
River Sand Ct. ... Pg.29 ... T2
River's Bend Dr. ... Pg.29 ... U2
Rolling Green Dr. ... Pg.30 ... T4
Rolling Wood Ct. ... Pg.29 ... U3
Schooner Ln. ... Pg.29 ... U1
Shore Line Rd. ... Pg.29 ... U3
Stonehenge Ln. ... Pg.30 ... T4
Thornhill ... Pg.30 ... U4
Thornhill Ct. ... Pg.30 ... U4
Timber Ridge ... Pg.29 ... U3
Tioga Tr. ... Pg.22 ... T2
Tuscarora Ct. ... Pg.22 ... T2
Twin Pond Rd. ... Pg.22 ... S3
Valley View ... Pg.29 ... U3
Vance ... Pg.29 ... U2
Vista Ln. ... Pg.29 ... V2
Waterview Ct. ... Pg.29 ... U3
Wedgewood Ln. ... Pg.29 ... U3
Wellington Ct. ... Pg.29 ... U3
Welsh Cir. ... Pg.29 ... U1
West Dr. ... Pg.29 ... T3
West Ln. ... Pg.29 ... T3
White Oak Dr. ... Pg.29 ... T3
White Pine Dr. ... Pg.29 ... T3
Wienecke Ct. ... Pg.29 ... V3
Woodland Dr. ... Pg.29 ... V2
Woodridge Ct. ... Pg.29 ... T3
Woodview Rd. ... Pg.29 ... U3
Wynstone Dr., N. ... Pg.30 ... T5

**FOREST PRESERVES**
Grassy Lake F.P. ... Pg.29 ... U3

**GOLF COURSES**
Barrington Shores G.C.
... Pg.29 ... U3
Stonehedge G.C. ... Pg.29 ... V2

**MISCELLANEOUS**
Village Hall ... Pg.29 ... U2

## LAKE BLUFF
Pages 21,27,28

**STREETS**
Albrecht Dr. ... Pg.27 ... Q16
Arbor Ct. ... Pg.28 ... P17
Arbor Dr. ... Pg.28 ... P17,18
Arden Shore Rd. ... Pg.21 ... P18
Arden Shore Rd., S.
... Pg.21 ... P18
Armour Dr. ... Pg.28 ... P17
Ascott Ct. ... Pg.28 ... P17
Ashington Cir. ... Pg.28 ... P17
Bath & Tennis Club Rd.
... Pg.28 ... Q17
Belle Foret Cir. ... Pg.28 ... N19
Belle Foret St. ... Pg.28 ... P17
Birch Rd. ... Pg.28 ... Q18
Birkdale Rd. ... Pg.28 ... Q17
Blodgett Ave. ... Pg.28 ... Q17
Bluff Rd. ... Pg.28 ... Q18
Boardman Ct. ... Pg.28 ... Q18
Bradford Ct. ... Pg.28 ... Q17
Briar Ln. ... Pg.28 ... Q18
Brierfield Ct. ... Pg.28 ... P17
Bristol Ct. ... Pg.28 ... P17
Buckminster Ct. ... Pg.28 ... P17
Cambridge Rd. ... Pg.28 ... Q18
Carlyle Cir. ... Pg.28 ... P17
Coventry Ct. ... Pg.28 ... P17
Crab Tree Ln. ... Pg.28 ... Q17
Cresent Dr. ... Pg.28 ... Q18
Eastway ... Pg.21 ... N18
Eva Terr. ... Pg.28 ... Q17
Evanston Ave. ... Pg.28 ... Q17
Fairhill Dr. ... Pg.28 ... Q18
Forest Cove Rd. ... Pg.28 ... Q18
Forest Hills Rd. ... Pg.28 ... Q18
Foss Ct. ... Pg.28 ... Q18
Fountain Ct. ... Pg.28 ... Q18
Garfield ... Pg.28 ... Q17
Glen Ct. ... Pg.28 ... Q18
Grafton Ct. ... Pg.28 ... P17
Greenwich Ct. ... Pg.28 ... P17
Gurney Ave. ... Pg.28 ... Q18
Haas Cir. ... Pg.21 ... N18
Hamilton Ct. ... Pg.28 ... P17
Hancock Ave. ... Pg.28 ... Q17
Hawthorne Ct. ... Pg.28 ... Q17
Hawthorne Ct., W. ... Pg.28 ... Q17
Hearthrow Ct. ... Pg.28 ... P17
Henrietta ... Pg.28 ... Q17
Hickory Ct. ... Pg.28 ... Q17
Hirst St. ... Pg.28 ... Q18
Indian Rd. ... Pg.28 ... Q18
Inverness Ct. ... Pg.28 ... P17
James Ct. ... Pg.28 ... P17
Kohl Rd. ... Pg.28 ... P17
Lake Ave. ... Pg.28 ... Q18
Lakeland Rd. ... Pg.28 ... Q18
Lancaster Ct. ... Pg.28 ... P17
Leeds Ct. ... Pg.28 ... Q17
Lillian Dells Rd. ... Pg.28 ... Q18
Lincoln Ave. ... Pg.28 ... Q17
Main St. ... Pg.28 ... Q17
Maple Ave. ... Pg.28 ... Q18
Margate Ct. ... Pg.28 ... P17
Market Sq. East ... Pg.28 ... Q16
Market Sq. West ... Pg.28 ... Q16
Marvin Rd. ... Pg.28 ... Q17
Mawman Ave. ... Pg.28 ... Q17
McClaren Ln. ... Pg.28 ... Q17
Moffett Rd. ... Pg.28 ... Q18
Mountain Ave. ... Pg.28 ... Q17
Neuman Ct. ... Pg.28 ... Q18
North Ave. ... Pg.28 ... Q18
Norwich Ct. ... Pg.28 ... P17
Oak Ave. ... Pg.28 ... Q17
Oak Ridge Ct. ... Pg.28 ... N19
Oak Terr. ... Pg.28 ... Q18
Park Ln. ... Pg.28 ... Q17
Park Pl. ... Pg.28 ... Q18
Phillip Ct. ... Pg.28 ... N19,P17
Pine Ct. ... Pg.28 ... Q17
Prospect Ave. ... Pg.28 ... Q18
Prospect Ave., W. ... Pg.28 ... Q17
Railroad ... Pg.28 ... Q17
Ravine Ave. ... Pg.28 ... Q17
Ravine Forest Dr. ... Pg.28 ... Q17
Rebecca Terr. ... Pg.28 ... P17
Ridge Oak Ct. ... Pg.28 ... P17
Rockland Ave. ... Pg.28 ... Q17
Rockland Rd. ... Pg.28 ... Q17
Roselle Terr. ... Pg.28 ... Q17
Rothbury Ct. ... Pg.28 ... P17
Scranton Ave. ... Pg.28 ... Q18
Sheridan Pl., E. & W.
... Pg.28 ... Q17
Sheridan Rd. ... Pg.28 ... Q17
Sherwood Dr. ... Pg.27 ... Q16
Sherwood Terr. ... Pg.27 ... Q16
Shore Acres Dr. ... Pg.28 ... N,P18
Shore Dr., N. ... Pg.27 ... Q16
Signe Ct. ... Pg.28 ... Q17
Simpson Ave. ... Pg.28 ... Q18
Skokie Hwy. ... Pg.28 ... P16
State St. ... Pg.28 ... Q16
Sunrise Ave. ... Pg.28 ... Q18
Sunset Pl. ... Pg.28 ... Q17
Sunset Terr. ... Pg.28 ... Q17
Sylvan Park Rd. ... Pg.28 ... Q18
Thorn Valley Ln. ... Pg.28 ... P17
Thornwood Ln. ... Pg.27 ... Q17
Trowbridge Cir. ... Pg.28 ... P17
Vincent ... Pg.28 ... P17
Walnut Ave. ... Pg.28 ... Q17
Warrington Ct. ... Pg.28 ... P17
Warrington Dr. ... Pg.28 ... P17
Washington Ave. ... Pg.28 ... Q18
Washington St. ... Pg.28 ... Q17
Weatherford Ct. ... Pg.28 ... P17
Wimbledon Ct. ... Pg.28 ... Q17
Wimbledon Rd. ... Pg.28 ... Q17
Winchester Ct. ... Pg.28 ... P17
Witchwood Ln. ... Pg.28 ... Q17-18
Witchwood Ln., W. ... Pg.28 ... Q17
Woodland Rd. ... Pg.28 ... Q18

**FOREST PRESERVES**
Lake Bluff F.P. ... Pg.28 ... Q17

**GOLF COURSES**
Knollwood C.C. ... Pg.28 ... Q15,16
Lake Bluff C.C. ... Pg.28 ... P16,17

**PARKS**
Artesian Lake Pk. ... Pg.28 ... Q17
Lake Park ... Pg.28 ... Q18
Ravine Park ... Pg.28 ... Q18

**SCHOOLS**
Lake Bluff Central Sch.
... Pg.28 ... Q17
Lake Bluff Elem. Sch.
... Pg.28 ... Q17
Lake Bluff Jr. H.S. ... Pg.28 ... Q17

**MISCELLANEOUS**
Childrens Home ... Pg.28 ... Q18
City Hall ... Pg.28 ... Q18

## LAKE FOREST
Pages 27,28,34-36

**STREETS**
Abington Combs Dr.
... Pg.27 ... T16
Academy Rd. ... Pg.27 ... S15
Academy Woods ... Pg.27 ... R15
Ahwahnee Ln. ... Pg.28 ... S17
Ahwahnee Rd. ... Pg.28 ... S17
Alden Ln. ... Pg.28 ... R17
Alison Ln. ... Pg.27 ... R16
Andover Ct. ... Pg.27 ... T15
Arbor Ln. ... Pg.34-35 ... U16
Arcady Dr. ... Pg.34 ... U16
Arlington Combs Dr.
... Pg.27 ... T16
Armour Cir. ... Pg.27 ... S16
Arrowhead Ln. ... Pg.27 ... T16
Ash Lawn Dr. ... Pg.27 ... S16
Ashland Ln. ... Pg.27 ... T15
Ashlawn Dr. ... Pg.27 ... S16
Ashley Rd. ... Pg.28 ... S18
Aspen Dr. ... Pg.34 ... U16
Atteridge Rd. ... Pg.28 ... R17
Bank Ln. ... Pg.28 ... S18
Barat Ct. ... Pg.28 ... S18
Barberry Ln. ... Pg.28 ... R18
Bark Clay Cir. ... Pg.27 ... R16
Barkclay Cir. ... Pg.27 ... R16
Barn Swallow Rd. ... Pg.27 ... T16
Barrys Ct. ... Pg.27 ... T16
Basswood Rd. ... Pg.27 ... T16
Bear Ct. ... Pg.27 ... S16
Berkshire Dr. ... Pg.27 ... S15
Beverly Pl. ... Pg.28,35 ... T18
Big Oak Ct. ... Pg.34-35 ... U16
Birch Ct. ... Pg.28 ... T17
Blackthorn Ln. ... Pg.28 ... T17
Bluff's Edge Dr. ... Pg.28 ... T19
Bluff's Edge Ln. ... Pg.28 ... T18
Bowling Green Dr. ... Pg.34 ... U15
Breckenridge Ave. ... Pg.34,35 ... T17
Breckenridge Ct. ... Pg.35 ... U17
Briar Ln. ... Pg.28 ... T18
Bridgeview Ln. ... Pg.34 ... U16
Bridle Ln. ... Pg.35 ... T17
Broadland Ln. ... Pg.27 ... T15
Broadsmore Dr. ... Pg.35 ... S17
Buena Rd. ... Pg.28,35 ... T17
Burr Oak Rd. ... Pg.28 ... R17
Burton Dr. ... Pg.27 ... S16
Butler Dr. ... Pg.28 ... T17
Carroll Rd. ... Pg.27 ... R16
Cascade Ct., N. & S.
... Pg.34 ... U16
Castlegate Ct. ... Pg.27 ... R16
Cherokee Rd. ... Pg.35 ... T18
Cherry Ave. ... Pg.28 ... S18
Chiltern Dr. ... Pg.28 ... S16
Christina Ln. ... Pg.35 ... U17
Church Rd. ... Pg.28 ... R18
Circle Ln. ... Pg.28 ... T19
Clover Ave. ... Pg.28 ... S17
College Rd. ... Pg.28 ... S18
Concord Dr. ... Pg.27 ... S15
Conway Farms Dr. ... Pg.27,34 ... S,T15
Conway Ln. ... Pg.34 ... T15
Conway Rd. ... Pg.34 ... T16
Cornell Ct. ... Pg.27 ... S15
Country Pl. ... Pg.34 ... T17
Coventry Dr. ... Pg.34 ... T16
Crab Tree Ln. ... Pg.28 ... R18
Crest Ct. ... Pg.35 ... U18
Deerpath Ave. ... Pg.27,28
... S16,R18
Deerpath Sq. ... Pg.27 ... S16
Deerpath Woods ... Pg.27 ... S16
Devonshire Ct. ... Pg.34 ... U15
Devonshire Ln. ... Pg.34 ... U15
Douglas Dr. ... Pg.28 ... T18
Dover Rd. ... Pg.35 ... U17
East Ln. ... Pg.27 ... T15
Edge Field Ln. ... Pg.27 ... T15
Edgecote Ln. ... Pg.28 ... S17
Edgewood Rd. ... Pg.28 ... R18
Efner Ave. ... Pg.28 ... R17-18
Elm Tree Rd. ... Pg.28 ... R18
Elmwood Ave. ... Pg.27 ... R14
Estate Ln., E. ... Pg.34-35 ... U16
Estate Ln. ... Pg.34 ... U15
Estes Ave. ... Pg.34 ... U17
Everett Rd. ... Pg.34 ... T16
Everett School Rd. ... Pg.34 ... U16
Evergreen Dr. ... Pg.34-35 ... U16
Exeter Pl. ... Pg.27 ... S16
Fairview Ave. ... Pg.35 ... T17
Fairway Dr. ... Pg.34 ... T16
Falls Cir. ... Pg.35 ... T17
Farm Rd. ... Pg.34 ... U15
Farnham Ln. ... Pg.35 ... U17
Field Ct. ... Pg.27 ... T15
Field Dr. ... Pg.27 ... T15
Fiore Dr. ... Pg.34 ... U16
Fletcher Cir. ... Pg.27 ... S16
Football Dr. ... Pg.27 ... R15
Forest Ave. ... Pg.28 ... S18
Forest Dr. ... Pg.28 ... R14
Forest Hill Rd. ... Pg.28,35 ... T18
Foster Pl. ... Pg.28 ... T17
Fox Trail Ct. ... Pg.34 ... T16
Franklin Pl. ... Pg.28 ... R17
Franz Dr. ... Pg.34-35 ... U16
Frost Pl. ... Pg.28 ... S18
Gage Ln. ... Pg.28 ... R16
Gavin Ct. ... Pg.27 ... T16
George Bell Rd. ... Pg.35 ... U19
Glenwood Rd. ... Pg.35 ... T18
Gloucester Crossing
... Pg.34 ... U16
Goldenrod Ln. ... Pg.34 ... U16
Golf Ln. ... Pg.28 ... S17,U15
Granby Rd. ... Pg.28 ... R18
Grandview Ln. ... Pg.35 ... U18
Green Bay Rd. ... Pg.28 ... R17,T18
Greenbriar Ln. ... Pg.28 ... S18
Greenleaf Ave. ... Pg.28 ... R18
Greenvale Rd. ... Pg.27 ... S16
Greenview Pl. ... Pg.28 ... S18
Greenway Dr. ... Pg.34 ... T15
Greenwood Ave. ... Pg.35 ... T18
Griffith Rd. ... Pg.28 ... R18
Grove Ct. ... Pg.34 ... U16
Hackberry Ln. ... Pg.34 ... U15
Halligan Cir. ... Pg.27 ... S16
Harlan Ct. ... Pg.35 ... U17
Harlan Ln. ... Pg.35 ... U17
Harvard Ct. ... Pg.27 ... S15
Hastings Rd. ... Pg.28 ... S17
Hathaway Cir. ... Pg.27 ... S16
Havenwood Ln. ... Pg.28 ... T18
Hawkweed Ln. ... Pg.28 ... R17
Hawthorn Dr. ... Pg.27 ... R14
Hawthorne Ave. ... Pg.27 ... R14
Hawthorne Pl. ... Pg.28 ... R18
Heather Ln. ... Pg.28 ... S18
Heritage Ct. ... Pg.34 ... U16
Heron Rd. ... Pg.28 ... T17
Hickory Ct. ... Pg.35 ... T17
High Holborn ... Pg.27 ... S16
Highland Ave. ... Pg.35 ... T17
Highview Terr. ... Pg.28 ... S18
Hilldale Pl. ... Pg.28 ... T18
Holland Ct. ... Pg.28 ... S17
Honeysuckle Rd. ... Pg.28 ... T17
Hospital Dr. ... Pg.27 ... R16
Hunter Ln. ... Pg.28 ... T17
Illinois Rd. ... Pg.28 ... S18
Illinois West Rd. ... Pg.28 ... S17
Inverlieth Rd. ... Pg.27 ... S16
Inverlieth Terr. ... Pg.27 ... S16
Ivy Ct. ... Pg.35 ... T18
Jacqulyn Ln. ... Pg.28 ... T17
James Ct. ... Pg.34 ... U16
James St. ... Pg.34 ... U16
Jennifer Ct. ... Pg.34-35 ... U16
June Terr. ... Pg.28 ... S18
Kajer Ln. ... Pg.35 ... U16
Katheryn Ln. ... Pg.34-35 ... U16
Keith Ln. ... Pg.28 ... T18
Kendler Ct. ... Pg.35 ... T18
Kennedy Rd. ... Pg.28 ... S16
Kennett Ln. ... Pg.34 ... U16
Kennington Terr. ... Pg.28 ... S17
Kimberly Ln. ... Pg.35 ... U17
Kimmer Ct. ... Pg.34 ... U16
King Muir Rd. ... Pg.27 ... S16
Kirk Hill Ln. ... Pg.27 ... R16
Knights Bridge Ct. ... Pg.34 ... T16
Knollwood Cir. ... Pg.27 ... Q16
Knollwood Ln. ... Pg.27 ... Q16
Knollwood Rd. ... Pg.27 ... Q16
Kurtis Ln. ... Pg.34-35 ... U16
Lake Forest Pl. ... Pg.27 ... R16
Lake Forest Place ... Pg.34 ... T16
Lake Lorraine Ln. ... Pg.27 ... R16
Lake Rd. ... Pg.28 ... R18
Lakewood Dr. ... Pg.34 ... T16
Larchmont Ln. ... Pg.27 ... S16
Larkspur Ct. ... Pg.34 ... U16
Laurel Ave. ... Pg.28 ... R17
Lawrence Ave. ... Pg.34 ... U16
Leland Ct. ... Pg.34 ... T16
Lexington Dr. ... Pg.27 ... S16
Linden Ave. ... Pg.35 ... T18
Lindsey Cir. ... Pg.27 ... S15
Littlefield Ct. ... Pg.34 ... U15
Loch Ln. ... Pg.28 ... T19
Longmeadow Ln. ... Pg.27 ... S16
Longwood Dr. ... Pg.27,35
... S14,T18
Louis Ave. ... Pg.35 ... T17
Lowell Ln. ... Pg.34 ... U16
Mallard Ln. ... Pg.28 ... T17
Maple Ct. ... Pg.28 ... S18
Maplewood Rd. ... Pg.28 ... S18
Mar Ln. ... Pg.34 ... T16
Marion Ave. ... Pg.35 ... T17
Market Sq. ... Pg.28 ... S18
Marlane Dr. ... Pg.34 ... T16
Marquette Ct. ... Pg.27 ... S15
Mayflower Rd. ... Pg.28 ... S18
Maywood Rd. ... Pg.28 ... S18
McCormick Dr. ... Pg.28 ... T18
McKinley Rd. ... Pg.28 ... R-S18
Meadow Lake Ln. ... Pg.27 ... T15
Meadow Ln. ... Pg.28 ... R18
Meadowood Dr. ... Pg.27 ... S16
Melody Rd. ... Pg.27 ... S16
Merritt Ln. ... Pg.34 ... V16
Michgamme Ln. ... Pg.28 ... S17
Milburne Rd. ... Pg.35 ... U17
Mills Ct. ... Pg.28 ... R18
Minthaven Rd. ... Pg.34 ... U15
Monticello Cir. ... Pg.27 ... R16
Morningside Dr. ... Pg.35 ... U18
Mt. Vernon Ave. ... Pg.34 ... U17
Nagaunee Ln. ... Pg.28 ... S17
Newcastle Dr. ... Pg.34 ... T16
Nickolson Rd. ... Pg.35 ... U19
Niles Ave. ... Pg.35 ... U17
Noble Ave. ... Pg.28 ... R17
North Ave. ... Pg.35 ... T17
North Cliff Way ... Pg.27 ... S16
North Gate ... Pg.28 ... S18
North Point Dr. ... Pg.27 ... T15
Northcroft Ct. ... Pg.34 ... T17
Northmoor Rd. ... Pg.28 ... S18
O'Leary Ln. ... Pg.27 ... S16
Oak Knoll Dr. ... Pg.27,34,36
... R-T16
Oak Trail Ln. ... Pg.27 ... S16
Oakdale Ave. ... Pg.35 ... T18
Oakwood Ave. ... Pg.28 ... S17-18
Old Barn Ln. ... Pg.34 ... T15
Old Colony Rd. ... Pg.34 ... U17
Old Elm Rd. ... Pg.35,37 ... U17
Old Mill Rd. ... Pg.34 ... U15-16
Overlook Dr. ... Pg.28 ... T19
Owentsia Rd. ... Pg.28 ... R17
Oxford Rd. ... Pg.28 ... R17
Paddock Ln. ... Pg.34 ... U16
Park Ave. ... Pg.28 ... R17
Park Mead Ln. ... Pg.27 ... S16
Parliament Ct. ... Pg.34 ... U15
Pembroke Dr. ... Pg.28 ... S17
Pine Croft Ln. ... Pg.27 ... S16
Pine Ln. ... Pg.28 ... R18
Pine Oak Cir. ... Pg.28 ... T16
Pine Oaks Cir. ... Pg.34 ... T16
Polo Dr. ... Pg.34 ... U17
Poplar Rd. ... Pg.28 ... T17
Prairie Ave. ... Pg.34 ... U17
Prairie View Ln. ... Pg.34 ... T14
Princeton Ct. ... Pg.27 ... S15
Private Rd. ... Pg.28 ... S17,18
Quail Dr. ... Pg.35 ... T17
Ranch Rd. ... Pg.34 ... U15
Ravine Park Dr. ... Pg.28 ... R18
Red Fox Ln. ... Pg.28 ... T17
Regency Ln. ... Pg.27 ... Q16
Reilly Ln. ... Pg.27 ... T16
Ridge Ln. ... Pg.28 ... S17
Ridge Rd. ... Pg.28 ... S-U17
Ridgefield Ln. ... Pg.27 ... T15
Ringwood Rd., N. ... Pg.28 ... S18
Ringwood Rd., S. ... Pg.28 ... T18
Riparian Dr. ... Pg.28 ... T19
Rockefeller Rd. ... Pg.28 ... T18
Rose Terr. ... Pg.28 ... R18
Rosemary Rd. ... Pg.28 ... S18
Rue Foret ... Pg.27 ... S16
Ryan Pl. ... Pg.28 ... S18
Saddle Run ... Pg.28 ... T17
Salisbury Ln. ... Pg.34 ... T15
Sandpiper Ln. ... Pg.28 ... T17
Saunders Rd. ... Pg.27 ... T15
Savana Ct. ... Pg.27 ... S16
Savanna Ct. ... Pg.27 ... S16
Scott St. ... Pg.28 ... R18
Sequoia Ct. ... Pg.28 ... S17
Shawford Way ... Pg.35 ... U17
Shawnee Ln. ... Pg.28 ... S17
Sheffield Ct. ... Pg.34 ... U16
Sheridan Rd. ... Pg.34 ... R-S18
Sir William Ln. ... Pg.34 ... U16
Skokie Hwy. ... Pg.34 ... T16
South Gate ... Pg.28 ... S18
South Meadow Ln. ... Pg.34 ... T15
South Shore Ln. ... Pg.27 ... T15
Spring Ln. ... Pg.28 ... R18
Spruce Ave. ... Pg.28 ... R18
Stable Ln. ... Pg.27 ... T16,17
Stablewood Dr. ... Pg.27 ... T15
Stablewood Ln. ... Pg.27 ... T15
Stanford Ct. ... Pg.27 ... S15
Stockbridge Ct. ... Pg.27 ... T15
Stone Ave. ... Pg.35 ... T17
Stone Gate Ln. ... Pg.28 ... S19
Stone Gate Rd. ... Pg.28 ... S19
Stonebridge Rd. ... Pg.27 ... T16
Stoneleigh Ct. ... Pg.34 ... U15
Stratford Ct. ... Pg.34 ... U15
Suffolk Ln. ... Pg.35 ... U18
Summerfield Dr. ... Pg.27 ... S16
Summit Ave. ... Pg.28 ... R17
Summit Pl. ... Pg.28 ... R17
Sunset Pl. ... Pg.28 ... R17
Surrey Ln. ... Pg.35 ... U17
Sussex Ln. ... Pg.27 ... S16
Symphony Dr. ... Pg.27 ... R16
Tanglewood Ct. ... Pg.27 ... T16
Tara Ln. ... Pg.34 ... U16
Telegraph Rd. ... Pg.34 ... R17
Thomas Pl. ... Pg.28 ... R17
Thorne Ln. ... Pg.28 ... S18
Timber Ln. ... Pg.35 ... T18
Tisbury Ln. ... Pg.27 ... S16
Tiverton Rd. ... Pg.27 ... S16
Town Line Rd. ... Pg.27 ... S15
Tri-State Tollway ... Pg.34 ... U15
Trillium Ln. ... Pg.34 ... U15
Turicum Rd. ... Pg.28 ... T18
Valley Rd. ... Pg.28,35
... T17-18
Vatman Rd. ... Pg.35 ... U19
Verda Ln. ... Pg.27 ... S16
Vine Ave. ... Pg.28 ... S18
Vore Rd. ... Pg.34-35 ... U16
Walden Ln. ... Pg.28 ... T18
Wallace Rd. ... Pg.27 ... T16
Walnut Rd. ... Pg.28 ... S18
Warwick Rd. ... Pg.27,28 ... S16
Washington Cir. ... Pg.28 ... S18
Washington Rd. ... Pg.28 ... S18
Waukegan Rd. ... Pg.27,34 ... S,U16
Waveland Rd. ... Pg.35 ... T18
Wedgewood Ct. ... Pg.34 ... U15
Wedgewood Dr. ... Pg.34 ... U15
West Fork Dr. ... Pg.34 ... U15
Western Ave. ... Pg.28
... R,S17,T18
Westleigh Rd. ... Pg.28 ... T16-18
Westminster Ave. ... Pg.28 ... R17
Westmoreland Rd. ... Pg.28 ... S17
Wharton Dr. ... Pg.34 ... T15
White Oak Rd. ... Pg.34 ... U16
Whitmore Ct. ... Pg.27 ... S16
Wild Rose Ln. ... Pg.34 ... U16
Wildwood Rd. ... Pg.28 ... S18
Willow St. ... Pg.28 ... R18
Wilshire Rd. ... Pg.35 ... U17
Wilson Dr. ... Pg.34 ... U15
Wimbledon Ct. ... Pg.34 ... U15
Windhaven Ct. ... Pg.34 ... U16
Windridge Dr. ... Pg.34 ... U16
Winston Rd. ... Pg.28 ... T18
Winthrop Ln. ... Pg.28 ... R18
Winwood Dr. ... Pg.27 ... R16
Wisconsin Ave. ... Pg.28 ... R17
Woodbine Ln. ... Pg.28 ... R18
Woodbine Pl. ... Pg.28 ... R18
Wooded Ln. ... Pg.28 ... S18
Woodhill Ln. ... Pg.34 ... U16
Woodland Rd. ... Pg.28 ... R17-18
Woodlawn Ave. ... Pg.28 ... S18
Woodridge Dr. ... Pg.34 ... U16
Woodstream Ct. ... Pg.34 ... T17
Woodward Ct. ... Pg.27 ... T15
Yale Ct. ... Pg.27 ... S15
Yore Rd. ... Pg.34 ... U16
Yorktowne Ln. ... Pg.27 ... T16
12th Rd. ... Pg.35 ... U19

**CEMETERIES**
Cemetery ... Pg.35 ... U19
Lake Forest Cem. ... Pg.28 ... R18
St. Mary's Cem. ... Pg.28 ... R18
St. Patrick's Cem. ... Pg.34 ... U16

**FOREST PRESERVES**
Lake County Nature Preserve
... Pg.35 ... T19
Middle Fork Savana F.P.
... Pg.27 ... S16
Prairie Wolf Slough ... Pg.34 ... U17

**GOLF COURSES**
Conway Farms G.C. ... Pg.34 ... T15
Deerpath Golf Course and Park
... Pg.28 ... R-S17
Fort Sheridan G.C. ... Pg.35 ... T19
Knollwood Country Club
... Pg.27 ... Q15
Onwentsia Club ... Pg.28 ... S17

**PARKS**
Buena Park ... Pg.35 ... U17
Deerpath Comm. Play Field
... Pg.28 ... S17
Everett Park ... Pg.34 ... U16
Forest Park ... Pg.28 ... R18
Meadowood Park ... Pg.27 ... R16
Norcroft Park ... Pg.35 ... U17
South Park ... Pg.28 ... S18
Triangle Park ... Pg.28 ... R18
Waveland Park ... Pg.28 ... T18
West Park ... Pg.28 ... R17

**SCHOOLS**
Barat College ... Pg.28 ... T18
Cherokee Sch. ... Pg.35 ... T18
Country Day Sch. ... Pg.18 ... S18
Deerhaven Sch. ... Pg.27 ... R16
Deerpath Intermediate Sch.
... Pg.28 ... S17
Deerpath Jr. H.S. ... Pg.28 ... S17
Everett Sch. ... Pg.34 ... U16
Ferry Hall Sch. for Girls
... Pg.28 ... S19
Gorton Sch. ... Pg.28 ... S18
Lake Forest Academy
... Pg.27 ... S15
Lake Forest College ... Pg.28 ... S18
Lake Forest H.S. East Campus
... Pg.28 ... R18
Lake Forest H.S. West Campus
... Pg.27 ... S16
Lake Forest Intermediate Sch.
... Pg.27 ... T16
Sheridan Sch. ... Pg.28 ... R18
St. Mary's Sch. ... Pg.28 ... R18
The Grove Sch. ... Pg.35 ... U17
Woodlands Academy of the
Sacred Heart ... Pg.28 ... T18

**MISCELLANEOUS**
Chicago Bears Football Club
... Pg.27 ... R15
City Hall ... Pg.28 ... R17
Compost Center ... Pg.27 ... S16
Havenwood Franciscan Fathers
... Pg.28 ... S18
Lake Forest Fitness Center
... Pg.27 ... R16
Lake Forest Hosp. ... Pg.28 ... R16
Lake Forest Oasis ... Pg.27 ... S15
Metra Station ... Pg.34 ... T16
R.R. Stations ... Pg.28,34
... R18,U16
Recreation Center ... Pg.28 ... S17
West Side Fire Station
... Pg.34 ... T16

## LAKE VILLA
Pages 2,3,9,10

**STREETS**
Alpine Ct. ... Pg.9 ... F5
Amber Ln. ... Pg.9 ... F5
Amherst Dr. ... Pg.10 ... F7
Apache Tr. ... Pg.9 ... F6
Arapaho Tr. ... Pg.10 ... E7
Baxter Ct. ... Pg.3 ... D7
Belmont Ave. ... Pg.10 ... E7
Blackberry Ln. ... Pg.9 ... G5
Blackstone Ct. ... Pg.3 ... D7
Boardwalk ... Pg.10 ... F7
Bradford Ct. ... Pg.10 ... E7
Breeze Rd., S., E. & W.
... Pg.9 ... F6
Briar Ridge Ln. ... Pg.10 ... F7
Brooking Ct. ... Pg.3 ... D7
Burnett Ave. ... Pg.10 ... E6-7
Carlyle Ct. ... Pg.3 ... D7
Cedar Ave. ... Pg.10 ... E6
Cedar Lake Ave., N. ... Pg.2 ... E6
Cedarwood Dr. ... Pg.9 ... G5
Central Ave. ... Pg.10 ... E6
Charlton Ct. ... Pg.10 ... F7
Charlton Rd. ... Pg.10 ... F7
Chelsea Cir. ... Pg.10 ... F6
Cherokee Ln. ... Pg.9 ... F5
Clayton Ave. ... Pg.10 ... E7
Clearview Ln. ... Pg.3 ... D7
Cleveland Ave. ... Pg.9 ... E6
Corona Dr. ... Pg.10 ... F8
Coventry Cove Ln. ... Pg.10 ... F6
Crabapple Dr. ... Pg.2 ... D5
Crabtree Ln. ... Pg.9 ... G5
Cremin Dr. ... Pg.10 ... E7
Deep Lake Rd. ... Pg.3 ... D7
Dellwood Ave. ... Pg.9 ... E,F6
Fairway Dr. ... Pg.2 ... D5
Farmhill Ct. ... Pg.10 ... F7
Farmhill Ln. ... Pg.10 ... F7
Fieldstone Ct. ... Pg.10 ... F7
Fieldstone Dr. ... Pg.10 ... F7
Frontage Rd. ... Pg.2 ... E6
Grace Ln. ... Pg.9 ... F5
Grand Ave. ... Pg.10 ... E7
Grass Lake Rd. ... Pg.3 ... D7
Haidi Ln. ... Pg.9 ... F5
Hampton Dr. ... Pg.10 ... F7
Harbor Ridge ... Pg.2 ... D5
Hazelwood Dr. ... Pg.9 ... G5
Hubbard Ln. ... Pg.3 ... D7
Huntington Cir. ... Pg.10 ... F7
Indian Ridge Ln. ... Pg.10 ... F7
Juniper Way ... Pg.10 ... F7
Kenz Ct. ... Pg.10 ... E7
Kevin Ave. ... Pg.10 ... F6
Lake Ave. ... Pg.10 ... E6
Lake Shore Dr. ... Pg.2 ... E6
Larch Way ... Pg.10 ... F7
Laurie Ct. ... Pg.9 ... F6
Lincoln Dr. ... Pg.9 ... F4
Majestic Ln. ... Pg.9 ... F5
McKenzie Ct. ... Pg.10 ... D7
McKinley Ave. ... Pg.10 ... E6
Meadowview Ct. ... Pg.10 ... F7
Milwaukee Ave. ... Pg.3 ... E6
Monaville Rd. ... Pg.9 ... F6
Monica Dr. ... Pg.10 ... F7
Nes Perce Dr. ... Pg.9 ... F5
North Ave. ... Pg.2 ... E6
Northwind Dr. ... Pg.9 ... F6
Oak Knoll Dr. ... Pg.9 ... F6
Oak Ln. ... Pg.9 ... F6
Oakton Ln. ... Pg.10 ... F7
Oakwood Ave. ... Pg.9 ... F6
Overlook Ct. ... Pg.10 ... F7
Painted Lakes Blvd. ... Pg.3 ... D7
Painted Lakes Ct. ... Pg.3 ... D7
Park Ave. ... Pg.10 ... F7
Petite Lake Rd. ... Pg.9 ... K6
Pine View Pass ... Pg.10 ... F7
Private Rd. ... Pg.2 ... E6
Rae Ave. ... Pg.2 ... E6
Rainy Lakes Ct. ... Pg.3 ... D7
Red Spruce Tr. ... Pg.10 ... F7
Rosemont Ln. ... Pg.2 ... E6
Rosselle Ct. ... Pg.10 ... F7
Rushing Ct. ... Pg.10 ... D7
Savanna Springs Dr.
... Pg.10 ... F7
Saxon Dr. ... Pg.9 ... F5
Sheeham Dr. ... Pg.10 ... F7
Sherwood Ave. ... Pg.10 ... E6
Shore Dr., N. ... Pg.2 ... E6
Shoshoni Tr. ... Pg.10 ... E7
Southwind Ct. ... Pg.9 ... F6
Southwind Dr. ... Pg.9 ... F6
Stonebridge Dr. ... Pg.2 ... D5
Summerfield Dr. ... Pg.9 ... F4
Summit Ct. ... Pg.10 ... F7
Sun Lake Rd. ... Pg.3 ... D7
Sun Lakes Ct. ... Pg.3 ... D7
Tallgrass Ln. ... Pg.10 ... F6
Twin Oaks Dr. ... Pg.2 ... E6
Tyler Ct. ... Pg.10 ... F7
Villa Ave. ... Pg.10 ... E7
Walden Ln. ... Pg.10 ... F6
Waterbury Cir. ... Pg.10 ... F6
Waters Edge Dr. ... Pg.10 ... F7
Wesley Ave. ... Pg.10 ... E6
White Pine Ln. ... Pg.10 ... F7
Winchester Ct. ... Pg.3 ... D7
Winchester Ln. ... Pg.3 ... D7
Winddance Ct. ... Pg.9 ... F6
Winddance Dr. ... Pg.9,10 ... F6,7
Woodhead Dr. ... Pg.10 ... E7
Woodhill Ct. ... Pg.10 ... F7
Woodhill Ln. ... Pg.10 ... F7

**CEMETERIES**
Angola Cem. ... Pg.10 ... F7

**FOREST PRESERVES**
Sun Lake Forest Preserve
... Pg.3 ... D7

**SCHOOLS**
Allendale Sch. ... Pg.9 ... E6
Calvary Christian Sch.
... Pg.9 ... F6
Intermediate Sch. ... Pg.10 ... F7
Pleviak Sch. ... Pg.10 ... E7
Prince of Peace Sch.
... Pg.10 ... E7
Round Lake H.S. ... Pg.9 ... K6

**MISCELLANEOUS**
Lake Villa Library ... Pg.9 ... E8
Railroad Station ... Pg.9 ... E6
Village Hall ... Pg.9 ... E6

## LAKE VILLA TOWNSHIP
Pages 2,3,9-11

**STREETS**
Academy Blvd. ... Pg.9 ... E4
Academy Dr. ... Pg.9 ... E4
Albert Ave. ... Pg.9 ... F5
Alice Ln. ... Pg.10 ... F8
Alpine Ct. ... Pg.9 ... F5
Alpine Ln. ... Pg.9 ... F5
Anderle Ave. ... Pg.3 ... E8
Antonio Ave. ... Pg.10 ... F8

**LAKE VILLA TOWNSHIP**

Apollo Ct. ......... Pg.2 ... D6
Arcade Dr., N. & S. Pg.9 .. F4
Ardmore Ln. ...... Pg.9 .... E5
Ash Ave. .......... Pg.9 .... E8
Avon Dr. .......... Pg.9 .... F4
Aztec Ct. .......... Pg.9 .... D5
Balboa Dr. ........ Pg.2 .... D5
Bald Eagle Rd. .... Pg.9 .... F4
Bay Shore Rd. ..... Pg.9 .... F4
Beach Ave. ........ Pg.2 .... D5
Beck Rd. ..... Pg.9,10 ... E8
Belmoral Park ..... Pg.2 .... E6
Black Cherry Ln. .. Pg.9 .... G5
Blackstone Pl. ..... Pg.9 .... F4
Brentwood Ln. ..... Pg.9 .... D7,8
Buena Ave. ........ Pg.9 .... E4
Busse Ln. ......... Pg.9 .... F4
Caine Rd. ......... Pg.9 .... G5
Capilo Ave. ....... Pg.10 ... F8
Carol Ln. ......... Pg.10 ... F4
Carson Dr. ........ Pg.9 .... F4
Cedar Ave. ........ Pg.2 .... F4
Cedar Crest Ln. ... Pg.9 .... F4
Cedar Lake Rd. .... Pg.9 .... F6
Cedar Lake Way ... Pg.9 .... F4
Cedar Valley Dr. .. Pg.9 .... F5
Cedarwood Dr. .... Pg.9 .... F7
Central Ave. ...... Pg.9 .... E6
Chesney St. ....... Pg.9 .... E4
Christiansen Ave. . Pg.10 .. E8
Columbia Bay Dr. . Pg.9 .... F7-8
Columbia Bay Dr., N. Pg.9 . E4

Columbus Ave. .... Pg.9 .... F9
Corona Dr. ........ Pg.9 .... F4
Cortey Dr. ........ Pg.2 .... D5
Crabapple Dr. ..... Pg.2 .... D5
Crabtree Ln. ...... Pg.9 .... G5
Cremana Ave. ..... Pg.10 ... G8
Deep Lake Rd. .... Pg.3 .... D7
Dering Ln. ........ Pg.9 .... E5
Diana Ave. ........ Pg.9 .... F5
Douglas Ln. ....... Pg.10 ... F5
Eagle Ct. .......... Pg.9 .... F4
Eastmoor Ave. .... Pg.9 .... F5
Edgewood Ave. ... Pg.10 ... E7
Edward Ave. ...... Pg.10 ... F-G8
Elizabeth Ct. ...... Pg.9 .... F4
Elizabeth Dr. ...... Pg.10 ... F-G7
Elm Ave. .......... Pg.2 .... D5
Elm St. ............ Pg.3 .... E8
Engle Rd. ......... Pg.9 .... F7-8
Entrance Dr. ...... Pg.9 .... E4
Fairfield Rd. ...... Pg.9 .... E-G5
Fairview Ave. ..... Pg.9 .... F4
Fairview Ct. ....... Pg.9 .... F4
Fairway Dr. ....... Pg.10 ... V5
Fox Tr. ............ Pg.10 ... F8
Garcia Dr. ......... Pg.10 ... F8
Gelden Ln. ........ Pg.3 .... D8
Gelden Ct. ........ Pg.3 .... D8
Genoa Ave. ....... Pg.10 ... F8
George Ct. ........ Pg.10 ... F7
Gillian Rd. ........ Pg.2 .... E5
Glade Dr. ......... Pg.9 .... F4
Glen Lake Rd. ..... Pg.2 .... D5
Glen Lake Rd. ..... Pg.9 .... F6
Golf Ln. ........... Pg.2 .... D5
Granada Blvd. ..... Pg.9 .... F4
Grand Ave. ... Pg.9,11 E5,F4,9
Grand Blvd. ....... Pg.9 .... E9-10
Grass Lake Rd. .... Pg.4 .... E9-10
Gratton Rd. ... Pg.10,13 .. E7
Harding Ave. ...... Pg.9 .... F4
Harlem Ave. ....... Pg.9 .... F4
Harbor Ridge Dr. .. Pg.2 .... D5
Harold Ct. ........ Pg.10 ... G8
Helen Ct. ......... Pg.10 ... F-G7
Helen Dr. ......... Pg.10 ... F-G7
Hickory St. ........ Pg.3 .... D8
Highwood Ave. .... Pg.2 .... D5
Highwoods Dr. .... Pg.2 .... D5
Hilda Ave. ........ Pg.10 ... F-G8
Hill Ct. ............ Pg.9 .... K5
Hillside Ave. ...... Pg.9 .... D8
Honey Ln. ......... Pg.9 .... E4
Inca Ln. ........... Pg.2 .... D5
Isola Ave. ......... Pg.10 ... F9
James Ct. ......... Pg.10 ... G8
James Dr. ......... Pg.10 ... F-G7
Kelly Rd. .......... Pg.4 .... D10
Lake Ave. ......... Pg.2,3 .. E6,8
Lake Shore Dr. ... Pg.2,9 .. E6,F4
Lakeview Ct. ...... Pg.9 .... F4
Lakeview Dr. ... Pg.2,9,10
Lakeview Ln. ...... Pg.9 .... D5,F4,8
Lakewood Ave. .... Pg.2 .... E6
Laurel St. ......... Pg.3 .... D7
Lawrence Ct. ...... Pg.9 .... F4
Lawrence Dr. ...... Pg.10 ... F-G7
Lehmann Blvd. .... Pg.9 .... F4
Liberty Ave. ....... Pg.2 .... D5
Lincoln Dr. ........ Pg.9 .... F4
Linda Ln. .......... Pg.2 .... D5
Linden Ave. ....... Pg.3 .... D7
Loon Lake Rd. .... Pg.3 .... D7
Loretto Ave. ...... Pg.10 ... F8
Maple Ave. ... Pg.3,9 .. F8
Marilyn Ln. ....... Pg.10 ... F-G8
Mary Ct. .......... Pg.10 ... F-G8
Mary Dr. .......... Pg.10 ... F8
Merriwood Ln. .... Pg.10 ... H7
Milburn Rd. ...... Pg.4 .... D-E10
Miller Rd. ......... Pg.2 .... D5
Milwaukee Ave. Pg.2,10 D6,F7
Montaville Rd. .... Pg.10 ... F6,G7
Montrose Dr. ...... Pg.2 .... F4
Morey Ln. ......... Pg.9 .... G5
Morton Dr. ........ Pg.10 ... F7-8
Munn Rd. ......... Pg.2 .... D5
Nathan Hale Dr., N. Pg.10 . F4
Nathan Hale Dr., S. Pg.9 .. F4
Newberry Ln. ..... Pg.9 .... F4
Nicklaus Way ...... Pg.2 .... D5
Nielson Ave. ...... Pg.10 ... F8
Nielson Dr. ........ Pg.10 ... F8
Normandy Ave. ... Pg.10 ... F-G8
North Ave. ........ Pg.3 .... E6
North Rd. ......... Pg.2 .... D5
North Way Ave. ... Pg.2 .... E6
Oak Ave. ...... Pg.2,3 .. D5,E8
Oak Creek Ln. .... Pg.9 .... D8
Oak Dr. ........... Pg.2 .... D5
Oakwood Dr. ...... Pg.9 .... D8
Obermaier Ln. .... Pg.9 .... D5
Paradise Dr. ...... Pg.9 .... D5
Park Ave. ...... Pg.2,10 D5,G8

Park Ave., W. ..... Pg.2 .... E6
Park Ct. .......... Pg.2 .... E6
Park Dr. .......... Pg.9 .... G7
Park Forest Ave. .. Pg.10 ... G9
Park Ln. .......... Pg.2 .... D5
Park Ln., E. & W. .. Pg.9 .... F4
Parma Ave. ....... Pg.10 ... F4
Peninsula Rd. ..... Pg.2 .... D5
Petite Ct. ......... Pg.2 .... D5
Petite Lake Rd. ... Pg.2 .... D5-6
Petite Terr. ....... Pg.2 .... D5
Pine St. ........... Pg.3 .... E7
Piper Ln. .......... Pg.9 .... F4
Ponce Ave. ........ Pg.10 ... G7
Poplar St. ......... Pg.3 .... D,E7
Prairie View Dr. ... Pg.1 .... F8
Raska Ln. ......... Pg.2 .... D5
Ravine Ave. ....... Pg.2 .... D5
Ravine Crest Dr. .. Pg.2 .... D5
Ravine Ct. ........ Pg.2 .... D5
Ravine Dr. ........ Pg.2 .... D5
Richard Ln. ....... Pg.9 .... F7
Riviera Dr. ........ Pg.10 ... F8
Romeroa Ave. .... Pg.9 .... D5
Rose Ave. ......... Pg.9 .... E5
Rose Ct. .......... Pg.9 .... F7
Rustic Dr. ......... Pg.3 .... D8
San Rem .......... Pg.10 ... F8
Sand Lake Rd. .... Pg.11 ... F10
Sarah Dr. ......... Pg.10 ... F7-8
Savage Rd. ........ Pg.3 .... D8
Saxony Dr. ........ Pg.9 .... F5
Sheridan Rd. ...... Pg.9 .... F4
Sistina Ave. ....... Pg.10 ... G8
Short St. .......... Pg.9 .... F4
Sienna Dr. ........ Pg.9 .... F9
Sunset Ln. ........ Pg.2 .... E4
South Ave. ........ Pg.9 .... D5
South Dr. ......... Pg.2 .... D5
Spruce St. ........ Pg.3 .... D7
St. John Dr. ....... Pg.2 .... D5
Stonebridge Ct. ... Pg.9 .... D5
Stonebridge Dr. ... Pg.2 .... D5
Summerfield Dr. .. Pg.9 .... E7
Sunnyside ......... Pg.2 .... E4
Sunset Ln. ........ Pg.2 .... E4
Sunshine Ave. .... Pg.10 ... F8
Terry Ave. ........ Pg.10 ... F8
Terry Dr. .......... Pg.10 ... F7
Thorndale Pl. ..... Pg.9 .... F4
Timber Ln. ........ Pg.9 .... F4
Trenker Rd. ....... Pg.2 .... D5
Valina Ave. ....... Pg.2 .... F4
Verona Ave. ...... Pg.10 ... F8-9
Villa Ct. ........... Pg.3 .... E7
Villa Dr. ........... Pg.3 .... E7
Wacker Dr. ........ Pg.9 .... F7
Wall St. ........... Pg.10 ... F8
Walnut Ave. ...... Pg.3 .... D7
Washington Ave. .. Pg.2 .... E5
Wayside Pl. ....... Pg.9 .... F4
West Dr. .......... Pg.3 .... D8
Westmoor Ave. ... Pg.9 .... D5
Wildwood Dr. ..... Pg.10 ... G8
Willow St. ........ Pg.3 .... E8
Wilton Way ....... Pg.2 .... E6
Winthrop Pl. ...... Pg.9 .... E4
Wittenberg Rd. ... Pg.3 .... D8
Woodland Ave. ... Pg.10 ... F4
Woodland Terr. ... Pg.9 .... F4
Woods Ave. ....... Pg.3 .... E7
1st St. ............ Pg.3,10 . F7
2nd St. ........... Pg.3,10 . C7
3rd St. ........... Pg.3 .... E7
4th St. ............ Pg.9 .... F4
5th St. ............ Pg.9 .... F4
5th St. ............ Pg.1 .... F7
6th St. ............ Pg.9 .... F4
7th Ave. .......... Pg.3 .... E7

CEMETERIES
Angolian Cemetery Pg.10 ... F7
Fox Lake Cemetery Pg.9 .... F5
Home Oaks Cemetery
........................ Pg.3 .... D7
Sand Lake Cem. .. Pg.10 ... E8

FOREST PRESERVES
Duck Hill Farm F.P. Pg.9 ... F8
Fourth Lake F.P. ... Pg.9 .... F8
Grant Woods F.P. .. Pg.9 .... F5
McDonald Woods F.P.
........................ Pg.11 ... E9
Sun Lake F.P. ..... Pg.3 .... D7

SCHOOLS
Gavin North Elem. Sch.
Oakland Sch. ...... Pg.3 .... D7

MISCELLANEOUS
Antioch Township Offices
........................ Pg.2 .... D6

**LAKE ZURICH**

Pages 30,31
STREETS
Aldine Rd. ........ Pg.30 ... U5
Alpine Dr. ......... Pg.30 ... U5
Amherst Ct. ....... Pg.30 ... W7
Andrew Ln. ....... Pg.30 ... V8
Apache Ct. ........ Pg.30 ... V6
Applegate Cir. .... Pg.30 ... W5
Applegate Ln. .... Pg.30 ... V5
Ascot Ct. .......... Pg.30 ... V6
Ash Ave. .......... Pg.30 ... V6
Ash St. ............ Pg.30 ... V6
Bayview Dr. ....... Pg.30 ... V5
Beach Dr. ......... Pg.30 ... V5
Beaubien Ct. ...... Pg.30 ... U6
Beauteau St. ...... Pg.30 ... V7
Beechwood Dr. ... Pg.30 ... W6
Berkley Rd. ....... Pg.30 ... V7
Berkshire ......... Pg.30 ... V6
Bern Ct. ........... Pg.30 ... U6
Betty Dr. .......... Pg.30 ... V5
Black Twig Cir. ... Pg.30 ... W5
Braemer Ln. ...... Pg.30 ... W5
Breckenridge Dr. . Pg.30 ... U6
Briar Point ........ Pg.30 ... V8
Bristol Trail Rd. ... Pg.30 ... W7
Brittany Rd. ....... Pg.30 ... W7
Broadway Ct. ..... Pg.30 ... W7
Brookfield Ct. ..... Pg.30 ... V6
Browning Ln. ..... Pg.30 ... V6
Brush Hill Ct. ..... Pg.30 ... V8
Buckingham Ct. ... Pg.30 ... W7
Buesching Rd. .... Pg.30 ... V6
Buffalo Gr. Rd. .... Pg.30 ... V6
Burr Oak Ct. ...... Pg.30 ... V6
Burr Oak Dr. ...... Pg.30 ... V6
Bushrun Ct. ....... Pg.30 ... W5
Butterfield Ln. .... Pg.30 ... U5
Carolyn Ct. ........ Pg.30 ... V6

Carriage ........... Pg.30 ... V5
Cedar Creek Dr. .. Pg.30 ... V7
Cedar St. .......... Pg.30 ... V6
Centoni Dr. ....... Pg.30 ... V5
Century Ct. ........ Pg.30 ... W5
Chancery Ln. ...... Pg.30 ... W6
Chasewood Dr. ... Pg.30 ... W6
Cherokee Rd. ..... Pg.30 ... V7
Chesterfield Ln. ... Pg.30 ... W6
Cheswick Ln. ...... Pg.30 ... U5
Chris Ct. .......... Pg.30 ... U5
Church St. ......... Pg.30 ... U5
Clearwater Ct. .... Pg.30 ... X7
Club House Ln. ... Pg.30 ... V6
Colonial Ct. ....... Pg.30 ... W5
Columbine Ct. .... Pg.30 ... W6
Coral Reef Way ... Pg.30 ... X6
Courtland Ct. ..... Pg.30 ... V6
Courtland Dr. ..... Pg.30 ... V6
Craig Terr. ........ Pg.30 ... V6
Crescent Rd. ...... Pg.30 ... W5
Cromwell Ct. ...... Pg.30 ... W6
Crystal Springs ... Pg.30 ... W6
Cuba Rd. .......... Pg.30 ... V5
Cypress Bridge Rd. Pg.30 . X6
Danvera Ln. ....... Pg.30 ... U7
Dearborn Ct. ...... Pg.30 ... VR
Deerchase Rd. .... Pg.30 ... W6
Deerpath Rd. ...... Pg.30 ... W6
Denberry Ct. ...... Pg.30 ... V6
Denberry Dr. ...... Pg.30 ... V6
Denise Rd. ........ Pg.30 ... V6
Donegal Ln. ....... Pg.30 ... V5
Dunwick Ct. ....... Pg.30 ... W5
Eastman Rd. ...... Pg.30 ... V7
Eddy Ln. ........... Pg.30 ... X6
Ela Rd. ............ Pg.30 ... W5
Elm Pl. ............ Pg.30 ... W5
Enterprise Pkwy. .. Pg.30 ... U5
Eric Ct. ............ Pg.30 ... W7
Eric Ln. ............ Pg.30 ... W7
Evanston Terr. .... Pg.30 ... U5
Evergreen St. ..... Pg.30 ... V6
Fairway Rd. ....... Pg.30 ... V5
Farm Bridge Rd. .. Pg.30 ... V7
Ferdare Ct. ........ Pg.30 ... V7
Fern Ct. ........... Pg.30 ... V7
Fern Dr. ........... Pg.30 ... V7
Fescue Ct. ......... Pg.30 ... V5
Fescue Dr. ......... Pg.30 ... V5
Fieldstone Dr. ..... Pg.30 ... W6
Forest Ave. ........ Pg.30 ... V6
Foxfire Ct. ......... Pg.30 ... W6
Foxfire Dr. ......... Pg.30 ... W6
Foxmoor Ln. ...... Pg.30 ... W7
Franson Ct. ........ Pg.30 ... U7
Garland Ct. ........ Pg.30 ... V7
Genesee St. ....... Pg.30 ... V6
Ginger Ln. ......... Pg.30 ... V8
Glen Farm Ln. .... Pg.30 ... V7
Glencoe Terr. ..... Pg.30 ... U5
Golf View Rd. ..... Pg.30 ... U5
Greenbay Ct. ...... Pg.30 ... W7
Grethe Ct., N. & S. Pg.30 . W7
Grever Ct. ......... Pg.30 ... W6
Grove St. .......... Pg.30 ... V6
Hampshire Ln. .... Pg.30 ... U5
Harbor Dr., E. ..... Pg.30 ... X6
Harbor Dr., N., S. & W. Pg.30 X6
Harvest Dr. ........ Pg.30 ... W7
Heartwood Ln. .... Pg.30 ... V7
Hickory Rd. ....... Pg.30 ... V6
Hidden Creek Rd. . Pg.30 ... V7
Highlands Ct. ...... Pg.30 ... V6
Hillside Ct. ........ Pg.30 ... V6
Hillside Dr. ........ Pg.30 ... T8
Hobbie Bush Dr. .. Pg.30 ... V7
Hollycourt Terr. ... Pg.30 ... U5
Honey Lake Rd. ... Pg.30 ... F5
Hunters Ln. ....... Pg.30 ... V5
Huntington Ct. .... Pg.30 ... W7
Huntington Way ... Pg.30 ... W7
Indigo Ct. ......... Pg.30 ... W4
Interlaken Dr. ..... Pg.30 ... W6
Ironwood Ct. ...... Pg.30 ... V6
Ivy Ct. ............. Pg.30 ... W7
Jamia Ln. .......... Pg.30 ... W7
Jean Terr. ......... Pg.30 ... U5
Joan Rd. ........... Pg.30 ... V5
Johnathan Rd. .... Pg.30 ... U5
Joyce Ln. .......... Pg.30 ... W5
June Terr. .......... Pg.30 ... U5
Juneway Terr. ..... Pg.30 ... U5
Kaplin St. .......... Pg.30 ... V6
Kenilworth Terr. .. Pg.30 ... U5
Kim Trail ........... Pg.30 ... V5
Kingwood Ln. ..... Pg.30 ... V7
Knox Park St. ..... Pg.30 ... V6
Kylenore Dr. ...... Pg.30 ... W6
Lake St. ........... Pg.30 ... V6
Lake Forest Rd. ... Pg.30 ... V5
Lakeview Pl. ....... Pg.30 ... V5
Lancaster Ln. ...... Pg.30 ... U5
Lexington Ln. ..... Pg.30 ... W7
Linden Rd. ........ Pg.30 ... U5
Lions Dr. .......... Pg.30 ... V5
Lismore Ct. ....... Pg.30 ... V6
Lorraine Ct. ....... Pg.30 ... U5
Main St. ........... Pg.30 ... V6
Manchester Ct. ... Pg.30 ... U5
Manchester St. ... Pg.30 ... U5
Manor Rd. ........ Pg.30 ... U5
March Ct. .......... Pg.30 ... W7
Marble Hill Dr. .... Pg.30 ... V7
March St. .......... Pg.30 ... V7
Marcus Ct. ........ Pg.30 ... U7
Meadow Ave. ..... Pg.30 ... W6
Meadow Brook Ct. Pg.30 . U6
Meadow Brook Ln. Pg.30 . U6
Meadow Ln. ....... Pg.30 ... U6
Midlothian Rd. .... Pg.30 ... U6
Millbrook Dr. ...... Pg.30 ... V7
Miller Rd. .......... Pg.30 ... U5
Mionske Dr. ....... Pg.30 ... U6
Mohawk Trail Ln. . Pg.30 ... V7
Newgate Ct. ....... Pg.30 ... W7
North County Ridge Rd. Pg.30 W6
Northcrest Rd. .... Pg.30 ... W6
O'Malley Ct. ....... Pg.30 ... W7
O'Malley Dr. ....... Pg.30 ... W7
Oak St. ............ Pg.30 ... V6
Oakwood Rd. ..... Pg.30 ... W6
Old Mill Grove Rd. Pg.30 . W-V7
Old Hard Rd. ...... Pg.30 ... V5
Old Rand Rd., N. . Pg.30 ... V6
Old Rand Rd., S. . Pg.30 ... V6
Orrington Ct. ...... Pg.30 ... W7
Oxford Ct. ......... Pg.30 ... W7
Oxford Ln. ......... Pg.30 ... W7

Paine St. .......... Pg.30 ... V6
Pamela Rd. ....... Pg.30 ... V5
Park Ave. ......... Pg.30 ... V6
Parkway Ave. ..... Pg.30 ... V6
Partridge Ln. ...... Pg.30 ... W5
Peachtree Ln. ..... Pg.30 ... W6
Pearlman Dr. ...... Pg.30 ... U7
Pebble Creek Dr. . Pg.30 ... V7
Pembridge Rd. .... Pg.30 ... W7
Peter's Ct. ........ Pg.30 ... U7
Pheasant Ridge Dr. Pg.30 W6-7
Pine Ave. ......... Pg.30 ... V6
Pine Tree Run ..... Pg.30 ... U5
Pleasant Rd. ...... Pg.30 ... U5
Pleasant Ridge Ct. Pg.30 . W7
Pohlman Ct. ....... Pg.30 ... U6
Portren Ln. ........ Pg.30 ... U7
Potowatomie St. . Pg.30 ... V6
Prairie Crossings .. Pg.30 ... V6
Prairie Ln. ......... Pg.30 ... V6
Prospect Rd. ...... Pg.30 ... U6
Queen Anne Ln. . Pg.30 ... W6
Quentin Rd. ....... Pg.30 ... W7
Racine Ct. ......... Pg.30 ... U6
Ramblewood Ct. . Pg.30 ... W6
Ramblewood Ln. . Pg.30 ... W6
Rand Rd. .......... Pg.30 ... V6
Ravenswood Ct. .. Pg.30 ... W7
Redline Terr. ...... Pg.30 ... VR
Red Bridge Ct. .... Pg.30 ... W,V7
Red Bridge Rd. ... Pg.30 ... W,V7
Red Haw Ln. ...... Pg.30 ... V6
Regency Dr. ....... Pg.30 ... W5
Regent Ct. ......... Pg.30 ... U5
Richmond Cir. ..... Pg.30 ... W5
Richmond Ct. ..... Pg.30 ... W5
Ridgewood Ct. .... Pg.30 ... V7
Ripple Brook Ct. .. Pg.30 ... W6
Robertson Ave. ... Pg.30 ... V6
Rock Rose Dr. ..... Pg.30 ... W6
Rodgers Ct. ....... Pg.30 ... U7
Rodgers Ln. ....... Pg.30 ... U7
Rose Rd. .......... Pg.30 ... V7
Rugby Rd. ......... Pg.30 ... U5
Russel Cir. ......... Pg.30 ... W5
Sandlewood Ct. .. Pg.30 ... W7
Sandy Ln. ......... Pg.30 ... V5
Schiller St. ........ Pg.30 ... U6
Schuldt Dr. ........ Pg.30 ... U6
Sedgwick Ct. ...... Pg.30 ... V8
Shaker Ln. ......... Pg.30 ... W7
Shallow Cove Rd. . Pg.30 ... X6
Sheffield Ct. ....... Pg.30 ... V5
Sheridan Ct. ....... Pg.30 ... V7
Shore Ln. S. ....... Pg.30 ... U5
Shore View ........ Pg.30 ... V5
Silverwood Ct. .... Pg.30 ... W6
South County Ridge Ct. Pg.30 W6
Spring Ct. .......... Pg.30 ... W6
Spruce St. ......... Pg.30 ... V6
Stanton Ct. ........ Pg.30 ... V7
Stanton Rd. ....... Pg.30 ... V7
Stillwater Ct. ...... Pg.30 ... W7
Stone Ave. ......... Pg.30 ... V7
Stratford Ct. ...... Pg.30 ... V7
Stratford Ln. ...... Pg.30 ... V7
Sugartree Ct. ...... Pg.30 ... V7
Summit Dr. ........ Pg.30 ... U5-6
Summit Terr. ...... Pg.30 ... U5
Sunrise Ln. ........ Pg.30 ... V6
Sunset Dr. ......... Pg.30 ... V6
Surryse Rd. ....... Pg.30 ... W6
Sussex Ct. ......... Pg.30 ... W7
Tall Grass Cir. ..... Pg.30 ... W6
Tara Ct. ........... Pg.30 ... W6
Telsel Rd. .......... Pg.30 ... V7
Terrace Ave. ...... Pg.30 ... W5
Thistle Ln. ......... Pg.30 ... V7
Thorndale Ct. ..... Pg.30 ... V7
Thorndale Ln. ..... Pg.30 ... V7
Timberwood ...... Pg.30 ... W7
Towne Mall Dr. ... Pg.30 ... V6
Trailside Dr. ....... Pg.30 ... W5
Trillium Tr. ......... Pg.30 ... W7
Tudor Ct. .......... Pg.30 ... W5
Turtle Pond Dr. ... Pg.30 ... W6
View Rd. ........... Pg.30 ... U5
Village Dr. ......... Pg.30 ... U5
Village Rd. ........ Pg.30 ... U5
Warwick Ct. ....... Pg.30 ... V6
Warwick Ln. ....... Pg.30 ... V6
Washo Cir. ........ Pg.30 ... V6
Washo Ct. ......... Pg.30 ... V6
Washo Ln. ......... Pg.30 ... V6
Waterbury Ct. ..... Pg.30 ... V7
Waterford Dr. ..... Pg.30 ... V7
Waterford Pl. ...... Pg.30 ... V7
White Birch Ln. ... Pg.30 ... V7
Whitehall Ct. ...... Pg.30 ... V7
Whitney Rd. ....... Pg.30 ... V5
Wilkes Ct. ......... Pg.30 ... W6
William Dr. ........ Pg.30 ... V7
Willmer Terr. ...... Pg.30 ... V5
Wilmette Terr. .... Pg.30 ... V5
Windemere Ln. ... Pg.30 ... V5
Winnetka Terr. .... Pg.30 ... V5
Woodbine Ctr. .... Pg.30 ... W6
Yorkshire Ln. ...... Pg.30 ... W7
Zurikh Dr. ......... Pg.30 ... V5

CEMETERIES
Lake Zurich Cem. . Pg.30 ... V6

GOLF COURSES
Lake Zurich G.C. .. Pg.30 ... U5

PARKS
Braemar Park ..... Pg.30 ... W5
Bristol Trails Park . Pg.30 ... V7
Chestnut Corners Park Pg.30 X7
Countryside West Park Pg.30 X7
Countryside West Soccer Field X7
Kuechmann Park . Pg.30 ... V6
Lions Park ......... Pg.30 ... V6
Manor Park ........ Pg.30 ... V5
North Athletic Field Pg.30 ... V6
Oak Ridge Marsh Nature Park V6
Paulus Park ........ Pg.30 ... V6
Quail Run Park .... Pg.30 ... W7
Sandlewood Park . Pg.30 ... W7
Sparrow Ridge Park Pg.30 ... W5
Warwick Park ...... Pg.30 ... V6
Zurites Field ....... Pg.30 ... V5

SCHOOLS
Isaac Fox Elem. Sch. Pg.30 . W6
Lake Zurich H.S. .. Pg.30 ... V7
Lake Zurich Middle Sch. South V6
Saint Adams Sch. Pg.30 ... W7
Seth Pine Sch. .... Pg.30 ... U5
St. Francis De Sales Sch. ... U7
Whitney Sch. ...... Pg.30 ... V7

MISCELLANEOUS
Kit's Sports Complex ...... Pg.30 V6

**LIBERTYVILLE**

Richard Staples Youth Sports
  Complex ......................... W7
The Barn Recreation Office ... V5
Village Hall ...................... V6

**LAKEMOOR**
Page 15
(For additional listings,
see Section 7)
STREETS
Bakers Ct. ................ L1
Beacon Bay .............. L1
Blacksmith St. ........... L1
Buoy ..................... L1
Captains Cove ........... L1
Carriage Way ............ M1
Concrete Dr. ............. L2
Darrell Rd. ............... M1
Dry Dock ................. L1
Fishook ................... L1
Fox Lake Rd. ............. M2
Gilmer Rd. ............... L1
Honeysuckle Ct. ........ M1
Hornblower .............. M1
Leaward .................. L1
McNally Ln. .............. M2
Mysty Ridge ............. L1
Neptune Cove ........... L1
Oyster Bay ............... L1
Portside .................. L1
Prairieview Ln. .......... M1
Rusty Scupper ........... L1
Sandbar .................. L1
Sandpiper ............... L1
Sawmill Ln. .............. L1
Shady Grove Ct. ......... L1
Sinker Bay ............... L1
South Lake Shore Dr. .. L2
Spring Creek Ct. ........ M1
Stowaway Bay .......... L1
Sullivan Lake Blvd. ..... L,M2
Sullivan Lake Rd. ....... L2
Wagon Trail Ct. ......... M1
Wagon Trail Rd. ........ M1
Wegner Rd. .............. M1
Windward ............... L1

**LAMBS CORNER**
Page 12....G12

**LIBERTYVILLE**
Pages 18,19,25,26
STREETS
Abbey Ct. .......... Pg.18 ... P11
Acorn Ln. .......... Pg.26 ... Q12
Adler Dr. ........... Pg.18 ... N12
American Way ..... Pg.18 ... P10
Ames St. .......... Pg.26 ... Q11
Amy Ln. ........... Pg.26 ... P11
Annie Ln. .......... Pg.18 ... P11
Apple Tree Pkwy. .. Pg.26 ... R13
Appley Ave. ....... Pg.26 ... R13
Arbor Ct. .......... Pg.26 ... Q13
Ardmore Terr. ..... Pg.26 ... R13
Artaius Pkwy. ..... Pg.26 ... R13
Arthur Ave. ........ Pg.26 ... R13
Ascot Ct. .......... Pg.26 ... R13
Ash St. ............ Pg.26 ... P13
Ashbury Ln. ....... Pg.26 ... Q13
Ashley Ln. ......... Pg.26 ... Q13
Austin Ave. ........ Pg.26 ... R13
Bartlett Terr. ....... Pg.26 ... P13
Bedford Ln. ....... Pg.25 ... Q11
Bell Ln. ............ Pg.25 ... Q11
Blackberry Ct. ..... Pg.18 ... N11
Blackburn Cir. ..... Pg.26 ... P11
Blueberry Hill Rd. . Pg.25 ... Q11
Brainard Ave. ..... Pg.26 ... P10
Brandywine Rd. ... Pg.25 ... Q11
Brian Cir. .......... Pg.18 ... N11
Briar Pl. ........... Pg.26 ... P13
Briarwood Ln. ..... Pg.26 ... R13
Bridle Ct. .......... Pg.26 ... R13
Broadway St. ...... Pg.26 ... P13
Buckingham Pl. ... Pg.26 ... R13
Buckley Rd. ....... Pg.19 ... N13
Burdick St. ......... Pg.26 ... P13
Burridge Ct. ....... Pg.26 ... Q13
Bush Ct. ........... Pg.18 ... N11
Butterfield Ln. ..... Pg.26 ... Q13
Butterfield Rd. ..... Pg.26 ... Q13
Caliente Ct. ........ Pg.18 ... N11
Cambridge Dr. .... Pg.26 ... Q13
Camelot Ln. ....... Pg.26 ... R13
Canterbury Ct. .... Pg.26 ... Q13
Carriage Hill Dr. ... Pg.19 ... Q13
Carter St. .......... Pg.26 ... P13
Cass Ave. .......... Pg.19 ... N12
Cass Ct. ........... Pg.26 ... P13
Catalpa Ln. ........ Pg.26 ... Q13
Chatham Ct. ....... Pg.26 ... R13
Checkerberry Ct. .. Pg.18 ... N11
Church St. ......... Pg.26 ... P13
Circle Dr. .......... Pg.26 ... Q13
Cleveland Ave. .... Pg.26 ... R13
Commerce Dr. ..... Pg.18 ... P12
Concord Ln. ....... Pg.18 ... Q14
Cook Ave. ......... Pg.26 ... Q12
Coolidge Ave. ..... Pg.26 ... P13
Coolidge Pl. ....... Pg.26 ... Q13
Country Club Dr. .. Pg.19 ... N12
Crabtree Ln. ....... Pg.26 ... R13
Crane Blvd. ........ Pg.26 ... R13
Crestfield Ave. ..... Pg.26 ... R13
Cypress Ln. ........ Pg.26 ... R13
Dancer Ct. ......... Pg.26 ... R13
Dawes St. .......... Pg.26 ... Q-R12
Deborah Ct. ....... Pg.18 ... N11
Dever Ct. .......... Pg.25 ... Q11
Douglas Ave. ...... Pg.26 ... P13
Dover Ct. ....... Pg.25,26 Q12
Downing Rd. ...... Pg.25 ... Q11
Downs Pkwy. ...... Pg.26 ... R13
Drake St. .......... Pg.26 ... Q12
Dymond Ave. ..... Pg.26 ... R13
Dymond Rd. ....... Pg.26 ... R13
Easy St. ............ Pg.25 ... Q11
Eaton Ct. .......... Pg.26 ... R13
Elderberry Dr. ..... Pg.18 ... N11
Ellis Ave. .......... Pg.26 ... P13
Ellis Ave., E. ....... Pg.26 ... R13
Ely Ln. ............. Pg.26 ... R13
Emerson Ln. ....... Pg.26 ... R13
Enterprise Dr. ...... Pg.18 ... N10
Eric Ln. ............ Pg.18 ... P12
Eston Ct. ........... Pg.26 ... Q13
Evergreen Ct. ...... Pg.26 ... P13
Fairlawn Ave. ...... Pg.26 ... P13
Fairview Ave. ...... Pg.26 ... P11
Flamingo Pkwy. ... Pg.26 ... R13

Florence Ave. ...... Pg.26 ... Q12
Florsheim Dr. ...... Pg.26 ... R13
Forest Ln. .......... Pg.26 ... P12
Forever Ave. ....... Pg.18 ... P11
Furlong Dr. ........ Pg.26 ... R13
Furlong Dr., E. ..... Pg.26 ... Q13
Garfield Ave. ...... Pg.26 .. Q12,13,R12
Glendale Rd. ....... Pg.26 ... Q12,13
Golf Ct. ............ Pg.26 ... Q12,13
Golf Rd. ........... Pg.26 ... Q12,13
Gracewood Dr. .... Pg.26 ... R13
Grant Ct. .......... Pg.26 ... P13
Greentree Pkwy. .. Pg.26 ... R13
Gulf Stream Pkwy. Pg.26 ... R13
Hackberry Ct. ..... Pg.18 ... N11
Hampton Terr. ..... Pg.26 ... P13
Harding Ave. ...... Pg.26 ... P13
Harms Ave. ........ Pg.26 ... Q11
Harris Rd. .......... Pg.18 ... N10
Harrison St. ........ Pg.26 ... Q13
Harvard Ln. ........ Pg.26 ... R13
Havenwood Dr. ... Pg.26 ... Q12
Hayes Ave. ......... Pg.26 ... Q12
Hemlock Ln. ....... Pg.26 ... Q11
Highgate Ct. ....... Pg.26 ... Q11
Hillcrest Dr. ........ Pg.25 ... Q11
Homefort Dr. ...... Pg.26 ... Q12
Homewood Dr. .... Pg.26 ... Q12
Hunter Ln. ......... Pg.26 ... R13
Hurlburt Dr. ....... Pg.26 ... Q12
Industrial Dr. ...... Pg.18 ... N10
Innsbruck Ct. ...... Pg.25 ... P11
Interlaken Ct. ...... Pg.25 ... P11
Interlaken Ln. ...... Pg.25 ... P11
Jackson Ave. ...... Pg.26 ... Q12
Jaimee Ln. ......... Pg.18 ... N11
James Ct. .......... Pg.26 ... R13
Jaimee Ln. ......... Pg.25 ... P11
Jeremy Ln. ........ Pg.18,26 P12
Johnson Ave. ...... Pg.26 ... P12
Joslyn Ct. .......... Pg.26 ... N11
Julie Ln. ........... Pg.18 ... N11
Juliet Cir. .......... Pg.18 ... P11
Juniper Pkwy. ..... Pg.26 ... R13
Juniper St. ......... Pg.26 ... P12
Kempton Dr. ....... Pg.26 ... R13
Kenloch Ave. ...... Pg.25 ... Q11
Kenwood Ave. .... Pg.25 ... Q11
Kildare Ave. ....... Pg.26 ... R13
Kristen Dr. ......... Pg.18 ... P11
Lake Shore Dr., N. . Pg.25 ... Q11
Lake St. ............ Pg.25 ... P11-P12
Lange Ct. .......... Pg.26 ... P12
Laurel Ave. ........ Pg.26 ... P12
Liberty Bell Ln. .... Pg.26 ... P13
Liberty Lake Dr. ... Pg.26 ... P13
Lilac Ct. ........... Pg.26 ... R12
Lincoln Ave. ....... Pg.26 ... Q12,13
Linden Ln. ......... Pg.26 ... Q12
Lingonberry Ct. ... Pg.18 ... N11
Lisa Ct. ............ Pg.18 ... N11
Loatonia Ct. ....... Pg.26 ... R13
Lothair Dr. ......... Pg.25 ... P11
Loyola Dr. ......... Pg.26 ... P11
Magnolia Ln. ...... Pg.26 ... R12
Maple Ave. ........ Pg.26 ... P13
Margate Ln. ....... Pg.26 ... Q13
Mayfair Dr. ........ Pg.26 ... Q13
Maywood Ct. ...... Pg.26 ... Q12
McKinley Ave. ..... Pg.26 ... P13
Meadow Ln. ....... Pg.26 ... Q13
Merill Ct. .......... Pg.26 ... Q12
Michaels Ln. ....... Pg.26 ... R13
Midlothian Rd. ..... Pg.18 ... P10
Mill Ct. ............ Pg.26 ... Q13
Miller Ct. .......... Pg.26 ... P12
Milwaukee Ave. ... Pg.26 ... Q13
Minear Dr. ......... Pg.26 ... P11
Mulberry Dr. ....... Pg.18 ... N11
Mullady Pkwy. .... Pg.26 ... P11
Nathan Ln. ........ Pg.18 ... P11
Newberry Ave. .... Pg.26 ... P13
Newgate Ct. ....... Pg.26 ... R13
Nita Ln. ........... Pg.18 ... P11
Nordic Ct. ......... Pg.25 ... P11
North Ave. ......... Pg.26 ... P13
Oak I. n. ........... Pg.26 ... Q13
Oak Spring Rd. .... Pg.25 ... Q11
Oak St. ............ Pg.26 ... P13
Oak Trail Dr. ....... Pg.26 ... R13
Old Barn Cir. ...... Pg.18 ... N11
Old Buckley Rd. ... Pg.18 ... N12
Old Hickory Ln. .... Pg.26 ... P13
Opal Dr. ........... Pg.26 ... P12
Orchard Ct. ........ Pg.26 ... P13
Oxford Ct. ......... Pg.18 ... N11
Oxford Pl. ......... Pg.26 ... R13
Paddock Ct. ....... Pg.26 ... R13
Paddock Ln. ....... Pg.26 ... R13
Paradise Ln. ....... Pg.25 ... Q11
Park Ave. .......... Pg.26 ... P11
Park Ave., W. ...... Pg.26 ... P11
Park Pl. ........... Pg.26 ... Q13
Parkview Dr. ....... Pg.17 ... P12
Parliament St. ..... Pg.26 ... R13
Paul Revere Ln. ... Pg.26 ... P13
Pembrooke Rd. ... Pg.26 ... R13
Peterson Rd. ...... Pg.18 ... N10
Pimlico Pkwy. ..... Pg.26 ... R13
Pine Meadow Dr. . Pg.25 ... P11
Pine Meadow Ln. . Pg.25 ... P11
Pine Tree Ln. ...... Pg.25 ... Q11
Pleasant Dr. ....... Pg.18 ... N11
Pondridge Rd. ..... Pg.26 ... R13
Poplar Ct. ......... Pg.26 ... P13
Portwine Dr. ....... Pg.25 ... Q11
Prairie Ave. ........ Pg.26 ... Q12
Quaker Hill Ln. .... Pg.18 ... N11
Red Top Dr. ....... Pg.26 ... R13
Regency Ln. ....... Pg.26 ... R13
Ridgeway Ln. ...... Pg.26 ... R13
Ridgewood Ln. .... Pg.26 ... R13
Riva Ridge Dr. ..... Pg.26 ... R13
Riverside Dr. ....... Pg.26 ... P12
Rockland Ave. ..... Pg.26 ... Q12
Rockland Rd. ...... Pg.26 ... P12
Romeo Ct. ......... Pg.18 ... P11
Roosevelt Dr. ...... Pg.26 ... R13
Rosewood Terr. ... Pg.26 ... R13
Ruidoso Ct. ........ Pg.26 ... R13
Sandstone Dr. ..... Pg.26 ... R13
Saxon Ln. ......... Pg.26 ... Q12
School St. ......... Pg.26 ... P13
Second Ave. ....... Pg.26 ... P11
Sedgwick Dr. ...... Pg.26 ... R13
Shari Ln. .......... Pg.18 ... P11
Springhaven Dr. ... Pg.26 ... R13
Spruce Ln. ......... Pg.26 ... R12

St. James Pl. ...... Pg.25 ... P11
St. William Dr. ..... Pg.25 ... P11
Stevenson Dr. ..... Pg.25 ... Q11
Stewart Ave. ...... Pg.26 ... P13
Stonegate Ct. ..... Pg.26 ... P12
Stonegate Rd. ..... Pg.26 ... P12
Suffolk Ct. ......... Pg.26 ... R13
Sunnyside Ave. .... Pg.26 ... Q13
Sunnyside Pl. ...... Pg.26 ... Q12
Sunnyview Rd. .... Pg.18 ... N11
Sunset Dr. ......... Pg.26 ... P12
Sussex Ln. ......... Pg.18 ... P11
Tall Tree Terr. ...... Pg.26 ... P12
Tamarack Ln. ...... Pg.26 ... R13
Technology Way ... Pg.18,25 P10
Thomas Ct. ........ Pg.25 ... P11
Thornapple Ln. .... Pg.26 ... P14
Thornbury Ln. ..... Pg.26 ... R13
Tiffany Ln. ......... Pg.18 ... N11
Tracy Ln. .......... Pg.26 ... R12
Trevor Cir. ......... Pg.18 ... P11
Trinity Pl. .......... Pg.18 ... P11
Tyler Ct. ........... Pg.26 ... R12
USG Dr. ........ Pg.18,25 P10
Valley Park Dr. ..... Pg.26 ... Q13
Victory Dr. ......... Pg.25 ... P11
Virginia Ave. ....... Pg.18 ... P10-11
Walnut St. ......... Pg.19 ... P12
Warwiak Ln. ....... Pg.26 ... Q10
Wedgemere Pl. ... Pg.26 ... Q13
Weeping Willow Ln. ......... P12
Wellington Ave. ... Pg.18 ... P12
West St. ........... Pg.26 ... P12
Wexford Ct. ....... Pg.26 ... Q11
Wheeler Ct. ....... Pg.26 ... P12
White Blvd. ........ Pg.18 ... N11
Willow Dr. ......... Pg.26 ... Q11
Wilshire Ct. ........ Pg.26 ... Q13
Wilshire Dr. ........ Pg.26 ... P12
Winchester Rd. Pg.19,25,26 ...
Winchester Rd., E. Pg.19 ... P11-12
Windhaven Rd. ... Pg.18,25 P11
Windsor Terr. ...... Pg.26 ... P13
Winners Cir. ....... Pg.26 ... R13
Woodfield Ln. ..... Pg.26 ... R13
Woodland Ln. ..... Pg.26 ... Q11
Wright Ave. ........ Pg.26 ... P12
Wrightwood Terr. . Pg.26 ... P13
Young Dr. ......... Pg.19 ... N12
1st St. ............. Pg.26 ... P,Q12
2nd Ave. .......... Pg.26 ... Q13
3rd St. ............ Pg.26 ... Q13
4th Ave. ........... Pg.26 ... Q13
4th St. ............ Pg.26 ... Q12
5th Ave. ........... Pg.26 ... Q13
7th Ave. ........... Pg.26 ... Q13

CEMETERIES
Lakeside Cem. .... Pg.26 ... P12

GOLF COURSES
Libertyville G.C. at Riverside Park
........................ Pg.26 ... R13
Pine Meadows Pvt. G.C. Pg.25 . P11

PARKS
Adler Park ......... Pg.19 ... P13
Blueberry Park .... Pg.18 ... N11
Butler Lake Pk. .... Pg.26 ... P12
Canterbury Park ... Pg.26 ... R13
Charles Brown Pk. Pg.26 ... P11
Cook Mem. Park .. Pg.26 ... P12
Dymond Annex Park ......... Q12
Gilbert Stiles Park . Pg.19 ... N12
Greentree Park ... Pg.26 ... H12
Interlaken Park .... Pg.25 ... P11
Minear Preserve .. Pg.26 ... P13
Nicholas Dowden Park North
........................ Pg.26 ... Q12
Nicholas Dowden Park South
Paradise Park ..... Pg.25 ... Q11
Paul Neal Park .... Pg.26 ... P11
Red Top Park ..... Pg.26 ... R13
Riverside Park ..... Pg.26 ... R13
Timber Creek Park Pg.26 ... R13
Willis Overhoser Park
........................ Pg.10 ... P11

SCHOOLS
Adler Park Sch. ... Pg.19 ... N12
Butterfield Sch. ... Pg.26 ... P11
Copeland Manor Sch.
........................ Pg.26 ... Q13
Cyd Lash Academy Pg.26 ... Q12
Highland Sch. ..... Pg.26 ... Q12
Libertyville H.S. ... Pg.26 ... Q12
Libertyville H.S. South Campus
........................ Pg.33 ... T13
Marytown a Retreat
........................ Pg.26 ... Q11
Rockland Sch. .... Pg.26 ... Q12
St. Joseph Sch. ... Pg.26 ... Q12

SHOPPING CENTERS
Liberty Mill Shopping Plaza
........................ Pg.26 ... Q13
Shopping Center .. Pg.26 ... P13

MISCELLANEOUS
Abbott Laboratories
........................ Pg.27 ... P15
Brainerd Building . Pg.26 ... Q12
Condell Memorial Hosp.
Cook Mem. Library Pg.26 ... P12
Fire Station North Pg.19 ... N12
Lake County Division of
  Transportation ... Pg.26 ... P12
Libertyville Business Park
Libertyville Township Office
........................ Pg.26 ... P12
Marytown Kolbe Shrine
........................ Pg.25 ... Q11
North Fire Station . Pg.19 ... P12
Police Dept. ....... Pg.26 ... P12
Post Office ......... Pg.26 ... P12
Public Works ...... Pg.26 ... P12
R.R. Station ........ Pg.26 ... M9
Railroad Station ... Pg.18 ... P11
Sewage Plant ..... Pg.26 ... R13
South Fire Station Pg.26 ... R13
St. Mary of the Lake Seminary
St. The Civic Center ......... Q11
Train Depot ........ Pg.26 ... P12
Village Hall ........ Pg.26 ... P12

## LIBERTYVILLE TOWNSHIP

Pages 18-20,25-27

**STREETS**

Allyson Ct. Pg.19 P14
Almond Rd. Pg.18 M11
Arcadia Rd. Pg.27 Q15
Arlington Dr. Pg.19 N13
Atkinson Ave. Pg.27 P15
Baker Rd. Pg.27 Q15
Ballard Dr. Pg.27 Q15
Bayonne Ave. Pg.27 Q15
Bell Ln. Pg.18 N12
Birchwood Ln. Pg.19 N13
Bob-O-Link Ln. Pg.18 N11
Borde Ct. Pg.19 P14
Bradley Rd. Pg.27 Q-S15
Brockwood Ln. Pg.19 P13
Brookhill Rd. Pg.18 N12
Brookside Ct. Pg.19 N12
Bruce Ct. Pg.26 P13
Buckley Rd. Pg.19 N13
Bull Creek Dr. Pg.18 N11
Butterfield Rd. Pg.25 R11
Casey Rd. Pg.19 M12
Center Dr. Pg.19 N13
Cherrywood Ln. Pg.19 N13
Clover Ct. Pg.19 N14
Clover Ln. Pg.19 N13
Country Ct. Pg.18 N11
Countryside Dr. Pg.18 N11
Crescent Knoll Dr. Pg.26 Q14
Daisy Ln. Pg.25 S10
Dan Patch Cir. Pg.19,20 M14
Des Plaines Dr. Pg.19 N13
East End Dr. Pg.19 N13
Egidi Rd. Pg.19 M12
Ellen Way Pg.19 P13
Elm Rd. Pg.27 Q15
Elmwood Ave. Pg.27 R14
Energy Dr. Pg.27 Q15
Fair Ln. Pg.19 N13
Fair Way Pg.19 P13
Fairhill Dr. Pg.18 N12
Finstead Dr. Pg.19 N12
Forest Dr. Pg.27 R14
Foster Ave. Pg.27 Q15
Foster Knoll Rd. Pg.27 P15
Green St. Pg.25 S10
Greenacre Dr. Pg.18 N12
Guerin Rd. Pg.19 N13-14
Hamilton Ct. Pg.25 R11
Hamilton Ln. Pg.25 R11
Haven Ln. Pg.19 N14
Hawthorne Ave. Pg.27 R14
Hawthorne Ln. Pg.26 P13
Herkey Dr. Pg.27 Q15
Hickory Ave. Pg.25 S10
Huntington Ct. Pg.25 R11
Huntington Dr. Pg.25 R11
Idlewood Ln. Pg.19 N13
Imperial Dr. Pg.27 S14
Ivy Ln. Pg.26 Q13
Janas Ct. Pg.19 N12
Jensen Ln. Pg.19 N13
Keith Dr. Pg.27 Q15
Kildare Ave. Pg.18 N12
Laurel Dr. Pg.27 Q15
Leesley Ct. Pg.18 N10
Leola Dr. Pg.27 Q15
Liberty Rd. Pg.18 M10
Lilac Dr. Pg.25 S10
Linden Ln. Pg.27 Q14
Longwood Dr. Pg.27 S14
Margate Ln. Pg.26 Q14
Melody Ln. Pg.27 S14
Milwaukee Ave. Pg.19,26 M,Q12
Minard Ln. Pg.26 Q14
Morgan Ct. Pg.26 M14
Muir Ave. Pg.27 P15
Nells Rd. Pg.19 P14
North Woods Dr. Pg.26 P13
O'Plaine Rd. Pg.19 N14
Oak Ave. Pg.25,27 R14
Oak Grove Ave. Pg.19 N,P13
Oak Ln. Pg.19,26 P,Q13
Oak Pond Ln. Pg.26 P13
Oak Spring Ln. Pg.26 P13
Oak Spring Rd. Pg.26 P13
Old Buckley Rd. Pg.18 N12
Old Hickory Ln. Pg.26 P13
Old School Rd. Pg.26 R13
Park Pl. Pg.19 P13
Parkhill Pg.26 Q14
Parliament Dr. Pg.25 R11
Peterson Rd. Pg.18 N10
Petronella Dr. Pg.27 Q14
Pinehurst Ct. Pg.18 N10
Pinewood Ln. Pg.19 N14
Plaister Ave. Pg.27 P16
Providence Dr. Pg.18 P12
Quassey Ave. Pg.27 P15
Ranch Rd. Pg.18 M10
Redwoods Ln. Pg.19 N14
Rein Ct. Pg.20 M14
Revere Dr. Pg.19 N13
River Dr. Pg.19 P13
River Rd. Pg.19 M,N13
Rockland Ln. Pg.26 Q13
Rockland Rd. Pg.26 Q13
Rose Ave. Pg.25 S10
Scotland Ct. Pg.20 M14
Shagbark Ln. Pg.26 Q14
Sprucewood Ln. Pg.19 P13
St. Andrews Dr. Pg.18 N11
St. Mary's Rd. Pg.19,26,27 N,P,S14
Steger Rd. Pg.18 M10
Sunnyview Rd. Pg.18 N11
Talbot Rd. Pg.27 P15
Tanglewood Ct. Pg.26 Q13
Tanya Tr. Pg.19 P13
Terre Dr. Pg.19 P13
Timber Ln. Pg.19 P13
Toni Ct. Pg.27 Q14
Town Line Rd. Pg.27 S14
Tri-State Tollway Pg.20,27 N15,Q14
U.S. Hwy. 176 Pg.27 Q15
Valley Ct. Pg.18 N11
Vernon Ct. Pg.26 Q13
Victoria Ln. Pg.26 P14
Violet Dr. Pg.25 S10
Waukegan Rd. Pg.20,27 M,P15
Whitman Ct. Pg.26 P14
Wildwood Ct. Pg.19 N,P13
Windsor Ln. Pg.25 R11
Wood Hollow Ln. Pg.18 N11
Wooddale Ln. Pg.26 Q13
Woodland Ln. Pg.27 T15
Woodview Dr. Pg.19 M14
22nd Pg.20 M15

**CEMETERIES**

Ascension Cem. Pg.19 N14

**FOREST PRESERVES**

Lake Co. Forest Preserve Dist. Hdqts. Pg.19 N12
MacArthur Woods Forest Preserve Pg.26 S13
Middle Fork Savanna Pg.27 R15
Old School F.P. Pg.26,27 Q14
Site 15 F.P. Pg.20 P15
Wilmot Wood F.P. Pg.19 P13

**GOLF COURSES**

Knollwood C.C. Pg.27 Q15

**PARKS**

Adler Park Pg.19 P13
Green Tree Park Pg.26 R12
Soccer Complex Pg.18 N10

**SCHOOLS**

Rondout Sch. Pg.27 Q15

**MISCELLANEOUS**

Canoe Launch Preserve Pg.26 Q13
Fire Station Pg.27 P15
Lambs Farm Petting Zoo and Amusement Park Pg.27 Q14
Mundelein Adv. Waste Water Treatment Fac. Pg.26 S13

## LINCOLNSHIRE

Pages 33,34

**STREETS**

Abbey Rd. Pg.33 V13
Andover Ct. Pg.34 V13
Anglican Ln. Pg.33 V15
Ashford Ct. Pg.33 U13
Astor Ct. Pg.33 U14
Barclay Blvd. Pg.34 W13
Bedford Ct. Pg.34 W15
Berkshire Ln. Pg.34 V15
Berwick Ct. Pg.34 V15
Bond St. Pg.33 W13
Book Ln. Pg.34 V15
Brampton Ct. Pg.34 U15
Brampton Ln. Pg.34 U14
Briarwood Ln. Pg.34 U15
Bristol Ct. Pg.34 V15
Brunswick Ln. Pg.34 V15
Buckingham Pl. Pg.34 V15
Bucks Co. Ct. Pg.34 V15
Buxton Ct. Pg.34 V15
Cambridge Ln. Pg.33 V14
Camden Ct. Pg.34 V15
Canterbury Rd. Pg.34 V15
Carlysle Dr. Pg.34 V13
Cedar Ln. Pg.33 V14
Cherrywood Ln. Pg.34 V15
Choate Ct. Pg.33 V13
Cold Stream Cir. Pg.33 W14
Conn. River Valley Ct. Pg.34 V15
Cornell Dr. Pg.34 V15
Coventry Ln. Pg.33 W14
Cumberland Dr. Pg.33 V14
Darby Ln. Pg.33 V14
Dartmouth Ct. Pg.33 V13
Dawson Ct. Pg.34 V15
Deer Run Pg.36 V15
Devonshire Ln. Pg.34 V15
Dover Dr. Pg.34 V14
Dukes Cir. Pg.34 V15
Dukes Ct. Pg.34 V15
Dukes Ln. Pg.34 V15
Durham Ct. Pg.34 U15
Elmwood Ln. Pg.33 V14
Elsinoor Dr. Pg.33 V14
Essex Ln. Pg.33 V14
Exeter Ct. Pg.33 V13
Exmoor Ln. Pg.34 W15
Fairfax Ln. Pg.34 W15
Fallstone Dr. Pg.34 V15
Farrington Cir. Pg.34 U15
Farrington Dr. Pg.34 U15
Fox River Ct. Pg.34 V15
Fox Trail Pg.34 W15
Friar Tuck Ct. Pg.34 V15
Gloucester Ct. Pg.33 U13
Grenedier Ct. Pg.34 V15
Groton Ct. Pg.33 V13
Half Day Rd. Pg.34 V15
Hastings Ln. Pg.34 V15
Heathrow Dr. Pg.33 W13
Hewitt Dr. Pg.34 V15
Hickory Ln. Pg.33 V14
Holtz Rd. Pg.33 V13
Hotchkiss Ct. Pg.33 V13
Jamestown Ln. Pg.33 U14
Jamestown Ln., N. Pg.33 U13
Kensington Dr. Pg.33 W14
Kenswick Ct. Pg.34 V15
Kent Ct. Pg.34 V15
Keswick Ct. Pg.34 V15
Kings Cross Dr. Pg.34 V15
Knightsbridge Pkwy. Pg.33 V13
Lake Zurich Hwy. Pg.33 V13
Lancaster Ln. Pg.33 V14
Leeds Ct. Pg.34 U15
Lincolnshire Dr. Pg.34 V14
Londonderry Ln. Pg.34 V14
Margate Dr. Pg.34 W13
Marriott Dr. Pg.34 V13
Mayfair Ln. Pg.34 V15
Melrose Ln. Pg.33 V14
Middlebury Ln. Pg.34 W15
Middlesex Ct. Pg.33 V13
Millbrook Dr. Pg.33 V13
Mohawk Valley Ct. Pg.34 V15
Nantucket Ct. Pg.34 V15
Natchez Ct. Pg.34 V15
Northfield Ct. Pg.33 V13
Northhampton Ln. Pg.34 U14
Nottingham Dr. Pg.34 V15
Oakwood Ln. Pg.33 V14
Old Mill Rd. Pg.34 V15
One Stevenson Dr. Pg.33 U13
Overlook Pt. Pg.33 W13
Oxford Dr. Pg.33 V14
Park Pl. Pg.33 W13
Parkway Dr. Pg.33 W13-14
Parton Ct. Pg.34 U15
Pembroke Ct. Pg.34 V14
Pembroke Dr. Pg.34 V14
Pheasant Row Pg.34 W15
Plymouth Ct. Pg.33 V14
Portshire Dr. Pg.34 V15
Provincetown Ct. Pg.33 U13
Queens Way Pg.34 V15
Regent Ln. Pg.34 V15
Reliance Ln. Pg.34 V15
Riverside Ln. Pg.33 V14
Riverside Rd. Pg.33 W14
Riverwoods Rd. Pg.34 U15
Robinhood Ct. Pg.34 V15
Royal Ct. Pg.34 V15
Sheffield Ct. Pg.33 V14
Shelter Rd. Pg.33 V13
Sherwood Dr. Pg.34 V15
Stafford Ct. Pg.34 U15
Stafford Ln. Pg.34 U15
Stonegate Cir. Pg.33 V14
Storybrook Ln. Pg.34 V15
Surrey Ln. Pg.34 U15
Sutton Ct. Pg.34 V15
Tidewater Ct. Pg.34 V15
Tower Pkwy. Pg.33 V13
Victoria Ln. Pg.33 W14
Warwick Ct. Pg.34 V15
Wellington Ct. Pg.34 V15
Westgate Pg.33 V13
Westminster Way Pg.34 V15
Westwood Ln. Pg.34 W15
Whitby Cir. Pg.34 V15
Whitby Ct. Pg.34 V15
Whitmore Ln. Pg.34 U14
Whytegate Ct. Pg.34 U14
William St. Pg.33 W13
Williamsburg Ln. Pg.33 U13
Wilmington Ct. Pg.34 V15
Wiltshire Dr. Pg.33 V14
Wimbledon Ct. Pg.33 U13
Windsor Dr. Pg.34 V15
Yorkshire Dr. Pg.33 V14

**FOREST PRESERVES**

Ryerson Woods Forest Preserve Pg.33 W14

**GOLF COURSES**

Lincolnshire Resort & G.C. Pg.33 V14

**PARKS**

Florsheim Nature Preserve Pg.34 U15
Prairie View Pk. Pg.33 U12
Rivershire Park Pg.33 V14
Balzer Park Pg.34 V15
Bicentennial Park Pg.34 W15
Memorial Park Pg.34 V15
Spring Lake Park Pg.33 V14
Whytegate Park Pg.34 U14

**SCHOOLS**

Daniel Wright Sch. Pg.33 U14
Half Day Sch. Pg.33 V13
Laura Sprague Sch. Pg.34 V15
Stevenson H.S. Pg.33 W13

**MISCELLANEOUS**

Lincolnshire Corporate Center Pg.33 V13
Marriott Resort Pg.33 V14
Post Office Pg.33 U13
Public Works Pg.33 U13
Vernon Area F.D. Hdqts. Pg.33 U13
Village Hall Pg.33 V14

## LINDENHURST

Pages 3,4,10,11

**STREETS**

Adam Dr. Pg.4 D9
Arrowhead Ct. Pg.11 F10
Ashwood Ct. Pg.11 F10
Astor Ct. Pg.11 F10
Auburn Ln. Pg.3 D9
Autumn Cir. Pg.3 D9
Beck Rd. Pg.4,10,11 D-F9
Beechwood Ln. Pg.11 F10
Blue Spruce Ct. Pg.11 F10
Bonner Ln. Pg.11 F9
Briar Ln. Pg.10 F9
Bridgeport Terr. Pg.4 D9
Brittany Ln. Pg.3 E9
Brook Ln. Pg.10 E9
Burr Oak Ln. Pg.10 E9
Cardinal Ct. Pg.1 E8
Carmen Ct. Pg.11 F9
Carriage Ln. Pg.11 E9
Catalina Ct. Pg.3 D8
Cherrywood Ln. Pg.10 E8
Chestnut Cir. Pg.10 E9
Clover Ct. Pg.3 D9
Colony Ave. Pg.1,4 D9
Colony Ct. Pg.4 D9
Constitution Dr. Pg.11 D9
Coral Ct. Pg.3 D8
Country Place Pg.11 F10
Countryside Ln. Pg.10 F9
Crabtree Ct. Pg.10 F9
Crooked Lake Ln. Pg.10 E8
Crosswind Ln. Pg.3 D8
Deep Lake Rd. Pg.10 E7
Deerpath Dr. Pg.11 F9
Delaware Ct. Pg.4 D10
Delaware Ln. Pg.4 D9
Dittmer Ln. Pg.1 E8
Dover Ct. Pg.11 G9
Elmwood Dr. Pg.10 E9
Emerald Ln. Pg.11 F9
Evergreen Ct. Pg.3 D8
Fairfield Rd. Pg.10 E8,9
Federal Cir. Pg.3 D9
Federal Pkwy. Pg.3 D9
Forest Ct. Pg.11 G9
Forest View Rd. Pg.4 E9
Franklin Ct. Pg.11 D9
Franklin Ln. Pg.11 D9
Gelden Ln. Pg.3 D8
Gettysburg Ct. Pg.11 D9
Glendale Ct. Pg.10 F9
Grand Ave. Pg.10,11 F8-9
Grand Cir. Pg.11 F9
Grass Lake Rd. Pg.4 E9
Great Oak Dr. Pg.11 E9
Green Briar Ln. Pg.11 F9
Green Tree Ct. Pg.11 E9
Hamilton Dr. Pg.4 D9
Hancock Ct. Pg.4 D10
Harbor Ridge Way Pg.4 D9
Harrisburg Ct. Pg.4 D9
Harvard Ct. Pg.4 D9
Hastings Pl. Pg.3 D9
Hawthorn Dr. Pg.10 E8
Hazelwood Pg.10 E8
Heather Ct. Pg.11 F10
Heritage Dr. Pg.4 D9
Hickory Ct. Pg.10 E8
Hickory Dr. Pg.10 E8
Highland Cir. Pg.11 F9
Highland Dr. Pg.11 F9
Highpoint Dr. Pg.3,10 E9
Hillcrest Ln. Pg.10 F9
Honeysuckle Ct. Pg.10 F9
Horizon Ct. Pg.3 D8
Independence Blvd. Pg.4 D10
Independence Ct. Pg.11 D9
Ironwood Dr. Pg.11 F9
Ivy Cir. Pg.3 D9
Jefferson Dr. Pg.3 D9
Lake Shore Dr. Pg.10 E9
Lakeview Ct. Pg.4 D9
Larksdale Rd. Pg.10 E8
Laurel Dr. Pg.11 E9
Liberty Ln. Pg.4 D9
Lindenhurst Dr. Pg.10 F9
Longmeadow Dr. Pg.10 E9
Madison Ln. Pg.4 D9
Magnolia Ln. Pg.11 F9
Mallard Dr. Pg.11 E9
Mallard Ridge Dr. Pg.10 E8
Maplewood Ct. Pg.10 E8
Maplewood Dr. Pg.10 E9
Meadow Dr. Pg.10 E9
Monroe Dr. Pg.4 D9
Munn Rd. Pg.10 E8
Newport Ct. Pg.3 D8
Nightingale Ln. Pg.10 E8
Northgate Rd. Pg.10 E9
Old Elm Rd. Pg.10 F9
Orchard Ln. Pg.11 E9
Oriole Ct. Pg.10 E8
Oxford Ct. Pg.4 D10
Paine Ave. Pg.4 D9
Partridge Cir. Pg.10 E8
Penn Blvd. Pg.4 D9
Penn Ct. Pg.4 D9
Pheasant Ridge Ct. Pg.11 E9
Pinecrest Ln. Pg.10 E9
Plum Tree Dr. Pg.11 F9
Poplar Ct. Pg.11 F10
Potomas Ct. Pg.4 D9
Prospect Dr. Pg.10 E8
Providence Ln. Pg.11 D9
Ptarmigan Pl. Pg.11 F10
Quail Ct. Pg.10 E8
Quincy Ct. Pg.4 D9
Red Rock Dr. Pg.3 E9
Ridge Ct. Pg.10 E9
Ridgeland Dr. Pg.10 E9
Robincrest Ln. Pg.10 E8
Rolling Ridge Ln. Pg.10 E9
Rose Tree Ln. Pg.11 E9
Rosewood Crossing Pg.11 F10
Sand Lake Rd. Pg.11 F9,10
Shag Bark Ln. Pg.3 E9
Skyline Cir. Pg.3 D9
Spring Hill Ln. Pg.11 E9
Sprucewood Ln. Pg.10 E8,9
Sumac Ct. Pg.11 F10
Summit Ct. Pg.3 D8
Sunset Ln. Pg.11 F9
Surrey Ln. Pg.3 E9
Sycamore Ct. Pg.11 F10
Tamarack Ct. Pg.11 F10
Teal Rd. Pg.4,11 E9
Thornwood Dr. Pg.11 F9
Timber Ln. Pg.11 E9
Timbercreek Dr. Pg.11 F10
Valley Dr. Pg.10 F9
Vista Terr. Pg.3 D9
Waterford Dr. Pg.4 E9
Whispering Pines Rd. Pg.4 E9
White Birch Rd. Pg.4 E9
White Oak Dr. Pg.10 E9
Willow Way Pg.11 F10
Windsor Ct. Pg.4 D9
Witchwood Ln. Pg.10 E9
Woodlane Dr. Pg.10 F9

**PARKS**

Elmwood Tot Lot Pg.3 E9
Engle Memorial Park Pg.3 D9
Forest View Park Pg.3 E9
Gibbs Clove Park Pg.11 F9
Lakewood Park Pg.4 D9
Lewis Park Pg.11 E9
Mallard Ridge Park Pg.10 E8
Willow Park Pg.10 E9

**SCHOOLS**

Hooper Sch. Pg.11 F9

**MISCELLANEOUS**

Beck Basin Pg.10 E9
Lindens Landing Pg.10 E9
Meyers Beach Pg.10 E9
Police Dept. Pg.10 F9
Village Hall Pg.11 F9

## LONG GROVE

Pages 24,25,31-33
(For additional listings, see Section 2)

**STREETS**

Albert Ln. Pg.31 W8
Alfred Ct. Pg.32 T11
Allison Ln.(Pvt.) Pg.32 W9
Antietam Dr. Pg.32 X10
Aptakisic Rd. Pg.32 W10-11
Arlington Hts. Rd. Pg.32 W11
Arrowhead Ct. Pg.32 T9
Ashley Ct. Pg.32 W9
Balsam Ct. Pg.32 U10
Barclay Ct. Pg.32 U11
Beaver Run Dr. Pg.31 W8
Bedfordshire Dr. Pg.32 U11
Bellisle Ln. Pg.32 T11
Berkshire Cir. Pg.32 U11
Black Walnut Tr. Pg.32 U11
Blue Heron Dr. Pg.33 U12
Blue Spruce Ct. Pg.32 U10
Blue Stem Ct. Pg.32 U10
Bob-O-Link Ln. Pg.32 W10
Boulder Ct. Pg.24 S9
Boulder Ct. Pg.24 S9
Breckenridge Dr. Pg.24 S8
Breckinridge Dr. Pg.24 S8
Breese Rd. Pg.32 W10
Brentwood Cir. Pg.32 W11
Briarcrest Ln. Pg.32 V,W11
Bridgewater Ct. Pg.32 X10
Bridlewood Ct. Pg.32 W11
Bridlewood Ln. Pg.32 W11
Brittany Ct. Pg.32 X11
Brittany Ln. Pg.32 X11
Brookbank Ln. Pg.32 V11
Brookhill Dr. Pg.32 V10
Butler Ln. Pg.32 V11
Carriage Way Pg.32 T9
Charles Ct. Pg.32 T11
Chickamauga Ln. Pg.32 X10
Churchill Ct. Pg.32 V11
Clearwater Pg.31 W8
Coach Rd. Pg.32 X9
Cobblestone Ln. Pg.32 T9
Collier Cir. Pg.32 T10
Connor Dr. Pg.24 S8
Country Ln. Pg.32 W10
Creekside Dr. Pg.25 T9
Crestview Dr. Pg.32 W9
Cripple Creek Dr. Pg.24 S8
Cuba Rd. Pg.32 W9,10
Cumberland Cir. Pg.32 X9
Danbury Ct. Pg.32 W11
Deerwood Dr. Pg.31 W9
Diamond Lake Rd. Pg.32 T10
Doncaster Ct. Pg.32 U10
Dorchester Cir. Pg.32 U11
Driftwood Ln. Pg.32 W9
Eleanor Dr. Pg.32 V9
Ellie Dr. Pg.25 T9
Endwood Dr. Pg.32 U11
Estate Ln. Pg.25 T10
Fairfield Dr. Pg.32 W11
Fairview Ln. Pg.32 W10
Farmcrest Ln. Pg.32 V11
Farmwood Dr. Pg.32 U10
Fenview Ln. Pg.32 V11
Finch Ln. Pg.32 U11
Forest Edge Ln. Pg.32 U10
Forest Fork Pg.31 W8
Forest Glen Pg.32 V11
Forest Tr. Pg.32 V10
Forest Way Cir. Pg.32 U10
Gentry Ct. Pg.32 V11
Gilmer Rd. Pg.32 U10
Goldeneye Dr. Pg.32 U12
Golf Ln. Pg.32 V,W11
Grant Ct. Pg.32 W10
Grant Pl. Pg.32 W10
Greenwiche Cir. Pg.32 U11
Hamilton Ct. Pg.32 V10
Hampton Dr. Pg.32 V11
Heartmoor Ct. Pg.32 V10
Heatherknoll Ct. Pg.32 V11
Heatherwood Ln. Pg.32 V11
Hedgewood Ct. Pg.32 V11
Heritage Ln. Pg.32 V10
Hickory Ct. Pg.32 V10
Hicks Rd. Pg.32 X9
Hidden Hills Pg.31 W8
Hidden Valley Rd. Pg.32 W9
Hiddencreek Ct. Pg.32 T11
High Meadow Ct. Pg.32 U10
High Point Ct. Pg.32 V10
Hilgers Ct. Pg.32 T11
Hilltop Rd. Pg.32 V11
Holly Ct. Pg.32 X10
Indian Ln. Pg.32 T10
Insignia Ct. Pg.24 S8
Kettering Dr. Pg.32 V11
Killdeer Ct. Pg.32 U11
Kimberly Ct. Pg.32 V10
Krueger Ct. Pg.32 V10
Krueger Ln. Pg.32 V10
Lake Pointe Cir. Pg.32 U10
Lake Zurich Hwy. Pg.32 V10
Lakeridge Ct. Pg.25 T9
Lakeridge Dr. Pg.25 T10
Lakeview Ct. Pg.31 W8
Lexington Dr. Pg.32 X9
Lincoln Ave. Pg.32 X10
Long Grove Rd. Pg.32 X9,10
Manassas Ln. Pg.32 X10
Manasses Ct. Pg.32 X10
Mardan Dr. Pg.32 X9
Mardan Dr., E. & W. Pg.32 X9
Marilynn Dr. Pg.32 V10
Mayflower Ln. Pg.32 X9
Meadow Creek Pg.32 T11
Meadow Ln. Pg.25 T10
Meadowknoll Ct. Pg.32 V11
Meadowlark Dr. Pg.32 X10
Medford Cir. Pg.32 U11
Merrimac Ln. Pg.32 W9
Middlesex Dr. Pg.32 W9
Millwood Farm Rd. Pg.32 W10
Monitor Dr. Pg.32 W9
Monitor Ln. Pg.32 W9
Monticello Ln. Pg.32 X9
Muirwood Ct. Pg.32 W9
Mundelein Rd. Pg.32 U10
N. Ridge Pl. Pg.32 T10
Normandy Ct. Pg.32 V10
North Krueger Rd. Pg.32 V10
Nottingham Dr. Pg.31 W9
Oak Grove Cir. Pg.32 V11
Oak Grove Dr. Pg.32 V11
Oak Hill Ln. Pg.31 X9
Oakleaf Pg.32 V10
Oakwood Cir. Pg.32 U11
Oakwood Rd. Pg.32 U11
Old Field Ct. Pg.32 V11
Old Field Ln. Pg.32 V11
Old McHenry Rd. Pg.32 V10
Old Wood Ln. Pg.32 V11
Olde Creek Ln. Pg.32 V11
Orchard Commons Pg.24 S8
Osage Rd. Pg.25 T10
Pamela Ct. Pg.32 V9
Partridge Ln. Pg.32 U11
Patricia Dr. Pg.32 V9
Pebble Creek Ln. Pg.32 V10
Picardy Ct. Pg.32 X11
Picardy Ln. Pg.32 X11
Pine Cone Ct. Pg.32 U10
Pine Ct. Pg.32 W10
Pine Grove Ct. Pg.32 V11
Pine Tree Ct. Pg.32 U10
Pine Tree Dr. Pg.32 U10
Pineham Ct. Pg.32 W11
Pintail Ln. Pg.33 U12
Pottowatomie Ct. Pg.32 X10
Prairie Crossing Pg.32 V11
Prairie Wind Rd. Pg.32 V10
Prairiemoor Ln. Pg.32 V11
Promontory Dr. Pg.32 V10
Red Oak Dr. Pg.32 V10
Redwing Ln. Pg.32 U10
Roanoke Ct. Pg.32 X10
Robert Parker Coffin Rd. Pg.32 W10
Robertson Blvd. Pg.32 V9
Rock Dove Ct. Pg.33 U12
Rolling Glen Dr. Pg.32 W9
Rosehedge Dr. Pg.32 T9
Rosos Pkwy. Pg.32 U11
Royal Melbourne Dr. Pg.32 V10,11
Saddle Ridge Ct. Pg.32 U10
Saddle Ridge Ln. Pg.32 U10
Salem Ct. Pg.32 T10
Salem Lake Blvd. Pg.31 V,N9
Saugatuck Tr. Pg.32 T11
Schaeffer Rd. Pg.32 X10
September Blvd. Pg.25 T9
Shagbark Ln. Pg.32 W10
Shaheen Ct. Pg.32 V9
Shiloh Dr. Pg.32 X9
Sinclaire Ct. Pg.32 T11
Sky Ln. Pg.32 V10
Southwell Ct. Pg.32 W11
Spring Valley Pg.31 W9
St. Clair Ln. Pg.32 T11
Stanford Cir. Pg.32 U11
Sterling Hts. Dr. Pg.32 T11
Stockbridge Ln. Pg.32 T10
Stonehaven Dr. Pg.32 V10
Sumter Dr. Pg.32 X10
Sunshine Ln. Pg.32 V10
Surrey Ln.(Pvt.) Pg.31 W,X9
Taggart Ct. Pg.32 U11
Tall Forrest Tr. Pg.32 V11
Tall Oaks Dr. Pg.32 V10
Tanager Way Pg.32 X10
Teal Ct. Pg.33 U12
Teal Ln. Pg.33 U12
Thorne Grove Dr. Pg.32 T11
Three Lakes Ct. Pg.32 W11
Three Lakes Dr. Pg.32 W10
Torrey Pine Cir. Pg.32 V11
Tremont Cir. Pg.32 U11
Trenton Ct. Pg.32 V10
Tribal Ct. Pg.25 T9
Turnberry Ln. Pg.31 W9
Twin Knolls Ln. Pg.32 W10
Twin Lakes Ln. Pg.32 U10
Union Ct. Pg.32 X10
Val Ct. Pg.24 S8
Valley View Cir. Pg.32 U10
Valley View Ln. Pg.32 U10
Victorian Dr. Pg.32 W9
Wakefield Ln. Pg.32 W11
Waterfowl Way Pg.32 U9
Wellington Dr. Pg.32 U,V10
Westbury Dr. Pg.32 V10
Westchester Cir. Pg.32 U11
Westmoreland Dr. Pg.32 T10
Wildflower Ct. Pg.32 T11
Wildwood Ct. Pg.32 V10
Wildwood Dr. Pg.32 V10
Wildwood Ln. Pg.32 W11
Williams Way Pg.32 T11
Willow Spring Rd. Pg.25 T10
Willow Valley Rd. Pg.31 X8
Willowbrook Rd. Pg.32 V10
Windham Ct. Pg.32 T10
Windham Ln. Pg.32 T10
Woodbine Ln. Pg.32 W10
Woodland Lane Pg.31 X9
Woods End Rd. Pg.32 V10
Woodview Ct. Pg.32 V11
Wynncrest Dr. Pg.32 X9

**GOLF COURSES**

Hillcrest C.C. Pg.32 W10
Indian Valley C.C. Pg.32 T10
Royal Melbourne Golf Center Pg.32 U,V10
Twin Orchard C.C. Pg.32 X10

**SCHOOLS**

Kildeer Sch. Pg.32 W10

**MISCELLANEOUS**

Fire Dept. Pg.32 W10
Long Grove Historical Village Pg.32 W11
Village Hall Pg.32 W10
Wooden Bridge Pg.32 W10

## LONG LAKE

Page 9...H4

## LOON LAKE

Page 2...C6

## METTAWA

Pages 26,27,33,34

**STREETS**

Bradley Rd. Pg.27 S15
Everett Rd. Pg.34 T14
Indian Ridge Rd. Pg.27 S14
Little St. Mary's Rd. Pg.26 R13
Maureen Ln. Pg.27 R14
Meadowood Ct. Pg.26 R14
Meadowood Ln. Pg.26 R14
Melody Ln. Pg.27 S14
Mettawa Dr. Pg.27 R15
Northwoods Ln. Pg.26 R14
Oak Hill Ln. Pg.27 R14
Old School Rd. Pg.26,27 R13,14
Prairie View Ln. Pg.27 T14
Put Rd. Pg.27 T14
Riverwoods Rd. Pg.27,34 T15
St. Mary's Rd. Pg.26 T14
Town Line Rd. Pg.26,27 T14
Twin Dr. Pg.27 R15
Westwood Ln. Pg.26 R14

**FOREST PRESERVES**

Granger Woods F.P. Pg.26 T14
MacArthur F.P. Pg.26 S13
Old School F.P. Pg.26 Q14

## MILLBURN

Page 4...E10

## MONAVILLE

Page 9...F5

## MUNDELEIN

Pages 18,24,25

**STREETS**

Aberdeen Ln. Pg.25 Q9
Aderley Ln. Pg.25 P9
Agnes Ave. Pg.25 R10
Albion Ln. Pg.25 R9
Alemeda Ln. Pg.25 P9
Alexandra Ct. Pg.25 R9
Allanson Rd. Pg.25 R10
Ambria Ct. Pg.25 P9
Ambria Dr. Pg.25 P10
Ambria Ln. Pg.25 P9
Amour Blvd. Pg.25 S11
Andover Dr. Pg.25 P9
Ansley Ct. Pg.25 R9
Anthony Ave. Pg.25 R10
Appleby Ct. Pg.25 Q9
Arbour Ct. Pg.25 Q10
Archer Ave. Pg.25 R10
Armwood Ln. Pg.24 Q9
Ashbrook Ln. Pg.25 R9
Aster Ct. Pg.25 P9
Atwater Dr. Pg.25 R9
Babcock Ct. Pg.25 R9
Ballantrae Pl. Pg.25 R11
Balmoral Dr. Pg.25 R9
Banbury Rd. Pg.25 P,Q10
Barlow Ln. Pg.25 R9
Barnhill Dr. Pg.25 Q9
Baskin Rd. Pg.25 T11
Beach Pl. Pg.25 Q10
Beach Walk Pg.25 R10
Bedford Rd. Pg.25 R11
Beechwood Dr., N. Pg.25 R8
Benbridge Ct. Pg.24 Q9
Bingham Cir. Pg.25 R9
Bingham Ct. Pg.25 R9
Bio-Logic Plaza Pg.25 S10
Bishop Way Pg.25 Q9
Blackburn Dr. Pg.25 R9
Blue Spruce Ln. Pg.25 Q10
Bobby Ave. Pg.25 Q10
Bonniebrook Ave. Pg.25 Q10
Bradford Ln. Pg.25 R9
Bradwell Ln. Pg.25 R11
Braeburn Rd. Pg.25 Q9
Braemar Ct. Pg.25 Q10
Braemar Dr. Pg.25 Q10
Brentwood Dr. Pg.25 R9
Brice Ave. Pg.25 R11
Bridgewater Ln. Pg.25 R9
Brighton Dr. Pg.25 R9
Bristol Ct. Pg.25 R11
Buckingham Ct. Pg.25 Q9
Buckingham Rd. Pg.24 Q9
Burnham Ct. Pg.25 R9
Butterfield Rd. Pg.25 T11
Cairo Ct. Pg.25 Q10
California Ave. Pg.25 R9
Cambridge Rd. Pg.25 P9
Campus Dr. Pg.25 S11
Canterbury Ln. Pg.25 T11
Cardinal Ct. Pg.25 R10
Castillian Way Pg.25 P10
Castleton Ct. Pg.25 Q9
Cedar St. Pg.25 R10
Chadwick Way Pg.25 P9
Chandler Dr. Pg.25 Q10
Charlotte Pl. Pg.25 Q10
Chestnut Ave. Pg.25 R10
Chetwood Ct. Pg.25 R9
Chicago Ave. Pg.25 Q,R10
Churchill Ct. Pg.25 T11
Clarewood Ln. Pg.25 P9
Clearbrook Park Dr. Pg.25 S10
Compton Ln. Pg.25 R9
Concord Cir. Pg.25 R11
Countryside Hwy. Pg.25 R11
Courtland St. Pg.25 R10
Crane Ave. Pg.25 S10
Cross Meadow Dr. Pg.25 R10
Crystal St. Pg.25 R9,10
Dairy Ln. Pg.25 Q10
Dalton Ave. Pg.25 R11
Darnell Dr. Pg.25 P9
Dean Pl. Pg.25 R10
Deepwoods Dr. Pg.25 S10
Derby Ln. Pg.25 T11
Diamond Pointe Dr. Pg.25 S10
Division St. Pg.25 R10
Dorchester Ct. Pg.25 P9
Dorchester Dr. Pg.25 P9
Dowing Pl. Pg.25 T11
Dublin Dr. Pg.25 Q9-10
Dunbar Rd. Pg.25 Q9-10
Dunleer Dr. Pg.25 Q10
Dunton Ct. Pg.25 R9
Eaton Way Pg.25 R11
Edgar A. Poe Ln. Pg.25 S10
Edgemont St. Pg.25 Q10
Edington Ln. Pg.25 R9
Elm Ave. Pg.25 S10
Emerald Ave. Pg.25 Q,R10
Emerson Ln. Pg.25 S10
Evergreen Ct. Pg.25 P9
Evergreen St. Pg.25 P9
Fairhaven Ln. Pg.25 Q10
Fairlawn Ave. Pg.25 Q,R9
Farina Ct. Pg.25 R9
Fieldcrest Dr. Pg.25 P9
Firth Rd. Pg.25 Q10
Fitch Rd. Pg.25 Q9
Fontana Pl. Pg.25 P9
Forest Ave. Pg.25 R10
Fountainview Dr. Pg.25 S10
Franklin St. Pg.25 P9
French Ct. Pg.25 R11
French Dr. Pg.25 R11
Friars Ln. Pg.24 Q9
Garfield Ave. Pg.25 R10
Garfield Ave., W. Pg.25 R10
George Dr. Pg.25 R11
Gifford Ct. Pg.25 R11
Glendale Pl. Pg.25 Q10
Glenview Ave. Pg.25 Q9
Goodwin Pl. Pg.25 Q10
Grace Ave. Pg.25 Q10
Granville Ave. Pg.25 Q10
Greenview Ave., E. Pg.25 Q,R10
Greenview Ave., W. Pg.25 R10
Greenwood Ave. Pg.25 Q10
Grove St. Pg.25 R10
Groveland Blvd. Pg.25 R9
Halifax Dr. Pg.25 P9
Hammond St. Pg.25 R10
Hampton Ct. Pg.25 R11
Hampton Dr. Pg.25 R11
Hampton Ln. Pg.25 R11
Handley Ct. Pg.25 Q9
Harrison Ave. Pg.25 P9
Harvard Ave. Pg.25 P9
Haverton Dr. Pg.25 P9
Hawley Ct. Pg.25 R10
Hawley St. Pg.24 Q9
Hawthorne Blvd. Pg.25 R10
Hawthorne Pl. Pg.25 R10
Hickory St. Pg.25 R10
High St. Pg.25 R10,11
Highland Dr. Pg.25 Q9
Hilgers Ct. Pg.25 T10
Hillside Dr. Pg.25 R10
Holcomb Dr. Pg.25 Q10
Hunt Ct. Pg.25 S11
Huntington Ct. Pg.25 R11
Huntington Dr. Pg.25 R11
Idlewild Ave. Pg.25 Q,R9
Ivanhoe Rd. Pg.25 P8
James Ave. Pg.25 Q10,11
James Pl. Pg.25 R10
Jeanette Pl. Pg.25 Q10
Kari (Birch) Ct. Pg.25 R10
Kari Ct. Pg.25 R10
Kensington Dr. Pg.25 P9
Keswick Dr. Pg.25 R9
Killarney Pass Pg.25 Q9
Killarney Pass Cir. Pg.25 Q9
Kings Way Pg.24 Q9
Knightsbridge Ct. Pg.25 R11
Knightsbridge Dr. Pg.25 R11
Lake Shore Dr., N. & S. Pg.25 R10
Lake St. Pg.25 R,S10
Lake Terr. Pg.25 R10

Lake View Dr. .... Pg.25 .... R10
Lange St. .... Pg.25 .. R10,11
Laramie St. .... Pg.25 .... Q10
Laurel St. .... Pg.25 .... Q10
Lawrence Dr. .... Pg.25 .... S10
Leeds Ct. .... Pg.25 .... T11
Leithton Rd. .... Pg.25 .... S11
Lenox Ln. .... Pg.25 .... R11
Lexington Ct. .... Pg.25 .... Q9
Lincoln Ave. .... Pg.25 .... R10
Linden St. .... Pg.25 .... R10
Liverpool Ln. .... Pg.25 .... P9
Lomond Dr. .... Pg.25 .... Q10
Londonderry Ln. .... Pg.25 .... Q10
Longfellow Ln. .... Pg.25 .... R9
Longwood Terr. .... Pg.25 .... S10
Louis Dr. .... Pg.25 .... T11
Lucerne Ct. .... Pg.25 .... Q10
Lucerne Rd. .... Pg.25 .... Q10
Lyndale St. .... Pg.25 .... Q10
Manchester Dr. .... Pg.25 .... P9
Manor Ln. .... Pg.24 .... Q9
Maple Ave. .... Pg.25 .... Q10
Maple Rd. .... Pg.24 .... Q8
Maplewood Ln. .... Pg.25 .... R10
Margaret .... Pg.25 .... R9
Marlborough Ct. .... Pg.25 .... R9
Mayfair Pl. .... Pg.25 .... T11
McCormick Ave. .... Pg.25 .... R10
McKinley Ave. .... Pg.25 .... R10
McRae Ln. .... Pg.24 .... Q8
Modline Pl. .... Pg.25 .... S11
Michael Ave. .... Pg.25 .... R10
Midland Ave. .... Pg.25 .... R10
Midlothian Ave. .... Pg.25 .... R9
Midlothian Rd. .... Pg.18 .... Q9
Midway Dr. .... Pg.25 .... R9
Morris St. .... Pg.25 .... Q10
Nelson C. White Pkwy. .... Pg.24 .... Q8
New Castle Ct. .... Pg.25 .... R11
Newbury Ln. .... Pg.25 .... R9
Newport St. .... Pg.25 .... T11
Noel Dr. S. .... Pg.25 .... P9
North Shore Dr. .... Pg.25 .... R10
Norton Dr. .... Pg.25 .... Q10
Norton Pl. .... Pg.25 .... Q10
Nottingham Ln. .... Pg.25 .... T11
Oak Ave. .... Pg.25 .... S10
Oak Creek Plaza .... Pg.25 .... S10
Oak Ln. .... Pg.25 .... R9
Oak St. .... Pg.25 .... R10
Oakdale Ave. .... Pg.25 .... R10
Olga St. .... Pg.25 .... S10
Orchard Ave. .... Pg.25 .... R11
Orchard St. .... Pg.25 .. R10,11
Orleans Dr. .... Pg.25 .... T11
Oslo Ct. .... Pg.25 .... T11
Oxford Dr. .... Pg.25 .... R10
Park Ave. .... Pg.25 .... Q9-10
Park St. .... Pg.25 .... Q10
Parliament Way .... Pg.25 .... R11
Pass Circle .... Pg.25 .... Q10
Patrick Dr. .... Pg.25 .... P9
Patti Ln. .... Pg.25 .... Q10
Pembrook Ln. .... Pg.25 .... R11
Perry Dr. .... Pg.25 .... R10
Pershing Ave. .... Pg.25 .... Q,R10
Pickford Ct. .... Pg.25 .... P9
Pine Meadow Ln. .... Pg.25 .... P11
Pinehurst Ct. .... Pg.25 .... R9
Pinehurst Dr. .... Pg.25 .... R9
Pleasure Dr. .... Pg.25 .... S10
Prairie Ave. .... Pg.25 .... R10
Prairie Ave., N. .... Pg.25 .... R10
Principal Ave. .... Pg.25 .... Q10
Prospect Ave. .... Pg.25 .... Q,R10
Quigley St. .... Pg.25 .... R10
Quigs Orchard .... Pg.25 .... R9
Racine Pl. .... Pg.25 .... Q10
Rays Ln. .... Pg.25 .... S10
Regent Dr. .... Pg.25 .... R9
Reidel Rd. .... Pg.25 .... T11
Richard Ct. .... Pg.25 .... T11
Ridge Ave. .... Pg.25 .... S10
Ridgeland Ave. .... Pg.25 .... R9
Ridgemoor Ave. .... Pg.25 .... Q,R9
Rouse Ave. .... Pg.25 .... R10
Russell Pl. .... Pg.25 .... R10
Rye Rd. .... Pg.25 .... P10
Salceda Ct. .... Pg.25 .... P9
Salceda Dr. .... Pg.25 .... P10
Salceda Ln. .... Pg.25 .... P10
Sandhurst Rd. .... Pg.25 .... R11
Scott St. .... Pg.25 .... R9
Seymour Ave. .... Pg.25 .... Q,R10
Shaddle Ave. .... Pg.25 .. R10-11
Shady Ln. .... Pg.25 .... S10
Shadydell Ave. .... Pg.25 .... R9
Shari Ln. .... Pg.25 .... Q10
Shaun Dr. .... Pg.25 .... T11
Sheffield Ave. .... Pg.25 .... P9
Sherwood Ct. .... Pg.25 .... R11
Shetland Dr. .... Pg.25 .... P9
Simpson Dr. .... Pg.25 .... S10
Somerset Ct. .... Pg.25 .... R9
Somerset Ln. .... Pg.25 .... R9
South Ave. .... Pg.25 .... S10
Southport Rd. .... Pg.25 .... R9
Spalding Dr. .... Pg.25 .... R9
Springbrook Dr. .... Pg.25 .... R9
Stafford Dr. .... Pg.25 .... R9
Sterling Dr. .... Pg.25 .... R9
Stone Dr. .... Pg.25 .... T11
Stonebridge Way .... Pg.25 .... R9
Stratford Ln. .... Pg.25 .... S10
Summerhill Dr. .... Pg.25 .... R9
Sunridge Ct. .... Pg.25 .... R9
Sunset Beach Walk .... Pg.25 .... R10
Sunset Ln. .... Pg.25 .... R9
Surridge Ct. .... Pg.25 .... R9
Templeton Ct. .... Pg.25 .... Q9
Terrace Dr. .... Pg.25 .... R11
Thomas Blvd. .... Pg.25 .... R11
Thomas Ct. .... Pg.25 .... R11
Thornton Way .... Pg.25 .... R9
Thorntree Rd. .... Pg.25 .... R8
Timothy Tr. .... Pg.25 .... P4
Tower Rd. .... Pg.25 .... S10
Town Line Rd. .... Pg.25 .... S11
Trescott St. .... Pg.25 .... S9
Tudor Dr. .... Pg.25 .... P9
Turret Ct. .... Pg.25 .... P9
US. Rte. 45 .... Pg.25 .... P-S10
Valencia Way .... Pg.25 .... A15
Verde Ct. .... Pg.25 .... P9
Verde Ln. .... Pg.25 .... P9
Victoria Rd. .... Pg.24 .... Q9
Wakefield Ct. .... Pg.25 .... S10
Walker Pl. .... Pg.25 .... R9
Walnut Ct. .... Pg.25 .... R,S10
Walnut St. .... Pg.25 .... R10
Warwick Ln. .... Pg.25 .... R9

Washington Blvd. .... Pg.25 .... R11
Washington Ct. .... Pg.25 .... R11
Waterview Dr. .... Pg.25 .... T11
Waverley Dr. .... Pg.25 .... T11
Wellington Ave. .... Pg.25 .... Q10
Wellington Ct. .... Pg.25 .... Q10
Wellington Dr. .... Pg.25 .... Q10
Westerfield Way .... Pg.25 .... P9
Westminster Dr. .... Pg.25 .... Q9
Weston Ln. .... Pg.25 .... Q9
White Hall Dr. .... Pg.25 .... T11
Whittler Ln. .... Pg.25 .... P10
Wilcox St. .... Pg.25 .... R10
Wildwood Ave. .... Pg.25 .... R10
Wilhelm Rd. .... Pg.25 .... T11
Wilton Ln. .... Pg.25 .... R9
Wimpole St. .... Pg.25 .... T11
Winchester Rd. .... Pg.18 .... P9
Windsor Pl. .... Pg.25 .... R11
Wingate Dr. .... Pg.25 .... R9
Winsted Pl. .... Pg.25 .... R9
Winston Ct. .... Pg.25 .... P9
Winthrop Dr. .... Pg.25 .... S10
Woodcrest Cir. .... Pg.25 .... Q9
Woodcrest Ct. .... Pg.25 .... Q9
Woodhaven Ct. .... Pg.25 .... Q9
Woodhaven Dr. .... Pg.25 .... Q9
Woodlawn Dr. .... Pg.25 .... R10
Wortham Ct. .... Pg.25 .... R9
Wortham Dr. .... Pg.25 .... R9
Wren's Gate .... Pg.25 .... P9
Yale Dr. .... Pg.24 .... Q8
Yardley Tr. .... Pg.25 .... P10
York Ct. .... Pg.25 .... S9
Yorkshire Dr. .... Pg.25 .... R10

CEMETERIES
Diamond Lake Cem. .... Pg.25 .... T11

GOLF COURSES
Village Green G.C. .... Pg.24 .... P9

PARKS
Clearbrook Park .... Pg.25 .... S11
Community Park .... Pg.25 .... P9
Hanrahan Park .... Pg.25 .... R11
Krocklauer Park .... Pg.25 .... R10
Lions Field Pk. .... Pg.25 .... R10
Memorial Park .... Pg.25 .... R10
Parks .... Pg.25 .. R9,11

SCHOOLS
Carl Sandburg Sch. .... Pg.25 .... R9
Carmel H.S. .... Pg.25 .... Q11
Fairhaven Sch. .... Pg.25 .... R9
Fairhaven Sch. .... Pg.25 .... P9
Jefferson Sch. .... Pg.25 .... R9
Lincoln Sch. .... Pg.25 .... Q10
Mechanics Grove Sch. .... Pg.25 .... Q9
Mundelein H.S. .... Pg.25 .... Q9
St. Maria Sch. .... Pg.25 .... Q9
St. Mary's of the Lake Seminary .... Pg.25 .... Q10
Washington Sch. .... Pg.25 .... R10

SHOPPING CENTERS
Diamond Lake S.C. .... Pg.25 .... R10
Fairhaven Plaza .... Pg.25 .... R9
Maple Tree Mall .... Pg.25 .... R10
Mundelein S.C. .... Pg.25 .... R10

MISCELLANEOUS
Fremont Twp. Library .... Pg.25 .... Q10
Marytown Klobe Shrine .... Pg.25 .... Q11
Mundelein Youth Ctr.
Post Office .... Pg.25 .... R10
Quigg Orchard .... Pg.25 .... R9
Village Hall .... Pg.25 .... R10

MYLITH PARK
Pg. 08,04

NEWPORT TOWNSHIP
Pages 4-6,11-13
STREETS
Adams Rd. .... Pg.6 .... D15
Bayonne Ave. .... Pg.6,13 .... D15,E16
Belle Plaine Ave. .... Pg.6,13 .... E15
Boulevard View Ave. .... Pg.6,13 .... E15
Crawford Rd. .... Pg.4 .... B10
Dale Ave. .... Pg.6,13 .... E15
Delany Rd. .... Pg.6,13 .... B-C,E15
Dilley's Rd. .... Pg.12 .... E13
Edwards Rd. .... Pg.5 .. A11,12
Green Bay Rd. .... Pg.6 .... A15
Hickory Rd. .... Pg.5 .... A14
Hunt Club Rd. .... Pg.11 .... E11
Kaiser Rd. .... Pg.5 .... C14
Kazmer Rd. .... Pg.5 .... C14
Kilbourne Rd. .... Pg.5 .... B13
Magnolia Ave. .... Pg.6,13 .... E16
Martin St. .... Pg.6 .... D15
McCarthy Rd. .... Pg.12 .... E13
Mill Creek Rd. .... Pg.5 .... C12
Millburn Rd. .... Pg.4 .... E10
Northwestern Ave. .... Pg.6,13 .... E15
Oak Knoll Cir., E. .... Pg.12 .... H12
Old Woodford Rd. .... Pg.5 .... B13
Pine Grove Ave. .... Pg.6,13 .... E16
Plaza Ln. .... Pg.5 .... D12
Red Oak Dr. .... Pg.12 .... T4
Rosecrans Rd. .... Pg.5 .... B13
Rosedale Ave. .... Pg.6,13 .... E15
Russell Rd. .... Pg.5 .... A13
Sharon St. .... Pg.6 .... D15
Sheridan Oaks Dr. .... Pg.4 .... A11
Skokie Hwy. .... Pg.5 .. A12,E13
Sunset Rd. .... Pg.5 .... D15
Sylvan Ave. .... Pg.6,13 .... E15
Town Line Rd. .... Pg.12 .... E12
Tri-State Tollway .... Pg.5 .... C12
Waveland Ave. .... Pg.6,13 .... E15
Waverly St. .... Pg.6 .... C15
Winthrop Harbor Rd.

PARKS
Woodland Ave. .... Pg.6,13 .... E16
9th St. .... Pg.5 .... C14
21st St. .... Pg.5,6 .... C15

CEMETERIES
Mount Rest Cem. .... Pg.5 .... A12
Oakdale Cem. .... Pg.5 .... A15
St. Patrick's Cem. .... Pg.5 .... C12

FOREST PRESERVES
Sterling Lake F.P. .... Pg.5 .... A13
Van Patton Woods .... Pg.5 .... A13

GOLF COURSES
Orchard Hills C.C. .... Pg.13 .... E15

SCHOOLS
Browe Sch. .... Pg.5 .... D12
Newport Sch .... Pg.5 .... B13
Townline Sch. .... Pg.13 .... E15

MISCELLANEOUS
Big Z Riding Club Arena .... Pg.6 .... A15
Camp Oakarro .... Pg.5 .... C12

NORTH BARRINGTON
Pages 23,29,30
STREETS
Aburdour Ct. .... Pg.23 .... T5
Apex Ct. .... Pg.30 .... U4
Arrow Head Ln. .... Pg.30 .... U4
Averill Ct. .... Pg.23 .... T5
Beachview Ln. .... Pg.30 .. U-V4
Biltmore Dr. .... Pg.30 .. U-V4
Blanche Ct. .... Pg.30 .... V4
Border L. .... Pg.29 .... U3
Border L., W. .... Pg.29 .... U3
Brook Forest Ct. .... Pg.30 .... W4
Brook Forest Ln. .... Pg.30 .... W4
Brookmont Ln. .... Pg.30 .... U4
Brookside Rd. .... Pg.30 .... U4
Candlewood Dr. .... Pg.23 .... T5
Carriage Rd. .... Pg.30 .... V4
Castleton Ct. .... Pg.30 .... T5
Castleview Ot. .... Pg.30 .... V4
Century Oaks Dr. .... Pg.30 .... V4
Cherry Hill Rd. .... Pg.29 .... V3
Christopher Dr. .... Pg.30 .... W5
Clarington Way .... Pg.30 .... T5
Concord Ln. .... Pg.30 .... U4
Coventry Ln. .... Pg.30 .... U4
Crooked Ln. .... Pg.30 .... U4
Crosswicks Ct. .... Pg.30 .... T5
Deverell Dr. .... Pg.30 .... U4
Drury Ln. .... Pg.30 .... U4
Duck Pond Ln. .... Pg.30 .... W4
Duxbury Dr. .... Pg.30 .... T5
Edgewood Pl. .... Pg.30 .... U4
Essex Ln. .... Pg.30 .... U4
Eton Dr. .... Pg.30 .... U4
Glen Circle .... Pg.30 .... U4
Golfview Dr. .... Pg.29 .. U-V4
Grassmere Ct. .... Pg.30 .... V4
Graystone Ln. .... Pg.30 .... V4
Halcyon Ln. .... Pg.30 .... U4
Halibrath Ct. .... Pg.30 .... T5
Haversham Ln. .... Pg.30 .... U4
Haverton Way .... Pg.30 .... W4
Hewes Dr. .... Pg.30 .... W4
Hidden Brook Dr. .... Pg.30 .... T4
Hidden Oaks Ln. .... Pg.30 .... T4
Hillandale Ct. .... Pg.30 .... U4
Hillburn Ct. .... Pg.30 .... T4
Hillburn Ln. .... Pg.30 .... T4
Homewood Ln. .... Pg.30 .... W4
Honey Lake Ct. .... Pg.30 .... W4
Honey Lake Rd. .... Pg.30 .... W4
Hunting Dr. .... Pg.30 .... U4
Iroquois Dr. .... Pg.30 .... U4
Kathleen Ct. .... Pg.30 .... V4
Kensington Dr. .... Pg.30 .... U4
Kettering Ct. .... Pg.30 .... V4
Kimberley Dr. .... Pg.30 .... U4
Lake Blvd. .... Pg.30 .. U-V3
Lake Zurich-Highwood Rd.
Lakeside Ct. .... Pg.23 .... T5
Lakeside Dr. .... Pg.23 .... T5
Lakeview Pl. .... Pg.30 .... U3
Larkins Ln. .... Pg.30 .... W4
Marbridge Ct. .... Pg.30 .... V4
Masland Ct. .... Pg.30 .... W5
Mockingbird Ln. .... Pg.30 .... U4
North Hill Dr. .... Pg.30 .... U4
Old Oak Rd. .... Pg.30 .... U4
Onondaga Dr. .... Pg.30 .... V3
Orchard Rd. .... Pg.30 .. U-V4
Osage Dr. .... Pg.30 .... V3
Ottawa Dr. .... Pg.30 .... V3
Oxford Rd. .... Pg.30 .... V4
Oxford Rd., E. .... Pg.30 .... V4
Pheasant Run Tr. .... Pg.30 .... U4
Piermont .... Pg.30 .... U5
Pinewood Dr. .... Pg.30 .... V4
Pooks Hill Rd. .... Pg.30 .... U4
Rainbow Rd. .... Pg.30 .... W4
Rand Rd. .... Pg.30,31 .. U5,X7
Randolph Ct. .... Pg.30 .... W4
Ravine Dr. .... Pg.30 .... T4
Ravine Ln. .... Pg.23 .... T5
Red Wing Ln. .... Pg.30 .... T4
Riderwood Rd. .... Pg.30 .... T5
Rugby Rd. .... Pg.30 .... U4
Rustic Dr. .... Pg.30 .... U4
Saddle Tree Ln. .... Pg.30 .... W4
Schafler Ln. .... Pg.30 .... W5
Seminole Dr. .... Pg.29 .... V4
Shady Ln. .... Pg.30 .. U-V4
Signal Hill Rd. .... Pg.30 .... V3
Signal Hill Rd., N. .... Pg.30 .... V3
Sioux Dr. .... Pg.30 .... V3
Stone Marsh Ln. .... Pg.23 .... T5
Stratham Dr. .... Pg.30 .... U4
Thomas Dr. .... Pg.30 .... U3
View Ct. .... Pg.30 .... T4
Weybridge Ln. .... Pg.30 .... T4
Woodbine Pl. .... Pg.30 .... U4
Wooded Ln. .... Pg.29 .... U4
Woodland Dr. .... Pg.30 .... U4
Wynstone Dr., N. .... Pg.29 .... V3
Wynstone Dr., S. .... Pg.30 .. U4-5
Wynstone Way .... Pg.30 .... U4

FOREST PRESERVES
Grassy Lake F.P. .... Pg.29 .... U3

GOLF COURSES
Biltmore C.C. .... Pg.30 .... V4
Wynstone G.C. .... Pg.30 .. T,U,4,5

PARKS
Haverton Conservation Area

MISCELLANEOUS
Fire Station .... Pg.30 .... T4
Village Hall .... Pg.30 .... U4
Village Sports Field .... Pg.30 .... U4
Village Wildlife Refuge .... Pg.30 .... V3

NORTH CHICAGO
Pages 20,21,27
STREETS
Adams St. .... Pg.21 .... L18

Amstutz Expwy. .... Pg.21 .... M18
Argonne Dr. .... Pg.20 .. M16-17
Arrington Ave. .... Pg.21 .... M17
Atkinson .... Pg.21 .... P15
Barry Ave. .... Pg.20 .... N16
Beacon Ave. .... Pg.20 .... N16
Beechnut Ave. .... Pg.20 .... L16
Beethoven St. .... Pg.20 .... N16
Berwyn Ave. .... Pg.20 .... N16
Birch Ave. .... Pg.27 .... P16
Broadway Ave. .... Pg.21 .... M17
Buckley Rd. .... Pg.20 .... P15
Butterfly Ct. .... Pg.21 .... M17
Carver Ave. .... Pg.21 .... L17
Casmir Pulaski Memorial Dr. .... Pg.21 .... L15
Commonwealth Ave. .... Pg.21 .... M17
Davis St. .... Pg.21 .... M17
Dickey Ave. .... Pg.21 .... M17
Dugdale Rd. .... Pg.20 .... M16
Elizabeth Ave. .... Pg.21 .... M17
Environ Cir. .... Pg.21 .... M17
Evergreen Ave. .... Pg.20 .... M16
Fellows Pl. .... Pg.21 .... M18
Foss Park Ave. .... Pg.20 .... M16
Frontenac Ave. .... Pg.20 .... N16
Golf Course Dr. .... Pg.21 .... N16
Grant Pl. .... Pg.21 .... M17
Graves Ct. .... Pg.21 .... M17
Green Bay Rd. .... Pg.20 .... M16
Greenfield Ave. .... Pg.21 .... M17
Greenleaf Ave. .... Pg.21 .... M17
Greenwood Ave. .... Pg.21 .... M17
Hampton Blvd. .... Pg.21 .... P15
Hempstead St. .... Pg.20 .... M16
Honore Ave. .... Pg.21 .... M17
Hunting St. .... Pg.20 .... P15
Jackson Ave. .... Pg.21 .... L17
Jackson St. .... Pg.21 .... L17
Jones Dr. .... Pg.21 .... L17
Kemble Ave. .... Pg.21 .... M17
Kennedy Dr. .... Pg.21 .... M17
King, Dr. Martin Luther, Jr. .... Pg.21 .... M17
Kristan Ave. .... Pg.21 .... M17
Lakeside Ave. .... Pg.21 .... P15
Laurelton St. .... Pg.20 .... M16
Lenox Ave. .... Pg.21 .... L17
Lenzini Dr. .... Pg.20 .... N16
Leslie Ave. .... Pg.21 .... N17
Lewis Ave. .... Pg.21 .... M17
Lincoln Ave. .... Pg.21 .... M17
Main St. .... Pg.20 .... M18
Maple Ave. .... Pg.20 .... L16
Marion .... Pg.21 .... M17
McKee Rd. .... Pg.20 .... L16
Meadow Ave. .... Pg.20 .... M16
Meadow Cir. .... Pg.27 .... P16
Meadowbrook Ln. .... Pg.20 .... N16
Merril Ave. .... Pg.20 .... M16
Morrow Ave. .... Pg.21 .... M17
Nagel Ct. .... Pg.20 .... Q15
Natoma Ave. .... Pg.21 .... M17
Nek Ave. .... Pg.21 .... M17
Northern Ave. .... Pg.20 .... M16
Oak Ave. .... Pg.21 .... M17
Pembroke Cir. .... Pg.27 .... P15
Prospect Ave. .... Pg.21 .... M17
Renken Ave. .... Pg.20 .... L16
Ridge Ave. .... Pg.21 .... M17
Sanctuary Ct. .... Pg.27 .... P16
Sanctuary Ln. .... Pg.27 .... P16
Seymour Ave. .... Pg.21 .... M17
Sheridan Rd. .... Pg.21 .... N17
Sherman Ave. .... Pg.21 .. L,M17
South Park Ave. .... Pg.21 .... L17
South Route 137 .... Pg.20 .... P16
Templeton St. .... Pg.20 .... M18
Vermont Ave. .... Pg.20 .... M16
Victoria St. .... Pg.21 .... L18
Wadsworth Ave. .... Pg.27 .... P16
Wallace Ave. .... Pg.21 .... M17
Walnut Ave. .... Pg.20 .... L16
Waukegan Rd. .... Pg.27 .... P15
Wellyen Ct. .... Pg.21 .... P15
Wellyen St. .... Pg.20 .... P16
Willow Ave. .... Pg.20 .... M16
Wright Ave. .... Pg.21 .... M17
Woodbury Ln. .... Pg.20 .... L15
2nd Ave. .... Pg.20 .... M18
11th St. .... Pg.20 .... L16
14th Pl. .... Pg.21 .... M18
14th St. .... Pg.21 .... M18
16th Pl. .... Pg.20 .. L16-18
16th St. .... Pg.20 .... M18
17th Pl. .... Pg.20 .. M16-18
17th St. .... Pg.20 .. M16-18
18th Pl. .... Pg.20 .. M16-18
18th St. .... Pg.20 .... N16
20th Pl. .... Pg.20 .... M16
20th St. .... Pg.20 .... M16
21st Pl. .... Pg.20 .. M16-18
21st St. .... Pg.20 .... M18
22nd Pl. .... Pg.20 .... M16
22nd St. .... Pg.21 .... M17
23rd Pl. .... Pg.20 .... M16
23rd St. .... Pg.20 .. M16-18
24th Pl. .... Pg.20 .. M16-17
24th St. .... Pg.20 .. M16-17
25th Pl. .... Pg.20 .. M16-17
25th St. .... Pg.21 .... N17

CEMETERIES
North Shore Gardens of
Memories .... Pg.20 .... L16

PARKS
Foss Park .... Pg.21 .... M18

SCHOOLS
Central Sch. .... Pg.21 .... M17
Community H.S. .... Pg.21 .... M17
Green Bay Sch. .... Pg.21 .... M17
Holy Rosary Sch. .... Pg.21 .... M18
Lake Shore Cath. Academy S.

MISCELLANEOUS
Commuter Sta. .... Pg.21 .... M18
Public Library .... Pg.21 .... M18

Public Works Bldg. Pg.21 .... L17
U.S. Naval Training Ctr.
FBI Range .... Pg.21 .... M18
Youth Center .... Pg.21 .... M17

OLD MILL CREEK
Pages 4,5,11,12
STREETS
Crawford Rd. .... Pg.4 .... D10
Hunt Club Rd. .... Pg.4,11 .. D-E11
Hutchins Rd. .... Pg.11 .... F11
Kelly Rd. .... Pg.11 .... F12
Milburn Rd. .... Pg.11,12 .... E11,12
Plaza Ln. .... Pg.5 .... D12
Sand Lake Rd. .... Pg.11,12 .... F11-12
Skokie Hwy. .... Pg.12 .... E13
Town Line Rd. .... Pg.12 .... E12
Wadsworth Rd. .... Pg.5 .... D12

PARK CITY
Page 20
STREETS
Ann Ave. .... Pg.20 .... K15
Barb Ave. .... Pg.20 .... K15
Bedford .... Pg.20 .... K15
Belvidere Rd. .... Pg.20 .... K15
Betty Ave. .... Pg.20 .... K15
Birch Ave. .... Pg.20 .... K15
Brym Mawr Ave. .... Pg.20 .... K15
Cambridge Dr. .... Pg.20 .... K15
Cornell .... Pg.20 .... K15
Crestwood .... Pg.20 .... K15
Devonshire Dr. .... Pg.20 .... K15
Diana Ave. .... Pg.20 .... K15
Docs Ln. .... Pg.20 .... K15
Dorsett Ct. .... Pg.20 .... K15
Dromley Ave. .... Pg.20 .... K15
Eastwood Pl. .... Pg.20 .... K15
Elaine Ave. .... Pg.20 .... K15
Ell St. .... Pg.20 .... L16
Eric Blvd. .... Pg.20 .... L16
Eva Ave. .... Pg.20 .... K15
Everett Pl. .... Pg.20 .... K15
Green Bay Rd. .... Pg.20 .... L16
Greenleaf St. .... Pg.20 .... K15
Greenleaf .... Pg.20 .... K15
Greenview Dr. .... Pg.20 .... K15
Harvey .... Pg.20 .... K15
Harwick .... Pg.20 .... K15
Hillcrest Dr. .... Pg.20 .... L16
Hood Ave. .... Pg.20 .... L16
Howard Ave. .... Pg.20 .... K15
Ingleside Pl. .... Pg.20 .... K15
Jeanette Ave. .... Pg.20 .... K15
Jen Ave. .... Pg.20 .... K15
Joy Ave. .... Pg.20 .... K15
Judy Ln. .... Pg.20 .... K15
June Ave. .... Pg.20 .... K15
Kehm Blvd. .... Pg.20 .... K15
Keller .... Pg.20 .... K15
Kenilworth Ave. .... Pg.20 .... L15
Knight Ave. .... Pg.20 .... K15
Lake Park Ave. .... Pg.20 .... K15
Longview Dr. .... Pg.20 .... L16
Lowe St. .... Pg.20 .... L16
Main St. .... Pg.20 .... K15
Marshfield Ave. .... Pg.20 .... K15
Mary Ave. .... Pg.20 .... K15
Meadow Dr. .... Pg.20 .... L16
Michael Ave. .... Pg.20 .... K15
Mobile Blvd. .... Pg.20 .... K15
Murphy .... Pg.20 .... K15
Noll Dr. .... Pg.20 .... L16
Northwood Ave. .... Pg.20 .... K15
Oak Dr. .... Pg.20 .... L16
Old Plank Rd. .... Pg.20 .... L16
Oldsmar .... Pg.20 .... K15
Pace Ave. .... Pg.20 .... K15
Palmer Cir. .... Pg.20 .... L16
Park Blvd. .... Pg.20 .... K15
Patricia Ln. .... Pg.20 .... K15
Richard Ave. .... Pg.20 .... K15
Roger Ave. .... Pg.20 .... K15
Rollo Blvd. .... Pg.20 .... K15
Rosedale Ave. .... Pg.20 .... K15
Sharon Ave. .... Pg.20 .... L16
Sunnyside Ave. .... Pg.20 .... L15
Susan Cir. Blvd. .... Pg.20 .... K15
Susan Cir., S. .... Pg.20 .... K15
Sussex Ct. .... Pg.20 .... K15
Ted Ave. .... Pg.20 .... K15
Telegraph Rd. .... Pg.20 .... K15
Teske Blvd. .... Pg.20 .... K15
Thorndale Ave. .... Pg.20 .... K15
Troy .... Pg.20 .... K15
Warren Ave. .... Pg.20 .... K15
Washington St. .... Pg.20 .... K15
West Mead
West St. .... Pg.20 .... K15
Wood St. .... Pg.20 .... L16
7th St. .... Pg.20 .... L16
8th St. .... Pg.20 .... L16
9th St. .... Pg.20 .... L16

PRAIRIE VIEW
Page 33...V12

QUENTIN'S CORNERS
Page 31...X7

RIVERWOODS
Pages 33,36
STREETS
Arrow Ln. .... Pg.36 .... W16
Baneberry Ln. .... Pg.33 .... X14
Bay Hill Ct. .... Pg.36 .... X15
Big Oak Ln. .... Pg.36 .... X15-6
Blackhawk Ln. .... Pg.36 .... X16
Blackhawk Ln. .... Pg.33 .... X14
Blackthorn Rd. .... Pg.33 .... X14
Brae Burn Ct. .... Pg.33 .... X14
Brae Burn Dr. .... Pg.33 .... X14
Buckthorn .... Pg.33 .... X14
Calvin Ct. .... Pg.36 .... W15
Camden Ct. .... Pg.36 .... X15
Chapel Gate .... Pg.36 .... X15
Cherokee Ln. .... Pg.33 .... X14
Chianti Tr. .... Pg.33 .... X14
Chicory Ln. .... Pg.33 .... X14
Chippewa Pkwy. .... Pg.33 .... X14
Clendenin Ln. .... Pg.36 .... X15
Columbine Ln. .... Pg.33 .... X14

Congressional Ln. .... Pg.36 .... X15
Corporate Dr. .... Pg.36 .... V15
Crestwood Ln. .... Pg.36 .... W15
Daquiri Dr. .... Pg.36 .... X15
Dawson Ct. .... Pg.36 .... X15
Deepwood Terr. .... Pg.36 .... V16
Deerfield Rd. .... Pg.36 .... W15
Duffy Dr. .... Pg.36 .... V15
Eagle Ct. .... Pg.36 .... X15
East Course Dr. .... Pg.36 .... X15
Edgewood Ct. .... Pg.36 .... W15
Edgewood Ln. .... Pg.36 .... W15
Estonian Ct. .... Pg.33 .... W14
Farmer Ct. .... Pg.36 .... X15
Forest Glen Ct. .... Pg.36 .... X15
Forest Glen Tr. .... Pg.36 .... X15
Fox Tail Ct. .... Pg.33 .... X14
Gemini Ln. .... Pg.36 .... X15
Glen Eagles Ln. .... Pg.36 .... X15
Greenbrier Ln. .... Pg.36 .... X15
Hazelnut Ln. .... Pg.36 .... X15
Hiawatha Ln. .... Pg.36 .... X15
Hill Ln. .... Pg.36 .... W16
Hoffman Ln. .... Pg.36 .... X15
Indian Trail Dr. .... Pg.33 .... X14
Interlocken Ct. .... Pg.36 .... X15
Julie Ln. .... Pg.36 .... X15
Juneberry Rd. .... Pg.36 .... X15
Kenilwood Ct. .... Pg.36 .... W15
Kenilwood Ln. .... Pg.36 .... W15
Kingswood Dr. .... Pg.36 .... X15
Knollwood Way .... Pg.36 .... W15
Legends Ct. .... Pg.36 .... X15
Links Ct. .... Pg.36 .... X15
Long Cove Ct. .... Pg.36 .... X15
Lyndale .... Pg.36 .... X15
Lyngby Ct. .... Pg.33 .... X14
Maple Pl. .... Pg.36 .... X15
Meredith Dr. .... Pg.36 .... X15
Mettawa Ln. .... Pg.33 .... X14
Muirfield Ln. .... Pg.36 .... X15
Oakhurst Ln. .... Pg.36 .... X15
Orange Brace Rd. .... Pg.36 .... X15
Palmer Ct. .... Pg.36 .... X15
Pebble Beach Ln. .... Pg.36 .... X15
Pine Tree Ln. .... Pg.36 .... X15
Port Wine Rd. .... Pg.33 .... X14
Portwine Rd. .... Pg.36 .... W15
Ringland Ln. .... Pg.36 .... X15
Riverwoods Ct. .... Pg.36 .... W15
Riverwoods Rd. .... Pg.36 .... W15
Robinwood Ln. .... Pg.36 .... W15
Rose Terr. .... Pg.36 .... X15
Royal Troon Ct. .... Pg.36 .... X15
Saunders Rd. .... Pg.36 .... V15
Sawgrass Ct. .... Pg.36 .... X15
Scotch Ln. .... Pg.36 .... X15
Seminole Ct. .... Pg.36 .... X15
Shadow Creek Ln. .... Pg.36 .... X15
Shawnee Tr. .... Pg.33 .... X14
Sherry Ln. .... Pg.36 .... X15
Shoal Creek Ct. .... Pg.36 .... X15
Somerset Hill Ct. .... Pg.36 .... X15
Spyglass Hill Ct. .... Pg.36 .... X15
Strenger Ln. .... Pg.36 .... X15
Studio Ln. .... Pg.36 .... X15
Suffield Sq. .... Pg.36 .... V15
Thornapple Ln. .... Pg.36 .... X15
Thornwood Ln. .... Pg.36 .... W15
Timber Hill Ln. .... Pg.36 .... X14
Timberline Ln. .... Pg.36 .... X15
Timberwood Ln. .... Pg.36 .... X15
Tour Ct. .... Pg.36 .... X15
Treasure Ln. .... Pg.36 .... X15
Trillium Ln. .... Pg.36 .... X15
Vernon Tr. .... Pg.36 .... X15
West Course Dr. .... Pg.36 .. W15-16
Whigam Ln. .... Pg.36 .... X15
Whigam Rd. .... Pg.36 .... X15
White Oak Ln. .... Pg.36 .... X15
Wild Dunes Ct. .... Pg.36 .... X15
Windlake Trail .... Pg.36 .... V16
Woodland Ct. .... Pg.36 .... W15
Woodland Lake, N. .... Pg.36 .... W15
Woodland Ln. .... Pg.36 .... W15
Yasmine Dr. .... Pg.36 .... X15

FOREST PRESERVES
Ryerson Wood F.P. .... Pg.33 .... W14

GOLF COURSES
Deerfield Park Dist. G.C.
Ravina Green C.C. .... Pg.36 .... X16

SCHOOLS
Riverwood Montessori Sch. .... Pg.36 .... W15

MISCELLANEOUS
Brentwood Nursing Home .... Pg.36 .... X14
Orphans of the Snow .... Pg.36 .... X16
Village Hall .... Pg.36 .... W16

ROSECRANS
Page 5...B12

ROUND LAKE
Pages 9,16,17
STREETS
A-OK Dr. .... Pg.9 .... K5
Alma Cir. .... Pg.9 .... K5
Alma Ct. .... Pg.9 .... K5
Alpine Dr. .... Pg.16 .... K5
Antares Cir. .... Pg.9,16 .. K5,6
Apollo Ct. .... Pg.9 .... K5
Applegate Ct. .... Pg.16 .... L6
Arrowhead Ct. .... Pg.16 .... L6
Avilon Ave. .... Pg.16 .... L6
Balmoral Dr. .... Pg.16 .... K5
Barnwood Ct. .... Pg.16 .... L6
Basswood Ct. .... Pg.16 .... L6
Beachfront Dr. .... Pg.16 .... K5
Belvidere Rd. .... Pg.16 .... L6
Bernice Ct., N. & S. .... Pg.9 .... K5
Bernice Ln. .... Pg.9 .... K5
Biminy Bay .... Pg.16 .... L6
Blackhorn Ct. .... Pg.16 .... L6
Boxwood Ct. .... Pg.16 .... L6
Buckthorn Ln. .... Pg.16 .... L6
Bugle Ct. .... Pg.9 .... K5
Cadro Dr. .... Pg.16 .... L6
Chapel Gate .... Pg.16 .... L6
Chicory Ln. .... Pg.16 .... K,L6
Clearview Cir. .... Pg.16 .... L6
Cranberry Ct. .... Pg.16 .... L6
Dawn Marie Terr. .... Pg.16 .... L6
Deerwood Ct. .... Pg.16 .... L6

Dell Ct. .... Pg.16 .... K6
Dogwood Ct. .... Pg.16 .... K6
Dorothy Ct. .... Pg.16 .... K6
Dorothy Ln. .... Pg.16 .... K6
Fairfield Ave. .... Pg.16 .... K6
Fairfield Rd. .... Pg.16 .... L5
Farmwood Ct. .... Pg.16 .... K6
Forest Ave. .... Pg.16 .... K6
Garden Ct. .... Pg.16 .... K6
Goodnow Ave. .... Pg.16 .... K6
Hackberry Ct. .... Pg.16 .... L6
Hart Rd. .... Pg.16 .... K5
Haywood Cir. .... Pg.16 .... K5
Haywood Dr. .... Pg.16 .... K5
High Point Rd. .... Pg.16 .... K6
High School Rd. .... Pg.16 .... K6
Hillandale Ave. .... Pg.16 .... K6
Hillside Dr. .... Pg.9 .... K6
Holly Ct. .... Pg.16 .... K6
Honey Ct. .... Pg.16 .... L6
Houston Ct. .... Pg.16 .... L6
Kitty Hawk Dr. .... Pg.9 .... K6
LEM Dr. .... Pg.9 .... K6
Lake Ct. .... Pg.16 .... K6
Lakewood Terr. .... Pg.16 .... K6
Laurel Ave. .... Pg.16 .... K5
Lincoln Ave. .... Pg.16 .... K6
Linden Dr. .... Pg.16 .... K6
Long Lake Dr. .... Pg.16 .... K6
Lunar Dr. .... Pg.16 .... K6
Lunga Dr. .... Pg.9 .... K6
Mac Gillis Dr. .... Pg.16 .... K5
Magna Dr. .... Pg.16 .... K6
Maple Ln. .... Pg.16 .... K6
Moon Rover Dr. .... Pg.9 .... K6
NASA Cir. .... Pg.9 .... K6
Nippersink Rd. .... Pg.16 .... K5
Old Farm Rd. .... Pg.16 .... K6
Orbiter Dr. .... Pg.9 .... K6
Orchard St. .... Pg.16 .... L6
Osage Ct. .... Pg.16 .... L6
Park Ave. .... Pg.16 .... K6
Petite St. .... Pg.16 .... L6
Pineview Ln. .... Pg.16 .... L6
Prairie Ln. .... Pg.16 .... L6
Primrose Ln. .... Pg.16 .... L6
Quail Hollow Ct. .... Pg.16 .... L6
Railroad Ave. .... Pg.16 .... K6
Ravine Ave. .... Pg.16 .... K6
Ridge Wood Dr. .... Pg.16 .... L6
Roberta Ct. .... Pg.16 .... L6
Rosedale Ct., N. & S. .... Pg.9 .... K6
Round Lake Rd. .... Pg.16 .... K6
Sagebrush Ct. .... Pg.16 .... L6
School Ct. .... Pg.16 .... K6
School Dr. .... Pg.16 .... L6
Spankey Ct. .... Pg.16 .... K6
Sunset Dr. .... Pg.16 .... K6
Sweet Clover Rd. .... Pg.16 .... L6
Sycamore Dr. .... Pg.16 .... L6
Tanglewood Ct. .... Pg.16 .... L6
Thistle Ct. .... Pg.16 .... L6
Treehouse Ln. .... Pg.16 .... L6
Valentine Dr. .... Pg.16 .... K6
Valley View Dr. .... Pg.16 .... L4
Wagonwood Rd. .... Pg.16 .... L6
Washington St. .... Pg.16 .... K6
Wedgewood Rd. .... Pg.16 .... K6
Weeping Willow Rd. .... Pg.16 .... L6
Whispering Oak Ln.
Wildrose Ct. .... Pg.16 .... K6
Wildspring Rd. .... Pg.16 .... L6
Wilson Rd. .... Pg.16 .... L6

CEMETERIES
Fort Hill Cemetery .... Pg.16 .... L5

PARKS
Cedar Valley Park .... Pg.16 .... K6
Country Lake Resort
Harts Park .... Pg.16 .... L5
Recreational Vehicle Park .... Pg.16 .... L5
Viking Park .... Pg.16 .... K6

SCHOOLS
Magee Middle Sch. .... Pg.16 .... K5
Round Lake H.S. .... Pg.16 .... K6
Round Lake Jr. H.S. .... Pg.16 .... K6
St. Josephs Sch. .... Pg.16 .... K6

SHOPPING CENTERS
Round Lake S.C. No. 1 .... Pg.16 .... K5
Round Lake S.C. No. 2 .... Pg.16 .... K6

MISCELLANEOUS
Library .... Pg.16 .... K5
Park District .... Pg.16 .... K5
Public Utility Bldg. .... Pg.16 .... K5
R.R. Station .... Pg.16 .... K5

ROUND LAKE BEACH
Pages 9,10
STREETS
Acorn Ct. .... Pg.9 .... G6
Acorn Dr. .... Pg.9 .... G7
Alma Cir. .... Pg.9 .... G7
Alma Ct. .... Pg.9 .... G7
Amber Prairie Gr. .... Pg.9 .... G7
Amber Prairie Way .... Pg.9 .... G7
Apache Tr. .... Pg.9 .... G6
Ardmore Dr. .... Pg.9 .... H6
Aster Ct. .... Pg.9 .... G6
Aster Dr. .... Pg.9 .... G6
Barberry Ln. .... Pg.9 .... H6
Bayview Dr. .... Pg.9 .... H6
Beachview Dr. .... Pg.9 .... H6
Beacon St. .... Pg.9 .... G6
Beverly Dr. .... Pg.9 .... H5
Beverly Ln. .... Pg.9 .... H5
Birchwood Ct. .... Pg.9 .... H5
Blackberry Ln. .... Pg.9 .... G5
Blue Grass Ct. .... Pg.9 .... H6
Bluebelle Ct. .... Pg.9 .... H6
Bonniebrook Ln. .... Pg.9 .... H6
Brentwood Dr. .... Pg.9 .... H7
Briar Ln. .... Pg.9 .... H6
Bridle Cir. .... Pg.10 .... G8
Bridle Ct. .... Pg.10 .... G8
Brighton Ln. .... Pg.10 .... H8
Buena Vista Ct. .... Pg.9 .... G7
Bugle Ln. .... Pg.9 .... G6
Butternut Ct. .... Pg.9 .... G6
Camden Ln. .... Pg.10 .... G7

Canbury Ln. Pg.10 G7
Carl Ct. Pg.9 H6
Carl Dr. Pg.9 G,H6
Carriage Ct. Pg.10 H7
Carriage Ln. Pg.10 H7
Castlebar Ct. Pg.10 G7
Cedar Lake Rd. Pg.9 H6
Center Dr. Pg.10 H7
Central Park Dr. Pg.9 H5
Channel Dr. Pg.9 H6
Channel Dr., N. & S. Pg.9 H6
Cherokee Dr. Pg.9 H5
Cherry Cove Ct. Pg.9 G6
Cherry Cove Ln. Pg.9 G6
Chestnut Dr. Pg.9 H6
Cheswick Ct. Pg.10 G7
Chicory Ln. Pg.10 G7
Christopher Ct. Pg.9 G6
Churchill Ct. Pg.10 G7
Circle Dr. Pg.10 H7
Circuit Dr. Pg.9 G,H6
Clarendon Dr. Pg.9 H6-7
Clarendon East End Dr. Pg.10 H7
Comanche Pg.9 G6
Corona Ct. Pg.9 H5
Country Walk Dr. Pg.9 G6
Countryside Ln. Pg.9 G6
Covington Ln. Pg.10 G7
Crescent Ct. Pg.9 H5
Dahlia Ln. Pg.9 G6
Daisy Ln. Pg.10 H7
Dakota Ct. Pg.9 G6
Deer Tr. Pg.10 G7
Deerpath Ct. Pg.9 H6
Diana Ct. Pg.9 H5
Eagle Creek Pg.9 G6
East End Ave. Pg.10 H7
Elm Ave. Pg.10 H7
Evergreen Ct. Pg.9 G6
Fairfield Terr. Pg.9 H6
Farifield Rd. Pg.9 H5
Ferndale Ct. Pg.9 H6
Foxchase Ct. Pg.10 G7
Foxchase Dr. Pg.10 G7
Fruitwood Dr. Pg.9 G6
Geneva Terr. Pg.9 H6
Glenview Ct. Pg.9 H6
Glenview Dr. Pg.9 H6
Glenwood Dr. Pg.9 H6
Goldenrod Terr. Pg.9 H6
Golfview Ct. Pg.9 H5-6
Golfview Dr. Pg.9 H5,6
Green Valley Ct. Pg.9 G6
Green Valley Ln. Pg.9 G6
Grove Dr. Pg.9 H6
Hainesville Rd. Pg.10 H7
Hardwood Path Pg.10 G8
Harvest Hill Pl. Pg.9 G6
Hawthorne Dr. Pg.9 H6
Heartland Path Pg.10 G7
Heather Terr. Pg.10 H7
Hickory Ave. Pg.9 H6
Hickory St. Pg.10 H7
Highland Pkwy. Pg.9 H6
Highland Terr. Pg.9 H6
Hillcrest Ct. Pg.9 G6
Hillside Ave. Pg.9 H5
Hillside Dr. Pg.9 H6
Hillwood Cir. Pg.9 H5
Honeysuckle Ct. Pg.9 G6
Honeysuckle Dr. Pg.9 G6
Hunters Ln. Pg.10 G8
Idlewild Dr. Pg.9 H6
Ivy Ct. Pg.10 H7
Juneway Terr. Pg.9 H6
Juniper Terr. Pg.9 H6
Karen Ln. Pg.9 G6
Kellycain Ct. Pg.10 G7
Kenilworth Dr. Pg.9 H6
Kenmore Ave. Pg.10 H7
Kildeer Dr. Pg.9 H5
Lagoon Terr. Pg.9 H6
Lake Ave. Pg.10 H7
Lake Shore Dr. Pg.9 H6
Lakewood Pkwy. Pg.9 H6
Lancaster Ln. Pg.10 G7
Laurel Ct. Pg.9 H6
Lenox Ct. Pg.10 G7
Leslie Ave. Pg.10 H7
Lexington Dr. Pg.10 G7
Lilac Ln. Pg.10 H7
Lindsay Dr. Pg.9 G6
London Ct. Pg.10 G7
Long Lake Rd. Pg.9 H5
Lotus Dr. Pg.9 H5
Mallard Creek Dr. Pg.10 H7
Mallard Ln. Pg.9 G6
Maple Dr. Pg.9 H6
Martingale Ln. Pg.10 G7,8
Mary Ct. Pg.9 G6
Masters Ln. Pg.10 G7
Mayfield Dr. Pg.9 H5
Meadow Green Ln. Pg.9 G6
Meadow Ln. Pg.10 G8
Meadowbrook Dr. Pg.9 H6
Meadowhill Ln. Pg.9 G6
Melrose Ave. Pg.10 H7
Milestone Cir. Pg.10 G7
Monaville Rd. Pg.10 G7
Morningside Dr. Pg.9 H5
Nicole Ln. Pg.9 G6
Nielsen Ave. Pg.9 H5
Norelius Ave. Pg.9 H5
Normandie Ln. Pg.9 G6
North Ave. Pg.10 H7
Oak Ave. Pg.10 H7
Oak St. Pg.10 H7
Oakleaf Cir. Pg.10 G8
Oakleaf Ct. Pg.10 G8
Oakleaf Ln. Pg.10 G8
Oaktree Cir. Pg.10 G8
Oaktree Tr. Pg.10 G7
Oakwood Dr. Pg.9 H5
Old Pond Ct. Pg.9 G6
Old Pond Ln. Pg.9 G6
Old Rollins Rd. Pg.10 G7
Orchard Ct. Pg.9 H6
Orchard Ln. Pg.9 G6,7
Palm Ct. Pg.10 G7
Park Dr. Pg.9 H6
Partridge Ct. Pg.9 H6
Passavant Ave. Pg.9 H5
Peachtree Ln. Pg.10 G7
Pembrook Ct. Pg.10 G7
Pennsbury Ct. Pg.10 G7
Periwinkle Way Pg.9 G6
Persimmon Ct. Pg.10 G7
Pheasant Ct. Pg.9 H6
Pheasant Ridge Ct. Pg.9 G6
Pine Grove Ave. Pg.10 H7
Pleasant Dr. Pg.9 H6
Plymouth Ct. Pg.10 G7
Poplar Ave. Pg.10 H7
Poplar St. Pg.9 H5
Princeton Ct. Pg.10 G7
Quaker Hollow Ln. Pg.10 G7
Red Wood Pg.9 G6
Redhead Ct. Pg.9 G6
Redwing Dr. Pg.10 H7
Regency Ln. Pg.10 H8
Ridgeway Ave. Pg.10 H7
Rollins Rd. Pg.10 H7
Ronald Terr. Pg.9 H5
Rosewood Ct. Pg.9 G6
Rosewood Ln. Pg.9 G6,7
Round Lake Dr. Pg.9 H6
Rustic Ct. Pg.9 G6
Rustic Ln. Pg.9 G6
Saddle Ln. Pg.10 G7
Salem Ln. Pg.10 G7
Sauk Ct. Pg.9 G6
Scott Ct. Pg.10 G7
Sedgefield Ct. Pg.10 G7
Shady Ln. Pg.9 H5
Shady Ln. Ct. Pg.9 H6
Shaker Ct. Pg.10 G7
Sheffield Ct. Pg.10 G7
Shoreland Ct. Pg.9 H6
Shorewood Rd. Pg.10 H7
Silver Oaks Dr. Pg.9 G6
Somerset Ct. Pg.10 G7
Southmoor Ln. Pg.9 H5
Springwood Ct. Pg.10 G7
Sprucewood Ct. Pg.9 G6
Sprucewood Ln. Pg.9 G6
Stanton Ct. Pg.10 G7
Sterling Ct. Pg.10 G7
Stockton Ct. Pg.10 G7
Stonehedge Ct. Pg.10 G7
Stratford Ln. Pg.10 G7
Sugar Run Ln. Pg.10 G7
Sunnyside Dr. Pg.9 H6
Sunrise Dr. Pg.9 G6
Sunset Dr. Pg.9 H6
Tall Grass Ct. Pg.9 G6
Turnbull Dr. Pg.9 H5
Villa Dr. Pg.9 G6
Villa Vista Pg.9 H5
Vine Ave. Pg.10 H7
Vineyard Ln. Pg.9 G6
Walnut Dr. Pg.9 H6
West End Dr. Pg.9 H6
Weston Ct. Pg.10 G7
Westview Ln. Pg.9 G6
Whitehall Ct. Pg.10 G7
Wildflower Ct. Pg.9 G6
Wildflower Ln. Pg.9 G6
Wildwood Dr. Pg.9 H6
William Ave. Pg.10 H7
Willow Ridge Pg.9 G6
Witchwood Ln. Pg.9 H6
Woodbine Dr. Pg.9 H6
Woodland Dr. Pg.9 H6
Woodmoor Dr. Pg.10 H7
Woodoak Cir. Pg.10 G8
Woodoak Dr. Pg.10 G8
Woodridge Dr. Pg.9 H5
Woodside Dr. Pg.9 G6
Yvonne Ct. Pg.9 G6

**GOLF COURSES**

Renwood C.C. Pg.10 H7

**PARKS**

Fairview Park Pg.9 H6
Jaycee Park Pg.9 H6

**SCHOOLS**

Avon Sch. Pg.10 H7
Raymond Ellis Sch. Pg.9 H6
Round Lake Beach Sch. Pg.9 H6

**SHOPPING CENTERS**

Eagle Creek S.C. Pg.9 H6
Mallard Creek S.C. Pg.10 H7
Rollins Plaza Pg.10 H7
The Commons S.C. Pg.10 H7

**MISCELLANEOUS**

Fire Station No. 2 Pg.9 H6
Railroad Station Pg.10 G7
Village Hall Pg.9 H6

## ROUND LAKE HEIGHTS

Page 9

**STREETS**

Arrowhead Dr. H6
Blackburn Ave. G5
Brentwood Dr. H5
Cambridge Dr. G5
Cedarwood Cir., N. & E. G6
Cedarwood Cir., S. & W. G5
Crossland Ave. G5
Flintwood Ct. G5
Hiawatha Tr. H5
Huntington Ave. G5
Keswick Ave. G5
Lotus Dr. H5
Meadowbrook Dr. H6
Mohawk Dr. G5
Partridge Ct. H6
Paxton Ave. G5
Pontiac Dr. H6
Scott Ave. G5
Southport Ave. G5
Summit Ct. G6
Summit Ct., N. G6
Tomahawk G5
Trent Dr. G5
Turkey Run Dr. G5
Warrior Dr. G5

**FOREST PRESERVES**

Shag Bark Nature Preserve G5

**PARKS**

Long Lake Woods G5
Shag Bark Park G5

**SCHOOLS**

Indian Hill Sch. G5

**MISCELLANEOUS**

Police Dept. H5
Village Hall C6

## ROUND LAKE PARK

Pages 10,16,17

**STREETS**

Abbey Ln. Pg.16 K6
Admiral Ct. Pg.17 K7
Amendola Way Pg.17 N7
Arabian Pg.17 N7
Arbor Dr. Pg.17 K7
Arlington Pg.17 N7
Augusta Dr. Pg.16 K6
Barbara Ct. Pg.16 L6
Bellevue Dr. Pg.17 K7
Belmont Pg.17 N7
Belvidere Rd. Pg.17 L6
Bengson Ct. Pg.16 L6
Betsy Pg.17 N7
Bison Dr. Pg.16 L6
Briar Hill Dr. Pg.17 K6
Canterbury Pg.17 N7
Cedar Dr. Pg.10 H7
Cedar Mound Rd. Pg.16 L6
Center Dr. Pg.17 L6
Citation Ln. Pg.17 N7
Clifton Dr. Pg.17 K6
Colony Dr. Pg.16 K6
Creekside Ln. Pg.16 L6
Dartmoor Dr. Pg.16 K6
Davis Ct. Pg.16 K6
Delmar Pg.17 N7
Derby Pg.17 N7
Derby Ct. Pg.17 N7
Devonshire Pg.17 N7
Elder Dr. Pg.17 K7
Elm Ave. Pg.10 K7
Fairlawn Dr. Pg.17 K7
Filly Ln. Pg.17 N7
Forest Glen Dr. Pg.17 K7
Furlong Pg.17 N7
Grandview Dr. Pg.17 K7
Greenwood Dr. Pg.17 K6
Hialeah Pg.17 N7
Highmoor Dr. Pg.17 K7
Jorgensen Ln. Pg.16 L6
Kenwood Dr. Pg.17 K6
Knollwood Dr. Pg.17 K7
Lake Ave. Pg.10 K7
Lake Shore Dr. Pg.17 K7
Linden Dr. Pg.16 K6
Locust Dr. Pg.17 K7
Lyle Ave. Pg.10 K7
Main St. Pg.17 K6
Maple Ave. pG.10 K7
Mayflower Terr. Pg.10 K7
Midland Dr. Pg.16 K6
Model Ct. Pg.16 L6
Mustang Pg.17 N7
Newhouse Dr. Pg.17 L6
Oak St. Pg.10 K7
Palomino Pg.17 N7
Parkview Ct. Pg.17 K7
Peterson Rd. Pg.17 N7
Pineview Dr. Pg.17 K7
Porter Dr. Pg.17 K6
Prospect Dr. Pg.17 K7
Ravine Dr. Pg.17 K7
Saddlebrook Dr. Pg.17 N7
Sandy Point Ln. Pg.17 K7
Saratoga Pg.17 N7
Schooner Ct. Pg.17 K7
Secretariat Pg.17 N7
Shetland Pg.17 N7
Surrey Ct. Pg.17 N7
Sylvan Dr. Pg.10 K7
Timber Creek Dr. Pg.16 L6
Trotter Pg.17 N7
Washington St. Pg.17 K6
Waterview Dr. Pg.17 K7
Willow Dr. Pg.17 K6
Windridge Dr. Pg.16 K6

**PARKS**

Bengson Park Pg.17 K7
Parrott Park Pg.17 K7

**SCHOOLS**

Round Lake Park Sch. Pg.17 K6
St. Paul Lutheran Sch. Pg.17 K6
W.J. Murphy Elem. Sch. Pg.16 K6

**MISCELLANEOUS**

Campbell Airport Pg.17 M7
Village Hall and Police Dept. Pg.17 K7

## RUSSELL

Page 5...A14

## SHIELDS TOWNSHIP

Pages 20,21,27,28

**STREETS**

Adelphia Ave. Pg.27 P-Q16
Ballard Dr. Pg.27 Q15
Basil Rd. Pg.27 Q16
Bayonne Ave. Pg.27 Q16
Bayshore Dr. Pg.21 P17
Beacon Ave. Pg.20 N16
Berwyn Ave. Pg.20 N16
Birch Ave. Pg.27 Q16
Blodgett Ave. Pg.27 Q16
Broadway Ave. Pg.21 P17
Brompton Ave. Pg.20 N16
Buckley Rd. Pg.20 N16
Burris Ave. Pg.27 P16
Clover Ln. Pg.27 Q16
Eastway Pg.21 N18
Fairbank Ave. Pg.20 N16
Forest View Dr. Pg.21 P17
Glendell Ave. Pg.28 P17
Green Ave. Pg.27 P-Q16
Green Bay Rd. Pg.28 P17
Herky Dr. Pg.27 Q15
Hillside Ave. Pg.20 P17
Jenkisson Ave. Pg.27 Q16
Juneway Rd. Pg.21 P17
Keith Dr. Pg.27 Q15
Kohl Rd. Pg.28 P17
Laurel Dr. Pg.27 Q15
Lawn Ave. Pg.20 N16
Leola Dr. Pg.27 Q15
Mawman Blvd. Pg.28 P17
Melvin Rd. Pg.21 P17
North Ave. Pg.27 Q16
Northern Ave. Pg.27 Q16
Northshore Dr. Pg.28 P17
Plaister Ave. Pg.27 P16
Private Rd. Pg.28 Q16
Quassey Ave. Pg.27 Q16
Rivers Dr. Pg.21 P17
Rockland Rd. Pg.27 Q16
Safford Ave. Pg.27 P16
Shagbark Rd. Pg.27 Q16
Sheridan Rd. Pg.21 P17
Shore Acres Rd. Pg.21 P18
Skokie Blvd. Pg.27 Q16
Skokie Hwy. Pg.27 P16
Smith Ave. Pg.27 Q16
St. Louis Pg.28 P17
Talbot Ave. Pg.27 P16
Thorn Valley Ln. Pg.28 P17
Thorntree Rd. Pg.27 Q16
Washington Ave. Pg.27 Q16
Washington St. Pg.27 Q16
Woodland Rd. Pg.27 Q16

**GOLF COURSES**

Shore Acres G.C. Pg.21 N-P18

## SPAULDING CORNERS

Page 13...H15

## SYLVAN LAKE

Page 24...S8

## THIRD LAKE

Pages 11,18

**STREETS**

Brigantine Ln. K10
Clipper Ct. K10
Coral Reef Ct. K10
Cottage St. H10
Crows Nest Ct. K10
Galleon Dr. H10
Grant Ave. H10
Lake Ave. H10
Lakeview Dr. H9
Lighthouse Ln. H10
Mainsail Dr. H10
Portside Ct. K10
Schooner Ln. H10
Seafarer Dr. K10
Sextant Dr. K10
Spinnaker Ct. H10
Starboard Ct. K10
Sunshine Ave. H10
Washington St. K10
Whaler Ct. K10
Windjammer Ct. K10
Windjammer Ln. K10

**FOREST PRESERVES**

Rollings Savana F.P. H10

## TOWER LAKES

Pages 22,29,30

**STREETS**

Abbot Pl. Pg.22 S3
Barrington Lakes Pg.22 T3
Barsumian Dr. Pg.22 T3
Bays Pl. Pg.22 S3
Blue Stem Ct. Pg.29 T3
Bridge Ln. Pg.22 T3
Cambridge Dr. Pg.22 T3
Circle Dr. Pg.22 S3
Devonshire Rd. Pg.22 T3
Edward Ln. Pg.22 T3
Essex Pl. Pg.22 T3
Esther Dr. Pg.22 S3
Fenview Dr. Pg.29 T3
Indian Grass Ct. Pg.29 T3
Indian Trails Rd. Pg.23 T4
Kelsey Rd. Pg.29 T3
Lake Shore Dr., N., W. & E. Pg.22 T3
Lake Shore Terr. Pg.22 T3
Leon Dr. Pg.22 S3
Medinah Ln. Pg.30 T4
Melrose Dr. Pg.22 T3
Murray Dr. Pg.22 T3
Nooding Flower Ct. Pg.29 T3
Oak St. Pg.22 T3
Oxford Rd. Pg.22 T3
Paddock Ln. Pg.22 T3
Pebble Creek Dr. Pg.23 T3
Raleigh Pl. Pg.22 T3
Roberts Rd. Pg.22 T3
Robin Rd. Pg.22 T3
Rolling Green Dr. Pg.30 T4
Rose Terr. Ct. Pg.29 T3
Roslyn Pl. Pg.22 T3
Scenic Dr. Pg.22 T3
South Dr. Pg.29 T3
South Hills Dr. Pg.29 T3
Stonehedge Ln. Pg.30 T4
Summit Dr. Pg.22 T3
Timber Ct. Pg.29 T3
Tomahawk Dr. Pg.22 S3
Tower Dr., E. & W. Pg.22 T3
Warwick Rd. Pg.22 T3
West Dr. Pg.22 S3
Wren Rd. Pg.22 T2

**PARKS**

Barsumian Park Pg.22 S3
Bays Park Pg.22 S3
Garden Lewis Park Pg.22 S3
Hussissian Park Pg.22 S3
Murray Park Pg.22 S3
Roses Park Pg.22 S3

## VERNON HILLS

Pages 25,26,32,33

**STREETS**

Abbey Ln. Pg.26 T12
Abilene Ln. Pg.26 T12
Adair Ct. Pg.26 T12
Adams Pg.25 S11
Adrian Ct. Pg.25 T11
Albany Ln. Pg.26 T12
Albert Dr. Pg.25,26 T12
Albright Ct. Pg.25 T11
Alexandria Dr. Pg.26 T12
Alfred Ct. Pg.32 T11
Alice Ct. Pg.25 T12
Allentown Ct. Pg.26 T12
Almond Ct. Pg.26 T12
Alpine Dr. Pg.26 T12
Altoona Ct. Pg.26 T12
Amber Ln. Pg.26 T12
Amherst Ct. Pg.26 T12
Angela Ct. Pg.26 T12
Ann Arbor Ln. Pg.25 T11
Ann Ct. Pg.33 T12
Annapolis Dr. Pg.33 T12
Apollo Ct. Pg.32 T12
Appian Way Pg.25 T12
Apple Orchard Pg.33 U13
Appleton Dr. Pg.26 T12
April Ave. Pg.26 T12
Aqua Ct. Pg.25 T12
Arcadia Ct. Pg.26 T12
Ardmore Ct. Pg.26 T12
Arlington Ct. Pg.26 T12
Aron Ct. Pg.33 T12
Aronomick Rd. Pg.26 R12
Ashland Ct. Pg.26 T12
Ashville Ct. Pg.33 T12
Ashwood Ct. Pg.33 T13
Aspen Dr. Pg.26 S,T12
Astoria Ct. Pg.26 T12
Athens Ct. Pg.26 T12
Atlantic Dr. Pg.26 T12
Atrium Dr. Pg.26 S12
Auburn Ct. Pg.33 T12
Augusta Dr. Pg.26 T12
Aurora Ct. Pg.26 T12
Austin Ct. Pg.33 T12
Autumn Ln. Pg.26 T12
Avon Ct. Pg.26 T12
Baltimore Dr. Pg.25,26 S12
Balustrol Dr. Pg.26 R12
Barn Swallow Ln. Pg.33 T,U12
Barton Dr. Pg.26 R12
Basswood Dr. Pg.33 T13
Beaver Creek Dr. Pg.26 R12
Bedford Rd. Pg.26 T12
Belle Isle Ln. Pg.32 T11
Birch Pg.32 T11
Birchwood Ct. Pg.33 T13
Birmingham Pl. Pg.33 T12
Blackwolfe Ct. Pg.26 R12
Bloomfield Ct. Pg.25 T11
Bluewater Ln. Pg.32 S12
Brandywine Pg.26 S12
Briarwood Ct. Pg.25 T11
Broadmoor Ln. Pg.26 R12
Broken Sound Pkwy. Pg.26 R12
Brook Hill Ln. Pg.33 T12
Brook Ln. Pg.26 S12
Brookwood Ct. Pg.33 T13
Browning Ct. Pg.26 S12
Bryant Pl. Pg.25 S11
Buchanan Ct. Pg.25 S11
Bunker Ct. Pg.26 T12-13
Burnside Ct. Pg.26 S12
Butler Ct. Pg.26 S11
Butterfield Rd. Pg.25 T11
Camargo Ct. Pg.26 R12
Camden Pl. Pg.32 U11,12
Cascade Dr. Pg.25 R11
Castlegate Ct. Pg.26 T12
Cedar Ct. Pg.26 S12
Center Dr. Pg.26 S12
Central Park Pl. Pg.33 U12
Centurion Ln. Pg.26 S12
Chatham Ct. Pg.26 S12
Cherokee Rd. Pg.26 T12
Cherry Valley Rd. Pg.32 T,U11
Cherrywood Ct. Pg.33 T13
Chesapeake Ct. Pg.26 S12
Chesterfield Ln. Pg.32 U12
Clairmont Ct. Pg.26 S12
Club Ln. Pg.33 U12
Cog Hill Ct. Pg.26 S11
Colonial Dr. Pg.26 R12
Colony Ct. Pg.26 S12
Commonwealth Pg.26 S12
Conachie Ct. Pg.32 T11
Congressional Ct. Pg.26 S12
Constitution Pg.26 S12
Continental Dr. Pg.26 T13
Corey's Ct. Pg.26 R12
Corporate Woods Pkwy. Pg.33 U13
Country Club Ln. Pg.32 T12
Court of Ash Pg.32 U11
Court of Elm Pg.32 U11
Court of Shorewood, S., E. & W. Pg.32 U11
Coventry Cir. Pg.26 S12
Crabtree Ln. Pg.26 T12
Creek Bend Dr. Pg.32 U12
Creek View Dr. Pg.32 U12
Creekside Dr. Pg.25 T11
Crestview Ln. Pg.26 S12
Cromwell Ct. Pg.26 S12
Crooked Stick Ct. Pg.26 S11
Cumberland Ct. Pg.26 S12
Cypress Pointe Dr. Pg.26 R12
Danbury Dr. Pg.32 U12
Dawson Ct. Pg.32 T11
Dearborn Ln. Pg.25 T11
Debill Ct. Pg.33 T12
Deerbrook Ln. Pg.32 U11
Deerpath Dr. Pg.33 T12
Depot St. Pg.33 U12
Dickinson Ct. Pg.26 S12
Dillons Ct. Pg.26 R12
Dogwood Ln. Pg.33 T13
Donnelley Pl. Pg.33 U12
Donnelly Pl. Pg.33 U12
Dover Ct. Pg.26 S12
Echo Ct Pg.26 S12
Edgewood Rd. Pg.26 T12
Elm Tree Ln. Pg.26 T12
Emerson Pl. Pg.25 S11
End Ct., W. Pg.25 S11
End Ln., W. Pg.25 S11
Eugene Terr. Pg.26 R12
Evergreen Dr. Pg.32 T12
Executive Way Dr. Pg.26 T13
Exeter Pl. Pg.26 T12
Fairview Dr. Pg.26 S,T12
Fairway Dr. Pg.26 S12
Farmindale Cir. Pg.25 S11
Farmington Ln. Pg.25 S11
Faulkner Pl. Pg.26 S12
Fernwood Ct. Pg.33 T13
Fiore Pkwy. Pg.25 T11
Forest Edge Dr. Pg.33 U13
Franklin Pl. Pg.25 S11
Georgetown Way Pg.33 U13
Gladstone Dr. Pg.26 S12
Golfview Ct. Pg.26 T13
Grant Pl. Pg.26 S12
Greenbriar Ln. Pg.32 U11
Greenleaf Dr. Pg.25 S11
Greenvale Rd. Pg.26 T12
Greenview Ct. Pg.26 T13
Gregg's Pkwy. Pg.26 R11
Grosse Pointe Blvd. Pg.32 T11
Haddon Cir. Pg.32 U11
Haig Point Ln. Pg.26 R12
Hamilton Pl. Pg.26 S12
Hampton Pl. Pg.26 S12
Hanover Pl. Pg.26 S12
Harbor Dr. Pg.26 T12
Harding Ct. Pg.26 S12
Harrison Ct. Pg.25 S11
Harvest Ct. Pg.25 T11
Harvey Lake Dr. Pg.26 S12
Hastings Ct. Pg.26 S12
Hawthorn Center Dr. Pg.26 S,T12
Hawthorne Pky. Pg.25,26 S12
Hayes Ct. Pg.25 S11
Hazel Crest Rd. Pg.31 X8
Hazel Time Dr. Pg.25 R11
Hemingway Ct. Pg.26 S12
Hickory Hill Dr. Pg.33 U13
Hobble Bush Ln. Pg.33 U12
Hughes Pl. Pg.26 S12
Hunter Ct. Pg.25 T11
Huntington Dr. Pg.25 R11
Huron St. Pg.33 U12
Indianwood Dr. Pg.26 S12
Interlaken Dr. Pg.26 R12
Inverness Dr. Pg.25 R11
Jackson Ct. Pg.25 S11
Jefferson Pg.25 S11
Jensen Ln. Pg.32 T11
Julie Ln. Pg.32 T11
Justins Ct. Pg.26 R12
Kalamazoo Cir. Pg.25 T11
Kennedy Pl. Pg.25 S11
Keswick Pg.33 T12
Kingston Ct. Pg.26 S12
Knollwood Ln. Pg.26 T12
LaSalle St. Pg.33 U12
Lafayette Pg.25,26 S12
Lakeside Dr., N. & E. Pg.32 T11
Lakeview Pkwy. Pg.26 T12-13
Landcaster Ct. Pg.26 S12
Lansing Ct. Pg.25 T11
Larchmont Ln. Pg.26 T12
Laurel Valley Dr. Pg.26 R12
Lexington Dr. Pg.26 T12
Lincoln Dr. Pg.25 S11
Lindenwood Ct. Pg.33 T13
Lindon Ln. Pg.33 T12
Locke Ln. Pg.25 R11
Lowell Pl. Pg.25,26 S,T12
Macarthur Ct. Pg.25 S11
Maidstone Dr. Pg.26 S11
Mallard Ct. Pg.25 T11
Malvern Ln. Pg.33 T12
Manchester Ln. Pg.33 T12
Maplewood Dr. Pg.33 T13
Market Pg.26 S12
Marlowe Pl. Pg.25 S11
Marquette Ct. Pg.32 T11
Marseilles St. Pg.33 U12
Mayflower Rd. Pg.26 T12
Meadow Ct. Pg.25 T11
Melody Ln. Pg.26 T12
Memphis Pl. Pg.33 T12
Meredith Pl. Pg.25 S11
Merimal Ln. Pg.33 T12
Michigan Ct. Pg.26 S12
Midway Ln. Pg.33 T12
Milwaukee Ave. Pg.26 S13
Monroe Pg.26 S12
Montauk Ln. Pg.33 T12
Montclair Rd. Pg.33 U12
Montebello Dr. Pg.33 T12
Monteith Ct. Pg.32 T11
Monterry Dr. Pg.33 T12
Montgomery Ln. Pg.33 T12
Muirwood Ct. Pg.25 T11
Mundelein Rd. Pg.32 T10
Museum Blvd. Pg.26 S12
Muskegan Ct. Pg.25 T11
Mystic Dr. Pg.33 T12
Napier Ct. Pg.32 T11
Nardis Dr. Pg.33 U12
Nicklaus Ct. Pg.26 R12
Noble Cir. Pg.33 U12
Northfield Dr. Pg.32 T10
Old Creek Rd. Pg.33 T12
Old Wood Ct. Pg.33 U12
Olympic Dr. Pg.25 R11
Ontario St. Pg.33 U12
Onwentsia Rd. Pg.26 T12
Palmer Cir. Pg.26 R12
Palmer Cir. Pg.26 R12
Parkside Ct. Pg.26 S12
Peachtree Pg.26 S12
Pebble Beach Way Pg.26 R12
Phillip Rd. Pg.26 S12
Pierce Ct. Pg.25 S11
Pine Lake Cir. Pg.26 S12
Pinehurst Dr. Pg.26 S12
Plainfield Ct. Pg.26 R12
Player Ct. Pg.26 R12
Plumwood Ln. Pg.33 T13
Plymouth Farm Rd. Pg.25 T11
Polk Ct. Pg.25 S11
Pontiac Ln. Pg.25 T11
Portage Ct. Pg.25 T11
Prairie Meadow Ln. Pg.32 U11
Princeton Ct. Pg.26 S12
Quaker Ridge Ct. Pg.26 S11
Ranney Ave. Pg.33 U12
Redwood Ct. Pg.25 T11
Regency Dr. Pg.26 S12
Revere Pl. Pg.26 S12
Richmond Pl. Pg.32 U11
Ridgewood Ct. Pg.26 S11
Ring Dr. Pg.26 T12,13
River Grove Ct. Pg.33 U12
River Grove Ln. Pg.33 U12
Roosevelt Dr. Pg.25 S11
Royal Birkdale Dr. Pg.26 R12
Royal Oaks Dr. Pg.32 T11
Saddle Back Ln. Pg.33 T12
Saddlebrook Ln. Pg.26 S12
Sarasota Ct. Pg.26 S12
Sarazen Dr. Pg.25 R11
Saugatuck Tr. Pg.32 T11
Sawgrass St. Pg.26 R12
Sheffield Ln. Pg.32 U11
Shelby Ct. Pg.32 T11
Shoal Creek Terr. Pg.25 R11
Sinclaire Ct. Pg.32 T11
Skylar Ct. Pg.26 R12
Somerset Ln. Pg.25 T11
Southfield Dr. Pg.25 T11
Southgate Dr. Pg.32 U12
Southwick Ct. Pg.26 S12
Sparta Ct. Pg.25 T11
Spring Ln. Pg.26 T12
Spruce Pg.32 T11
Spruce Ct. Pg.32 U11
St. Andrews Dr. Pg.25 R11
St. Clair Ln. Pg.32 T11
St. Ives Ln. Pg.33 T12
Stanwich Rd. Pg.25 R11
Sterling Hts. Rd. Pg.32 T11
Stevenson Pl. Pg.25 S11
Stockton Ct. Pg.26 S12
Stone Fence Rd. Pg.33 T,U12
Streamwood Ln. Pg.26 S12
Sullivan Dr. Pg.32,33 T11-12
Summer Ct. Pg.32 W11
Sunset Ct. Pg.25 T11
Superior St. Pg.33 U12
Sussex Cir. Pg.33 U12
Sutcliffe Cir. Pg.32 U11
Sutton Ct. Pg.26 S12
Swinburne Pl. Pg.25 S11
Sycamore St. Pg.25 S11
Tally Ho Dr. Pg.32 U11
Tanglewood Ct. Pg.33 T13
Tanwood Ct. Pg.25 T11
Taylor Ct. Pg.25 S11
Televista Pg.33 T12
Tennis Ln. Pg.32 T11
Tennyson Pl. Pg.25 S11
Timber Ln. Pg.26 S12
Torrey Pines Pg.26 S11
Town Line Rd. Pg.26 S12
Trevino Terr. Pg.25 R11
Tryall Ln. Pg.26 R12
Turtle Bay Rd. Pg.26 R12
Tyler Ct. Pg.25 S11
Tyrell Ln. Pg.26 R12
Valhalla Terr. Pg.25 R11
Van Buren Ct. Pg.25 S11
Vernon Ct. Pg.26 S12
Vernon Dr. Pg.26 S12
Wadsworth Pl. Pg.25 S12
Warren Ln. Pg.25 T11
Warrington Rd. Pg.26 T12
Warson Ct. Pg.26 R12
Washington Pg.25 S11
Waterview Cir. Pg.32 T11
Webster Pl. Pg.26 S12
Wentworth Ct. Pg.26 S12
Westmoreland Dr. Pg.32 U11
Westwood Ct. Pg.33 T13
White Barn Rd. Pg.33 U12
White Fence Ct. Pg.33 T12
Whiting Ct. Pg.26 R12
Whitman Pl. Pg.25 S12
Whitney Ct. Pg.26 S12
Whitney Pl. Pg.25 S11
Wildwood Ct. Pg.33 T13
Williams Way Pg.32 T11
Wilshire Ct. Pg.26 S12
Windsor Dr. Pg.26 S12
Winfield Ct. Pg.25 T11
Woodlands Pkwy. Pg.33 U13

**CEMETERIES**

Cemetery Pg.33 U12
Willow Lawn Cem. Pg.33 U12

**FOREST PRESERVES**

Buffalo Creek F.P. Pg.33 X10-11
Granger Woods F.P. Pg.26 T14
MacArthur Woods F.P. Pg.26 S13

**GOLF COURSES**

Vernon Hills G.C. Pg.32,33 U12
White Deer Run G.C. Pg.26 R12

**PARKS**

Aquatic Park Pg.26 T12
Aspen Backyard Park Pg.32 T12
Augusta Park Pg.26 T12
Century Park Pg.26 S12
Deerpath Park Pg.26 T12
Gross Point Park Pg.32 T11
Hawthorn Club Park Pg.33 U12
Miramac Park Pg.33 T12
Oakwood Park Pg.32 T11
Stone Fence Park Pg.33 T12
Sullivan Woods Pg.33 U12

**SCHOOLS**

College of Lake Co. Southlake Educational Ctr. Pg.26 U13
Hawthorne Jr. H.S. Pg.26 S12
Libertyville H.S. South Campus Pg.26 T12

**SHOPPING CENTERS**

Fashion Square S.C. Pg.26 S13
Hawthorn Village Commons Pg.26 S12
Hawthorne S.C. Pg.26 S13
Market Place S.C. Pg.26 S13
Rivertree S.C. Pg.26 S13
Townline S.C. Pg.26 S13

**MISCELLANEOUS**

Continental Executive Business Park Pg.33 U13
Corporate Woods Business Park Pg.33 U13
Cuneo Museum & Gardens Pg.26 S13
Hartman Pavillion Pg.32 T11
Mundelein Primary Sewage Treatment Plant Pg.26 S12
Park District Office Pg.32 T11
Police Dept. Pg.26 S12
Post Office Pg.26 S12
R.R. Station Pg.33 U12
Sullivan Center Park Dist. Office Pg.26 S12
Sullivan Comm. Center Pg.26 T12
Vernon Twp. Offices Pg.33 V12
Village Hall Pg.32 U11

## VERNON TOWNSHIP

Pages 25-27,32-34,36
(For additional listings, see Section 2)

**STREETS**

Apple Hill Ln. Pg.33 V13
Apple Orchard Ln. Pg.33 U13
Arlyd Rd. Pg.33 W12
Ash St. Pg.33 X14
Bride Trail Rd. Pg.33 U14
Brittany Ln. Pg.33 V14
Brockman Ave. Pg.33 V12
Busch Rd. Pg.25 X12
Buxton Ct. Pg.34 V15
Calvin Ct. Pg.34 W15
Caren Ct. Pg.32 W12
Carton Ave. Pg.33 W13
Catalpa St. Pg.33 X14
Cemetery Rd. Pg.33 V13
Chapel Gate Pg.36 X15
Cherrywood Ln. Pg.34 V15
Concordia Ln. Pg.33 U14
Conway Rd. Pg.27 T15
County Line Rd. Pg.36 X15
Dell Ln. Pg.34 V15
Depot Pl. Pg.33 W13
Devonshire Ln. Pg.34 V15
Diamond Lake Rd. Pg.25 T10
Dogwood St. Pg.33 X14
Duffy Lane Pg.34 V15
Durham Ct. Pg.34 U15
East Ln. Pg.34 T15
East Mill Rd. Pg.33 W14
Easton Ave. Pg.33 V12
Elm Rd. Pg.33 U14
Estonian Ln. Pg.33 W14
Farner Ct. Pg.34 W15
Frank Ave. Pg.33 X13
G.K. Ln. Pg.33 W13
Gail Dr. Pg.32 W11
Garden Ct. Pg.33 X13
Golf Rd. Pg.32 W11
Gregg Rd. Pg.33 U14
Hawthorne Ln. Pg.27 T15

Hidden Lake Dr. Pg.33 X12
Hilgers Ct. Pg.25 T10
Hilltop Rd. Pg.32 V10
Holtz Rd. Pg.33 V13
Indian Creek Rd. Pg.33 V13
James Cir. Pg.36 X14
Juneway Ave. Pg.33 X13
Kingston Ct. Pg.33 U12
Kingston Row Pg.33 U12
Lake Zurich Hwy. Pg.32 V10
Lee Lane Pg.33 V12
Leeds Ct. Pg.34 U15
Lita Ave. Pg.33 X13
Long Beach Dr. Pg.36 X14
Long Grove-Aptakisic Rd. Pg.32 W11
Loyola Ave. Pg.36 X14
Main St. Pg.33 V12
Maple Ct. Pg.33 X13
Maple Pl. Pg.34 V15
Marie Ave. Pg.33 X13
Mayland Villa Rd. Pg.33 U14
Meadow Ln. Pg.34 T15
Menna Ln. Pg.33 V12
Michael Ave. Pg.33 X13
Myvil Dr. Pg.33 X14
Newman St. Pg.36 X14
North Woodbine Cir. Pg.33 U13
Oak Ln Pg.33 U14
Old Half Day Rd. Pg.33 V13
Old Mill Rd. Pg.34 U15
Olsen Ct. Pg.33 V13
Orchard Hill Rd. Pg.27 T15
Osage Rd. Pg.25 T10
Park Ave. Pg.33 V12
Park Pl. Pg.33 W13
Parton Ct. Pg.34 U15
Pekara Dr. Pg.33 X14
Pet Ln. Pg.33 W12
Pope Blvd. Pg.33 X13
Port Clinton Rd. Pg.33 U12
Portwine Rd. Pg.36 X15
Prairie Ln. Pg.33 V12
Prairie Rd Pg.33 V12
Raabe Ln. Pg.33 W13
Raleigh Dr. Pg.33 U12
Richard Ct. Pg.33 V12
River Oaks Dr. Pg.33 U14
Riverside Rd. Pg.33 W14
Robinhood Ln. Pg.34 V15
Ronnie Dr. Pg.33 W12
Rose Terr. Pg.34 V15
Saunders Rd. Pg.27 T15
Saunders Rd. Pg.27 T15
Story Book Ln. Pg.34 V15
Styrenge Ln. Pg.34 W15
Sunridge Ln. Pg.33 X12
Sunshine Ln. Pg.32 W11
Surrey Ct. Pg.34 U15
Surrey Ln. Pg.34 U15,V15
Thompson Blvd. Pg.32 W12
Trail Way Pg.33 U14
Valdon Rd. Pg.33 U14
Walnut Dr. Pg.33 X13
Weiland Rd. Pg.33 W13
Westwood Ln. Pg.34 W15
William St. Pg.33 W13
Willow Springs Rd. Pg.25 T10
Woodbine Cir., N. & S. Pg.33 U13
Woodbine Dr. Pg.33 U13
Woodland Ln. Pg.27 T15
1st St. Pg.33 V12
2nd St. Pg.33 V12

**CEMETERIES**
Vernon Cem. Pg.33 V14

**FOREST PRESERVES**
Granger Woods Forest Preserve Pg.27 T14
Half Day F.P. Pg.33 U14
Wright Woods Forest Preserve Pg.33 U14

**SCHOOLS**
Adlai Stevenson H.S. Pg.33 V13
Daniel Wright Sch. Pg.34 U14
Diamond Lake Sch. Pg.25 S10
Half Day Sch. Pg.33 V13

**MISCELLANEOUS**
Didier Farms Pg.33 W12
Ryerson Cabin Pg.33 W14
Smith River Cabin Pg.33 W14

## VOLO

Page 15...M2

## WADSWORTH

Pages 5,6,12,13

**STREETS**
Adams Rd. Pg.6 D15
Andover Rd. Pg.5 D14
Anna Dr., N., S., E. & W. Pg.12 F13
Arbor Ct. Pg.12 E14
August Zupec Rd. Pg.6 D15
Bartlett Ln. Pg.6 C,D15
Birch Ln. Pg.12 E14
Blue Spruce Ct. Pg.5 E14
Bryn Mawr Pg.6 E15
Burr Oak Ln. Pg.5 E14
Caroline Ave. Pg.6 D14
Cashmore Rd. Pg.12 E-F14
Chaplin St. Pg.6 E15
Cherrywood Ln. Pg.5 C12
Chicago Ave. Pg.5 E14
Concord Ln. Pg.5 D14
Country Lane Dr. Pg.12 E14
Crabapple Dr. Pg.12 E14
Deer Creek Pg.5 D15
Dilley's Rd. Pg.12 E13
Elm Ln. Pg.6 E15
Forest View Rd. Pg.6 C15
Foxglove Ln. Pg.5 C12
Goldenrod Ln. Pg.5 C,D13
Golf Ln. Dr. Pg.12 E14
Gorham Ln. Pg.5 A13
Greenview Dr. Pg.6 C15
Hansen Rd. Pg.12 F13
Harmony Ct. Pg.5 D14
Hunt Club Tr. Pg.5 C12
Jody Ln. Pg.5 D14
Juniper Ct. Pg.5 E14
Kilbourne Rd. Pg.5 D14
Leslie Ln. Pg.6 C15
Mauser Dr. Pg.6 D15
McCarthy Rd. Pg.12 E13
Meadow Ln. Pg.6 D15
Mulberry Ln. Pg.12 F13
Nature Ct. Pg.5 D14
Northwestern Ave. Pg.6 E15
Northwoods Dr. Pg.5 E14
Oak Knoll Rd. Pg.6 D14
Oak Tree Ln. Pg.6 E14
Oakcrest Ln. Pg.5 E14
Old Orchard Dr. Pg.5 C12
Pickord St. Pg.6 E15
Prairie View Dr. Pg.5 D14
Pratum Terra Dr. Pg.6 D14
Primrose Ln. Pg.12 E14
Public Rd. Pg.5 C12
Red Oak Terr. Pg.5 E14
Reed Ct. Pg.5 C12
Rosedale Ave. Pg.6 E15
Sand Ct. Pg.5 F13
Sandy Ct. Pg.12 E14
Schlosser Ct. Pg.12 E14
Sedge Ct. Pg.5 C13
Shagbark Ln. Pg.13 E14
Shelley Ln. Pg.13 E14
Sheryl Lynn Dr. Pg.5 D14
Sterling Ln. Pg.5 A13
Stiehr Rd. Pg.6 C15
Stonegate Rd. Pg.6 C15
Thornapple Ln. Pg.12 F13
Thorne Meadow Cir. Pg.5 C12
Timberland Terr. Pg.6 C15
Trillium Ct. Pg.5 D13
Valley View Rd. Pg.12 F13
Wadsworth Rd. Pg.6 D15
Walden Ln. Pg.5 D14
Wedgewood Ct. Pg.5 D14
Willow Ln. Pg.12 F13
Winchester Rd. Pg.6 D15
Woodland Ave. Pg.6 E15
Yorkhouse Rd. Pg.12 E14

**CEMETERIES**
St. Patrick's Cem. Pg.5 C12

**FOREST PRESERVES**
Des Plaines River Trail Pg.5,12 A-E13

**SCHOOLS**
St. Patrick's Sch Pg.5 D14

## WARREN TOWNSHIP

Pages 11-13,18-20

**STREETS**
Adelaide Ave. Pg.13 F15
Algonquin St. Pg.18 L11
Almond Ln. Pg.18 K11
Almond Rd. Pg.18 M11
Apple Ln. Pg.12 H12
Applewood Ct. Pg.12 H12
Arbor Ave. Pg.18 M10
Ash Ct. Pg.11 G10
Ash St. Pg.11 G10
Aspen Ct. Pg.11 K11
Atlantic Ave. Pg.13 G15
Audrey Ave. Pg.13 F15
Avon Ct. Pg.18 L11
Back Bay Ct. Pg.11 G11
Bairstow St. Pg.13 F15
Banbury Ct. Pg.11 G11
Banbury Dr. Pg.11 G11
Barberry Ln. Pg.13 G15
Batter Shall Dr. Pg.18 L11
Bayonne Ave. Pg.13 F16
Belle Plaine Ave. Pg.13 F-G15
Belvidere Rd. Pg.18,19 L11-12
Beverly Ave. Pg.11 G10
Beverly Rd. Pg.11 G10
Big Oaks Rd. Pg.18 L11
Birch Ln. Pg.11 G12
Black Velvet Ln. Pg.11,12 F12
Blackhawk Pg.18 L11
Blanchard Rd. Pg.13 F15
Blossom St. Pg.13 F15
Bluff Ct. Pg.18 L12
Bough Ct. Pg.12 H13
Boulevard View Pg.13 F-G15
Branch Rd. Pg.12 H13
Bridal Tr. Pg.12 G12
Bridle Ct. Pg.11,18 K11
Bridle Ln. Pg.11,18 K11
Bridlewood Ave. Pg.11 G11
Brigantine Ln. Pg.18 K10
Brooke Ave. Pg.18 M10
Brookside Dr. Pg.11 G11
Buck Ct. Pg.11 F10
Carvis Pl. Pg.11 H10
Cemetery Rd. Pg.12 H12
Center Dr. Pg.11 G10
Cherokee Ct. Pg.18 K11
Cheyenne Ave. Pg.13 G15
Cheyenne Ct. Pg.18 L11
Chippewa Rd. Pg.18 L11
Circle Ct. Pg.18 L10
Clearview Ave. Pg.13 G15
Clipper Ct. Pg.18 K10
Cornell Ave. Pg.20 K15
Cottage St. Pg.11 H10
Cottonwood Ct. Pg.18 L11
Country Ln. Pg.18 L10
Country Meadows Ln. Pg.19 K13
Cove Rd. Pg.18 L11
Dady Ct Pg.18 K11
Dartmoor Dr. Pg.18 L11
Dawn Ct. Pg.18 K11
Deer Trail Dr. Pg.11 F10
Deerpath Rd. Pg.18 L10
Deerview Dr. Pg.11 F10
Devon Ct. Pg.12 G12
Devonshire Ln. Pg.20 K15
Dillys Rd. Pg.12 F13
Douglas Terr. Pg.11 G11
Eastview Ave. Pg.18 K,L10
Eastview Rd. Pg.18 L11
Eastwood Ave. Pg.19 L14
Eastwood Pl. Pg.20 K15
Edgewood Dr. Pg.11,12 G11,H12
Elizabeth St. Pg.13 F15
Elm St. Pg.18 L11
Elsbury St. Pg.11 G11
Elsie Ave. Pg.12 H13
Everett Pl. Pg.20 K15
Evergreen Dr. Pg.18 K11
Fairfield Ln. Pg.18 L11
Fairview Ln. Pg.18 L11
Fernview Ln. Pg.11 F10
Field View Dr. Pg.11 G11
Florida Ave. Pg.13 G15
Forest Ave. Pg.20 L15
Forest Dr. Pg.18 K11,M10
Fox Hill Dr. Pg.12 F12
Gagemere Pg.18 K11
Gages Lake Dr. Pg.18 K11
Gages Lake Rd. Pg.18,19 K10-12
Gagewood Ln. Pg.19 K12
Glen Dr. Pg.18 K10
Gold Springs Ct. Pg.11 G11
Grand Ave. Pg.11 G11
Grand Dr. Pg.18 K11
Grandwood Dr. Pg.11 G10-11
Grant Ave. Pg.11 H10
Greentree Dr. Pg.18 L11
Greentree Rd. Pg.18 L11
Greenwood Ave. Pg.13 G15
Greier Rd. Pg.11 G10
Hampshire Dr. Pg.11 G11
Hansen Rd. Pg.12 F13
Hawk Ct. Pg.18 K11
Heather Ct. Pg.18 K10
Hendee St. Pg.13 F15
Hickory Ct. Pg.11 K11
Hickory Ln. Pg.18 L12
Hickory Pl. Pg.18 L10
Highfield Dr. Pg.11 G10
Highfield Dr., W. Pg.11 G10
Highland Ave. Pg.13 G15
Hill Ave. Pg.20 L15
Homestead Pg.18 K11
Homestead Ct. Pg.18 K11
Horseshoe Ln. Pg.11 J11
Hunt Club Rd. Pg.19 L12
Huntington Cir. Pg.19 L12
Hutchins Rd. Pg.11 F11
Hyatt Ln. Pg.20 K15
Idlewild Ave. Pg.18 K11
Indian Pl. Pg.18 L10
Ingleside Pl. Pg.20 K15
Iroquois Ave. Pg.18 K11
Island Ave. Pg.18 L11
Island Ct. Pg.18 K10
Ivy Ct. Pg.18 K11
Ivy Ln. Dr. Pg.18 K11
Jasmine Ct. Pg.18 K10
John Mogg Rd. Pg.18 L10
Jonathan Rd. Pg.12 H12
Judy Dr. Pg.11 G10
Julie Ct. Pg.18 K11
Julie Ln. Pg.18 K11
Juniper St. Pg.12 H13
Karelia Ln. Pg.12 H12
Karen Ln. Pg.11 G10
Kennedy Dr. Pg.20 L14
Kewaunee Dr. Pg.18 K11
Kimberwick Ln. Pg.12 F12
Knowles Rd. Pg.11 H10
Lake Park Ave. Pg.20 K15
Lake Rd. Pg.18 K10
Lake Shore Dr. Pg.18 K10,L11
Lake St. Pg.11 H10
Lakeview Ct. Pg.18 L10
Lakeview Terr. Pg.11 G11
Lark Dr. Pg.18 K13
Larkspur Ct. Pg.18 K11
Lavender Cir. Pg.11 K10
Lawn Ave. Pg.20 L15
Lee Ave. Pg.13 H15
Lee Cir. Pg.11 G11
Limb Ct. Pg.12 H13
Lincoln Ave. Pg.11 H10
Linda Ln. Pg.11 G11
Linden Ln. Pg.18 M10
Lindenwood Dr. Pg.18 L11
Lone Rock Dr. Pg.18 L11
Lovers Ln. Pg.18 K10
Magnolia Ave. Pg.13 F-H15
Main St. Pg.18 K10
Mainsail Dr. Pg.18 K10
Manitowoc Ct. Pg.18 K11
Maple Ave. Pg.18 L10
Maple Ln. Pg.19 K12
Mawman St. Pg.13 F15
McGaw Rd. Pg.20 L15
Meadow Brook Dr. Pg.18 K11
Meadow Ln. Pg.11,18 G11,L10
Meadow Ridge Dr. Pg.11 G11
Meadowgrass Dr. Pg.11 F10
Meander Dr. Pg.18 K11
Melody Rd. Pg.20 L15
Mill Creek Crossing Pg.11 G11
Mill Creek Dr. Pg.11 G11
Mill Ct. Pg.11 G10
Mill Rd. Pg.18 L11
Milwaukee Ave. Pg.19 M12
Nemesis Ave. Pg.13 F15
Noreen Ct. Pg.18 K11
Northwestern St. Pg.13 F15
Northwoods Pg.20 K15
O'Plaine Rd. Pg.19 K14
Oak Ave. Pg.18 L10
Oak Knoll Cir. Pg.12 H12
Oak St. Pg.18 K10
Oakland Ave. Pg.18 K11
Oakwood Dr. Pg.11 G10
Old Creek Ct. Pg.11 G11
Old Gages Lake Rd. Pg.18 K10
Old Pine Ct. Pg.11 K11
Old Plank Rd. Pg.18 L10
Old Walnut Cir. Pg.11 K11
Old Woods Tr. Pg.12 G11,12
Orchard Ln. Pg.18 K10
Orchard Valley Rd. Pg.12,18 H12
Overbrook Ct. Pg.11 G11
Pacific Ave. Pg.13 G15
Paddock St. Pg.13 F15
Pamela Pl. Pg.11 G10
Park Crescent Pg.11 F10
Park Dr. Pg.11 G11
Park Pl. Pg.11,18 H,L10
Park St. Pg.18 L10
Parkway Ave. Pg.20 L15
Pin Oak Ln. Pg.11 H12
Pine Ave. Pg.18 M10
Pine Creek Tr. Pg.18 K11
Pleasant Pl. Pg.11 H10
Pond Ridge Cir. Pg.11 G11
Prospect Pg.18 K10
Rae Ln. Pg.11 G10
Red Oak Ln. Pg.11 H12
Redbud Ln. Pg.11 K11
Ridge Rd. Pg.18 L11
River Rd. Pg.19 L13
Robert Ct. Pg.18 K11
Rolling Hills Pg.18 L10
Roosevelt Rd. Pg.11 H10
Rosedale Ave. Pg.13 F15
Rosemont Ave. Pg.11 H10
Royal Oak Ln. Pg.18 K11
Rule Ct. Pg.18 L10
Running Creek Ct. Pg.11 G11
Rush St. Pg.18 K10
Saddle Ct. Pg.11,18 J-K11
Saddle Ln. Pg.18 K11
Salisbury Dr. Pg.11 G11
Sallmon Ave. Pg.13 F15
Sand Lake Rd. Pg.11 F11
Sandy Ct. Pg.11,18 K11
Seafarer Dr. Pg.18 K10
Sears Blvd. Pg.18 L10
Shannon Dr. Pg.19 L12
Shawnee Ave. Pg.18 K11
Sheridan Ave. Pg.11 H10
Sibelius Ln. Pg.12 H12
Skokie Hwy. Pg.12,19 F,K13
South Rd. Pg.12 H13
Springbrook Dr. Pg.11 G11
Springwood Dr. Pg.11 K11
Spruce St. Pg.12 H13
Stearns School Rd. Pg.11,12 G11,12
Sterling Ct. Pg.18 K10
Still Water Ct. Pg.11 G11
Stonebridge Ln. Pg.11 K10
Streamwood Ct. Pg.11 G11
Streamwood Dr. Pg.11 G11
Sulkey Dr. Pg.18 K11
Sumac Ln. Pg.11 K11
Summit Dr. Pg.18 K11
Sunnyside Ave. Pg.19 K14
Sunset Ave. Pg.18 L10
Sunset Dr. Pg.18 L10
Tangueray Dr. Pg.18 K10
Telegraph Rd. Pg.20 L15
Tempest Way Pg.11 K9
Thornapple Dr. Pg.18 L11
Thoroughbred Dr. Pg.12 F12
Tiger Tail Ct. Pg.18 K12
Timber Ln. Pg.18 L11
Tomahawk Ct. Pg.18 L11
Traer Terr. Pg.11 G11
Treeline Ct. Pg.18 K11
Twin Lakes Blvd. Pg.18 L11
Tyler Ave. Pg.13 F15
Valley Dr. Pg.18 L11
Valley Rd. Pg.12 H12
Valley View Dr. Pg.18 L10
Verco Ave. Pg.13 F15
Vermont Ave. Pg.13 F15
Walden Way Pg.11 G11
Wall Ave. Pg.13 F15
Walnut Ln. Pg.11,18 K11
Warren Ave. Pg.18 K11
Washington St. Pg.11,12 H12,K11,14
Waukee Ave. Pg.12 G14
Wayside Pl. Pg.18 L10
West Ave. Pg.20 L15
West Wind Dr. Pg.12 G12
Westwood Pl. Pg.11 G10
White Oak Ln. Pg.11 J11
Wildberry Ct. Pg.11 F10
Willow Ct. Pg.11 G10
Willow Point Dr. Pg.18 L10
Windjammer Ct. Pg.11 H10
Windslow Dr. Pg.18 K11
Winnebago Ct. Pg.18 K11
Winnebago Dr. Pg.18 K11
Winslow Dr. Pg.18 K11
Wooddale Tr. Pg.11 F10
Wooded Glen Dr. Pg.18 K11
Woodhill Dr. Pg.12 H13
Woodland Ct. Pg.11 G11
Woodland Dr. Pg.18 L11
Woodland Terr. Pg.18 L10
Wright Ave. Pg.18 K10
Wright Rd. Pg.18 K10
Yearling Dr. Pg.12 F12
Yew Tree Dr. Pg.11 F10
Yorkhouse Rd. Pg.13 F15
Yorkshire Dr. Pg.11 G11
1st St. Pg.18 K10
2nd St. Pg.18 K10

**CEMETERIES**
Highland Memorial Cemetery Pg.19 L12
Warren Cem. Pg.12 G12

**FOREST PRESERVES**
Almond Marsh Forest Preserve Pg.10 L11
Gurnee Woods Pg.12 G14

**SCHOOLS**
Spaulding North Sch. Pg.13 E15
Warren Twp. H.S. (Proposed) Pg.12 K12
Woodland Jr. H.S. Pg.18 K12
Woodland Sch. Pg.18 K12
Laremont Sch. Pg.18 K11

**MISCELLANEOUS**
Ct. Cava Monastery Pg.19 L12
Warren Township Offices Pg.11 K11

## WAUCONDA

Pages 22,23

**STREETS**
Adams Ave. Q4
Anthony Dr. S3,4
Appaloosa Tr. S3
Arabian Ct. S3
Baldwin Ln. Q5
Bangs St. R3
Barbara Ln. Q4
Barrington Rd. S3
Bonner Rd. Q4
Brett Ln. R4
Briar Rd. Q3
Brown St. Q,R3
Chestnut Cir. R3
Church St. R3
Clearview Ave. R4
Clover Rd. R3
Cook St. Q3
Cortland Ln. Q5
Cortland Terr. Q5
Country Lane Ct. R4
Crescent Terr. Q3
Crestview Dr. R4
Daniel St. R3
Dato Ln. Q3
Delia Dr. R4
Delo Dr. S4
Dunbar Rd. R3
Earls Ct. Q4
Edgewater Ln. R4
Edgewater Pkwy. Q4
Edward Pl. Q4
Erica Dr. Q5
Farmhill Cir. R3
Farmhill Ct. R3
Foster Dr. R4
Francis St. R3
Garland Rd. Q4
George Ave. R3
Gossell Rd. Q5
Grand Blvd. Q5
Grant Pl. Q4
Hammond St. R4
Harrison Ave. Q4
Helena Ave. R3
Henri Ln. Q3
High St. R4
Highland Ave. R4
Hill St. R4
Hollow Hill Dr. Q3
Horseshoe Cir. S3
Hubbard Ct. R3
Indian Ridge Tr. R3
Industrial Dr. Q3
Jackson Ave. Q4
Jackson Ct. Q4
James Ave. Q4
Jamie Ln. Q3
Jessica Dr. Q5
Jonathon Ct. Q5
Karl Ct. Q4
Kent Ave. R4
Kimball Ave. R4
Kyle Ct. Q3
Lake Ct. R4
Lake Shore Blvd. R4
Lake Shore Dr. Q4
Lakeview Ave. R4
Larkdale Row Q3
Laurel Ave. Q3
Legion St. R4
Lewis Ave. R3
Liberty St. R3
Lincoln Ave. Q4
Linden Ln. R3
Lipizan Ln. S3
Lotus St. R4
Macintosh Dr. Q5
Madison Ave. Q4
Main St. R3
Maple Ave. R3
Marina Ct. R4
Marina St. R4
Marine Rd. Q3
Marlene Ct. R4
Meadowview Dr. R3
Middle Ave. S3
Mill St. R3
Mill St., E. R4
Minerva Ave. R3
Monroe Ave. Q4
Nancy Ct. Q4
Neil Ave. Q4
North Ave. R3
North Shore Dr. Q4
Oak Bluff Ct. R4
Oak Dr. Q4
Oakdale Ave. Q5
Oaks Ave. R4
Oakwood Rd. R3
Old Country Way R3
Orton Ave. R3
Osage St. R3
Osage Terr. Q3
Pamela Ct. Q4
Park Ave. Q4
Park Pl. Q4
Park St. R4
Pershing Dr. Q4
Pleasant View Dr. Q5
Ridge Ave. Q4
Ridge Ct. R4
Ridge St. R4
Road Way R4
Roosevelt Rd. R3
Ross St. R3
Roxbury Ln. Q5
Saddlewood Dr. S3
Sheridan Dr. Q4
Shiela Ct. Q4
Shore Ct. Q4
Sky Hill Rd. R4
Slocum Lake Rd. R3
South St. R4
Summit Ave. Q5
Sunnyside Ave. R4
Surf Terr. R3
Sutton Cir. Q5
Sycamore Cir. R3
Thomas Ct. R3
Van Buren Ave. Q4
Walnut Rd. R3
Washington Ave. Q4
Wauconda Rd. R3
Wethington Cir. R4
Wethington Dr. R4
Willow Rd. R3
Wilson Ave. R4
Woodland Ave. R4
Woodland Rd. Q4

**PARKS**
Cook Park R3

**SCHOOLS**
Robert Crown Sch. Q3
Transfiguration Sch. R3
Wauconda Grade Sch. R3
Wauconda H.S. R3
Wauconda Jr. H.S. R3

**MISCELLANEOUS**
Lake County Museum R5
Library R3
Lindy's Landing R4
The Golf Farm P3
Village Hall R4
Wauconda Industrial Park Q4

## WAUCONDA TOWNSHIP

Pages 15,16,22,23

**STREETS**
Ada St. Pg.22 R,S1
Alemeda Pg.15 M1
Alvina St. Pg.23 R4
Anderson Rd. Pg.22 R,S3
Ann Ct. Pg.22 S3
Ash St. Pg.22,23 R4,S1
Barrington Rd. Pg.22 S3
Bay View St. Pg.22 R1
Beech St. Pg.22 R1
Belvidere Rd. Pg.15 M3-4
Berkley Ct. Pg.23 Q4
Bernice St. Pg.22 R,S1
Blakley Pkwy. Pg.23 S4
Bluff St. Pg.23 Q4
Bonner Rd. Pg.22,23 Q2,4
Brooks St. Pg.22 S2
Brown Rd. Pg.23 S4
Burnett Rd. Pg.22 Q1
Callahan Rd. Pg.22 P3
Cary Plaza Pg.23 Q4
Casé Rd. Pg.22 P2
Channel St. Pg.22 R1
Clark St. Pg.22 R1
Converse Rd. Pg.22 R1
Cook St. Pg.23 Q4
Crest Rd. Pg.22 Q2
Darrell Rd. Pg.15,22 M,N1,N2
Division Pg.22 R1
Dowell Rd. Pg.15 M2,N1,2
Ellen St. Pg.22 R,S1
Elm St. Pg.22 R1
Elmwood Ave. Pg.23 R4
Fairview Rd. Pg.22 S1
Fish Lake Rd. Pg.15 M3
Fisher Rd. Pg.15 N2
Forest Garden Rd.(Pvt.) Pg.22 R3
Fox Lake Rd. Pg.15 M2
Gardner Rd. Pg.23 Q4
Garland Dr. Pg.22 Q3
Genesee St. Pg.22 R1
Geraldine Ln. Pg.22 S1
Gilmer Rd. Pg.15 N3-4
Gossell Rd. Pg.16,23 P4
Grace St. Pg.22 R1
Grace Wells Dr. Pg.23 Q4
Gravel Pit Rd. Pg.22 Q1
Greenview Dr. Pg.23 S4
Harrison Ave. Pg.23 Q4
Hermosa Ave. Pg.23 S4
Hickory Ln. Pg.23 Q4
Hickory St. Pg.22 R1-2
Highview Rd. Pg.22 Q2
Hill Ave. Pg.23 S4
Hill St. Pg.22 R1
Hillside Ave. Pg.23 R4
Hillside Dr. Pg.15 M1
Huston Ave. Pg.22 R1
Ivanhoe Rd. Pg.22,23 S3,4
Karen Dr. Pg.22 S3
Lake Dr. Pg.22,23 Q4,R1
Lake Pkwy. Pg.23 Q4
Lake Shore Ct. Pg.23 S4
Lake Shore Dr., E. Pg.23 S4
Lake Shore Dr. Pg.23 S4
Lake St. Pg.23 Q4
Lake View Cir. Pg.22 Q2
Lake Vista Dr. Pg.22 Q1
Lakeview Ave. Pg.23 R4
Lakeview Ct. Pg.22 R1
Lakeview Dr. Pg.22 R1
Lamphere St. Pg.22 R1
Langley Ct. Pg.22 R1
Laurel Ave. Pg.23 S3
Laurel Ct. Pg.22 S3
Laurel Ln. Pg.22 R1
Lexington Ct. Pg.22 R1
Leyte Ct. Pg.22 R1
Liberty St., W. Pg.22 R3
Lily Lake Rd. Pg.15 M1
Lindy Ln. Pg.22 R1
Locust Dr. Pg.22 S1
Longacre Ct. Pg.22 Q1
Mac St. Pg.22 R2
Madison Ave. Pg.23 Q4
Main St. Pg.22 R2
Maple Ave. Pg.22 S1
Maple St. Pg.22 R1
Marilyn Meadow Pg.23 P4
Marion St. Pg.22 S2
May St. Pg.22 R2
Mead Ave. Pg.23 S4
Meadow Lane Rd. Pg.22 Q2
Meadow Ln. Pg.23 S4
Meeker Ct. Pg.22 R1
Morey St. Pg.22 S1
Morningside Dr. Pg.15 M1
Mylith Rd. Pg.22 R1
Myrtle St. Pg.23 R4
Neville Rd. Pg.15 P1
North St. Pg.22 R2
Oak Knoll Rd. Pg.22 Q2
Oak St., E. Pg.22 R1-2
Orchard Dr. Pg.22 R2
Orchard Rd. Pg.22 S1
Park Ave., E. & W. Pg.22 R1
Parkview Dr. Pg.22 R1
Parkview Dr. Pg.22 R1
Pheasant Ct. Pg.22 S3
Pheasant Tr. Pg.22 S3
Pleasant View Ave. Pg.23 Q4
Poplar Dr. Pg.22 R1
Poplar St. Pg.22 R-S1
Rand Rd. Pg.15,22,23 P,Q3,R4
Ridge Ct. Pg.23 R4
Ridge St. Pg.23 R4
River Oaks Dr. Pg.22 Q1
Roberts Rd. Pg.22 S1
Robin Ct. Pg.23 P4
Shady Ln. Pg.22 R1
South Ave. Pg.22 S2
Sunset Dr. Pg.15 M1
Swift Ct. Pg.22 S3
Tamarack Dr. Pg.23 S4
Timothy Tr. Pg.23 P4
Valentine Rd. Pg.23 Q4
Valley View Dr. Pg.15 M1
Virginia Ln. Pg.23 P4
Wade St. Pg.23 Q4
Walnut St. Pg.22 R1
Wegner Rd. Pg.15 M1
Werden Ave. Pg.23 R4
West End Rd. Pg.23 Q4
West St. Pg.23 Q4
Williams Park Rd Pg.22 R2
Willow Rd. Pg.22 S1
Wilson Ave. Pg.23 R4
Wilton Rd. Pg.23 S4
Winding Lane Dr. Pg.23 Q4
Wood Creek Dr. Pg.22 Q1
York Rd. Pg.23 S4

**FOREST PRESERVES**
Illinois Nature Preserve & Nat'l. Landmark Pg.23 R4
Singing Hills F.P. Pg.22 P3

## WAUKEGAN

Pages 6,7,13,14,19-21

**STREETS**
Abington Ct. Pg.13 G14
Adams St. Pg.21 L18
Adelaide Ave. Pg.13 F16
Adelphi Ave. Pg.13 G16
Agusta Dr. Pg.12 F14
Alexander Ct. Pg.14 G18
Alta Vista Dr. Pg.14 G18
Amhurst Pkwy. Pg.20 M15
Amstutz Expwy. Pg.14 G18
Apache Rd. Pg.13 G17
Apple Ave. Pg.20 K16
Archer Ave. Pg.21 K18
Arizona Dr. Pg.13 G16
Armory Pl. Pg.14 G17
Arthur Ct. Pg.13 K16
Arthur Dr. Pg.13 E17
Ash St. Pg.14 G,H,K18
Ashley Ln. Pg.13 G16
Atlantic Ave. Pg.13 G16,17
Audrey Ave. Pg.13 F16
Augusta Dr. Pg.12 F14
Austin Ave. Pg.13 H16
Aviation Dr. Pg.6 E16
Baldwin Ave. Pg.13 K16
Ballentine St. Pg.14 F17
Bank Ct. Pg.7 E17
Bank Ln. Pg.7 D17
Bayberry Ct. Pg.19 M14
Beach Rd. Pg.13 E17
Beech Ave. Pg.14 G18
Belle Plaine Ave. Pg.13 F15
Belmont Ct. Pg.19 M13
Belvidere Rd. Pg.20 K16
Belvidere St. Pg.20 K16-18
Benny Ave. Pg.21 K17
Berry Ct. Pg.13 H17
Bertrand Ave. Pg.7 D,E17
Berwick Blvd. Pg.13 G-H17
Besley Pl. Pg.21 K18
Birchwood Dr. Pg.20 M16
Blanchard Rd. Pg.14 F17-18
Blossom Ave. Pg.12 F14
Bluff Ct. Pg.21 K18
Bluff St. Pg.21 K18
Boardman St. Pg.14 F17
Bob O'Farrell Ln. Pg.7 E17
Bonnie Brook Ln. Pg.13 G16
Bonnie Brook Ln., S. Pg.13 G17
Bonnie Brook Ln., W. Pg.13 F16
Bonnie Brook Ln., N. & E. Pg.13 F17
Bonnie Brook Rd. Pg.13 G15-16
Bordman St. Pg.11 F17
Boulevard View Pg.13 F15
Brentwood Ln. Pg.13 G14
Briar Ln. Pg.13 G17
Bristol Rd. Pg.13 F17
Brnot Ave. Pg.13 F16
Brooke Ave. Pg.13 G16
Brookside Ave. Pg.13 H16
Browne Ct. Pg.7 D17
Browning St. Pg.21 L18
Brownstone Way Pg.20 L14
Buck Ave. Pg.14 G17-18
Buck St. Pg.14 G17
Buckingham Rd. Pg.14 E17
Buirick N. Pg.14 G17
Bur Wood Dr. Pg.20 M15
Burr Oak Dr. Pg.12 F14
Burris Ave. Pg.13 G16
Burton Ave. Pg.14 H17
Bush Ct. Pg.21 L17
Butrick St. Pg.14,21 F,H-K17
Butternut Ln. Pg.20 L14
Campbell Ln. Pg.20 M14
Campus Cir. Pg.13 H16
Candlestick Way Pg.19 L14
Cardinal Ct. Pg.20 M14
Carnation Ct. Pg.21 K18
Carney Ave. Pg.20 L17
Caroline Pl. Pg.21 K18
Carriage Ln. Pg.13 H16
Caryn Ln. Pg.13 K16
Cashmore Rd. Pg.12 F14
Casmir Pulaski Dr. Pg.20 L15
Castle Ct. Pg.13 F17
Catalpa Ave. Pg.20 K17
Cedar Ave. Pg.20 L17
Celano Dr. Pg.19 M14
Center St. Pg.14 H18
Central Ave. Pg.20 K16
Chapel St. Pg.21 K18
Chaplin St. Pg.6 E16
Charleston Rd. Pg.14 F17
Charron Ln. Pg.20 K17
Chatham Rd. Pg.13 E16
Cherokee Rd. Pg.13 G17
Cherry Tree Ct. Pg.12 E14
Chestnut Ave. Pg.20 L16
Chestnut St. Pg.14 G-H18
Cheyenne Rd. Pg.13 G16
Chinook Rd. Pg.13 G16
Chippewa Rd. Pg.13 G17
Choctaw Rd. Pg.13 G17
Churchill Ct. Pg.19 M13
Churchill Ln. Pg.19 M13
Circle Ct. Pg.14 G18
Clarke Ave. Pg.21 K18
Clarkson St. Pg.14 H17
Clayton St. Pg.14 K18
Clearview Ave. Pg.13 G16
Clinton St. Pg.21 K18
Colbert Rd. Pg.13 K16
Collier Ct. Pg.21 L17
Colorado Ave. Pg.13 G16
Colville Pl. Pg.14 G18
Comanche Ct. Pg.13 G17
Commonwealth Ave. Pg.21 L17
Continental Dr. Pg.13 F14
Cook Ct. Pg.20 K17
Cornelia Ave. Pg.13,14 K16-17
Cornelia St. Pg.13 K16
Cornell Rd. Pg.14 F17
Corona Rd Pg.14 G18
Cory Ave. Pg.14 H18
Country Club Ave. Pg.13 G15-16
Country Ln. Pg.12 F14
Country Pl. Pg.12 F14
County St. Pg.14,21 H,K18
Coventry Way Pg.19 L14
Creek Rd. Pg.13 G17
Crescent Pl. Pg.13 H17
Crest Ct. Pg.12 F14
Cummings Ave. Pg.21 K18
Cypress Ave. Pg.21 K18
Cypress St. Pg.12,21 F14,K18
Dahringer Rd. Pg.14 H18
Dakota Rd. Pg.13 G16
Dale Ln. Pg.13 G16
Dana Ave. Pg.13 F16
Darla Ct. Pg.19 L14
Darrow Ln. Pg.20 K16
Day Break Dr. Pg.19 M13
Day Break Farm Rd. Pg.19 M13
Delany Rd. Pg.13 G15
Delaware Rd. Pg.13 G17
Devonshire Rd. Pg.13 E17
Dewoody Rd. Pg.14 F17
Dickinson St. Pg.14 F17
Dilger Ave. Pg.20 K-L16
Dixie Ave. Pg.20 K16
Dodge Ave. Pg.20,21 K17
Dorchester Ave. Pg.13 H16
Dorchester Ct. Pg.21 K17
Dorothy Ct. Pg.12 E14
Dorothy Rd. Pg.13 E16
Douglas Ave. Pg.14 H18

## WAUKEGAN

Douglas Cir. Pg.13 H16
Douglas Ct. Pg.14 H18
Dover Rd. Pg.13 E17
Drew Ln. Pg.13 K16
Dromey Ave. Pg.20 L16
Dugan St. Pg.21 K18
Dugdale Rd. Pg.21 K17
Dunley Ct. Pg.13 K17
East Dr. Pg.13 K18
East End Ave. Pg.14 F17
Eastview Dr. Pg.14 H18
Eastwood Ave. Pg.19 L14
Eastwood Ct. Pg.12 F14
Eastwood Rd. Pg.14 E17
Edgewood Rd. Pg.13 E17
Edison Ct. Pg.14 K17
Edwards St. Pg.14 H17
Egidi Ln. Pg.19 M12
Egret Ct. Pg.20 M14
Elder Ln. Pg.20 L14
Elizabeth Ave. Pg.21 L17
Elizabeth Ln. Pg.14 F17
Ellis Ave. Pg.13 H16
Elmwood Ave. Pg.14,21 F-L17
Elmwood Ave., N. Pg.14,20,21 G,K17
Emmanuel Ave. Pg.6 E16
Ernie Krueger Cir. Pg.13 G15
Ernie Krueger Dr., S. Pg.13 G15
Everett Rd. Pg.14 E17
Evergreen Ave. Pg.13 E-H16
Evergreen Ct. Pg.13 H16
Fairfield Cir. Pg.14 H17
Fairfield Ct., E. Pg.14 H18
Fairfield Ct., W. Pg.14 H17
Fairmont Rd. Pg.19 M13
Falcon Dr. Pg.20 M14
Ferry St. Pg.14 F17
Finch Ct. Pg.20 M14
Florence Ave. Pg.13 H16
Florida Ave. Pg.13 G16
Florida Rd. Pg.13 G16
Flossmoor Ave. Pg.13 G-H17
Foam Forms Pl. Pg.14 H18
Forest Ave. Pg.19,21 K18,L14
Forest Ct. Pg.14 G18
Forest Ln. Pg.13 F17
Forest View Ln. Pg.19 M13
Forrest Hills Ct. Pg.12 F14
Foster McGaw Dr. Pg.6 E16
Franklin St. Pg.14 H18
Frazier St. Pg.14 F17
Frolic Ave. Pg.13 K16
Fulton Ave. Pg.21 K,L17
Gallagher Rd. Pg.14 G18
Garden Pl. Pg.13 H17
Garrick Ave. Pg.13 F16
Gavin Ln. Pg.19 M14
Genessee St. Pg.21 K18
Gent Dr. Pg.13 F15
George Ave. Pg.21 K18
George St. Pg.13 K16
Georgetown Ave. Pg.13 G17
Gillett Ave. Pg.14 H18
Gladstone Ave. Pg.21 K17
Gladys Ct. Pg.7 D17
Glen Ct. Pg.21 K18
Glen Dr. Pg.21 L17
Glen Flora Ave. Pg.14 H17
Glen Rock Ave. Pg.21 K17
Glendenning Pl. Pg.14 G18
Glendower Ave. Pg.13 H17
Golf Rd. Pg.14 G18
Golfmoor Ave. Pg.13 G17
Grand Ave. Pg.14 H18
Grandmore Ave. Pg.13 H16
Grandview Ave. Pg.13 H16
Grandville Ave. Pg.13 H16
Graves Ave. Pg.13 F16
Gray Ct. Pg.20 K16
Green Ave. Pg.13 H16
Green Bay Pl. Pg.20 L16
Green Bay Rd. Pg.13 H,K16
Greenfield Ave. Pg.21 L17
Greenwood Ave. Pg.13,14 G16-18
Greenwood Terr. Pg.14 G17
Gretta Ave. Pg.20 K-L17
Griffith Ave. Pg.7 E17
Grove Ave. Pg.13,14 G17,H18
Grove St. Pg.14 H18
Guerin Rd. Pg.19 N13
Hamilton Ct. Pg.14 K17
Hampshire Ln. Pg.12 F14
Hanlon Rd. Pg.19 M13
Harbor Pl. Pg.14 K18
Harding Ave. Pg.13,14 G17,18
Harrison Ave. Pg.13 H16
Harrison Pl. Pg.13 H16
Hart St. Pg.13 E16
Hawk Ct. Pg.20 M14
Hawthorne Ct. Pg.13 G15
Hawthorne Ln. Pg.13 F17
Hayley Ct. Pg.20 K16
Hazel Ct. Pg.21 K18
Hemholz Ave. Pg.21 K18
Henry Pl. Pg.14 G18
Herbert Dr. Pg.13 G17
Heritage Ln. Pg.12 F14
Hickory Hill Rd. Pg.13 F13
Hickory St. Pg.14 G-H18
Hidden Glen Dr. Pg.20 K16
Highland Ave. Pg.14 H17
Highland Cir. Pg.14 H17
Hillman Ct. Pg.14 K17
Hills St. Pg.21 K18
Hillside Ave. Pg.20 K16
Hilltop Ln. Pg.19 M13
Hollis Ave. Pg.13 H16
Home Ave. Pg.13,21 H16,K18
Hope Ln. Pg.13 G16
Howard St. Pg.13 E16
Hull Ct. Pg.14 H18
Huntington Lakes Dr. Pg.19 M13
Huron Terr. Pg.13 G16
Hyde Park Ave. Pg.13,14 H16-17
Illini Rd. Pg.13 G16
Indian Rd. Pg.13 G16
Indiana Ave. Pg.14 H17
Indiana St. Pg.14 H17
Iroquois Rd. Pg.13 G16
Irving Pkwy. Pg.13 E17
Jackson Ct. Pg.14 H17
Jackson St. Pg.14,21 H18,K17
James Ct. Pg.14 H18
James St. Pg.14 K18
Jaquelyn Ln. Pg.13 F16
Jefferson Ave. Pg.14 K17
Jefferson Dr. Pg.19 M13
Jenkinson Ct. Pg.13 K17
Jensen Ct. Pg.21 K18
Jensen Ln. Pg.19 M13
Johnson Rd. Pg.6 D17
Jolley Ave. Pg.20 K16
Joseph Dr. Pg.13 F15
Judge Ave. Pg.14 H-K17
Judge Pl. Pg.14 H17
Julian St. Pg.14 H18
Kathy Ln. Pg.13 K16
Kehil North Ave. Pg.20 L15
Keith Ave. Pg.13,14 G16-18
Keller Ave. Pg.20 K-L17
Kellogg Ave. Pg.13 G17
Kennard St. Pg.21 K18
Kennedy Dr. Pg.19 M13
Kingston Rd. Pg.13 F16
Knight Ave. Pg.20 L16
Kyle Dr. Pg.20 K16
Lake Ct. Pg.21 K18
Lake St. Pg.21 K18
Lakehurst Rd. Pg.20 L15
Lakeside Dr. Pg.20 L15
Lakeview Ave. Pg.21 K18
Lakeview Terr. Pg.19 M13
Lakewood Ave. Pg.13 K16
Laurel Ave. Pg.21 K17
Laurel Ln. Pg.13 F17
Lawn Ave. Pg.19 L14
Lawn Ct. Pg.14 H18
Le Baron St. Pg.13 K16
Leith Ave. Pg.13 H17
Lenox Ave. Pg.21 L18
Leo Singer Ln. Pg.7 E17
Lewis Ave. Pg.13,14,20,21 F-K17
Lewis Pl. Pg.14 H17
Liberty St. Pg.21 K18
Lincoln Ave. Pg.21 K18
Linden Ave. Pg.14 G17
Linden St. Pg.14 H17
Lindsay Ave. Pg.14 H18
Little Foot Rd. Pg.13 G16
Lloyd Ave. Pg.20 K17
Longview Rd. Pg.14 G17-18
Lorene Ct. Pg.13 E17
Lorraine Ave. Pg.14 F-K17
Lorraine Pl. Pg.14 H17
Low Ave. Pg.14 H17
Lucia Ave. Pg.20,21 K16,17
Lydia St. Pg.13 H17
Lynn Terr. Pg.13 H17
Lyons Ct. Pg.21 L17
MacArthur Dr. Pg.14 F17
Madison St. Pg.14 K18
Magnolia Ln. Pg.12 F14
Maple Ave. Pg.21 K17
Maple Tree Ln. Pg.13 F14
Marian Ct. Pg.21 K18
Mariflores Ave. Pg.14 G18
Mariposa Ave. Pg.14 G18
Market St. Pg.21 K18
Marshall Pkwy. Pg.20 L17
Martin Ave. Pg.20 K,L17
Martin Luther King, Jr. Dr., Dr. Pg.20 M15
Mary Jane Ln. Pg.7 E17
Massena Ave. Pg.14 H18
Mathon Dr. Overpass Pg.14 H18
Matthew Ct. Pg.19 M13
May St. Pg.21 L18
McAlister Ave. Pg.21 K18
McAree Rd. Pg.13 F-H16
McGaw Rd. Pg.20 L15
McKay St. Pg.14 F17
McKinley St. Pg.21 K18
Meadowlark Ln. Pg.13 F17
Meadowview Cir. Pg.19 M13
Meagan Ct. Pg.19 M13
Melrose Ave. Pg.20 K16
Menominee Rd. Pg.13 G16
Merton Ave. Pg.14 G17
Metropolitan Ave. Pg.13 H16
Meyer Rd. Pg.13 F15
Miami Rd. Pg.13 G16
Midlane Dr. Pg.13 F15
Mill Ct. Pg.14 H18
Milwaukee Ave. Pg.19 M12
Mini Dr. Pg.13 F14
Minoque Ave. Pg.20 L16
Miraflores Ave. Pg.14 G18
Mohawk Rd. Pg.13 G16
Mohican Rd. Pg.13 G16
Monroe St. Pg.13 K16-17
Montesana Ave. Pg.14 F17,18
Morris Ct. Pg.7 D17
Muirfield Ave. Pg.13 H17
Muirfield Dr. Pg.12 F14
Muncey Ave. Pg.14 G18
Myrtle St. Pg.14 H18
Navajo Rd. Pg.13 G16
Nemery Ct. Pg.13 H16
Nemesis Ave. Pg.13 G16
New York Ave. Pg.14 E17
New York St. Pg.14 G-H17
Newcastle Ct., E. & W. Pg.13 F17
Newcastle Rd. Pg.13 E-F17
Niva Ct. Pg.13 G17
Noll St. Pg.13 K16
Nordigan Dr. Pg.14 F18
Norma Pg.13 K16
Norman Dr. Pg.20 M15
Normandy Ct. Pg.19 L14
North Ave. Pg.14 G-H18
North Park Ave. Pg.14 K18
Northern Ave. Pg.13 G16
Northfield Ave. Pg.13 H16
Northmoor Ave. Pg.13 H17
Northpoint Blvd. Pg.20 L15
Northwest St. Pg.14 K18
Northwestern Ave. Pg.13 G15
O'Plaine Rd. Pg.19 M13
Oak Ave. Pg.6 E17
Oak Crest St. Pg.14 H17
Oak St. Pg.21 K17-18
Oak Tree Ln. Pg.14 H17
Oakland Ave. Pg.13 H16
Oakley Ave. Pg.14 H18
Oakwood Ave. Pg.13 K16
Oneida Pl. Pg.13 G16
Orchard Ave. Pg.13 H16,K17
Orchard Ln. Pg.13 H16
Orchard Rd. Pg.14 F17
Osage Cir. Pg.13 G16
Osprey Ln. Pg.20 M14
Otto Graham Ln. Pg.7 E17
Ottowa Rd. Pg.13 G16
Pacific Ave. Pg.13,14 G-H17
Palmer Pl. Pg.14 H18
Park Ave. Pg.21 K18
Park Ave., N. Pg.14 K18
Parkway Ave. Pg.20 L15
Parmalee Pl. Pg.14 G18
Partridge St. Pg.14 F17
Paul St. Pg.14 H17
Pawnee Rd. Pg.13 G16
Pearsall Pkwy. Pg.20 L17
Pebble Beach Dr. Pg.12 F14
Peppertree Ln. Pg.13 H16
Pershing Rd. Pg.14 H18
Phillippa Ave. Pg.14 K18
Pigeon Ave. Pg.13 K16
Pikoi Ln. Pg.19 N13
Pine St. Pg.14 F-H17
Pioneer Ave. Pg.13 H16
Pioneer Ct. Pg.13 H16
Pioneer Rd. Pg.13 H-L16
Pleasant Hill Gate Pg.20 L14
Polo Ave. Pg.13 G16
Poplar St. Pg.14 F-H18
Porter St. Pg.14 H17
Powell Ave. Pg.21 K18
Prairie Ave. Pg.20 K16
Prescott St. Pg.21 L18
Prestwick Ln. Pg.12 F14
Princeton Ct. Pg.19 L14
Prospect Ct. Pg.21 K18
Public Rd. Pg.14 H18
Public Service Ave. Pg.13 H16
Quill Ln. Pg.19 L14
Ravine Ave. Pg.21 K18
Regency Ln. Pg.20 M14
Renier St. Pg.13 E16
Rice St. Pg.14 F17
Ridge Ave. Pg.20 K16
Ridgeland Ave. Pg.13 H16-17
River Bend Dr. Pg.19 M13
River Park Dr. Pg.19 M13
River Rd. Pg.19 M13
Roberts Ave. Pg.13 F16
Robin Ct. Pg.20 M14
Rock Pkwy. Pg.13 E17
Rodger Edwards Ave. Pg.14 G17
Rogers Ct. Pg.14 H18
Roundstone Way Pg.19 L14
Rudd Ct. Pg.19 M14
Rugby Ct. Pg.13 F17
Runyard Pl. Pg.21 K17
Salem Ave. Pg.21 K17
Sallmon Rd. Pg.13 F16
Sand St. Pg.14 H18
Sea Horse Rd. Pg.14 H18
Seminole Rd. Pg.13 G16
Seneca Rd. Pg.13 G16
Sequoit Rd. Pg.13 G17
Service Ave. Pg.13 H16
Shadow Brook Ct. Pg.19 M13
Shawnee Rd. Pg.13 G16
Sheeler Ave. Pg.13 H16
Sheridan Ct. East Pg.14 G18
Sheridan Rd. Pg.14,21 F,L18
Sherman Ave. Pg.13 H16
Sherman Pl. Pg.14 K18
Shields Dr. Pg.20 M15
Shirley Dr. Pg.13 F15
Shoshone Rd. Pg.13 G16
Sioux Pg.13 G16
Skokie Highway Pg.20 M16
South Ave. Pg.21 K18
South Park Ave. Pg.14 K18
Southern Hills Dr. Pg.12 F14
Southview Ave. Pg.13 H16
Southview Ave. Pg.13 F16
Sparrow Ct. Pg.20 M14
Spaulding Ave. Pg.13 K16
Spring St. Pg.21 K18
Spruce Ave. Pg.14 G18
St. James St. Pg.14 K18
St. Rte 120 Pg.20 L16
St. Rte 21 Pg.19 M12
St. Rte 43 Pg.20 M15
Staben Ave. Pg.20 L16
Stanley Ave. Pg.14 G18
Steele Ct. Pg.14 H18
Steeple Chase Circle Dr. Pg.19 M13
Stewart Ave. Pg.14 H18
Stonegate Rd. Pg.14 E17
Stripe Ct. Pg.13 K16
Sumac Ave. Pg.20 K-L17
Sunderlin St. Pg.21 L18
Sunset Ave. Pg.13 G15-17
Sunset Terr. Pg.14 G18
Swallowtail Dr. Pg.19 L14
Sycamore Dr. Pg.13 H16
Talcott Dr. Pg.19 L14
Tamara Ct. Pg.14 H17
Tannahill Dr. Pg.13 G15
Telegraph Rd. Pg.20 L15
Ten Pin Ln. Pg.7 E17
Terrace Ave. Pg.14 G-H18
Tewes Ln. Pg.7 E17
Thaxter Ave. Pg.20 K16
Theresa Ave. Pg.13 H16
Thompson Ave. Pg.14 G18
Thorneberry Ct. Pg.19 M14
Tiffany Dr. Pg.13 H17
Timber Woods Ln. Pg.19 M13
Tobin Ct. Pg.21 L17
Town Line Rd. Pg.13 E16
Tremont Ct. Pg.19 M13
Trenton Ct. Pg.19 M13
Tucker Ln. Pg.19 L14
Twyford Rd. Pg.13 F17
Tyler Ave. Pg.13 F16
University Ave. Pg.13 H16-17
Utica St. Pg.14,21 H,K18
Varonen Ave. Pg.13 G16
Vercoe Ave. Pg.13 F16
Vermont Ave. Pg.13 F16
Victor Ln. Pg.19 N13
Victoria Ln. Pg.12 E14
Victoria St. Pg.21 K18
Victory St. Pg.21 K17
Wadsworth Ave. Pg.21 L18
Wadsworth Rd. Pg.6 D16
Wainlow Ave. Pg.21 K17
Wall Ave. Pg.13 F16
Walnut St. Pg.14 G-H18
Warbler Ct. Pg.20 M14
Washington Park Pg.21 K-L17
Washington St. Pg.14 K17
Washington Terr. Pg.13 K16
Water St. Pg.21 K18
Waukee, W. Pg.13 K16
Waukegan Rd. Pg.20 M15
Waverly Pl. Pg.13 H17
Waxwing Ln. Pg.20 M14
Wellington Rd. Pg.19 L14
West Ave. Pg.19 L14
West Dr. Pg.13 K16
West Park St. Pg.21 K18
West St. Pg.21 K18
West Waukee Pg.13 K16
Western Ave. Pg.14 G17
Westmoreland Ave. Pg.13,14 H17
Wetzel Ct. Pg.14 K17
Whidden Ave. Pg.20 K17
Whispering Willows Ct. Pg.19 M13
White Oak Dr. Pg.20 M15
Whitney St. Pg.14 F17
Williamsburg Ave. Pg.13 G17
Willow Ave. Pg.20 L16
Willow Ct. Pg.13 H16
Willow Dr. Pg.14 G18
Wilson Ave. Pg.14 F17
Windsor Ct. Pg.19 L14
Winhaven Dr. Pg.14 E17
Winnebago Rd. Pg.13 G16
Wisconsin Ave. Pg.20 K-L17
Witchwood Ln. Pg.13 F17
Wood Ave. Pg.20 K16
Woodlawn Ave. Pg.14 H17
Woodlawn Cir. Pg.14 H17
Worack Pl. Pg.21 K17
Wren Ct. Pg.20 M14
Yeoman St. Pg.14 F-H17
York House Rd. Pg.13 F16
Zepher St. Pg.13 E16
1st St. Pg.14 H18
2nd St. Pg.14 H18
3rd St. Pg.14 G18
4th St. Pg.14 G-H18
5th St. Pg.14 G18
6th St. Pg.20 K17
7th St. Pg.20 L16
8th St. Pg.21 L17
9th Pkwy. Pg.20 L17
9th St. Pg.20,21 L17
10th Ct. Pg.21 L17
10th St. Pg.20 L16-17
11th Ct. Pg.21 L17
11th St. Pg.20 L17
12th St. Pg.20 L17
13th St. Pg.20 L17
14th St. Pg.20 L17

### CEMETERIES

Oakwood Cem. Pg.21 L18
St. Mary's Cem. Pg.21 L18

### FOREST PRESERVES

Almond Road F.P. Pg.19 L13
Green Belt F.P. Pg.20 L16
Independence Grove F.P. Pg.19 N13
Lyons Woods Pg.14 F18
Waukegan Savana Forest Preserve Pg.13 E15

### GOLF COURSES

Bonnie Brook Muni. G.C. Pg.13 F17
Glen Flora C.C. Pg.14 G18
Midlane G.C. Pg.12,13 F14

### PARKS

Armory Park Pg.13 H17
Beach Park Pg.14 K18
Bedrosian Park Pg.21 K18
Belvidere Park Pg.20 K17
Ben Diamond Mem. Park Pg.13 G17
Bevier Park Pg.14 F17
Callahan Park Pg.13 F16
City Park Pg.14 K18
Clark Park Pg.14 F18
Clearview Park Pg.14 G17
Dugdale Park Pg.21 K17
Edward Field Pg.14 G17
Foss Park Pg.21 L17
Glen Flora Park Pg.14 G18
Hinkston Park Pg.13 H16
Illinois Beach State Park Pg.14 F19
King Park Pg.21 K18
Kirk Park Pg.21 K18
North Beach Park Pg.14 H19
Powell Park Pg.14 K18
Roosevelt Park Pg.21 K18
Smith Park Pg.21 L18
Upton Park Pg.14 H18
Victory Park Pg.14 H18
Village Park Pg.13 F14
Washington Park Pg.21 K18
Weiss Field Pg.13 K17
Yeoman Park Pg.14 H17

### SCHOOLS

Andrew Cooke Sch. Pg.21 K18
Bonnie Brook Sch. Pg.14 F17
Clark Sch. Pg.14 F18
Clearview Sch. Pg.13 G17
Daniel Webster Jr. H.S. Pg.14 H17
Gertrude Carman Sch. Pg.21 K18
Glen Flora Sch. Pg.14 H18
Glenwood Sch. Pg.13 H17
Greenwood Sch. Pg.14 G18
Hyde Park Sch. Pg.14 H17
Immaculate Conception Sch. Pg.14 H18
Immanual Evangelical Lutheran Sch. Pg.13 H16
Jack Benny Jr. H.S. Pg.14 G17
Jackson Sch. Pg.21 K17
Lakeshore Cath. Acad. Central Pg.21 L18
Lakeshore Cath. Acad. N. Pg.21 K18
Lincoln School Pg.14 H18
Little Fort Sch. Pg.14 F17
Lyon Sch Pg.21 L17
McCall Sch. Pg.13 F16
North Sch. Pg.14 H18
Oakdale Sch. Pg.13 G16
Spaulding Sch. Pg.13 H16
St. Anatasia Sch. Pg.14 H18
Thomas Jefferson Jr. H.S. Pg.20 K17
Washington Sch. Pg.20 K17
Waukegan Twp. H.S. East Pg.21 K17
West Sch. Pg.21 K17
Whittier Sch. Pg.14 H17
Waukegan West H.S. Pg.13 H17

### SHOPPING CENTERS

Belvidere Mall Pg.21 K17
Lakehurst S.C. Pg.20 L15

### MISCELLANEOUS

Commuter Sta. Pg.21 K18
County Health Dept. Pg.13 H16
St. Therese Hosp. Pg.20 H16
Victory Memorial Hosp. Pg.14 H18
Waukegan Yacht Club Pg.14 K19

## WAUKEGAN TOWNSHIP

Pages 13,14

### STREETS

Adelphi Ave. H16
Arizona Ave. G16
Atlantic Ave. G15
Austin Ave. H16
Brooke Ave. G16
Cheyenne Rd. G15
Clearview Ave. G16
Colorado Ave. G16
Cornell Rd. E17
Country Club Ave. G15
Crescent Ave. E15
Duggald Ave. H16
Florida Ave. G15
Garnett Ave. F18
Garrick Ave. F,G16
Glen Flora Ave. G15
Grandmore Ave. H16
Grandview Ave. H16
Grandville Ave. H16
Green Bay Rd. F16
Green Pl. G16
Greenwood Ave. G15
Grove Ave. G15
Harrison Ave. H16
Hendee Rd. F15
Highland Ave. G15
Hyde Park Ave. H16
Johns Manville Ave. G16
Keith Ave. G15
Lee Ave. G15
Metropolitan Ave. G16
Morton Ave. E18
Nemesis Ave. F16
North Ave. F18
Northern Ave. G,H16
Northfield Ave. H16
Oakwood Ave. H16
Pacific Ave. G15
Paddock St. F15
Polo Ave. G16
Public Service Ave. H16
Sherman Ave. G16
Southview Ave. H16
Tyler Ave. F16
University Ave. H16
Vermont Ave. F16
Wall Ave. F16
York House Rd. F16

### PARKS

Bevier Park F17
Callahan Park F16

### MISCELLANEOUS

Commonwealth Edison Co. Sta. No. 16 G19

## WEST DEERFIELD TOWNSHIP

Pages 27,28,34-37

### STREETS

Birchwood Ln. Pg.37 V17
Chris Ct. Pg.36 W16
County Line Rd. Pg.36 X16
Deer Run Dr. Pg.36 X16
Elmwood Pl. Pg.37 V17
Forest Ct. Pg.37 V17
Half Day Rd. Pg.36 V16
Hawthorne Ln. Pg.36 X16
Hickory Knoll Ln. Pg.36 W16
Montgomery Dr. Pg.36 W16
Oakwood Pl. Pg.37 V17
Saunders Rd. Pg.36 X16
Tri-State Tlwy. (I-94) Pg.36 X16
Wildwood Ln. Pg.37 V17
Woodview Ln. Pg.36 X16

## WILDWOOD

Page 18...L10

## WILLIAMS PARK

Page 22...S1

## WILSON

Page 20...L15

## WINTHROP HARBOR

Pages 6,7

### STREETS

Adams Ave. B18
Aiken Ct. B18
Alison St. A19
Alton Ct. A18
Beckett St. A19
Ben Ct. B18
Berrong Ct. A17
Broadway Ave., E. & W. B17
Burke Dr. B18
Camden Cove A18
Cargo Bay A18
Casco Bay A17
Cavin Ave. A18
Cedar Ct. A19
Charles Ave. A18
Chatham Cove A17
Chestnut Cir. A18
Clearmer Ct. A17
Clearview Ct. A17
College Ave. A18
Compton Ct. A17
Cornerstone Dr. A17
Deerpath Cir. A19
Deerpath Dr. A19
East End B19
Ellis Ave. A18
Fairhaven Dr. A18
Franklin Ave. B18
Franklin St. B19
Frans Ct. A18
Fulton Ave. B18
Funkerburk Dr. B18
Garnett Ave. A18
Geddes Ave. A18
Har-Bar Cir. A17
Harbor Ct. A18
Highland Ct. A18
Holdridge Ave. A18
Ivy Ct. A17
Ja-lor Ct. A18
James Ave. A18
Judith Ct. A18
Kimberly Ln. A18
Kirkwood Ave. A18
Lake Shore Rd. B19
Lake Vista Rd. A19
Landon Ave. B19
Laurie Ave. A19
Lawrence St. A19
Madison Ave. A18
Mae Ct. B18
Main St. A18
Marion St. A19
Mary Ave. B18
Meadow Ct. A17
Meadow Ln. A18
Monroe Ave. B18
North Ave. A18
Oak Shore Dr. A19
Old Darty Ln. A18
Park Ave. B19
Park Ave., N. A18
Park View Dr. A17
Potash St. A19
Prairie Ave. A18
Ravine Dr. A18
Roberts Rd. A18
Rose Ct. A17
Runyard Ave. A18
Russell Ave. A18
Sheridan Pl. A18
Sheridan Rd. A18
Sherman Dr. A19
Shields Ave. A18
Stonegate Dr. A16
Thompson Ave. A18
Valley Rd. A17
Vista Ln. A18
Vista Rd. B19
Washington Ave. A17
West Dr. B18
Whitney Ave. A18
Wilson Ave. A18
4th St. A18
5th St. A17-18
6th St. A18
8th St. A18
9th St. A18
10th St. A17-18
11th St. A18
12th St. B18
13th St. B17
14th St. B18
15th St. B17-19

### PARKS

Illinois Beach State Pk. B19

### SCHOOLS

Spring Bluff Sch. A18
West Field Jr. H.S. A18

### MISCELLANEOUS

City Hall A19
Post Office A18

## ZION

Pages 6,7

### STREETS

Barnhart Ave. C18
Bethany Ave. C18
Bethel Blvd. D18
Bethesda Blvd. C18
Bethlehem Ave. C18
Brigadoon Dr. B16
Burnett Ave. B19
Butterfield Ln. B16
Caledonia Ave. D18
Caledonia Blvd. D19
Calvary Ln. D18
Carmel Blvd. D17
Champart St. D18
Clover Ln. D18
Cloverdale Ave. D18
Colgate Ave. D18
Dawn Ln. D18
Daybreak Ln. B16
Deborah Ave. C19
Douglas Dr. A16
Dowie Memorial Dr. C18
Dusk Dr. B16
Ebenezer Ave. C19
Eden Ave. C19
Edina Blvd. C18
Eli Ave. C19
Elim Ave. C18
Elisha Ave. C,D18
Elizabeth Ave. C18
Elijah Ave. D18
Emmaus Ave. C18
Emden Ave. C18
Enoch Ave. C,D18
Eshcol Ave. C,D18
Ezekiel Ave. D18
Ezekiel Pl. C,D18
Ezra Ave. C,D18
Fago Ave. B17
Fleming Ave. B17
Forest Bi-Way B16
Fossland Ave. B17
Francis Ct. B16
Franklin Ct. B16
Franklin St. B16
Fulton C19
Gabriel Ave. C18
Galilee Ave. C17
George Ct. B16
Gideon Ave. C18
Gilboa Ave. C17
Gilead Ave. C17
Green Bay Rd. A16
Gregory St. A16
Hampson Ct. C17
Harbor Ridge Dr. B17
Hayner Ave. B17
Heather Ct. B16
Hebron Ave. C,D17
Hermon Ave. C,D17
Highland Rd. B16
Hill Dr. B16
Hillside Ave. C19
Hilltop Ave. B19
Horeb Ave. C17
Horizon Ct. C16
Industrial Ave. B17
James Ct. B16
Jethro Ave. C17
Joanna Ave. C17
Joppa Ave. C17
Kedron Blvd. B18
Kenosha Rd. B16
Kensington Ln. B17
Lake View Ave. C18
Leah Ave. C17
Lebanon Ave. D17
Lewis Ave. B17
Logan Ct. B18
Lorelei Dr. A,B16
Lowery Ct. C17
Lucile Ct. A16
Luckie Ct. A16
Lydia Ave. B,C17
Lydia Pl. C17
May-Kay Ln. D18
Midday Dr. B16
Northlawn Ave. B16
Pamela Ct. B16
Parkway Ln. B16
Pelican Ct. B17
Portsmouth Dr. B17
Primrose Ct. B16
Ravina Ave. B18
Ridge Ct. B16
Ridge Dr. B16
Salem Blvd. C17
Schooner Ct. B17
Sharon Pl. D18
Sheridan Rd. D18
Shetland B16
Shiloh Blvd. C18
Southport Ct. B17
Stella Ct. C17
Sunshine Ln. B16
Swager Ln. B16
Tallgrass Ct. B16
Tartan Tr. B16
Thistle Ln. B16
Thompson B18
Thorpe Ave. B17
Timet St. A16
Timothy A16
Wemberly Dr. B17
Westside Tr. B16
Willow Crest Dr. B16
Willow Ln. B17
Wilson Ct. B18
Wilson St. B18
Winthrop Ct. B18
9th St. A16
13th St. B16
16th St. B16
17th St. B17
18th St. B17
19th St. B17
20th St. B17
21st St. C17-18
22nd St. C17-18
23rd St. C17-19
24th St. C17-18
25th St. C17-18
26th St. C17-18
27th St. C17-18
28th St. C18-19
29th St. D17
30th St. D17
31st St. D17
32nd St. D17
33rd St. D17
34th St. D17-18

### CEMETERIES

Lake Mound Cem. D18
Mount Olivet Memorial Cem. B16

### GOLF COURSES

Shiloh Park G.C. C18

### PARKS

Beulah Park B18
Carmel Park D18
Davis Park C17
Dow Creek Pk. D18
Edina Park C19
Galilee Park C17
Hermon Park C17
Hosah Park C19
Illinois Beach State Pk. B-D19
Joanna Park C17
Offner Park D17
Ophir Park D18
Sharon Park D18
Shiloh Park C18

### SCHOOLS

Beulah Sch. B17
Central Jr. H.S. C18
East Sch. C18
Elmwood Sch. C17
Our Savior's Lutheran Sch. C18
Shiloh Park Sch. C18
Spirit of Life Christian Sch. A16
Waukegan Christian Sch. C18
West Sch. C17
Zion Benton H.S. East Campus C18
Zion Benton H.S. West Campus C16
Zion Christian Sch. B17

### MISCELLANEOUS

Chamber of Commerce C19
City Hall D18
Civil Defense Bldg. C19
Historical Society C18
Hospital C18
Leisure Center C18
Library C18
Post Office C18
Recycling Center C17

# MC HENRY COUNTY
## SECTION 7

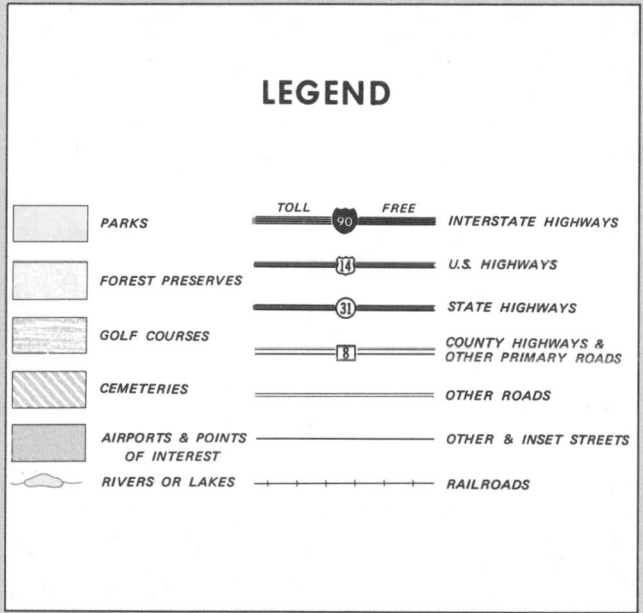

## LEGEND

| | |
|---|---|
| PARKS | **TOLL** **FREE** — 90 — INTERSTATE HIGHWAYS |
| FOREST PRESERVES | — 14 — U.S. HIGHWAYS |
| GOLF COURSES | — 31 — STATE HIGHWAYS |
| CEMETERIES | — 8 — COUNTY HIGHWAYS & OTHER PRIMARY ROADS |
| AIRPORTS & POINTS OF INTEREST | OTHER ROADS |
| RIVERS OR LAKES | OTHER & INSET STREETS |
| | RAILROADS |

**TURN PAGE FOR ORIENTATION MAP**

# SECTION 7
# ORIENTATION MAP

Information on this page is to be used for general reference only.
For definitve listings of all information, see index at end of this section.

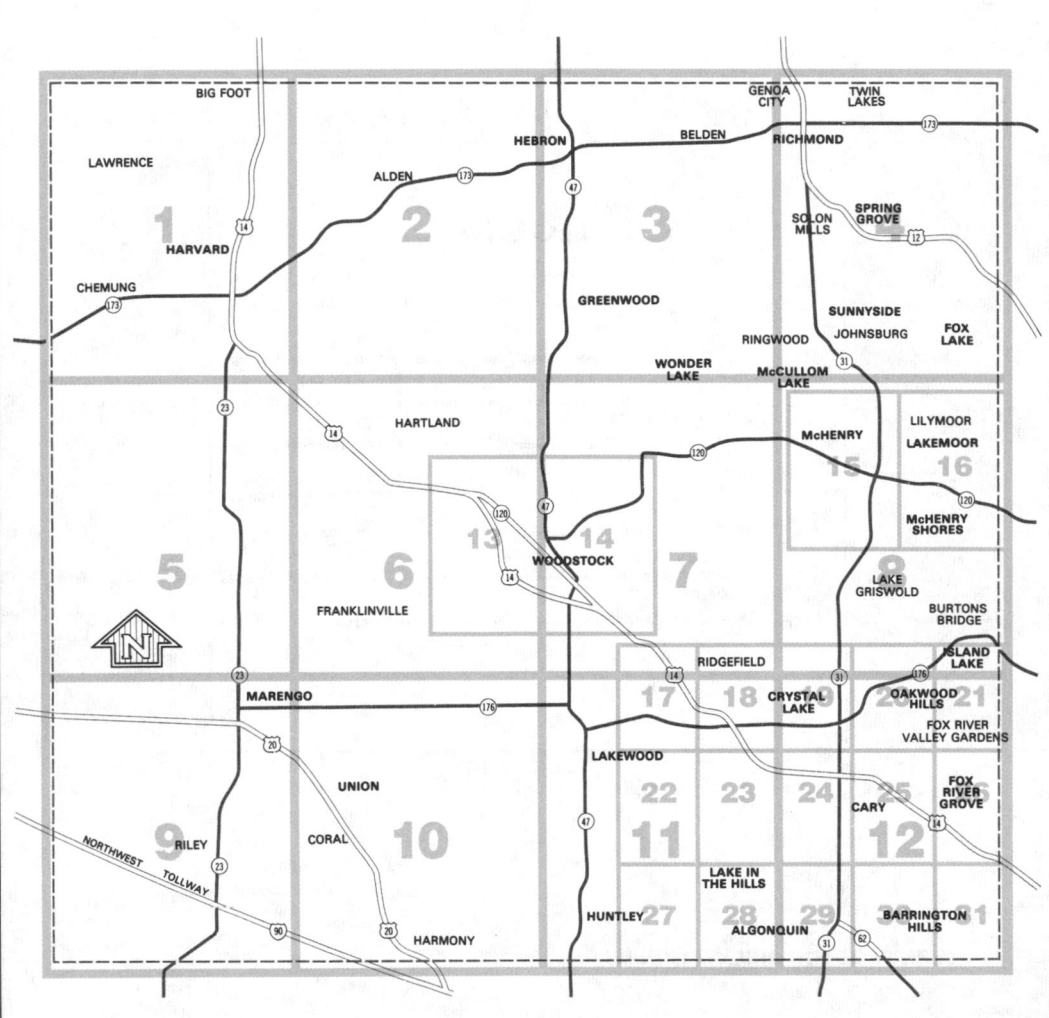

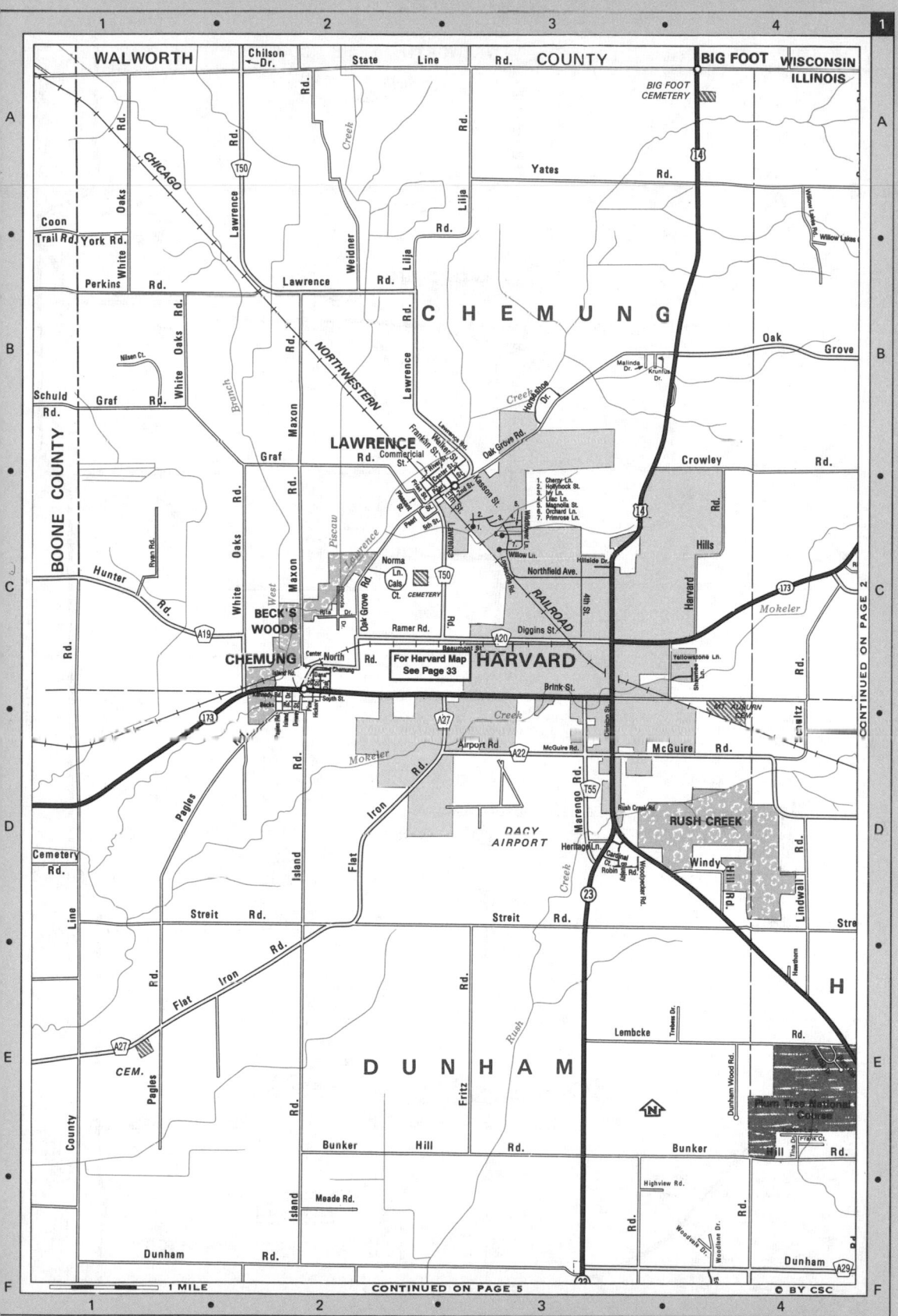

WALWORTH
Chilson Dr.
State Line Rd. COUNTY
BIG FOOT
WISCONSIN
ILLINOIS

BIG FOOT CEMETERY

Chilson Dr.

Creek

Yates Rd.

CHICAGO

Coon Trail Rd.
York Rd.
White
Oaks
Perkins Rd.
Lawrence
Lawrence
Rd.
Weidner
Lilja
Lilja
Rd.

CHEMUNG

Oak Grove

Nilsen Ct.
Schuld Rd.
Graf Rd.
White Oaks Rd.
Maxon Rd.
Lawrence
Graf Rd.
NORTHWESTERN
Creekshoe Dr.
Malinda Dr.
Krunlus Dr.
Horseshoe Dr.
Oak Grove Rd.

LAWRENCE
Commercial St.
Franklin St.
Walter St.
Crowley Rd.

Hills

1. Cherry Ln.
2. Hollyhock St.
3. Ivy Ln.
4. Lilac Ln.
5. Magnolia St.
6. Orchard Ln.
7. Primrose Ln.

BOONE COUNTY

Branch

Piscaw

Maxon Rd.
White Oaks Rd.
West
Lawrence

Hunter Rd.
Ryan Rd.
A19

BECK'S WOODS

Oak Grove Rd.
Norma Ln.
Cals Ct.
T50
CEMETERY
Willow Ln.
Northfield Ave.
Hillside Dr.
Harvard
173
Mokeler

Ramer Rd.
Diggins St.
4th St.
A20
RAILROAD

CHEMUNG

Center Rd.
North
For Harvard Map See Page 33
HARVARD
Brink St.
Yellowstone Ln.
Sholes Ln.

173
South St.

Mokeler
Creek
Airport Rd.
A22
McGuire Rd.
McGuire Rd.
Schultz

Pagles
Iron
Flat
Rd.
A27
Marengo Rd.
T55
Rush Creek Rd.
RUSH CREEK
Windy
Lindwall Rd.

Cemetery Rd.
DACY AIRPORT
Heritage Ln.
Cardinal Ct.
Robin Rd.
Aspen Rd.
Woodpecker Rd.
Hill Rd.

Line
Streit Rd.
Streit Rd.
23
H

Flat Iron Rd.
Rd.
Fritz Rd.
Lembcke Rd.
Trebes Dr.
Stre

A27
CEM.
Pagles
DUNHAM
Dunham Wood Rd.
Rush Tree National Cobra

County
Bunker Hill Rd.
Bunker Rd.
Hill Rd.
Ting Ct.
Frank Ct.

Island Rd.
Meade Rd.
Highview Rd.
Woodland Dr.
Woodside Dr.

Dunham Rd.
Dunham
A29

CONTINUED ON PAGE 2

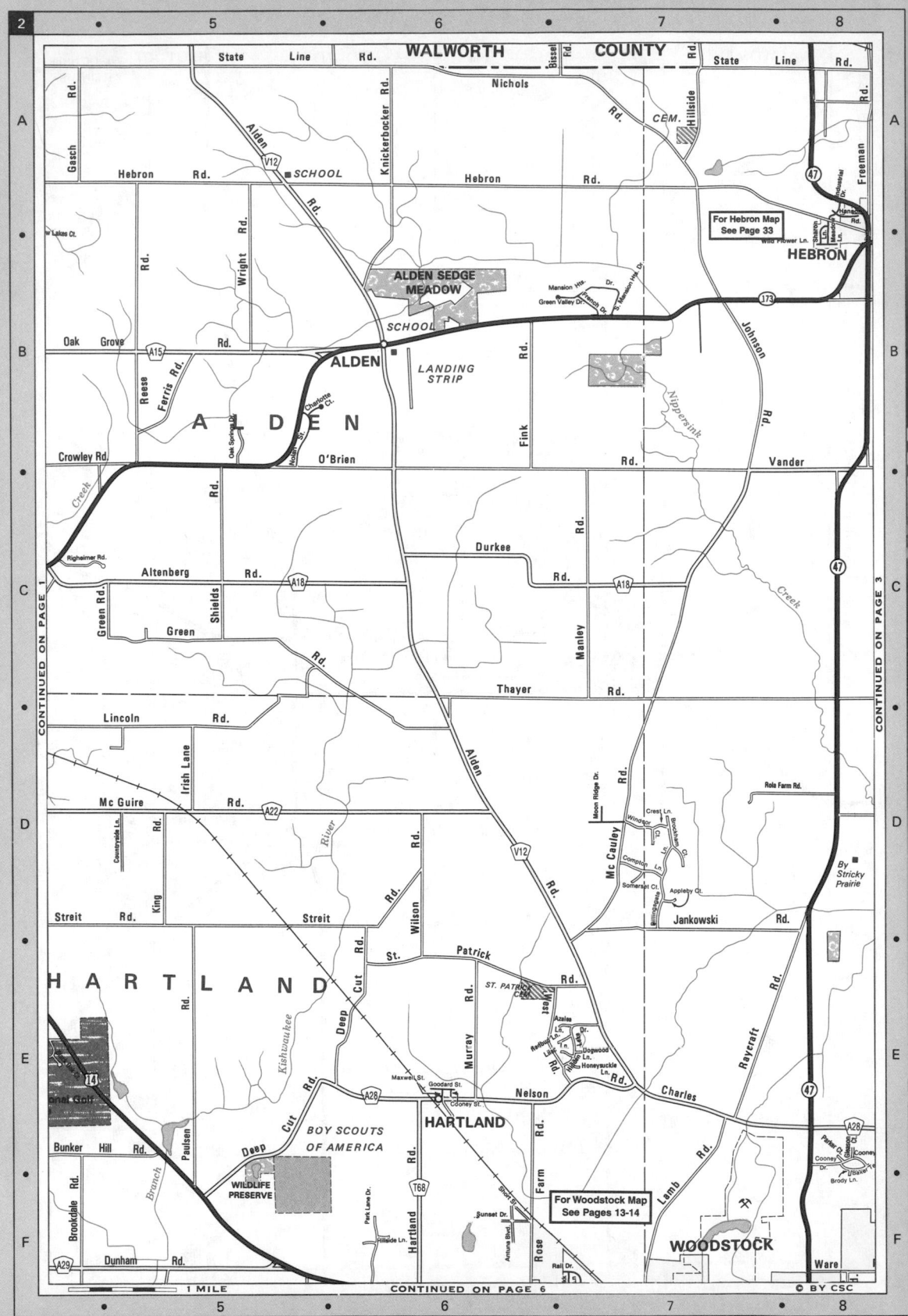

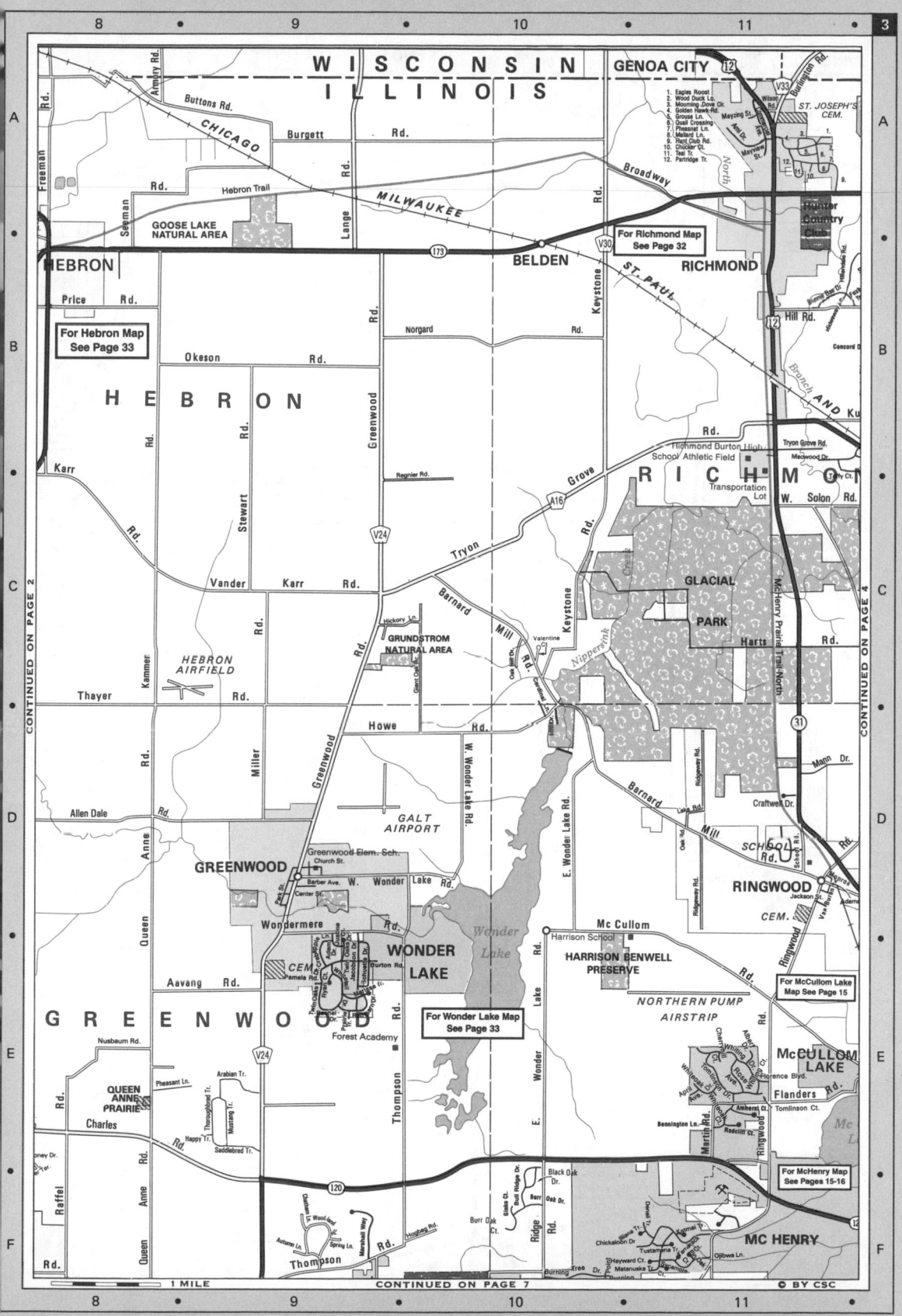

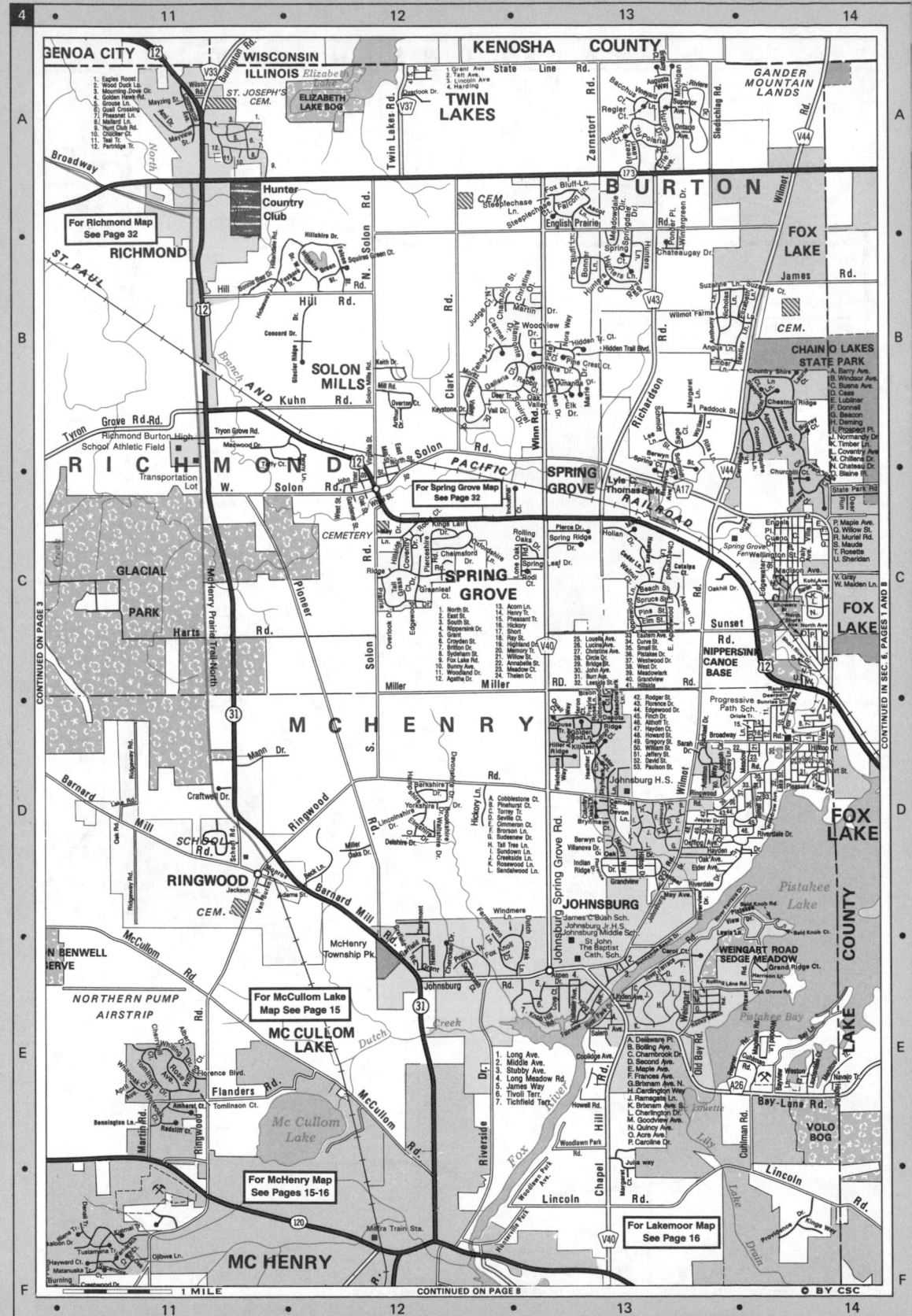

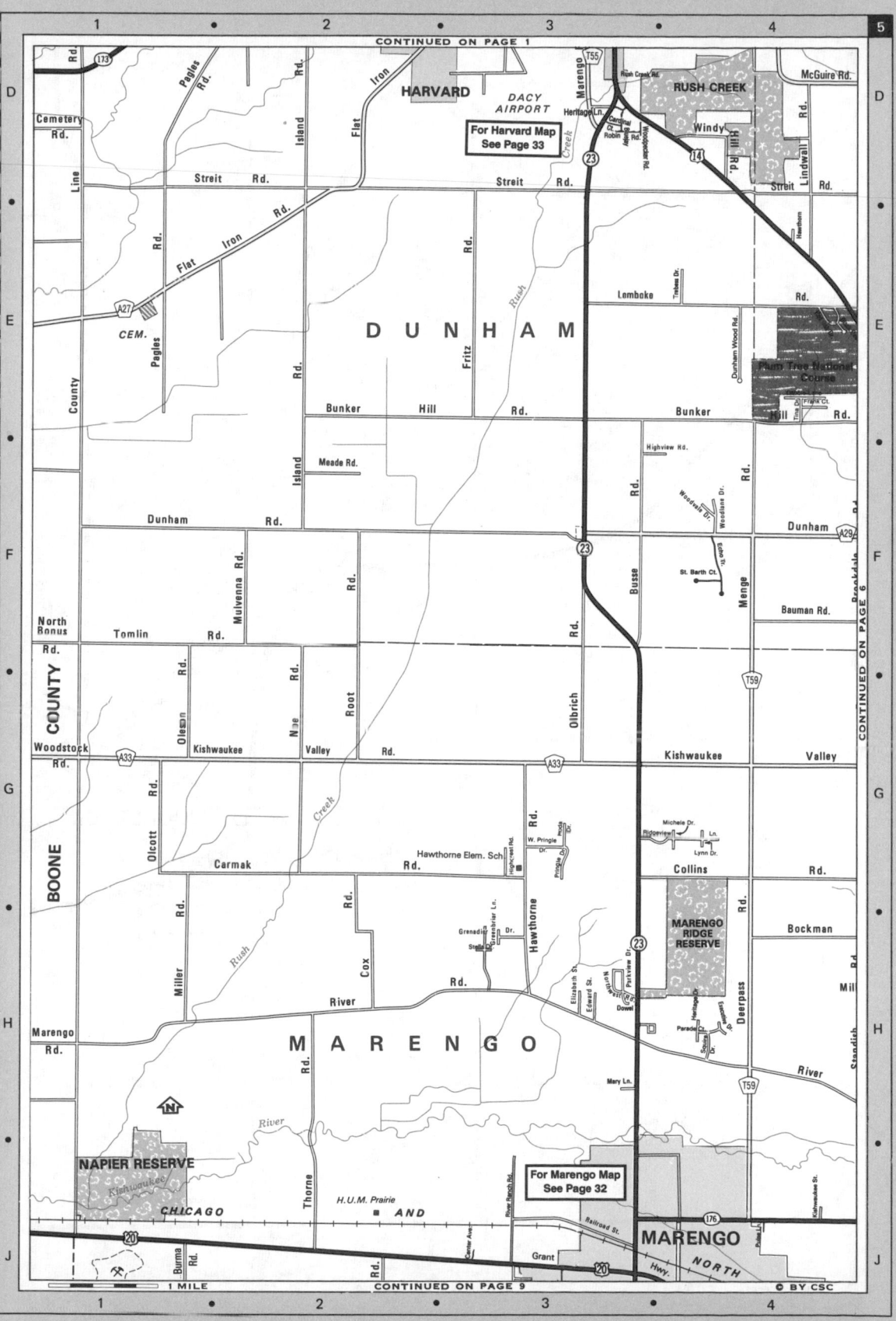

CONTINUED ON PAGE 1

HARVARD

DACY
AIRPORT

For Harvard Map
See Page 33

RUSH CREEK

McGuire Rd.

Cemetery
Rd.

Streit    Rd.

Streit    Rd.

Windy

Streit    Rd.

Lindwall    Rd.

CEM.

Pagles
Rd.

Island    Rd.

Flat    Iron

Flat    Iron    Rd.

Line

County

Pagles

Rd.

D U N H A M

Lembcke

Rush    Creek

Bunker    Hill    Rd.

Fritz    Rd.

Island    Rd.

Meade Rd.

Dunham    Rd.

Bunker    Hill    Rd.

Plum Tree National
Course

Frank Ct.

Highview Rd.

Woodfall Dr.

Woodland Dr.

Dunham    Rd.

St. Barth Ct.

Menge    Rd.

Bauman    Rd.

North
Bonus
Rd.

Tomlin    Rd.

Mulvenna    Rd.

Rd.

Rd.

Busse    Rd.

C O U N T Y

Woodstock

Oleson    Rd.

Nae    Rd.

Root    Rd.

Kishwaukee    Valley    Rd.

Olbrich    Rd.

Kishwaukee

Valley

Olcott    Rd.

Carmak    Rd.

Hawthorne Elem. Sch.

W. Pringle

Highcrest Rd.

Pringle Dr.

Ridgeview

Michele Dr.

Lynn Dr.

Collins    Rd.

Bockman

B O O N E

Rush    Creek

Miller    Rd.

Cox    Rd.

Hawthorne    Rd.

Grenadier
Dr.

Stella

Elizabeth St.

Edward St.

Parkview Dr.

MARENGO
RIDGE
RESERVE

Rd.

Deerpass

Mil

River    Rd.

River    Rd.

Dowel

Parade

Stella

Heritage Rd.

River

Standish Rd.

Marengo
Rd.

M A R E N G O

Mary Ln.

NAPIER RESERVE

Kishwaukee

River

Thorne    Rd.

H.U.M. Prairie

C H I C A G O        A N D

River Ranch Rd.

For Marengo Map
See Page 32

Kishwaukee St.

Burma    Rd.

Rd.

Center Ave.

Grant

Railroad St.

Hwy.

M A R E N G O

N O R T H

CONTINUED ON PAGE 9

1 MILE

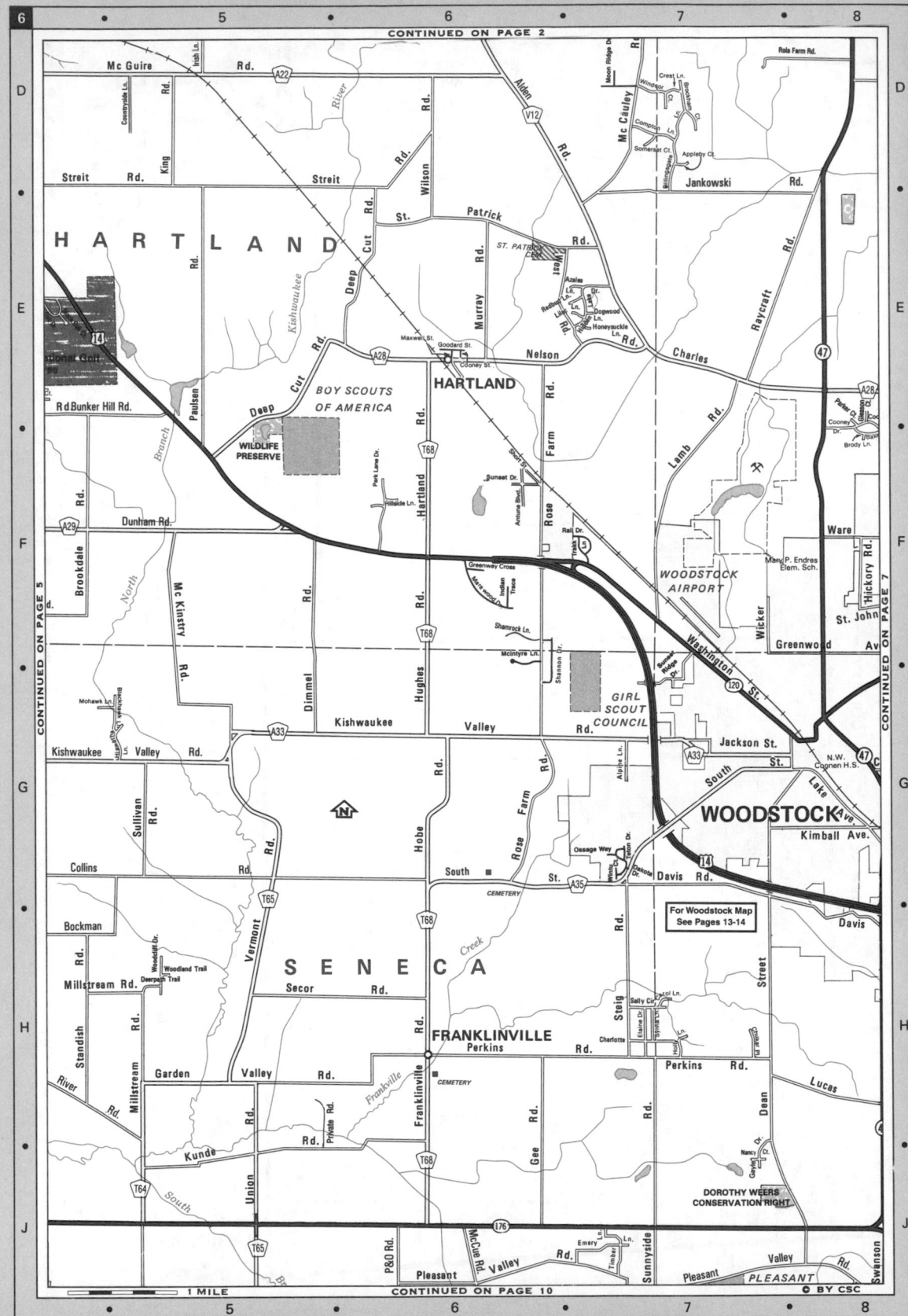

CONTINUED ON PAGE 2

McGuire Rd.

Irish Ln.

A22

River

V12

Countryside Ln.

King Rd.

Streit Rd.

Streit

Wilson Rd.

Streit

Cut Rd.

Deep Cut Rd.

St. Patrick

Patrick

Murray Rd.

ST. PATRICK CEM.

West

St. PATRICK Rd.

Azalea Dr.

Redbud Ln.

Birch Ct.

Dogwood Dr.

Honeysuckle Ln.

Rd.

Charles Rd.

Moon Ridge Dr.

Crest Ln.

Rola Farm Rd.

McCauley

Windsor

Compton Ln.

Somerset Ct.

Appleby Ct.

Billingsgate Ln.

Jankowski Rd.

Raycraft Rd.

47

A28

# H A R T L A N D

Rd.

Paulsen

Bunker Hill Rd.

Rd.

A29

Maxwell St.

A28

Goddard St.

Cooney St.

**HARTLAND**

Nelson Rd.

Rose Farm Rd.

BOY SCOUTS
OF AMERICA
WILDLIFE
PRESERVE

Park Lane Dr.

Hartland Rd.

Hillside Ln.

Sunset Dr.

Antuna Blvd.

Short St.

Lamb Rd.

Mary P. Endres
Elem. Sch.

A28

Parker Ct.

Cooney Dr.

Brody Ln.

Ware

Hickory Rd.

North Branch

Brookdale

Dunham Rd.

Rd.

McKinstry Rd.

Rd.

Rd.

T68

Greenway Cross

Mars Indian Trace

Indian Trace

Rall Dr.

Tracks

14

WOODSTOCK
AIRPORT

St. John

Greenwood Av.

CONTINUED ON PAGE 5

CONTINUED ON PAGE 7

Mohawk Ln.

Blackhawk Ln.

Dimmel Rd.

Hughes Rd.

Shamrock Ln.

McIntyre Ln.

Shannon Dr.

T68

Washington St.

120

Bonnie
Ridge Dr.

Kishwaukee

Valley

Rd.

Sullivan Rd.

Rd.

A33

Kishwaukee

Valley

Rd.

Hobe Rd.

Rose Farm Rd.

GIRL
SCOUT
COUNCIL

Rd.

Alpine Ln.

Jackson St.

A33

St.

N.W.
Coonen H.S.

47

C

Lake Ave.

**WOODSTOCK**

Kimball Ave.

Collins

Rd.

Rd.

South

St.

A35

Ossage Way

Dakota Dr.

Winterberry Ln.

Davis Rd.

14

Davis

Bockman Rd.

Woodcliff Dr.

Woodland Trail

Deerpath Trail

Millstream Rd.

Vermont Rd.

T65

# S E N E C A

Secor Rd.

T68

CEMETERY

Creek

Steig Rd.

Sally Cir.

Carol Ln.

Charlotte Rd.

Elaine Ct.

For Woodstock Map
See Pages 13-14

Street

Lucas

Standish Rd.

Milstream Rd.

River Rd.

Garden Valley Rd.

Secor Rd.

Rd.

**FRANKLINVILLE**
Perkins

Franklinville Rd.

CEMETERY

Perkins Rd.

Dean Rd.

Kunde Rd.

Rd.

Private Rd.

Rd.

Gee Rd.

Rd.

Nancy Dr.

Garden Ct.

DOROTHY WEERS
CONSERVATION RIGHT

T64

South

Br.

T65

176

P&O Rd.

McCue Rd.

Valley Rd.

Emery

Timber Ln.

Sunnyside

Pleasant

Valley Rd.

Swanson

Pleasant

**PLEASANT**

© BY CSC

1 MILE

CONTINUED ON PAGE 10

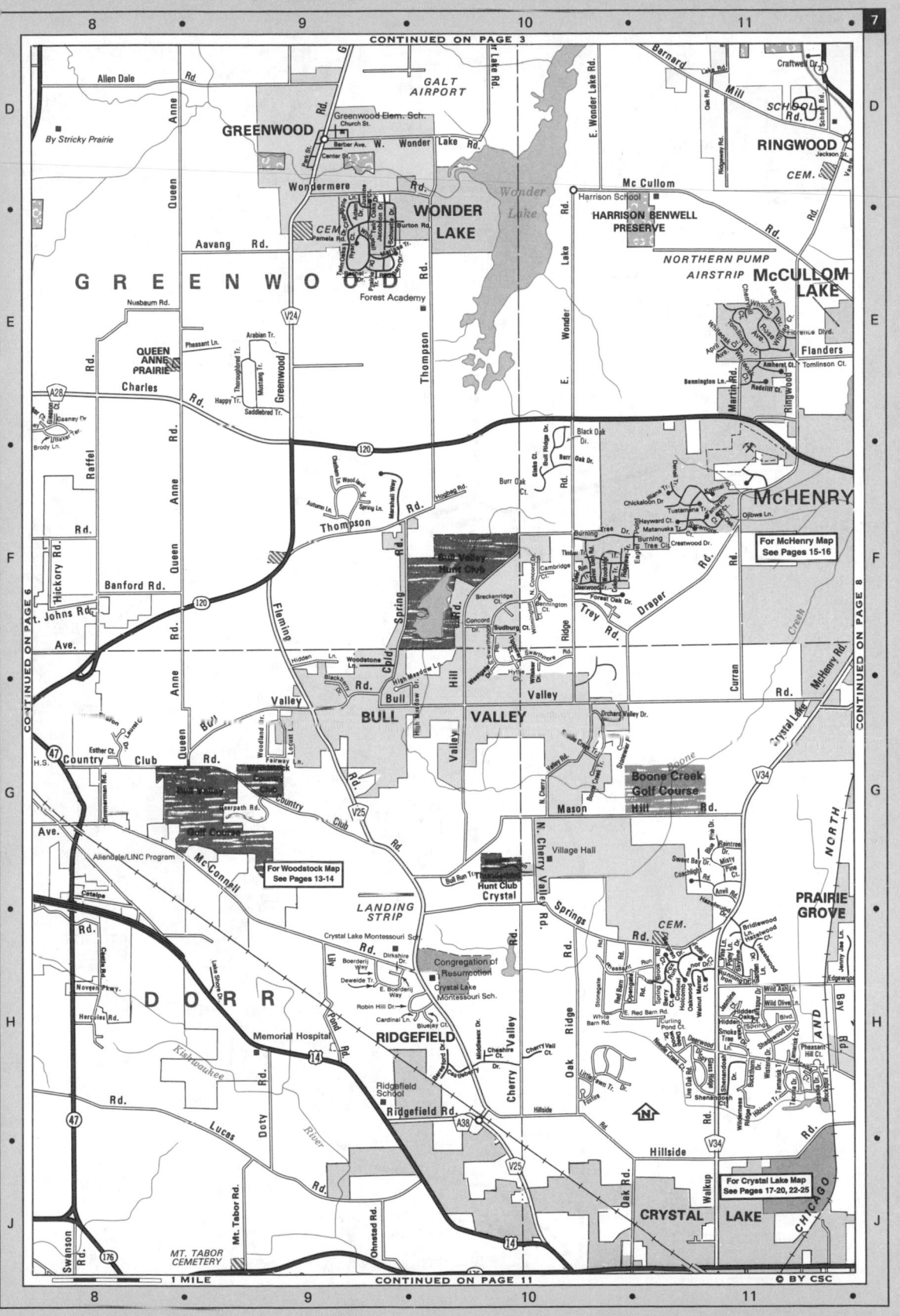

CONTINUED ON PAGE 3

8  9  10  11

D

By Stricky Prairie

Allen Dale Rd.

GREENWOOD

Greenwood Elem. Sch.
Church St.
Barber Ave.  W. Wonder Lake Rd.
Center St.
Wondermere  Rd.

GALT
AIRPORT

GREENWOOD

Queen Anne Rd.

Aavang Rd.

CEM.
Pamela Ct.
Jacobs Dr.
Burton Rd.

WONDER
LAKE

Wonder
Lake

Forest Academy

E. Wonder Lake Rd.

Barnard Rd.
Mill

Craftwell Rd.
SCHOOL Rd.

RINGWOOD
Jackson St.
CEM.

McCullom

Harrison School

HARRISON BENWELL
PRESERVE

NORTHERN PUMP
AIRSTRIP

McCULLOM
LAKE

Whiting Dr.
Florence Blvd.
Flanders

April Ave.
Amherst Ct.  Tomlinson Ct.
Radcliff Ct.
Ringwood Rd.

E

GREENWOOD

Nusbaum Rd.

QUEEN
ANNE
PRAIRIE

Arabian Tr.
Pheasant Ln.
Thoroughbred Tr.
Mustang Tr.
Happy Tr.
Saddlebred Tr.

V24

Charles Rd.

Kearney Dr.
Brody Ln.

A28

Thompson Rd.
Greenwood Rd.

120

Bennington Ln.

Martin Rd.

E

Raffel Rd.

Hickory Rd.

Banford Rd.

Queen Anne Rd.

120

Thompson Rd.

Chelsea Ln.
Wood Ave.
Autumn Ln.
Spring Ln.
Marshall Way

Thompson

Hogback Rd.

Black Oak
Dr.
Gloria Ct.
Bull Ridge Dr.
Burr Oak Dr.

Burr Oak
Ct.

Chickaloon Dr.
Tustamena Ct.
Hayward Ct.
Matanuska Ct.
Forest Oak Dr.
Crestwood Dr.
Ojibwa Ln.

McHENRY

Cambridge
Ct.
N. Concord Dr.

Draper Rd.

Creek

For McHenry Map
See Pages 15-16

F

F

St. Johns Rd.
Ave.

Fleming Rd.

Child Hill Rd.

Spring Hill Rd.

Bull Valley
Hunt Club

Hidden Ln.
Woodstone Dr.
Black

High Meadow Ln.

Breckenridge Dr.
Concord
Sudburg Dr.
Hytfie
Swarthmore

Burning Tree

Burning
Tree

Bennington
N. Concord Dr.
Ridge Rd.
Trey Rd.
Curran Rd.

McHenry Rd.

CONTINUED ON PAGE 8

Bull
Valley

Valley

Valley

Valley

BULL

VALLEY

Orchard Valley Dr.

Boone

Boone Creek
Golf Course
Hill Rd.

V34

NORTH

G

47

Country Club

Esther Ct.

Queen Bull Rd.

Deerpath Rd.

Woodland Dr.
Fairway
Locust Ln.

Country Club Rd.

V25

Mason

Village Hall

Coachlight Dr.
Sweet Bay Dr.
Brie Dr.
Raintree
Mistly Pine Ct.
Anvil Rd.

PRAIRIE
GROVE

G

Allendale/LINC Program

Catalpa

Noveen Pkwy.

McConnell Rd.

For Woodstock Map
See Pages 13-14

LANDING
STRIP

Crystal Lake Montessori Sch.

Bull Run Trl.

Hunt Club
Crystal

Hazelwood Ct.
Bridlewood
Hazelwood

Stonegate
Red Barn
White Barn Rd.
E. Red Barn Rd.

CEM.

Springs Rd.

N. Cherry Valley Rd.

Wild Ash Ln.
Wild Olive Ln.
Hidden Oaks
Smoke Tree
Deerwood
Edgewood

H

DORR

Rd.

Hercules Rd.

Memorial Hospital

Boerderij
Way
Deweide Tr.
E. Boerderij
Way
Robin Hill Dr.
Cardinal Ln.
Bluejay Ct.

Lily Rd.
Dirkshire
Dr.

Congregation of
Resurrection
Crystal Lake
Montessori Sch.

Middlesex Dr.
Cheshire
Ct.
Cherry Vail
Ct.

Oak
Ridge Rd.

Shenandoah

Pheasant
Hill Ct.

H

14

Kishwaukee

River

RIDGEFIELD

Ridgefield
School

Ridgefield Rd.

A38

Hillside

Cherry Valley Rd.

Hillside

V25

V34

J

47

176

Swanson Rd.

Mt. Tabor Rd.

MT. TABOR
CEMETERY

Olmstead Rd.

Doty Rd.

Pond Rd.

1 MILE

14

Oak Rd.

Oak Ridge Rd.

CRYSTAL LAKE

Walkup

For Crystal Lake Map
See Pages 17-20, 22-25

© BY CSC

J

CONTINUED ON PAGE 11

8  9  10  11

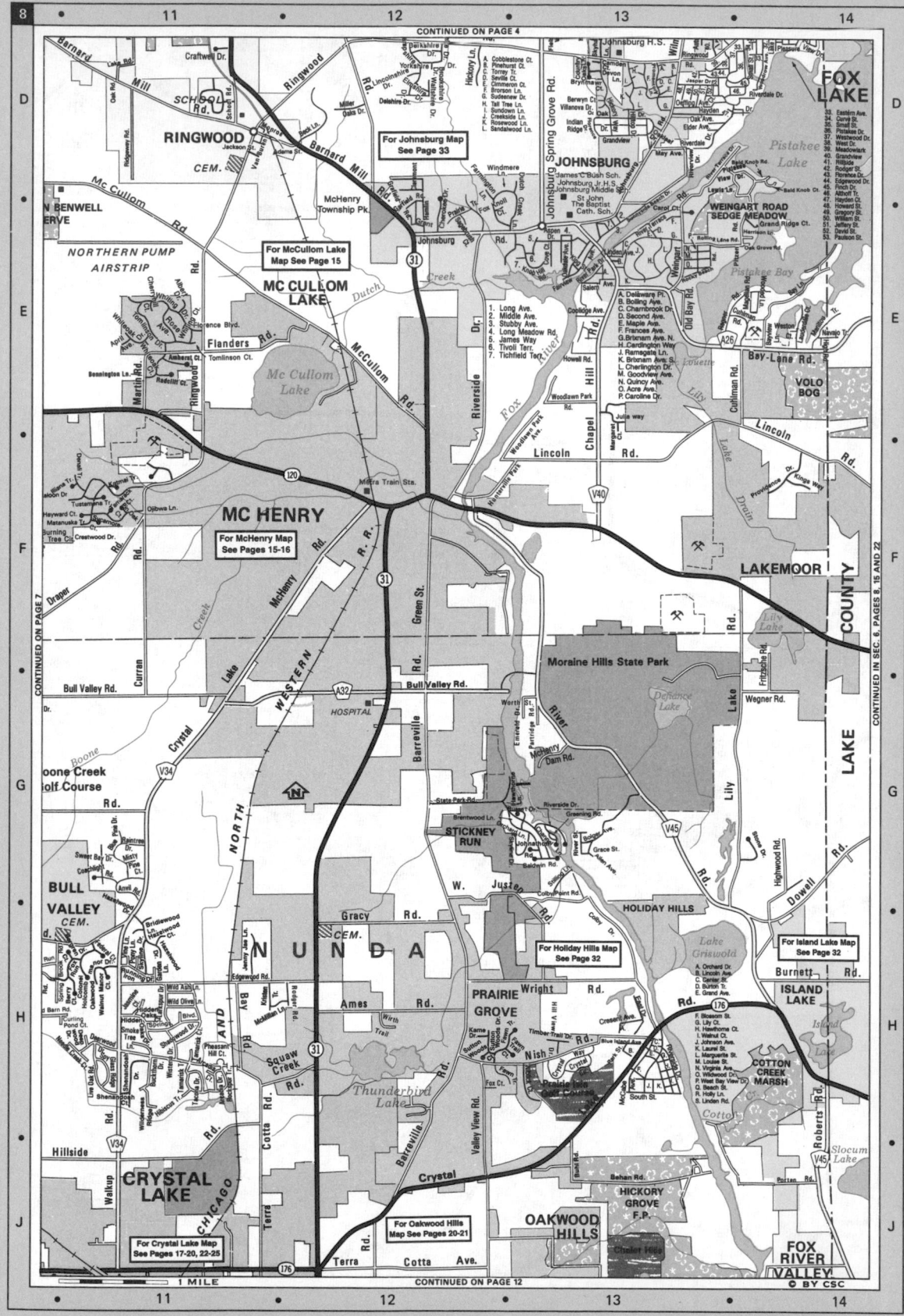

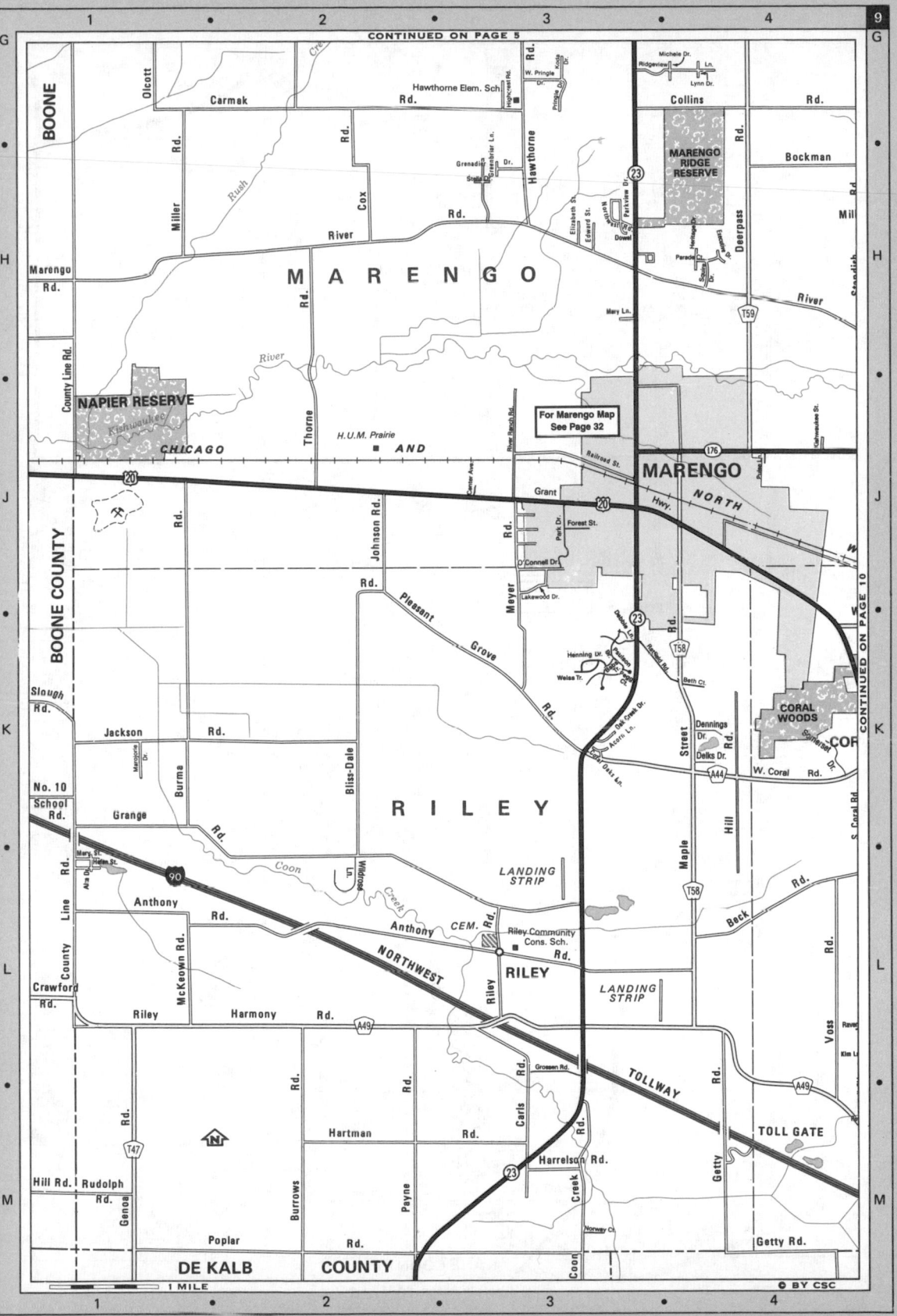

9

CONTINUED ON PAGE 10

BOONE

MARENGO

Olcott

Carmak
Rd.

Miller
Rd.

Cox
Rd.

River
Rd.

Hawthorne Elem. Sch.

Highpoint Rd.

W. Pringle
Dr.

Pringle
Dr.

Koda
Rd.

Michele Dr.

Ridgeview
Ln.

Lynn Dr.

Collins
Rd.

Rd.

Bockman
Rd.

MARENGO
RIDGE
RESERVE

Grenadier
Dr.

Greenbriar Ln.

Stella Rd.

Hawthorne

Elizabeth St.

Edward St.

Parkview St.

Dowel

Heritage Dr.

Parade
Dr.

Deerpass
Rd.

Mill

Marengo
Rd.

River
Rd.

Thorne
Rd.

Rush

River

H.U.M. Prairie

Mary Ln.

T59

River

Standish

County Line Rd.

NAPIER RESERVE

Kishwaukee

CHICAGO

AND

For Marengo Map
See Page 32

River Ranch Rd.

Railroad St.

MARENGO

NORTH

176

Calwaukee St.

20

Center Ave.

Grant

20

Hwy.

Johnson Rd.

Rd.

Meyer

Park Dr.

Forest St.

O'Connell Dr.

Lakewood Dr.

Pleasant

Grove

Rd.

Henning Dr.

Weiss Tr.

Debbie St.

23

T58

Rittbera Rd.

Beth Ct.

Oak Creek Dr.

Acorn Ln.

Oaks Ln.

Dennings
Dr.

Delks Dr.

Rd.

A44

W. Coral

CORAL
WOODS

Somerset

COR

Rd.

BOONE COUNTY

Slough
Rd.

Jackson
Rd.

Burma
Rd.

Rd.

Bliss-Dale
Rd.

RILEY

Street

Maple

Hill

Rd.

No. 10
School
Rd.

Grange

Rd.

Marjorie
Dr.

Coon

Wildrose
Ln.

Creek

LANDING
STRIP

T58

Beck
Rd.

90

Mary St.
Helm St.

Ara Dr.

Anthony

Rd.

Anthony

CEM.
Rd.

Riley Community
Cons. Sch.
Rd.

LANDING
STRIP

Voss
Rd.

Kim Ln.

County
Line
Rd.

Crawford
Rd.

Riley

McKeown Rd.

Harmony

Rd.

A49

NORTHWEST

Riley

RILEY

TOLLWAY

Rd.

A49

TOLL GATE

T47

Genoa

Rudolph
Rd.

Hill Rd.

Burrows

Rd.

Hartman

Payne

Rd.

Carls
Rd.

Rd.

Grossen Rd.

Rd.

Harrelson Rd.

23

Getty
Rd.

River

Poplar

Rd.

DE KALB

COUNTY

Norway Ct.

Coon

Creek

Getty Rd.

1 MILE

© BY CSC

G
H
J
K
L
M

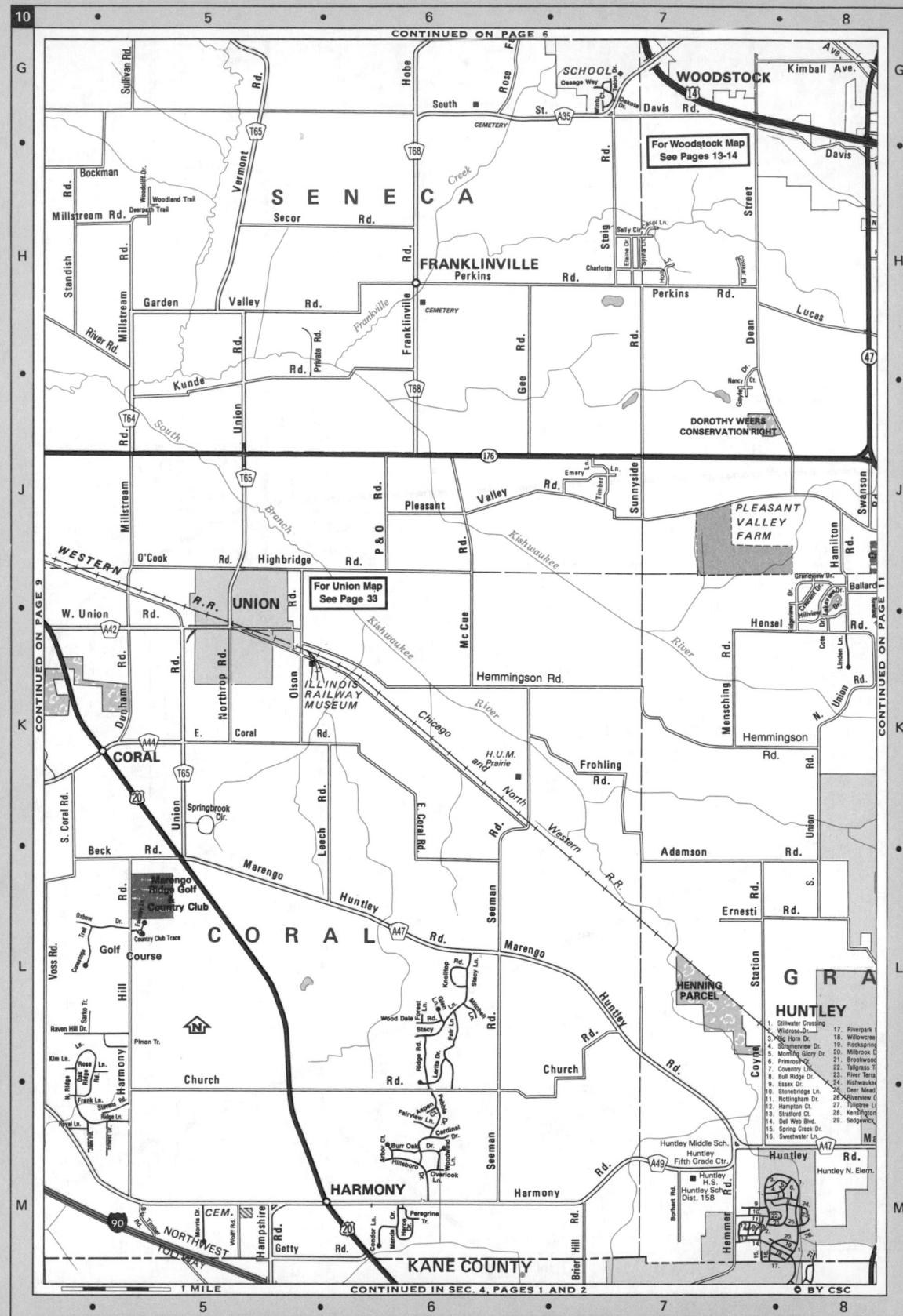

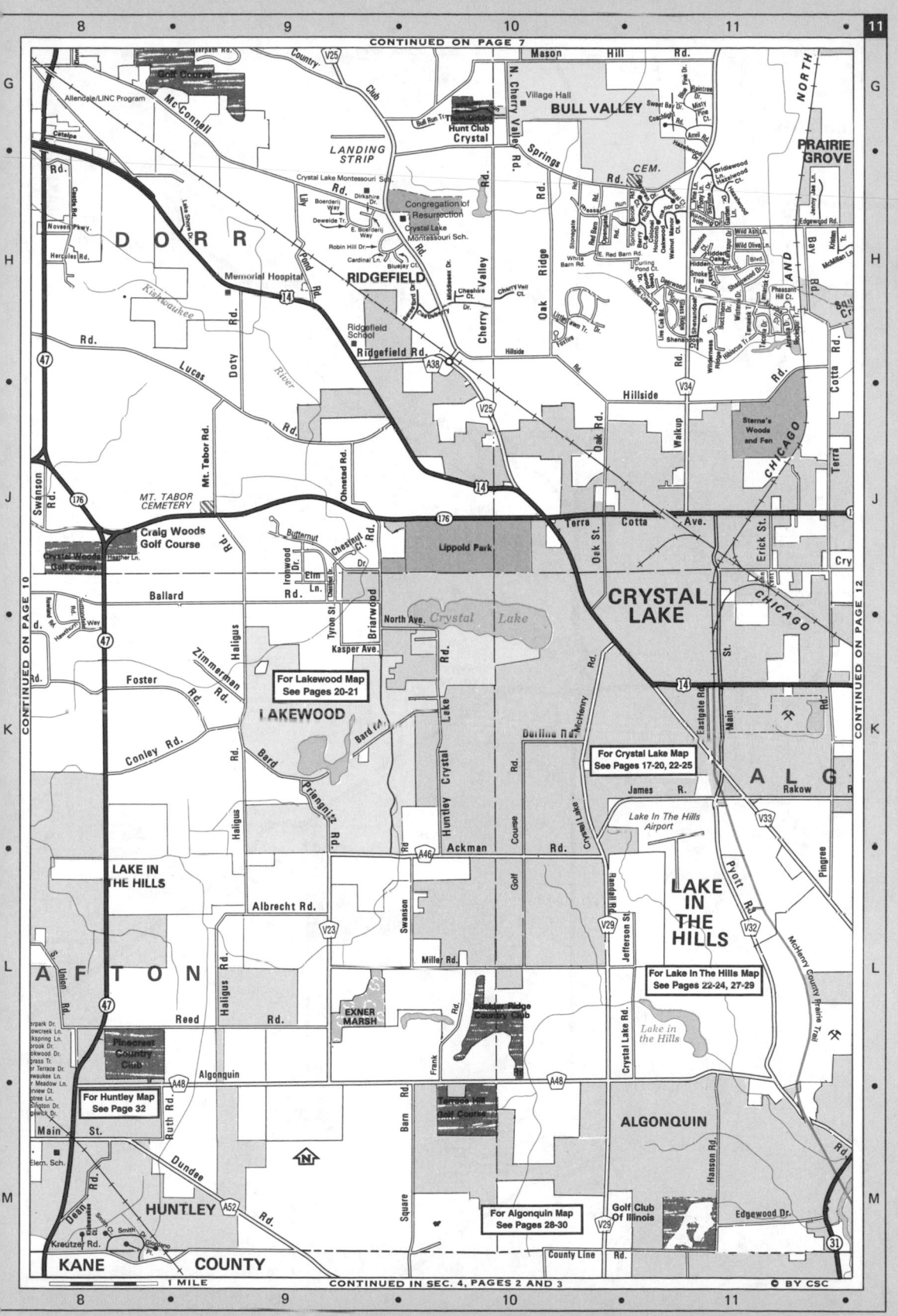

CONTINUED ON PAGE 7

G

**BULL VALLEY**

*LANDING STRIP*

Hunt Club
Crystal

CEM.

**PRAIRIE GROVE**

NORTH

Allendale/LINC Program

McConnell

Golf Course

Mason Hill Rd.

N. Cherry Valley Rd.

Village Hall

Bull Run Tr.

Springs

Rd.

Sweet Bay Ln.

Coachlight Rd.

Misty Pine Ct.

Anvil Rd.

Bridlewood
Lakelewood
Ct.

Catalpa

Novean Pkwy.

Hercules Rd.

DORR

Rd.

Castle Rd.

Laas Shore Dr.

Crystal Lake Montessori Sch.

Dirkshire Dr.

E. Boerderij Way

Deweide Tr.

Robin Hill Dr.

Cardinal Ln.

Bluejay Ct.

Congregation of
Resurrection
Crystal Lake
Montessori Sch.

Cheshire Ct.

Boerderij Rd.

Middlesex Dr.

Cherry Veil Dr.

Cherry Valley Rd.

Pheasant Rd.

Ruth Rd.

Red Barn Rd.

White Barn Rd.

Little Fawn Tr.

Oak Ridge Rd.

Stonegate

Red Barn Ct.

Spring Berry

Oakwood Rd.

Darwood Tr.

Hidden Oaks

Shenandoah Rd.

Wild Ash Ln.

Wild Olive Ln.

Hidden Oaks Blvd.

Smoke Tree Ln.

Sherwood Dr.

Pheasant Hill Ct.

Wilderness Ridge

Rebecca Tr.

Memorial Hospital

Kishwaukee

Rd.

14

Pond Rd.

Doty Rd.

Lucas Rd.

River

RIDGEFIELD

Ridgefield School

Ridgefield Rd.

A38

Ohnstad Rd.

Hillside

Oak Ridge Rd.

Hillside

Walkup

V34

V25

14

Sterne's
Woods
and Fen

CHICAGO

Cotta Rd.

Terra

47

176

Swanson Rd.

MT. TABOR
CEMETERY

Mt. Tabor Rd.

Craig Woods
Golf Course

Crystal Woods
Golf Course

Heather Ln.

Hawthorne Trail

Way

47

Ballard

Foster

Butternut

Chestnut Ct. Rd.

Ironwood Dr.

Elm Ln.

Daisler St.

Briarwood

Tyron St.

Lippold Park

North Ave.

Kasper Ave.

*Crystal Lake*

Terra Cotta Ave.

Oak St.

CHICAGO

Erick St.

Cry

**CRYSTAL
LAKE**

14

Main St.

Eastgate Rd.

**For Lakewood Map
See Pages 20-21**

**LAKEWOOD**

Zimmerman Rd.

Haligus Rd.

Rd.

Conley Rd.

Bard

Bard Ct.

Preiengnitz Rd.

Haligus Rd.

Crystal Lake Rd.

Huntley Rd.

North Ave.

Darline Rd.

McHenry Rd.

Golf Course Rd.

Ackman

A46

James R.

Lake In The Hills
Airport

Rakow

V33

**For Crystal Lake Map
See Pages 17-20, 22-25**

**ALG**

**LAKE
IN
THE
HILLS**

Albrecht Rd.

V23

Swanson Rd.

Miller Rd.

A52

Randall Rd.

V29

Jefferson St.

Main St.

Pyott Rd.

V32

Pingree

McHenry County Prairie Trail

Lake in
the Hills

**For Lake In The Hills Map
See Pages 22-24, 27-29**

**LAKE
IN
THE HILLS**

Union Rd.

47

Reed

Haligus Rd.

EXNER
MARSH

Boulder Ridge
Country Club

Crystal Lake Rd.

Frank

Barn Rd.

Square Rd.

Pinecrest
Country
Club

A48

Algonquin

**For Huntley Map
See Page 32**

Main St.

Elem. Sch.

**AFTON**

Ruth Rd.

Dundee Rd.

Terrace Hill
Golf Course

A48

**ALGONQUIN**

Hanson Rd.

Golf Club
Of Illinois

31

Edgewood Dr.

**HUNTLEY**

A52

Rd.

Dean Rd.

Kreutzer Rd.

Smith Rd.

Elmwood Pl.

**For Algonquin Map
See Pages 28-30**

V29

County Line Rd.

**KANE          COUNTY**

CONTINUED ON PAGE 10

CONTINUED ON PAGE 12

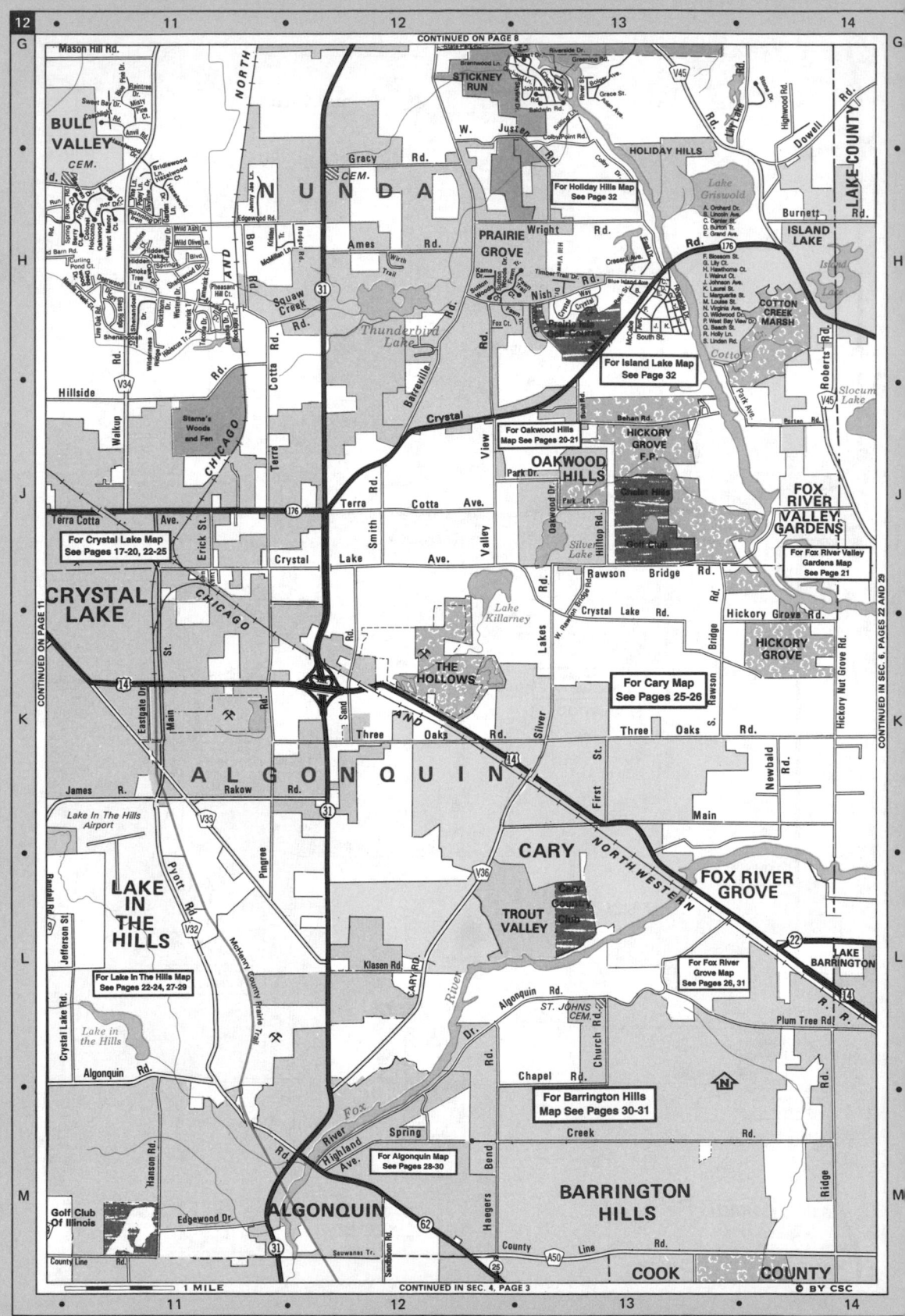

CONTINUED ON PAGE 8
CONTINUED ON PAGE 11
CONTINUED IN SEC. 6, PAGES 22 AND 29
CONTINUED IN SEC. 4, PAGE 3

BULL VALLEY

NUNDA

STICKNEY RUN

PRAIRIE GROVE

HOLIDAY HILLS

ISLAND LAKE

COTTON CREEK MARSH

OAKWOOD HILLS

HICKORY GROVE F.P.

FOX RIVER VALLEY GARDENS

CRYSTAL LAKE

THE HOLLOWS

HICKORY GROVE

ALGONQUIN

CARY

FOX RIVER GROVE

LAKE IN THE HILLS

TROUT VALLEY

LAKE BARRINGTON

BARRINGTON HILLS

ALGONQUIN

COOK COUNTY

For Holiday Hills Map See Page 32

For Island Lake Map See Page 32

For Oakwood Hills Map See Pages 20-21

For Fox River Valley Gardens Map See Page 21

For Crystal Lake Map See Pages 17-20, 22-25

For Cary Map See Pages 25-26

For Lake In The Hills Map See Pages 22-24, 27-29

For Fox River Grove Map See Pages 26, 31

For Barrington Hills Map See Pages 30-31

For Algonquin Map See Pages 28-30

LAKE COUNTY

1 MILE

© BY CSC

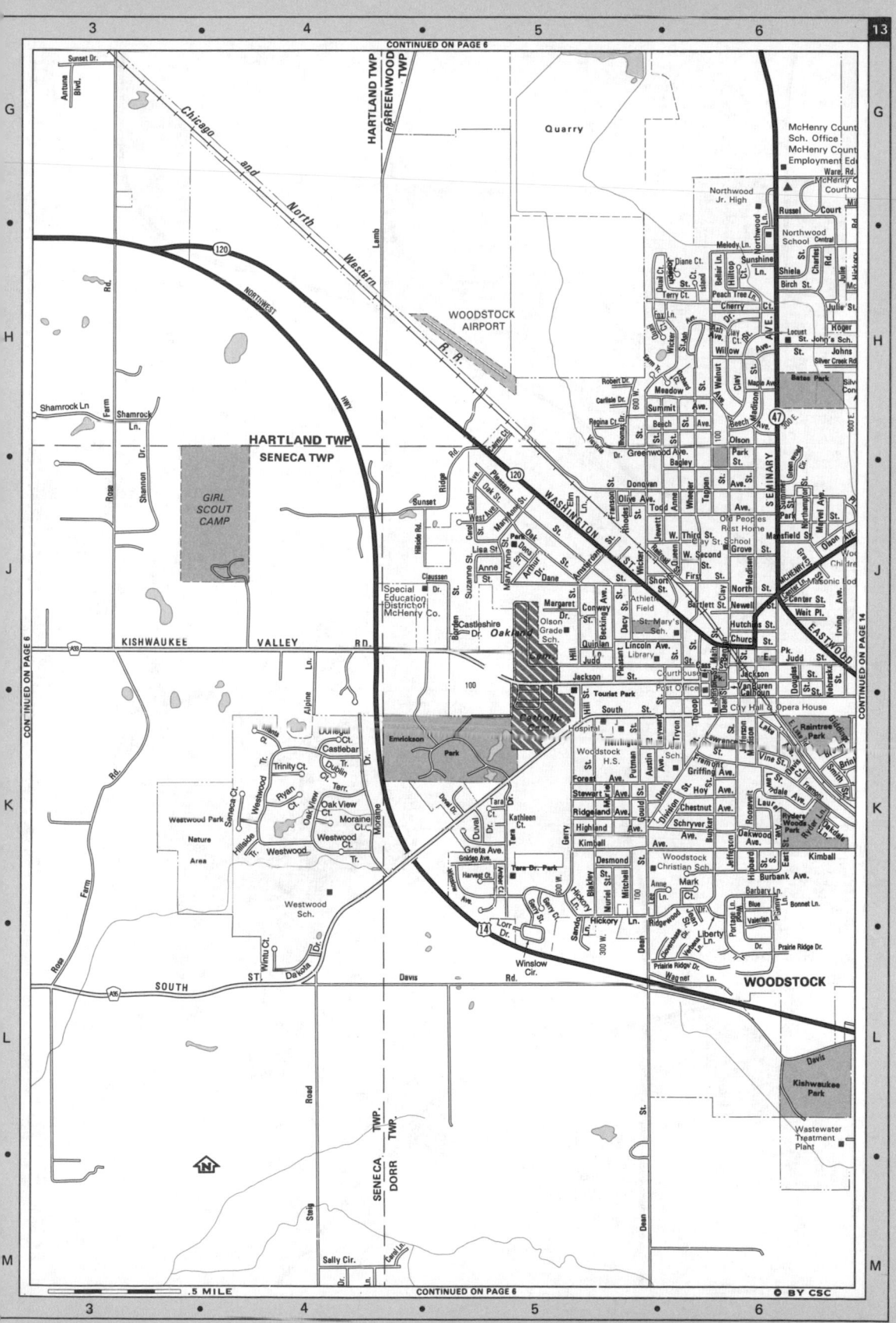

CONTINUED ON PAGE 6

G

HARTLAND TWP

GREENWOOD TWP

Quarry

McHenry County
Sch. Office
McHenry County
Employment Ed.
Ware Rd.
McHenry C.
Courthou

Northwood
Jr. High

Northwood
School   Central

120

Chicago   and   North   Western

NORTHWEST   HWY

WOODSTOCK
AIRPORT

R.   R.

Russel   Court

Sunset Dr.
Antuna Blvd.

Melody Ln.
Sunshine
Ln.

Diane Ct.
Quail Ct.

Shiela
St.
Birch St.
Julie St.
Charles Rd.
Bellair St.
Hilltop
St.

Terry Ct.
Peach Tree Ln.
Cherry
Ct.
Roger

Locust

St. John's Sch.
St.
Johns
Silver Creek Rd.

Bates Park

47

H

Shamrock Ln.

Shamrock
Ln.

Rose Farm Rd.

Shannon Dr.

Robert Dr.
Meadow
St.
Carlisle Dr.
Summit
St.
600 E.

Walnut
St.
Clay St.
Maple Ave.

Regina Ct.
Beach
Ave.
Beech St.
100
Olson
Dr.
300 E.

HARTLAND TWP

SENECA TWP

Sunset

Ridge Rd.

Carol St.

West St.

Maryland St.

120

WASHINGTON  ST.

Greenwood Ave.
Bagley
St.
Park
St.

SEMINARY

Green Ln.

GIRL
SCOUT
CAMP

Hillside Rd.

Lisa St.

Suzanne St.

Mary Ann St.

Oak St.

Donovan
St.
Fremont St.
Todd St.
Wheeler St.
Tappan St.
Ave.

Olive Ave.
Pleasant St.

Mansfield St.

Marvel Ave.
Northington St.

Claussen
Dr.

Anne
St.

Arthur St.

Dane St.
W. Third St.
W. Second St.
First St.
North St.
Grove St.

Old Peoples
Rest Home

Lily St.
School
Queen St.

Madison St.

Center Dr.

KISHWAUKEE  VALLEY  RD.

Special
Education
District of
McHenry Co.

Castleshire
Dr.

Oakland

Biden St.

Margaret
Dr.
Olson
Grade Sch.
Quintlan
Hill
St.
Judd St.

Conway
St.
Becking St.
Dacy St.

Short
Bartlett St.

Newell St.
Hutchins
St.
Masonic Lod

Weit Pl.

EASTWOOD

J

100

Alpine

Donegal
Ct.
Castlebar
Tr.

Trinity Ct.

Ryan
Ct.

Oak View
Ct.

Dublin
Terr.

Moraine
Ct.

Jackson
St.

Catholic
Cemetery

Lincoln Ave.
Library

Courthouse

Jackson
St.

Douglas
St.
Nebraska
St.
Pk. Judd
St.

Church St.

E.

K

CONTINUED ON PAGE 6

Seneca Ct.

Westwood Park
Nature
Area

Hillside

Westwood
Ct.

Westwood
Tr.

Oak View
Ct.

Montana

Oval Ct.

Enrickson
Park

Tara
Ct.

Doveal
Dr.

Kathleen
Ct.

Tara St.

Tourist Park
South

Woodstock
H.S.

Hospital

Harrington
St.
Putnam St.

Fremont Ave.
Griffing Ave.
Stewart St.
Ridgeland Ave.

Hoy Ave.

Chestnut St.

Schryver
Ave.

Austin
St.
Sch.

Tryon St.

Lawrence
Ave.

Vine St.

Raintree
Park

CONTINUED ON PAGE 14

Westwood
Sch.

Greta Ave.

Harvest Ct.
Gnideo Ave.

Tara Dr. Park

Barry St.

Sandy St.

Hickory
Ct.

Highland Ave.
Kimball
St.

Desmond
St.

Muriel St.
Mitchell St.

Baxley St.

100

Woodstock
Christian Sch.

Anne
Ln.
Mark
Ct.

Hubbard St.
Burbank Ave.

Jefferson St.

Oakwood
Ave.

Kimball

Laurel Ave.

Ryders
Woods
Park

L

14

Lorr
Dr.

Winslow
Cir.

Hickory
Ln.
Ridgewood

Prairie Ridge Dr.
Wagner Ln.

Liberty
Dr.
Prairie Ridge Dr.

Barbary Ln.
Blue
St.
Valerian
Ln.
Bonnet Ln.

Portage Ln.
Dean
St.

WOODSTOCK

SOUTH

Wintu Ct.

Devola
Dr.

Davis

Rd.

Davis

Kishwaukee
Park

Wastewater
Treatment
Plant

Rose Farm Rd.

Road

SENECA TWP.

DORR TWP.

Steig Rd.

Sally Cir.

Carol Ln.

Dean St.

M

N

CONTINUED ON PAGE 6

© BY CSC

3   4   5   6

CONTINUED ON PAGE 7

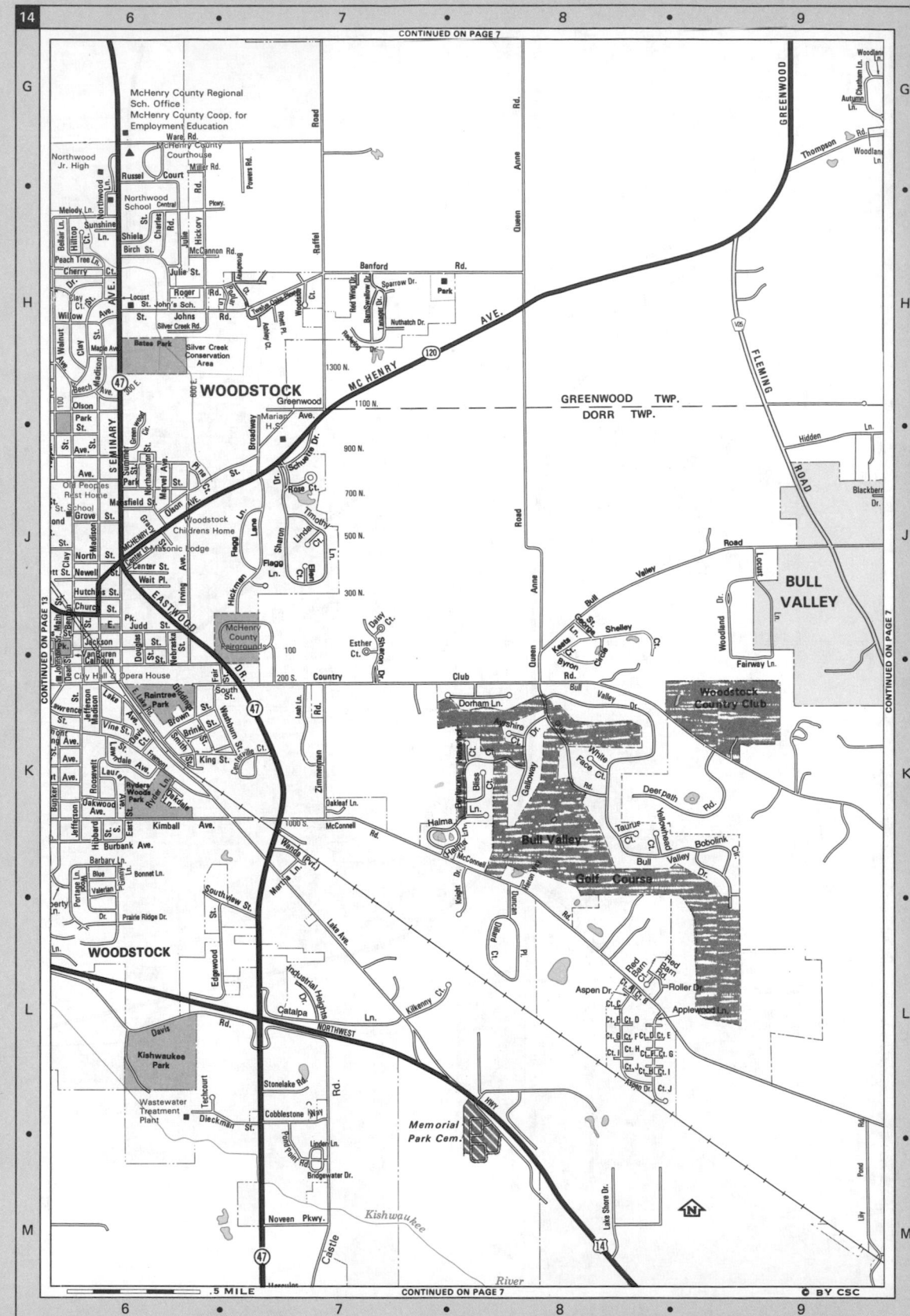

McHenry County Regional
Sch. Office
McHenry County Coop. for
Employment Education

Northwood
Jr. High

Northwood
School

McHenry County
Courthouse

**WOODSTOCK**

Silver Creek
Conservation
Area

Bates Park

**GREENWOOD TWP.**
**DORR TWP.**

Woodstock
Childrens Home

McHenry County
Fairgrounds

City Hall & Opera House

Raintree Park

**WOODSTOCK**

Ryders Woods
Park

Kishwaukee
Park

Wastewater
Treatment
Plant

**BULL VALLEY**

Woodstock
Country Club

Bull Valley
Golf Course

Memorial
Park Cem.

Kishwaukee

River

.5 MILE

© BY CSC

CONTINUED ON PAGE 13

CONTINUED ON PAGE 7

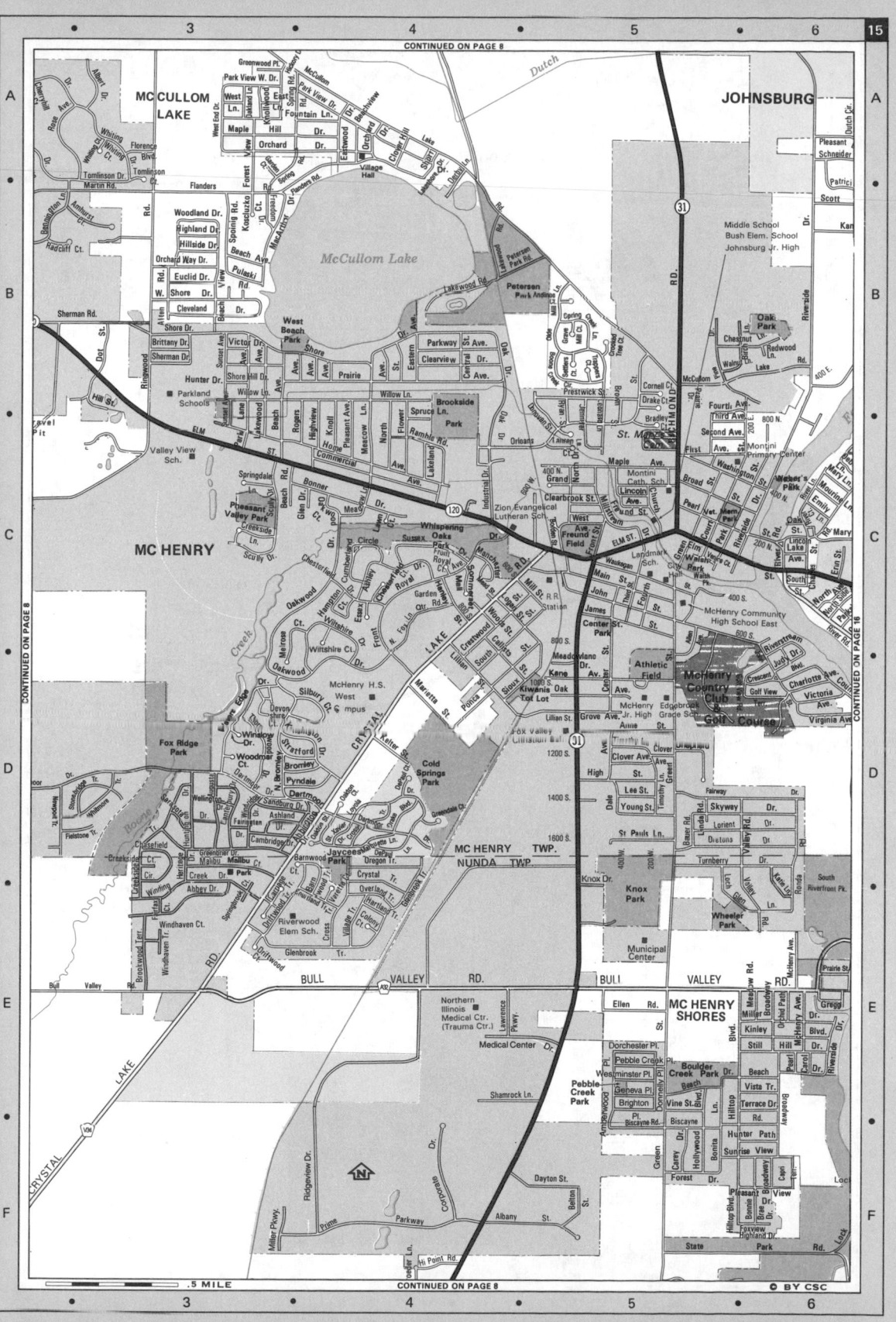

CONTINUED ON PAGE 8

CONTINUED ON PAGE 8

CONTINUED ON PAGE 16

CONTINUED ON PAGE 8

© BY CSC

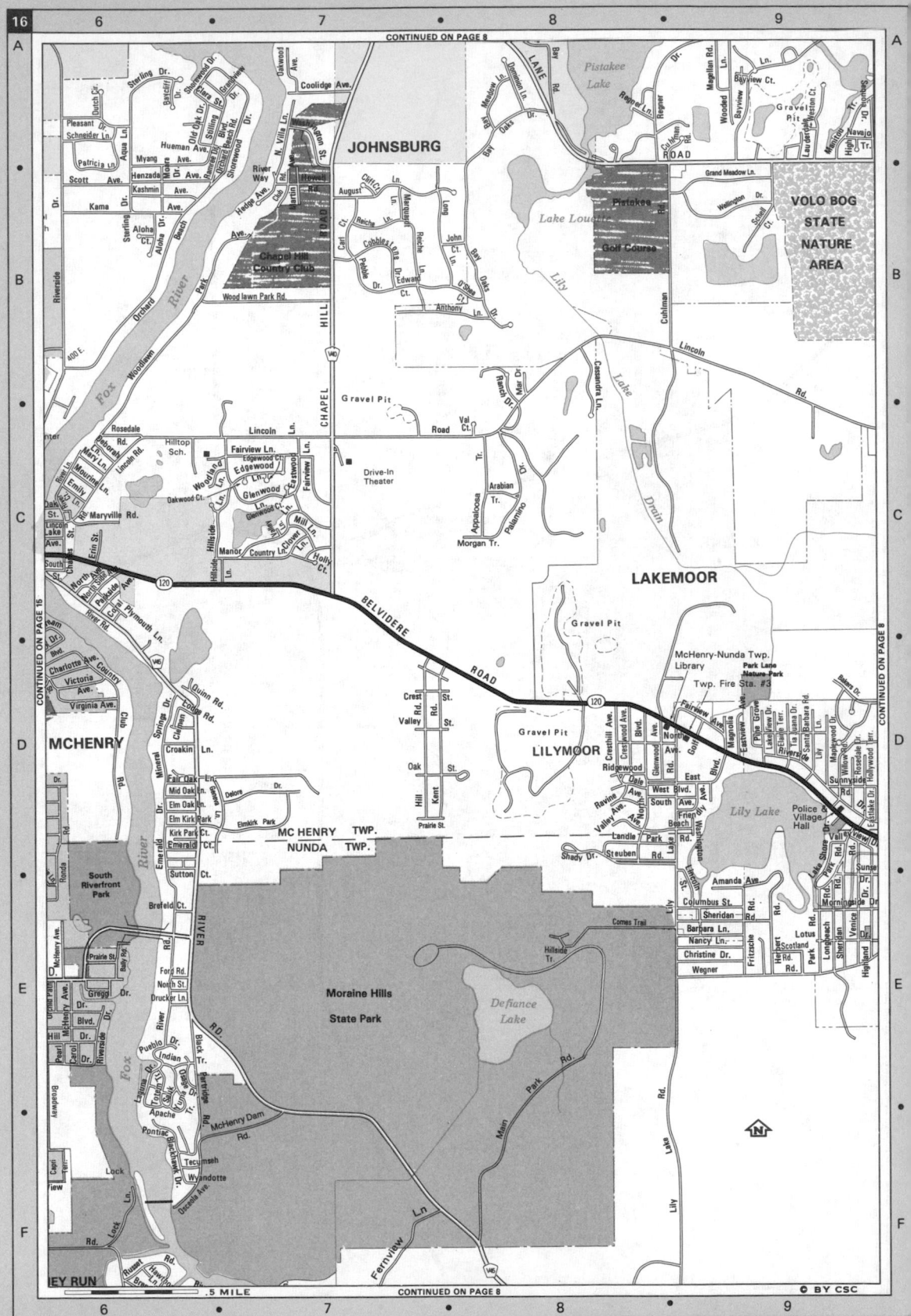

**16**

CONTINUED ON PAGE 8

JOHNSBURG

Pistakee Lake

Lake Louise

Pistakee Golf Course

VOLO BOG STATE NATURE AREA

Chapel Hill Country Club

Wood lawn Park Rd.

Fox River

Drive-In Theater

Gravel Pit

Lincoln Rd.

LAKEMOOR

BELVIDERE ROAD

120

McHenry-Nunda Twp. Library

Park Lane Nature Park

Twp. Fire Sta. #3

Gravel Pit

LILYMOOR

MCHENRY

Crest Valley

Oak

Prairie St.

MC HENRY TWP.
NUNDA TWP.

Lily Lake

Police & Village Hall

South Riverfront Park

Moraine Hills State Park

Defiance Lake

Comes Trail

Fox River

McHenry Dam Rd.

Main Park Rd.

Lily Lake Rd.

CONTINUED ON PAGE 15

CONTINUED ON PAGE 8

EY RUN

.5 MILE

© BY CSC

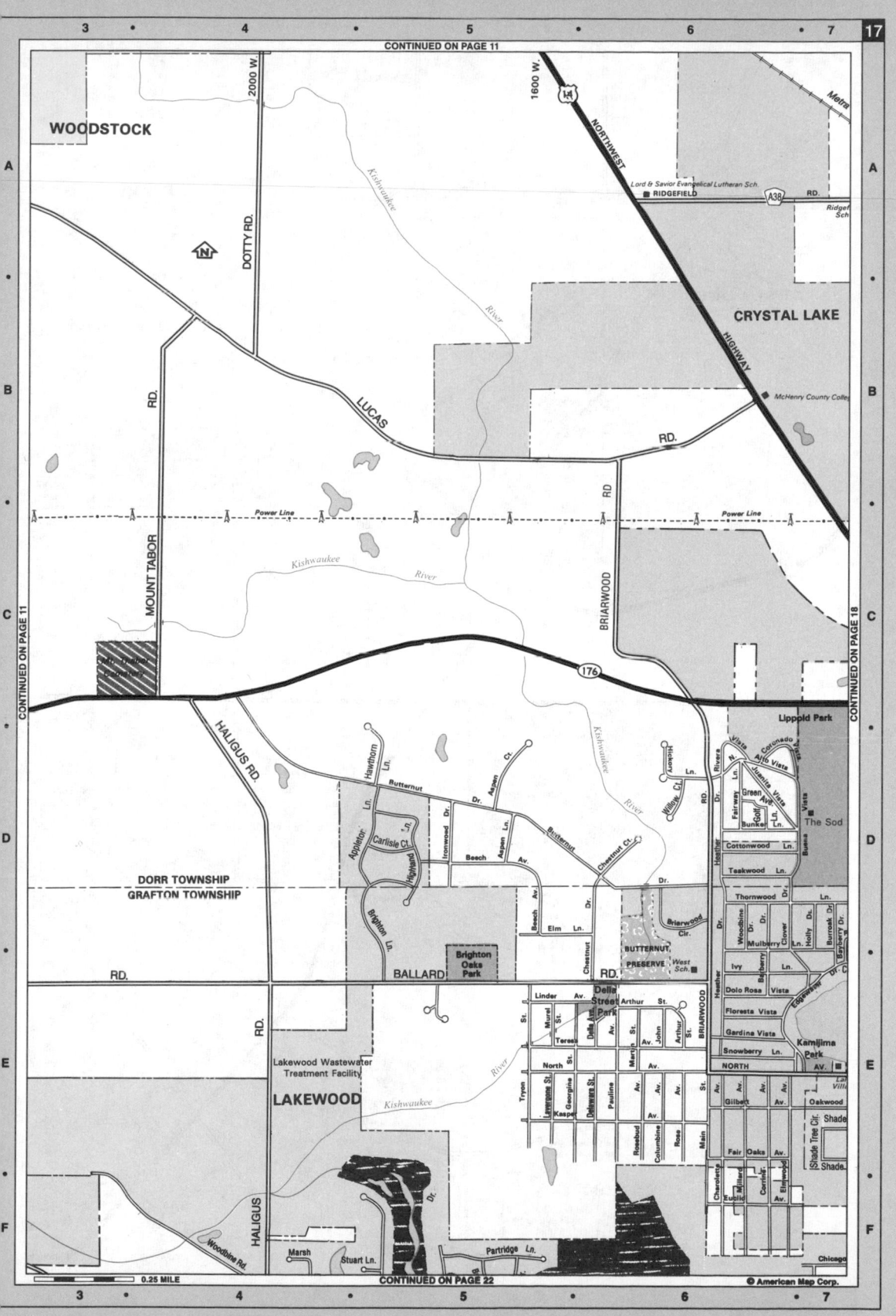

WOODSTOCK

CRYSTAL LAKE

CONTINUED ON PAGE 11

CONTINUED ON PAGE 11

CONTINUED ON PAGE 18

2000 W.

1600 W.

NORTHWEST

HIGHWAY

Metra

Lord & Savior Evangelical Lutheran Sch.
RIDGEFIELD
A38
RD.
Ridgef.
Sch.

McHenry County Colle.

DOTTY RD.

RD.

MOUNT TABOR

LUCAS

RD.

RD.

Kishwaukee

River

Power Line

Power Line

Kishwaukee

River

BRIARWOOD

176

Lippold Park

HALIGUS RD.

Hawthorn

Ln.

Butternut

Appleton

Ln.

Carlisle Ct.

Highland

Ln.

Ironwood

Dr.

Beech

Aspen

Dr.

Aspen

Ln.

Butternut

Dr.

Chestnut

Ct.

Aspen

Ct.

Willow

Ct.

Highland

Ln.

Rivera

Vista

Coronado

Fairway

Ln.

Juanita

Vista

Alta Vista

Golf

Ln.

Green

Av.

Bunker

Ln.

Buena

Vista

The Sod

Heather

Cottonwood

Ln.

Teakwood

Ln.

Thornwood

Dr.

Woodbine

Dr.

Clover

Holly

Dr.

Burr Oak

Dr.

Bayberry

Dr.

Mulberry

Dr.

Barberry

Ivy

Ln.

Dolo Rosa

Vista

Floresta

Vista

Gardina Vista

Snowberry

Ln.

NORTH

Kamijima

Park

AV.

Edgewood

Dr.

DORR TOWNSHIP

GRAFTON TOWNSHIP

Brighton

Ln.

Beech

Av.

Butternut

Dr.

Chestnut

Briarwood

Cir.

Elm

Ln.

Briarwood

PRESERVE

West

Sch.

RD.

RD.

BALLARD

Brighton
Oaks
Park

Della
Street
Park

Linder

Av.

Murel

St.

Teresa

St.

Linden

St.

Della Ave.

Arthur

St.

Martin

St.

John

St.

Arthur

St.

BRIARWOOD

Kishwaukee

River

Lakewood Wastewater
Treatment Facility

LAKEWOOD

Kishwaukee

River

North

St.

Tryon

St.

Lawrence St.

Kasper

St.

Georgina

St.

Delaware St.

Pauline

St.

Rosebud

Av.

Columbine

Av.

Rose

Av.

Main

St.

Av.

Av.

Av.

Av.

Gilbert

Av.

Fair Oaks

Av.

Av.

Av.

Av.

Shade Tree Cir.

Shade

Shade

Cherokee

Av.

Eufalia

Av.

Hilliard

Av.

Cornhet

Av.

Elmwood

Av.

Oakwood

Lake
Villa

HALIGUS

Dr.

Marsh

Stuart Ln.

Partridge Ln.

Woodbine Rd.

Chicago

CONTINUED ON PAGE 22

0.25 MILE

© American Map Corp.

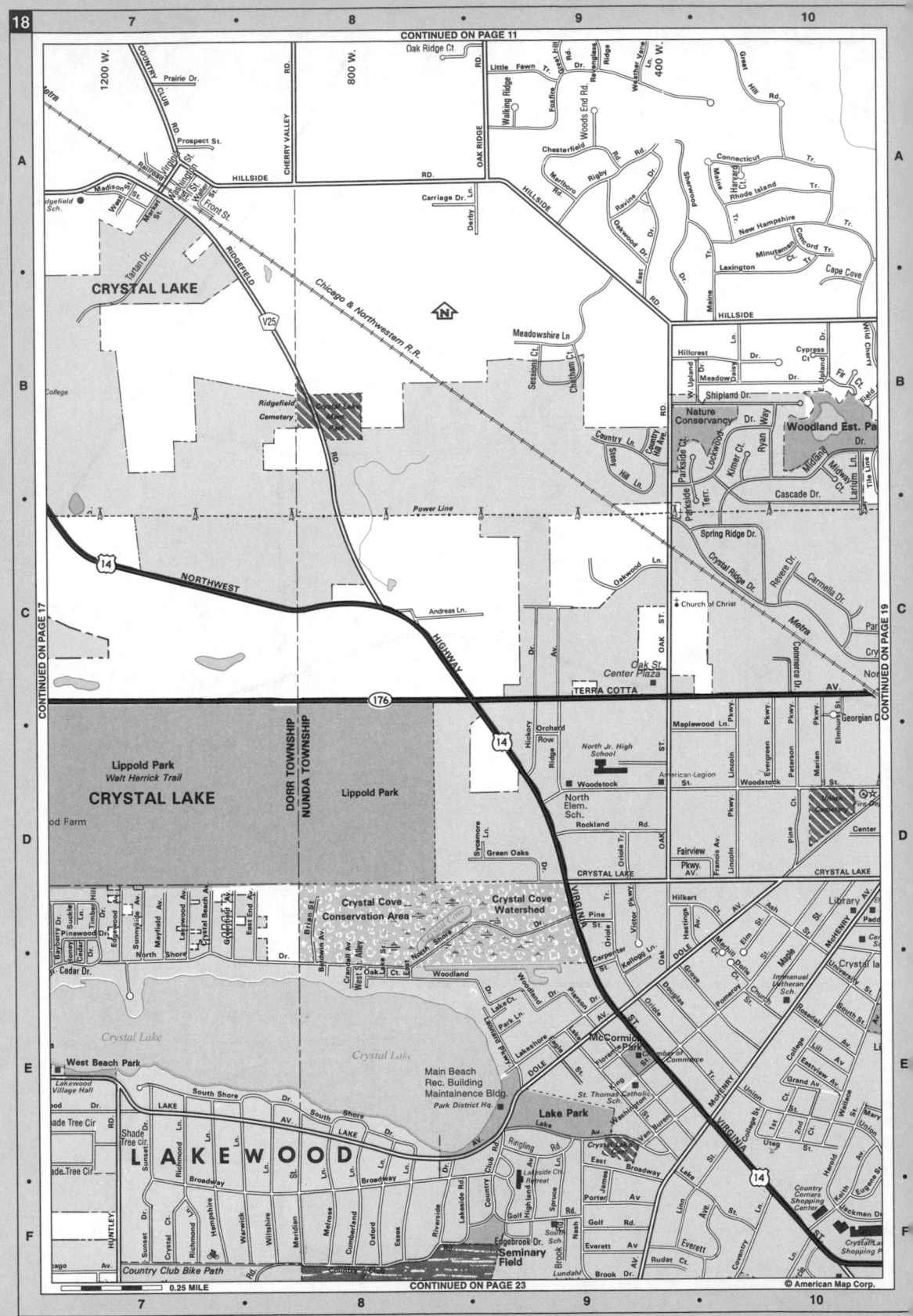

CONTINUED ON PAGE 11

7     8     9     10

A

B

C

D

E

F

CONTINUED ON PAGE 17

CONTINUED ON PAGE 19

CONTINUED ON PAGE 23

0.25 MILE

© American Map Corp.

CRYSTAL LAKE

LAKEWOOD

CRYSTAL LAKE

Lippold Park
Walt Herrick Trail

Lippold Park

7     8     9     10

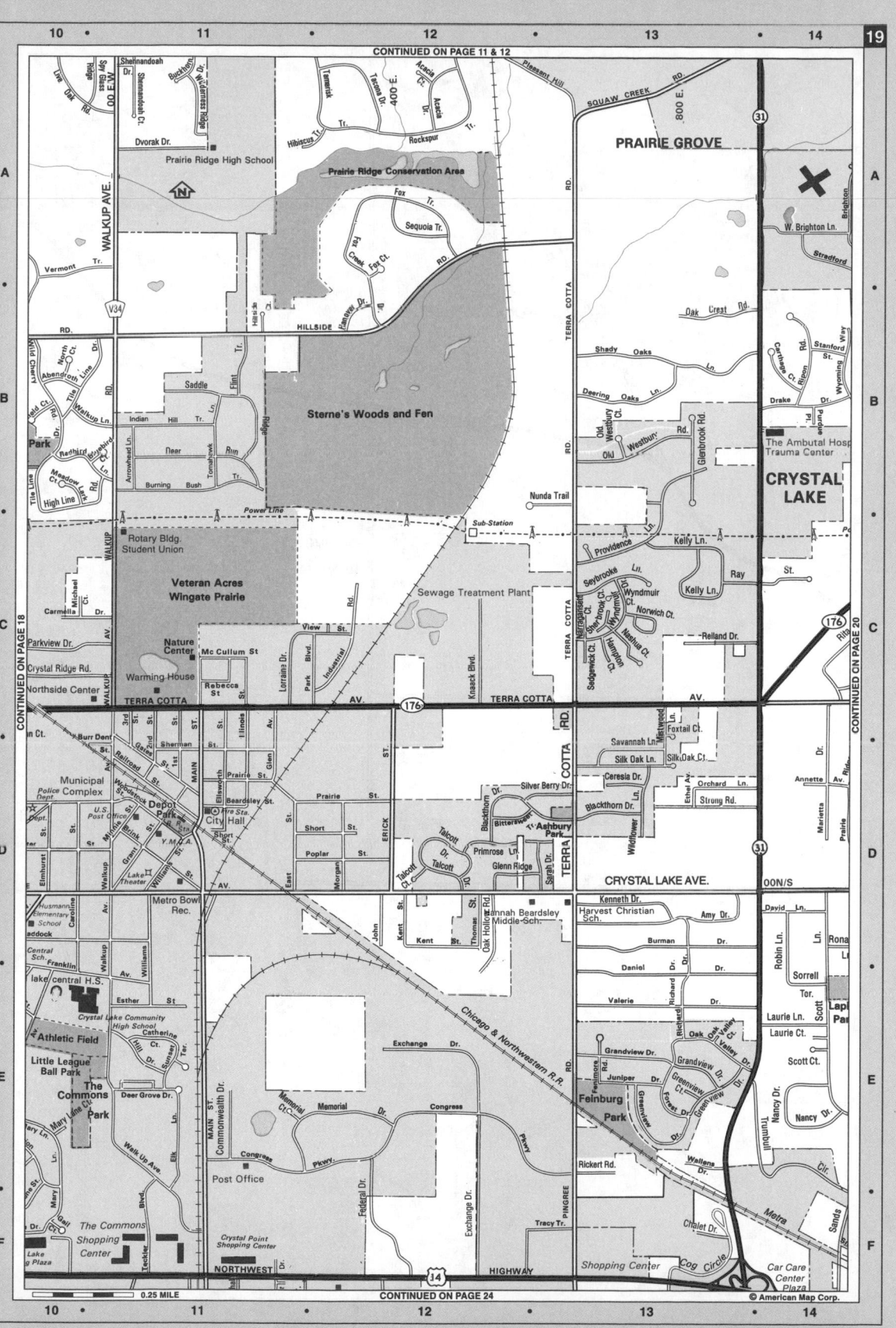

CONTINUED ON PAGE 11 & 12
CONTINUED ON PAGE 18
CONTINUED ON PAGE 20
CONTINUED ON PAGE 24

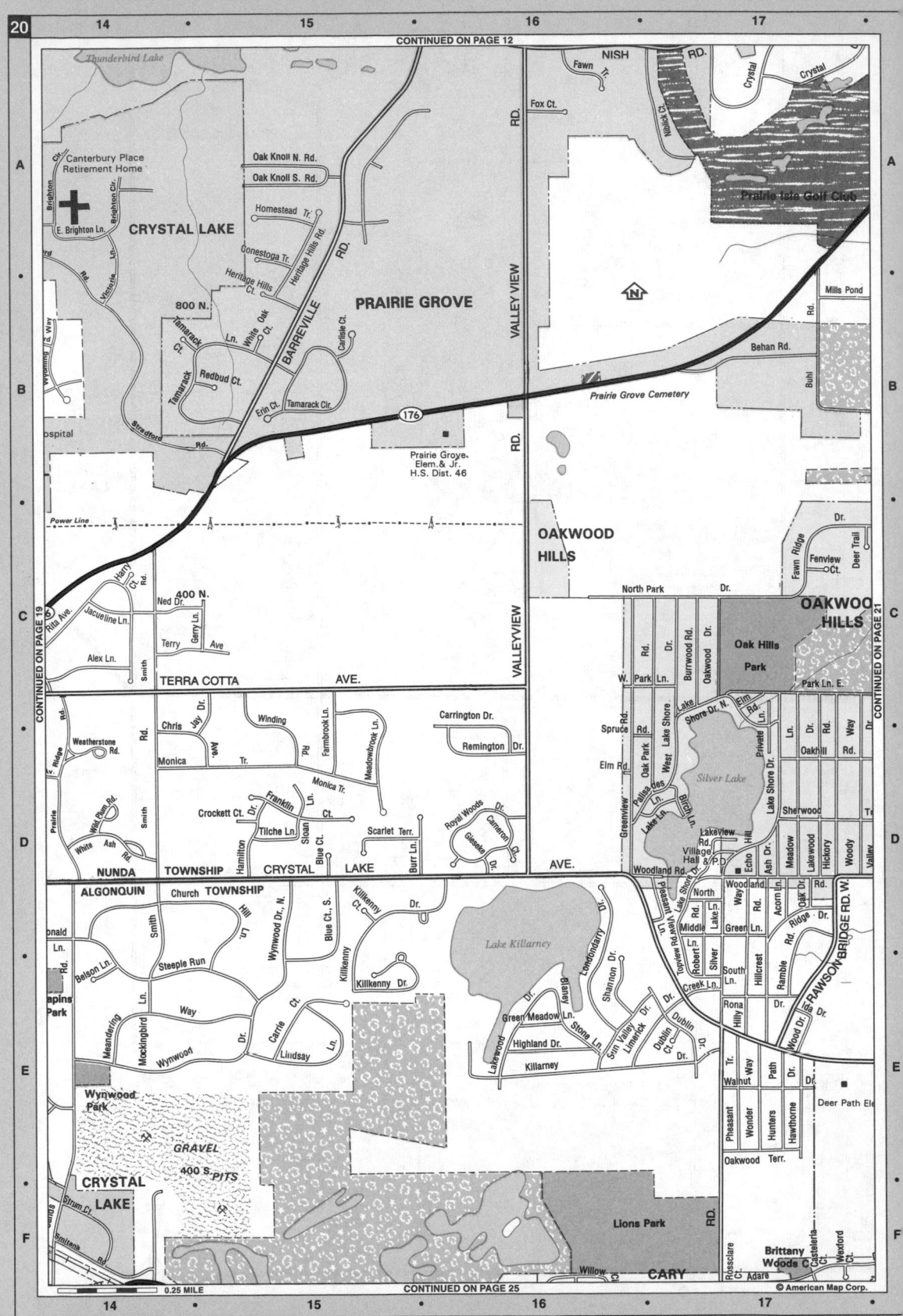

**20**

CONTINUED ON PAGE 12

14    15    16    17

*Thunderbird Lake*

NISH RD.

Fawn Tr.

Crystal

Crystal

Fox Ct.

**A**

Canterbury Place
Retirement Home

E. Brighton Ln.

Brighton Cir.

**CRYSTAL LAKE**

Oak Knoll N. Rd.
Oak Knoll S. Rd.

Homestead Tr.

Conestoga Tr.

Heritage Hills Ct.

Heritage Hills Rd.

800 N.

BARREVILLE RD.

White Oak Ln.

Carlisle Ct.

**PRAIRIE GROVE**

VALLEY VIEW

Prairie Isle Golf Club

Mills Pond

Behan Rd.

Buhl

**B**

Tamarack Ct.

Redbud Ct.

Tamarack

Erin Ct.

Tamarack Cir.

176

Prairie Grove Cemetery

Prairie Grove.
Elem. & Jr.
H.S. Dist. 46

Stradford

*Power Line*

Hospital

**C**

CONTINUED ON PAGE 19

Rita Ave.

Harry Ct. Rd.

Jacqueline Ln.

400 N.
Ned Dr.

Gerry Ln.

Terry

Ave

Alex Ln.

Smith

**TERRA COTTA AVE.**

RD.

VALLEYVIEW

**OAKWOOD
HILLS**

North Park Dr.

W. Park Ln.

Burrwood Rd.

Oakwood Dr.

**OAKWOOD
HILLS**

Oak Hills
Park

Park Ln. E.

Fawn Ridge

Fenview Ct.

Deer Trail

CONTINUED ON PAGE 21

**D**

Weatherstone Rd.

Prairie Ridge Rd.

Wild Plum Rd.

White Ash Rd.

Smith Rd.

Chris Jay Dr.

Monica

Tr.

Winding

Farmbrook Ln.

Meadowbrook Ln.

Monica Tr.

Crockett Ct. Dr.

Franklin Ct.

Tilche Ln.

Sloan

Blue Ct.

Scarlet Terr.

Hamilton

**CRYSTAL**

Burr Ln.

Carrington Dr.

Remington Dr.

Royal Woods Dr.

Gieseke

Cameron

AVE.

Spruce

Elm Rd.

Greenview

Palisades

Oak Park

Lake Ln.

West Lake Shore

Lake Shore Dr. N.

Birch Ln.

*Silver Lake*

Lakeview
Rd.

Village
Hall & P.D.

Woodland Rd.

Elm Rd.

Private

Oakhill Rd.

Sherwood

Lake Shore Dr.

Ash Dr.

Meadow

Lakewood

Hickory

Woody

**LAKE**

**NUNDA**

**TOWNSHIP**

**CRYSTAL LAKE**

**E**

ALGONQUIN

Church

**TOWNSHIP**

Belson Ln.

Smith

Steeple Run

Way

Meandering

Mockingbird

Wynwood

Hill Ln.

Wynwood Dr. N.

Blue Ct. S.

Killkenny

Killkenny Ct.

Dr.

Killkenny Dr.

Carrie Ct.

Lindsay Ln.

*Lake Killarney*

Londondairy Dr.

Shannon Dr.

Green Meadow Ln.

Highland Dr.

Stone Dr.

Son Valley Dr.

Limerick Dr.

Killarney

Lakewood

Topview Rd.

Lake View Dr.

Pleasant

North Ln.

Middle Ln.

Robert Dr.

Creek Ln.

Rona

Hilly

Dublin Ct.

Dublin Dr.

Woodland

Oak Ln.

Acorn Ln.

Green Ln.

Silver Ln.

Hillcrest

Ramble Dr.

Ridge

RAWSON BRIDGE RD. W.

Ida Rd.

Wood Dr.

South Ln.

**F**

Wynwood
Park

Chapins
Park

**CRYSTAL
LAKE**

Strum Ct.

*GRAVEL
PITS*

400 S.

*Lions Park*

Willow

**CARY**

Walnut Way

Path

Pheasant

Wonder

Hunters

Hawthorne

Oakwood Terr.

Deer Path Ele

Rosselare Ct.

Adare

**Brittany
Woods C**

Castlefid

Wexford Ct.

RD.

N

© American Map Corp.

0.25 MILE

CONTINUED ON PAGE 25

14    15    16    17

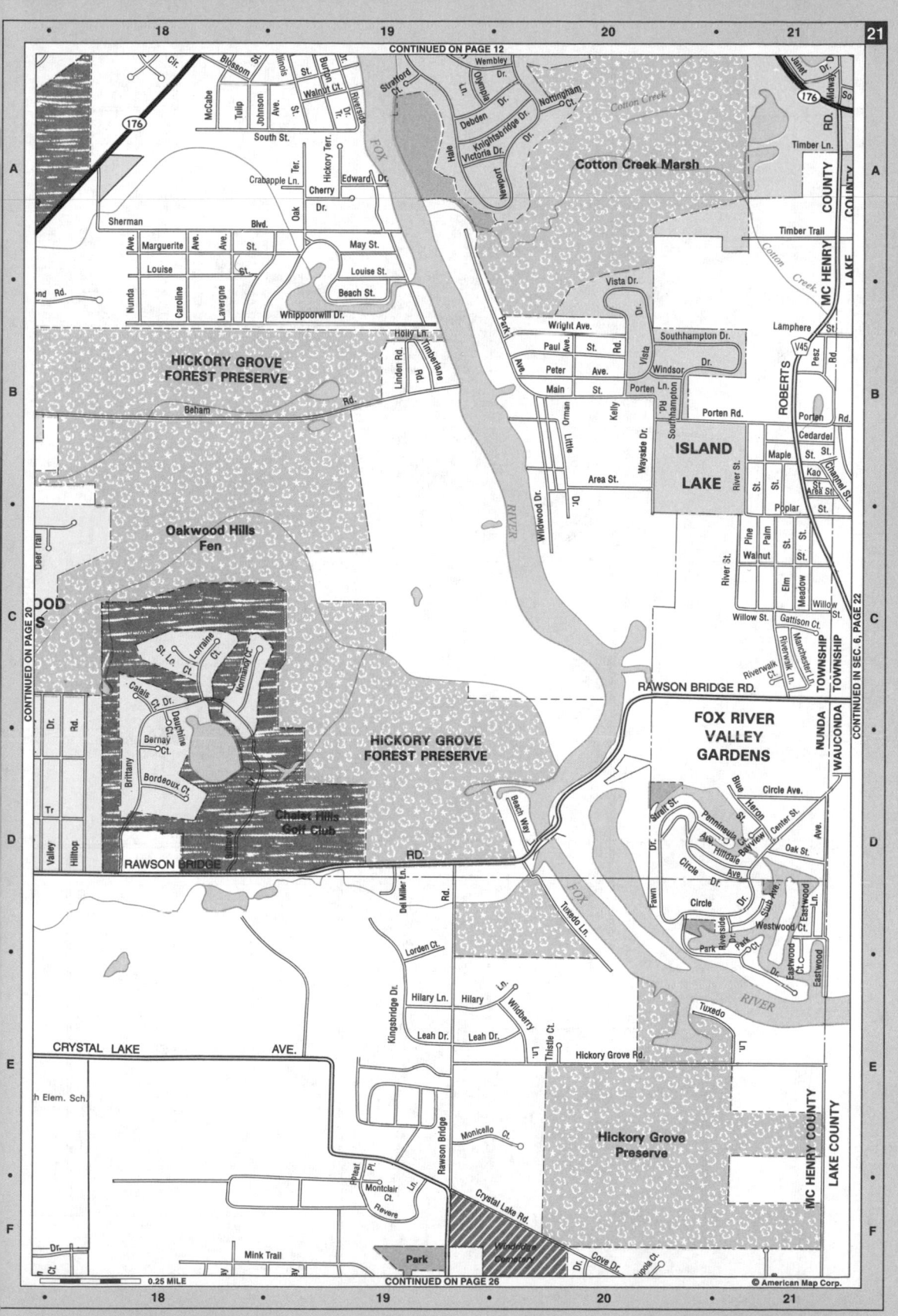

CONTINUED ON PAGE 12

CONTINUED ON PAGE 26

CONTINUED ON PAGE 20

CONTINUED IN SEC. 6, PAGE 22

18    19    20    21

**Cotton Creek Marsh**

**HICKORY GROVE FOREST PRESERVE**

**Oakwood Hills Fen**

**HICKORY GROVE FOREST PRESERVE**

**ISLAND LAKE**

**FOX RIVER VALLEY GARDENS**

**Chalet Hills Golf Club**

RAWSON BRIDGE

RAWSON BRIDGE RD.

CRYSTAL LAKE AVE.

**Hickory Grove Preserve**

MC HENRY COUNTY

LAKE COUNTY

NUNDA TOWNSHIP

WAUCONDA TOWNSHIP

0.25 MILE

© American Map Corp.

A B C D E F

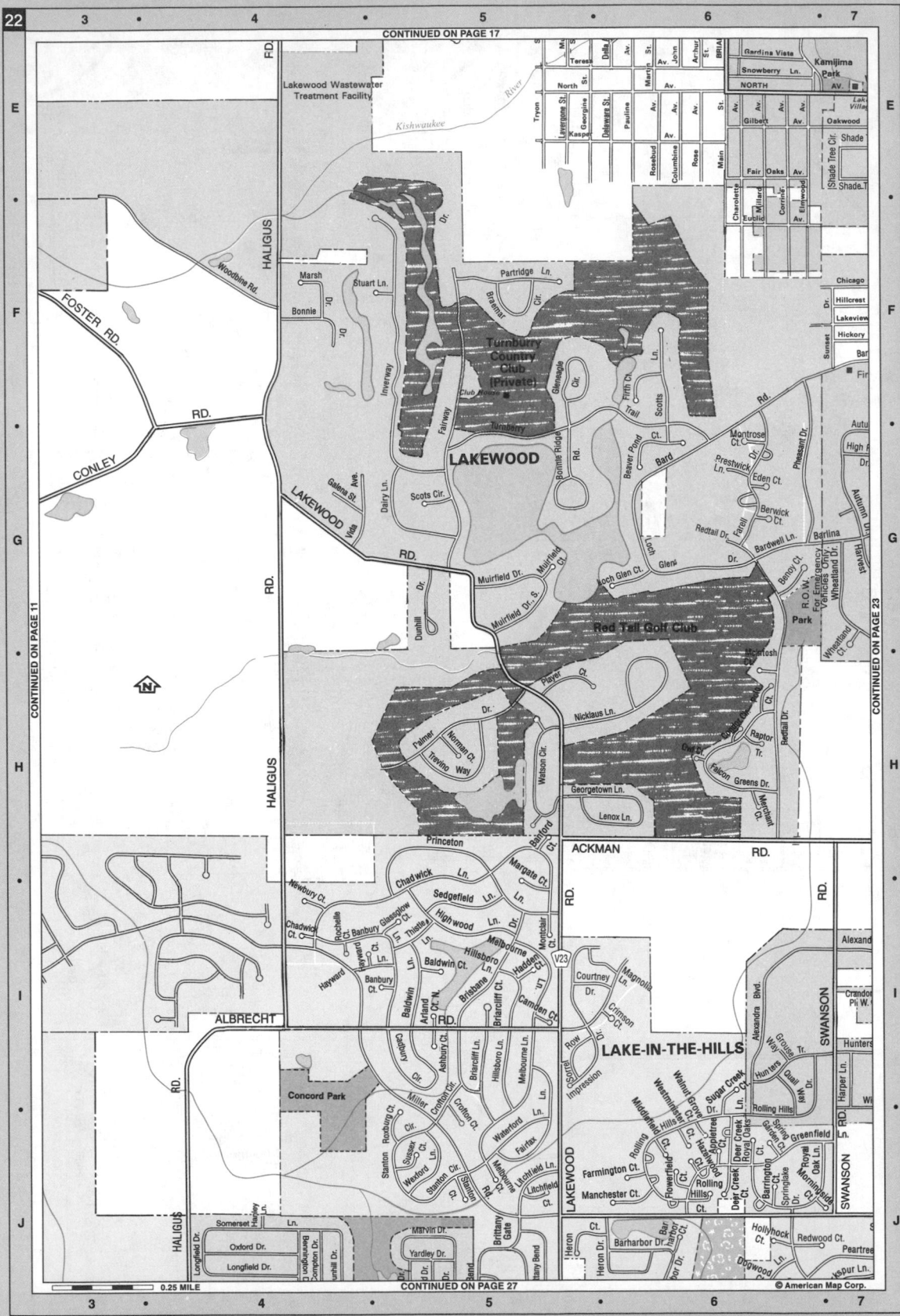

CONTINUED ON PAGE 17

CONTINUED ON PAGE 11

CONTINUED ON PAGE 23

CONTINUED ON PAGE 27

Lakewood Wastewater
Treatment Facility

Kishwaukee

Turnbury
Country
Club
(Private)

LAKEWOOD

Red Tail Golf Club

Park

R.O.W.
For Emergency
Vehicles Only

ACKMAN                    RD.

LAKE-IN-THE-HILLS

Concord Park

ALBRECHT

0.25 MILE

© American Map Corp.

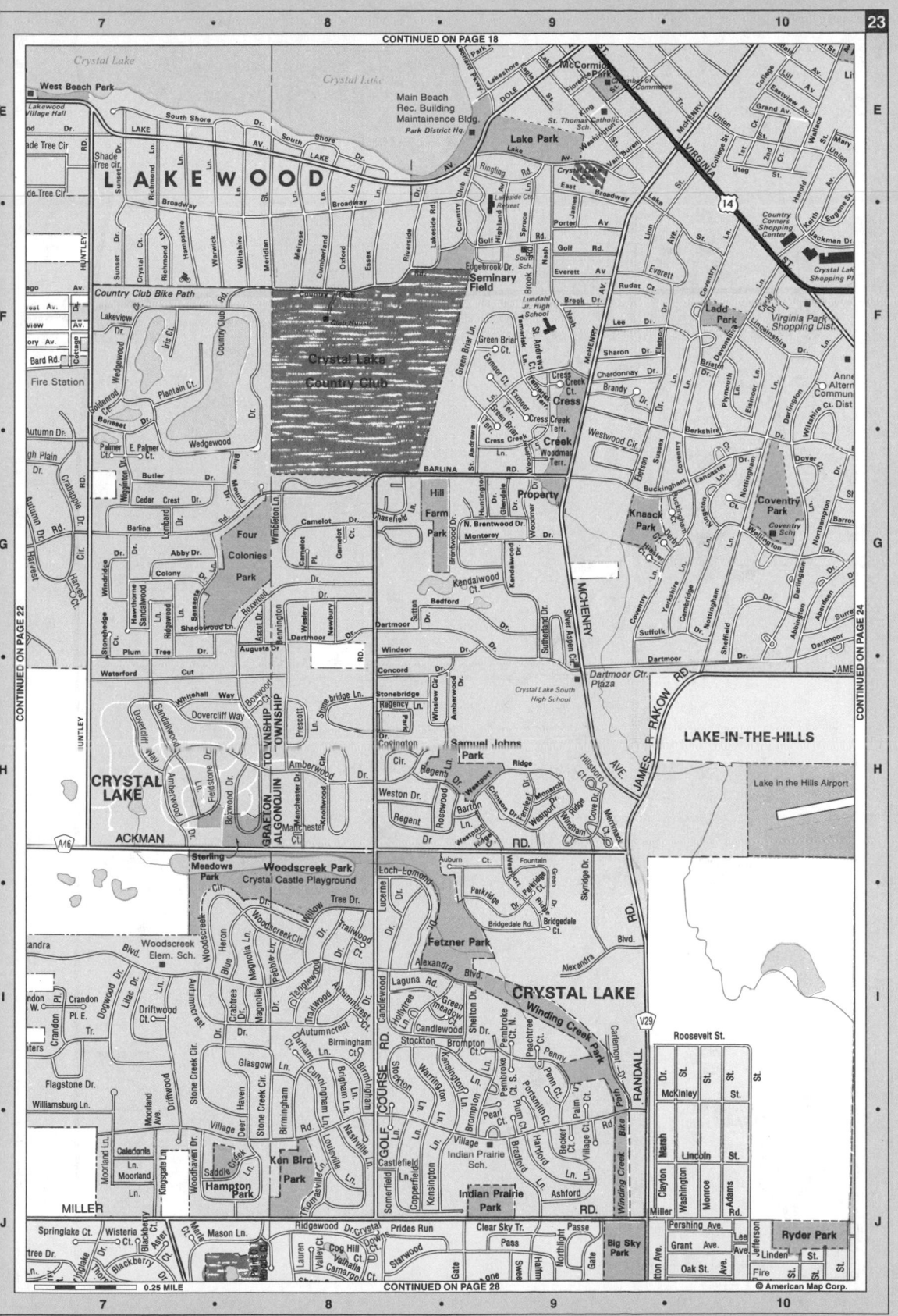

CONTINUED ON PAGE 18

CONTINUED ON PAGE 22

CONTINUED ON PAGE 24

CONTINUED ON PAGE 28

© American Map Corp.

0.25 MILE

CONTINUED ON PAGE 19

CONTINUED ON PAGE 23

CONTINUED ON PAGE 25

CONTINUED ON PAGE 29

© American Map Corp.

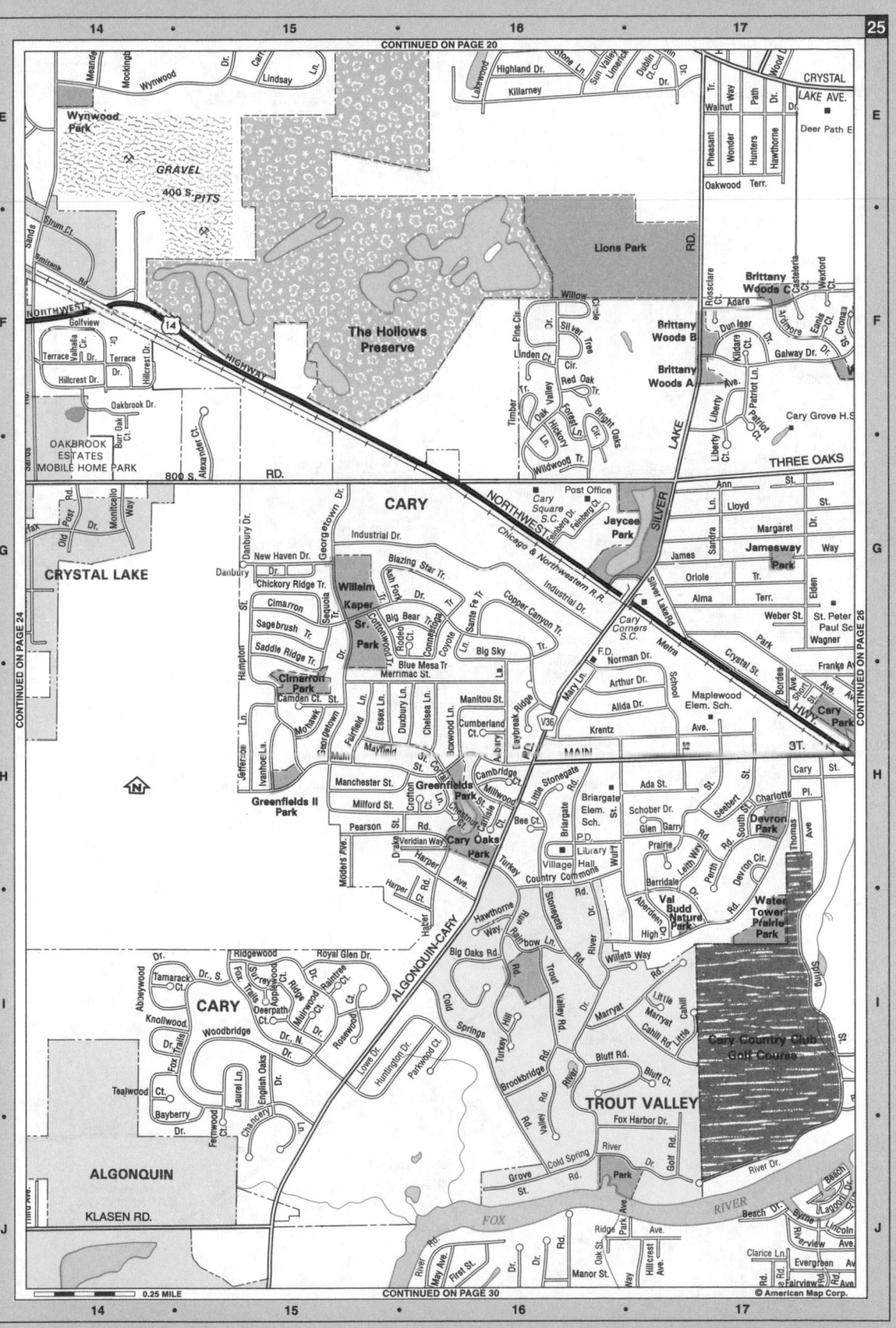

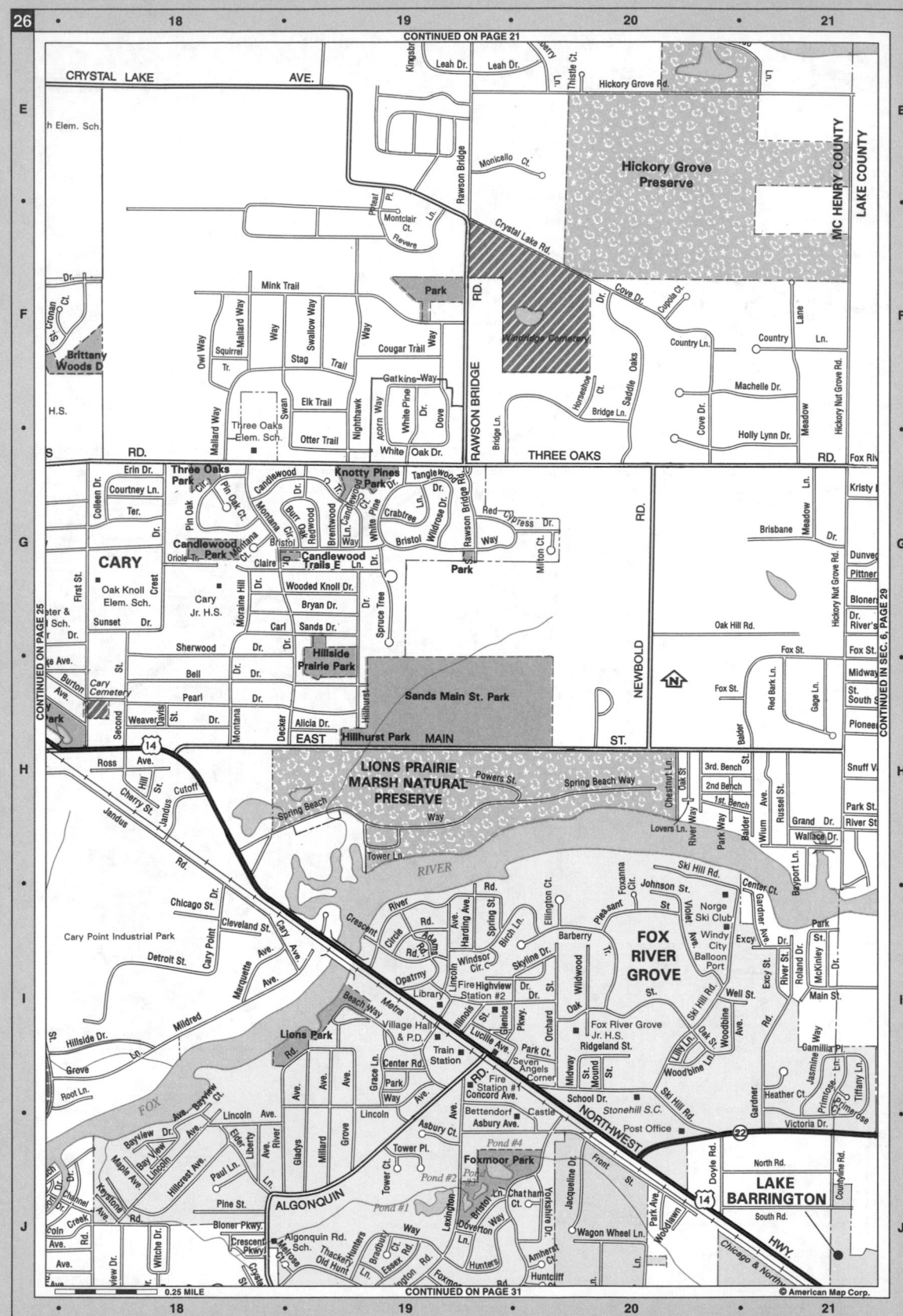

CONTINUED ON PAGE 21

CRYSTAL LAKE AVE.

h Elem. Sch.

Hickory Grove Rd.

Hickory Grove
Preserve

MC HENRY COUNTY

LAKE COUNTY

Brittany
Woods D

H.S.

Mink Trail

Park

Mallard Way
Owl Way
Squirrel

Swallow Way
Stag
Way

Cougar Trail

Gatkins Way

Elk Trail

Otter Trail

Three Oaks
Elem. Sch.

White Pine
Dr.
Dove

Oak Dr.

Crystal Lake Rd.

Cove Dr.
Cuppla Ct.

Country Ln.

Country
Lane
Ln.

Machelle Dr.

Cove Dr.

Holly Lynn Dr.

Meadow

Hickory Nut Grove Rd.

Wauridge Cemetery

RAWSON BRIDGE RD.

THREE OAKS

RD.

Fox Riv

Erin Dr.
Colleen Dr.
Courtney Ln.
Ter.

Three Oaks
Park

Knotty Pines
Park Cr.

Tangle wood
Dr.

Red Cypress Dr.

Kristy

Brisbane

Meadow

Dunweg
Pittner
Bloners

RD.

NEWBOLD

CARY

Oak Knoll
Elem. Sch.

Pin Oak

Candlewood
Park

Montana

Bristol

Claire

Candlewood
Trails E

Crabtree

Bristol
Wildrose Dr.

White Pine

Milton Ct.

Oak Hill Rd.

Fox St.

Hickory Nut Grove Rd.

River's
Dr.

Fox St.
Midway
St.
South

Pioneer

CONTINUED ON PAGE 25

First St.

Crest

Sunset

Dr.

Moraine Hill

Dr.

Cary
Jr. H.S.

Wooded Knoll Dr.

Bryan Dr.

Carl
Sands Dr.

Dr.

Spruce Tree

Red Bark Ln.

Fox St.

Gage Ln.

Cary
Cemetery

Burton
Ave.
Park

Second

Weaver

Davis
St.
Dr.

Sherwood

Bell

Pearl

Dr.

Montana

Decker

Alicia Dr.

Hillside
Prairie Park

Sands Main St. Park

EAST

Hillhurst Park

MAIN

ST.

Ross

Ave.

Cherry St.

Jandus
Cutoff

Hillhurst

LIONS PRAIRIE
MARSH NATURAL
PRESERVE

Spring Beach

Powers St.

Spring Beach Way

Way

Chestnut Ln.

3rd Bench

2nd Bench
1st Bench

Oak St.

Russel St.

Grand
Dr.
Wallace Dr.

Snuff V

Park St.
River St

Jandus

Rd.

RIVER

Tower Ln.

Lovers Ln.

River
Way

Park Way

Balder

Wlium

Bayport Ln.

Chicago St.
Dr.

Cleveland St.

Cary Ave.

Crescent
Circle
Rd.

River

Rd.

Adams

Spring St.

Birch Ln.

Ellington Ct.

Barberry

Pleasant

Foxanna
Cir.

Johnson St.

Ski Hill Rd.

Norge
Ski Club

Center Ct.

Gardner
Dr.

Excy

Park

Cary Point Industrial Park

Detroit St.

Cary Point

Marquette

Ave.

Windsor
Cir.

Harding Ave.

Skyline Dr.

Glenice

Wildwood

FOX
RIVER
GROVE

Violet

Windy
City
Balloon
Port

Excy
St.

River St.

Roland Dr.

McKinley

Main St.

Hillside Dr.

Mildred

Beach Way

Metra

Village Hall
& P.D.

Opatrny

Library

Fire
Station #2

Highview

Illinois

Lincoln

St.

St.

St.

Oak

Orchard

Fox River Grove
Jr. H.S.
Ridgeland St.

Midway

Ski Hill Rd.

Well St.

Woodbine

Camilla Pl.

Jasmine

Primrose
Tiffany

Lions Park

Grove

Root Ln.

Lincoln

Ave.

Grace Ln.

Center Rd.

Lucille Ave.

Park Ct.

Seven
Angels
Corner

St.
Mound

Wood'bine

Heather Ct.

Primerose

FOX

BayView
Bay View
Bay Lincoln
Maple Ave.

Elder

Liberty

Hillcrest Ave.

Paul Ln.

Ave.

River

Gladys
Millard

Grove

Lincoln

Asbury Ct.

Tower Pl.

Fire
Station #1
Concord Ave.

Bettendorf
Asbury Ave.

Castle

NORTHWEST

School Dr.
Stonehill S.C.

Post Office

Gardner

Victoria Dr.

Doyle Rd.

North Rd.

Countyline Rd.

LAKE
BARRINGTON

Channel

Keystone

Pine St.

ALGONQUIN

Bloner Pkwy.

Algonquin Rd.
Sch.

Crescent
Pkwy.

Melrose

Thackery
Old Hunt

Way

Lexington

Overton

Bristol Ln.

Chatham
Ct.

Pond #4
Pond

Foxmoor Park

Jacqueline Dr.

Yorkshire Dr.

Front
St.

Park Ln.

Woodlawn

South Rd.

Chicago & North

HWY.

Pond #2

Pond #1

Hunters

Bradley

Essex
Rd.

Foxmo

Hunters
Rd.

Amherst

Huntcliff

Wagon Wheel Ln.

0.25 MILE

CONTINUED ON PAGE 31

© American Map Corp.

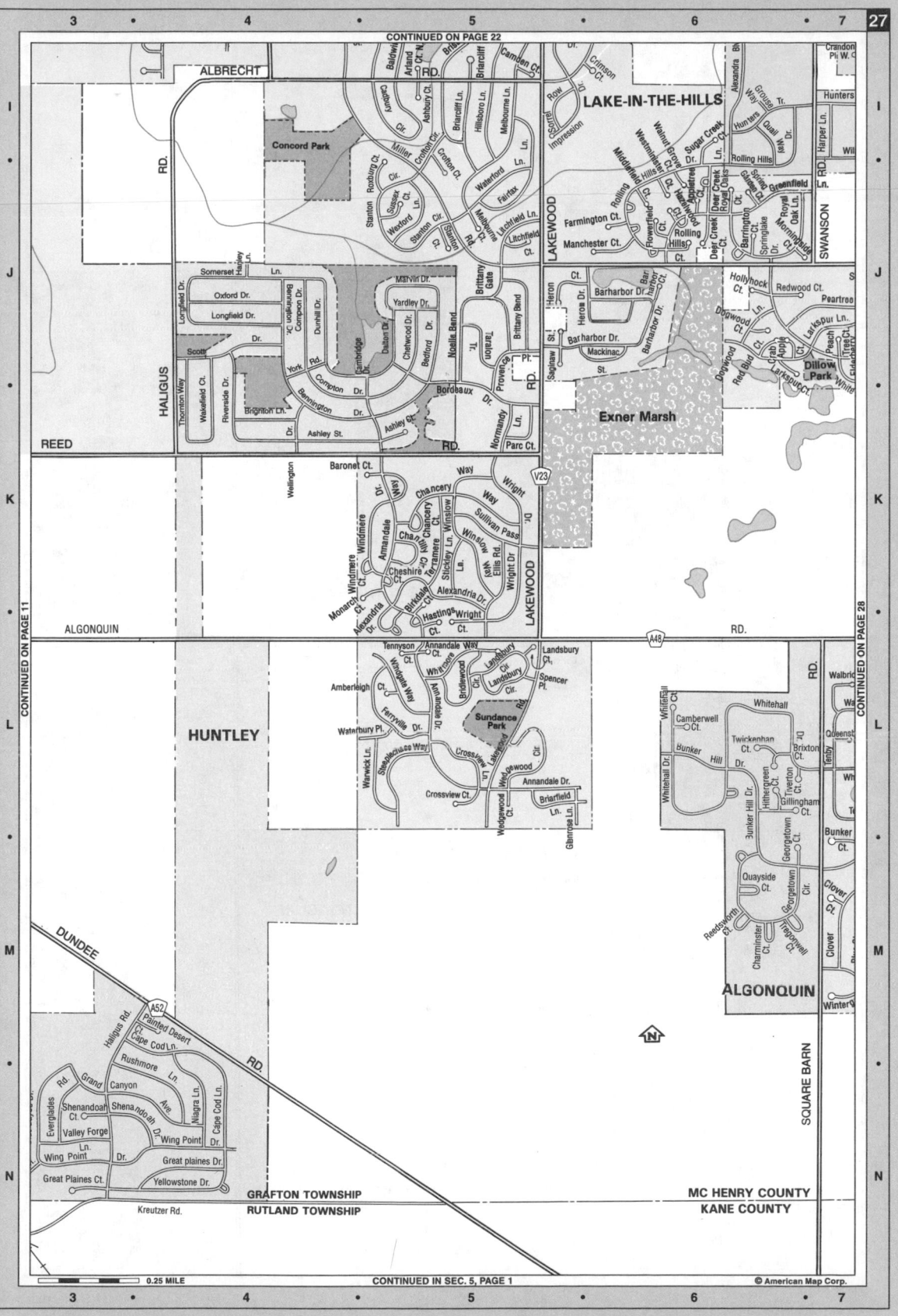

CONTINUED ON PAGE 22

LAKE-IN-THE-HILLS

Concord Park

ALBRECHT

RD.

Baldwin
Arland
Camden Ct.
Briarcliff
Cadbury
Ashbury Ct.
Ct.
Briarcliff Ln.
Hillsboro Ln.
Melbourne Ln.
Miller
Croton Ct.
Croton Dr.
Crimson
Row
Sorrel
Impression
Walnut Grove
Sugar Creek
Deer Creek
Alexandra
Grouse
Quail
Hunters
Hunters
Hunters
Tr.
Dr.
Harper Ln.
Will

RD.

Roxbury Ct.
Waterford
Fairfax
Westmeadow
Middlefield Hills
Squirrel
Spring
Royal Oak
Garner
Greenfield
Ln.

Stanton
Sussex
Melbourne
Ct.
Litchfield
Ct.
Litchfield
Rolling
Flowerfield
Deer Creek
Ct.
Springlake
Morningside
Rolling Hills
Royal Oak
Swanson

Wexford
Stanton Cir.
Cir.
Farmington Ct.
Manchester Ct.
Rolling
Hills
Deer Creek
Ct.
Barrington
Ct.

LAKEWOOD

Somerset
Hagley
Ln.
Marvin Dr.
Brittany
Gate
Heron
Ct.
Barharbor Dr.
Hollyhock
Redwood Ct.
Peartree

Longfield Dr.
Oxford Dr.
Yardley Dr.
Brittany Bend
Heron
St.
Barharbor
Barharbor Dr.
Dogwood
Larkspur Ln.

Longfield Dr.
Compton Dr.
Dunhill
Chatwood Dr.
Noelle Bend
Heron Dr.
Barharbor Dr.
Mackinac
Dogwood
Crab Apple
Dillow

HALIGUS
Scott
Dr.
Dalton Dr.
Cambridge
Bedford
Tanton
Provence
Pt.
Saginaw
St.
Red Bud
Peach
Park
White

Thornton Way
Wakefield Ct.
York
Rd.
Compton
Dr.
Bordeaux
Dr.
RD.
Exner Marsh

Riverside Dr.
Brighton Ln.
Bennington
Dr.
Ashley Ct.
Normandy

REED
RD.
Ashley St.
Parc Ct.
Ln.

Baronet Ct.
Wellington
Way
Wright
V23

Windemere
Amandale
Way
Chancery
Sullivan Pass
Way
Wright Dr.

Windemere
Cheshire
Terramere
Winslow
Stickley Ln.
Ellis Rd.
Ct.

Monarch
Birkdale
Alexandria Dr.
Wright
LAKEWOOD

ALGONQUIN
Alexandria
Hastings
Ct.
Wright
Ct.
A48
RD.

Tennyson
Annandale Way
Landsbury
Ct.
Landsbury

Whitmore
Landsbury
Cir.
Spencer
Pl.
Walbrk
Wa

Amberleigh
Windgate Way
Bridlewood
Cir.
Whitehall
Camberwell
Ct.
Whitehall
Queensb

HUNTLEY
Waterbury Pl.
Ferryville
Dr.
Sundance
Park
Bunker
Hill
Twickenham
Dr.
Brixton
Ct.
Tenby
Wh

Warwick Dr.
Shadowhouse Way
Crossview Ln.
Wedgewood
Annandale Dr.
Whitehall Dr.
Hithergreen
Tiverton
Gillingham
Ct.
Bunker
Te
Ct.

Crossview Ct.
Briarfield
Bunker Hill Dr.
Georgetown
Clover
Ct.

Wedgewood Dr.
Glenreal Ln.
Quayside
Ct.
Georgetown
Cir.

Reedsworth
Ct.
Charminster
Tregonwell
Ct.
ALGONQUIN
Clover
Ct.

DUNDEE
RD.
Winter

A52
Painted Desert
Halligus Rd.
Cape Cod Ln.
Ct.
SQUARE BARN

Rushmore
Ln.
Canyon
Ave.

Grand
Shenandoah
Shenandoah
Niagra Ln.
Cape Cod Ln.

Everglades
Rd.
Valley Forge
Ln.
Wing Point
Dr.

Wing Point
Great plaines Dr.

Great Plaines Ct.
Yellowstone Dr.
GRAFTON TOWNSHIP
MC HENRY COUNTY

Kreutzer Rd.
RUTLAND TOWNSHIP
KANE COUNTY

CONTINUED ON PAGE 11

CONTINUED ON PAGE 28

0.25 MILE

CONTINUED IN SEC. 5, PAGE 1

© American Map Corp.

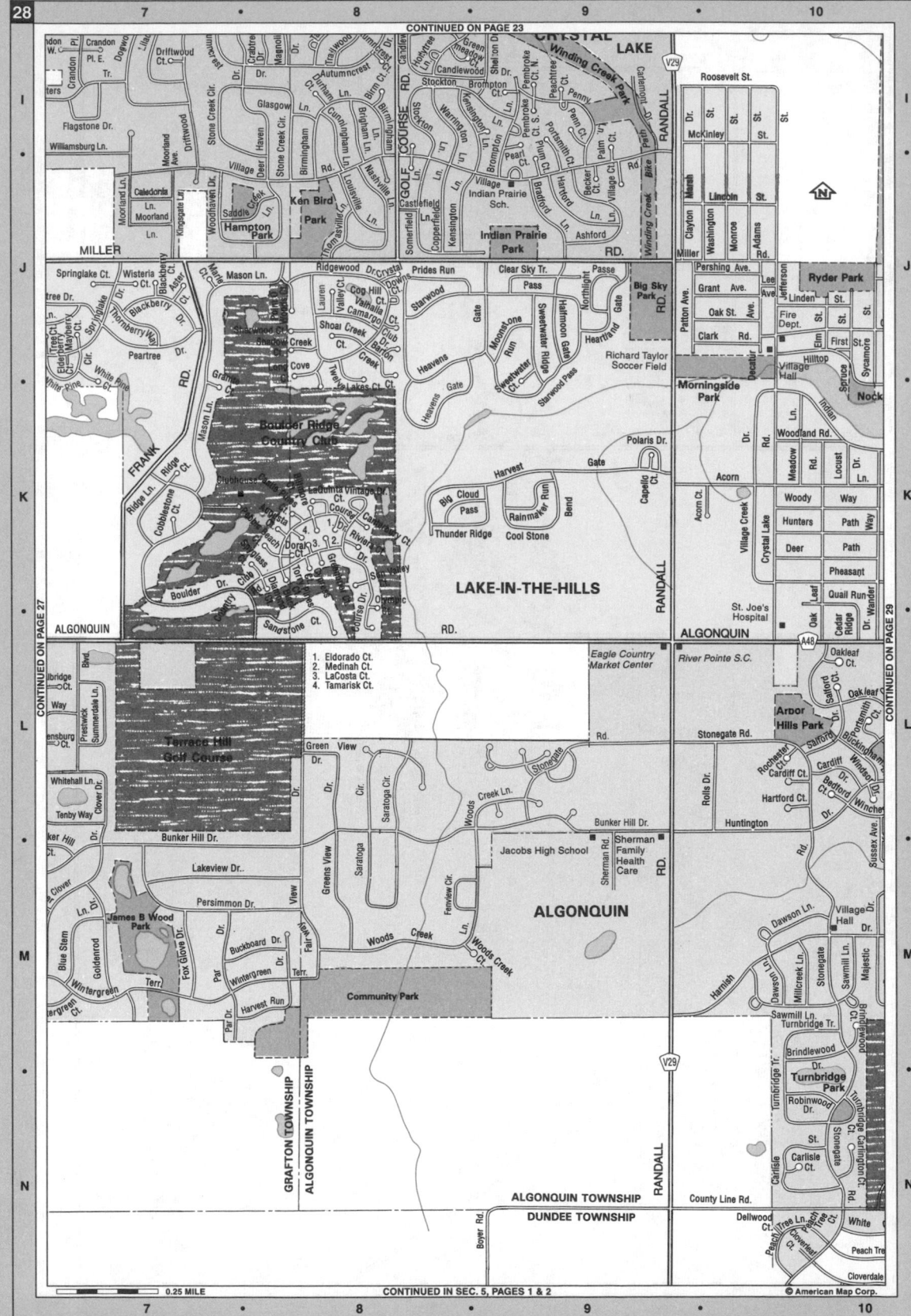

CONTINUED ON PAGE 23

CRYSTAL LAKE

CONTINUED ON PAGE 27

CONTINUED ON PAGE 29

MILLER

FRANK

ALGONQUIN

LAKE-IN-THE-HILLS

1. Eldorado Ct.
2. Medinah Ct.
3. LaCosta Ct.
4. Tamarisk Ct.

Boulder Ridge Country Club

Terrace Hill Golf Course

Hampton Park

Ken Bird Park

Indian Prairie Park

Big Sky Park

Richard Taylor Soccer Field

Morningside Park

Ryder Park

Village Hall

Fire Dept.

Crystal Lake

St. Joe's Hospital

Eagle Country Market Center

River Pointe S.C.

Arbor Hills Park

James B Wood Park

Jacobs High School

Sherman Family Health Care

ALGONQUIN

Community Park

Village Hall

Turnbridge Park

GRAFTON TOWNSHIP

ALGONQUIN TOWNSHIP

ALGONQUIN TOWNSHIP

DUNDEE TOWNSHIP

ALGONQUIN TOWNSHIP Rd.

County Line Rd.

RANDALL RD.

0.25 MILE

CONTINUED IN SEC. 5, PAGES 1 & 2

© American Map Corp.

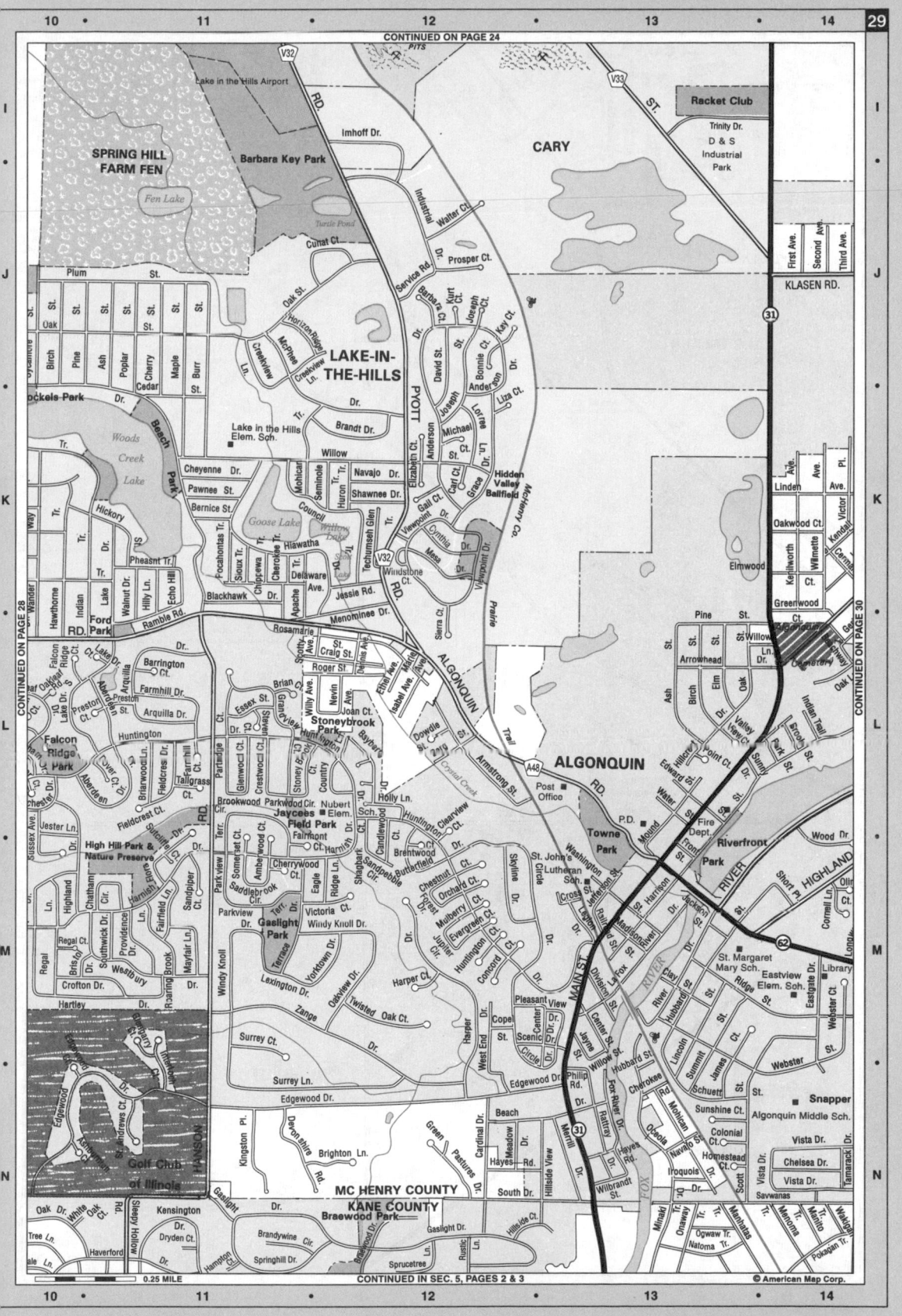

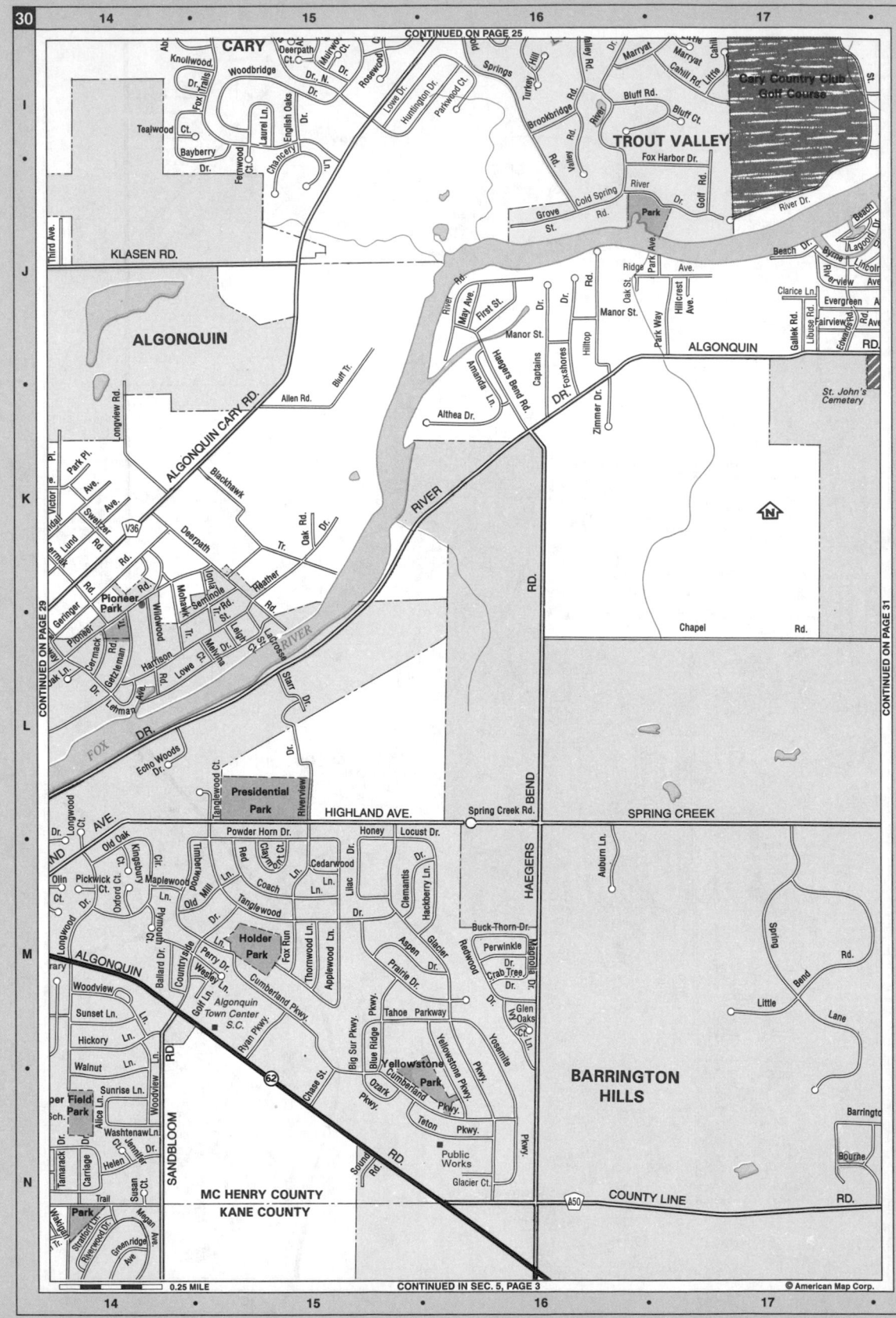

CONTINUED ON PAGE 25

CARY

TROUT VALLEY

Cary Country Club
Golf Course

KLASEN RD.

ALGONQUIN

ALGONQUIN

St. John's
Cemetery

CONTINUED ON PAGE 29

CONTINUED ON PAGE 31

Pioneer
Park

Chapel                    Rd.

Presidential
Park

HIGHLAND AVE.

Spring Creek Rd.          SPRING CREEK

Holder
Park

Algonquin
Town Center
S.C.

ALGONQUIN

BARRINGTON
HILLS

Yellowstone
Park

Field
Park

Public
Works

Park

MC HENRY COUNTY
KANE COUNTY

COUNTY LINE          RD.

0.25 MILE

CONTINUED IN SEC. 5, PAGE 3

© American Map Corp.

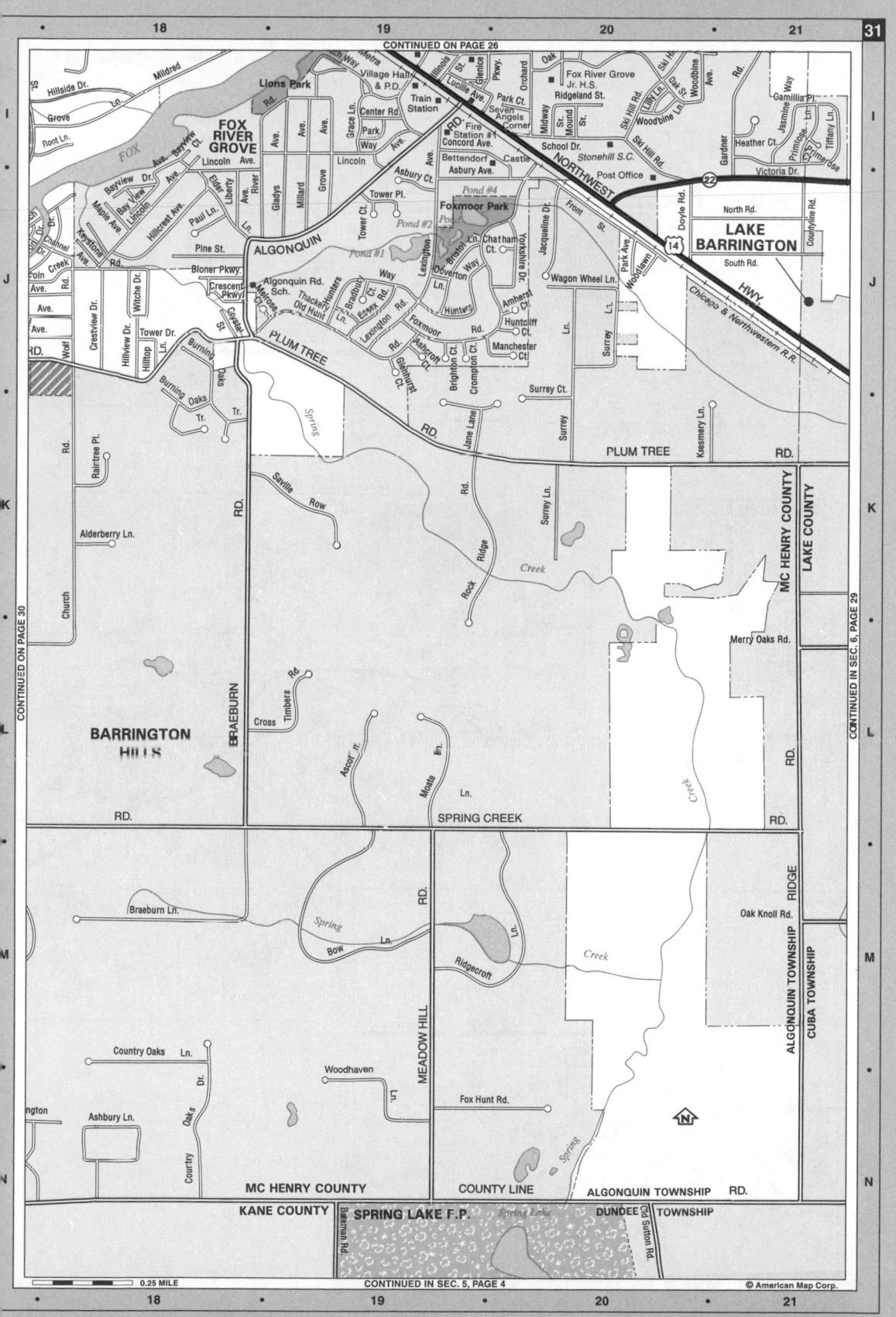

CONTINUED ON PAGE 26

CONTINUED ON PAGE 30

CONTINUED IN SEC. 6, PAGE 29

CONTINUED IN SEC. 5, PAGE 4

0.25 MILE

© American Map Corp.

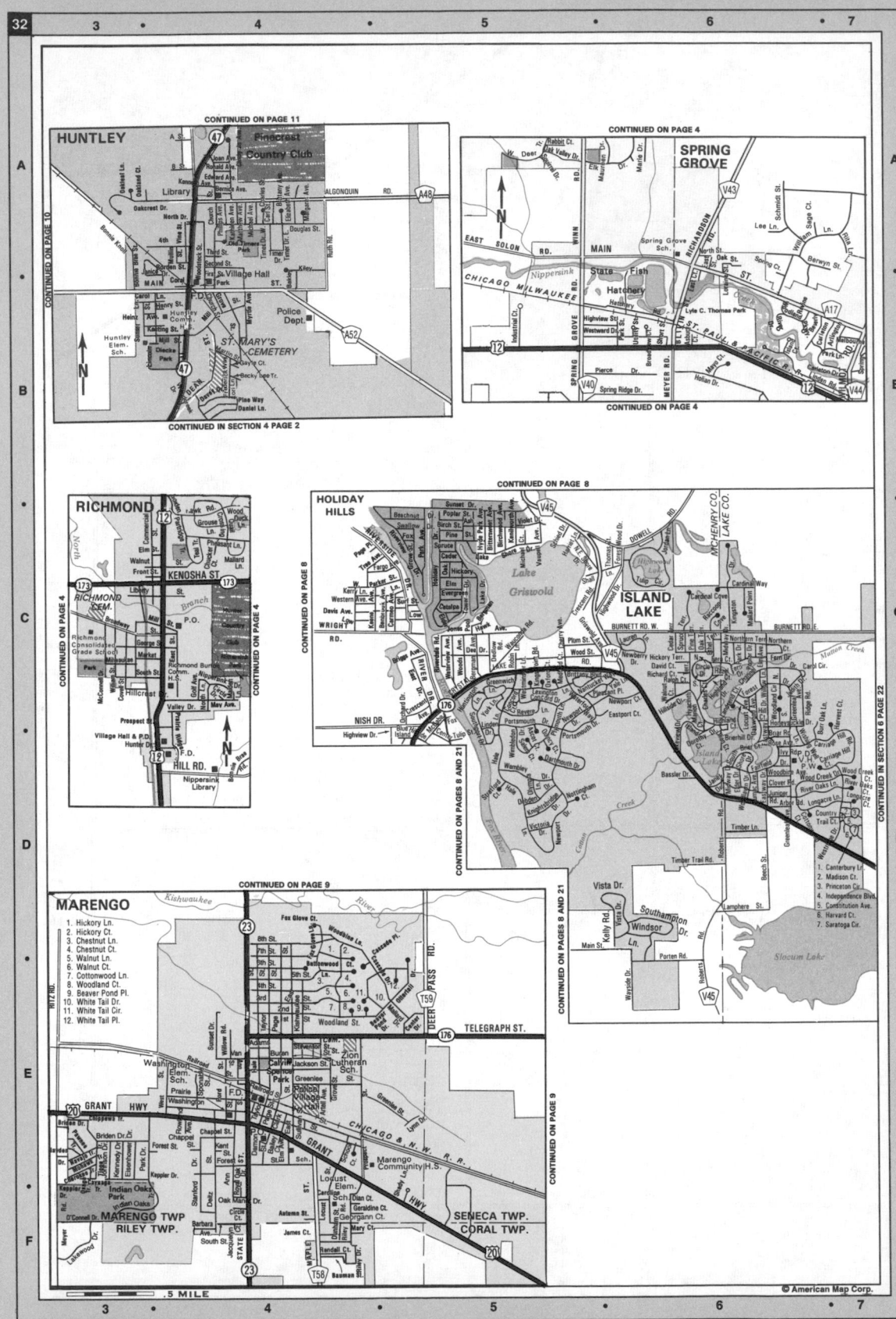

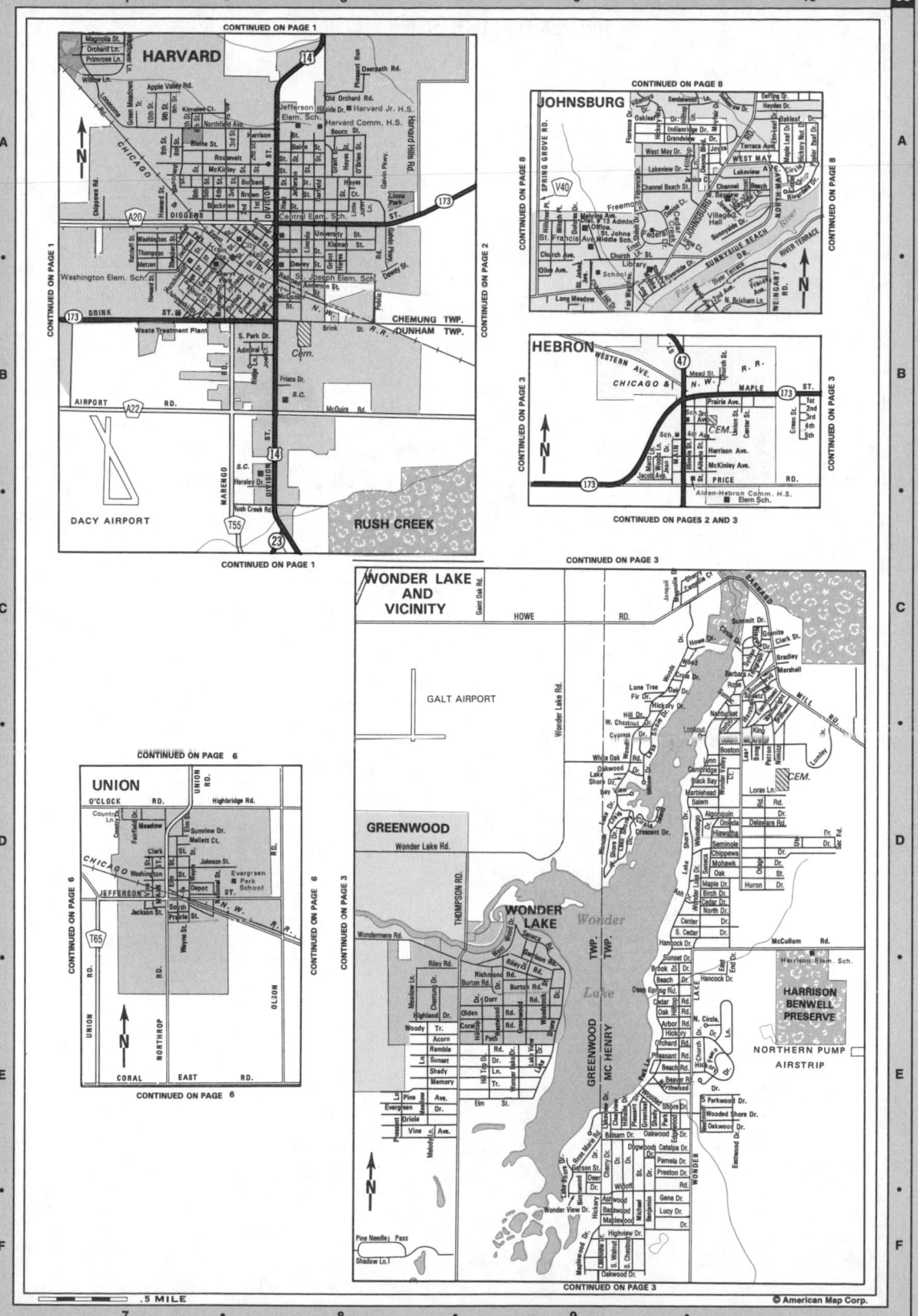

HARVARD

CONTINUED ON PAGE 1

Magnolia St.
Orchard Ln.
Primrose Ln.

Willow Ln.

Green Meadows
Tr.

Apple Valley Rd.

Old Orchard Rd.

Deerpath Rd.

Pleasant Run

Jefferson
Elem. Sch.

Harvard Jr. H.S.
Harvard Comm. H.S.
Bourn St.

Harrison

Roosevelt

McKinley

Burbank

Brown

Blackman

Central Elem. Sch.

CHICAGO

A20

Diggens

University St.
Kleiner St.

St. Joseph Elem. Sch.

Dewey St.

Anderson St.

Lions
Park

173

N.W.

Lincoln

Hall

McComb

CHEMUNG TWP.
DUNHAM TWP.

173 DRINK ST.

Waste Treatment Plant

Cem.

S. Park Dr.

Admiral Ct.

S.C.

Friace Dr.

AIRPORT RD.

McGuire Rd.

A22

S.C.

Hartley Dr.

Rush Creek Rd.

DACY AIRPORT

14

T55

23

MARENGO RD.

DIVISION ST.

RUSH CREEK

CONTINUED ON PAGE 1

CONTINUED ON PAGE 1

CONTINUED ON PAGE 2

JOHNSBURG

CONTINUED ON PAGE 8

SPRING GROVE RD.

V40

WEST MAY

Freemont

St. Francis
Ave.

St. Johns
Middle Sch.

Church Ave.
Olive Ave.

Long Meadow

Library

School

Fox River

SUNNYSIDE BEACH

WEINGART RD.

RIVER TERRACE

CONTINUED ON PAGE 8

CONTINUED ON PAGE 8

HEBRON

CONTINUED ON PAGE 3

WESTERN AVE.
CHICAGO &

47

Mead St.

Prairie Ave.

MAPLE

173 ST.

N.W.

CEM.

Harrison Ave.
McKinley Ave.

PRICE RD.

Alden-Hebron Comm. H.S.
Elem. Sch.

173

1st
2nd
3rd
4th
5th

CONTINUED ON PAGE 3

CONTINUED ON PAGES 2 AND 3

CONTINUED ON PAGE 3

WONDER LAKE
AND
VICINITY

GANT OAK Rd.

HOWE RD.

GALT AIRPORT

Wonder Lake Rd.

Lone Tree Dr.
Fir Dr.

W. Chestnut

Cypress Dr.

White Oak Rd.

Oakwood
Lake
Shore Dr.
Bay View

Summit Dr.

Granite
Clark St.

Bradley
Marshall

MILL RD.

CEM.

Loras Ln.

Cambridge Dr.
Black Bay
Marblehead
Salem

Algonquin
Omega
Hiawatha
Chippewa
Seminole
Mohawk
Oak

Ute

Delaware Rd.

Maple Dr.
Birch Dr.
Cedar Dr.
North Dr.

Center Dr.
S. Cedar

Hancock Dr.

McCullom Rd.

Harrison Elem. Sch.

HARRISON
BENWELL
PRESERVE

NORTHERN PUMP
AIRSTRIP

GREENWOOD

Wonder Lake Rd.

THOMPSON RD.

WONDER
LAKE

Wonder

Lake

GREENWOOD TWP.
MC HENRY TWP.

Wondermere Rd.

Riley Rd.

Richmond
Burton Rd.
Olden
Coral

Acorn
Ramble
Sunset
Shady
Memory

Pine Ave.
Oriole Dr.
Vine Ave.

Elm St.

Sunset Dr.
Brook Dr.
Beach
Deep Spring Rd.
Cedar Rd.
Oak Rd.
Arbor Rd.
Hickory
Pleasant Rd.
Beach Rd.
Beaver
Driftwood

S. Parkwood Dr.

Wooded Shore Dr.
Oakwood Dr.

Balsam Dr.
Dogwood
Catalpa Dr.
Pamela Dr.
Preston Dr.
Gene Dr.
Lucy Dr.

Highview Dr.

Pine Needle Pass
Shadow Ln.

Cherry Dr.
Deer Dr.

Ashwood
Basswood
Maplewood

Wonder View Dr.

UNION

O'CLOCK RD.

UNION RD.

Highbridge Rd.

Country
Ln.

Fairfield Dr.
Meadow

Sunview Dr.
Mallett Ct.

Clark

Johnson St.

Evergreen
Park School

Depot

Washington

Jefferson

Jackson St.

South
Prairie St.

Wayne St.

CHICAGO

N.W. R.R.

T65

UNION RD.

NORTHROP RD.

OLSON RD.

CORAL EAST RD.

CONTINUED ON PAGE 6

CONTINUED ON PAGE 6

CONTINUED ON PAGE 6

CONTINUED ON PAGE 6

CONTINUED ON PAGE 3

CONTINUED ON PAGE 3

.5 MILE

© American Map Corp.

# INDEX TO MCHENRY COUNTY

**ALDEN**
Page 2 .... B6

**ALDEN TOWNSHIP**
Pages 1,2
**STREETS**
Alden Rd. . . . . Pg.2 . . A5
Altenberg Rd. . Pg.2 . . C5
Bissell Rd. . . . Pg.2 . . A7
Charlotte Ct. . . Pg.2 . . B5
Crowley Rd. . . Pg.2 . . B4
Durkee Rd. . . . Pg.2 . . C6
Ferris Rd. . . . . Pg.2 . . B5
Fink Rd. . . . . . Pg.2 . . B7
French Dr. . . . Pg.2 . . B7
Gasch Rd. . . . Pg.2 . . A4
Green Rd. . . . . Pg.2 . . C5
Green Valley Dr. Pg.2 . . B7
Hebron Rd. . . . Pg.2 . . A5,6
Knickerbocker Rd.
. . . . . . . . . . . . Pg.2 . . A6
Manley Rd. . . . Pg.2 . . C7
Mansion Hts. Dr.
. . . . . . . . . . . . Pg.2 . . B7
Mansion Hts. Dr., S.
. . . . . . . . . . . . Pg.2 . . B7
Nichols Rd. . . . Pg.2 . . A6
Nolan St. . . . . Pg.2 . . B5
O'Brien Rd. . . . Pg.2 . . B6
Oak Grove Rd. . Pg.2 . . B5
Oak Springs Dr. Pg.2 . . B5
Reese Rd. . . . . Pg.2 . . B5
Righeimer Rd. . Pg.2 . . C4
Schultz Rd. . . . Pg.1 . . C4
Shields Rd. . . . Pg.2 . . C5
State Line Rd. . Pg.2 . . A5
Thayer Rd. . . . Pg.2 . . C6
Willow Lakes Ct.
. . . . . . . . . . . . Pg.1 . . B4
Willow Lakes Ln.
. . . . . . . . . . . . Pg.1 . . A4
Wright Rd. . . . Pg.2 . . B5

**FOREST PRESERVES**
Alden Sedge Meadow
. . . . . . . . . . . . Pg.2 . . B6

**SCHOOLS**
Schools . . . . . . Pg.2 . . A5,B6

**MISCELLANEOUS**
Landing Strip . Pg.2 . . B6

**ALGONQUIN**
Pages 11,12,24,25,28-30
(For additional listings,
see Sections 4 and 5)
**STREETS**
Aberdeen Dr. . Pg.29 . L11
Algonquin Cary Rd.
. . . . . . . . . . . . Pg.30 . L15
Algonquin Rd. . Pg.29 . L13
Alice Ln. . . . . . Pg.30 . N14
Amberwood Ct. Pg.29 . M11
Applewood Ln. . Pg.30 . M15
Armstrong St. . Pg.29 . L12
Arquilla Dr. . . . Pg.29 . L11
Arrowhead Dr. . Pg.29 . L13
Ash St. . . . . . . Pg.29 . L13
Ashburton Ct. . Pg.29 . N11
Aspen Dr. . . . . Pg.30 . M15
Ballard Dr. . . . . Pg.30 . M14
Barrington Ct. . Pg.29 . L11
Bayberry Dr. . . Pg.29 . L12
Beach Dr. . . . . Pg.29 . N12
Beachway Dr. . Pg.29 . L14
Bedford Ct. . . . Pg.28 . L10
Berg St. . . . . . . Pg.29 . L12
Big Sur Pkwy. . Pg.30 . M15
Birch St. . . . . . Pg.29 . L13
Blue Ridge Pkwy.
. . . . . . . . . . . . Pg.30 . M15
Blue Stem Ln. . Pg.28 . N14
Braewood Dr. . Pg.29 . N12
Brandywine Cir. Pg.29 . N11
Brentwood Dr. . Pg.29 . M12
Brian Ct. . . . . . Pg.29 . L11
Briarwood Ln. . Pg.29 . L11
Brindlewood Ct. Pg.28 . M10
Brindlewood Dr. Pg.28 . M10
Bristol Dr. . . . . Pg.29 . M12
Brixton Ct. . . . . Pg.27 . L6
Brook St. . . . . . Pg.29 . L14
Brookwood Cir. Pg.29 . L11
Buck Thorn Dr. Pg.30 . M16
Buckboard Dr. . Pg.28 . M8
Buckingham Dr. Pg.28 . L10
Bunker Hill Ct. . Pg.28 . M7
Bunker Hill Dr. . Pg.28 . M7
Butterfield Dr. . Pg.29 . M12
Camberwell Ct. Pg.27 . L6
Candlewood Ct. Pg.29 . L12
Cardiff Ct. . . . . Pg.28 . L10
Cardiff Dr. . . . . Pg.28 . L10
Cardinal Dr. . . . Pg.29 . M11
Carlington Ct. . Pg.28 . M11
Carlisle Ct. . . . . Pg.28 . N10
Carlisle St. . . . . Pg.28 . N10
Carriage Dr. . . . Pg.29 . M13
Cedarwood Ln. Pg.30 . M15
Center Dr. . . . . Pg.29 . M13

Center St. . . . . Pg.29 . M13
Cermak Rd. . . . Pg.30 . L14
Charminster Ct. Pg.27 . M6
Chase St. . . . . Pg.30 . N15
Chatham Cir. . . Pg.29 . M11
Chelsea Dr. . . . Pg.29 . L14
Cherokee Rd. . . Pg.29 . N13
Cherrywood Ct. Pg.29 . M11
Chestnut Ct. . . Pg.29 . M12
Circle Dr. . . . . . Pg.29 . M13
Clay St. . . . . . . Pg.29 . M13
Claymont Ct. . . Pg.30 . M15
Clearview Ct. . . Pg.29 . L12
Clemantis Dr. . Pg.29 . M15
Clematis Dr. . . Pg.29 . M7
Clover Ct. . . . . Pg.28 . L7
Cloverdale Ct. . Pg.29 . N10
Colonial Ct. . . . Pg.29 . N13
Concord Ct. . . . Pg.29 . M12
Copel St. . . . . . Pg.29 . M12
Cornell Ln. . . . . Pg.29 . L14
Country Ln. . . . Pg.29 . L14
Countryside Dr. Pg.30 . M14
County Line Rd. Pg.30 . M14
Crab Tree Dr. . . Pg.30 . M16
Crestwood Ct. . Pg.29 . N12
Crofton St. . . . . Pg.29 . M18
Cross St. . . . . . Pg.29 . M13
Cumberland Pkwy.
. . . . . . . . . . . . Pg.30 . M15
Dawson Ln. . . . Pg.28 . M10
Deerpath Rd. . . Pg.28 . K15
Dellwood Ct. . . Pg.28 . N10
Division St. . . . Pg.29 . M13
Dover Ct. . . . . . Pg.29 . L11
Dowdle St. . . . . Pg.29 . L12
Dryden Ct. . . . . Pg.29 . N11
Eagle Ridge Ln. Pg.29 . M12
Eastgate Dr. . . Pg.29 . L14
Echo Woods Dr.
. . . . . . . . . . . . Pg.29 . L14
Edgewood Ave. Pg.30 . K15
Edgewood Ct. . Pg.29 . N12
Edgewood Dr. . Pg.29 . N12
Edward St. . . . . Pg.29 . L13
Elm St. . . . . . . Pg.29 . L13
Essex St. . . . . . Pg.29 . M8
Evergreen Ct. . Pg.29 . M12
Fairfield Ln. . . . Pg.29 . M11
Fairmont Ct. . . Pg.29 . M11
Fairway View Dr.
. . . . . . . . . . . . Pg.28 . M8
Falcon Ridge Ct.
. . . . . . . . . . . . Pg.29 . L10
Farmhill Ct. . . . Pg.29 . L11
Farmhill Dr. . . . Pg.29 . L11
Fenview Ct. . . . Pg.28 . M8
Fieldcrest Ct. . . Pg.29 . L11
Fieldcrest Dr. . . Pg.29 . L11
Flora Dr. . . . . . Pg.29 . M11
Forest Dr. . . . . Pg.29 . M12
Fox Glove Dr. . . Pg.28 . M7
Fox River Dr. . . Pg.29 . M13
Fox Run Ln. . . . Pg.30 . M15
Front St. . . . . . Pg.29 . M13
Gaslight Dr. . . . Pg.29 . N11
Georgetown Cir.
. . . . . . . . . . . . Pg.27 . M6
Gerlinger Rd. . . Pg.30 . K14
Getzleman Tr. . Pg.30 . L14
Gillingham Ct. . Pg.27 . L6
Glacier Ct. . . . . Pg.30 . M16
Glacier Pkwy. . Pg.30 . M16
Glen Oaks Ct. . Pg.29 . M11
Glengarry Ct. . . Pg.29 . M11
Glenwood Ct. . Pg.29 . L11
Goldenrod Dr. . Pg.28 . M7
Golf Ln. . . . . . . Pg.30 . L15
Grandview Ct. . Pg.29 . L12
Greens View Dr. Pg.28 . L13
Hackberry Ln. . Pg.30 . M16
Haegers Bend Rd.
. . . . . . . . . . . . Pg.30 . N16
Hanson Rd. . . . Pg.29 . M10
Harnish Dr. . . . Pg.29 . M11
Harper Ct. . . . . Pg.29 . M12
Harper Dr. . . . . Pg.29 . M12
Harrison St. . . . Pg.29 . M13
Hartford Ct. . . . Pg.28 . L10
Hartley Dr. . . . . Pg.29 . M11
Harvest Run Dr. Pg.28 . M8
Hayes Rd. . . . . Pg.29 . N13
Heather Dr. . . . Pg.30 . L15
Helen Dr. . . . . . Pg.30 . N14
Hickory Ln. . . . Pg.30 . N14
Highland Ave. . Pg.29 . M11
Highland Dr. . . Pg.30 . M10
Hillcrest Dr. . . . Pg.29 . L13
Hillside Dr. . . . . Pg.29 . L11
Hillside View . . Pg.29 . N13
Hithergreen Ct. Pg.27 . L6
Holly Ln. . . . . . Pg.29 . L12
Homestead Ct. Pg.29 . M13
Honey Locust Dr.
. . . . . . . . . . . . Pg.30 . M15
Hubbard St. . . . Pg.29 . M13
Huntington Ct. . Pg.28 . L10
Huntington Dr. . Pg.28 . L10
Indian Trail . . . Pg.29 . L14
Interloch Ct. . . Pg.29 . N11

Ionia Tr. . . . . . Pg.30 . K15
Ivy Ln. . . . . . . . Pg.30 . K16
Jackson St. . . . Pg.29 . M13
James Ct. . . . . Pg.29 . M13
Jayne St. . . . . . Pg.29 . M13
Jefferson St. . . Pg.29 . M13
Jennifer Ct. . . . Pg.30 . N14
Jester Ln. . . . . Pg.29 . L10
Jupiter Cir. . . . . Pg.29 . M12
Kensington Dr. Pg.29 . N11
Kingsbury Ct. . Pg.30 . M15
Klasen Rd. . . . Pg.30 . J14
La Fox River Dr.
. . . . . . . . . . . . Pg.29 . M13
LaCrosse St. . . Pg.29 . M13
Lake Dr. E. . . . Pg.29 . L11
Lake Dr., S. . . . Pg.29 . L10
Lakeview Dr. . . Pg.28 . M7
Legion Dr. . . . . Pg.30 . L14
Lehman Ave. . . Pg.30 . L14
Leigh Ct. . . . . . Pg.30 . L15
Lexington Ave. Pg.29 . M11
Lilac Dr. . . . . . . Pg.29 . M13
Lincoln St. . . . . Pg.29 . M13
Longview Rd. . . Pg.30 . M14
Longwood Ct. . Pg.30 . M14
Longwood Dr. . Pg.30 . M14
Lowe Dr. . . . . . Pg.29 . L15
Madison St. . . . Pg.29 . M13
Magnolia Dr. . . Pg.30 . M16
Main St. . . . . . . Pg.29 . M13
Majestic Ct. . . . Pg.30 . M15
Maplewood Ln. Pg.30 . M14
Mayfair Ln. . . . Pg.29 . M11
Meadow Dr. . . . Pg.29 . N12
Melvina Ct. . . . Pg.30 . L15
Merrill Dr. . . . . Pg.29 . M11
Millcreek Ln. . . Pg.28 . M10
Mohawk St. . . . Pg.29 . L14
Mound St. . . . . Pg.29 . L13
Mulberry St. . . Pg.29 . M12
Oak Ln. . . . . . . Pg.29 . L13
Oak St. . . . . . . Pg.29 . L13
Oakleaf Ct. . . . Pg.28 . L10
Oakleaf Dr. . . . Pg.28 . L10
Oakleaf Rd. . . . Pg.28 . L10
Oakview Dr. . . . Pg.29 . M12
Oceola Dr. . . . . Pg.29 . N13
Old Mill Ln. . . . Pg.30 . M15
Old Oak Cir. . . Pg.29 . M14
Olin Ct. . . . . . . Pg.29 . L14
Orchard Ct. . . . Pg.29 . M12
Oxford Ct. . . . . Pg.30 . M14
Ozark Pkwy. . . Pg.29 . N15
Par Dr. . . . . . . Pg.28 . M7
Park St. . . . . . . Pg.29 . M13
Parkview Terr. . Pg.28 . M8
Parkwood Ct. . Pg.29 . L11
Parkwood Dr. . Pg.29 . M11
Partridge Ct. . . Pg.29 . L11
Peach Tree Ct. Pg.28 . N10
Peach Tree Ln. Pg.28 . N10
Peachtree Ct. . Pg.28 . N10
Perry Dr. . . . . . Pg.29 . N13
Persimmon Dr. Pg.30 . M15
Perwinkle Dr. . Pg.30 . M16
Philip Dr. . . . . . Pg.29 . N13
Pickwick Ct. . . Pg.30 . M14
Pine St. . . . . . . Pg.29 . L13
Pioneer Rd. . . . Pg.29 . L14
Pleasant View Dr.
. . . . . . . . . . . . Pg.29 . L14
Plymouth Ct. . . Pg.29 . M13
Point Ct. . . . . . Pg.29 . M14
Portsmith Ct. . . Pg.28 . L10
Powder Horn Dr.
. . . . . . . . . . . . Pg.28 . M8
Prairie Dr. . . . . Pg.30 . M15
Preston Ct. . . . Pg.29 . L11
Preston St. . . . Pg.29 . L11
Prestwick Blvd. Pg.28 . L7
Providence Dr. . Pg.29 . M14
Quayside Ct. . . Pg.27 . M6
Queensbury Ct. Pg.28 . L7
Randall Rd. . . . Pg.29 . M11
Rattray Dr. . . . . Pg.29 . N13
Red Coach Ln. Pg.28 . M8
Redwood Dr. . . Pg.30 . M16
Reedsworth Ct. Pg.27 . M6
Regal Ct. . . . . . Pg.29 . M10
Regal Ln. . . . . . Pg.29 . M10
Ridge St. . . . . . Pg.29 . M13
River Dr. . . . . . Pg.29 . M13
Riverview Dr. . . Pg.30 . L15
Riverwood Dr. . Pg.30 . N14
Riverwood Ln. . Pg.30 . N14
Roaring Brook Ln.
. . . . . . . . . . . . Pg.29 . M11
Robinwood Dr. Pg.28 . L10
Rochester Ct. . Pg.28 . L10
Rolls Dr. . . . . . Pg.29 . N13
Ryan Pkwy. . . . Pg.30 . M15
Saddlebrook Cir.
. . . . . . . . . . . . Pg.30 . M15
Salford Ct. . . . Pg.29 . L10
Salford Dr. . . . . Pg.28 . L10
Sandbloom Rd. Pg.30 . N14
Sandpebble Ct.
. . . . . . . . . . . . Pg.29 . M11
Sandpiper Ct. . Pg.29 . M11
Saratoga Cir. . . Pg.28 . M8

Savwanas Tr. . Pg.30 . N14
Sawmill Ln. . . . Pg.28 . M10
Scenic Dr. . . . . Pg.29 . M13
Schuett St. . . . Pg.29 . M13
Scott St. . . . . . Pg.29 . N13
Seminole Rd. . . Pg.30 . K15
Shagbark Ct. . . Pg.30 . M12
Sherman Rd. . . Pg.28 . M9
Short Pl. . . . . . Pg.29 . L14
Skyline Dr. . . . . Pg.29 . M12
Sleepy Hollow Rd.
. . . . . . . . . . . . Pg.29 . N11
Somerset Ct. . . Pg.29 . L11
Sound Rd. . . . . Pg.30 . N15
South Dr. . . . . . Pg.30 . M13
Southwick Dr. . Pg.29 . N13
Springhill Dr. . . Pg.29 . N12
Square Barn Rd.
. . . . . . . . . . . . Pg.30 . M7
St. Andrews St. Pg.29 . N11
St. Route 31 . . Pg.29 . M13
St. Route 62 . . Pg.29 . M13
Starr Dr. . . . . . Pg.30 . L15
Steven Ct. . . . . Pg.29 . N13
Stonegate Rd. . Pg.28 . L10
Stoneybrook Ct.
. . . . . . . . . . . . Pg.29 . L12
Stratford Ln. . . Pg.30 . N14
Summerdale Ln.
. . . . . . . . . . . . Pg.28 . L7
Summit St. . . . Pg.29 . M13
Sunny Dr. . . . . Pg.29 . M13
Sunrise Ln. . . . Pg.30 . N14
Sunset Ln. . . . . Pg.30 . N14
Sunshine Ct. . . Pg.29 . N13
Surrey Ct. . . . . Pg.29 . N11
Surrey Ln. . . . . Pg.29 . N11
Susan Ct. . . . . Pg.30 . N14
Sussex Ave. . . Pg.29 . L10
Sutcliff Ct. . . . . Pg.29 . N13
Tahoe Pkwy. . . Pg.30 . M15
Tallgrass Ct. . . Pg.30 . M15
Tamarack Dr. . Pg.30 . N14
Tanglewood Dr. Pg.30 . L15
Tanglewood Dr. Pg.30 . N14
Tenby Way . . . Pg.28 . L7
Terrace Dr. . . . Pg.29 . M11
Teton Pkwy. . . Pg.30 . N16
Thornwood Ln. Pg.30 . M15
Timberwood Ln.
. . . . . . . . . . . . Pg.30 . M15
Tiverton Ct. . . . Pg.27 . L6
Tregonwell Ct. . Pg.27 . M6
Turnbridge Ln. . Pg.28 . N10
Turnbridge Tr. . Pg.28 . N10
Twickenham Ct.
. . . . . . . . . . . . Pg.27 . L6
Twisted Oak Ct. Pg.29 . M12
Valley View Ct. Pg.29 . L13
Victoria Ct. . . . Pg.29 . M7
Vista Dr. . . . . . Pg.29 . N14
Walbridge Ct. . Pg.28 . L7
Walnut Ln. . . . . Pg.30 . N14
Washington St. Pg.29 . M13
Washtenaw Ln. Pg.29 . N14
Water St. . . . . . Pg.29 . L13
Waverly Dr. . . . Pg.29 . L14
Webster Dr. . . . Pg.29 . L14
Webster St. . . . Pg.29 . L14
Wesley Ln. . . . Pg.30 . M15
Westbury Dr. . . Pg.29 . M11
Westend Dr. . . Pg.29 . M12
White Oak Ct. . Pg.29 . N10
White Oak Dr. . Pg.28 . N10
White Oak St. . Pg.28 . N10
Whitehall Ct. . . Pg.27 . L6
Whitehall Dr. . . Pg.27 . L6
Whitehall St. . . Pg.27 . L7
Wilbrandt St. . . Pg.29 . M13
Wildwood Rd. . Pg.30 . L14
Willow Ln. . . . . Pg.29 . L14
Willow St. . . . . Pg.29 . M13
Winchester Dr. Pg.28 . L10
Windsor Ct. . . . Pg.28 . L10
Windy Knoll Dr. Pg.28 . M7
Wintergreen Ct. Pg.28 . M7
Wintergreen Terr.
. . . . . . . . . . . . Pg.28 . M7
Wood Dr. . . . . . Pg.29 . L14
Woods Creek Ct.
. . . . . . . . . . . . Pg.28 . M8
Woods Creek Ln.
. . . . . . . . . . . . Pg.28 . M8
Woodview Ln. . Pg.30 . M14
Yellowstone Pkwy.
. . . . . . . . . . . . Pg.30 . N16
Yorktown Dr. . . Pg.29 . M12
Yosemite Pkwy.
. . . . . . . . . . . . Pg.30 . N16
Zange Dr. . . . . Pg.29 . M11

**CEMETERIES**
Algonquin Cemetery
. . . . . . . . . . . . Pg.29 . L14

**GOLF COURSES**
Golf Club of Illinois
. . . . . . . . . . . . Pg.11,29
. . . . . . . . . . . . M,N11
Terrace Hill Golf Course
. . . . . . . . . . . . Pg.11,28
. . . . . . . . . . . . L7,M10

**PARKS**

Braewood Park Pg.29 . N12
Community Park
. . . . . . . . . . . . Pg.28 . M8
Falcon Ridge Park
. . . . . . . . . . . . Pg.29 . L10
Gaslight Park . . Pg.29 . M11
High Hill Park . Pg.29 . M11
Holder Park . . . Pg.30 . M15
James B. Wood Park
. . . . . . . . . . . . Pg.28 . M7
Jaycees Field Park
. . . . . . . . . . . . Pg.29 . L11
Pioneer Park . . Pg.30 . L14
Presidential Park
. . . . . . . . . . . . Pg.29 . L11
Riverfront Park Pg.29 . M13
Snapper Field Park
. . . . . . . . . . . . Pg.30 . N14
Stoneybrook Park
. . . . . . . . . . . . Pg.29 . L12
Towne Park . . . Pg.29 . L13
Turnbridge Park
. . . . . . . . . . . . Pg.28 . N10
Yellowstone Park
. . . . . . . . . . . . Pg.30 . N16

**SCHOOLS**
Algonquin Middle Sch.
. . . . . . . . . . . . Pg.29 . N14
Eastview Elem. Sch.
. . . . . . . . . . . . Pg.29 . L14
Fairview Ave. . . Pg.30 . J17
Jacobs H.S. . . . Pg.28 . M9
Nubert Elem. Sch.
. . . . . . . . . . . . Pg.29 . L12
St. John's Lutheran Sch.
. . . . . . . . . . . . Pg.29 . M13
St. Margaret Mary Sch.
. . . . . . . . . . . . Pg.29 . M13

**SHOPPING CENTERS**
Algonquin Town Center
. . . . . . . . . . . . Pg.30 . K15
Eagle Country Market
  Center . . . . . . Pg.28 . L9
River Pointe S.C.
. . . . . . . . . . . . Pg.28 . L9

**MISCELLANEOUS**
Fire Department
. . . . . . . . . . . . Pg.29 . L13
Library . . . . . . . Pg.29 . L14
McHenry Co. Prairie Trail
. . . . . . . . . . . . Pg.29 . M13
Police Department
. . . . . . . . . . . . Pg.29 . L13
Post Office . . . . Pg.29 . L13
Public Works . . Pg.30 . N16
Railroad Station
. . . . . . . . . . . . Pg.29 . M13
Sherman Family Health
  Care . . . . . . . Pg.28 . M9
Village Hall . . . Pg.29 . L13
Village Hall (future site)
. . . . . . . . . . . . Pg.28 . L10

**ALGONQUIN TOWNSHIP**
Pages 11,12,18-21,
23-26,28-31
**STREETS**
Acron St. . . . . . Pg.20 . D17
Algonquin Rd. . Pg.30 . J17
Allen Rd. . . . . . Pg.30 . K15
Althea Dr. . . . . Pg.30 . K16
Amanda Ln. . . . Pg.30 . J17
Amy Dr. . . . . . . Pg.19 . D13
Balder . . . . . . . Pg.26 . H21
Balder St. . . . . Pg.26 . H21
Bayport Ln. . . . Pg.26 . H21
Beach Dr. . . . . Pg.30 . J17
Belson Ln. . . . . Pg.20 . E14
Bioner Pkwy. . . Pg.26 . J18
Birch St. . . . . . Pg.24 . G13
Blackhawk Dr. . Pg.30 . K15
Blarney Stone Ln.
. . . . . . . . . . . . Pg.20 . E16
Bloner Pkwy. . . Pg.31 . J19
Blue Ct., S. . . . Pg.20 . D15
Bluff Rd. . . . . . Pg.20 . D17
Bluff Tr. . . . . . . Pg.26 . K15
Braeburn Rd. . . Pg.31 . K18
Bridge Ln. . . . . Pg.26 . F20
Bridle Ln. . . . . . Pg.26 . F20
Brighton Ln. . . . Pg.29 . N12
Brisbane Dr. . . Pg.20 . G21
Burman Dr. . . . Pg.19 . D13
Byrne Dr. . . . . . Pg.30 . J18
Captain's Dr. . . Pg.30 . J16
Cardinal Dr. . . . Pg.29 . N12
Carrie Ct. . . . . Pg.20 . E15
Center Ct. . . . . Pg.26 . H21
Cermak Dr. . . . Pg.30 . K14
Channel Dr. . . . Pg.30 . J17
Chapel Rd. . . . Pg.30 . K17
Chestnut Ln. . . Pg.20 . H20
Church Hill Ln. . Pg.26 . F20
Claire St. . . . . . Pg.24 . G13
Clarice Ln. . . . . Pg.30 . J17
Cogs Cir. . . . . . Pg.19 . F13
Congress Pkwy.
. . . . . . . . . . . . Pg.19 . F12
Cougar Tr. . . . . Pg.20 . F19

Country Ln. . . . Pg.26 . F21
County Line Rd. Pg.28 . N9
Cove Dr. . . . . . Pg.21 . F20
Cowlin St. . . . . Pg.24 . F13
Craig St. . . . . . Pg.29 . L12
Creek Ln. . . . . Pg.20 . E17
Crescent Pkwy. Pg.31 . J18
Crestview Dr. . . Pg.31 . J18
Crystal Lake Ave.
. . . . . . . . . . . . Pg.20 . D15
Crystal Lake Rd.
. . . . . . . . . . . . Pg.21 . F20
Crystal St. . . . . Pg.31 . J18
Cupola Ct. . . . . Pg.26 . F20
Daniel Dr. . . . . Pg.19 . E13
David Ln. . . . . . Pg.19 . D14
Deerpath Rd. . . Pg.30 . K15
Del Miller Ln. . . Pg.26 . D19
Dennis Ave. . . Pg.29 . L12
Devonshire Rd. Pg.20 . N11
Dove Way . . . . Pg.26 . F19
Doyle Rd. . . . . Pg.26 . J20
Drive-in Ln. . . . Pg.24 . F13
Dublin Dr. . . . . Pg.30 . K15
Dublin Dr. . . . . Pg.20 . E17
Edwards Rd. . . Pg.30 . J17
Elk Tr. . . . . . . . Pg.20 . F19
Elmwood Ct. . . Pg.29 . K14
Ethel Ave. . . . . Pg.29 . L12
Evergreen Ave. Pg.30 . J17
Fairview Ave. . . Pg.30 . J17
Federal Dr. . . . Pg.19 . F12
First Ave. . . . . . Pg.29 . J14
First St. . . . . . . Pg.30 . J16
Fox Shore Dr. . Pg.30 . J16
Fox St. . . . . . . Pg.26 . H21
Gage Ln. . . . . . Pg.26 . H21
Gallek Rd. . . . . Pg.30 . J17
Gardener Ave. . Pg.26 . I21
Geringer Rd. . . Pg.30 . K14
Grand Dr. . . . . Pg.26 . H21
Green Ln. . . . . Pg.20 . D17
Green Meadow Ln.
. . . . . . . . . . . . Pg.20 . E16
Green Pastures Dr.
. . . . . . . . . . . . Pg.29 . N12
Greenwood Dr. Pg.29 . L12
Grove Lane . . . Pg.25 . J16
Haegers Bend Rd.
. . . . . . . . . . . . Pg.30 . J16
Hanson Rd. . . . Pg.29 . N12
Hawthorne Dr. . Pg.30 . K15
Hayes Rd. . . . . Pg.29 . N12
Heather Dr. . . . Pg.30 . K15
Hemlock St. . . Pg.24 . G13
Hickory Nut Grove Rd.
. . . . . . . . . . . . Pg.21 . E20
Highland Ave. . Pg.30 . L15
Highland Dr. . . Pg.24 . G14
Hillary Ln. . . . . Pg.21 . E19
Hillcrest Ave. . . Pg.30 . J17
Hillcrest Rd. . . Pg.24 . G13
Hilltop Dr. . . . . Pg.31 . J18
Hilltop Ln. . . . . Pg.31 . J18
Hillview Dr. . . . Pg.31 . J18
Hilly Way . . . . . Pg.20 . E17
Holly Lynn Dr. . Pg.26 . F21
Horseshoe Dr. . Pg.26 . F20
Hunters Path . . Pg.26 . E17
Ida Dr. . . . . . . . Pg.20 . E17
Iroquois Dr. . . . Pg.29 . N13
Isabel Ave. . . . Pg.30 . K15
Jefferson St. . . Pg.23 . J10
Joan Ct. . . . . . Pg.29 . J12
John St. . . . . . . Pg.19 . D12
Kenilworth Ave. Pg.30 . K14
Kenneth Dr. . . . Pg.30 . N14
Kent St. . . . . . . Pg.19 . D13
Killarney Dr. . . Pg.20 . E16
Killkenny Ct. . . Pg.20 . D15
Killkenny Dr. . . Pg.20 . D15
Kingsbridge Dr. Pg.21 . E19
Kingston Pl. . . . Pg.29 . M11
Klasen Rd. . . . Pg.30 . J15
Lagoon Dr. . . . Pg.30 . J17
Lake Shore Dr. Pg.20 . D17
Lakewood Dr. . Pg.20 . E14
Laurie Ct. . . . . Pg.19 . F14
Laurie Ln. . . . . Pg.19 . F14
Leah Dr. . . . . . Pg.31 . J17
Libuse Rd. . . . . Pg.30 . J17
Limerick Dr. . . . Pg.20 . E16
Lincoln Creek Dr.
. . . . . . . . . . . . Pg.31 . J18
Linden Ave. . . . Pg.30 . K14
Lindsay Ln. . . . Pg.20 . E15
Londonary Dr. . Pg.20 . E16
Longview Rd. . . Pg.30 . N15
Lorden Ct. . . . . Pg.26 . K19
Lovers Ln. . . . . Pg.26 . H20
Lund Ave. . . . . Pg.30 . K14
Machelle Dr. . . Pg.26 . F21
Main St. . . . . . . Pg.26 . I20
Main St. E. . . . Pg.26 . H20
Mallard Ln. . . . Pg.20 . F18
Manor St. . . . . Pg.24,30
. . . . . . . . . . . . G13,J16
Marie Ave. . . . Pg.29 . L12
May Ave. . . . . . Pg.30 . K14
McKinley St. . . Pg.26 . I21

Meadow Lane . Pg.26 . F21
Meandering Way
. . . . . . . . . . . . Pg.20 . E14
Middle Ln. . . . . Pg.20 . D17
Mink Tr. . . . . . . Pg.20 . F19
Mockingbird Ln.
. . . . . . . . . . . . Pg.20 . E14
Mohican Dr. . . Pg.29 . N13
Monticello Way Pg.25 . G14
Nancy Dr. . . . . Pg.19 . E14
Navajo St. . . . . Pg.29 . N13
Nevin Ave. . . . Pg.29 . L12
Newbald Rd. . . Pg.26 . G20
Nighthawk Way Pg.20 . F19
North Ln. . . . . . Pg.20 . D17
North Rd. . . . . Pg.31 . J21
Northwest Hwy.
. . . . . . . . . . . . Pg.19 . F13
Oak Dr. . . . . . . Pg.26 . D17
Oak Hill Rd. . . . Pg.26 . G20
Oak St. . . . . . . Pg.30 . K15
Oak St. . . . . . . Pg.25 . J16
Oak St. . . . . . . Pg.20,25
. . . . . . . . . . . . H20,J16
Oakwood Ct. . . Pg.29 . K14
Oakwood Terr. . Pg.26 . E17
Old Post Rd. . . Pg.25 . G14
Olw Way . . . . . Pg.20 . F18
Otter Tr. . . . . . Pg.20 . E17
Park Ave. . . . . Pg.26,30
. . . . . . . . . . . . J17,20
Park Pl. . . . . . . Pg.30 . K14
Park St. . . . . . . Pg.26 . J20
Park Way . . . . Pg.26,30
. . . . . . . . . . . . H20,J17
Pheasant Tr. . . Pg.26 . E17
Pingree Rd. . . . Pg.19 . F13
Pleasant View Ln.
. . . . . . . . . . . . Pg.20 . D17
Plumtree Rd. . . Pg.31 . J17
Powers St. . . . Pg.26 . H19
Pyott Rd. . . . . . Pg.24 . F13
Ramble Rd. . . . Pg.20 . E17
Randall Rd. . . . Pg.28 . N9
Rawson Bridge Rd.
. . . . . . . . . . . . Pg.29 . N12
Rawson Bridge Rd., S.
. . . . . . . . . . . . Pg.26 . F19
Rawson Bridge Rd., W.
. . . . . . . . . . . . Pg.20 . E17
Raymond Dr. . . Pg.24 . G14
Red Bark Ln. . . Pg.26 . H21
Redwood St. . . Pg.24 . G13
Richard Dr. . . . Pg.19 . E13
Ridge Ave. . . . Pg.30 . J17
Ridge Dr. . . . . Pg.20 . D17
Ridge Rd. . . . . Pg.31 . N21
River Rd. . . . . . Pg.25 . J17
River St. . . . . . Pg.26 . I21
River Way . . . . Pg.30 . J17
Riverview Ave. Pg.30 . J17
Riverview Dr. . . Pg.20 . D17
Robert Rd. . . . Pg.20 . D17
Robin Ln. . . . . Pg.19 . D14
Roger St. . . . . Pg.29 . L12
Roland Dr. . . . Pg.26 . I21
Rona Dr. . . . . . Pg.26 . F20
Ronald Ln. . . . Pg.19 . D14
Roosevelt Rd. . Pg.23 . I10
Rosamarie Ln. Pg.29 . L12
Rose St. . . . . . Pg.24 . F13
Russel St. . . . . Pg.30 . H21
Saddle Oaks Dr. Pg.26 . F20
Sagger Ln. . . . Pg.26 . G13
Sandbloom Rd. Pg.30 . N14
Sands Rd. . . . . Pg.19 . F14
Sauwanas Tr. . Pg.30 . N14
Scott Ct. . . . . . Pg.19 . L12
Scotty Ave. . . . Pg.29 . L12
Second Ave. . . Pg.29 . J14
Shales St. . . . . Pg.24 . F13
Shannon Dr. . . Pg.20 . E17
Silver Lakes Rd.
. . . . . . . . . . . . Pg.20 . D17
Smitana Rd. . . Pg.25 . F14
Smith Rd. . . . . Pg.20 . D14
Sorrell Ter. . . . Pg.20 . E14
South Dr. . . . . Pg.29 . N12
South Ln. . . . . Pg.20 . E17
South Rd. . . . . Pg.31 . J17
Spring Beach Way
. . . . . . . . . . . . Pg.26 . H20
Spring Creek Rd.
. . . . . . . . . . . . Pg.31 . L20
Squirrel Tr. . . . Pg.20 . F18
St. Route 22 . . Pg.26 . J21
St. Route 31 . . Pg.19 . E13
St. Route 62 . . Pg.30 . N15
Stag Tr. . . . . . . Pg.20 . F18
State St. . . . . . Pg.26 . I20
Steeple Run . . Pg.20 . E14
Sun Valley Dr. . Pg.20 . E16
Swallow Way . . Pg.20 . F18
Swan Way . . . . Pg.20 . E17
Sweitzer Rd. . . Pg.25 . K14
Third Ave. . . . . Pg.29 . J14
Third Bench . . Pg.20 . H20
Thistle Ct. . . . . Pg.21 . E20
Thomas St. . . . Pg.19 . D12
Three Oaks Rd. Pg.26 . G14

**ALGONQUIN TOWNSHIP**

Topview Rd. .... Pg.20 . E17
Tower Dr. .... Pg.31 . J18
Tower Ln. .... Pg.26 . H19
Trumbull Cir. . Pg.19 . E14
Tuxedo Ln. ... Pg.21 . D20
US Route 14 . Pg.19 . F13
Valerie Dr. ... Pg.19 . E13
Valley Rd. .... Pg.25 . I16
Victor Pl. .... Pg.30 . K14
Virginia St. ... Pg.24 . H12
Wallace Dr. .. Pg.26 . H21
Wallens Dr. .. Pg.19 . E13
Walnut Dr. ... Pg.20 . E17
Wildberry Ln. . Pg.21 . E20
Willy Ave. .... Pg.29 . L12
Wilmette Ave. Pg.29 . K14
Witche Dr. ... Pg.31 . J18
Wium Ave .... Pg.20 . H21
Wolf Rd. ..... Pg.31 . J18
Wonder Way .. Pg.20 . E17
Woodland Rd. Pg.20 . D17
Woodlawn .... Pg.26 . J20
Woods Dr. ... Pg.20 . J17
Wynwood Dr .. Pg.20
.............. D15,E14
Zimmer Dr. ... Pg.30 . K16
Zimmer Rd. ... Pg.30 . J16
1st Bench ... Pg.20 . H20
2nd Bench ... Pg.20 . H20

**AIRPORTS**
Lake in the Hills Airport
.............. Pg.24 . H11

**CEMETERIES**
Wind Ridge Cemetery
.............. Pg.26 . F20

**FOREST PRESERVES**
Hickory Grove Preserve
.............. Pg.26 . E20
Lions Prairie Marsh Natural
  Preserve .... Pg.26 . H19
McHenry Co. Prairie Trail S.
.............. Pg.24 . L11
Oakwood Hills Fen
.............. Pg.12,21
The Hollows Preserve
.............. C18,J13
.............. Pg.25 . F15

**GOLF COURSES**
Cary C.C. .... Pg.25 . I17

**PARKS**
Lapins Park ... Pg.19 . E14
Park ......... Pg.21,25
.............. F19,J16
Wynwood Park Pg.20 . E14

**SHOPPING CENTERS**
Car Care Center Plaza
.............. Pg.19 . F14

**MISCELLANEOUS**
Crystal Lake Theater
.............. Pg.24 F13
McHenry County Prairie
  Trail ....... Pg.29 . N13
Oakwood Estates Mobile
  Home Park .. Pg.25 . F14
Y.M.C.A. ..... Pg.25 . F13

**BARRINGTON HILLS**
Page 12,30,31
(Portions within Lake, Cook
& Kane Counties, for
additional listings,
see Sections 4, 5 and 6)

**STREETS**
Alderberry Ln. . Pg.31 . K18
Algonquin Rd. . Pg.30 . J17
Asbury Ave. .. Pg.31 . J20
Ascot Ln. .... Pg.31 . L19
Ashbury Ln. .. Pg.31 . N18
Auburn Ln. ... Pg.30 . M16
Barrington .... Pg.30 . N17
Bourne ....... Pg.30 . N17
Bow Ln. ...... Pg.31 . M19
Braeburn Ln. . Pg.31 . M18
Braeburn Rd. . Pg.31 . K18
Burning Oaks Tr.
.............. Pg.31 . K18
Chapel Ln. ... Pg.30 . L17
Church Rd. ... Pg.31 . K18
Country Oaks Dr.
.............. Pg.31 . N18
Country Oaks Ln.
.............. Pg.31 . M18
County Line Rd.
.............. Pg.31 . N20
Cross Timber Rd.
.............. Pg.31 . L19
Fox Hunt Ln. . Pg.31 . N19
Front St. ..... Pg.31 . J20
Haegers Bend Rd.
.............. Pg.31 M16
Jacqueline Dr. Pg.31 . J20
Jane Lane .... Pg.31 . K21
Kresmery Ln. . Pg.31 . K21
Little Bend Rd. Pg.30 M17
Meadow Hill Rd.
.............. Pg.31 N19
Moate Ln. .... Pg.31 . L19
Plum Tree Ln. . Pg.31 . K18
Raintree Pl. .. Pg.31 . L18
Ridge Rd. .... Pg.31 . L21
Ridgecroft Ln. Pg.31 M20

River Dr. .... Pg.30 . K16
Rock Ridge Rd. Pg.31 . K19
Saville Row .. Pg.31 . K19
Spring Creek Rd.
.............. Pg.30 . L17
Spring Lane .. Pg.30 M17
Surrey St. ... Pg.31 . K20
Surrey Ln. ... Pg.31 J,K20
Wagon Wheel Ln.
.............. Pg.31 . K20
Woodhaven Ln. Pg.31 . N19

**CEMETERIES**
St. John's Cemetery
.............. Pg.31 . J18

**BELDEN**
Page 3...B10

**BIG FOOT**
Page 1...A4

**BULL VALLEY**
Page 7
**STREETS**
Blackberry Dr. ......... C9
Boone Creek Ter. ...... G10
Bull Valley Rd. ...... G9,10
Cherry Valley Rd., N. ... G10
Cold Spring Rd. ........ F9
Fleming Rd. ........... F9
Happy Tr. ............ E9
Hidden Ln. ........... G10
High Meadow Dr. ...... G10
High Meadow Ln. ...... G9
Locust Ln. ............ G9
Marshland Way ........ F9
Mason Hill Rd. ...... G10,11
Orchard Valley Dr. ..... G10
Ridge Rd. ............ G10
Saddle Creek Ct. ...... G10
Saddle Creek Tr. ...... G10
Stickney Run .......... G10
Sudbury Ct. ........... F10
Valley Hill Rd. ...... F,G10
Woodstone Ln. ........ F9

**CARY**
Pages 12,25,26
**STREETS**
Abbeywood Dr. Pg.25 . I14
Aberdeen .... Pg.25 . I17
Acorn Way ... Pg.26 . F19
Ada St. ...... Pg.25 . H17
Adare Dr. .... Pg.25 . F17
Alexander Ct. Pg.25 . G15
Algonquin-Cary Rd.
.............. Pg.25 . H16
Alicia Dr. .... Pg.25 . H17
Alida Dr. ..... Pg.25 . H17
Alma Terr. ... Pg.25 . G17
Ann St. ...... Pg.25 . G17
Applewood Ct. Pg.26 . I15
Ardmore Dr. . Pg.25 . F17
Arthur Dr. ... Pg.25 . H17
Asbury Ln. ... Pg.25 . H16
Ash Fork Tr. . Pg.26 . I16
Bayberry Dr. . Pg.25 . I15
Bee Ct. ...... Pg.26 . H18
Bell Dr. ...... Pg.25 . G17
Berridale Ave. Pg.25 . G17
Big Bear Tr. .. Pg.26 . I16
Big Sky Tr. ... Pg.26 . I16
Blazing Star Tr. Pg.26 . I16
Blue Mesa Tr. Pg.26 . I16
Borden Ave. .. Pg.25 . H16
Boxwood Ln. . Pg.26 . I16
Brentwood Ln. Pg.26 . G19
Briargate Rd. Pg.25 . I16
Bright Oaks Cir. Pg.25 . F16
Bristol Way .. Pg.26 . G19
Bryan Dr. .... Pg.25 . G19
Burr Oak Ct. . Pg.26 . G19
Burton Ave. .. Pg.25 . H18
Cambridge Ct. Pg.26 . G19
Camden Ct. .. Pg.25 . I16
Candlewood Ct. Pg.26 . G19
Candlewood Tr. Pg.26 . G18
Carl Sands Dr. Pg.26 . G19
Cary Ave. .... Pg.25 . I18
Cary Point Dr. Pg.25 . G17
Cary St. ..... Pg.25 . H17
Castelaria Cl. Pg.25 . F17
Catkins Way .. Pg.26 . F19
Chancery Ln. . Pg.25 . H15
Charlotte Pl. . Pg.25 . H17
Chelsea Ln. .. Pg.25 . H18
Cherry St. ... Pg.25 . H18
Chestnut Ct. . Pg.25 . H17
Chicago St. .. Pg.26 . I18
Chickory Ridge Tr.
.............. Pg.25 . G15
Cimarron Ln. . Pg.26 . I16
Claire Ln. .... Pg.26 . I18
Cleveland St. Pg.25 . G17
Cold Springs Rd.
.............. Pg.25 . I16
Colleen Dr. .. Pg.26 . G19
Connestoga Tr. Pg.25 . G16
Copper Canyon Tr.
.............. Pg.25 . G16
Cornell Ln. ... Pg.25 . H16
Cottonwood Tr. Pg.25 . G15
Country Commons Rd.
.............. Pg.25 . H16
Courtney Ln. . Pg.26 . H16
Coyote Ln. ... Pg.26 . I16
Crabtree Ln. . Pg.26 . H16
Crest Dr. .... Pg.26 . H17
Crofton Ct. .. Pg.25 . F17
Cronan St. ... Pg.25 . F17
Crystal Lake Ave.
.............. Pg.25 . E17
Crystal St. ... Pg.25 . G17
Cumberland St. Pg.25 . H16
Danbury Dr. .. Pg.25 . G15
Davis St. ..... Pg.26 . H18
Daybreak Ridge Pg.25 . H17
Decker Ln. ... Pg.26 . H19

Deerpath Ct. . Pg.25 . I15
Detroit St. ... Pg.26 . I18
Deveron Ct. .. Pg.25 . H17
Drake St. .... Pg.26 . G19
Dunleer Dr. .. Pg.25 . F17
Duxbury Ln. .. Pg.25 . H16
Elden Dr. .... Pg.25 . G17
English Oaks Dr.
.............. Pg.25 . I15
Ennis Ct. .... Pg.25 . F17
Erin Dr. ...... Pg.26 . G18
Essex Ln. .... Pg.25 . I14
Fairfield Ln. .. Pg.25 . H15
Feinberg Ct. . Pg.25 . F16
Feinberg Dr. . Pg.25 . G16
Fernwood Ct. . Pg.25 . F16
First St. ...... Pg.26 . G18
Forest Ln. ... Pg.25 . F16
Fox Trails Dr. . Pg.25 . I15
Franke Ave. .. Pg.25 . H16
Galway St. ... Pg.25 . F17
Georgetown Dr. Pg.25 . F17
Glen Garry Rd. Pg.25 . H17
Habel Rd. .... Pg.25 . H16
Hampton St. . Pg.25 . G15
Harper Ave. .. Pg.26 . G10
Harper Ct. ... Pg.25 . F16
Hickory Ln. .. Pg.25 . F16
High Rd. ..... Pg.25 . I17
Hill St. ...... Pg.25 . H18
Hillhurst Dr. . Pg.26 . I18
Hillside Dr. .. Pg.25 . I18
Industrial Dr. . Pg.25 . G15
Ivanhoe Ln. .. Pg.25 . I18
James Way ... Pg.25 . G17
Jandus Cutoff Pg.26 . H18
Jandus Rd. ... Pg.26 . H16
Jefferson Ln. . Pg.25 . H15
Kildare Ct. ... Pg.25 . F17
Knollwood Dr. Pg.25 . I14
Krentz Ave. .. Pg.25 . H17
Laurel Ln. ... Pg.25 . I15
Leith Way .... Pg.25 . F17
Liberty Ave. .. Pg.25 . F17
Liberty Ct. ... Pg.25 . F17
Linden Ct. ... Pg.25 . F16
Little Stonegate
.............. Pg.25 . H16
Lloyd St. ..... Pg.25 . H16
Lowe Dr. ..... Pg.25 . I16
Main St. ..... Pg.25 . H17
Manchester St. Pg.25 . H15
Manitou Ct. .. Pg.25 . H16
Margaret Ter. Pg.25 . G17
Marquette Ave. Pg.25 . I18
Mary Ln. ..... Pg.25 . F16
Mayfield St. .. Pg.25 . H16
Merrimac St. . Pg.25 . H16
Mildred Ave. . Pg.26 . I18
Milford St. ... Pg.25 . H16
Millwood St. . Pg.25 . H16
Milton Ct. .... Pg.26 . G20
Moders Ave. . Pg.25 . H15
Mohawk St. .. Pg.25 . G16
Montana Ct. . Pg.26 . H,G18
Montana Dr. . Pg.26 . G18
Moraine Hills Dr.
.............. Pg.26 . G18
Muirwood St. Pg.25 . I15
New Haven Dr. Pg.25 . G15
Norman Dr. .. Pg.25 . G16
Northwest Hwy.
.............. Pg.25 . G15
Oak Valley Dr. Pg.26 . F16
Oriole Ct. .... Pg.26 . G18
Oriole Tr. .... Pg.25 . G17
Park Ave. .... Pg.25 . G17
Patriot Ct. ... Pg.25 . F17
Patriot Ln. ... Pg.25 . F17
Pearl Dr. ..... Pg.25 . F16
Pearson Rd. . Pg.25 . H15
Perth Rd. .... Pg.25 . F17
Pin Oak Cir. .. Pg.26 . G18
Pin Oak St. .. Pg.26 . G18
Pine Cir. ..... Pg.25 . F16
Prairie St. ... Pg.25 . H17
Raintree Ct. . Pg.25 . I15
Rawson Bridge Rd.
.............. Pg.2b . G19
Red Cypress Dr.
.............. Pg.26 . G19
Red Oak Tr. .. Pg.25 . F16
Red Wood Dr. Pg.25 . G17
Ridgewood Dr. Pg.25 . I15
Rodeo Ct. ... Pg.26 . I16
Rosewood Ct. Pg.25 . I15
Ross Ave. .... Pg.26 . H18
Rossclare Ct. Pg.25 . F17
Royal Glen Dr. Pg.25 . I15
Saddle Ridge Tr.
.............. Pg.25 . G16
Sagebrush Tr. Pg.25 . G15
Sandra Ln. ... Pg.25 . G16
Sante Fe Tr. . Pg.25 . G16
Schober Dr. .. Pg.25 . H17
School St. .... Pg.25 . H17
Second St. ... Pg.26 . H18
Seebert St. .. Pg.25 . H17
Sequoia Tr. .. Pg.25 . G15
Sherwood Dr. Pg.25 . G18
Short St. ..... Pg.25 . H16
Silver Lakes Rd.
.............. Pg.25 . F17
Silver Tree Cir. Pg.25 . F16
South St. ..... Pg.25 . H17

Spring Beach Way
.............. Pg.26 . H18
Spring St. ... Pg.25 . I17
Spruce Tree Dr. Pg.26 . G19
St. Route 31 . Pg.25 . I14
Stonegate Rd. Pg.26 . H16
Sunset Dr. ... Pg.26 . G18
Surrey Ridge Dr.
.............. Pg.25 . I15
Tamarack Ct. Pg.25 . I14
Tanglewood Dr. Pg.26 . G18
Tealwood Ct. . Pg.25 . I14
Thomas Ave. . Pg.25 . H17
Three Oaks Rd. Pg.25 . G17
Timber Tr. ... Pg.25 . I15
Turkey Run Rd. Pg.26 . H16
US Route 14 . Pg.25 . H16
Veridian Way . Pg.25 . H16
Wagner Dr. .. Pg.25 . F16
Weaver Dr. .. Pg.25 . H18
Weber St. .... Pg.25 . F17
Wexford St. .. Pg.25 . F17
White Oaks Dr. Pg.25 . F17
White Pine Dr. Pg.25 . G16
Wildrose Dr. . Pg.25 . G16
Wildwood Tr. . Pg.25 . G16
Willow Cir. ... Pg.25 . F16
Woodbridge Dr. Pg.25 . I15
Wooded Knoll Dr.
.............. Pg.25 . H16
Wulff St. ..... Pg.25 . H16

**CEMETERIES**
Cary Cemetery Pg.26 . H18

**GOLF COURSES**
Cary Country & Golf Course
.............. Pg.25 . I17

**PARKS**
Brittany Woods Park A
.............. Pg.25 . I16
Brittany Woods Park B
.............. Pg.25 . H16
Brittany Woods Park C
.............. Pg.25 . H16
Brittany Woods Park D
.............. Pg.25 . F18
Candlewood Park
.............. Pg.26 . G19
Candlewood Trail E. Park
.............. Pg.26 . G19
Cary Oaks Park Pg.25 . H17
Cary Park. ... Pg.25 . H17
Cimarron Park Pg.26 . I16
Devron Park . Pg.25 . H17
Greenfield 2 Park
.............. Pg.25 . H16
Greenfield Park Pg.25 . H16
Hillhurst Park Pg.26 . H17
Hillside Prairie Park
.............. Pg.26 . G19
James Way Park
.............. Pg.25 . G16
Jaycee Park . Pg.25 . G16
Knotty Pines Park
.............. Pg.26 . G19
Lions Park ... Pg.25 . F16
Park ......... Pg.25 . I16
Sands Main St. Park
.............. Pg.26 . I18
Three Oaks Park
.............. Pg.25 . G17
Val Budd Nature Park
.............. Pg.25 . H16
Water Tower Prairie Park
.............. Pg.25 . G15
William Caper Sr. Park
.............. Pg.25 . G15

**SCHOOLS**
Briargate Elem. Sch.
.............. Pg.25 . H16
Cary Grove H.S.
.............. Pg.25 . F17
Cary Jr. H.S. Pg.26 . G18
Deer Path Elem. Sch.
.............. Pg.26 . E18
Maplewood Elem. Sch.
.............. Pg.25 . H17
Oak Knoll Elem. Sch.
.............. Pg.25 . H16
St. Peter & Paul Sch.
.............. Pg.25 . G17
Three Oaks Elem. Sch.
.............. Pg.25 . G17

**SHOPPING CENTERS**
Cary Corners S.C.
.............. Pg.25 . H16
Cary Square S.C.
.............. Pg.25 . G17

**MISCELLANEOUS**
Cary Point Industrial Park
.............. Pg.26 . H16
Fire Department
.............. Pg.25 . G16
Library ....... Pg.25 . H16
Police Department
.............. Pg.25 . H16
Post Office ... Pg.25 . H16
Village Hall .. Pg.25 . H16

**CHEMUNG**
Page 1...C2

**CHEMUNG TOWNSHIP**
Page 1
**STREETS**
Becks Rd. ............ C2
Brink St. ............ C4
Cals Ct. ............. C2
Center St. ........... C2
Chemung ............. C2
Commercial St. ....... C3
Countryside Dr. N. ..... B1
Crowley Rd. .......... B4
Dana .............. C2
Dewey St. ........... C2
Elm St. ............. B2
First St. ............ C2
Graf Rd. ........... B1,2
Harvard Hills Rd. ..... C4
Hickory St. .......... C2
Hillside Dr. .......... C2
Horseshoe Dr. ....... B3
Hunter Rd. ........... C1
Island Dr. ......... D,C2
Island Rd. ........... C2
Kennedy Rd. ......... C2
Krunfus ............ B3
Lawrence Rd. ...... A,B2
Lilja Rd. .......... A3,B2
Malinda Dr. .......... B3
Maxon Rd. ........ B,C2
Nilsen Ct. ........... B1
Norma Ln. ........... C2
North Rd. ........... C2
Oak ............... C2
Oak Grove Rd. ..... B3,C2
Pagles Rd. .......... C2
Pearl St. ............ C3
Perkins Rd. .......... B1
Pine St. ............ D2
Pleasant St. ......... C2
Ramer Rd. ........... C2
Rhonda Dr. ......... C2
Rita Dr. ............ C2
River St. ............ B2
Ryan Rd. ............ C1
South St. ............ C2
Southport Rd. ........ A2
State Line Rd. ........ A2
Weidner Rd. .......... B2
White Oaks Rd. .. A,B1,C2
Yates Rd. ........... A3
York Rd. ............ B1
2nd St. ............. C3
5th St. .............. C2

**CEMETERIES**
Big Foot Cemetery ..... A4

**FOREST PRESERVES**
Becks Woods .......... C2

**CORAL**
Page 10...K5

**CORAL TOWNSHIP**
Pages 9,10
**STREETS**
Arbor Ct. .... Pg.10 . M6
Aspen Ct. .... Pg.10 . M6
Beck Rd. ..... Pg.9 . L5
Big Timber Rd. Pg.10 . M5
Brier Hill Rd. . Pg.10 . M7
Burr Oak Dr. . Pg.10 . M5
Cardinal Dr. . Pg.10 . M6
Church Rd. ... Pg.10 . L7,M5
Condor Ln. ... Pg.10 . M6
Conestoga Trail Pg.10 . L4
Coral East Rd. Pg.33 . E7
Coral Rd. .... Pg.10 . K4-6
Country Club Trace
.............. Pg.10 . L5
Dunham Rd. .. Pg.10 . K5
Ernest Dr. ... Pg.10 . L4
Fair Ln. ...... Pg.10 . L6
Fairview Ln. .. Pg.10 . M6
Fairway Ln. .. Pg.10 . L5
Forest Ln. ... Pg.10 . L6
Frank Ln. .... Pg.10 . M4
Frohling Rd. . Pg.10 . K7
Getty Rd. .... Pg.9 . M4
Glen Ln. ..... Pg.10 . L6
Hampshire Rd. Pg.10 . M5
Harmony Hill Rd.
.............. Pg.10 . L6
Harmony Rd. . Pg.10 . M6
Hemmingson Rd.
.............. Pg.10 . K6,7
Heron Dr. ... Pg.10 . M6
Hillsboro Ln. . Pg.10 . M6
Jani Rd. ..... Pg.10 . M4
Kim Ln. ...... Pg.10 . L4
Knolltop Rd. . Pg.10 . L6
Leech Rd. ... Pg.10 . K6
Lerita Dr. ... Pg.10 . L6
Manda Dr. ... Pg.10 . M4
Marengo-Huntley Rd.
.............. Pg.10 . L5,7
McCue Rd. ... Pg.10 . K6
Mitchell Ln. . Pg.10 . L6
Morris Dr. ... Pg.10 . M5
O'Cook Rd. .. Pg.10 . J5
Oak Ridge Rd. Pg.10 . L4
Olson Rd. ... Pg.10 . K5
Overlook Ln. . Pg.10 . M4
Oxbow Dr. ... Pg.10 . L4
Pebble Rd. ... Pg.10 . M6

**CRYSTAL LAKE**

Peregrine Tr. . Pg.10 . M6
Pinon Tr. .... Pg.10 . L5
Raven Hill Dr. Pg.10 . L4
Ridge Rd. .... Pg.10 . L4,6
Riley Hamony Rd.
.............. Pg.10 . M4
Rose Ln. ..... Pg.10 . L4
Royal Ln. .... Pg.10 . M4
Sarko Tr. .... Pg.10 . L4
Seeman Rd. .. Pg.10 . L,M6
Somerset Dr. Pg.9 . K4
Springbrook Cir.
.............. Pg.10 . L5
Stacy Ln. .... Pg.10 . L6
Stevens Rd. . Pg.10 . M5
Union Rd. .... Pg.10,33
.............. D,E7,K5
Voss Rd. .... Pg.9 . L4
Wolff Rd. .... Pg.10 . M5
Wooddale Rd. Pg.10 . L6
Woodwind Ln. Pg.10 . M6

**CEMETERY**
Cemetery .... Pg.4 . M5

**FOREST PRESERVES**
Coral Woods . Pg.9 . L7
H.U.M. Prairie Pg.10 . K6

**GOLF COURSES**
Marengo Ridge Golf &
  Country Club Pg.10 . L5

**MISCELLANEOUS**
Illinois Railway Museum
.............. Pg.10 . K5

**CRYSTAL LAKE**
Pages 11,12,17-20,
22-25,27,28
**STREETS**
Abbington Dr. Pg.23 . G10
Abby Dr. ..... Pg.23 . G7
Aberdeen Dr. Pg.23 . G10
Ackman Rd. .. Pg.23 . H7
Alexandra Blvd. Pg.23 . I2
Amberwood Dr. Pg.23 . H7,9
Arrowhead Ln. Pg.19 . B11
Ascot Dr. .... Pg.23 . G8
Ash St. ...... Pg.18 . D10
Ashford Ln. .. Pg.23 . J9
Auburn Ct. .. Pg.23 . H9
Augusta Dr. . Pg.23 . G8
Augusta Rd. . Pg.23 . G7
Autumncrest Ct.
.............. Pg.23 . I8
Autumncrest Dr.
.............. Pg.23 . I7
Baldwin Ave. Pg.18 . E8
Bard Rd. .... Pg.17 . E6
Barberry Dr. . Pg.17 . E6
Barlina Rd. .. Pg.23 . G9
Barreville Rd. Pg.19 . B15
Barrow Dr. .. Pg.24 . G10
Barton Dr. ... Pg.23 . J9
Bayberry Dr. Pg.18 . D7
Beardsley Tr. Pg.24 . D11
Becker Ct. ... Pg.23 . J9
Bedford Dr. . Pg.23 . G9
Bennington Dr. Pg.23 . G10
Berkshire Dr. Pg.23 . G10
Biringham Ln. Pg.23 . I8
Bittersweet Tr. Pg.19 . D12
Blackthorn Dr. Pg.19 . D12
Blue Heron Dr. Pg.23 . I8
Blue Mound Dr. Pg.23 . G8
Boneset Dr. .. Pg.23 . F7
Boxwood Ct. Pg.23 . H8
Boxwood Dr. Pg.23 . G8
Bradford Ln. . Pg.23 . J9
Brandy Dr. ... Pg.23 . H9
Brentwood Dr. Pg.23 . G9
Brian St. .... Pg.18 . D8
Briarwood Cir. Pg.17 . D6
Briarwood Rd. Pg.17 . D6
Bridgedale Ct. Pg.23 . I9
Bridgedale Rd. Pg.23 . I9
Brigham Ln. . Pg.23 . I7
Brighton Cir. . Pg.23 . A14
Brighton Dr. . Pg.20 . A14
Brink St. ..... Pg.19 . D11
Bristol Dr. ... Pg.23 . F10
Broadway ... Pg.23 . F8
Brompton Ct. Pg.23 . I9
Brompton Ln. Pg.23 . I9
Brook Dr. .... Pg.23 . F9
Brook Rd. ... Pg.23 . F9
Buckingham Dr. Pg.23 . G10
Buckingham Dr. Pg.23 . G9
Buena Vista .. Pg.17 . D6
Burning Bush Tr.
.............. Pg.19 . B11
Burr Dent Dr. Pg.23 . D11
Burr Oak Dr. Pg.25 . F14
Burr Oak Dr. Pg.17 . D7
Butler Dr. ... Pg.23 . G7
Cademia Ln. . Pg.17 . D6
Caledonia Dr. Pg.23 . I7
Cambridge Ln. Pg.23 . G10
Camelot Ct. . Pg.23 . G8
Camelot Ln. . Pg.23 . G8
Camelot Rd. . Pg.23 . G8
Candlewood Dr. Pg.23 . G8
Canterbury Dr. Pg.24 . G11
Cardiff Dr. ... Pg.24 . G11
Carlemont Dr. Pg.23 . I9

**CRYSTAL LAKE (streets)**

Carmella Dr. . Pg.18 . C10
Caroline St. . . Pg.19 . D10
Carpenter St. . Pg.18 . C10
Cascade Dr. . . Pg.18 . C10
Castlefield Ln. . Pg.23 . J8
Catherine Ct. . Pg.24 . E11
Cedar Crest Dr. Pg.18 . E9
Cedar Dr. . . . Pg.18 . D7
Center St. . . . Pg.18 . D10
Ceresia Dr. . . Pg.19 . D13
Chalet Dr. . . . Pg.23 . F9
Chardonnay Dr. Pg.19 . F9
Charlotte Ave. . Pg.17 . E6
Chasefield Ln. . Pg.23 . G8
Chesterfield Ln. Pg.23 . G8
Church St. . . . Pg.18 . D10
Circle Dr. . . . Pg.23 . F10
Clover Dr. . . . Pg.17 . D6
College St. . . . Pg.18 . D10
Colony Dr. . . . Pg.23 . G7
Commerce Dr. . Pg.18 . C10
Commercial Rd.
. . . . . . . . . . Pg.24 . F11
Commonwealth Dr.
. . . . . . . . . . Pg.24 . E11
Concord Dr. . . Pg.23 . F9
Congress Pkwy.
. . . . . . . . . . Pg.24 . E11
Copperfield Ln. Pg.23 . J8
Coronado Vista Pg.17 . D6
Corrine Ave. . . Pg.17 . E6
Cottage Dr. . . Pg.23 . F7
Cottonwood Ln.
. . . . . . . . . Pg.17 . . D6
Country Club Rd.
. . . . . . . . . . Pg.23 . . F8
Country Hill Ave.
. . . . . . . . . . Pg.18 . . B9
Country Ln. . . Pg.18 . . B9
Coventry Ln. . . Pg.23 . F10
Covington Cir. . Pg.23 . H8
Crab Tree Dr . . Pg.23 . . I8
Crabapple Dr. . Pg.23 . G7
Crandall Ave. . Pg.18 . E8
Crandon Pl. . . Pg.23 . . I7
Cress Creek Ct. Pg.23 . F9
Cress Creek Ln. Pg.23 . G7
Cress Creek Ter.
. . . . . . . . . . Pg.23 . . F9
Crimson Dr. . . Pg.23 . H9
Crystal Beach Ave.
. . . . . . . . . . Pg.18 . . D7
Crystal Lake McHenry Rd.
. . . . . . . . . . Pg.18 . . D9
Crystal Point Dr.
. . . . . . . . . . Pg.24 . F11
Crystal Ridge Dr.
. . . . . . . . . . Pg.18 . C10
Crystal Ridge Rd.
. . . . . . . . . . Pg.19 . C10
Cumberland Ln.
. . . . . . . . . . Pg.23 . . F8
Cunningham Ln.
. . . . . . . . . . Pg.23 . . I8
Darlington Ln. . Pg.23 . F10
Dartmoor Dr. . Pg.23 . G10
Deer Grove Dr. Pg.24 . E11
Deer Haven Dr. Pg.23 . I8
Deer Run . . . Pg.19 . B11
Denton Ct. . . . Pg.24 . G11
Derby Ct. . . . Pg.23 . G10
Devonshire Ln. Pg.23 . F10
Dogwood Dr. . Pg.23 . . I7
Dole Ave. . . . Pg.18 . D10
Dolle Ct. . . . . Pg.18 . E10
Dolo Rosa Vista
. . . . . . . . . . Pg.17 . . E6
Douglas Ave. . Pg.18 . E9
Dover Ct. . . . Pg.23 . G10
Dovercliff Way . Pg.23 . . H7
Driftwood Ct. . Pg.23 . . I7
Driftwood Dr. . Pg.23 . . I7
Duffy Dr. . . . . Pg.23 . G13
Durham Ct. . . Pg.23 . F10
Dvorak Dr. . . . Pg.23 . A11
Eagle St. . . . . Pg.18 . E9
East Broadway St. Pg.18 . E9
East End Ave. . Pg.18 . D8
East St. . . . . Pg.24 . D11
Eastgate Rd. . Pg.24 . F11
Eastview Ave. . Pg.18 . E10
Edgebrook Dr. . Pg.18 . E9
Edgewater Dr. . Pg.17 . E6
Edgewood Ave. Pg.18 . E10
Eletson Dr. . . Pg.23 . F9
Elisnoor Ln. . . Pg.23 . F10
Elk Ln. . . . . . Pg.24 . D11
Ellsworth St. . . Pg.19 . D11
Elm St. . . . . . Pg.18 . D10
Elmhurst St. . . Pg.18 . D10
Elmwood Ave. . Pg.17 . E6
Erick St. . . . . Pg.19 . D12
Essex Ln. . . . Pg.23 . F8
Esther St. . . . Pg.24 . E11
Euclid Ave. . . Pg.17 . F6
Eugene St. . . Pg.23 . F10
Everett Ave. . . Pg.18 . F9
Evergreen Pkwy.
. . . . . . . . . . Pg.18 . D10
Exchange Dr. . Pg.24 . E12
Exmoor Ct. . . Pg.23 . F9
Exmoor Terr. . Pg.23 . F9
Factory Rd. . . Pg.24 . E11
Fair Oaks Ave. Pg.18 . E6
Fairfax Dr. . . . Pg.24 . G14
Fairview Pkwy Pg.18 . D9

Faringdon Dr. . Pg.24 . G10
Federal Dr. . . Pg.24 . E12
Fenimore Rd. . Pg.24 . E13
Fernleaf Dr. . . Pg.23 . H9
Fernwald Dr. . Pg.23 . . I7
Flagstone Dr. . Pg.23 . . I7
Flint Tr. . . . . . Pg.19 . B11
Florence St. . . Pg.18 . E9
Floresta Vista . Pg.17 . E6
Forest Dr. . . . Pg.24 . E13
Fountain Green Dr.
. . . . . . . . . . Pg.E6,F11
Foxtall Ct. . . . Pg.19 . C13
Francis Ave. . . Pg.18 . D10
Gail Ct. . . . . . Pg.24 . F10
Gardina Vista . Pg.17 . E6
Gates St. . . . Pg.19 . D11
Georgian Ct. . Pg.18 . D10
Gilbert Ave. . . Pg.17 . E6
Glasgow Ln. . . Pg.23 . . I8
Glen Ave. . . . Pg.24 . D11
Glen Ridge . . Pg.19 . D12
Glenbrook Rd. Pg.19 . B13
Glendale Dr. . . Pg.23 . G9
Goldenrod Ct. . Pg.23 . . F7
Golf Course Rd. Pg.23 . . I8
Golf Rd. . . . . Pg.18 . . F9
Golfview Dr. . . Pg.25 . F14
Grand Ave. . . Pg.18 . C10
Grandview Dr. . Pg.24 . E13
Granville St. . . Pg.19 . D11
Green Brier Ct. Pg.23 . F9
Green Brier Ln. Pg.23 . F9
Green Brier Ter. Pg.23 . F9
Green Meadow Ct.
. . . . . . . . . . Pg.23 . . I8
Green Oaks Dr. Pg.23 . J8
Greenfield Dr. . Pg.18 . D7
Greenview Ct. . Pg.24 . E13
Greenview Dr. . Pg.24 . E13
Grouse Way . . Pg.23 . . I6
Grove St. . . . Pg.18 . C9
Hampton Ct. . Pg.19 . C13
Harold St. . . . Pg.18 . D10
Harper Ln. . . . Pg.23 . . I7
Hartford Ln. . . Pg.23 . J9
Harvest Cir. . . Pg.23 . G7
Harvest Ct. . . Pg.23 . G7
Hastings Ave. . Pg.18 . D9
Hawthorne Dr. Pg.23 . G7
Heather Dr. . . Pg.17 . D6
Heisler Ct. . . . Pg.23 . G9
Heritage Dr. . . Pg.24 . F11
Hickory Dr. . . Pg.18 . C9
High Plaine Dr. Pg.22 . F7
Highland Ave. . Pg.18 . F9
Hilkert Ct. . . . Pg.18 . D10
Hill Dr. . . . . . Pg.24 . E11
Hillcrest Dr. . . Pg.25 . F14
Hillsboro Ct. . . Pg.23 . H9
Hillside Rd. . . Pg.19 . B11
Holly Dr. . . . . Pg.17 . D7
Hollytree Ln. . . Pg.23 . . I8
Honey Suckle Ln.
. . . . . . . . . . Pg.18 . . D7
Hull Ln. . . . . Pg.24 . D10
Hunters Tr. . . Pg.23 . . I7
Huntington Dr. Pg.23 . . I8
Huntley Crystal Lake Rd.
. . . . . . . . . . Pg.19 . B13

Illinois St. . . . Pg.19 . C11
Indian Hill Tr. . Pg.19 . B11
Industrial Rd. . Pg.24 . D10
Iris Ct. . . . . . Pg.23 . . F7
Ivy Ln. . . . . . Pg.17 . . E6
Jackman Dr. . . Pg.23 . F10
James R Rakow Rd.
. . . . . . . . . . Pg.23 . H10
Juniper Ln. . . Pg.24 . E13
Keith Ave. . . . Pg.23 . F10
Kellogg Ln. . . Pg.18 . D9
Kelly Ln. . . . . Pg.19 . C13
Kendalwood Ct. Pg.23 . G9
Kendalwood Dr. Pg.23 . G9
Kensington Ln. Pg.18 . B10
King St. . . . . Pg.18 . D10
Kingsgate Ln. . Pg.23 . . I9
Kingston Ln. . Pg.23 . G10
Knaack Blvd. . Pg.19 . C12
Knollwood Cir. Pg.23 . H8
Laguna Rd. . . Pg.23 . J8
Lake Ave. . . . Pg.18 . E9
Lake Ct. . . . . Pg.18 . D9
Lake St. . . . . Pg.18 . E8,9
Lakeshore Dr. . Pg.18 . E9
Lakeside Rd. . Pg.23 . F8
Lakeview Dr. . Pg.23 . F7
Lakewood Ave. Pg.18 . D7
Lancaster Ct. . Pg.24 . E12
Lancaster Dr. . Pg.23 . G10
Larium Ln. . . . Pg.18 . B10
Lee Dr. . . . . . Pg.23 . G13
Leonard Pkwy. Pg.18 . E10
Liberty Dr. . . . Pg.24 . E11
Lilac Dr. . . . . Pg.23 . . I7
Lill Ave. . . . . Pg.18 . D10
Lincoln Pkwy. . Pg.18 . D10
Lincolnshire Dr.
. . . . . . . . . . Pg.23 . . I9
Linn Ave. . . . Pg.23 . . F9
Loch Lomond Dr.
. . . . . . . . . . Pg.23 . . I8
Lochwood Dr. . Pg.18 . B10
Lombard Dr. . . Pg.23 . G7

Lorraine Dr. . . Pg.19 . C11
Lou St. . . . . . Pg.24 . F11
Louisville Ln. . Pg.23 . J8
Lucas Rd. . . . Pg.17 . B5
Lucerne Dr. . . Pg.18 . . I8
Lutter Dr. . . . . Pg.24 . G14
Magnolia Ct. . Pg.23 . J8
Magnolia Ln. . Pg.23 . . J8
Main St. . . . . Pg.18,24
Manchester Ct. Pg.23 . J8
Manchester Dr. Pg.23 . J8
Maple St. . . . Pg.18 . D10
Maplewood Ln. Pg.18 . D10
Marhil Ct. . . . Pg.24 . D10
Marian Pkwy. . Pg.18 . D10
Mary Lane Ct. Pg.24 . E10
Mary St. . . . . Pg.18 . E10
Mayfield Ave. . Pg.18 . D7
McArdle Dr. . . Pg.24 . G13
McCulom St. . Pg.19 . C11
McHenry Ave. . Pg.18 . E10
Melrose Dr. . . Pg.23 . G9
Memorial Ct. . Pg.24 . E11
Memorial Dr. . Pg.24 . E12
Meridian Ln. . . Pg.23 . C13
Merrimack Dr. . Pg.23 . H9
Meyer Dr. . . . Pg.24 . G14
Midlane Dr. . . Pg.18 . B10
Midway Ct. . . Pg.18 . B10
Mill Rd. . . . . . Pg.23 . J9
Millard Ave. . . Pg.17 . E6
Minnie St. . . . Pg.19 . C13
Mistwood Ln. . Pg.19 . C13
Monarch Dr. . . Pg.23 . H9
Monterey Dr. . Pg.23 . G9
Monticello Way Pg.25 . G14
Moorland Ln. . Pg.23 . . I7
Morgan St. . . Pg.19 . D12
Mulberry Ln. . Pg.23 . . I6
Narragansett Dr.
. . . . . . . . . . Pg.17 . D6
Nash Rd. . . . Pg.23 . . F9
Nashua Ct. . . Pg.19 . C13
Nashua St. . . Pg.19 . C13
New Castle Ct. Pg.24 . G10
Newbury Dr. . . Pg.23 . G8
Nimco Dr. . . . Pg.24 . G13
North Ave. . . . Pg.17 . E6
North Shore Dr.
. . . . . . . . . . Pg.18 . . D9
Northampton Dr.
. . . . . . . . . . Pg.23 . G10
Northwest Hwy.
. . . . . . . . . . Pg.24 . F11
Norwich Ct. . . Pg.19 . C13
Nottingham Ct. Pg.23 . G10
Nottingham Ln. Pg.23 . G10
Oak Ct. . . . . Pg.18 . E8
Oak Hollow Rd. Pg.19 . D13
Oak St. . . . . . Pg.18 . D9
Oak Valley Ct. Pg.24 . E13
Oak Valley Dr. Pg.24 . E13
Oakbrook Dr. . Pg.25 . F14
Official Rd. . . Pg.24 . F11
Old Post Rd. . Pg.25 . G14
Old Westbury Dr.
. . . . . . . . . . Pg.19 . B13
Orchard Row . Pg.18 . D7
Oriole Tr. . . . . Pg.18 . D9
Oxford Ln. . . . Pg.23 . F7
Paddock St. . . Pg.18 . D10
Palm Ct. . . . . Pg.23 . F9
Palmer Ct. . . . Pg.23 . G7
Park Blvd. . . . Pg.19 . C13
Parish Ln. . . . Pg.18 . E9
Parkridge Ct. . Pg.23 . H8
Parkridge Dr. . Pg.23 . H8
Parkside Ct. . . Pg.18 . B9
Parkside Terr. . Pg.18 . C9
Parkview Dr. . Pg.19 . C13
Peachtree Ct. . Pg.23 . H9
Pearl Ct. . . . . Pg.23 . G9
Pebble Ln. . . . Pg.23 . I8
Pembrook Ct. . Pg.19 . D13
Penn Ct. . . . . Pg.23 . I9
Penny Ln. . . . Pg.23 . I9
Peterson Pkwy. Pg.18 . D10
Pine Ct. . . . . Pg.18 . D7
Pine St. . . . . Pg.18 . D9
Pinewood Dr. . Pg.18 . D7
Pingree Rd. . . Pg.24 . F13
Plantain Ct. . . Pg.23 . . I8
Plum Ct. . . . . Pg.23 . . J9
Plum Tree Dr. . Pg.23 . . I8
Plymouth Ln. . Pg.23 . F9
Pomeroy St. . Pg.18 . E10
Poplar St. . . . Pg.19 . D12
Porter Ave. . . Pg.23 . F9
Portsmith Ct. . Pg.23 . F10
Prairie St. . . . Pg.19 . D11
Prescott Ln. . . Pg.18 . E9
Primrose Ln. . Pg.23 . H9
Providence Ln. Pg.19 . C12
Pyott Rd. . . . Pg.24 . E11
Quail Way . . . Pg.23 . . I6
Railroad St. . . Pg.19 . D11
Randall Rd. . . Pg.24 . E11
Raymond Dr. . Pg.24 . G14
Rebecca St. . . Pg.19 . C11
Regency Park Dr.

Regent Dr. . . Pg.23 . H8
Reiland Dr. . . Pg.19 . C13
Revere Dr. . . Pg.18 . C10
Rickert Rd. . . Pg.24 . E13
Ridge Ave. . . Pg.18 . D9
Ridgefield Rd. . Pg.17 . A6
Ridgewood Ln. Pg.23 . G7
Ringling Rd. . . Pg.18 . E9
Rivera Vista . . Pg.17 . D6
Riverside Dr. . Pg.23 . F8
Rockland Rd. . Pg.18 . D9
Rosedale Ave. Pg.18 . E10
Rosenthal Dr. . Pg.24 . F11
Rosewood Ln. Pg.23 . H8
Rudat Ct. . . . Pg.23 . J8
Ryan Way . . . Pg.18 . B10
Saddle Creek Ln.
. . . . . . . . . . Pg.23 . . J8
Saddle Ridge . Pg.19 . B11
Sandalwood Ln.
. . . . . . . . . . Pg.23 . . G7
Sands Rd. . . Pg.24 . F14
Sarah Dr. . . . Pg.19 . C13
Sarasota Ct. . Pg.23 . G7
Savannah Ln. . Pg.19 . C13
Sedgewick Ct. Pg.19 . D13
Seybrooke Ln. Pg.19 . C13
Shadowood Ln.
. . . . . . . . . . Pg.23 . . G7
Sharon Dr. . . Pg.23 . G10
Sheffield Dr. . . Pg.23 . G10
Shelton Ln. . . Pg.23 . . I9
Sherbon Ln. . . Pg.24 . G11
Sherbrooke Ct. Pg.19 . C13
Sherman St. . . Pg.19 . C11
Shipland Dr. . . Pg.18 . B10
Short St. . . . . Pg.19 . D13
Silk Oak Ct. . . Pg.19 . D13
Silk Oak Ln. . . Pg.19 . D13
Silver Aspen Cir.
. . . . . . . . . . Pg.23 . . G9
Silver Berry Dr. Pg.19 . D13
Skyridge Dr. . . Pg.23 . . I9
Smitana Rd. . . Pg.24 . F14
Snowberry Ln. Pg.17 . E6
Somerset Ln. . Pg.24 . E10
South St. . . . Pg.18 . E10
Spring Ridge Dr.
. . . . . . . . . . Pg.18 . C10
Spruce Ln. . . Pg.17 . E6
St. Andrews Ct. Pg.23 . F9
St. Andrews Ln.
. . . . . . . . . . Pg.23 . . F9
St. Route 176 Pg.19 . D12
St. Route 31 . Pg.24 . F13
State St. . . . . Pg.23 . G10
Stockton Ln. . Pg.23 . . I8
Stonebridge Ln.
. . . . . . . . . . Pg.23 . . H8
Stonecreek Cir. Pg.23 . . I7
Stonefield Ln. . Pg.23 . J8
Stonehedge Ct. Pg.23 . G7
Stony Hill Ln. . Pg.18 . B9
Stratford Ln. . Pg.20 . B14
Strum Ct. . . . Pg.24 . F11
Suffolk Dr. . . Pg.23 . G9
Sunnyside Ave. Pg.18 . E10
Sunset Ter. . . Pg.24 . E11
Surrey Ln. . . . Pg.24 . G10
Sussex Ln. . . Pg.23 . F10
Sutherland Dr. Pg.23 . G8
Sutton Dr. . . . Pg.23 . G8
Sycamore Ln. Pg.18 . D9
Talcott Ave. . . Pg.19 . D12
Talcott Ct. . . . Pg.19 . D12
Tamarisk Ln. . Pg.23 . F9
Tamarisk Terr. Pg.23 . F9
Tanglewood Dr. Pg.23 . . I8
Tartan Dr. . . . Pg.23 . . I4
Teakwood Ln. . Pg.17 . D6
Teckler Blvd. . Pg.24 . F11
Tek Dr. . . . . . Pg.24 . G13
Terra Cotta Ave. Pg.18 . C13
Terra Cotta Rd. Pg.19 . C13
Terrace Dr. . . Pg.25 . F14
Teverton Ln. . Pg.24 . G10
Thatchery Rd. Pg.24 . F11
Thomasville Ln.
. . . . . . . . . . Pg.23 . . J9
Thornwood Ln. Pg.17 . D6
Three Oaks Rd. Pg.24 . E13
Timber Hill Dr. Pg.18 . D7
Tomahawk Ln. Pg.19 . B11
Tracy Tr. . . . . Pg.24 . F13
Trailwood Ct. . Pg.23 . . I8
Trailwood Dr. . Pg.23 . . I8
Trumball Ct. . Pg.24 . E14
US Route 14 . Pg.18 . E12
Union St. . . . Pg.18 . E10
University St. . Pg.18 . E10
Upland Dr. . . Pg.18 . B10
Uteg St. . . . . Pg.18 . E10
Valhalla Ln. . . Pg.25 . F14
Van Buren St. Pg.18 . E9
Victor Pkwy. . Pg.18 . D9
Victoria Ln. . . Pg.20 . D14
View St. . . . . Pg.19 . C12
Village Ct. . . . Pg.23 . J9
Village Rd. . . . Pg.23 . J9
Virginia St. . . Pg.18 . E9
Walk Up Ave. . Pg.24 . E11
Walk Up Rd. . Pg.19 . E12
Wallace Ave. . Pg.19 . E10
Walt Herrick Trail

Warrington Ln. Pg.23 . . I8

Washington St. Pg.18 . . E9
Waterford Cut . Pg.23 . H7
Wedgewood Dr.
. . . . . . . . . . Pg.23 . . F7
Wellington Dr. Pg.23 . G11
Wesley Dr. . . Pg.23 . G8
West St. Alley . Pg.18 . E8
Weston Dr. . . Pg.23 . G8
Westport Ridge Pg.23 . H9
Westport Ridge Ct.
. . . . . . . . . . Pg.23 . . H9
Westwood Ct. Pg.23 . G9
Wheatland Ct. Pg.22 . G7
Wheatland Dr. Pg.23 . G7
Whitehall Way Pg.23 . H7
Wiggington Dr. Pg.23 . G7
Wildflower Ln. Pg.19 . D13
Williams St. . . Pg.24 . D11
Williamsburg Ln.
. . . . . . . . . . Pg.23 . . I7
Willowtree Dr. . Pg.23 . I8
Wiltshire Ct. . . Pg.23 . F10
Wimbleton Ln. Pg.23 . G8
Windham Cove Dr.
. . . . . . . . . . Pg.23 . . H9
Windridge Dr. Pg.23 . H9
Windsor Dr. . . Pg.23 . G9
Winslow Cir. . . Pg.23 . H8
Woodbine Dr. . Pg.17 . D6
Woodcreek Cir. Pg.23 . . I7
Woodhaven Dr. Pg.23 . J7
Woodland Dr. Pg.18 . E9
Woodmar Dr. . Pg.23 . G9
Woodmar Ln. . Pg.23 . G9
Woodmar Terr. Pg.23 . G9
Woodstock St. Pg.18 . D9
Wyndmuir Ct. Pg.19 . C13
Wyndmuir Dr. Pg.19 . C13
Yorkshire Ln. . Pg.23 . G10
1st Ct. . . . . . Pg.18 . E10
1st St. . . . . . Pg.18 . E10
2nd Ct. . . . . Pg.18 . E10
2nd St. . . . . Pg.18 . E10
3rd St. . . . . . Pg.24 . C11

**SCHOOLS**
Annex Alternative Sch.
. . . . . . . . . . Pg.24 . . F11
Canterbury Sch.
. . . . . . . . . . Pg.23 . . F7
Community H.S. Dist. 155
. . . . . . . . . . Pg.24 . F10
Coventry Sch. Pg.23 . G10
Crystal Lake Central H.S.
. . . . . . . . . . . H7,M4
Crystal Lake S. H.S.
. . . . . . . . . . Pg.23 . . H9
Crystal Lake Sch. Dist. 47
. . . . . . . . . . Pg.24 . . F11
Hannah Beardsley Middle
Sch. . . . . . . Pg.19 . D13
Harvest Christian Sch.
. . . . . . . . . . Pg.19 . D13
Husmann Elem. Sch.
. . . . . . . . . . Pg.18 . . D10
Immanual Lutheran Sch.
. . . . . . . . . . Pg.23 . . I7
Indian Prairie Sch.
. . . . . . . . . . Pg.23 . J9
Lundahl Jr. H.S.
. . . . . . . . . . Pg.23 . . F9
McHenry County College
. . . . . . . . . . Pg.17 . . B6
North Elem. Sch.
. . . . . . . . . . Pg.18 . D9
North Jr. H.S. Pg.23 . G10
Prairie Ridge High Sch.
. . . . . . . . . . Pg.19 . A11
South Sch. . . Pg.23 . F9
St. Thomas Cath. Sch.
. . . . . . . . . . Pg.18 . . F9
The Academy Pg.24 . F11
West Sch. . . . Pg.17 . E6
Woods Creek Elem. Sch.
. . . . . . . . . . Pg.23 . . I7

**SHOPPING CENTERS**
Commons S.C. Pg.24 . F11
Country Corners S.C.
. . . . . . . . . . Pg.23 . . F9
Coventry Plaza Pg.24 . G11
Crystal Court S.C.
. . . . . . . . . . Pg.24 . . E12
Crystal Lake Shopping
Plaza . . . . . Pg.23 . F10
Crystal Point S.C.
. . . . . . . . . . Pg.24 . . F11
Dartmoor Center Plaza
. . . . . . . . . . Pg.23 . . H9
Oak Street Center Plaza
. . . . . . . . . . Pg.18 . . C9
Precision Plaza Pg.23 . G13
. . . . . . . . . . Pg.24 . F13
Twin Ponds Market Place S.C.
. . . . . . . . . . Pg.24 . . E14
Virginia Park Shopping
District . . . Pg.23 . F10

**MISCELLANEOUS**
Ambutal Hospital Trauma
Center . . . . . Pg.19 . B14
American Legion
. . . . . . . . . . Pg.18 . . D9
Canterbury Place Retirement
Home . . . . Pg.20 . A14
Chamber of Commerce
. . . . . . . . . . Pg.18 . . E9
City Hall . . . . Pg.19 . D11
Fire Station . . Pg.19,22,24
. . . . . . . . . D11,F7,G11
Lake Theater . Pg.19 . D11
Library . . . . . Pg.18 . D10
Metra Bowl Recreation
. . . . . . . . . . Pg.19 . . D11
Municipal Complex
. . . . . . . . . . Pg.19 . . C11
Nature Center Pg.19 . C11
Nature Conservancy
. . . . . . . . . . Pg.18 . . B10
Northside Center
. . . . . . . . . . Pg.19 . . C11
Park District Hq.
. . . . . . . . . . Pg.18 . . E9
Police Dept. . . Pg.19 . D11
Post Office . . Pg.24 . E11
Railroad Station
. . . . . . . . . . Pg.19 . . D11
Rotary Building Student
Union . . . . . Pg.18 . E9
Sewage Treatment Plant
. . . . . . . . . . Pg.19 . . C12
Warming House
. . . . . . . . . . Pg.19 . . C11
Winding Creek Bike Path
. . . . . . . . . . Pg.23 . J9
YMCA . . . . . Pg.19,24
. . . . . . . . . D11,F13

**DORR TOWNSHIP**
Pages 6,7,10,11,13,14,17,18

**STREETS**
Alto Vista N. . Pg.17 . D6
Aspen Ct. . . . Pg.17 . D5
Aspen Ln. . . . Pg.17 . D5
Beech Ave. . . Pg.17 . D5
Beresford Dr. . Pg.7 . H10
Bluejay Ct. . . Pg.11 . H9
Boerberij Way Pg.11 . H9
Briarwood Rd. Pg.17 . D6
Buena Vista . Pg.17 . D6

**CEMETERIES**
Crystal Lake Cemetery
. . . . . . . . . . Pg.23 . . E9
Crystal Lake Memorial Park
Cem. . . . . . Pg.18 . . B8
Ridgefield Cemetery
. . . . . . . . . . Pg.18 . . B8
Union Cem. . . Pg.18 . D10

**FOREST PRESERVES**
Butternut Forest Preserve
. . . . . . . . . . Pg.17 . . D6
Crystal Cove Conservation
Area . . . . . . Pg.18 . E8
Stearns Woods & Fens
. . . . . . . . . . Pg.19 . . C12
Veterans Acres Wingate
Prairie . . . . Pg.19 . C11

**GOLF COURSES**
Crystal Lake C.C.
. . . . . . . . . . Pg.23 . . F8

**PARKS**
Ashbury Park . Pg.19 . D13
Athletic Field . Pg.24 . E11
Canterbury Park
. . . . . . . . . . Pg.24 . . G11
Conventry Park Pg.23 . G10
Cress Creek Property
. . . . . . . . . . Pg.23 . . G8
Crystal Castle Playground
. . . . . . . . . . Pg.23 . . H8
Crystal Cove Watershed
. . . . . . . . . . Pg.23 . . D9
Depot Park . . Pg.19 . D11
Edgewater Park Pg.17 . E7
Feinburg Park Pg.24 . E13
Fetzner Park . Pg.23 . . I9
Four Colonies Park
. . . . . . . . . . Pg.23 . . G8
Hampton Park Pg.23 . G9
Hill Farm Park Pg.23 . G8
Indian Prairie Park
. . . . . . . . . . Pg.23 . . J9
Ken Bird Park Pg.23 . G9
Ladd Park . . Pg.23 . G9
Lake Park . . . Pg.18 . E9
Lakeside Center Retreat
. . . . . . . . . . Pg.18 . . E9
Lippold Park . Pg.23 . D7
Little League Ballpark
. . . . . . . . . . Pg.24 . . E11
McCormick Park
. . . . . . . . . . Pg.18 . . E9
Park . . . . . . Pg.23 . G9
Samuel John's Park
. . . . . . . . . . Pg.23 . . H8
Seminary Field Pg.23 . F9
Spoerl Park . Pg.24 . E11
Sterling Meadows Park
. . . . . . . . . . Pg.23 . . H8
The Commons Park
. . . . . . . . . . Pg.24 . . E11
Winding Creek Park
. . . . . . . . . . Pg.23 . . I9
Woodland Estate Park
. . . . . . . . . . Pg.18 . . B10
Woods Creek Park
. . . . . . . . . . Pg.23 . . H8

Bull Run Trail . Pg.10 . G10
Bull Valley Rd. Pg.7,14
. . . . . . . . . . . G9,J8
Bunker Ln. . . Pg.17 . . D6
Butternut Dr. . Pg.17 . D5
Butternut Rd. . Pg.11 . J9
Byron Cir. . . . Pg.14 . J8
Cardinal Ln. . Pg.11 . H9
Carol Ln. . . . Pg.10,13
. . . . . . . . . . . H7,M4
Castle Rd. . . Pg.7,14
. . . . . . . . . . . H8,M7
Castleberry Dr. Pg.7 . H10
Catalpa Ln. . . Pg.7,14
. . . . . . . . . . . G8,L7
Cherry Valley Rd.
. . . . . . . . . . Pg.18 . . A8
Cheshire Ct. . Pg.7 . H10
Chestnut Ct. . Pg.17 . D6
Chestnut Dr. . Pg.17 . D6
Chukar Pl. . . Pg.6 . H7
Church St. . . Pg.23 . A7
Coronado Vista Pg.17 . D6
Country Club Rd.
. . . . . . . . . . Pg.18 . . A7
Davis St. . . . Pg.13 . L5,6
Dean St. . . . Pg.10,13
. . . . . . . . . . . H7,M5
Deerpath Rd. . Pg.7,14
. . . . . . . . . . . G9,K8
Deweide Tr. . . Pg.11 . H9
Dieckman Dr. Pg.14 . L6
Dirkshire Dr. . Pg.11 . H9
Doty Rd. . . . Pg.17 . A4
East End Ave. Pg.18 . E4
Edgewood St. Pg.14 . L6
Esther Ct. . . . Pg.7 . J8
Fairway Ln. . . Pg.7,14,17
. . . . . . . . . . . D4,J9
Fleming Rd. . Pg.14 . H9
Front St. . . . . Pg.18 . A7
Gayle Dr. . . . Pg.6,10 . J7
Golf Ln. . . . . Pg.17 . D6
Green Ave. . . Pg.17 . D6
Haligus Rd. . . Pg.17 . D4
Hamilton Rd. . Pg.10 . J8
Hawthorn Ln. Pg.17 . E6
Heather Ln. . . Pg.17 . E6
Hercules Rd. . Pg.7 . H8
Hickory Ln. . . Pg.17 . D6
Hidden Ln. . . Pg.7 . G9
High Meadow Dr.
. . . . . . . . . . Pg.7 . G9
High Meadow Ln.
. . . . . . . . . . Pg.7 . G9
Hillside Rd. . . Pg.18 . A8
Holly Ln. . . . Pg.10 . H7
Hythe Cir. . . Pg.7 . F10
Ironwood Dr. . Pg.17 . D6
Juanita Vista Pg.17 . D6
Keats Ct. . . . Pg.14 . J8
Laurel Ct. . . Pg.7,14
. . . . . . . . . . . G8,J7
Lily Pond Rd. Pg.7 . H9
Locust . . . . . Pg.14 . J9
Lucas Rd. . . Pg.17 . A4
Madison St. . Pg.17 . A7
Market St. . . Pg.17 . A7
McConnel Rd. Pg.7,14
. . . . . . . . . . . G9,K8
McHenry Rd. . Pg.14 . J7
Middlesex Dr. Pg.7 . H10
Mt. Thaber Rd. Pg.17 . C4
Nancy Ct. . . Pg.10 . J7
Northwest Hwy.
. . . . . . . . . . Pg.18 . . A6
Noveen Pkwy. Pg.7,11,14
. . . . . . . . . . . H8,M7
Ohnstad Rd. . Pg.17 . C6
Perkins Rd. . Pg.10 . H7
Pond Rd. . . . Pg.11 . H9
Prairie Dr. . . Pg.18 . A7
Prospect St. . Pg.18 . A7
Queen Anne Rd.
. . . . . . . . . . Pg.7,14 . G8,J7
Railroad Ave. Pg.17 . G,J8
Ridgefield Rd. Pg.18 . A7
Rivera Vista . Pg.17 . D6
Robin Hill Dr. Pg.11 . H9
Sando Ln. . . Pg.13 . L5
Sharon Dr. . . Pg.7,14
. . . . . . . . . . . G8,J7
Shelly Ct. . . . Pg.14 . J8
Southview St. Pg.14 . J8
St. George Ln. Pg.14 . J8
St. Route 176 Pg.17 . C6
St. Route 47 . Pg.14 . M7
Sunset Ridge Dr.
. . . . . . . . . . Pg.13 . . J8
Swanson Rd. . Pg.11 . J8
Tipperary Ct. . Pg.17 . D6
US Route 14 . Pg.18 . A6
Valley Hill Rd. Pg.7 . G10
Virginia St. . . Pg.17 . A7
Waller St. . . . Pg.17 . A7
Washington St. Pg.18 . A7
West St. . . . . Pg.17 . A7
Westgate Dr. . Pg.7 . F10
Willow Ct. . . Pg.17 . D6
Woodland Dr. Pg.7,14 . G,J9
Zimmerman Rd.
. . . . . . . . . . Pg.7,14

**AIRPORTS**
Landing Strip . Pg.11 . G9

# DORR TOWNSHIP

**CEMETERIES**
Memorial Park Cemetery ........ Pg.14 .. M8
Mt. Tabor Cemetery ........ Pg.17 .. C4
Ridgefield Cemetery ........ Pg.18 .. E2

**FOREST PRESERVES**
Dorothy Weers Conservation Right ..... Pg.14 .. H8

**GOLF COURSES**
Bull Valley G.C. Pg.7 .. G8
Crystal Woods Golf Course ........ Pg.11 .. J8
Turnberry C.C. Pg.20 .. C6
Woodstock C.C. ........ Pg.7 .. G9

**SCHOOLS**
Crystal Lake Montessori Sch. ........ Pg.11 .. G9
Lord & Savior Evangelical Luth. Sch. Pg.18 .. A6
Ridgefield Sch. Pg.18 .. A7

**MISCELLANEOUS**
Congre. of Resurrection ........ Pg.11 .. H10
Landing Strip. Pg.7 .. G9
Pleasant Valley Farm ........ Pg.10 .. J7
Thunderbird Hunt Club ........ Pg.11 .. G10

## DUNDEE TOWNSHIP
**STREETS**
Manhatas Tr. . Pg.29 .. N13
Manito Tr. . Pg.29 .. N14
Menoma Tr. . Pg.29 .. N13
Minaki Tr. . Pg.29 .. N13
Onaway Tr. . Pg.29 .. N13
Wakigan Tr. . Pg.29 .. N14

## DUNHAM TOWNSHIP
Pages 1,5
**STREETS**
Airport Rd. .. Pg.1 .. D3
Bluejay Rd. . Pg.1 .. D3
Bunker Hill Rd .. Pg.1 .. E2,4
Busse Rd. .. Pg.5 .. F3
Cardinal Ct. .. Pg.1 .. F3
County Line Rd. ........ Pg.1 .. E1
Dunham Rd. . Pg.1 .. E4
Dunham Wood Rd ........ Pg.1 .. E4
Echo Tr. .. Pg.5 .. F4
Flat Iron Rd. .. Pg.1 .. D,E2
Fritz Rd. .. Pg.1 .. E3
Hawthorn .. Pg.5 .. F4
Heritage Ln. .. Pg.1 .. D3
Highview Rd. .. Pg.1 .. D2
Inland Dr. .. Pg.1 .. D2
Island Rd. .. Pg.1 .. E3
Lembeke Rd. .. Pg.1 .. E3
Marengo Rd. .. Pg.1 .. F3
McGuire Rd. .. Pg.1 .. D4
Menge .. Pg.5 .. F4
Mulvenna Rd. . Pg.5 .. F2
Pagles Rd. .. Pg.1 .. D,E1
Robin Rd. .. Pg.1 .. D3
Schultz Rd. .. Pg.1 .. D4
St. Barth Ct. .. Pg.1 .. F4
Streit Rd. .. Pg.1 .. D1,3
Tomlin Rd. .. Pg.5 .. F1
Trebess Dr. .. Pg.1 .. E4
Windy Hill Rd. .. Pg.1 .. D4
Woodlane Dr. . Pg.1 .. E4
Wondpecker Rd. ........ Pg.1 .. D3
Woodvale Dr. . Pg.1 .. F4

**AIRPORTS**
Dacy Airport . Pg.1 .. D3

**CEMETERIES**
Cemetery .... Pg.1 .. E1
Mt. Auburn Cemetery ........ Pg.1 .. D4

**FOREST PRESERVES**
Rush Creek .. Pg.1 .. D4

## FOX LAKE
Page 4
(Portions within Lake County, for additional listings, see Section 6)
**STREETS**
Appaloosa Ln. ...... C13
Carriage Ln. ........ B14
Chelsey Ct. ........ B14
Chestnut Ridge ..... B14
Churchill St. ........ B14
Country Shire Ln. ... B14
Country Squire Ln. .. B14
Deer Run ........ C14
Heather Ridge ...... B14
Jomes Rd. ........ B14
Laurie Ct. ........ C13
Morgan Cir. ........ C13
Park Vista Ln. ...... B14
Steeple Ct. ........ B14
Sundial Ln. ........ B14
Surrey Ct. .......... B14
Wilmot Rd. .......... A14

## FOX RIVER GROVE
Pages 12,26,31
(For additional listings, see Section 6)
**STREETS**
Adams Rd. .. Pg.26 .. I19
Algonquin Rd. Pg.31 .. J19
Amherst Ct. . Pg.31 .. J20
Asbury Ave. .. Pg.31 .. J19
Asbury Ct. .. Pg.31 .. J19
Ashcroft Ct. . Pg.31 .. J19
Bay View Ave. Pg.31 .. J18
Bayberry Tr. .. Pg.26 .. I20
Bayview St. .. Pg.31 .. I18
Bayview Dr. .. Pg.31 .. J18
Beach Way .. Pg.31 .. I19
Birch Ln. .... Pg.26 .. I19
Bradbury Ct. . Pg.31 .. J19
Brighton Ct. . Pg.31 .. J19
Bristol Ln. .. Pg.31 .. I21
Camilla Pl. .. Pg.31 .. I21
Center Rd. .. Pg.31 .. I19
Chatham Ct. . Pg.31 .. J20
Circle Rd. .. Pg.26 .. I19
Concord Ave. .. Pg.31 .. I19
Crescent Rd. . Pg.31 .. J18
Crompton Ct. . Pg.31 .. J19
Doverton Ave. Pg.31 .. J18
Elder Ln. .. Pg.31 .. J18
Ellington Ct. . Pg.31 .. J19
Essex Rd. .. Pg.31 .. J19
Excy Dr. .. Pg.31 .. I21
Excy St. .... Pg.31 .. I21
Foxanna Cir. . Pg.31 .. I20
Foxmoor Rd. . Pg.31 .. J19
Gardner Ave. .. Pg.31 .. I21
Gardner Rd. .. Pg.31 .. I21
Gladys Ave. .. Pg.31 .. J19
Glenhurst Ct. . Pg.31 .. J19
Glenice Pkwy. Pg.31 .. I19
Grace Ln. .. Pg.31 .. I19
Grove Ave. .. Pg.31 .. I19
Harding Ave. . Pg.26 .. I19
Heather Ct. .. Pg.31 .. I19
Highview Ct. . Pg.31 .. I19
Hillcrest Ave. . Pg.31 .. J18
Huntcliff Ct. . Pg.31 .. J20
Hunters Way . Pg.31 .. J19
Illinois St. .. Pg.31 .. I19
Jasmine Way . Pg.31 .. I21
Johnson St. .. Pg.26 .. I20
Keystone Ave. . Pg.31 .. J18
Lexington Ave. Pg.31 .. J19
Lexington Rd. . Pg.31 .. J19
Liberty Ave. .. Pg.31 .. J18
Lilly Ln. .... Pg.31 .. I20
Lincoln Ave. .. Pg.31 .. J19
Lincoln Creek Rd. ........ Pg.31 .. J18
Lucille Ave. .. Pg.31 .. I19
Manchester Ct. Pg.31 .. J20
Maple Ave. .. Pg.31 .. J18
Melrose St. .. Pg.31 .. I19
Midway St. .. Pg.31 .. I20
Millard Ave. .. Pg.31 .. I19
Mound St. .. Pg.31 .. I20
Northwest Hwy. ........ Pg.31 I19,20
Oak Ln. .. Pg.31 .. J19
Old Hunt Rd. . Pg.26 .. J19
Opalrny Dr. .. Pg.26 .. I19
Orchard St. .. Pg.31 .. I20
Park Ct. .. Pg.31 .. I20
Park Way .. Pg.31 .. I19
Paul Ln. .. Pg.31 .. J18
Pine St. .. Pg.31 .. J18
Pleasant St. .. Pg.31 .. J19
Plum Tree Rd. . Pg.31 .. J19
Primrose Ct. .. Pg.31 .. I21
Primrose Ln. .. Pg.31 .. I21
Ridgeland St. . Pg.31 .. I20
River Rd. .. Pg.31 .. I20
School Dr. .. Pg.31 .. I20
Ski Hill Rd. .. Pg.31 .. I20
Skyline St. .. Pg.26 .. I20
Spring St. .. Pg.26 .. I10
St. Route 22 . Pg.31 .. I19
Thackery Ln. .. Pg.31 .. J19
Tiffany Ln. .. Pg.31 .. I21
Tower Ct. .. Pg.31 .. J19
Tower Pl. .. Pg.31 .. J19
US Route 14 . Pg.31 .. I19,I20
Victoria Dr. .. Pg.31 .. I21
Violet Ave. .. Pg.26 .. I20
Well St. .... Pg.31 .. I20
Wildwood .. Pg.31 .. I20
Windsor Cir. .. Pg.26 .. I19
Woodbine Ave. Pg.31 .. I20
Woodbine Ln. . Pg.31 .. I20
Yorkshire Dr. . Pg.31 .. J20

**PARKS**
Foxmoor Park . Pg.31 .. J19
Lions Park .. Pg.31 .. I19

**SCHOOLS**
Algonquin Rd. Sch. ........ Pg.31 .. J18
Fox River Grove Jr. H.S. ........ Pg.31 .. I20

**SHOPPING CENTERS**
Stonehill S.C. . Pg.31 .. I20

**MISCELLANEOUS**
Bettendorf Castle ........ Pg.31 .. I20
Fire Station #1 Pg.31 .. I19
Fire Station #2 Pg.31 .. I19
Library ...... Pg.31 .. K7
Norge Ski Jump ........ Pg.26 .. I20
Police Department ........ Pg.31 .. I20
Post Office .. Pg.31 .. J20
Seven Angels Corner ........ Pg.26 .. I19
Train Station . Pg.31 .. I19
Village Hall . Pg.31 .. I19
Windy City Balloon Port ........ Pg.26 .. I20

## FOX RIVER VALLEY GARDENS
Pages 12,21
(For additional listings, see Section 6)
**STREETS**
Bayview Dr. .. Pg.21 .. D21
Blue Heron St. Pg.21 .. D21
Center St. .. Pg.21 .. D21
Circle Ave. .. Pg.21 .. D21
Circle Dr. .. Pg.21 .. D21
........ Pg.21 D20,21
Eastwood Ave. Pg.21 .. D21
Eastwood Ct. . Pg.21 .. D21
Eastwood Ln. . Pg.21 .. D21
Fawn Dr. .. Pg.21 .. D20
Gattison Ct. .. Pg.21 .. C21
Hilldale Ave. .. Pg.21 .. C21
Manchester Tr. Pg.21 .. C21
Oak St. .... Pg.21 .. D21
Park Ct. .. Pg.21 .. C21
Park Dr. .. Pg.21 .. E21
Peninsula Ave. Pg.21 .. D20
Rawson Bridge Rd. ........ Pg.21 .. C21
River St. .. Pg.21 .. C21
Riverside Dr. . Pg.21 .. C21
Riverwalk Ct. . Pg.21 .. C21
Riverwalk St. . Pg.21 .. C21
Straight St. .. Pg.21 .. D20
Strait St. .. Pg.21 .. D20
Stub Ave. .. Pg.21 .. C21
Westwood Ct. . Pg.21 .. C21
Willow St. .. Pg.21 .. C21

## FRANKLINVILLE
Page 6...H6

## GENOA CITY
Pages 3,4...A11

## GRAFTON TOWNSHIP
Pages 10,11,22,23,27,28
**STREETS**
Ackman Rd .. Pg.23 .. H7
Adamson Rd . Pg.10 .. L7
Albrecht Rd. . Pg.22 .. I4
Algonquin Rd. Pg.22 .. L6
Arthur St. .. Pg.17 .. E6
Ballard Rd. .. Pg.22 .. F7
Bard Rd. .... Pg.22 .. F7
Beech Ave. .. Pg.17 .. E6
Briarwood Rd. Pg.17 .. E6
Butternut Dr. . Pg.17 .. D5
Charlotte Ave. Pg.17 .. F6
Chestnut Dr. . Pg.22 .. F6
Chicago Ave. . Pg.23 .. F7
Columbine Ave. Pg.17 .. E6
Conley Rd. .. Pg.22 .. G4
Cote Dr. .. Pg.10 .. K8
Cottage Ave. . Pg.22 .. F7
Cottage Dr. .. Pg.23 .. F7
County Line Rd. ........ Pg.27 .. N4
Coyne Station Rd. ........ Pg.10 .. L7
Crescent Dr. . Pg.10 .. J8
Crystal Lake Rd. ........ Pg.11 .. L9
Delaware St. . Pg.17 .. E6
Della Ave. .. Pg.22 .. F6
Dundee Rd. .. Pg.27 .. N4
East End Ave. Pg.17 .. D5
Elm Ln. .... Pg.17 .. D5
Ernesti Rd. .. Pg.17 .. D7
Foster Rd. .. Pg.24 .. F4
Frank Rd. .. Pg.28 .. K7
Georgine St. . Pg.17 .. E5
Grandview Dr. Pg.17 .. J8
Greenfield Ave. Pg.17 .. E4
Haligus Rd. .. Pg.17 .. L4
Hamilton Rd. . Pg.10 .. J8
Hawthorn Way Pg.10 .. K8
Hemmer Rd. .. Pg.10 .. M7
Hemmingson Rd. ........ Pg.10 .. K7
Hensel Rd. .. Pg.22 .. F7
Hillcrest Ave. . Pg.22 .. F7
Hillview Dr. .. Pg.10 .. K8
Huntley Rd. .. Pg.22 .. F7
John ...... Pg.17 .. C7
Kasper Ave. .. Pg.17 .. E6
Kreutzer Rd. .. Pg.11 .. M8
Lakeview Ave. Pg.22 .. F7
Lakeview Dr. . Pg.10 .. J8
Lakewood Rd. Pg.22 .. I5
Lavergone St. Pg.17 .. E5
Linden Ln. .. Pg.10 .. K8
Linder Ave. .. Pg.17 .. E6
Main St. .... Pg.17 .. E6
Martin St. .. Pg.17 .. E6
Mensching Rd. Pg.10 .. K7
Miller Rd. .. Pg.23 .. J7
Murel St. .. Pg.17 .. E6
North Ave. .. Pg.17 .. E6
Pauline Ave. . Pg.17 .. E6
Priengnitz Rd. Pg.11,22 .. H5,K9
Reed Rd. .. Pg.27 .. K4
Ridgeview Dr. Pg.10 .. K8
Rose Ave. .. Pg.17 .. E6
Rosebud Ave. Pg.17 .. E6
Rowland St. .. Pg.11 .. K8
Ruth Rd. .... Pg.11 .. M8
Square Barn Rd. ........ Pg.27 .. L7
Sunnyside Ave. Pg.20 .. D4
Sunset Ave. . Pg.17 .. E6
Suttondale Rd. Pg.10 .. K8
Swanson Rd. . Pg.22 .. I7
Teresa Ave. .. Pg.17 .. E6
Tyron St. .. Pg.28 .. E5
Union Rd. .. Pg.10 .. K8

**FOREST PRESERVES**
Butternut Forest Preserve ........ Pg.17 .. D6
Exner Marsh . Pg.27 .. K6
Henning Parcel Pg.10 .. A13

**GOLF COURSES**
Terrace Hill Golf Course ........ Pg.28 .. L7

**PARKS**
Della St. Park . Pg.17 .. E6

## GREENWOOD
Pages 3,33
**STREETS**
Aavang Rd. . Pg.3,7 .. E9
Allendale Rd. . Pg.3 .. D9
Barber Ave. .. Pg.3 .. D9
Center St. .. Pg.3 .. D9
Church St. .. Pg.3 .. D9
Greenwood Rd. Pg.3 .. D9
Miller Rd. .. Pg.3 .. D9
Park St. .. Pg.3 .. D9
Thompson Rd. Pg.3,33 .. D9
Wondermere Rd. ........ Pg.3,33 .. D9

**AIRPORTS**
Galt Airport . Pg.3 .. D9

**FOREST PRESERVES**
Bystricky Prairie ........ Pg.7 .. D8
Queen Ann Prairie ........ Pg.7 .. E8

**SCHOOLS**
Greenwood Elem. Sch. ........ Pg.3 .. D9

## GREENWOOD TOWNSHIP
Pages 2,3,7,13,14,33
**STREETS**
Aavang Rd. .. Pg.3 .. E9
Acorn Path .. Pg.3 .. D8
Allen Dale Rd. Pg.3 .. D8
Appleby Ct. .. Pg.2 .. D7
Arabian Tr. .. Pg.7 .. E9
Autumn Ln. .. Pg.7,14 .. F,G9
Baker Ter. .. Pg.14 .. G9
Banford Rd. .. Pg.7,14 .. F0,H7
Billingsgate Ln. Pg.2 .. D7
Birchwood Dr. Pg.33 .. F9
Breckenridge Ct. ........ Pg.7 .. F10
Brockman Ct. . Pg.2 .. D7
Brody Ln. .. Pg.2 .. F8
Central Parkway Rd. ........ Pg.14 .. H6
Charles Rd. .. Pg.2 .. E7
Chatham Ln. . Pg.7,14 .. F,G9
Cold Spring Rd. ........ Pg.7 .. F9
Compton Ln. . Pg.6 .. D7
Cooney Dr. .. Pg.2 .. E8
Crest Ln. .. Pg.2 .. D7
Deer Dr. .. Pg.33 .. E9
Elm St. .... Pg.33 .. E9
Evergreen Dr. Pg.33 .. E8
Fleming Rd. .. Pg.14 .. H9
Gerson St. .. Pg.33 .. E9
Giant Oak Rd. Pg.33 .. C9
Gleason Ct. .. Pg.2 .. E8
Greenwood Rd. Pg.3,14 D,G9
Hickory Dr. .. Pg.33 .. F9
Hickory Rd. .. Pg.7,14 .. F8,H6
Hill Top Dr. .. Pg.33 .. F9
Hogbag Rd. .. Pg.3,7 .. F10
Howe Rd. .... Pg.33 .. C9
Jankowski Rd. Pg.2 .. D7
Lake Shore Dr. Pg.33 .. E9
Lake View Dr. Pg.33 .. E9
Lamb Rd. .. Pg.2,13 .. F7,H4
Maplewood Dr. Pg.33 .. E9
McCannon Rd. Pg.14 .. H6
McHenry Rd. . Pg.14 .. H7
Meadow Ln. .. Pg.33 .. E8
Melody Dr. .. Pg.33 .. E8
Memory Tr. .. Pg.33 E8-9
Miller Rd. .. Pg.3,14 .. D9,G6
Mustang Tr. .. Pg.7 .. E9
Nusbaum Rd. . Pg.3 .. E8
Oriole ...... Pg.33 .. E8
Parker Ct. .. Pg.2 .. E8
Pheasant Ln. . Pg.33 .. E8
Pine Ave. .. Pg.33 .. E8
Pine Needle Pass ........ Pg.33 .. F8
Pleasant Ln. . Pg.33 .. E8
Powers Rd. .. Pg.14 .. G7
Queen Anne Rd. ........ Pg.3,7,14 .. D,F,H8
Raffel Rd. .. Pg.7,14 .. F8,H7
Ramble Rd. .. Pg.33 .. E8
Raycraft Rd. .. Pg.3 .. E8
Roger Rd. .... Pg.14 .. H6
Rola Farm Rd. Pg.2 .. D8
Rose Marie Rd. Pg.33 .. E9
Saddle Bred Tr. Pg.7 .. E9
Shadow Ln. .. Pg.33 .. F8
Shady Ln .. Pg.33 .. E8
Somerset Ct . Pg.6 .. F7
Spring Ln. .. Pg.3 .. F9
St. Route 120 Pg.13 .. H4
St. Route 47 . Pg.13 .. G6
Sunburg Ct. .. Pg.7 .. F10
Sunset Dr. .. Pg.33 .. E8
Swarthmore S. Pg.7 .. F10
Thompson Rd. Pg.7,14,33 .. D,E,F,G9
Vine Ave. .. Pg.33 .. E8
Ware Rd. .. Pg.7,14 .. F8,G9
Windsor Rd. .. Pg.6 .. D7
Wonder Lake Dr. ........ Pg.33 .. E9
Wonder Lake Rd. ........ Pg.3,33 .. D9,D,E10
Wonder View Dr. ........ Pg.33 .. F9
Wondermere Rd. ........ Pg.3,33 D8,F9
Woodland Ln. . Pg.3 .. F9
Woody Tr. .. Pg.33 .. E8

**AIRPORTS**
Galt Airport . Pg.3 .. D9

**FOREST PRESERVES**
Bystricky Prairie ........ Pg.7 .. D8
Queen Ann Prairie ........ Pg.7 .. E8

**SCHOOLS**
Forest Academy ........ Pg.7 .. E9

**MISCELLANEOUS**
Bull Valley Hunt Club ........ Pg.7 .. F10
Bohart Rd. .. Pg.10 .. M7

## HARMONY
Page 10...M6

## HARTLAND
Page 6...E6

## HARTLAND TOWNSHIP
Pages 1,2,5,6,13
**STREETS**
Alden Rd. .. Pg.2 .. D6
Antuna Blvd. . Pg.6,13 .. F6,G3
Bauman Rd. .. Pg.5 .. F4
Black Oak Ct. Pg.6 .. E7
Brookdale Rd. Pg.1 .. C4
Bunker Hill Rd. Pg.1 .. E4
Compton Ln. . Pg.6 .. D6
Cooney St. .. Pg.6 .. E6
Countryside Ln. Pg.6 .. D5
Debbie Ln. .. Pg.1 .. C4
Deep Cut Rd. . Pg.6 .. E5,6
Dogwood Ln. . Pg.6 .. E7
Dunham Rd. .. Pg.1 .. E4
Frank Ct. .. Pg.2 .. D6
Goddard St. .. Pg.6 .. E6
Greenway Cross ........ Pg.13 .. H3
Hartland Rd. . Pg.2 .. D6
Hawthorn St. . Pg.1 .. E4
Hidden Ln. Dr. ........ Pg.2 .. E7
Hillside Ln. .. Pg.2,6 .. F6
Honeysuckle Ln. ........ Pg.6 .. E7
Indian Trace . Pg.6,13 .. F6,H3
Irish Ln. .. Pg.2 .. D6
King Rd. .. Pg.6 .. D5
Lake Dr. .. Pg.1 .. C4
Lamb Rd. .. Pg.13 .. H4
Lilac Ln. .. Pg.2 .. D7
Lincoln Rd. .. Pg.2 .. D5
Lindwall Rd. .. Pg.2 .. E6
Marwood Dr. . Pg.6 .. F6
Maxwell St. .. Pg.6 .. E6
McCauley Rd. . Pg.6 .. E6
McGuire Rd. .. Pg.6 .. D5
McKinstry Rd. . Pg.6 .. F5
Menge Rd. .. Pg.5 .. F4
Moon Ridge Dr. Pg.6 .. D7
Murray Rd. .. Pg.6 .. E6
Nelson Rd. .. Pg.6 .. E6
Northwest Hwy. (US 14) ........ Pg.13 .. H4
Park Lane Dr. Pg.2,6 .. F6
Paulsen Rd. .. Pg.2 .. E5
Rail Dr. .. Pg.6 .. F7
Red Oak Dr. .. Pg.1 .. E4
Redbud Ln. .. Pg.6 .. E7
Rose Farm Rd. Pg.6,13 .. F6,H3
Saint Patrick Rd. ........ Pg.6 .. E6
Schultz Rd. .. Pg.1 .. D4
Shamrock Ln. . Pg.6,13 .. H3,L6
Shannon Dr. .. Pg.13 .. H3
Short St. .... Pg.2,6 .. F6
Somerset Ct. . Pg.6 .. F7
St. Route 120 Pg.13 .. H4
Strait Rd. .. Pg.6 .. D4,0
Sunset Dr. .. Pg.6,13 .. F6,G3
Tina Dr. .... Pg.1 .. E4
Trakk Ln. .. Pg.6 .. E7
US Route 14 . Pg.13 .. H4
West Rd. .. Pg.6 .. E8
Wilson Rd. .. Pg.6 .. D6
Windsor Ct. .. Pg.6 .. D7

**CEMETERIES**
St. Patrick Cemetery ........ Pg.6 .. E6

**FOREST PRESERVE**
Wildlife Preserve ........ Pg.6 .. F5

**GOLF COURSES**
Plum Tree National Golf Course ...... Pg.6 .. F6

**MISCELLANEOUS**
Boy Scouts of America ........ Pg.6 .. E6

## HARVARD
Pages 1,33
**STREETS**
Admiral .... Pg.33 .. B8
Airport Rd. .. Pg.33 .. B7
Anderson St. . Pg.33 .. B8
Ayer St. .... Pg.33 .. B8
Beaumont St. Pg.1 .. C3
Blackman St. . Pg.33 .. A7
Blaine St. .. Pg.33 .. A7
Blanchard St. . Pg.33 .. A,B7
Bourn St. .. Pg.33 .. A8
Brainard St. .. Pg.33 .. A8
Brink St. .. Pg.33 .. B7,8
Brown St. .. Pg.33 .. A8
Burbank St. .. Pg.33 .. A8
Cambell .... Pg.33 .. A8
Cherry Ln. .. Pg.1 .. C3
Chippewa Rd. Pg.33 .. A7
Church St. .. Pg.33 .. A8
Deerpath Rd. . Pg.33 .. A7
Dewey St. .. Pg.33 .. B8
Diggens St. .. Pg.33 .. A7
Division St. .. Pg.33 .. A,B8
Dunlap St. .. Pg.33 .. B8
Eastman St. . Pg.33 .. B7
Finney St. .. Pg.33 .. B8
Frisco Dr. .. Pg.33 .. B8
Front St. .. Pg.33 .. A7
Galvin Pkwy. . Pg.33 .. A8
Garfield St. .. Pg.33 .. A8
Grant St. .. Pg.33 .. A,B8
Harrison St. .. Pg.33 .. A8
Hart St. .. Pg.33 .. B8
Harvard Hills Rd. ........ Pg.33 .. A8
Hayes Ct. .. Pg.33 .. A8
Hayes St. .. Pg.33 .. A,B8
Hereley Dr. .. Pg.33 .. B8
Hillside Dr. .. Pg.33 .. A8
Hollyhock St. . Pg.1 .. C3
Horseshoe Dr. Pg.1 .. B3
Howard St. .. Pg.33 .. A,B7
Hutchinson St. Pg.33 .. A7
Ivy Ln. .... Pg.1 .. C3
Jackman St. . Pg.33 .. A7
Janowski St. . Pg.33 .. A8
Jefferson St. . Pg.33 .. A8
Joel Ct. .. Pg.33 .. B8
Johnson St. .. Pg.33 .. B7
Killeen St. .. Pg.33 .. B8
Kimalee Ct. .. Pg.33 .. A8
Klaman St. .. Pg.33 .. A8
Kleen ...... Pg.33 .. B8
Lawrence Rd. Pg.1 .. C2
Lilac Ln. .. Pg.1 .. C3
Lincoln St. .. Pg.33 .. A8
Little John Ln. Pg.33 .. A8
Lonesome Rd. Pg.1 .. C3
Magnolia St. . Pg.1 .. C3
Marengo St. . Pg.33 .. B7
McComb St. . Pg.33 .. B8
McGuire Rd. .. Pg.33 .. A8
McKinley St. . Pg.33 .. A7
Metzen St. .. Pg.33 .. B7

# HEBRON TOWNSHIP

Myer St. .... Pg.33 .. B7
Northfield Ave. Pg.1 .. C3
O'Brien St. .. Pg.33 .. A8
Oak Grove Rd. Pg.1 .. B2
Old Orchard Rd. ........ Pg.33 .. A8
Orchard Ln. .. Pg.1 .. C3
Page St. .... Pg.33 .. B7
Park Dr., S. .. Pg.33 .. B8
Park St. .... Pg.33 .. A7
Pheasant Run Pg.1 .. C3
Primrose Ln. . Pg.1 .. C3
Public Rd. .. Pg.33 .. B8
Railroad St. .. Pg.33 .. B8
Randall St. .. Pg.33 .. B8
Ratzlaff St. .. Pg.33 .. A,B7
Ridge Ln. .. Pg.33 .. B8
Roosevelt St. . Pg.33 .. A7
Rush Creek Rd. Pg.33 .. A8
Shawnee Ln. . Pg.1 .. C4
Summer St. .. Pg.33 .. A8
Thompson St. Pg.33 .. A8
University St. . Pg.33 .. A8
Washington St. Pg.33 .. A7
Wildflower Ln. Pg.1 .. C3
Willow Ln. .. Pg.1 .. C3
Yellowstone Ln. Pg.1 .. C4
1st St. .... Pg.33 .. A8
2nd St. .... Pg.33 .. A8
3rd St. .... Pg.33 .. A7
4th St. .... Pg.33 .. A7
5th St. .... Pg.33 .. A7
6th St. .... Pg.33 .. A7
7th St. .... Pg.33 .. A7
8th St. .... Pg.33 .. A7
9th St. .... Pg.33 .. A7
10th St. .... Pg.33 .. A7

**AIRPORTS**
Dacy Airport . Pg.33 .. C7

**CEMETERIES**
Cemetery .... Pg.25 .. E18

**PARKS**
Lions Park .. Pg.33 .. A8
Marys Park .. Pg.33 .. B7

**SCHOOLS**
Central Elem. Sch. ........ Pg.33 .. A8
Harvard Comm. H.S. ........ Pg.33 .. A8
Harvard Jr. H.S. ........ Pg.33 .. A8
Jefferson Elem. Sch. ........ Pg.33 .. A8
St. Joseph Elem. Sch ........ Pg.33 .. A8
Washington Elem. Sch. ........ Pg.33 .. A7

**MISCELLANEOUS**
City Hall .... Pg.33 .. A8
Train Station . Pg.33 .. A7

## HEBRON
Pages 2,3,33
**STREETS**
Center St. .. Pg.33 .. B10
Church St. .. Pg.33 .. B10
Hanson Rd. .. Pg.2 .. B8
Harrison Ave. Pg.33 .. B10
Illinois St. .. Pg.33 .. B10
Industrial Dr. . Pg.2 .. B8
Jacob Ave. .. Pg.33 .. B9
Jean Dr. .. Pg.33 .. B9
Main St. .... Pg.33 .. B9
Maple St. .. Pg.33 .. B10
Marci Ln. .. Pg.33 .. B9
McKinley Ave. Pg.33 .. B10
Mead St. .. Pg.33 .. B10
Meadow Ln. .. Pg.2 .. B8
Prairie Ave. .. Pg.33 .. B9
Price Rd. .. Pg.2 .. B8
Sharon Ln. .. Pg.2 .. B8
St. Albans St. Pg.33 .. B10
Union St. .. Pg.33 .. B10
Western Ave. Pg.33 .. B9
Wild Flower Way ........ Pg.2 .. B8
Woods Ln. .. Pg.33 .. B9
3rd Ave. .. Pg.33 .. B10
4th Ave. .. Pg.33 .. B10

**CEMETERIES**
St. Albans St. and 3rd Ave. Cem. ...... Pg.33 .. B10

**SCHOOLS**
Alden-Hebron Elem. Sch. ........ Pg.33 .. B8
Alden-Hebron Middle Sch. ........ Pg.33 .. B10

## HEBRON TOWNSHIP
Pages 2,3,33
**STREETS**
Armory Rd. .. Pg.2,3 .. A8
Barnard Mill Rd. ........ Pg.2,3 .. C10
Burgett Rd. .. Pg.2,3 .. A9
Buttons Rd. .. Pg.2,3 .. A8
Freeman Rd. . Pg.2,3 .. A8
Giant Oak Rd. Pg.2,3 .. C10
Green St. .. Pg.33 .. B10
Greenwood Rd. Pg.2,3 .. B9

Hickory Ln. . . . Pg.2,3 . . C9
Hillside Rd. . . . Pg.2,3 . . A7
Johnson Rd. . . . Pg.2,3 . . B,C7
Kemman Rd. . . Pg.2,3 . . A7
Lange Rd. . . . Pg.2,3 . . A9
McCauley Rd. . . Pg.2,3 . . C7
Norgard Rd. . . . Pg.2,3 . . B10
Okeson Rd. . . . Pg.2,3 . . B9
Price Rd. . . . Pg.2,3 . . B8
Queen Anne Rd. . Pg.2,3 . . C8
Regnier Rd. . . . Pg.2,3 . . C10
Seeman Rd. . . . Pg.2,3 . . A8
State Line Rd. . . Pg.2,3 . . A7
Stewart Rd. . . . Pg.2,3 . . A7
Thayer Rd. . . . Pg.2,3 . . A7
Tryon Grove Rd.
. . . . . Pg.2,3 . . C10
Vander Karr Rd.
. . . . . Pg.2,3 . . B8,C9
1st Ave. . . . . Pg.33 . . B10
2nd Ave. . . . . Pg.33 . . B10
5th Ave. . . . . Pg.33 . . B10

AIRPORTS
Hebron Airfield . . Pg.3 . . C9

CEMETERIES
Cemetery . . . . Pg.2 . . A7

FOREST PRESERVES
Grund Strom Natural Area
. . . . . Pg.3 . . C10

HOLIDAY HILLS
Pages 8,32
STREETS
Ash Ln. . . . . Pg.32 . . C5
Beachnut Dr. . . Pg.32 . . C5
Birch St. . . . . Pg.32 . . C5
Birchwood Ave. . Pg.32 . . C5
Bittersweet Ave.
. . . . . Pg.32 . . C5
Catalpa . . . . Pg.32 . . C5
Cedar . . . . . Pg.32 . . C5
Elder . . . . . Pg.32 . . C5
Elm . . . . . . Pg.32 . . C5
Evergreen . . . Pg.32 . . C5
Fox . . . . . . Pg.32 . . C5
Grove St. . . . . Pg.32 . . C5
Hickory . . . . . Pg.32 . . C5
Holiday Dr. . . . Pg.32 . . C5
Hyde Park Dr. . . Pg.32 . . C5
Kenilworth Ave. . Pg.32 . . C5
Lake Dr. . . . . Pg.32 . . C5
Lake Shore Dr. . Pg.32 . . C5
Low . . . . . . Pg.32 . . C4,5
Oak . . . . . . Pg.32 . . C5
Park Ave. . . . . Pg.32 . . C5
Pine St. . . . . Pg.32 . . C5
Poplar St. . . . Pg.32 . . C5
Riverview Dr. . . Pg.32 . . C5
Spruce . . . . . Pg.32 . . C5
Sunset Dr. . . . Pg.32 . . C5
Swallow Dr. . . . Pg.32 . . C5
Tower Dr. . . . . Pg.32 . . C5
Violet Dr. . . . Pg.32 . . C5
Wauconda Rd. . . Pg.32 . . C5

HUNTLEY
Pages 10,11,32
STREETS
A St. . . . . . Pg.32 . . A4
Algonquin Rd. . . Pg.32 . . A4
Ashley Ct. . . . Pg.27 . . K5
Ashley St. . . . Pg.27 . . K5
B St. . . . . . Pg.32 . . A4
Bakley . . . . . Pg.32 . . A,B4
Bayou Ct. . . . Pg.27 . . N3
Becky Lee Tr. . . Pg.32 . . B4
Bedford Dr. . . . Pg.27 . . J5
Bennington Dr. . Pg.27 . . J4
Bernice Ave. . . Pg.32 . . A4
Big Horn Dr. . . Pg.10 . . L8
Blue Bayou Dr. . Pg.27 . . N3
Bohart Rd. . . . Pg.10 . . L8
Bonnie Brae St. . Pg.32 . . A,B3
Bonnie Knoll . . Pg.32 . . A3
Bordeaux Dr. . . Pg.27 . . J5
Borden St. . . . Pg.27 . . K4
Brighton Ln. . . Pg.27 . . K4
Brittany Ave. . . Pg.32 . . A4
Brookwood Dr. . Pg.10 . . L8
Bull Ridge Dr. . Pg.10 . . L8
Cambridge Dr. . Pg.27 . . K5
Cape Cod Ln. . . Pg.27 . . N4
Carl St. . . . . Pg.32 . . A4
Carol Ln. . . . . Pg.32 . . B3
Charles St. . . . Pg.32 . . A4
Chetwood Dr. . . Pg.27 . . J5
Church St. . . . Pg.32 . . A4
Cindy Jo Ave. . . Pg.27 . . J4
Compton Dr. . . Pg.27 . . J4
Coral . . . . . Pg.32 . . B4
Coventry Ln. . . Pg.10 . . L8
Dalton Dr. . . . Pg.27 . . J5
Daniel Ln. . . . Pg.32 . . A4
Davey Dr. . . . Pg.32 . . B4
Dean St. . . . . Pg.11,32
. . . . . B4,M8
Deer Meadow Ln.
. . . . . Pg.10 . . L8
Del Webb Blvd. . Pg.10 . . L8
Douglas St. . . . Pg.32 . . A4
Dundee Rd. . . . Pg.11 . . M9
Dunhill Dr. . . . Pg.27 . . A4
Edward Ave. . . Pg.32 . . A4

Elizabeth Ave. . Pg.32 . . A4
Essex Dr. . . . Pg.10 . . L8
Everglades Rd. . Pg.27 . . N3
First St. . . . . Pg.32 . . A4
Frederick Way . . Pg.32 . . B4
Gayle Ct. . . . . Pg.32 . . B4
Giordano Pl. . . Pg.11 . . M8
Grand Canyon Ave.
. . . . . Pg.27 . . N3
Grand Plaines Ct.
. . . . . Pg.27 . . N3
Great Plaines Dr.
. . . . . Pg.27 . . N4
Grove St. . . . . Pg.32 . . B4
Haligus Rd. . . . Pg.27 . . N4
Hampton Ct. . . Pg.10 . . L8
Hanley Ln. . . . Pg.27 . . J4
Heinz Ave. . . . Pg.32 . . B3
Henry St. . . . Pg.32 . . B4
Janice Dr. . . . Pg.32 . . A4
Joan Ave. . . . Pg.32 . . A4
Kathleen Ave. . . Pg.32 . . A4
Keating St. . . . Pg.32 . . A4
Kenneth Ave. . . Pg.32 . . A4
Kensington Dr. . Pg.10 . . L8
Kiley . . . . . Pg.32 . . A4
Kishwaukee Ct. . Pg.11 . . M8
Kishwaukee Ln.
. . . . . Pg.10 . . L8
Kreautzer Rd. . . Pg.11 . . M8
Lincoln St. . . . Pg.32 . . B4
Longfield Dr. . . Pg.27 . . J4
Lori Ln. . . . . Pg.32 . . B4
Main St. . . . . Pg.32 . . B4
Margaret Ave. . . Pg.32 . . B4
Martin St. . . . Pg.32 . . B4
Marvin Dr. . . . Pg.27 . . J5
Matthew Ave. . . Pg.32 . . A4
Michael Ave. . . Pg.32 . . A4
Milbrook Dr. . . Pg.10 . . L8
Mill St. . . . . Pg.32 . . B4
Morning Glory Ln.
. . . . . Pg.10 . . L8
Myrtle Ave. . . . Pg.32 . . B4
Niagra Ln. . . . Pg.27 . . N4
North Dr. . . . . Pg.32 . . A4
Nottingham Dr. . Pg.10 . . L8
Oakcrest Dr. . . Pg.32 . . A3,4
Oakleaf Ct. . . . Pg.32 . . A3
Oakleaf Ln. . . . Pg.32 . . A3
Oxford Dr. . . . Pg.27 . . J4
Painted Desert Ct.
. . . . . Pg.27 . . N4
Phillips Ave. . . Pg.32 . . A4
Pine Way . . . . Pg.32 . . B4
Primrose Ct. . . Pg.10 . . L8
River Terrace Dr.
. . . . . Pg.10 . . L8
Riverpark Ln. . . Pg.10 . . L8
Riverside Dr. . . Pg.27 . . K4
Riverview Ct. . . Pg.10 . . L8
Rocksprings Ln.
. . . . . Pg.10 . . L8
Ronald Ave. . . . Pg.32 . . A4
Rushmore Ln. . . Pg.27 . . N4
Ruth Rd. . . . . Pg.32 . . A4
Scott Dr. . . . . Pg.27 . . J4
Second St. . . . Pg.32 . . A4
Sedgewick St. . . Pg.10 . . L8
Shenandoah Ct. . Pg.27 . . N3
Shenandoah Dr.
. . . . . Pg.27 . . N4
Smith Ct. . . . . Pg.11 . . M8
Smith Dr. . . . . Pg.11 . . M8
Somerset Ln. . . Pg.27 . . J4
Spring Creek Dr.
. . . . . Pg.10 . . L8
Stillwater Crossing
. . . . . Pg.10 . . L8
Stonebridge Ln.
. . . . . Pg.10 . . L8
Stratford Dr. . . Pg.10 . . L8
Summerview Dr.
. . . . . Pg.10 . . L8
Sunset Ln. . . . Pg.32 . . A4
Sweetwater Ln. . Pg.10 . . L8
Tallgrass Tr. . . Pg.10 . . L8
Third St. . . . . Pg.32 . . A4
Thornton Way . . Pg.27 . . K4
Timer Dr. . . . . Pg.32 . . A4
Tuliptree Ln. . . Pg.10 . . L8
Union Special Plaza
. . . . . Pg.32 . . A4
Valley Forge Ln.
. . . . . Pg.27 . . N3
Vine St. . . . . Pg.32 . . A4
Wakefield Ct. . . Pg.27 . . K4
Wellington Dr. . Pg.27 . . K4
Wildrose Dr. . . Pg.10 . . L8
Willowcreek Ln.
. . . . . Pg.10 . . L8
Wing Point Dr. . Pg.27 . . N3
Woodcreek Dr. . Pg.32 . . B4
Woodstock St. . . Pg.32 . . B4
Yardley Dr. . . . Pg.27 . . J5
Yellowstone Dr. . Pg.27 . . N3
York Rd. . . . . Pg.27 . . J4
4th St. . . . . Pg.32 . . A4

CEMETERIES
St. Mary's Cemetery
. . . . . Pg.32 . . B4

GOLF COURSES
Pinecrest G.C. . Pg.11,32
. . . . . A4,L8

PARKS
Diecke Park . . Pg.32 . . B4
Old Timers Park
. . . . . Pg.32 . . A4

SCHOOLS
Huntley N. Elem. Sch.
. . . . . Pg.11 . . M8
Huntley Comm. H.S.
. . . . . Pg.11 . . M8
Huntley Elem. Sch.
. . . . . Pg.32 . . B3
Huntley Fire Grade Ctr.
. . . . . Pg.10 . . M7
Huntley H.S. . . Pg.10 . . M7
Huntley Middle Sch.
. . . . . Pg.10 . . M7
Huntley Sch. Dist. 158
. . . . . Pg.10 . . M7

MISCELLANEOUS
Library . . . . . Pg.32 . . A4
Police Dept. . . Pg.32 . . B4
Village Hall . . . Pg.32 . . A4

ISLAND LAKE
Page 8,21,32
(For additional listings,
see Section 6)
STREETS
Arbor Rd. . . . . Pg.32 . . D6
Ascot Ln. . . . . Pg.32 . . D5
Bassler Dr. . . . Pg.32 . . D6
Beech St. . . . . Pg.32 . . D6
Briar Ct. . . . . Pg.32 . . D6
Briar Rd. . . . . Pg.32 . . D6
Brierhill Dr. . . Pg.32 . . D6
Brittany Blvd. . Pg.32 . . C5
Burnett Rd. . . . Pg.32 . . C5
Burr Oak Ln. . . Pg.32 . . C,D6
Canterbury Ln. . Pg.32 . . D7
Cardinal Cove . . Pg.32 . . D7
Cardinal Way . . Pg.32 . . D7
Carol Circle . . . Pg.32 . . D7
Carriage Hill Ct. Pg.32 . . D6,7
Carriage Hill Rd.
. . . . . Pg.32 . . D6,7
Cedar Terr. . . . Pg.32 . . C6
Channel Dr. . . . Pg.32 . . C6
Charles Ct. . . . Pg.32 . . C6
Circle Dr. . . . . Pg.32 . . C6
Clover Rd. . . . Pg.32 . . C6
Concord Ct. . . . Pg.32 . . C5
Concord Dr. . . . Pg.32 . . C6
Constitution Ave.
. . . . . Pg.32 . . D7
Cottonwood Ct. . Pg.32 . . D6
Country Trail Ct.
. . . . . Pg.32 . . D6-7
Dartmouth Dr. . Pg.32 . . D5
David Ct. . . . . Pg.32 . . D6
Debden Dr. . . . Pg.21,32
Dorothy Ct. . . . Pg.32 . . D6
Dorothy Dr. . . . Pg.32 . . D6
Dowell Rd. . . . Pg.32 . . C5
Eastport Ct. . . Pg.32 . . D6
Eastway Dr. . . . Pg.32 . . C,D6
Elder Dr. . . . . Pg.32 . . D6
Elm Ave. . . . . Pg.32 . . C5
Ethel Terr. . . . Pg.32 . . C6
Fairfield Dr. . . Pg.32 . . C6
Fern Ct. . . . . Pg.32 . . C6
Fern Dr. . . . . Pg.32 . . C6
Forest Dr. . . . Pg.32 . . C6
Greenleaf Ave. . Pg.32 . . C,D6
Greenwich Ln. . Pg.32 . . C6
Hale Ln. . . . . Pg.21,32
. . . . . A19,C5,6
Harvard Ct. . . . Pg.32 . . D7
Hazel Ct. . . . . Pg.32 . . C6
Hickory Terr. . . Pg.32 . . C6
Highland Ct. . . Pg.32 . . C6
Highland Dr. . . Pg.32 . . C6
Hill Ct. . . . . Pg.32 . . C6
Hillside Dr. . . . Pg.32 . . C6
Honeysuckle Ln.
. . . . . Pg.32 . . C6
Huntington Ln. . Pg.32 . . C5
Hyacinth Terr. . Pg.32 . . C6
Ilene Ln. . . . . Pg.32 . . C6
Independence Blvd.
. . . . . Pg.32 . . D7
Island Dr. . . . Pg.32 . . D6
Ivy Rd. . . . . Pg.32 . . D6
Janet Dr. . . . . Pg.21,32
Jordan Ln. . . . Pg.32 . . A21,D6
Judith Dr. . . . Pg.32 . . C6
Juniper Rd. . . . Pg.32 . . D6
Kelly Rd. . . . . Pg.21,32
. . . . . B20,D6
Kings Point Rd. . Pg.32 . . C5
Kingston Dr. . . Pg.32 . . C5
Knightsbridge Dr.
. . . . . Pg.21,32
. . . . . A19,20,D5
Lakeview Dr. . . Pg.32 . . D6
Lampsher St. . . Pg.32 . . D6
Landsend Ct. . . Pg.32 . . D6
Lauren Ln. . . . Pg.32 . . C6
Lexington Ln. . . Pg.32 . . D6
Lilian Ct. . . . Pg.32 . . C6
Linden Dr. . . . Pg.32 . . C,D5
Locust Ave. . . . Pg.32 . . C6
Longacre Ln. . . Pg.32 . . D7

Longacre Ln. . . Pg.32 . . D6,7
Madison St. . . . Pg.32 . . D7
Main St. . . . . Pg.32 . . D5
Mallard Pt. . . . Pg.32 . . C6
Marion Ct. . . . Pg.32 . . C6
Medford Ct. . . . Pg.32 . . C5
Midway Dr. . . . Pg.21,32
. . . . . A21,E6
Nantucket Way . Pg.32 . . C5,6
Newberry Dr. . . Pg.32 . . C6
Newport Ct. . . . Pg.32 . . C6
Newport Dr. . . . Pg.21,32
. . . . . A20,C,D5
Northern Ct. . . Pg.32 . . C6
Northern Ter. . . Pg.32 . . C6
Nottingham Ct. . Pg.21,32
. . . . . A20,D5
Oak Terr. . . . . Pg.32 . . C6
Oakwood Ave. . . Pg.32 . . C,D6
Olympia Ln. . . . Pg.21,32
. . . . . A19,D5
Oxford Ct. . . . Pg.32 . . C6
Park Dr. . . . . Pg.32 . . C6
Pine Terr. . . . Pg.32 . . C6
Pleasant Pl. . . Pg.32 . . C5,6
Plymouth Ln. . . Pg.32 . . C6
Poplar Dr. . . . Pg.32 . . C6
Porten Rd. . . . Pg.21,32
. . . . . B20,21,E6
Portsmouth Cir. Pg.32 . . C,D5
Princeton Cir. . Pg.32 . . D7
Quincy Ct. . . . Pg.32 . . D6
Raccoon Cove . . Pg.32 . . C6
Ralph Ct. . . . . Pg.32 . . C6
Revere Ln. . . . Pg.32 . . C6
Richard Ct. . . . Pg.32 . . C6
Ridge Rd. . . . . Pg.32 . . C6
River Oaks Ct. . Pg.32 . . D6,7
River Oaks Ln. . Pg.32 . . D7
River St. . . . . Pg.32 . . B21
Roberts Rd. . . . Pg.32 . . D,E6
Rose Ave. . . . . Pg.32 . . C6
Salem Ct. . . . . Pg.32 . . C6
Saratoga Cir. . . Pg.32 . . D7
South Shore Dr.
. . . . . Pg.32 . . D6
Southampton Dr.
. . . . . Pg.21,32
. . . . . B20,D6
Southern Terr. . Pg.32 . . A21
Southport Dr. . . Pg.32 . . C,D5
Spruce Terr. . . Pg.32 . . C6
St. Route 176 . . Pg.21,32
. . . . . A21,C5
Stratford Ct. . . Pg.21,32
. . . . . A19,D5
Sumac Ave. . . . Pg.32 . . C5
Timber Ln. . . . Pg.32 . . C6
Timber Trail Rd.
. . . . . Pg.21,32
. . . . . A21,D6
Tulip Cir. . . . Pg.32 . . C6
Victoria Dr. . . Pg.21,32
. . . . . A19,D5
Vista Dr. . . . . Pg.21,32
. . . . . B20,C5,6
Walnut Ct. . . . Pg.32 . . C6
Waterford Way . Pg.32 . . C5
Wayside Dr. . . . Pg.21,32
. . . . . B20,E6
Wembley Dr. . . Pg.21,32
. . . . . A19,20,D5
Westminister Ln.
. . . . . Pg.32 . . C6
Willow Ln. . . . Pg.32 . . C6
Wimbledon Dr. . Pg.32 . . D5
Windsor Ln. . . . Pg.21,32
. . . . . B20,D6
Wishing Well Ln.
. . . . . Pg.32 . . D6
Wood Creek Dr. Pg.32 . . D6,7
Woodbine Ave. . Pg.32 . . D6
Woodland Cir. . Pg.32 . . D6
Woodlawn Dr. . Pg.32 . . D6
Yale Ln. . . . . Pg.32 . . C6
York Ln. . . . . Pg.32 . . C5

FOREST PRESERVES
Cotton Creek Marsh
. . . . . Pg.21 . . A20

JOHNSBURG
Page 4,16,33
STREETS
Acre Ave. . . . . Pg.4 . . E13
Amber Way . . . Pg.4 . . D13
Aspen Dr. . . . . Pg.4 . . D13
Aster Ct. . . . . Pg.4 . . D13
Autumn Way . . . Pg.4 . . D13
Bald Knob Rd. . . Pg.4 . . D14
Bayview Dr. . . . Pg.33 . . A10
Berwyn Ct. . . . Pg.4 . . E13
Bison Ln. . . . . Pg.4 . . E13
Bitsch Pl. . . . Pg.33 . . A9
Bolling Ave. . . Pg.4 . . E13
Brixham Ln., N. Pg.4,33
. . . . . B10,E13
Brixham Ln., S. Pg.4 . . E13
Broson Ct. . . . Pg.4 . . D12
Bryn Mawr Ct. . Pg.4 . . D12
Brynmawr Ct. . Pg.4,8 . . D13
Camden St. . . . Pg.4 . . D13
Cardington Way
. . . . . Pg.33 . . A9,10
Carol Ct. . . . . Pg.4 . . E13
Caroline Ct. . . Pg.4 . . E13

Cedar Creek Dr. Pg.33 . . A9
Channel Beach St.
. . . . . Pg.33 . . A,B9
Chapel Hill Rd. . Pg.33 . . B9
Charnbrook Dr. . Pg.4 . . E13
Cherokee Dr. . . Pg.3 . . E12
Church Ave. . . . Pg.33 . . A9
Church St. . . . Pg.33 . . A9
Cimmeron Ct. . Pg.4 . . D12
Claremont . . . . Pg.4 . . E12
Cobblestone Ct. Pg.4 . . D12
Cottonwood Ct. Pg.4 . . D12
Country Oaks Ln.
. . . . . Pg.4,8 . . D13
Cove Ct. . . . . Pg.4 . . D12
Creekside Ln. . . Pg.4 . . E13
Dakota Ridge . . Pg.4 . . D13
Delaware Pl. . . Pg.4 . . E13
Denise Ct. . . . Pg.33 . . A9
Dennis Blvd. . . Pg.33 . . A9
Devon Ln. . . . Pg.4 . . D12
Dolores Dr. . . . Pg.33 . . A9
Dutch Creek Ln.
. . . . . Pg.4 . . E12
Ernst Ln. . . . . Pg.33 . . A9
Fair Way Ave. . . Pg.33 . . B9
Fairview Ave. . . Pg.4 . . D12
Farmington Ln. . Pg.4 . . E13
Federal . . . . . Pg.33 . . A9
Fieldstone Way . Pg.4 . . D13
Florence Dr. . . Pg.4 . . D13
Frances Ave. . . Pg.4,33
. . . . . B10,E13
Freemont Ln. . . Pg.33 . . A9
Garfield Rd. . . Pg.3 . . E12
Golden Rod Ln. Pg.4 . . D13
Goodview Ave. . Pg.4 . . D13
Grand Ridge Ct.
. . . . . Pg.4 . . E14
Grant . . . . . . Pg.3 . . E12
Grouse Tr. . . . Pg.4 . . E13
Hamlin . . . . . Pg.4 . . E12
Harrison Ln. . . Pg.4 . . E14
Hayden Dr. . . . Pg.33 . . A10
Heather Ln. . . . Pg.4 . . D13
Heron Ct. . . . . Pg.4 . . D12
Hickory Way . . Pg.4,33
. . . . . A9,D13
Hillcrest Pl. . . Pg.33 . . A9
Hiller Ridge . . Pg.4 . . D13
Hilltop Ln. . . . Pg.4,33
. . . . . A10,D13
Indigo Ct. . . . Pg.4 . . D13
Irene Ct. . . . . Pg.33 . . A9,10
James Way . . . Pg.4 . . D13
Janice Ct. . . . Pg.33 . . A10
Jewel Dr. . . . . Pg.33 . . A10
Joesph Cir. . . . Pg.4 . . E13
Johnsburg Rd. . Pg.4,33
. . . . . A10,E13
Johnsburg Spring Grove Rd.
. . . . . Pg.33 . . A9
Kildeer Ln. . . . Pg.4 . . D13
King St. . . . . Pg.4 . . E13
Knob Hill Rd. . . Pg.4 . . E13
Lakeview Dr. . . Pg.33 . . A,B9
Lewis Ln. . . . . Pg.4 . . D13
Linden Ave. . . . Pg.4 . . E13
Long Ave. . . . . Pg.4,33
. . . . . B9,E13
Long Meadow Ave.
. . . . . Pg.4,33
. . . . . B9,E13
Maple Ave. . . . Pg.4,33
. . . . . A10,E13
May Ave. . . . . Pg.4,8 . . D13
Meadowlark Ln.
. . . . . Pg.4 . . D13
Mehring Ave. . . Pg.33 . . A9
Middle Ave. . . . Pg.4 . . E12
North May . . . Pg.33 . . A10
Oak Ct. . . . . Pg.4 . . D13
Oak Grove Rd. . Pg.4 . . E14
Oakdale Ave. . . Pg.4 . . E13
Oeffling Dr. . . Pg.33 . . A10
Old Bay Rd. . . Pg.4 . . E13
Olive Ave. . . . Pg.33 . . A9
Pinehurst Ct. . . Pg.4 . . D12
Pistakee View Dr.
. . . . . Pg.4 . . D12
Prairie Rose Ln.
. . . . . Pg.4 . . D13
Prairie Tr. . . . Pg.4 . . D13
Quail Ct. . . . . Pg.4 . . D13
Quincy Ave. . . . Pg.4 . . D13
Rachael Dr. . . . Pg.4 . . D13
Ramsgate Ln. . . Pg.4 . . D13
River Park Dr. . Pg.4 . . E13
River Terr. . . . Pg.4,33
Riverside Dr. . . Pg.33 . . B9
Riverview Dr. . . Pg.4,8 . . D13
Rolling Lane Rd.
. . . . . Pg.4 . . E14
Rosewood Ln. . . Pg.4 . . D12
Sagebrush Ct. . Pg.4 . . D13
Salem Ave. . . . Pg.4,16
Sandalwood Ln.
. . . . . Pg.33 . . A9,10
Sarah Dr. . . . . Pg.4 . . E13
Second Ave. . . Pg.4 . . D13
Seville Ct. . . . Pg.4 . . D12

Shiloh Dr. . . . Pg.33 . . A9
Skyhawk Ln. . . Pg.4 . . D13
St. Francis Ave. Pg.33 . . B9
St. Johns Ave. . Pg.33 . . B9
Stubby Ave. . . Pg.4,33
. . . . . B9,E13
Sudenaw Dr. . . Pg.4,33
. . . . . A10,D12
Sundown Ln. . . Pg.4 . . D13
Sunnyside Beach Dr.
. . . . . Pg.33 . . A9
Sunnyside Dr. . Pg.33 A,B10
Sunset . . . . . Pg.4 . . D12
Terrace Ave. . . Pg.33 . . A9
Tichfield Terr. . Pg.4 . . E13
Tivoli Terr. . . Pg.4 . . E13
Torrey Tr. . . . Pg.4 . . D12
Villanova Dr. . . Pg.4 . . D13
Villanova Dr. . . Pg.4 . . A9
Weingart Rd. . . Pg.33 . . A10
West May Ave. . Pg.33 . A9,10
Windmere Ln. . Pg.4 . . D12
2nd Ave. . . . . Pg.33 . . B10

FOREST PRESERVES
Wiengart Road Sedge
Meadow . . . Pg.4 . . E13

SCHOOLS
District #12 Admin. Office
. . . . . Pg.33 . . A9
James C. Bush Sch.
. . . . . Pg.8 . . E13
Johnsburg Jr. H.S.
. . . . . Pg.8 . . E13
Johnsburg Middle Sch.
. . . . . Pg.8 . . E13
School . . . . . Pg.33 . . B9
St. John the Baptist Cath.
Sch. . . . . . Pg.8 . . E13
St. John's Middle Sch.
. . . . . Pg.33 . . A9
Library . . . . . Pg.33 . . B9
Village Hall . . . Pg.33 . . A10

LAKE-IN-THE-HILLS
Pages 11,12,22-24,27-29
STREETS
Acorn Ct. . . . . Pg.28 . . K10
Acorn Ln. . . . . Pg.28 . . K10
Adams St. . . . . Pg.27 . . J10
Albrecht Rd. . . Pg.27 . . I5
Alcoff Ct. . . . Pg.11,22
Alexandria Dr. . Pg.27 . . K5
Algonquin Rd. . Pg.27 . . L5
Amberleigh Ct. Pg.27 . . L5
Anderson Dr. . . Pg.29 . . J12
Annandale Ct. . Pg.27 . . I5
Annandale Dr. . Pg.27 . . I5
Apache Tr. . . . Pg.29 . . K11
Appletree Ct. . . Pg.27 . . J6
Arland Ct., N. . . Pg.27 . . I5
Ash St. . . . . Pg.29 . . J11
Ashbury Ct. . . Pg.22 . . I5
Aster Ct. . . . . Pg.28 . . J7
Augusta Ct. . . Pg.28 . . K9
Aurora Ct. . . . Pg.11,22
. . . . . I4,K8
Aurora Ln. . . . Pg.11,22
. . . . . I4,K8
Avaton Ct. . . . Pg.11,22
Avaton Ln. . . . Pg.11,22
. . . . . I4,K9
Baldwin Ct. . . Pg.22 . . I5
Baldwin Ln. . . Pg.22 . . I5
Banbury Ct. . . Pg.22 . . I5
Banbury Ln. . . Pg.22 . . I4
Banford Ct. . . Pg.22 . . I5
Barbara Ct. . . Pg.29 . . J12
Barbarbor Ct. . Pg.27 . . J6
Barbarbor Dr. . Pg.27 . . J6
Baronet Ct. . . Pg.27 . . K5
Barrington Ct. . Pg.27 . . J6
Barton Creek Ct.
. . . . . Pg.28 . . J8
Bernice St. . . . Pg.29 . . K11
Big Cloud Pass . Pg.28 . . K8
Biltmore Ct. . . Pg.28 . . K8
Birch St. . . . . Pg.29 . . J10
Birkdale Ct. . . Pg.28 . . K8
Black Diamond Ct.
. . . . . Pg.28 . . K8
Blackberry Ln. . Pg.28 . . J7
Blackberry Dr. . Pg.28 . . J7
Blackhawk Dr. . Pg.29 . . K11
Bonnie Ct. . . . Pg.29 . . J12
Bordeaux Dr. . . Pg.27 . . I5
Boulder Dr. . . . Pg.28 . . K7
Brandt Dr. . . . Pg.29 . . K12
Briarcliff Ct. . . Pg.27 . . I5
Briarcliff Ln. . . Pg.27 . . I5
Briarfield In. . . Pg.27 . . L5
Bridlewood Cir. Pg.27 . . L5
Brindlewood Way
. . . . . Pg.28 . . J8
Brisbane Ct. . . Pg.27 . . I5
Brittany Bend . Pg.27 . . J6
Burr St. . . . . Pg.29 . . J11
Cadbury Ct. . . Pg.22 . . I5
Camargo Club Dr.
. . . . . Pg.28 . . J8

Capello Ct. . . . Pg.28 . . K9
Carl Ct. . . . . Pg.29 . . K12
Castle Pines Ct. Pg.28 . . K8
Cedar Ridge Dr. Pg.28 . . K10
Cedar St. . . . . Pg.29 . . K11
Chadwick Ct. . . Pg.22 . . I5
Chadwick Ln. . Pg.22 . . H5
Chancery Ct. . . Pg.27 . . K5
Chancery Way . . Pg.27 . . K5
Chantilly Cir. . Pg.27 . . K5
Cherokee Tr. . . Pg.29 . . K11
Cherry St. . . . Pg.29 . . J11
Chesire Ct. . . . Pg.27 . . K5
Cheyenne Dr. . . Pg.29 . . K11
Chippewa Tr. . . Pg.29 . . K11
Clark Rd. . . . . Pg.28 . . J10
Clayton Marsh Dr.
. . . . . Pg.28 . . J9
Clear Sky Tr. . . Pg.28 . . J8
Cobblestone Ct.
. . . . . Pg.28 . . K7
Cog Hill Ct. . . Pg.28 . . J8
Cool Stone Bend
. . . . . Pg.28 . . K9
Council Tr. . . . Pg.29 . . K12
Country Club Rd.
. . . . . Pg.28 . . K8
Course Dr. . . . Pg.28 . . K8
Courtney Dr. . . Pg.27 . . I5
Crab Apple Ct. . Pg.27 . . J6
Creekview Ln. . Pg.29 . . J11
Crimson Ct. . . Pg.22 . . I5
Crofton Cir. . . Pg.22 . . I5
Crofton Ct. . . Pg.22 . . I5
Crossview Ct. . Pg.27 . . L5
Crossview Ln. . Pg.27 . . L5
Crystal Downs Ct.
. . . . . Pg.28 . . J8
Crystal Lake Rd.
. . . . . Pg.28 . . K10
Cunat Ct. . . . Pg.29 . . J12
Cynthia Dr. . . Pg.29 . . K12
Cypress Ct. . . Pg.28 . . K8
Danbury Cir. . . Pg.11,22
David St. . . . . Pg.29 . . J12
Decatur Ave. . . Pg.27 . . J6
Deer Creek Ct. Pg.27 . . J6
Deer Creek Ln. Pg.27 . . J6
Deer Path . . . Pg.28 . . K10
Delaware Ave. . Pg.29 . . K11
Dogwood Ct. . . Pg.27 . . J6
Dogwood Ln. . . Pg.27 . . J6
Doral Ct. . . . Pg.28 . . K8
Echo Hill . . . . Pg.29 . . J12
Elderberry Ct. . Pg.28 . . J7
Eldorado Ct. . . Pg.28 . . L8
Elizabeth Ct. . Pg.29 . . K12
Ellis Rd. . . . . Pg.27 . . K5
Elm St. . . . . Pg.29 . . J10
Fairfax St. . . . Pg.27 . . J5
Farrington Ct. . Pg.27 . . J6
Ferryville Ct. . Pg.27 . . J6
First St. . . . . Pg.29 . . J10
Flowerfield Ct. Pg.27 . . J6
Frank Rd. . . . Pg.28 . . K7
Gail Ct. . . . . Pg.29 . . K12
Geneva Ct. . . . Pg.11,22
. . . . . I4,K9
Geneva Ln. . . . Pg.11,22
Glasgow Ct. . . Pg.29 . . I5
Glenrose Ln. . . Pg.27 . . L5
Grace Dr. . . . Pg.29 . . K12
Granite Ct. . . . Pg.28 . . K7
Grant Ave. . . . Pg.28 . . J10
Greenbrier Ct. . Pg.28 . . K8
Greenfield Ct. . Pg.27 . . J6
Hadden Ct. . . . Pg.22 . . I5
Halfmoon Gate Pg.28 . . J9
Haligus Rd. . . Pg.27 . . I4
Harvest Gate . . Pg.28 . . K9
Hastings Ct. . . Pg.27 . . L5
Hawthorne Tr. . Pg.29 . . K12
Hayward Ct. . . Pg.22 . . I4
Hayward Ln. . . Pg.22 . . I4
Hazelwood Ct. . Pg.27 . . J6
Heartland Gate Pg.28 . . J9
Heavens Gate . Pg.28 . . J9
Hensley Ln. . . Pg.11,22
Heron Ct. . . . Pg.27 . . J5
Hiawatha Dr. . Pg.29 . . K11
Hickory St. . . . Pg.29 . . J11
Highwood Ct. . Pg.11 . . I4
Highwood Ln. . Pg.22 . . I4
Hillsboro Ln. . Pg.27 . . I5
Hilltop Dr. . . . Pg.28 . . J10
Hilly Ln. . . . . Pg.29 . . K11
Hollyhock Ct. . Pg.27 . . J6
Horizon Ridge . Pg.28 . . J9
Hunters Path . Pg.28 . . K10
Impression Dr. . Pg.22 . . I5
Indian Tr. . . . Pg.29 . . K11
Industrial Dr. . Pg.29 . . J9
James R. Rakow Rd.
. . . . . Pg.24 . . H11
Jefferson St. . . Pg.29 . . J10
Jessie Rd. . . . Pg.28 . . K10
Joesph Ct. . . . Pg.29 . . J12
Joesph St. . . . Pg.29 . . J12
Kay Ct. . . . . Pg.29 . . J10
Kurt Ct. . . . . Pg.29 . . K12
LaCosta Ct. . . Pg.28 . . L8

LaQuinta Ct. ... Pg.28 .. K8
Lake Dr. ... Pg.29 .. K11
Lakewood Rd. ... Pg.28 .. I5
Landsbury Cir. ... Pg.27 .. L5
Landsbury Ct. ... Pg.27 .. L5
Larkspur Ct. ... Pg.27 .. J6
Larkspur Ln. ... Pg.27 .. J6
Lauren Valley Ct.
.......... Pg.28 .. J8
Lee Ave. ... Pg.28 .. J10
Lincoln St. ... Pg.28 .. J10
Linden St. ... Pg.28 .. J10
Litchfield Ct. ... Pg.27 .. J5
Litchfield Ln. ... Pg.27 .. J5
Liza Ct. ... Pg.29 .. K12
Locust ... Pg.28 .. K10
Long Cove Ct. ... Pg.28 .. J8
Lorree Ln. ... Pg.29 .. K12
Lucerne Cir. ... Pg.11,22 .. I3,K8
Lucerne St. ... Pg.11 .. K8
Mackinac St. ... Pg.27 .. J6
Manchester Ct. ... Pg.27 .. J6
Maple St. ... Pg.29 .. J11
Margate Ct. ... Pg.22 .. H5
Marlo Ct. ... Pg.28 .. J7
Mason Ln. ... Pg.28 .. K7
Mayberry Ct. ... Pg.28 .. J7
McKenzie Dr. ... Pg.11,22 .. H3,K8
McKinley St. ... Pg.28 .. I10
McPhee Dr. ... Pg.29 .. J11
Meadow Ln. ... Pg.28 .. K10
Medinah Ct. ... Pg.28 .. L8
Melbourne St. ... Pg.27 .. J5
Melbourne Ln. ... Pg.22 .. I5
Menominee Dr. ... Pg.29 .. K12
Mesa Dr. ... Pg.20 .. L12
Michael Ct. ... Pg.29 .. K12
Middlefield Ct. ... Pg.27 .. J6
Miller Rd. ... Pg.28 .. J7
Mohican Tr. ... Pg.29 .. K11
Monarch Ct. ... Pg.27 .. K5
Monroe St. ... Pg.28 .. J10
Montclair Ct. ... Pg.29 .. K12
Montgomery Dr.
.......... Pg.11,22 .. I4,K8
Montrose Dr. ... Pg.11,22 .. I3,K8
Moonstone Run ... Pg.28 .. J9
Morningside Ct. ... Pg.27 .. J6
Navajo Dr. ... Pg.29 .. K12
Newbury Ct. ... Pg.22 .. I4
Noelle Bend ... Pg.22 .. I5
Normandy Ln. ... Pg.27 .. L5
Northlight Pass ... Pg.28 .. J9
Oak Leaf Rd. ... Pg.28 .. K10
Oak St. ... Pg.28 .. J10
Olympic Ct. ... Pg.28 .. K8
Parc Ct. ... Pg.27 .. J6
Patton Ave. ... Pg.28 .. J9
Pawnee Ct. ... Pg.29 .. K11
Peach Tree Ct. ... Pg.27 .. J7
Peartree Dr. ... Pg.27 .. J6
Pebble Beach Ct. ... Pg.28 .. J8
Pershing Ave. ... Pg.28 .. J10
Pheasant Tr. ... Pg.28 .. K10
Pine St. ... Pg.29 .. I10
Pingree Rd. ... Pg.29 .. I13
Plum St. ... Pg.29 .. J11
Pocahontas Tr. ... Pg.29 .. K11
Point O Woods Ct. ... Pg.28 .. J8
Polaris Dr. ... Pg.29 .. K9
Poplar St. ... Pg.29 .. J11
Prides Run ... Pg.28 .. J8
Princeton Ln. ... Pg.22 .. H5
Prosper Ct ... Pg.29 .. J12
Provence Pl. ... Pg.27 .. J5
Pyott Rd. ... Pg.24 .. H11
Quail Run ... Pg.28 .. K10
Rainmaker Run ... Pg.28 .. K9
Ramble Rd. ... Pg.29 .. L11
Randall Rd. ... Pg.28 .. J9
Red Bud Ct. ... Pg.27 .. J6
Redwood Ct. ... Pg.27 .. K5
Reed Rd. ... Pg.27 .. K5
Ridge Ct. ... Pg.28 .. K7
Ridge Ln. ... Pg.28 .. K7
Ridgewood Dr. ... Pg.28 .. J8
Riviera Ct. ... Pg.28 .. K8
Rochelle Ct. ... Pg.22 .. I4
Rolling Hills Ct. ... Pg.27 .. J6
Rolling Hills Dr. ... Pg.27 .. J6
Roosevelt St. ... Pg.28 .. I10
Roxburg Ct. ... Pg.27 .. J6
Royal Oak Ct. ... Pg.27 .. J6
Royal Oak Ln. ... Pg.27 .. J6
Saginaw St. ... Pg.29 .. J7
Sandstone Ct. ... Pg.28 .. L8
Savon Ct. ... Pg.11,22 .. I3,K8
Savon Dr. ... Pg.11,22 .. I3,K8
Sedgefield Ln. ... Pg.22 .. I5
Seminole St. ... Pg.29 .. K12
Service Rd. ... Pg.29 .. J12
Shadow Creek Ct. ... Pg.28 .. J8
Shawnee Dr. ... Pg.29 .. K12
Sherwood Ct. ... Pg.28 .. J10
Shoal Creek Ct. ... Pg.28 .. J8

Sienna Dr. ... Pg.11 .. K8
Sierra Ct. ... Pg.29 .. L12
Sioux Tr. ... Pg.29 .. K11
Sorrel Row ... Pg.29 .. L12
Spencer Ct. ... Pg.27 .. L5
Spencer Place ... Pg.27 .. L5
Spriing Garden Ct. ... Pg.27 .. J6
Spring Lake Dr. ... Pg.22 .. J6
Springlake Ct. ... Pg.28 .. J7
Springlake Dr. ... Pg.28 .. J7
Spruce St. ... Pg.28 .. J10
Spyglass Ct. ... Pg.28 .. K8
St. Route 31 ... Pg.29 .. I13
Stanton Cir. ... Pg.27 .. J5
Stanton Ct. ... Pg.27 .. J5
Starwood Pass ... Pg.28 .. J8,9
Steeplechase Way ... Pg.27 .. K5
Stickley Ln. ... Pg.27 .. K5
Sugar Creek Ct. ... Pg.27 .. I6
Sullivan Pass ... Pg.27 .. K5
Sun Valley Ct. ... Pg.28 .. K8
Succox Ct. ... Pg.28 .. J8
Swanson Rd. ... Pg.27 .. J7
Sweetwater Ct. ... Pg.28 .. J9
Sweetwater Ridge ... Pg.28 .. J9
Sycamore St. ... Pg.28 .. J10
Tamarisk Ct. ... Pg.28 .. L8
Taralon Tr. ... Pg.27 .. J5
Techumseh Glen Tr. ... Pg.29 .. K12
Tennyson Ct. ... Pg.27 .. K5
Terramere Ln. ... Pg.27 .. I5
Thistle Ln. ... Pg.22 .. I5
Thornberry Way ... Pg.20 .. J7
Thunder Ridge ... Pg.28 .. K9
Torry Pines Ct. ... Pg.28 .. J8
Trinity Dr. ... Pg.29 .. I13
Twelve Lakes Ct. ... Pg.28 .. J8
Valhalla Ct. ... Pg.28 .. J8
Viewpoint Dr. ... Pg.29 .. K12
Village Creek Tr. ... Pg.28 .. K10
Vintage Dr. ... Pg.28 .. K8
Virginia St. ... Pg.29 .. I13
Walnut Dr. ... Pg.29 .. K11
Walnut Grove Ct. ... Pg.27 .. J6
Walter Ct. ... Pg.29 .. J12
Wander Way ... Pg.28 .. K10
Warwick Ct. ... Pg.27 .. L5
Washington St. ... Pg.28 .. J10
Waterbury Pl. ... Pg.27 .. L5
Wedgewood Cir ... Pg.27 .. L5
Wedgewood Ct. ... Pg.27 .. L5
Westminister Ct. ... Pg.27 .. J6
Wexford Ct. ... Pg.27 .. J5
White Pine Cir. ... Pg.28 .. J7
White Pine Ln. ... Pg.28 .. J7
Whitmore Way ... Pg.27 .. L5
Willow St. ... Pg.29 .. K12
Windgate Way ... Pg.27 .. K5
Windmere Ct. ... Pg.27 .. K5
Windmere Dr. ... Pg.27 .. K5
Windmere Way ... Pg.27 .. K5
Windstone Ct. ... Pg.29 .. K8
Winslow Way ... Pg.27 .. K5
Wisteria Ct. ... Pg.28 .. K8
Woodland Rd. ... Pg.28 .. K10
Woody Way ... Pg.28 .. K10
Worthington Ln.
.......... Pg.11,22 .. I4,K8
Wright Dr. ... Pg.27 .. K5

**FOREST PRESERVES**
Exner Marsh ... Pg.27 .. K6
Spring Hill Farm Fen ... Pg.29 .. J11

**GOLF COURSES**
Boulder Ridge C.C. ... Pg.28 .. K8

**PARKS**
Barbara Key Park ... Pg.29 .. J11
Beach Park ... Pg.29 .. K11
Big Sky Park ... Pg.28 .. J8
Concord Park ... Pg.22 .. I4
Dillow Park ... Pg.27 .. J6
Ford Park ... Pg.29 .. L11
Hidden Valley Ballfield ... Pg.29 .. K12
Morningside Park ... Pg.28 .. J10
Nockels Park ... Pg.28 .. J10
Richard Taylor Soccer Field ... Pg.28 .. J9
Ryder Park ... Pg.28 .. J10
Sundance Park ... Pg.28 .. J9

**SCHOOLS**
Lake in the Hills Elem. Sch. ... Pg.29 .. K11

**MISCELLANEOUS**
D & S Industrial Park ... Pg.29 .. I13
Fire Department ... Pg.28 .. J10
Lake in the Hills Airport ... Pg.24 .. H11
McHenry County Prairie Trail
South ... Pg.24 .. H11
Racket Club ... Pg.28 .. I13
Village Hall ... Pg.28 .. J10

**LAKEMOOR**
Pages 8,16
**STREETS**
Anthony Ln. ... Pg.16 .. B8
Bakers Ct. ... Pg.16 .. D9
Bay Meadow Ln. ... Pg.16 .. A8
Bay Oaks Dr. ... Pg.16 .. A8
Dominion Ln. ... Pg.16 .. D9
Elmaine Terr. ... Pg.16 .. D9
Fritzche Rd. ... Pg.16 .. E9
Herbert Rd. ... Pg.16 .. E9
Highland Dr. ... Pg.16 .. E9
Hollywood Terr. ... Pg.16 .. E9
Julia Way ... Pg.8 .. E13
Kings Way ... Pg.8 .. F14
Lake Rd., N. ... Pg.16 .. D9
Lake Shore Dr. ... Pg.16 .. D9
Lakeview Dr. ... Pg.16 .. D0
Lilly Ln. ... Pg.16 .. D9
Lily Lake Pkwy ... Pg.16 .. E9
Longbeach Rd. ... Pg.16 .. E9
Lotus Dr. ... Pg.16 .. E9
Maplewood Dr. ... Pg.16 .. D9
Margaret Ct. ... Pg.8 .. E13
Morningside Dr. ... Pg.16 .. E9
North Lake Rd. ... Pg.16 .. D9
Park Rd. ... Pg.16 .. D,E9
Pine Grove ... Pg.16 .. E9
Providence Dr. ... Pg.8 .. F14
Riverside Dr. ... Pg.16 .. E9
Rosedale Dr. ... Pg.16 .. D9
Santa Barbara Rd. ... Pg.16 .. E9
Scotland Rd. ... Pg.16 .. E9
Sheridan Rd. ... Pg.16 .. E9
Sunnyside Rd. ... Pg.16 .. D9
Sunset Dr. ... Pg.16 .. D9
Tia Junda Dr. ... Pg.16 .. D9
Valleyview Dr. ... Pg.16 .. E9
Venice Rd. ... Pg.16 .. E9
Wegner Rd. ... Pg.16 .. E9
Willow Rd. ... Pg.16 .. D9

**FOREST PRESERVES**
Volo Bog ... Pg.4 .. E14

**PARKS**
Park Lane Nature Park ... Pg.16 .. D9

**MISCELLANEOUS**
McHenry-Nunda Township
Library ... Pg.16 .. D9
Police & Village Hall ... Pg.16 .. D9
Township Fire Station #3 ... Pg.16 .. D9

**LAKEWOOD**
Pages 11,22,23
**STREETS**
Ackman Rd. ... Pg.22 .. H6
Appleton Ln. ... Pg.17 .. E4
Rallard Rd. ... Pg.17 .. E4
Bard Rd. ... Pg.22 .. F6
Bardwell Ln. ... Pg.22 .. G6
Beaver Pond Ct. ... Pg.22 .. G6
Beech Ave. ... Pg.17 .. U5
Benoy Ct. ... Pg.22 .. G6
Berwick Ct. ... Pg.22 .. G6
Bonnie Dr. ... Pg.22 .. F4
Bonnie Ridge Rd. ... Pg.22 .. F4
Braemar Cir. ... Pg.22 .. F5
Brighton Ln. ... Pg.17 .. D5
Broadway ... Pg.23 .. F7
Carlisle Ln. ... Pg.17 .. D5
Center Ave. ... Pg.23 .. F7
Chicago Ave. ... Pg.23 .. E7
Condor Cir. ... Pg.22 .. H6
Country Club Rd. ... Pg.23 .. F7
Crystal Ct. ... Pg.23 .. F7
Cumberland Ln. ... Pg.23 .. E8
Dairy Ln. ... Pg.22 .. G5
Dunhill Dr. ... Pg.22 .. G6
Eden Ct. ... Pg.22 .. G6
Essex Ln. ... Pg.23 .. E8
Fairway Dr. ... Pg.22 .. F5
Falcon Greens Dr. ... Pg.22 .. H6
Farell Dr. ... Pg.22 .. G6
Firth Ct. ... Pg.22 .. F6
Foster Rd. ... Pg.11 .. K8
Galena St. ... Pg.22 .. G4
Georgetown Ln. ... Pg.22 .. H6
Gleneagle Cir. ... Pg.22 .. F5
Haligus Rd. ... Pg.22 .. F4
Hampshire Ln. ... Pg.23 .. F7
Highland Ln. ... Pg.17 .. D5
Huntley Rd. ... Pg.23 .. E7
Inverway ... Pg.22 .. F4
Lake Ave. ... Pg.22 .. G5
Lakewood Rd. ... Pg.22 .. G5
Lenox Ln. ... Pg.23 .. F7
Loch Glen Ct. ... Pg.22 .. G6
Loch Glen Dr. ... Pg.22 .. G6
Main St. ... Pg.22 .. F6
Marsh Dr. ... Pg.22 .. F4
McIntosh Ct. ... Pg.22 .. H6
Melrose Ln. ... Pg.23 .. F7
Merchant Ct. ... Pg.22 .. H6
Meridian St. ... Pg.22 .. G6
Muirfield Ct. ... Pg.22 .. G5
Muirfield St. ... Pg.22 .. G5
Nicklaus Ln. ... Pg.22 .. H6
Norman Ct. ... Pg.22 .. G6
Oakwood Dr. ... Pg.22,23 .. E7
Owl Ct. ... Pg.22 .. H6
Oxford Ln. ... Pg.22 .. G6
Palmer Dr. ... Pg.22 .. H5
Park ... Pg.22 .. G6
Partridge Ln. ... Pg.22 .. F5
Pheasant Dr. ... Pg.22 .. G6
Player Ct. ... Pg.22 .. H5-6
Polo Ct. ... Pg.22 .. H6
Prestwick Ln. ... Pg.22 .. G6
Raptor Tr. ... Pg.22 .. H6
Redtail Dr. ... Pg.22 .. H6
Richmond Ln. ... Pg.23 .. E7
Scots Cir. ... Pg.22 .. G5
Scotts Ln. ... Pg.22 .. H6
Shade Tree Cir. ... Pg.22,23 .. E7
South Shore Dr. ... Pg.23 .. E7
State Rte. 47 ... Pg.11 .. K8
Stuart Ln. ... Pg.22 .. F5
Sunset Dr. ... Pg.23 .. E7
Turnberry Trail ... Pg.22 .. G5
Vida Ave. ... Pg.23 .. F7
Warwick Ln. ... Pg.23 .. F7
Watson Ct. ... Pg.22 .. H5
Wiltshire Ln. ... Pg.22 .. E,F8
Woodbine Rd. ... Pg.17 .. F4

**GOLF COURSES**
Red Tail Golf Club ... Pg.22 .. G6
Turnberry Country Club ... Pg.22 .. F6

**PARKS**
Brighton Oaks Park ... Pg.17 .. E5
Kamijima Park ... Pg.17 .. E7
West Beach Park ... Pg.23 .. E7

**MISCELLANEOUS**
Lakewood Village Hall ... Pg.23 .. E7
Water Treatment Facility ... Pg.22 .. E4

**LAWRENCE**
Page 1...C3
**LILYMOOR**
Page 16...D8
**MARENGO**
Pages 9,32
**STREETS**
Adams ... Pg.32 .. E4
Ann St. ... Pg.32 .. E4
Autumn St. ... Pg.32 .. E4
Bailey ... Pg.32 .. E4
Bailey Ct. ... Pg.32 .. E4
Barbara Ct. ... Pg.32 .. E4
Bauman St. ... Pg.32 .. E4
Beaver Pond Dr. ... Pg.32 .. E5
Beaver Pond Pl. ... Pg.32 .. E3
Briden Dr. ... Pg.32 .. E3
Buttonwood Dr. ... Pg.32 .. E4
Buttonwood Ln. ... Pg.32 .. E4
Caroline ... Pg.32 .. F4
Cascade Dr. ... Pg.32 .. E4,5
Cascade Pl. ... Pg.32 .. E5
Cayuyga ... Pg.32 .. E5
Center Dr. ... Pg.32 .. E5
Chappel St. ... Pg.32 .. E4
Cherokee Tr. ... Pg.32 .. E3
Chestnut Ct. ... Pg.32 .. D3
Chestnut Ln. ... Pg.32 .. D3
Chippewa Tr. ... Pg.32 .. E3
Circle Ct. ... Pg.32 .. E4
Clark ... Pg.32 .. E4
Cottonwood Ln. ... Pg.32 .. E3
Damon St. ... Pg.32 .. E4
Deer Pass Rd. ... Pg.32 .. E3
Deitz St. ... Pg.32 .. E,F4
Dian Ct. ... Pg.32 .. F4
Dunham St. ... Pg.32 .. F4
East St. ... Pg.32 .. E4
Eisenhower Dr. ... Pg.32 .. E3
Elm Ave. ... Pg.32 .. E4
Elm St. ... Pg.9,32
Fox Glove Ct. ... Pg.32 .. E4,J3
Fox Glove Ln. ... Pg.32 .. D4
Georgann Ct. ... Pg.32 .. F4
Geraldine Ct. ... Pg.32 .. F4
Grace St. ... Pg.32 .. F4
Grant Hwy. ... Pg.9,32 .. E3,4
Greenlee St. ... Pg.32 .. E4
Hale St. ... Pg.32 .. E4
Hayden Dr. ... Pg.32 .. E4
Hickory Ct. ... Pg.32 .. D3
Hickory Ln. ... Pg.32 .. D3
Indian Oaks Tr. ... Pg.32 .. F3
Jackson St. ... Pg.32 .. E4
Jacquelyn Ct. ... Pg.32 .. E4
James Ct. ... Pg.32 .. E4
Johnson Dr. ... Pg.32 .. E3
Kennedy Dr. ... Pg.32 .. E3
Kent St. ... Pg.32 .. E4
Keppler Dr. ... Pg.32 .. E4
Kishwaukee ... Pg.32 .. E4
Locust St. ... Pg.32 .. E5
Lynn Dr. ... Pg.32 .. E5
Mallard Dr. ... Pg.32 .. E4
Maple St. ... Pg.32 .. E4
Mary Ct. ... Pg.32 .. F4
Mohawk Dr. ... Pg.32 .. E4
Navaho Tr. ... Pg.32 .. E3
O'Connell Dr. ... Pg.32 .. E4
Oak Manor Dr. ... Pg.32 .. F4
Osage Tr. ... Pg.32 .. E3
Ottertail Dr. ... Pg.32 .. E3
Ottertail Pl. ... Pg.32 .. E3
Page St. ... Pg.32 .. E4
Park Dr. ... Pg.9,32 .. E3
Pawnee Dr. ... Pg.32 .. E3
Prairie St. ... Pg.32 .. L4
Prospect St. ... Pg.32 .. E4
Pulse Lane ... Pg.5,9 .. E4
Railroad St. ... Pg.9,32 .. E4,J3
Randall Ct. ... Pg.32 .. F4
Riley Dr. ... Pg.32 .. E4
Riley Rd. ... Pg.32 .. E,F4
Ritz Rd. ... Pg.32 .. E4
Rowland Ave. ... Pg.32 .. E4
Royal Oak Dr. ... Pg.32 .. E,F4
School Ct. ... Pg.32 .. E4
Shady Ln. ... Pg.32 .. E4
South St. ... Pg.32 .. E4
Spoonable St. ... Pg.32 .. E4
Stanford Dr. ... Pg.32 .. E3
State St. ... Pg.32 .. E,F4
Stevenson St. ... Pg.32 .. E4
Sullivan St. ... Pg.32 .. E4
Sunset Dr. ... Pg.32 .. E4
Taylor St. ... Pg.32 .. E4
Telegraph St. ... Pg.32 .. E4
Tioga Tr. ... Pg.32 .. E3
Van Buren St. ... Pg.32 .. E4
Walnut Cir. ... Pg.32 .. E4
Walnut Ln. ... Pg.32 .. E4
Washington St. ... Pg.32 .. E4
West St. ... Pg.32 .. E4
White Tail Cir. ... Pg.32 .. E3
White Tail Dr. ... Pg.32 .. E3
White Tail Pl. ... Pg.32 .. E3
Willow Rd. ... Pg.32 .. E4
Woodbine Ln. ... Pg.32 .. D4
Woodland Ct. ... Pg.32 .. D4
Woodland St. ... Pg.32 .. E4

**CEMETERIES**
Cemetery ... Pg.32 .. E4

**PARKS**
Calvin Spencer Park ... Pg.32 .. E4
Indian Oaks Park ... Pg.32 .. F3

**SCHOOLS**
Locust Sch. ... Pg.32 .. E4
Marengo Comm. H.S. ... Pg.32 .. E3
Washington Elem. Sch. ... Pg.32 .. E4
Zion Lutheran Sch. ... Pg.32 .. E4

**MISCELLANEOUS**
Fire Dept. ... Pg.32 .. E4
Police/Village Hall ... Pg.32 .. E4
Post Office ... Pg.32 .. E4

**MARENGO TOWNSHIP**
Pages 5,9
**STREETS**
Carmak Rd. ... Pg.5 .. G2
Collins Rd. ... Pg.5 .. G2
Cox Rd. ... Pg.5 .. G3
Deerpass Rd. ... Pg.5 .. G3
Edward St. ... Pg.5 .. H3
Elizabeth St. ... Pg.5,9 .. H4
Executive Dr. ... Pg.5 .. H3
Greenbriar Ln. ... Pg.5 .. H3
Grenadier Dr. ... Pg.5 .. H3
Hawthorne Rd. ... Pg.5 .. H3
Heritage Dr. ... Pg.5,9 .. H4
Highcrest Rd. ... Pg.5 .. G3
Johnson Rd. ... Pg.9 .. J3
Kishwaukee Valley Rd. ... Pg.5,9 .. H3
Koda Dr. ... Pg.5 .. H3
Lynn Dr. ... Pg.5 .. H3
Mary Ln. ... Pg.5 .. H3
Meyer Rd. ... Pg.9 .. J3
Michele Dr. ... Pg.5 .. H3
Miller Rd. ... Pg.5 .. H1
Noe Rd. ... Pg.5 .. G2
Northwest Rd. ... Pg.5 .. H3
O'Connell Rd. ... Pg.9 .. J3
Olbrich Rd. ... Pg.5 .. G3
Olcott Rd. ... Pg.5 .. G1
Oleson Rd. ... Pg.5 .. G1
Parade Ct. ... Pg.5,9 .. H4
Parkview Dr. ... Pg.5 .. H3
Pringle Dr. ... Pg.5 .. H3
Ridgeview Ln. ... Pg.5 .. G4
River Ranch Rd. ... Pg.5,9 .. J3
River Rd. ... Pg.5 .. H2
Root Rd. ... Pg.5 .. G2
Squire Dr. ... Pg.5,9 .. H4
Stella Dr. ... Pg.5 .. H3
Thorne Rd. ... Pg.5,9 .. J2

**FOREST PRESERVES**
H.U.M. Prairie ... Pg.5 .. J2
Marengo Ridge Reserve ... Pg.5 .. H3

**SCHOOLS**
Hawthorn Elem. Sch. ... Pg.5 .. G3

**McCULLOM LAKE**
Pages 8,15
**STREETS**
Beachview ... Pg.15 .. A4
Clover Hill ... Pg.15 .. A4
East Ln. ... Pg.15 .. A3
Eastwood Dr. ... Pg.15 .. A3
Forest View ... Pg.15 .. A3
Fountain Ln. ... Pg.15 .. A3
Garden Ct. ... Pg.15 .. A3
Greenwood Pl. ... Pg.15 .. D5
Hickory Dr. ... Pg.15 .. A3
Knollwood ... Pg.15 .. A3
Lakeshore Dr. ... Pg.15 .. A4
Maple Hill Dr. ... Pg.15 .. A4
McCullom Lake Rd. ... Pg.15 .. A4
Oak St. ... Pg.15 .. A3
Oakland Ln. ... Pg.15 .. A3
Oakview West ... Pg.15 .. A3
Orchard Dr. ... Pg.15 .. A3,4
Park View Dr. ... Pg.15 .. A3
Sarina Rd. ... Pg.15 .. A3
Short ... Pg.15 .. A3
Spring Rd. ... Pg.15 .. A3
West End Dr. ... Pg.15 .. A3
West Ln. ... Pg.15 .. A3

**MISCELLANEOUS**
Village Hall ... Pg.15 .. A4

**McHENRY**
Pages 3,4,7,8,15,16
**STREETS**
Abbey Dr. ... Pg.15 .. E3
Abbington Dr. ... Pg.15 .. D3,4
Albany St. ... Pg.15 .. F5
Albert Dr. ... Pg.4,15 .. A3,E13
Allen Ave. ... Pg.15 .. C5
Amberwood Pl. ... Pg.15 .. C5
Amherst Dr. ... Pg.15 .. B3
Anderson Dr. ... Pg.15 .. C5
Andinos Ct. ... Pg.15 .. B5
Anne St. ... Pg.15 .. D5
April Ave. ... Pg.4 .. E13
Ashland ... Pg.15 .. C3
Ashley Dr. ... Pg.15 .. C4
Augusta Dr. ... Pg.15 .. C4
Bally Dr. ... Pg.16 .. E6
Bally Rd. ... Pg.16 .. E6
Barnwood Ct. ... Pg.15 .. E1
Barnwood Tr. ... Pg.15 .. E1
Bauer Rd. ... Pg.15 .. D5
Beach Ave. ... Pg.15 .. C3
Beach Ct. ... Pg.15 .. C3
Beach Rd. ... Pg.15 .. C3
Belden St. ... Pg.15 .. B2
Bennington Ln. ... Pg.15 .. B5
Benton Dr. ... Pg.15 .. C5
Birch Ln. ... Pg.15 .. B6
Biscayne Dr. ... Pg.15 .. E5
Bonita Ln. ... Pg.15 .. F5
Bonner Dr. ... Pg.15 .. C4
Bonnie Brae ... Pg.15 .. E6
Boone ... Pg.15 .. C5
Boone Creek Cir. ... Pg.15 .. B5
Bradley Ct. ... Pg.15 .. B5
Brighton Pl. ... Pg.15 .. C5
Brittany Dr. ... Pg.15 .. C5
Broad St. ... Pg.15 .. C4
Broadway ... Pg.15 .. E,F6
Broden St. ... Pg.15 .. D3
Bromley, N. ... Pg.15 .. D3
Brookwood Tr. ... Pg.15 .. B3
Brown St. ... Pg.15 .. C4
Burning Tree Dr. ... Pg.7 .. F10
Callista St. ... Pg.15 .. C4
Cambridge Dr. ... Pg.15 .. C4
Canterbury Dr. ... Pg.15 .. C5
Capri Terr. ... Pg.15 .. F6
Carey Dr. ... Pg.15 .. F5
Carol ... Pg.15 .. C3
Carriage Tr. ... Pg.15 .. E5
Center St. ... Pg.15 .. D5
Central St. ... Pg.15 .. B2
Chapel Hill Rd. ... Pg.8 .. F13
Charlotte Ave. ... Pg.15 .. D6
Chasefield Cir. ... Pg.15 .. D3
Cherry Hill Ct. ... Pg.16 .. A2
Cherryhill Ct. ... Pg.4 .. E13
Chesapeake Dr., W. ... Pg.15 .. B3
Chesterfield Ct. ... Pg.15 .. C4
Chesterfield Dr. ... Pg.15 .. C4
Chestnut Ln. ... Pg.15 .. B5
Chickaloon Dr. ... Pg.7,15 .. C2,F11
Church ... Pg.15 .. C5
Clearbrook St. ... Pg.15 .. C5
Clearview Dr. ... Pg.15 .. B4
Clover Ave. ... Pg.15 .. D5
Colony Ct. ... Pg.15 .. C4
Colony Tr. ... Pg.7 .. F10
Commercial Ave. ... Pg.15 .. C4
Cornell Ct. ... Pg.15 .. B5
Corporate Dr. ... Pg.15 .. C4
Country Ln. ... Pg.16 .. C7
Court St. ... Pg.15 .. C5
Courtland Tr. ... Pg.15 .. C4
Creekside Cl. ... Pg.15 .. D3
Creekside Ln. ... Pg.15 .. D3
Creekside Tr. ... Pg.15 .. D3
Crescent Blvd. ... Pg.16 .. C6
Crestwood Dr. ... Pg.7,8 .. F11
Crestwood St. ... Pg.15 .. C4
Crooked Tree Ct. ... Pg.15 .. B5
Cross Tr. ... Pg.15 .. E4
Crystal Lake Rd. ... Pg.15 .. D4
Cumberland Cir. ... Pg.15 .. C4
Dale Ave. ... Pg.15 .. D5
Dart Moor Rd. ... Pg.15 .. D3
Dayton St. ... Pg.15 .. F5
De Paul Ct. ... Pg.15 .. B5
De Paul St. ... Pg.15 .. C4
Deer Run Tr. ... Pg.7 .. F10
Deerwood Tr. ... Pg.7 .. F10
Denali Trail ... Pg.3,4,7,8 .. F11
Derby Ln. ... Pg.15 .. F6
Devonshire Ct. ... Pg.15 .. D3
Donnelly Pl. ... Pg.15 .. C5
Donovan St. ... Pg.15 .. B,D5
Dorchester Pl. ... Pg.15 .. C5
Dot St. ... Pg.15 .. B3
Drake Blvd. ... Pg.15 .. C4
Drake Ct. ... Pg.15 .. B5
Driftwood Tr. ... Pg.15 .. E3
Eaglewood Tr. ... Pg.15 .. D3
Eastern Ave. ... Pg.15 .. B4
Elm Ave. ... Pg.15 .. C5
Elm St. ... Pg.15 .. C3,5
Emily Ln. ... Pg.15 .. C6
Erin St. ... Pg.15 .. C6
Essex ... Pg.15 .. C4
Fairfax Ct. ... Pg.15 .. E3
Fairfax Dr. ... Pg.15 .. E3
Fairway Dr. ... Pg.15 .. D6
Farington Dr. ... Pg.15 .. D3
Fieldstone Tr. ... Pg.15 .. D5
Florence Blvd. ... Pg.4,15 .. A3,E13
Flower Ave. ... Pg.15 .. C4
Flower St. ... Pg.15 .. C4
Foolish Pleasure Dr. ... Pg.15 .. B4
Forest Dr. ... Pg.15 .. E6
Fourth ... Pg.15 .. C5
Fox Ln., N. ... Pg.15 .. C4
Freund St. ... Pg.15 .. C4
Front Royal Ct. ... Pg.15 .. D6
Front Royal Dr. ... Pg.15 .. D6
Front St. ... Pg.15 .. C5
Garden Qtr. Rd. ... Pg.15 .. D4
Geneva Pl. ... Pg.15 .. C5
Glen ... Pg.15 .. D5
Glen Dr. ... Pg.15 .. C4
Glenbrook Tr. ... Pg.15 .. E4
Golfview Ave. ... Pg.15 .. C6
Grand Ave. ... Pg.15 .. C5
Grave Mill Ct. ... Pg.15 .. B5
Green St. ... Pg.15 .. C5
Greenbrier Dr. ... Pg.15 .. D6
Greendale Ct. ... Pg.15 .. E6
Gregg Dr. ... Pg.15 .. E6
Grove Ave. ... Pg.15 .. C4
Hampton Ct. ... Pg.15 .. B3
Hanley St. ... Pg.15 .. B3
Harrington ... Pg.15 .. B5
Hartland Tr. ... Pg.15 .. D3
Hartman Ln. ... Pg.15 .. C2
Hayward Dr. ... Pg.3,4,7 .. F11
Heritage Dr. ... Pg.15 .. F6
Hi Point Rd. ... Pg.15 .. F5
High St. ... Pg.15 .. C4
Highview Ave. ... Pg.15 .. C4
Hill St. ... Pg.15 .. B3
Hilltop Blvd. ... Pg.15 .. C6
Holly Ct. ... Pg.16 .. C7
Hollywood Blvd. ... Pg.15 .. F5
Home Ave. ... Pg.15 .. C3
Hunter Dr. ... Pg.15 .. B3
Hunter Path ... Pg.15 .. F6
Huntington Dr. ... Pg.15 .. D3
Idyle Dell Rd. ... Pg.15 .. E5
Illiana Tr. ... Pg.3,4,7,8 .. F11
Industrial Rd. ... Pg.15 .. C4
James St. ... Pg.15 .. C5

**MC HENRY**

Jennifer Ln. .. Pg.15 .. C5
John St. .. Pg.15 .. C5
Judy Dr. .. Pg.15 .. C5
Kane Ave. .. Pg.15 .. D5
Katie Ln. .. Pg.15 .. D5
Katmai Tr. .. Pg.3,4,7,8 .. F11
Kelter St. .. Pg.15 .. D4
Kensington Dr. Pg.15 .. D3
Kinley Blvd. .. Pg.15 .. E6
Knoll Ave. .. Pg.15 .. C4
Knox Rd. .. Pg.15 .. D5
Lake Ave. .. Pg.15 .. C5
Lakeland .. Pg.15 .. C3
Lakewood Ave. .. Pg.15 .. C3
Lakewood Rd. .. Pg.15 .. B4
Lawn Ct. .. Pg.15 .. C6
Lawrence Pkwy. .. Pg.15 .. E5
Lee St. .. Pg.15 .. D5
Leonard Ave. .. Pg.15 .. C5
Lillian St. .. Pg.15 .. D4,5
Lincoln Ave. .. Pg.15 .. C5
Lincoln Rd. .. Pg.15 .. D5
Linda Rd. .. Pg.15 .. D5
Loch Glen Ln. .. Pg.15 .. B5
Logan St. .. Pg.15 .. C4
Lorient Dr. .. Pg.15 .. D5
Loyola Dr. .. Pg.15 .. D4
Main St. .. Pg.15 .. C5
Malibu Dr. .. Pg.15 .. D3
Manchester .. Pg.15 .. A3,E13
Manor Ave. .. Pg.16 .. C7
Maple Ave. .. Pg.15 .. C5
Marietta St. .. Pg.15 .. D4
Marquette Ln. .. Pg.15 .. D4
Maryetta St. .. Pg.15 .. D4
Maryville Rd. .. Pg.15 .. D4
Matanuska Tr. Pg.3,4,7,8 .. F11
McCullom Lake Rd. .. Pg.15 .. B5
McHenry Ave. .. Pg.15 .. B5
McHenry Rd. .. Pg.15 .. C3
Mead St. .. Pg.15 .. C4
Meadow Ln. .. Pg.15 .. C4
Meadow Rd. .. Pg.15 .. E6
Meadowlane Dr.
Medical Ctr. Dr. Pg.15 .. E5
Melrose St. .. Pg.15 .. C3
Milfred St. .. Pg.15 .. D3
Mill St. .. Pg.15 .. C5
Miller Dr. .. Pg.15 .. E6
Miller Pkwy. .. Pg.15 .. F3
Millstream Dr. .. Pg.15 .. D5
Newport Tr. .. Pg.15 .. E6
North Ave. .. Pg.15 .. C4
Oak Ave. .. Pg.15 .. C4
Oak St. .. Pg.15 .. C4
Oak Point Rd. Pg.15 .. F4
Oak St. .. Pg.15 .. C4
Oakton St. .. Pg.15 .. D4
Oakton St. .. Pg.15 .. C4
Oakwood Ct. .. Pg.15 .. C4
Oakwood Rd. .. Pg.15 .. C,D4
Ojibwa Ln. .. Pg.3,4,7,8,15 C2,F11
Olde Mill Ln. .. Pg.15 .. B5
Orchard Path .. Pg.15 .. E6
Orleans St. .. Pg.15 .. D5
Overland Tr. .. Pg.15 .. E4
Park Lane Ave. Pg.15 .. C5
Park St. .. Pg.15 .. C5
Parkway Ave. .. Pg.15 .. B4
Pearl .. Pg.15 .. E6
Pearl St. .. Pg.15 .. E5
Pebble Creek Pl. Pg.15 .. E5
Petersen Park Rd. .. Pg.15 .. B4
Pin Oak Ln. .. Pg.3,4,7,8 .. F11
Pine Dr. .. Pg.15 .. B5
Pleasant Ave. .. Pg.15 .. C4
Pleasant View Dr. .. Pg.15 .. F6
Ponca St. .. Pg.15 .. D4
Prairie Ave. .. Pg.15 .. B4
Prairie St. .. Pg.15 .. E6
Prestwick St. .. Pg.15 .. B5
Prime Pkwy. .. Pg.15 .. D4
Pydale .. Pg.15 .. D4
Radcliff Ct. .. Pg.15 .. B5
Ramble Rd. .. Pg.15 .. E6
Rhonda Rd. .. Pg.15 .. D5
Richmond Rd. .. Pg.15 .. C4
Ridgeview Dr. .. Pg.15 .. D3
Ringwood Rd. .. Pg.15 .. B3
Riverside Dr. .. Pg.15,16 .. C,E6
Riverstream .. Pg.15 .. C6
Rogers Ave. .. Pg.15 .. C4
Ronda Rd. .. Pg.15 .. D5
Rose Ave. .. Pg.4,15 .. A3,E13
Ryan St. .. Pg.15 .. B5
Sandburg Dr. .. Pg.15 .. D4
Sarasota Dr. .. Pg.15 .. C3
Schroeder Ln. .. Pg.15 .. F4
Scully Dr. .. Pg.15 .. C3
Settlers Ct. .. Pg.15 .. B5
Shamrock Ln. .. Pg.15 .. C4
Shepherd Hill Ln.
Sherman Dr. .. Pg.15 .. B5
Shore Dr. .. Pg.15 .. B4

Shorehill Dr. .. Pg.15 .. B3
Silbury Ct. .. Pg.15 .. D4
Silver Glen Rd. .. Pg.7 .. F10
Sioux .. Pg.15 .. D4
Skyway Dr. .. Pg.15 .. D5
Somerset Mall .. Pg.15 .. C4
South St. .. Pg.15 .. D4
Spring Creek Ln. .. Pg.15 .. B5
Springbrook Ct. .. Pg.15 .. E3
Springdale Ln. .. Pg.15 .. C3
Spruce Ln. .. Pg.15 .. B4
St. Pauls Ln. .. Pg.15 .. D4
St. Xavier Dr. .. Pg.15 .. D4
Still Hill Dr. .. Pg.15 .. E6
Stonebridge Tr. Pg.15 .. D3
Strattford Ct. .. Pg.15 .. D3
Sunrise View .. Pg.15 .. F6
Sunset Ave. .. Pg.15 .. B3
Sussex Dr. .. Pg.15 .. C4
Sycamore Ct. .. Pg.3,4,7,8 .. F11
Tamarack Ct. .. Pg.3,4,7,8 .. F11
Terrace Dr. .. Pg.15 .. E6
Third St. .. Pg.15 .. D5
Thornwood Dr. Pg.15 .. D3
Timber Tr. .. Pg.7 .. F10
Timothy Ln. .. Pg.15 .. C5
Tomlinson Dr. .. Pg.4,15
Tomlinson Dr. .. Pg.4,15 .. A3,E13
Trappers Ct. .. Pg.15 .. D5
Tustamena Tr. Pg.3,4,7,8 .. F11
Valley Rd. .. Pg.15 .. D6
Venice Ct. .. Pg.15 .. C5
Verette Ct. .. Pg.15 .. E4
Victor Dr. .. Pg.15 .. D6
Victoria Ave. .. Pg.15 .. D6
Village Tr. .. Pg.15 .. A5
Vine St. .. Pg.15 .. C5
Virginia Ave. .. Pg.15 .. D6
Vista Trail .. Pg.15 .. B5
Walnut Ln. .. Pg.15 .. B5
Washington St. Pg.15 .. C5
Waters Edge Dr.
Waukegan Rd. .. Pg.15 .. D3
Wellington Dr. .. Pg.15 .. D3
West Ave. .. Pg.15 .. C5
Westminster Pl. Pg.15 .. E5
Whiteoak Ct. .. Pg.15 .. E13
Whiteoak Dr. .. Pg.4 .. E13
Whiting Ct. .. Pg.4,15
Whiting Dr. .. Pg.4,15 .. A2,E13
Whitmore Tr. .. Pg.15 .. D3
Willow Rd. .. Pg.15 .. D3
Wiltshire Ct. .. Pg.15 .. D4
Wiltshire Dr. .. Pg.15 .. D4
Windhaven Ct. .. Pg.15 .. E3
Windhaven Tr. Pg.15 .. E3
Winding Creek Dr.
Winslow Dr. .. Pg.15 .. D3
Winslow Cir. .. Pg.15 .. D3
Woodmar Ct. .. Pg.15 .. C3
Woodridge Dr. Pg.7 .. F10
Woods St. .. Pg.15 .. C4
Young St. .. Pg.15 .. C5

**CEMETERIES**
St. Mary's Cemetery .. Pg.15 .. B5

**GOLF COURSES**
McHenry C.C. .. Pg.15 .. D5

**PARKS**
Boulder Creek Park
Brookside Park Pg.15 .. B4
Center Street Pk. .. Pg.15 .. C5
Cold Springs Park .. Pg.15 .. D4
Fox Ridge Park Pg.15 .. D3
Freund Park .. Pg.15 .. C5
Jaycees Park .. Pg.15 .. C5
Kiwanis Tot Lot Pg.15 .. D5
Knox Park .. Pg.15 .. C5
Malibu Park .. Pg.15 .. D3
Oak Park .. Pg.15 .. B6
Pebble Creek Park
Petersen Park Pg.15 .. B4
Pleasant Valley Park .. Pg.15 .. C3
South Riverfront Park .. Pg.15 .. D6
Veterans Mem. Park .. Pg.15 .. C5
Walsh Park .. Pg.15 .. C5
West Beach Park .. Pg.15 .. B3
Wheeler Park .. Pg.15 .. E5
Whispering Oaks Park .. Pg.15 .. C4

**SCHOOLS**
Bush Elem. Sch.
Edgebrook Grade Sch .. Pg.15 .. D5
Fox Valley Christian Sch. .. Pg.15 .. D5
Johnsburg Jr. H.S. .. Pg.15 .. B5
Landmark Sch. Pg.15 .. C5
McHenry Comm. H.S. East .. Pg.15 .. D4
McHenry Comm. H.S. West .. Pg.15 .. D4
McHenry Jr. H.S. .. Pg.15 .. C5
Middle Sch. .. Pg.15 .. B5
Montini Cath. Sch. .. Pg.15 .. C5
Parkland Sch. Pg.15 .. C5
Riverwood Elem. Sch. .. Pg.15 .. E4
Valley View Sch. .. Pg.15 .. C3
Zion Ev. Lutheran Sch. .. Pg.15 .. C5

**MISCELLANEOUS**
McHenry Co. Prairie Trail .. Pg.15 .. A-F4
Municipal Center .. Pg.15 .. E5
Northern Ill. Medical Ctr. .. Pg.15 .. E5

**McHENRY TOWNSHIP**
Pages 3,4,7,8,15,16,33

**STREETS**
Acorn Ln. .. Pg.4 .. C13
Agatha Dr. .. Pg.4 .. C13
Algonquin Dr. Pg.33 .. D10
Aloha Ct. .. Pg.16 .. B6
Aloha Dr. .. Pg.16 .. B6
Althoff Terr. .. Pg.4 .. F11
Alton Rd. .. Pg.15 .. B3
Amby Ln. .. Pg.4 .. D13
Annabelle St. .. Pg.4 .. D13
Appaloosa Trail Pg.16 .. C8
Aqua Ln. .. Pg.16 .. A6
Arabian Spur .. Pg.16 .. C8
Arbor Rd. .. Pg.33 .. D9
Ash Dr. .. Pg.4 .. D13
Ashwood .. Pg.33 .. D9
Aspen Dr. .. Pg.4 .. E13
August Ln. .. Pg.16 .. B7
Bakers Dr. .. Pg.4 .. C13
Bald Knob Ct. .. Pg.8 .. D14
Bald Knob Rd. Pg.8 .. D14
Balsam Dr. .. Pg.33 .. C9
Barbara .. Pg.33 .. C10
Barnard Mill Rd. .. Pg.33 .. C10
Baron Dr. .. Pg.8 .. C14
Basswood .. Pg.33 .. F9
Bay Dr. .. Pg.16 .. A6
Bay Ln. .. Pg.4 .. E14
Bay View .. Pg.33 .. D9
Bayview Dr. .. Pg.16 .. A9
Bayview Ln. .. Pg.4,16
Beach Ave. .. Pg.15,16 .. B3,D8
Beach Dr. .. Pg.33 .. E9
Beach Rd. .. Pg.33 .. E9
Beach View .. Pg.15 .. B3
Beaver Rd. .. Pg.33 .. E9
Beck Ln. .. Pg.4 .. D12
Belvidere Rd. .. Pg.16 .. C7
Benjamin Dr. .. Pg.4 .. D13
Bennington Ct. Pg.7 .. F10
Berkshire Dr. .. Pg.4 .. D12
Birch Dr. .. Pg.33 .. D10
Black Bay .. Pg.33 .. D10
Black Oak Dr. Pg.7 .. F10
Blue Pine Dr. Pg.7,11 G11
Bolling Ave. .. Pg.4 .. E13
Bong .. Pg.33 .. D10
Boston .. Pg.33 .. D10
Bradley .. Pg.4 .. D13
Bridge St. .. Pg.4 .. D13
Britton Dr. .. Pg.4 .. C13
Broadway Rd. Pg.4 .. D13
Brook Dr. .. Pg.33 .. E9
Brookshire Dr. Pg.4 .. D12
Brorson Ln. .. Pg.4 .. C13
Bull Ridge Dr. Pg.7 .. F10
Bunny Ave. .. Pg.4 .. C13
Burr Ave. .. Pg.4 .. C13
Burr Oak Ct. .. Pg.7 .. F10
Burr Oak Dr. .. Pg.7 .. F10
Cambridge .. Pg.4 .. D12
Cambridge Dr. Pg.7 .. F10
Camellia Ct. .. Pg.33 .. C9
Cardinal Ln. .. Pg.3 .. D10
Carl Ct. .. Pg.16 .. B7
Cassandra Rd. Pg.16 .. C7
Catalpa Dr. .. Pg.33 .. C9
Cedar Dr. .. Pg.33 .. D10
Cedar Rd. .. Pg.15 .. D3
Center Dr. .. Pg.33 D9,10
Chapel Hill Rd. Pg.4 .. E13
Charles St. .. Pg.16 .. C6
Cherokee Dr. .. Pg.4 .. E12
Cherry Dr. .. Pg.16 .. C6
Chestnut Dr., S. Pg.33 .. F9
Chestnut Dr., W.
Chippewa Dr. .. Pg.33 .. D10

Christine Ave. .. Pg.4 .. D13
Church St. .. Pg.33 .. E10
Cimmeron Ct. .. Pg.4 .. D12
Circle Ct. .. Pg.33 .. A10
Circle Dr. .. Pg.33 .. C10
Circle Island .. Pg.33 .. D9
Circle N. .. Pg.33 .. E10
Clara St. .. Pg.16 .. A6
Claremont .. Pg.4 .. D12
Clark St. .. Pg.33 .. C10
Clearview .. Pg.33 .. E9
Clemen .. Pg.16 .. D6
Cleveland Dr. .. Pg.15 .. B3
Cliff Ct. .. Pg.16 .. B7
Clover Ln. .. Pg.16 .. C7
Club Rd. .. Pg.16 .. B7
Club Rd. .. Pg.16 .. B7
Cobblestone Ct. .. Pg.4 .. D12
Cobblestone Dr. .. Pg.16 .. B7
Concord Dr., N. Pg.7 .. F10
Coolidge Ave. .. Pg.4,16 .. A7,E13
Coral .. Pg.16 .. C6
Country Club Rd. .. Pg.16 .. D6
Country Ln. .. Pg.16 .. C6
Court St. .. Pg.15 .. C5
Craftwell Dr. .. Pg.3,4,8 D11
Craig .. Pg.33 .. D9
Creekside Ln. .. Pg.33 .. D12
Crescent Dr. .. Pg.33 .. D9
Crest St. .. Pg.16 .. D7
Cresthill Ave. .. Pg.16 .. D8
Crestwood Ave. Pg.16 .. D8
Croakin Ln. .. Pg.16 .. D7
Cross Dr. .. Pg.33 .. C9
Croyden St. .. Pg.4 .. C13
Culhman Rd. .. Pg.4,16
Curran Rd. .. Pg.8 .. F11
Curve Ct. .. Pg.4 .. D13
Cypress Dr. .. Pg.33 .. D9
Dale Ave. .. Pg.16 .. D8
David St. .. Pg.4 .. D13
Deborah Ln. .. Pg.16 .. C6
Deep Spring Rd. .. Pg.33 .. E9
Deerpath .. Pg.4 .. D14
Delaware Rd. .. Pg.33 .. D10
Delore Dr. .. Pg.16 .. D7
Delshire Dr. .. Pg.4 .. D12
Devonshire Dr. Pg.4 .. D12
Dogwood Dr. .. Pg.33 .. E9
Dot St. .. Pg.15 .. B3
Draper Rd. .. Pg.4,15
Dutch Cir. .. Pg.16 .. A6
East Blvd. .. Pg.16 .. D9
East St. .. Pg.4 .. C13
Eastern Ave. .. Pg.4 .. C13
Eastview Ave. .. Pg.16 .. D9
Eastview Ln. .. Pg.16 .. C7
Edgebrook Ct. .. Pg.33 .. E10
Edgewood .. Pg.33 .. E9
Edgewood Ct. .. Pg.4 .. C13
Edgewood Dr. Pg.16 .. C7
Edgewood Ln. .. Pg.16 .. B7
Edward Ct. .. Pg.16 .. B7
Eisenhower .. Pg.33 .. C10
Elder Ave. .. Pg.4 .. D13
Elm Leaf Dr. .. Pg.33 .. A10
Elm Ln. .. Pg.8 .. C13
Elm Oak Dr. .. Pg.16 .. D6
Elmshire Ln. .. Pg.4 .. C13
Emerald .. Pg.16 .. C6
Enfield Dr. .. Pg.15 .. B3
Fair Oak Ln. .. Pg.16 .. D8
Fairview Ln. .. Pg.16 .. C7
Fairway Rd. .. Pg.15 .. D5
Farm Ln. .. Pg.16 .. C7
Fawn Ln. .. Pg.33 .. E10
Fernwood Dr. Pg.4 .. D13
Fir Dr. .. Pg.33 .. D9
First Ave. .. Pg.15 .. C5
Flanders Rd. .. Pg.4,15
Florence Dr. .. Pg.4 C,D13
Forest View .. Pg.15 .. A3
Fourth Ave. .. Pg.15 .. C5
Fox Lake Rd. .. Pg.4 .. C13
Fox River Ave. Pg.16 .. A7
Freedom Dr. .. Pg.15 .. B3
Friendly Ave. .. Pg.4 .. E13
Garfield Rd. .. Pg.4 .. E12
Gene Dr. .. Pg.33 .. E10
Geneva Ln. .. Pg.16 .. D7
Ginko Ct. .. Pg.7 .. F10
Glenwood Ave. Pg.16 .. C6
Glenwood Ct. .. Pg.16 .. C7
Glenwood Ln. .. Pg.16 .. C7
Golf .. Pg.16 .. D9
Grafield Rd. .. Pg.4 .. D12
Grandview .. Pg.4,16 .. A7,D13
Grandview Dr. Pg.4,33 .. A9,10,D13
Granite .. Pg.33 .. C10
Grant Ave. .. Pg.4 .. C13
Grant Ave. .. Pg.4 .. C13
Green St. .. Pg.15 .. C5
Greenleaf .. Pg.33 .. C9
Gregory St. .. Pg.4 .. D13
Hamlin .. Pg.4 .. E12
Hampshire Dr. Pg.4 .. D12

Hancock Dr. .. Pg.33 .. D9
Harbor .. Pg.33 C,D10
Harrison Ln. .. Pg.8 .. E14
Hayden Dr. .. Pg.4 .. D13
Hayden Ln. .. Pg.4 .. D13
Hedge Ave. .. Pg.16 .. B7
Hedge Pl. .. Pg.16 .. B7
Henry Tr. .. Pg.4 .. C13
Henzada Ave. .. Pg.16 .. B6
Hiawatha Dr. .. Pg.33 .. D10
Hickory Dr. .. Pg.33 .. C,F9
Hickory Ln. .. Pg.4 .. D12
Hickory Nut Dr. Pg.33 .. A10
Hickory Way .. Pg.8 .. D12
High .. Pg.16 .. A9
High Rd. .. Pg.4 .. E14
Highland Dr. .. Pg.4,15 .. B3,D13
Highview Dr. .. Pg.33 .. F9
Hill Dr. .. Pg.33 .. F9
Hill Rd. .. Pg.16 .. D6
Hillside .. Pg.4 .. C13
Hillside Dr. .. Pg.33 .. E9
Hillside Ln. .. Pg.16 .. C6
Hilltop Dr. .. Pg.24 .. F16
Hilltop Ln. .. Pg.4,8
Holly Ct. .. Pg.16 .. C7
Howard St. .. Pg.4 .. E13
Howe Dr. .. Pg.33 .. C10
Howe Rd. .. Pg.33 .. C9
Howell Rd. .. Pg.16 .. A6
Hueman Ave. .. Pg.16 .. A6
Hunter Ridge .. Pg.32 .. D11
Huron Dr. .. Pg.33 .. D10
Indianridge Dr. Pg.4,33
Ivy Ln. .. Pg.4,8 .. E12
Jasper Dr. .. Pg.4 .. D13
Jeffery St. .. Pg.4 .. D13
John Ave. .. Pg.4 .. C13
John Ct. .. Pg.16 .. B8
Johnsburg Rd. .. Pg.4
Jonquil .. Pg.33 .. C9
Joyce .. Pg.33 .. A10
Kama Ave. .. Pg.16 .. A6
Kashmin Ave. .. Pg.16 .. B6
Kelter St. .. Pg.15 .. D4
Kent Rd. .. Pg.16 .. D7
King St. .. Pg.33 .. D10
Kirk Park Ct. .. Pg.16 .. D6
Knob Hill Rd. .. Pg.4
Kosciuzko Rd. .. Pg.15 .. B3
Lake Ave. .. Pg.16 .. C6
Lake Shore Dr. Pg.33
Lake St. .. Pg.4 .. D13
Lakeshore Dr. .. Pg.15 .. B3
Lakeview Dr. .. Pg.33 E,F9
Lakewood Rd. .. Pg.15 .. B4
Landle Park Rd. Pg.16 .. C7
Lauderdale .. Pg.16 .. A9
Lauderdale St. Pg.4 .. E14
Lear .. Pg.33 .. D10
Leeside St. .. Pg.4 .. C13
Lily Ave. .. Pg.16 .. D9
Lily Lake Rd. .. Pg.16 .. D9
Lincoln Rd. .. Pg.4,15
Lincolnshire Dr. Pg.4 .. D13
Linda Rd. .. Pg.15 .. D5
Linden Ave. .. Pg.4 .. E13
Lodge Rd. .. Pg.4 .. E13
Lone Tree .. Pg.16 .. B7
Long Ln. .. Pg.16 .. C7
Lookout Dr. .. Pg.4 .. E14
Loras Ln. .. Pg.33 .. D10
Louella Ave. .. Pg.4 .. D13
Lucina Ave. .. Pg.4 .. D13
Lucy Dr. .. Pg.33 .. F9
Lumley Dr. .. Pg.33 .. E10
Lynn .. Pg.4 .. D13
MacArthur Dr. Pg.15 .. B3
Magellan Rd. .. Pg.16 .. A9
Magnolia .. Pg.16 .. C6
Magnolia Dr. .. Pg.33 .. C9
Manitou Tr. .. Pg.4,16
Mann Dr. .. Pg.4 .. D11
Manor Ln. .. Pg.16 .. C7
Maple Dr. .. Pg.33 .. D10
Maple Leaf Dr. Pg.33 .. A10
Mar Dr. .. Pg.4 .. E13
Marblehead .. Pg.33 .. D9
Marietta St. .. Pg.15 .. D4
Marquart St. .. Pg.16 .. A7
Marshall .. Pg.33 .. C10
Martin Ave. .. Pg.16 .. C6
Martin Rd. .. Pg.33 .. A10
Mary Ln. .. Pg.15 .. C5
Maryville Rd. .. Pg.16 .. C6
Mayfair Dr. .. Pg.33 .. A10
Mayfield Dr. .. Pg.4 .. D12
McArthur .. Pg.33 .. F9
McCullom Rd. Pg.7,8,33 .. D10,11,E12
Meadow Ct. .. Pg.4 .. C13
Meadow Dr. .. Pg.4 .. C13
Meadowlark .. Pg.33 .. C9
Memory Tr. .. Pg.4 .. D13
Michael St. .. Pg.33 .. E9
Mid Oak Dr. .. Pg.16 .. D6
Mill Dr. .. Pg.4 .. D13
Mill Ln. .. Pg.16 .. C7

Miller Oaks Dr. Pg.4 .. D12
Mineral Springs Dr. .. Pg.16 .. D6
Misty Pine Ct. Pg.7,11 G11
Mogra Dr. .. Pg.16 .. A6
Mohawk Dr. .. Pg.33 .. D10
Morgan Tr. .. Pg.16 .. C8
Mouraine Ln. .. Pg.16 .. A6
Myang Ave. .. Pg.16 .. A6
Nantucket .. Pg.33 .. C10
Navajo Tr. .. Pg.4,16
Niagara Dr. .. Pg.33 .. D10
Nimitz .. Pg.33 .. D10
Nippersink Dr. .. Pg.4 .. D12
North Ave. .. Pg.16 C6,D8
North Blvd. .. Pg.16 .. D8
North Dr. .. Pg.33 .. D10
Northside Ave. .. Pg.16 .. D8
Northwood Dr. Pg.33 .. E9
O'Shea Ct. .. Pg.16 .. B8
Oak Ave. .. Pg.16 .. D13
Oak Dr. .. Pg.33 .. C10
Oak Grove Rd. Pg.4 .. E14
Oak St. .. Pg.33 .. D10
Oakleaf Dr. .. Pg.16,33
Oakwood Ct. .. Pg.16 .. C6
Oakwood Dr. .. Pg.33
Oeffling Ct. .. Pg.4 .. D13
Oeffling Dr. .. Pg.4 .. D13
Old Oak Dr. .. Pg.16 .. A6
Oneida .. Pg.33 .. D10
Orchard Beach Pg.16 .. D10
Orchard Ln. .. Pg.4 .. D13
Orchard Rd. .. Pg.33 .. D10
Orchardway Dr. Pg.15 .. B3
Oriole Tr. .. Pg.4 .. D14
Osage Rd. .. Pg.33 .. D10
Palomino Dr. .. Pg.16 .. C8
Pamela Dr. .. Pg.33 .. A10
Park Ln. .. Pg.33 .. D10
Parkside Ave. .. Pg.16 .. C8
Parkwood Dr. .. Pg.33 .. E10
Patricia Ln. .. Pg.16 .. A6
Patton .. Pg.33 .. D10
Paulson St. .. Pg.4 .. D13
Pebble Dr. .. Pg.16 .. B7
Pheasant Rd. .. Pg.33 .. C9
Pheasant Tr. .. Pg.4 .. D14
Pinehurst Ct. .. Pg.4 .. D13
Pistakee Dr. .. Pg.4 .. C13
Pistakee Ln. .. Pg.16,33
Pleasant View Dr. .. Pg.4 .. C13
Plymouth Ln. .. Pg.16 .. C6
Ponca .. Pg.15 .. D4
Poplar Leaf Dr. Pg.33 .. A10
Prairie St. .. Pg.16 .. D7
Prairie Ridge .. Pg.32 .. C,D4
Preston Dr. .. Pg.33 .. E10
Promontory Ln. Pg.4 .. D13
Pulaski St. .. Pg.16 .. C7
Quinn Rd. .. Pg.15 .. B3
Raintree Dr. .. Pg.7,11 G11
Rand Dr. .. Pg.16 .. B6
Ranch Dr. .. Pg.16 .. C6
Ravine Ave. .. Pg.16 .. C6
Ray St. .. Pg.4 .. D13
Reed Kent Ave. Pg.4 .. E13
Regner Dr. .. Pg.16 .. C6
Regner Ln. .. Pg.16 .. A8
Regner Rd. .. Pg.4 .. E14
Relche Ln. .. Pg.16 .. D7
Rhonda Rd. .. Pg.16 .. D6
Richard Ln. .. Pg.4 .. D13
Richmond Rd. .. Pg.15 .. C5
Ridge Rd. .. Pg.7 .. F10
Ridgeway Rd. .. Pg.4 .. D11
Ringwood Rd. .. Pg.4 .. B,C6
River Ln. .. Pg.16 .. B7
River Ln. .. Pg.15 .. C6
River Rd. .. Pg.16 B,C6
River Way .. Pg.16 .. C6
Riverdale Dr. .. Pg.4,33
Riverside Dr. .. Pg.4 A10,D13
Rocky Beach Rd.
Rodger St. .. Pg.4 .. E13
Rolling Ln. Rd. Pg.4 .. E13
Rose .. Pg.33 .. C10
Rosedale .. Pg.16 .. C6
Rosewood Ct. Pg.4,8 .. D12
Sac Rd. .. Pg.33 .. D10
Salem Rd. .. Pg.33 .. D10
Sandalwood Ln. .. Pg.4 .. D12
Schneider .. Pg.4 .. D11
School Rd. .. Pg.33 .. A10
Scott Ave. .. Pg.15 .. C5
Second Ave. .. Pg.15 .. C5
Seminole Dr. .. Pg.33 .. D10
Seneca Dr. .. Pg.33 .. D10
Sequoia Dr. .. Pg.16 .. A9
Seville Ct. .. Pg.4 .. D12
Shennandoah Dr. .. Pg.33 .. D10
Shore Dr., W. .. Pg.33 .. F9
Shorewood Dr. Pg.33 .. A7
Short .. Pg.16 .. C7
Short Ln. .. Pg.4 .. D13

Skyway Dr. .. Pg.15 .. D5
Small St. .. Pg.4 .. C13
South St. .. Pg.4,15 .. C6,13
Southside Ave. Pg.16 .. D8
Spaatz .. Pg.33 .. C10
Spojnia .. Pg.15 .. B3
Spring Grove Rd. .. Pg.4 .. D13
Spring Rd. .. Pg.15 .. B3
St. Pauls Ln. .. Pg.15 .. D5
Sterling Dr. .. Pg.16 .. A,B6
Stilling Blvd. .. Pg.16 .. A7
Stillwell .. Pg.33 .. C10
Sudeenew Dr. Pg.4 .. D12
Sumac .. Pg.33 .. C10
Summervil Ave. Pg.16 .. D8
Summit Dr. .. Pg.4 .. D12
Sundown Ln. .. Pg.4 .. D12
Sunnyside Beach Dr. .. Pg.4,8 .. E13
Sunrise Dr. .. Pg.4 .. D14
Sunset Dr. .. Pg.33 .. D9
Sweet Bay Dr. Pg.7,11 G11
Sydenham St. Pg.4 .. C13
Sylvan .. Pg.33 .. C10
Tall Tree Ln. .. Pg.4 .. D12
Telegraph .. Pg.33 .. C10
Thelan Rd. .. Pg.4 .. D13
Thelen Dr. .. Pg.4 .. D13
Third Ave. .. Pg.15 .. B5
Torrey Tr. .. Pg.4 .. D12
Trey Rd. .. Pg.7 .. F10
Ute .. Pg.33 .. D10
Valle Lo Lane .. Pg.16 .. A6
Valley Ave. .. Pg.16 .. C8
Valley Ct. .. Pg.33 .. C8
Valley Ln. .. Pg.16 .. C6
Valley Rd. .. Pg.16 .. D6
Valley St. .. Pg.16 .. D7
Vern St. .. Pg.4 .. D13
Victoria Ave. .. Pg.4 .. D13
Villa Ln., N. .. Pg.16 .. A7
Virginia Ave. .. Pg.16 .. A6
Wainwright .. Pg.33 .. C10
Walnut Dr. .. Pg.33 .. F9
Walnut St. .. Pg.33 .. F9
Waltshire Ln. .. Pg.4 .. D12
Washington .. Pg.33 .. D9
Washington St. Pg.16 .. A7
Weingart Rd. .. Pg.4 .. E13
West Blvd. .. Pg.16 D8,9
West Dr. .. Pg.4 .. D13
Westmoor Dr. Pg.33 .. D10
Weston Ct. .. Pg.4 .. E14
Westshore Dr. Pg.15 .. B3
Westwood Dr. Pg.4 .. D13
White Oak Rd. Pg.33 .. D9
Widoff Rd. .. Pg.33 .. E9
William St. .. Pg.4 .. D13
Willow Dr. .. Pg.33 .. D9
Willow Rd. .. Pg.15 .. B3
Willow St. .. Pg.4 .. D13
Wilmington Ct. Pg.7 .. F10
Wilmot Rd. .. Pg.4 .. D13
Winnebago Dr. Pg.33 .. D10
Wonder Lake Dr. .. Pg.33 .. D9
Wonder Lake Rd., E. .. Pg.3 .. E10
Wonder Valley Ct.
Wonder Wood Dr. .. Pg.4 .. D13
Wood Lawn Park Ave. .. Pg.33 C,D9
Wooded Ln. .. Pg.4 .. B6,F13
Wooded Ln. .. Pg.4 A9,E14
Wooded Shore Dr.
Woodland Dr. .. Pg.33 E9,10
Woodland Ln. .. Pg.16 .. C6
Woodlawn Park Rd. .. Pg.16 .. B7
Woodrow Ave. Pg.4 .. D14
Yorkshire Dr. .. Pg.4 .. D12

**CEMETERIES**
Cemetery .. Pg.4 .. D11

**FOREST PRESERVES**
Harrison Benwell Preserve .. Pg.3 .. D11
Volo Bog State Nature Area .. Pg.16 .. B9
Wiengart Rd. Sedge Meadow .. Pg.8 .. E13

**GOLF COURSES**
Chapel Hill Country Club .. Pg.16 .. B7
Pistakee Golf Course .. Pg.16 .. B8

**SCHOOLS**
Harrison Elem. Sch. .. Pg.33 .. E10
Hilltop Sch. .. Pg.16 .. C6
Johnsburg H.S. Pg.4 .. D13
Progressive Path Sch. .. Pg.4
Ringwood Sch. Pg.4 .. D11

**MISCELLANEOUS**
Northern Pump Airstrip .. Pg.3 .. E11

## NUNDA TOWNSHIP

**NUNDA TOWNSHIP**
Pages 7,8,11,12,15,16,
18-21
(For additional listings,
see detail maps)

**STREETS**
Abendroth . . Pg.19 . . B10
Acacia Ct. . . . Pg.19 . . A12
Acacia Dr. . . . Pg.19 . . A12
Alex Ln. . . . . . Pg.20 . . C14
Allen Ave. . . Pg.8,12 G13
Amada Ave. . . Pg.16 . . E9
Andreas Ln. . . Pg.18 . . C8
Annette Ave. . . Pg.19 . D14
Anvil Rd. . . . Pg.7,11,12
. . . . . . . . . . . . . . . . . . . . G11
Apache . . . . . Pg.16 . . E6
Area St. . . . . . Pg.21 . . B21
Baldwin Rd. . . Pg.8,12 G13
Bally Dr. . . . . Pg.16 . . E6
Barbara Ln. . . Pg.16 . . E9
Barreville Rd. . Pg.8 . . H12
Bay Rd. . . . . . Pg.8 . . H11
Beach St. . . . . Pg.21 . . B19
Beach Way . . . Pg.21 . . D20
Beech Ln. . . . . Pg.21 . . B19
Belden St. . . . Pg.15 . . F5
Benbrook Ave. . Pg.32 . . C5
Bergen Ct. . . . Pg.11 . . H11
Bergman Ave. . Pg.32 . . C5
Berry Ct. . . . . Pg.11 . . H11
Black Partridge Rd.
. . . . . . . . . . . Pg.16 . . E6
Blackhawk Dr. . Pg.16 . . F6
Blossom St. . . Pg.21 . . A18
Blue Ct. . . . . . Pg.20 . D15
Blue Island Ave.
. . . . . . . . . . . . . . . Pg.8,32
Blue Pine Dr. . Pg.7 . . G11
Bluebird Ct. . . Pg.19 . . B11
Bolger Ave. . Pg.8,12 G13
Brefeld Ct. . . . Pg.16 . . E6
Brentwood Lane
. . . . . . . . . . Pg.8,12 G13
Bridlewood Ln. Pg.11 . . H11
Briggs Ave. . . Pg.32 . . C5
Buckthorn Dr. . Pg.19 . . A11
Buhl Rd. . . . . . Pg.20 . B17
Bull Valley Rd. Pg.16 . . E6
Burnett Rd. . . Pg.8 . . H14
Burr Lane . . . Pg.20 . D16
Burton St. . . . Pg.21 . . A19
Cameron Ct. . . Pg.20 . D16
Cape Cove . . . Pg.18 . . B10
Carmella Dr. . . Pg.19 . . C10
Carmeo Ave. . . Pg.32 . . C5
Caroline Ave. . Pg.21 . . B18
Carriage Dr. . . Pg.18 . . A9
Carriage Tr. . . Pg.15 . . E4
Carrington Dr. . Pg.20 . C16
Carthage Ct. . . Pg.19 . . B14
Catalpa St. . . . Pg.8 . . J14
Cedar St. . . . . Pg.8 . . J14
Cedardell St. . Pg.21 . . B21
Center . . . . . . Pg.32 . . D5
Center St. . . . . Pg.8 . . H13
Channel Ln. . . Pg.8,12 G13
Channel St. . . . Pg.21 . . B21
Chatham Ct. . . Pg.18 . . B9
Cherry Ave. . . Pg.32 . . C5
Cherry Dr. . . . Pg.21 . . A19
Cherry Vail Ct. Pg.7 . . H10
Cherry Valley Rd.
. . . . . . . . . . . Pg.18 . . A8
Cherry Valley Rd., N.
. . . . . . . . . . . Pg.7 . . G10
Chesterfield Rd.
. . . . . . . . . . . Pg.18 . . A9
Chris Ave. . . . Pg.20 . D15
Christine Dr. . . Pg.16 . . E9
Coachlight Rd. Pg.7,11,12
. . . . . . . . . . . . . . . . . . . G11
Colby Dr. . . . . Pg.8 . . G13
Colby Point Rd. Pg.8,12 G13
Columbus St. . Pg.16 . . E9
Comes Trail . . Pg.16 . . E8
Concord Tr . . Pg.18 . . A10
Connecticut Tr. Pg.18 . A10
Country Club Rd.
. . . . . . . . . . . Pg.18 . . E2
Crabapple Dr. . Pg.8 . . H13
Crabapple Ln. . Pg.21 . . A19
Crescent Ave. Pg.8,12,32
. . . . . . . . . . . . . . . . . . C5,H13
Crocket Ct. . . . Pg.20 . D15
Crystal Cir. . . . Pg.20 . A17
Crystal Lake Ave.
. . . . . . . . . . . Pg.19 . D13
Crystal Lake McHenry Rd.
. . . . . . . . . . . Pg.19 . . B11
Crystal Lake Rd.
. . . . . . . . . . . . . . Pg.8,32
. . . . . . . . . . C5,H13,J12
Crystal Springs Rd.
. . . . . . . . . . . Pg.7 . . H10
Crystal Way . . Pg.20 . A17
Curling Pond Ct.
. . . . . . . . . . . Pg.7 . . H11
Cypress Dr. . . Pg.18 . . B10
Daisy Ln. . . . . Pg.19 . . B11
Davis Ave. . . . Pg.32 . . C4
Dayton St. . . . Pg.15 . F4,5
Dedlow Ct. . . . Pg.33 . . C5

Dee Dr. . . . . . Pg.32 . . C5
Deep Wood Dr. Pg.32 . . C5
Deering Oaks Ln.
. . . . . . . . . . . Pg.19 . . B13
Derby Ln. . . . . Pg.18 . . A9
Dowell Rd. . . . Pg.8,32
. . . . . . . . . . . . . . C6,G14
Drake Dr. . . . . Pg.19 . . B14
Driftwood Tr. . . Pg.15 . . E4
Drucker Ln. . . Pg.16 . . E6
Dvorak Dr. . . . Pg.19 . . A11
East Dr. . . . . . Pg.18,32
. . . . . . . . . . . . . . A9,C5
Edgewood Rd. Pg.7 . . H11
Edward Dr. . . . Pg.21 . . A19
Elgin . . . . . . . Pg.15 . E,F5
Elm Rd. . . . . . Pg.15 . . E5
Elm St. . . . . . . Pg.21 . . C21
Emerald Ct. . . Pg.16 . . D6
Emerald St. . . Pg.8,16
. . . . . . . . . . . . . . D6,G13
Erick St. . . . . . Pg.19 . D12
Ethel Ave. . . . Pg.19 . D13
Fargo Ave. . . . Pg.32 . . C5
Farmbrook Ln. Pg.20 . D15
Fern View Ln. . Pg.8 . . G13
Fernwood Ln. . Pg.8 . . G13
Field Ct. . . . . . Pg.19 . D14
Fir Ct. . . . . . . . Pg.18 . . B10
Ford Rd. . . . . . Pg.16 . . E6
Forest Blvd. . . Pg.8 . . J14
Forestwood Dr. Pg.32 . . C6
Fox Creek Dr. . Pg.19 . . A12
Fox Ct. . . . . . . Pg.19 . . A12
Fox Run . . . . . Pg.7 . . H11
Fox St. . . . . . . Pg.8 . . H13
Fox Tr. . . . . . . Pg.19 . . A12
Fox View Dr . . Pg.18 . . A9
Foxfire Dr. . . . Pg.18 . . A9
Franklin Ct. . . . Pg.20 . D15
Fritzsche Rd. . Pg.7 . . H13
Garden Ln. . . . Pg.8 . . H11
Gerry Ln. . . . . Pg.20 . C15
Gieseke Dr. . . Pg.20 . D16
Glenbrook Tr. . Pg.15 . . E4
Grace St. . . . . Pg.8,12 G13
Grand Ave. . . . Pg.18 . . A10
Great Hill Rd. . Pg.18 A9,10
Groat Hill Rd., G.
. . . . . . . . . . . Pg.18 . . F1
Green St. . . . . Pg.15 . . F5
Greening Rd. . Pg.8,12 G13
Griswold Ave. . Pg.32 . . C5
Hamilton Dr. . . Pg.20 . D15
Hanover Dr. . . Pg.19 . . B12
Harriet Ln. . . . Pg.32 . . C5
Harry Ct. . . . . Pg.20 . C14
Harvard Ct. . . Pg.18 . . A10
Hawk . . . . . . . Pg.32 . . C5
Hawthorne Ct. Pg.8 . . H13
Hawthorne Ln. Pg.12,16
. . . . . . . . . . . . . . F6,G13
Hazelwood Ct. Pg.8 . . H13
Hazelwood Dr. Pg.4 . . H11
Hibiscus Tr. . . Pg.19 . . A12
Hickory Terr. . . Pg.7 . . H13
Hidden Oaks Ct.
. . . . . . . . . . . Pg.11 . . H11
Hidden Springs Blvd.
. . . . . . . . . . . Pg.8 . . H11
Highland Ave. . Pg.8 . . H13
Highline Rd. . . Pg.19 . . B10
Highview Dr. . . Pg.32 . . D4
Highwood Dr. . Pg.32 . . C6
Highwood Rd. Pg.8 . . G14
Hillcrest Dr. . . Pg.18 . . B10
Hillside . . . . . . Pg.32 . . C5
Hillside Dr. . . . Pg.19 . . B11
Hillside St. . . . Pg.19 . . B11
Hillside Tr. . . . Pg.19 . . B10
Hillview Dr. . . . Pg.8 . . H13
Holly Ln. . . . . . Pg.21 . . B19
Idyl Dell Rd. . . Pg.8 . . G12
Illinois St. . . . . Pg.21 . . B19
Indian Tr. . . . . Pg.16 . . E6
Industrial Rd. . Pg.19 . C12
Jacaline Ln. . . Pg.20 . C14
Jasmine Ln. . . Pg.19 . . B11
Jay Dr. . . . . . . Pg.20 . C15
Jenny Jae Ln. . Pg.8 . . H11
Johnathon Rd. Pg.12 . G13
Johnson Ave. . Pg.21 . . A18
Jones Ave. . . . Pg.32 . . C5
Justen Rd., W. Pg.8 . . G12
Kao St. . . . . . . Pg.21 . . B21
Keene Ave. . . Pg.19 . C13
Kelly Ave. . . . . Pg.8 . . J14
Kelly Rd. . . . . . Pg.21 . . B20
Kerry Ln. . . . . Pg.32 . . C4
Knox Dr. . . . . . Pg.15 . . D5
Kristen Tr. . . . Pg.16 . . E6
Laguna Dr. . . . Pg.16 . . E6
Lamphere St. . Pg.21 . . B21
Larkspur Dr. . . Pg.8 . . H11
Lavergne Ave. Pg.18 . . B10
Lexington Tr. . Pg.18 . . B10
Lily Ct. . . . . . . Pg.8 . . H11
Lily Lake Rd. . Pg.8,16
Lincoln Ave. . . Pg.8 . . H13
Lincoln St. . . . Pg.16 . . D9
Linden Rd. . . . Pg.21 . . B19
Little Dr. . . . . . Pg.21 . . B20
Little Fawn Tr. Pg.19 . . A9
Live Oak Rd. . Pg.19 . . A10
Lock Ln. . . . . . Pg.16 . . F6

Louise St. . . . . Pg.21 . . B19
Main Park Rd. Pg.16 . . F8
Main St. . . . . . Pg.21 . . B20
Maine Tr. . . . . Pg.18 . . B10
Maple St. . . . . Pg.21 . . C21
Marguerite St. Pg.21 . . A18
Marietta Dr. . . Pg.19 . D14
Marlboro Rd. . Pg.18 . . A9
Mason Hill Rd. Pg.7 . . G10
May St. . . . . . . Pg.21 . . A19
McCabe Ave. . Pg.20,32
McHenry Dam Rd.
. . . . . . . . . . . . . . Pg.8,16
. . . . . . . . . . . . . . F7,G13
McMillian Ln. . Pg.8 . . H11
Meadow Dr. . . Pg.21 . . B18
Meadow Lark Ct.
. . . . . . . . . . . Pg.18 . . B10
Meadow St. . . Pg.21 . . C21
Meadowbrook Ln.
. . . . . . . . . . . Pg.20 . D15
Meadowshire Ln.
. . . . . . . . . . . Pg.18 . . B9
Michael Ct. . . Pg.19,32
Mills Pond Rd. Pg.20,21
. . . . . . . . . . . . . . B17,18
Minuteman Ct. Pg.18 . . G2
Mistwood Ln. . Pg.19 . D13
Misty Pine Ct. Pg.7 . . G11
Monica Ave. . . Pg.20 . B14
N.E. Shore Dr. Pg.32 . . C5
Nancy Ln. . . . Pg.16 . . E9
Ned Dr. . . . . . . Pg.21 . . A18
New Hampshire Tr.
. . . . . . . . . . . Pg.18 . . A10
North Dr. . . . . Pg.32 C4,5
North Park Dr. Pg.20 . C17
Northwest Hwy.
. . . . . . . . . . . Pg.18 . . C8
Nunda Ave. . . Pg.19 . . B13
Oak Crest Rd. Pg.8 . . H13
Oak Dr. . . . . . . Pg.21 . . B21
Oak Fire Dr. . . Pg.7 . . H10
Oak Rd. . . . . . Pg.11 . . H10
Oak Ridge Ct. Pg.18 . . A9
Oak Ridge Rd. Pg.18 . . B9
Oak St. . . . . . . Pg.19 . . B11
Oak Ter. . . . . . Pg.21 . . A19
Oakwood Dr. . Pg.8 . . H13
Oakwood Ln. . Pg.18 . . C9
Oakwood Manor Dr.
. . . . . . . . . . . . . . . . . . . . 
Opengate Rd. Pg.11 . . H11
Orchard Rd. . . Pg.8,12 H13
Orchard St. . . Pg.19 . D13
Orman Ave. . . Pg.21 . . B20
Osasge Dr. . . Pg.16 . . E6
Page Pl. . . . . . Pg.32 . . C4
Palm St. . . . . . Pg.21 . . C21
Park Ave. . . . . Pg.21 . . A19
Park St. . . . . . Pg.8 . . H13
Parker St., W. Pg.32 C4-5
Partridge Rd. . Pg.8 . . H11
Paul St. . . . . . Pg.21 . . B21
Pesz Rd. . . . . Pg.21 . . B21
Peter St. . . . . Pg.21 . . B21
Pheasant Ln. . Pg.18 . . G2
Pheasant Run Pg.7 . . H10
Pine St. . . . . . Pg.21 . . C21
Pleasant Hill Rd.
. . . . . . . . . . . Pg.19 . . A13
Plum St. . . . . . Pg.32 . . C5
Point Rd. . . . . Pg.15 . . F4
Pontiac . . . . . . Pg.16 . . F6
Pony Ln. . . . . . Pg.8 . . H11
Pool . . . . . . . . Pg.33 . . C5
Poplar St. . . . . Pg.21 . . C21
Porten Rd. . . . Pg.21 . . B21
Prairie . . . . . . Pg.16 . . E6
Prairie Ridge Rd.
. . . . . . . . . . . Pg.20 . B14
Pueblo Dr. . . . Pg.16 . . E6
Purdue Pl. . . . Pg.19 . D14
Raintree Dr. . . Pg.7 . . G11
Ravenglass Ridge
. . . . . . . . . . . Pg.18 . . A9
Ravine Dr. . . . Pg.18 . . A9
Rawson Bridge Rd.
. . . . . . . . . . . . . . . . . . . . 
Ray St. . . . . . . Pg.19 . C14
Raylander Rd. Pg.19 . C13
Red Barn Rd., E.
. . . . . . . . . . . . . . . . . . . . 
West Bay View Dr.
. . . . . . . . . . . . . . . . . . . . 
Redbird Ln. . . Pg.19 . . B11
Remington Dr. Pg.20 . D16
Rhode Island Tr.
. . . . . . . . . . . . . . . . . . . . 
Ridgefield Ave. Pg.18 . . B8
Rieland St. . . . Pg.19 . . K3
Rigby Rd. . . . . Pg.18 . . A9
Ripon Rd. . . . . Pg.19 . B14
Rita Ave. . . . . Pg.20 . C14
River Dr. . . . . . Pg.32
River Rd. . . . . Pg.8,16
River St. . . . . . Pg.8,12,21
. . . . . . . . . . . . . . C21G13
Riverdale Rd. . Pg.32 . . C5
Riverside Dr. . Pg.21,32
. . . . . . . . . . . . . . A19,C4,5

Roberts Rd. . . Pg.21 . . A21
Robin Ln. . . . . Pg.32 . . C5
Rockspur Tr. . . Pg.19 . . A12
Rodger Rd. . . . Pg.8 . . H12
Royal Woods Dr.
. . . . . . . . . . . Pg.20 . D16
Running Iron Dr.
. . . . . . . . . . . Pg.8 . . H11
Russet Ct. . . . Pg.8,12 G13
Russet Rd. . . . Pg.16 . . F6
Sauk . . . . . . . . Pg.16 . . E6
Scarlet Trail . . Pg.20 . D15
Schied Dr. . . . Pg.32 . . C5
Schroder Ln. . . Pg.15 . . F4
Sequoia Tr. . . Pg.19 . . A12
Sessions Ct. . Pg.18 . . A9
Shadowood Dr. Pg.8 . . H11
Shady Dr. . . . . Pg.16 . . D8
Shady Oaks Ln. Pg.19 . . B13
Shall Ln. . . . . . Pg.32 . C5,6
Shenandoah Ct. Pg.4 . . H11
Shennandoah Dr.
. . . . . . . . . . . Pg.19 . . A11
Shennandoah Tr.
. . . . . . . . . . . Pg.19 . . A11
Sheridan Rd. . Pg.16 . . E9
Shorman Blvd. Pg.21 . . A19
Sherman Rd. . Pg.8 . . H13
Sherwood Dr. Pg.18 . . A9
Shore Dr., NE. Pg.33 . . C5
Short . . . . . . . . Pg.8 . . H13
Skyline Dr. . . . Pg.8,12 G13
Sloan Ln. . . . . Pg.20 . D15
South St. . . . . Pg.21 . . A18
Spring Brook Rd.
. . . . . . . . . . . Pg.7 . . H11
Spyglass Ridge Pg.19 . . A11
Squaw Creek Rd.
. . . . . . . . . . . Pg.19 . . A13
Squaw Valley Rd.
. . . . . . . . . . . Pg.19 . . K1
St. Route 176 Pg.8,20
St. Route 31 . Pg.19 . B14
Stanford St. . . Pg.19 . B14
State Park Rd. Pg.8 . . G12
Steuben Rd. . . Pg.19 . . A11
Stilling Ln. . . . Pg.8,12 G13
Stone Dr. . . . . Pg.19 . C14
Stonegate Rd. Pg.7 . . H10
Strong Rd. . . . Pg.19 . D13
Surf St. . . . . . . Pg.32 . . C5
Sutton Ct. . . . . Pg.18 . . D6
Swarthmore Rd.
. . . . . . . . . . . Pg.7 . . F10
Sweet Bay Dr. Pg.7 . . G11
Tacoma Dr. . . Pg.21 . . A19
Tamarisk Tr. . . Pg.19 . . A12
Tecumseh . . . Pg.16 . . F6
Terra Cotta Ave.
. . . . . . . . . . . . . . . . . . . . 
Terra Cotta Rd. Pg.19 . B13
Terry Ave. . . . Pg.20 . C16
Thomas Ct. . . Pg.32 . . C6
Tilden Ln. . . . . Pg.20 . D15
Tile Line Dr. . . Pg.19 . . B11
Timber Trail . . Pg.21 . . A19
Timberland Rd. Pg.21 . . B19
Totem Tr. . . . . Pg.16 . . E6
Tree Ave. . . . . Pg.32 C4-5
Tulip St. . . . . . Pg.21,32
US Route 14 . Pg.18 . . C8
Upland Dr. . . . Pg.18 . . B10
Valley View Rd. Pg.20 . B16
Vaupell Ave. . . Pg.8 . . H13
Vermont Tr. . . Pg.19 . . A10
Vine Ln. . . . . . Pg.8 . . H11
Virginia Ave. . Pg.8 . . H13
Walking Ridge Pg.18 . . A9
Walkup Ave . . Pg.18 . . H2
Walkup Ln. . . . Pg.8 . . J11
Walkup Rd. . . Pg.8 . . J11
Walnut Ct. . . . Pg.21 . . A19
Walnut Manor Ct.
. . . . . . . . . . . . . . . . . . . . 
Walnut Ln. . . . Pg.11 . . H11
Walnut St. . . . Pg.21 . . C21
Waterview Ave. Pg.32 . . C5
Wayside Dr. . . Pg.21 . . B20
Weather Stone Rd.
. . . . . . . . . . . . . . . . . . . . 
Weather Vane Ln.
. . . . . . . . . . . Pg.20 . B14
Wegner Rd. . . Pg.8,16
. . . . . . . . . . . . . . E9,G14
West Bay View Dr.
. . . . . . . . . . . . . . . . . . . . 
Western Ave. . Pg.8 . . H13
Whippoorwill Dr.
. . . . . . . . . . . . . . . . . . . . 
White Ash Rd. Pg.20 . B14
White Barn Rd. Pg.7 . . H10
Wild Ash Dr. . Pg.19 . . L4
Wild Cherry Rd. Pg.19 . . B10
Wild Plum Rd. Pg.20 . B14
Wilderness Ridge
. . . . . . . . . . . Pg.19 . . A11
Wildwood Dr. Pg.21 . . B20
Willow St. . . . . Pg.21 . . C21
Wiltberger Rd. Pg.7,18
. . . . . . . . . . . . . . E,F1,H10
Winding Rd. . . Pg.20 . D15
Windy Knoll . . Pg.7 . . H11
Wisteria Dr. . . Pg.8 . . H11
Witaker Rd. . . Pg.7 . . F10

Woodland . . . Pg.18 . . F1
Woods Ave. . . Pg.32 . . C5
Woods End Rd. Pg.18 . . A9
Worth St. . . . . Pg.8 . . G13
Wright Ave. . . Pg.21 . . B20
Wright Rd. . . . Pg.32
. . . . . . . . . . . . . . C4,H13
Wyandotte . . . Pg.16 . . F6
Wyoming Way Pg.20 . B14
Yuma Tr. . . . . Pg.16 . . E6

**CEMETERIES**
Ridgefield Cemetery
. . . . . . . . . . . Pg.18 . . E2

**FOREST PRESERVES**
Cotton Creek Marsh
. . . . . . . . . . . Pg.21 . . B20
Hickory Grove Forest
Preserve . . . Pg.19 . . B19
Oakwood Hills Fen
. . . . . . . . . . . Pg.4 . . H11
Sterne's Woods & Fen
. . . . . . . . . . . Pg.19 . . B12

**GOLF COURSES**
Boone Creek Golf Course
. . . . . . . . . . . Pg.7 . . G11
Chalet Hills Golf Club
. . . . . . . . . . . Pg.7 . . D19
Prairie Isle Golf Course
. . . . . . . . . . . Pg.12 . H13

**PARKS**
Crystal Lake Memorial Park
. . . . . . . . . . . Pg.18 . . B8
Moraine Hills State Park
. . . . . . . . . . . Pg.8,16
. . . . . . . . . . . . . . E7,G13
Squaw Creek Property
. . . . . . . . . . . Pg.19 . . A11
Squaw Creek Woods
. . . . . . . . . . . . . . . . . . . . 
Woodland Estate Park
. . . . . . . . . . . . . . . . . . . . 

## OAKWOOD HILLS
Pages 12,20,21
**STREETS**
Ash Dr. . . . . . Pg.20 . D17
Bernay Ct. . . . Pg.21 . . D18
Birch Ln. . . . . Pg.20 . D17
Bordeoux Ct. . Pg.21 . . D18
Brittany Dr. . . Pg.21 . . D18
Burrwood Rd. Pg.20 . D17
Calais Ct. . . . . Pg.21 . . C18
Crystal Lake Ave.
. . . . . . . . . . . Pg.20 . D16
Dauphine Ct. . Pg.21 . . D18
Deer Trail . . . . Pg.21 . . C18
Echo Hill . . . . Pg.20 . D17
Elm Rd. . . . . . Pg.20 . D17
Fawn Ridge Dr. Pg.20 . C17
Fenview Ct. . . Pg.20 . D16
Greenview Rd. Pg.20 . D16
Hickory Rd. . . Pg.20 . D17
Hilton Rd. . . . Pg.20 . D18
Lake Ln. . . . . Pg.20 . D17
Lake Shore Dr. Pg.20 . D17
Lakeview Rd. . Pg.20 . D17
Lakewood Dr. Pg.20 . D17
Lorraine Ct. . . Pg.21 . . C18
Meadow Ln. . . Pg.20 . D17
Normandy Ct. Pg.21 . . C18
North Park Dr. Pg.20 . C17
Oak Dr. . . . . . Pg.20 . D17
Oak Park Rd. . Pg.21 . . C18
Oakhill Rd. . . . Pg.20 . D17
Oakwood Dr. . Pg.20 . D17
Palisades Ln. . Pg.20 . D17
Park Ln. . . . . . Pg.20 . D17
. . . . . . . . . . . . . . . . . C16,17
Pleasant View Ln.
. . . . . . . . . . . . . . . . . . . . 
Rawson Bridge W.
. . . . . . . . . . . . . . . . . . . . 
Sherwood Tr. . Pg.20 . D18
Spruce Rd. . . Pg.20 . D17
St. Lo Ct. . . . . Pg.21 . . C18
Valley Dr . . . . Pg.21 . D18
Valley View Rd. Pg.20 . C16
West Lake Shore Dr.
. . . . . . . . . . . Pg.20 . C17
Woodland Rd. Pg.20 . D17
Woody Way . . Pg.20 . D17

**GOLF COURSES**
Chalet Hills G.C.
. . . . . . . . . . . Pg.21 . . D18

**PARKS**
Oak Hills Park Pg.20 . C17

**MISCELLANEOUS**
Police Department
. . . . . . . . . . . Pg.20 . D17
Village Hall . . Pg.20 . D17

## PRAIRIE GROVE
Pages 8,19,20
**STREETS**
Barreville Rd. . Pg.20 . A15
Behan Rd. . . . Pg.20 . B17
Buhl Rd. . . . . Pg.20 . B17
Carlisle Ct. . . Pg.20 . B15
Conestoga Tr. Pg.19 . . A15
Crystal Cir. . . Pg.20 . A17
Cypress Way . Pg.20 . A17

Erin Ct. . . . . . Pg.20 . B15
Fawn Tr. . . . . Pg.20 . A16
Fawn Trail Ct. Pg.8 . . H13
Fox Ct. . . . . . . Pg.20 . A16
Gracy Rd. . . . Pg.8,20
. . . . . . . . . . . . . . A15,H12
Heriatge Hills Rd.
. . . . . . . . . . . Pg.20 . A15
Heritage Hills Ct.
. . . . . . . . . . . . . . . . . . . . 
Homestead Tr. Pg.8 . . H12
Kame Dr. . . . . Pg.20 . A17
Niblick Ct. . . . Pg.20 . A17
Nish Rd. . . . . . Pg.20 . A16
Oak Knoll Rd. Pg.20 . B15
Pleasant Hill . Pg.19 . . A13
Redbud Ct. . . Pg.20 . B15
Squaw Creek Rd.
. . . . . . . . . . . Pg.19 . . A13
St. Route 176 Pg.19 . . B16
St. Route 31 . Pg.19 . . A14
Sutton Woods Ct.
. . . . . . . . . . . Pg.8 . . H12
Tamarack Cir. Pg.20 . B15
Tamarack Ct. Pg.20 . B15
Tamarack Ln. Pg.20 . B15
Timber Trail Dr. Pg.8 . . H13
Valley View Rd. Pg.20 . B16
White Oak Dr. Pg.20 . B15

**CEMETERIES**
Priaire Grove Cemetery
. . . . . . . . . . . Pg.20 . B16

**GOLF COURSES**
Prairie Isle Golf Course
. . . . . . . . . . . Pg.12,20
. . . . . . . . . . . . . . A17,H13

**SCHOOLS**
Prairie Grove Elem. & Jr. H.S.
Sch. Dist. 46
. . . . . . . . . . . Pg.20 . B16

## RICHMOND
Pages 4,32
**STREETS**
Ami Dr. . . . . . Pg.3,4 . A11
Bonnie Brae Rd.
. . . . . . . . . . . Pg.32 . . D4
Broadway St. . Pg.32 . . C3
Chucker Ct. . . Pg.4,32
. . . . . . . . . . . . . . A11,C3
Circle Dr. . . . . Pg.32 . . C4
Commercial Ave.
. . . . . . . . . . . Pg.3,4 . A11
Commercial St. Pg.32 . . C4
Covell St . . . . Pg.32 . . C4
Eagles Roost . Pg.4 . . A11
East St. . . . . . Pg.32 . . C4
Elm St. . . . . . . Pg.32 . . C4
Front St. . . . . Pg.32 C3,4
George St. . . Pg.32 C3,4
Golden Hawk Rd.
. . . . . . . . . . . . . . . . Pg.4,32
Gulf Ave. . . . . Pg.3E . . A11,C3
Grouse Ln. . . Pg.4,32
. . . . . . . . . . . . . . A11,C3
Hill Rd. . . . . . Pg.32 . . D4
Hillcrest Dr. . . Pg.32 C3,4
Kenosha Ave. Pg.32 . . C4
Liberty St. . . . Pg.32 C3,4
Maiden Ln. . . Pg.32 . . C4
Mallard Ln. . . Pg.4,32
. . . . . . . . . . . . . . A11,C3
Market St. . . . Pg.32 C3,4
May Ave. . . . . Pg.32 . . C4
May Ln. . . . . . Pg.4 . . C12
Mayview St. . . Pg.3,4 . A11
Mayzing St. . . Pg.3,4 . A11
McConnel Dr. Pg.32 . . C3
Mill St. . . . . . . Pg.32 . . C4
Milwaukee . . Pg.32 . . C4
Mourning Dove Cir.
. . . . . . . . . . . Pg.4 . . A11
Nippersink Dr. Pg.32 . . C4
North Ln. . . . . Pg.32 . . C4
Partridge Tr. . Pg.4,32
. . . . . . . . . . . . . . A11,C3
Pheasant Ln. . Pg.4,32
. . . . . . . . . . . . . . A11,C3
Prospect St. . Pg.32 . . C3
Quail Crossing Pg.4,32
. . . . . . . . . . . . . . A11,C3
Solon Mills Rd. Pg.32 . . C4
South St. . . . . Pg.32 C3,4
Springdale Dr. Pg.4 . . A11
Teal Tr. . . . . . Pg.4,32
. . . . . . . . . . . . . . A11,C3
Tryon Grove Rd.
. . . . . . . . . . . Pg.4 . . C11
Twin Lakes Rd. Pg.4 . . A12
Valley Dr. . . . . Pg.32 . . C3
Walnut St. . . . Pg.32 C3,4
William St. . . . Pg.32 . . C3
Wilson Rd. . . . Pg.3,4 . A11
Wood Duck Ln. Pg.4,32
. . . . . . . . . . . . . . A11,C3

**CEMETERIES**
Richmond Cemetery
. . . . . . . . . . . Pg.32 . . C3

**GOLF COURSES**
Hunter Country Club
. . . . . . . . . . . Pg.32 . . C4

## RILEY TOWNSHIP

**PARKS**
Park . . . . . . . . Pg.32 . . C4

**SCHOOLS**
Richmond Burton Comm.
H.S. . . . . . . . Pg.32 . . C4
Richmond Cons. Grade School
. . . . . . . . . . . Pg.32 . . C3

**MISCELLANEOUS**
Fire Dept. . . . Pg.32 . . C4
Hunt Club . . . Pg.4 . . A11
Nippersink Library
. . . . . . . . . . . Pg.32 . . C4
Police Dept. . . Pg.32 . . D3
Village Hall . . Pg.32 . . D4

## RICHMOND TOWNSHIP
Pages 3,4,32
**STREETS**
Arthur Dr. . . . Pg.4 . . B12
Bonnie Brae Dr. Pg.4 . . B11
Broadway . . . Pg.4 . . A11
Burlington Rd. Pg.4 . . A11
Clark Rd. . . . . Pg.4 . . B12
Concord Dr. . . Pg.4 . . B11
East St. . . . . . Pg.4 . . C12
English Prairie Rd.
. . . . . . . . . . . Pg.4 . . A12
Falcon Dr. . . . Pg.4 . . B12
Foxboro Tr. . . Pg.4 . . B12
Gardner St. . . Pg.4 . . C12
Glacier Ridge Dr.
. . . . . . . . . . . Pg.4 . . B11
Grant Ave. . . . Pg.4 . . A12
Green St. . . . . Pg.4 . . A12
Harding Ave . . Pg.4 . . A12
Harts Rd. . . . . Pg.4 . . C11
Hideaway Ln. . Pg.4 . . B11
Hill Rd. . . . . . Pg.4 . . B12
Hillandale Rd. Pg.4 . . B11
Hillshire Dr. . . Pg.4 . . B11
John St. . . . . . Pg.4 . . B12
Keith Dr. . . . . Pg.4 . . B12
Keystone Rd. . Pg.3 B,C10
Kuhn Rd. . . . . Pg.4 . . B12
Lakeview Rd. . Pg.4 . . A12
Lincoln Ave. . . Pg.4 . . B11
Macwood Dr. Pg.4 . . B11
May Ln. . . . . . Pg.4 . . C12
Mill Rd. . . . . . Pg.4 . . B12
Mill St. . . . . . . Pg.4 . . C12
Miller Rd. . . . . Pg.4 . . C12
Norgard Rd. . . Pg.3 . . B10
North St. . . . . Pg.4 . . C12
Oak Hill Dr. . . Pg.3 . . C10
Oak St. . . . . . Pg.4 . . B12
Overlook Dr. . Pg.4 . . A12
Overton Dr. . . Pg.4 . . B12
Penny Ln. . . . Pg.32 . . A13
Pioneer Rd. . . Pg.4 . . C12
Solon Rd. . . . Pg.4 B,C12
Squires Green Ct.
. . . . . . . . . . . Pg.4 . . B12
State Line Rd. Pg.4 . . A13
Taffy Ct. . . . . Pg.4 . . A12
Taft Ave. . . . . Pg.4 . . A12
Tryon Grove Rd.
. . . . . . . . . . . . . . . . . . . . 
. . . . . . . . . . . Pg.4 . . C11
Turner St. . . . Pg.4 . . C12
Tyron Grove Rd.
. . . . . . . . . . . . . . . . . . . . 
Valentine Ct. . Pg.3 . . C10
Virginia St. . . Pg.4 . . C12
West St. . . . . . Pg.4 . . C12
White St. . . . . Pg.4 . . C12
Winn Rd. . . . . Pg.4 . . B13
Zarnstorff Rd. Pg.4 . . A13

**CEMETERIES**
Cemetery . . . Pg.4 A,C12

**FOREST PRESERVES**
Elizabeth Lake Bog
. . . . . . . . . . . Pg.4 . . A12
Glacial Park . . Pg.4 . . C11
McHenry Co. Prairie Trail N.
. . . . . . . . . . . Pg.4 . . B11

## RIDGEFIELD
Page 11...H10

## RILEY
Page 9...L3

## RILEY TOWNSHIP
Page 9
**STREETS**
Acorn Ln. . . . Pg.9 . . K3
Alta Dr. . . . . . Pg.9 . . L1
Anthony Rd. . Pg.9 . . L1,2
Beck Rd. . . . . Pg.9 . . L4
Beth Ct. . . . . . Pg.9 . . K4
Bliss-Dale Rd. Pg.9 . . K2
Burma Rd. . . . Pg.9 . . K1
Burrows Rd. . Pg.9 . . M2
Carls Rd. . . . . Pg.9 . . M3
Coon Creek Rd. Pg.9 . . M3
Coral Oaks Ln. Pg.9 . . K3
Coral West Rd. Pg.9 . . K3
County Line Rd.
. . . . . . . . . . . . . . . . . . . . 
Delks Dr. . . . . Pg.9 . . L1
Demings Dr. . Pg.9 . . K4
Genoa Rd. . . . Pg.9 . . M1
Getty Rd. . . . . Pg.9 . . M4

## RILEYTOWNSHIP

Grange Rd. . . . Pg.9 . . . K1
Grossen Rd. . . Pg.9 . . . L3
Harrelson Rd. . . Pg.9 . . M3
Hartman Rd. . . Pg.9 . . . M2
Helen St. . . . . Pg.9 . . . L1
Hill Rd. . . . . . Pg.9 . . . K4
Jackson Rd. . . Pg.9 . . . K1
Lakewood Dr. . Pg.9,32
. . . . . . . . . . . . . . . . . F3,J2
Maple Street Rd.
. . . . . . . . . . . Pg.9 . . . K4
Marjorie Dr. . . Pg.9 . . . K1
Mary St. . . . . . Pg.9 . . . L1
McKeown Rd. . Pg.9 . . . L1
Meyer Rd. . . . Pg.9 . . . J3
Northwest Tollway
. . . . . . . . . . . Pg.9 . . . L2
Norway Ct. . . . Pg.9 . . . M3
Oak Creek Dr. . Pg.9 . . . K3
Payne Rd. . . . Pg.9 . . . M2
Pleasant Grove Rd.
. . . . . . . . . . . Pg.9 . . . K3
Poplar Rd. . . . Pg.9 . . . M2
Ratfield Rd. . . Pg.9 . . . K3
Riley Rd. . . . . Pg.9 . . . L3
Rily Harmony Rd.
. . . . . . . . . . . Pg.9 . . . L2
Rudolph Rd. . . Pg.9 . . . M1
Voss Rd. . . . . Pg.9 . . . L2
Wildrose Ln. . . Pg.9 . . . L2

**AIRPORTS**
Landing Strip . Pg.9 . . . L3

**CEMETERIES**
Cemetery . . . . Pg.9 . . . L3

**SCHOOLS**
Riley Comm. Cons. Sch.
. . . . . . . . . . . Pg.9 . . . L3

## RINGWOOD

Pages 4,8

**STREETS**
Adams St. . . Pg.3,4,8 D11
Barnard Mill Rd.
. . . . . . . . . . . Pg.4 . . D11
Craftwell Dr. . . Pg.4 . . D11
Jackson St. . Pg.3,4,8 D11
Lake Rd. . . . . Pg.4 . . D11
Mann Dr. . . . . Pg.4 . . D11
Monroe . . . . . Pg.4 . . D11
Ridgeway Rd. . Pg.8 . . D11
Ringwood Rd. . Pg.4 . . D11
School Rd. . . . Pg.4 . . D11
State Route 31 Pg.4 . . D11
Van Buren . . . Pg.4 . . D11

## SENECA TOWNSHIP

Pages 5,6,9,10,13

**STREETS**
Aine Dr. . . . . Pg.13 . . M4
Alpine Ln. . . . Pg.6,13
. . . . . . . . . . . . . . . . . G7,K4
Blackhawk Ln. Pg.6 . . . G5
Bockman Rd. . Pg.5 . . . H4
Carol Ln. . . . . Pg.6 . . . H7
Charlotte . . . . Pg.6 . . . H7
Chukar Pl. . . . Pg.10 . . H7
Collins Rd. . . Pg.6 . . . G6
Dean St. . . . . Pg.10 . . H7
Davis Rd. . . . Pg.13 . . L4
Deerpath Trail Pg.6 . . . H5
Dimmel Rd. . . Pg.6 . . . G5
Elaine Dr. . . . Pg.6 . . . H7
Emery Ln. . . . Pg.10 . . J7
Franklinville Rd. Pg.6 . . H6
Garden Valley Rd.
. . . . . . . . . . . Pg.6 . . . H5
Gayle Dr. . . . Pg.6 . . . H7
Gee Rd. . . . . Pg.6 . . . J6
Hiawatha Ln. . Pg.6 . . . G5
Highbridge Rd. Pg.6 . . . J5
Hobe Rd. . . . Pg.6 . . . G6
Holly Ln. . . . Pg.6,10 . H7
Hughes Rd. . . Pg.6 . . . G6
Kishwaukee St. Pg.5 . . . J3
Kishwaukee Valley Rd.
. . . . . . . . . . . Pg.6,13
. . . . . . . . . . . . . . . . . G6,J3
Kunde Rd. . . . Pg.6 . . . J5
Lucas Rd. . . . Pg.6 . . . H8
McIntyre Ln. . Pg.6 . . . G6
Millstream Rd. Pg.6 H4,5,J5
Mohawk Ln. . . Pg.5 . . . G4
Nancy Ct. . . . Pg.6 . . . H7
Ocock Rd. . . . Pg.6 . . . J5
P & O Rd. . . . Pg.10 . . J6
Perkins Rd. . . Pg.10 . . H6
Pleasant Valley Rd.
. . . . . . . . . . . Pg.10 . . J6
Private Rd. . . Pg.6 . . . J5
River Rd. . . . . Pg.5 . . . H4
Rose Farm Rd. Pg.6,13
. . . . . . . . . . . . . . . . . G6,J3
Sally Cir. . . . Pg.6,13
. . . . . . . . . . . . . . . . . H7,M4
Sayle Dr. . . . Pg.6 . . . H7
Secor Rd. . . . Pg.6 . . . H5

Shannon Dr. . Pg.6,13
South St. . . . . Pg.6,13
. . . . . . . . . . . . . . . . . G6,J3
Standish Rd. . Pg.5 . . . H4
Steig Rd. . . . . Pg.6,13
. . . . . . . . . . . . . . . . . H7,M4
Sullivan Rd. . . Pg.6 . . . G5
Sunnyside Rd. Pg.10 . . J7
Sylvia Ln. . . . Pg.6 . . . H7
Telgraph St. . . Pg.26 . . L16
Timber Ln. . . . Pg.10 . . J7
US Route 14 . Pg.13 . . K4
Union Rd. . . . Pg.6 . . . J5
Vermont Rd. . Pg.6 . . . H5
Woodcliff Dr. . Pg.6 . . . H5
Woodland Trail Pg.6 . . . H5

**MISCELLANEOUS**
Girl Scout Camp
. . . . . . . . . . . Pg.6,13
. . . . . . . . . . . . . . . . . G7,J4

## SOLON MILLS

Page 4 . . . B12

## SPRING GROVE

Pages 4,32

**STREETS**
Altamonte Dr. . Pg.4 . . B12
Amanda Dr. . . Pg.4 . . B13
Angus Ln. . . . Pg.4 . . B13
Anthony Ln. . . Pg.4 . . B13
Applewood Ln. Pg.4 . . C13
Asbury Ct. . . Pg.32 . . B6
Ascot Ln. . . . Pg.4 . . A13
Aspen Ct. . . . Pg.4 . . C13
Beach St. . . . Pg.4 . . C13
Bellevue Dr. . Pg.32 . . B6
Bentley Ln. . . Pg.4 . . B14
Blivin St. . . . Pg.32 . . B6
Clark Rd. . . . Pg.4 . . B12
Bonner Ln. . . Pg.4 . . B13
Broadview Ct. Pg.32 . . B6
Carmel Ct. . . Pg.4 . . B12
Catalpa Ct. . . Pg.4 . . C13
Cedar Ln. . . . Pg.4 . . C13
Champion St. . Pg.4 . . B12
Chateaugay Dr. Pg.4 . . B12
Chlemsford Dr. Pg.4 . . C12
Christine Ct. . Pg.4 . . B12
Clark Rd. . . . Pg.4 . . B12
Coventry Dr. . Pg.4 . . C12
Deer Tr., W. . . Pg.4 . . B12
East Ct. . . . . Pg.32 . . B6
East Solon Rd. Pg.4 . . A5
East St. . . . . Pg.32 . . A6
Edgewood Dr. Pg.4 . . C12
Elizabeth Ln. . Pg.4 . . B14
Elk Dr. . . . . . Pg.4,32
. . . . . . . . . . . . . . . . A5,6,B13
Elk St. . . . . . Pg.4 . . B13
Elm St. . . . . . Pg.4 . . B13
Ember Ln. . . . Pg.4 . . B13
English Prairie Rd.
. . . . . . . . . . . . . . . . . G7,K4
Erie Ave. . . . . Pg.4 . . A13
Falcon Ln. . . . Pg.4 . . A13
Fox Bluff Ln. . Pg.4 . . A,B13
Fox Tr. . . . . . Pg.4 . . B13
Fox Trail Dr. . . Pg.4 . . B13
Galleria Dr. . . Pg.4 . . B12
Greenleaf Ct. . Pg.4 . . B12
Hatchery Rd. . Pg.32 . . B6
Hawthorne Ln. Pg.4 . . C13
Hidden Tr. Blvd. Pg.4 . . B13
Hidden Tr. Ct. Pg.4 . . B13
Highview St. . Pg.32 . . B5,6
Hillside Dr. . . Pg.4 . . C12
Holian Dr. . . . Pg.4,32
. . . . . . . . . . . . . . . . . B6,C13
Hunters Ct. . . Pg.4 . . B13
Hunters Ln. . . Pg.4 . . B13
Huron Dr. . . . Pg.4 . . A13
Industrial Ct. . Pg.32 . . B5
Judge Ct. . . . Pg.4 . . B12
Kings Lair Dr. Pg.4 . . C12
Lone Oak Rd. Pg.4 . . C13
Loraine St. . . Pg.32 . . A,B6
Main St. . . . . Pg.32 . . A6
Marie Dr. . . . Pg.4,32 . A6
Martin Dr. . . . Pg.4 . . B12
Maureen Dr. . Pg.32 . . A6
May Ln. . . . . Pg.4 . . C12
Mayo Ct. . . . Pg.4,32
. . . . . . . . . . . . . . . . . B6,C13
Meadowdale Cir.
. . . . . . . . . . . Pg.4 . . B13
Meyer Rd. . . . Pg.32 . . B6
Michigan Dr. . Pg.4 . . A13
Monterra Dr. . Pg.4 . . B13
Nicholas Ln. . Pg.4 . . B13
Nora Way . . . Pg.4 . . B13
North St. . . . . Pg.32 . . A6
Oak St. . . . . . Pg.32 . . A5
Ontario Ave. . Pg.4 . . A13
Overlook Dr. . Pg.4 . . C12
Oxfordshire Ln. Pg.4 . . B13
Park St. . . . . Pg.32 . . B6

Pater Ct. . . . Pg.4 . . B13
Pierce Dr. . . Pg.4,32
. . . . . . . . . . . . . . . . . B6,C13
Pierceshire Rd. Pg.4 . . C12
Pine Crest Ct. Pg.4 . . B13
Pine St. . . . . Pg.4 . . C13
Polaris Rd. . . Pg.4 . . A13
Ponder Ln. . . Pg.4 . . B13
Prairie Dr. . . . Pg.4 . . B12
Rabbit Ct. . . . Pg.4,32
. . . . . . . . . . . . . . . . . A5,B13
Richardson Rd. Pg.4,32
. . . . . . . . . . . . . . . . . A6,B13
Ridge Rd. . . . Pg.4 . . B12
Robin Ct. . . . Pg.4 . . C12
Rodi Ct. . . . . Pg.4 . . C13
Rolling Oaks Dr.
. . . . . . . . . . . Pg.4 . . C13
Short St. . . . Pg.32 . . B6
Spring Ct. . . . Pg.4 . . B13
Spring Grove Rd.
. . . . . . . . . . . Pg.32 . . B5
Spring Leaf Dr. Pg.4 . . C13
Spring Ridge Dr.
. . . . . . . . . . . Pg.4,32
. . . . . . . . . . . . . . . . . B6,C13
Springdale Dr. Pg.4 . . B13
Spruce St. . . Pg.4 . . C13
Squirrel Dr. . . Pg.32 . . A5
Steeplechase Ct.
. . . . . . . . . . . Pg.4 . . A13
Steeplechase Ln.
. . . . . . . . . . . Pg.4 . . A13
Superior Ave. . Pg.4 . . A13
Suzanne Ct. . Pg.4 . . B14
Suzanne Ln. . Pg.4 . . B14
Tahoe Ln. . . . Pg.4 . . B12
Tall Grass Ct. Pg.4 . . B12
Utility St. . . . Pg.32 . . B6
Walnut Ct. . . Pg.4 . . C13
Westward Dr. . Pg.32 . . B5,6
Wilmot Farms Ln.
. . . . . . . . . . . Pg.4 . . B14
Winn Rd. . . . . Pg.4,23
. . . . . . . . . . . . . . . . . A5,C13
Wintergreen Dr.
. . . . . . . . . . . Pg.4 . . B13
Woodview Dr. Pg.4 . . B13

**PARKS**
Lyle C. Thomas Park
. . . . . . . . . . . Pg.4 . . C13

**SCHOOLS**
Spring Grove Sch.
. . . . . . . . . . . Pg.32 . . A6

**MISCELLANEOUS**
State Fish Hatchery
. . . . . . . . . . . Pg.32 . . A,B6

## TROUT VALLEY

Pages 12,25,30

**STREETS**
Algonquin Cary Rd.
. . . . . . . . . . . Pg.25 . . I16
Big Oaks Rd. . Pg.25 . . I16
Bluff Ct. . . . . Pg.30 . . I17
Bluff Rd. . . . . Pg.30 . . I17
Brookbridge Rd.
. . . . . . . . . . . Pg.25 . . I16
Cahill Rd. . . . Pg.25 . . I17
Cold Spring Rd.
. . . . . . . . . . . Pg.25 . . I16
Country Commons Rd.
. . . . . . . . . . . Pg.25 . . I16
Fox Harbor Dr. Pg.30 . . J17
Golf Rd. . . . . Pg.30 . . I17
Grove Rd. . . . Pg.25 . . I16
Hawthorne Way
. . . . . . . . . . . Pg.25 . . I16
High Rd. . . . . Pg.25 . . I16
Little Cahill . . Pg.30 . . I17
Little Marryat . Pg.25 . . I17
Marryat Rd. . . Pg.25 . . I17
Rainbow Ln. . Pg.25 . . I16
River Dr. . . . . Pg.30 . . J17
Stonegate Rd. Pg.25 . . I16
Trout Valley Rd.
. . . . . . . . . . . Pg.25 . . I16
Turkey Hill . . Pg.25 . . I16
Turkey Run Rd. Pg.25 . . I16
Willets Way . . Pg.25 . . I17

## TWIN LAKES

Page 4 . . . A12

## UNION

Pages 10,33

**STREETS**
Clark St. . . . . Pg.33 . . D7
Country Ln. . . Pg.33 . . D7
Depot . . . . . . Pg.33 . . D7
Elm St. . . . . . Pg.33 . . D7
Fairfield Dr. . . Pg.33 . . D7
Highbridge Rd. Pg.33 . . D7,8
Jackson St. . . Pg.33 . . D7
Jefferson St. . Pg.33 . . D7,8
Johnson St. . . Pg.33 . . D7,8
Main St. . . . . Pg.33 . . D7
Mallett Dr. . . Pg.33 . . D7

Meadow . . . . Pg.33 . . D7
National St. . . Pg.33 . . D7
Northrop Rd. . Pg.33 . . D7
O'Clock Rd. . . Pg.33 . . E7
Olson Rd. . . . Pg.33 . . D-E8
Prairie St. . . . Pg.33 . . D7
South . . . . . . Pg.33 . . D7
Sunview Dr. . . Pg.33 . . D7
Vine St. . . . . Pg.33 . . D7
Washington St. Pg.33 . . D7
Wayne St. . . . Pg.33 . . D7

**SCHOOLS**
Evergreen Park Sch.
. . . . . . . . . . . Pg.33 . . D8

## WONDER LAKE

Pages 7,33

**STREETS**
Adam Dr. . . . Pg.3,7 . . E9
Burton Rd. . . . Pg.33 . . E9
Chemung Dr. . Pg.33 . . E8
Coral Rd. . . . Pg.33 . . E9
Crabapple Ln. Pg.3,7 . . E9
Dorr Rd. . . . . Pg.33 . . E9
Garrison Rd. . Pg.33 . . D,E9
Greenwood Dr. Pg.33 . . E9
Highland Dr. . Pg.33 . . E8
Hilltop Dr. . . . Pg.33 . . E9
Jacobson Dr. Pg.3,7 . . E9
Justine Ct. . . Pg.33 . . E9
Lake Shore Dr. Pg.33 . . E9
Marissa Tr. . . Pg.3 . . . E9
Meadow Ln. . Pg.33 . . E8
Olden Rd. . . . Pg.33 . . E9
Pamela Rd. . . Pg.33 . . E9
Prairie Tr. . . . Pg.3 . . . E9
Rachel Dr. . . Pg.3 . . . E9
Red Barn Dr. . Pg.3 . . . E9
Richmond Rd. Pg.33 . . E9
Riley Rd. . . . . Pg.33 . . E8,9
Ryan Ct. . . . . Pg.3 . . . E9
Schuette Dr. . Pg.3,7 . . E9
Seneca Rd. . . Pg.3 . . . D9
Thompson Rd. Pg.33 . . E9
Twin Oaks Dr. Pg.33 . . E9
West Wood Dr. Pg.33 . . E,D9
Whitetail Dr. . Pg.3 . . . E9
Woodmere Rd. Pg.33 . . F9
Woodstock St. Pg.33 . . E9

## WOODSTOCK

Pages 6,7,13,14

**STREETS**
Amber St. . . . Pg.13 . . K5
Amsterdam St. Pg.13 . . J5
Anne St. . . . . Pg.13 . . J5
Applewood Ln. Pg.14 . . L8
Arthur Dr. . . . Pg.13 . . J6
Ash Ave. . . . . Pg.13 . . H6
Ashley Ct. . . . Pg.14 . . H7
Aspen Dr. . . . Pg.14 . . L8
Austin Ave. . . Pg.13 . . K6
Ayrshire Ct. . Pg.13 . . K8
Bagley St. . . . Pg.14 . . J6
Banford Rd. . . Pg.14 . . H7
Barbary Ln. . . Pg.13 . . L6
Barn Swallow Dr.
. . . . . . . . . . . . . . . . . . H7
Bartlett St. . . Pg.13 . . J6
Becking Ave. . Pg.14 . . J5
Beech Ave. . . Pg.13 . . J5
Bell Air Ln. . . Pg.13 . . K6
Benton . . . . . Pg.13 . . J7
Bertsum Ln. . Pg.14 . . K8
Birch Rd. . . . Pg.14 . . K8
Blakley St. . . Pg.13 . . K5
Bliss Ct. . . . . Pg.14 . . K6
Blue Bonnet Ln.
. . . . . . . . . . . Pg.13 . . K6
Bobolink Cir. . Pg.13 . . K6
Borden St. . . Pg.13 . . J5
Bridgewater Dr. Pg.14 . . M7
Brink St. . . . . Pg.14 . . K6
Broadway Ave. Pg.14 . . J7
Broadway Ct. Pg.14 . . J7
Broadway Rd. Pg.14 . . H7
Brown St. . . . Pg.13 . . J6
Bull Valley Dr. Pg.13 . . K8
Bunker St. . . Pg.13 . . K6
Burbank Ave. . Pg.14 . . K6
Cains St. . . . Pg.13 . . H5
Cairns Ct. . . . Pg.14 . . J6
Calhoun St. . Pg.13 . . H5
Carlisle Dr. . . Pg.14 . . K7
Carol Ave. . . Pg.13 . . J5
Carol St. . . . . Pg.13 . . J5
Cass St. . . . . Pg.13 . . J6
Castlear Tr. . . Pg.14 . . M7
Castlear Tr. . . Pg.13 . . K7
Castleshire Dr. Pg.13 . . J5
Catalpa Ln. . . Pg.14 . . L7
Center Ln. . . Pg.13 . . J6
Center Ct. . . . Pg.14 . . J6
Centerville Ct. Pg.14 . . K7
Central Pkwy. . Pg.14 . . H6
Charles Rd. . . Pg.14 . . J6
Cherry Ct. . . . Pg.13 . . J6
Chestnut Ave. Pg.14 . . K6
Church St. . . Pg.13 . . J6

Claussen Dr. . Pg.13 . . J5
Clay St. . . . . Pg.13 . . H,J6
Cloverchase Cir.
. . . . . . . . . . . Pg.13 . . L6
Club Rd. . . . . Pg.14 . . K7
Cobblestone Way
. . . . . . . . . . . Pg.14 . . L7
Conway St. . . Pg.13 . . J5
Country Club Rd.
. . . . . . . . . . . Pg.14 . . L8
Ct. A . . . . . . Pg.14 . . L8
Ct. B . . . . . . Pg.14 . . L8
Ct. C . . . . . . Pg.14 . . L8
Ct. D . . . . . . Pg.14 . . L8
Ct. E . . . . . . Pg.14 . . L8
Ct. F . . . . . . Pg.14 . . L8
Ct. G . . . . . . Pg.14 . . L8
Ct. H . . . . . . Pg.14 . . L8
Ct. I . . . . . . . Pg.14 . . L8
Ct. J . . . . . . Pg.14 . . L8
Dacy St. . . . . Pg.13 . . J5
Dakota Dr. . . Pg.13 . . L4
Dane St. . . . Pg.13 . . J4,5
Davis Ct. . . . Pg.14 . . K6
Davis Rd. . . . Pg.14 . . L6
Dean St. . . . Pg.13 K6,L5
Desmond St. . Pg.14 . . J6
Diana Ct. . . . Pg.13 . . H5
Dieckman St. Pg.13 . . L8
Dillard Ct. . . . Pg.14 . . L8
Division St. . . Pg.13 . . J6
Dona Ct. . . . Pg.13 . . J5
Donegal Ct. . Pg.13 . . J5
Donovan Ave. Pg.13 . . J5
Dorham Ln. . . Pg.13 . . K8
Douglas St. . Pg.13 . . J6
Dublin Ct. . . . Pg.13 . . K4
Duncan Pl. . . Pg.13 . . L8
Duvall Dr. . . . Pg.13 . . K5
East St. S. . . Pg.13 . . J6
Eastwood Dr. Pg.14 . . H6
Edgewood St. Pg.14 . . L6
Ellen Ct. . . . . Pg.14 . . J7
Fair St. . . . . . Pg.14 . . K7
Farm Tr. . . . . Pg.14 . . H6
First St. . . . . Pg.13 . . J6
Flagg Ln. . . . Pg.14 . . J7
Forest Ave. . . Pg.13 . . K6
Fox Ln. . . . . . Pg.14 . . H6
Franson St. . . Pg.13 . . J5
Fremont St. . . Pg.13 . . K6
Galloway Dr. . Pg.13 . . K8
Gerry Ct. . . . Pg.13 . . J5
Gerry St. . . . Pg.13 . . J5
Giddings St. . Pg.14 . . K6
Ginny Ln. . . . Pg.13 . . K6
Golden Ave. . Pg.14 . . J5
Gould St. . . . Pg.13 . . K5
Gracy St. . . . Pg.14 . . J6
Grant St. . . . Pg.13 . . J6
Greenwood Ave.
. . . . . . . . . . . . . . . . . . H6
Greenwood Cir. Pg.13 . . H6
Grove St. . . . Pg.14 . . J6
Halma . . . . . Pg.14 H8,K7
Halma . . . . . Pg.14 H7,8
Harvest Ct. . . Pg.13 . . K5
Hayward St. . Pg.13 . . K6
Heron Way . . Pg.14 . . K8
Herrington Pl. Pg.14 . . K5
Hibbard St. . . Pg.13 . . K6
Hickman Ln. . Pg.14 . . J7
Hickory Ln. . . Pg.13 . . K5
Highland Ave. Pg.13 . . K5
Hill St. . . . . . Pg.13 . . J,K5
Hillside Rd. . . Pg.13 . . J5
Hillside Tr. . . . Pg.13 . . K6
Hilltop Ct. . . . Pg.13 . . H6
Hoy Ave. . . . Pg.13 . . K6
Huffman St. . Pg.14 . . J6
Hutchins St. . Pg.14 . . J6
Industrial Heights Dr.
. . . . . . . . . . . Pg.14 . . L7
Infanta Ct. . . Pg.13 . . K4
Irving Ave. . . Pg.13 . . J6
Island Ct. . . . Pg.13 . . H6
Jackson St. . Pg.13 . . J5,6
Jean St. . . . . Pg.13 . . K6
Jefferson St. . Pg.13 K5,7
Jewett St. . . . Pg.14 . . J6
Johnson . . . . Pg.13 . . J6
Joseph St. . . Pg.13 . . H6
Judd St. . . . . Pg.13,14
. . . . . . . . . . . . . . . . . . J5,6
Julie St. . . . . Pg.14 . . K6
Kathleen . . . Pg.13 . . K5
Kimball Ave. . Pg.13 K5,6
King St. . . . . Pg.14 . . K6
Kinkenny Ct. . Pg.14 . . L7
Knight Dr. . . . Pg.14 . . K8
Lake Ave. . . . Pg.13 . . K6
Lake Rd., E. . Pg.14 . . J6
Lake Shore Dr. Pg.7,14
Laurel Ave. . . Pg.14 . . K7
Lawndale St. . Pg.14 . . K6
Lawrence St. Pg.13 . . K6
Leah St. . . . . Pg.14 . . K7

Lee Ann Ln. . Pg.13 . . K5
Liberty Ln. . . Pg.13 . . L6
Lincoln Ave. . Pg.13 . . L6
Linda Ct. . . . Pg.14 . . J7
Linden Ln. . . Pg.14 . . J6
Lisa St. . . . . . . . . . . J5
Locust . . . . . Pg.13 . . H6
Locust St. . . . Pg.14 . . H6
Lorr Dr. . . . . Pg.13 . . K5
Madison . . . . Pg.13 . . K5
Madison St. . Pg.13 H,J6
Main St. . . . . Pg.13 . . J6
Mansfield St. Pg.14 . . J6
Maple Ave. . . Pg.13 . . H6
Margaret Dr. . Pg.13 . . J5
Mark Ct. . . . . Pg.13 . . J5
Martha Ln. . . Pg.14 . . K7
Marvel Ave. . Pg.14 . . J6
Mary Ann St. Pg.14 . . K7
McCannon . . Pg.13 . . H6
McConnell Rd. Pg.14 . . K5
McCoy St. . . . Pg.13 . . J5
McHenry Ave. Pg.14 . . J7
Meadow Ave. Pg.13 . . J6
Melody Ln. . . Pg.14 . . K5
Miller Rd. . . . Pg.13 K6,L5
Mitchell . . . . Pg.13 . . K5
Moraine Ct. . Pg.13 . . J6
Moraine Dr. . Pg.13 . . J6
Muriel St. . . . Pg.13 . . K5
Nebraska St. . Pg.14 . . J6
Neuwhof Ct. . Pg.13 . . J6
Newell St. . . . Pg.13 . . J6
North Hampton Pg.14 . . J6
North St. . . . Pg.13 . . J6
Northwest Hwy.
. . . . . . . . . . . . . . . . Pg.13,14
Northwood Ln. Pg.13 . . H6
Nuthatch Dr. . Pg.14 . . H7
Oak Ave. . . . Pg.13 . . J5
Oak Ct. . . . . Pg.13 . . J5
Oak View Ter. Pg.13 . . K4
Oakdale Ln. . Pg.14 . . K8
Oakleaf Ln. . . Pg.13 . . K7
Oakwood Ave. Pg.13 . . K6
Olive Ave. . . . Pg.13 . . K6
Olson St. . . . Pg.14 . . H6
Orchard Ct. . Pg.14 . . H6
Ossage Way . Pg.6 . . G7
Park St. . . . . . . . . . . . L6
Peachtree Ln. Pg.13 . . K4
Pine Ct. . . . . Pg.14 . . J6
Pleasant St. . Pg.13 . . J5
Pond Point Rd. Pg.13 . . M7
Poplar Ln. . . Pg.14 . . H7
Portage Ln. . . Pg.13 . . L6
Prairie Ridge Ln.
. . . . . . . . . . . Pg.13 . . L6
Putnam St. . . Pg.14 . . K5
Quail Ct. . . . Pg.14 . . K5
Queen Anne St. Pg.13 . . J6
Quinlan Ln. . . Pg.13 . . J5
Raffel Rd. . . . Pg.14 G,H7
Railroad St. . Pg.13 . . J6
Red Barn St. . Pg.14 . . L8
Red Barn Rd. Pg.14 . . L8
Redwing Dr. . Pg.14 . . H7
Regina Ct. . . Pg.13 . . J5
Rhett Pl. . . . . Pg.14 . . H7
Rhodes St. . . Pg.13 . . J5
Ridgeland Ave. Pg.13 . . K8
Ridgewood Dr. Pg.13 . . K6
Robert Dr. . . Pg.13 . . H5
Roller Dr. . . . Pg.14 . . J5
Roosevelt . . . Pg.14 . . K6
Rose Ct. . . . Pg.14 . . J7
Russel Court . Pg.14 . . G6
Ryan Ct. . . . . Pg.13 . . K4
Ryder Woods . Pg.14 . . J5
Sando Ln. . . . Pg.13 . . K5
Schryver Ave. Pg.13 . . K6
Schuette Dr. . Pg.14 . . J7
Second St., W. Pg.13 . . J6
Seminary Ave. Pg.13 . . J6
Seneca Ct. . . Pg.14 . . J6
Sharon Dr. . . Pg.14 . . J7
Shiela St. . . . Pg.14 . . J6
Short St. . . . Pg.13 . . J6
Smith St. . . . Pg.14 . . K6
South St. . . . Pg.13 K5,7
Southview St. Pg.14 . . L7
Sparrow Dr. . Pg.14 . . H7
St. Johns Rd. Pg.14 . . J6
Stewart Ave. . Pg.13 . . L7
Stonelake Rd. Pg.14 . . J3
Summit Ave. . Pg.13 . . J6
Sumner St. . . Pg.13 . . J6
Sunshine Ln. Pg.13 . . J6
Suzanne St. . Pg.13 . . J5
Tanager Dr. . Pg.13 . . H7
Tappan St. . . Pg.13 . . K5
Tara Ct. . . . . Pg.13 . . K5
Tara Dr. . . . . Pg.13 . . K5
Taurus Ct. . . Pg.13 . . K8
Techcourt . . . Pg.14 . . J5
Terry Ct. . . . . Pg.13 . . J6
Teton Dr. . . . Pg.6 . . G7
Third St., W. . Pg.13 . . J6
Thomas Dr. . Pg.13 . . H5

Throop St. . . Pg.13 . . K0
Timothy Ln. . Pg.14 . . J7
Todd Ave. . . Pg.13 . . J6
Tryon St. . . . Pg.13 . . K6
Twelve Oaks Pkwy.
. . . . . . . . . . . . . . . . . . H7
Valerian Ln. . Pg.13 . . L6
Van Buren . . Pg.13 . . J6
Verbena Ln. . Pg.13 . . L6
Victoria Dr. . . Pg.13 . . H5
Vine St. . . . . Pg.13 . . K6
Wait Pl. . . . . Pg.13 . . J6
Walnut Dr. . . Pg.13 . . H6
Wanda (Pvt) . Pg.14 . . K7
Washburn St. Pg.13 . . K7
Washington St. Pg.13 . . J5
Westwood Ct. Pg.13 . . J5
Westwood Tr. Pg.13 . . K4
Wheeler St. . Pg.13 . . J5
White Face Ct. Pg.14 . . K8
White Fence Ct. Pg.13 . . J6
Wicker St. . . Pg.14 H6,J5
Willow Ave. . Pg.13 . . H6
Winslow Ave. Pg.13 . . K5
Winslow Cir. . Pg.13 . . K5
Wintu Ct. . . . Pg.13 . . L4
Wood Dr. . . . Pg.13 . . L6
Woodside Ct. Pg.13 . . H7
Yellowhead Ct. Pg.13 . . K8
Zimmerman Rd. Pg.14 . . K7

**AIRPORTS**
Woodstock Airport
. . . . . . . . . . . Pg.13 . . H5

**CEMETERIES**
Catholic Cem. Pg.13 . . K5
Memorial Park Cemetery
. . . . . . . . . . . Pg.14 . . L7
Oakland Cem. Pg.13 . . J5

**GOLF COURSES**
Bull Valley Golf Course
. . . . . . . . . . . Pg.13 . . K8
Woodstock C.C. Pg.14 . . K9

**PARKS**
Emricson Park Pg.13 . . K4
Kishwaukee Park
. . . . . . . . . . . . . . . . . . L6
Olson Park . . Pg.13 . . H6
Raintree Park Pg.14 . . J5
Ryders Woods Park
. . . . . . . . . . . . . . . . . . J5
Silver Creek Conservation
. . . . . . . . . Area Pg.13 . . H6
Silver Creek Park
. . . . . . . . . . . . . . . . . . J5
Tara Dr. Park . Pg.13 . . K5
Tourist Park . Pg.13 . . J5
Westwood Park Nature Area
. . . . . . . . . . . Pg.13 . . K3

**SCHOOLS**
Allendale/LINC Program
. . . . . . . . . . . Pg.7 . . G8
Clay St. Sch. Pg.13 . . J6
Dean St. Sch. Pg.13 . . K6
Marian Central H.S.
. . . . . . . . . . . Pg.14 . . H7
Mary P. Endres Elem. Sch.
. . . . . . . . . . . Pg.6 . . F8
N.W. Coonen H.S.
. . . . . . . . . . . Pg.6 . . G8
Northwood Jr. H.S.
. . . . . . . . . . . Pg.13 . . G6
Northwood Sch.
. . . . . . . . . . . . . . . . . . H6
Olson Middle Sch.
. . . . . . . . . . . Pg.13 . . J5
St. John St. Sch. Pg.13 . . J6
St. Mary Sch. Pg.13 . . J6
Westwood Sch. Pg.14 . . K4
Woodstock Christian Sch.
. . . . . . . . . . . Pg.13 . . K5
Woodstock H.S.
. . . . . . . . . . . Pg.13 . . K5

**MISCELLANEOUS**
Athletic Field . Pg.13 . . J5
City Hall and Opera House
County Fairground
. . . . . . . . . . . Pg.14 . . J6
Courthouse . Pg.13 . . J6
Girl Scout Camp
. . . . . . . . . . . . . . . . . . J3
Hospital . . . . Pg.13 . . K5
Masonic Lodge Pg.14 . . J6
McHenry Co. Courthouse
. . . . . . . . . . . . . . . . Pg.14 . . G6
McHenry Co. Regional Sch.
. . . . . . . . . Office Pg.13 . . G6
Old Peoples Rest Home
. . . . . . . . . . . . . . . . . . J6
Public Library Pg.13 . . J6
Waste Water Treatment
. . . . . . . . . Plant Pg.13 . . L6
Woodstock Children's
. . . . . . . . . . Home Pg.14 . . J8

# JOLIET AND VICINITY
## SECTION 8

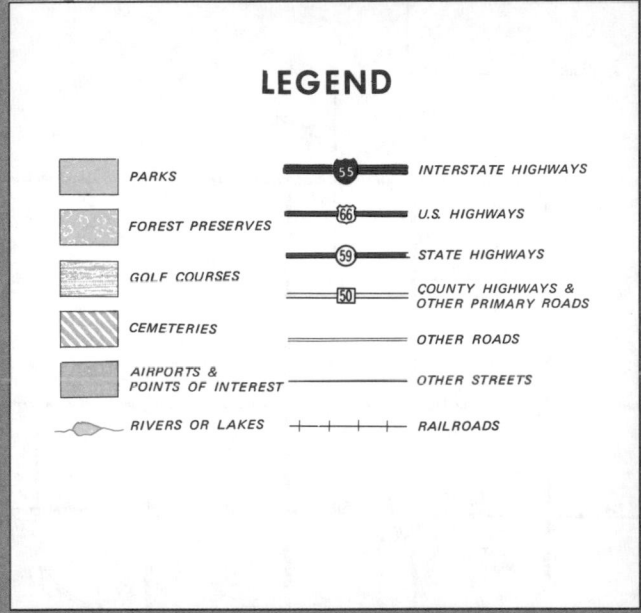

## LEGEND

| | | | |
|---|---|---|---|
| PARKS | | 55 | INTERSTATE HIGHWAYS |
| FOREST PRESERVES | | 66 | U.S. HIGHWAYS |
| GOLF COURSES | | 59 | STATE HIGHWAYS |
| CEMETERIES | | 50 | COUNTY HIGHWAYS & OTHER PRIMARY ROADS |
| AIRPORTS & POINTS OF INTEREST | | | OTHER ROADS |
| RIVERS OR LAKES | | | OTHER STREETS |
| | | | RAILROADS |

**TURN PAGE FOR ORIENTATION MAP**

# SECTION 8
## ORIENTATION MAP

Information on this page is to be used for general reference only.
For definitve listings of all information, see index at end of this section.

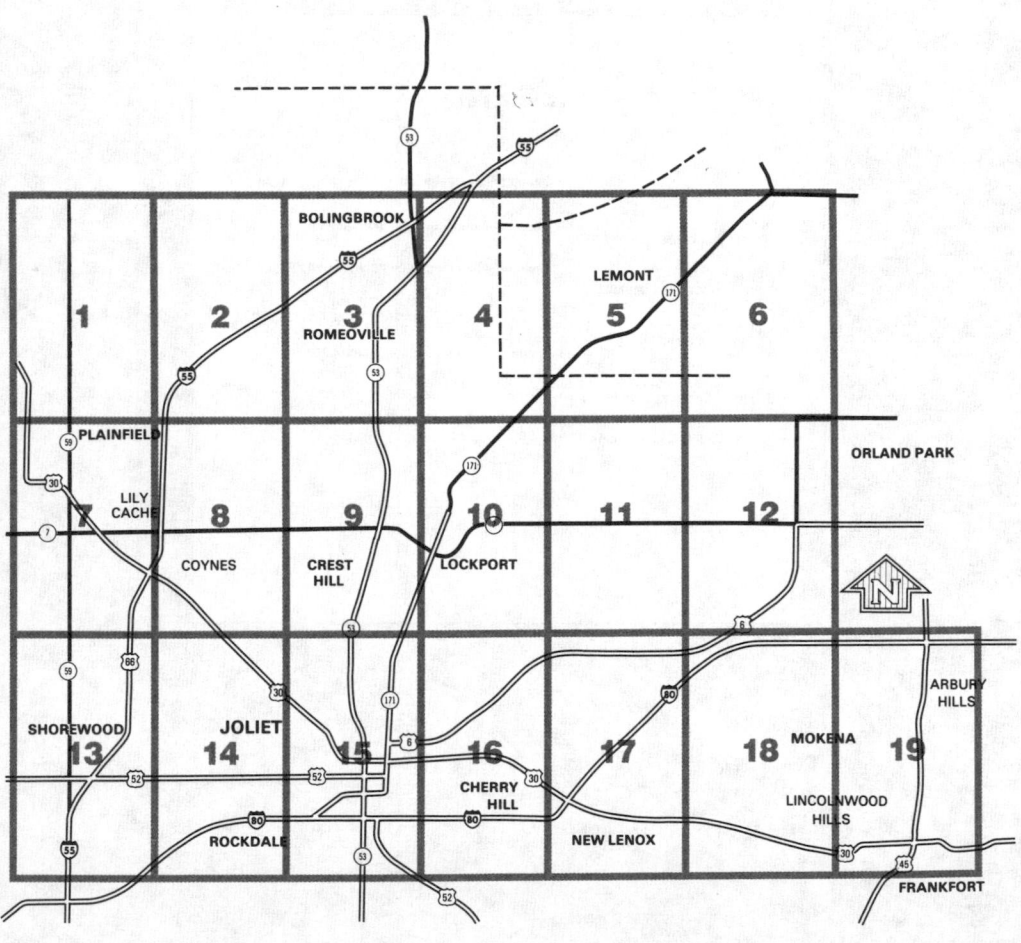

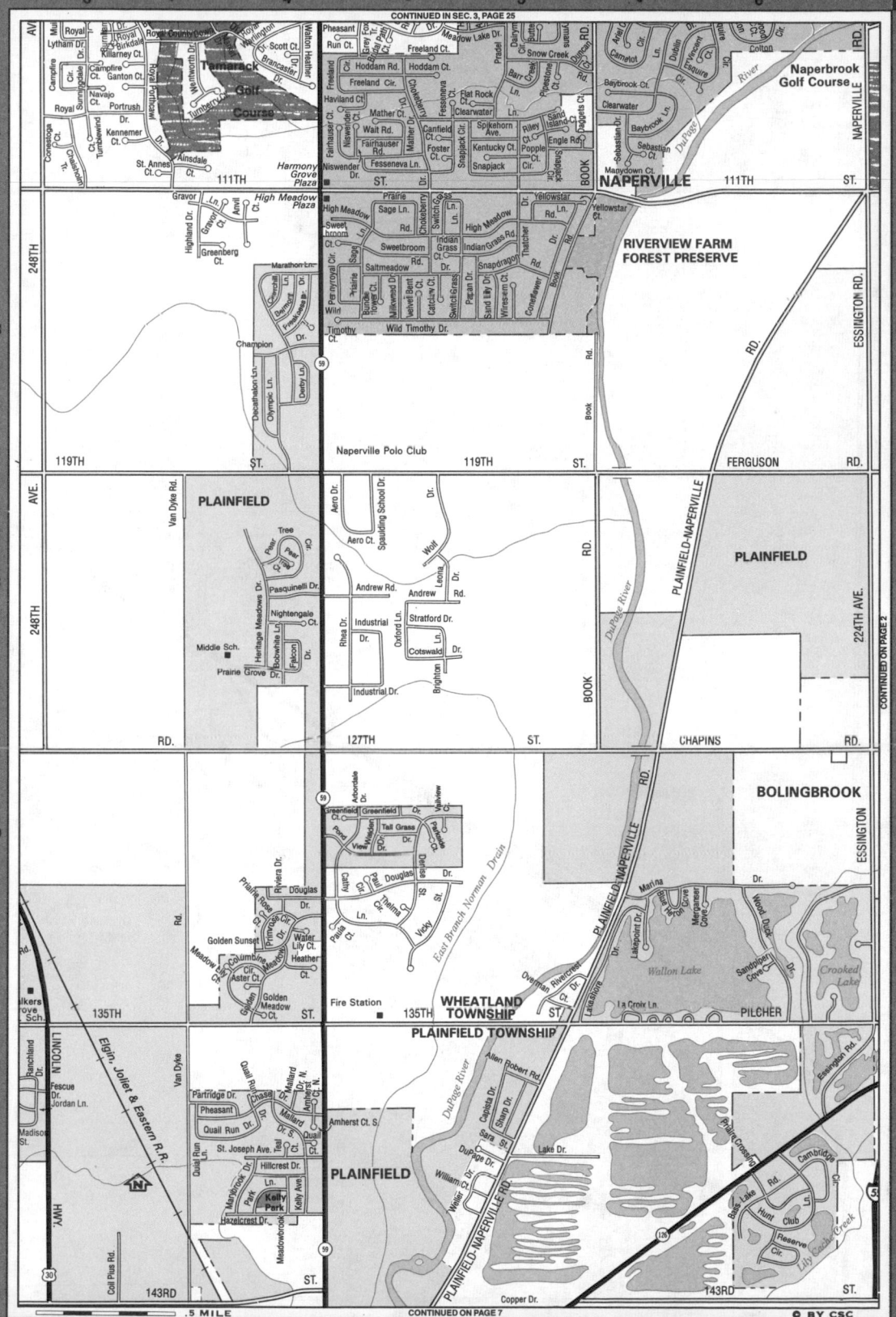

CONTINUED ON PAGE 2

© BY CSC

.5 MILE

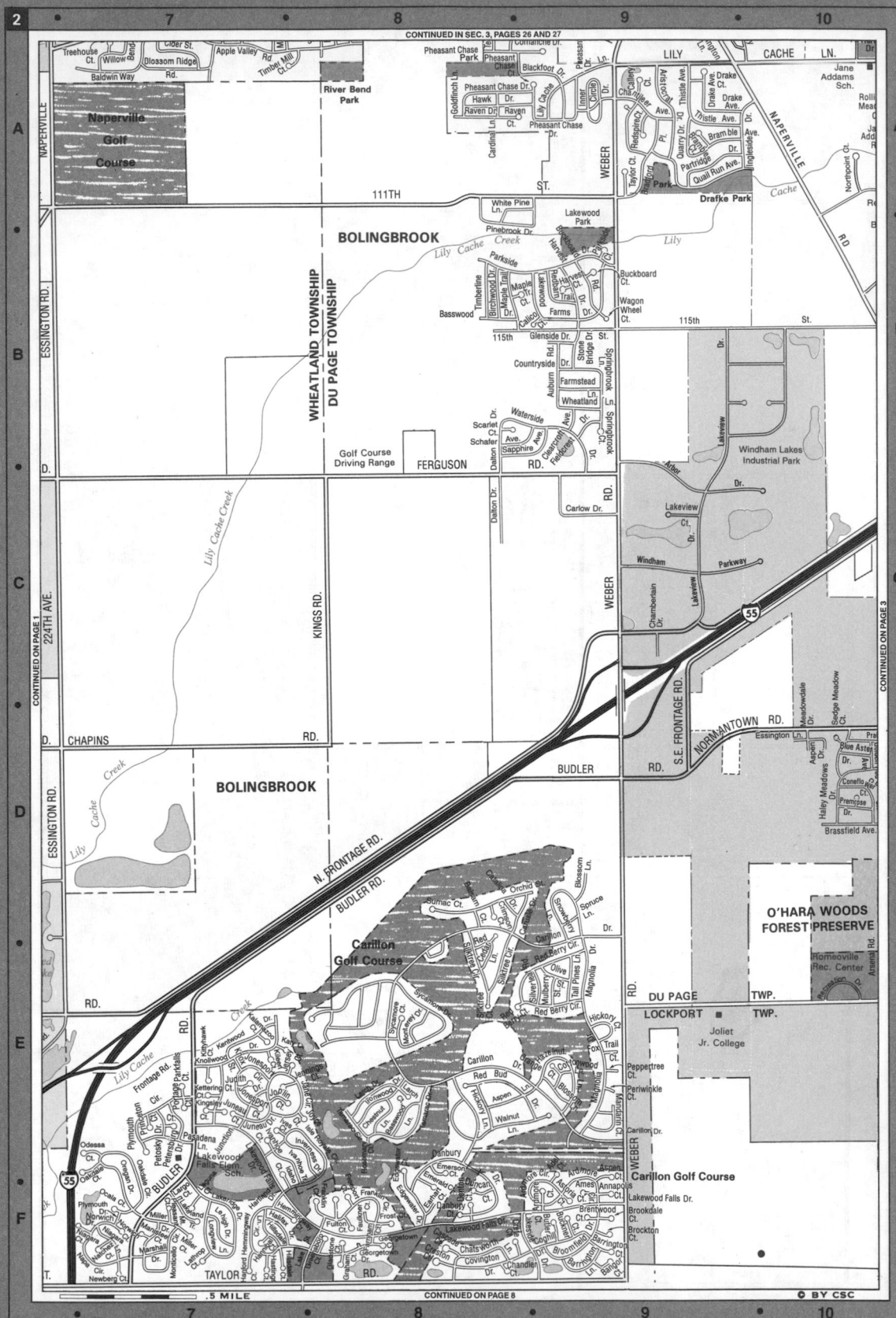

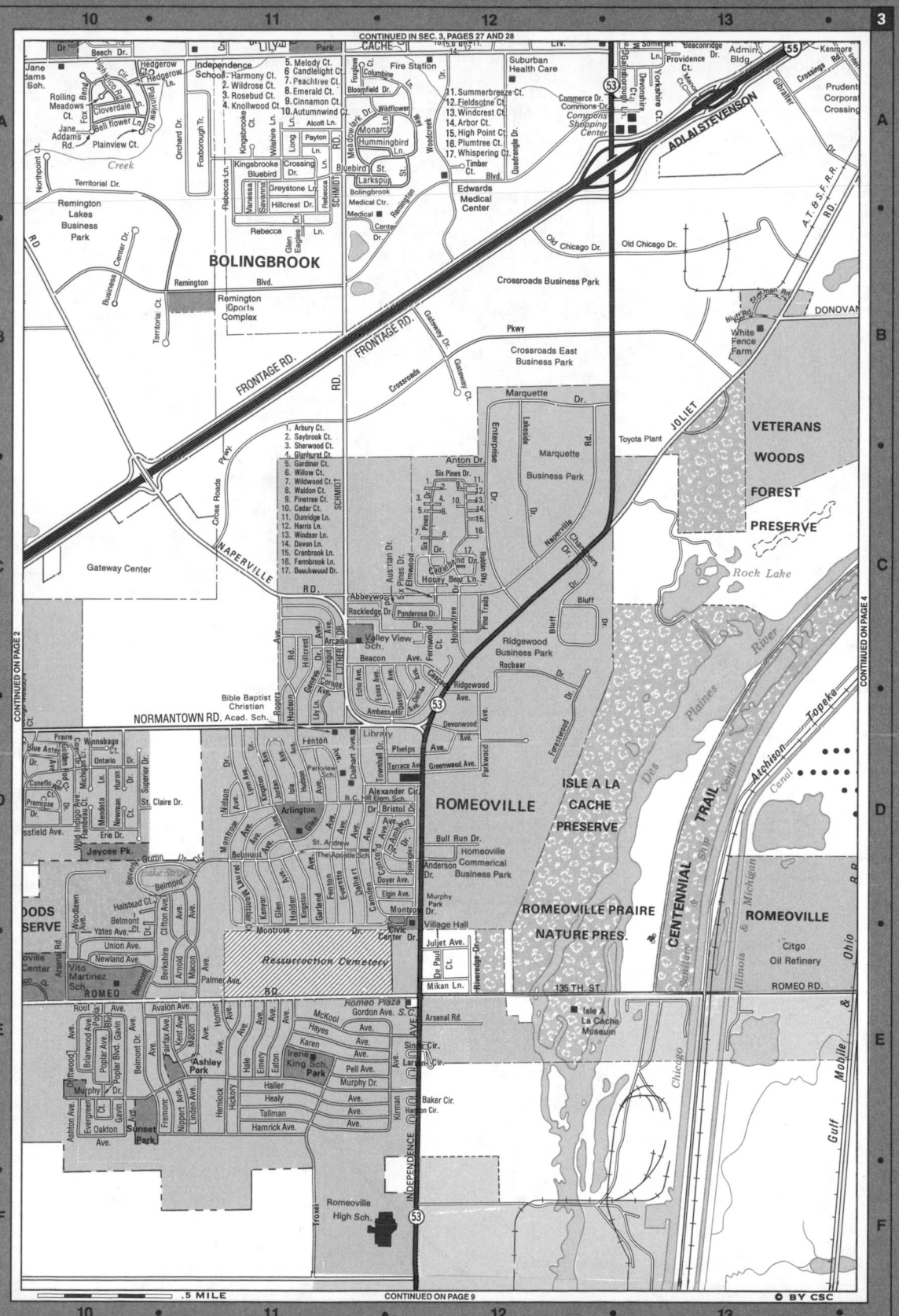

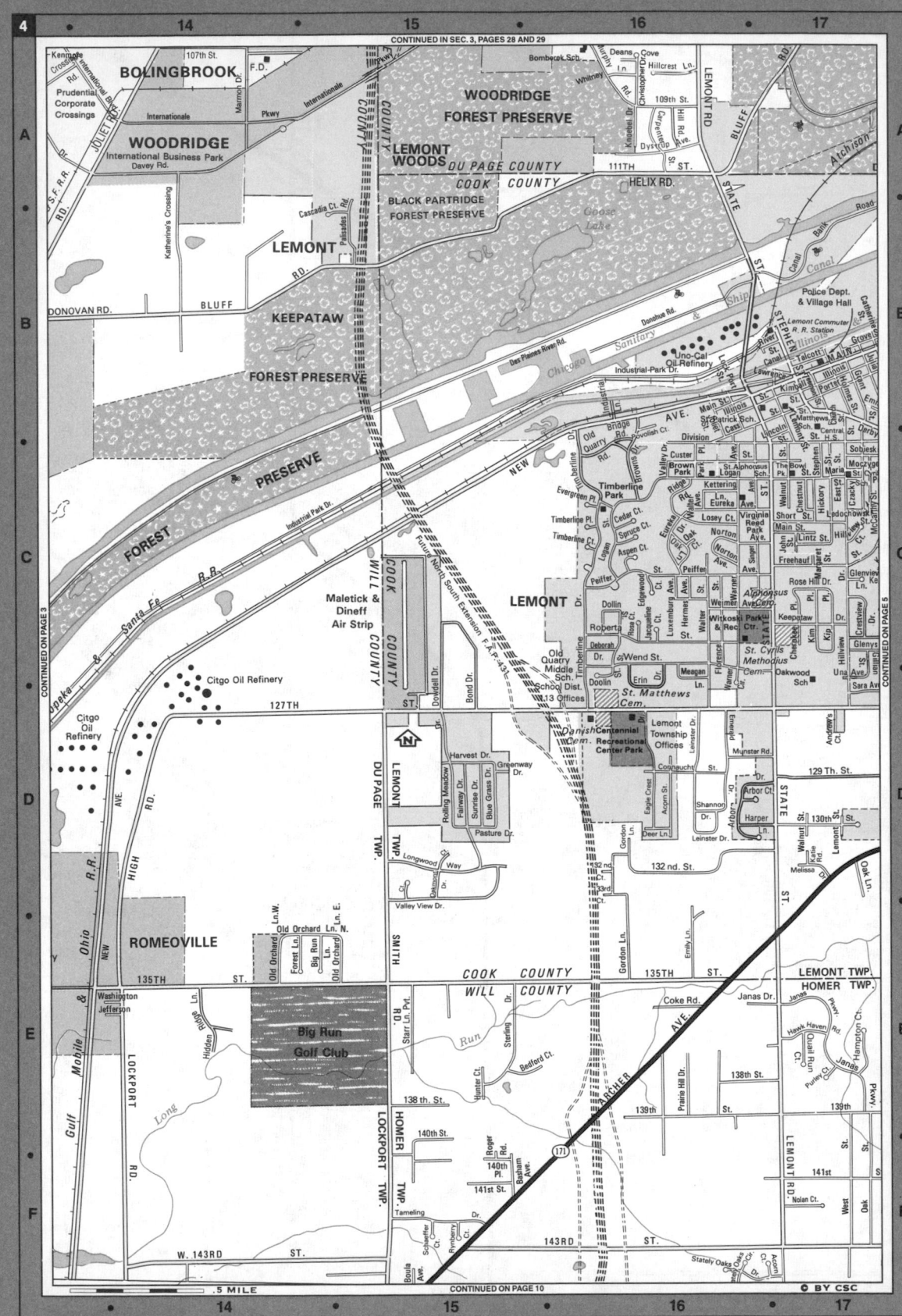

CONTINUED IN SEC. 3, PAGES 28 AND 29

BOLINGBROOK

107th St.

Prudential
Corporate
Crossings

WOODRIDGE

International Business Park
Davey Rd.

WOODRIDGE
FOREST PRESERVE

LEMONT
WOODS

DU PAGE COUNTY
COOK COUNTY

BLACK PARTRIDGE
FOREST PRESERVE

HELIX RD.

Goose
Lake

Police Dept.
& Village Hall

Lemont Commuter
R. R. Station

LEMONT

BLUFF

DONOVAN RD.

KEEPATAW

FOREST PRESERVE

FOREST

PRESERVE

Des Plaines River Rd.

Uno-Cal
Oil Refinery

Industrial-Park Dr.

Santa Fe R.R.

Topeka

Citgo Oil Refinery

Citgo
Oil
Refinery

Maletick &
Dineff
Air Strip

127TH

LEMONT

Timberline
Park

Old Quarry
Middle Sch.
School Dist.
#13 Offices

St. Matthews
Cem.

Danish Centennial
Cem.

Recreational
Center Park

Lemont Township
Offices

129 Th.St.

Harvest Dr.

Rolling Meadow

Fairway Dr.

Sunrise Dr.

Blue Grass Dr.

Greenway
Dr.

Pasture Dr.

132 nd. St.

130th St.

Longwood
Way

Valley View Dr.

ROMEOVILLE

135TH

Old Orchard

Forest Ln.

Big Run
Ln.

COOK COUNTY
WILL COUNTY

135TH

LEMONT TWP.
HOMER TWP.

Washington
Jefferson

Big Run
Golf Club

Long Run

138th St.

Coke Rd.

Janas Dr.

ARCHER

138th

139th

141st

Hunter Ct.

Bedford Ct.

140th St.

Roger
Rd.

140th
Pl.

Basham
Ave.

141st St.

171

139th

Prairie Hill Dr.

141st

Nolan Ct.

Tameling
Dr.

W. 143RD

143RD

ST.

CONTINUED ON PAGE 3
CONTINUED ON PAGE 5

.5 MILE

© BY CSC

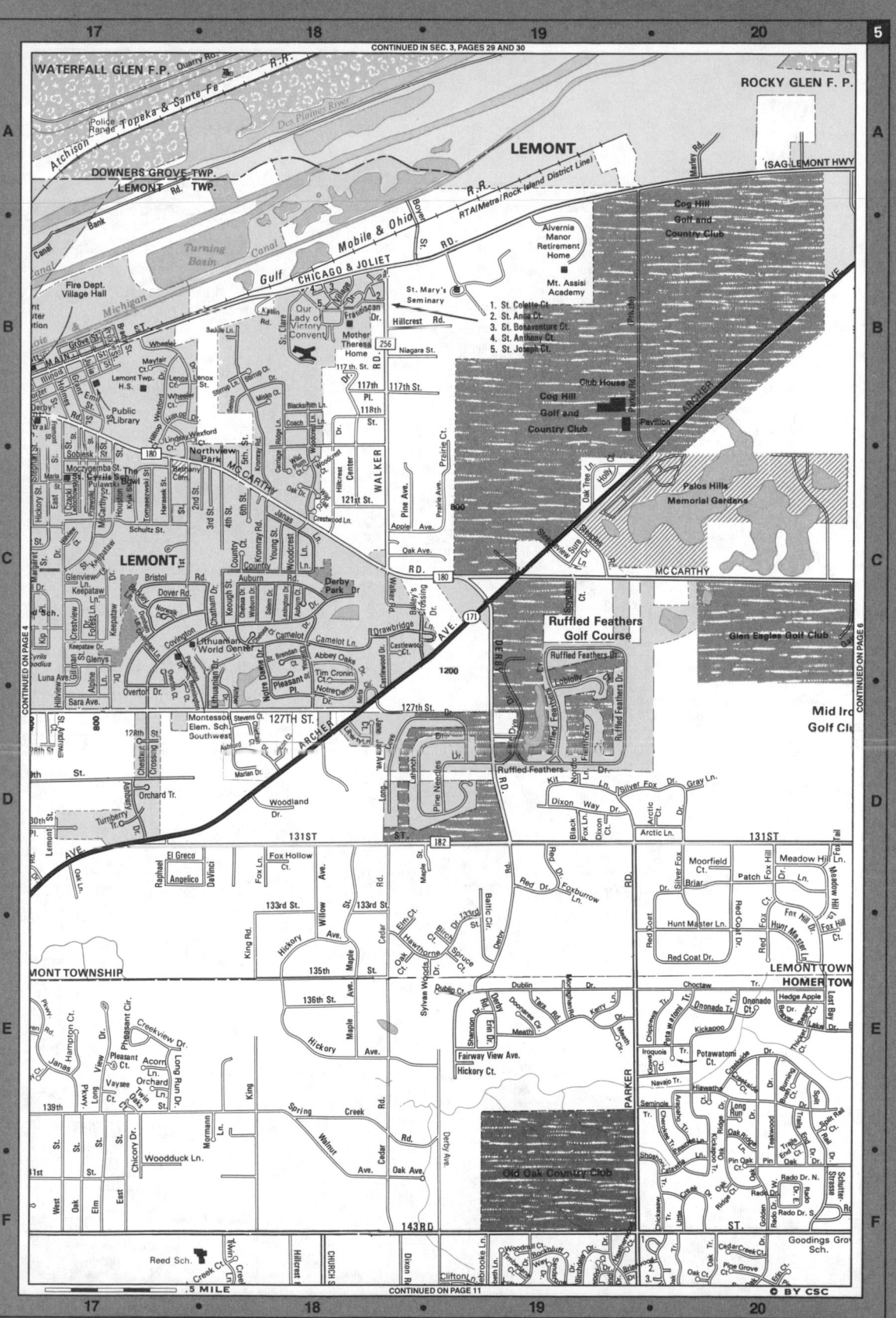

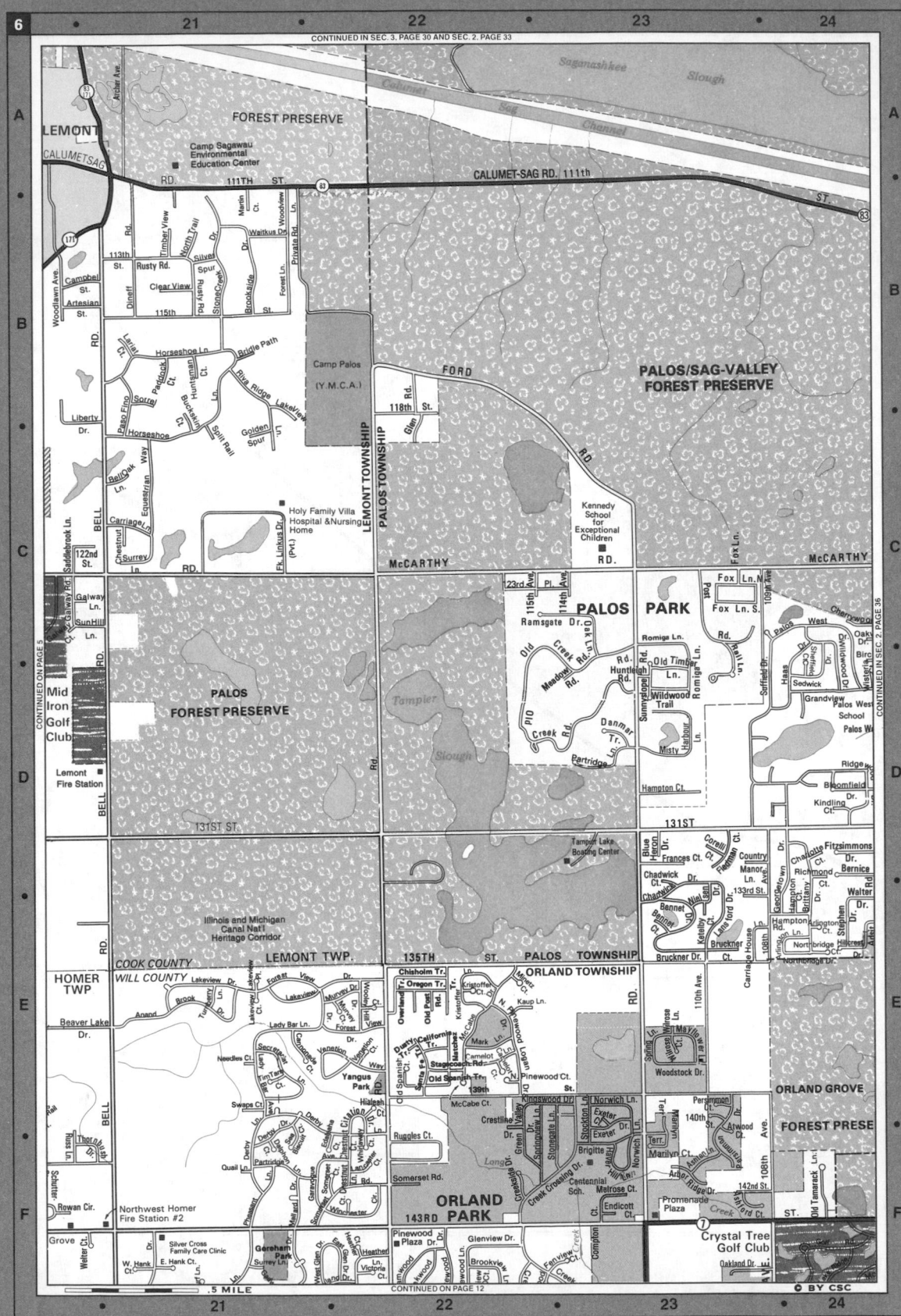

CONTINUED IN SEC. 3, PAGE 30 AND SEC. 2, PAGE 33

**LEMONT**

CALUMET SAG

FOREST PRESERVE

Camp Sagawau Environmental Education Center

RD. 111TH ST.

CALUMET-SAG RD. 111th ST.

Archer Ave.

Timber View
North Trail
Martin Ct.
Woodview
Waitkus Dr.
Silver Spur
Private Rd.
Forest Ln.
113th St.
Rusty Rd.
Clear View
Rusty Rd.
StoneCreek
Brookside
115th St.
Dineff

Woodlawn Ave.
Campbell St.
Artesian St.
RD.
Liberty Dr.
Saddlebrook Ln.
122nd St.
BELL

Horseshoe Ln.
Leisl
Paddock Ct.
Hummingbird
Bridle Path
Rive Ridge
LakeView
Palo Fino
Sorral
Buckskin
Split Rail
Golden Spur
Horseshoe
BellOak Ln.
Equestrian Way
Carriage
Chestnut Ln.
Surrey
RD.

Camp Palos
(Y.M.C.A.)

FORD RD.

118th St.
Glen Rd.

Holy Family Villa Hospital & Nursing Home
Fk. Linkus Dr. (Pvt.)

LEMONT TOWNSHIP

PALOS TOWNSHIP

McCARTHY

**PALOS / SAG-VALLEY FOREST PRESERVE**

Fox Ln.

Kennedy School for Exceptional Children

McCARTHY RD.

CONTINUED ON PAGE 5

Galway Ln.
Galway Rd.
SunHill Ln.

**Mid Iron Golf Club**

Lemont Fire Station

BELL RD.

**PALOS FOREST PRESERVE**

131ST ST.

Tampier

Slough

Tampier Lake Boating Center

**PALOS PARK**

23rd Ave.
14th Pl.
115th Ave.
114th Ave.
Ramsgate Dr.
Oak Ln.
Old Creek Rd.
Meadow Rd.
PLO Creek Rd.
Danmar Tr.
Partridge
Hampton Ct.

Romiga Ln.
Sunnyslope Rd.
Old Timber Ln.
Huntleigh Rd.
Romiga Rd.
Wildwood Trail
Misty Harbour

131ST

Post Rd.
Fox Ln. N.
Fox Ln. S.
Bell Dr.

109th Ave.
Palos West
Cherryhill
Oaky Dr.
Suffield Dr.
Shelfield
Haas
Sedwick
Birch
Grandview
Palos West School
Palos W
Ridge
Bloomfield Dr.
Kindling Ct.

CONTINUED IN SEC. 2, PAGE 36

Blue Heron
Frances Ct.
Corah Ct.
Country Manor Ave.
Fitzsimmons Dr.
Chadwick Dr.
Charles Dr.
Niall
133rd St.
Richmond
Charlotte
Bernice
Walter
Bennet Ct.
Bennet
Lane ford Dr.
Keelby
Bruckner
Hampton Rd.
Arlington
George town
Brittany Ct.
Northbridge
108th
Northbridge Dr.

135TH ST.
PALOS TOWNSHIP
Bruckner Dr.
Carriage House
Ct.

COOK COUNTY
WILL COUNTY
LEMONT TWP.

Illinois and Michigan Canal Nat'l Heritage Corridor

**HOMER TWP**

Beaver Lake Dr.

Anand
Brook Ln.
Lakeview Dr.
Forest View
Lakeview Ct.
Murray Dr.
Lakeview
Forest View
Lady Bar Ln.

Needles Ct.
Secretariat
Canyon
Venetian
Wimbledon Way
**Yangus Park**
Hialeah
McCabe Ct.

Swaps Ct.
Derby
Citation
Chestnut
Quail
Partridge
Winchester

ORLAND TOWNSHIP

Chisholm Tr.
Oregon Tr.
Overland Tr.
Old Post Rd.
Kristoffen
Kristoffer
Kaup Ln.
Mark Ln.
Mertz
Santa Fe
Old California Tr.
Stagecoach Rd.
Camelot Ln.
Old Spanish Tr.
Old Spanish Tr.
139th
Pinewood Ct.
Pinewood Ct.
Kingswood Dr.
Crestline Dr.
Green Valley Dr.
Norwich Ln.
Stockton Ln.
Exeter Dr.
Exeter
Springwood
Stonegate Ln.
Brigitte
Hill
Creek Crossing Dr.
Creekside Dr.
Lang Dr.
Ruggles Ct.
Somerset Rd.
Centennial Sch.
Melrose Dr.
Endicott Ct.

RD.
110th Ave.
Melrose
Spring Melrose
Woodstock Dr.

**ORLAND GROVE**
**FOREST PRESE**

Persimmon St.
140th St.
Marilyn
Terr.
Atwood Ave.
Ardle Ridge Dr.
142nd St.
Ford Ct.
Old Tamarack
Promenade Plaza

**ORLAND PARK**
143RD

**HOMER TWP**

Beaver Lake Dr.
BELL RD.
Thorn bush
Rowan Cir.
Schiller
Grove Ct.
Welter Ct.

**Northwest Homer Fire Station #2**

Silver Cross Family Care Clinic
W. Hank Ct.
E. Hank Ct.

**Gareham Park**
Surrey Ln.

Pinewood Plaza Dr.
Glenview Dr.
Brookview
Fenview
Compton
West Glen
Victoria
Heather

**Crystal Tree Golf Club**
Oakland Dr.

Old Tamarack
142nd St.

CONTINUED ON PAGE 12

.5 MILE

© BY CSC

CONTINUED ON PAGE 1

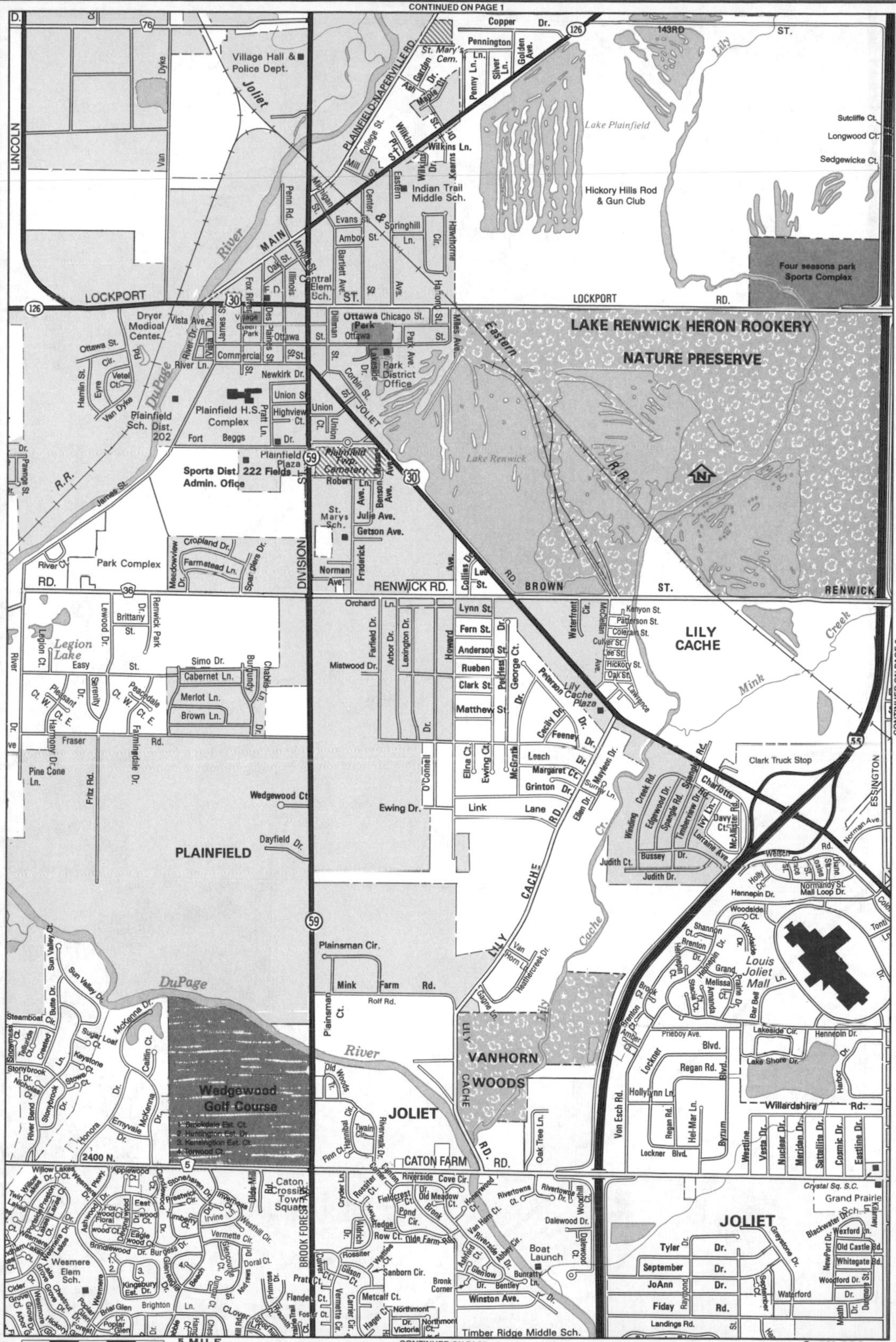

CONTINUED ON PAGE 8

LAKE RENWICK HERON ROOKERY
NATURE PRESERVE

Lake Renwick

Lake Plainfield

Hickory Hills Rod & Gun Club

Four seasons park Sports Complex

LILY CACHE

Village Hall & Police Dept.

Dryer Medical Center

Plainfield H.S. Complex

Plainfield Sch. Dist. 202

Sports Dist. 222 Fields Admin. Office

Legion Lake

Renwick Park

PLAINFIELD

DuPage

Wedgewood Golf Course

JOLIET

VANHORN WOODS

CATON FARM

Louis Joliet Mall

Clark Truck Stop

Crystal Sq. S.C.

Grand Prairie

JOLIET

Caton Crossing Town Square

Wesmere Elem. Sch.

Timber Ridge Middle Sch.

Indian Trail Middle Sch.

RENWICK RD.

LOCKPORT RD.

LINCOLN

MAIN

DIVISION

BROOK FORK RD.

Mink Creek

Lily Cache

LILY CACHE RD.

CONTINUED ON PAGE 13

.5 MILE

© BY CSC

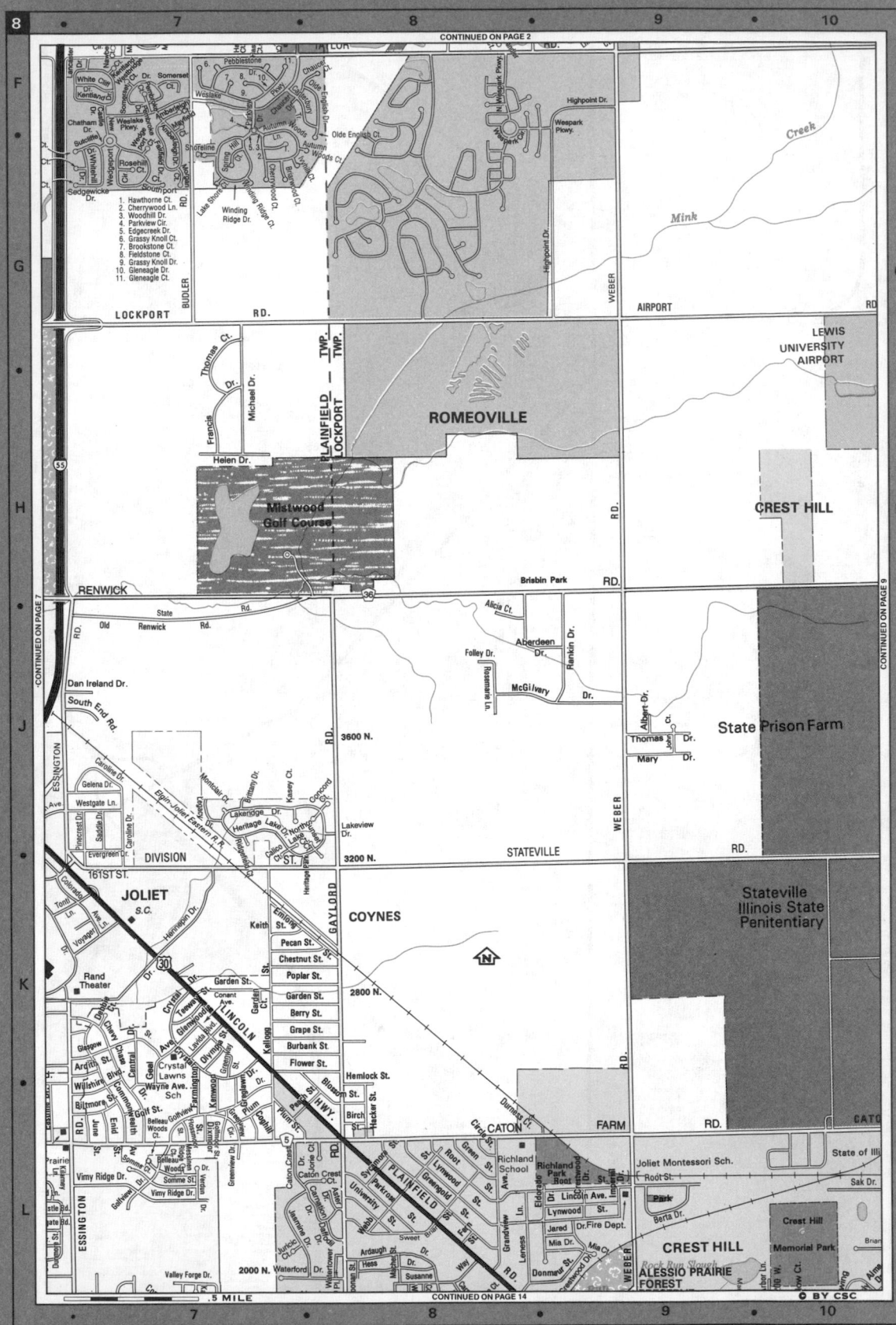

F

G

H

J

K

L

CONTINUED ON PAGE 7
CONTINUED ON PAGE 9

1. Hawthorne Ct.
2. Cherrywood Ln.
3. Woodhill Dr.
4. Parkview Cir.
5. Edgecreek Dr.
6. Grassy Knoll Ct.
7. Brookstone Ct.
8. Fieldstone Ct.
9. Grassy Knoll Dr.
10. Gleneagle Dr.
11. Gleneagle Ct.

LOCKPORT RD.

BUDLER RD.

AIRPORT RD.

ROMEOVILLE

LEWIS UNIVERSITY AIRPORT

Mink

Creek

CREST HILL

Mistwood Golf Course

RENWICK

Old Renwick Rd.

State Rd.

Brisbin Park RD.

State Prison Farm

Dan Ireland Dr.

South End Rd.

ESSINGTON

3600 N.

3200 N.

STATEVILLE

JOLIET
S.C.

Rand Theater

DIVISION

161ST ST.

COYNES

N

Stateville Illinois State Penitentiary

2800 N.

Pecan St.
Chestnut St.
Poplar St.
Garden St.
Berry St.
Grape St.
Burbank St.
Flower St.

Hemlock St.

Birch St.

CATON

FARM RD.

CATON

Richland School

Richland Park

Joliet Montessori Sch.

State of Illi

CREST HILL
Memorial Park

2000 N.

Valley Forge Dr.

PLAINFIELD RD.

CREST HILL
ALESSIO PRAIRIE FOREST

WEBER RD.

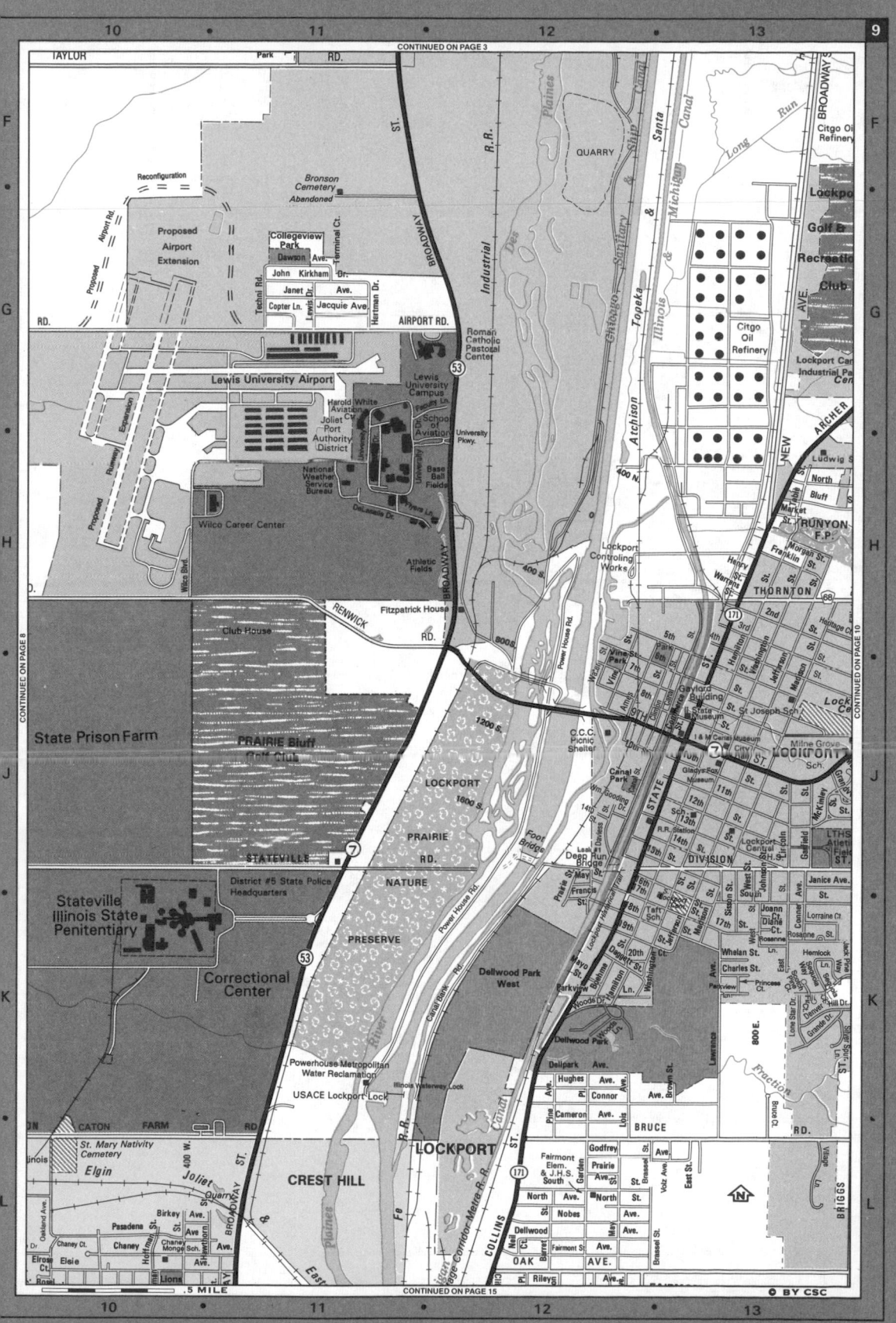

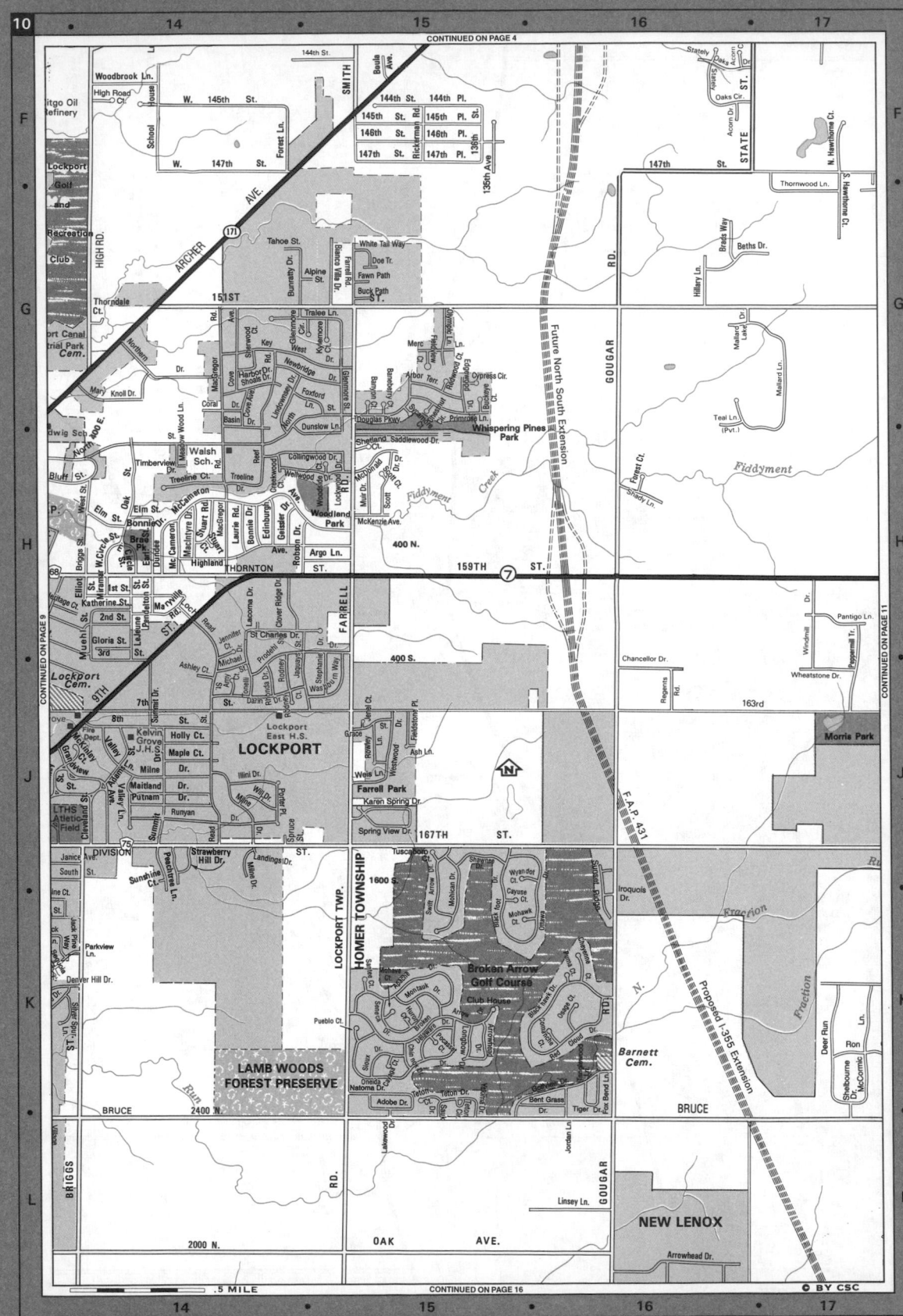

CONTINUED ON PAGE 4

CONTINUED ON PAGE 9

CONTINUED ON PAGE 11

LOCKPORT

LOCKPORT TWP.

HOMER TOWNSHIP

Broken Arrow
Golf Course

LAMB WOODS
FOREST PRESERVE

Morris Park

NEW LENOX

CONTINUED ON PAGE 16

.5 MILE

© BY CSC

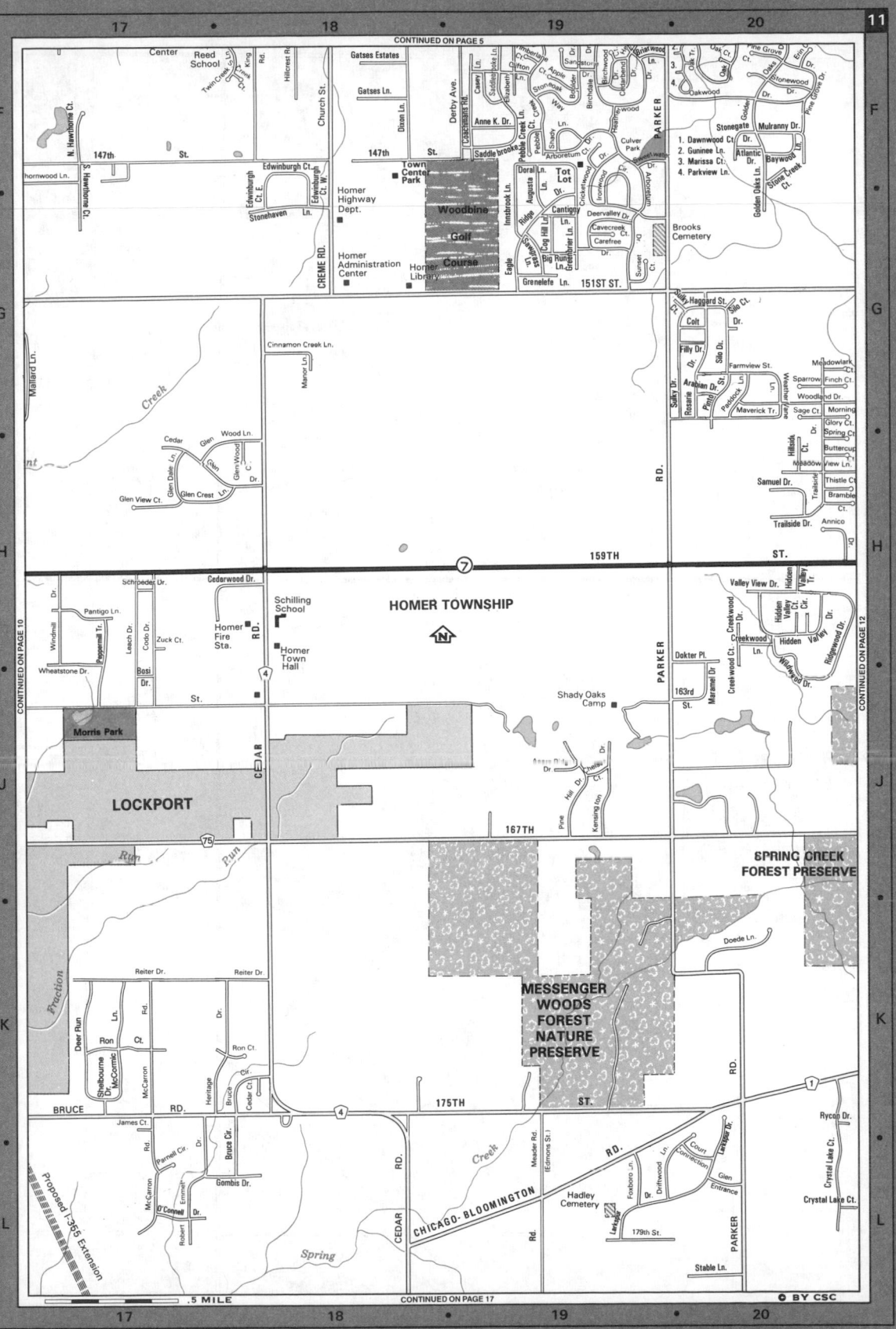

CONTINUED ON PAGE 5

17 · 18 · 19 20

F

Center  Reed School
TwinCreek Ln.  King  Rd.
Hillcrest R.
Church St.
Gatses Estates
Gatses Ln.
Dixon St.
Derby Ave.
COACHMANS RD.
Imberloe Dr.
Clifton Ct. Apple  Briarwood Dr.
Beechwood  Oak  Oak Ct.  Pine Grove Dr.
Oaks  Glen  Oaks Ct.  Stonewood
Oakwood  Dr.  Dr.
N. Hawthorne Ct.
147th  St.
Edwinburgh Ct.
Stonehaven
Edwinburgh Ct. E.  Edwinburgh Ct. W.
147th  St.
Town Center Park
Homer Highway Dept.
Homer Administration Center
Homer Library

Stonegate  Golden
Mulranny Dr.
1. Dawnwood Ct.
2. Guninee Ln.
3. Marissa Ct.
4. Parkview Ln.
Atlantic  Baywood
Golden Oaks Ln.  Stone Creek Ct.

Saddle brooks Rd.
Anne K. Dr.
Saddlestoke Ln.
Pebble Creek Ln.
Pebble Ct. Shady  Ct.
Arboretum Ct.
Culver Park
PARKER
Woodbine Golf Course
Doral St.  Tot Lot
Innsbrook Ln.  Cantigny  Deervalley Dr.
Augusta  Ridge  Cavecreek Dr.
Cwg Hill Ln.  Carefree
Eagle  Big Run  Greenbriar
Grenelefe Ln.  151ST ST.  Sunset Ct.
Brooks Cemetery

G

Mallard Ln.
Creek
Cinnamon Creek Ln.
Manor Dr.
Cedar  Wood Ln.
Glen  Glen-Wood  Dr.
Glen Dale  Glen
Glen View Ct.  Glen Crest

Haggard St.  Silo Ct.
Colt  Silo Dr.
Filly Dr.  Farmview St.
Arabian Dr.  Paddock  Maverick Tr.
Sully Dr.  Rosarie  Petit  Sage Ct.
Meadowlark
Sparrow  Finch Ct.
Woodland Dr.
Weather Vane  Morning
Glory Ct.
Spring Cr
Buttercup
Hillside  Meadow  View Ln.
Thistle Ct
Bramble
Samuel Dr.  Trailside  Ct.
Trailside Dr.  Annico

RD.

H

159TH  (7)  ST.

CONTINUED ON PAGE 10

Schroeder Dr.
Cedarwood Dr.
Schilling School
Pantigo Ln.  Zuck Ct.
Windmill  Dr.  Leach Dr.  Codo Dr.
Wheatstone Dr.  Bosi Dr.
Homer Fire Sta.
RD.
4
Homer Town Hall
St.

HOMER TOWNSHIP
N

Valley View Dr.  Hidden  Valley Tr.
Creekwood Dr.
Hidden Valley Ct.
Creekwood Ct.  Hidden  Valley Wy.
Dokter Pl.  Creekwood  Hidden
Maramel Dr.  Ln.  Wildwood Dr.  Ridgewood Dr.
163rd St.

PARKER

CONTINUED ON PAGE 12

J

Morris Park

LOCKPORT

CEDAR  RD.

Shady Oaks Camp
Angus Ridge Dr.
Hill Dr.  Chelsea
Pine  Kensington

167TH  ST.

SPRING CREEK FOREST PRESERVE

75
Run  Run
Fraction

Reiter Dr.  Reiter Dr.
Deer Run
Ron  Ln.
McCormic  Rd.  Dr.  Ron Ct.
Shelbourne  McCarron
Dr.

Heritage
Bruce Cir.
Cedar Ln.

Doede Ln.

MESSENGER WOODS FOREST NATURE PRESERVE

RD.

1

K

BRUCE  RD.
James Ct.
McCarron  Rd.  Parnell Cir.  Bruce Cir.
O'Connell  Emmell  Gombis Dr.
Robert  Dr.

4  175TH  ST.

Creek

CEDAR  RD.

CHICAGO-BLOOMINGTON  RD.

Meader Rd.
(Edmons St.)
Hadley Cemetery
Foxboro Jn.
Driftwood  Glen  Entrance
Court Connection
Lamppost Dr.  Glen
179th St.
Stable Ln.

PARKER  RD.

Rycon Dr.
Crystal Lake Ct.

Proposed I-355 Extension
Spring

L

.5 MILE

CONTINUED ON PAGE 17

© BY CSC

17 · 18 · 19 20

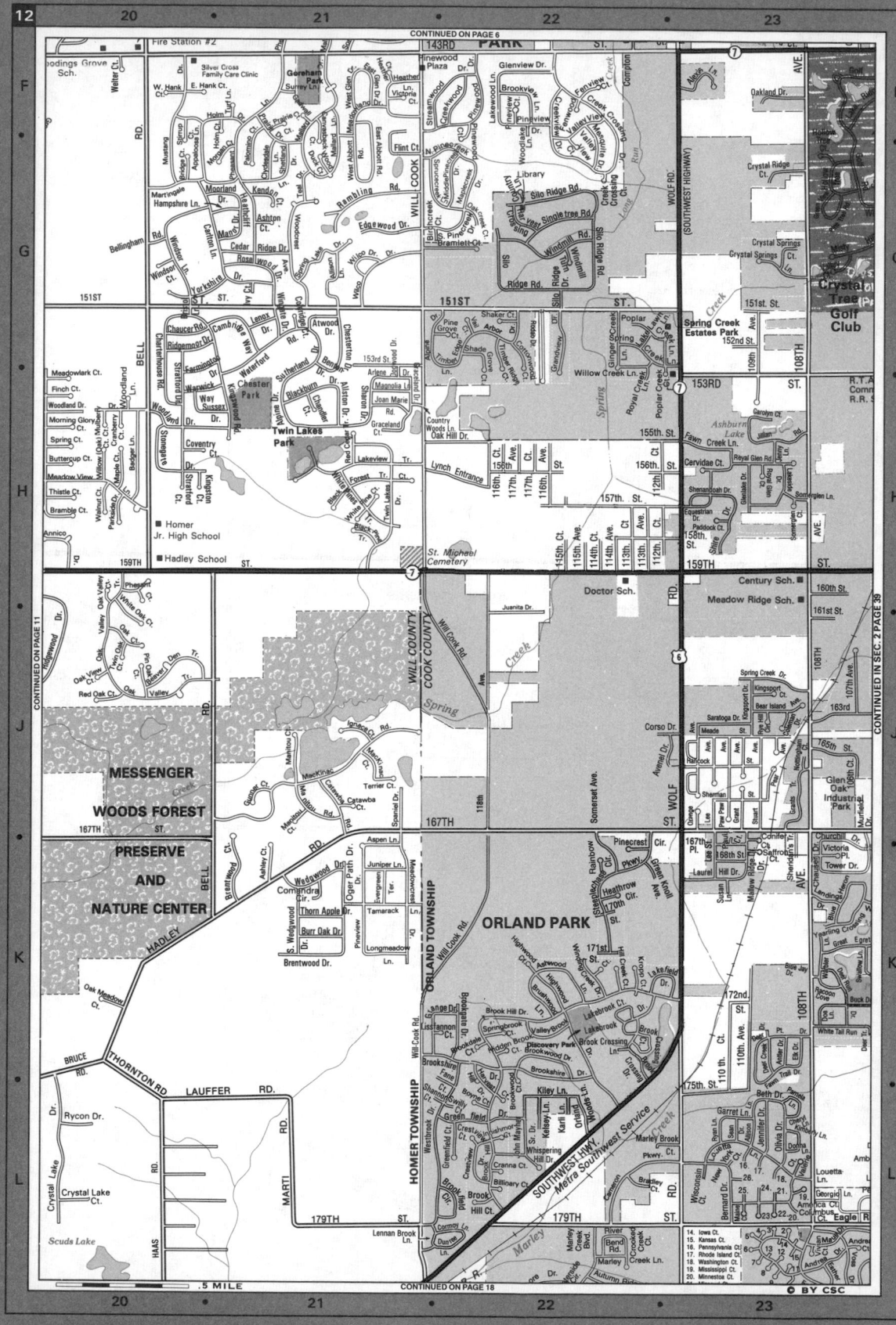

CONTINUED ON PAGE 7

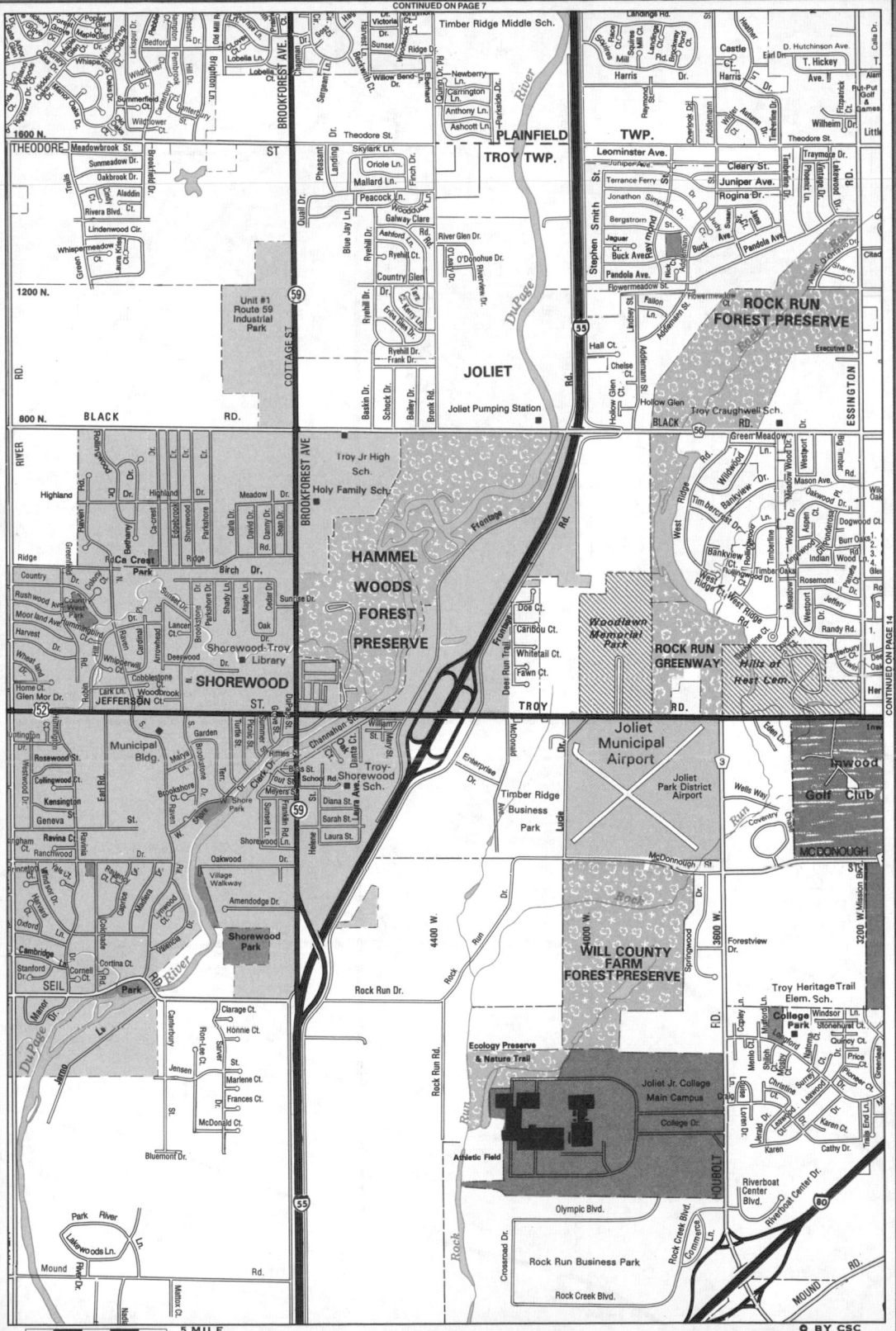

CONTINUED ON PAGE 14

© BY CSC

CONTINUED ON PAGE 8

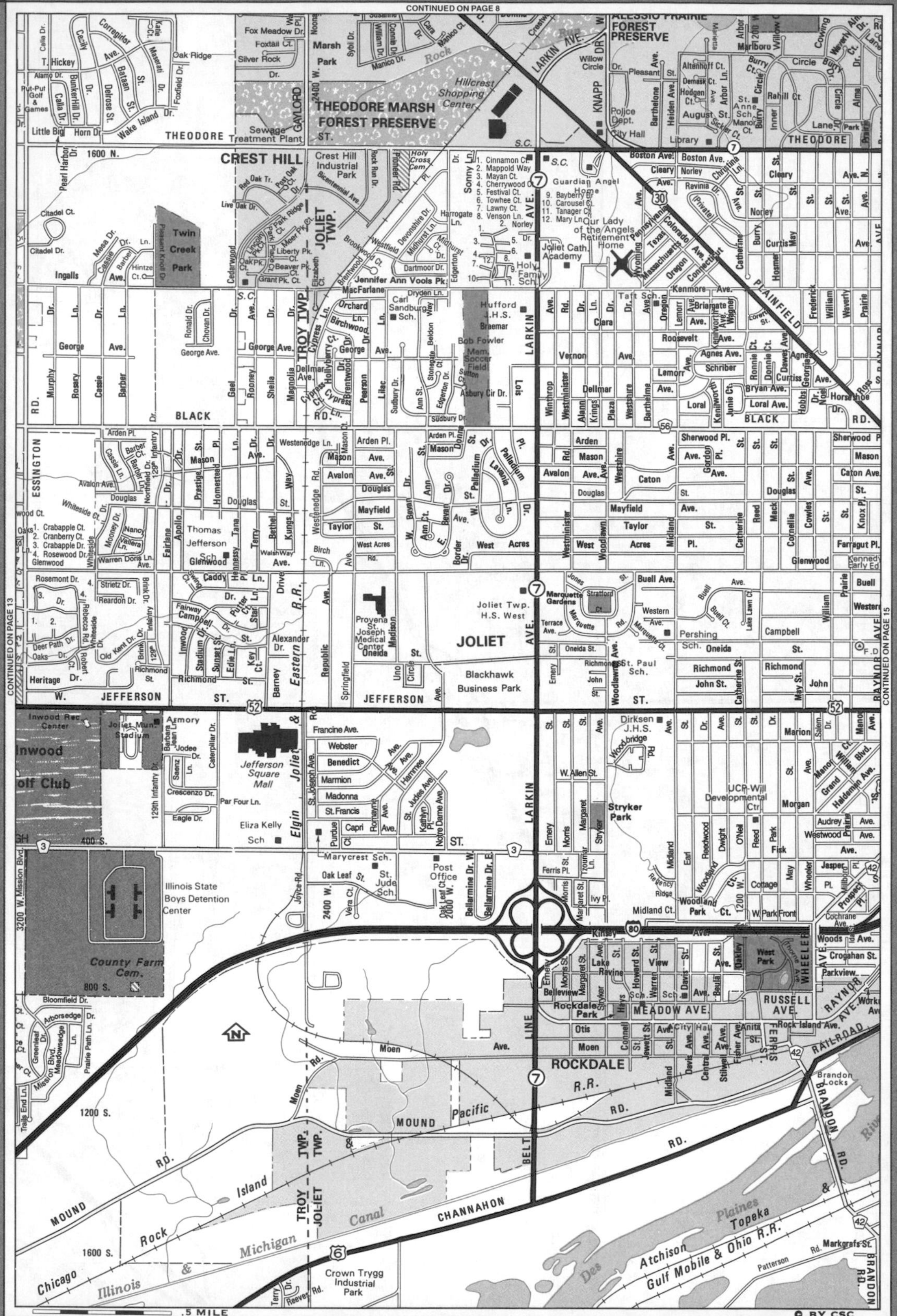


CONTINUED ON PAGE 13

CONTINUED ON PAGE 15

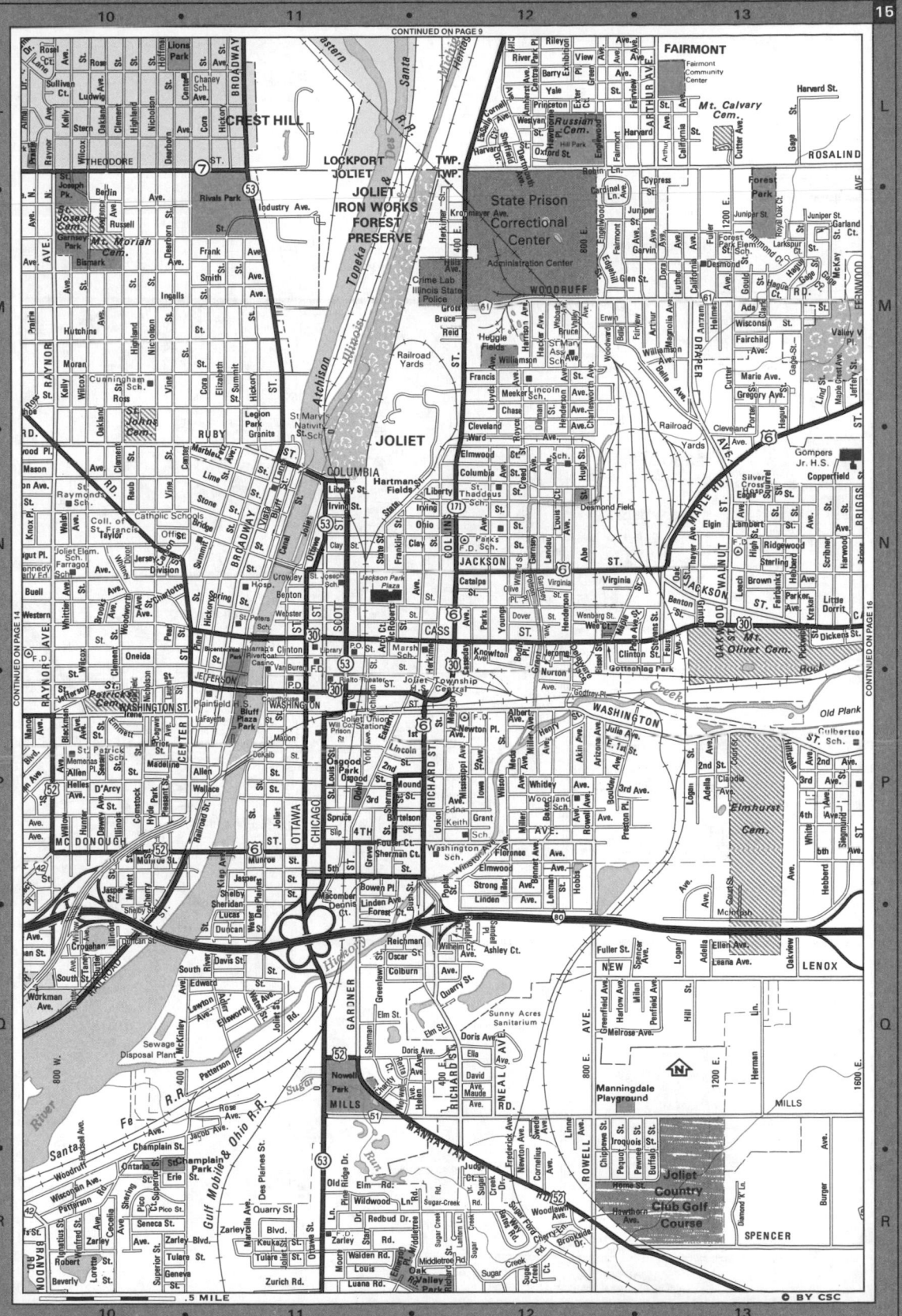

CONTINUED ON PAGE 9

CONTINUED ON PAGE 14

CONTINUED ON PAGE 16

.5 MILE

© BY CSC

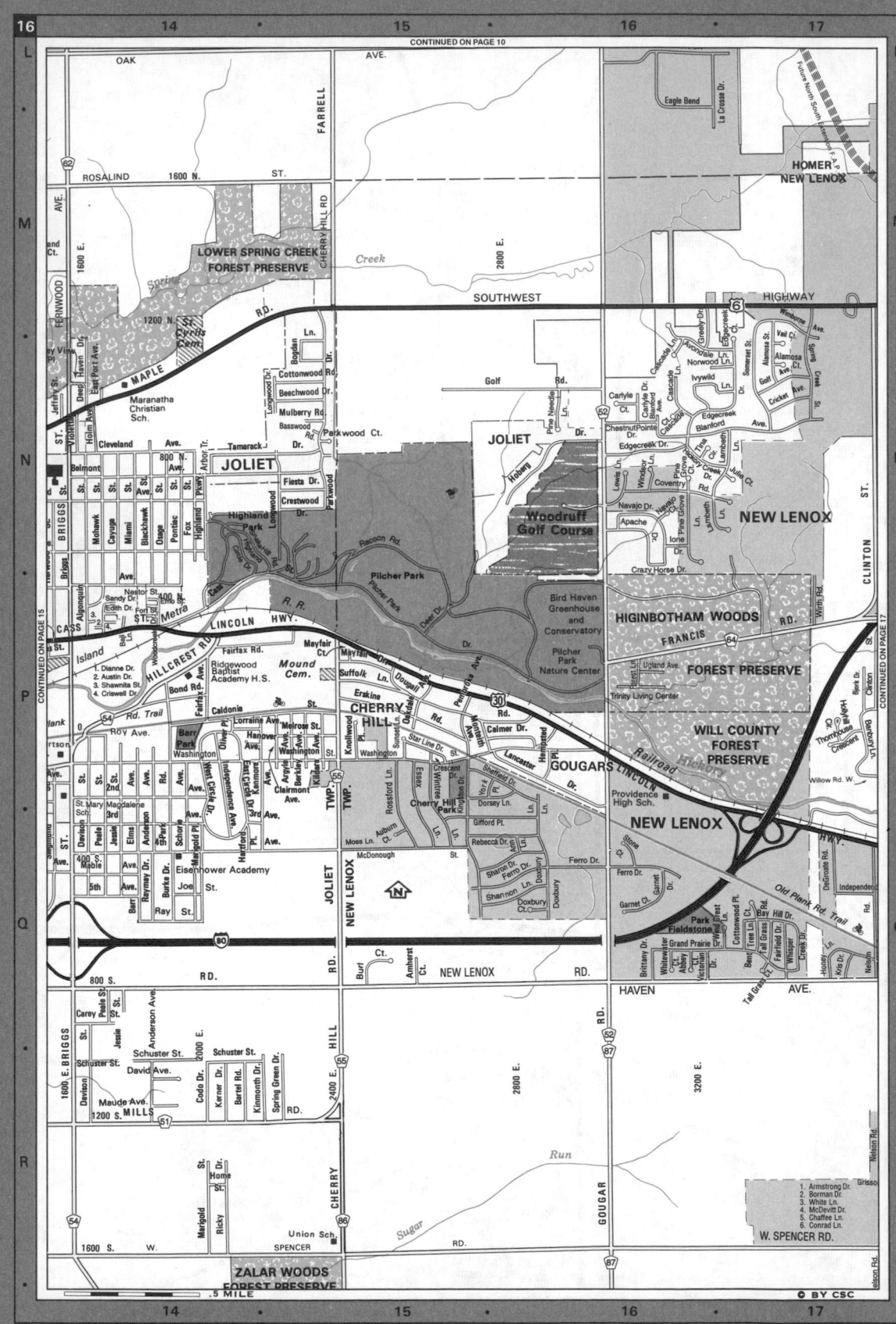

CONTINUED ON PAGE 10

CONTINUED ON PAGE 15

CONTINUED ON PAGE 17

© BY CSC

.5 MILE

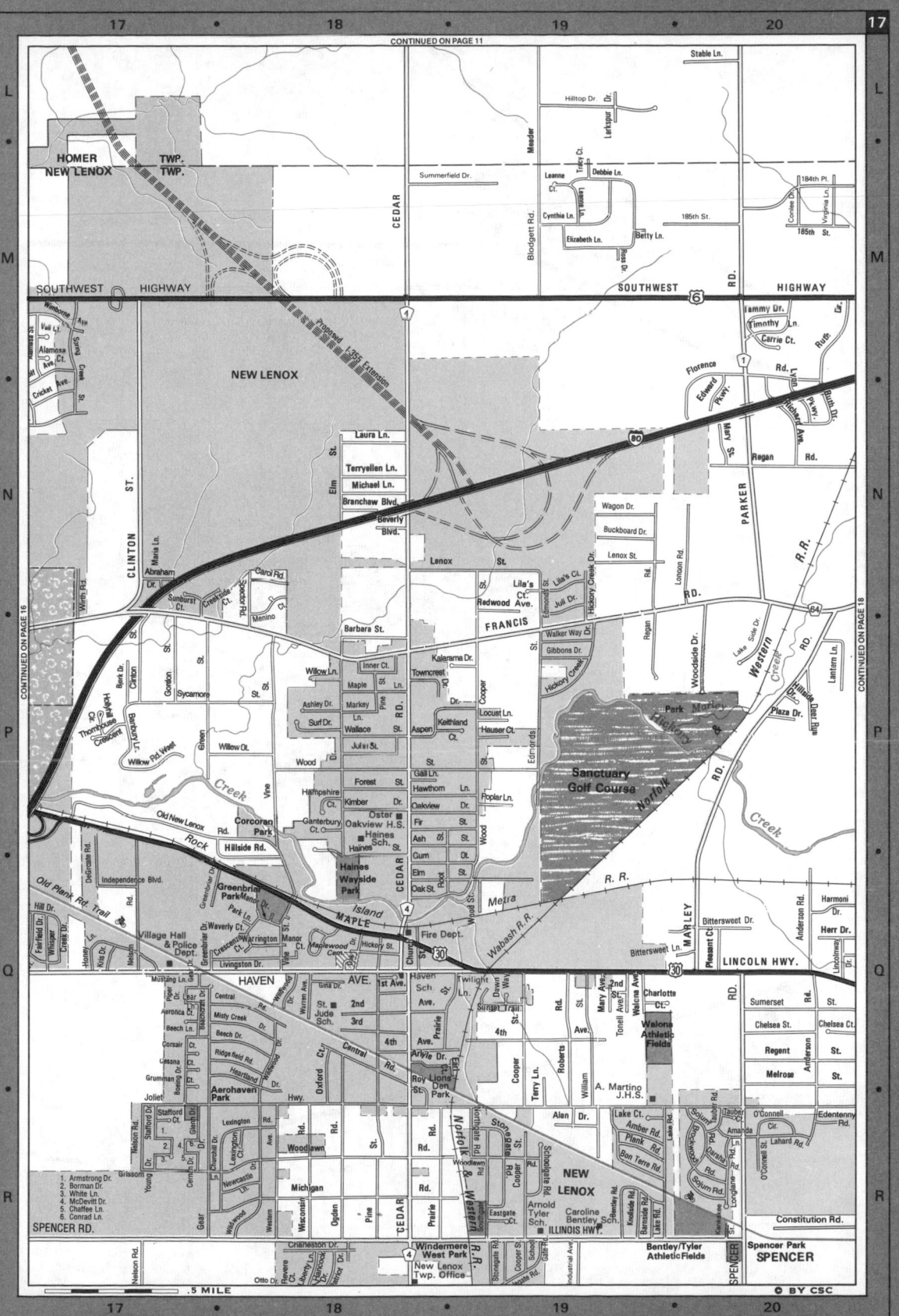

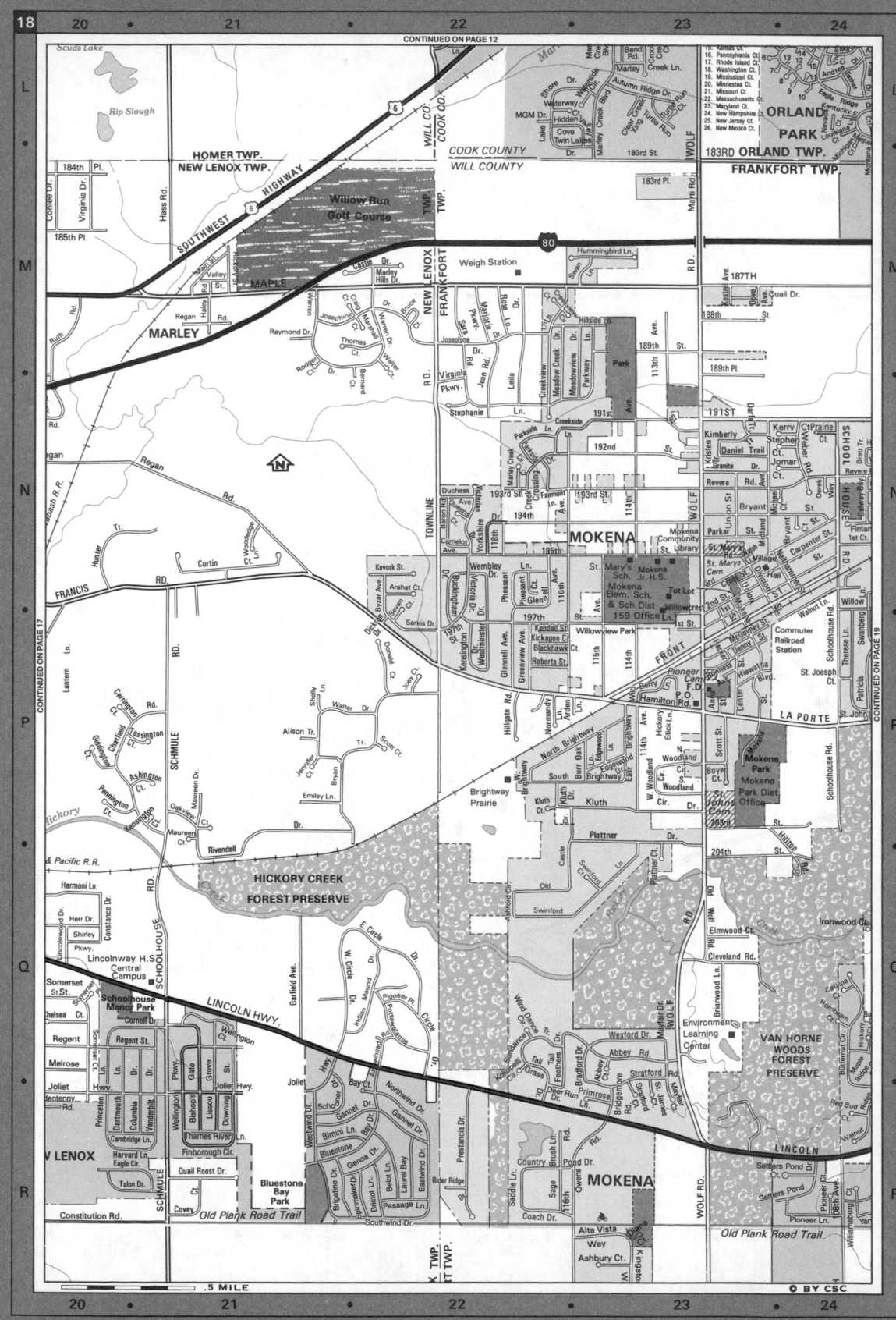

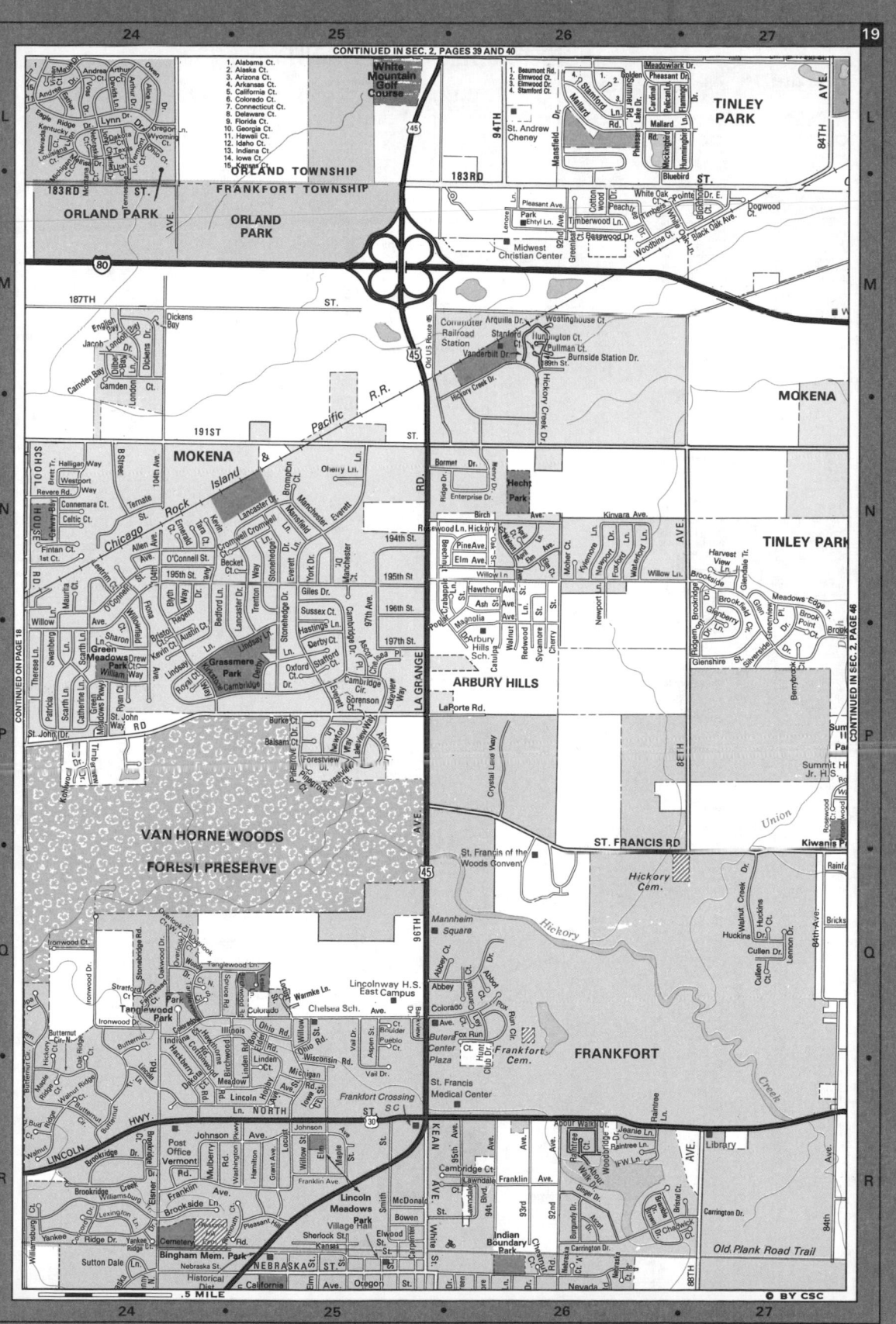

# INDEX TO JOLIET AND VICINITY

## ARBURY HILLS
Page 19 .... N26

## BOLINGBROOK
Pages 1-4
(For additional listings, see Section 3)

### STREETS
- Alcott Ln. ... Pg.3 ... A11
- Apple Valley Rd. ... Pg.2 ... A7
- Arbor Dr. ... Pg.3 ... A12
- Aristocrat Dr. ... Pg.2 ... A8
- Auburn Rd. ... Pg.2 ... B9
- Autumnwind Ct. ... Pg.3 ... A12
- Baldwin Way ... Pg.2 ... A7
- Basswood Dr. ... Pg.2 ... B8
- Beaconridge Dr. ... Pg.3 ... A13
- Bellflower Ln. ... Pg.3 ... A11
- Birchwood Dr. ... Pg.2 ... B8
- Blackfoot Dr. ... Pg.2 ... A8
- Bloomfield Dr. ... Pg.3 ... A11
- Blossom Ridge Rd. ... Pg.2 ... A7
- Bluebird Dr. ... Pg.2 ... A8
- Bluebird St. ... Pg.3 ... A11
- Bradford Pl. ... Pg.2 ... B9
- Bramble Ave. ... Pg.2 ... A8
- Bramble Ct. ... Pg.2 ... B9
- Bristol Way ... Pg.3 ... A10
- Business Center Dr. ... Pg.3 ... B10
- Calico Ct. ... Pg.2 ... B9
- Callery Ct. ... Pg.2 ... B9
- Callery Dr. ... Pg.2 ... B9
- Candlelight Ct. ... Pg.3 ... A12
- Cardinal Ln. ... Pg.8 ... C9
- Chanticleer Ave. ... Pg.2 ... A9
- Chapins Rd. ... Pg.2 ... D7
- Cider St. ... Pg.3 ... A12
- Cinnamon Ct. ... Pg.3 ... A12
- Clearcroft Ave. ... Pg.2 ... B9
- Cloverdale Ln. ... Pg.3 ... A11
- Columbine Ln. ... Pg.3 ... A12
- Commerce Dr. ... Pg.3 ... A12
- Commons Dr. ... Pg.3 ... A13
- Countryside Dr. ... Pg.2 ... B9
- Coventry Ln. ... Pg.2 ... A9
- Cross Roads Pkwy. ... Pg.3 ... B12
- Crossings Rd. ... Pg.3 ... A11
- Crossroads Pkwy. ... Pg.3 ... B11
- Dalton Dr. ... Pg.2 ... C8
- Devonshire Ct. ... Pg.3 ... A13
- Drake Ave. ... Pg.2 ... A9
- Drake Ct. ... Pg.2 ... A9
- Emerald Ct. ... Pg.3 ... A12
- Farmstead Ln. ... Pg.2 ... B9
- Ferguson Rd. ... Pg.1,2 ... C6,7
- Fieldcrest Dr. ... Pg.3 ... A12
- Fieldstone Ct. ... Pg.3 ... A11
- Fox Bend Cir. ... Pg.2 ... A9
- Foxborough Tr. ... Pg.3 ... A11
- Foxglove Ct. ... Pg.3 ... A12
- Frontage Rd. ... Pg.3 ... B11
- Frontage Rd., N. ... Pg.2 ... D8
- Gainsborough Ln. ... Pg.3 ... A12
- Gateway Ct. ... Pg.3 ... B12
- Gateway Dr. ... Pg.3 ... B12
- Gibraltar Dr. ... Pg.3 ... A13
- Glen Eagles Dr. ... Pg.3 ... A11
- Glenside Dr. ... Pg.2 ... B9
- Goldfinch Ln. ... Pg.2 ... A8
- Greystone Ln. ... Pg.3 ... A11
- Harmony Ct. ... Pg.3 ... A11
- Harvest Ct. ... Pg.2 ... B9
- Harvest St. ... Pg.3 ... A11
- Hawk Dr. ... Pg.2 ... A8
- Hedgerow Ct. ... Pg.3 ... A10
- Hedgerow Ln. ... Pg.3 ... A10
- High Knob Rd. ... Pg.3 ... A11
- High Point Ct. ... Pg.3 ... A12
- Hillcrest Dr. ... Pg.3 ... A11
- Hummingbird Ln. ... Pg.3 ... A11
- Ingleside Dr. ... Pg.2 ... A8
- Inner Cricle Dr. ... Pg.2 ... A9
- Internationale Dr. ... Pg.3 ... A10
- Interstate 55 ... Pg.2,3 ... A13,D8
- Jane Adams Rd. ... Pg.3 ... A10
- Joliet Rd. ... Pg.2 ... C8
- Kings Rd. ... Pg.2 ... C8
- Kingsbrooke Crossing ... Pg.3 ... A11
- Kingsbrooke Dr. ... Pg.3 ... A11
- Knollwood Ct. ... Pg.3 ... A12
- Lakewood Farms Dr. ... Pg.2 ... B9
- Larkspur St. ... Pg.3 ... A11
- Lily Cache Ln. ... Pg.2,3 ... A10-11
- Long Ln. ... Pg.3 ... A11
- Manor Ct. ... Pg.3 ... A13
- Maple Tr. ... Pg.2 ... B5
- Maple Tr. Ct. ... Pg.2 ... B5
- Marina Dr. ... Pg.1 ... D6
- Marmon Dr. ... Pg.2 ... A14
- Meadowlark Dr. ... Pg.3 ... A11
- Medical Center Dr. ... Pg.3 ... B11
- Melody Ct. ... Pg.3 ... A12
- Monarch Ln. ... Pg.3 ... A11
- Naperville Rd. ... Pg.2,3 ... A-D6
- Northpoint Ct. ... Pg.3 ... A11
- Old Chicago Dr. ... Pg.3 ... B12
- Orchard Dr. ... Pg.3 ... A11
- Parkside Ct. ... Pg.2 ... B9
- Parkside Dr. ... Pg.2 ... B8
- Partridge Dr. ... Pg.3 ... A11
- Payton Ln. ... Pg.3 ... A11
- Peachtree Ct. ... Pg.3 ... A11
- Pheasant Chase Ct. ... Pg.2 ... A8
- Pheasant Chase Dr. ... Pg.2 ... A8
- Pilcher Rd. ... Pg.2 ... E7
- Pinebrook Dr. ... Pg.2 ... B9
- Plainfield Naperville Rd. ... Pg.1 ... B6
- Plainview Ct. ... Pg.3 ... A11
- Plainview Dr. ... Pg.3 ... A11
- Plumtree Ct. ... Pg.3 ... A12
- Providence Ct. ... Pg.3 ... A13
- Quadrangle Dr. ... Pg.3 ... A12
- Quail Run Ave. ... Pg.3 ... A11
- Quarry Dr. ... Pg.2 ... A9
- Raven Ct. ... Pg.2 ... A8
- Raven Dr. ... Pg.2 ... A8
- Rebecca Ln. ... Pg.3 ... A11
- Redbarn Tr. ... Pg.2 ... L7
- Redspire Ct. ... Pg.2 ... A9
- Remington Blvd. ... Pg.3 ... B10-12
- Rolling Meadows Ct. ... Pg.3 ... A10
- Rosebud Ct. ... Pg.2 ... A12
- Sapphire Ave. ... Pg.2 ... B9
- Savanna ... Pg.2 ... A11
- Scarlet Ct. ... Pg.2 ... B9
- Schafer Ave. ... Pg.2 ... B9
- Schmidt Rd. ... Pg.2 ... B11
- Springbrook Ct. ... Pg.2 ... B9
- Springbrook Ln. ... Pg.2 ... B9
- Stone Bridge Dr. ... Pg.2 ... B9
- Summerbreeze Ct. ... Pg.3 ... A12
- Taylor Ct. ... Pg.2 ... A8
- Territorial Ct. ... Pg.3 ... B11
- Territorial Rd. ... Pg.3 ... B10
- Thistle Ave. ... Pg.2 ... A9
- Timber Ct. ... Pg.3 ... B12
- Timberline ... Pg.2 ... B8
- Vanessa ... Pg.3 ... A11
- Wagon Wheel Ct. ... Pg.2 ... B9
- Weber Rd. ... Pg.2 ... A9
- Wheatland Ln. ... Pg.2 ... A8
- Whispering Ct. ... Pg.3 ... A12
- White Pine Ln. ... Pg.2 ... B9
- Wildflower Way ... Pg.3 ... A12
- Wildrose Ct. ... Pg.3 ... A12
- Wilshire Ln. ... Pg.3 ... A12
- Windcrest Ct. ... Pg.3 ... A12
- Woodcreek Dr. ... Pg.3 ... B12
- Yorkshire Ct. ... Pg.3 ... A13
- 111th St. ... Pg.2 ... A8-9
- 115th St. ... Pg.2 ... B10

### GOLF COURSES
- Golf Course Driving Range ... Pg.2 ... B8
- Naperville G.C. ... Pg.2 ... A7

### PARKS
- Drafke Park ... Pg.2 ... A8
- Lakewood Park ... Pg.2 ... B9
- River Bend Park ... Pg.2 ... A8

### SCHOOLS
- Independence Sch. ... Pg.3 ... A10
- Jane Addams Middle Sch. ... Pg.2 ... A10

### SHOPPING CENTERS
- Commons S.C. ... Pg.3 ... A12

### MISCELLANEOUS
- Bolingbrook Medical Center ... Pg.3 ... B11
- Crossroads East Business Park ... Pg.3 ... B12
- Driving Range ... Pg.2 ... B10
- Edwards Medical Center ... Pg.3 ... B12
- Fire Station ... Pg.3,4 ... A11,14
- Gateway Center ... Pg.3 ... C10
- Prudential Corporate Crossings ... Pg.4 ... A13
- Remington Lakes Business Park ... Pg.3
- Remington Sports Complex ... Pg.3 ... B11
- Suburban Health Care ... Pg.3 ... A12
- Toyota Plant ... Pg.3 ... B13

## COYNES
Page 8 .... K8

## CREST HILL
Pages 8,9,14,15

### STREETS
- Alma Dr. ... Pg.14 ... L10
- Altenhoff Ct. ... Pg.14 ... L9
- Arbor Ln. ... Pg.14 ... L8
- Ardaugh Dr. ... Pg.8 ... L8
- Aster Dr. ... Pg.8 ... L7
- August St. ... Pg.14 ... M9
- Barthelone Ave. ... Pg.14 ... L9
- Beaver Park Ct. ... Pg.14 ... M7
- Berta Dr. ... Pg.8 ... L8
- Bicentennial Ave. ... Pg.14 ... M8
- Birkey Ave. ... Pg.9 ... L11
- Brian Dr. ... Pg.8 ... L10
- Broadway St. ... Pg.15 ... L11
- Burry Circle Dr. ... Pg.14 ... L10
- Burry Ct. ... Pg.14 ... L10
- Cara Dr. ... Pg.8 ... L8
- Carnation Dr. ... Pg.8 ... L7
- Caton Crest Ct. ... Pg.8 ... L8
- Caton Crest Dr. ... Pg.8 ... L8
- Caton Farm Rd. ... Pg.8 ... L8
- Cedarwood Dr. ... Pg.14 ... L9
- Center St. ... Pg.15 ... L11
- Chaney Ave. ... Pg.9 ... L10
- Chaney Ct. ... Pg.9 ... L10
- Circle St. ... Pg.8 ... L8
- Clement St. ... Pg.15 ... L10
- Connie Dr. ... Pg.14 ... L8
- Cora St. ... Pg.15 ... L11
- Cowing Ln. ... Pg.14 ... L10
- Crestwood Dr. ... Pg.14 ... L9
- Daffodil Dr. ... Pg.8 ... L7
- Dearborn St. ... Pg.15 ... M11
- Demask Ct. ... Pg.14 ... L9
- Donmaur St. ... Pg.8 ... L8
- Durness Ct. ... Pg.8 ... L8
- Eldorado Dr. ... Pg.14 ... L9
- Elrose Ct. ... Pg.9 ... L10
- Elsie Ave. ... Pg.14 ... L8
- Fern St. ... Pg.8 ... L8
- Fox Meadow Dr. ... Pg.14 ... L7
- Foxtail Ct. ... Pg.14 ... L7
- Gladiola Ln. ... Pg.8 ... L7
- Grandview Ave. ... Pg.14 ... L8
- Grant Park Ct. ... Pg.14 ... M7
- Green St. ... Pg.8 ... L8
- Greengold St. ... Pg.14 ... L9
- Hawthorn St. ... Pg.14 ... L11
- Heiden Ave. ... Pg.8 ... L8
- Hess Dr. ... Pg.15 ... L8
- Hickory St. ... Pg.15 ... L11
- Highland St. ... Pg.14 ... L10
- Hodgen Ct. ... Pg.14 ... L9
- Hoffman St. ... Pg.9 ... L11
- Hosmer ... Pg.14 ... L7
- Imperial Dr. ... Pg.8 ... L8
- Inner Circle Dr. ... Pg.14 ... L10
- Jared Dr. ... Pg.8 ... L7
- Jasmine Dr. ... Pg.8 ... L7
- Jorie Ct. ... Pg.8 ... L7
- Juricic Ct. ... Pg.8 ... L7
- Kelly Ave. ... Pg.15 ... L10
- Knapp Dr. ... Pg.14 ... M9
- Larkin Ave. ... Pg.14 ... L8
- Leness Ct. ... Pg.14 ... L8
- Liberty Park Ct. ... Pg.14 ... M7
- Lincoln Ave. ... Pg.8 ... L8
- Lincoln Park St. ... Pg.14 ... M7
- Live Oak Dr. ... Pg.14 ... L7
- Ludwig Ave. ... Pg.15 ... L10
- Lynwood Ave. ... Pg.8 ... L9
- Mache St. ... Pg.8 ... L8
- Manico Ct. ... Pg.14 ... L8
- Manico Dr. ... Pg.14 ... L8
- Manor Ct. ... Pg.15 ... L10
- Marietta Ave. ... Pg.14 ... L9
- Maryknoll Ln. ... Pg.14 ... L10
- Mia Ct. ... Pg.8 ... L8
- Mia Dr. ... Pg.8 ... L9
- Nicholson St. ... Pg.15 ... L11
- Noonan St. ... Pg.8 ... L8
- Oak Park Ct. ... Pg.14 ... M7
- Oakland Ave. ... Pg.9 ... L10
- Park Pl. Ct. ... Pg.14 ... M7
- Park Ridge Ct. ... Pg.14 ... M7
- Parkrose St. ... Pg.8 ... L8
- Pasadena Ave. ... Pg.9 ... L10
- Pioneer Rd. ... Pg.14 ... L10
- Plainfield Rd. ... Pg.8 ... L8
- Pleasant St. ... Pg.14 ... L9
- Post Oak Ct. ... Pg.14 ... M8
- Prairie Ave. ... Pg.15 ... M10
- Rahill Ct. ... Pg.14 ... L10
- Raynon Ave. ... Pg.14 ... M10
- Red Oak Tr. ... Pg.14 ... L7
- Rock Run Dr. ... Pg.14 ... L8
- Rose Ave. ... Pg.15 ... L10
- Rose Ct. ... Pg.8 ... L9
- Rosel Ct. ... Pg.15 ... L10
- Sak Dr. ... Pg.8 ... L10
- Sickler Ct. ... Pg.14 ... M9
- Silver Rock Dr. ... Pg.14 ... L7
- Stern Ave. ... Pg.15 ... L10
- Sullivan Ct. ... Pg.8 ... L10
- Susanne Way ... Pg.8 ... L8
- Sweet Briar St. ... Pg.8 ... L8
- Sybil Dr. ... Pg.14 ... L8
- Sycamore St. ... Pg.14 ... L8
- Theodore St. ... Pg.15 ... M10
- University St. ... Pg.8 ... L8
- Waterford Dr. ... Pg.8 ... L7
- Watertower Pl. ... Pg.14 ... L7
- Waverly Ct. ... Pg.14 ... L10
- Webb St. ... Pg.14 ... L10
- Weber Rd. ... Pg.8 ... L9
- Wilcox St. ... Pg.15 ... M10
- William Dr. ... Pg.14 ... L8
- Willow Circle Dr. ... Pg.14 ... L9
- Willow Ct. ... Pg.14 ... L10

### CEMETERIES
- St. Mary Nativity Cem. ... Pg.15 ... L10
- St. Mary's Cem. ... Pg.9 ... L10

### FOREST PRESERVES
- Alessio Prairie F.P. ... Pg.8 ... L9
- Theodore Marsh F.P. ... Pg.8 ... L8

### GOLF COURSES
- Priairie Bluff G.C. ... Pg.9 ... J11

### PARKS
- Crest Hill Mem. Pk. ... Pg.14 ... L10
- Lions Park ... Pg.8,15 ... L9,M10
- Richland Park ... Pg.14 ... M7

### SCHOOLS
- Chaney Sch. ... Pg.19 ... L11
- Juliet Montessori H.S. ... Pg.
- Richland Sch. ... Pg.14 ... L8
- St. Anne Sch. ... Pg.14 ... L9

### SHOPPING CENTERS
- Hillcrest S.C. ... Pg.14 ... M7
- Shopping Center ... Pg.14 ... M7

### MISCELLANEOUS
- City Hall ... Pg.14 ... M9
- Crest Hill Industrial Park ... Pg.14 ... M8
- Fire Department ... Pg.14 ... M8
- Library ... Pg.14 ... M9
- Police Dept. ... Pg.14 ... M9

## DOWNERS GROVE TOWNSHIP
(DuPage County)
Pages 4,5
(For additional listings, see Section 3)

### STREETS
- Bluff Rd. ... A16
- Carpenter St. ... A16
- Christopher Dr. ... A16
- Davey Rd. ... A16
- Deans Cove ... A16
- Dystrup Ave. ... A16
- Hill Rd. ... A16
- Hillcrest Ln. ... A16
- Knoebel Dr. ... A16
- Lennon Dr. ... A16
- Lincoln Ln. ... A16
- Ley Ct. ... A16
- Lincoln Hwy. ... A16
- Linden Ct. ... A16
- Linden Rd. ... A16
- Maple Ridge Ct. ... A16
- Maple St. ... A16
- McDonald Ln. ... A16
- Meadow Ave. ... A16
- Mulberry Rd. ... A16
- Nebraska Ct. A ... A16
- Nebraska Ct. B ... A16
- Nebraska St. ... A16
- Nevada St. ... A16
- North St. ... A16
- Oakridge Ct. ... A16
- Oakwood Dr. ... A16
- Oregon St. ... A16
- Overlook Ct. E & W ...

### FOREST PRESERVES
- Waterfall Glen F.P. ... A17

### SCHOOLS
- Bromberek Sch. ... A15

### MISCELLANEOUS
- Argonne National Laboratory Reservation ... A17

## DU PAGE TOWNSHIP
Pages 2-4
(For additional listings, see Section 3)

### STREETS
- Balsam Ct. ... Pg.2 ... D8
- Big Run Ln. ... Pg.4 ... E14
- Blossom Ln. ... Pg.2 ... D9
- Bluff Rd. ... Pg.3 ... B13-14
- Carlisle Dr. ... Pg.2 ... D8
- Catalina Dr. ... Pg.2 ... D8
- Crimson Ct. ... Pg.2 ... D9
- Davey Rd. ... Pg.2
- De Paul Ct. ... Pg.3 ... E12
- Donovan Rd. ... Pg.3 ... B13
- Forest Ln. ... Pg.4 ... E14
- Frontage Rd. ... Pg.3 ... B11
- High Rd. ... Pg.4 ... C13
- Joliet Rd. ... Pg.3 ... C13
- Juliet Ave. ... Pg.3 ... E12
- Lily Cache Ln. ... Pg.2 ... A9
- Mikan Ln. ... Pg.3 ... E12
- Naperville Rd. ... Pg.2 ... C10
- New Ave. ... Pg.2 ... C14
- Normantown Rd. ... Pg.2 ... D10
- Old Orchard Ln. E. ... Pg.4 ... E15
- Old Orchard Ln. N. & W.
- Orchid St. ... Pg.3 ... D8
- Riveredge Dr. ... Pg.3 ... E12
- Romeo Rd. ... Pg.2 ... E10
- Schmidt Rd. ... Pg.3 ... C11
- Snowberry Ln. ... Pg.2 ... D9
- Spruce Ln. ... Pg.2 ... D9
- Sumac Ct. ... Pg.2 ... D9
- 107th St. ... Pg.1 ... A10
- 111th St. ... Pg.1 ... A12
- 115th St. ... Pg.2 ... B9
- 127th St. ... Pg.4 ... D14
- 135th St. ... Pg.2 ... E14

### FOREST PRESERVES
- Keepataw F.P. ... Pg.4 ... B14
- Romeoville Prairie Nature Pres.
- Veterans Woods F.P. ... C13

## FRANKFORT
Pages 18,19
(For additional listings, see Section 2)

### STREETS
- Abbey Ct. ... Pg.19 ... Q26
- Abbey Dr. ... Pg.19 ... Q26
- Abbott Ct. ... Pg.19 ... R26
- Abour Walk Dr. ... Pg.19 ... R26
- Ashley Ct. ... Pg.19 ... Q26
- Aspen Ct. ... Pg.19 ... Q25
- Aspen St. ... Pg.19 ... R25
- Azalea Rd. ... Pg.19 ... R26
- Bankview Dr. ... Pg.19 ... Q25
- Birchwood Rd. ... Pg.19 ... Q25
- Boulder Ct. ... Pg.19 ... Q25
- Bowen St. ... Pg.19 ... R25
- Box Elder Rd. ... Pg.19 ... Q25
- Brookridge Creek Dr. ... R24
- Brookridge Ct. ... Pg.19 ... R24
- Brookridge Dr. ... Pg.19 ... R24
- Brookside Ln. ... Pg.19 ... R24
- Butternut Cir. ... Pg.18 ... Q,R24
- Butternut St. ... Pg.19 ... Q24
- Butternut Tr. ... Pg.19 ... R24
- Cambridge Ct. ... Pg.19 ... Q26
- Cardina Ct. ... Pg.19 ... Q26
- Cardinal Ct. ... Pg.19 ... R25
- Carpenter ... Pg.19 ... R25
- Catalpa Ct. ... Pg.19 ... R26
- Cemetery Rd. ... Pg.18 ... Q24
- Chestnut Ct. ... Pg.19 ... R26
- Colorado Ave. ... Pg.19 ... R24
- Concord Dr. ... Pg.19 ... R24
- Cottonwood Rd. ... Pg.19 ... R24
- Crystal Lake Way ... Pg.19 ... P26
- Cullen Ct. ... Pg.19 ... Q27
- Cullen Dr. ... Pg.19 ... Q27
- Dakota Ct. ... Pg.19 ... R25
- Elm St. ... Pg.19 ... R25
- Elsner Rd. ... Pg.19 ... N26
- Elwood St. ... Pg.19 ... R25
- Evergreen Dr. ... Pg.19 ... Q26
- Fox Run Cir. ... Pg.19 ... Q26
- Fox Run Ct. ... Pg.19 ... Q26
- Franklin Ave. ... Pg.19 ... R24,25
- Grant Ave. ... Pg.19 ... R25
- Hackberry Rd. ... Pg.19 ... R25
- Hamilton Ave. ... Pg.19 ... R25
- Hawthorne Rd. ... Pg.19 ... Q25
- Hawthorne Rd. ... Pg.19 ... R25
- Hickory Ct. ... Pg.19 ... Q24
- Hobby Ave. ... Pg.19 ... R25
- Hornbeam Ct. ... Pg.19 ... R24
- Huckins Ct. ... Pg.19 ... Q27
- Huckins Dr. ... Pg.19 ... Q27
- Hunt Club Dr. ... Pg.19 ... R26
- IFW Ln. ... Pg.19 ... R26
- Illinois Rd. ... Pg.19 ... R24
- Indiana Ct. ... Pg.19 ... Q24
- Iowa Ct. ... Pg.19 ... R25
- Ironwood Dr. ... Pg.19 ... Q24
- Jeanie Ln. ... Pg.19 ... R26
- Johnson Ave. ... Pg.19 ... R24
- Kansas St. ... Pg.19 ... R25
- Kean Ave. ... Pg.19 ... R25
- La Grange Rd. ... Pg.19 ... R25
- LaPorte Rd. ... Pg.19 ... R26
- Lawndale Blvd. ... Pg.19 ... R26
- Lawndale Ct. ... Pg.19 ... R26
- Lennon Dr. ... Pg.19 ... Q27
- Leslie Ln. ... Pg.19 ... R26
- Lexington Ln. ... Pg.19 ... R24
- Ley Ct. ... Pg.19 ... R26
- Lincoln Hwy. ... Pg.19 ... R26
- Linden Ct. ... Pg.19 ... R25
- Linden Rd. ... Pg.19 ... R25
- Maple Ridge Ct. ... Pg.19 ... R26
- Maple St. ... Pg.19 ... R25
- McDonald Ln. ... Pg.19 ... R25
- Meadow Ave. ... Pg.19 ... R25
- Mulberry Rd. ... Pg.19 ... R24
- Nebraska Ct. A ... Pg.19 ... R26
- Nebraska Ct. B ... Pg.19 ... R26
- Nebraska St. ... Pg.19 ... R24,25
- Nevada St. ... Pg.19 ... R25
- North St. ... Pg.19 ... R26
- Oakridge Ct. ... Pg.19 ... Q24
- Oakwood Dr. ... Pg.19 ... Q24
- Oregon St. ... Pg.19 ... R25
- Overlook Ct. E & W ... Pg.19 ... Q24
- Overlook Dr. ... Pg.19 ... Q24
- Penny Ct. N. ... Pg.19 ... R26
- Penny Ln. ... Pg.19 ... R26
- Pioneer Ct. ... Pg.19 ... R26
- Pioneer Dr. ... Pg.19 ... R26
- Pleasant Hill Rd. ... Pg.19 ... Q24
- Plymouth Ct. ... Pg.19 ... R25,S29
- Pueblo Ct. ... Pg.19 ... Q25
- Raintree Ln. ... Pg.19 ... R26
- Red Bud Ct. ... Pg.18 ... R24
- Sangmeister Rd. ... Pg.19 ... R24
- Settlers Pond Ct. ... Pg.18 ... R24
- Settlers Pond Dr. ... Pg.18 ... R24
- Sherlock St. ... Pg.19 ... R25
- Smith St. ... Pg.19 ... R25
- Spruce Rd. ... Pg.19 ... R26
- St. Francis Rd. ... Pg.19 ... Q26
- Sutton Dale Ln. ... Pg.19 ... R26
- Sycamore Dr. ... Pg.19 ... R26
- Tanglewood Ct. N. & S. ... Pg.19 ... Q24
- Tanglewood Rd. ... Pg.19 ... Q24,25
- Utah St. ... Pg.19 ... R24
- Vail Dr. ... Pg.19 ... R26
- Vermont Rd. ... Pg.19 ... R24
- Walnut Creek Dr. ... Pg.19 ... R24
- Walnut Ridge ... Pg.19 ... R24
- Walnut Ridge Ct. ... Pg.19 ... R24
- Warmke Ln. ... Pg.19 ... R24
- Washington Pkwy. ... Pg.19 ... R25
- White St. ... Pg.19 ... R24
- Williamsburg Ct. ... Pg.19 ... R24
- Williamsburg Tr. ... Pg.19 ... R24
- Willow St. ... Pg.19 ... Q,R25
- Wood Ct. ... Pg.19 ... R24
- Woodbridge Dr. ... Pg.19 ... R24
- Yankee Ridge Ct. ... Pg.19 ... R24
- Yankee Ridge Dr. ... Pg.19 ... R24
- 85th Ct. ... Pg.19 ... R27
- 88th Ave. ... Pg.19 ... R26
- 95th Ave. ... Pg.19 ... Q26
- 96th Ave. ... Pg.19 ... Q25
- 108th Ave. ... Pg.19 ... Q25

### CEMETERIES
- Frankfort Cem. ... Pg.19 ... Q26
- Hickory Cemetery ... Pg.19 ... Q26
- Pleasant Hill Cem. ... Pg.19 ... R26

### PARKS
- Bingham Mem. Park ... Pg.19 ... R24
- Lincoln Meadow Park ...
- Tanglewood Park ... Pg.19 ... Q24

### SCHOOLS
- Chelsea School ... Pg.19 ... Q25

### SHOPPING CENTERS
- Butera Center Plaza ...
- Frankfort Crossing S.C. ... Pg.19 ... R25
- Mannheim Square ... Pg.19 ... Q26

### MISCELLANEOUS
- Historical Dist. ... Pg.19 ... R25
- St. Francis Medical Center ...
- Village Hall ... Pg.19 ... R25

## FRANKFORT TOWNSHIP
Pages 18,19
(For additional listings, see Section 2)

### STREETS
- Arden Ln. ... Pg.18 ... P23
- Ash Ave. ... Pg.19 ... N26
- Beechnut Dr. ... Pg.19 ... N26
- Birch Ave. ... Pg.19 ... N26
- Briarwood Ln. ... Pg.18 ... P26
- Catulpa St. ... Pg.19 ... P26
- Cherry St. ... Pg.19 ... N26
- Cleveland Ave. ... Pg.19 ... N26
- Cleveland Rd. ... Pg.18 ... Q23
- Colorado Ave. ... Pg.19 ... N25
- Crabapple Ln. ... Pg.19 ... N26
- Elm Ave. ... Pg.19 ... N26
- Elmwood Ct. ... Pg.18 ... Q23
- Ethyl Ln. ... Pg.18 ... M26
- Francis Rd. ... Pg.18 ... Q23
- Franklin Ave. ... Pg.19 ... N26
- Hamilton Rd. ... Pg.18 ... P23
- Hawthorn Ave. ... Pg.19 ... N26
- Hickory St. ... Pg.19 ... N26
- Hilgate Rd. ... Pg.18 ... Q23
- Hillcrest Dr. ... Pg.19 ... N26
- Interstate 80 ... Pg.18 ... M25
- Ironwood Ct. ... Pg.18 ... N22
- Ironwood Dr. ... Pg.18 ... N22
- Jean Rd. ... Pg.18 ... N22
- Kluth Dr. ... Pg.18 ... P23
- Kohlwood Dr. ... Pg.19 ... P24
- La Grange Rd. ... Pg.19 ... P24
- La Porte Rd. ... Pg.18 ... N22
- Leila Dr. ... Pg.18 ... N22
- Lexington Ave. ... Pg.19 ... N26
- Lincoln Hwy. ... Pg.19 ... P26
- Magnolia Ave. ... Pg.19 ... N26
- Marjorie Pkwy. ... Pg.18 ... M22
- Normandy Ln. ... Pg.18 ... M22
- Oak St. ... Pg.19 ... N26
- Osage Rd. ... Pg.18 ... P23
- Park Dr. ... Pg.19 ... P24
- Pine Ave. ... Pg.19 ... N26
- Pleasant Ave. ... Pg.19 ... N26
- Poplar St. ... Pg.19 ... N26
- Redwood Ln. ... Pg.19 ... N26
- Rose Ln. ... Pg.18 ... M22
- Rosewood Ln. ... Pg.19 ... N26
- Sara Rd. ... Pg.19 ... N26
- School House Rd. ... Pg.18 ... P24
- Stephanie Ln. ... Pg.19 ... N26
- Sycamore St. ... Pg.19 ... N26
- Town Line Rd. ... Pg.19 ... N22
- Virginia Pkwy. ... Pg.18 ... M22
- Walnut St. ... Pg.19 ... P26
- Willow Ln. ... Pg.19 ... N26
- Wolf Rd. ... Pg.19 ... N26
- Woodland Cir. N, S & W ...
- 88th Ave. ... Pg.19 ... P23
- 92nd Ave. ... Pg.19 ... N26
- 93rd Ave. ... Pg.19 ... R26
- 94th Ave. ... Pg.18 ... N26
- 104th Ave. ... Pg.19 ... N26
- 108th Ave. ... Pg.18 ... N25
- 113th Ave. ... Pg.19 ... N26
- 114th Ave. ... Pg.19 ... N,P23
- 115th Ave. ... Pg.19 ... N26
- 183rd St. ... Pg.18 ... M24
- 187th St. ... Pg.18 ... M23
- 189th St. ... Pg.18 ... M23
- 191st St. ... Pg.18 ... N23
- 192nd St. ... Pg.18 ... M23
- 193rd St. ... Pg.18 ... N22
- 203rd St. ... Pg.18 ... P23
- 204th St. ... Pg.18 ... Q23

### FOREST PRESERVES
- Brightway Prairie ... Pg.19 ... P22
- Van Horne Woods ... Pg.19 ... Q25

### SCHOOLS
- Arbury Hills Sch. ... Pg.19 ... P26
- Lincolnway H.S. East Campus ... Pg.19 ... Q25

### MISCELLANEOUS
- Enviornmental Learning Center ...
- Library ... Pg.19 ... R27
- St. Francis of the Woods Convent ... Pg.19 ... Q26
- Weigh Station ... Pg.18 ... M22

## HOMER TOWNSHIP
Pages 4-6,10-12

### STREETS
- Acorn Ct. ... Pg.10 ... F16
- Acorn Dr. ... Pg.10 ... F16
- Acorn Ln. ... Pg.5 ... E17
- Acorn Ridge Dr. ... Pg.11 ... J19
- Allison Ln. ... Pg.12 ... G21
- Aliston Dr. ... Pg.11 ... H21
- Anand Brook Dr. ... Pg.6 ... E21
- Anne K. Dr. ... Pg.11 ... F19
- Annico Dr. ... Pg.11 ... H20
- Appaloosa Ln. ... Pg.12 ... G20
- Arabian Dr. ... Pg.11 ... F20
- Arapaho Tr. ... Pg.12 ... G21
- Arboretum Dr. ... Pg.11 ... G19
- Archer Ave. ... Pg.10 ... F15
- Arlene Dr. ... Pg.12 ... G21
- Ashley Ct. ... Pg.12 ... K21
- Aspen Ln. ... Pg.12 ... K21
- Aston Ct. ... Pg.12 ... G21
- Atlantic Dr. ... Pg.11 ... F20
- Atwood Dr. ... Pg.12 ... G21
- Augusta Ln. ... Pg.11 ... G19
- Badger Ln. ... Pg.12 ... G21
- Basham Ave. ... Pg.4 ... F15
- Baywood Ln. ... Pg.11 ... F20
- Beaver Ct. ... Pg.5 ... E20
- Beaver Den Tr. ... Pg.12 ... J20
- Beaver Lake Dr. ... Pg.5,6 ... E20
- Bedford Ln. ... Pg.4 ... E15
- Bell Rd. ... Pg.6,12 ... E-H20
- Bellingham Rd. ... Pg.12 ... G20
- Benton Dr. ... Pg.12 ... G21
- Big Run Ln. ... Pg.11 ... G19
- Birchdale Dr. ... Pg.11 ... F19
- Birchwood Ct. ... Pg.11 ... F19
- Black Forest Ct. ... Pg.12 ... H21
- Black Forest Tr. ... Pg.12 ... H21
- Black Pine Tr. ... Pg.12 ... H21
- Blackburn Dr. ... Pg.12 ... H21
- Bosi Dr. ... J17
- Boula Ave. ... Pg.10 ... F15
- Boulder Dr. ... Pg.11 ... F19
- Brads Way ... Pg.10 ... G16
- Bramble Ct. ... Pg.12 ... K21
- Brentwood Dr. ... Pg.12 ... K21
- Briarwood Ln. ... Pg.11 ... F19
- Bristol Ln. ... Pg.12 ... G21
- Bruce Cir. ... Pg.11 ... K18
- Bruce Rd. ... Pg.11 ... K20
- Burning Bush Ct. ... Pg.5 ... E20
- Burr Oak Dr. ... Pg.12 ... H20
- Buttercup Ct. ... Pg.12 ... H21
- Cambridge Way ... Pg.12 ... G21
- Cannonade Ct. ... Pg.6 ... E21
- Cantigny Ln. ... Pg.11 ... G19
- Canvasback Ct. ... Pg.12 ... J20
- Carefree Dr. ... Pg.11 ... H20
- Carlton Ln. ... Pg.12 ... G20
- Casey Ln. ... Pg.11 ... F19
- Catawba Ln. ... Pg.12 ... J21
- Catawba Ln. ... Pg.5 ... F20
- Catawba Rd. ... Pg.12 ... J21
- Cavecreek Ct. ... Pg.12 ... J21
- Cedar Creek Ct. ... Pg.12 ... J20
- Cedar Ct. ... Pg.11 ... L18
- Cedar Glen Dr. ... Pg.11 ... H17
- Cedar Rd. ... Pg.5,11 ... E,F,J18
- Cedar Ridge Dr. ... Pg.12 ... G19
- Cedarbend Dr. ... Pg.11 ... F19
- Cedarwood Dr. ... Pg.11 ... H18
- Chancellor Dr. ... Pg.10 ... J16
- Chandler Ct. ... Pg.12 ... J21
- Charterhouse Rd. ... Pg.12 ... G20
- Chaucer Rd. ... Pg.12 ... G20
- Chelsea Ct. ... Pg.11 ... J19
- Cherokee Tr. ... Pg.5 ... F20
- Chesterton Dr. ... Pg.12 ... F21
- Chestnut Ct. ... Pg.5 ... F21
- Chestnut Ln. ... Pg.6 ... E21
- Chicago-Bloomington Tr. ... Pg.9 ... L19
- Chickasaw Tr. ... Pg.5 ... F20
- Chicory Tr. ... Pg.5 ... F17
- Chippewa Tr. ... Pg.5 ... E18
- Choctaw Tr. ... Pg.5 ... E20
- Church St. ... Pg.11 ... H21
- Cinnamon Creek Ln. ...
- Citation Ct. ... Pg.6 ... E19
- Citation Dr. ... Pg.6 ... E19
- Clifton Ln. ... Pg.11 ... F18
- Clydesdale Ln. ... Pg.12 ... G20
- Coachmans Rd. ... Pg.11 ... F19
- Codo Dr. ... Pg.11 ... J17
- Cog Hill Ln. ... Pg.11 ... J17
- Cokes Rd. ... Pg.12 ... G18
- Coleridge Ct. ... Pg.12 ... G20
- Comandra Ct. ... Pg.12 ... K21
- Country Woods Ln. ...
- Court Connection ... Pg.12 ... H21
- Coventry Ct. ... Pg.12 ... H20
- Cranberry Ct. ... Pg.12 ... G20
- Creekside Ct. ... Pg.5 ... F20
- Creekside Dr. ... Pg.11 ... G17
- Creekwood Ct. ... Pg.11 ... J20
- Creekwood Dr. ... Pg.11 ... J20
- Creekwood Ln. ... Pg.11 ... J21
- Creme Rd. ... Pg.12 ... G17
- Crestwood Dr. ... Pg.5 ... F18
- Cricketwood Ct. ... Pg.11 ... G19
- Cricketwood Dr. ... Pg.11 ... G19
- Crystal Lake Ct. ... Pg.12 ... L20
- Crystal Lake Dr. ... Pg.12 ... L20
- Dalphon Ct. ... Pg.6 ... F21
- Dawnwood Ct. ... Pg.11 ... G20
- Deer Run ... Pg.11 ... K17
- Deervalley Dr. ... Pg.11 ... H21
- Derby Ave. ... Pg.5 ... F18
- Derby Dr. ... Pg.5 ... F21
- Derby Rd. ... Pg.11 ... F18
- Dixon Ln. ... Pg.11 ... F18
- Doede Ln. ... Pg.11 ... H20
- Dogwood Dr. ... Pg.12 ... G21
- Dokler Pl. ... Pg.11 ... J20
- Doonaree Ct. ... Pg.5 ... E19
- Doral Ln. ... Pg.11 ... G19
- Driftwood Ln. ... Pg.11 ... J19
- Dublin Ct. ... Pg.5 ... E19
- Dublin Dr. ... Pg.5 ... E19
- Eagle Bend ... Pg.10 ... L16
- East Abbott Rd. ... Pg.12 ... G21
- East Glen Dr. ... Pg.12 ... G21
- East St. ... Pg.5 ... F17
- Edaleaha Ct. ... Pg.5 ... F21
- Edgewood Dr. ... Pg.12 ... G21
- Edinburgh E. & W. ... Pg.11 ... G18
- Elizabeth Ln. ... Pg.11 ... F18
- Elm St. ... Pg.5 ... F21
- Erin Ct. ... Pg.6 ... F20
- Erin Dr. ... Pg.6 ... E19
- Evergreen Terr. ... Pg.12 ... K21
- Fairway View Ave. ... Pg.5 ... E19
- Farmington Dr. ... Pg.12 ... H21
- Farmview St. ... Pg.11 ... F21
- Farrell Rd. ... Pg.10 ... H15
- Fairfield Way ... Pg.12 ... G21
- Filly Dr. ... Pg.12 ... G21
- Finch Ct. ... Pg.12 ... H20
- Flint Dr. ... Pg.12 ... G21
- Forest View Dr. ... Pg.6 ... H16
- Foxboro Ln. ... Pg.11 ... J19
- Gadwall Ct. ... Pg.12 ... K21
- Garavogue Ave. ... Pg.6 ... F21
- Gatses Estates ... Pg.11 ... F18
- Gatses Ln. ... Pg.11 ... F18
- Glen Crest Ln. ... Pg.11 ... H17
- Glen Dale Ln. ... Pg.11 ... H17
- Glen Entrance ... Pg.11 ... G20
- Glen View Ct. ... Pg.11 ... H17
- Glen Wood Ct. ... Pg.11 ... H18
- Glen Wood Ln. ... Pg.11 ... H18
- Golden Oak Dr. ... Pg.11 ... H17
- Golden Oaks Dr. ... Pg.11 ... F,G20
- Gombis Dr. ... Pg.11 ... L18
- Gougar Rd. ... Pg.10 ... L16
- Graceland Dr. ... Pg.12 ... H21
- Greenbrier Ln. ... Pg.11 ... G19
- Grenelefe Ln. ... Pg.11 ... G19
- Gunilee Ln. ... Pg.11 ... G20
- Gunner Ct. ... Pg.12 ... J21
- Haas Rd. ... Pg.12 ... L20
- Hadley Rd. ... Pg.12 ... K18
- Hagard St. ... Pg.11 ... G20
- Hampshire Ln. ... Pg.12 ... G20
- Hampton Ct. ... Pg.5 ... E17
- Hawk Haven Rd. ... Pg.4 ... E17
- Hawthorne Ct. N. & S. ... Pg.11 ... G17
- Heathcliff Rd. ... Pg.12 ... G21
- Heather Ct. ... Pg.12 ... F21
- Heather Ln. ... Pg.12 ... F21
- Heatherwood Ct. ... Pg.11 ... F19
- Heatherwood Dr. ... Pg.11 ... F19
- Hedge Apple Dr. ... Pg.5 ... E20
- Heritage Dr. ... Pg.11 ... L18
- Hiawatha Ct. ... Pg.5 ... F20
- Hiawatha Dr. ... Pg.5 ... F20
- Hickory Ave. ... Pg.5 ... E18
- Hidden Valley Cir. ... Pg.11 ... J20
- Hidden Valley Dr. ... Pg.11 ... J20
- Hidden Valley Dr. ... Pg.11 ... H20
- Hidden Valley Tr. ... Pg.11 ... J20
- Hilary Ln. ... Pg.10 ... G16
- Hillcrest Rd. ... Pg.5,11 ... F18
- Hillside Ct. ... Pg.11 ... H20
- Hilltop Dr. ... Pg.11 ... L19
- Holm Ct. ... Pg.12 ... G21
- Holm Dr. ... Pg.12 ... G21
- Hunter Ct. ... Pg.4 ... E15
- Ignace Ct. ... Pg.12 ... G21
- Innisbrook Ln. ... Pg.11 ... G19
- Ironwood Cir. ... Pg.11 ... J19
- Iroquois Tr. ... Pg.5 ... E19
- Ivy Ct. ... Pg.12 ... G21
- James Ct. ... Pg.11 ... L17
- Janas Ct. ... Pg.12 ... G20
- Kensington Dr. ... Pg.12 ... G20
- Kerry Ln. ... Pg.5 ... E19
- Kickapoo Tr. ... Pg.5 ... F20
- King Rd. ... Pg.5,11 ... E,F18
- Kingston Ct. ... Pg.12 ... F21
- Kingston Dr. ... Pg.12 ... F21
- Kiowa Ct. ... Pg.5 ... E20
- Kundrat Ln. ... Pg.10 ... F16
- Lady Bar Ave. ... Pg.5 ... F21
- Lady Bar Ln. ... Pg.5 ... F21
- Lakeview Ct. ... Pg.5 ... E21
- Lakeview Dr. ... Pg.5 ... E21
- Lakeview Pl. ... Pg.5 ... E21
- Lakeview Rd. ... Pg.5 ... E21
- Lancaster Ct. ... Pg.12 ... F21
- Larkspur Ct. ... Pg.11 ... J19
- Larkspur Dr. ... Pg.11 ... L20,M19
- Leafit Dr. ... Pg.11 ... J17
- Lemont Rd. ... Pg.11 ... G19
- Lenox Dr. ... Pg.12 ... G21
- Little Creek Dr. ... Pg.11 ... F20
- Long Run Ct. ... Pg.12 ... G20
- Long Run Dr. ... Pg.12 ... E17
- Long View Dr. ... Pg.11 ... F18
- Longmeadow Ln. ... Pg.12 ... G20
- Lost Boy Ln. ... Pg.5 ... E20
- MacKinac Rd. ... Pg.12 ... J21
- Magnolia Ln. ... Pg.12 ... G20
- Mallard Ct. ... Pg.12 ... K21
- Mallard Lake Dr. ... Pg.11 ... G17
- Mallard Ln. ... Pg.11 ... H17
- Manitou Ct. ... Pg.5 ... F20
- Manitou Rd. ... Pg.12 ... J21
- Manor Dr. ... Pg.11 ... J20
- Maple Ave. ... Pg.5 ... E18

Maple Ct. ... Pg.12 ... H20
Maramel Dr. ... Pg.11 ... J20
Marissa Ct. ... Pg.11 ... G20
Marti Rd. ... Pg.12 ... L21
Martingale Ln. ... Pg.12 ... G20
Maverick Tr. ... Pg.11 ... H20
McCarron Rd. ... Pg.11 ... L18
McCormick Ln. ... Pg.11 ... K17
McDonald Dr. ... Pg.10 ... H15
McKenzie Ave. ... Pg.10 ... H15
Meader Rd. ... Pg.11 ... M19
Meadow View Ln. ... Pg.11 ... H20
Meadowcrest Dr. ... Pg.12 ... K21
Meadowland Dr. ... Pg.12 ... F21
Meadowlark Ct. ... Pg.12 ... H20
Meath Cir. ... Pg.5 ... E19
Meath Dr. ... Pg.5 ... G15
Merc Ln. ... Pg.12 ... G15
Monaghan Rd. ... Pg.5 ... E19
Moorland Dr. ... Pg.12 ... G20
Morgan Ct. ... Pg.12 ... G21
Mormann Ln. ... Pg.5 ... E17
Morning Glory Ct. ... Pg.12 ... H20
Muir Dr. ... Pg.10 ... H15
Mulberry Ct. ... Pg.10 ... H20
Mulranny Dr. ... Pg.11 ... J21
Murvey Ct. ... Pg.6 ... E21
Murvey Dr. ... Pg.6 ... E21
Mustang Dr. ... Pg.7 ... E20
Navajo Tr. ... Pg.5 ... E20
Needles Ct. ... Pg.6 ... E21
Nolan Ct. ... Pg.4 ... F17
O'Connell Dr. ... Pg.11 ... L18
Oak Ave. ... Pg.5,10 ... F19
Oak Ct. ... Pg.5 ... F20
Oak Meadow Ct. ... Pg.12 ... K20
Oak Ridge Ct. ... Pg.5 ... F19
Oak Ridge Dr. ... Pg.5 ... F20
Oak Ridge Ln. ... Pg.5 ... F20
Oak St. ... Pg.4 ... F17
Oak Tr. ... Pg.11 ... F20
Oak Valley Ct. ... Pg.12 ... H20
Oak Valley Tr. ... Pg.12 ... H20
Oak View Ct. ... Pg.12 ... J20
Oakwood Dr. ... Pg.12 ... F20
Uger Path Dr. ... Pg.12 ... K21
Olympia Ln. ... Pg.10 ... G15
Onondaga Ct. ... Pg.5 ... E20
Onondaga Tr. ... Pg.5 ... E20
Orchard Ln. ... Pg.5 ... E17
Paddock Ln. ... Pg.11 ... H20
Palomino Ct. ... Pg.12 ... G20
Pantigo Ln. ... Pg.11 ... J17
Parker Rd. ... Pg.5 ... F19
Parkside Dr. ... Pg.12 ... H20
Parkview Ln. ... Pg.11 ... G20
Parnell Cir. ... Pg.11 ... L18
Partridge Ln. ... Pg.6 ... F21
Pawnee Ln. ... Pg.5 ... F20
Pebble Creek Ct. ... Pg.6 ... G19
Pebble Creek Dr. ... Pg.6 ... F19
Peppermill Tr. ... Pg.11 ... J17
Pheasant Cir. ... Pg.5 ... E17
Pheasant Ct. ... Pg.12 ... H20
Pheasant Ln. ... Pg.6 ... F21
Pin Oak Ct. ... Pg.5,11 ... F20
Pin Oak Dr. ... Pg.5 ... F20
Pine Grove Ct. ... Pg.12 ... F20
Pine Grove Dr. ... Pg.11 ... F20
Pine Hill Dr. ... Pg.7 ... J19
Pineview Dr. ... Pg.12 ... K21
Pinto Ct. ... Pg.12 ... F20
Pleasant Ct. ... Pg.5 ... E17
Potawatomi Ct. ... Pg.5 ... E20
Potawatomi Tr. ... Pg.5 ... E20
Prairie Ct. ... Pg.12 ... G21
Prairie Dr. ... Pg.12 ... G21
Prairie Hill Dr. ... Pg.4 ... E16
Provencal Dr. ... Pg.11 ... F20
Purley Ct. ... Pg.4 ... E17
Quail Ln. ... Pg.6 ... F21
Quail Run Ct. ... Pg.4 ... E17
Rado Dr. (N.S.E.W)
Rambling Rd. ... Pg.12 ... G21
Red Cedar Tr. ... Pg.12 ... H21
Red Oak Ct. ... Pg.12 ... G20
Regents Rd. ... Pg.10 ... J16
Reiter Dr. ... Pg.11 ... K18
Rickerman Rd. ... Pg.10 ... G15
Ridgemoor Dr. ... Pg.12 ... G20
Ridgewood Dr. ... Pg.12 ... J20
Robert Emmett Dr.
Rockbluff Way ... Pg.11 ... L18
Roger Rd. ... Pg.4 ... F15
Ron Ct. ... Pg.12 ... K18
Rosarie Dr. ... Pg.11 ... G20
Hosewood Dr. ... Pg.12 ... G21
Rowan Ct. ... Pg.4 ... F20
Russ Ln. ... Pg.6 ... H20
Rycon Dr. ... Pg.11 ... H19
Rynberk Ct. ... Pg.4 ... F20
Saddle Brook Ln. ... Pg.11 ... F19
Sage Ct. ... Pg.11 ... H20
Samuel Dr. ... Pg.11 ... L19
Sandstone Dr. ... Pg.11 ... F19
Sawgrass Ln. ... Pg.7 ... G19
Schaeffer Ct. ... Pg.4 ... F15
Schroeder Dr. ... Pg.11 ... H17
Schutter Strasse ... Pg.4 ... F15
Scott Ave. ... Pg.12 ... H15
Scott Rd. ... Pg.10 ... H15
Sea Biscuit Ct. ... Pg.12 ... F20
Secretariat Ln. ... Pg.6 ... F21
Seminole Tr. ... Pg.11 ... K19
Shady Ln. ... Pg.11 ... G19,H16
Sharon Dr. ... Pg.12 ... H21
Shelbourne Dr. ... Pg.11 ... F20
Shetland Ct. ... Pg.10 ... H15
Shetland Dr. ... Pg.12 ... F20
Shoshoni Tr. ... Pg.5 ... F20
Silo Ct. ... Pg.11 ... G20
Silo Dr. ... Pg.11 ... G20
Somerset Ct. ... Pg.6 ... F21
Somerset Rd. ... Pg.6 ... F21
South Creek Ct. ... Pg.11 ... F18
Southwest Hwy. ... Pg.12 ... L21
Spaniel Dr. ... Pg.12 ... H20
Sparrow Ct. ... Pg.11 ... H20
Split Rail Ct. ... Pg.5 ... F20
Split Rail Dr. ... Pg.5 ... F20
Spring Creek Rd. ... Pg.5 ... E18
Spring Ct. ... Pg.12 ... H20
Spring Lake Dr. ... Pg.12 ... G21
Stable Ln. ... Pg.11 ... L20
Starr Ln. (Pvt) ... Pg.4 ... E15
State St. ... Pg.11 ... G17
Stately Oaks Cir. ... Pg.10 ... F17

Stately Oaks Dr. ... Pg.10 ... F16
Sterling Dr. ... Pg.4 ... E15
Stirrup Ct. ... Pg.12 ... H20
Stonecreek Ct. ... Pg.11 ... G20
Stonegate Ct. ... Pg.11,12 ... F20
Stonehaven Ln. ... Pg.11 ... G18
Stoneoak Way ... Pg.11 ... F19
Stonewood Dr. ... Pg.11 ... F20
Stratford Ct. ... Pg.6 ... F21
Stratford Dr. ... Pg.12 ... H20
Sulky Ct. ... Pg.12 ... H20
Sulky Dr. ... Pg.11 ... H20
Sunset Ct. ... Pg.12 ... H20
Sussex Ln. ... Pg.12 ... F21
Sutherland Dr. ... Pg.12 ... H21
Swaps Ct. ... Pg.12 ... F21
Sweetwater Dr. ... Pg.11 ... G20
Tamarack Ln. ... Pg.12 ... K21
Tameling Dr. ... Pg.4 ... F15
Tara Dr. ... Pg.5 ... E19
Teakwood Dr. ... Pg.5 ... F20
Teal Dr. ... Pg.11 ... H17
Teal Ln. ... Pg.11 ... H17
Terrier Ct. ... Pg.12 ... J21
Thicket Ct. ... Pg.5 ... E20
Thistle Ct. ... Pg.11 ... P15
Thorn Apple Dr. ... Pg.12 ... M3
Thornburn Dr. ... Pg.6 ... F20
Thornton Rd. ... Pg.12 ... K20
Thornwood Ln. ... Pg.11 ... M17
Tim Tam Ct. ... Pg.12 ... F21
Timberlane Ct. ... Pg.11 ... F19
Trails End Ct. ... Pg.5 ... F20
Trails End Dr. ... Pg.5 ... F20
Trailside Dr. ... Pg.11 ... H20
Turf Ln. ... Pg.12 ... F20
Turnberry Ln. ... Pg.6 ... E21
Twin Lakes Ln. ... Pg.11 ... F18
Twin Lakes Dr. ... Pg.12 ... H21
Twin Oak Ct. ... Pg.12 ... H20
Twin Oaks Ct. ... Pg.5 ... E17
Valley View Dr. ... Pg.11 ... H20
Vaysee Ct. ... Pg.5 ... E17
Venetion Ct. ... Pg.6 ... F22
Venetion Way ... Pg.6 ... E22
Vost Dr. ... Pg.11 ... J17
Walnut Ave. ... Pg.5 ... E19
Walnut Ct. ... Pg.12 ... G21
Warwick Way ... Pg.12 ... H20
Waterford Rd. ... Pg.12 ... H20
Weather Vane Ln. ... Pg.11 ... H20
Wedgwood Dr. ... Pg.12 ... K21
Welter Ct. ... Pg.6 ... F20
West Abbott Rd. ... Pg.12 ... N7,8
West Glen Dr. ... Pg.12 ... K21
West St. ... Pg.5 ... F17
Wheatstone Dr. ... Pg.11 ... J17
Whirlaway Ct. ... Pg.6 ... F21
White Oak Ct. ... Pg.11 ... J20
Wick Dr. ... Pg.11 ... F19
Wilco Dr. ... Pg.12 ... G21
Wildwood Ln. ... Pg.11 ... H20
Will-Cook Rd. ... Pg.12 ... G21
Willow (Oak) Ct. ... Pg.11 ... H20
Winchester Cir. ... Pg.6 ... F22
Winchester Ct. ... Pg.6 ... F22
Windmill Dr. ... Pg.11 ... J17
Windsor Ct. ... Pg.12 ... G20
Windsor Dr. ... Pg.12 ... G20
Wingate Dr. ... Pg.11 ... K21
Wood Duck Ct. ... Pg.12 ... G21
Woodcrest Ave. ... Pg.12 ... G21
Woodduck Ln. ... Pg.5 ... F17
Woodland Ct. ... Pg.12 ... G21
Woodland Ln. ... Pg.12 ... G21
Woodmill Dr. ... Pg.5 ... F20
Wooley Hill Ct. ... Pg.4 ... E16
Wooley Hill Dr. ... Pg.4 ... E16
Yorkshire Dr. ... Pg.12 ... G21
Zuck Ct. ... Pg.11 ... J17
135th Ave. ... Pg.10 ... G15
135th St. ... Pg.4,5 ... E15,18
136th St. ... Pg.10 ... E18
136th St. ... Pg.4 ... E15,16
139th St. ... Pg.4 ... E16,17
140th St. ... Pg.4 ... F15
141st St ... Pg.4 ... F16
143rd St. ... Pg.5 ... F18
144th St. ... Pg.10 ... F16
144th St. ... Pg.10 ... G17
145th Pl. ... Pg.10 ... F15
145th St. ... Pg.10 ... F15
146th Ct. ... Pg.10 ... F15
146th St. ... Pg.10 ... F15
147th St. ... Pg.10 ... F15,16
151st St. ... Pg.10 ... G20
153rd St. ... Pg.12 ... G21
159th St. ... Pg.11 ... H19
163rd St. ... Pg.11 ... J17,20
175th St. ... Pg.11 ... J19
175th St. ... Pg.11 ... L19
179th St. ... Pg.12 ... L21

**CEMETERIES**
Barnett Cem. ... Pg.10 ... K16
Brooks Cem. ... Pg.11 ... L19
Hadley Cem. ... Pg.11 ... L19
St. Michael's Cem. ... Pg.12

**FOREST PRESERVES**
Messenger Woods

**GOLF COURSES**
Old Oak G.C. ... Pg.11 ... F19
Woodbine G.C. ... Pg.11 ... J19

**PARKS**
Chester Park ... Pg.12 ... H21
Culver Park ... Pg.12 ... G20
Gireham Park ... Pg.12 ... F21
Morris Park ... Pg.12 ... J17
Town Center Park ... Pg.12 ... G18
Twin Lakes Park ... Pg.12 ... L21
Yangus Park ... Pg.6 ... F22

**SCHOOLS**
Gooding Grove Sch.
Hadley Sch. ... Pg.5 ... F20
Homer Jr. H.S. ... Pg.11 ... H21
Reed Sch. ... Pg.12 ... F18
Schilling Sch. ... Pg.11 ... J18

**MISCELLANEOUS**
Admin. Center ... Pg.11 ... G18
Fire Station ... Pg.11 ... J18
Library / Highway Dept. ... Pg.11 ... G19
N.W. Fire Station No. 1
N.W. Fire Station No. 2 ... Pg.4 ... F16
Shady Oaks Camp ... Pg.11 ... J19
Silver Cross Family Care Clinic
Town Hall ... Pg.11 ... H18

**JOLIET**
Pages 7,8,13-16
**STREETS**

Abbey Cir. ... Pg.7 ... L5
Abe St. ... Pg.15 ... N12
Ada St. ... Pg.15 ... M13
Adelman St. ... Pg.13 ... M6
Adella Ave. ... Pg.15 ... P13
Alder St. ... Pg.15 ... Q11
Agnes ... Pg.15 ... M10
Agnes Ave. ... Pg.14 ... N6
Akin Ave. ... Pg.15 ... P12
Aladdin Ct. ... Pg.13 ... M3
Alamo Dr. ... Pg.13 ... M6
Alamosa Ct. ... Pg.13 ... M17
Alamosa Dr. ... Pg.13 ... M6
Albert Ave. ... Pg.13 ... M17
Alaun Dr. ... Pg.14 ... N9
Albert Ave. ... Pg.15 ... P12
Aldrich Dr. ... Pg.7 ... L4
Alexander Dr. ... Pg.14 ... N3
Algonquin St. ... Pg.14 ... N14
Allen St. ... Pg.15 ... P10,11
Allen St. W. ... Pg.7 ... P9
Amanda Ct. ... Pg.7 ... K6
Amber Ct. ... Pg.7 ... K6
Ann Ct. ... Pg.14 ... N8
Anthony Ln. ... Pg.13 ... L5
Antral ... Pg.13 ... M13
Apache Dr. ... Pg.16 ... N6
Apollo Dr. ... Pg.13 ... N6
Applewood Ct. ... Pg.7 ... L3
Arbor Gate Dr. ... Pg.13 ... L3
Arbor Glen Dr. ... Pg.13 ... L3
Arbor Tr. ... Pg.16 ... N14
Arborsedge Dr. ... Pg.13 ... Q6
Arch Ct. ... Pg.15 ... P12
Arden Pl. ... Pg.14 ... N7,8
Ardith St. ... Pg.8 ... K7
Arizona Ave. ... Pg.15 ... P13
Arthur Ave. ... Pg.15 ... M13
Asbury Cir. Dr. ... Pg.14 ... N14
Ashcott Ln. ... Pg.13 ... L5
Ashford Ct. ... Pg.7 ... L4
Ashford Ln. ... Pg.7 ... L4
Ashley Ct. ... Pg.15 ... Q12
Ashwood Dr. ... Pg.7 ... L3
Aspen Ct. ... Pg.13 ... N6
Audrey Ave. ... Pg.15 ... P10
Austin Dr. ... Pg.16 ... P14
Autumn Dr. ... Pg.13 ... M6
Avalon Ave. ... Pg.14 ... N8
Avondale Ln. ... Pg.13 ... M16
Babylon Ave. ... Pg.16 ... P8
Baker Ave. ... Pg.15 ... P12
Balmoral Dr. ... Pg.13 ... M6
Bankview Ct. ... Pg.13 ... M13
Bar Bell Ln. ... Pg.7 ... K6
Barbara Jean Ln. ... Pg.14 ... P7
Barber Ln. ... Pg.14 ... N,7,7
Barber Ln. ... Pg.14 ... M7,N6
Barney Dr. ... Pg.14 ... N7
Bartelson Rd. ... Pg.13 ... M5
Bartelson St. ... Pg.15 ... P12
Bartlett Ln. ... Pg.14 ... N9
Basswood Rd. ... Pg.16 ... N14
Bataan St. ... Pg.15 ... L7
Bayberry Dr. ... Pg.14 ... M8
Beckwith Ct. ... Pg.13 ... L4
Bedford Dr. ... Pg.13 ... L4
Beechwood Ct. ... Pg.16 ... N15
Beldon Way ... Pg.14 ... M8
Bellarmine Dr., E & W ... Pg.13 ... Q8
Belle Ave. ... Pg.15 ... M,N13
Belleau Wood Dr. ... Pg.8 ... L3
Belleau Woods Ct. ... Pg.8 ... L7
Belmont Ave. ... Pg.16 ... N14
Benedict Ave. ... Pg.14 ... P8
Bennet Ave. ... Pg.15 ... M13
Benton ... Pg.15 ... N11-13
Bergstrom St. ... Pg.13 ... M5
Bernadette Ln. ... Pg.15 ... M10
Bethel Dr. ... Pg.14 ... N8
Betula St. ... Pg.16 ... Q9
Bevan Dr., E & W ... Pg.13 ... N8
Big Timber Rd. ... Pg.13 ... L6
Biltmore St. ... Pg.8 ... K7
Birch Ln. ... Pg.14 ... N8
Birchwood Ct. ... Pg.16 ... N14
Bismark Ave. ... Pg.14 ... M10
Bissell St. ... Pg.15 ... P13
Black St. ... Pg.13 ... N6,10
Blackman Ave. ... Pg.7 ... L4
Blackwater Dr. ... Pg.7 ... L3
Blandford Ave. ... Pg.15 ... N17
Bloomfield Dr. ... Pg.13 ... Q6
Blue Jay Ln. ... Pg.13 ... M5
Bodio Pl. ... Pg.15 ... M11
Bodio Pl. ... Pg.16 ... P12
Bogdan Ln. ... Pg.16 ... M15
Border Dr. ... Pg.14 ... N8
Boston Ave. ... Pg.14 ... M9
Boulder Ave. ... Pg.15 ... N13
Bowen Pl. ... Pg.15 ... Q12
Brenton Ct. ... Pg.13 ... K6
Brenton Dr. ... Pg.13 ... L4
Brentwood Dr. ... Pg.14 ... M8
Brentwood Pl. ... Pg.14 ... M8
Briar Glen Dr. ... Pg.7 ... L2
Briargate ... Pg.14 ... M9
Brighton Ln. ... Pg.7 ... L3
Brindlewood Dr. ... Pg.7 ... L3
Brink Dr. ... Pg.14 ... N7
Brittany Dr. ... Pg.8 ... J7
Broadway ... Pg.15 ... N11
Brockway Pond Ct.
Bronk Corner ... Pg.13 ... L6
Bronk Rd. ... Pg.13 ... L6
Bronk St. ... Pg.7 ... M3
Brookfield Dr. ... Pg.7 ... M3
Brooks St. ... Pg.16 ... N10

Brookwood Ct. ... Pg.14 ... M8
Brown Ave. ... Pg.15 ... N13
Bruce ... Pg.15 ... M12
Bryan Ave. ... Pg.14 ... N9
Buck Ave. ... Pg.13 ... M13
Buell Ave. ... Pg.14 ... N8
Buell Ct. ... Pg.14 ... N8
Buffalo St. ... Pg.15 ... R12
Bunker Hill Dr. ... Pg.14 ... L7
Bunratty Ln. ... Pg.7 ... L5
Burgess Dr. ... Pg.7 ... L3
Burr Oaks Rd. ... Pg.13 ... N6
Burry St. ... Pg.15 ... N12
Butler ... Pg.15 ... Q12
Cagwin Ave. ... Pg.15 ... P10
Calico Ct. ... Pg.8 ... J7
California Ave. ... Pg.15 ... M13
Calla Dr. ... Pg.14 ... N2
Campbell St. ... Pg.14 ... P7,9,10
Canal St. ... Pg.15 ... N11
Candlewood Ct. ... Pg.7 ... L3
Candlewood Dr. ... Pg.7 ... L3
Canterbury Ct. ... Pg.13 ... L3,P6
Canterbury St. ... Pg.13 ... L3
Capri Ave. ... Pg.14 ... P8
Cardinal Ln. ... Pg.15 ... M13
Caribou Ct. ... Pg.13 ... P5
Carlyle Ct. ... Pg.16 ... N9
Carlyle Dr. ... Pg.16 ... N9
Carousel Ct. ... Pg.14 ... M8
Carrier Ct. ... Pg.7 ... L4
Carrington Ln. ... Pg.13 ... L5
Carson St. ... Pg.15 ... N11
Cascade Ct. ... Pg.16 ... N6
Cascade Ln. ... Pg.16 ... N6
Cass St. ... Pg.15 ... P12
Casseday Ave. ... Pg.15 ... P12
Cassie Ln. ... Pg.13 ... N6
Catalpa Pl. ... Pg.16 ... Q9
Caterpillar Dr. ... Pg.14 ... L7
Catherine St. ... Pg.14 ... M9
Cathy Dr. ... Pg.13 ... R6
Caton Corner ... Pg.7 ... L4
Caton Farm Rd. ... Pg.7 ... L4
Cayuga Ct. ... Pg.16 ... N14
Cayuga St. ... Pg.13 ... N6
Cecily Dr. ... Pg.14 ... L7
Cedar Lakes Ct. ... Pg.7 ... L3
Center St. ... Pg.15 ... N11
Chapman Dr. ... Pg.13 ... L3
Charlesworth Ave. ... Pg.15 ... N12
Chase Ave. ... Pg.15 ... N11
Chelse Ct. ... Pg.15 ... N5
Cherry St. ... Pg.15 ... N11
Chestnut Hill Dr. ... Pg.13 ... L4
Chestnut Pointe Dr.
Chicago St. ... Pg.15 ... P11
Chippewa St. ... Pg.13 ... N6
Chovan Dr. ... Pg.14 ... M7
Christina Ln. ... Pg.14 ... M9
Christine Ave. ... Pg.13 ... Q6
Cider Grove Ct. ... Pg.13 ... L3
Cindy Ct. ... Pg.13 ... M3
Cinnamon Ct. ... Pg.8 ... L3
Citadel Ct. ... Pg.13 ... M6
Citadel Dr. ... Pg.14 ... M6
Clara Ave. ... Pg.14 ... N9
Clark St. ... Pg.13 ... M13
Claudia Ave. ... Pg.16 ... P5
Clay St. ... Pg.15 ... N11
Cleary Ave. ... Pg.15 ... M10
Cleveland Ave. ... Pg.15 ... N12,14
Clinton St. ... Pg.15 ... P11,13
Clover Ct. ... Pg.7 ... K4
Clover Ln. ... Pg.7 ... K4
Cochrane Ave. ... Pg.15 ... N12
Colburn Ave. ... Pg.15 ... Q12
College Dr. ... Pg.13 ... R5
Colorado Ave. ... Pg.8 ... K7,M9
Columbia St. ... Pg.15 ... N11,12
Commerce Ln. ... Pg.13 ... R6
Comstock St. ... Pg.15 ... P10
Concord Ct. ... Pg.8 ... K7
Connecticut ... Pg.14 ... M9
Copley Ln. ... Pg.13 ... M5
Copperfield Ave. ... Pg.16 ... N14
Corella Ave. ... Pg.15 ... N10
Cornelia St. ... Pg.15 ... N10
Corregidor St. ... Pg.14 ... L7
Cottage Pl. ... Pg.14 ... N7
Cotter Ln. ... Pg.13 ... M5
Country Glen Dr. ... Pg.13 ... L5
Country Oak Dr. ... Pg.7 ... L3
Coventry Chase ... Pg.13 ... L4
Coventry Ct. ... Pg.13 ... L4
Coventry Rd. ... Pg.16 ... N14
Cowles Ave. ... Pg.15 ... N10
Crabapple Ct. ... Pg.14 ... P7
Crabapple Dr. ... Pg.14 ... P7
Craig Dr. ... Pg.13 ... L3
Cranberry Ct. ... Pg.14 ... P7
Crazy Horse Dr. ... Pg.16 ... N6
Creed St. ... Pg.15 ... N12
Crescenzo Dr. ... Pg.14 ... N8
Crested Butte Tr. ... Pg.4 ... M3
Criswell Dr. ... Pg.16 ... P14
Croghan St. ... Pg.15 ... Q10
Crossroad Dr. ... Pg.13 ... M5
Crowley ... Pg.15 ... N11
Cryder Ln. ... Pg.7 ... L4
Culver St. ... Pg.7 ... L4
Curtis Ave. ... Pg.15 ... N10
Cutter Ave. ... Pg.15 ... M13
Cypress Ln. ... Pg.14 ... N8
Cypress Ln. ... Pg.14 ... N8
D'Arcy ... Pg.14 ... P10
D. Hutchinson Ave.
Dalewood Dr. ... Pg.7 ... L3
Dalewood Dr. ... Pg.7 ... L3
Dartmoor Dr. ... Pg.14 ... M8
David Ave. ... Pg.15 ... P12
Dawes Ave. ... Pg.15 ... M10
DeKalb St. ... Pg.15 ... P11
Dearborn St. ... Pg.15 ... N11
Deer Run Dr. ... Pg.7 ... M3
Deer Run Trail ... Pg.15 ... P5

Delaware Pl. ... Pg.15 ... P12
Dellmar Ave. ... Pg.15 ... N8,9
Delrose St. ... Pg.14 ... L7
Demmond Ct. ... Pg.15 ... M13
Dennis Ct. ... Pg.15 ... Q11
Der Dr. ... Pg.16 ... P15
Des Plaines St. ... Pg.15 ... Q11
Desmond St. ... Pg.15 ... M13
Devonshire Dr. ... Pg.14 ... M8
Dewey Ave. ... Pg.15 ... P10
Diane St. ... Pg.7 ... J6
Dianne Dr. ... Pg.16 ... P14
Dillman Ave. ... Pg.15 ... N12
Division St. ... Pg.15 ... N11
Division St. ... Pg.8 ... J7
Dixon ... Pg.15 ... N10
Doe Ct. ... Pg.13 ... P5
Dogwood Ct. ... Pg.13 ... N6
Dolores St. ... Pg.14 ... M7
Donna St. ... Pg.14 ... N8
Donnie Ct. ... Pg.15 ... N10
Dora Ave. ... Pg.15 ... M13
Doral Ct. ... Pg.7 ... L3
Doris Ave. ... Pg.15 ... N13
Douglas St. ... Pg.13 ... N6,8,10
Dover St. ... Pg.15 ... P12
Draper Ave. ... Pg.15 ... M13
Dryden Ln. ... Pg.14 ... N8
Dunbar Ct. ... Pg.7 ... L3
Duncan St. ... Pg.15 ... Q11
Dunmore St. ... Pg.7 ... L6
Dwight Ave. ... Pg.14 ... P8
Eagle St. ... Pg.15 ... N13
Eaglewood Ct. ... Pg.7 ... L3
Earl St. ... Pg.15 ... Q9
Eastern Ave. ... Pg.15 ... P12
Eastwood Ct. ... Pg.7 ... L3
Eberhard Ln. ... Pg.7 ... L4
Edgehill St. ... Pg.16 ... N16
Edgerton Dr. ... Pg.14 ... M8
Edie Ln. ... Pg.14 ... L7
Edith Dr. ... Pg.16 ... N14
Edward St. ... Pg.15 ... Q11
Eigin Ave. ... Pg.15 ... N13
Elizabeth St. ... Pg.14 ... N8
Ella Ave. ... Pg.15 ... Q12
Elm St. ... Pg.15 ... Q12
Elmwood Ave. ... Pg.15 ... Q12
Elmwood St. ... Pg.15 ... N12
Emery St. ... Pg.14 ... P9
Emmet ... Pg.15 ... P10
Emo St. ... Pg.14 ... N8
Engelwood ... Pg.16 ... M13
Enterprise Dr. ... Pg.13 ... P5
Erins Glen Dr. ... Pg.13 ... M3
Erwin ... Pg.15 ... N13
Essington Rd. ... Pg.13 ... L3
Executive Dr. ... Pg.13 ... L6
Fairbanks St. ... Pg.15 ... M10
Fairchild Ave. ... Pg.15 ... N9
Fairfield Ave. ... Pg.15 ... P13
Fairlane Dr. ... Pg.14 ... N6
Fairmont Ave. ... Pg.15 ... M13
Fairview Ave. ... Pg.14 ... M13
Fairway Ln. ... Pg.14 ... P7
Fallon Ln. ... Pg.13 ... Q6
Faragut Pl. ... Pg.15 ... N10
Farrell Rd. ... Pg.16 ... N15
Fawn Ct. ... Pg.13 ... P5
Ferris Pl. ... Pg.14 ... M9
Festival Ct. ... Pg.8 ... J8
Fetz Ave. ... Pg.15 ... N11
Finch Dr. ... Pg.16 ... N6
Fiesta Dr. ... Pg.16 ... N6
Finn Ct. ... Pg.7 ... R12
Fisk Ave. ... Pg.15 ... P13
Fitzpatrick Ct. ... Pg.7 ... L4
Flanders Ct. ... Pg.7 ... L3
Floralwood Ct. ... Pg.13 ... M3
Florence Ave. ... Pg.15 ... Q12
Flowermeadow Dr.
Flowermeadow St.

Forest St. ... Pg.13 ... Q12
Forest Grove Dr. ... Pg.7 ... L3
Forestview Dr. ... Pg.13 ... M5
Fort St. ... Pg.15 ... N14
Foster Ct. ... Pg.7 ... L4
Fouser Ct. ... Pg.15 ... P12
Foxfield Dr. ... Pg.7 ... L4
Foxwood Ct. ... Pg.7 ... L3
Francine Ave. ... Pg.14 ... P8
Francis St. ... Pg.15 ... N12
Frank Ave. ... Pg.15 ... M11
Frank St. ... Pg.15 ... N12
Frank Turk Dr. ... Pg.7 ... L2
Franklin St. ... Pg.15 ... N12
Frederick St. ... Pg.15 ... M10
Fuller ... Pg.15 ... N11
Fuller St. ... Pg.15 ... Q13
Gaensel Ln. ... Pg.7 ... L4
Gage Ct. ... Pg.15 ... N11
Gage St. ... Pg.15 ... N11
Galway Rd. ... Pg.13 ... M4,5
Gardner St. ... Pg.15 ... P13
Garfield ... Pg.15 ... N13
Garnsey Ave. ... Pg.15 ... M13
Garvin St. ... Pg.15 ... P13
Gaylord Rd. ... Pg.13 ... J6
Gebhard St. ... Pg.15 ... N13
Georgia ... Pg.15 ... N10
Gibson Ct. ... Pg.7 ... L3
Glasgow St. ... Pg.13 ... K7
Glen St. ... Pg.15 ... M13
Glencourte Ct. ... Pg.7 ... L3
Glenn Ave. ... Pg.15 ... N12
Glenlow Dr. ... Pg.7 ... L3
Glenwood Ave. ... Pg.13 ... N6,8
Glenwood Green Dr.
Godfrey Dr. ... Pg.15 ... P12
Golf Ave. ... Pg.15 ... M17
Golfview Dr. ... Pg.13 ... N13
Goodhue Ln. ... Pg.13 ... L3
Gordon St. ... Pg.13 ... M6
Gore St. ... Pg.15 ... L4
Gougar Rd. ... Pg.16 ... N16
Gould St. ... Pg.7 ... M3
Grace St. ... Pg.7 ... J6
Grand Blvd. ... Pg.15 ... P10
Grand Highland Dr.
Grand Prairie Dr. ... Pg.7 ... K6
Granite ... Pg.15 ... N11
Grant Ave. ... Pg.15 ... N17

Graystone Dr. ... Pg.7 ... L6
Greeley Dr. ... Pg.16 ... M16
Green St. ... Pg.13 ... M3
Green Trails ... Pg.13 ... M3
Greenlawn St. ... Pg.15 ... Q11
Greenleaf Dr. ... Pg.13 ... Q6
Gregoire ... Pg.13 ... Q11
Griffin ... Pg.15 ... M12
Grinton ... Pg.15 ... L3
Hacker Ave. ... Pg.15 ... M12
Hager Ct. ... Pg.7 ... L3
Hague Ct. ... Pg.15 ... N13
Hague Pl. ... Pg.15 ... N13
Haldeman Ave. ... Pg.15 ... P10
Hall Ct. ... Pg.15 ... M5
Hammes Ave. ... Pg.14 ... P8
Hampton Ct. ... Pg.12 ... K8
Hannibal Ct. ... Pg.12 ... L4
Harbor Dr. ... Pg.7 ... K6
Harris Dr. ... Pg.7 ... L2
Harrison Ave. ... Pg.15 ... M12
Harrogate Ln. ... Pg.14 ... M8
Harvest Ln. ... Pg.7 ... L4
Harwood St. ... Pg.16 ... N14
Hebbend St. ... Pg.15 ... N13
Hebberd Ave. ... Pg.16 ... P15
Hedge Row Ct. ... Pg.7 ... L3
Helen Ave. ... Pg.15 ... P8
Henderson Ave. ... Pg.15 ... N12
Hennepin Dr. ... Pg.7 ... K4
Hennessy Pl. ... Pg.13 ... N6
Henry St. ... Pg.15 ... P12
Heritage Lake Dr. ... Pg.8 ... J7
Heritage Park ... Pg.8 ... J7
Herkimer St. ... Pg.15 ... Q12
Herman Ln. ... Pg.15 ... Q13
Hickory Creek Dr. ... Pg.16 ... N16
Hickory St. ... Pg.15 ... N13
Highland Circle Dr.
Highland Woods Ct. ... Pg.13 ... N14
Higley Pl. ... Pg.15 ... P13
Hills Ave. ... Pg.15 ... M12
Hillsdale Rd. ... Pg.15 ... P13
Hobbs Dr. ... Pg.15 ... N16
Hollow Glen Ct. ... Pg.13 ... M5
Hollow Glen Dr. ... Pg.13 ... M5
Holly Ct. ... Pg.7 ... L4
Hollyberry Ct. ... Pg.14 ... N8
Holm Ave. ... Pg.16 ... N14
Holmes ... Pg.15 ... N11
Homestead Pl. ... Pg.15 ... N11
Honeywood Ct. ... Pg.7 ... L4
Horseshoe Dr. ... Pg.15 ... N10
Hosmer St. ... Pg.15 ... M10
Houbolt Rd. ... Pg.13 ... R6
Hutchins St. ... Pg.15 ... M13
Hyacinth Ct. ... Pg.13 ... L4
Hyde Park ... Pg.11 ... P11
Ida St. ... Pg.15 ... Q6
Illinois St. ... Pg.7 ... P,Q10
Indian Wood Ln. ... Pg.13 ... M6
Industry Ave. ... Pg.15 ... N11
Ingalls Ave. ... Pg.14 ... M8,11
Interstate 55 ... Pg.7 ... L3
Interstate 80 ... Pg.13 ... Q9
Inverness Dr. ... Pg.7 ... L4
Inwood St. ... Pg.14 ... N7
Iowa Ave. ... Pg.15 ... P12
Irene ... Pg.15 ... N9
Iroquois St. ... Pg.15 ... R12
Irvine Ln. ... Pg.7 ... L2
Irving St. ... Pg.15 ... N11,12
Ivy Pl. ... Pg.7 ... K4
Ivywild Ln. ... Pg.15 ... M13
Jackson St. ... Pg.15 ... N12,13
Jane Ct. ... Pg.13 ... M5
Jasper Pl. ... Pg.15 ... M5
Jasper St. ... Pg.15 ... Q10,11
Jefferson St. ... Pg.13 ... P7-10
Jeffery Dr. ... Pg.13 ... Q6
Jerald Dr. ... Pg.13 ... N6
Jersey ... Pg.15 ... N12
Jodee Dr. ... Pg.14 ... N8
Joe St. ... Pg.15 ... P10
Joliet St. ... Pg.15 ... N11
Jonathan Simpson Dr.

Landau Ave. ... Pg.15 ... N12
Landings Ct. ... Pg.13 ... L5
Landings Rd. ... Pg.13 ... L5
Langsford Dr. ... Pg.7 ... K2
Larkin Ave. ... Pg.15 ... M9
Larkspur Ct. ... Pg.16 ... N14
Laura Dr. ... Pg.13 ... M3
Laura Friss Ct. ... Pg.13 ... M3
Laurel St. ... Pg.15 ... P11
Lauren Dr. ... Pg.13 ... R6
Lavanie Ln. ... Pg.14 ... N8
Lawny Ct. ... Pg.14 ... N8
Lawrence Ave. ... Pg.15 ... M10
Lawton Ave. ... Pg.15 ... Q11
Leach Ln. ... Pg.15 ... N13
Leawood Ct. ... Pg.13 ... R6
Leawood Dr. ... Pg.13 ... R6
Legacy Dr. ... Pg.8 ... J7
Lehman St. ... Pg.15 ... Q12
Lemoor Ave. ... Pg.14 ... N9
Leominster Ave. ... Pg.13 ... M5
Liberty St. ... Pg.15 ... N11,12
Lilac Ln. ... Pg.14 ... N8
Lime St. ... Pg.15 ... N11
Lincoln Hwy. ... Pg.8 ... K7
Lincoln St. ... Pg.15 ... P12
Linden Ave. ... Pg.15 ... P13
Linderwood Cir. ... Pg.13 ... M3
Lindsay St. ... Pg.15 ... M5
Linne Ave. ... Pg.15 ... R12
Lillie Big Horn Dr. ... Pg.16 ... M7
Lloyds Ave. ... Pg.15 ... N13
Lobelia Ct. ... Pg.7 ... K4
Lobelia Ln. ... Pg.13 ... L4
Logan St. ... Pg.15 ... P13
Lois Pl. ... Pg.14 ... N9
Longford Dr. ... Pg.13 ... L3
Loomis Ave. ... Pg.14 ... N9
Loran Dr. ... Pg.15 ... L3
Loretta St. ... Pg.15 ... M10
Louise Ln. ... Pg.13 ... L3
Louise St. ... Pg.7 ... J6
Lucas ... Pg.15 ... Q11
Lucie Dr. ... Pg.13 ... P5
Luis Ct. ... Pg.15 ... N12
Luther Ave. ... Pg.15 ... M13
MacFarlane Dr. ... Pg.14 ... M8
Mack St. ... Pg.15 ... N10
Macomber ... Pg.15 ... Q11
Madeline ... Pg.15 ... P11
Madison St. ... Pg.15 ... N11
Madonna Ave. ... Pg.15 ... P8
Magnolia Ave. ... Pg.15 ... M13
Mail Loop St. ... Pg.7 ... K6
Mailard Ln. ... Pg.15 ... M4
Manhattan Rd. ... Pg.15 ... P13
Manor Ave. ... Pg.7 ... P10
Manor Ct. ... Pg.7 ... P10
Manor Oaks Ct. ... Pg.7 ... L3
Maple Glen Ct. ... Pg.7 ... L3
Maple Glen Dr. ... Pg.7 ... L3
Maple Rd. ... Pg.15 ... N13
Maple St. ... Pg.15 ... Q12
Mappold Way ... Pg.12 ... M8
Marble St. ... Pg.15 ... N11
Margaret St. ... Pg.7 ... L3
Marion St. ... Pg.15 ... P10,11
Mark Ct. ... Pg.7 ... L4
Market St. ... Pg.15 ... Q10
Marmion Ave. ... Pg.7 ... P8
Marquette Ct. ... Pg.14 ... N8
Marquette St. ... Pg.7 ... K4
Mary Ln. ... Pg.7 ... Q9
Maserati Dr. ... Pg.14 ... L7
Mason Ave. ... Pg.13 ... N6,8
Mason Ct. ... Pg.13 ... L3
Massachusetts ... Pg.14 ... M9
Mathewson Ave. ... Pg.15 ... R12
May St. ... Pg.15 ... N11
Mayan Ct. ... Pg.12 ... M8
Mayfield Ave. ... Pg.14 ... N8-9
McDonald Ave. ... Pg.13
McDonough St. ... Pg.14 ... P7,10
McKay St. ... Pg.15 ... L3
McKenna Dr. ... Pg.7 ... L3
McKinley Ave. ... Pg.15 ... N13
McRoberts St. ... Pg.15 ... N12
Meadow Wood Dr. ... Pg.13 ... N6
Meadowbrook Ln. ... Pg.12
Meadowsedge Ln. ... Pg.16
Meath Dr. ... Pg.15 ... L6
Meda Ave. ... Pg.15 ... P12
Meha Ct. ... Pg.7 ... L4
Meksor Ct. ... Pg.15 ... P12
Melchor ... Pg.15 ... P12
Melissa Ct. ... Pg.7 ... L3
Memenas Pl. ... Pg.15 ... P10
Menlo Ct. ... Pg.13 ... Q6
Menlo St. ... Pg.13 ... Q6
Messinger Ridge Dr. ... Pg.8 ... L7
Metcalf Ct. ... Pg.15 ... L4
Miami St. ... Pg.16 ... N14
Midhurst Ln. ... Pg.14 ... M8
Midland Ave. ... Pg.15 ... N9
Midiand Ct. ... Pg.14 ... N2
Miles Ave. ... Pg.15 ... Q12
Millborn Pl. ... Pg.14 ... N8
Mission Blvd. ... Pg.13 ... L3
Mississippi Ave. ... Pg.15 ... P12
Mohawk St. ... Pg.15 ... N14
Montclair Ct. ... Pg.8 ... J7
Mooney Dr. ... Pg.14 ... N7
Morgan St. ... Pg.15 ... N11
Morgan St. ... Pg.15 ... P10
Morningside Ct. ... Pg.14 ... N14
Morris St. ... Pg.7 ... P9
Mosby Rd. ... Pg.7 ... L3
Mound Rd. ... Pg.15 ... R12
Mount St. ... Pg.15 ... P12
Mulberry Rd. ... Pg.16 ... N15
Mulford Ln. ... Pg.13 ... M8
Munroe Ave. ... Pg.18 ... Q11
N. Lake Ct. ... Pg.7 ... L2
Nancy Vallera Ln. ... Pg.7 ... L2
Natoma Ct. ... Pg.13 ... Q6
Navajo Dr. ... Pg.16 ... N6
Neal Ave. ... Pg.16 ... N16
Neal St. ... Pg.15 ... N13
New Lenox Rd. ... Pg.15 ... Q13
Newberry Ln. ... Pg.7 ... L4
Newell Ave. ... Pg.15 ... M12
Newton Pl. ... Pg.15 ... P12
Nicholas Ct. ... Pg.7 ... L3
Nicholson St. ... Pg.15 ... M,P11
Noel ... Pg.15 ... N11
Norley Ave. ... Pg.14 ... M9,10

**JOLIET (continued)**

Norley Dr. .... Pg.14 .... M8
Norman Ave. .... Pg.7 .... J6
Normandy St. .... Pg.7 .... J7
North Lake Ct. .... Pg.8 .... J7
Northfield Dr. .... Pg.14 .... N7
Northmont Ct. .... Pg.7 .... L4
Northmont Dr. .... Pg.7 .... L4
Norton .... Pg.15 .... P12
Norwood Ln. .... Pg.14 .... M16
Notre Dame Ave. .... Pg.13 .... M5
O'Donohue Dr. .... Pg.13 .... M5
O'Leary Ct. .... Pg.15 .... P13
O'Neil St. .... Pg.15 .... P10
Oak Leaf Ct. .... Pg.14 .... Q8
Oak Leaf St. .... Pg.14 .... Q8
Oak Ridge .... Pg.14 .... L7
Oak St. .... Pg.15 .... N13
Oak Tree Ln. .... Pg.7 .... K5
Oakbrook Dr. .... Pg.13 .... M3
Oakland Ave. .... Pg.15 .... N10
Oakwood Dr. .... Pg.7 .... L6
Oakwood St. .... Pg.15 .... N13
Ohio St. .... Pg.15 .... N12
Old Castle Rd. .... Pg.7 .... L6
Old Kent Dr. .... Pg.14 .... P7
Old Meadow Ct. .... Pg.7 .... L6
Old Oaks Ct. .... Pg.13 .... L3
Old Woods Tr. .... Pg.7 .... K4
Olde Farm Rd. .... Pg.7 .... L4
Olde Mill Rd. .... Pg.7 .... L4
Olive Pl. .... Pg.15 .... N12
Olympic Blvd. .... Pg.13 .... P6,10
Oneida St. .... Pg.13 .... P8,10
Orchard Ln. .... Pg.14 .... M8
Oregon .... Pg.14 .... M9
Oriole Ln. .... Pg.7 .... M4
Oscar Ave. .... Pg.15 .... Q12
Osgood St. .... Pg.15 .... P11
Ottawa St. .... Pg.15 .... N,P11
Outer Loop St. .... Pg.7 .... K5
Overlook Dr. .... Pg.13 .... M5
Page Ave. .... Pg.15 .... P13
Palladium Dr. .... Pg.14 .... M9
Pamela Ct. .... Pg.13 .... L4
Pandola Dr. .... Pg.13 .... M6
Par Four Ln. .... Pg.14 .... P7
Park Dr. .... Pg.15 .... P10
Parker Ave. .... Pg.15 .... N15
Parks Ave. .... Pg.15 .... N12
Parkside Dr. .... Pg.13 .... L5
Parkwood Ct. .... Pg.14 .... N15
Parkwood Dr. .... Pg.14 .... N16
Pawnee St. .... Pg.15 .... R12
Peacock Ln. .... Pg.13 .... M4
Pearl Harbor Dr. .... Pg.14 .... M7
Pearson Dr. .... Pg.14 .... M6
Pembrook Ct. .... Pg.13 .... L4
Pennsylvania .... Pg.14 .... M9
Pequot St. .... Pg.15 .... R12
Pheasant Landing Dr.
Phoenix Ln. .... Pg.14 .... M8
Pilcher Park Dr. .... Pg.16 .... P15
Pine Grove Ct. .... Pg.9 .... N16
Pine Needle Ln. .... Pg.14 .... N16
Pine St. .... Pg.15 .... P11
Pioneer Ct. .... Pg.13 .... Q6
Plainfield Rd. .... Pg.13 .... M10
Plaza Dr. .... Pg.14 .... N9
Pleasant St. .... Pg.15 .... N12
Polson Pl. .... Pg.15 .... N12
Pond Ct. .... Pg.7 .... L4
Ponderosa Pl. .... Pg.13 .... N6
Poplar Glen Ct. .... Pg.7 .... L3
Poplar St. .... Pg.15 .... M10
Prairie Ave. .... Pg.15 .... M10
Prairie St. .... Pg.15 .... N10
Prairie Trail Ct. .... Pg.13 .... M3
Pratt Ct. .... Pg.14 .... N8
Prestige St. .... Pg.13 .... N6
Preston Pl. .... Pg.15 .... P13
Prestwick Cir. .... Pg.7 .... L3
Priaire Path Ln. .... Pg.13 .... J7
Price Ct. .... Pg.13 .... Q6
Prieboy Ave. .... Pg.7 .... J6
Primrose Ct. .... Pg.14 .... N8
Prior St. .... Pg.15 .... P11
Prospect Pl. .... Pg.15 .... Q10
Purdue Ct. .... Pg.14 .... P8
Putter Ct. .... Pg.13 .... M4
Quail Dr. .... Pg.13 .... M4
Quincy Ct. .... Pg.13 .... Q6
Quinn Dr. .... Pg.14 .... N15
Raccoon Rd. .... Pg.15 .... N15
Race Ct. .... Pg.13 .... L4
Racshall St. .... Pg.15 .... P11,Q10
Randall Ct. .... Pg.15 .... Q12
Randy Rd. .... Pg.13 .... P6
Raub St. .... Pg.14 .... M8
Ravinia Dr. .... Pg.14 .... M9
Raymor Ave. .... Pg.15 .... M,P10
Reardon Dr. .... Pg.14 .... N7
Rebecca Rd. .... Pg.14 .... P7
Reed St. .... Pg.14 .... N,P10
Reedwood Dr. .... Pg.7 .... L6
Reeves Rd. .... Pg.14 .... N7
Regency Ridge .... Pg.14 .... Q9
Reichman .... Pg.13 .... L5
Reid .... Pg.14 .... M12
Republic Ave. .... Pg.14 .... P8
Richards St. .... Pg.15 .... P,Q12
Richmond St. .... Pg.14 .... P7,9,10
Rick Ct. .... Pg.13 .... M6
Ridge Ct. .... Pg.13 .... N6
Ridgefield Ct. .... Pg.8 .... J7
Ridgewood .... Pg.15 .... N13
River Bend Ln. .... Pg.7 .... K3
River Glen Dr. .... Pg.13 .... M3
River St. .... Pg.15 .... Q11
Riverboat Center Blvd. .... Pg.13
Riverboat Center Dr.
.... Pg.13 .... R6
Riverside Dr. .... Pg.7 .... L3
Rivertowne Ct. .... Pg.13 .... L5
Rivertowne Dr. .... Pg.13 .... L5
Riverview Dr. .... Pg.13 .... M5
Riverwalk Dr. .... Pg.13 .... M5
Riviera Blvd. .... Pg.13 .... M5
Robert Ct. .... Pg.14 .... N8
Robin Ln. .... Pg.15 .... M13
Rock Creek Blvd. .... Pg.13 .... R6
Rock Run Dr. .... Pg.13 .... L3
Rogina Dr. .... Pg.13 .... L3
Rollingwood Ln. .... Pg.13 .... N6
Romayne Ave. .... Pg.14 .... P8
Ronald Dr. .... Pg.14 .... M7

Ronnie Ct. .... Pg.15 .... N10
Roosevelt Ave. .... Pg.14 .... M9
Rosemont Dr. .... Pg.13 .... N6
Rosewood Dr. .... Pg.13 .... N6,P7
Ross St. .... Pg.15 .... N10
Rossiter Ct. .... Pg.7 .... L4
Rossiter Pkwy. .... Pg.7 .... L4
Rowell Ave. .... Pg.15 .... P,R12
Royal Oak Ct. .... Pg.16 .... N14
Royce Ave. .... Pg.15 .... N12
Russell St. .... Pg.15 .... M10
Ryehill Ct. .... Pg.13 .... M4
Ryehill Dr. .... Pg.13 .... M4
Saenz Ln. .... Pg.14 .... P7
Salem Dr. .... Pg.15 .... P10
Sandy Dr. .... Pg.16 .... N14
Schribner St. .... Pg.14 .... N9
Scott St. .... Pg.15 .... N11
Seeser St. .... Pg.15 .... P13
September Ct. .... Pg.7 .... L6
Sergeant Ln. .... Pg.13 .... L4
Shannon Ct. .... Pg.7 .... K6
Sharen Ct. .... Pg.13 .... M6
Shawnita .... Pg.16 .... N14
Sheridan .... Pg.15 .... Q11
Sherman Ct. .... Pg.15 .... Q12
Sherman St. .... Pg.15 .... P12
Sherwood Pl. .... Pg.14 .... N9,10
Shiloh Ct. .... Pg.13 .... Q6
Siegmund St. .... Pg.16 .... P14
Sierra Highlands Dr. .... Pg.13 .... L3
Sierra Highlands Dr. .... Pg.13 .... L3
Skylark Ln. .... Pg.13 .... M4
Slalom St. .... Pg.15 .... M11
Snomass Ct. .... Pg.7 .... K3
Somerset St. .... Pg.13 .... M17
Somme Ct. .... Pg.8 .... L7
Somme St. .... Pg.8 .... L7
Sonny Ln. .... Pg.15 .... Q10
South St. .... Pg.15 .... Q10,11
Southwest Hwy. .... Pg.16 .... M17
Spring St. .... Pg.15 .... N11
Springfield Ave. .... Pg.14 .... N8
Springwood Dr. .... Pg.13 .... Q6
Spruce Slip .... Pg.15 .... P11
Squires Mill Ct. .... Pg.13 .... L5
Squires Mill Rd. .... Pg.13 .... L5
Squirrel St. .... Pg.15 .... N13
St. Andrews Dr. .... Pg.7 .... L4
St. Francis .... Pg.14 .... P8
St. Joseph Ave. .... Pg.14 .... P8
St. Judes Ave. .... Pg.14 .... P8
St. Louis St. .... Pg.15 .... P11
Stacia Ct. .... Pg.7 .... K6
Stadium Dr. .... Pg.14 .... P7
Star Ln. .... Pg.14 .... P7
State St. .... Pg.15 .... N12
Steamboat Cir. .... Pg.13 .... R6
Stein Ave. .... Pg.15 .... N13
Stephen Smith St. .... Pg.13 .... M5
Sterling Ave. .... Pg.15 .... N13
Stevens St. .... Pg.15 .... N15
Stone St. .... Pg.15 .... N11
Stonegate Ct. .... Pg.14 .... N8
Stonehaven Dr. .... Pg.13 .... L3
Stonehurst Ct. .... Pg.13 .... Q6
Stonybrook Dr. .... Pg.7 .... K3
Stowe Ct. .... Pg.7 .... K3
Stratford Ct. .... Pg.14 .... N9
Streitz Dr. .... Pg.14 .... N7
Strong Ave. .... Pg.15 .... Q12
Stryker St. .... Pg.14 .... P8
Sudbury Dr. .... Pg.14 .... N8
Sugarloaf Ct. .... Pg.7 .... K3
Summerfield Ct. .... Pg.13 .... M3
Summit St. .... Pg.15 .... N11
Sun Valley Ct. .... Pg.7 .... K3
Sun Valley Dr. .... Pg.7 .... K3
Summeadow Dr. .... Pg.7 .... M3
Sunrise Ct. .... Pg.8 .... J7
Sunset Ct. .... Pg.8 .... J7
Sunset Ridge Dr. .... Pg.13 .... L3
Surrey Ct. .... Pg.14 .... P7
Surry St. .... Pg.15 .... Q6
Susan St. .... Pg.15 .... M6
Sutton Ct. .... Pg.14 .... N8
Swede Ave. .... Pg.15 .... R12
Swing Ct. .... Pg.13 .... M4
T. Hickey Ave. .... Pg.14 .... L6
Tamarack Dr. .... Pg.16 .... N15
Tana Ln. .... Pg.14 .... N7
Tanager Ct. .... Pg.14 .... N8
Taney .... Pg.15 .... Q10
Tara Ct. .... Pg.13 .... M5
Taylor St. .... Pg.7 .... N8-10
Telluride Ct. .... Pg.7 .... K3
Terrace Ave. .... Pg.7 .... P9
Terrence Ferry Dr. .... Pg.13 .... M5
Terry Dr. .... Pg.14 .... M9
Texas .... Pg.14 .... M9
Thayer Ave. .... Pg.15 .... N13
Theodore St. .... Pg.13 .... M3-4
Timber Oaks Dr. .... Pg.13 .... N6
Timber Oaks St. .... Pg.13 .... N6
Timberline Ct. .... Pg.13 .... N,P6
Timberline Dr. .... Pg.13 .... M6
Tina Cir. .... Pg.13 .... N17
Tonti Ln. .... Pg.7 .... K6
Torwood Ct. .... Pg.7 .... L2
Towhee Ct. .... Pg.14 .... M8
Trails End Ln. .... Pg.13 .... Q6
Traymore Dr. .... Pg.13 .... M6
Troy Rd. .... Pg.13 .... P5
Twain Ct. .... Pg.7 .... L4
Twin Lakes Dr. .... Pg.7 .... L3
Twin Oaks Dr. .... Pg.13 .... L3
Tzoumar Ln. .... Pg.14 .... P9
Union St. .... Pg.15 .... P12
Uno Circle .... Pg.14 .... P8
Vail Ct. .... Pg.15 .... M17
Valley Ave. .... Pg.15 .... N12
Valley Forge Dr. .... Pg.8 .... L7
Van Horn Ct. .... Pg.14 .... L5
VanBuren St. .... Pg.15 .... N11
Venson Ln. .... Pg.14 .... M8
Vera Ct. .... Pg.14 .... Q8
Verdun Dr. .... Pg.8 .... L7
Vermette Ct. .... Pg.7 .... L4
Vernon Ave. .... Pg.14 .... N8
Victoria Dr. .... Pg.13 .... L4
Victoria Lakes Ct. .... Pg.13 .... L3
Victoria Lakes Dr. .... Pg.13 .... L3
Vintage Dr. .... Pg.15 .... N11
Violetta .... Pg.14 .... N14
Virginia St. .... Pg.15 .... N12

Virmy Ridge Dr. .... Pg.8 .... L7
Vista Ln. .... Pg.15 .... N11
Voyager Ln. .... Pg.8 .... K7
Wabash Ave. .... Pg.15 .... M12
Wagner .... Pg.14 .... M9
Wake Island Dr. .... Pg.14 .... M7
Wallace St. .... Pg.14 .... N8
Walnut St. .... Pg.15 .... N13
Walsh Ave. .... Pg.14 .... N8
Walsh Way .... Pg.14 .... N8
Ward Ave. .... Pg.15 .... N12
Warren Doris Ln. .... Pg.14 .... M8
Washington St. .... Pg.15 .... P11,13
Water St. .... Pg.15 .... Q11
Waterford Dr. .... Pg.13 .... L6
Wattles Ct. .... Pg.7 .... L4
Waverly St. .... Pg.15 .... N14
Webster St. .... Pg.14 .... P8
Webster St. .... Pg.15 .... N11
Wee Ct. .... Pg.15 .... P13
Welsch Rd. .... Pg.7 .... K6
Wenberg .... Pg.15 .... P13
Wesmere Dr. .... Pg.13 .... L3
Wesmere Lake Dr.
Wesmere Pkwy. .... Pg.7 .... L3
West Park Front .... Pg.15 .... P13
West Ridge .... Pg.13 .... N6
Western Ave. .... Pg.14 .... N9
Westfield Dr. .... Pg.14 .... N8
Westhill Cir. .... Pg.7 .... L4
Westminster Rd. .... Pg.14 .... N9
Westmore Grove Dr.
Westnedge Ln. .... Pg.14 .... N8
Westnedge Rd. .... Pg.14 .... N8
Westport Dr. .... Pg.13 .... L4
Westshire Dr. .... Pg.14 .... N9
Westwood Ave. .... Pg.15 .... P10
Westwood Ln. .... Pg.7 .... L6
Wheeler Ave. .... Pg.15 .... Q10
Whispering Oaks Dr. .... Pg.7 .... L3
Whispering Oaks Dr. .... Pg.7 .... L3
Whispermeadow Ct.
White Ave. .... Pg.13 .... P13
Whitegate Rd. .... Pg.7 .... L6
Whiteside Ct. .... Pg.14 .... N7
Whiteside Dr. .... Pg.14 .... N7
Whitetail Ct. .... Pg.15 .... P13
Whitley Ave. .... Pg.15 .... P5
Whitney St. .... Pg.15 .... N10
Whittier Ave. .... Pg.15 .... N10
Wilcox St. .... Pg.15 .... N,P10
Wild Oak Ct. .... Pg.15 .... N6
Wildflower Ct. .... Pg.13 .... M3
Wildflower Dr. .... Pg.14 .... M3
Wildwood .... Pg.13 .... N6
Wilhelm Dr. .... Pg.13 .... N6
Wilhelm Ct. .... Pg.15 .... Q12
Willard St. .... Pg.14 .... N7
William St. .... Pg.14 .... M,N10
Williamson Ave. .... Pg.15 .... M12,13
Willow Ave. .... Pg.15 .... N11
Willow Lakes Ct. .... Pg.7 .... L3
Willow Lakes Dr. .... Pg.7 .... L3
Willowbend Dr. .... Pg.13 .... M4
Wilshire Blvd. .... Pg.8 .... L7
Wilson St. .... Pg.15 .... P12
Wiltshire Dr. .... Pg.13 .... M17
Winding Lakes Dr.
Windsor Ln. .... Pg.13 .... N6
Winston Ave. .... Pg.15 .... Q12
Winter Ct. .... Pg.13 .... M6
Winthrop Ave. .... Pg.14 .... N9
Wisconsin St. .... Pg.15 .... N11
Woodbridge Rd. .... Pg.14 .... N9
Woodcreek Dr. .... Pg.16 .... N14
Woodcock Ln. .... Pg.13 .... M4
Woodford Dr. .... Pg.14 .... L6
Woodhill Ct. .... Pg.7 .... L6
Woodland Ave. .... Pg.14 .... N9
Woodland Ct. .... Pg.14 .... Q9
Woodland Dr. .... Pg.14 .... N,P9
Woodruff Pl. .... Pg.14 .... M12
Woods Ct. .... Pg.15 .... Q10
Woodside Ct. .... Pg.7 .... M4
Woodside Dr. .... Pg.7 .... M4
Woodstock Ln. .... Pg.7 .... L4
Woodward .... Pg.15 .... M13
Woodworth Ave. .... Pg.15 .... N10
Wyoming Ave. .... Pg.14 .... M8
York Ave. .... Pg.15 .... Q10
Youngs Ave. .... Pg.15 .... P12
1st Ave. .... Pg.14 .... P12
1st St. E. .... Pg.15 .... P13
2nd St. .... Pg.15 .... P13
3rd Ave. .... Pg.15 .... P13
4th Ave. .... Pg.15 .... P13
5th St. .... Pg.15 .... Q12
129th Infantry Dr. .... Pg.14 .... P7

**AIRPORTS**
Joliet Municipal Airport .... Pg.13 .... P5,6
Joliet Park Dist. Airport .... Pg.13 .... P11

**CEMETERIES**
County Farm Cem.
Elmhurst Cem. .... Pg.14 .... Q7
Hills of Rest Cem. .... Pg.13 .... P13
Mt. Moriah Cem. .... Pg.13 .... M10
Mt. Olivet Cemetery
St. Johns Cem. .... Pg.15 .... N10
St. Josephs Cem. .... Pg.14 .... N10
St. Patricks Cem. .... Pg.15 .... N10
Woodlawn Memorial Cem.

**FOREST PRESERVES**
Ecology Preserve & Nature Trail .... Pg.13 .... Q5
Joliet Iron Work Forest Preserve .... Pg.15 .... M11
Rock Run F.P. .... Pg.13 .... P6
Rock Run Greenway

**GOLF COURSES**
Inwood Golf Club
Joliet C.C. .... Pg.13 .... P13
Wedgewood G.C. .... Pg.7 .... K4
Woodruff G.C. .... Pg.16 .... N16

**PARKS**
Athletic Field .... Pg.13 .... Q5
Bluff Plaza Park .... Pg.15 .... P11
Bob Fowler Mem. Soccer Fields
College Park .... Pg.13 .... Q8
Desmond Field .... Pg.15 .... N12
Forest Park .... Pg.15 .... M13
Garnsey Park .... Pg.15 .... M10
Gottschalg Park .... Pg.15 .... P13
Hartman Field .... Pg.15 .... N12
Heggie Field .... Pg.14 .... M12
Jennifer Ann. Vools Park
Legion Park .... Pg.14 .... M8
Longleaf Park .... Pg.13 .... M6
Manningdale Playground
Marquette Gardens .... Pg.14 .... N9
Nowell Park .... Pg.15 .... Q11
Osgood Park .... Pg.15 .... P11
Rivals Park .... Pg.15 .... M11
St. Joseph Park .... Pg.15 .... N14
Stryker Park .... Pg.14 .... P9
Twin Creek Park .... Pg.14 .... M7
West Park .... Pg.15 .... Q10

**SCHOOLS**
Carl Sandburg Sch. .... Pg.14 .... M8
Catholic Sch. Office .... Pg.15 .... N11
College of St. Francis .... Pg.15 .... N10
Culbertson Sch. .... Pg.16 .... P14
Cunningham Sch. .... Pg.15 .... N10
Dirksen Jr. High .... Pg.14 .... P9
Edna Keith Sch. .... Pg.15 .... P12
Eliza Kelly Sch. .... Pg.14 .... P8
Farragut Sch. .... Pg.15 .... P10
Gompers Jr. H.S. .... Pg.16 .... N14
Hufford Jr. H.S. .... Pg.14 .... M9
Hufford Jr. H.S. .... Pg.15 .... P13
Joliet Cath. Academy .... Pg.14 .... M9
Joliet Jr. College Main Campus .... Pg.13 .... R5
Joliet Twp. H.S. Central .... Pg.15 .... P12
Joliet Twp. H.S. West .... Pg.14 .... M8
Lincoln Sch. .... Pg.15 .... N12
Marsh Sch. .... Pg.15 .... P12
Marycrest Sch. .... Pg.14 .... P8
Parks Sch. .... Pg.15 .... N12
Pershing Sch. .... Pg.14 .... P9
St. Joseph Sch. .... Pg.15 .... Q8
St. Jude Sch. .... Pg.14 .... P9
St. Mary Nativity Sch. .... Pg.15 .... N11
St. Marys Assumption Sch.
St. Patricks Sch. .... Pg.15 .... M12
St. Paul Sch. .... Pg.15 .... P10
St. Peters Sch. .... Pg.15 .... P11
St. Raymond Sch. .... Pg.15 .... N10
St. Thaddeus Sch. .... Pg.15 .... N12
Taft Sch. .... Pg.14 .... M9
Thomas Jefferson Sch. .... Pg.14 .... N7
Timber Ridge Middle Sch. .... Pg.7 .... L5
Troy Craughwell Sch. .... Pg.13 .... N6
Troy Heritage Trail Elem. Sch.
UCP-Will Development Ctr. .... Pg.15 .... P10
Washington Sch. .... Pg.15 .... P12
Wesmere Elem. Sch.
Woodland Sch. .... Pg.15 .... P12

**SHOPPING CENTERS**
Caton Crossing Town Square
Jackson Park Plaza .... Pg.9 .... N11
Jefferson Mall .... Pg.15 .... P7
Louis Joliet Mall .... Pg.7 .... K6
Shopping Center .... Pg.14 .... M8

**MISCELLANEOUS**
Armory .... Pg.14 .... P7
Blackhawk Business Park
Clark Truck Stop .... Pg.7 .... J6
Crime Lab Illinois State Police .... Pg.15 .... M12
Guardian Angel Home .... Pg.14 .... M9
Harrah's Riverboat Casino .... Pg.15 .... P11
Illinois State Boys Detention Center .... Pg.14 .... Q7
Inwood Rec. Center .... Pg.7 .... P7
Joliet Muni. Stadium .... Pg.15 .... P11
Joliet Pumping Station .... Pg.13 .... N5
Joliet Union Station .... Pg.15 .... P11
Library .... Pg.15 .... P11
Provena St. Joesph Medical Center .... Pg.14 .... N11
Rand Theater .... Pg.15 .... K6
Reformatory .... Pg.14 .... Q7
Rock Run Business Park .... Pg.15 .... R5
Silver Cross Hosp. .... Pg.15 .... N13
State Prison .... Pg.15 .... M12
State Prison Correctional Administration Ctr. .... Pg.15 .... M12
Sunny Acres Sanitarium .... Pg.15 .... Q12
Timber Ridge Business Park .... Pg.15 .... P5

**JOLIET TOWNSHIP**
Pages 14-16
STREETS
Adella Ave. .... Pg.15 .... Q13
Anderson Ave. .... Pg.16 .... P,Q14
Argyle Ave. .... Pg.15 .... P15
Barr .... Pg.14 .... Q14

Dartol Rd. .... Pg.16 .... Q14
Bates Rd. .... Pg.15 .... R12
Belmont Ave. .... Pg.16 .... N14
Berkley Ave. .... Pg.15 .... P15
Beverly St. .... Pg.15 .... P13
Blackhawk St. .... Pg.16 .... N16
Bond Rd. .... Pg.7 .... R12
Brandon Rd. .... Pg.15 .... R10
Briggs St. .... Pg.16 .... Q14
Brookside Dr. .... Pg.15 .... R10
Burger Ave. .... Pg.16 .... N14
Burke Dr. .... Pg.15 .... P14
Caldonia St. .... Pg.16 .... Q14
Carey St. .... Pg.16 .... Q14
Cecelia Ave. .... Pg.16 .... N14
Champlain St. .... Pg.15 .... Q11
Charity .... Pg.16 .... Q14
Cherry Hill Rd. .... Pg.15 .... Q15
Cherry Ln. .... Pg.15 .... R12
Circle Dr., E & W .... Pg.15 .... P14
Clairmont Ave. .... Pg.16 .... P15
Cleveland Ave. .... Pg.16 .... N14
Condo Dr. .... Pg.15 .... Q14
Cornelius Ave. .... Pg.15 .... R11
David Ave. .... Pg.16 .... N16
Davidson St. .... Pg.16 .... Q14
Dennis Ave. .... Pg.16 .... N16
Des Plaines St. .... Pg.15 .... Q11
Diamond "K" Ln. .... Pg.16 .... Q14
Dickens St. .... Pg.16 .... N16
Doris Ave. .... Pg.15 .... Q12
East Port Ave. .... Pg.16 .... Q14
Ellen Ave. .... Pg.15 .... Q13
Ellsworth Ave. .... Pg.15 .... N10
Elm St. .... Pg.16 .... P14
Elms Ave. .... Pg.16 .... N14
Erie St. .... Pg.15 .... P14
Fairfax Ave. .... Pg.15 .... P14
Fairfax Rd. .... Pg.15 .... P14
Fernwood Ave. .... Pg.16 .... N14
Fox St. .... Pg.16 .... N16
Frederick Ave. .... Pg.15 .... R12
Fuller St. .... Pg.16 .... Q14
Garfield Ave. .... Pg.16 .... N14
Geneva St. .... Pg.15 .... Q11
Greenfield Ave. .... Pg.15 .... Q13
Hanover Ave. .... Pg.16 .... N14
Harlow Ave. .... Pg.15 .... Q13
Hartford Pl. .... Pg.16 .... Q14
Helen Ave. .... Pg.15 .... Q13
Herman Ln. .... Pg.15 .... Q13
Highland Pkwy. .... Pg.16 .... N14
Hill St. .... Pg.15 .... Q13
Hillcrest Rd. .... Pg.15 .... Q14
Hunter Rd. .... Pg.16 .... R14
Ignatius St. .... Pg.16 .... N16
Independence Ave. .... Pg.15 .... P14
Interstate 80 .... Pg.15 .... B14
Jacob Ave. .... Pg.15 .... Q13
Jeffery St. .... Pg.16 .... N14
Jessie St. .... Pg.16 .... P,Q14
Joe St. .... Pg.16 .... N14
Joliet St. .... Pg.15 .... Q11
Judge Ct. .... Pg.15 .... Q11
Juliet St. .... Pg.15 .... Q11
Kenmore Ave. .... Pg.15 .... P15
Kerner Dr. .... Pg.16 .... N14
Keuka St. .... Pg.15 .... Q11
Kildare Ave. .... Pg.15 .... Q15
Kinmonth Dr. .... Pg.16 .... N16
Lantern Ln. .... Pg.15 .... R12
Leana Ave. .... Pg.16 .... Q14
Lewis Rd. .... Pg.15 .... R12
Lincoln Hwy. .... Pg.16 .... N14
Logan Ave. .... Pg.15 .... Q13
Lorette Ave. .... Pg.16 .... N14
Lorraine Ave. .... Pg.15 .... R10
Luana Rd. .... Pg.15 .... Q13
Mable Ave. .... Pg.16 .... N14
MacIntosh .... Pg.15 .... Q13
Maple Crest Ave. .... Pg.16 .... N14
Marcella Ave. .... Pg.15 .... Q13
Marigold Ct. .... Pg.16 .... N14
Marigold St. .... Pg.16 .... N14
Maude Ave. .... Pg.15 .... R10
Maude Ave. .... Pg.16 .... N14
Melrose St. .... Pg.16 .... P15
Middletree Rd. .... Pg.16 .... N14
Milan .... Pg.15 .... Q13
Mills Rd. .... Pg.16 .... N16
Moore Ln. .... Pg.15 .... Q11
Nannan Ln. .... Pg.16 .... Q14
New Lenox Rd. .... Pg.16 .... R8
Newton Ave. .... Pg.15 .... Q13
Nowell Ave. .... Pg.15 .... Q13
Oakview Ave. .... Pg.15 .... Q13
Old Elm Rd. .... Pg.15 .... Q11
Oliver Pl. .... Pg.16 .... N14
Osage St. .... Pg.16 .... N14
Ottawa St. .... Pg.15 .... Q11
Overton Dr. .... Pg.16 .... N16
Patterson Rd. .... Pg.15 .... Q11,R10
Peale St. .... Pg.16 .... Q14
Penfield Ave. .... Pg.15 .... Q13
Pico Ct. .... Pg.15 .... Q11
Pico Dr. .... Pg.15 .... Q11
Pine Ridge Dr. .... Pg.15 .... R12
Pontiac St. .... Pg.15 .... Q11
Quarry St. .... Pg.15 .... Q11,12
Ray St. .... Pg.16 .... Q14
Raymay Dr. .... Pg.16 .... N14
Retta Ct. .... Pg.15 .... Q12
Richard St. .... Pg.15 .... R12
Ricky Dr. .... Pg.16 .... N14
Robert St. .... Pg.15 .... R10
Rosalie St. .... Pg.16 .... N14
Rosebud Dr. .... Pg.15 .... R12
Roy Ave. .... Pg.15 .... R12
Sandell Pl. .... Pg.16 .... Q14
Schorie Ave. .... Pg.16 .... P14
Schuster St. .... Pg.16 .... Q14
Seneca St. .... Pg.15 .... Q11
Sherring St. .... Pg.15 .... Q13
Snake Hill Rd. .... Pg.16 .... N14
Spencer Ave. .... Pg.15 .... R12
Spencer Rd. .... Pg.15 .... R14
Spring Green Dr. .... Pg.15 .... R12
Starr .... Pg.15 .... Q11
Sugar Creek Ct. .... Pg.15 .... R12
Sugar Creek Rd. .... Pg.15 .... R12
Sugar Ford Way .... Pg.15 .... R12
Superior St. .... Pg.15 .... Q11
Tulare .... Pg.15 .... Q11
Valley View Pl. .... Pg.16 .... M14

Walden Rd. .... Pg.15 .... Q11
Washington St. .... Pg.16 .... P15
White Ave. .... Pg.15 .... P13
Wildwood Ln. .... Pg.15 .... R12
Winfred St. .... Pg.15 .... R10
Wisconsin Ave. .... Pg.15 .... R10
Woodlawn Ave. .... Pg.15 .... N14
Woodruff Ave. .... Pg.15 .... R12
Zarley Blvd. .... Pg.15 .... Q11
Zurich Rd. .... Pg.15 .... P14
2nd Ave. .... Pg.16 .... P14
3rd Ave. .... Pg.16 .... P14
4th Ave. .... Pg.15 .... P14
5th Ave. .... Pg.16 .... P14

**CEMETERIES**
Mound Cemetery Pg.16 .... P15

**FOREST PRESERVES**
Lower Spring Creek Pres.
Sugar Creek F.P. .... Pg.16 .... R14,15

**PARKS**
Barr Park .... Pg.14 .... Q14
Champlain Park .... Pg.15 .... R11
Highland Park .... Pg.15 .... R11
Oak Valley Pk. .... Pg.15 .... R12

**SCHOOLS**
Eisenhower Academy .... Pg.16 .... Q14
Marinatha Christian Sch. .... Pg.15 .... Q13
Ridgewood Baptist Academy Sch.
Union Sch. .... Pg.16 .... P14

**LEMONT**
Pages 4,5
STREETS
Abbey Oaks Dr. .... C18
Acorn St. .... D16
Alpine Ln. .... D17
Amber Dr. .... D18
Andrews Ct. .... D17
Arbor Ct. .... D16
Arbor Dr. .... D16
Archer Ave. .... D17
Ashbury Dr. .... C17
Asheford Dr. .... D18
Aspen Ct. .... D17
Auburn Ct. .... C17
Auburn Rd. .... D18
Bailey's Crossing Dr. .... C18
Bennington Ct. .... D17
Berkley Ln. .... D17
Blacksmith Ln. .... B18
Blue Grass Dr. .... D15
Bluff Rd. .... B14
Brady St. .... B17
Bridge Rd. .... C16
Bristol Rd. .... C17
Brown's Ct. .... C16
Camelot Ln. .... C18
Canal .... B16
Canal Bank Rd. .... B17
Carriage Ridge Ln. .... B18
Cascadia Ct. .... B14
Cass St. .... C16
Castlewood Ct. .... D18
Castlewood Dr. .... D18
Catherine St. .... B17
Cedar Ct. .... C16
Chatham Dr. .... C17
Chelsea Ct. .... C17
Chelsea Dr. .... C17
Cherokee Pl. .... D16
Chestnut .... C16
Chestnut Crossing .... D17
Chestnut Crossing Dr. .... D17
Chieftan Ct. .... C18
Church St. .... B17
Coach Ln. .... B18
Connacht St. .... D16
Country Ct. .... C17
Country Ln. .... C18
Covington Ct. .... C17
Covington Dr. .... C17
Crestview Dr. .... C17
Crestwood Ln. .... C18
Custer St. .... C16
Czacky St. .... C16
Davey Rd. .... A14
Deborah Dr. .... C16
Deer Ln. .... E16
Derby Rd. .... C17
Division St. .... C16
Doolin St. .... C16
Dover Rd. .... C17
Drawbridge Ln. .... D18
Dunham Ln. .... C17
Eagle Crest .... C18
East St. .... C17
Edgewood Ct. .... D16
Emerald Dr. .... D16
Emil St. .... C17
Erin Dr. .... C16
Eureka Ave. .... C18
Eureka Dr. .... C18
Evergreen Pl. .... C16
Fairway Dr. .... D15
Falcon Ct. .... D18
Firebom Ct. .... D17
Florence Ave. .... C18
Forest Ln. .... D17
Fransiscan Dr. .... C18
Freehauf St. .... C16
Freemont St. .... B17
Gillian St. .... C17
Glenview Ln. .... C17
Glenys Dr. .... C17
Grant St. .... C17
Greenway Dr. .... D15
Grove St. .... C17
Harasek St. .... C18
Harper Ln. .... C18
Harvest Dr. .... D15
Hermes Ave. .... C18
Hickory St. .... C16
Hilltop Ct. .... D17
Hilltop Dr. .... D17
Hilview Dr. .... D17
Hilview Dr. .... C17
Holmes St. .... C18
Houston St. .... C18
Illinois St. .... C17
Industrial Dr. .... B16
Industrial Park Dr. .... C17

Jacqueline Ct. .... D16
Janas Ln. .... D18
Jane Ave. .... D18
Jane Ct. .... D18
John St. .... C16
Joliet St. .... C16
Julia St. .... B17
Katlin Rd. .... B18
Keepataw Dr. .... C17
Keepataw Ct. .... C17
Keepataw Dr. .... C,D17
Keepotaw Ln. .... C17
Keough St. .... C16
Kettering Ln. .... C16
Kern Rd. .... D17
Kimball St. .... C16
Kip Pl. .... D17
Kromray Dr. .... B17
Kromray Rd. .... C18
Kruk St. .... C17
Lahinch Dr. .... D18
Lawrence .... C16
Ledochowski St. .... C16
Lemont St. .... C16
Lenox Ct. .... C17
Lenox St. .... C17
Lexington Dr. .... C18
Lincoln St. .... C16
Lindsay Ct. .... C17
Lisle Ave. .... C16
Lithuanian Dr. .... D17
Loblolly Ct. .... D19
Lockport St. .... C16
Logan St. .... C16
Long Cove Dr. .... C18
Losey Ct. .... C16
Luna Ave. .... D17
Luxemburg Ave. .... B17
Main St. .... B17
Margaret St. .... C17
Maria St. .... C17
Mariam Dr. .... C18
Mayfair Ct. .... B17
McCarthy St. .... C18
Meagan Ln. .... C16
Mirta Cir. .... C16
Misko Ct. .... B17
Moczygemba .... D17
Munster Rd. .... D16
New Ave. .... C15
Norton Ave. .... C16
Norwalk Ct. .... C17
Norwalk Rd. .... C17
Notre Dame Ln. .... C17
Oak Ct. .... C16
Oak Ln. .... C16
Old Quarry Rd. .... C16
Orchard Tr. .... D17
Overton Ct. .... D17
Overton Dr. .... D17
Palisades Rd. .... B16
Park Pl. .... D15
Pasture Dr. .... D15
Peiffer St. .... C17
Pendelton Dr. .... C17
Pete Dye Dr. .... D18
Pine Needles Dr. .... D18
Pleasant Pl. .... C18
Porter St. .... C17
Poxhook Ct. .... C16
Pruyne St. .... B17
Przewloki St. .... C17
Pulawski St. .... C17
Quarry St. .... C16
River St. .... B16
Roberts St. .... D15
Rolling Meadow Dr. .... D15
Rose Ct. .... C16
Rosehill Dr. .... C18
Route 171 .... C19
Ruffled Feathers Dr. .... D18
Saddle Ln. .... B17
Sag-Lemont Hwy. .... A20
Salem Dr. .... C17
Sara Ave. .... D17
Sawgrass Dr. .... C18
Schultz St. .... C17
Senon Dr. .... B17
Short St. .... C16
Singer Ave. .... C18
Sobieski St. .... C17
Spruce Ct. .... C16
Spyglass Ct. .... C19
St. Anne Ct. .... B19
St. Anthony Ct. .... B19
St. Bonaventure Ct. .... C18
St. Brendan's Ct. .... C18
St. Clare .... B19
St. Colette Ct. .... B19
St. Joesph Ct. .... C18
St. Vincent's Dr. .... C18
Ste. St. .... B-D16
Stephen St. .... C16
Steven Ct. .... C18
Stirrup Ct. .... B17
Sunrise Dr. .... C17
Talcott .... B16
Tim Cronin Ct. .... C18
Timberline Dr. .... C,D16
Timberline Pl. .... C18
Tomaszewski St. .... C17
Turnberry Tr. .... C17
Valley Dr. .... B18
Village Dr. .... B18
Walnut Ct. .... C16
Walnut St. .... C16
Walter Ave. .... C16
Warner Ave. .... C16
Warner Cir. .... C16
Wend St. .... C16
Wexford Ct. .... C17
Wheeler Ct. .... C17
Wheeler Dr. .... B17
Wild Oak St. .... C18
Wild Plum Ct. .... C18
Woburn Dr. .... C17
Woodcrest Ct. .... C18
Woodcrest Ln. .... B,C18
Young St. .... C17
1st St. .... C17
2nd St. .... C17
3rd St. .... C17
4th St. .... C17
5th St. .... C17
6th St. .... C17

## LEMONT

119th St. ... C18
127th St. ... D17
128th St. ... D17
129th St. ... D17
130th St. ... D18
131st St. ... D18

**CEMETERIES**
Alphonsus Cemetery ... C16
Bethany Cemetery ... C17
Danish Cemetery ... D16
St. Cyril's Methodius Cemetery C17
St. Matthews Cemetery ... D16

**GOLF COURSES**
Ruffled Feathers G.C. ... C19

**PARKS**
Brown Park ... C16
Centennial Rec. Area & Park . D16
Derby Park ... C18
Hilltop Park ... C17
Jaycee Park ... D17
Northview Park ... C18
Public Park ... C17
The Bowl Park ... C17
Timberline Park ... C16
Virginia Reed Park ... C16
Witkoski Rec. Ctr. & Park .. D16

**SCHOOLS**
Central H.S. ... C17
Lemont Township H.S. ... B17
Montessori Elem. Sch.
  Southwest ... D17
Oakwood Sch. ... D17
Old Quarry Middle Sch. ... D16
School Dist. 133 Offices ... D16
St. Alphonsus Sch. ... C16
St. Cyrils Sch. ... C17
St. Matthews Sch. ... C16
St. Patricks Sch. ... C16

**MISCELLANEOUS**
Lemont Township Offices .... D16
Library ... B17
Lithuanian World Ctr. ... D17
Mother Theresa Home ... B18
Our Lady of Victory Convent .. B18
Police Department ... B17
R.R. Station ... B16
Uno-Cal Oil Refinery ... B16
Village Hall ... B17

## LEMONT TOWNSHIP
Pages 4-6
**STREETS**
Angelico ... Pg.5 ... D17
Apple Ave. ... Pg.5 ... C18
Archer Ave. ... Pg.5 ... D18
Arctic Ct. ... Pg.5 ... E20
Arctic Ln. ... Pg.5 ... E20
Artesian Dr. ... Pg.5 ... B20
Baltic Cir. ... Pg.5 ... E19
Bell Oak Ln. ... Pg.6 ... C20
Bell Rd. ... Pg.6 ... C20
Birch Ct. ... Pg.5 ... E18
Black Fox Ln. ... Pg.4 ... E19
Bond Dr. ... Pg.4 ... D15
Boyer Rd. ... Pg.5 ... B18
Briar Patch Ln. ... Pg.5 ... B21
Bridle Path ... Pg.5 ... B21
Brookside Dr. ... Pg.6 ... B21
Buckskin Ct. ... Pg.6 ... B21
Campbell St. ... Pg.6 ... B20
Canal Bank Rd. ... Pg.5 ... B21
Carriage Ln. ... Pg.6 ... C21
Cedar Rd. ... Pg.5 ... E,F18
Center Dr. ... Pg.5 ... C18
Chestnut ... Pg.6 ... C20
Clear View ... Pg.5 ... E18
DaVinci ... Pg.5 ... D18
Derby Rd. ... Pg.5 ... C18
Des Plaines River Rd. ... Pg.4 ... B15
Dineff Rd. ... Pg.5 ... A15
Dixon Ct. ... Pg.5 ... E19
Dixon Way Dr. ... Pg.5 ... A15
Donohue Rd. ... Pg.4 ... B16
Dowdell Dr. ... Pg.4 ... D15
El Green ... Pg.5 ... D17
Elm Ct. ... Pg.5 ... E18
Emerald Dr. ... Pg.4 ... D16
Emily Ln. ... Pg.4 ... E16
Equestrian Way ... Pg.6 ... C21
Fairway Dr ... Pg.4 ... E15
Fk. Linkus Dr. (Pvt.) ... Pg.6 ... C21
Forest Ln. ... Pg.6 ... B21
Fox Hill Ct. ... Pg.5 ... E20
Fox Hill Dr. ... Pg.5 ... E20
Fox Hollow Ct. ... Pg.5 ... E18
Fox Ln. ... Pg.5 ... E20
Fox Tail ... Pg.5 ... E20
Foxburrow Ln. ... Pg.5 ... E20
Galway Ct. ... Pg.6 ... D20
Galway Ln. ... Pg.6 ... D20
Galway Rd. ... Pg.6 ... D20
Golden Spur ... Pg.6 ... C21
Gordon Ln. ... Pg.4 ... E16
Gray Ln. ... Pg.5 ... D20
Hawthorne Dr. ... Pg.5 ... E18
Helix Rd. ... Pg.4 ... A16
Hickory Ave. ... Pg.5 ... E18
Hillcrest Dr. ... Pg.5 ... C18
Hillcrest Rd. ... Pg.5 ... B18
Holly Ct. ... Pg.5 ... C19
Holly Ln ... Pg.5 ... C19
Horseshoe Ln. ... Pg.6 ... B21
Hunt Master Ln. ... Pg.6 ... B20
Huntsman Ct. ... Pg.4 ... E17
Katie Rd. ... Pg.4 ... E17
Katlin Rd. ... Pg.5 ... B18
King Rd. ... Pg.5 ... E18
Kit Ln. ... Pg.5 ... D19
Klotz Ave. ... Pg.5 ... C19
Lake View ... Pg.5 ... E18
Lariat Ct. ... Pg.4 ... B21
Leinster Dr. ... Pg.4 ... D16
Lemont St. ... Pg.4 ... E17
Liberty Dr. ... Pg.6 ... E15
Longwood Way ... Pg.4 ... E15
Main St. ... Pg.5 ... B18
Maple St. ... Pg.5 ... E18
Martin Ct. ... Pg.6 ... B21
McCarthy Rd. ... Pg.5,6 ... C19-21
Meadow Hill Ln. ... Pg.5 ... D18
Melissa Dr. ... Pg.4 ... E17
Moorfield Ct. ... Pg.5 ... E20
Munster Dr. ... Pg.4 ... D16

New Rd. ... Pg.4 ... C15
Niagara St. ... Pg.5 ... B18
Nordic Ln. ... Pg.5 ... E20
North Trail ... Pg.6 ... D21
Oak Ave. ... Pg.5 ... C18
Oak Ct. ... Pg.5 ... C18
Oak Ln. ... Pg.4 ... E17
Oakmont Ct. ... Pg.4 ... E15
Oakmont Dr. ... Pg.4 ... E15
Paddock Ct. ... Pg.4 ... B21
Parker Rd. ... Pg.5 ... C19
Paso Fino ... Pg.6 ... B20
Pine Ave. ... Pg.5 ... C18
Prairie Ave. ... Pg.5 ... E18
Prairie Ct. ... Pg.5 ... C18
Raphael ... Pg.5 ... D17
Red Coat Dr. ... Pg.5 ... E19
Red Dr. ... Pg.5 ... E19
Red Fox Ct. ... Pg.5 ... E20
Riva Ridge Ln. ... Pg.6 ... B21
Rusty Rd. ... Pg.4 ... B21
Saddlebrook Ln. ... Pg.6 ... C20
Sag-Lemont Hwy. ... Pg.5 ... A20
Shannon Dr. ... Pg.4 ... D16
Silver Fox Dr. ... Pg.5 ... D20
Silver Spur ... Pg.6 ... B21
Smith Rd. ... Pg.4 ... D15
Smitty Ave. ... Pg.5 ... E21
Sorrel ... Pg.6 ... B21
Split Rail ... Pg.6 ... D18
Spruce Ct. ... Pg.5 ... E18
Slate St. ... Pg.4 ... D,E16
Stone Creek Dr. ... Pg.5 ... B21
Sun Hill Ln. ... Pg.6 ... C20
Surrey Ln. ... Pg.6 ... C18
Sylan Woods Dr. ... Pg.5 ... E18
Timber View ... Pg.6 ... B21
Valley View Ct. ... Pg.4 ... E15
Valley View Dr. ... Pg.4 ... E15
Watkus Dr. ... Pg.6 ... B21
Walker Rd. ... Pg.6 ... B,C18
Walnut St. ... Pg.4 ... E17
Willow Ave. ... Pg.5 ... E18
Woodland Dr. ... Pg.5 ... D18
Woodlawn Ave. ... Pg.6 ... B20
Woodview Ln. ... Pg.5 ... B21
111th St. ... Pg.4 ... A16
113th St. ... Pg.6 ... B21
115th St. ... Pg.6 ... B21
117th Pl. ... Pg.5 ... C18
117th St. ... Pg.5 ... C18
118th St. ... Pg.5 ... C18
119th St. ... Pg.6 ... C18
121st St. ... Pg.5 ... C18
122nd St. ... Pg.6 ... C20
127th St. ... Pg.4 ... D17
129th St. ... Pg.4 ... D17
130th Pl. ... Pg.4 ... E17
131st St. ... Pg.5,6 ... D18-21
132nd Ct. ... Pg.4 ... E18
133rd Ct. ... Pg.4 ... E16
133rd St. ... Pg.5 ... E18
135th St. ... Pg.4 ... E16,18

**CEMETERIES**
Palos Hills Mem. Gardens ... Pg.5 ... C20

**FOREST PRESERVES**
Black Partridge F.P. ... Pg.5 ... B15
Palos F.P. ... Pg.6 ... D21
Rocky Glen F.P. ... Pg.6 ... A20

**GOLF COURSES**
Cog Hill Golf & Country Club ... Pg.5
Glen Eagles G.C. ... Pg.5 ... B19
Mid Iron G.C. ... Pg.6 ... D20
Ruffled Feather G.C. ... Pg.5 ... C19

**SCHOOLS**
Mt. Assisi Academy ... Pg.5 ... B19
St. Mary's Seminary ... Pg.5 ... B18

**MISCELLANEOUS**
Alvernia Manor Retirement Home ... Pg.6 ... B19
Camp Palos (YMCA) ... Pg.6 ... C21
Holy Family Villa ... Pg.6 ... C21
Illinois & Michigan Canal Nat'l Heritage Corr ... Pg.6 ... E21
Lemont Fire Station ... Pg.5
Maletick & Dineff Air Strip ... Pg.4 ... D20
Our Lady of Victory Convent ... Pg.5 ... B18

## LILY CACHE
Page 7...J6

## LOCKPORT
Pages 9,10
**STREETS**
Adams St. ... Pg.10 ... J14
Adobe Dr. ... Pg.10 ... L15
Alpine St. ... Pg.10 ... J14
Ames ... Pg.9 ... J13
Amy Ct. ... Pg.10 ... H15
Apache Dr. ... Pg.10 ... H15
Arbor Tr. ... Pg.10 ... H15
Archer Ave. ... Pg.9 ... J13
Arrowhead Dr. ... Pg.10 ... H15
Ash Ln. ... Pg.10 ... J15
Ashley Ct. ... Pg.10 ... H15
Baneberry Ct. ... Pg.10 ... H15
Banyon Ct. ... Pg.10 ... H15
Basin Dr. ... Pg.10 ... H14
Bent Grass Dr. ... Pg.10 ... L16
Blackfoot Dr. ... Pg.10 ... H15
Blackhawk Dr. ... Pg.10 ... K16
Boehme St. ... Pg.9 ... J13
Broken Arrow Dr. ... Pg.10 ... H15
Bruce Rd. ... Pg.10 ... K16
Buck Path ... Pg.10 ... H15
Buckeye Ct. ... Pg.10 ... H15
Bunratty Dr. ... Pg.10 ... H15
Canal Bank Rd. ... Pg.10 ... K12
Canal St. ... Pg.9 ... J13
Cayuga Ct. ... Pg.10 ... K15
Cayuga St. ... Pg.10 ... K15
Cedar Rd. ... Pg.11 ... H14
Charles St. ... Pg.9 ... K13
Chestnut Cir. ... Pg.10 ... H15

Cheyenne Ct. ... Pg.10 ... K16
Chinook Dr. ... Pg.10 ... K15
Cleveland St. ... Pg.9 ... J14
Clifton St. ... Pg.9 ... J13
Clover Ridge Dr. ... Pg.10 ... H14
Comanche Ct. ... Pg.10 ... K16
Conner Ave. ... Pg.9 ... K13
Coral Dr. ... Pg.10 ... H14
County Lane Rd. ... Pg.10 ... G14
Cove Ave. ... Pg.10 ... G15
Cypress Cir. ... Pg.10 ... G15
Daggett St. ... Pg.9 ... K16
Darrin Dr. ... Pg.10 ... J14
Daviess St. ... Pg.9 ... J13
Delaware Dr. ... Pg.10 ... K15
Dellpark Ave. ... Pg.9 ... K12
Denver Hill Dr. ... Pg.10 ... G14
Diane Ct. ... Pg.10 ... K13
Division St. ... Pg.9 ... K13
Doe Tr. ... Pg.10 ... H15
Douglas Pkwy. ... Pg.10 ... H15
Dunslow Ln. ... Pg.10 ... H13
East St. ... Pg.9 ... K13
Edgewood Dr. ... Pg.10 ... H15
Elliott St. ... Pg.10 ... J14
Farrell Rd. ... Pg.10 ... J15
Fawn Path ... Pg.10 ... H15
Fieldview Ct. ... Pg.10 ... G15
Fielstone Pl. ... Pg.10 ... J15
Fir Ct. ... Pg.9 ... J13
Fox Bend Ln. ... Pg.10 ... L16
Foxford Ln. ... Pg.10 ... H15
Francis St. ... Pg.9 ... K12
Garfield St. ... Pg.9 ... J13
Glenmore Cir. ... Pg.10 ... G14
Gloria St. ... Pg.10 ... H14
Golfview Dr. ... Pg.10 ... L16
Gougar Rd. ... Pg.10 ... K16
Grace St. ... Pg.10 ... J14
Grandview Ave. ... Pg.9 ... K13
Hamilton St. ... Pg.9 ... J13
Harbor Dr. ... Pg.10 ... J14
Hemlock Ln. ... Pg.10 ... H15
Heritage Ct. ... Pg.10 ... I10
Holly Ct. ... Pg.10 ... H14
Huron Ct. ... Pg.10 ... K15
Illini Dr. ... Pg.10 ... K15
Industrial Dr. ... Pg.9 ... J13
Iroquois Dr. ... Pg.10 ... K16
Jack Pine Way ... Pg.10 ... L16
Janice Ave. ... Pg.10 ... J14
Jaquarlys St. ... Pg.10 ... J15
Jefferson St. ... Pg.9 ... J13
Jenel Ct. ... Pg.10 ... J13
Jennifer Ct. ... Pg.10 ... J14
Joam Ct. ... Pg.9 ... K13
Johnson St. ... Pg.10 ... K13
Jordan Ln. ... Pg.10 ... J14
Joseph Dr. ... Pg.10 ... J14
Karen Springs Dr. ... Pg.10 ... J15
Katherine St. ... Pg.10 ... J14
Key West Dr. ... Pg.10 ... G14
Kylemore Ct. ... Pg.10 ... H15
LaJeune St. ... Pg.10 ... J14
Lacoma Dr. ... Pg.10 ... J14
Lakewood Dr. ... Pg.10 ... L15
Landings Dr. ... Pg.10 ... K12
Lawrence Ave. ... Pg.9 ... K13
Lincoln St. ... Pg.9 ... J13
Lindoversey Dr. ... Pg.10 ... H14
Lone Star Dr. ... Pg.9 ... K13
Longbow Dr. ... Pg.10 ... L15
Lorraine Ct. ... Pg.10 ... J14
MacGregor Rd. ... Pg.10 ... H14
Madison St. ... Pg.9 ... J13
Maitland Dr. ... Pg.10 ... H14
Maple Ct. ... Pg.10 ... J14
Mary Ann Ln. ... Pg.9 ... K13
Mary Knoll Dr. ... Pg.10 ... K12
May St. ... Pg.9 ... K13
Mayo St. ... Pg.9 ... K13
McKinley St. ... Pg.10 ... J14
McKinley St. ... Pg.10 ... J14
Meadow Wood Ln. ... Pg.10 ... H14
Merc Ln. ... Pg.10 ... G15
Michael St. ... Pg.10 ... J14
Milne Dr. ... Pg.10 ... J14
Mohave Ct. ... Pg.10 ... K15
Mohawk Ln. ... Pg.10 ... K16
Mohican Dr. ... Pg.10 ... K15
Montauk Dr. ... Pg.10 ... K16
Morring Pl. ... Pg.10 ... H14
Muehl St. ... Pg.10 ... J14
Natamo Dr. ... Pg.10 ... L15
Newbridge Dr. ... Pg.10 ... H14
North St. ... Pg.10 ... J14
Northern Dr. ... Pg.10 ... G15
Olympic Ln. ... Pg.10 ... G15
Onieda Dr. ... Pg.10 ... K15
Ottawa Dr. ... Pg.10 ... K15
Parkview Ln. ... Pg.9 ... K12,13
Peachtree Ln. ... Pg.10 ... K15
Pocasset Ct. ... Pg.10 ... K15
Porter Pl. ... Pg.10 ... J14
Prairie St. ... Pg.10 ... H15
Primrose Ln. ... Pg.10 ... H15
Princess Ct. ... Pg.10 ... H15
Prodehl Dr. ... Pg.10 ... J15
Pueblo Ct. ... Pg.10 ... K16
Puma Ct. ... Pg.10 ... L16
Putnam Dr. ... Pg.10 ... K12
Read St. ... Pg.9 ... K13
Red Cloud Dr. ... Pg.10 ... K16
Redwood Ct. ... Pg.10 ... H15
Reef Rd. ... Pg.10 ... H14
Renwood Ct. ... Pg.10 ... J15
Rhonda Dr. ... Pg.10 ... J15
Rio Grande Dr. ... Pg.9 ... K13
Rodney Ct. ... Pg.10 ... J15
Rodney St. ... Pg.10 ... J15
Rosanne Ct. ... Pg.9 ... K13
Rosanne St. ... Pg.9 ... K13
Rowley Ln. ... Pg.10 ... H14
Runyan Dr. ... Pg.10 ... F15
Saddlewood Dr. ... Pg.10 ... H15
Santee Ct. ... Pg.10 ... K15
Sauk Dr. ... Pg.10 ... K15
Scotch Pine Ct. ... Pg.10 ... H15
Seneca Dr. ... Pg.10 ... K15
Sequoia Ct. ... Pg.10 ... H15
Sequoia Way ... Pg.10 ... H15
Shawnee Dr. ... Pg.10 ... K15
Sherwood Ct. ... Pg.10 ... H14
Shetland Ct. ... Pg.10 ... H15
Shoals Dr. ... Pg.10 ... H14
Silver Spur Ln. ... Pg.10 ... H15
Sioux Ct. ... Pg.10 ... K15

Sisson St. ... Pg.9 ... K13
South St. ... Pg.10 ... J14
Spring View Dr. ... Pg.10 ... H15
Spruce St. ... Pg.10 ... J14
St. Charles Dr. ... Pg.10 ... J14
St. Charles Dr. ... Pg.10 ... J14
State St. ... Pg.10 ... H14
Stephanie Dr. ... Pg.10 ... J14
Strawberry Hill Dr. ... Pg.10 ... J14
Summit Dr. ... Pg.10 ... G14
Sunset Ridge Ct. ... Pg.10 ... K16
Sunshine Ct. ... Pg.10 ... H15
Swift Arrow Dr. ... Pg.10 ... L15
Sycamore Ct. ... Pg.10 ... H15
Taft Sch. ... Pg.9 ... J13
Tahoe St. ... Pg.10 ... G14
Tanglewood Ln. ... Pg.10 ... L16
Teton Cir. ... Pg.10 ... L15
Teton Dr. ... Pg.10 ... L15
Teton Dr. ... Pg.10 ... L15
Thornton St. ... Pg.10 ... H13
Tiger Dr. ... Pg.10 ... L16
Timberview Dr. ... Pg.10 ... H14
Torelli Dr. ... Pg.10 ... L16
Tralee Ln. ... Pg.10 ... G14
Treeline Ct. ... Pg.10 ... H14
Tuscaboro Ct. ... Pg.10 ... H15
Valley Ln. ... Pg.10 ... J14
Village Ln. ... Pg.9 ... J13
Vine St. ... Pg.9 ... J13
Washburn Way ... Pg.10 ... J15
Washington St. ... Pg.9 ... J13
Water St. ... Pg.9 ... J13
Weis Ln. ... Pg.10 ... H15
West St. ... Pg.9 ... K13
Westwood Dr. ... Pg.10 ... L16
Whelan St. ... Pg.9 ... K13
Will Dr. ... Pg.10 ... L16
Woods Dr. ... Pg.10 ... K13
Woods Ln. ... Pg.9 ... K13
Wyandot Ct. ... Pg.10 ... K16
Yakima Dr. ... Pg.10 ... L15
1st St. ... Pg.10 ... H14
2nd St. ... Pg.10 ... H14
3rd St. ... Pg.9 ... J13,14
4th St. ... Pg.9 ... F9
5th St. ... Pg.9 ... J13
6th St. ... Pg.9 ... J13
7th St. ... Pg.9 ... J13,14
8th St. ... Pg.9 ... J13
9th St. ... Pg.10 ... J14
10th St. ... Pg.10 ... J14
11th St. ... Pg.10 ... J14
12th St. ... Pg.10 ... J14
13th St. ... Pg.9 ... J14
15th St. ... Pg.10 ... J15
16th St. ... Pg.10 ... K13
17th St. ... Pg.10 ... K13
18th St. ... Pg.10 ... K13
19th St. ... Pg.10 ... K13
20th St. ... Pg.10 ... K13
151st St. ... Pg.10 ... G14
163rd St. ... Pg.11 ... J18

**CEMETERIES**
S. Suburban Cem. ... Pg.9

**GOLF COURSES**
Broken Arrow Golf Course ... Pg.10 ... K15
Lockport Golf & Rec. Club ... Pg.10 ... G14

**PARKS**
Athletic Fld ... Pg.10 ... J14
Canal Park ... Pg.10 ... J14
Dellwood Park West ... Pg.10 ... K12
Dellwood Pk. ... Pg.10 ... K13
Farrell Park ... Pg.10 ... J14
Vine St. Pk. ... Pg.10 ... J14
Woodland Park ... Pg.10 ... H15

**SCHOOLS**
Kelvin Grove Sch. ... Pg.10 ... J14
Lockport Central H.S. ... Pg.10 ... J13
Lockport East H.S. ... Pg.10 ... J13
Ludwig Sch. ... Pg.10 ... H14
Milne Grove Sch. ... Pg.10 ... J14
St. Joseph Sch. ... Pg.9 ... J13
Walsh Sch. ... Pg.10 ... H14

**MISCELLANEOUS**
C.C.C. Picnic Shelter ... Pg.9 ... J12
City Hall ... Pg.10 ... J14
Fire Department ... Pg.10 ... J14
Gladys Fox Museum ... Pg.9 ... J13
Illinois & Michigan Canal Museum ... Pg.9 ... J13
Illinois State Museum ... Pg.9 ... J13
Lockport Canal Industrial Pk. ... Pg.9 ... G13
Lockport Historical Trail ... Pg.9 ... J13
Railroad Station ... Pg.9 ... J13

## LOCKPORT TOWNSHIP
Pages 2-4,8-10,14-16
**STREETS**
Aberdeen Dr. ... Pg.8 ... J9
Adel Ct. ... Pg.10 ... L12
Airport Rd. ... Pg.9 ... G11
Albert Dr. ... Pg.8 ... H8
Alice Ct. ... Pg.8 ... J8
Alpine Ct. ... Pg.2 ... E8
Ames Ct. ... Pg.2 ... F9
Amhurst Ave. ... Pg.10 ... L12
Annapolis Ct. ... Pg.2 ... F9
Ardmore Ct. ... Pg.10 ... H14
Ardmore Dr. ... Pg.10 ... H14
Arthur Ave. ... Pg.15 ... L13
Aspen Ct. ... Pg.2 ... F9
Astoria Ct. ... Pg.2 ... F9
Bangor Ct. ... Pg.2 ... F9
Barret St. ... Pg.8 ... L12
Barrington Ln. ... Pg.8 ... F8
Barrington Ln. ... Pg.2 ... F9
Barry Ave. ... Pg.15 ... L13
Basswood Ln. ... Pg.2 ... E8

Bayberry Ct. ... Pg.2 ... E8
Bayberry Rd. ... Pg.2 ... E8
Birch St. ... Pg.8 ... L8
Bloomfield Dr. ... Pg.2 ... F9
Blossom St. ... Pg.8 ... J8
Blue Blossom Ln. ... Pg.2 ... E8
Bluff St. ... Pg.10 ... H14
Bonnie Dr. ... Pg.10 ... H14
Brassel St. ... Pg.9 ... L13
Brentwood Ct. ... Pg.2 ... F9
Briggs St. ... Pg.10 ... L14
Brisbin Park ... Pg.8 ... H8
Broadway St. ... Pg.8 ... G11
Brockton Ct. ... Pg.2 ... F9
Brookdale Ct. ... Pg.2 ... F9
Brown St. ... Pg.9 ... K13
Bruce Ave. ... Pg.9 ... L13
Bruce Rd. ... Pg.9 ... L13
Buckner Ct. ... Pg.2 ... F9
Butler Ct. ... Pg.2 ... F9
California Ave. ... Pg.15 ... L13
Cameron Ave. ... Pg.9 ... L12
Canton Farm Rd. ... Pg.8 ... L8
Carillon Dr. ... Pg.2 ... E8
Cascade Ct. ... Pg.2 ... F9
Central Park Pl. ... Pg.15 ... L12
Chandler Ct. ... Pg.2 ... F9
Chatsworth Ln. ... Pg.2 ... F8
Cherry Ln. ... Pg.2 ... E8
Chestnut Ln. ... Pg.2 ... F8
Circle St. ... Pg.10 ... H14
Cliff Ave. ... Pg.15 ... L12
Coghill Dr. ... Pg.2 ... F9
Collins St. ... Pg.9 ... L12
Connor Ave. ... Pg.9 ... L13
Copter Ln. ... Pg.9 ... G11
Cornell Ave. ... Pg.15 ... L12
Cottonwood Ln. ... Pg.2 ... E8
County Lane Rd. ... Pg.10 ... G14
Covington Dr. ... Pg.2 ... F8
Creston Ct. ... Pg.2 ... F9
Crete Ct. ... Pg.2 ... F9
Cutter Ave. ... Pg.8 ... L13
Danbury Ct. ... Pg.2 ... F9
Danbury Pl. ... Pg.2 ... F9
Dartmouth Ave. ... Pg.15 ... M12
Dawson Ave. ... Pg.9 ... G11
Dellwood Ave. ... Pg.10 ... L12
Denton Ct. ... Pg.2 ... F8
Duncan Ct. ... Pg.2 ... F8
Dundee Dr. ... Pg.10 ... H14
Earhart Ct. ... Pg.2 ... F8
Earl St. ... Pg.10 ... H14
East St. ... Pg.15 ... L13
Edgewater Ct. ... Pg.2 ... F8
Edgewater Dr. ... Pg.9 ... J13
Edgewood Ave. ... Pg.9 ... J13
Edinburgh ... Pg.10 ... H15
Elm St. ... Pg.16 ... E8
Emerald Ct. ... Pg.2 ... E8
Emerson Ct. ... Pg.2 ... F8
Exhibition Pl. ... Pg.15 ... L12
Exter Ct. ... Pg.15 ... L12
Fairmount St. ... Pg.15 ... L13
Fairview Ave. ... Pg.15 ... L13
Farnham Ct. ... Pg.2 ... F8
Farrell Rd. ... Pg.16 ... E13
Faulkner Ct. ... Pg.2 ... F8
Folley Dr. ... Pg.2 ... J8
Forest Ln. ... Pg.8 ... G15
Fox Trail Ct. ... Pg.2 ... F8
Franklin Ct. ... Pg.2 ... F8
Franklin Dr. ... Pg.2 ... F8
Franklin St. ... Pg.9 ... H13
Freeport Ct. ... Pg.2 ... F9
Frost Ct. ... Pg.2 ... F8
Fulton Ct. ... Pg.2 ... F9
Gage St. ... Pg.10 ... L13
Gaylord Rd. ... Pg.8 ... K8
Georgetown Ln. ... Pg.2 ... F8
Georgetown Dr. ... Pg.2 ... F8
Giessler Dr. ... Pg.10 ... H15
Gladstone Ct. ... Pg.2 ... F8
Godfrey Ave. ... Pg.9 ... L12
Graham Ct. ... Pg.2 ... F8
Green Garden Pl. ... Pg.9,15 ... L12
Greensboro Ct. ... Pg.2 ... F8
Hacker St. ... Pg.8 ... L13
Hartman Dr. ... Pg.2 ... F8
Harvard St. ... Pg.15 ... L13,M12
Hawthorne Ave. ... Pg.15 ... L12
Hazelnut Ln. ... Pg.2 ... E8
Hemlock St. ... Pg.8 ... L8
Henry St. ... Pg.9 ... H13
Hickory Ct. ... Pg.2 ... E9
Hickory Ln. ... Pg.2 ... E8
Hidden Ridge Ln. ... Pg.4 ... E14
High Road Ct. ... Pg.10 ... F14
Highland Ave. ... Pg.10 ... L14
Hughes Ave. ... Pg.9 ... K12
Interstate 55 ... Pg.2 ... F9
Ironwood Dr. ... Pg.2 ... E9
Jacquie Ave. ... Pg.9 ... G11
Janet Ave. ... Pg.9 ... G11
John Ct. ... Pg.8 ... J9
John Kirkham Dr. ... Pg.9 ... G11
LaSalle Ct. ... Pg.15 ... L12
Lakeside Dr. ... Pg.2 ... F9
Lakewood Falls Dr. ... Pg.2 ... F9
Larch Ct. ... Pg.2 ... E8
Larch Dr. ... Pg.2 ... F8
Laurie Rd. ... Pg.10 ... H14
Lewis Dr. ... Pg.9 ... H11
Loch ... Pg.10 ... J14
Lois Ave. ... Pg.15 ... L12
Magnolia Dr. ... Pg.2 ... E8
Mahagony Ln. ... Pg.2 ... E8
Market St. ... Pg.9 ... H13
Mary Dr. ... Pg.9 ... J9
Maryville Rd. ... Pg.8 ... H14
May St. ... Pg.9 ... H14
McCameron Ave. ... Pg.10 ... H14
McGivary Dr. ... Pg.8 ... H14
McGregor Rd. ... Pg.10 ... H14
McIntyre Dr. ... Pg.2 ... F8
Miramar ... Pg.10 ... H14
Monterey Dr. ... Pg.2 ... E8
Morgan St. ... Pg.9 ... H13
Mulberry St. ... Pg.8 ... E9
Neil Ct. ... Pg.2 ... F9
New St. ... Pg.9 ... H13
Notes Ave. ... Pg.15 ... L12
North St. ... Pg.2 ... E8
Oak Ave. ... Pg.2 ... F9
Oak St. ... Pg.15 ... L12
Olive St. ... Pg.8 ... N22
Orange Blossom Ln. ... Pg.2 ... E9

## MOKENA

Oxford St. ... Pg.15 ... M12
Peach St. ... Pg.8 ... L7
Pendleton St. ... Pg.10 ... H14
Pine Ave. ... Pg.9 ... L12
Powerhouse Rd. ... Pg.9 ... J12
Prairie Ave. ... Pg.9 ... L13
Princeton St. ... Pg.15 ... L12
Red Berry Cir. ... Pg.2 ... E8
Red Berry Ln. ... Pg.2 ... E8
Red Bud Dr. ... Pg.2 ... E8
Red Bud Ln. ... Pg.2 ... E8
Red Cedar Ln. ... Pg.2 ... E8
Renkin Dr. ... Pg.8 ... J9
Renwick Rd. ... Pg.9 ... H10
Riley Ave. ... Pg.15 ... L12
River View Ave. ... Pg.15 ... L12
Rosemarie Ln. ... Pg.8 ... J8
Rosemary Ct. ... Pg.2 ... E8
Roslind St. ... Pg.15 ... M13
School House Ln. ... Pg.10 ... F14
Sheffield Dr. ... Pg.15 ... M12
Shetland Ct. ... Pg.10 ... H14
Silktree Ct. ... Pg.2 ... E8
Silktree Ln. ... Pg.2 ... E9
Silver Leaf Rd. ... Pg.2 ... E8
Smith Rd. ... Pg.4,10 ... E,F15
Stateville Rd. ... Pg.9 ... J11
Stewart Ct. ... Pg.10 ... H14
Sycamore Ct. ... Pg.2 ... E8
Table St. ... Pg.9 ... H13
Tall Pines Ln. ... Pg.2 ... E8
Tamarack Ct. ... Pg.2 ... E9
Tamarack Dr. ... Pg.2 ... E8
Taylor Rd. ... Pg.9 ... F10
Terminal Ct. ... Pg.9 ... G11
Thomas Dr. ... Pg.8 ... J8
Thorndale Ct. ... Pg.10 ... G14
Turkey Pines ... Pg.2 ... E9
Volz Ave. ... Pg.9 ... L12
Walnut Ln. ... Pg.2 ... E8
Warrens St. ... Pg.9 ... H13
Weber Rd. ... Pg.8 ... G9
Weslyan St. ... Pg.15 ... L12
Wilco Blvd. ... Pg.9 ... H10
Woodbrook Ln. ... Pg.10 ... H14
Yale St. ... Pg.15 ... L12
144th St. ... Pg.10 ... F15
145th St. ... Pg.10 ... G14
147th St. ... Pg.10 ... G14
151st St. ... Pg.10 ... G14

**CEMETERIES**
Mt. Calvary Cem. ... Pg.15 ... L13
Russian Cem. ... Pg.15 ... L12

**FOREST PRESERVES**
Lambs Woods Forest Preserve ... Pg.10 ... L14
Lockport Prairie Nature Preserve ... Pg.9 ... J12
Runyon Woods Forest Preserve ... Pg.9 ... H13

**GOLF COURSES**
Carillon Ct. ... Pg.2 ... E8

**PARKS**
Bonnie Brae Pk. ... Pg.10 ... H14
College View Park ... Pg.9 ... G11
Fairmont Comm. Ctr. ... Pg.9 ... L13
Romeo Shores ... Pg.8 ... H9

**SCHOOLS**
Fairmont Jr. H.S. ... Pg.9 ... L12
Fairmont Sch. ... Pg.9 ... L12

**MISCELLANEOUS**
Illinois Water Lock ... Pg.9 ... J11
Lewis Univ. Airport ... Pg.9 ... H11
Lockport Prairie Nature Preserve Front Bridge ... Pg.9 ... J12
Powerhouse Metropolitan Water Reclamation ... Pg.9 ... J12
Stateville Prison ... Pg.9 ... K10

## MOKENA
Pages 18,19
**STREETS**
Abbey Ct. ... Pg.18 ... Q23
Abbey Rd. ... Pg.18 ... Q23
Aileen Ave. ... Pg.19 ... N24
Alta Vista Way ... Pg.18 ... P23
Anna St. ... Pg.18 ... P23
April Ct. ... Pg.19 ... N26
April Ln. ... Pg.19 ... N26
Arahat Ct. ... Pg.18 ... P23
Arbor Ln. ... Pg.19 ... P26
Arquilla Dr. ... Pg.19 ... M26
Asbbury Ct. ... Pg.18 ... R23
Ashford Ce. ... Pg.18 ... Q22
Austin Ct. ... Pg.19 ... N24
Balsam Ct. ... Pg.19 ... P25
Baron Rd. ... Pg.18 ... R22
Beckett Ct. ... Pg.19 ... N24
Bedford Ln. ... Pg.19 ... N26
Birch Ave. ... Pg.19 ... N26
Blackhawk Ct. ... Pg.18 ... P22
Blyth Way ... Pg.18 ... R22
Bonness Ave. ... Pg.18 ... P23
Bornet Dr. ... Pg.19 ... N25
Boyer Ct. ... Pg.18 ... R23
Bradford Dr. ... Pg.18 ... R23
Bridgemore Rd. ... Pg.18 ... R23
Brightway, N. S. & W. ... Pg.18 ... R23
Bristol ... Pg.18 ... P22
Brompton Ct. ... Pg.19 ... N25
Brush Ln. ... Pg.18 ... P23
Bryant Ct. ... Pg.18 ... N24
Bryant St. ... Pg.18 ... N24
Buckingham Dr. ... Pg.18 ... Q23
Burke Ct. ... Pg.19 ... N23,24
Burnside Station Dr. ... Pg.19 ... M26

Camden Ct. ... Pg.19 ... M24
Camelot Ave. ... Pg.18 ... N22
Carpenter St. ... Pg.18 ... N24
Catherine Ln. ... Pg.19 ... P24
Celtic Ct. ... Pg.19 ... N18
Center St. ... Pg.18 ... P23
Cherry Ln. ... Pg.19 ... N25
Coach Dr. ... Pg.18 ... R22
Connemara Ct. ... Pg.18 ... R22
Country Pond Dr. ... Pg.18 ... R22
Creek Crossing Dr. ... Pg.18 ... N22
Creekside Ln. ... Pg.18 ... N22
Creekview Cir. ... Pg.18 ... M22
Creekview Ct. ... Pg.18 ... M22
Creekview Ln. ... Pg.18 ... M22
Cromwell Ct. ... Pg.19 ... N24
Cromwell Ln. ... Pg.19 ... N25
Cross St. ... Pg.18 ... N24
Daniel Tr. ... Pg.18 ... N23
Darla Tr. ... Pg.18 ... N23
Deer Run Dr. ... Pg.18 ... Q22
Denny St. ... Pg.18 ... P23
Derby Ct. ... Pg.19 ... N24
Derby Ln. ... Pg.19 ... N23
Derek Way ... Pg.18 ... N24
Diana Ct. ... Pg.18 ... R23
Dickens Bay Ct. ... Pg.18 ... M24
Dickens Dr. ... Pg.18 ... M24
Dickran Dr. ... Pg.19 ... N24
Dilber Dr. ... Pg.19 ... P24
Division St. ... Pg.18 ... N23
Duchess Ave. ... Pg.18 ... N22
Edgewood Dr. ... Pg.18 ... P23
Edgewood Ln. ... Pg.18 ... Q23
Elm Ct. ... Pg.19 ... N26
Elm Ln. ... Pg.19 ... N26
English Bay ... Pg.18 ... M24
Enterprise Dr. ... Pg.18 ... N26
Everett Ln. ... Pg.18 ... P25
Fairmont Ln. ... Pg.18 ... N26
Fintan Ct. ... Pg.19 ... N24
Fiona Ave. ... Pg.18 ... N24
Ford Ct. ... Pg.19 ... P25
Forestview Ct. ... Pg.18 ... P25
Forestview Dr. ... Pg.19 ... P25
Foxford Ln. ... Pg.2 ... E9
Francis Rd. ... Pg.18 ... P22
Front St. ... Pg.18 ... P23
Galway Bay ... Pg.18 ... M24
Galway Rd. ... Pg.19 ... N24
Glenneil Ave. ... Pg.18 ... N,P22
Granite Dr. ... Pg.18 ... P23
Greenview Ave. ... Pg.18 ... P22
Hacker ... Pg.18 ... R22
Halligan Way ... Pg.19 ... N24
Hamilton Rd. ... Pg.18 ... R23
Hastings Ln. ... Pg.19 ... N26
Henry Dr. ... Pg.19 ... N26
Hiawatha Blvd. ... Pg.18 ... N26
Hickory Creek Dr. ... Pg.19 ... N26
Hickory Stick Ln. ... Pg.18 ... P22
Hillside Ln. ... Pg.18 ... M23
Humingbird Ln. ... Pg.18 ... M23
Huntington Ct. ... Pg.18 ... M26
Jacob Dr. ... Pg.19 ... N18
Jomar Ct. ... Pg.19 ... N24
Keith Ave. ... Pg.19 ... N25
Keith Ct. ... Pg.18 ... P24
Kendall St. ... Pg.19 ... P24
Kensington Dr. ... Pg.18 ... P23
Kerry Ct. ... Pg.19 ... N24
Kevin Ave. ... Pg.19 ... P24
Kickapoo Ct. ... Pg.18 ... N23
Kimberly Tr. ... Pg.18 ... N23
Kingston Way ... Pg.19 ... N26
Kinvara Ave. ... Pg.19 ... N26
Kirkstone Way ... Pg.19 ... P26
Kluth Ct. ... Pg.18 ... P23
Kluth Dr. ... Pg.18 ... P23
Kovok St. ... Pg.18 ... Q22
Kristen Tr. ... Pg.18 ... N23
Kvork St. ... Pg.18 ... Q22
Kylemore Ln. ... Pg.19 ... N26
La Grange Rd. ... Pg.19 ... N26
Lancaster Dr. ... Pg.19 ... N24
Lee Trim Ct. ... Pg.18 ... N26
Lincoln Hwy. ... Pg.18 ... P22
Lindsay Ln. ... Pg.19 ... P24
London Bay Ct. ... Pg.18 ... M24
London Ln. ... Pg.19 ... N24
Manchester Dr. ... Pg.19 ... N26
Mansfield Ln. ... Pg.19 ... N24
Marley Creek Ct. ... Pg.18 ... N24
Maurita Ct. ... Pg.19 ... N24
Mayfair Ct. ... Pg.18 ... N23
Mayfair Dr. ... Pg.18 ... N23
Mcklovney's St. ... Pg.18 ... M22
Meadow Creek Dr. ... Pg.18 ... M22
Meadow View Dr. ... Pg.19 ... N23
Michael Ct. ... Pg.19 ... N24
Midland Ave. ... Pg.18 ... P23
Midland Rd. ... Pg.18 ... P23
Moher Ct. ... Pg.2 ... N26
Mokena St. ... Pg.18 ... P24
Newport Dr. ... Pg.18 ... N26
Newport Ln. ... Pg.2 ... N26
Newton Way ... Pg.19 ... P24
O'Connell Ave. ... Pg.18 ... N24
Old Castle Dr. ... Pg.18 ... Q22
Old U.S. Route 45 ... Pg.18 ... M25
Owens Rd. ... Pg.18 ... N26
Oxford Ct. ... Pg.19 ... P23
Parker St. ... Pg.18 ... N25
Parkside Ct. ... Pg.18 ... N24
Parkside Ln. ... Pg.18 ... N24
Parkway Ln. ... Pg.18 ... N24
Patricia Ln. ... Pg.19 ... P24
Pheasant Ct. ... Pg.18 ... N24
Pheasant Ln. ... Pg.18 ... N24
Pinegrove Ct. ... Pg.18 ... P25
Pinegrove Dr. ... Pg.18 ... P25
Plattner Ct. ... Pg.18 ... P23
Plattner Dr. ... Pg.18 ... P23
Prairie Ct. ... Pg.19 ... N24
Prestancia Dr. ... Pg.18 ... N24
Primrose Ln. ... Pg.18 ... N23
Pullman Ln. ... Pg.19 ... M26
Quail Dr. ... Pg.18 ... N23
Queens Ct. ... Pg.18 ... N24
Regent Dr. ... Pg.19 ... N24
Revere Rd. ... Pg.18 ... N23,24
Rider Ridge Dr. ... Pg.5 ... N24
Ridge Ct. ... Pg.18 ... N25
Roberts St. ... Pg.18 ... N24
Rose Wood Ln. ... Pg.18 ... N22
Royal Ct. ... Pg.19 ... P24
Saddle ... Pg.18 ... R22

## MOKENA

Sarkis Dr. ... Pg.18 ... P22
Scarth Ave. ... Pg.19 ... P24
Scarth Ln. ... Pg.19 ... P24
School House Rd. ... Pg.19 ... N24
Scott St. ... Pg.19 ... P23
Sevan Ct. ... Pg.18 ... P22
Sorenson Ct. ... Pg.19 ... P25
St. James Ct. ... Pg.18 ... P24
St. John Dr. ... Pg.19 ... P24
St. Joseph Ct. ... Pg.19 ... P24
St. Mary's Rd. ... Pg.18 ... N23
Stafford Ct. ... Pg.19 ... P25
Stanford Ct. ... Pg.19 ... N26
Stephen Ct. ... Pg.19 ... N24
Stonehenge Dr. ... Pg.19 ... P25
Stratford Dr. ... Pg.18 ... P25
Stratford Rd. ... Pg.18 ... G22
Sundance Ct. ... Pg.18 ... G22
Sussex Ct. ... Pg.19 ... N25
Swan Ln. ... Pg.19 ... P24
Swanburg Ln. ... Pg.19 ... P24
Swinford Ct. ... Pg.18 ... G23
Swinford Ln. ... Pg.18 ... G22
Tall Feathers Dr. ... Pg.18 ... Q22
Tall Grass Dr. ... Pg.19 ... Q22
Therese Ln. ... Pg.19 ... P24
Town Line Rd. ... Pg.18 ... N22
Trenton Way ... Pg.19 ... N25
Union St. ... Pg.19 ... N23
Vanderbilt Dr. ... Pg.18 ... P22
Victoria Dr. ... Pg.18 ... P22
Victorian Dr. ... Pg.18 ... N22
Walnut Ln. ... Pg.19 ... P24
Walnut St. ... Pg.19 ... N24
Walsh Ln. ... Pg.18 ... N26
Waterford Ln. ... Pg.2 ... N26
Weber Rd. ... Pg.19 ... N24
Wembley Dr. ... Pg.18 ... P22
Westinghouse Ct. ... Pg.19 ... N26
Westminster Dr. ... Pg.19 ... N24
Westport Way ... Pg.19 ... N24
Wexford Dr. ... Pg.18 ... G23
Wid Berry Ln. ... Pg.18 ... P23
Willow Ave. ... Pg.19 ... N26
Willow Ln. ... Pg.19 ... N26
Willowcrest Ln. ... Pg.18 ... N26
Willowfield Ct. ... Pg.19 ... N24
Wild Dance Cir. ... Pg.18 ... G22
Wolf Rd. ... Pg.18 ... N23
Yorkshire Dr. ... Pg.19 ... N24
1st Ct. ... Pg.18 ... N23
1st St. ... Pg.18 ... N23
2nd St. ... Pg.18 ... N23
3rd St. ... Pg.18 ... N23
97th Ave. ... Pg.19 ... N24
116th Ave. ... Pg.19 ... N22
183rd Pl. ... Pg.18 ... M23
188th St. ... Pg.18 ... N23
191st St. ... Pg.18 ... N23
193rd St. ... Pg.19 ... N23
194th St. ... Pg.19 ... N25
195th St. ... Pg.18 ... N23
196th St. ... Pg.19 ... N25
197th Pl. ... Pg.19 ... P25
197th St. ... Pg.18 ... P22,25
198th St. ... Pg.19 ... P25

### CEMETERIES
Pioneer Cem. ... Pg.18 ... P23
St. John's Cem. ... Pg.18 ... N23
St. Mary's Cem. ... Pg.18 ... N23

### PARKS
Grassmere Park ... Pg.19 ... P25
Green Meadows Park ... Pg.19 ... P24
Hecht Park ... Pg.19 ... P24
Mokena Park ... Pg.18 ... P23
Mokena Park Dist. Headquarters ... Pg.18 ... P23
Tot Lot ... Pg.18 ... P23
Willowview Park ... Pg.18 ... P23

### SCHOOLS
Mokena Elem. Sch. ... Pg.18 ... P23
Mokena Elem. Sch. & Sch. Dist 159 Office ... Pg.18 ... P23
Mokena Jr. H.S. ... Pg.18 ... N23
St. Mary's Sch. ... Pg.18 ... N23

### MISCELLANEOUS
Commuter R.R. Station ... Pg.18 ... M26,N23
Fire Dept. ... Pg.18 ... P23
Library ... Pg.18 ... N23
Mokena Park Dist. Office ... Pg.18 ... P23
Post Office ... Pg.18 ... P23
Village Hall ... Pg.18 ... P23

## NAPERVILLE
Page 1
(For additional listings, see Section 3)
### STREETS
Barr Creek Ln. ... A5
Baybrook Ct. ... A5
Baybrook Ln. ... A5
Book Rd. ... A5
Bundleflower Dr. ... A5
Canfield Ct. ... A5
Catclaw Ct. ... B4
Chokeberry Dr. ... B4
Clearwater Ln. ... A5
Coneflower Dr. ... B5
Daggets Ct. ... A5
Duncan Ct. ... A5
Engle Rd. ... A5
Fairhauser Ct. ... A4
Fairhauser Rd. ... A4
Fesseneva Ct. ... A5
Fesseneva Ln. ... A5
Flat Rock Ct. ... A5
Foster Ct. ... A5
Freeland Cir. ... A4
Freeland Ct. ... A5
Haviland Ct. ... A5
High Meadow Rd. ... B4
Hoddam Ct. ... A5
Hoddam Rd. ... A5
Indian Grass Ct. ... B5
Indian Grass Rd. ... B5
Kentucky Ct. ... A5
Manydown Ct. ... A5
Mather Ct. ... A5
Mather Dr. ... A5
Milkweed Dr. ... B4
Naperville Rd. ... A4
Niswender Ct. ... A4
Niswender Dr. ... A4
Papan Dr. ... B5
Pennryoyal Ct. ... B4
Pigeston Ct. ... A5
Popple Ct. ... A5
Prairie Sage Ln. ... A5
Riley Ct. ... A5
Route 59 ... B4
Saltmeadow Dr. ... A5
Sand Island Ct. ... A5
Sand Lily Dr. ... B5
Sebastian Ct. ... A6
Sebastian Dr. ... A5
Snapdragon Rd. ... B5
Snapjack Cir. ... A5
Snow Creek Rd. ... A5
Spikehorn Ave. ... A5
Sweetbroom Ct. ... B4
Sweetbroom Dr. ... B4
Switchgrass Ln. ... B5
Thatcher Dr. ... A5
Velvet Bent Ct. ... A5
Wait Rd. ... A4
Wild Timothy Dr. ... B4
Wild Timothy Dr. ... B4
Wirestem Ct. ... B5
Yellowstar Ct. ... A5
Yellowstar Ln. ... B5
111th St. ... A4

### FOREST PRESERVES
Riverview Farm F.P. ... B5

### SHOPPING CENTERS
Harmony Grove Plaza ... A4
High Meadow Plaza ... A4

## NEW LENOX
Pages 16-18
### STREETS
Abbey Ct. ... Pg.17 ... Q16
Abraham Dr. ... Pg.17 ... N17
Aeronca Ct. ... Pg.17 ... Q17
Amanda Ln. ... Pg.17 ... R20
Amber Rd. ... Pg.17 ... R19
Ann Ln. ... Pg.16 ... Q15
Arlyle Dr. ... Pg.17 ... Q18
Armstrong Ln. ... Pg.17 ... P20
Arrowhead Dr. ... Pg.10 ... L16
Ash St. ... Pg.17 ... P19
Ashley Dr. ... Pg.17 ... P18
Aspen Dr. ... Pg.17 ... R19
Auburn Ct. ... Pg.16 ... Q15
Barbara St. ... Pg.17 ... P18
Barnside Rd. ... Pg.17 ... R19
Bay Ct. ... Pg.17 ... R20
Bay Hill Dr. ... Pg.16 ... Q17
Beech Ln. ... Pg.17 ... Q17
Beechcraft Dr. ... Pg.17 ... Q17
Belot Ln. ... Pg.18 ... R22
Ben Tree Ln. ... Pg.18 ... Q17
Bentley Rd. ... Pg.17 ... R19
Bimini Ln. ... Pg.17 ... R20
Bishop's Gate ... Pg.18 ... R21
Bluestone Way Dr. ... Pg.17 ... R20
Bon Terre Rd. ... Pg.17 ... R19
Borman Dr. ... Pg.17 ... Q17
Brigatine Dr. ... Pg.18 ... R22
Bristol Ln. ... Pg.18 ... R22
Brittany Dr. ... Pg.17 ... R16
Brockwood Rd. ... Pg.17 ... R20
Cambridge Ln. ... Pg.18 ... R21
Canterbury Ct. ... Pg.17 ... P18
Carol Rd. ... Pg.17 ... N18
Cedar Rd. ... Pg.17 ... R18
Central Rd. ... Pg.17 ... Q18
Cessna Ct. ... Pg.17 ... Q17
Chaffee Ln. ... Pg.17 ... R18
Charleston Dr. ... Pg.18 ... R18
Church St. ... Pg.17 ... Q18
Churchill Dr. ... Pg.17 ... R17
Clinton St. ... Pg.17 ... P19
Columbia Dr. ... Pg.18 ... R21
Conrad Ln. ... Pg.17 ... Q17
Cornell Dr. ... Pg.18 ... Q20
Corsair Ct. ... Pg.17 ... Q17
Cottonwood Pl. ... Pg.16 ... N17
Coventry Rd. ... Pg.16 ... N16
Creekside Ct. ... Pg.17 ... N17
Crescenzo Ct. ... Pg.17 ... Q18
Darsha Rd. ... Pg.17 ... R20
Dartmouth Ln. ... Pg.18 ... R21
Dawn Way ... Pg.17 ... Q19
DeGroate Rd. ... Pg.17 ... Q17
Dorsey Ln. ... Pg.17 ... P16
Downing St. ... Pg.18 ... R21
Doxbury Ct. ... Pg.18 ... R16
Doxbury Ln. ... Pg.18 ... R16
Eagle Cir. ... Pg.18 ... R21
Eagle Ridge Dr. ... Pg.11 ... G19
Earl Ct. ... Pg.17 ... Q19
Eastgate Ct. ... Pg.17 ... R19
Eastwind Dr. ... Pg.18 ... R21
Edentenny Rd. ... Pg.17 ... R20
Edmonds St. ... Pg.17 ... P19
Elm St. ... Pg.17 ... N,P,Q18
Essex Ln. ... Pg.18 ... R15
Fairfield Dr. ... Pg.17 ... Q17
Ferro Dr. ... Pg.16 ... Q16
Finborough Dr. ... Pg.17 ... P19
Fir St. ... Pg.17 ... P18
Forest St. ... Pg.17 ... P18
Francis Rd. ... Pg.17 ... N17
Gail Ln. ... Pg.17 ... Q17
Garnet Dr. ... Pg.17 ... R20
Garnet Ct. ... Pg.16 ... Q16
Garnet Dr. ... Pg.16 ... Q16
Gear Dr. ... Pg.17 ... Q17
Genoa Dr. ... Pg.18 ... R22
Gibbons Dr. ... Pg.17 ... P16
Gifford Pl. ... Pg.16 ... P16
Gina Dr. ... Pg.17 ... Q18
Glenn Dr. ... Pg.17 ... R17
Grand Prairie Dr. ... Pg.17 ... Q16
Greenbriar Dr. ... Pg.17 ... R19
Grissom Ln. ... Pg.17 ... R17
Grumman Ct. ... Pg.17 ... Q17
Gum St. ... Pg.17 ... Q19
Haines St. ... Pg.17 ... Q18
Hampshire Cir. ... Pg.17 ... P18
Hancock Dr. ... Pg.17 ... R18
Harvard Ln. ... Pg.18 ... R21
Hauser Ct. ... Pg.17 ... Q17
Haven Ave. ... Pg.17 ... Q18
Hawthorn Ln. ... Pg.17 ... P19
Heartland Dr. ... Pg.17 ... P19
Hickory Green Dr. ... Pg.17 ... P19
Hickory St. ... Pg.17 ... Q18
Honey Ln. ... Pg.17 ... Q17
Independence Blvd. ... Pg.17 ... P18
Inner Ct. ... Pg.17 ... P18
Interstate 80 ... Pg.17 ... N18
Ione Dr. ... Pg.16 ... N16
John St. ... Pg.17 ... P18
Joliet Hwy. ... Pg.17 ... R17
Juli Dr. ... Pg.17 ... R18
Keithland Ct. ... Pg.17 ... Q18
Kimber St. ... Pg.17 ... P18
Kingston Dr. ... Pg.17 ... P15
Knollside Rd. ... Pg.17 ... R19
Kris Dr. ... Pg.17 ... Q17
LaCrosse Dr. ... Pg.10 ... L16
Lahard Rd. ... Pg.17 ... R20
Lake Ct. ... Pg.17 ... R19
Lake Rd. ... Pg.17 ... R19
Lambeth Ln. ... Pg.17 ... N17
Laurel Bay ... Pg.18 ... R22
Lear Ln. ... Pg.17 ... Q17
Lenox St. ... Pg.17 ... N19
Lewis Ln. ... Pg.16 ... N16
Lexington Ct. ... Pg.18 ... R18
Lexington Rd. ... Pg.17 ... R18
Liberty Ln. ... Pg.17 ... R18
Lila's Ct. ... Pg.17 ... R18
Lincoln Hwy. ... Pg.16 ... P16
Lissou Grove ... Pg.18 ... R21
Livingston Dr. ... Pg.17 ... P19
Longlane Rd. ... Pg.17 ... R20
Manor Ct. ... Pg.17 ... R18
Manor Dr. ... Pg.17 ... R18
Maple Ave. ... Pg.17 ... P18
Maple Ln. ... Pg.17 ... P18
Maria Ln. ... Pg.17 ... N17
Markey Ln. ... Pg.17 ... P18
McDevitt Dr. ... Pg.17 ... R17
McDonough St. ... Pg.16 ... Q15
Misty Creek Dr. ... Pg.17 ... Q18
Mustang Ln. ... Pg.17 ... Q17
Nelson Rd. ... Pg.17 ... Q,R17
New Castle Ln. ... Pg.17 ... R18
New Lenox Rd. ... Pg.16 ... N16
Northgate Rd. ... Pg.17 ... R19
Northwind Dr. ... Pg.18 ... R22
O'Connell Dr. ... Pg.17 ... R20
O'Connell St. ... Pg.17 ... Q20
Oak Dr. ... Pg.17 ... P19
Oak St. ... Pg.17 ... Q19
Oakview Dr. ... Pg.17 ... P19
Old New Lenox Rd. ... Pg.17 ... Q18
Omar Rd. ... Pg.17 ... M17
Otto Dr. ... Pg.17 ... N17
Oxford Cir. ... Pg.18 ... R21
Oxford Ct. ... Pg.17 ... Q17
Park Ln. ... Pg.17 ... Q18
Passage Ln. ... Pg.18 ... R22
Patriot Dr. ... Pg.17 ... Q17
Pine Grove Ln. ... Pg.16 ... N16
Pine Ridge Dr. ... Pg.17 ... R18
Piper Dr. ... Pg.17 ... Q17
Plank Rd. ... Pg.17 ... R19
Poplar Ln. ... Pg.17 ... R18
Prairie Ave. ... Pg.17 ... P19
Princeton Ln. ... Pg.17 ... R20
Rebecca Dr. ... Pg.16 ... Q15
Regan Rd. ... Pg.17 ... R17
Regert St. ... Pg.18 ... Q20
Revere Ct. ... Pg.17 ... R18
Ridgefield Rd. ... Pg.17 ... R19
Root St. ... Pg.17 ... Q19
Rossford Ln. ... Pg.16 ... P15
Schoolgate Ct. ... Pg.17 ... Q15
Schooner Dr. ... Pg.18 ... R21
Shannon Ln. ... Pg.17 ... Q16
Sharon Dr. ... Pg.16 ... Q15
Sheffield Dr. ... Pg.17 ... N18
Sojourn Rd. ... Pg.17 ... R20
Southwest Hwy. ... Pg.16 ... M17
Southwind Dr. ... Pg.2 ... R22
Spector Rd. ... Pg.17 ... N18
Spencer Rd. ... Pg.17 ... N18
Spinmaker Dr. ... Pg.18 ... R21
Spring Creek St. ... Pg.16 ... N17
Stafford Ct. ... Pg.17 ... R17
Stafford Dr. ... Pg.17 ... R17
Stone Ct. ... Pg.17 ... R18
Stonegate Rd. ... Pg.17 ... R19
Sunburst Ct. ... Pg.17 ... N18
Sunset Tr. ... Pg.17 ... Q19
Surf Dr. ... Pg.17 ... P18
Tall Grass Ln. ... Pg.16 ... Q17
Tall Grass Rd. ... Pg.16 ... Q17
Talon Dr. ... Pg.18 ... R20
Tauber Rd. ... Pg.17 ... R20
Thames River Ln. ... Pg.18 ... R21
Towncrest Dr. ... Pg.17 ... Q18
Twilight Ln. ... Pg.17 ... P18
Vanderbilt Dr. ... Pg.18 ... R21
Victorian Dr. ... Pg.17 ... Q16
Vine St. ... Pg.17 ... P18
Walker Way ... Pg.17 ... P19
Wallace St. ... Pg.17 ... P19
Warren Ave. ... Pg.17 ... Q18
Warrington Dr. ... Pg.17 ... R19
Washington St. ... Pg.16 ... P15
Waverly Ct. ... Pg.17 ... R18
Wellington Pkwy. ... Pg.18 ... Q21
West Haven Ave. ... Pg.17 ... R17
Western Ave. ... Pg.17 ... R18
Westwind Dr. ... Pg.17 ... R17
Whisper Creek Dr. ... Pg.17 ... R17
White Ln. ... Pg.17 ... R17
Whitewater Ct. ... Pg.17 ... R18
Wildwood Dr. ... Pg.17 ... R18
Willow Ln. ... Pg.17 ... R18
Wimborne Ave. ... Pg.17 ... M17
Wind Crest Ln. ... Pg.18 ... R20
Windsor Ln. ... Pg.16 ... N16
Wintree Ln. ... Pg.16 ... N16
Wirth Rd. ... Pg.17 ... N17
Wood Cooper St. ... Pg.17 ... P18
Woodlawn Rd. ... Pg.17 ... R18
York Pl. ... Pg.16 ... Q16
Young Dr. ... Pg.17 ... P18
1st Ave. ... Pg.17 ... Q18
2nd Ave. ... Pg.17 ... Q18
3rd Ave. ... Pg.17 ... Q18
4th Ave. ... Pg.17 ... Q18

### CEMETERIES
Maplewood Cem. ... Pg.17 ... Q18

### GOLF COURSES
Sanctuary G.C. ... Pg.17 ... P19

### PARKS
Aerohaven Park ... Pg.17 ... N19
Bentley/Tyler Athletic Fields ... Pg.17 ... R20
Bluestone Bay Park ... Pg.18 ... R21
Cherry Hill Park ... Pg.17 ... Q18
Corcoran Park ... Pg.17 ... Q18
Fieldstone Park ... Pg.17 ... Q16
Green Briar Park ... Pg.17 ... Q18
Haines Wayside Park ... Pg.17 ... Q18
Lions Den Park ... Pg.17 ... P15
New Lenox Park District ... Pg.17 ... P19
Schoolhouse Manor Park ... Pg.17 ... Q20
Spencer Park ... Pg.17 ... N19
Walona Athletic Fields ... Pg.17 ... Q19
Windermere West Park ... Pg.17 ... R19

### SCHOOLS
Alex Martino Jr. H.S. ... Pg.17 ... Q20
Arnold Tyler Sch. ... Pg.17 ... P18
Caroline Bentley Sch. ... Pg.17 ... R20
Haines Elem. Sch. ... Pg.17 ... Q18
Haven Sch. ... Pg.18 ... R18
Martino Jr. H.S. ... Pg.17 ... Q20
Oster Oakview Sch. ... Pg.17 ... N18
St. Jude Sch. ... Pg.17 ... Q18

### MISCELLANEOUS
Fire Dept. ... Pg.17 ... Q18
New Lenox Twp. Office ... Pg.17 ... Q20
Old Plank Rd. Trail ... Pg.17 ... Q17
Village Hall & Police Dept. ... Pg.17 ... Q18

## NEW LENOX TOWNSHIP
Pages 16-18
### STREETS
Alison Tr. ... Pg.18 ... P21
Allen Dr. ... Pg.17 ... R19
Amanda Rd. ... Pg.17 ... R20
Amhurst Ct. ... Pg.16 ... Q15
Anderson Rd. ... Pg.17 ... Q20
Arrowhead Rd. ... Pg.18 ... Q22
Ashington Ct. ... Pg.18 ... P21
Banbury Ln. ... Pg.17 ... P17
Banchaw Blvd. ... Pg.17 ... N18
Bernard Ct. ... Pg.18 ... M21
Betty Ln. ... Pg.17 ... M19
Beverly Blvd. ... Pg.17 ... N18
Bishop's Gate ... Pg.18 ... R21
Bittersweet Dr. ... Pg.18 ... P21
Bittersweet Ln. ... Pg.17 ... P17
Bjork Dr. ... Pg.17 ... P17
Blodgett Rd. ... Pg.17 ... M19
Branchaw Blvd. ... Pg.17 ... N18
Brisbane Rd. ... Pg.17 ... Q20
Brivendell Dr. ... Pg.18 ... R21
Bruce Ct. ... Pg.18 ... M22
Bryan Tr. ... Pg.18 ... M21
Buckboard Dr. ... Pg.18 ... P21
Burl Ct. ... Pg.16 ... Q15
Calmer Dr. ... Pg.16 ... N18
Carol Rd. ... Pg.17 ... N18
Carrie Ct. ... Pg.17 ... M20
Carrington Ct. ... Pg.18 ... P21
Castle Dr. ... Pg.18 ... P21
Cedar Rd. ... Pg.17 ... R18
Charlotte Ct. ... Pg.17 ... Q20
Chatfield Rd. ... Pg.18 ... P21
Chelsea Ct. ... Pg.17 ... Q18
Chelsea St. ... Pg.17 ... Q18
Cherry Hill Rd. ... Pg.17 ... N18
Circle Dr. (E&W) ... Pg.18 ... Q22
Clifton St. ... Pg.17 ... N17
Clinton St. ... Pg.17 ... P17
Conlee Dr. ... Pg.17 ... M20
Constitution Rd. ... Pg.17 ... P18
Cooper St. ... Pg.17 ... P,Q19
Cornell Dr. ... Pg.17 ... Q20
Covey Ct. ... Pg.18 ... P21
Craig Ct. ... Pg.18 ... M22
Crescent Dr. ... Pg.16 ... P15
Curtin Ct. ... Pg.18 ... M18
Cynthia Ln. ... Pg.17 ... M19
Debbie Ln. ... Pg.17 ... M19
Deer Run ... Pg.17 ... R20
Donald Ct. ... Pg.18 ... P22
Downing St. ... Pg.18 ... R21
Edmonds St. ... Pg.17 ... P19
Edward Pkwy. ... Pg.17 ... N20
Elizabeth Ln. ... Pg.17 ... M19
Emiley Ln. ... Pg.18 ... P21
Erskine Rd. ... Pg.16 ... P15
Florence Rd. ... Pg.17 ... M20
Francis Rd. ... Pg.17 ... P19,20
Garfield Ave. ... Pg.17 ... Q18
Giddington Ct. ... Pg.18 ... P21
Gordon St. ... Pg.17 ... P17
Gougall Rd. ... Pg.16 ... Q15
Gouger Rd. ... Pg.16 ... N16
Green St. ... Pg.17 ... P18
Haley Rd. ... Pg.18 ... M21
Harmoni Ln. ... Pg.17 ... M19
Hass Rd. ... Pg.18 ... M18
Hempsted Pl. ... Pg.17 ... P16
Herr Dr. ... Pg.17 ... N18
Hickory St. ... Pg.18 ... M18
Hillside Dr. ... Pg.17 ... P20
Hillside Rd. ... Pg.17 ... P20
Hoberg Dr. ... Pg.16 ... N16
Hollyhill Ct. ... Pg.17 ... P17
Hunter Tr. ... Pg.18 ... P21
Illinois Hwy. ... Pg.17 ... N18
Indian Mound Dr. ... Pg.18 ... Q22
Interstate 80 ... Pg.17 ... R19
Jennifer Ct. ... Pg.17 ... M19
Joey Ct. ... Pg.18 ... P22
Joliet Hwy. ... Pg.17 ... N20
Josephine Dr. ... Pg.18 ... M21
Kalarama Dr. ... Pg.17 ... P19
Kankakee St. ... Pg.17 ... N20
Kensington Ct. ... Pg.18 ... R21
Knollwood Pl. ... Pg.16 ... N19
Lake Ct. ... Pg.17 ... R19
Lake Side Dr. ... Pg.17 ... P20
Lancaster Dr. ... Pg.16 ... P16
Laura Ln. ... Pg.17 ... N18
Leanne Ct. ... Pg.17 ... M19
Leanne Ln. ... Pg.17 ... M19
Lenox St. ... Pg.17 ... N19
Lila's Ct. ... Pg.17 ... R18
Lincoln Hwy. ... Pg.17 ... Q20,21
Lincolnway Dr. ... Pg.17 ... Q20
Lincolnwood Dr. ... Pg.17 ... Q20
Lisson Grove ... Pg.18 ... R21
Locust Ln. ... Pg.17 ... P19
London Rd. ... Pg.17 ... N20
Longlane Rd. ... Pg.17 ... N20
Lynn Pkwy. ... Pg.17 ... P20
Maeley Rd. ... Pg.17 ... P20
Main St. ... Pg.18 ... M21
Marley Hills Dr. ... Pg.18 ... M22
Marshall Ct. ... Pg.18 ... M22
Mary Ave. ... Pg.17 ... Q20
Mary St. ... Pg.17 ... N20
Maureen Ct. ... Pg.18 ... M20
Maureen Dr. ... Pg.18 ... P21
Mayfan Ln. ... Pg.16 ... P15
Maynard Rd. ... Pg.17 ... N18
Melrose St. ... Pg.17 ... Q20
Menno Ct. ... Pg.18 ... N18
Menno Dr. ... Pg.17 ... P18
Michael Ln. ... Pg.17 ... N18
Michigan Rd. ... Pg.17 ... N18
Monteith Ave. ... Pg.16 ... P15
Oakdale Ave. ... Pg.16 ... P15
Oakview Ct. ... Pg.18 ... P21
Ogden Rd. ... Pg.17 ... R18
Parker Rd. ... Pg.17 ... N18
Pembrook Ave. ... Pg.16 ... P15
Pennington Ct. ... Pg.18 ... P21
Pine St. ... Pg.17 ... R18
Pioneer Pl. ... Pg.18 ... Q22
Plaza Dr. ... Pg.17 ... Q20
Pleasant Ct. ... Pg.17 ... Q20
Pottawatamie ... Pg.18 ... Q22
Prairie Rd. ... Pg.17 ... N20
Quails Roost Dr. ... Pg.18 ... R21
Raymond Dr. ... Pg.18 ... M21
Redwood Ave. ... Pg.17 ... N19
Regan Rd. ... Pg.17 ... R17
... Pg.17 ... M21,N19,20
Regent St. ... Pg.18 ... Q20
Richard Ave. ... Pg.17 ... N19
Roberts Rd. ... Pg.17 ... Q19
Rodger Ct. ... Pg.18 ... N17
Ross Dr. ... Pg.17 ... N19
Ruth Rd. ... Pg.17 ... M20
Schmule Rd. ... Pg.17 ... Q20
Schoolhouse Rd. ... Pg.18 ... Q21
Scott Ct. ... Pg.18 ... P22
Shelly Ln. ... Pg.18 ... P21
Solourn Rd. ... Pg.17 ... R20
Somerset Pl. ... Pg.17 ... Q20
Somerset St. ... Pg.17 ... Q20
Southwest Hwy. ... Pg.17 ... M20,21
Spector Rd. ... Pg.17 ... N18
Spencer Rd. ... Pg.17 ... N18
Star Line Dr. ... Pg.16 ... P15
Suffolk Ln. ... Pg.17 ... P17
Summerfield Dr. ... Pg.17 ... N19
Sunset Ln. ... Pg.16 ... P15
Sycamore St. ... Pg.17 ... P17
Tammy Dr. ... Pg.17 ... M20
Tauber Ct. ... Pg.17 ... R20
Tauber Rd. ... Pg.17 ... R20
Terry Ln. ... Pg.17 ... M20
Terryellen Ln. ... Pg.17 ... N18
Tessington Ct. ... Pg.18 ... P21
Thames River Ln. ... Pg.18 ... R21
Thomas Ct. ... Pg.18 ... M22
Thornhouse Crescent ... Pg.17 ... P17
Timothy Ln. ... Pg.17 ... P17
Tonell Ave. ... Pg.17 ... P19
Town Line Rd. ... Pg.18 ... N22
Tracy Ct. ... Pg.17 ... M19
Valley St. ... Pg.17 ... P17
Vine St. ... Pg.17 ... P18
Virginia Dr. ... Pg.17 ... M20
Wagon Dr. ... Pg.17 ... N19
Walona Ave. ... Pg.17 ... P17
Walter Dr. ... Pg.18 ... M21
Walter Dr. ... Pg.17 ... N20
Warren Dr. ... Pg.18 ... M21
Wellington Pkwy. ... Pg.18 ... M21
William St. ... Pg.17 ... P17
Willow Rd. W. ... Pg.17 ... P17
Willow St. ... Pg.17 ... P18
Wisconsin Rd. ... Pg.17 ... R19
Woodedge Ln. ... Pg.18 ... N21
Woodlawn Rd. ... Pg.17 ... R18
Woodside Dr. ... Pg.17 ... N20
2nd St. ... Pg.17 ... Q19
184th Pl. ... Pg.17 ... M20
185th Pl. ... Pg.17 ... M20
185th St. ... Pg.17 ... M20

### CEMETERIES
St. Cyrils Cem. ... Pg.10 ... H14

### FOREST PRESERVES
Hickory Creek ... Pg.18 ... Q21
Zalar Woods F.P. ... Pg.16 ... R15

### GOLF COURSES
Willow Run G.C. ... Pg.18 ... N18
Woodruff G.C. ... Pg.16 ... N16

### PARKS
Higginbotham Woods ... Pg.16 ... P16

### SCHOOLS
Lincoln Way H.S. ... Pg.18 ... Q21
Providence Catholic H.S. ... Pg.16 ... P16

### MISCELLANEOUS
New Lenox Park District ... Pg.17 ... P19
Old Plank Road Trail ... Pg.17 ... R19

## ORLAND PARK
Page 19
(For additional listings, see Section 2)
### STREETS
Interstate 80 ... M25
La Grange St. ... M25
U.S. Route 45 ... M25
104th Ave. ... M24
183rd St. ... M24

## PLAINFIELD
Pages 1,7
### STREETS
Allen Robert Dr. ... Pg.1 ... E5
Allen Robert Rd. ... Pg.1 ... E5
Amboy Ave. ... Pg.7 ... G4
Amherst Ct., N & S ... Pg.1 ... E5
Arbor Dr. ... Pg.7 ... J4
Ardordale Dr. ... Pg.7 ... J4
Arnold St. ... Pg.7 ... G4
Ash St. ... Pg.7 ... H4
Aster Ct. ... Pg.1 ... E4
Bartlett St. ... Pg.7 ... G4
Bass Lake Rd. ... Pg.7 ... H4
Belmont Dr. ... Pg.1 ... B4
Benson Ave. ... Pg.7 ... G4
Blue Heron Cove ... Pg.7 ... D4
Bobwhite Ln. ... Pg.1 ... C4
Book Rd. ... Pg.7 ... C5
Brett St. ... Pg.1 ... E3
Brown Ln. ... Pg.7 ... J4
Burgundy Dr. ... Pg.7 ... G3
Bussey Dr. ... Pg.7 ... J4
Cabernet Ln. ... Pg.7 ... H4
Cambridge Ct. ... Pg.1 ... E6
Capista Dr. ... Pg.7 ... G4
Cathy Ln. ... Pg.7 ... G4
Center St. ... Pg.7 ... G4
Chablis Ln. ... Pg.7 ... H4
Champion Dr. ... Pg.1 ... E4
Chapins Rd. ... Pg.7 ... D6
Chelsea Ln. ... Pg.7 ... E3
Chicago St. ... Pg.7 ... G4
Churchill Ln. ... Pg.7 ... B4
Coilplus Rd. ... Pg.7 ... J3
College St. ... Pg.7 ... H4
Columbine Cir. ... Pg.1 ... E4
Commercial St. ... Pg.7 ... G4
Corbin St. ... Pg.7 ... H4
Dayfield Dr. ... Pg.7 ... H4
Decathalon Ln. ... Pg.1 ... D5
Deer Path Cir. ... Pg.7 ... F3
Denise St. ... Pg.7 ... G4
Derby Ln. ... Pg.1 ... B4
Des Plaines St. ... Pg.7 ... G4
Diana Ct. ... Pg.1 ... E3
Dillman St. ... Pg.7 ... G4
Douglas Dr. ... Pg.1 ... E4
Eastern St. ... Pg.7 ... G4
Easy St. ... Pg.7 ... J3,4
Edgewood Dr. ... Pg.7 ... J6
Essington Rd. ... Pg.1 ... D6
Evans St. ... Pg.7 ... G4
Eyre Cir. ... Pg.1 ... E4
Fairfield Dr. ... Pg.7 ... H4
Falcon Dr. ... Pg.7 ... D4
Ferguson Rd. ... Pg.7 ... C6
Fescue Dr. ... Pg.7 ... H4
Fort Beggs Dr. ... Pg.7 ... H4
Fox River St. ... Pg.7 ... G4
Fraser Rd. ... Pg.1 ... E3
Fritz Rd. ... Pg.7 ... J3
Getson Ave. ... Pg.7 ... G4
Golden Meadow Dr. ... Pg.1 ... E4
Golden Sunset Dr. ... Pg.1 ... E4
Greenfield Ct. ... Pg.1 ... D4
Greenfield Dr. ... Pg.1 ... D4
Hamlin St. ... Pg.7 ... G3
Hartong St. ... Pg.7 ... G4
Hawthorn Cir. ... Pg.7 ... G4
Hazelcrest Dr. ... Pg.1 ... E4
Heather Ct. ... Pg.1 ... E4
Heritage Meadows Dr. ... Pg.1 ... E4
Heron St. ... Pg.7 ... D4
Highview Ct. ... Pg.7 ... E4
Hillcrest Dr. ... Pg.1 ... E4
Hunt Club Ln. ... Pg.7 ... F6
Illini Dr. ... Pg.7 ... H3
Illinois St. ... Pg.7 ... G4
James St. ... Pg.7 ... H4
Jordan Ln. ... Pg.1 ... E3
Judith Ct. ... Pg.1 ... J5
Judith Ln. ... Pg.1 ... J5
Julie Ave. ... Pg.7 ... H4
Kelly Ave. ... Pg.7 ... G4
La Croix Ln. ... Pg.7 ... E5
Lakepoint Dr. ... Pg.1 ... D6
Lakeshore Dr. ... Pg.7 ... E4
Lakeside Ave. ... Pg.7 ... G4
Lakeside Dr. ... Pg.7 ... H4
Landwood Dr. ... Pg.7 ... J3
Lewood Dr. ... Pg.7 ... J3
Lexington Dr. ... Pg.7 ... H4
Lily Cache Rd. ... Pg.7 ... C4
Lincoln Hwy. ... Pg.7 ... F3
Lynn St. ... Pg.7 ... H4
Madison St. ... Pg.7 ... G4
Main St. ... Pg.7 ... G4
Maple St. ... Pg.7 ... G4
Marathon Ln. ... Pg.1 ... D4
Marina Dr. ... Pg.7 ... E4
Marybrook Dr. ... Pg.7 ... E4
Massay Ave. ... Pg.7 ... J4
McClellan Ave. ... Pg.7 ... G4
Meadow Lily Ct. ... Pg.7 ... C4
Meadowbrook ... Pg.7 ... E4
Merlot Ln. ... Pg.7 ... H4
Michigan St. ... Pg.7 ... G4
Miles Ave. ... Pg.7 ... J4
Mill St. ... Pg.7 ... G4
Mink Farm Rd. ... Pg.7 ... D4
Mistwood Dr. ... Pg.7 ... J6
Naperville Rd. ... Pg.7 ... D6
Newkirk Dr. ... Pg.7 ... H4
Nightengale Ct. ... Pg.7 ... H4
Norman Ave. ... Pg.7 ... J4
O'Connell Dr. ... Pg.7 ... H4
Oak St. ... Pg.7 ... G4
Orchard Ln. ... Pg.7 ... E4
Ottawa St. ... Pg.7 ... G4
Park Ave. ... Pg.7 ... G4
Park Ln. ... Pg.1 ... E3
Parkside Ct. ... Pg.7 ... D5
Pasquinelli Dr. ... Pg.7 ... D4
Pawnge St. ... Pg.7 ... H3
Pear Tree Cir. ... Pg.1 ... C4
Pear Tree Rd. ... Pg.1 ... C4
Penn Rd. ... Pg.7 ... G4
Pheasant Chase Dr. ... Pg.1 ... C4
Pheasant Dr. ... Pg.1 ... E3-4
Pilcher Rd. ... Pg.1 ... E3
Plainfield-Naperville Rd. ... Pg.1,7
Plainsman Cir. ... Pg.7 ... K4
Plainsman Dr. ... Pg.7 ... K4
Pond View Dr. ... Pg.7 ... K4
Prairie Crossing ... Pg.7 ... D4
Prairie Dr. ... Pg.7 ... H3
Prairie Grove Dr. ... Pg.1 ... E4
Pratt Ln. ... Pg.7 ... H4
Preakness Dr. ... Pg.7 ... B4
Prairie Crossing ... Pg.7 ... E6
Prairie Rose Ct. ... Pg.7 ... D4
Primrose Cir. ... Pg.1 ... D4
Quail Ct. ... Pg.7 ... D4
Quail Run Ln. ... Pg.7 ... C4
Ranchland Dr. ... Pg.7 ... E4
Reserve Cir. ... Pg.7 ... E5
Richland Dr. ... Pg.1 ... E3
River Dr. ... Pg.7 ... G4
River Ln. ... Pg.7 ... G3
Rivera Dr. ... Pg.7 ... H4
Robert Ln. ... Pg.7 ... J4
Robin Ct. ... Pg.7 ... H3
Route 126 ... Pg.7 ... H4
Route 30 ... Pg.1,7 ... F3,G4,H5
Route 59 ... Pg.7 ... C4
Sandpiper Cove ... Pg.7 ... E6
Sara St. ... Pg.7 ... G3
Sharp Dr. ... Pg.7 ... E5
Simo Dr. ... Pg.7 ... J4
Spring Hill Ln. ... Pg.7 ... J6
Spring Hill Ln. ... Pg.7 ... E4
St. Joesph Ave. ... Pg.1 ... E4
Tall Grass Dr. ... Pg.1 ... D4
Teal Ct. ... Pg.7 ... D4
Timberview Dr. ... Pg.7 ... C4
Union Ct. ... Pg.7 ... H4
Union St. ... Pg.7 ... H4
Vailview Ct. ... Pg.1 ... D5
Van Dyke Rd. ... Pg.7 ... F3
Vetel Ct. ... Pg.7 ... G3
Vista Dr. ... Pg.7 ... G4
Vista Ln. ... Pg.7 ... G4
Walden Dr. ... Pg.7 ... G4
Water Lily Ct. ... Pg.7 ... D4
Waterfront Cir. ... Pg.7 ... D4
Winding Creek Rd. ... Pg.7 ... J5
Wood Duck Dr. ... Pg.1 ... D6
Wood Ct. ... Pg.7 ... G4
119th St. ... Pg.1 ... B4
143rd St. ... Pg.1,7 ... C6
224th Ave. ... Pg.1 ... C6

### CEMETERIES
Plainfield Cem. ... Pg.7 ... H4

### PARKS
Kelly Park ... Pg.7 ... F4
Ottawa Park ... Pg.7 ... G4
Village Green Park ... Pg.7 ... G4

### SCHOOLS
Indian Trail Jr. H.S. ... Pg.7 ... G4
Middle Sch. ... Pg.1 ... C4
Plainfield H.S. Complex ... Pg.7 ... G4
Plainfield Sch. Dist 202 ... Pg.7 ... E5
School ... Pg.1 ... E5
St. Mary's Sch. ... Pg.7 ... G4
Walkers Grove Elem. Sch. ... Pg.1 ... E3

### SHOPPING CENTERS
Lily Cache Plaza ... Pg.7 ... J5
Plainfield Plaza ... Pg.7 ... E5

### MISCELLANEOUS
Fire Department ... Pg.7 ... G4
Park District Offices ... Pg.7 ... G4
Plainfield Park Dist. ... Pg.7 ... E5
Police Dept. ... Pg.7 ... F4
Village Hall ... Pg.7 ... F4

## PLAINFIELD TOWNSHIP
Pages 1,2,7,8,13,14
### STREETS
Addleman St. ... Pg.13 ... L6
Anderson St. ... Pg.7 ... J5
Ardith St. ... Pg.13 ... L6
Benson Ave. ... Pg.7 ... K4
Bentley Dr. ... Pg.7 ... L5
Berry St. ... Pg.7 ... K7
Biltmore Ave. ... Pg.1 ... K4
Brittany St. ... Pg.7 ... J4
Bronk Rd. ... Pg.7 ... H5
Brown St. ... Pg.7 ... J4
Butler Rd. ... Pg.2,8 ... E-G7
Burbank St. ... Pg.13 ... L6
Byrum Blvd. ... Pg.13 ... L6
Caroline Dr. ... Pg.8 ... J7
Castle Ct. ... Pg.13 ... L6
Catlin Ct. ... Pg.7 ... K3
Caton Farm Rd. ... Pg.8 ... J7
Cecily Dr. ... Pg.7 ... J4
Central Dr. ... Pg.8 ... K7
Charlotte Rd. ... Pg.7 ... J6
Chestnut St. ... Pg.8 ... K4
Chevy Chase Dr. ... Pg.7 ... J6
Clark St. ... Pg.7 ... J5
Cog Hill ... Pg.7 ... L7
Colerlain St. ... Pg.7 ... J5
Collins St. ... Pg.7 ... H5
Commonwealth Ave. ... Pg.8 ... L7
Conant Ave. ... Pg.7 ... L7
Copper Dr. ... Pg.7 ... J6
Cosmic Dr. ... Pg.7 ... J4
Crystal Dr. ... Pg.7 ... J6
Culver St. ... Pg.7 ... J5
Dan Ireland Dr. ... Pg.7 ... J7
Dan O'Connell Dr. ... Pg.7 ... J7
Davy Ct. ... Pg.7 ... J6
Debbie Ct. ... Pg.7 ... J4
Division St. ... Pg.8 ... K4
Dixmoor St. ... Pg.7 ... L7
DuPage St. ... Pg.1 ... E5

## PLAINFIELD TOWNSHIP

Earl Dr. ......... Pg.7 ... L6
Eastline St. ..... Pg.7 ... L6
Easy St. ......... Pg.7 ... J3
Edgewood Ct. ..... Pg.7 ... J4
Ellen Dr. ........ Pg.7 ... J5
Ellina Ct. ....... Pg.7 ... J5
Emlong St. ....... Pg.8 ... K7
Emyvale Dr. ...... Pg.7 ... L3
Enid St. ......... Pg.8 ... L7
Essington Rd. .... Pg.7 ... J6
Evergreen Dr. .... Pg.8 ... L7
Ewing Ct. ........ Pg.7 ... J5
Ewing Dr. ........ Pg.7 ... J5
Farmindale Dr. ... Pg.8 ... J3
Farmington ....... Pg.8 ... L7
Feeney Dr. ....... Pg.7 ... J3
Fern St. ......... Pg.7 ... J5
Flossmoor St. .... Pg.8 ... L7
Flower St. ....... Pg.8 ... K7
Francis Dr. ...... Pg.8 ... H7
Fraser Rd. ....... Pg.7 ... J3
Frederick Ave. ... Pg.7 ... H4
Friday Rd. ....... Pg.7 ... J3
Frontage Rd. ..... Pg.2 ... E7
Gagne Ln. ........ Pg.2 ... K5
Galena Dr. ....... Pg.8 ... J7
Garden Ct. ....... Pg.8 ... K7
Garden Dr. ....... Pg.13 .. F5
Garden St. ....... Pg.8 ... K7
Geal Ave. ........ Pg.7 ... J5
George Dr. ....... Pg.7 ... J5
Getson Ave. ...... Pg.7 ... H4
Glasgow St. ...... Pg.8 ... K7
Glenwood Blvd. ... Pg.8 ... K7
Golden Ave. ...... Pg.7 ... F5
Golf St. ......... Pg.8 ... L7
Golf View Dr. .... Pg.8 ... L7
Golfmoor St. ..... Pg.8 ... K7
Grape St. ........ Pg.8 ... K7
Greenview Cir. ... Pg.8 ... L7
Greenway St. ..... Pg.8 ... K7
Greglawn ......... Pg.8 ... L7
Grinton Dr. ...... Pg.7 ... J5
Halifax Dr. ...... Pg.2 ... E7
Hanford Ct. ...... Pg.2 ... E7
Hannibal Ct. ..... Pg.2 ... F7
Harmony Dr. ...... Pg.7 ... J3
Harris Dr. ....... Pg.13 .. M6
Hartland Dr. ..... Pg.2 ... E7
Hastings Ct. ..... Pg.2 ... E7
Heather Ln. ...... Pg.13 .. L6
Heathercreek Dr. . Pg.7 ... K5
Hel-Mar Ln. ...... Pg.13 .. L6
Helen Dr. ........ Pg.8 ... H7
Hemmingway Cir. .. Pg.2 ... E7
Hemmingway St. ... Pg.2 ... E7
Hickory St. ...... Pg.7 ... J5
Hillsdale Ct. .... Pg.2 ... F7
Hillsdale Ln. .... Pg.2 ... F7
Hillsdale Rd. .... Pg.2 ... F7
Hollylynn Ln. .... Pg.7 ... K5
Honora Dr. ....... Pg.7 ... J5
Howard Ave. ...... Pg.7 ... H5
Idaho Ct. ........ Pg.2 ... E7
Inverness Dr. .... Pg.2 ... E7
Isle Royale Cir. . Pg.2 ... E7
Ivanhoe Ct. ...... Pg.2 ... E7
Ivanhoe Tr. ...... Pg.2 ... E7
Ives Ct. ......... Pg.2 ... E7
Ivy Ln. .......... Pg.7 ... J6
Jane Cir. ........ Pg.2 ... E7
Jay St. .......... Pg.8 ... E7
Jennings Ct. ..... Pg.2 ... E7
Jersey Ct. ....... Pg.2 ... E7
Jo Ann Dr. ....... Pg.7 ... L6
Jonesport Cir. ... Pg.2 ... E7
Jonesport Ct. .... Pg.2 ... E7
Juplin Ct. ....... Pg.2 ... E7
Joyce Ct. ........ Pg.2 ... E7
Judith St. ....... Pg.1 ... L7
Julie Ave. ....... Pg.2 ... E7
Junction Dr. ..... Pg.2 ... E7
June St. ......... Pg.7 ... L6
Juneau Ct. ....... Pg.2 ... E7
Kalamazoo Ct. .... Pg.2 ... E7
Katy Ct. ......... Pg.2 ... F7
Kearns Dr. ....... Pg.7 ... G5
Keith St. ........ Pg.8 ... K7
Kellogg St. ...... Pg.8 ... K7
Kendall Dr. ...... Pg.2 ... E7
Kentwood Dr. ..... Pg.2 ... E7
Kenwood .......... Pg.8 ... K7
Kenyon St. ....... Pg.7 ... J5
Kettering Ct. .... Pg.2 ... E7
Kileen Ct. ....... Pg.2 ... E7
Kingsley Ct. ..... Pg.2 ... E7
Kitty Hawk Ct. ... Pg.2 ... E7
Knollwood Dr. .... Pg.2 ... E7
Knox St. ......... Pg.2 ... E7
Laguna Ct. ....... Pg.2 ... E7
Lake Dr. ......... Pg.1 ... E5
Lake Ridge Dr. ... Pg.2 ... E7
Lake St. ......... Pg.7 ... J3
Lakeland St. ..... Pg.2 ... E7
Lakeridge Dr. .... Pg.2 ... E7
Lakewood Falls Dr.
Largo Ct. ........ Pg.2 ... E7
Lathrop Ct. ...... Pg.2 ... E7
Lavida ........... Pg.8 ... K7
Lawrence St. ..... Pg.7 ... J5
Leach Ct. ........ Pg.7 ... J5
Lee St. .......... Pg.8 ... H,J5
Legion Ct. ....... Pg.7 ... J3
Lehigh Dr. ....... Pg.7 ... J5
Lewood Dr. ....... Pg.7 ... J5
Lincoln Hwy. ..... Pg.7,8 .. F3,K7
Linden Ct. ....... Pg.7 ... L6
Lockner Blvd. .... Pg.7 ... L6
Lockport Rd. ..... Pg.8 ... G7
Longview Ln. ..... Pg.7 ... J5
Lorraine Ave. .... Pg.7 ... J5
Manassa Ln. ...... Pg.7 ... J5
Manistee Ct. ..... Pg.2 ... E7
Margaret Ct. ..... Pg.7 ... J5
Marshall Dr. ..... Pg.2 ... E7
Matthew St. ...... Pg.7 ... J5
Mayleon Dr. ...... Pg.2 ... E7
McGrath Dr. ...... Pg.7 ... J5
McKenna Dr. ...... Pg.7 ... K3
Meridian Dr. ..... Pg.7 ... L6
Michael Dr. ...... Pg.8 ... H7
Miller Ct. ....... Pg.7 ... J5
Miller Dr. ....... Pg.2 ... E7
Monticello Cir. .. Pg.7 ... F7
Mt. Pleasant Ct. . Pg.2 ... F7

Napa Cir. ........ Pg.2 ... F7
Natcher Ct. ...... Pg.2 ... F7
Newberg Ct. ...... Pg.2 ... F7
Niagara Ct. ...... Pg.2 ... F7
Niagara Ln. ...... Pg.2 ... F7
Norman Ave. ...... Pg.7 ... H4
Norwich Ct. ...... Pg.2 ... F7
Norwich Dr. ...... Pg.2 ... F7
Nuclear Dr. ...... Pg.7 ... L6
Oak St. .......... Pg.7 ... J5
Oakdale Cir. ..... Pg.2 ... F7
Oakdale Ct. ...... Pg.2 ... F7
Ocala Ct. ........ Pg.2 ... F7
Odessa Ct. ....... Pg.2 ... F7
Old Renwick Rd. .. Pg.8 ... H7
Olympia St. ...... Pg.8 ... K7
Oregon Dr. ....... Pg.2 ... F7
Overland Dr. ..... Pg.7 ... J5
Overman St. ...... Pg.1 ... E5
Parkfalls Ct. .... Pg.2 ... F7
Pasadena Ln. ..... Pg.2 ... E7
Patterson St. .... Pg.7 ... J5
Peacedale Ct. .... Pg.2 ... J3
Pearless Dr. ..... Pg.2 ... E7
Pecan St. ........ Pg.2 ... K5
Pennington Ln. ... Pg.2 ... F5
Penny Ln. ........ Pg.7 ... F5
Petersburg Dr. ... Pg.2 ... E7
Peterson Dr. ..... Pg.7 ... E7
Petosky Dr. ...... Pg.2 ... E7
Pike Cove ........ Pg.7 ... J3
Pilcher Rd. ...... Pg.1 ... E5
Pinecone Ln. ..... Pg.2 ... E7
Pinecrest Dr. .... Pg.8 ... J7
Pleasant Ct., E. & W. Pg.7 .. J3
Plum St. ......... Pg.8 ... L7
Plymouth Cir. .... Pg.2 ... F7
Plymouth Ct. ..... Pg.2 ... F7
Poplar St. ....... Pg.8 ... K7
Portage Ct. ...... Pg.2 ... F7
Princeton Ct. .... Pg.2 ... F7
Raymond Dr. ...... Pg.7 ... J5
Raymond St. ...... Pg.7 ... L6
Regan Rd. ........ Pg.2 ... E7
Renwick Park Dr. . Pg.7 ... J3
Renwick Rd. ...... Pg.7 ... H3-7
River Ct. ........ Pg.7 ... H3
River Rd. ........ Pg.2 ... J3
Rivercrest Dr. ... Pg.1 ... L6
Robert Ln. ....... Pg.7 ... H4
Route 126 ........ Pg.1 ... L6
Route 59 ......... Pg.1 ... L6
Rubin ............ Pg.2 ... J6
Saddle Dr. ....... Pg.7 ... L6
Satellite Dr. .... Pg.8 ... J7
September Dr. .... Pg.7 ... L6
Serenity Dr. ..... Pg.7 ... J3
Silver Ln. ....... Pg.7 ... F3
South End Rd. .... Pg.7 ... J7
Spangle Rd. ...... Pg.7 ... J6
State Rd. ........ Pg.8 ... K7
Stateville Rd. ... Pg.8 ... K7
Surrey Ln. ....... Pg.7 ... J5
Teeway St. ....... Pg.7 ... L6
Thomas Ct. ....... Pg.8 ... H7
Tyler Dr. ........ Pg.2 ... E7
Van Horn Ln. ..... Pg.7 ... L6
Vesta Dr. ........ Pg.7 ... L6
Von Esch Rd. ..... Pg.7 ... K5
Wayne Ave. ....... Pg.7 ... H4
Weller Ct. ....... Pg.1 ... L6
Westgate Ln. ..... Pg.8 ... J7
Westline Dr. ..... Pg.7 ... L6
Whiskey Rd. ...... Pg.1,7 .. J3
Wilkins Dr. ...... Pg.7 ... G5
Wilkins Ln. ...... Pg.7 ... G5
Wilkins Pl. ...... Pg.7 ... L6
Willardshire Rd. . Pg.7 ... K6
William Ct. ...... Pg.1 ... L7
Wilshire Blvd. ... Pg.8 ... L7
Winston Ave. ..... Pg.7 ... L5

### SCHOOLS
Lake Renwick Heron Rookery
  Nature Preserve

### GOLF COURSES
Carillon G.C. .... Pg.2 ... E8

### PARKS
Romeo Shores Fishing Area
Vanhorn Woods .... Pg.7 ... K5

### SCHOOLS
Lakewood Falls Elem. Sch.

### MISCELLANEOUS
Fire Station ..... Pg.1 ... E4

## ROCKDALE
Pages 14,15
### STREETS
Anita St. ............ Q10
Belleview Ave. ....... Q9
Belt Line ............ Q9
Centra Ave. .......... Q9
Connell Ave. ......... Q9
Davis Ave. ........... Q9
Davis St. ............ Q9
Emery St. ............ Q9
Ferris St. ........... Q10
Fisher Ave. .......... Q9
Howard St. ........... Q9
Jewett St. ........... Q9
Lake View Ave. ....... Q9
Margaret St. ......... Q9
Meadow Ave. .......... Q9
Midland St. .......... Q9
Moen Ave. ............ Q9
Morris St. ........... Q9
Otis Ave. ............ Q9
Railroad St. ......... Q10
Ravine ............... Q9
Raynor Ave. .......... Q10
Rimsey Ave. .......... Q9
Rock Island Ave. ..... Q10
Russell Ave. ......... Q9
Stillwell Ave. ....... Q9
Stryker St. .......... Q9
Warren St. ........... Q9
Workman Ave. ......... Q10

### PARKS
Rockdale Pk. ......... Q9

## ROMEOVILLE
Pages 2-4,8,9
### STREETS
Abbeywood Dr. .... Pg.3 ... C11
Airport Rd. ...... Pg.3 ... G11
Alexander Ln. .... Pg.3 ... D11
Ambassador Ave. .. Pg.3 ... D11
Amberleigh Ct. ... Pg.8 ... F7
Amberleigh Dr. ... Pg.8 ... F7
Amherst Dr. ...... Pg.3 ... D11
Anderson Rd. ..... Pg.3 ... D12
Anton Dr. ........ Pg.3 ... C12
Arbor Dr. ........ Pg.2 ... C9
Arbury Ct. ....... Pg.3 ... B11
Arcadia .......... Pg.3 ... C11
Arlington Dr. .... Pg.3 ... D11
Arnold Ave. ...... Pg.3 ... E10
Arsenal Rd. ...... Pg.3 ... E10
Ashton Ave. ...... Pg.3 ... E10
Aspen Dr. ........ Pg.2 ... D10
Austrian Dr. ..... Pg.3 ... C12
Avalon Ave. ...... Pg.3 ... E10
Baker Cir. ....... Pg.3 ... E12
Beacon Ave. ...... Pg.3 ... E11
Beechwood Dr. .... Pg.3 ... C11
Belmont Ct. ...... Pg.3 ... E10
Belmont Dr. ...... Pg.3 ... D10,11
Berkshire Ave. ... Pg.3 ... E11
Beverly Griffin Dr. Pg.3 .. D10
Blue Aster Dr. ... Pg.2 ... D10
Bluff Dr. ........ Pg.3 ... C12
Brassfield Ave. .. Pg.3 ... D11
Briarwood Ave. ... Pg.2 ... E10
Bristol Ave. ..... Pg.3 ... D11
Brookstone Ct. ... Pg.8 ... F7
Budler Rd. ....... Pg.2 ... D9
Bull Run Dr. ..... Pg.3 ... D,E11
Camden Ave. ...... Pg.3 ... D11
Canterbury Trail . Pg.8 ... F7
Cascade .......... Pg.3 ... D11
Cedar Ct. ........ Pg.3 ... D11
Cedarbend Dr. .... Pg.3 ... C11
Chamberlain Dr. .. Pg.2 ... C9
Chambers Dr. ..... Pg.3 ... C12
Chatham Dr. ...... Pg.8 ... F7
Chauncer Ct. ..... Pg.8 ... F7
Chauncer Dr. ..... Pg.8 ... F7
Civic Center Dr. . Pg.3 ... E11
Clifton Ave. ..... Pg.3 ... E10
Concord Ave. ..... Pg.3 ... D11
Coneflower Ct. ... Pg.2 ... D10
Coneflower Dr. ... Pg.3 ... D10
Corona Ave. ...... Pg.3 ... D11
Cranbrook Ct. .... Pg.3 ... D10
Dalhart Ave. ..... Pg.3 ... D-E11
Dalhart Ave. ..... Pg.3 ... D11
Delta Ave. ....... Pg.3 ... D11
Devon Ln. ........ Pg.3 ... C11
Devonwood Ave. ... Pg.8 ... F7
Dexter Ave. ...... Pg.3 ... D11
Donovan Rd. ...... Pg.3 ... B13
Doyer Ave. ....... Pg.3 ... C11
Driftwood Ave. ... Pg.3 ... E10
Dunridge Ln. ..... Pg.3 ... C11
Eaton Ave. ....... Pg.3 ... E11
Echo Ave. ........ Pg.3 ... D11
Edgecreek Dr. .... Pg.8 ... F7
Elgin Ave. ....... Pg.3 ... E11
Elmwood Dr. ...... Pg.3 ... B13
Emery Ave. ....... Pg.3 ... E11
Enterprise Dr. ... Pg.3 ... E10
Erie Ln. ......... Pg.3 ... D11
Essex Ave. ....... Pg.3 ... D11
Essington Ln. .... Pg.2 ... D10
Everette Ave. .... Pg.3 ... E11
Evergreen Ct. .... Pg.3 ... C12
Faculty Ln. ...... Pg.9 ... G11
Fairfax Ave. ..... Pg.3 ... E10
Fairview Ct. ..... Pg.8 ... F7
Farmbrook Ln. .... Pg.3 ... C11
Farmngt Ave. ..... Pg.3 ... D11
Fenton Ave. ...... Pg.3 ... D,E11
Fernwood Ct. ..... Pg.3 ... C11
Fieldstone Dr. ... Pg.8 ... F7
Flambeau Ct. ..... Pg.3 ... D10
Forestwood Dr. ... Pg.3 ... D12
Fremont Ave. ..... Pg.3 ... E10
Frontage Rd., S.E.
Gardiner Ct. ..... Pg.2 ... D9
Garland Ave. ..... Pg.3 ... E11
Gavin Ave. ....... Pg.3 ... E10
Geneva Ave. ...... Pg.3 ... D11
Glen Ave. ........ Pg.3 ... D,E11
Gleneagle Ct. .... Pg.8 ... F7
Gleneagle Dr. .... Pg.8 ... F7
Glenhurst Ct. .... Pg.3 ... B11
Golden Rod Ave. .. Pg.3 ... D10
Gordon Ave. ...... Pg.3 ... D11
Greenwood Ave. ... Pg.3 ... E11
Hale Ave. ........ Pg.3 ... E11
Haley Meadows Dr.
Haller Ave. ...... Pg.3 ... E11
Halstead Ct. ..... Pg.3 ... E10
Hamrick Ave. ..... Pg.3 ... F10,11
Hanson Ct. ....... Pg.3 ... C11
Harris Ln. ....... Pg.3 ... C11
Hayes Ave. ....... Pg.3 ... E11
Healy Ave. ....... Pg.3 ... E11
Hemlock Ave. ..... Pg.3 ... E11
Hickory Ave. ..... Pg.3 ... E11
High Rd. ......... Pg.3 ... E13
Highpoint Dr. .... Pg.8 ... G7
Hillcrest Dr. .... Pg.3 ... C11
Holden Ave. ...... Pg.3 ... E11
Homer Ave. ....... Pg.3 ... C11
Honey Bear Ln. ... Pg.3 ... C11
Honeytree Dr. .... Pg.3 ... C11
Hudson Ave. ...... Pg.3 ... E11
Huron Dr. ........ Pg.3 ... D10
Independence Ave.
Interstate 55 .... Pg.2 ... C9
Iola Ave. ........ Pg.3 ... D-F11
Jackson St. ...... Pg.3 ... E13
Jefferson ........ Pg.4 ... E14
Joliet Rd. ....... Pg.3 ... B13
Jordan Ave. ...... Pg.3 ... E10

Karen Ave. ....... Pg.3 ... E11
Kent Ave. ........ Pg.3 ... E10
Kentland Ct. ..... Pg.8 ... F7
Kenyon Ave. ...... Pg.3 ... E11
Kingston Dr. ..... Pg.3 ... D11
Kirman Ave. ...... Pg.3 ... E11
Lake Shore Ct. ... Pg.8 ... G7
Lake Shore Dr. ... Pg.8 ... G7
Lakeside Dr. ..... Pg.3 ... C12
Lakeview Ct. ..... Pg.2 ... C9
Lakeview Dr. ..... Pg.2 ... C9
Lancaster Dr. .... Pg.8 ... F7
Larsen Cir. ...... Pg.3 ... E11
Laurel Ave. ...... Pg.3 ... D11
Lily Ln. ......... Pg.3 ... D11
Linden Ave. ...... Pg.3 ... E11
Lockport Rd. ..... Pg.2 ... E13
Longwood Ct. ..... Pg.8 ... F7
Luther Dr. ....... Pg.3 ... D11
Lynn Ave. ........ Pg.3 ... E11
Macon Ave. ....... Pg.3 ... B12
Marquette Dr. .... Pg.3 ... B12
Mayfield Ct. ..... Pg.8 ... F7
McKool Ave. ...... Pg.3 ... E11
Meadowdale Dr. ... Pg.3 ... D10
Mendota Ln. ...... Pg.3 ... D10
Michigan Dr. ..... Pg.3 ... D10
Montclair Ct. .... Pg.3 ... D11
Montrose Dr. ..... Pg.3 ... E11
Morgan Ct. ....... Pg.8 ... F7
Murphy Dr. ....... Pg.3 ... E11
Nashville Dr. .... Pg.3 ... D11
Nelson Ave. ...... Pg.3 ... D11
New Ave. ......... Pg.3 ... E13
New Castle Dr. ... Pg.8 ... F7
Newland Ave. ..... Pg.3 ... E10
Newman Ct. ....... Pg.3 ... D10
Nippert Ave. ..... Pg.3 ... E11
Normantown Rd. ... Pg.2,3 .. D9-11
Oakton Ave. ...... Pg.3 ... E10
Old Orchard Ln., W.
Olde English Ct. . Pg.8 ... F7
Olde English Dr. . Pg.8 ... F7
Ontario Dr. ...... Pg.3 ... D10
Palmer Ave. ...... Pg.3 ... E11
Parkview Ct. ..... Pg.8 ... F7
Parkview Dr. ..... Pg.8 ... F7
Parkwood Ave. .... Pg.3 ... D12
Pebblestone Dr. .. Pg.8 ... F7
Pell Ave. ........ Pg.3 ... E11
Pembroke Ct. ..... Pg.8 ... F7
Pembroke Dr. ..... Pg.8 ... F7
Pine Trails ...... Pg.3 ... C12
Ponderosa Dr. .... Pg.3 ... C11
Poplar Ave. ...... Pg.3 ... D10
Prairie Clover Dr. Pg.3 .. D10
Premrose Ct. ..... Pg.3 ... D10
Premrose Dr. ..... Pg.3 ... D10
Recreation Dr. ... Pg.2 ... E13
Ridgewood Ave. ... Pg.3 ... D12
Robbin Dr. ....... Pg.3 ... C12
Rocbaar Dr. ...... Pg.3 ... D12
Rockledge Dr. .... Pg.3 ... C11
Rogers Rd. ....... Pg.3 ... D11
Romeo Rd. ........ Pg.2 ... C11
Roof Ave. ........ Pg.3 ... E11
Roschill Ct. ..... Pg.3 ... C11
Saybrook Dr. ..... Pg.8 ... F7
Schmidt Rd. ...... Pg.3 ... C11
Sedge Meadow Dr.
Sedgewicke Ct. ... Pg.8 ... F7
Sedgewicke Dr. ... Pg.8 ... F7
Sherman Rd. ...... Pg.3 ... B13
Sherwood Ct. ..... Pg.3 ... E11
Shoreline Ct. .... Pg.8 ... F7
Slide Ln. ........ Pg.3 ... C11
Six Pines Dr. .... Pg.3 ... C11
Somerset Ct. ..... Pg.3 ... E11
Somerset Dr. ..... Pg.8 ... F7
Southport Ct. .... Pg.8 ... F7
Spangler Ave. .... Pg.3 ... E11
Springhill Ct. ... Pg.8 ... F7
St. Claire Dr. ... Pg.3 ... D10
Superior Dr. ..... Pg.3 ... D10
Sutcliffe Ct. .... Pg.3 ... C11
Sutcliffe Dr. .... Pg.8 ... F7
Tallman Ave. ..... Pg.3 ... E11
Taylor ........... Pg.3 ... F7-10
Terrace Ave. ..... Pg.3 ... D11
Townhall Dr. ..... Pg.3 ... C11
Troxel Ave. ...... Pg.3 ... F11
Union Ave. ....... Pg.3 ... E10
University Dr. ... Pg.9 ... H11
University Pkwy. . Pg.9 ... H11
Waldon Ct. ....... Pg.3 ... B11
Washington ....... Pg.3 ... F7
Weber Rd. ........ Pg.2 ... E,F9
Wedgeport Cir. ... Pg.8 ... G7
Wedgeport Ct. .... Pg.8 ... G7
Wesark Ct. ....... Pg.3 ... B11
Wesark Pkwy. ..... Pg.3 ... B11
Wesark Pkwy., N.
Westlake Pkwy. ... Pg.3 ... B11
White Cliff Dr. .. Pg.8 ... F7
Whitehill Dr. .... Pg.3 ... C11
Wild Indigo Ave. . Pg.3 ... D10
Wildwood Ct. ..... Pg.3 ... D11
Willow Ct. ....... Pg.3 ... C11
Windham Pkwy. .... Pg.3 ... C12
Winding Ridge Dr. Pg.8 ... F7
Winding Ridge Dr. Pg.8 ... F7
Winnebago Ct. .... Pg.3 ... D10
Woodhill Dr. ..... Pg.8 ... F7
Woodlawn Ave. .... Pg.3 ... E11
Yates Ave. ....... Pg.3 ... E10
115th St. ........ Pg.2 ... E11
135th St. ........ Pg.2 ... E12

### AIRPORTS
Lewis Lockport Airport Pg.9 .. G11

### CEMETERIES
Resurrection Cemetery Pg.3 .. E11

### FOREST PRESERVES
Centennial Trail Forest Preserve
Isle A-La Cache Preserve Pg.3 . D12
O'Hara Woods .... Pg.2 ... E10

Romeoville Prairie Nature
  Preserve ...... Pg.3 ... E12
Veteran's Woods F7
  ............. Pg.3 ... C13

### GOLF COURSES
Mistwood G.C. .... Pg.8 ... H7-8

### PARKS
Ashley Park ...... Pg.3 ... E11
College View Park Pg.9 ... G11
Jaycee Park ...... Pg.3 ... E10
Murphy Park ...... Pg.3 ... E11
Romeoville Rec. Ct.
  ............. Pg.2 ... E10
Sunset Park ...... Pg.3 ... E10

### SCHOOLS
Bible Baptist Christian Academy
  Sch. ......... Pg.3 ... D11
Irene King Sch. .. Pg.3 ... E11
Joliet Jr. College Pg.9 ... G11
Lewis University . Pg.9 ... G11
Parkview Sch. .... Pg.3 ... D11
R.C. Hill Elem. Sch.
Romeoville H.S. .. Pg.3 ... F11
St. Andrew The Apostle Sch.
Valley View Sch. . Pg.3 ... D11
Vito Martinez Sch.
  ............. Pg.3 ... F10

### SHOPPING CENTERS
Romeo Plaza S.C. . Pg.3 ... E11

### MISCELLANEOUS
Fitzpatrick House Pg.3 ... H12
Harold White Aviation Center
  ............. Pg.9 ... G11
Isle A La Cache Museum
Joliet Port Authority District
  ............. Pg.9 ... H11
Library .......... Pg.3 ... D11
Marquette Business Park
  ............. Pg.3 ... C12
National Weather Bureau
  ............. Pg.9 ... H11
Roman Catholic Pastoral Center
Romeoville Commercial Business
  Park ......... Pg.3 ... C11
School of Aviation Pg.9 ... H11
Uno-Ven Chicago Oil Refinery
Village Hall ..... Pg.3 ... E11
White Fence Farm Pg.3 ... B13
Will County Area Career Center
Windham Lakes Industrial Park
  ............. Pg.2 ... C9

## SHOREWOOD
Page 13
### STREETS
Amendodge Dr. ........ Q4
Arrowhead Dr. ........ P4
Bass St. ............. P3
Beith Rd. ............ P3
Berkley Ct. .......... P3
Bethany Dr. .......... N4
Black Rd. ............ N4
Brookforest Ave. ..... N4
Brookshore Ct. ....... P4
Brookshore Dr. ....... P4
Buckingham Ct. ....... P4
Buckingham Pl. ....... P4
Ca-Crest Dr. ......... N4
Cambridge Ln. ........ Q3
Caprice Dr. .......... Q3
Cardinal Pl. ......... P4
Carlisle Dr. ......... N4
Cedar Ln. ............ N4
Channahon St. ........ P4
Chartwell Trace ...... P4
Chartwell Trace Ct. .. P4
Clark Dr. ............ P4
Cobblestone Ct. ...... P4
Collingwood Ct. ...... Q3
Colonade Rd. ......... Q3
Colony Ct. ........... P4
Cornell Ct. .......... P3
Cortina Ct. .......... Q3
Cottage St. .......... M,P4
Country Dr. .......... N3
County Farm Rd. ...... N3
Danny Dr. ............ N4
Dante Ct. ............ P4
David Dr. ............ N4
Deerwood Dr. ......... P4
Diana Ave. ........... P4
Du Page St. .......... N4
Edgebrook Dr. ........ N4
Franklin Rd. ......... P3
Frontage Rd. ......... N5
Garden Terr. ......... P3
Geneva St. ........... P3
Greenfield Rd. ....... N3
Grove St. ............ N4
Harvard Ct. .......... Q3
Harvest Dr. .......... P3
Helene St. ........... N4
Highland Dr. ......... N4
Home Ct. ............. P3
Hummingbird Ct. ...... P3
Hunter Dr. ........... P3
Huntington Ct. ....... N4
Huntington Dr. ....... P4
Jarno Ln. ............ Q3
Jefferson St. ........ P3
Kensington St. ....... N3
Lancer Dr. ........... P3
Lark Ln. ............. Q3
Laura St. ............ P3
Lynwood Ct. .......... N4
Madiera Dr. .......... Q3
Manor Dr. ............ N4
Maple Ln. ............ N4
Marly Ln. ............ P4
Mayra Ln. ............ Q3
Meadow Dr. ........... N4
Meyer St. ............ N4
Moorland Ave. ........ Q3
Oak Ct. .............. P4
Oak Dr. .............. P3
Oakwood Dr. .......... P4
Oxford Ln. ........... Q3

## TINLEY PARK
Page 19
(For additional listings, see Section 2)
### STREETS
Basswood Ct. ......... M26
Berrybrook Ct. ....... P27
Blackoak Ave. ........ M27
Brook Point Ct. ...... N27
Brookfield Ct. ....... N27
Brookridge Dr. ....... N27
Brookside Glen Ct. ... N28
Brookside Glen Dr. ... N28
Brushwood Ln. ........ N28
Burchfront Dr. ....... M27
Camelot Dr. .......... Q3
Dogwood Ct. .......... M27
Eagleridge Ln. ....... M27
Enclave Ln. .......... N28
Glenberry Ln. ........ M27
Glenbrook Ct. ........ N28
Glenbrook Ln. ........ N28
Glendale Tr. ......... P27
Glenshire St. ........ N27
Graphics Dr. ......... M26
Greenleaf Ct. ........ M26
Greenview Pl. ........ N27
Greenway Blvd. ....... M28
Harvest View Ln. ..... P4
Meadows Edge Tr. ..... M27
North Star Ct. ....... M28
Peachtree Dr. ........ M27
Ridgemont Dr. ........ N27
Silverside Dr. ....... P27
Timbers Pointe Dr. ... M27
Timbers Pointe Dr.,E. M27
Timbers Pointe Dr.,W. M26
Timberwood Ln. ....... P4
White Oak Ln. ........ M26
White Oak Ln. ........ N28
Woodbine Ct. ......... M27
81st Ave. ............ M28
88th Ave. ............ M27
92nd Ave. ............ M26
183rd St. ............ N28
186th St. ............ M28

### GOLF COURSES
St. Andrew Chaney Sch. .. L26

### MISCELLANEOUS
Midwest Christian Center .. M26

## TROY TOWNSHIP
Pages 13,14
### STREETS
Appaloosa Ln. .... Pg.13 .. M2
Bailey Dr. ....... Pg.13 .. N6
Bankview ......... Pg.14 .. N6
Barber Ln. ....... Pg.14 .. N7
Baskin Dr. ....... Pg.13 .. N4
Black Rd. ........ Pg.13 .. N3,4
Bluemont Dr. ..... Pg.13 .. N4
Brook Rd. ........ Pg.13 .. N5
Canterbury St. ... Pg.13 .. Q4
Cassie Ln. ....... Pg.14 .. N7
Chestnut Dr. ..... Pg.13 .. M2
Clarage Ct. ...... Pg.13 .. Q4
Country Farm Rd. . Pg.13 .. Q4
Eden Ln. ......... Pg.13 .. M2
Equestrian Ct. ... Pg.13 .. M2
Francis Ct. ...... Pg.13 .. Q4

## WOODRIDGE

Frank Dr. ........ Pg.13 .. M4
Gael Dr. ......... Pg.14 .. N7
George Ave. ...... Pg.14 .. N7
Glenwood Ave. .... Pg.14 .. N7
Green Meadow Ln.
Houbold Rd. ...... Pg.13 .. N6
Interstate 55 .... Pg.13 .. N3
Interstate 80 .... Pg.13 .. R6
Jensen St. ....... Pg.13 .. Q4
Lakewoods Ln. .... Pg.13 .. R3
Magnolia Dr. ..... Pg.14 .. N8
Marlene Ct. ...... Pg.13 .. Q4
Mattox Ct. ....... Pg.13 .. N4
McDonald Ct. ..... Pg.13 .. Q4
Mound Rd. ........ Pg.13 .. R3
Murphy Dr. ....... Pg.14 .. N7
Nada Dr. ......... Pg.13 .. N3
Palamino Ct. ..... Pg.13 .. M2
Palamino Dr. ..... Pg.13 .. M2
Park River Ln. ... Pg.13 .. M2
River Dr. ........ Pg.13 .. N3
River Rd. ........ Pg.13 .. M,N3
Roan Ln. ......... Pg.13 .. M2
Rock Run Dr. ..... Pg.13 .. Q5
Rollingwood Ct. .. Pg.13 .. N6
Rollingwood Dr. .. Pg.13 .. N6
Ron-Lee Ct. ...... Pg.13 .. Q4
Roney Ave. ....... Pg.14 .. N7
Ronnie Ct. ....... Pg.13 .. N4
Rosary Ln. ....... Pg.14 .. N7
Saddlebrook Ln. .. Pg.13 .. N4
Sarver Dr. ....... Pg.13 .. Q4
Schock Dr. ....... Pg.13 .. N4
Theodore St. ..... Pg.13 .. M5
Timberline ....... Pg.13 .. N6
Timberline Ct. ... Pg.13 .. N6
Troy Rd. ......... Pg.13 .. P6
Wells Way ........ Pg.13 .. P6
West Ridge Rd. ... Pg.13 .. N6

### FOREST PRESERVES
Will County F.P. . Pg.13 .. Q5

## WHEATLAND TOWNSHIP
Pages 1,2
### STREETS
Aero Ct. ......... Pg.1 ... C4
Aero Dr. ......... Pg.1 ... C4
Ainsdale Ct. ..... Pg.1 ... A4
Andrew Rd. ....... Pg.1 ... A4
Anvil Ct. ........ Pg.1 ... A4
Book Rd. ......... Pg.1 ... C5
Brighton Ln. ..... Pg.1 ... A3
Callandar Ct. .... Pg.1 ... A3
Campfire Ct. ..... Pg.1 ... A3
Campfire Ct. ..... Pg.1 ... A3
Cathy Ln. ........ Pg.1 ... C5
Catswald Dr. ..... Pg.1 ... C5
Chaisholm Tr. .... Pg.1 ... A3
Chapins Rd. ...... Pg.1 ... C4
Conestoga Dr. .... Pg.1 ... A3
Denise St. ....... Pg.1 ... D5
Douglas Dr. ...... Pg.1 ... D4
Ferguson Rd. ..... Pg.1,2 .. C6
Gamton Ct. ....... Pg.1 ... A3
Gravor Ct. ....... Pg.1 ... A3
Gravor Ln. ....... Pg.1 ... A3
Greenburg Ct. .... Pg.1 ... B4
Highland Dr. ..... Pg.1 ... B4
Industrial Dr. ... Pg.1 ... C4
Kennemer Ct. ..... Pg.1 ... C8
Kings Rd. ........ Pg.1 ... C5
Leona Dr. ........ Pg.1 ... A3
Littlestone Ln. .. Pg.1 ... A3
Naperville Rd. ... Pg.1 ... D7
Navajo Ct. ....... Pg.1 ... A3
Oxford Ln. ....... Pg.1 ... C4
Paul Cir. ........ Pg.1 ... A3
Paula Ct. ........ Pg.1 ... A3
Plainfield Naperville Rd.
  ............. Pg.1 ... C6
Port Marnock Ct. . Pg.1 ... A3
Rhea Dr. ......... Pg.1 ... C4
Royal Porthcawl Dr.
  ............. Pg.1 ... A3
Royal Portrush Dr.
  ............. Pg.1 ... A3
Spaulding School Dr.
St. Annes Ct. .... Pg.1 ... C4
Stratford Dr. .... Pg.1 ... C5
Sunningdale Dr. .. Pg.1 ... C5
Thelma Ct. ....... Pg.1 ... U4
Torphin Hill Ct. . Pg.1 ... A3
Tumbleend Ct. .... Pg.1 ... A3
Turnberry Dr. .... Pg.1 ... A4
Van Dyke Rd. ..... Pg.1 ... C4
Vicky St. ........ Pg.1 ... D5
Wentworth Dr. .... Pg.1 ... A3
Wolf Dr. ......... Pg.1 ... C5
113th St. ........ Pg.1,2 .. O4
119th St. ........ Pg.1 ... C5
127th St. ........ Pg.1 ... D5
135th St. ........ Pg.1 ... E5
248th Ave. ....... Pg.1 ... C3

### GOLF COURSES
Naperbrook G.C. .. Pg.2 ... A6
Tamarack G.C. .... Pg.1 ... A4

### MISCELLANEOUS
Fire Station ..... Pg.1 ... E4
Naperville Polo Club
  ............. Pg.1 ... B5

## WOODRIDGE
Page 4
### STREETS
Bluff Rd. ............ B15
Davey Rd. ............ A14
Davey Rd. ............ A14
International Pkwy. .. A13-15
Joliet Rd. ........... A14
Katherine's Crossing  B14
Marmon Dr. ........... A14
107th St. ............ A14

### FOREST PRESERVES
Woodridge F.P. ....... A15

### MISCELLANEOUS
International Business Park .. A14

# ZIP CODE DIRECTORY
## SECTION 9

### ILLINOIS INDEX

60001 .. Alden ............. B3
60002 .. Antioch ............ B6
60004 .. Arlington Heights .. F7
60005 .. Arlington Heights .. F7
60006 .. Arlington Park ..... F6
60007 .. Elk Grove Village .. G6
60008 .. Rolling Meadows ... F6
60010 .. Barrington/ Deer Park/
          So. Barrington ..... E5
60012 .. Crystal Lake ..... D4
60013 .. Cary ............. E5
60014 .. Crystal Lake ..... E4
60015 .. Deerfield/
          Riverwoods ........ E7
60016 .. Des Plaines ...... F8
60018 .. Des Plaines/
          Rosemont ........ G7
60020 .. Fox Lake ......... C5
60021 .. Fox River Grove .. E5
60022 .. Glencoe .......... F9
60025 .. Glenview ......... F8
60026 .. Glenview N.A.S. ... F8
60029 .. Golf ............. G8
60030 .. Grayslake ........ D6
60031 .. Gurnee ........... C7
60033 .. Harvard .......... C3
60034 .. Hebron ........... C3
60035 .. Highland Park .... B4
60037 .. Fort Sheridan .... E8
60040 .. Highwood ......... E8
60041 .. Ingleside ........ C5
60042 .. Island Lake ...... D5
60043 .. Kenilworth ....... F9
60044 .. Lake Bluff ....... D8
60045 .. Lake Forest ...... E7
60046 .. Lake Villa ....... C6
60047 .. Lake Zurich/
          Long Grove/ Kildeer E6
60048 .. Libertyville ..... D7
60050 .. McHenry .......... C5
60053 .. Morton Grove ..... G8
60056 .. Mount Prospect ... F7
60060 .. Mundelein ........ D6
60061 .. Vernon Hills ..... E7
60062 .. Northbrook ....... F8
60064 .. North Chicago .... D8
60067 .. Palatine/ Inverness F6
60068 .. Park Ridge ....... G8
60069 .. Lincolnshire/
          Prairie View ..... E7
60070 .. Prospect Heights . F7
60071 .. Richmond ......... B4
60072 .. Ringwood ......... C4
60073 .. Round Lake ....... C6
60074 .. Palatine ......... E6
60075 .. Russell .......... B7
60076 .. Skokie ........... G9
60077 .. Skokie ........... G9
60080 .. Solon Mills ...... B5
60081 .. Spring Grove ..... B5
60082 .. Techny ........... F8
60083 .. Wadsworth ........ B7
60084 .. Wauconda ......... D5
60085 .. Waukegan ......... C8
60087 .. Waukegan ......... C8
60088 .. Great Lakes ...... D8
60089 .. Buffalo Grove .... E7
60090 .. Wheeling ......... E7
60091 .. Wilmette ......... F9

60093 .. Wilmette/ Northfield F9
60096 .. Winthrop Harbor ... B8
60097 .. Wonder Lake ...... C4
60098 .. Woodstock ........ D3
60099 .. Zion ............. B8
60101 .. Addison .......... H6
60102 .. Algonquin/
          Lake In The Hills .. E4
60103 .. Bartlett/
          Hanover Park ..... G5
60104 .. Bellwood ......... H7
60106 .. Bensenville ...... G7
60107 .. Streamwood ....... G5
60108 .. Bloomingdale ..... G6
60109 .. Burlington ....... G3
60110 .. Carpentersville .. F4
60118 .. Dundee ........... F4
60119 .. Elburn ........... H3
60120 .. Elgin ............ F5
60123 .. Elgin ............ G4
60126 .. Elmhurst ......... H7
60130 .. Forest Park ...... H8
60131 .. Franklin Park .... H7
60134 .. Geneva ........... H4
60136 .. Gilberts ......... F4
60137 .. Glen Ellyn ....... H6
60139 .. Glendale Heights . H6
60140 .. Hampshire ........ F3
60141 .. Hines ............ J8
60142 .. Huntley .......... E3
60143 .. Itasca ........... G6
60144 .. Kaneville ........ J2
60147 .. LaFox ............ H3
60148 .. Lombard .......... H6
60151 .. Maple Park ....... H2
60152 .. Marengo .......... E2
60153 .. Maywood/ BroadviewH8
60154 .. Westchester ...... J7
60157 .. Medinah .......... G6
60160 .. Melrose Park ..... H7
60162 .. Hillside ......... H7
60163 .. Berkeley ......... H7
60164 .. Northlake ........ H7
60165 .. Stone Park ....... H8
60170 .. Plato Center ..... G3
60171 .. River Grove ...... H8
60172 .. Roselle/ Keeneyville G6
60173 .. Schaumburg ....... F6
60174 .. St. Charles ...... H4
60175 .. St. Charles....... G4
60176 .. Schiller Park .... G8
60177 .. South Elgin ...... G4
60180 .. Union ............ E2
60181 .. Villa Park/
          Oakbrook Terrace . H7
60182 .. Virgil ........... G3
60183 .. Wasco ............ G3
60184 .. Wayne ............ G5
60185 .. West Chicago ..... H5
60187 .. Wheaton .......... H5
60188 .. Carol Stream ..... H6
60190 .. Winfield ......... H5
60191 .. Wood Dale ........ G7
60193 .. Schaumburg ....... G6
60194 .. Schaumburg/
          Hoffman Estates . F6
60195 .. Hoffman Estates .. F6
60201 .. Evanston ......... F9
60202 .. Evanston ......... G9
60203 .. Evanston ......... F9
60301 .. Oak Park ......... H8

60302 .. Oak Park.......... H8
60304 .. Oak Park.......... H8
60305 .. River Forest ..... H8
60401 .. Beecher .......... O9
60402 .. Berwyn/ Stickney.. J8
60406 .. Blue Island ...... L9
60408 .. Braidwood ........ P5
60409 .. Calumet City ..... L10
60410 .. Channahon ........ N5
60411 .. Chicago Heights/
          Lynwood/
          Sauk Village .... M10
60415 .. Chicago Ridge .... K8
60417 .. Crete ............ N9
60419 .. Dalton ........... L10
60421 .. Elwood ........... N5
60422 .. Flossmoor ........ M9
60423 .. Frankfort ........ M8
60425 .. Glenwood ......... M10
60426 .. Harvey/ Markham . L9
60428 .. Hazel Crest ...... L9
60430 .. Homewood ......... M9
60431 .. Joliet ........... M6
60432 .. Joliet ........... M6
60433 .. Joliet ........... M6
60435 .. Joliet/Crest Hill .. L5
60436 .. Joliet ........... M5
60438 .. Lansing .......... M10
60439 .. Lemont ........... K7
60440 .. Bolingbrook ...... K6
60441 .. Lockport ......... L6
60442 .. Manhattan ........ N7
60443 .. Matteson ......... M8
60445 .. Midlothian/
          Crestwood ....... L9
60446 .. Romeoville ....... L5
60447 .. Minooka .......... N5
60448 .. Mokena ........... M7
60449 .. Monee ............ N8
60451 .. New Lenox ........ M7
60452 .. Oak Forest ....... L8
60453 .. Oak Lawn ......... K9
60455 .. Bridgeview ....... K8
60456 .. Hometown ......... K9
60457 .. Hickory Hills .... K8
60458 .. Justice .......... K8
60459 .. Burbank .......... K8
60461 .. Olympia Fields ... M9
60462 .. Orland Park ...... L7
60463 .. Palos Heights .... L8
60464 .. Palos Park ....... K7
60465 .. Palos Hills ...... K8
60466 .. Park Forest ...... M9
60468 .. Peotone .......... O8
60469 .. Posen ............ L9
60471 .. Richton Park ..... M8
60472 .. Robbins .......... L9
60473 .. South Holland .... L9
60475 .. Steger ........... M9
60476 .. Thorton .......... M9
60477 .. Tinley Park/
          Orland Hills .... M8
60478 .. Country Club Hills . L9
60480 .. Willow Springs ... K7
60481 .. Wilmington ....... O6
60482 .. Worth ............ K8
60501 .. Summit/ Argo ..... J8
60504 .. Aurora ........... J5
60505 .. Aurora ........... K4
60506 .. Aurora ........... J4
60510 .. Batavia .......... K4

60511 .. Big Rock ......... K2
60512 .. Bristol .......... K3
60513 .. Brookfield ....... J8
60514 .. Clarendon Hills/
          Willowbrook ...... K7
60515 .. Downers Grove .... J6
60516 .. Downers Grove .... J6
60517 .. Woodridge ........ J6
60519 .. Eola ............. J5
60521 .. Hinsdale/ Oak Brook/
          Burr Ridge ....... J7
60525 .. LaGrange/ Countryside/
          Indian Head Park/
          Burr Ridge ....... J7
60532 .. Lisle ............ J6
60534 .. Lyons ............ J8
60538 .. Montgomery ....... K4
60539 .. Mooseheart ....... J4
60540 .. Naperville ....... J5
60542 .. North Aurora ..... J4
60543 .. Oswego ........... L4
60544 .. Plainfield ....... K5
60546 .. Riverside/
          North Riverside ... J8
60554 .. Sugar Grove ...... J3
60555 .. Warrenville ...... J5
60558 .. Western Springs .. J7
60559 .. Westmont/ Darien . J7
60560 .. Yorkville ........ L3
60561 .. Westmont/ Darien . J7
60563 .. Naperville ....... J5
60564 .. Naperville ....... K5
60565 .. Naperville ....... K5
60601 .. Prudential Plaza . H10
60602 .. Downtown Station . H10
60603 .. Downtown Station . H10
60604 .. Downtown Station . H10
60605 .. Downtown Station . H10
60606 .. Main P.O. ........ H9
60607 .. Main P.O. ........ H9
60608 .. Pilsen ........... J9
60609 .. Stockyards ....... J9
60610 .. Fort Dearborn .... H9
60611 .. Fort Dearborn .... H9
60612 .. Midwest .......... H9
60613 .. Lakeview ......... G9
60614 .. Lincoln Park ..... H9
60615 .. Hyde Park ........ J10
60616 .. 22nd Street ...... J9
60617 .. South Chicago .... K10
60618 .. Kedzie/ Grace .... H9
60619 .. Grand Crossing ... K10
60620 .. Auburn Park ...... K9
60621 .. Englewood ........ J9
60622 .. Wicker Park ...... H9
60623 .. Hawthorne ........ J9
60624 .. Garfield Park .... H9
60625 .. Ravenswood ....... G9
60626 .. Rogers Park ...... G9
60627 .. Riverdale ........ L9
60628 .. Roseland ......... K9
60629 .. Chicago Lawn ..... J9
60630 .. Jefferson ........ G8
60631 .. Norwood Park ..... G8
60632 .. Elsdon ........... J9
60633 .. Hegewisch ........ L10
60634 .. Dunning .......... G8
60635 .. Elmwood Park ..... H8
60636 .. Ogden Park ....... J9
60637 .. Jackson Park ..... J10
60638 .. Clearing ......... J8

60639 .. Cragin ........... H8
60640 .. Uptown ........... G9
60641 .. Irving Park ...... H8
60643 .. Morgan Park ...... K9
60644 .. Austin ........... H8
60645 .. Northtown ........ G9
60646 .. Edgebrook ........ G8
60647 .. Logan Square ..... H9
60649 .. South Shore ...... J10
60650 .. Cicero Branch .... J8
60651 .. Division St. ..... H8
60652 .. Ashburn .......... K9
60653 .. Hyde Park ........ J10
60655 .. Mount Greenwood... K9
60656 .. Harwood Heights .. G8
60657 .. Graceland ........ H9
60658 .. Alsip ............ K9
60659 .. Northtown ........ G9
60660 .. Rogers Park ...... G9
60666 .. O'Hare Int'l Airport . G7
60714 .. Niles ............ G8
60805 .. Evergreen Park ... K9

### INDIANA INDEX

46302 .. Boone Grove ...... O13
46303 .. Cedar Lake ....... N10
46304 .. Chesterton ....... L14
46307 .. Crown Point ...... N11
46311 .. Dyer ............. M10
46312 .. East Chicago ..... K11
46319 .. Griffith ......... M11
46320 .. Hammond .......... L10
46321 .. Munster .......... M10
46322 .. Highland ......... M11
46323 .. Hessville ........ L11
46324 .. South Calumet Ave L10
46327 .. Hammond .......... L10
46341 .. Hebron ........... O13
46342 .. Hobart ........... M13
46347 .. Kouts ............ O14
46348 .. LaCrosse ......... O14
46349 .. Lake Village ..... Q11
46355 .. Leroy ............ N12
46356 .. Lowell ........... P11
46360 .. Michigan City .... L14
46368 .. Portage .......... L13
46373 .. St. John ......... N11
46375 .. Schereville ...... M14
46376 .. Schnieder ........ P11
46377 .. Shelby ........... P11
46383 .. Valparaiso ....... N13
46390 .. Wanatah .......... N14
46391 .. Westville ........ M14
46392 .. Wheatfield ....... P14
46393 .. Wheeler .......... M13
46394 .. Whiting .......... L10
46402 .. Gary/ Downtown ... L12
46403 .. Gary/ Miller Station L12
46404 .. Gary/ Tolleston .. L12
46405 .. Gary/ Lake Station L12
46406 .. Gary/ Brunswick
          Station/ Buffington. L11
46407 .. Gary/ 15th Ave Station
          .................. L12
46408 .. Gary/ Glen Park Station
          (West) .......... M11
46409 .. Gary/ Glen Park Station
          (East) .......... M12
46410 .. Gary/ Merrillville . M12

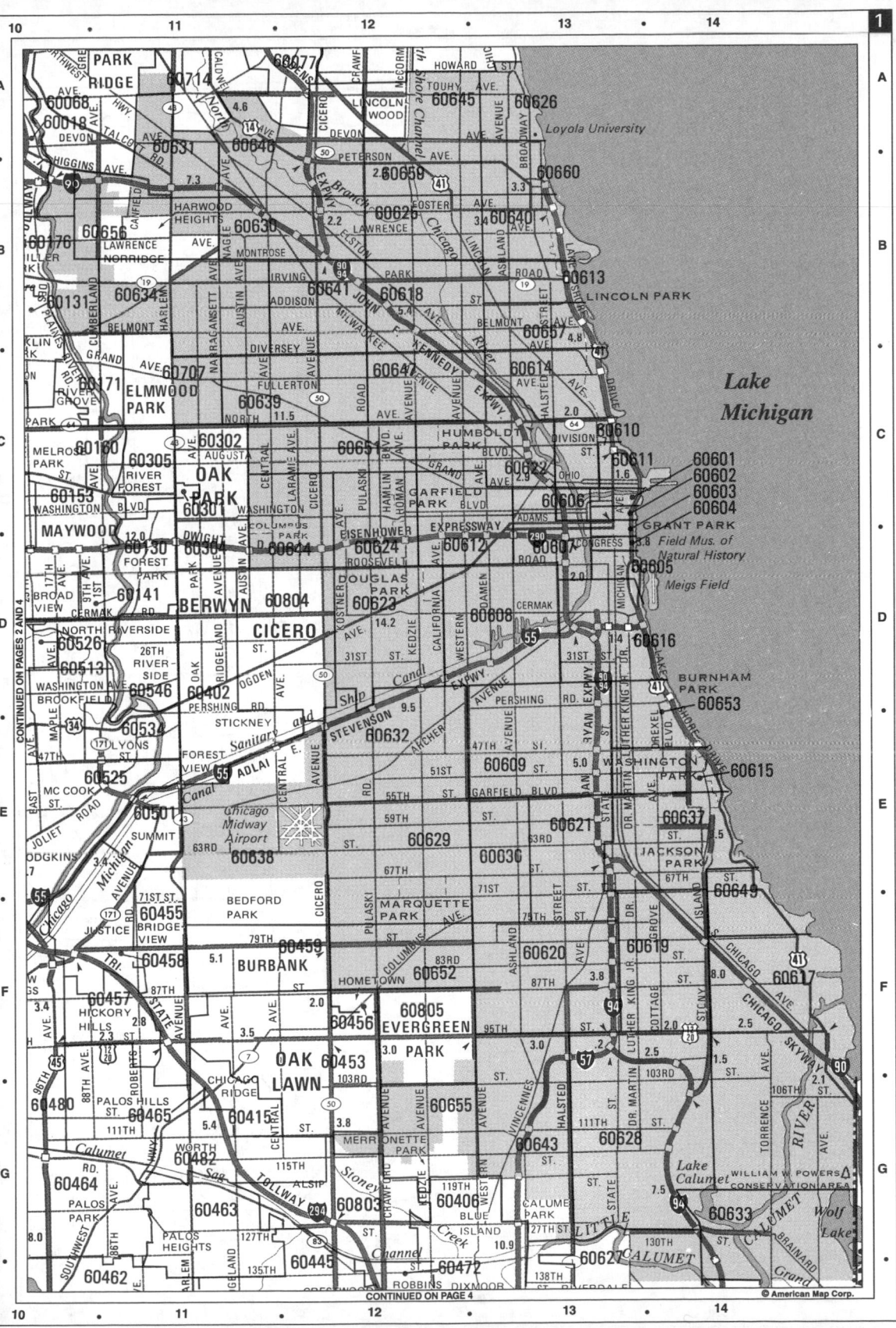

© American Map Corp.

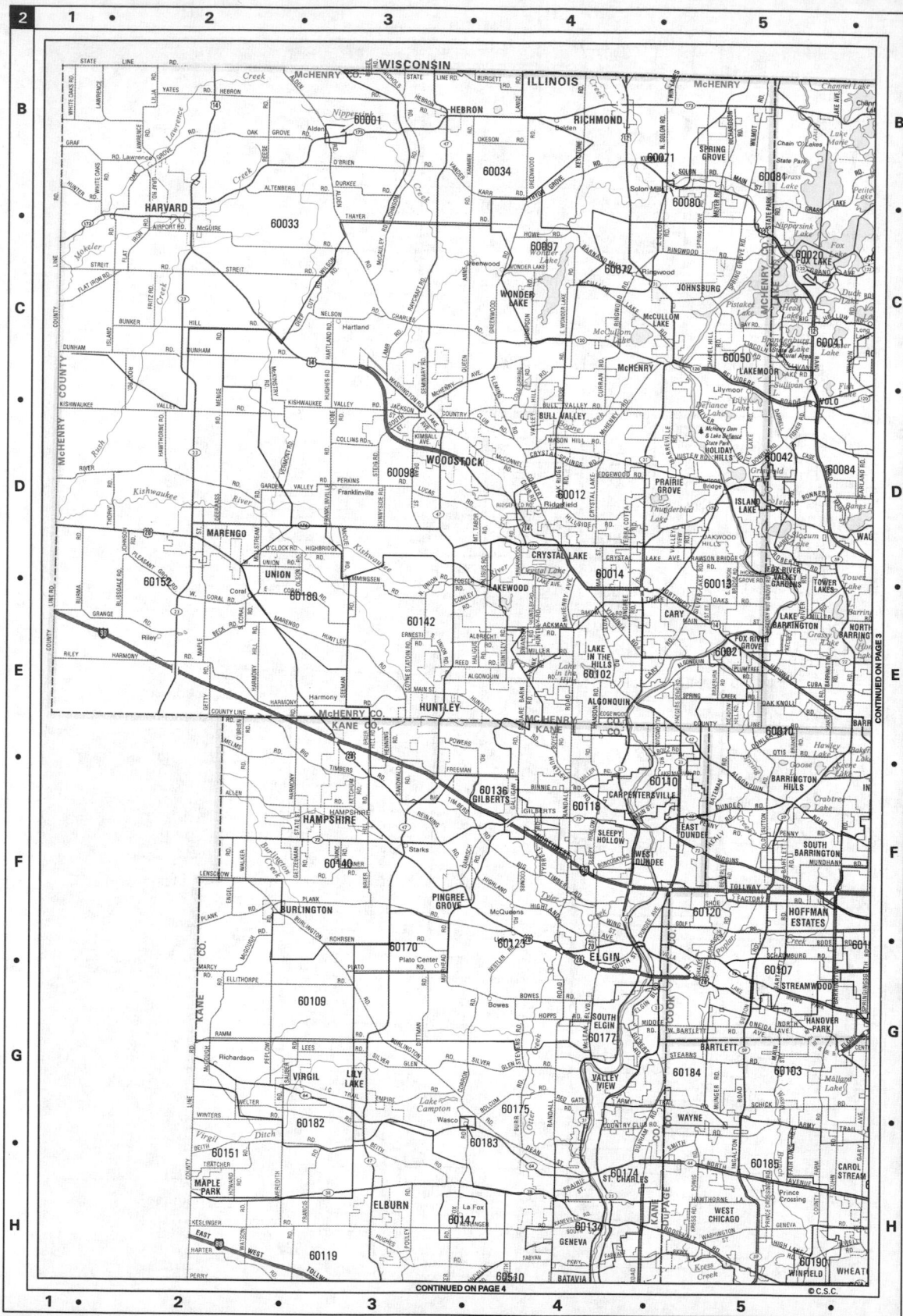

CONTINUED ON PAGE 3

CONTINUED ON PAGE 4

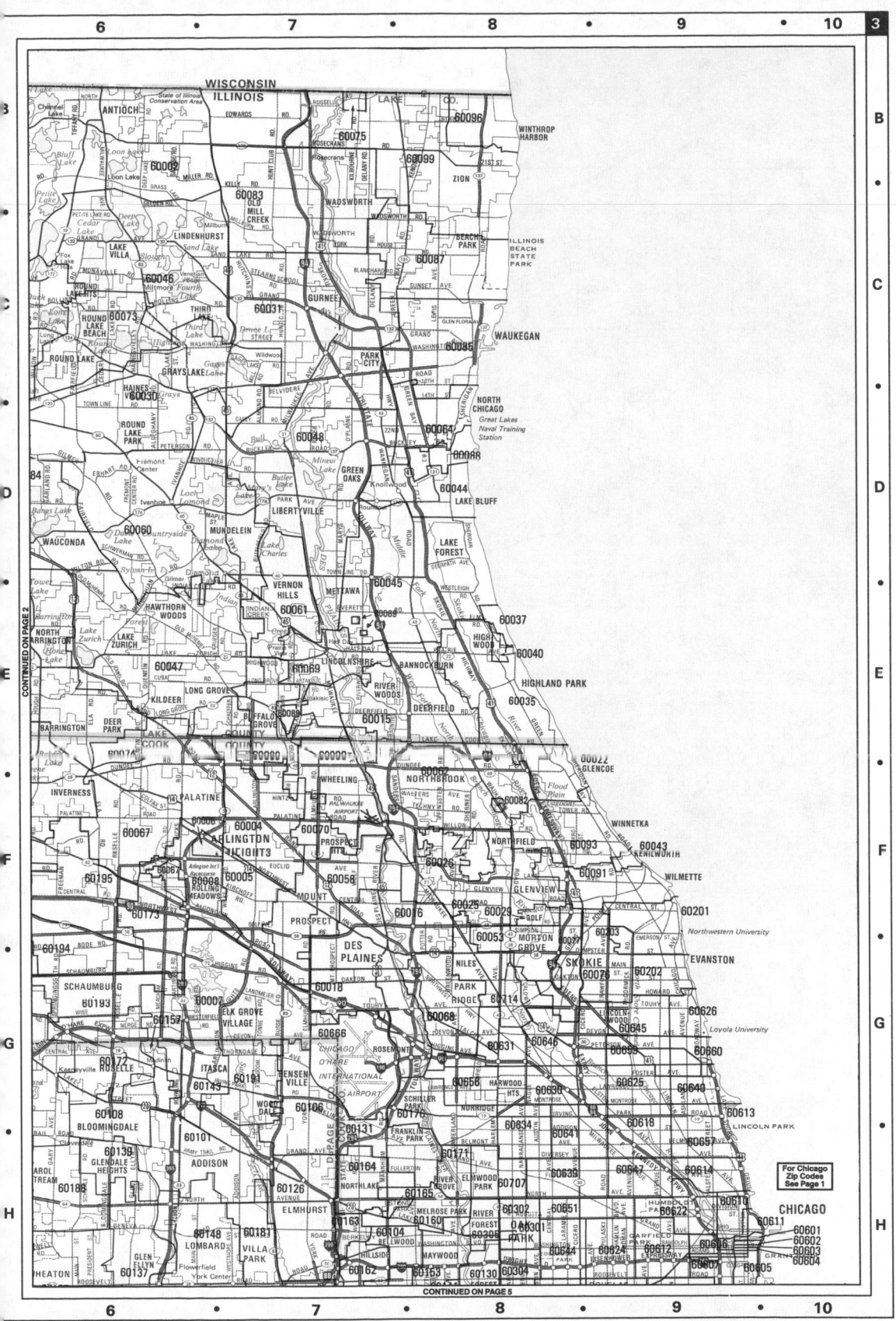

CONTINUED ON PAGE 2
CONTINUED ON PAGE 5

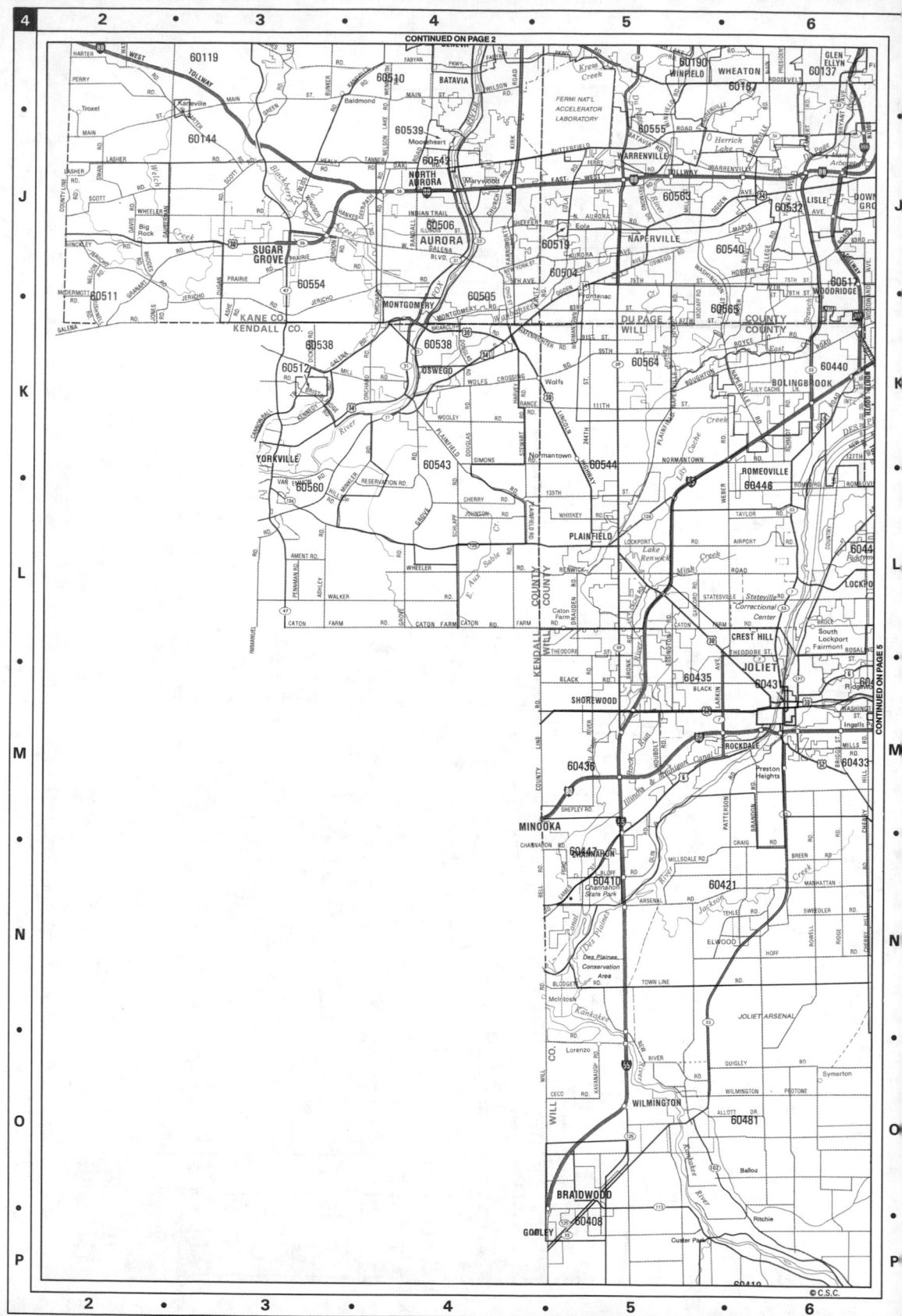

CONTINUED ON PAGE 2

CONTINUED ON PAGE 5

© C.S.C.

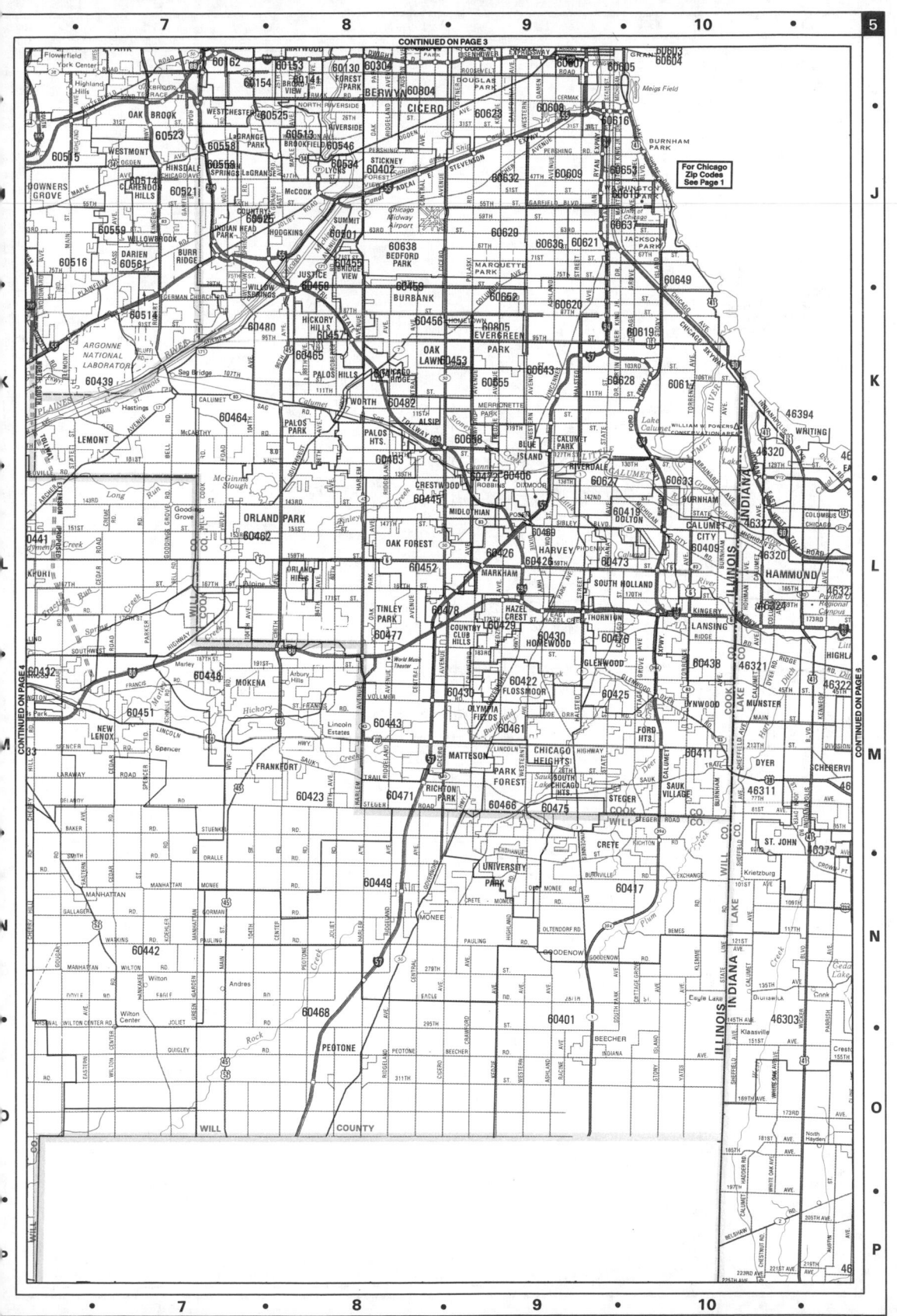

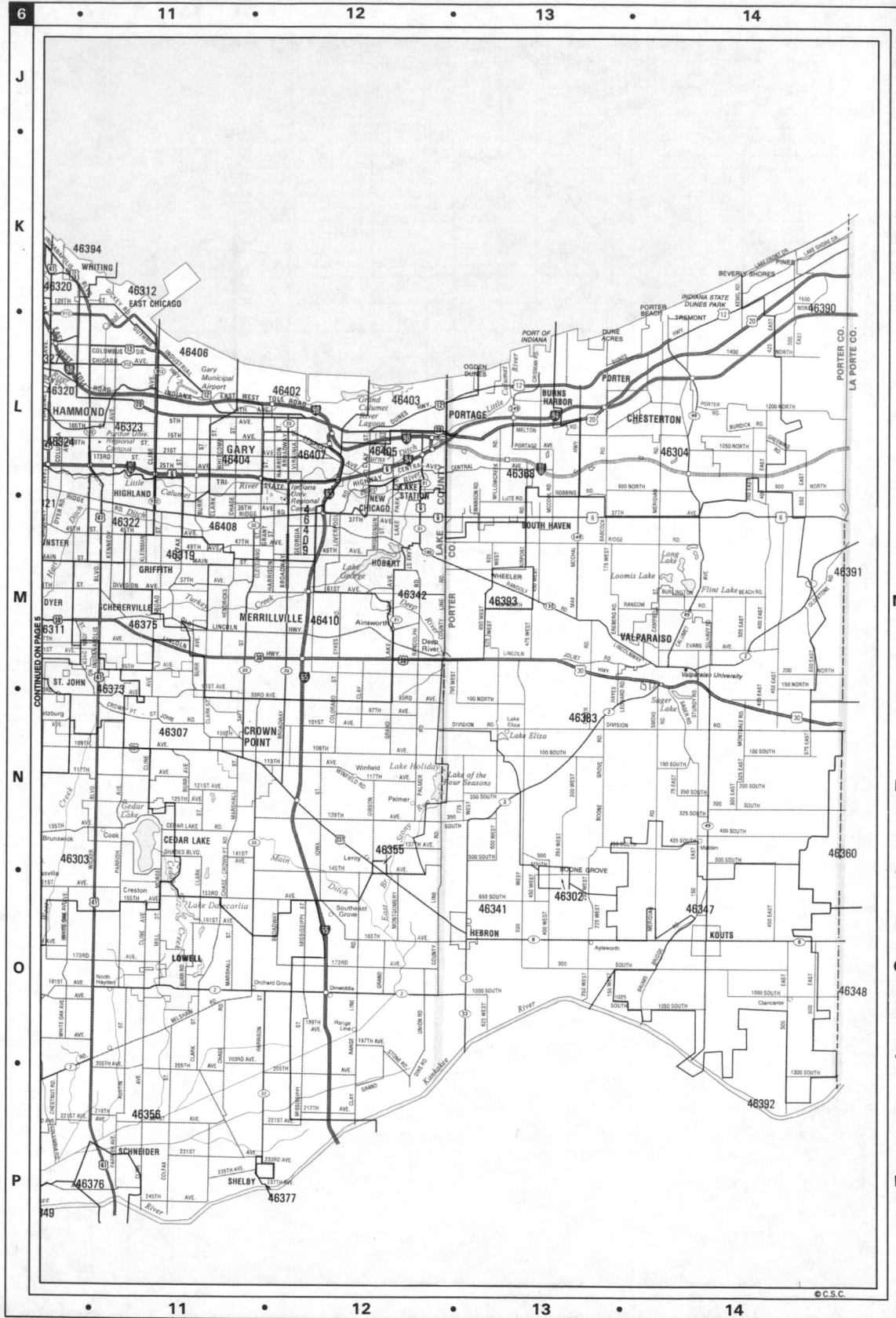

# CHICAGO AND VICINITY
## SECTION 10

## LEGEND

### Road Classifications

| | |
|---|---|
| Toll Expressways | ▬▬▬▬ |
| Free Expressways | ▬▬▬▬ |
| Principal Routes | ▬▬▬ |
| Secondary Routes | ▬▬ |
| Other Roads | ▬ |
| Under Construction | ▭▭▭▭▭ |

### Boundaries

| | |
|---|---|
| City | ——————— |
| County | – – – – – – |
| State | — — — — |

### Highway Markers

| | |
|---|---|
| Interstate Highways | 🛡 |
| Federal Highways | Ⓜ |
| State Highways | ㉕ |

**TURN PAGE FOR ORIENTATION MAP**

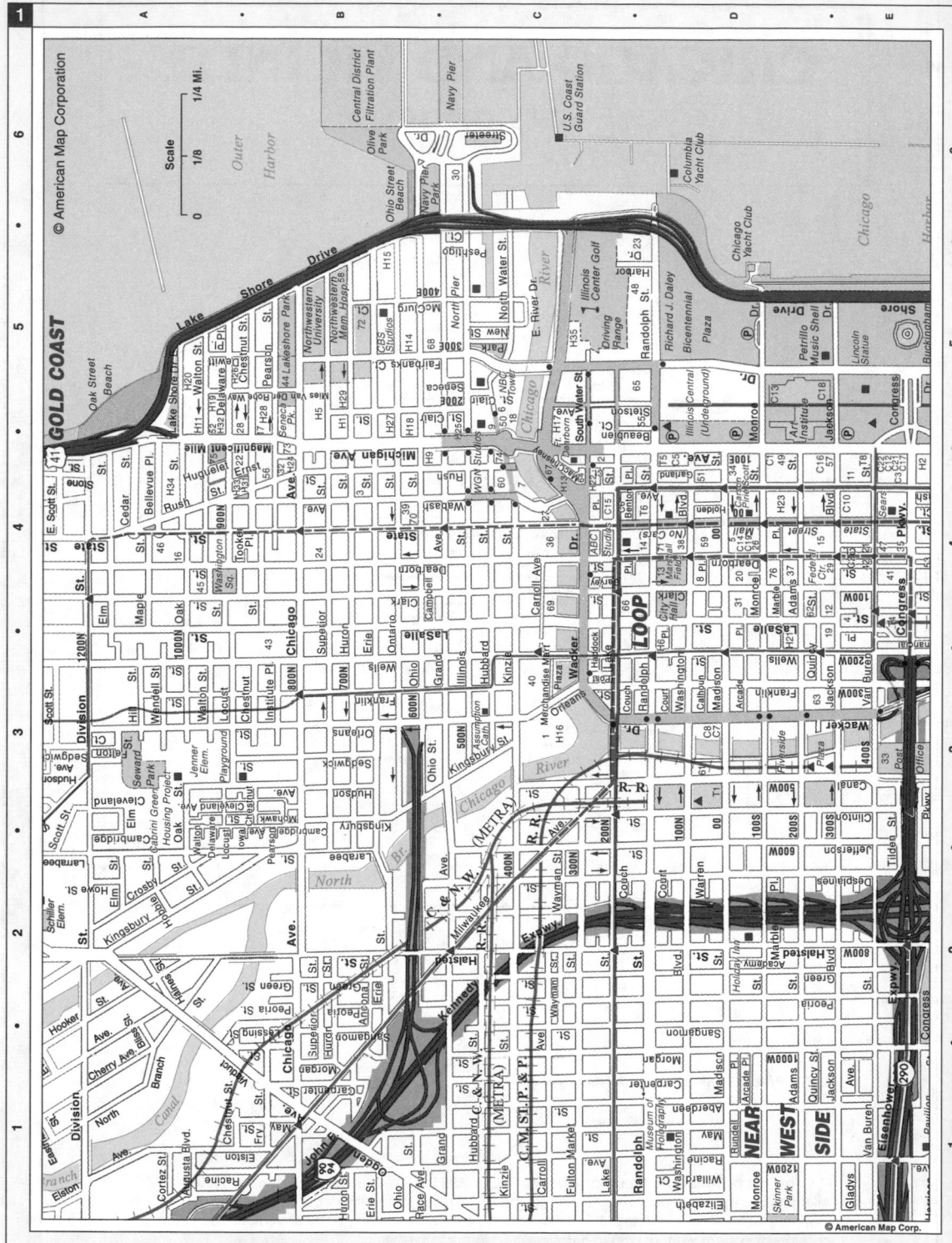

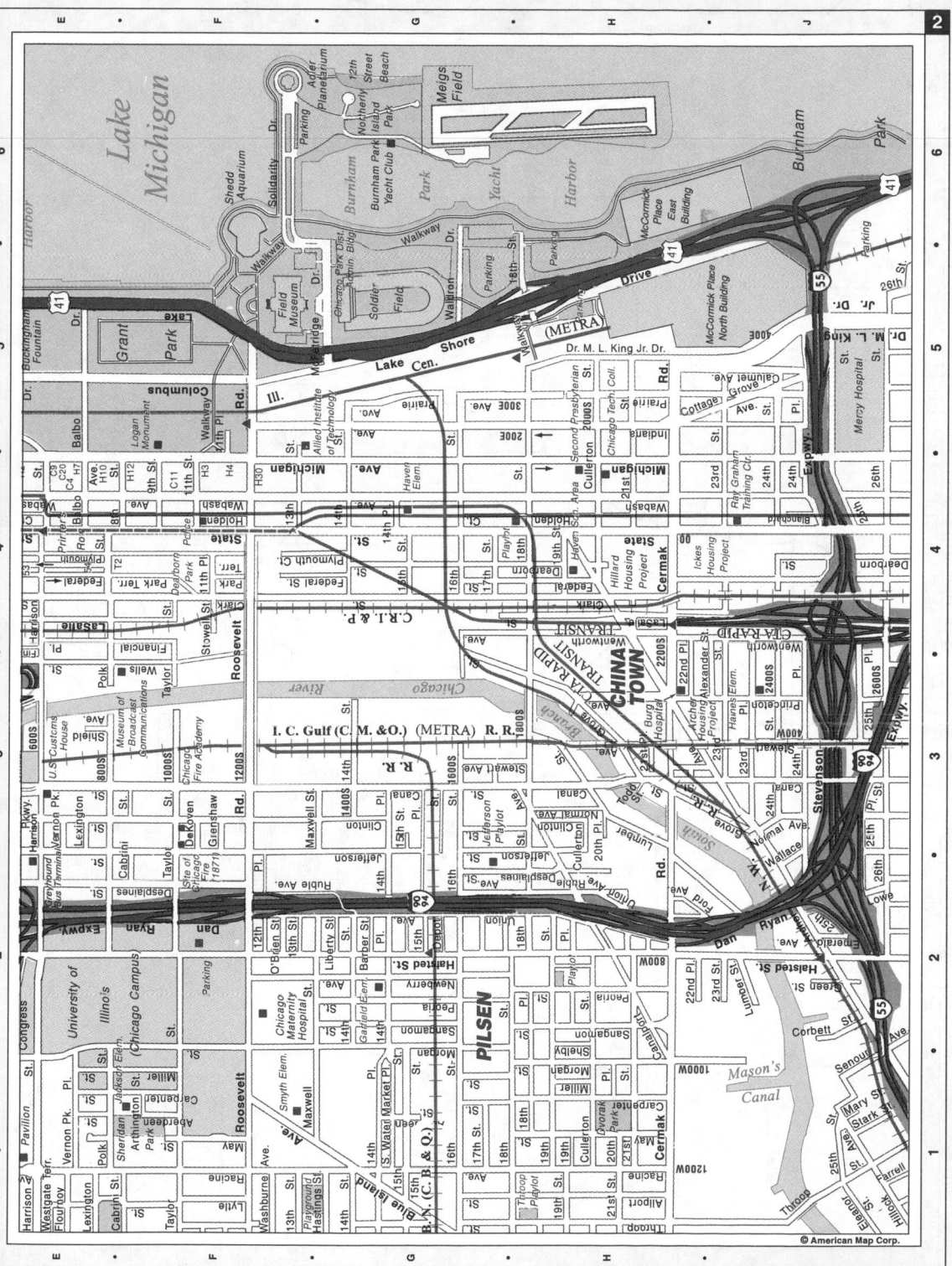

**2**

Lake Michigan

Harbor

Shedd Aquarium

Adler Planetarium

12th Street Beach

Netherland

Northerly Island Park

Meigs Field

Burnham Park

Burnham Park Yacht Club

Burnham Park

Chicago Park Dist. Admin. Bldg.

Harbor

Yacht Harbor

McCormick Place East Building

Burnham Park

U.S. 41

55

26th

Parking

Parking

Parking

Parking

Walkway

Solidarity Dr.

Walkway

Walkway Dr.

18th St.

41 Drive

McCormick Place North Building

300E

Lake Shore

(METRA)

Dr. M. L. King Jr. Dr.

Lake Cen.

Grant Park

Buckingham Fountain

Lake

Columbus Rd.

Ill.

Balbo

Logan Monument

11th Pl.

Walkway

Prairie Ave.

300E Ave.

St.

Second Presbyterian

2000S

Chicago Tech. Coll.

Prairie Ave.

Calumet Ave.

Cottage Grove Ave.

St.

26th

Mercy Hospital

Dr. M. King

Allied Institute of Technology

300E

St.

Indiana

2000S

23rd

24th

24th

Expwy.

26th

C9 C20 C4 C11

Balbo Ave.

H10 H7 H12

9th St.

11th St.

H3 H4

H30

Michigan Ave.

Haven Elem.

Culleton

21st St.

Michigan

Wabash

Ray Graham Training Ctr.

Wabash Ave.

Roosevelt Rd.

13th

14th

Holden

Holden

18th St.

19th St.

State

Blanchard

Dearborn

State

Police

Plymouth Ct.

14th St.

16th

17th

Playlot

Hilliard Housing Project

Cermak

Ickes Housing Project

St.

00

Federal St.

Plymouth Ct.

Federal

Federal

Clark

Dearborn

Primer Row

Park Terr.

Park

11th Pl.

Park Terr.

Dearborn

Stowell

Clark Ave.

C.R.I. & P.

Ave.

East

CTA RAPID

TRANSIT

Wentworth

22nd Pl.

2500S

2400S

2600S

Financial Pl.

LaSalle Pl.

Financial

Stowell St.

St.

CHINA TOWN

CTA RAPID TRANSIT

Archer Housing Project

Princeton Ave.

400W

25th

Federal

Harrison

Polk

Wells

Taylor

Museum of Broadcast Communications

Chicago River

St.

1800S

Branch

Burg Hospital

Archer Ave.

Wentworth Ave.

Alexander St.

Haines Elem.

Pl.

Stewart Ave.

Expwy.

U.S. Customs House

600S

Shield

800S

St.

Chicago Fire Academy

1000S

1200S

I. C. Gulf (C. M. &O.) (METRA) R. R.

14th St.

R. R.

1600S

Stewart Ave.

23rd

24th

Canal

Canal

Stevenson

94

25th Pl.

Expwy.

Harrison Pkwy.

Vernon Pk.

Lexington

DeKoven

Grenshaw

Maxwell St.

Clinton

15th St.

Jefferson St.

Clinton

Normal Ave.

20th Pl.

Lumber

Todd

Grove

23rd Pl.

Stevenson

24th

25th Pl.

Lowe

Cabrini

Taylor

Desplaines

Site of Chicago Fire (1871)

Grenshaw Pl.

14th

Jefferson

16th

Union Ave.

Rubie Ave.

Desplaines Ave.

Culleton

Jefferson

Ford Ave.

Normal Ave.

Wallace

26th

Greyhound Bus Terminal

Dan Ryan Expwy.

Parking

12th

O'Brien St.

Liberty St.

Barber St.

16th

94

Depot St.

Union St.

Dan Ryan

Emerald Ave.

22nd St.

23rd St.

Lumber St.

Halsted St.

Green St.

Corbett St.

Senour Ave.

55

Pavilion

Congress Pkwy.

University of Illinois (Chicago Campus)

St.

St.

St.

St.

Roosevelt

Newberry Ave.

Chicago Maternity Hospital

Garfield Elem.

14th St.

Halsted St.

Peoria

Sangamon

Morgan

18th

Playlot

Peoria

Sangamon

Shelby

Morgan

Miller

800W

1000W

Mason's Canal

Mary St.

Stark St.

Miller

Sheridan Jaksrd Elem.

Arthington

Pavilion

Vernon Pk.

Polk

Carpenter

Park St.

Smyth Elem.

PILSEN

18th St.

Culleton

Dvorak Park

Cermak

Carpenter

1000W

St.

St.

Mary

Ave.

25th

Senour

Harrison

Westgate Terr. Flournoy

Lexington

Cabrini St.

Aberdeen St.

Roosevelt

May

St.

Maxwell

14th St.

17th St.

18th

19th St.

20th

21st St.

Racine

1200W

St.

Throop

Eleanor St.

Hillock

Lyle

Taylor

13th St.

14th

Washburne Ave.

15th

(S. Water Market Pl.)

Blue Island Ave.

B. N. (C. B. & Q.)

16th

17th St.

18th

19th St.

Throop Playlot

20th

21st St.

Racine

Throop

© American Map Corp.

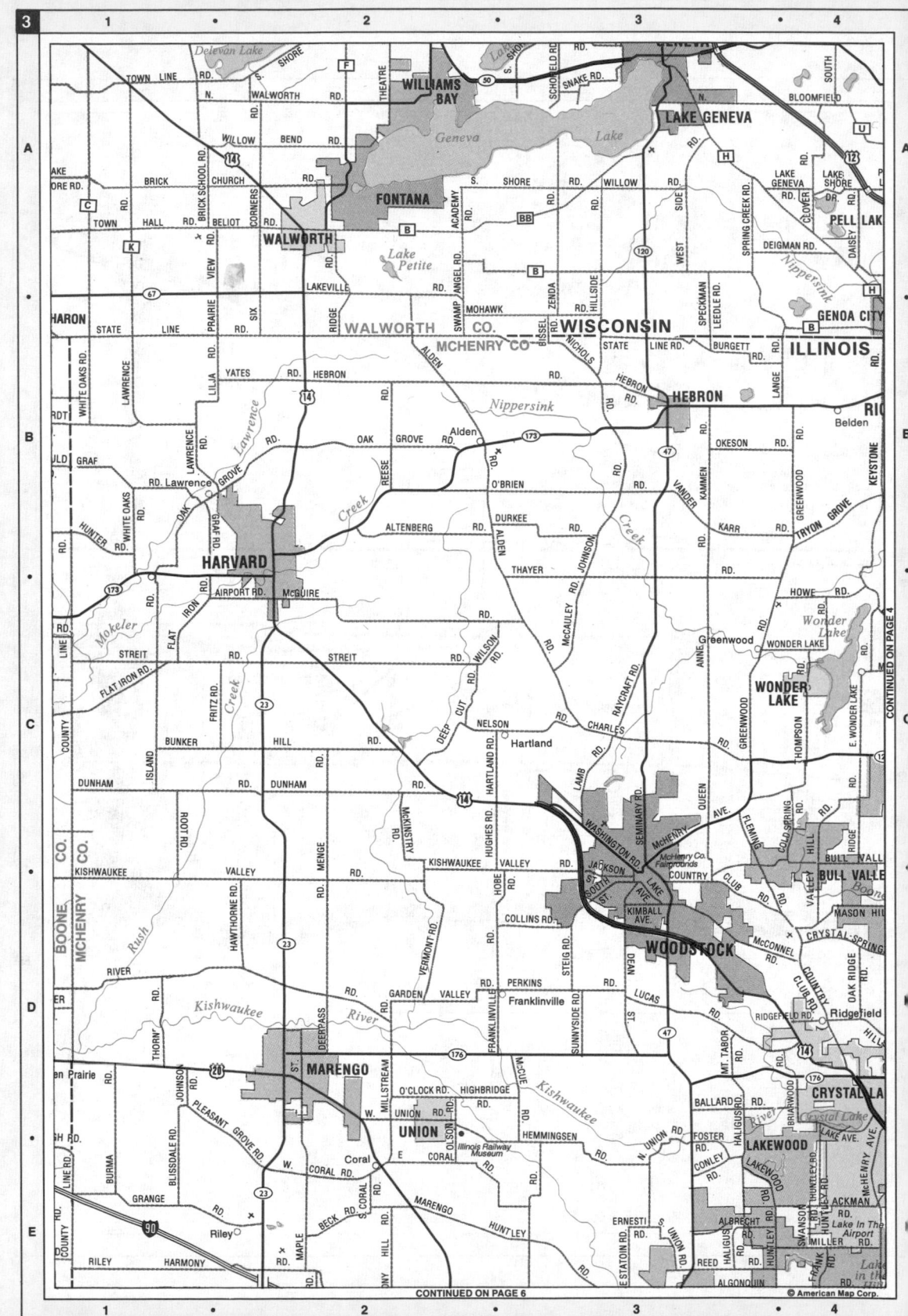

CONTINUED ON PAGE 4

CONTINUED ON PAGE 6

© American Map Corp.

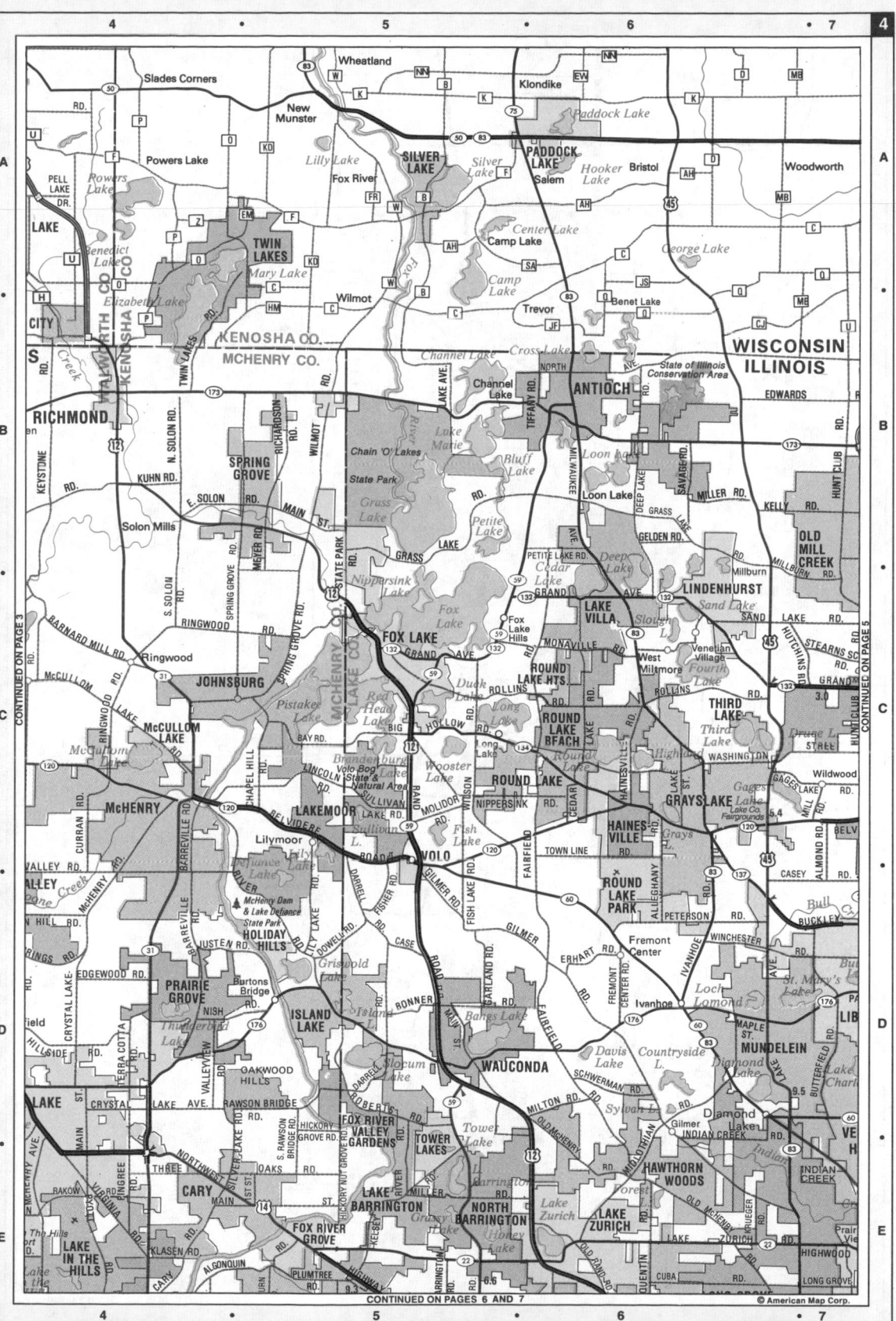

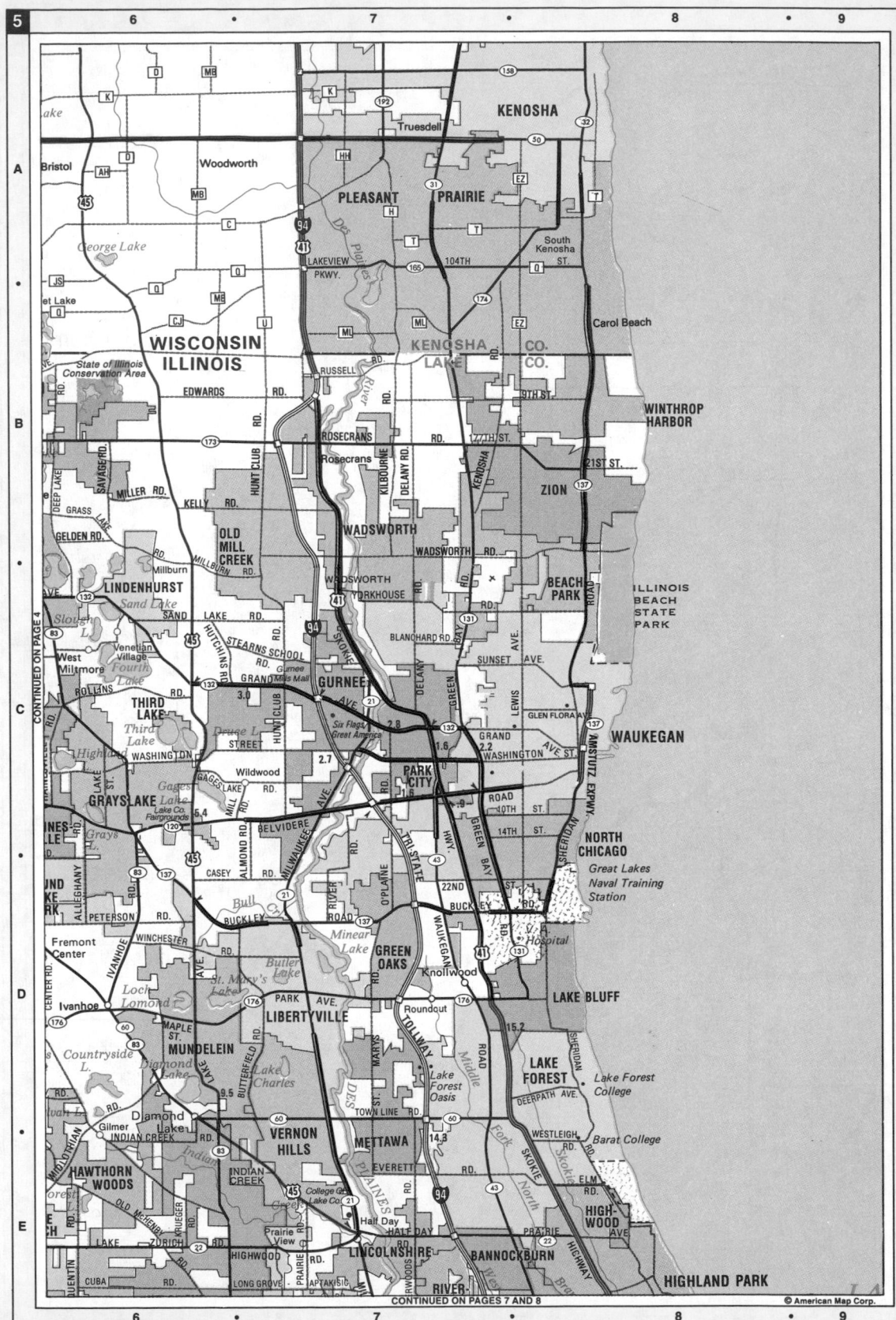

**KENOSHA**

Truesdell

Bristol

Woodworth

**PLEASANT**     **PRAIRIE**

LAKEVIEW PKWY.

104TH

South Kenosha St.

George Lake

State of Illinois Conservation Area

**WISCONSIN**
**ILLINOIS**

EDWARDS     RD.

Carol Beach

**KENOSHA     CO.**
**LAKE     CO.**

**WINTHROP HARBOR**

Russell     RD.

ROSECRANS     RD.     177TH ST.

Rosecrans

Kilbourne     Delany Rd.

21ST ST.

**ZION**

Savage Rd.
Miller Rd.
Kelly     Rd.

Hunt Club

**OLD MILL CREEK**

Millburn

Millburn

**WADSWORTH**

WADSWORTH     RD.

**BEACH PARK**

Deep Lake
Grass Lake
Gelden Rd.

**LINDENHURST**

Sand Lake
Sand     Lake     Rd.

WADSWORTH
YORKHOUSE

**ILLINOIS BEACH STATE PARK**

Slough L.

West Miltmore

Venetian Village
Fourth Lake

Stearns School Rd.

Gurnee Mills Mall

Blanchard Rd.

Sunset Ave.

**THIRD LAKE**

Third Lake

Druce L.

Grand Ave.
Gilmee

**GURNEE**

3.0

2.8

**WAUKEGAN**

Highland L.

WASHINGTON

Wildwood

Six Flags Great America

1.6

Glen Flora Ave.
Lewis

137

**GRAYSLAKE**

Gages Lake

Lake Co. Fairgrounds

**PARK CITY**

2.7

2.2

GRAND     AVE. ST.
WASHINGTON

5.4

BELVIDERE

.9

40TH     ST.

14TH     ST.

**NORTH CHICAGO**

Great Lakes Naval Training Station

Grays L.

CASEY     RD.

22ND     ST.

BUCKLEY     RD.

Fremont Center

WINCHESTER     RD.

Minear Lake

Butler Lake

**GREEN OAKS**

Knollwood

Hospital

**LAKE BLUFF**

Ivanhoe

176

Loch Lomond

St. Mary's Lake

PARK     AVE.

Roundout

176

15.2

**MUNDELEIN**

**LIBERTYVILLE**

Countryside L.

Diamond Lake

Lake Charles

Lake Forest Oasis

**LAKE FOREST**

Lake Forest College

9.5

DEERPATH AVE.

Barat College

Diamond Lake
Gilmer
**INDIAN CREEK**

**VERNON HILLS**

**METTAWA**

TOWN LINE     RD.

14.8

WESTLEIGH

**HAWTHORN WOODS**

**INDIAN CREEK**

EVERETT     RD.

College Gr.
Lake Co.

**HIGH-WOOD**

Prairie View

Half Day
Half Day

**LINCOLNSHIRE**

**BANNOCKBURN**

**HIGHLAND PARK**

CUBA

LONG GROVE

APTAKISIC

RIVER     RD.

CONTINUED ON PAGES 7 AND 8

CONTINUED ON PAGE 4

© American Map Corp.

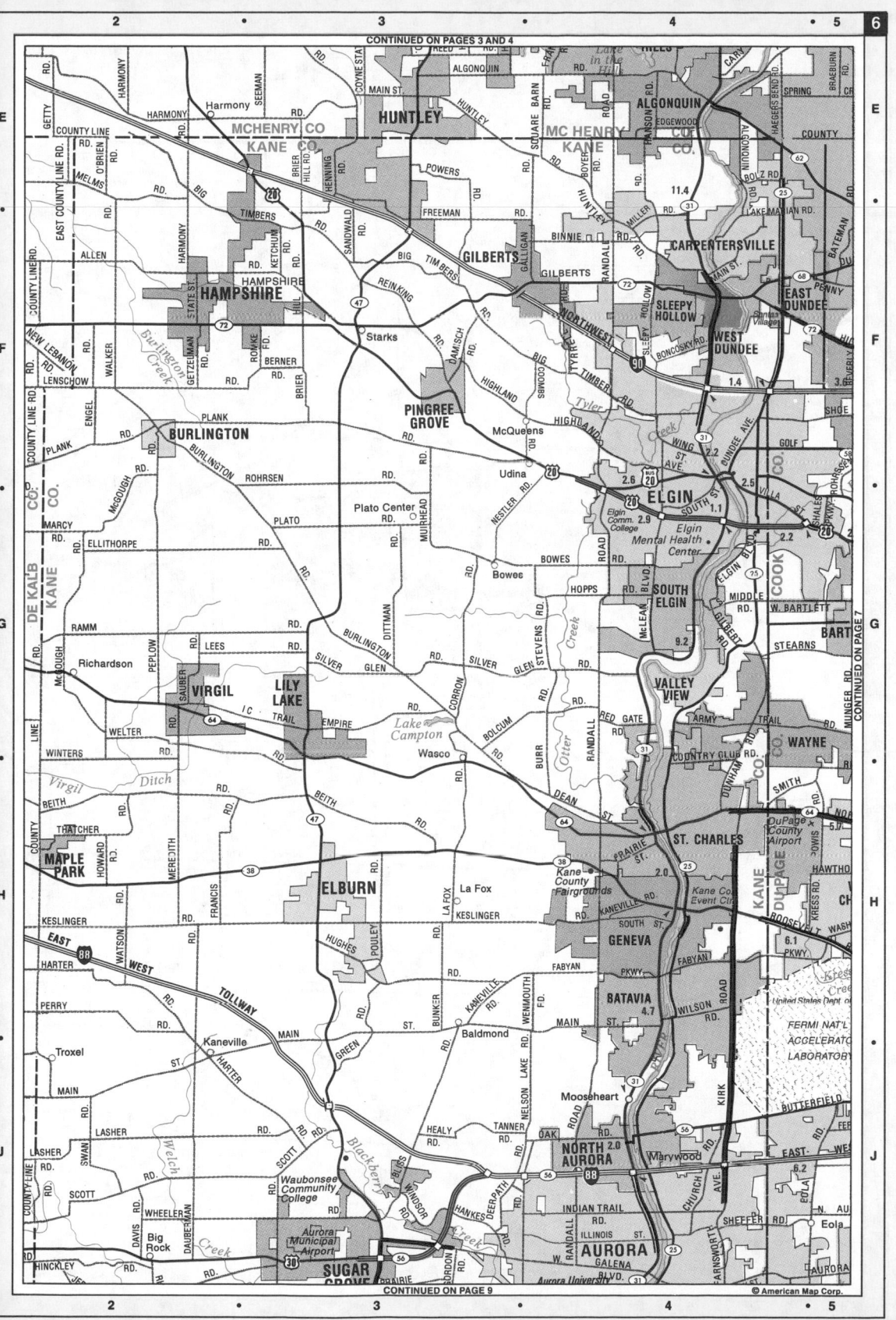

CONTINUED ON PAGES 3 AND 4

**MCHENRY CO**
**KANE CO.**

HUNTLEY

MC HENRY
KANE CO.

ALGONQUIN

CARPENTERSVILLE

SLEEPY
HOLLOW

EAST
DUNDEE

WEST
DUNDEE

GILBERTS

HAMPSHIRE

Starks

PINGREE
GROVE

McQueens

Udina

ELGIN

Elgin
Comm.
College

Elgin
Mental Health
Center

SOUTH
ELGIN

BURLINGTON

Plato Center

Bowes

HOPPS

VALLEY
VIEW

Richardson

VIRGIL

LILY
LAKE

Lake
Campton

Wasco

WAYNE

Empire

DuPage
County
Airport

ST. CHARLES

MAPLE
PARK

ELBURN

La Fox

Kane
County
Fairgrounds

Kane Co.
Event Ctr.

GENEVA

Troxel

Kaneville

Baldmond

BATAVIA

FERMI NAT'L
ACCELERATOR
LABORATORY

United States Dept. of

EAST
HARTER    WEST
TOLLWAY

Mooseheart

Big
Rock

Waubonsee
Community
College

Aurora
Municipal
Airport

SUGAR
GROVE

NORTH
AURORA

Marywood

INDIAN TRAIL

Eola

AURORA

Aurora University

CONTINUED ON PAGE 9

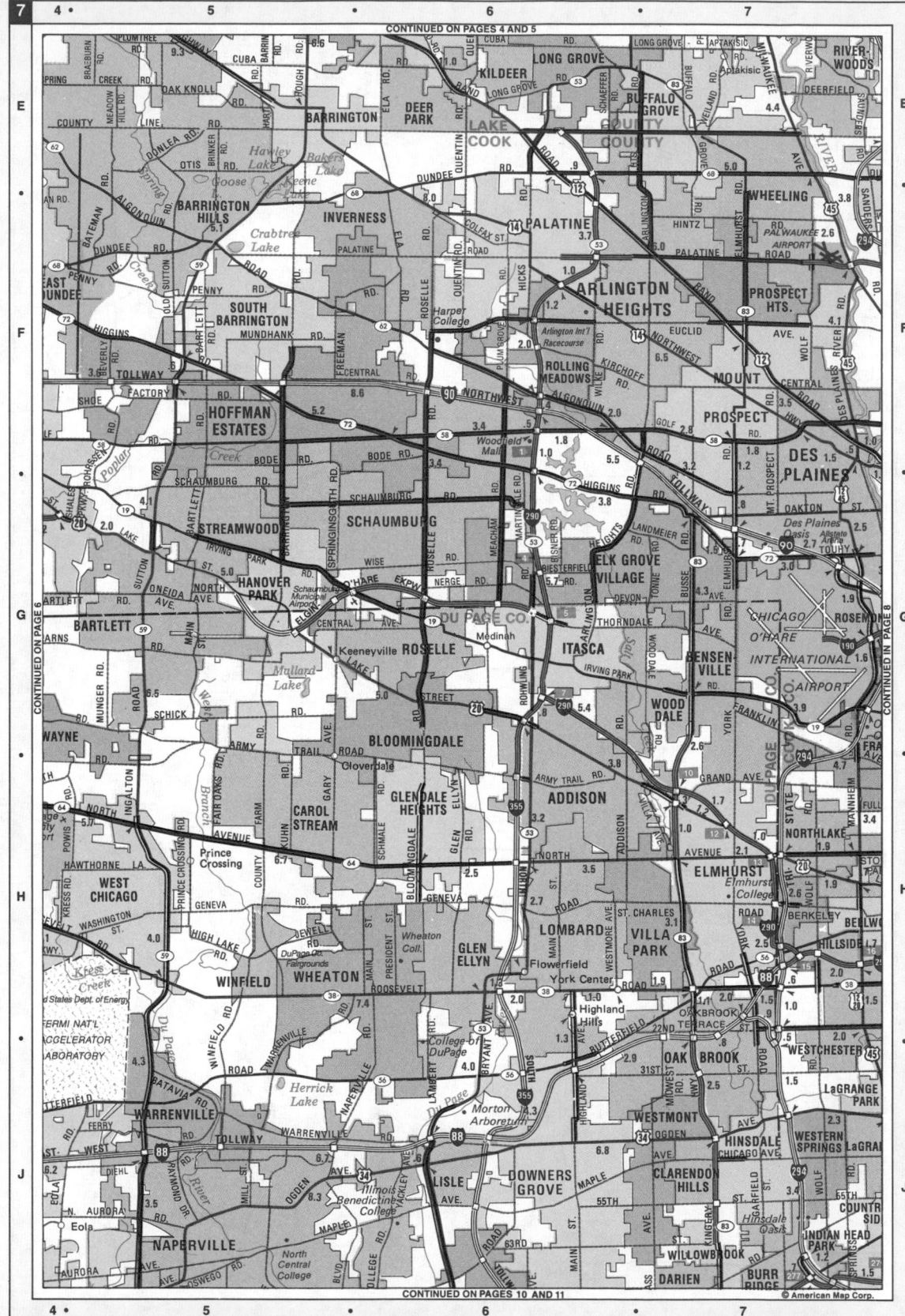

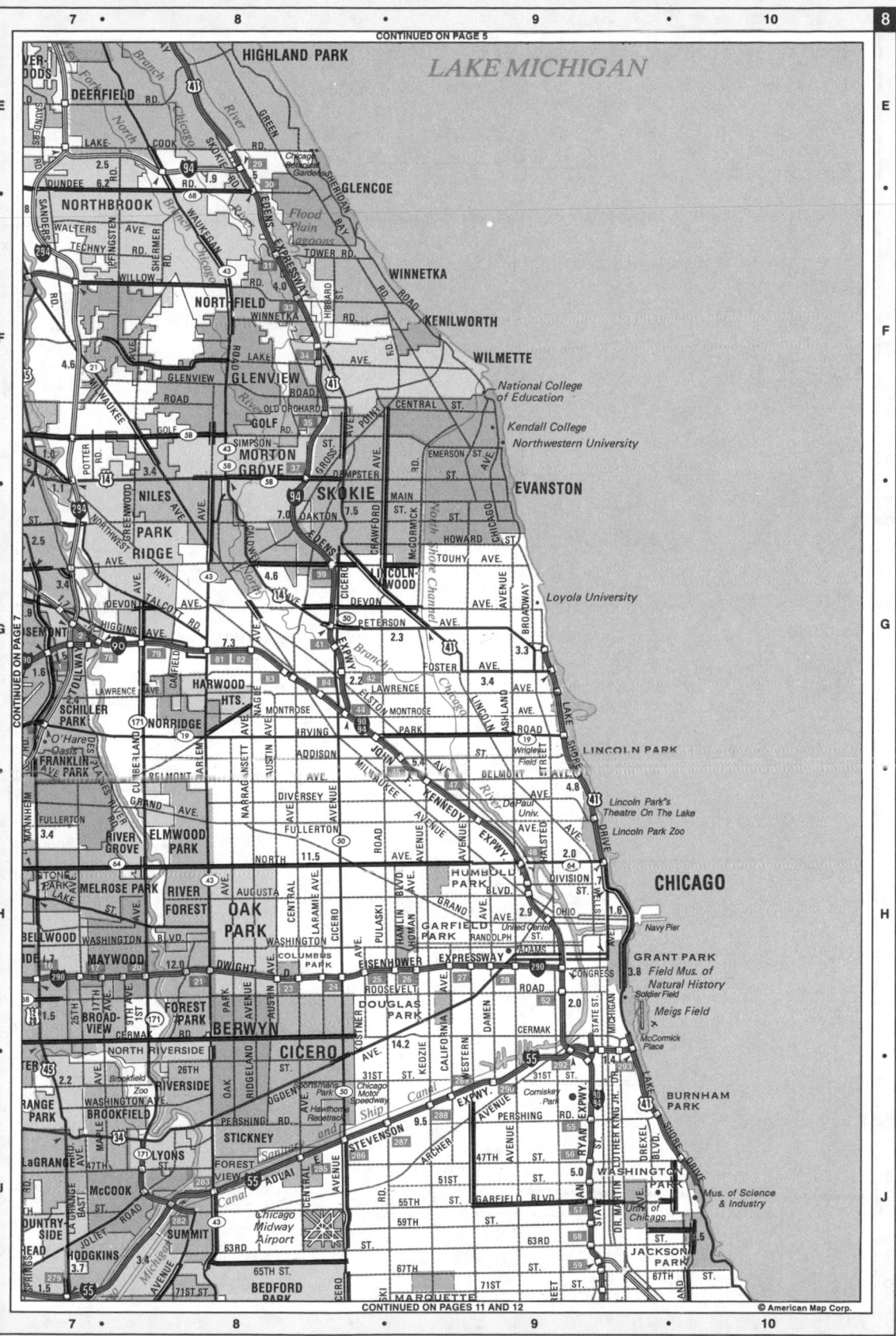

LAKE MICHIGAN

HIGHLAND PARK

DEERFIELD

NORTHBROOK

GLENCOE

NORTHFIELD

WINNETKA

KENILWORTH

WILMETTE

GLENVIEW

National College of Education

GOLF

MORTON GROVE

Kendall College

Northwestern University

NILES

SKOKIE

EVANSTON

PARK RIDGE

LINCOLNWOOD

Loyola University

Broadway

Harwood Hts.

SCHILLER PARK

NORRIDGE

LINCOLN PARK

FRANKLIN PARK

O'Hare Oasis

Wrigley Field

DePaul Univ.

Lincoln Park's Theatre On The Lake

RIVER GROVE

ELMWOOD PARK

Lincoln Park Zoo

MELROSE PARK

RIVER FOREST

OAK PARK

HUMBOLDT PARK

DIVISION

CHICAGO

Navy Pier

BELLWOOD

MAYWOOD

GARFIELD PARK

United Center

GRANT PARK

Field Mus. of Natural History

Soldier Field

FOREST PARK

BROADVIEW

BERWYN

CICERO

DOUGLAS PARK

Meigs Field

McCormick Place

NORTH RIVERSIDE

RIVERSIDE

BROOKFIELD

Brookfield Zoo

Chicago Motor Speedway

Hawthorne Racetrack

Comiskey Park

BURNHAM PARK

ORANGE PARK

STICKNEY

WASHINGTON PARK

LaGRANGE

LYONS

FOREST VIEW

McCOOK

SUMMIT

Chicago Midway Airport

Mus. of Science & Industry

Univ. of Chicago

JACKSON PARK

COUNTRYSIDE

HODGKINS

BEDFORD PARK

MARQUETTE

© American Map Corp.

CONTINUED ON PAGE 7

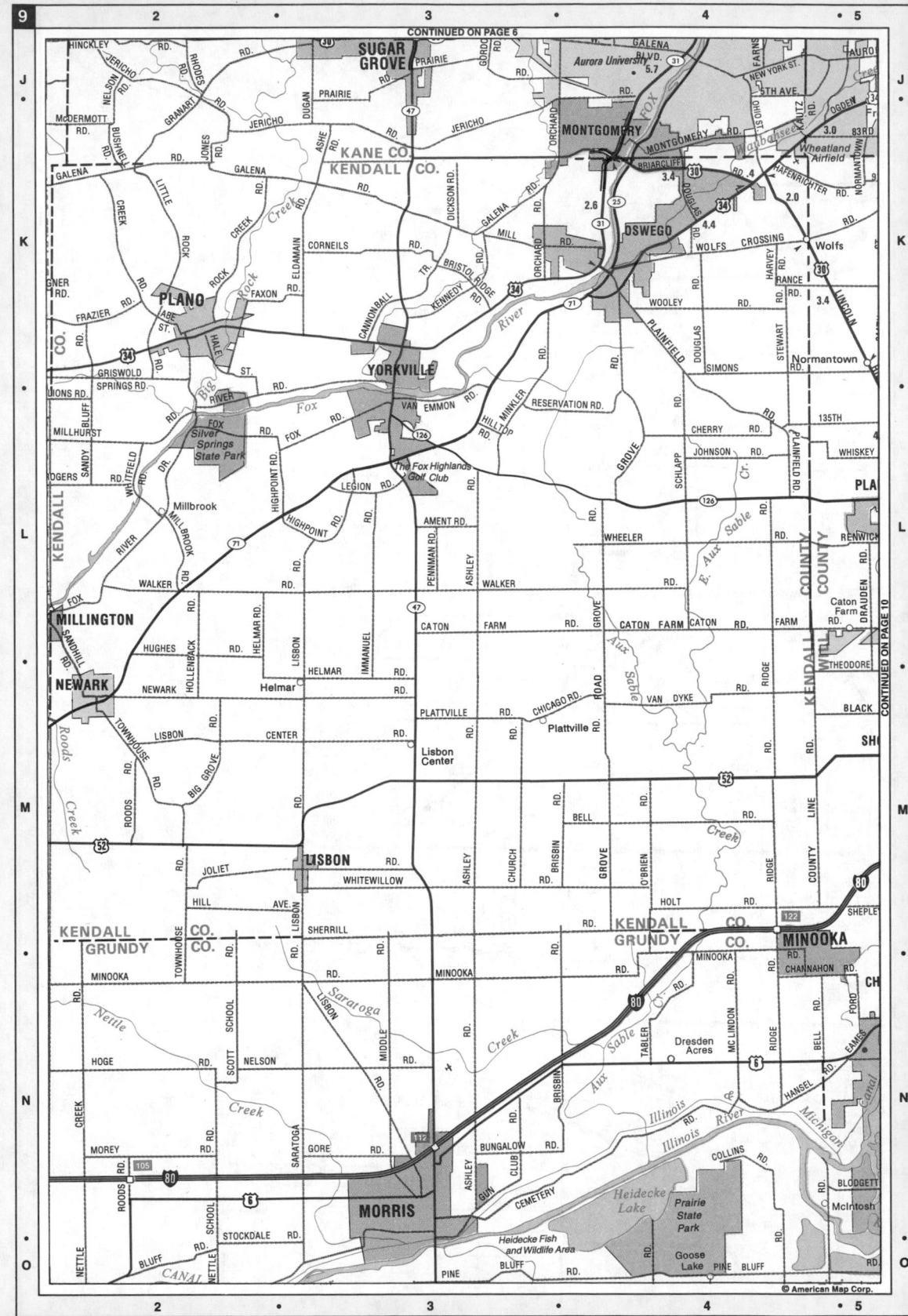
CONTINUED ON PAGE 6

CONTINUED ON PAGE 10

© American Map Corp.

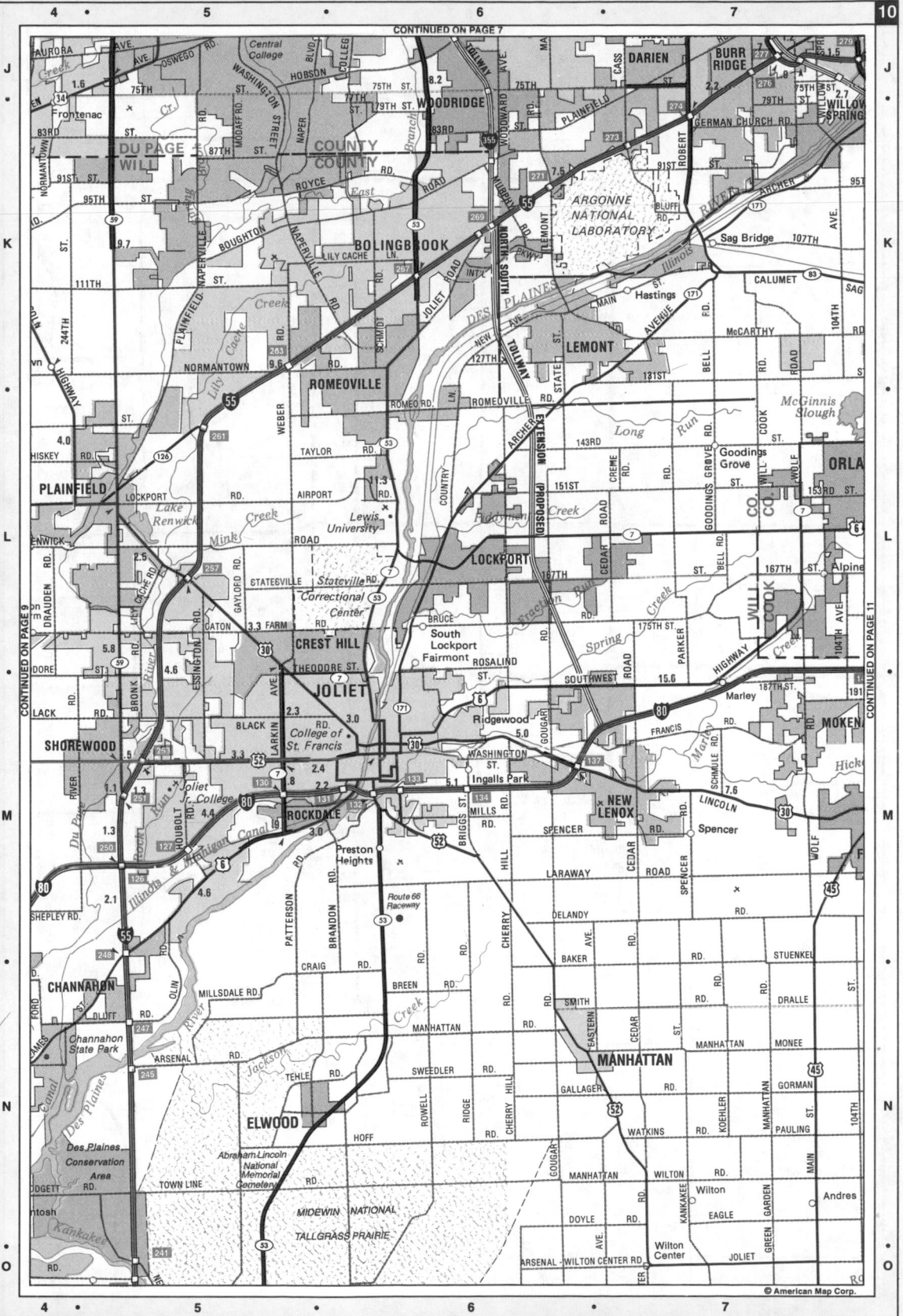

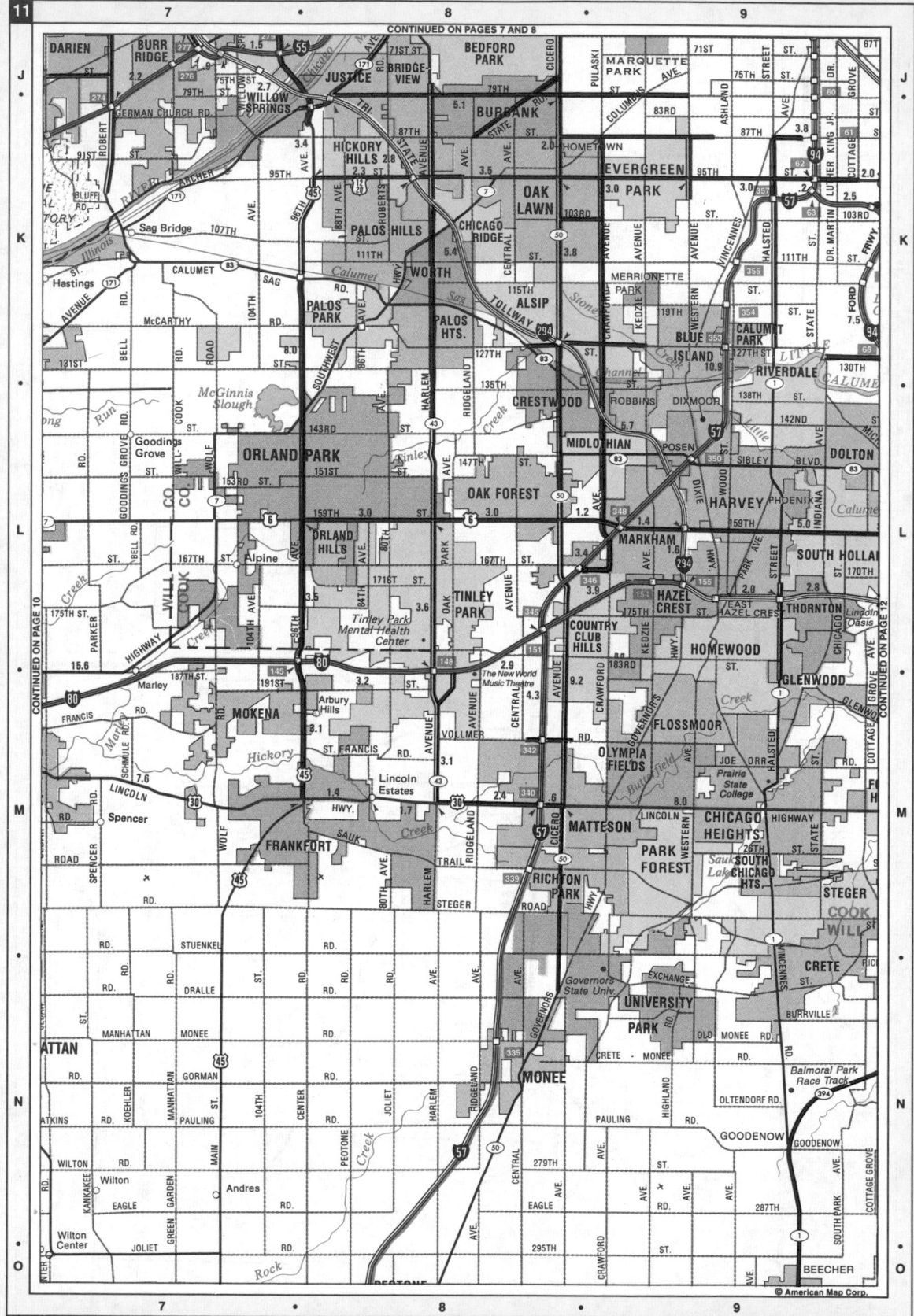

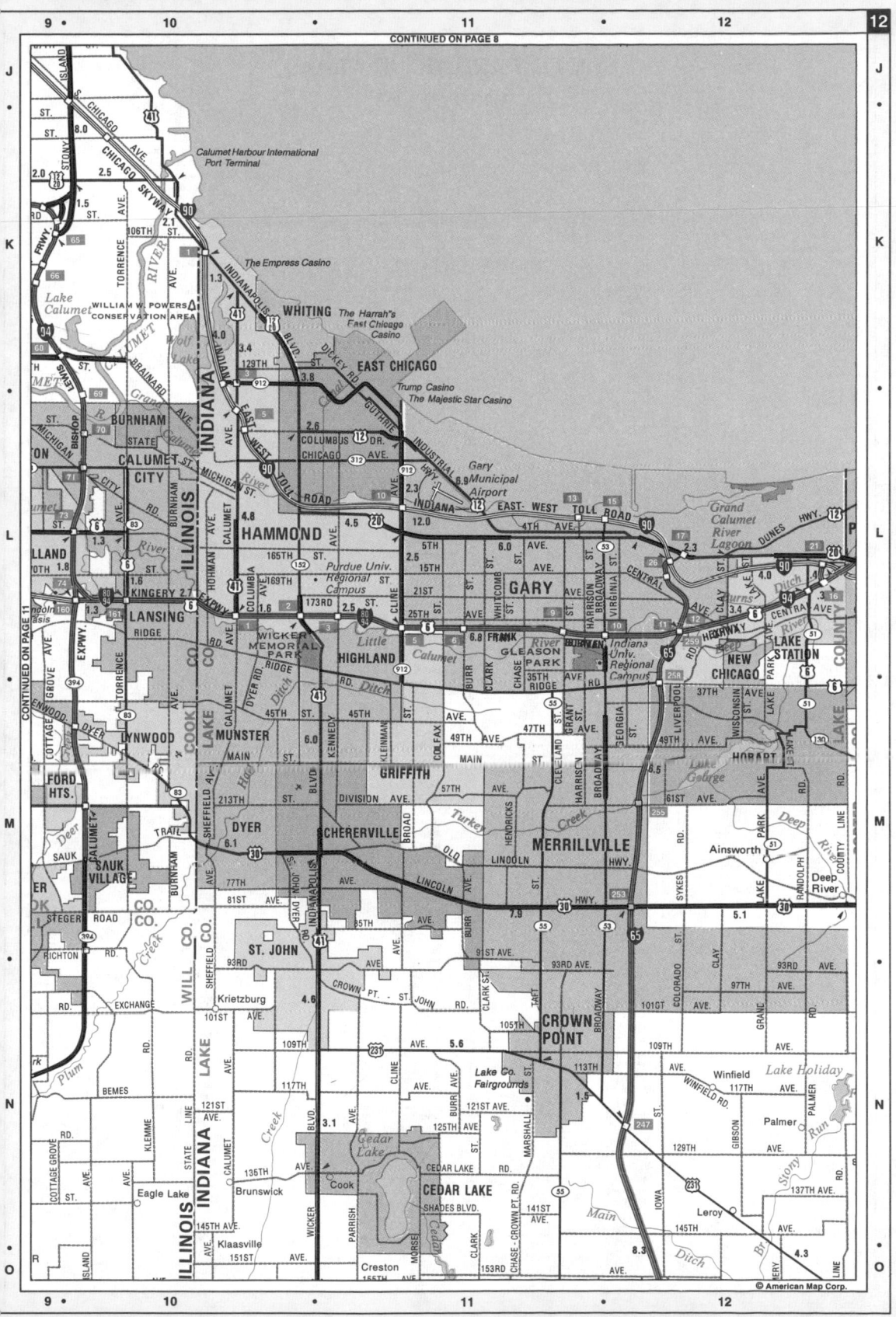

CONTINUED ON PAGE 8

CONTINUED ON PAGE 11

© American Map Corp.

# CHICAGO AND VICINITY INDEX

### See Map Pages 3-12

## ILLINOIS

| | |
|---|---|
| Addison | H4 |
| Algonquin | E2 |
| Alpine | L5 |
| Alsip | K6 |
| Antioch | B4 |
| Aptakisic | E5 |
| Arbury Hills | M6 |
| Arlington Heights | F4 |
| Aurora | J2 |
| Baldmond | H1 |
| Bannockburn | E5 |
| Barrington | E3 |
| Barrington Hills | F3 |
| Bartlett | G3 |
| Batavia | H2 |
| Beach Park | C6 |
| Bedford Park | J6 |
| Belden | B2 |
| Bellwood | H5 |
| Bensenville | G5 |
| Berkeley | H5 |
| Berwyn | H6 |
| Bloomingdale | G4 |
| Blue Island | K7 |
| Bolingbrook | K4 |
| Bridgeview | J6 |
| Broadview | H5 |
| Brookfield | J6 |
| Buffalo Grove | E4 |
| Bull Valley | D2 |
| Burbank | K6 |
| Burnham | L8 |
| Burr Ridge | J5 |
| Burtons Bridge | D3 |
| Calumet City | L8 |
| Calumet Park | K7 |
| Carol Stream | H3 |
| Carpentersville | F2 |
| Cary | E2 |
| Caton Farm | L3 |
| Channel Lake | B3 |
| Chicago Heights | M7 |
| Chicago Ridge | K6 |
| Cicero | H6 |
| Clarendon Hills | J5 |
| Country Club Hills | L6 |
| Countryside | J5 |
| Crest Hill | L3 |
| Crestwood | L6 |
| Crete | M7 |
| Crystal Lake | D2 |
| Darien | J5 |
| Deer Park | E4 |
| Deerfield | E5 |
| Des Plaines | F5 |
| Diamond Lake | D4 |
| Dixmoor | L7 |
| Dolton | L7 |
| Downers Grove | J4 |
| East Dundee | F2 |
| East Hazelcrest | L7 |
| Elburn | H1 |
| Elgin | F2 |
| Elk Grove Village | G4 |
| Elmhurst | H5 |
| Elmwood Park | H6 |
| Eola | J3 |
| Evanston | G7 |
| Evergreen Park | K7 |
| Fairmont | L4 |
| Flossmoor | M7 |
| Flowerfield | H4 |
| Ford Heights | M7 |
| Forest Park | H6 |
| Forest View | J6 |
| Fox Lake | C3 |
| Fox Lake Hills | C3 |
| Fox River Grove | E3 |
| Fox River Valley Gardens | D3 |
| Frankfort | M5 |
| Franklin Park | H5 |
| Fremont Center | D4 |
| Frontenac | K3 |
| Gages Lake | C4 |
| Geneva | H2 |
| Gilberts | F1 |
| Gilmer | D4 |
| Glen Ellyn | H4 |
| Glencoe | E6 |
| Glendale Heights | H4 |
| Glenview | F6 |
| Glenwood | M7 |
| Golf | F6 |
| Goodings Grove | L5 |
| Grayslake | C4 |
| Green Oaks | D5 |
| Greenwood | C1 |
| Gurnee | C5 |
| Hainesville | C4 |
| Half Day | E5 |
| Hanover Park | G3 |
| Harvey | L7 |
| Harwood Heights | G6 |
| Hastings | K5 |
| Hawthorn Woods | E4 |
| Hazel Crest | L7 |
| Hebron | B1 |
| Hickory Hills | K6 |
| Highland Hills | H4 |
| Highland Park | E6 |
| Highwood | E6 |
| Hillside | H5 |
| Hinsdale | J5 |
| Hodgkins | J5 |
| Hoffman Estates | F3 |
| Holiday Hills | D3 |
| Hometown | K6 |
| Homewood | L7 |
| Huntley | E1 |
| Indian Creek | E4 |
| Indian Head Park | J5 |
| Ingalls Park | M4 |
| Inverness | F4 |
| Island Lake | D3 |
| Itasca | G4 |
| Ivanhoe | D4 |
| Johnsburg | C2 |
| Joliet | M4 |
| Justice | J6 |
| Keeneyville | G3 |
| Kenilworth | F7 |
| Kildeer | E4 |
| Knollwood | D5 |
| La Fox | H1 |
| LaGrange | J5 |
| LaGrange Park | J5 |
| Lake Barrington | E3 |
| Lake Bluff | D6 |
| Lake Forest | D6 |
| Lake In The Hills | E2 |
| Lake Villa | C4 |
| Lake Zurich | E4 |
| Lakemoor | C3 |
| Lakewood | E1 |
| Lansing | L8 |
| Lemont | K4 |
| Libertyville | D5 |
| Lily Lake | H1 |
| Lincoln Estates | M6 |
| Lincolnshire | E5 |
| Lincolnwood | G6 |
| Lindenhurst | C4 |
| Lisbon Center | M1 |
| Lisle | J4 |
| Lockport | L4 |
| Lombard | H4 |
| Long Grove | E4 |
| Long Lake | C3 |
| Loon Lake | B4 |
| Lynwood | M8 |
| Lyons | J6 |
| Markham | L7 |
| Marley | M5 |
| Marywood | J2 |
| Matteson | M6 |
| Maywood | H6 |
| McCook | J6 |
| McCullom Lake | C2 |
| McHenry | C2 |
| McQueens | F1 |
| Medinah | G4 |
| Melrose Park | H5 |
| Merrionette Park | K7 |
| Mettawa | D5 |
| Midlothian | L6 |
| Millburn | B4 |
| Minooka | M2 |
| Mokena | M5 |
| Montgomery | K2 |
| Mooseheart | J2 |
| Morton Grove | F6 |
| Mount Prospect | F5 |
| Mundelein | D4 |
| Naperville | J3 |
| New Lenox | M5 |
| Niles | G6 |
| Normantown | K2 |
| Norridge | G6 |
| North Aurora | J2 |
| North Barrington | E3 |
| North Chicago | D5 |
| North Riverside | H6 |
| Northbrook | F5 |
| Northfield | F6 |
| Northlake | H5 |
| Oak Brook | J5 |
| Oak Forest | L6 |
| Oak Lawn | K6 |
| Oak Park | H6 |
| Oakbrook Terrace | H5 |
| Oakwood Hills | D3 |
| Old Mill Creek | B4 |
| Olympia Fields | M7 |
| Orland Hills | L6 |
| Orland Park | L5 |
| Oswego | K2 |
| Palatine | F4 |
| Palos Heights | K6 |
| Palos Hills | K6 |
| Palos Park | K6 |
| Park City | C5 |
| Park Forest | M7 |
| Park Ridge | G6 |
| Phoenix | L7 |
| Pingree Grove | F1 |
| Plainfield | L3 |
| Plato Center | G1 |
| Plattville | M1 |
| Posen | L7 |
| Prairie Grove | D2 |
| Prairie View | E5 |
| Preston Heights | M4 |
| Prince Crossing | H3 |
| Prospect Heights | F5 |
| Richmond | B2 |
| Richton Park | M6 |
| Ridgefield | D2 |
| Ridgewood | M4 |
| Ringwood | C2 |
| River Forest | H6 |
| River Grove | H6 |
| Riverdale | L7 |
| Riverside | J6 |
| Riverwoods | E5 |
| Robbins | L7 |
| Rockdale | M3 |
| Rolling Meadows | F4 |
| Romeoville | K4 |
| Rondou | D5 |
| Rosecrans | B5 |
| Roselle | G4 |
| Rosemont | G5 |
| Round Lake | C3 |
| Round Lake Beach | D4 |
| Round Lake Heights | C4 |
| Round Lake Park | C4 |
| Sag Bridge | K5 |
| Sauk Village | M8 |
| Schaumburg | G4 |
| Schiller Park | G5 |
| Shorewood | M3 |
| Skokie | F6 |
| Sleepy Hollow | F2 |
| Solon Mills | B2 |
| South Barrington | F3 |
| South Chicago Heights | M7 |
| South Elgin | G2 |
| South Holland | L7 |
| South Lockport | L4 |
| Spencer | M5 |
| Spring Grove | B2 |
| St. Charles | H2 |
| Starks | F1 |
| Steger | M7 |
| Stickney | J6 |
| Stone Park | H5 |
| Streamwood | G3 |
| Sugar Grove | J1 |
| Summit | J6 |
| Third Lake | C4 |
| Thornton | L7 |
| Tinley Park | L6 |
| Tower Lakes | E3 |
| Udina | F1 |
| University Park | M6 |
| Valley View | G2 |
| Venetian Village | C4 |
| Vernon Hills | D5 |
| Villa Park | H5 |
| Volo | C3 |
| Wadsworth | B5 |
| Warrenville | J3 |
| Wasco | G1 |
| Wauconda | D3 |
| Waukegan | C6 |
| Wayne | G3 |
| West Chicago | H3 |
| West Dundee | F2 |
| West Miltmore | C4 |
| Westchester | H5 |
| Western Springs | J5 |
| Westmont | J5 |
| Wheaton | H3 |
| Wheeling | F5 |
| Wildwood | C5 |
| Willow Springs | K5 |
| Willowbrook | J5 |
| Wilmette | F7 |
| Winfield | H3 |
| Winnetka | F6 |
| Winthrop Harbor | B6 |
| Wolfs | K2 |
| Wonder Lake | C2 |
| Wood Dale | G4 |
| Woodridge | K4 |
| Woodstock | D1 |
| Worth | K6 |
| York Center | H4 |
| Yorkville | K1 |
| Zion | B6 |

## INDIANA

| | |
|---|---|
| Ainsworth | C8 |
| Deep River | C8 |
| Dyer | M8 |
| East Chicago | A7 |
| Gary | B7 |
| Griffith | C7 |
| Hammond | L8 |
| Highland | B7 |
| Hobart | C8 |
| Lake Station | B8 |
| Merrillville | C8 |
| Munster | M8 |
| New Chicago | B8 |
| Schererville | C7 |
| St. John | C6 |
| Whiting | K8 |

## WISCONSIN

| | |
|---|---|
| Benet Lake | B4 |
| Bristol | A4 |
| Camp Lake | A3 |
| Carol Beach | B6 |
| Fox River | A3 |
| Genoa City | B2 |
| Kenosha | A5 |
| Lake Geneva | A1 |
| Paddock Lake | A2 |
| Pell Lake | A2 |
| Pleasant Prairie | A5 |
| Powers Lake | A2 |
| Salem | A3 |
| Silver Lake | A3 |
| South Kenosha | A6 |
| Trevor | B4 |
| Truesdell | A5 |
| Twin Lakes | A3 |
| Wilmot | B3 |
| Woodworth | A4 |

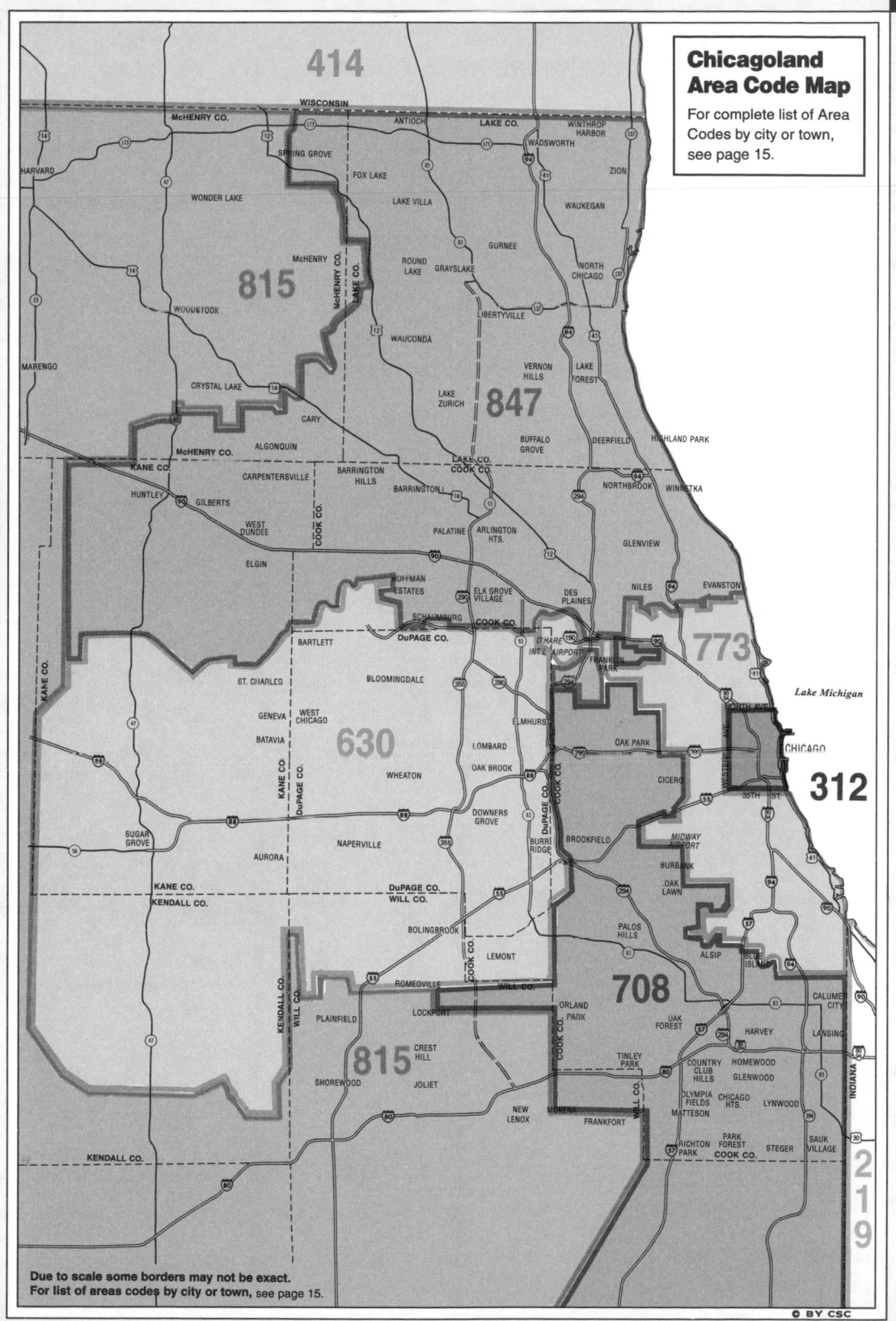

Chicagoland Area Code Map

For complete list of Area Codes by city or town, see page 15.

Due to scale some borders may not be exact.
For list of areas codes by city or town, see page 15.

© BY CSC

# TELEPHONE AREA CODES BY CITY

### See Map on Page 14

## ILLINOIS

| CITY | AREA CODE |
|---|---|
| Abbott Park | 847 |
| Addison | 630 |
| Alden | 815 |
| Algonquin | 847 |
| Alsip | 708 |
| Antioch | 847 |
| Aptakisic | 847 |
| Arbury Hills | 815 |
| Arlington Heights | 847 |
| Aurora | 630 |
| Baldmond | 630 |
| Bannockburn | 847 |
| Barrington | 847 |
| Barrington Hills | 847 |
| Bartlett | 630 |
| Batavia | 630 |
| Beach Park | 847 |
| Bedford Park | 708 |
| Belden | 815 |
| Bellwood | 708 |
| Bensenville | 630 |
| Berkeley | 708 |
| Berwyn | 708 |
| Big Foot | 815 |
| Big Rock | 630 |
| Bloomingdale | 630 |
| Blue Island | 708 |
| Bolingbrook | 630 |
| Bowes | 630 |
| Bridgeview | 708 |
| Broadview | 708 |
| Brookfield | 708 |
| Buffalo Grove | 847 |
| Bull Valley | 815 |
| Burbank | 708 |
| Burlington | 847 |
| Burnham | 708 |
| Burr Ridge | 630 |
| Burtons Bridge | 847 |
| Calumet City | 708 |
| Calumet Park | 708 |
| Carney Corners | 847 |
| Carol Stream | 630 |
| Carpentersville | 847 |
| Cary | 847 |
| Cedar Lake | 847 |
| Channel Lake | 847 |
| Chemung | 815 |
| Chicago | 312,773 |
| Chicago Heights | 708 |
| Chicago Ridge | 708 |
| Cicero | 708 |
| Clarendon Hills | 630 |
| Coral | 815 |
| Country Club Hills | 708 |
| Countryside | 708 |
| Coynes | 815 |
| Crest Hill | 815 |
| Crestwood | 708 |
| Crystal Lake | 815 |
| Darien | 630 |
| Deep Lake | 847 |
| Deer Park | 847 |
| Deerfield | 847 |
| Des Plaines | 847 |
| Diamond Lake | 847 |
| Dixmoor | 708 |
| Dolton | 708 |
| Downers Grove | 630 |
| East Dundee | 847 |
| East Hazelcrest | 708 |
| Eddy | 847 |
| Elburn | 630 |
| Elgin | 847 |
| Elk Grove Village | 847 |
| Elmhurst | 630 |
| Elmwood Park | 708 |
| Evanston | 847 |
| Evergreen Park | 708 |
| Fairfield | 847 |
| Flossmoor | 708 |
| Flowerfield | 630 |
| Ford Heights | 708 |
| Forest Park | 708 |
| Forest View | 708 |
| Fox Lake | 847 |
| Fox Lake Hills | 847 |
| Fox River Grove | 847 |
| Fox River Valley Gardens | 847 |
| Frankfort | 708,815 |
| Franklin Park | 847 |
| Franklinville | 815 |
| Gages Lake | 847 |
| Geneva | 630 |
| Gilberts | 847 |
| Gilmer | 847 |
| Glen Ellyn | 630 |
| Glencoe | 847 |
| Glendale Heights | 630 |
| Glenview | 847 |
| Glenwood | 708 |
| Golf | 847 |
| Grayslake | 847 |
| Green Oaks | 847 |
| Greenwood | 815 |
| Gurnee | 847 |
| Hainesville | 847 |
| Half Day | 847 |
| Hampshire | 847 |
| Hanover Park | 630 |
| Harmony | 815 |
| Hartland | 815 |
| Harvard | 815 |
| Harvey | 708 |
| Harwood Heights | 708 |
| Hawthorn Woods | 847 |
| Hazel Crest | 708 |
| Hebron | 815 |
| Hickory Hills | 708 |
| Highland Park | 847 |
| Highwood | 847 |
| Hillside | 708 |
| Hinsdale | 630 |
| Hodgkins | 708 |
| Hoffman Estates | 847 |
| Holiday Hills | 815 |
| Hometown | 708 |
| Homewood | 708 |
| Huntley | 847 |
| Indian Creek | 847 |
| Indian Head Park | 708 |
| Ingals Park | 815 |
| Ingleside | 847 |
| Inverness | 847 |
| Island Lake | 847 |
| Itasca | 630 |
| Ivanhoe | 847 |
| Johnsburg | 815 |
| Joliet | 815 |
| Justice | 708 |
| Kaneville | 630 |
| Kenilworth | 847 |
| Kildeer | 847 |
| La Fox | 630 |
| LaGrange | 708 |
| LaGrange Park | 708 |
| Lake Barrington | 847 |
| Lake Bluff | 847 |
| Lake Forest | 847 |
| Lake Villa | 847 |
| Lake Zurich | 847 |
| Lake in the Hills | 847 |
| Lakemoor | 815 |
| Lakewood | 815 |
| Lambs Corners | 847 |
| Lansing | 708 |
| Lawrence | 815 |
| Lemont | 630 |
| Libertyville | 847 |
| Lily Cache | 815 |
| Lily Lake | 630 |
| Lilymoor | 815 |
| Lincolnshire | 847 |
| Lincolnwood | 847 |
| Lindenhurst | 847 |
| Lisle | 630 |
| Lockport | 815 |
| Lombard | 630 |
| Long Grove | 847 |
| Long Lake | 847 |
| Loon Lake | 847 |
| Lynwood | 708 |
| Lyons | 708 |
| Maple Park | 630 |
| Marengo | 815 |
| Markham | 708 |
| Marywood | 630 |
| Matteson | 708 |
| Maywood | 708 |
| McCook | 708 |
| McCullom Lake | 815 |
| McHenry | 815 |
| McQueens | 630 |
| Medinah | 630 |
| Melrose Park | 708 |
| Merrionette Park | 708 |
| Mettawa | 847 |
| Midlothian | 708 |
| Millburn | 847 |
| Mokena | 708,815 |
| Monaville | 847 |
| Montgomery | 630 |
| Mooseheart | 630 |
| Morton Grove | 847 |
| Mount Prospect | 847 |
| Mundelein | 847 |
| Mylith Park | 847 |
| Naperville | 630 |
| New Lenox | 815 |
| Niles | 847 |
| Norridge | 708 |
| North Aurora | 630 |
| North Barrington | 847 |
| North Chicago | 847 |
| North Riverside | 708 |
| Northbrook | 847 |
| Northfield | 847 |
| Northlake | 708 |
| Oak Brook | 630 |
| Oak Forest | 708 |
| Oak Lawn | 708 |
| Oak Park | 708 |
| Oakbrook Terrace | 630 |
| Oakwood Hills | 847 |
| Old Mill Creek | 847 |
| Olympia Fields | 708 |
| Orland Hills | 708 |
| Orland Park | 708 |
| Oswego | 630 |
| Palatine | 847 |
| Palos Heights | 708 |
| Palos Hills | 708 |
| Palos Park | 708 |
| Park City | 847 |
| Park Forest | 708 |
| Park Ridge | 847 |
| Phoenix | 708 |
| Pingree Grove | 847 |
| Plainfield | 815 |
| Plato Center | 847 |
| Posen | 708 |
| Prairie Grove | 815 |
| Prairie View | 847 |
| Prospect Heights | 847 |
| Quentin's Corners | 847 |
| Richardson | 815 |
| Richmond | 815 |
| Richton Park | 708 |
| Ridgefield | 815 |
| Ridgewood | 815 |
| Riley | 815 |
| Ringwood | 815 |
| River Forest | 708 |
| River Grove | 708 |
| Riverdale | 708 |
| Riverside | 708 |
| Riverwoods | 847 |
| Robbins | 708 |
| Rockdale | 815 |
| Romeoville | 815 |
| Rosecrans | 847 |
| Roselle | 630 |
| Rosemont | 847 |
| Round Lake | 847 |
| Round Lake Beach | 847 |
| Round Lake Heights | 847 |
| Round Lake Park | 847 |
| Russell | 847 |
| Sauk Village | 708 |
| Schaumburg | 847 |
| Schiller Park | 847 |
| Scraper-Moecherville | 630 |
| Shorewood | 815 |
| Skokie | 847 |
| Sleepy Hollow | 847 |
| Solon Mills | 815 |
| South Barrington | 847 |
| South Chicago Heights | 708 |
| South Elgin | 847 |
| South Holland | 708 |
| South Park | 630 |
| Spaulding Corners | 847 |
| Spring Grove | 847 |
| St. Charles | 630 |
| Starks | 847 |
| Steger | 708 |
| Stickney | 708 |
| Stone Park | 708 |
| Streamwood | 630 |
| Sugar Grove | 630 |
| Summit | 708 |
| Sylvan Lakes | 847 |
| Third Lake | 847 |
| Thornton | 708 |
| Tinley Park | 708 |
| Tower Lakes | 847 |
| Troxel | 708 |
| Twin Lakes | 815 |
| Udina | 847 |
| Union | 815 |
| Valley View | 847 |
| Vernon Hills | 847 |
| Villa Park | 630 |
| Virgil | 630 |
| Volo | 815 |
| Wadsworth | 847 |
| Warrenville | 630 |
| Wasco | 630 |
| Wauconda | 847 |
| Waukegan | 847 |
| Wayne | 630 |
| West Chicago | 630 |
| West Dundee | 847 |
| Westchester | 708 |
| Western Springs | 708 |
| Westmont | 630 |
| Wheaton | 630 |
| Wheeling | 847 |
| Wildwood | 847 |
| Williams Park | 708 |
| Willow Springs | 708 |
| Willowbrook | 630 |
| Wilmette | 847 |
| Wilson | 847 |
| Winfield | 630 |
| Winnetka | 847 |
| Winthrop Harbor | 847 |
| Wonder Lake | 815 |
| Wood Dale | 630 |
| Woodridge | 630 |
| Woodstock | 815 |
| Worth | 708 |
| Zion | 847 |

## INDIANA

| CITY | AREA CODE |
|---|---|
| Ainsworth | 219 |
| Deep River | 219 |
| Dyer | 219 |
| East Chicago | 219 |
| Gary | 219 |
| Griffith | 219 |
| Hammond | 219 |
| Highland | 219 |
| Hobart | 219 |
| Lake Station | 219 |
| Merrillville | 219 |
| Munster | 219 |
| New Chicago | 219 |
| Schererville | 219 |
| St. John | 219 |
| Whiting | 219 |

## WISCONSIN

| CITY | AREA CODE |
|---|---|
| Benet Lake | 414 |
| Bristol | 414 |
| Camp Lake | 414 |
| Carol Beach | 414 |
| Fox River | 414 |
| Genoa City | 414 |
| Kenosha | 414 |
| Lake Geneva | 414 |
| Paddock Lake | 414 |
| Pell Lake | 414 |
| Pleasant Prairie | 414 |
| Powers Lake | 414 |
| Salem | 414 |
| Silver Lake | 414 |
| South Kenosha | 414 |
| Trevor | 414 |
| Truesdell | 414 |
| Twin Lakes | 414 |
| Wilmot | 414 |
| Woodworth | 414 |

# Notes

# Notes